Routledge
Encyclopedia of
PHILOSOPHY

General Editor
EDWARD CRAIG

London and New York

First published 1998
by Routledge
New Fetter Lane, London EC4P 4EE
Simultaneously published in the USA and Canada
by Routledge
29 West 35th Street, New York, NY 10001

©1998 Routledge

Typeset in Monotype Times New Roman by
Routledge

Printed in England by
T J International Ltd, Padstow, Cornwall, England

Printed on acid-free paper which conforms to ANS1.Z39, 48-1992 and ISO 9706 standards

British Library Cataloguing-in-Publication Data
A catalogue record for this book is available from the British Library

The Library of Congress Cataloguing-in-Publication data is given in volume 10.

ISBN: 0415-07310-3 (10-volume set)
ISBN: 0415-18706-0 (volume 1)
ISBN: 0415-18707-9 (volume 2)
ISBN: 0415-18708-7 (volume 3)
ISBN: 0415-18709-5 (volume 4)
ISBN: 0415-18710-9 (volume 5)
ISBN: 0415-18711-7 (volume 6)
ISBN: 0415-18712-5 (volume 7)
ISBN: 0415-18713-3 (volume 8)
ISBN: 0415-18714-1 (volume 9)
ISBN: 0415-18715-X (volume 10)

ISBN: 0415-16916-X (CD-ROM)
ISBN: 0415-16917-8 (10-volume set and CD-ROM)

Contents

Using the *Encyclopedia*

List of entries

Using the *Encyclopedia*

The *Routledge Encyclopedia of Philosophy* is designed for ease of use. The following notes outline its organization and editorial approach and explain the ways of locating material. This will help readers make the most of the *Encyclopedia*.

SEQUENCE OF ENTRIES

The *Encyclopedia* contains 2,054 entries (from 500 to 19,000 words in length) arranged in nine volumes with a tenth volume for the index. Volumes 1–9 are arranged in a single alphabetical sequence, as follows:

Volume 1: A posteriori *to* Bradwardine, Thomas

Volume 2: Brahman *to* Derrida, Jacques

Volume 3: Descartes, René *to* Gender and science

Volume 4: Genealogy *to* Iqbal, Muhammad

Volume 5: Irigaray, Luce *to* Lushi chunqiu

Volume 6: Luther, Martin *to* Nifo, Agostino

Volume 7: Nihilism *to* Quantum mechanics, interpretation of

Volume 8: Questions *to* Sociobiology

Volume 9: Sociology of knowledge *to* Zoroastrianism

Alphabetical order

Entries are listed in alphabetical order by word rather than by letter with all words including *and*, *in*, *of* and *the* being given equal status. The exceptions to this rule are as follows:

- biographies: where the forenames and surname of a philosopher are inverted, the entry takes priority in the sequence, for example:

Alexander, Samuel (1859–1938)
Alexander of Aphrodisias (*c.* AD 200)
Alexander of Hales (*c.* 1185–1245)

- names with prefixes, which follow conventional alphabetical placing (see Transliteration and naming conventions below).

A complete alphabetical list of entries is given in each of the Volumes 1 to 9.

Inverted titles

Titles of entries consisting of more than one word are often inverted so that the key term (in a thematic or signpost entry) or the surname (in a biographical entry) determines the place of the entry in the alphabetical sequence, for example:

Law, philosophy of *or*
Market, ethics of the *or*
Hart, Herbert Lionel Adolphus (1907–93)

Conceptual organization

Several concerns have had a bearing on the sequence of entries where there is more than one key term.

In deciding on the sequence of entries we have tried, wherever possible, to integrate philosophy as it is known and studied in the USA and Europe with philosophy from around the world. This means that the reader will frequently find entries from different philosophical traditions or approaches to the same topic close to each other, for example, in the sequence:

Political philosophy [signpost entry]
Political philosophy, history of
Political philosophy in classical Islam
Political philosophy, Indian

Similarly, in entries where a philosophical tradition or approach is surveyed we have tried, whenever appropriate, to keep philosophical traditions from different countries together. An example is the sequence:

Confucian philosophy, Chinese
Confucian philosophy, Japanese
Confucian philosophy, Korean
Confucius (551–479 BC)

Finally, historical entries are usually placed with contemporary entries under the topic rather than the historical period. For example, in the sequence:

Language, ancient philosophy of
Language and gender
Language, conventionality of
Language, early modern philosophy of
Language, Indian theories of
Language, innateness of

DUMMY TITLES

The *Encyclopedia* has been extensively cross-referenced in order to help the reader locate their topic of interest. Dummy titles are placed throughout the alphabetical sequence of entries to direct the reader to the actual title of the entry where a topic is discussed. This may be under a different entry title, a synonym or as part of a larger entry. Wherever useful we have included the numbers of the sections (§§) in which a particular topic or subject is discussed. Examples of this type of cross-reference are:

AFRICAN AESTHETICS *see*
AESTHETICS, AFRICAN

CANGUILHEM, GEORGES *see*
FRENCH PHILOSOPHY OF SCIENCE §§3–4

TAO *see* DAO

GLOSSARY OF LOGICAL AND MATHEMATICAL TERMS

A glossary of logical and mathematical terms is provided to help users with terms from formal logic and mathematics. 'See also' cross-references to the glossary are provided at the end of entries where the user might benefit from help with unfamiliar terms. The glossary can be found in Volume 5 under L (LOGICAL AND MATHEMATICAL TERMS, GLOSSARY OF).

THE INDEX VOLUME

Volume 10 is devoted to a comprehensive index of key terms, concepts and names covered in Volumes 1–9, allowing readers to reap maximum benefit from the *Encyclopedia*. A guide to the index can be found at the beginning of the index. The index volume includes a full listing of contributors, their affiliations and the entries they have written. It also includes permission acknowledgements, listed in publisher order.

STRUCTURE OF ENTRIES

The *Routledge Encyclopedia of Philosophy* contains three types of entry:

- 'signpost' entries, for example, METAPHYSICS; SCIENCE, PHILOSOPHY OF; EAST ASIAN PHILOSOPHY. These entries provide an accessible overview of the sub-disciplines or regional coverage within the *Encyclopedia*; they provide a 'map' which directs the reader towards and around the many entries relating to each topic;
- thematic entries, ranging from general entries such as KNOWLEDGE, CONCEPT OF, to specialized topics such as VIRTUE EPISTEMOLOGY;
- biographical entries, devoted to individual philosophers, emphasizing the work rather than the life of the subject and with a list of the subject's major works.

Overview

All thematic and biographical entries begin with an overview which provides a concise and accessible summary of the topic or subject. This can be referred to on its own if the reader does not require the depth and detail of the main part of the entry.

Table of contents

All thematic and biographical entries over 1000 words in length are divided into sections and have a numbered table of contents following the overview. This gives the headings of each of the sections of the entry, enabling the reader to see the scope and structure of the entry at a glance. For example, the table of contents in the entry on HERACLITUS:

1 Life and work
2 Methodology
3 Unity of opposites and perspectivism
4 Cosmology
5 Psychology, ethics and religion
6 Influence

Cross-references within an entry

Entries in the *Encyclopedia* have been extensively cross-referenced in order to indicate other entries that may be of interest to the reader. There are two types of cross-reference in the *Encyclopedia*:

1. 'See' cross-references

Cross-references within the text of an entry direct the reader to other entries on or closely related to the topic under discussion. For example, a reader may be directed from a conceptual entry to a biography of the philosopher whose work is under discussion or vice versa. These internal cross-references appear in small capital letters, either in parentheses, for example:

Opponents of naturalism before and since Wittgenstein have been animated by the notion that the aims of social science are not causal explanation and improving prediction, but uncovering rules that make social life intelligible to its participants (see EXPLANATION IN HISTORY AND SOCIAL SCIENCE).

or sometimes, when the reference is to a person who

has a biographical entry, as small capitals in the text itself, for example:

> Thomas NAGEL emphasizes the discrepancy between the objective insignificance of our lives and projects and the seriousness and energy we devote to them.

For entries over 1,000 words in length we have included the numbers of the sections (§) in which a topic is discussed, wherever useful, for example:

> In *Nicomachean Ethics*, Aristotle criticizes Plato's account for not telling us anything about particular kinds of goodness (see ARISTOTLE §§ 21–6).

2. 'See also' cross-references

At the end of the text of each entry, 'See also' cross-references guide the reader to other entries of related interest, such as more specialized entries, biographical entries, historical entries, geographical entries and so on. These cross-references appear in small capitals in alphabetical order.

References

References in the text are given in the Harvard style, for example, Kant (1788), Rawls (1971). Exceptions to this rule are made when presenting works with established conventions, for example, with some major works in ancient philosophy. Full bibliographical details are given in the 'List of works' and 'References and further reading'.

Bibliography

List of works

Biographical entries are followed by a list of works which gives full bibliographical details of the major works of the philosopher. This is in chronological order and includes items cited in the text, significant editions, dates of composition for pre-modern works (where known), preferred English-language translations and English translations for the titles of untranslated foreign-language works.

References and further reading

Both biographical and thematic entries have a list of references and further reading. Items are listed alphabetically by author's name. (Publications with joint authors are listed under the name of the first author and after any individual publications by that author). References cited in the text are preceded by an asterisk (*). Further reading which the reader may find particularly useful is also included.

The authors and editors have attempted to provide the fullest possible bibliographical information for every item.

Annotations

Publications in the 'List of works' and the 'References and further reading' have been annotated with a brief description of the content so that their relevance to readers' interests can be quickly assessed.

EDITORIAL STYLE

Spelling and punctuation in the *Encyclopedia* have been standardized to follow British English usage.

Transliteration and naming conventions

All names and terms from non-roman alphabets have been romanized in the *Encyclopedia*. Foreign names have been given according to the conventions within the particular language.

Arabic

Arabic has been transliterated in a simplified form, that is, without macrons or subscripts. Names of philosophers are given in their Arabic form rather than their Latinate form, for example, IBN RUSHD rather than AVERROES. Arabic names beginning with the prefix 'al-' are alphabetized under the substantive part of the name and not the prefix, for example:

> KILWARDBY, ROBERT (d. 1279)
> AL-KINDI, ABU YUSUF YAQUB IBN ISHAQ (d. *c*.866–73)
> KNOWLEDGE AND JUSTIFICATION, COHERENCE THEORY OF

Arabic names beginning with the prefix 'Ibn' are alphabetized under 'I'.

Chinese, Korean and Japanese

Chinese has been transliterated using the Pinyin system. Dummy titles in the older Wade–Giles system are given for names and key terms; these direct the reader to the Pinyin titles.

Japanese has been transliterated using a modified version of the Hepburn system.

Chinese, Japanese and Korean names are given in Asian form, that is, surname preceding forenames, for example:

> WANG FUZHI
> NISHITANI KEIJI

The exception is where an author has chosen to present their own name in conventional Western form.

Hebrew

Hebrew has been transliterated in a simplified form, that is, without macrons or subscripts.

Russian

Cyrillic characters have been transliterated using the Library of Congress system. Russian names are usually given with their patronymic, for example, BAKUNIN, MIKHAIL ALEKSANDROVICH.

Sanskrit

A guide to the pronunciation of Sanskrit can be found in the INDIAN AND TIBETAN PHILOSOPHY signpost entry.

Tibetan

Tibetan has been transliterated using the Wylie system. Dummy titles in the Virginia system are given for names and key terms. A guide to Tibetan pronunciation can be found in the INDIAN AND TIBETAN PHILOSOPHY signpost entry.

European names

Names beginning with the prefixes 'de', 'von' or 'van' are usually alphabetized under the substantive part of the name. For example:

BEAUVOIR, SIMONE DE
HUMBOLDT, WILHELM VON

The exception to this rule is when the person is either a national of or has spent some time living or working in an English-speaking country. For example:

DE MORGAN, AUGUSTUS
VON WRIGHT, GEORG HENRIK

Names beginning with the prefix 'de la' or 'le' are alphabetized under the prefix 'la' or 'le'. For example:

LA FORGE, LOUIS DE
LE DOEUFF, MICHÈLE

Names beginning with 'Mc' or 'Mac' are treated as 'Mac' and appear before Ma.

Historical names

Medieval and Renaissance names where a person is not usually known by a surname are alphabetized under the forename, for example:

GILES OF ROME
JOHN OF SALISBURY

List of entries

Below is a complete list of entries in the order in which they appear in the *Routledge Encyclopedia of Philosophy.*

An alphabetical list of contributors, their affiliations and the entries they have written can be found in the index volume (Volume 10).

DESCARTES, RENÉ
(1596–1650)

René Descartes, often called the father of modern philosophy, attempted to break with the philosophical traditions of his day and start philosophy anew. Rejecting the Aristotelian philosophy of the schools, the authority of tradition and the authority of the senses, he built a philosophical system that included a method of inquiry, a metaphysics, a mechanistic physics and biology, and an account of human psychology intended to ground an ethics. Descartes was also important as one of the founders of the new analytic geometry, which combines geometry and algebra, and whose certainty provided a kind of model for the rest of his philosophy.

After an education in the scholastic and humanistic traditions, Descartes' earliest work was mostly in mathematics and mathematical physics, in which his most important achievements were his analytical geometry and his discovery of the law of refraction in optics. In this early period he also wrote his unfinished treatise on method, the Rules for the Direction of the Mind, *which set out a procedure for investigating nature, based on the reduction of complex problems to simpler ones solvable by direct intuition. From these intuitively established foundations, Descartes tried to show how one could then attain the solution of the problems originally posed.*

Descartes abandoned these methodological studies by 1628 or 1629, turning first to metaphysics, and soon afterwards to an orderly exposition of his physics and biology in The World. *But this work was overtly Copernican in its cosmology, and when Galileo was condemned in 1633, Descartes withdrew* The World *from publication; it appeared only after his death.*

Descartes' mature philosophy began to appear in 1637 with the publication of a single volume containing the Geometry, Dioptrics *and* Meteors, *three essays in which he presented some of his most notable scientific results, preceded by the* Discourse on the Method, *a semi-autobiographical introduction that outlined his approach to philosophy and the full system into which the specific results fit. In the years following, he published a series of writings in which he set out his system in a more orderly way, beginning with its metaphysical foundations in the* Meditations *(1641), adding his physics in the* Principles of Philosophy *(1644), and offering a sketch of the psychology and moral philosophy in the* Passions of the Soul *(1649).*

In our youth, Descartes held, we acquire many prejudices which interfere with the proper use of our reason. Consequently, later we must reject everything we believe and start anew. Hence the Meditations *begins with a series of arguments intended to cast doubt upon everything formerly believed, and culminating in the hypothesis of an all-deceiving evil genius, a device to keep former beliefs from returning. The rebuilding of the world begins with the discovery of the self through the 'Cogito Argument' ('I am thinking, therefore I exist') – a self known only as a thinking thing, and known independently of the senses. Within this thinking self, Descartes discovers an idea of God, an idea of something so perfect that it could not have been caused in us by anything with less perfection than God Himself. From this he concluded that God must exist which, in turn, guarantees that reason can be trusted. Since we are made in such a way that we cannot help holding certain beliefs (the so-called 'clear and distinct' perceptions), God would be a deceiver, and thus imperfect, if such beliefs were wrong; any mistakes must be due to our own misuse of reason. This is Descartes' famous epistemological principle of clear and distinct perception. This central argument in Descartes' philosophy, however, is threatened with circularity – the Cartesian Circle – since the arguments that establish the trustworthiness of reason (the Cogito Argument and the argument for the existence of God) themselves seem to depend on the trustworthiness of reason.*

Also central to Descartes' metaphysics was the distinction between mind and body. Since the clear and distinct ideas of mind and body are entirely separate, God can create them apart from one another. Therefore, they are distinct substances. The mind is a substance whose essence is thought alone, and hence exists entirely outside geometric categories, including place. Body is a substance whose essence is extension alone, a geometric object without even sensory qualities like colour or taste, which exist only in the perceiving mind. We know that such bodies exist as the causes of sensation: God has given us a great propensity to believe that our sensations come to us from external bodies, and no means to correct that propensity; hence, he would be a deceiver if we were mistaken. But Descartes also held that the mind and body are closely united with one another; sensation and other feelings, such as hunger and pain, arise from this union. Sensations cannot inform us about the real nature of things, but they can be reliable as sources of knowledge useful to maintaining the mind and body unity. While many of Descartes' contemporaries found it difficult to understand how mind and body can relate to one another, Descartes took it as a simple fact of experience that they do. His account of the passions is an account of how this connection leads us to feelings like wonder, love, hatred, desire, joy and sadness, from which all other passions derive. Understanding these passions helps us to control them, which was a central aim of morality for Descartes.

Descartes' account of body as extended substance led to a physics as well. Because to be extended is to be a body, there can be no empty space. Furthermore, since all body is of the same nature, all differences between bodies are to be explained in terms of the size, shape and motion of their component parts, and in terms of the laws of motion that they obey. Descartes attempted to derive these laws from the way in which God, in his constancy, conserves the world at every moment. In these mechanistic terms, Descartes attempted to explain a wide variety of features of the world, from the formation of planetary systems out of an initial chaos, to magnetism, to the vital functions of animals, which he considered to be mere machines.

Descartes never finished working out his ambitious programme in full detail. Though he published the metaphysics and the general portion of his physics, the physical explanation of specific phenomena, especially biological, remained unfinished, as did his moral theory. Despite this, however, Descartes' programme had an enormous influence on the philosophy that followed, both within the substantial group that identified themselves as his followers, and outside.

1 Life

René Descartes was born on 31 March 1596 in the Touraine region of France, in the town of La Haye, later renamed Descartes in his honour. In 1606 or 1607 he was sent to the Collège Royal de La Flèche, run by the Jesuit order. Here he received an education that combined elements of earlier Aristotelian scholasticism with the new humanistic emphasis on the study of language and literature. But the core of the collegiate curriculum was the study of Aristotelian logic, metaphysics, physics and ethics. Descartes left La Flèche in 1614 or 1615, and went to the University of Poitiers, where he received his *baccalauréat* and his *licence en droit* in late 1616. In Part I of the *Discours de la méthode* (*Discourse on the Method*) (1637), he discusses his education in some detail, explaining why

he found it increasingly unsatisfactory. In the end, he reports, he left school, rejecting much of what he had been taught there. He chose the life of the military engineer, and set out across Europe to learn his trade, following the armies and the wars. On 10 November 1618, in the course of his travels, he met Isaac Beeckman. An enthusiastic scientific amateur since his early twenties, Beeckman introduced Descartes to some of the new currents in science, the newly revived atomist ideas, and the attempt to combine mathematics and physics (see ATOMISM, ANCIENT). Despite the fact that they only spent a few months together, Beeckman put Descartes on the path that led to his life's work. A number of discussions between them are preserved in Beeckman's extensive notebooks (1604–34), which still survive, and include problems Beeckman set for Descartes, as well as Descartes' solutions. It was for Beeckman that Descartes wrote his first surviving work, the *Compendium musicum*, a tract on music theory, then considered a branch of what was called mixed mathematics, along with other disciplines such as mathematical astronomy and geometric optics. Exactly a year after first meeting Beeckman, this new path was confirmed for Descartes in a series of three dreams that he interpreted as a call to settle down to his work as a mathematician and philosopher.

During the 1620s, Descartes worked on a number of projects including optics and the mathematics that was eventually to become his analytic geometry. In optics, he discovered the law of refraction – the mathematical law that relates the angle of incidence of a ray of light on a refractive medium, with the angle of refraction. Though some claim that Descartes learned this law from Willebrod Snel, after whom the law is now named, it is generally thought that Descartes discovered it independently. In his mathematical programme, he showed how algebra could be used to solve geometric problems, and how geometric constructions could be used to solve algebraic problems.

Descartes' most extensive writing from this period is the *Regulae ad directionem ingenii* (*Rules for the Direction of the Mind*), a treatise on method that he worked on between 1619 or 1620 and 1628, when he abandoned it incomplete. He continued to travel extensively throughout Europe, returning to Paris in 1625, where he was to stay until spring 1629. In Paris, Descartes became closely associated with Marin Mersenne who later became a central figure in the dissemination of the new philosophy and science in Europe, the organizer of a kind of scientific academy and the centre of a circle of correspondents, as well as Descartes' intellectual patron (see MERSENNE, M.). Through his voluminous correspondence with

Mersenne, Descartes remained connected to all the intellectual currents in Europe, wherever he was to live in later years. An important event in this period took place at a gathering at the home of the Papal Nuncio in Paris in 1627 or 1628, where Descartes, responding to an alchemical lecture by one M. Chandoux, took the occasion to present his own ideas, including his 'fine rule, or natural method' and the principles on which his own philosophy was based (letter to Villebressieu, summer 1631; Descartes 1984–91 vol 3: 32). This attracted the attention of the Cardinal Bérule, who in a private meeting, urged Descartes to develop his philosophy.

In spring 1629 Descartes left Paris and moved to the Low Countries, where he set his methodological writing aside and began his philosophy in earnest. The winter of 1629–30 was largely occupied with the composition of a metaphysical treatise, which, as we shall later see, represents the foundations of his philosophy. The treatise is now lost, but Descartes told Mersenne that it had tried to 'prove the existence of God and of our souls when they are separated from the body, from which follows their immortality' (letter to Mersenne, 25 November 1630; Descartes 1984–91 vol 3: 29). This was followed by the drafting of *Le Monde* (*The World*), Descartes' mechanist physics and physiology, a book intended for publication. In the first part, also called the 'Traité de la lumière' (Treatise on Light), Descartes begins with a general account of the distinction between a sensation and the motion of tiny particles of different sizes and shapes that is its cause, followed by an account of the foundations of the laws of nature. After then positing an initial chaos of particles in motion (not *our* cosmos, but one made by God in some unused corner of the world), Descartes argues that by means of the laws of nature alone, this cosmos will sort itself into planetary systems, central suns around which swirl vortices of subtle matter which carry planets with them. He concludes the 'Traité de la lumière' with an account of important terrestrial phenomena, including gravity, the tides and light, showing how much like our cosmos this imaginary mechanist cosmos will appear. The second part, the 'Traité de l'homme' (Treatise on Man), begins abruptly by positing that God made a body that looks exactly like ours, but which is merely a machine. Presumably missing – or never written – is a transition between the two treatises that shows how by the laws of nature alone this human body could arise in our world. (This part of the argument is noted in Part V of the later *Discourse on the Method*.) In the text that we now have, Descartes then went on to argue that all phenomena that pertain to life (thought aside) can arise in this body in a purely mechanical way, including nutrition and digestion, the circulation of blood, the movement of the muscles and the transmission of sensory information to the brain.

By 1633 Descartes had in hand a relatively complete version of his philosophy, from method, to metaphysics, to physics and biology. But in late 1633, he heard of the condemnation of Galileo's Copernicanism in Rome, and cautiously decided not to publish his *World*, which was evidently Copernican (see GALILEO GALILEI). Indeed, he first decided never to publish anything at all. But the despair did not last. Between 1634 and 1636, Descartes collected some of the material he had been working on, and prepared three essays for publication, the Géométrie, the Météors and the Dioptrique. These scientific essays were preceded by a general introduction, the *Discours de la méthode pour bien conduir sa raison et chercher la vérité dans les sciences* (*Discourse on the Method for Properly Conducting Reason and Searching for Truth in the Sciences*). The *Discourse* presents itself as autobiography, an account of the path the young author (the book was published anonymously) followed in his discoveries, including a summary of his method (Part II), of his early metaphysical speculations (Part IV) and of the programme of *The World* (Part V). In the scientific essays, Descartes presented some of his most striking results, hiding the foundational elements (such as his apparent Copernicanism and his rejection of scholastic form and matter) that would be most controversial.

While not uncontroversial, the *Discourse* and *Essays* were very successful, and induced Descartes to continue his programme for publishing his philosophy. The next work to appear was the *Meditationes* (*Meditations*) of 1641, which included an extensive selection of objections to the *Meditations* from various scholars in learned Europe, including HOBBES, GASSENDI, ARNAULD, and Mersenne himself, along with Descartes' responses, a total of seven sets in all (these are cited in this entry as the First Objections, Second Replies, and so on). This was followed in 1644 by the publication of the *Principia Philosophiae* (*Principles of Philosophy*) in which, after a review of his metaphysics, Descartes gives an exposition of his physics adapted and expanded from *The World*. French translations of the *Meditations* and the *Principles* done by others, but with important variants from the original Latin (presumably introduced by Descartes himself), appeared in 1647.

By the late 1630s, Descartes' work had entered the Dutch universities, and was taught at the University of Utrecht by Henricus Reneri and, following him, by Henricus REGIUS. Descartes' un-Aristotelian views called down the wrath of Gisbertus Voëtius, who

3

started a pamphlet war against Descartes and Regius that raged for some time. Descartes supported Regius, and gave him advice as to how to respond and contain the affair. Eventually, however, Descartes broke with him when Regius wrote and in 1646 published his *Fundamenta physices*, about which Descartes had severe reservations. Regius responded with a broadsheet, a kind of summary of his main theses, emphasizing their differences. Descartes, in turn, responded in 1648 with the Notae in programma quoddam (Comments on a Certain Broadsheet). There was a similar incident in Leiden, where Descartes had disciples (François du Ban, Adriaan Heereboord) as well as an influential enemy (Revius).

In the late 1640s Descartes was working on drafting and publishing more of his philosophy. Two additional parts of the *Principles* were planned, extending the work to cover elements of human biology. While notes remain in the form of an incomplete treatise on the human body (*La description du corps humain – Description of the Human Body*) and on the foetus (*Prima cogitationes circa generationem animalium – First Thoughts on the Generation of Animals*), the larger work was never finished. There are also important works concerning morals and moral psychology dating from these years. Some of this material is found in the letters to the Princess ELISABETH OF BOHEMIA, with whom he had a long and important correspondence, starting in 1643. Descartes' account of the passions is found in the last work he published in his lifetime, the short *Passions de l'âme* (*Passions of the Soul*), which appeared in 1649.

With the exception of a few short trips to Paris in 1644, 1647 and 1648, Descartes remained in the Low Countries until October 1649, when he was lured to Stockholm to be a member of the court of Queen Christina. There he fell ill in early 1650, and died on 11 February of that year.

2 The programme

Descartes' thought developed and changed over the years. But even so, there are a number of threads that run through it. Like most of his lettered contemporaries, Descartes was educated in a scholastic tradition that attempted to combine Christian doctrine with the philosophy of Aristotle. Indeed, at La Flèche, where he first learned philosophy, Aristotle as interpreted by Aquinas was at the centre of the curriculum. What he learned was an interconnected system of philosophy, including logic, physics, cosmology, metaphysics, morals and theology.

On his own account, Descartes rejected the Aristotelian philosophy as soon as he left school. From the notes Beeckman took on their conversations, it is probable that what dissatisfied him most in what he had been taught was natural philosophy. For an Aristotelian, the understanding of the natural world was grounded in a conception of body as composed of matter and form. Matter was that which remained constant even during the generation and corruption of bodies of different kinds, and that which all bodies of all sorts have in common; form was that which was responsible for the characteristic properties of particular sorts of bodies. For example, form was to explain why earth falls and tends to be cold, and why fire rises and tends to be hot. In contrast, though he came to reject Beeckman's rather strict atomism, Descartes seems to have been attracted to the kind of mechanistic view of the world that his mentor espoused. Descartes held from then on that the manifest properties of bodies must be explained in terms of the size, shape and motion of the tiny parts that make them up, and rejected the appeal to innate tendencies to behaviour that lay at the foundation of the Aristotelian view (see ARISTOTLE §8).

But even though he rejected much of the philosophy of the schools, there was one element that remained with him: like his teachers at La Flèche, Descartes always held that knowledge has a kind of systematic coherence. In Rule 1 of the *Rules* Descartes wrote that 'everything is so interconnected that it is far easier to learn all things together than it is to separate one from the others.... All [sciences are] connected with one another and depend upon one another'. Later, when he read Galileo's *Two New Sciences* (1638), Descartes dismissed the Italian scientist because his work lacked that kind of coherence (letter to Mersenne, 11 October 1638; Descartes 1984–91 vol 3: 124–8). His own project was to build his own interconnected system of knowledge, a system comprising an account of knowledge, a metaphysics, a physics and other sciences. This ambition is summarized in one of his last writings, the Preface to the French edition of the *Principles*, where he wrote that 'all philosophy is like a tree, whose roots are metaphysics, whose trunk is physics, and whose branches, which grow from this trunk, are all of the other sciences, which reduce to three principle sciences, namely medicine, mechanics, and morals'. In this way, Descartes saw himself as reconstituting the Aristotelian–Christian synthesis of the scholastics, grounded not in a natural philosophy of matter and form, but in a mechanist conception of body, where everything is to be explained in terms of size, shape and motion.

Certain important features of the Cartesian programme are worth special mention. The Aristotelian–Christian synthesis is founded in a variety of kinds of authority: the authority of the senses, the authority of ancient texts and the authority of his teachers. Descartes wanted to ground his thought in himself alone, and in the reason that God gave him. Since, Descartes claimed, reason gives us genuine certainty, this means that true knowledge is certain. In Rule 3 of the *Rules* he wrote that 'concerning things proposed, one ought to seek not what others have thought, nor what we conjecture, but what we can clearly and evidently intuit or deduce with certainty; for in no other way is knowledge acquired'. The rejection of the authority of the senses, texts and teachers shaped Descartes' thought in fundamental ways. Because of it, his philosophical system began with the Cogito Argument, which establishes the self as the starting-place of knowledge. Moreover, his two most influential works, the *Discourse* and the *Meditations*, were written in the first person so as to *show* the reader how Descartes did or might have come to his own state of knowledge and certainty, rather than *telling* readers what they are to believe, and thus setting himself up as an authority in his own right. Despite his rejection of authority, however, Descartes always claimed to submit himself to the authority of the Church on doctrinal matters, separating the domain of revealed theology from that of philosophy.

Another important feature of Descartes' tree of knowledge was its hierarchical organization. Throughout his career he held firmly to the notion that the interconnected body of knowledge that he sought to build has a particular order. Knowledge, for Descartes, begins in metaphysics, and metaphysics begins with the self. From the self we arrive at God, and from God we arrive at the full knowledge of mind and body. This, in turn, grounds the knowledge of physics, in which the general truths of physics (the nature of body as extension, the denial of the vacuum, the laws of nature) ground more particular truths about the physical world. Physics, in turn, grounds the applied sciences of medicine (the science of the human body), mechanics (the science of machines) and morals (the science of the embodied mind).

3 Method

Before beginning an account of the individual parts of Descartes' tree of knowledge, it is necessary to discuss his method. Method was the focus of his earliest philosophical writing, the *Rules*, and appeared prominently in his first published writing, the *Discourse on the Method*. But what exactly that method was is somewhat obscure.

In the second part of the *Discourse*, the method is presented as having four rules: (1) 'never to accept anything as true if I did not have evident knowledge of its truth: that is, carefully to avoid precipitate conclusions and preconceptions'; (2) 'to divide each of the difficulties I examined into as many parts as possible'; (3) 'to direct my thoughts in an orderly manner, by beginning with the simplest and most easily known objects in order to ascend little by little...to knowledge of the most complex'; and (4) 'throughout to make enumerations so complete and reviews so comprehensive, that I could be sure of leaving nothing out'. Given the general nature and apparent obviousness of these rules, it is not surprising that many of Descartes' contemporaries suspected him of hiding his *real* method from the public.

But Descartes' account of the method in the *Rules* is somewhat fuller. In Rule 5 he says: 'We shall be following this method exactly if we first reduce complicated and obscure propositions step by step to simpler ones, and then, starting with the intuition of the simplest ones of all, try to ascend through the same steps to a knowledge of all the rest'. This method is illustrated with an example in Rule 8. There Descartes considers the problem of the anaclastic line, the shape of a lens which will focus parallel lines to a single point. The first step in the solution of the problem, Descartes claims, is to see that 'the determination of this line depends on the ratio of the angles of refraction to the angles of incidence'. This, in turn, depends on 'the changes in these angles brought about by differences in the media'. But 'these changes depend on the manner in which a ray passes through the entire transparent body, and knowledge of this process presupposes also a knowledge of the nature of the action of light'. Finally, Descartes claims that this last knowledge rests on our knowledge of 'what a natural power in general is'. This last question can, presumably, be answered by intuition alone, that is, a purely rational apprehension of the truth of a proposition that has absolute certainty. Once we know what the nature of a natural power is, we can, Descartes thought, answer one by one all the other questions raised, and eventually answer the question originally posed, and determine the shape of the lens with the required properties. These successive answers are to be connected deductively (in a way outlined in the *Rules*) with the first intuition, so that successive answers follow intuitively from the first intuition.

The example of the anaclastic line suggests that Descartes' method proceeds as follows. One starts with a particular question, q_1. The reductive moment in the method then proceeds by asking what we have to know in order to answer the question originally posed. This leads us from q_1 to another question, q_2, whose answer is presupposed in order for us to be able to answer q_1; it is in this sense that q_1 is said to be reduced to q_2. This reductive process continues until we reach a question whose answer we are capable of knowing through intuition, say q_n. At that point, we begin what might be called the constructive moment of the method, and successively answer the questions we have posed for ourselves, using the answer to q_n to answer q_{n-1}, the answer to q_{n-1} to answer q_{n-2}, and so on until we arrive at q_1, the question originally posed, and answer that.

Understood in this way, the method has some very interesting properties. First, it results in knowledge that is completely certain. When we follow this method, the answer to the question originally posed is grounded in an intuition; the answers to the successive questions in the series are to be answered by deducing propositions from propositions that have been intuitively grasped as well. Second, the method imposes a certain structure on knowledge. As we follow the series of questions that constitute the reductive step of the method, we proceed from more specific questions to more general, from the shape of a particular lens to the law of refraction, and ultimately to the nature of a natural power. The answers that are provided in the constructive stage follow the opposite path, from the metaphysically more general and more basic to the more specific.

The *Rules* was written over a long period of time, and there are numerous strata of composition evident in the work as it survives. In a passage from Rule 8 that is probably in one of the last strata of composition, Descartes raises a problem for the method itself to confront, indeed the *first* problem that it should confront: 'The most useful inquiry we can make at this stage is to ask: What is human knowledge and what is its scope?... This is a task which everyone with the slightest love of truth ought to undertake at least once in life, since the true instruments of knowledge and the entire method are involved in the investigation of the problem'. While it is not entirely clear what Descartes had in mind here, it is not implausible to interpret him as raising the problem of the justification of intuition itself, the epistemological foundation of the method. In framing the method in the *Rules*, Descartes takes for granted that he has a faculty, intuition, by which he is capable of grasping truth in some immediate way, and that what he knows by intuition is worthy of trust. But why *should* we trust intuition? This, in essence, is one of the central questions in the *Meditations*, where Descartes argues that whatever we perceive clearly and distinctly is true.

Method was a central concern of Descartes' earlier writings, in both the *Rules* and the *Discourse*. In later writings it seemed to play little explicit role in his thought, but the hierarchical structure of knowledge with which the method is closely connected – the idea that knowledge is grounded in a structure of successively more metaphysically basic truths, ultimately terminating in an intuition – remained basic to his thought. In his later work, that ultimate intuition is not the nature of a natural power, as it was in the anaclastic line example, but the intuition that establishes the existence of the knowing subject, the Cogito Argument.

4 Doubt and the quest for certainty

In the *Rules for the Direction of the Mind*, Rule 2 reads: 'We should attend only to those objects of which our minds seem capable of having certain and indubitable cognition'. While, as we shall later see, Descartes seemed to relax this demand somewhat in his later writings, the demand for certainty was prominent throughout many of his writings. Historically, this can be seen as a reaction against important sceptical currents in Renaissance thought, the so-called 'Pyrrhonist Crisis'. In the face of the rapidly expanding boundaries of the European world in the sixteenth century, from new texts to new scientific discoveries to the discoveries of new worlds, contradictions and tensions in the intellectual world abounded, making it more and more attractive to hold, with the classical sceptics, that real knowledge is simply beyond the ability of human beings to acquire (see SCEPTICISM, RENAISSANCE; PYRRHONISM). Against this, Descartes asserted that real, certain knowledge is possible; though his name is associated with scepticism, it is as an opponent and not an advocate.

But though certainty was central to Descartes, the path to certainty begins with doubt. In Meditation I, entitled 'What can be called into doubt', Descartes says that 'I realised that it was necessary, once in the course of my life, to demolish everything completely and start again right from the foundations if I wanted to establish anything at all in the sciences that was stable and likely to last'. Following that, he presents a series of three sceptical arguments designed to eliminate his current beliefs in preparation for replacing them with certainties. The strategy is to undermine the beliefs, not one by one but by undermining 'the basic principles' on which they rest. While at least some of these arguments can be found in versions in the *Discourse* and in other writings by Descartes, they receive their fullest exposition in the *Meditations*.

The first argument is directed at the naïve belief that everything learned via the senses is worthy of belief. Against this Descartes points out that 'from time to time I have found that the senses deceive, and it is prudent never to trust completely those who have deceived us even once'. The second, the famous dream argument, is directed against the somewhat less naïve view that the senses are at least worthy of belief when dealing with middle-sized objects in our immediate vicinity: 'A brilliant piece of reasoning! As if I were not a man who sleeps at night. I plainly see that there are never any sure signs by means of which being awake can be distinguished from being asleep'. But even if I doubt the reliability of what the senses seem to be conveying to me right now, Descartes supposes, the dream argument still leaves open the possibility that there are some general truths, not directly dependent on my present sensations, that I can know. Descartes replies to this with his deceiving God argument.

This complex argument has two horns. Descartes first supposes 'the long-standing opinion that there is an omnipotent God who made me the kind of creature that I am'. Because God is omnipotent, he might have made me in such a way that I go wrong in even the simplest and most evident beliefs that I have – for example, that $2 + 3 = 5$, or that a square has four sides. Though God is thought to be good, the possibility that I am so deeply prone to error seems as consistent with his goodness as the fact that I go wrong even occasionally, at least at this stage of the investigation. But what if there is no God, or what if I arose by 'fate or chance or a continuous chain of events, or by some other means'? In this case, Descartes argues, the less powerful my original cause, 'the more likely it is that I am so imperfect as to be deceived all the time'.

With this, the sceptical arguments of Meditation I are complete: 'I am finally compelled to admit that there is not one of my former beliefs about which a doubt may not properly be raised'. But, Descartes notes, 'my habitual opinions keep coming back'. It is for that reason that Descartes posits his famous evil genius: 'I will suppose therefore that not God, who is supremely good and the source of truth, but rather some evil genius of the utmost power and cunning has employed all his energies in order to deceive me'. The evil genius (sometimes translated as the 'evil demon') is introduced here not as a separate argument for doubt, but as a device to help prevent the return of the former beliefs called into doubt.

These arguments have a crucial function in Descartes' project. As he notes in the introductory synopsis of the *Meditations*, these arguments 'free us from all our preconceived opinions, and provide the easiest route by which the mind may be led away from the senses'. In this way the sceptical doubt of Meditation I prepares the mind for the certainty to which Descartes aspired. But in the Third Replies,

responding to criticisms from Hobbes, Descartes notes two other roles that the sceptical arguments play in his thought. Descartes remarks that they are introduced 'so that I could reply to them in the subsequent Meditations'. As considered below, the deceiving God argument is answered in Meditations III and IV, and the dream argument is answered in the course of his discussion of sensation in Meditation VI. (Since Descartes, quite rightly, continued to maintain that sensation is not entirely trustworthy as a guide to how things really are, the first sceptical argument is never fully answered, though in Meditation VI he carefully sets out the conditions under which we can trust the senses.) Finally, he notes that the arguments are there as a kind of standard against which he can measure the certainty of his later conclusions: 'I wanted to show the firmness of the truths which I propounded later on, in the light of the fact that they cannot be shaken by these metaphysical doubts'. In all these ways, Descartes presented himself as addressing the sceptic, and defending a kind of dogmatic philosophy.

5 The Cogito Argument

Descartes' philosophy begins in doubt. The first step towards certainty, the Archimedean point from which the whole structure will grow, is the discovery of the existence of the self. At the beginning of Meditation II, reflecting on the evil genius posited at the end of Meditation I, Descartes observes: 'Let him deceive me as much as he can, he will never bring it about that I am nothing so long as I think that I am something. I must finally conclude that this proposition, *I am, I exist*, is necessarily true whenever it is put forward by me or conceived in my mind'. In the earlier *Discourse* (Part IV) and the later *Principles of Philosophy* (Part I §7), this proposition has the more familiar form, 'I am thinking, therefore I exist,' or, 'ego cogito, ergo sum,' in its Latin formulation. Here, it is called the Cogito Argument.

There is considerable discussion about how exactly Descartes thought this argument functions. There are two strains of interpretation that derive directly from his texts. In the Second Replies, Descartes observes that 'when we become aware that we are thinking things, this is a primary notion which is not derived by means of any syllogism'. This suggests that the Cogito Argument is known immediately by direct intuition. In the *Principles* (Part I §10), however, Descartes notes that before knowing the Cogito, we must grasp not only the concepts of thought, existence and certainty, but also the proposition that 'it is impossible that that which thinks should not exist'. This suggests that the Cogito *is* a kind of syllogism, in which I infer my existence from the fact that I am thinking, and with the premise that whatever thinks must exist. Recent analytic philosophers have also been attracted to the Cogito, trying to understand its obvious allure through speech act theory and theories of demonstratives (Hintikka 1967; Markie 1992). These accounts, however, are distant from anything that Descartes himself conceived.

There is also some confusion about what the conclusion of the Cogito Argument is supposed to be. In the body of Meditation II, Descartes clearly establishes the existence of the self as a thinking thing or a mind. But the title of Meditation II, 'The nature of the human mind, and how it is better known than the body' suggests that Descartes believed that he had established that the nature of the human mind is thought. Further still, in parallel texts in the *Discourse* (Part IV) and the *Principles* (Part I §7-8), Descartes suggests that the Cogito establishes the existence of a thinking substance distinct from the body, though in the text of Meditation II, this seems to be denied.

Though most closely associated with Descartes, the Cogito Argument may not be altogether original. A number of Descartes' contemporaries, both during his life and afterwards, noticed the connection between the Cogito and similar formulations in Augustine (see AUGUSTINE §2). However, what was important to Descartes about the Cogito is the foundational role it plays in his system. For Descartes, it is 'the first thing we come to know when we philosophise in an orderly way' (*Principles*: Part I §7). Common sense might think that the physical world of bodies, known through sensation, is more accessible to us than is the mind, a thinking thing whose existence is established, even though we have rejected the senses. But, as Descartes argues in Meditation II using the example of a piece of wax, despite our prejudices, bodies are not conceived through the senses or the imagination but through the same process of purely intellectual conception that gives us the conception of ourselves as thinking things. Furthermore, knowledge of the external world is less certain than knowledge of the mind, since whatever thought could lead us to a probable belief in the existence of bodies will lead us to believe in the existence of the self with certainty.

The project, then, is to build the entire world from the thinking self. It is important here that it is not just the mind that is the foundation, but *my* mind. In this way, the starting place of philosophy for Descartes was connected with the rejection of authority that is central to the Cartesian philosophy. In beginning with the Cogito, we build a philosophy detached from history and tradition.

6 God

The next stage in the system, as outlined in the *Meditations*, seeks to establish that God exists. In his writings, Descartes made use of three principal arguments. The first (at least in the order of presentation in the *Meditations*) is a causal argument. While its fullest statement is in Meditation III, it is also found in the *Discourse* (Part IV) and in the *Principles* (Part I §§17-18). The argument begins by examining the thoughts contained in the mind, distinguishing between the formal reality of an idea and its objective reality. The formal reality of any thing is just its actual existence and the degree of its perfection; the formal reality of an idea is thus its actual existence and degree of perfection as a mode of mind. The objective reality of an idea is the degree of perfection it has, considered now with respect to its content. (This conception extends naturally to the formal and objective reality of a painting, a description or any other representation.) In this connection, Descartes recognized three fundamental degrees of perfection connected with the capacity a thing has for independent existence, a hierarchy implicit in the argument of Meditation III and made explicit in the Third Replies (in response to Hobbes). The highest degree is that of an infinite substance (God), which depends on nothing; the next degree is that of a finite substance (an individual body or mind), which depends on God alone; the lowest is that of a mode (a property of a substance), which depends on the substance for its existence. Descartes claims that 'it is manifest by the natural light that there must be at least as much reality in the efficient and total cause as in the effect of that cause'. From that he infers that there must be as much *formal* reality in the cause of an idea as there is *objective* reality in the idea itself. This is a bridge principle that allows Descartes to infer the existence of causes from the nature of the particular ideas that are in the mind, and thus are effects of some causes or another. In Meditation III, Descartes discusses various classes of ideas, one by one, and concludes that, as a finite substance, he can conceivably be the cause of all the ideas he has in his mind except for one: the idea of God. Since the idea of God is an idea of something that has infinite perfection, the only thing that can cause that idea in my mind is a thing that formally (actually) has the perfection that my idea has objectively – that is, God himself.

Descartes used two other arguments for the existence of God in his writings. In Meditation III, following the causal argument, he offers a version of the cosmological argument for those who, still blinded by the senses, may be reluctant to accept the bridge principle that his causal argument requires. (Versions of this argument are also found in *Discourse* Part IV, and in *Principles* Part I §§20–1.) This argument begins with the author's own existence, as established in Meditation II. But, the author might ask, what could have created me? It will not do, Descartes argues, to suggest that I have been in existence always, and thus I do not need a creator, since it takes as much power to sustain me from moment to moment as it does to create me anew. I could not have created myself because then I would have been able to give myself all the perfections that I so evidently lack. Furthermore, if I could create myself, then I could also sustain myself, which I do not have the power to do; being a thinking thing, if I had such a power, I would be aware of having it. My parents cannot be my creators, properly speaking, since they have neither the ability to create a thinking thing (which is all I know myself to be at this stage of the *Meditations*), nor to sustain it once created. Finally, I could not have been created by another creature of lesser perfection than God, since I have an idea of God, an idea I could not acquire from a lesser being. (Here one suspects that this cosmological argument really collapses into the first causal argument.) From this Descartes concludes 'that the mere fact that I exist and have within me an idea of a most perfect being...provides a very clear proof that God indeed exists'.

These first two arguments for the existence of God play a central role in the validation of reason, as discussed below. But after reason has been validated on theological grounds, Descartes presents in Meditation V a version of the ontological argument (see GOD, ARGUMENTS FOR THE EXISTENCE OF §§2–3). After reflecting on the basis of geometric reasoning, the fact that 'everything which I clearly and distinctly perceive to belong to that thing really does belong to it', Descartes concludes that this applies to the idea of God as well. Hence he concludes that 'it is quite evident that existence can no more be separated from the essence of God than the fact that its three angles equal to two right angles can be separated from the essence of a triangle, or than the idea of a mountain can be separated from the idea of a valley'. Though apparently circular in so far as its validity seems to depend on the prior arguments for the existence of God, it is not; Descartes' point is that 'even if it turned out that not everything on which I have meditated in these past days is true, I ought still to regard the existence of God as having at least the same level of certainty as I have hitherto attributed to the truths of mathematics'. As with the other two arguments, Descartes' ontological argument is also found in the *Discourse* (Part IV) and in the *Principles* (Part I §§14–16); indeed, in the *Principles* it is the first argument he gives.

As noted above, the existence of God plays a major role in the validation of reason. But it also plays a major role in two other parts of Descartes' system. As we shall later see in connection with Descartes' physics, God is the first cause of motion, and the sustainer of motion in the world. Furthermore, because of the way he sustains motion, God constitutes the ground of the laws of motion. Finally, Descartes held that God is the creator of the so-called eternal truths. In a series of letters in 1630, Descartes enunciated the view that 'the mathematical truths which you call eternal have been laid down by God and depend on Him entirely no less than the rest of His creatures' (letter to Mersenne, 15 April 1630; Descartes 1984–91 vol 3: 23), a view that Descartes seems to have held into his mature years. While it never again gets the prominence it had in 1630, it is clearly present both in correspondence (for example, letter to Arnauld, 29 July 1648; Descartes 1984–91 vol 3: 358–9) and in published writings (for example, in the Sixth Responses).

Various commentators have proposed that Descartes was really an atheist, and that he includes the arguments for the existence of God as window dressing. While this is not impossible, the frequent appeal to God in philosophical contexts, both in private letters and in published work, suggests that it is rather unlikely.

7 The validation of reason

With the existence of God established, the next stage in Descartes' programme is the validation of reason. At the beginning of Meditation III, before proving God's existence, Descartes notes that the uncertainty that remains is due only to the fact that the meditator does not know whether or not there is a God and, if there is, if he can be a deceiver. This suggests that all one must do to restore reason and defeat the third and most general sceptical argument presented in Meditation I is to prove that there is a benevolent God. And at the end of Meditation III, after two proofs for the existence of God, Descartes concludes directly that this God 'cannot be a deceiver, since it is manifest by the natural light that all fraud and deception depend on some defect'. But this is not enough. In the course of the deceiving-God argument of Meditation I, Descartes notes that if some deception is consistent with divine benevolence, then total deception would be as well. Since it is undeniable that we do make mistakes from time to time, and are thus deceived, this raises a problem for Descartes: what, if anything, does God's benevolence and veracity guarantee?

Descartes answers this question by way of an account of error in Meditation IV. Roughly speaking, the mistakes I make are due to myself and my (improper) exercise of my free will, while the truths I come to know are because of the way God made me. More exactly, Descartes asserts that judgments depend on two faculties of the mind, 'namely, on the faculty of knowledge [or intellect] which is in me, and on the faculty of choice or freedom of the will'. A judgment is made when the will assents to an idea that is in the intellect. But the intellect is finite and limited in the sense that it does not have ideas of all possible things. On the other hand, the will is indefinite in its extent, Descartes claims: 'It is only the will or freedom of choice which I experience within me to be so great that the idea of any greater faculty is beyond my grasp'. It is in our free will that we most resemble God. In certain circumstances, Descartes held, 'a great light in the intellect is followed by a great inclination in the will', and in this way the intellect determines the will to assent. This, he thought, is a proper use of the will in judgment. In this situation, where the intellect determines the will to assent, Descartes talks of our having a clear and distinct perception of a truth. In this case, God has made us in such a way that we cannot but assent. (Clear and distinct perceptions are very close to what he calls 'intuitions' in the *Rules*, as discussed above.) But because the will has a greater extent than the intellect, and is not restrained by it, sometimes things outside the intellect move the will to assent. This is where error enters: 'The scope of the will is wider than that of the intellect; but instead of restricting it within the same limits, I extend its use to matters which I do not understand. Since the will is indifferent in such cases, it easily turns aside from what is true and good, and this is the source of my error and sin'. In this way, I am responsible for error by extending my will beyond where it belongs. God can in no way be held accountable for my mistakes any more than he can be responsible for my sins. I cannot reproach my maker for not having given me more ideas in the intellect than I have, nor can I fault him for having made me more perfect by giving me a free will. But as a result of a limited intellect and a free will, it is possible for me both to make mistakes and to sin.

As a result of this analysis of error, Descartes is able, in Meditation IV to assert his famous principle of clear and distinct perception, an epistemological principle to replace the principles that were rejected as a result of the sceptical arguments of Meditation I: 'If I simply refrain from making a judgement in cases where I do not perceive the truth with sufficient clarity and distinctness, then it is clear that I am behaving correctly and avoiding error. But if in such cases I either affirm or deny, then I am not using my free will correctly'. With this, reason is validated, and the deceiving-God argument answered. Yet, this does not end Descartes' engagement with the sceptical arguments of Meditation I, and in Meditation VI he also addresses the question of the reliability of the senses, presents a limited validation of sensory knowledge, and answers the dream argument.

The validation of reason, central as it is to Descartes' project in the *Meditations*, has one apparent flaw: it seems to be circular. The validation of reason in Meditation IV depends on the proof of the existence of God which, in turn, depends on the proof of the existence of the self as a thinking thing. But evidently we must assume that clear and distinct perceptions are trustworthy in order to trust the Cogito and the proofs for the existence of God that ground the validation of reason – the so-called 'Cartesian Circle'. Two of the objectors to the *Meditations* noticed this point, and elicited responses from Descartes, in the Second and the Fourth Replies. Descartes' answer is not altogether clear. In the *Second Replies* he remarks, in answer to one such objection, that 'when I said that we can know nothing for certain until we are aware that God exists, I expressly declared that I was speaking only of knowledge of those conclusions' deduced by long arguments, and not of 'first principles', such as the Cogito Argument. This suggests that Descartes would exempt immediately intuitable (self-evident) propositions from the scope of the doubt of Meditation I, and use them as tools for establishing the premises of the argument that leads to the validation of reason in Meditation IV. There are serious problems with this approach. For one, it seems arbitrary to exempt self-evident propositions from the scope of doubt. Such propositions would seem to fall quite naturally among those most obvious of things that Descartes calls into doubt there; if God could create me in such a way that I go wrong when I add two and three, he could create me in such a way that I go wrong with any other self-evident belief. Furthermore, even if those propositions that are immediately evident are outside the scope of doubt, Descartes' proofs for the existence of God, necessary premises of his validation of reason, are not self-evident. These apparent problems might be either weaknesses in Descartes' response, or reasons to doubt that we have understood Descartes correctly in his responses.

The problem of circularity and the obvious problems in Descartes' apparent answer have elicited numerous examinations of the issue in the commentary literature. It is not clear just what Descartes' own solution was, nor whether or not there is a good response to the Cartesian Circle. But whatever the answer, the problem is not a superficial oversight on Descartes' part. It is a deep philosophical problem that will arise in some form or another whenever one attempts a rational defence of reason.

8 Mind and body

One of Descartes' most celebrated positions is the distinction between the mind and the body. Descartes did not invent the position. It can be found in various forms in a number of earlier thinkers. It is a standard feature of Platonism and, in a different form, is common to most earlier Christian philosophers, who generally held that some feature of the human being – its mind or its soul – survives the death of the body (see PLATO §13). But the particular features of Descartes' way of drawing the distinction and the arguments that he used were very influential on later thinkers.

There are suggestions, particularly in the *Discourse* (Part IV) and in the *Principles* (Part I §§7–8) that the distinction between mind and body follows directly from the Cogito Argument, as discussed above. However, in the *Meditations* Descartes is quite clear that the distinction is to be established on other grounds. In Meditation VI he argues as follows: I have a clear and distinct idea of myself as a thinking non-extended thing, and a clear and distinct idea of body as an extended and non-thinking thing. Whatever I can conceive clearly and distinctly, God can so create. So, Descartes argues, the mind, a thinking thing, can exist apart from its extended body. And therefore, the mind is a substance distinct from the body, a substance whose essence is thought.

Implicit in this argument is a certain conception of what it means to be a substance, a view made explicit in the *Principles* (Part I §51) which defines a substance as 'nothing other than a thing which exists in such a way as to depend on no other thing for its existence', no other thing but God, of course. In so far as the mind can exist independently of the body, it is a substance on this definition. (God is the third kind of substance, along with mind and body, though because of his absolute independence, he is a substance in a somewhat different sense.) On Descartes' metaphysics, each substance has a principal attribute, an attribute that characterizes its nature. For mind it is thought, and for body it is extension. In addition, substances have modes, literally ways of instantiating the attributes. So, for Descartes, particular ideas, particular volitions, particular passions are modes of mind, and particular shapes, sizes and motions are modes of body.

Descartes' conception of mind and body represents significant departures from the conceptions of both notions in the late scholastic thought in which he was educated. For the late scholastics, working in the Aristotelian tradition, body is composed of matter and form. Matter is that which remains constant in change, while form is that which gives bodies the characteristic properties that they have. For Descartes, however, all body is of the same kind, a substance that contains only geometric properties, the objects of geometry made concrete. The characteristic properties of particular forms of body are explained in terms of the size, shape and motion of its insensible parts (see §11 below). For the late scholastics, the mind is connected with the account of life. On the Aristotelian view, the soul is the principle of life, that which distinguishes a living thing from a dead thing; it is also taken to be the form that pertains to the living body. The mind is the rational part of the soul, that which characterizes humans, and not usually considered a genuine substance, though by most accounts, with divine aid, it can survive the death of the body (see NOUS; PSYCHE). For Descartes, the majority of the vital functions are explained in terms of the physical organization of the organic body. The mind, thus, is not a principle of life but a principle of thought. It involves reason, as does the rational soul of the Aristotelians, but it also involves other varieties of thought, which pertain to other parts of the Aristotelian soul (see ARISTOTLE §17). Furthermore, it is a genuine substance, and survives the death of the body naturally and not through special divine intervention.

Mind and body are distinct because they can exist apart from one another. However, in this life, they do not. In Meditation VI Descartes observed: 'Nature also teaches me, by these sensations of pain, hunger, thirst and so on that I am not merely present in my body as a sailor is present in a ship, but that I am very closely and, as it were, intermingled with it, so that I and the body form a unit'. He sometimes went so far as to say that the human mind is the form of the human body, the only kind of form that he recognizes in nature, and that the human being – the union of a mind and a body – constitutes a genuine substance, though the context of these statements suggests that they may be made more for orthodoxy's sake than an expression of his own views (see, for example, the letter to Regius, January 1642 (Descartes 1984–91 vol 3: 208), where he is advising Regius on the best way to answer the attacks made by the more orthodox Aristotelian Gisbertus Voëtius in connection with the controversy at Utrecht.) But be that as it may, he was clearly committed to holding that the mind and the body are united. Some of his contemporaries found it difficult to understand how two such different substances could interact and be joined. Sometimes Descartes dismissed this objection by saying that it is no more difficult than understanding how form and matter unite for the Aristotelians, something that everyone learns at school (letter to Arnauld, 29 July 1648; Descartes 1984–91 vol 3: 358). But elsewhere, particularly in an important exchange of letters with the Princess Elisabeth of Bohemia, Descartes offered a different explanation, remarking that it is simply an empirical fact that they do unite and interact, something that we learn from everyday experience, and suggesting that just as we have innate notions that allow us to understand the notions of thinking and extended substance, we also have an innate notion that allows us to comprehend how mind and body interact, and how together they can constitute a unity (letters to Elisabeth, 21 May 1643 and 28 June 1643; Descartes 1984–91 vol 3: 217–20, 226–9).

According to Descartes, the mind is joined to the body in one specific place: the pineal gland, a single gland in the centre of the brain, between the two lobes. This is the spot in which interaction takes place. The mind has the ability to move the pineal gland, and by doing so, to change the state of the brain in such a way as to produce voluntary motions. Similarly, the sensory organs all transmit their information to the pineal gland and, as a result of that, sensation is transmitted to the attached mind. However, because of the interconnection of the parts that make up the organic body, by virtue of being connected to the pineal gland, the mind can properly be said to be connected with the body as a whole (*Passions*: §§30–2) (see PERSONS).

9　The external world and sensation

The argument for the distinction between mind and body in Meditation VI establishes the nature of body as extension, but it does not establish the real existence of the world of bodies outside of the mind. This is the focus of the last series of arguments in the *Meditations*. The argument begins in Meditation VI with the recognition that I have 'a passive faculty of sensory perception', which would be useless unless there was also an 'active faculty, either in me or in something else' which produces the ideas of sensation. Descartes has already established in Meditation IV that the mind has only two faculties – a passive faculty of perception, and the active faculty of will. Since it is passive, perception cannot be the source of my ideas of sensation, and since sensations are involuntary, they cannot be the product of my will. So, the ideas of sense must come from somewhere else. God 'has given me a great propensity to believe that they are produced by corporeal things', and no means to correct my error if that propensity is deceptive. So, Descartes concluded, God would be a deceiver if my sensory ideas come from anything but from bodies. This argument does not prove that everything we sense about bodies is reliable, but only that 'they possess all the properties which I clearly and distinctly understand, that is, all those which, viewed in general terms, are comprised within the subject-matter of pure mathematics'. (In the *Principles* Part II §1 there is also an argument for the existence of the external world, but it is somewhat different.)

The proof of the existence of the external world tells us that, in general, bodies are the causes of our sensations and it tells us, in general, what the nature of body is. But it does not seem to tell us much about what we can (and cannot) learn about specific bodies in the world around us in specific circumstances. These questions are addressed at the end of Meditation VI in a general discussion of the reliability of sensation, the most extensive such discussion in Descartes' writings. He argues there that the senses are given to me 'simply to inform the mind of what is beneficial or harmful for the composite of which the mind is a part; and to this extent they are sufficiently clear and distinct'. That is, while they cannot tell me anything about the real nature of things – that is for the intellect or reason to determine – they can inform me about specific features of my environment that relate to maintaining the union of my mind and body. So, for example, when the senses tell us that some particular apples are red and others green, this can give us reliable information that some may be ripe (and thus nutritious) and others not, but it cannot tell us that the one is, in its nature, red, and the other really green. Similarly, when I feel a pain in my toe, this tells me that there is damage to my toe, not that there is something resembling the sensation that is actually in the toe. Even in this, the sensation may be misleading. As Descartes points out, people sometimes feel pain in limbs even after they have been amputated.

Given the nature of the extended body, and the causal process by which pains (and other sensations) are transmitted through the body to the pineal gland, where the non-extended mind is joined to the extended body, such misleading sensations are inevitable; similar sensations in the mind can be the result of very different causal processes in the body. For example, a sensation of pain-in-the-toe can be caused either by a change in the state of the toe itself, or by an appropriate stimulation of the nerve connecting the toe to the brain at any point between the two. But, Descartes claims, though sensation is fallible, 'I know that in matters regarding the well-being of the body, all my senses report the truth much more frequently than not'. Furthermore, I can use multiple senses and memory, together with the intellect, 'which has by now examined all the causes of error' in order to weigh the evidence of the senses and use it properly. And with this, Descartes is finally able to answer the dream argument of Meditation I. For my waking experience is interconnected in a way in which my dreaming experience is not; the things I see in waking life, unlike those in dreams, come to me through all my senses, and connect with my memory of other objects. I can use this interconnectedness of waking experience, together with my intellect and my knowledge of the causes of error, to sort out veridical sensations and distinguish them from the deceptive sensory experiences of dreams. Sometimes even my waking experiences will be deceptive, of course, but we are capable of determining specific circumstances in which the senses are worthy of our trust. And so, contrary to the original doubts raised by the dreaming argument in Meditation I, there is no general reason to reject waking experience as such.

Though subordinated to reason, sensation, cast into doubt in Meditation I, re-enters as a legitimate source of knowledge about the world by the end of Meditation VI.

10 Philosophical psychology and morals

Morality was a concern of Descartes' in a variety of texts. In the third part of his *Discourse* he presents what he calls a 'provisional morality', a morality to govern our behaviour while we are in the process of revising our beliefs and coming to certainty. In the tree of philosophy in the Preface to the French edition of the *Principles*, morals is listed as one of the fruits of the tree, along with medicine and mechanics. It is also a theme in the letters he exchanged with the Princess Elisabeth of Bohemia in the mid-1640s, together with another concern – the passions, what they are and, more importantly, how to control them. These themes are intertwined again in Descartes' last major work, the *Passions of the Soul* (1649).

In one of the letters that serves as a preface to the *Passions*, Descartes announces that he will treat the passions 'only as a natural philosopher [*en physicien*], and not as a rhetorician or even as a moral philosopher'. Accordingly, the bulk of the *Passions* is taken up with detailed accounts of what the passions are, and how they arise from the connection between the human body and the human mind. As Descartes conceived them, the passions are grouped with sensation and imagination, perceptions of the mind that arise from external impulses. In this respect, Descartes differed radically from the Aristotelian scholastic philosophers who attached the passions to the appetitive faculty rather than the perceptive. But though grouped with other perceptions, the ones that

concern Descartes in this treatise are a special group of perceptions, 'those whose effects we feel as being in the soul itself, and for which we do not normally know any proximate cause to which we can refer them', those 'which are caused, maintained, and strengthened by some movement of the spirits' (*Passions*: §§25, 27). (The 'spirits' in question are the animal spirits, a fluid matter that played a major role in Descartes' biology.) The principal effect of the passions is to 'move and dispose the soul to want the things for which they prepare the body. Thus the feeling of fear moves the soul to want to flee, that of courage to want to fight' and so on (*Passions*: §40). As with sensations, the passions of the soul play a role in the preservation of the mind–body union: 'The function of all the passions consists solely in this, that they dispose our soul to want the things which nature deems useful for us, and to persist in this volition; and the same agitation of the spirits which normally causes the passions also disposes the body to make movements which help us to attain these things' (*Passions*: §52).

For the schoolmen, the passions pertained to the appetitive faculty, and were principally organized around a distinction between the 'irascible' and the 'concupiscent' appetites. Descartes, however, was attempting to fashion a conception of the passions based on a very different conception of the soul, one in which there is no distinction among appetites (*Passions*: §68). His categorization of the passions was based on a list of six primitive passions, which pertain to the perceptive rather than to the appetitive faculty: wonder, desire, love and hatred, joy and sadness – 'all the others are either composed from some of these six or they are species of them' (*Passions*: §69). Much of his attention in the short book is directed at accounts of what each of these basic passions is, what it feels like and its physiological causes and effects in the body, and how all the other passions can be understood in terms of the six basic ones.

But although Descartes presents himself as examining the passions '*en physicien*', there is a moral dimension to the discussion as well. Part of the motivation for the examination of the passions is their control. While the passions, like everything given to us by God, can contribute to our well-being, they can also be excessive and must be controlled (*Passions*: §211). While the passions are not under our direct control, by understanding what they are and how they are caused we can learn indirect means for controlling them (*Passions*: §§45–50; 211). This, Descartes asserts, is the 'chief use of wisdom, [which] lies in its teaching us to be masters of our passions and to control them with such skill that the evils which they cause are quite bearable, and even become a source of joy' (*Passions*:

§212). Important in this process is what Descartes calls *générosité*, best translated as 'nobility'. *Générosité* is the knowledge that all that belongs to us, properly speaking, is our own free will, and the resolution to use it well, 'that is, never to lack the will to undertake and carry out whatever one judges to be best' (1649: §53). Understood in this way, *générosité* is both a passion (an immediate feeling) and a virtue ('a habit of the soul which disposes it to have certain thoughts') (*Passions*: §§160–1). The person who has *générosité* 'has very little esteem for everything that depends on others', and as a result, Descartes claims, is able to control their passions (*Passions*: §156).

11 Physics and mathematics

To his contemporaries, Descartes was as well-known for his system of physics as he was for the metaphysical views that are now more studied. Indeed, as he indicates in the Preface to the French edition of the *Principles*, metaphysics constitutes the roots of the tree of philosophy, but the trunk is physics.

Descartes' physics was developed in two main places. The earliest is in the treatise *Le Monde* (*The World*) which he suppressed when Galileo was condemned for Copernicanism in 1633, though summarized in Part V of the *Discourse*. Later, in the early 1640s, he presented much of the material in a more carefully worked-out form, in Parts II, III and IV of the *Principles*. Like the physical thought of many of his contemporaries, his physics can be divided into two parts – a general part, which includes accounts of matter and the general laws of nature, and a specific part, which includes an account of particular phenomena.

The central doctrine at the foundations of Descartes' physics is the claim that the essence of body is extension (discussed in §8 above). This doctrine excludes substantial forms and any sort of sensory qualities from body. For the schoolmen there are four primary qualities (wet and dry, hot and cold) which characterize the four elements. For Descartes, these qualities are sensations in the mind, and only in the mind; bodies are in their nature simply the objects of geometry made real. Descartes also rejected atoms and the void, the two central doctrines of the atomists, an ancient school of philosophy whose revival by Gassendi and others constituted a major rival among contemporary mechanists. Because there can be no extension without an extended substance, namely body, there can be no space without body, Descartes argued. His world was a plenum, and all motion must ultimately be circular, since one body must give way to another in order for there to be a place for it to enter (*Principles* II: §§2–19, 33). Against

atoms, he argued that extension is by its nature indefinitely divisible: no piece of matter is in its nature indivisible (*Principles* II: §20). Yet he agreed that, since bodies are simply matter, the apparent diversity between them must be explicable in terms of the size, shape and motion of the small parts that make them (*Principles* II: §§23, 64) (see LEIBNIZ, G.W. §4).

Accordingly, motion and its laws played a special role in Descartes' physics. The essentials of this account can be found in *The World*, but it is set out most clearly in the *Principles*. There (*Principles* II: §25), motion is defined as the translation of a body from one neighbourhood of surrounding bodies into another. Descartes is careful to distinguish motion itself from its cause(s). While, as we have seen, motion is sometimes caused by the volition of a mind, the general cause of motion in the inanimate world is God, who creates bodies and their motion, and sustains them from moment to moment. From the constancy of the way in which God sustains motion, Descartes argues, the same quantity of motion is always preserved in the world, a quantity that is measured by the size of a body multiplied by its speed (*Principles* II: §36). To this general conservation law he adds three more particular laws of nature, also based on the constancy by which God conserves his creation. According to the first law, everything retains its own state, in so far as it can. As a consequence, what is in motion remains in motion until interfered with by an external cause, a principle directly opposed to the Aristotelian view that things in motion tend to come to rest (*Principles* II: §§37–8). According to the second law, bodies tend to move in rectilinear paths, with the result that bodies in circular motion tend to move away at the tangent (*Principles* II: §39). The first and second laws together arguably constitute the first published statement of what NEWTON, later called the law of inertia. Descartes' third law governs the collision between bodies, specifying when one body imposes its motion on another, and when two bodies rebound from one another without exchanging motion. The abstract law is followed by seven specific rules covering special cases (*Principles* II: §§40–52). Though the law of collision turns out to be radically inadequate, it casts considerable light on Descartes' conception of the physical world. One of the determinants of the outcome of a collision is what Descartes calls the 'force' of a body, both its force for continuing in motion, and its resistance to change in its motion (*Principles* II: §§43). The role of such forces in Descartes' mechanist world has generated much discussion, since they would seem to be completely inconsistent with Descartes' view that the essence of body is extension alone.

These general accounts of matter and motion form

the basis of Descartes' physical theories of particular phenomena. The *Principles* goes on to explain how the earth turns around the sun in an enormous fluid vortex and how the light that comes from the sun is nothing but the centrifugal force of the fluid in the vortex, with ingenious explanations of many other particular phenomena in terms of the size, shape and motion of their parts. Other works contain further mechanistic explanations, for example of the law governing the refraction of light (*Dioptrics* II) and the way colours arise in the rainbow (*Meteors* VIII).

Descartes' hope was that he could begin with an assumption about how God created the world, and then deduce, on the basis of the laws of motion, how the world would have to have come out (*Discourse* V, VI; *Principles* III: §46). But this procedure caused some problems. It is not easy to specify just how God might have created the world – whether the particles that he first created were of the same size, for example, or of every possible size. Furthermore, any hypothesis of this sort would seem to be inconsistent with the account of creation in Genesis (*Principles* III: §§43–7). These difficulties aside, it seemed obvious to Descartes how to proceed. For example, from his denial of the vacuum it would seem to follow that bodies in motion would sort themselves out into circular swirls of matter, the vortices which were to explain the circulation of the planets around a central sun. Similarly, Descartes used the tendency to centrifugal motion generated by the circular motion of the vortex to explain light, which, he claimed, was the pressure of the subtle matter in the vortex. But the very complexity of the world militates against the full certainty that Descartes originally sought, particularly when dealing with the explanation of particular phenomena, such as the magnet. Indeed, by the end of the *Principles*, it can seem that he has given up the goal of certainty and come to accept the kind of probability that he initially rejected (*Principles* IV: §§204–6).

Central to Descartes' physics is his rejection of final causes: 'When dealing with natural things we will, then, never derive any explanations from the purposes which God or nature may have had in view when creating them. For we should not be so arrogant as to suppose that we can share in God's plans' (*Principles* I: §28). The emphasis on efficient causes was to prove very controversial later in the century.

One especially curious feature of Descartes' physics, however, is the lack of any substantive role for mathematics. Descartes was one of the great mathematicians of his age. While it is, perhaps, anachronistic to see modern analytic geometry and so-called Cartesian coordinates in his *Geometry* (1637), there is no question but that it is a work of real depth and influence. In it he shows how one could use algebra to solve geometric problems and geometry to solve algebraic problems by showing how algebraic operations could be interpreted purely in terms of the manipulation and construction of line segments. In traditional mathematics, if a quantity was represented as a given line, then the square of that quantity was represented as a square constructed with that line as a side, and the cube of the quantity represented as a cube constructed with that line as an edge, effectively limiting the geometric representation of algebraic operations to a very few. By demonstrating how the square, cube (and so on) of a given quantity could all be represented as other lines, Descartes opened the way to a more complete unification of algebra and geometry. Also important to his mathematical work was the notion of analysis. Descartes saw himself as reviving the work of the ancient mathematician, Pappus of Alexandria, and setting out a methodology for the solution of problems, a methodology radically different from the Euclidean style of doing geometry in terms of definitions, axioms, postulates and propositions, which he regarded as a method of presentation rather than a method of discovery. According to the procedure of analysis, as Descartes understood it, one begins by labelling unknowns in a geometric problem with letters, setting out a series of equations that involve these letters, and then solving for the unknowns to the extent that this is possible.

Unlike his contemporary, Galileo, or his successors, Leibniz and Newton, Descartes never quite figured out how to apply his mathematical insights to the physical world. Indeed, it is a curious feature of his tree of knowledge that, despite the central place occupied by mathematics in his own accomplishments, it seems to have no place there.

12 Life and the foundations of biology

The last part of the Cartesian programme was his biology. First presented in the Treatise on Man, part of *The World* project which was abandoned in 1633 when Galileo was condemned, Descartes intended to rework some of that material and publish it – as Parts V and VI of the *Principles* under the title 'De Homine'. Although he never finished this rewriting, it is clear from the notes left behind that it was very much on his mind in years that preceded his sudden and premature death.

His hope seems to have been to show how, from matter and the laws of motion alone, life would arise spontaneously as matter came to organize itself in an appropriate way (Discourse V). Unfortunately he never worked out this view, suggestive of later theories of evolution, in any detail. Yet, he was quite clear that all the functions of life (with the exception of thought and reason in humans) are to be explained not in terms of the soul, the principle of life, but in terms of matter in motion. Accordingly, in the Treatise on Man, he accounts for a variety of phenomena, including digestion, involuntary motion, the action of the heart, and sense perception, in purely mechanical terms. (Summarized in *Discourse* Part V, with special emphasis on the circulation of the blood.)

While Descartes' biology was controversial among his contemporaries, one aspect was especially so. According to his account, there is only one kind of soul in the world, the rational soul, which humans and angels have and animals do not. Humans are organic machines, collections of matter organized so as to be able to perform vital functions, attached to rational souls. Animals, on the other hand, are just machines: their behaviour is purely mechanical and they are, strictly speaking, incapable of conscious experience of any sort (Discourse V).

13 The Cartesian heritage

It is difficult to overestimate the influence of Descartes. In philosophy, the Cogito Argument signalled the centrality of the self and the rejection of authority from without, the authority of both texts and teacher. For physics, Descartes represented the rejection of the scholastic physics of matter and form, and its replacement by a mechanistic physics of matter and motion. So in biology, he stood for mechanism and the rejection of Aristotelian vitalism.

Descartes had many followers who took his ideas (as they understood them) as dogma, and developed them as they thought he would have wanted them to do. The most important centres of Cartesian thought were France, where he was remembered as a countryman, despite his long absence, and the Netherlands, where he had lived. In France, his thought was carried on by a circle around Claude Clerselier, who gathered and published his letters as well as other works. Louis de LA FORGE commented on Descartes' physiology, and wrote a Cartesian treatise on the mind, extending Descartes' ideas. Gerauld de CORDEMOY, tried to blend Cartesian philosophy with atomism, to the puzzlement of most of his contemporaries. Jacques ROHAULT was influential in Cartesian physics well after Newton had published the work that would eventually eclipse such theories. Other followers, mainly in the Low Countries, include Henricus REGIUS, considered Cartesian by many despite Descartes' public rejection; Adriaan Heereboord, one of Descartes' partisans in Leiden; Johannes de Raey, one of those who attempted to reconcile Descartes with the true philosophy of Aristotle; and Johannes

CLAUBERG, who recast Cartesianism into more scholastic garb. There were many more minor Cartesians of various nationalities. Late seventeenth-century Europe was flooded with paraphrases of and commentaries on Descartes' writings.

Other more independent thinkers were strongly influenced by Descartes without explicitly being followers. The best-known such figure is probably Nicolas MALEBRANCHE. While his thought owes much to other influences, particularly to seventeenth-century Augustinianism, in his *Recherche de la vérité* (*Search after Truth*) (1674–5) he follows Descartes in offering a critique of the senses, rejecting the authority of tradition, and appealing to clear and distinct perceptions. Descartes was also an important influence on the Cambridge Platonist Henry MORE, who regarded Descartes' philosophy, in particular his distinction between mind and body, as support for his own attacks on materialism (see CAMBRIDGE PLATONISM). SPINOZA, too, was influenced by Descartes. His first published book was a commentary on Descartes' *Principles*, and although he later moved well outside the Cartesian camp, Descartes' doctrines helped to structure his mature thought. Spinoza's metaphysical vocabulary (substance, attribute and mode) is borrowed from Descartes, as is the centrality of the attributes of thought and extension in his metaphysics.

While many of Descartes' partisans tried to remain orthodox, there is at least one doctrine characteristic of later Cartesianism that Descartes himself probably did not hold, namely, occasionalism (see OCCASIONALISM). Malebranche and the Flemish Cartesian Arnold GEULINCX are most often associated with the doctrine, but it appears in Cartesian writings long before theirs. According to occasionalism, God is the only active causal agent in the world; finite minds and bodies are not real causes, but only occasions for God to exercise his causal efficacy. Motivated by the picture of divine sustenance from moment to moment that underlies Descartes' derivation of the laws of motion, together, perhaps, with general worries about the efficacy of finite causes and specific worries about mind – body interaction, occasionalism became a standard doctrine. Though often also attributed to Descartes himself, the grounds for doing so are rather slim.

Descartes' mark can also be seen among his opponents. He was clearly a target of Hobbes' materialism and sensationalism in, for example, Part I of *Leviathan* (1651). His epistemology and treatment of God were explicitly targeted by PASCAL in the *Pensées* (1658–62, published 1670). Leibniz, too, attacked his physics, his rejection of formal logic, his conception of body and his conception of the mind, among many other things. The inadequacy of the Cartesian philosophy is a constant subtext to Locke's *Essay Concerning Human Understanding* (1689), particularly in his discussion of our knowledge of mind and his rejection of the dogmatic claim to know the essences of substances. In natural philosophy, Newton's early writings show a careful study of Descartes' writings, particularly those on motion, and book II of his *Principia* was devoted to a refutation of the vortex theory of planetary motion. Between around 1650 and the eclipse of Cartesian philosophy some time in the early eighteenth century, it was simply impossible to write philosophy without reacting in some way to Descartes.

See also: ARISTOTELIANISM IN THE 17TH CENTURY; CERTAINTY; DOUBT; DUALISM; LOCKE, J.; ARISTOTELIANISM, MEDIEVAL; PERCEPTION, EPISTEMIC ISSUES IN; RATIONALISM; RÉGIS, P.-S.; SCEPTICISM; SUBSTANCE

List of works

Descartes, R. (1964–74) *Oeuvres de Descartes*, ed. C. Adam and P. Tannery, Paris: CNRS/Vrin, new edn, 11 vols. (Originally published 1897–1913, and more recently updated, this is still the standard edition of Descartes' writings in the original languages. It contains editions of all of the writings listed below, as well as his letters. The incomplete *La description du corps humain* and *Prima cogitationes* are included in volume 11.)

—— (1984–91) *The Philosophical Writings of Descartes*, ed. and trans. J. Cottingham, R. Stoothoff, D. Murdoch and A. Kenny, Cambridge: Cambridge University Press, 3 vols. (The now-standard English translation of Descartes' writings. It contains the entire *Rules, Discourse, Meditations* and *Passions*, as well as selections from his other writings and letters.)

—— (1620–c.28) *Regulae ad directionem ingenii* (Rules for the Direction of the Mind), in vol. 1 of *The Philosophical Writings of Descartes*, ed. and trans. J. Cottingham, R. Stoothoff, D. Murdoch and A. Kenny, Cambridge: Cambridge University Press, 1984–91. (Descartes' early treatise on method, left unpublished at his death. Manuscripts were widely circulated, and it was published first in Dutch translation in 1684 and in the Latin original in 1701.)

—— (c.1630–3) *Le Monde* (The World), excerpted in vol. 1 of *The Philosophical Writings of Descartes*, ed. and trans. J. Cottingham, R. Stoothoff, D. Murdoch and A. Kenny, Cambridge: Cambridge University Press, 1984–91. (Descartes' first draft of

a scientific system, including general physics, cosmology, terrestrial physics, and human physiology. Withdrawn from publication when Galileo was condemned, the *Treatise on Man* was first published in Latin translation in 1662, then in the French original in 1664; the *Treatise on Light* was first published in French in 1664.)

—— (1637) *Discours de la méthode pour bien conduir sa raison et chercher la vérité dans les sciences plus la dioptrique, les meteores, et la geometrie, qui sont des essais de cete methode* (Discourse on the Method for Properly Conducting Reason and Searching for Truth in the Sciences, as well as the Dioptrics, the Meteors, and the Geometry, which are essays in this method), in vol. 1 of *The Philosophical Writings of Descartes*, ed. and trans. J. Cottingham, R. Stoothoff, D. Murdoch and A. Kenny, Cambridge: Cambridge University Press, 1984–91. (Descartes' first publication: three scientific treatises, together with an introduction that was to become more famous and widely read than the essays that it introduced.)

—— (1641) *Meditationes de prima philosophia* (Meditations on First Philosophy), in vol. 2 of *The Philosophical Writings of Descartes*, ed. and trans. J. Cottingham, R. Stoothoff, D. Murdoch and A. Kenny, Cambridge: Cambridge University Press, 1984–91. (Descartes' main metaphysical work, it was published with a series of objections together with Descartes' replies, six sets in the 1641 edition; a seventh was added in the 1642 edition. Also important is the 1647 French translation, published with some changes.)

—— (1644) *Principia philosophiae* (Principles of Philosophy), excerpted in vol. 1 of *The Philosophical Writings of Descartes*, ed. and trans. J. Cottingham, R. Stoothoff, D. Murdoch and A. Kenny, Cambridge: Cambridge University Press, 1984–91. (After Part I, which deals with metaphysics, this mainly deals with Descartes' physics. Also important is the 1647 French translation, with a new preface and some significant changes.)

—— (1649) *Les passions de l'âme* (The Passions of the Soul), in vol. 1 of *The Philosophical Writings of Descartes*, ed. and trans. J. Cottingham, R. Stoothoff, D. Murdoch and A. Kenny, Cambridge: Cambridge University Press, 1984–91. (Descartes' last published work, this deals with philosophical psychology and morals.)

References and further reading

The journal *Archives de Philosophie* annually publishes a report from the Centre d'études cartésiennes (Université de Paris IV (Sorbonne)), which contains full bibliographies of recent work on Descartes and Cartesianism, together with selective reviews.

Baillet, A. (1691) *La Vie de M. Descartes* (Life of Descartes), Paris: Daniel Horthemels, 2 vols. (The most important source on Descartes' life. It was his 'official' biography, commissioned by a circle of Descartes' followers. Baillet had access to numerous papers that are no longer extant.)

Beck, L.J. (1952) *The Method of Descartes: A Study of the Regulae*, Oxford: Oxford University Press. (Detailed study of Descartes' method, as presented in the *Rules*.)

—— (1965) *The Metaphysics of Descartes: A Study of the Meditations*, Oxford: Oxford University Press. (A careful study of Descartes' *Meditations*.)

* Beeckman, I. (1604–34) *Journal tenu par Isaac Beeckman de 1604 à 1634*, ed. C. de Waard, The Hague: Nijhoff, 4 vols, 1939–53. (Excerpts from the journals, which include discussons between Descartes and Beeckman, are also included in *Oeuvres de Descartes*, ed. C. Adam and P. Tannery, Paris: CNRS/Vrin, 1964–74, vol 10: 41–78, 151–69.)

Bouillier, F. (1868) *Histoire de la philosophie cartésienne (History of Cartesian philosophy)*, Paris: Durand, 3rd edn, 2 vols; repr. New York: Garland, 1987. (After more than a century, this remains the best study of Descartes' influence on his contemporaries and followers.)

Chappell, V. and Doney, W. (eds) (1987) *Twenty-five years of Descartes Scholarship 1960–1984. A Bibliography*, New York: Garland. (An update of Sebba's earlier bibliography.)

Clarke, D.M. (1982) *Descartes' Philosophy of Science*, Manchester: Manchester University Press. (A study of Descartes' science and its philosophy, from the point of view of Descartes' actual practice.)

Cottingham, J.G. (1986) *Descartes*, Oxford: Blackwell. (Good introductory study of Descartes' philosophical thought.)

—— (ed.) (1992) *The Cambridge Companion to Descartes*, Cambridge: Cambridge University Press. (This collection has good, up-to-date overviews of current thought on a variety of topics in Descartes' philosophy.)

Curley, E.M. (1978) *Descartes against the Skeptics*, Cambridge, MA: Harvard University Press. (A study of Descartes' philosophical writings as a response to classical scepticism.)

Des Chene, D. (1996) *Physiologia: Natural philosophy in late Aristotelian and Cartesian thought*, Ithaca, NY: Cornell University Press. (An up-to-date study of Descartes' relation to scholastic philosophy, progressively becoming a central theme in Cartesian studies.)

Doney, W. (ed.) (1967) *Descartes: A Collection of Critical Essays*, Garden City, NY: Doubleday. (Collection of classic and often-cited articles on Descartes' philosophy.)

Frankfurt, H. (1970) *Demons, Dreamers and Madmen: The Defense of Reason in Descartes' Meditations*, Indianapolis, IN: Bobbs-Merrill. (An imaginative and highly influential reading of Descartes' epistemology, particularly the Cartesian circle.)

* Galilei, G. (1638) *Discorsi e dimostrazioni matematiche, intorno à due nuove scienze*, trans. S. Drake, *Two New Sciences*, Madison, WI: University of Wisconsin Press, 1974. (The work dismissed by Descartes as lacking systematic coherence.)

Garber, D. (1992) *Descartes' Metaphysical Physics*, Chicago, IL: University of Chicago Press. (This concentrates on Descartes' natural philosophy and its relation to his more philosophical interests.)

Gaukroger, S. (ed.) (1980) *Descartes: Philosophy, Mathematics and Physics*, Sussex: Harvester Press. (This collection contains a number of now-classic essays on Descartes' physics and mathematics in relation to his more philosophical concerns.)

—— (1995) *Descartes: An Intellectual Biography*, Oxford: Oxford University Press. (This biography also serves as a historically sensitive commentary on Descartes' thought. It is especially good on Descartes' earlier period.)

Gilson, É (1930) *Études sur le rôle de la pensée médievale dans la formation du système cartésien* (Studies on the role of Medieval thought in the formation of the Cartesian system of philosophy), Paris: Vrin. (A classic discussion of Descartes' relations to the scholastic thought which dominated earlier philosophy.)

Grosholz, E. (1991) *Cartesian Method and the Problem of Reduction*, Oxford, Oxford University Press. (Study of Cartesian method, particularly good for its discussion of Descartes' mathematics.)

Gueroult, M. (1984) *Descartes' Philosophy Interpreted According to the Order of Reasons*, trans. R. Ariew, Minneapolis, MN: University of Minnesota Press, 2 vols. (Though Gueroult has certain interpretative biases, this remains one of the great close commentaries on Descartes' philosophy in the French tradition.)

* Hintikka, J. (1968) 'Cogito, Ergo Sum: Inference or Performance', in W. Doney (ed.) *Descartes: A Collection of Critical Essays*, Garden City, NY: Doubleday, 108–139. (The main adherent of the approach to the Cogito through speech act theory and theories of demonstratives, mentioned in §5 above.)

Kenny, A. (1968) *Descartes*, New York: Random

House. (Classic introduction to Descartes' thought.)

Marion, J.-L. (1975) *Sur l'ontologie grise de Descartes* (On Descartes' hidden ontology), Paris: Vrin, 2nd edn, 1981. (A study of Descartes' *Rules* in opposition to Aristotle, arguing that Descartes smuggles in a kind of secret ontology. This and the following two books constitute a trilogy, offering a somewhat idealistic interpretation of Descartes' thought. They have been widely read, and enormously influential on recent Cartesian studies.)

—— (1981) *Sur la théologie blanche de Descartes* (On Descartes' blank theology), Paris: Presses Universitaires de France. (A study of Descartes' conception of God and the role he plays in the Cartesian system, focusing on the conception of God as the creator of eternal truths.)

—— (1986) *Sur le prisme métaphysique de Descartes. Constitution et limites de l'onto-théo-logie dans la pensée cartésienne* (On Descartes' metaphysical prism: the constitution and limits of onto-theo-logy in Cartesian thought), Paris: Presses Universitaires de France. (A Heideggerian interpretation of the metaphysics of the *Meditations*, concentrating on the relation between God and the self.)

* Markie, P. (1992) 'The Cogito and its importance', in J. Cottingham (ed.) *The Cambridge Companion to Descartes*, Cambridge: Cambridge University Press. (A general survey of analytic interpretations of the Cogito.)

* Regius, H. (1646) *Fundamenta physices* (Foundations of physics), Amsterdam. (Regius' main presentation of his natural philosophy, about which Descartes had serious reservations.)

Rodis-Lewis, G. (1971) *L'oeuvre de Descartes* (The work of Descartes), Paris: Vrin, 2 vols. (A chronological study of Descartes' thought and writings that also serves as an intellectual biography. Elegantly written, it shows an unusually broad knowledge of Descartes' writings. Also useful for its encyclopedic discussion of the French literature on Descartes before 1971.)

Rorty, A.O. (ed.) (1986) *Essays on Descartes' Meditations*, Berkeley, CA: University of California Press. (This collection of essays, all on themes from the *Meditations*, serves as a collective commentary on the work.)

Sabra, A.I. (1961) *Theories of Light from Descartes to Newton*, London: Oldbourne; 2nd edn, Cambridge: Cambridge University Press, 1981. (Study of seventeenth-century optics, particularly good on Descartes contribution to the subject.)

Sebba, G. (1964) *Bibliographia Cartesiana. A Critical Guide to the Descartes Literature 1800–1960*, The Hague: Matinus Nijhoff. (The standard source for the older literature on Descartes. In addition to a listing by author, it contains some commentary on the more important items.)

Shea, W.R. (1991) *The Magic of Numbers and Motion: The Scientific Career of René Descartes*, Canton, MA: Science History Publications. (This study of Descartes' scientific thought is particularly good on his early years.)

Verbeek, T. (1992) *Descartes and the Dutch: Early Reactions to Cartesianism (1637–1650)*, Journal of the History of Philosophy Monograph Series, Carbondale, IL: Southern Illinois University Press. (Excellent study of Descartes' intellectual and personal relations with the people among whom he lived for the better part of his adult life.)

Voss. S. (ed.) (1993) *Essays on the Philosophy and Science of René Descartes*, New York and Oxford; Oxford University Press. (Collection of articles that gives a good idea of current/recent work.)

Vuillemin, J. (1960) *Mathématiques et métaphysique chez Descartes* (Descartes' mathematics and metaphysics), Paris: Presses Universitaires de France. (A very valuable study of Descartes' mathematics understood in the context of his philosophy.)

Williams, B. (1978) *Descartes: the Project of Pure Enquiry*, Hassock: Harvester. (Classic introduction to Descartes' philosophical thought from an analytic point of view.)

Wilson, M. (1978) *Descartes*, London: Routledge. (An excellent and influential commentary, centred on the *Meditations*.)

DANIEL GARBER

DESCRIPTION, KNOWLEDGE BY *see* KNOWLEDGE BY ACQUAINTANCE AND DESCRIPTION

DESCRIPTIONS

'Definite descriptions' are noun phrases of the form 'the' + noun complex (for example, 'the finest Greek poet', 'the cube of five') or of the form possessive + noun complex (for example, 'Sparta's defeat of Athens'). As Russell realized, it is important to philosophy to be clear about the semantics of such expressions. In the sentence 'Aeschylus fought at Marathon', the function of the subject, 'Aeschylus', is to refer to something; it is a referential noun phrase (or

'singular term'). By contrast, in the sentence 'Every Athenian remembers Marathon', the subject noun phrase, 'every Athenian', is not referential but quantificational. Definite descriptions appear at first sight to be referential. Frege treated them referentially, but Russell held that they should be treated quantificationally in accordance with his theory of descriptions, and argued that certain philosophical puzzles were thereby solved.

1 Frege
2 Russell's theory of descriptions: informal characterization
3 Russell's theory of descriptions: formal characterization
4 Strawson's theory and criticisms of Russell
5 Ambiguity theories

1 Frege

Gottlob Frege provided the first systematic account of quantification in natural language and the first systematic theory of reference (1892). The class of 'singular terms' (referential noun phrases), for Frege, was delimited by a set of logical tests (for example, the licensing of existential generalization) and was recursive. It included ordinary proper names and definite descriptions. Thus '5', 'the cube of 5', 'Aeschylus' and so on were all singular terms.

If a description ⌜the F⌝ is referential, then it is natural to take its reference to be the unique entity satisfying 'F'; a sentence ⌜The F is G⌝ is true if and only if that entity is G. But what if no entity, or more than one entity, satisfies the descriptive condition, as in (1) or (2)?

(1) *The largest prime number* lies between 10^{23} and 10^{27}.

(2) *The man who landed on the moon* was American.

Such descriptions are said to be 'improper'. Frege considered it a defect of natural language that it permits the possibility of improper terms. As far as his own logical system was concerned, he thought it essential that every formula have a truth-value, and so he insisted that every singular term have a reference (or meaning): he stipulated that a specified object in the range of the quantifier(s) serve as the referent of every improper description. While this stipulation proved useful for his formal system, Frege recognized that some other account of improper descriptions in ordinary language was needed. Once he had made his distinction between the 'sense' and 'reference' of an expression, he suggested that an improper term has a sense but no reference (see FREGE, G. §3; SENSE AND REFERENCE §1). The main problem with this proposal is that it predicts, rather counterintuitively, that any sentence containing an improper term (in a transparent context) lacks a truth-value. For example, it predicts that (1) and (2) above lack truth-values.

2 Russell's theory of descriptions: informal characterization

Like Frege, Bertrand RUSSELL thought it important to explain how a sentence such as (1) or (2) could be meaningful. At one time he entertained the idea of a realm of non-existent entities to serve as the referents of descriptions such as 'the largest prime number' and 'the round square'; but by 1905 he thought this idea conflicted with a 'robust sense of reality' and his theory of descriptions came about, in part as an attempt to purify his ontology (see EXISTENCE §2).

On Russell's account, descriptions are not singular terms at all but phrases that logical analysis reveals to be quantificational: if ⌜the F⌝ is a definite description and ⌜…is G⌝ is a predicate phrase, then the proposition expressed by an utterance of ⌜The F is G⌝ is equivalent, says Russell, to the proposition expressed by an utterance of ⌜There is exactly one F, and everything that is F is G⌝. That is, ⌜The F is G⌝ is analysed as

(3) $(\exists x)((\forall y)(Fy \leftrightarrow y = x) \mathbin{\&} Gx)$.

The proposition expressed by ⌜The F is G⌝ is 'general' ('object-independent') rather than 'singular' ('object-dependent') in the sense that there is no object for which its grammatical subject stands; upon whose existence that of the proposition expressed depends. Unlike a singular term, a definite description, even if it is in fact satisfied by a unique object, does not actually *refer* to that object. It is as wrong, on Russell's account, to inquire into the referent of ⌜the F⌝ as it is to inquire into the referent of ⌜every F⌝ or ⌜no F⌝.

On Russell's account, sentences containing improper descriptions have truth-values. For example, (1) above is false as it is not the case that there exists a largest prime number. Similarly, sentence (2) is false as it is not the case that there exists exactly one man who landed on the moon.

Russell's theory opens up the possibility of accounting for certain *de dicto/de re* ambiguities in terms of scope permutations (see DE RE/DE DICTO). For example, (4) below may be analysed as either (5) or (6), according to whether the description 'the largest prime number' is given large or small scope with respect to 'John thinks that':

(4) John thinks that the largest prime number lies

between 10^{23} and 10^{27}.

(5) $(\exists x)((\forall y)(\text{largest-prime } y \leftrightarrow y = x)$ & John thinks that: x lies between 10^{23} and 10^{27}).

(6) John thinks that: $(\exists x)((\forall y)(\text{largest-prime } y \leftrightarrow y = x)$ & x lies between 10^{23} and 10^{27}).

(5) is false; but (6) may be true. Thus Russell is able to explain the intuitive ambiguity of (4) and avoid positing an ontology that includes such things as a largest prime number. Smullyan (1948) points out that Russell's theory similarly explains *de dicto*/*de re* ambiguities in modal contexts, for example, in 'The number of planets is necessarily odd' (see DE RE/DE DICTO §2; MODAL LOGIC).

Russell came to treat ordinary proper names as 'disguised' or 'truncated' descriptions. For example, the name 'Cicero' might be analysed as the description 'the greatest Roman orator' while the coreferential name 'Tully' might be analysed as the description 'the author of *De Fato*'. On the face of it, this provided Russell with accounts (not dissimilar to Frege's) of why 'Cicero was bald' and 'Tully was bald' differ in informativeness, and of why (7) and (8) need not agree in truth-value:

(7) John believes Cicero was bald.

(8) John believes Tully was bald.

In the light of Kripke's work on names and necessity (1980), it is widely held that descriptive analyses of proper names cannot succeed (see PROPER NAMES). There is good reason, however, to think that at least some pronouns anaphorically linked to (referring back to), but not bound by, quantified noun phrases are understood in terms of definite descriptions (see Neale 1990).

3 Russell's theory of descriptions: formal characterization

On Russell's account, descriptions are 'incomplete' symbols; they have 'no meaning in isolation', that is, they do not stand for things. In *Principia Mathematica* (1910–13), descriptions are represented by quasi-singular terms of the form '$(\imath x)(Fx)$', which can be read as 'the unique x which is F'. Superficially, the iota-operator is a variable-binding device for forming a term from a formula. A predicate symbol 'G' may be prefixed to a description '$(\imath x)(Fx)$' to form a formula '$G(\imath x)(Fx)$', which can be expanded in accordance with a suitable 'contextual definition'. (To define an expression ζ contextually is to provide a procedure for converting any sentence containing occurrences of ζ into an equivalent sentence that is ζ-free.)

The analysis in (3) above does not constitute a final

contextual definition of '$G(\imath x)(Fx)$' because of the possibility of scope ambiguity where a formula containing a description is itself a constituent of a larger formula (see SCOPE). Scope ambiguity is conveniently illustrated with descriptions in the context of negation. For a genuine singular term α, there is no difference between wide and narrow scope negation: α is not-F just in case it is not the case that α is F. For a description, however, there is a formal ambiguity. Let 'Kx' represent 'x is a king of France' and 'Wx' represent 'x is wise'. Then the formula '$\neg W(\imath x)(Kx)$' ('The king of France is not wise') is ambiguous between (9) and (10):

(9) $(\exists x)((\forall y)(Ky \leftrightarrow y = x)$ & $\neg Wx)$

(10) $\neg(\exists x)((\forall y)(Ky \leftrightarrow y = x)$ & $Wx)$.

These are not equivalent: only (10) can be true when there is no king of France. In *Principia Mathematica*, the scope of a description is specified by appending a copy of it within square brackets to the front of the formula that constitutes its scope. Thus (9) and (10) are represented as (11) and (12) respectively:

(11) $[(\imath x)(Kx)]\neg\{W(\imath x)(Kx)\}$

(12) $\neg\{[(\imath x)(Kx)]W(\imath x)(Kx)\}$.

In (11) the description has what Russell calls a 'primary occurrence' by virtue of having scope over the negation; in (12) the description has a 'secondary occurrence' by virtue of lying within the scope of the negation. Where a description has smallest possible scope, it is conventional to omit the scope marker; thus (12) can be reduced to '$\neg W(\imath x)(Kx)$'.

With the matter of scope behind us, the theory of descriptions can be stated exactly:

$$[(\imath x)(\phi x)]G(\imath x)(\phi x) =_{df} (\exists x)((\forall y)(\phi y \leftrightarrow y = x) \, \& \, Gx)$$

where ϕ is a formula. On Russell's account, there is no possibility of a genuine referring expression failing to refer, so no predicate letter in the language of *Principia Mathematica* stands for 'exists'. Russell introduces a symbol '$E!$' ('E shriek') that may be combined with a description to create a well-formed formula. Thus

$$E!(\imath x)(\phi x) =_{df} (\exists x)(\forall y)(\phi y \leftrightarrow y = x)$$

'$E!$' allows a treatment of negative existentials. (According to Russell, an utterance of 'The king of France does not exist' made today would be true precisely because there is no king of France.) Successive applications will allow any well-formed formula containing a definite description to be replaced by an equivalent formula that is description-free.

It is often objected that Russell's theory, which

21

substitutes complex quantificational structure for 'the', is unfaithful to surface syntax. The objection is engendered by an insufficiently keen appreciation of the distinction between a theory and its formal implementation. The extent of the mismatch between 'The king is wise' and its analysis

(13) $(\exists x)((\forall y)(\text{king } y \leftrightarrow y = x) \,\&\, \text{wise } x)$

has nothing to do with descriptions *per se*. In order to characterize the logical forms of even 'some philosophers are wise' and 'every philosopher is wise' in the predicate calculus we have to use formulas containing sentence connectives, no counterparts of which occur in the surface forms of the sentences:

(14) $(\exists x)(\text{philosopher } x \,\&\, \text{wise } x)$

(15) $(\forall x)(\text{philosopher } x \rightarrow \text{wise } x)$.

And when we formalize sentences such as 'Just two philosophers are wise', we find much more complexity than there is in surface syntax:

(16) $(\exists x)(\exists y)[\text{philosopher } x \,\&\, \text{philosopher } y \,\&\, \text{wise } x \,\&\, \text{wise } y \,\&\, (\forall z)((\text{philosopher } z \,\&\, \text{wise } z) \rightarrow z = x \vee z = y)]$.

The supposed problem about descriptions, then, is in fact a symptom of a larger problem involving the application of first-order logic to sentences of ordinary language.

Work on 'generalized' quantification provides a solution to the larger problem (as well as treatments of quantifiers such as 'most' that cannot be handled within first-order logic; see QUANTIFIERS, GENERALIZED). Natural language quantification is normally restricted: we talk about all philosophers or most poets, not about all or most entities. A simple modification of the predicate calculus yields a language – call it 'RQ' – that captures this fact while retaining the precision of regular first-order logic. In RQ, a determiner such as 'some', 'every' or 'no' combines with a formula to create a restricted quantifier such as '[every x: philosopher x]'. And such a quantifier may combine with a formula to form a formula:

(17) [every x: philosopher x] (wise x).

The viability of such a language shows that the language of *Principia Mathematica* is not essential to the theory of descriptions. Since the word 'the' is a one-place quantificational determiner (as are 'some', 'every', 'no' and so on), RQ can treat 'the' as combining with a formula 'king x' to form a restricted quantifier '[the x: king x]'. The sentence 'The king is wise' will then be represented as

(18) [the x: king x] (wise x).

Different scope possibilities are easily captured. For instance, 'The king is not wise' is ambiguous between (19) and (20):

(19) [the x: king x] $\neg$(wise x)

(20) $\neg$[the x: king x](wise x).

Using a formal language in which descriptions are treated as restricted quantifiers does not mean abandoning Russell's view that descriptions are 'incomplete symbols' that 'disappear on analysis'. Rather, treating descriptions as restricted quantifiers results in an explanation of where his theory of descriptions fits into a systematic account of natural language quantification, a theory in which 'every', 'some', 'most', 'a', 'the' and so on are members of a unified syntactic and semantic category.

4   Strawson's theory and criticisms of Russell

As part of a broad critique of the idea that the semantics of formal languages can be used to analyse the meanings of statements of natural language, P.F. STRAWSON argued against Russell's theory of descriptions on the grounds that (1) it fails to recognize that referring is something done by speakers and not expressions, (2) it fails to do justice to the way speakers ordinarily use sentences containing descriptions to make statements (speakers use descriptions to refer, not to quantify) and (3) it rides roughshod over important distinctions, such as the distinction between the meaning of a sentence (and the statement made by a particular use of σ (see PROPOSITIONS, SENTENCES AND STATEMENTS).

Using as an example 'The present king of France is wise', Strawson argues that Russell's theory is thwarted because the same sentence can be used to say something true on one occasion and something false on another. It is certainly true that Russell paid little attention to the distinction between the linguistic meaning of a sentence type and the proposition expressed by a particular dated utterance of that sentence type; but it was the latter that actually concerned him, and Strawson could get no mileage out of Russell's inattention to the distinction. The fact that a description (or any other quantified noun phrase) may contain an indexical component ('the *present* king of France', 'every man *here*', and so on) illustrates that some descriptions are subject to both the theory of descriptions and a theory of indexicality (see DEMONSTRATIVES AND INDEXICALS). Thus contextual features play a role in fixing the proposition expressed. And this can be true also if the overt indexical element is missing, as in 'The king of France is wise'.

This appreciation of contextual factors forms the basis of the Russellian response to a second Strawsonian objection. According to this, someone who uses a description ⌜the F⌝ typically intends to refer to some object or other and say something about it; there is no question of claiming that some object uniquely satisfies F. Someone who says 'The table is covered with books', for instance, does not express a proposition that entails the existence of exactly one table. But, Strawson claimed, it is a part of the meaning of ⌜the F⌝ that such an expression is used correctly only if there is an F. If this condition is not satisfied – if the 'presupposition' that there is an F is false – a use of ⌜The F is G⌝ cannot be considered to express a proposition that is either true or false. The Russellian response to Strawson is that descriptions such as 'the table' are often understood as elliptical uses of fuller descriptions such as 'the table over there', 'the table in front of me' and so on; or else they are evaluated with respect to a restricted domain of discourse. Again the phenomenon is not confined to descriptions, but is found with quantified noun phrases more generally.

Strawson's original statement (1950) of his own theory contains an interesting ambiguity. He can be understood as claiming either that no proposition is expressed, or that a proposition which is neither true nor false is expressed, when someone uses a sentence containing an empty description. A second ambiguity comes with the notion of 'presupposition'. This can be viewed as an epistemological or pragmatic relation between a person and a statement, or as a logical relation between two statements (see PRESUPPOSITION). An epistemological or pragmatic notion of presupposition appears to have no bearing on the semantic issues Strawson wanted to address when he challenged Russell.

The Strawsonian position faces some serious obstacles. If someone were to utter (21) right now, they would unquestionably say something false.

(21) The king of France shot my cat last night.

But on Strawson's account, the speaker will have expressed no proposition because the presupposition that there is a unique king of France is false. Descriptions occurring in the context of attitude verbs create a similar problem. For example, someone might utter a true statement using (22):

(22) Ponce de León thought the fountain of youth was in Florida,

so the presence of an empty description does not always result in a failed speech act. This is something Strawson (1964) came to concede. In order to reduce the number of incorrect predictions made by his earlier theory, he suggested that the presence of an empty description sometimes renders the proposition expressed false and at other times prevents a proposition from being expressed at all (sometimes ⌜The F is G⌝ *entails* the existence of a unique F, and at other times it (only) *presupposes* it).

5 Ambiguity theories

Consideration of the behaviour of descriptions in non-extensional contexts and the possibility of misdescribing an individual as the F, but successfully communicating something about that individual, has led some philosophers (for example, Donnellan 1966) to suggest that descriptions are sometimes quantificational, at other times referential. When ⌜the F⌝ is used in the Russellian way, the proposition expressed is general (object-independent); when it is used referentially the proposition expressed is singular (object-dependent). Donnellan considers examples such as the following: (1) A detective discovers Smith's mutilated body but has no idea who killed him. Looking at the body, he exclaims, 'The murderer is insane'. (2) Jones is on trial for Smith's murder; I am convinced of his guilt; hearing Jones ranting in court, I say, 'The murderer is insane'. On Donnellan's account, in case (1) the description is being used attributively; in case (2) it is being used referentially. Cases such as (2), it is argued, cannot be treated in accordance with Russell's theory. Following Grice (1969), however, many have argued (1) that so-called referential uses of descriptions can usually be accommodated within Russell's theory by invoking a distinction between the proposition expressed by (an utterance of) a sentence on a given occasion and the proposition the speaker primarily intends to communicate on that occasion; (2) that the phenomenon of referential usage is not specific to definite descriptions, but arises with quantified noun phrases quite generally; (3) that the referential/attributive distinction is neither exclusive nor exhaustive; and (4) that no such distinction can do the work of Russell's notion of the scope of a description. It would seem, then, that something very close to Russell's theory will probably form a component of any finally acceptable theory.

See also: FREE LOGICS, PHILOSOPHICAL ISSUES IN §3; LOGICAL AND MATHEMATICAL TERMS, GLOSSARY OF; REFERENCE §6

References and further reading

Carnap, R. (1947) *Meaning and Necessity*, Chicago, IL: University of Chicago Press. (Discussion of views presented in §§1–2.)

Davies, M. (1981) *Meaning, Quantification and Necessity*, London: Routledge. (Discussion of views presented in §5.)

* Donnellan, K. (1966) 'Reference and Definite Descriptions', *Philosophical Review* 77: 281–304. (Discussion of views presented in §5.)

* Frege, G. (1892) 'Über Sinn und Bedeutung', *Zeitschrift für Philosophie und philosophische Kritik* 100: 25–50; trans. 'On Sense and Reference', in *Translations from the Philosophical Writings of Gottlob Frege*, trans. and ed. P.T. Geach and M. Black, Oxford: Blackwell, 3rd edn, 1980. (Source of views presented in §1. The page numbers of the original publications appear in the text.)

* Grice, H.P. (1969) 'Vacuous Names', in D. Davidson and J. Hintikka (eds) *Words and Objections: Essays on the Work of W.V. Quine*, Dordrecht: Reidel, 118–45. (Discussion of views presented in §§2, 5.)

* Kaplan, D. (1978) 'Dthat', in P. Cole (ed.) *Syntax and Semantics*, vol. 9, *Pragmatics*, New York: Academic Press, 221–43. (Discussion of views presented in §5.)

Kripke, S.A. (1979) 'Speaker Reference and Semantic Reference', in P.A. French, T.E. Uehling and H.K. Wettstein (eds) *Contemporary Perspectives in the Philosophy of Language*, Minneapolis, MN: University of Minnesota Press, 6–27. (Discussion of views presented in §§2, 5.)

* —— (1980) *Naming and Necessity*, Cambridge, MA: Harvard University Press. (See §2.)

* Neale, S. (1990) *Descriptions*, Cambridge, MA: MIT Press. (Discussion of views presented in §§2–5. Extensive bibliography.)

—— (1994) 'Grammatical Form, Logical Form, and Incomplete Symbols', in A.D. Irvine and G.A. Wedeking (eds) *Russell and Analytic Philosophy*, Toronto, Ont.: University of Toronto Press, 97–139. (Discussion of views presented in §2.)

* Russell, B.A.W. (1905) 'On Denoting', *Mind* 14: 479–93; repr. in *Logic and Knowledge: Essays 1901–1950*, ed. R.C. Marsh, London: Routledge, 1992. (Source of views presented in §2.)

* —— (1911) 'Knowledge by Acquaintance and Knowledge by Description', in *Mysticism and Logic*, London: Routledge, 1986. (Source of views presented in §2.)

Sainsbury, R.M. (1979) *Russell*, London: Routledge & Kegan Paul. (Discussion of views presented in §§2, 5.)

Sellars, W.S. (1954) 'Presupposing', *Philosophical Review* 63: 197–215. (Discussion of views presented in §4.)

* Smullyan, A.F. (1948) 'Modality and Description', *Journal of Symbolic Logic* 13: 31–7; repr. in L. Linsky (ed.) *Reference and Modality*, Oxford: Oxford University Press, 1971, 35–43. (Discussion of views presented in §2.)

* Strawson, P.F. (1950) 'On Referring', *Mind* 59: 320–44. (Source of views presented in §4.)

—— (1954) 'Reply to Mr. Sellars', *Philosophical Review* 63: 216–31. (Source of views presented in §4.)

* —— (1964) 'Identifying Reference and Truth-Values', *Theoria* 30: 96–118. (Source of views presented in §4.)

—— (1972) *Subject and Predicate in Logic and Grammar*, London: Methuen. (Source of views presented in §4.)

* Whitehead, A.N. and Russell, B.A.W. (1910–13) *Principia Mathematica*, Cambridge: Cambridge University Press, 3 vols; 2nd edn, 1925–7, esp. vol. 1, *14. (Source of views presented in §3.)

STEPHEN NEALE

DESERT AND MERIT

The ideas of desert and merit are fundamental to the way we normally think about our personal relationships and our social institutions. We believe that people who perform good deeds and display admirable qualities deserve praise, honours and rewards, whereas people whose behaviour is anti-social deserve blame and punishment. We also think that justice is in large part a matter of people receiving the treatment that they deserve. But many philosophers have found these ways of thinking hard to justify. Why should people's past deeds determine how we should treat them in the future? Since we cannot see inside their heads, how can we ever know what people really deserve? How can we reconcile our belief that people must be responsible for their actions in order to deserve credit or blame with the determinist claim that all actions are in principle capable of being explained by causes over which we have no control?

1 **Desert and merit**
2 **Desert and personal responsibility**
3 **Critics of desert**
4 **Desert and justice**

1 Desert and merit

We use the concepts of desert and merit when we are thinking about how it is appropriate to treat people in a wide range of contexts. We say that Einstein deserved the Nobel prize for his work in theoretical physics, that Nixon deserved to be impeached for his role in the Watergate cover-up, that Jane deserves more thanks from her children than she is getting, that nurses deserve to have their pay increased. All of these claims have essentially the same structure (see Feinberg 1970): there is a subject, either an individual like Einstein or a set of people like the nurses, who are said to be deserving; there is a characteristic or an activity in virtue of which they are said to be deserving, which I shall call the *desert base* – Einstein's researches, or the work that nurses do; and there is something that is deserved, a burden or a benefit that it is appropriate or fitting for the subject to have on account of the desert base – the Nobel prize, a pay award (see PRAISE AND BLAME).

Both the treatment deserved and the desert base vary a great deal from case to case, and mistakes in analysing the concept of desert often arise from considering only one kind of example. We can say in general that the characteristic or activity that forms the desert base must be something that we value positively or, in the case of deserved blame or punishment, negatively (see VALUES). But the valuing can be of many different kinds. Sometimes people are said to deserve rewards for activities that are morally valuable – we might say, for instance, that the charitable work done by a great philanthropist deserves to be honoured. In other cases – such as those of athletes or scientists who are awarded prizes – we value someone's accomplishments without giving them moral credit. To suppose that all desert must be moral desert is to shrink the range of possible desert bases unwarrantably.

The concepts of desert and merit are linked closely, and some languages have only a single word where English has two. The main difference is that we tend to use desert when talking about someone's performance, and merit when talking about their personal capacities and abilities (see Lucas 1980). Thus when we say that appointments should be made on the basis of merit, we mean that the candidate who shows the greatest capacity to fill the position should be awarded it. On the other hand, when somebody has performed a courageous act or written an excellent essay, we usually say that they deserve something in return, a decoration or a grade. Desert also conveys the sense that the subject is responsible for what he does, whereas in pre-modern systems of thought, including that of ancient Greece, people were judged meritorious according to the quality of their actions, and with little regard to individual responsibility as we understand it (see Adkins 1960).

2 Desert and personal responsibility

What are the implications of saying that people deserve rewards, punishments and other modes of treatment only when they are responsible for the performance that forms the basis of desert (see RESPONSIBILITY)? It means first of all that they must have intended to do what they did. If I gun down a desperado thinking that he is the sheriff, I do not deserve the price that has been put on his head. Moreover my deserts are lessened or even removed entirely to the extent that my performance depends on luck. I may win a competition through a lucky series of guesses, but the person who really deserved to win was the person who knew the answers all along. This link between desert and responsibility is particularly tight when punishment is at stake (see CRIME AND PUNISHMENT). When legal systems punish people for occurrences they could have done nothing to prevent, we regard these punishments as undeserved and unfair. The driver who runs over a child even though he was taking good care and could have done nothing to avoid the accident does not deserve blame or punishment, but sympathy.

Problems arise, however, when we reflect that people's performances depend in nearly every case not only on their intentions and efforts but on circumstances beyond their control, including the natural talents that they bring to the performance. Einstein's achievement in developing the theory of relativity required considerable innate mathematical ability as well as a stimulating early education in science. Many philosophers have concluded that genuine desert must be based only on those parts of people's actions or characteristics for which they are responsible, for instance the efforts they make or the talents they have chosen to develop. Whatever stems from natural causes beyond their control is irrelevant.

But this conclusion, too, faces difficulties. For willingness to make an effort, or a decision to develop a talent, is likely to be affected by initial circumstances and natural abilities. Would Einstein have decided to work on the theory of relativity if he had not known that he had a talent for theoretical physics? As John Rawls puts it, the character that enables someone to make an effort 'depends in large part upon fortunate family and social circumstances for which he can claim no credit' (1971: 104).

It seems, then, that the notion of desert collapses if we insist that a deserving person must be personally responsible for all of the conditions necessary for their performance. To keep the link between desert and personal responsibility we must substitute a weaker understanding of responsibility, such that a person can be responsible for a performance even though that performance depends upon circumstances and capacities for which they were not responsible. So long as they intended to perform the activity, and were sufficiently in control of it (it wasn't a lucky accident), they may deserve benefits on account of it, even though their performance depended on natural capacities that others might lack (see MORAL LUCK).

3 Critics of desert

An alternative response is to insist that desert requires responsibility in the stronger sense, and then to say that, because no one is ever fully responsible in this sense for what they do, the concept of desert as ordinarily understood should be scrapped. This is often thought to follow from determinism (see FREE WILL §1). If every human action and decision has ultimately a set of causes beyond the agent, the idea of desert must either be abandoned or be given a new meaning. Utilitarians have argued that to say of someone that they deserve something is only to say that it is socially useful to reward them for performing a certain service (see UTILITARIANISM).

The same conclusion – that desert is at best a secondary idea – has been arrived at in other ways too. As we have seen, desert as ordinarily understood very often looks to the past as a reason for assigning a benefit or burden now: criminals deserve punishment for their past misdeeds; Einstein deservedly won the Nobel prize in 1921 for work done fifteen years earlier. But this appears to collide with the principle that in deciding how to act, we should consider only the future effects of our actions, which many have taken to be a requirement of practical rationality. On this view, we must reinterpret desert in forward-looking terms – we must estimate people's deserts by considering the consequences of different ways of allocating our resources, rather than looking back at what they have already done – if we are to have any good reason to give people what they deserve.

A third line of attack is to suggest that we cannot establish what people deserve until we know which institutions are fair. It is an illusion to suppose that people have deserts in advance of social institutions like competitions, honours systems, or property systems, which are conventional in nature (see PROPERTY). When we say that people deserve things, what we mean is that they are legitimately entitled to them; these are the benefits they would expect to get, or the burdens they would expect to suffer, if the institutions were fair and working as they should. Once again the effect is to relegate desert to the status of a secondary moral idea.

We can now see what is required in order to defend something like our ordinary concept of desert. First, we must either reject determinism, or else argue that determinism is compatible with personal responsibility in a sense strong enough to support desert.

Second, we must defend what Sher (1987) has called 'antecedentialism', the view that an act or occurrence may be called for because it would stand in a certain relation to some antecedent act or event. Third, we must show that our judgments about desert are sufficiently independent of institutional conventions for desert to function as a critical standard which we can appeal to when deciding which institutions to adopt.

4 Desert and justice

Justice often requires us to give people what they deserve (see JUSTICE). Where it does not, this is usually because it is beyond our power to bring about the deserved outcome, or because attempting to do so would have unjust side effects (we cannot ensure that the best athlete wins the race or that good people find the partners they deserve). But if a society allows women to be paid less than men for doing the same job, or punishes lesser crimes more severely than greater crimes, it is to that extent unjust, and we have an obligation to change it.

The assumptions underlying this claim have been challenged both by conservatives and by radicals, who converge in thinking that 'desert' and 'merit' are too subjective to stand as independent criteria of distribution. Hume argued that merit might seem the most natural basis of distribution but 'so great is the uncertainty of merit, both from its natural obscurity, and from the self-conceit of each individual, that no determinate rule of conduct would ever result from it' (1751: 193). More recently, Hayek (1960) has argued along similar lines (see HUME, D.; HAYEK, F.A.). They both make two errors. One is to suppose that desert must mean moral desert; the difficulty of making objective estimates of moral deservingness does not imply that other measures of desert – such as economic productivity – are equally obscure. The other error is to suppose that desert must supplant all other forms of entitlement, rather than serving as a critical standard by which existing entitlements can be judged, and new ones created.

Radicals claim that standards of desert and merit are socially constructed to support existing practices and institutions (see Young 1990). We can see this claim deployed in debates over affirmative action. When it is argued that giving preference to women or racial minorities in the allocation of jobs or college places conflicts with the principle of merit, the critics reply that 'merit' here merely refers to qualities which existing (male, white) society has chosen to designate as relevant. This criticism is likely to backfire, however, because if merit is abandoned altogether, it appears to open the door to practices that discriminate more openly and directly against disadvantaged groups (see DISCRIMINATION).

Justice is more than the requital of desert. It sometimes demands rule-following and respect for existing entitlement, sometimes equal treatment, or distribution according to need (see EQUALITY; NEEDS AND INTERESTS). But to divorce justice and desert entirely would be to abandon some of our most deeply held convictions for reasons which may be less than compelling.

See also: RECTIFICATION AND REMAINDERS; MORAL SENTIMENTS

References and further reading

* Adkins, A.W.H. (1960) *Merit and Responsibility*, Oxford: Oxford University Press. (Explores ideas of merit in classical Greek thought.)
* Feinberg, J. (1970) 'Justice and Personal Desert' in *Doing and Deserving*, Princeton, NJ: Princeton University Press. (A valuable analysis drawing attention to the variety of claims we make about people's deserts.)
* Hayek, F.A. (1960) *The Constitution of Liberty*, London: Routledge & Kegan Paul, ch. 6. (Argues that distribution according to merit cannot be reconciled with a market economy.)
  Honderich, T. (1990) *The Consequences of Determinism: A Theory of Determinism*, Oxford: Clarendon Press, vol. 2, ch. 4. (Considers carefully the implications of determinism for desert as a ground of punishment, and other kinds of desert.)
* Hume, D. (1751) *An Enquiry Concerning the Principles of Morals*, in *Enquiries Concerning the Human Understanding and Concerning the Principles of Morals*, ed. L.A. Selby-Bigge, revised by P.H. Nidditch, Oxford: Clarendon Press, 3rd edn, 1975. (Argues that merit has no place among the rules of justice, which are merely useful conventions.)
* Lucas, J. (1980) *On Justice*, Oxford: Clarendon Press. (Defends desert, and claims that it is central to our thinking about justice.)
  MacIntyre, A. (1981) *After Virtue*, London: Duckworth. (Claims that justice must be understood in terms of desert, but that modern societies lack the practices that sustain desert.)
* Rawls, J. (1971) *A Theory Of Justice*, Cambridge, MA: Harvard University Press, sections 17, 48. (Dismisses desert as basic moral idea, and reinterprets it as legitimate entitlement.)
* Sher, G. (1987) *Desert*, Princeton, NJ: Princeton University Press. (The best recent discussion of desert, exploring possible justifications for a wide range of desert claims.)
  Sidgwick, H. (1874) *The Methods of Ethics*, London: Macmillan; 7th edn, 1907, book III, ch. 5, book IV, ch. 3. (A classic review of ordinary thinking about desert, together with proposals for reconstructing the concept along utilitarian lines.)
* Young, I.M. (1990) 'The Myth of Merit' in *Justice and the Politics of Difference*, Princeton, NJ: Princeton University Press. (Radical attack on the principle of merit.)

DAVID MILLER

DESGABETS, ROBERT (1610–78)

Although he is now little known, Desgabets was an important seventeenth-century French philosopher, theologian, scientist and mathematician. An early defender of Cartesian philosophy, his physical explication of transubstantiation created such an uproar that he complied with a public order and renounced his views. He defended the essential union and interaction of soul and body, and the free creation of the eternal truths. The latter view led him to an empiricist epistemology: all ideas have a sensory basis and are essentially related to existing objects. Despite his originality, he is best known for his polemic with Foucher.

Robert Desgabets, Benedictine monk and early defender of Cartesian philosophy, was born in Ancemont, France. He was active in the Cartesian circles of Paris and Toulouse, well known to Clerselier, ROHAULT, MALEBRANCHE, CORDEMOY, Retz and RÉGIS. Despite his busy ecclesiastical career, he was *au courant* with the latest scientific discoveries. His pioneering work on blood transfusion inspired the French physician Jean Denis to attempt the procedure for the first time on a human subject (the subject lived, but the procedure was not successful). During his lifetime, only three small works were published: *'Discourse de la communication ou transfusion du sang'* (Discourse on the communication or transfusion of blood) (1668), *Considérations sur l'état présent de la controverse touchant le Très Saint-Sacrement de l'autel* (Considerations on the present state of the controversy concerning the Holy Sacrament) (1671) and *Critique de la Critique de la Recherche de la vérité* (Critique of the Critique of the Search After Truth) (1675). However, many of his philosophical manuscripts are known to have circulated widely in Cartesian circles; Régis was greatly influenced by his ideas.

Desgabets' writings deal with a broad range of philosophical, scientific and theological issues. His *Traité de l'indéfectibilité des créatures* (c.1654) (Treatise on the indefectibility of created beings), contains 'the indefectibility thesis', his most original thesis, drawn from Descartes' doctrine that God is the free and indifferent cause of everything, including the eternal truths and essences. Desgabets reasoned that if everything was created by an immutable, indivisible act of God's will then substances were created in their essence as well as their existence. There is no priority of intelligible essence over material existence since both are equally contingent on the omnipotent will of God. Thus, every substance is equally indestructible, necessary and real in both its essence and existence. The epistemological upshot of favouring divine omnipotence over divine wisdom is empiricism, since if God's will is not constrained by rational considerations then any a priori basis for knowledge is upset, leaving experience as the only means for knowing what God actually created. Desgabets thus lays the metaphysical foundation for the Cartesian empiricism which he subsequently developed over twenty years.

His *Le guide de la raison naturelle* (Guide to Natural Reason) (1671) is an examination of the principles and limits of reason. On the assumption that substances are created, he argues that conceivability itself has its source in created substance. He concludes that to conceive of an object is to have an idea of an actually existing object. It is the essential intentionality of ideas which ensures that simple conceptions are always true.

His important *Supplément à la philosophie de M. Descartes* (Supplement to the philosophy of Descartes) (1675) is an examination of the basic principles of Cartesianism, with corrections of Descartes' alleged errors. In this work his empiricism is fully developed. From Descartes' doctrines of soul–body union and interaction, he derives the empiricist claims that all that is in the soul passes through the senses, that all thoughts are accompanied by sensible signs or words, and that our thoughts have succession and duration which are inseparable from bodily movement. Even the *Cogito* involves the succession of ideas, which itself presupposes the idea of extension or body. Thus, the mind is not better known than body. Nor is the first principle of philosophy the *Cogito*, but rather, that all simple conceptions are always true and conform to their objects.

In physics, Desgabets' fidelity to Descartes' ideas is readily evident. He praises Descartes' system of physics against that of GASSENDI, arguing that the essence of matter is extension, that sensible qualities belong to mind, and that a void is impossible. Moreover, he rejects Cordemoy's atomist revision of Cartesianism as one based on a false conception of the continuum and infinite divisibility: if atoms have extension, then they have parts, and if they have parts then they are divisible.

Critique of the Critique of the Search After Truth is a polemical defence of Malebranche against the sceptic FOUCHER. Desgabets challenges Foucher's 'most odious' doctrine that ideas must resemble their objects in order to represent them. Both Malebranche and Desgabets follow Descartes in the belief that resemblance is not necessary for representation. However, Desgabets opts for a different account to that of Malebranche, explicating the relation between ideas and their objects in terms of an 'essential and intentional relation' (see MALEBRANCHE, N. §3).

Desgabets did not believe that reason and faith are opposed, but thought that theological revelation should be made consistent with philosophy. In *Considerations on the present state of the controversy concerning the Holy Sacrament* he argues that the new philosophical reformation is a product of joining mathematics to philosophy, which has enabled the explication of theological mysteries such as that of the Eucharist. That matter and quantity are the same thing means that there cannot be quantity without substance. This entails that if the body of Christ is present in the Host then it is actually present, that is, locally extended. Not surprisingly, Desgabets' views were judged by fellow ecclesiastics – notably ARNAULD – to be completely against tradition. After a public trial and retraction, which resulted in a future ban on his writings, he retreated from public life to a monastery at Breuil, France. Fortunately, under the protection of Cardinal de Retz, he produced some of his best philosophical writings and participated in Cartesian conferences at Commercy.

Desgabets' system is erected on two basic and connected theses: the free creation of the eternal truths and essences, and the principle that simple conceptions contain a demonstrative proof of the reality and existence of their objects. His significance lies in his development and defence of a form of empiricism that, despite its anti-rationalist tendencies, has a clear basis in the work of Descartes himself and constitutes a respectable strain of Cartesianism.

See also: DESCARTES, R.

List of works

Desgabets, R. (1983) *Oeuvres philosophiques inédites*, Analecta Cartesiana 2, ed. J. Beaude, intro. by G. Rodis-Lewis, Amsterdam: Quadratures. (An essential but not widely available collection of Desgabets' philosophical writings, including works previously available only in manuscript. It includes *Traité de l'indéfectibilité des créatures* (Treatise on the indefectibility of created beings) (1653–74), *Le guide de la raison naturelle* (The Guide to Natural Reason) (1671) and *Supplément à la philosophie de M. Descartes* (Supplement to the Philosophy of Descartes) (1675), as well as rich bio-bibliographical information superseding all previous compilations.)

—— (1668) *'Discourse de la communication ou transfusion du sang'* (Discourse on the communication or transfusion of blood), Paris: J.B. Denis. (This scientific piece describes an apparatus and procedure for blood transfusion, invented by Desgabets.)

—— (1671) *Considérations sur l'état présent de la controverse touchant le Très Saint-Sacrement de l'autel* (Considerations on the present state of the controversy concerning the Holy Sacrament), Holland. (This work, published anonymously, stirred up controversy for Cartesians because of its theologically sensitive thesis that the body of Christ is locally extended.)

—— (1675) *Critique de la Critique de la Recherche de la vérité (Critique of the Critique of the Search After Truth)*, Paris. (A response to Foucher's sceptical critique of the first edition of Malebranche's *Search After Truth* (1674) – although Malebranche did not welcome Desgabets' defence. Desgabets attacks Foucher's position that ideas must resemble their objects in order to represent them.)

References and further reading

Armogathe, J.-R. (1977) *Theologia Cartesiana: L'Explication physique de l'Euchariste chez Descartes et dom Desgabets* (Cartesian theology: the physical explication of the Eucharist according to Descartes and dom Desgabets), The Hague: Martinus Nijhoff. (A detailed history of the controversy surrounding Cartesian explications of the mystery of the Eucharist, with an examination of Descartes' and Desgabets' physical explication of transubstantiation.)

Beaude, J. (1974) 'Desgabets et son oeuvre' (Desgabets and his work), *Revue de sythèse* 95:7–17. (A solid bio-bibliographical piece.)

—— (1979) 'Cartésianisme et anticartésianisme de Desgabets' (The Cartesianism and anti-Cartesianism of Desgabets), *Studia Cartesiana 1*, Amsterdam: Quadratures, 1–24. (An insightful analysis of the Cartesian and anti-Cartesian tendencies of Desgabets' thought.)

—— (1980) 'Le Guide de la raison naturelle dans l'oeuvre de Desgabets' (The guide to natural reason in the writings of Desgabets) *Recherches sur le XVIIe siècle IV*, Paris: Centre National de la Recherche scientifique. (This work, establishing Desgabets as author of the unpublished manuscript *The Guide of Natural Reason* (1671), includes a useful discussion of some of Desgabets' primary precepts.)

Cousin, V. (1852) *Fragments de philosophie cartésienne* (Fragments of the Cartesian philosophy), Paris: Didier; repr. Geneva: Slatkine Reprints, 1970. (Volume 3 includes selections from unpublished exchanges between Retz, Malebranche and Corbinelli on Desgabets. Due to incompleteness and emphasis on Retz, these fragments do not serve as an introduction to Desgabets, but the work includes rare manuscript material and a good bibliography.)

Lemaire, P. (1901) *Le Cartésianisme chez les Bénédictins: Dom Robert Desgabets son système, son influence et son école*, (Cartesianism according to the Benedictines: Dom Robert Desgabets, his system, his influence, and his school) Paris: Alcan. (Despite some bio-bibliographical errors and unreliable inferences about the significance of Desgabets' ideas, this remains an important full-length study with many quotations from unpublished manuscripts and a comprehensive bibliography.)

Robinet, A. (1974) 'Dom Robert Desgabets, le conflit philosophique avec Malebranche et son l'oeuvre métaphysique' (Dom Robert Desgabets, his philosophical conflict with Malebranche and his metaphysical work), *Journée Desgabets, Revue de synthèse* 95: 65–83. (This article examines Desgabets' influence on Malebranche, found in Malebranche's views on occasionalism, the non-materiality of thoughts and the nature of the eternal truths.)

Rodis-Lewis, G. (1993) 'Der Cartesianismus in Frankreich' (The diffusion of Cartesianism in France), in J-P. Schobinger ed. *Grundriss der Geschichte der Philosophie, Die Philosophie des 17. Jahrhunderts*, Band II, Basel/Stuttgart, 398–445. (One section of this chapter is devoted to Desgabets, including a summary of his main philosophical theses.)

—— (1981) 'Polémiques sur la création des possibles et sur l'impossible dans l'école cartésienne' (Polemics in the Cartesian School on the creation of possibles and on the impossible), *Studia Cartesiana 2*, Amsterdam: Quadratures, 105–23. (Discusses Desgabets' role in the Cartesian debate on Descartes' doctrine of the free creation of essences and truths.)

—— (1966) *The Downfall of Cartesianism 1673–1712*,

The Hague: Martinus Nijhoff. (Includes an examination of Foucher's critique of Desgabets' account of ideas as intentional representations.)

PATRICIA A. EASTON

DESIGN, ARGUMENT FROM
see GOD, ARGUMENTS FOR THE EXISTENCE OF

DESIGNATORS *see* PROPER NAMES

DESIRE

If an agent is to be moved to action, then two requirements have to be fulfilled: first, the agent must possess beliefs about the way things actually are, about the actions possible given the way things are, and about the likely effects of those actions on how things are; and, second, the agent must have or form desires to change the way things are by resorting to this or that course of action. The beliefs tell the agent about how things are and about how they can be altered; the desires attract the agent to how things are not but can be made to be.

This rough sketch of beliefs and desires is widely endorsed in contemporary philosophy; it derives in many ways from the seminal work of the eighteenth century Scottish philosopher David Hume. The striking thing about it, from the point of view of desire, is that it characterizes desire by the job desire does in collaborating with belief and thereby generating action: it characterizes desire by function, not by the presence of any particular feeling. The account raises a host of questions. Is desire an entirely different sort of state from belief, for example, and from belief-related states like habits of inference? Does desire have to answer to the considerations of evidence and truth that are relevant to belief and inference? How does desire relate to preference and choice? And how does desire relate to the values that we ascribe to different courses of action and that influence us in what we do?

1   **Desire and belief**
2   **Desire and inferential habit**
3   **Desire and preference**
4   **Desire and evaluation**

1   Desire and belief

In ordinary parlance we speak of desiring to go to Paris, or desiring a meal, as well as desiring *that* something happen or be the case. But a more or less agreed point in discussions of desire is that despite these various usages desire is always, at bottom, an attitude towards a possible way things may be, towards a possible state of affairs. If I desire to go to Paris, then I have a desiderative attitude – a 'pro-attitude' – towards the possibility that I go to Paris; if I desire a meal then I have a similar attitude towards the possibility that I eat a meal.

Attitudes towards possibilities, designated by that-clauses such as 'that I go to Paris', are usually described as propositional or intentional attitudes. The feature that links desire with belief, the feature that makes them two of a kind, is that they are both propositional attitudes. The belief 'that p' is one attitude towards the proposition 'that p'; the desire 'that p' is a different attitude towards the same proposition or content. If I believe that I am in Paris, then I have one attitude towards that possibility; if I desire that I be in Paris, I have another (see PROPOSITIONAL ATTITUDES).

What, then, distinguishes desires and beliefs? Here the general line is that the two sorts of attitudes have different roles to play in the agent's psychology. The role of a belief 'that p' – at least if it is a 'descriptive' belief (see §4) – is to prompt the agent to act in the way that is appropriate for realizing their desires in a world where, other things being equal, it is the case that p. The role of a desire 'that p' is to prompt the agent to act in the way that is believed appropriate, given how things are otherwise believed to be, for bringing it about that p. My belief that I am in Paris leads me to drive on the right: given a desire to avoid accidents, it leads me to act in a way that is appropriate in a world where I am now in Paris. My desire to be in Paris leads me to book a flight, given a belief that I am not now in Paris and that booking a flight is the appropriate way of bringing it about that I am in Paris.

The different roles of belief and desire are reflected nicely in the fact that what it means for a belief to be successful – what it means for my belief that I am in Paris to be correct – is that the mind comes to correspond to the world; whereas what it means for a desire to be succcessful – what it means for my desire to get to Paris to be effective - is that the world, the relevant part of the world involving me and Paris, comes to correspond to the mind. Belief has a world-to-mind direction of fit, desire a mind-to-world direction of fit (see BELIEF).

2 Desire and inferential habit

To say that desires have a world-to-mind direction of fit is to hold that desires are goal-seeking: their satisfaction requires that the world conform to a certain ideal. But desires are not the only goal-seeking states that have to be posited by intentional psychologists. Any subject that is to count as a believer must be credited with learned or ingrained habits of inference, whereby they are led from the formation of certain new beliefs to the formation of other beliefs that the new beliefs support: for example they are led from the formation of the belief 'that p', given the belief 'that if p then q', to the belief 'that q'; or from the formation of the belief that someone is a bachelor to the belief that he is a man; or from the belief that this is Australia to the belief that such and such an animal is probably a marsupial. Such habits of inference operate like desires in the sense that when they are successful or effective, then the relevant part of the world – the pattern in the subject's beliefs – comes to correspond to them, not they to the world: the subject comes to believe what they require that the subject should believe. Habits of inference, like desires, are orientated towards the realization of certain goals.

What, then, is the distinction between desires and habits of inference? If a desire leads to a certain type of response – say, my hand moving upwards in greeting a friend – that is because I believe that that sort of response is designed to make the world fit the desire: it realizes my desire to greet my friend. The belief about the suitability of the response for realizing the goal channels the impact of the desire. But when a habit of inference leads to a suitable response – the formation of a new belief – it does so without any need for a belief on the subject's part about a connection between that response and the goal towards which the habit is orientated. Thus my habit of inferring 'male' from 'bachelor' can issue in the belief that someone is unmarried without my registering that by forming that belief I satisfy the inferential goal: that by forming that belief I come to believe something entailed by my belief that the person is a bachelor.

Desire is not only a goal-seeking state, then; it is also a belief-channelled one. That desires are belief-channelled, and habits of inference not, should be no surprise. With the choices that desires serve to generate, there are different responses that the agent can make by way of realizing the goal in question: if my goal is to greet my friend, then I may raise the palm of my hand in a subdued way or gesticulate more wildly. With the responses that habits of inference serve to produce, on the other hand, the agent is not aware of different ways in which the relevant goal may be realized: different ways in which the required belief may be formed. Whereas a belief in the suitability of the particular response chosen – a belief that moving my hand thus and so is a way of greeting – is necessary to explain why desire leads to that particular response, no such belief need figure in the inferential case.

3 Desire and preference

To prefer one option to another is to be disposed to choose it in a two-way contest. That means that successful preference, like successful desire, requires that the world come to fit it, and not the other way around: it requires that the agent come to act in the manner preferred. Preference, in a word, is a goal-seeking state of mind. Furthermore, preference, like desire, is a belief-channelled state. If an agent acts so as to realize a preferred option, that always involves a belief that the particular action taken is a way of realizing the option. So what distinguishes desire from preference?

Preference may mean preference between features or properties, as in someone's saying that they prefer honesty to politeness, or that they prize friendship above patriotism. With respect to such features, the relation between preference and desire is best expressed by saying that what we call 'desire' can also be called 'degree of preference'. We can know all about someone's 'feature-preferences' without knowing anything about the intensity with which different features are preferred to others. When we know about their 'feature-desires', we learn about these intensities: we learn about how much the agent prefers each feature relative to others; we learn about the person's degrees of preference as well as their order of preference. To know that someone prefers living in a warm climate to living in a cold climate is not to know much about them; to know that they have such and such a desire for living in a warm climate – that they prefer it with such and such an intensity – is to know quite a lot.

But preference may also mean, not feature-preference, but preference between different mutually exclusive, jointly exhaustive ways things may be; in particular it may mean preference between different ways an agent may make things be: preference between the rival options in a decision. 'Desire' is used ambiguously in relation to 'preference' in this sense. We may ask how much you desire this or that alternative – whether you feel any desire for this or that alternative – and then we are asking, as in the other case, about your degree of preference: about what decision theorists call your 'subjective utility' for that alternative. Or we may ask which of the alternatives you desire, which of the alternatives you want, and then we are asking which alternative you prefer overall, without regard to degrees – which alternative you prefer in the sense, roughly, of 'intend'.

This latter usage is relatively special, however; and generally we can say that while desires and preferences are both goal-seeking, belief-channelled states, there is no difficulty about the distinction between them. Preferences rank features or alternatives against one another, and desires represent degrees of intensity in those rankings – degrees, as we say, of preference. The notion of degrees of preference is in need of further elaboration, of course. Decision theory, for instance, is an attempt to explicate the notion systematically for preferences between alternatives. It measures a person's degree of preference for an alternative by the choices they would make with regard to different probabilistic packages involving that alternative – different gambles, as one version has it – on the assumption that they are rational in this sense: they try to maximize the expectation of 'subjective utility' (see DECISION AND GAME THEORY §2).

4 Desire and evaluation

It appears that if desire is defined after the fashion described here, then desire is indispensable for belief-mediated action. Beliefs serve to give the subject a descriptive sense of the environment and they do not on their own predispose the agent in any particular direction of change. The sort of state that is necessary for that, by the account given, is what we call 'desire'.

The ubiquity of desire that is thereby established raises a problem. For it appears that certain *nondescriptive* beliefs appear in the genesis of at least some actions and play precisely the sort of goal-seeking, belief-channelled role that we have associated with desires. I may be moved on occasion, not just by the desire for fun, but by the *judgment* that fun is desirable. More generally, I may be moved by a variety of evaluative judgments: say, the judgment that it is best or right that p, or that it would be just if p, or enjoyable if p, or whatever. The problem is how such evaluations can serve to direct an action at the same time that desires serve in this role. How are evaluation and desire supposed to relate when they are both present?

It will not do in response to deny the appearances and say that evaluation is not an important phenomenon or even that it is an illusion. Deliberative reflection and argument often plays a role in leading the human agent to a certain decision and action, and it is evaluation, not desire, that figures in deliberation.

I argue from the fact that it is desirable that p, and the fact that I can make it the case that p by X-ing, to the conclusion that I should X. I do not argue from the premise that I desire that p: that premise in itself would give me no reason for fulfilling the desire, unless I assumed that it was desirable to fulfil it. I see good grounds for helping an elderly person across the street in the thought that it would be kind to do so, or that it would make their crossing less hazardous. I do not find such grounds in the thought that I have a certain desire to help them.

A different response to the problem is to deny that evaluation is a species of belief. According to expressivist theories, evaluations are simply expressions of desire, or expressions of desire that meet certain standards, or something of the kind; they are not beliefs. The utterances 'It is right that p,' or 'It is desirable that p,' do nothing more than mark the fact that the utterer is well disposed; they are tantamount to saying 'P: wow!' (see EMOTIVISM). The explanation, then, of how evaluative attitudes play the same role as desires is that there is little or no difference between evaluative attitudes and desires. But expressivist theories are rejected by many, on the ground that evaluations have all the hallmarks of belief, being well or ill supported, being true or false, being capable of figuring in the antecedents of conditionals – if torture is wrong, we should outlaw it – and so on. Expressivist theories are rejected in favour of a cognitivist view of evaluations: a view that represents evaluations as varieties of belief or judgment. What are we to say, on this approach, about how evaluations and desires relate to one another?

A general schema would have it that evaluations – evaluative beliefs or judgments – are attended by corresponding desires, and lead to action, in just those conditions that count as normal. This schema means that there is a very intimate linkage between evaluation and desire, on any plausible explication of normal conditions – a linkage tighter than one of mere inductive association. Some versions of the schema will construe normal conditions as cognitively faultless conditions – conditions where there is no lack of understanding, no illogic, or whatever, associated with the evaluation. Other versions will be less inclined to have desires dance to such a purely cognitive tune (though they may still think that desires are subject to constraints of reason similar to those governing cognitive states); they will be cognitivist about evaluation without being cognitivist about desires as well. Such versions of the schema will say that evaluative belief certainly involves desire under certain independently specifiable conditions, but that those conditions are not guaranteed of fulfilment just by the fact that the belief is cognitively irreproachable; it may also be required that the subject holds in the ordinary, spontaneous way by the evaluations, is not overwhelmed by passion, and so on.

A theory of desire that deals with its relation to belief, inference, preference and evaluation will be able to answer the questions raised in the introduction. But it should also give us pointers on a number of other issues raised in discussions of desire. When is a desire for an option just a *prima facie* or *pro tanto* desire, for example? Answer: when it is simply a desire for a feature that is ascribed to the option, not a desire for the option itself. When is a desire a visitation on the agent, not a desire autonomously held – not a desire with which the agent identifies? Answer: when it fails to correspond with the agent's mature evaluations, or perhaps with the agent's higher-order desires about which lower-order desires to hold: when, for some such reason, it prevails, as we say, in a compulsive or obsessive way. As such issues confront us, so we may hope that answers will generally suggest themselves.

See also: ACTION; INTENTION; RATIONALITY, PRACTICAL; VALUES

References and further reading

Anscombe, G.E.M. (1957) *Intention*, Oxford: Blackwell. (Classic discussion of the mind-to-world direction of fit of desire.)

Bratman, M. (1987) *Intention, Plans, and Practical Reason*, Cambridge, MA: Harvard University Press. (An argument that intention cannot be assimilated to desire.)

Frankfurt, H. (1988) *The Importance of What We Care About*, New York: Cambridge University Press. (Discusses autonomously held desires and introduces higher-order desires as the key to autonomy.)

* Hume, D. (1739–40) *A Treatise of Human Nature*, ed. L.A. Selby-Bigge, Oxford: Clarendon Press, 1888, revised P.H. Nidditch, Oxford: Oxford University Press, 1978. (Book II, part 3 is the classic presentation of reason and belief as existence distinct from passion and desire.)

Jackson, F. (1984) 'Internal Conflicts in Desires and Morals', *American Philosophical Quarterly* 22: 105–14. (Distinguishes desires for features and desires for alternative prospects.)

Marks, J. (ed.) (1986) *The Ways of Desire*, Chicago, IL: Precedent. (Useful collection of articles on various aspects of desire.)

Pettit, P. (1993) *The Common Mind: An Essay on Psychology, Society and Politics*, New York: Oxford University Press. (Chapter 1 distinguishes desires and inferential habits.)

Pettit, P. and Smith, M. (1990) 'Backgrounding Desire', *Philosophical Review* 99: 565–92. (Discusses the roles of desire and evaluation.)

—— (1993) 'Practical Unreason', *Mind* 102: 53–80. (Discusses the ways in which desire and evaluation may come apart.)

Smith, M. (1987) 'The Humean Theory of Motivation', *Mind* 96: 36–61. (Very useful and accesssible discussion of the mind-to-world direction of fit of desire.)

—— (1994) *The Moral Problem*, Oxford: Blackwell. (Shows the broad significance of the question of how desire and evaluation relate.)

Watson, G. (1975) 'Free Agency' *Journal of Philosophy* 72: 205–20. (Casts autonomously held desires as desires that accord with evaluation.)

PHILIP PETTIT

DETERMINISM AND INDETERMINISM

Over the centuries, the doctrine of determinism has been understood, and assessed, in different ways. Since the seventeenth century, it has been commonly understood as the doctrine that every event has a cause; or as the predictability, in principle, of the entire future. To assess the truth of determinism, so understood, philosophers have often looked to physical science; they have assumed that their current best physical theory is their best guide to the truth of determinism. It seems that most have believed that classical physics, especially Newton's physics, is deterministic. And in this century, most have believed that quantum theory is indeterministic. Since quantum theory has superseded classical physics, philosophers have typically come to the tentative conclusion that determinism is false.

In fact, these impressions are badly misleading. The above formulations of determinism are unsatisfactory. Once we use a better formulation, we see that there is a large gap between the determinism of a given physical theory, and the bolder, vague idea that motivated the traditional formulations: the idea that the world in itself is deterministic. Admittedly, one can make sense of this idea by adopting a sufficiently bold metaphysics; but it cannot be made sense of just by considering determinism for physical theories.

As regards physical theories, the traditional impression is again misleading. Which theories are deterministic turns out to be a subtle and complicated matter, with many open questions. But broadly speaking, it turns out that much of classical physics, even much of Newton's physics, is indeterministic. Furthermore, the alleged indeterminism of quantum theory is very controversial: it enters, if at all, only in quantum theory's account of measurement processes, an account which remains the most controversial part of the theory.

1 **Consensus**
2 **Controversy**
3 **Defining determinism**
4 **The notion of state**

1 Consensus

Over the centuries, the doctrine of determinism has been understood, and its truth or falsity assessed, in different ways. (We follow the nearly universal practice of taking 'indeterminism' as simply the negation of determinism; so our discussion can focus on determinism.) Since the rise of modern science in the seventeenth century, it has been commonly understood as the 'law of universal causation', that every event has a cause; or as the predictability, in principle, of all of the future, given full knowledge of the present.

What evidence a philosopher takes to count for or against this doctrine varies immensely from one philosopher to another, according to their philosophical project. For example, many assess determinism in the light of their opinions about such metaphysical topics as free will or God (see FREE WILL; OMNISCIENCE §3). Others see connections between determinism and broadly logical topics about time (see MANY-VALUED LOGICS, PHILOSOPHICAL ISSUES IN §1). But this entry is restricted to formulating determinism, and assessing whether it is true, by considering the deliverances of physical theory. Of course, this restriction does not mean that our discussion only applies to wholly secular philosophers: many theistic philosophers, for example Kant, have discussed determinism in terms of the physics of their day. Some have even endorsed it, as part of their philosophy of nature; again Kant provides the outstanding example (see KANT, I. §7).

Making this restriction, we can say that since the seventeenth century, philosophers have typically taken their current best physical theory as their guide to the truth of determinism. And during the second half of this period, there has been a remarkable consensus about what that best theory is, and what it indicates about determinism.

During the nineteenth century, most of the educated public took Newtonian mechanics, and especially the Newtonian theory of gravitation, to be their best physical theory. Indeed, many took it to be

an unrevisable foundation for physical theorizing. At its simplest, the idea was that Newton had laid down in his mechanics a schema for the mechanical explanation of the physical world. The schema was encapsulated in Newton's second law, that the force on a body is equal to its mass times its acceleration. Knowing the force and the mass, one could calculate the acceleration, and thus how the body moved. So to get a mechanical explanation of a given phenomenon, one had only to 'fill in the schema' by finding the forces involved. The paradigm case was of course gravitation; here Newton himself had discovered the nature of the force, and had calculated with stunning success how the planets and other celestial bodies move. Accordingly, many believed that Newtonian mechanics could in principle describe any phenomenon, perhaps by postulating strange forces (see MECHANICS, CLASSICAL §2).

They also believed that all the theories that could arise by thus filling in the schema would be deterministic; for the motion of a body would be determined by the forces on it (together with its initial position and velocity). The *locus classicus* for this view is a passage by Laplace, in which he not only states the doctrine that Newtonian mechanics is deterministic, but also provides formulations of determinism – first, in terms of causation, and then in terms of prediction; we shall later have reason to criticize both the doctrine and the formulations.

> We ought then to regard the present state of the universe as the effect of its anterior state and as the cause of the one which is to follow. Given for one instant an intelligence which could comprehend all the forces by which nature is animated and the respective situation of the beings who compose it – an intelligence sufficiently vast to submit these data to analysis – it would embrace in the same formula the movements of the greatest bodies of the universe and those of the lightest atom; for it, nothing would be uncertain and the future, as the past, would be present to its eyes. The human mind offers, in the perfection which it has been able to give to astronomy, a feeble idea of such an intelligence.

(Laplace [1820] 1951: 4)

During the twentieth century, quantum theory and relativity theory became our best physical theories; by 1930, they had superseded classical physics. Since these theories are comparatively new and technically demanding, they have not become part of 'educated common sense' in the way in which Newtonian theories did (at least eventually, say by the mid-nineteenth century). But most philosophers who have addressed the topic have concluded that while relativity theory is deterministic, quantum theory is indeterministic. Indeterminism is taken to be the lesson of the much-cited uncertainty principle. This conclusion also has authority on its side: the great majority of the discoverers of quantum theory endorse it. So philosophers have typically come to the tentative conclusion that determinism is false.

2 Controversy

But this consensus has been badly misleading. First of all, formulations of determinism in terms of causation or predictability are unsatisfactory. And once we use a correct formulation, it turns out that much of classical physics, even much Newtonian physics, is indeterministic; and that parts of relativity theory are indeterministic (owing to singularities). Furthermore, the alleged indeterminism of quantum theory is very controversial – for it enters only, if at all, in quantum theory's account of measurement processes, an account which remains the most controversial part of the theory.

Formulations of determinism in terms of causation or predictability are unsatisfactory, precisely because of philosophers' interest in assessing determinism by considering physical theories. That interest means that determinism should be formulated in terms that are clearly related to such theories. But 'event', 'causation' and 'prediction' are vague and controversial notions, and are not used (at least not univocally) in most physical theories. Prediction has the further defect of being an epistemological notion – hence Laplace's appeal to an 'intelligence'; while the intuitive idea of determinism concerns the ontology or 'world-picture' of a given theory (see CAUSATION; EVENTS).

Fortunately, the intuitive idea of determinism can be formulated quite precisely, without these notions. The key idea is that determinism is a property of a theory. Imagine a theory that ascribes properties to objects of a certain kind, and claims that the sequence through time of any such object's properties satisfies certain regularities. In physics, such objects are usually called 'systems'; the properties are called 'states'; and the regularities are called 'the laws of the theory'. Then we say that the theory is deterministic if and only if for any two such systems: if they are in exactly the same state as one another at a given time, then according to the theory (for example, its laws about the evolution of states over time), they will at all future times be in the same state as one another. (Montague 1974, pioneered this kind of formulation.)

We can make determinism even more precise in the context of specific physical theories, by using their notions of system, state and law (regularity). But the classification of theories as deterministic or indeterministic is not completely automatic. For the notions of system, and so on, are often not precise in a physical theory as usually formulated. So various different formulations of determinism are often in principle legitimate for a given theory; and there is room for judgment about which formulation is interpretatively best.

However, it is well-established that the main conclusions are as reported above. The philosopher who has done most to classify physical theories in this way is Earman (1986), who upholds these main conclusions. We shall just briefly support these conclusions with two points that his book does not cover. (The details of the above formulation of determinism will not be needed for these points.)

First, much Newtonian physics is indeterministic. Indeed, indeterminism is lurking in the paradigm case discussed by Laplace: point-masses influenced only by their mutual gravitational attraction, as described by Newton's law of gravitation.

But surely the motion of each point-mass is determined by thus forces on it, in this setting the gravitational force (together with its initial position and velocity) (see MECHANICS, CLASSICAL §2)? Indeed it is, *locally*. That is: given the initial positions, velocities and forces, the motion of each point-mass is determined, for *some* interval of time extending into the future. But it might be a very short interval. (Technically, the equations of the theory have a unique solution for some interval of time, perhaps a very short one.) Furthermore, as time goes on, the interval of time for which there is such a solution might get shorter, shrinking to zero, in such a way that after some period of time, the solution does not exist any more. In effect, determinism might hold locally in time, and yet break down globally.

One way this might happen is by collisions: in general, Newtonian mechanics is silent about what would happen after two or more point-masses collide. But more interestingly, it seems that it might also happen *without* collisions. Thus it was conjectured in 1897 that one might somehow arrange for one of the point-masses to accelerate in a given spatial direction, ever more rapidly and at so great a rate, during a period of time, in such a way that it does not exist in space at the end of the period! By that time, it has disappeared to 'spatial infinity'. (The source for the energy needed by the acceleration is the infinite potential well-associated with Newton's inverse-square law of gravitation.) That this can indeed happen with just Newtonian gravity was finally proved true by Xia in 1992 (using a system of five point-masses). So now we know that, even setting aside collisions, Laplace's vision of Newtonian determinism is only valid for local intervals of time.

Second, quantum theory can be interpreted as being deterministic. De Broglie and Bohm showed that such an interpretation of elementary quantum theory is possible, despite the alleged proofs that it was impossible (given in the 1930s by some of the discoverers of quantum theory). The basic idea is that a quantum system consists of both a wave and a particle. The wave evolves deterministically over time according to the fundamental equation of quantum theory (the Schrödinger equation) and it determines the particle's motion, which therefore also moves deterministically, given the wave (hence this interpretation is also called the pilot wave interpretation). This contrasts with the orthodox interpretation. Roughly speaking, the orthodox interpretation accepts only the wave, and accommodates particle-like phenomena by having the wave evolve indeterministically (violating the Schrödinger equation) during processes of measurement (see QUANTUM MECHANICS, INTERPRETATION OF §3; QUANTUM MEASUREMENT PROBLEM). In recent years, the de Broglie–Bohm approach has been greatly developed so as to yield a deterministic interpretation of more and more of advanced quantum theory, including quantum field theory (see Cushing 1994). Suffice it to say, a deterministic interpretation of quantum theory is entirely coherent.

There remain two other controversial matters; which return us to general metaphysics and philosophy of science. First, should we apply the idea of determinism, as we have formulated it, to theories of the whole universe, that is, cosmologies? If so, then the 'systems' in question will be universes or 'possible worlds', that is, total possible courses of history. So one will in general not require that the systems whose states one compares must lie in the same possible world (see POSSIBLE WORLDS).

Second, should we accept the idea, for a given kind of system, of a complete theory, a theory that in some sense describes the whole truth about the systems? Some philosophers hold that this idea is incoherent: at least if it is filled out as allowing that such a theory is never formulated by humans; or at least if it allows that humans might be in principle incapable of formulating such a theory (see SCIENTIFIC REALISM AND ANTIREALISM §1). But if we accept some version of this idea, then we can reasonably talk of the systems, or perhaps the kind of system, being deterministic: namely, if and only if the systems' final theory is deterministic.

So the cautious answer to these questions is No. To answer Yes is to be bold: (some would say, incoherent). In particular, if we answer Yes to both questions,

we are in effect accepting that it is meaningful to talk of the whole universe being deterministic. For we are accepting the idea of a complete theory of a given possible world (a total possible course of history). So we can reasonably call this theory the 'theory of the world', and its general propositions 'the laws of nature' (see LAWS, NATURAL §1). (Again, humans are unlikely to have much idea of this theory or its laws.) And then we can say that the given world is deterministic if and only if its theory is. That is, the given world is deterministic if and only if any two worlds, obeying this theory, that have exactly the same state (in the sense of this theory) as one another at a given time also have exactly the same state at all later times.

The rest of this entry is restricted to discussing determinism for given physical theories. It thereby answers No to the second question; and, cosmological theories apart, it also answers No to the first question. But before embarking on this cautious strategy, we should briefly note that, historically, the bold (perhaps incoherent) idea of the entire world being deterministic, irrespective of any theory, has been very important; it has been the focus of countless philosophers' discussions of determinism (both for and against it).

3 Defining determinism

In §2 we said that a theory is deterministic if and only if for any two systems of the kind described by the theory: if they are in exactly the same state as one another at a given time, then according to the theory, they will at all future times be in the same state as one another. But this formulation is still rough.

The main problem is that, whatever theory one considers, its systems are continually interacting with their environment: as physicists put it, no system is 'completely isolated'. For example, each system feels the gravitational pull of other objects. These interactions make determinism, as just formulated, an impossibly tall order. For, first, it will be very rare for two systems to be in exactly the same state at a given time. And even if they are, it will be virtually impossible that their subsequent interactions with their environments match so exactly that they are also in the same state as one another at all future times. But surely, determinism should not be so formulated that it will fail because of the vagaries of interactions with other systems: whether it fails or holds should be a matter internal to the theory considered.

The remedy is clear enough. To set aside such interactions, we need to formulate determinism in terms of completely isolated systems. But we cannot just think in terms of two systems in an otherwise empty universe. For in general the theory will take these two systems to interact with each other; so that again determinism can fail in a spurious way. That is to say, even if we suppose that at a given time the two systems are in the same state, at some future time they may well not be: their interaction, as described by the theory, might lead to their states differing. (The problem is of course aggravated if we think of the systems as also interacting in other ways, not described by the theory.)

To avoid this kind of spurious failure of determinism, we need to think of the theory as describing single completely isolated systems, each one alone in its universe. Let us say that a sequence of states for such a single system, that conforms to the laws of the theory, is a *model* of the theory. So a model contains a system of the theory's kind, undergoing a history allowed by the theory: the model is a 'toy universe' or 'toy possible world', according to the theory. (This use of 'model' is common in general philosophy of science. In particular, it is often useful to consider a scientific theory as the class of its models in this sense, rather than in the traditional manner of logicians – as a set of sentences closed under deduction; see MODELS; THEORIES, SCIENTIFIC.) Using this notion of model, we can give a better definition of determinism, which avoids the problem of interactions. We say that a theory is deterministic if and only if: any two of its models that agree at a time t on the state of their objects, also agree at all times future to t.

(This definition returns us to the first of the two questions at the end of §2: namely, should we apply the idea of determinism to theories of the whole universe, for example cosmologies? We now see that our strategy for avoiding spurious violations of determinism, due to interactions between systems, commits us to answering Yes to this question. For by taking a model of any theory to describe a single completely isolated system, alone in its universe, we are in a sense treating any theory as a cosmology. But since each of a theory's possible universes contains just one system of the kind treated by the theory, it is typically a humble, even a dull, cosmology!)

This definition is still a bit vague: precisely how should we understand a single time t in two models, and two models 'agreeing' on their states at t? The answers to these questions lie in the idea of isomorphism of models, or parts of models; in the usual sense used by logicians. (There is no need for a 'meta-time' outside the two models, in terms of which their time series can be compared: thank goodness, since that would be very questionable!). Thus we can speak of an 'instantaneous slice' of one model (that is, the part describing the system at a single time) being isomorphic to an instantaneous slice of another

model. And similarly, we can speak of isomorphism of 'final segments' of two models: that is, isomorphism of parts of two models, each part describing the system at all times future to some time within the model. Determinism is then a matter of isomorphic instantaneous slices implying that the corresponding final segments are isomorphic (where 'corresponding' means 'starting at the time of the instantaneous slice'). That is: we say that a theory is deterministic if, and only if: for any two of its models, if they have instantaneous slices that are isomorphic, then the corresponding final segments are also isomorphic.

4 The notion of state

To a philosopher, our definition of determinism looks very formal. And indeed, it is closely related to purely mathematical questions. For a physical theory is often presented as a set of equations, so-called 'differential equations', governing how physical magnitudes (for example, numerically measurable quantities like distance, energy and so on) change with time, given their values at an initial time. Our definition then corresponds to such a set of equations having a unique solution for future times, given the values at the initial time; and whether a set of differential equations has a unique solution (for given initial values) is a purely mathematical property of the set.

But we should beware of identifying determinism with this purely mathematical property: there are conceptual, indeed metaphysical, matters behind the mathematics. The reason lies in the notion of state. We have taken states to be simply the properties ascribed by a theory to objects of a certain kind (the theory's 'systems'); and so as varying from one theory to another. But there are two general features which the notion of state needs to have if our definition of determinism is to be sure of capturing the intuitive idea. These features are vague, and cannot be formalized: but without them, there is a threat that our definition will be intuitively too weak.

First, states need to be intrinsic properties. It is notoriously hard to say exactly what is meant by 'intrinsic', but the idea is to rule out properties which might code information about how the future just happens to go, and thus support a spurious determinism. Thus, to take an everyday example, 'Fred was mortally wounded at noon' implies that Fred later dies. But the property ascribed at noon is clearly extrinsic: it 'looks ahead' to the future. And so this implication does not show that there is any genuine determinism about the processes that led to Fred's later death.

Second, states need to be 'maximal', that is they need to be the logically strongest consistent properties the theory can express (compatibly with their being intrinsic). For in an intuitively indeterministic theory, there might well be some properties (typically, logically weak ones) such that models agreeing on these properties at one time implies their agreeing on them at all later times.

Do physical theories' notions of state have these two features? The question is vague because there is no agreed analysis of the ideas of an intrinsic, or a maximal, property. Perhaps 'maximal' can be readily enough analysed in terms of logical strength, as just hinted. But it is notoriously hard to analyse 'intrinsic'. But, by and large, the answer to this question is surely Yes. Physics texts typically define, or gloss, 'state' and similar words as a system's maximal (or 'complete') set of intrinsic (or 'possessed') properties; and in philosophy, the most commonly cited examples of intrinsic properties are the magnitudes figuring in the states of familiar physical theories, such as mass or electric charge. So it seems there is no widespread problem of spurious satisfactions of determinism.

But although there is not a problem, the need for these features brings out the main point: determinism is not a formal feature of a set of equations. Indeed, there are many examples of a set of differential equations which can be interpreted as a deterministic theory, or as an indeterministic theory, depending on the notion of state used to interpret the equations.

The idea of states as intrinsic also brings out two other points, one philosophical and one technical. The philosophical point concerns the ideas at the end of §2 about laws of nature, and the whole universe (as against a given theory) being deterministic. One of course expects that making sense of the idea of laws of nature will involve the theory of properties. But we now see a more specific point: that making sense of the universe being deterministic will involve the general analysis of 'intrinsic'.

The technical point concerns theories that treat all the states up to the given time, taken together, as contributing to determining the future states. (There are a few such theories. It does not matter here whether all these earlier states taken together do determine all the future states: as, one might say, whether there is determinism of the future by the whole past.) At first sight, it looks as if such theories add to the usual intrinsic notion of state, a highly extrinsic notion – for which the state at a given time encodes some of the information in all earlier intrinsic states. What is going on?

In fact, in all such theories (so far as this author knows) the extrinsic notion is a technical convenience, rather than a new notion of state. The theory refers to the arbitrarily distant past (typically in some time-integral from minus infinity to the given time) just as

a mathematically tractable way of stating information about the state at the given time, information that contributes to the future development of the system. (Wanting to state this information of course reflects the idea of states as maximal.) For example: in statistical physics, some such time-integrals define correlations in the present state; and in theories that study systems interacting with their environment, the past states of the system yield useful information about the present influence of the environment (which is otherwise not represented in the formalism).

Note that this explanation accords with a familiar tenet about causation: that past states influence the future, but only via their influence on the current state – there is thus no 'action at a temporal distance'. This tenet is widely held by philosophers; and to the extent that one can talk about causation in physical theories, it is upheld in physics. This is especially true of relativity theory; for relativity both unifies space and time, and upholds the principle of contact-action (see RELATIVITY THEORY, PHILOSOPHICAL SIGNIFICANCE OF §3; SPACETIME). The tenet is also closely related to a very common property (being Markovian) of probabilistic theories, both in physics and beyond. Indeed, according to some probabilistic theories of causation, the tenet is equivalent to the theory being Markovian.

Theories that refer to past states are relevant to our final topic: the fact (mentioned in §2) that there are some uncontroversial variations on our definition of determinism. So far we have for simplicity assumed that there is a single intuitive idea of determinism: the idea of the present state determining future states. But as we have just seen, there is an analogous idea: that all the states up to the present, taken together, determine future states. It just so happens that (using an intrinsic, maximal notion of state!) this idea is not obeyed in known physical theories: they have no 'action at a temporal distance'. But that is no reason to deny to the idea the name 'determinism'; or, more clearly, 'determinism of the future by the past' (rather than by the present).

This point is reinforced by other analogous ideas, ideas which *are* obeyed in known physical theories. Thus in general relativity, and in quantum field theory, diverse technical reasons make it much easier to define a state on an interval of time (called a 'sandwich' of spacetime!) than at an instant of time (a 'slice' of spacetime). There is no hint here of action at a temporal distance: the interval can be arbitrarily short – it is just that for technical reasons it must have some duration. But such states prompt rather different definitions of determinism, requiring (roughly speaking) that for any interval, no matter how short, states to the future of that interval are determined by the state on it. And these definitions are often satisfied.

One can instead strengthen the definition of determinism, requiring the state at the given time to determine not only future states, but also past states. Many important physical theories have a property called 'time-symmetry' or 'time-reversal invariance', which implies that they satisfy this stronger definition, if they satisfy our first one. A famous example is Newtonian mechanics. Indeed, it may well be that Laplace had in mind this point (rather than just the intelligence having a memory), when he said in the quotation above 'as the past' (see MECHANICS, CLASSICAL; THERMODYNAMICS §§4–5).

References and further reading

Bohm, D. (1957) *Causality and Chance in Modern Physics*, London: Routledge & Kegan Paul. (Discussion of determinism and chance, by one of the two inventors of a deterministic interpretation of quantum theory; see end of §2.)
* Cushing, J. (1994) *Quantum Mechanics: Historical Contingency and the Copenhagen Hegemony*, Chicago, IL: University of Chicago Press. (Discussion of historical, philosophical and physical aspects of the de Broglie–Bohm interpretation.)
* Earman, J. (1986) *A Primer on Determinism*, Dordrecht: Reidel. (The best single book on determinism in the physical sciences. It wages a fine campaign against the false consensus, discussed in §§1, 2.)
* Laplace, P. (1820) Essai philosophique sur les probabilités; forming the introduction to his *Théorie analytique des probabilités*, Paris: V Courcier; repr. F.W. Truscott and F.L. Emory (trans.) *A Philosophical Essay on Probabilities*, New York: Dover, 1951. (The page reference is from the reprint. This work is famous as a treatise on probability theory and its philosophy, quite apart from its statement of determinism in the introduction.)
* Montague, R. (1974) 'Deterministic Theories', in R. Thomason (ed.) *Formal Philosophy*, New Haven, CT: Yale University Press. (Technical paper pioneering the kind of definition given in §2–3. This collection was posthumous published.)
* Xia, Z. (1992) 'The Existence of Noncollision Singularities in Newtonian Systems', *Annals of Mathematics* 135: 411–68. (Mathematical paper proving indeterminism in Newtonian gravitation.)

JEREMY BUTTERFIELD

DEVELOPMENT ETHICS

Development ethics is ethical reflection on the ends and means of socioeconomic change in poor countries and regions. It has several sources: criticism of colonialism and post-Second World War development strategies; Denis Goulet's writings; Anglo-American philosophical debates about the ethics of famine relief; and Paul Streeten's and Amartya Sen's approaches to development.

Development ethicists agree that the moral dimension of development theory and practice is just as important as the scientific and policy components. What is often called 'development' – economic growth, for instance – may be bad for people, communities and the environment. Hence, the process of development should be reconceived as beneficial change, usually specified as alleviating human misery and environmental degradation in poor countries.

Development ethicists do not yet agree on whether their ethical reflection should extend to destitution in rich *countries or aspects of North–South relations apart from development aid. Other unresolved controversies concern the status and content of substantive development norms. Finally, agreement does not yet exist as to how the benefits of and responsibilities for development should be distributed within and between countries.*

1   **The nature of development ethics**
2   **Sources**
3   **Areas of consensus**
4   **Controversies and agenda**

1   The nature of development ethics

National policy makers, project managers and international aid donors involved in development in poor countries often confront moral questions in their work. Development scholars recognize that social-scientific theories of 'development' and 'underdevelopment' have ethical as well as empirical and policy components. Development philosophers and other ethicists formulate ethical principles relevant to social change in poor countries, analyse and assess the moral dimensions of development theories and seek to resolve the moral quandaries raised in development policies and practice: In what direction and by what means should a society 'develop'? Who is morally responsible for beneficial change? What are the obligations, if any, of rich societies (and their citizens) to poor societies?

2 Sources

There are several sources for moral assessment of the theory and practice of development. First, beginning in the 1940s, activists and social critics – such as Gandhi in India, Raúl Prébisch in Latin America, and Frantz Fanon in Africa – criticized colonial and orthodox economic development (see GANDHI, M.K.; FANON, F.). Second, since the early 1960s, American Denis Goulet, influenced by French economist Louis-Joseph Lebret and social scientists such as Gunner Myrdal, has argued that '"development" needs to be redefined, demystified, and thrust into the arena of moral debate' (1971: xix). Drawing on his training in continental philosophy, political science and social planning as well as on his grassroots experience in numerous projects in poor countries, Goulet was a pioneer in addressing 'the ethical and value questions posed by development theory, planning, and practice' (1977: 5). One of the most important lessons taught by Goulet (1971) is that so-called 'development', owing to its costs in human suffering and loss of meaning, can amount to 'anti-development' (see Berger 1974).

A third source of development ethics is the effort of Anglo-American moral philosophers to deepen and broaden philosophical debate about famine relief and food aid. Beginning in the early 1970s, often in response to Peter Singer's utilitarian argument for famine relief (1972) and Garrett Hardin's 'lifeboat ethics' (1974), many philosophers debated whether affluent nations (or their citizens) have moral obligations to aid starving people in poor countries and, if they do, what are the nature, bases and extent of those obligations (see Aiken and LaFollette (eds) 1976). By the early 1980s, however, moral philosophers, such as Nigel Dower, Onora O'Neill and Jerome M. Segal, had come to agree with those development specialists who for many years had believed that famine relief and food aid were only one part of the solution to the problems of hunger, poverty, underdevelopment and international injustice. These philosophers have argued that what is needed is not merely an ethics of aid but a more comprehensive, empirically informed, and policy relevant 'ethics of Third World development'. The kind of assistance and North–South relations called for depend on how (good) development is understood.

A fourth source of development ethics is the work of Paul Streeten and Amartya Sen. Both of these economists have addressed the causes of global economic inequality, hunger and underdevelopment, and attacked these problems with, among other things, a conception of development formulated explicitly in terms of ethical principles. Building on Streeten's 'basic human needs' strategy (1981), Sen argues that development should be understood ultimately not as economic growth, industrialization or modernization, which are at best means (and sometimes not very good means), but as the expansion of people's valuable capabilities and functionings: 'what people can or cannot do, e.g., whether they can live long, escape avoidable morbidity, be well nourished, be able to read and write and communicate, take part in literary and scientific pursuits, and so forth' (1984: 497) (see Nussbaum and Sen (eds) 1993; Nussbaum and Glover (eds) 1995).

These four sources have been especially influential in the work of Anglo-American development ethicists. When practised by Latin Americans, Asians, Africans and non-Anglo Europeans, development ethics often draws on philosophical and moral traditions distinctive of their cultural contexts (see, for example, Luis Camacho (1993) on Costa Rica, and Godfrey Gunatilleke (1988) on Asia).

3 Areas of consensus

Although differing on a number of matters, development ethicists exhibit a wide consensus about the commitments that inform their enterprise, the questions they are posing and the unreasonableness of certain answers. Development ethicists typically ask the following related questions. What should count as (good) development? Should we continue using the concept of development instead of, for example, 'progress', 'transformation', 'liberation', or 'postdevelopment alternatives to development' (Escobar 1995)? What should be a society's basic economic, political and cultural goals and strategies, and what principles should inform their selection? What moral issues emerge in development policy making and practice and how should they be resolved? How should the burdens and benefits of development be conceived and distributed? Who or what should be responsible for bringing about development? A nation's government, civil society or the market (see MARKET, ETHICS OF THE)? What role – if any – should more affluent states, international institutions, and nongovernmental associations and individuals have in the self-development of poor countries? What are the most serious local, national and international impediments to good development? To what extent, if any, do moral scepticism, moral relativism, national sovereignty and political realism pose a challenge to this boundary-crossing ethical inquiry? Who should decide these questions and by what methods (see MORAL EXPERTISE)?

In addition to accepting the importance of these

questions, most development ethicists share ideas about their field and the general parameters for ethically-based development. First, development ethicists contend that development practices and theories have ethical dimensions and can benefit from explicit ethical analysis and criticism. Second, development ethicists tend to see development as a multidisciplinary field with both theoretical and practical components that intertwine in various ways. Hence, they aim not merely to understand development, conceived generally as desirable social change, but also to argue for and promote specific conceptions of such change. Third, although they may understand the terms in somewhat different ways, development ethicists are committed to understanding and reducing human deprivation and misery in poor countries. Fourth, a consensus exists that development projects and aid givers should seek strategies in which both human wellbeing and a healthy environment jointly exist and are mutually reinforcing (Engel and Engel (eds) 1990). Fifth, these ethicists are aware that what is frequently called 'development' – for instance, economic growth – has created as many problems as it has solved. 'Development' can be used both descriptively and normatively. In the descriptive sense, 'development' is usually identified as the processes of economic growth, industrialization, and modernization that result in a society's achieving a high (per capita) gross domestic product. So conceived, a 'developed' society may be either celebrated or criticized. In the normative sense, a developed society, ranging from villages to national and regional societies, is one whose established institutions realize or approximate (what the proponent believes to be) worthwhile goals – most centrally, the overcoming of economic and social deprivation. To avoid confusion, when a normative sense of 'development' is meant, the noun is often preceded by a positive adjective such as 'good' or 'ethically justified'.

A sixth area of agreement is that development ethics must be conducted at various levels of generality and specificity. Just as development debates occur at various levels of abstraction, so development ethics should assess (1) basic ethical principles, (2) development goals and models such as 'economic growth', 'growth with equity', 'basic needs' and, in the 1990s, 'sustainable development', 'structural adjustment' and 'human development' (United Nations Development Programme), and (3) specific institutions and strategies.

Seventh, most development ethicists believe their enterprise should be international in the triple sense that the ethicists engaged in it come from many nations, including poor ones; that they are seeking to forge an international consensus; and that this consensus emphasizes a commitment to alleviating worldwide deprivation.

Eighth, although many development ethicists contend that at least some development principles or procedures are relevant for any poor country, most agree that development strategies must be contextually sensitive. What constitutes the best means – for instance, state provisioning, market mechanisms, civil society and their hybrids – will depend on a society's history and stage of social change as well as on regional and global forces.

Ninth, this flexibility concerning development models and strategies is compatible with the uniform rejection of certain extremes. For example, most development ethicists would repudiate two models: (1) the maximization of economic growth in a society without paying any direct attention to converting greater opulence into better human living conditions for its members, what Sen and Jean Drèze call 'unaimed opulence', and (2) an authoritarian egalitarianism in which physical needs are satisfied at the expense of political liberties.

4 Controversies and agenda

In addition to these points of agreement, there are several divisions and unsettled issues. A first unresolved issue concerns the scope of development ethics. Development ethics originated as the 'ethics of Third World Development'. There are good reasons to drop – as a Cold War relic – the 'First–Second–Third World' trichotomy. There is no consensus, however, on whether or not development ethics should extend beyond its central concern of assessing the development ends and means of poor societies.

Some argue that development ethicists should criticize human deprivation wherever it exists and that rich countries, since they too have problems of poverty, powerlessness, and alienation, are 'underdeveloped' and, hence, fall properly within the scope of development ethics. Perhaps the socioeconomic model that the North has been exporting to the South results in the underdevelopment of both. Others contend that since development ethicists address questions of rich country responsibility and global distributive justice, they should not restrict themselves to official development assistance but should also treat international trade, capital flows, migration, environmental pacts, military intervention, and responses to human rights violations committed by prior regimes. The chief argument against extending the boundaries in these ways is that development ethics would thereby become too ambitious and diffuse. If development ethics grew to be identical with all social ethics or all international ethics, the result might be that insufficient attention would be paid to alleviating poverty and powerlessness in *poor* countries. Both sides agree that development ethicists should assess various kinds of North–South (and South–South) relations with respect to their effects on economic and political inequality in poor countries. What is unresolved, however, is whether development ethics also should address such topics as the ethics of trade, military intervention and international institutions.

Development ethicists are divided also on the status of the moral norms that they seek to justify and apply. Three positions have emerged. Universalists, such as utilitarians and Kantians, argue that development goals and principles are valid for all societies (see UNIVERSALISM IN ETHICS §3; UTILITARIANISM; KANTIAN ETHICS). Particularists, especially communitarians and postmodern relativists, reply that universalism masks ethnocentrism and (Northern) cultural imperialism (see COMMUNITY AND COMMUNITARIANISM; POSTMODERNISM). Pro-development particularists either eschew all universal principles or affirm only the *procedural* principle that each nation or society should draw only on its own traditions and decide its own development ethic and path. (Anti-development particularists, rejecting both change brought from the outside and public reasoning about social change, condemn all development discourse and practice.) A third approach – advanced, for example, by Martha Nussbaum, Jonathan Glover, Seyla Benhabib and David Crocker – tries to avoid the standoff between the first two positions (see Nussbaum and Glover (eds) 1995). On this view, development ethics should forge a cross-cultural consensus in which a society's own freedom to make development choices is one among a plurality of fundamental norms and in which these norms are of sufficient generality so as not only to permit but also to require sensitivity to societal differences (see MORAL PLURALISM).

Next is a question related to the universalism-particularism debate: to what extent, if any, should development ethicists propose visions committed to a certain conception of human wellbeing, and how 'thick' or extensive should this vision be? There is a continuum here: at one end, there is more commitment to the values of individual choice, tolerance of differences, and public deliberation about social ends and means; and, at the other, more normative guidance about the good human life but less room for individual and social choice.

Supposing that development principles should have some substantive content (beyond the procedural principle that each society or person should decide for itself), there are disagreements about that content.

Assuming that social development concerns human development, with what moral categories should it be conceived? Candidates include: utility (preference satisfaction); social primary goods, such as income; negative liberty; basic human needs; autonomy; valuable capabilities and functionings; and rights. Although some think that a development ethic ought to include more than one of these moral concepts, development ethicists differ with respect to which ones to embrace and how to relate them. One alternative would be to work out a concept of human wellbeing that combines, on the one hand, a Neo-Kantian commitment to autonomy, critical dialogue and public deliberation with, on the other hand, neo-Aristotelian beliefs in the importance of physical health and social participation. Development duties might then flow from the idea that all humans should have a right to at least a minimal level of wellbeing.

There is also an ongoing debate about how development's benefits, burdens and responsibilities should be distributed within poor countries and between rich and poor countries. Utilitarians prescribe simple aggregation and maximization of individual utilities. Rawlsians advocate that income and wealth be maximized for the least well-off (individuals or nations) (see RAWLS, J.). Libertarians contend that a society should guarantee no form of equality apart from equal freedom from the interference of government and other people. Capabilities ethicists defend governmental responsibility to enable everyone to be able to advance to a level of sufficiency with respect to the valuable functionings.

Development ethicists also differ with respect to whether (good) social development should have – as an ultimate goal – the promotion of values other than the present and future human good. Some development ethicists ascribe intrinsic value, equal to or even superior to the good of individual human beings, to human communities of various kinds, for instance, family, nation or cultural group. Others argue that nonhuman individuals and species, as well as ecological communities, have equal and even superior value to human individuals (see ANIMALS AND ETHICS). Those committed to 'ecodevelopment' or 'sustainable development' do not yet agree on what should be sustained as an end in itself and what should be maintained as an indispensable or merely helpful means (see ENVIRONMENTAL ETHICS). Nor do they agree on how to surmount conflicts among intrinsic values.

See also: FUTURE GENERATIONS, OBLIGATIONS TO; JUSTICE, INTERNATIONAL; POSTCOLONIALISM

References and further reading

* Aiken, W. and LaFollette, H. (eds) (1976) *World Hunger and Morality*, Upper Saddle River, NJ: Prentice Hall; 2nd edn, 1996. (The first edition comprises philosophical debates in the early 1970s over the ethics of food aid; as well as retaining three of these articles, the second edition contains later pieces that either address responsibilities for aid or, especially in parts III and IV, recast the ethics of food aid to an ethics of development and international justice.)

Aman, K. (ed.) (1991) *Ethical Principles for Development: Needs, Capacities or Rights?*, Upper Montclair, NJ: Institute for Critical Thinking. (Outlines diverse approaches to the question of whether development ethics should emphasize needs, capabilities or rights.)

Attfield, R. and Wilkins, B. (eds) (1992) *International Justice and the Third World*, London: Routledge. (British essays on development ethics and international justice.)

* Berger, P. (1974) *Pyramids of Sacrifice: Political Ethics and Social Change*, New York: Basic Books. (Challenging essay linking 'political ethics' and Third World poverty.)

Camacho, L. (1993) *Ciencia y tecnología en el subdesarrollo*, Cartago: Editorial Tecnológica de Costa Rica. (A leading Latin American philosopher addresses ethical issues concerning science and technology in developing countries.)

Crocker, D.A. (1991) 'Toward Development Ethics', *World Development* 19: 457–83. (An introductory survey and bibliography of the nature, methods, and value of development ethics.)

* Dower, N. (1988) 'What is Development? A Philosopher's Answer', *Centre for Development Studies Occasional Paper Series* 3, Glasgow: University of Glasgow. (Argues for the role of philosophers in development studies and for the normative meaning of development as socioeconomic change that ought to occur.)

* Engel, J.R. and. Engel, J.G. (eds) (1990) *Ethics of Environment and Development: Global Challenge, International Response*, Tucson, AZ: University of Arizona Press. (An international collection that explores different ways of relating environmental and development ethics.)

* Escobar, A. (1995) *Encountering Development: The Making and Unmaking of the Third World*, Princeton, NJ: Princeton University Press. (Postmodernist 'deconstruction' of development theory and practice as imperialist and destructive of traditional life.)

Gasper, D. (1994) 'Development Ethics – An Emergent Field? A Look at Scope and Structure, with Special Reference to the Ethics of Aid', in R. Prendergast and F. Stewart (eds) *Market Forces and World Development*, London: Macmillan, New York: St Martin's Press. (A helpful stocktaking that defends development ethics as a 'multidisiciplinary field' that closes the gap between abstract philosophy and practical experience in order to promote desirable change in poor countries.)

* Goulet, D. (1971) *The Cruel Choice: A New Concept in the Theory of Development*, New York: Athenaeum. (In this seminal work, the pioneer in development ethics applies ethical reflection to development theory, policy and practices.)

* —— (1977) *The Uncertain Promise: Value Conflicts in Technology Transfer*, New York: IDOC/North America. (With many concrete examples, this work shows that technology transfer can be both an obstacle and an aid to authentic development.)

Gunatilleke, G., Tiruchelvam, N. and Coomaraswamy, R. (eds) (1988) *Ethical Dilemmas of Development in Asia*, Lexington, MA: Lexington Books. (Accessible international collection addressing ethical, empirical and political aspects of Asian development.)

* Hardin, G. (1974) 'Lifeboat Ethics: The Case Against Helping the Poor', *Psychology Today* 8: 38–43, 123–6. (Argues on utilitarian and prudential grounds that affluent nations are morally obliged not to help famine-stricken countries.)

* Nussbaum, M. and Glover, J. (eds) (1995) *Women, Culture and Development*, Oxford: Clarendon Press. (A valuable international collection of advanced essays explaining, assessing and applying the capabilities ethic to the issue of gender equality in developing countries.)

* Nussbaum, M. and Sen, A. (eds) (1993) *The Quality of Life*, Oxford: Clarendon Press. (Advanced essays that clarify and evaluate the capabilities and other approaches to quality of life in both rich and poor countries.)

O'Neill, O. (1980) 'The Moral Perplexities of Famine Relief', in T. Regan (ed.) *Matters of Life and Death: New Introductory Essays in Moral Philosophy*, New York: Random House; repr. as 'Ending World Hunger', in T. Regan (ed.) *Matters of Life and Death: New Introductory Essays in Moral Philosophy*, New York: McGraw-Hill, 1993, 3rd edn. (A critique of utilitarian approaches to world hunger and an accessible statement of the author's Kantian duty-based ethic of aid and development.)

Segal, J.M. (1991) 'What is Development?', in C.V. Blatz (ed.) *Ethics and Agriculture: An Anthology on Current Issues in World Context*, Moscow, ID: University of Idaho Press. (An influential paper that argues for an ethically based concept of development and evaluates three development models: growth, growth with equity, and basic needs.)

* Sen, A. (1984) *Resources, Values and Development*, Oxford: Blackwell, Cambridge, MA: Harvard University Press. (Contains several of Sen's important papers on the capabilities approach to development.)
* Singer, P. (1972) 'Famine, Affluence and Morality', *Philosophy and Public Affairs* 1: 229–43; repr. in W. Aiken and H. LaFollette (eds) *World Hunger and Morality*, Upper Saddle River, NJ: Prentice Hall, 2nd edn, 1996. (Argues on utilitarian grounds affluent individuals are morally obliged to contribute to famine relief.)
* Streeten, P. with Burki, S.J., Haq, M., Hicks, N., and Stewart, F. (1981) *First Things First: Meeting Basic Needs in Developing Countries*, Oxford: Oxford University Press. (The classic statement of the basic needs approach to change in poor countries.)

DAVID A. CROCKER

DEVLIN, LORD *see* LAW AND

MORALITY

DEWEY, JOHN (1859–1952)

The philosophy of John Dewey is original and comprehensive. His extensive writings contend systematically with problems in metaphysics, epistemology, logic, aesthetics, ethics, social and political philosophy, philosophy and education, and philosophical anthropology. Although his work is widely read, it is not widely understood.

Dewey had a distinctive conception of philosophy, and the key to understanding and benefiting from his work is to keep this conception in mind. A worthwhile philosophy, he urged, must be practical. Philosophic inquiry, that is, ought to take its point of departure from the aspirations and problems characteristic of the various sorts of human activity, and an effective philosophy would develop ideas responsive to those conditions. Any system of ideas that has the effect of making common experience less intelligible than we find it to be is on that account a failure. Dewey's theory of inquiry, for example, does not entertain a conception of knowledge that makes it problematic whether we can know anything at all. Inasmuch as scientists have made extraordinary advances in knowledge, it behoves the

philosopher to find out exactly what scientists do, rather than to question whether they do anything of real consequence.

Moral philosophy, likewise, should not address the consternations of philosophers as such, but the characteristic urgencies and aspirations of common life; and it should attempt to identify the resources and limitations of human nature and the environment with which it interacts. Human beings might then contend effectively with the typical perplexities and promises of mortal existence. To this end, Dewey formulated an exceptionally innovative and far-reaching philosophy of morality and democracy.

The subject matter of philosophy is not philosophy, Dewey liked to say, but 'problems of men'. All too often, he found, the theories of philosophers made the primary subject matter more obscure rather than less so. The tendency of thinkers is to become bewitched by inherited philosophic puzzles, when the persistence of the puzzle is a consequence of failing to consider the assumptions that created it. Dewey was gifted in discerning and discarding the philosophic premises that create needless mysteries. Rather than fret, for instance, about the question of how immaterial mental substance can possibly interact with material substance, he went to the root of the problem by challenging the notion of substance itself.

Indeed, Dewey's dissatisfaction with the so-called classic tradition in philosophy, stemming at least from Plato if not from Parmenides, led him to reconstruct the entire inheritance of the Western tradition in philosophy. The result is one of the most seminal and fruitful philosophies of the twentieth century.

1   **Life**
2   **Philosophical anthropology**
3   **Metaphysics**
4   **Theory of inquiry**
5   **Moral philosophy: the construction of good**
6   **Moral philosophy: the democratic way of life**

1   Life

Dewey was born in Burlington, Vermont in 1859. He earned his BA degree at the University of Vermont, where he was particularly drawn to Scottish common-sense realism. He took his Ph.D. at the Johns Hopkins University, writing his dissertation on the psychology of Kant. At Hopkins he was much influenced by the experimental psychology of G. Stanley Hall, but he was taken above all by the philosophy of Hegel, taught by George Sylvester Morris. Hegel's philosophy, Dewey later said, answered his craving for a unified vision of reality, as distinguished from dualistic and reductive philosophies and those that were content with providing isolated analyses of particular phenomena.

After holding appointments at the University of Michigan and the University of Minnesota, he moved to the University of Chicago in 1894, where he was head of the Department of Philosophy, Psychology and Pedagogy. There he founded the University Elementary School (better known as the Laboratory School or the Dewey School), where he introduced experimental educational practices that both stemmed from and modified his philosophy of education. During this period Dewey began a decided shift away from Hegelian idealism in the direction of his naturalistic experimentalism. In 1904 he moved to Columbia University in New York City, where he developed his mature philosophy. He retired in 1930 but continued to teach as Professor Emeritus at Columbia until 1939. Thereafter he continued to be active, mostly in New York City, until his death in 1952.

Dewey's production of philosophic works was prodigious: forty books and more than 700 articles. After the death of William James in 1910, he was without peer in philosophy in the USA and became a figure of exceptional national and international prominence. He was frequently invited to lecture abroad; he did so in Mexico, China, Japan, Turkey, France, Scotland and the USSR. He was called to several major lectureships, including the Carus Lectures in 1922, the Gifford Lectures in 1929, the William James Lecture in 1930 and the Terry Lectures in 1934. He received honorary degrees from several major universities world-wide and was a founder and the first President of the American Association of University Professors and President of the American Philosophical Association.

Inasmuch as he took seriously the notion of philosophy as a guide to conduct, it was fitting that he devoted much of his time to practical causes. He took a leading role in numerous associations devoted to political and educational reforms, and at the same time contributed frequently to public discourse in such journals of opinion as *The New Republic*, *Commentary*, *The Nation* and *Christian Century*. In 1937, at the age of 78, he accepted the chairmanship of the Commission of Inquiry to investigate the charges of Josef Stalin against Leon Trotsky. The question of Trotsky's guilt or innocence was second-ary to the question of whether Stalin was the leader of a great democratic and economic revolution or the perpetrator of massive and brutal oppression. Dewey and the Commission found Trotsky not guilty and Stalin guilty, for which he was viciously criticized by a host of intellectuals sympathetic to Stalin.

2 Philosophical anthropology

Dewey's thinking about human nature is profoundly indebted to the theory of biological evolution as well as to James' *Principles of Psychology* (1890), which itself owed much to the Darwinian view. The classical idea of species implies changeless essence. It was also taken to imply that there is a perfectly definite end and station in life that each human being ought to achieve in order to fulfil their nature. Darwin's theory that species come into existence and undergo change was, therefore, truly revolutionary: the potentialities of human nature are not fixed, and there is no predetermined outcome or definite social role towards which each and every person ought to aim (see DARWIN, C.R. §§2–3; JAMES, W. §2).

According to the Darwinian conception, the human being is not understood primarily as a spectator of nature, but as a participant in it. Like any living organism, we are caught up in processes of change whose tendencies are fateful for our weal and woe. All human practices and aims are conceived with this assumption foremost in mind. Any form of human endeavour – including moral, cognitive and artistic activity – is elucidated as a mode of practice in which the individual acts with multiple agencies of the surrounding environment. Any experience is a con-joint effect of the organism and environment acting together, rather than a passive registration of external stimuli.

Dewey's notion of habit is fundamental to his analysis of human nature. A habit is not the private possession of an individual. It is the product of interactions inclusive of organism and environment, in which the resultant habit is determined as much by particular features of the environment as by the impulses of the organism. The habits appropriate to agricultural practice, for example, could not arise in the individual in isolation from the conditions in which farming occurs. The soil, the seasons and the elements dictate forms of action as much as the physiological and intellectual capacities of the farmer. The habits of farming are a collaborative result of organism and environment.

An impulse by itself does not constitute a form of action. It is plastic, and a formed habit of thought or action can only result from interaction. Dewey believed that a person's nature can take a plurality of possible forms, depending on environmental conditions. While he acknowledged that there are native differences in human beings, Dewey regarded such variations as highly malleable and subject to change as a consequence of learning. For everyone, then, there are multiple opportunities and possible directions for growth. Growth implies that our basic dispositions, our virtues, intelligence, talents and traits of personality are subject to the formations of home, school, church and every manner of human association. It is no surprise, then, that Dewey devoted so much study and experiment to the practice of education.

There is no mind or self antecedent to the formation of habit. The self, according to Dewey, is a dynamic complex of habits. It is an outcome, not an original existence. Mind consists of habits. Every idea is a habit of action; it is an anticipation of definite ways of behaving. The idea of a table, for example, consists of all the ways one can act with the object so designated. To have an idea of a table is not necessarily to have an image, nor is it to envisage the inherent essence of tablehood. It is to be prepared to act with such objects in ways to bring about predictable outcomes. Such outcomes are originally learned by means of active participation with objects, hence mind is derivative of behaviour. But the meanings which constitute mind are mostly (perhaps exclusively, Dewey sometimes seems to say) provided by language. Language, too, is derivative of conduct, but it is necessarily social conduct. The public meanings conveyed by language could not arise except in shared activity with shared features of an environment. According to Dewey's thinking, consequently, mind can arise only within a social condition. Actual thinking is a function of acquired habits and the promptings of a specific situation.

In accordance with these conceptions, Dewey distinguished a form of conduct that could be common to all human activities. This form he called, generically, art. It is a deliberate practice with the environment, by means of which an individual transforms conditions that are initially disordered and troubling into a situation that is unified and directed. The individual must identify the nature of the problematic conditions, formulate possible plans of action that would utilize the instrumentalities of the particular situation, and execute the plan that seems to hold most promise for success. In conduct as art, individuals move from an initial condition of alienation from the environment to one in which they have effectively engaged their powers with those of their surroundings and have brought the two to consummation. Dewey thought that conduct of this sort characterizes all forms of effective activity. This type of conduct is natural to a living being striving to cope with processes of change, and it provides a consummation of effort that human beings find intrinsically fulfilling (see PRAGMATISM §1; ANTHROPOLOGY, PHILOSOPHY OF).

3 Metaphysics

Dewey did not think of metaphysics as a foundational discipline, conjuring up principles to certify value judgments and cognitive claims. On the contrary, he was very critical of metaphysics which had such pretensions; such endeavours were part of the obnoxious heritage of the classic tradition.

The classic tradition originating in ancient Greek philosophy is above all characterized by the assumption of disparate realms of being, Dewey contended. These realms are conceived in notably different ways, but they have in common the belief that there is a world of 'true' being, the most real being: that of changeless perfection, which is juxtaposed to a world of becoming, where all things come into existence, undergo change and pass away. The classic notion of being is not only false but pernicious, for it provides the rationale for moral absolutes, whose actual effect is to demand a conformity that is injurious to human flourishing (see PLATO §10).

A universal assumption of the reigning tradition, Dewey observed, was that true being is conceived as the object of rational knowledge as such. That alone is the really real. Prior philosophies accordingly had been typically reductive, declaring with the idealists, for example, that reality *per se* is nothing but a rational order of ideas, or with the materialists that nature is nothing but matter in motion, possessing none of the other traits commonly experienced: such fateful events as immediate quality, disorder and ends. With these reductive assumptions, philosophers attributed to subjective mind within itself the plural and varying properties that would otherwise be predicated of nature (see IDEALISM §1; MATERIALISM §3).

Dewey's metaphysical thought is an attempt to restore to the world the integrity of which philosophers had divested it. He provides a characterization of the most prominent features of the natural world in their continuities with human experience. This is a world of becoming, in the classic vernacular; there is no changeless being. Such phenomena as experience, human nature, mind, knowledge, art and value are conceived as natural functions of the biological organism interacting with an environment marked by change, order and disorder, obstacles, instrumentalities and episodic fulfilments.

The restoration of integrity of vision is consequent upon the continuity of experience and nature. We experience real events in their relations to ourselves and to each other. We accept our experience as disclosing real traits of the world. The varying qualities of events are natural functions. Not only are sensations of colours and sounds the outcomes of natural processes, but also the full panoply of characteristics that we refer to with such predicates as 'lovely', 'hateful', 'wicked' and 'admirable'. Genuine potentialities of nature are thus exhibited. The potentiality is neither in the organism alone nor in the object alone, but in the situation inclusive of both.

With such assumptions, Dewey insists, for example, on the reality of what he calls the precarious: events that are threatening, disordered, baffling and the like, which were formerly excluded from the really real. We experience such things as terrorist attacks, avalanches, lost keys, droughts and stubbed toes. These are not simply mental occurrences, unrelated to nature. They are public phenomena, and if we cannot accord them appropriate ontological status, philosophy can offer no clue as to how we can contend with them.

Qualitative change, likewise, is as real as anything else and it is one of the traits of nature that Dewey discerned and analysed with telling effect. He calls these changes 'histories'. Phenomena that had been regarded in the classic tradition as original entities or substances are treated by Dewey as the outcomes of histories. Mind, intelligence, knowledge, human nature and moral and aesthetic values are such outcomes. Dewey frequently analysed them in detail, believing that to possess knowledge of such change is invaluable in contending deliberately and effectively with the processes in which we are mortally implicated.

A further significant trait is what Dewey calls 'the stable'. This expression refers not only to conditions that are relatively constant and enduring, but, fundamentally, to the correlations between processes of change. So-called laws of nature are not self-subsistent beings; they are the correlations between one process of change and another, as are those involving pressure and temperature in an enclosed volume of gas, for example. Both pressure and temperature undergo change, and the change in one is correlated in a measurable and predictable way with change in the other. As such correlations are determined, it becomes possible to introduce deliberate variations in natural events for the sake of directing them to predictable outcomes. Knowledge, then, is neither a direct grasp of essences nor a summary of antecedently received sensations. It is an instrument for directing processes of change.

The purpose of Dewey's metaphysics is practical. Its main intent, he declared, is to exhibit the nature and function of intelligence. Contrast the classic model with Dewey's: if the nature of the world is thought to be morally and cognitively determined by a pattern of changeless perfection, then the role of intelligence is to attain a direct grasp of such principles. Subsequently, events in the world of becoming are classified as conforming or not con-

forming to the antecedent pattern. This is a classificatory and deductive logic, formalized by Aristotle. According to such a logic, moral action consists of the attempt to constrain processes of change to conform to the antecedent absolute. If, however, the object of knowledge is the correlation between processes of change, and if the constituents of these processes can be varied, then it becomes possible to direct such processes towards welcome fulfilments. This procedure Dewey calls 'experimental logic'. These are distinctly different procedures of practical action, and if the assumptions of the classic tradition are false, then conduct is pointlessly straitjacketed. When Dewey says it is the task of philosophy to characterize the nature of things in a way that illuminates possible harmonies between our ambitions and aspirations and the realities of the world, he has in mind the substitution of an experimental logic for the stultifying anachronisms of the classic tradition (see PROCESSES §4; WHITEHEAD, A.N. §4).

4 Theory of inquiry

The heart of Dewey's pragmatism – or 'instrumentalism', as he preferred – is his theory of inquiry. It is most significant that the explicit guiding assumption of this theory is that logical distinctions and methods of inquiry develop out of the process of problem-solving activities. The logic of inquiry is not a set of norms existing independently of and prior to our cognitive efforts. Rather, procedures and logical distinctions introduced by inquirers prove themselves in their successes in resolving cognitively problematic situations. 'Successful' is not to be defined by philosophers, but by the aims of modern science itself, which Dewey took to be the prediction and control of natural phenomena. Ultimately at stake in disputes about the nature and possibility of knowledge is the capacity of human beings to act in concert with ongoing events. Such action is dependent upon the determination of how changes in one process are correlated with changes in another.

Science, then, does not get its credentials from philosophy. Instead, the philosopher studies science for a number of worthy purposes: to understand the nature of effective inquiry, the nature of the valid object of knowledge and the possible extensions of scientific methods to domains of problem-solving that are not exclusively scientific. Dewey also appropriates scientific results as indispensable constituents in his particular analyses of human nature, social processes and methods of education. (This is not to say that scientists themselves do not sometimes misunderstand the nature of their own activity, as Dewey on occasion points out.)

According to any philosophy at the turn of the twentieth century, all experience is exclusively subjective: it takes place within the mind, rather than being a consciousness of events external to the sentient being. Traditional dualistic epistemology, then, treats experience as a private, self-enclosed domain that is only problematically (if at all) related to anything beyond itself. Epistemologists laboured to conceive how a purely subjective mental event might possibly correspond to something external to it. If experience is continuous with nature, however, the real problem is of an entirely different sort: to determine how variations in one natural and public event (or set of events) are related to variations in other such events.

This is a problem not for philosophers, but scientists, and scientists have proved very successful in reaching such determinations. They perform experiments and make observations in accordance with a hypothesis. The hypothesis states that if specified changes are introduced under controlled conditions, predictable effects will ensue. If the inquiry is conducted as the hypothesis prescribes, and if the effects occur as predicted, then the hypothesis is tentatively confirmed. Dewey always insisted that warrant for the putative knowledge is dependent upon confirmation from the community of relevant inquirers. Such warrant is always a matter of degree and it is always fallible.

Inquiry involves the deliberate manipulation of the conditions within which it occurs. The very subject matter of the investigation might be controlled, as in laboratory work; or the conditions of observation might be controlled, as in astronomy. In any case, the inquirer introduces deliberate change in the cognitive situation in order to produce the object of knowledge.

The object of knowledge as such is the outcome of a process; it does not exist antecedently to inquiry. Natural events, with their own potentialities, powers and limitations, exist prior to inquiry, of course, but they do not in that condition constitute an object of knowledge. When such an object is produced, its character is dependent upon the specific conditions of inquiry that have been introduced, including the subject matter under scrutiny. The investigator has responded to a specific problematic situation, has contrived an inquiry of a particular sort, and makes observations and measurements in terms of concepts that are largely characteristic of the existing state of the science. Inquiry is inevitably theory-laden – or, in Dewey's parlance, meaning-laden. Inquiry constitutes, in identifiable and specifiable ways, a transformation of antecedent subject matter.

Inasmuch as Dewey regards the object of knowledge as a deliberate construction, some readers have concluded that he is an antirealist. This conclusion is mistaken. Dewey repudiated the archaic idea that knowledge is a correspondence between an object and a mental image, but that does not make him an antirealist. Indeed, whatever 'realism' is taken to mean, Dewey's study of inquiry concludes that our ideas are determined by the nature of real events to a far greater extent than was recognized in any pre-pragmatic philosophy. The meaning of any object consists of the conception of all that object can do in relation to other objects. In other words, we know how objects function as constituents of processes of change; and in that form alone can we utilize them for practical purposes. Mere images cannot do so; nor can Platonic forms or Cartesian essences. Our conceptual systems, moreover, have arisen from the very processes of effective inquiry. Although our concepts are subject to revision, it can hardly be said that they are arbitrary impositions on nature. While it must be insisted that the successes of science are always open to refinement and revision, it is unmistakable that our ability to function with formerly inscrutable and overwhelming natural powers has undergone astounding advancement. Dewey calls this shift a revolution from arts of acceptance to arts of control (see SCIENTIFIC REALISM AND ANTIREALISM §4).

5 Moral philosophy: the construction of good

The classic tradition has supposed the existence of something essentially changeless and perfect in the nature of things, ranging from Platonic forms to natural law, and from Kantian reason to the nature of the Absolute. Even utilitarianism shares in that tradition in supposing a single criterion of good, as does Marxism in holding that there is but a single pattern that describes all historical change. Many philosophers have thought that they espy a moral absolute; and many have believed that such an absolute is of supreme value in human conduct. Many others would like to agree, but they have despaired of discerning such a rationally incontrovertible standard.

The classic tradition assumes a changeless principle or goal for all moral action, yet the real world is marked by change. It presents the continuing occurrence of unique situations, each of which can yield a variety of possible outcomes. There is likewise an indefinite plurality of human possibilities. Adherence to the classic tradition, then, constitutes a demand for unyielding conformity to prevailing cultural requirements, which are given a specious authority by religious or philosophic speculations. The tradition enforces conditions in which human possibilities are denied for the sake of maintaining precedent, custom or arbitrary authority. Historically, the feudal system has been the most prominent example. The contemporary demand that women and men should not be confined to their traditional roles is, in effect, a repudiation of the classic tradition.

As Dewey conceived it, the moral life is suffused with innumerable possibilities of enjoyment and happiness, as well as of disaster. Ordinary life revolves around familiar attachments, ambitions and fears. The philosophic task, Dewey believed, is to place at the disposal of human beings the assumptions and methods that would facilitate the efforts in which they will be engaged in any case. It is a project of enabling and liberating. Each situation might be approached to identify its unique opportunities for fulfilment. The precarious values of the situation might be clarified and united into more inclusive wholes and made more secure against obstacles and threats.

This procedure Dewey calls the 'construction' of good. No phrase encapsulates so well both his opposition to the classical tradition and his alternative to it. Rather than conform to an antecedently given pattern of right conduct, one actively constructs a new situation, intending to discriminate its particular tendencies and to contrive a consummation of the energies of the organism and environment – the practice referred to in §3 as 'conduct as art'. Dewey can be eloquent in characterizing such experience as one of deeply enriched qualities and cherished meanings. It is a cumulative experience, enhancing human powers. The continuation of this process over time Dewey denominates 'growth'.

There is no absolute consummation in life, nor any exact station determined a priori by one's nature. Rather, one may treasure the very process of conduct as art. Dewey says that growth itself is the only moral end, and he identifies it primarily as a social process. Our behaviour is characteristically interpersonal; as such, it is the source of most of our learning, and our participation with others is the source of our most profound satisfactions. As a constituent of growth, 'shared experience is the greatest of human goods'. The construction of good is typically a shared activity, greatly facilitated by deliberate cooperation.

The activity requires appropriate habits of thought and conduct, including those of communication and cooperation. Above all, Dewey believes, it requires the habits of experimental inquiry. The situations to be transformed are often of a complex and comprehensive nature, such as, for example, the reconstruction of educational institutions; so we must possess reliable knowledge of how such practices actually work. We must also possess the imaginative habits of the experimenter to formulate hypotheses about how

such conditions might be reconstructed. We might hypothesize that certain innovations in practice would eventuate, say, in more alert, reflective and well-motivated students. The hypothesis guides conduct by prescribing the changes that would effect such results: the introduction of specified procedures would transform educational activity in such a way as to produce the desired outcomes. This is the manner in which scientific hypotheses guide conduct, not – by contrast – in deducing a prescription for action from an alleged moral absolute. That would be a reversion to the logic of the classical tradition (see PRAGMATISM IN ETHICS §3).

6 Moral philosophy: the democratic way of life

Dewey was convinced that modern society is swamped in the modes of thought inherited from the classic tradition. Instead of using experimental logic, we depend on putative moral absolutes. Our conduct is governed, in effect, by precedent, which largely represents, according to Dewey, the entrenched prerogatives of privileged groups. The most beneficent change that could be introduced into society, consequently, would be the teaching and widespread adoption of experimental habits of thought (see EDUCATION, HISTORY OF PHILOSOPHY OF §9). We would not just address our several problematic situations with greater promise of success, but we would re-evaluate our economic and political behaviour with a view to what that behaviour really does and to what any alternatives to it might do.

Dewey sometimes called deliberation and action of this sort 'social intelligence' and sometimes 'democracy as a way of life'. Democracy as a way of life, he said, could be a norm for all forms of human association. Surprisingly, Dewey never provided a systematic exposition of the norms of this life, but its constituents can be extracted from his writings. It consists of several habits or virtues, foremost among them experimental habits of inquiry. These include fallibilism, rather than dogmatism, and an insistence that we follow the evidence of inquiry wherever it leads, rather than cling to preconceived ideas. Experimentalism implies both a willingness to entertain novel hypotheses and the personal flexibility to try out unaccustomed modes of action. The dissemination of the results of inquiry as widely as possible is also indispensable to the democratic ethos.

Democratic life, as Dewey conceives it, also implies respect for persons. Respect of this sort does not entail policy prescriptions, but it means that every person has a right to participate in the formation of goods. It implies that individuals should be seriously receptive to each other's concerns, taking them into account – at least initially – as deserving an honest hearing. It also implies that persons communicate with each other freely and honestly to convey their concerns and to propose their tentatively preferred plans of action. Out of such virtue and discourse, leavened with scientific knowledge, shared proposals for action would emerge and would be honoured. It should go without saying that democratic virtue excludes deliberately antisocial behaviour.

On a small scale, these procedures are familiar. In our personal relations – friendships, marriages and voluntary associations of all kinds – we do not presume to enforce our views on other participants in a unilateral way. We assume that there will be differences of opinion, great and small, and we typically assume that we will talk these problems over in a civil manner and try to arrive at some more or less amicable agreement about what to do. We do not always succeed in doing so, but when we fail, we do not generally bolt the association. Our common activities are usually too precious for anything so shortsighted. Our treasured relationships do not survive such intransigence. Dewey believed that the virtues exhibited in such relations might be extended to incorporate much wider groups.

No philosopher before Dewey had conceived moral discourse as essentially communicative. The democratic virtues, after all, are impertinent to the various incarnations of the classic tradition. If the good and the right are known absolutely, the discourse of social intelligence is superfluous. One must concede that such discourse does not guarantee that consensus will always occur. Conflict and frustration are inevitable; but Dewey believed that they would be substantially less than they are when immovable oppositions are generated by moral absolutes.

The disciplines of the democratic way of life are demanding, and they can easily be corrupted. Dewey urged that schooling of all kinds incorporate the procedures of cooperative intelligence as a matter of routine. Indeed, all forms of association might be conducted in a manner to make democratic values habitual. Were such favourable conditions to exist, he thought, this way of life could be reasonably approximated.

It is a way of life that can be criticized for providing insufficient finality to moral judgment. It is true: the democratic/scientific virtues do not ensure the unanimity craved by adherents to the classic tradition. On the other hand, their exercise precludes the source of most of our torments: deliberately hurtful conduct. And it promises a release of human possibilities from needless subservience to moral absolutes. In fact, the verdict on Dewey's moral philosophy might be that it makes excessive demands of human flesh, not that it is too permissive. In any case, if the classic tradition is indeed a relic, then perhaps Dewey's thought points the way to a more pertinent philosophy than any other currently offered to our candid judgment (see SOCIAL DEMOCRACY §2).

List of works

Dewey, J. (1969–90) *The Early Works of John Dewey, 1882–1898*; *The Middle Works of John Dewey, 1899–1924*; *The Later Works of John Dewey, 1925–1953*, ed. J.A. Boydston, Carbondale, IL: Southern Illinois University Press, 37 vols. (Contains the entirety of Dewey's published work. Does not include his correspondence, which is being edited for eventual publication.)

—— (1887) *Psychology*; repr. in *Early Works*, vol. 2, Carbondale, IL: Southern Illinois University Press, 1969–90. (Dewey's text draws on Helmholz, Wundt, Lotze, Herbart, Bain, Spencer, James, Hall and others in a defence of idealism; criticized by James and others for its Hegelianism, it was eclipsed three years later by the publication of James' *The Principles of Psychology*.)

—— (1896a) 'The Reflex Arc Concept in Psychology', *Psychological Review* 3: 357–70; repr. in *Early Works*, Carbondale, IL: Southern Illinois University Press, 1969–90, vol. 5, 96–106. (Important transitional work between Dewey's early Hegelianism and his later experimentalism and pragmatism.)

—— (1896b) 'Interest in Relation to the Training of the Will', *Second Supplement to the First Yearbook of the National Herbart Society*, 209–46; repr. in *Early Works*, Carbondale, IL: Southern Illinois University Press, 1969–90, vol. 5, 111–50. (Dewey's revolutionary educational philosophy.)

—— (1916) *Democracy and Education*, New York: Macmillan. (Dewey's most systematic statement of his philosophy of education. Good introduction to his entire philosophy. Contained in *Middle Works*, vol. 9.)

—— (1922) *Human Nature and Conduct*, New York: Holt. (A comprehensive statement of Dewey's philosophy of human nature, including its bearing on moral conduct. Contained in *Middle Works*, vol. 12.)

—— (1925) *Experience and Nature*, Chicago, IL, and London: Open Court. (Dewey's metaphysics. Contained in *Later Works*, vol. 1.)

—— (1927) *The Public and Its Problems*, New York: Holt. (Principally on the nature of democratic life. Contained in *Later Works*, vol. 2.)

—— (1929) *The Quest for Certainty*, New York: Minton Balch. (Sustained critique of the classic tradition in philosophy. Contrasts absolutistic and experimental approaches to ethics. Contained in *Later Works*, vol. 4.)

Dewey, J. and Tufts, J.H. (1932) *Ethics*, New York: Holt. (An account of the distinctive values of the moral life, their sources, functions and interrelations. Contained in *Later Works*, vol. 7.)

Dewey, J. (1934) *Art as Experience*, New York: Minton Balch. (Superb statement of the nature of art and its significance for all human conduct. Contained in *Later Works*, vol. 10.)

—— (1938) *Logic: The Theory of Inquiry*, New York: Holt. (Magisterial elaboration of Dewey's instrumentalism. Contained in *Later Works*, vol. 12.)

References and further reading

Alexander, T. (1987) *John Dewey's Theory of Art, Experience, and Nature: The Horizons of Feeling*, Albany, NY: State University of New York Press. (Elucidates the prominence of aesthetic experience in all conduct. Excellent antidote to the treatment of Dewey as technocrat.)

Boisvert, R. (1988) *Dewey's Metaphysics*, New York: Fordham University Press. (Clearly written exposition displays the sophistication of Dewey's metaphysics.)

Campbell, J. (1995) *Understanding John Dewey*, Chicago, IL: Open Court. (The best general introduction to Dewey's philosophy.)

Gouinlock, J. (1972) *John Dewey's Philosophy of Value*, New York: Humanities Press. (Exhibits Dewey's moral thought as organic to his philosophical anthropology and metaphysics.)

—— (1986) *Excellence in Public Discourse: John Stuart Mill, John Dewey, and Social Intelligence*, New York: Teachers College Press. (Systematic exposition of Dewey's philosophy of social intelligence.)

* James, W. (1890) *The Principles of Psychology*, Cambridge, MA: Harvard University Press, 1981, 3 vols. (A brilliant and exhaustive study of psychological theory as it existed in the late nineteenth century. Includes the extensive elaboration of James' own views.)

Rockefeller, S. (1991) *John Dewey: Religious Faith and Democratic Humanism*, New York: Columbia University Press. (A rich account of Dewey's moral philosophy and philosophy of religion in the context of Dewey's own life experience.)

Sleeper, R. (1986) *The Necessity of Pragmatism*, New Haven, CT: Yale University Press. (Excellent study of Dewey's theory of inquiry.)

JAMES GOUINLOCK

DHARMA *see* DUTY AND VIRTUE, INDIAN CONCEPTIONS OF

DHARMAKĪRTI (*c.*600–60)

Dharmakīrti represents the philosophical apex of the Buddhist contribution to Indian thought of the post-systematic period. On the basis of Dignāga's late works he developed a system of epistemology with a strong emphasis on logic, propounding it both as an explanation and defence of Dignāga's thought. His logic, particularly, was new; in order to create a system of Buddhist logic proper, it clearly established the general Indian idea that logical relations are founded in reality. Buddhist epistemology as shaped by Dharmakīrti became a strong and influential rational tradition in late Indian Buddhism and has been studied and continued in Tibet up to the present time.

1 Writings
2 Epistemology and logic

1 Writings

According to legend, Dharmakīrti was born a South Indian Brahman and taught at the monastic 'university' of Nālanda. He was a pupil of Īśvarasena and, in the words of the Chinese pilgrim Yijing, 'brought further progress in the field of logic after Dignāga' ([671–95] 1966: 182). He was also an acknowledged poet. The later Buddhist tradition followed Dharmakīrti's interpretation of DIGNĀGA, and he strongly influenced the Brahmanical logicians as well. His theories have been studied and transmitted by Tibetan epistemologists and logicians up to the present time and remain part of the traditional higher education curriculum in Tibet.

Possibly all Dharmakīrti's philosophical works, four major and three minor, are extant in their original Sanskrit in China, but due to the inaccessibility of these sources, in the case of the *Pramāṇaviniścaya* and the *Hetubindu* we are still forced to rely on Tibetan translations, fragments and reconstructions. Research on Dharmakīrti has shifted from an earlier, more doxographic attitude towards an investigation of his work in context, focusing on the problems he was concerned with and the answers developed in his major works. An early attempt at interpretation by Stcherbatsky (1932) provided a fascinating overview, but was hampered by a too limited textual basis and a strong neo-Kantian bias in interpretation.

Dharmakīrti's first work, a treatise consisting of verses and partly explanatory, partly elaborative prose, is an audacious statement of his new logical theory, which he openly presents as a new interpretation of Dignāga's teaching, superior to that of his teacher Īśvarasena. This early work (called *Hetu prakaraṇa* by Frauwallner) is basically a study of the definition of logical reason (*hetu*) which may have been intended to supersede a similar work by Dignāga that is now lost (the *Hetumukha*), although it is not, in character, a commentary on Dignāga's treatise. It was incorporated by Dharmakīrti into the great verse-compendium of the *Pramāṇavārttika* (Commentary on Valid Cognition) as its first chapter ('On Inference'), and the parts in prose were regarded as Dharmakīrti's own commentary on this chapter. The other chapters of the *Pramāṇavārttika* are, in fact, conceived as a commentary on Dignāga's *Pramāṇasamuccaya* (Collected Writings on Valid Cognition), the second chapter dealing with the proof of the Buddha's authority, the third with perception and the fourth with proof. Much is new in this work but, because it is structurally unbalanced, Dharmakīrti left it unfinished.

Drawing heavily on the earlier work, Dharmakīrti chose to compose a new statement of his ideas as an independent text in three chapters (on valid cognition and perception, on inference, and on proof), the *Pramāṇaviniścaya* (Analytical Determination of Valid Cognition), of which the *Nyāyabindu* (Drop of Logic) is an abstract. Dharmakīrti returned to his first subject with the *Hetubindu* (Drop of Logical Reason), treating it in a more formal way, with digressions devoted to the proof of momentariness, to a detailed presentation of his theory of causality, and to a final refutation of his teacher's attempt at developing an alternative logic in order to 'save' Dignāga's theory (see MOMENTARINESS, BUDDHIST DOCTRINE OF §§1, 5). In his last work, the *Vādanyāya* (Rule for Disputations), he applied the results of his work on the logical reason to interpretations of the forms and rules governing public disputations, and refuted the canon of the Nyāya school that had seemingly been in use for that purpose up to his time (see NYĀYA-VAIŚEṢIKA §6). In the context of Indian polemical practice, Dharmakīrti is unique in emphasizing that disputations have their purpose in the search for truth. Two small works, the *Sambandhaparīkṣā* (Examination of Relations) and the *Santānāntarasiddhi* (Proof of Other Mental Continua), have not yet been attributed to a definite period of production.

2 Epistemology and logic

Except for the second and third chapters of the *Pramāṇavārttika* and the two small treatises just mentioned, Dharmakīrti's work is mainly concerned with developing Dignāga's epistemology and logic. He presents new ideas in the traditional way as the correct interpretation of the latter's thought. Epistemological thought, in this context, is an attempt at providing a rational frame for human practice, meaningful both in everyday life and in the pursuit of the ultimate goal indicated by the Buddha. In the second chapter of the *Pramāṇavārttika*, the Buddha is proven to be an authority on the value of all human activity and the final goals of spiritual aspiration. The third chapter, 'On Perception', is a critical analysis of the nature and possibility of perception. While elsewhere in his work, especially when dealing with epistemological issues, Dharmakīrti takes his stand on an ontology of 'critical realism' (the Sautrāntika tradition) and develops empirical models and categories for his theories, when analysing perception the option of a reality independent of cognition is dissolved, and an idealistic ontology (of the Yogācāra kind) remains (see EPISTEMOLOGY, INDIAN SCHOOLS OF §1; BUDDHISM, YOGĀCĀRA SCHOOL OF §§1–4).

Dharmakīrti's theory of meaning is nominalistic. Words and concepts refer only to the difference from others (*anyāpoha*) that is common to individual realities. This common character is unreal, but in human experience realities evoke a like judgment of their capacities, and thereby a link is provided between the false realm of beginningless constructs and the momentary instants of reality experienced (see UNIVERSALS, INDIAN THEORIES OF §3).

Like Dignāga, Dharmakīrti accepts two kinds of valid cognition which hold good in practice: perception and inference. Perception is a cognition devoid of conceptual construction and is nonerroneous. Inferential cognition, being conceptual, is by nature erroneous, but if attained under the strict formal conditions of logic may be necessarily true. Verbal cognition based on authority or scripture is also inferential when it can be established as being trustworthy with regard to its specific, totally imperceptible object.

In the field of logic, Dharmakīrti transforms Dignāga's theory, which emphasized the formal aspects of logical reason, by insisting, like pre-Dignāga Sāṅkhya logic, on the need for the necessary logical relation to have a foundation in reality. In fact, he interprets Dignāga's logic through his own, arguing that the former is not possible without implying the latter. The three marks of a logical reason required by Dignāga are fulfilled only by Dharmakīrti's three kinds of logical reason. Two possible connections in reality, real identity and causality, restrict the kinds of concepts from which others can be inferred to three: 'essential property' (*svabhāva*) and 'nonperception' (*anupalabdhi*), based on real identity, and 'effect' (*kārya*), based on causality. When these real connections are ascertained, inference is a valid cognition, although because it is conceptual by nature it is essentially problematic. However, when inference is correctly applied it may serve to remove or correct erroneous concepts and replace them with others more appropriate to reality (see INFERENCE, INDIAN THEORIES OF §§5–6).

In Dharmakīrti's thought, logical theory and application are tightly interwoven. For example, he develops a new form of the proof of universal momentary destruction (*kṣaṇabhaṅga*), deriving it, in the *Pramāṇaviniścaya*, from the concept of being (*sattva*). In elaborating this proof for the first time, he applies a new method for ascertaining the logical relation between the two concepts involved. Subsequently, in the later *Hetubindu*, this new method is also incorporated into the theory of logic.

See also: BUDDHIST PHILOSOPHY, INDIAN §§4–5; NOMINALISM, BUDDHIST DOCTRINE OF

List of works

Most translations and studies are in German and Japanese (by E. Frauwallner, T. Vetter, H. Tosaki, E. Steinkellner, C. Oetke).

Steinkellner, E. and Much, M.T. (1995) *Texte der erkenntnistheoretischen Schule des Buddhismus* (Texts of the Buddhist Epistemological Schools), Göttingen: Vandenhoek & Ruprecht, 23–44. (Bibliographical survey of the Dharmakīrti's texts in Sanskrit or Tibetan translation, and their translations into European languages and Japanese.)

References and further reading

Bijlert, V.A. van (1989) *Epistemology and Spiritual Authority*, Vienna: Arbeitskreis für Tibetische und Buddhistische Studien Universität Wien. (An annotated translation of *Pramāṇavārttika* ch. 2, verses 1–7, containing the definition of validity in cognitions.)

Dreyfus, G.B. (1997) *Recognizing Reality, Dharmakīrti's Philosophy and its Tibetan Interpretations*, Albany, NY: State University of New York Press. (A comprehensive study of the Tibetan philosophical work in continuation of Dharmakīrti's ontology, philosophy of language and epistemology.)

Franco, E. (1997) *Dharmakīrti on Compassion and Rebirth*, Vienna: Arbeitskreis für Tibetische und Buddhistische Studien Universität Wien. (An annotated translation of *Pramāṇavārttika* ch. 2, verses 34–72, together with Prajñākaragupta's Commentary and five relevant studies.)

* Stcherbatsky, T. (1930, 1932) *Buddhist Logic*, Leningrad: Izdatel'stvo Akademii Nauk SSSR, 2 vols; Osnabrück: Biblio Verlag, 1970; Delhi: Motilal Banarsidass, 1992. (An introduction to Buddhist logic on the basis of the *Nyāyabindu* and its commentary by Dharmottara; written with a heavy Neo-Kantian bias, it is a largely out-of-date, but still useful, survey and has been reprinted many times.)

Steinkellner, E. (ed.) (1991) *Studies in the Buddhist Epistemological Tradition. Proceedings of the Second International Dharmakīrti Conference, Vienna, June 11–16, 1989*, Vienna: Verlag der Österreichischen Akademie der Wissenschaften. (Conference proceedings giving a clear impression of the state of Dharmakīrti studies.)

Vetter, T. (1984) *Der Buddha und seine Lehre in Dharmakīrtis Pramāṇavārttikam* (The Buddha and his Theory in Dharmakīrti's *Pramāṇavārttikam*), Vienna: Arbeitskreis für Tibetische und Buddhistische Studien Universität Wien, 1990. (An annotated translation of *Pramāṇavārttika* ch. 2, verses 131–285 with a concise introduction on Dharmakīrti's religious thought.)

* Yijing (671–95) *A Record of the Buddhist Religion as Practised in India and the Malay Archipelago*, trans. J. Takakuru, London, 1896; repr. Delhi, 1966. (Referred to in §1.)

ERNST STEINKELLNER

DIALECTICAL MATERIALISM

Dialectical materialism is the official name given to Marxist-Leninist philosophy by its proponents in the Soviet Union and their affiliates elsewhere. The term, never used by either Karl Marx or Friedrich Engels, was the invention of the Russian Marxist Georgii Plekhanov, who first used it in 1891. Engels, however, favourably contrasted 'materialist dialectics' with the 'idealist dialectics' of Hegel and the German idealist tradition, and the 'dialectical' outlook of Marxism with the 'mechanistic' or 'metaphysical' standpoint of other nineteenth-century materialists.

Dialectical materialism proclaims allegiance to the methods of empirical science and opposition to all forms of scepticism which deny that science can know the nature of reality. Dialectical materialists reject religious belief generally, denying the existence of non-material or supernatural entities (such as God or an immortal human soul). Unlike other forms of materialism, however, dialectical materialists maintain that the fundamental laws governing both matter and mind are dialectical *in the sense in which that term is used in the philosophy of G.W.F. Hegel.*

Although dialectical materialism is supposed to constitute the philosophical underpinnings of Marxism, Marx's only major contribution to it was his materialist conception of history. The more fundamental philosophical views of dialectical materialism have their main source in the writings of Engels, especially Anti-Dühring *(1878),* Dialectics of Nature *(1875–82) and* Ludwig Feuerbach and the End of Classical German Philosophy *(1886). To this last work Engels appended the eleven 'Theses on Feuerbach' written by Marx in 1845, which contrasted the 'old' or 'contemplative' materialism with the practically oriented materialism which was to be the basis of the proletarian movement. Further developments of dialectical materialism are found in writings by V.I. Lenin and subsequent Soviet writers. Lenin's chief additions were his critique of 'empirio-criticism' (the empiricist phenomenalism of certain Russian followers of Ernst Mach, who argued that matter was to be reduced to sense data), and his conception of the 'partisanship' of all philosophical views.*

1 **Materialism**
2 **Dialectics**
3 **Dialectical laws**
4 **Historical materialism**
5 **Materialism and practice**
6 **The fate of dialectical materialism**

1 Materialism

According to Engels, the fundamental question of all philosophy is 'Which is primary, matter or consciousness?' The question of 'primacy' is also put this way: 'Which, matter or consciousness, is the source of the other?' Materialism holds to the primacy of matter, idealism to the primacy of consciousness. Theism, which maintains that matter was created by a supernatural (divine) consciousness, is taken to be the chief form of idealism; under the title 'objective idealism' this is sometimes distinguished from 'subjective idealism,' the view that the material world exists only for the individual mind (see IDEALISM). Although these two versions of idealism do not appear to make consciousness the 'source' of matter in the same sense, it is even less clear in what way

materialism takes matter to be the 'source' of consciousness. Dialectical materialists apparently mean to endorse whatever account of mind results from empirical scientific investigations; but they are confident that we already know enough to exclude supernaturalist, dualist or idealist accounts.

Dialectical materialists sometimes also give the 'primacy of matter over consciousness' an epistemological interpretation. Idealists are charged with a tendency to scepticism concerning knowledge of the material world, whereas materialists maintain that the material world is knowable through empirical science. This confidence is supported by appeal to the practical successes of empirical science, by which is meant both the results of experimentation (which involve the experimenter's practical interaction with the world) and the technological fruits of empirical science. Practice is asserted to be the sole criterion of truth; doubts and questions which cannot be given a practical significance are to be dismissed. The sceptical doubts of idealistic philosophy are held to be refutable in this way.

Dialectical materialists also insist that thought bears a certain determinate relation to matter, serving as its 'image' or 'reflection'. The world of consciousness is the material world 'translated into forms of thought'. The point of this last phrase seems to be that thought is given in certain determinate forms, which bear determinate relationships (especially developmental ones) to each other, whose subject matter is 'dialectics'. The epistemology of dialectical materialism opposes some traditional forms of empiricism in that it emphasizes the independent importance of determinate (dialectical) forms of thinking in the theoretical process through which science comes to know reality. Engels, for example, argues that Marx's theory of capitalism is 'dialectical' by emphasizing structural parallels between Hegel's *Science of Logic* and Marx's *Capital*.

2 Dialectics

If the opposition of idealism and materialism concerns the fundamental question of philosophy, the opposition between metaphysics and dialectics concerns the fundamental issue of method. The 'metaphysical' method (as Engels calls it, borrowing the term from Hegel's critique of pre-Kantian philosophy) is identified with the mechanistic programme of early modern science, which is taken to have been discredited by such nineteenth-century discoveries as electromagnetic field theory. But following Engels, dialectical materialism upholds (at least a modified version of) the critique of early modern science presented by German idealism and its 'philosophy of nature', which opposes formalism and reductionism and emphasizes phenomena of organic interconnection and qualitative emergence. Early modern mechanism was a form of atomistic reductionism, which takes the world to consist fundamentally of material corpuscles interacting and combining in various ways according to unchanging laws. Essences or natural kinds no longer have any fundamental role to play in science, since all qualitative differences are ultimately to be reduced to quantitative differences at the fundamental level of explanation.

This picture was rejected by German idealists such as SCHELLING and HEGEL. Under the title 'philosophy of nature' (*Naturphilosophie*) they attempted to develop a comprehensive picture of nature as the expression of an absolute reality transcending nature. Although Engels could not accept the anti-naturalist form of idealist philosophy of nature, he shared many of its aims and wanted to vindicate its 'dialectical' principles against contemporary materialists such as Ludwig BÜCHNER and Erich HAECKEL, whom he regarded as still fettered by the old mechanism or 'metaphysics'. From the idealists, Engels retained the idea that the natural world involves forms of organization that are essentially different in quality, each with its own distinctive regularities; they are irreducible to any fundamental form of matter or unchanging set of laws. Engels' new materialism holds that new essences or forms of organization may emerge in the course of history. Thus the commonest charges dialectical materialists bring against metaphysical materialism are that it ignores the fundamentally developmental nature of matter, that it tries to reduce all change to quantitative change, and that it fails to recognize internal contradictions in the nature of material things as the fundamental source of change. The antidote is to recognize and employ the dialectical laws of thought.

3 Dialectical laws

First law: the unity of opposites. The nature of everything involves internal opposition or contradiction. This is probably the most obscure dialectical idea, because it is the most wilfully paradoxical, seeming at times to amount to a flat denial of the logical law of non-contradiction. Echoing Hegel's 'resolution' of Zeno's paradoxes, for example, Engels writes: 'Motion itself is a contradiction . . . coming about through a body at one and the same moment of time being both in one place and in another place, being at one and the same place and also not in it'. Regarded as an attempted solution to Zeno's paradoxes, such remarks are at best extremely obscure; they do apparently intend to challenge the canonical

status of traditional logic, and put in question even the law of non-contradiction.

Hegel, however, sometimes draws a distinction between the way the principles of traditional logic as they are 'meant' (so understood, he regards them as trivially true and of no philosophical interest) and a deeper 'metaphysical' significance that may be discovered in them (see HEGEL, G.W.F. §6). Understood in the latter way the laws are false, but importantly so, because they represent the standpoint of the abstract 'understanding' which fails to comprehend the essential interrelatedness of things and their necessary development. Understood as a denial of traditional logic on this metaphysical interpretation, the law of the unity (or interpenetration) of opposites claims something which, if not always entirely clear, is at least plainly not (in the traditional sense) logically self-contradictory: namely, that the essences of things include differing and opposed, often complementary, elements or processes, and that essential change or development in the world occurs through the conflict of these opposed moments. It is not hard to see how an emphasis on the organic could give rise to such a view, since the life of an organism often consists in a dynamic equilibrium of opposed processes (Engels' example is nutrition and excretion). Further, it is not difficult to see how a representation of changes in the world as resulting from conflicting local tendencies deemed essential to a certain organization constitutes a clear alternative to a reductive mechanistic explanation in terms of unchanging basic elements following general laws. Some later dialectical materialists distinguish 'non-antagonistic' contradictions from 'antagonistic' ones: that is, opposed processes that harmonize and reinforce one another from those which tend towards the essential destruction of the complex they constitute. They also distinguish 'internal' contradictions from 'external' ones, the former constituting the essential nature of a phenomenon and the latter involving the contingent collision of things with different natures.

Second law: quantity and quality. Quantitative change always eventually leads to qualitative change or development. Engels cites such phenomena as the suddenness of the transition between the solid, liquid and gaseous states of substances as their temperatures change. The important thing in such examples is that purely quantitative changes lead to the emergence of new qualities which cannot be adequately grasped in terms of the concepts in which the purely quantitative changes can be formulated. Once again, the rejection of mechanistic reductionism is evident both in the insistence on the existence and importance of qualitative differences and in the idea that what is ultimately important, even about the quantitative changes studied by the mechanists, is the way they lead to qualitative differences.

Third law: negation of the negation. Change negates what is changed, and the result is in turn negated, but this second negation leads to a further development and not a return to that with which we began. MARX, in Volume 1 of *Capital* (1865), famously described capitalist property as the 'negation' of individual property based on the labour of the proprietor, and communist property as the 'negation' of capitalist property, hence as the 'negation of the negation'. The point once again is to emphasize the emergence of what is qualitatively new, and the fact that this emergence is to be understood in terms of the specific essence of that which is in process rather than in terms of general laws applying to simple elements of which it is composed.

The three dialectical laws are often seen to operate in close association, as when 'negation' is the result of antagonistic or 'contradictory' tendencies essential to something, which thereby change it into something qualitatively different. In general, dialectical thinking tries to explain change as the outcome of conflicts which emerge from the essence of something, which are resolved when its essence is transformed and it attains a new stage of its development. This last idea is sometimes presented by popular expositors of 'dialectics' in the jargon of 'thesis–antithesis–synthesis'. This particular bit of grotesque jargon, however, is almost never found in the writings of dialectical materialists themselves. It was never used by Hegel or Engels, and was used by Marx only once, solely for the purpose of ridicule. Its employment nearly always betrays either ignorance of dialectical thinking or contemptuous hostility to it – usually both these at once.

4 Historical materialism

The most prominent application of dialectical materialism is to the historical development of society, in the shape of Marx's 'materialist conception of history'. It has sometimes been made a matter of controversy how far Marx's economic theory of the history of capitalism and his shrewd analyses of contemporary political events actually embody his theoretical programme, the main lines of which are stated in the *German Ideology* (1845) and the Preface to *Toward a Critique of Political Economy* (1859). The fundamental thing in human history is the productive powers of society and their tendency to grow. Productive powers at a given stage of development determine the nature of human labouring activity because labour consists in the exercise of precisely those powers. A given set of productive powers also thereby favours certain 'material relations of production', forms of human cooperation or division of labour, which are not directly part of them, but facilitate their employment to a greater degree than rival forms would do. They thereby also favour certain 'social relations of production', systems of social roles relating to the control of the production process and the disposition of its fruits. It is this system of social relations of production which Marx calls the 'economic structure of society' which forms the 'real basis' of social life on the materialist theory, conditioning 'superstructures' such as the political state and the 'ideological' forms of consciousness found in religion, philosophy, morality and art.

Within the framework of any system of social relations of production, society's productive powers expand at a greater or lesser rate, depending on the historical circumstances, including the social relations themselves. Eventually, however, a given set of social relations of production are outgrown or rendered obsolete by the productive powers. The prevailing relations either make it difficult to employ the existing powers or else fetter the further development of these powers. Powers and relations of production thus come into conflict or 'contradiction'; an 'epoch of social revolution' begins. The outcome of the conflict is the transformation of the relations of production to bring them into line with the productive powers so as to facilitate the further expansion of these powers. Changes in the superstructure of society, including its political and legal institutions, are to be explained by the required changes in the social relations of production. The mechanism by which these adjustments are to be carried out is the class struggle. At a given stage of history, that class is victorious whose class interests consist in the establishment of that set of production relations which best suits the productive powers at that stage.

Historical materialism exemplifies the principles of dialectical materialism: each mode of production has its own essential laws and tendencies; each has inherent tendencies to undermine itself and change into something new, and these tendencies operate through oppositions or contradictions essential to it. Although Marx occasionally applies it to pre-modern societies, this theory of history was obviously suggested to him by the rise of capitalism; Marx envisages the overthrow of capitalism and the rise of socialism as following the same pattern of historical development.

5 Materialism and practice

Beginning with Marx's 'Theses on Feuerbach' (1845), one prominent claim made by dialectical materialists is that their view alone provides for an adequate relation of philosophy to 'practice'. In the 'Theses', Marx meant to side with Hegelian philosophy against the empiricism of Feuerbach and eighteenth-century mechanistic materialism, holding that its conception of our relation to nature is exclusively contemplative, while until now only idealism has grasped the 'active side' of this relation (albeit inadequately). An adequate grasp of practice, in his view, is based on the understanding of philosophy's involvement in the fundamental social struggles brought to light by historical materialism. Only in this way do we become fully conscious of ourselves as natural, and naturally historical, beings.

Lenin's theory of 'partisanship' was an attempt to develop this important side of Marxism: the recognition that all philosophical thinking must be understood in its social significance and its relation to historical struggles. The 'partisanship' of philosophy is all too easy for us to stigmatize as simply an excuse for constraining philosophical thought through party dogma. But the philosophical import of the doctrine (as distinct from its political abuses) is rather to liberate thinking by making it more self-aware as regards its class basis and social situatedness (see LENIN, V.).

6 The fate of dialectical materialism

The plausibility of any theory as programmatic as dialectical materialism must finally depend on how fruitful it is in its actual employment. As the official philosophy of Soviet Marxism-Leninism, however, dialectical materialism was doomed to stasis and sterility by the repressive and authoritarian political conditions under which its practitioners were forced to operate. Thus a philosophy whose spirit was to challenge traditional religious authority and to exalt the fact of qualitative novelty and ceaseless progressive development has become our century's most notorious example of ossified dogmatism, incapable either of internal development or of response to external change, often degenerating into the mechanical repetition of empty phrases borrowed from the science and philosophy of an earlier century. Yet this historical irony too easily obscures the important fact that the basic aims and principles of dialectical materialism are very much in harmony with any outlook which perceives a fundamental opposition between scientific theories and religious myths, tries to address the scientific challenges posed by the failure of the seventeenth and eighteenth century mechanistic programme, and seeks a scientific metaphysics as the basis for an enlightened view of the world.

See also: ENGELS, F; MARX, K; MATERIALISM; PLEKHANOV, G.V.

References and further reading

Acton, H.B. (1955) *The Illusion of the Epoch: Marxism-Leninism as a Philosophical Creed*, London: Cohen & West. (An informed but critical discussion of Marxist philosophy.)

Afanasyev, V.G. (1980) *Marxist Philosophy*, 4th edn, Moscow: Progress. (Standard exposition of Soviet Marxist-Leninist philosophy.)

Bochenski, J.M. (1963) *Dialectical Materialism*, Dordrecht: Nijhoff. (A very polemical discussion of Soviet dialectical materialism.)

Cohen, G.A. (1978) *Karl Marx's Theory of History*, Princeton, NJ: Princeton University Press. (An influential interpretation/defence of Marxian historical materialism.)

Cornforth, M. (1971) *Dialectical Materialism*, New York: International Publishers. (A standard survey of Marxist-Leninist philosophy by an important British exponent.)

* Engels, F. (1878) *Anti-Dühring*, Moscow: Progress, 1962. (The major philosophical work by Engels.)

—— (1875–82) *Dialectics of Nature*, New York: International Publishers, 1973. (The chief source of Engels' philosophy of nature.)

* —— (1886) *Ludwig Feuerbach and the End of Classical German Philosophy*, in K. Marx and F. Engels, *Selected Works in One Volume*, London: Lawrence & Wishart, 1968, 584–622. (First published as a review, this is a history of German philosophy, placing Marx's materialism at its culmination.)

* Hegel, G.W.F. (1812–16) *Science of Logic*, trans. A.V. Miller, Atlantic Highlands, NJ: Humanities Press, 1993. (Mentioned in §1 above. Engels parallelled this work to Marx.)

Lenin, V.I. (1960) *Collected Works*, Moscow: Progress. (Vol. 38 contains the *Philosophical Notebooks* which contain his sympathetic reflections on Hegelian speculative logic.)

—— (1909) *Materialism and Empirio-Criticism*, trans. A. Fineberg, New York: International Publishers, 1948. (Lenin's critique of the Russian Machists contains some of his main discussion of philosophical questions.)

* Marx, K. and Engels F. (1975–) *Marx Engels Collected Works*, New York: International Publishers. (The comprehensive edition in English.)

Oizerman, T. (1984) *The Main Trends in Philosophy*, Moscow: Progress. (A survey of philosophy from a Marxist-Leninist standpoint during the last years of the Soviet period.)

Plekhanov, G. (1961) *Selected Philosophical Works*,

trans. A. Rothstein, New York: International Publishers. (The chief Russian source of much of Marxist-Leninist thought.)

Ruben, D. (1979) *Marxism and Materialism*, 2nd edn, Brighton: Harvester. (A sympathetic but critical discussion of Marxist materialism.)

Wetter, G. (1959) *Dialectical Materialism*, trans. P. Heath, New York: Praeger. (A critical study of Marxism-Leninism.)

Wood, A. (1981) *Karl Marx*, London: Routledge & Kegan Paul. (A comprehensive study of Marx's philosophical thought.)

ALLEN W. WOOD

DIALECTICAL SCHOOL

An offshoot of the Megarian school, and active c.350–250 BC, the Dialectical school was an important precursor of Stoic logic. Its leading members were Diodorus Cronus and Philo. Its interests included modality, conditionals and logical puzzles. Its primary allegiance was probably Socratic, but with some additional debt to the Eleatic Zeno.

The Dialecticians have regularly been assumed to be identical with the Megarians (see MEGARIAN SCHOOL), but several testimonies show them to be a distinct and rival school. The Megarians are even reported to have filched pupils from them (Diogenes Laertius, II 113). Although linked by a common interest in sophisms, by a shared Socratic background tinged with Eleaticism and by the fact that Clinomachus of Thurii, official founder of the Dialectical school, had been a pupil of the Megarian founder Euclides, the two schools exhibited largely different philosophical outlooks. Where the Megarians emphasized and developed Socrates' specifically moral teachings, the Dialecticians seem to have stressed the intrinsic value of dialectical activity – argument by question and answer. Since SOCRATES himself had called dialectical discussion the greatest human good (Plato, *Apology* 38a), the school's stance can be seen as a bid for Socrates' mantle, in direct competition with the Megarians and other Socratic schools (see SOCRATIC SCHOOLS). The school's appearance in a list of 'ethical' sects (Diogenes Laertius, I 18) can therefore be taken seriously. If Diodorus, in devising his own four arguments against motion, was also indicating allegiance to Zeno of Elea, the acknowledged founder of dialectic, the move was perhaps legitimized by Plato's *Parmenides*, where the young Socrates welcomes a lesson in Zenonian dialectic.

What united the school was its commitment to dialectical virtuosity as such. On individual points of logical theory they differed widely.

Clinomachus is reported as 'the first author of treatises on propositions, predicates etc.' (Diogenes Laertius, II 112). The school's pioneering work on the nature of predicates is confirmed by Seneca (*Letters* 117.12), but it is also clear from Diodorus' and Philo's work on conditionals and modal logic that they anticipated the Stoics, and differed from Aristotle, in treating entire propositions rather than terms as the basic units in logic on this and on Diodorus' other work, see DIODORUS CRONUS and PHILO THE DIALECTICIAN). Their theory of sign inference also paved the way for Stoicism, as did their analysis of inferential validity if, as Ebert (1991) has argued, a number of references to 'the dialecticians' in Sextus Empiricus are to this school. Zeno of Citium, founder of Stoicism, studied under Diodorus.

Diodorus' Master Argument, defending his definition of 'possible' as 'what is or will be true', was their most celebrated product. A less known companion piece, also attributed to the school, is the Mowing Argument, which tries to devalue the word 'perhaps' by arguing that every prediction must be either simply true or simply false. Although both arguments lent themselves to deterministic interpretations, the different modal views of Philo and the little-known Panthoides did not, and the school as such clearly had no commitment to determinism.

Another area of dialectical activity, with strong Socratic antecedents, was the framing of definitions. A Dialectical definition of 'expertise' (*technē*) is recorded, and Aristotle (*Topics* VI 10) criticizes that of 'life' by the early Dialectician Dionysius of Chalcedon.

References and further reading

* Aristotle (c. mid 4th century BC) *Topics*, trans. in J. Barnes (ed.) *The Complete Works of Aristotle*, vol. 1, Princeton, NJ: Princeton University Press, 1984. (Aristotle's handbook on dialectics.)

* Diogenes Laertius (c. early 3rd century AD) *Lives of the Philosophers*, trans. R.D. Hicks, *Diogenes Laertius Lives of Eminent Philosophers*, Loeb Classical Library, Cambridge, MA: Harvard University Press and London: Heinemann, 1925, 2 vols. (Book II 106–12 in volume 1 covers the main Dialectical philosophers.)

* Ebert, T. (1991) *Dialektiker und frühe Stoiker bei Sextus Empiricus* (Dialectians and Early Stoics in Sextus Empiricus), Göttingen: Vandenhoeck & Ruprecht. (Pioneering attempt to recover evidence on the Dialectical school; an earlier version of

Part 1, on signs, had appeared in English in *Oxford Studies in Ancient Philosophy* 5 (1987): 83–126.)

Giannantoni, G. (1990) *Socratis et Socraticorum Reliquiae* (The Fragments of Socrates and the Socratics), Naples: Bibliopolis. (Volume 1 includes the fullest available collection of Greek and Latin testimonies on the Dialecticians, although there classed as 'Megarians'; many testimonies on the school are still missing.)

Primavesi, O. (1992) 'Dionysios der Dialektiker und Aristoteles über die Definition des Lebens' (Dionysius the Dialectician and Aristotle on the Definition of Life), *Rheinisches Museum für Philologie* 135: 246–61. (Discovers a Dialectical definition in Aristotle, I VI 10.)

Sedley, D. (1977) 'Diodorus Cronus and Hellenistic philosophy', *Proceedings of the Cambridge Philological Society* 203: 74–120. (On the separation of the Dialectical from the Megarian school, and on Diodorus' influence.)

* Sextus Empiricus (2nd century AD) *Works*, trans. R.G. Bury, Loeb Classical Library, Cambridge, MA: Harvard University Press and London: Heinemann, 1933–49, 4 vols. (The main passages in which Ebert (1991) has detected reports of the Dialectical school are Outlines of Pyrrhonism II 110–11, 146–50, 229–35 and Against the Professors VIII (Against the Logicians II) 93–8, 108–17, 124–8.)

DAVID SEDLEY

DIALOGICAL LOGIC

Dialogical logic characterizes logical constants (such as 'and', 'or', 'for all') by their use in a critical dialogue between two parties: a proponent who has asserted a thesis and an opponent who challenges it. For each logical constant, a rule specifies how to challenge a statement that displays the corresponding logical form, and how to respond to such a challenge. These rules are incorporated into systems of regimented dialogue that are games in the game-theoretical sense. Dialogical concepts of logical consequence can then be based upon the concept of a winning strategy in a (formal) dialogue game: B is a logical consequence of A if and only if there is a winning strategy for the proponent of B against any opponent who is willing to concede A. But it should be stressed that there are several plausible (and non-equivalent) ways to draw up the rules.

1   **Main characteristics**
2   **An example**
3   **Motivations and applications**

1   Main characteristics

Logic is to provide us with viable concepts of logical consequence, logical truth, consistency and so on, and to that end to elucidate the meaning of logical constants (see LOGICAL CONSTANTS). Dialogical logic, which is the logical part of dialogue theory, goes about this by assigning to each logical constant a clear 'meaning-in-use', where the context of use is one of critical dialogue arising from a conflict of opinions about a statement: the initial thesis. This thesis – the question at issue, one might say – is challenged by the opponent (*O*) and defended by the proponent (*P*). The opponent may or may not have granted some statements in advance: the initial concessions or hypotheses of the dialogue. The dialogical approach is to be compared to, and contrasted with, semantic or model-theoretic characterizations of the logical constants (see MODEL THEORY) and deduction-theoretic characterizations (see PROOF THEORY; NATURAL DEDUCTION, TABLEAU AND SEQUENT SYSTEMS).

Each logical constant is characterized by the specific modes of challenge of which the participants may avail themselves to attack or question a statement with that particular logical constant as its principal operator; as well as by the specific responses to these challenges. For instance, a conjunctive statement '*A* and *B*' can be challenged in two ways: by questioning *A* and by questioning *B*. The response to the first type of challenge consists of *A*, whereas the response to the second type of challenge consists of *B*. In the case of a disjunctive statement '*A* or *B*', however, the only type of challenge pertains to this statement in its totality, but the responses are the same, with the distinctive difference that in this case the choice between *A* and *B* is the respondent's, rather than the challenger's. A survey of these so-called logical rules is given in the table.

The logical rules are not sufficient, for the meaning of each logical constant also depends on global characteristics of the dialogues. Structural rules stipulate who may challenge what and how often, whether responses may be repeated, and so on. Finally, rules for winning and losing determine the situations in which a participant may be declared to be the winner (or loser) of the dialogue. A full set of rules of all three types (see the table and lists of rules below) defines a 'dialogue game', or 'dialectic system'.

If a dialogue game makes use of an interpreted nonlogical vocabulary, the game and its dialogues are called material; otherwise they are called formal. In material games, typically, elementary statements can be defended by pointing out their (extra-dialogical) truth. Thus observation and other ways of fact-finding are connected with material dialogues. In formal dialogue games these material modes of defence are not available.

2 An example

The following formal dialogue game yields intuitionistic (constructive, effective) predicate logic (see INTUITIONISM). It is based on a first-order language for predicate logic with an infinity of individual constants $a, b, \ldots$. Formulas are denoted as $A, B, \ldots$. The result of substituting an individual constant a for the free variable x in the formula A is denoted as $A[a/x]$.

This game is asymmetric in the following sense: at all times P has a statement to defend, whereas O never has a thesis to defend. However, P must have some means to exploit the initial concessions. To that end P is allowed to question the concessions in order to generate more detailed concessions. The corresponding moves of question (by P) and answer (by O) are formally identical to the moves of challenge (properly so called) by O and response (or, defence) by P, but the intuitive motivation is different. Thus the asymmetry of the game remains hidden as far as the logical rules are concerned. It is clearly borne out, however, by the structural rules and by the very different ways P and O can win a dialogue.

Structural Rules

1 There are two participants: the proponent, P, who defends a thesis, and the opponent, O, who

may or may not have granted a number of concessions.

2 The participants move alternately. O makes the first move: a challenge of the thesis.

3 Each move by O is a challenge or an answer according to a logical rule.

4 Each move by P is a question or a defence according to a logical rule, or a winning remark, that is, either '*Ipse dixisti!*' ('You said so yourself!') or '*Absurdum dixisti!*' ('You said something absurd!').

5 P is not allowed to question O's elementary statements.

6 A winning remark '*Ipse dixisti!*' is allowed only if the most recently challenged statement of P's can also be found among O's concessions.

7 A winning remark '*Absurdum dixisti!*' is allowed only if $\perp$ can be found among O's concessions.

8 The only statement P is allowed to defend is the one that was most recently attacked by O.

9 Except for the initial challenge, each move by O is to consist of a reaction to the immediately preceding move by P (answering P's question, or challenging a newly introduced statement).

10 Before the onset of the dialogue proper, P is to announce a limit on the number of P-moves. P is not allowed any moves beyond that number.

Rules for Winning and Losing

1 P wins by making a winning remark.

2 O wins whenever it is P's turn to make a move but no legal move is available.

Logical Rules

	Statement	*Challenge/question*	*Defence/answer*
Rule$_\rightarrow$	$A \rightarrow B$	A	B
Rule$_\neg$	$\neg A$	A	$\perp$ (elementary statement of absurdity)
Rule$_\vee$	$A \vee B$	?	A or B (defender/answerer chooses)
Rule$_\wedge$	$A \wedge B$	A? or B? } (challenger/questioner chooses)	A B
Rule$_\forall$	$\forall x A$	a? (challenger/questioner selects constant)	$A[a/x]$
Rule$_\exists$	$\exists x A$	?	$A[a/x]$ (defender/answerer selects constant)
Rule$_{EI}$	elementary statement	?	none

3 Motivations and applications

The connection between dialogues and logic, which goes back to Aristotle's *Topics*, was reintroduced by Paul Lorenzen in 1958 (see Lorenzen and Lorenz 1978). Originally, the motivation was to be found in the philosophy of mathematics: the dialogues were to yield a criterion of constructivity and to justify a constructive logic without recourse to Brouwerian solipsism (see INTUITIONISM). But studies by Kuno Lorenz and others were not slow to point out that with a little fiddling of the structural rules the dialogue games could be forced to yield classical logic instead, although constructive logic seemed more 'natural' from the dialogical point of view.

In the meantime it had become clear how logical concepts were to be defined dialogically. We have seen above how a definition of logical consequence can be framed in terms of the existence of a winning strategy for the proponent in a formal game. The case of an empty set of concessions gives us a definition of logical truth. Consistency of a set of statements can be defined as the existence of a winning strategy for an opponent who concedes these statements against a proponent who defends ⊥. This strategy shows how *O* can maintain this position without conceding absurdity. Clearly, different formal dialogue games may give rise to different concepts of logical consequence; to different logics, one might say.

The challenges and responses given in the logical rules of dialogical logic are closely similar and often identical to those given in Hintikka's rules for game-theoretic semantics (see SEMANTICS, GAME-THEORETIC). But in game-theoretic semantics one tries to exploit the concept of a game to construct a semantic theory (for natural language), whereas dialogical logic is rather to be conceived as providing an alternative to the semantic approach. Even so, the two approaches are closely related.

Later on dialogical logic came to be part of a programme for a normative reconstruction of the language of science, ethics, philosophy and politics that was worked out by Paul Lorenzen and others (see Lorenzen and Schwemmer 1973) in the so-called Erlangen school of German constructivism (see LORENZEN, P.). The dialogue rules contribute to this programme by giving us reconstructed versions of the logical constants.

More generally, dialogical logic has been influential in the development of argumentation theory, including the theory of argumentative discussions and fallacy theory.

See also: LOGICAL AND MATHEMATICAL TERMS, GLOSSARY OF

References and further reading

Barth, E.M. and Krabbe, E.C.W. (1982) *From Axiom to Dialogue: A Philosophical Study of Logics and Argumentation*, Berlin and New York: De Gruyter. (Chapters 3 and 4 provide normative foundations, from the point of view of a theory of argumentative discussions, for a number of dialectic systems. Chapters 5, 7 and 11 discuss the metatheory of dialectic systems and present proofs of equivalence with model-theoretic and deduction-theoretic systems. A standard introductory course in logic is presupposed.)

Felscher, W. (1986) 'Dialogues as a Foundation for Intuitionistic Logic', in D. Gabbay and F. Guenthner (eds) *Handbook of Philosophical Logic*, vol. 3, *Alternatives to Classical Logic*, Dordrecht: Reidel, 341–72. (A useful and concise introduction to the subject, with a useful bibliography. A bit more technical.)

Haas, G. (1984) *Konstruktive Einführung in die formale Logik* (A Constructive Introduction to Formal Logic), Mannheim: Bibliographisches Institut, Wissenschaftsverlag. (This is both an introduction to logic and an introduction to dialogical logic, with many examples, detailed explanations and proofs.)

Krabbe, E.C.W. (1985) 'Formal Systems of Dialogue Rules', *Synthese* 63 (3): 295–328. (Includes a survey of options in constructing a dialectic system, with a closer study of constructive systems and equivalence proofs. Only the last part is highly technical. Useful bibliography.)

Lorenzen, P. (1969) *Normative Logic and Ethics*, Mannheim: Bibliographisches Institut. (An early and brief exposition in English.)

—— (1986) *Lehrbuch der konstruktiven Wissenschaftstheorie* (Textbook of Constructive Philosophy of Science), Mannheim: Bibliographisches Institut, Wissenschaftsverlag. (Contains the first part of Lorenzen and Schwemmer (1973).)

* Lorenzen, P. and Lorenz, K. (1978) *Dialogische Logik*, Darmstadt: Wissenschaftliche Buchgesellschaft. (The essential writings of Lorenzen and Lorenz from the genesis of contemporary dialogical logic in 1958 to 1973.)

* Lorenzen, P. and Schwemmer, O. (1973) *Konstruktive Logik, Ethik und Wissenschaftstheorie* (Constructive Logic, Ethics and Philosophy of Science), Mannheim: Bibliographisches Institut, 2nd edn, 1975. (The 'bible' of Erlangen constructivism. The first part has a mature exposition of Lorenzen's dialogical logic and the way it functions in the Erlangen programme mentioned in §3.)

Walton, D.N. and Krabbe, E.C.W. (1995) *Commitment*

in *Dialogue: Basic Concepts of Interpersonal Reasoning*, Albany, NY: State University of New York Press. (Pursues the integration of dialogical logic with other dialogue theory, especially Charles Hamblin's formal dialectic.)

ERIK C.W. KRABBE

DICEY, ALBERT VENN (1835–1922)

A. V. Dicey, who held the Vinerian Chair of English Law at Oxford University between 1882 and 1909, is widely regarded as the high priest of orthodox constitutional thought in Britain. Living through a period of great political and economic change, Dicey recognized that the duty of the constitutional lawyer could no longer be one of simply venerating Britain's ancestral, unwritten constitution. He appreciated the need to try to lay bare its legal foundations and to identify its fundamental principles. In embarking on this exercise, Dicey, a follower of John Austin, employed an analytical method which treated law as a datum to be analysed and classified and which served to furnish a descriptive account of how law's various divisions fit together to provide an ordered whole. Dicey was the first to apply this legal positivist method to the study of constitutional law in Britain. The method became so ensconced in legal thought in twentieth-century Britain that today lawyers scarcely acknowledge any work in constitutional law which predates Dicey's work. It is as though he invented the subject.

In his classic text, *The Law of the Constitution* (1885), Dicey defined the subject of constitutional law as the study of the rules which affect the distribution or the exercise of the sovereign power of the state. These rules comprise two sets: laws in the strict sense which are enforced by courts; and conventions, understandings, habits and practices which are not so enforced but which regulate the conduct of the members of the sovereign power. Through this formalistic and positivistic distinction between law and convention, Dicey was able authoritatively to demarcate the boundaries of the subject.

Dicey's influence, however, has not been confined to his method. His view of the character of constitutional law was shaped by a particular political outlook which, on the face of it, seemed far removed from an Austinian method. This outlook was a form of 'diffused Burkeanism' (see BURKE, E.) which was a characteristic of much of nineteenth-century English political thought. He believed that the English system

– resting on a love of order, a Conservative spirit, and a belief in ordinary morality as a guide to public life – represented the climax of political achievement. These qualities were to be found, above all, in the common law heritage and, owing to the fact that it is a judge-made constitution, within the British constitution itself.

In *The Law of the Constitution* Dicey identified three guiding principles underpinning the British constitution: the legislative sovereignty of the Queen-in-Parliament; the universal rule throughout the constitution of ordinary law (otherwise understood as the rule of law); and the ultimate dependence of constitutional conventions on the law of the constitution. His objective was to show how, once their interlocking nature is understood, these principles were conducive to the promotion of liberty. Parliamentary sovereignty, the right of Parliament to make or unmake any law whatsoever, was the dominant characteristic of the political institutions. Though an instrument well adapted for the establishment of democratic despotism, Dicey argued that the sovereignty of Parliament, as contrasted with other forms of sovereign power, favoured the supremacy of law: first, because the constituent parts of Parliament provided checks and balances (the idea of 'self-correcting democracy'); and, second, because the rule of law implies the predominance of rigid legality throughout institutions and thus increases the authority of Parliamentary sovereignty (see SOVEREIGNTY §§2–3).

Dicey's formulation of the idea of the rule of law has been viewed as the most influential restatement of the principle since the eighteenth century. Nevertheless, it is not without its ambiguities. Dicey suggested that the concept had three meanings: the absolute supremacy of regular law as opposed to the influence of arbitrary power; the principle of equality before the law; and, finally, that the constitution is a product of ordinary law and thus that constitutional law is not the source but the consequence of individual rights. Running throughout these meanings, there lies a relatively specific conception of law as a universal body of general rules which have evolved through time and which are enunciated by judges. Also implicit within, but fundamental to, the conceptual structure of Dicey's constitutional thought is the idea of the separation of powers. Dicey's view that Parliamentary sovereignty favours the supremacy of law seems to hold sway only in so far as we regard the legislative function as that of laying down general rules for society rather than incorporating the vesting of discretionary powers in executive agencies. Similarly, Dicey's notorious view that administrative law undermined the rule of law can readily be understood once administrative law is viewed as an infringement of the principle of the separation of judicial and executive powers (see RULE OF LAW (RECHTSSTAAT) §§1–2).

The Law of the Constitution, though masquerading as an introductory treatise of positivist legal science, is in reality a work of considerable intellectual imperialism. The Whig interpretation of history which underpins it was later laid bare in *Law and Opinion in England during the Nineteenth Century* (1905), a work much criticized by historians and which in actuality simply explicates Dicey's intellectual and political assumptions. These assumptions, however, did not survive Dicey's own times. In 1914 he wrote a long introduction to the eighth edition of *The Law of the Constitution*. Taking the form of a lament, it mourned a loss of faith in Parliamentary government and a decline in veneration for the rule of law which Dicey believed had occurred since the mid-Victorian era and which he suggested were threatening the principles of the British constitution which he had first sought to formulate in 1885. However, Dicey's actual concerns mattered little. By this stage, the historical figure had more or less disappeared, to be replaced by an entity known as 'Dicey' which has lived on through successive generations of lawyers as the expositor of the fundamental principles on which the British constitution is founded.

See also: AUSTIN, J.; CONSTITUTIONALISM; LAW, PHILOSOPHY OF; LEGAL POSITIVISM

List of works

Dicey, A.V. (1885) *An Introduction to the Study of the Law of the Constitution*, 8th edn, London: Macmillan, 1915. (The last edition which Dicey edited of his classic work.)

—— (1905) *Lectures on the Relation between Law and Opinion in England during the Nineteenth Century*, London: Macmillan. (Based on lectures delivered at Harvard on the history of English law in the nineteenth century.)

References and further reading

Collini, S. (1991) *Public Moralists: Political Thought and Intellectual Life in Britain 1850–1930*, Oxford: Clarendon Press, ch. 7. (Subtle interpretation of Dicey's thought.)

Cosgrove, R.A. (1980) *The Rule of Law: Albert Venn Dicey, Victorian Jurist*, Chapel Hill, NC: University of North Carolina Press. (Competent intellectual biography.)

Craig, P.P. (1990) *Public Law and Democracy in the United Kingdom and the United States of America*, Oxford: Clarendon Press, ch. 2. (On Dicey and the idea of 'self-correcting democracy'.)

Lawson, F.H. (1959) 'Dicey Revisited', *Political Studies* 7: 109–26, 207–21. (General and orthodox appraisal.)

Loughlin, M. (1992) *Public Law and Political Theory*, Oxford: Clarendon Press, chaps 1, 7. (On Dicey's method, principles and values.)

MARTIN LOUGHLIN

DIDEROT, DENIS (1713–84)

Chief editor of the great eighteenth-century Encyclopédie *(1751–72), Diderot set out a philosophy of the arts and sciences which took the progress of civilization to be a measure of mankind's moral improvement. He did not regard that progress as having produced universal benefits, however, and perceived the Christian religion which had accompanied it as morally harmful to those who subscribed to it and even more dangerous to societies thus far untouched by it. Religious dogmas tended to pervert the organic development of human passions, and secular education which presumed that all minds were equally receptive to instruction threatened to thwart the natural evolution of human faculties in other ways.*

Like Rousseau, Diderot subscribed to a philosophy of education which encouraged curiosity rather than promoted truth. He stressed the need for the adaptability of moral rules to the physiological characteristics of the individuals to whom they applied, pointing to a connection between human cultures and biology in a manner that would influence fresh outlooks upon the sciences of man at the end of the Age of Enlightenment.

1 **Encyclopedic polymath**
2 **Speculating about politics**
3 **On primitivism, religion and sexuality**
4 **Theory of education**
5 **Vitalist materialism**
6 **Central tenets in oblique articulations**

1 Encyclopedic polymath

One of the most central figures of the European Enlightenment, Diderot was chiefly renowned in his own lifetime as the principal editor of the *Encyclopédie* (1751–72), constructed as a monument of human reason and invention, like the Crystal Palace that would be built in London a century later in celebration of an age of industry and commerce. More than any other philosopher of the eighteenth century, he shaped his intellectual career around the production and circulation of books, which in progressive circles were held to be both the vehicle and measure of enlightenment for an epoch of greater literacy and prosperity than Europe had ever known before.

Appointed with Jean Le Rond D'ALEMBERT as joint editor of the *Encyclopédie* in 1747, Diderot initially undertook to write more articles himself than any other contributor to this reasoned dictionary of the arts and sciences, whose publishing history from 1751 would eventually extend over a period of thirty years, and whose thirty-five volumes would come to embrace 20 million words and more than 2,000 plates. As the guiding spirit of that collective enterprise of men of letters, Diderot often reassembled the ideas of other thinkers, drawing upon ancient and modern sources alike, from Lucretius to Shaftesbury. Having begun his literary career around 1743 as a translator, he proved the Enlightenment's most expert literary ventriloquist, sometimes passing off borrowed material as if he had written it himself, sometimes ascribing his own ideas to others.

In part because so much of his best work was to appear posthumously, often in the form of fictional dialogues, Diderot came to be regarded as the Enlightenment's most eclectic thinker, displaying a special fondness for the pluralist dimensions of eclecticism in general in his own entry on that very subject for the *Encyclopédie*, itself indebted to other authors. In *Le Neveu de Rameau* (Rameau's Nephew) (1762–74) in particular, deemed by Hegel, Goethe and Marx to be the finest work of the whole Enlightenment, he portrays the character of the most explosively original and romantic personality of eighteenth-century European literature as at odds with itself and also with Diderot, who figures both as the author of the dialogue and a personage within it, depicted as conventional in upholding a bourgeois code of morals. As distinct from some of his equally celebrated contemporaries – such as Montesquieu, Voltaire or Rousseau – Diderot elaborated no single overriding doctrine, nor did he devote himself to one great intellectual crusade.

Especially well versed in the history of philosophy, he extolled its ancient and modern achievements alike, from Epicurean doctrines of continual flux, to Spinozistic conceptions of selfsufficiency, to the atheistic materialism of La Mettrie and Maupertuis. In his *Pensées philosophiques* (Philosophical Thoughts) of 1746, largely inspired by Shaftesbury, he put forward a set of aphorisms that expressed notions of natural law and ideals of natural religion, which could be engraved in the human heart without need of Christian scruples. In his *Lettre sur les aveugles* (Letter on the Blind) of 1749, he set out a case for the adaptability of the senses as evidenced by the fact that mental images could be formed without sight or conversations pursued without sound, believing that powers of perception were transitive across human faculties and did not themselves spring from sensory experience. The late eighteenth-century teaching of sign languages to the deaf, and the deep structural grammars of modern Chomskian linguistics, were to draw inspiration from such claims that fundamental human capacities are not determined by the contingencies of their exercise. At the time of its publication, however, Diderot's *Lettre sur les aveugles* only managed to invite the suspicion that he was a materialist and atheist, on which grounds he was to be imprisoned in Vincennes for over three months.

In the longest of the contributions to the work of which he was chief editor, the article 'encyclopédie' itself, he expounded themes of practical or applied philosophy that could bring the arts and sciences of civilization together, by encouraging the interpenetration of the liberal with the mechanical arts and the cooperation of specialists across disciplines, along lines that bridged what we have come to term 'the two cultures'. In showing how science had been rendered useful to the public interest or common good through such inventions as the compass and the printing press, Diderot sought to provide tangible illustrations of a Platonic ideal of promoting virtue through knowledge. His goal, like that of so many other *philosophes* of the eighteenth century, was to cast off the veil of ignorance and lift the yoke of precedence, thus overcoming dead dogma. Almost as much as D'Alembert's preliminary discourse to the *Encyclopédie*, Diderot's own article on that very subject could be read as a general manifesto of the Enlightenment.

2 Speculating about politics

His political philosophy was first propounded in the *Encyclopédie*, particularly in articles such as *autorité politique*, which offers a theory of the social compact that binds both the prince and his subjects to one another without recourse to theological sanctions; and *droit naturel* (natural law), which sets out a theory of universal justice with respect to mankind's 'general will', a term of scant significance in the history of political thought before Diderot gave it fresh impetus. In 1774, in his *Observations sur le Nakaz*, or commentary on a new code of law for Russia as proposed by the empress Catherine the Great, he called for a programme of secular education to stimulate the civilization and selfreliance of that country through indigenous and small-scale enterprises, opposing the importation of Western physiocratic doctrines and their schemes of wholesale agrarian reform within a cultural environment to which they were ill-suited. Catherine had purchased Diderot's library and had invited him to St Petersburg, but she failed to convince him of the wisdom of her efforts to reform the political system of her nation along lines she imagined had already been achieved in the West. While advocating the emancipation of serfs, which was not to her liking, Diderot was convinced that material progress in Russia should proceed apace with its intellectual development rather than in accordance with alien precepts of modernity.

As editorial spokesman for the cause of enlightenment and a major contributor on political subjects to the *Encyclopédie*, Diderot stood for principles which appear to differ sharply from those of ROUSSEAU, for fifteen years his closest companion, who had conceived the central idea of his own philosophy of history – which forms a moral critique of the progress of the arts and sciences – en route to visit his friend in prison. Whereas Rousseau decried the moral consequences of the progress of the arts and sciences, Diderot applauded them. Whereas Rousseau subscribed to ideals of spartan republicanism, Diderot was cosmopolitan and willing to encourage monarchical regimes so long as their authority was tolerant and benign, directed to the promotion of the public interest. Rousseau's notion of the general will, as an ideal of public engagement only conceivable to the citizens of selfgoverning states, was largely designed to contradict Diderot's conception of the same term as pertaining to the common humanity of individuals even when motivated by self-interest, in so far our notions of what is right and good do not, Diderot supposed, depend upon our political identities.

If, for Rousseau, men's morals were shaped by their politics, Diderot was instead convinced that politics were fundamentally shaped by morality. In his article *hobbisme* for the *Encyclopédie*, he contrasted Rousseau's idea that society rendered mankind malicious with a Hobbesian notion that war was our species' natural state, rejecting them both (see HOBBES, T.). Believing that conflict was not inescapable either in nature or in society, he upheld an alternative doctrine, which he drew ultimately from Pufendorf's *De iure naturae et gentium* (1672), that human frailties had rendered civil society necessary, while the natural sociability of selfishly motivated persons had rendered it possible and, at least in principle, beneficial as well (see PUFENDORF, S.).

3   On primitivism, religion and sexuality

In his *Supplément au Voyage de Bougainville* (Supple-
ment to the Bougainville Journey), dating from the early 1770s but largely unpublished until after his death, Diderot was to portray the virtues of a primitive society in colours so attractive as to seem to shed doubt upon his allegiance to the moral splendours of civilization. This text, purporting to serve as an appendix to one of the earliest descriptions of Tahiti, contrasts an exotic world characterized by the zealous satisfaction of bodily appetites with a familiar world wherein it is dictated that they should be repressed. Diderot's depiction of a society in which sexuality is celebrated, and within which incest, adultery and fornication are not held to be either criminal or sinful, forms a critique of monogamy, celibacy and sexual repression in the West at the same time as it offers tribute to the promiscuity of Polynesians.

The *Supplément*'s fictional opposition of two cultures – one stirred naturally by libidinous desire, the other artificially held in check by religion and hypocrisy – owes a debt to the *Lettres persanes* (The Persian Letters) (1721) of MONTESQUIEU and more generally to eighteenth-century travellers' tales, either real or imaginary, which found European, and most particularly Christian, civilization to be at fault in the light of Oriental alternatives. In granting tangible presence and geographical specificity in the modern world to a population that still enjoyed the freedom of its state of nature, Diderot also seems to have drawn inspiration from Rousseau's *Discours sur l'inégalité* (Discourse on the Origin of Inequality) (1755). Like Rousseau, he judged that the moral values which prevailed in the West were often contrary to human nature, which they distorted through artifice, subterfuge and selfdeception.

Especially with respect to the sexual longings of individuals in Christian communities, and above all the warped personalities of their monastic priests, Diderot was convinced that in Western cultures there had arisen a great gulf between human physicality and morality. But he did not share Rousseau's view that such a gulf was unbridgeable. He imagined that Tahitian society showed how it could be overcome, in promoting the public interest out of individuals' sexual proclivities, thereby stimulating a socially welcome growth in population. The irreverent, sensuous, liberal, anti-colonial and utilitarian themes of the *Supplément au Voyage de Bougainville* pursue, in different idioms, a philosophy which springs from the same point of view that informed Diderot's contributions to the *Encyclopédie* and to which he was to subscribe virtually all his life – the belief that great public benefits may spring from unconstrained selfish sociability. In holding to such a doctrine, more often associated in diverse formulations with Bernard

MANDEVILLE and Adam SMITH, Diderot espoused one of the most central moral philosophies of the whole Enlightenment.

4 Theory of education

At least some of the tensions which are manifest in his writings reflect the clash of principles and personalities that he perceived in the world at large. At once a materialist and an atheist, Diderot was determined to describe the behaviour of individuals empirically, in all their diverse, contrasting and irregular forms. Such diversity and contrast were features of human nature as much as of human history, he supposed and, in his *Réfutation de l'ouvrage d'Helvétius intitulé 'L'Homme'* (Refutation of Helvétius' Work *Man*) of 1774, he accordingly took issue with the famous dictum of Helvétius' *De l'homme*, published posthumously in 1773, that 'l'éducation peut tout' (see HELVÉTIUS, C.-A.). The proposition that education can achieve everything was false, according to Diderot, because it presumed that men and women were everywhere identical and that differences in character depended entirely upon the circumstances of a person's upbringing.

Because this supposition appealed to a notion of human equality, it was tempting to believe, in the light of it, that all individuals at birth shared the same capacities. But that was a delusion, Diderot contended, based on the false premise that each person was motivated only by his or her sensations which, through instruction and refinement, would become the grounds of every sort of rational and moral judgment. It was impossible, Diderot insisted, to pass directly from sensation to judgment or, in effect, from animal reflexes to human design. Intraspecifically, it had to be noted that only humans possess the capacity to reason and thus to formulate ideas and combine them into judgments. Interspecifically, it was necessary to remark that individuals exhibit their reason in different degrees, mental capacity as a whole being unequally distributed. In allowing with Helvétius that vices do not spring from human nature but are generally attributable to harmful social practices and teachings, there should be no presumption that all individuals have good minds, endowed with a latent natural genius just awaiting cultivation and training.

Diderot's critique of the philosophy of education of Helvétius bears a striking resemblance to Rousseau's challenge, made in *Émile* a decade earlier, of much the same theory of the formation of the human intellect and character already sketched in Helvétius' *De l'esprit* (1758). Rousseau and Diderot were each convinced that genius cannot be instilled by tuition and that education ought to nourish the natural dispositions and qualities of children rather than impose their tutors' designs and expectations upon them. Their common objections to Helvétius nevertheless took different forms. While Rousseau decried materialism in general, Diderot took issue only with that crude variant which, on his understanding, reduced all thought to pure sensation. Whereas Rousseau mistrusted teachers who either believed or pretended that they spoke on God's behalf, Diderot was persuaded that God himself had been invented by man. He judged that Rousseau had fundamentally confused unsociability for selfreliance, and he showed no interest in promoting any scheme of negative education that might be fit for children freed from all dependence on others, like Robinson Crusoe learning to fend for himself.

Diderot's conception of human nature differs from Rousseau's in attributing more dynamic potentialities for change and self-improvement to each individual's seminal personality. If he had coined the term *perfectibilité*, which was in fact invented by Rousseau, it would have encapsulated his understanding of the spark of genius, the impulse of creativity and the moral formation of character. Yet both men agreed, in contrast with Helvétius, that education ought fundamentally to accord with human nature instead of recasting it. Each subscribed essentially to a belief in self-education, aiming to encourage children to follow their intuitions and thereby attain intellectual and moral maturity by being true to themseves. They also shared a profound mistrust of the superstitious idolatry that passed for a Christian education, proffered in priestly interpretations of the mysteries of Holy Writ. As opposed to the arcane dogmas of a revealed religion, they were drawn to the spectacle of creation and to the open book of nature. They both thought that education ought to be pursued endogenously, out of natural curiosity, accompanying the development of the human faculties, and never by indoctrination.

5 Vitalist materialism

It is hardly surprising that a philosopher who advocated that moral principles should be true to Nature, which he believed to be in a state of continual flux, should have found himself suspected of lack of consistency. Like his colleague and co-editor of the *Encyclopédie*, D'Alembert, he saw his own Age of Enlightenment as committed to a systematic spirit but not the spirit of system which had distinguished the principal contributions of seventeenth-century European philosophy. Although he was the author of a treatise on mathematics and geometry, he was more interested in matters of style, particularly with respect to painting, music and the theatre. His *Salons* (1759–81) comprise perhaps the principal contribution to art criticism in the eighteenth century, and his posthumously published *Essai sur la peinture* (Essay on Painting) (written in 1765) was to stir the imagination of Baudelaire and other admirers in the Age of Romanticism.

He is better described as an empiricist than as a rationalist, indebted more to the philosophical methods of Bacon and Locke than to those of Descartes and Leibniz. He was a materialist in denying the existence in man of an intangible spirit or soul, and over the course of his life he became a progressively more outspoken atheist, in rejecting all notions of either a transcendent or immanent God. As is most conspicuous from his so-called *Lettre à Landois* (1756) and his novella *Jacques le fataliste* (written in 1773) he was at once a philosophical determinist, convinced that Nature left no room for unpredictability or caprice, and at the same time a libertarian, who identified the fundamental dignity of human conduct in terms of autonomous agency and choice, in poignant recognition of the bittersweet paradox that to choose is to act from a motive beyond one's control.

Diderot's materialism drew more inspiration from the sciences of physiology and medicine of his day than from physics, since he perceived matter not as inert but as inherently active and self-animating, as a collecton of atoms in a seminal fluid in continual fermentation. He was struck by Haller's research on the sensitivity and irritability of organic matter and was most particularly impressed by Bordeu and the Montpellier School of physiological medicine, which excited his interest in the internal mechanisms that gave impetus to such matter and regulated its health. Like Montesquieu, he sought to investigate the dynamic forces and tensions which shape the conduct of both living bodies and social systems. To the extent that a number of human sciences would around the end of the eighteenth century come to address such issues as apparently more fundamental than the constitutional and legislative programmes of Enlightenment political theorists, Diderot may be regarded as a philosophical precursor of such change.

Michel Foucault's depiction in *Les mots et les choses: une archéologie des sciences humaines* (The Order of Things) (1966) of certain epistemic metamorphoses within the sciences of man that may be dated from around 1770 to 1800 could have embraced the materialist philosophy of Diderot in addition to the examples offered from economics, linguistics and biology (see FOUCAULT, M.). Diderot's reflections on the organic forms and forces of social life and on the growth and decadence of civilizations might in the twentieth century have come to be termed 'structural-functionalism'. In his own day they illustrate an approach to the science of society which would progressively displace speculations about the moral dimensions of human conduct with investigations into its underlying, bodily or material, causes. They herald the advent of 'sociology' in the nineteenth century in so far as it was modelled upon eighteenth-century 'physiology'.

6 Central tenets in oblique articulations

Diderot's reflections on the arts, human nature and society were not only to strike his readers among romanticists and scientists alike as particularly modern. By virtue of his irregular and sometimes fitful literary style, his preference for the cut and thrust of the dialogue over the discursive finality of the treatise, and his pursuit of anonymity as the mysteriously unidentified author of his own texts, he anticipated some of the philosophical issues raised by postmodernist thinkers today, often in criticism of the so-called 'Enlightenment Project' as a whole. No major writer of the eighteenth century left so many of his principal works unpublished in his lifetime, even though several, including the best among them, had been drafted long before his death. No encyclopedist ever managed better to convey his own thoughts by way of plagiarism, insinuation, multiple cross-references and deliberately misleading notes and commentaries. In assuming the personae of historical figures whose ideas he transcribed in his own fashion, and of characters he invented in order to contradict himself, he succeeded more than any other eighteenth-century writer in bestowing independent life upon his work, in the act of creation releasing it from the pen of its author. Like Socrates in Plato's *Phaedrus* or Derrida in *De la grammatologie*, he sought to ensure that the dead hand of script would not count as his last word. Even through his writings Diderot's voice appears to speak aloud, weaving a conversation without end.

If coming to final conclusions was not his chief aim either as a philosopher or as an encyclopedist, a number of unsettled doctrines may nevertheless be ascribed to him as among his most significant contributions to eighteenth-century thought across several disciplines. First, he supposed that civilizations were like socially organic forms of life, marked by cyclical patterns of growth, maturity and decay, and by institutions which reflected the dynamic or repressive character of their moral or religious principles. In these beliefs, which above all inform his contributions, dealing with global history, to Abbé Raynal's *Histoire des Deux Indes* (History of Two

Indias) (1772–80), he was guided both by Buffon's *Histoire naturelle* (Natural History) (1749–88) and by Montesquieu's *Esprit des lois* (The Spirit of the Laws) (1748).

Second, he held that biological attributes of human nature – including instincts for survival and companionship but also bodily weaknesses and mental stupidity endemic to solitary existence – made society both necessary and possible. His *Apologie de l'abbé de Prades*, together with several of his articles on political subjects for the *Encyclopédie*, make plain the influence upon him with respect to this subject of Pufendorf, as well as the double-edged nature of his rejection of Hobbes's and Rousseau's differing perspectives on mankind's isolated state of nature.

Third, he was convinced that moral rules which dictate human conduct could promote the general interest of a society only if they accorded with and gave free rein to the physical desires of its members. Both in *Le Rêve de d'Alembert* (1769) and the *Supplément au Voyage de Bougainville*, he put a case for the ultimate physicality of human nature, whose constituent matter he believed to be moved by vital forces which would ensure its natural development towards an appropriate morality unchecked by extraneous rules. Convinced that liberty and necessity went hand in hand, he saw certain features of Western civilization as injurious to freedom when they attempted to obstruct the determinate mechanisms of natural law, as was the case most particularly with religions whose codes of duty stifled the expression of usefully pleasurable passions, thereby harming both individual wellbeing and public peace. In the light of his philosophy, he would have emblazoned our churches and their attendant institutions with warnings of the hazards they pose to our health. He thought Christianity was not only the opiate of the people but a spiritually carcinogenic poison.

Fourth, he believed that political and social institutions needed to correspond as well to a population's national or regional temperament and to its level of development. Just as punishments would be tailored to crimes, so laws should fit the communities they serve and direct. In his *Observations sur le Nakaz* he claimed that the character of the Russian peasantry was ill-suited to the drastic reforms proposed by French physiocrats, while in the *Histoire des Deux Indes* he argued that the fresh freedoms won in America were unlikely to take root in the acidic old soil of Europe. If he would not categorically exclude a favourable meaning for the term 'enlightened despotism', Diderot believed that good government was never harsh and that no people ought to be governed too much.

All of these principles of organic growth and adapatibility led Diderot to perceive human liberty in much the same way that Montesquieu described laws – that is, as a set of necessary relations deriving from the nature of things. The character of individuals must not be forced, he thought, but, in passing gradually and without impediment through the seasonal changes of their constitutions, whole populations naturally change themselves. As their nature changes, so too should their political systems. The metamorphoses of human development ought only to record the various stages of our species' spontaneous generation.

See also: EDUCATION, HISTORY OF PHILOSOPHY OF; ENLIGHTENMENT, CONTINENTAL; ENCYCLOPEDISTS, EIGHTEENTH-CENTURY; MATERIALISM; NATURAL LAW

List of works

Diderot's numerous works include: *Pensées philosophiques* (1746); *Les Bijoux indiscrets* (1748); *Lettre sur les aveugles* (1749); *Lettre sur les sourds et muets* (1751); the *Encyclopédie* (1751–72); *Pensées sur l'interprétation de la nature* (1754); *Lettre à Landois* (1756); *Le Fils naturel* (1757); *Salons* (1759–81); *Le Neveu de Rameau* (1762–74); *Essai sur la peinture* (1765); *Le Rêve de d'Alembert* (1769); *Supplément au Voyage de Bougainville* (1772); contributions to *Histoire des Deux Indes* (1772–80); *Observations sur le Nakaz* (1773–4); *Réfutation de l'ouvrage d'Helvétius intitulé L'Homme* (1774); *Éléments de physiologie* (1774–80); *Essai sur la vie de Sénèque* (1778). Listed below are the most notable collections of his work.

Diderot, D. (1875–7) *Oeuvres complètes*, ed. J. Assézat and M. Tourneux, Paris. (The best more or less complete edition.)
—— (1956) *Oeuvres philosophiques*, Paris: Garnier.
—— (1963) *Oeuvres politiques*, ed. P. Vernière, Paris: Garnier.
—— (1975–) *Oeuvres complètes*, ed. H. Dieckmann, J. Proust and J. Varloot, Paris: Hermann. (Still in progress, the most accurate edition.)
—— (1982) *The Irresistible Diderot*, ed. J. Hope Mason, London: Verso. (Extensive extracts in translation, with introductions.)
—— (1992) *Diderot's Political Writings*, ed. J. Hope Mason and R. Wokler, Cambridge: Cambridge University Press.

References and further reading

Benot, Y. (1970) *Diderot: De l'athéisme à l'anticolonialisme*, Paris: François Maspero. (A notable interpretation of Diderot's politics, with a detailed chronology.)

Chouillet, A.-M. (ed.) (1985) *Colloque International Diderot (1713–1784)*, Paris: Aux amateurs de livres. (A major collection of essays reflecting the state of Diderot scholarship today.)

Chouillet, J. (1973) *La Formation des idées esthétiques de Diderot*, Paris: Armand Colin. (The fullest treatment of Diderot's philosophy of art.)

—— (1977) *Diderot*, Paris: Société d'édition d'enseignement supérieur. (An introduction to Diderot's thought across the spectrum of his interests and enthusiasms.)

Crocker, L. (1966) *Diderot: The Embattled Philosopher*, New York: Free Press. (A well-informed intellectual portrait intended for a popular readership.)

Duchet, M. (1971) *Anthropologie et histoire au siècle des lumières*, Paris: François Maspero. (Contains a chapter on Diderot's anthropology.)

Gordon, D. and Torrey, N. (1947) *The Censoring of Diderot's 'Encyclopédie' and the Re-established Text*, New York: Columbia University Press. (On the tribulations of the publishing history of Diderot's chief work.)

France, P. (1983) *Diderot*, Oxford: Oxford University Press. (A brief survey in English of Diderot's literary career.)

Furbank, P.N. (1992) *Diderot: A Critical Biography*, London: Secker & Warburg. (Locates Diderot's interest in the arts at the centre of his life.)

Lough, J. (1968) *Essays on the 'Encyclopédie' of Diderot and d'Alembert*, London: Oxford University Press. (A detailed commentary on the compilation of a work of reference.)

Mauzi, R. (1960) *L'idée du bonheur dans la littérature et la pensée française au XVIIIe siècle*, Paris: Armand Colin. (Treats Diderot's ideas on happiness in the context of eighteenth-century French philosophy.)

Proust, J. (1967) *Diderot et l'Encyclopédie*, Paris: Armand Colin. (The most comprehensive discussion of Diderot's contributions.)

Strugnell, A. (1973) *Diderot's Politics*, The Hague: Nijhoff. (Includes a commentary on Diderot's contributions to the *Histoire des Deux Indes*.)

Wilson, A. (1972) *Diderot*, New York: Oxford University Press. (The fullest intellectual biography in any language.)

ROBERT WOKLER

DIETRICH OF FREIBERG (*c.*1250–after 1310)

In his work on the rainbow, De iride et radialibus impressionibus *(On the Rainbow and Radial Impressions), Dietrich makes extensive use of experimental observation. He also wrote a number of other, more theoretical works including* De esse et essentia *(On Existence and Essence) and* De intellectu et intelligibili *(On Intellect and the Intelligible). In these works, Dietrich's emphasis varies; his theological works tend to be heavily Neoplatonic, while his more secular philosophical works are more Aristotelian. Dietrich disagreed with Aquinas on certain metaphysical issues, and seems to have written in opposition to particular works by Aquinas.*

A Dominican from Germany, Dietrich studied at the University of Paris *c.*1275–7 and became master of theology at St Jacques in Paris before 1303. He was named provincial of Teutonia in 1293 and vicar provincial in 1310. He is best known for his investigations on the rainbow, put into writing by special request of the meeting of the general chapter of the Dominican order at Toulouse in 1304. The resulting work, *De iride et radialibus impressionibus* (On the Rainbow and Radial Impressions) draws on the optical theories of Alhazen, but in addition takes a new approach to researching the causes of the rainbow. Dietrich's innovation, as Boyer (1959) explains, was to see the value of investigating the reflective and refractive properties of individual raindrops rather than of the rain cloud taken as a whole. Extensive experimental observations of the paths of light rays through glass spheres and beakers filled with water enabled him to deduce how light passes through raindrops to produce both the lower and upper bows of rainbows. This part of his theory would not be further refined until the time of Descartes. His explanation of how colours are produced in the rainbow was less enduring, but is well thought out and closely argued (see NATURAL PHILOSOPHY, MEDIEVAL).

Dietrich also wrote on a wide range of other topics in natural philosophy, logic, psychology, metaphysics and theology. Other works in natural philosophy are less oriented toward experimental evidence: they include short works on the four elements and their compounds, on light and colour, on time and on astronomy. In his less experimental works, and particularly in his theological works, Dietrich displays extensive knowledge of and interest in Neoplatonic as well as Aristotelian theories. In the theological work *De intellectu et intelligibili* (On Intellect and the

Intelligible), for example, Dietrich describes creation as intellectual emanation through a hierarchy of Intelligences beginning with the primary intelligence – the soul of the first firmament – and progressing down to the world of man. Gilson (1955) has characterized the cosmology Dietrich sets forth here as a restatement of PROCLUS using Aristotelian terminology. This aspect of Dietrich's thught was to influence German Dominican mystics such as MEISTER ECKHART.

In his psychology, Dietrich rejects the Averroistic notion of a separate, shared agent intellect (see AVERROISM). Instead, Dietrich argues that there is an individual agent intellect always in action within each person. Thus far most thinkers of his time would have agreed, but Dietrich's account of the role of the agent intellect in human knowledge is once more strongly Neoplatonic. In his view, intellectual knowledge cannot be explained by the process of abstraction alone; an act of the agent intellect is required to make the object of cognition intelligible. The agent intellect is able to carry out this operation of intuitive cognition because it is made in the image of the divine intellect, proceeding from the divine ideas as an image and likeness of total being. Since, as an image of the divine, the human agent intellect comprehends all being, it is capable of knowing all other things by virtue of its knowledge of itself and as a feature of its orientation toward God (see PLATONISM, MEDIEVAL).

Dietrich disagrees with AQUINAS on certain important metaphysical issues. Maurer (1956), in his edition of Dietrich's *De quidditatibus entium* (On The Essential Natures of Things), has argued that both this work and *De esse et essentia* (On Existence and Essence) were written in opposition to Aquinas' *De esse et essentia*. Dietrich denies Aquinas' argument that there is a distinction between essence (*essentia*) and existence (*esse*) in reality. The fact that we can understand a rose without knowing if one exists does not force us to acknowledge a real distinction between the rose's existence and its essence, by Dietrich's account, but merely shows that there are two ways of knowing about the rose. The only difference between essence and existence that Dietrich allows is in their manner of signifying being: *esse* signifies being as actuality, while *essentia* signifies it as disposition to actuality. Several other differences with Aquinas follow from this important fundamental disparity. To give one important example, Dietrich denies that it is in any way possible for accidents to exist without a subject, an argument that puts in question Aquinas' explanation of transubstantiation.

List of works

Dietrich of Freiberg (*c.*1280–1310) Scientific Works, in W.A. Wallace (ed.) *The Scientific Methodology of Theodoric of Freiberg*, Studia Friburgensia, new series 26, Fribourg: Fribourg University Press, 1959, 306–76. (Includes texts of three minor scientific works (*De miscibilis in mixto*, *De luce et eius origine* and *De coloribus*) and parts of two others (*De accidentibus*, excerpts from chapters 1–5 and 8–15; *De elementis corporum naturalium inquantum sunt partes mundi*, excerpts from chapters 1–8), plus a full list of minor works available in modern editions up to 1959.)

—— (*c.*1280–1310) *De esse et essentia* (On Existence and Essence), ed. E. Krebs, 'Le Traité *De Esse et Essentia* de Thierry de Fribourg', *Revue néoscolastique de philosophie* 18: 516–36, 1911. (Philosophical work, possibly written in opposition to Aquinas.)

—— (*c.*1280–1310) *De quidditatibus entium* (On The Essential Natures of Things), ed. and trans. A. Maurer, 'The *De quidditatibus entium* of Dietrich of Freiberg and its Criticism of Thomistic Metaphysics', *Mediaeval Studies* 18: 173–203, 1956. (A further work on essence, also possibly written in opposition to Aquinas.)

—— (*c.*1280–1310) *De intellectu et intelligibili* (On The Intellect and the Intelligible), printed as *Tractatus de intellectu et intelligibili* in E. Krebs, *Meister Diestrich (Theodoricus Teutonicus de Vriberg). Sein Leben, seine Werke, seine Wissenschaft*, Beiträge zur Geschichte der Philosophie und Theologie des Mittelalters XII, 5–6, Munster: Aschendorff, 1914, 119–206. (Dietrich's major work on the intellect.)

—— (1304–10) *De iride et radialibus impressionibus*, ed. and trans. J. Würschmidt, *Dietrich von Freiberg: Über den Regenbogen und die durch Strahlen erzeugten Eindrücke*, Beiträge zur Geschichte der Philosophie und Theologie des Mittelalters XII, 5–6, Munster: Aschendorff, 1914. (Dietrich's best known work. Excerpts are also translated in W.A. Wallace (ed. and trans.) 'On the Rainbow and Radiant Impressions', in E. Grant (ed.) *A Source Book in Medieval Science*, Cambridge, MA: Harvard University Press, 1974.)

References and further reading

* Boyer, C.B. (1959) *The Rainbow: From Myth to Mathematics*, New York: T. Yoseloff, 110–24. (Explains the importance and the influence of Dietrich's work on the rainbow.)
* Gilson E. (1955) *History of Christian Philosophy in the Middle Ages*, London: Sheed & Ward, 433–7,

753–5. (Discusses three of Dietrich's strongly Neoplatonic theological works.)

Wallace, W.A. (1981) 'Dietrich von Freiberg', in C.C. Gillispie (ed.) *Dictionary of Scientific Biography*, New York: Scribner, vol. 4, 92–5. (A more detailed introduction to Dietrich's scientific writings.)

FIONA SOMERSET

DIGAMBARA JAINISM

see JAINA PHILOSOPHY

DIGBY, KENELM (1603–65)

Seventeenth-century English Catholic, original member of the Royal Society, and one of the first philosophers to produce a fully developed system of mechanical philosophy, Sir Kenelm Digby cut a dashing figure as a poet, privateer and philosopher. As a Catholic and royalist, he spent much of his life in semi-exile on the continent where he conversed with many of the political and intellectual leaders of his time; as a philosopher, he was favourably compared to René Descartes and John Locke. He attempted to wed the philosophy of Aristotle to the new mechanical physics, which maintained that every event in the material world is reducible to matter in motion. His interests and writings cover a wide range, from religion and magic to vegetative growth and literary commentary. The explicit goal of his most significant book, Two Treatises *(1644), was to prove the immortality of the human soul. To this end, the first treatise constitutes an exhaustive study of bodies and their features. By showing that all corporeal qualities are to be explained in strictly material terms, he prepares the way for a thorough discussion of the soul. Digby argues that the soul must be immaterial (and hence immortal) because otherwise its features cannot be explained. He went on to apply the mechanical principles which he developed in this work to a variety of topics, including some traditionally associated with the occult. His works on alchemical, medical and religious topics were also widely read.*

1   Life
2   The *Two Treatises*
3   Other works

1   Life

Sir Kenelm Digby was one of the most colourful and impressive figures of his generation. He was not yet three when his father, Sir Everard Digby, was tortured and executed for his role in the Gunpowder Plot. As a Catholic at Oxford (1618–20), the young man was forced to remain on the periphery of the university. He studied there with the mathematician and astronomer, Thomas Allen, who probably introduced him to alchemical experiments. He travelled to France, Spain and Italy (1620–3) where a prince considered him 'the just measure of perfection' and Marie de Medici made immodest advances. A friend to such writers and artists of his era as Ben Jonson and Anthony van Dyck, and to members of the English royal family, Digby was knighted by James I, was a successful privateer for Charles I, and chancellor to Queen Henrietta Maria. In 1625 he married Venetia Stanley, famous for her beauty and intellectual achievements, with whom he had five children, and whose sudden death in 1633 turned his attention from public concerns to philosophical contemplation. The first two years of a lengthy period of mourning were spent in secluded study at Gresham College, London, in whose laboratories he conducted experiments. Digby converted to Anglicanism in 1630 (possibly for political reasons), but reconverted before he moved to France in 1635, where he felt more comfortable as a Catholic.

Although under suspicion in England as a Catholic and ardent royalist, and briefly imprisoned there (1642–3), he often travelled from France and even negotiated with Cromwell in 1648 and 1654–5 for toleration of Catholicism in England. After his reconversion, he turned his attention to religious and ecumenical issues and published *A Conference with a Lady about Choyce of Religion* (1638) and a response to Thomas Browne's popular *Religio Medici* entitled *Observations upon Religio Medici*, the latter written in 1643 while he was in prison. During his many years in Paris, he was part of the MERSENNE circle, studied anatomy and chemistry, published his *Two Treatises* (1644), and was one of the early admirers of Descartes' *Discourse on Method*. He conversed and corresponded with HOBBES and DESCARTES, both of whom seem to have thought well of him. Along with his mentor and fellow English Catholic, Thomas WHITE, Digby was one of the first Englishmen to produce a fully developed system of mechanical philosophy. He applied the mechanical principles which he developed in his *Two Treatises* to a variety of topics. He collected medical, chemical, and household remedies as well as books and manuscripts. Many of his recipes and remedies, which he exchanged with other natural philosophers including Robert BOYLE, were published after his death. Digby went to Montpellier in 1657 to take the waters and there gave his famous account of the powder of sympathy. This led to his most popular book, *A late Discourse Made in a Solemne Assembly... touching the Cure of Wounds by the Powder of Sympathy* (1658 – originally in French), which was reprinted often and translated into a number of languages. Digby travelled to Germany, the Low Countries and Scandinavia; in 1660, after the Restoration, he returned to England, where he was one of the original members of the Royal Society. He presented his *A Discourse Concerning the Vegetation of Plants* to the Society in 1661. Although Digby's works were soon superseded, he was highly regarded in his day. As a contemporary wrote, he was: 'This Ages Wonder for his Noble Parts, Skilled in six Tongues, and learned in all the Arts'.

2   The *Two Treatises*

Digby published his *Two Treatises* in Paris in 1644 with the professed goal of proving the immortality of the soul. In the dedicatory epistle he makes plain that he desires to analyse bodies because 'the knowledge of them serveth to the knowledge of the soul', that is, through an exhaustive account of the nature of bodies and their qualities, he hopes to show that features of the human soul are not 'effected by corporeall agents', and hence must have something immaterial as their source. In his preface, Digby is particularly clear about his method. Against the scholastics who achieve neither science nor certitude, but attribute to bodies 'hidden qualities that mans witt cannot reach unto', Digby intends to begin with 'the commonest things' in nature so as 'to shew from what principles, all kindes of corporeall operations do proceed; and what kind of operations all these must be, which issue out of these principles'. By arguing in his first treatise that corporeal qualities can be explained wholly in terms of the material constituents of bodies and without any reference to occult powers, Digby prepares the way in his second treatise for his argument for the immortality of the soul. As he puts it in his preface, he intends to 'raise' his discussion in the second treatise 'to the contemplation of the soule; and shew, that her operations are such, as cannot proceed from those [mechanical] principles; which being adequate and common to all bodies, we may rest assured, that what cannot issue from them, cannot have a body for its source'.

In the *Two Treatises* Digby interweaves ancient and modern principles into an Aristotelian fabric. He has unmitigated scorn for the scholastics and high esteem for contemporaries like Descartes and GALILEO. But whereas the latter mechanists explicitly reject the Aristotelian philosophy, Digby embraces it (see ARISTOTLE). He asserts in the conclusion to the first treatise that his proposals 'are built upon the same foundations' as Aristotle whom he describes as: 'the greatest Logician, Metaphysitian and Universall scholler... that ever lived'. Aristotle's 'name must never be mentioned among schollers, but with reverence, for his unparalleled worth; and with gratitude for the large stocke of knowledge he hath enriched us with'. But Digby is equally explicit about the fact that for the true science, we must inform Aristotelian principles with the new discoveries: 'Let us then admire him for what he has deliver'd us: and where he falls short or is weary in his search... let us seek to supply and relieve him' (1644: ch. XX).

Defining body in terms of quantity, and quantity in terms of divisibility, Digby offers an account of bodies and their qualities in mechanical terms. He uses rarity and density, which he describes as the different ways in which something is divisible, to explain the four elements of Aristotle. He maintains that his analyses of Aristotle's four elements are 'the proper notions of the four elements... which are, the notions of Quantity' (1644: ch. IV). He applies the principles of force and velocity to these elements and then 'deduces' the principles 'which govern Mechanics' (1644: ch. IX). From the features of these 'most simple bodies' or elements, Digby intends to explain the qualities and operations of all the 'compounded' bodies of nature, both animate and inanimate. He acknowledges in his conclusion that he departs from Aristotle on a 'few points', but insists that his fundamental principles are Aristotle's: 'all the difference between us is, that we enlarge ourselves to more particulars then he hath done'.

In his criticism of the scholastic philosophy, Digby nicely exemplifies the transformation under way in seventeenth-century thought. The mechanical physics had brought about a radical re-evaluation of a number of doctrines which the scholastics had promulgated for centuries. Digby was particularly articulate concerning the ontology of the objects of perception. On this topic, he shares many of the same doctrines, if not the same depth of thought, of John Locke (see LOCKE, J. §§4–5). According to the scholastic tradition, sensible qualities were treated as irreducibly distinct attributes of the object of perception. The sensible quality of colour, for instance, was believed to exist in essential relation to sight and was not considered reducible to any other attribute in the object. Digby rejected as unintelligible this tendency 'to give actual Beings to the quantity, figure, colour, smell, taste and other accidents' of the object, 'each of them distinct one from another, as also from the substance which they clothe'. His point was that just 'because I find the notions of them really distinguished... in my mind' I should not act 'as if there were different Entities' (1644: ch. I). According to Digby (and Locke), the sensible accidents of the scholastics in fact have no separate or distinct existence in reality. Rather, 'what is but one entire thing in it self, seemeth to be many things in my understanding'. However separate these qualities may be in the mind, they are but aspects of a single, unitary thing in reality. According to Digby, this unitary thing consists of corpuscles of matter in motion which in turn cause motions in the surrounding matter. Some of these motions pass through both the medium and the sense organs until they reach the brain of the perceiver and there cause an appropriate idea in the mind. The multiplicity of the qualities which we perceive are therefore due not to a multiplicity in the object but rather to one in the sense organs. According to Digby, the senses 'make severall and distinct pictures of what entereth by their doors' and thereby constitute a different way in which the object can cause motions and hence ideas in us (1644: ch. I).

Having made an exhaustive study of bodies and their features in his first treatise, Digby turns his attention to matters immaterial in his second. By showing that all corporeal qualities are to be explained in strictly material terms, he has prepared the way for his discussion of the rational soul and its qualities. At this point he acknowledges that we 'have passed the Rubicon of experimental knowledge' so that 'henceforth, we must in all our searches and conclusions rely upon the single evidence of Reason'. Digby claims that when we are stripped of everything material 'there still remaineth a *substance*, a *thinker*, an *Ego* or *I*' (1644: ch. IX). His argument for immortality is fairly standard. He defines the soul as that which is immaterial and indivisible and notes that only something material can undergo the decay and dissolution which mortality requires. That is, since 'no change at all can happen to an abstracted soul', it is incapable of mortality (1644: ch. XII).

Digby's *Two Treatises* was widely read and generally well received by his contemporaries. His physical proposals, however, did not make a lasting contribution. Digby himself offers the most likely explanation for their failure in his dedicatory epistle: 'a gallant man, whose thoughts flye att the highest game... deemeth it farre too meane for him, to dwell upon the subtilest of their mysteries for science sake'. In the end, Digby's mechanical physics was too imprecise and incomplete; the treatises could not compete with the more fully articulated physical systems of Galileo, Descartes and GASSENDI.

3 Other works

Digby applied himself to topics ranging from alchemy and plant growth to religion and literature. Of special interest to philosophers is the fact that he was prepared to extend the mechanical principles developed in the *Two Treatises* to all of his scientific and philosophical studies, even to topics traditionally associated with the occult. He practised alchemy, but agreed with many of his contemporaries that its language and method should be made more precise. He studied and conversed with Nicolas le Fèvre and other chemists-alchemists on the continent and, like them, was inclined to turn alchemical experiments into precise chemical events. Some of the results of his studies appear in his *A Choice Collection of Rare Chymical Secrets and Experiments in Philosophy*, published posthumously in 1682.

Digby also studied medicine: he both collected and experimented with medicinal recipes and, like many of his contemporaries, he was interested in the Paracelsian tradition of sympathetic medicine (see PARACELSUS). Digby agreed with his Paracelsian predecessors that a wound could be healed by treating an object that contained blood from it (say, the sword that had caused the wound or bandage that had bound it). He was convinced that the Paracelsians were correct, since he had successfully cured a serious wound by such means. He diverged significantly from the tradition, however, in his explanation of the effectiveness of the treatment: whereas the Paracelsian explanation was based on occult virtues and hidden sympathies, Digby's explanation relies on mechanical principles. In his book on the powder of sympathy, Digby presents the seven physical principles from which his explanation is supposed to follow and then proposes that because the medicine 'being incorporated with the blood cannot choose but make the same voyage together with the atoms of blood', and because 'there will be a kind of current of air drawn round about the wound', it follows that the blood on the object treated with the medicine will find 'the proper source and original root whence they [the atoms of blood] issue' and 'will joyntly be imbibed together [with the medicine] within all the corners, fibres, and orifices of the Veins which lye open about the wound; when it must of necessity be refresht, and in fine imperceptibly cured'. Thus Digby explains the traditional medical 'fact' by modern means.

While some of his alchemical and medical opinions placed him in a tradition that was soon supplanted, Digby was at the forefront of the science of biology. In his *A Discourse Concerning the Vegetation of Plants*, which he presented to the nascent Royal Society in 1661, he attempts to explain plant growth by chemical and mechanical means. In his analysis of the growth and decay of plants, he relies on his notions of the four elements and their characteristic 'actions'. He gives a very clear description of the germination, development, and reproduction of plants and uses an observational technique very accurate for the time. While neither so colourful nor so popular as his book on the powder of sympathy, this work was probably his most significant scientific offering.

See also: ALCHEMY; ARISTOTELIANISM IN THE 17TH CENTURY

List of works

Digby, K. (1638) *A Conference with a Lady about Choyce of Religion*, Paris.
—— (1643) *Observations upon Religio Medici*, London.
—— (1644) *Two Treatises, In the one of which the Nature of Bodies; in the other, the Nature of Mans Soule; is looked into: in the way of discovery, of the Immortality of Reasonable Soules*, Paris; repr. New York: Garland, 1978.
—— (1652) *A Discourse, Concerning Infallibility in Religion*, Paris.
—— (1658) *Discours fait en une célèbre assemblée, par le Chevalier Digby... touchant la guérison des playes par la poudre de sympathie*, Paris; trans. E. White as *A late Discourse Made in a Solemne Assembly... touching the Cure of Wounds by the Powder of Sympathy*, London, 1658.
—— (1661) *A Discourse Concerning the Vegetation of Plants*, London.
—— (1668) *Choice and Experimented Receipts in Physick and Chirurgery... Collected by the Honourable and truly Learned Sir Kenelm Digby Kt. Chancellour to her Majesty the Queen Mother*, London.
—— (1682) *A Choice Collection of Rare Chymical Secrets and Experiments in Philosophy, as also Rare and unheard-of Medicines*, ed. G. Hartman, London.

References and further reading

Ayers, M. (1991) *Locke*, London: Routledge, 2 vols. (Contains an account of Digby on the ontology of the object of perception and on other matters related to Locke and the generation of British philosophers after Digby.)
Ayers, M. and Garber, D. (eds) (1997) *The Cambridge History of Seventeenth-Century Philosophy*, Cambridge: Cambridge University Press. (Contains several discussions of Digby.)
Bligh, E.W. (1932) *Sir Kenelm Digby and his Venetia*, London: Sampson Low & Co., Ltd. (This also includes the 'expurgated passages' from Digby's memoirs, and a bibliography.)

* Browne, T. (1643) *Religio Medici*, London; repr. ed. W.A. Greenhill, La Salle, IL: Open Court, 1991. (A reprint of an 1881 imprint, this edition also includes correspondence between Brown and Digby, notes and an index.)
Dobbs, B.J. (1971–4) 'Studies in the Natural Philosophy of Sir Kenelm Digby', *Ambix* 18: 1–25; 20: 143–63; 21: 1–28. (The most thorough summary available of Digby's work in natural philosophy and alchemy.)
Henry, J. (1982) 'Atomism and Eschatology: Catholicism and Natural Philosophy in the Interregnum', *British Journal for the History of Science* 15: 211–39. (A discussion of the ecumenism of Digby and his mentor, Thomas White.)
Krook, D. (1993) *John Sergeant and his Circle*, Leiden: Brill. (A discussion of Digby's Aristotelianism and his relation to Sergeant and to other progressive English Catholics. Chapter 3 is especially relevant.)
Petersson, R.T. (1956) *Sir Kenelm Digby: The Ornament of England, 1603–65*, Cambridge, MA: Harvard University Press. (A thorough and colourful account of Digby's life and work, with a complete bibliography of his works, including some not listed above.)

CHRISTIA MERCER

DIGNĀGA (*c.*480–*c.*540)

A logician and epistemologist, Dignāga is traditionally regarded as the founder of a Buddhist school that sought to avoid divisive controversies over which Buddhist writings were authentic by emphasizing logic and epistemology rather than the study of scriptures and their commentaries. His principal contributions consisted of refining the theory of inference and tightening the forms of argument commonly used in debate and polemics. His theories became the basis on which the influential philosopher Dharmakīrti built his system, which became the standard Buddhist scholastic system in India and later in Tibet.

1 Epistemology
2 Theory of language
3 Influence

1 Epistemology

According to traditional hagiographies, Dignāga was born around 480 into a Brahman family near Kāñcī in south India, where he was ordained a Buddhist monk as a young man. Dissatisfied with his teachers in the south, he is supposed to have travelled north and become a disciple of VASUBANDHU. Celebrated for his debating skills, he was nicknamed the 'Bull in debate'.

At the beginning of his principal work, *Pramāṇasamuccaya*, Dignāga stated that his purpose was to resolve several controversies that other philosophers had generated about the means of acquiring knowledge. Whereas his predecessors had enumerated several methods by which knowledge may be acquired, Dignāga took the position that there are in fact only two methods. These two methods are distinguished from one another in virtue of the kinds of object that can be their subject matters. The first method of securing new knowledge is described as pure sensation (*pratyakṣa*), a form of cognition that is free of all judgment (*kalpanā*). The subject matter of this type of cognition is particular instances (*svalakṣana*) of colour, sound and other sensible properties. The second method is described as inferential reasoning. The subject matter of this type of cognition is universals (*sāmānyalakṣaṇa*). In contrast to most Brahmanical philosophers who had preceded him, Dignāga held that only the senses can be aware of particular sensations, and only the intellect can be aware of universals. The view that there are exactly two types of knowledge, and that there is no subject matter common to both of them, came to be a hallmark of Buddhist doctrine, since it was accepted by most Buddhist philosophers writing in Sanskrit and rejected by the majority of Brahmanical and Jaina philosophers (see EPISTEMOLOGY, INDIAN SCHOOLS OF §1).

Before Dignāga, most Indian treatises dealing with reasoning were primarily devoted to outlining the rules of debate between opposing parties. Consequently, discussions of the formal properties of correct lines of argument were mingled with discussions of which errors on a discussant's part would result in defeat. Dignāga is usually given credit for being the first Indian philosopher to make a clear distinction between the formal properties of correct reasoning and the rules of debate. Debate, he said, is merely the articulation for the benefit of another person of a conclusion that one has arrived at by oneself through correct reasoning.

A correct inference, said Dignāga, is one that makes use of an observable property that serves as a sign (*liṅga*) of an unobserved property. The object to which the signifiable property can be inferred to belong is called the subject (*pakṣa*) of the inference. One property can serve as the sign of a second property only if three conditions are met. First, the sign must be observed to be a property of the subject of the inference. Second, the sign must be known to occur together with the signified property in objects other than the subject of the inference. And third, the sign must not be known to occur in objects in which the signified property is absent (see INFERENCE, INDIAN THEORIES OF).

2 Theory of language

In contrast to the Brahmanical philosophical traditions, Buddhist and Jaina philosophers denied the authority of the Veda, the sacred texts on which the Brahmanical religion was based. According to Brahmanical philosophers, these sacred texts came from a nonhuman source and were infallible. Brahmanical philosophers tended to argue that human perception and reasoning are always liable to error, and human beings must therefore appeal to superhuman sources of knowledge if they are ever to have certainty. Moreover, human knowledge is ultimately limited to what can be known through the senses, and it requires a special source of knowledge such as the Veda to make people aware of duty, the merit that attends doing one's duties, and the rewards of earning that merit. The language of the Veda was regarded as different from all ordinary human languages in that it is eternal (see MĪMĀṂSĀ §3). All of these Brahmanical doctrines were repudiated by Dignāga, who held that all sentences, including those of the Veda, are merely a special kind of sign that function in essentially the same ways as any other kind of inferential sign. Since language is merely a species of inference, information communicated through language is no more reliable than information gained through reasoning. And like all other inferential knowledge, the knowledge communicated through language does not convey positive information about things but merely eliminates certain states of affairs from consideration. Dignāga argued that language cannot express the particulars that are known through the senses; rather, verbal symbols express only concepts generated by the mind. These concepts are formed not by observing universals or similarities that are sensed in particulars, but by ignoring the differences in what is observed.

3 Influence

Although Dignāga was honoured for centuries in India and Tibet as the founder of the Buddhist epistemological movement, his works were eventually superseded by his followers, the most notable of whom were DHARMAKĪRTI, Dharmottara, Śāntarakṣita and Kamalaśīla in India, and TSONG KHA PA BLO BZANG GRAGS PA and MKHAS GRUB DGE LEGS DPAL BZANG PO in Tibet. Although a few of Dignāga's minor works were translated from Sanskrit into Chinese, none of his most important writings, and virtually none of the writings of his followers, were studied in China. Consequently, the epistemological school of Buddhism never developed in China and other parts of East Asia. After the demise of Buddhism in Northern India, the Sanskrit originals of most of Dignāga's works were gradually lost and nearly forgotten. In the early twentieth century, historians of Indian philosophy began to take a renewed interest in studying his works (mostly in Tibetan translations) and assessing his place in the evolution of Indian theories of inference.

See also: BUDDHIST PHILOSOPHY, INDIAN §4; KNOWLEDGE, INDIAN VIEWS OF §3; NOMINALISM, BUDDHIST DOCTRINE OF; UNIVERSALS, INDIAN THEORIES OF

List of works

Over twenty philosophical writings have been attributed to Dignāga. Of these, seven are no longer extant. The remaining works are extant only in Tibetan or Chinese translation. The following list includes only those for which studies or translations in European languages are available.

Dignāga (*c.* 520) *Ālambanaparīkṣa* (Examination of the Object of Awareness), trans. S. Yamaguchi, 'Examen de l'objet de la connaissance (*Ālambanaparīkṣa*): textes tibétains et chinois et traduction des stances et du commentaire éclaircissements et notes d'après le commentaire tibétain de Vinītadeva' (Examination of the Object of Awareness: Tibetan and Chinese texts, with translation of illuminating stanzas and commentary, and notes after Vinītadeva), *Journal Asiatique* (January–March): 1–59, Paris: Imprimerie Nationale, 1929; also trans. F. Tola and C. Dragonetti, 'Dignāga's *Ālambanaparīkṣavṛtti*', *Journal of Indian Philosophy* 10: 105–34, 1982. (A brief work in eight verses that investigates various possibilities for what the exact nature of the content of a sensory cognition is.)
—— (*c.* 525) *Nyāyamukha* (Introduction to Systematic Reasoning), trans. G. Tucci, *The Nyāyamukha of Dignāga*, Heidelberg: Materialien zur Kunde des Buddhismus, 1930. (An introductory work on the methods of correct reasoning.)
—— (*c.* 530) *Pramāṇasamuccaya* (Collected Writings on the Acquisition of Knowledge), first chapter translated in Hattori, M., *Dignāga, On Perception*, Cambridge, MA: Harvard University Press, 1968; excerpts of chapters two and five translated in Hayes, R.P., *Dignāga on the Interpretation of Signs*, Dordrecht: Kluwer Academic Publishers, 1988. (A

collection of writings on epistemology, with sections on sense perception, inference, debate and theory of language.)

References and further reading

Frauwallner, E. (1959) 'Dignāga, sein Werk und seine Entwicklung' (Dignāga, his Work and its Development), *Wiener Zeitschrift für die Kunde Süd- und Ostasiens* 3: 83–164. (An attempt to place Dignāga's writings in chronological order.)
Hattori, M. (1968) *Dignāga, On Perception*, Cambridge, MA: Harvard University Press. (Introduction includes biography of Dignāga and a complete list of works attributed to him.)
Hayes, R.P. (1988) *Dignāga on the Interpretation of Signs*, Dordrecht: Kluwer Academic Publishers. (A study of several of Dignāga's works on epistemology, with an attempt to place his theories in the context of earlier Buddhist philosophers.)
Herzberger, R. (1986) *Bhartṛhari and the Buddhists*, Dordrecht: Kluwer Academic Publishers. (A study of the relationship between the Brahmanical philosopher Bhartṛhari and the Buddhists Dignāga and Dharmakīrti. Rather complex and technical, but informative.)
Matilal, B.K. and Evans, R.D. (1986) *Buddhist Logic and Epistemology: Studies in the Buddhist Analysis of Inference and Language*, Dordrecht: Reidel. (A collection of papers, some quite technical. Matilal's introduction is accessible to the nonspecialist and offers a good overview of issues addressed by Dignāga and his followers.)
Mookerjee, S. (1935) *The Buddhist Philosophy of Universal Flux: an Exposition of the Philosophy of Critical Realism as Expounded by the School of Dignāga*, Delhi: Motilal Banarsidass, repr. 1975. (Although somewhat dated, this is still one of the best introductions to the philosophical issues at the centre of the epistemological school founded by Dignāga.)
Shastri, D.N. (1964) *Critique of Indian Realism: A Study of the Conflict Between the Nyāya-vaiśeṣika and the Buddhist Dignāga School*, Agra: Agra University. (A thorough study of the Brahmanical reactions to the Buddhist criticisms of their ontological and epistemological positions.)
Warder, A.K. (1980) *Indian Buddhism*, Delhi: Motilal Banarsidass. (A good survey of Buddhism in classical India that has a substantial chapter on Dignāga and the epistemological school of Buddhism.)

RICHARD P. HAYES

DILTHEY, WILHELM (1833–1911)

Wilhelm Dilthey saw his work as contributing to a 'Critique of Historical Reason' which would expand the scope of Kant's Critique of Pure Reason *by examining the epistemological conditions of the human sciences as well as of the natural sciences. Both kinds of science take their departure from ordinary life and experience, but whereas the natural sciences seek to focus on the way things behave independently of human involvement, the human sciences take account of this very involvement. The natural sciences use external observation and measurement to construct an objective domain of nature that is abstracted from the fullness of lived experience. The human sciences (humanities and social sciences), by contrast, help to define what Dilthey calls the historical world. By making use of inner as well as outer experience, the human sciences preserve a more direct link with our original sense of life than do the natural sciences. Whereas the natural sciences seek explanations of nature, connecting the discrete representations of outer experience through hypothetical generalizations and causal laws, the human sciences aim at an understanding that articulates the fundamental structures of historical life given in lived experience. Finding lived experience to be inherently connected and meaningful, Dilthey opposed traditional atomistic and associationist psychologies and developed a descriptive psychology that has been recognized as anticipating phenomenology.*

Dilthey first thought that this descriptive psychology could provide a neutral foundation for the other human sciences, but in his later hermeneutical writings he rejected the idea of a foundational discipline or method. Thus he ends by claiming that all the human sciences are interpretive and mutually dependent. Hermeneutically conceived, understanding is a process of interpreting the 'objectifications of life', the external expressions or manifestations of human thought and action. Interpersonal understanding is attained through these common objectifications and not, as is widely believed, through empathy. Moreover, to fully understand myself I must analyse the expressions of my life in the same way that I analyse the expressions of others.

Not every aspect of life can be captured within the respective limits of the natural and the human sciences. Dilthey's philosophy of life also leaves room for a kind of anthropological reflection whereby we attempt to do justice to the ultimate riddles of life and death. Such reflection receives its fullest expression in worldviews, which are overall perspectives on life encompassing the way we perceive and conceive the world, evaluate it aesthetically and respond to it in action. Dilthey discerned many typical worldviews in art and religion, but in Western philosophy he distinguished three recurrent types: the worldviews of naturalism, the idealism of freedom and objective idealism.

1 Foundation of the human sciences
2 Descriptive psychology
3 The formation of the historical world
4 Anthropological reflection on life and types of worldview

1 Foundation of the human sciences

Dilthey initially studied theology at Heidelberg and Berlin, but increasingly devoted his attention to history and philosophy. Before completing his dissertation on Schleiermacher's ethics in 1864, he had already written a long prize-essay, 'Das hermeneutische System Schleiermachers in der Auseinandersetzung mit der älteren protestantischen Hermeneutik' (Schleiermacher's Hermeneutic, A System in Relation to Earlier Protestant Hermeneutics) (see SCHLEIERMACHER, F.D.E.). After teaching at Basel, Kiel and Breslau, Dilthey was appointed in 1882 to the chair in philosophy in Berlin that Hegel had once occupied. His more empirical approach to the understanding of history departs from Hegel in being radically multidisciplinary. Dilthey's contributions to cultural and social history, to literary criticism and to the history of the human sciences in general found their philosophical grounding in a major, although unfinished, theoretical work, *Einleitung in die Geisteswissenschaften* (*Introduction to the Human Sciences*) (1883, 1982).

In 1883, Dilthey published the first of two projected volumes of this work. Book One of the *Einleitung* was devoted to an overview of the human sciences; Book Two to a history of the rise and fall of metaphysics in relation to the project of grounding the natural and human sciences. At the end of this history he maintains that both metaphysics and the modern natural sciences have established false models for the human sciences by constructing abstract intelligible worlds independent of lived experience. A new epistemology is needed which will show that the modern scientific conception of nature is a mere phenomenal abstraction from the more inclusive reality of life. Dilthey introduces the idea of a life-nexus (*Zusammenhang des Lebens*) as the original matrix of reality, not only for the human sciences, but also for the natural sciences. If the natural sciences find it useful to explain phenomena by means of elemental entities and universal mechanistic laws, this does not entail that they possess a more ultimate reality than the human sciences or that the latter should be constrained to drop the idea of purposiveness from their understanding of history and society.

Dilthey shows that in the past the human sciences were blinded by the success of natural science to adopt its mechanistic approach. Inspired by the ideas of Hobbes, Spinoza and Hume, a natural system of the human sciences was formed (see HOBBES, T. §2; HUME, D. §1; SPINOZA, B.). A theoretical analysis of human nature was to establish 'a few general psychic elements to explain the facts of human historical life'. These psychological elements and a finite number of non-teleological laws, like that of self-preservation, were supposed to explain the mysteries of life, the intricacies of human action, and the complexities of social interaction.

Even more problematic than the reductive character of this natural system of the human sciences is the fact that from the traditional epistemological perspective the separate foundations of the natural and the human sciences mark a division within theory alone. This has the unfortunate effect of relegating practical philosophy to a secondary concern. Dilthey disapproves of the abstract way in which a purely theoretical approach to the human sciences seeks the explanative basis for the value judgments and the imperatives that regulate the life of the individual and society. The proper foundation of the system of the sciences must be located in 'self-reflection' in contrast to 'theory of knowledge'. Self-reflection based on our experience of life provides the foundation for action as well as for thought. This philosophical self-reflection renders theory and practice equiprimordial.

The real task of founding both the natural and the human sciences was left for the second volume of the *Einleitung*, but Dilthey did not publish it during his lifetime. He did, however, work out a large part of it, which first appeared in 1982 in Volume 19 of the *Gesammelte Schriften* (Collected Works). Dilthey examines the conditions of consciousness involved in our prescientific awareness of reality. He begins Book Four with a first principle, that of phenomenality, according to which everything real is accessible as a fact of consciousness without being reduced to a mere representation of consciousness. It is important to point out that Dilthey's conception of phenomenality should be contrasted to phenomenalism, which reduces all reality to facts of consciousness (see PHENOMENALISM). Nor is it to be confused with the view that facts of consciousness are mere phenomena as distinct from external reality. Dilthey shows how the facts of our consciousness possess a primordial reality that already contains a reference to things beyond consciousness. When we become aware of something *as* a fact of consciousness we possess what Dilthey calls *Innewerden* or 'reflexive awareness'. This

reflexive awareness is pre-reflective and involves a felt self-givenness but no explicit sense of self. *Innewerden* is thus not to be equated with an objectifying self-consciousness, for it precedes any subject–object, act–content distinction. Reflexive awareness is proto-intentional in that it is oriented towards the world even if the world is not yet thematized as an external objective domain. It is this sense of being already a part of the world that is lost in the natural sciences, but must be preserved in the human sciences. Dilthey's initial descriptions of the facts of consciousness constitute an empirical phenomenology and are at the level of prescientific *Wissen* or immediate knowledge.

Dilthey's second principle, that of self-reflection, allows him to move to the level of scientific *Erkenntnis* or conceptual knowledge. In reflexive awareness we possess the felt reality of the facts of consciousness, but this does not entitle us to posit their reality conceptually. The move from the first level of prescientific reflexive awareness to conceptualization is one of explication, where the reflexive becomes reflective. The principle of self-reflection explicates the facts of consciousness into an overall nexus that encompasses all aspects of psychic life.

Within this framework of total consciousness, self-reflection then begins to differentiate between facts of self-consciousness and facts of the world. Facts that are perceived as existing in my consciousness are grasped as part of inner perception. Those facts that are independent of my self are considered facts of outer perception. But the distinction between self and world is not one that can be derived from the intellect alone. The reality of the external world is not an inference based on causal hypotheses, but is felt primarily through resistance to the practical impulses of the will.

Dilthey proceeds to show that a reflexive or felt awareness accompanying acts of will provides a crucial step in the process of differentiating self and world. Through the felt tension between efficacy of the will and resistance to it we learn to distinguish the reality of inner perception from outer perception. This dynamic relation to the external world is more fundamental than the static epistemological relation of a representation to an object. Whereas representational consciousness projects the world as a theoretical horizon for objects of natural science, reflexive awareness possesses the world as a temporal nexus in which I participate, but which is also full of things and persons actively resisting my will. A new, reflective epistemology of the human sciences must reclaim our original access to life and thus cannot be merely an extension of the epistemology of the natural sciences.

Book Five again does not restrict itself to the

human sciences, but considers the logical conditions that determine all acts of representing reality. It provides Dilthey's logic, not as a formal logic that abstracts from reality, but as an intermediary between the epistemological and methodological approaches to all the sciences that represent reality. Being representational, thought leaves behind the immediate certainty of reflexive awareness, but gains the capacity to apprehend truth. Thought is the attentive 'positing of reality' (*das Wirkliche*) not simply as that which momentarily resists, but as that which 'realizes a constant effect' (*das Wirkende*). Whereas perception posits as the real the shifting contents of what happens to be present, thought creates a nexus of representations that is in agreement with a system of reality that remains more or less constant.

The sixth and last book of the *Einleitung* begins with a general discussion of method and how it makes explicit the procedures for grasping reality inherent in the logical operations of thought. Dilthey distinguishes methods recurring in every domain of human knowledge from those peculiar to particular problems. The latter kind of method constitutes what Dilthey calls a higher logic which establishes 'rules of procedure that arise when a particular set of real conditions is introduced'. Dilthey is still speaking of both natural and human sciences, for he claims that 'aspects of mathematics, higher criticism, hermeneutics, jurisprudence [and] statistics belong to this higher logic'. It is only at the level of higher logic that we can begin to differentiate methodologically between the natural and the human sciences in specific ways.

The task of analysis and synthesis in the sciences is to simplify reality conceptually and to reorganize it in more systematic terms. Related to the process of analysis is the process of abstraction. The difference is that abstraction starts with a complex whole, 'singles out one fact and disregards the others, whereas [analysis] seeks to apprehend the majority of the facts that make up the factors of a complex whole'. Abstraction can occur in both the natural and the human sciences, but applies especially to the former. To the extent that analysis moves from a whole to its parts without isolating them from this whole, it can be said to engender understanding in the human sciences.

2 Descriptive psychology

Dilthey's 'Ideen über eine beschreibende und zergliedernde Psychologie' ('Ideas Concerning a Descriptive and Analytic Psychology') (1894) aims to wean psychology away from naturalistic models and redefine it as a human science. This new psychology would be 'first' within the system of the human sciences in the sense that it provides neutral descriptions of experience. It must suspend the general hypotheses of traditional psychology as much as possible, whether they be psychophysical or associationist. Such hypotheses strive to explain all psychic processes as different constructions from certain basic mental elements, such as representations. However, these elements cannot be well-determined or measured, with the result that hypotheses relating them have remained largely untestable.

Most psychological hypotheses about the association of representations are dispensable because inner experience is already interconnected. Whereas outer experience presents us with many unconnected phenomena which can only be related through the hypotheses of the natural sciences, psychology must consult the data of inner experience which are given as parts of a real continuum. This means that connectedness in psychic life does not need to be explained hypothetically, but can be experienced directly.

However, Dilthey does not altogether rule out hypotheses from his descriptive psychology. They are merely prevented from assuming the fundamental role they play in the natural sciences. It is clearly necessary to construct particular hypotheses when the continuity that normally exists among psychic processes is broken or interrupted. Also in cases where we were not fully attentive, questions of detail may remain problematic and thus require hypotheses to clarify what might have happened. Whereas explanative psychology *qua* natural science begins with general hypotheses, descriptive psychology may end with particular explanative hypotheses.

So far psychology has been considered mainly in relation to the description of inner experience. It should be pointed out that for Dilthey inner experience is not purely inwardly directed or introspective. Inner experience is often about external objects, but focuses on our attitude towards them. It is therefore in some way more encompassing than outer experience, which excludes subjective attitudes. To move beyond this paradox Dilthey developed a new conception of experience that replaces the Kantian term *Erfahrung* with *Erlebnis* (lived experience). Lived experience is experience in its most inclusive sense and 'contains a relation of inner and outer'.

Because lived experience discloses the original continuum of psychic life, it becomes necessary to reformulate the traditional conception of understanding which had been oriented primarily to our discrete outer experiences of natural phenomena. According to Kant, our experience of nature involves a discursive faculty of understanding (*Verstand*) that proceeds synthetically from partial representations to construct objective wholes (see KANT, I. §§6–7). Dilthey's attack on faculty psychology undermines Kant's pure intellectual conception of *Verstand*, which constructs the world in terms of fixed, abstract categories. When Dilthey speaks of understanding he means a very different process of *Verstehen*, which is concrete and develops historically. In so far as the *Verstehen* (understanding) of psychic life is based on lived experience it can be intuitive and proceed from the whole to the parts.

Kant's *Verstand* as intellectual faculty was really geared to the scientific explanation of natural events. It allows us to relate the phenomena of nature, but provides no insight into their underlying reality. Dilthey accepts this limit for our knowledge of nature, but not for the understanding of ourselves and others. We cannot really understand nature, because it is not of our own making. Dilthey aligns himself with Vico by claiming that we can only truly know what we have ourselves made or contributed to (see VICO, G. §6). We thus have an access to psychological, social and historical reality – a recognition of ourselves in others, so to speak – which is impossible in relation to nature. Understanding constitutes the main goal of the human sciences in the way that explanation defines the natural sciences.

The fact that Dilthey points to the limits of scientific explanation has given some the mistaken impression that understanding is irrational. While explanation may be conceived as a purely intellectual process, understanding should not be characterized antithetically as a product of mere feeling or empathy. Lived experience does provide an immediate sense of the whole, but understanding, in appealing to all the powers of the psyche, does not overlook the intellectual processes. Sometimes understanding and explanation converge. Since understanding is contextual, it may need to bring external factors to bear which will then play a subordinate explanatory role. Similarly, the description of lived experience must go over into analysis to bring out implicit structural relations more clearly.

There is an interdependence between the cognitive, emotive and volitional aspects of our consciousness which is at once structural and dynamic. While Dilthey begins with a discussion of representations, they are not considered as the underlying elements, with feelings and acts of will reduced to mere functions of representations. In some cases, representations may produce certain feelings which lead to a disposition to act. But in turn, representations themselves receive retroactive influences from our feelings and volitions. Clearly no aspect of psychic life can be understood in isolation or as most basic.

Dilthey regards development as a process of articulation whereby an indeterminate psychic continuum is differentiated into more distinctly related parts of a structural whole. The psychological concept especially formulated to define this formation of the self is that of the 'acquired nexus of psychic life' (*erworbener Zusammenhang des Seelenlebens*). This acquired psychic nexus embodies the history of the development of an individual and reveals the structural ordering of past experience. Encompassing knowledge of the world, evaluations and dispositions to act, it orients all present and future experience.

The individuality of the self is defined in terms of the structural articulation of the acquired psychic nexus. No qualitative uniqueness need be posited to explain individuality. What serves to distinguish individuals from one another is that the commonly held traits are manifested with differing forcefulness. In a given person, some qualities may be so faintly exhibited as to be, in effect, unobservable, others with such strength that we tend to notice them alone.

Dilthey's discussion of individuality reflects one of the most pervasive themes of his philosophy – the understanding of human individuality as an essential goal of history and the human sciences. Dilthey meant to further such understanding with a comparative psychology, but he never completed it as he went through a transition in which he reconsidered some of his assumptions about the role of psychology and began to develop his later hermeneutic approach to the human sciences.

3   The formation of the historical world

With his 'Entstehung der Hermeneutik' ('The Rise of Hermeneutics') in 1900, Dilthey began to sketch out a position which would define his work until his death. While he does not abandon the psychological description of lived experience, Dilthey comes to view its ability to capture the meaning of our life as more limited. Much of the meaning of our experience remains unconscious until it is expressed. Thus the description of the life of the subject cannot be done without the interpretation of its expressed objectifications. Dilthey resumed the task of a Critique of Historical Reason from this hermeneutical perspective, publishing *Der Aufbau der geschichtlichen Welt in den Geisteswissenschaften* (*The Formation of the Historical World in the Human Sciences*) in 1910.

There is a further problem which occasioned Dilthey's move to hermeneutics and underscores the limitations of description. The descriptions of psychology seem to function primarily on the scientific level of representational consciousness which – however well-integrated – stands apart from the world. How do we deal with prescientific reflexive awareness according to which we are already part of the world? Can description also be applied to its more inclusive life-nexus? Here Dilthey found inspiration in Husserl's *Logische Untersuchungen* (*Logical Investigations*) and its theory of intentionality. Dilthey had given a seminar on this work in the Winter Semester 1904/5. Husserl in turn visited Dilthey and wrote that this meeting inspired him to occupy himself extensively with the problems of the human sciences (see HUSSERL, E. §2).

In Dilthey's 'Ideen', understanding was used to describe the connectedness of facts of consciousness. According to his later hermeneutical writings, understanding must clarify these connections as meaning-relations. Since the meaning-relations of our experience and expressions are not necessarily measurable in terms of the framework of the psychic nexus, Dilthey turns to historical life as the ultimate framework for interpretation. Whereas the acquired psychic nexus incorporated the objective sphere into the life of the individual subject, in the *Aufbau* Dilthey becomes equally concerned to conceive the inverse way in which subjects are intentionally related to objective and public spheres. To do so Dilthey appropriates the Hegelian term 'objective spirit' as the overall historical context for understanding. He rejects Hegel's particular definition of objective spirit as the socio-historical stage of the self-realization of absolute spirit in favour of a concept consistent with a reinterpretation of spirit as human activity. 'Objective spirit' designates the whole range of human objectifications, whether they be expressions in language and other media meant to communicate, or practices and deeds meant to influence. This objective spirit is at once the embodiment of human thought and action as well as the medium within which they occur. It includes the contexts we share to make interaction possible: not only the sociopolitical institutions originally considered by Hegel, but also the cultural institutions of art, religion and philosophy which he had classified as absolute spirit (see HEGEL, G.W.F. §8).

Objective spirit provides the kind of overall framework for Dilthey's hermeneutics that tradition comes to provide in Gadamer's hermeneutics. But objective spirit is not as dominant as tradition in Gadamer, for Dilthey articulates it into more specific *Wirkungszusammenhänge* (systems of reciprocal influence), whether they be historical epochs or social and cultural systems. This is relevant to Dilthey's distinction between elementary and higher understanding. The former orients an expression to the common context of objective spirit. That is, the elementary understanding of a sentence focuses only on what it explicitly asserts and is commonly assumed to mean.

Problems concerning the implicit meaning of expressions call for higher understanding, which requires us to refer to more specific systems of reciprocal influence. Thus we attempt to determine any ambiguous expressions in a legal document by considering the particular legal system of the period in which it was drawn up. Only after having exhausted what the appropriate public contexts of expressions can do to clarify their objective meaning, should we turn to the subjective or psychological context. Now psychology is no longer the first of the human sciences, but the last. The highest or last mode of understanding is the *Nacherleben* or re-experiencing of an expression of lived experience. This re-experiencing does not involve reproducing the state of mind of the author. Hermeneutics expects us to understand authors not as they understood themselves, but better.

Although his hermeneutics ultimately focuses on the relation between lived experience, expression, and understanding (*Erlebnis, Ausdruck, Verstehen*), Dilthey admits that many expressions such as mathematical formulas and handshakes expressing agreement can be understood apart from relating them to lived experience. But when an expression does articulate our lived experience, as in a work of art, it can enrich our understanding of life in immeasurable ways. This is why Dilthey's writings on the imagination of artists bear importantly on his theory of interpretation.

4 Anthropological reflection on life and types of worldview

Dilthey's aesthetic writings play a central role in his philosophy. They not only contribute to his conception of interpretation as it functions in the theory of the human sciences, but they also explicate the way in which we reflect about the meaning of life in everyday existence. There are many levels at which we try to understand what happens in life. Both pre-scientific anthropological reflection and scientific psychological description contribute to the understanding of order in our lives. Similarly, the categories whereby we establish order in the world are by no means purely scientific, but can in some cases be traced back to the 'syntactical articulation of language'. Sometimes the same category (for example, Aristotle's acting and suffering) can receive varying formulations as it functions at the level of ordinary experience (for example, efficacy), of the human sciences (for example, influence), and of the natural sciences (for example, causality). Other categories such as value, purpose and meaning are distinctive of the human sciences. The peculiar fascination of the arts, especially the literary arts, is that they can somehow relate all these levels in the search for order, without, however, producing a conceptual system. Like philosophers and religious thinkers, certain great poets have the capacity to articulate a comprehensive worldview.

One of Dilthey's last essays was *Die Typen der Weltanschauung und ihre Ausbildung in den metaphysischen Systemen* (*Types of Worldview and their Development in Metaphysical Systems*) (1911). Whereas the kinds of worldview found in art and religion are quite diverse, worldviews in Western philosophy have received a more conceptual, metaphysical formulation that allows them to be distinguished into three main types: naturalism, the idealism of freedom and objective idealism. Naturalism as found in Democritus, Hobbes and others, reduces everything to what can be perceived or determinately cognized and is pluralistic in structure; the idealism of freedom as found in Plato, Kant and others insists on the irreducibility of the will and is dualistic; objective idealism as found in Heraclitus, Leibniz and Hegel affirms reality as the embodiment of a harmonious set of values and is monistic. Each of these metaphysical types of worldview is a perspectival interpretation of reality respectively emphasizing either our cognitive or representational capacities, our volitional ends, or what is felt to be valuable. Despite being totalistic, these types of worldview cannot attain absolute knowledge, according to Dilthey.

Because Dilthey analyses three incommensurable types of worldview that recur, he is often considered a relativist. In his essay 'Philosophie als strenge Wissenschaft' ('Philosophy as a Rigorous Science'), Husserl quotes some passages from this essay that also seem to lead Dilthey down the path of historicism. In one of them, Dilthey uses 'the development of the historical consciousness' to question the universal validity of any metaphysical worldview that claims to comprehend conceptually how everything in the world is interconnected. By appealing to historical consciousness, Dilthey is not, as Husserl thinks, making a mere factual claim about the inability of past metaphysical speculative systems to gain universal acceptance. Historical consciousness is for Dilthey a broadening perspective that takes claims out of their actual local contexts and locates them in the sphere of universal history. It is a product of the Enlightenment and could even be considered the counterpart of the transcendental point of view. Indeed, Dilthey's stance here is analogous to Kant's in rejecting metaphysical speculation and is no more relativistic or historicist than Kant's standpoint.

Dilthey's historical consciousness makes possible a critical analysis of worldviews, and it is this kind of analysis that shows that metaphysical worldviews cannot be scientifically adjudicated. Any effort to provide a comprehensive scientific account of reality would have to synthesize the results of the natural sciences and the human sciences. But ultimately the approaches of these two kinds of science are so different that they cannot in principle be synthesized. Dilthey's appeal to historical consciousness is thus not at all a challenge to the objective validity of science. It is instead an attempt to preserve the objectivity of scientific *Erkenntnis*. Worldviews, in turn, have their main value for Dilthey as reflective articulations of the meaning of our own life-nexus as given in prescientific *Wissen*.

See also: HEGELIANISM §6; HERMENEUTICS; HISTORICISM §1; HISTORY, PHILOSOPHY OF §4; PHENOMENOLOGICAL MOVEMENT; SOCIAL SCIENCE, HISTORY OF PHILOSOPHY OF §8

List of works

Dilthey, W. (1914–90) *Gesammelte Schriften* (Collected Works), Göttingen: Vandenhoeck & Ruprecht, 20 vols. (The standard complete works.)

—— (1985–) *Selected Works*, ed. R.A. Makkreel and F. Rodi, Princeton, NJ: Princeton University Press, 6 vols. (Vol. 1 (1989), vol. 4, *Hermeneutics and the Study of History* (1996), and vol. 5, *Poetry and Experience* (1985), are the three volumes now in print.)

—— (1883, 1982) *Einleitung in die Geisteswissenschaften*, trans. R.A. Makkreel and F. Rodi, *Introduction to the Human Sciences*, in *Selected Works*, ed. R.A. Makkreel and F. Rodi, Princeton, NJ: Princeton University Press, vol. 1, 1989. (Includes all of Book One and materials from Books Two, Four, Five, and Six.)

—— (1894) 'Ideen über eine beschreibende und zergliedernde Psychologie', trans. R. Zaner and K. Heiges, 'Ideas Concerning a Descriptive and Analytic Psychology', in *Descriptive Psychology and Historical Understanding*, with intro. by R.A. Makkreel, The Hague: Martinus Nijhoff, 1977. (The translated volume also contains 'The Understanding of Other Persons'.)

—— (1900) 'Entstehung der Hermeneutik', trans. R.A. Makkreel and F. Rodi, 'The Rise of Hermeneutics', in *Hermeneutics and the Study of History*, vol. 4 of *Selected Works*, ed. R.A. Makkreel and F. Rodi, Princeton, NJ: Princeton University Press, 1996. (This volume of the *Selected Works* also contains 'Das hermeneutische System Schleiermachers in der Auseinandersetzung mit der älteren protestantischen Hermeneutik' (Schleiermacher's

Hermeneutic, A System in Relation to Earlier Protestant Hermeneutics) (1960).)

—— (1910) *Der Aufbau der geschichtlichen Welt in den Geisteswissenschaften*, trans. R.A. Makkreel and F. Rodi, *The Formation of the Historical World in the Human Sciences*, in *Selected Works*, ed. R.A. Makkreel and F. Rodi, Princeton, NJ: Princeton University Press, vol. 3, (forthcoming). (Here Dilthey comes closest to working out his Critique of Historical Reason.)

—— (1911) *Die Typen der Weltanschauung und ihre Ausbildung in den metaphysischen Systemen*, trans. W. Kluback and M. Weinbaum, *Types of Worldview and their Development in Metaphysical Systems*, in *Dilthey's Philosophy of Existence*, New York: Bookman Associates, 1957. (Relates worldviews in poetry, religion and philosophy.)

—— (1976) *Selected Writings*, ed. H.P. Rickman, Cambridge: Cambridge University Press. (Contains excerpts from various works, including *The Formation of the Historical World in the Human Sciences* (1910).)

References and further reading

Ermarth, M. (1978) *Wilhelm Dilthey: The Critique of Historical Reason*, Chicago, IL: University of Chicago Press. (A comprehensive account of Dilthey's thought with a good historical background.)

* Husserl, E. (1900–1) *Logische Untersuchungen*, trans. J.N. Findlay, *Logical Investigations*, London and New York: Routledge, 1977. (Classical formulation of the theory of the intentionality of consciousness and of such phenomenological concepts as act, content and object, expression and meaning.)

* —— (1910–11) 'Philosophie als strenge Wissenschaft', trans. G. Laver, 'Philosophy as a Rigorous Science', in *Phenomenology and the Crisis of Philosophy*, New York: Harper & Row, 1965. (An attack on worldview philosophy as lacking in rigour.)

Makkreel, R.A. (1975, 1992) *Dilthey: Philosopher of the Human Studies*, Princeton, NJ: Princeton University Press. (A developmental examination of Dilthey's philosophy with special attention to its relation to Kant; updated to deal with recently published posthumous writings.)

Makkreel, R.A. and Scanlon, J. (eds) (1987) *Dilthey and Phenomenology*, Washington, DC: Center for Advanced Research in Phenomenology and University Press of America. (Exploration of Dilthey's relation to phenomenology by ten international scholars.)

Orth, E.W. (ed.) (1985) *Dilthey und die Philosophie der Gegenwart* (Dilthey and Contemporary Philosophy), Freiburg, Alber Verlag. (Exploration of Dilthey's relevance to a variety of topics by twelve scholars, including Apel and Gadamer.)

Owensby, J. (1994) *Dilthey and the Narrative of History*, Ithaca, NY: Cornell University Press. (A topical study focusing on recently published posthumous writings.)

Rodi, F. (ed.) (1983–) *Dilthey-Jahrbuch für Philosophie und Geschichte der Geisteswissenschaften* (Dilthey-Yearbook for Philosophy and the History of the Human Sciences), Göttingen: Vandenhoeck & Ruprecht. (Published essays on Dilthey and related figures and themes. Also provides bibliography updates.)

Rodi, F. and Lessing, H.-U. (eds) (1984) *Materialien zur Philosophie Wilhelm Diltheys* (Materials Relevant to the Philosophy of Wilhelm Dilthey), Frankfurt am Main: Suhrkamp. (A collection of classical essays on Dilthey by such thinkers as Scheler, Landgrebe, Bollnow, Plessner, Marcuse, Misch, Habermas and Gadamer.)

RUDOLF A. MAKKREEL

DIODORUS CRONUS
(late 4th–early 3rd centuries BC)

The most famous member of the Dialectical school, the Greek philosopher Diodorus Cronus maintained various paradoxical theses. He argued that any attempt to divide space, time or matter must end with little regions, periods or bodies that cannot further be divided; hence, he inferred, things cannot be in motion. Diodorus also contributed to the contemporary debate on conditionals: one proposition implies another, he held, if and only if it never has been possible, and is not now possible, to have the former proposition true and the latter proposition false. Diodorus is however most famous for inventing the master argument. The master argument relied on two assumptions: that every past truth is necessary, and that the impossible does not follow from the possible. It concluded, on these assumptions, that no proposition is possible unless it either is true or will be. The master argument was designed to support Diodorus' definition of possibility: a proposition is possible if and only if it either is or will be true. This definition is not exactly tantamount to the fatalist doctrine that all truths are necessary, but it was felt to come too close to fatalism for comfort.

1   Life and reputation
2   Atomism and change
3   Conditionals and consequence

4 The definition of possibility
5 The master argument

1 Life and reputation

Born in Iasos, in Asia Minor, during the last half of the fourth century BC, Diodorus died around 284 BC. The abusive nickname 'Cronus' ('Old Fogey') he inherited from his teacher Apollonius Cronus. Diodorus was the greatest showman among the Dialecticians (see DIALECTICAL SCHOOL), a school to which, it is said, his five daughters also belonged. He held that words get their meaning not from nature nor even from convention, but instead from the intention with which they are uttered; and that in consequence none of his words were ambiguous unless uttered with the intention of saying more things than one. His views on meaning he illustrated by giving a daughter the male name 'Theognis', and by naming a slave with the Greek equivalent of 'In fact however'. He helped refine various already current paradoxes such as the liar paradox ('What I am saying is false'), the veiled paradox ('You don't know who the man behind the veil is. He is your father. So you don't know who your father is') and the paradox of the Sorites (which in Diodorus' hands became 'If two in a trio of atoms are in motion, then the trio are predominantly in motion; if the trio are predominantly in motion, then a quartet to which that trio belong are also predominantly in motion; and so on; so a myriad of atoms will be predominantly in motion, even if only two of them are actually moving'). Diodorus' most celebrated contributions were his arguments against change, his theory of logical consequence and the views on modality which he defended with his master argument. It was said that 'even the crows on the roof-tops caw' about the issues Diodorus raised; and conversation about the master argument was a notoriously effective way of blighting dinner parties. In modern times, the master argument has become the subject of a massive literature, much of it highly speculative.

2 Atomism and change

Diodorus held that all things consist of 'minimal and partless bodies' so small as to be indivisible, but big enough for there to be only finitely many of them in any finitely sized body. He held similar views about time and space: any larger stretch of time may be divided into short periods, each of length greater than zero but with no smaller parts into which it can be divided; and each finite space consists of finitely many indivisible volumes.

Diodorus concluded that nothing is ever moving.

Sextus Empiricus gives the fullest single report of Diodorus' many arguments on these matters:

> If something is moving, it is moving now. If it is moving now, it is moving in the present time. If it is moving in the present time, it is moving in a partless time. For if the present time is divided, it will be divided completely into the past and future, and so will no longer be present. If something is moving in a partless time, it traverses partless places. If it traverses partless places, it is not moving. For when it is in the first partless place, it is not moving; for it is still in the first partless place. And when it is in the second partless place, again it is not moving, but has moved. So nothing is moving.

(Against the Professors X 119–20)

Although Diodorus denies that things move, he concedes that they are not now where they were, and that they therefore have moved. If we wonder how a thing can have moved without ever moving, Diodorus points out that Helen had three husbands, even though the present-tensed 'Helen has three husbands' was never true; for her husbands were successive, not simultaneous.

3 Conditionals and consequence

It was widely agreed that the relation between antecedent and consequent in a true conditional is the same as that between premises and conclusion in a valid argument: the conclusion (or consequent) was said to 'follow from' the premises (or antecedent). This was unfortunate. It implies that in an argument like:

It is day.

If it is day, it is light.

So, it is light.

the conditional premise is either false or redundant. The parties to the unfortunate agreement that these two relations are identical did however dispute about what the single relation was (see PHILO THE DIALECTICIAN §2).

Diodorus was party to the agreement, and also to the dispute. He declared that one proposition follows from another if and only if it neither was nor is possible for the former to be false while the latter is true.

An immediate consequence of Diodorus' definition is that if one proposition now follows from another, then it has always done so. This consequence is a defect if Diodorus' definition is taken as an account of which conditionals are true. For by holding out my right arm I can make true a previously false conditional: 'If I hold out my left arm, both my arms will be held out'. This consequence is however a virtue if Diodorus' definition is taken as an account of which arguments are valid. For it would be astonishing if a previously invalid argument should become valid.

On Diodorus' definition, everything follows from a proposition that is and always has been impossible; and a proposition that is and always has been necessary follows from everything. Diodorus' atomism was invoked to give a piquant illustration of both points simultaneously: on Diodorus' account, 'There are minimal and partless bodies' follows from its own negation, 'There are no minimal and partless bodies'.

Diodorus' explanation of following can be explained further. The result is: one proposition follows from another if and only if there is no time when the former is false and the latter is true. This result is reached by applying, to Diodorus' original definition of following, his definition of possibility.

4 The definition of possibility

Diodorus defined the possible as what is or will be true (for example, it is possible for me to be in Corinth if and only if I am or will be there), and the necessary as what, being true, will never be false. Diodorus therefore disagreed both with the Aristotelian idea that the necessary is what is true at every time, and with the Megaric idea that the possible is what is true now (see MEGARIAN SCHOOL).

One curious consequence concerns change of modalities. On Diodorus' definitions, what was once contingent can become either necessary or impossible. The reverse change cannot take place: once something is either necessary or impossible it remains so for ever. As time passes, previously open possibilities therefore get closed off. Moreover, the only way a previously open possibility can get closed off is by being actualized: if something once was possible but is no longer so, then it has been actually true in the meantime.

A second curious consequence concerns 'future contingents', propositions of the form 'So-and-so will happen' that are neither necessary nor impossible. Suppose that 'Adam will sin' is such a proposition. If 'Adam will sin' is not impossible, then, on Diodorus' definition, it either is true now or will be true in the future; either way, Adam will sin. If 'Adam will sin' is not necessary, then, on Diodorus' definition, it either is or will be false. But since Adam will sin, the first alternative can be eliminated. Hence 'Adam will sin' will be false at some time in the future. Moreover, once such a proposition is false, it will remain false for

ever thereafter. Hence, on Diodorus' definition, 'Adam will sin' will become and remain impossible. This reasoning is generally applicable: on Diodorus' definition, each future contingent is now true and will eventually become permanently impossible.

A third curious consequence concerns past necessities. If a proposition has been true, then it always will have been so. By Diodorus' definition, past truths are therefore necessary. This applies only to simple past tensed truths, like 'Diodorus was born in Iasos'. The more complex truth 'Diodorus' fragments have never yet been properly edited' is contingent if his fragments will be properly edited in future. And the metric truth 'Diodorus was born nearly 25 centuries ago' can also be false, for it will be.

Why should Diodorus' definition be accepted? It is obvious enough that if something is or will be true, then it is possible. More controversial is the converse, that if something is possible, then it is or will be true. To establish the converse, Diodorus devised the master argument.

5 The master argument

According to Epictetus:

> The master argument seems to have been put forward from some such starting points as these. There is a mutual inconsistency of these three propositions with one another:
>
> Every past truth is necessary;
>
> The impossible does not follow from the possible;
>
> Something is possible which neither is true nor will be.
>
> Diodorus saw this inconsistency and used the plausibility of the first two propositions to establish that nothing is possible which neither is true nor will be.
>
> (*Discourses* II 19.1)

The word translated 'past' is the most general term for verbs in any of Greek's various past tenses. Hence Diodorus' first premise presumably means that each true proposition in a past tense is necessarily true. This interpretation is that of CHRYSIPPUS, who accepted the first premise (Epictetus, *Discourses* II 19.2–5) and who defended it on the grounds that past truths cannot change from true to false (Cicero, *On Fate* 14): Chrysippus' reasoning is entirely cogent if by 'past truth' we mean only simple past tensed truths, like 'Diodorus was born in Iasos'.

How did Diodorus reason from his first two premises to the negation of the third? We learn of the first two premises because they were disputed by Stoics, who rejected Diodorus' conclusion but who could find nothing other than these two premises to contest (see CLEANTHES). Hence our reconstruction should not make obvious use of other premises more likely to be contested by the Stoics than these first two. Here is one reconstruction to meet this standard.

Let us take the proposition 'Diodorus snores'. From this proposition, it follows that 'Diodorus snores' never was at any past time going to be false for ever thereafter. Hence, if this proposition is possible, then it is possible also that 'Diodorus snores' never was at any past time going to be false for ever thereafter (for the impossible does not follow from the possible). If however our proposition now is and always will be false, then 'Diodorus snores' was at some past time going to be false for ever thereafter; indeed, it is necessary that 'Diodorus snores' was at some past time going to be false for ever thereafter (for every past truth is necessary). Hence if the same proposition is and always will be false but is nevertheless possible, we have a contradiction: that the proposition will always be false has necessarily been so at some time, and also has possibly never been so.

See also: LOGIC, ANCIENT §5; PRIOR, A.N.; TENSE AND TEMPORAL LOGIC

References and further reading

Denyer, N. (1981a) 'The Atomism of Diodorus Cronus', *Prudentia* 13: 33–45. (An expansion of the material in §2.)

—— (1981b) 'Time and Modality in Diodorus Cronus', *Theoria* 47: 31–53. (An earlier version of the material in §§3–5.)

Döring, K. (1972) *Die Megariker* (The Megarians), Amsterdam: Grüner. (Collection of ancient sources, together with some German commentary.)

Gaskin, R. (1995) *The Sea Battle and the Master Argument*, Berlin and New York: de Gruyter. (Contains ample discussion of rival interpretations, together with a massive bibliography.)

Giannantoni, G. (1990) *Socratis et Socraticorum Reliquiae* (The Remains of Socrates and the Socratics), Naples: Bibliopolis. (Volume 1 pages 413–35 contains an almost complete collection of the ancient evidence about Diodorus.)

Long, A.A. and Sedley, D.N. (1987) *The Hellenistic Philosophers*, Cambridge: Cambridge University Press. (Contains some of the main sources, together with English commentaries and translations.)

Prior, A. (1967) *Past, Present and Future*, Oxford: Clarendon Press. (Chapter 2 axiomatizes Diodoran modal logic.)

Sedley, D. (1977) 'Diodorus Cronus and Hellenistic Philosophy', *Proceedings of the Cambridge Philological Society* 203, new series, 23: 74–120. (Comprehensively sets Diodorus in his historical context.)

White, M.J. (1992) *The Continuous and the Discrete: Ancient Physical Theories from a Contemporary Perspective*, Oxford: Clarendon Press. (Expounds, sometimes rather technically, Diodoran atomism and its ancient rivals.)

NICHOLAS DENYER

DIOGENES LAERTIUS
(*c.* AD 300–50)

Diogenes Laertius is the author of a famous work entitled Lives of the Philosophers *consisting of nearly one hundred accounts of individual philosophers. These contain mainly biographical information, but sometimes also include doctrinal summaries. The work is extremely valuable because it preserves much information on Greek philosophers from sources now lost.*

Diogenes Laertius is the author of the only work to come down to us from antiquity that gives a comprehensive account of the Greek philosophical tradition. It consists of ten books, which contain eighty-four accounts of individual Greek philosophers, varying in length from an entire book to a few lines. Very little is known about the author. A disputed text (IX 109) suggests that his home town was Nicaea in Bithynia (not far from Byzantium). This provincial location might explain the somewhat dated quality of his erudition. Diogenes scarcely mentions philosophers of the Roman period except for a list of Sceptics at IX 116. The last-named of these is a pupil of Sextus Empiricus, which indicates that he wrote the book no earlier than the first half of the third century AD. Diogenes himself does not belong to any philosophical school, but does appear to have sympathy for the philosophy of Epicurus (X 29).

An older title of Diogenes' work, known since the Middle Ages simply as *Lives of the Philosophers*, gives a more accurate indication of its content: *Lives and Maxims of Those who Gained Fame in Philosophy and the Doctrines of Each School*. The overall structure of the work is determined by the theory of successions in Greek philosophical historiography (see DOXOGRAPHY), as the following summary shows:

Book I the seven sages, including Thales;

Book II the Ionian succession, including Anaximander, Anaxagoras, Socrates and the Socratics;

Book III Plato;

Book IV Plato's successors in the Academy;

Book V Aristotle and his successors in the Lyceum;

Book VI Antisthenes, Diogenes and the Cynic philosophers;

Book VII Zeno and the Stoic philosophers (some twenty chapters have gone missing at the end);

Book VIII the Italian succession, headed by Pythagoras and Empedocles;

Book IX the 'scattered' philosophers, including Heraclitus, Parmenides and Democritus;

Book X Epicurus.

Only one woman philosopher receives a separate chapter: Hipparchia the Cynic (VI 96–8).

The work is in an unfinished state. Individual chapters or 'biographies' contain a remarkable variety of material, giving the work an uneven and compilatory quality. Doctrines are only presented in detail when the chapter deals with the founder of a school (for example, the extremely valuable doxography on the Stoics in Book VII). A typical chapter includes the origin of the philosopher and who his teachers were, the date when he flourished (*akmē*), anecdotes illustrating his life, maxims, lists of works (extremely valuable), other documents such as wills and letters (the latter usually fictitious), an epigram by the author on the philosopher's death, and a list of other persons with the same name. Diogenes does not write a history of philosophy in the modern sense. He combines biographical and doctrinal material because he is convinced, like most writers on philosophy in antiquity, that there is a intrinsic relation between the *bios* (life) and the *logos* (doctrine) of every philosopher.

The value of the information supplied by Diogenes is entirely dependent on the quality of his sources. The nature and extent of these has long been the subject of debate. It is now thought that he has excerpted and stitched together material from widely scattered sources. These date mainly from the Hellenistic period, and include many important works in the historiography of ancient philosophy which are no longer extant. Since the Byzantine period Diogenes' work has been extensively used. No other work provides us with so much information on ancient philosophers. Despite its undeniable mediocrity, it is truly priceless.

List of works

Diogenes Laertius (*c*. early 3rd century AD) *Lives of the Philosophers*, trans. R.D. Hicks, *Diogenes Laertius Lives of Eminent Philosophers*, Loeb Classical Library, Cambridge, MA: Harvard University Press and London: Heinemann, 1925, 2 vols; revised H.S. Long, 1972. (English translation with Greek text facing; outdated edition, but not yet superseded.)

References and further reading

Knoepfler, D. (1991) *La vie de Ménédème d'Érétrie de Diogène Laërce: contribution à l'histoire et à la critique du texte des Vie des Philosophes* (Diogenes Laertius' Life of Menedemus of Eretria: A Contribution to the History and Evaluation of the Text of the *Lives of the Philosophers*), Basle: Friedrich Reinhardt. (Important remarks on the state of the textual tradition.)

Mansfeld, J. (1986) 'Diogenes Laertius on Stoic Philosophy', *Elenchos* 7: 295–382. (Includes important general remarks on Diogenes' method, together with a detailed analysis of how he proceeds in Book VII on the Stoics.)

Mejer, J. (1978) *Diogenes Laertius and his Hellenistic Background*, Hermes Einzelschriften 40, Wiesbaden: Franz Steiner. (Very good on Diogenes' mediated use of Hellenistic sources.)

DAVID T. RUNIA

DIOGENES OF APOLLONIA (5th century BC)

Diogenes was the last of the early Greek physicists. He claimed that interactions between things would be impossible unless all were forms of one basic substance. Adapting ideas of Anaximenes and Anaxagoras, he identified the basic substance as air, which in its optimal form possesses intelligence and thereby controls the universe at large and animal life in particular. Diogenes worked out a detailed psychology and physiology, explaining sense perception as an exercise of intelligence due to interaction between air in the region of the brain and atmospheric air. This theory was mocked by Aristophanes, but influenced various Hippocratic writings.

1 Life and work
2 Monism
3 Psychology and physiology

1 Life and work

Almost nothing is known of Diogenes' life. His birthplace Apollonia was probably the Milesian colony of that name on the Black Sea. Diogenes

87

Laertius (IX 57) dates him to the same period as Anaxagoras (500–428 BC). Aristophanes' allusion to his ideas (*Clouds* 227–33) and Theophrastus' statement that he was pretty much the last of the Presocratics (A5) suggest someone younger. Simplicius attributes the surviving fragments to a general work on nature (A4), but the sequence of topics would seem to point to another of the treatises by Diogenes – *On the Nature of Man* – as their probable source.

Diogenes is elsewhere credited like the atomists with belief in an infinite number of worlds, and with a cosmogony and account of the earth and the heavenly bodies which largely recapitulate Anaxagoras' theories (A1, A6, A12) (see ANAXAGORAS §4). Indeed, Theophrastus explicitly represented him as drawing eclectically from these two major fifth-century systems (A5). But the work from which Simplicius quotes evidently had a quite different theme. It began with metaphysical argument for the fundamental identity of all physical things (fr. 2). Then, consequent upon proofs that the universe is permeated with intelligence (frs 3 and 4), it contended that the seat of intelligence is air, which is a single substance, despite variations in temperature, moisture and mobility etc. (fr. 5). Simplicius assures us that this substance is the eternal imperishable body whose existence was derived a priori in the opening argument (frs 7 and 8).

There followed a sequence of proofs designed to substantiate the dependence of animal life and intelligence upon air. Simplicius mentions demonstrations that sperm is aerated and that acts of intelligence occur when air via blood takes possession of the whole body. He refers to an anatomy of the human veins, which is preserved more or less verbatim by Aristotle (*History of Animals* III 2, see Diogenes fr. 6). Diogenes probably gave his account of sense perception, extensively reported by Theophrastus (A19), at this point in the book, along with discussions of physiological phenomena like sleep and digestion.

These detailed explanations appear to have constituted the real focus of the work. Its structure is just what one might expect of a fifth-century book 'on the nature of man': Polybus, author of the Hippocratic treatise bearing this title, complains of the way some writers on human physiology preface their accounts with grandiose claims, supported by meaningless proofs, about a single basic substance.

2 Monism

Ancient and modern historians of philosophy alike see Diogenes' theory as reviving the system of a century earlier (see ANAXIMENES §1). But it is a revival informed by reflection on more recent philosophy. Thus the argument for MONISM found in fragment 2 has clear affinities with theses of Anaxagoras and Democritus, although Democritus may depend on Diogenes; there are also verbal echoes of Melissus and Empedocles. Diogenes proposes that two objects cannot mix with or benefit or harm each other, nor can one grow or be born from another, unless they are really – 'in their nature' – the same. Since he assumes that the four elements all do interact with one another, he concludes that all of them, and therefore all things whatsoever, are forms of the same basic substance. Diogenes' monism therefore allows for a world of variety and change. Nor does he acknowledge any need to rebut Melissus' proofs of the logical impossibility of alteration, even if the wording of fragment 2 betrays his familiarity with them.

Diogenes' arguments that there is 'much intelligence' in the basic substance recall HERACLITUS as well as Anaxagoras. He appeals principally to the optimal disposition of day and night and the seasons, but also to the role of soul and intelligence in sustaining animal life (frs 3 and 4). Yet this is only preparatory to enunciation of his main thesis: the identification of air as what possesses intelligence. Once again Diogenes echoes Anaxagoras (fr. 12: see ANAXAGORAS §4), but this time to subvert his insistence that mind (*nous*) is something pure from admixture with any other kind of substance. For Diogenes it is not mind, but the air that is its physical seat which permeates all things and thereby organizes and controls them. It is accordingly air that is to be regarded as what is strong and eternal and 'knowing many things' (fr. 8), and as thereby deserving ascription of the divinity Anaxagoras effectively predicated of mind. Mind is in fact an attribute, not a substance at all. Hence no doubt the substitution of *noēsis*, 'intelligence', for Anaxagoras' *nous*.

Only air in a particular state has the power of intelligence; namely, when hotter than atmospheric air, but cooler than that in the vicinity of the sun (fr. 5). The surviving fragments say nothing of how air can take the form of, for example, earth or water (although the doxography speaks of compression; A1, A6). We might wonder why evidence that air pervades and controls everything should suggest that it is the basic substance. No doubt the underlying thought is simply that no substance *could* be dominant without being basic.

3 Psychology and physiology

If Diogenes conceived his chief general contribution to philosophy as rescuing Anaxagorean metaphysics from dualism, his work in psychology and physiology was, as noted, more influential. Diogenes' systematic treatment of these topics challenges comparison with those of Anaxagoras and Empedocles. Following the argument given in fragment 2, he made sense perception a product of interaction between air within and air without (Theophrastus, *On the Senses* 39–45). His exposition began unusually but understandably with the best cases for his theory: smell and then hearing. A weaker explanation is provided for sight and taste however. Diogenes' fanciful analysis of the vascular system allowed him to argue that air was conveyed by blood throughout the body to various destinations, including notably the head. Following Alcmaeon he conceived of the brain as the principal seat of sensations, which were apparently construed as functions of intelligence: Diogenes observed that when we have our minds on other things, we neither see nor hear. In general, the finer the air within and the more delicate the passages through which it is conveyed, the more acute the associated perceptions.

This explanatory scheme was applied to a great variety of phenomena. To take just one, pleasure is viewed as the result of efficient mixture of air and blood in the veins permeating the whole body. Many undesirable conditions are put down to the effect of moisture or *ikmas*. Evidently a key Diogenean notion, this was used to explain such phenomena as magnetism and the flooding of the Nile (A18, A33). Its action upon internal air inhibits intelligence, as manifested in sleep and drunkenness, and may also (to Aristophanes' amusement) be evidenced in animals which breathe air close to the ground.

See also: PNEUMA §I

References and further reading

Barnes, J. (1979) *The Presocratic Philosophers*, London: Routledge & Kegan Paul. (The final chapter is an unorthodox but philosophically stimulating account of Diogenes.)

* Diogenes of Apollonia (5th century BC) Fragments, in H. Diels and W. Kranz (eds) *Die Fragmente der Vorsokratiker* (Fragments of the Presocratics), Berlin: Weidemann, 6th edn, 1952, vol. 2, 51–69. (The standard collection of the ancient sources both fragments and testimonia, the latter designated by 'A'; includes Greek texts with translations in German.)

Guthrie, W.K.C. (1962–78) *A History of Greek Philosophy*, Cambridge: Cambridge University Press, 6 vols. (The most detailed and comprehensive English-language history of early Greek thought; a serviceable treatment of Diogenes can be found in volume 2 pages 362–81.)

Kirk, G.S., Raven, J.E. and Schofield, M. (1983) *The Presocratic Philosophers*, Cambridge: Cambridge University Press, 2nd edn. (A valuable survey of Presocratic philosophy, including texts and translations; contains an engaged but judicious evaluation of Diogenes.)

Laks, A. (1983) *Diogène d'Apollonie,* Lille: Presses Universitaire de Lille and Paris: Éditions de la Maison des sciences de l'homme. (The fullest modern account of Diogenes, fundamental for further scholarly work; includes all the texts in Diels and Kranz (1952) with French translations.)

MALCOLM SCHOFIELD

DIOGENES OF OENOANDA (*c.* 2nd century AD)

The Epicurean philosopher Diogenes came from the Greek town Oenoanda in Lycia (Turkey). He is known exclusively for his massive philosophical inscription, erected in a colonnade there. Its remains contain sayings of Epicurus, plus Diogenes' own writings, mainly on physics and ethics. His Epicureanism is largely traditional, but possible innovations include talk of a future Epicurean golden age.

Diogenes is known for the inscription he erected in a colonnade in the town of Oenoanda, Lycia (Turkey), his birthplace. Most probably the inscription belongs to the second century AD. Diogenes informs the reader that he was already old and sick when he set up the inscription. We also learn that he was in contact with Epicurean friends in Athens, Chalcis, Thebes and Rhodes. The fact that he could afford to set up this enormous inscription in a public place testifies that he was a wealthy and influential man in Oenoanda.

Since 1884, 212 blocks or fragments have been discovered. The inscription probably covered a wall about 80 metres in length in the town's south stoa or colonnade, on the so-called esplanade. The text was arranged in either five or seven courses, carrying treatises on ethics, physics and old age. The ethics section (frs 28–61) was the lowest inscribed course and was underwritten by a course of maxims of EPICURUS. They support Diogenes' argument, and are clearly meant to establish its Epicurean authenticity. The physics treatise, on the next course, starts with an introduction to the whole inscription. Higher courses carried letters of Diogenes (to his friends Antipater, Dionysius, Carus and Menneas) and his maxims, as well as letters attributed to Epicurus. Above stood Diogenes' treatise *On Old Age* (frs 137–79). Each section of the text looks like an opened papyrus scroll.

Diogenes wants the physics part to be read first, and at the beginning he announces the aim of his inscription: to help those who are 'well-constituted'. Like Epicurus he regards philosophy as a therapy, and intends to offer his philosophy as a medicine not only for his fellow citizens but also for foreigners: they are all citizens of one country, the world. The inscription, closely following traditional Epicureanism, attests its author's humanity and cosmopolitanism.

The physics and ethics treatises deal mainly with standard Epicurean topics. However, one remarkable fragment of the ethics treatise describes an Epicurean golden age, a future in which justice and friendship will render the protection of citizens by institutions unnecessary (fr. 56).

In the treatise on old age (frs 137–79) Diogenes addresses young readers and repudiates their negativity about old age, in which, he maintains, the mind remains active. Homer shows that old men are excellent speakers. If slow like the elephant, the old also resemble it in intelligence. The absence of sensual desires is not a disadvantage. Poverty is more valuable than wealth.

Among the letters and maxims, the letter to Antipater (imitating Epicurus' *Letter to Pythocles* in form and content; see EPICURUS §2) sheds some light on Diogenes' life and his contacts with Epicurean friends in Greece. Philosophically, it deals with the infinite number of worlds. Other of Diogenes' fragments contain the remains of a letter to Dionysius (and Carus?) whose topics were epistemological, ethical and biographical. It speaks of Epicurus 'the herald who brought you complete salvation' (fr. 73 III 13), and we learn of Epicurus' narrow escape from death after a shipwreck. Most important are the fragments of a letter by Epicurus to his mother, which deals with visions of absent persons, the author's happiness and the fear of death, along with a plea not to send money any more since the author has sufficient (frs 125–6).

See also: EPICUREANISM §1

References and further reading

Clay, D. (1990) 'The Philosophical Inscription of Diogenes of Oenoanda: New Discoveries 1969–1983', in W. Haase (ed.) *Aufstieg und Niedergang der römischen Welt*, Berlin and New York: de Gruyter, II 36: 4, 2446–559. (Valuable survey of Diogenes' Stoa, the inscribed wall and individual documents of the inscription.)
* Diogenes of Oenoanda (*c.* 2nd century AD) Fragments, ed. M.F. Smith, *Diogenes of Oinoanda, The Epicurean Inscription*, Naples: Bibliopolis, 1993.

(Up-to-date edition, with English translation and lucid commentary, by the scholar who has discovered numerous new fragments of the inscription.)
Puech, B. and Goulet, R. (1994) 'Diogène d'Oinoanda', in R. Goulet (ed.) *Dictionnaire des Philosophes Antiques*, Paris: CNRS Éditions, vol. 2, 803–6. (Guide to the modern scholarship, with extensive bibliography.)

MICHAEL ERLER

DIOGENES OF SINOPE (412/403–324/321 BC)

Diogenes of Sinope was considered, along with Antisthenes, the founder of Cynicism. His nickname 'Cynic', literally 'doglike', reflects the highly unconventional lifestyle he lived and advocated. Radically re-evaluating mankind's relation to both nature and civilization, Diogenes redefined the individual's freedom and self-sufficiency, advocating a training (askēsis) for achieving both.

Although a historical figure, Diogenes quickly became a literary character – probably in his own lost works, certainly in those of others. Hence his life, lost writings and oral teachings are intertwined in a complex tradition comprising: (1) a biographical strand transmitted by Diogenes Laertius – itself a collage of literary and oral traditions about Diogenes; (2) the more overtly literary representations by writers such as Lucian and Dio Chrysostom (*Discourses*). Contemporary evidence for Diogenes is virtually nil.

Critical assessment of the biographical tradition is more than usually important in Diogenes' case, since his thought is transmitted to us primarily in the form of pointed anecdotes and aphorisms (*chreiai*). Diogenes was exiled from Sinope (on the southern coast of the Black Sea) for defacing the city's coins. 'Defacing the currency' was to become a central metaphor for the Cynics' critique of the tradition – driving out the counterfeit coin of conventional wisdom to make room for the authentic Cynic life lived 'according to nature'. Surprisingly, numismatic evidence discovered in the twentieth century appears to confirm the story of Diogenes' exile, but that may be the only trustworthy part of the biography. The tradition also claims that Diogenes (1) studied with ANTISTHENES, (2) discovered his vocation ('defacing the currency') by consulting an oracle and (3) was sold into slavery and spent the rest of his life as a private tutor to his master's children. Claim (1) may be chronologically impossible, and was perhaps fabricated by Stoics eager to give their school a Socratic pedigree via the Cynics. Claim (2) is suspiciously reminiscent of stories told of Socrates and of Zeno of Citium. Claim (3) conflicts with the tradition that Diogenes grew old spending his summers in Corinth and winters in Athens living in his *pithos*, a large wine-jar. In all probability, both (2) and (3) are based on literary works by or about Diogenes that were later treated biographically.

Similarly, there are several conflicting versions of Diogenes' literary activity. Two authorities denied that Diogenes had left anything in writing, yet we have two lists of works attributed to him. The first consists of thirteen dialogues (including a *Republic*), some epistles and seven tragedies. A second list, probably of Stoic origin, consists of twelve dialogues (eight of which are absent from the first list) and some letters and sayings (*chreiai*), thus implicitly denying the authenticity of Diogenes' *Republic* and of his tragedies.

Diogenes' philosophical significance was a product of the manifold traditions purporting to represent him as much as it was of the facts of his life, of which we know few. Diogenes' unconditional pursuit of happiness in the face of exile and poverty led him to challenge the most fundamental ideas and taboos of Greek civilization and to valorize nature as a source of moral insight greater than that of custom or of the existing philosophical schools. The consequences of his experiment were remarkable and lasting, not only for philosophy – Stoicism and Epicureanism emerge in the philosophical context Diogenes helped to create – but for the literary and social traditions that antiquity transmitted to Europe.

See also: CYNICS

References and further reading

* Dio Chrysostom (*c.* AD 100) *Discourses*, vol. 1, trans. J.C. Cahoon and H. Crosby, Loeb Classical Library, Cambridge, MA: Harvard University Press and London: Heinemann, 1932. (Parallel Greek text and English translation; Diogenes is represented in Orations 4, 6, 8–10.)
* Diogenes Laertius (*c.* early 3rd century AD) *Lives of the Philosophers*, trans. R.D. Hicks, *Diogenes Laertius Lives of Eminent Philosophers*, Loeb Classical Library, Cambridge, MA: Harvard University Press and London: Heinemann, 1925, 2 vols. (Parallel Greek text and English translation; Book VI is our most important source for Diogenes of Sinope.)
Giannantoni, G. (1990) *Socratis et Socraticorum Reliquiae*, Naples: Bibliopolis, 4 vols. (Ancient sources in Greek and Latin, with discussion in Italian; includes all the documentation relevant to Diogenes.)
Paquet, L. (1988) *Les Cyniques grecs: Fragments et témoinages*, Ottawa, Ont.: Les Presses de l'Université d'Ottawa. (An annotated French translation of the main Cynic fragments and testimonia.)

R. BRACHT BRANHAM

DISCOURSE SEMANTICS

Discourse and its interpretation have interested philosophers since ancient times, and have been studied in different areas of philosophy such as rhetoric, the philosophy of language and the philosophy of literature. Discourse has attracted interest from philosophers working in the continental tradition, and it received considerable attention in the 1980s from analytic philosophers, philosophers of language, linguists, cognitive scientists and computer scientists; within these fields a formal, logical analysis of discourse interpretation, or discourse semantics, has emerged.

Discourse semantics arose in an attempt to solve certain problems that affected formal theories of meaning for single sentences. These problems had to do with the interpretation of pronouns and other 'anaphoric' elements in language. A detailed examination of the data showed that the meaning of an individual sentence in a discourse could depend upon information given by previous sentences in the discourse. To analyse this dependence, discourse semantics developed a formal analysis of a discourse context and of the interaction between the meaning of a sentence and the discourse context in which it is to be interpreted. The essential idea of discourse semantics is that the meaning of a sentence is a relation between contexts. The 'input' discourse context furnishes the information needed to interpret the anaphoric elements in the sentence; the information conveyed by the sentence when added to the input context yields a new, or 'output', discourse context that can serve to interpret the next sentence in the discourse.

1   **Static semantics for discourse and its difficulties**
2   **Dynamic semantics for discourse**
3   **More elaborate discourse semantics**
4   **Conclusions**

1   Static semantics for discourse and its difficulties

To understand the development of discourse semantics, one must look at the problems that motivated its development. To do this, one must know something about the interpretation of the constituents of discourse – the constituent sentences and their constituent phrases as treated in standard formal semantics. In the 1960s, Richard MONTAGUE developed a very influential framework, Montague Grammar, for analysing how the meaning of a complex expression depends on the meanings of its constituents (see COMPOSITIONALITY; POSSIBLE WORLDS; SEMANTICS). One might think that there is nothing more to the interpretation of a discourse than simply building up the meanings of its constituent sentences and then combining them. But once a clear and precise proposal for the semantics of sentences was given by Montague Grammar, several problems emerged that showed that the interpretation of discourse would not be so simple. There are two related phenomena in semantics that cause difficulty for Montague Grammar, namely pronominal anaphora and temporal anaphora, and these have spurred advances in the analysis of discourse.

Pronominal anaphora. One problem for the Montague Grammar approach to discourse is the interpretation of anaphoric pronouns. Pronominal anaphora occurs when a pronoun refers back to some word or phrase in the preceding discourse. In the discourses below, the anaphoric pronouns 'he' and 'it' refer back respectively to a 'farmer' and a 'donkey'.

(1) A farmer owns a donkey and he beats it.
(2) A farmer owns a donkey. He beats it.
(3) If a farmer owns a donkey, he beats it.

In semantics the meaning of a discourse like (1) can be given by a formula of some logical language with a clear model-theoretic interpretation – this formula is known as the logical form of the sentence. Montague Grammar uses the language of intensional, higher-order logic, but for our purposes the only thing we need to know about this language is that indefinite noun phrases like 'a farmer' are translated as existential quantifiers and pronouns are translated as bound variables. Thus, a sentence such as (1) has the translation:

$$\exists x \exists y \, (\text{farmer}(x) \,\&\, \text{donkey}(y) \,\&\, \text{owns}\,(x, y)$$
$$\&\, \text{beats}\,(x, y))$$

The first problem for Montague Grammar is that since it gives the meaning of a discourse sentence by sentence, it is unclear how to connect the pronouns in the second sentence of (2) with the existential quantifiers that bind them in the first sentence. Another problem emerges with the attempt to treat (3), which is an example of the 'donkey sentence

problem' originally discovered by Geach (1963). The meaning of (3) is captured by the formula:

$$\forall x \forall y ((\text{farmer}(x) \,\&\, \text{donkey}(y) \,\&\, \text{owns}\,(x, y))$$
$$\rightarrow (\text{beats}\,(x, y))$$

But Montague Grammar has no uniform translation of the indefinite determiner *a* that yields a correct treatment of (1) and (3) satisfactorily; it does not provide any explanation of why the translation of indefinites is context-sensitive in this way, nor does it handle inter-sentential anaphora (see ANAPHORA).

Temporal structure of discourse. Observations by Barbara Partee and people working on the analysis of French tense in discourse first brought attention to a facet of the meaning of tenses that was missing from the best analyses of tense of the day. Those analyses took tenses to be temporal operators of the sort found in tense logic. In a French discourse like:

(4) Pierre entra dans le salon. Il s'assit sur la banquette. Il s'endorma.
(Pierre entered the room. He sat down on the sofa. He fell asleep.)

the three events introduced (Pierre's entering, his sitting down, and his falling asleep) all occur in the past if (4) is true. This much the analyses of tense were able to capture. But they miss a crucial generalization about texts like (4). The events described there are portrayed as occurring not only in the past but also in a definite sequence – that in which they are introduced in the discourse. We naturally understand the story as telling us that Pierre's entering the room occurred prior to his sitting down which in turn occurred prior to his falling asleep. On the operator view of tenses, a past-tensed sentence of the (logical) form $P\varphi$ is true just if φ holds for some time prior to the moment of speech; this view is incapable of capturing the contextual sensitivity shown in (4). Similarly incapable are views on which verbs are treated as predicates of events and the past tense introduces a relation of 'earlier than' between the event and the moment of speech (see TENSE AND TEMPORAL LOGIC).

2 Dynamic semantics for discourse

Motivated by the problems with the interpretation of pronouns in discourse, Hans Kamp (1981) and Irene Heim (1982) independently proposed not only a solution to the interpretation of anaphoric elements but a new way of looking at discourse semantics. They redefined the semantic contributions in a discourse of a sentence and its constituents. In Montague Grammar, among other accounts of discourse interpretation, the contribution of a sentence is a proposition, or, formally, a set of possible worlds in which the sentence is true. Such a proposition contributes to the content of a discourse in a simple way: the meaning of a discourse is just the intersection of all the propositions that are the meanings of the discourse's constituent sentences. For Kamp and Heim, a sentence S when interpreted in a discourse D no longer simply yields a set of worlds; S may also yield a set of discourse entities or 'discourse referents' to which elements of subsequent discourse may refer. This approach came to dominate semantics in linguistics during the 1980s and 1990s. What follows develops Kamp's approach to discourse semantics, known as 'Discourse Representation Theory' or DRT.

DRT assigns a truth-conditional meaning to a natural language discourse in two steps: the 'DRS construction procedure' and the 'correctness definition'. The first step is to construct a representation of the content of the discourse (known as a 'Discourse Representation Structure' or DRS). The ontological status of a DRS has been subject to some debate: some view it as a partial model of the discourse, others view it merely as an alternative logical form for English, still others as some sort of conceptual structure. Nevertheless, the structure of a DRS is precisely defined. It consists of a pair of sets: (1) a set, or 'universe', of discourse referents, and (2) a set of 'conditions'. Discourse referents are analogous to the domain of a partial model – they are objects talked about in the discourse – while conditions are property ascriptions to these discourse individuals. The technical definition of a DRS and DRS condition is given through a doubly recursive definition. In thinking of DRSs as partial models, DRSs as abstract structures should be distinguished from the language used to describe them. The DRS language uses a box notation – the upper part of the box lists the discourse referents in the universe of the DRS, while the bottom part of the box describes the conditions. Kamp's notation is in fact reminiscent of Peirce's existential graphs. For instance, the DRS for 'a farmer owns a donkey' is given in (K1); it tells us that the discourse speaks of two entities, one a farmer (x), one a donkey (y), and

(K1)

$x\ \ y$
farmer(x)
donkey(y)
owns(x,y)

that, according to the discourse, the farmer owns the donkey.

While Kamp develops a top-down approach to DRS construction, Wada and Asher (1986), Zeevat (1989) and Asher (1993) develop a construction procedure whereby each lexical element contributes some sort of DR-theoretic structure. These then combine following the syntactic structure of the sentence to produce the DRS for the sentence in a manner that is in the tradition of compositional Montague semantics. Noun phrases like 'a farmer' or 'a donkey' introduce a novel discourse referent into the DRS as well as a condition on that discourse referent; verbs introduce conditions on the discourse referents introduced by the noun phrases that are their syntactic arguments. Anaphoric pronouns, following the original Kamp treatment of DRT (see Kamp 1981), are treated as bound variables; they introduce new occurrences of discourse referents that have been introduced by noun phrases in antecedent discourse.

The construction of a DRS for a discourse proceeds incrementally, sentence by sentence, exploiting the syntactic parse of each sentence, and building a DRS for the discourse as a whole from DRSs for each constituent sentence. More precisely, if $\mathbf{K}_m$ is the DRS derived from the first m sentences and K_{m+1} is the DRS derived from the $m+1$st sentence, then the DRS for the discourse of $m+1$ sentences is just the DRS that combines the universes of $\mathbf{K}_m$ and K_{m+1} and their condition sets:

$$\langle(U_{\mathbf{K}_m} \cup U_{K_{m+1}}), (Con_{\mathbf{K}_m} \cup Con_{K_{m+1}})\rangle$$

So in constructing a DRS for (2), for instance, we would add to the DRS in (K1) simply the condition 'beats(x,y)' to get a correct representation for (2):

(K2)

$x\ \ y$
farmer(x)
donkey(y)
owns(x,y)
beats(x,y)

Let us now briefly look at DRT's treatment of sentence (3) given in §1. We use the same analysis of indefinite noun phrases and pronouns as introduced above, together with construction procedures for conditionals and universal quantifiers (such as the quantifier expressed by 'every farmer'). Both constructions introduce what is known as a 'complex condition' in a DRS; complex conditions consist of DRSs as arguments to some operator. For instance, 'if..., then...' introduces the following relation on DRSs, where P and Q are variables for DRSs.

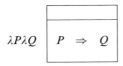

So when we have two clauses linked by 'if..., then...', the first clause gives us a DRS bound by P, while the second gives us a DRS which replaces Q. For example, 'if Mary is happy, then Fred is happy' would yield the following DRS:

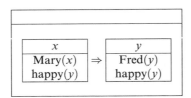

If we choose the right discourse referents for the pronouns 'he' and 'it', we get the right DR-theoretic translation for (3) in a uniform way from the treatment of the indefinite noun phrase and pronouns:

(K3)

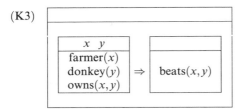

Several forms of complex conditions have been proposed in DRT to handle various connectives and quantifiers. Most prevalent are those of the form $K \Rightarrow K'$ used to represent sentences that contain a conditional or universal quantifier, and those of the form $\neg K$ which result from processing sentences in which a verbal or sentence-level negation occurs.

In order to understand what these complex conditions mean we must look at the second component of DRT, the correctness definition. The correctness definition tells us what conditions must obtain in order for a DRS, thought of as a partial model, to be properly embedded in a Tarskian model of the sort familiar from first-order logic (see MODEL THEORY). If the DRS for a discourse can be properly embedded in a model M, then we say that the discourse is true in M. A 'DRS model' is a pair

$< D, I >$ where D is a non-empty set (a domain of individuals) and I is a function that assigns n-tuples from D^n to atomic n-ary conditions of DRSs. Atomic conditions are those conditions that are derived from natural-language nouns, verbs and some adjectives – the sort that are contained in the DRSs for (1) and (2). A DRS K is properly embedded in a DRS model M if and only if there is a function f from the universe of K into the universe of M such that all the conditions of K are satisfied in M. What we have to do now is to define satisfaction of a condition in K. Intuitively the idea is simple: for a condition in the DRS to be satisfied in a model, there must be a mapping or embedding of the universe of K in the universe of M such that the objects $f(x_1), \ldots, f(x_n)$ bear the relation that the DRS condition predicates of $x_1, \ldots, x_n$. For an atomic DRS condition of the form $\Psi(\alpha_1, \ldots, \alpha_n)$, where $\alpha_1, \ldots, \alpha_n$ are discourse referents, $\Psi(\alpha_1, \ldots, \alpha_n)$ is satisfied in a DRS model M relative to an embedding function f if and only if $\langle f(\alpha_1), \ldots, f(\alpha_n) \rangle$ is an element of the interpretation of Ψ in M. A complex condition of the form $K \Rightarrow K'$ is satisfied in a DRS model M relative to an embedding function f if and only if for every function g that extends f to a proper embedding of K there is an extension h of g that is a proper embedding of K'. A complex condition of the form $\neg K$ is satisfied in a DRS model M relative to an embedding function f if and only if there is no function g that extends f to a proper embedding of K. Intuitively, we see how the interpretation of these DRS conditions captures the definition of a material conditional, a universal quantifier and negation. Technically we have a simultaneous recursive definition of proper embedding of a DRS in a model and of the satisfaction of a DRS condition with respect to a model. (For details see Kamp and Reyle 1993.)

In applying this definition of truth to (K3), we get the intuitively right truth-conditions for the sentence: for every pair of objects such that one is a farmer and the other is a donkey and the farmer owns the donkey, the farmer beats the donkey. These truth-conditions are the same as those for the universally quantified sentence, 'every farmer who owns a donkey beats it'. While some problems in the interpretation of pronouns have been uncovered in further studies on anaphora in a dynamic semantic setting, the dynamic semantic approach represents a considerable advance over Montague Grammar's approach to the interpretation of pronouns in discourse.

DRT and temporal anaphora. Following Davidson (1967), DRT takes verbs to introduce conditions on eventualities (events or states) (see DAVIDSON, D. §2). DRT postulates a complex algorithm that serves to connect by means of temporal relations the eventuality introduced by the main verb of a sentence with the eventualities already present in the DRS built up from previous discourse. In declarative form, we formulate the results of the algorithm as follows. If α and β are two sentences that follow one after another in the discourse and both introduce eventualities with a verb in the *passé simple*, we have (where $<$ is the 'earlier than' relation):

$$PS(\alpha) \& PS(\beta) \rightarrow e_\alpha < e_\beta$$

If past tense also implies that the event described by the verb occurs prior to the speech time, this rule in effect predicts just the right temporal interpretation of discourse (4). The complex DRS construction procedure has been applied to basic tense forms of French and English (see Kamp and Reyle 1993 for an extensive discussion and bibliography).

Limitations of dynamic semantics. DRT makes an important contribution to our understanding of how the discourse context affects pronominal and temporal interpretation. But DRT does not do justice to the complex interaction of pragmatic and semantic factors in discourse, and this leads to incorrect predictions about the way anaphora, both temporal and pronominal, is treated in DRT.

A clear example of where DRT goes wrong is with its analysis of temporal anaphora. DRT is right to make the contributions of tense depend upon the discourse context. But it attempts to make the temporal structure of a text almost completely dependent on the tense forms used in the text. In most natural languages, however, the temporal structure of the events introduced in a text is underdetermined by the sequence of tense forms. In particular, the rule above, which is a consequence of the DRS construction procedure, is false for French – a point of which some of the earliest workers on tense in DRT were aware – or English. Consider the following examples (from Lascarides and Asher 1993):

(5a) John entered the room. Fred greeted him.

(5b) John fell. Fred pushed him.

These two discourses employ the same sequence of tense forms, yet they suggest different temporal structures. DR-theorists have been forced to revise the construction procedure and to abandon the view that the tense forms and the order of the sentences in a discourse alone determine temporal structure. This conclusion follows not only from an examination of the English simple past but also from a careful look at the data concerning the French *plus que parfait* (see Asher and Bras 1992) and the English pluperfect (Lascarides and Asher 1992).

One might ask, what in combination with tense sequences determines the temporal structure? One proposal is that a more developed view of discourse structure is needed. Originally suggested by the computer scientist and artificial intelligence (AI) researcher Jerry Hobbs (1985), this thesis has been worked out in the context of a formal discourse semantics by Lascarides and Asher (1993). This approach to tense is part of a more general view: discourse structure has systematic effects on discourse interpretation, which it is the task of discourse semantics to study. As we shall see, both temporal and pronominal anaphora require a more elaborate discourse semantics.

3 More elaborate discourse semantics

When interpreters read a text, they naturally understand it as divided into parts related in various ways. Some parts form a narrative, others furnish a background to a narrative or an explanation of some action, still others may elaborate other parts of the text. Sometimes these divisions and the relations between them are signalled by punctuation and the presence of certain words in the text. But often interpreters infer the appropriate divisions and discourse relations without these cues. This sort of structure is completely missing from the treatment of discourse in DRT, but it has been recognized as an important aspect of discourse in other disciplines – for example, literary theory and the natural language processing (NLP) area of AI (see ARTIFICIAL INTELLIGENCE). In the mid-1970s, computer scientists like Roger Shank claimed text-understanding systems and text-information retrieval systems to be one of the central goals of NLP research in AI. This early interest led to a substantial amount of research on discourse structure in the mid to late 1980s (Polanyi 1988; Hobbs 1985; Grosz and Sidner 1985). This work has concentrated on the discourse structure of written texts, though analyses of highly structured, task-oriented dialogues have yielded important insights. Many divergent positions have been taken, but several uncontroversial conclusions have been drawn from these studies: (1) discourse is structured and can be represented by a set of objects (propositions or bits of text) related by discourse relations; (2) this structure is hierarchical and recursive. For discourse semantics, we must integrate the view of discourse structure elaborated by these authors with a theory of meaning. This connection between semantics and discourse structure, however, is lacking in most of the discourse theories in AI.

A richer notion of discourse structure is incorporated into the framework of dynamic semantics in

Asher (1993), resulting in a nontrivial extension of DRT known as 'segmented Discourse Representation Theory' or SDRT. SDRT is one way to integrate discourse structure for texts and semantics. Another approach can be found in the works of Scha and his colleagues, but it exploits a different version of dynamic semantics.

According to SDRT, every discourse is analysed into a representational structure called a 'segmented DRS' or SDRS, and this is in turn embedded into a complete model that furnishes truth-conditions for the discourse. The model theory for SDRSs is somewhat involved, because the models must allow for quantification over and reference to dynamic propositions (for details see Asher 1993 or Asher 1996). An SDRS, like a DRS, is a pair of sets; but unlike a DRS the elements of the first set are either DRSs or SDRSs, while the second pair consists of a set of conditions in which discourse relations are predicated of elements in the first set. In comparing an SDRS for a narrative text with a DRS for the same text, we would see that the DRS is segmented into elements of the first set in the SDRS with discourse relations holding between these elements. These elements or 'constituents' of an SDRS serve several useful functions. First of all, they constitute referents for anaphoric pronouns (like 'this' in the example below) whose antecedents are facts or propositions:

(6) One plaintiff was passed over for promotion. Another didn't get a pay increase for five years. A third received a lower wage than men doing the same work. But the jury didn't believe this (any of this).

In the example above, we appear to have two possible antecedents (depending to some degree on how this is stressed): the proposition formed by the discourse as a whole and the proposition given by the last sentence. In SDRT these two anaphoric possibilities and only these two anaphoric possibilities are predicted; they result from two different, acceptable places to which the new information contained in the last sentence can be attached to the SDRS built up from the previous three sentences. Below we have a pictorial representation of the two SDRSs that could be constructed for (6). $K_1, \ldots, K_4$ represent the DRSs derived from the four sentences of the discourse; K_0' is a topic that results from the SDRS construction and the constraints on Narration (every Narration must have a nontrivial topic); the shadowed letters represent complex constituents or constituents that are SDRSs. The lines represent membership, while $\Downarrow$ represents a particular type of discourse relation (like Elaboration) that introduces a hierarchical structure into an SDRS. Narr stands for Narration, Elab for

Elaboration, and Contr for Contrast. Notice the two different positions of attachment for K_4.

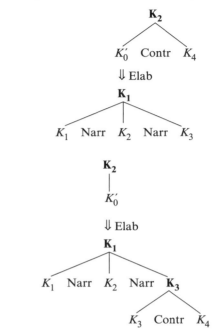

The crucial task for a discourse semantics like SDRT is to specify a procedure that will enable us to construct a discourse representation. In DRT the discourse representation is built up from the syntactic structure and a translation procedure for syntactic elements in the parse tree. SDRT exploits the DRS construction procedure to build DRSs for clauses, and it also makes use of the constraints DRT places on anaphora resolution. But in SDRT we need more information to be able to deduce where to attach new information in the antecedently built-up representation and by means of which discourse relation to attach it. The constraints on appropriate attachment sites are defined configurationally, following much of the work on discourse structure in AI. But the difficult part is to infer the appropriate discourse relation. Sometimes certain cue words or phrases indicate the presence of particular discourse relations, but those discourse relations may be present even when there are no cues. For instance, consider the following pairs:

(7a) John went to jail. He embezzled funds from the pension account.

(7b) John went to jail, because he embezzled funds from the pension account.

(8a) Mary went to school. She met with her students. She went home.

(8b) Mary went to school. Then she met with her students. Afterwards she went home.

Discourses (7a) and (7b) on the one hand and (8a) and (8b) on the other, lend themselves to the same interpretation. In the examples in (7), the second clause or sentence gives us the explanation for what happened in the first; while in (8), we read the clauses in each as narrating a sequence of events that are in the order that they are introduced in the text. Yet only in (7b) and (8b) are these interpretations fully determined by the semantic contributions of special 'clue' words like 'because' or the temporal adverbials in (8b). In (7a) and (8a), we infer the presence of an Explanation relation or a Narration relation based on pragmatic principles and the contents of the constituents the discourse relations tie together in the SDRSs for these discourses. However, this inference is not deductively valid; within a richer discourse context, we can cancel, for instance, the inference that the second sentence in (7a) offers an explanation of what happened in the first:

(7c) John went to jail. He embezzled funds from the pension account. But that is not why he went to jail.

But it also seems that the explanation relation is undeniably there in (7a). Thus, we must have a means of inferring discourse relations by default; the default or 'nonmonotonic' inference of a discourse relation R can be overridden in cases where we have information in the context that is inconsistent with our conclusion that R holds. SDRT uses facts about the discourse context, the contents of the constituents including the lexical contents of particular words, world knowledge and pragmatic principles, to infer discourse relations nonmonotonically. An attempt to code all of this knowledge explicitly for certain simple examples is given in Lascarides and Asher (1993).

Once we have inferred that some discourse relation R relates new information to some available attachment point in the SDRS constructed from the preceding discourse, we can update this SDRS with the new information. But this updating does not consist in simple addition. It also requires in many cases the revision of the contents of the constituents in the SDRS. It is in the process of constituent revision that anaphora resolution and the determination of temporal structure are accomplished in SDRT. For instance, consider again the discourse in (4). The *passé simple* of the verbs in this text all introduce the simple DRS condition saying that the eventuality described by the verb occurred prior to the speech point. There is no attempt in the semantics to link up the eventuality with the temporal structure built up antecedently, as there is in DRT. But now the underlying logical inference mechanisms of SDRT discussed above lead us to conclude that Narration relates the constituents α and β derived from the first two sentences and the constituents β and χ derived from the second and third sentence. According to SDRT, Narration has certain temporal effects: Narration $(\alpha, \beta) \rightarrow e_\alpha < e_\beta$. So once we have attached the three constituents in (4) with Narration, we immediately conclude that the text gives us a sequence of events that follows the order in which these events are introduced in the text. The effect of Narration is one way to formulate precisely part of Grice's maxim 'be orderly'. The order of presentation of the events in the text reflects their temporal order (see IMPLICATURE §4). But the pragmatic principles appealed to in the formalization of Lascarides and Asher (1993) and used to infer that Narration holds between these constituents are a good deal more specific than the general Gricean maxims of conversation, and they are expressed in logic.

In (5b) additional information contained in the two clauses leads us to defeat the inference to Narration and to conclude that a different discourse relation – Explanation – holds between the two constituents of the SDRS. Explanation has different temporal consequences from Narration: Explanation $(\alpha, \beta) \rightarrow \neg(e_\alpha < e_\beta)$ and, where ' > ' is a weak conditional used to represent default patterns, Explanation $(\alpha, \beta) > (e_\beta < e_\alpha)$. So we conclude that in (5b) the pushing came *before* the falling, as intuitions would dictate. Thus, while DRT attempted to derive the temporal structure of a text from the semantics of the sequence of tenses in a discourse alone, SDRT exploits not only the compositional semantics but also many other sources of information that contribute to discourse structure to determine temporal structure.

4 Conclusions

Because of the rapidity with which the field of discourse semantics has evolved, it is hard to say exactly where the field will develop or even whether it will continue as a field. It is quite unclear whether DRT or SDRT will remain active research areas. SDRT has been applied not only to the central discourse semantic concerns of temporal and pronominal anaphora, but it has also helped in analysing the spatiotemporal structure of texts (Asher *et al.* 1994), the role of discourse structure in lexical disambiguation (Asher and Lascarides 1995), and the interactions between discourse structure and speakers' and interpreters' cognitive states – in particular their beliefs and discourse goals (Asher and Lascarides 1994). To advance further, SDRT and other formalisms for discourse semantics require a better understanding of the organization of the lexicon and of the role of general world knowledge. As discourse semantics moves to give a formally precise analysis (capitalizing on empirical studies) of discourse interpretation in dialogue, other factors like the interaction between semantics and speech acts will have to be taken into account (see SPEECH ACTS).

See also: PRAGMATICS

References and further reading

* Asher, N. (1993) *Reference to Abstract Objects in Discourse*, Dordrecht: Kluwer. (This book (referred to in §3) introduces SDRT to take account of rhetorical relations and their effects on truth-conditional content. It applies SDRT to propositional anaphora and VP ellipsis.)

* —— (1996) 'Mathematical Treatments of Discourse Contexts', *Proceedings of the Tenth Amsterdam Conference on Formal Semantics*, Amsterdam: ILLC Publications, vol. 1, 21–40. (This article gives a revised, improved version of SDRT. It is a much shorter introduction to SDRT than Asher 1993.)

* Asher, N., Aurnague, M., Bras, M., Sablayrolles, P. and Vieu, L. (1994) 'Computing the Spatiotemporal Structure of Discourse', in H. Hunt, R. Muskens and G. Rentier (eds) *Proceedings of the First International Workshop on Computational Semantics*, Tilburg: Tilburg University Publications, 11–20. (This article uses SDRT to model the spatio-temporal structure of discourse.)

* Asher, N. and Bras, M. (1992) 'The Temporal Structure of French Texts within Segmented Discourse Representation Theory', in M. Aurnague, A. Borillo and M. Bras (eds) *Semantics of Time, Space, Movement and Spatio-Temporal Reasoning*, Working Papers of the 4th International Workshop on Time and Space, IRIT Working Papers, Toulouse: Université Paul Sabatier, 203–18.

* Asher, N. and Lascarides, A. (1994) 'Intentions and Information in Discourse', *Annual Proceedings of the American Computational Linguistics Meetings*, 34–41. (This paper addresses the information flow between discourse structure and cognitive states in a couple of examples. Referred to in §4.)

* —— (1995) 'Lexical Disambiguation in a Discourse Context', *Journal of Semantics* 12 (1): 69–108. (This paper applies SDRT to lexical disambiguation and

shows how discourse structure can affect this task. Referred to in §4.)

* Davidson, D. (1967) 'The Logical Form of Action Sentences', in N. Rescher (ed.) *The Logic of Decision and Action*, Pittsburgh, PA: The University Press, 81–95. (In this article, Davidson proposes that verbs are predicates of events.)

* Geach, P.T. (1963) *Reference and Generality*, Ithaca, NY: Cornell University Press. (This book is a collection of Geach's influential articles, in which among other things the puzzle about donkey sentences (referred to in §1) is introduced.)

* Grice, H.P. (1967) *Logic and Conversation. William James Lectures*, repr. in *Studies in the Ways of Words*, Cambridge, MA: Harvard University Press, 1989. (The introduction of conversational 'maxims', which are referred to in §3.)

Groenendijk, J. and Stokhof, M. (1990) 'Dynamic Predicate Logic', in H. Kamp (ed.) *Dyana Deliverable*, 2.5a. (This paper introduces an alternative approach to dynamic semantics from DRT as presented in Kamp 1981.)

* Grosz, B. and Sidner, C. (1985) 'The Structure of Discourse Structure', Palo Alto: SRI, SRI Technical Note 369. (This paper gives a very influential view of discourse structure and argues for a parallel between discourse structure and the intentions of the speaker. Referred to in §3.)

* Heim, I. (1982) *The Semantics of Indefinite and Definite Noun Phrases*, Amherst, MA: University of Massachusetts Press. (Referred to in §2; Heim's Ph.D. thesis offers an alternative way of developing dynamic semantics to Kamp 1981 and is close to the views presented in Groenendijk and Stokhof 1990.)

* Hobbs, J. (1985) 'On the Coherence and Structure of Discourse', Stanford, CA: Center for the Study of Language and Information, report no. CSLI-85-37. (This paper introduces and argues for the idea that various anaphoric phenomena may be dependent upon discourse structure. Referred to in §§2–3.)

* Kamp, H. (1981) 'A Theory of Truth and Semantic Representation', in J. Groenendijk, T. Janssen and M. Stokhof (eds) *Formal Methods in the Study of Language*, Amsterdam: Mathematisch Centrum Tracts, 277–322; repr. in J. Groenendijk *et al.* (eds) *Truth, Interpretation and Information*, Dordrecht: Foris, 1984, 1–41. (This article (referred to in §2) contains the original presentation of DRT. It is difficult to read but is the principal source for many of the developments in dynamic semantics.)

* Kamp, H. and Reyle, U. (1993) *From Discourse to Logic; Introduction to Model-Theoretic Semantics of Natural Language, Formal Logic and Discourse Representation Theory*, Dordrecht: Kluwer. (This

book is an introductory textbook to DRT that extends considerably the semantic coverage of the theory from that given in Kamp 1981. Referred to in §2.)

* Lascarides, A. and Asher, N. (1992) 'The Pluperfect in Narrative Discourse', in M. Aurnague, A. Borillo, M. Borillo and M. Bras (eds) *Semantics of Time, Space, Movement and Spatio-Temporal Reasoning*, Working Papers of the 4th International Workshop on Time and Space, IRIT Working Papers, Toulouse: Université Paul Sabatier, 183–217. (A condensed version of this paper called 'A Semantics and Pragmatics of the Pluperfect' appears on pages 250–9 of *Proceedings of the 6th Conference of the European Chapter of Computational Linguistics*, published in Utrecht in 1993. These papers discuss the pluperfect in narrative discourse from the perspective of SDRT.)

* —— (1993) 'Temporal Interpretation, Discourse Relations, and Commonsense Entailment', *Linguistics and Philosophy* 16: 437–93. (This paper criticizes the analysis of tense within DRT and proposes a new simplified account using the SDRT framework. Referred to in §§2 and 3.)

* Partee, B. (1973) 'Some Structural Analogies between Tenses and Pronouns in English', *Journal of Philosophy* 70: 601–9. (In this article Partee argues that tenses like the simple past exhibit a contextual sensitivity in interpretation similar to that of anaphoric pronouns.)

* Polanyi, L. (1988) 'A Formal Model of the Structure of Discourse', *Pragmatics* 1–88. (This article contains another influential approach to discourse structure, with powerful treatments of interruptions and discourse repairs. Referred to in §3.)

Prust, J. and Scha, R. (1990) 'A Discourse Perspective on Verb Phrase Anaphora', in M. Stokhof and L. Torenvliet (eds) *Proceedings of the Seventh Amsterdam Colloquium*, Amsterdam: ITLI Publications, 451–74. (This article develops the theory of discourse parallelism in detail and points to the use of dynamic semantics as developed by Groendijk and Stokhof as the interpretive component.)

* Scha, R. and Polanyi, L. (1988) 'An Augmented Context Free Grammar for Discourse', *Proceedings of COLING*, Budapest. (This article proposes a 'discourse syntax', in which trees model discourse structures, together with an interpretation of the leaves of those trees. The interpretation uses Montague Grammar, however, and is not dynamic.)

* Wada, H. and Asher, N. (1986) 'BLDRS: A Prolog Implementation of LFG and DR Theory', *Proceedings of the 11th International Conference on Computational Linguistics*, Bonn, 540–5. (This was one early implementation of DRT and suggested a compositional treatment of dynamic semantics.)

* Zeevat, H. (1989) 'A Compositional Approach to Discourse Representations', *Linguistics and Philosophy* 12: 95–131. (This paper gives a detailed treatment of how to build up DRSs in a compositional way, similar to the construction of formulas representing meanings of expressions in Montague Grammar. Referred to in §2.)

NICHOLAS ASHER

DISCOVERY, LOGIC OF

Bacon, Descartes, Newton and other makers of the Scientific Revolution claimed to have found and even used powerful logics or methods of discovery, step-by-step procedures for systematically generating new truths in mathematics and the natural sciences. Method of discovery was also the prime method of justification: generation by correct method was something akin to logical derivation and thus the strongest justification a claim could have. The 'logic' of these methods was deductive, inductive or both. By the mid-nineteenth century, logic of discovery was yielding to the more flexible and theory-tolerant method of hypothesis as the 'official' method of science. In the twentieth century, Karl Popper and most logical positivists completed the methodological reversal from generativism to consequentialism by setting their hypothetico-deductive method against logic of discovery. What is epistemologically important, they said, is not how new claims are generated but how they fare in empirical tests of their predictive consequences. They demoted discovery to the status of historical anecdote and psychological process. Since the late 1950s, however, there has been a revival of interest in methodology of discovery on two fronts – logical and historical. An earlier explosion of work in symbolic logic had led to automata theory, computers, and then artificial intelligence. Meanwhile, a maturing history of science was furnishing information on science as a process, on how historical actors and communities actually discovered or constructed their claims and practices. Now, in the 1980s and 1990s, liberal epistemologists once again admit discovery as a legitimate topic for philosophy of science. Yet attempts to both naturalize and to socialize inquiry pose new challenges to the possibility of logics of discovery. Its strong associations with 'the' method of science makes logic of discovery a target of postmodernist attack, but a more flexible construal is defensible.

1   Logic and method

A logic of discovery in the narrowest sense would be a valid reasoning procedure that leads to new knowledge. More broadly, 'logic of discovery' includes routine methods and research techniques that contain inductive or heuristic steps and sometimes produce new knowledge claims that need further justification. A heuristic procedure is a shortcut that compromises the reliability of an algorithm for greater speed or efficiency. In the broadest sense of discovery as an achievement, 'logic of discovery' or the discovery process includes the entire research effort from the first tentative posing of a problem to the 'final' testing and accepting of a solution as adequate.

Does deductive logic constitute a logic of discovery in the narrow sense? The usual objection – that deductive argument is not ampliative – confuses logical with epistemic novelty and 'amplification'. True, the conclusion contains no more logical content than the premises collectively, but it may contain more epistemic content, relative to the current state of knowledge. Strictly deductive arguments in mathematics, logic and the sciences have led to astounding (epistemically novel) conclusions. Since deductive arguments may have empirical premises, and hence empirical conclusions, this reply also blunts the related objection that deductive methodology is a priori and so cannot generate new empirical claims. Deductive reasoning from what we already 'know' can yield empirical conclusions that are epistemically novel, even revolutionary; for example, the Lorentz transformation is derivable from a mathematically generalized form of the Galilean transformation plus the 'empirical fact' that the speed of light is constant (see RELATIVITY THEORY, PHILOSOPHICAL SIGNIFICANCE OF §1).

A more serious objection to deductive logic of discovery is that it is not a method or procedure and hence provides no guidance to discovery. It is a logic of justification that tells us whether a proof is valid, but it does not show us how to find such proofs.

Relaxing deductive strictures to allow inductive methods does yield low-level logics of discovery. An example is Reichenbach's inductive method, based on repeated self-correcting applications of his 'straight rule' (see REICHENBACH, H. §3). Factor analysis and other probabilistic and statistical methods furnish inductive discovery procedures, but we cannot expect these methods alone to produce novel, deep-structural theories.

Another way in which to 'relax' deductive logic into a useful method is to add heuristic rules, for example, rules that instruct us to search first for an answer here or to try A, B and C, in that order. Heuristic rules in the form of 'production rules' (if the situation is X, then do Y) are central to the work of Allen Newell, Herbert Simon and others in artificial intelligence (AI) (see ARTIFICIAL INTELLIGENCE §2). Their motivating idea is that discovery is problem-solving behaviour; hence, what we already know about problem solving can be transferred to methodology of discovery. And we know that problem solving typically involves heuristic search through spaces or 'trees' of possible solutions. They claim that their BACON and KEKADA programs have rediscovered laws of Kepler, Black, Ohm, Krebs and others (see Langley et al. 1987).

While Simon's group prefers to employ very general heuristics, others employ heuristics that are highly content- and context-specific. In effect they answer the above a priori objection by employing heuristics laden with theoretical and empirical content specific to the discipline or even the particular problem at hand. In AI this corresponds to the move from general problem solvers to knowledge-based or 'expert' and case-based systems. This move is motivated by the quest for greater problem-solving power. Roughly speaking, the more powerful the program, the more specific its sphere of application.

Developments in AI represent the 'logical' wing of methodology of discovery. The 'historical' wing was inspired by a post-war 'internalist' history of science, which showed that typical discoveries are discursive, structured in time. Accordingly, historical philosophers reject as overly romantic the view that discoveries are momentary, irrational inspirations. But finding no uniform logic of discovery, some defend the epistemic interest of discovery by retreating from logic to claiming the rationality of discovery and by contending that mode of discovery can be relevant to justification and hence to epistemology. Some writers interpose a third stage – prior appraisal, preliminary evaluation or heuristic appraisal – between original generation of ideas and 'final' justification. Few historicists fully embrace AI accounts of discovery. Historicists doubt whether we do know enough about problem solving in general to capture the richness of historical investigations in the form of AI programs.

AI advocates retort that the historical approach is too vague to explain much. An adequate explanation of historical discoveries must be 'computational': it must furnish a program capable of actually re-making the discovery in question, given the historically relevant problems and data. On strong versions of this view, an adequate discovery explanation posits something akin to a constructive proof already available to the historical actors and used by them to make that discovery! Historicists reply that this demand puts the cart before the horse and imputes foreknowledge to the actors; that, typically, routinized problem-solving procedures are later, refined products or parts of the total discovery rather than antecedently available explainers of it. Historicists complain that the AI programs employ cleaned-up textbook versions of Kepler's and others' problems and data and thus illegitimately reverse the order of knowing by imposing present conceptions on the past. They whiggishly sacrifice historical reality to AI production values.

2   Is there a logic of discovery?

The question is ambiguous and has been understood in at least three ways.

(1) Does there exist, in the abstract mathematical sense, one or more logics (routine methods) of discovery?

(2) Do/did scientists actually possess one or more logics of discovery?

(3) If so, does their knowledge of methods of discovery explain any historical discoveries?

To those who engage in highly formal studies of type (1), for example machine learning theory, historical issues are simply irrelevant. For them the question of existence is mathematical-ontological, not historical. However, a formal existence proof does not in itself produce a method actually usable on the frontier of research. Accordingly, most methodologists have been more interested in (2) and (3). (2) puts the question in epistemological rather than ontological terms, while (3) concerns historical and historiographic application.

Is there a logic or method of discovery in senses (2) or (3), a systematic and routine way of attaining new knowledge? Can the Scientific Revolution be partially explained in terms of new methods of discovery? Most methodologists agree that there is no single method of discovery, let alone a single 'method of science', understood as something that gives precise direction to inquiry. However, in a weaker and more local sense, we surely do possess numerous routinized problem-solving methods, procedures that would immensely impress a Descartes or a Newton. While these procedures do not, all by themselves, generate deep new theories, they do help us organize in fruitful ways both extant knowledge and our knowledge-productive powers; and the semi-automated (computer-aided) modelling techniques available in many

sciences can guide the construction of serious, deep theory candidates (see MODELS).

Actually, the epistemic importance of discovery, here understood as initial generation of a claim, would seem to be secure, whether or not there is a method or even a rationality of discovery in some pre-specified sense. For if we are ever to find true, correct or adequate claims and techniques, they must first be generated in some way, whether by a rational, methodical process or not. A correct claim has no chance of being selected (justified) unless a discovery process first puts it on the table for further consideration. Thus, manner of generation is relevant to epistemology. But this point must not be overrated, for the epistemic importance of discovery in this broad sense does not entail the existence of a method or logic, or even the rationality, of discovery.

The principal objection to there being rules for discovery is that 'creative routine' is a contradiction-in-terms. Romantic poets long ago raised this objection: originality, by definition, cannot be a product of rules. (They do have a point, but do they not also confuse epistemic and logical novelty?) More recently, from a different quarter, evolutionary epistemologists such as Karl POPPER (1959) and Donald Campbell (1960) have contended that 'logic of discovery' is an oxymoron. They in effect raise the a priori objection of §1 from the opposite side: a genuine logic of discovery is impossible, for it would require prescience or clairvoyance – knowing now what we shall only find out later. On the frontier of knowledge, says Campbell, we can only proceed blindly. At the absolute frontier of research, there can be no method to guide us. All genuine creativity in the arts and sciences amounts to blind variation plus selective retention (BV + SR), which is basically the mechanism of biological evolution. This claim threatens both AI and historical methodologies of discovery.

Methodologists of discovery respond that actual research, even on the frontier, looks more directed than this; hence, there remains some scope for method, with its concern for economy of research. From the perspective of methodology as a sort of managerial science of our limited epistemic resources, BV + SR is the most wasteful form of production there is. It introduces no 'quality control at the source' but instead tests and discards almost everything at the justificatory 'selection' stage. Reducing discovery to blind luck is precisely what Bacon and Descartes wished to avoid. And, in fact, historical investigators have nearly always been guided by powerful constraints at the generation stage. Evolutionary epistemologists reply that guiding heuristics are often available but that we must consider them, in turn, as ultimately products of previous hierarchies of

BV + SR. Thus it would be wrong to see Campbell and Simon as being totally opposed.

3 Some problems and prospects

Many critics dismiss logic of discovery as a historically dated subject; yet, understood as a broad topic area rather than a specific method, it engages several intellectual developments. We can conceive logic of discovery as the study of knowledge amplification in all its forms; whence it embraces all the ways in which scientific claims are constructed. We need not cast the issues in terms of false dilemmas such as history versus logic, social constructivism versus realism and logic versus rhetoric. On the contrary, discovery logics (routinized modes of problem solving, model construction, and data analysis) are themselves discovered or constructed and maintained as succeeding generations reconstruct and refine the work of their predecessors. And the rhetoric of inquiry (including problem representation, modelling, learning by example, and point-of-view in problem solving) is crucial to creative cognition. Rhetoric helps both to familiarize the unfamiliar and to de-familiarize the familiar. KUHN (1962) and current AI and cognitive psychological work on learning by example, by exemplars rather than rules, suggests that the rhetoric of inquiry is, in part, a sort of fuzzy logic of discovery. Kuhnian exemplars constitute a system of rhetorical places or concrete models for ongoing work at the frontier. It is noteworthy that nearly every philosophical account of learning, theory structure, theory reduction, modelling, and so on, ultimately depends on analogy, metaphor, similarity relations, and other rhetorical tropes.

Heuristic appraisal, the evaluation of the promise or fertility of a problem, theory, technique or research proposal is a 'discovery' topic that deserves more study. It is immensely important, as scientists and funding committees must base nearly all of their decisions on heuristic appraisal. But how is it possible to go beyond an item's 'track record' to evaluate its future promise? Here discovery intersects the central epistemological problems of futurology: what can we know about possible futures, and how?

A related issue, the more important insofar as successful logics of discovery are local and content-specific, is to what extent these methods can be applied in other areas. This is one form of the problem of transfer of technology and connects with problems of standardization. There may be no scientific method that is at once universal and deeply instructive, but scientists nonetheless want to generalize the more modest results that they do have, to make as much of the world as possible scientifically intelligible. Far

from presupposing the existence of a fixed scientific method, logics of discovery are themselves products of discovery/construction. Even the logical and rhetorical discovery and constitution of new sciences falls under discovery, broadly understood.

See also: HANSON, N.R.; SCIENTIFIC METHOD

References and further reading

Baird, D. (1992) *Inductive Logic: Probability and Statistics*, Englewood Cliffs, NJ: Prentice Hall. (Accessible text with a chapter on factor analysis and discovery.)

Bechtel, W. and Richardson, R. (1993) *Discovering Complexity: Decomposition and Localization as Strategies in Scientific Research*, Princeton, NJ: Princeton University Press. (A study of research strategies in the biological and behavioural sciences.)

* Campbell, D.T. (1960) 'Blind Variation and Selective Retention in Creative Thought as in Other Knowledge Processes', *Psychological Review* 67: 380–400. (A classic, readable presentation of an evolutionary epistemological account of creativity.)

Darden, L. (1991) *Theory Change in Science: Strategies from Mendelian Genetics*, Oxford: Oxford University Press. (Theory construction in twentieth-century biology, informed by AI.)

Kelly, K. (1996) *The Logic of Reliable Inquiry*, Oxford: Oxford University Press. (An excellent, technical treatment of the formal learning theory approach to discovery.)

Kantorovich, A. (1993) *Scientific Discovery: Logic and Tinkering*, Buffalo, NY: SUNY Press. (An attempt to work out a naturalistic account in detail.)

Kleiner, S. (1993) *Scientific Discovery: A Theory of the Rationality of Science*, Dordrecht: Kluwer. (Logic of questions applied to Darwin's work.)

* Kuhn, T.S. (1962) *The Structure of Scientific Revolutions*, Chicago, IL: University of Chicago Press; 2nd edn, 1970. (The contemporary classic that marks the transition from logical positivism and Popper to historical philosophy, sociology and psychology of science.)

* Langley, P., Simon, H.A., Bradshaw, G. and Zytkow, J. (1987) *Scientific Discovery*, Cambridge, MA: MIT Press. (An accessible presentation of largely data-driven AI discovery programs such as BACON.)

Laudan, L. (1981) *Science and Hypothesis*, Dordrecht: Reidel. (Essays on the emergence of 'the' method of hypothesis, in opposition to methodologies of discovery.)

Newell, A. and Simon, H.A. (1972) *Human Problem*

Solving, Englewood Cliffs, NJ: Prentice Hall. (A classical, reconstructed summary of their work since the 1950s.)

Nickles, T. (1980) 'Scientific Discovery, Logic, and Rationality' and 'Scientific Discovery', in *Case Studies*, Dordrecht: Reidel. (Conference papers, mostly taking an historical approach; extensive introduction and references.)

—— (1998) 'Discovery', in W. Newton-Smith (ed.) *A Companion to the Philosophy of Science*, Oxford: Blackwell. (Expands on several points in this entry.)

* Popper, K.R. (1959) *The Logic of Scientific Discovery*, New York: Basic Books. (Popper defends his hypothetico-deductive method against inductivist and other methods of discovery.)

Shrager, J. and Langley, P. (eds) (1990) *Computational Models of Scientific Discovery and Theory Formation*, San Mateo, CA: Morgan Kaufmann. (A good sample of 1980s work in AI, including Kulkarni and Simon's KEKADA.)

Wimsatt, W. (1980) 'Reductionistic Research Strategies and their Biases in the Units of Selection Controversy', in T. Nickles (ed.) *Case Studies*, 213–59. (A biological case study of heuristics and their limits; combines insights of Simon and Campbell.)

THOMAS NICKLES

DISCRIMINATION

A principle forbidding discrimination is widely used to criticize and prohibit actions and policies that disadvantage racial, ethnic and religious groups, women and homosexuals. Discriminatory actions often rely on unfavourable group stereotypes and the belief that members of certain groups are not worthy of equal treatment. A prohibition of discrimination applies to the distribution of important benefits such as education and jobs, and says that people are not to be awarded or denied such benefits on grounds of characteristics such as race, ethnicity, religion or gender. Attempts have been made to expand this principle to cover institu-institutional discrimination. Discrimination is morally wrong because its premise that one group is less worthy than another is insulting to its victims, because it harms its victims by reducing their self-esteem and opportunities, and because it is unfair.

1   The anti-discrimination principle
2   Institutional discrimination
3   What makes discrimination wrong?

1   The anti-discrimination principle

Prejudice and ethnic hostility, and the discrimination and other forms of intolerance that they generate, are found in all parts of the world. Prejudice typically involves a negative attitude towards a group based on a belief that members of the group are undeserving of equal treatment because they are somehow inferior or morally deficient. Prejudice often relies on stereotypes – simplified and negatively slanted conceptions of the typical characteristics and activities of members of the group. Racism is one species of prejudice; other species include bigotry, sexism, extreme nationalism and homophobia.

The moral norm that makes discrimination wrong can be formulated as follows:

The anti-discrimination principle. When distributing educational opportunities and jobs [*list of items*], never exclude whole groups of persons or choose one person over another on grounds of race, ethnicity, religion, or race [*list of excluded characteristics*] unless the use of these characteristics in particular circumstances is demonstrably legitimate and important.

This anti-discrimination norm is presupposed by most condemnations of discrimination, and is found in most civil rights legislation (Brest 1976). It rejects ways of thinking that assume the inferiority or depravity of certain groups, and forbids some of the most important ways of acting and deliberating that flow from such assumptions. Because it is concerned with the grounds on which decisions are made (and thus with people's reasons and intentions), proving that discrimination has occurred is often difficult.

The anti-discrimination principle forbids those distributing certain benefits and burdens to 'choose...on the basis of...certain excluded characteristics. This regulates the process of selection, but only indirectly regulates its outcomes. It does not forbid an employer to deny employment to a Muslim, if that is the outcome of a non-discriminatory selection process, but it blocks the employer from using an applicant's Muslim beliefs as a reason in deciding whether or not to employ the applicant. Formal or informal statements of qualifications cannot mention religion or other excluded characteristics. The anti-discrimination principle says how *not* to allocate certain important benefits, but it does not say how they should be allocated. It does not, for example, prescribe that these benefits should be allocated in accordance with competency or qualifications. Goldman (1979) has defended the additional principle that employment and selection for advanced education should always be on the basis of competence.

The formulation of the anti-discrimination principle given above is too narrow. The two bracketed clauses (the 'list of items' and the 'list of excluded characteristics') mark slots that need to be filled in more adequately. The list of items could be expanded by listing, along with educational opportunities and jobs, matters such as housing, public accommodation, legal rights, opportunities for political participation, public assistance and military service. Perhaps the underlying idea here is to focus on benefits and burdens that have a major impact on people's prospects, long-term welfare and self-respect, and whose distribution can be regulated without deeply invading people's liberties. The anti-discrimination principle does not apply to the distribution of all benefits and burdens. It does not forbid, for example, choosing someone who shares one's religion as a friend, or using gender as a factor in choosing a spouse.

The list of excluded characteristics could be expanded beyond race, ethnicity, religion and gender to include national origin, political beliefs, being a non-citizen, sexual orientation, income and age. It is sometimes suggested that an anti-discrimination principle should exclude reliance on characteristics that are 'irrelevant' or 'arbitrary'. What makes this plausible is the fact that one's religious beliefs, for example, have little bearing on one's qualifications to work in a construction company. Choosing people for construction work on the basis of their religion just seems irrational. But if the owners of a large construction company seek to employ only fellow Christians because they think they are more likely to be honest and hard-working, or because they want to create a certain religious atmosphere within the company, they cannot be faulted for making arbitrary choices or using irrelevant criteria. The problem is rather that these selection procedures are inappropriate for a large company in a diverse country because they are unfair to non-Christians.

2 Institutional discrimination

The anti-discrimination principle is narrow in its scope and the occurrence of discrimination is often hard to prove. Thus it is unlikely that widespread acceptance and legal enforcement of the principle will quickly stop discrimination or eliminate the consequences of past discrimination. Affirmative action programmes, which go beyond anti-discrimination, are intended to do these things more rapidly (see AFFIRMATIVE ACTION). But many have attempted to expand the scope of the anti-discrimination principle to cover *institutional* discrimination (Banton 1991; Ezorsky 1991). There are at least five sorts of

phenomena that a norm addressing institutional discrimination might cover.

(1) *Unconscious discrimination.* To engage in discriminatory behaviour one does not have to be aware that one is doing so. One can discriminate by relying on stereotypes one is unaware of or by unconsciously following old customs. This sort of discrimination can be brought under the anti-discrimination principle by defining 'choose... on grounds of...' in a broad enough way to cover decisions that unconsciously rely on stereotypes and discriminatory customs.

(2) *Statistical discrimination.* Characteristics that are relevant to selection for a position often are statistically correlated to some degree with characteristics such as race, ethnicity and gender. An employer may refuse, for example, to employ a woman in a warehouse because they believe correctly that most women are unable to lift the heavy boxes stored in the warehouse. Although the likelihood that one can do a certain kind of job is generally an appropriate basis for selection, it is discriminatory to exclude all women from jobs requiring heavy lifting on the grounds that most women are unable to do it. Lifting abilities are easy to test on an individual basis, and hence it is fairer to require that people be selected as individuals rather than on the basis of some class to which they belong. Statistical discrimination can be excluded by the anti-discrimination principle if we specify that 'choose... on the basis of...' covers and thus forbids using the excluded characteristics as statistical indicators of the presence or absence of qualifications.

(3) *Reaction qualifications.* When the customers of a business are prejudiced it may be rational for the business to conform to those prejudices in choosing its employees. It is not in general wrong to select people for positions on the basis of the preferences of the people they will serve. If customers like travel agents with pleasant personalities there is nothing wrong with making the possession of such a personality a job qualification for travel agents. Thus we cannot say that it is arbitrary to select people on the basis of reaction qualifications, but in some contexts it is discriminatory to do so. Wertheimer (1983) argues that relying on reaction qualifications based on race and gender often leads to injustices. It may be possible to bring reaction qualifications under the anti-discrimination principle by extending 'choose... on the grounds of...' to cover choosing on the basis of one's customers' prejudices.

(4) *Personal connections.* Ezorsky (1991) argues that finding new employees by word-of-mouth advertising within the social networks of one's present employees is discriminatory towards blacks in contexts where blacks have been excluded from employment by past discrimination and where residential segregation persists. Although this method of recruiting employees might be unobjectionable in some circumstances, it is discriminatory in societies with a history of racism. To prohibit this sort of discrimination we probably have to go beyond the negative anti-discrimination principle to a supplementary requirement that jobs be advertised publicly and that employment through personal connections be avoided.

(5) *Legacy of discrimination.* Allocative decisions can transmit a legacy of discrimination even though they themselves are not discriminatory in the standard sense. Black people growing up in the southern states of the USA in the 1950s were likely to have had educational opportunities inferior to those of whites and to have faced substantial discrimination in seeking employment when they left school. Thirty years later, when such a person sought a job from a company that had fully non-discriminatory hiring policies, they could well have had a less good record of work experience than a white who was not disadvantaged early on by discrimination in education and employment. Choosing a white person because of better work experience in such a case would not be directly discriminatory, but it would transmit the legacy of discrimination. How to address this sort of case seems more a matter of affirmative action than anti-discrimination.

3 What makes discrimination wrong?

Consider a clear violation of the anti-discrimination principle, such as an employer prejudicially refusing to hire or even consider blacks for work in a restaurant. What is wrong with such an action? First, it is insulting to blacks because of its underlying premise that some racial groups are less worthy than others. Second, it is harmful to blacks because it often reduces self-esteem and produces a sense of inferiority, and because it deprives people of opportunities that would have allowed them to live better lives and make greater contributions to society. Discrimination in education and employment will tend to reduce a group's aspirations and productivity by reducing the payoff of investments in education and work experience. Third, discrimination is often irrational. It frequently relies on unjustified beliefs and stereotypes, and selects people on irrelevant and arbitrary

grounds. Although it is not in general morally wrong to act irrationally, irrational actions that distribute important goods in ways that harm and disadvantage other people may indeed be wrong because they are unfair. Finally, the most important reason why discrimination is wrong is that it is unfair. Victims of racial discrimination in employment, for example, can legitimately complain that as full members of society who have done their part in preparing to participate in and contribute to society it is unfair for them to be handicapped in areas such as education, employment and politics by discrimination flowing from other people's prejudices.

See also: LINGUISTIC DISCRIMINATION

References and further reading

Alexander, L. (1992) 'What Makes Wrongful Discrimination Wrong?: Biases, Preferences, Stereotypes, and Proxies', *University of Pennsylvania Law Review* 141 (November): 149–219. (A clear but complicated exploration of the morality of various types of discriminatory preferences.)

* Banton, M. (1992) 'The Nature and Causes of Racism and Racial Discrimination', *International Sociology* 7 (1): 69–84. (Contrasts discrimination, which is 'universal and normal', with racism, which is 'historically and geographically specific'. Also discusses the United Nations 1965 *Convention on the Elimination of all Forms of Racial Discrimination*.)

Boxill, B. (1984) *Blacks and Social Justice*, Totowa, NJ: Rowman & Allenheld. (Chapter one criticizes views that equate non-discrimination with colour blindness.)

* Brest, P. (1976) 'Foreward: In Defense of the Anti-discrimination Principle', *Harvard Law Review* 90 (2): 1. (An attempt to define, limit and defend a principle prohibiting discrimination based on race.)

* Ezorsky, G. (1991) *Racism and Justice: The Case for Affirmative Action*, Ithaca, NY: Cornell University Press. (Chapter one contains a good discussion of 'overt and institutional racism'.)

* Goldman, A. (1979) *Justice and Reverse Discrimination*, Princeton, NJ: Princeton University Press. (Chapter two constructs a philosophical defence of awarding positions by competence.)

King, M. (1969) 'Letter from Birmingham City Jail', in H. Bedau (ed.) *Civil Disobedience*, New York: Pegasus. (The late civil rights leader's indictment of racism and racial discrimination.)

Thomas, L. (1980) 'Sexism and Racism: Some Conceptual Differences', *Ethics* 90 (2): 239–50.

(Argues that racist attitudes are 'relatively easier to give up' than sexist ones.)

* Wertheimer, A. (1983) 'Jobs, Qualifications, and Preferences', *Ethics* 94 (2): 99–112. (A thorough discussion of qualifications based on client preferences.)

JAMES W. NICKEL

DISCRIMINATION AND LANGUAGE *see* LINGUISTIC DISCRIMINATION

DISSOI LOGOI

Dissoi logoi *('Twofold Arguments') is the title scholars apply to a short anonymous collection of arguments for and against various theses. The work, in Greek, is (questionably) dated around 400 BC, and regarded as an interesting, if second-rank, product of the Sophistic age.*

The opening sentence of *Dissoi logoi* announces 'twofold arguments' about good and bad: one set to show that good and bad are the same, another to show they are different. Chapters 2–4 follow the same pattern for the opposites seemly and shameful, just and unjust, true and false, respectively. Chapters 5–7 argue for and against a thesis, respectively: 'The demented and the sane, the wise and the ignorant, both do and say the same things', 'Wisdom and virtue cannot be taught or learned' and 'Public offices should be assigned by lot'. Chapter 8 argues positively for the idea that a good speaker will know everything. Chapter 9 recommends the art of memorization, but the manuscripts break off leaving both chapter and treatise incomplete.

This is a mere summary of the document. Nothing can be said with certainty about it. Not only its author, but its text, date, overall purpose and intellectual affiliations remain matters for scholarly speculation. Speculation has run riot.

To begin with the text: its Doric dialect is marred by intrusions of Attic and some Ionic forms. Is this due to the tendency of scribes to normalize the texts they copy? To a non-Doric speaker writing for a Doric-speaking audience? Or did a Doric author rewrite an earlier text? Imperfect Doric betrays numerous forgeries ascribed to early Pythagoreans but produced long *after* 400 BC. The antique feel to the text could be misleading.

What of the standard dating? This rests largely on a mention of the Peloponnesian war (431–404 BC) as the most recent of a series of notable wars going back, via the Persian and Trojan wars, to the battle of the gods and giants. Was there a comparable war between 404 BC and Rome's conquest of the Hellenistic kingdoms? If not, the *Dissoi logoi* could have been written centuries after 404 BC.

Concerning the overall purpose of the piece, on the standard dating, the best guide is Aristotle's description (*Sophistical Refutations* 183b36–184a1) of earlier methods of teaching rhetoric and dialectic: the idea was that memorizing specimen arguments would somehow equip the student to produce, at the appropriate juncture, new instances of a typical pattern. On this hypothesis, the author's intellectual affiliations are not discernible from first-person remarks like 'I assert this latter view' (4.2). These belong to the argumentative strategies a student must memorize. That sometimes the author appears to endorse both sides of the dispute must be disregarded: 'I' does not refer to the author but to the speaker in some imaginary debate.

It is not a high-powered debate. Many of the arguments for and against do not even manage to contradict each other. Good and bad are the same because the same thing is good in some circumstances, bad in others; they are different because 'good' and 'bad' mean different things. 'I am an initiate' is both false (in your mouth) and true (in mine); yet 'false' and 'true' mean different things.

Scholars seek influences and sources for particular arguments in the collection: Protagoras and Hippias are especially popular. But most of what we 'know' about individual Sophists is itself speculation (see HIPPIAS; PROTAGORAS; SOPHISTS). Besides, time moves slower in philosophy than in life: arguments and examples get repeated for centuries after their first appearance. The arguments in chapter 6 for and against the teachability of wisdom and virtue show numerous points of contact with Plato's *Protagoras* (319a–328d) and *Meno* (89e–96d). Is Plato drawing on themes already broached in the *Dissoi logoi* or did our author draw on Plato? Neither conclusion is safe. Philosophy being what it is, statements like 'before now people have frequented sophists and gained no benefit' (6.5) could easily be written when the 'Sophists' were a phenomenon of the distant past.

So why were these feeble arguments preserved? The *Dissoi logoi* survives in fact as an appendix to the manuscripts of SEXTUS EMPIRICUS, who regularly argues for and against a thesis to induce suspension of judgment about it. This suggests the collection was of interest to Pyrrhonian sceptics, either for historical reasons or because, according to these sceptics, even feeble arguments are useful as the appropriate cure for milder cases of dogmatism (Sextus Empiricus, *Outlines of Pyrrhonism* III 280–1). A sceptic called Zeuxis, a friend of AENESIDEMUS, wrote *On Dissoi Logoi* (Diogenes Laertius, IX 106). Both Pyrrho himself and his follower Aenesidemus came from Doric-speaking regions. Could Zeuxis be commenting on the *Dissoi logoi*, supposing or pretending it was antique?

Like all suggestions about the *Dissoi logoi*, the above is speculation. Sober readers will suspend judgment on every question about the work.

References and further reading

Barnes, J. (1979) *The Presocratic Philosophers*, London: Routledge & Kegan Paul. (The account of the *Dissoi logoi* in volume 2, pages 214–20 improves some of the feebler relativistic arguments.)

Diels, H. and Kranz, W. (eds) (1952) *Die Fragmente der Vorsokratiker* (Fragments of the Presocratics), Berlin: Weidmann, 6th edn. (The standard collection of the ancient sources. Full Greek text of *Dissoi logoi* is in volume 2, pages 405–16.)

Guthrie, W.K.C. (1969) *A History of Greek Philosophy*, Cambridge: Cambridge University Press, vol. 3, 316–19; part 1 is repr. as *The Sophists*, Cambridge: Cambridge University Press, 1971. (Helpful account from the standard viewpoint.)

Robinson, T.M. (1979) *Contrasting Arguments: An Edition of the Dissoi Logoi*, New York: Arno Press. (The first and only full-length edition, with translation, commentary and bibliography of previous work.)

Ryle, G. (1966) *Plato's Progress*, Cambridge: Cambridge University Press, ch. 4. (Entertaining account of the background and point of the work on the conventional dating.)

Sprague, R.K. (1968) 'Dissoi Logoi or Dialexeis', *Mind* 77: 155–67; repr. in *The Older Sophists*, Columbia, SC: University of South Carolina Press, 1972. (English translation of the text from Diels and Kranz (1952).)

M.F. BURNYEAT

DODGSON, CHARLES LUTWIDGE (LEWIS CARROLL) (1832–98)

Dodgson, an Oxford teacher of mathematics, is best known under his pseudonym, Lewis Carroll. Although not an exceptional mathematician, his standing has risen somewhat in the light of recent research. He is also of note as a symbolic logician in the tradition of Boole and De Morgan, as a pioneer in the theory of voting, and as a gifted amateur photographer. His literary output, ranging from satirical pamphleteering, light verse and puzzle-making to an immense correspondence, is again largely amateur in nature, and would hardly have survived without the worldwide success of his three master-works, Alice's Adventures in Wonderland *(1865),* Through the Looking-Glass *(1871) and* The Hunting of the Snark *(1876). Together with portions of his two-volume fairy-novel* Sylvie and Bruno *(1889/93) they are the only writings, ostensibly for children, to have attracted or deserved the notice of philosophers.*

Dodgson was the eldest son of a North-of-England clergyman. From Rugby School he went on to Christ Church, Oxford, where he obtained a first in mathematics and, in due course, a lectureship which he held for the rest of his working life. A prim, sentimental bachelor clergyman, Dodgson himself was no philosopher; his diaries and letters record the banalities of his London theatre-going, child friendships and contacts with the art world, but reflect throughout a busily inventive rather than a deeply thoughtful mind. Mainly through photography, he got to know a number of eminent people, from Tennyson, Ruskin and the Rossettis to Lord Salisbury, the Prime Minister, but never himself figured as a literary lion, still less a Victorian sage. As Dodgson the mathematician, he would even disclaim authorship of the *Alice* books, never suspecting that these would be the works to bring him philosophical fame, not merely as a fount of allusion for logical analysts but also as an ample wabe for the gyrings and gimblings of literary theorists across the English Channel.

To the analytical philosopher, *Wonderland* provides a wealth of bad arguments on such themes as the criteria of reality and personal identity, the relativity of space and size, the effects of arrested time and causality-reversal, the theory of types, the status of nonentities and the paradoxes of solipsism and idealism. Although nobody imagines that the Mad Hatter, Tweedledee or the White Queen have any serious light to shed on these matters, their dicta remain perennially useful as a model of how not to think, and are freely cited by the likes of Russell, Moore, Broad and even Wittgenstein.

By French neo-structuralists, on the other hand (notably DELEUZE and Lecercle), the Carrollian corpus is elevated to a far more solemn significance, and taken to afford genuine insight into the logic of dreams and madness, the nature of nihilism and nonsense, the collapse of all differences between names and things, the deconstruction of language by puns and portmanteau-words, and its ultimate subjugation under the stipulative dictatorship of a Humpty-Dumptyan subject. Like the Freudian commentators of an earlier generation, who found cannibalism and psychosis everywhere they looked in *Alice*, the postmodern critics have discovered in it themes and purposes that would have horrified the author, supposing that anyone could have explained them to him.

That *Alice* has influenced a host of modernist writers, from Kafka and Joyce to Borges, Ionesco, Nabokov, Beckett, Artaud and the entire surrealist movement, it would be idle to dispute. But before Mr Dodgson, the pedantic Oxford logician, is thereupon canonized as an apostle of anarchy and irrationalism, it needs to be stated in his defence that the Carrollian absurd, whatever its consequences, is so far from being morbidly antirational in origin that it issues directly from the nature of logic. Formal logicians care nothing for the content of their propositions; they only want to know the consequences. As arbitrary class-names, snarks and boojums, cabbages and kings, bats and tea-trays, beavers and butchers and things that begin with an 'M' are all equally serviceable as terms for the syllogisms that Dodgson delighted in, and what is the harm, then, in animating them with a touch of fictional life? Carroll, so regarded, is in no way a deconstructor of the established order. He is simply one more in the long line of logical humorists, stretching from Zeno, Euthydemus and Buridan to his own mentor, De Morgan, and continuing thereafter via F.C.S. Schiller to Russell, Jourdain, Quine and Raymond Smullyan. It should be no surprise to anyone, therefore, that all five of the last-mentioned are known devotees of *Alice*.

List of works

For details of the following works, the reader is advised to consult *The Lewis Carroll Handbook*, ed. S. Williams *et al.*, listed in References and further reading.

Carroll, Lewis (1865) *Alice's Adventures in Wonderland*, London: Macmillan, 1866.

—— (1871) *Through the Looking-Glass*, London: Macmillan.

—— (1876) *The Hunting of the Snark*, London: Macmillan.

Dodgson, C.L. (1879) *Euclid and his Modern Rivals*, London: Macmillan.

Carroll, Lewis (1885) *A Tangled Tale*, London: Macmillan.

—— (1886) *The Game of Logic*, London: Macmillan.

—— (1889) *Sylvie and Bruno*, London: Macmillan.

—— (1893) *Sylvie and Bruno Concluded*, London: Macmillan.

—— (1896) *Symbolic Logic*, Part I, London: Macmillan.

References and further reading

Abeles, F. (ed.) (1994) *The Mathematical Pamphlets, etc., of C.L. Dodgson*, New York: The Lewis Carroll Society of North America. (The sole collection of its kind, indispensable to the study of Dodgson the mathematician.)

Bakewell, M. (1996) *Lewis Carroll*, London: Heinemann. (Well-written general biography by a competent media professional.)

Bartley, W.W., III (ed.) (1977) *Lewis Carroll's Symbolic Logic*, New York: Clarkson Potter, 1986. (Carroll's unfinished treatise on logic, in an adroitly edited modern reconstruction.)

Clark, A. (1979) *Lewis Carroll: A Biography*, London: Dent, and New York: Schocken. (A sensible account of the life, providing new details, with relatively little speculation.)

Cohen, M.N. (ed.) (1979) *The Letters of Lewis Carroll*, London and New York: Oxford University Press, 2 vols. (Fourteen-hundred letters, annotated with immense care and learning.)

—— (1995) *Lewis Carroll: a Biography*, London: Macmillan, and New York: Knopf. (Full-length portrait, over-solicitous in places, but still a work of great authority. The treatment of Dodgson's religious opinions is particularly worthy of note.)

Collingwood, S.D. (1898) *The Life and Letters of Lewis Carroll*, London: Fisher Unwin, and New York: Century. (The authorized biography, by Dodgson's nephew. Although written in haste, it has lasted well and supplies a foundation for all the rest.)

Deleuze, G. (1969) *Logique du sens*, Paris: Editions de Minuit; trans. M. Lester as *The Logic of Sense*, New York, Columbia University Press, 1990. (None too much of either for the uninitiated reader; but its post-Freudian ruminations on language are heavily indebted to *Alice*.)

Gardner, M. (1960) *The Annotated Alice*, New York: Clarkson Potter, and London: Penguin; revised edn, 1993. (Along with Hudson's biography, this work is largely responsible for the widespread modern-day interest in *Alice*.)

—— (1962) *The Annotated Snark*, New York: Simon & Schuster, and London: Penguin. (Lively and informative guide.)

—— (1990) *More Annotated Alice*, New York:

Random House. (Another gleaning of Alician lore, much of it supplied by correspondents.)

Green, R.L. (ed.) (1953) *The Diaries of Lewis Carroll*, London: Cassell, and New York: Oxford University Press, 2 vols. (Full but inevitably selective edition, since it omits mathematical and logical entries. Wakeling's new version will supersede it.)

Guiliano, E. (ed.) (1976) *Lewis Carroll Observed*, New York: Clarkson Potter. (Useful anthology of critical essays and reviews.)

—— (ed.) (1982) *Lewis Carroll: A Celebration*, New York: Clarkson Potter. (Critical essays and reviews by various hands; worthwhile, but somewhat leaden as a birthday tribute.)

—— (1980) *Lewis Carroll: An Annotated Bibliography, 1960–1977*, Charlottesville, VA: University of Virginia Press. (For the period it covers, this is a great improvement on the *Handbook*.)

Guiliano, E. and Kincaid, J. (eds) (1982) *Soaring with the Dodo*, New York: The Lewis Carroll Society of North America. (A further selection of original articles and reviews.)

Heath, P. (1974) *The Philosopher's Alice*, New York: St Martin's Press, and London: Academy Editions. (A not-entirely-serious vade mecum to the logico-philosophic undertones of *Alice*.)

Hudson, D. (1954) *Lewis Carroll: An Illustrated Biography*, London: Constable; new edn, New York: Clarkson Potter, 1977. (An updated and much embellished version of a life generally considered the most level-headed of its day.)

Lecercle, J.-J. (1985) *Philosophy through the Looking Glass*, London: Hutchinson, and La Salle, IL: Open Court. (More lucid and coherent foray into the territory frequented by Deleuze, and a useful means of access to his thought.)

—— (1994) *Philosophy of Nonsense*, London and New York: Routledge. (*Alice* under deconstruction once more, in the vain hope of finding a philosophy of language in the wreckage.)

Phillips, R. (ed.) (1971) *Aspects of Alice*, New York: Vanguard. (Reprints a wide range of articles from the earlier critical literature.)

Sutherland, R.D. (1970) *Language and Lewis Carroll*, The Hague: Mouton. (Academic in tone but a very thorough and perceptive study, by a well-read professional linguist.)

Thomas, D. (1996) *Lewis Carroll*, London: John Murray. (A darker portrait than that of Bakewell, lit by stage fire from the Victorian underworld.)

Wakeling, E. (ed.) (1993) *The Oxford Pamphlets, etc., of C.L. Dodgson*, Charlottesville, VA: University of Virginia Press. (Assembles virtually the entire literary output of Dodgson the Oxford don, college worthy and public nuisance.)

—— (ed.) (1993–) *Lewis Carroll's Diaries*, Luton: The Lewis Carroll Society. (An ongoing multi-volume edition of material not hitherto published in full.)

Williams, S. and Madan, F. (1924) *The Lewis Carroll Handbook*, Folkestone: Dawson, and Hamden, CT: Archon Books; revised edn, ed. R.L. Green, 1962; revised edn, ed. D. Crutch, 1979. (Long past its prime, despite revisions. Rambling and undependable, it remains, for all that, the chief source of bibliographical information and a necessity for the serious student or collector.)

PETER HEATH

DŌGEN (1200–53)

Dōgen Kigen, the founder of Japanese Sōtō Zen Buddhism, is most noted for his argument that meditation is the expression or enactment of enlightenment, not the means to attaining it. Dōgen believed that even a novice might achieve insight, however fleeting. The difficulty, however, is in expressing that insight in one's daily acts, both linguistic and non-linguistic. In developing his position, Dōgen articulated a phenomenology of incarnate consciousness and a sophisticated analysis of meaning. His theories of mind–body unity, contextualized meaning, temporality and theory–praxis influenced many prominent modern Japanese philosophers such as Watsuji Tetsurō, Tanabe Hajime and Nishitani Keiji.

Tradition states that Dōgen was of aristocratic background and orphaned at the age of seven. A few years later he entered the Tendai Buddhist monastery on Mount Hiei, one of Japan's great spiritual and intellectual centres of the time. He left the monastery at seventeen because he could not resolve an apparent contradiction in Tendai doctrine, the idea that spiritual practice to achieve enlightenment is necessary even though we are all already somehow inherently enlightened. His quest took him to China in 1223 where he studied under the Chinese Chan (Zen) master Rujing (1163–1228). Dōgen returned to Japan in 1227 with Rujing's verification that he had achieved enlightenment and was a Zen master in his own right. In Japan, Dōgen wrote a series of innovative essays, many on philosophical subjects, later collected as *Shōbōgenzō* (Treasury of the True Dharma Eye). He spent the final decade of his life establishing a comprehensive monastic community in the isolated mountain regions of today's Fukui prefecture. Sōtō eventually became the most popular form of Zen Buddhism in Japan with a strong following among the laity.

Dōgen was a philosophical realist insofar as he maintained we have access to 'presencing of things as they are' (*genjōkōan*). However, that presence is inherently meaningless. Meaning only arises within context, and context always involves an act of human consciousness. Hence, a simple correspondence between what-is and what-is-thought is not possible (see TRUTH, CORRESPONDENCE THEORY OF). The nature and function of context must also enter into the consideration of truth and falseness.

Dōgen sometimes drew on the traditional Buddhist example of the ocean. To a fish the ocean is a translucent palace; to a person at sea, it is a great circle extending to the horizon in all directions; to a heavenly being, it is a shimmering string of jewel-like reflections. What is the ocean in itself? Dōgen maintained it is intrinsically none of those things, yet has the capacity to be all of them. The meaningless presence is expressed by such vacuous Buddhist terms as 'suchness', 'thusness' or 'emptiness'. Yet, in the fish's context, the sea truly becomes a palace; in the person's it is a circle, and in the heavenly being's it is jewel-like reflections. In itself, the presence (the ocean) is simply the not-yet-conceptualized, meaningless reality that can be contextualized and made meaningful in an infinite number of ways.

For Dōgen, therefore, error is possible by either overly absolutizing or overly relativizing meaning. Fixed in only one context of understanding, one may absolutize its meanings, assuming them to exist independently of consciousness as the things themselves. For example, although the fish would be correct to think in its context that the presence is a palace, it would be wrong to think that it can *only* be a palace. Alternatively, one may err in the direction of extreme relativism. Because there are a limitless number of contexts giving meaning to the presence as, for example, 'palace', 'circle' or 'jewels', this does not imply the presence can assume any meaning whatsoever. Such extreme relativism would be wrong on two counts. First, in each specific context there is only one correct meaning; to the person at sea, for example, the presence is not a palace. Second, there can be some attributed meanings that cannot be correct in any context. Dōgen gave the example of time as 'flying away'. Since the idea itself is logically incoherent (at what rate does time fly?), it can never be true in any context.

For Dōgen these ruminations on presence, context and meaning had implications for Zen practice. He believed the anxiety of everyday life arises from misunderstanding meaning and misreading contexts. We become fixed in interpreting the world as if there

were only a very limited number of possibilities. We force our interpretations to fit that limited repertoire of contexts. This inhibits our capacity to adjust to change, and in fact encourages us to deny the reality or importance of both change and context. Zen practice addresses this predicament in two ways.

First, Dōgen believed that Zen meditation, 'just sitting', is a method for disengaging the normal meaning-bestowing function of consciousness. In the non-affirming, non-negating mode he called 'without thinking', one can encounter phenomena in their contextless, meaningless state. In this respect, insight into presence is immediately available to anyone. Yet, human life requires meaning; thus the second function of Zen meditation is to be aware of the contextualizing, meaning-bestowing process, watching it structure the formerly inchoate 'presence'.

It is extremely difficult to distinguish whether one is watching a spontaneous unfolding of contextual meaning or a projection of a previous meaning on to the phenomena. Therefore, the student benefits from a master who continually shifts the context of discourse and action, requiring the student to express new meanings appropriate to the shifts. To the extent the master does the unexpected, the student becomes aware of having had an expectation, a contextual presupposition about what is meaningful in the situation. The master's actions deconstruct those expectations, those fixed meanings. In Dōgen's terminology, the 'master and student practise together' by opening each other to new vistas of expressive meaning, each true to the newly emergent context. This type of practice, Dōgen maintained, is the expression or enactment of enlightenment, not the test or method used to achieve it. In this responsive openness to meaning, one breaks free of the delusory idea that truth is fixed and reality static.

See also: BUDDHIST PHILOSOPHY, JAPANESE; JAPANESE PHILOSOPHY; MEANING AND TRUTH; TRUTH, DEFLATIONARY THEORIES OF

List of works

Dōgen (1200–53) *Dōgen zenji zenshū* (Complete Works of Zen Master Dōgen), ed. Ōkubo Dōshū, Tokyo: Chikuma Shōbō, 1969–70, 2 vols. (The standard critical edition with manuscript variants noted.)

—— (1200–53) *Shōbōgenzō* (Treasury of the True Dharma Eye), trans. Kim Hee-jin, *Flowers of Emptiness: Selections from Dōgen's Shōbōgenzō*, Studies in Asian Thought and Religion 2, Lewiston, NY: The Edwin Mellen Press, 1985; trans. Yokoi Yūhō, *The Shōbō-genzō*, Tokyo: Sankibō Busshorin,

1985. (Yokoi is currently the best complete translation of Dōgen's *magnum opus*, but flawed somewhat by lack of philosophical subtlety and inadequate explanatory apparatus. Kim's edition is a translation of the bulk of the text with the aim of capturing in English some of the philosophical wordplay of Dōgen's distinctive style of writing.)

—— (1231) *Bendōwa*, trans. N. Waddell and Abe Masaro, 'Dōgen's Bendōwa', *The Eastern Buddhist* 5, 1970 (1): 124–57. (Technical, excellent translation of one of Dōgen's more philosophical essays.)

—— (1233) *Genjōkōan*, trans. N. Waddell and Abe Masaro, 'Shōbōgenzō Genjōkōan', *The Eastern Buddhist* 6, 1973 (2): 115–28. (Technical, excellent translation of one of Dōgen's more philosophical essays.)

—— (1241) 'Shōbōgenzō Buddha-nature', *The Eastern Buddhist* 8 (2): 94–112; 9 (1): 87–105; 9 (2): 71–87. (Technical, excellent translation of one of Dōgen's more philosophical essays.)

References and further reading

Abe Masao (1992) *A Study of Dōgen: His Philosophy and Religion*, ed. S. Heine, Albany, NY: State University of New York Press. (A collection of essays on Dōgen's philosophy by an important Japanese scholar writing in a comparative context mainly for a Western audience.)

Bielefeldt, C. (1988) *Dōgen's Manuals of Zen Meditation*, Berkeley, CA: University of California Press. (Meticulous, historical study comparing the technical details of Dōgen's theory of meditation with his Zen Buddhist predecessors and rivals.)

Heine, S. (1985) *Existential and Ontological Dimensions of Time in Heidegger and Dōgen*, Albany, NY: State University of New York Press. (Detailed analysis of Dōgen's theory of temporality in comparison with that of Heidegger.)

Kasulis, T.P. (1981) *Zen Action/Zen Person*, Honolulu, HI: University of Hawaii Press. (Chapters 6–7 explain more fully the aspects of Dōgen's thought presented in this entry.)

Kim Hee-jin (1975) *Dōgen Kigen Mystical Realist*, Association for Asian Studies Monograph XXIX, Tucson, AZ: University of Arizona Press. (Pioneering work in making Dōgen's philosophical perspective available to Western readers.)

LaFleur, W.R. (ed.) (1985) *Dōgen Studies*, Honolulu, HI: University of Hawaii Press. (Good collection of essays by several Dōgen scholars on a variety of points, many philosophical.)

Nagatomo Shigenori (1992) *Attunement Through the Body*, Albany, NY: State University of New York Press. (A provocative theory of mind–body unity, drawing on traditional and modern Japanese philosophical ideas. Chapters 4–7 deal specifically with Dōgen.)

Shaner, D.E. (1985) *The Bodymind Experience in Japanese Buddhism: A Phenomenological Study of Kūkai and Dōgen*, Albany, NY: State University Press of New York. (Using Western phenomenological categories, a good analysis of Dōgen's theory of the oneness of body and mind.)

Tanahashi Kazuaki (ed.) (1985) *Moon in a Dewdrop: Writings of Zen Master Dōgen*, San Francisco, CA: North Point Press. (A readable translation of a broad sampling of Dōgen's writings with copious annotations for technical terms; useful introduction to Dōgen's writings.)

THOMAS P. KASULIS

DONG ZHONGSHU (195–115 BC)

Tradition hailed Dong Zhongshu as the 'father of Han Confucianism' because of his influential theories that posit a perfect congruence between divine and human realms kept in balance by the true king, who functions as mediator, moral exemplar and lawmaker. Undoubtedly the most famous exegete in the 'Gongyang' commentarial tradition to the Chunqiu *(Spring and Autumn Annals), Dong is also credited by convention with the composition of the* Chunqiufanlu *(Luxuriant Dew of the Annals), though recent scholarship questions this attribution.*

Major revisions in the conventional assessment of Dong Zhongshu are under way for several reasons. First, no early evidence supports the view of Dong as architect responsible for adapting pre-Qin Confucian thought to the needs of the centralized imperial Chinese state. Second, many theoretical innovations once tied to Dong can now be shown to either predate (sometimes by millennia) or postdate Dong, requiring a systematic reconsideration of Dong's distinctive contributions. For example, it now seems that Dong did not introduce either Five Phases theory or the Red–White–Black 'three ages' historical cycle into Confucianism. Third, the *Chunqiufanlu* is now more often seen as a composite text that may represent some 150 years of Gongyang scholarship, compelling scholars to begin the arduous task of isolating those passages assignable to Dong alone.

A review of all the extant material that is indisputably authentic shows the central importance for Dong of Heaven's relation to the king (see TIAN).

According to Dong, Heaven originates and embodies the impulse towards perfection in all things, then works through impersonal natural forces (specifically, the cycles of *yinqi* and *yangqi* (see QI; YIN–YANG)) to foster good rule by suasive virtue, thereby obviating the need for harsh punishments. A perfect congruence between the natural (*tiandi*) and human worlds means that change in one sphere produces comparable change in the other, so that human acts (especially those of the ruler and his immediate circle) influence cosmic harmony for good or for ill. This triadic correspondence is exemplified by the Chinese character for 'king', in which three parallel horizontal lines (for heaven–earth–man) are connected by a single vertical signifying the mediating 'king'. Implicit in Dong's simple vision are three important presumptions: (1) in cosmos and society, hierarchy is 'natural'; (2) rule by moral suasion can be perfectly effective because it partakes of the divine; and (3) unusual events (such as floods, droughts and fires) are to be analysed according to set rules imbedded in the *Chunqiu*, for they convey Heaven's encoded messages to the ruler.

Dong's thought may be reconstructed in three additional areas for which sufficient reliable material survives, namely his theories on law, human nature and economic policy. As jurist, Dong argued that the Han statutes should be modified in light of the Confucian principle of 'rectifying names' (see LOGIC IN CHINA §1; CONFUCIAN PHILOSOPHY, CHINESE). In essence, Dong asserted that subordinates are obligated only to those superiors who have properly fulfilled their ascribed societal roles. (This assertion, of course, had important implications for legitimacy theory.) With regard to human nature, Dong believed that all humans at birth have the potential for both good and evil because Heaven endows both *yinqi* and *yangqi*; the transforming influence of the ruler and of ritual is needed if ordinary persons are fully to realize Heaven's intention. At one stroke, Dong thereby resolved the quarrel between MENCIUS and XUNZI over human nature and the origin of evil (see XING). In his memorials on the economy, Dong urged the state to induce commoners to return to the 'basic occupation' of agriculture, while minimizing the gross inequalities in wealth that inevitably prove divisive to society. The ruler must insure his subjects' economic and physical security, and then moral education, if he is to fulfill his sacred obligations as Son of Heaven.

Internal contradictions abound in Dong's thought. For example, both Heaven and the sage seem at once omnipotent and sharply constrained, not only by great cosmic and historical cycles but also by the others' will to take the moral initiative. Thus it remains unclear which of several factors (such as the reigning monarch's character, receipt of the Mandate from Heaven or the operation of impersonal cycles) is primarily responsible for the state of the empire at any one time. Moreover, Dong's call for the total abolition of punishment for the common people is at odds with his firm belief that even sage-rulers provide less than perfect moral models for their subjects. Given such apparent confusion, Dong is often remembered best for three memorials urging the Han throne to reserve imperial patronage for Confucianism alone, since continued competition among contending ways of thought would preclude any attempts to forge a truly unified political and social system.

See also: CHINESE CLASSICS; CONFUCIAN PHILOSOPHY, CHINESE; TIAN; YIN–YANG

List of works

Dong Zhongshu (195–115 BC) *Dong Zhongshu jueshi* (Legal Decisions of Dong Zhongshu), in Ma Guohan, *Yuhanshan fangji yishu*, Taibei: Shijie shuju, 1967, vol. 2, 1180–1. (This contains fragments of Dong's legal pronouncements. The bulk of the *Dong Zhongshu* (123 chapters) is now lost. It has been erroneously identified since the 6th century AD with the extant *Chunqiufanlu*, which includes material from the earlier *Gongyang* interpretive tradition, as well as material postdating Dong.)

References and further reading

Arbuckle, G. (1991) 'Restoring Dong Zhongshu (BCE 195–115): An Experiment in Historical and Philosophical Reconstruction', Ph.D. thesis, University of British Columbia. (An excellent overview of Dong's life and work.)

Dai Jun-ren. (1968) 'Dong Zhongshu bushuo wuxing kao', *Guoli zhongyang tushuguan guankan* 2 (2): 9–19. (An early challenge to the authenticity of the *Chunqiufanlu*.)

Keimatsu Mitsuo (1959) 'Shunjū Hanrigogyō shohen gisaku kō', *Kanazawa Daigaku hōbun gakubu ronshū* 6: 25–46. (The first systematic argument alleging the spurious nature of the Five Phases chapters of the *Chunqiufanlu*.)

Pankenier, D. (1990) 'Sandai Astronomical Origins of Heaven's Mandate', paper prepared for the 6th International Conference on the History of Science in China, Cambridge, 2–7 August 1990. (Discusses the early origins of Five Phases and the Black–White–Red cyclical scheme of history.)

Queen, S. (1996) *From Chronicle to Canon: The Hermeneutics of the Spring and Autumn, According* to *Tung Chung-shu*, Cambridge: Cambridge University Press. (A fine introduction to Dong, with special emphasis on his elaboration of *Gongyang* theories.)

MICHAEL NYLAN

DOOYEWEERD, HERMAN (1894–1977)

A Dutch philosopher and legal theorist, Herman Dooyeweerd challenged the Enlightenment ideal of autonomous rational thought and sought a religious foundation for philosophy. Religious self-knowledge, he contended, is the necessary condition of all knowing. Dooyeweerd proposed an elaborate ontology of physical and social reality based on the Christian doctrine of creation. His thought has been influential among Calvinists in The Netherlands, North America and South Africa.

Dooyeweerd was a Dutch neo-Calvinist philosopher and professor of law at the Free University of Amsterdam (1926–65). His most notable achievement was his lifelong effort to develop a distinctly Christian philosophy that included an epistemology which directly challenged modern Kantian rationalism and an ontology rooted in the Christian doctrine of creation. With D.H.T. Vollenhoven he founded the international Society for Calvinist Philosophy in 1935. His full philosophical statement, *A New Critique of Theoretical Thought*, anticipates a number of late-twentieth-century philosophical interests, including postmodern critiques of Enlightenment rationalism.

Dooyeweerd's work self-consciously builds on the late-nineteenth-century Dutch Calvinist revival movement inspired and directed by Abraham Kuyper (1837–1920). This neo-Calvinism had as its goal the full rechristianizing of Dutch culture and society, and proceeded from a strong Augustinian sense of spiritual antithesis between Christian and secular culture. For Dooyeweerd, as for Kuyper, all theorizing was rooted in religious presuppositions; the Enlightenment prejudice against prejudice was itself rooted in personal commitments. All thought is engaged and interested thought. Dooyeweerd's method of exposing the Enlightenment bias – his 'transcendental critique' – is one of his truly creative and significant accomplishments.

Unlike some Christian philosophers who attempt transcendent or external critiques of the pretended autonomy of modern thought and simply *assert* bias,

Dooyeweerd tried to show that an immanent examination of thought itself reveals its religious presuppositions. Analogously to Kant's critical method, Dooyeweerd, who was decisively influenced by Neo-Kantian philosophy as well as by the phenomenology of Husserl, argued that a consideration of the necessary conditions of thought discloses a supratheoretical or religious starting point. Philosophy's concern about meaning directs all thought to questions of origin, and these questions cannot be answered by theoretical thought itself. This awareness of the boundary limits of theoretical thought forces the philosopher to confront the integrating capacity of the human ego or, in biblical terms, the heart. Self-knowledge is thus the basis of all epistemology, and pure presuppositionless rationalism is an impossibility.

Religion is thus the integrative reality of all thought. Dooyeweerd did not restrict his understanding of 'religion' to concrete, particular, historical religions, but, like TILLICH (§4), understood it to be whatever human beings might give ultimate allegiance or value to. In his judgment, four religious, integrative 'ground-motives' dominate the history of Western thought: the Greek 'form–matter' motive, the medieval synthesis of 'nature–grace', the modern dialectic of 'nature' ('necessity') and 'freedom', and the biblical motive of 'Creation–Fall–Redemption'. For Dooyeweerd, as for neo-Calvinism, redemption is the restoration of creation.

Dooyeweerd's own ontology is rooted in Christian convictions about creation, particularly the conviction that creation is meaningfully diverse and structured by God's law. In Dutch his philosophy is called *Wijsbegeerte der Wetsidee* ('Philosophy of the Law-Idea'). Here Dooyeweerd also built on Kuyper's thought, this time on the notion of 'sphere-sovereignty': the idea that physical and social reality exhibits an irreducible diversity which is grounded in divine ordinances. While Kuyper utilized this doctrine primarily for political purposes (to free social structures such as the family and the school from the hegemony of the state), Dooyeweerd expanded it to a full ontology of 'modal aspects'. These modal aspects of created reality (including numerical, spatial, biotic, psychical, lingual, economic, jural-legal) are the investigative areas of the special sciences. The task of philosophy is to examine and explain how the modalities relate to each other. Dooyeweerd also developed a complex theory of whole 'entities' – termed 'individuality structures' – each of which in a unique configuration exhibits all the modal aspects.

Emphasizing the doctrine of creation also led Dooyeweerd to a rather positive attitude towards human culture and history. Strongly affirming Calvin's and Kuyper's doctrine of 'common grace' – God's non-saving favour towards all humanity – Dooyeweerd articulated a philosophy of history that was very appreciative of cultural development (see CALVIN, J. §§2–3). Cultural products and social institutions were perceived as organically unfolding and differentiating from their creational roots. Both this differentiation and cultural diversity are to be respected.

In addition to his native country, Dooyeweerd has had significant attention and influence in North America and South Africa. A 'Dooyeweerd Center for Christian Philosophy', which will concentrate on publishing Dooyeweerd's works in English and stimulating the study of his thought, was opened at Redeemer College, Canada, in 1994.

List of works

Dooyeweerd, H. (1953–8) *A New Critique of Theoretical Thought*, Amsterdam: H.J. Paris and Philadelphia, PA: Presbyterian & Reformed Publishing Company, 3 vols. (The full and mature expression of Dooyeweerd's epistemology and modal ontology.)
—— (1960) *In the Twilight of Western Thought*, Philadelphia, PA: Presbyterian & Reformed Publishing Company. (A series of lectures given by Dooyeweerd on a North American tour, this remains the most accessible introduction to Dooyeweerd's writing.)
—— (1979) *Roots of Western Culture*, Toronto, Ont.: Wedge. (This is a more elaborate introduction to Dooyeweerd's cultural analysis, including the four ground-motives.)

References and further reading

Kalsbeek, L. (1975) *Contours of a Christian Philosophy: An Introduction to Herman Dooyeweerd's Thought*, Toronto, Ont.: Wedge. (A very readable entry into Dooyeweerd's often complex thought.)
Kuyper, A. (1931) *Lectures in Calvinism*, Grand Rapids, MI: Eerdmans. (Originally delivered as the Stone Lectures at Princeton University in 1898, these are indispensable background reading for understanding Dooyeweerd's neo-Calvinist vision.)
McIntire, C.T. (1985a) 'Herman Dooyeweerd in North America', in D. Wells (ed.) *Reformed Theology in America*, Grand Rapids, MI: Eerdmans, 172–85. (Traces Dooyeweerd's philosophical influence among Calvinists in North America.)
—— (ed.) (1985b) *The Legacy of Herman Dooyeweerd*, Lanham, MD: University Press of America. (Contains a series of explorations of Dooyeweerd's thought by the faculty of the Institute for Christian Studies, Toronto, Canada. It also contains a thorough bibliography.)

JOHN BOLT

DOSTOEVSKII, FËDOR MIKHAILOVICH (1821–81)

Dostoevskii, regarded as one of the world's greatest novelists, is especially well known for his mastery of philosophical or ideological fiction. In his works, characters espouse intriguing ideas about theology, morality and psychology. Plots are shaped by conflicts of ideas and by the interaction of theories with the psychology of the people who espouse them. Indeed, Dostoevskii is usually considered one of the greatest psychologists in the history of Western thought, not only because of the accounts of the mind his characters and narrators elucidate in detail, but also because of the peculiar behaviour betraying the depths of their souls. Dostoevskii is particularly well known for his description of the irrational in its many modes.

Deeply engaged with the political and social problems of his day, Dostoevskii brought his understanding of individual and social psychology to bear on contemporary issues and gave them a lasting relevance. His predictions about the likely consequences of influential ideas, such as communism and the social theory of crime, have proven astonishingly accurate; he has often been regarded as something of a prophet of the twentieth century.

His reputation rests primarily on four long philosophical novels – Prestuplenie i nakazanie (Crime and Punishment) *(1866),* Idiot (The Idiot) *(1868–9),* Besy (The Possessed, *also known as* The Devils) *(1871–2) and* Brat'ia Karamazovy (The Brothers Karamazov) *(1879–80) – and on one novella,* Zapiski iz podpol'ia (Notes From Underground) *(1864). In his day, Dostoevskii was as famous for his journalistic writing as for his fiction, and a few of his articles have remained classics, including 'Mr. D–bov and the Question of Art' (1861) – a critique of utilitarian aesthetics – and 'Environment' (1873).*

Dostoevskii's works have had major influence on Western and Russian philosophy. In Russia, his novels inspired numerous religious thinkers, including Sergei Bulgakov and Nikolai Berdiaev; existentialists, such as Lev Shestov; and literary and ethical theorists, most notably Mikhail Bakhtin. In the West, his influence has also been great. Here, too, his writings are repeatedly cited (along with Kierkegaard's) as founding works of existentialism. Perhaps because of a misreading, they influenced Freud and Freudianism. Directly and through the medium of Bakhtin, his ideas have played a role in the rethinking of mind and language. And his rejection of utopianism and socialism has been repeatedly cited in twentieth-century political debates and theories.

Dostoevskii's influence has been diverse and at times contradictory, in part because of the different genres in which his ideas are expressed. Not only the overall meanings of his novels but also the views of his characters, including those he meant to refute, have been attributed to him. Moreover, his essays sometimes express ideas at variance with his novels. Most recently, philosophical significance has been discovered not only in the content but also in the very form of his novels. Their odd plot structure has been shown to have implications for an understanding of authorship, responsibility and time.

1 Life
2 Core ideas
3 Major works before *The Brothers Karamazov*
4 *The Brothers Karamazov*
5 Time, form and ethics

1 Life

The son of a military surgeon, Dostoevskii grew up in a pious household to which he attributed his (rather tortured) religious faith. Celebrated at a young age for his early fiction, he became involved in a secret socialist society, the Petrashevskii Circle, which was infiltrated by the tsarist secret police. In 1849 he was arrested and, after spending months in prison, was sentenced to be executed, a sentence reduced at the last possible moment. The experience of mock-execution shaped both his sense of how the human mind works in extreme situations and his obsession with temporality. Dostoevskii then spent years in a Siberian prison camp, which he later described in his short novel *Notes From the House of the Dead* (1860–1), and several more years in internal exile before being allowed to return to European Russia. By his own account, his time in Siberia changed his views decisively. He rediscovered his religious faith and decisively rejected Western utopian socialism. Imprisonment itself led him to appreciate the importance of privacy and of individual choice, which he felt were rejected by socialists. Attending to the psychology of criminals, he came to see more clearly the irrational in everyone and rejected rationalist and utilitarian models of the psyche. Above all, his experience living among common people developed in him a deep distaste for the condescension of

intellectuals who professed to save 'the people', whom they hardly knew. In the process, he came to reject the intellectuals' principal tool, abstract theory, as inadequate to the complexity of real human needs and motives.

Upon returning to Russia, Dostoevskii worked alternately as a journalist and a novelist. During this time, he suffered from a variety of misfortunes, including the epilepsy that first struck him in Siberia, compulsive gambling and constant indebtedness. He was forced to travel abroad to escape creditors and developed a deep distaste for the West. During his epileptic seizures, he experienced an extraordinary sense of universal harmony and of the cessation of all temporal processes, topics that appear prominently in his fiction (especially *The Idiot*) and fed his interest in time. His gambling led him to explore the human need for the radically uncertain and (a favourite problem) the nature of self-destructive behaviour performed by people who recognize it as such. His indebtedness and poverty, which reached extremes, sometimes forced him to write and publish his novels serially without an advance plan. Consequently, he was at times as uncertain as his characters about their destiny. He eventually made a virtue of this process, and by so doing discovered new ways to represent the openness of the future and the palpability of choice. He managed to transfer the excitement of the creative process to the novels themselves as he wrote them and as the readers read them.

His politics grew increasingly conservative, or rather anti-revolutionary, as he wrote novels about people possessed by extreme and radical ideologies. Although for most of his life Dostoevskii was severely sceptical about the possibility of a substantive philosophy of history, for a period of about two years (1876–7), he reversed his stance and imagined he had discovered the key to history and the signs of an imminent apocalypse, after which Russia would assume a messianic role and lead the world. These views appear in *Dnevnik pisatelia* (*A Writer's Diary*) (published intermittently from 1873 to 1881), a work that also experimented with turning a one-person periodical into a peculiar literary genre open to the contingencies of current events. Some articles written during this period, which occasionally included anti-Semitic diatribes, remain the greatest embarrassment to his contemporary admirers. Having come to his senses, he produced his greatest and probably most humane work, *The Brothers Karamazov*, shortly before his death in 1881.

2 Core ideas

Perhaps the core idea of Dostoevskii's works is human

freedom. Famous as a psychological writer, he declared that he was not in fact a psychologist, if by that term one meant a person who regards human behaviour as governed by laws that make it in principle predictable. He described the historical process as not subject to laws and decisively rejected any theory guaranteeing progress (or any other outcome). In his theology, he insisted that the essence of Christianity was free choice, and so any religion that offered 'miracle, mystery, and authority' (a phrase in *The Brothers Karamazov*) as ways of allaying doubt were in fact anti-Christian. Thus uncertainty and striving without guarantees was essential, not detrimental, to Christian belief. For a similar reason, utopian politics promising to offer a final solution to ensure happiness would deprive us of our humanity, which is essentially a matter of effort, of choices that can be mistaken, and of processes without guaranteed outcomes.

Dostoevskii's novels consequently develop an anti-deterministic theory of time in which each moment possesses the potential for multiple futures. Whatever did happen at a given moment something else might have. In his articles on crime he argued, and in his novels he illustrated, that human intentions are often essentially processual: there may never be a moment when a decision is made, even subconsciously. Rather, a shifting and always incomplete process governs behaviour from moment to moment. In such cases, the ascription of an intention in the usual sense is a retrospective activity oversimplifying the facts. If a crime committed in this way could be repeated, the result might well be different, because the process allows for many possibilities at each moment of choice. One meaning of the image of the devil, who appears as a character in *The Brothers Karamazov*, is the personification of the forces introducing radical uncertainty into the world.

It followed for Dostoevskii that all ethical philosophy aspiring to iron-clad rules for moral action must be mistaken; for if such rules could be provided, action according to them would lack the quality of choosing the good in the face of uncertainty. Christ's image, not an abstract philosophy, must be our guide. The unknowability of the future also explains the fallacy behind utilitarian views of art. Dostoevskii agrees that art should be useful, but he contends that utility should apply to an uncertain future, when our purposes may be far from those of the present. Great art lasts because it is capable of affecting us in radically different times and places. Among the qualities that allow art to be unforeseeably useful is beauty.

Insisting on human unpredictability, Dostoevskii rejected utopian schemes because they were based on too great a confidence in the needs of humanity as a whole and too little concern for individuals to make their own varying choices. Indeed, thinkers who place too much faith in an abstract theory are unlikely to recognize that people are essentially processual. Nevertheless, Dostoevskii believed that utopians with an unjustifiable faith in salvationist theories would likely seize control. As a result, he was probably unique among nineteenth-century writers in predicting that the twentieth century would be the era of what we have come to call totalitarianism, the features of which he described (especially in *The Possessed*) in remarkably accurate detail.

Dostoevskii's distrust of theory, especially his rejection of materialist and rationalist definitions of humanity, led him to another prescient prediction, this one pertaining to Western liberal societies. Whereas others typically assumed that increasing wealth and expanding freedoms would lead to reduced crime, Dostoevskii predicted the opposite. What would swamp liberal progress would be a decline in religious belief and the conviction that moral norms transcend utilitarian purposes. The more people come to accept that good and evil are merely social constructs, the less restraint they will feel. If God is dead, then all is permitted, as Ivan Karamazov says (in *The Brothers Karamazov*). No amount of law enforcement could ever compensate for the inner conviction that crime is simply morally wrong in the eyes of God or from the perspective of some transcendent value. Moreover, the very theory that crime is merely the product of the social environment is itself part of the social environment. Its acceptance is bound to increase crime. Dostoevskii repeatedly performs this self-reflexive act on theories, a move that fits well with his novelistic technique of examining ideas by their lived consequences.

3 Major works before *The Brothers Karamazov*

Zapiski iz podpol'ia (*Notes From Underground*) (1864) consists of two parts, a paradoxical philosophical diatribe by the narrator and a series of reminiscences of his earlier life. Part I argues, and both parts illustrate, the complexity of psychological processes that transcend all theories presuming human rationality. His critique of all rational choice models can still stand as a useful corrective today. These models fail for two important reasons. First, they are false to actual experience. The underground man cites witty examples from daily life and history that only the most tortured or tautological reasoning could subsume under a model of rationality. Second, the most important human preference does not resemble the others and cannot be listed along with them: the desire to choose unpredictably. Any model that makes human action in principle predictable deprives us of our very selves. Satisfy all our desires, and we will desire to harm ourselves, simply to show that we are people and not 'organ stops' or 'piano keys'. That is, our greatest desire is a meta-desire, a longing to desire unpredictably. That is the source of the underground man's 'spite', a concept to which he gives metaphysical significance.

In the course of his tirade, the underground man also rejects the existence of any historical laws and all models discerning an inner rationality to history. Alluding to Hegel, he observes: 'The only thing one cannot say [about history] is that it is rational'. Polemicizing with Buckle and liberal faith in a law of progress, he observes that civilization has given humanity more efficient and crueller ways to kill and torture each other (another passage anticipating the twentieth century). Thinkers invent historical and social laws because they have decided in advance that only such an approach is truly scientific, which is ironic because science involves fidelity to the facts. 'But man is so fond of systems and abstract deductions that he is ready to distort the truth intentionally, he is ready to deny what he can see and hear just to justify his logic' ([1912–20] 1960: 21).

If determinism were correct and if scholars really could know the true laws of history and psychology, then human life would turn into 'extracting square roots' and behaving according to 'a table of logarithms'. Life would then be simply a finished product, but it can be meaningful only as a process. All utopian schemes, with their image of a finished and perfected world, would, if realized, become prisons, houses of the dead. Nevertheless, Dostoevskii also rejects the underground man's way of opposing such rationalism by pure spite. Spite, the novel demonstrates, also has its own iron-clad, if perverse, logic. Real freedom cannot be found simply by inverting determinism, as the underground man does. Rather, the work implies, it demands the Christian concept of humanity as free and the self as developing in relation to others.

In *Crime and Punishment* (1866), Dostoevskii explores the psychology of an intellectual who wants to live according to various theories justifying murder. The novel shows each of these theories to be inadequate to the way people actually live and feel. Indeed, the theories motivating the hero contradict each other, as one justifies killing as moral on utilitarian grounds while another denies that morality is anything but an empty social construct. Moreover, the hero finds himself unable to account, after the crime, for his decision to commit it, the reason being that he never actually made a decision. He was, rather, possessed by a state of mind that guided him

processually, moment by moment, in a dream-like state. Taken as a whole, the novel refutes ideology – not just particular theories, but the ideological cast of mind itself – by psychology.

One of the hero's theories is that humanity is divided into two groups, a majority of ordinary people who serve as mere breeders and a minority of innovators who have the right to transgress all moral codes. Dostoevskii suggests that the desire to be a superman in this way is typical of any intelligentsia that takes its theories too seriously. Even, or especially, if such schemes promise to make people happy, they will lead to killing and cause more harm than good. But they exert an almost irresistible appeal for intelligentsias.

The Idiot (1868–9) written without an advance plan with the author discovering the course of events along with his characters, may be taken as a kind of thought experiment. The author creates a perfectly good man and sees what effect he would have on real people, whose psychology includes the perverse and irrational as well as more normal human motivations. People often react to the Idiot's goodness by feeling resentful at their own moral inferiority, which leads them to still worse behaviour. The result is that, because of his very goodness, he destroys both himself and almost everyone around him.

In effect turning its own processual composition into a theme, this novel also explores the nature of time, arguing (in what is probably the work's most famous passage) that 'Columbus was happy not when he had discovered America, but when he was discovering it.... It's life that matters, nothing but life – the process of discovering, the everlasting and perpetual process, not the discovery itself, at all' ([1912–20] 1962: 21).

The Possessed, often considered the greatest European political novel, explores the mentality of revolutionaries and fashionable liberals. Almost as critical of liberals as of radicals, Dostoevskii saw the former as the progenitors of the latter, even though they are often horrified by them. Both share the mentality of the intelligentsia, which views itself as entrusted with the salvation of humanity. The novel criticizes the tendency of utopians to reason down from abstract principles, which leads them to absurd but dangerous social conclusions. Arguably the most quoted line of the novel belongs to one radical theoretician: 'Starting from unlimited freedom, I arrive at unlimited despotism'. In a passage that seems to anticipate the Chinese Cultural Revolution, the novel attacks radical egalitarianism as an ideal. Under socialism, one revolutionary declares, 'All are slaves and equal in their slavery... the great thing about it is equality... Cicero will have his tongue cut out, Copernicus will have his eyes put out, Shakespeare will be stoned' ([1912–20] 1963: 424).

4   *The Brothers Karamazov*

More extensively than any other work of Dostoevskii, *The Brothers Karamazov* explores the nature of Christian truth. Developing an idea in *The Idiot*, Dostoevskii demonstrates that goodness consists of small, kindly actions, rather than great and heroic deeds. Small actions may have a concatenating effect no one can foresee. Evil, too, is conceived as consisting primarily of day-to-day actions. Thus in one chapter, when the devil appears as a character, he is not grand, Satanic and alien, but ordinary and banal. This 'petty devil' is one of Dostoevskii's most famous creations.

The height of Dostoevskii's achievement appears in a sequence of three chapters, in which the intellectual brother, Ivan, tries to seduce his pious younger brother, Alësha, from religion by refuting Christianity on moral grounds. It is remarkable that these arguments, coming from the pen of a Christian author, have often been considered to be the strongest pages ever written against faith. In 'Rebellion', Ivan contrasts all conceivable theodicies with the reality of innocently suffering children. Ivan has also composed 'The Grand Inquisitor', a story in which Christ returns to earth during the Spanish Inquisition and is arrested by the Grand Inquisitor, who contends that Christ should have accepted the temptations of the devil just as (he says) the Catholic Church actually has. The Inquisitor reasons that people do not want to be free, only to think they are free. They can be happy only when their consciences are held by others and their choices are made for them, so they will not feel guilt or regret whatever happens. The Inquisitor's ideals evidently represent socialism as well as Catholicism, two apparently antagonist movements that, in Dostoevskii's view, were really the same because they share an anthropology.

Christ never replies to the Inquisitor, and the Inquisitor's arguments appear irresistible, and yet the reader, for reasons that are hard to specify, adheres all the more strongly to the Christian ideal of freedom. Ivan has 'refuted' God the Father in 'Rebellion' and God the Son in 'The Grand Inquisitor', but he has unwittingly adhered to the Holy Spirit in 'The Brothers Make Friends'. Here his sheer love of 'the sticky green leaves that open in the spring' expresses a love of God's world. As elsewhere in the novel, Dostoevskii's point is that faith comes not from doctrine but from how one lives moment to moment. It is not doctrine that leads to faith, but faith, born of good living, that may lead to acceptance of doctrine,

which is not the content of true religion but its expression.

The novel's plot turns on Ivan's theory that moral responsibility, if it exists at all, pertains only to actions, not to wishes. Ivan will do nothing to harm his thoroughly noxious father, but 'in my wishes I reserve myself full latitude'. When his father is killed, Ivan comes to feel guilty precisely for wishing his father's death. He is right to do so, because the novel demonstrates that most evil happens indirectly, because a climate of evil is created by our evil wishes. In such a climate, crime is bound to happen one way or another. The proximate cause of such crimes is less important than the climate. Because all of us indulge such wishes, 'everyone is responsible for everyone and for everything', as the novel's holy Father Zosima contends ([1912–20] 1950: 244). This logic also explains why the devil, as the personification of evil, is thoroughly ordinary.

We are reminded of the Sermon on the Mount, where Jesus says that we are responsible for our wishes. In this way, the novel demonstrates the truth of the Gospel psychologically. Ivan's doctrines, whatever their strength as dialectic, run counter to the human spirit. Of course, Dostoevskii's psychological 'proof' of Christianity does not demonstrate the existence of God or the doctrine of the Trinity. But it does show that faith is grounded not in some philosophical propositions, but existentially and anthropologically, in the depths of our being.

Like *Notes From Underground* and *The Possessed*, *The Brothers Karamazov* explores the psychology of 'the insulted and the humiliated', a trade mark theme of Dostoevskii. If one understands this spiritual state, one will see that those afflicted with the psychology of their own victimization are precisely the ones who understand best how to inflict pain on others and who are most likely to seek revenge by doing so. It follows that such people, for all their claims to the moral high ground, are the last ones in whom one should entrust political power.

5   Time, form and ethics

Deeply concerned with describing time as open, Dostoevskii remained suspicious that the well-structured plots of traditional novels implicitly endorse determinism or fatalism. The problem is that in these works everything fits and events take place not only because of prior causation, as in life, but also in order to fit a pattern visible when the work is over. Thus, contingency is ruled out. Dostoevskii therefore developed a method of writing ensuring that the reader senses at each moment that whatever happens, something else easily could have. Time therefore becomes a field of possibilities. Nothing is tending to a pregiven ending – which, in fact, Dostoevskii himself sometimes did not know. The unstructured quality of some of his works, which often contain numerous loose ends, results from this technique. On the other hand, the extraordinary suspense of his novels derives from this method of representing time the way it is experienced in life, as truly open. Thus the very form of Dostoevskii's novels became an instrument of his argument for freedom in an open world containing 'an infinite multitude of ramifications' (as one character in *The Idiot* says) and countless possibilities, shaped by chance and by our own actions.

The sense of open time is also reflected in Dostoevskii's ethical tenets. If people are fundamentally free, then they always have the ability to be surprising. It followed for Dostoevskii that one thing we must never do is treat others as if they were fully known quantities, as if we could be sure what they are going to do, as the various schools of psychology in principle do. In rejecting determinism, materialism, nihilism, historicism and psychologism, while rethinking the nature of narrative art, Dostoevskii explored the meaning of human freedom.

See also: BAKHTIN, M.M.; BERDIAEV, N.A.; BULGAKOV, S.N.; EXISTENTIALISM; SHESTOV, L.

List of works

Dostoevskii, F.M. (1972–90) *Polnoe sobranie sochinenii F.M. Dostoevskogo* (The Complete Works of F.M. Dostoevskii), Leningrad: Nauka, 30 vols. (The standard Russian edition of Dostoevskii's works.)

—— [Dostoevsky] (1912–20) *The Novels of Fyodor Dostoevsky*, trans. C. Garnett, 12 vols; repr. New York: Modern Library, 1950; repr. New York: Dutton, 1960. (The best translation of Dostoevskii's novels, reissued and revised many times.)

—— (1860–1) *Zapiski iz mërtvogo doma in Vremia*, trans. C. Garnett, *Notes From the House of the Dead*, New York: Dutton, 1960. (Describes Dostoevskii's years in a Siberian prison camp.)

—— (1864) *Zapiski iz podpol'ia*, trans. C. Garnett, revised R. Matlaw, *Notes From Underground*, New York: Dutton, 1960. (Examined in §3.)

—— (1866) *Prestuplenie i nakazanie*, in *Russkii vestnik*; trans. C. Garnett, *Crime and Punishment*, New York: Dutton, 1960. (Exploration of the psychology of an intellectual who wants to live according to various theories justifying murder.)

—— (1868–9) *Idiot*, in *Russkii vestnik*; trans. C. Garnett, *The Idiot*, New York: Modern Library, 1962. (Examined in §3.)

—— (1871–2) *Besy*, trans. C. Garnett, *The Possessed*, New York: Modern Library, 1963. (Often considered to be the greatest European political novel. Explores the mentality of revolutionaries and fashionable liberals.)

—— (1873, 1876–7, 1880, 1881) *Dnevnik pisatelia*, trans. K. Lantz, A Writer's Diary, Evanston, IL: Northwestern University Press, 1993, 1994, 2 vols. (Referred to in §1.)

—— (1879–80) *Brat'ia Karamazovy*, in *Russkii vestnik*; trans. C. Garnett, *The Brothers Karamazov*, New York: Modern Library, 1950. (Examined in §4.)

—— (1963) *Dostoevsky's Occasional Writings*, ed. and trans. D. Magarshack, New York: Random House. (A collection of Dostoevskii's nonfictional works.)

References and further reading

Bakhtin, M. (1929) *Problemy poetiki Dostoevskogo*; expanded 2nd edn 1963; ed. and trans. C. Emerson, *Problems of Dostoevsky's Poetics*, Minneapolis, MN: University of Minnesota Press, 1984. (The most influential book on Dostoevskii, this theoretical study explores the significance of his invention of 'the polyphonic novel', develops a theory of language and relates Dostoevskii's work to ethics, psychology and authorship.)

Frank, J. (1986) *Dostoevsky: The Stir of Liberation, 1860–65*, Princeton, NJ: Princeton University Press. (Part of Frank's five-volume biography, this book situates Dostoevskii's ideas about nihilism, socialism and materialism in the intellectual milieu of his time. It discusses *Notes From Underground*.)

—— (1995) *Dostoevsky: The Miraculous Years, 1865–71*, Princeton, NJ: Princeton University Press. (This volume of Frank's biography deals with *Crime and Punishment*, *The Idiot* and *The Possessed*.)

Jackson, R.L. (1966) *Dostoevsky's Quest for Form: A Study of His Philosophy of Art*, New Haven, CT: Yale University Press. (Explores Dostoevskii's aesthetics as expressed in his articles and embodied in his work.)

Morson, G.S. (1994) *Narrative and Freedom: The Shadows of Time*, New Haven, CT: Yale University Press. (An exploration of the philosophy of time and narrative form in Dostoevskii and other writers.)

GARY SAUL MORSON

DOUBLE EFFECT, PRINCIPLE OF

'Double effect' refers to the good and bad effects which may foreseeably follow from one and the same act. The principle of double effect originates in Aquinas' ethics, and is supposed to guide decision about acts with double effect where the bad effect is something that must not be intended, such as the death of an innocent person. The principle permits such acts only if the bad effect is unintended, not disproportionate to the intended good effect, and unavoidable if the good effect is to be achieved. The principle has wide relevance in the moral evaluation of acts which have foreseen double effects. Controversy arises over the identification of the agent's intention in difficult cases, and over the use of the principle to resolve issues such as abortion, euthanasia, the use of pain-relieving drugs which hasten death, self-defence, and the killing of certain sorts of non-combatants in war.

1 The role of the principle
2 Origin, development, conditions and application
3 Criticisms, difficulties and further applications

1 The role of the principle

The principle, or doctrine, of double effect is important in the application of moral theory to practical cases. The principle asserts the moral relevance of a distinction between those effects of our acts which are intended and those effects which are foreseen but unintended. Sometimes in acting for the best we bring about an unavoidable yet foreseen bad effect which is not part of what we are aiming to achieve. For instance, a doctor prescribes chemotherapy for cancer, knowing that this treatment also causes hair loss; a driver whose brakes fail swerves in order to avoid a group of children on a pedestrian crossing, foreseeing that the car will hit someone standing at the side of the road; a teacher fails an essay that does not deserve to pass, knowing that the student will be upset. 'Double effect' refers to the two foreseen effects of acts such as these: the good effect (eliminating cancer, saving lives, maintaining academic standards) which the agent intends, and the bad effect (hair loss, injuring or killing someone, causing distress) which the agent foresees but does not act in order to bring about.

Many acts with double effect can be characterized as instances of bringing about the lesser of two evils: opting for what is morally more important, at the expense of foreseeably causing a bad effect which is outweighed by the intended good effect. Where the foreseen bad effect is itself morally serious (such as the death of an innocent person), the principle of double effect holds that the bad effect must be unintended: it must not be what the agent aims to achieve in the circumstances nor a means to bringing about the intended good effect. The principle could permit the driver to swerve in order to avoid hitting the children on the crossing, even though the person standing at the side of the road is thereby seriously endangered. But the principle does not permit an agent to kill an innocent person as a means of saving others; the driver must not aim to kill the person at the side of the road as part of a plan.

2 Origin, development, conditions and application

The principle is traceable to Aquinas' justification, in *Summa theologiae*, of homicide in self-defence. Aquinas held that a private person must never kill anyone intentionally; hence his appeal to 'double effect' in justifying foreseen killing in self-defence. The use of lethal force in self-defence has two foreseen effects: saving oneself (good effect) and the death of the aggressor (bad effect). Aquinas maintained that, provided one's intention is only to use necessary and proportionate force in warding off an unjust attack, the aggressor's death is unintended.

The principle of double effect has been developed subsequently as a general precept of nonconsequentialist ethics. The principle is central to absolutist moral theories which hold that some intended acts are always intrinsically evil and that it is never permissible to use an evil means to achieve a good end. The combination of these two tenets can make moral decision very difficult in some cases in which agents will foreseeably bring about a serious bad effect whatever they do. If the driver whose brakes fail does not swerve, the children on the crossing will probably be killed; if the driver does swerve, the person at the side of the road will probably be killed. As a guide to decision in such cases, the principle holds that under strict conditions it is permissible foreseeably to bring about an effect of a type that it is never permissible to intend. These conditions are: that the act itself (in this case, swerving the car) be morally good or indifferent; that the bad effect (killing the one person) be an unavoidable, unintended effect of the act which also achieves the good effect (saving the children); and that the good effect be sufficiently weighty to warrant causing the bad effect. The last condition, proportionality, must always be taken into account. The agent's good intention, and the fact that the bad effect is unintended, are on their own insufficient to permit foreseeably causing serious harm. Evaluation of the relative seriousness of good and bad foreseen effects is sometimes reasonably straightforward, but sometimes can be difficult.

The distinction between intended and unintended effects is also more widely invoked as part of nonabsolutist, nonconsequentialist moral theories which hold that the agent's intention is important to the moral evaluation of acts which have both good and bad foreseen effects.

3 Criticisms, difficulties and further applications

Critical discussions of the principle focus on the distinction between incidental and intended effects and on its relevance to practical moral problems. According to the principle, a foreseen bad effect is unintended provided it is incidental to what the agent aims to achieve in the circumstances and to the means of bringing about the intended good effect. If we return to the example of the swerving car, incidental and intended effects are distinguished easily: the driver does not swerve the car in order to hit the person at the side of the road, but in order to avoid hitting the children; the children are saved not by that person's being harmed but by the car's swerving. Exponents of the principle often invoke the so-called 'test of failure' in maintaining that particular foreseen bad effects are incidental both to the agent's aim and to the means of its achievement in the circumstances. This test, which Duff (1990) points out must be applied in the light of the agent's beliefs at the time of acting, asks: would agents fail to achieve what they intend if, contrary to expectation, the foreseen bad effect does not occur? To this question, the swerving driver can answer sincerely, 'No, I intend to harm as few people as possible; my aim will be achieved if the person at the side of the road somehow escapes injury.' However, both the identification of the agent's intention and the distinction between the foreseen good and bad effects, on which the principle relies, can be difficult. For instance, if I can stop an aggressor only by shooting through an innocent person whom the aggressor is using as a shield, do I intend harm to the innocent shield or not? If the 'test of failure' is plausibly to identify particular foreseen bad effects as incidental, such effects must be distinguishable in a defensible way both from the good effect and from the means of achieving it in the circumstances. As has been suggested by Foot (1967), the principle cannot allow one to maintain that one does not intend to kill someone, but only to blow them to pieces. The characterization of the agent's intention in the context of some traditional applications of the principle, such as termination of ectopic pregnancy and homicide in self-defence, is problematic. These

important difficulties have been addressed by both advocates and critics of the principle.

The principle of double effect is relevant to critical legal thinking about, for instance, the mental element of murder, and the appropriateness of the defence of necessity in cases of justified risk taking. In paradigm acts of double effect the agent foresees both the good and bad effects as certain or highly probable. The distinction between intended and foreseen effects, however, is also applicable to acts of justifiable risk taking, in which the good and bad effects are incompatible possible outcomes; in such cases the bad effect can even be the more likely to occur. For example, a surgeon might justifiably operate in a desperate attempt to save someone's life, foreseeing that the surgery or its effects may well kill the patient; a parent might justifiably throw a child out of a burning building as its only hope of survival, realizing that the fall may well kill it.

See also: INTENTION; RESPONSIBILITY

References and further reading

Anscombe, G.E.M. (1961) 'War and Murder', in W. Stein (ed.) *Nuclear Weapons: A Catholic Response*, London, Merlin Press; repr. in *Collected Philosophical Papers*, Oxford: Blackwell, 1981, vol. 3, 51–61. (Clear absolutist defence of the principle; critical discussion of its application to killing non-combatants in war.)

* Aquinas, T. (1266–73) *Summa theologiae* (Synopsis of Theology), London: Eyre & Spottiswood, 1966, vol. 38, IIa.IIae.64, esp. answer 7. (Formulation of the principle in context of self-defence.)

Connell, F.J. (1967) 'Double Effect, Principle of', in *New Catholic Encyclopedia*, New York: McGraw-Hill, vol. 4, 1020–2. (Clear traditional statement of the principle and its conditions.)

* Duff, R.A. (1990) *Intention, Agency and Criminal Liability*, Oxford: Blackwell, chaps 3–5. (Detailed discussion of the distinction between intention and foresight and its legal significance.)

Finnis, J. (1991) 'Intention and Side-Effects', in R.G. Frey and C.W. Morris (eds) *Liability and Responsibility*, Cambridge: Cambridge University Press, 32–64. (Considers the legal significance of distinction between intention and foresight.)

* Foot, P. (1967) 'The Problem of Abortion and the Doctrine of Double Effect', *Oxford Review* 5; repr. in *Virtues and Vices*, Oxford: Blackwell, 1978, 19–32. (Critique of the principle and its application to abortion.)

Grisez, G. (1970) 'Towards a Consistent Natural Law Ethics of Killing', *The American Journal of*

Jurisprudence 15: 64–96. (Complex interpretation of the principle, in terms of its application to abortion and self-defence.)

Mangan, J. (1949) 'An Historical Analysis of the Principle of Double Effect', *Theological Studies* X (1): 41–61. (Outlines the historical beginnings of the principle, and its development through to modern times.)

Quinn, W. (1989) 'Actions, Intentions, and Consequences: The Doctrine of Double Effect', *Philosophy and Public Affairs* 18 (4): 334–51. (Nonabsolutist defence of the principle.)

Uniacke, S. (1984) 'The Doctrine of Double Effect', *The Thomist* 48 (2): 188–218. (General critical discussion of the principle.)

—— (1994) *Permissible Killing: The Self-Defence Justification of Homicide*, Cambridge: Cambridge University Press, ch. 4. (Detailed critique of the principle's application to self-defence.)

SUZANNE UNIACKE

DOUBT

Doubt is often defined as a state of indecision or hesitancy with respect to accepting or rejecting a given proposition. Thus, doubt is opposed to belief. But doubt is also contrasted with certainty. Since it seems intelligible to say that there are many things we believe without being completely certain about them, it appears that we may not have a unitary concept of doubt.

Although doubt is often associated in philosophy with scepticism, historically the relation between the two is complex. Moreover, some philosophers deny that sceptical arguments have any essential connection with inducing doubts.

Sceptical doubts, as philosophers understand them, differ from ordinary doubts in their depth and generality. We all have doubts about some things. But the philosophical sceptic wonders whether we ever have the slightest reason to believe one thing rather than another. However, the reasonableness of such doubts – and even their intelligibility – remains controversial. The various attitudes philosophers adopt with respect to the status of sceptical doubts characterize the main approaches to epistemological theory.

1   **Doubt, belief and certainty**
2–3   **Philosophical doubt**

1   Doubt, belief and certainty

Dictionaries typically run together concepts such as indecision and hesitancy, contrasting doubt with both belief and certainty. But as we can evidently believe something without being certain about it, it seems that our concept of doubt itself may not be clear-cut. It is tempting to speculate that this seeming duality is a result of competing epistemological traditions: an older tradition that identifies knowledge with demonstrative knowledge, hence with rational certainty (see CERTAINTY), and a newer tradition for which probabilistic justification is sufficient. But it is also worth noting that 'belief' has become a term of art. Outside philosophy, reference to a person's 'beliefs' is likely to mean their fundamental convictions and not just anything they might be said to accept. Even in philosophy, much discussion of doubt has had in the background questions about religious faith, which might also contribute to a dictionary's associating belief with certainty.

Thinking of belief in the modern philosopher's wide sense, how should we understand the relations between belief, certainty and doubt? One question concerns whether belief is an all-or-nothing matter or whether it admits of degrees. For Bayesians, although there are some beliefs to which we assign the highest possible strength, most belief is partial (see PROBABILITY THEORY AND EPISTEMOLOGY). So from a Bayesian standpoint, although there is a natural contrast between doubt and certainty, doubt is not opposed to belief.

What if we insist that belief is all-or-nothing? It is widely held that there are two types of certainty: subjective (which applies to persons), and objective (which applies to propositions). So we might say that, when we assent to propositions on inconclusive evidence, we recognize *them* to be less than certain but *we* have made up our minds. To assent is to eliminate subjective uncertainty – that is, doubt.

This is not conclusive. Even if belief is all-or-nothing, some beliefs are more firmly rooted than others. If we think of these degrees of entrenchment as degrees of subjective certainty, 'doubt versus belief' and 'doubt versus certainty' will draw different distinctions. In reply, we might say that a shallowly rooted proposition is one I regard as doubt*ful* – that is, open to reasonable doubt – which does entail its being doubt*ed*. But it seems equally natural to say that this would be something I accept, while still having doubts about it. Our concept of doubt just may not be unitary.

2   Philosophical doubt

In philosophy, doubt has often been connected with scepticism. However, for the ancient sceptics, suspension of judgment is not doubt but its cure (see

PYRRHONISM). This makes sense if we think of doubt as an *uncomfortable* state of indecision, the discomfort arising from a persisting desire to decide. If systematic suspension of judgment attenuates this desire, it eliminates the anxiety of doubt.

Scepticism can vary in strength. A fairly weak form of scepticism denies that anything is certain (doubt versus certainty again). By contrast, radical scepticism attacks the possibility of our being able to justify a belief to even the slightest degree. Scepticism can also vary in scope: it can be narrowly focused; it can pertain to certain broad classes of beliefs (for example, all beliefs about the external world); it can be universal. The sceptic's 'philosophical' doubts are distinguished from ordinary doubts by both their unusual depth and their generality: they extend to matters that are not ordinarily doubted, or even considered open to doubt.

Philosophers have been interested mainly in *reasonable* doubt – doubt for which one has a good reason – and particularly with the *limits* of reasonable doubt. Since sceptical arguments suggest that the scope for reasonable doubt is much wider than we normally suppose, exploring the limits of reasonable doubt is very much a matter of exploring the limits of scepticism.

The fundamental argument for universal scepticism goes back to the classical Greek sceptics and centres on a deadly trilemma: that any attempt to justify a belief leads to a vicious regress, reasoning in a circle, or reliance on brute assumptions. This argument would be defeated if we could identify beliefs which could not rationally be doubted. The quest for such 'basic' beliefs is characteristic of foundationalism (see FOUNDATIONALISM). However, philosophical opinion has moved steadily away from regarding any beliefs as strictly indubitable. Contemporary foundationalists mostly favour a more modest conception of basic beliefs, according them some intrinsic but defeasible credibility (see KNOWLEDGE, DEFEASIBILITY THEORY OF).

It would be desirable to defeat universal scepticism without resort to the idea of intrinsically credible basic beliefs. Beliefs that can plausibly be accorded this privileged status tend to be unambitious with respect to their content, which makes problematic their adequacy as a basis for reasonable belief. Thus foundationalism meets one kind of scepticism only at the cost of threatening us with others. Consider scepticism with respect to knowledge of the external world. The argument for this form of scepticism famously occurs in Descartes, who claims that, since his entire experience of the world could be a kind of systematic hallucination induced by an evil demon, all his beliefs about external reality can reasonably be doubted, at least until he sees how the possibility of such deception can be eliminated (see DESCARTES, R. §4). But the thought that experiential knowledge underdetermines what it is reasonable to believe about the world makes a sceptical point only if, in the last analysis, experiential beliefs are intrinsically 'epistemologically prior' to beliefs about the world. Generalized doubts depend on generalized relations of justificatory dependence.

If this is correct, 'Cartesian' doubts depend essentially on foundationalism. However, many philosophers, including Stroud (1984b) and Nagel (1986), deny that any sceptical arguments depend on such highly specific and controversial epistemological commitments. They see scepticism as 'natural' or intuitive in the sense of arising out of the most ordinary and everyday epistemological considerations; but this conception of scepticism is more difficult to defend than is often thought.

Since by ordinary standards the error-possibility Descartes cites as a ground for doubt is remote, how reasonable are his doubts? The answer to this question is complicated by the fact that the 'reasonableness' of doubt is affected by other than purely epistemological considerations. For example, in a situation where the costs of making a mistake are very high, it might be reasonable to remain in doubt about something even though in possession of evidence that would ordinarily be considered sufficient (see CONTEXTUALISM, EPISTEMOLOGICAL). This suggests a defence of the reasonableness of doubts based on the remote error-possibilities that figure in sceptical arguments. True, such possibilities are not to be taken seriously in ordinary contexts of inquiry. But Descartes' project – a systematic, reconstruction of human knowledge from the ground upwards – is far from ordinary. This project, which requires setting aside all practical concerns, enforces a higher standard of certainty than would be reasonable in everyday contexts. However, this argument, because of its emphasis on certainty, is not clearly a defence of the reasonableness of radical scepticism, which is the most interesting type.

Hume claims that sceptical 'doubts' are not just unreasonable but entirely fictitious. According to Hume, no one seriously doubts that there is an external world because it is psychologically impossible to doubt such 'natural' beliefs. Having a theoretical answer to scepticism is neither here nor there. (This line of thought has recently been endorsed by Strawson (1985).) There are two replies. One draws on the point made above: that sceptical doubts arise only in the context of a distinctive kind of theoretical inquiry. To be sure, no one ordinarily doubts the things the sceptic questions; but why does this show that they are always and everywhere immune from doubt? Even Hume admits to being overwhelmed by sceptical doubts when he withdraws from ordinary concerns and reflects on their rational basis. The second reply (see, for example, Harman 1973) defends the interest of sceptical arguments by denying that they have any essential connection with doubt. We do not need to refute the sceptic to assuage anyone's actual doubts. Rather, the hope is to learn something about knowledge by seeing how such arguments go wrong. At bottom, these two replies are not all that different. Not even Descartes claims to be able permanently to strip himself of his ordinary beliefs. His doubting them in the course of philosophical inquiry consists in not taking them for granted. In this sense, even the most purely methodological sceptic may be said to doubt his commonsense convictions.

3 Philosophical doubt (cont.)

Highlighting the context-sensitivity of sceptical doubts raises interesting and unresolved issues about the relationship between the results of philosophical reflection and everyday practices of inquiry. The traditional view has been that philosophical reflection brings into view fundamental epistemological facts which 'practical' concerns lead us to ignore. So, if sceptical arguments are irrefutable, we have discovered, under the conditions of philosophical inquiry, that no belief about, say, the external world can be adequately justified. But if philosophical inquiry imposes extraordinary constraints on knowledge and justification, we may only have discovered that knowledge is impossible under the (self-imposed) conditions of philosophical inquiry.

There is a deep disagreement here. Is sceptical doubt rooted in fundamental, context-invariant facts, like the supposed epistemological priority of experiential beliefs over beliefs about the world, so that it points to something about knowledge in general? Call the view that it is 'epistemological realism' and note that it is far from obvious that ordinary epistemic practices commit us to such a conception of justificational relations. Or does what it is reasonable or even possible to doubt depend on contextually variable factors, most notably the kind of inquiry in which we are involved, so that sceptical doubt may be an artefact of a certain conception of epistemological investigation, hence (again) not at all 'natural'? This much is sure: if doubt is strongly contextually constrained, it is not a merely psychological fact that doubts which seem so compelling in the study dissipate in the street.

Traditional epistemological theories such as foundationalism and the coherence theory take sceptical doubts at face value and try to provide reassurance (see KNOWLEDGE AND JUSTIFICATION, COHERENCE THEORY OF; FOUNDATIONALISM). But some philosophers question the very intelligibility of universal doubt. This results from philosophy's having taken 'the linguistic turn'. Whereas language used to be regarded as a medium for the communication of thought, which was conceived to exist independently of language, the currently dominant view is that language is a *vehicle* of thought. This conception leads many philosophers to see an essential connection between truth and meaning: what our words mean – hence what thoughts we have – is a function of what sentences we hold true (see CHARITY, PRINCIPLE OF). To entertain all the thoughts we currently have while universally doubting their truth may not be as straightforward as once was supposed. Such ideas mesh nicely with a contextualized conception of doubt and justification. *Anything* may be dubitable, but not *everything* at once. We can keep doubt as a spur to inquiry without worrying that it is in permanent danger of getting out of hand.

See also: ERROR AND ILLUSION, INDIAN CONCEPTIONS OF; FALLIBILISM; RATIONAL BELIEFS; SCEPTICISM

References and further reading

Burnyeat, M. (1983) 'Can the Sceptic Live his Scepticism?', in M. Burnyeat (ed.) *The Skeptical Tradition*, Berkeley, CA: University of California Press. (Argues that the Pyrrhonian ideal of a life without belief cannot be realized.)

Cavell, S. (1979) *The Claim of Reason*, Oxford: Oxford University Press. (Part 2 is especially relevant. Claims that although the sceptic seems to adapt ordinary doubting procedures, his doubts are less than fully intelligible.)

Clarke, T. (1972) 'The Legacy of Skepticism', *Journal of Philosophy* 69 (20): 754–69. (Influential paper exploring a distinction between 'plain' and 'philosophical' doubts.)

Descartes, R. (1641) *Meditations on First Philosophy*, in J. Cottingham, R. Stoothoff and D. Murdoch (eds) *The Philosophical Writings of Descartes*, Cambridge: Cambridge University Press, 1975, vol. 2. (The most important discussion of sceptical doubts in early modern philosophy.)

Dewey, J. (1929) *The Quest for Certainty: Gifford Lectures 1929*, New York: Capricorn, 1960. (Fundamental text of US pragmatism, tracing sceptical worries to a misguided 'spectator' conception of knowledge.)

Fogelin, R. (1995) *Pyrrhonian Reflections on Knowledge and Justification*, Princeton, NJ: Princeton University Press. (Argues that Pyrrhonian doubts admit of no theoretical resolution.)

* Harman, G. (1973) *Thought*, Princeton, NJ: Princeton University Press. (Chapter 1 argues that 'refuting the sceptic' is purely a matter of understanding where sceptical arguments go wrong.)

Hume, D. (1751) *Enquiries Concerning Human Understanding and the Principles of Morals*, ed. L.A. Selby-Bigge, 3rd edition revised by P.H. Nidditch, Oxford: Oxford University Press, 1975. (A pivotal text in the sceptical tradition, claiming that our most fundamental beliefs are groundless but unshakeable.)

Moore, G.E. (1925) 'A Defence of Common Sense', in *Philosophical Papers*, London: Allen & Unwin, 1959. (Much-discussed paper, though critics disagree sharply over its intent and significance.)

* Nagel, T. (1995) *The View from Nowhere*, Oxford: Oxford University Press. (See especially chapter 10 where Nagel argues that sceptical doubts arise inevitably from our tendency to take an 'objective' view of our epistemic situation.)

Sextus Empiricus (*c.*200) *Outlines of Pyrrhonism (Sextus Empiricus Vol. 1)*, trans. R.G. Bury, London: Heinemann, 1933. (The most important source for ancient Greek scepticism.)

* Strawson, P. (1985) *Skepticism and Naturalism: Some Varieties*, London: Methuen. (See especially chapter 1. Defends the view that our resistance to sceptical doubts is at bottom psychological because our most fundamental beliefs are not a matter of 'reason'.)

Stroud, B. (1984a) *The Significance of Philosophical Scepticism*, Oxford: Oxford University Press. (Important critical examination of the main anti-sceptical strategies.)

* —— (1984b) 'Skepticism and the Possibility of Knowledge', *Journal of Philosophy* 81 (10): 545–51. (Denies that sceptical problems reflect commitment to epistemological foundationalism.)

Williams, M. (1988) 'Scepticism without Theory', *Review of Metaphysics* 41 (3): 547–88. (Argues that the difference between 'Pyrrhonian' and 'Cartesian' scepticism has been widely misunderstood.)

—— (1992) *Unnatural Doubts*, Oxford: Blackwell; corrected edn, Princeton, NJ: Princeton University Press, 1996. (Claims that sceptical problems depend on an antecedent commitment to contentious philosophical ideas.)

Wittgenstein, L. (1969) *On Certainty*, Oxford, Blackwell. (Argues that doubt can arise only within contexts in which other beliefs are held certain: hence global doubt is impossible.)

MICHAEL WILLIAMS

DOXOGRAPHY

*Doxography is a term describing the method of recording opinions (*doxai*) of philosophers frequently employed by ancient Greek writers on philosophy. It can also refer to texts or passages consisting of such accounts. The ancient tradition of doxographical writing finds its origin in the dialectical method of Aristotle and Theophrastus. Later works by authors such as Aëtius and Arius Didymus record much valuable material on ancient philosophers, although usually with little analysis or argumentation. Doxographical passages are also found in other ancient philosophical works, usually as a prelude to the discussion of a theme.*

The term 'doxography' is derived from the neologism *doxographus* introduced by the German scholar Herman Diels. Literally it means 'writer of opinions (*doxai*)'. In his great work *Doxographi Graeci* (1879) Diels collected various ancient documents which summarize the philosophical doctrines of ancient philosophers (particularly in the area of natural philosophy). He meant the term to contrast with *biographus*, 'writer of lives', although in practice it is difficult to make an absolute distinction between the two kinds of writings (see DIOGENES LAERTIUS).

If we examine the documents collected by Diels and others more closely, we can see that at least three different kinds of writing are found:

(1) In the so-called 'Placita' literature the organizing principle is systematic. Groups of *placita* (views) or *doxai* (opinions) are collected on particular subjects, each attributed to a philosopher or school: for example, 'Plato declared that the cosmos is unique. Democritus and Epicurus affirmed that there are infinite worlds', etc. The most famous example of such a collection is by Aëtius, first reconstructed by Diels on the basis of a Pseudo-Plutarchean *epitome* and extracts preserved by the anthologist Johannes Stobaeus.

(2) In the so-called 'On the Schools' (*Peri haereseōn*) literature, the doxographical information is collected in order to present the thought of a school of thought (for example, the Stoa) or an important philosopher (for example, its founder Zeno). Good examples of such doxographies are found in the surviving fragments of Arius Didymus and in Diogenes Laertius.

(3) A third genre that is related to doxography is the so-called 'Successions' (*diadochai*) literature, in which the generations of philosophers are linked to each other by way of a teacher–pupil relation, both prior to and during the development of the philosophical schools in the Hellenistic period: for example, Anaximander was the pupil of Thales in the so-called Ionian succession. The best surviving examples are the works on the Academy and the Stoa found in the library of PHILODEMUS at Herculaneum. Although in these works relatively little information is given on the doctrines of the philosophers, the principle of the succession is a feature shared with other doxographical accounts.

Apart from these specific doxographical writings, doxographies are frequently found in authors when they deal with particular philosophical topics. A famous example is found in Cicero's work *On the Nature of the Gods* (I 18–41), which begins with a long doxographical survey of theological opinions inserted in a piece of Epicurean polemic (see CICERO §3). This reflects the origin of the practice, which, as Mansfeld (1992) has shown, is to be located in the dialectical method introduced by Aristotle. When embarking on the examination of a philosophical theme, Aristotle often first collects and examines the so-called *endoxa* (reputable opinions). For example at the beginning of *On the Soul* (I 2.403b20) he states: 'For our study of soul it is necessary, when formulating the problems of which in our further advance we are to find the solutions, to summon the opinions (*doxai*) of our predecessors, so that we may profit by whatever is sound in their suggestions and avoid their errors'.

Aristotle's practice was continued and extended by his colleague and successor THEOPHRASTUS (§8). Especially influential appears to have been his large collection of *Physical Opinions* in eighteen books, which gave a systematic presentation of the views of the philosophers up to Plato on natural philosophy. This lost work is thought to have been the source of much material in later doxographical works and accounts, although the precise contours of its influence have proved difficult to trace.

From its origins in the Peripatetic school, the doxographical method became widely used in ancient philosophical writings. It is particularly common in Patristic sources, since it gives a quick overview of pagan thinking. A defect of doxography is that in the course of time it tends to become rather schematic, eschewing both argument and analysis, and concentrating chiefly on the juxtaposition of views or on a thin skeleton of doctrine. This lack of argumentation has given the doxographical tradition a bad name.

Nevertheless it should be recognized that it has distinctive methods (especially involving the use of disjunction and diaeresis), which give us important insights into the way that ancient philosophers handled their own history. Moreover it has preserved a great amount of invaluable information on the views of philosophers which would otherwise have been lost.

In modern scholarship on ancient philosophy the term 'doxography' is also often used in a broader, less technical sense. In such cases it describes all forms of presentation of philosophers' views by means of summaries without direct reference to the philosopher's own words. Because this broader usage invites confusion with the doxographical tradition proper as described in the main body of this article, it is not to be recommended.

References and further reading

* Diels, H. (1879) *Doxographi Graeci* (Greek Doxographers), Berlin: de Gruyter; repr. 1976. (Main collection of doxographical writings; includes Aëtius, Arius Didymus and fragments of Theophrastus.)

Hahm, D.E. (1990) 'The Ethical Doxography of Arius Didymus', in W. Haase (ed.) *Aufstieg und Niedergang der römischen Welt Part II: Principate*, vol. 36.4: 2935–3055. (Fine analysis of an important doxographical source on Peripatetic and Stoic ethics.)

Lachenaud, G. (1993) 'Plutarque', in *Œuvres morales*, vol. 12 (2): *Opinions des Philosophes*, Paris: Les Belles Lettres, 2nd edn. (Useful for the writings of Aëtius, although Diels' reconstruction of the original, for all its imperfections, is still indispensable.)

* Mansfeld, J. (1992) '*Physikai doxai* and *Problēmata physica* from Aristotle to Aëtius (and Beyond)', in W.W. Fortenbaugh and D. Gutas (eds) *Theophrastus: His Psychological, Doxographical and Scientific Writings*, Rutgers University Studies in the Classical Humanities 5, New Brunswick, NJ, and London: Transaction Publishers, 63–111. (Valuable research on the philosophical background of the doxographical method.)

Mansfeld, J. and Runia, D.T. (1996) *Aëtiana: The Method and Intellectual Context of a Doxographer*, volume 1: *The Sources, Philosophia Antiqua* 73, Leiden: Brill. (First volume of a thorough analysis of the Diels hypothesis and the entire doxographical tradition.)

Runia, D.T. (1989) 'Xenophanes on the Moon: A *Doxographicum* in Aëtius', *Phronesis* 34: 245–69.

(Gives an example of how doxographical material needs to be analysed.)

DAVID T. RUNIA

DREAMING

We naturally think of dreams as experiences very like perceptions or imaginings, except that they occur during sleep. In prescientific thought the interpretation of dreams played a role in divining the future, and it plays a role, albeit a much more limited one, in modern psychology (although in Freudian psychoanalysis dreams have been considered to give access to some of the hidden operations of the mind). Dreaming is puzzling in many respects. We do not have ready-to-hand criteria for checking dream reports, not even our own; conscious or lucid dreams are the exception rather than the rule; and there is the puzzle of how we distinguish waking experience from a very lifelike dream. Furthermore, the nature of dreams is doubtful – some have even denied that to dream is to undergo an experience during sleep: dreams on this view are to be understood in terms of what happens when we 'recall' them.

1 The ordinary account of dreams
2 Dreaming and scepticism
3 Are dreams experiences?
4 Content and role of dreams

1 The ordinary account of dreams

The common-sense theory of dreams is that they are mental experiences; that most of them are delusive; and that they are distinct from other delusive experiences, like hallucinations, in virtue of the fact that they occur during sleep. Our conscious access to dreams is effected mainly via memory; upon waking, most dreams are recalled as having occurred to us, without any interaction between us and them. There are, however, reports of lucid dreams, in which subjects feel that they can deliberate about actions they take in dreams, or are conscious of dreaming as it occurs.

A natural classification would see dreaming as akin to hallucinating and imagining, but also to remembering; as a consequence, some of the philosophical problems posed by dreams will be inherited from the class of problems posed by these other types of experience. You dreamt for instance of a concert given by Rubinstein (a concert you did actually attend), and of a sudden metamorphosis of Rubinstein on stage

into a huge rabbit. That this is a dream about Rubinstein and not about another pianist is likely to be explained in the same way in which one explains that your recollections of Rubinstein are recollections of *him* (see MEMORY §3). That this is specifically a fancy-like hallucinatory episode goes hand in hand with the fact that its content is similar to that of fancies, and, like the latter, might be disconfirmed by memory, inconsistent with other experiences, and contrary to the laws of the actual world.

Sometimes external circumstances influence a dream; but the lack of a systematic agreement between the contents of our dreams and states of the external world indicates that dreams are mostly generated from within the mind. There has to be something like a dream engine – independent of conscious control – responsible for the production of our dreams (internal movements of the soul, according to Plato, and, for Aristotle, a sort of inertia of sensible impressions, similar to that explaining the formation of after-images).

Common-sense evidence that dreams are datable episodes in the mental life of a subject is given by phenomena such as external stimuli, like the sound of an alarm-clock, entering into the content of the subject's dreams. During the 1950s and 1960s, experiments by W. Dement (1958), D. Foulkes (1966), N. Kleitman, M. Jouvet and others, established a correlation between dreaming and phases of so-called 'paradoxical sleep' (PS), characterized by intense brain activity, muscular atony, and, in some animals, rapid eye movements (hence the term 'REM sleep', which is somewhat imprecise, for animals like the mole or the owl have PS but no REMs). PS is periodical – it recurs after phases of orthodox (or NREM) sleep – and takes about one quarter of the time of the entire period of sleep. Subjects woken during PS can easily and vividly recall a detailed, picture-like, ongoing dream.

2 Dreaming and scepticism

Descartes used the dream argument in the *Meditations* (1641) in order to shake our belief in the reliability of the senses (see DESCARTES §4). Is it possible to describe our waking life as a dream? If so, how could we distinguish dreaming from perceiving? Of course, nothing depends specifically on dreams in the dream argument for the possibility of mistrust in perception; hallucinatory experiences would do as well. Moreover, perception is normally accompanied by reflexive awareness, whereas dreaming is normally not, and thus dreaming is not the best candidate for the sceptical argument, unless it be lucid dreaming. But these differences are hardly necessary differences, and the *epistemological* question of establishing how dreaming may be distinguished from perceiving remains open. (1) One might try a phenomenological answer, pointing out that our waking experience is distinguished by the fact that we believe it to begin upon awakening, and to end upon falling asleep. But – the sceptic will answer – nothing excludes that we dream that we both wake up and fall asleep. (2) Descartes proposed that clarity and distinctness of contents is a sign of veracity, but one has to admit that even the clearest and most distinct perceptions might turn out to be delusive. (3) Descartes, in the *Sixth Meditation* (1641), suggested that some form of the coherence criterion would allow, in some cases, a distinction between dreams and non-dream experiences; Leibniz, however, thought the knowledge provided through the application of this criterion not certain but only probable. But this criterion cannot exclude a certain set of coherent experiential reports being about an especially coherent great dream; as Hobbes remarked in his *Objections* to Descartes (see Descartes [1641] 1969), we might be dreaming of an all-encompassing coherent connection between experiences. It thus seems that the distinction between dreaming and waking is epistemologically not available.

An attack on scepticism, grounded in an argument against the received view that dreams are experiences, which is itself based on a very strong and controversial version of the principle of verification, has been put forward by Norman Malcolm (1959). Malcolm links (criterially) the occurrence of a dream with the (possibility of an) utterance of a dream report. Indeed, according to Malcolm, the only acceptable criterion for the occurrence of any experience or state is that one be able to provide a report thereof, a position which clearly relies on an extreme verificationist conception of meaning and truth (see CRITERIA §1). Malcolm's main argument is that: (1) if one dreams, then one is asleep; (2) as there is no possibility of applying any criterion during sleep and the occurrence of a dream during sleep cannot therefore be verified, the question of whether a dream occurred during one's sleep is meaningless; (3) for the same reason the question of whether a certain experience took place during one's sleep is also meaningless. The conclusion is (4) that dreams cannot contain (or be identical with) experiences occurrring during sleep.

This is of some consequence for scepticism: if dreams are not experiences occurring during sleep, then the sceptic's question of how we can tell dream experience from waking experience does not even arise. Moreover, the debate over the principle of coherence would be revealed as senseless, for it would presuppose that we can make sense of comparing contents and finding out that some do not cohere with most others (thereby discovering that we are not dreaming); this is, by Malcolm's lights, absurd, for to compare is to judge, and no judgments occur during sleep.

3 Are dreams experiences?

Malcolm's theory invites an account that loosens the dreaming process from experiencing, and ties it to dream-recall. The account asserts that a dream, though apparently long, might be condensed in a short time span, and be triggered upon awakening. Freud reports Maury's 'guillotine dream' (a complex series of events related to the French revolution and concluded by the dreamer's own beheading) which was triggered by the fall of a small board on the dreamer's neck. In order to avoid ascribing premonitory abilities to the mind, Freud suggested that in such a case the dream was already available in the form of a mental plot and that it was only recalled as a result of the accident. More recently, this view has been developed into the cassette theory of dreams (Dennett 1976). According to this theory, the composition of dreams would be temporally independent of the remembering or the performance of dreams; dream plots could be conscious for the first time upon recalling. Further evidence for this theory is provided by the fact that dreams often recur; it is plausible to think that such dreams are not composed each night, but that they are already available and simply played back once again.

4 Content and role of dreams

What are dreams good for? Ancient philosophers often assimilated dreaming to perceiving: its function was to foresee future events, and, accordingly, its aetiology envisaged the intervention of the gods. Aristotle, conscious of the delusory content of dreams, held that they are purposeless and simply the concomitant of things purposive: they are *symptomata* or by-products. Modern psychology has struggled up to now inconclusively with the function of dreams. It has been conjectured that dreams are the safety-valve of an overloaded mind; that dreams are used to clear the neural network of superfluous information acquired during the time we are awake; that dreams keep the organism in a state of constant alertness; that dreams stabilize memory traces after learning; that they have the role of preserving mental identity.

Neurophysiologists often study dreams independently of all questions of content, though an ideally complete science of dreams should be able to account for this aspect, too. For whatever their nature (whether they are experiences, or pre-composed plots), it is indisputable that dreams have content and, taken at face value, a reference. They are *about* objects and persons, and they represent these objects and persons as having certain properties. We express the content of our dreams by using 'that'-clauses (as in 'I dreamt that she was ill') in the same way in which we express the content of beliefs, of intentions that rationalize actions, of perceptual states. But the very fact that dreams have content is puzzling. The content of beliefs, intentions and perceptual states has the power to provide an explanation of other psychological states and of actions; it also expresses the satisfaction-condition for wishes. Freud suggested that the content of dreams indicates a (suppressed or repressed) wish, which the occurrence of the dream fulfils in hallucinatory fashion, and in a disguised form (see FREUD, S. §4). Of course this form of wish-fulfilment is not standard, for it not only does not eliminate the ground for the wish, but it may also hinder the latter's being satisfied (if your wish is to drink, your dream that you drink may prevent you from waking up and actually drinking). A function should be found, then, for these vicarious and incomplete wish-fulfillings exemplified by dreams. Freud's account of the role of the dream, an account which accommodates its having the content it has, is to protect our sleep from being disturbed by a troublesome wish. A persisting wish, repressed beneath the threshold of consciousness, associates with some occasional thoughts or impressions, and surfaces during sleep. Because this wish would be intolerable to the dreamer, and would disturb their sleep, its 'latent content' receives an elaboration and becomes 'manifest' in an acceptable, non-disturbing form.

It should finally be noted that a less ambitious theory constructed along Aristotelian lines could ascribe a primary, physiological function to dreams, and a secondary, concomitant function associated with their content. The empirical discovery that dreams have a certain purely neurophysiological function by no means excludes the proposition that they also fulfil, in subordination thereto, a common-sense psychological function which necessarily involves their content.

See also: PROPHECY §1–2; SCEPTICISM

References and further reading

* Aristotle (*c.*350 BC) *On Dreams*, in W.D. Ross (ed.) *The Works of Aristotle*, London: Oxford University Press, 1931, vol. 3. (The first complete small treatise on dreams.)

Debru, C. (1990) *Neurophilosophie du rêve*, Paris: Hermann. (Overview of the main neurophysiological theories.)

* Dement, W. and Kleitmann, N. (1957) 'Cyclic Variations of EEG during Sleep and their Relations to Eye Movements, Bodily Motility and Dreaming', *Electroenceph. Clin. Neurophysiol.* 3: 673–90. (The title says it all.)

* Dennett, D. (1976) 'Are Dreams Experiences?', *Philosophical Review* 73: 151–71; repr. in D. Dennett, *Brainstorms*, Cambridge, MA: MIT Press. (Tries to do justice to both Malcolm's insights and neurophysiological evidence.)

* Descartes, R. ([1641] 1969) *Meditations on First Philosophy*, trans. E.S. Haldane and G.R.T. Ross, in *The Philosophical Works of Descartes*, Cambridge: Cambridge University Press, vol. 1. (The famous 'dream argument' and its anti-sceptical criticism.)

* Foulkes, D. (1966) *The Psychology of Sleep*, New York: Scribner's. (Standard source.)

Hopkins, J. (1991) 'The Interpretation of Dreams', in J. Neu (ed.) *The Cambridge Companion to Freud*, Cambridge: Cambridge University Press, 86–135. (A lucid synopsis of Freud's theory of dreams in an analytic framework.)

* Jouvet, M. (1991) 'Le someil paradoxal: Est-il le gardien de l'individuation psychologique?' (Paradoxical Sleep: Is it the Guardian of Psychological Individuation?), *Revue Canadienne de Psychologie* 45: 148–68

* Malcolm, N. (1959) *Dreaming*, London: Routledge & Kegan Paul. (Important monograph on the concept of dreaming, with some of the most debated arguments, and useful excerpts from the philosophical literature.)

Putnam, H. (1962) 'Dreaming and "Depth Grammar"', in R. Butler (ed.) *Analytical Philosophy. First Series*, Oxford: Blackwell; repr. in *Mind, Language and Reality*, Cambridge: Cambridge University Press, 1975, 304–24. (Anti-verificationist criticism of Malcolm.)

ROBERTO CASATI

DU BOIS-REYMOND, EMIL (1818–96)

Emil du Bois-Reymond conducted pioneering research in electrophysiology which established him as a major figure in German science in the second half of the nineteenth century. His influence extended further through his more general writings in politics and philosophy of science, in which he argued for theoretical restraint and for the recognition that certain problems (for example, the mind–body problem) fell beyond scientific modes of inquiry and explanation.

Du Bois was born in Berlin and educated there in medicine and physiology. His distinctions in experimental science resulted in election to the Berlin Academy of Sciences; he was later honoured as its perpetual secretary from 1867. Holder of the chair of Physiology at Berlin from 1858 and co-editor of *Archiv für Anatomie* from 1857 to 1877, du Bois exercised great influence in the biological sciences throughout the second half of the nineteenth century.

Du Bois is of interest as a result of two distinguishable but interconnected projects. The first is that body of research and theory concerned with basic principles in neurophysiology. The second is his more general and accessible writings in philosophy of science. It was through his standing within the scientific community that these latter productions came to enjoy great authority.

At the start of his career, Du Bois was a researcher in Johannes Müller's laboratory, as one of a group of young scientists who in a matter of years would become leading figures, namely Carl Ludwig, Ernst Brücke and Herman von Helmholtz. These four entered into something of a pact: they were to reject any theory in biology that was not grounded in the basic sciences of physics and chemistry. The graduation thesis du Bois had submitted to the Berlin faculty reported the results of his research on electric fish. In 1841, Müller passed along Carlo Matteucci's recent 'Note sur les phénomènes électrique des animaux' (*C.R. Acad. Sci.*, Paris, 1841, (13): 540–), in which Matteucci had shown that electrical currents could be recorded between a point on the surface of a muscle and one deep within it. Taking this as his starting point, du Bois proceeded to investigate electrophysiological phenomena under a wide variety of conditions, publishing the results and their theoretical implications in his influential two-volume *Untersuchungen über Thierische Elektricität* (*On Animal Electricity*) (1848–9). In later years, du Bois criticized Matteucci's methods and resented his failure to cite those of du Bois' studies on which Matteucci's work depended. Du Bois explained his findings in terms of a wave of polarization created by what he called 'electromotive molecules' of positive and negative charge. He scrupulously avoided taking a firm position on the actual physical nature of these hypothetical entities, stating only that they should be understood as 'foci of chemical change'. Subsequent

developments in neurophysiology disconfirmed some of the details of du Bois' theory, but his general perspective was redeemed.

As a statesman of science eager to establish its proper place within the larger contexts of culture and thought, du Bois contributed two books of considerable interest and importance. In his *Über die Grenzen des Naturerkennens* (On the Limits of the Knowledge of Nature) (1872) a modest and restrained positivism can be identified, the echo of the early pact barely audible. He acknowledges the inability of experimental science to settle issues of an essentially metaphysical nature, and is prepared to accept the possibility that even certain natural phenomena will never disclose their most fundamental principles. The mind–body problem illustrates this well. This problem, as he understood it, exemplifies the general problem of reconciling different 'substances'. A distinguished neurophysiologist, du Bois fully appreciated the dependence of mental life on the integrity and functional capacities of the nervous system. But on the question of just how these functions do give rise to mental life – just how physicochemical processes influence, determine or regulate mental life – du Bois offered his famous one-word answer: *'Ignorabimus!'* ('We will be ignorant!'). It is interesting that du Bois would illustrate the general problem further by noting the (substantial) difference between matter and energy.

A later edition of this work, published in 1880, includes his *Die Sieben Weltrathsel* (The Seven Riddles of the Universe). Here du Bois defends the overarching perspective of the scientist, which includes not only the commitment to disinterested and objective inquiry, but also the modesty of the fallibilist. In acknowledging at once the power and the limits of scientific knowledge, he preserved room for philosophy to bring its quite different methods of analysis and inquiry to bear upon vexed questions, even as he liberated science from the burden of having to explain what in the end may well be inexplicable.

Du Bois also expressed himself publicly on matters of political and social importance. On the Franco-Prussian War, for example, his 1870 published address at the University of Berlin, *Über den Deutschen Krieg* (*The German War*), was widely cited and discussed.

See also: SCIENCE, 19TH CENTURY PHILOSOPHY OF §6

List of works

Du Bois-Reymond, E. (1848–84) *Untersuchungen über Thierische Elektricität*, Berlin: G. Reimer, 2 vols; trans. *On Animal Electricity*, H.B. Jones (ed.), London, Churchill, 1852. (In this work du Bois takes early steps towards what would become the ionic theory of the formation and propagation of the neural impulse.)

—— (1870) *Über den deutschen Krieg*, trans. G. Solling, *The German War*, Berlin, J. Sittenfeld, 1870. (Here, du Bois as citizen expresses his judgment of the Franco-Prussian War.)

—— (1872) *Über die Grenzen des Naturerkennens* (On the Limits of the Knowledge of Nature), Leipzig: Veit. (The limits and power of natural science are discussed with a calm and seasoned criticality.)

—— (1880) *Über die Grenzen des Naturerkennens. Die sieben Welträthsel* (On the Limits of the Knowledge of Nature; The Seven Riddles of the Universe), Leipzig: Veit. (One of the riddles, the connection between mind and body, is recognized as a source of enduring perplexity. 'Ignorabimus!' – we will be ignorant.)

—— (1883) *Sitzungsberichte der Königlich-preussischen Academie der Wissenschaften zu Berlin* 16; trans. L. Brunon, as *On Secondary Electromotive Phenomena in Muscles, Nerves and Electrical Organs*, in *Translation of Biological Memoirs*, Oxford: Oxford University Press, 161–225, 1887. (The electrical theory of nerve and muscle excitability is developed in this work and illustrated by way of experimental measurements.)

References and further reading

Cranefield, P.F. (ed.) (1982) *Two Great Scientists of the Nineteenth Century: Correspondence of Emil Du Bois-Reymond and Carl Ludwig*, trans. S.L. Ayed, Baltimore, MD: Johns Hopkins University Press. (This volume presents letters collected by Estelle Du Bois-Reymond and contains a foreword by Paul Cranefield as well as notes and indexes.)

DANIEL N. ROBINSON

DU CHÂTELET-LOMONT, GABRIELLE-ÉMILIE (1706–49)

The name of this aristocratic woman, a true intellectual with a passion for mathematics, philosophy and science, is linked to that of Voltaire, whose life and interests she shared for fifteen years. In the rural retreat of Cirey they studied, disagreed, wrote and published. She was introduced to Newtonian science by Maupertuis and Voltaire but departed from their views, when she tried to combine Leibnizian metaphysics with Newton's empirically based science in her Institutions de physique *(1740). She translated Newton's* Principia *from Latin into French and added a commentary on the system of the world (1745–9, published 1756).*

Gabrielle-Émilie de Breteuil was born into an aristocratic family in Paris and showed an early interest in intellectual pursuits. As an adolescent she translated Virgil's *Aeneid* into French. Later she learned Italian and English. She developed a passion for astronomy and physics, and studied mathematics seriously in order to understand these sciences.

In 1725 she married Florent-Claude, Marquis du Châtelet and Comte de Lomont, by whom she had three children. The marquis, often away with his regiment, was tolerant of his wife's behaviour. She was able to combine an intellectual life with the worldly, social life of the aristocracy. Among her lovers were the Duc de Richelieu, the mathematician and early French Newtonian Pierre-Louis de Maupertuis, who taught her mathematics, and Voltaire, who, risking arrest after the publication of his *Lettres philosophiques* in 1734, took refuge at her family property at Cirey-sur-Blaise in Champagne. There they created a centre of learning and pleasure. They set up a well-equipped laboratory and performed experiments on light, fire, optics, and so forth. Among their visitors were the popularizer of Newton's optics, Francesco Algarotti, Maupertuis, Johann (II) Bernoulli and Samuel König, a Swiss mathematician and philosopher, who spent most of 1739 with the Cirey household and taught Madame du Châtelet mathematics and the metaphysics of Leibniz and Wolff.

At Cirey Voltaire composed his *Éléments de la philosophie de Newton* and *Traité de métaphysique* (published 1738 and 1784 respectively). When he submitted an essay on the nature of fire for the 1738 competition of the Academy of Sciences, her disagreement with his views led her to submit, without Voltaire's knowledge, her own entry. She especially criticized his material view of light and fire. For her, fire – which had no weight – justified Descartes's subtle matter, which Voltaire had consistently attacked. Although neither Voltaire nor Madame du Châtelet won, their entries were published by the Academy.

Madame du Châtelet's most lasting contribution to learning was her translation into French of Sir Isaac Newton's *Philosophiae Naturalis Principia Mathematica*, to which she devoted the last years of her life. It was published posthumously in 1756, seven years after her death. She also wrote an original work, her *Institutions de physique* (Instruction in Physics) (1740), a textbook written to introduce her son to science, in which she presented metaphysics as a necessary introduction to physics. She admitted her debt to Christian Wolff's *Ontologia* (1729) and to summaries by König of works by Wolff. The manuscript, in the Bibliothèque Nationale de France, shows she had prepared an earlier version before König's arrival which was not Leibnizian, except for the chapter on *vis viva* (kinetic energy). König converted her to the Leibniz–Wolff philosophy, for her the only satisfactory metaphysics. She rewrote the metaphysical chapters accordingly. Voltaire liked to believe she never was really convinced by this philosophy. However, she was very firm in her Leibnizian views. She had adopted the Leibnizian view of the force of moving objects and was reading Wolff's Latin works in 1738 before König's arrival (see LEIBNIZ, G.W.; WOLFF, C.).

Her disagreements with Voltaire led to a sort of public dialogue between them. She reviewed his *Éléments de la philosophie de Newton* in the *Journal des savants* (September 1738); he published an article on her *Dissertation sur la nature du feu* in the *Mercure de France* (June 1739) and a critical review of her *Institutions de physique* also in the *Mercure de France* (June 1741). Voltaire kept reaffirming his Newtonian views against her attacks. The Leibnizian principle of sufficient reason had caused her to abandon attraction at a distance, empty space and atoms, all part of Voltaire's Newtonianism.

While never denying that the world behaved according to Newtonian principles, she felt that science had to discover mechanical causes for all phenomena. She followed Leibniz and Wolff in adopting non-material monads, which contained force, the sufficient reason for change in the material world. Force was conserved in a perfectly functioning universe. Voltaire remained very sceptical of metaphysics, and was particularly hostile to monads, since he was committed to attraction at a distance as the mysterious but divine force that kept the universe in operation.

Her stand on *vis viva* in the final chapter of her *Institutions* gave rise to a public dispute with Dortous de Mairan and indirectly with Voltaire. Was the force of moving bodies equal to the mass times the velocity squared, as Leibniz claimed, or to the mass times the simple velocity, the traditional view, supported aggressively by Mairan? Both Mme du Châtelet and Voltaire became involved in the dispute.

In her *Institutions* she attacked Mairan's view. Mairan, obviously piqued, about the time he became secretary of the Academy of Sciences (January 1741) replied in an open *Lettre à Madame la marquise Du Chastellet, sur la question des forces vives....* She then published her *Réponse...à la lettre de M. de Mairan sur la question des forces vives* (1741), an attack both personal and insulting. Finally Voltaire submitted to the Academy his *Doutes sur la mesure des forces motrices* (1741), in support of Mairan, and attacking the Leibnizian view of his mistress, without mentioning her name.

Voltaire, like the periodicals of the period, admitted that Madame du Châtelet had given the French a clear, elegant account of the Leibniz–Wolff philosophy, which was little known in France.

Madame du Châtelet was also the author of a *Discours sur le bonheur*, written about 1747 and first published in 1779, and is considered the author of an unpublished manuscript of biblical criticism entitled *Examen de la Genèse*, in another area of interest she shared with Voltaire.

In 1748 Mme du Châtelet fell in love with the minor poet, Jean-François de Saint-Lambert, became pregnant by him at the age of 43 and died of childbed fever in Lunéville at the court of Lorraine.

See also: NEWTON, I.; VOLTAIRE

List of works

Du Châtelet-Lomont, G.-É. (1739) *Dissertation sur la nature et la propagation du feu* (Dissertation on the Nature and Propagation of Fire), in *Pièces qui ont été présentées à l'Académie des sciences, pour concourir au prix de l'année 1738* (Entries presented to the Academy of Sciences for the competition of 1738), Paris: Imprimerie royale.

—— (1740) *Institutions de physique* (Instruction in Physics), Paris: Prault fils; *Institutions physiques*, Amsterdam: Au dépens de la compagnie, 2nd edn, 1742; repr. of 2nd edn, Hildesheim: Olms, 1988.

—— (1741) *Réponse de madame la marquise du Châtelet, à la lettre que M. de Mairan, secrétaire perpétuel de l'Académie des sciences, &c. lui a écrit le 18 février 1741 sur la question des forces vives* (Reply from Mme du Châtelet to the letter of M. de Mairan, permanent secretary to the Academy of Sciences, of 18 February 1741, on the question of *vis viva*), Brussels: Foppens.

—— (c.1747) *Discours sur le bonheur* (Discourse on Happiness), ed. R. Mauzi, Paris: Les Belles Lettres, 1961. (First published 1779.)

Newton, I. (1745–9) *Principes mathématiques de la philosophie naturelle* (Mathematical Principles of Natural Philosophy), trans. G.-É. du Châtelet-Lomont, Paris: Desaint et Saillant, partial edn, 1756; complete edn, 1759; repr. Paris: Blanchard, 1966; repr. Paris: Jacques Gabay, 1990. (Du Châtelet-Lomont's translation of Newton's *Principia*.)

References and further reading

Barber, W.H. (1955) *Leibniz in France from Arnauld to Voltaire*, Oxford: Clarendon Press. (A French enthusiast; Mme du Châtelet and the general French hostility to Leibniz.)

——— (1967) 'Mme du Châtelet and Leibnizianism: The Genesis of the *Institutions de physique*', in W.H. Barber, J.D. Brumfitt *et al.* (eds) *The Age of the Enlightenment, Studies Presented to Theodore Besterman*, Edinburgh: Oliver & Boyd, 200–22.

Janik, L.G. (1982) 'Searching for the Metaphysics of Science: The Structure and Composition of Madame Du Châtelet's *Institutions de physique*, 1737–1740', *Studies on Voltaire and the Eighteenth Century*, 201: 85–113. (A thorough analysis of the manuscript in the Bibliothèque Nationale de France and the stages that led Mme du Châtelet to present Leibnizian metaphysics as an introduction to science.)

Taton, R. (1969) 'Madame du Châtelet, traductrice de Newton', *Archives internationales d'histoire des sciences* 22: 185–210.

Vaillot, R. (1978) *Madame du Châtelet*, Paris: Michel. (A readable biography, which examines the various aspects of her life.)

Wade, I.O. (1947) *Studies on Voltaire with some unpublished papers of Mme du Châtelet*, Princeton, NJ: Princeton University Press. (Contains her translation of Mandeville's *Fable of the Bees*, her fragmentary *Essai sur l'optique*, and three chapters of a *Grammaire raisonnée*; analysis of these texts and Voltaire's *Traité de métaphysique*.)

——— (1969) *The Intellectual Development of Voltaire*, Princeton, NJ: Princeton University Press. (Part III, pages 253–570, examines the intellectual activity at Cirey.)

ROBERT L. WALTERS

DUALISM

Dualism is the view that mental phenomena are, in some respect, nonphysical. The best-known version is due to Descartes (1641), and holds that the mind is a nonphysical substance. Descartes argued that, because minds have no spatial properties and physical reality is essentially extended in space, minds are wholly nonphysical. Every human being is accordingly a composite of two objects: a physical body, and a nonphysical object that is that human being's mind. On a weaker version of dualism, which contemporary thinkers find more acceptable, human beings are physical substances but have mental properties, and those properties are not physical. This view is known as property dualism, or the dual-aspect theory.

Several considerations appear to support dualism. Mental phenomena are strikingly different from all others, and the idea that they are nonphysical may explain just how they are distinctive. Moreover, physical reality conforms to laws formulated in strictly mathematical terms. But, because mental phenomena such as thinking, desiring and sensing seem intractable to being described in mathematical terms, it is tempting to conclude that these phenomena are not physical. In addition, many mental states are conscious states – states that we are aware of in a way that seems to be wholly unmediated. And many would argue that, whatever the nature of mental phenomena that are not conscious, consciousness cannot be physical.

There are also, however, reasons to resist dualism. People, and other creatures with mental endowments, presumably exist wholly within the natural order, and it is generally held that all natural phenomena are built up from basic physical constituents. Dualism, however, represents the mind as uniquely standing outside this unified physical picture. There is also a difficulty about causal relations between mind and body. Mental events often cause bodily events, as when a desire causes an action, and bodily events often cause mental events, for example in perceiving. But the causal interactions into which physical events enter are governed by laws that connect physical events. So if the mental is not physical, it would be hard to understand how mental events can interact causally with bodily events. For these reasons and others, dualism is, despite various reasons advanced in its support, a theoretically uncomfortable position.

1   Mental and physical

Underlying dualism is the strong intuition that the ordinary functioning of people is of two fundamentally different kinds. Much of what happens to us is thoroughly physical, on a par with the properties and behaviour of things such as stones, houses and planets. But we also engage in thinking, we desire and perceive things, and we feel emotions such as joy and anger. In these ways we seem to be dramatically different from such purely physical objects as stones and planets. It is natural to want to epitomize these observations by positing the idea that all concrete reality is either mental or physical, and nothing is both. Not only do the mental and the physical exhaust everything; they are also mutually exclusive. This conclusion points to some form of dualism. Either every person consists of a nonphysical substance operating in tandem with a purely physical body, or people at least have certain states or properties that are not physical.

It is worth stressing that dualism requires the mental and the physical to be mutually exclusive. If they were not, mental substances might also be physical, and mental states such as thoughts and sensations might be not just mental, but also physical as well. Moreover, the common-sense contrast between mental and physical does not by itself imply that mental phenomena lie outside the physical realm. We often contrast a special range of phenomena with the physical, even though the phenomena under consideration are strictly speaking physical; consider the contrast in computer talk between physical and logical disk drives. Mental phenomena are unlike any others, but highly distinctive phenomena are not, just on that account, nonphysical.

Still, there are reasons to think that mental and physical are indeed disjoint categories. For one thing, it is held that if they were not disjoint we could not capture what it is that is distinctive about mind. If people were just physical substances, and their mental states just special sorts of physical states, we would not be able to explain the striking difference between people and paradigmatically physical objects such as stones and houses. Some have gone so far as to urge that what is distinctive about being mental is, at bottom, simply that it is nonphysical.

But this argument is open to challenge, since we can explain the contrast between stones and people without supposing that mental and physical are mutually exclusive categories. Consider a parallel case. When we focus on living things, it is natural to contrast biological phenomena with such physical objects as stones and stars. But that does not lead us to conclude that the biological and the physical are mutually exclusive categories, and that living things are not purely physical. Rather, living organisms are physical objects, though of a very special sort, and we need not posit anything nonphysical to characterize what is special about them (see VITALISM).

Dualism implies that things are different in the case of the mind; that is, it implies that to capture what is distinctive about mental functioning we must posit substances or properties that are not physical. If, on the other hand, we can characterize the mind without positing anything nonphysical, dualism is wrong. The hypothesis that this is possible is mind–body materialism, and it has been championed especially forcefully in a version called the identity theory of mind (see MIND, IDENTITY THEORY OF).

Can such a characterization be given? According to Descartes, it is essential to everything physical that it has spatial extension, and being spatially extended implies having parts. So we can conceive of any physical object as being divided into parts; those parts would themselves be extended, and hence physical objects. But Descartes held that the same is not true about minds. Minds, he claimed, are not mere collections of mental states, as the bundle theory maintains (see MIND, BUNDLE THEORY OF); rather, minds are essentially unified. So we cannot even conceive of a mind's being divided into parts. A satisfactory characterization of the mental, therefore, implies that minds are nonphysical (see DESCARTES, R. §8).

The bundle theory put to one side, however, there is reason to question this argument. Surgically sectioning the neural pathways that connect the two cerebral hemispheres results in striking experimental behaviour, which some researchers believe indicates the presence after surgery of two distinct conscious minds (see SPLIT BRAINS). Also, brain lesions sometimes result in dissociation of mental functions, which also suggests that a normally unified mind may come to be divided. Such results cast doubt on traditional ideas about mental unity, and the very possibility of these interpretations undermines Descartes' claim that we cannot even conceive of a mind's being divided into parts. To sustain dualism, therefore, we would need some other reason to hold that a satisfactory characterization of mind must proceed in nonphysical terms.

According to Descartes' well-known *cogito*, the statement 'I am, I exist' is true whenever I assert it or mentally conceive it, and the 'I' whose existence I thereby establish is my mind, not my body. But Descartes explicitly recognizes that these considerations do not constitute an argument for dualism. Rather, as he saw, they establish at best only a conceptual difference between mind and body, and not the 'Real Distinction' for which he argues independently by appeal to divisibility.

2 Dualism and physical science

To show that the mind is nonphysical, we need to know not only what being mental amounts to, but also what it is to be physical. Descartes relied on the alleged indivisibility of mind, and on a conception of the physical as divisible. That conception of physical reality, in turn, rested on Descartes' conviction that the essential properties of physical reality are all geometrical properties.

But there is another conception of physical reality that seems to support dualism. Scientific developments over the last four centuries present a picture in which the laws governing physical reality are invariably formulated in strict mathematical terms. As Galileo put it, the book of nature is 'written in the language of mathematics' (1623: 238).

This idea captures the mathematical character of the physical in terms that are more general than Descartes' claim that the essential properties of physical reality are all geometrical. So it allows for a less constrained argument for dualism, independently of particular claims about what is essential to the mind. Whatever the nature of thinking, sensing, desiring and feeling, one might well deny that there could be strictly mathematical laws that govern such states. On this conception of the physical, then, mental states would not be physical.

The argument as just formulated supports property dualism, according to which no mental states or properties are physical. But we can adjust the argument to support substance dualism as well. If mental substances exist, their behaviour would presumably not be governed by mathematically formulable laws; so such substances would not be physical. The argument is therefore more flexible than Descartes' appeal to indivisibility, which adapts less readily to the case of property dualism. This is important, since contemporary concern about dualism is almost always about dualism of properties, not substances. Partly that is because of doubts about whether the traditional notion of a substance is useful. But it is also partly because of a tendency to think of people's minds not as any kind of substance at all but rather as the totality of their mental functioning, including their dispositions and abilities to function mentally.

There are various reasons to think that mental states cannot be the subjects of mathematically formulable laws. We describe our thoughts and desires in terms of the objects they are about. The property of being about something, and its related properties, are called intentional properties (see INTENTIONALITY). Mental states can be about things that do not exist; we all sometimes think about and desire nonexistent things. So thinking and desiring are somewhat like relations one can bear to nonexistent objects. But such ostensible relations, which can hold even to nonexistent things, cannot figure in mathematical descriptions of things.

There are other sorts of mental states that aren't strictly speaking about anything; examples are bodily sensations such as pains and tickles, and perceptual states such as visual experiences. The distinguishing properties of these states are not their intentional properties, but rather certain qualitative properties – for example, the redness of a visual experience or the dull, throbbing character of a pain (see QUALIA). Again, it seems unlikely that these properties could figure in mathematically formulable laws.

These intentional and qualitative properties are, arguably, the distinguishing properties of mental states – the properties in terms of which we identify those states and distinguish them from everything else. We cannot argue that mental states are physical simply by denying that they have these properties.

But our intuitive sense that these properties resist mathematical description may not be reliable. Compare our intuitions about ordinary macroscopic objects. We ordinarily take such objects to have various common-sense properties, such as colour, taste and smell. And we conceive of these common-sense physical properties in qualitative terms that seem resistant to mathematical description. Yet we can understand these properties mathematically: for example, we can construe the colours of bodies in terms of physical reflectance (see COLOUR, THEORIES OF; SECONDARY QUALITIES). Perhaps, then, we can explain the intentional and qualitative properties of mental states in ways that allow for mathematical description of those properties.

The general outline such explanations would have, moreover, is clear enough. Some have argued, for example, that a thought's being about something is a matter of its having a certain content (see PROPOSITIONAL ATTITUDES), and that we can explain content, in turn, in a scientifically satisfactory way. And there is much about qualitative mental states that succumbs to quantitative treatment, as any standard textbook on perception reveals. So a successful theory of mental properties may show how to render those properties scientifically acceptable. The intuition that mental properties resist scientific treatment may therefore reflect only the current state of theorizing, just as many common-sense physical properties seemed recalcitrant to mathematical treatment before suitable scientific advances had occurred.

3 Qualitative states

Nonetheless, many would insist that, whatever science may show, qualitative properties cannot be physical. All physical objects are composed of colourless microparticles; so it is tempting to hold that no physical objects are coloured. We do, however, describe visual sensations in colour terms, for example as red or green sensations. And if nothing physical is coloured but visual sensations are, those sensations cannot be physical. Indeed, if no physical objects are coloured, colour is arguably not a physical property.

But when we describe a physical object as red, for

example, this colour is a distinct property from that which we sometimes attribute to visual sensations. Physical colour is a property of a certain kind of object, namely, physical objects. Visual sensations, however, are not objects at all; they are states of people and other sentient creatures. Since the properties objects have are distinct from those of states, the colour of visual sensations is a different property from any property physical objects might have. Denying colour of physical objects does not show, therefore, that to have colour properties visual sensations must be nonphysical.

It is sometimes argued that, unless we construe sensations as objects as opposed to states, we will not be able to distinguish among the various sensations we have at any moment. And sensations are plainly not physical objects; so if they are objects of any sort, they must be nonphysical objects (see Jackson 1977). But it is likely that whatever distinctions we can draw among sensations construed as objects can be preserved if we construe them as states instead (see MENTAL STATES, ADVERBIAL THEORY OF; SENSE-DATA).

Since bodily and perceptual sensations are not objects of any kind, but rather states of sentient creatures, there is indeed a categorial difference between sensations and physical objects. But that categorial difference is only that between objects and their states, and so by itself is irrelevant to dualism.

4 Objections to dualism

Although the character of physics underlies one major argument for dualism, a specific principle of physics is sometimes thought to show that dualism is wrong. That principle states that in a closed physical system (that is, closed to other physical systems) the total energy remains constant. But if mental events are nonphysical, then, when mental events cause bodily events, physical motion occurs uncaused by anything physical. And this, it seems, would result in an increase of the total energy in the relevant closed physical system. Mental causation of bodily events would conflict with the principle of the conservation of energy.

No such problem arises, even if dualism is true, when bodily events cause mental events. When bodily events cause mental events, presumably they cause other physical events as well, which enables energy to be conserved. In part because this problem seems to arise only in one causal direction, some theorists have adopted a version of dualism known as epiphenomenalism, according to which mental events are nonphysical and are caused by bodily events, but are themselves causally inert (see EPIPHENOMENALISM).

Epiphenomenalism thus avoids the difficulty about conservation of energy. An even more extreme variant of dualism, known as parallelism, also avoids this difficulty, by denying that any causal interaction between mental and bodily events occurs at all. To distinguish these variants from the standard view, on which causal interaction occurs in both directions, this view is sometimes called interactionism.

But the dualist need not adopt the unintuitive idea that mental events never cause bodily events. Conservation of energy dictates only that the energy in a closed physical system is constant, not also how that energy is distributed within the system. Since mental events could effect bodily changes by altering that distribution of energy, the conservation principle does not preclude minds' having bodily effects.

A second difficulty sometimes raised also has to do with the causal interaction between the physical and the nonphysical. We seem to understand well enough how physical events cause one another, but it is held that causal interaction between mind and body is simply unintelligible, and so cannot occur. We have, it is objected, no conception whatever of how nonphysical events could cause or be caused by physical events.

But we understand how things happen only relative to a theory that governs the relevant events and tells us how those phenomena fit with various others. Understanding does not require a scientific theory; we often rely on informal, common-sense folk theories. But some theory or other is needed. So physical causation seems intelligible only because we have theories that cover those cases. And because we have no theory that governs mind–body interactions, we have no way to understand how they could occur. The appearance of unintelligibility here shows not that such interactions cannot occur, but only that we have at present no useful theory that would cover them if they do occur. Moreover, even if we cannot develop such a theory, that need not be because mind–body interaction is impossible; it might instead be due only to some limitation on our ability to understand things (see McGinn 1991).

A third objection pertains again to causal interaction. For nonphysical events to cause bodily events, those nonphysical events must intervene in the normal sequence of bodily causes and effects. And it is argued that this would result in a detectable time lag somewhere in that sequence of bodily events. Because there is no such lag, dualism is mistaken. But causal intervention need not result in any relevant time lag. Consider the effects of gravitational force, the propagation of which is undetectable on the time scale relevant for brain and other bodily events. All in all, standard objections to dualism seem to fare no better than the standard arguments used to establish its truth.

5 Dualism and consciousness

Descartes defined mental states as conscious states, that is as states of which we are immediately conscious. Few today would endorse this definition, since it is generally held that mental states can and do occur without being conscious (see UNCONSCIOUS MENTAL STATES). But Descartes' definition fits well with dualism, because mental states provide intuitive support for dualism only when they are conscious.

Consider Descartes' argument for dualism. He held that minds are such unqualified unities that we cannot even conceive of their being divided into parts. This claim is tempting only when we focus on conscious mental states. We represent our conscious states as all belonging to a single subject, and so as inseparable from one another. But not all mental states are conscious. So this unity of consciousness does not confer a similar unity on the mind generally.

Another example concerns bodily and perceptual sensations. Dualism strikes many as most plausible for these states, because their qualitative properties seem intuitively not to be physical. But this intuition concerns only those qualitative states which are conscious. Sensations do occur of which we are in no way conscious, for example in subliminal perception or peripheral vision. And although not conscious, these sensations belong to the same types as conscious sensations; we subliminally sense various standard colours, for example, and sounds of various types. Since we distinguish types of sensation by their qualitative properties, the non-conscious sensations that occur in subliminal perception must have the same distinguishing properties as conscious sensations have, namely qualitative properties. The only difference is that in these cases we are in no way conscious of being in states that have those properties.

But when sensations are not conscious, there is no reason to think they resist being described in terms appropriate for the physical sciences. And the same holds for mental states of whatever sort, when they are not conscious. Dualism is intuitively plausible only for conscious mental states.

Considerations raised in the previous section also help disarm this last argument. Our failure to understand how neural processes could have qualitative properties reflects only our lack of a suitable theory of how neural processes could have such properties; it does not show that they do not have those properties.

Consider a related argument. We have, it seems, no conception of how bodily states could have the qualitative properties in terms of which we characterize sensations. It seems simply unintelligible that neural occurrences, or any other physical events, could have the qualities exhibited by a conscious sensation of pain, or a conscious experience of seeing red. This has led some to argue that qualitative mental states cannot be physical. But, again, the argument has force only for conscious states. When qualitative states are not conscious, we have no intuitive problem understanding how their distinguishing properties could belong to physical states.

Consciousness is presupposed even in empirical arguments for dualism. Libet (1985), for example, has experimentally isolated certain anomalies about the subjective timing of mental events, which he thinks suggest causal intervention by nonphysical factors. But these anomalies are detectable only when subjects report their mental states, and thus only when those states are conscious. In addition, a mental state's being conscious consists in a subject's being conscious of that state in a way that seems immediate. So anomalies about subjective timing may be due not to intervention by nonphysical causes, but to differences between when mental events occur and when subjects become conscious of them.

Evidently dualism derives no support from mental states that are not conscious. But then it is unclear why cases in which we are conscious of our mental states should make dualism more plausible.

One reason sometimes offered is the subjective differences among conscious experiences, which seem to resist treatment in physicalist terms (see Nagel 1986). But these differences can very likely be explained by appeal to differences in the circumstances and perceptual apparatus of various sentient creatures. Once it is clear that non-conscious mental states lend no plausibility to dualism, it is unlikely that conscious states will either (see CONSCIOUSNESS §4).

6 Dualism and the concept of mind

Because dualism conflicts with the scientific consensus that at bottom everything is physical, it receives little endorsement today. But among those who reject dualism, there are some who nonetheless find compelling certain reasons for holding that mental phenomena are nonphysical. They deny, for example, that the distinguishing properties of thoughts and sensations can be construed so as to conform to the dictates of physicalist description, or they have some other reason to hold that mental phenomena are nonphysical. They combine a dualist conception of what mental states are with a rejection of dualism.

The only option for such theorists is to deny that

anything mental exists. This denial, known as eliminative materialism, adopts a traditional, dualist concept of mind, but insists that this dualist conception does not apply to anything. Though certain nonmental, physical phenomena may enable us to explain and predict things we usually explain and predict by appeal to mental states, on this view nothing mental exists (see ELIMINATIVISM).

Because eliminativism relies on a dualist concept of mind, we can very likely avoid this extravagant result. As argued above, we need not construe mental states and their properties in ways that imply the dualist claim that mental phenomena are nonphysical. Accordingly, we can resist both dualism and the eliminativist alternative.

See also: MENTAL CAUSATION

References and further reading

Chisholm, R.M. (1957) *Perceiving: A Philosophical Study*, Ithaca, NY: Cornell University Press. (Especially chapter 11; classic argument that the mental and physical are mutually exclusive.)

* Descartes, R. (1641) *Meditations on First Philosophy*, in *The Philosophical Writings of René Descartes*, trans. by J. Cottingham, R. Stoothoff and D. Murdoch, Cambridge: Cambridge University Press, 1984, vol. 2, 1–62. (Classic statement and defence of dualism; influences all subsequent discussions.)

* Galilei, G. (1623) *The Assayer*, in *Discoveries and Opinions of Galileo*, trans. S. Drake, Garden City, NY: Anchor Books, 1957. (Classic statement of the conception of physics often used in defending dualism.)

* Jackson, F. (1977) *Perception: A Representative Theory*, Cambridge: Cambridge University Press. (Important argument that perceiving requires nonphysical, mental objects.)

Kripke, S.A. (1980) *Naming and Necessity*, Cambridge, MA.: Harvard University Press, 127–32, 144–55 (Contains important argument that mental phenomena are not physical.)

* Libet, B. (1985) 'Unconscious Cerebral Initiative and the Role of Conscious Will in Voluntary Action', *The Behavioral and Brain Sciences* 8 (4): 529–66. (Argument that experimental situations reveal the operation of nonphysical factors.)

* McGinn, C. (1991) *The Problem of Consciousness*, Oxford: Blackwell. (Argument that we are constitutionally unable to understand the interaction of mind and body.)

* Nagel, T. (1986) *The View From Nowhere*, New York: Oxford University Press. (Especially chapters 1–7; highly influential argument for property dualism, based on the nature of consciousness.)

O'Shaughnessy, B. (1980) *The Will: A Dual Aspect Theory*, Cambridge: Cambridge University Press. (Detailed, extensive development of a property-dualist theory.)

Popper, K.R. and Eccles, J.C. (1977) *The Self and Its Brain*, Berlin: Springer. (Dualist arguments, based in part on neuroscientific findings.)

Robinson, H. (ed.) (1993) *Objections to Physicalism*, Oxford: Oxford University Press. (Fine collection of articles defending dualism.)

Rosenthal, D.M. (1986) 'Two Concepts of Consciousness', *Philosophical Studies* 49 (3): 329–59. (Theory of the nature of consciousness; argues that explaining consciousness does not require adopting dualism.)

Shoemaker, S. and Swinburne, R. (1984) *Personal Identity*, Oxford: Blackwell. (Swinburne's essay defends a dualist theory.)

Strawson, P. F. (1959) *Individuals*, London: Methuen. (Especially chapter 3. Statement and defence of a classic version of property dualism.)

DAVID M. ROSENTHAL

DUCASSE, CURT JOHN (1881–1969)

Ducasse was a highly systematic philosopher and scarcely any field or topic escaped his attention. He criticized Hume's account of causality, advocated 'soft determinism' and developed an 'adverbial' realist account of our knowledge of the external world. He was a dualist on the mind–body relation, a 'progressive hedonist' in ethics, a defender of the 'will to believe', an expressionist in the philosophy of art, a scourge of art critics and a critic of theism. He also wrote on propositions, truth, signs, liberal education, linguistic metaphilosophy and paranormal phenomena. His influence on younger philosophers has been greatest, however, in the areas of causality, adverbial realism, progressive hedonism, the will to believe and aesthetics. Ducasse died in 1969, but his work remains significant, especially through his influence on Roderick Chisholm and Wilfred Sellars.

1 Life

Born in Angoulême, France, in 1881, Ducasse was educated at the Bordeaux Lycée, Abbotsholme School in England and, after emigrating to the USA, at the University of Washington and Harvard University. He received the Ph.D. from Harvard in 1912, having done his dissertation under the direction of Josiah ROYCE. He taught at University of Washington from 1912 to 1926, then at Brown University until 1958, when he retired. Ducasse helped establish the *Journal of Symbolic Logic*, and was the first president of the Association for Symbolic Logic. He was one of the clearest philosophical writers in the United States and always sought to avoid obscurity.

2 Causality and necessity

Ducasse was a perceptive critic of Hume's analysis of causality, according to which, objectively considered, 'cause' means only regularity among contiguous sequences of logically independent impressions: having observed without exception that one object follows another object, we thereby acquire a habit of mind, namely, the 'propensity, which custom produces to pass from an object to the idea of its usual attendant' (Hume 1739–40: 165). Ducasse was unimpressed with Hume's view. Two of his many criticisms are particularly effective. First, Hume's phenomenalism deprives him of the right to use the distinction between 'perceptions' and 'objects', without which his own rendition of the causal relation could not even be stated. Second, Hume's own position undermines his use of the concept of propensity. In Hume's world there can be only perceptions (impressions) which *are* but cannot *act*, while a propensity refers to what a thing or substance is capable of doing or is likely to do. Hence perception is too narrow a concept to sustain the ideas of propensity (see HUME, D. §2).

As an alternative Ducasse referred to the method of single difference: the strict experiment. He defined causation as the observable relation that holds between the three terms of a strict experiment – the complete state of affairs (S) wherein occur two and *only two* changes in a given time-period, one of which occurs immediately after and adjacent to the other, the second qualifying as proximate effect (E) of the first, the proximate cause. Both Hume and Ducasse, it would seem, confused the reasons we have for saying that x and y are causally related with the meaning of the term 'cause'. Hume saw the method of agreement as the primary way causal propositions are confirmed and so interpreted the meaning of 'cause' as 'constant conjunction'. On the other hand, Ducasse saw the method of single difference as the most reliable way

causal propositions are known to be true and hence interpreted the meaning of 'cause' as 'the only change in S immediately prior to E'. It is clear that both methods under different conditions provide good reasons for saying that x is the cause of y, but if so they cannot also be given as definitions of the concept 'cause'.

For Ducasse, there are other necessities besides logical ones – the blow of a hammer physically necessitates breaking the glass, the death of John's wife psychologically necessitates his depression, and so on. His inclusive concept of necessity he labelled 'etiological necessity'. Though usually clear, Ducasse wrote ambiguously about this concept, sometimes portraying it as an ontological ingredient of the world and at other times denying it. On one hand, he wrote that when King Charles lost his head the swing of the axe *forced* his head to be severed from his body; that people directly perceive a bird perching on a branch to *cause* the branch to bend; and so on. Moreover he often referred to the distinction between agents and patients among the particulars of the worlds. On the other hand, he wrote that any 'power' analysis of causality would introduce a mysterious, ineffable element into causality and thus must be rejected. Ducasse had apparently caught something of the Humean virus when he least expected it. He certainly believed in the agent–patient view of causality, yet there was no possibility of justifying this distinction unless he conceived some particulars to have the power to produce certain effects.

3 Adverbial realism

Ducasse's greatest contribution to philosophy is probably his 'adverbial' view of perceiving physical objects, a view developed by his student Roderick Chisholm and others (see MENTAL STATES, ADVERBIAL THEORY OF §2). According to Ducasse, in everyday life, as we all agree, we directly perceive physical objects and some of their properties and we cannot avoid believing in their independent existence. Many philosophers, however, point out that we sometimes experience illusions and hallucinations and hence, at least in some cases, must be directly aware of our own sensations and impressions and are not apprehending physical objects. Further, since perception is the result of a long causal chain of physical and physiological stimulation which ends in the brain as a sensation, it would seem that we are *always* directly aware of our own sensations and impressions, and never of physical objects. Like Thomas Reid before him, Ducasse dismissed these arguments because they spawned an unsolvable dilemma: either the physical world becomes unknowable, or 'physical object' takes on a meaning radically different from what people ordinarily do in fact mean by the term.

It was to escape from this dilemma that Ducasse developed his adverbial view of sensation. He proposed that we reject sensations as entities and think of them instead as ways of sensing an object, expressed by adverbs, not nouns: 'I see bluely', not 'I see this blue colour'. Thus when a person sees something which looks blue, they are not directly aware of a blue sensation but are being appeared to bluely by an object. The adverbial view, Ducasse claimed, not only avoids the traditional dilemma; it also shows that it is impossible to state the sensationalist view without referring to physical objects as basic epistemic entities. How an object appears to people must make some reference to the physiological states of the observer and the physical conditions of observation; such reference to specific people and conditions is required *before* one can construct a substantive vocabulary of sensations. Ducasse also used the concept of variable appearings to counter the sensationalist argument from illusion and hallucination by accounting for them in terms of variability in the state of the observer and the physical conditions of observation.

4 Progressive hedonism

According to Ducasse various social contexts exemplify different moral codes, but none of the codes can itself be established as the right one and the others as wrong ones, because every code is equally tenable in its context, each being as logically arbitrary as the others. Ducasse called his view 'ethical liberalism' and, though it sounds like straightforward relativism, it is somewhat distinct from this traditional doctrine.

Since no ethical code can be proved to be the correct one, there is no way of establishing either egoism or altruism as the right attitude. Nevertheless there are other ways of changing attitudes than by argumentation; egoists may have their horizons broadened and come to empathize with other people. The point of a liberal education is precisely that of widening horizons by enlarging the range of ideas to be apprehended by students and by making them familiar with a wider range of people with whom they can learn to identify. According to Ducasse egoists have not been convinced by arguments in any shift from egoism to altruism; the point is that widening horizons and the knowledge of what it is possible to enjoy or care about have changed the egoist into a person who *in fact* cares about others. This view has come to be called Ducasse's 'progressive hedonism' (see HEDONISM §1).

Progressive hedonism is a form of universal hedonism and hence, minus the relativism, is akin to utilitarianism (see UTILITARIANISM §5). Numerous criticisms have been made of utilitarianism, one of which is particularly relevant to Ducasse: a person may have to be dishonest in order to avoid starvation, but how is this situation compatible with progressive hedonism? Ducasse answered that, instead of saying that one should contribute to the general welfare, the progressive hedonist should recommend that one commit the smallest amount of evil commensurate with continued existence. Ducasse, then, became an early advocate of what has come to be called 'negative utilitarianism'.

5 The will to believe

What are the moral requirements in epistemology when there is insufficient evidence to decide an issue? Dickenson Miller (1942) argued that it is a moral duty to suspend judgment until further evidence becomes available. His friend Ducasse, however, believed that the only *moral* responsibility is to consult all available evidence impartially; if the evidence is in balance, then one has the right, but not the duty, either to suspend judgment or to accept whatever alternative has life-sustaining value.

Ducasse insisted that this was the legitimate core of William James' article 'The Will to Believe' (1897), which Ducasse thought should have been called 'The Right to Believe'. Against Ducasse, Miller argued that believing without adequate evidence would relax one to the point of believing propositions for practical reasons when the evidence was sufficient to substantiate the denial of that belief. But Ducasse countered by pointing out an opposite spreading effect. He feared that Miller's 'sceptical' condemnation of belief where there is no preponderance of evidence might spread to areas where there is a supporting preponderance in the form of probabilities. Should we insist on near certainties and ignore acting on probabilities?

In later correspondence, however, Ducasse made the same mistake that James had made earlier and committed himself to the strong view that one *ought* to accept life-sustaining beliefs if the evidence is inconclusive – indeed, it is one's duty to do so. In Ducasse's words a 'fool's paradise' is preferable to a 'fool's hell'. He even suggested that in order to avoid the latter a person is justified in using psychological devises to strengthen commitment to the former. Miller was horrified at this suggestion, since such psychological conditioning, he claimed, would make it impossible to look for new evidence and evaluate it properly if encountered. Miller's criticism can be forcefully paraphrased thus: 'Is there a great difference between self-inflicted brainwashing and political brainwashing?'

6 Aesthetics

Ducasse formulated an expressionist theory of art according to which an artist's feelings or emotions, some quite subdued and nameless, are embodied in words, lines, colours, forms, sounds and motion. This self-expression of artists is objective in the sense that they create works of art which when contemplated yield back the feelings of which they are the attempted expression. This objectification of feelings must be consciously done and critically controlled to distinguish it from expressive activities such as sighing and yawning. The critical control usually involves much trial and error as artists experiment within their different media. The trial-and-error procedure helps to clarify and refine the feeling, and in this respect also gives to art creation an objective dimension. The feeling that a work of art expresses, then, is not identical with the original feeling of the artist but is a 'feeling image', a concept not clearly articulated by Ducasse but one which seems to be a recollection of a feeling rather than the feeling itself (see ARTISTIC EXPRESSION §5). There are many definitions of fine art which Ducasse flatly rejected, including Tolstoi's view that communication of feeling is an essential part of fine art (see TOLSTOI, L.N.). For Ducasse it is no essential aspect of a work of art that consumers of it should have its feeling dimension communicated to them. Ducasse also separated art from the concept of beauty; for him art was wholly defined as objective self-expression. No doubt he established one sense of art which is independent of such traditional aesthetic concepts as beauty and communication; however, restricting the meaning of 'art' to objective self-expression seems as unnecessarily restrictive as it would be to limit the meaning of 'religion' to varieties of monotheism.

Outside academic circles Ducasse was well known for his criticism of art critics. They give biographical facts about artists, collate their pieces in chronological or stylistic orders and refer to previous artists who influenced them and those whom they subsequently influenced. Though this may be interesting discursive information, most of it does not help in forming artistic judgments. None the less Ducasse never denied that discursive scholarship can be an aid to appreciation and evaluation, if it serves as a guide for perceiving more acutely and for discriminating in greater detail. The proper role of the critic, Ducasse thought, is that of a guide in a foreign city who, on the basis of their thorough knowledge of the city, points out what onlookers might easily have missed on their own.

List of works

Ducasse, C.J. (1924) *Causation and the Types of Necessity*, Seattle, WA: University of Washington Press. (The most complete and thorough presentation of Ducasse's non-Humean analysis of causality. Unlike Hume's constant conjunction view, Ducasse argues that propositions are singular in nature.)

—— (1930) *The Philosophy of Art*, New York: The Dial Press. (Ducasse's classic statement of his expressionist view of art in which a work of art embodies some subtle nuance of feeling that can be captured by a viewer as well as recaptured by the artist. This and his other popular writings on art led to his election to the presidency of the American Society of Aesthetics.)

—— (1944) *Art, the Critics and You*, New York: Oskar Piest. (A popular presentation of his aesthetic theory, but more importantly a stinging criticism of art critics who think that scholarly information about works of art is necessary for appreciation of art.)

—— (1951) *Nature, Mind, and Death*, The 1949 Carus Lectures, La Salle, IL: Open Court. (Ducasse's most elaborate and profound book, touching, as it does, on all the major areas of his interest from technical epistemology and metaphysics through a host of other issues culminating in a section on paranormal phenomena.)

—— (1968) *Truth, Knowledge and Causation*, London: Routledge & Kegan Paul. (A republication of the most important articles written by Ducasse in epistemology and metaphysics. It is a fruitful book for anyone who wants the technical philosophy of which Ducasse was such a master.)

References and further reading

Dommeyer, F.C. (ed.) (1966) *Current Philosophical Issues: Essays in Honour of Curt John Ducasse*, Springfield, IL: Charles C. Thomas. (Includes the editor's charming biography of Ducasse and a thorough bibliography of his work, as well as essays related to Ducasse's philosophy by Alice Ambrose, Charles Baylis, Brand Blanshard, Roderick Chisholm, Marvin Farber, Charles Hartshorne, Morris Lazerowitz, E.H. Madden, A.I. Melden, H.H. Price and Vincent Tomas, among others. Many of Ducasse's articles and reviews are available only in the journals in which they originally appeared, and Dommeyer's bibliography of Ducasse's work is indispensable.)

Hare, P.H. and Madden, E.H. (1975) *Causing, Perceiving and Believing: An Examination of the Philosophy of C.J. Ducasse*, Dordrecht: Reidel. (A full-scale examination of Ducasse's life including bibliographical references to his own work and to the secondary literature. Contains a guide to Ducasse's unpublished writings in the Archives of Brown University, John May Library.)

* Hume, D. (1739–40) *A Treatise of Human Nature*, ed. L.A. Selby-Bigge and P. Nidditch, Oxford: Oxford University Press, 1975. (Hume argues here that the concept of natural necessity is a function of repeated associations that lead to a mental expectation of B when presented with A. In this way he eliminates power as a basic metaphysical category.)

* James, W. (1897) 'The Will to Believe', in *The Will to Believe and Other Essays in Popular Philosophy*, Cambridge, MA: Harvard University Press. (The definitive edition of the works of William James.)

* Miller, D. (1942) 'James's Doctrine of the "Right to Believe"', *Philosophical Review* 51. (Miller's most powerful attack on James's will to believe doctrine.)

Murphy, G. *et al.* (1970) 'A Tribute to C.J. Ducasse', *Journal of the American Society for Psychical Research* 64: 139–47. (Tributes to Ducasse by Brand Blanshard, C.D. Broad, Antony Flew and Gardner Murphy.)

EDWARD H. MADDEN

DUHEM, PIERRE MAURICE MARIE (1861–1916)

Duhem was a French Catholic physicist, historian of science and philosopher of science. Champion of a programme of generalized thermodynamics as a unifying framework for physical science, he was a pioneer in the history of medieval and renaissance science, where he emphasized a continuity between medieval and early modern science. Duhem was also one of the most influential philosophers of science of his day, thanks to his opposition to mechanistic modes of explanation and his development of a holistic conception of scientific theories, according to which individual empirical propositions are not tested in isolation but only in conjunction with other theoretical claims and associated auxiliary hypotheses. Such a view of theory testing entails that there are no 'crucial experiments' deciding unambiguously for or against a given theory and that empirical evidence therefore underdetermines theory choice. Theory choice is thus partly a matter of convention.

Duhem's conventionalism is similar in kind to that later advocated by Otto Neurath and by W.V. Quine.

1 Life
2 Physics
3 History of science
4 Philosophy of science

1 Life

Born in Paris and educated at the École Normale Supérieure, Duhem took his doctorate (in mathematics) from the Sorbonne in 1888 with a thesis on the theory of magnetization by induction. He had made a first attempt at the doctorate (in physics) in 1884, while only a third-year student at the École Normale, with a thesis on the concept of the 'thermodynamic potential'. This concept was later to become the centrepiece of most of his work in physics. Although published two years later as Duhem's first book, the 1884 thesis was rejected mainly due to the opposition of Marcelin Berthelot, whose principle of maximum work – which wrongly asserts that chemical changes tend spontaneously to produce maximum heat – was criticized by Duhem. Undaunted by this rejection, Duhem took first place in the *concours d'agrégation*, the competitive examination for university teaching positions in France, in 1885. Two years later he began work as a lecturer in physics at Lille, where he met his wife, Marie-Adèle Chayet, whom he married in late October 1890 in Paris. A daughter, Hélenè, was born in September 1891, but the great tragedy of Duhem's life occurred in July 1892, when Marie-Adèle died after giving birth prematurely to a second daughter. Duhem never remarried, keeping household in later years with his devoted daughter and future biographer, Hélenè, who also arranged for the posthumous publication of the last five volumes of Duhem's ten-volume historical magnum opus, *Le système du monde*.

Duhem's conservative, Catholic orientation, his stubborn and contentious manner and the continuing opposition of politically influential, anti-clerical, senior French scientists like Berthelot all combined to prevent his ever winning an academic position in Paris. In 1893, he left Lille for Rennes, moving the following year to Bordeaux, where he remained until his death in 1916. Duhem deeply resented this lack of recognition. When asked whether he would be interested in a newly created chair in the history of science at the Collége de France in 1893, he replied that he would go to Paris as a physicist or not at all, but he was pleased when, in 1913, he was finally elected a non-resident member of the Académie des Sciences.

Few thinkers can match Duhem's breadth and versatility, for he made contributions of fundamental importance in three different areas – thermodynamics and physics, philosophy of science and history of science. His work in these areas divided roughly into three overlapping phases. First, from the mid-1880s to 1900, thermodynamics and physics were his dominant interest, but with treatises on elasticity and energetics still being published as late as 1906 and 1911, respectively. In 1892, Duhem began publishing a series of essays on questions of methodology that would culminate in the publication in book form of his most influential work in the philosophy of science, *La théorie physique. Son objet et sa structure* in 1906. It was also in the mid-1890s that Duhem published his first essays in the history of science, starting on the path that would lead him to such important historical works as his *Études sur Léonard de Vinci* (1906–13) and *Le système du monde* (1913–59).

A curious denouement to Duhem's prodigious literary outpouring was his publication a few months after the outbreak of the First World War, and shortly before his death, of a series of lectures under the title *La science allemande*. He regarded this work as his patriotic contribution to the French war effort. Drawing upon Pascal's distinction between *l'esprit géométrique* and *l'esprit d'finesse* (see PASCAL, B. §5), Duhem excoriated what he characterized as the axiomatizing, deductive excess of the German scientific intellect, contrasting this with the healthy good sense (*bon sens*) displayed by the French mind in its choice of first principles. This good sense is alleged to provide French thinkers with an anchor in intuitively apprehended truth not to be found in German science. However much one might lament this dubious excursion into national scientific typology, *La science allemande* can and should also be read as an intellectual autobiography, as Duhem's mature statement about his own preferred way of doing science.

2 Physics

Duhem's most important contributions to physics were in the areas of thermodynamics and physical chemistry (see THERMODYNAMICS; CHEMISTRY, PHILOSOPHICAL ASPECTS OF §3). Indeed his entire scientific programme was driven by the conviction that a generalized thermodynamics would be the proper unifying scheme for physical theory, with all of chemistry and physics, including mechanics, electricity and magnetism, being derivable from thermodynamic first principles. The intellectual style evinced in this project could be characterized as a balanced combination of the abstract, axiomatizing geometric

spirit and a *bon sens* not too rigidly controlled by empirical constraints in the choice of axioms, along with a total unconcern for mechanical models and a thoroughgoing scepticism about any underlying atomistic ontology.

Strongly influenced by the work of J.W. Gibbs and H. VON HELMHOLTZ, Duhem started from the concept of the 'thermodynamic potential', related to the Gibbs and Helmholtz free energies, which he deployed in a manner formally analogous to potentials in mechanics for the purpose of representing all physical and chemical changes. The programme, which finds its mature statement in Duhem's *Traité d'énergétique* of 1911, was not ultimately successful, but along the way Duhem made a number of enduring contributions to thermodynamics and physical chemistry. Among these were the Duhem–Margules and Gibbs–Duhem equations, the first clear definition of a reversible process in thermodynamics as a quasi-static limiting process, and the first general proof of the Gibbs phase rule. That these results were obtained in the context of a programme of generalized thermodynamics was sufficient to earn Duhem's work a warm reception among late-nineteenth-century German energeticists, such as Wilhelm Ostwald and Georg Helm. Duhem was also one of the first continental scientists to appreciate the work of Gibbs, penning the earliest critical examination of Gibbs' 'On the Equilibrium of Heterogenous Substances' (1876, 1878) in 1887 and promoting the French translation of Gibbs' works with his pamphlet, *Josiah Willard Gibbs, à propos de la publication de ses mémoires scientifiques* (1907).

3 History of science

In the mid-1890s Duhem began publishing some shorter papers on the history of mechanics and thermodynamics in the *Revue des deux mondes* and the *Revue des questions scientifiques*. In 1902 he published two major historical studies, *Le mixte et la combinaison chimique. Essai sur l'évolution d'une idée* and *Les théories électriques de J. Clerk Maxwell. Étude historique et critique*, the first of a series of such works that was also to include *L'évolution de la mécanique* (1903a), *Les origines de la statique. Les sources des théories physiques* (1905–6), *Études sur Léonard de Vinci, ceux qu'il a lus et ceux qui l'ont lu* (1906–13), and his greatest historical work, the ten-volume *Le système du monde. Histoire des doctrines cosmologiques de Platon à Copernic* (1913–59).

It was in the history of medieval and Renaissance science that Duhem made his most important contribution. Here his name is associated with the thesis that most of the important innovations of early modern science had roots in the medieval period sufficient to warrant our viewing the science of that later period as a continuous outgrowth of the earlier one and not as a radical, revolutionary break with a scholastic dark age, as had standardly been assumed by previous historians of science, such as William WHEWELL.

As late as the time of his 1903 *L'évolution de la mécanique*, Duhem still subscribed to the dominant view of the Middle Ages as a fallow period in the history of science between the Greeks and the revival of science in the late Renaissance. It was in the course of his work on his *Origines de la statique* (1905–6) that he first came to suspect otherwise, when his tracking down a few references to the then all but unknown Jordanus de Nemore led to his discovery of a rich medieval tradition, centred at the University of Paris, that was known to and influenced later authors. Most importantly, in his *Études sur Léonard de Vinci* (1906–13) and *Le système du monde* (1913–59), Duhem began to reconstruct the neglected science of the Middle Ages, including the work of such figures as Jean Buridan, Albert of Saxony, and Nicole Oresme, attempting to document the manner in which the pivotal contributions of Leonardo, in particular, drew upon these earlier thinkers.

A theological motivation was never far from the surface in Duhem's historical writings. In addition to seeking to undercut the popular anti-clerical modernism of the Third Republic by disputing claims to revolutionary novelty on behalf of modern science, Duhem also sought to reveal the role in intellectual history of divine providence in the form of what he termed an 'ideè directrice' leading science forward to a 'natural classification' as the endpoint of inquiry.

4 Philosophy of science

Duhem's philosophy of science is a species of conventionalism (see CONVENTIONALISM). It was first developed in a series of essays appearing in the early to mid-1890s in the *Revue des questions scientifiques*, but is best known from the presentation in Duhem's *La théorie physique. Son objet et sa structure*. This first appeared in 1904 and 1905 as a series of articles in the *Revue de philosophie*, and then in book form in 1906. The essential content of Duhem's position is also to be found adumbrated in his *ΣΩZEIN TA ΦAINOMENA, Essai sur la notion de théorie physique, de Platon á Galilée* (1908).

According to Duhem: 'A physical theory is not an explanation. It is a system of mathematical propositions, deduced from a small number of principles, which aim to represent as simply, as completely, and as accurately as possible a set of experimental laws'.

Moreover, from a purely logical point of view, there will always be a multiplicity of different physical theories equally capable of representing a given set of experimental laws. The argument for this conclusion starts from the doctrine of epistemological holism, according to which a scientific hypothesis is tested not in isolation, but only as part of an entire body of scientific theory (see THEORIES, SCIENTIFIC). Duhem exemplified this through his critique of the Newtonian idea of the *experimentum crucis*, an experiment the outcome of which would, by itself, determine unambiguously the truth or falsity of a given scientific hypothesis. There can be no crucial experiment, according to Duhem, because in order to derive a testable prediction from a hypothesis we must draw upon a set of auxiliary assumptions concerning such matters as the functioning of the experimental apparatus and the absence of extraneous physical influences (see CRUCIAL EXPERIMENTS). It follows that a negative experimental result could be explained by rejecting either the hypothesis in question or one or more of the auxiliary assumptions. Hence there will always be a multiplicity of empirically-equivalent total theories for representing any set of experimental laws, meaning that theory choice is underdetermined by empirical evidence, and that the community's choice of one among these alternative theoretical representations will have the status of a convention (see UNDERDETERMINATION §3).

Nevertheless, there is progress in science, the history of a field like optics or mechanics revealing continuous convergence towards what Duhem terms a 'natural classification'. An analysis of scientific method proves that science does not provide explanations; it is an 'act of faith' that convinces us that such an order in our theoretical representations corresponds to the real order in nature. Duhem quotes his favourite philosopher, Pascal: 'We have an impotence to prove, which cannot be conquered by any dogmatism; we have an idea of truth which cannot be conquered by any Pyrrhonian scepticism'.

Here lies the explanation for the generally anti-metaphysical tendency of Duhem's thinking about scientific method. Thus, he criticizes what he alleges to be a typically English penchant for seeking mechanical models of physical phenomena, as illustrated by Maxwell's search for mechanical models of the electromagnetic ether, arguing that the search for models is as often as not an impediment to the progress of scientific inquiry (see ELECTRODYNAMICS; MODELS §3). By contrast, he commends what he regards as the typically French geometric or axiomatic/formal approach to science, as exemplified in his own work in thermodynamics and other areas.

Duhem's avowed purpose in denying to empirical

science the capacity to determine unambiguously the deepest truth about nature was thereby to reserve a place for theology as the arbiter of truth in metaphysics. This emerges with special clarity from his 1905 essay, 'Physique de Croyant', which he added as an appendix to the second edition of *La théorie physique*. But whatever Duhem's conservative, Thomistic, theological aims might have been, it was the anti-metaphysical bent of his philosophy of science that was prized by many of his postivistically inclined scientific and philosophical contemporaries, from Édouard LE ROY, who characterized Duhem's philosophy as an instance of the 'new positivism', to Ernst MACH, who was so taken by *La théorie physique* that he promoted its translation into German in 1908.

Duhem's philosophy of science differs in crucial respects from the conventionalism of H.J. POINCARÉ. Most importantly, Duhem did not follow Poincaré in characterizing conventions in science as merely 'apparent hypotheses' that are, in fact, 'disguised definitions', to be distinguished from genuine empirically verifiable hypotheses. Duhem's holism entails that all of the propositions constituting a body of scientific theory are on an epistemic par, any possible differences in susceptibility to revision in the face of new evidence being a matter, not of principle – as in the difference between analytic definitions and synthetic empirical propositions – but rather a contingent, practical matter of the community's historically and sociologically conditioned degree of commitment to different pieces of the total body of scientific theory. This difference between the conventionalism of Poincaré and that of Duhem is reflected in the different varieties of conventionalism that grew up in later twentieth-century philosophy of science. Moritz SCHLICK and Hans REICHENBACH adopted an essentially Poincaréan conception of the conventionality of coordinating definitions, while Otto NEURATH, Albert EINSTEIN and W.V. QUINE adopted Duhem's holism, the latter two thinkers extending holism about the empirical content of theories to a holism about the meanings of individual terms in science.

See also: CRUCIAL EXPERIMENTS; LOGICAL POSITIVISM; SCIENTIFIC METHOD

List of works

Duhem, P.M.M. (1886) *Le potential thermodynamique et ses applications à la mécanique chimique et à la étude des phénomènes électriques* (The Thermodynamic Potential and Its Applications to Mechanics, Chemistry and the Study of Electrical Phenomena), Paris: A. Hermann. (Duhem's dissertation.)

—— (1892a) 'Quelques réflexions au sujet des théories physiques' ('Some Reflections on the Subject of Physical Theories'), *Revue des questions scientifique*, 2nd series, 31: 139–77. (Duhem's first paper on the philosophy of science.)

—— (1892b) 'Notation atomique et hypothèse atomistique' ('Atomic Notation and the Atomistic Hypothesis'), *Revue des questions scientifique*, 2nd series, 31: 391–454.

—— (1893a) 'Physique et métaphysique' ('Physics and Metaphysics'), *Revue des questions scientifique*, 2nd series, 34: 55–83. (On the difference between the methods and objects of physics and metaphysics.)

—— (1893b) 'L'école anglaise et les théories physiques, à propos d'un livre de W. Thomson' ('The English School and Physical Theories: apropos a Book by W. Thomson'), *Revue des questions scientifique*, 2nd series, 34: 345–78. (Critique of mechanistic explanation.)

—— (1894) 'Quelques réflexions au sujet de la physique expérimentale' ('Some Reflections on the Subject of Experimental Physics'), *Revue des questions scientifique*, 2nd series, 36: 179–229. (The first clear statement of Duhem's underdeterminationism.)

—— (1895a) 'Les théories de la chaleur. I. Les précurseurs de la thermodynamique' ('Theories of Heat. I. The Precursors of Thermodynamics'), *Revue des deux mondes* 129: 869–901. (On the history of thermodynamics.)

—— (1895b) 'Les théories de la chaleur. II. Les créateurs de la thermodynamique' ('Theories of Heat. II. The Creators of Thermodynamics'), *Revue des deux mondes* 130: 379–415. (Continuation of 1895a.)

—— (1895c) 'Les théories de la chaleur. III. Chaleur et movement' ('Theories of Heat. III. Heat and Motion'), *Revue des deux mondes* 130: 851–68. (Continuation of 1895a.)

—— (1896) 'L'évolution des théories physiques du XVIIᵉ siècle jusqu'à nos jours' ('The Evolution of Physical Theories from the Seventeenth Century to Our Day'), *Revue des questions scientifique*, 2nd series, 40: 463–99. (On the history of physical theory in the modern period.)

—— (1902a) *Le mixte et la combinaison chimique. Essai sur l'évolution d'une idée* (Mixture and Chemical Combination: An Essay on the Evolution of an Idea), Paris: C. Naud; repr. Paris: Fayard, 1985. (On the history of the idea of chemical combination.)

—— (1902b) *Les théories électriques de J. Clerk Maxwell. Étude historique et critique* (The Electrical

Theories of J. Clerk Maxwell: A Historical and Critical Study), Paris: A. Hermann. (Critial history of Maxwell's work on electrodynamics.)

—— (1903a) *L'évolution de la mécanique*, Paris: A. Joanin; German trans. P. Frank *Die Wandlungen der Mechanik und der mechanischen Naturerklärung*, Leipzig: J.A. Barth, 1912; trans. M. Cole *The Evolution of Mechanics, Monographs, and Textbooks on Mechanics of Solids and Fluids*, Alphen aan den Rijn, The Netherlands and Germantown, MD: Sijthoff & Noordhoff, 1980. (Duhem's major study of the history of mechanics.)

—— (1903b) 'Analyse de l'ouvrage de Ernst Mach: *Le mécanique. Étude historique et critique de son développement*' ('Analysis of the Ernst Mach's Work: *Le mécanique. Étude historique et critique de son développement*'), *Bulletin des sciences mathématiques*, 2nd series, 27: 261–83. (Review of the French translation of Mach's *Science of Mechanics*.)

—— (1905) 'Physique de croyant', *Annales de philosophie chrétienne* 155: 44–67, 133–159; repr. in *La théorie physique*, 2nd edn, 413–47; trans. as 'Physics of a Believer', included in *La théorie physique*, 2nd edn, 1914, 273–311.

—— (1905–6) *Les origines de la statique. Les sources des théories physiques*, Paris: A. Hermann, 2 vols; trans. G.F. Leneaux, V.N. Vagliente and G.H. Wagener, *The Origins of Statics: The Sources of Physical Theory*, Boston and Dordrecht: Kluwer, 1991. (On the history of statistics.)

—— (1906a) *La théorie physique. Son objet et sa structure*, Paris: Chevalier et Rivière; 2nd edn, 1914; repr. Paris: Vrin, 1989; German trans. F. Adler, intro. by E. Mach *Ziel und Struktur der physikalischen Theorien*, Leipzig: J.A. Barth, 1908; trans. P.P. Wiener, *The Aim and Structure of Physical Theory*, Princeton, NJ: Princeton University Press, 1954. (Originally published in the *Revue de philosophie* 4, 1904; 5, 1904; and 6, 1905. Duhem's major essay on the philosophy of science.)

—— (1906b) *Recherches sur l'élasticité* (Investigations on Elasticity), Paris: Gauthier-Villars. (One of Duhem's last major scientific works.)

—— (1906–13) *Études sur Léonard de Vinci, ceux qu'il a lus et ceux qui l'ont lu* (Studies on Leonardo da Vinci: Those Whom He Had Read and Those Who Have Read Him), Paris: A. Hermann, 3 vols. (Historical study of Leonardo da Vinci.)

—— (1907) *Josiah Willard Gibbs, à propos de la publication de ses mémoires scientifiques* (Josiah Willard Gibbs: On the Occasion of the Publication of His Scientific Writings), Paris: A. Hermann. (Duhem's brief on behalf of Gibb's approach to thermodynamics.)

—— (1908) *ΣΩZEIN TA ΦAINOMENA, Essai sur la notion de théorie physique, de Platon á Galilée*, Paris: A. Hermann; repr. Paris: Vrin, 1990; trans. E. Dolan and C. Maschier, *To Save the Phenomena: An Essay on the Idea of Physical Theory from Plato to Galileo*, Chicago, IL: University of Chicago Press, 1969. (Briefer historical statement of Duhem's philosophy of science.)

—— (1911) *Traité d'énergétique ou de thermodynamique générale* (Treatise on Energetics or General Thermodynamics), Paris: Gauthier-Villars, 2 vols. (Late statement of Duhem's programme of generalized thermodynamics.)

—— (1913–59) *Le système du monde. Histoire des doctrines cosmologiques de Platon à Copernic* (The System of the World: A History of Cosmological Doctrines from Plato to Copernicus), Paris: A. Hermann, 10 vols; selected portions, mainly from vol. 7, trans. R. Ariew *Medieval Cosmology*, Chicago, IL: University of Chicago Press, 1985. (Duhem's most important study of the history of ancient and medieval cosmology.)

—— (1915) *La science allemande*, Paris: A. Hermann; trans. J. Lyon, *German Science*, La Salle, IL: Open Court, 1991. (Wartime critique of the German way of doing science.)

—— (1996) *Essays in the History and Philosophy of Science*, trans. R. Ariew and P. Barker, Indianapolis, IN and Cambridge: Hackett. (A collection of essays in translation, includes 1892a, 1893a, 1893b, 1894, 1903b and selections from 1908.)

References and further reading

Ariew, R. and Barker, P. (eds) (1990) 'Pierre Duhem: Historian and Philosopher of Science', special issue of *Synthèse* 83 (2–3). (A very rich collection representative of the best recent work on Duhem's history and philosophy of science.)

Brenner, A. (1990) *Duhem: Science, réalité et apparence. La relation entre philosophie et histoire dans l'œuvre de Pierre Duhem* (Duhem: Science, Reality and Appearance. The Relation between Philosophy and History in the Work of Pierre Duhem), Paris: Vrin. (A reliable and accessible recent critical study that stresses the systematic unity of Duhem's work.)

Brouzeng, P. (1987) *Duhem, 1861–1916. Science et providence* (Duhem, 1861–1916: Science and Providence), Paris: Belin. (A recent biographical study.)

Diederich, W. (1974) *Konventionalität in der Physik. Wissenschaftstheoretische Untersuchungen zum Konventionalismus* (Conventionality in Physics: Investigations in the Philosophy of Science Concerning on Conventionalism), Berlin: Duncker & Humblot. (A little-known but still very helpful study of the conventionalist tradition, emphasizing Poincaré and Duhem and their reception by logical empiricists.)

Duhem, H.-P. (1936) *Un savant français: Pierre Duhem* (A French Scholar: Pierre Duhem), Paris: Librairie Plon. (Biography by Duhem's daughter.)

Jaki, S.L. (1987) *Uneasy Genius: The Life and Work of Pierre Duhem*, Dordrecht: Nijhoff. (The most comprehensive recent biography; also contains the most complete bibliography.)

Lowinger, A. (1941) *The Methodology of Pierre Duhem*, New York: Columbia University Press. (The first study to introduce Duhem's philosophy of science to an American audience.)

Maiocchi, R. (1985) *Chimica e Filosofia, Scienza, Epistemologia, Storia e Religione nell' Opera di Pierre Duhem* (Chemistry and Philosophy, Science, Epistemology, History and Religion in the Work of Pierre Duhem), Florence: La Nuova Italia Editrice. (A provocative reading of Duhem's philosophy of science as aiming to defend the place of theory in science rather than a statement of instrumentalistic conventionalism.)

Martin, R.N.D. (1991) *Pierre Duhem: Philosophy and History in the Work of a Believing Physicist*, La Salle, IL: Open Court. (A very helpful study that pays special attention to the religious side of Duhem's thinking.)

Picard, E. (1921) *La vie et l'oeuvre de Pierre Duhem* (The Life and the Work of Pierre Duhem), Paris: Gauthier-Villars. (One of the earliest biographies.)

DON HOWARD

DUHEM-QUINE THESIS

see Crucial experiments (§6); Duhem, Pierre Maurice Marie; Quine, Willard Van Orman; Underdetermination (§3)

DUḤKHA *see* Suffering, Buddhist views of origination of

DÜHRING, EUGEN KARL (1833–1921)

Versatile and prolific, Eugen Dühring constructed a metaphysical system uniting naturalism with a priori principles, such as a 'law of definite number' which asserts that everything countable must be finite; hence, the natural world must be limited, and past time must have a beginning. Value judgments are based on natural drives and feelings: in particular, the concept of injustice arises from the resentment produced by injury. Since criminal law is 'a public administration of revenge', the deterrent function of punishment is irrelevant to its rightness. In politics, Dühring combined his socialism with a fervent racism, chauvinism and anti-Semitism.

Dühring was born in Berlin, the only child of a civil servant. He studied law, but when an eye complaint led to complete blindness, shifted to philosophy and political economy. Dühring gained his doctorate in 1861 and became *Privatdozent* at the University of Berlin in 1863, but his campaign against 'spiritual corruption' in universities and his attacks on professors led to his dismissal in 1877. Quarrelsome and litigious, Dühring continued to feud with editors and publishers, produced books on many topics, and championed Robert Mayer's claim for priority in establishing the conservation of energy. Having outlived his enemies, he died at Nowawes, near Potsdam, in 1921.

Dühring constructed a realistic and naturalistic system which he called *Wirklichkeitsphilosophie* ('philosophy of reality'), based on 'principles', which are not really universal propositions but indications of the conditions for gaining knowledge. The most important task for metaphysics, Dühring claims, is to eliminate false conceptions of infinity. The only meaningful concept of infinity is that of a succession which never reaches an end: a completed infinity is an absurdity or 'chimaera', even a self-contradiction. Dühring's finitism is expressed in what he terms 'the law of definite number'. Everything that can be counted must be finite in number. Since this mathematical axiom must apply to reality, the number of world-bodies at any given moment is a particular determinate number.

The most striking consequence of this principle is a denial of the eternity of the world. Because an infinite series of past events would be a completed infinity, there must be a first state of the world, a timeless stability or original chaos, though how this gave rise to a succession of change is a problem. Only for future time is infinite meaningful, as it is no more than the absence of any final state. Similarly, space can be thought of as infinite only negatively, as the unlimited possibility of going further; and infinite divisibility cannot be imagined as a process leading to infinitesimal quantities.

Dühring's moral philosophy is a version of naturalism. Since thinking by itself can never produce an 'ought' out of an 'is', he argues, all ideas of right and wrong must be based on drives and feelings. In particular, our notion of injustice arises out of the natural impulse to retaliate against those who have harmed us. The reactive feeling of *ressentiment*, as Dühring terms it, which finds expression in the drive for revenge, is not produced by some moral judgment made on other grounds; on the contrary, it is what supplies the material content needed for any concept of justice. Civilized society has taken over the task of acting against offenders, rather than leaving it to individual vengeance; yet however universal and impersonal our conceptions of right and wrong may become, their underlying impulse remains the same. Criminal justice, even in its ideal form, is a public administration of revenge. Hence the death penalty is appropriate for murder, whether or not it discourages further crime: the employment of legal punishment for deterrence is a 'terroristic system', having nothing to do with justice (see CRIME AND PUNISHMENT §§1–2).

More broadly, Dühring proposes an alternative to both pessimism and optimism by surveying the feelings and emotions that give value to life. Injustice is the greatest evil in the world, while the greatest good is harmonious interaction with others: here Dühring shows the influence of Ludwig FEUERBACH in emphasizing human sympathy, love and mutual respect. He condemns asceticism for devaluing the natural side of human nature, and separating the spiritual from the sensuous. Satisfaction comes from striving for real goals, and trusting in the value of life; but religion is harmful, since it diverts attention from actuality to an imaginary world.

As a political economist, Dühring followed Henry Carey in suggesting a 'harmony' of labour and capital, and advocating measures to improve the worker's condition. His own 'socialitarian' programme envisaged future society as a network of egalitarian communes. However, Dühring opposed the International and its 'Jewish ringleader' Karl Marx. A fervent racist, he called for the exclusion of Jews and the elimination of 'asiatism' in all its forms – including Christianity – from German culture, while rejecting Darwinism as a brutal, immoral and typically English doctrine.

Ironically, Dühring's most important influences were negative ones. Interest in his ideas among German socialists impelled Karl Marx and Friedrich Engels to construct a comprehensive philosophy of their own. Encouraged by Marx, Engels subjected Dühring's system to a detailed critique in *Herr Eugen Dühring's Revolution in Science* (1878), commonly known as *Anti-Dühring*, which became an official text for later Marxism. Engels rejects Dühring's apriorism in favour of an empiricist and inductivist approach and, perhaps provoked by Dühring's attack on the Hegelian aspects of Marx's *Kapital*, defends the 'laws' of dialectic as general descriptions of natural processes, even affirming the presence of contradictions in reality (see ENGELS, F.).

Another contemporary to oppose Dühring was Friedrich NIETZSCHE. In Nietzsche's view, Dühring is right in tracing our familiar concepts of good and evil back to vengefulness, but wrong in overlooking other drives which are spontaneous and active rather than reactive, embody strength rather than weakness, and belong to conquerors and rulers rather than the oppressed. Nietzsche proposes to establish new values which express this 'will to power'; and when he condemns socialism as a politics of *ressentiment* it is, rightly or wrongly, Dühring that he has in mind.

See also: NATURALISM IN ETHICS

List of works

Dühring, E. (1865a) *Capital und Arbeit* (Capital and Labour), Berlin: A. Eichhoff. (Programme for a reformist socialism.)

—— (1865b) *Carey's Umwälzung der Volkswirthschaftslehre und Socialwissenschaft* (Carey's Revolution in Economic Theory and Social Science), Munich: E.A. Fleischmann. (Defence of the American writer's economic and political ideas.)

—— (1865c) *Natürliche Dialektik* (Natural Dialectic), Berlin: E.S. Mittler. (Theory of the principles of thinking.)

—— (1865d) *Der Werth des Lebens* (The Value of Life), Breslau: E. Trewendt. (Dühring's answer to pessimism.)

—— (1869) *Kritische Geschichte der Philosophie von ihren Anfängen bis zur Gegenwart* (Critical History of Philosophy from its Beginnings to the Present), Berlin: L. Heimann. (A survey from Thales to Feuerbach and Mill.)

—— (1871)*Kritische Geschichte der Nationalökonomie und des Socialismus* (Critical History of Political Economy and Socialism), Berlin: T. Grieben. (An attempted synthesis of economic theory and socialist practice.)

—— (1873a) *Cursus der National- und Socialökonomie*

(Course of Political and Social Economy), Berlin: T. Grieben. (Systematic presentation of economic theory.)

—— (1873b) *Kritische Geschichte der allgemeinen Principien der Mechanik* (Critical History of the General Principles of Mechanics), Berlin, T. Grieben. (Interpretation of modern physics as based on axiomatic universal principles.)

—— (1875) *Cursus der Philosophie* (Course of Philosophy), Leipzig: E. Koschny. (Exposition of Dühring's metaphysical system.)

—— (1880) *Robert Mayer der Galilei des neunzehnten Jahrhunderts* (Robert Mayer, the Galileo of the Nineteenth Century), Chemnitz: E. Schmeitzner. (Biographical defence of the controversial scientist.)

—— (1881) *Die Judenfrage als Racen-, Sitten- und Culturfrage* (The Jewish Question as a Question of Race, Morality and Culture), Karlsruhe: H. Reuter. (A violently anti-Semitic polemic.)

—— (1882) *Sache, Leben und Feinde* (Cause, Life and Enemies), Karlsruhe: H. Reuter. (Dühring's autobiography.)

—— (1883) *Der Ersatz der Religion durch Vollkommeneres* (The Replacement of Religion by Something Higher), Karlsruhe: H. Reuter. (Proposes a 'spiritual leadership' more suited to the German race than Christianity.)

References and further reading

Binder, H. (1933) *Das sozialitäre System Eugen Dührings*, Jena: G. Fischer. (A study of Dühring's version of socialism.)

Bois, H. (1909) 'Le finitisme de Dühring', *L'Année philosophique* 20: 93–124. (Discusses Dühring's finitism.)

* Engels, F. (1878) *Herrn Eugen Dühring's Umwälzung der Wissenschaft*, Leipzig: Genossenschaftsdruckerei; 3rd edn, 1894, trans. E. Burns *Herr Eugen Dühring's Revolution in Science*, in F. Engels and K. Marx, *Collected Works* vol. 25, London: Lawrence & Wishart, 1987. (Engels' polemic against Dühring.)

Small, R. (1990) 'Nietzsche, Dühring, and Time', *Journal of the History of Philosophy* 28: 229–50. (Analysis of debate about infinite time.)

Vaihinger, H. (1876) *Hartmann, Dühring und Lange*, Iserlohn: J. Baedeker. (A balanced contemporary assessment.)

Venturelli, A. (1986) 'Asketismus und Wille zur Macht. Nietzsches Auseinandersetzung mit Eugen Dühring', *Nietzsche-Studien* 15: 107–39. (Surveys Dühring's influence on Nietzsche.)

ROBIN SMALL

DUMMETT, MICHAEL ANTHONY EARDLEY (1925–)

For Michael Dummett, the core of philosophy lies in the theory of meaning. His exploration of meaning begins with the model proposed by Gottlob Frege, of whose work Dummett is a prime expositor. A central feature of that model is that the sense (content) of a sentence is given by a condition for its truth, displayed as deriving from its constituent structure. If sense so explicated is to explain linguistic practice, knowledge of these truth-conditions must be attributed to language users by identifying features of use in which it is manifested. Analysis of truth suggests we seek such manifestation in patterns of assertion. But scrutiny of those patterns shows that there is no distinction between use which manifests knowledge of classical truth-conditions, and use which manifests knowledge of a weaker kind of truth – for example, one which holds whenever we possess a potential warrant for a statement.

Such considerations motivate reconstruing sense as given by conditions for this weaker kind of truth. But rejigging Fregean semantics in line with such a conception is highly nontrivial. Mathematical intuitionism, properly construed, gives us models for doing so with mathematical language; Dummett's programme is to extend such work to everyday discourses. Since he further argues that realism consists in defending the classical semantics for a discourse, this programme amounts to probing the viability of antirealism about such things as the material world, other minds and past events.

1   Sense
2   Truth, use and inference
3   Realism and antirealism

1   Sense

Michael Dummett, English logician and philosopher of language, was educated at Oxford, where he spent almost all his academic career, and occupied the Wykeham Chair of Logic from 1979 to 1992. His numerous papers in books and journals began appearing in the early 1950s; major longer works stretch from *Frege: Philosophy of Language* (1973) to *The Origins of Analytical Philosophy* (1993a).

While at odds with most Oxford philosophers of his own generation and of its predecessor in the importance he attaches to formal techniques, Dummett preserves a fundamental Oxford perspective by insisting on the centrality of the theory of meaning. Pure philosophy, as an a priori discipline, he argues, can do no more than clarify thought. But we cannot take our access to thoughts as unproblematic. (Ignoring this is the error of 'code' conceptions of language, which in Dummett's view include that of H.P. GRICE (§§2–3); for these take such access for granted, and then try to explain meaning by correlating utterances with thoughts as thus (mis)conceived.) For we need to explain the compositional nature of thoughts, and so to display them as structures of thought-elements (concepts). There is, however, no mental process consisting of the bare apprehension of a concept. Rather, thought for us requires a vehicle; and our only access to the structure of thought is through the structure of some such vehicle. Further, though images and so on may serve as vehicles for simple thoughts, language is the paradigmatic thought-vehicle, and essential for sophisticated thought. So a theory of thoughts is best based on a theory of a language apt to express them.

Dummett derives his guiding conception of such a theory of language from FREGE, in a profound interpretation of the work of that philosopher, to the elaboration and defence of which many of his publications are devoted. This paradigm puts a theory of sense at the core of the theory of meaning for a language, charged with articulating how sentences express thoughts; it supplements this with a theory of force, which spells out the conventions enabling utterances to be classified as assertions, orders, questions and so on. The dichotomy, Dummett argues, is an essential one; the later Wittgenstein repudiated it at the cost of neglecting the systematicity of language (see WITTGENSTEIN, L.J.J. §9).

The core theory of sense is founded on a syntax and a semantic theory. The former reads into each sentence of the language a structure out of finitely-many primitive syntactic elements. Then, relative to a given domain of objects, the semantic theory specifies, for each kind of primitive expression the syntax discerns, a sort of entity apt to count as the semantic value of expressions of that kind. Finally, rules of the theory explain how complex expressions, and in particular sentences, systematically assume semantic values in a way determined by their syntactic structure and the semantic values of their syntactic parts. Frege provided the detail of a model syntax apt for a wide range of languages, and of a semantic theory suited to such a syntax. Crucially, his account takes the semantic value of a singular term to be a specific object from the domain (its referent), and that of a sentence to be a truth-value, classically conceived.

Given a semantic theory, an 'interpretation' for a language consists of a domain along with an assignment of semantic values to primitive expressions. With some sentence value(s) distinguished as 'desig-

nated', these interpretations fix a logic: C follows from premises X if and only if on any interpretation in which all members of X take a designated value, so does C. Specifying an interpretation, and so presenting the semantic values of primitive expressions in a specific way, gives them a sense; 'the' sense of the primitives of a functioning language is given by a specification sensitive to the antecedent meanings. Senses for complex expressions are then given by the specifications of their derivative semantic values which the semantic theory generates on the basis of their constituent structure; in particular, on the Fregean model at least, the sense of a sentence is given by that condition for its truth which is derived on the basis of its constituent structure.

How does sense, thus explicated, relate to linguistic ability? Dummett argues that the latter is not merely practical, like the ability to swim, but that it involves a substantial theoretical component, which the theory of sense spells out. Thus speakers are to be credited with knowledge of the truth-conditions of sentences as deriving from constituent structure, and it is in such knowledge that their grasp of the sense of a sentence consists. Attribution of such knowledge is unproblematic where the speaker can supply a non-circular verbal explanation of the truth-condition of a sentence, so that the knowledge concerned can be regarded as explicit and actual. But, on pain of circularity, not all cases can be like this. For the rest, we must reckon the knowledge involved either actual but implicit, that is, unconscious; or else explicit but hypothetical (so that our theory articulates only what *would* suffice to account for linguistic capacity, were it known explicitly, saying nothing of the mechanisms which actually underpin the capacity it characterizes). Either way, the theory of sense must justify such attributions, by showing how they meet but do not exceed what is required to account for features of the linguistic practice they purport to explain. Indeed, by pointing to the way the knowledge it attributes is manifested in use, it explains in what this knowledge consists (see SENSE AND REFERENCE §§1–3).

2 Truth, use and inference

Scrutiny of the relationship between key notions in the theories of force and of sense, Dummett thinks, reveals the point of contact between the speaker's knowledge of sense and linguistic practice. For the archetype of the sort of force which an utterance may carry is the basic one of assertion, so a major task for the theory of force will be to articulate the conventions governing that practice, and in particular to delineate the conditions under which an assertion is correct, that is, unimpeachable *qua* assertion (even if still liable to more general criticism, for example, *qua* obscenity). In doing so, it links assertion with truth: for an assertion is correct if and only if made by a speaker possessed of what is conventionally counted an adequate warrant for its truth. This connection, suitably communalized, might almost serve to characterize the most primitive notion of truth: truth at its most primitive is the property a sentence has if and only if among us we possess a warrant which would render an assertion of it correct.

Almost; for in fact the condition for truth even at its most minimal must extend beyond our actual possession of a warrant. This follows from the logical behaviour sentences exhibit when embedded in more complex contexts, such as the antecedent of a conditional: 'if some even number exceeding 2 is not the sum of two primes, Goldbach was in error' says that Goldbach was in error under a condition including, but more generous than, that in which we possess a warrant for the antecedent because we can actually produce an instance of an even number of the relevant sort. Again, truth is what deductive reasoning preserves; and we can learn something new by drawing a deductive inference. But that would be impossible if reaching a true conclusion always meant reaching one for which we already possessed a warrant.

Classical truth is the concept obtained by widening the core notion of actual warranted assertibility until a statement is counted true if and only if a warrant for it could be obtained by a being able to transcend the limitations which restrict our observations to the local and the gross, and our surveys to finite domains. While Dummett sometimes reserves the word 'true' for classical truth, he also makes it clear that less radical widenings may produce concepts deservedly called truth-concepts. The one he discusses most is verificationist truth, which retains the human measure of warrants, but counts a statement true when our warrant for it is merely potential, not actual. Another is pragmatist truth, under which a statement is reckoned true if we potentially possess a warrant for everything following from the statement as a consequence. Evidently, a logic based on either of these alternative truth-concepts would differ from the classical one, in ways it remains for theory to detail, though some points of difference are obvious immediately. In particular, the existence of undecidable statements – statements for which we possess neither a potential warrant, nor a guarantee that we will never possess one, such as statements about the remote past or future, or ones involving counterfactual conditionals or quantification over infinite domains – means that neither will follow the classical

conception in validating the Bivalence Principle (that every proposition is either true or false).

The primordial connection of truth-concepts with assertion suggests that we look to patterns of assertive practice for behavioural expression of a speaker's grasp of truth-conditions. If, moreover, the grasp of truth-conditions is to be constitutive of attaching sense, the pattern of assertive practice associated with grasp of the truth-condition of a given sentence must be so structured as not to include assertions already presupposing understanding of the sentence itself. Thus Dummett rejects meaning holism, and postulates instead the existence of a hierarchy of sentences, with understanding of a given sentence presupposing a prior grasp only of sentences occupying a lower place in the hierarchy.

Now let a 'canonical' warrant for a statement at the lowest level of this hierarchy be some cognitive state – paradigmatically an observational one – determined by the semantic structure of the statement, and certified by the theory of force as sufficient for its correct assertion; and let a canonical warrant for a higher-level statement be a set of lower-level statements jointly providing adequate grounds for the statement in question, by the lights of the deductive logic of the underlying semantic theory, or such looser standards as the theory of force approves. Then a speaker may manifest grasp of verificationist truth-conditions by a disposition to assert a lowest-level statement when possessed of a canonical warrant for it, and a higher-level one when disposed to assert lower-level sentences constituting one of its canonical warrants. Similarly, a grasp of the pragmatist truth-conditions of a statement is manifested by a disposition to assert such lower-level statements as are guaranteed to be canonically warranted if the given one is. (And to act in ways consonant with such warrants, we may add. But such action too is reflected in patterns of assertion, because acting warrants the assertion that one has acted.)

Critically, however, there is no additional assertive pattern which unambiguously certifies that a speaker's grasp is of a *classical* truth-condition, as distinct from one of these weaker substitutes. The sole plausible candidate is that it is manifested in the additional propensity to reason with the full strength of classical logic. This is, however, an unreliable indicator, since we allow our deductive practices to be shaped by our semantic theorizing – including, perhaps, an illegitimate attribution to ourselves of a grasp of classical truth-conditions.

The inability of a theory of sense based on classical truth to meet the manifestation requirement suggests founding the theory on an alternative truth-concept. The matter of choosing between the verificationist and pragmatist concepts for this role is less substantial than may appear, Dummett argues; for the aspects of linguistic practice which each emphasizes – justification of and commitment by assertion – are so intertwined that, to the extent our practice forms a whole which is harmonious (in a sense apt for formal characterization), the same ultimate end will be reached from either beginning. What is unclear is how to frame a semantic theory apt to underpin a theory of sense based on either concept. Construing the semantic value of a sentence as a truth-value works only in the classical case. We can still take the sense of a sentence to be given by a condition for nonclassical truth; but the elaborating theory must proceed indirectly, and assign to sentences semantic values not themselves truth-values, but in whose terms truth may be defined. One paradigm is provided by Heyting's semantics for mathematical sentences, which takes as the semantic value of a sentence an effective division of mathematical constructions into those which do, and those which do not, prove the sentence, and defines verificationist truth in terms of such values. The urgent task for the theory of meaning is to find analogous nonclassical semantics apt to found theories of sense for less rarified areas of discourse. In the absence of these, our most detailed account of language rests unsatisfactorily on a suspect attribution to its users of a shady concept.

3 Realism and antirealism

Whereas, in Dummett's view, further philosophical issues typically arise through applying insights of the core theory of meaning to the language of specialist disciplines, the metaphysical issue of realism is distinctive inasmuch as, properly diagnosed, it is directly concerned with themes in the theory of meaning, and hence a semantic issue (see REALISM AND ANTIREALISM §4).

The leading idea is that the essence of a realist thesis is not the independent existence of a range of entities, but the objectivity of the truth of a set of sentences. The earlier Dummett seeks to cash objectivity in terms of bivalence, but baulks at classifying all rejections of bivalence as rejections of realism, citing in illustration Strawson's doctrine that sentences containing vacuous singular terms lack truth-value (see STRAWSON, P.F. §2). Hence his earlier writings seek to distinguish deep and shallow rejections of bivalence, Strawson's typifying the shallow; and regard realism as compromised only when rejection goes deep. His later view is that even Strawson's rejection of bivalence does repudiate a realism, namely Meinong's unlovely realism concerning nonexistent objects (see MEINONG, A. §3); but

further, that rejecting *any* feature of the classical semantic theory, not just bivalence, marks a departure from realism. So Russell's alternative to Strawson's treatment of vacuous singular terms also involves antirealism, since his Theory of Descriptions treats (apparent) singular terms nonclassically in not giving their semantic values by an assignment of referents (see DESCRIPTIONS §2). In so far as the analysis of the theory of meaning sketched in preceding sections militates against classical semantics, therefore, it constitutes a case for global antirealism, though an incomplete one pending details of a suitable anti-realist alternative.

In Dummett's terms, reductionism involves repudiating realism only when the semantics of the reducing theory, or the details of the reduction, preclude reading classical semantics into sentences of the reduced theory; notably, when they determine that truth as applied to such sentences is not bivalent, or that the semantic value of a singular term is other than its referent. Central-state materialism thus involves no antirealism: sentences and singular terms of mental discourse assume respectively the determinate truth-values and referents of the neurophysiological expressions to which they are reduced. A common reductive pattern which *does* entail antirealism arises out of subjunctive conditionals. Let 'Were A the case, B would be' and 'Were A the case, B would not be' be called 'opposites'. Then there is no general guarantee that one of a pair of opposites must always hold. Yet often reduction proceeds by reducing a sentence to a subjunctive conditional, and its negation to the opposite; so bivalence for the reduced sentences is flouted and realism rejected, unless special circumstances can be pleaded. Behaviourism and phenomenalism both exemplify this pattern and, lacking grounds for special pleading, qualify as antirealisms, though the commitment to rejecting bivalence was not recognized by historical phenomenalists.

Sundering the link between antirealism and reductionism allows for non-reductionist antirealisms, an exemplar of which Dummett finds in mathematical intuitionism. True, many formulations of intuitionism link it with reductionist doctrines of mathematics as the study of solipsistic mental constructions. But these, Dummett argues, are best construed metaphorically; he construes intuitionism as advocating a semantics for mathematical language based upon verificationist truth, embodying suggestions for the detail of such a semantics, and a mine of ideas for its extension beyond mathematics. These intuitionist sympathies fall short of open espousal, though Dummett is committed to mathematical antirealism in some form – his careful examination of Frege's philosophy of mathematics concludes that paradox is inevitable when classical logic combines with 'indefinitely extensible concepts' such as that of number. Tensed discourse constitutes another area for which any antirealism must be non-reductionist. Rejection of bivalence for future-tensed statements is familiar enough; a further Dummettian theme is that the apparent fixity of the past is not the barrier it may seem to a similar rejection for past-tensed ones.

See also: ANTIREALISM IN THE PHILOSOPHY OF MATHEMATICS §2; INTUITIONIST LOGIC AND ANTIREALISM §4; MANY-VALUED LOGICS, PHILOSOPHICAL ISSUES IN §4–5; MEANING AND VERIFICATION §5; KNOWLEDGE, TACIT

List of works

This list comprises only books on philosophical themes; these include anthologies, in which almost all of Dummett's philosophical essays are collected.

Dummett, M.A.E. (1973) *Frege: Philosophy of Language*, London: Duckworth; 2nd edn, 1981. (Detailed discussion of Frege's philosophy of language, and themes arising therefrom.)

—— (1977) *Elements of Intuitionism*, Oxford: Clarendon Press. (Text on intuitionist logic and mathematics, with much philosophical motivation.)

—— (1978) *Truth and Other Enigmas*, London: Duckworth. (Anthology containing almost all philosophical papers published before 1976. See especially Essay 1, on truth; Essay 14, on philosophical motivations of intuitionism; Essay 21, on antirealism about the past.)

—— (1981) *The Interpretation of Frege's Philosophy*, London: Duckworth. (Further defence of the interpretation of Frege put forward in Dummett 1973.)

—— (1991a) *Frege and Other Philosophers*, Oxford: Clarendon Press. (Anthology of papers entirely or largely about Frege and not previously anthologized.)

—— (1991b) *Frege: Philosophy of Mathematics*, London: Duckworth. (Detailed examination of Frege's philosophy of mathematics.)

—— (1991c) *The Logical Basis of Metaphysics*, Cambridge, MA: Harvard University Press. (The most systematic statement of Dummett's own overall position. Not for beginners.)

—— (1993a) *The Origins of Analytical Philosophy*, London: Duckworth. (Traces the origins of the analytical movement, emphasizing the contribution of Frege.)

—— (1993b) *The Seas of Language*, Oxford: Clarendon Press. (Anthology of almost all papers on metaphysics and philosophy of language not previously anthologized. See especially Essay 2 on meaning; Essay 8, on truth; Essay 18, on mathematics; Essay 20, the best introduction to realism and antirealism; Essay 11, for more detail on the same theme.)

References and further reading

Heck, R. (ed.) (forthcoming) *Logic, Language, and Reality: Essays in Honour of Michael Dummett*, Oxford: Oxford University Press. (Collection of papers on all aspects of Dummett's work.)

McGinn, C. (1980) 'Truth and Use', in M. Platts (ed.) *Reference, Truth and Reality*, London, Boston, MA, and Henley: Routledge & Kegan Paul, 19–40. (Lucid exposition of Dummett's position combined with critical evaluation.)

McGuinness, B. and Oliveri, G. (eds) (1994) *The Philosophy of Michael Dummett*, Dordrecht: Kluwer. (Collection of papers on Dummett's work, with replies by Dummett.)

Peacocke, C. (1986) *Thoughts: An Essay on Content*, Oxford: Blackwell. (See especially Chapters 1–3. An illuminating if at times difficult attempt to reconcile the manifestability requirement with classical truth.)

Taylor, B. (ed.) (1987) *Michael Dummett*, Dordrecht: Martinus Nijhoff. (Collection of papers on Dummett's work, with replies by Dummett.)

Wright, C. (1993) *Realism, Meaning and Truth*, Oxford and Cambridge, MA: Blackwell, 2nd edn. (Collection of papers elaborating and expounding a position deeply influenced by Dummett's work.)

BARRY TAYLOR

DUNS SCOTUS, JOHN (*c.*1266–1308)

Duns Scotus was one of the most important thinkers of the entire scholastic period. Of Scottish origin, he was a member of the Franciscan order and undertook theological studies first at Oxford and later at Paris. He left behind a considerable body of work, much of which unfortunately was still undergoing revision at the time of his death. Notable among his works are questions on Aristotle's Metaphysics, *at least three different commentaries on the* Sentences *of Peter Lombard (the required text for a degree in theology) and a lengthy set of university disputations, the quodlibetal questions. A notoriously difficult and highly* original thinker, Scotus was referred to as 'the subtle doctor' because of his extremely nuanced and technical reasoning. On many important issues, Scotus developed his positions in critical reaction to the Parisian theologian Henry of Ghent, the most important thinker of the immediately preceding generation and a severe Augustinian critic of Aquinas.

Scotus made important and influential contributions in metaphysics, epistemology and ethics. In metaphysics, he was the first scholastic to hold that the concepts of being and the other transcendentals were univocal, not only in application to substance and accidents but even to God and creatures. In this, Scotus broke with the unanimous view based on Aristotle that being could not be predicated of both substance and accident, much less of, except by analogy, God and creature. Scotus argued in general that univocity was required to underwrite any natural knowledge of God from creatures or of substance from accidents. Given univocity, he concluded that the primary object of the created intellect was being, rejecting Aquinas' Aristotelian view that it was limited to the quiddity of the sense particular and Henry of Ghent's Augustinian view that it was God. That is, Scotus argues that even the finite intellect of the creature is by its very nature open to knowing all being.

Scotus' proof of the existence of God is the most ambitious of the entire scholastic period. Prior efforts at demonstrating the existence of God showed little concern with connecting the eclectic body of inherited arguments. Scotus' proof stands apart as an attempt to integrate logically into a single demonstration the various lines of traditional argument, culminating in the existence of God as an actually infinite being. As a result, his demonstration is exceedingly complex, establishing within a sustained and protracted argument God as first efficient cause, as ultimate final cause and as most eminent being – the so-called triple primacy – the identity within a unique nature of these primacies, and finally the actual infinity of this primary nature. Only with this final result of infinity is Scotus prepared to claim he has fully demonstrated the existence of God. Notable features of the proof include Scotus' rejection of Aristotle's argument from Physics VIII (the favoured demonstration of Aquinas), the reduction of exemplar cause to a species of efficient cause, important clarifications about the causal relations at issue in arguments against infinite regress, an a priori proof constructed from the possibility of God similar to that proposed by Leibniz, and the rejection of the traditional argument that the infinity of God can be inferred from creation ex nihilo.

Scotus is a realist on the issue of universals and one of the main adversaries of Ockham's programme of nominalism. He endorsed Avicenna's theory of the common nature, according to which essences have an independence and priority to their existence as either universal in the mind or singular outside it. Intepreting Avicenna, Scotus argued that natures as common must have their own proper unity which is both real and less than the numerical unity of a singular; that is, natures are common prior to any act of the intellect and possess their own real, lesser unity. They are accordingly not of themselves singular, but require a principle of individuation. Rejecting the standard views that essences are individuated by either actual existence, quantity or matter, Scotus maintained that the principle of individuation is a further substantial difference added to the species. This 'individual difference' is the so-called haecceitas or 'thisness', a term used seldom by Scotus himself. The common nature and individual difference were said by Scotus to be really identical in the individual, but 'formally distinct'. The 'formal distinction,' developed by Scotus chiefly in connection with the Trinity and the divine attributes, is an integral part of his realism and was as such attacked by Ockham. It admits within one and the same thing a distinction between realities, formalities or entities antecedent to any act of the intellect to provide an objective foundation for our concepts. These formalities are nonetheless really identical and inseparably united within the individual.

In epistemology, Scotus is important for his demolition of Augustinian illumination, at least in the elaborate defence of it given by Henry of Ghent, and the distinction between intuitive and abstractive cognition. Scotus rejected Henry's defence as leading to nothing but scepticism, and set about giving a complete account of certitude apart from illumination. He grounded certitude in the knowledge of self-evident propositions, induction and awareness of our own states. After Scotus, illumination never made a serious recovery. Scotus' other epistemological contribution was the allocation to the intellect of a direct, existential awareness of the intelligible object. This was called intuitive cognition, in contrast to abstractive knowledge, which seized the object independently of whether it was present to the intellect in actual existence or not. This distinction, credited to Scotus by his contemporaries, was invoked in nearly every subsequent scholastic discussion of certitude.

While known primarily for his metaphysics, the importance and originality of Scotus' ethical theory has been increasingly appreciated. Scotus is a voluntarist, holding for example that not all of the natural law (the decalogue) is absolutely binding, that prudence and the moral virtues are not necessarily connected and that the will can act against a completely correct judgment of the intellect. It is Scotus' theory of will itself, however, that has attracted the most attention. He argues that *the will is a power for opposites, not just in the sense that it can have opposite acts over time but in the deeper sense that, even when actually willing one thing, it retains a real, active power to will the opposite. In other words, he detaches the notion of freedom from those of time and variability, arguing that if a created will existed only for an instant its choice would still be free. In this, he has been heralded as breaking with ancient notions of modality that treated contingency principally in terms of change over time. Scotus argued that the will, as a capacity for opposites, was the only truly rational power, where the rational was opposed to purely natural agents whose action was determined. In this sense, the intellect, as a purely natural agent, was not a rational power. Finally, Scotus endowed the will with an innate inclination to the good in itself apart from any advantage it might bring to the agent. This inclination or affection for the just (*affectio iustitiae, as it was termed by Anselm), enabled the will to escape the deterministic inclination of natures toward their own perfection and fulfilment.*

1 Career
2 Works
3 Sources and method
4 The place of Scotus in medieval philosophy
5 Univocity of the transcendental concepts
6 Primary object of the intellect
7 Proofs for the existence of God
8 The proof from efficient causality
9 Essentially-ordered causes
10 Proof from possibility
11 Actual infinity of first efficient cause
12 Universals and individuation
13 Intuitive and abstractive cognition
14 Theory of will

1 Career

Despite his importance and influence, little is known with certainty about the life and career of Duns Scotus. The commonly reported details of his family origins, early education and entry into the Franciscan order are now regarded as suspect owing to their origin in a partially fabricated eighteenth-century chronicle. More reliable is the date of his ordination to the priesthood in 1291, from which it is inferred that he must have been born about 1266. Scotus probably began his theological studies at Oxford about 1288, although it is debated whether he also studied at Paris prior to 1302. In any event, it is certain that he was present in Oxford in 1300 as a bachelor in theology, at which time he was participating in disputations and beginning to revise his lectures given there on the *Sentences* of Peter LOMBARD.

Scotus, however, never became master of theology at Oxford. At the recommendation of the English provincial, he was instead sent to Paris to lecture on the *Sentences* for a second time, which he began to do in the autumn of 1302. His Paris lectures were interrupted in June 1303 when King Philip the Fair required declarations of allegiance from religious houses at the university during his dispute with Pope Boniface VIII over taxation of church property. Scotus was among some eighty Franciscans from the Paris convent expelled from France by Philip for siding with the pope. During his exile from Paris Scotus is thought to have returned to Oxford, at which time he may have held his Oxford *Collations*. Scotus was back in Paris to resume his lectures on the *Sentences* by the autumn of 1304, when he was nominated by the Franciscan minister-general, Gonsalvus of Spain, as next in line for the Franciscan chair in theology. In his recommendation, Gonsalvus attested that Scotus' reputation had already 'spread everywhere'. Scotus is accordingly thought to have incepted as master by early 1305.

As regent in theology at Paris, Scotus disputed one set of quodlibetal questions and perhaps his Paris *Collations*. For reasons that are unclear, he was soon transferred from Paris to the Franciscan house of studies in Cologne, where a document dated February 1307 names him as a lector. Nothing is known of his activities at Cologne, where he appears to have remained until his early death, traditionally given as 8 November 1308. Remarkably, Scotus produced the bulk of his substantial writings in a period of barely ten years.

2 Works

As with the details of his career, Scotus' works suffered greatly in transmission. It is fair to say that no scholastic thinker of his stature has been so burdened by misattribution and textual confusion. While much progress has been made in untangling Scotus' corpus, fundamental questions remain, particularly concerning chronology.

Scotus' works can be divided into philosophical and theological writings, with the latter generally regarded as later and more definitive. The philosophical writings consist first of all of questions on PORPHYRY and on the *Categories, Peri hermeneias* and *Sophistical Refutations* of ARISTOTLE. These logical works are all presumed to be early products of his arts training, and they appear to have exercised little influence. Much more important are Scotus' lengthy questions on the *Metaphysics* (only books I–IX are authentic), also traditionally regarded as an early work dating from his arts career. The questions on the *Metaphysics* are notorious for their difficulty, arising in part from the hundreds of revisions, additions and intrusions made to the text. Their traditionally early dating has been somewhat tempered in light of research indicating that certain sections appear to have been later. Finally, a much shorter set of questions on Aristotle's *On the Soul* is attributed to Scotus, but its chronology is uncertain.

Scotus' reputation, however, rests on his longer and more developed theological writings, and principal among these are his commentaries on the *Sentences*. A major advance of textual research on Scotus has been to tease apart the various versions of his *Sentences* that had been conflated even by his earliest disciples. At least three commentaries are now recognized: the *Lectura*, which are his earliest lectures on the *Sentences* at Oxford; the *Ordinatio*, a greatly expanded revision of the *Lectura*; and the *Reportatio parisiensis*, which are students' reports of his Parisian lectures. Of capital importance for the interpretation of Scotus is the chronological relationship of the *Ordinatio* and *Reportatio parisiensis*, because the treatment of important issues in the Paris lectures differs markedly from that in the Oxford commentaries. A governing thesis of the critical edition of this work has been that the *Ordinatio* formed the latest and most definitive of Scotus' commentaries, incorporating both his early Oxford *Lectura* and his Paris lectures. A revised tendency, however, has been to see the first book of the *Ordinatio* as earlier than the *Reportatio parisiensis*. In other words, it is increasingly thought that Scotus must have begun work on the *Ordinatio* before he left Oxford for Paris in 1302. Resolution of this must await further study of the Paris reports, which remain unedited for the first book.

In addition to his commentaries on the *Sentences*, Scotus left two sets of theological disputations. The first, his *Quaestiones quodlibetales* (Quodlibet Questions), certainly date from his regency at Paris and should be regarded as the mature work of a master at the height of his career. A second set of university disputations, the *Collationes* (Collations) are also important but have been little studied. As with the *Sentences*, Scotus has *Collations* from both Oxford and Paris. Finally, Scotus wrote two treatises, the *De primo principio* (On the First Principle) and the *Theoremata*. The former is a lengthy and systematic deduction of the existence and nature of God according to axiomatic method. Nearly two-thirds of the *De primo principio*, however, comes directly from the *Ordinatio*, which suggests that Scotus may not have finished the treatise himself. The authenticity of the *Theoremata* has been contested owing to a section which argues, among other things, that

natural reason cannot demonstrate the existence of God. The *Theoremata* is a work nonetheless attributed to Scotus both by manuscripts and by his contemporaries.

3 Sources and method

After nearly fifty years of publication and research, the critical edition of Scotus' works has resulted in two general findings important for the exegesis of his thought. The first is that Scotus' single, most important source by far was HENRY OF GHENT, the leading theologian at the University of Paris in the generation after AQUINAS. On one major issue after another, Scotus begins with an extensive analysis and criticism of Henry's position only to develop his own view in reaction to it. At least for his Oxford commentaries, Scotus' real textbook was not Peter Lombard's *Sentences* but, in effect, Henry of Ghent's *Summa*. The relation of Scotus to Henry, however, is complex and does not simply consist in the former rejecting Henry's conclusions. Scotus' own position is often indebted to Henry's vocabulary, distinctions and general philosophical framework. Even when he does not have Henry's opinion under direct consideration, he will presume Henry's prior discussion of the matter. Accordingly, Henry should be properly viewed as the major intellectual influence on Scotus as much as his principal adversary.

A second finding is that Scotus revised his works heavily by way of additions, annotations and insertions, termed *extra*, or 'outside Scotus' original text'. This method is especially apparent in the first book of the *Ordinatio* and in the questions on the *Metaphysics*. Scotus' additions and insertions to his initial text can run to pages and typically record further objections and replies, often lodged by a contemporary, and note cross-references to related arguments elsewhere. Consequently, at these places Scotus' texts cannot be read as finished products but as work in progress containing several chronological layers.

4 The place of Scotus in medieval philosophy

Scotus occupied a pivotal place in scholastic thought, closing the thirteenth century and opening the fourteenth intellectually as well as chronologically. First of all, Scotus' focus on Henry of Ghent, quite apart from its obvious exegetical importance, was otherwise significant for the period. By in effect making a contemporary work the object of his commentary on the *Sentences*, Scotus fundamentally changed the programme and form of scholastic literature itself. While this change was already underway in the previous generation, Scotus nonetheless marks a clear divide between the thirteenth-century project of incorporating Greek and Arabic sources, as exemplified by ALBERT THE GREAT, BONAVENTURE and AQUINAS, and the fourteenth-century focus on contemporary opinion evident in WILLIAM OF OCKHAM.

However, Scotus' greater contribution lies in his philosophical innovations, which not only became frequently discussed opinions – Scotus is one of the most cited authors in the fourteenth century – but defined the very issues and terms of analysis for the next century. Among the important concepts introduced by Scotus must be considered the following: in metaphysics, the univocity of the transcendental concepts, proofs for the existence of God and the principle of individuation; in epistemology, the distinction between intuitive and abstractive cognition; and in ethics, the will as a rational power for contraries and the interpretation of Anselm's distinction between affection for justice (*affectio iustitiae*) and affection for what is advantageous (*affectio commodi*).

5 Univocity of the transcendental concepts

One of Scotus' most striking metaphysical positions was that being and the other transcendentals could be conceived as univocally common to God and creatures, substance and accident. In this, he broke with the unanimous view of the thirteenth century that being could not be predicated univocally of substance and accident, much less of God and creatures. The common scholastic opinion, based directly on ARISTOTLE, was that being was predicated of God and creatures neither univocally nor equivocally but according to analogy (see BEING). Univocal predication was taken to violate God's transcendence over creatures and equivocity to render natural knowledge of God impossible. Rather, being was said to be predicated according to analogy, which meant that it was asserted of God in a primary sense and of creatures in a related but derived sense. Analogy was therefore construed as a middle way between the extremes of univocity and equivocity, balancing the competing demands of God's transcendence and knowability.

In general, Scotus' position was that some univocal concept of being common to God and creatures was presumed by the traditional conviction that knowledge of the divine nature or attributes was naturally attainable. Scotus singled out Henry of Ghent for sustained attack on this score as part of a comprehensive and critical appraisal of his entire theory of knowledge, which was in general Augustinian (see AUGUSTINIANISM). In his treatment of analogy, Henry was much more emphatic and explicit than

previous discussions had been in claiming that being, when conceived in its utmost generality, did not form a single, common notion (*ratio*), but only two exclusive and proper concepts, one applicable only to God and the other only to creatures. He repeatedly stressed that there could be no separate notion of being distinct from those proper to either God or creature, so that being could be conceived only as either finite or infinite, created or uncreated. To admit an absolute concept of being apart from these two would simply be an admission of one common to both. Scotus argued from several angles that Henry could not consistently maintain that being resolved only into two proper notions, having no conceptual element in common, and at the same time uphold the possibility of natural knowledge of God.

Of Scotus' several arguments for univocity – at one point he outlines ten – the one labelled 'from certain and doubtful concepts' was regarded by his contemporaries as the most compelling. This argument was aimed squarely at Henry's repeated insistence that there could be no concept of being apart from the analogous and proper notions of infinite and finite being applicable exclusively to God and creature (see HENRY OF GHENT). An intellect certain about one concept but doubtful about others, has a concept about which it is certain that is different from the concepts about which it is doubtful. We can be certain that God is a being, while doubting whether God is infinite or finite being. Therefore, the concept of being is different from, and hence univocal to, the concepts of infinite or finite being. Scotus takes the first premise to be evident, for a given intellect cannot be both certain and doubtful of the same concept. The second premise is true *de facto* because past thinkers, such as the Presocratics, disagreed as to whether the first principle was finite or infinite. Yet, in attempting to establish one of these alternatives, no philosopher ever doubted that the first principle was a being. Being must therefore have a separate, distinct concept.

Put more generally, Scotus' point is that prior to demonstration, the intellect is doubtful whether God is an infinite or finite being. Yet, such a demonstration must be based upon something certain about God, for otherwise it would proceed from premises doubtful in all respects. Thus, unless the concept of being is admitted as certain, apart from the doubtful concepts of infinite and finite which are themselves the object of demonstration, no certain reasoning about God will be possible. Henry's refusal to admit a concept of being distinct from any proper to God therefore entails that the intellect is either certain and doubtful of the same notion or certain of none at all.

In a similar line of attack, Scotus is more explicit still that Henry's denial of a univocal concept of being renders natural knowledge of God impossible. A creature causes a concept that is either common to it and God or proper to God alone. Since Henry denies the former, he must hold the latter to explain the natural origin of our concepts of God. Scotus, however, argues that it is impossible for a creature to cause directly any concept wholly proper to God. In general, an object can only produce a concept of what it contains either as an essential part or an essential property, as is evident from the traditional division of essential predicates. Obviously, the creature can contain nothing proper to God as either a part or property of its essence without violating divine transcendence. Thus, if a creature can directly produce any concept applicable to God at all, it must be one that is common rather than proper.

Finally, Scotus applies these same criticisms to the very foundations of all scholastic accounts for natural knowledge of God, the Anselmian doctrine of pure perfections and the Pseudo-Dionysian procedure of removal and eminence. According to Scotus, both of these presuppose univocity, so that 'All the masters and theologians seem to use a concept common to God and creature, although they deny this verbally when they apply it' (*Lectura* 1 d.3 n.29). Anselm's doctrine holds that we attribute to God those perfections found in creatures which are pure in the sense that, conceived in themselves, they entail no imperfection, such as will, intellect or wisdom. These perfections are defined by Anselm generally as 'what absolutely is better to be than not' (see ANSELM OF CANTERBURY). But by this definition, something is first determined to constitute a pure perfection and then on that basis attributed to God, not the reverse. Pure perfections abstracted from creatures must therefore have some meaning that is prior to any they have as proper to God alone. Scotus makes the same point regarding the Pseudo-Dionysian methods of removal and eminence (see PSEUDO-DIONYSIUS). According to Scotus, all metaphysical inquiry about God proceeds by taking some formal notion (*ratio formalis*) and removing from it all imperfections with which it is found in a creature. For example, we take the formal notion of the will – the power for opposites – and remove any limitations connected with its existence in a creature, such as variability. We then attribute it to God by conceiving of it not just as lacking imperfection, but as possessing the greatest degree of perfection, such that it is omnipotent. This process presumes that the formal notion of the will stripped of creaturely limitations is the same notion of will assigned the highest degree of perfection; otherwise the first step of the procedure would simply have no relevance to the second. If nothing of the notion abstracted from creatures remains when we attribute

it to God, then perfections in creatures have nothing to say about the perfection of God.

The outcome of the above arguments is Scotus' revision of the structure of the concept of transcendental being. In place of Henry's scheme, where being taken in its ultimate generality resolves into a pair of simple notions proper to God and proper to creatures, Scotus admits a single, simple concept which is common to both. As a result, the analogous concepts of being proper to God and proper to creatures, which for Henry were simple and irreducible, became for Scotus composite, comprising the common notion of being and the determining concepts of infinite and finite.

It is important to stress that in these arguments Scotus does not entirely set aside the received doctrine of analogy. He of course admitted that the concepts of being proper to God and proper to creature were analogous. His fundamental point is rather that unless there is some underlying concept of being common to these analogous ones, then they will in fact turn out not to be analogous at all but purely equivocal, thus rendering natural knowledge of God impossible. What Scotus did set aside was reliance on the analogous relationship itself as sufficient to account for any proper concept of God. Since knowledge of a relation is posterior, not prior, to any knowledge of the terms related, analogy does not explain but presupposes a knowledge of being as proper to God. Accordingly, some univocal, conceptual community between God and creatures is demanded by the traditional project of natural knowledge of the divine nature or attributes.

6 Primary object of the intellect

Given univocity, it seems to follow directly that being is the primary object of the intellect, for the concept of being is common to, and hence more primitive than, any notion proper to either God or creatures. Scotus in fact draws this conclusion, arguing that unless the concept of being is univocal, there can be no object encompassing all that the intellect can know. Thus, in addition to ensuring the possibility of natural knowledge of God, the other important epistemological function of univocity is to provide the intellect with a primary or defining object.

To avoid what he saw as equivocation on the issue, Scotus distinguished three different viewpoints from which an object of the intellect could be considered primary: generation or origin, perfection and adequation. The first two were relatively uncontroversial, since there was broad agreement that all knowledge originated from the senses and that God constituted the highest knowable object. Accordingly, Scotus concluded that the specific nature of the sense particular was first in terms of the generation or origin of knowledge. In a similarly conventional position, Scotus put God as the first object in the order of perfection absolutely speaking, while the most perfect object proportioned to our intellect was the sensible nature. (Scotus, like most, refined these positions with various qualifications and distinctions.) The order of adequation, however, was more disputed, for here the primary object defined the nature of the intellectual power as such.

By 'adequate' Scotus meant what Aristotle called the 'commensurately universal', which formed one of the conditions of strict demonstration outlined in the *Posterior Analytics*. The adequate object of a power is that which is coextensive and commensurate with all objects over which that power ranges. It is in this sense that the primary object circumscribes the scope of a power and hence marks it off as distinct from other powers. In general, Scotus recognizes two ways in which an object may be adequate: either because it forms a universal nature or aspect (*ratio*) found in all things which a power surveys, such as colour in the case of sight, or because it is a single, most perfect object that includes within itself all the other objects governed by a power. In the case of the intellect, Scotus says that an object is adequate in the first way by community or predication, for it is common to and hence predicable of all that is intelligible; in the second way, an object is adequate virtually, for by understanding it, the intellect is moved to understand all else that is intelligible.

Scotus reports two competing opinions on the adequate object of the intellect, representing broadly Aristotelian and Augustinian theories of knowledge. The first is the well-known position of AQUINAS, taken to represent the Aristotelian orientation, that the adequate object of the human intellect is the essence or quiddity of the sense particular. Scotus argues against Aquinas' position on both theological and philosophical grounds, maintaining in each case that the adequate object concerns the nature of the power as such. Theologically, Scotus rejects Aquinas' position because, in limiting the scope of the created intellect in its nature to the material quiddity, it rendered the knowledge of the immaterial essence of God promised in beatitude impossible. On the same grounds, Scotus rejects Aquinas' explanation that, since 'grace perfects nature', the intellect will be elevated by a supernatural quality that will enable it to attain an immaterial object. While Scotus of course holds that a supernatural grace is required for our intellect to have direct vision of God, he denies that any supervening quality can modify a power so as to change its adequate object. In that case, the power is

not simply perfected but, by definition, transformed into a power of an altogether different nature. Philosophically, Scotus argues that on Aquinas' position the science of metaphysics would be impossible, for the intellect cannot acquire a science whose object exceeds the scope of the primary object of the intellect itself. But the object of metaphysics, being *qua* being, is more universal than material natures.

The second opinion, which represents an Augustinian approach, is that of HENRY OF GHENT, who posited God as the primary object of the intellect. As indicated above, Henry held that being and the other transcendentals taken in their utmost generality resolved into two distinct notions, one proper to God and the other to creatures. Henry had to designate one of the two as primary as regards our intellect, and he argued that those proper to God were prior. This followed from his strong commitment to an Augustinian theory of illumination, according to which the essence of a creature was truly known only by reference to its eternal archetype or idea in the mind of God (see AUGUSTINIANISM). Scotus replies that, as indicated, if God is the adequate object of the created intellect, the divine nature must either be common to or virtually include all that is intelligible. The divine essence is obviously not universally common to all intelligible objects, since God cannot be predicated of creatures. Although the divine essence does virtually include all that is intelligible, God is not on this account the adequate object of any created intellect. If this were the case, then the human intellect would be moved to understanding all intelligibles by a single object, namely the divine essence, rather than directly by those intelligibles themselves. The divine essence, of course, can function as an object in this way only for the divine intellect, which is to say that God is the adequate object of the divine mind alone. By way of a corollary to his refutation of Henry, Scotus also excludes on similar grounds substance as the adequate object of the intellect in the sense that it virtually contains accidents. This would mean that accidents could only be known through substance, which is false, since accidents themselves can move the intellect as intelligible objects.

Having excluded both God and substance in his refutation of Henry, Scotus concluded that no single object can be primary for the created intellect in the sense that it virtually contains all else that is intelligible. Therefore, if there is a primary, adequate object of the intellect, it must be such owing to its community. Since nothing is more common than being, it must be the primary object of the intellect. Scotus notes that this presupposes a univocal concept of being, so that if univocity is denied the intellect can have no adequate object.

In making being the primary object of the intellect, Scotus was in fact tacitly advancing yet a third opinion, that of Avicenna (see IBN SINA). In central passages of his *Metaphysics*, Avicenna had made being both a primary conception of the mind and, in explicit contradistinction to either God or substance, the proper subject of a universal science of metaphysics. These texts strongly implied that Avicenna had seen being as the primary object of the intellect, prior to both God and creatures. Henry of Ghent had already explicitly raised just this interpretation of Avicenna in order to reject it forcefully on the grounds that it entailed a univocal concept of being. Henry's analysis was not lost on Scotus, who adopted the Avicennian position as a consequence of his doctrine of univocity.

7 Proofs for the existence of God

Duns Scotus' argument for the existence of God was perhaps the most ambitious of the scholastic period. Running to hundreds of pages and comprising dozens of interim conclusions and corollaries, it exists in at least four significantly modified versions, one in each of his three commentaries on the *Sentences* and separately as the treatise *De primo principio*. Among its distinctive features are the demonstration of the so-called 'triple primacy', the rejection of Aristotle's proof from motion, the definition of essentially ordered causes, the argument from possibility and the demonstration of God as infinite being.

According to Scotus, the highest naturally attainable concept of God is that of an actually infinite being. Consequently, Scotus holds that a complete argument for the existence of God can demonstrate nothing less than that some being is actually infinite. For Scotus a proof for a first efficient cause, such as Aquinas' second way, would not itself fully constitute a demonstration that God exists, but, as will be evident, would be merely a preliminary step in such a demonstration. Thus whereas most scholastics, like AQUINAS, first establish that God exists and only later derive infinity as a divine attribute, Scotus requires the demonstration of infinity as logically necessary to establish God's existence itself. As a result, the structure of Scotus' proof is exceedingly complex, involving a good portion of his entire natural theology.

The overall structure of Scotus' demonstration comprises three large, principal steps divided into two main articles. The first step establishes that there is a first efficient and final cause and a most perfect being, the second that these three coincide in a unique nature, and the third that this nature is actually infinite. The first two steps together constitute the first article, which Scotus says establishes God according to the relative properties of causality and eminence (in other words, perfection), and the third step forms the second article, which reaches God according to the absolute property of actual infinity. The establishment in the first half of the proof of something primary according to each of the relative properties of efficiency, finality and eminence is referred to as the demonstration of the 'triple primacy.' All of these steps are intricately argued and supported by sometimes large preliminary results, such as that God has both an intellect and will as preparatory to the proof of actual infinity.

As in other areas of his thought, Scotus' proof reveals the influence of HENRY OF GHENT. Scotus took over the structure of the triple primacy directly from Henry's attempt to schematize the eclectic body of received arguments for the existence of God according to the Pseudo-Dionysian ways of causality and eminence (see PSEUDO-DIONYSIUS). By subdividing causality into efficient, formal or exemplar, and final causes and interpreting eminence in terms of degrees of perfection, Henry sought to reconcile the disparate arguments from the Aristotelian (efficient and final cause) and Augustinian (exemplar cause and eminence) traditions. In an otherwise important metaphysical step, Scotus maintained against Henry that exemplar cause was simply a species of efficienct cause, and therefore eliminated it as a separate class of argument for the existence of God on the grounds of logical economy. He thereby streamlined Henry's original divisions of causality and eminence to the three of the triple primacy.

8 The proof from efficient causality

Each of Scotus' proofs for a primacy in efficient cause, final cause and eminence contains three main conclusions: that there is a first in that order, that it is uncaused and that it actually exists. Because Scotus establishes these three results principally for efficienct causation and then applies them to the other two cases, it will be sufficient to examine each of these three conclusions leading to a first efficient cause.

Before beginning the proof from efficienct causation proper, Scotus explains that he is demonstrating a first efficient cause of being and explicitly discards Aristotle's argument for a prime mover in *Physics* VIII. Scotus does so not because he thinks Aristotle's proof invalid but, again, on grounds of economy. To prove a first cause of motion is not necessarily to prove a first efficient cause of being. While the two may coincide in reality, further demonstration is required to establish this identity. Including Aristotle's physical proof would therefore necessitate a further step. Prior to Scotus, Aristotle's approach had been increasingly seen as inferior to Avicenna's strictly metaphysical proof based on necessity and possibility, especially by Henry of Ghent. Scotus, however, represents the final step where *Physics* VIII is omitted altogether from the standard corpus of arguments for God.

The first conclusion under efficient causation, then, is that there is some efficient cause absolutely first, so that it neither exists nor exercises its causal power by virtue of some prior cause. Scotus' main argument for this first conclusion is brief. He formulates the initial premise broadly to include even possible effects: some being can be caused efficiently (*aliquod ens est effectibile*). It is therefore either caused by itself, by nothing or by another. Since it cannot be caused by nothing or by itself, it is caused by another. This other is either a first efficient cause in the way explained or it is a posterior agent, either because it can be an effect of, or can cause in virtue of, another efficient cause. Again, either this is first, or we argue as before, and some prior cause is required. Thus, there is either an infinity of efficient causes, so that each has some cause prior to it, or there is a first cause posterior to none. Since an infinity of causes is impossible, there must be a primary cause that is posterior to none.

This argument immediately encounters two objections, and Scotus' replies to them contain the bulk of his proof. The first is that the argument begs the question because it assumes that an infinite regress of causes is impossible. Here is it observed that the philosophers (that is, Aristotle and Avicenna) admitted an infinite series of causes, for they held that the generation of individuals could proceed to infinity, and hence every generating agent would have some prior cause. The second objection is that Scotus' argument is not strictly demonstrative because it is based on premises that are contingent, namely, that some effect exists. As such, the proposed proof lacks the necessity required of Aristotelian demonstration in the proper sense.

9   Essentially-ordered causes

In response to the first objection, Scotus defines the precise nature of causal relations at issue in arguments against infinite regress. According to Scotus, they do not concern simply essential as opposed to accidental causes, but rather essentially-ordered as opposed to accidentally-ordered causes. The former concern only the relationship that a single cause bears to its given effect, namely, that the effect arises from the nature of the cause rather than from something incidental to it. Essentially-ordered causes, however, concern the relationship of several causes to each other in jointly producing an effect. As defined by Scotus, there are three features of essentially-ordered as opposed to accidentally-ordered causes. The first is that the posterior cause depends upon the prior for the very exercise of its causality and not just for its being, which can be the case in accidentally-ordered causes. The second is that essentially-ordered causes always differ in nature so that the prior cause is more perfect in kind. This is a consequence of the first feature, for given two causes of the same nature, either is sufficient to produce the same effect. Finally, essentially-ordered causes must be simultaneously present to produce their effect, for otherwise from the second feature, some perfection in causality required for that effect would be missing.

Given this distinction, Scotus excludes the counter-example drawn from the philosophers, since it concerns an infinite series of temporally successive, generating causes. The causes in such a series are therefore not essentially but only accidentally ordered to each other in producing a given effect, for the posterior cause does not depend upon the prior for its causal action itself, but only for its existence. This is clear, for all the generating causes in the series are individual agents of the same nature or species, and thus not all are required simultaneously to produce the same effect. For instance, parents can produce a child whether or not their own parent or grandparent is alive. Rather, Scotus directs his argument against an infinite series of causes upon which the entire succession of individual agents itself would depend. Scotus claims that no philosopher admitted an infinite series of such essentially ordered or 'ascending' causes.

Having so defined the notion of causality operative in the proof, Scotus remains content to give five brief arguments against infinite regress, based in part upon the received reasoning of Aristotle's *Metaphysics* II and Avicenna. An exception is the fifth of these arguments, for here Scotus establishes the possibility of a first efficient cause, the actual existence of which he deduces later. Scotus argues that since efficient causality does not of itself imply imperfection, it is possible for it to exist in some nature without imperfection. That is, efficient causality, like wisdom or intellect, is a 'pure perfection'. However, if there is an infinite regress in efficient causes, then all would be dependent on some prior cause and efficiency could never be found without imperfection, contrary to assumption. Therefore, a first efficient cause in the sense defined must be possible. While seemingly weaker than the other arguments against infinite regress in that it establishes only the possibility of a first efficient cause, this result enables Scotus to construct a strict demonstration which he claims is necessary.

10 Proof from possibility

To the second objection, that the proof began from contingent premises and thus was not a true demonstration, Scotus replies that his argument for a first efficient cause can be formulated with either existential or modal premises. In the first way, the argument begins with the actual existence of some effect or change and argues directly to the existence of a cause owing to the correlative nature of effect and cause. Formulated in this fashion, the argument is based on contingent but evidently true premises. In the second way, the argument takes its premise from the possibility of some effect and concludes to the possibility of a cause. The actual existence of a first efficient cause is then deduced from its possibility. In this way, the argument can be recast so as to be a necessary demonstration, for the premises are statements not about the actual existence of some effect but about its nature or possibility. Scotus draws out the necessary argument from possibility in the last conclusion concerning efficient cause.

Having answered these two objections, Scotus proceeds to the remaining two of three conclusions necessary to establish a primacy in efficient causality. The second is that the first efficient cause is uncausable, with respect to both its own existence and its ability to cause. As Scotus indicates, this conclusion simply makes explicit the notion of 'first' already demonstrated in the arguments against infinite regress. The third and final conclusion is that an efficient cause first in this sense actually exists. As established in the fifth argument against infinite regress, a first efficient cause is possible. Scotus then argues that if such a cause is possible, it must actually exist. If it does not exist, then it could only be possible if some other cause was able to bring it into existence. But such a first efficient cause is absolutely uncausable, so that if it does not actually exist, it is impossible for it to exist. Therefore, if the first efficient cause can exist, it does exist. Alternatively, Scotus says, the same conclusion can be reached by the other traditional arguments recorded against infinite regress, although, as indicated in the above reply to the second objection, they begin from contingent premises.

11 Actual infinity of first efficient cause

After establishing the existence of a first efficient and

final cause and most perfect being, and their identity in a unique nature, Scotus then moves to the actual infinity of that nature. As indicated, Scotus does not consider the existence of God to have been proven until actual infinity has been demonstrated. He derives the infinity of this primary nature from its properties of efficienct causality, final causality and eminence. The demonstrations based on efficient causality are notable.

Scotus considers two standard arguments for the infinity of the first efficient cause, both treated in some detail by Henry of Ghent in his question on divine infinity, and then constructs a third of his own. The first, based on Aristotle's *Physics* VIII, is that since the first mover causes an infinite (that is, beginningless) motion, it must be infinite in power. Scotus, however, sees the argument as needing considerable expansion to establish infinity in the sense desired. First of all, to avoid basing the argument on the false assumption of an eternal world, he argues that the antecedent could be changed to the weaker claim that it is possible for God to cause an infinite motion. (Scotus, like Aquinas, regarded the eternity of the world as factually false but not impossible (see ETERNITY OF THE WORLD, MEDIEVAL VIEWS OF).) Scotus claims that the consequent equally follows if God can, but in fact does not, produce an eternal motion. Second, he recognizes that a cause is not infinite in power simply because it produces an effect or succession of like effects – in this case the uniform rotations of the outermost heaven – for an infinite duration. Given a finite effect of infinite duration or an infinite succession of such effects, it only follows that their cause is also infinite in duration, not necessarily in power or perfection. Thus, Scotus revises Aristotle's original reasoning by arguing that the prime mover is causally responsible for the entire infinite succession of motions and derived effects taken together and in their totality. This he does in several ways, all of which depend upon recognizing that the prime mover, since it is the first efficient cause, depends on nothing else for its causal power. As such, the prime mover must possess within itself all at once the total power required to produce all of its effects realizable over an infinite time, for it can receive no power from any external cause. Since these effects are infinite in number, it must be infinite in power.

In addition to the Aristotelian approach based upon the prime mover as the first efficient cause of motion, Henry advanced a second argument for divine infinity based on God as the first efficient cause of being, that is, on God as creator. Henry argued that since the distance traversed from nothing to being in the act of creation *ex nihilo* was infinite (for a finite distance presupposes two finite beings), God had to be infinite in power. Whereas Scotus found the first approach based on Aristotle's *Physics* salvageable, he rejected outright this second argument based on creation. First of all, he noted that the argument requires that creation be taken in the revealed sense of a temporal beginning of the world, which is a matter of religious belief, rather than in the philosophically demonstrable sense of causal dependence. Secondly, Scotus denies that there is an infinite 'distance' between being and nothing. Contradictories are not distant in the sense that there is some interval between them, for they are immediate, but only in the sense that one extreme is more perfect than the other. Thus, two opposed extremes cannot be more 'distant' than the more perfect of the two. But the more perfect extreme in creation is merely finite. Thus, while a creature is infinitely distant from God, since the more perfect extreme is infinite, it is not so distant from nothing.

Scotus' third and preferred argument for infinity is drawn from exemplar causation, that is, from the efficient cause considered as an intellective agent. Prior to this proof, Scotus first establishes three necessary preliminary results: that the first cause has an intellect and will, that its intellectual and voluntary acts are identical to its essence and that it knows all that can be known both distinctly and actually. From this he argues that since the divine intellect knows distinctly and actually all that can be known, it knows these things all at once, for an intellect knows successively only if it moves from confused to distinct or from potential to actual knowledge. The things that can be known are infinitely many; therefore, since the intellect of the first efficient cause knows infinitely many things at once, it is actually infinite.

In sum, then, Scotus accepts proofs for infinity based upon the first efficient cause as prime mover and exemplar but not as creating cause. After completing further proofs for infinity based on finality and eminence, he concludes that the existence of God has been demonstrated according to the highest attainable concept (see GOD, ARGUMENTS FOR THE EXISTENCE OF).

12 Universals and individuation

Generally speaking, Scotus is regarded as a realist on the issue of universals because he admits that the universal has some reality and unity prior to any act of the intellect and accordingly that it has some sort of real distinction – the so called formal distinction – from the individual. On this score, he was attacked by WILLIAM OF OCKHAM, who, committed to a thorough nominalism, denied any sort of distinction within the individual that would grant the universal a reality of its own (see NOMINALISM; UNIVERSALS). As such, Scotus and Ockham are typically viewed as poles in the fourteenth-century strain of the realist–nominalism debate. Scotus, however, was not an extreme realist. For instance, he argued at length against Henry of Ghent's theory which accorded the essences of things a real being in the mind of God antecedent to their creation (see HENRY OF GHENT). Even Ockham places Scotus next to last in his series of opinions ranked according to their degree of realism.

Scotus does not directly treat the problem of the reality of universals, as one finds it treated in the commentaries of BOETHIUS and ABELARD, but rather addresses it in the course of determining the principle of individuation. By Scotus' time, the thirteenth-century discussion of individuation had become highly involved, leading Peter OLIVI to remark that there was 'an endless forest of opinions on the matter'. Scotus reaches his own position after a lengthy examination and rejection of five possible views: a common opinion that there is no need to posit a separate principle of individuation, followed by four specific views: negation (Henry of Ghent), actual existence (a common view), quantity (Giles of Rome) and matter (a common view attributed to Aristotle). Scotus devotes a separate question to the elimination of each of these opinions, leaving him to conclude in a sixth view what the principle of individuation must be.

The greatest burden of Scotus' entire discussion is the refutation of the first view that there is no need to posit a distinct principle of individuation. The issue is whether a common nature, such as equinity or humanity, is of itself individual. This first view holds that the nature is individual of itself, so that there is no need to account for its individuality by any other factors than those that bring the nature itself into actual existence, namely, the generating causes themselves. It is not, in this view, that the nature is first produced as universal and then some intervening causes are required to contract it to a singular instance, for the nature is produced and exists only as singular. To the contrary, what is required is an explanation of the nature's universality, for this does not belong to the nature as it exists absolutely and in reality but only in relation to the intellect.

In essence, what Scotus is combating is the nominalistic position that reality is thoroughly singular and hence individuality requires no explanation. Scotus mounts two main arguments against this view, both of which bring out his realism. The first is that the object of a power, insofar as it functions as its object, is naturally prior to the act of that power. The reason is that a cause is prior to its effect, and the object is a cause of the act of a power. However, if the nature is of itself singular insofar as it is prior to an act of the intellect, then the intellect in its act of understanding will grasp its object in a way contrary to the very nature of that object itself, namely, as common rather than singular. Therefore, the nature cannot be of itself singular but must be the common antecedent to an act of the intellect.

Scotus' second argument issues in his doctrine of a lesser or 'minor' unity. He maintains that the nature must have its own proper unity which is both real and less than the numerical unity of the singular. Otherwise, every real unity would be numerical, which is false. The reason is that many relationships are recognized as real in the sense that they are not mind-dependent, yet are not based on things numerically one but on species, genera and other common classes. Therefore, these must have unity which is less than numerical but nonetheless real. For instance, the basis of all physical change, which is real, is contrariety; but things are not contrary insofar as they are numerically one, for then there would be as many contraries as individuals. Thus contraries – hot and cold, up and down – must each be one by a unity that is real but less than numerical. Or again, the relation of similarity is real in the sense that it is not simply the product of the mind. It cannot be based on what is numerically one, for then all things would be equally similar. Conversely, there are degrees of diversity that are not merely mind-imposed, so that Socrates differs more from rock than from Plato. This would not follow, however, if all unity were numerical, for then all individuals would be equally diverse.

Accordingly, Scotus concludes that the natures of things, such as equinity and humanity, are not of themselves individual but are the common antecedent to any act of the intellect. From this it follows that natures taken in themselves are not, strictly speaking, universal either, for universality in the strict sense is a relation of reason resulting from an act of the intellect. Quoting Avicenna's famous text on the common nature (*natura communis*), Scotus says that the nature taken in itself is neither universal nor singular: 'Equinity is nothing else but equinity alone. Of itself it is neither one nor many, neither universal nor particular' (*Ordinatio* 2 d.3 n.31) That is, according to Scotus, although the nature is never found except as universal in the mind or as singular outside the mind, it cannot of itself be either. If equinity were in itself universal, so as to include the note of universality in its definition, it could not be predicated of any singular instance, for no individual is a universal. If it were singular of itself, it could be asserted of only one instance. Thus, in order to be

capable of realization in either state, the nature taken in itself must be neutral with respect to both. It is this common nature that forms the proper object of the intellect, functions as the predicate in true, universal statements, and has the real, lesser unity demonstrated above.

Given that the natures or essences of things are not of themselves singular, they must be made such by some individuating factor, just as they are made universal in the strict sense by an intervening act of the intellect. As indicated, Scotus rejects four candidates for this individuating principle. The first is Henry of Ghent's position that a nature is individual when it cannot be pluralized further (for example, Socrates cannot be multiplied) and is not identified with another (Socrates is not Plato).Thus, Henry concluded that a nature is individuated by a twofold negation. Scotus argues that an individual is something positive and thus cannot be caused by negation. In any event, Henry's theory does not give an exact cause, for every negation presupposes something positive. What is sought then is the positive factor that causes these two negative properties of an individual.

The next opinion is that actual existence individuates, which is based upon the principle that actuality distinguishes. Since existence is the ultimate act, it must cause the ultimate distinction, namely, individuality (see HENRY OF GHENT). Against this, Scotus argues that while existence is an act, it is not an act relevant to individuation. At issue is what makes some substance, such as a horse or stone, individual. Existence is an act outside of and posterior to the whole predicamental line of substance; it is in this sense that existence is often said to be 'accidental', for it lies outside the essence or natures of things. One of the more common views was that individuation was caused by quantity, since a form was taken to be pluralized insofar as it was found in an extended, material substrate. Scotus replies that if accidents are posterior to substance, this holds *a fortiori* of individual substance, since ARISTOTLE identifies this as substance in the primary sense. Therefore, quantity as an accident is posterior to whatever makes a substance individual. Elsewhere, Scotus deploys this same line of reasoning against the Boethian theory that a collection of accidents individuates (see BOETHIUS, A.M.S.). Finally, he rejects the standard Aristotelian view that matter individuates, since matter is in itself indeterminate and indistinct. It cannot therefore be a principle of distinction.

From all of this, Scotus concludes that the principle of individuation must be something real and positive in the substantial order as opposed to any kind of accident, whether existential or categorical, and, while not a substantial form itself, the ultimate reality or perfection of that form. In other words, the principle of individuation is a further substantial difference added to the specific nature; indeed, Scotus calls it an 'individual difference'. While the individual difference is of course not a further specific difference, Scotus depicts it as functioning metaphysically in a closely analogous way. Thus, just as the specific difference renders the nature of which is it a part incapable of division into any further species, so the individual difference renders the singular absolutely indivisible. Further, the specific difference is a reality formally distinct from, and actual with respect to, the reality of the genus. Also, the individual difference is actual with respect to the reality of the specific nature and formally distinct from it. Finally, the individual difference is irreducibly simple and hence wholly diverse from any other individual difference. In this it is comparable to ultimate specific differences, which are absolutely simple and diverse. The individual difference, however, is unlike any specific difference, because it adds no further quidditative or essential reality. If the nature or essence of a thing be considered its form, then the individuating difference may be considered 'material' in the extended sense that it contributes no common essence or nature but rather contracts such a nature to an ultimate subject. Posterity has labelled this individual difference *haecceitas* or 'thisness', a term used sparingly by Scotus himself and then usually to mean the state of being singular (*singularitas*) rather than the principle of individuation itself.

The significance of Scotus' theory of individuation is that it breaks with the fundamental Greek conception of the species as the principal locus of both being and intelligibility, codified in the Latin tradition by the Boethian dictum that 'The species is the entire being of an individual.' As schematized in the so called Porphyrian tree, differences proper in the category of substance were seen to end with the final species and individuation was explained through something extrinsic, whether by way of accidents or matter. Scotus, however, extends the process of division and differentiation in the substantial line past the species and down into the constitution of the individual itself, going so far as to place the species and individual difference in a relation of potency and act akin to that of genus and specific difference. He thus accords the individual a true reality and admits as a consequence that the individual is *per se* intelligible. In so elevating both the reality and intelligibility of the individual, Scotus' realism on the issue of universals is decidedly un-Platonic.

13 Intuitive and abstractive cognition

In the area of epistemology, Scotus' most influential contributions were the distinction between intuitive and abstractive cognition and the demolition of Augustinian illumination, at least in the highly sophisticated form given to it by HENRY OF GHENT. While the latter is of broader philosophical interest, virtually every scholastic discussion in epistemology after Scotus utilizes his distinction between abstraction and intuition, which contemporaries claimed originated with him. Scotus' notion especially of intuitive cognition was, of course, subjected to refinement and revision in subsequent discussions, but always with Scotus' original definition in mind.

As defined technically by Scotus, intuitive cognition is knowledge of an object insofar as it is actually existing and present to the intellect. Abstractive cognition is knowledge of the object insofar as it is abstracted from actual existence or non-existence. A number of clarifications are in order. First of all, as will be clear from Scotus' argument for the distinction, both intuitive and abstractive cognition are acts of the intellect proper and do not differ in that intuition grasps the sense particular and abstraction the universal. Both types of cognition have as their object the essence or quiddity as opposed to the sense particular. In intuition, the quiddity is known as being caused by what is existing and present, in abstractive cognition by the intelligible species residing in the intellect as surrogate for the existing object itself. In this context, then, 'abstractive' does not for Scotus refer to Aristotelian abstraction of the universal. Second, Scotus is specific that 'intuitive' is not here equated with 'non-discursive', the common epistemological sense associated with the Augustinian term *intuitus* (glance), particularly in the context of divine knowledge or the beatific vision (see AUGUSTINIANISM). Some abstractive knowledge can be 'intuitive' in this sense, since it can be non-discursive. Scotus says that he is here taking 'intuitive' absolutely, as when we say that we 'see (*intueri*) a thing as it really is'.

Scotus argues that the intellect must possess both types of cognition based upon its commonly admitted functions. Thus, the intellect must be capable of abstractive cognition, for otherwise scientific knowledge in the strict Aristotelian sense would be impossible. The reason is that an object is contingent insofar as it is actually existent and present to the intellect. If therefore the intellect cannot grasp an object in abstraction from its existence, all knowledge would be contingent. In other words, the intellect could know no statements about an object as true or false independent of that object's existential state. Conversely, the intellect must be capable of intuitive cognition, for a perfection found in a lower power must be found in a higher power of the same type. However, the senses, which are cognitive faculties like the intellect, seize the sensible particular as present and existing. Therefore, the intellect must also have this capacity. As Scotus explains, the particular senses have intuitive, sensible cognition of the particular, while the imagination knows the same object abstractively by means of the sensible species which can remain in the absence of the sensible thing itself. The same twofold cognitive capacity must, by parity, be found in the intellect. At the level of sense, however, two separate powers are required for these two different cognitive acts because the sense powers are distinguished by having different material organs. Owing to its greater perfection as an immaterial power, the intellect possesses both capacities in a united way. Furthermore, intuitive cognition is also required to account for the beatific vision, where the divine essence will be known, according to scripture, 'face to face'; that is, as existentially present to the intellect.

For Scotus, then, the intellect has a direct apprehension of an intelligible object insofar as it is the actually existing and present cause of its cognitive act. The chief philosophical use to which Scotus puts intuitive cognition is to supply certitude for contingent propositions. For example, he claims that by means of intuitive cognition we are as certain about our own acts as we are about necessary, self-evident propositions. After Scotus, the entire fourteenth-century preoccupation with certitude was regularly cast in terms of intuitive cognition. For instance, a common problem discussed was whether God could cause an intuitive cognition of a non-existent object (see WILLIAM OF OCKHAM §4).

14 Theory of will

While perhaps better known for his metaphysics than his ethics, Scotus' ethical theory has attracted increasing attention for being innovative and even radical. For example, he departs from fundamental thirteenth-century positions by holding that not all of the natural law (the decalogue) is absolutely binding, that prudence is not necessarily connected to moral virtue and that the will can act contrary to a fully correct moral judgment of the intellect. These and other such conclusions arise from Scotus' strong notion of will itself, which is complex and the focus of much of the attention given to his ethical theory. Three features of Scotus' conception of will have been seen as particularly important: the will as a power for opposites, the will as rational power and the dual inclination or 'affection' (*affectio*) of the will.

Scotus holds that there is a twofold freedom arising from the will as a power for opposites. The will is free in an evident way, says Scotus, since it is capable of opposite acts successively, such as loving and hating. This type of freedom, however, is not a perfection, since it pertains to the will as changeable and variable. In a second, less evident way, Scotus argues, the will is also free apart from any succession or change, for at the very moment at which it is willing an act, it remains a real, active power to will the opposite. Obviously Scotus does not mean by this that the will is capable of willing contrary acts simultaneously. Rather, he means that, if there is to be a contingent and free cause called the will, an act must be consistent with the real possibility of its opposite at the same time. (Scotus goes to considerable lengths to clarify the logical ambiguities of his position.)

Scotus argues for this 'less evident' sense of freedom and contingency by means of his famous hypothetical case of an instantaneously existent will, which in fact derived from the standard scholastic question of whether an angel could have sinned at the first instant of its creation. Consider a created will that has been brought into existence only for an instant and at that instant has a determinate act of willing. Scotus argues that, despite existing only for an instant, this will cannot produce its volition necessarily, but must do so freely and contingently. The reason is that a cause, when it actually causes, must do so either necessarily or contingently. That is, a cause is not now contingent because it existed previously and then, at that previous time, was able either to cause or not, but only because it is such at the moment when it actually operates. Thus, if a will existing at an instant causes necessarily, it would cause in that way at every instant, and thus never be a free or contingent cause. Therefore, since the will causes contingently and freely at that instant, it must have a real power for the opposite at that same instant. The will is thus a power for opposites apart from any succession, for there is no succession at an instant.

In arguing that the will is a power for opposites apart from any succession or change, Scotus departed from a long standing conception of free choice, such as represented by the standard discussion of freedom in Lombard's *Sentences*. There, LOMBARD states that choice is not free with respect to what is past or present, but only with respect to the future. The reason is that what is present is already determined, and it is not within our power to make what already is not be the case. Rather, we are only free to change what will be in the future. Scotus denies this on the above grounds that it would render the will a necessary rather than contingent and free cause, for the causal nature of the will is determined only when it operates as a cause. To be free, therefore, the will must be contingently related to its act of volition even at the moment of that act. This means that the will must have a real power for the opposite of what it wills at that very moment (see FREE WILL).

The notion of contingency resulting from this particular aspect of Scotus' doctrine of will is regarded by some as his most important philosophical contribution of all. In this connection, Scotus is regularly portrayed as breaking with Aristotelian conceptions of modality that persisted until the scholastic period. As the above account indicates, something is contingent according to Scotus if, at the moment it occurs, there is a real possibility for its opposite. This is in contrast to Aristotle's construction of contingency, where something is contingent if its opposite can actually occur at some other time. In this, Scotus is seen as ushering in a modern conception of possibility previously thought to have begun with LEIBNIZ. While Scotus' originality on this score has been overstated – the basic doctrine of will behind this new notion of contingency is found in Peter OLIVI – there can be little doubt that the extended analysis given to it by Scotus ensured its influence.

In a position related to the above conception of the will, Scotus maintained that the will was a rational power. Commenting on the text of Aristotle in which rational powers are defined as those capable of producing contrary effects, Scotus made the primary division of all active powers the natural versus the voluntary. A natural agent is one that is of itself determined to act. That is, a natural power will issue in a determinate act necessarily and to its greatest capacity unless impeded. A voluntary or free power is not determined of itself to act, so that it may issue in a contrary act or no act at all. By this Scotus really means that the will is self-determining. Its indeterminacy to act is not a defect owing to an insufficiency of power but a perfection that results from an abundance of power capable of contrary effects. Given this primary division of nature and will, Scotus places the intellect on the side of natural powers so that, in Aristotle's definition, it is not strictly speaking rational. The will consequently became the only truly rational power, where 'rational' was contrasted with 'naturally determined'. In a complete reversal of the intellectualist and Aristotelian model accepted by AQUINAS, Scotus concluded that the intellect was rational only in the qualified sense that it is required as a precondition for the action of the will.

The will, however, is not only an active power, but an appetite with inclinations. Here too, Scotus sought to protect the will from natural determinism by adopting Anselm's distinction between an affection or inclination for the advantageous (*affectio commodi*) and an affection for justice (*affectio iustitiae*) (see ANSELM OF CANTERBURY §6). As interpreted by Scotus, the former is the inclination to self-fulfilment characteristic of natural desire. What is sought is the perfection of the agent. The latter is an inclination not for the good of the agent but for the good in itself. Scotus claims that the will has an 'innate' affection for the just and that this is the basis of its liberty. The affection for the just enables the will to transcend the determination of natural appetite to self-fulfilment by loving the supreme good, God, for its own sake or other lesser goods for their own worth (see RIGHT AND GOOD §2).

See also: ARISTOTELIANISM, MEDIEVAL; AUGUSTINIANISM; BEING; FRANCIS OF MEYRONNES; GOD, ARGUMENTS FOR THE EXISTENCE OF; GOD, CONCEPTS OF; HENRY OF GHENT; WILLIAM OF OCKHAM

List of works

Duns Scotus, John (*c.*1290–1308) *Opera omnia. Editio nova iuxta editionem Waddingi XII tomos continentem*, Paris: Vivès, 1891–5, 26 vols; selections ed. and trans. A.B. Wolter, *Duns Scotus on the Will and Morality*, Washington, DC: Catholic University, 1987; ed. and trans. A.B. Wolter and W.A. Frank, *Duns Scotus, Metaphysician*, Lafayette, IL: Purdue University Press, 1995. (The Vivès edition is a typographically enlarged reprint of the Wadding edition (Lyons, 1639). Contains many spurious works. For the certainly authentic works, see C. Balić (1966) *John Duns Scotus. Some Reflections on the Occasion of the Seventh Centenary of his Birth*, Rome: Scotistic Commission, 29–44. Since the critical Vatican edition is far from complete, this is still the only text for many of Scotus' writings. Even for those texts which have been critically edited, the edition remains valuable for the scholia, parallel citations and commentaries by later Scotists. Wolter (1987) contains extensive selections with facing Latin and substantial introductions; Wolter and Frank provide a re-translation of selected texts with commentary.)

—— (*c.*1290–1308) *Opera omnia studio et cura Commissionis Scotisticae ad fidem codicum edita*, Vatican City: Typis Polyglottis Vaticanis, 1950–, 11 vols to date. (Planned critical or Vatican edition of Scotus' writings. Published to date are vols 1–7 (*Ordinatio* to bk 2, dist. 3), vols 16–19 (*Lectura*).)

—— (before 1300) *Lectura*, in *Opera omnia studio et cura Commissionis Scotisticae ad fidem codicum edita*, Vatican City: Typis Polyglottis Vaticanis,

1950–, vols 16–19. (The questions on divine foreknowledge are translated by A. Vos, *Contingency and Freedom: John Duns Scotus, Lectura I 39*, Dordrecht: Kluwer, 1994.)

—— (after 1300) *Ordinatio*, in *Opera omnia studio et cura Commissionis Scotisticae ad fidem codicum edita*, Vatican City: Typis Polyglottis Vaticanis, 1950–, vols 1–7. (The prologue is translated by A. Wolter in 'Duns Scotus on the Necessity of Revealed Knowledge', *Franciscan Studies* 11: 231–71, 1951. The question on whether God's existence is self-evident is translated in E. Fairweather, *A Scholastic Miscellany: Anselm to Ockham*, Philadelphia, PA: Westminster Press, 1956, 428–39. The questions on the principle of individuation are translated by P.V. Spade in *Five Texts on the Medieval Problem of Universals*, Indianapolis, IN: Hackett Publishing Company, 1994, 57–113. *Duns Scotus, Philosophical Writings*, trans. A. B. Wolter, Indianapolis, IN, and Cambridge: Hackett Publishing Company, 1987, is a translation of selections from the *Ordinatio* with facing Latin text of the Vivès edition.)

—— (*c.*1302–5) *Reportatio parisiensis*, part trans. A. Wolter and M. Adams, 'Duns Scotus' Parisian Proof for the Existence of God', *Franciscan Studies* 42: 248–321, 1982. (Translation and edition of the Parisian verison of the proof for the existence of God.)

—— (*c.*1306) *Quodlibetal Questions*, ed. F. Alluntis, *Obras del Doctor Sutil, Juan Duns Escoto: Cuestiones Cuodlibetales*, Madrid: Biblioteca De Autores Cristianos, 1968; trans. F. Alluntis and A.B. Wolter, *God and Creatures: The Quodlibet Questions*, Princeton, NJ: Princeton University Press, 1975; repr. Washington, DC: Catholic University of America Press, 1987. (Alluntis' edition is a revision of Vivès text of the *Quodlibetal Questions*. Alluntis and Wolter's translation includes a helpful glossary of Scotistic vocabulary.)

Duns Scotus (*c.*1308) *De primo principio* (On First Principle), ed. and trans. A.B. Wolter, *John Duns Scotus: A Treatise on God as First Principle*, Chicago, IL: Franciscan Herald Press, 1966; 2nd revised edn, 1983. (An edition and translation of De primo principio. The revised edition adds an extensive commentary.)

References and further reading

In addition to the works noted below, the proceedings of the International Scotistic Congress (*Congressus Scotisticus Internationalis*) contain many articles on all aspects of Scotus' thought. See *De doctrina Ioannis Duns Scoti*, Rome: Cura Commissionis Scotisticae,

1968, 4 vols; *Deus et homo ad mentem I. Duns Scoti*, Rome: Societas Internationalis Scotisticae, 1972; *Regnum hominis et regnum Dei*, ed. C. Bérubé, Rome: Societas Internationalis Scotistica, 1978, 2 vols; *Homo et Mundus*, ed. C. Bérubé, Rome: Societas Internationalis Scotistica, 1981.

Adams, M.M. (1982) 'Universals in the Fourteenth Century', in N. Kretzmann, A. Kenny and J. Pinborg (eds) *The Cambridge History of Later Medieval Philosophy*, Cambridge: Cambridge University Press, 411–39. (Includes comparison of Scotus and Ockham on universals.)

Boler, J. (1993) 'Transcending the Natural: Duns Scotus on the Two Affections of the Will', *American Catholic Philosophical Quarterly* 67: 109–22. (Discussion of *affectio commodi* and *affectio iustitiae*.)

Brown, J. (1976) 'Duns Scotus on Henry of Ghent's Arguments for Divine Illumination: The Statement of the Case', *Vivarium* 14 (1): 94–113. (Detailed examination of Scotus' rejection of illumination.)

Brown, S. (1965) 'Avicenna and the Unity of the Concept of Being: The Interpretations of Henry of Ghent, Duns Scotus, Gerard of Bologna and Peter Aureoli', *Franciscan Studies* 25: 117–50. (History of the problem of univocity.)

Cress, D. (1975) 'Toward a Bibliography on Duns Scotus on the Existence of God', *Franciscan Studies* 35: 45–65. (Scholarship on this topic in Scotus is nearly the size of that for Descartes.)

Dumont, S.D. (1984) 'The *quaestio si est* and the Metaphysical Proof for the Existence of God according to Henry of Ghent and Duns Scotus', *Franziskanische Studien* 66: 335–67. (General metaphysical background in Henry of Ghent assumed by Scotus' proof.)

—— (1987–9) 'The Univocity of Being in the Fourteenth Century', *Mediaeval Studies* 49: 1–75; 50: 186–256; (with S. Brown) 51: 1–129. (Technical and detailed history of univocity among Scotus' followers. Contains previously unedited texts.)

—— (1988) 'The Necessary Connection of Prudence to the Moral Virtues according to John Duns Scotus – Revisited', *Recherches de théologie ancienne et médiévale* 55: 184–206. (Refutes Lottin's interpretation that Scotus subscribes to the Aristotelian theory of the connection of the virtues.)

—— (1989) 'The Scientific Character of Theology and the Origin of Duns Scotus' Distinction between Intuitive and Abstractive Cognition', *Speculum* 64 (3): 579–99. (Argues primary application of the distinction is theological.)

—— (1992) 'Transcendental Being: Scotus and Scotists', *Topoi* 11: 135–48. (Interpretation given to univocity by Scotus' followers.)

—— (1995a) 'The Origin of Scotus' Theory of Synchronic Contingency', *The Modern Schoolman* 72 (January–March) 149–68. (Peter Olivi's influence on Scotus' doctrine of will.)

—— (1995b) 'The Question on Individuation in Scotus' *Quaestiones in Metaphysicam*', in L. Sileo (ed.) *Vita Scoti. Methodologica ad mentem Joannis Duns Scoti*, Rome: Edizioni Antonianum, vol. 1.193–227. (Against the traditional view that the version of the theory in the *Metaphysics* is earlier than that of the *Sentences*.)

Frank, W.A. (1992) 'Duns Scotus on Autonomous Freedom and Divine Co-Causality', *Medieval Philosophy and Theology* 2: 142–64. (Interesting analysis of an acute difficulty for Scotus' notion of free will.)

Gilson, É. (1952) *Jean Duns Scot. Introduction à ses positions fondamentales* (John Duns Scotus: Introduction to His Fundamental Positions), Paris: Vrin. (The most recent comprehensive book on Scotus' philosophy, but of limited value owing to its failure to take account of Henry of Ghent.)

Honnefelder, L. (1979) *Ens inquantum ens. Der Begriff des Seienden als solchen als Gegenstand der Metaphysik nach der Lehre des Johannes Duns Scotus* (Being *qua* Being: The Concept of Being as such as the Object of Metaphysics in the Thought of John Duns Scotus), Beiträge zur Geschichte der Philosophie und Theologie des Mittelalters, Neue Folge 16, Münster: Aschendorff. (Extensive work on Scotus' conception of the science of metaphysics.)

Ingham, M.E. (1989) *Ethics And Freedom: An Historical–Critical Investigation Of Scotist Ethical Thought*, Washington, DC: University Press of America. (Argues that Scotus' ethics emphasizes efficient rather than final cause.)

Kent, B. (1996) *Virtues of Will: The Transformation of Ethics in the Late Thirteenth Century*, Washington, DC: Catholic University of America Press. (Excellent study referring to Scotus throughout. Argues that Scotus is more moderate and indebted over his doctrine of will than commonly portrayed.)

King, P. (1992) 'Duns Scotus on the Common Nature and the Individual Difference', *Philosophical Topics* 20 (2): 51–76. (Detailed philosophical analysis of theory of individuation.)

Marenbon, J. (1987) *Later Medieval Philosophy (1150–1350)*, London: Routledge, 154–68. (Contains chapter on Scotus' epistemology addressing issue of 'intellective memory'.)

Marrone, S. (1983) 'The Notion of Univocity in Duns Scotus' Early Works', *Franciscan Studies* 43: 347–95. (Traces evolution of the doctrine in Scotus, who appears to have initially denied univocity.)

—— (1988) 'Henry of Ghent and Duns Scotus on the Knowledge of Being', *Speculum* 63 (1): 22–57. (Argues than Henry and Scotus are closer than usually admitted.)

Owens, J. (1948) 'Up to What Point is God Included in the Metaphysics of Duns Scotus?', *Mediaeval Studies* 10: 163–77. (Analysis of Scotus' difficult opening question in his *Metaphysics* on the subject of metaphysics.)

—— (1957) 'Common Nature: A Point of Comparison between Thomistic and Scotistic Metaphysics', *Mediaeval Studies* 19: 1–14. (Influential article on the treatment of Avicennian common nature by Aquinas and Scotus.)

The Monist (1965) *Philosophy of John Duns Scotus in Commemoration of the 700th Anniversary of His Birth*, The Monist 49. (Collection of articles.)

Prentice, R. (1968) 'The Voluntarism of Duns Scotus as seen in his Comparison of the Intellect and the Will', *Franciscan Studies* 28: 63-103. (Detailed examination of Scotus' analysis of Henry of Ghent's position that the will is higher than the intellect and Aquinas' position to the opposite.)

Ryan, J.K. and Bonansea, B. (eds) (1965) 'John Duns Scotus, 1265–1965', in J.K. Ryan and B. Bonansea (eds) *Studies in Philosophy and the History of Philosophy* 3, Washington, DC: Catholic University of America. (Very useful and now standard collection of articles.)

Schaefer, O. (1955) *Bibliographia de vita operibus et doctrina Ioannis Duns Scoti, Saec. XIX-XX* (Bibliography of the Life, Works and Doctrine of John Duns Scotus), Rome: Orbis Catholicus-Herder. (Standard bibliography that includes anything remotely to do with Scotus.)

—— (1967) 'Resenha abreviada da bibliographia escotista mais recente (1954–1966)' (A Short List of More Recent Scotistic Bibliography), *Revistas Portuguesa de Filosofia* 23: 338–63. (Addendum to above.)

Sileo, L. (ed.) (1995) *Via Scoti. Methodologica ad mentem Joannis Duns Scoti* (The Way of Scotus: Methodology in the Thought of John Duns Scotus), Rome: Edizioni Antonianum, 2 vols. (Massive collection of articles on Scotus in all languages.)

Wolter, A.B. (1946) *The Transcendentals and Their Function in the Philosophy of Duns Scotus*, St. Bonaventure, NY: The Franciscan Institute. (A study still regarded as the best introduction to Scotus' metaphysics.)

—— (1990) *The Philosophical Theology of John Duns Scotus*, ed. M. Adams, Ithaca, NY: Cornell University Press. (Collection of many of Wolter's excellent and clear articles on Scotus covering main topics in his epistemology, metaphysics and theory of will.)

—— (ed.) (1993) *Duns Scotus*, special issue of *American Catholic Philosophical Quarterly* 67. (Dedicated issue of the journal. Contain excellent and up-to-date introduction to Scotus' life and works by Wolter.)

Wood, R., Honnefelder, L. and Dreyer, M. (eds) (1996) *John Duns Scotus: Metaphysics and Ethics*, Leiden: Brill. (Collection of articles.)

STEPHEN D. DUMONT

DUPLEIX, S. *see* ARISTOTELIANISM IN THE 17TH CENTURY

DURAN, PROFIAT (d. *c*.1414)

Duran, known also as Efodi, produced a wide variety of works displaying a considerable understanding of Christian culture, which he then used to criticize Christianity from a Jewish perspective. Heavily influenced by both Maimonides and Abraham ibn Ezra, he stressed the dual nature of the Torah as a system of belief and practice. His work includes Neoplatonic and astrological ideas, and sought to emphasize the salvific force of the Torah.

Profiat Duran's given name was Isaac ben Moses Levi, but he is perhaps best known as Efodi. He was a Spanish-Jewish theologian and polemicist of the later fourteenth and early fifteenth centuries. An active anti-Christian polemicist, he was also the author of two philosophical works, the 'Introduction' to his grammatical work, *Ma'aseh Efod* (The Making of the Ephod) and a popular commentary to Maimonides's *Guide to the Perplexed*. In the former, Duran maintains that the Torah teaches true science (logic, physics, metaphysics) and is the best way to learn it. Such knowledge is important, but true felicity in this world and in the next depends upon proper fulfillment of the Torah's commandments (*mitzvot*). Duran deals with the different ways in which thinkers have analysed how the Torah is to be observed. Some had argued that all that is important is carrying out the *mitzvot*. It is not necessary to know why these commandments ought to be followed beyond recognizing that they are commandments, on the model of medical treatment where someone may not understand the workings of the treatment, yet undertake it and as a result be cured of the ailment. Duran disagrees with this view, arguing that the Torah has two parts, knowledge and practice. These parts are

intimately connected, since it is necessary to have knowledge to understand how to carry out the commandments. Duran criticizes the view that religion and philosophy are in opposition to each other. Carrying out one's religious obligations, he argues, serves to attract the emanation of heaven, along the Neoplatonic pattern. Worship achieves the heights of perfection only in the Land of Israel, since it lies closer to the powerful forces of grace than anywhere else in the world. Nonetheless, the commandments must be obeyed wherever one is, and their fulfillment brings about happiness in this life.

Duran considers the claims of the Kabbalists and concludes that they are closer to the spirit of the Torah than are the philosophers, even more so if they are right in their claims to be able to affect the course of nature through their practices. Yet they also disagree among themselves a great deal, which is hardly an indication of a secure repository of truth. So, although philosophy and Kabbalah both have merits, the proper object of study is really the Torah, which is the only sure route to eternal happiness. In the Torah one is working with a holy language, and in studying it one participates in the holiness of the names which are to be found there. When the Temple existed, it was the conduit through which the divine emanation flowed to the people of Israel, and when it was destroyed (because the Jews had stopped studying Scripture) it was replaced by the Torah. The Torah is the only path to the highest happiness, and the only route to God is through carrying out its commandments. Theoretical knowledge in itself is incapable of attaining this eternal and complete happiness, and only the Jews are really able to carry out the proper role of human beings in serving God through carrying out his commandments. The Torah represents the source of divine providence for the Jews and guarantees their survival, despite the many dangers and disasters which they undergo. Duran was no doubt reflecting from his own experience here, for he had been forced to convert to Christianity and was able to practice openly as a Jew only later in his life. Although he defended stoutly the study of the Torah, he also accepted the importance of the natural sciences so long as they do not contradict the foundations of the faith.

Duran's *Commentary on the Guide to the Perplexed* is printed in the standard editions of that work. It is brief, literal and very conservative, trying to present MAIMONIDES as a thinker well within the mainstream of received Judaism. In places where Maimonides seems to interpret Judaism in too thoroughly Aristotelian a manner, Duran sands down the rough edges, pulling Maimonides back in the direction of traditionalist orthodoxy. On the other hand, he frankly acknowledges the dangers of some of Maimonides's arguments as far as religion is concerned. His conservatism is in many ways typical of the Jewish philosophers of the late fourteenth and early fifteenth centuries. He did, after all, have to respond both to the continual spiritual crises in the Spanish Jewish community as a result of the conversionary pressures of the Christians, and to the impact of the Jewish Averroist movement (see AVERROISM, JEWISH). On the other hand, his arguments for the role of the Torah in reconciling the physical and spiritual aspects of humanity was to play a large role in Jewish philosophy in the fifteenth century on its approach to modernity.

See also: IBN EZRA, A.; MAIMONIDES, M.

List of works

Duran, P. (before *c.*1414) *Commentary on the Guide to the Perplexed*, Venice, 1551. (Duran's treatment of the *Guide*.)
—— (before *c.*1414) 'Introduction' to *Ma'aseh Efod*, ed. D. Raffel in *Sinai* 100, 1987: 749–95. (Duran's defence of the Torah.)

References and further reading

Lasker, D. (1977) *Jewish Philosophical Polemics Against Christianity in the Middle Ages*, New York: Ktav. (An excellent account of Duran's anti-Christian writings.)
Sirat, C. (1985) *A History of Jewish Philosophy in the Middle Ages*, Cambridge: Cambridge University Press, 352–7. (General discussion of Duran's life and works, linking him closely with Abraham ibn Ezra and Moses Maimonides.)

MENACHEM KELLNER
OLIVER LEAMAN

DURAN, SIMEON BEN TZEMACH (1361–1444)

Simeon Duran was chiefly a religious thinker who incorporated a variety of philosophical traditions into his thought. He argues that revelation is the only certain route to knowledge. Following this principle, he criticizes those who argued that some of the principles of religion are more important or basic than others. To reject any aspect of religious law is to abandon the whole, and on this point Duran sets himself against Maimonides.

1 Life and works
2 Dogma and the nature of Judaism

1 Life and works

Simeon ben Zemah Duran, Spanish *halakhist* and theologian, fled the anti-Jewish outbreaks of 1391 and spent the rest of his life in North Africa. Duran is best known as the author of numerous responsa (written answers to *halakhic* inquiries), from which much can be learned concerning the history of the Jews of Spain and North Africa in general and in particular of conversos (Jews forcibly converted to Christianity). He is also the author of a number of theological and polemical works that reflect a moderate Maimonideanism: Duran accepts the basic naturalism of Maimonides's Aristotelian view of the world while moderating its intellectualism. Duran's polemic against Christianity and Islam (*Keshet u-Magen*) is not philosophical in character. His most important contribution to Jewish thought is in the area of dogmatics, found primarily in two commentaries, *Ohev Mishpat* (Lover of Justice) – a work on Job and *Magen Avot* (Shield of the Fathers) – a work on Tractate Avot. The introduction to the former includes an extensive discussion of divine providence.

2 Dogma and the nature of Judaism

The issue of dogma had been introduced into medieval Judaism by Moses MAIMONIDES (1138–1204), who formulated thirteen articles of belief in his commentary on the Mishnaic tractate Sanhedrin. Maimonides's enormously influential account of these doctrines of Judaism was presented, in effect, as an answer to the question: who is a Jew? In his discussions, Duran approaches the issue from a number of perspectives, not one of them that of Maimonides. In one place, Duran asks a structural question: construing Judaism as a deductive science, what are its axioms? His answer is: creation and providence. Providence, however, can be derived from creation, so in fact creation is the only basic principle of Judaism. In a second place, Duran seeks to explicate and defend Maimonides's account of the Jewish creed, reducing his thirteen dogmas to three: God's existence, Torah from heaven (that is, divine revelation as manifested in the giving of the Torah), and divine retribution. This account seems to have decisively influenced Joseph ALBO (fifteenth century) in his *Sefer ha-'Iqqarim* (Book of Principles). This second account, however, is not merely a summary of Maimonides, since it depends upon and even derives from Duran's third discussion, which diverges crucially from Maimonides. In this discussion Duran makes the claim that Judaism has only one principle – to believe what the Torah teaches – or, alternatively, that Judaism has as many principles as there are commandments in the Torah. It is in the context of this discussion that Duran defines heresy, not as false belief, but as the conscious rejection of a belief known to be taught by the Torah or the conscious adoption of a belief known to be denied by the Torah. The relative liberalism represented by Duran's departure from the idea of a fixed set of dogmas constitutive of Jewish faith is extremely rare in medieval religion.

Duran's three accounts answer three different questions:

(1) Construing Judaism as a deductive science, what are its axioms?
(2) Why did Maimonides posit the beliefs he did in his 'Thirteen Principles'?
(3) What is heresy?

Many of Duran's ideas were new and unprecedented but his influence was modest at best, both because his views were not adequately understood in his own day and because he wrote near the end of the period of active medieval Jewish philosphical discussion.

See also: MAIMONIDES, M.

List of works

Duran, S. ben Tzemach (1361–1444) *Ohev Mishpat* (Lover of Justice), Venice, 1590. (A commentary on the Book of Job.)
—— (1361–1444) *Keshet u-Magen* (Bow and Shield), Livorno, 1762. (A defence of Judaism against the attacks of Christianity and Islam.)
—— (1361–1444) *Magen Avot* (Shield of the Fathers), Livorno, 1785. (A commentary on the mishnaic tractate *Avot*.)

References and further reading

* Albo, J. (*c.*1425) *Sefer ha-'Iqqarim* (Book of Principles), ed. and trans. I. Husik, *Sefer ha-'Iqqarim: Book of Roots*, Philadelphia, PA: Jewish Publications Society, 1946, 5 vols. (Presentation of the dogmas of Judaism according to Albo.)
Bleich J. (1929) 'Duran's view of the Nature of Providence', *Jewish Quarterly Review* 69: 208–25. (Summary of Duran's theory of providence.)
Kellner, M. (1986) *Dogma in Medieval Jewish Thought*, Oxford: Oxford University Press, ch. 3. (Contains translations of Duran's writings on dogma and analyses of them; the notes contain full references to studies on Duran.)
Sirat, C. (1985) *A History of Jewish Philosophy in the Middle Ages*, Cambridge: Cambridge University Press. (Chronological history of Jewish philosophy in the Middle Ages.)

MENACHEM KELLNER

DURANDUS OF ST POURÇAIN (1275?–1334)

Although strongly Aristotelian in outlook, Durandus rejected certain classic points of Thomist doctrine such as the speculative 'scientific' and unique nature of theology, the theory of the active intellect and the doctrine of species. After carrying out a detailed examination of the Thomist theses, Durandus decided firmly in favour of theology being faith in revelation, something aenigmatica *and therefore meritorious. In this way, in the opinion of some modern scholars, he anticipated the position of William of Ockham; the position later known as 'Ockham's razor' appears more than once in his writings.*

The date of Durandus' birth is uncertain, but is believed to be about 1275. Early references speak of his presence in the convent of St Jacques in Paris, where he obtained a *licentia docendi* in 1312, and of the fact that as early as 1306 he had been criticized by a brother Dominican, HERVAEUS NATALIS, for an assertion contained in his *Commentariorum* (commentary on the *Sentences* of Peter LOMBARD), a work that was probably unfinished at the time but was no doubt already in circulation among the 'curious', as Durandus himself complained. In 1313, Pope Clement V made Durandus lector of the Holy Palace, and four years later, Pope John XXII made him bishop of Limoux, thus freeing him from his vow of obedience to the Dominican Order. In 1318 he became bishop of Le Puy and, in 1326, bishop of Meaux. He died in Meaux in 1334.

Following further criticism of his *Commentariorum* in 1314 and 1316, the Dominican Order carried out two formal inquiries, which concluded that certain theses contained in the work were dangerous and likely to impair that unity of doctrine which legitimized the intellectual independence of the Dominicans. At this time the teaching of the doctrines of AQUINAS was becoming increasingly dominant; Thomist doctrine was defended repeatedly as being 'the soundest', while anyone who 'acted in a contrary manner and in spite of warnings failed to withdraw from his position' was severely censured. The disagreement between Durandus and his order continued, and the second edition of his commentary on the *Sentences* appeared in a reduced and expurgated form in 1310–11. In a later third edition (1317?–27), the censured points were to some extent restored.

In addition to three editions of his commentary on the *Sentences*, Durandus' works include the *Quodlibeta*, the *Quaestiones de habitibus* (Questions About States), *De libero arbitrio* (On Free Will) and *De natura cognitionis* (On the Nature of Cognition), written in Paris, three further *Quodlibeta* written in Avignon, and the *De origine jurisdictionum* (The Origins of Jurisdictions), written while he was bishop of Meaux. In 1333, after being consulted by the pope and asked to express his opinion on the theory of the beatific vision, Durandus wrote *De visione Dei* (The Vision of God), but this failed to win the approval of John XXII, who submitted it to a committee of censors.

The originality of Durandus as a theologian lies in the fact that he remained fundamentally faithful to Aristotelian–Thomist subjects and terminology, while diverging from that tradition in his conclusions. At the same time, he appears to have stood outside the anti-Thomist Augustinian tradition of the Franciscans (see AUGUSTINIANISM). The chief problem for the historian is how to interpret the accusations of 'aversion to Thomism' which his contemporaries launched against him and which were later repeated in sixteenth century editions of the *Commentariorum* (Lyon 1558, Venice 1589). There is a theoretical consistency in Durandus' opposition to Aquinas, which emerges particularly over the question of the scientific nature of theology discussed in the commentary, showing that Durandus possessed his own clear-cut epistemology. Articles of faith, which Aquinas likened to the principles of knowledge, in Durandus' view are not 'rational', nor can they be referred to other self-evident principles, but 'only believed'. Faith is unconnected both with knowledge based on reasoning and with that obtained by way of experience. The subject of theology is supernatural and therefore not to be examined by man with his natural cognitive faculty; and it follows that the theological process itself cannot be rational. 'It is unreal to postulate a supernatural light that does not exist in all men and cannot be given to those who do not possess it' (*Commentariorum* 1, f.5 v.17).

Such statements are linked with fundamental points of Durandus' metaphysics and epistemology. The intellectual act itself is able to apprehend reality without the mediation of images (the 'species' of the Thomists), and *in se* can perceive individuals. Universals do not exist since everything that exists is individual. The formal distinction drawn by DUNS SCOTUS between real beings and conceptual beings is 'frivolous' and leads to the conclusion that man's knowledge of God is purely nominal. Truth may be defined as the formal condition of the object of knowledge, the relation between being and being perceived. It may be added that more than once in the course of discussion Durandus appealed to what was later to be known as Ockham's razor by asserting that *frustra ponuntur plura ubi pauciora sufficiunt* (it is futile to do with more what can be done with fewer) (see WILLIAM OF OCKHAM).

Durandus' principal thesis is that the theology of a human being who is a *viator* (one who has not yet attained the beatific vision) is based on belief in Scripture, which speaks in the language of metaphor capable of imparting not knowledge but moral teaching. Theology, Durandus remarks, is like rules of navigation which must be observed by sailors if they are to voyage in safety even 'if the stars are not of interest to them in themselves'. If the theologian exceeds these limits and launches into demonstrations that are no more than apparent, 'he assumes the capacity of the philosopher and loses his definition of theologian'. For Durandus, theology was an enigmatic body of knowledge and therefore meritorious for men, since 'it is not true that theologians or simple believers know the will of God and from this draw further knowledge' (*Commentariorum* f.11 r.10).

See also: ARISTOTELIANISM, MEDIEVAL

List of works

Durandus of St Pourçain [Durandus de Sancto Porciano] (before 1313) *Quaestiones de habitibus* (Questions About States), ed J. Koch, *Durandi de Sancto Porciano, O.P. Tractatus de habitibus, quaestio quarta [De subiectis habituum]*, Opuscula et textus historiam ecclesiae eiusque vitam atque doctrinam illustrantia. Series scholastica 8, Monasterii: Typis Aschendorff, 1930. (Edition of Durandus' *Quaestiones*.)

—— (1313?–17) *Quodlibeta* (Quodlibetal Questions), ed. P.T. Stella, *Qudolibeta avenionensia tria, additis correctionibus Hervei Natalis supra dicta Durandi in primo quolibet*, Textus et studia in historium scholasticae, cura Pontificii Athenaei Salesiani I, Zurich: Pas-Verlag, 1965; *Quodlibeta Paris I (Q.I–Q.IV)*, ed. T. Takada, Series of Hitherto Unedited Texts of Medieval Thinkers IV, Kyoto, 1968. (Editions of Durandus' quodlibetal questions.)

—— (1317?–27) *Sententias theologicas Commentarium* (Commentary on the Sentences); Latin edition published as *D. Durandi a Sancto Porciano In Petri Lombardi Sententias theologicas Commentarium libri 4*, Venice, ex typographia Guerraea, 1571; facsimile reprint, Ridgewood, NJ: Gregg, 1964. (This is an edition of the later third edition of the *Commentarium*.)

—— (1333) *De visione Dei* (The Vision of God), ed. G. Cremascoli, 'Il "Libellus de visione dei" di Durando di S. Porziano', *Studi medievali* Ser. III 25, 1984, 393–443. (Durandus on beatific vision.)

References and further reading

Fournier, P. (1938) 'Durand de S. Pourçain', Histoire littéraire de la France, vol. XXXIV, Paris: Imprimerie Nationale. (Study of his life and works.)

Fumagalli Beonio-Brocchieri, M. (1969) *Durando di S. Porziano. Elementi filosofici della terza redazione del 'Commento alle Sentenze'* (Durandus of St Pourçain: Philosophical Elements in the Third Redaction of the Commentary on the *Sentences*), Florence: La Nuova Italia. (An account of the principal philosophical and theological conceptions in the *Commentary*.)

Godet, P. (1924) 'Durand de S. Pourçain', *Dictionnaire de théologie catholique*, vol. IV, Paris: Letouzey et Ane, 1964–6. (Short biography.)

Hervaeus Natalis (c.1308) *De relatione contra Durandum et Durandi de S. Porciano, O.P., Quol. Paris. I. Q. 2 (3)*, ed. T. Takada, Kyoto, 1966. (Hervaeus' criticism of Durandus' commentary on the Sentences.)

Hinnebusch, W.A., and Bedouelle, G. (1990) *Brève histoire de l'ordre dominicain* (Short History of the Dominican Order), Paris: Éditions du Cerf. (History of the Dominican Order including passages on Durandus.)

Koch, J. (1927) *Durandus de S. Porciano, O.P.: Forschungen zum Streit um Thomas von Aquin zu Beginn des 14. Jahrhunderts* (Introduction to the Opposition to Thomas Aquinas at the Beginning of the Fourteenth Century), vol. 1: *Literargeschichtliche Grundlegung*, Beiträge zur Geschichte der Philosophie des Mittelalters: Texte und Undersuchungen 26, Münster: Aschendorff. (A fundamental study of Durandus' life, works and thought.)

Mandonnet, P. (1947) 'Frères prêcheurs', *Dictionnaire de théologie catholique*, Paris: Letouzey et Ane, vol. 6, 863–924. (Short history of the Dominican Order.)

Martin, R.M. (1930) *La controverse sur le péché originel au début du XIVe siècle. Textes inédits* (The Dispute About Original Sin at the Beginning of the Fourteenth Century), Louvain: 'Spicilegium sacrum lovaniense'. (Includes the views of Durandus.)

Müller, E. (1941) 'Quaestionen der ersten Redaktion von I und II Sententiarum des D. de S.P.' (Questions about the First Version of Books I and II of the Sentences by Durandus of St Pourçain), *Divus Thomas*, Freiburg: Albertinum, 435–40. (Study of Durandus' commentary on the *Sentences*.)

Synan, E.A. (1990) Sensibility and Science in Mediaeval Theology: the Witness of Durandus of Saint-Pourçain and Denis the Carthusian, in R. Työrinoja, A.I. Lehtinen and D. Føllesdal (eds) *Knowledge and the Sciences in Mediaeval Philosophy: Proceedings of the Eighth International Congress of Mediaeval Philosophy (SIEPM) Helsinki 24–9 August 1987*, Helsinki: Finnish Society for Missiology, vol. III. (Durandus' views on knowledge.)

Tabarroni, A. (1990) *'Paupertas Christi et apostolorum'. L'ideale francescano in discussione (1322–1324)* (The Poverty of Christ and the Apostles: The Dispute about the Franciscan Ideal 1322–4), Rome: Istituto Storico Italiano per il Medio Evo. (The early fourteenth-century dispute on apostolic poverty.)

MARIATERESA FUMAGALLI BEONIO-
BROCCHIERI

DURKHEIM, ÉMILE (1858–1917)

Émile Durkheim is generally recognized to be one of the founders of sociology as a distinct scientific discipline. Trained as a philosopher, Durkheim identified the central theme of sociology as the emergence and persistence of morality and social solidarity (along with their pathologies) in modern and traditional human societies. His distinctive approach to sociology was to adopt the positivistic method in identifying and explaining social facts – the facts of the moral life. Sociology was to be, in Durkheim's own words, a science of ethics.

Durkheim's sociology combined a positivistic methodology of research with an idealistic theory of social solidarity. On the one hand, Durkheim forcefully claimed that the empirical observation and analysis of regularities in the social world must be the starting point of the sociological enterprise; on the other hand, he was equally emphatic in claiming that sociological investigation must deal with the ultimate ends of human action – the moral values and goals that guide human conduct and create the essential conditions for social solidarity. Accordingly, in his scholarly writings on the division of labour, on suicide, on education, and on religion, Durkheim sought to identify through empirical evidence the major sources of social solidarity and of the social pathologies that undermine it.

1 Intellectual biography

Émile Durkheim was born in Epinal (France) in 1858 to a three-generation family of Jewish rabbis. From an early age he was being trained to become a rabbi, but in his youth he first had a passing religious crisis, and later broke away from Judaism and became agnostic. Durkheim was trained in philosophy at the École Normale Supérieure in Paris, influenced by such thinkers as Charles Renouvier and Émile Boutroux, and obtained his *agregation de philosophie* in 1882. He taught philosophy at various Parisian *lycées* early in his career. In 1887 he first taught and later became professor of social sciences at the University of Bordeaux, a position he held until 1902 when he became first professor of education and later professor of education and sociology at the prestigious Sorbonne in Paris until the year of his death.

During his tenure at the University of Bordeaux, Durkheim published in quick succession three major works that qualified him as one of sociology's founders: *The Division of Labor in Society* (1893), *The Rules of Sociological Method* (1895), and *Suicide: A Study in Sociology* (1897). During that same period Durkheim established the *Année sociologique*, France's first sociology journal, and directed a social science research group that gravitated around the journal. Durkheim's years at the Sorbonne were characterized by a focus on the broad philosophical and ethical themes he recognized to be at the centre of the sociological enterprise. He lectured extensively on his philosophy of human nature, on value judgments in the social sciences, on epistemology, on the history of pedagogy, on moral education, and on religion. His last major monograph, *The Elementary Forms of the Religious Life* was published in 1912. Greatly saddened by the loss of his own son and close friends during the First World War, Émile Durkheim died in 1917, aged 59.

2 The sociological method

In his attempt to establish sociology as an academic discipline, Durkheim sought to identify early in his work the distinctiveness of the sociological approach and its unique methodology of sociological research. First, Durkheim established that society was not simply equivalent to the sum of its individual members; using a chemical metaphor, he viewed it as an organic compound endowed with qualities that surpassed the qualities of its constituting elements. While advocating that sociology should follow the path of the natural sciences and life sciences in developing a scientific standing, Durkheim realized that social facts – the phenomena of the moral life – were very different from the phenomena observed in the natural world. Social facts were representations of the collective life of society: laws, religious beliefs, norms, myths, customs. But the sociologist should treat them with the same empirical scrutiny natural scientists afforded to the phenomena of nature. According to Durkheim, we must treat social facts as things, and to identify social facts we must rely on the two characteristics they display: they are external to individuals and they constrain them. Social facts are obligatory, and their transgressions are punished with appropriate social sanctions.

Social facts are independent of individuals, and as such they are not affected by individuals' behaviour. The causes of social facts, instead, must be sought in antecedent social facts; for instance, the social fact of punishment is causally explained by the strong collective sentiments felt by a society against a particular kind of behaviour. At the same time, social facts also perform a function in society – they are the means for the achievement of societal ends. The social fact of punishment, for instance, seeks to maintain and reinforce the collective sentiments that sanction the improper conduct of society's members. Durkheim acknowledged the importance of investigating both the causes and the functions of social facts, but he emphasized that functional analysis is distinctively sociological in that it seeks to relate a social fact to the larger social organism.

Following through his metaphor of society as an organism, Durkheim classified social facts as normal or pathological, in terms of their relation with the larger social environment – with the social organism as a whole. The adequacy of a social fact like a social norm must be evaluated in terms of the social ends such a norm fosters – this requires that the sociologist evaluate the desirability of social ends. Durkheim argued that value judgments are inevitable in the social sciences, since the facts of society are the values and beliefs of the collectivity (see VALUE JUDGMENTS IN SOCIAL SCIENCE §1). Thus, a scientific sociology must be able to identify desirable social goals before it can identify the best means to achieve them. Here, I believe, Durkheim's positivistic methodology and idealistic social theory show their greatest strain as he tries to make value judgments amenable to direct scientific investigation (see POSITIVISM IN THE SOCIAL

SCIENCES). Such strain is reflected in Durkheim's substantive sociological research on the division of labour and on suicide.

3 Social solidarity and social pathologies

Durkheim's empirical research on the division of labour and on suicide demonstrated the potential of sociology as an academic discipline by taking up topics that had been previously analysed by other social sciences, and showing that sociology's distinctive approach shed a new light on them.

The division of labour was considered an economic phenomenon that led to increased production and wealth. Durkheim argued that the division of labour was also an important moral phenomenon that described the changing foundations of social solidarity from traditional to modern societies. On the one hand, traditional societies exhibited relatively undifferentiated roles of individuals in economic life; individuals were able to perform a variety of tasks and were basically interchangeable with each other. Social solidarity in traditional societies emerged from the unmediated identity of its members. Durkheim called this traditional form of social solidarity mechanical solidarity. On the other hand, modern societies are characterized by a high degree of differentiation of tasks in economic life, and individuals are highly interdependent in their economic activities. Social solidarity in modern societies emerges from the functional interdependence of individuals' differentiated roles; this modern form of social solidarity he calls organic solidarity. Thus, the increase in the division of labour was not detrimental in modern societies, but rather provided a new organic source of solidarity to replace the waning mechanical solidarity of traditional societies. But Durkheim was also concerned with the social pathologies manifested in highly differentiated societies; specifically, he identified a condition of 'anomic' division of labour whereby the norms that bind the economic activities of individuals are greatly weakened. The anomic division of labour led to a loss of social solidarity, and society as a whole suffered from it. Guided by his idealistic standard of social solidarity, Durkheim failed to consider the possibility that the weakening of social norms was in fact a normal and inevitable feature of modernity.

Suicide was another topic Durkheim claimed as rightfully sociological. While psychological, biological, and ecological explanations had been provided, Durkheim argued that suicide was also a significant social phenomenon to be explained sociologically. Suicide rates illustrated how insufficient or excessive regulation and integration in the social organism led to a predictable quota of voluntary deaths, year after year. Durkheim was particularly concerned with the social pathologies of modernity, as he identified two pertinent types of suicide: egoistic suicide and anomic suicide. Egoistic suicide was prompted by the insufficient integration and attachment of individuals to society, demonstrated by the higher rates of suicide observed in Protestant countries as compared to Catholic countries. Anomic suicide was prompted by society's weakened regulation of individuals' conduct, especially in economic life, as demonstrated by the higher rates of suicide found in industrial societies as compared to agricultural societies. Egoistic and anomic suicide shared the spotlight in Durkheim's study because they both illustrated his concern with the underlying pathology of modernity: the loosening of individuals' attachment to society and the breakdown of the social norms that should restrain individuals' asocial behaviour. As with his theory of the anomic division of labour, Durkheim's theory of egoistic and anomic suicide failed to consider suicide as, possibly, a normal phenomenon of our times, deriving from the collectivity's value of the freedom and autonomy of individuals as the cornerstone of modernity.

4 Moral education and religion

In the last two decades of his life Durkheim turned his attention away from the pathologies of modernity, to focus on the central role of education and religion in creating, renewing and sustaining social solidarity.

In his lectures on moral education (published posthumously in 1925) Durkheim argued that education should provide individuals with discipline, attachment to society, and autonomy of judgment. The first element guaranteed society's successful role in regulating the conduct of its members; the second gave individuals a sense of belonging and of successful integration with the collectivity; the third equipped the competent member of society with the ability autonomously to discern the desirability of society's moral values and to subscribe to them spontaneously. The themes of insufficient regulation and social integration that characterized Durkheim's work on suicide were recast here in a positive form: how to achieve successful regulation and social integration in modern societies. The theme of autonomy, then, echoed Durkheim's repeated emphasis that the dignity of the individual was unquestionably the central moral value of modernity.

Durkheim's work on religion brought to full circle his characterization of society as centred on collective representations. Criticizing the Marxist approach, Durkheim rejected the view that economic life preceded religious phenomena; instead he argued that in primitive societies everything was religious. In *The Elementary Forms of the Religious Life* Durkheim demonstrated the centrality of religion in providing the cognitive, intellectual and moral foundations of social life. He argued that since religious phenomena were the earliest expression of social life they were also the source of our rules of logic and of our system of thought. The categories of time and space, of class and number, and of genus and species must have originated in the early experience of the collectivity, manifested through religious life. Thus, for example, the idea of time and of its division of years and seasons emerged, in Durkheim's view, from the religious distribution of ceremonies, rituals and holidays in primitive societies.

By demonstrating that cognitive and moral phenomena found their roots in primitive religious life Durkheim sought to prove that everything is social in its origins. This was, in the end, Durkheim's master thesis, that society is the source of everything that makes us human – moral rules, altruism, rules of logic, cognitive categories, and ultimate beliefs and values. Accordingly, he constantly downplayed the role of psychology, of economics, of history, and constantly emphasized the role of collective representations in shaping the life of society and of its members. Perhaps Durkheim's philosophy was exceedingly sociocentric; it was certainly unambiguous and forceful in making the case for sociology as the science of moral life.

See also: RELIGION AND POLITICAL PHILOSOPHY; SOCIAL SCIENCE, METHODOLOGY OF §2

List of works

Durkheim, É. (1893) *De la division du travail social*, Paris: Alcan; trans. G. Simpson, *The Division of Labor in Society*, New York: Macmillan, 1933. (Discussed in §3 of this entry.)

—— (1895) *Les regles de la methode sociologique*, Paris: Alcan; trans. S.A. Solovay and J.H. Mueller, *The Rules of Sociological Method*, Chicago, IL: University of Chicago Press, 1938. (Discussed in §2 of this entry.)

—— (1897) *Le Suicide: etude de sociologie*, Paris: Alcan; trans. J.A. Spaulding and G. Simpson, *Suicide: A Study in Sociology*, Glencoe, IL: Free Press of Glencoe, 1951. (Discussed in §3 of this entry.)

—— (1912) *Les Formes elementaires de la vie religieuse*, Paris: Alcan; trans. J.W. Swain, *The Elementary Forms of the Religious Life*, New York: Macmillan, 1915. (Discussed in §4 of this entry.)

—— (1925) *L'Education morale*, Paris: Alcan; trans. E.K. Wilson and H. Schnurer, *Moral Education*, New York: Free Press, 1961. (Discussed in §4 of this entry.)

References and further reading

Fenton, S. (1984) *Durkheim and Modern Sociology*, Cambridge and New York: Cambridge University Press. (Discusses Durkheim's sociology within its disciplinary context.)

Hall, R.T. (1987) *Émile Durkheim: Ethics and the Sociology of Morals*, New York: Greenwood Press. (Systematic analysis of Durkheim's thought on morality and ethics.)

Jones, R.A. (1986) *Émile Durkheim: An Introduction to Four Major Works*, Beverly Hills, CA: Sage. (An introduction to *Division of Labor*, *Rules*, *Suicide* and *Elementary Forms*.)

LaCapra, D. (1972) *Émile Durkheim: Sociologist and Philosopher*, Ithaca, NY: Cornell University Press. (Discusses Durkheim's major works and highlights their philosophical framework.)

Lukes, S. (1973) *Émile Durkheim: His Life and Work*, New York: Harper & Row. (Exhaustive presentation of Durkheim's work within the context of his intellectual biography.)

Parkin, F. (1992) *Durkheim*, Oxford and New York: Oxford University Press. (A short introduction to Durkheim.)

Pickering, W.S.F. (1984) *Durkheim's Sociology of Religion*, London: Routledge & Kegan Paul. (A detailed treatment of themes and theories in Durkheim's sociology of religion.)

Pope, W. (1975) *Durkheim's Suicide: A Classic Analyzed*, Chicago, IL: University of Chicago Press. (Analyses *Suicide*'s theory and data.)

Thompson, K. (1982) *Émile Durkheim*, New York: Tavistock. (An introductory overview of Durkheim.)

Turner, S.P. (ed.) (1993) *Émile Durkheim: Sociologist and Moralist*, London: Routledge. (A collection on Durkheim's science of morality.)

Wallwork, E. (1972) *Durkheim: Morality and Milieu*, Cambridge, MA: Harvard University Press. (Describes the evolution and shifts in Durkheim's science of ethics.)

MARCO ORRÚ

DUTCH BOOK ARGUMENT

see PROBABILITY THEORY AND

EPISTEMOLOGY

DUTY

To have a duty is, above all, to be subject to a binding, normative requirement. This means that unless there are exculpating reasons someone who has a duty is required to satisfy it, and can be justifiably criticized for not doing so. Having a duty to do something is like having been given a command by someone who has a right to be obeyed: it must be done.

Sometimes we speak as if we have duties to individuals (such as persons and institutions). So, for example, if Jones makes a promise to Smith, then Jones has a duty to Smith to keep the promise. We also talk as if we have duties to perform, or to refrain from performing, types of actions, for instance, a duty to help those in need. Even if the performance of such a duty involves treating an individual in a certain way, the duty may not be to that individual. For example, a duty to be charitable might not be a duty to anyone, not even the recipient of the charity.

An important feature of duties is that they provide some justifying reason for action. If we explain why we did something by saying that it was our duty, we are offering a justification for the action. Such a justifying reason does not depend on the entire nature of the action. For example, if we make a promise, we have some justifying reason for keeping it, regardless of what was promised, or to whom the promise was made. Again it is like a command. If we are given a command by someone with a right to be obeyed, we have some justification for obeying it, no matter what we are commanded to do. On some views, however, the justifying reason we have for doing something because it is required by duty may not be decisive: we may have an even better reason for doing something else. None the less, that something is required by duty provides some justifying reason for doing it.

Talk about duties is found in many areas; we speak, for example, of legal duties, moral duties, professional duties, the duties of a scholar and, even, matrimonial duties. This discussion will focus on moral duty, but may have wider application.

1   **Duty and other normative concepts**
2   **Kinds of duties**
3   **The grounds of duties**

1   Duty and other normative concepts

Related to the concept of duty are a number of other important normative concepts. Among these are the concepts of obligation, right, permission and prohibition. The relations between permissions, prohibitions and duties are fairly straightforward: if we are permitted to do something, then we do not have a duty not to do it; if we are prohibited from doing something, we have a duty not to do it (see DEONTIC LOGIC). The relationships between duties, obligations and rights are not as obvious.

According to most modern use, obligation and duty are taken to be coextensive, if not identical. So, to have a duty to do something is the same as to have an obligation to do it. However, there is a narrower view concerning duty. According to this, duties must result from roles, namely, from status, occupation or position. For example, subjects are said to have duties to their sovereign, physicians to their patients and parents to their children. The duty arises from the role (being a subject, physician or parent). Obligations are distinct from duties on this view. Obligations result only from voluntary actions; for instance, an obligation might result from the making of a promise. It may be that the distinction between duties and obligations is currently seldom recognized because many of our roles are taken on voluntarily. Although there is much to be said for the narrower view, for the rest of this essay current usage will be followed and it will be assumed that duties and obligations are substantially the same.

One important view about the relationship between rights and duties is that there is a correlation between, at least, some rights and duties. A version of this thesis is expressed in the two following principles (Ross 1930: 48).

1   A right of *A* against *B* implies a duty of *B* to *A*.
2   A duty of *B* to *A* implies a right of *A* against *B*.

It should be noted that accepting these principles does not force us to accept the less plausible view that there is a general correlation between rights and duties, such that every right implies a duty and every duty implies a right. As has been pointed out, there may be duties concerning individuals which are not duties to those individuals. Likewise, individuals may have rights which are not rights against anyone in particular. About such cases the above principles are silent. Rather, the proposal is that there is a correlation between, for example, Smith's having a duty to Jones, and Jones' having a right against Smith (see RIGHTS).

An evaluation of these principles requires that we examine the following questions. (1) What can have duties? (2) To what can there be duties? (3) What can have rights? (4) Against what can there be rights?

The answers to (1) and (4) are fairly clear. It is reasonable to think that in order for an entity to have a duty, or for there to be a right against it, that entity must be able to recognize that it is subject to a normative requirement, a cognitive ability lacked by beings that are not rational (see MORAL AGENTS). Consequently, only persons (rational beings), such as humans, can have duties and we can have rights only against persons. This still leaves open whether non-persons can have rights and whether we can have duties to non-persons. Can we, for example, have duties to nonhuman animals, or, perhaps, the biosphere? Can such things have rights against us (see ANIMALS AND ETHICS; ENVIRONMENTAL ETHICS)?

One important view is that non-rational beings cannot have rights and we cannot have duties to them. Again, the thought is that a required cognitive capacity is lacking. It is sometimes argued that having any right, let alone a right against someone, requires the ability to claim it. Even according to this view, however, we might have duties concerning non-persons, or with respect to them. We could, for example, have a duty not to cause non-persons unnecessary pain, without its being a duty to anyone. Accepting this view would not require rejection of either of the principles.

An alternative view argues that for an individual to have a right, or for us to have a duty to that individual, does not require that individual to have anything like the cognitive capacity needed to have a duty, or to be the sort of thing against whom others can have rights. The standards are different. Perhaps all that is needed is being sentient, or having interests. If so, then we could accept that some non-persons can have rights against us and that we can have duties to some non-persons. This also is consistent with both of the principles.

One possible reason for rejecting the principle that a duty of *B* to *A* implies a right of *A* against *B* is the thought that we can have duties to ourselves, but cannot have rights against ourselves. The idea that persons can have rights against themselves is difficult to accept. That persons can have duties to themselves, such as that of self-improvement, seems much more plausible. However, if we take it that a duty to a person involves what is owed to that person, then the idea is much less plausible: can we really owe anything to ourselves? Alternatively, it might be that we have duties that concern ourselves, without their actually being duties to ourselves. If this is so, then no reason has been offered for rejecting the two principles (see MORAL STANDING).

2 Kinds of duties

A number of distinctions have been offered between types or kinds of duties. The most important of these distinctions are those between positive and negative duties, *prima facie* and 'all-in' duties or 'all things considered' duties, perfect and imperfect duties, and subjective and objective duties.

The distinction between positive and negative duties is supposed to rest on a more fundamental difference between acting and refraining from acting. The idea is that positive duties concern what we are required to do, while negative duties concern what we are required to refrain from doing. Examples of positive duties might be the duties to help others and to develop our talents. Examples of negative duties might be the duties not to lie and not to kill.

A concentration on negative duties is often associated with deontological theories (see DEONTO-LOGICAL ETHICS). According to such theories, morality consists largely of constraints on action, none of which we can morally violate, but which may be relevant only in a limited number of situations. Deontologists often hold that the distinction between positive and negative duties can be morally significant: the negative duties are more important or more stringent than the positive ones. Indeed, it is sometimes held that there can be a duty not to bring about something, while there is no duty to prevent it from occurring (see DOUBLE EFFECT, PRINCIPLE OF). For example, there might be a very stringent duty not to kill someone, while there is, at best, a much less stringent duty to save that person's life (see LIFE AND DEATH).

Teleological theories, especially consequentialist ones, even if they recognize a distinction between positive and negative *actions*, generally do not consider it to underpin a difference between negative and positive *duties* that has any moral significance (see TELEOLOGICAL ETHICS; PERFECTIONISM; CONSEQUENTIALISM). Such theories are concerned with the promoting of values, and it does not matter whether the values are promoted by acting or refraining from acting. For example, if the value is respect for life, then it can be promoted equally well either by refraining from killing or by saving lives.

While it seems reasonable to think that there is some difference between positive and negative actions, that this involves a morally significant difference is much more contentious. Views about this divide roughly along the same lines as do those concerning the relative advantages of deontological and teleological theories. No doubt this will remain controversial as long as these approaches to duty compete.

An equally controversial and perhaps equally important distinction can be drawn, as it was by Ross (1930), between *prima facie* duties and 'all-in' duties (see ROSS, W.D.). (*Prima facie* duties are sometimes called 'pro tanto duties' or 'duties other things being equal', while all-in duties are sometimes called 'duties proper' or 'duties all things considered'.) A *prima facie* duty is not, contrary to its literal meaning, something that merely *appears* to be a duty. Rather, to say that we have a *prima facie* duty to perform some action expresses the idea that the action involves an important moral consideration, but one that can be (morally) outweighed, or overridden, by other moral considerations. For example, assume that an agent has a choice between keeping a promise and helping someone in need, but cannot do both. Keeping the promise is a *prima facie* duty because it involves the morally important consideration of fidelity; helping the person in need is also a *prima facie* duty as it involves the morally important consideration of beneficence. The agent's all-in duty depends on the nature of all the relevant *prima facie* duties. That is, an all-in duty is what duty requires all things considered, in particular, given all *prima facie* duties.

Part of the motivation for this distinction is the idea that (all-in) duties can always be satisfied: there are never any real conflicts of duties. Using this distinction, we can attempt to explain apparent conflicts of duties in terms of conflicts of *prima facie* duties. When it seems that we have a duty to do two things, and we cannot do both, this distinction allows us to say that they are not really competing duties, but merely competing *prima facie* duties. (In some cases, of course, we would be permitted to do either, but would not have a duty to do either.) However, that all apparent conflicts of duties or moral dilemmas can be explained away in this fashion is not obvious. There seem to be situations where agents have to choose between courses of action that are so horrible that none is acceptable and the agent should feel regret no matter what is done. Whether such cases involve real conflicts of duties depends on two things. First, it depends on whether we take dilemmas to exclude there being a correct answer to the question of what duty requires. It may be that what we call something a dilemma simply because the choices are so awful. Second, it depends on whether there is some inconsistency in feeling regret for doing something that was required by duty.

Regardless of the attitude that is taken to possible conflicts of duty, the notion of a *prima facie* duty faces difficulties. Foremost among these is the lack of a persuasive account of how all-in duty results from diverse *prima facie* duties. No satisfactory account has

been given of the conditions under which one *prima facie* duty 'overrides' another.

The view that there is a distinction between perfect and imperfect duties is attributed to KANT (§10) (see KANTIAN ETHICS). He said that a perfect duty 'allows no exception in the interest of inclination' ([1785] 1903: 421). Although it is not clear exactly what he had in mind, one plausible view is that the distinction is between duties owed to particular individuals and duties that are not owed to anyone but which merely concern them. If we have a duty to someone, then that person has a right against us. (Kant thought that we can have duties to ourselves and may even have thought that we can have rights against ourselves.) If we have a duty that is not to anyone, then that duty does not involve a right against us. This, arguably, gives us more latitude in how to satisfy the duty. A duty not to kill is owed to each person, while a duty of charity is not owed to anyone, and can be satisfied by helping any of a number of persons. Perfect duties are usually associated with negative, stringent duties, while imperfect duties are associated with positive, less stringent duties.

Finally, if a theory allows for a difference between what a person sincerely considers to be required by duty and what is actually required by duty, then it can allow for a distinction between subjective and objective duty. Subjective duty is that which one sincerely takes to be one's duty, while objective duty is that which is actually required by duty. There are other notions closely related to subjective obligation, which are sometimes offered as accounts of subjective duty. One is the notion of that which duty probably requires; another is that which it would be most reasonable to think that duty requires. Each of the latter is distinct from subjective duty, as I have characterized it. One may be sincere but incorrect about what duty probably requires. Also, one may have a sincere belief about what duty requires, which is not the most reasonable belief one can have.

3 The grounds of duties

Given that to have a duty is to be subject to a binding normative requirement, we might naturally wonder how it is that we could become subject to such a requirement. Who or what binds us? This, perhaps, is the most difficult and most interesting question concerning duties.

One tradition says that only God could be the source of our duties (see RELIGION AND MORALITY §1; NATURAL LAW). Given God's existence, it might be thought that God has authority over us and can impose duties on us. God would then have a right to our obedience. Giving us the Ten Commandments can be thought of as one way that God has imposed duties on us. If this is correct, then we have a duty to obey them. A problem with this view is that it has the implication that if God does not exist, then there are no duties. Another problem with it is that it is unclear why we are required to do as God commands. That is, it is unclear why God has authority over us. Indeed, a similar question can be asked about anyone or anything else, whether a person, institution or society, that is supposed to be able to impose duties on us. Why should we think that they have the authority to impose duties on us, or what gives them the right to tell us what to do?

Perhaps instead of having duties imposed on us by other humans, it is the structure of the universe itself that imposes the duties. On this view, duties (or moral laws) would be analogous to physical laws. Just as we are subject to physical laws, such as Newton's law of gravitation, we are subject to binding normative requirements, for example, the duty to help others who are in need. It is not that the universe has authority over us and we must obey its command, rather it is that normativity is part of the very fabric of the universe.

Various problems with this view have been raised. One is that the features of the universe that produce the duty would be very strange, unlike anything else about which we know (see NATURALISM IN ETHICS; MORAL REALISM §6). A second is that it is difficult to see how we could learn about these duties. We do not have any perceptual experience of them, and perceptual experience is widely thought to be the way that we gain knowledge about the world (see MORAL KNOWLEDGE). The third objection rests on the action-guiding nature of duty. The idea is that it is a necessary feature of accepting something as being required by duty that we are to some extent motivated to do it. How is it that duties imposed on us by the structure of the world motivate us (see MORAL MOTIVATION)?

If duties are not imposed by things independent of us, perhaps we impose them on ourselves. Indeed, as Kant argued, it might be that a duty can only be imposed by the person having it (see KANT, I. §9). A non-Kantian expression of a similar idea is this. Only moral agents can have moral duties. Moral agents are responsible for their actions, and being responsible for an action requires that the agent does it (see RESPONSIBILITY). However, freedom is not sufficient for moral agency. For example, it seems that children are free, but not moral agents. Moral agency also requires that agents act rationally, that they act on reasons that they accept as adequate. This means an action is performed because of the nature of the action. If duties could be imposed on us by others –

God, society, or the universe – then we would not be moral agents. We would not be acting on adequate reason because our reason for acting would not be the nature of the action. Instead, we would be acting because the action was imposed as a duty. It would be like obeying a command simply because it was a command and not because what was commanded was appropriate for the situation. So for something to be someone's duty, it must result from that person – only we can impose duties on ourselves. A similar point is this: moral agents have authority over themselves, but are subject to no other authority (see AUTONOMY, ETHICAL).

Numerous questions can be raised about the idea that we impose duties on ourselves. Why is giving ourselves reasons for actions imposing duties on ourselves? After all, if we have authority over ourselves, can we not change our duties at will? Indeed, what is it to have authority over ourselves? A possible answer to these questions is that the second condition of moral agency, that we act rationally or act from adequate reason, provides additional normative constraints on what we can do as moral agents. In particular, this condition may require a sort of impartiality: a reason for a rational agent acting in a certain way in a particular situation must be a reason for any rational agent to act in the same way in similar situations (see IMPARTIALITY; UNIVERSALISM IN ETHICS §5).

If we were to accept that others cannot impose duties on us and we cannot impose duties on ourselves, would there be any use for the notion of duty? Is the idea of a duty, of morality itself, a fiction to be discarded? Not necessarily. There could be other explanations of why we think that the notion of duty is relevant to our actions.

One position is that we cannot do without some notion of duty: it is a useful instrument. On such an account, the reasons for accepting a system of morality would not be moral reasons. Instead, the reasons would be ones of self-interest, or a combination of self-interest and interest in others (see PRUDENCE §3). The idea is that people will generally be better off living in a society where there are social institutions and conventions regulating behaviour (see CONTRACTARIANISM). For example, killing might be proscribed because it is to everyone's mutual advantage not to have to worry about being killed. A problem for this view is that there may be some people in a society who contribute such a small amount to the society that there is no reason to cooperate with them. Indeed, some may contribute so little that there is not even any reason to refrain from killing them.

Another approach suggests that what seem to be

claims about duties, for example, that there is a duty to refrain from killing, actually are not claims at all. Since they are not claims, they cannot be true or false. They are merely expressions of attitudes. For example, if someone says, 'We have a duty to help those in need', no claim is being made; the utterance is merely the expression of a positive attitude towards helping those in need. It is as if the person said, 'Hooray for helping others' (see EMOTIVISM). The main challenge for this view is to explain why much of moral conversation seems like reasoned argument. One strategy for dealing with this challenge is to argue that there is a logic of attitudes that mirrors the logic of claims or propositions.

In addition to the difficulties in giving an account of how we come to be subject to duties, the entire project of trying to characterize ethical concerns in terms of duties has come under criticism. One main objection is that the idea of duty is so closely connected to the idea of God as a lawmaker or imposer of duties that the concept has no place in secular philosophy (see Anscombe 1958). Another is that concentrating on duty blinds us to the rich diversity of considerations that are relevant to ethics. Instead of asking what our duties are, we should be asking how we should live (Williams 1985) (see VIRTUE ETHICS).

See also: CONSCIENCE; DUTY AND VIRTUE, INDIAN CONCEPTIONS OF

References and further reading

Some of these items involve intricate argument but few are technical.

* Anscombe, G.E.M. (1958) 'Modern moral philosophy', *Philosophy* 33: 1–19. (A powerful attack on the use of the concept of duty in secular philosophy.)
Bennett, J. (1995) *The Act Itself*, Oxford: Clarendon Press. (A discussion of the nature of action, including whether there is a morally significant difference between positive and negative actions.)
Frazier, R.L. (1995) 'Moral relevance and *ceteris paribus* principles', *Ratio* 8: 115–27. (A modern account of *prima facie* duties.)
Gauthier, D. (1986) *Morals By Agreement*, Oxford: Oxford University Press. (A modern defence of contractarianism.)
Gowans, C. (ed.) (1987) *Moral Dilemmas*, Oxford: Oxford University Press. (A collection of articles concerning the possibility of moral dilemmas.)
Helm, P. (ed.) (1981) *Divine Commands and Morality*, Oxford: Oxford University Press. (A collection

containing articles on the proposal that God imposes duties on us.)
Hobbes, T. (1651) *Leviathian*, ed. J.P. Plamenatz, London: Collins, 1962. (The classic statement of contractarianism.)
Hume, D. (1739/40) *A Treatise of Human Nature*, ed. L.A. Selby-Bigge, revised by P.H. Nidditch, Oxford: Clarendon Press, 2nd edn, 1978. (The classic account of the view that what seem to be moral claims are actually expressions of moral sentiments.)
* Kant, I. (1785) *Grundlegung zur Metaphysik der Sitten*, in *Kants gesammelte Schriften*, ed. Königlichen Preußischen Akademie der Wissenschaften, Berlin: Reimer, vol. 4, 1903; trans. with notes by H.J. Paton, *Groundwork of the Metaphysics of Morals* (originally *The Moral Law*), London: Hutchinson, 1948; repr. New York: Harper & Row, 1964. (References made to this work in the entry give the page number from the 1903 Berlin Akademie volume; these page numbers are included in the Paton translation. This classic work contains the argument that we impose duties on ourselves.)
Korsgaard, C.M. (1996) *The Sources of Normativity*, Cambridge: Cambridge University Press. (A Neo-Kantian account of the grounds of duty, with a good discussion of alternative proposals.)
Mackie, J.L. (1977) *Ethics: Inventing Right and Wrong*, Harmondsworth: Penguin. (Contains a good introductory discussion of the problems with thinking that duty can be imposed on us by the nature of the universe.)
Sayre-McCord, G. (ed.) (1988) *Essays on Moral Realism*, Ithaca, NY: Cornell University Press. (A collection of articles concerning whether the nature of the universe can provide the grounds of duty. It contains a very good introductory chapter.)
Sinnott-Armstrong, W. and Timmons, M. (eds) (1996) *Moral Knowledge? New Readings in Moral Epistemology*, Oxford: Oxford University Press. (A collection of articles on the possibility of moral knowledge, containing a very good annotated bibliography.)
Rawls, J. (1971) *A Theory of Justice*, Cambridge, MA: Harvard University Press. (A very influential defence of a position which is an interesting combination of a contractarian and a Neo-Kantian approach to ethics.)
* Ross, W.D. (1930) *The Right and the Good*, Oxford: Oxford University Press. (The source of a notion of a *prima facie* duty.)
Thomson, J.J. (1990) *The Realm of Rights*, Cambridge, MA: Harvard University Press. (Includes a discussion of the relationship between duties and

rights, and a discussion of who (or what) can have rights and duties.)

White, A.R. (1984) *Rights*, Oxford: Clarendon Press. (Includes a discussion of the relationship between duties and rights, and a discussion of who (or what) can have rights and duties.)

* Williams, B. (1985) *Ethics and the Limits of Philosophy*, Cambridge, MA: Harvard University Press and London: Fontana. (A collection of articles supporting the view that duty-based moral systems are not sensitive to a wide range of important ethical considerations.)

Zimmerman, M.J. (1996) *The Concept of Moral Obligation*, Cambridge: Cambridge University Press. (A very general and comprehensive account of obligation (or duty), which gives close consideration to many of the topics discussed in this entry.)

ROBERT L. FRAZIER

DUTY AND VIRTUE, INDIAN CONCEPTIONS OF

Two principal strains of ethical thought are evident in Indian religious and philosophical literature: one, central to Hinduism, emphasizes adherence to the established norms of ancient Indian culture, which are stated in the literature known as the Dharmaśāstras; another, found in texts of Buddhism, Jainism and Hinduism alike, stresses the renunciation of one's familial and social obligations for the sake of attaining enlightenment or liberation from the cycle of rebirth. The Dharmaśāstras define in elaborate detail a way of life based on a division of society into four 'orders' (varṇas) – priests, warriors, tradesmen and servants or labourers – and, for the three highest orders, four 'stages of life' (āśramas). Renunciation is valid only in the final two stages of life, after one has fulfilled one's responsibilities as a student of scripture and as a householder. The various traditions that stress liberation, on the other hand, advocate total, immediate commitment to the goal of liberation, for which the householder life presents insuperable distractions. Here, the duties of the householder are replaced by the practice of yoga and asceticism. Nevertheless, specific ethical observances are also recommended as prerequisites for the achievement of higher knowledge through yoga, in particular, nonviolence, truthfulness, not stealing, celibacy and poverty. The liberation traditions criticized the system of the Dharmaśāstras for being overly concerned with ritual and external forms of purity and condoning – indeed, prescribing – the killing of living beings in Vedic sacrifices; but it was only in the

Dharmaśāstras that the notion of action solely for duty's sake was appreciated. The Hindu scripture the Bhagavad Gītā (Song of God) represents an effort to synthesize the two ideals of renunciation and the fulfilment of obligation. It teaches that one should integrate yoga and action in the world. Only when acting out of the state of inner peace and detachment that is the culmination of the practice of yoga can one execute one's duty without regard for the consequences of one's actions. On the other hand, without the cultivation of inner yoga, the external forms of renunciation – celibacy, mendicancy, asceticism – are without significance. It is inner yoga that is the essence of renunciation, yet yoga is quite compatible with carrying out one's obligations in the world.

1 **Introduction**
2 **Duty**
3 **Renunciation**
4 **Renunciation in action**

1 Introduction

Ethics was not a prominent topic of sectarian controversy in classical Indian philosophy. While Hindu, Buddhist and Jaina philosophers debated such things as the existence of universals, the reality of the external world and the existence of a self, they did not often argue directly about the nature of the good or right action. Each religious-philosophical tradition had its own body of sacred texts to which it appealed in defining *dharma* – that is, duty or righteousness, the way of conducting one's life so as to achieve happiness on earth and salvation after death. Given allegiance to a particular scripture, the question of how one should live was largely moot; debate centred, rather, on the epistemological question of how one can be confident that a particular scripture is authoritative. At the same time, two distinct ethical ideals are found espoused, explicitly or implicitly, throughout Indian religious and philosophical literature – the observance of duty, and renunciation. The ideal of renunciation cuts across all three major traditions. Especially in the Hindu tradition, where both ideals are represented, their conflict is an important theme and an attempt was made, in the *Bhagavad Gītā* (Song of God), to reconcile them.

2 Duty

The emphasis on duty is represented primarily, if not exclusively, by texts of the Hindu tradition. In the *Ṛg Veda*, the oldest stratum of text (*c.*2000 BC), virtue is conformity to cosmic law (*ṛta*). That involves not only

183

the performance of various obligatory rites on behalf of the gods, but also the observance of fidelity and rectitude in human relationships. In the Brāhmaṇas, later texts devoted to analysing and interpreting rituals, virtue is narrowly conceived as ritual excellence. The sacrifice is understood to yield its result through its own magic, by directly effecting what it symbolizes, not by honouring or ingratiating the gods to whom it is addressed. Transgression is thus merely a ritual mistake, a blunder or negligence – not an offence against a personal being to whom one owes an obligation – either in the context of the sacrifice itself or in human affairs seen as an extension thereof; and it produces a defilement, materially conceived as a taint or miasma, that can only be ritually removed. The Brāhmaṇas declare, for example, that the impurity of the most heinous deeds, even the killing of a Brahman (priest), can be wiped away by performing a horse sacrifice.

This ritualistic conception of virtue was significantly modified in the Dharmaśāstras, 'treatises on *dharma*' (composed from about 600 BC onward), the most famous of which is the *Mānavadharmaśāstra* (Laws of Manu). The correct performance of rituals is still important, but the highest *dharma*, according to this literature, is 'good conduct' in the broadest sense: 'Neither austerities nor [the study of] the Veda, nor [the performance of] the Agnihotra [rite], nor lavish liberality [to priests] can ever save him whose conduct is vile and who has strayed from the path [of *dharma*]' (*Vasiṣṭha dharmasūtra* 6.3). Nevertheless, *dharma* still fundamentally involves *doing* (and avoiding) certain things; it is implicitly defined as the adherence to certain norms, specifically, the norms of the ancient Indian society that referred to itself as 'the Aryas', which transmitted the Vedic literature. The Dharmaśāstras lay down the occupations of the various classes or 'orders' (*varṇas*, commonly referred to as 'castes') of Aryan society. Brahmans serve as priests and teachers; *kṣatriyas* as princes and warriors, *vaiśyas* as tradesmen and *śūdras* as labourers and servants. For the three highest, or 'twice-born', orders they prescribe four 'stages of life' (*āśramas*) – studentship, marriage, forest residence and renunciation – and specify that they are to be observed only in succession. Thus, although renunciation is part of the scheme, it is still to be undertaken only at a certain time and in a certain way, and so falls under the rubric of duty. (A well-known verse of the *Mānavadharmaśāstra* states, 'A twice-born man who seeks final liberation without having studied the Vedas, without having begotten sons, and without having offered sacrifices, sinks downwards' (6.37).) For the Brahman order in particular, the Dharmaśāstras spell out numerous restrictions intended to preserve its

unique 'purity' – the avoidance of polluting agents, especially contact with people of lower orders, the avoidance of certain foods, and so forth. They also specify rules bearing on marriage and inheritance and other matters of civil law. They prescribe various sacraments to be undergone at certain junctures of life, the most important being the investiture of the sacred thread at the beginning of the period of studentship. They go into a plethora of matters of etiquette, even prescribing how to have sex and answer the calls of nature.

Western scholars have criticized the Brahmanical system of the Dharmaśāstras (so called because it was composed by Brahman literati in ancient times and describes a society in which Brahmans have ultimate authority) for considering virtue to be mere conformity to established practices without attempting to arrive at more fundamental principles by which such practices could be justified or criticized. But the Dharmaśāstras speak of, besides the *dharma* of the specific *varṇas*, 'the *dharma* common to all orders' (*sarvāśramadharma*). That includes such things as forgiveness, self-control, not stealing or lying, non-violence, restraint of the senses, compassion, patience, freedom from anger, envy and avarice, and so on. Thus, while there is indeed a lack of reflection on the nature of virtue in general in the Dharmaśāstras, or for that matter in Indian thought as a whole, a step in that direction can be seen in the attempt to identify these more general duties – which, however, are considered to apply only to Aryas; other 'barbarian' societies are condemned simply for being non-Aryan. At the same time, the influential Mīmāṃsā school of Hindu philosophy explicitly asserted that, *dharma* being supersensible and thus unknowable by unaided reason, we can learn about it only from revelation. Moreover, one's state of mind is clearly recognized as essential to right conduct in the Dharmaśāstras; mere external conformity is not enough. The psychological sources of transgression – desire, greed, anger and delusion – are identified, and intention is said to add weight to the deed. Although mechanical expiation is still provided for – misconduct is still conceived to produce a defilement that can be washed away, and numerous purification rituals are described – remorse is also part of expiation.

The various Hindu schools of philosophy engaged in an extensive discussion of the nature of the scriptural injunction (*vidhi*) that commands one to carry out or avoid a certain act. Nyāya philosophers held that the injunction makes one aware of a means (the dharmic act) by which a certain desirable purpose can be achieved; that is, it motivates the hearer to act by implicitly appealing to the hearer's self-interest, whether it be spiritual or hedonistic. In general, a dharmic, pious life was thought to be conducive to happiness and prosperity on earth and the attainment of heaven after death; but, as we shall see, it was also considered instrumental in attaining ultimate salvation in the form of liberation from the cycle of rebirth. Bhāṭṭa Mīmāṃsā philosophers, on the other hand, believed that the *vidhi*, specifically, the ending of the optative verb of the injunctive sentence, actually *impels* the agent toward acting by virtue of its own peculiar efficacy (referred to as *śabdabhāvanā*). At the same time, an awareness of some purpose to be achieved through the act is also necessary. Prābhākara Mīmāṃsā philosophers, finally, held that a *vidhi* motivates one to act neither by *causing* one to act through the potency of its language, nor by *persuading* one to do so by suggesting the achievement of a desired end, but simply by making one aware of an obligation (*niyoga*) that one feels bound to carry out; it is followed for its own sake, without regard for the result of the act it prescribes. Understood in this way, the scriptural injunction resembles the Kantian categorical imperative. This theory also implies that the will of the agent who carries out an injunction is free (see MĪMĀṂSĀ).

3 Renunciation

The ideal of the renunciation (*sannyāsa*) of all familial and social obligations for the sake of enlightenment or liberation (*mokṣa*, *nirvāṇa*) from the cycle of rebirth was espoused in various classical Indian traditions and represents a rejection of the Brahmanical ideal. Already in the late Vedic texts called the Upaniṣads (800–300 BC) the sacrificial cult is called into question. Residence in heaven, to be achieved through ritual acts, is declared undesirable because it is impermanent: after the merit of one's good deeds (karma) is exhausted the soul must return to the physical world, where one again experiences suffering. The only possibility of fulfilment is to transcend embodied existence altogether; this is conceived in the Upaniṣads and the Vedānta school of philosophy, which based itself on the Upaniṣads, as a merging of the individual soul with Brahman, the ultimate reality of the universe. For the Hindu Nyāya-Vaiśeṣika school, it was the dissociation of the self from the mind and body, and hence from all conditions of consciousness. The Buddha refused to characterize *nirvāṇa* at all, suggesting that it is simply beyond human conception (see VEDĀNTA §§1, 3; NYĀYA-VAIŚEṢIKA §7; NIRVĀṆA). Almost all liberation traditions emphasized techniques of yoga and asceticism along with renunciation – withdrawal from society and life as a celibate monk, hermit or wandering mendicant – as means of reducing the

factors that determine rebirth, variously identified as ignorance, karma or desire. Even the commission of good acts was believed to bind the soul further in *saṃsāra* (the cycle of rebirth); for every action, whether bad or good, must eventually yield a retribution in the form of pleasure or pain, both of which require a body. (An exception is the case of an enlightened being, whose actions have no consequences because such a being has overcome the state of individuality.) Jainism, especially, recommended asceticism and self-mortification as means of directly reducing the load of accumulated karma (see JAINA PHILOSOPHY §3).

However, the liberation traditions also acknowledged that the observance of certain moral precepts is essential for spiritual advancement. The texts of Buddhism, Jainism and Hinduistic yoga state the same pentad of commandments: nonviolence, truthfulness, not stealing, celibacy and nonpossession. It was generally believed that such observances reduce the tendencies towards passion that serve as the conditions of the fruition of karma. Overall, this list of virtues represents a critique of the ethical system of the Dharmaśāstras; it recommends universal principles over traditional, caste-specific norms and stresses intention over overt performance. (For each of the five virtues there corresponds a mental attitude to be cultivated; one should, for example, not only refrain from taking what does not belong to oneself, but also not have covetous thoughts.) Buddhist and Jaina texts in particular ridicule the *dharma* of the Brahmans because it not only reflects an obsession with external forms of purity but also actually involves injury to living beings. It is puzzling how a man could think himself good just because he bathes every time he comes into contact with a *śūdra*; it is even more incomprehensible that he could think so because he slaughters an animal in a sacrifice! One can see, however, that this critique of Brahmanical ethics is not entirely fair. Though they emphasize specific caste obligations, the Dharmaśāstras also recommend the cultivation, by all members of society, of most of the same virtues stressed in the liberation traditions (the notable exception being nonpossession, which precludes existence as a householder; celibacy in the Brahmanical scheme was reinterpreted as sexual restraint in marriage). They even advocate nonviolence, though typically they recommend it *outside* the context of the sacrifice; and it is the killing of a Brahman that is especially condemned.

It should also be kept in mind that the virtues recognized by the liberation traditions were understood chiefly as means to an end – enlightenment or liberation. It was only within the tradition of the Dharmaśāstras, specifically in the Mīmāṃsā discussions of *vidhi* and, as we shall see, in the *Bhagavad Gītā*, that an appreciation of the ideal of action simply for duty's sake was attained. However, the emphasis Buddhism placed on nonviolence (*ahiṃsā*) and compassion (*karuṇā*) indicates that at least those virtues had more than instrumental value there. The Mahāyāna writings, in particular, stress that compassion is not to be practised out of any interest – certainly not for the sake of worldly delights, but also not even for the sake of liberation. The saints of Mahāyāna Buddhism, the Bodhisattvas, postpone disappearance into *nirvāṇa* until they have helped to enlighten all other beings: 'By his own person, like a baited hook, without partaking of any enjoyment himself, he attracts others and saves them. Thus it is said … "Charity is the enlightenment of the Bodhisattva"' (*Śikṣāsamuccaya*, BST edn, 22). The Buddhists came close to deriving nonviolence explicitly from the Golden Rule. While nonviolence is sometimes treated purely instrumentally in Indian thought – it is said in certain Jaina texts that violence must be avoided because it causes injury to *oneself*, in so far as the passions that engender it prevent the soul from attaining liberation – there is none the less a marked tendency to view it as a duty grounded on a law of reason or insight into one's kinship with all creatures.

4 Renunciation in action

The Hindu scripture the *Bhagavad Gītā*, perhaps the single most important Indian text that relates to ethics, can be seen as an attempt to reconcile the two ideals of duty and renunciation. Contained in the epic poem the *Mahābhārata* (c.200 BC–AD 200, traditionally attributed to Vyāsa), the *Gītā* relates a dialogue between Kṛṣṇa (Krishna), an incarnation of the Supreme Being Viṣṇu, and the warrior Arjuna. The issue of the dialogue is whether Arjuna should participate in the great battle that is about to take place, for his own cousins lead the opposing side. Arjuna knows that his cause is just – his cousins are violent and despotic; they have deprived him and his brothers of their due portion of the kingdom – but he nevertheless feels that it would be a violation of *dharma* to be an agent of the destruction of his own friends and relatives, no matter how wrong they are. Filial duty has come into conflict with Arjuna's duty as a prince (*kṣatriya*) to preserve order in society and defend it against its enemies. In response to Arjuna's quandary, Kṛṣṇa does not enter into a discussion of the nature of virtue or universal principles of right action (as perhaps Socrates would have done) but tells Arjuna to cultivate yoga, which will enable him to rise above his situation. Yoga will provide Arjuna with clarity and equanimity, so that he is no longer

confused about his duty – which Kṛṣṇa suggests is obvious, anyway: to defend society against evil – or overcome with remorse about the pain he must inflict in doing what he must do. It will bring about a state of calm and centredness from which he can carry out right action undistracted by passion; 'Yoga is skill in action', says Kṛṣṇa (2.50). Moreover, it will transform the personality, so that Arjuna will no longer act as an individual agent but yield to the forces of nature – ultimately, to God – acting through his body: 'He who thinks this self is a killer and he who thinks it is killed, both fail to understand; it does not kill, nor is it killed' (2.19). The yogin is not 'bound' by what he does; his actions do not necessitate further rebirth.

Thus the *Gītā* works out a synthesis of the ideals of duty and renunciation, proposing a new ideal of renunciation in action. Especially in the third, fourth and fifth chapters the theme of renunciation is taken up. Merely external forms of renunciation are criticized: one who physically refrains from acting but still yearns after sensual pleasures in his mind is a hypocrite (3.6). Thus, the tables are turned on the liberation traditions, which had criticized Brahmanical ethics for being formalistic. True renunciation is the state of inner yoga, a condition of complete calm, contentment and detachment. This is compatible with acting so as to carry out one's responsibilities in the world, even with observing the specific prescriptions of the Dharmaśāstras – indeed, the *Gītā* upholds the *varṇa-āśrama* system. In reality, all creatures are driven to act in so far as they are part of nature, which is subject to constant change – the fluctuations of 'the three *guṇas*' (basic ingredients of material nature). Kṛṣṇa, the Supreme Being, refers to his own case: 'These worlds would collapse if I did not perform action' (3.24). It is stressed, however, that action should be undertaken only for its own sake, out of a sense of duty: 'You have a right to action alone, not the fruits [of action]' (2.47). Thus, the state of yoga is essential for right action, because only in that state is one not driven by inclination. It is the detachment of yoga that makes it possible for one to act only for duty's sake. The *Gītā* also describes this state of mind in terms of considering one's actions as a sacrifice and surrendering one's actions to God.

The *Bhagavad Gītā* contains many religious teachings that do not relate directly to ethics but reflect the sectarian (Vaiṣṇava) origins of the poem. It stresses above all that Viṣṇu is the ultimate reality and that salvation can be attained only by worshipping Viṣṇu in his true form. Yet in the end, this metaphysical knowledge provides the solution to Arjuna's ethical dilemma. At a certain point Kṛṣṇa, who until then has appeared just as a fellow warrior, reveals himself to Arjuna as God. Arjuna sees the infinite within his body – innumerable gods, creatures and universes; the physical and psychological constituents of all beings; the past and the future, including even the outcome of the battle he is about to fight. Overwhelmed by Kṛṣṇa's infinite splendour, he now sees his own concerns as trivial. Realizing that his own actions are part of a vast panorama of life directed by God, he surrenders himself completely to Kṛṣṇa and prepares to fight.

See also: FA; FATALISM, INDIAN; KARMA AND REBIRTH, INDIAN CONCEPTIONS OF

References and further reading

* *Bhagavad Gītā* (Song of God) (*c.*200 BC), trans. F. Edgerton *The Bhagavad Gītā*, Harvard Oriental Series 38–9, Cambridge, MA: Harvard University Press, 1944. (A readable and accurate translation of the most important text of Hinduism.)
Bühler, G. (ed.) (1879–92) *The Sacred Laws of the Aryas: As Taught in the Schools of Āpastamba, Gautama, Vasiṣṭham, and Baudhāyana*, Sacred Books of the East 2, 14, Oxford: Clarendon Press. (A collection of important Dharmaśāstras.)
Dhammapada (6th–5th century BC), trans. F.M. Müller, *The Dhammapada*, Sacred Books of the East 12, New York: Scribner, 1901. (A foundational treatise on Buddhist practice.)
Hopkins, E.W. (1924) *Ethics of India*, New Haven, CT: Yale University Press. (Still the best survey of Indian ethics.)
Kane, P.V. (1968–77) *History of the Dharmaśāstras*, Poona: Bhandarkar Oriental Research Institute, 5 vols. (A comprehensive guide to Hindu legal and ethical literature.)
Maitra, S.K. (1978) *The Ethics of the Hindus*, Delhi: Asian Publication Services. (Contains in-depth discussions of the views of the Hindu philosophical schools on various topics.)
* *Mānavadharmaśāstra* (*c.*600 BC), trans. W. Doniger and B.K. Smith, *Laws of Manu*, New York: Viking Penguin, 1992. (The most influential of the Dharmaśāstras.)

JOHN A. TABER

DWORKIN, RONALD (1931–)

Ronald Dworkin's early, highly controversial, thesis that there are right answers in hard cases in law, coupled with his attack on the idea that law is simply a system of rules, gained him a prominent and distinct place in the anti-positivist strand of legal theory. He has developed and enriched his earlier insights by tying his notion of law-as-interpretation to the ideals of community and equality. Dworkin is an influential representative of liberal thought, who combines clear and analytical thinking with political involvement expressed in decisive and timely interventions in many of the important political debates of our time.

Ronald Dworkin, born in Massachusetts, read philosophy and law at Harvard and Oxford; after a brief period in legal practice he became a professor of law at Yale in 1962. In 1969 he succeeded H.L.A. HART as Professor of Jurisprudence at Oxford University and since 1975 has also been Professor at New York University. His ideas have been profoundly influential in developing British and US jurisprudential thought.

Since very early in his career Dworkin has queried the positivist (and particularly the Hartian) concept of law as a system of rules. Dworkin criticizes positivism for its limited and impoverishing account of law that necessarily entails judicial law-making and retrospectivity in hard cases. Dworkin argues that every judicial decision requires discretion understood as the exercise of judgment, as interpretation, and yet none requires discretion of the unrestricted type envisaged by positivists. The right legal answer cannot be 'read off' a rule but requires a justification (that subsumes the rule under it) in terms of discussing principles embodied in the law (see LEGAL POSITIVISM §5; LEGAL REASONING AND INTERPRETATION §§2–4).

To his first distinction, 'rules/principles' – that underlies his attack on positivism – Dworkin adds a second, that of 'principles/policies', that underlies his attack on utilitarianism. Principles are propositions that describe rights, and to 'take rights seriously' (1978) means to always allow them to 'trump' policies. In every case a requirement of justice or fairness embodied in principle should override any competing consideration of policy associated with the pursuit of collective goals.

Both distinctions, both attacks, are present in *Law's Empire* (1986), which integrates the earlier insights in a theory of law-as-interpretation fundamentally enriched by the notion that the law is a practice and occurs in a community of interpreters. Legal interpretation requires us to appreciate that law is a practice that involves us as participants in arguing its meaning. For the interpretive attitude to take hold people must try to view the practice 'in its best light' and reconceive its requirements in the light of what would most fully realize its implied purpose. This is a requirement performed on objective ground: not by imposing upon the practice outside moral or personal purposes, but by retrieving purpose from within the practice, as it is intelligible to the people participating in the common form of life, the community.

Dworkin's theory of law-as-interpretation focuses precisely on the junction of law with the notion of community. First, as horizon and inventory, community circumscribes the ambit of possibilities of what a practice may require, locating each attempt at the best interpretation of the requirements of the practice within the context we share of its possible meanings. But debating the best among possible understandings involves the participants in an argument over the purpose or point of the practice; interpretation is always justification for Dworkin, the imputation of justificatory principle, but a principle that is already embodied in the past record of the practice, retrieved not posited. It is a kind of reflexive equilibrium between what fits the community's legal record and what morally justifies it – a balancing undertaken against the background of the whole body of the law – that yields for each case in law the right answer, which Dworkin calls 'integrity'. With neither unreflective adherence nor contempt for past legal decisions – a contempt of which Dworkin accuses his prime adversaries, the critical legal scholars – Dworkin's ideal judge secures that the community act in a consistent manner in applying its conception of justice (see CRITICAL LEGAL STUDIES). Through the notion of integrity Dworkin can construct a concept that is true to demands of interpretation and community. Interpreting a set of social practices under the demands of integrity sustains the unity of community, elevates it from a bare to a true community and allows the fraternal attitude within to flourish.

Dworkin's work has attracted a great deal of criticism, of which we may identify four axes. The first contests his account of interpretation. It has been argued here that Dworkin falsely assumes that interpretation ought to be a 'best' reconstruction when the point of interpretation is to show the practice as it actually is; that making the law more attractive than it is performs a mystifying, ideological function; and that it allows the meaning of laws to become relativized since 'best justifications' are – to some extent at least – subjective. The second questions the 'dialectical' relationship between community and the law. Why assume with Dworkin that law is constitutive of the texture of our communities, and provides the terms in which we argue our normative commitments? A third line contests the fundamental distinctions that Dworkin employs. The rules/principles distinction, it has been argued, cannot serve to refute positivism because nothing in positivism precludes principles understood in a justificatory role and as rationalizations behind rules. The privile-

ging of principle over policy runs into the frequent difficulty of keeping the two types of political aim apart in practice. Finally it has been argued that fit cannot be meaningfully divorced from justification – a 'fit' is always already justified as such – and as an integral part of justification it could not at the same time constrain it. The fourth line questions Dworkin's theory's liberal underpinning, one that is best captured in his advocacy of law as an institution that elevates conflicts from the battleground of politics to the forum of principle (1985) in such a way that with its insistence on the maintainance of unity and of 'fit' within the system precludes the possibility of radical critique and change.

Dworkin's suggestion about what it means to treat people as equals informs his intervention in the debate over reverse discrimination. His theory of distributive justice is explored in a series of articles on equality (1981a, 1981b, 1991) where he argues for equality of resources rather than equality of welfare. Dworkin is known for his interventions in many heated controversies of our time over civil disobedience, pornography, freedom of speech (1985) and abortion and euthanasia (1993). The latter is an attempt to shift the debate from the seemingly intractable disputes in the battlefield of politics towards the common ground that we share: a commitment to the sanctity of life. Thus recasting the debate unifies our political communities around a common commitment while allowing principled disagreement on the morality of abortion and euthanasia that in turn yields greater tolerance for individual choice and renews Dworkin's image as one of the most important liberal theorists of our time.

See also: JUSTICE, EQUITY AND LAW §6; LAW AND MORALITY §4; LEGAL IDEALISM

List of works

Dworkin, R. (1978) *Taking Rights Seriously*, London: Duckworth. (A collection of early articles, including his attack on positivism.)

—— (1981a) 'What Is Equality? Equality of Welfare' (part I), *Philosophy and Public Affairs* 10: 185–246. (In both this article and the following article (1981b) Dworkin argues for an 'endowment-insensitive' equality of resources rather than for equality of welfare. There are two further parts to his theory of equality, also in 1991.)

—— (1981b) 'What is Equality? Equality of Resources' (part II), *Philosophy and Public Affairs* 10: 283–345. (See Dworkin 1981a.)

—— (1985) *A Matter of Principle*, Cambridge, MA: Harvard University Press. (A collection of articles on, among others, 'the political basis of law', the nature of interpretation, the economic view of law, reverse discrimination and censorship.)

—— (1986) *Law's Empire*, London: Fontana. (Dworkin's major work in legal theory on the nature of law as an interpretive practice and his prescription as to how legal interpretation should be undertaken.)

—— (1991) 'Foundations of Liberal Equality', *Tanner Lectures of Human Values*, Salt Lake City, UT: University of Utah Press, 3–119. (Restatement of the theory of equality.)

—— (1993) *Life's Dominion*, London: HarperCollins. (Dworkin's thesis on abortion, euthanasia and the sanctity of life.)

—— (1996) *Freedom's Law*, Harvard, MA: Belknap. (A collection of interventions on political and constitutional issues.)

References and further reading

Cohen, M. (ed) (1983) *Ronald Dworkin and Contemporary Jurisprudence*, London: Duckworth. (A collection of important critiques; see especially Fish, Postema. Includes a 'Reply' by Dworkin.)

Guest, S. (1992) *Ronald Dworkin*, Edinburgh: Edinburgh University Press. (Sympathetic and comprehensive account of the life and the works; includes full bibliography.)

Hunt, A. (ed) (1992) *Reading Dworkin Critically*, New York: Berg. (An uneven collection, containing some interesting critiques; see especially Hunt.)

Kerruish, V. (1991) *Jurisprudence as Ideology*, London: Routledge. (A feminist critique of legal liberalism that contains a critique of Dworkin's work.)

EMILIOS A. CHRISTODOULIDIS

DYNAMIC LOGICS

Dynamic logics have been designed by Pratt as formal systems for reasoning about computer programs. The main ingredients discussed are programs, operations on programs, states and properties of states. In particular one can formalize that every execution of a program p starting in state s terminates in a state with a given property. Thus correctness statements for programs can be dealt with. According to Segerberg (1980) programs might be viewed more generally as actions of some agent so that certain aspects of human action theory can also be formulated and studied in these systems.

1 **Motivation**
2 **Propositional dynamic logic**
3 **Dynamic predicate logic**

1 Motivation

In Pratt's (1976) setting the meaning of a program p with respect to an abstract machine $\mathcal{M}$ is taken as the transition relation $\mathcal{M}_p$ between states of $\mathcal{M}$, so that $\mathcal{M}_p$ holds for states s and s' (symbolized by $s\mathcal{M}_p s'$) if and only if there is a machine run according to p starting in state s and terminating in state s'. The execution of programs can be non-deterministic – another run of $\mathcal{M}$ according to p might well lead from the same initial state to quite a different final state. Deterministic programs are therefore special programs where the transition relation is actually a (partial) function. From already given programs one can obtain other programs by applying operations like 'first do p_1 and then p_2' (*composition*), 'do p_1 or p_2' (*nondeterministic choice*) or 'apply p a finite number of times' (*iteration* or *looping*). Given a certain stock of basic propositions, i.e. properties of states, one can build new propositions by taking boolean combinations of already given propositions or asking modal questions like 'does every terminating run of a program p starting in state s necessarily end in a state with property Q?'. Thus to every program p naturally corresponds a modal operator $[p]$... to be read: 'after (each terminating execution of) p it is the case that ...' The proposition '*not* : $[p]$ *false*' expresses for instance at s that at least one run of p starting in s will terminate. Every proposition Q induces a test programme 'if Q proceed, otherwise skip' (*test*). The corresponding relation holds for s and s' if and only if $s = s'$ and s satisfies Q. Formalizing this situation leads immediately to propositional dynamic logic.

2 Propositional dynamic logic

The above remarks suggest the following formal language where formulas and program terms (for short: programs) are simultaneously built up from propositional and program variables with the aid of the usual propositional connectives, say ¬ (not) and → (implies), the p-necessity operator $[p]$ for programs p, and the program forming operations; (composition) ∪ (choice), * (iteration) and ? (test). The formation rules for formulas and programs are as follows:

- propositional variables are formulas and if φ and ψ are formulas and p is a program variable then $\neg\varphi$, $(\varphi \rightarrow \psi)$ and $[p]\varphi$ are formulas

- program variables are programs and if p and q are programs and φ is a formula then $(p;q)$, $(p \cup q)$, $p*$ and $\varphi?$ are programs.

Other propositional connectives and the p-possibility operator $\langle p \rangle$ are introduced by definition. For instance $\langle p \rangle$ stands for $\neg[p]\neg$. A Kripke-semantics is now easily established. A model $\mathcal{M} = (S, I)$ for this language consists of a nonempty set S (the set of states or 'possible worlds' of $\mathcal{M}$) and a function I which assigns to every propositional variable a property in S, i.e. a subset of S, and to every program variable a two-place relation in S, an accessibility relation. Then the truth of formulas φ in $\mathcal{M}$ at state s (symbolically: $\mathcal{M} \models_s \varphi$) and the interpretation of programs p (symbolically: $\mathcal{M}_p$) can be simultaneously defined. The interesting cases are:

- $\mathcal{M} \models_s [p]\varphi$ iff for every s', $s\mathcal{M}_p s'$ implies $\mathcal{M} \models_{s'} \varphi$
- $\mathcal{M}_{(p;q)} = \mathcal{M}_p \circ \mathcal{M}_q$, $\mathcal{M}_{(p \cup q)} = \mathcal{M}_p \cup \mathcal{M}_q$, $\mathcal{M}_{p*} = (\mathcal{M}_p)*$
- $\mathcal{M}_{\varphi?} = \{(s,s) \mid \mathcal{M} \models_s \varphi\}$

where $R_1 \circ R_2$ denotes the product of R_1 and R_2, i.e. $sR_1 \circ R_2 s'$ holds iff there is an s_1 such that $sR_1 s_1$ and $s_1 R_2 s'$, $R_1 \cup R_2$ denotes the set theoretical union of R_1 and R_2, and $R*$ denotes the reflexive and transitive closure of R, i.e. $sR*s'$ holds iff either $s = s'$ or for some natural number n there are $s_1, \ldots, s_n$ such that sRs_1 and $\ldots$ and $s_n R s'$ hold. A lot of constructs known from ordinary programming languages can now be formalized, for instance 'if φ then p else q' is $((\varphi?;p) \cup (\neg\varphi?;q))$ or 'while φ do p' is $((\varphi?;p)*;\neg\varphi?)$. The set of valid formulas, i.e. formulas which are true in every model at all states, can be generated (in Hilbert-style) from certain axioms by *modus ponens* and the necessititation rule. The set of all tautologies together with the formulas given by the schemas below could be chosen (after Segerberg 1980) as axioms:

- $[p](\varphi \rightarrow \psi) \rightarrow ([p]\varphi \rightarrow [p]\psi)$
- $[(p;q)]\varphi \leftrightarrow [p][q]\varphi$
- $[(p \cup q)]\varphi \leftrightarrow ([p]\varphi \wedge ([q]\varphi)$
- $[\varphi?]\psi \leftrightarrow (\varphi \rightarrow \psi)$
- $[p*]\varphi \rightarrow (\varphi \wedge [p][p*]\varphi)$
- $[p*](\varphi \rightarrow [p]\varphi) \rightarrow (\varphi \rightarrow [p*]\varphi)$

Correctness of the system is easily verified and completeness has been proved by Gabby, Parikh and Segerberg (see Goldblatt 1987). There are also correct and complete Gentzen-type systems. The question of general validity of a formula turns out to be decidable (Fischer and Ladner 1979).

3 Dynamic predicate logic

Viewing states as the content of certain storage units $x_0, x_1, x_2, \ldots$ they can be identified with functions assigning to each x_n its contents $s(x_n)$. Thus $s(x_n)$ denotes the object (for instance a string over an alphabet) that occupies in state s the n-th storage unit. The set of objects that are allowed to appear in some storage unit constitutes a one- (or many-) sorted domain in which certain basic first- (or higher-) order properties and functions are fixed. Using these initial data a first- (or higher-) order possibly many-sorted modal language, known as dynamic predicate logic, can be used to describe transition phenomena initiated by programs in state sets. Simple assignments of the form $x := t$ (to be read: 'set x equal to t') are often taken as the only basic programs from which all others are derived by program forming operations. A run of such a simple assignment $x := t$ starting in state s has the effect that only the content of the storage unit x is 'updated' by the value of t and every other unit is left untouched. The resulting state s' will be denoted by $s(x/t)$. Simple assignment programs are obviously deterministic and universally terminating. Fixing a first order language with individual variables $x_0, x_1, x_2, \ldots$ and certain relation and function symbols, a model $\mathcal{M} = (D, I)$ for such a language consists of a nonempty domain D and an interpretation function I which associates with every relation and function symbol of the language an appropriate relation or function in D. Every formula φ then defines a property in S, the set of all assignments to the variables – that is the set of all functions from $\{x_0, x_1, x_2, \ldots\}$ to D. An element s in S has the φ-property iff φ is true in $\mathcal{M}$ under the assignment s, symbolically $\mathcal{M} \models_s \varphi$. The essential new case in defining truth is:

- $\mathcal{M} \models_s [x := t]\varphi$ iff $\mathcal{M} \models_{s(x/t)} \varphi$

Therefore $[x := t]\varphi$ is (under certain syntactical conditions) equivalent to $\varphi(x/t)$ which arises from φ by substituting t for every free occurrence of x in φ. Using the iteration operation it is possible to express things which in general cannot be said by any fixed number of applications of the substitution operation. For instance $[(x_1 := f(x_1))*]Q(x_1)$ expresses in $\mathcal{M}$ at s that all of

$$s(x_1), f^{\mathcal{M}}(s(x_1)), f^{\mathcal{M}}(f^{\mathcal{M}}(s(x_1))), \ldots$$

have the property corresponding to Q in $\mathcal{M}$. In such a language the natural numbers can now be characterized up to isomorphism by a formula. The main part of this formula says that for every y the program

$$(x := 0; \text{ while } x \neq y \text{ do } x := x + 1)$$

terminates (at least once). This means that every element can be reached in finitely many steps from 0 by adding 1 each time. Here iteration is used essentially. From the characterizability of the natural numbers it follows in particular that the set of valid formulas is not recursively enumerable so that no usual proof system can be correct and complete. However, by adding an infinitary rule (a sort of ω-rule) correctness and completeness can be re-established.

Dynamic predicate logic can be viewed as a sublogic of an extended predicate logic in which countable conjunctions and disjunctions are allowed. That is because a formula $[p*]\varphi$ is obviously equivalent of the disjunction over the set of formulas.

$$\varphi, \ [p]\varphi, \ [(p;p)]\varphi, \ [((p;p);p)]\varphi, \ [(((p;p);p);p)]\varphi, \ldots$$

Many variations of the core formalism are possible; for instance tests are often restricted to Boolean combinations of atomic formulas. This seems to be more realistic since tests of the form $(\forall x\varphi)$? might involve a search through an infinite domain. Also, random assignments (written as $x:=?$) are sometimes introduced. In a model $\mathcal{M}=(D,I)$ such a basic random assignment denotes the relation which holds between two assignments s and s' if and only if $s'=s(x/d)$ for some $d \in D$. The formula $\forall x\varphi$ can then be expressed by $[x:=?]\varphi$.

See also: LOGICAL AND MATHEMATICAL TERMS, GLOSSARY OF

References and further reading

* Fischer, M.J. and Ladner, R.E. (1979) 'Propositional dynamic logic of regular programs', *Journal of Computer and System Sciences* 18, 194–211. (Presents the first proof of decidability for propositional dynamic logic.)
* Goldblatt, R. (1987) 'Logics of Time and Comutation', *CSLI Lecture Notes Number 7*, Stanford. (Good general reference for modal, tense and dynamic logic.)
  Harel, D. (1984) 'Dynamic logic', in D. Gabbay and F. Guenthner (eds) *Handbook of Philosophical Logic* vol. 2, Dordrecht: Reidel, 497–60.(Extensive handbook article presenting many results and some proofs. Contains valuable bibliographic information.)
  Kozen, D. and Tiuryn, J. (1990) 'Logics of programs', in J. v. Leeuwen (ed.) *Handbook of Theoretical Computer Science* vol. B, Amsterdam: Elsevier, 789–840. (Another, perhaps more accessible, handbook of articles.)
* Pratt, V.R. (1976) 'Semantical considerations on Floyd-Hoare logic', *Proceedings of 17th IEEE Symposium on Foundations of Computer Science*, 109–21. (Work initiating the subject.)
* Segerberg, K. (1980) 'Applying modal logic', *Studia Logica* vol. 39, 275–95. (A good introduction to dynamic logic.)

ULF FRIEDRICHSDORF

E

EARLY CHRISTIAN PHILOSOPHY *see* PATRISTIC PHILOSOPHY

EAST ASIAN PHILOSOPHY

Sinitic civilization, which includes the Chinese-influenced cultures of Japan and Korea, established an early lead over the rest of the world in the development of its material culture – textiles, iron casting, paper, maritime arts, pottery, soil sciences, agricultural and water technologies, and so on. For centuries after the first sustained incursions of Europe into East Asia, there were more books printed in the classical Chinese language – the 'Latin' of East Asia – than in all of the rest of the world's languages combined. As recently as the beginning of the industrial revolution in the eighteenth century, it was China rather than Europe which, by most standards, was the arbiter of science and civilization on this planet.

If 'philosophy' – the pursuit of wisdom – is an aspiration of high cultures generally, why then was it not until the late nineteenth century, in response to a growing relationship with Western learning, that an East Asian term for 'philosophy' was coined, first by the Japanese (*tetsugaku*), and then introduced into Chinese (*zhexue*) and Korean (*ch'ôlhak*)? If it would be absurd to suggest that East Asian cultures have no history, no sociology, no economics, then how do we explain the fact that Asian philosophy is a subject neither researched nor taught in most Anglo-European seats of higher learning?

1 Uncommon assumptions, common misconceptions

The prominent French sinologist Jacques Gernet (1985) argues that when the two civilizations of China and Europe, having developed almost entirely independently of each other, first made contact in about 1600, the seeming resistance of the Chinese to embracing Christianity and, more importantly, the philosophic edifice that undergirded it was not simply an uneasy difference in the encounter between disparate intellectual traditions. It was a far more profound difference in mental categories and modes of thought, and particularly, a fundamental difference in the conception of human agency. Much of what Christianity and Western philosophy had to say to the East Asians was, quite literally, nonsense – given their own philosophic commitments, they could not think it. In turn, the Jesuits interpreted this difference in ways of thinking quite specifically as ineptness in reasoning, logic and dialectic.

The West has fared little better in its opportunity to appreciate and to appropriate Sinitic culture. In fact, it has fared so badly that the very word 'Chinese' in the English language, found in illustrative expressions from 'Chinese revenge' and 'Chinese puzzle' to 'Chinese firedrill', came to denote 'confusion', 'incomprehensibility' or 'impenetrability', a sense of order inaccessible to the Western mind. The degree of difference between a dominant Western metaphysical sense of order and the historicist 'aesthetic' order prevalent in the radial Sinitic world view has plagued the encounter between these antique cultures from the start. When seventeenth-century European savants such as LEIBNIZ and WOLFF were looking to corroborate their universal indices in other high cultures – the one true God, impersonal rationality, a universal language – China was idealized as a remarkable and 'curious land' requiring the utmost scrutiny. In the course of time, however, reported on by philosophers such as KANT, HEGEL, MILL and EMERSON, Western esteem for this 'curious land' plummeted from such 'Cathay' idealizations to the depths of disaffection for the inertia of what, in the context of the Europe-driven industrial revolution, was recast as a moribund, backward-looking and fundamentally stagnant culture.

In classical Chinese there is an expression: 'We cannot see the true face of Mount Lu because we are standing on top of it.' Although virtually all cultural traditions and historical epochs are complex and diverse, there are certain fundamental and often unannounced assumptions on which they stand that give them their specific genetic identity and continuities. These assumptions, extraordinarily important as they are for understanding the cultural narrative, are often concealed from the consciousness of the participants in the culture who are inscribed by them, and become obvious only from a perspective external to the particular tradition or epoch. Often a tradition suspends within itself competing and even conflicting elements which, although at odds with one another, still reflect a pattern of importances integral to and constitutive of its cultural identity. These underlying strands are not necessarily or even typically logically coherent or systematic, yet they do have a coherence as the defining fabric of a specific and unique culture.

Looking at and trying to understand elements of the East Asian cultural narrative from the distance of Western traditions, then, embedded as we are within our own pattern of cultural assumptions, has both advantages and disadvantages. One disadvantage is obvious and inescapable. To the extent that we are unconscious of the difference between our own fundamental assumptions and those that have shaped the emergence of East Asian philosophies, we are sure to impose upon this geographical area our own presuppositions about the nature of the world, making what is exotic familiar and what is distant near. On the other hand, a clear advantage of an external perspective is that we are able to see with greater clarity at least some aspects of 'the true face of Mount Lu': we are able to discern, however imperfectly, the common ground on which the Confucian and the Buddhist stand in debating their differences, ground which is in important measure concealed from they themselves by their unconscious assumptions.

2 One-world natural cosmology

In the dominant world view of classical East Asia, we do not begin from the dualistic 'two-world' reality/ appearance distinction familiar in classical Greek metaphysics, giving rise as it does to ontological questions such as: 'What is the Being behind the beings?' Rather, we begin from the assumption that there is only the one continuous concrete world that is the source and locus of all of our experience, giving rise to cosmological and ultimately ethical questions such as: 'How do these myriad beings best hang together?' Order within the classical East Asian world view is 'immanental' and 'emergent', an indwelling regularity in things themselves. It is the always unique yet continuous graining in wood, the distinctive striations in a piece of jade, the regular cadence of the surf, the peculiar veining in each and every leaf. The power of creativity resides in the world itself. The order and regularity this world evidences is neither derived from nor imposed upon it by some independent, activating power, but inheres in the world itself. Change and continuity are equally 'real'; time itself is the persistence of this self-transformation.

The 'one' world, then, is the efficient cause of itself. Situation takes priority over agency; process and change take priority over form and stasis. The context itself is resolutely dynamic, autogenerative, self-organizing and, in a real sense, alive. This one world is constituted as a sea of qi, psychophysical energy that disposes itself in various concentrations, configurations and perturbations (see QI). There is an intelligible pattern (see LI) that can be discerned and mapped from each different perspective within the world (see DE) that is its dao, a 'pathway' which can, in varying degrees, be traced out to make one's place and one's context coherent (see DAO). Dao is, at any given time, both what the world is and how it is, always as entertained from some particular perspective or another. In this tradition, there is no final distinction between some independent source of order, and what it orders. There is no determinative beginning or presumptive teleological end. The world and its order at any particular time is self-causing, 'so-of-itself' (ziran) (see CHINESE PHILOSOPHY; DAOIST PHILOSOPHY; DAODEJING; ZHUANGZI). Truth, beauty and goodness as standards of order are not 'givens': they are historically emergent, something done, a cultural product. Given the priority of situation over agency, there is a continuity between nature and nurture, a mutuality between context and the human being. In such a world, it is not unexpected that the Yijing (Book of Changes) is the first among the ancient classics (see YIJING).

3 Ars contextualis: the art of contextualizing

The 'two-world' metaphysical order inherited out of classical Greece has given the Western tradition a theoretical basis for objectivity – the possibility of standing outside and taking a wholly external view of things – a 'view from nowhere'. Objectivity is not only the basis for such universalistic claims as objective truth, impersonal reason and necessity, but further permits the decontextualization of things as 'objects' in our world. It is the basis on which we can separate objective description from subjective prescription.

By contrast, in the 'one world' of classical East Asia, instead of starting abstractly from some underlying, unifying and originating principle, one begins from one's own specific place within the world. Without objectivity, 'objects' dissolve into the flux and flow, and existence becomes a continuous, uninterrupted process. Each person is invariably experiencing the world as one perspective within the context of many. Since there is only the one world, we cannot get outside of it. From the always unique place one occupies within the cosmos of classical East Asia, one construes and interprets the order of the world around one as contrasting 'thises' and 'thats'– 'this person' and 'that person' – more or less proximate to oneself. Since each and every person or thing or event is perceived from some position or other, and hence is continuous with the position that entertains it, each thing is related to and a condition of every other.

In the human world, all relationships are continuous from ruler and subject to friend and friend, relating everyone as an extended 'family'. Similarly, all 'things', like all members of a family, are correlated and thus interdependent. Every thing is holographic in entailing all other things as conditions for its continued existence, and is what it is at the pleasure of everything else. Whatever can be predicated of one thing or one person is a function of a network of relationships, all of which combine to give it its role and to constitute its place and its definition.

There is no strict notion of identity that issues forth as some essential defining feature – a divinely endowed soul, rational capacity or natural locus of rights – that makes all human beings equal. In the absence of such equality, the various relationships which define one thing in relation to another are qualitatively hierarchical and contrastive: bigger or smaller, more noble or more base, harder or softer, stronger or weaker, more senior or more junior. Change in the quality of relationships between things always occurs on a continuum as movement between such polar oppositions.

The general and most basic language for articulating such correlations among things is metaphorical: in some particular aspect at some specific point in time, one person or thing is 'overshadowed' by another; that is, made *yin* to another's *yang*. Literally, *yin* means 'shady' and *yang* means 'sunny', defining in the most general terms those contrasting and hierarchical relationships which constitute indwelling order and regularity (see YIN–YANG).

It is important to recognize the *interdependence* and correlative character of the *yin–yang* kind of polar opposites, and to distinguish this contrastive tension from the dualistic opposition implicit in the vocabulary of the classical Greek world, where one primary member of a set such as Being transcends and stands *independent* of, and thus is more 'real' than the world of Becoming. The implications of this difference between dualism and correlativity contrast are fundamental and pervasive.

To continue the 'person' example, generally in East Asian philosophy, a particular person is not a discrete individual defined in terms of some inherent nature, but is a centre of constitutive roles and relationships. These roles and relationships are dynamic, constantly being enacted, reinforced and ideally deepened through the multiple levels of natural, cultural and social discourse. By virtue of these specific roles and relationships, a person comes to occupy a place and posture in the context of family, community and world. The human being is not shaped by some given design which underlies natural and moral order in the cosmos, and which stands as the ultimate objective of human growth and experience. Rather, the 'purpose' of the human experience, if it can be so described, is more immediate; it is to coordinate the various ingredients which constitute one's particular world here and now, and to negotiate the most productive harmony out of them. Simply put, it is to get the most out of what you have here and now.

4 Radial harmony

A major theme in Confucianism, foundational throughout East Asia, is captured in the phrase from *Analects* 13.23, 'the exemplary person pursues harmony (*ho*), not sameness' (see CONFUCIAN PHILOSOPHY, CHINESE; CONFUCIAN PHILOSOPHY, JAPANESE; CONFUCIAN PHILOSOPHY, KOREAN; NEO-CONFUCIAN PHILOSOPHY). This conception of 'harmony' is explained in the classical commentaries by appeal to the culinary arts. In the classical period, a common food staple throughout northern Asia was *keng*, a kind of a millet gruel in which various locally available and seasonal ingredients were brought into relationship with one another. The goal was for each ingredient – the cabbage, the radish, the bit of pork – to retain its own colour, texture and flavor, but at the same time to be enhanced by its relationship with the other ingredients. The key to this sense of harmony is that it begins from the unique conditions of a specific geographical location and the full contribution of those particular ingredients readily at hand – *this* piece of cabbage, *this* fresh, young radish, *this* tender bit of pork and so on – and relies upon artistry rather than recipe for its success.

The Confucian distinction between an inclusive harmony and an exclusive sameness has an obvious social and political application, underscoring the fertility of the kind of harmony that maximizes difference. This 'harmony' is not a given in some preassigned cosmic design, but is the quality of the combination at any one moment created by effectively correlating and contextualizing the available ingredients, whether they be foodstuffs, farmers or infantry. It is not a quest of discovery, grasping an unchanging reality behind the shadows of appearance, but a profoundly creative journey where the quality of the journey is itself the end. It is the attempt to make the most of any situation.

In summary, at the core of the classical East Asian world view is the cultivation of radial harmony, a specifically 'centre-seeking' or 'centripetal' harmony which is productive of consensus and orthodoxy. This harmony begins from what is most concrete and immediate – that is, from the perspective of any particular human being – and draws through patterns of deference from the outside in toward its centre. Hence there is the almost pervasive emphasis on personal cultivation and refinement as the starting point for familial, social, political and cosmic order (see SELF-CULTIVATION IN CHINESE PHILOSOPHY). A preoccupation in classical East Asian philosophy, then, is the cultivation of this centripetal harmony as it begins with oneself, and radiates outward.

The East Asian world view is thus dominated by this 'bottom-up' and emergent sense of order which begins from the coordination of concrete detail. It can be described fairly as an 'aestheticism', exhibiting concern for the artful way in which particular things can be correlated efficaciously to thereby constitute the *ethos* or character of concrete historical events and cultural achievements. Order, like a work of art, begins with always unique details, from 'this bit' and 'that', and emerges out of the way in which these details are juxtaposed and harmonized. As such, the order is embedded and concrete – the colouration that differentiates the various layers of earth, the symphony of the morning garden, the wind piping through the orifices of the earth, the rituals and roles that constitute a communal grammar to give community meaning. Such an achieved harmony is always particular and specific, and is resistant to notions of formula and replication.

5 Philosophical syncreticism

As one might expect in a cultural narrative which privileges interdependence and the pursuit of radial harmony, orthodoxy is neither exclusive nor systematic. Rather, traditions are porous and syncretic. In the Han dynasty, for example, Confucianism is first fortified by elements appropriated from the competing schools of pre-Qin China such as Daoism and Legalism (see LEGALIST PHILOSOPHY, CHINESE). Later it absorbs into itself an increasingly Sinicized Buddhist tradition, evolving over time into a neo-Confucianism (see NEO-CONFUCIAN PHILOSOPHY). At the same time, the *shuyuan* academies established by the great neo-Confucian syncretist ZHU XI are modelled on Buddhist monastic schools. In more recent years the Western heresy, Marxism, and other elements of Western learning such as the philosophy of KANT and HEGEL, are being appropriated by China and digested to produce what today is being called the 'New Confucianism' (see MARXISM, WESTERN; MARXISM, CHINESE).

The indigenous shamanistic tradition of Korean popular religion absorbed first Buddhism and then Confucianism from China, reshaping these traditions fundamentally to suit the uniqueness of the Korean social and political conditions (see BUDDHIST PHILOSOPHY, KOREAN; CONFUCIAN PHILOSOPHY, KOREAN). Native Japanese Shintoism emerges as a distinction made necessary by the introduction of first Buddhism and then Confucianism, where each tradition assumes a complementary function within the culture (see SHINTŌ; CONFUCIAN PHILOSOPHY, JAPANESE; BUDDHIST PHILOSOPHY, JAPANESE). More recently, in the work of Kyoto School thinkers such as NISHIDA, TANABE and NISHITANI, German idealism is mined and alloyed with the Japanese Buddhist tradition to produce new directions.

Although Confucianism, Buddhism and Daoism – the dominant traditions of East Asia – have certainly been rivals at one level, it has been characteristic of the living philosophical traditions defining of East Asian culture to pursue mutual accommodation through an ongoing process of encounter and appropriation; hence the familiar expression *sanjiao weiyi*, 'the three teachings (Confucianism, Buddhism and Daoism) are as one'. A continuation of this process is presently underway with the ongoing East Asian appropriation of Western philosophy.

See also: ANCIENT PHILOSOPHY; CHINESE PHILOSOPHY; INDIAN AND TIBETAN PHILOSOPHY; JAPANESE PHILOSOPHY

References and further reading

* Gernet, J. (1985) *China and the Christian Impact*, Cambridge: Cambridge University Press. (A reconstructed conversation between the Jesuits and Chinese intellectuals on their first encounters in the sixteenth and seventeenth centuries.)

Hall, D.L and Ames, R.T. (1995) *Anticipating China: Thinking Through the Narratives of Chinese and Western Culture*, Albany, NY: State University of New York Press. (A comparative study of the uncommon assumptions that ground the Chinese and Western philosophical traditions.)

—— (1997) *Thinking From the Han: Self, Truth, and Transcendence in China and the West*, Albany, NY: State University of New York Press. (An examination of several fundamental themes that distinguish the Chinese cultural narrative from the Western philosophical tradition.)

Mungello, D.E. (1985) *Curious Land: Jesuit Accommodation and the Origins of Sinology*, Honolulu, HI: University of Hawaii Press. (A discussion of the inquiry of the seventeenth-century European intellectuals into Sinitic culture.)

ROGER T. AMES

EBERHARD, JOHANN AUGUST (1739–1809)

A German philosopher and theologian, Eberhard was trained in the rationalist tradition of Christian Wolff, but was also influenced by the more empirical 'popular philosophy' of the Enlightenment. Although a prolific author, who wrote on virtually every area of philosophy, he is best known today for his controversies with the two foremost German thinkers of his time, Gotthold Ephraim Lessing and Immanuel Kant.

Born in Halberstadt, Eberhard studied theology at Halle and entered the ministry in 1763. In 1778 he was appointed professor of philosophy at Halle and in 1786 he became a member of the Berlin Academy.

The controversy with LESSING was initiated by the publication of his first work, *Neue Apologie des Socrates* (New Apology of Socrates) (1772–8). Here Eberhard defended the heretical doctrine of the salvation of virtuous pagans (such as Socrates) and attacked the orthodox doctrines of original sin and eternal punishment. He also accused LEIBNIZ of insincerity for his defence of the latter doctrine in his *Theodicy*. The attack on Leibniz occasioned Lessing's reply, which consists of an ironical defence of both Leibniz and the doctrine of eternal punishment, as well as a critique of what he took to be Eberhard's superficial rationalism. Eberhard responded to Lessing in the second volume of the *Neue Apologie*.

After this, Eberhard turned his interest to philosophy and published his *Allgemeine Theorie des Denkens und Empfindens* (General Theory of Thinking and Sensing) (1776). Although deeply influenced by Leibniz's *Nouveaux essais* (New Essays) (1704), he criticized Leibniz's account of innate ideas and defended Locke's view that all ideas derive from experience (see LOCKE, J.). The work was immediately successful, resulting in a prize from the Berlin Academy and the appointment at Halle. He was also quite successful as a teacher and exerted considerable influence on the young Friedrich SCHLEIERMACHER. He also published several handbooks on various aspects of philosophy, based largely on his lectures.

Eberhard initiated the controversy with KANT through his editorship of the *Philosophisches Magazin* (1789–91) and the *Philosophische Archiv* (1792–5). In these journals, which were created expressly to attack the Kantian philosophy, he published numerous articles, mostly written by himself and his colleague, J.G. Maass, criticizing major tenets of the *Critique of Pure Reason* (1781/1787) from a Leibnizian standpoint. The central theme of these articles is the superiority of the Leibnizian to the Kantian philosophy. It is claimed that whatever is true in Kant is already to be found in Leibniz and that wherever Kant departs from Leibniz he is wrong. In the course of arguing for this, however, Eberhard and Maass also raise important objections to Kant's distinction between analytic and synthetic judgments, the doctrine of the ideality of space and time, and the concept of an unknowable thing in itself. Kant, who usually refrained from engaging in direct polemics, made an exception in this case and responded in his *On a Discovery According to which Any New Critique of Pure Reason is Rendered Dispensable by an Older One* (1790). Eberhard is thus to be credited with occasioning this very significant clarification of Kant's views.

See also: ENLIGHTENMENT, CONTINENTAL

List of works

Eberhard, J.A. (1772–8) *Neue Apologie des Socrates* (New Apology of Socrates), Berlin, 2 vols.
—— (1776) *Allgemeine Theorie des Denkens und Empfindens* (General Theory of Thinking and Sensing), Berlin.
—— (1783) *Theorie der schönen Künste und Wissenschaften* (Theory of Fine Arts and Sciences), Berlin.
—— (1787) *Vernunftlehre der natürlichen Theologie* (Rational Doctrine of Natural Theology), Berlin.
—— (ed.) (1789–91) *Philosophisches Magazin*, 4 vols.

References and further reading

Allison, H.E. (1966) *Lessing and the Enlightenment*, Ann Arbor, MI: The University of Michigan Press. (Contains analysis of both Eberhard's theological views and Lessing's critique.)
—— (1973) *The Kant–Eberhard Controversy*, Baltimore, MD and London: Johns Hopkins University Press. (Contains an English translation of Kant's response to Eberhard and an analysis of the controversy.)
Beiser, F. (1987) *The Fate of Reason, German Philosophy from Kant to Fichte*, Cambridge, MA: Harvard University Press. (Chapter 7 contains an account of the controversy with Kant.)

HENRY E. ALLISON

ECOLOGICAL PHILOSOPHY

In the early 1970s a small number of academic philosophers in the English-speaking world began to turn their attention to questions concerning the natural environment. Environmental philosophy initially encompassed various types of inquiry, including applied ethics oriented to issues such as nuclear power and the deployment of toxic chemicals; more abstract extrapolations of traditional ethical theories, such as Kantianism and utilitarianism, into environmental contexts; and, also, a far more radical project involving the reappraisal of basic presuppositions of Western thought in the light of their implications for our relation to the natural world. The first two were basically extensions of existing areas of philosophy, and it is arguably the third project – often described as 'ecological philosophy' or 'ecophilosophy' – which constitutes a distinctively new branch of philosophy. It is to environmental philosophy in this third sense that the present entry is devoted.

Although the ecophilosophical project was explicitly normative in intent, it was quickly found to entail far-reaching investigations into the fundamental nature of the world. Indeed it was seen by many as entailing a search for an entirely new ecological paradigm – a worldview organized around a principle of interconnectedness, with transformative implications for metaphysics, epistemology, spirituality and politics, as well as ethics. Moreover, the process of elaborating a new ecological view of the world was found to uncover the contours of an already deeply embedded worldview, organized around a principle of separation or division, underlying and shaping the traditional streams of modern Western thought.

1   **Origins of ecophilosophy**
2   **The classical scientific worldview**
3   **Ecological worldviews**
4   **Three streams of ecophilosophy**
5   **Foundations of the ecological view**

1   Origins of ecophilosophy

In its earlier phases ecophilosophy was primarily (though not exclusively) associated with a movement known as 'deep ecology', a term coined in 1973 by the Norwegian philosopher Arne NAESS. Naess contrasted 'shallow environmentalism', which sought environmental reform within existing philosophical and ideological parameters, with the 'deep, long-range ecology movement', which involved challenging prevailing philosophical and ideological assumptions about our relation to the natural world. Naess provided his own versions of these challenges and

gave his own responses to them, but arguably his most important contribution to environmental philosophy has been to open up this new horizon and to reveal the radical potential of the ecological approach.

Ecophilosophy can no longer be encompassed within the various 'platforms' of deep ecology initially enunciated by Naess and his followers. However, although the 'deeper' questions that ecology poses are now being explored in a variety of ways, many ecophilosophers agree on the broad outlines of the hitherto dominant worldview and its emerging ecological alternatives.

2   The classical scientific worldview

The dominant worldview is sometimes called Newtonian, sometimes Cartesian. It was forged during the scientific revolution of the seventeenth and eighteenth centuries, though it is often seen as having antecedents in both classical Greek thought and Christianity. It is Newtonian insofar as it is atomistic and mechanistic, and Cartesian insofar as it is dualistic. From a Newtonian point of view, the natural world is made up of *atoms* – discrete particles, units that exist independently of one another. It is built like a machine out of aggregates held together not by any mutual affinity or intrinsic dynamism but purely *mechanically*, by blind, external laws of motion. (Gravitation was an anomaly for Newton, an 'occult' force which vitiated the simplicity of the mechanistic picture.) Such an atomistic world is fully quantifiable and hence describable in mathematical terms, since it can be reduced to nothing but countable units in measurable spatial relations. It is nothing but the mechanical sum of its inert parts.

To characterize the natural world in this way drained it of all of the attributes associated with mind – attributes such as agency, the power of self-mobilization, subjectivity, soul, meaning and purpose. It followed either that mind was illusory, a phenomenon which, as Hobbes argued, could be reduced to mechanism, or that mind was no part of the natural system, but, as Descartes claimed, a distinct category of substance, ontologically independent of matter (see SUBSTANCE §2).

It was the Cartesian *dualism*, rather than the Hobbesian reduction, which came to inform the worldview that emerged from classical science. Mind, banished from matter, took up its dwelling place in us. Because the world in which we exist was considered to be made up of discrete parts, none of which was intrinsically connected with any other, mind could indeed be sealed away in human brains in this way, and, so to speak, not leak out into the surrounding world. This cultural preference for the Cartesian over the Hobbesian view might perhaps be attributed to the fact that the nihilism implicit in Hobbes was relatively unlivable, whereas the Cartesian approach was ideologically appealing.

For if humanity was the repository of all meaning and purpose, then it was also the exclusive locus of value; matter as the inert and dead, the purposeless and blind, possessed only the meaning and hence value that we projected onto it This flattering image of humanity as categorically elevated above the rest of nature had an obvious appeal in an expansive and ambitious age. Moreover, the natural world, divested of intrinsic value, was rendered a fit object for human use, significant only as a reservoir of resources for humankind. This dissolution of traditional constraints on the exploitation of the natural environment obviously suited the mercantile ends of the early modern era.

In reinforcing the assumption that humanity is the only proper object of moral concern and the only yardstick of meaning and value in life, the scientific worldview is seen by ecophilosophers as entrenching the human centredness or *anthropocentrism* that was to a certain extent already, in the pre-modern period, characteristic of Western thought, with its Judaeo-Christian and classical Greek and Roman origins.

Ultimately, the classical scientific worldview and the anthropocentrism which accompanies it may be seen to rest on a fundamental principle of division or separation: reality at every level, indeed thought itself, is separated out into units, or divided into opposing categories. Not only is the natural world divided into atoms, and mind divorced from body, but God, as spirit, stands apart from and above the realm of matter; the epistemic subject is constituted by its separation and strict 'detachment' from the object; society is seen as the sum of the discrete and autonomous individuals which are its units; thought proceeds by analysis, by the consideration of parts.

3   Ecological worldviews

If the 'dominant worldview' emphasizes separation, alternative, ecological worldviews rest on a principle of interconnectedness. 'Ecology' is not intended here in its literal sense, as denoting merely a branch of biological science. The science of ecology, with its representation of the living world as a system of relationships, is in itself neutral with respect to its deeper metaphysical implications. In ecophilosophy, however, this science serves as a *model* – an appropriate theoretical image for a set of irreducible ontological interdependencies.

From this ecological perspective, the world is not seen as divided into mutually independent parts and mutually exclusive attributes: everything is seen as implicating, and being implicated in, the identities of other things, reality being a relational system of shared, interpenetrating essences. Since the properties of a given individual are a function of its relations with individuals of countless other kinds, these properties do not belong exclusively to it: each individual owes its nature to others in the network. It follows that meaning-giving and value-endowing qualities such as mind or subjectivity or soul, and the value that accompanies them, cannot be monopolized by human beings, but must be diffused throughout the systems of the natural world.

In restoring to reality its intrinsic interconnectedness, the ecological perspective implies that since non-human others are implicated in our identity, they are also implicated in our ends and interests, and hence in our conception of the good. In reanimating the world with a quality analogous to mind, this perspective furthermore implies that nature is morally significant in its own right, and is not merely a stockpile of resources for humankind. Such an *ecocentric* perspective situates humanity *in* nature rather than apart from and above it, and thereby removes the traditional justification for anthropocentric attitudes. The idea of interconnectedness can function as an organizing principle not only within metaphysics and ethics, but in many different theoretical and practical contexts. For example, from the interconnected perspective, the epistemic subject is not constituted by way of separation or detachment from its object. Rather, the subject seeks understanding of 'the other' through empathy, affinity, a sense of kinship – through dialogue rather than the objectifying gaze of traditional science. In the theological context, spirit is seen as immanent in matter, body, Nature. Spirituality thus involves celebration of and reverence for our corporeal existence, and affirmation of the natural world and our enmeshment in it. In the sociopolitical context, society is seen not as an aggregate of social atoms – essentially mutually independent individuals – but as a collective, in which individuals are constituted through their relations with one another.

The idea of interconnectedness, however, has been interpreted in different ways by different authors. Perhaps the most important divergence is that between broadly holistic and relational interpretations. According to the more holistic interpretations, interconnectedness implies that individuals exist or are significant only at the level of appearance: individuality lacks ultimate ontological significance. In this case, the individual may be seen as 'one with' the greater whole.

The holistic interpretation can itself be read in two

ways. Either I see nature as an extension of myself, so that its interests become indistinguishable from my interests, and 'eco-defence' becomes a matter of self-defence. Or I see myself as an outgrowth or expression of nature, a purely natural phenomenon, so to speak, without independent identity or interests In this case I substitute nature's interests for my own. From this holistic point of view then, I either absorb nature conceptually into myself, or lose myself in nature. Holistically oriented ecophilosophers have tended to opt for the former reading.

According to the more relational interpretations of interconnectedness, individuals are real, but their reality is a function of their relationships: it is through their interactions that they maintain themselves and define their boundaries. The natural world thus appears not as a field or continuum, but as a community, in which individuals are internally related, in the manner of a family, but are nevertheless distinct. It is incumbent on us, from this point of view, to recognize our kinship with other individuals, but also to respect their otherness. Empathy is required, but not outright identification.

The holistic interpretation of interconnectedness has been identified, by certain critics, with deep ecologists. Some feminists have argued that metaphysics recapitulates psychology, in the sense that different views of the structure of the world emanate from different ego psychologies. In particular, the atomistic outlook is taken to reflect a psychology of separateness associated, in certain ('object rleations') branches of feminist psychoanalytic theory, with the masculine self, while a relational outlook is taken to reflect a relational psychology associated with the feminine self. Some feminists argue that when ecophilosophers postulate an holistic metaphysic, in an attempt to escape the alienation of the atomistic self, they inadvertently perpetuate this alienation, by replacing the isolated local self with an inflated but still isolated global self. From this point of view, then, true interconnectedness calls for relationality rather than holism, for self-in-relation rather than the expansion of self into a greater unity.

Alhough there is much ongoing ambivalence among ecophilosophers as to the exact nature of ecological interconnectedness, the holistic and relational interpretations (and the relational form of individualism that the latter interpretation implies) may be construed as complementary: interconnectedness may be seen as entailing the identities of both wholes and (relational) individuals. Individuals may be seen as energy configurations or sub-systems which maintain their integrity by continuous give and take with the wider system within which they are nested. Their relationality thus entails their individuality, but the relational constitution of the wider system ensures that that system, too, possesses an inherent unity and integrity which makes it an indivisible whole.

4 Three streams of ecophilosophy

Three broad streams of ecophilosophy have emerged to date, though a number of individual ecophilosophers remain unaffiliated with any of them. These streams are deep ecology, ecofeminism and social ecology, and though all are broadly ecocentric in their outlook, their critiques of the dominant worldview and their elaborations of the idea of ecological interconnectedness differ to a certain extent. They each impute the contemporary environmental crisis to the anthropocentric underpinnings of Western thought; but they offer somewhat competing analyses of this anthropocentric premise and differently nuanced remedies for it.

While deep ecologists have been most effective in bringing the problem of anthropocentrism to light, they have generally been less concerned than either ecofeminists or social ecologists with analysing its origins in the Western tradition. This relative lack of concern reflects a shying away, in deep ecology, from systematic approaches generally. Early in the development of deep ecology, Naess drew a distinction between deep ecology as a 'platform', on the one hand, and deep ecology as a collection of 'ecosophies', on the other. The deep ecology platform, which served as the manifesto for deep ecology as a radical political movement, consisted of an (evolving) set of principles on which all who counted themselves deep ecologists could agree. These principles have in the past included such propositions as that all beings have an equal right to live and blossom ('biocentric egalitarianism'), and that the wellbeing and flourishing of nonhuman life on earth has intrinsic value. 'Intrinsic value' is here understood as value which is independent of the usefulness of nonhuman life for narrow human purposes (see VALUES). An ecosophy is any philosophical theory or tradition which can ground this set of principles (see Drengson and Inoue 1995).

Naess' own ecosophy is an amalgam of various influences, including Spinoza, Gandhi, logical positivism and the nature-centredness of the Norwegian folk tradition. It is articulated by Naess as a philosophy of 'self-realization', according to which individuals can overcome their culturally acquired alienation from the natural world by recognizing the ultimate ontological seamlessness of reality, and gradually identifying themselves with wider and wider circles of being, until their sense of self encompasses not only the personal ego, but family, community, bio-region, land, society at large and eventually the planet as a whole. As they realize this larger Self, individuals will perceive their own interests as converging with those of the rest of life.

Ecofeminists tend to trace the human/nature split that defines anthropocentrism to a mind/body dualism which has its earliest origins in antiquity. Like ecophilosophers generally, they recognize the importance of resolving this schism, of making the partitioned world whole again, and of re-animating a 'dead' nature. However, ecofeminists identify the mind/body divide as part of a wider, indeed comprehensive system of dualistic thought, the purpose of which is to divide the world conceptually into mutually opposing and hierarchically ranked categories. This system revolves around certain core dichotomies, which, in addition to mind/body, include spirit/matter, subject/object, culture/Nature, reason/emotion and reason/instinct. Under the influence of these dualistic categories, Western culture has, over approximately the last 2000 years, developed a view of the world as divided into things which possess mind or reason and things which lack it, where the former are set above the latter, and the moral significance of the latter is discounted. Reason is paradigmatically aligned with humankind, and unreason with a mechanical nature, which can accordingly then be subjected to the kinds of instrumental and exploitative attitudes that have led to the current environmental crisis.

Ecofeminists, unlike deep ecologists, offer a political analysis of the dualistic system of thought: this system serves as the naturalizing and legitimating framework for hierarchical political regimes. Theorists such as Val Plumwood (1993) show that the reason/nature dichotomy is used not only to elevate humanity above nature, but to rank one group above another within society: different social groups are assessed according to their perceived relative identifiability, or otherwise, with reason or mind. Thus, in Western cultures, men have traditionally appropriated reason (and hence mind, spirit, intellect and the subject position), while women have been consigned to nature (and hence to the body, matter, emotion, instinct and the object position). White colonizers have identified themselves with reason (civilization, science, enlightenment) and adopted the masculine subject position, while identifying the colonized with nature (primitivism, superstition, barbarism), thereby relegating them to the object position. So, too, with the ruling classes in capitalist societies; they have defined themselves in terms of reason (mental work), while defining workers in terms of the body or nature (manual work). Other groups of oppressors characterize themselves, and those they oppress, according to the same self-serving dualistic logic.

The dualistic construction of nature, with its disastrous consequences for the environment, can thus be seen as an ideological instrument of political oppression. From this point of view nature cannot be ideologically rehabilitated until the political agenda that is served by its being rendered inferior is exposed and addressed. At the same time, however, political oppression cannot be eliminated until the assumption that there exists anything corresponding to the idea of a pure object, to which subordinated groups can be conceptually assimilated, is rejected. In other words, we must respect and engage with nature as a subject in its own right, before we can respect and engage with the social 'other' whose subjectivity has also been denied.

From this kind of ecofeminist perspective, environmentalism is inextricably linked with other social movements, such as those against sexism, racism and class oppression: ideologies of gender and race and class cannot be recast without an overhaul of our understanding of nature, and the ideological rehabilitation of nature cannot be achieved without the concurrent rehabilitation of women, colonized races, and other oppressed groups.

The approach of social ecology to the problem of anthropocentrism closely parallels that of the kind of ecofeminism just outlined. Murray Bookchin, the main architect of social ecology, argues (1982) that the human impulse to dominate Nature is formed in hierarchical societies, and will not be overcome until the social conditions which generate 'epistemologies of rule' or psychologies of domination are corrected. This will not occur, according to Bookchin, until hierarchy in all its forms – familial, gerontological, institutional as well as political – is eradicated from society.

Like ecofeminists and deep ecologists, Bookchin regards nature as a field of relations holistically imbued with an active attribute which confers upon it meaning and moral significance. He describes this attribute as 'subjectivity'. However, unlike ecofeminists and deep ecologists, Bookchin emphasizes the evolutionary aspect of ecology: Nature is not just an assemblage of interrelated parts but a process whereby new and more complex unities are continually being generated through increased differentiation of their elements. In other words, an ecosystem is constituted not only through its internal relations, but also through its history and its telos. In light of this recognition of the evolutionary drive towards ever greater complexity, Bookchin draws a qualitative line between humankind and nature. While human subjectivity ('second nature') is ontologically continuous with the subjectivity of the nonhuman realm ('first nature'), inasmuch as it derives from and recapitulates the latter, it nevertheless transcends it, in the sense that subjectivity has in us attained new levels of complexity and self-organization. For Bookchin then, harmony with the natural environment is achieved not by a simple identification with Nature, such as deep ecologists prescribe, nor merely by a resolution of dualistic opposites – putting mind back into matter – as ecofeminists recommend. From his evolutionary point of view, we achieve harmony with nature, and save the planet, by allowing our own nature the freedom to unfold in its own essential way. Since our nature was formed in a thoroughly ecological system, and since the telos of such a system is the continual elaboration of greater complexity and further diversity, this is also the telos of our nature. We can accordingly only flourish in a society which preserves or recreates, or even enhances, at both social and biological levels, the ecological dynamic of our original matrix. Social relations as well as relations with the natural environment will have to be ecological, and therefore nonhierarchical, if we are to continue to evolve more complex and diverse forms of subjectivity or mentality. Our own self-realization, as individuals, and the further evolution of humanity, thus in fact call for the very kind of nonhierarchical society which, by eliminating psychologies of domination, ensures that our relations with the natural world are reciprocal and benign.

5 Foundations of the ecological view

The intuition of ecological interconnectedness has been epistemologically grounded and philosophically elaborated in ways beyond those already canvassed. For some authors any attempt to provide a theoretical foundation for this intuition is seen as misguided, since a sense of ecological interconnectedness is, according to them, properly derived from direct experience of nature in the field. Other authors appeal for justification to certain 'minority traditions' within Western philosophy, such as pantheism, Romanticism, the monism of Spinoza or the process philosophy of Alfred North Whitehead. Eastern traditions, such as Daoism and Buddhism, and the spiritual traditions of indigenous peoples, are also invoked. Developments in disciplines other than philosophy, including the 'new physics' (Capra 1983; Bohm 1980), systems theory (Bateson 1979; Lovelock 1979), biology (Maturana and Varela 1988) and cultural studies (Roszak 1973; Berman 1981) are cited by yet other authors. In all these areas, traditional assumptions about nature are being overturned and reorganized along more holistic or relational lines. Naess' reminder that many different traditions and theories can provide the starting point for an ecological view of the world can be considered an essential aspect of the ecophilosophical project. His invitation to people to construct their own 'ecosophies', drawing on direct experience and philosophical ideas that are familiar and congenial to them, implies that premises couched in terms as different as mythology, religion, science and mathematics may yet lead to conclusions convergent in relevant respects. Commitment to an ecological worldview, then, is not inconsistent with a high degree of epistemological pluralism and a rich diversity of cultural expression.

The idea that everything to a certain extent shares the fate of everything else is in fact the spiritual axiom of many pre-modern and non-Western societies. It may have been the rejection of this idea, in favour of the idea of division or separation, that helped to bring about the estrangement between Western philosophy and spirituality in the modern period. Perhaps – though some ecophilosophers would disagree – ecophilosophy represents a first step toward the reunion of these two pathways to understanding.

See also: ENVIRONMENTAL ETHICS; GREEN POLITICAL PHILOSOPHY; MONISM; NATURPHILOSOPHIE; PANTHEISM

References and further reading

* Bateson, G. (1979) *Mind and Nature*, London: Wildwood House. (Systems approach to mind and nature.)
* Berman, M. (1981) *The Re-enchantment of the World*, Ithaca, NY: Cornell University Press. (Study of the place of science in the history of consciousness.)
* Bohm, D. (1980) *Wholeness and the Implicate Order*, London: Routledge & Kegan Paul. (A holistic cosmology based on the new physics.)
* Bookchin, M. (1982) *The Ecology of Freedom*, Palo Alto, CA: Cheshire Books. (A source book for the metaphysical foundations of social ecology.)
  Brennan, A. (1988) *Thinking About Nature*, London: Routledge. (Includes account of the metaphysical implications of scientific ecology.)
  Callicott, J.B. (1989) *In Defense of the Land Ethic*, Albany, NY: State University of New York Press. (Part II includes discussion of metaphysical implications of ecology; Part IV examines material relevant to §§2 and 5.)
* Capra, F. (1983) *The Turning Point*, London: Fontana. (An influential popular account of the new physics.)
* Drengson, A. and Inoue, Y. (eds) (1995) *The Deep*

Ecology Movement, Berkeley, CA: North Atlantic Books. (An anthology of seminal deep ecology articles by Arne Naess and others. For Naess bibliography see Rothenberg, 1993.)

Fox, W. (1990) *Toward a Transpersonal Ecology*, Boston, MA and London: Shambhala. (Overview of deep ecology literature.)

* Lovelock, J. (1979) *Gaia: A New Look at Life on Earth*, Oxford and New York: Oxford University Press. (A systems account of the biosphere.)

Mathews, F. (1991) *The Ecological Self*, London: Routledge. (Expansion of material in §§2–3.)

* Maturana, H. and Varela, F. (1988) *The Tree of Knowledge: the Biological Roots of Human Understanding*, Boston, MA: Shambhala. (A systems account of living things.)

* Plumwood, V. (1993) *Feminism and the Mastery of Nature*, London: Routledge. (An ecofeminist analysis of dualistic patterns of thought and critique of traditional philosophies of nature.)

Rolston, H. (1986) *Philosophy Gone Wild*, Buffalo, NY: Prometheus Books. (See especially Section I.)

—— (1988) *Environmental Ethics*, Philadelphia, PA: Temple University Press. (This seminal environmental philosopher interweaves ethical and ontological questions, and offers a distinctively evolutionary perspective on ecology.)

* Roszak, T. (1973) *Where the Wasteland Ends: Politics and Transcendence in Postindustrial Society*, Garden City, NY: Anchor/Doubleday. (Nature from the viewpoint of the cultural history of the West.)

* —— (1979) *Person/Planet: The Creative Disintegration of Industrial Society*, London: Victor Gollancz. (Cultural study of human identity in light of environmental crisis.)

Rothenberg, D. (1993) *Is it Painful to Think? Conversations with Arne Naess*, Minneapolis, MN: University of Minnesota Press. (Extensive Naess bibliography.)

Taylor, P. (1986) *Respect for Nature*, Princeton, NJ: Princeton University Press. (Chapter 3 is relevant to material in §3 on individual identity from the ecological viewpoint.)

Whitehead, A.N. (1929) *Process and Reality: An Essay in Cosmology*, New York: Macmillan, and Cambridge: Cambridge University Press; corrected edn, with comparative readings and detailed index, by D.R. Griffin and D.W. Sherburne, New York: The Free Press, 1978. (Whitehead's central work in speculative metaphysics, presented in axiomatized form with extensive applications.)

FREYA MATHEWS

ECOLOGY

Philosophers of science have paid relatively little attention to ecology (compared to other areas of biology like evolution and genetics), but ecology poses many interesting foundational and methodological problems. For example, the problems of clarifying the differences and causal connections between the various levels of the ecological hierarchy (organism, population, community, ecosystem...); the issue of how central evolutionary biology is to ecology; long-standing issues concerning the extent to which the domain of ecology is more law-governed or more a matter of historical contingency, and the related question of whether ecologists should rely more on laboratory/manipulative versus field/comparative methods of investigation.

1   **The ecological hierarchy**
2   **Superorganisms**
3   **Methodological issues**

1   The ecological hierarchy

Ecology is most often characterized as the study of the 'distribution and abundance of organisms'. For example, ecologists ask, what biotic factors (for example, predation, interspecific competition for resources) and/or abiotic factors (for example, climate) are responsible for the presence or absence of a species in a particular location, or for the diversity of species in a particular area? More specifically (to pose a few famous ecological questions), why are there so many different species on the face of the earth? Are there just as many species as there are niches (and what are 'niches', anyway)? Why are there so many different species of plankton in a lake? Why are big, fierce animals rare?

Ecology is also characterized in terms of the hierarchy of entities that constitute its domain: organisms, populations (for example, the population of a particular species of bass in a lake), communities (for example, the interacting populations of bass, minnows and plankton in a lake), ecosystems (for example, the lake, including the bass, minnows and plankton),... the biosphere. (For the sake of comparison or contrast, the genetic/evolutionary hierarchy consists of genes, organisms, populations, species, genera, families, orders, classes... kingdoms.)

The ecological hierarchy imposes or affords two directions of causal analysis for each level. Thus, for example, ecology includes the study of changes in population size as influenced by traits of the organisms that compose the populations ('upward' causation, in the sense of 'up' the hierarchy), and the study of changes in population size in the context of the communities to which the populations belong ('downward' causation). Ecologists study changes in community structure as influenced by the populations that compose the communities, and in the context of the ecosystems to which the communities belong. And so on. Among the most basic foundational issues that arise in ecology are the problems of clarifying the differences and causal connections between the different levels of the ecological hierarchy.

The diversity of spatial and temporal scales associated with the variety of ecological entities and processes is also an important consideration in many of the foundational and methodological issues that arise in ecology. Consider for instance the difficulty in characterizing the nature of 'communities' – a maple-birch forest together with the deer that inhabit it may be considered one community, and the various interacting species of microorganisms that inhabit the gut of any one of those deer may be considered another community. To make matters more difficult, the species' composition of a community may change over time as new species colonize the area in question and outcompete other species, and so on. At what point do we say that one community has been replaced by another?

2 Superorganisms

The upper levels of the ecological hierarchy have from time to time been conceived quite holistically, even as higher level organisms or 'superorganisms'. For instance, just as organisms of a particular species undergo a fairly regular sequence of developmental stages to adulthood, so too the species' composition of a disturbed area has been thought to undergo a fairly regular sequence of 'successional' stages back to the 'mature' state (for example, from the weedy annuals that first colonize a forest clearing, to the perennial herbs, to the shrubs, and ultimately to the trees that reconstitute the mature forest). Just as individual organisms display self-regulatory abilities (like the ability to maintain body temperature within a narrow range), so too populations, communities and ecosystems have been conceived as having self regulatory properties (like the ability of a population to regulate its size). Just as organisms of different species have distinctive metabolisms, so too different communities and ecosystems have distinctively different energy flows and nutrient cycles. Still more analogies have been pursued.

The superorganism concept was also motivated by methodological considerations. Ecology emerged as a self-conscious discipline in the early twentieth century when the methodological model for biology was experimental physiology, with its emphasis on the repeatable, the manipulable and the verifiable. This was considered the best antidote to excessive interest in evolution, which seemed bound-up with the historically unique, the nonmanipulable and the nonrecoverable. Early ecologists advocated the investigation of superorganisms in the manner in which experimental physiologists investigated organisms.

That is not to say that the superorganism concept is, or was, inherently anti-evolutionary. It has played an important role in 'group selection' theories (see EVOLUTION, THEORY OF; SOCIOBIOLOGY). For example, just as Darwinians have traditionally explained the prevalence of a type of organism in terms of natural selection for organisms of that type, so too some ecologists have explained the prevalence of some types of populations, communities and ecosystems in terms of the selective persistence of systems of those types. Superorganismal, group-selectionist concepts in ecology have been the target of considerable criticism from some evolutionary biologists, who argue that the concepts reflect a lack of understanding of evolution. However, these issues have been a fruitful source of discussion concerning the conceptual relationships of ecology to evolutionary biology (more about the connections between ecology and evolutionary biology later).

Many who have rejected superorganism concepts in ecology have nonetheless also rejected the idea that the higher level entities are merely interacting collections of the lower level components. They have held instead that the lower level components interact in such a way as to contribute to the integrity of the upper level entity. So for example, communities and ecosystems are understood by many to be integrated into food webs, which are in turn structured largely by predator–prey relations and interspecific competition for available prey/resources. This integrity has been characterized most generally as 'stability'. But this stability has proved difficult to characterize in a general way. Numerous variants of the concept have been elaborated: neighbourhood stability, global stability, dynamic stability, bounded stability, cyclic stability, trajectory stability, resistance, resiliency, constancy, elasticity, persistence, inertia, and more. Compounding the difficulty of specifying the nature of the integrity of higher level ecological entities is the scale – temporal and spatial – at which, and during which, the supposed stability is maintained.

3 Methodological issues

Proponents of the importance of evolutionary thinking in ecology have emphasized the role of natural selection in contributing to community and ecosystem integrity and stability. That is, to the extent that natural selection results in the mutual adaptation of the member species of a community, the community becomes a more integrated and stable whole. Arguments for the importance of evolutionary thinking in ecology have hinged on several issues, one of which concerns 'evolutionary time' versus 'ecological time'. Ecological time is often considered much shorter – too short for ecological processes to be influenced by evolutionary changes. Proponents of the importance of evolutionary thinking in ecology have challenged the distinction, arguing, for example, that evolution by natural selection occurs in a short enough time period to have a significant effect on the outcome of an ecological process. Consider for instance an ecological process like interspecific competition for resources. One possible outcome would be extirpation of one of the species from the area – a purely ecological phenomenon. But this is not the only possible outcome: one of the species could evolve in a direction that allows its members to make use of a resource not utilized by the other species. In this case, evolution would allow both species to coexist within a community.

The connections between ecology and economics may be as significant as the connections between ecology and evolutionary biology. Those connections are well evidenced by the importance within ecology of such concepts as resource, competition, consumer, producer, productivity, efficiency, energy budget, guild, and so on.

One of the major conceptual divides in ecology has been between those who view upper level entities of the ecological hierarchy as real entities having some characterizable integrity, and those who view the upper levels more as combinations of populations that coincidentally migrated to the same area and that coincidentally have the same range of environmental tolerances. Of course, this is a continuum, not a strict dichotomy of outlooks. Not only might any particular community lie between the extremes, but some communities might lie more towards one end of the spectrum, while other communities lie towards the other end. But many ecologists have pursued (and continue to pursue) the extremes.

Associated with this difference in perspective are other conceptual and methodological differences. Proponents of the more holistic viewpoint have tended to emphasize and focus on optimal equilibrium states in which higher level entities persist, and/or towards which they develop, and/or towards which they return when disturbed. Proponents of equilibrium viewpoints tend to belittle the importance of historical contingency, inasmuch as equilibrium states can be reached by different routes. Proponents of the alternative viewpoint tend to question the reality of equilibrium states, and stress the importance of historical contingencies. Although, again, this is a continuum of perspectives, not a strict dichotomy. And once again, the temporal and spatial scale of the investigation is relevant to the apparent importance of historical accident. While ecology distanced itself from history in its early days, and while leading ecologists continued to stress the differences between ecology and the historical sciences through the 1970s, there are now calls for a 'new ecology' that takes historical contingency more seriously.

Discussions of the merits and implications of historical contingency versus equilibrium approaches often involve discussions of the predictiveness and nomic status of ecological theory. That is, to the extent that historical contingency prevails, it has been suggested, ecological theory will be less predictive and less law-like. Equilibrium theories are not the only way to bring predictiveness and law-like order to ecology; but they have long been held as the best hope. After all, equilibrium points are by definition predictable/inevitable as long as specifiable 'disturbing' conditions do not obtain. Equilibrium specifications thus have just the right form for *ceteris paribus* laws.

A re-evaluation of the importance of historical contingency is also occurring in evolutionary biology. In ecology, as in evolutionary biology, concerns about history have led to discussions of methodology, and to criticism of the idea that the only proper methodological models are laboratory-based sciences such as particle physics and molecular biology. While ecology aligned itself methodologically with laboratory experimental physiology in its early days, it has recently been suggested that it might as well or better model itself on historical disciplines like astronomy and geology (see GEOLOGY, PHILOSOPHY OF). A wide range of experimental methodologies, from laboratory to field, and from manipulative to comparative, is employed in such disciplines and seems to have an important place in ecology as well.

See also: ECOLOGICAL PHILOSOPHY; ENVIRONMENTAL ETHICS; HOLISM AND INDIVIDUALISM IN HISTORY AND SOCIAL SCIENCE; SPECIES; TAXONOMY

References and further reading

Diamond, J. and Case, T.J. (eds) (1986) *Community Ecology*, New York: Harper & Row. (Still a fairly state-of-the-art collection of essays addressing and exhibiting the 'plurality' of theories and methods appropriate to understanding this central level of the ecological hierarchy. Included are excellent essays on the equilibrium/law versus the nonequilibrium/history continuum of theories, and the laboratory manipulation versus field/comparative continuum of methodologies.)

Hagen, J.B. (1992) *An Entangled Bank: The Origins of Ecosystem Ecology*, New Brunswick, NJ: Rutgers University Press. (An historical introduction to foundational issues in community and ecosystems ecology.)

Keller, E.F. and Lloyd, E.A. (eds) (1992) *Keywords in Evolutionary Biology*, Cambridge, MA: Harvard University Press. (Includes entries for a number of ecological concepts, including 'Community', 'Competition', 'Environment', 'Group Selection', 'Niche', 'Resource', 'Unit of Selection'.)

Kingsland, S.E. (1985) *Modelling Nature: Episodes in the History of Population Ecology*, Chicago, IL: University of Chicago Press. (A historical introduction to foundational and methodological issues in population ecology; the 'Afterword' to the second edition, 1996, includes a discussion of the new emphasis of history in ecology.)

Kormondy, E.J. (ed.) (1965) *Readings in Ecology*, Englewood Cliffs, NJ: Prentice Hall. (A nice collection of classic papers, with short commentaries.)

McIntosh, R.P. (1985) *The Background of Ecology: Concept and Theory*, Cambridge: Cambridge University Press. (A comprehensive survey – somewhat historical, somewhat philosophical – of foundational and methodological issues in ecology.)

Peters, R.H. (1991) *A Critique for Ecology*, Cambridge: Cambridge University Press. (A somewhat old-fashioned but comprehensive criticism of – rather than an attempt to understand – the level of generality and predictiveness in ecology.)

Real, L.A. and Brown, J.H. (eds) (1991) *Foundations of Ecology: Classic Papers with Commentaries*, Chicago, IL: University of Chicago Press. (Just as the title says.)

Shrader-Frechette, K.S. and McCoy, E.D. (1993) *Method in Ecology: Strategies for Conservation*, Cambridge: Cambridge University Press. (Discussion of difficulties surrounding the concepts of 'community' and 'stability', as well as the problems of generalization in ecology.)

JOHN BEATTY

ECONOMIC APPROACH TO LAW *see* LAW, ECONOMIC APPROACH TO

ECONOMICS AND ETHICS

Unlike many other sciences, economics is linked both to ethics and to the theory of rationality. Although many economists regard economics as a 'positive' science of one sort of social phenomena, economics is built around a normative theory of rationality, and has a special relevance to policy making and the criticism of social institutions. Economics complements and intersects with moral philosophy in both the concepts it has constructed and in its treatment of normative problems.

Fundamental to modern economics is its conception of human beings as rational agents, whose choices are determined by complete and transitive preferences. Although economists stress the usefulness of this notion of rationality in explaining human behaviour, rationality is clearly also a normative notion. The mathematical tools economists have developed to represent and study the implications of rational action in collective and interactive contexts are thus of immediate relevance to moral philosophers.

Also of interest to moral philosophy is the problematic attempt in welfare economics to fashion a normative theory of economic institutions and policies around the goal of helping people satisfy their subjective preferences. This project relies, controversially, on equating people's wellbeing with the degree of satisfaction of their subjective preferences; an individual's 'utility' on this view is no more than an index of how well their subjective preferences are satisfied. Furthermore, since most welfare economists assume that there is no meaningful way to compare degrees of preference satisfaction across people, the project also requires a scheme for weighing the effectiveness of alternative economic arrangements in satisfying preferences without weighing the comparative satisfaction levels of different individuals. Central to the project is Pareto optimality – the notion of an 'efficient' arrangement as one in which no individual can achieve higher preference satisfaction without someone else undergoing a reduction in their satisfaction level.

Economic policies and institutions can be appraised in terms of a variety of values other than efficiency. Notable both in historical and contemporary discussions are the values of liberty, justice and equality. Since a large part of economics is carried out with a view to its possible application to policy, ethics has a significant part to play in economics. By the same token, economics may be of great importance to ethics, both through its exploration of consequences and through the development of mathematical and conceptual tools.

1 **Rationality**
2 **Utility theory and welfare**
3 **Alternative views of wellbeing**

1 Rationality

At the foundation of both positive and normative economics lies a normative theory of individual rationality (see RATIONAL CHOICE THEORY). The theory is very thin, because it raises no questions about the rationality of ultimate ends and few questions about the rationality of beliefs. The standard view of rationality concerns only the internal completeness and consistency of an individual's preferences and the connection between preference and choice. In 'revealed-preference theory' preferences are derived from choices, and rationality is in effect taken to be a condition on choices (actions) only. In the standard theory of rationality (and implicitly in revealed-preference theory, too), preferences are subjective states that lead to actions.

An agent A chooses (acts) rationally if A's preferences are rational, and A never prefers an available option to the option chosen. A's preferences are rational only if they are complete and transitive. A's preferences are transitive if and only if, for all options x, y, and z, if A prefers x to y and y to z, then A prefers x to z. The same stands where A is indifferent. Transitivity is a plausible, although not completely uncontroversial, requirement of rationality. A's preferences are complete if, for all options x and y, either A prefers x to y, or A prefers y to x, or A is indifferent between x and y. If A's preferences are complete, then A is never unable to rank x and y. It is questionable whether completeness is a condition of rationality.

If an agent's preferences are rational, one can assign numbers to the objects of preference. These numbers, which are arbitrary apart from their order, merely indicate preference ranking. They are 'ordinal utilities', and the theory of rationality may be restated: agents are rational if and only if their preferences may be represented by ordinal utility functions, and their choices maximize utility. (Representation by a continuous utility function presupposes an additional technical condition.) One should avoid saying that they act 'in order to maximize utility'. In contemporary economic theory, utility is merely an index or indicator. It is not a substantive aim or an object of preference. One cannot sensibly pursue utility or take more or less utility in exchange for more or less of some genuine object of preference. Maximizing utility is just doing what one most prefers to do.

This standard theory of rationality is silent concerning what to do in circumstances of risk or uncertainty. Someone who prefers $10 to $5 but who prefers a gamble with a $5 prize to an identical gamble with a $10 prize violates none of the axioms of the standard theory (see RISK). To extend the standard theory requires (apart from additional technical conditions) one further substantive axiom, the so-called 'independence condition' or 'sure-thing principle'. This condition says that when an individual faces a choice between two bets that are identical except for one prize, then they will prefer the bet with the preferred prize. When one's preferences satisfy this additional independence condition, then they can be represented by an 'expected utility function'. Such functions have three important features. First, the expected utility of a lottery, $U(L)$, that pays off R with probability p and S with probability $(1-p)$ is $pU(R) + (1-p)U(S)$. Second, if U and U' are expected utility functions representing the preferences of an agent, then $U' = aU + b$, where a is a real number greater than zero and b is any real number. Expected utility functions are thus said to be 'unique up to a positive affine transformation'. Third, the requirement that subjective degrees of belief conform to the axioms of the probability calculus is implicit in the application of expected utility theory in conditions of uncertainty. Hence expected utility theory also contains a thin theory of rational belief. Expected utilities, like ordinal utilities, only provide information concerning preference and are not themselves goals or objects of preference. In expected utility theory, as in ordinal utility theory, choice is determined by preference.

The standard views of rationality and the theorems that permit their mathematical representation provide a framework in which to pose questions about the relations between morality and rationality. Their importance to moral philosophy depends in addition on the links between this view of rationality and a particular view of welfare.

2 Utility theory and welfare

All plausible moral views assign an important place to individual wellbeing. This is most obviously true of utilitarianism, which takes morality as maximizing some function of the welfare of individual members of society (see UTILITARIANISM §§1–3). Non-utilitarian views that emphasize notions of rights, fairness and justice also need a conception of human wellbeing. These views not only recognize the virtue of benevolence, which requires some notion of human good, but even their core notions make reference to wellbeing. Thus, for example, justice is understood in terms of treating the interests of different persons properly, and acting rightly often involves avoiding harm to other individuals. Notions of harm and of interest are plainly connected to notions of human wellbeing.

Given the commitments of economists to utility theory in explaining human choices, it is natural that they would look also to levels of utility or of preference satisfaction as the fundamental measure of human wellbeing for evaluative purposes. And indeed it is easy to reason as follows. Rational people have complete and transitive preference rankings and choose from among the available alternatives what they most prefer. Rational people also choose from the available options whatever they believe to be best. If one assumes in addition (as is common in positive economics) that individuals have correct beliefs and that they are self-interested, then it follows that (among the available options) what rational people most prefer is what rational people choose, which is the same thing as what is best for them. In other words, wellbeing is the satisfaction of preference.

Philosophers are less happy than economists with the idealization involved in assuming correct beliefs, and they are less convinced that people are always self-interested. Hence, they generally reject a view of welfare as the satisfaction of actual preferences. A view of welfare as the satisfaction of 'informed' and self-interested preferences is however common in contemporary philosophy and suffices to make the tools and explorations of economists relevant to philosophical concerns (see WELFARE §1).

As both economists and philosophers have noticed, preference-satisfaction theories of wellbeing are problematic, even if one insists that the preferences be informed and self-directed. For preferences that are not based on indisputably false beliefs may nevertheless be based on highly contestable beliefs. Even if the preferences of people who beg for money to make a sacrifice to their god are well-informed, others may question whether satisfying them will make these people better off. If the notion of individual wellbeing is to be employed in weighing the strength of claims for social provision, it must permit reasoned social agreement on basic components of wellbeing and on the relative 'urgency' of claims to different goods (Scanlon 1975). One might acknowledge a moral obligation to feed such people, but not to finance their worship.

There are other reasons, too, to question whether the conception of wellbeing as the satisfaction of preferences is suitable for assessing claims to scarce resources. For example, a person who has cultivated a taste for exotic foods may be miserable without them and, in one sense, worse off than someone in similar circumstances who delights in junk food. But one may

question whether social policy should be responsive to such preferences. Similarly, it is questionable whether satisfying racist, sadistic and other antisocial preferences should count as contributing to individual wellbeing. Also of concern are 'adaptive preferences' and the effects of culture on preferences (Elster 1983; Sen 1987). For example, women who are systematically denied roles in public life, or equal shares of consumption goods, may learn not to want what they have not got. Their utility may be reasonably high, but objectively their level of wellbeing may be low.

Despite these difficulties, most economists prefer to cling to a preference-satisfaction view as a reasonable approximation. Philosophical proponents of these views (for example, Griffin 1986) have worked hard to deflect some of the objections and have defended the view that wellbeing is the satisfaction of 'informed' or 'rational' preferences. The commitment most economists have to a preference-satisfaction view derives from the links between a preference-satisfaction view of welfare and the explanatory uses of utility theory, and it is strengthened by the strong aversion many economists feel to anything that smacks of paternalism. Even though recognizing that individuals may be wrong about what is good for them does not imply that one should support paternalistic policies; it permits the question of paternalism to come up.

3 Alternative views of wellbeing

On the other hand, the difficulties with a subjective preference-satisfaction view of wellbeing have led many philosophers and a few economists to propose different conceptions of wellbeing: traditional hedonistic views and hybrids such as Sidgwick's (1901) view that certain mental states are intrinsically good yet are good because they are intrinsically desired, 'perfectionist' views in which the desires that count and their weight depend on the objective value of their objects (Griffin 1986; Parfit 1984; Raz 1986), Rawls' 'primary goods' (1971) and Amartya Sen's 'capabilities' (1987, 1992).

In Sen's view, a capability is the ability to achieve a certain sort of 'functioning' – literacy is a capability; reading is a functioning. People may value capabilities for their own sake as well as for the functionings they permit – you are glad to know you can walk around even if you are inclined to stay put. In Sen's view, preference satisfaction is too crude and too insensitive to the variety of values to serve as the basis for social evaluation. Rawls' primary-goods approach also fails to include a wide-enough range of relevant 'capabilities'. In focusing on primary social goods, Sen argues that it leaves out more internal features of persons' circumstances, such as physical handicaps, which may profoundly affect wellbeing. Rawls' account also may not work well for comparing the wellbeing of persons who are much above the minimum.

Sen's alternative is to define wellbeing in terms of the set of functionings a person achieves. Being well nourished is an example of a functioning whose achievement may be impaired either by internal obstacles (such as a digestive disorder) or external ones (a lack of money to buy food). Functionings are of course a vector (being well nourished, reading books, sleeping well) and combining them into a measure of wellbeing requires settling on the relative weight to be given to different capabilities and functionings. Obviously the problems of weighing different capabilities and functionings are serious. But even if they are insuperable and it turns out that focusing on capabilities and functionings sometimes leaves one unable to rank social alternatives, such an approach still leads one to focus on the morally relevant features of social alternatives. Particularly in the context of poor people and poor countries, measuring the extent of certain basic capabilities, like literacy or health-related capabilities, may be an effective way of gauging levels of wellbeing.

One important advantage of more objective approaches is that they avoid the problems of interpersonal comparison that derive from identifying wellbeing and utility (construed as an index of preference satisfaction). Formerly, economists such as Pigou (1920) argued that overall welfare would be maximized by equalizing incomes as much as was consistent with retaining incentives to produce. Citing diminishing marginal utility of income, they maintained (not implausibly), that $100 contributes less to the wellbeing of someone with an income of $50,000 than to the wellbeing of someone with an income of $5,000. Other things being equal, a more equal distribution of income would increase total welfare.

This argument supposes that one can compare the contributions income makes to the wellbeing of different people. Once one takes seriously the preference-satisfaction view of wellbeing, these comparisons become problematic. Lionel Robbins (1932) argued compellingly that since preference rankings are entirely subjective and introspective, there is no way to compare where A is in A's preference ranking with where B is in B's ranking. The fact that people nevertheless make interpersonal comparisons of wellbeing depends, Robbins argues, on the value judgment that the preferences of people in similar circumstances are similarly satisfied. (One might instead question whether these comparisons of wellbeing are comparisons of preference satisfaction.)

Robbins' argument did not convince everyone. One

approach has been to build up interpersonal welfare judgments from individual judgments of the form: 'I would prefer to be person P with consumption bundle x than Q with consumption bundle y' (see Kolm 1972 and Harsanyi 1977). If there is widespread agreement among individuals on such extended preferences, they can be used to construct interpersonally comparable welfare measures. Alternatively such 'extended preferences' may summarize what a perfected psychological theory would say about the relationship between the causal factors that lead people to have the preferences they have and the states of the world that satisfy preferences.

Although preference-satisfaction views of welfare do permit one to make use of the technical apparatus economists have developed, one should note the many problematic features of such views. The identification of wellbeing with the satisfaction of preferences is questionable in itself. It gives rise to serious problems of interpersonal comparisons. It is biased by adaptive preferences, and it fails to link up with the normative terms of policy debate.

4 Efficiency and Pareto optimality

Economists have given the common-sense notion of 'efficiency' a precise technical meaning: adopt the metric of utility (preference satisfaction) to measure a person's wellbeing. Consider some allocation of resources which yields a certain distribution of utility. A different allocation is a 'Pareto improvement' if and only if it makes at least one person better off (in terms of preference satisfaction) and makes no one worse off. An allocation is 'efficient' or 'Pareto optimal' if no other allocation is a Pareto improvement compared to it. In other words, in a Pareto optimal allocation, every alternative that satisfies someone's preferences better leads to someone else's preferences being less well satisfied. The great attraction of this notion for economists is that it permits a partial ranking of resource allocations or of social states which is responsive to individual preferences without employing any interpersonal comparisons of utility.

If one is minimally benevolent and favours making people better off, then, other things being equal, one should favour prospects that are better for someone and worse for no one. If in addition one identifies being better off with having a higher utility, then (other things being equal) one will endorse Pareto improvements and Pareto optimal allocations. Moreover, one can offer an argument in terms of these concepts for regarding a perfectly competitive equilibrium as a sort of moral ideal, other things being equal. What economists call 'the first welfare theorem' shows that competitive equilibria under certain idealized conditions (no externalities, no public goods, no informational limits, and so on) are Pareto efficient. Minimal benevolence then implies that competitive equilibria are (other things being equal) morally good economic states, and that market failures are bad. Furthermore, the 'second welfare theorem' shows that an efficient economic outcome producing any desired distribution of welfare can be attained by the workings of a competitive market, given the right initial distribution of endowments to agents. So with no ethical premise more controversial than minimal beneficence, albeit with a controversial conception of individual wellbeing, economists can offer moral evaluations along one significant dimension.

However, the Pareto principle may be unappealing when it involves honouring people's intrusive preferences regarding others' consumption patterns or levels of wellbeing. Moreover, it has been shown that the Pareto principle is inconsistent with the conjunction of individual and collective rationality in conditions of uncertainty (Seidenfeld *et al.* 1989). The problem lies in the fact that unanimity in individual rankings may rest on disagreements in subjective probability judgments and disagreements in preferences among options involving no uncertainty. Should unanimity in individual preference for *A* over *B* require that *A* be judged better, if the unanimity depends on disagreements in values and probability judgments? Quite apart from these problems, the Pareto principle has very limited applicability, since economic changes usually involve winners and losers. Economists have been reluctant to accept these severe limitations and have struggled for many years over the issue of whether, without invoking interpersonal utility comparisons, some device could be found that would permit judgments in cases involving trade-offs among individuals. The hope was that one could find a way to endorse 'potential Pareto improvements', in which the gains to the winners were sufficient to compensate the losers in utility terms, without actually making the compensation (Hicks 1939; Kaldor 1939). The conclusion has been that no such blanket endorsement is possible, partly owing to technical failings in the proposed devices for identifying 'improvements', but more fundamentally because there simply is no way to judge changes that affect distributions while remaining neutral on distributive questions (Little 1957; Streeten 1953; Samuelson 1950). But to stop here would leave welfare economists with little to say, and practical applications of welfare economics in the form of cost–benefit analysis need to go on (see Pareto principle).

The difficulties seem to have been dealt with in two ways. One is by increasing modesty: one cannot

always endorse potential Pareto improvements, but at least economists can identify them and leave the endorsing to politicians. Second, it seems that welfare economists have moved implicitly towards reuniting considerations of efficiency and equity. Blanket endorsements of potential Pareto improvements are unjustifiable, but since there are various theoretical ways to adjust such measures for equity concerns, one can suggest that equity-adjusted potential Pareto improvements can consistently be endorsed. (Stimulated partly by an interest in making inequality comparisons and equity judgments more precise, economists have devoted extensive energy to developing a variety of statistical techniques for measuring and describing inequality (Sen 1992).) Economists remain queasy about the final step of actually endorsing any one way of adjusting for equity concerns.

5 Economics and 'moral mathematics'

There are currently many areas in which the tools and theories of economists have contributed to moral philosophy. The two areas of economics that have been of the most immediate relevance to moral philosophy have been social choice theory and game theory (see Social choice theory §3; Rational choice theory §§2–3). Economists and philosophers have used social choice theory and game theory mainly to investigate questions concerning the aggregation of individual preferences and judgments and concerning justice in social coordination and bargaining. But the tools of economics may apply to a much wider range of ethical issues. For example, there has been an energetic debate concerning conceptions of equality that has depended on formal concepts and arguments developed by economists (see Equality). When two individuals do not have exactly the same bundles of commodities, what could economic equality mean? One answer is 'welfarist': economic equality is equality of preference satisfaction. But economists seek to avoid making interpersonal utility comparisons, and it is questionable whether egalitarians should be concerned to equalize welfare. Another way to give sense to the notion of equality is to suppose that individuals acquired their different commodity bundles by means of voluntary exchanges beginning from a situation in which all had identical bundles (Dworkin 1981). In that case the allocation will be 'envy-free' in the sense that no one will prefer the commodity bundle of anyone else. It is then possible to investigate formally a number of questions: when will envy-free allocations exist? When will they be Pareto optimal? What sorts of events will upset or preserve the envy-freeness of a distribution? Is there any alternative formal characterization of equality? Here is an area in which inquiries of moral philosophers and economists are closely interwoven. There are others, too, ranging from John Roemer's (1988) formal explorations into concepts of exploitation to recent work attempting to give a formal characterization of freedom.

6 Conclusion

Economists and moral philosophers share interests in rationality and in the evaluation and criticism of social institutions. Although the theoretical precommitments and starting points of scholars trained in these disciplines are often different, the two subjects have a great deal to offer one another. To the extent that moral philosophers want to bring their work to bear on the criticism and reform of social institutions, they have much to learn from economists, who have long been concerned with working out the consequences of alternative policies and with finding operational measures of theoretical concepts. Economists offer moral philosophers a range of powerful tools. At the same time, economists concerned with evaluating institutions and policies can hardly avoid a concern with ethics.

See also: DECISION AND GAME THEORY; ECONOMICS, PHILOSOPHY OF; GUANZI; MARKET, ETHICS OF THE

References and further reading

Buchanan, A.E. (1985) *Ethics, Efficiency, and the Market*, Totowa, NJ: Rowman & Allanheld. (A discussion of ethics and economics by a contemporary moral philosopher.)

Dworkin, G., Bermant, G. and Brown, P.G. (eds) (1977) *Markets and Morals*, Washington, DC: Hemisphere, and New York: Halsted Press. (An anthology of essays on issues in ethics and economics.)

* Dworkin, R. (1981) 'What is Equality? Part 2: Equality of Resources', *Philosophy and Public Affairs* 10 (4): 283–345. (A seminal discussion of equality of resources.)

* Elster, J. (1983) *Sour Grapes: Studies in the Subversion of Rationality*, New York: Cambridge University Press. (A study of the notion of rationality and of failures of rationality.)

Elster, J. and Roemer, J. (eds) (1991) *Interpersonal Comparisons of Wellbeing*, Cambridge: Cambridge University Press. (An anthology of essays on the problems of making interpersonal utility comparisons.)

Gauthier, D. (1986) *Morals by Agreement*, Oxford: Oxford University Press. (An ambitious and influential attempt to derive a theory of justice from bargaining theory.)

* Griffin, J. (1986) *Wellbeing: Its Meaning, Measurement and Moral Importance*, Oxford: Clarendon Press. (A major restatement of utilitarianism arguing for an informed-preference view of wellbeing.)

* Harsanyi, J. (1977) *Rational Behavior and Bargaining Equilibrium in Games and Social Situations*, Cambridge: Cambridge University Press. (A general development of rational choice theory and game theory with a systematic discussion of interpersonal utility comparisons.)

Hausman, D. and McPherson, M. (1993) 'Taking Ethics Seriously: Economics and Contemporary Moral Philosophy', *Journal of Economic Literature* 31 (2): 671–731. (A comprehensive survey of literature on ethics and economics.)

Hausman, D. and McPherson, M. (1996) *Economic Analysis and Moral Philosophy*, Cambridge: Cambridge University Press. (A nontechnical introduction to major issues in economics and ethics.)

* Hicks, J. (1939) 'The Foundations of Welfare Economics', *Economic Journal* 49 (196): 696–712. (A classic statement of 'new welfare economics' based on the compensation criterion.)

* Kaldor, N. (1939) 'Welfare Propositions of Economics and Interpersonal Comparisons of Utility', *Economic Journal* 49 (195): 549–52. (The first presentation and application of the notion of a potential Pareto improvement.)

* Kolm, S.-C. (1972) *Justice et équité* (Justice and Equality), Paris: Éditions du Centre National de la Recherche Scientifique. (A groundbreaking work, with the first systematic treatment of extended sympathy judgments.)

* Little, I. (1957) *A Critique of Welfare Economics*, Oxford: Oxford University Press, 2nd edn. (A classic discussion of the difficulties of welfare economics without interpersonal comparisons.)

McClennen, E. (1990) *Rationality and Dynamic Choice: Foundational Explorations*, Cambridge: Cambridge University Press. (A general development of the theory of rational choice, including a critique of the standard theory and the development of an alternative theory.)

* Parfit, D. (1984) *Reasons and Persons*, Oxford: Oxford University Press. (A major study of relations between rationality, personal identity and consequentialism.)

* Pigou, A.C. (1920) *The Economics of Welfare*, London: Macmillan. (The classic statement of traditional utilitarian welfare economics.)

* Rawls, J. (1971) *A Theory of Justice*, Cambridge, MA:

Harvard University Press. (A development of a contractualist theory of justice and the most important work of social philosophy of the last century.)

* Raz, J. (1986) *The Morality of Freedom*, Oxford: Oxford University Press. (A defence of liberalism and perfectionism.)

* Robbins, L. (1932) *An Essay on the Nature and Significance of Economic Science*, London: Macmillan; 2nd edn, 1935. (A major methodology overview with a classical argument in chapter 6 against the possibility of interpersonal comparisons.)

* Roemer, J. (1988) *Free to Lose*, Cambridge, MA: Harvard University Press. (An accessible introduction to Roemer's analytically sophisticated restatement of themes in Marxian economics and social philosophy.)

* Samuelson, P.A. (1950) 'Evaluation of Real National Income', *Oxford Economic Papers*, new series, 2 Jan (1): 1–29. (A technical demonstration of the impossibility of disentangling efficiency and distributional questions.)

* Scanlon, T. (1975) 'Preference and Urgency', *Journal of Philosophy* 72 (22): 655–70. (An argument that questions of justice cannot be decided only by considerations involving preference satisfaction.)

* Seidenfeld, T., Kadane, J. and Schervish, M. (1989) 'On the Shared Preferences of Two Bayesian Decision Makers', *Journal of Philosophy* 86 (5): 225–44. (Proof of the inconsistency of individual and social Bayesian rationality in circumstances of uncertainty.)

Sen, A.K. (1982) *Choice, Welfare and Measurement*, Cambridge, MA: MIT Press. (This collection of essays contains many of Sen's principal earlier contributions to ethics and welfare economics.)

* —— (1987) *On Ethics and Economics*, Oxford: Blackwell. (A concise and lucid but demanding introduction to the subject.)

* —— (1992) *Inequality Reexamined*, Cambridge, MA: Harvard University Press. (An introduction to Sen's more recent work on inequality, capabilities and welfare.)

Sen, A. and Williams, B. (eds) (1982) *Utilitarianism and Beyond*, Cambridge: Cambridge University Press. (An influential and useful anthology of essays on economics and ethics, with particular reference to utilitarianism.)

* Sidgwick, H. (1901) *The Methods of Ethics*, London: Macmillan, 6th edn. (One of the most important works in ethics of the past two centuries, containing a classical restatement and defence of utilitarianism.)

* Streeten, P. (1953) 'Appendix: Recent Controversies', in G. Myrdal *The Political Element in the Development of Economic Theory*, trans. P. Streeten, London: Routledge & Kegan Paul, 208–17. (A brief overview of the interdependence of questions of efficiency and distribution.)

DANIEL HAUSMAN
MICHAEL S. McPHERSON

ECONOMICS, PHILOSOPHY OF

People have thought about economics for as long as they have thought about how to manage their households, indeed Aristotle compared the study of the economic affairs of a city to the study of the management of a household. During the two millennia between Aristotle and Adam Smith, one finds reflections concerning economic problems mainly in the context of discussions of moral or policy questions. For example, scholastic philosophers commented on money and interest in inquiries concerning the justice of 'usury' (charging interest on money loans), and in the seventeenth century there was a great deal of discussion of policy concerning foreign trade. Economics only emerged as a distinct field of study with the bold eighteenth-century idea that there were 'economies' – that is autonomous law-governed systems of human interaction involving production, distribution and exchange. This view was already well developed in Adam Smith's Wealth of Nations, *from which much of economics derives.*

Economics is of philosophical interest in three main regards: it raises moral questions concerning welfare, justice and freedom; it raises foundational questions concerning the nature of rationality; and it raises methodological or epistemological questions concerning the character and possibility of knowledge of social phenomena. The fundamental theory of standard orthodox economics is of particular epistemological interest because of its resemblance to theories in the natural sciences coupled with its uneven empirical performance.

More than 150 years ago John Stuart Mill confronted the problem of how to reconcile his high regard for economics (despite its empirical adequacies) with his commitment to empiricism. His solution, which was accepted by most economists until the 1930s, held that the basic principles of economics are well established by introspection or everyday experience. One can thus justifiably have confidence in economics, despite the inexactness of its implications, which is only to be expected, since economics deals only with the most important determinants of economic phenomena.

In the 1930s Mill's views were rejected as too dogmatic and insufficiently empirical. But the views that succeeded Mill's during the generation after the Second World War, most notably the position of Milton Friedman and views deriving from the work of Karl Popper and Imre Lakatos, were less able to deal satisfactorily with the empirical inadequacies of economic theories than were Mill's. Since the mid 1980s there have been several new approaches, ranging from Donald McCloskey's rejection of methodological assessment at one extreme to Alexander Rosenberg's conclusion that economics cannot be a successful empirical science at the other.

1   **What is economics?**
2   **Why is economics of philosophical interest?**
3   **Classic discussions of philosophical foundations**
4   **Milton Friedman's views**
5   **Popperian perspectives**
6   **Contemporary directions in economic methodology**
7   **Conclusions**

1   What is economics?

Contemporary economics is divided into many schools and branches. The main 'orthodox', 'neoclassical', or 'neo-Walrasian' school models economic outcomes as equilibria in which individuals have done as well for themselves as they could given their preferences and the constraints on their choices. Common to all branches of orthodox economics are standard assumptions concerning technological possibilities and individual choice. Production is subject to diminishing returns to additional units of any given input, other inputs held constant, and is assumed not to show increasing returns to scale. The rational choices of individual agents are constrained by their initial endowment with resources and goods and by the technological possibilities. Agents are rational in the sense that their choices are determined by their preferences, which are complete and transitive. An agent's preferences are complete if they can rank all alternatives. An agent's preferences are transitive if for all alternatives x, y and z, they prefer x to z, whenever they prefer x to y and y to z (and similarly for indifference). Agents are typically assumed to want more consumption or leisure for their households and greater net returns for their firms. In competitive markets it is assumed that firms and individuals cannot influence prices, but economists and game theorists are also interested in strategic interactions, in which the rational choices of separate individuals are interdependent.

Orthodox economics has four main branches and many sub-specialities. The view of economic phenomena as equilibria resulting from constrained rational individual choice has a greater prominence in some branches and subspecialities than in others. It is central in the most theoretical branch, which consists of microeconomics, general equilibrium theory and game theory. Econometrics, in contrast, is as much statistics as economics. It uses data and statistical techniques to determine the values of parameters and to test specific models. Macroeconomics, the third branch, is concerned with whole economies and particularly with the causes of the business cycle and economic growth. In John Maynard Keynes' *General Theory* (1936) its links with individual choice are tenuous. Contemporary economists in contrast have defended alternative macroeconomic theories in which the view of economic phenomena as equilibria resulting from constrained rational choices is central. The fourth branch, consisting of orthodox work in 'applied economics' (which is what most economists do), is consistent with the general theoretical picture of economic equilibrium, but applied theories make further simplifications to facilitate application. Within particular sub-specialities, such as international trade theory, labour economics or financial economics, one may find work lying along all of the four main branches.

There are also many other schools of economics. Austrian economists accept orthodox views of choices and constraints, but they emphasize uncertainty and question whether one should regard outcomes as equilibria. Institutionalist economists question the value of abstract general theorizing. They emphasize the importance of generalizations concerning norms and behaviour within particular institutions. Applied work in orthodox economics is sometimes very similar to applied institutionalist economics. Marxian economists traditionally articulated and developed Karl Marx's economic theories, but recently many Marxian economists have revised traditional Marxian concepts and themes with tools borrowed from orthodox economic theory. There are also socioeconomists, behavioural economists, chaos theorists, post-Keynesians, and neo-Ricardians. Within orthodox economics itself, there are also many different schools or approaches, such as agency theorists, the Chicago school, constitutional political economy, new institutional economics, and public choice theory. Economics is not one homogeneous enterprise. This entry will focus on neoclassical economic theory because the orthodox neoclassical school is the best known and most influential and because its central theory has attracted the most philosophical attention.

2   Why is economics of philosophical interest?

Economics has been of philosophical interest in three main regards. First, it raises moral questions concerning freedom, social welfare and justice. Although economists often deny that their theories have ethical content, they are ready with advice about how to make life better. Markets, which are the central institutions with which economics has traditionally been concerned, involve voluntary interactions, yet they are simultaneously mechanisms that regulate individual activities and allocate goods to people. They thus raise intricate moral questions concerning coercion, voluntary action, and social justice (see ECONOMICS AND ETHICS). All of the leading figures in contemporary social and political philosophy comment on and are influenced by work in economics (Hausman and McPherson 1996).

Second, contemporary theoretical economics is largely a theory of rational choice. This may seem surprising, since economics is supposed to be an explanatory and predictive science of the actual interactions among people rather than a normative discipline studying how people ought rationally to choose, but it is indeed a fact. This fact joins the interests of economists to the interests of those philosophers concerned with rational choice (see RATIONAL CHOICE THEORY; SOCIAL CHOICE).

Third, economics raises important questions in philosophy of science. In part this is because all significant cognitive enterprises raise questions for epistemology or philosophy of science. But orthodox theory is of particular methodological interest for seven reasons.

Positive and normative. The extent to which economics appears to be permeated with normative concerns raises methodological questions about the relationships between a positive science (of 'what is') and a normative science (of 'what ought to be'). The standard view is that the positive science of economics, like engineering, helps policy-makers to choose the means to accomplish their ends, but it has no bearing on the choice of ends itself. This view is questionable, because economists have to interpret and articulate the incomplete specifications of goals and constraints provided by policy makers (see VALUE JUDGMENTS IN SOCIAL SCIENCE).

Reasons and causes. It is of philosophical interest that orthodox theoretical economics is as much a theory of rational choices as it is a theory that explains and predicts economic outcomes. Although economists are more interested in the aggregate results of individual choices than in the choices themselves, their theories offer both causal explanations for why individuals choose as they do and

accounts of the reasons for their choices. Embedded within orthodox economics is a specific variant of 'folk psychology', and orthodox economics provides a specific context in which to question whether folk-psychological explanations in terms of reasons can also be causal explanations (see PSYCHOLOGY, THEORIES OF; EXPLANATION IN HISTORY AND SOCIAL SCIENCE).

Naturalism. Of all the social sciences, economics most closely resembles the natural sciences. Economic theories have been axiomatized, and essays and books of economics are full of theorems. Of all the social sciences, only economics boasts a Nobel Prize. Economics is thus a test case for those concerned with the extent of the similarities and differences between the natural and social sciences (see NATURALISM IN SOCIAL SCIENCE §2).

Abstraction and idealization. Economics raises questions concerning the legitimacy of severe abstraction and idealization. For example, economic models often stipulate that everyone is perfectly rational and has perfect information or that commodities are infinitely divisible. Such claims are exaggerations, and they are clearly false. Can good science make such false claims (see SCIENTIFIC REALISM AND SOCIAL SCIENCE)?

Ceteris paribus clauses. Because economists attempt to study economic phenomena as constituting a separate domain, influenced only by a small number of causal factors, the claims of economics are true only *ceteris paribus* – that is, they are true only if there are no interferences or disturbing causes. What are *ceteris paribus* clauses, and when if ever are they legitimate in science (see SOCIAL LAWS)?

Causation. Many important generalizations in economics make causal claims. For example, the law of demand asserts that a price increase will (*ceteris paribus*) diminish the quantity demanded. Yet economists are wary of causal language because of its suggestion that outcomes have single causes and because of difficulties in integrating talk of causation and talk of mutual determination. Econometricians have also been deeply concerned with the possibilities for determining causal relations from statistical evidence and with the relevance of causal relations to the possibility of consistent estimation of parameter values (see CAUSATION §3).

Structure and strategy. During the past generation philosophers of science have been concerned to comprehend the larger theoretical structures that unify and guide research within particular research traditions or research programmes. Since orthodox economics is systematically unified, though not in quite the way that Kuhn (1970) or Lakatos (1970) discuss, it poses interesting puzzles about what guides research. Since the success of orthodox economics is controversial, this 'research tradition' also poses questions about how unified and constrained research ought to be.

These are the seven most significant philosophical issues concerning neoclassical economic theory, and many of these issues arise concerning all schools of economics.

3 Classic discussions of philosophical foundations

Explicit methodological reflection on economics dates back to the 1830s to the work of Nassau Senior (1836) and John Stuart Mill (1836). Their methodological reflections must be understood against the backdrop of the economic theory with which they were familiar. That theory ('classical economics') said comparatively little concerning the choices of consumers and supposed that people seek more wealth and are overly inclined to reproduce. With diminishing returns in agriculture and an increasing population, the rate of return in agriculture (and, given the mobility of capital, elsewhere) will diminish, and the ultimate result will be a stationary state in which profits are low, workers receive subsistence wages, and landlords receive large rents. On account of this view of the future, economics was called 'the dismal science'. Classical economics, like contemporary theory, relied on bold simplifications and it had empirical difficulties. Although populations grew considerably, the rate of return in the nineteenth century did not fall sharply, and wages increased dramatically.

Mill was firmly committed to the economics of his day, yet he was a strict empiricist (see MILL, J.S.; EMPIRICISM §5). Since economics faced such major empirical difficulties, it might appear that Mill would have to change his epistemology or disavow his economics. Call this conflict between empiricism and economics, which arises from the apparent disconfirmations of economics and the difficulty of testing it, 'Mill's problem'. Mill attempted to solve it by maintaining that the basic premises of economics are empirically well established by introspective psychology or by experimental testing of technical claims such as the law of diminishing returns. These well-supported premises state how specific causal factors operate. If the only causal factors influencing economic phenomena were those specified in these premises, then the predictions of economic theory would be correct. But economic phenomena depend on many causal factors that are left out of economic theories. Consequently, the implications are inexact. They are always imprecise, and when the factors left out are of particular importance, the predictions of the theories may be completely mistaken. This inexactness explains why the implications of economic theories are so poorly confirmed, and consequently the problems do not show that there is anything mistaken in the fundamental generalizations of economics. In Mill's view, the empirical confirmation of economic theories is indirect and 'deductive'. It derives from the confirmation of their premises. The inductive method of 'specific experience' cannot be employed because of the multiplicity of causes. Furthermore, since there is no way to incorporate a much larger number of causal factors without destroying the 'separateness' of economics and subsuming it into a general social science, this inexactness is an inevitable feature of economics as a distinct discipline. Economics is unavoidably a science of 'tendencies' only.

Mill's view was tremendously influential until the 1930s, although there were always critics who argued for a more directly empirical approach to assessing economic theories. The most important methodological works of the late nineteenth century, J.E. Cairnes' *The Character and Logical Method of Political Economy* (1875) and John Neville Keynes' *The Scope and Method of Political Economy* (1891) defend Mill's view, and one can still find it clearly expressed in Lionel Robbins' classic *An Essay on the Nature and Significance of Economic Science* (1932). Some have also argued that Mill is, in fact, essentially right (Hausman 1992, chaps 8, 12). But by the 1940s most of those writing on economic methodology had repudiated Mill's view of economics as a separate and inexact science justified by a deductive method.

Methodological challenges to Mill's view before the 1930s came mainly from those working outside the orthodox mainstream. The most important challenge came from the German Historical School in the nineteenth century and from the American Institutionalists in the twentieth century. These critics argued that theories should apply more directly to specific historical circumstances and should be tested more directly through these applications. Members of the German Historical School also questioned whether it is possible to separate a positive economic science from normative issues of policy making. Mill accepts the positive/normative division, though not in quite its modern form, and it is explicit in later followers such as J.N. Keynes. Members of the German Historical School wanted economic theorizing to be more explicitly normative and oriented toward specific historical circumstances and policy recommendations.

Although these objections did not shake the views on theory assessment accepted by mainstream economists, views which remained stable for the century after Mill, changes in philosophical conceptions did accompany the significant changes that occurred during that century in economic theory itself. Neoclassical economics, unlike its classical predecessor, focuses on individual choices, which unavoidably reflect subjective preferences and beliefs. This fact disturbed critics of neoclassical economics, such as Thorstein Veblen, who saw it as a departure from the general trend of science away from teleological concerns and towards objective causal relations (1898). Defenders such as Frank Knight, Ludwig von Mises and Lionel Robbins agreed that the role of subjective factors sets economics apart from the natural sciences. But they denied that the methodological distinctiveness of economics demonstrates any methodological error. Indeed von Mises and his followers saw this peculiarity of economics as a virtue that provides a special certainty to the conclusions of economics (1949). In their view (though not in the view of other so-called 'Austrian' economists such as Hayek), the conclusions of economics are beyond rational dispute, because they result from the privileged access people have to their preferences and beliefs or because they derive from the meaning of rationality (see CERTAINTY).

The neoclassical focus on individual choice also led to a redefinition of the discipline. Mill and the classical economists had seen economics as concerned with specific causal factors – essentially acquisitive motives, diminishing returns, and the propensity to reproduce – which preponderate in a specific domain of social life (1836: 323). Robbins, in contrast, defined economics as 'the science which studies human behaviour as a relationship between ends and scarce means which have alternative uses' (1932: 15). In Robbins' view, economics is not concerned with production, consumption, distribution or exchange as such. It is instead concerned with an aspect of all human action. The causal factors with which economics is concerned – rational self-interest – have a role in all human affairs. This vision of economics has been vindicated to some extent by applications of economic models to matters such as decisions to marry (Becker 1981) and by the development of game theory (see DECISION AND GAME THEORY). To regard the subject matter of economics as an aspect of all human action is nevertheless an exaggeration, since economists continue to focus on a particular domain of social phenomena and on causal factors – such as diminishing returns – that are of particular importance only in that domain.

The methodological reflections of Knight, Robbins, and the Austrians reinforced Mill's views of economics as an inexact science, whose conclusions are credible because they follow deductively from well-established premises. Yet this view of theory

assessment in economics, which was virtually unchallenged within mainstream economics in 1930, was almost without defenders by the end of the 1950s. During this short period economists came to believe that Mill's view of confirmation was insufficiently empirical. Economics could be scientific only if its theories were subjected to empirical testing, and its theories could be rationally acceptable only if they passed these tests. It looks as if economists became familiar with the work of the logical positivists (see LOGICAL POSIVITISM) and applied their views to economics. But there is little solid evidence that the methodological changes were the result of the influence of logical positivism. The general changes in intellectual climate that gave rise to logical positivism may have separately caused this revolution in economic methodology. Books by Lesley Fraser (1937), Terence Hutchison (1938) and Felix Kaufmann (1944) made the case for such a methodological reorientation. Hutchison's was the most influential of these books (probably because of Frank Knight's lengthy attack on Hutchison's views in the *Journal of Political Economy* (1940)). Hutchison had studied in Germany and was familiar with the work of the logical positivists and of Karl Popper, and he complained that statements qualified with vague *ceteris paribus* clauses cannot be refuted.

Paul Samuelson's work on the theory of revealed preference (1938) was especially influential. Samuelson showed that if consumer choices in simplified models satisfy a consistency condition, then it is possible in principle to construct from the choices a preference ordering over commodity bundles. His work thus suggested that it might be possible to reformulate economic theory without relying on hard-to-test claims about subjective states of choosers. In teasing out the 'operationally significant' content of economics from its mentalistic formulation, one might be able to make economics conform to demanding empiricist strictures. Samuelson was himself more influenced by the work of scientists such as Gibbs and Bridgman than by the logical positivists, and his own view of methodology (1963), which essentially repudiates all generalizations that are not themselves separately and directly testable, is more extreme than are the views of the logical positivists.

Whatever the cause, Mill's views were eclipsed. Methodologists no longer defended them, although it is arguable that economists continued to rely on them in practice. But Mill's problem remained. Neoclassical economic theory, like its classical predecessor, is hard to test and often apparently disconfirmed. Unless one is prepared to reject the theory or to deny that theories ought to fit the data, one needs to provide some defence of the empirical credentials of economics.

4 Milton Friedman's views

Since the mid twentieth century a large literature devoted to economic methodology has emerged. That literature explores many methodological approaches and applies its conclusions to many schools and branches of economics. Most of the literature focuses on the fundamental theory of mainstream economics – the theory of the equilibria resulting from constrained rational individual choice. This section focuses on Milton Friedman's extremely influential views. Two particularly significant alternatives to Friedman not discussed here can be found in Machlup (1978) and Samuelson (1963).

In his 1953 essay, 'The Methodology of Positive Economics', Friedman argued that the only relevant test of an economic theory is its success in predicting the phenomena that economists are concerned with. He believes that standard microeconomic theories and the quantity theory of money pass such tests well. He responds to criticisms of theories that point out that they contain 'unrealistic assumptions' (such as the assumption that firms are profit maximizers) by arguing that the criticisms presuppose mistakenly that theories can be tested by their assumptions. In Friedman's view, Mill's problem evaporates as soon as one recognizes that scrutinizing the realism of assumptions is a methodological mistake.

Friedman begins his essay by distinguishing sharply between positive and normative economics (see ECONOMICS AND ETHICS §5). He dismisses the possibility of rational argument concerning values, but maintains that disagreements about economic policy result more from disagreements concerning the consequences of alternative policies than from disputes about values. The goal of positive economics is, in Friedman's view, exclusively predictive: 'The ultimate goal of a positive science is the development of a "theory" or "hypothesis" that yields valid and meaningful (i.e., not truistic) predictions about phenomena not yet observed' (1953: 7). Friedman thus defends an instrumentalist view of science. Note that 'predictions' here are simply implications of a theory whose truth is not yet known.

Friedman's central claim that the realism of 'assumptions' is irrelevant to the assessment of a theory does not follow from a standard instrumentalist perspective, in which the correctness or incorrectness of all the observable consequences of a theory bear on its acceptability. For the assumptions of economics (for example that firms maximize profits) are testable, and a standard instrumentalist would not dismiss apparent disconfirmations as irrelevant. To make sense of Friedman's position, one must recognize that he rejects a standard instrumentalist concern with all the predictions of a theory. Friedman denies that the goal of economics is predictive success in general. The practical point of an economic theory is correct prediction only for 'the phenomena it purports to explain' (1953: 30). A good tool need not be an all-purpose tool. The fact that survey results are inconsistent with predictions derived from the hypothesis that firms are profit maximizers is irrelevant, because survey results are not among the phenomena that the theory of the firm is intended to explain.

From his thesis that the goal of economics is such 'narrow' predictive success, Friedman jumps to the conclusion that narrow predictive success is the only relevant test. Although tempting, this inference is a mistake. It is like arguing that the only relevant way to check a computer program is to run it and see whether it does what it is supposed to. If it is possible to tell for sure by running a program whether it will always do what it is supposed to, then there is indeed no point to studying the code (though studying the code might be cheaper and easier than investigating what happens when one runs the program). But with economic theories, as with complicated computer programs, one can only look at a small sample of their performance, and success in the sample is no guarantee of success in general. One cannot look and see how well the theory performs with respect to the full range of phenomena it was designed to account for. Indeed, the point of a theory is precisely to provide guidance when one does not yet know how the theory's predictions come out. Just as one can assess computer programs by studying their code or examining how they work in uninteresting applications, so one can assess theories by examining their assumptions and attending to the success or failure of uninteresting predictions. Such scrutiny of the 'realism of assumptions' is of particular importance when extending a theory to new circumstances or when modifying a theory in the face of predictive failure.

Friedman's narrow view of the goals of economics is also contestable. Even though economics has a crucial policy mission, many economists are concerned to explain economic phenomena, and many simply want to know the truth about various aspects of economies. Those economists obviously cannot accept Friedman's view that the realism of assumptions does not matter. The argument above shows that economists who accept Friedman's narrow view of the goals of economics cannot dismiss criticisms of the realism of assumptions either. Friedman does not solve Mill's problem.

5 Popperian perspectives

A second modern approach to Mill's problem derives from Karl Popper's philosophy of science and is more critical of economics (see POPPER, K. §§2–3). Popper defends a 'falsificationist' methodology. Scientists should formulate theories that are 'logically falsifiable' – that is, inconsistent with some possible observation reports. 'All crows are black' is logically falsifiable, since it is inconsistent with (and would be falsified by) an observation report of a red crow. Second, Popper maintains that scientists should subject theories to harsh tests and should be willing to reject them when they fail the tests. Third, scientists should regard theories as, at best, interesting conjectures. Passing a test does not confirm a theory or provide one with reason to believe it. All it does is to justify continuing to employ it (since it has not yet been falsified) and devoting increased efforts to attempting to falsify it (since it has thus far survived testing). Popper has also written in defence of what he calls 'situational logic' (which is basically rational choice theory) as the correct method for the social sciences. There appear to be serious tensions between Popper's falsificationism and his defence of situational logic, and his discussion of situational logic has not been as influential as his falsificationism. For discussion of this aspect of Popperian economic methodology, see Hands (1985).

Given Popper's philosophy of science, there seems little hope of solving Mill's problem without rejecting contemporary economic theory and condemning its practitioners as behaving in scientifically illegitimate ways. For specific economic theories are rarely logically falsifiable. When they are, they are rarely subjected to tests, let alone harsh tests. When they fail the tests, they are rarely repudiated. Worst of all, economic theories, which have not even been well tested, are taken to be well-established, perhaps even unquestionable guides to policy, rather than merely conjectures. Some critics of neoclassical economics have made these criticisms (Eichner 1983). But most of those who have espoused Popper's philosophy of science have not repudiated mainstream economics and have not been harshly critical of its practitioners.

Mark Blaug (1992) and Terence Hutchison (1938), who are the most prominent Popperian methodologists, criticize particular features of economics, and they both call for more testing and a more critical attitude. But both understate the radicalism of Popper's views and take his message to be merely that scientists should be critical and concerned to test their theories. Blaug's and Hutchison's criticisms have sometimes been challenged on the grounds that economic theories cannot be tested, because of their *ceteris paribus* clauses and the many subsidiary assumptions required to derive testable implications (Caldwell 1984). But this response ignores Popper's insistence that testing requires methodological decisions not to attribute failures of predictions to mistakes in subsidiary assumptions or to 'interferences'. For views of Popper's philosophy and its applicability to economics, see de Marchi (1988) and Caldwell (1991).

Applying Popper's views on falsification literally would be destructive. Not only neoclassical economics, but all known and probably all imaginable economic theories would be condemned as unscientific, and there would be no way to discriminate among economic theories. One major problem is that one cannot derive testable implications from theories by themselves. To derive testable implications, one also needs subsidiary assumptions or hypotheses concerning distributions, measurement devices, proxies for unmeasurable variables, the absence of various interferences, and so forth (see DUHEM, P.; QUINE, W.V. §1). These problems arise generally and Popper proposes that they be solved by a methodological decision to regard a failure of the deduced testable implication to be a failure of the theory. But in economics the subsidiary assumptions are extremely uncertain and in many cases known to be false. Making the methodological decision that Popper requires is unreasonable and would lead one to reject all economic theories.

Imre Lakatos (1970), who was for most of his philosophical career a follower of Popper, offers a broadly Popperian solution to this problem (see LAKATOS, I.). Lakatos denies that one tests individual theories. When theories face empirical difficulties, as they always do, one attempts to modify them. Scientifically acceptable (in Lakatos' terminology 'theoretically progressive') modifications always have some additional testable implications and are thus not purely *ad hoc*. If some of the new predictions are confirmed, then the modification is 'empirically progressive' and one has reason to reject the unmodified theory and to employ the new theory, regardless of how unsuccessful, in general, either theory may be. Though progress may be hard to come by, Lakatos' views do not have the same destructive implications as Popper's. Lakatos appears to solve Mill's problem by arguing that what matters is empirical progress or retrogression rather than empirical success or failure. It is thus easy to see why Lakatos' views have become more widespread among economic methodologists than Popper's. Developing Kuhn's notion of a 'paradigm' (1970) and some hints from Popper, Lakatos also developed a view of the global theory structure of whole theoretical enterprises, which he called 'scientific research programmes'. Lakatos emphasized that there is a 'hard core' of basic theoretical propositions that are not to be questioned and that substantial heuristics guide members of a research programme in the articulation and modification of specific theories. These views were also attractive to economic methodologists, since theory development in economics is so sharply constrained and directed, and since economics appears at first glance to have a hard core. The fact that economists do not give up basic theoretical postulates that appear to be false might be explained and justified by regarding them as part of the hard core of the neoclassical research programme.

Yet Lakatos' views do not provide a satisfactory solution to Mill's problem. For it is questionable whether the development of neoclassical economic theory has demonstrated empirical progress. For example, the replacement of 'cardinal' utility theory by 'ordinal' utility theory in the 1930s, which is generally regarded as a major step forward, involved the replacement of one theory by another that was strictly weaker and which had no additional empirical content. Furthermore, despite his emphasis on heuristics as guiding theory modification, Lakatos still emphasizes testing. Science is for Lakatos a much more empirically driven enterprise than is contemporary economics (Hands 1991). It is also doubtful whether research enterprises in economics have hard cores (Hoover 1991; Hausman 1992, ch. 6). For attempts to apply Lakatos' views to economics, see Latsis (1976) and Weintraub (1985). As is apparent in de Marchi and Blaug (1991), writers on economic methodology have in recent years become increasingly disenchanted with Lakatos' philosophy.

There is a second major problem with Popper's philosophy of science, which plagues Lakatos' views as well. Both defend the startling thesis that there is no such thing as empirical confirmation. Popper and Lakatos deny that the results of testing can give one reason to believe that statements are true, and both deny that results of tests can justify relying on statements in practical endeavours or in theoretical inquiry. They would accordingly regard as mistaken any claim that there is better evidence for one unfalsified proposition than for another. Someone who questions whether there is enough evidence for some proposition to justify relying on it in theoretical studies or for policy purposes would be making the methodological 'error' of supposing that there can be evidence in support of hypotheses. With the notable exception of Watkins (1984), few philosophers within the Popperian tradition have faced up to this radical consequence.

6 Contemporary directions in economic methodology

The failure of Friedman's, Popper's, and Lakatos' views to solve Mill's problem has had little impact on most economists, who are little concerned with methodology and who, when pressed, typically defend a position like Friedman's. But those specifically concerned with methodology have turned in many new directions, of which only three will be discussed here. Especially notable among the projects not discussed here are Lawrence Boland's neo-Popperian views (1989), Bruce Caldwell's 'methodological pluralism' (1982), Uskali Mäki's realist philosophy of economics (1990), Phillip Mirowski's exploration of the metaphorical structure of economics (1990), and E. Roy Weintraub's social constructivism (1991). There has also been a substantial effort to apply structuralist views of scientific theories to economics (Stegmüller et al. 1982; Balzer and Hamminga 1989), and recently there have been some discussions of economics from feminist perspectives (Ferber and Nelson 1993).

One radical reaction to the failure to solve Mill's problem is to deny that it can be solved. In Alexander Rosenberg's view (1992), economics can only make imprecise 'generic' predictions, and it cannot make progress, because it is built around folk psychology, which is a mediocre theory of human behaviour which (owing to the irreducibility of intentional notions) cannot be improved. Complex economic theories ought to be valued as applied mathematics, not as empirical theory. Since economics, despite its many well-trained practitioners, does not show the same consistent progress as the natural sciences, one cannot dismiss out of hand Rosenberg's suggestion that economics is an empirical dead end. But his view that it has made no progress and that it does not permit quantitative predictions is hard to accept. For example, it seems that contemporary economists can do a much better job of predicting the revenue consequences of a change in tax rates than could economists of even a century ago.

An equally radical but opposite reaction is Donald McCloskey's. He would solve Mill's problem by repudiating methodology. In McCloskey's view, the only relevant and significant criteria for assessing the practices and products of a discipline are those accepted by the practitioners. Apart from a few general standards such as honesty and a willingness to listen to criticisms, the only justifiable criteria for any conversation are those of the participants. The pretensions of philosophers to judge the discourse of scientists are arrogant and may be dismissed. Mill's problem dissolves when economists recognize that philosophical standards of empirical success may be safely ignored. Those who are interested in understanding the character of economics and in contributing to its improvement should eschew methodology and study instead the 'rhetoric' of economics – that is, the means of argument and persuasion that succeed among economists.

McCloskey's studies of the rhetoric of economics have been valuable and influential (1985, esp. ch. 5–7), but much of his work consists not of such studies but of philosophical critiques of the pretensions of methodology. These are more problematic, because the position sketched in the previous paragraph is hard to defend and potentially self-defeating. It is hard to defend, because epistemological standards for good science have already infected the conversation of economists. The standards of predictive success which give rise to Mill's problem are standards that economists already accept. Mill's problem can be dissolved only if economists can be persuaded to surrender the standards that gave rise to it. But the position sketched in the previous paragraph makes it difficult to argue for any changes in standards. Furthermore, as Alexander Rosenberg has argued, it seems that economists would doom themselves to irrelevance if they were to surrender standards of predictive success, for it is upon such standards that policy decisions are made. McCloskey does not, in fact, want to preclude all 'external' criticisms, which maintain that economists are sometimes persuaded when they should not be or are not persuaded when they should be. For he criticizes the conflations of statistical significance with economic importance, which are, as he documents, nevertheless extremely common (1985, ch. 9). Sometimes McCloskey characterizes rhetoric descriptively as the study of what in fact persuades, but sometimes he characterizes it normatively as the study of what ought to persuade (1985, ch. 2). And if rhetoric is the study of what ought to persuade, then it is methodology, not an alternative to methodology. Mill's problem cannot be conjured away.

A third approach is to return to Mill's own solution. Many of the basic principles of economics are plausible and are borne out in everyday experience. Although such plausibility does not place these principles beyond question, it does provide some warrant for them and some warrant for what may be deduced from them. Given the weakness of tests involving market data, in which there is an uncontrolled multiplicity of causal factors, it may be reasonable to hang on to orthodox theory in the face of disconfirmation. This thought can be rigorously supported in terms of Bayesian confirmation theory (Hausman 1992, ch. 12).

Yet this restoration of something like Mill's solution is in many ways as close to Rosenberg's and McCloskey's views as it is to Mill's. For the recognition that market tests will generally be too weak to shake the initial plausibility of the basic principles is simultaneously a recognition that there is little to be learned from market data. Although not quite as hostile to the empirical claims of economics as is Rosenberg's position, this view holds out few hopes for major improvements in economics. (By seeking higher quality data from observational studies and particularly experiments (see Roth 1988), economists may however be able to find a way out of this impasse.) On the other hand, in its insistence that one study the specific problems and constraints that economists face, this view joins McCloskey's in calling for less philosophically blinded studies of the rhetoric of economics (although it does not, of course, accept McCloskey's condemnation of epistemology).

7 Conclusions

Contemporary economic methodology is in turmoil. It has become an active area of research engaging major efforts by dozens of economists and a small group of philosophers. Economics presents a tantalizing list of puzzles, with Mill's problem at the core. And these problems have a special philosophical interest because of the connections between economics and ethics and between economics and the theory of rationality. There is much that is unknown and puzzling about how much people can learn about the character of their interactions and about what methods are most likely to help them to learn more. Economics is one exciting venue in which these general problems can be raised, but it has not, as yet, provided any easy solutions.

See also: GUANZI; SOCIAL SCIENCE, HISTORY OF PHILOSOPHY OF

References and further reading

Backhouse, R. (ed.) (1994) *New Perspectives on Economic Methodology*, London: Routledge. (An accessible collection of recent essays.)

* Balzer, W. and Hamminga, B. (eds) (1989) *Philosophy of Economics*, Dordrecht: Kluwer. (Contains mainly applications to economics of the structuralistic view of theories; cited in §6.)

* Becker, G. (1981) *A Treatise on the Family*, Cambridge, MA: Harvard University Press. (Applications of economic theory to the family; cited in §3.)

* Blaug, M. (1992) *The Methodology of Economics: Or How Economists Explain*, Cambridge: Cambridge

University Press, 2nd edn. (An influential discussion from a Popperian perspective; cited in §5.)

* Boland, L. (1989) *The Methodology of Economic Model Building: Methodology after Samuelson*, London: Routledge. (One of a series of books developing a distinctive neo-Popperian view of economic methodology; cited in §6.)

Buchanan, J. and Vanberg, V. (1991) 'The Market as a Creative Process', *Economics and Philosophy* 7: 167–86. (A classic statement of an 'Austrian' perspective.)

* Cairnes, J.E. (1875) *The Character and Logical Method of Political Economy*, New York: A.M. Kelley, 2nd edn, 1965. (One of the major nineteenth-century works on economic methodology by a follower of John Stuart Mill; cited in §3.)

* Caldwell, B. (1982) *Beyond Positivism: Economic Methodology in the Twentieth Century*, London: Allen & Unwin. (An extremely influential introduction to economic methodology; cited in §6.)

* —— (ed.) (1984) *Appraisal and Criticism in Economics*, London: Allen & Unwin. (A useful collection of roughly positivist or Popperian essays on economic methodology; cited in §5.)

* —— (1991) 'Clarifying Popper', *Journal of Economic Literature* 29: 1–33. (A major summary of Popper's views as applicable to economics; cited in §5.)

—— (ed.) (1993) *The Philosophy and Methodology of Economics*, Cheltenham: Edward Elgar. (A three-volume collection of essays on economic methodology.)

Dugger, W. (1979) 'Methodological Differences between Institutional and Neoclassical Economics', *Journal of Economic Issues* 13: 899–909. (A further discussion of the character of institutionalist economics; mentioned in §3.)

* Eichner, A. (1983) 'Why Economics is not yet a Science', in A. Eichner (ed.) *Why Economics Is not yet a Science*, Armonk, NY: M.E. Sharpe, 205–41. (An example of a Popperian critique of orthodox economics; cited in §5.)

* Ferber, M. and Nelson, J. (eds) (1993) *Beyond Economic Man: Feminist Theory and Economics*, Chicago, IL: University of Chicago Press. (A collection of essays examining economics from a feminist perspective; cited in §6.)

* Fraser, L. (1937) *Economic Thought and Language. A Critique of Some Fundamental Concepts*, London: A. & C. Black. (Calls for a more positivistic view of economics; cited in §3.)

* Friedman, M. (1953) 'The Methodology of Positive Economics', in *Essays in Positive Economics*, Chicago, IL: University of Chicago Press, 3–43. (The most influential single essay on economic methodology; discussed in §4.)

* Hands, D. (1985) 'Karl Popper and Economic Methodology', *Economics and Philosophy* 1: 83–100. (A discussion of the relevance of Popper's situational logic to economic methodology; cited in §5.)

* —— (1991) 'The Problem of Excess Content: Economics, Novelty and a Long Popperian Tale', in N. de Marchi and M. Blaug (eds), *Appraising Modern Economics: Studies in the Methodology of Scientific Research Programs*, Cheltenham: Edward Elgar, 38–75. (A discussion of empirical emphasis in Lakatos' philosophy of science; cited in §5.)

* Hausman, D. (1992) *The Inexact and Separate Science of Economics*, Cambridge: Cambridge University Press. (A general account of the philosophy of economics that defends a reformulation of J.S. Mill's views; cited in §§5, 6.)

Hausman, D. (ed.) (1984) *The Philosophy of Economics: An Anthology*, Cambridge: Cambridge University Press. (A collection of both classic and recent essays in the philosophy of economics.)

* Hausman, D. and McPherson, M. (1996) *Economic Analysis and Moral Philosophy* Cambridge: Cambridge University Press. (An introduction to work at the boundaries of economics and ethics; cited in §2.)

* Hoover, K. (1991) 'Scientific Research Program or Tribe? A joint Appraisal of Lakatos and the New Classical Macroeconomics', in N. de Marchi and M. Blaug (eds) *Appraising Modern Economics: Studies in the Methodology of Scientific Research Programs*, Cheltenham: Edward Elgar, 364–94. (A discussion of the structure of new classical economics with a critique of Lakatos' philosophy of science; cited in §5.)

* Hutchison, T. (1938) *The Significance and Basic Postulates of Economic Theory*, New York: A.M. Kelley, repr. with a new preface, 1960. (Probably the most important methodological work calling for a more positivistic or Popperian view; cited in §3.)

* Kaufmann, F. (1944) *Methodology of the Social Sciences*, London: Oxford University Press. (Call for a more positivistic approach; cited in §3.)

* Keynes, J.M. (1936) *The General Theory of Employment, Interest and Money*, London: Macmillan. (The work that announced the Keynesian revolution in economics; cited in §1.)

* Keynes, J.N. (1891) *The Scope and Method of Political Economy*, New York: A.M. Kelley, 4th edn, 1917. (A classic work on economic methodology heavily influenced by J.S. Mill; cited in §3.)

Klamer, A., McCloskey, D. and Solow, R. (eds) (1988) *The Consequences of Economic Rhetoric*, New York: Cambridge University Press. (Essays containing further discussion of McCloskey's views on the rhetoric of economics; discussed in §6).

* Knight, F. (1940) 'What is "Truth" in Economics?', *Journal of Political Economy* 48: 1–32. (An influential review of Hutchison (1938) that defends an old-fashioned Millian view of economic methodology; cited in §3.)

Koopmans, T. (1957) *Three Essays on the State of Economic Science*, New York: McGraw-Hill. (The most important book on economic methodology of the 1950s; defends a moderate empiricist position.)

* Kuhn, T. (1970) *The Structure of Scientific Revolutions*, Chicago, IL: University of Chicago Press, 2nd edn. (A recent classic in philosophy of science defending the importance of 'paradigms'; cited in §2.)

* Lakatos, I. (1970) 'Falsification and the Methodology of Scientific Research Programmes', in I. Lakatos and A. Musgrave (eds), *Criticism and the Growth of Knowledge*, Cambridge: Cambridge University Press, 91–196. (The major statement of Lakatos' philosophy of science; cited in §§2, 5.)

* Latsis, S. (ed.) (1976) *Method and Appraisal in Economics*, Cambridge: Cambridge University Press. (A collection of essays applying Lakatos' philosophy to economics; cited in §5.)

Leijonhufvud, A. (1973) 'Life Among the Econ', *Western Economic Journal* 11: 327–37. (A humorous commentary on economic methodology.)

Leontief, W. (1971) 'Theoretical Assumptions and Nonobserved Facts', *American Economic Review* 61: 1–7. (An influential critique of the abstractness and empirical weakness of contemporary economics.)

Little, D. (ed.) (1993) *On the Reliability of Economic Models: Essays in the Philosophy of Economics*, Boston, MA: Kluwer. (A recent collection of essays on economic methodology.)

* McCloskey, D. (1985) *The Rhetoric of Economics*, Madison, WI: University of Wisconsin Press. (This contains the major statement of McCloskey's views; cited in §6.)

* Machlup, F. (1978) *Methodology of Economics and Other Social Sciences*, New York: Academic Press. (A collection of Machlup's essays on economic methodology; cited in §4.)

* Mäki, U. (1990) *Studies in Realism and Explanation in Economics*, Helsinki: Suomalainen Tiedeakatemia. (Essays clarifying notions of realism and defending its importance in understanding economics; cited in §6.)

* Marchi, N. de (ed.) (1988) *The Popperian Legacy in Economics*, Cambridge: Cambridge University Press. (Contains essays and debate concerning Popperian economic methodology; cited in §5.)

—— (ed.) (1992) *Post-Popperian Methodology of Economics: Recovering Practice*, Boston, MA: Kluwer. (A collection with examples of new directions in economic methodology.)

* Marchi, N. de and Blaug, M. (eds) (1991) *Appraising Modern Economics: Studies in the Methodology of Scientific Research Programs*, Cheltenham: Edward Elgar. (A collection devoted to essays appraising Lakatosian economic methodology; cited in §5.)

Marx, K. (1857–8) *Grundrisse*, trans. M. Nicolaus, New York: Random House, 1973. (The introduction contains Marx's most extensive discussion of economic methodology.)

Menger, C. (1883) *Problems of Economics and Sociology*, ed. L. Schneider, trans. F. Nock, Urbana, IL: University of Illinois Press, 1963. (A critique of the views of the German Historical School discussed in §3.)

* Mill, J.S. (1836) 'On the Definition of Political Economy and the Method of Investigation Proper to it', in *Collected Works of John Stuart Mill*, vol. 4, Toronto, Ont.: University of Toronto Press, repr. 1967. (The first presentation of Mill's influential views on economic methodology; cited in §3.)

—— (1843) *A System of Logic*, London: Longmans, Green & Co., 1949. (Book VI contains a significant reworking of Mill's views on economic methodology; discussed in §3.)

* Mirowski, P. (1990) *More Heat Than Light*, Cambridge: Cambridge University Press. (A recent discussion of the history and methodology of economics that emphasizes the use of analogies to physics; cited in §6.)

* Mises, L. von (1949) *Human Action. A Treatise on Economics*, New Haven, CT: Yale University Press. (Mises' major work, which defends a view of the basic principles of economics as known a priori; cited in §3.)

Morgan, M. (1990) *History of Econometric Ideas*, Cambridge: Cambridge University Press. (A historical account of econometrics that highlights its methodological problems.)

Popper, K. (1968) *The Logic of Scientific Discovery*, London: Hutchinson & Co, rev. edn. (Popper's major work discussed in §5.)

Redman, D. (1989) *Economic Methodology: A Bibliography with References to Works in the Philosophy of Science, 1860–1988*, New York: Greenwood Press. (A useful source for further references.)

* Robbins, L. (1932) *An Essay on the Nature and Significance of Economic Science*, London: Macmillan, 1935. (One of the most important books on methodology; cited in §3.)

Roscher, W. (1874) *Geschichte der National-oekonomik in Deutschland* (The History of the National

Economy in Germany), Munich: R. Oldenbourg. (One statement of the views of the German Historical School mentioned in §3.)

* Rosenberg, A. (1992) *Economics – Mathematical Politics or Science of Diminishing Returns?* Chicago, IL: University of Chicago Press. (Denies the possibility of empirical progress in economics; cited and discussed in §6.)

* Roth, A. (1988) 'Laboratory Experimentation in Economics: a Methodological Overview', *Economic Journal* 98: 974–1031. (A survey emphasizing methodological issues; cited in §6.)

Samuels, W. (ed.) (1980) *The Methodology of Economic Thought: Critical Papers from the Journal of Economic Thought (Issues)*, New Brunswick, NJ: Transaction Books. (A collection of methodological essays from an institutionalist perspective.)

* Samuelson, P. (1938) 'A Note on the Pure Theory of Consumer's Behavior', *Economica* 5: 61–71. (An influential presentation of revealed-preference theory that led economists to take a more positivistic view of economic methodology; cited in §3.)

* —— (1963) 'Problems of Methodology – Discussion', *American Economic Review Papers and Proceedings* 53: 232–6. (A presentation of Samuelson's views on economic methodology; cited in §4.)

* Senior, N. (1836) *Outline of the Science of Political Economy*, New York: A.M. Kelley, repr. 1965. (Contains one of the first discussions of economic methodology. Senior's position is similar to Mill's and cited in §3.)

* Smith, A. (1776) *An Inquiry into the Nature and Causes of the Wealth of Nations*, Oxford: Oxford University Press, 1976. (One of the most important economics books ever written; cited in introduction.)

* Stegmüller, W., Balzer, W. and Spohn, W. (eds) (1982) *Philosophy of Economics: Proceedings, Munich, July 1981*, New York: Springer. (Applications of the structuralist view of scientific theories to economics; cited in §6.)

* Veblen, T. (1898) 'Why is Economics not an Evolutionary Science?', *Quarterly Journal of Economics* 12: 373–97. (A classic institutionalist critique of neoclassical economics.)

* Watkins, J. (1984) *Science and Scepticism*, Princeton, NJ: Princeton University Press. (A sophisticated account of philosophy of science in the Popperian tradition; cited in §5.)

Weber, M. (1975) *Roscher and Knies: The Logical Problem of Historical Economics*, trans. G. Oakes, New York: Macmillan. (A discussion of the German Historical School; cited in §3.)

* Weintraub, E. (1985) *General Equilibrium Analysis: Studies in Appraisal*, Cambridge: Cambridge University Press. (An influential application of Lakatos' philosophy of science; cited in §5.)

* —— (1991) *Stabilizing Dynamics*, Cambridge: Cambridge University Press. (A history of recent work on dynamics defending postmodern, social constructivist views.)

(Essays on economic methodology are conveniently indexed in *The Journal of Economic Literature* and in the *Index of Economic Articles in Journal and Collective Volumes* under the number, 036 prior to 1991 and under the number B4 since then. Redman (1989) is an annotated bibliography of essays on economic methodology published before 1988.)

DANIEL HAUSMAN

EDUCATION, HISTORY OF PHILOSOPHY OF

The philosophy of education may be considered a branch of practical philosophy, aimed ultimately at the guidance of an important aspect of human affairs. Its questions thus arise more or less directly from the features of educational practice and the role of education in the promotion of individual and social wellbeing, however much its answers may be conditioned by the larger philosophical and historical settings in which they are posed. Philosophers have concerned themselves with what the aims of education should be, and through what forms of instruction, inquiry and practice those aims might be attained. This demands attention to the contents of instruction and who shall have authority over it. It demands attention to the nature of instruction itself, its epistemic dimensions and what is entailed by its reliance on language; the nature of learning and human development, both moral and intellectual; and how all of these are interrelated. The philosophy of education thus stands at the intersection of moral and political philosophy, epistemology, and the philosophy of mind and language, as they bear on the foundations of educational practice.

The philosophy of education began in classical antiquity with the challenges posed by Socrates to the educational claims of the sophists. Plato and Aristotle developed systematic theories of education guided by an ethic of justice and self-restraint, and by the goal of promoting social harmony and the happiness or wellbeing of all citizens. The Stoic descendants of Socrates were expelled from Rome and the oratorical model of higher education given official sanction, but Augustine re-established the philosophical model through a synthesis of Platonism and Christianity, and in his mature educational thought brought elements of the oratorical and Platonic models together in his account of the Christian teacher's training.

The religious wars of the Reformation inspired several philosophical stances toward the relationships of Church, state, school and conscience. Hobbes argued for a consolidation of ecclesiastical and civil authority, with full sovereign authority over education; Locke for liberty, religious toleration, and private education aiming at self-governance in accordance with reason; and Rousseau not just for the free development and exercise of the full array of human faculties, but for the establishment of a civic religion limited to the core of shared Christian beliefs which Enlightenment figures from Descartes onward had thought evident to natural reason.

The Enlightenment's embrace of science and reason yielded efforts towards the development of a science of learning and pedagogy in the nineteenth century, but Rousseau's romantic reaction to it and defence of democracy were also powerful influences. In the twentieth century, Dewey produced a new synthesis of Enlightenment and Rousseauian themes, drawing on Hegel, the experimentalism of Mill, evolutionary theory and psychology, and aspects of the substance and intent of Rousseau's pedagogy.

1   Socrates and the sophists
2   Plato and Aristotle
3   Hellenistic and Roman education
4   Augustine and Aquinas
5   The Renaissance and Reformation
6   Descartes and Locke
7   Rousseau and Kant
8   The nineteenth century
9   John Dewey

1   Socrates and the sophists

Educational philosophy began in the Greek classical period with the examination of the educational claims of the sophists undertaken by Socrates. The sophists brought higher education to the democratized Athens of the fifth and fourth centuries BC, offering those who aspired to political leadership a training in political *aretē* (the goodness, excellence or virtue required for success in pursuing appropriate ends) or *phronēsis* (sound judgment or practical wisdom) (see ARETĒ; SOPHISTS). This form of education suggested that most citizens lacked the virtue and judgment required for a life in public affairs, and one can detect a concession to the political dangerousness of this in the claims of Protagoras that cities and their citizens do indeed teach virtue to the young, but that his own teaching could refine and develop it by degrees. In Plato's *Protagoras*, Socrates exposes the tensions in

this view by distinguishing between the habitual virtue of good or obedient citizens, and true virtue which involves intellectual insight and sound judgment (that is, *phronēsis*), noting that a skill which merely refines and enlarges the former cannot yield the latter.

More generally, the Socratic response to the sophists was above all cautionary. As we encounter Socrates in the *Protagoras* and other early dialogues of Plato, he dedicated himself to showing through his method of questioning (*elenchus*) that those who claimed to be teachers of *aretē* lacked the expert knowledge of it which its teaching would require. The possession of such knowledge would allow one to defend and explain the truths one believes through a reasoned account (*aitias logismos*), and Socrates denied that he was himself a teacher, apparently on the grounds that he was unable to give such an account of his own beliefs. He advocated the individual care of one's own soul, and embraced an ethic of justice, wisdom and self-restraint, in opposition to the competitive ethic of the warrior heroes portrayed by Homer and embraced by Greek popular morality. How far he thought his own elenctic method would carry one in this care of the soul, or in the search for the best way to live, is unclear (see SOCRATES).

2   Plato and Aristotle

The adequacy of the Socratic *elenchus* was evidently one of Plato's concerns in the *Meno*, for the work presents us with a Socratic interlocutor who is purged of misplaced confidence and ready to join Socrates in a search for the nature of virtue, but asking how the search is to go forward without the benefit of any knowledge of the object of the search. This prompts the introduction of Plato's theory that all learning is recollection, and a demonstration of an *elenchus* arriving, without recourse to prior knowledge, at the discovery of a geometrical fact. The theory of recollection underwrites the hope that a search will yield truth, by suggesting that one can count on having enough true beliefs to drive out the false, as one's beliefs become more coherent under questioning. Plato implies that one ascends from there to knowledge as one reasons through the relationships among all the truths in the relevant domain and can thereby understand and provide an explanatory account of any one of them.

In the *Republic*, Plato envisages the inculcation of self-restraint through a comprehensive system of compulsory education for each social class, and develops an elaborate defence of the Socratic thesis that justice is a virtue indispensable for a happy life. Plato was evidently concerned that the education of his time, which was dominated by the study of Homer, was inconsistent with the inculcation of these virtues, and regarded an education which would eliminate unnecessary desires for contested goods as the one way to eliminate wars of conquest and the political instability so prevalent in Greek life. He envisages a craft training for members of the labouring class, which will free them from the dominance of desires for unnecessary consumption and prepare them for a happy life of efficient money making. Members of the 'guardian' class are to be given a communal upbringing which will eliminate conflict arising from clan loyalties, and a primary education in music, athletics and stories which will enable them to be happy in their pursuit of honour by making them courageous and gentle towards each other and those they protect. The philosopher-kings must know what is good for the city, and Plato proposes an education which will not only elevate their minds through the study of abstract sciences to dialectic and apprehension of the transcendent 'Form' of goodness, but also provide many years of experience in the affairs of the city.

Plato's *Laws* describes a city which resembles that of the *Republic* in aiming at the virtue and happiness of all citizens, but is quite unlike it in being a constitutional rule of law grounded in reason and informed consent. The insistence on consent, and an unwavering commitment to the idea that every institution, including legislation and its enforcement, is educative, leads to the proposal that all laws be prefaced with 'preludes' that are both moving and explanatory, and that these 'preludes' should serve as models for the literary substance of state-operated day schools. Two noteworthy aspects of the theory of learning and instruction at work in the *Laws* are the prominent role assigned to guided practice, and its rich use of the model of a good doctor who communes with and earns the trust and cooperation of a patient before prescribing a remedy. It shares with the *Republic* the view that rational self-control and the ability to perceive what is good can only develop under the influence of good upbringing and education.

Aristotle's *De Partibus Animalium* (On the Parts of Animals) opens with a characterization of a complete education as one which enables a person to form reasonable judgments of the goodness or badness of reasoning in all branches of knowledge. This requires an understanding of the manner and canons of investigation in the various branches of knowledge, and it is fair to say that Aristotle dedicated himself not only to the discovery and elaboration of those canons of investigation, but also to making them known through his lectures and the wide-ranging scientific investigations of his 'school', the Lyceum.

Of the works of Aristotle that have survived, it is the *Politics* and *Nicomachean Ethics*, the works of 'political science' intended as guides to political practice, that are most revealing of his educational philosophy. They suggest that he thought a higher education for political *phronēsis* should provide leaders and their advisors with systematic knowledge of how to pursue the proper aim of the state (namely, the best kind of life for all its citizens), and a knowledge of the causes of dissolution of states which would provide corrupt leaders with the motivation to pursue reforms. Plato had argued that unjust regimes tend to be short-lived, and Aristotle offered his own comparative study of 158 constitutional histories as confirmation.

Aristotle shared Plato's view that justice and human wellbeing require systematic educational efforts to make citizens virtuous and to create social unity, but his accounts of education for good character and unity are interestingly different. His view of *aretē* is that what is essential to it, beyond being disposed to desire the right ends and take pleasure in their attainment, is judging and acting from a well-rounded grasp of the morally important particulars of the situations one faces. The beginnings of *aretē* must be established through exposure to good models and habitual obedience to good law, but its refinement requires practice guided by coaching and correction. This progress in perception, responsiveness and judgment reaches its highest development through conversation with trusted and exemplary companions who can best enable one to know oneself.

Aristotle was critical of the communism of the *Republic*, and followed the Plato of the *Laws* in proposing the establishment of state-sponsored day schools. He seems to have regarded common schooling, and its proposed education for virtue, as the natural culmination of reforms by which a city can be unified through the cultivation of goodwill, common non-competitive aspirations, and friendships which bridge the divides between different social classes.

3 Hellenistic and Roman education

The conquests of Alexander the Great brought an end to any hope that the fulfilment of human nature could be achieved through the educational and political efforts of an autonomous *polis* or city-state. Philosophy of education thereby lost its connection to public life in the Hellenistic Age, and what remained of it in Stoicism was the doctrine that an understanding of divine reason allows one to be happy, good and free of the tyranny of unnecessary desires, by enabling one to accept the inevitability of lacking what one does not have and cannot possess.

The Stoics took divine reason to be manifested in the order of nature, and Chrysippus and others apparently held that an adequate understanding of nature is best attained through a study of logic and physics (see STOICISM §3).

Rome had no need for a philosophy withdrawn from public life, and when the Emperor Vespasian granted the first public subsidy for higher learning in the first century, it went to the school of rhetoric operated by Quintilian. His work, the Institutio Oratoria (The Training of the Orator), is both a textbook of rhetoric and a treatise on the principles of education, and it exercised a powerful influence on Western educational ideals well into the nineteenth century. Quintilian took the highest aim of education to be the formation of a perfect orator, a person made both eloquent and good through exercises in composition and declamation, and a broad study of the liberal arts and rhetorical theory.

4 Augustine and Aquinas

AUGUSTINE is regarded, with justice, as not only the primary architect of the synthesis of Christianity and Platonism on which Christian theology was built, but also the foremost philosopher of education of late antiquity and of Catholicism generally. He was trained as an orator and held teaching posts in rhetoric for twelve years, but upon his conversion to Christianity in 386 he renounced the shallow worldliness of the oratorical ideal, setting himself and the philosophy of education upon a new course. Fundamental to Augustine's view of education is the idea that its proper goals are first of all conversion and repentance, or the acceptance on faith of Christian beliefs and a commitment and effort of will to live without sin; and secondly, for the few who can achieve it, a wisdom consisting of direct knowledge of the soul and God through reason, or the insight of an intellect directed inwardly.

Augustine's view of the course of higher studies preparatory for the attainment of this wisdom, and for its use by the Christian teacher, underwent a marked development between the educational works written in the first years after his conversion and those finished after he was consecrated bishop of Hippo in 395. The mainsprings of this development were a dramatic growth in his respect for biblical Scriptures as the word of God, which led him to revise his view of the role and value of liberal studies, and an appreciation for the value of rhetoric which grew with his responsibilities in the Church.

In his De ordine (On Order), Augustine affirms the existence of an all-embracing Divine order, knowable through liberal studies which allow one to grasp the pervasive reasonableness in things emanating from God's intellect or Logos. It is dialectic or philosophical reasoning which teaches one how to learn and how to teach, he says, and this is compatible both with his view that the soul must prepare itself to see God through the exercise of its own reason, and his view in De magistro (The Teacher) that knowledge of a thing is achieved in seeing it, not in hearing someone name or describe it. He argues there through a theory of signs and language that teaching through words cannot enable us to know things by displaying them, but can only remind or prompt us to consult our own divinely illuminated reason, or else induce us to believe things on trust without understanding or knowledge.

Augustine's De catechizandis rudibus (Catechizing the Uninstructed) develops a curriculum for the uneducated which is intended to induce moral behaviour and faith in God sufficient for salvation. His De doctrina christiana (Christian Instruction) explicates the training and methods through which Christian teachers may properly interpret biblical Scripture and teach the truths discovered in them. He prescribes a course of studies encompassing languages, history, geography, natural science, technology, logic and mathematics, all as an aid to understanding Scripture, and offers canons of interpretation by which the Christian teacher may distinguish the literal from the allegorical, and find the hidden meaning in the latter. Rhetoric returns in the service of faith and love of God and neighbour, in the training of the Christian teacher and in detailed guidance on how the truths discovered in scripture are best presented.

The embrace of Aristotle by Thomas AQUINAS produced a second major synthesis of classical and Christian thought, and a philosophy of teaching which owes much to both Aristotle and Augustine. Aquinas argues that acquiring knowledge by discovery and by instruction are alike in that a teacher can only lead a student to knowledge by making manifest to them the discursive reasoning through which discoveries are made. 'Outward' teaching may thus produce knowledge by aiding the student in reasoning through the application of self-evident general principles to particular matters, though it is God who teaches 'inwardly' by endowing the mind with the 'light of reason' and a knowledge of these first principles.

5 The Renaissance and Reformation

The Renaissance and Reformation are noteworthy in educational history on many grounds, including the incorporation of the educational ideals and programme of Quintilian into the Christian humanism of Desiderius ERASMUS and others; Martin Luther's translations and promotion of universal, publicly-funded elementary education, so that the common people might read and thereby consult for themselves the Scriptures (see LUTHER, M.); and the founding of the Jesuit order and its system of colleges by Ignatius Loyola. What inspired the most weighty philosophical response, however, was the turbulent course of the Reformation itself, and the urgent questions it raised about the relationships between church, state, school and individual conscience.

Thomas HOBBES has been neglected by histories of philosophy of education, but a central concern of his *Leviathan* was to establish the desirability of uniting civil and ecclesiastical authority in a sovereign empowered to use public education to inculcate correct religious and moral beliefs. In both *Leviathan* and *Behemoth*, his history of the English Civil War, he attributed social disorder, including conflict and civil war arising from the exercise of individual judgment in religious matters, to faulty instruction from the pulpit and in the universities. This instruction not only incited conflict over theological questions without answers, he argued, but spread doctrines contrary to the natural law of civil and moral duty. Because these doctrines shaped a conception of religious interests linked to the expectation of an afterlife, Hobbes regarded attempts to suppress rebellion by force as futile, and argued that sovereign authority over education and the interpretation of scripture was desirable and necessary to ensure peace.

6 Descartes and Locke

René Descartes' remarks on education are continuous with the classical tradition in identifying universal wisdom as the greatest good and proper aim of instruction, but he turned a deeply Augustinian account of reason against the curricula of Augustine, Aquinas and the scholastic university, and championed the free and methodical exercise of individual reason or self-instruction as the surest path to wisdom and the progress of science and human emancipation. He regarded the unrestrained use of reason in the pursuit of understanding as a natural and desirable expression of human nature, and held that the individual intellect can easily discover within itself a knowledge of God, the soul and good actions. Thus, he regarded the inward gaze of reason itself as the best guide for the conduct of life, and the means through which theological disagreements and the conflict arising from them may be resolved. However, he held that the purging of prejudice through doubt

or the suspension of belief is a necessary prerequisite to the effective employment of reason.

With regard to the curricular proposals of Augustine, Descartes maintained that the revealed truths of Scripture are beyond the intelligence of even the best trained interpreter, and that in general it takes more skill to find what is true in books than to discover the truth for oneself. In answer to Aquinas and the scholastic tradition, he argued that instruction through syllogistic deductions undermines both the freedom and power of reason, because syllogistic deduction does not ensure any intellectual grasp of the propositions involved and does not enable one to discover new knowledge. Exercise with inquiries conducted on his own more natural method of reasoning is the recommended alternative (see DESCARTES, R. §2).

Descartes laid the foundations for the educational philosophy of the Enlightenment, but it remained to John Locke to provide an influential articulation of it. Locke deepened Descartes' attack on second-hand knowledge by combining the latter's view that knowledge can only be obtained through the perception of 'clear and distinct' ideas, with his own systematic development of the claim that one can only acquire ideas through one's own experience. With this epistemic individualism as his starting point, he took the fundamental and humanizing goal of education to be the development of rational abilities and the habits of doubt, reflection and foresight required to form children into adults who will judge and act in accordance with the dictates of reason. This is consistent with his having put virtue, wisdom, and 'breeding' (that is, respect for self and others) before learning or the acquisition of knowledge, since he regarded virtue as a disposition to follow one's desires only when doing so accords with the dictates of reason or natural moral law. Autonomy of judgment and action are thereby reconciled with virtue and sociability through the concept of self-mastery, and education is to be first and foremost a process of habituation to self-mastery.

Locke held that parents have a natural duty to educate their children to be self-governing and able to provide for themselves, but he proposed public action to ensure that even children of paupers would receive instruction in Christian morality and a trade: those who will never have the leisure for knowledge or science would have little use for more than this, he suggested. For the sons of landed gentry he counselled a general education through private tutelage, aimed to produce gentlemen ready to contribute to the wellbeing of the community. This education should encourage a breadth of experience and inquiry reaching down to the foundations of beliefs, and promote reflection on desires by refusing to gratify those that are excessive. It should exercise firm but gentle authority over the child, appeal early and often to the child's reason, and make education enjoyable since autonomous learning cannot be coerced (see LOCKE, J.).

7 Rousseau and Kant

The concern that animates the educational and political thought of Jean-Jacques Rousseau is the preservation of the freedom and goodness which he took to define human nature, in opposition to the Enlightenment conception of humanity as essentially rational, progressing towards happiness and the perfection of its nature through the cultivation of reason. Rousseau argued in his first and second *Discourses* that what the arts and sciences encourage are sentiments of self-love and ambition which are destructive of our goodness and freedom, leading us to an insatiable pursuit of private gain at the expense of the common good. To this image of fallen humans, rooted in the orthodox identification of pride as the 'root of all evil', he coupled a further challenge to the hope that progress might be achieved through the ascendancy of reason, observing that in such a state of society the voice of individual reason will counsel free-riding, the unjust enjoyment of the rights of citizenship without the discharge of corresponding duties.

Rousseau held in his *Émile*, the most influential educational tract of the modern era, that in order to educate a boy both for himself and for society, one must preserve his natural freedom and goodness by conforming the education of 'humans' and 'things' to nature's timetable for the development of his faculties and motives. Children are moved first by the expectation of pleasure and pain, later by a grasp of what is useful, and finally by reason; and they should learn at each stage through experience and feeling, not through books or the imposition of discipline or teaching. The tutor need do little but shield the child from the corrupting influence of society and organize his activities (and thereby his experiences and feelings) in order to nurture the growth of moral sentiments and conscience, of a self-sufficiency grounded in prudence and mastery of a craft, and of his faculties and knowledge of the world, God and moral law. Freedom from material reliance on others and from the domination of excessive desires is thus assured.

By contrast with Locke, Rousseau held that freedom from domination by others requires that the child's behaviour be corrected solely by the experience of the natural consequences of actions, and that

adults make law for themselves through a form of democracy in which the citizens retain and exercise direct legislative sovereignty. Good citizenship requires, however, that they aim at the common good when it conflicts with their private ends, and Rousseau envisages in *On The Social Contract* a 'Great Legislator' who proposes good laws and persuades the public to enact and obey them through neither force (which would negate freedom) nor rational argument (which wouldn't solve the free-rider problem). The legislator must teach by example and through a 'natural' civil religion, established not as dogma but as sentiments of sociability (see ROUSSEAU, J.-J. §3).

Immanuel Kant's philosophy of education is like Rousseau's in being grounded in a philosophy of history, but it reaffirms not only the essential rationality of human nature, but also original sin and the naturalness of discord and competitive self-love. His conception of the end for which we were created is that our rational nature should find full expression, that we should achieve moral perfection through effort and the grace it occasions, and that we should thereby become both happy and worthy of that happiness. This future kingdom of heaven on earth is what children should be educated for, but the stages of their education must first recapitulate the stages of human history already traversed. The first of these is nurture; the second discipline, to counterbalance natural unruliness; the third is culture (information and instruction), to develop ability and prudence; the last (for the world order yet to come) is moral training, to encourage respect for moral law and an acceptance of its priority over self-love as the principle of one's will.

8 The nineteenth century

The nineteenth century was a period of unprecedented innovation in the theory of learning and the theory and practice of pedagogy, particularly in Germany. From a philosophical standpoint this activity can be described most simply as a playing-out of Enlightenment ideas and of the romantic and aesthetic reactions to them initiated by Rousseau and Friedrich von SCHILLER. Johann Heinrich Pestalozzi (1746–1827) and Friedrich Wilhelm Froebel (1782–1852) were the most prominent of those strongly influenced by Rousseau, the former being known for a pedagogy grounded in the analysis of tasks into simple components, his advocacy of universal educational rights and efforts to educate the poor 'organically' in a family-like setting; the latter for founding the kindergarten as a place of growth in unity with God and nature. Johann

Friedrich HERBART is noteworthy for his attempts to develop the experimental science of pedagogy envisaged by Kant, and for a theory of ideas and learning which held that it is 'apperceptive masses' formed by past experience that structure new experiences, allowing the assimilation of ideas that are compatible but driving from consciousness those that are not.

Though not a philosopher of education himself, Karl MARX has figured importantly in the subsequent history of the field through, among other things, his theory of ideology, an exceedingly influential if unsystematic account of the way in which socioeconomic roles and the ideas that structure them are learned through contact with a society and its institutions. Contraposed to the radical egalitarianism of Marx was the radical elitism of Friedrich NIETZSCHE, the other great immoralist of the nineteenth century, who condemned the democratization of the universities on the grounds that the reversal of cultural decadence and advancement of human wellbeing through the free play of creativity requires that higher education remain the exclusive province of 'higher types'.

9 John Dewey

John Dewey is regarded with justice as the preeminent philosopher of education of the twentieth century. Like Marx and Nietzsche, he understood the function of philosophy to be social and cultural reconstruction, and like Marx he aspired to reconstruct philosophy itself by bringing science into it. But he rejected the teleological conceptions of history embraced by Marx, Hegel and Kant in favour of a kind of evolutionary naturalism. He took this naturalism to preclude the existence of absolute norms of conduct, and to warrant recognition of a plurality of goods and moral criteria. If there is any 'end' entailed by human nature it is growth itself, he argued and, following Rousseau, he held that a good society is one in which growth is maximized, harmonized with that of others, and reconciled with the collective work of citizenship. He argued, much as Rousseau did, that democracy is the one form of political life in which the convergence of these goals is possible, and he adopted and developed John Stuart Mill's idea that social progress is possible through the freedom of individuals to engage in social experimentation, or the application of the methods of science to the problems of social existence (see MILL, J.S.). Dewey insists that this experimentation or application of 'social intelligence' must be cooperative, governed by the norms of respectful communication, and guided by the plurality of goods and

criteria valued by those whose interests are at stake. He thought that in this way the Enlightenment promise of social progress through the application of scientific method might be achieved simultaneously with enacting democracy as 'a way of life' in which human growth and quality of experience can be optimized.

Experience became for Dewey both the goal and means of education: the richness of future experience its goal, and present experiences which engage the student's activity and improve the prospect of desirable experiences in the future its means. His methodological Hegelianism, or strategy of undercutting the dualisms dividing one school of opinion against another, is as evident in his philosophy of education as elsewhere. He resisted the duality of thought and action, book learning and vocationalism, pedagogy driven by a preconceived curriculum and pedagogy driven by the antecedent interests of the child. Above all, he held that the social world of the school and of a properly democratic society must coincide, and that the exercise of intelligence and engagement in adaptive conduct are inseparable. Classrooms must therefore be devoted to the collaborative activity of inquiry, he concluded (see DEWEY, J.).

See also: EDUCATION, PHILOSOPHY OF; KAIBARA EKKEN

References and further reading

Aquinas (*c.*1257) 'De Magistro' (The Teacher), question 11 in *Quaestiones Disputatae de Veritate* (Truth), vol. 2, trans. J.V. McGlynn, Indianapolis, IN: Hackett Publishing Co., 1994. (Aquinas' treatise on teaching.)

* Augustine (386) *De ordine* (On Order or Divine Providence and the Problem of Evil), trans. R.P. Russell in *The Fathers of the Church: The Writings of Saint Augustine*, vol. 1, ed. L. Schopp, New York: Cima Publishing Co., 1948, 229–332. (An early work on liberal studies and knowledge of God.)

* —— (386–9) *Contra Academicos* (Against the Academicians) and *De magistro* (The Teacher), trans., intro. and notes by P. King, Indianapolis, IN: Hackett Publishing Co., 1995. (A critique of scepticism and an account of knowledge and teaching.)

* —— (397–426) *De doctrina christiana* (Christian Instruction), trans. J.J. Gavigan in *Fathers of the Church: The Writings of Saint Augustine*, vol. 4, ed. R. Deferrari, Washington, DC: The Catholic University of America Press, Inc., 1947–66,

19–235. (A treatise on the Christian teacher's training and methods of teaching.)

* —— (400) *De catechizandis rudibus* (Catechizing the Uninstructed), trans. J.P. Christopher, Washington, DC: Catholic University Press, 1926. (Proposes a course of instruction for the uneducated.)

* Aristotle (*c.*330 BC) *De Partibus Animalium* (On the Parts of Animals), Greek text with trans. A. Peck in *Aristotle*, vol. 12, Loeb Classical Library, Cambridge, MA: Harvard University Press. (Opens with remarks on the nature of education.)

* —— (*c.*330 BC) *Nicomachean Ethics*, trans. and notes T. Irwin, Indianapolis, IN: Hackett Publishing Co., 1985. (Aristotle's main ethical work and an important source of his educational thought.)

* —— (*c.*330 BC) *Politics*, trans., intro. and notes by C. Lord, Chicago, IL: University of Chicago Press, 1984. (Aristotle's lectures on politics and the place of education in a good city.)

Ashcraft, R. (ed.) (1991) *John Locke: Critical Assessments*, vol. 2, London: Routledge. (Includes articles on Locke's educational thought and related topics such as reason, natural law and toleration.)

Bacon, F. (1605–10) *The Advancement of Learning and New Atlantis*, ed. A. Johnston, Oxford: Clarendon Press, 1974. (Seminal works of the modern era on the condition and advancement of knowledge and human progress – they shaped the pedagogical proposals of J.A. Comenius and others.)

Beck, F.A.G. (1964) *Greek Education*, London: Methuen. (A historical account of Greek education and its leading theorists.)

Beck, L.W. (1978) 'Kant on Education', in *Essays on Kant and Hume*, New Haven, CT: Yale University Press. (A valuable introduction and guide to the relevant texts.)

Curren, R. (1997) *Aristotle on the Necessity of Public Education*, Savage, MD: Rowman & Littlefield. (A study in Aristotle's educational politics which gives close attention to the influence of Plato's *Laws*.)

Descartes (1628–49) *The Philosophical Writings of Descartes*, vols 1 and 2, trans. J. Cottingham *et al.*, Cambridge: Cambridge University Press, 1984–5. (See his *Rules For the Direction of The Mind*; *Discourse on Method*, parts 1 and 2; *The Search For Truth By Means of the Natural Light*; and the 'Author's Letter' or preface to the *Principles of Philosophy*.)

Dewey, J. (1899) *The School and Society*, Chicago, IL: University of Chicago Press. (A good introduction to Dewey's educational thought.)

—— (1902) *The Child and the Curriculum*, Chicago, IL: University of Chicago Press. (Another early and accessible statement of Dewey's educational philosophy.)

—— (1909) *Moral Principles in Education*, Boston, MA: Houghton Mifflin. (On moral education in the schools.)

—— (1916) *Democracy and Education*, New York: Macmillan. (Dewey's most systematic work on education.)

—— (1927) *The Public and Its Problems*, New York: Henry Holt. (On social intelligence and related ideas.)

—— (1938) *Experience and Education*, New York: Macmillan. (An introductory restatement of his educational views which looks back critically on the progressive education movement.)

Epictetus (*c.*120) *The Discourses as Reported by Arrian, The Manual, and Fragments*, Greek text with trans. by W. Oldfather, 2 vols, Cambridge, MA: Harvard University Press, 1966–7. (An example of late Stoicism with extended commentary on moral instruction.)

Flower, E. and Murphey, M.G. (1977) *A History of Philosophy in America*, vol. 2, New York: Putnam. (The long chapter on Dewey provides an excellent overview of his thought.)

Froebel, F. (1826) *Die Menschenerziehung* (*The Education of Man*), trans. W.N. Hailmann, Clifton, NJ: Keeley, 1974. (The earliest and most systematic of Froebel's educational works.)

Garforth, F.W. (1980) *Educative Democracy: John Stuart Mill on Education in Society*, Oxford: Oxford University Press. (A detailed account of Mill's views on education and its role in society.)

Herbart, J.H. (1804–6) *Über die ästhetische Darstellung der Welt als das Hauptgeschäft der Erziehung; Allgemeine Pädagogik aus dem Zweck der Erziehung abgeleitet* (*The Science of Education, Its General Principles Deduced From Its Aim, and the Aesthetic Revelation of the World*), trans. with intro. H.M. Felkin and E. Felkin, Boston, MA: Heath, 1892. (A work of practical pedagogical theory.)

—— (1836) *Umriß von pädagogischen Vorlesungen* (*Outlines of Educational Doctrine*), trans. A.F. Lange, notes C. De Garmo, London: Macmillan, 1901. (A theoretical enquiry into how education is possible.)

* Hobbes, T. (1651) *Leviathan: Or The Matter, Form, and Power of a Commonwealth Ecclesiastical and Civil*, ed., intro. and notes E. Curley, Indianapolis, IN: Hackett Publishing Company, 1994. (The most important of Hobbes' works of political philosophy.)

* —— (1668) *Behemoth*, ed. W. Molesworth, Source Works Series No. 38, New York: Burt Franklin Research, 1962. (Reveals Hobbes' view of the role of the universities in the English Civil War.)

Hook, S. (1946) *Education For Modern Man: A New*

Perspective, New York: Alfred A. Knopf. (An elaboration and defence of Dewey's philosophy of education.)

Kant, I. (1775–80) *Eine Vorlesung Kants Über Ethik im Auftrage der Kantgesellschaft* (*Lectures on Ethics*) trans. L. Infield, Indianapolis, IN: Hackett Publishing Company, 1980. (See especially 'The Ethical Systems of the Ancients'; 'Conscience'; 'Self-Mastery'; 'Duties Towards Particular Classes of Human Beings'; 'Duties Arising From Differences of Age'; and 'The Ultimate Destiny of the Human Race'.)

—— (1784–98) *Political Writings*, ed., intro. and notes H. Reiss, trans. H.B. Nisbet, Cambridge: Cambridge University Press, 1991. (See especially the essays 'Idea For a Universal History With a Cosmopolitan Purpose'; 'An Answer to the Question: "What is Enlightenment?"'; 'The Contest of Faculties'; and 'Conjectures on the Beginning of Human History'.)

—— (1803) *Über Pädagogik* (*Kant on Education*), trans. A. Churton, Bristol: Thoemmes Press, 1992. (A compilation of Kant's notes and published remarks on education.)

Kraut, R. (ed.) (1992) *The Cambridge Companion to Plato*, Cambridge: Cambridge University Press. (Many important aspects of Plato's educational philosophy are examined in this accessible guide to his thought.)

Lloyd, S.A. (1992) *Ideals as Interests in Hobbes's Leviathan*, Cambridge: Cambridge University Press. (An interpretation which takes seriously the important role of education in the *Leviathan*.)

Locke, J. (1689) *Essay Concerning Human Understanding*, ed. P.H. Nidditch, Oxford: Clarendon Press, 1975. (A seminal work in the theory of ideas and knowledge.)

—— (1690) *Second Treatise of Government*, ed. and intro. C.B. Macpherson, Indianapolis, IN: Hackett Publishing Company, 1980. (A political work which includes remarks on the educational duties of parents.)

—— (1693) *Some Thoughts Concerning Education*, ed., intro. and notes J.W. Yolton and J.S. Yolton, Oxford: Clarendon Press, 1989. (Locke's principal work on education.)

—— (1706) *Of the Conduct of the Understanding*, ed., intro. and notes T. Fowler, New York: Burt Franklin, 1971. (Reprint of 1882 edition. A treatise on the cultivation of the intellect.)

Maritain, J. (1943) *Education at the Crossroads*, New Haven, CT: Yale University Press. (An influential elaboration of a twentieth-century Catholic philosophy of education.)

Marrou, H. (1956) *A History of Education in Antiquity*, trans. G. Lamb, London: Sheed & Ward. (A readable account of educational theory and practice down through the Hellenistic, Roman and early medieval periods.)

—— (1957) *St. Augustine and His Influence Through the Ages*, New York: Harper & Brothers. (Standard interpretation of the educational aspects of Augustine's thought and influence.)

Marx, K. (1845–6) *Die deutsche Ideologie* (*The German Ideology*), pt 1, with selections from pts 2 and 3, ed. C.J. Arthur, trans. W. Lough, C. Dutt and C.P. Magill, New York: International Publishers, 1974. (The only work by Marx expressly concerned with ideology.)

—— (1867) *Das Kapital* (*Capital*), vol. 1, ed. F. Engles, trans. S. Moore and Aveling, New York: International Publishers, 1967. (An important source of Marx's ideas about ideology.)

Masters, R.D. (1968) *The Political Writings of Rousseau*, Princeton, NJ: Princeton University Press. (A general and very readable commentary offering an extended examination of *Émile* as its point of departure.)

Mill, J.S. (1859) *On Liberty*, ed. E. Rapaport, Indianapolis, IN: Hackett Publishing Company, 1978. (An important source of liberal, educational and cultural theory.)

—— (1867) 'Inaugural Address at the University of St. Andrews', in *John Stuart Mill on Education*, ed., intro. and notes F.W. Garforth, New York: Teachers College Press, 1971. (This volume also contains the parts of Mill's *Autobiography* which are of educational interest.)

—— (1873) *Autobiography*, ed. R. Howson, New York: Columbia University Press, 1944. (Includes a lengthy account of Mill's own education and commentary on it.)

Nehamas, A. (1992) 'What Did Socrates Teach And To Whom Did He Teach It?', *Review of Metaphysics* 46 (4): 279–306. (An examination of Socrates' denial that he was a teacher, with useful discussion of other interpretations.)

Nietzsche, F. (1872) *Über die Zukunft unserer Bildungsanstalten* (*On the Future of Our Educational Institutions*), in *The Complete Works of Friedrich Nietzsche*, vol. 3, ed. O. Levy, trans. J.M. Kennedy, New York: Russell & Russell, 1924. (A critique of the democratization of the universities.)

—— (1874) *Schopenhauer als Erzieher* (*Schopenhauer as Educator*), trans. J.W. Hillesheim and M.R. Simpson, Chicago, IL: Regnery Gateway, Inc., 1965. (On what it means to be a teacher of mankind.)

Painter, F. (1889) *Luther on Education*, St. Louis, MO: Concordia Publishing House. (A readable but not impartial history with translations of Luther's two notable educational works.)

Pestalozzi, J. (1777–1826) *Pestalozzi's Educational Writings*, ed. J.A. Green and F. Collie, London: Longmans, 1912. (A selection of his diverse educational works.)

* Plato (390s–350s BC) *Complete Works*, ed. J. Cooper, Indianapolis, IN: Hackett Publishing Company, 1996. (The dialogues of most direct relevance are the *Euthydemus, Protagoras, Meno, Gorgias, Symposium, Republic, Theaetetus* and *Laws*.)

Price, K. (1967) *Education and Philosophical Thought*, Boston, MA: Allyn & Bacon, 2nd edn. (An introductory but dated history, with selections from major figures.)

* Quintilian (Marcus Fabius Quintilianus) (*c.*92) *Institutio Oratoria* (*The Education of an Orator*), vols. 1–4, text and trans. H.E. Butler, London: Heinemann, 1920–2. (On rhetoric and the principles of education.)

Reeve, C.D.C. (1988) *Philosopher-Kings*, Princeton, NJ: Princeton University Press. (An excellent treatment of the *Republic* and its educational proposals.)

* Rousseau, J.-J. (1750–62) *The Basic Political Writings of Jean–Jacques Rousseau*, trans. D.A. Cress, Indianapolis, IN: Hackett Publishing Company, 1987. (Includes the first and second *Discourses, Political Economy*, and *On the Social Contract*.)

* —— (1762) *Émile*, (or *On Education*), trans. A. Bloom, New York: Basic Books, 1979. (Rousseau's principal work on education.)

Schiller, F. (1795) *Briefe über die ästhetische Erziehung des Menschen* (*On The Aesthetic Education of Man: In a Series of Letters*), trans. E.M. Wilkinson and L.A. Willoughby, Oxford: Clarendon Press, 1967. (A seminal defence of aesthetic education as the means to develop both sensibility and rationality. See §8 above.)

Schouls, P. (1989) *Descartes and the Enlightenment*, Edinburgh: Edinburgh University Press. (A detailed discussion of the aspects of Descartes' thought bearing on his concept of good instruction, and their influence on the Enlightenment.)

Sherman, N. (1989) *The Fabric of Character*, Oxford: Oxford University Press. (A sophisticated account of Aristotle's theory of virtue and character education.)

Sullivan, R. (1989) *Immanuel Kant's Moral Theory*, Cambridge: Cambridge University Press. (A comprehensive and lucid interpretation, with an appendix on moral education.)

Ulich, R. (ed.) (1954) *Three Thousand Years of Educational Wisdom: Selections From Great Documents*, Cambridge, MA: Harvard University Press. (Useful as an introduction to texts and traditions in educational thought which could not be included here.)

Whitehead, A.N. (1929) *The Aims of Education*, New York: Macmillan. (Apart from Dewey, possibly the most significant work in philosophy of education from the first half of the twentieth century.)

Woodward, W. (1904) *Desiderius Erasmus: Concerning the Aim and Method of Education*, Cambridge: Cambridge University Press. (A historical and expository essay and translations of the major educational writings.)

RANDALL R. CURREN

EDUCATION, PHILOSOPHY OF

The philosophy of education is primarily concerned with the nature, aims and means of education, and also with the character and structure of educational theory, and its own place in that structure. Educational theory is best regarded as a kind of practical theory which would ideally furnish useful guidance for every aspect and office of educational practice. Such guidance would rest in a well-grounded and elaborated account of educational aims and the moral and political dimensions of education, and also in adequate conceptions and knowledge of teaching, learning, evaluation, the structure and dynamics of educational and social systems, the roles of relevant stake-holders and the like.

Philosophers of education often approach educational issues from the vantage points of other philosophical sub-disciplines, and contribute in a variety of ways to the larger unfinished project of educational theory. These contributions may be divided into work on the nature and aims of education, on the normative dimensions of the methods and circumstances of education, and on the conceptual and methodological underpinnings of its methods and circumstances – either directly or through work on the foundations of other forms of research relied upon by education theory.

Philosophical analysis and argument have suggested certain aims as essential to education, and various movements and branches of philosophy, from Marxism and existentialism to epistemology and ethics, have suggested aims, in every case controversially. Thus, one encounters normative theories of thought, conduct and the aims of education inspired by a broad consideration of epistemology, logic, aesthetics and ethics, as well as Marxism, feminism and a host of other '-isms'. In this mode of educational philosophizing, the objects of various branches of philosophical study are proposed as the ends of education, and the significance of pursuing those ends is elaborated with reference to those branches of study.

A second form of educational philosophy derives from substantive arguments and theories of ethics, social and political philosophy and philosophy of law, and concerns itself with the aims of education and the acceptability of various means to achieve them. It revolves around arguments concerning the moral, social and political appropriateness of educational aims, initiatives and policies, and moral evaluation of the methods, circumstances and effects of education. Recent debate has been dominated by concerns about children's rights and freedom, educational equality and justice, moral and political education, and issues of authority, control and professional ethics.

The philosophy of education has also sought to guide educational practice through examining its assumptions about the structure of specific knowledge domains and the minds of learners; about learning, development, motivation, and the communication and acquisition of knowledge and understanding. Philosophy of science and mathematics have informed the design of curriculum, pedagogy and evaluation in the teaching of science and mathematics. Philosophy of mind, language and psychology bear on the foundations of our understanding of how learning occurs, and thus how teaching may best promote it.

1 **Philosophical analysis and theory**
2 **Epistemology and the curriculum**
3 **Logic and critical thinking**
4 **Aesthetics, perception and creativity**
5 **Ethics**
6 **Political philosophy**
7 **Philosophy of law and education policy**
8 **Philosophy of science**
9 **Philosophy of mind, language and psychology**

1 Philosophical analysis and theory

Philosophy of education emerged in the second half of the twentieth century as a distinct branch of philosophy, devoted to the systematic study of education through the methods of conceptual analysis and the methods and findings of other, more established philosophical sub-disciplines and movements. This was evident in the creation of journals and societies of philosophy of education, but more importantly in the work of Richard Peters, Israel Scheffler and others who recast philosophy of education in an analytical mould and brought educational philosophizing in the schools and departments of education of the English-speaking world into closer contact with mainstream philosophy.

This process of recasting the methods of philosophy of education had begun in the 1940s with the work of C.D. Hardie, but at mid-century what mostly passed for educational philosophy was a lengthy menu of 'educational philosophies' consisting of little more than restatements of a common stock of wisdom about schooling in the vocabularies of various 'schools' of thought. These pragmatist, idealist, realist and other philosophies of education were grounded in the conviction that a philosophy of education can be derived from the tenets of any 'philosophical school', a mistake whose continuing influence is evident in more recent attempts to develop existentialist, phenomenological, hermeneutical, postmodernist and other philosophies of education.

As it developed from the late 1950s to the 1970s, analytical philosophy of education was centrally concerned with the analysis of educational concepts such as 'teaching', 'learning', and 'understanding'. A good example of this kind of work is Scheffler's (1960) analysis of teaching as involving an intent to bring about learning, the use of instructional strategies reasonably calculated to engender it, and a manner respectful of the learner's rationality. An extensive literature developed around this 'standard thesis', generating alternative analyses and accounts of quality in teaching, the boundaries between indoctrination and teaching, and the nature of learning. Some of this was illuminating and may have helped to clear away confusions and false assumptions about teaching in the literature of educational studies and reform, but conceptual analysis was a tool of limited efficacy in a domain lacking the sorts of metaphysical problems that Wittgenstein, Austin and Ryle had been at pains to resolve. The analysis of educational concepts went forward with neither the larger philosophical purposes of the formal and ordinary language movements themselves, nor the normative resources which the great educational theories of philosophy's past had brought to bear on practice (see ANALYTICAL PHILOSOPHY; ORDINARY LANGUAGE PHILOSOPHY, SCHOOL OF).

Work on this core of distinctly educational concepts had declined so substantially by the 1980s that one might reasonably judge that philosophy of education had lost its identity as a distinct sub-discipline and been reabsorbed into the parent discipline and its sturdier progeny. In any case it has been relatively inconspicuous in an era when other domains of practical philosophy have enjoyed spectacular growth and development, even as its scattered remains have been reinvigorated by the richer methods and bodies of work that have developed in ethics, political philosophy, informal logic and philosophy of the sciences, and by an outpouring of scholarship on the history of philosophy that is both philosophical and seriously historical. Philosophers of education had never ceased to engage the history of their field, but they are now in a position to do so more profitably.

The rich and largely untapped opportunities at hand are best pursued with a reasonable conception in view of the ways in which the philosophy of education can appropriately contribute to the larger enterprise of educational theory. This requires a model of the structure of a theory of education and of the place of philosophy of education within it.

Frankena (1965) and others have defended the view that philosophy of education must be regarded as principally an offshoot of ethics, and Hirst (1983) has formulated a plausible view of educational theory as a systematic body of practical principles generated, tested and justified by practice as much as through research in the disciplines. But a full account of the ways in which philosophy can contribute to the development of educational theory has yet to be synthesized. Broadly speaking, one can say that a fully elaborated theory of education would span education's aims and means, its patients, practitioners and beneficiaries, its manner, mode and circumstances of provision, providing practical guidance which both explains and justifies what is to be done. The subdivisions of philosophy contribute to this enterprise through suggesting and illuminating the character of possible goals of education (see §§2–4), justifying educational aims and providing normative guidance for various aspects of the provision of education (§§5–7), and through guidance regarding assumptions of fact about learning, development and the character of specific subject domains (§§8–9).

2 Epistemology and the curriculum

Philosophical theories of the curriculum have generally been guided either by ethical or political-theoretic arguments about the proper aims and constraints of education (see §§5–6), or by an embrace of the concerns of one or another of the philosophical sub-disciplines or movements. Existentialists have proposed authenticity and freedom as the aims which should guide teaching and the curriculum, Marxists and critical theorists propose social reconstruction or the abandonment of hierarchically imposed curricula, feminists a more girl-centred curriculum (see EXISTENTIALISM; FEMINISM; MARX, K.). Epistemology commends knowledge as a worthy object of instruction, and provides some basic guidance in how to make it one.

Peters (1966) held in his early writings that education consists in initiation into the forms of knowledge evolved by society, both to develop the mind and to transmit a valuable heritage. Dewey had rejected knowledge-transmission models of education in favour of an emphasis on experimentation, problem-solving and critical thinking rooted in the child's prior interests (see DEWEY, J.); Peters argued in response that the disciplines themselves supply the various forms of critical thinking and problems to be addressed, and that it is the teacher's job to lead children beyond their present interests to a love of knowledge. Hirst (1973) developed a similar view of *liberal* education, arguing that the development of a rational mind is inseparable from initiation into the forms of knowledge, and that this initiation should involve an 'immersion' in the concepts and methods of the various forms sufficient to yield an understanding of how each works and to allow the learner to experience the world through their distinctive structures.

Epistemology clearly lacks the wherewithal to warrant such a narrow view of the curriculum, as Peters later recognized, but it may still provide guidance for education to the extent that knowledge or the development of an ability to acquire it is an acknowledged aim. Scheffler (1965) has perhaps made the most of what analytical epistemology has to offer, by developing the distinction between knowing-that and knowing-how, and examining the implications for teaching of the *belief* and *evidence* conditions for knowing-that. The former demands that classrooms engage students' beliefs, rather than merely train them to give the right answers; the latter demands that they encourage internalization of the methods and forms of evidence by which knowledge is generated if students are to be epistemically autonomous.

Most of the recent literature has taken its cue not so much from philosophical epistemology as from a variety of movements built on unwitting adherence to remnants of logical positivism, confusion over the significance of debates about foundationalism, and epistemological scepticism rooted in theories of ideology and the incommensurability of paradigms (see §8). The dominant concern is that authority in school and society has rested illicitly on claims of epistemic authority.

3 Logic and critical thinking

Logic would seem to commend rationality as an educational goal or ideal, much as epistemology does, and to suggest that there are skills of reason or rational inference that can be isolated and taught independently of other aspects of the curriculum. Since the 1960s, however, there has developed a large body of work on critical thinking predicated on the inadequacy of formal deductive logic as an account of quality in inference, argumentation and reasoning. Formal logic has thus been largely set aside as a model for the teaching of critical thinking, though something of its spirit has been preserved in the idea of subject-neutral principles of reason assessment advocated even by those who regard critical thinking as no less epistemic than logical. This critical thinking movement has produced not only one of the more important streams of theoretical analysis undertaken in recent philosophy of education, but also innovations in curriculum and evaluation procedures at all levels of instruction.

Debate about the nature, teaching and evaluation of critical thinking was strongly influenced through the 1960s and 1970s by the work of Ennis (1962), who first conceived of critical thinking as correctly assessing statements, later as thinking that is reasonable, reflective and concerned with assessing not only beliefs, but also actions. His focus on discrete skills of reasoning has drawn a variety of criticisms.

McPeck (1990) has argued, against not only Ennis but the critical thinking movement generally, that there is no significant body of general critical thinking skills which can be taught. Citing Hirst, he argues that the subject-specific forms of inquiry we engage in have too little in common for us to extract a common logic which can be profitably taught as a subject in its own right.

Other philosophers have rebutted McPeck's grounds for denying the existence of a robust set of subject-neutral critical thinking skills, while also arguing that there is more to being a critical thinker than possessing such skills. Paul (1982) has insisted that the mastery of atomic thinking skills only makes one a 'weak sense' critical thinker with the ability to criticize the views of others and reinforce one's own. Exchanges of arguments involve clashes between opposing perspectives or world views, so to be a 'strong sense' critical thinker involves being able to take a sympathetic view of perspectives and world views one does not hold, he argues. Resisting the potential relativism in Paul's view (see RELATIVISM), Siegel (1988) has argued that it is 'atomistic' criteria of appraisal that we must rely on in judging worldviews. He holds that a critical thinker is one who is appropriately moved by reasons, one who possesses not only the abilities of rational assessment but a willingness, desire and disposition to follow reason. Lipman (1991) has argued that philosophy itself affords the best training in reasonableness and judiciousness guided by the ideal of rationality, and that it requires that we convert classrooms at all grade levels into 'communities of inquiry' through conversation governed by norms of reasonableness and mutual respect.

These developments lay useful groundwork for an integration of work in philosophy of education with broader philosophical investigations of the nature of rationality and good judgment.

4 Aesthetics, perception and creativity

The precarious position of the arts and the aesthetic in contemporary education has lent urgency to questions about the aims and value of education in the arts. Philosophers of education have sought to answer these questions through engagement with philosophical aesthetics and the philosophy of art and literature. Their primary concern has been to elaborate a compelling vision of the value of a proper education in the arts; their assertions of value have rested sometimes in direct appeals to the quality of human experience, but more often in accounts of the contributions of the aesthetic to the cognitive, practical and productive aspects of human existence.

In work first published in the 1970s, Scheffler held that aesthetic experience is not simply emotional but also cognitive, and that in interpreting both art and the situations which confront us in life our feelings guide our perceptions (see Scheffler 1991). Greene (1995) and Nussbaum (1990) have taken related lines of thought farther in arguing that education in the arts develops a perceptiveness which equips one well for life. The former has argued that the visual and performance arts embody distinct representational symbol systems whose mastery 'releases' the learner's perception and imagination, thereby liberating both judgment and action. The latter has brought an Aristotelian account of the development of virtue and practical judgment in defence of literary art, and the novel especially, for its value in cultivating the capacity to discern and respond to what is morally salient in concrete situations.

Philosophical interest in the productive and performance aspects of arts instruction has focused on the nature of creativity and how best to promote it. In opposition to the widespread belief that creative and rational thought are mutually exclusive, the tendency of recent philosophical work, such as Bailin (1988), has been to view significant achievement as the measure of creativity, and productive imagination as resting on knowledge and skill.

5 Ethics

Ethics holds a central place in philosophy of education through its role in justifying not only the aims and priorities of education, but education itself.

Peters (1966) shaped the course of debate with an argument for eschewing talk of aims and a non-instrumental justification of education, but by the 1970s the landscape was crowded with 'de-schoolers' and child liberationists who denied that imposing education on children is justified. The liberationists argued that children must be assigned the same liberty rights as adults, and held that the consequences of doing so would be benign. Purdy (1992) has refuted this most effectively, with a review of the evidence against the liberationists' optimistic assumptions about children's rationality and development in the absence of constraint, and with a defence of the legitimacy of moral education in government-run schools. She, Callan (1988) and others have nevertheless defended the importance of autonomy as a central goal of education, arguing in various ways that the development of autonomy is promoted by upbringing and teaching which nurture self-control, critical thinking, self-examination and related traits. Others have appealed to children's rights and wellbeing, the duties of adults and other forms of moral premises in defending educational aims ranging from various conceptions of the individual student's good to promotion of environmental responsibility.

R.M. HARE stimulated interest in moral education with his view, first adumbrated in *The Language of Morals* (1952), that what is important is that children should learn the *form* of morality so that they may find and embrace a set of moral principles of their own. Other prominent moral theorists followed his lead, generating a debate largely defined by the tensions between Kantian and Aristotelian views (see KANTIAN ETHICS). Kurt Baier (1973) and others took positions sympathetic to Lawrence Kohlberg's conception of moral development as a sequence of stages toward mature moral reasoning. Resisting both 'moral indoctrination' and treating the child's intuited 'values' as authoritative, they advocated instruction in moral reasoning that would enable a child to become morally autonomous or able to identify and apply rationally acceptable moral principles. Taking a more Aristotelian view, Pincoffs (1986) defended moral habituation from the charge of indoctrination with the argument that it is only through such habituation that one can perceive and appreciate the moral qualities of things (see ARISTOTLE §§21–3). He and Nussbaum have developed virtue-centred accounts of moral education which regard the development of perception, affect and judgment as interrelated. Recent work has sought to join such approaches with accounts of care, trust and the psychosocial foundations of moral learning.

Educational ethics has become increasingly visible as a branch of professional and practical ethics not unlike medical or business ethics. This is particularly true of the ethics of higher education, which has flourished in eras of crisis in the universities such as the 1960s and 1990s. The topics that dominate current debate include curricular multiculturalism; university neutrality in the face of injustice or political controversy; university–business partnerships and other arrangements that may compromise academic integrity; the proper management of student life in the face of sexual harassment and violence, alcohol and drug abuse, and racism. Multiculturalism has also become an important focus of debate in the ethics of primary and secondary education, joining such topics as the ethics of student evaluation, discipline and classroom management, and the ethics of educational research (see MULTICULTURALISM).

6 Political philosophy

Political philosophy has been a perennial source of reflection on the significance of education for civic life, and on the proper role of the state in overseeing and sponsoring education. The classical tradition took education to be an important instrument of statesmanship and civic wellbeing, while liberals such as John Stuart MILL regarded state sponsorship of education as a threat to liberty. Modern liberal democracies have neither fully accepted nor fully rejected either of these views in practice, nor have they fully accepted or rejected the liberal egalitarian idea that equal educational opportunity is essential to social justice. The tensions and tradeoffs involved in these compromised commitments generate ongoing debate, and provide an important context for assessing the import of the ethical endorsements of education for autonomy noted in §5.

A 'liberal education' is defined by 'comprehensive liberals', such as Ackerman (1980), as one that would provide children with the resources to develop their own self-conceptions and choose their own courses in life. This requires that it be nondirective with respect to substantive conceptions of the good, and promote autonomy grounded in rational scrutiny of the alternatives. 'Political liberals', such as Macedo (1995), argue in response that this requirement is not easily reconciled with liberalism's own acceptance of diversity. Can one coherently endorse individual autonomy while denying parents the right to bring their children up in their own traditions and religion? Another line of argument which rejects comprehensive liberalism concerns itself with a perceived decline in civic commitment and a sense of sharing in a common good and belonging to a common social order (see COMMUNITY AND COMMUNITARIANISM; LIBERALISM).

Gutmann's liberal democratic view of education (1987) is built on an uneasy alliance between this communitarian view and comprehensive liberalism. She holds that democracy requires that communities be able to shape their futures through democratic control of education, subject to the limits set by principles which demand, among other things, that all children be enabled through education to participate 'effectively' in democratic deliberations. In the face of widely divergent views of the prospects for creating an 'educated public' able to rationally engage in such deliberations, MacIntyre (1987) has derived an account of the conditions that are required, from a historical instance in which they were arguably present.

Marxist critiques of schooling and liberal meritocracy begin by noting the persistence of inequality, and historical connections between the rise of government-run school systems and the factory system. They conclude that the perpetuation of inequality has been essential to the role of schools in capitalist societies, their function being to sort students for different economic positions, in a way that masks the intergenerational transmission of class behind an ideology of individual effort and desert. Many variants of this view have developed around different conceptions of the assets which schools provide to those bound for economic and social privilege, but their recommendations for practice seem invariably to follow Gramsci's vision of offering whatever resistance to the dominant ideology one can, in whatever institutional setting one can (see Gramsci 1971).

The most recent work in the Marxist tradition attempts to overcome its preoccupation with class stratification, by emphasizing the importance of other dimensions of social cleavage and oppression, such as race, gender and sexual orientation. A related feminist criticism of liberal educational theory and reform, which bears importantly on the care and upbringing of children, is that they have opened up greater opportunity for women to choose traditionally male paths in life, but have done little to elevate domestic work or prepare anyone to do it well (see FEMINIST POLITICAL PHILOSOPHY).

7 Philosophy of law and education policy

In philosophy of education there are two kinds of work which involve a direct concern with law and draw significantly upon work in the history and philosophy of law. One addresses the general relationships between law and education, the other treats educational issues as problems of public policy whose resolution may be aided by legal argument and reform.

Ancient Greek thought was acutely attuned to questions about the relationships between law and education, and understood both that compliance with law must rest for the most part in an informed acceptance of its demands, and that the laws themselves and all the institutions of a city are educative and must be so regarded to ensure civic wellbeing. The re-evaluation of these views is evident in Curren's examination of the role of education in the foundations of just law (1995b), in connection with the ideal of rule by consent, and in the work of Sandel (1996) and other communitarians who have reasserted the claim that national policy and law should be shaped by a sensitivity to their educative import. This latter development is particularly important for educational philosophy, inasmuch as there are compelling reasons to think that schooling is not the whole of education, and that its prospects for success are limited by the broader educational forces in a society.

Education is an important arena of public policy debate, and an appropriate though underdeveloped object of philosophical public policy studies. Some of the most important topics of current discussion are educational equality, freedom of speech and religion in government-run education, proposals to create arrangements which would allow parents a choice of schools at the public expense, and school safety and security. These debates bring a consideration of common law principles and fundamental constitutional rights to bear on some of the issues at stake in debates about liberal and democratic education.

Debate over educational equality has focused on alternative conceptions of its form, the educational goals it should be concerned with, and the principles which demand it. Is full equalization the appropriate aim, for instance, or is the relative equality inherent in assuring that all students reach some specified threshold acceptable? Or should one only be concerned, as the courts of the USA are, to ensure that race, native language, learning disabilities and other 'suspect' factors are not barriers to equal educational opportunity? With regard to the justification of equality (see EQUALITY), does the principle of 'equal protection' in the free enjoyment of fundamental political rights provide grounds for insisting on equality, as some, including Gutmann (1987) and Curren (1995a), have argued?

An important line of argument regarding children's rights begins with the conviction that the free speech rights of adults are meaningless if the state can control through education what one thinks as a child. If this is correct, then one might conclude that inculcation of community values beyond a core of essential civic commitments is a breach of fundamental rights. One might also conclude, as Arons (1986) does, that taking freedom of speech and religion seriously requires that parents be provided with a financially feasible choice among schools. An important issue in the philosophy and policy of higher education at present, is how constitutional protection of free speech should be understood to apply to attempts to draft speech codes to suppress racist 'hate speech'.

A debate which invokes common-law principles, rather than constitutional ones, is how we should understand the framework of fundamental legal principles bearing on the school's responsibility for the safety of students. How should one regard the elements of sovereign immunity to liability still present in the legal systems of common-law countries, given the role of compulsory attendance laws in placing children in a position of danger, if school personnel fail to provide adequate security against assault by third parties?

8 Philosophy of science

In order to teach a subject with sensitivity to its epistemic structure, teachers must grasp and be guided by the same kind of understanding which philosophers of science, mathematics, history or economics aim at – that is, a secure (if nontechnical) sense of the methods of discovery or investigation, of the methods and logic of confirmation, and of the forms of explanation and theory which define it as a mode of inquiry, and they must attend to these in both teaching and evaluating students. Philosophy of science in particular has been called into service in efforts to reshape pedagogy, curriculum and methods of assessment, though the lessons drawn could be applied in the teaching of other subjects as well.

An international 'crisis' in science education was declared in the 1980s in a series of reports citing dismal levels of both learning and interest in science, and further concern about the inadequacy of science instruction has been generated since then by neo-romantic attacks on science by postmodernists and some feminists. Government calls for revision of science curricula have become more receptive to the idea that students should not only learn science, but learn *about* science, giving encouragement to the idea that introducing history and philosophy of science into the science curriculum would give students not only a more accurate appreciation of science as an enterprise, but a far more engaging one as well.

Two important related topics in current debates about science instruction are constructivism and multiculturalism. Constructivists promote 'discovery' learning in science in the belief that scientific thinking develops naturally in children, a belief rooted in a form of empiricism according to which science finds order in experience, and (in the radical versions of constructivism) has access to nothing beyond immediate experience. Versions of relativism originating in selective readings of Kuhn's work have also become pervasive in educational theory and found their way into proposals for multicultural curricula which would present ethno-sciences as no less rationally confirmed than Western science. Matthews (1994) and others have responded with observations about the distinctiveness of Western science, reminders of Kuhn's insistence that science *is* rational (though not in a way that can be adequately represented as rule following), and by identifying the empiricist and positivistic premises relied upon by constructivists, even as they denounce positivism (see KUHN, T.).

Philosophers of education have also made use of work in philosophy of science in offering methodological critiques of social science research in education, and have relied on models of explanation drawn from action theory and philosophy of the social sciences in evaluating and offering alternatives to the explanatory models underlying educational critiques and policy proposals. Green (1980) has been among the most ambitious in this regard in developing what amounts to a rational-choice model of the dynamics of educational systems.

9 Philosophy of mind, language and psychology

It is widely assumed within the educational research community that psychology, cognitive science, psychometrics and social learning theory have largely displaced philosophy from its historical role in formulating theories of the mind, language and human development, and determining what implications (if any) those theories have for educational practice (see COGNITIVE DEVELOPMENT; LEARNING). Nevertheless, at least two roles related to this empirical aspect of educational theory remain appropriate for philosophy, one foundational and critical, the other interpretative and synthetic.

Gilbert RYLE gave encouragement in *The Concept of Mind* to the possibility of a 'philosophy of learning', but the analyses of mental concepts which this inspired in the 1950s and 1960s have given way more recently to interest in the foundations and adequacy of the bodies of psychological and measurement research which educational researchers have looked to for guidance in the conduct of educational practice. Behaviourist learning theory and cognitive and moral stage theories have been subjected to critical scrutiny by a number of philosophers. Wren (1982) has examined social learning theory and found its accounts of self-regulation inadequate. Block and Dworkin (1974) have produced a notable critique of 'general intelligence' as a theoretical construct and identified deficiencies in the validation of IQ tests as a measure of it. Norris (1995) and others have contributed in a variety of ways to conceptual, experimental and development efforts pertaining to validity, test formats and the measurement of critical and 'higher-order' thinking in classroom and standardized tests of achievement.

Even when psychological findings can be accepted at face value, however, their relevance to educational practice can only be settled by recourse to a theory of education concerned with the kinds of persons we should want students to become. A psychological theory is not itself such a theory, despite the recent dominance of psychology in educational studies. There remains the interpretive and synthetic task of building a cogent educational theory, drawing on whatever facts and practical know-how may be available, which a philosopher is as well-equipped as anyone to undertake. It is a task as important as it is difficult, and if the results of past efforts often fall short, both philosophically and practically, that is all the more reason for capable philosophers to turn their attention to it.

See also: EDUCATION, HISTORY OF PHILOSOPHY OF

References and further reading

* Ackerman, B.A. (1980) *Social Justice in The Liberal State*, New Haven, CT: Yale University Press. (Referred to in §6. Includes a 'comprehensive liberal' theory of education.)
* Arons, S. (1986) *Compelling Belief*, Amherst, MA: University of Massachusetts Press. (Referred to in §7. A good introduction to issues of free speech, religion and values, and parental versus community control of education.)
* Baier, K. (1973) 'Moral Autonomy as an Aim of Moral Education', in G. Langford and D.J. O'Connor (eds) *New Essays in the Philosophy of Education*, London: Routledge & Kegan Paul. (Referred to in §5. Defence of a Kantian view by a leading moral theorist.)
* Bailin, S. (1988) *Achieving Extraordinary Ends: An Essay on Creativity*, Dordrecht: Kluwer Academic Publishers. (Referred to in &4. An essay on the nature and teaching of creativity.)
* Block, N. and G. Dworkin (1974) 'IQ, Heritability and Inequality' pts I and II, *Philosophy and Public Affairs* 3 (4): 331–409; 4 (1): 40–99. (Referred to in §9. Combines philosophy of psychology and ethics.)
Burgess, R.G. (ed.) (1989) *The Ethics of Educational Research*, New York: The Falmer Press. (Topics in educational research ethics.)
Cahn, S. (ed.) (1990) *Morality, Responsibility, and the University*, Philadelphia, PA: Temple University Press. (Essays in the ethics of higher education.)
* Callan, E. (1988) *Autonomy and Schooling*, Montreal, Que.: McGill-Queen's University Press. (Referred to in §5. A defence of autonomy as an aim of education.)
Cooper, D.E. (1986) *Education, Values and Mind: Essays for R.S. Peters*, London: Routledge & Kegan Paul. (Provides a good picture of Peters' formative role in the field and a bibliography of his work.)
* Curren, R. (1995a) 'Justice and the Threshold of Educational Equality', in M. Katz (ed.) *Philosophy of Education 1994*, Urbana, IL: Philosophy of Education Society. (Referred to in §7. On the form of equality, problems in Gutmann's view, an alternative to hers linked to Curren 1995b.)
* —— (1995b) 'Punishment and Inclusion', *Canadian Journal of Law & Jurisprudence* 8 (2): 259–74. (Referred to in §7. On the role of education in the foundations of law.)
—— (1995c) 'Coercion and the Ethics of Grading and Testing', *Educational Theory* 45 (4): 425–41. (A moral argument for changes in both standardized and classroom testing.)
* Ennis, R. (1962) 'A Concept of Critical Thinking', *Harvard Educational Review* 32 (1): 81–111. (Referred to in §3. An influential conception of critical thinking and its role in education.)
* Frankena, W. (1965) *Philosophy of Education*, New York: Macmillan. (Referred to in §1. An account of the structure of a philosophy of education derived from J.S. Mill, and a sampling of twentieth-century theories.)
Fuller, T. (ed.) (1989) *The Voice of Liberal Learning: Michael Oakeshott on Education*, New Haven, CT: Yale University Press. (A prominent conservative's major writings on education.)
Fullinwider, R. (ed.) (1996) *Public Education in a Multicultural Society*, Cambridge: Cambridge University Press. (On the philosophical issues pertaining to multicultural schooling.)
* Gramsci, A. (1971) *Selections From the Prison Notebooks*, London: Lawrence & Wishart. (Referred to in §6. A classic of twentieth-century Marxism.)
* Green, T.F. (1980) *Predicting The Behavior of the Educational System*, Syracuse, NY: Syracuse University Press. (Referred to in §8. Develops an explanatory model inspired by Anscombe's work on the explanation of action.)
* Greene, M. (1995) *Releasing the Imagination: Essays on Education, the Arts, and Social Change*, San

Francisco, CA: Jossey-Bass Publishers. (Referred to in §4. Essays by a leading US proponent of aesthetic education.)

* Gutmann, A. (1987) *Democratic Education*, Princeton, NJ: Princeton University Press. (Referred to in §§6–7. An influential work and useful guide to debates in education politics and policy.)

* Hardie, C.D. (1942) *Truth and Fallacy in Educational Theory*, Cambridge: Cambridge University Press. (Referred to in §1. A pioneering work in analytical philosophy of education.)

* Hare, R.M. (1952) *The Language of Morals*, Oxford: Clarendon Press. (Referred to in §5. A major meta-ethical work of the mid-twentieth century.)

—— (1992) *Essays on Religion and Education*, Oxford: Clarendon Press. (Essays on education and religion by a leading moral theorist.)

* Hirst, P.H. (1973) 'Liberal Education and the Nature of Knowledge', in R.S. Peters (ed.) *The Philosophy of Education*, Oxford: Oxford University Press. (Referred to in §2. An influential theory of the curriculum. The volume is a landmark in the emergence of the field and contains a helpful discursive bibliography.)

* —— (1983) 'Educational Theory', in *Educational Theory and Its Foundation Disciplines*, London: Routledge & Kegan Paul. (Referred to in §1. On the character and development of educational theory.)

Hoekema, D. (1994) *Campus Rules and Moral Community: In Place of In Loco Parentis*, Lanham, MA: Rowman & Littlefield. (On the ethics of college student life.)

Kaminsky, J.S. (1993) *A New History of Educational Philosophy*, London: Greenwood Press. (A controversial but informative history of educational philosophy as a field of study in the education schools of Australasia, the UK and the USA.)

Kleinig, J. (1982) *Philosophical Issues in Education*, London: Croom Helm. (A good survey of issues with an excellent bibliography.)

* Lipman, M. (1991) *Thinking In Education*, Cambridge: Cambridge University Press. (Referred to in §3. Good judgment as an aim of education, and Lipman's community of inquiry model for teaching it.)

* Macedo, S. (1995) 'Liberal Civic Education and Religious Fundamentalism: The Case of God v. John Rawls?' *Ethics* 105 (3): 468–96. (Referred to in §6. Lead article in a symposium on citizenship, democracy and education.)

* MacIntyre, A. (1987) 'The Idea of an Educated Public', in G. Haydon (ed.) *Education and Values*, London: Institute of Education, University of London. (Referred to in §6. Identifies the requirements for creating an educated public.)

* Martin, J.R. (1994) *Changing the Educational Landscape: Philosophy, Women, and Curriculum*, London: Routledge. (Essays in feminist philosophy of education.)

* Matthews, M.R. (1994) *Science Teaching: The Role of History and Philosophy of Science*, London: Routledge. (Referred to in §8. The best piece of work on science and education to date.)

* McPeck, J. (1990) *Teaching Critical Thinking*, New York: Routledge. (McPeck's essays and an exchange between him and other leading figures.)

* Norris, S. (1995) 'Format Effects on Critical Thinking Test Performance', *Alberta Journal of Educational Research* 41 (4): 378–406. (Referred to in §9. A philosopher's multidisciplinary work on alternative measures of performance in critical thinking.)

* Nussbaum, M. (1990) *Love's Knowledge: Essays on Philosophy and Literature*, Oxford: Oxford University Press. (Referred to in §§4–5. Essays on moral learning, the place of literary art in education and related topics.)

Passmore, J. (1980) *The Philosophy of Teaching*, London: Duckworth. (A comprehensive philosophy of pedagogy.)

* Paul, R.W. (1982) 'Teaching Critical Thinking in the "Strong" Sense', *Informal Logic Newsletter* 4 (2): 2–7. (Referred to in §3. A concise statement of Paul's view of critical thinking.)

* Peters, R.S. (1966) *Ethics and Education*, London: Allen & Unwin. (Referred to in §§2 and 5. Major statement of his early view, progressively modified in later works. For a list of his works see Cooper 1986.)

* Phillips, D.C. (1995) 'The good, the bad, and the ugly: The many faces of Constructivism', *Educational Researcher* 24 (7): 5–12. (A survey of the varieties of constructivist learning theory.)

* Pincoffs, E. (1986) *Quandries and Virtues*, Lawrence, KS: Kansas University Press. (Referred to in §5. Develops an account of moral education within a virtue-ethical framework.)

* Purdy, L. (1992) *In Their Best Interests? The Case Against Equal Rights For Children*, Ithaca, NY: Cornell University Press. (Referred to in §5. A feminist response to liberationist theories of education.)

* Ryle, G. (1949) *The Concept of Mind*, London: Hutchinson University Library. (Referred to in §9. A major work of the mid-twentieth century, and a significant influence on the course of philosophy of education.)

* Sandel, M. (1996) *Democracy's Discontent*, Cambridge, MA: Harvard University Press. (Referred to in §7. Takes a broad interdisciplinary view of the

educative significance of public institutions and policies.)

* Scheffler, I. (1960) *The Language of Education*, Springfield, IL: Charles C. Thomas. (Referred to in §1. An influential work in the analytic mode.)

* —— (1965) *Conditions of Knowledge: An Introduction to Epistemology and Education*, Glenview, IL: Scott, Foresman & Co. (Referred to in §2. Remains a good overview of the lessons of philosophical epistemology for education, even though its references are dated.)

* —— (1991) *In Praise of the Cognitive Emotions*, New York: Routledge. (Referred to in §4. Scheffler's essays in philosophy of education from the 1970s and 1980s.)

Sellers, M. (1994) *An Ethical Education*, Oxford: Berg Publishers. (Papers on the curriculum and aims of the university, campus speech and affirmative action.)

* Siegel, H. (1988) *Educating Reason: Rationality, Critical Thinking and Education*, New York: Routledge. (Referred to in §3. An important account of critical thinking as a goal of education.)

Strike, K. (1989) *Liberal Justice and the Marxist Critique of Education*, New York: Routledge. (A useful guide to Marxist theories of education.)

* Wren, T. (1982) 'Social Learning Theory, Self-Regulation, and Morality', *Ethics* 92 (3): 409–24. (Referred to in §9. Lead article in a symposium on moral development.)

RANDALL R. CURREN

EDWARDS, JONATHAN (1703–58)

Jonathan Edwards' work as a whole is an elaboration of two themes – God's absolute sovereignty and the beauty of his holiness. God's sovereignty is articulated in several ways. Freedom of the Will (1754) defends theological determinism. God is the complete cause of everything that occurs, including human volitions. Edwards is also an occasionalist, idealist and mental phenomenalist. God is the only real cause of events. Human volitions and 'natural causes' are mere 'occasions' upon which God produces the appropriate effects. Physical objects are collections of sensible 'ideas' of colour, shape, solidity, and so on, and finite minds are collections of 'thoughts' or 'perceptions'. God's production of sensible ideas and thoughts in the order which pleases him is the only 'substance' underlying them. God is thus truly 'being in general', the 'sum of all being'.

The beauty or splendour of God's holiness is the principal theme of two late works – End of Creation and True Virtue (both published posthumously in 1765). The first argues that God's end in creation is the external manifestation of his internal splendour. That splendour primarily consists in his holiness and its most perfect external expression is the holiness of the saints, which mirrors and depends upon it. True Virtue defines holiness as 'true benevolence' or 'the love of being in general' ([1765b] 1957–, vol. 8: 546), and distinguishes it from such counterfeits as rational self-love, instincts like parental affection and pity, and natural conscience. Since beauty is defined as 'agreement' or 'consent' and since true benevolence consents to being in general, true benevolence alone is truly beautiful. Natural beauty and the beauty of art are merely its image. Only those with truly benevolent hearts, however, can discern this beauty.

Edwards' projected History of Redemption would have drawn these themes together, for it is in God's work of redemption that his sovereignty, holiness and beauty are most effectively displayed.

1 **Life**
2 **Theological determinism**
3 **Idealism, mental phenomenalism, occasionalism and views on identity**
4 **God as being in general**
5 **God's end in creation**
6 **Ethics**
7 **Theological aesthetics**
8 **The sense of the heart**
9 ***The History of Redemption***

1 Life

Edwards was born into a family of Congregationalist clergymen in East Windsor, Connecticut in 1703. He entered Yale in 1716, where he read Locke and Newton and began 'The Mind' (1829a) and 'Natural Philosophy' (1829b). In 1725 the church in Northampton chose Edwards to succeed his grandfather, Solomon Stoddard. The most notable events of his tenure were the revivals of 1734 and 1740, the latter of which came to be known as the 'Great Awakening'. Edwards' defence of the revivals and criticisms of their excesses culminated in his first major treatise, the *Religious Affections* (1746). Worsening relations with his congregation came to a head in a dispute over qualifications for church membership, with Edwards rejecting the less rigorous standards of his grandfather and insisting on a public profession of saving faith. He was dismissed in 1750 by a margin of one vote. Refusing invitations to pulpits in North America and Scotland, Edwards retreated to the Indian mission at Stockbridge, where he completed his last major works – *Freedom of the Will* (1754), *Original Sin* (1758), *End of Creation* and *True Virtue* (both published posthumously in 1765). Edwards accepted an appointment as President of the College of New Jersey (now Princeton) in 1757. He died from smallpox in 1758, less than four weeks after his arrival.

2 Theological determinism

Edwards believed that indeterminism is incompatible with our dependence on God and hence with his sovereignty. If our responses to God's grace are contra-causally free, then our salvation partly depends on us and God's sovereignty is not 'absolute and universal'. *Freedom of the Will* is Edwards' defence of theological determinism. He first attempts to show that indeterminism is incoherent. For example, he argues that by 'self-determination' the indeterminist must mean either that one's actions (including one's acts of willing) are preceded by an act of free will or that one's acts of will lack sufficient causes. The first leads to an infinite regress while the second implies that acts of will happen accidentally. Edwards also contends that indeterminism is inconsistent with ordinary moral concepts. If, for instance, the necessity of sinning wholly excuses, then a bias to sin should partially excuse. But it does not; a person who acts from settled habits of maliciousness is deemed 'so much the more worthy to be detested and condemned' ([1754] 1957–, vol. 1: 360). Since indeterminism implies that necessity excuses, it is inconsistent with the way we attribute blame.

Edwards' principal reasons *for* theological determinism are God's sovereignty, the principle of sufficient reason (which requires that everything that begins to be have a complete cause), and God's foreknowledge (see OMNISCIENCE §3). God's foreknowledge is discussed at length. Call a decision I make at time t_n 'D'. God is omniscient and has therefore always believed that D occurs at t_n. Since God cannot be mistaken, the occurrence of D at t_n is entailed by his believing at some earlier time t_{n-m} that D occurs at t_n. But God's forebelief is past (in relation to t_n); therefore, it is 'now necessary' in the sense that nothing can be done at t_n to alter it. Now what is entailed by a necessary fact is itself necessary. Hence, D could not fail to occur at t_n. The conclusion cannot be evaded by appealing to God's timelessness and denying that God's forebeliefs precede their objects. For even though God's forebeliefs may be timeless, divinely inspired prophecies are not. Yet divinely inspired prophecies are necessarily connected with the acts of will they foretell and are clearly past (and

hence necessary) in relation to them. *Freedom of the Will* concludes by arguing that necessity is not incompatible with the ascription of praise and blame or with moral responsibility. We are responsible for our actions in the ordinary sense when we do what pleases us, and determinism does not deny that we often act as we please. And though God and Christ necessarily act for the best, their actions are eminently praiseworthy.

3 Idealism, mental phenomenalism, occasionalism and views on identity

Edwards' idealism, mental phenomenalism and occasionalism provide a philosophical interpretation of the doctrine of God's absolute sovereignty. If Edwards is correct, God is the only true substance and the only true cause.

True or real causes meet three conditions: (1) they cannot exist at different times or places from their effects; (2) they are total causes, in that nothing else is needed for their effects; and (3) they necessitate their effects. Now God is spatially and temporally omnipresent; nothing is separated from him by spatial or temporal distance. Furthermore, his activity is a necessary and fully sufficient condition for the occurrence of any spatiotemporal effect. Finally, God's will is necessarily effective. His will, therefore, is a true cause. Nothing else meets these conditions. Hence, God is the only real cause. Apparent causes (for example, striking a match) are simply the *occasions* upon which God produces effects (for example, the match's ignition) according to 'established methods and laws' (see OCCASIONALISM).

In an early paper ('Of Atoms') Edwards argued that the concept of a material substance underlying solidity, resistance and other physical properties is either empty or denotes God's causal activity. If material substance were real, it would be something which 'subsisted by itself, and stood underneath and kept up solidity and all other [physical] properties' ([1829b] 1957–, vol. 6: 215). God alone meets these conditions and is therefore the only 'substance' underlying physical properties. Deploying arguments analogous to (but apparently uninfluenced by) Berkeley's, Edwards further argues that a 'body is nothing but a particular mode of perception' and that 'the material universe exists only in the mind' ([1829a] 1957–, vol. 6: 368; 1957–, vol. 6: 398) (see BERKELEY, G. §§3, 6–7).

Edwards' mental phenomenalism is a natural extension of his occasionalism and views on material substance. God is the only real cause of 'thoughts' or 'perceptions'. If a substance is what 'subsists by itself', 'stands underneath' and 'keeps up' a set of properties, then the concept of mental substance too is either empty or denotes God's causal activity. A mind, therefore, 'is nothing but a composition and series of perceptions [mental events]...connected by...laws' ([1829a] 1957–, vol. 6: 398). Mental and physical substance are thus God's producing mental events and their objects (sensible ideas or 'sensations') 'according to...methods and laws' which he has freely established ([1829a] 1957–, vol. 6: 344).

God's sovereignty extends to criteria of identity. 'Species' (kinds or natures) are the ways we classify things. But our classifications depend on our needs and interests, and on the character of the world we live in. In determining these things, God has thus determined what counts as a 'species' or kind. Now criteria of identity are determined by a thing's nature. God, therefore, is the ultimate ground of these criteria (and hence can if he wishes treat Adam and his posterity as one thing, holding the children responsible for the sin of their progenitor).

4 God as being in general

As the only true substance and only true cause, God is 'being in general'. He 'is the sum of all being and there is no being without His being. All things are in Him and He in all' (1955: 87). Edwards does not mean that God is the power of being or being as such rather than an omniscient mind and omnipotent will. God 'is properly' a necessarily existing 'intelligent willing agent, such as our souls, only without our imperfections, and not some inconceivable, unintelligent, necessary agent' ([1955] 1957–, vol. 13: 452).

True Virtue associates being with capacity or power and asserts that 'degree of existence' is a function of 'greater capacity and power' ([1765b] 1957–, vol. 8: 546). 'Miscellany 94' (1890) assimilates perfect entity and perfect activity. 'An Essay on the Trinity' (1903) identifies God's perfect activity with his outflowing love or holy will. Other passages identify entity with mind or 'perceiving being'. The drift of these scattered observations is an identification of being with mind in action and of degree of being with degree of consciousness and the comparative perfection of the activity in which it is engaged. Because God's power and consciousness are unlimited, so too is his being.

In speaking of God as 'being in general', Edwards means more than that finite beings are totally dependent on God for their existence and properties. Because he is the only true substance and only true cause, created beings are no more than God's 'images' or 'shadows'. God is the 'head' of the system of beings, its 'chief part', an absolute sovereign whose being, power and perfection are so great 'that the whole system of created beings, in comparison of Him, is as the light dust of the balance' (1955: 142). 'Being in general' thus refers to the system of beings – principally to God but to 'particular beings' as well in so far as they depend upon and reflect him.

5 God's end in creation

End of Creation defines God's glory as 'the emanation and true external expression of God's internal glory and fullness'. It includes (1) 'the exercise of God's perfections to produce a proper effect', (2) 'the manifestation of his internal glory to created understandings', (3) 'the communication of the infinite fullness of God to the creature' and (4) 'the creature's high esteem of God, love to God, and complacence and joy in God; and the proper exercises and expressions of these' ([1765a] 1957–, vol. 8: 527).

The first and third 'parts' of God's glory are not ontologically distinct since the principal effect of God's exercise of his perfections is 'his fullness communicated'. And the third includes the second and fourth, as God's internal fullness or glory is the 'fullness of his understanding consisting in his knowledge' of himself 'and the fullness of his will consisting in his virtue and happiness'. God's 'external glory...consists in the communication of these', that is, in bringing it about that 'particular minds' know and love God and delight in him. One through four are thus 'one thing, in a variety of views and relations' ([1765a] 1957–, vol. 8: 527).

Edwards never doubted that God's end or aim must be that which is supremely good and excellent, namely himself. But he also thought that the essence of goodness is the communication of good for its own sake and that this implies that the creature's happiness is God's ultimate end. *End of Creation* reconciles these convictions by including human happiness (which consists in knowing and loving God, and rejoicing in him) in God's ultimate end, namely the communication of his internal glory 'ad extra'.

Now God is primarily glorious for his holiness and his will is holy because it exhibits true benevolence – the love of being in general in which 'true virtue' consists. The communication of his internal glory therefore principally consists in the holiness of the saints (the elect), which is identical with their love of being in general, that is, of God and their neighbour.

6 Ethics

Edwards' reflections on ethics culminate in *True Virtue* (1765b). True virtue's aim is the general good. Those who love the general good, however, also prize the disposition that promotes it. Truly benevolent people thus love two things – being and benevolence.

But truly virtuous people not only value benevolence because it promotes the general good; they also relish it for its own sake. Hence, while virtue 'most essentially consists in benevolence to Being in general' ([1765b] 1957–, vol. 8: 540), there is a wider sense in which it includes not only benevolence but also a delight or 'complacence' in benevolence's intrinsic excellence or beauty.

It is God that is 'infinitely the greatest being' and 'infinitely the most beautiful and excellent'. True virtue thus principally consists 'in a supreme love to God, both of benevolence and complacence' ([1765b] 1957–, vol. 8: 550–1). It follows that 'a determination of mind to union and benevolence to a *particular person or private system* [whether one's self, one's family, one's nation or humanity], which is but a small part of the universal system of being . . . is not of the nature of true virtue' unless it is dependent on, or 'subordinate to, benevolence to Being in general' ([1765b] 1957–, vol. 8: 554).

Things that ordinarily pass as virtue – rational self-interest, such natural instincts as parental affection and pity, and conscience – are counterfeits. These simulacra prompt us to promote the good of others and to approve virtue and condemn vice. But they fall 'short of the extent of true virtuous benevolence, both in . . . nature and object' ([1765b] 1957–, vol 8: 609). There is no more true virtue in loving others from self-love than in self-love itself. Natural instincts such as parental affection or pity are defective because 'they don't arise from any temper of benevolence to Being in general' ([1765b] 1957–, vol. 8: 610). (Thus I may pity the misfortune of someone whose good fortune would displease me.) Conscience is the product of a power of placing ourselves in the situation of others (which is necessary for mutual understanding), a sense of the natural fitness of certain responses (injury and punishment or disapproval, benefit and approval or reward), and self-love. Placing ourselves in the situation of those we have injured, we recognize that we would resent being treated in the same way and that we are therefore inconsistent in approving of treating others in ways we would not wish to be treated ourselves. The resulting sense of 'inconsistence' or 'self-opposition' makes us 'uneasy' since 'self-love implies an inclination to feel and act as one with ourselves' ([1765b] 1957–, vol. 8: 589).

7   Theological aesthetics

According to Edwards, beauty or 'excellency' 'consists in the similarness of one being to another – not merely equality and proportion, but any kind of similarness. . . . This is an universal definition of excellency: The consent of being to being' ([1829a] 1957–, vol. 6: 336). One who loves others, for example, or wishes them well 'agrees' with them or 'consents' to them. But love's scope can be narrower or wider. Agreement or consent is 'comprehensive' or 'universal' only when directed towards being in general. True benevolence alone, therefore, is truly beautiful. The beauty of a well-ordered society, of the natural fitness between actions and circumstances, 'of a building, of a flower, or of the rainbow' is an 'inferior, secondary beauty' which is a mere image of this. Secondary beauty consists in order, symmetry, harmony or proportion, that is, in 'uniformity in the midst of variety' ([1765b] 1957–, vol. 8: 561–2).

Only God's benevolence is perfect. Hence, God alone is (truly) beautiful without qualification. The fitness of God's dispensations, the harmony of his providential design, and so on, also exhibit the highest degree of secondary beauty. God, therefore, is 'infinitely the most beautiful and excellent' ([1765b] 1957–, vol. 8: 550).

God is also the 'foundation and fountain . . . of all beauty'. 'All the beauty to be found throughout the whole creation is . . . the reflection of the diffused beams of that Being who hath an infinite fullness of brightness and glory' ([1765b] 1957–, vol. 8: 550–1). God's world is saturated with beauty – not only the 'harmony of sounds, and the beauties of nature' to which Edwards was especially sensitive but also (and primarily) the beauty of the gospel, of God's providential work in history and of the saints. The saints alone, however, can discern true beauty.

8   The sense of the heart

Because the Holy Spirit dwells in them, the saints love being in general. Their benevolence is the basis of a new 'spiritual sense' whose 'immediate object' is the 'beauty of holiness' – a 'new simple idea' that cannot 'be produced by exalting, varying or compounding' other ideas and that truly 'represents' divine reality ([1746] 1957–, vol. 2: 205, 260; [1765b] 1957–, vol. 8: 622).

Edwards sometimes identifies beauty with the pleasure that holy things evoke in the saints or the tendency they have to evoke it, and at other times with the consent of being to being. His view, however, appears to be as follows. An idea of true beauty is similar to a Lockean idea of a primary or secondary quality. Feelings of spiritual delight are (to use Locke's words) simple 'sensations or perceptions in our understanding' like our ideas of colour or solidity. The tendency holy things have to evoke these ideas in the saints is what Locke calls a 'quality', that is, 'the power to produce those ideas in us' ([1689] 1894, vol.

1: 169). Benevolence is the objective 'mechanism' underlying this power. Like simple ideas of primary and secondary qualities, the spiritual sensation 'represents' or is a 'perception' of its object. Just as 'extension' can refer to the idea, the power or the configuration of matter which is the base of the power, so 'true beauty' can refer to the spiritual sensation, the relevant dispositional property or to benevolence.

Edwards calls the new mode of spiritual understanding a 'sense' because the apprehension of spiritual beauty is (1) immediate (non-inferential) and (2) involuntary. Furthermore, (3) it involves relish or delight and (following Locke) being pleased or pained is a kind of sensation or perception. Finally, (4) it is the source of a new simple idea and (as Locke says) all simple ideas come 'from experience'.

The saints alone are in a proper epistemic position to discern the truths of religion. Only those who are struck with the beauty of holiness can appreciate the 'hatefulness of sin', for example, and thus be convinced of the justice of divine punishment and our inability to make restitution. The new sense also helps us grasp the truth of the gospel as a whole. A conviction of the gospel's truth is an immediate inference from its beauty or splendour.

Edwards' defence of the objectivity of the new spiritual sense has four steps. (1) Benevolence agrees with the nature of things. The world is an interconnected system of minds and ideas in which the only true substance and cause is an infinite and omnipotent love. Human benevolence is thus an appropriate or fitting response to reality. (2) Benevolence delights in benevolence. Since benevolence is an appropriate response to reality, so too is delight in benevolence. (3) But delighting in benevolence just is perceiving its spiritual beauty. It follows that (4) the saints' spiritual perceptions are true 'representations' of something 'besides what [is] in [their] own minds' ([1765b] 1957–, vol. 8: 622).

9 The History of Redemption

In a letter of 1757 to the trustees of the College of New Jersey, Edwards said that he had long contemplated 'a great work, which I call a *History of the Work of Redemption*, a body of divinity in an entire new method, being thrown into the form of a history' ([1829–30, vol. 1: 569–70] 1957–, vol. 9: 62). Edwards' untimely death aborted the project, but a sermon series delivered in 1739 ([1774] 1957–, vol. 9) which traces the work of redemption 'from the fall of man to the end of the world' would have undoubtedly provided its basis. His proposed history would have been the natural culmination of the project begun in

True Virtue and *End of Creation*. For the redemption is 'the *summum* and *ultimum* of all the divine operations and decrees', the manifestation of God's internal glory in time ([1829–30, vol. 1: 569–70] 1957–, vol. 9: 62). It would have also provided a fitting climax to Edwards' intellectual career as a whole. For it is in his work of redemption that God most fully displays his sovereignty, holiness and splendour. Whether Edwards' work would have anticipated modern historiography, as some claim, is more doubtful. For the sermon series is essentially a doctrinal work. (The section on Christ's earthly ministry, for example, is not a life of Jesus but a discussion of the incarnation and atonement.) Nor does Edwards restrict himself to natural causes, but freely appeals to divine decrees and to typology to explain events. Whatever novelty the sermon series has consists in the rich skein of images by which Edwards connects the events of redemption history and in an emphasis on the objective side of God's act of redemption; this is comparatively rare in a Puritanism which stressed the redemption's application. (Edwards treats the subjective side in *Religious Affections*.)

List of works

Edwards, J. (1957) *The Works of Jonathan Edwards*, ed. P. Miller (vols 1–2), J. Smith (vols 3–9) and H.S. Stout (vols 10–), New Haven, CT: Yale University Press, 1957–. (The earlier Dwight edition is a widely available edition of Edwards' work. Miller *et al.* will supersede earlier editions when completed; the extensive introductions are especially helpful.)

—— (1746) *Religious Affections*, in *The Works of Jonathan Edwards*, New Haven, CT: Yale University Press, 1957–, vol. 2. (An analysis of the nature of holy affections and the criteria for distinguishing them from counterfeits.)

—— (1754) *Freedom of the Will*, in *The Works of Jonathan Edwards*, New Haven, CT: Yale University Press, 1957–, vol. 1. (A philosophically sophisticated defence of determinism.)

—— (1758) *Original Sin*, in *The Works of Jonathan Edwards*, New Haven, CT: Yale University Press, 1957–, vol. 3. (Part 3 (351–433) contains interesting discussions of inherited liability, identity and occasionalism.)

—— (1765a) *End of Creation*, in *The Works of Jonathan Edwards*, New Haven, CT: Yale University Press, 1957–, vol. 8, 405–536. (Discusses God's reasons for creating the world.)

—— (1765b) *True Virtue*, in *The Works of Jonathan Edwards*, New Haven, CT: Yale University Press,

1957–, vol. 8, 539–627. (Edwards' major treatise on ethics.)

—— (1774) *A History of the Work of Redemption*, in *The Works of Jonathan Edwards*, New Haven, CT: Yale University Press, 1957–, vol. 9. (The sermon series delivered in 1739.)

—— (1829a) 'The Mind', in *The Works of Jonathan Edwards*, New Haven, CT: Yale University Press, 1957–, vol. 6, 332–93. (Notes for a proposed treatise on the mind.)

—— (1829b) 'Natural Philosophy', in *The Works of Jonathan Edwards*, New Haven, CT: Yale University Press, 1957–, vol. 6, 192–295. (A collection of papers and notes that contains the important 'Of Being', 'Of the Prejudices of the Imagination' and 'Of Atoms'.)

—— (1890) 'Miscellany 94', in *The Works of Jonathan Edwards*, New Haven, CT: Yale University Press, 1957–, vol. 13, 256–63. (Edwards' first discussion of the Trinity.)

—— (1903) 'An Essay on the Trinity', in *Treatise on Grace and Other Posthumously Published Writings*, Cambridge: James Clarke & Co., 1971, 99–131. (Written in 1730. Edwards' second major discussion of the Trinity.)

—— (1817, 1847) *The Works of President Edwards*, ed. E. Williams and E. Parsons, New York: B. Franklin, 1968. (A reprint of the eight-volume 1817 edition and the two supplementary volumes published in 1847.)

—— (1829–30) *The Works of President Edwards*, ed. S.E. Dwight, New York: G. & C. & H. Carvill, 10 vols. (A widely available edition of Edwards' work.)

—— (1955) *The Philosophy of Jonathan Edwards from His Private Notebooks*, ed. H.G. Townsend, Eugene, OR: University of Oregon Monographs. (Contains philosophically important selections from the 'Miscellanies', a series of over 1300 entries on philosophical and theological topics begun in 1722.)

—— (1971) *Treatise On Grace and Other Posthumously Published Writings*, ed. P. Helm, Cambridge: James Clarke & Co. (Contains papers not included in the collected works, including 'Observations Concerning the Scripture Oeconomy of the Trinity and Covenant of Redemption' (Miscellany 1062).)

References and further reading

Delattre, R.A. (1968) *Beauty and Sensibility in the Thought of Jonathan Edwards*, New Haven, CT: Yale University Press. (The best study of Edwards' theological aesthetics.)

Fiering, N. (1981) *Jonathan Edwards' Moral Thought and its British Context*, Chapel Hill, NC: University of North Carolina Press. (An important study of Edwards' ethics and its sources.)

Jenson, R.W. (1988) *America's Theologian: A Recommendation of Jonathan Edwards*, New York: Oxford University Press. (An examination of Edwards' complex relations to Enlightenment thought.)

* Locke, J. (1689) *An Essay Concerning Human Understanding*, Oxford: Clarendon Press, 2 vols, 1894. (An important influence on Edwards' epistemology, philosophy of language and philosophical anthropology.)

Miller, P. (1949) *Jonathan Edwards*, New York: W. Sloane Associates. (A pioneering work that emphasizes Edwards' debt to Locke.)

Smith, J.E. (1992) *Jonathan Edwards, Puritan Preacher, Philosopher*, London: Geoffrey Chapman and Notre Dame, IN: University of Notre Dame Press. (A useful introduction.)

Wainwright, W.J. (1980) 'Jonathan Edwards and the Language of God', *Journal of the American Academy of Religion* 48: 520–30. (Examines Edwards' theory of images and types.)

—— (1982) 'Jonathan Edwards, Atoms, and Immaterialism', *Idealistic Studies* 12: 79–89. (A reconstruction of Edwards' argument for immaterialism.)

—— (1988) 'Original Sin', in T.V. Morris (ed.) *Philosophy and the Christian Faith*, Notre Dame, IN: University of Notre Dame Press. (Examines Edwards' views on responsibility and identity.)

—— (1995) *Reason and the Heart*, Ithaca, NY: Cornell University Press. (Chapter 1 expands the material of §8 of this entry and discusses Edwards' views on reason.)

—— (1996) 'Jonathan Edwards, William Rowe, and the Necessity of Creation', in J. Jordan and D. Howard-Snyder (eds) *Faith, Freedom and Responsibility*, Lanham, MD: Rowman & Littlefield. (Argues that Edwards' theistic metaphysics entails that God must create the actual world.)

Winslow, O.E. (1940) *Jonathan Edwards 1703–1758: A Biography*, New York: Macmillan. (Still the best biography.)

WILLIAM J. WAINWRIGHT

EFODI *see* DURAN, PROFIAT

EGOISM AND ALTRUISM

Henry Sidgwick conceived of egoism as an ethical theory parallel to utilitarianism: the utilitarian holds that one should maximize the good of all beings in the universe; the egoist holds instead that the good one is ultimately to aim at is only one's own. This form of egoism (often called 'ethical egoism') is to be distinguished from the empirical hypothesis ('psychological egoism') that human beings seek to maximize their own good. Ethical egoism can approve of behaviour that benefits others, for often the best way to promote one's good is to form cooperative relationships. But the egoist cannot approve of an altruistic justification for such cooperation: altruism requires benefiting others merely for their sake, whereas the egoist insists that one's ultimate goal must be solely one's own good.

One way to defend ethical egoism is to affirm psychological egoism and then to propose that our obligations cannot outstrip our capacities; if we cannot help seeking to maximize our own well being, we should not hold ourselves to a less selfish standard. But this defence is widely rejected, because psychological egoism seems too simple a conception of human behaviour. Moreover, egoism violates our sense of impartiality; there is no fact about oneself that justifies excluding others from one's ultimate end.

There is, however, a different form of egoism, which flourished in the ancient world, and is not vulnerable to this criticism. It holds that one's good consists largely or exclusively in acting virtuously, and that self-interest properly understood is therefore our best guide.

1 **Definitions of 'egoism'**
2 **Egoism's treatment of altruism**
3 **Arguments for and against**
4 **An ancient form of egoism**

1 Definitions of 'egoism'

The term 'egoism' was introduced into modern moral philosophy as a label for a type of ethical theory that is structurally parallel to utilitarianism (see UTILITARIANISM). The latter theory holds that one ought to consider everyone and produce the greatest balance of good over evil; egoism, by contrast, says that each person ought to maximize their own good. Both theories are teleological, in that they hold that the right thing to do is always to produce a certain good (see TELEOLOGICAL ETHICS). But the utilitarian claims that the good that one is to maximize is the universal good – the good of all human beings and perhaps all sentient creatures. The egoist, on the other

hand, holds that the good one is ultimately to aim at is only one's own (see GOOD, THEORIES OF THE).

This way of classifying ethical theories is due to Henry SIDGWICK, who regarded the choice between utilitarianism and egoism as one of the principal problems of moral philosophy. In *The Methods of Ethics* (1874), Sidgwick frames the issue in terms that assume that the good is identical to pleasure (a doctrine called 'hedonism') (see HEDONISM). He uses 'utilitarianism' for the view that one is to maximize the amount of pleasure in the universe, and holds that the only form of egoism worth considering is hedonistic egoism. Since few philosophers now accept the identity of pleasure and the good, the terms of the debate have changed. 'Egoism' is applied to any doctrine, whatever its conception of the good, that advocates maximizing one's own good.

Often this doctrine is called 'ethical egoism', to emphasize its normative status. By contrast, the term 'psychological egoism' is applied to an empirical hypothesis about human motivation. It holds that whenever one has a choice to make, one decides in favour of the action one thinks will maximize one's own good. It is possible to agree that we are inevitably selfish in this way, but to regard this as an evil element in our nature. Conversely, it is possible to hold that although people ought to maximize their own good, they seldom try to do so. (In the remainder of this entry, 'egoism' will refer to ethical egoism, unless otherwise indicated.)

2 Egoism's treatment of altruism

A defender of egoism need not frown upon attachments to others, feelings of compassion, or beneficent acts. For it is open to the egoist to argue that these social ties are an effective means to one's own ends. For example, it is a matter of common sense that altruistic behaviour – behaviour intended to help others – is often advantageous, when it motivates others to respond in kind (see RECIPROCITY). What little one loses in simple acts of kindness may be more than compensated when others reciprocate.

Although egoists may argue that benefiting others is generally in one's interests, they give a controversial justification for such beneficence. It is widely agreed that one should at times benefit others for *their* sake (Aristotle, for example, in *Nicomachean Ethics*, considers this essential to the best kind of friendship). To act for the sake of others is to take their good as a sufficient reason for action. But this is exactly what egoists cannot accept. They hold that ultimately the only justification for acts of beneficence is that they maximize one's own good. Ultimately, one is not to benefit others for their sake, but for one's own. If 'altruism' is used (as it often is) to refer to behaviour that not only benefits others, but is undertaken for their sake, then egoism is opposed to altruism.

3 Arguments for and against

Philosophers have sometimes tried to refute egoism by showing that it contains a contradiction or is in some way self-undermining. The best known attempt is that of G.E. MOORE in *Principia Ethica* (1903), but he has had few followers. Instead, Sidgwick's opinion that egoism is rational is generally accepted. But even if one agrees, one may ask whether there are good reasons for choosing egoism over other alternatives. Why must it always be a mistake to sacrifice one's good for the greater good of others? If a small loss in one's wellbeing can produce great gains for others, what is wrong with accepting that loss?

The egoist might at this point take refuge in psychological egoism. Although it is possible to affirm psychological egoism and reject ethical egoism – to agree that by nature we are ultimately self-seeking, and to condemn such behaviour as evil – few philosophers regard this as an appealing mix of theories. For what plausibility can there be in a standard of behaviour that we are incapable of achieving? The egoist may therefore respond to our question 'Why should we not sacrifice our good for the sake of others?' by urging us not to impose impossible standards upon ourselves. We do not in fact make such sacrifices, and should not blame ourselves for being the way we are.

The problem with this strategy is that psychological egoism has come under heavy attack in the modern period. Hobbes (1651) and Mandeville (1714) have been widely read as psychological egoists, and were criticized by such philosophers as Hutcheson (1725), Rousseau (1755) and Hume (1751), who sought to show that benevolence, pity and sympathy are as natural as self-love (see HOBBES, T.; MANDEVILLE, B.; HUTCHESON, F.; ROUSSEAU, J.-J.; HUME, D.). Kant held (1788), against psychological egoism, that the rational recognition of moral principles can by itself motivate us and overcome self-love (see KANTIAN ETHICS). Perhaps the most influential critique of psychological egoism is that of Butler (1726), who argued that by its nature self-love cannot be the only component of our motivational repertoire (see BUTLER, J.). He also pointed out that even if we feel gratification when we satisfy our desires, it cannot be inferred that such gratification is the object of those desires. The combined force of these attacks has left psychological egoism with few philosophical defenders.

At this point, an important challenge to ethical egoism should be noticed: although my circumstances, history, or qualities may differ from yours in morally significant ways, and these differences may justify me in seeking my good in preference to yours, the mere fact that I am myself and not you is not by itself a morally relevant difference between us. That my good is mine does not explain why ultimately it alone should concern me. So, if my good provides me with a reason for action, why should not your good, or the good of anyone else, also provide me with a reason – so long as there are no relevant differences between us? The ideal of impartiality seems to support the conclusion that we should have at least some concern with others (see IMPARTIALITY). In fact, egoists implicitly accept a notion of impartiality, since they say that just as my ultimate end should be my good, yours should be your good. So they must explain why they accept this minimal conception of impartiality, but nothing stronger. There is nothing morally appealing about excluding all others from one's final end; why then should one do so?

4 An ancient form of egoism

The kind of egoism we have been discussing can be called 'formal', in that it makes no claim about what in particular is good or bad for human beings. It holds instead that whatever the good is, it is one's own good that should be one's ultimate end. This is the conception one arrives at when one begins from Sidgwick's pairing of egoism with utilitarianism, then abstracts from his hedonism. A different kind of egoism, which might be called 'substantive', first proposes a concrete conception of the good, and then urges each of us to maximize our own good, so conceived. It is this form of egoism that flourished in the ancient world. Plato, Aristotle and the Stoics do not accept the formal principle that whatever the good is, we should seek only our own good, or prefer it to the good of others (see PLATO; ARISTOTLE; STOICISM). Instead, they argue for a specific conception of the good, and because the social virtues play so large a role in that conception, they regard self-love not as the enemy of virtue and the larger community but as an honourable motive, once it is developed in the proper direction (see EUDAIMONIA; VIRTUES AND VICES).

Even if psychological egoism is too simple a conception of human nature, it is undeniable that we normally have a deep concern for our own welfare. If self-love is a force that often conflicts with moral duty and inherently resists education, then human beings are necessarily and deeply divided creatures. This is the Augustinian and Kantian picture. By contrast, the dominant strand of ancient ethics proposes a more optimistic conception of the human situation. It does not claim that one should seek one's own good, come what may for others; rather, by arguing that acting virtuously and acting well coincide, it seeks to undermine the common assumption that at bottom the self must come into conflict with others.

See also: BUDDHIST CONCEPT OF EMPTINESS; MORAL MOTIVATION; MORAL SCEPTICISM; MORALITY AND IDENTITY §2; PRUDENCE

References and further reading

* Aristotle (*c.* mid 4th century BC) *Nicomachean Ethics*, trans. with notes by T. Irwin, Indianapolis, IN: Hackett Publishing Company, 1985, books VIII, IX. (Discusses friendship.)
* Butler, J. (1726) *Fifteen Sermons Preached at the Rolls Chapel*, Sermons I, II, III, XI, XII; repr. in S. Darwall (ed.) *Five Sermons Preached at the Rolls Chapel and A Dissertation Upon the Nature of Virtue*, Indianapolis, IN: Hackett Publishing Company, 1983, esp. Sermon XI. (Argues that self-love cannot be the only human motivation.)
  Gauthier, D. (ed.) (1970) *Morality and Rational Self-Interest*, Englewood Cliffs, NJ: Prentice Hall. (Selections by historical figures, contemporary essays and a bibliography.)
* Hobbes, T. (1651) *Leviathan*, ed. E. Curley, Indianapolis, IN: Hackett Publishing Company, 1994, part I, chaps 6–16. (Often read as a work of psychological egoism.)
* Hume, D. (1751) *An Enquiry Concerning the Principles of Morals*, ed. J.B. Schneewind, Indianapolis, IN: Hackett Publishing Company, 1983, sections 5, 9. (Seeks to show the naturalness of sympathy.)
* Hutcheson, F. (1725) *The Original of our Ideas of Beauty and Virtue*, excerpted in J.B. Schneewind (ed.) *Moral Philosophy from Montaigne to Kant*, vol. 2, Cambridge: Cambridge University Press, 1990. (Attempts to refute psychological egoism.)
* Kant, I. (1788) *Critik der practischen Vernunft*, trans. L.W. Beck, *Critique of Practical Reason*, New York: Macmillan, 1993, 36–8. (Argues that recognition of moral principles can overcome self-love.)
* Mandeville, B. (1714) *The Fable of the Bees: or, Private Vices, Publick Benefits*, ed. F.B. Kaye, Indianapolis, IN: Liberty Fund, 1988. (A portrait of human selfishness.)
* Moore, G.E. (1903) *Principia Ethica*, ed. T. Baldwin, Cambridge: Cambridge University Press, revised edn, 1993, sections 58–61, 63. (An attempt to refute egoism.)
  Nagel, T. (1970) *The Possibility of Altruism*, Oxford: Clarendon Press. (A difficult but widely discussed attack on egoism.)
  Plato (*c.*380–367 BC) *Republic*, trans. A.D. Lindsay, revised by T.H. Irwin, London: Dent, 1992. (The most elaborate attempt to show that it is in one's interest to be just.)
* Rousseau, J.-J. (1755) *Discours sur l'origine et les fondements de l'inégalité parmi les hommes*, trans. D.A. Cress, *Discourse on the Origin of Inequality*, Indianapolis, IN: Hackett Publishing Company, 1992. (Contains a discussion of self-love and compassion.)
  —— (1762) *Émile: ou, de l'éducation*, trans. A. Bloom, *Emile: or, On Education*, Harmondsworth: Penguin, 1991, esp. book IV. (Distinguishes healthy from destructive self-love, and describes an education in which healthy self-love flourishes.)
* Sidgwick, H. (1874) *The Methods of Ethics*, London: Macmillan; 7th edn, 1907. (Argues for the plausibility of both egoism and utilitarianism.)

RICHARD KRAUT

EGYPTIAN COSMOLOGY, ANCIENT

Ancient Egypt has left us no systematic philosophy in the modern sense. However, there is abundant evidence that the Egyptians were concerned with all the usual problems of existence. The answers to these questions were mostly expressed through the use of myth, or commentary upon myth. Though complex and polytheistic, Egyptian religion provided a subtle means of commentary upon a range of theological, ethical and psychological questions. The range and quality of Egyptian technical achievements presupposes a degree of theoretical knowledge, some of which has survived and some of which can be reconstructed, either from Egyptian texts themselves, or from commentaries in the classical authors. Until recently much of the latter has been dismissed as inaccurate, but modern scholars are increasingly inclined to agree with the high value which Greek commentators placed on Egyptian thinking.

1   Sources
2   Doctrines

1   Sources

Although Egyptian civilization lasted for almost thirty-five centuries, many texts survive only in fragments, or are lost completely. The small fraction which has come down to us is biased in favour of royal inscriptions or monumental texts. The loss of temple libraries, which are known to have contained technical manuals and catalogues, is especially unfortunate. The large quantity of administrative texts which survive are of more value to the social and economic historian than to the philosopher. On the other hand, a strong tradition of scribal education existed which has ensured the transmission of ethical and didactic works in some numbers. As a result, the broad principles of Egyptian thinking can be reconstructed with some confidence.

A good starting point can be found in the so-called *Memphite Theology*. In its present form this is a hieroglyphic inscription, now in the British Museum. It is dated to the reign of Shabaqo (*c*.710 BC), although the original text could date from 500 years earlier and a date in the third millennium BC has even been suggested. In the *Memphite Theology*, the god Ptah, patron of Memphis and of craftsmanship, is described as the creator of the world, which he does by means of his heart (the traditional seat of thought and feeling) and his tongue. In other words, the creator first conceptualizes the forms to be created and then brings them into being by means of articulate language.

The Egyptians attached great importance to names. They believed names contained the essence of the object or person to which they referred. They were also drawn to etymologies based on puns. These were considered not to be accidental, but to contain vital information about the meaning and purpose of words. Egyptian dictionaries were based on this principle and the hieroglyphic script itself arises from similar use of paronomasia, or play on words. Creation legends were common in Egypt as in other civilizations, but the sophistication and clarity of the *Memphite Theology* are remarkable. Parallels with the opening of Genesis are occasionally made, although these should be treated with caution.

Similar sophistication can be found unusually in the *Book of the Dead*. This is a mixture of spells, myths and apotropaic formulae (intended to prevent evil), designed to secure the survival of the deceased beyond the divine judgment which awaited them and into the afterlife. Although the ideas underlying the *Book of the Dead* are complex and sublime, the composition itself is not normally considered an intellectual triumph. Chapter 75 of the text contains impressive material which takes the form of a dialogue between the spirit of the deceased, often identified with the god Osiris, and a supreme creator named Atum. The dead man finds eternity incomprehensible because it lacks food and drink, human love and familiar landmarks of time or space. Atum's

reply is that all these have been superseded by the eternal contemplation of his own face, amounting to a communion with his presence beyond physical description. Here too there is evidence of serious questioning about the nature of existence and the problem of comprehending other dimensions of reality.

2 Doctrines

Egyptian religion was complex and its only modern parallel would be Hinduism. A multiplicity of gods was subdivided into local divinities. These were arranged in triads, broadly comparable with human families consisting of god, goddess and child (normally male, but sometimes female). The same gods could rearrange themselves into different families in differing localities. Most gods could be assimilated into the solar deity, which had various names, while some gods combined in pairs for certain functions. The god Osiris was thought of as an earthly god-king who had undergone death and been restored to immortality in the underworld. In many ways, Osiris and the sun-god are counterparts. This concept introduces us to one of the characteristics of Egyptian thought: the emphasis on duality and the need to reconcile opposing principles. The force which reconciled these opposites was *ma'at*, a concept embracing truth, justice and harmony, and which could be personified as a goddess in its own right.

A similar duality can be seen in the theology of kingship. Unlike the rulers of neighbouring states, the Pharaoh was both divine and human. The divine aspect of the ruler was expressed in the prenomen given to him (or occasionally her) at the coronation. This name was borne by him even after his death, when he became Osiris. His personal name, or nomen, was equally revered, but was not part of his immortal identity. (Conventionally, this duality was expressed in a double title, but wrongly translated as 'King of Upper and Lower Egypt'.) It is possible although not certain that this pattern of thought survived into the early Christian period, where it may have predisposed the Egyptians towards Monophysitism, the belief that the person of Christ has only one nature, which is divine and possesses human attributes.

A corresponding pattern of duality and immanence can be seen in the concept of the *ka*, essentially a birth-spirit similar to the Latin *genius*. However, the idea also encompassed the notion of the immortal essence humans were thought to possess and the individuality which distinguished them. Other living things possessed *kas*, a belief which conveniently allowed offerings of food or flowers to be presented to the gods, who would happily partake of their *kas* while leaving the physical objects to be consumed by the priesthood. However, the *ka* was also dependent on the survival of the earthly body after death. This tenet underwrote the entire death industry characteristic of the culture, although in the main it was concerned with immortality rather than morbidity. There is also a psychological link between the *ka* and the name. In later texts these two terms can be used interchangeably.

Later Neoplatonists, notably IAMBLICHUS, were fascinated by Egyptian religion, at least by the aspects which were accessible. Iamblichus saw the entire system as monotheistic and he and others were convinced that it foreshadowed the Platonic Theory of Forms (see PLATO §10). Most Egyptologists have been dismissive of these ideas, although they have begun to gain some credibility over time. Monotheism is compatible with much of what is known about Egyptian gods. The idea itself, and the broad outlines of the theory of Forms, might have been acceptable to an educated Egyptian at the earliest period. The Egyptian would have rejected the exclusive nature of such ideas as the sole explanation of thinking. Those who did try to impose such exclusivity upon Egyptian religion, such as the Pharaoh Akhenaten, were condemned. Some of these ideas, combined with themes from Hellenistic philosophy, resurfaced in the body of texts known as the *Corpus Hermeticum* (second century AD), where they are ascribed to the Graeco-Egyptian divine sage known as Hermes Trismegistos (see HERMETISM).

Egyptian technology was impressive as was the thinking which went with it. The formula for the area of a circle, $A = (8/9\ d)^2$, gives an excellent working value for π, and there are textual references to nanoseconds, the dependence of moonlight on sunlight and possibly the speed of light itself. The fact that such things could not be measured did not mean that they could not be envisaged. Astronomical methods of timekeeping were fairly accurate, as was the use of the water-clock. Astrology, however, was a late import from Mesopotamia, although one that soon became thoroughly naturalized.

Egyptian wisdom literature is a genre of its own. Primarily it is concerned with social and ethical problems of some complexity. As the genre developed, there was a growing emphasis away from questions of purely social behaviour and towards the problem of fate and its relation to individual guilt and responsibility. One answer to this dichotomy was to contrast the psychological impact of good behaviour with that of bad, thus internalizing moral responsibility. In a late text, *Papyrus Insinger*, good is externalized and seen as an absolute to be pursued regardless of consequences or the vicissitudes of

fortune. Here too the complexity and range of Egyptian writings are seen at their best. Egyptian thought, like Egyptian art and architecture, tolerates diversity and is characterized by both sophistication and simplicity.

See also: EGYPTIAN PHILOSOPHY: INFLUENCE ON ANCIENT GREEK THOUGHT

References and further reading

Assmann, J. (1995) *Egyptian Solar Religion in the New Kingdom*, London: Kegan Paul International. (Not an easy read, but an excellent example from one of the best authorities.)

Copenhaver, B.P. (1992) *Hermetica*, Cambridge: Cambridge University Press. (Translations of the *Corpus Hermeticum* and a very full commentary.)

Hornung, E. (1983) *Conceptions of God in Ancient Egypt: the One and the Many*, London: Routledge & Kegan Paul. (Thoughtful analysis of the main patterns of Egyptian thought.)

Griffiths, J. Gwyn (1995) *Triads and Trinity*, Cardiff: University of Wales Press. (Important study in comparative religion.)

Lichtheim, M. (1973–80) *Ancient Egyptian Literature*, 3 vols, Los Angeles, CA: University of California Press. (Clear translations and extracts from standard works.)

Ray, J.D. (1995) 'Egyptian Wisdom Literature', in J. Day *et al.* (eds) *Wisdom in Ancient Israel: Essays in Honour of J.A. Emerton*, Cambridge: Cambridge University Press. (Survey of Egyptian ethical writing.)

Shafer, B.E. (ed.) (1991) *Religion in Ancient Egypt*, London: Routledge. (A series of good essays with wide a variety of approaches.)

Shaw, I. and Nicholson, P. (1995) *The British Museum Dictionary of Ancient Egypt*, London: British Museum Press. (Useful individual entries.)

JOHN D. RAY

EGYPTIAN PHILOSOPHY: INFLUENCE ON ANCIENT GREEK THOUGHT

Before the decipherment of hieroglyphics (a process only completed in the 1830s), it was widely believed that many famous Greek philosophers had studied in Egypt and that Greek philosophy was ultimately derived

from a lost 'Egyptian mystery system'. This belief was derived in part from ancient sources, which described how certain Greek philosophers had studied with Egyptian priests. The notion that these individual sessions were part of an extensive formal programme of education derives from an historical novel, Séthos (1731), by the Abbé Jean Terrasson. This book, which pretended to be based on lost original sources, offered a detailed portrait of a complex Egyptian university system. It was translated into several European languages and widely popularized in the rituals and mythology of Freemasonry.

The existence of such a formal Egyptian mystery system of education was not confirmed by actual Egyptian sources once they could be read and translated. The myth has been given a new lease of life in revisionist histories of the ancient world composed by writers whose ancestors had been brought to the New World as slaves. These writers sought to show that Greek philosophy was derived from Egyptian philosophy and that what has been recognized as Western civilization stems from Africa. This entry reviews the evidence for these claims and concludes that although the Greeks had great respect for Egyptian wisdom and piety, what has always been known as Greek philosophy derives from the original work of Greeks. It finds moreover that if the Greek philosophers who lived in Ionia were influenced by any outside ideas, these came to them through the monotheistic religions of other peoples living in the Near East.

1   **Greek philosophers in Egypt**
2   **The myth of an Egyptian mystery system**

1   Greek philosophers in Egypt

Nothing in surviving Egyptian literature from the period before the founding of Alexandria in 332 BC resembles the dialectical methods and argumentative structures invented and used by Greek philosophers. Even after Greeks had been living in Egypt for some centuries, Egypto-Greek philosophical treatises, such as those preserved in the Hermetic Corpus, have a declarative format and theological character (see HERMETISM). If Greek philosophy were closely dependent on Egyptian models, we would expect to find evidence of parallel texts or direct echoes, as we do in the case of the Roman poets who from early times adapted and quoted Greek sources. However, we do not find this, in Egypt or in any other contemporary civilization, in the area of Greek philosophy. This is not to say that the Egyptians did not possess a profound theology and concept of justice, or that this theology and other wisdom is not impressively expressed in surviving Egyptian litera-

ture. It is simply that Egyptian (or Hebrew) wisdom literatures are different in nature from the philosophical writings of PLATO and ARISTOTLE. The writings of these philosophers are nontheological in character and reach their conclusions through argument and discussion. Nor is it likely that there was an Egyptian philosophy, similar to Greek philosophy, that is now lost. If there had been such an extensive body of literature some Greeks would have known about it and there would not have been any reason not to acknowledge it. Greeks tended to be so respectful of Egyptian learning that they were eager to refer to it whenever they could. The kind of Egyptian learning to which Plato refers in his works takes the form of wisdom narratives, the kind of moral tales of which we possess Egyptian examples. In the *Phaedrus* and the *Philebus*, Socrates tells a story about the god Theuth's invention of letters. In the *Timaeus* and the *Critias*, Plato's incomplete dialogue, Critias tells the story of Atlantis, which his ancestor Solon learned from an Egyptian priest during his visit to the Egyptian pharaoh Amasis. These stories are not told in the usual question-and-answer dialogue form, but as long didactic narratives almost certainly of Plato's own invention.

The ancient biographers who describe the philosophers' sojourns in Egypt never discuss in detail what philosophical ideas the Greeks might have learned from Egyptian priests. Rather, they imagine that the Greeks acquired from the Egyptians practical learning, often of a scientific nature. In the minds of the biographers, the acquisition of such Eastern wisdom provided a motivation for Greek philosophers to travel to Egypt and to the Near East. Foreign travel also helped to explain why particular philosophers contrived to be distinctive and original. When THALES (sixth century BC) conjectured that the first element was water he could have been drawing on Babylonian mythology, or reflecting on the importance of the river Maeander to his native city of Miletus. But his biographers supposed that he had also seen the most remarkable of all rivers, the Nile. In order to account for the originality of his ideas of mathematics and religion Greek writers assumed that PYTHAGORAS visited Egypt and the Near East before settling in southern Italy. A century after Pythagoras' death, historian Herodotus conjectured that Pythagoras' theory of the transmigration of souls, which has no parallel in early Greek thought, had an Egyptian origin. In fact Egyptian notions of the fate of the soul after death are completely different from the Greek. In the first century BC Egyptian priests told Diodorus that Pythagoras shared with the Egyptians the notion that animals had souls. They also claimed that Pythagoras learned about geometry in Egypt, without mentioning anything specific. Both Egyptians and Greeks were interested in geometry and this common interest was seen to be evidence of dependence. Still more was discovered about Pythagoras as time went on. The Greek Iamblichus specifies that Pythagoras spent twenty-two years in Egypt during which time he studied all aspects of Egyptian religion. He was also initiated into all the rites and learned astronomy and geometry. Iamblichus provides no specific information about what he actually learned. Rather, the point of the journey seems to be that he studied whatever it was he learned abroad. Before going to Egypt he visited Syria and after Egypt he studied with the Magi in Babylon. For ancient Greek biographers, foreign study was the most natural and convenient way to account for the originality of Pythagoras' ideas.

The priests told Diodorus that everything for which these Greeks were admired was brought from Egypt. They said that Greek philosopher DEMOCRITUS of Abdera (fifth century BC) spent five years studying astrology in Egypt. This connection seems tenuous because the Egyptians were interested in astronomy, the motion of the stars and not in astrology, predictions about human fate that might be derived from astronomical observation. Like many Greek writers Democritus was interested in the causes of the inundation of the Nile. However, according to astronomer Ptolemy (second century AD), Democritus did his research on weather indications in Macedonia and Thrace. Nothing that he is reported to have said suggests that he had a detailed personal knowledge of Egypt.

In the case of other Greek philosophers, interest in the Nile or geometry counts as 'evidence' of a visit to Egypt. The priests told Diodorus that the Greek astronomer Oenopides of Chios (fifth century BC) learned from Egyptian priests about the obliquity of the ecliptic of the sun. Diodorus does not indicate and perhaps did not know that the Pythagoreans already knew about the ecliptic before Oenopides discovered it, or that it had been recognized by the Babylonians around 700 BC. Earlier in his account of Egypt Diodorus gives Oenopides' explanation of the inundation of the Nile. He explained Oenopides' deduction that the temperature of well water feels warm in the winter and cold in the summer indicating that the Nile's subterranean waters maintain similar temperatures in the summer when there are no rains in Egypt. Again there is no reason to imagine that Oenopides needed to study in Egypt in order to form this false hypothesis. His reliance on analogy rather than on empirical evidence seems characteristically Greek.

Diodorus reports that the fourth-century Greek philosopher EUDOXUS of Cnidus, like Democritus, learned astrology from the Egyptian priests, although it was the Alexandrian Greeks rather than the Egyptians who were interested in that subject. No doubt Eudoxus could have learned geometry in Egypt. However, it was also possible and more likely that he learned the theory of axiomatic mathematics from his teacher the fouth-century Greek philosopher ARCHYTAS of Tarentum. In fact nothing in the surviving fragments suggests that Eudoxus had a highly specialized knowledge of Egypt judging from the fragments. He could have learned what he knew from Greek writers like Hecataeus and Herodotus without ever having visited Egypt. None the less, new details about his visit were added as time went on. The priests at Heliopolis showed the Greek geographer Strabo (first century BC) statues of Plato and Eudoxus and pointed out the places where they had studied, although no one was sure how long they had stayed there as there were several different versions of the story. Diogenes Laertius supplies the name of Eudoxus' Egyptian teacher, saying that while in Egypt Eudoxus shaved his beard and eyebrows like an Egyptian priest and that while there an Apis bull licked his cloak. Egyptian priests understood this to be an omen that he would be famous, but only for a short time. These anecdotes tell us nothing about what Eudoxus studied or did in Egypt. Instead, they portray him as a late antique holy man, in much the same way as Iamblichus described Pythagoras.

In view of the way Plato uses Egyptian lore, the presence of Egyptian tales in his dialogues does not necessarily indicate that he studied in Egypt, especially since the narration of these tales does not require the use of dialectic and argumentation. Plato never says in any of his writings that he went to Egypt and there is no reference to such a visit in the semibiographical *Seventh Letter*. The superficial knowledge of Egypt and vague chronology displayed in his dialogues resemble historical fiction more than history. Anecdotes about his visit to Egypt appear in the work of writers after the Hellenistic period (*c.*300 BC to the mid first century BC). Later biographers added details to the story of Plato's Egyptian travels in order to provide aetiologies for the Egyptian references in his writings. In a letter purportedly sent by Phaedrus to Plato in Sais, Plato studies the question of the 'all' and Phaedrus asks for information about the pyramids and unusual Egyptian animals. Plato was supposed to have heard from Sechnupis of Heliopolis the story of Theuth told in the *Phaedrus* and Diogenes Laertius says he went to Egypt to study with Egyptian seers.

The Church Father CLEMENT OF ALEXANDRIA (AD 150–215) suggested that Plato studied in Egypt with the Hermes Trismegistus, or 'thrice greatest Hermes'.

But in fact the collection of works attributed to Hermes could not have been written without the conceptual vocabulary developed by Plato and Aristotle. It is deeply influenced by Plato and the writings of Neoplatonist philosophers in the early centuries AD (see NEOPLATONISM). Plato seems never to have learned from these Egyptian teachers anything characteristically Egyptian, so far as is known about Egyptian theology from Egyptian sources. His notion of Egyptian theology and life remains similar to that of other Athenians. He did not so much change the Athenian notion of Egyptian culture as enrich and idealize it so that it could provide a dramatic and instructive contrast with Athenian customs in his dialogues.

2 The myth of an Egyptian mystery system

The Egyptians had an urgent reason for wanting to assert their priority over the Greeks. In Herodotus' day the country was under Persian domination and then was ruled by Greeks after Alexander's conquest, therefore one of the few remaining ways for them to maintain national pride was through their history. Similar assertions of priority over the Greeks were made by Jews living in Alexandria. These Jews were determined to show that despite being subject to Greeks, they not only understood Greek culture but had provided the inspiration for the authors of the sacred writings and cherished literature of their conquerors' civilization: the mythical Greek singer Musaeus was none other than Moses. Such claims were taken up by the Church Fathers who sought to show that Greek philosophy owed a considerable debt to Hebrew scripture. There was support for the notion of Egyptian influence on Greek thought in the syncretism of the early centuries AD, most particularly in the cult of Isis, which combined Egyptian ritual practices with the Greek notion of *mysteria*, or initiations.

Terrasson drew on these sources (and his own ideas about French Christian education) for his depiction in his novel *Séthos* (1731) of an elaborate series of Egyptian initiations. The process he described inspired the contemporary initiation rituals of Freemasonry and were perhaps parodied in Mozart's opera *Die Zauberflöte*. The belief persists that these fundamentally Greek ideas could have been Egyptian according to revisionist histories of writers who call themselves Afrocentrists. These writers have insisted that Greek philosophy originated in Egypt, although no direct connection can be found between Egyptian wisdom literature and work of writers like Heraclitus, Plato, or Aristotle.

One of the most influential of these writers, Marcus Garvey (1887–1940) stated that white Europeans had concealed the truth about the priority of Egyptian (or African) culture because of their hostility towards black people. M. Bernal supported these claims in his study *Black Athena* (1987). C.A. Diop in his influential *Civilisation ou Barbarie* (*Civilization or Barbarism: an Authentic Anthropology*) (1981) sought to show that there was widespread African influence on Western thought. G.G.M. James in *Stolen Legacy* (1954) and his pupil Y.A.A. ben-Jochannan in *Africa, Mother of Western Civilization* (1971) stated that Aristotle stole books from the library at Alexandria, which in fact was not built until after Aristotle's death. Moreover, no other ancient author says that Aristotle went to Egypt with Alexander. Such claims have no more substance than the assertions of the Hellenistic Egyptians and Jews who claimed that the Greeks borrowed all their ideas from their ancestors. There is no evidence that the Greeks stole or borrowed their philosophy from Egypt, or indeed from other peoples, such as the Phoenicians, Hittites, or Medes, with whom they came into contact. However, there was some Egyptian influence on Greek medicine, science and mathematics from the middle of the second millennium BC which continued after the Greeks re-established contact with the Egyptians in the sixth century BC. But, influence cannot be thought of as theft or borrowing and is usually a two-way process. If the early Greek philosophers drew their ideas from any foreign cultures, it was principally from the civilizations of the Near East.

See also: EGYPTIAN COSMOLOGY, ANCIENT

References and further reading

* ben-Jochannan, Y.A.A. (1971) *Africa, Mother of Western Civilization*, Baltimore, MD: Black Classic Press, repr. 1988. (Purports to show that Greek civilization was stolen from Egypt.)
* Bernal, M. (1987) *Black Athena: The Afro-Asiatic Roots of Classical Civilization*, vol. 1, *The Fabrication of Ancient Greece*, vol. 2, *The Archaeological and Documentary Evidence*, New Brunswick, NJ: Rutgers University Press. (Vol. 1 attempts to demonstrate that because of racism and anti-Semitism, European scholars failed to recognize the Egyptian and near Eastern origins of Greek civilization. Vol. 2 supplies factual evidence for the theories advanced in vol. 1.)
  Brisson, L. (1987) 'L'Égypte de Platon' (Plato's Egypt), *Les études philosophiques*, new series, 2–3: 101–31. (A brief account of the treatment of Egypt in Plato's philosophy.)

Burkert, W. (1987) *Ancient Mystery Cults*, Cambridge, MA: Harvard University Press. (Discusses the religious and social purposes of ancient Greek mystery cults.)

Copenhaver, B.P. (1992) *Hermetica*, Cambridge: Cambridge University Press. (An annotated translation of the treatises attributed to Hermes Trismegistus.)

Curto, S., Donadoni, S. and Donadoni Roveri, A.M. (eds) (1990) *L'Egitto dal mito all' Egittologia*, trans. E. Poore and F.L. Rossi, *Egypt from Myth to Egyptology*, Turin: Istituto Bancario San Paolo. (Describes how Egypt has been seen by Europeans from ancient times to the present day.)

Dent, E. (1960) *Mozart's Operas*, Oxford: Clarendon Press, 2nd edn. (Offers a detailed account of the Masonic elements in Mozart's opera *The Magic Flute*.)

* Diop, C.A. (1981) *Civilisation ou Barbarie*, Paris: Présence Africaine; trans. Y.-L. Meema Ngemi, *Civilization or Barbarism: an Authentic Anthropology*, Brooklyn, NY: Lawrence Hill Books, 1991. (Attempts to discover the origins of European thought in ancient Africa.)

Froidefond, C. (1971) *Le mirage égyptien dans la littérature grecque d'Homère à Aristote* (The Egyptian Mirage in Greek Literature From Homer to Aristotle), Aix-en-Provence: Ophrys. (Examines the Greeks' knowledge of Egypt before Alexander's conquest.)

Iversen, E. (1961) *The Myth of Egypt and its Hieroglyphs in European Tradition*, Princeton, NJ: Princeton University Press; repr. 1993. (Describes how the nature of the Egyptian system of writing was misunderstood by Europeans and was used by them to create a mythical Egypt.)

* James, G.G.M. (1954) *Stolen Legacy*, New York: Philosophical Library. (Claims that Greek philosophy was stolen from Egypt.)

Lefkowitz, M. (1996) *Not Out of Africa: How Afrocentrism Became an Excuse to Teach Myth as History*, New York: Basic Books. (Examines Afrocentric myths about Greek culture and the origins of Greek civilization.)

Morenz, S. (1973) *Egyptian Religion*, trans. A.E. Keep, Ithaca, NY: Cornell University Press. (A general account of Egyptian ritual practices and beliefs.)

Palter, R. (1996) 'Black Athena, Afro-Centrism, and the History of Science', in M.R. Lefkowitz and G.M. Rogers (eds) *Black Athena Revisited*, Chapel Hill, NC: University of North Carolina Press, 209–66. (Examines the extent of Egyptian influence on Greek science.)

Riginos, A.S. (1976) *Platonica: The Anecdotes Concerning the Life and Writings of Plato*, Leiden: E.J. Brill. (Analyses the ancient legends about the life of Plato.)

Rutherford, R.B. (1995) *The Art of Plato*, London: Duckworth. (Discusses Plato's use in his dialogues of stories about Egypt.)

* Terrasson, J. (1731) *Séthos*, Paris: Jacques Guérin; trans. T. Lediard, London: J. Walthoe, 1732. (An historical novel, based on Greek and Roman sources, about the education of an Egyptian prince.)

MARY LEFKOWITZ

EINSTEIN, ALBERT (1879–1955)

Albert Einstein was a German-born Swiss and American naturalized physicist and the twentieth century's most prominent scientist. He produced the special and general theories of relativity, which overturned the classical understanding of space, time and gravitation. According to the special theory (1905), uniformly moving observers with different velocities measure the same speed for light. From this he deduced that the length of a system shrinks and its clocks slow at speeds approaching that of light. The general theory (completed 1915) proceeds from Hermann Minkowski's geometric formulation of special relativity as a four-dimensional spacetime. Einstein's theory allows, however, that the geometry of spacetime may vary from place to place. This variable geometry or curvature is associated with the presence of gravitational fields. Acting through geometrical curvature, these fields can slow clocks and bend light rays.

Einstein made many fundamental contributions to statistical mechanics and quantum theory, including the demonstration of the atomic character of matter and the proposal that light energy is organized in spatially discrete light quanta. In later life, he searched for a unified theory of gravitation and electromagnetism as an alternative to the quantum theory developed in the 1920s. He complained resolutely that this new quantum theory was not complete. Einstein's writings in philosophy of science developed a conventionalist position, stressing our freedom to construct theoretical concepts; his later writings emphasized his realist tendencies and the heuristic value of the search for mathematically simple laws.

1   Life
2   Special relativity
3   General relativity
4   Quantum theory: early contributions

5 Quantum theory: critique of the standard
 interpretation
6 Philosophy of science

1 Life

Albert Einstein was born in Ulm in southern
Germany. He entered the Federal Polytechnical
School in Zurich, Switzerland, in 1896 to study
physics, after failing the entrance exam the previous
year. Upon completion of his studies in 1900, he was
unable to find an academic position. Having renounced German citizenship in 1896, he acquired
Swiss citizenship in 1901. From 1902 to 1909 he
worked as a patent examiner in Bern. He then moved
rapidly through a series of academic positions in
Zurich and Prague. Finally in 1914 Einstein moved to
a prestigious professorship without teaching obligations at the University of Berlin and also to the
directorship of the new Kaiser Wilhelm Institute for
Physics. In 1919, observations of the solar eclipse
provided confirmation of his general theory of
relativity. The success was trumpeted in the popular
press and Einstein became an unwilling celebrity. In
1922, he was awarded the Nobel Prize. After 1920,
Einstein became known as an advocate of cultural
Zionism, also a socialist and (until the rise of Hitler) a
pacifist. After fleeing Germany, from 1933 until his
death he was at the Institute for Advanced Study in
Princeton, New Jersey, adopting citizenship of the
USA in 1940.

2 Special relativity

Classical electrodynamics posited the ether as a
medium for carrying light and other electromagnetic
waves (see MAXWELL J.C. §2; ELECTRODYNAMICS;
OPTICS §§1, 4). Einstein based his 1905 special theory
of relativity on the conviction that the state of rest of
this medium was superfluous and could be eliminated
from an otherwise unaltered electrodynamics by
revising classical notions of space and time. These
revisions were developed as the consequences of two
postulates: the principle of relativity, which required
the equivalence of all uniform or inertial states of
motion, and the light postulate, which required that
the speed of light remain the same constant,
independent of the motion of the source, for observers
in any inertial motion.

At first, Einstein's two postulates seemed incompatible. As an observer proceeds through a sequence
of ever-faster inertial states of motion, the observer's
speed comes closer to that of light. However the light
postulate requires that they would see no reduction in
the speed of light. Einstein showed that the postulates

are compatible if rods and clocks do not behave
classically when they move close to the speed of light.
Similarly, he showed that no material system could be
accelerated up to the speed of light. As the system
approaches that speed its inertial mass would increase
without limit, precluding further acceleration. The
mass gained is proportional to the energy of motion
and provides one example of the inertia of energy, a
result that became famous under the rubric '$E = mc^2$'.

In his celebrated 1905 analysis, Einstein explained
the apparent incompatibility of the postulates as
resulting from an arbitrary conception about the
simultaneity of distant events. He described a
procedure involving light signals that would by
definition synchronize distant clocks. From this
definition and the postulates of his theory, Einstein
showed that inertially moving observers in relative
motion must disagree over which distant events are
simultaneous, in contradiction of classical expectations (see RELATIVITY THEORY, PHILOSOPHICAL
SIGNIFICANCE OF §§1–3).

3 General relativity

Einstein's general theory of relativity is a relativistic
theory of gravitation extending Minkowski's spacetime formulation of special relativity (see SPACETIME
§2). Its principal novelty is that gravitational fields
are not represented as entities like electric fields
distinct from the background spacetime. Rather they
appear as curvature in the background spacetime
geometry. Since Einstein's theory relegated gravitation
to this background structure, it could readily account
for the most distinctive property of gravitation: the
trajectories of bodies in free fall are essentially
independent of their masses and internal constitutions.

The theory agrees observationally with Newtonian
theory almost exactly in common domains. Marked
differences emerge only in very strong gravitational
fields or on cosmic scales. Early empirical successes of
the theory depended on very small effects: minute
deviations in the motion of the planet Mercury from
that expected classically, a small deflection of starlight
grazing the sun and the slight reddening of light from
a massive star due to the gravitational slowing of the
atom-clocks emitting the light.

Einstein's development of the theory over the
period 1907–15 was inspired by the hope that a
relativistic theory of gravitation might extend the
principle of relativity to acceleration. He hoped the
final theory would satisfy a principle he attributed to
Ernst Mach: inertial forces acting on accelerating
bodies are not due to acceleration through space but
to an interaction with all other masses (see RELATIV-

ITY THEORY, PHILOSOPHICAL SIGNIFICANCE OF §6). He also postulated the principle of equivalence, which required that the inertial field of uniform acceleration is equivalent to a homogeneous gravitational field. While Einstein's general theory remains without serious challenge as a relativistic theory of gravitation and cosmology, debate continues over all his heuristic principles.

General relativity is 'generally covariant': it employs arbitrary spacetime coordinates. From 1913 to 1915, on the basis of his 'hole argument', Einstein had doubted that such freedom was physically admissible. He answered these doubts with the 'point coincidence argument'. It supposed that the physical content of his theory was fully exhausted by a catalogue of spacetime coincidences, which remain unaltered under arbitrary changes of coordinate system. As early as 1917, Erich Kretschmann objected that general covariance cannot express a generalized principle of relativity since, under the suppositions of the point coincidence argument, any spacetime theory can be recast in a generally covariant form (see RELATIVITY THEORY, PHILOSOPHICAL SIGNIFICANCE OF §4).

One of Einstein's earliest applications of his new theory was his 1917 cosmological model. Its spatial geometry is spherical, so that space has a finite volume and no edge (see COSMOLOGY §3). Einstein's motivation in devising the model was to satisfy Mach's principle, which he felt was violated by stipulating the limiting cosmic geometry at the infinity of space. From the 1920s until his death, Einstein's work on general relativity was increasingly absorbed into his attempts to produce a unified field theory which would treat not just gravitational but also electromagnetic fields geometrically.

4 Quantum theory: early contributions

By 1905 Einstein was convinced of the failure of classical electrodynamics to account for black body radiation, and blamed the wave picture of radiation. His light quantum hypothesis proposed that high-frequency heat radiation behaves thermodynamically as though its energy were spatially localized in quanta whose size depends on Planck's constant. This hypothesis was at the heart of his Nobel prize-winning explanation of the photo-electric effect. The following year, Einstein treated the non-classical behaviour of specific heats at low temperatures with a similar assumption (implicit in Planck's work of 1900) of discreteness for the energy levels of atoms (see PLANCK, M.).

Einstein never integrated these discontinuities into a coherent theory. Such a theory could not merely replace the wave picture by a particle view, for, in

1909, he had demonstrated that both wave and particle views together were required for a complete account of radiation fluctuations. His 1916 theory of the emission and absorption of radiation was largely independent of the classical picture. It associated momentum as well as energy with the quanta and introduced stimulated emission, which governs the operation of lasers. His last contribution, before the quantum revolution of 1925–7, was to treat radiation as a quantum gas of indistinguishable particles by means of Einstein–Bose statistics.

Throughout, Einstein employed statistical methods, even representing emission and absorption of radiation as random processes. Yet he never broke with his belief that his treatment was defective since 'it leaves the time and direction of elementary processes to "chance"'.

5 Quantum theory: critique of the standard interpretation

Einstein reacted strongly against complementarity, the positivist interpretation of the new quantum theory that became standard (see BOHR, N.; LOGICAL POSITIVISM §4; HEISENBERG, W.), in particular to its indeterminism and irrealism. Einstein felt that no essentially statistical theory could be fundamental in physics (his determinism) and that every fundamental theory should allow one to describe individual objects and processes independently of acts or conditions of observation (his realism). Moreover, he thought that the collapse of the quantum wave function introduced a kind of non-local action that could not be reconciled with relativity and that one could not recover classical mechanics as a suitable limiting case of quantum mechanics.

The impressive empirical success of quantum mechanics led him to envisage a better relativistic theory from which both the quantum theory and ordinary mechanics would emerge as limiting cases. He believed that this new (realist and deterministic) theory would not employ the dynamical variables of mechanics but would require different concepts. Thus Einstein's vision was not that of a hidden variables' extension of the quantum theory (see QUANTUM MECHANICS, INTERPRETATION OF §3), as some have supposed. Instead, he worked to build a unified theory of the electromagnetic and gravitational fields that might be the starting point for the new physics. Toward the end of his life, with a unification programme not proceeding well, he may have abandoned his hope for a spacetime ('field') theory, looking instead to what he sometimes referred to as an 'algebraical physics'.

Einstein's scientific fame made him the quantum

theory's most important critic. He held that the theory was descriptively incomplete: that the quantum state function describes only ensembles of systems and, at best, provides an incomplete or partial description of the individual case. Einstein argued for this conclusion in a famous paper ('EPR') co-authored with his then assistants, Podolsky and Rosen (1935). The structure of EPR is complex and has given rise to a whole literature attempting to identify its errors and challenge its assumptions (see BELL'S THEOREM §1). Ironically, it turns out that EPR was actually written not by Einstein but by Podolsky, and that Einstein himself was critical of Podolsky's text, which he said 'buried' the main point. In subsequent publications Einstein gave his own versions. One version assumes that spatially separated quantum systems possess 'real physical states' (separability) and that these states are not immediately influenced by distant events (locality). Another version discharges these twin assumptions by focusing on macroscopic systems, for which separability and locality seem secure. This argument, developed in a correspondence that produced the similar 'cat paradox' of Erwin Schrödinger, challenges whether the quantum theory can accommodate gross macroscopic events, like an explosion due to radioactive decay (see QUANTUM MEASUREMENT PROBLEM).

6 Philosophy of science

The founders of Vienna Circle logical empiricism claimed Einstein as a supporter, arguing, for example, that Einstein's critique of absolute distant simultaneity implicitly assumed an empiricist criterion of meaningfulness (see LOGICAL POSITIVISM §2; VIENNA CIRCLE §3). Actually, from the 1920s, Einstein distanced himself from the anti-metaphysical tendencies of logical empiricism. Only in the 1960s, when logical empiricism's influence waned, did a balanced interpretation of Einstein's philosophy of science begin to emerge.

Einstein acknowledged Mach's influence, especially Mach's example of the historical and critical analysis of received scientific concepts. But from his early work on statistical physics to his late work on unified field theory, Einstein evinced no doubt about the reality of his underlying physical ontology, often representing proof of that reality as his aim, as in his claim that his work on statistical physics and Brownian motion aimed to establish the reality of atoms and molecules.

Einstein's realism is not, however, the scientific realism of the later twentieth century, nor the convergentist realism of Peirce or Popper (see SCIENTIFIC REALISM AND ANTIREALISM §1). Ein-

stein's mature philosophy of science combines a working physicist's realism with Duhemian underdetermination and conventionalism (see DUHEM, P.M.M. §4). For Einstein, there is, in principle, no unique determination of theory by empirical evidence, although, in practice, theory choice seems uniquely determined. Because of this underdetermination in principle that Einstein believed pervaded all physical theory, he held that scientific theories are 'free creations of the human intellect', whose predictions must conform to empirical evidence. After the early 1930s, Einstein's rationalist sentiments grew, for he increasingly viewed mathematical or logical simplicity as a guide in choosing among empirically equivalent theories, although he doubted that the relevant sense of simplicity could be precisely defined since it involved 'a reciprocal weighing of incommensurable qualities'. How an underdetermined deep ontology can be considered 'real' is clarified by the recognition that, for Einstein, realism was less a general semantic thesis about the interpretation of all theories and more a demand that spatio-temporal theories satisfy a few, specifically physical, requirements, chiefly determinism and separability.

Einstein's conventionalist realism was refined during the 1920s as he, Schlick and Reichenbach sought to construct a new empiricism opposing the Neo-Kantianism of thinkers like Ernst Cassirer, who tried to save Kant's doctrine of the a priori in the face of general relativity's assertion that the global geometry of spacetime is non-Euclidean. Einstein disputed Schlick and Reichenbach's declaration that only coordinating definitions are conventional, arguing that the coordinating definition– empirical proposition distinction was arbitrary (see GENERAL RELATIVITY, PHILOSOPHICAL RESPONSES TO).

One of Einstein's most original contributions to scientific methodology was his distinguishing between 'principle theories' and 'constructive theories'. The former are based upon well-confirmed high-level empirical generalizations, like the light and relativity principles in special relativity, or the first and second laws of thermodynamics, which function as regulative principles constraining the choice of constructive models. Ultimate understanding comes via a constructive theory, but early investigations in new domains will progress more rapidly by first seeking principle theories to guide the search for constructive models.

See also POINCARÉ, H.; SPACE; SPACETIME; TIME

List of works

Einstein's numerous works are available in a series of collections. The more accessible are referenced here.

Einstein, A. (1954) *Ideas and Opinions*, New York: Crown. (A collection of nonscientific and popular scientific writings. Includes writings and translations of central importance to §6.)

—— (1977) *Relativity: The Special and the General Theory*, London: Methuen, 15th edn. (A popularization of relativity theory.)

—— (1987–) *The Collected Papers of Albert Einstein*, J. Stachel, M. Klein, R. Schulmann, *et al.* (eds) Princeton, NJ: Princeton University Press. (Ongoing publication of a standard edition of Einstein's published and private papers with companion English translation volumes.)

—— (1990) *Out of My Later Years*, New York: Bonanza. (A collection of nonscientific and popular scientific writings.)

Einstein, A. and Infeld, L. (1938) *The Evolution of Physics: The Growth of Ideas from the Early Concepts to Relativity and Quanta*, Cambridge: Cambridge University Press. (Survey of the historical development of physics.)

Einstein, A., Podolsky, B. and Rosen, N. (1935) 'Can Quantum Mechanical Description of Physical Reality be Considered Complete?', *Physical Review* 47: 777–80. (The 'EPR' paper, written by Podolsky, discussed in §5.)

References and further reading

Fine, A. (1986) *The Shaky Game: Einstein, Realism and the Quantum Theory*, Chicago, IL: University of Chicago Press. (Realism in general and Einstein's realism (see §6) and expansion of material of §5.)

Holton, G. (1968) 'Mach, Einstein, and the Search for Reality', *Daedalus* 97: 636–73; repr. in *Thematic Origins of Scientific Thought: Kepler to Einstein*, Cambridge, MA: Harvard University Press, 1973, 219–59. (Significant early treatment of Einstein's realism. Compare with later treatments in Fine 1986 and Howard 1993. See §6.)

Howard, D. (1993) 'Was Einstein Really a Realist?' *Perspectives on Science* 1: 204–51. (Argues for significant realist moment even in Einstein's early philosophy of science, but distinguishes Einstein's marriage of conventionalism, holism and realism from scientific realism of later twentieth century; examines role of physical principles in Einstein's realism. See §6.)

Howard, D. and Stachel, J. (series eds) (1989–) *Einstein Studies*, Boston, MA: Birkhaueser. (Series devoted to Einstein and physics in his tradition.

Volumes 1 (1989), 3 (1992) and 5 (1993) treat the history of general relativity.)

Lorentz, H.A., Einstein, A., Minkowski, H. and Weyl, H. (eds) (1952) *The Principle of Relativity*, notes by A. Sommerfeld, trans. W. Perrett and G.B. Jeffrey, New York: Dover. (Collection of original papers in relativity theory by Einstein and others including the most-used English translations of *On the Electrodynamics of Moving Bodies* (1905) and *The Foundation of the General Theory of Relativity* (1916). See §§2 and 3.)

Nathan, O. and Norden, H. (1968) *Einstein on Peace*, New York: Schocken Books. (Comprehensive study of Einstein's social and political activities and writings, with lengthy excepts from writings. See §1.)

Norton, J.D. (1993) 'General Covariance and the Foundations of General Relativity: Eight Decades of Dispute', *Reports on Progress in Physics* 56: 791–858. (Review of the debate over the physical significance of general covariance. See §3.)

Pais, A. (1982) *Subtle is the Lord... The Science and the Life of Albert Einstein*, Oxford: Clarendon Press. (Biographical account of Einstein's scientific work.)

Paty, M. (1993) *Einstein Philosophe: La Physique comme philosophic practique* (Einstein, Philosopher: Physics as Practical Philosophy), Paris: Presses Universitaires de France. (Comprehensive study of Einstein's philosophy of science. See §6.)

Schilpp, P.A. (ed.) (1951) *Albert Einstein: Philosopher–Scientist*, New York, Tudor, 2nd edn. (Discussion of Einstein's work by leading scientists and philosophers of Einstein's later years; includes Einstein's Autobiographical Notes, Einstein's 'Reply to Criticisms' and bibliography of Einstein's writing.)

Seelig, C. (1960) *Albert Einstein. Leben und Werk eines Genies unserer Zeit* (Albert Einstein. Life and Work of a Genius of our Time), Zurich: Europa Verlag. (This biography draws on an extensive correspondence between the author, Einstein and others.)

ARTHUR FINE
DON HOWARD
JOHN D. NORTON

ELEATIC PHILOSOPHY

see GORGIAS; MEGARIAN SCHOOL; MELISSUS; PARMENIDES; PRESOCRATIC PHILOSOPHY; XENOPHANES; ZENO OF ELEA

ELECTRODYNAMICS

Electric charges interact via the electric and magnetic fields they produce. Electrodynamics is the study of the laws governing these interactions. The phenomena of electricity and of magnetism were once taken to constitute separate subjects. By the beginning of the nineteenth century they were recognized as closely related topics and by the end of that century electromagnetic phenomena had been unified with those of optics. Classical electrodynamics provided the foundation for the special theory of relativity, and its unification with the principles of quantum mechanics has led to modern quantum field theory, arguably our most fundamental physical theory to date.

As James Clerk Maxwell (1831–79) pointed out in the preface to his *A Treatise on Electricity and Magnetism* (1873), the ancients were aware that certain bodies, such as amber, once rubbed, attract other bodies. These and similar phenomena are termed electric after the Greek for amber, *ēlectron*. Similarly, the lodestone has long been known to attract pieces of iron at a distance. These and related phenomena are termed magnetic after Magnesia (Greek, *magnēs*), an ancient city in Asia Minor where the lodestone was found. A full historical background to electrodynamics would include the development of electric circuit theory and of optics (see OPTICS).

The modern science of electricity and magnetism can be conveniently dated by the publication in 1600 of William Gilbert's (1540–1603) great work on magnetic and electric phenomena. To him we owe the terms 'electric attraction', 'electrical force' and 'magnetic pole'. Gilbert associated electricity with a tenuous effluvium (or vapour) that was liberated from a body by the action of friction. René Descartes (1596–1650) attempted to explain magnetism in terms of vortices in a fluid that surrounded magnets. These ideas were consonant with a corpuscular theory of light and the caloric theory of heat. The electric effluvium was even conjectured to be associated with the effect of gravity. Such a plenum or ether would play a central role in the development of physical theory into the beginning of the twentieth century.

Stephen Gray (d. 1736) and Benjamin Franklin (1706–90) were among those who postulated various qualitative theories based on electrical fluids. Joseph Priestley (1733–1804), using an analogy with Newton's law of gravitation, suggested an inverse square law of attraction or repulsion between electric charges. Although there were earlier approximate verifications, by 1785 Charles-Augustin de Coulomb (1736–1806) made a fairly accurate direct experimental test of this law, which now bears his name.

A concise mathematical formulation of electrostatic theory was presented in 1812 by Siméon-Denis Poisson (1781–1840). Both he and Pierre-Simon Laplace (1749–1827) recognized that the vector electrostatic force (like the gravitational one) could be calculated from the potential energy of a system of charges. By 1828, the theory of the electric potential had been formalized by George Green (1793–1841). In 1820 Hans Christian Ørsted (1777–1851) discovered a new type of effect that arose when charges were set in motion to produce an electric current. These magnetic effects were soon given precise mathematical formulations by Jean-Baptiste Biot (1774–1862), Félix Savart (1791–1841) and, most elegantly, by André-Marie Ampère (1775–1836). In 1845, Franz Neumann (1798–1895) discovered a vector potential function for the magnetic field. Action at a distance remained the dominant mode of thought in this area until the time of Michael Faraday (1791–1867), who introduced the concept of electric and magnetic fields. Faraday's field, and his 1831 law of electromagnetic induction, formed the basis for Maxwell's unification of electric and magnetic phenomena. Maxwell's theory demonstrated that electric and magnetic phenomena are governed by a common set of equations and that optical phenomena are electromagnetic in nature (see FIELD THEORY, CLASSICAL; MAXWELL, J.C. §2). Heinrich Hertz (1857–94) contributed significantly to the acceptance of Maxwell's theory, not only by experimental verification in the 1880s of the electromagnetic nature of light, but also, in the 1890s, with a series of papers that gave a concise presentation of the axioms of Maxwell's theory and a clear explanation of electromagnetic phenomena by rigorous deduction from those principles. Hertz's often-quoted dictum that the essence of Maxwell's theory is the equations themselves would become a fair characterization of the attitude of one school of modern physicists toward theories in general (see HERTZ, H.). Even into the twentieth century 'continental'-style physicists prized theories of generality and mathematical abstractness, whereas models of specific phenomena were favoured in Great Britian.

So dominant had been Newtonian mechanics and the mechanical worldview, that even Maxwell and many of his contemporaries attempted to underpin electromagnetic phenomena with mechanical models. This was the programme of the electromagnetic ether, brought to its most complete mathematical formulation by Hendrik Lorentz (1853–1928) at the end of the nineteenth century. In fact, electromagnetic phenomena came to play such a central role in physics that, in the early years of the twentieth century, attempts were made to replace the mechanical worldview with an electromagnetic one, whereby mechanical properties such as mass were accounted for in terms of electromagnetic properties such as charge. It was out of these foundational struggles in electrodynamics that Albert Einstein's special theory of relativity emerged in 1905 (see EINSTEIN, A. §2). Subsequent efforts by Paul Dirac (1902–84) to apply the principles of quantum mechanics to electrodynamics led in 1928 to the first formulation of quantum electrodynamics and, through the work of Werner HEISENBERG (1901–76) and Wolfgang Pauli (1900–58), which began in 1929, to modern quantum field theory. Electrodynamics was central in quantum field theory coming to the fore and in replacing the old particle–field dualism with the quantum-field ontology (see FIELD THEORY, QUANTUM).

See also: MECHANICS, CLASSICAL; RELATIVITY THEORY, PHILOSOPHICAL SIGNIFICANCE OF

References and further reading

Buchwald, J.Z. (1985) *From Maxwell to Microphysics*, Chicago, IL: University of Chicago Press. (A history of electromagnetic theory during the last quarter of the nineteenth century.)

Faraday, M. (1839–55) *Experimental Researches in Electricity*, London: R. & J.E. Taylor. (An exhaustive account of Faraday's seminal work in electricity and magnetism.)

* Gilbert, W. (1600) *De Magnete*, London: Peter Short. (An early study of magnetism.)

Jackson, J.D. (1975) *Classical Electrodynamics*, New York: John Wiley & Sons, 2nd edn. (An authoritative modern textbook on the technical aspects of the subject.)

* Maxwell, J.C. (1873) *A Treatise on Electricity and Magnetism*, Oxford: Clarendon Press. (The classic text on electromagnetic theory.)

Sommerfeld, A. (1952) *Electrodynamics*, New York: Academic Press. (A technical presentation, accompanied by useful comments on the history of the subject.)

Tricker, R.A.R. (1965) *Early Electrodynamics: The First Law of Circulation*, London: Pergamon Press. (An elementary and detailed account of the discovery of the basic laws governing the interactions between electric currents and magnetic fields.)

Whittaker, E. (1973) *A History of the Theories of Aether and Electricity*, New York: Humanities Press. (A classic on the history of the subject from antiquity to the discovery of quantum mechanics.)

JAMES T. CUSHING

ELIADE, MIRCEA (1907–86)

Eliade was educated as a philosopher. He published extensively in the history of religions and acted as editor-in-chief of Macmillan's Encyclopedia of Religion *(1987). The influence of his thought, through these works and through thirty years as director of the history of religions department at Chicago University, is considerable.*

Eliade's analysis of religion assumes the existence of 'the sacred' as the object of worship of religious humanity. It appears as the source of power, significance and value. Humanity apprehends 'hierophanies' – physical manifestations or revelations of the sacred – often, but not only, in the form of symbols, myths and rituals. Any phenomenal entity is a potential hierophany and can give access to nonhistorical time, what Eliade calls illud tempus *('that time'). The apprehension of this sacred time is a constitutive feature of the religious aspect of humanity.*

1 Life
2 Thought

1 Life

Eliade was born in Bucharest, Romania. Despite a childhood interest in entomology and botany (which doubtless first attracted his attention to Goethe, a lifelong role model and inspiration), he developed an interest in world literature and was led from there to philology, philosophy and comparative religion. As a youth he read extensively in Romanian, French and German, and around 1924–5 he learned Italian and English to read Raffaele Pettazzoni and James George Frazer in the original.

In 1925 Eliade enrolled at the University of Bucharest, where he studied in the department of philosophy. The influence of Nae Ionescu, then an assistant professor of logic and metaphysics and an active journalist, was keenly felt by the young Eliade and the shadow which fell on the older scholar because of his involvement with the extreme right in interwar Romania has darkened Eliade's reputation.

Eliade's Master's thesis examined Italian Renaissance philosophers from Marcilio Ficino to Giordano Bruno, and Renaissance humanism was one of his major influences when he turned to India in order to 'universalize' the 'provincial' philosophy he had inherited from his European education. Finding that the Maharaja of Kassimbazar sponsored European scholars to study in India, Eliade applied and was granted an allowance for four years. In 1928 he sailed for Calcutta to study Sanskrit and philosophy under

Surendranath Dasgupta, a professor at the university there.

He returned to Bucharest in 1932 and successfully submitted an analysis of yoga as his doctoral thesis in 1933, which was published in French as *Yoga: essai sur les origines de la mystique Indienne* (Yoga: A Treatise on the Origins of Indian Mysticism). This was extensively revised and republished as *Yoga, Immortality, and Freedom* (1958a). As Ionescu's assistant, Eliade lectured on, among other things, Aristotle's *Metaphysics* and Nicholas of Cusa's *Docta ignorantia*. From 1933 to 1939 he was active with the Criterion group, which gave public seminars on a wide range of topics. They were strongly influenced by the philosophy of 'trairism' the search for the 'authentic' in and through lived experience (Romanian, *traire*), which was seen as the only source of 'authenticity'.

After the Second World War, during which he served with the Romanian Legation in the UK and Portugal, Eliade was unable to return to the newly communist Romania because of his connection with the right-wing Ionescu. In 1945 he moved to Paris, where his acquaintance with George Dumézil, an important scholar of comparative mythology, secured him a part-time post teaching comparative religion at the École des Hautes Études at the Sorbonne. From this time on almost all of Eliade's scholarly works were written in French.

At the prompting of Joachim Wach, director of the history of religions department at the University of Chicago, Eliade was invited to give the 1956 Haskell Lectures on 'Patterns of Initiation' at Chicago. These were later published as *Rites and Symbols of Initiation* (1958b). In 1958 Eliade was invited to assume the chair of the history of religions department at Chicago. There he stayed until his death in 1986, publishing extensively and writing largely unpublished fiction. He also launched the journals *History of Religions* and *The Journal of Religion*, and acted as editor-in-chief for Macmillan's *Encyclopedia of Religion* (1987).

2 Thought

Despite his focus on the history of religions, Eliade never relinquished his philosophical agenda. That said, he never fully clarified his philosophy. There has been radical disagreement over his thought, some seeing it as a crucial contribution to the study of religion, and some seeing him as an obscurantist whose normative assumptions are unacceptable.

In *Cosmos and History: The Myth of the Eternal Return* (1954), a book which he was tempted to subtitle *Introduction to a Philosophy of History*, Eliade distinguishes between religious and nonreligious humanity on the basis of the perception of time as heterogeneous and homogeneous respectively. This distinction will be immediately familiar to students of Henri BERGSON (§2) as an element of that philosopher's analysis of time and space. Eliade contends that the perception of time as a homogeneous, linear and unrepeatable medium is a peculiarity of modern and nonreligious humanity. Archaic or religious humanity (*homo religiosus*), in comparison, perceives time as heterogeneous; that is, as divided between profane time (linear) and sacred time (cyclical and reactualizable). By means of myths and rituals which give access to this sacred time, religious humanity protects itself against the 'terror of history', a condition of helplessness before the absolute *data* of historical time, a form of existential anxiety.

In the very process of establishing this distinction, however, Eliade undermines it, insisting that nonreligious humanity in any pure sense is a very rare phenomenon. Myth and *illud tempus* are still operative, albeit concealed, in the world of modern humanity and Eliade clearly regards the attempt to restrict real time to linear historical time as finally self-contradictory. He squarely sets himself against the historicism of HEGEL (§8).

'The sacred' has also been the subject of considerable contention. Some have seen Eliade's 'sacred' as simply corresponding to a conventional concept of deity, or to Rudolf Otto's *ganz andere* (the 'wholly other'), whereas others have seen a closer resemblance to Émile Durkheim's socially influenced sacred (see OTTO, R.; DURKHEIM, É. §4). Eliade himself repeatedly identifies the sacred as the real, yet he states clearly that 'the sacred is a structure of human consciousness' (1969: i; 1978: xiii). This would argue more for the latter interpretation: a social construction of both the sacred and of reality. Yet the sacred is identified as the *source* of significance, meaning, power and being, and its manifestations as hierophanies, cratophanies or ontophanies accordingly (appearances of the holy, of power or of being). Corresponding to the suggested ambiguity of the sacred itself is the ambiguity of its manifestations.

Eliade states that believers for whom the hierophany is a revelation of the sacred must be prepared by their experience, including their traditional religious background, before they can apprehend it. To others the sacred tree, for example, remains simply a tree. It is an indispensable element of Eliade's analysis that any phenomenal entity could be apprehended as a hierophany with the appropriate preparation. The conclusion must be that all beings reveal, and at the same time conceal, the nature of Being. A reprise of Nicholas of Cusa's 'coincidence of opposites' is evident here, as is a possible explanation of the systematic ambiguity of Eliade's writings (see NICHOLAS OF CUSA §2).

Finally, religion, systematically understood as the apprehension of relative worth conferred through nonhistorical realities (including all abstract and imaginary entities), but revealed and confirmed through historical phenomena, is seen as a unifying human universal. It is characteristic of Eliade's style of writing, both in his fictional and in his academic work, that this conclusion is nowhere clearly stated. Leading assertions are scattered throughout his publications on the history of religions, alchemy, symbolism, initiation, myth and so on inviting his readers either to make an immediate interpretation or to pursue the question further into the thicket of his *oeuvre*.

See also: MYSTICISM, NATURE OF; PHENOMENOLOGY OF RELIGION; RELIGIOUS EXPERIENCE §1

List of works

Eliade, M. (1954) *Cosmos and History: The Myth of the Eternal Return*, trans. W. Trask, Princeton, NJ: Princeton University Press. (Probably Eliade's most crucial and approachable short work. Contains his analysis of heterogeneous and homogeneous time, and his conception of the 'terror of history' and the ability to 'reactualize' religious time.)

—— (1958a) *Yoga, Immortality and Freedom*, trans. W. Trask, London: Routledge & Kegan Paul. (First published in French as *Yoga: essai sur l'origine de la mystique Indienne* in 1933, this informative and scholarly work analyses yoga as a concrete search for freedom from human limitations.)

—— (1958b) *Rites and Symbols of Initiation (Birth and Rebirth)*, trans. W. Trask, London: Harvill Press. (Eliade's 1956 Haskell Lectures at the University of Chicago. His analysis of initiatory themes implies their ubiquity and structure as a symbolic death and rebirth.)

—— (1958c) *Patterns in Comparative Religion*, trans. R. Sheed, London: Sheed & Ward. (An attempt to delineate the morphology of the sacred, this is frequently criticized for its cross-cultural and ahistorical approach, which organizes religious phenomena by structural similarities regardless of time or place of origin. A valuable source of data nevertheless.)

—— (1959) *The Sacred and the Profane: The Nature of Religion*, trans. W. Trask, London: Harcourt Brace Jovanovich. (Picking up where Otto's *The Idea of the Holy* left off, the sacred is explicated through its relation to its binary counterpart, the profane, and the complex dialectic of the two is outlined.)

—— (1960) *Myths, Dreams and Mysteries: The Encounter between Contemporary Faiths and Archaic Realities*, trans. P. Mairet, London: Harvill Press. (Eliade's understanding of myth in the modern world and the mythic prestige of origins, and his analysis, among other things, of the symbolism of ascension, flight, the labyrinth and swallowing by a monster.)

—— (1961) *Images and Symbols: Studies in Religious Symbolism*, trans. P. Mairet, London: Harvill Press. (More on symbolism, particularly the symbolism of the centre, knots, shells and pearls. Symbolism and history are discussed, as is method.)

—— (1963) *Myth and Reality*, trans. W. Trask, New York: Harper & Row. (The structure of myths. More on the prestige of origins and on the survival of myths and mythic themes in modern thought.)

—— (1964) *Shamanism: Archaic Techniques of Ecstasy*, trans. W. Trask, London: Routledge & Kegan Paul. (Long a standard work in the study of shamanism, this is a detailed and valuable source of information on the phenomenon.)

—— (1965) *The Two and the One*, trans. J.M. Cohen, Chicago, IL: University of Chicago Press. (An important analysis of the *coincidenta oppositorum* (coincidence of opposites), or binary oppositions, in religious ideas. Androgyny is explored, as are cosmogony and eschatology, the birth and death of the cosmos or worldview.)

—— (1969) *The Quest: History and Meaning in Religion*, London: University of Chicago Press. (This attempt at a more methodological work pulls together articles previously published on Eliade's methodological and theoretical presuppositions, including his 'new humanism' and his response to the quest for the 'origins' of religion.)

—— (1978) *A History of Religious Ideas*, vol. 1, *From the Stone Age to the Eleusinian Mysteries*, trans. W. Trask, Chicago, IL: University of Chicago Press. (Originally projected as a complete history of religion in one volume, this was an attempt to give Eliade's understanding of the entire history of religion from a unified perspective. It is a useful reference work, potentially readable in its entirety. Many of Eliade's categories survive in this mature work: the terror of history, the *coincidenta oppositorum*, the symbolism of the centre, and the *hieros gamos*, or symbolic heavenly marriage.)

—— (1982) *A History of Religious Ideas*, vol. 2, *From Gautama Buddha to the Triumph of Christianity*, trans. W. Trask, Chicago, IL: University of Chicago Press. (See note to volume 1 (1978).)

—— (1985) *The History of Religious Ideas*, vol. 3, *From Muhammad to the Age of the Reforms*, trans. A. Hiltebeitel and D. Apostolos-Cappadona, Chicago, IL: University of Chicago Press. (See note to volume 1 (1978).)

—— (ed.) (1987) *Encyclopedia of Religion*, New York: Macmillan. (Sixteen volumes of articles on every aspect of religion by leading scholars in the field. Currently the standard reference encyclopedia on religion.)

References and further reading

Allen, D. (1978) *Structure and Creativity in Religion: Hermeneutics in Mircea Eliade's Phenomenology and New Directions*, The Hague: Mouton. (An interesting philosophical study of Eliade's thought that perhaps overemphasizes Eliade's methodology as phenomenology of religion.)

Allen, D. and Doeing, D. (1980) *Mircea Eliade: An Annotated Bibliography*, New York and London: Garland. (An excellent polyglot bibliography, although a definitive posthumous bibliography is in preparation by M.L. Ricketts and M. Handoca.)

Baird, R.D. (1971) 'Phenomenological Understanding: Mircea Eliade', in *Category Formation and the History of Religion*, The Hague: Mouton, 74–91. (A critique of Eliade as making unwarranted ontological assumptions and normative judgments that should, however, be verified against a thorough reading of the primary sources.)

Cave, J.D. (1992) *Mircea Eliade's Vision for a New Humanism*, Oxford: Oxford University Press. (An accessible interpretation of Eliade's work in terms of humanism, which was one of Eliade's major foci.)

Dudley, G., III (1977) *Religion on Trial: Mircea Eliade and His Critics*, Philadelphia, PA: Temple University Press. (This readable and broadly favourable work reconceives Eliade's thought in terms of a research programme for the history of religion.)

Idinopulos, T.A. and Yonan, E. (eds) (1994) *Religion and Reductionism: Essays on Eliade, Segal, and the Challenge of the Social Sciences for the Study of Religion*, Leiden: E.J. Brill. (A variety of challenging articles on Eliade's status, and implications for the study of religion. Of particular interest is W. Paden's 'Before "The Sacred" Became Theological: Rereading the Durkheimian Legacy'.)

Olson, C. (1992) *The Theology and Philosophy of Eliade*, New York: St Martin's Press. (A general and readable consideration of Eliade's thought.)

Rennie, B. (1996) *Reconstructing Eliade: Making Sense of Religion*, New York: State University of New York Press. (A thorough explication of Eliade's work, which assumes that it has an internal coherence for the critic to uncover; includes an extensive bibliography.)

Ricketts, M.L. (1988) *Mircea Eliade: The Romanian Roots*, New York: Columbia University Press, 2 vols. (A massive and thorough piece of research into Eliade's life, thought and works up until 1945; a useful bibliography is provided.)

Strenski, I. (1987) 'Mircea Eliade', in *Four Theories of Myth in Twentieth-Century History*, London: Macmillan. (One of the earliest critiques to raise Eliade's political background; it attempts to trace the influence of that background in his theoretical constructs.)

BRYAN STEPHENSON RENNIE

ELIMINATIVISM

'Eliminativism' refers to the view that mental phenomena – for example, beliefs, desires, conscious states – do not exist. Although this can seem absurd on its face, in the twentieth century it has gained a wide variety of adherents, for example, scientific behaviourists, who thought that all human and animal activity could be explained in terms of the history of patterns of stimuli, responses and reinforcements; as well as some who have thought that neurophysiology alone is all that is needed.

Two immediate objections to eliminativism – for example, that it is incoherent because it claims there are no 'claims', and that it conflicts with data of which we are all immediately aware – arguably beg the question against the view. What is wanted is non-tendentious evidence for the mind. Contrary to behaviourism, this seems to be available in the intelligent behaviour of most higher animals.

1   The view and its appeal
2   Objections

1   The view and its appeal

Eliminativism about anything, *x*, is the view that *x*'s do not exist. Thus, atheists are eliminativists about God(s). However, the focus of most contemporary 'eliminativist' debates is on eliminativism about mental phenomena: for example, beliefs, desires, sensations, consciousness. Although the view seems to many absurd on its face, in the twentieth century it has gained a wide variety of adherents. Its earliest advocates were the scientific behaviourists such as J.B. Watson, who thought that all human and animal activity could be explained in terms of the history of patterns of stimuli, responses and reinforcements, mental states being 'needless way stations' (Skinner 1963). But there have also been those who have

263

thought that neurophysiology alone was all that was needed (see Rorty 1965; Churchland 1986; BEHAVIOURISM, METHODOLOGICAL AND SCIENTIFIC; CONNECTIONISM).

A crucial terminological point: *reduction* is not the same as *elimination*! If chemists succeed in 'reducing' claims about water to claims about H_2O, they have shown that water does exist just as much as those molecules do. Similarly, if a philosopher or psychologist succeeds in 'reducing' some mental to a physical phenomenon, that does not for a moment entail that that mental phenomenon is not perfectly real (see REDUCTIONISM IN THE PHILOSOPHY OF MIND).

Moreover, reductions themselves can be of many sorts: some (like that of 'water') involve identification of an ordinary with a scientific kind; others (like that of 'weeds') might involve what is scientifically a very arbitrary classification. 'Weeds' have not been *eliminated*, even if they are not scientifically interesting. (Sometimes, however, philosophers who deny that mental phenomena correspond to any scientifically interesting (causal) phenomena are also regarded as eliminativist; see MENTAL CAUSATION).

Two sorts of difficulty with the reduction of the mental to the physical lead many to eliminativism: (1) no one has yet been able to provide a satisfactory physical account of intentionality, or the fact that one's thoughts are 'about', for example, non-mental things (Chisholm 1957; Quine 1960; INTENTIONALITY); and (2) conscious, sensory experience has seemed to many to be essentially 'private', not located in physical space (Descartes 1973), and so not open to the public scrutiny required of an objective science (see PRIVACY). Of course, for some, these are all reasons to embrace dualism (see DUALISM); but, for the convinced physicalist, the failure of reduction is a reason for elimination.

The debate between dualists and eliminativists can be compared to either of two debates in the history of science: the debate over whether magnetic forces were needed in addition to gravitational ones; and the debate over whether vital forces were needed in addition to standard physio-chemical ones. However, this places the dualist in an extremely vulnerable position. For it seems to be a striking fact about people and animals that – putting aside the claims of 'parapsychology' – 'all of their non-tendentiously described behaviour could be explained in principle by reference to physical properties alone' (Quine 1960: 264; see PARAPSYCHOLOGY). If dualism is taken literally as the positing of non-physical mental phenomena in addition to the phenomena of physics, it risks the fate of vitalism (see VITALISM).

The need for 'non-tendentious' evidence, that is, evidence that is not described in terms that presuppose mentalism, is crucial here. Just as it is no argument against molecular biology that it does not explain the activity of a 'vital fluid', so it is no argument against an eliminativism that it does not explain 'inner experience' or 'intentional action'. These quoted descriptions simply assume without argument what the biologist and the eliminativist are challenging (Churchland 1981: 88–90).

It should be borne in mind that eliminativism is not a proposal about how people should ordinarily live and talk. It is an issue about whether there really are mental phenomena. Most eliminativists are quite happy to use mental talk *instrumentally*, just as they might be happy to speak in geocentric terms when navigating at sea (Quine 1960: §45).

2 Objections

Philosophers and psychologists have employed a number of strategies to meet the challenges posed by eliminativism. They range from claims of introspection, to purely philosophical ('transcendental') arguments about the position's incoherence, to arguments based upon empirical evidence of the sort gathered by natural science.

Introspective arguments. Mentalists often claim that people know immediately and indubitably that they have minds. Indeed, some would go so far as to claim that all knowledge depends upon knowledge of one's own mental states. One strategy for replying to such arguments is to show how to account for the activities of 'introspection' and science in appropriately sanitized terms, rather in the way the anti-vitalist might sanitize the vitalist's description of living things. A well-known such effort is Quine's replacement of 'belief' by 'dispositions to utter certain sentences in certain circumstances' (1960). Sentences, on this view, are just sequences of certain sounds, and theories just sets of sentences. Introspective claims may be replaced by dispositions to utter certain sentences as a result of physical events in one's body.

Transcendental arguments. Transcendental arguments attempt to show that eliminativism is incoherent because the theory itself presupposes the existence of mental phenomena (Baker 1987; Boghossian 1990): if eliminativism is *true* then the eliminativist must countenance an intentional property like truth.

At this point, however, the eliminativist can resort to deflationary semantic theories, that avoid analysing predicates like 'x is true' in any fashion that takes them to express a real property. Rather, they are construed as logical devices: asserting that a sentence is true is just a quoted way of asserting the sentence itself: to say, '"God exists" is true' is just to say, 'God exists'. In so far as dispositional replacements of 'claims', and deflationary accounts of 'true', are coherent, eliminativism is not self-refuting (see Devitt and Rey 1991; TRUTH, DEFLATIONARY THEORIES OF).

Empirical evidence. Is there any non-tendentious evidence for mentality? While it does seem that there is no denying that every motion of every animal could be explained in physical terms, it is by no means obvious that every non-accidental pattern in the behaviour of animals could be so explained. And these patterns can be described without using mentalistic language. Thus, the behaviour of rats in mazes and many animals in the wild has been studied in considerable detail: the *patterns* in that behaviour can be shown to resist any explanation that does not posit at least internal representational states (for example, rats trained to run a roundabout route in a maze will take shortcuts later made available). In the case of human beings, one need think merely of 'standardized' tests of mental capacities (like the SAT and GRE), on which the 'questions' and 'answers' can be physically specified: the patterns of graphite on the 'answer' sheets are overwhelmingly correlated with the 'questions' across the millions of students. It is virtually impossible to imagine an explanation of these correlations that does not posit mental states (for example, the students understand the instructions, are able to think, want to do well, and so fill in the correct answers).

However, these regularities seem to be evidence only for a propositional attitude psychology. Some have thought that this is enough to capture all the problematic phenomena about the mind (Lycan 1987). Others (Block 1978; Levine 1983) have thought more is required for conscious experiences of, for example, colours: what are called 'qualia' (see QUALIA). It is not obvious, however, that non-tendentious data can be adduced for such experiences regarded as more than propositional attitudes. Influenced by Wittgenstein (1953), some have defended eliminativism with respect to these further phenomena, even when other portions of the mental are accepted (Rey 1983; Dennett 1991).

See also: FOLK PSYCHOLOGY; MATERIALISM IN THE PHILOSOPHY OF MIND

References and further reading

* Baker, L. (1987) *Saving Belief: A Critique of Physicalism*, Princeton, NJ: Princeton University Press. (A criticism of various reductionist and eliminativist proposals; on pages 113–48 some (cautious) sympathy is expressed for a transcendental argument against eliminativism.)
* Block, N. (1978) 'Troubles with Functionalism', in C. Savage (ed.) *Minnesota Studies in the Philosophy of Science*, vol. 9, Minneapolis, MN: University of Minnesota Press; repr. in W. Lycan (ed.) *Mind and Cognition*, Oxford: Blackwell, 1990. (An important set of arguments against the leading recent reductionist approach to the mind; emphasizes particularly the difficulties in reducing sensations and qualia.)
* Boghossian, P. (1990) 'The Status of Content', *Philosophical Review* 99: 157–84. (A transcendental argument against the eliminativist denial of semantic properties.)
* Chisholm, R. (1957) *Perceiving: A Philosophical Study*, Ithaca, NY: Cornell University Press. (An influential defence of 'Brentano's thesis' of the irreducibility of the mental to the physical.)
* Churchland, Patricia (1986) *Neurophilosophy*, Cambridge MA: MIT Press, esp. 395–9. (A sketch of a neurophysiological approach to psychology in a way that takes eliminativism seriously.)
* Churchland, Paul (1981) 'Eliminativism and Propositional Attitudes', *Journal of Philosophy* 78 (2): 67–90; repr. in W. Lycan (ed.) *Mind and Cognition*, Oxford: Blackwell, 1990. (A bold attack on mentalism as a 'stagnant research program'.)
* Dennett, D. (1991) *Explaining Consciousness*, Boston, MA: Little, Brown. (A popular exposition of many eliminativist ideas, although Dennett often vacillates between eliminativism and reductionism.)
* Descartes, R. (1973) *The Philosophical Works of Descartes*, trans. E. Haldane and G. Ross, Cambridge: Cambridge University Press, 2 vols. (Classic defence of dualism; see especially the *Discourse on Method* part 5, the letters to the Marquis of Newcastle and Henry More, and the Sixth Meditation.)
* Devitt, M. and Rey, G. (1991) 'Transcending Transcendentalism: A Response to Boghossian', *Pacific Philosophical Quarterly* 72 (2): 87–100. (Defence of simply the coherence of eliminativism against transcendental arguments, specifically that of Boghossian (1990).)
* Hannan, B. (1993) 'Don't Stop Believing: The Case Against Eliminative Materialism', *Mind and Language* 8: 165–79. (Excellent survey of various arguments against eliminativism.)
* Levine, J. (1983) 'Materialism and Qualia: The Explanatory Gap', *Pacific Philosophical Quarterly* 64: 354–61. (Early, clear statement of the 'explanatory gap' problem that motivates some to eliminativism – others to dualism.)
* Lycan, W. (1987) *Consciousness*, Cambridge MA: MIT Press. (Attempt to defend a propositional attitude psychology adequate for the basic range of mental phenomena.)

—— (ed.) (1990) *Mind and Cognition*, Oxford: Blackwell. (Excellent anthology of many recent papers on eliminativism, dualism and reductionism.)

* Quine, W.V. (1960) *Word and Object*, Cambridge, MA: MIT Press. (Classic and influential statement of certain eliminativist doctrines, for example, his 'thesis of the indeterminacy of translation' (chapter 2 and §45) and his elimination of 'distinctive mental states and events behind behavior' (§54).)

* Rey, G. (1983) 'A Question About Consciousness', in N. Block, O. Flanagan and G. Guzeldere (eds) *The Nature of Consciousness: Philosophical Debates*, Cambridge, MA: MIT Press, 1997, 461–82. (An eliminativism about specifically certain common conceptions of qualia and consciousness, but within the framework of a reductionist 'language of thought' view of the mind.)

—— (1997) *Contemporary Philosophy of Mind: A Contentiously Classical Approach*, Oxford: Blackwell. (Chapters 3 and 4 present a lengthy exposition of eliminativism and of the evidence for and against it afforded by the history of behaviourism.)

* Rorty, R. (1965) 'Mind–Body Identity, Privacy and Categories', *Review of Metaphysics* 19 (1): 41–8. (One of the first philosophical defences of eliminativism in favour of neurophysiology.)

* Skinner, B.F. (1963) 'Behaviorism at Fifty', *Science* 140: 951–8; repr. with recent reactions in the light of the 'cognitive revolution', in *Behavioral and Brain Sciences* 7 (4): 615–65, 1984. (Classic statement of behaviourism, and its complaints against mentalism.)

Stich, S. (1983) *From Folk Psychology to Cognitive Science: The Case Against Belief*, Cambridge, MA: MIT Press. (Argues that 'belief' is not a natural kind, and so defends at least eliminativism to that extent.)

* Wittgenstein, L. (1953) *Philosophical Investigations*, Oxford: Blackwell, esp. §§230–308. (Although Wittgenstein himself would have resisted many of the 'isms' discussed here, his work provided an important inspiration for many eliminativist suggestions; particularly his attack on 'private objects' as 'grammatical fictions'.)

GEORGES REY

ELIOT, GEORGE (1819–80)

George Eliot is the pseudonym of the English writer Mary Ann Evans, whose mind was strongly influenced by the main philosophical currents of the time and who made a distinctive contribution of her own through her critical essays and fiction.

Although George Eliot was early seen to be intellectually gifted, she received little education of an institutional kind after leaving school at 16; from the age of nine, however, she was a prodigious reader, her appetite for learning being strengthened further by the religious conflicts of her youth. After a phase of intense Evangelical devotion she translated Strauss' *Life of Jesus* and turned to humanists such as Spinoza, finding Wordsworth's tempering of pantheism with moral insistence even more congenial (see STRAUSS, D.F. §1). She was well versed in traditional philosophy and at an early stage spoke of her aspiration that she might 'live to reconcile the philosophies of Locke and Kant'. Her primary concern, however, was with scientific naturalism and its implications. Her spell as assistant editor of the *Westminster Review* from 1851 to 1854 and then as contributor gave her the opportunity to meet and debate with some of the leading writers of the day and to write on topics such as human physiology and critical approaches to the Bible. She worked intimately with Herbert SPENCER for a time, respecting him particularly for his acknowledgment that the universe was ultimately unknowable. She admired Darwin's *Origin of Species* but declared herself to be more impressed by 'the mystery that underlies the processes'. She was also fascinated by the associationist psychology of Alexander Bain, its leading exponent, and by the positivism of Auguste COMTE, of whom G.H. Lewes, with whom she lived from 1854, was a devoted if critical follower. Her strongest sympathies were perhaps with the intellectual position of Ludwig Feuerbach, who saw religion as essentially an anthropological phenomenon, with Christianity providing the key to the subjective and moral nature of human beings (see FEUERBACH, L. §2).

George Eliot thought of herself primarily as an aesthetic teacher, arguing at the same time that 'if such teaching lapses anywhere from the picture to the diagram it becomes the most offensive of all teaching'. Feuerbach's example provided an attractive way of viewing her own role as a novelist, using her longer fictions both as a repository for observations tested by experience and a crucible for the exposition and testing of her own ideas. In *Middlemarch* (1871–2) she carried on this process in a study of provincial life forty years before she was writing, when the implications of the new biblical criticism and developments in the study of physiology were throwing former certainties into doubt, yet also creating exciting prospects. In her most complex fiction, *Daniel*

Deronda (1876), current work in physiology and psychology is caught up into the detail of her human observations, while her aspirations towards moral single-mindedness are reflected in the hero's embracing of the Zionist ideal. Her attempts to find a stance for him which could combine the cool rationality of an empiricist with scope for his fiery ardour suggests the ultimate contradiction within which her moral thinking was wrought.

List of works

Eliot, G. (1955, 1978) *The George Eliot Letters*, ed. G.S. Haight, New Haven, CT, and London: Yale University Press, vols 1–7, 1955; 8–9, 1978. (The comprehensive edition of the letters, with some extracts from the letters and journals of G.H. Lewes.)
—— (1984) *Daniel Deronda*, ed. G. Handley, Oxford: Clarendon Press. (The standard edition of this novel.)
—— (1986) *Middlemarch*, ed. D. Carroll, Oxford: Clarendon Press. (The standard edition of this novel.)
Byatt, A.S. and Warren, N. (eds) (1990) *Selected Essays, Poems and Other Writings*, Harmondsworth: Penguin. (The best selection from the essays, poems and other writings, with an introduction by A.S. Byatt.)

References and further reading

Ashton, R. (1980) *The German Idea: Four English Writers and the Reception of German Thought*, Cambridge: Cambridge University Press. (Chapter 4 deals with George Eliot.)
Beer, G. (1986) *George Eliot*, London: Routledge; Bloomington, IN: Indiana University Press. (On her feminism.)
Dodd, V.A. (1990) *George Eliot: An Intellectual Life*, London: Macmillan. (An account of her intellectual development.)
Haight, G.S. (1968) *George Eliot: A Biography*, Oxford and New York: Oxford University Press. (The standard biography.)
Karl, F. (1995) *George Eliot: A Biography*, London: HarperCollins. (A fuller and updated account.)
Myers, W. (1984) *The Teaching of George Eliot*, Leicester: Leicester University Press. (A good general guide.)
Newton, K.M. (1981) *George Eliot: Romantic Humanist*, London: Macmillan; Totowa, NJ: Barnes & Noble. (On her Romantic heritage as a thinker.)
Paris, B. (1965) *Experiments in Life: George Eliot's Quest for Values*, Detroit, MI: Wayne State University Press. (The impact of empirical philosophy on George Eliot's thought.)
Shaffer, E.S. (1975) *'Kubla Khan' and The Fall of Jerusalem*, Cambridge: Cambridge University Press. (Chapter 6 is 'George Eliot and the Higher Criticism of the Bible'.)
Shuttleworth, S. (1984) *George Eliot and nineteenth-century science: the make-believe of a beginning*, Cambridge: Cambridge University Press. (On George Eliot's attitude to physiology.)
Strauss, D.F. (1835–6) *Das Leben Jesu*, Tübingen: Osiander; trans. M.A. Evans (George Eliot, 1846), *Life of Jesus*, Philadelphia, PA: Fortress, 1972. (Strauss's 'quest' for the historical Jesus.)
Wright, T.R. (1986) *The Religion of Humanity: The Impact of Comtean Positivism on Victorian Britain*, Cambridge: Cambridge University Press. (Chapter 5 deals with George Eliot and positivism.)

JOHN BEER

ELISABETH OF BOHEMIA (1618–80)

Elisabeth of Bohemia, Princess Palatine, exerted an influence on seventeenth-century Cartesianism via her correspondence with Descartes. She questioned his accounts of mind–body interaction and free will, and persuasively argued that certain facts of embodiment, the unlucky fate of loved ones, and the demands of the public good, constitute serious challenges to Descartes' neo-Stoic view of the happy life of the autonomous will.

Eldest daughter of the exiled 'Winter King and Queen' of Bohemia, Princess Elisabeth was educated at the Prisenhof in Leiden. In 1644, DESCARTES dedicated his *Principles of Philosophy* to her, and two years later she attempted to introduce Descartes' work at the German courts. In 1670, as Abbess at Herford, she provided a haven for her correspondent, Anna Maria van SCHURMAN, and the persecuted Labadists. She corresponded and met with Quaker leaders William Penn and Robert Barclay. Near the end of her life, she was interested in the views of MALEBRANCHE and the mystical philosopher, Jacob BOEHME; she corresponded with LEIBNIZ via her sister Louise, Abbess of Maubuisson in France.

On 6 May 1643, Elisabeth began her correspondence with Descartes by arguing that voluntary motion is unintelligible in terms of Descartes' mechanical philosophy. For, determination of movement is due to (1) the impulsion of the moved object,

(2) the manner in which the mover impels the object, and (3) the qualification and figure of the surface of the moving object. (1) and (2) require contact; (3) requires extension. But souls are not extended and contact seems incompatible with their immateriality. Elisabeth urges that we need a more comprehensive definition of 'the soul' than simply a 'thinking thing'; we need to know what other properties the soul has, if we are to make its causal powers intelligible. She notes that while we suppose thought to be essential to the soul, this is difficult to prove in the cases of foetuses and deep faints – a challenge to Cartesianism that the Empiricists subsequently developed. To Descartes' rejoinder that we have a *per se* intelligible primitive notion, known by sense, of how an incorporeal soul can move a corporeal body, Elisabeth – prefiguring the position of LOCKE and HUME – responds that she has no such notion. She acknowledges that the senses show that the soul moves the body, but she denies that they, any more than imagination or understanding, show *how* this happens. She suggests that there might be unknown properties in the soul – even extension, which might belong to a faculty like sensation.

It is Elisabeth's personal problems, especially 'the weakness of my sex' (poor health due to afflictions of the soul) and the suffering of her family, that lead to discussion of *De Vita Beata* (On the Happy Life) by SENECA. Descartes' neo-Stoic solution requires that happiness depend only on what follows from the will guided by reason. But Elisabeth finds that her passions cannot be *immediately* controlled by her will and this often leads to her body becoming disordered. In addition, there are illnesses that diminish or deprive us of our reasoning power. Finally, regret, 'one of the principal obstacles to happiness', appears unavoidable when attempting to weight one's own goals along with the competing goods of others in society: 'To know all those [goods] about which one is constrained to make a choice in an active life, it would be necessary to possess infinite knowledge' (13 September 1645). Descartes replies that while we cannot know everything, we need only follow certain neo-Stoic principles for a happy life. One such principle is: the infallibility of God's decrees teaches us to accept in good spirit everything that happens to us, since it comes from God. Elisabeth replies that this principle does not help in the case of free decisions of the will; in such cases God's predetermination is not intelligible. She remained puzzled by Descartes' retort that the independence which we feel, which makes our actions sanctionable, is not incompatible with the dependence all things have on God. She argues that it is 'as impossible for the will to be at the same time free and attached to the decrees of Providence, as for the divine power to be both infinite and limited' (30

November 1645). Elisabeth's focus is on the will's liberty of indifference, which Descartes had stressed in his *Principles*, and its incompatibility with determination of any kind.

Some recent commentators have taken Elisabeth's use of her own body and female social role in her criticisms of the privileged, disembodied will as prefiguring contemporary feminist critiques of Cartesianism (Bordo 1998; Harth 1992; Thompson 1983).

See also: STOICISM

List of works

Elisabeth left no published treatises and her firm wish was that her letters should not be published. In consequence, none of her letters was published until 1862, and to date they have not been collected in a single volume; they may be found in the published works of her correspondents.

Barclay, Colonel D. (1870) *Reliquiae Barclaianae: Correspondence of Colonel D. Barclay and Robert Barclay of Urie and his son Robert, including Letters from Princess Elisabeth of the Rhine, the Earl of Perth, the Countess of Sutherland, William Penn, George Fox and others,* London: Winter & Bailey. (Contains Elisabeth's 1676–9 correspondence in English with Robert Barclay about religious matters and political events affecting the Quakers; also contains one letter in English from Elizabeth to Benjamin Furly.)

Descartes, R. (1964–74) *Oeuvres de Descartes,* vols 3, 4 and 5, ed. C. Adam and P. Tannery, nouvelle présentation, Paris: J. Vrin. (The standard edition of the Elisabeth–Descartes correspondence.)

—— (1978) *Descartes: His Moral Philosophy and Psychology,* ed. and trans. J. Blom, New York: New York University Press. (Contains English translations of fourteen philosophical letters of Elisabeth to Descartes and his responses.)

Hauck, K. (ed.) (1908) *Die Briefe der Kinder des Winterkönigs* (The letters of the children of the Winter King), Heidelberg: G. Koester. (Letters of Elisabeth and her siblings, which provide historical information about her family.)

Malebranche, N. (1958–84) *Oeuvres complètes de Malebranche,* vols 18 and 19, ed. A. Robinet, Paris: J. Vrin. (Contains synopses of the lost Elisabeth–Malebranche correspondence as well as discussion of Elisabeth in the Leibniz–Malebranche correspondence.)

References and further reading

* Bordo, S. (ed.) (1998) *Rereading the Canon: Descartes*, University Park, PA: Pennsylvania State University Press. (Contains several essays exploring Elisabeth's philosophical contributions.)

* Foucher de Careil, L. (1862) *Descartes et la Princesse Palatine, ou de l'influence du cartésianisme sur les femmes au XVIIe siècle* (Descartes and the Princess Palatine, or on the Cartesian influence seventeenth-century women), Paris: Auguste Durand. (One of the early discussions of Elisabeth and the Cartésiennes.)

Godfrey, E. (1909) *A Sister of Prince Rupert: Elizabeth Princess Palatine and Abbess of Herford*, London and New York: John Lane. (Written under a pseudonym by Jessie Bedford, this is one of the earliest book-length biographies of Elisabeth in English.)

* Harth, E. (1992) *Cartesian Women: Versions and Subversions of Rational Discourse in the Old Regime*, Ithaca, NY: Cornell University Press. (Focuses on Elisabeth's criticisms of Descartes' neo-Stoic view of the will and examines gender issues in their correspondence. Pages 67–78 are especially relevant.)

Penn, W. (1981) *The Papers of William Penn*, vol. 1, ed. M. Dunn and R. Dunn, Philadelphia, PA: University of Pennsylvania Press. (Includes biographical information about Elisabeth's meetings with Quaker and Labadist leaders.)

* Thompson, J. (1983) 'Women and the High Priests of Reason', *Radical Philosophy* 34: 10–14. (A feminist critique of Descartes' picture of rationality, in which Elisabeth's letters are read as an early version of this line of criticism.)

Zedler, B. (1989) 'The Three Princesses', *Hypatia* 4 (1): 28–63. (Provides bibliographies and a discussion of the philosophical correspondences of Elisabeth, her sister Sophie, Electress of Hanover, and the latter's daughter, Sophie Charlotte, Queen of Prussia.)

EILEEN O'NEILL

EMERSON, RALPH WALDO (1803–82)

The American philosopher and poet Ralph Waldo Emerson developed a philosophy of flux or transitions in which the active human self plays a central role. At the core of his thought was a hierarchy of value or existence, and an unlimited aspiration for personal and social progress. 'Man is the dwarf of himself', he wrote in his first book Nature *(1836). Emerson presented a dire portrait of humankind's condition: 'Men in the world of today are bugs or spawn, and are called "the mass" and "the herd"'. We are governed by moods which 'do not believe in one another', by necessities real or only imagined, but also, Emerson held, by opportunities for 'untaught sallies of the spirit' – those few real moments of life which may nevertheless alter the whole.*

Emerson's lectures drew large audiences throughout America and in England, and his works were widely read in his own time. He influenced the German philosophical tradition through Nietzsche – whose The Gay Science *carries an epigraph from 'History' – and the Anglo-American tradition via William James and John Dewey. Emerson's major works are essays, each with its own structure, but his sentences and paragraphs often stand on their own as expressions of his thought.*

1 Life
2 Emerson as philosopher
3 Early works
4 Mature philosophy

1 Life

Ralph Waldo (known to friends and family as 'Waldo') was the fourth of eight children born in Boston to the Reverend William Emerson and Ruth Haskins Emerson. He lost his father to tuberculosis just before his seventh birthday and was brought up by his mother and his father's sister Mary Moody Emerson. After four undistinguished years at Harvard, he became a schoolteacher and studied theology there, preparing for the ministry.

In 1829, Emerson was ordained pastor of the Second (Unitarian) Church of Boston and married Ellen Tucker. Ellen died of tuberculosis in 1831, and the following year Emerson resigned his position on the grounds that he could no longer administer the sacrament of the Last Supper, which he considered a 'dead form'. On Christmas Day, 1832, he set sail for Europe, where he toured Malta, Italy, France, Switzerland, England and Scotland. In Britain, he visited the ageing poets William Wordsworth and Samuel Taylor Coleridge, and the historian and philosopher of culture Thomas Carlyle, who became a lifelong friend.

Soon after his return in November 1833, Emerson gave his first lecture, 'The Uses of Natural History', at the Masonic Temple of Boston, embarking on a career as an orator that would continue for the next half-century. He married Lidian Jackson in 1835 and settled in Concord, Massachusetts, from which he set out on lecture tours through the northeastern United

States and later to England (1847–8 and 1872–3) and the American midwest.

Emerson's published works, derived from his lectures and journals, include *Nature* (1836), *Essays, First Series* (1841), *Essays, Second Series* (1844), *Representative Men* (1850), *English Traits* (1856), *The Conduct of Life* (1860) and *Society and Solitude* (1875).

2 Emerson as philosopher

There is no one to whom commentators, philosophers or not, are more apt to *deny* the title of philosopher than Emerson. Most twentieth-century discussions of his work have been by literary critics, with such notable exceptions as John Dewey's 1903 address 'Ralph Waldo Emerson – Philosopher of Democracy' and a series of papers by Stanley Cavell. Emerson is no system-builder in the mould of Descartes, Kant or Hegel, and his use of the essay form – inherited from his hero, MONTAIGNE – corresponds to the radical epistemological and metaphysical openness of his thought: towards the end of his great essay 'Experience', he writes, 'I know better than to claim any completeness for my picture. I am a fragment and this is a fragment of me.'

Emerson has a broadly Kantian outlook, according to which the world is in some way our construction. But like other Romantics, he finds that the 'lenses which paint the world' include our passions: 'Life is a train of moods like a string of beads, and as we pass through them they prove to be many-coloured lenses which paint the world their own hue, and each shows only what lies in its focus.' These moods 'do not believe in one another': each comes with 'its own tissue of facts and beliefs'. In one moment, we find ourselves bound by fate, in another real possibilities open up; in one moment we see a picture or read a book with a sense of adventure and understanding, in another we cannot see what interested us before. 'Our life', Emerson states, 'is March weather, savage and serene in one hour'.

At the centre of the series of moods lies the self – or, it would be better to say, the problem of the self. Emerson, like Kierkegaard and Nietzsche, finds the existence of the self to be a major issue. If the mass of men are 'bugs or spawn' and even the great or representative person is 'partial,' then the achievement of a fully developed human self is an enormous task. Emerson presents himself as having undertaken this task in 'Self-Reliance' (1841): 'Few and mean as my gifts may be, I actually am, and do not need for my own assurance or the assurance of my fellows any secondary testimony.'

Emerson's philosophy is a blend of classical and incipiently 'postmodern' or 'pragmatist' notions. With its references to the 'Unity' or 'Over-Soul, within which every man's particular being is contained', or to 'the Ideal journeying always with us, the heaven without rent or seam', Emerson's writing exhibits a strong Neoplatonic streak. Yet in a world of shifting moods and things that 'slip through our fingers... when we clutch hardest at them', Emerson finds no foundations, but only 'a house founded on the sea'. Even our language, far from reflecting permanent forms, is 'fluxional', 'vehicular and transitive... good, as ferries and horses are, for conveyance, not as farms and houses are, for homestead'. These Neoplatonic and pragmatic tendencies come together in Emerson's statement that 'the one thing in the world, of value, is the active soul'. Whether in history, philosophy or conversation, Emerson stresses the expansions or transitions of thinking the individual undergoes. Each of his major essays offers a series of such transitions.

3 Early works

Emerson's philosophy is often taken as starting with his first book *Nature* (1836), where he expresses a sense of 'decorum and sanctity in the woods' and of vast 'prospects' for a culture of new thought and 'new men'. The new culture can be achieved, and the beauty of the world restored, 'by the redemption of the soul', but this redemption takes place, Emerson emphasizes, according to no formula or model, but through 'untaught sallies of the spirit, by a continual self-recovery, and by entire humility'.

Emerson's distinctive philosophical voice emerges in 'The American Scholar' (1837) where, in one of the reversals characteristic of his thinking, he writes of the scholar less as a man in a library than as a complete 'Man Thinking', whose 'dictionary' is a life of free action. Influenced by but not 'warped out of his own orbit' by past writing, the scholar is an original source rather than 'the parrot of other men's thinking'. Emerson calls us back to ordinary life: to 'the literature of the poor, the feelings of the child, the philosophy of the street, the meaning of household life'. Although he is often termed a 'transcendentalist', Emerson does not wish to transcend the common world. 'I embrace the common, I explore and sit at the feet of the familiar, the low. Give me insight into today and you may have the antique and future worlds.'

'An Address Delivered Before the Senior Class in Divinity College, Cambridge', commonly known as the 'Divinity School Address' (1838), contains a fierce attack on institutional religion, but a defence of such 'holy bards' as Moses and Jesus. The 'eastern monarchy of a Christianity' that Emerson finds around him treats the revelation as something that happened 'long ago...as if God were dead'. But, Emerson insists, 'God is; not was'.

Emerson's first series of twelve essays contains some of his best-known work, including 'History', 'Self-Reliance', 'The Over-Soul' and 'Circles', as well as 'Friendship', 'Spiritual Laws', 'Intellect' and 'Compensation'. Emerson thinks of history, like scholarship, primarily as a matter of the personal and the present, as 'the desire to do away this wild, savage and preposterous There or Then, and introduce in its place the Here and the Now'. 'The Over-Soul' teaches a religion of the here and now to go along with Emerson's present-oriented history and scholarship: 'The simplest person, who in his integrity worships God, becomes God.' 'Circles' expresses Emerson's vision of flux and incompletion, in which 'permanence is but a word of degrees'. Especially in morality, 'there is no virtue which is final; all are initial'. Yet Emerson presents his own set of initial or experimental virtues, including especially 'abandonment' and 'enthusiasm'.

'Self-Reliance' offers an indictment of the crowd or public – a 'mob' of 'timorous, desponding whimperers' – and a radical defence of the individual. 'Whoso would be a man', Emerson states, 'must be a nonconformist'; and the healthy attitude of human nature is displayed in 'the nonchalance of boys who are sure of a dinner'. Anticipating Nietzsche's idea of the human creation of higher values, Emerson brazenly asks 'What have I to do with the sacredness of traditions if I live wholly from within?'

4 Mature philosophy

Emerson's 'Experience' dominates the second series of essays (1844), building an interpretation of human experience around the writer's grief at the death of his five-year-old son. The essay opens with the depiction of a series of stairs whose top and bottom we cannot see. This, Emerson tells us, is 'where we find ourselves'. Like many Emersonian essays, 'Experience' tells the story of 'the fall of man' and of rebirth or renewal – not through a foreign power but through contemporary 'men and women'. How can we make our way through 'the system of illusions' or the 'train of moods' in which we find ourselves, when there is no final, best view, no 'anchorage'? A newly pragmatic Emerson maintains that we can learn to skate over the surfaces of life; or, in a related metaphor, to find that 'everything good is on the highway'. The second series also includes 'Manners', where Emerson develops a philosophy of social relations that, anticipating Nietzsche, stresses the distance between individuals.

In 'Nominalist and Realist' the final essay in the series, he develops a perspectival metaphysics that complements his epistemology of moods.

Emerson's preoccupation with the heroic develops most fully in *Representative Men* (1850), which includes essays on Plato, Napoleon, Montaigne, Shakespeare, Swedenborg and Goethe. The sceptic in the Montaigne essay takes a position between those of 'the abstractionist and the materialist', each of whom treats the world as more solid than it is. We are in fact 'spinning like bubbles in a river...bottomed and capped and wrapped in delusions'. Montaigne, the wise sceptic, develops a philosophy of 'fluxions and mobility...a ship in these billows we inhabit... tight, and fit to the form of man'.

The greatest of Emerson's late essays, 'Fate' (1860), dwells on the biological, physical and psychological forces controlling our experience. Our individual fortunes are fated, Emerson holds, in that the events that 'seem to meet' us are as much 'exuded' from our character as encountered. Yet he insists that there is also liberty or freedom, and that this liberty rests on our powers of thinking: 'if there be irresistible dictation, this dictation understands itself'. As in all his work, from *Nature* onward, Emerson records both our subjection to necessity and our powers of overcoming it. The ideal life, he suggests, can be achieved through a controlled oscillation or balance between 'Nature' and 'Thought'.

See also: AMERICAN PHILOSOPHY IN THE 18TH AND 19TH CENTURIES §2; NEOPLATONISM; PRAGMATISM

List of works

Emerson, R.W. (1971–) *The Collected Works of Ralph Waldo Emerson*, ed. R. Spiller *et al.*, Cambridge, MA: Harvard University Press. (The new standard edition of Emerson's writings.)

—— (1903–4) *The Complete Works of Ralph Waldo Emerson*, ed. E.W. Emerson, Boston, MA: Houghton Mifflin, 12 vols. (Former standard edition.)

—— (1836) *Nature*; repr. in *Collected Works*, Cambridge, MA: Harvard University Press, 1971, vol. 1, 1–45. (Emerson's first book, advocating an 'original relation' to the universe.)

—— (1837) 'The American Scholar'; repr. in *Collected Works*, Cambridge, MA: Harvard University Press, 1971, vol. 1, 52–70. (Calls for active souls rather than slavish scholars or 'bookworms'.)

—— (1838) 'The Divinity School Address'; repr. in *Collected Works*, Cambridge, MA: Harvard University Press, 1971, vol. 1, 76–93. (Controversial graduation address at Harvard Divinity School, in which Emerson attacks the 'Monster' of institutional Christianity.)

—— (1841) *Essays, First Series*, in *Collected Works*, Cambridge, MA: Harvard University Press, 1971, vol. 2. (Contains 'Self-Reliance', 'Circles', 'The Over-Soul' and 'Intellect'.)

—— (1844) *Essays, Second Series*, in *Collected Works*, Cambridge, MA: Harvard University Press, 1971,vol. 3. (Contains 'Experience', 'The Poet' and 'Nominalist and Realist'.)

—— (1850) *Representative Men*, in *Collected Works*, Cambridge, MA: Harvard University Press, 1971, vol. 4. (Essays on Montaigne, Plato, Napoleon and others.)

—— (1860) *The Conduct of Life*, New York: Harcourt Brace, 1960. (Contains 'Fate', 'Power' and 'Illusions'.)

—— (1910–14) *The Journals of Ralph Waldo Emerson*, ed. E.W. Emerson and W.E. Forbes, Boston, MA, and New York: Houghton Mifflin, 10 vols. (Records of his reading and thinking from 1819 onwards, and the source for much in his essays.)

—— (1960–82) *The Journals and Miscellaneous Notebooks of Ralph Waldo Emerson*, ed. W. Gillman, *et al.*, Cambridge, MA: Belknap Press, Harvard University Press, 16 vols. (The standard edition.)

—— (1961–72) *The Early Lectures of Ralph Waldo Emerson*, ed. S.E. Whicher, R.E. Spiller and W.E. Williams, Cambridge, MA: Harvard University Press, 3 vols. (Includes Emerson's first lectures of 1833; and a course on 'The Present Age' given in 1839–40.)

—— (1964) *The Letters of Ralph Waldo Emerson*, ed. R.L. Rusk, New York: Columbia University Press, 6 vols. (Correspondence with family and friends, including Mary Moody Emerson, Margaret Fuller, Henry David Thoreau, Henry James Sr, Oliver Wendell Holmes Sr.)

Emerson, R.W. and Carlyle, T. (1964) *The Correspondence of Emerson and Carlyle*, ed. J. Slater, New York: Columbia University Press. (Transatlantic correspondence of two great figures of Romanticism.)

References and further reading

Allen, G.W. (1981) *Waldo Emerson*, New York: Viking Press. (A fine, readable biography of Emerson.)

Cavell, S. (1981) 'Thinking of Emerson' and 'An Emerson Mood', in *The Senses of Walden, An Expanded Edition*, San Francisco, CA: North Point Press. (Sets out Emerson's relation to Heidegger through discussion of his 'epistemology of moods'.)

—— (1988) *In Quest of the Ordinary: Lines of Skepticism and Romanticism*, Chicago, IL: University of Chicago Press. (Traces lines of thought from Kant to Coleridge and Emerson, and offers an existentialist reading of 'Self-Reliance'.)

—— (1989) 'Finding as Founding: Taking Steps in Emerson's "Experience"', in *This New Yet Unapproachable America*, Albuquerque, NM: Living Batch Press. (Argues that Emerson offers a proto-Heideggerian criticism of 'thinking as clutching', and a conception of foundation as 'finding' or 'taking the open road'.)

—— (1990) 'Introduction' and 'Aversive Thinking' in *Conditions Handsome and Unhandsome: The Constitution of Emersonian Perfectionism*, Chicago, IL: University of Chicago Press, 1990. (Emerson's thought in relation to issues discussed by Kant, Nietzsche, Heidegger and Rawls.)

Ellison, J. (1984) *Emerson's Romantic Style*, Princeton, NJ: Princeton University Press. (A close reading of Emersonian texts stressing the 'defensive and aggressive functions' of his irony, repetitions and contradictions.)

Firkins, O.W. (1915) *Ralph Waldo Emerson*, Boston, MA: Houghton Mifflin. (A superbly written general account of Emerson's life and writing.)

Goodman, R.B. (1990) *American Philosophy and the Romantic Tradition*, Cambridge: Cambridge University Press. (Discusses Emerson's relation to European Romanticism and American pragmatism.)

Kateb, G. (1995) *Emerson and Self-Reliance*, Thousand Oaks, CA: Sage Publications. (Emerson's social and political philosophy.)

Packer, B.L. (1982) *Emerson's Fall*, New York: Continuum. (The best contemporary literary treatment of Emerson's essays.)

Poirier, R. (1992) *Poetry and Pragmatism*, Cambridge, MA: Harvard University Press. ('Emersonian pragmatism' in William James, Robert Frost, Gertrude Stein and Wallace Stevens.)

Richardson, R.D., Jr (1995) *Emerson: The Mind on Fire*, Berkeley, CA: University of California Press. (An excellent, comprehensive biography of Emerson.)

Whicher, S. (1953) *Freedom and Fate: An Inner Life of Ralph Waldo Emerson*, Philadelphia, PA: University of Pennsylvania Press. (A classic discussion of Emerson's dialectic of freedom and fate.)

RUSSELL B. GOODMAN

EMOTION IN RESPONSE TO ART

The main philosophical questions concerning emotion in response to art are as follows. (1) What kind or type of emotions are had in response to works of art? (2) How can we intelligibly have emotions for fictional persons or situations, given that we do not believe in their existence? (This is known as 'the paradox of fiction'.) (3) Why do abstract works of art, especially musical ones, generate emotions in audiences, and what do audiences then have these emotions towards? (4) How can we make sense of the interest appreciators have in experiencing empathetically art that is expressive of negative *emotions? (A particular form of this query is 'the paradox of tragedy'.) (5) Is there a special* aesthetic *emotion, raised only in the context of experience of art? (6) Is there an irresolvable tension between an emotional response to art and the demands of aesthetic appreciation? Answers to these questions depend to some extent on the conception of emotion adopted.*

1   Introduction

Having emotions for art works or responding emotionally to them is a familiar enough occurrence, and hardly seems puzzling when recalled at that level of generality. Why should not works of art, in company with people, animals, natural objects and political events, produce emotions in us? Philosophers have, however, raised questions about emotional responses to art in particular contexts, where, viewed from certain angles, there is indeed something puzzling about them.

One such context is that of response to fictions (whether literary, dramatic or cinematic ones), where emotions appear to be had, not only for the work or representation itself, but for the fictional characters or situations represented therein, even though these are perfectly well understood not to exist. A second such context is that of abstract, or nonrepresentational art (music being the example *par excellence*), where it is unclear both what could elicit such a response and

what its object could be. A third context is that in which art works expressive of negative emotion (for example, tragedies, requiems and tales of horror) engender parallel responses in perceivers without thereby being avoided or disapproved of by them. And a fourth context in which emotional response to art has struck philosophers as problematic is where the proper appreciation of art is at issue, when it is asked whether such appreciation is compatible with undergoing emotions of the familiar sort that art seems capable of raising in us.

2   The nature of emotions

In order to assess fruitfully the varieties of emotional response to art it is obviously of use to have some account of exactly what emotions are – in the occurrent, as opposed to the dispositional, sense. Philosophical debate on the nature of emotions, informed to greater or lesser degree by available work in psychology, has in the past thirty years or so revolved around an opposition between feeling-based (or sensation-based) approaches and thought-based (or cognition-based) approaches. The former holds that at the core of an emotion is an internal feeling or set of sensations, while the latter holds that at its core an emotion is a particular kind of thought, judgment or evaluation. While the feeling approach has trouble with the intentionality (or object-directedness) and amenability to reason of many emotions, the thought approach has trouble with the experiential aspect of emotions (that is, with what it is to feel them, as opposed to merely having the beliefs or entertaining the thoughts that may be associated with them), with the evident inertia and passivity of many emotional conditions, and with states of desire, whose connection with many emotions seems more than contingent. Still, while the feeling approach can be faulted for too 'mindless' a picture of emotions, it is right to insist on bodily response and inner affect of some sort as a *sine qua non* of emotion, and while the thought approach can be faulted for too 'mindful' a picture of emotions, it is right to emphasize that many emotions include cognitive elements essentially: for example, thoughts with specific contents, which contents are in many cases socially shaped.

At present there appears to be some consensus that, in perhaps the majority of cases, an emotion is best thought of as a bodily response with a distinctive physiological, phenomenological and expressive profile, one that serves to focus attention in a given direction, and which involves cognition to varying degrees and at various levels. The level of cognitive involvement runs from mere registering of presence, to ways of seeing or regarding that which is registered, to propositional conceptions of the object responded to, to articulate beliefs about or attitudes toward the object of response. Alternatively put, an experienced emotion can be said to have as its core a bodily reaction – comprising physiological sensations, feelings of comfort and discomfort, and orientings of attention – which reaction is often caused or modified by, and is sometimes necessarily bound up with, cognitions of various sorts and strengths, depending on the type of emotion involved. Note that on such a view of emotion, in which cognitive representations on the order of beliefs (or for that matter, desires) are seen as characteristic of, but not essential to, experienced emotion, the intentionality or directedness of emotions (as opposed, say, to moods) is preserved by the root feature of orientation of attention to or focusing of concern on that which the subject registers as significant.

On the other hand, there is also a growing acknowledgment that the pre-theoretically recognized emotions constitute an irreducibly heterogeneous class, that is, that they do not form a 'natural kind'. It seems reasonable to recognize a spectrum of emotional states experienced by humans, from the startle reaction, involving minimal cognition, at one end, to pride, envy, shame, jealousy, grief, remorse, embarrassment and the like, involving complex and often morally conditioned cognitions, at the other end, with hunger, surprise, lust, fear, anger, joy, sorrow and so on filling the vast middle ground. The emotional responses typical of engagement with art, though, tend to be of a sort that has a moderate or high cognitive involvement – a fact relevant to some recent attempts to dissolve too quickly the paradox of fiction by appeal to what need not be true of all cases of emotion.

Although it is convenient to speak of emotions having elements or components of various sorts (for example, thoughts, sensations, desires, feelings, pleasures, pains, shifts of attention), these should not be thought of as merely bundled together, and the emotion as a mere conglomeration. The truth is rather that an emotion is an *ordered* complex or structure of the elements it is taken to comprehend, with *causal* relations prominent among those in which this order consists. My anger at my daughter for having carelessly misplaced my keys, for example, is a bodily response, rooted in physiology and reflected in countenance, involving a focusing of attention on her, and feelings of agitation and displeasure, which result jointly from my thought of her action and my desire that she should not have so acted, while fuelling, perhaps, my desire that she in some way pay for having so acted.

3 Emotional response to representational art: the paradox of fiction

The much-discussed paradox of fiction can be formulated as a set of three propositions, to each of which we seem to have strong allegiance, but which are jointly inconsistent, and thus impossible to maintain coherently as a set. Solutions to the paradox, then, typically take the form of a rejection of one or more of the propositions, with a reasoned justification for doing so. The propositions are these:

(a) We often have emotions for fictional characters and situations known to be purely fictional;
(b) Emotions for objects logically presuppose beliefs in the existence and features of the objects in question;
(c) We do not harbour beliefs in the existence and features of objects known to be fictional. In the extensive discussion in the literature of this conundrum, almost every possible solution to it has been aired. The following comprise most of the solutions that have found adherents.

(1) The Non-Intentionalist solution: emotional responses to fictions are not, despite appearances, instances of emotions as such, but rather of less complex states, such as moods (cheerfulness, for example) or reflex reactions (shock, for example), which lack the full intentionality and cognitivity of emotions *per se*. As is evident, this solution involves the denial of (a). But the diagnosis it offers seems to apply comfortably to only a small portion of the full range of sustained responses to fictions.

(2) The Suspension-of-Disbelief solution: while caught up in fictions, consumers thereof temporarily allow themselves to believe in the nonexistent characters and situations of the fiction, and thus to have bona fide emotions for them, reverting to standing beliefs in their nonexistence once the fiction no longer actively engages them. Such a solution, turning on a denial of (c), though popular in the nineteenth century, unacceptably depicts consumers of fiction as having both a rather tenuous grip on reality and an amazing ability to manipulate their beliefs at will.

(3) The Surrogate-Object solution: emotional responses to fictions take as their real objects not known-to-be-nonexistent persons and events in fictions, but other existent and believed-to-be-existent objects. This solution, in one way or another, thus calls (a) into question.

On one version of this solution, the object of response is simply the fictional work or artistic representation itself, or parts thereof. On another version, the objects of response are rather the descriptions, images, propositions or thought contents afforded *by* the fiction or representation. And on a third version, different enough from the preceding two to deserve a separate label – the Shadow-Object proposal – the objects of response are real individuals or phenomena from the subject's life experience, ones resembling the persons or events of the fiction, of which the fiction puts the subject covertly or indirectly in mind.

The Surrogate-Object solution in its first two guises distorts the logic and phenomenology of emotional response to fictions. Whatever the nature or status of our response to fictional characters or situations, it is an emotional response to *them*, not to something else. Our responses, however ultimately analysed, have those characters and situations as their evident objects, and not the vehicles that bring them to us or the thoughts through which they are delineated. Much the same complaint can be brought against the Shadow-Object proposal, though here it is clear that the sort of response to which the proposal draws attention does indeed often accompany and underlie the emotional response to fictional matters *per se*. Still, despising a fictional character, say, is not simply reducible to despising people of that sort generally, or to despising some actual similar individual of one's acquaintance.

(4) The Anti-Judgmentalist solution: emotional responses to objects do not logically require beliefs concerning the existence or features of such objects, but only weaker sorts of cognitions, for example, seeing a certain way, conceiving in a certain manner or regarding as if such and such; thus, there is no good reason not to categorize the emotional responses had towards fictions as standard emotions, since they satisfy the demands of a more relaxed cognitivism about emotions. This approach to the paradox, which directly challenges (b), has a growing number of proponents, and merits extended discussion.

The instances of emotional response that challenge judgmentalism – the view that the cognitive element involved in all emotions is a judgment or belief – are mostly of two types. The first type is where there is insufficient time for cognition as such, so that no real representation of the object responded to is formed, there being only a virtually instantaneous reaction, instinctive or reflexive in nature, unmediated by conscious thought (examples: apprehension at a suddenly looming shape, disgust at an accidentally felt slug). A second type is where, though cognition is involved in generating the response, the representation thus formed is either not propositional in nature, or else does not have the status of a judgment, or both (examples: phobic fear of garter snakes, unfounded resentment of female superiors).

As noted earlier, the emotions involved in responding to fictions (for instance, pity, sorrow, love, admiration, anger, hate, hope) lie in the main in the middle and upper ranges of cognitive complexity for emotions. It thus seems undeniable that, whether or not they involve beliefs, such emotions are centrally mediated by representations of various sorts, such as views, conceptions or evaluations, which serve to *characterize* the object of response.

However, even if emotions at this cognitive level do not necessarily involve beliefs of a *characterizing* sort about their objects, such emotions, it seems, must still involve *existential* beliefs in regard to those objects, or something very close to that; that is to say, attitudes or stances of the order of 'taking to exist' or 'regarding as existent'. Otherwise, the state attributed becomes unintelligible, whether as an emotion or anything else. How can one be said to pity, fear, admire or hate something that one does not, concurrently with one's emotion, at least take or regard as existing, now or at some other time? If indeed that cannot be said, then the problem resurfaces, despite what is right in the critique of judgmentalism: since sane consumers of fiction do not regard fictional characters as existing, even when fully engaged with them appreciatively, they cannot really be in the full-fledged emotional states they are casually said to inhabit. The paradox of fiction is proof against anti-judgmentalist dissolution, even if we grant that emotions can occur without characterizing beliefs.

The sticking-point of the paradox is the dimension of existence and nonexistence, as this connects to the cognitive characterization that emotions of the sort in question minimally require. When we view or conceive an object as having such and such properties, whether or not we strictly believe that it does, we must, on pain of incoherence, be taking it to exist or regarding it as existent. For nothing can coherently be viewed or conceived as having properties without at the same time being treated as existent. A case of genuine emotion of a cognitively mediated sort, unlike a corresponding emotional response to a fictional character, involves at least viewing or conceiving an object as having such and such features, which thus in turn presupposes regarding it as existent or taking it to exist.

But I do not, when reading Dostoyevsky's *The Brothers Karamazov*, take Smerdyakov to exist, and so cannot strictly be viewing or conceiving him as having properties, such as being base or being a murderer. And though my evaluative Smerdyakov-thoughts, generated as I read, may largely be what causes my hate response, directed ostensibly at him, for that response to strictly have *him* as its object, and so count clearly as an instance of hatred *of* Smerdyakov, requires, once more, that I take him to exist – which I clearly do not. It may, however, be the case both that I imagine or make-believe that someone to that effect exists, and that as a result I imaginarily, or make-believedly, experience for him an emotion of hate.

(5) The Surrogate-Belief solution: certain emotional responses to fictions (for instance, that of pity) require only beliefs that, *in the fiction*, the character exists and is or does such and such, and those beliefs are indeed widely held by rational consumers of fiction. This solution thus rejects (c), though not in the manner of Suspension-of-Disbelief theorists.

However, the beliefs this proposed solution highlights, beliefs about what is fictionally the case, can only ground the truth of one's fictionally or imaginarily pitying a character, not of one's literally doing so. Furthermore, that such beliefs play a role in generating emotional responses to fictions does not touch the heart of the paradox, which is that intelligible emotions for objects of the sort typical of engagement with fiction conceptually require beliefs in the existence of such objects, or at a minimum, an existential stance towards them. Beliefs about how things are fictionally can *cause* emotional reactions of some sort, to be sure, but they cannot logically ground intelligible emotions for entities whose existence is denied. Even where the emotion in question is such as to constitutively require beliefs, they are the wrong sort of beliefs partly to constitute such emotions. The beliefs I have 'about' Anna Karenina, say, cannot coherently make her the proper object of any pitiful reaction I might have. Pity involves concern for the welfare of some creature and distress at its suffering. If one does not believe such welfare or suffering is actual, what can one be concerned *for* or distressed *about*? Pity may likewise involve wishes or desires with respect to the thing pitied, but in the absence of a belief in the thing, or more loosely, an existential commitment to it, there cannot coherently be any such wishes or desires.

(6) The Irrationalist solution: while caught up in fictions, consumers of fiction become irrational, responding emotionally to objects that they know do not exist and thus do not have the features they are represented as having. Irrationalists either implicitly deny (c), proposing that we do in some manner endorse the existence of fictional characters and events – while apparently at the same time disavowing them – which qualifies as irrational, in the sense of being inconsistent, or else they implicitly deny (b), holding that we can have emotions for such as fictional characters and events, towards which we lack the usual beliefs, but qualifying such emotions

consequently as irrational, in the sense of being unwarranted.

On the first construal the Irrationalist solution closely approaches that of Suspension-of-Disbelief, with the difference, perhaps, that no attempt is made to mitigate the clash of existential stances involved by suggesting that they are not simultaneously in full force. On the second construal the Irrationalist solution holds appreciators of fiction at fault, not for believing what they already believe the negation of – that fictional characters and events exist – but for emotionally responding to such characters and events in ways contraindicated by their beliefs.

It might seem that the Irrationalist solution, on this second construal, is saved from being a non-starter by the rejection of judgmentalism, since otherwise it could be held to be simply impossible, rather than just possibly irrational, to experience full-fledged emotions in the absence of certain beliefs. But as suggested earlier, if the critique of judgmentalism, applied to emotions of the sort that fiction typically elicits, shows only that characterizing beliefs, as opposed to existential ones, may be absent in such cases, the logical space this construal hopes to occupy may not be available. In any event, in the judgment of most commentators, portraying the normal consumer of fiction as fundamentally enmeshed in irrationality, however this be understood, is too high a price to pay for this to be an acceptable solution to the paradox.

(7) The Make-Believe, or Imaginary, solution: emotional responses to fictions cannot, despite appearances, be instances of the ordinary emotions with whose names we tend to label them, but are instead instances of imaginary or make-believe emotions. For, first, the standard emotions of life arguably have belief or belief-like presuppositions, notably existential ones, that are not fulfilled in normal engagement with fictions; and second, such emotions have motivational or behavioural consequences that are not in evidence in the course of such engagement.

The proposal is that in our interactions with works of fiction we experience make-believe emotions, or make-believedly experience emotions, for fictional characters and situations; it is thus (a) that is rejected on this solution. Make-believedly experiencing fear, say, is sufficiently similar to really experiencing fear, especially internally, that it is easily confused with it, and yet make-believedly experiencing fear can be reconciled (while really experiencing fear cannot) with the absence of existential endorsement and motivational upshot *vis-à-vis* the fictions that are feared. In this way the paradox is finally resolved.

In considering this solution, it is important to distinguish the claim that what we feel for fictional characters is *some* kind of emotion, or constitutes emotional response in the *broad* sense, from the claim, here disputed, that what we feel for fictional characters and describe with some ordinary emotion-word is literally an example of such emotion. We are indeed moved, this solution affirms, but not strictly to the standard emotions whose names come to our lips. Note also that to qualify our emotions for fictions as imaginary is to say that they are ones we imagine ourselves to be having, on the basis of experiences contributory to emotion that we are *actually* having, but does not imply that such emotions are illusory or unreal.

Though the Make-Believe proposal probably provides the best resolution to the paradox of fiction as such, a full account of our emotional responses when engaged with fictions – as opposed to our emotions for fictional characters *per se* – will want to acknowledge what is called to our attention by the Non-Intentionalist and Surrogate-Object proposals as well. And even the Irrationalist proposal, on the first construal, may contain a grain of truth; for perhaps we are, at least at moments of maximum involvement, in the incoherent states of mind it postulates as ours throughout.

4 Emotional response to abstract art: music and feeling

Emotional response to abstract art is puzzling, principally because the strategies that provide obvious explanations of both why we respond emotionally, and what we are responding to, in the case of representational art, seem not to be available. A novel, film or Impressionist landscape gives me the image of a human world, elements of which I can empathize or identify with, react to sympathetically or antipathetically, or even mirror unthinkingly, by a sort of natural contagion. But with a symphony, sonata, minimalist sculpture or Abstract Expressionist painting such explanations appear to have no purchase. Human beings and their predicaments are notably absent, at least as far as representation is concerned. So why or how does perception of such art works raise emotion, and on what is such emotion directed? Concentrating for brevity's sake on the art of music, rough answers are as follows.

In so far as music is capable of eliciting emotions in listeners, this appears to work through two different routes or mechanisms, typically operating in tandem. The first we may label the sensory or cognitively unmediated route, and the second the perceptual–imaginative, or cognitively mediated route. It seems undeniable that music has a certain power to induce sensations, feelings and even moods in virtue of its basic musical properties, virtually without any interpretation or construal on the listener's part. Particular timbres, rhythms, intervals, dynamics and tempi exemplify this power most clearly. Such properties need only be registered, as it were, to have their effect, at least for one acclimatized to a given musical culture. The rise in heartbeat caused by rapid tempo, the discomfort occasioned by dissonant intervals, the kinetic impulses induced by dancing rhythms, the excitement produced by quick alternations of soft and loud, the relaxation engendered by a certain tone colour or manner of articulation, are all familiar phenomena. But if the capacity of music to elicit emotion were exhausted by the direct effects of sensing basic musical features, it would be a poor thing, falling far short of the evocation of emotions proper, or even the semblance of such. The gap is filled by the second, or cognitively mediated, route to such evocation.

In addition to presenting an array of sonic features, simultaneously and successively, much music offers the appearance of human emotion, or of persons outwardly manifesting emotional states; arguably, that is what the expressiveness of music largely consists in (see EXPRESSION, ARTISTIC). In other words, music is often heard as, or heard as if, or just imagined to be, the expression of emotion by an unspecified individual, whom we may call the music's 'persona'. The degree of resemblance between the shape of music and the behaviour through which emotions are commonly expressed in life will have something, though not everything, to do with our being disposed to hear music in such ways. In any event, once this occurs, the mechanisms mentioned above and familiar from appreciation of representational art – mirroring, identification, empathy, sympathy, antipathy – can come into play, resulting in the arousal in the auditor of those same emotions, or else the feelings characteristic of them, or else those emotions on an imaginary plane. The sensory aspect of music alone indeed seems capable of inducing in us at least a number of simple states of arousal ingredient in many emotions. But it is the perceptual–imaginative aspect, manifested in our disposition to hear emotion or emotional expression in music, that is surely primarily responsible for the complex, more robustly emotional responses to music, whether mirroring or reactive, that so many listeners report.

It remains to add that these mechanisms do not operate in total isolation from each other. The emotion which I hear a passage as expressing may soften or accentuate the particular psychological effect some basic musical feature produces on me, while the effect induced in me largely unthinkingly by some basic musical feature may influence and constrain the emotion of which I am disposed to hear an image in the music.

But if emotions are often produced in listeners in virtue of listening to emotionally expressive music, towards what are such emotions directed? Music neither supplies any objects, nor appears itself to be an appropriate object, for at least the vast majority of such emotions as are putatively aroused. In addition, music does not seem to provide anything that would justify the beliefs or attitudes towards objects that many objects can be held to require. Among the ways of responding to this difficulty are the following.

It can be held that music produces only moods in listeners, moods which intrinsically lack intentionality (anxiety or elation, for example), or else that it produces 'objectless' emotions, ones characteristically taking objects but somehow lacking them when aroused by music, for example, sadness or joy directed on nothing, or on nothing in particular.

Alternatively, it can be held that music produces in listeners just the *feeling* component of an emotion, together with the sense of focus or directedness inherent in the bodily response at the emotion's core, but not the cognitions which characteristically accompany or even partly constitute the emotion.

Finally, it could be maintained that what music occasions in many listeners are states of *imaginary* emotion. The idea is that listeners readily erect, upon a basis of feelings produced in them by music whose expressiveness they empathetically grasp, imagined emotions of a corresponding sort, and that they do this through imagining, usually tacitly, objects and thoughts suitable to the emotions in question. The object of musical emotion, then, is not missing, but merely indefinitely posited in imagination, or is perhaps logically appropriated, as it were, from the emotion imaginarily ascribed to the music's persona.

5 Emotional response to negatively emotional art: the paradox of tragedy

The paradox of negative emotion in art – of which the paradox of tragedy is a classical illustration – is this. Art that is negatively emotional, that is, art that represents, expresses or otherwise deals with emotions such as shame, grief, horror, sorrow, anger, remorse, despair and the like, seems to have a propensity to elicit parallel responses in appreciators. But if that is so, one would expect appreciators to avoid, or at any rate, judge as inferior, art of this nature. Yet not only do they not do so, but often they hold such art to be the highest or most rewarding of all.

A number of possible explanations have been given for how it is that persons rationally desire or value the empathic experience of negatively emotional art,

given the ostensibly negative character of that experience. Here is a general categorization of such explanations.

(1) Compensatory explanations: negative emotion aroused by negatively emotional art is, as such, unpleasant, but undergoing it offers other rewards that compensate for this. (2) Conversionary explanations: negative emotion, which is initially or ordinarily a disagreeable response, is transformed, in the context of artistic appreciation, into something that is in fact agreeable, or at any rate, capable of being enjoyed. (3) Organicist explanations: negative emotion aroused by negatively emotional art is an essential element in a total experience, an organic whole, that is desired or valued. (4) Revisionary explanations: neither negative emotions, nor the feelings they include, are intrinsically unpleasant or undesirable, and thus there is nothing odd about appreciating art that induces such emotions or feelings. (5) Deflationary explanations: despite appearances, neither negative emotions, nor the feelings they include, are really aroused in us by negatively emotional art.

Compensatory explanations include Aristotle's doctrine of catharsis, understood as a purging or purification of excess or unruly emotions of pity and fear through engagement with tragic drama, which justifies the raising of such emotions in the course of that engagement (see KATHARSIS). Another such explanation appeals to the value of knowledge of important truths of human existence that emotional engagement with negative art is said to afford. A third explanation endorses such engagement, not for the knowledge of life it may afford, but rather for the knowledge of the art work it facilitates, emotional engagement with a work being seen as a necessary cost, in many cases, of fully understanding it. A fourth such explanation invokes the moral exercise that is provided, or the moral deepening that results, as a benefit of engagement with negatively emotional art. And a fifth explanation appeals to purely aesthetic pleasures in the beauty, lifelikeness or virtuosity of the representation or expression itself, positing these as enough to outweigh whatever negative emotion is undergone in their appreciation.

Conversionary explanations include Hume's explanation of the appreciation of tragedy; like that just noted, Hume's explanation highlights the pleasure in artistic representation and expression as such, but premises that this pleasure, being greater than the pain of the negative emotions concomitantly raised, does not simply offset that pain, but rather overwhelms and absorbs it, leaving an experience of uniformly positive character (see HUME, D. §3). A rather different conversionary explanation proposes that since the negative emotions raised by a work of art have no life implications for spectators, calling for no actions and betokening no real harms, such emotions must evidently be so altered by the artistic conditions under which they issue that, though still recognizable as this or that negative emotion (disagreeable affects intact), they are yet capable of being relished or enjoyed for experience's sake.

An example of an organicist explanation would be one invoking a satisfaction in the raising of some negative emotion by a work of art, perhaps because the emotion strikes one as appropriately raised in such circumstances, and oneself as admirably human for being thus susceptible. Such a satisfaction would obviously be inseparable from the negative emotion raised, in the fact of which satisfaction is taken. Another such explanation would appeal to the value of working through negative emotions in connection with a work of art, via immersion in its formal, narrative or dramatic structure, the emotions raised thus being an essential element in the experience valued as a whole.

Revisionary explanations are something like this: the experience of negative emotions is not intrinsically unpleasant; the affects involved (that is, sensations and feelings) are not in themselves disagreeable, and can be unproblematically savoured as such, in appropriate contexts. What is negative about negative emotions is only the *evaluation* of their objects that is central to such emotions. Thus, there is no special difficulty about people seeking these emotions from art.

Deflationary explanations come in at least three varieties. One of these hypothesizes artistic analogues of the life emotions, distinct from them in hedonic tone, conative connectedness and behavioural implication, and proposes that only these are raised in us by engagement with emotional art, and not the life emotions themselves. Another deflationary explanation simply flatly denies that anything like the ordinary emotions are evoked in subjects in the course of engaging with emotional art, and suggests that the subject's response, in so far as it is emotional, is exhausted by properly *appreciative* reactions, such as being moved by a work's beauty of expression. A third deflationary explanation maintains that spectators are always only make-believedly in states of negative emotion in virtue of engaging with a work of art, and that on the assumption that make-believe emotions of the negative sort are not inherently displeasing, there is no special problem about people tolerating or even actively pursuing such experiences.

Lack of space prevents a detailed assessment of these proposals, but there would seem to be more merit in compensatory and organicist explanations, and in the second of the conversionary explanations sketched above, than in revisionary or deflationary ones.

6 Emotion for art and aesthetic appreciation of art

Are there emotions unique to the appreciation of art, or aesthetic emotions *per se*, had when and only when a work is apprehended aesthetically? Past theorists, notably Clive Bell, have posited something of this sort, but such a posit has not lately found favour, nor does it appear to answer to any pressing theoretical problem about art. On the other hand, there may be an interesting category of positive emotions that, if not had uniquely for art, are both distinctive of the appreciation of art and not of the sort that typically figure in the content of art. Candidates would be admiration for a work's skill, fascination with a work's form, delight in a work's beauty, or awe at a work's depth of insight or expression. What might also figure here are experiences, remarked by many, of momentary will-lessness or self-transcendence occasioned by intense absorption in a work of art.

The question may also be raised as to the appropriateness of emotional responses to art of the ordinary sort. One form of this question concerns an apparent tension between the familiar picture of an emotion as a disturbing derangement of the psyche and the image of aesthetic appreciation as a state of calm and unclouded attention to a work of art.

The traditional notion of the aesthetic attitude, whose roots are in Kant, Schopenhauer and the eighteenth-century theorists of taste, depicts a frame of mind characterized by disinterestedness, detachment and disengagement from the practical (see AESTHETIC ATTITUDE §3). But, charitably construed, such a notion demands only that one's personal situation or condition not be what primarily drives or directs one's response to a work, but instead, the humanly significant material that the work presents. In other words, such a notion need not call for suppression of emotional receptivity generally. So long as one's emotional response is a way of connecting to a work, of tracing its expressive outline or grasping its dramatic import, rather than a means of being distracted from it, or a springboard to wallowing in one's private concerns, then there is no conflict between responding to a work with a range of ordinary emotions on the basis of one's life experience and individual sensibility, and appreciating a work in an aesthetically appropriate manner as the specific embodiment of human content it is. By contrast, disinterestedness or detachment understood not as a principle for maintaining focus on a work rather than one's own circumstances, but as a desired end-state of impassivity or imperturbability, is nothing an account of artistic appreciation need embrace.

See also: ABSTRACT ART; ART, VALUE OF §6; EMOTIONS, PHILOSOPHY OF; EROTIC ART; FICTIONAL ENTITIES; HUMOUR; MUSIC, AESTHETICS OF §7; SUBLIME, THE; TRAGEDY

References and further reading

Budd, M. (1985) *Music and The Emotions*, London: Routledge. (A masterly and largely critical survey of influential theories of musical expression and evocation.)

—— (1995) *Values of Art*, Harmondsworth: Penguin. (Advances in its fourth chapter an important positive account of the relationship of music and emotion, and in its third chapter, a nuanced solution to the paradox of tragedy.)

Carroll, N. (1990) *The Philosophy of Horror*, London: Routledge. (A ground-breaking approach to issues of our response to horror fictions, including discussion of both the paradox of fiction and the paradox of tragedy.)

Currie, G. (1990) *The Nature of Fiction*, Cambridge: Cambridge University Press. (Develops a general theory of fictions and our response to them, one influenced by, but not coincident with, that of Walton.)

Davies, S. (1994) *Musical Meaning and Expression*, Ithaca, NY: Cornell University Press. (A painstaking and comprehensive survey of its topics, covering some of the same ground as Budd (1985).)

Deigh, J. (1994) 'Cognitivism in the Theory of Emotions', *Ethics* 104: 824–54. (A valuable survey article consolidating recent critiques of the cognitivist paradigm of emotions.)

Eaton, M.M. (1982) 'A Strange Kind of Sadness', *Journal of Aesthetics and Art Criticism* 41: 51–63. (Addresses the enjoyment of negative emotions from art, emphasizing the element of control of such emotions by the art work as key to such enjoyment.)

Feagin, S. (1983) 'The Pleasures of Tragedy', *American Philosophical Quarterly* 20: 95–104. (Proposes an approach to the paradox of tragedy in terms of pleasurable meta-responses had to intrinsically unpleasant first-order responses.)

Hjort, M and Laver, S. (eds) (1997) *Emotion and the Arts*, Oxford: Oxford University Press. (A collection of new essays on the present topic.)

Kivy, P. (1989) *Sound Sentiment*, Philadelphia, PA: Temple University Press. (Containing 'The Corded Shell' and supplementary essays, this is a well-known brief for cognitivism about musical expres-sion and musical appreciation, denying that normal listeners respond to expressive music by feeling ordinary emotions.)

Lamarque, P. (1981) 'How Can We Fear and Pity Fictions?', *British Journal of Aesthetics* 21: 291–304. (Proposes a form of the Surrogate-Object solution to the paradox of fiction, to the effect that thought-complexes are the objects of our emotional responses to fictional characters.)

Levinson, J. (1990) 'Music and Negative Emotion', in *Music, Art, and Metaphysics*, Ithaca, NY: Cornell University Press. (Proposes a pluralistic solution to the problem posed by appreciation of negatively emotional music, and explores the nature of a listener's imaginative engagement with expressive music).

Moran, R. (1994) 'The Expression of Feeling in Imagination', *Philosophical Review* 103: 75–106. (Emphasizes the importance of emotional modes of imagining, as opposed to the imagining of emotions, in understanding our emotions for art.)

Matravers, D. (1997) *Art and Emotion*, Oxford: Oxford University Press. (A sophisticated defence of the arousal theory of emotional content in art, with reference to both fiction and music.)

Morreall, J. (1993) 'Fear Without Belief', *Journal of Philosophy* 90: 359–66. (Critiques judgmentalism about emotions and suggests that this dissolves the paradox of fiction, obviating solutions such as that of Walton, which posit make-believe emotions centrally.)

Neill, A. (1991) 'Fear, Fiction, and Make-Believe', *Journal of Aesthetics and Art Criticism* 49: 47–56. (Discusses and criticizes Walton's approach to the problem of fearing fictions.)

—— (1993) 'Fiction and the Emotions', *American Philosophical Quarterly* 30: 1–13. (Develops a Surrogate-Belief solution to the paradox of fiction.)

Oatley, K. (1994) 'A Taxonomy of the Emotions of Literary Response and a Theory of Identification in Fictional Narrative', *Poetics* 23: 53–74. (Title is self-explanatory.)

Packer, M. (1989) 'Dissolving the Paradox of Tragedy', *Journal of Aesthetics and Art Criticism* 47: 212–19. (Critically reviews a number of proposals on the paradox and defends a form of compensatory theory in which the satisfaction of apprehending necessity and universality in human affairs is brought to the fore.)

Radford, C. (1975) 'How Can We Be Moved by the Fate of Anna Karenina?', *Proceedings of the Aristotelian Society* Supplement 49: 67–93. (The initiating paper in the modern series of responses to the paradox of fiction, which claims that in such responses we inescapably reveal ourselves as irrational.)

—— (1989) 'Emotions and Music: A Reply to the Cognitivists', *Journal of Aesthetics and Art Criticism* 47: 69–76. (A reply to Kivy (1989), arguing for the power of emotional music to induce at least simple emotions in listeners.)

Ridley, A. (1995) *Music, Value, and the Passions*, Ithaca, NY: Cornell University Press. (Defends a view of emotion in music that mediates between cognitivist and arousalist positions.)

—— (1992) 'Desire in the Experience of Fiction', *Philosophy and Literature* 16: 279–91. (Argues that we can and do have desires regarding fictional characters, thus making it more plausible that we straightforwardly have emotions for them.)

Robinson, J. (1994) 'The Expression and Arousal of Emotion in Music', *Journal of Aesthetics and Art Criticism* 52: 13–22. (Emphasizes the importance of feelings of a small-scale sort in the analysis of music's emotionality.)

—— (1995) 'Startle', *Journal of Philosophy* 92: 53–74. (Develops a bodily-response based conception of emotions, arguing convincingly that recent philosophy has overemphasized the cognitive dimension of emotions.)

Schaper, E. (1978) 'Fiction and the Suspension of Disbelief', *British Journal of Aesthetics* 18: 31–44. (Argues that suspension of disbelief cannot coherently explain our reactions to fictional characters, and endorses a variety of Surrogate-Belief solution to the paradox of fiction.)

Walton, K. (1990) *Mimesis as Make-Believe*, Cambridge, MA: Harvard University Press. (A defence of the role of making-believe and make-believe emotions in the understanding of fictions; widely influential, both in this form and in that of the articles that preceded it.)

Yanal, R. (1994) 'The Paradox of Emotion and Fiction', *Pacific Philosophical Quarterly* 75: 54–75. (Offers a categorization of different positions regarding the paradox of fiction, and endorses mainly a Surrogate-Belief solution to it.)

Zemach, E. (1996) 'Emotion and Fictional Beings', *Journal of Aesthetics and Art Criticism* 54: 41–8. (In response to the paradox of fiction, proposes that we have appropriate and rational beliefs toward nonexistents such as fictional characters.)

JERROLD LEVINSON

EMOTIONS AND MORALITY
see MORALITY AND EMOTIONS

EMOTIONS, NATURE OF

What is an emotion? This basic question was posed by William James in 1884, and it is still the focus for a number of important arguments in the philosophy of mind and ethics. It is, on the face of it, a quest for a definition, but it is also a larger quest for a way of thinking about ourselves: how should we think about emotions – as intrusive or as essential to our rationality, as dangerous or as indispensable to our humanity, as excuses for irresponsibility or, perhaps, as themselves our responsibilities? Where do emotions fit into the various categories and 'faculties' of the mind, and which of the evident aspects of emotion – the various sensory, physiological, behavioural, cognitive and social phenomena that typically correspond with an emotion – should we take to be essential? Which are mere accompaniments or consequences?

Many philosophers hold onto the traditional view that an emotion, as a distinctively mental phenomenon, has an essential 'subjective' or 'introspective' aspect, although what this means (and how accessible or articulate an emotion must be) is itself a subject of considerable dispute. Many philosophers have become sceptical about such subjectivism, however, and like their associates in the social sciences have turned the analysis of emotions to more public, observable criteria – to the behaviour that 'expresses' emotion, the physiological disturbances that 'cause' emotion, the social circumstances and use of emotion language in the ascription of emotions. Nevertheless, the seemingly self-evident truth is that, whatever else it may be, an emotion is first of all a feeling. But what, then, is a 'feeling'? What differentiates emotions from other feelings, such as pains and headaches? And how does one differentiate, identify and distinguish the enormous number of different emotions?

1   **The nature of emotion: feelings, physiology and behaviour**
2   **Emotions and their contents: intentionality**
3   **The individuation of emotions**
4   **The rationality of emotions**

1   **The nature of emotion: feelings, physiology and behaviour**

William James put his emphasis on the physiological and 'felt' nature of emotion, arguing that an emotion was a sensation (or set of sensations) caused by a physiological or 'visceral' disturbance which in turn was prompted by some disturbing perception. James did not adequately distinguish between involuntary physiological changes in the body and minimal expressions of emotion such as weeping and grimacing, but the virtue of the Jamesian theory, nevertheless, is that it specifies the nature of emotional sensation as quite particular and therefore verifiable by reference to its visceral cause. Unfortunately, the Jamesian theory turns out to be wrong, at least in its details. The physiologist W.B. Cannon, early in the century, showed clearly that emotions and changes in the body do not correspond in any convincing way. Moreover, one might feel flushed, uncomfortable and 'as if' one were afraid, but those feelings need not be fear. Some theorists have tried to save feeling theory by employing the vague, general (and technical) notion of 'affect', but such terms do no more than cover up the problem with a word. The challenge is to develop an 'adequate phenomenology' of felt emotion.

Recent advances in brain neurology disclose structural and functional patterns in the central nervous system which are correlated with and under experimental conditions bring about certain emotional reactions. Do these patterns dictate the structure of an adequate theory of emotion, or are those findings but one more set of (contingent) considerations for inclusion in an all-embracing theory? Whatever the case, it is now clear that philosophers cannot ignore or neglect the rich neurophysiological literature on emotions. Indeed, there is now a discipline in philosophy called 'neurophilosophy', which makes the new neurology central to any adequate analysis of emotion and 'the mind' (Churchland 1990). One of the factors that has altered the history of the philosophy of mind most radically has been new advances in previously unknown or undeveloped sciences. Nevertheless, an emotion cannot be *only* a neurological phenomenon. Neurology may provide the underlying cause, but it does not at present supply an adequate account of the content.

Virtually all emotions get expressed (however minimally) in behaviour. Should behavioural tendencies or sequences of actions or certain basic gestures be taken as essential? A great deal of detailed work in psychology has shown the enormous subtlety and the seemingly 'hard-wired' nature of basic patterns of facial expression. Many philosophers, following Wittgenstein's *Philosophical Investigations* (1953) and Gilbert Ryle's *Concept of Mind* (1949), have suggested that an emotion is nothing but its behavioural expression, though certainly not a single gesture but an open-ended sequence of actions. An emotion is not a 'ghostly inner event', Ryle tells us, but a 'multi-track disposition' to behave in any number of recognizable ways (see BEHAVIOURISM, ANALYTIC). Thus philosophers have tried to understand the difference between emotions not in terms of inner feeling but rather in terms of value-laden description of the relevant social situations. Errol Bedford (1956) suggested that the difference between shame and embarrassment, for example, was not some shade of difference between internal *qualia* (see QUALIA) but a difference in the descriptions of two different kinds of awkward situations. To be ashamed is to feel oneself blameworthy; to be embarrassed is to feel oneself a victim. In 1962 two psychologists, S. Schachter and J. Singer, agreed with James that an emotion begins with physiological 'arousal', but they also argued that an emotion requires 'labelling' on the basis of social context.

Although behaviour and the social circumstances no doubt have much to do with emotion, they alone cannot account for emotion. Behaviour counts as emotional expression just because it is the expression of something else, and the social circumstances do not define but only provide the context for the emotion. Thus Ryle finds himself discussing, even while dismissing, the various 'twitches and itches' that make up the mind, and Wittgenstein never denies the existence of inner feelings. He only insists that it is not on that basis that we identify our emotions. Feelings, physiology and behaviour, along with the social circumstances, all fit into the portrait of emotion, but what, nevertheless, seems missing is the emotion.

2 Emotions and their contents: intentionality

Emotions presuppose certain sorts of cognitions: an awareness of danger in fear, the judgment that one has been offended in anger, the belief that someone has died in grief, the conviction that someone or something is lovable in love. Emotions, in other words, involve concepts, judgments and beliefs, and they also include 'objects', persons, things, states of affairs and possibilities, which those concepts, judgments and beliefs are about. Love is love only insofar as it is love of something or someone, and anger is anger only insofar as it is anger about something or at someone. Freud's 'free-floating anxiety' counts as an emotion only insofar as it does indeed (as Freud (1935) argued) have an object, albeit 'unconscious'. Philosophers (following Aristotle and the scholastics) have come to call the essential nature of what an emotion is about the 'formal object' of emotion, and more recent philosophers have come to call the fact that an emotion is (and must be) about something its 'intentionality' (see INTENTIONALITY). It is the intentionality of emotions that provides the 'content' of emotions. But notice that this content is not an inner feeling, and it may or may not be correlated with any particular physiology or behavioural expression. Nor need it be defined by the immediate circumstances. A person can become embarrassed or angry on account of a sudden thought or association, quite apart from the present situation. Indeed, an emotion is often 'about' some nonexistent object: the object of fear may be imaginary; the person one still loves may be deceased.

An emotion, on this cognitive account, consists of a certain way of conceiving of and responding to the world, accompanied, perhaps, by certain feelings, expressed in certain typical types of behaviour and further explained by certain neurophysiological discoveries. But this means that emotions are prone to two very different types of explanation, two different kinds of answers to the question 'why?' Because they are intentional and involve cognitions, emotions seem to require an explanation that invokes a person's beliefs and attitudes towards the world. A person is angry because they believe that so-and-so wronged them; someone is saddened because they have found out that they have just lost a loved one. But this cannot be a complete account of emotional explanation. We also explain emotions by citing the fact that a person has been sleepless all week, or is ill, or has been given some medication. In other words, explanation of emotion may cite an underlying cause which may or may not make mention of the object of emotion. The cause may be physiological, for example – an underlying state of irritability, an ingested drug or a direct surgical stimulation of the brain. The cause may be some state of affairs, or incident, that triggered the person's emotion, but this may not be the object of the person's emotion nor need they have any memory or awareness of it. But how this causal explanation can be reconciled with an explanation in terms of beliefs and attitudes is not obvious, and many philosophers tend to emphasize the importance of one over the other. One provides a fuller account of the intentionality of an emotion by describing the specific details of the emotion and its content. The other provides an explanation in terms of an underlying cause which may or may not make mention of the contents of the emotion. And to make matters even more complicated, philosophers and psychologists at least since Darwin have also appealed to evolutionary accounts and more general theories of the function of emotions in species survival. Thus the best explanation of some emotions, at least, may be found neither in an immediate set of causes nor in the

evident beliefs and desires of the subject but in the evolutionary development of a certain built-in response to the world (De Sousa 1987, Gibbard 1990).

3 The individuation of emotions

The cognitive theory also allows a precise answer to the question of how we distinguish and identify different emotions. The difference between shame and embarrassment, for example, cannot be an extremely subtle difference in our sensations (which is not to say that there might not be such differences), nor does it lie in the fact that we tend to behave differently when we are embarrassed and when we are ashamed. The difference is to be found in the content, in the fact that in shame one feels responsible, while in embarrassment one finds oneself caught in but not in control of extremely awkward circumstances. But it is the subject's view, or perspective, of the circumstances, not the circumstances themselves, that defines the content of the emotion. Furthermore, the label that identifies the emotion is (in part) the subject's recognition of (what they take to be) the nature of the situation and their proper response to it. Take, for example, the very different emotions of fear and anger. Leaving aside any questions about respective physiological mechanisms and the obvious fact that their expressions ('flight versus fight') tend to be very different, it is nevertheless clear that the way one identifies one's own emotion is on the basis of whether the situation is fearful or offensive, respectively. This difference in turn can be explained by elaborating the various beliefs and desires that constitute each emotion.

Where the cognitive theory becomes most interesting and valuable, however, is in distinguishing and explaining the more subtle nuances between seemingly similar emotions, for example between hatred, indignation, resentment, contempt, scorn and loathing. These are not merely rhetorical differences. Consider hatred, resentment and contempt. Resentment, as Friedrich Nietzsche ([1887] 1967) explained at some length, is an emotion of inferiority, an emotion in which one conceives of oneself as an inferior being compared to those one resents. Contempt, on the other hand, is an emotion of superiority, an emotion in which one conceives of oneself as superior to the other. (Given this 'up–down' metaphor, consider the significance of finding someone 'beneath contempt'.) Hatred, finally, is an egalitarian emotion, hostile to be sure, but between equals. Hatred, unlike resentment and contempt, can even be an intimate emotion, which is why it so readily finds its place as the 'opposite' of love. And speaking of love, consider the very significant nuances between love and adoration, admiration and respect, not to mention the various degrees of liking and infatuation. Thus the analysis of emotion and emotion language becomes a detailed and subtle study in differences, a careful account of the very distinctive ways in which we relate to the world. It consists of much more than the crude and unspecified notion of feelings and their relation to the underlying physiology.

4 The rationality of emotions

The cognitive basis of emotions also raises another important question, and that is the *rationality* of emotions. Many thinkers have written as if the emotions were not only irrational but also non-rational, that is, not even candidates for intelligence. Defenders of the cognitive view insist that emotions involve at least a modicum of intelligence and therefore can be irrational. The Stoics, for example, taught that all emotions are mistaken (irrational) judgments. Aristotle, on the other hand, simply assumed that an emotion could be appropriate or inappropriate, foolish or prudent, not just on the basis of whether or not it was acceptable in the circumstance in question (though that social dimension was certainly essential) but on the basis of the perceptions, beliefs and desires of the individual. The fact that emotions consist at least in part of cognitions means that they can be evaluated in terms of the same epistemic and ethical criteria that we use to evaluate other beliefs and intentions: are they appropriate to the context? Do they consider the facts of the matter? Are their perceptions fair and their evaluations reasonable? Indeed the argument is now prevalent and persuasive that emotions cannot be understood without grasping their reasons, and these reasons in turn give us a basis for evaluation (De Sousa 1987, Greenspan 1988). The current debate, however, concerns how these reasons are to be understood, and whether the rationality of emotions can indeed be fairly compared to the evaluation of more fully deliberative, articulate activities. Indeed, to what extent are the emotions not merely suffered but in some sense wilful or voluntary? Jean-Paul Sartre, for example, suggests that emotions are really *strategies*, ways of coping with a difficult world (Sartre 1948).

The rationality of emotions also moves to centre-stage the relationship between emotions and ethics. Some philosophers, notoriously Immanuel Kant, tried to remove the emotions (and all such inclinations) from the realm of morality, but others, for example the 'moral sentiment theorists' who preceded him, made certain emotions, such as sympathy or compassion, the very heart of any adequate ethics. Today the role of the emotions in the formation and the expression of a person's character is becoming the focus of an extensive debate over the place of the personal virtues (as opposed to impersonal rules and principles) in ethics, and with this the question of how much control a person has over their emotions – whether we cultivate our emotional characters or simply find ourselves with a certain personality – is very much at issue. Indeed, to make this question all the more tantalizing, philosophers are now beginning to look carefully at the variation of emotions from culture to culture. Insofar as emotions are cognitive and based on concepts and ways of engaging the world, it is at least plausible to suggest that they may well differ considerably from one society to another. Too often philosophers have tried to answer such empirical questions a priori, but the facts seem to indicate that not only are different emotions appropriate at different times and in different places, but the emotions themselves differ as well. Some societies do not seem to have either the concept or the emotion of anger, or jealousy, or love, and others have emotions for which we do not even have names. There is nothing in the nature of emotion that assures universality, but neither is it self-evident that emotions differ all that much from place to place. We all share 'the human condition', after all, and there is good reason to suppose that certain basic emotions or emotion-types may be shared by everyone.

As for the question of emotions and choice, the supposed passivity of emotions, even those who do not share Sartre's insistence that emotions are wilful strategies might nevertheless agree that emotions are functional and not merely disruptions, that they are indeed ways of coping, whether inherited through natural selection, cultivated in the less articulate practices of a society or, perhaps, unconsciously mustered up by individuals as strategic responses. Obviously a good deal of ethics and our attitudes towards ourselves depend on this. Do we see ourselves as the victims of emotions, or are the emotions rather an essential part of our rationality, a key ingredient in the virtues and a significant part of our conception of ourselves and the world? The study of emotion in philosophy is, accordingly, not a detached and marginal discipline but the very core of our inquiry into ourselves and our own natures. It was Socrates, the great champion of reason, who took as his motto the slogan at Delphi, 'Know thyself', and the rather extreme injunction that 'the unexamined life is not worth living.' But part of that knowledge, surely, is our understanding and appreciation of our emotions, which are, after all, much of what makes life worth living.

See also: EMOTION IN RESPONSE TO ART; EMOTIONS, PHILOSOPHY OF

References and further reading

* Bedford, E. (1956) 'Emotion', *Proceedings of the Aristotelian Society* 57: 281–304. (An early attempt to give an analysis of emotion in terms of behaviour and social context.)

Calhoun, C. and Solomon, R. (eds) (1984) *What is an Emotion?*, New York: Oxford University Press. (A wide-ranging collection of original sources from Aristotle to contemporary philosophy and psychology, including James, Cannon, Bedford, Freud and Sartre.)

* Cannon, W. (1929) *Bodily Changes in Pain, Hunger, Fear and Rage*, New York: Appleton. (An early study of the physiology of emotion and a direct attack on the James–Lange theory.)

* Churchland, P.S. (1990) *Neurophilosophy*, Cambridge, MA: MIT (The most thoroughgoing exploration of the relevance of neurology to the philosophy of mind to date.)

* De Sousa, R. (1987) *The Rationality of Emotion*, Cambridge, MA: MIT (An original and often exciting exploration of these issues.)

Freud, S. (1915) 'The Unconscious' in *Freud Standard Edition*, London: Hogarth, 1935, vol. 14. (The question of 'unconscious emotions'.)

* Gibbard, A. (1990) *Wise Choices, Apt Feelings: A Theory of Normative Judgment*, Cambridge, MA: Harvard University Press. (An insightful revision of the 'emotivist' view of ethics using an evolutionary model.)

* Greenspan, P. (1988) *Emotions and Reasons*, New York: Routledge. (The most thorough examination of the role of reasons in emotion.)

* James, W. (1884) What is an Emotion?, *Mind* 19: 188–204.

Kenny, A. (1963) *Action, Emotion and Will*, London: Routledge & Kegan Paul. (A classic study of the notion of intentionality and the role of the formal object in emotion.)

Lyons, D. (1980) *Emotion*, Cambridge: Cambridge University Press. (An excellent physiological-cognitive analysis of emotion.)

Neu, J. (1977) *Emotion, Thought and Therapy*, Berkeley and Los Angeles, CA: University of California Press. (A thorough-going cognitive view of emotion.)

* Nietzsche, F. ([1887] 1967) *On the Genealogy of Morals*, New York: Random House.

Rorty, A. (ed.) (1980) *Explaining Emotions*, Berkeley and Los Angeles, CA: University of California Press. (An excellent collection of contemporary essays.)

* Ryle, G. (1949) *The Concept of Mind*, New York: Barnes and Noble. (An attempt to eliminate the emotions as aspects of the 'ghost in the machine'.)

* Sartre, J.-P. (1948) *The Emotions: Sketch of A Theory*, New York: Philosophical Library. (The innovative conception of emotions as 'magical transformations of the world'.)

* Schachter, S. and Singer, J. (1962) 'Cognitive, Social and Physiological Determinants of Emotional State', *Psychology Review* 69 (5). (The most influential contemporary response to William James in psychology.)

Solomon, R. (1993) *The Passions: Emotions and the Meaning of Life*, Indianapolis, IN: Hackett Publishing Company. (Expansion of the cognitive view discussed in this entry.)

Wilson, J.R.S. (1972) *Emotion and Object*, Cambridge: Cambridge University Press. (Perhaps the best and most extended discussion of the 'intentionality' of emotion.)

* Wittgenstein, L. (1953) *Philosophical Investigations*, London: Routledge & Kegan Paul.

ROBERT C. SOLOMON

EMOTIONS, PHILOSOPHY OF

Emotions have always played a role in philosophy, even if philosophers have usually denied them centre stage. Because philosophy has so often been described as first and foremost a discipline of reason, the emotions have often been neglected or attacked as primitive, dangerous or irrational. Socrates reprimanded his pupil Crito, advising that we should not give in to our emotions, and some of the ancient Stoic philosophers urged a life of reason free from the enslavement of the emotions, a life of apatheia (apathy). In Buddhism, too, much attention has been given to the emotions, which are treated as 'agitations' or klesas. Buddhist 'liberation', like the Stoic apatheia, becomes a philosophical ideal, freedom from the emotions.

Philosophers have not always downgraded the emotions, however. Aristotle defended the view that human beings are essentially rational animals, but he also stressed the importance of having the right emotions. David Hume, the eighteenth-century empiricist, insisted that 'reason is, and ought to be, the slave of the passions'. In the nineteenth century, although Hegel described the history of philosophy as the development of reason he also argued that 'nothing great is ever done without passion'. Much of the history of philosophy can be told in terms of the shifting relationship between the emotions (or 'passions') and reason, which are often at odds, at times seem to be at war, but ideally should be in harmony. Thus Plato painted a picture of the soul as a chariot with three horses, reason leading the appetites and 'the spirited part', working together. Nietzsche, at the end of the nineteenth century, suggested that 'every passion contains its own quantum of reason'.

Nietzsche's suggestion, that emotion and reason are not really opposites but complementary or commingled, has been at the heart of much of the debate about emotions since ancient times. Are emotions intelligent, or are they simply physical reactions? Are they mere 'feelings', or do they play a vital role in philosophy and in our lives?

1 **Reason, emotion: master and slave**
2 **Plato to the Stoics**
3 **Descartes to Nietzsche**
4 **The twentieth century**

1 Reason, emotion: master and slave

Perhaps the most striking and definitive metaphor in the history of the philosophy of the emotions is that of master and slave, the wisdom of reason firmly in control and the dangerous impulses of emotion safely suppressed, channelled or forced into submission. The master–slave metaphor displays two features that still determine much of the philosophical view of emotion today. First and foremost there is the inferior role of emotion, the idea that emotion is such more primitive, less intelligent, more dangerous and thus to be controlled by reason (an argument that Aristotle and other enlightened Athenians also used to justify the political institution of slavery). Second, and more profoundly, there is the reason–emotion distinction itself, as two different natural kinds, two conflicting and antagonistic aspects of the soul. Even those philosophers who sought to integrate them and reduce one to the other (typically reducing emotion to an inferior genus of reason, a 'confused perception' or 'distorted judgement') maintained the distinction and continued to insist on the superiority of reason. Hume, famously declaring that reason should be the slave of the passions, ultimately fell back on the same metaphor, simply turning it around.

Philosophical concerns about emotion are often part of some larger ethical or epistemological pursuit. For example, Descartes wrote his treatise *On the Passions of the Soul* in part because the emotions played an awkward but central role in his 'two substance' view of mind and body. In his *Ethics*, Spinoza, like the early Stoics, saw the passions – and

the misunderstanding of the passions – as the key to explaining much of human unhappiness. Hume devoted the middle third of his *Treatise of Human Nature* to an ingenious analysis of the passions, employing the same minimalist ontology of 'impressions', 'ideas' and 'associations' that he used to describe the workings of the mind in general. Immanuel Kant included virtually all the emotions as 'inclinations' in order to distinguish them sharply from reason, the proper realm of ethics. Nietzsche, on the other hand, celebrated the worldliness of the passions in order to chastize philosophical reason as 'other-worldly' escapism (see HUME, D.; KANT, I. §9; NIETZSCHE, F.).

Conceptions of emotion vary with ethical and religious convictions. Virtually every culture distinguishes between good emotions (which are healthy, virtuous and conducive to social harmony) and bad emotions (which tend to be unhealthy, vicious and socially disruptive). Some emotions are said to be pious – love, hope and faith, for example; others are designated as sinful – pride, envy and anger, for instance. How the emotions are viewed also depends on which emotions are taken as exemplary – violent or calm, selfish or other-directed, hostile or benevolent. Compassion and affection suggest a very different view of emotions than do outrage and jealousy. Conceptions of emotion are influenced by the virtues and vices of the time and culture. Consider warrior rage and physical courage in Homeric Greece, the concept of justice in Socratic Athens, the importance of faith in the middle ages, passionate love in twelfth-century France, the 'gentlemanly' virtues in eighteenth-century Britain, personal piety and the place of duty in early modern Germany, litigious anger and moral indignation in contemporary USA. In place of the opposition between reason and the emotions, in other words, perhaps we should ask which emotions play what roles in which culture.

2 Plato to the Stoics

The emotions as such do not form one of the aspects of Plato's tripartite soul. What we call emotion seems divided not only between spirit and appetite but, considering Plato's discussion of *eros* as the lot of the Good in *The Symposium*, the emotions are involved in reason as well (see PLATO §12). Aristotle, by contrast, did seem to have a view of emotion as such, and in his *Rhetoric* (Bk. II, Ch. 1) he defines emotion 'as that which leads one's condition to become so transformed that his judgment is affected, and which is accompanied by pleasure and pains. Examples of emotion include anger, fear, pity, and the like, as well as the opposites of these'.

Aristotle discussed certain emotions at length, notably anger which he describes in remarkably modern terms. In the *Rhetoric* he defines anger as 'a distressed desire for conspicuous vengeance in return for a conspicuous and unjustifiable contempt of one's person or friends'. He adds that 'anger is always directed towards someone in particular, for example Cleon, and not towards all of humanity', and mentions if only in passing the physical distress that virtually always accompanies such emotion. The key to his analysis, however, is the notion of a 'slight' as the cause of anger, which may be an instance of 'scorn, spite or insolence'. Aristotle makes allowances for only imagined slights (in other words, unwarranted anger is nevertheless anger), and he gives a central place to the desire for revenge, thus introducing a behavioural component at the heart of the emotion.

Aristotle's view of emotion developed in the context of broader ethical concerns. Anger is of interest to him because it is a natural reaction to offence as well as a moral force, which can be cultivated and provoked by reason and rhetoric. There are circumstances in which it is appropriate to get angry, those in which it is not, and only a certain intensity of anger is justified. Here, as elsewhere, Aristotle defines virtue as 'the mean between the extremes'. So too, courage is not fearlessness nor 'overcoming' fear so much as it is having just the right amount of fear, to be neither foolhardy nor a coward. But what is particularly instructive in Aristotle's accounts of emotion is the fact that the split between rationality and emotion is not much in evidence. The emotions are an essential part of the rational life (see ARISTOTLE §29).

In Roman times, we find a similar conjunction of ethics and emotion in the philosophy of the Stoics. But whereas Aristotle took emotion as essential to the good life, the Stoics analysed emotions as conceptual errors, conducive to misery. Seneca and Chrysippus, for example, developed a theory of the emotions as judgments, judgments about the world and one's place in it. The Stoics saw the world, however, as out of control and beyond any reasonable expectations, and so they viewed the emotions, which imposed such expectations on the world, as *misguided* judgments about life and our place in the world. The emotions, consequently, make us miserable and frustrated. The alternative was 'psychic indifference' or *apatheia*. The Stoics believed in a 'higher' reason, but – like the Buddhists thousands of miles away – they believed that the best life could be achieved only by realizing the pointlessness of emotional attachments and involvement (see STOICISM).

3   Descartes to Nietzsche

The study of emotion was central to Christian psychology and theories of human nature throughout the middle ages. But when René Descartes reviewed the literature on emotion in his *Passions of the Soul*, he concluded that what they taught was 'so far from credible, that I am unable to entertain any hope of approximating the truth excepting by shunning the paths they followed'. Descartes, accordingly, tried to start anew, but he was fundamentally a scientist and a mathematician, awed by 'the natural light of reason'. He also tended to disdain the bodily and the bestial, and the emotions, he argued, were caused by agitations in the 'animal spirits', minute particles of blood. The emotions involve sensations caused by this agitation, as well as perceptions, desires and beliefs. Thus, over and above the physical agitation and familiar sensations, the emotion of hatred, for example, ultimately arises from the perception of an object's potential harmfulness, and involves a desire to avoid it. Accordingly, an emotion is not merely a perception of the body – it may also be 'a perception of the soul' and an essential ingredient in wisdom: 'The utility of the passions consist alone in their fortifying and perpetuating the soul thoughts which it is good that it should preserve'. Bad emotions, by contrast, are those which 'fortify these thoughts more than necessary, or conserve others on which it is not good to dwell'. Descartes' six 'primitive' passions – wonder, love, hatred, desire, joy and sadness – are thus not mere agitations of the animal spirits but ingredients in the good life as well (see DESCARTES, R. §10).

Baruch (Benedict) Spinoza might well be considered a latter-day Stoic, for he also regarded emotions as misguided 'thoughts' about life and our place in the world (see SPINOZA, B. DE §9). But unlike the Stoics, Spinoza did not aspire to that 'psychic indifference' known as *apatheia*. Rather, he urged the attainment of a certain sort of 'bliss', which could be achieved only by getting straight one's thinking about the world. In particular, we had to give up the idea that we were or could be in control of our own lives, and adopt instead the all-embracing idea of ourselves and our minds as part of God. Most of the emotions, which are passive reactions to our unwarranted expectations of the world, will leave us hurt, frustrated and enervated. The active emotions, by contrast, emanate from our own true natures and heighten our sense of activity and awareness.

David Hume attacked superstition and irrationality in all quarters, defending the virtues of reason (see HUME, D. §3). But reason, Hume argued, does not have the power to motivate even the most minimal moral behaviour. 'It is not contrary to reason', he declared in one of his outrageous proclamations in the *Treatise of Human Nature* (Bk II, Pt 3, Sect. iii) 'to prefer the destruction of the whole world to the scratching of my finger'. What motivates us to right (and wrong) behaviour, Hume insisted, were our passions, the moral sentiments. Rather than being relegated to the margins of ethics and philosophy, the passions deserve central respect and consideration.

Hume's theory is especially important not only because he challenged the inferior place of passion in philosophy and questioned the role of reason. He also advanced a theory of the passions which, although limited and encumbered by his general theory of mind, displayed dazzling insight and a precocious attempt to account for the place of reason in emotion. Like many of his contemporaries and predecessors, Hume defined an emotion as a certain kind of sensation – what he called an 'impression' – whether pleasant or unpleasant, which was physically stimulated by the movement of the 'animal spirits' in the blood (as in Descartes). But the impressions that constituted our emotions were always to be located within a causal network of other impressions and, more importantly, of ideas. Ideas caused our emotional impressions, and were caused in turn by them. The pleasant impression of pride, for example, was caused by the idea that one had achieved or accomplished something significant, and the impression in turn caused another idea, which Hume describes as an idea of the self, *simpliciter*. The emotion, in other words, could not be identified with the impression or sensation alone but could only be identified by virtue of the whole complex of impressions and ideas.

Immanuel Kant was, like Hume, a champion of the Enlightenment, but although he also questioned the capacities and limits of reason, he was uncompromising in its defence against any attempt to replace reason by irrational faith or to ground ethics on fleeting human feeling instead of the universal and necessary dictates of reason (see KANT, I. §2). Thus Kant reinforced the crucial distinction between reason and the 'inclinations' and dismissed the latter (including the moral sentiments) as inessential to morals at best, as intrusive and disruptive or worse. And yet although Kant felt no need to develop a theory of emotion, his position on the 'inclinations' is more ambiguous than is usually supposed, and his respect for 'feeling' more significant. It was Kant, a quarter century before Hegel, who insisted that 'nothing great is ever done without passion', and it was Kant, in his *Critique of Judgment*, who celebrated the importance of shared feeling in the appreciation of beauty and the awe with which we try to comprehend the wonder of God's creation (see KANT, I. §12). Indeed, even Kant's central notions of respect and human dignity, the very heart of his rationalist ethics, are sometimes argued to be matters of feeling as well as reason, thus calling into question the harshness of his ruthlessly divided self. When his successor Hegel took over the reins of German philosophy in the early nineteenth century, Kant's distinction between reason and emotion was again called into question, and Hegel's own odyssey of reason (in *The Phenomenology of Spirit*) has rightly been called a 'logic of passion' as well.

Friedrich Nietzsche was a philosopher for whom passion was the watchword and reason a source of suspicion (see NIETZSCHE, F. §5). He was the culmination of a long line of 'Romantics', beginning with the *Sturm und Drang* poets of the previous century and continuing through the philosophy of his own favourite influence, the Neo-Kantian pessimist Arthur SCHOPENHAUER. Nietzsche anticipated the global scepticism and conceptual chaos of the twentieth century and, like Freud who admired him, he described (and celebrated) the darker, more instinctual and less rational motives of the human mind. Accordingly, he praised the passions and, in an ironic twist, described the passions as themselves having more reason than Reason. But this was not to say that all passions are wise. Some, he declares, 'drag us down with their stupidity', and others, notably the 'slave' emotion of *resentment*, are devious and clever but to a disastrous end: the 'levelling' of the virtuous passions and the defence of mediocrity.

4 The twentieth century

In the twentieth century one can trace the fate of emotion in Western philosophy through two very different tracks. In the USA and England, the emotions were given short shrift, in large part because of the emphasis on logic and language. The British philosopher Bertrand Russell elaborately praises love and passion in the opening pages of his autobiography, but in his philosophy says virtually nothing about them. The nature of emotion was a major concern of William JAMES and the young John DEWEY in the early years of the century, but it was James, with his emphasis on the physiological nature of emotion, who determined much of the bias against emotion in philosophy and psychology for years to come. James argued that an emotion was a sensation (or set of sensations) caused by a 'visceral' disturbance which in turn was prompted by some disturbing 'perception'. Perhaps the first major attention to emotion in Anglo-American philosophy came in mid-century, when an ethical theory named 'emotivism' came to dominate both the English and the US scene (see EMOTIVISM). But emotivism, which was part and parcel of a cross-the-board philosophical purgative known as 'logical positivism', was essentially a dismissal of ethical (and many other) questions in philosophy as 'meaningless' (that is, unscientific and without verifiable solutions). Emotion came back onto the stage of philosophy but only as the butt of the argument: ethical statements are meaningless, so they can therefore be *nothing but* expressions of emotion.

During the same period in Europe, however, the emotions enjoyed more attention. Franz BRENTANO succeeded the British moral sentiment theorists in attempting to base an ethics on a foundation of emotions. Max Scheler, Martin HEIDEGGER and, more recently, Paul RICOEUR developed ambitious philosophies in which emotions were given central place in human existence and accorded considerable respect. In the shadow of the Second World War, Jean-Paul Sartre offered a slim but important *'Sketch' of a Theory of Emotions*, followed by his *Being and Nothingness* which includes within its many pages a number of detailed 'phenomenological' analyses of emotion. Sartre's conception of emotions as 'magical transformations of the world' – wilful strategems for coping with a difficult world – added a new 'existential' dimension to the investigation of emotion (see SARTRE, J.P. §2).

In Anglo-American philosophy, the fortunes of emotion changed slowly. In an article simply entitled 'Emotion' (indicating how rarely the topic had even been broached), Errol Bedford addressed the Aristotelian Society in 1956 on the nature of emotion and the errors of thinking of emotions as 'feelings'. The essay might have sat on the shelves gathering dust except for the fact that the then dean of Oxford philosophers, J.L. AUSTIN, took it upon himself to remark on one of Bedford's claims. The subsequent attention kept the article alive, and in the 1960s the subject seemed to come to life again. Today, emotions are no longer at the margins of philosophy, and there is a rich variety of debates about the nature and the conceptual structure of emotions, their rationality and their place in the good life

See also: EMOTIONS

References and further reading

* Aristotle (*c.* mid 3rd century BC) *Rhetoric*, trans. R. McKeon in *The Works of Aristotle*, New York: Random House, 1941. (See especially his acute analysis of anger at Book II, Chapter 1.)

Augustine (*c.*400) *Confessions*, trans. J.K. Ryan, New York: Doubleday, 1960. (One of the world's most famous treatises on faith and temptation.)

* Bedford, E. (1956) 'Emotion', *Proceedings of the Aristotelian Society* 57 (1956–7): 281–304. (A classic piece of analytic philosophy on emotion.)

Brentano, F. (1874) *Psychology from the Empirical Standpoint*, trans. D.B. Terrell, London: Routledge & Kegan Paul, 1971. (Discusses the modern notion of 'intentionality' which influenced Freud and phenomenology.)

Calhoun, C. and Solomon, R. (eds) (1984) *What is an Emotion?*, New York: Oxford University Press. (A wide-ranging collection of classic sources on emotion.)

* Descartes, R. (1649) *Passions of the Soul*, trans. S. Voss, Indianapolis, IN: Hackett, 1989. (Descartes' most illuminating work on the 'mind–body problem' and the nature of emotion.)

* Hegel, G.W.F. (1807) *Phenomenology of Spirit*, trans A.V. Miller, Oxford: Oxford University Press, 1977. (An extremely difficult but essential defence of the 'dialectic' – the overcoming of contradictions – in philosophy. See, for example, Chapter 4, 'Master and Slave'.)

Heidegger, M. (1927) *Being and Time*, trans. J. Macquarrie and E. Robinson, New York: Harper & Row, 1962. (Equally obscure and important master-text by the most controversial of German authors. See the section on moods.)

* Hume, D. (1738) *A Treatise of Human Nature*, ed. L.A. Selby-Bigge, Oxford: Oxford University Press, 1978. (Book 2, Part 3, Section 3 contains one of the most insightful and elegantly-written defences and analyses of emotion in the English language.)

James, W. (1890) *What is an Emotion?*, New York: Dover. (One of the classic work by the great American philosopher-psychologist, the basis of much debate about emotions ever since.)

* Kant, I. (1790) *Critique of Judgment*, trans. W.S. Pluhar, Indianapolis, IN: Hackett Publishing Company, 1987. (The third of Kant's Critiques, in part devoted to the analyses of aesthetic judgment and feeling.)

* Nietzsche, F. (1887) *On the Genealogy of Morals*, trans. W. Kaufmann, New York: Random House, 1967. (His discussion of resentment in Book I is particularly relevant.)

* Plato (*c.*380s BC) *Symposium*, trans. P. Woodruss and A. Nehamas, Indianapolis, IN: Hackett Publishing Company, 1989. (The classic discussion of love.)

—— (*c.*370s BC) *The Republic*, trans. G.M.A. Grube, Indianapolis, IN: Hackett Publishing Company, 1974. (One of the greatest works in philosophy. The analogy between the 'parts of the soul' and the harmonious state are in Book IV.)

Ricoeur, P. (1950) *The Voluntary and the Involuntary*, trans E. Kohak, Evanston, IL: Northwestern University Press, 1966. (An original contribution to phenomenology.)

* Sartre, J.P. (1938) *The Emotions: Sketch of a Theory*, trans. B. Frechtman, New York: Philosophical Library, 1948. (A remarkably clear, single-minded exploration of the 'existentialist' view of emotion, focusing on emotions as 'magical transformations'.)

* —— (1943) *Being and Nothingness*, trans. H. Barnes, New York: Washington Square, 1956. (An extremely difficult gigantic tome of a work, devoted to defending in full Sartre's 'existentialist' view of being human, being free and responsible.)

Scheler, M. (1970) *The Nature of Sympathy*, trans. P. Heath, New York: Archon, 1970. (A modern defence of the 'moral sentiments' in ethics and an original contribution to phenomenology.)

Seneca (AD 41) *De Ira* (On Anger), trans. J. Cooper, Cambridge: Cambridge University Press, 1995. (A classic defence of the Stoic 'extirpation' of the passions.)

* Spinoza, B. de (1677) *Ethics*, trans. S. Shirley, Indianapolis, IN: Hackett Publishing Company, 1982. (A moving and sensitive work on the emotions, despite the mathematico-deductive style and the early books on metaphysics.)

ROBERT C. SOLOMON

EMOTIVE MEANING

Emotive meaning contrasts with descriptive meaning. Terms have descriptive meaning if they do the job of stating facts: they have emotive meaning if they do the job of expressing the speaker's emotions or attitudes, or exciting emotions or attitudes in others. Emotivism, the theory that moral *terms have only or primarily emotive meaning, is an important position in twentieth-century ethics. The most important problem for the idea of emotive meaning is that emotive meaning may not really be a kind of meaning: the jobs of moral terms supposed to constitute emotive meaning may really be performed by speakers using moral terms, on only some of the occasions on which they use them.*

There are two components in emotivist accounts of the function and meaning of moral terms. One is a matter of relations to the speaker: moral assertions serve to express the speaker's emotions or attitudes. The other is a matter of relations to the audience: moral assertions serve to commend things, or to arouse emotions or attitudes in the audience.

The most celebrated accounts of emotive meaning were developed by A.J. AYER and C.L. STEVENSON. Ayer (1936) argued on general metaphysical and epistemological grounds that moral terms can only express and excite emotions. Stevenson (1937) developed a more detailed theory, relying more on distinctively ethical considerations (see EMOTIVISM). These theories are liable to make moral discussion seem irrational, and to make no distinction between moral argument and propaganda. R.M. HARE developed a theory designed to remedy these defects. He argued that sentences using paradigm moral terms like 'good', 'right' and 'ought' are really disguised imperatives. Since there is a logic of imperatives, there is room for rational moral argumentation, and moral argument can be distinguished from propaganda, even though moral assertions do not primarily state facts (see PRESCRIPTIVISM).

The most important difficulties for the idea of emotive meaning can be raised by asking whether the emotive meaning of moral terms is a matter of speech act performed by someone using these terms, and, if so, what kind of speech act? One can distinguish between locutionary, illocutionary, and perlocutionary acts (or force). Locutionary acts are simply a matter of uttering certain words with certain senses and referents. Illocutionary acts are done *in* saying things; what illocutionary act one performs in uttering a sentence is determined together by the senses and referents of the words in the sentence and the context. Perlocutionary acts are done *by* saying things. That one performs a certain perlocutionary act is not guaranteed by performing an appropriate illocutionary act: it depends on further variable features of the context. Suppose Bob utters the words 'Down with the aristocrats!' before a large crowd in a revolutionary situation. Bob performs a locutionary act just by saying words with that meaning. In this context, Bob also performs the illocutionary act of *inciting* revolution. Bob's words may also, in that context, have the perlocutionary effect of *provoking* revolution; but this is not guaranteed by the locutionary or the illocutionary force of Bob's utterance. If Bob is sufficiently unpopular, his advocating revolution may actually dampen revolutionary enthusiasm. This classification suggests that the order of explanation typically goes from the locutionary to the illocutionary and the perlocutionary: it is in virtue of the sense and reference of the words one utters and the context that one performs a certain illocutionary act, and that one performs certain perlocutionary acts. The presumption is that an account of meaning will begin with sense and reference; if it begins with illocutionary or perlocutionary acts, it may begin in the wrong place (see SPEECH ACTS).

Some early accounts of emotive meaning seem to identify the meaning of moral assertions with perlocutionary acts (for example, arousing emotions). But this seems both to be the wrong place to begin and to raise a further concern. If we think of meaning as a matter of convention, not (mere) causal variation, then causal correlations between utterances and the production of certain effects are not really meanings. Perhaps then emotive meaning is a matter of illocutionary force. Unfortunately, seeing emotive meaning as illocutionary force is also problematic; in addition to the general problem that an account of meaning apparently should not begin with the illocutionary, there is the specific problem that moral terms do not seem *always* to have the right kinds of illocutionary force. Consider the suggestion that 'good' is used to commend. While it may be true that the term 'good' as used in 'This is a good tennis racket', uttered in a sports shop has the illocutionary force of commending a tennis racket, 'good' as used in 'If you can't get a good one there, try the shop down the street', does not obviously seem to commend anything.

Moral arguments raise especially acutely a version of the same problem for the view that emotive meaning is illocutionary force. Consider the argument: 'Telling the truth is good; if telling the truth is good, getting your little brother to tell the truth is good; so getting your little brother to tell the truth is good.' This argument looks valid. But while 'telling the truth is good' in its occurrence as the first premise commends telling the truth, in its occurrence in the second premise it does not seem to commend anything. So, the suggestion is, emotivists cannot account for the validity of some moral arguments, because if meaning is understood as illocutionary force, it is not the same between different occurences of the same words in arguments. This problem is often called 'the problem of unasserted contexts' (in the second premise, 'telling the truth is good' occurs unasserted).

Fans of emotive meaning can respond to these criticisms. Hare (1952), Blackburn (1984) and Gibbard (1990) have all offered solutions to the problem of unasserted contexts. It is certainly true that the meanings of *some* words (like 'promise') seem well explained by explaining the illocutionary act one performs in using them. Moreover, it is not an accident that, for instance, 'good' is often used to commend, while it is an accident if 'fast' is used to commend. Still, an attractive alternative to the theory that 'good' has emotive meaning is that 'good' *means*

something like 'meets the relevant standards'. It is by virtue of this meaning that 'good' is often used to commend. Emotive force is then explained by meaning, not vice versa.

See also: EMOTIVISM; PRESCRIPTIVISM

References and further reading

* Ayer, A.J. (1936) *Language, Truth and Logic*, New York: Dover. (Chapter 6 is Ayer's classic argument for and presentation of emotivism.)
Alston, W. (1967) 'Emotive Meaning', in P. Edwards (ed.) *The Encyclopedia of Philosophy*, New York: Macmillan and the Free Press, vol. 2, 486–93. (A trenchant critique of the idea of emotive meaning.)
* Blackburn, S. (1984) *Spreading The Word*, Oxford: Oxford University Press. (Chapters 5 and 6 defend a theory giving moral words emotive meaning.)
* Gibbard, A. (1990) *Wise Choices, Apt Feelings*, Cambridge, MA: Harvard University Press. (A sophisticated and wide ranging recent defence of, *inter alia*, a kind of emotive meaning.)
* Hare, R.M. (1952) *The Language of Morals*, Oxford: Oxford University Press. (Classic defence of the view that moral terms are disguised imperatives.)
* Stevenson, C.L. (1937) 'The Emotive Meaning of Ethical Terms', *Mind* 46: 14–31. (Stevenson's initial presentation of emotivism.)
—— (1944) *Ethics and Language*, New Haven, CT: Yale University Press. (Book-length development of Stevenson's view.)
Urmson, J.O. (1968) *The Emotive Theory of Ethics*, London: Hutchinson & Co. (Balanced consideration and development of emotive theory.)
Ziff, P. (1960) *Semantic Analysis*, Ithaca, NY: Cornell University Press. (Chapter 6 is an early and trenchant development of the kind of critique of emotive meaning given above.)

DAVID PHILLIPS

EMOTIVISM

Emotivists held that moral judgments express and arouse emotions, not beliefs. Saying that an act is right or wrong was thus supposed to be rather like saying 'Boo!' or 'Hooray!' Emotivism explained well the apparent necessary connection between moral judgment and motivation. If people judge it wrong to lie, and their judgment expresses their hostility, then it comes as no surprise that we can infer that they are disinclined to lie. Emotivism did a bad job of explaining the important role of rational argument in moral practice, however.

Indeed, since it entailed that moral judgments elude assessment in terms of truth and falsehood, it suggested that rational argument about morals might be at best inappropriate, and at worst impossible.

In the early part of the twentieth century, under the influence of logical positivism, a new view about the nature of morality emerged: emotivism (see LOGICAL POSITIVISM). Emotivists held that when people say, 'It is wrong to tell lies', they express their hostility towards lying and try to get others to share that hostility with them. Moral claims were thus supposed to be very different from claims expressing beliefs. Beliefs purport to represent the world, and so are assessable in terms of truth and falsehood. Emotions, by contrast, do not purport to represent the world, so moral claims were supposed to elude such assessment (see ANALYTIC ETHICS §1; MORAL JUDGMENT §1). Judging acts right and wrong was thus rather like saying 'Boo!' and 'Hooray!'

Emotivism had evident appeal. It is widely agreed that there is a necessary connection of sorts between moral judgment and motivation. If someone judges telling lies to be wrong then they are motivated, to some extent, not to lie. But what people are motivated to do depends on what they approve of, or are hostile towards, not simply on what they believe (see MORAL MOTIVATION). Imagine, then, that someone's judgment that telling lies is wrong expressed a belief. In order to know whether they are inclined to lie or not we would then need to know, in addition, whether they approve of, or are hostile towards, telling lies. But we need to know no such thing. Knowing that they judge lying wrong suffices to know that they are disinclined to lie. This fits well with the idea that the judgment itself simply expresses hostility.

Emotivism also had its difficulties, however. Though emotivists admitted that rational argument about morals had an important role to play, their view entailed that this role was strictly limited. Since they agreed that less fundamental moral claims are entailed by more fundamental claims along with factual premises, and since they agreed that factual premises could be criticized rationally, they held that less fundamental moral claims must be rationally-based. Someone who judges lying wrong because they think that lies are harmful must, they thought, change their mind on pain of irrationality if shown that lying is harmless. But at the same time they insisted that fundamental moral claims – those that are not so derived like, perhaps, the claim that it is wrong to cause harm – are immune from such rational criticism. This was the so-called 'fact/value gap' (see FACT/VALUE DISTINCTION; LOGIC OF ETHICAL DISCOURSE).

It is unclear whether emotivists were consistent in allowing even this limited role for rational argument, however.

1   If it is wrong to cause harm and lying causes harm then it is wrong to tell lies

2   It is wrong to cause harm

3   Lying causes harm

Therefore, it is wrong to tell lies

This argument is valid only if 'It is wrong to cause harm' in premises (1) and (2) means the same thing. If this phrase means different things then there is an equivocation and the argument is straightforwardly invalid. Emotivism entails that someone who asserts (2) expresses hostility towards causing harm. Yet whatever 'It is wrong to cause harm' means in (1), it most certainly does not serve to express such hostility. In (1) the phrase appears in the antecedent of a conditional. Someone who asserts (1) may thus even deny that it is wrong to cause harm. They need therefore have no hostility to express towards causing harm.

Philosophers sympathetic to emotivism have tried to rescue it from this objection. There is a real question whether emotivists themselves should ever have been interested in preserving an important role for rational argument about morals, however. If the function of moral judgment is simply to express emotions and arouse like emotions in others then it follows that rational argument is at best one way, and perhaps not a very good way, of achieving these aims. We might be more effective if we distracted people from the facts and used rhetoric, humiliation and brainwashing instead. It is hard to see how emotivists could find fault with the idea that a practice in which the use of such technologies was widespread could still constitute a perfectly proper *moral* practice.

The best emotivists could say at this point was, 'Boo for persuasion and brainwashing!' Philosophers who thought this response failed to acknowledge the central and defining role played by rational argument in moral practice concluded that emotivism extracted too high a price for its explanation of the necessary connection between moral judgment and motivation. Subsequent theorists have focused on whether an alternative explanation of the necessary connection is available, one which also accommodates the idea that rational argument plays such a central and defining role. No consensus on this issue has emerged, however.

If nothing else, emotivism succeeded in making clear how difficult it is to explain the necessary connection between moral judgment and motivation, together with the idea that rational argument plays a central and defining role in moral practice, if the emotions that cause our actions are assumed to be beyond rational criticism. Much recent work about the nature of morality proceeds by calling this assumption into question.

See also: AYER, A.J.; EXPRESSION, ARTISTIC; MORAL KNOWLEDGE; MORAL REALISM; MORALITY AND EMOTIONS §§1–2; PRESCRIPTIVISM; STEVENSON, C.L.

References and further reading

Ayer, A.J. (1936) *Language, Truth and Logic*, London: Gollancz; 2nd edn, 1946, ch. 6. (Contains a classic statement of emotivism by a logical positivist.)

Blackburn, S. (1984) *Spreading the Word*, Oxford: Oxford University Press, ch. 6. (Shows how modern versions of emotivism attempt to avoid the problems faced by their ancestor.)

Smith, M. (1994) *The Moral Problem*, Oxford: Blackwell. (Argues that, contrary to the standard assumption, emotions can be rationally criticized. Ch. 2 contains a critical discussion of Ayer's emotivism and more modern versions.)

Stevenson, C.L. (1944) *Ethics and Language*, New Haven, CT: Yale University Press. (Another classic statement of emotivism and explanation of the difference between disagreements about values and disagreements about facts.)

Warnock, G. (1967) *Contemporary Moral Philosophy*, London: Macmillan, ch. 3. (Contains a critical discussion of emotivism.)

MICHAEL SMITH

EMPEDOCLES (*c.*495–*c.*435 BC)

Empedocles, born in the Sicilian city of Acragas (modern Agrigento), was a major Greek philosopher of the Presocratic period. Numerous fragments survive from his two major works, poems in epic verse known later in antiquity as On Nature *and* Purifications.

On Nature *sets out a vision of reality as a theatre of ceaseless change, whose invariable pattern consists in the repetition of the two processes of harmonization into unity followed by dissolution into plurality. The force unifying the four elements from which all else is created – earth, air, fire and water – is called Love, and Strife is the force dissolving them once again into plurality. The cycle is most apparent in the rhythms of plant and animal life, but Empedocles' main objective is to tell the history of the universe itself as an exemplification of the pattern.*

The basic structure of the world is the outcome of disruption of a total blending of the elements into main masses which eventually develop into the earth, the sea, the air and the fiery heaven. Life, however, emerged not from separation but by mixture of elements, and Empedocles elaborates an account of the evolution of living forms of increasing complexity and capacity for survival, culminating in the creation of species as they are at present. There followed a detailed treatment of a whole range of biological phenomena, from reproduction to the comparative morphology of the parts of animals and the physiology of sense perception and thinking.

The idea of a cycle involving the fracture and restoration of harmony bears a clear relation to the Pythagorean belief in the cycle of reincarnations which the guilty soul must undergo before it can recover heavenly bliss. Empedocles avows his allegiance to this belief, and identifies the primal sin requiring the punishment of reincarnation as an act of bloodshed committed through 'trust in raving strife'. Purifications accordingly attacked the practice of animal sacrifice, and proclaimed prohibition against killing animals to be a law of nature.

Empedocles' four elements survived as the basis of physics for 2,000 years. Aristotle was fascinated by On Nature; *his biology probably owes a good deal to its comparative morphology. Empedocles' cosmic cycle attracted the interest of the early Stoics. Lucretius found in him the model of a philosophical poet. Philosophical attacks on animal sacrifice made later in antiquity appealed to him as an authority.*

1   **Life and work**
2   **Pythagoreanism**
3   **The cycle of change**
4   **The biological paradigm**
5   **Cosmic history**
6   **Biological explanations**
7   **Sacrifice**

1   Life and work

The first lines of Empedocles' poem *Purifications* give a flavour of the man:

> Friends, who live in the great city of the yellow Acragas, up on the heights of the citadel, caring for good deeds, I give you greetings. An immortal god, mortal no more, I go about honoured by all, as is fitting, crowned with ribbons and fresh garlands.
>
> (fr. 115)

Men and women followed him in their thousands, Empedocles says, wanting prophecies or remedies for diseases. Not surprisingly there accumulated in antiquity a huge conglomeration of fact and fantasy about the life and death of such a figure, summarized by Diogenes Laertius (VIII 51–75). A cautious sifting yields the following picture.

Empedocles was born of aristocratic family, a little after Anaxagoras. He died aged sixty. He was active in the political life of Acragas as a fierce opponent of oligarchy and tyranny. He had a reputation as an orator: Aristotle even makes him the inventor of rhetoric. He is described as a physician, but despite his profound interest in human physiology, anecdotes of his miracle working and the supernatural powers he claimed his teaching would impart (fr. 111) both strongly suggest a practitioner of magic, an activity doubtless to be seen in the context of his Pythagorean religious beliefs.

Among various writings ascribed to him, the two most important were *On Nature* and *Purifications*, hexameter poems probably in three and two books respectively. *On Nature* was at the time of its composition very likely the longest work of philosophy ever written and Empedocles' fragments constitute the largest corpus of original extracts to survive of any Presocratic. Scholars disagree about which of the fragments belong to which of the two major works – the sources seldom supply specific information on this point. In the age of Victorian rationalism it was supposed that *On Nature* presented a sober materialist philosophy of nature, subsequently abandoned in *Purifications* for the intoxications of mystery religion. Fragments were assigned to the two poems accordingly. The basis for this division of the material has long since collapsed, and more recent study (notably by Kahn 1960) has suggested that *On Nature* itself draws religious morals from a philosophy which was always conceived in religious terms. Indeed, it has been argued that the great majority of the fragments, including those on religious themes, belong to *On Nature*, *Purifications* being simply a collection of oracles and ritual prescriptions designed to satisfy the desire for healing and salvation Empedocles mentions in its opening verses.

2 Pythagoreanism

Empedocles praises Pythagoras as a man of surpassing knowledge and 'wise works', with powers of foresight extending to ten or twenty generations ahead (fr. 129). What prompted this extravagant admiration was evidently Pythagoras' analysis of the human condition: to atone for sin the soul is subject to a cycle of reincarnations into a variety of living forms (since all life is akin) until release is eventually achieved (see PYTHAGORAS §2). On this view animal sacrifice counts as unwitting slaughter of one's kin.

Empedocles dramatizes the implication in some gothic hexameters:

> Father lifts up a beloved son changed in form, and butchers him with a prayer, helpless fool.... Similarly son seizes father and children their mother, and tearing out the life they consume the flesh of those they love.
>
> (fr. 137)

Further verses spell out the penalty bloodshed incurs, invoking an 'oracle of Necessity' which condemns guilty spirits (*daimones*) to wander apart from the blessed for 30,000 years, in all manner of mortal forms. They conclude with a dramatic confession: 'Of these I too am now one, an exile from the gods and a wanderer, having put my trust in raving Strife' (fr. 115).

Fragment 115 is said by Plutarch to have formed part of the preface to Empedocles' philosophy. Is this a reference to *Purifications* (the usual supposition)? 'Philosophy' rather suggests *On Nature*; and Empedocles announces the *recovery* of his divinity at the start of *Purifications* (see §1). On the basis of comparison with the proem to Lucretius' *On the Nature of Things* Sedley (1989) argues persuasively that the entire sequence of fragments just summarized helped to launch *On Nature*. Whether this is right or not, Empedocles' Pythagoreanism is the best clue we have to his intentions in *On Nature*. The poem should be seen as an attempt to exhibit the cycle of incarnation as an instance of a general pattern of repetition governing all change: plurality is converted into unity by the power of Love and unity is then broken into plurality by Strife, until the process is reversed and conversion of plurality into unity begins once again. What *On Nature* works out in detail is the realization of this pattern in the rhythms of plant and animal life and the design and dissolution of the body, but above all in the history of the universe itself (see PYTHAGOREANISM §3).

3 The cycle of change

The cycle of change is announced in fragment 17.1–2: 'A twofold tale I shall tell: at one time they grew to be one alone out of many, at another again they grew apart to be many out of one'. These lines deliberately echo and defiantly contradict the assertion of PARMENIDES (§3) that there is only *one* tale to tell, that of changeless and timeless being and unity (fr. 8.1–6). The language of growth is not accidental. Empedocles has already indicated that the subjects of the dual process are what he calls the 'roots': earth, air, fire and water. Subsequent philosophy would speak of these as 'elements', but Empedocles chooses a designation which captures the idea that they are not merely the basis of everything else, but themselves have a potentiality for development. He is emphatic in his agreement with the Parmenidean thesis that nothing comes into being from non-existence or perishes into it: mixture and separation of roots are what humans mistakenly call birth and death (frs 8–12).

After amplification of the twofold tale Empedocles continues: 'And these things never cease their continual interchange, now through love all coming together into one, now again each carried apart by strife's hatred' (fr. 17.6–8). Mixture and separation would not occur without the agency of forces bringing them about. Are Love and Strife physical or psychological forces? For us it is counterintuitive to envisage earth or fire as capable of psychological responses. But *On Nature* is permeated with expressions of the hatred the roots have for each other, of their desire for one another. Empedocles does not write as though he wants the reader to construe them metaphorically. On the other hand, the operation of Love in creating mixtures of the roots is often also described in the language of craftsmanship: she welds (frs 34, 96) and rivets (fr. 87) and fires like a potter (fr. 73). Here Love seems to represent whatever physical force makes for the assimilation of things. However we are to conceive of Love and Strife, they are certainly treated as existing independently of the roots. But there is a difference between them: Love is 'among' the roots, Strife 'apart from' them (fr. 17.19–20). The implication is presumably that Love works with the grain, Strife against it: roots have a natural tendency to join together, whether earth with earth or in mixture with air, fire and water, whereas their separation is unnatural (fr. 22). Aristotle, however, found Empedocles thoroughly confusing on this issue (*Generation and Corruption* II 6).

Fragment 17.9–13 sums up the two key features of change – its oscillating duality and its ceaseless repetition – in a surprisingly Heraclitean conclusion (compare HERACLITUS §3):

So insofar as they have learned to grow one from many, and again they grow many as the one grows apart, thus far do they come into being and have no stable life; but insofar as they never cease their continual interchange, thus far they exist always, changeless in the cycle.

The implication is that Parmenides looked for changeless existence in the wrong place: it is not to be found in being (not even the being of the roots), but in the regularity of the cycle of unending flux.

4 The biological paradigm

The initial presentation of the cycle of change in fragment 17 is entirely general and abstract in its formulations. The evidence for the structure and content of the following section of *On Nature* is inadequate, although newly discovered fragments may clarify the matter (see Martin and Primaveri 1997). However Empedocles seems to have taken the creation of plants and animals as a paradigm of the way mixture of roots generates a huge variety of other forms (fr. 21). He appealed to the analogy of a painter, using a few pigments with many potentialities:

When they seize pigments of many colours in their hands, mixing in harmony more of some and less of others, they produce from them forms resembling all things, creating trees and men and women, beasts and birds and water-bred fish, and long-lived gods, too, highest in honour.

(fr. 23)

If this is how art achieves its effects, why should we look for any other explanation of the way nature produces the originals copied by the painter?

It may be that the paradigm of animal creation, once established, was subsequently invoked in later sections of the poem. For example, the following lines from fragment 20 might well have been written to support the notion expressed in fragment 31 of the disintegration of the limbs of the cosmic sphere:

This is well-known in the mass of mortal limbs: at one time, in the maturity of a vigorous life, all the limbs that are the body's portion come into one through love; at another time again, torn asunder by evil strifes, they wander, each apart, on the shore of life. So it is too for shrubs and water-housed fish and mountain-laired beasts and wing-progressing gulls.

5 Cosmic history

Mention of the cosmic sphere brings us to Empedocles' boldest application of the concept of a cycle of change: to the history of the universe. He conceived that just as harmonization by Love and decomposition by Strife constitute the common pattern for the biological development of plants and animals, there must be a similar story to tell about the universe as a whole. But here he supposed that the unity achieved at one pole of the cycle and the division at the other took more radical and absolute forms than in the biological realm. When – as he described first as usual – the influence of Love is at its strongest, all distinctions disappear as reality becomes a perfect divine sphere (frs 27–9). Strife for its part generates a vortex which not only breaks the sphere down into its constituent roots, but achieves their complete separation. It is under Strife's domination that the world as we are familiar with it comes into being (A37, 42).

Empedocles' account of this development was evidently extensive, and included full discussions of all the topics by now traditional in philosophical cosmogony: notably, the formation of the earth, the sea, and the heavenly bodies, and the evolution of life. Strife divides the roots into four great isolated masses. What happens next is obscure, but the key process was physical interaction between these masses: some of its effects inevitable, some pure chance (see, for example, fr. 53). In particular, misty air heated by fire rises up and forms a nocturnal hemisphere balanced by a diurnal counterpart of fire. The sun is a reflection of this fire, the moon compacted air. The earth too sweats under the heat of the sun, which is the origin of the sea (A30, 49, 66).

The power of Strife is clearly not what it was, but we hear nothing yet of Love. Its influence begins to be apparent with the emergence of life. A clear example is the creation of bone, ascribed to *harmonia*, one of Empedocles' synonyms for Love: 'And kindly earth received in its broad melting-pots two parts of the gleam of Nestis [water] out of eight, and four of Hephaestus [fire], and they became white bones, marvellously joined by the gluing of harmonia' (fr. 23). The creatures to which bodily parts such as this belonged were described subsequently, in Empedocles' memorable theory of evolution:

> Empedocles held that the first generations of animals and plants were not complete, but consisted of separate limbs not joined together; the second, arising from the joining of these limbs, were like creatures in dreams; the third was the generation of whole-natured forms. The fourth arose no longer from the homogeneous substances such as earth or water, but by intermingling, in some cases as the result of the compacting of their food, in others because female beauty excited the sexual urge. And the various species of animal were distinguished by the quality of the mixture in them.
> (A72)

Surviving fragments give vivid details of the bizarre beings of the first three stages (frs 57–62). From these it is clear that in the first two especially chance was made responsible for a great deal. Empedocles may have talked in this context of the survival of the fittest: a remarkable anticipation of Darwinism, although criticized by Aristotle for its inability to account for the regular teleological patterns of nature (*Physics* II 8). It is only with the animals of the fourth (that is, present) stage that Love begins to exercise a control over the whole structure and pattern of life (fr. 71). The evidence suggests that at this point in the poem Empedocles included a full-scale comparative biology of plant and animal species, focused on explanation of the formation and function of the parts of the body.

Ultimately all this diversity would be reabsorbed into the divine sphere. *On Nature* may have concluded with some verses which foreshadow this, speaking of god as a mind, 'holy and beyond description, darting through the whole universe with swift thoughts' (fr. 134).

Aristotle sometimes talks as if he thinks two cosmogonies were envisaged: one occurring as Strife grew more powerful, another as its influence ebbed. He then complains that Empedocles said and could say nothing about the second (A42). Some modern commentators have reinforced this idea of a double cosmogony, adding a double zoogony and appealing to some obscure lines which speak of a 'double birth and double failing of mortal things' (fr. 17.3–5). But it seems likely that this is just a reference to the growth of unity, then of plurality, both 'mortal' conditions persisting only for a while. In any event, the reduplicating interpretation is hard to reconcile with the shape of the cosmic history as it emerges from the rest of the fragments.

Another way of reading Empedocles' history of the universe is as an arbitration and synthesis between two approaches to cosmogony adopted by different among his philosophical predecessors. Broadly speaking, the Ionians from Anaximander on explain the emergence of a world or worlds as the outcome of separation from an original undifferentiated condition, and of the consequent interaction between the physical forces released by the separation. By contrast, in the cosmological part of his poem Parmenides had posited an original duality of fire and night, and explained the development of cosmic order and life on earth as the work of Aphrodite mixing the two basic forms (Parmenides fr. 13). Empedocles implies that each strategy is half right: separation produces a differentiated universe, but mixture the biosphere.

There is in fact reason to think that Empedocles wanted to be read as among other things an encyclopedist of previous thought. For example, the forms generated in the early phases of evolution are not just the stuff of dreams, but also recapitulate and rationalize myth. Most notable of these is the figure of the Minotaur, surely the model of Empedocles' 'ox-headed man-natured' being (fr. 61). At the opposite extreme, his verses describing the divine sphere deliberately recall Xenophanes' god (see XENOPHANES §3) – 'No twin branches spring from his back, no feet, no nimble knees, no fertile parts'

(Empedocles, fr. 29) – and that of Parmenides' being – 'Thus he is held fast in the close obscurity of *harmonia*, a rounded sphere rejoicing in joyous solitude' (Empedocles, fr. 27).

6   Biological explanations

The power of Empedocles as a thinker and his gifts as a poet are most happily married in the surviving extracts of his biology, where he shows an extraordinary capacity to get the reader to *see* the kinship of all nature. Sometimes parts of animals with homologous functions are just listed: 'The same things are hair and leaves and close-packed wings of birds and scales, coming into being on sturdy limbs' (fr. 82). Sometimes metaphor makes the point: 'Thus do tall trees lay eggs: first olives...' (fr. 79). Other animals are armed with horns or teeth or stings, but 'Sharp-speared hairs bristle on hedgehogs' backs' (fr. 83).

Perception was explained by an ingenious theory of pores and effluences. It occurs when pores in the sense organ are just the right size to admit effluences of shape, sound, etc. given off by things (A92). The theory was employed to account for other phenomena also, such as chemical mixture (frs 91–2, A87) and magnetism (A89). Only like things (or things made like by Love) could have symmetrical pores and effluences. Empedocles posits fire in the eye for perception of light colours, a resounding bell in the ear to account for hearing, and breath in the nose for smelling (A86). Little of this material survives in his own words, except for an extended simile:

As when someone planning a journey through the wintry night prepares a light, a flame of blazing fire, kindling for whatever the weather a linen lantern, which scatters the breath of the winds when they blow, but the finer light leaps through outside and shines across the threshold with unyielding beams: so at that time did she [Aphrodite] give birth to the round eye, primeval fire confined within membranes and delicate garments, and these held back the deep water that flowed around, but they let through the finer fire to the outside.

(fr. 84)

Empedocles made thinking a function of blood around the heart (fr. 105). Of all physical substances blood comes closest to an equal blending of all the elements, even though its origin still owes something to chance (fr. 98). This is what equips it to grasp the nature of things: earth with earth, and so on – but also Love with Love and Strife with Strife (fr. 109).

7   Sacrifice

Empedocles relates his guilt over bloodshed to 'trust in raving strife' (fr. 115). As all creation of plants and animals is due to the power of Love, so Strife is the invariable cause of their dissolution and death. It is in his account of blood that Empedocles describes the mixture of the roots as 'anchored in the perfect harbours of Kypris [Love]' (fr. 98). Hence to kill by spilling blood is to act against the principle that makes for all that flourishes and enjoys harmony. It is no surprise that Empedocles conceives it as madness.

Theophrastus tells us that in his account of 'sacrifices and theogony', usually taken to belong to *Purifications*, Empedocles portrayed a golden age when humans recognized only Love as a god: 'They did not count Ares a god nor Battle-cry, nor was Zeus their king nor Kronos nor Poseidon, but Kypris [that is, Aphrodite] was queen' (fr. 128). There was no animal sacrifice:

Her they propitiated with holy images, with paintings of living creatures, with perfumes of varied fragrance and sacrifices of pure myrrh and sweet-scented frankincense, throwing to the ground libations of yellow honey. The altar was not drenched with the unspeakable slaughters of bulls, but this was held among humans the greatest defilement – to tear out the life from noble limbs and eat them.

(fr.128, continued)

Empedocles envisages this golden age as a time when humans were in fact friends with the rest of animal creation: 'All things were tame and gentle to humans, both beasts and birds, and friendship burned bright' (fr. 130). Is the image of harmony painted in these passages intended as part of the cosmic history? According to Empedocles' theory of evolution Strife was more, not less, dominant in the past. We should infer that like most pictures of primal bliss, this too is designed to function principally as an ideal measure of contemporary misery and wickedness.

What Empedocles lays down for all time is a moral rule against killing living things, whose expression led Aristotle to treat it as a paradigm of how natural law is to be conceived: 'That which is the law for all extends unendingly throughout wide-ruling air and the boundless sunlight' (fr. 135). Particular Pythagorean injunctions against touching beans and laurel leaves are recorded as Empedoclean (frs 140–1). As for the future, other verses promise the repentant sinner eventual release from the burden of reincarnation entailed by committing bloodshed:

At the end they come among humans on earth as prophets, bards, doctors and princes; and thence they arise as gods highest in honours, sharing with the other immortals their hearth and table, without part in the sorrows of men, unwearied.

(frs 146–7)

Empedocles no doubt found the killing of other humans as horrific as animal sacrifice – the lines in which he represents sacrifice *as* infanticide etc. trade on a particular form of revulsion on the part of the reader. But he directs his outrage at violence to life as such, and more specifically at the assumption that blood-shedding can form part of a proper form of worship. In other words, his protest aims both to broaden our moral horizons and to reform religion. It should be seen as a radical challenge to the entire cultural framework of the ancient Greek city-state.

References and further reading

Bollack, J. (1965–9) *Empédocle*, Paris: Les Éditions de Minuit, 4 vols. (An edition of fragments of *On Nature* and associated testimonia, with Greek text, French translation and commentary; champions the interpretation of the cosmic cycle adopted here; sometimes eccentric, but contains a wealth of insight, particularly on Empedocles' vocabulary.)

* Empedocles (*c.*495–*c.*435 BC) Fragments, in H. Diels and W. Kranz (eds) *Die Fragmente der Vorsokratiker* (Fragments of the Presocratics), Berlin: Weidemann, 6th edn, 1952, vol. 1, 276–375. (The standard collection of the ancient sources, both fragments and testimonia, the latter designated by 'A'; includes Greek text of the fragments with translations in German.)

Guthrie, W.K.C. (1962–78) *A History of Greek Philosophy*, Cambridge: Cambridge University Press, 6 vols. (The most detailed and comprehensive English-language history of early Greek thought; the long and sympathetic account of Empedocles, in volume 2 pages 122–265, is still the best treatment in English.)

* Kahn, C.H. (1960) 'Religion and Natural Philosophy in Empedocles' Doctrine of the Soul', *Archiv für Geschichte der Philosophie* 42: 3–35; repr. in A.P.D. Mourelatos (ed.) *The Pre-Socratics*, Garden City, NY: Doubleday, 1974, 397–425. (A seminal article on the coherence of Empedocles' thought.)

Kirk, G.S., Raven, J.E. and Schofield, M. (1983) *The Presocratic Philosophers*, Cambridge: Cambridge University Press, 2nd edn. (A valuable survey of Presocratic philosophy, including texts and translations; the account of Empedocles presented in the biographical entry largely follows its interpretations.)

Kingsley, P. (1995) *Ancient Philosophy, Mystery and Magic: Empedocles and Pythagorean Tradition*, Oxford: Clarendon Press. (On Empedocles' physical system and its connection with Pythagorean traditions.)

* Martin, A. and Primaveri, O. (1997) *L'Empédocle de Strasbourg*, Berlin: de Gruyter. (An edition of papyrus fragments of Empedocles in the possession of the library of the University of Strasbourg.)

* Sedley, D.N. (1989) 'The Proems of Empedocles and Lucretius', *Greek, Roman and Byzantine Studies* 30: 269–96. (An attractive reconstruction of the proem to *On Nature*; revises the allocation of fragments between *On Nature* and *Purifications*.)

Solmsen, F. (1965) 'Love and Strife in Empedocles' Cosmology', *Phronesis* 10: 123–45; repr. in R.E. Allen and D.J. Furley (eds), *Studies in Presocratic Philosophy*, London: Routledge & Kegan Paul, vol. 2, 221–64. (The best argument for the single-cosmogony interpretation.)

Wright, M.R. (1981) *Empedocles: The Extant Fragments*, New Haven, CT, and London: Yale University Press. (An edition with translations, commentary and glossary; an indispensable aid to deeper study; contains a useful statement of the double-cosmogony interpretation.)

Zuntz, G. (1971) *Persephone*, Oxford: Clarendon Press. (A study of western Greek mystery religion; part 2 pages 181–274 re-edits *Purifications* and offers a powerfully suggestive interpretation.)

MALCOLM SCHOFIELD

EMPIRICISM

In all its forms, empiricism stresses the fundamental role of experience. As a doctrine in epistemology it holds that all knowledge is ultimately based on experience. Likewise an empirical theory of meaning or of thought holds that the meaning of words or our concepts are derivative from experience. This entry is restricted to epistemological empiricism. It is difficult to give an illuminating analysis of 'experience'. Let us say that it includes any mode of consciousness in which something seems to be presented to the subject, as contrasted with the mental activity of thinking about things. Experience, so understood, has a variety of modes – sensory, aesthetic, moral, religious and so on – but empiricists usually concentrate on sense experience, the modes of consciousness that result from the stimulation of the five senses.

It is obvious that not all knowledge stems directly from experience. Hence empiricism always assumes a stratified form, in which the lowest level issues directly from experience, and higher levels are based on lower levels. It has most commonly been thought by empiricists that beliefs at the lowest level simply 'read off' what is presented in experience. If a tree is visually presented to me as green I simply 'register' this appearance in forming the belief that the tree is green. Most of our beliefs – general beliefs for example – do not have this status but, according to empiricism, are supported by other beliefs in ways that eventually trace back to experience. Thus the belief that maple trees are bare in winter is supported by particular perceptual beliefs to the effect that this maple tree is bare and it is winter.

Empiricism comes in many versions. A major difference concerns the base on which each rests. A public version takes beliefs about what we perceive in the physical environment to be directly supported by experience. A phenomenalist version supposes that only beliefs about one's own sensory experience are directly supported, taking perceptual beliefs about the environment to get their support from the former sort of beliefs. The main difficulties for a global empiricism (all knowledge is based on experience) come from types of knowledge it is difficult to construe in this way, such as mathematical knowledge.

1 **Versions of epistemic empiricism**
2 **A phenomenalist empirical base**
3 **A public empirical base**
4 **Problems about the superstructure**
5 **Criticisms of empiricism**

1 Versions of epistemic empiricism

There are broad distinctions within epistemology that affect empiricism as well as other positions. One can think of *knowledge* or of *justified belief* as based on experience. To simplify the discussion we concentrate on the latter whenever we get into the details, though it is sometimes convenient to speak in terms of knowledge. If, as is often supposed, knowledge is justified belief that meets further conditions, then the necessity of an empirical basis for justified belief will extend to knowledge as well. There is also the question of whether the justification of belief depends on what the belief is *based on* (what gives rise to it), or whether it simply depends on what the believer *has* in the way of possible grounds, reasons or evidence, whether made use of or not. We take the former as a basis for discussion. Thus the empiricism under consideration here holds that all justified beliefs acquire their justification from being based, directly or indirectly, on experience.

Although empiricism typically concentrates on sense experience, this is not the only possibility. It is

plausible to suppose that one's introspective knowledge of one's feelings, desires and other mental states derives from one's experience of those states (see INTROSPECTION, EPISTEMOLOGY OF). There is also a religious empiricism that takes certain beliefs about God to be justified by being based on a (frequently non-sensory) experiential presentation of God (see JAMES, W. §4; RELIGIOUS EXPERIENCE). This entry is restricted to sensory empiricism.

Empiricism comes in stronger and weaker forms. One such distinction has to do with scope – whether the view takes all knowledge to be based on experience, or restricts this claim to knowledge of the physical universe, excluding, for example, mathematical and/or religious knowledge. There are also differences regarding the strength of support lower levels must give higher levels in order that the beliefs at the higher levels be justified.

2 A phenomenalist empirical base

A common-sense form of empiricism takes perceptual beliefs about the physical environment (external beliefs) to be directly supported by experience – such beliefs as 'that house is on fire', 'a rabbit just ran across the yard' or 'a car is parked in front of the house'. But there are considerations that have driven philosophers to retreat to phenomenal beliefs about one's own sensory experience as constituting the base. For one thing, external beliefs are often not solely based on experience, but rest, at least in part, on other beliefs. Thus I typically recognize a book as my copy of *Principia Ethica* not just by the way it looks (many other copies look just like that), but also by the fact that it is on a shelf in a study that belongs to me. For another thing, external beliefs can be mistaken even if confidently based on sense experience. I may unhesitatingly form the perceptual belief that the car in front of the house is a Pontiac when it is a Buick. Many philosophers have felt that if empirical knowledge is to be worthy of the name, at least the foundations on which it rests must consist of absolutely certain knowledge that cannot possibly be mistaken (Lewis 1946). Finally, it has been held that since, when I form an external perceptual belief, I would, if I reflected on the matter, take the justification of that belief to be the sensory experience on which it is based, that shows that beliefs about sensory experience are more basic in our empirical knowledge. All this can drive one to take phenomenal beliefs as the only ones that are directly supported by experience, with external beliefs supported by the phenomenal beliefs.

And yet these considerations do not require that conclusion. It remains to be shown that beliefs must be mistake-proof to constitute an empirical base. And the fact that external perceptual beliefs are based on sense experience should not be confused with the claim that they are based on beliefs about sense experience. Finally, even if my belief that this is my copy of *Principia Ethica* is partly based on other beliefs, that would prevent it from figuring in the empirical base only on an extreme form of empiricism, one that requires knowledge to be based on beliefs that are justified solely by experience. There are also more moderate forms that take the empirical base to include beliefs that are partly based on experience. An alternative way of handling this point would be to restrict the empirical base to those external beliefs that are justified solely by experience, leaving others for the superstructure.

It is just as well that those considerations are not conclusive, for there are serious difficulties in resting empirical knowledge of the world on a purely phenomenal base. Despite centuries of strenuous effort, no one has succeeded in showing how knowledge of the public physical world can be derived from knowledge of one's own experience, at least if we confine ourselves to generally recognized modes of inference. It has been widely recognized at least since the time of Hume that if we try to base an inference from sensory appearances to external objects on an empirically established correlation between them, we cannot establish that the correlation holds unless we already have knowledge of each side of it (see HUME, D. §2). And how can we get knowledge of the external side without already having established some such correlations to go on? Some have tried to side-step this difficulty by arguing that our experience is best explained by supposing that it is due to public physical objects in the ways we usually suppose (BonJour 1985). But that argument has never been developed in a thoroughly convincing way. Finally, some have turned in desperation to phenomenalism, the view that physical object statements are to be analysed in terms of what experiences one would have under certain circumstances. To say that there is a car parked in front of my house is to say something about what sensory experiences a sentient subject would have under certain conditions (Lewis 1946). The hope of the phenomenalist is that if the physical world is not radically different in nature from sense experience, it will not be impossible to infer the former from the latter. But apart from problems that attach to even these inferences, the programme runs afoul of the fact, classically pointed out by Chisholm (1948), that when we try to give a phenomenalist interpretation of, for example, 'There is a car parked in front of my house', we cannot specify the conditions in which a subject would have the relevant experiences without using physical-object language to do so. For example, we must include in those conditions the physical orientation and physical condition of the subject. We have to presuppose what we are trying to analyse in order to give the analysis (see PHENOMENALISM).

3 A public empirical base

These considerations drive us back to taking external perceptual beliefs to be, at least in part, directly justified by sense experience. There are many ways of spelling this out. The major differences come from differences in the analysis of sensory experience. We can distinguish three traditional views on this:

(1) Sense-datum theory. It consists of immediate awareness of non-physical entities that are, so to speak, reifications of the ways external objects appear to our experience. Thus, on this view, a typical visual experience of a round, red ball would involve being directly aware of a round, red sense-datum, which is distinct from the ball itself in being non-physical and existing only as an object for sensory awareness (Price 1932).
(2) Theory of appearing. A sense experience is an awareness of an object (in veridical perception an external object) appearing to one in a certain way (looking, sounding, tasting... a certain way).
(3) Adverbial theory. Sense experience should not be construed as the direct awareness of any object – internal or external. It is rather a way or mode of awareness, a way of being conscious. When I see a red round ball, my consciousness is a matter of sensing redly, roundly, and, perhaps, 'ball-ly' (Chisholm [1966] 1977).

It has been held that sense experience is to be understood as a process of acquiring perceptual beliefs or inclinations to such beliefs (Armstrong 1961). Others have advocated physicalist construals in terms of the stimulation of sense organs. But these innovations have not had much effect on empiricist epistemology.

One might think that on the sense-datum theory one could not suppose external perceptual beliefs to be directly justified by sense experience. For this theory postulates the awareness of an internal object that, so to speak, stands between the subject and the external object. Does that not imply that any beliefs about the external object would have to be based on beliefs about the sense datum? Not necessarily. Several of the most prominent sense-datum theorists in the first part of this century – G.E. Moore, C.D. Broad and H.H. Price – emphatically denied that any inference from sense-data to external objects is involved. Instead they maintained that when one forms the usual external belief upon becoming aware of a certain sense-datum, that belief is justified just by virtue of being so formed. This is, in effect, to take the belief to be justified by the sense experience in question.

In considering the accounts of direct empirical justification one gets on these different construals of sense experience it will be helpful to recognize that in every case we need to draw a connection between features of the sense experience and the content of the belief. A belief will be justified by an experience only if there is the right kind of 'match' between the two. The details of the match will vary, depending on the account of sense experience. The sense-datum theory will have to work out some way of 'projecting' characteristics of external objects from features of sense-data. No one has ever done this in a convincing way for a realist (non-phenomenalist) account of physical objects. With phenomenalism it is a different ball game, for there the only entities referred to even in external beliefs are sense-data. The other views of sense experience have an easier time of it here. Since the theory of appearing construes sense experience as a matter of the way objects (usually external objects) appear, there can be a direct match between what an object appears to be and what it is. If an object looks like a two-storey wooden house, one is justified in believing it to be a two-storey wooden house. The only complexity here comes from complete hallucinations – Macbeth supposing himself to see a dagger in front of him when there is no dagger there. The theory can deal with such cases by saying that one is justified in the perceptual belief that X is P if and only if it is just as if X appears to one as P. (To Macbeth it was just as if a dagger appeared before him, the handle towards his hand.) The adverbial theory does not have this problem, since it does not construe sense experience as consisting in some *object* appearing in a certain way. It can read the content of the belief directly off the way of sensing, assuming, as may not be the case, that it is intelligible to convert all perceivable features of external objects into *ways* of sensing.

The complexity involved in formulating principles of justification that relate belief content to experiential content is so staggering that more than one philosopher has sought to cut the Gordian knot by simply granting *carte blanche* to all perceptual beliefs (Chisholm [1966] 1977). To be sure, one cannot deny that some perceptual beliefs are ill formed, and even among those that are not some can be shown to be false. We must not forget the many contradictions between witnesses to automobile accidents, as well as the proverbial drunkard who 'sees snakes'. A great help at this point is the distinction between *prima facie* and unqualified justification. To say that a subject is *prima facie* justified in believing that p is to say that this belief will be justified provided there is nothing to invalidate that status – either sufficient reasons for regarding the belief as false or sufficient reasons for supposing that the justifying grounds do not do the job in this instance (see KNOWLEDGE, DEFEASIBILITY THEORY OF). If I have a visual presentation of an elephant sitting on my lawn, I am justified in supposing that there is an elephant on my lawn, unless I have sufficient reasons for supposing that there are no elephants in the vicinity, or sufficient reasons for supposing that my visual experience was produced in such a way as to make it an unreliable indication of what is before me. Thus we can reasonably hold that all perceptual beliefs are *ipso facto prima facie* justified, even though this status may be overridden in some cases (see PERCEPTION, EPISTEMIC ISSUES IN).

4 Problems about the superstructure

As we have been characterizing empiricism, it would seem to be committed to foundationalism, the doctrine that all knowledge (justified belief) rests on a foundation of beliefs that are justified otherwise than by other beliefs, for example, by experience (see FOUNDATIONALISM). The 'empirical base' of which we have been speaking is simply a special case of the 'foundations' of foundationalism. It is only a special case because there are other possibilities for foundations, for example, rationally self-evident truths. But remember that we have acknowledged forms of empiricism that do not restrict the empirical base to beliefs justified solely by experience. Do these forms count as foundationalism? Well, we can also recognize stronger and weaker forms of foundationalism along the same lines (BonJour 1985). Strong foundationalism holds that all knowledge rests on beliefs that are wholly justified by something other than beliefs. Weaker forms require of foundational beliefs only that they are at least partially justified by something other than beliefs. Thus a weaker empiricism will also be a weaker foundationalism.

Continuing in the foundationalist vein, an empiricist epistemology will include not only a doctrine of the empirical base, but also a doctrine of the ways in which other beliefs are justified by their relations to that base. Traditional accounts have concentrated on deductive and inductive inference. Any beliefs that can be deductively or inductively inferred from that base are, or can be, justified. How this works out depends on the scope of inductive inference. If it is restricted to simple enumeration (inferring a generalization from instances), much of what we ordinarily consider to be empirical knowledge will fail to pass the test. Consider testimony: much of what we think we know has been acquired by taking someone's word for it. Are we always or usually in possession of inductive evidence that the testifier is reliable? That is, have we checked out the person's testimony in a sufficient number of cases and found it to be usually accurate? Obviously not. With most of the information we glean from books we have no evidence worthy of the name for the reliability of the author. We simply take it that the author is to be trusted unless we have reason to the contrary (see TESTIMONY). Here too we give *prima facie* credence to certain beliefs, supposing them to be justified in the absence of sufficient reasons to think otherwise. Something similar can be said of the arguments to the best explanation that we constantly employ in a variety of contexts, for example, in arriving at an explanation of Jim's recent unfriendliness towards me. Once again we take the fact that this seems to us the best explanation of the empirical facts in question to justify us in accepting it, even though, in most cases, we lack any significant deductive or inductive reasons for that acceptance (see INFERENCE TO THE BEST EXPLANATION). Thus, if empiricism is to be at all plausible, it will have to recognize modes of building up the superstructure other than the traditional deductive and enumeratively inductive modes (Chisholm [1966] 1977).

5   Criticisms of empiricism

Criticisms of empiricist epistemology have mostly been of two types. First, there are areas of generally accepted knowledge that seem not to be accounted for by empiricism. Most prominently and most obviously, there is a priori knowledge, knowledge based on something other than experience (see A PRIORI). The least controversial examples of this are logic and mathematics. To take a simple example, it seems for all the world as if our knowledge that '2 + 2 = 4' does not rest at all on sense experience. It seems that we can know this to be true just by considering the proposition. The proposition is *self-evident*. There is no need to support it by empirical evidence, nor could it be overthrown by empirical evidence. If we seem to perceive two apples and two more apples making a sum of five apples rather than four, we would reject the supposed perception rather than the arithmetical truth. Other empirically recalcitrant areas include high-level theory in science, aesthetic knowledge and religious knowledge. But perhaps these latter cases can be handled by sufficiently extended ways of getting the superstructure from the base (high-level theoretical science) or by recognizing modes of justifying experience other than sense experience (aesthetic and religious experience). Still, logic and mathematics remain a stumbling block.

Some empiricists, like John Stuart Mill, have sought to show that mathematical knowledge, contrary to first impressions, rests on empirical evidence after all (see MILL, J.S. §§2–4). But a more common empiricist tack in the twentieth century has been that such knowledge is a matter of tracing out the logical implications of the meanings of the constituent terms. We know that '2 + 2 = 4' just by virtue of realizing that its truth follows from what is meant by '2', '+', '=' and so on. We know that 'p' logically follows from 'p and q' just because of what is meant by 'and' (Ayer 1936). But how does this show it to be *empirical* knowledge? It would seem that knowledge that owes its status to our grasp of the meanings of words is as far from being supported by *experience* as knowledge of self-evident propositions. The answer is that those who take this line do not suppose themselves to have shown that the knowledge in question is empirical, but rather that it is not knowledge 'of the world', not knowledge of what things are like independent of our conceptual arrangements. They take this line to imply that so-called logical and mathematical knowledge is restricted to the consequences of the way we conceptualize the world, and hence not the sort of thing we should expect to be based on experience. In the most radical version of this position, the claim is that this (so-called) knowledge falls outside the empiricist net because it is not really knowledge at all.

The second criticism is of an internal kind. Whereas the first objection was that there are areas of knowledge that empiricism cannot accommodate, the second objection is that even on the empiricist's home field knowledge claims rest, in part, on non-empirically based principles. The most widely advertised example concerns induction. Many philosophers have concluded that we cannot rationally infer generalizations from instances without assuming some principle of regularity. Suppose we have examined 5,000 samples of copper all of which are ductile. How does that warrant us in inferring that copper is always (or even almost always) ductile? How do we know that the next 5,000 samples will not fail to exhibit ductility? When we make inferences like this, are we not assuming some such general principle as that 'Regularities that hold in a large and varied sample will hold universally', or 'The future will resemble the past', or 'Properly chosen samples are representative of the whole class of which they are samples'? And are such principles themselves justified by experience? If we were to suppose they are, would that not require us to assume such principles in order to validate the inference? And that would make the empirical justification circular. Hence it seems that empirical induction depends for its validity on principles that cannot be empirically justified. And that would seem to be an absolute limit on the extent to which we can take knowledge, even in the 'empirical' sphere, to be wholly justified by experience (Russell 1948) (see INDUCTION, EPISTEMIC ISSUES IN).

See also: A POSTERIORI; EPISTEMOLOGY, HISTORY OF; INNATE KNOWLEDGE; RATIONALISM

References and further reading

Alston, W.P. (1991) *Perceiving God: The Epistemology of Religious Experience*, Ithaca, NY: Cornell University Press. (A defence of the thesis, mentioned in §1 above, that religious experience is a source of epistemic justification for certain kinds of beliefs about God.)

—— (1993) *The Reliability of Sense Perception*, Ithaca, NY: Cornell University Press. (A fairly technical criticism of attempts to establish the reliability of sense perception without relying on sense perception to do so.)

* Armstrong, D.M. (1961) *Perception and the Physical World*, London: Routledge & Kegan Paul. (General account of perception.)

* Ayer, A.J. (1936) *Language, Truth, and Logic*, London: Victor Gollancz Ltd, 2nd edn, 1948. (Classic presentation of logical empiricism.)

Bealer, G. (1992) 'The Incoherence of Empiricism', *The Aristotelian Society*, supplementary vol. 66: 99–138. (Powerful internal criticism of empiricism.)

* BonJour, L. (1985) *The Structure of Empirical Knowledge*, Cambridge, MA: Harvard University Press. (An accessible presentation of a coherentist account of empirical knowledge.)

* Chisholm, R.M. (1948) 'The Problem of Empiricism', *Journal of Philosophy* 45 (19): 512–17. (The classic critique of phenomenalism.)

* —— (1966) *Theory of Knowledge*, Englewood Cliffs, NJ: Prentice Hall, 2nd edn, 1977. (The second edition provides a very influential, concise presentation of a foundationalist epistemology.)

* Lewis, C.I. (1946) *An Analysis of Knowledge and Valuation*, La Salle, IL: Open Court. (The definitive account of a phenomenalist theory of empirical knowledge.)

Moser, P. (1989) *Knowledge and Evidence*, Cambridge: Cambridge University Press. (A difficult but comprehensive presentation of an empiricist foundationalism.)

Pollock, J. (1974) *Knowledge and Justification*, Princeton, NJ: Princeton University Press. (An advanced presentation of a foundationalist account of empirical knowledge.)

* Price, H.H. (1932) *Perception*, London: Methuen, 2nd edn, 1950. (A classic presentation of the sense-datum theory of perception.)

* Russell, B.A.W. (1948) *Human Knowledge: Its Scope and Limits*, London: Allen & Unwin. (The distillation of decades of Russell's thought about empirical knowledge.)

WILLIAM P. ALSTON

EMPIRIOCRITICISM, RUSSIAN *see* RUSSIAN EMPIRIOCRITICISM

EMPTINESS, BUDDHIST CONCEPT OF *see* BUDDHIST CONCEPT OF EMPTINESS

ENCYCLOPEDISTS, EIGHTEENTH-CENTURY

The Encyclopédie, ou dictionnaire raisonné des sciences, des arts et des métiers *was published in seventeen folio volumes (about 20 million words) between 1751 and 1765, accompanied by eleven volumes of engravings (1762–72). Its chief editor was Diderot, with D'Alembert acting as co-editor for the first seven volumes. The work was an expression of the Enlightenment belief in improvement through knowledge.*

From the outset the *Encyclopédie* attracted hostile criticism, especially from ecclesiastical circles; publication was halted twice and the last ten volumes had to be collected by subscribers from outside Paris. Because of its comprehensive scope, the wide range of its contributors, and the prominence which it owed as much to its critics as its supporters, the work came to be regarded as an embodiment of the French Enlightenment. Numerous editions (and volumes of extracts) were published in the 1770s and 1780s, as well as four supplementary volumes and two volumes of indices.

In his article 'Encyclopédie' in volume V (1755), DIDEROT expressed an intention 'of changing the general way of thinking'; in his *Discours préliminaire* to volume I (1751), D'ALEMBERT provided the fullest account of the principles guiding this ambition. They were epitomized by the phrases 'esprit philosophique' or 'esprit systématique', by which was meant a critical, enquiring, rational approach, opposed to prejudice, obscurity, superstition, intolerance and dogmatism (whether that emanating from established institutions or that evident in the 'esprit de système' of a priori philosophical doctrines). The empirical method of LOCKE, the scientific principles of NEWTON, and the practical benefits of knowledge advocated by Francis BACON, were held up as models; the writings of BAYLE, FONTENELLE and MONTESQUIEU were significant influences. The practical application of thought, in terms of both social reform and the mechanical arts, received particular emphasis; a humanitarian concern and a desire for freedom (intellectual, civil, economic, political) were recurring themes, although the work was not politically radical. The philosophical articles were not notable for their originality (although the occasional discussion of materialist ideas was seen as dangerously new by some); many took the form of a historical survey, written by Diderot but drawing heavily on J.J. Brucker's *Historia critica philosophiae*.

The title-page announced that the *Encyclopédie* was written by 'une société de gens de lettres', over a hundred and thirty of whom have been identified. Apart from contributions from VOLTAIRE, who wrote over forty articles of minor interest, and some by figures who later became famous – such as the editors themselves, Rousseau, Turgot, d'Holbach, Quesnay, or Marmontel – most were by individuals who were little known or of whom we otherwise know nothing (see ROUSSEAU, J.-J.). Generally speaking they seem to have been experts in their fields: professional men, academicians, civil servants, scientists, doctors, men of letters, engineers, manufacturers, and so on. Almost a quarter of the work was written by one dedicated, indefatigable and (regrettably) undistinguished contributor, the Chevalier de Jaucourt. The diversity of these figures, the variety of views expressed and the unevenness of the articles prevent any easy categorization of these writers, but their participation in the enterprise itself demonstrated a widespread faith in the power of ideas to bring about human improvement.

See also: ENLIGHTENMENT, CONTINENTAL

List of works

Diderot, D. and D'Alembert, J. Le R. (eds) (1751–65) *Encyclopédie, ou dictionnaire raisonné des sciences, des arts et des métiers*, Paris; trans. N. Hoyt *et al.*, *Encyclopedia*, New York, 1965. (The translation contains 39 articles.)

D'Alembert, J. Le R. (1751) *Discours préliminaire*, intro. and trans. by R.N. Schwab, *Preliminary Discourse*, New York, 1963.

Hope Mason, J. (1982) *The Irresistible Diderot*, London. (Contains extracts from 60 articles by Diderot, in translation.)

References and further reading

Kafker, F.A. and S.L. (1988) *The Encyclopedists as individuals: a biographical dictionary of the Encyclopédie*, Studies on Voltaire and the Eighteenth Century, Oxford: The Voltaire Foundation. 257. (Comprehensive study of the contributors.)

Lough, J. (1968) *Essays on the Encyclopédie of Diderot and D'Alembert*, Oxford. (Detailed study of certain articles.)

—— (1971) *The Encyclopédie*, London. (Best general survey.)

Proust, J. (1962) *Diderot et l'Encyclopédie*, Paris. (Masterly account of Diderot's thought in relation to his articles.)

—— (1965) *L'Encyclopédie*, Paris. (Good introduction.)

Schwab, R.N. *et al.* (1971–84) *Inventory of the Encyclopédie*, Studies on Voltaire and the Eighteenth Century, Oxford: The Voltaire Foundation. 80, 83, 85, 91–3, 223.

Wilson, A.M. (1972) *Diderot*, New York. (Detailed biography.)

JOHN HOPE MASON

ENCYCLOPEDISTS, MEDIEVAL

The modern encyclopedic genre was unknown in the classical world. In the grammar-based culture of late antiquity, learned compendia, by both pagan and Christian writers, were organized around a text treated as sacred or around the canon of seven liberal arts and sciences, which were seen as preparatory to divine contemplation. Such compendia, heavily influenced by Neoplatonism, helped to unite the classical and Christian traditions and transmit learning, including Aristotelian logic, to the Middle Ages.

Writers in the encyclopedic tradition include figures such as Augustine and Boethius, both of whom were extremely influential throughout the medieval period. Other important writers included Macrobius, whose Saturnalia *spans a very wide range of subjects; Martianus Capella, whose* De nuptiis Philologiae et Mercurii *(The Marriage of Philology and Mercury) covers the seven liberal arts and sciences; Cassiodorus, who presents the arts as leading towards the comtemplation of the heavenly and immaterial; and Isidore, whose* Etymologies *became one of the most widely referred-to texts of the Middle Ages. These writers also had a strong influence which can be seen later in the period, particularly in the Carolingian Renaissance and again in the twelfth century.*

1 **Learned compendia and the encyclopedic tradition**
2 **Augustine**
3 **Macrobius**
4 **Martianus Capella**
5 **Boethius**
6 **Cassiodorus**
7 **Isidore of Seville**
8 **Conclusion**

1 Learned compendia and the encyclopedic tradition

The classical world produced nothing like the modern encyclopedia with its universal range and disconnected entries in alphabetical order. Instead, ancient scholars preferred to unify their knowledge by literary or philosophical means. By the first century BC the term 'encyclopedia' was often used, but it generally denoted a set of interconnected disciplines fit for upper class freemen (hence 'liberal') and propaedeutic in nature. The philosophers might see such disciplines as leading the mind from the material to the immaterial world, and thence to metaphysical philosophy. For most, the set included both mathematical and linguistic arts. With much fluctuation, there evolved a canon of seven interrelated liberal arts and sciences: grammar, rhetoric and dialectical logic (the medieval trivium), and arithmetic, geometry, music and astronomy (the medieval quadrivium). During the first three centuries AD, Middle Platonist and Neoplatonist philosophers strongly influenced the solidifying of this canon; indeed, it has been seen (controversially) as primarily their invention (Hadot 1984) (see NEOPLATONISM; PLATONISM, EARLY AND MIDDLE).

Various types of learned compendium existed, and it is possible to distinguish three particular types or genres. Genre A can be described as miscellaneous information, presented haphazardly, perhaps in the attractive and memorable dialogue form, as a gentleman's 'learned baggage' (to use Macrobius' phrase) and handbook of civilized conversation. An example is the *Attic Nights* of Aulus Gellius, written in the second century AD. In genre B, information is organized by disciplines, whether in a sequence of treatises or as a unitary work. Varro (116–27 BC) probably composed an encyclopedic sequence of volumes on the seven arts and sciences, with medicine and architecture added. Varro allegedly saw the

mathematical four as leading to contemplation of the immaterial; in this he may have been influenced by Neopythagorean philosophy (see NEO-PYTHAGOREANISM). In the first century AD, in his *Natural History*, the elder Pliny united his subject by themes of nature's divinity and human partnership with it; this allowed expansion into a wide range of information.

In the culture of late antiquity, dominated by the grammarian, a third type of compendium developed. In genre C, compendia were centred around some revered text, classical or biblical. These texts, which were often seen as inspired, could be allegorically interpreted and used as a source of cosmological, spiritual and metaphysical wisdom. Isidore, for example, drew extensively for his encyclopedia on both the *Hexaemeron* (Commentary on Genesis) of Ambrose (AD 339–97) and the commentaries on Vergil of Servius (*fl. c.*AD 400), whom Macrobius depicted as the model grammarian. To understand such sacred texts, encyclopedic learning, especially the skill in literary analysis owed to grammar and rhetoric, was seen as necessary and the texts themselves might serve as educational exemplars (see PATRISTIC PHILOSOPHY).

2 Augustine

As a young man, AUGUSTINE was strongly influenced by the Neoplatonists. Following his conversion to mainstream Christianity, he proposed a sequence of works on the seven arts and sciences, perhaps substituting philosophy for astronomy. He saw these as propaedeutic to a theology of Christian Neoplatonist type (Hadot 1984). He also increasingly saw them as handmaids to biblical exegesis (see his very influential *De doctrina christiana* (On Christian Instruction)). He apparently completed works on grammar and music only (the latter in dialogue form), but his *De civitate Dei* (The City of God) transmitted a vast range of learning in its replies to polytheists and pagan Neoplatonists.

3 Macrobius

Macrobius' *Saturnalia*, written *c.*AD 430, but set in the 380s, belongs partly to genre A. In their form, and as an exemplar of scholarly manners, these prandial conversations between Roman gentlemen owe much to Cicero and Aulus Gellius. However, their core (Books III–VI) consists of discussions of Vergil, seen as universally learned and inspired. Partly through and around these discussions, Macrobius transmitted views and information on literary style, allegorical technique, pagan ritual and theology, astronomy, physiology, etymology and general antiquarian topics.

For Macrobius, the other three inspired authors were HOMER, PLATO and CICERO. His Platonizing commentary on *The Dream of Scipio* (from Cicero's *Republic*) helped to transmit classical cosmological science to the Middle Ages, integrating it with Neoplatonist theology. This work is also important for its numerology, classification of the virtues and presentation of Platonist and Aristotelian disputes on the nature of the soul. It owed much to commentaries on Plato's *Timaeus* and *Republic* by PORPHYRY, and notably influenced the thirteenth-century encyclopedist Vincent of Beauvais.

4 Martianus Capella

Like Macrobius, Martianus was probably a pagan; he wrote at Carthage, perhaps around AD 470. His *De nuptiis Philologiae et Mercurii* (The Marriage of Philology and Mercury) belongs partly to genre B, systematically expounding and summarizing the Varronian canon of arts and sciences (omitting medicine and architecture). However, the work (a 'Menippean' mixture of prose and verse, like Varro's satires) also depicts, in an allegorical myth, the Neoplatonic apotheosis of the learned human soul, which returns to its heavenly home to become the bride of a god; on this marriage the arts and sciences attend as bridesmaids. Thus Martianus audaciously improved on Macrobius by creating his own sacred text: 'With its description of the kosmos, the fall and ascent of the soul, theurgic initiation, and an apotheosis, the work can be seen as a summa of pagan knowledge, religious and secular' (Shanzer 1986: 28).

Paradoxically, this was a work which, in terms of both form and content, had a profound influence on the Christian Middle Ages. In the ninth century, Johannes Scottus ERIUGENA drew extensively on it for his cosmology; in the tenth century, GERBERT OF AURILLAC made much use of the books on the quadrivium. Its influence was especially strong on the Platonists and cosmographers associated with the twelfth-century School of Chartres (see CHARTRES, SCHOOL OF). Alan of Lille owed much to it in his *De planctu naturae*, and also in his *Anticlaudianus*, a summa of the seven arts and sciences which depicts the ascent of Phronesis, with their help, to the Empyrean. BERNARD OF TOURS similarly has an ascent of Natura in his Menippean *De mundi universitate*.

Book IV of *De nuptiis*, on dialectic, was especially influential in the ninth to eleventh centuries. Martianus' logic was basically Aristotelian and syllogistic, depending much on Porphyry's *Isagoge*, which he perhaps knew in the fourth-century translation by MARIUS VICTORINUS; he may well have used a *Perihermeneias* (perhaps that of Apuleius in the second century) for categorical propositions, and the categorical syllogism. He was also affected by Stoic development of the hypothetical syllogism and by Stoic propositional logic, derived ultimately from Varro (see STOICISM). Like Boethius and Cassiodorus, Martianus transmitted the so-called *logica vetus* (old logic); this was partly superseded during the twelfth century by the *logica nova* (new logic), through the discovery of more sophisticated works of Aristotle (see ARISTOTELIANISM, MEDIEVAL; LANGUAGE, MEDIEVAL THEORIES OF; LOGIC, MEDIEVAL).

5 Boethius

BOETHIUS, writing in sixth-century Italy, was much influenced by the Neoplatonism of Macrobius and the fifth century Alexandrians. He planned, but never finished, complete translations of Plato and Aristotle and a series of introductions and translations for the seven arts and sciences; he is therefore another encyclopedic author. His *Institutio arithmetica* (Introduction to Arithmetic) and *Institutio musica* (Introduction to Music) survive, as do a commentary on Cicero's Topics, translations and commentaries for Porphyry's *Isagōgē* and Aristotle's *Prior Analytics*, *Categories* and *Perihermeneias*, and translations of Aristotle's *Topics* and *Sophistic Refutations*. In five treatises, he gave his own introduction to Peripatetic logic.

Eriugena, Gerbert of Aurillac, Abbo of Fleury, ANSELM and ABELARD all owed much to Boethius. His logic influenced the debate between realists and nominalists, and remained popular until the end of the fifteenth century. He also transmitted Pythagorean musical theory and Euclidean geometry.

6 Cassiodorus

Boethius' kinsman Cassiodorus, writing also in the sixth century, was a rhetorician rather than a philosopher and was an encyclopedist in all three genres. His *Variae* (letters drafted for barbarian monarchs) digress into a wide range of learning offering a model of cultivated discourse between ruler and subject, and were exploited later in the Middle Ages. His *Expositio Psalmorum* (Exposition on the Psalms) is partly conventional exegesis, but also developed the Psalms for Christians as an encyclopedic exemplar of the arts and sciences, especially rhetoric.

Cassiodorus' *Institutiones*, partly an intellectual rule for his monastery of Vivarium, were also meant for a wider audience, superseding a project for a

Roman school of Christian higher education. Book I is a kind of patristic and monastic encyclopedia. It gives an expanded bibliography of biblical texts, commentaries and works of relevant theology, as well as advice on exegesis, a list of church councils and information on history, geography, medicine, gardening and textual copying. Book II, which achieved a separate and wider circulation, is devoted to the seven arts and sciences. Like Augustine, Cassiodorus regarded these as essential to scriptural study; he also presents them as leading the soul towards the heavenly and immaterial, to the point where the Bible will deepen awareness of God. He treats the seven methodically, analysing and summarizing their salient points and advising on further reading. His canon is that of Varro and Martianus Capella, but he owes something also to the tradition of the fifth century Neoplatonists (especially, perhaps, AMMONIUS). From the latter he derives the order of his treatment, his influential distinction between the arts of the trivium and the disciplines of the quadrivium (the former deal with contingent matters, the latter with necessities) and his analysis of the subjects of philosophy: the disciplines belong to doctrinal or mathematical philosophy, which is in turn a branch of speculative philosophy.

His section on dialectic is based partly on the translations and commentaries of Boethius and Marius Victorinus, but perhaps also on Ammonius' commentary on Porphyry's *Isagōgē*. *Institutiones* II proved a highly valuable handbook in the early Middle Ages, and specially influenced two major figures of the Carolingian Renaissance, Alcuin and Hrabanus Maurus. The latter's *De institutione clericorum* integrated the arts and sciences into clerical education, as Cassiodorus had done (see CAROLINGIAN RENAISSANCE).

7 Isidore of Seville

Isidore's *Etymologies* or *Origins*, written in the early seventh century, was a new – though still grammar-based – departure, organizing knowledge around the histories and definitions of individual words. Indebted ultimately to Stoic theories of etymology, but more directly to Augustine's remarks on semiotics (especially in *De doctrina Christiana* II), Isidore assumed that the name of a thing gives a key to its nature. On this principle (partly rational, but also reflecting Neo-Pythagorean and biblical mysticism) he founded a twenty-book compendium, encyclopedic in range even by modern standards. Only the first four books deal with the seven arts and sciences (medicine is added as a second philosophy, healing the body as

philosophy does the soul), and the dictionary method precludes extensive expositions.

Following the tradition, Isidore sees the canon as steps to divine contemplation. From Book V onwards the work is less systematic, though by no means random in construction. Isidore follows trains of thought in which (for example) Christian studies (Books VI–VIII) conclude with a catalogue of heresies; heresies suggest pagan philosophies, philosophies suggest classical poetry and poetry suggests sibyls, mages and diviners. Book II, on rhetoric and dialectic, is based mainly on Cassiodorus, but Isidore made additions: there is a section on law, based on TERTULLIAN, and another on opposites (ultimately Aristotelian, and also treated by Martianus Capella). Etymologies in this book yielded useful translations of Greek technical terms.

Second-hand Stoicism influenced Isidore's views on cosmology and morality (see STOICISM). Although condemning EPICUREANISM, he retained the atomic theory, and extended it to numbers and language (Book XIII). He gave a brief survey of ancient philosophy (Book VIII), valuable despite its crudities. Also valuable was his exclusion of Christian theology and revelation from his logical definitions, and his strong assertion of the worth of dialectic (Book II); he affirmed the continuing relevance of philosophy, despite its dangers to the Christian (Books IV and VIII). The simple Latin, brief entries and lists of contents made the *Etymologies* ideal for reference; its survival in over 1,000 manuscripts attests its popularity. Curtius (1953: 23) has called it the basic book of the entire Middle Ages. Hrabanus Maurus adopted Isidore's method, and much of his contents, in his encyclopedia *On the Nature of Things*.

8 Conclusion

Late antiquity was a period of translations, florilegia, abridgements and other short guides to a variety of disciplines. As Boethius saw, these were vital when Greek east and Latin west were drifting apart, and educational institutions declining. It was also a time of tension between Christianity and the classical tradition. In the preservation of learning and eventual combination of the two roads to wisdom, the encyclopedists, pagan and Christian, played an essential part, thanks largely to the adaptability and spiritual attractions of the Neoplatonic philosophy which so strongly influenced their subject matter.

See also: MARIUS VICTORINUS; PATRISTIC PHILOSOPHY

References and further reading

Augustine (386) *De musica* (On Music), ed. J.-P. Migne, *Patrologia Latina*, vol. 32, Paris: J.-P. Migne, 1861; trans. R.C. Taliaferro in *Fathers of the Church*, vol. 4, New York: Fathers of the Church Inc., 1947.

—— (*c*.395–8) *De doctrina Christiana* (On Christian Doctrine), ed. J. Martin, *Corpus Christianorum*, Series Latina 32, Turnhout: Brepols, 1962; trans. J.J. Garrigan, Christian Instruction, in *Fathers of the Church*, vol. 2, New York: Fathers of the Church Inc., 1947. (A Bible-centred treatise on Christian education and rhetoric.)

—— (413–27) *De civitate Dei* (The City of God), ed. B. Dombart and A. Kalb, Leipzig: Teubner, 1928–9; trans. H. Bettenson, *The City of God*, Harmondsworth: Penguin Books, 1972. (A wide-ranging response to pagan criticism of Christianity, and exposition of Christian political theology.)

Boethius, A.M.S. (*c*.500–*c*.522) *Collected Works*, ed. J.-P. Migne, *Patrologia Latina*, Paris: J.-P. Migne, 1860, vols 63–4.

—— (*c*.500–*c*.522) *Institutio arithmetica* (Introduction to Arithmetic), ed. G. Friedlein, Leipzig: Teubner, 1867; trans. M. Masi, *Boethian Number Theory: A Translation of the 'De Institutione Arithmetica'*, in Studies in Classical Antiquity, vol. 6, Amsterdam: Rodopi, 1983.

—— (*c*.500–*c*.522) *Institutio musica* (Introduction to Music), ed. G. Friedlein, Leipzig: Teubner, 1867; trans. C.M. Bower, New Haven, CT: Yale University Press, 1989.

—— (*c*.500–*c*.522) *Commentarii in librum Aristotelis Peri hermenias* (Commentary on Aristotle's Perihermeneias), ed. K. Meiser, Leipzig: Teubner, 1887–90.

—— (*c*.500–*c*.522) *In Isagogen Porphyrii Commenta* (Commentaries on Porphyry's *Isagōgē*), ed. S. Brandt, Corpus Scriptorum Ecclesiasticorum Latinorum 48, Vienna and Leipzig: Tempsky & Freytag, 1906.

—— (*c*.500–*c*.522) *De hypotheticis syllogismis* (On Hypothetical Syllogisms), ed. L. Obertello, *Logicalia*, vol. 1, Brescia: Paideia editrice, 1969.

—— (*c*.500–*c*.522) Aristotelian translations and translation of Porphyry's *Isagoge*, ed. L. Minio-Paluello and B. Dod, *Aristoteles Latinus*, Brussels, Leiden, Bruges and Paris: Desclée De Brouwer, Brill, 1961–75.

—— (*c*.500–*c*.522) *De topicis differentiis* (On Topical Differences), trans. and commentary by E. Stump, *Boethius's De topicis differentiis*, Ithaca, NY: Cornell University Press, 1978.

Cassiodorus (506–37) *Variae*, ed. T. Mommsen, Berlin: Weidmann, 1894; selection trans. S.J.B. Barnish, *Variae*, Liverpool: Liverpool University Press, 1992. (State documents with learned digressions, written for the Ostrogothic kings of Italy.)

—— (*c*.540–*c*.555) *Expositio Psalmorum* (Exposition of the Psalms), ed. M. Adriaen, Corpus Christianorum, Series Latina 97–8, Turnhout: Brepols, 1958; trans. P.G. Walsh, *Explanation of the Psalms*, New York and Mahwah, NJ: Paulist Press, 1990–1. (A commentary on the Psalms which uses them as a textbook of rhetoric, logic and miscellaneous learning.)

—— (*c*.562) *Institutiones* (Institutes), ed. R.A.B. Mynors, Oxford: Clarendon Press, 1937; trans. L.W. Jones, *An Introduction to Divine and Human Readings by Cassiodorus Senator*, New York: Columbia University Press, 1946. (A Christian guide to sacred and secular learning.)

Cahiers d'Histoire Mondiale (1966), 9 (3). (A useful volume of articles on the history of encyclopedias; see especially articles by P. Grimal (459–82), M. de Gandillac (483–518) and J. Fontaine (519–38).)

Courcelle, P. (1969) *Late Latin Writers and their Greek Sources*, Cambridge, MA: Harvard University Press. (Translation from a French original. The work has chapters on Macrobius, Augustine, Boethius and Cassiodorus; influential, but to be used with caution.)

* Curtius, E.R. (1953) *European Literature and the Latin Middle Ages*, London: Routledge & Kegan Paul. (Translation from a German original by W.R. Trask. Useful on the role of rhetoric and etymology, and the afterlives of the encyclopedists; a literary rather than philosophical treatment.)

Fontaine, J. (1984) *Isidore de Séville et la Culture Classique dans l'Espagne Wisigothique* (Isidore of Seville and Classical Culture in Visigothic Spain), 2nd edn, Paris: Études Augustiniennes. (The fundamental study of Isidore in his own time.)

Gibson, M.T. (ed.) (1981) *Boethius: His Life, Thought and Influence*, Oxford: Blackwell. (Valuable chapters by J. Barnes, J. Caldwell, O. Lewry, and D. Pingree on Boethius as philosopher, musicologist and geometer, and his influence.)

* Hadot, I. (1984) *Arts Libéraux et Philosophie dans la Pensée Antique* (The Liberal Arts and Philosophy in Ancient Thought), Paris: Études Augustiniennes. (Controversially ascribes the canon of the seven arts and sciences to the Neoplatonists and Augustine; highly critical of Marrou (1938).)

Irvine, M. (1994) The Making of Textual Culture: 'Grammatica' and Literary Theory, 350–1100, Cambridge: Cambridge University Press. (An imaginative study, putting the encyclopedists in the context of a grammarian's world.)

Isidore (c.620–35) *Etymologiae* (Etymologies), ed. W.M. Lindsay, Oxford: Clarendon Press, 1911. (An encyclopedia organised around the histories and definitions of words. Translations of the separate books in various languages are in progress under the auspices of the Centre National des Recherches Scientifiques; among these note P.K. Marshall's English translation of Book II, Paris: Éditions des Belles Lettres, 1983.)

Laistner, M.L.W. (1957) *Thought and Letters in Western Europe, A.D. 500–1900*, London: Methuen. (Has material on Hrabanus Maurus, Cassiodorus and Isidore. Standard work, but should be used with caution.)

Macrobius (probably c.430) *Saturnalia*, ed. J. Willis, Leipzig: Teubner, 1970; trans. P.V. Davies, New York: Columbia University Press, 1969. (A symposiastic dialogue whose core is devoted to Vergil.)

—— (probably c.430) *Commentarii in Somnium Scipionis* (Commentary on the *Dream of Scipio*), trans. W.H. Stahl, New York: Columbia University Press, 1952. (A Platonizing commentary on a myth from Cicero's *Republic*.)

Marrou, H.-I. (1938) *Saint Augustin et la Fin de la Culture Antique* (Saint Augustine and the End of Ancient Culture), Bibliothèque des Écoles Françaises d'Athènes et de Rome, vol. 45, Paris: Éditions de Boccard. (Fundamental on the evolution of the canon of the seven arts and sciences in relation to Augustine.)

Martianus Capella (perhaps c.470) *De nuptiis Philologiae et Mercurii* (The Marriage of Philology and Mercury), ed. J. Willis, Leipzig: Teubner, 1983; trans. W.H. Stahl and E.L. Burge, *The Marriage of Philology and Mercury*, vol. II, trans. W.H. Stahl and E.L. Burge, *Martianus Capella and the Seven Liberal Arts*, New York: Columbia University Press, 1977. (Encyclopedic learning presented in an allegorical myth. Volume I of this work (with R. Johnson) gives a full introduction to Martianus Capella.)

O'Donnell, J.J. (1979) *Cassiodorus*, Berkeley, CA: University of California Press. (Useful, but uninspired.)

* Shanzer, D.R. (1986) *A Philosophical and Literary Commentary on Martianus Capella's De Nuptiis Philologiae et Mercurii*, Book I, Berkeley, CA: University of California Press. (As an introduction to Martianus, less comprehensive but more intelligent than Stahl and Burge's first volume.)

SAMUEL BARNISH

ENGELS, FRIEDRICH (1820–95)

Until the 1970s the most influential framework for understanding Marx's career and ideas was the one established by Engels. This framework was crucially related to his understanding of philosophy and its supposed culmination in Hegel's systematic and all-encompassing idealism.

Engels claimed that Marx had grounded Hegel's insights in a materialism that was coincident with the physical and natural sciences of his day, and that Marx had identified a dialectical method applicable to nature, history and thought. With respect to history, Marx was said to have formed a 'materialist conception', from which his analysis of capitalist society and its 'secret' of surplus value were derived. Together these intellectual features were the core of the 'scientific socialism' which, Engels argued, should form the theory, and inform the practice, of the worldwide socialist or communist movement. This was to abolish the poverty and exploitation necessarily engendered, he claimed, by modern industrial production.

Philosophically the tenets of dialectical and historical materialism have been defended and modified by orthodox communists and non-party Marxists, and expounded and criticized by political and intellectual opponents. The three laws of dialectics, and the doctrine that history is determined by material factors in the last instance, have been attacked as tautologous and indeterminate. Engels's view that scientific socialism is a defensible representation of Marx's project has also been challenged by textual scholars and historians.

1 Life and works
2 Political theory
3 Scientific socialism

1 Life and works

Engels rightly described himself as an 'autodidact in philosophy', and neither planned nor realized a career as a philosopher in his lifetime. Yet his works represent the founding texts of Marxism and of Marxist philosophy, in that they set an authoritative context through which to interpret the ideas of Karl MARX in a specifically philosophical way.

Born into a wealthy Rhineland family, and growing up amidst the disruption of rapid industrialization, the teenage Friedrich embarked on a paradoxical career. All his life he was reluctantly associated with the family's business interests, though politically he sympathized with the plight of the industrial working classes. Pursuing his political interests as a revolutionary populist required him to address intellectual elites and doctrinaires, particularly those within the burgeoning socialist movement and tiny communist parties. Yet the issues addressed in those works became ever more rarified and philosophical, despite the scorn that he always evinced for 'mere' philosophers and dabbling cranks, and his enthusiasm for political action.

Most paradoxically of all, Engels pronounced himself 'junior partner' to Marx, yet for many years the only way to identify, explicate and defend the *philosophical* content of Marx's work was through *Herrn Eugen Dührings Umwälzung der Wissenschaft* (*Anti-Dühring*), *Socialisme utopique et socialisme scientifique* (*Socialism: Utopian and Scientific*) and *Ludwig Feuerbach und der Ausgang der klassischen deutschen Philosophie* (*Ludwig Feuerbach and the End of Classical German Philosophy*), all written by Engels and published under his name alone. The claim that those works represent the views of Marx rests on retrospective textual exegesis, theories of 'partnership' and 'division of labour' between the two, and negative 'evidence' that Marx, who was Engels's economic dependent from the 1850s until his death in 1883, had opportunities to repudiate what Engels was saying. Engels himself contributed to this narrative, establishing his own works as the authoritative interpretation of Marx. Hence his self-description as 'second fiddle' is in reality somewhat paradoxical.

Bizarrely, Engels is also given credit for 'assuming paternity' for the illegitimate son of the Marx family's housemaid, supposedly to save Marx embarrassment and his wife the scandal. But the documentary evidence for this tale is highly suspect, and the view that paternity of this child was an issue for anyone at all before the 1960s, when the story first surfaced, rests on reading this lurid narrative back into the ambiguities of contemporary correspondence (Carver 1989: 162–71).

Engels had the image of a lifelong bachelor in public and a discreet bohemian in private, and his successive liaisons with the working-class Burns sisters (Mary and 'Lizzie') are well attested. Yet they now seem to fit all too easily into the nineteenth-century pattern wherein bourgeois males could 'keep' women of an inferior class in the suburbs or employ them in a respectable function as housekeeper, whilst presuming in every way on their economic dependence. Engels married 'Lizzie' only when it was clear that she was dying and could not be Mrs/Frau Engels in his Anglo-German milieu, nor survive him as a claimant on his estate. These liaisons were childless, and it is likely that both women were lifelong illiterates, or nearly so.

Engels himself was an accomplished writer from his early twenties in German and English, fluent in French, and later a student and correspondent in numerous other languages. His library and papers, including the collection of manuscripts and other materials inherited from Marx, represented an important intellectual resource for the socialist and communist movement from his death until the dissolution of Soviet-style communism in the 1980s, not least the notebooks posthumously published as *Dialektik der Natur* (*The Dialectics of Nature*), from which an 'official' philosophy of science was derived (see DIALECTICAL MATERIALISM).

2 Political theory

By the time he was nineteen, Engels's intellectual and political interests had moved from a heady combination of revolutionary liberalism and romantic nationalism to the Young Hegelian perspective then current in the universities, though he was never officially able to be a student. From a twentieth-century perspective this movement seems an intellectual cabal, but Engels's apprehension of these debates was overwhelmingly political. In a regime where politics itself was almost wholly an illegitimate activity, any form of criticism was by definition subversion and inevitably confined to a small circle of writers, publishers and readers.

Engels can be distinguished from others in the school by his unusual interest in modern technology and applied sciences, and in his preoccupation with the industrial working classes, existing and prospective. Within a short time he was contributing to the *Rheinische Zeitung*, most notably on the social science of political economy, as yet little appreciated in Germany, and on attempts to discern its place within Hegel's overall system. Thus Engels first met the earnest Dr Marx and the communist Moses Hess on a brief visit to the editorial collective at Cologne in 1842, whilst *en route* to a further posting with the family manufactures at Manchester.

In England Engels wrote in both German and English on 'the social question' and the politics of class conflict, giving particular attention to socialism or communism (the terms were largely indistinguishable then). This was conceived as a system of cooperative ownership of productive resources and an egalitarian, non-monetary system of distribution applicable to society at large, combined with institutions for democratic decision-making. Engels's *Umrisse zu einer Kritik der Nationalökonomie* (*Outlines of a Critique of Political Economy*) argued that a developing rationality in history could be discerned in both economic theory and practice. Applying a Hegelian dialectic of successive negations to the concepts 'free trade' and 'competition', he derived the necessity of worsening economic crises as his result, and the tenets of communism and the politics of class struggle as a resolution. Moreover in *Die Lage der arbeitenden Klasse in England* (*The Condition of the Working Class in England*) he produced an impassioned documentary and eyewitness survey of proletarian poverty and exploitation in modern industry.

On his return to Germany in 1844 Engels continued his career as a political agitator and socialist pamphleteer, this time in particular association with Marx, and the two produced three collaborative works: *Die heilige Familie* (*The Holy Family*) (by Engels and Marx, though with separately signed chapters), the manuscript *Die deutsche Ideologie* (*The German Ideology*) (posthumously published as the work of Marx and Engels), and their joint, though unsigned, masterpiece *Manifest der kommunistischen Partei* (*Manifesto of the Communist Party*).

During the revolutionary events of 1848–9 Engels assisted Marx, who had assumed editorship of the *Neue Rheinische Zeitung* in Cologne. Although Engels took advantage of the need to flee political repression from resurgent monarchists by making a walking tour through Burgundy in the autumn of 1848, he also saw active service in the spring of 1849 as liberal insurgents retreated in a more or less orderly way to the Swiss border. Making his way to England, Engels settled gradually but firmly into a life away from Germany, from partisan politics in either country, and from direct engagement with economic theory or social conditions, other than through a role, largely self-assumed, as publicist, popularizer and eventually editor for Marx.

3 Scientific socialism

Philosophically, Engels's distinctive contributions were the terms 'materialist conception of history' and the 'laws of dialectics', which were assigned to Marx but explicated in various reviews, letters, introductions and texts. The assignment of these terms to Marx is itself questionable, and the explications by Engels are neither as full nor as tightly written as his reputation suggests.

Marx formulated and employed an 'outlook', occasionally self-identified as 'materialist' (in opposition to both idealism and 'traditional' materialism), and used terms such as 'science', 'law' and 'dialectic' in his works (though much more rarely than most commentaries suggest). But it was Engels who insisted that Marx's presuppositions included a matter–consciousness dichotomy, that his works were part of a system of Hegelian proportions, that his politically engaged social science was inclusive of the

natural sciences of the day (including Darwinian biology as well as physical chemistry), and that a methodology derived from Hegel's presumed 'dialectic' was crucial for Marx and for understanding his achievements.

In Engels's commentaries, Marx's 'materialist conception of history' included both the quoted view that 'the mode of production of material life conditions the social, political and intellectual life-process in general', and the gloss that 'political action and its results originated in material causes'. Thus Marx's 'guiding thread' was said to be the 'great law of motion in history', but in Engels's version it emerged with a further layer of philosophical ambiguity. Engels's qualifications – that 'the production and reproduction of real life' is the 'ultimately', but not the only, 'determining element' in history – could never allay the additional difficulties that he imposed on what were already problematic, and arguably for Marx, quite marginal formulations.

The 'laws of dialectics' assigned to Marx were formulated by Engels as reworkings of Hegel's insights into a modern 'science of interconnections, in contrast to metaphysics'. He suggested three: 'transformation of quantity into quality and vice versa', 'interpenetration of opposites' and 'negation of the negation'. He described these as causal and invariable laws of motion forcing their way through the innumerable changes that can be observed in natural phenomena, human history, and 'thought' or logic, and maintained that they were validated by deduction. The circularity of such observations and the tautologous character of such laws were not apparent to Engels, and his more extravagant claims to link those ideas to a Marxian 'system' were not in fact published until after Marx's death (Carver 1983: 129–41).

Engels's 'scientific socialism' grounded the intellectual wing of the socialist and communist movement firmly in German philosophy, which he presumed had culminated in Hegel. The overarching project of his life was to link the world of progressive politics with the truths that he believed could be discerned from a philosophical system spanning the material, social and conceptual worlds, conceived developmentally. Among those truths, he alleged, was Marx's concept of 'surplus value'. This and other truths identified by Marx were said by Engels to be critical elements in a revolutionary political strategy. But Engels was not himself expert at the practicalities of getting from philosophical ideas to political action, nor was his philosophy capable of generating a concept of human agency that was philosophically defensible or politically useful.

See also: HEGELIANISM §3; MARXISM, WESTERN §1; MARXIST PHILOSOPHY OF SCIENCE; MARXIST PHILOSOPHY, RUSSIAN AND SOVIET; SOCIALISM;

List of works

Engels, F. (1844) *Umrisse zu einer Kritik der Nationalökonomie*, trans. M. Milligan, *Outlines of a Critique of Political Economy*, in K. Marx and F. Engels, *Collected Works*, London: Lawrence & Wishart, 1975, vol. 3, 418–43. (Pioneering attempt to subject political economy to philosophical analysis.)

—— (1845) *Die Lage der arbeitenden Klasse in England*, trans. F. Kelly-Wischnewestzky, *The Condition of the Working Class in England*, in K. Marx and F. Engels, *Collected Works*, London: Lawrence & Wishart, 1975, vol. 4, 295–583. (A survey, still very readable, of the horrors of early nineteenth-century industrialization.)

—— (1878–9) *Herrn Eugen Dührings Umwälzung der Wissenschaft*, trans. E. Burns, *Anti-Dühring*, in K. Marx and F. Engels, *Collected Works*, London: Lawrence & Wishart, 1987, vol. 25, 5–309. (Polemical work incorporating Engels's influential interpretation and defence of Marx.)

—— (1880) *Socialisme utopique et socialisme scientifique*, trans. *Socialism: Utopian and Scientific*, in K. Marx and F. Engels, *Selected Works in One Volume*, London: Lawrence & Wishart, 1968, 375–428. (Three chapters of *Anti-Dühring* revised, published as a pamphlet and very widely translated and circulated.)

—— (1884) *Der Ursprung der Familie, des Privateigentums und des Staats*, trans. *The Origin of the Family, Private Property and the State*, in K. Marx and F. Engels, *Selected Works in One Volume*, London: Lawrence & Wishart, 1968, 449–583. (Engels's attempt to account for the origin of women's oppression and the evolution of private property in prehistory by using a social Darwinian theory of sexual selection as well as gendered explanations of economic development.)

—— (1886) *Ludwig Feuerbach und der Ausgang der klassischen deutschen Philosophie*, trans. *Ludwig Feuerbach and the End of Classical German Philosophy*, in K. Marx and F. Engels, *Selected Works in One Volume*, London: Lawrence & Wishart, 1968, 584–622. (First published as a review, this is a history of German philosophy, placing Marx's materialism at its culmination and identifying it as an inversion of Hegelian idealism and arguing its coincidence with natural science.)

—— (1925) *Dialektik der Natur*, trans. C. Dutt, *The Dialectics of Nature*, in K. Marx and F. Engels,
Collected Works, London: Lawrence & Wishart, 1987, vol. 25, 311–588. (Notes comprising a philosophical analysis of the subject matter and methods of nineteenth-century natural science, including the 'laws of dialectics'.)

Engels, F. and Marx, K. (1845) *Die heilige Familie*, trans. R. Dixon and C. Dutt, *The Holy Family*, in K. Marx and F. Engels, *Collected Works*, London: Lawrence & Wishart, 1975, vol. 4, 5–209. (An attack on romantic, utopian and philosophical socialists of the 1840s, but incorporating interesting early formulations of Marx's 'outlook'.)

—— (1932) *Die deutsche Ideologie*, trans. W. Lough, *The German Ideology*, in K. Marx and F. Engels, *Collected Works* vol. 5, London: Lawrence & Wishart, 1976, 19–581. (Foundational manuscript, still not accessible in a properly edited version, nor adequately interpreted yet as an integrated work, but essential reading as an important exposition of Marx's 'outlook' in Part One.)

—— (1848) *Manifest der kommunistischen Partei*, trans. S. Moore, *Manifesto of the Communist Party*, in K. Marx and F. Engels, *Collected Works*, London: Lawrence & Wishart, 1976, vol. 6, 477–519. (Still the best introduction to Marx's 'outlook', particularly the centrality of class struggle, and innocent of Engels's later interpretive framework, save in the footnotes.)

References and further reading

Arthur, C. J. (ed.) (1996) *Engels Today: A Centenary Appreciation*, London: Macmillan. (Collection of original articles covering aspects of Engel's work that are currrently of interest.)

* Carver, T. (1983) *Marx and Engels: The Intellectual Relationship*, Brighton: Harvester Wheatsheaf. (A detailed textual study of similarities and differences between the works of the two men).

* —— (1989) *Friedrich Engels: His Life and Thought*, Basingstoke: Macmillan. (Intellectual biography focusing on Engels's career before he met Marx, and including a detailed guide to further reading.)

Henderson, W.O. (1976) *The Life of Friedrich Engels*, London: Frank Cass, 2 vols. (Valuable for factual detail.)

Mayer, G. (1934) *Friedrich Engels*, The Hague: Martinus Nijhoff, 2 vols; repr. Cologne: Kiepenheuer & Witsch, 1971. (Inspirational but out of date and somewhat uncritical 'classic' biography in German.)

Rubel, M. (1981) 'The "Marx Legend", or Engels, Founder of Marxism', in *Rubel on Marx*, ed. Joseph O'Malley and Keith Algozin, Cambridge and New York: Cambridge University Press, 15–25. (Courageous paper dating from 1970 questioning Engels's own account of his role *vis-à-vis* Marx, and thus casting doubt on all 'standard' accounts of Marxism.)

Stedman Jones, G. (1973) 'Engels and the End of Classical German Philosophy', *New Left Review* 79: 17–36. (Brief but promising inquiry into Engels's appropriation of idealist philosophy.)

—— (1977) 'Engels and the Genesis of Marxism', *New Left Review* 106: 79–104. (Brief but detailed study of Engels's framework for interpreting Marx.)

Steger, M and Carver, T. (eds) (1997) *Engels after Marx*, College Park, PA: Pennsylvania University Press. (Collection of original articles covering 'identity', 'philosophy', 'politics' and 'legacy'.)

TERRELL CARVER

ENGINEERING AND ETHICS

Engineering ethics is that form of applied or professional ethics concerned with the conduct of engineers. Though engineers do many different things, they share a common history, which includes codes of ethics. Most codes explicitly declare public health, safety and welfare to be 'paramount'. Many questions of engineering ethics concern interpretation of 'public', 'safety' and 'paramount'. Engineers also have important obligations to client and employer, including confidentiality, proper response to conflict of interest, stewardship of resources, and honesty (not only avoiding false statements but volunteering certain information). Each engineer also has obligations to other engineers and to the profession as a whole.

1 The profession of engineering
2 Ethics and engineering
3 Topics in engineering ethics

1 The profession of engineering

'Engineering' as an honorific term suggesting both precision and success is often used where it does not belong. The pyramids are sometimes described as 'works of engineering', though engineers had nothing to do with them. 'Social engineering', 're-engineering' and even 'genetic engineering' – though technologies or applied sciences – are no more engineering than architecture or medicine is.

What, then, is 'engineering'? Unfortunately, there is no wholly satisfactory answer. It is, of course, what engineers do, but engineers do many things. They design machinery, chemical plants, harbours, bridges,

office buildings, electrical grids, and other complex systems, manage their construction, oversee their operation, and plan their disposal. Though other occupations may do such things too (for example, architects also design buildings), engineers differ from these others in how they do it. Engineering is a certain way of doing such things. This way of doing things has a history; it is that history, rather than any abstract idea, that defines engineering.

The English word 'engineer' comes from French. The first people to be called 'engineers' were soldiers associated with 'engines of war' (such as cannons and siege towers). They were engineers only in the sense that they operated (or otherwise worked with) an 'engine' (that is, a complex device for some useful purpose). In 1676, the French organized these 'engineers' into a special unit, the *corps du génie*. Within two decades, the *corps* was known all over Europe for unusual achievements in military construction. When another country borrowed the French word 'engineering' for use in its own army, it was for the sort of activity the *corps du génie* engaged in.

At first, the *corps du génie* was more like an organization of masters and apprentices than a modern profession. Only during the 1700s did the French slowly come to understand what they wanted in an *officier du génie* and how to get it by formal education. By the end of the 1700s, they had a curriculum from which today's engineering curriculum differs only in detail; they had also invented engineering as an occupation distinguished from that of other builders by its knowledge of modern physics, chemistry and mathematics, its skill in organization, and its concern with utility rather than beauty, and from the sciences by its focus on making rather than knowing. Civilian engineering is a branch of this (originally) military tree.

So far, this is a history of an occupation. The history of a profession tells how people engaged in a certain occupation organized to hold each other to standards beyond what law, market, and morality would otherwise demand. The history of a profession is the history of organizations, standards of competence, and standards of conduct. For engineering, that history tells of a slow shift from granting membership based on connection with large construction projects, practical invention, or other technological achievements to granting it based on two more demanding requirements. One requirement – a certain sort of knowledge – is occupational. This requirement is now typically identified with a degree in engineering. The other requirement – a commitment to use that knowledge in certain ways (that is, according to engineering's code of ethics) – is professional (see PROFESSIONAL ETHICS).

2 Ethics and engineering

'Ethics' (in this context) can be used in three senses: (a) as a synonym for ordinary morality; (b) as the name of a philosophical study attempting to understand morality as a rational undertaking; or (c) as the name of certain special standards of conduct governing members of a group in virtue of their membership (see MORALITY AND ETHICS §§1–2).

In the first sense, engineering ethics is the application of ordinary moral rules, principles, or ideals to circumstances involving engineering. Neither philosophers nor codes of professional ethics have more than an educational or heuristic role. In the second sense, engineering ethics consists of attempts to offer a reasoned understanding (a theory) of how ordinary morality should guide engineering. In this sense, engineering ethics is just a subdivision of moral theory ('philosophical ethics'). But in the third sense, engineering ethics resembles law. Just as a law (or legal system) applies only to certain moral agents, those within its jurisdiction, so engineering ethics would apply only to certain moral agents, engineers. And just as law includes the interpretation, application, and justification of particular laws, so engineering ethics would include the interpretation, application and justification of engineering's special standards. The philosophical contribution to engineering ethics (in this sense) resembles legal philosophy's contribution to law, more a sorting of concepts and arguments than an application of moral theory.

Formal codes of engineering ethics did not appear in England before the mid-1800s, in the United States before 1900, or in Germany before the 1950s. While many professions, especially law and medicine, make a commitment to the profession's code of ethics a formal requirement for admission, engineering has not, except for licensed Professional Engineers. Instead, the expectation of commitment reveals itself when an engineer is found to have violated the code of ethics. The defence, 'I'm an engineer but I didn't promise to follow the code and therefore did nothing wrong', is never accepted. The profession answers, 'You committed yourself to the code when you claimed to be an engineer.'

While engineering ethics (in our third sense) dates from the 1800s, its philosophical study (ethics in our second sense) dates only from the 1970s. The field is still taking shape, working out its relation with moral theory, philosophy of technology, and philosophy of the professions.

Engineering ethics does not yet have a settled place in the college curriculum. In philosophy departments, classes in engineering ethics are often called 'Moral Problems in Engineering'; in engineering departments, 'Issues in Professionalism'. A course in engineering ethics, whether taught in a philosophy or an engineering department, will cover much about the history and organization of engineering.

3 Topics in engineering ethics

One topic of engineering ethics is the status of the code of ethics itself. (There are, in fact, several codes, though differences are relatively small.) Is a code just a statement of what morality would require of engineers, code or no code, or does it demand more of engineers than morality does? If it demands more, on what basis, if any, can it claim obedience from engineers? Is the claim legal or moral? If moral, does it rest on an implicit promise or on some other moral consideration (see PROMISING)?

Almost any code of engineering ethics provides a good checklist of major topics of engineering ethics. We may divide the other topics into four large categories. The first category concerns obligations to the public. Though the first codes of ethics emphasized personal honour and loyalty to client or employer, today most emphasize the public health, safety and welfare. Indeed, many codes make that consideration 'paramount'. Among questions dealt with under this obligation are: Who are the public? (Citizens of other countries or just fellow citizens? Employees of one's own company or just 'ordinary people'?) How safe is 'safe' (see RISK)? What is the public welfare? Does treating the public health, safety or welfare as paramount mean that an engineer must sometimes blow the whistle on his employer?

The second category concerns obligations to employer or client. Engineers are supposed to be faithful agents or trustees of their employer or client. Not only should they protect trade secrets, maintain confidentiality, avoid (or, at least, reveal) conflicts of interest, make clear the limits of their expertise, and try to use resources efficiently, they should also make sure that an employer or client understands the full implications of any decision in which an engineer is involved. Where an employer or client is a large corporation, there are special problems of determining *who* must understand for the employer or client to understand.

The third category concerns obligations to other engineers. Not only should engineers not discriminate against one another or compete unfairly; they have an obligation to provide engineers under their supervision with opportunities for professional development.

The fourth category, obligations to the profession, is a miscellany of questions. Engineers have an obligation to increase the competence and prestige of the engineering profession. Are they then sometimes obliged to reveal their employer's trade secrets to the profession? Engineers have an obligation to make public statements on engineering matters only in an objective and truthful manner. How forceful can an engineer's manner become without ceasing to be objective? Do engineers have an obligation to participate in engineering societies? What is the relation of this obligation to that of faithful agent and trustee of the employer or client?

See also: RESPONSIBILITIES OF SCIENTISTS AND INTELLECTUALS; TECHNOLOGY AND ETHICS

References and further reading

Board of Ethical Review, National Society of Professional Engineers (1965–3) *Opinions of the Board of Ethical Review*, Arlington, VA: NSPE Publications, National Society of Professional Engineers, vols I–II. (Several hundred ethics cases, indexed by subject and with (official) discussion, applying NSPE Code.)

Davis, M. (1991) 'Thinking Like an Engineer: The Place of a Code of Ethics in the Practice of a Profession', *Philosophy & Public Affairs* 20 (2): 150–7. (Defends role of codes in engineering ethics, using the case of the 'Challenger' explosion (January 1986); example of what is being done.)

Elbaz, S.W. (1990) *Professional Ethics and Engineering: A Resource Guide*, Arlington, VA: National Institute of Engineering Ethics. (Designed for someone thinking of teaching engineering ethics; includes useful bibliography.)

Harris, C.E., Pritchard, M.S., and Rabins, M.J. (1995) *Engineering Ethics: Concepts and Cases*, Belmont, CA: Wadsworth Publishing. (Code-based approach to field; good bibliography.)

Johnson, D.G. (1991) *Ethical Issues in Engineering*, Englewood Cliffs, NJ: Prentice Hall. (Standard collection of readings, useful for introduction to issues.)

Ladenson, R.F., Choromokos, J., d'Anjou, E., Pimsler, M., and Rosen, H. (1980) *A Selected Bibliography of Professional Ethics and Social Responsibility in Engineering*, Chicago, IL: Center for the Study of Ethics in the Professions at Illinois Institute of Technology. (Old, but extensive and wide-ranging bibliography.)

Martin, M.W. and Schinzinger, R. (1983) *Ethics in Engineering*, New York: McGraw-Hill, revised 2nd edn, 1989. (Treats engineering as social experimentation.)

Schlossberger, E. (1993) *The Ethical Engineer*, Philadelphia, PA: Temple University Press. (Emphasizes

morality, rather than codes, in analyzing issues in engineering ethics.)

MICHAEL DAVIS

ENLIGHTENMENT, CONTINENTAL

The Enlightenment is frequently portrayed as a campaign on behalf of freedom and reason as against dogmatic faith and its sectarian and barbarous consequences in the history of Western civilization. Many commentators who subscribe to this view find the Enlightenment's cosmopolitan opposition to priestly theology to be dangerously intolerant itself, too committed to uniform ideals of individual self-reliance without regard to community or diversity, or to recasting human nature in the light of science. Modern debates about the nature of the Enlightenment have their roots in eighteenth-century controversies about the arts and sciences and about ideas of progress and reason and the political consequences of promoting them. Even when they shared common objectives, eighteenth-century philosophers were seldom in agreement on substantive issues in epistemology or politics. If they were united at all, it was by virtue only of their collective scepticism in rejecting the universalist pretensions of uncritical theology and in expressing humanitarian revulsion at crimes committed in the name of sacred truth.

1   **Modern assessments**
2   **Appraisals in the eighteenth century**
3   **Its diversity and contrasts**

1   Modern assessments

The eighteenth-century Enlightenment is the only period of modern history described, most often by its detractors but sometimes also by its admirers, as a single intellectual movement or campaign, orchestrated around a common set of themes. Its leading thinkers, comprising Europe's first intelligentsia, are perceived as jointly committed to liberating mankind from the tyrannies of dead dogma and blind faith. They held that the barbarism of European culture in its Dark Ages had been due to ignorance and bigotry, and that the Crusades, the Inquisition and sectarian wars had been responsible for retarding the moral development of individuals and fragmenting their political communities. Unlike earlier philosophers who had sought to interpret the world, the advocates of Enlightenment were determined to change it. Their frequent engagement in public policy or status as civil servants and advisors to princes, their esteem for science over tradition, their empiricism and apparent preference for applied philosophy over metaphysics, have made them seem wedded to a belief in the unity of theory and practice. These same features of their doctrines or professions have in turn inspired the opposition of critics who, like Edmund BURKE among their contemporaries, judged Enlightenment philosophy responsible for the French Revolutionary overthrow of the *ancien régime*, or who, like Alasdair MacIntyre today, blame it for inaugurating the monolithic philosophical trappings of modernity. Such charges against a so-called 'Enlightenment Project' have figured centrally in hostile interpretations of its significance over the past 200 years. On the one hand, both its conservative and liberal critics, such as Hegel at the turn of the nineteenth century or Jacob Talmon in the mid-twentieth century, have condemned its universalist philosophy of the rights of man, which they see as having been unsheathed in the Jacobin Terror and subsequently in the totalitarian regimes of our own day, whose vast schemes of social engineering are said to be inspired by its supposition that human nature may be recast like pliant clay. On the other hand, communitarian and postmodernist opponents of the Enlightenment, such as Charles Taylor in the first instance and Michel FOUCAULT in the second, have equally decried its moral atomism and superficial understanding of the self, or alternatively its espousal of uniformitarian doctrines which leave scant room for individual diversity or cultural pluralism (see COMMUNITY AND COMMUNITARIANISM; POSTMODERNISM). Most hostile of all are those commentators who have followed the contention of Max HORKHEIMER and Theodor ADORNO that the Enlightenment's purely instrumental grasp of scientific rationality paved the way to the organization of genocide in the Second World War.

Much of the criticism of the Enlightenment Project has been concentrated upon two of its most seminal figures – Adam SMITH and Immanuel KANT – the first because his liberal philosophy appears to remove all notions of absolute value from interpersonal relations, the second because his account of moral duty and autonomy seems to disregard the complex motives which actually inspire human action. In his attachment to universal rules legislated in the light of abstract reason; in his insistence (in modern parlance) upon preferring the right over the good; in his impartiality and essentially cosmopolitan indifference to difference, Kant in particular has come to be regarded as the principal spokesman for the vacuous subjectivism and empty formalism of the whole Enlightenment Project. The philosophical hermeneu-

tics of Hans-Georg GADAMER takes up a fundamentally Hegelian position in criticizing Kant's, and therefore the Enlightenment's, abstract notion of individual self-awareness on account of its deracination from real experience. But Jürgen HABERMAS, in reaffirming the critical stance of Kant's philosophy, equally upholds the emancipatory aims of that same Enlightenment in its subjection of traditional beliefs to the scrutiny of reason, which cannot but undermine tradition's authority.

Among modern social philosophers, Habermas is particularly well-disposed to what he takes to be mainstream Enlightenment thought, but the *Oxford English Dictionary* suggests an anti-Enlightenment bias within the English language itself, in identifying much the same perspective which Habermas applauds as 'superficial intellectualism' marked by 'insufficient respect for authority and tradition', adding that a *philosophe* – in the French language associated above all with the Enlightenment – is 'one who philosophizes erroneously'. Among eighteenth-century figures, only Hume and Kant, and occasionally Berkeley or Condillac, have been acknowledged by historians of philosophy as genuinely first-rate thinkers. The contributions of Hume and Kant to modern empiricism and rationalism, respectively, have nevertheless been considerable. When MacIntyre takes issue with Alfred Ayer and Richard Hare, he challenges contemporary Oxford exponents of two perspectives of an Enlightenment Project which he claims was bound to fail. The liberal principles of John Rawls' influential *Theory of Justice* (1971) also spring above all from the moral philosophy of Kant (see RAWLS, J.).

2 Appraisals in the eighteenth century

Debates of the nineteenth and twentieth century about the Enlightenment's significance in European intellectual history take up themes already pursued in the eighteenth century by both its protagonists and critics, particularly in France in the 1750s in connection with the *Encyclopédie* of DIDEROT and D'ALEMBERT (1751–72) and in Prussia in the 1780s and 1790s with regard to the limits of reason and the political implications of promoting its use. More than any other work of the eighteenth century the *Encyclopédie* may be regarded as the centrepiece of the Enlightenment, representing the self-image of an age of reason and invention much like the Crystal Palace would exhibit the character of an age of science and industry a century later. Assembled by contributors who formed an international republic of letters or party of humanity, the *Encyclopédie* was conceived as a reasoned dictionary of the arts and sciences, a modern monument to a classical ideal, inherited above all from Plato, that the promotion of knowledge and the pursuit of virtue should go hand in hand (see ENCYCLOPEDISTS, EIGHTEENTH-CENTURY).

In his preliminary discourse published in its first volume in 1751, D'Alembert, with Diderot the *Encyclopédie*'s joint overall editor, delivered what has sometimes been described as the manifesto of the Enlightenment as a whole. Taking stock of the achievements of the human mind through works of individual genius, D'Alembert lavished praise upon his precursors, including Bacon, Descartes and Leibniz among the philosophical and scientific giants of the seventeenth century. But no previous age had made such great progress along the path of knowledge as his own, he argued, in part because men of genius had turned their attention to the liberal and mechanical arts with the same enthusiasm as others had embraced pure science, in part because the human mind's productions had come to form a veritable library of useful information for a world in which prejudice could be overcome through reading. The *Encyclopédie* was an agent of general enlightenment, he thought, because it was accessible to a literate audience, transmitted in a vulgar rather than arcane language.

Some of these notions were borrowed from FONTENELLE and other progressively-minded contributors to the early eighteenth-century *Querelle des anciens et des modernes*, and Diderot was to develop them further in his own article, *encyclopédie*, which appeared in volume five, of comparable length to D'Alembert's discourse, and equally designed to pay tribute to human industry and scientific inventiveness, which pushed back the frontiers of knowledge and thereby roused mankind from the dogmatic slumbers of its fundamentalist faiths. Such principles articulated one of the most central doctrines of French *philosophes* in particular, who like their patron saint, Voltaire, warmed to the achievements of English science, civility and toleration, which they characteristically took to be more robust guides to enlightenment than the predominantly classical, more archaic, forms of French culture and taste.

They were to figure as well as in the celebrations of the progress of the human mind produced by Turgot around the same time as D'Alembert's discourse, and above all, in the course of the French Revolution by CONDORCET, D'Alembert's successor as permanent secretary of the French Académie des Sciences. Condorcet's sketch of the nine historical epochs through which civilization has passed, and of the tenth epoch to come, is particularly notable for its anticlericalism, its devotion to science, its faith in the power of reason to bring about societal change, and

its optimistic tone adopted at the darkest moment of the French Revolution. For the past 200 years it has been regarded as the most characteristic expression of the idea of progress in Enlightenment thought, turning D'Alembert's focus upon books and treatises to more political ends and wider social objectives.

Just before D'Alembert's preliminary discourse was published, another work appeared, however, which he cites because it pursues an altogether different line of argument about the connection between virtue and knowledge. This was Rousseau's *Discourse on the Arts and Sciences* (1750), in which he contends that the trappings of civilization are but garlands of flowers around the iron chains by which mankind is weighed down (see ROUSSEAU, J.-J.). The philosopher of nature as opposed to culture thus launched the first of his many attacks upon his own age of enlightenment. Although neither Nietzsche nor Foucault would ever recognize a debt to Rousseau in their own conjunctions of *savoir* with *pouvoir*, their critiques of the Enlightenment followed a path already mapped by him, which challenged the main thrust of the *Encyclopédie* at the moment of its birth.

The German debate on the meaning of enlightenment was launched more than thirty years later, by way of an article by the theologian Johann Friedrich Zöllner which appeared in the *Berlinische Monatsschrift* in December 1783. To the question he put, 'What is enlightenment?', numerous replies were submitted by correspondents in the course of the next several years, some published in other journals. The most important of these were by Moses MENDELSSOHN, who was one of Rousseau's German translators, and by Immanuel Kant. Mendelssohn sought to meet the objections to enlightenment posed by those most anxious to protect human society from overwrought change, and he argued that the discretion of each individual was a better censor of dangerous ideas than the full force of the law. To keep the inventiveness of enterprising persons in check on account of the hazards they raised was to legislate against human progress, which was a matter not for man but for Providence, he maintained, admitting that there were nevertheless certain truths useful to individuals but harmful to citizens.

In his short essay 'Was ist Aufklärung?', which appeared in the *Berlinische Monatsschrift* in December 1784, Kant introduced a similar distinction between the individual and the citizen, claiming that enlightenment was more difficult to achieve in the private than in the public domain, because of each person's ingrained immaturity or lack of courage to rely upon their own understanding. It was in the public sphere, however, rather than in private that it was most imperative for enlightenment to be gained, he insisted, and what was needed above all for its triumph was freedom. The century of Frederick the Great was not yet an enlightened age, but it was, Kant remarked, an age of enlightenment in which the obstacles to mankind's self-reliance and self-guidance were being gradually lifted. Over a decade later, he was to draw a still more optimistic portrait of the disinterested sympathy which would be felt by all mankind as it sought to live under republican constitutions which could have no interest in wars. In his essay *The Contest of the Faculties* (1798) he argued, in prophetic voice, that the human race was continually improving and that even apparent reversals like the Jacobin Terror would not arrest its further moral progress.

3 Its diversity and contrasts

Such differences of emphasis between French and German asessments of the Enlightenment lend warrant to the proposition, most often put forward by historians against philosophers, that any notion of a coherent and collective 'Enlightenment Project' is little more than a myth. French *philosophes*, Scottish moralists and German pietists, even when they managed to agree amongst themselves, were not committed to the same cause, it is suggested – French thinkers in particular proving characteristically more radical than their counterparts elsewhere, not least because, for the most part writers without university appointments or official duties as state servants, they were more free to speak their minds. The undeniable truth of that contention points towards greater specificity in identifying Enlightenment philosophies without obscuring the genuinely collective enterprise in which their authors were often engaged.

Thanks to a variety of moral weeklies, literary periodicals and eventually newspapers, and to an international book trade, both authorized and clandestine, philosophical essays, discourses, treatises and encyclopedias circulated on a scale unprecedented in human history and at a speed which enabled Scottish writings indebted to Montesquieu and German commentaries on those same works to cross-fertilize one another in appearing within a matter of months, as if electronically linked to the Internet today. Political thinkers of the Enlightenment served as ministers in the courts of Maria Theresa, Joseph II, Leopold II, George III, Gustav III, Frederik VI, and Louis XVI, while kings corresponded with philosophers, sought their company and solicited their advice. Literacy made the spread of enlightenment possible, granting to experts in all subjects a political presence and power in society they had not earlier enjoyed. This command of publicity by the friends of the Enlightenment makes the notion of their collective project credible, even allowing for the diverse and sometimes conflicting objectives of its adherents.

It is nevertheless imperative that due weight be placed on the substantive differences between those objectives, however much they were pursued in concert. CONDILLAC, the most influential of the French empiricists of the Enlightenment, came to revise his own views substantially in the course of his intellectual career, attempting at first to correct Locke's epistemology by way of refining the doctrine of the association of ideas so as to explain the generation of self-awareness without recourse to intuition, while later, in his account of the statue-man, putting forward a more physiological notion of psychic life as rooted in the senses, particularly the sense of touch. The French materialists, in turn – principally Maupertuis, La Mettrie and d'Holbach – put forward a number of claims about the physical determination of morality which were similar to those of the later Condillac, although their works were received differently and came to be regarded, especially by the Church, as the most incendiary of the philosophies of the Enlightenment on account of their denial of the existence of an immaterial and immortal soul (see LA METTRIE, J.O. DE).

When political thinkers of the Enlightenment agreed that their aim should be to devise a set of rules for the proper management of human affairs in the light of the known tendencies of human nature, they were sometimes drawn to utilitarianism in the manner of HUTCHESON, HELVÉTIUS, Beccaria or BENTHAM, who advocated policies which promoted the greatest happiness or least pain of the greatest number, by way of constitutional reforms which abolished physical torture and all civil retribution for moral crimes (see UTILITARIANISM). But from much the same premises other philosophers advocated instead sumptuary laws in order to promote economic equality and the collective ownership of property such as were proposed by Dom Deschamps, Morelly and Mably, while still others adopted the wholly contrary stance of Turgot, Antonio Genovesi and Giuseppe Palmieri, who perceived the social benefits of economic inequality and held that the state could best promote economic development by exercising as little control as possible over the liberties and initiative of its citizens.

In criticizing monolithic notions of a science of the human mind, perceived as subject to the laws of nature in a universe which it reflects, critics of the Enlightenment Project often overlook the richness and diversity of its various themes. No major thinker of the eighteenth century was more persuaded of physicalist explanations of social behaviour and culture than MONTESQIEU, who plainly fits the description offered by Richard Rorty, for instance, of a philosopher convinced that objective knowledge of all things, including human conduct, is possible and that mind is a mirror of nature. Yet from the single dimension of his belief in the scientific study of both matter and mind, there springs no universalism or cosmopolitanism of any kind, since above virtually all his contempories Montesquieu was specially sensitive to local variety, specificity and the uniqueness of social institutions, customs and mores.

Enlightenment philosophers – empiricists and rationalists together – are perhaps best described as sceptics who collectively framed fundamentally liberal objections to what they took to be the universalist bigotry of sacred truth. If their principal battlecry was Voltaire's 'Ecrasez l'infâme', they were, on account of their commitment to toleration, drawn by an ideal of peaceable assembly such as Voltaire himself in his *Philosophical Letters* (1734) had found among the traders of the London Stock Exchange, where no church was supreme and individuals of different faiths could deal with one another as if they were of the same religion (see VOLTAIRE). In opposing the ethnic cleansers of their day, the philosophers of the Enlightenment contributed to our understanding of what we now call crimes against humanity.

See also: CLANDESTINE LITERATURE; ENLIGHTENMENT, JEWISH; ENLIGHTENMENT, RUSSIAN; ENLIGHTENMENT, SCOTTISH

References and further reading

Cassirer, E. (1932) *Philosophie der Aufklärung*, Boston: Beacon Press; trans. A. Koelin and J. Pettegrove, *The Philosophy of the Enlightenment*, Princeton, NJ: Princeton University Press, 1951. (Originally published in German in 1932, a high-minded account of critical philosophy in the eighteenth century, addressing its systematic spirit as distinct from the spirit of system of seventeenth-century metaphysics.)

Darnton, R. (1982) *The Literary Underground of the Old Regime*, Cambridge, MA: Harvard University Press. (An account of Grub Street hacks, publishers and peddlers of forbidden books in eighteenth-century France, who pursued wordly success more often than philosophical truth.)

Fox, C., Porter, R. and Wokler, R. (eds) (1995) *Inventing Human Science: Eighteenth-Century Domains*, Berkeley, CA: University of California Press. (Commentaries on the Enlightenment sciences of natural history, medicine, anthropology, psychology and politics.)

Gay, P. (1966, 1969) *The Enlightenment: An Interpretation*, vol. 1, *The Rise of Modern Paganism*, vol. 2, *The Science of Freedom*, New York: Knopf. (Assesses the Enlightenment as an intellectual movement of diverse political reformers committed to secularism, humanity, cosmopolitanism and freedom.)

Hampson, N. (1968) *The Enlightenment*, Harmondsworth: Penguin. (A general study of eighteenth-century thinkers within their particular backgrounds.)

Havens, G.R. (1955) *The Age of Ideas: From Reaction to Revolution in Eighteenth-Century France*, New York: Holt. (A detailed study of leading thinkers of the French Enlightenment from Bayle and Fontenelle to Diderot and Beaumarchais.)

Hazard, P. (1954) *European Thought in the Eighteenth Century*, London: Hollis & Carter. (Originally published in French in 1946, a comprehensive account of Christianity, unbelief and educational and moral doctrines in the Enlightenment's republic of letters.)

Manuel, F.E. (1959) *The Eighteenth Century Confronts the Gods*, Cambridge, MA: Harvard University Press. (A studyof the place of pagan mythology, polytheism and deism in the Enlightenment, and of eighteenth-century critiques of religious fanaticism.)

Outram, D. (1995) *The Enlightenment*, Cambridge: Cambridge University Press. (A general treatment, addressing recent commentaries on the social production and marketing of ideas, with chapters on science, religion, exoticism, gender and government.)

Porter, R. and Mikuláš T. (eds) (1981) *The Enlightenment in National Context*, Cambridge: Cambridge University Press. (Assesses literary and professional elites of the eighteenth century in their diverse social and political environments.)

Reill, P.H. (1975) *The German Enlightenment and the Rise of Historicism*, Berkeley, CA: University of California Press. (Interprets the German Aufklärung as an intellectual movement shaped by Leibnizian philosophy, the Ständestaat tradition and the contending claims of Pietism and rationalism.)

Schmidt, J. (ed.) (1996) *What is Enlightenment? Eighteenth-Century Answers and Twentieth-Century Questions*, Berkeley, CA: University of California Press. (Reassembles eighteenth-century German interpretations of and twentieth-century commentaries on the meaning of enlightenment, with a notable introduction.)

Scott, H.M. (ed.) (1990) *Enlightened Absolutism: Reform and Reformersin Later Eighteenth-Century Europe*, London: Macmillan. (Addresses the importance of the particular national and provincial environments in which philosophical kingship was pursued.)

Venturi, F. (1972) *Italy and the Enlightenment: Studies in a Cosmopolitan Century*, London: Longman. (Learned essays on Italian contributors to the Enlightenment theory and practice of cosmopolitanism, patriotism and socialism, from Radicati and Paoli to Filangieri and Pagano.)

Wade, I.O. (1938) *The Clandestine Organization and Diffusion of Philosophic Ideas in France from 1700 to 1750*, Princeton, NJ: Princeton University Press. (A study of the circulation of philosophical and theological manuscripts which prefigured the predominant philosophical currents of the period 1750–89.)

Yolton, J.W., Porter, R., Rogers, P. and Stafford, B.M. (eds) (1991) *The Blackwell Companion to the Enlightenment*, London: Blackwell. (An illustrated encyclopedic treatment of political and literary doctrines and their authors, and of the arts and sciences in the eighteenth century.)

ROBERT WOKLER

ENLIGHTENMENT, JEWISH

The eighteenth century in Europe saw the beginnings of Jewish emancipation, and this led to an intellectual development which came to be known as the Jewish Enlightenment or Haskalah. This movement emphasized the rational individual, the notion of natural law, natural religion and toleration, and natural rights. The effect of this form of thought was to provide a justification for the equality of the Jews with other citizens of national entities. The most important exponent of this movement was Moses Mendelssohn, who dominated the debate on the role Jews should play in the state and the rationality of Judaism as a religion. Ultimately the Jewish Enlightenment moved east and became connected with such movements as Zionism. In Germany it led to the development of the Reform movement. The Jewish Enlightenment very much set the agenda for the next two centuries of debate about Jewish ideas by seeking to analyse the links between religion and reason in Judaism.

1   Haskalah and philosophy
2   The Haskalah and the history of philosophy
3   The afterlife of the Haskalah

1   Haskalah and philosophy

Haskalah (Jewish Enlightenment) is the name given to a series of movements at times resembling and often modelled on the various Enlightenment movements in western and central Europe. The Haskalah first took root in the major Prussian cities of Berlin and Königsberg in the latter half of the eighteenth century. It spread to other German cities and to Vienna; and from there, throughout the nineteenth century, to Bohemia, Galicia, Podolia, Lithuania and the southern Ukraine, especially the city of Odessa. Although each area of Haskalah had its own unique features, the *maskilim* (the adherents of Haskalah) of Europe were all committed to the social and intellectual revitalization of the Jewish communities of Europe. Their programme included the learning of European languages and developing familiarity with European culture, including philosophy, as well as a transformation of the Jewish economic profile and educational system. While *maskilim* were often few in number the Haskalah had an important impact on Jewish culture in central and eastern Europe in the nineteenth century.

The Haskalah in Prussia produced one major philosopher: Moses MENDELSSOHN (1729–86). Mendelssohn became one of the most important philosophers of the German *Aufklärer*, even while he remained central to the development of Jewish thought and ideological modernization. In his *Briefe über die Empfindungen* (Letters on Feeling) (1755b) and *Philosophische Schriften* (Philosophical Writings) (1761) he redirected aesthetic discussion by insisting that judgments about beauty are independent of ethical purpose or logical criteria. In 1763 he published *Abhandlung über die Evidenz in metaphysischen Wissenschaften* (Treatise on Evidence in Metaphysical Knowledge), in which he tried to shield metaphysics from the claim that its proofs for the existence of God and morality do not attain the certainty of mathematics. His reputation as a major German philosopher was assured with the publication of his Platonic dialogue *Phädon, oder über die Unsterblichkeit der Seele* (Phaedo, or on the Immortality of the Soul) in 1767. The dialogue was a philosophical best-seller and adumbrated the quintessential Enlightenment statement of belief in the immortality of the soul. Even after the publication of Kant's critical works, Mendelssohn remained a staunch defender of the demonstrability of the existence of God, as is shown in his last work, *Morgenstunden, oder Vorlesungen über das Dasein Gottes* (Morning Hours, or Lectures on the Existence of God) (1786), a work intended, among other things, to defend Mendelssohn's friend LESSING from charges of atheism and Spinozism.

Even as he took full and active part in the European Enlightenment, Mendelssohn remained committed to the development of Jewish culture and thought, as can be seen by his numerous Hebrew works, especially his commentary on Exodus, and his book *Jerusalem, oder über religiöse Macht und Judentum* (Jerusalem, or on Religious Power and Judaism) (1783). In this work, Mendelssohn applied theories of natural right to the political status of the Jews and to European societies generally. He insisted on a clear delineation of the prerogatives of Church and state in (what ought to be) a secular society. In the second half of the book he developed a philosophy of Judaism that defended his ancestral faith against charges of immorally excluding non-Jews from salvation. He insisted that Judaism embodied a revealed legislation, rather than a revealed religion and argued that Judaism does not coerce its adherents in matters of religion any more than it excludes non-Jews from salvation.

Mendelssohn used his Bible commentary to disseminate some of his ideas regarding metaphysics and politics to a larger Jewish audience. In addition, we find in his Bible commentary a distinct contribution to the emerging field of philosophical linguistics, although this side of Mendelssohn's work remained largely unknown beyond the Jewish community, as it was written in Hebrew. Here Mendelssohn tried to develop the notion that language was a vehicle for mediating more than one intended significance. The search for authorial intention, then, although a standard concern at the time, could not proceed simply on a philological and literal level. Texts needed to be interpreted more broadly to appreciate fully the intended significance of their words, phrases and sentences. In practice, for Mendelssohn, this meant the submission of the interpreter to the ancient interpretative traditions. The recognition of the polyvalency of meanings in a text might have led Mendelssohn to a more historically rooted view of texts and their appropriate interpretations. But he tended to rest content with the traditional subtleties of the rabbinic midrashic method (see MIDRASH).

Mendelssohn was the only important Jewish philosopher in German-speaking lands who remained committed to Haskalah throughout his life. But mention should be made of two other members of the Berlin Jewish community who were associated with the Haskalah movement for a time. Salomon MAIMON (1753/4–1800), a Polish Jew, came to Berlin in quest of opportunities for the free pursuit of knowledge. He was associated for a time with the *maskilim* of Berlin and wrote a Hebrew work designed to reconcile scientific principles with the study of the Torah. He translated Mendelssohn's *Morgenstunden* into Hebrew and wrote a philosophical commentary, also in Hebrew, on Maimonides' *Guide to the Perplexed* (see MAIMONIDES, M.). Eventually, Maimon rejected the notion that Jewish culture could be reconciled with modern philosophy and devoted the rest of his career to writing several philosophical works critical of Kant's transcendental philosophy.

The stimulus of Kantian thought was to lead yet another, albeit far less original, philosophical voice away from Haskalah, that of Marcus Herz (1747–1803). Herz was briefly associated with the Haskalah movement, but went on to become one of Kant's earliest disciples – he was chosen by KANT to be a respondent in the defence of his inaugural dissertation. Herz thanks Kant for helping to liberate him from a life of 'dragging a burden of prejudices', a reference to his Jewish cultural background. His *Betrachtungen aus der spekulativen Weltweisheit* (Meditations Drawn from Speculative Wisdom), written in 1771, represents an early commentary on Kant's inaugural dissertation, which, like the work of so many commentators and popularizers, shows distinct misunderstanding of the Kant's work. Ultimately, Herz made a name for himself as an important scientist and physician. As with Maimon, the Haskalah made possible his encounter with European philosophy. But unlike Maimon, he did little to advance the cause of Jewish enlightenment.

The various other centres of Haskalah produced only one other important philosopher, Nachman KROCHMAL of Galicia (1785–1840). Unlike the Prussians, Krochmal advanced philosophical discussion within the Jewish community alone. Although the leading intellectual of the Haskalah in Galicia, far from the German 'intellectual marketplace' as he put it, he became an astute observer of the German philosophical environment. Krochmal provided one of the first Jewish responses to, and adaptations of, elements of the philosophical work of Spinoza, Kant, Herder, Schelling and Hegel. In his posthumously published *Moreh nevukhei ha-Zeman* (Guide to the Perplexed of Today) (1851), Krochmal adapted Kantian epistemological concepts to demonstrate the need to interpret religious sources with an eye to their deeper philosophical significance. He then proceeded to show that the deeper philosophical significance of traditional Jewish sources, both ancient and medieval, corresponded to the most recent discoveries of the German Idealist philosophers. Using his interpretative method, Krochmal argued that a range of traditional Jewish concepts – such as belief in a personal God who created the world and revealed a desired way of life – remained philosophically coherent, for, when properly interpreted, they were shown to be concrete representations of the abstract metaphysics of HEGEL and SCHELLING.

Krochmal responded to the regnant philosophy of history that considered Jewish culture – among many others – to be sublated in the onward march of history, by arguing that Jewish religion, because of its apprehension of the absolute, stood outside the historical 'laws' that mandated the eventual cultural demise of all nations and states. Although he was an important model for aspiring Jewish intellectuals in eastern Europe, his philosophical work was of limited influence. His lasting contribution would seem to lie in his implicit exposure of the unstated and culturally biased assumptions of modern idealist philosophy. His work showed that different cultural assumptions would lead to the application of idealist concepts in a way that yielded philosophical and religious conclusions that diverged significantly from those reached by the German Idealists themselves.

2 The Haskalah and the history of philosophy

The Haskalah, not unlike the Enlightenment movements of western and central Europe, produced few original philosophical minds (see ENLIGHTENMENT, CONTINENTAL). But there were many lesser lights and still more followers of their guidance in the quest for an enlightened way of life and thought. For this reason at least, the Haskalah remains an important, although largely unmined, resource for the student of the history of philosophy. The hundreds of *maskilim* throughout Europe were avid consumers of French and German philosophy. They were also eager readers of Spinoza's works as well (see SPINOZA, B. DE). Knowing what they read and how they understood it is vital to an understanding of the spread and impact of the modernizing trends of European thought. The earliest Prussian *maskilim* emerge at a time when Christian WOLFF was one of the leading philosophers of Germany. In the works of these early *maskilim*, including Mendelssohn, one can discern Wolff's distinct influence. Similarly, the ethical writings of *maskilim* in Germany display familiarity with Enlightenment ethics. One result is a turning away from the pessimistic tone of many traditional Jewish ethical writings. The influences that we observe show that the German *maskilim* were the most acculturated, and most at home, linguistically and culturally, in the world of European philosophy.

Yet the Haskalah moved eastward just as European philosophy was undergoing a revolution reflected in the works of the post-Enlightenment Idealists, and the works of HERDER as well. The derivative thinking of the Eastern *maskilim* remained rooted in Enlightenment thought even as it embraced the new idealism. This often difficult combination produced fascinating tensions, facilitated by the fact that, with the exception of Krochmal, Jewish readers in central and eastern Europe tended to read popularizations of Kant rather than Kant himself. What this meant in practice was that the eastern European Jewish writers and thinkers of the Haskalah often developed 'Kantian' ideas in ways that were quite consistent with central Enlightenment ideals – with assumptions and consequences that would have been unrecognizable to the master. Similarly, Jewish writers embraced certain Rousseauian notions regarding education and ethics (see ROUSSEAU, J.-J.). Again, though, they tended to receive this material second-hand. Especially important as a popularizer of Kant and Rousseau was the Swiss writer, thinker and historian Heinrich Zschokke (1771–1848). The dependence on Zschokke for knowledge of Kant and Rousseau is particularly manifest among the *maskilim* of Lithuania.

In examining the *maskilim* as consumers of European thought, we find several matters especially worthy of note to the historian of philosophy. The first is that post-Kantian *maskilim* tended to find Kant's ethical thought thoroughly compelling, despite its overtly anti-Judaic component. Yet these *maskilim* separated Kant's ethics from his critical metaphysics. They had little use for the latter, and tended to reduce even Kant's ethics to the principles of duty and autonomy. They then went about showing how such ethics were compatible with the biblical *mitzvot*, despite the fact that these divine commandments might readily seem thoroughly heteronomous, and certainly seemed so to Kant. Here Kant's ethical thinking was removed from its place within his thought and enlisted on behalf of a very different, modernizing cum apologetic cultural project.

Post-Hegelian *maskilim* tended to have a very limited understanding of Hegel. Here again Krochmal is the exception. Yet thinkers who had no apparent understanding of Hegel's metaphysics, ethics or politics were drawn to his philosophy of history. Once again we find these thinkers drawing selectively from Hegel's thought. Even when some paid rhetorical lip service to the dialectical movement of history, what interested the *maskilim* most was the teleological view of history that Hegel's thought seemed to legitimate. This view in turn allowed the *maskilim* to conceptualize observed changes in Jewish history as part of a larger drama that they could interpret as pointing towards the fulfilment of their own cultural aspirations. The continued influence of Enlightenment ideals is manifest here.

Eclectic borrowing from Spinoza may be discerned

in the work of some of the more religiously radical *maskilim*. They wanted to re-enact the drama of Spinoza's liberation from the Jewish religious tradition. Yet they sought to do so without adopting Spinoza's universalism.

3 The afterlife of the Haskalah

Throughout the encounter with post-Enlightenment European thought in the various centres of Haskalah, the movement in some ways remained very much modelled on the European Enlightenment. Everywhere and always committed to Enlightenment rationalism, the *maskilim* remained thoroughly optimistic regarding the ability of the Jewish community to generate a rational culture even as they expressed deep contempt for the Jewish masses, and often for its rabbinic elite. But European thought and politics moved on, and for some the efforts of the *maskilim* to graft more recent thinking onto the tree of rationalism and optimism came to appear hopelessly naïve. Many others, like Maimon and Herz, came to see the effort to reconcile European thought – however well or poorly understood – with Judaism, traditional or reformed, as irrelevant at best, dishonest at worst. Thus, in each of its centres, the Haskalah, like the Enlightenment itself, tended to be of limited duration. Yet in its own limited way it helped bring about fundamental intellectual change in the Jewish communities of Europe. It promoted and legitimized new areas of inquiry among Jews and contributed mightily to the emergence of new philosophical and political ideologies as Jews entered the twentieth century.

See also: ENLIGHTENMENT, CONTINENTAL; JEWISH PHILOSOPHY IN THE EARLY 19TH CENTURY; MENDELSSOHN, M.

References and further reading

Altmann, A. (1973) *Moses Mendelssohn: A Biographical Study*, Philadelphia, PA: Jewish Publications Society. (Magisterial study of all aspects of his life, including his personal and intellectual relationships to many of the leading philosophical voices of the day.)

Arkush, A. (1994) *Moses Mendelssohn and the Enlightenment*, Albany, NY: State University of New York Press. (An effort to situate Mendelssohn within the context of the thought of Leibniz, Wolff, Kant and Lessing, based almost exclusively on Mendelssohn's German writings.)

Dubin, L. (1997) 'The Social and Cultural Context: Eighteenth-Century Enlightenment', in D. Frank and O. Leaman (eds) *History of Jewish Philosophy*,

London: Routledge. (A comprehensive guide to the period, including a detailed bibliography.)

Harris, J. (1991) *Nachman Krochmal: Guiding the Perplexed of the Modern Age*, New York: New York University Press. (An intellectual biography which treats his complex relationship with the major schools of German Idealism, as well as the thought of Herder and Spinoza.)

* Krochmal, N. (1851) *Moreh Nevukhei ha-Zeman* (Guide to the Perplexed of Today), ed. with Hebrew introduction by S. Rawidowicz, Berlin: Einot, 1924; repr. Waltham, MA: Ararat, 1961. (Adapts Kantian epistemological methods to interpret the Jewish religious sources with an eye to discovering their inner, philosophical meaning. Krochmal argues that at their deeper level these sources, both ancient and medieval, anticipated the discoveries of the German Idealist philosophers.)

Mendelssohn, M. (1755a) *Philosophische Gespräche* (Philosophical Speeches), Berlin. (In this work, Mendelssohn declares himself a disciple of the school of Leibniz and takes sides with Spinoza.)

* —— (1755b) *Briefe über die Empfindungen* (Letters on Feeling), Berlin. (Contains a philosophy of the beatiful and forms a chief basis of all philosophical-aesthetic criticism in Germany.)

* —— (1763) *Abhandlung über die Evidenz in metaphysischen Wissenschaften* (Treatise on Evidence in Metaphysical Knowledge), Berlin: Mande und Spener, 1786. (Essay comparing the demonstrability of metaphysical propositions with that of mathematical ones.)

* —— (1767) *Phädon, oder über die Unsterblichkeit der Seele* (Phaedo, or on the Immortality of the Soul), Wien: C.F. Schade, 1812. (His chief philosophical work, dealing with the immortality of the soul, following Plato's dialogue of the same name.)

* —— (1783) *Jerusalem, oder über religiöse Macht und Judentum* (Jerusalem, or on Religious Power and Judaism), trans. with notes by A. Arkush, *Jerusalem*, Hanover, NH: University Press of New England, 1983. (His epoch-making work calling for the emancipation of the Jews and setting out the conditions of religious freedom in a pluralistic state.)

* —— (1785) *Morgenstunden, oder Vorlesungen über das Dasein Gottes* (Morning Hours, or Lectures on the Existence of God), Berlin: C. Voss, 1786. (Sets forth Mendelssohn's fundamental metaphysical beliefs and argues against pantheism.)

Rotenstreich, N. (1984) *Jews and German Philosophy*, New York: Schocken. (A useful and thorough consideration of the relationship between Jewish and German thought in the eighteenth to twentieth centuries.)

Sorkin, D. (1996) *Moses Mendelssohn and the Religious Enlightenment*, Berkeley, CA: University of California Press. (Complements and challenges Arkush by relying on both the Hebrew and Jewish writings of Mendelssohn within the context of theological Wolffianism.)

JAY M. HARRIS

ENLIGHTENMENT, RUSSIAN

When Russia embraced secular European ways of thought under Peter the Great, its educated elite came into contact first with the German Enlightenment, which combined the rationalism of Descartes and Leibniz with the emotionalism of Protestant pietism. With its acknowledgement of established authority, and emphasis on a person's responsibility to the community rather than individual rights, this strand of early Enlightenment thought suited the state-building of Peter.

By the second half of the eighteenth century, the universality of the French language, the influence of geniuses such as Montesquieu and Voltaire, and the formation of a conscious Enlightenment party among the French philosophes *meant that their polemical writings carried the mainstream of progressive thought. It was this Enlightenment that was embraced by Catherine the Great, who professed its tenets: tolerance and the conviction that perfecting social organization would ensure human happiness. She encouraged the growth of an intellectual elite to spread the ideas of the* philosophes *and form an enlightened public opinion.*

Russia's tradition of absolutism and the institution of serfdom, however, proved inimical to Enlightenment values. Nevertheless, the Russian Enlightenment engendered an elite of individuals eager to act as critics and moral leaders of their society who would determine the future course of Russian social thought.

1 **State Enlightenment**
2 **Enlightenment of society**
3 **Means of Enlightenment**
4 **Consequences of Russian Enlightenment**

1 State Enlightenment

The ground was prepared for the Russian Enlightenment when Peter the Great reshaped Muscovy, with its Orthodox religious culture, into a modern, secular European state. In order to achieve his reforms, the Russian service elite were obliged to immerse themselves in the contemporary currents of European thought, science, social progress and literature. Some were sent abroad for training, but most learned from the technicians and educators imported from the West to modernize the state. The majority came from Germany and brought with them the philosophical outlook of their homeland. This outlook, forged in the West's recent scientific revolution, also underpinned the modern technology imported by these specialists. Consequently, Petrine Russia sought advice on education from LEIBNIZ and Christian WOLFF, and it was their pupils who were recruited for the new Academy of Sciences: G.F. Müller, Schlözer and Stählin, the historians; Euler, the mathematician; and Pallas, the biologist, geographer, linguist and explorer – these were the leading scholars and scientists in eighteenth-century Russia.

The intellectual framework which these teachers brought with them was constructed from the rationalism of Descartes and the natural-law ideas of Leibniz and Pufendorf. The rationalism and legalism were imbued, however, with the emotionalism of Protestant pietism, whose proponent was Christian Wolff. Both the pietist emphasis on the acceptance of properly constituted authority, whether religious or political, and its stress on a person's obligation to serve the community rather than on selfish individual rights, suited the requirements for state-building initiated by Peter. The influence of this particular German strand of Enlightenment was reinforced by the prestige of the eighteenth-century polymath M.V. Lomonosov (1711–65) whose work and writings reflected the scientific education he had received in the universities of Marburg and Freiburg, with their strong pietist tradition. A constant promoter of the 'common good', he was instrumental in the founding in 1755 of Moscow University, where the employment of a number of influential German professors ensured the persistence of the German outlook.

Despite the influx of Western patterns of thought the essence of Enlightenment – and accumulation of knowledge permitting the critical appraisal of social relationships in order to improve human life – was not assimilated by Russia in the first half of the eighteenth century. It was in fact negated when Peter exploited the means of Enlightenment as an instrument to transform society from above in order to augment the state's military, economic and administrative efficiency. Nevertheless, some of the prerequisites for Enlightenment, such as the founding of scientific, educational and publishing institutions, had been established. And crucially, a secular conceptual framework had been created outside traditional Orthodoxy.

2 Enlightenment of society

The mainstream of the European Enlightenment, represented by the works of the French *philosophes*, penetrated into Russia from the 1740s, but the progress and development of the Enlightenment in Russia is intimately connected with the person and the reign (1762–96) of Catherine the Great, who declared her allegiance to the ideals and aims of the Enlightenment in her memoirs. In 1767 she published her *Nakaz*, or the *Instruction* provided to guide the deliberations of the deputies summoned to a Legislative Commission. Although the rational precepts of Bielfeld and Justi and the pietist morality of Christian Wolff are present in the document as reminders of the German influence, the *Instruction* was mainly composed of liberal ideas taken from the *Encyclopédie*, from Beccaria's *Dei delitti e delle pene* (*On Crimes and Punishments*) (1764) and above all from MONTES-QUIEU, whose *De l'esprit des lois* (*The Spirit of the Laws*) (1748) was called by Catherine her 'prayer book'. The *Instruction* demonstrated the sovereign's respect for Enlightenment thought and gave it imperial sanction.

Another Enlightenment initiative of Catherine's was the 1766 essay competition on the peasant question organized by the Free Economic Society, Russia's first independent cultural institution, and inspired by the economic arguments of the *Encyclopédie* and the physiocrats. Few Russians competed, but among the 164 entries were essays by Voltaire and Marmontel.

The Free Economic Society competition and the *Instruction* linked Russia with the wider European Enlightenment in two ways. First, it provided Europe with another example of an 'enlightened despot' in the person of Catherine. It was important in the eyes of the *philosophes* that sovereigns themselves should understand the lack of justice in the existing social order. In Catherine the Great the French *philosophes* discovered an empress prepared to play the part of an 'enlightened monarch', eager to buy their books, to correspond with them, to invite them to visit her, to give them patronage and even to carry out the reformation of society they proposed. Proof of this was her declaration of admiration for Montesquieu in a letter to d'Alembert where she explained that she had plagiarized him 'for the good of twenty million people, which must come of it'.

Second, the consultative assembly called to consider the Instruction was an example of the involvement of broader sections of society in the Enlightenment. It supplied a precondition for the spread of the Enlightenment: the establishment of public forums for debate and publicity, permitting individuals to participate in the process of social reform. One of the striking propositions in the Instruction (article 58) was the need 'to prepare the Minds of People' before the implementation of improved legislation.

European Enlightenment was no longer exploited merely as an instrument to strengthen the efficiency of the state; the welfare of society and that of its members was now the objective. 'The happiness of one and all' was the motto on the medal given to the deputies summoned to respond to the *Instruction*, and one of its closing articles (521) stated that its propositions were 'the Choice of those Means, whereby the Russians may be rendered the most happy possible of Mankind'.

3 Means of Enlightenment

After the suspension of the Legislative Commission, as a result of the outbreak of the Turkish War, other channels were found for the diffusion of Enlightenment thought. In 1768 Catherine founded a 'Society for the Translation of Foreign Books' which by 1772 had published over forty titles, including extracts from the *Encyclopédie*, Montesquieu and Voltaire. Meanwhile she had called into being the publication of moral weeklies, modelled on the *Spectator* of Addison and Steele, that popularized Enlightenment attitudes. She opened state archives to aid private historiographical enterprises. Licensing requirements for presses and publishing houses were abolished in 1783. In Catherine's approval for private charitable initiatives in popular education, and particularly for Ivan Betskoi's plans for foundling homes that would produce a new type of citizen, support was given to the institutionalization of the social vision of the Enlightenment.

Although these means were all under imperial tutelage, there seems to have been a policy of encouraging a class of intellectuals who would guide society, correct its defects and help eradicate the obstacles frustrating the creation of an enlightened society. Eventually, with the emergence of a social elite that was not an official part of state authority, public opinion began to take on a corrective function and became a power factor with which the state had to contend.

In this a leading role was played by writers, aware of themselves as forming a 'republic of letters', as Mikhail Kheraskov, Director of Moscow University's Press and Library, called the group of young men who had gathered around him. No original contribution, however, was made by them to European Enlightenment philosophy. For these Russian writers, Enlightenment meant initially the reception and later the adaptation of Western developments, and the participation of Russia in the general cultural development of Europe. Their own function was that of the mediator, spreading the ideas of the French *philosophes* of the previous generation. This insinuation of Enlightenment ideas into the consciousness of Europeanized Russians was as essential a part of the Enlightenment as the composition of the key works had been.

The most prominent director of this process was Nikolai Novikov (1714–1818), originally a minute-taker at the Legislative Commission where he would have noted the shaping of a rudimentary public opinion. Following the Commission's disbandment, Novikov appealed to that newly aware public as editor of a series of moral weeklies which castigated obscurantism and promoted the image of the truly enlightened citizen. The 1770s saw Novikov making a significant contribution to the development of publishing, and in 1779 he obtained the lease of Moscow University Press, which dominated Russian publishing for the next decade. Simultaneously he created the Typographical Company, a significant independent publishing concern.

Novikov was also a leading figure in Russian Freemasonry, one of the principal channels for the dissemination of Enlightenment values. In the 1770s the outlook of the Russian Freemason was broadly that of the approved *philosophes* and for Russians at that time the terms 'Voltairean' and 'Freemasonic' were synonymous. But later, Russian Freemasonry, under the influence of pietism, shunned the radical trends of the *philosophes* and nurtured a moderate Enlightenment which refused to become anti-Christian.

The fusion of Enlightenment values with a heightened moral awareness and religious and spiritual sympathies could prove a powerful amalgam. This was shown by another significant figure of the Russian Enlightenment, Aleksandr Radishchev (1748–1802). Radishchev studied at Leipzig, a centre of pietism, where he was also influenced by the later radical generation of *philosophe* writers: Mably, Raynal, Helvetius and Rousseau, who argued that there was a need to change institutions in order for humanity to be able to realize its true potential. This combination of spiritual enthusiasm, moral commitment and a desire for institutional change, particularly for the abolition of serfdom, was crystallized in Radishchev's *Puteshestvie iz Peterburga v Moskvu* (Journey from St Petersburg to Moscow) (1790), the most radical statement of the Russian Enlightenment.

4 Consequences of Russian Enlightenment

For publishing his *Journey from St Petersburg to Moscow* Radishchev received a death sentence, commuted to ten years of exile. Novikov was also sentenced in 1792 to fifteen years of imprisonment for his involvement with Freemasonry. This repression signalled the end of Catherine's enthusiasm for the Enlightenment, which had been blighted by the Pugachev rebellion and the French Revolution. At the end of her reign it seemed the Enlightenment had left little trace on Russia's official institutions. However, a cultural elite among the nobility had emerged as a self-conscious civil society, steeped in Enlightenment values and yearning to be free from the shackles of the state. The Enlightenment had taught them to question Russia's traditional political structure, particularly autocracy and serfdom. The Enlightenment belief in the perfectibility of society, the pursuit of happiness, and the prospect of a rational code of laws persisted. It was a faith protested with fervour by men nurtured in the Masonic lodges which imparted a particular spiritual earnestness to the Russian Enlighteners. Here was the breeding ground for the Russian intelligentsia of the nineteenth century.

See also: ENLIGHTENMENT, CONTINENTAL; LEIBNIZ, G.W.; MONTESQUIEU; NATURAL LAW; PIETISM; VOLTAIRE; WOLFF, C.; LIBERALISM, RUSSIAN §1

References and further reading

* Beccaria, C.B. (1764) *Dei delitti e delle pene*, ed. F. Venturi, Turin: Einaudi, 1965; R. Bellamy (ed.), trans. R. Davies, V. Cox, R. Bellamy, *On Crimes and Punishments and Other Writings*, Cambridge: Cambridge University Press, 1995.

Billington, J.H. (1966) *The Icon and the Axe: An Interpretive History of Russian Culture*, London: Weidenfeld & Nicolson. (The chapter 'The Troubled Enlightenment' (213–68) examines the Enlightenment in the context of Russia's general cultural history.)

* Catherine the Great (1767) *Nakaz* (Instruction); P. Dukes (ed.) *Catherine the Great's Instruction (Nakaz) to the Legislative Commission, 1767*, Newtonville, MA: Oriental Research Partners, 1977. (A contemporary eighteenth-century English translation of the *Nakaz* with a balanced introduction and bibliography.)

Dukes, P. (1981) 'The Russian Enlightenment', in R. Porter and M. Teich (eds), *The Enlightenment in National Context*, Cambridge: Cambridge University Press, 176–91. (Examines the Russian national variant of the European Enlightenment.)

Jones, W.G. (1984) *Nikolay Novikov: Enlightener of Russia*, Cambridge: Cambridge University Press. (Expansion of §3.)

McConnell, A. (1964) *A Russian Philosophe: Alexander Radishchev 1749–1802*, The Hague: Martinus Nijhoff. (Expansion of §3.)

* Montesquieu, C. de S., Baron de (1748), *De l'esprit des lois*, ed. G. Truc, Paris: Garnier, 1949; trans. T. Nugent, *The Spirit of the Laws*, New York: Hafner, 1949.

Raeff, M. (1966) *The Origins of the Russian Intelligentsia: the Eighteenth-Century Nobility*, New York: Harcourt, Brace & World. (The contribution of the nobility to the Enlightenment; expansion of §4.)

—— (1973) 'The Enlightenment in Russia and Russian Thought in the Enlightenment', in J.G. Garrard (ed.) *The Eighteenth Century in Russia*, Oxford: Clarendon Press, 25–47. (Particularly useful for its expansion of §1.)

Robel, G. (1992) 'Zur Aufklärung in Adelsgesellschaften: Rußland und Polen' (On the Enlightenment in Nobility Societies: Russia and Poland), in S. Juttner and J. Schlobach (eds) *Europäische Aufklärung(en): Einheit und nationale Vielfalt*, Hamburg: Felix Meiner Verlag, 152–71. (An excellent survey, the comparison with Poland being used to highlight the particular nature of the Russian experience.)

W. GARETH JONES

ENLIGHTENMENT, SCOTTISH

This term refers to the intellectual movement in Scotland in roughly the second half of the eighteenth century. As a movement it included many theorists – the best known of whom are David Hume, Adam Smith and Thomas Reid – who maintained both institutional and personal links with each other. It was not narrowly philosophical, although in the Common Sense School it did develop its own distinctive body of argument. Its most characteristic feature was the development of a wide-ranging social theory that included pioneering 'sociological' works by Adam Ferguson and John Millar, socio-cultural history by Henry Home (Lord Kames) and William Robertson as well as Hume's Essays (1777) and Smith's classic 'economics' text The Wealth of Nations (1776). All these works shared a commitment to 'scientific' causal explanation and sought, from the premise of the uniformity of human nature, to establish a history of social institutions in which the notion of a mode of subsistence played a key organising role. Typically of the Enlightenment as a whole this explanatory endeavour was not divorced from explicit evaluation. Though not uncritical of their own commercial society, the Scots were in no doubt as to the superiority of their own age compared to what had gone before.

1   Overview
2   Social theory
3   Civilized society

1   Overview

The Scottish Enlightenment may be conveniently dated from the publication of Hume's *Treatise of Human Nature* (1739–40; see HUME, D.) to the revised sixth edition of Smith's *Theory of Moral Sentiments* (1790; see SMITH, A.) It can be fairly described as a 'movement' since it was not confined to a handful of authors but encompassed upwards of fifty participants, who all either knew or were aware of each other. Unlike in France, the Enlightenment in Scotland had strong institutional and establishment roots being based in the universities and the various satellite groups and societies to which even non-academics like Hume and James Hutton or law-lords like Henry HOME (Lord Kames) and James Burnett (Lord Monboddo) belonged. As a movement it was also multifaceted. Scientific theory and experiment were well represented. Some of Isaac Newton's earliest disciples were Scottish, including, notably, Colin Maclaurin. Important work was undertaken by William Cullen and Joseph Black in chemistry and at the end of the period Hutton laid the foundation for uniformitarian geology. Literary theory was also prominent with treatises on rhetoric by George CAMPBELL (1776); and Hugh BLAIR (1783); disquisitions on taste by Alexander GERARD (1759), and many others, plus pioneering works of literary criticism by Thomas Blackwell (notably Blackwell 1735). In philosophy a number of Scots, led by Reid, developed their own Common Sense School, which was stimulated by Hume's perceived scepticism and was critical of the entire 'way of ideas' (see COMMON SENSE SCHOOL; REID, T.).

2   Social theory

Perhaps the most characteristic aspect of the Scottish Enlightenment was its social theory and it is upon that aspect that this entry focuses, taking the term to include historical and moral theory.

The Scots took human sociality to be an evidentially warranted fact. A common explanation of it was

327

that humans possessed a social instinct or appetite. This was seen as 'social' rather than simply familial, and Kames (1774), among others, undertook a detailed comparison between human and animal association. Despite some similarities, the distinctiveness of human sociality was insisted upon especially in the form of non-instrumental social ties such as friendship and loyalty. Part of the significance of this commitment to evidence was the deliberate rejection, most notably by Hume (see HUME, D. §§4–5), of the conceptions of a state of nature and a social contract.

Not only were these notions fanciful but they over-emphasized the role of purposive rationality. Here the Scots' views differed from those typical of the French Enlightenment and of English thinkers like PRIESTLEY. For these latter thinkers Lockean epistemology (see LOCKE, J.) had laid the foundations for an essentially optimistic 'perfectibilist' philosophy. Since to mould experience is to mould human character, then, informed by the findings of reason, it becomes possible to set humans irrevocably on the right track. Accordingly, the more rational society becomes, the more rational will be the experience that it passes on to the next generation. For the Scots this was simplistic. In practice, the scope of reason was circumscribed by habit and social convention; social norms, for example, were the product of socialization not rational insight. In the case of government this meant that although they all had their origin in violence, 'time by degrees...accustoms the nation to regard as their lawful or native princes, that family which at first they considered as usurpers' (Hume [1741–77] 1987: 474–5). Legitimacy in practice was the work of sentiments over time rather than the correspondence (or not) to some rational principle, like consent.

This link between social experience and normative judgments was the linchpin of Smith's Theory of Moral Sentiments (1757). To Smith the effects of social intercourse teach what behaviour is acceptable and in due course individuals internalise these social judgments as conscience, viewing their own actions and motives as an 'impartial well-informed spectator' would (see SMITH, A. §3). The assumptions in Smith's moral philosophy were widely shared. Following the lead of Francis Hutcheson they sought on the one hand to dismiss 'rationalist' accounts of morality (it was 'more properly felt than judg'd of' (Hume 1739–40 III.1.2)) and, most especially, on the other to undermine the egocentric assimilation of 'morality' to self-interest as in the work of Thomas HOBBES and Bernard MANDEVILLE. Against the pretended naturalism of Hobbes and Mandeville, all the Scots insisted on a true naturalism, the facts of human nature testifying in their view to the presence of truly moral

experience, a disinterested concern for the wellbeing of others. Hutcheson invoked a special 'moral sense' (as did, though not identically, Kames (1751) to explain this concern, while both Hume and Smith (without being in total agreement) rejected this recourse to a direct sense, referring instead to a concurrence of sentiments by means of a principle of sympathy (see HUME, D. §3; SMITH, A. §2).

This sensitivity to socialization also meant the Scots were sceptical of the supposed achievements of Great Legislators like Lycurgus in moulding social institutions. Instead the Scots drew attention to the accidental and gradual formation of these institutions; in a phrase of Adam Ferguson's, co-opted by later critics of rationalism like, for example, Hayek (1960), 'nations stumble upon establishments which are indeed the result of human action, but not the execution of any human design' (Ferguson 1767); see FERGUSON, A.). This is an exemplification of the 'law of unintended consequences', of which the other classic formulation in the Scottish Enlightenment was Smith's 'invisible hand', whereby pursuit of self-interest by individuals furthered the public interest. While this has a clear bearing on the operation of markets, it was also used more generally – by John MILLAR, for example (1787, volume 1), to account for the development of the jury system.

This diminution of the role of rationalistic individualism was part of the Scots' endeavour to explain social institutions as the effects of correspondingly social causes. They sought to go beyond the mere cataloguing of facts and provision of indiscriminate historical narrative to the tracing of the chain of causes and effects (see the Preface to Kames (1758)). This was typically executed by writing 'natural histories' (as in Hume (1757)). The key assumption was that human nature was constant and uniform in its principles and operations (see HUMAN NATURE, SCIENCE OF IN THE 18TH CENTURY). From that premise the theorists traced the development of key institutions, such as property, government, ranks, the status of women and religion, from simplicity to complexity or from rudeness to civilization. As a means of organizing this development, emphasis was laid, as Robertson said, on different 'modes of subsistence' (1777 Book 4). With Smith's account seemingly seminal, social development was seen to fall into four stages – hunting, herding, farming and exchanging (see SMITH, A. §4). In outlining this development, evidence from contemporary ethnography and classical history was combined in a deliberate utilization of the comparative method. Such comparisons, as well as being a way of checking the validity of any particular report, enabled them both to sift out 'chance' or random associations from truly causal conjunctions and to supply the missing links in the causal chain. This permitted them self-consciously to write universal histories. The title of James Dunbar's *Essays on the History of Mankind in Rude and Cultivated Ages* (1780) captured what was typical of this general enterprise. The overall aim of these inquiries was to render the 'amazing diversity' (as Millar termed it (1779, 3rd edition, Introduction) of social life explicable. While later philosophers like Collingwood (see Collingwood 1961) have heavily criticized this view of the past, for the Scots of the Enlightenment, history was (in Hume's phrase) a branch of the 'science of man'. It was also openly evaluative.

3 Civilized society

The Scots regarded their own society as belonging to the fourth commercial stage. Given that 'industry, knowledge and humanity' are indissolubly linked (see Hume (1752) 1741–77), and present in commercial societies, then, in contrast, earlier savage societies were indolent, ignorant and cruel. Commercial society was 'polished'; moral sentiments were refined; taste was delicate; religion had lost much of its superstitious overlay. These features fitted together to characterize not only their own 'civilized' society but also their theoretical comprehension of it. In this way their social theory meshed with their moral, aesthetic and religious thought. A nation of savages would live in small scattered groups, worship many gods, have a dull moral sense and a crude taste. But refinement in all these linked spheres develops as humans gradually succeed in triumphing over the dictatorship of needs.

What was seen especially to distinguish a civilized society was the operation of the rule of law, and this was reflected in the salience the Scots attached to justice. Hume, Smith and Kames, though differing in details, all agreed in regarding justice as indispensable to social life. What made this fourth stage 'commercial' was that within it everyone was 'in some measure a merchant' (Smith (1776) Book 1, Chapter 4). As Smith argued, the decisive ingredient of this stage was the extent of the division of labour, which, in its turn, depended on the extent of the market (see SMITH, A. §4). Although bartering was a natural disposition it required the stability wrought by the rule of law to become decisively effective. Once the division of labour was established it greatly increased the material wellbeing of the inhabitants, but that it also had deleterious effects was widely recognised. Ferguson and Kames evaluated these using the long-standing vocabulary of 'corruption'. For Ferguson these effects were part of a more pervasive weakness of commercial societies. He was most especially concerned about the passivity – the preoccupation with 'private' affairs – that these societies engendered. Liberty, he believed, could not be secure if all it meant was obeying just laws; it also needed active involvement. It was to this end that he wished to see a revival of public spirit in the form of militias. Smith, like Hume, did believe that 'modern liberty' came from rule-following, since a stable framework, provided by the inflexible administration of justice, permitted individuals to pursue their own interests in their own way. He did nonetheless recognize, as an unintended consequence of the specialization attendant on the division of labour, that it affected adversely the labourer's virtues. His remedy was the provision, at the public's expense, of primary education. This mixture of analysis and judgment by the Scots in their treatment of their own society is characteristic of the Enlightenment in general and demonstrates that for all their undoubted distinctiveness there truly was a Scottish Enlightenment.

See also: ABERDEEN PHILOSOPHICAL SOCIETY; COMMENSENSISM; ENLIGHTENMENT, CONTINENTAL; MORAL SENSE THEORIES; NATURALISM IN ETHICS; NATURALISM IN SOCIAL SCIENCE

References and further reading

Berry, C. (1997) *The Social Theory of the Scottish Enlightenment*, Edinburgh: Edinburgh University Press. (Provides both a detailed analysis and a synoptic overview, including a survey of interpretations.)

* Blackwell, T. (1735) *An Enquiry into the Life and Writings of Homer*, repr. Menston: Scolar Press 1972. (Investigates the reciprocal relationships between the poet, his poetry and his socio-cultural context.)

Blair, H. (1783) *Lectures on Rhetoric and Belles-Lettres*, ed. H.F. Harding, Carbondale, IL: Southern Illinois University Press, 2 vols, 1965. (A largely derivative but for that reason valuably indicative assembly of contemporary views on literary and aesthetic topics.)

Campbell, G. (1776) *The Philosophy of Rhetoric*, ed. L. Bitzer, Carbondale, IL and Edwardsville, IL: Southern Illinois University Press. (Investigates how language, widely understood, is linked to the faculties of human nature.)

Campbell, R. and Skinner, A. (eds) (1982) *The Origins and Nature of the Scottish Enlightenment*, Edinburgh: Donald. (A collection which deals both with the institutional setting, precursors and aspects of the Scots' thought).

* Collingwood, R. (1961) *The Idea of History*, Oxford:

Oxford University Press. (Outlines his idealist philosophy of history and criticizes alternative views.)

* Dunbar, J. (1780) *Essays on the History of Mankind in Rude and Cultivated Ages*, Bristol: Thoemmes Press, 2nd edn, 1781. (Develops a distinctive view of psychological and social development.)

* Ferguson, A. (1767) *An Essay on the History of Civil Society*, ed. D. Forbes, Edinburgh: Edinburgh University Press, 1966. (Frequently interpreted as a pioneering work of sociology, it is a wide-ranging moralistic assessment of commercial society in a broad historical sweep.)

Gerard, A. (1759) *An Essay on Taste*, facsimile repr. of 3rd edn (1780), Gainsville, FL: Scholars' Facsimiles & Reprints, 1963. (Applies associationist principles to literary criticism.)

* Hayek, F. (1960) *The Constitution of Liberty*, London: Routledge & Kegan Paul. (Important statement of Hayek's philosophy where his debt to the Scots is acknowledged.)

Hont, I. and Ignatieff, M. (eds) (1983) *Wealth and Virtue: The Shaping of Political Economy in the Scottish Enlightenment*, Cambridge: Cambridge University Press. (A collection of articles focusing on the Scots' analyses of commerce.)

* Hume, D. (1739–40) *A Treatise of Human Nature*, ed. L.A. Selby-Bigge; revised P.H. Nidditch, Oxford: Clarendon Press, 1978. (One of philosophy's great books that Hume himself later dismissed in preference for his subsequent writing)

* —— (1741–77) *Essays Moral Political and Literary*, ed. E.F. Miller, Indianapolis, IN: Liberty Press, revised edn. 1987. (Important collection, especially for Hume's economic and political thinking.)

* —— (1757) *Natural History of Religion* , ed. W. Colver, Oxford: Clarendon Press, 1976. (Traces the development of religious belief from its roots in human nature)

Hutcheson, F. (1725) *Inquiry into the Original of our Ideas of Beauty and Virtue*, London and Dublin. (Contains his first formulation of the philosophy of moral sense.)

* Kames, Lord (Home, H.) (1751) *Essays on the Principles of Morality and Natural Religion*, Edinburgh: Kincaid & Donaldson; revised London: Hitch & Hawes; Dodsley, Rivington, Fletcher & Richardson, 1758; Edinburgh: Bell & Murray, 1779. (Contains critiques of Hutcheson, Hume and Smith, late editions amended the necessitarianism of the first edition.)

* —— (1758) *Historical Law Tracts*, Edinburgh: Kincaid & Bell; London: Millar, 2 vols; revised and enlarged, Edinburgh: Bell & Creech; London: Cadell, 1776, 1 vol. (Traces the evolution of legal

thinking, important for its evocation of stages of social development.)

* —— (1774) *Sketches on the History of Man*, Edinburgh: Creech; London: Strahan & Cadell; 3rd edn with Kames' last additions and corrections, Edinburgh: Creech; London: Strahan & Cadell, 1778. (A rambling comendium that deals idiosyncratically with most aspects of social life.)

* Millar, J. (1779) *The Origin of the Distinction of Ranks*, 3rd amended edn, repr. in W. Lehmann (ed.), *John Millar of Glasgow*, Cambridge: Cambridge University Press, 1960. (The Ranks is another work that has been identified as a significant early sociological treatise.)

—— (1787–1803) *Historical View of the English Government*; excerpts repr. in W. Lehmann (ed.), *John Millar of Glasgow*, Cambridge: Cambridge University Press, 1960. (The last 4 vols were published posthumously.)

Reid, T. (1764) *Inquiry into the Human Mind, On the Principles of Common Sense*, Edinburgh. (The seminal statement of Common Sense philosophy.)

* Robertson, W. (1777) *The History of America*, ed. D. Stewart, in 1 vol., London: William Ball, 1740. (Book 4 contains an important discussion of Amerindian society.)

Sher, R. (1985) *Church and University in the Scottish Enlightenment*, Edinburgh: Edinburgh University Press. (Contains a lengthy bibliography.)

* Smith, A. (1757) *The Theory of Moral Sentiments* ed. A.Macfie and D. Raphael, Indianapolis, IN: Liberty Press, 1982. (A major work that outlines a philosophical psychology of moral judgment.)

* — (1776) *An Inquiry into the Nature and Causes of the Wealth of Nations*, ed. R.Campbell and A. Skinner, Indianapolis, IN: Liberty Press, 1981. (Epoch-making work that laid the foundation for analytical economics and advocated free trade.)

Stewart, M.A. (ed.) (1990) *Studies in the Philosophy of the Scottish Enlightenment*, Oxford: Clarendon Press. (A mix of general and specific – especially on Hume – essays.)

CHRISTOPHER J. BERRY

ENTAILMENT *see* RELEVANCE
LOGIC AND ENTAILMENT

ENTHUSIASM

For much of the seventeenth and eighteenth centuries, enthusiasm denotes a state of (claimed) divine inspiration. The claimed inspiration is almost always seen by those who employ the term as delusory, and enthusiasm is almost always seen as bad, akin to fanaticism, irrationality, and madness. The term is most commonly applied to Protestants outside the Church of England and, at times, to Catholics and pre-Christian mystics. Throughout the period, enthusiasm much less often denotes devotion and zeal or poetic inspiration. In the nineteenth century, concern with enthusiasm declines.

There are various debates about enthusiasm, understood as claimed divine inspiration. One concerns its causes. Thomas HOBBES (1651) suspected that much enthusiasm was hypocritical, a political ploy. Others linked enthusiasm with melancholy. Henry MORE (1662) argued that melancholy causes both overheated passions and an overheated imagination; enthusiasts suppose that anything extraordinary, such as the state of their passions, must be due to God, and so conclude that they are inspired. Later, Isaac Taylor (1823) drops the reference to melancholy but leaves an excessive imagination, trespassing on the terrain of reason, as the etiology. Of the cases where no explanation is obvious, Meric Casaubon (1656) argues that the cause is likely still natural; there are many extraordinary yet natural events. All note that attention and admiration from others discourages critical thought about one's claims to inspiration.

More, Casaubon and Taylor proceed by cataloging varieties of enthusiasm, treating each as a natural and medical rather than supernatural and possibly heretical phenomenon. Although they see that their approach could, in other hands, furnish a thoroughly sceptical account of religious experience, they do not intend to rule out true divine inspiration. They merely quarrel with contemporary claims to it.

Another debate concerns why enthusiasm is bad. Enthusiasm can be criticized on epistemic grounds. Enthusiasts justify their claims, not by reason or faith, but by citing direct communication from God. John LOCKE (1700) asks why we should believe that such communication has occurred. This cannot be proven by citing the feeling that the claim is from God, nor by noting that we cannot explain why the claim is made, nor by citing our strength of conviction, nor by showing by reason that the claim is true. One needs reason to show that the claim comes from God. Locke thinks this is possible: Moses's doubts were dispelled by the burning but unconsumed bush and the transformation of the rod into a serpent. But Locke supposes contemporary enthusiasts have no such assurance.

Enthusiasm can be criticized on religious grounds. It leads to schisms in the Church, and an opposition to church government, since mediators between oneself and God are unnecessary. It leads one to read, or even ignore, Scripture in light of one's own fancy, rather than in light of scholarly interpretation. Jeremy Taylor ([c.1640–1670] 1854) worries that enthusiasts bypass the established ways to grace. More's attack on enthusiasm is motivated by his desire to defend Christian belief and experience as rational. Enthusiasts, by abandoning reason for an 'inner light,' make this impossible.

Enthusiasm can also be criticized on moral and political grounds. Enthusiasm was often seen as a leading cause of the Anabaptist Peasants' Revolt and the English civil war. On the standard view, enthusiasts foist their views on others with force and intolerance, since they are convinced that they act in God's name. They are rarely up for reasoned discussion with others, particularly given the private nature of their inspiration. They ignore common morality for 'higher' concerns. And in opposing church government, they bring anarchy, since church government is vital to civil government.

Against this, David HUME (1741) gives an idiosyncratic analysis: religions based on enthusiasm have violent beginnings, given the presumptuous character of those prone to enthusiasm. But in time, these religions become calm and innocuous, since there is little church government and ritual to support their practices. In their pride and resistance to church government, Hume argues, enthusiasts become friends to civil liberty.

A third debate centres on the best way of combating enthusiasm. Some favour state coercion. The Third Earl of SHAFTESBURY (1711) replies that religious enthusiasm flourishes under oppression. He favours free public debate, featuring ridicule of enthusiasts. (Swift's *A Tale of a Tub* (1704) is the most notable example.) To defend *oneself* against enthusiasm, Shaftesbury recommends self-knowledge sufficient to identify the true causes of any supposed inspiration. For those infected, More recommends temperance, humility, and reason. Jeremy Taylor recommends prudence.

A fourth debate centres on distinguishing good and bad enthusiasm. More, Locke and Isaac Taylor suggest various tests for true divine inspiration. In addition to public phenomena such as the burning bush, the beliefs and actions which proceed from the inspiration must be moral, reasonable and consistent with Scripture. Worries about what happens should only some of these tests be fulfilled, like worries about

Biblical instances of enthusiasm that do not meet these tests, are largely ignored. The emphasis is on exposing the bad, not identifying the good.

Here Shaftesbury is an exception. He argues in favour of enthusiasm, largely because he treats any divine inspiration not as a matter of supernatural prophesying, quaking, or speaking in tongues, but as a natural raising of the imagination in the presence of beauty and goodness. Enthusiasm, he argues, is needed for any extraordinary achievement. Without it, life is dull and brutish.

In the nineteenth century, enthusiasm comes to be usually understood as mere devotion and zeal, without implying divine inspiration as their cause. The term 'enthusiasm' largely ceases to name an object of philosophical debate, since whether devotion and zeal are good or bad depends largely on the ends to which they are put. Debate about divine inspiration continues in literature on the epistemology of religion. But in the nineteenth century the issue becomes less pressing – perhaps because the Evangelical movement brought enthusiasm into the Church of England, perhaps because enthusiasts were seen as less of a political threat, or perhaps because increased scepticism about defending Christianity on rational grounds made the contrast between rational and enthusiastic believer less sharp.

See also: MYSTICISM, NATURE OF; RELIGION AND EPISTEMOLOGY; RELIGIOUS EXPERIENCE

References and further reading

Alston, W. P. (1991) *Perceiving God*, Ithaca, NY: Cornell University Press. (A sympathetic, analytic treatment of the epistemology of religious experience.)

* Casaubon, M. (1656) *A Treatise Concerning Enthusiasme*, Gainesville, FL: Scholars' Facsimiles and Reprints, 1970. (A naturalistic etiology and taxonomy. A shorter edition was published in 1655.)

* Hobbes, T. (1651) *Leviathan*, ed. C.B. Macpherson, Harmondsworth: Penguin, 1968. (For Hobbes's scepticism concerning divine possession, see especially chapters 8, 12, 32 and 34.)

* Hume, D. (1741) 'Of Superstition and Enthusiasm', in *Essays: Moral, Political, and Literary*, ed. E.F. Miller, Indianapolis, IN: Liberty, 1985. (A contrast between enthusiasm and superstition, with respect to etiology and consequences. The essay appeared in the first (1741) edition of Hume's *Essays*.)

Knox, R.A. (1950) *Enthusiasm*, Oxford: Clarendon Press. (A detailed history of the subject, concentrating on the seventeenth and eighteenth centuries.)

* Locke, J. (1700) *An Essay Concerning Human Understanding*, 2nd edn, ed. P.H. Nidditch, Oxford: Clarendon Press, 1979. (See 'Of Enthusiasm', IV.xix. Epistemic tests for divine inspiration. Locke added this chapter to the second (1700) edition of the *Essay*, first published 1689.)

* More, H. (1662) *Enthusiasmus Triumphatus*, Los Angeles, CA: Augustan Reprint Society, 1966. (A shorter early edition was published in 1656. Another naturalistic etiology and taxonomy. Snappier than Casaubon.)

* Shaftesbury, A., 3rd Earl of (1711) *Characteristics of Men, Manners, Opinions, Times, etc.*, ed. J.M. Robertson, Glouster, MA: Peter Smith, 1963, 2 vols. (For defence of enthusiasm, understood as a quality necessary for any extraordinary achievement, see especially *A Letter Concerning Enthusiasm, The Moralists*, part 3, section 2, and *Miscellaneous Reflections* II, chapter I.)

Steffan, T.G. (1941) 'The Social Argument Against Enthusiasm (1650–1660)', *Texas Studies in English*, 21: 39–63. (An excellent summary.)

* Swift, J. (1704) *A Tale of a Tub and other works*, ed. A. Ross and D. Woolley, Oxford: Oxford University Press, 1986. (The most famous instance of enthusiasm ridiculed.)

* Taylor, I. (1823) *The Natural History of Enthusiasm*, London: Holdsworth. (The emphasis is on errors of religion rather than errors of rationality.)

* Taylor, J. (1854) *The Whole Works of the Right Reverend Jeremy Taylor*, ed. R. Herber and C.P. Eden, London: Longman, Brown, Green, and Longmans, 10 vols. (Taylor wrote in the 1640s through the 1660s. His references to enthusiasm are scattered; Steffan (1941) gives a short account and references.)

Tucker, S.I. (1972) *Enthusiasm*, Cambridge: Cambridge University Press. (A clear history of the word 'enthusiasm,' with a fine bibliography.)

ROBERT SHAVER

ENTSCHEIDUNGSPROBLEM

see CHURCH'S THEOREM AND THE DECISION PROBLEM

ENVIRONMENTAL AESTHETICS *see* NATURE, AESTHETIC APPRECIATION OF

ENVIRONMENTAL ETHICS

Theories of ethics try to answer the question, 'How ought we to live?'. An environmental ethic refers to our natural surroundings in giving the answer. It may claim that all natural things and systems are of value in their own right and worthy of moral respect. A weaker position is the biocentric one, arguing that living things merit moral consideration. An ethic which restricts the possession of moral value to human persons can still be environmental. Such a view may depict the existence of certain natural values as necessary for the flourishing of present and future generations of human beings. Moral respect for animals has been discussed since the time of the pre-Socratic philosophers, while the significance to our wellbeing of the natural environment has been pondered since the time of Kant and Rousseau. The relation of the natural to the built environment, and the importance of place, is a central feature of the philosophy of Heidegger. Under the impact of increasing species loss and land clearance, the work on environmental ethics since the 1970s has focused largely on one specific aspect of the environment – nature in the wild.

1   Respect for life and the 'natural'
2   Radical environmental ethics
3   Applications and environmental politics
4   A contested project

1   Respect for life and the 'natural'

Living things are characterized by a tendency to preserve and maintain themselves in the face of environmental challenge. Aristotelian and Stoic thinkers regarded such self-preservation as an 'end' or *telos* at which living things aim. A weaker conception of the endeavour to maintain life is found in Spinoza's conception of *conatus* (see SPINOZA, B. DE §§9–11). The term 'autopoeitic' has been coined more recently to refer to those processes which are self-producing and self-maintaining. Are living things – characterized as having *telos*, *conatus*, or being autopoeitic – worth respecting for themselves (see MORAL STANDING §§1–2)? And would such respect be moral? Only in the present century has an affirmative answer to both questions been argued in detail (see Taylor and Mathews, in Brennan (ed.) 1995; O'Neill 1993).

This contrasts with moral concern for animals, which can be traced back to the pre-Socratic philosophers of ancient Greece (see PRESOCRATIC PHILOSOPHY). The Renaissance essayist Montaigne referred to them as our 'brothers and companions', while Jaques, in Shakespeare's *As You Like It*, made a striking plea for the rights of deer to graze in the forest undisturbed by hunters. A peak of concern for animals was reached in the eighteenth century when there was great debate over whether orang-utans should be classified as a kind of human. Since then, various forms of animal liberation have been proposed on both consequentialist and deontological grounds (see CONSEQUENTIALISM; DEONTOLOGICAL ETHICS).

It was also in the eighteenth century that the Swiss philosopher Jean-Jacques Rousseau urged extending our moral concern beyond animals to include care for plants and all living things. Deploring the utilitarian preoccupation with medicinal uses of herbs, he quips: 'It is no use seeking garlands for shepherdesses among the ingredients of an enema' (1782: 110). At roughly the same time, Immanuel Kant's *Critik der Urteilskraft (Critique of Judgment)* (1790) emphasized the importance of aesthetic experiences of nature to human wellbeing (see KANT. I. §12). Kant does not, however, suggest that animals or other natural things have any moral worth in their own right. If it is morally wrong to beat a dog or damage a beautiful landscape, this will be because of the damage these acts do to human sensibilities and character.

Rousseau was the inspiration for French romanticism and can claim to be the first environmental ethicist. Two centuries later, Aldo Leopold, professor of forestry at the University of Wisconsin unconsciously echoes him: 'Examine each question in terms of what is ethically and aesthetically right, as well as what is economically expedient. A thing is right when it tends to preserve the integrity, stability and beauty of the biotic community' (Leopold, in Zimmerman *et al.* (eds) 1993). Leopold's land ethic has been philosophically influential since its revival by American writers in the 1970s and 1980s.

2   Radical environmental ethics

The best-known radical ethic, Arne Naess' 'deep ecology', argues that human self-realization depends on identification with nature (see SELF-REALIZATION). Deep ecology started as a doctrine of biospheric egalitarianism – that all living things have the same claim to live and flourish. It evolved into a platform meant to embrace all those who recognize the inherent value of natural things and who share a concern to preserve natural diversity whatever their differences in underlying philosophies (see Zimmerman *et al.* (eds) 1993). A key point of deep ecology is that all living things are members of larger biotic or ecological communities. The larger community may then be regarded as a place of value, with individual needs and projects assessed in terms of their contribution to the good of the larger whole.

333

Other radical positions are already aligned with well-known political standpoints. Murray Bookchin's 'social ecology' is a type of Green anarchism, while some ecofeminists regard the destruction of nature as intimately linked to the oppressive structures of patriarchy (see ANARCHISM). Although these latter positions are associated with what Michael Zimmerman (1994) calls 'countercultural' movements, they need not be morally radical in the sense of advocating an ecocentric or biocentric ethic. Most eco-anarchists hold anthropocentric value theories, and different feminist theories give contrasting accounts of the value of nature and the position of women with respect to it. As a result, there is no generally agreed radical platform. Instead, there is often strife among competing interests. For example, deep ecology has been attacked by ecofeminists as a form of patriarchal imposition (Salleh, in Brennan (ed.) 1995) or as embodying masculine egoism (Plumwood 1993).

3 Applications and environmental politics

In an applied turn for the subject, several writers have studied the philosophy of policy and the limits of economic methods in application to environmental valuation. Typical work in this area is by Mark Sagoff, Bryan Norton and Kristin Shrader-Frechette. For the applied workers, issues about nuclear wastes, pollution, cost-benefit analysis and the working of the global economy are of central importance (see TECHNOLOGY AND ETHICS). However, for many of these writers, the 'environment' in question is still the wilderness. Others, such as Henry David THOREAU and Martin HEIDEGGER have found nature closer to home. Heidegger's work has been taken up and applied by some writers on architecture, especially Christian Norberg-Schulz (1988).

For Heidegger human life takes place 'between earth and sky' (see Norberg-Schulz 1988: 38–42). Architecture and engineering are means of bringing a landscape into being: 'The bridge gathers the earth as landscape around the stream.... It does not just connect banks that are already there. The banks emerge as banks only as the bridge crosses the stream.' The concepts of place, orientation and identification are central to his account of humans as dwelling in a land. It can also be argued that an ethic of care for the earth is derivable from Heidegger's work: the contribution of the individual to the greater totality is to protect and articulate the place they have been given to take care of. This may be the meaning of Heidegger's statement that 'mortals dwell inasmuch as they save the earth...' (1971). This account accepts the inevitability of, and necessity for, human intervention in nature. Despite Heidegger's

problematic association with German National Socialism, Norberg-Schulz provides a detoxified interpretation which permits his ideas to resonate with those of ecofeminists, Leopoldians and 'deep' ecologists.

Bertrand Russell comments in his *History of Western Philosophy* that Hitler is an outcome of Rousseau. Certainly, there are well-known connections between ecologistic thinking and the political right, not just confined to Heidegger. Ernest HAECKEL, who coined the term 'ecology', was associated with the extreme right, the Hitler youth were taught to value nature and the SS training manual declared the forests of Germany to be of special value (Pois 1986). Although followers of the deep ecology platform are typically vague about the political solutions they put forward, the position has on occasion been accused of supporting 'eco-fascism'. The fear behind this accusation is that biocentrism or ecocentrism may motivate the state to be unacceptably coercive towards individuals for the sake of some larger environmental good. Usually, however, supporters of deep ecology take pains to distance themselves from fascistic or totalitarian solutions to environmental problems. It should be noted that one of the best-known published defences of environmental totalitarianism is in the work of Hans Jonas (1985), an avowed anthropocentric theorist.

4 A contested project

Since the 1970s, acceptance that living things, and possibly all natural things, have value in their own right has been the touchstone to distinguish those who are 'deeper' Green theorists from those of a 'shallower' style (see Sylvan and Bennett 1994). It very soon appeared that the animal protection movement and the 'new' environmental consciousness were on a collision course (see ANIMALS AND ETHICS). While animal liberationists focused on freeing animals from various human oppressions, the new ecological sensibility was less concerned about the evils of the intensive farm than with the fate of its waste stream. Extreme animal advocates thought up schemes for reducing the total amount of animal suffering by the abolition of predation and parasitism; meantime the new ecological thinkers recognized the naturalness of suffering and death in the struggle for existence.

Behind this difference lay a lack of clarity about the concept of nature. Should humans in some sense 'follow nature' despite the presence of pain and harm throughout the living world (see Mill 1874; Rolston, in Brennan (ed.) 1995)? The French theorist Michel Serres (1995) diagnosed the environmental crisis as stemming in part from the inability to state coherently the distinction between 'nature' and 'culture' (see

FRENCH PHILOSOPHY OF SCIENCE §7). In a related vein, Jean-François Lyotard has suggested that animals can be wronged in a way that forbids restitution: their difference from humans means that the rules of human justice, and for the assigning of damages, cannot be applied legitimately to them. So animals are forever barred from the possibility of bearing witness according to human rules (see LYOTARD, J.-F.). If Lyotard's suggestion were extended to nonhuman objects in general, then there would arguably be no viewpoint from which a comprehensive ethic of the environment could be formulated. Notice that the grounds for such pessimism seem overstated. Even if the rules of human justice do not, literally, apply to dogs, cats and rabbits, we have no difficulty in describing actions towards animals as 'kind', 'unfair', 'cruel' and so on.

Maintaining a narrow perspective, the agenda set by many American, Australian and Norwegian writers was focused firmly on issues concerned with wilderness and the reasons for its preservation. Virtually no attention was paid to the built environment. Outside the cities, the environment of most people is the savannah. But it was seldom mentioned either. Instead, most environmental philosophers were concerned with the forest and the mountain, places of recreation for the elite and of permanent abode of only a few humans. Perhaps the new sub-discipline should have been called 'the philosophy of wild places' or 'jungle ethics'.

Writers like Naess and Rolston have followed the eighteenth-century romantics – especially Kant and Rousseau – by emphasizing the importance of wilderness experience to the human psyche. Lifestyles in which such enthusiasms can be indulged demand a standard of living far beyond the dreams of most of the world's population. Travel to wild places often uses the jet aircraft and motor transport. It has been argued that the motor car is at the heart of many of the most serious environmental problems, including pollution and resource depletion. The economic structures which support elite access to wilderness seem to be implicated in the destruction and pollution which provoked environmental concern in the first place. Yet there is seldom much discussion of car-dependency in the literature.

This is not the only area of silence. The exploitation, oppression and war associated with securing oil supplies and other resources are not normally discussed. A similar silence hangs over toxic waste dumping, forced movements of populations, civil war, the causes of world poverty and the other social features that have damaging environmental impact. In the absence of a discussion of the unequal use of resources and energy across different groups of people

and different nations, the focus on wilderness preservation led to a suspicion that Western-style radical environmentalism had a bias against the developing countries. Perhaps, indeed, it was another aspect of the imperialist or colonizing projects of the rich countries (as suggested in Guha, in Brennan (ed.) 1995) (see DEVELOPMENT ETHICS).

The project of environmental ethics involves intense scrutiny of the foundations of value theory. As a result, there is the potential for engagement with mainstream moral philosophy as well as with rational actor theory and economics. Questions about the aesthetics of nature resonate with many topics in literary and art theory, including the significance of originals as opposed to fakes (see Elliot, in Elliot (ed.) 1995). Finally, the project provides a route into discussions of the general predicaments of modernity and postmodernism, as evidenced by Zimmerman (1994) and Serres (1995) (see POSTMODERNISM).

See also: AGRICULTURAL ETHICS; ECOLOGICAL PHILOSOPHY; ENGINEERING AND ETHICS; FUTURE GENERATIONS, OBLIGATIONS TO

References and further reading

* Brennan, A. (ed.) (1995) *The Ethics of the Environment*, London: Dartmouth. (A selection of essays aimed at the researcher and advanced student, covering the central areas of the field. Among the articles included are: 'The Ethics of Respect for Nature', by Paul Taylor; 'Conservation and Self-Realization: A Deep Ecology Perspective', by Freya Mathews; 'The Ecofeminism/Deep Ecology Debate', by Ariel Salleh; 'Can and Ought We to Follow Nature?', by Holmes Rolston; and 'Radical American Environmentalism and Wilderness Preservation: A Third World Critique', by Ramachandra Guha.)

Elliot, R. (ed.) (1995) *Environmental Ethics*, Oxford: Oxford University Press. (This collection includes material critical of radical and 'deep' approaches. Includes the editor's own essay, 'Faking Nature'.)

* Heidegger, M. (1971) *Poetry, Language, Thought*, trans. and with an introduction by A. Hofstadter, New York: Harper & Row. (Three essays in this volume – 'The Origin of the Work of Art', 'The Thing' and 'Building, Dwelling, Thinking' – outline Heidegger's theory that our buildings can both disclose and appropriate our natural surroundings. When we build poetically, we dwell in and belong to the places we occupy.)

* Jonas, H. (1985) *The Imperative of Responsibility: In Search of An Ethics for the Technological Age*, Chicago, IL: University of Chicago Press, 128–38.

(Although arguing that natural things have a good of their own, Jonas insists that we only have a responsibility to care for nonhuman things to the extent that their good impinges on human flourishing.)

* Kant, I. (1790) *Critik der Urteilskraft*, trans. W.S. Pluhar, *Critique of Judgment*, Indianapolis, IN: Hackett Publishing Company, 1987. (Places emphasis on the importance of aesthetic experiences of nature to human wellbeing.)
* Mill, J.S. (1874) 'Nature', in *Three Essays on Religion*, London: Longmans, Green, Reader and Dyer; repr. in *Collected Works of John Stuart Mill*, ed. J.M. Robson, London: Routledge and Toronto, Ont.: University of Toronto Press, 1991, vol. 10. (Poses a classic dilemma: the injunction to follow nature is either empty or wicked. Anyone who advocates 'following nature' needs to consider Mill's arguments.)
* Norberg-Schulz, C. (1988) *Architecture, Meaning and Place*, New York: Electa/Rizzoli. (Provides a reading of Heidegger enriched by his own striking turns of phrase. An easy introduction to difficult subject-matter.)
* O'Neill, J. (1993) *Ecology, Policy and Politics*, London: Routledge. (A useful study of environmental ethics and policy informed by an Aristotelian conception of human wellbeing.)
* Plumwood, V. (1993) *Feminism and the Mastery of Nature*, London: Routledge. (A sophisticated and philosophically-challenging study of ecofeminism.)
* Pois, R.A. (1986) *National Socialism and the Religion of Nature*, London: Croom Helm. (A cautionary historical survey of how ideas about nature were partly constitutive of the myth of the Herrenvolk.)
* Rousseau, J.-J. (1782) *Rêveries du promeneur solitaire*, trans. P. France, *Reveries of the Solitary Walker*, Harmondsworth: Penguin, 1979. (In this neglected work, Rousseau dreams of touching nature, identifying with it and so becoming free from 'the memory of men and the attacks of the wicked'. The solitariness of the walker reminds the reader that such identification requires withdrawal from society and the social contract.)
* Serres, M. (1992) *The Natural Contract*, trans. E. MacArthur and W. Paulson, Ann Arbor, MI: University of Michigan Press, 1995. (Stimulating, if obscure, attempt to explain why a global environmental problem may elude both human description and social legislation.)
* Sylvan, R. and Bennett, D. (1994) *Greening Ethics*, Cambridge: White Horse Press (A defence of a radical environmental ethic with attention to its political consequences.)
* Zimmerman, M., Callicott, J.B., Sessions, G., Warren, K.J., Clark, J. (eds) (1993) *Environmental Philosophy: From Animal Rights to Radical Ecology*, Englewood Cliffs, NJ: Prentice Hall. (A typical introductory collection focusing on often-quoted material. Includes Aldo Leopold's 'The Land Ethic'.)
* Zimmerman, M. (1994) *Contesting Earth's Future*, Berkeley, CA: University of California Press. (This work discusses countercultural movements in the United States in the context of the postmodern predicament.)

ANDREW BRENNAN

ENVIRONMENTALISM
see GREEN POLITICAL PHILOSOPHY

EPICHARMUS (*c.* early 5th century BC)

One of the earliest Greek dramatists, Epicharmus wrote mostly comedies with mythological content in Sicily around 500 BC. A number of philosophical passages were attributed to him in antiquity; their authenticity, sometimes doubted even then, has remained controversial, but the quotations were widely influential and remain of interest.

Although Epicharmus' comedies are lost, fragments provide tantalizing hints of their character: short farces filled with slapstick, stock characters, lively language and sententious maxims; mythological burlesques, often involving Hercules and Odysseus. His appreciation for the comic possibilities of all aspects of contemporary Greek culture led him on occasion to introduce and parody such recent developments as rhetorical theory and philosophical speculation; for example, Aristotle reports that he attacked Xenophanes, and one of his mythological plays was entitled *Logos and Logina* ('Mr and Mrs Reason').

In later antiquity, Epicharmus' frequent aphorisms and occasional (pseudo-) philosophical passages encouraged the popular view that he was a Pythagorean sage. Treatises on physics and medicine were attributed to him and 'authenticated' by acrostics, and collections of useful but largely spurious maxims circulated under his name (one introduction to such a collection survives on a papyrus); as early as the fourth century BC the Aristotelian Aristoxenus recognized that at least one philosophical work attributed to Epicharmus was not genuine. Doubters remained a minority however.

Also in the fourth century BC, the Sicilian author Alcimus accused Plato of having plagiarized the theories of Epicharmus (whom Plato twice cites with respect); four passages cited as evidence by Alcimus and said by him to derive from Epicharmus are transmitted by Diogenes Laertius. Only the first one (fr. 1) seems likely to be by Epicharmus. Its high-flown, seemingly serious contrast between the constant mutability of human beings and the eternal changelessness of the gods in fact probably served to make a ludicrous comic point: yesterday's borrower owes no money today, and the guest invited yesterday may be refused entrance today, since in the meantime each has become a different person; a man who promised payment yesterday but refuses payment on these grounds today can be beaten by his creditor with impunity – the defaulter's complaint can be refuted on these very same grounds. On the basis of this passage, Epicharmus was later said to have invented the so-called 'growing argument': if growth is the addition of new matter, whoever grows is constantly becoming a different individual, in which case there is no enduring individual who can be said to have grown (see STOICISM §6).

The other fragments distinguish the Good in itself from good people, who show by their actions that they have learned what it is, attribute wisdom to animals, and assert that beauty is in the eye of the beholder. It is unlikely that Epicharmus is the author, and they are certainly not the source of Plato's doctrines; but they do provide fascinating evidence of the degree to which philosophical discourse could find a place on the comic stage.

References and further reading

Cassio, A.C. (1985) 'Two Studies on Epicharmus and his Influence', *Harvard Studies in Classical Philology* 89: 37–51. (Discusses Alcimus' use of passages from Epicharmus to attack Plato and Aristoxenus' Pythagorizing interpretation of Epicharmus.)

* Epicharmus (c. early 5th century BC) Fragments, in H. Diels and W. Kranz (eds) *Die Fragmente der Vorsokratiker* (Fragments of the Presocratics), Berlin: Weidmann, 1952, 6th edn, vol. 1, 190–210. (The standard collection of the ancient sources; includes Greek texts with translations in German.)

Freeman, K. (1957) *Ancilla to The Pre-Socratic Philosophers*, Cambridge, MA: Harvard University Press, 34–40. (An English translation of the fragments in Diels' collection.)

Kaibel, G. (ed.) (1899) *Comicorum Graecorum Fragmenta. I.1: Doriensium Comoedia Mimi Phlyaces* (Fragments of the Greek Comic Poets. I.1: The Comedy of the Dorians, Mimes, Phlyacean Farces), Berlin: Weidmann, 88–147. (Provides the fullest collection of surviving reports and fragments.)

Pickard-Cambridge, Sir A. (1927) *Dithyramb Tragedy and Comedy*, revised T.B.L. Webster, Oxford: Clarendon Press, 2nd edn, 1962. (Chapter 4 pages 230–88, especially 247–55, presents an excellent survey of the material and its difficulties.)

Sedley, D. (1982) 'The Stoic Criterion of Identity', *Phronesis* 27: 255–75. (An important and stimulating analysis of the growing argument.)

GLENN W. MOST

EPICTETUS (AD *c.*50–*c.*120)

*Epictetus was a Greek Stoic philosopher of the late first and early second centuries AD. He developed Stoic ideas of responsibility into a doctrine of autonomy and inner freedom based on his concept of moral personality (*prohairesis*). Ethics and practical moral training are central to his thought, but he was also responsible for innovations in epistemology. He emphasized the need to achieve freedom from the passions and to maintain equanimity in the face of a world determined by a providential, though often inscrutable, fate. He frequently treats the Stoic Zeus as a personal deity, and his distinctive combination of personal piety and stringent rationalism (together with his pungent style) have contributed to his enduring influence.*

1 **Life and works**
2 **Teachings**
3 **Ethics**

1 Life and works

Born in Hierapolis of Phrygia, Epictetus was a slave owned by a powerful freedman at the court of Nero. He became a follower of the Stoic MUSONIUS RUFUS and a philosopher in his own right. At around the age of 40 he was banished and moved to Nicopolis on the Adriatic coast of Greece; there he taught until his death some time after 120. His thought owed most to early Stoicism, especially its third head CHRYSIPPUS, on whom he lectured. Epictetus wrote nothing for publication, but his student Arrian (a Roman aristocrat) recorded and published his informal lectures, mostly on ethics (the *Discourses*, of which four books survive). Epictetus' formal teaching consisted of the exegesis of early Stoic texts and possibly those of other philosophers. Arrian also compiled a *Handbook* of Epictetus' teaching (the *Enchiridion*). The Neoplatonic commentator SIMPLICIUS wrote a commentary on it, and it has been widely read since its revival in the Renaissance.

2 Teachings

The central idea of Epictetus' moral teaching is the distinction between what is in our power (*eph' hēmin*) and what is not. This contrast goes back to early Stoic discussions of determinism and moral responsibility (see STOICISM §21). For Epictetus, only our mental life (thoughts, beliefs, decisions, emotions) is in our power and so 'free'; hence it and the moral state dependent on it (virtue or vice) are the key to happiness. Everything else, including bodily pleasure and pain, is subject to control by external forces and so irrelevant to genuine moral welfare.

Epictetus did not organize his teaching around the traditional triad of logic, physics and ethics. Rather (*Discourses* III 2) he developed a scheme of three topics or areas of practice. First, desires and aversions must be managed, so as never to desire the unattainable nor to flee the inevitable. Two mental techniques are recommended to achieve this: the rational anticipation of possible negative outcomes and 'reservation' (*hupexairesis*, a restriction of desires with the proviso 'if that is what Zeus wills for me'). Since the only truly valuable things are in our power, this goal can be achieved by learning the difference between what is good and what is merely 'preferred'. Second, one must learn to manage impulses and choices and learn what the appropriate thing to do is in different circumstances; one must also learn the importance of living in an orderly, well-thought-out manner. The third topic aims at gaining control over one's own assent so that all error and precipitancy are avoided.

The first topic will free us from irrational passions (*pathē*). The second will guide us in our dealings with others. The third topic – based essentially on logic and epistemology – is reserved for those who have progressed through the first two. The intellectual strength it yields should be put to use in supporting a moral life, not indulged in for its own sake – a conception of the purpose of logic which goes back to the earliest generations of the Stoic school. In the *Discourses* Epictetus stresses that logic is of no value in its own right, but that it must serve ethical needs. (He makes the same point about virtually every form of learning, whether the expertise of professional literary critics and grammarians or even his own ability to expound the classical texts of early Stoicism.) The role of logic, then, is to help us

understand the workings of the world and our place in it – which requires the ability to make reliable inferences from careful observations.

Epictetus made one important innovation, which concerns the so-called 'preconceptions' (*prolēpseis*), the antecedent notions which most humans share. Earlier Stoics too were committed to the task of examining them and rendering them consistent with each other, with their experience, and with the common conceptions of other people. But for earlier Stoics the origin of these preconceptions lay in the normal experience of the world which virtually everyone shares. Epictetus converts these preconceptions into something approaching innate ideas. The impact of this change on ethics was negligible, but it foreshadowed important epistemological developments and the openness to Platonism which one senses in MARCUS AURELIUS.

We may form an impression of Epictetus' competence in logic and dialectic from his account of the master argument of DIODORUS CRONUS §5, which shows first-hand familiarity with several different Stoic views as well as with Diodorus, and from his many references to the technicalities of Stoic logic (*Discourses* II 19).

Physics, the second traditional branch of philosophy, is largely taken over from earlier Stoic theory. The key point is the providential organization of the world by nature (which Epictetus often regards as a personal god, Zeus). Nature is a rational organizing force and the principles which guide it are similar in kind to our own rationality. Hence, like earlier Stoics, Epictetus regards it as the perfection of our own rationality to accommodate ourselves willingly to the inevitable operations of the world. Where Chrysippus had spoken of the goal of life as learning to live in accordance with an understanding of what happens by nature, Epictetus speaks more often of following the will of Zeus. This more religious tone may be due to the nature of the *Discourses*, addressed as they were to a non-specialist audience; there is no reason to believe that Epictetus' views on the importance of physics or theology to ethics differed much from those of Chrysippus or CLEANTHES (whose *Hymn to Zeus* he quotes at the end of the *Enchiridion* alongside Plato's *Crito* and *Apology*, and Euripides).

3 Ethics

Ethics is clearly the core of Epictetus' teaching. Following a trend which is also apparent in the work of SENECA and Musonius, and which culminates perhaps in the *Meditations* of Marcus Aurelius, Epictetus emphasizes the importance of inner mental life. All philosophers who claimed Socrates as their basic inspiration held that happiness (EUDAIMONIA) was the goal of life and that it depended on the care of the soul. But later Stoics put more emphasis on the autonomy of our inner life, its independence of the contingencies of our bodily and social experience. Several features of Epictetus' thought flow from this:

(1) The contrast between what is in our power (*eph' hēmin*) and what is not: 'In our power are belief, impulse to action, desire, aversion – in a word, everything that *we* do; not in our power are our body, possessions, reputation, political office – in a word, everything that is not our own doing' (*Enchiridion* 1.1).

(2) The focus on *prohairesis*, or moral personality. Earlier Stoics seldom mention this term (which is important for ARISTOTLE (§20), though in a different sense); Epictetus adopted it to express the idea that their moral identity is something which rational agents can control and for which they are wholly responsible. In this respect it recalls Seneca's novel emphasis on will (Latin *voluntas*). Epictetus does not refer to anything which could not be expressed by referring to the commanding faculty (*hēgemonikon*) and to assent as earlier Stoics did, but the new term permits an emphasis on inner mental life.

(3) The polarization between our impressions (*phantasiai*) and the critical use which we make of them. Impressions can be external, such as the appearance of a possible source of pleasure or pain, or internal, such as our own opinions and notions, but all must be subjected to critical scrutiny before we accept them. This process, the 'use of impressions', is, like the Socratic *elenchos* (see SOCRATES §§2–3), internalized, and it is the most important moral practice which Epictetus urges on his audience.

Other philosophical schools appear frequently in Epictetus' lectures; he does not merely preach to the converted. He takes an anti-Epicurean stance, attacking Epicurus' neglect of logic, his denial of providence, his hedonism, and most of all the anti-social implications of his egoism (see ARCESILAUS; CARNEADES; EPICUREANISM §§10–11). The Academics are also attacked for their scepticism. As one might expect, Epictetus has an ambivalent attitude to CYNICS. He rejected the extremes of their life-style. But from another point of view, their moral autonomy made them an ideal for which to strive. It was inevitable that Epictetus should look up to the Cynics, whose very extremism turned them into symbols of the values which he held most dear. All human beings, he thought, must strive for inner freedom; the independent and even anti-social beha-viour of the Cynics expressed in a socially visible form the ultimate goal of moral life for Epictetus.

See also: STOICISM

List of works

Epictetus (*c.* early 2nd century AD) *Discourses*, trans. W.A. Oldfather, Loeb Classical Library, Cambridge, MA: Harvard University Press and London: Heinemann, 1925–8; trans. J. Souilhé, *Epictète: Entretiens*, Paris: Les Belles Lettres, 1941. (Greek text with, respectively, English translation and French translation; the latter edition is the more up to date.)

—— (*c.* early 2nd century AD) *The Handbook (Enchiridion)* , trans. W.A. Oldfather, Loeb Classical Library, Cambridge, MA: Harvard University Press and London: Heinemann, 1925–8; trans. N. White, *The Handbook of Epictetus*, Indianapolis, IN: Hackett, 1983. (The former includes Greek text; the latter is the best available translation, with a good introduction to Epictetus.)

References and further reading

Arnold, E.V. (1911) *Roman Stoicism*, Cambridge: Cambridge University Press. (Standard work, somewhat dated but still useful.)

Bonhöffer, A. (1890) *Epictet und die Stoa*, Stuttgart: Enke. (Still fundamental.)

—— (1894) *Die Ethik des Stoikers Epictet*, Stuttgart: Enke. (Still fundamental.)

Hershbell, J.P (1989) 'The Stoicism of Epictetus: Twentieth Century Perspectives', in W. Haase (ed.) *Aufstieg und Niedergang der römischen Welt*, Berlin: de Gruyter, II 36.3: 2, 148–63. (Excellent literature review; includes discussion of Epictetus' relation to other philosophers.)

Hijmans, B.L. (1959) *Askēsis: Notes on Epictetus' Educational System*, Assen: Van Gorcum. (Epictetus' life and work; focuses on moral education.)

Long, A.A. (1991) 'Representation and the Self in Stoicism', in S. Everson (ed.) *Psychology*, Cambridge: Cambridge University Press, 102–20. (Emphasizes the philosophical interest of Epictetus' psychology.)

BRAD INWOOD

EPICUREANISM

Epicureanism is one of the three dominant philosophies of the Hellenistic age. The school was founded by Epicurus (341–271 BC). Only small samples and indirect testimonia of his writings now survive, supplemented by the poem of the Roman Epicurean Lucretius, along with a mass of further fragmentary texts and secondary evidence. Its main features are an anti-teleological physics, an empiricist epistemology and a hedonistic ethics.

Epicurean physics eveloped out of the fifth-century atomist system of Democritus. The only per se existents are bodies and space, each of them infinite in quantity. Space includes absolute void, which makes motion possible, while body is constituted out of physically indissoluble particles, 'atoms'. Atoms are themselves further measurable into sets of absolute 'minima', the ultimate units of magnitude. Atoms are in constant rapid motion, at equal speed (since in the pure void there is nothing to slow them down). Stability emerges as an overall property of compounds, which large groups of atoms form by settling into regular patterns of complex motion. Motion is governed by the three principles of weight, collisions and a minimal random movement, the 'swerve', which initiates new patterns of motion and obviates the danger of determinism. Atoms themselves have only the primary properties of shape, size and weight. All secondary properties, for example, colour, are generated out of atomic compounds; given their dependent status, they cannot be added to the list of per se existents, but it does not follow that they are not real. Our world, like the countless other worlds, is an accidentally generated compound, of finite duration. There is no divine mind behind it. The gods are to be viewed as ideal beings, models of the Epicurean good life, and therefore blissfully detached from our affairs.

The foundation of the Epicurean theory of knowledge ('Canonic') is that 'all sensations are true' – that is, representationally (not propositionally) true. In the paradigm case of sight, thin films of atoms ('images') constantly flood off bodies, and our eyes mechanically register those which reach them, neither embroidering nor interpreting. These primary visual data (like photographs, which 'cannot lie') have unassailable evidential value. But inferences from them to the nature of external objects themselves involves judgment, and it is there that error can occur. Sensations thus serve as one of the three 'criteria of truth', along with feelings, a criterion of values and psychological data, and prolēpseis, naturally acquired generic conceptions. On the basis of sense evidence, we are entitled to infer the nature of microscopic or remote phenomena. Celestial phenomena, for example, cannot be regarded as divinely engineered (which would conflict with the prolēpsis of

god as tranquil), and experience supplies plenty of models adequate to explain them naturalistically. Such grounds amount to consistency with directly observed phenomena, and are called ouk antimarturēsis, 'lack of counterevidence'. Paradoxically, when several alternative explanations of the same phenomenon pass this test, all must be accepted as true. Fortunately, when it comes to the foundational tenets of physics, it is held that only one theory passes the test.

In ethics, pleasure is the one good and our innately sought goal, to which all other values are subordinated. Pain is the only bad, and there is no intermediate state. Bodily pleasure becomes more secure if we adopt a simple lifestyle which satisfies only our natural and necessary desires, with the support of like-minded friends. Bodily pain, when inevitable, can be outweighed by mental pleasure, which exceeds it because it can range over past, present and future enjoyments. The highest pleasure, whether of soul or of body, is a satisfied state, 'static pleasure'. The short-term ('kinetic') pleasures of stimulation can vary this state, but cannot make it more pleasant. In striving to accumulate such pleasures, you run the risk of becoming dependent on them and thus needlessly vulnerable to fortune. The primary aim should instead be the minimization of pain. This is achieved for the body through a simple lifestyle, and for the soul through the study of physics, which offers the most prized 'static' pleasure, 'freedom from disturbance' (ataraxia), by eliminating the two main sources of human anguish, the fears of god and of death. It teaches us that cosmic phenomena do not convey divine threats, and that death is mere disintegration of the soul, with hell an illusion. Being dead will be no worse than not having yet been born. Physics also teaches us how to evade determinism, which would turn moral agents into mindless fatalists: the indeterministic 'swerve' doctrine (see above), along with the logical doctrine that future-tensed propositions may be neither true nor false, leaves the will free.

Although Epicurean groups sought to opt out of public life, they respected civic justice, which they analysed not as an absolute value but as one perpetually subject to revision in the light of changing circumstances, a contract between humans to refrain from harmful activity in their own mutual interest.

1 The Epicureans

For the foundation and nature of the Epicurean school, and for Epicurus' own writings, see EPICURUS. After Epicurus' death in 271 BC the school continued to flourish, at Athens and in other centres around the Mediterranean, for at least five centuries. Although there were numerous developments and schisms, these were always moderated by appeals to the scriptural authority of Epicurus' own writings and those of his close collaborators Metrodorus, Polyaenus and Hermarchus.

The surviving writings of Epicurus include *Letter to Herodotus, Letter to Pythocles, Letter to Menoeceus, Kyriai doxai* (*Key Doctrines*) – all preserved in Book X of Diogenes Laertius – and parts of *On Nature*. In addition, we have from the first century BC the Epicurean poem of LUCRETIUS, dealing mainly with physics, and numerous fragmentary papyri of the Epicurean PHILODEMUS, excavated from a villa at Herculaneum. Finally, there is the second-century AD philosophical inscription of the Epicurean DIOGENES OF OENOANDA, which contains much supplementary information.

2 Foundations of physics

Whatever the universe consists of must be permanent. Nothing comes into being out of nothing or perishes into nothing – two fundamental principles widely regarded as indubitable, but defended by the Epicureans on empirical grounds (Lucretius I 159–264): literal generation would be incompatible with the observed regularities of natural processes, such as the dependence of organic growth on the right material conditions; and literal annihilation would, given the infinity of past time, by now have ensured that nothing at all was left. Nor can the universe (the 'all') be changed by addition or subtraction, since by definition it has nothing outside it that could enter or into which bits could escape.

Next comes a statement of what the universe does consist of: bodies and space (*Letter to Herodotus* 39–40). This is taken to be self-evident, that is, underivatively known and unchallengeable. The reasoning is no doubt that bodies are the things which most obviously have independent existence; and that since that independence is most evident in their ability

to move in space, the bits of space which they vacate as they move must exist independently of *them*.

Space is at this stage simply presented as what the bodies are in, and what they move through – a three-dimensional extension which persists whether occupied or unoccupied. When occupied it gets called 'place', when unoccupied 'void' (*kenon*, literally the 'empty'), and when things move through it 'room' (*chōra*, etymologically linked by Epicurus with *chōrein*, 'go'). Epicurus prefers to use these familiar terms rather than a generic one for 'space', for which Greek has no precise word (the concept itself being one which had emerged only gradually, with Epicurus perhaps the first to isolate it clearly), and which he manages to capture only by his invented phrase 'intangible nature' (*anaphēs physis*). That there is void, that is, that contrary to the majority ancient view some space is altogether empty, is argued by appeal to such phenomena as motion and permeation. Motion cannot be accounted for, it is argued (Lucretius I 370–83), by the alternative hypothesis of complementary redistribution of matter on the model of a fish exchanging places with the water when it swims. Even the fish would be stuck fast unless there were some void to break the deadlock. Otherwise it would be unable to move until the water had cleared a path for it, or the water until the fish had cleared a path for it.

As for body, it remains for now largely unanalysed, beyond a set of arguments to show that it must exist microscopically as well as macroscopically: its underlying atomic structure cannot be demonstrated until it has been shown that body and space are the sole constituents of the universe. And the next move is to show just that. First, body and space are analysed as contradictory opposites: only three-dimensional things exist *per se*, and if these are resistant they must be body, if non-resistant void (Lucretius I 430–9). This is the positive proof that body and space are not only irreducibly distinct but also jointly exhaustive. There then follows a supplementary argument (Lucretius I 449–82), in which all other contenders for *per se* existence – including properties and time – are written off as secondary attributes, parasitic on body and/or space. None of these could exist independently of bodies and/or space. Time is dependent on change, that is, on moving bodies. And even facts about the past (for example, that there was a Trojan War), which might seem to outlive the bodies (Agamemnon and others) of which they are true and therefore to acquire independent existence, are truths about places which still persist (Troy, Mycenae and so on), or, if you prefer, about the universe.

Only now that it is fully established can the body–space dualism be deployed to show that at the lowest level of analysis there will be not only portions of empty space uninterrupted by body but also portions of body uninterrupted by empty space – and therefore, since there is no third thing, totally uninterrupted. Being perfectly solid, these are 'atoms', literally 'uncuttables'. The capacity of a body to disintegrate is directly correlated to the amount of void within it; therefore a body containing no void at all is altogether indestructible (Lucretius I 511–39). That there are such bodies is confirmed both by the evident fact that matter is not completely annihilated by fragmentation, and by the observed regularities of nature, which imply that something altogether unchanging underlies them.

Having mapped the universe out into space occupied by discrete portions of body, Epicurus adds that both space and body are infinite in extent (*Letter to Herodotus* 41–2, Lucretius I 958–97). First, the infinity of the universe itself (a highly controversial thesis in antiquity, rejected by both the Platonist and the Aristotelian tradition) is argued by appeal to the notion of a limit: it could only be limited if there were something beyond it to limit it, and the notion of the universe (the 'all') precludes that. (Lucretius adds the time-honoured argument: what if I go to the supposed edge of the universe and throw something?) Second, it is argued that each of the two constituents of the universe must also, taken on its own, be infinite: finite body in infinite space would be too dissipated to form compounds, while infinite body in finite space would simply not fit.

3 Minima

The fifth-century atomists (see ATOMISM, ANCIENT; LEUCIPPUS; DEMOCRITUS §2) had first introduced atoms at least partly to circumvent the puzzles that ZENO OF ELEA (§§4–6) had derived from the supposition of infinite divisibility: any magnitude will, as the sum of infinitely many parts, be infinitely large; and motion will be impossible, since it will require the traversal of infinitely many sub-distances. But if atoms, as seems inevitable given their varying shapes and sizes, are not the smallest possible magnitudes but simply indissoluble lumps, it is hard to see that this kind of indivisibility can do anything to thwart Zeno: each atom will consist of infinitely many parts, and threaten to be infinitely large and/or untraversable.

Epicurus (*Letter to Herodotus* 56–9) starts by making the first clear distinction in ancient thought between (1) things which are physically indivisible, and (2) those which modern scholarship sometimes calls theoretically, conceptually or mathematically indivisible, but which in ancient usage are called either 'minimal' (*elachista*) or 'partless' (*amerē*). (For Epicurus' main predecessor in a theory of type (2), see DIODORUS CRONUS §2.) Not only, Epicurus says (*Letter to Herodotus* 56), (1) can things not be 'cut' to infinity (a reference to atoms, which are physically 'uncuttable'), as proved earlier, 'but also (2) we must not consider that in finite bodies there is *traversal* [moving along something part by part] to infinity, not even through smaller and smaller parts [that is, not even in a convergent series such as $\frac{1}{2}, \frac{1}{4}, \frac{1}{8}, \ldots$]'. Otherwise, he warns, Zenonian consequences will ensue.

By showing that a finite body cannot contain an infinite number of parts, Epicurus considers that he has established the existence of an absolutely smallest portion of body, which henceforward he calls 'the minimum (*elachiston*) in the atom'. Clearly it cannot be larger than an atom, or it would not be a minimum, so it must be either an entire atom or part of one. (For reasons which emerge later, it must in fact be the latter.) The idea that an extended magnitude like an atom consists of minimal or partless units is designed to avoid Zenonian paradoxes, but, as Aristotle had pointed out in *Physics* VI, it generates paradoxes of its own. In particular, it is hard to see how two partless items can be adjacent, since they cannot touch either part to part (they do not have parts) or whole to whole (or they would be co-extensive, not adjacent). Epicurus answers brilliantly with the analogy of the 'minimum in sensation' – the smallest magnitude you can see. Any larger visible magnitude consists of a precise number of these minima, which are seen as adjacent without touching in either of the two ways offered by Aristotle, but, as Epicurus puts it, 'in their own special way'. This provides a model which is readily transferable to the 'minimum in the atom'.

But it also follows, of course, that *any* extended magnitude will consist of an exact number of minima, since after analysis into minima there could not be a fraction of a minimum left over. This makes all magnitudes commensurable, and conflicts with the geometers' recognition of incommensurable lengths, for example, the side and diagonal of a square. So much the worse for geometry, was the conclusion of Epicurus and his collaborator Polyaenus, himself formerly a distinguished geometer. They concluded, at least provisionally, that geometry is false.

In one respect the analogy between the sensible and actual minimum fails. Visible minima are capable of independent motion (for example, a falling object viewed at a suitable distance might be a sensible minimum), but actual minima are not, says Epicurus. This perhaps reflects Aristotle's argument in *Physics* VI 10 that a partless entity (he is thinking especially of a geometric point) could not move except incidentally to the motion of a larger body. At all events, it follows that, since atoms move, no atom consists of just one minimum.

Atoms must vary widely in shape and size in order to account for the large range of phenomena (Lucretius II 333–477). But they cannot vary indefinitely, since out of a finite set of minima only a finite number of shapes can be formed. Being partless, minima cannot be partly adjacent, so two minima can only be arranged in one shape, three minima in only two shapes, and so on (Lucretius II 478–531).

4 Motion

Surprisingly, atoms never stop moving, even within a compound object, since the medium through which they move is void, which can offer them no resistance. More surprisingly, for the same reason they move at a vastly greater speed than any familiar motion through an obstructive medium such as air; even than sunlight, which is seen to spread from horizon to horizon virtually instantaneously (Lucretius II 142–64). More surprisingly still, they all move at equal speed, since in a vacuum, unlike air, there is no resistance from the medium to slow down the lighter ones more than the heavier ones (*Letter to Herodotus* 61). In stating all these claims, Epicurus is accepting paradoxical consequences of the hypothesis that void exists, consequences which Aristotle had drawn (*Physics* IV) in the belief that they were sufficiently absurd to discredit the hypothesis. Moreover, the equal speed of atoms was confirmed by another objection Aristotle thought he had found to atomism (*Physics* VI 2): if there is a minimal magnitude, there can be no differences of speed, because then in the time the faster object took to travel one minimum the slower one would, impossibly, have to travel less than one minimum. Epicurus welcomed this argument, along with the conclusion Aristotle thought absurd, because his theories of void and minima now offered two independent grounds for the same conclusion, that atoms move at equal speed.

The apparent lack of fit between these findings about atoms and the variable speed of macroscopic motions is explained as follows (*Letter to Herodotus* 62). Even in a compound object the individual atoms are perpetually moving, but in tight and regular cyclical patterns which make the complex as a whole stable. Phenomenal differences of speed, say between two runners, represent merely the aggregate motions of the atoms in each over an observed period of time.

There are three causes of an atom's motion. The first is its own weight, interpreted as an inherent tendency to move downwards (see §8). The second is collisions with other atoms, which can deflect an originally downward motion along any number of new rectilinear trajectories, thus generating the patterns of motion of which compounds are born.

The third cause of atomic motion is the 'swerve' (*parenklisis*), whereby an atom may shift from its rectilinear trajectory onto an adjacent one – a displacement sideways by a distance of one minimum (there being no smaller distance). This happens 'at no fixed place or time', meaning that the occurrence of a swerve is causally undetermined. The theory, derided by Epicurus' opponents but now recognized as comparable in its implications to modern quantum indeterminism, looks like a drastic solution requiring a drastic problem. Two such problems are recorded (Lucretius II 216–93). First, since all atomic motion starts out as vertical and equal in speed, without a swerve no collisions would ever have started, and hence no world could have been formed. It may be doubted whether this was a sufficiently pressing problem to motivate an abandonment of universal causality: given the infinite past history of the universe, Epicurus had no need to posit a very first collision; in which case every collision could have been explained as the effect of previous ones. The second problem seems to have been the real motivation of the swerve: if all atomic motion is causally determined, free will becomes impossible (see §12).

5 Qualities

Atoms themselves have only the primary or ineliminable features of body: size, shape and weight. They lack the secondary properties of colour, flavour and so on. The ground for this parsimony is (*Letter to Herodotus* 54–5) that secondary properties are in their nature changeable, whereas atoms have been posited as the enduring entities which underlie change. Atomism instead treats colour and the like as purely macroscopic properties, caused by the individual shapes and overall arrangement of the constituent atoms in a compound body, and changed if that arrangement changes. Lucretius frequently compares the explanatory economy of this system to that of the alphabet, capable of generating endless different words simply by rearranging a modest stock of letters. In practice the crudely sketched atomistic explanations of macroscopic properties owe more to the shapes than to the arrangement of a thing's constituent atoms (fluids consist of smaller and rounder atoms, sweet things of smoother ones...), although the degree of separation between atoms plays some part.

There are two kinds of properties (*symbebēkota*). 'Permanent accompaniments' (Greek *ta aidion parakolouthounta*, Latin *coniuncta*) are essential to a thing's very existence, for example, tangibility for body and heat for fire, while accidents (*symptōmata*) are non-essential, for example, slavery or poverty for a human being. It is crucial to note that no ontological priority is implied for the properties of atoms over those of phenomenal bodies. The earlier atomist tradition had tended to treat atoms and void alone as real, with phenomenal properties mere arbitrary constructions placed upon them by the human mind and sense organs. This had led atomism in the direction of epistemological scepticism, a tendency which Epicurus himself strenuously resists. In discussing the status of properties (*Letter to Herodotus* 68–71), he emphasizes that although undoubtedly different from the *per se* existents, body and void, they are no less real for that. (The second-generation Epicurean Polystratus adds that even relative properties such as 'beneficial' and 'harmful', often decried as unreal by sceptics, have clear causal effects.) Accidents, in fact, have no existence at the microscopic level (*Letter to Herodotus* 70), and yet are real. This is a clear indication that Epicurus is consciously opposed to the atomist reductionism of his predecessors: colours and other accidents are real, yet irreducibly different from atomic structures. Although atomic structures are *causally* prior to the phenomena which they generate, they are in no way *ontologically* privileged over them.

6 The criteria of truth

Since, then, Epicurus' version of atomism allows the reality of sensible properties, he does not inherit Democritus' motive for casting doubt on the veracity of sense–perception (see DEMOCRITUS §3). And indeed for Epicurus the primary 'criterion of truth' is the senses: 'All sensations are true.'

The soul is an atomic structure spread throughout the body, but with a command centre which houses rational thought (these can be considered functionally, although not anatomically, equivalent to the nervous system and brain, respectively). A sensation is the soul's mechanical but conscious registering of the phenomenal properties of an external body. In the paradigm case of sight, this occurs because the outer layers of bodies are constantly streaming off them in all directions, taking the form of 'images' (Greek *eidōla*, Latin *simulacra*), atom-thin films of matter which more or less preserve their colour and shape in transit (*Letter to Herodotus* 49–52, Lucretius IV 26–268). Streams of these can enter the eye, producing vision; isolated ones can also directly enter the mind, asleep or awake, and enable it to visualize objects (Lucretius IV 722–822, 962–1036). Importantly, *any* act of picturing, by the eyes or the mind,

is the registration of one or more images arriving from outside. The infallibility of the senses consists in their mechanical registering of these images, without adding, subtracting, embroidering or interpreting. A useful analogy is photography, which 'cannot lie' because it merely records mechanically the patterns of light arriving at the camera lens, and leaves it to us to interpret what they represent. All sensations are bona fide evidence about the external world. All error lies in the 'added opinion' (*to prosdoxazomenon*) by which the mind interprets these data. Note that truth here is representational, not propositional: the sensation is true because it accurately represents the physical data reaching the sense organ. The opinion based on it may be regarded as true or false according to whether or not it succeeds in representing accurately the state of affairs which caused the sensation. Even in a case of outright delusion it is the mind which, because deranged, misinterprets the perfectly accurate impressions which reach it. As for the more important counterexamples to the theory, those of optical illusions, the paradigmatic case is the square tower which looks round at a distance. The images start out square, but because of the distance which they must travel through obstructive air they are rounded on arrival at the eyes (if this is too crude to be credible, substitute the image of a coin, oval due to perspective). Therefore vision is accurately registering the images as they are on arrival. This is a correct, not a misleading, view of a distant tower, and to call it a case of mis-seeing, says Epicurus (Sextus Empiricus, *Against the Professors* VII 206–10), is like saying that you are mishearing someone across the room just because you are not hearing their voice as it would sound inside their mouth.

The veracity of the senses is not, as many hold, impugned by their ability to conflict with each other. Strictly speaking, no two sensations are commensurable. If sight and touch differ about the shape of an object, that is because sight reports the shape of a colour patch, touch the shape of a body. If two visual sensations of the same object conflict, as in the case of the tower, that is because they are reporting two different kinds of colour patch, mediated by different quantities of intervening air.

The photographic reliability of the senses is what makes them not only true but a criterion of truth. However, when Epicurus appeals to the evidence of the senses as his ultimate criterion, it is not usually to these raw sensations, still awaiting interpretation by the mind, but to facts directly attested by them, for example, that things move, or that round objects move more readily than jagged ones. He regularly talks as if these interpreted sensations acquire the self-evident veracity which initially belongs only to the raw impressions.

The second criterion of truth is *prolēpsis*, or 'preconception' – a key term in ancient epistemology, first introduced by Epicurus. The *prolēpsis* of a thing is an instinctively acquired generic grasp of its nature, which enables you to recognize instances of it and is available for analysis in conceptual inquiries. Your *prolēpsis* of a human being, acquired unreflectively by accumulated past experience, enables you both to recognize humans when you meet them, and in the course of an inquiry to establish their essential features, for example, rationality and mortality. (When *prolēpseis* are said to be built up from past sensory experiences, these must again be interpreted sense–impressions, not raw ones.) Other *prolēpseis* appealed to in Epicurean arguments include those of god, body, utility and responsibility. *Prolēpseis* are taken to be common to all human beings, and therefore to function like a set of shared intuitions which we can hope to rediscover beneath our acquired false beliefs and to use as common ground for joint philosophical inquiry

The third criterion of truth is feelings (*pathē*), which generically divide up into just two kinds: pleasure and pain. As such, feelings certainly function as criteria of *value*, since Epicurus equates good with pleasant, bad with painful. But they also provide the introspective data on which Epicurus founds his psychological theory (*Letter to Herodotus* 63).

7 Scientific method

Starting from the direct data of the senses, broader and less accessible truths can be established. Epicurus apparently divided the accessing process into two classes, 'attestation' (or 'witnessing', 'confirmation', and so on: *epimarturēsis*) and 'non-contestation' (or 'lack of counterevidence', 'non-confirmation', and so on: *ouk antimarturēsis*). Attestation plays a relatively minor part in scientific inference, since it seems confined, if not to truths directly supplied by the senses, at most to inductive generalizations derived from these. The main concern of Epicurean science is the extension of such knowledge beyond the realm of direct experience, into inaccessibly remote regions of the universe such as the heaven or other worlds, and into the microscopic realm of atoms and void. Here theories cannot be directly confirmed, but are tested instead by their *consistency* with empirical data: hence 'non-contestation' by phenomena.

Not that *mere* consistency with experience is enough to establish truth. A theory is only entertained in the first place if it has some explanatory power or recommends itself in some comparable way. But there may be several alternative theories of equal merit in this regard, and if so each must be tested for 'non-contestation' by phenomena, to see which survives. There are many intrinsically credible general theories of matter, for example, including the four-element theory and the monistic fire theory of Heraclitus, and likewise many intrinsically plausible theories of vision, and so on. But all except the Epicurean theory fail somehow to be consistent with the entire range of phenomena against which they are tested.

In some other cases, however, especially astronomical ones, Epicurus admits that two or more rival theories survive the test. This might be considered an indication that the consistency test can at best prove a theory possible, not true. But Epicurus insists that in such cases all the successful theories are indeed true. Sometimes this means that several different explanations of the same phenomenon – for example, thunder, or the generation of perceptual 'images' (see §6) – operate concurrently in our world. In other cases it means no more than that, given the intrinsic possibility of the hypothesized causal process, it must operate *somewhere* in the infinite universe, even if not here.

All such 'sign-inferences' (*sēmeiōseis*) are from something evident to something non-evident. Often this is from the macroscopic to the microscopic: either causal inference from a macroscopic effect to a microscopic cause (for example, from the observed regularities of nature to the existence of unchangeable elements; see §2), or analogical inference (for example, from the mobility of observed spheres to that of spherical atoms, see §5). Others are from the macroscopic to the macroscopic: either from accessible to inaccessible entities or events (for example, from the mechanism of the water-wheel to the rotation of the stars), or from the present to the past or future (for example, from the current structure of a social institution like law or language to its historical origin, or from the impermanence of familiar compounds to the future destruction of the world).

The nature and validity of such sign-inferences is debated between the Epicureans and the Stoics in Philodemus, *On Signs*, including an important controversy about the justification of induction.

8 Cosmology

Epicurus argues that there can be no creating or controlling divinity (see §9), and that our world, one of infinitely many, is an accidental and temporary product of large-scale atomic collisions (for the role of the 'swerve' in this, see §4). Apparent evidence of divine creation can be explained mechanistically. Animal parts, for instance, however well suited to their uses, came into existence accidentally before those uses were conceived. In the early days of life on earth many non-viable creatures were generated, but did not survive (Lucretius V 837–77; a widely admired anticipation of Darwinian survival of the fittest). Even human institutions such as language and law, often attributed to divine benefactors, are formalized versions of modes of behaviour with purely natural origins in human need and instinct.

Epicurus' account of the world's structure is largely Presocratic in inspiration. Since atoms have no inherent attractive powers, he cannot accept the geocentric cosmologies of Plato, Aristotle and others, in which heavy stuffs tend not strictly downwards but inwards towards the centre. The direction 'down' is itself taken to be an absolute one, so that throughout the universe objects fall parallel to each other, rather than towards the centre of a spherical earth. For him the earth's stability depends not on its being at the centre (in infinite space there is no centre) but on the cushioning effects of the air beneath it. In a notorious passage (I 1052–82) Lucretius dismisses as ill-conceived the geocentrists' impressively accurate description of the antipodes.

9 God

That our world cannot be a product of divine craftsmanship is argued on several grounds (especially Lucretius V 156–234). Quite apart from the world's obvious imperfection, and the difficulty of finding a motive for its creation by already blissfully happy beings, the true conception of a god is incompatible with the role of cosmic administrator. A god is a supremely tranquil being, whereas the burdens of government include attitudes of anger, favour and worry.

How do we know that god is like this? In Epicurus' view there is a natural conception (*prolēpsis*: see §6) of god as a blessed and immortal anthropomorphic being, a conception shared by all human beings, even though in most it has been obscured by a veneer of false beliefs, for example, that the gods are vengeful, or that they govern our lives, turn the heavens and so on. People tend to endow god with their own moral values, especially the competitive values of political society, and by the same token the Epicurean reversion to the true conception of divinity as tranquil and detached is also a rediscovery of the natural human goal, tranquillity (see §10). Epicurus is insistent that 'there are gods', and even that they should be worshipped, but as an act of veneration for a life to which we ourselves aspire, not in the hope of appeasement.

But how can there be gods, if that means literally (that is, biologically) immortal beings? If according to Epicureanism nothing exists independently except bodies and void, and a god can hardly be either void or a single atom, a god must be an atomic complex. But it is a cardinal tenet that no compound body can be everlasting (Lucretius III 806–18).

Here scholarly opinion divides. The majority seek special ways in which an Epicurean god can nevertheless be literally immortal, by living in sheltered regions beyond our world and by consisting of constantly replenished streams of visual 'images' (on which see §6). Others (following Sextus Empiricus, *Against the Professors* IX 43–7) favour an idealist interpretation of Epicurean theology, whereby god, properly understood, just is our own idealization of a happy human life. On this view, when god is said by the sources to consist of visual 'images', this is simply because according to Epicurean cognitive psychology (§6) *all* imagination consists in the apprehension of images which enter us from outside. The images which provide the raw material for our conception of god need not flow to us from any objectively real divine being, but may be ordinary locally generated human images. Epicurus' main point in identifying god with a stream of images was apparently the negative one of denying that god is a 'solid body' at all (Cicero, *On the Nature of the Gods* I 49).

Epicurus seems to have spoken repeatedly about how we should *think* of god as being, behaving and so on, which in itself is equally compatible with the realist and the idealist interpretation. Equally powerless to settle the dispute is the insistence of Epicurus and his followers that their position is theistic, or that of his critics that it is atheistic. But on either reading it should be clear that the importance of god in Epicurus' system is not cosmological but ethical. Having a correct conception of god is identical with moral enlightenment.

10 Hedonism

Another 'innate' human attitude, along with the *prolēpsis* of god, is the pursuit of pleasure as the only positive value, or 'end' (*telos*). Epicurus argues that the behaviour of the newborn, and even of non-human animals, confirms that to maximize pleasure and minimize pain is the natural and primal drive (Cicero, *On Ends* I 30). Just as physics began with the crude mapping out of *per se* existents into bodies and space (§2), so ethics starts with the mapping out of all intrinsic values into pleasure and pain. And again as in physics, the next move consists in showing these two items to be jointly exhaustive: the absence of pain is itself pleasure, and there is therefore no intermediate state (Cicero, *On Ends* I 37–9).

This controversial thesis goes to the heart of

Epicurus' ethics. In his view, most human misery results from ignorance of how to quantify pleasure. Where some hedonists, especially the contemporary Cyrenaic School (see CYRENAICS §4), had recommended the constant renewal of pleasure through self-indulgence, Epicurus observes that this accumulation does not increase the total of pleasure beyond that achieved when all pain has gone, but only 'varies' it. Freedom from pain is itself already a supremely pleasant state. The pursuit of luxury, far from increasing pleasure, enlarges your desires and leaves you needlessly vulnerable to the whims of fortune.

In his physics, Epicurus had completed the division of *per se* existents into bodies and void by showing that other claimants to *per se* existence, such as properties and time, are in fact parasitic on bodies for their existence. Likewise in ethics, he now examines the non-hedonic values which others assert, such as virtue, and argues that they are in fact valued not for their own sake but as instrumental means to pleasure (Cicero, *On Ends* I 42–54).

It remains to fill out the prescription for the maximization of pleasure, that is, to sketch the ideal Epicurean life. This involves calculating the relative roles of bodily and mental pleasures, and of static and 'kinetic' pleasures. Bodily feeling is in a way focal, since mental pleasure and pain consist ultimately in satisfaction and dissatisfaction, respectively, about bodily feeling. For instance, the greatest mental pain, namely fear, is primarily the expectation of future bodily pain (which is the main ground, and a mistaken one, for the fear of death). But although mental feelings ultimately depend on bodily ones, and not vice versa, mental feelings are a more powerful ingredient in an overall good life. Someone in bodily pain – which may be unavoidable – can outweigh this by the mental act of reliving past pleasures and looking forward to future ones. It is this ability to range over past and future that gives mental feeling its greater power. But misused, especially when people fear everlasting torture after death, it can equally well become a greater evil than its bodily counterpart.

Static pleasure is the absence of pain. The bodily version of it is called 'painlessness' (*aponia*), the mental version 'tranquillity' (*ataraxia*, literally 'non-disturbance'). Tranquillity depends above all on an understanding of the universe, which will show that contrary to the beliefs of the ignorant it is unthreatening. (This is, strictly speaking, the sole justification for the study of physics.) Kinetic pleasure is the process of stimulation by which you either arrive at static pleasure (for example, drinking when thirsty) or 'vary' it (for example, drinking when not thirsty). There are mental as well as bodily kinetic pleasures, for example, (perhaps) the 'joy' of resolving a

philosophical doubt or holding a fruitful discussion with friends. Although kinetic pleasures have no incremental value, Epicurus does apparently consider them an essential part of the good life. This is particularly because the mental pleasure which serves to outweigh present pain will inevitably consist in reliving past *kinetic* pleasures and anticipating future ones. So a successful Epicurean life cannot be monotonous, but must be textured by regular kinetic pleasures. In the letter written on his deathbed, Epicurus claimed that despite the intense bodily pains this was the happiest day of his life, because of all the past joys of philosophical discussion that he could relive.

At the same time, these kinetic pleasures must be carefully managed. Some desires are natural, others empty. The latter – for example, thirst for honours – should not be indulged, because their satisfaction will bring either no pleasure or a preponderance of pain over pleasure. Even of the natural ones, some are non-necessary. For instance, the desire for food is necessary, but the desire for luxurious food is not. In order to be maximally independent of fortune, it is important to stick primarily to the satisfaction of natural and necessary desires. But occasional indulgence in those kinetic pleasures which are natural but non-necessary has a part to play, so long as you do not become dependent on them. True to this principle, Epicurean communities lived on simple fare, and even trained themselves in asceticism, but held occasional banquets (see EPICURUS §3).

11 Social values

Ancient ethics does not problematize altruism as such, but it does seek the moral foundations of two specific forms of altruism: justice, that is, respecting the interests of your fellow citizens; and friendship. Given that Epicurean hedonism is egoistic – that all your choices as an agent aim at your own pleasure – is it possible to put someone else's pleasure before your own?

Epicurus analyses justice not as an absolute value but as a contractual relation between fellow citizens, its precise character engendered by current social circumstances (*Key Doctrines* 31–7). Sometimes it proves mutually advantageous to abstain from forms of behaviour which harm others, in return for a like undertaking from them. So long as such a contract proves socially advantageous, it is correctly called 'justice'. It imposes no moral obligation as such, and the ground for respecting it is egoistic – that even if you commit an injustice with impunity the lingering fear of being found out will disrupt your tranquillity (*Key Doctrines* 17, 35).

With regard to his own philosophical community, Epicurus attached positive value to justice and to the specific laws which enforced it not because philosophers need any restraint from wrongdoing but because they need protection from the harm that others might inflict. 'Do not take part in politics' was an Epicurean injunction, political ambition being a misguided and self-defeating quest for personal security. But the school nevertheless upheld the need for legal and political institutions, and sought to work within their framework.

Where the political life fails to deliver personal security, friendship can succeed. The very foundation of the Epicurean philosophical community was friendship, of which the mutual dealings of Epicurus and his contemporaries were held up as an ideal model by their successors. Unlike justice, friendship is held to have intrinsic value – meaning not that it is valuable independently of pleasure, but that it is intrinsically pleasant, not merely instrumentally pleasant like justice. Moreover, the pleasure lies in altruistic acts of friendship, not merely in the benefits received by way of reciprocation.

Later Epicureans were pressed by their critics for a more precise reconciliation of friendship with egoism, and developed the position as follows (Cicero, *On Ends* I 66–70). According to one group, it is indeed for our own pleasure that we form friendships, and it is as a means to this, not ultimately for our friends' sake, that we share their pleasure and place it on a par with our own. A second group veered away from egoism: although friendship starts out as described by the first group, the outcome is something irreducibly altruistic, whereby we come to desire our friends' pleasure purely for their sake. A third group sought to restore egoism: the second group is right, but with the addition that friendship is a symmetrical contract, analogous to justice: *each* friend is committed to loving the other for the other's own sake.

12 Free will

Epicurus was arguably the first to make free will a central philosophical issue (see FREE WILL). He takes it that determinism must be false. It is incompatible with basic moral attitudes; the data of self-awareness falsify it; and it is a position which cannot even be argued coherently, since to enter an argument is to assume that both parties to the debate are responsible for their beliefs and could adopt others (*On Nature* XXV).

Determinism is arrived at by two routes, each of which must therefore contain a false supposition. The first route is via a logical law, that of bivalence: since all propositions, including those about the future, are either true or false, if it is already false that a given event will occur, it cannot occur, and if true, it cannot fail to occur. Therefore everything that occurs occurs of necessity. Epicurus' response is (like Aristotle's in *De interpretatione* 9, as widely interpreted) to reject the law of bivalence as regards future-tensed propositions. Predictions whose accuracy depends on human decisions yet to be made are, at the time of utterance, neither true nor false.

The second route is physical. We – our souls as well as our bodies – consist entirely of atoms, which move according to mechanical laws. How then can anything be genuinely 'up to us'? Are we not automata, our actions the outcome of infinite atomic causal chains? This time the Epicurean response is that the laws of atomic motion are not after all entirely deterministic. Atoms' motion through weight and blows is mechanical and invariable, but there must be a third, indeterministic, aspect of their motion, the minimal 'swerve' (see §4).

But how do swerves help explain free will? The question is much debated by scholars. Epicurus may appear to be merely substituting an unpredictable mechanism for a predictable one, not putting *us* in charge. Perhaps, as with the denial of bivalence, he is merely attempting to remove an obstacle to free will, not to explain it. Whether the swerve enters more directly than this into his account of volition will depend partly on whether he thinks that mental events such as volition are reducible to atomic changes in the soul, in which swerving atoms could play a part. There is in fact strong evidence (*On Nature* XXV) that he regarded mental events as irreducibly different from the soul atoms underlying them, and even as having their own causal efficacy *on* the atoms. (For his rejection of atomic reductionism, see §5 above.) If so, it may be safest to conclude that volition is already by its own nature autonomous – not part of an antecedent causal chain at all – and that this is the primary explanation of free will. Unfortunately its autonomy would be rendered impotent if either the laws of logic or those of physics had already determined our future actions independently of it. Therefore both sets of laws must be so rewritten as to circumvent this danger, and to keep alternative possibilities genuinely open. In the case of physics, the indeterministic swerve just is the most economical realization of that requirement.

13 Death

That the soul must itself be composed of atoms has, in Epicurus' judgment, one very cheering implication. It can easily be shown to perish with the body. Lucretius (III 417–829) presents a whole battery of arguments for this, based not only on the evidence for the soul's dissolubility but also on other indications, such as the continuous parallelism between its development and decay and those of the body. From the finding that there is no conscious survival after death Epicurus concludes that 'death is nothing to us'. To fear your own future non-existence is as groundless as to regret the time when you had not yet been born, and involves the absurdity of imagining yourself being there to witness and lament your own non-existence. To regret that your pleasures will be cut short is to make the computational mistake of supposing that a finite lifespan is *ipso facto* less pleasant than an infinite one. In a brilliant diatribe against the fear of death, Lucretius (III 830–1094) interprets the myths of punishment in the afterlife as allegories for moral malaise in this life, and portrays much human unhappiness, manifested in the vain search for security through wealth and power, as subconsciously nourished by the fear of death.

14 Influence

Epicureanism enjoyed exceptionally widespread popularity, but unlike its great rival Stoicism it never entered the intellectual bloodstream of the ancient world. Its stances were dismissed by many as Philistine, especially its official rejection of all cultural and intellectual activities not geared to the Epicurean good life. It was also increasingly viewed as atheistic, and its ascetic hedonism misrepresented as crude sensualism (hence the modern use of 'epicure'). The school nevertheless continued to flourish down to and well beyond the end of the Hellenistic age. The poets Virgil and Horace had Epicurean backgrounds, and other prominent Romans such as Cassius, the assassin of Julius Caesar, called themselves Epicureans. In the first three centuries of the Roman Empire many writers show some debt to Epicurean thought, including not only the novelist Petronius but even the Stoic Seneca and the Platonist Porphyry. When MARCUS AURELIUS (§1), Roman emperor AD 161–80, established four official chairs of philosophy at Athens, a chair of Epicureanism was among them. In later antiquity Epicureanism's influence declined, although it continued to provide a target for thinkers, both Christian and pagan, in search of a godless philosophy to attack. Serious interest in it was revived by Renaissance humanists, and its atomism was an important influence on early modern physics, especially through Gassendi.

See also: HELLENISTIC PHILOSOPHY

References and further reading

* Aristotle (*c.* mid 4th century BC) *Physics*, trans. in J. Barnes (ed.) *The Complete Works of Aristotle*, Princeton, NJ: Princeton University Press, 1984. (Book VI, especially chapters 1 and 10, contains challenges to 'partless' constituents of magnitude, to which Epicurus seems to be responding.)

Asmis, E. (1986) *Epicurus' Scientific Method*, Ithaca, NY: Cornell University Press. (The fullest account of Epicurean epistemology.)

* Cicero (45 BC) *On Ends*, trans. H. Rackham in *De finibus bonorum et malorum* (On the Ends of Good and Evil), Loeb Classical Library, Cambridge, MA: Harvard University Press and London: Heinemann, 1914. (Latin text with English translation; Epicurean ethics is expounded in Book I and criticized in Book II.)

* —— (45 BC) *On the Nature of the Gods*, trans. H. Rackham, Loeb Classical Library, Cambridge, MA: Harvard University Press and London: Heinemann, 1933. (Latin text with English translation; Book I is a report and critique of Epicurean theology.)

* Diogenes Laertius (*c.* early 3rd century AD) *Lives of the Philosophers*, trans. R.D. Hicks, *Diogenes Laertius Lives of Eminent Philosophers*, Loeb Classical Library, Cambridge, MA: Harvard University Press and London: Heinemann, 1925, 2 vols. (Book X, in volume 2, contains the life of Epicurus, along with complete texts of his three letters and the *Key Doctrines*.)

Festugière, A.J. (1946) *Epicure et ses dieux*, Paris: Presses Universitaires de France;; trans. C.W. Chilton, *Epicurus and his Gods*, Oxford: Blackwell, 1955. (Brilliant and accessible portrayal of Epicureanism's philosophical mission.)

Furley, D.J. (1967) *Two Studies in the Greek Atomists*, Princeton, NJ: Princeton University Press. (Classic investigation of Epicurus' theories of minima and free will; fairly technical.)

Jones, H. (1989) *The Epicurean Tradition*, London: Duckworth. (Useful guide to the influence of Epicureanism in antiquity and after.)

Long, A.A. (1974) *Hellenistic Philosophy*, London: Duckworth. (Includes the best introductory account of Epicureanism.)

Long, A.A. and Sedley, D.N. (1987) *The Hellenistic Philosophers*, Cambridge: Cambridge University Press, 2 vols. (Volume 1 contains translations of the principal texts, with commentary, volume 2 the original Greek and Latin; Epicureanism is in §§4–25.)

* Lucretius (*c.*55 BC) *On the Nature of Things*, trans. W.H.D. Rouse, Loeb Classical Library, Cambridge,

MA: Harvard University Press and London: Heinemann, 1975. (Latin text with English translation, revised by M.F. Smith.)

Mitsis, P. (1988) *Epicurus' Ethical Theory*, Ithaca, NY: Cornell University Press. (Lucid philosophical critique.)

Philodemus (*c*.40 BC) *On Signs*, ed. P. De Lacy and E. De Lacy, *Philodemus on Methods of Inference*, Naples: Bibliopolis, 1978. (With English translation and notes; a classic record of a Stoic Epicurean debate on scientific inference.)

Usener, H. (1887) *Epicurea*, Stuttgart: Teubner. (Still the major collection of Epicurean texts and testimonia, but without translation.)

DAVID SEDLEY

EPICURUS (341–271 BC)

Epicurus of Samos founded the Epicurean school of philosophy. Initially a Democritean, he overhauled Democritus' atomism so radically that his system was soon considered an independent one. He formed three Epicurean communities, the final one at Athens where his school, the Garden, became synonymous with Epicureanism. He and his three leading colleagues wrote voluminously, and their collective works became the school's canonical texts in later generations. Those of Epicurus alone amounted to 300 books (scrolls), including his seminal treatise On Nature. *Most were long and technical, but he also composed short digests as an* aide memoire.

1   Life
2   Writings
3   The school

1   Life

Although born on the Aegean island of Samos, Epicurus was the son of an Athenian, Neocles, and hence an Athenian citizen; this entitled him to own land at Athens, where he later established his principal school. While still in Samos he took lessons with a Platonist, Pamphilus, and much of his eventual philosophy can be seen as a reaction against Platonism. Equally formative was his period of study at Teos, although he violently disapproved of Nausiphanes, his Democritean teacher there, and may have been reacting against him in setting out to reshape the atomist tradition (see ATOMISM, ANCIENT; DEMOCRITUS). Epicurus famously professed to be self-taught. This was a denial that he had learnt anything from his

teachers, Pamphilus and Nausiphanes, and he certainly never disguised his debt to Democritus and other forerunners. He also, in these formative years, developed an admiration for PYRRHO, later to become the patron saint of Scepticism, and may have acquired from his model of practical conduct the ideal of tranquillity which was to become the primary ethical goal in his own system (see EPICUREANISM §10).

At the age of 31 Epicurus set up his first school, in Mytilene on the island of Lesbos. Soon after that, he moved to Lampsacus (on the west coast of modern Turkey), where he established a second school. There he acquired many of the pupils who were to remain his closest associates for the remainder of his life, including Polyaenus, Metrodorus and his eventual successor Hermarchus. These communities continued to flourish even after 307 BC, when Epicurus and a number of his colleagues moved on to Athens to establish the Garden, thereafter the headquarters of Epicureanism, on a plot of land which he bought just outside the city walls.

2   Writings

Epicurus' writings were voluminous, but now only a few short works survive, along with fragments of others and a great mass of secondary testimonies. *On Nature*, of which fragments survive on papyrus, was his major treatise, written in thirty-seven books over many years, and covering much more than the physical topics which the title suggests. Books I–XIII, probably written before the move to Athens, covered the principal subject matter of physics. Books XIV–XV (dated 301–300 BC) seem to have contained a refutation of other physical theories. Another book (perhaps XXV) is devoted to psychology. Book XXVIII (dated 296 BC) discusses the philosophical role of language. These texts, although difficult and stylistically clumsy, show Epicurus actively at work on his philosophy, responding to opponents and colleagues and entertaining doubts.

Just four short works by Epicurus survive entire, preserved verbatim by the historian of philosophy Diogenes Laertius. The *Letter to Herodotus* is an epitome of *On Nature* I–XIII, on basic physics. The *Letter to Pythocles* epitomizes those parts of his work which dealt with astronomy, meteorology and kindred phenomena. The *Letter to Menoeceus* is an ethical epitome. Finally, the *Kyriai doxai* – 'Key Doctrines' – is a set of maxims on ethics and epistemology, apparently excerpted from individual works. The first four of these were held to sum up the aims of the system, and ran, in the abbreviated form known as 'the fourfold remedy' (*tetrapharmakos*): 'God presents no fears, death no worries. And while good is readily attainable, evil is readily endurable'. The object of these short digests was to aid Epicurus' pupils not so much in understanding his teachings as in memorizing them. They are nevertheless often the best evidence we have to go on. (Another preserved anthology of maxims, the *Vatican Sayings*, less structured than the *Kuriai doxai*, is someone's compilation from the works of Epicurus and other early school members.) None of these digests has a firm date, but there are reasons for placing the *Letter to Herodotus* around 305 BC, and the *Letter to Pythocles* shortly after.

Of his lost works, the most important seem to have been the *Canon*, on the principles of epistemology, and *On the End*, on ethics.

3 The school

In later generations, Epicureans worked from a set of school texts with virtually biblical status. These were the work of four founding fathers – 'the men' (*hoi andres*), as they were known in the school, meaning roughly 'the great men'. The infallible four were Epicurus, Metrodorus, Hermarchus and Polyaenus. Their texts were endlessly scrutinized in disputes about orthodoxy, and their correspondence, along with that of other early Epicureans, was anthologized and studied as a model of the philosophical life. Hermarchus is particularly notable for his detailed account of the origins of law, preserved by Porphyry (*On Abstinence* I 7–12), and Polyaenus was a former mathematician who, in joining the school, came to renounce all geometry as false (see EPICUREANISM §3).

The Epicurean community was a close-knit one, based on the cult of friendship and the communal study of philosophy, detached from political society without actively opposing it. Unusually for the time, women, children and even slaves and prostitutes participated on equal terms with men. Epicurus taught philosophy to his slave Mys, and Leontion was a prostitute who became a leading member of the group and wrote a work against Theophrastus.

In later generations Epicurus' portrait was ubiquitous, along with the often strikingly similar images of his co-founders. In the manner of the 'hero cults' of classical Greece, regular celebrations were held in their memory – a ritual which Epicurus had already instituted in his own lifetime in remembrance of Metrodorus, Polyaenus and others. It was a cardinal tenet that dead friends should be remembered and celebrated, never mourned. Aside from the feasting on these occasions, the Epicurean lifestyle was an ascetic one, belying the modern meaning of 'epicure'.

See also: EPICUREANISM

References and further reading

Arrighetti, G. (1968) *Epicuro, opere*, Turin: Einaudi, 2nd edn, 1973. (At present the only comprehensive collection of Epicurus' surviving writings with Italian translation and commentary.)

Bailey, C. (1926) *Epicurus, The Extant Remains*, Oxford: Clarendon Press. (Unfortunately still the best English edition of Epicurus' main surviving writings; includes Greek text.)

Clay, D. (1983) 'Individual and Community in the First Generation of the Epicurean School', in '*SUZHTHSIS. Studi sull'epicureismo greco e romano offerti a Marcello Gigante*, Naples: Macchiaroli, I, 255–79.

* Diogenes Laertius (*c.* early 3rd century AD) *Lives of the Philosophers*, trans. R.D. Hicks, *Diogenes Laertius Lives of Eminent Philosophers*, Cambridge, MA: Loeb Classical Library, Harvard University Press and London: Heinemann, 1925, 2 vols. (Book X, in volume 2, contains the life of Epicurus, along with complete texts of his three letters and the *Kyriai doxai*.)

Frischer, B. (1982) *The Sculpted Word*, Berkeley, CA: University of California Press. (Intriguing investigation of Epicurean portraiture as a means of recruitment.)

Sedley, D. (1976) 'Epicurus and his Professional Rivals', in J. Bollack and A. Laks (eds) *Études sur l'epicurisme antique (Cahiers de Philologie I)*, 119–59. (On Epicurus' attitude to other philosophers.)

DAVID SEDLEY

EPIPHENOMENALISM

Epiphenomenalism is a theory concerning the relation between the mental and physical realms, regarded as radically different in nature. The theory holds that only physical states have causal power, and that mental states are completely dependent on them. The mental realm, for epiphenomenalists, is nothing more than a series of conscious states which signify the occurrence of states of the nervous system, but which play no causal role. For example, my feeling sleepy does not cause my yawning – rather, both the feeling and the yawning are effects of an underlying neural state.

Mental states are real, and in being conscious we are more than merely physical organisms. Nevertheless, all our experiences, thoughts and actions are determined by our physical natures. Mental states are actually as smoke from a machine seems to be, mere side effects making no difference to the course of Nature.

1 Epiphenomenalism
2 The principal objections to epiphenomenalism

1 Epiphenomenalism

Epiphenomenalism is a version of dualism, rejecting reduction of the mental to the physical (see DUALISM, REDUCTIONISM IN THE PHILOSOPHY OF MIND). Unlike other dualist theories, however, it denies that conscious mental states are ever causes. It is never pain that makes us wince, nor anger that makes us shout. Remembering our childhood plays no part in the writing of our memoirs. What has caused philosophers to propose a theory which is such an affront to common sense?

On the one hand, the rise early in the seventeenth century of the conception of the physical realm as a closed system, in which the forces of material nature are the only influences that determine the course of events, when combined with the naturalistic view that human beings are a part of material nature, and governed by its laws, seems to leave no room for a realm of mental states having a role in fixing the course of events. With the demise of vitalism (see VITALISM) regarding the forces governing animate life, the case for the physical causal closure of the material realm has seemed compelling.

On the other hand, philosophers have held that it is a fact of experience that we *do* enjoy conscious states, whose features are incompatible with a purely physical nature. The appeal of epiphenomenalism lies in its capacity to resolve this dilemma.

The theory can, as in its classical form, be applied to all mental states. Other versions can admit physical, and effective, subconscious mental states. Even among conscious states, a theory can be epiphenomenalist about some, such as the phenomenal qualia of sensory awareness (see QUALIA), and yet reductively materialist regarding memories or thoughts.

The term 'epiphenomenon' – meaning a secondary symptom – was first applied to consciousness in 1890 by William James, but the position which he was attacking had already existed for some time.

Simmias, in Plato's Phaedo, asserts that body stands to mind as a musical instrument stands to its 'harmonia' (85e3 –86d4). If we interpret the latter as meaning the music produced by an instrument, Simmias's theory has epiphenomenalist overtones.

In the eighteenth century Charles Bonnet discussed in his *Essai de Psychologie* (1735) a theory according to which 'the soul is a mere spectator of the movements of its body', though it 'believes itself to be the author of them', while the body 'performs of itself all that series of actions which constitutes life'.

In 1865 Shadworth Hodgson's *Time and Space* provided the first full formulation of epiphenomenalism. 'States of consciousness', he wrote, 'are not produced by previous states of consciousness, but both are produced by the action of the brain; and, conversely, there is no ground for saying that . . . states of consciousness react upon the brain or modify its action.' In 1870 Hodgson became epiphenomenalism's first explicit supporter (in *Theory of Practice*). Thomas Huxley soon followed; and his 1874 essay 'On the Hypothesis that Animals are Automata, and its History', with its famous phrase 'we are conscious automata', is the classic statement of the theory.

In the twentieth century epiphenomenalism was not widely supported, although George Santayana (1905) and C.D. Broad (1925) both have epiphenomenalist leanings, and John Lachs (1963) vigorously defended the theory. In 1970 Keith Campbell proposed a 'New Epiphenomenalism', which combines aspects of epiphenomenalism with the view that mental states are brain states (see MIND, IDENTITY THEORY OF). Frank Jackson later defended a similar view. Where classical epiphenomenalism asserts that mental states are non-physical and causally inert, the new epiphenomenalism asserts that mental states are causally potent physical states of the brain, but that in addition to their physical properties some of these states possess phenomenal properties or *qualia* which are non-physical and non-causal.

For epiphenomenalism to be a doctrine distinct from both dualism and materialism, it must involve a very strong conception of causality as productive power or efficacy. No 'Humean' or regularity theory of causation will be sufficient. For the epiphenomenalist admits that many conscious states are regularly followed by other conscious states or by actions, yet denies that the former ever cause the latter.

It will not do, furthermore, to move from mere de facto regularities to *necessary* sequences. For conscious states figure in necessary sequences just as much as neural ones do. If necessary sequence is necessary and sufficient for the causal link, then the neural states will be followed, of necessity, both by the conscious states and by the actions to which the neural states give rise. So the conscious states will also be linked necessarily with the actions, and so will be causes of the actions.

It will not be sufficient, either, to offer a merely counterfactual account of the causal link. Provided the conscious states are effects of the neural states alone, if the conscious states had not existed, nor would the neural states. Then the actions would not have existed either. So if the conscious states had not existed, nor would the actions, and so once again the conscious states count as causes of the actions.

The epiphenomenalist needs to insist that the sequences, and necessary sequences, and counterfactual linkages are indeed there, connecting conscious states with actions, but that these links are not present *on account of any causal activity in the conscious states*. Only insofar as such a strong conception of causation can be sustained, can epiphenomenalism be maintained as a distinctive position in the theory of mind.

2 The principal objections to epiphenomenalism

The evidence problem. The standard way in which we obtain evidence for the existence and nature of something is from its effects on the mind, either directly, or through traces. If epiphenomenalism is true, then conscious states leave no effects, not even on the mind in which they occur. How then can we ever have any reason to believe that we are, or were, in any conscious state?

The epiphenomenalist can appeal here to indirect causal chains. The neural state which produces the conscious epiphenomenon also produces awareness, and recall, of that conscious state. Because the neural state is a reliable indicator of the existence of the conscious state, the evidence we have for the existence of the neural state is *ipso facto* evidence for the existence of the conscious one.

A further problem concerns evidence for epiphenomenalism as a theory. Epiphenomenalism would be refuted – and perhaps a strong dualism established – by the discovery of mental efficacy which is *not* neural efficacy. But to confirm the theory requires proving the absence of mental causal power, and a negative is notoriously difficult to establish conclusively. The case for epiphenomenalism is the case for physical closure – a global proposition supported only by overall theoretical power – combined with the case against the reduction of mental states to physical ones.

The evolution problem. One of the most persistent criticisms of epiphenomenalism, associated especially with Sir Karl Popper (see Popper and Eccles 1977), is the claim that it is incompatible with the theory of evolution.

According to the epiphenomenalist, creatures with consciousness will behave in exactly the same way as creatures with the same neural organization, but without consciousness. So consciousness can confer no reproductive advantage. Accordingly, there can be no natural mechanism which selects for consciousness, no matter what the processes that drive selection may be. So consciousness cannot emerge in an evolutionary development.

The argument as it stands is faulty; for it may be that although there can be no selection *for consciousness*, there may well be selection for something else – complex neural organization – of which consciousness is an inevitable by-product. The argument does retain some force, however, as an impotent consciousness seems to be such a gratuitous and inexplicable addendum. If consciousness is genuinely impotent, it is hard to see why neural organizations that match conscious ones in power, but lack consciousness, should not have evolved alongside the existing ones. And if epiphenomenalism is true, we have a further epistemic problem here. How could we know that consciousness does always accompany neural complexity (see OTHER MINDS)?

The problem of meaning. The thought is widespread that, at least in fundamental cases, the referential part of the meaning of reports of the existence of a state or an event depends on a causal chain from the state or event in question to the report (see REFERENCE §4). Can epiphenomenalists accept this principle? According to them mental states and events do not feature in the causal history of any utterance. Thus if the principle were true, the vocabulary of mental descriptions would be critically defective, and all reports concerning mental states and events would be meaningless.

While the epiphenomenalist's strong notion of causation prevents an appeal to a direct causal link in explaining the meaning of mental reports, an appeal might be made to counterfactual dependencies. A certain neural state causes me to feel like a million dollars, and also to utter the words 'I feel like a million dollars'. The feeling does not cause the utterance, but if I did not feel this way then the neural state would not have existed, and neither, therefore, would the utterance have occurred.

The problem here is the symmetry of the counterfactual dependency in question. Neither the feeling nor the utterance would have existed without the other. Yet the epiphenomenalist needs to hold that the utterance is *about* the feeling, while the feeling is not *about* the utterance.

Faced with the options of no semantic relation between utterance and mental item, or a semantic relation obtaining both ways, the epiphenomenalist chooses the former. All mental reports *are* meaningless – but only when considered as purely physical noises. For the epiphenomenalist, meaning and reference are *mental* phenomena, and hence are *epi*phenomena: when you say to me 'I've had an idea,' I act upon your words purely mechanically, as a computer at a telephone exchange responds to a sequence of tones. Meaning does not enter here, and were none of us conscious we would all behave – linguistically and non-linguistically – exactly as we do now. However, in addition to the causal relations involved in this automatic process there are semantic relations obtaining between the mental effect of the neural state caused in me when I hear your words, and the idea which you have had.

For the epiphenomenalist, meaning does not span the gap between mental and physical; meaning remains on the mental side, causation on the physical. While this is a consistent position, it does underline the counterintuitive nature of epiphenomenalism.

See also: CONSCIOUSNESS; MENTAL CAUSATION

References and further reading

* Bonnet, C. (1755) *Essai de Psychologie*, London, ch. 32. (Sympathetic discussion, using the possibility of an automaton to replicate human behaviour.)
* Broad, C.D. (1925) *The Mind and its Place in Nature*, London: Routledge & Kegan Paul, esp. chaps 3, 10 and 12. (Clear and judicious, but ultimately non-commital, exposition.)
* Campbell, K. (1984) *Body and Mind*, Notre Dame, IN: University of Notre Dame Press, 2nd edn. (Classic source for new epiphenomenalism.)
* Hodgson, S. (1865) *Time and Space: A Metaphysical Essay*, London: Longmans, Green, part 1, ch. 5, §30. (Earliest explicit presentation of epiphenomenalism.)
—— (1870) *Theory of Practice: An Ethical Enquiry*, London: Longmans, Green, book I, ch. 3. (First explicit defence of the theory.)
* Huxley, T. (1874) 'On the Hypothesis that Animals are Automata, and Its History' in *Collected Essays*, London: Macmillan, 1893, vol. 1, *Method and Results*, 199–250. (Classic presentation of the theory and the grounds for it.)
* Jackson, F. (1982) 'Epiphenomenal Qualia', *Philosophical Quarterly* 32: 127–36. (Influential article defending the legitimacy of epiphenomena.)
* James, W. (1890) *The Principals of Psychology*, New York: Holt, ch. 5. (Extended, ultimately critical discussion.)
* Lachs, J. (1963) 'The Impotent Mind', *Review of Metaphysics* 17: 187–99. (Defends the theory by responding to many leading objections.)
* Plato (*c.* 370 BC) *Phaedo*, trans. D. Gallop, Oxford: Clarendon Press, 1975. (Suggests, but does not support, the dependence of mind on matter.)
* Popper, K. and Eccles, J. (1977) *The Self and its Brain*, London: Springer International. (Adopts a dualist position and presents the evolution objection to.)
* Santayana, G. (1905) *The Life of Reason*, London: Constable, vol. 1. (Expresses the view that consciousness cannot produce, but only confer, meaning on events.)

KEITH CAMPBELL
NICHOLAS J. J. SMITH

EPISTEMIC LOGIC

Modern treatment of epistemic logic began in the 1950s when some philosophers noticed (as scholastics had done before them) certain regularities in the logical behaviour of the concept of knowledge (for example, that knowing a conjunction is equivalent to knowing all its conjuncts) and began to systematize them. Initially these regularities were presented in the form of an axiomatic-deductive system, as in other branches of logic. Later, questions began to be asked concerning the model theory on which such an 'epistemic logic' is based. Still later, the concrete interpretation of this model theory has become an issue. In this way, gradually a bridge has begun to be forged from purely logical questions to such central epistemological questions as those concerning the objects of knowledge, different kinds (or even senses) of knowledge (and their interrelations), the intensional character of knowledge, the de dicto *versus* de re *distinction, and so on.*

1 Propositional epistemic logic
2 The semantics of quantified epistemic logic
3 Rules for quantified epistemic logic
4 Wider perspectives

1 Propositional epistemic logic

Epistemic logic began as a study of the logical behaviour of the expression 'knows that' (see PROPOSITIONAL ATTITUDE STATEMENTS). One of the main aims of this study is to be able to analyse other constructions in terms of 'knows' by means of 'b knows that'. This basic notion will be expressed in the notation used here by 'K_b'. (This symbolization is slightly misleading in that, in a formula of the form $K_b S$, the term 'b' for the agent (knower) is intended to be outside the scope of 'K', not inside, as the notation might suggest.) When the knower is the same throughout a sentence (or an argument), the 'b' is often omitted.

The logic of 'K' ('knows that') is based on certain

simple, pragmatic and epistemological insights. First, what is the use of the notion of knowledge? In what way are you better off when you come to know that S? The basic answer is clear. When you know that S, you can legitimately omit from consideration all possibilities under which it is not the case that S; in other words, you can restrict your attention to the situations in which it is true that S. (What is meant by 'legitimately' here is a major philosophical problem. It is essentially tantamount to the well-known problem of defining knowledge (see KNOWLEDGE, CONCEPT OF). For the purposes of epistemic logic, however, we do not have to solve this problem. The structural characterization just given suffices for our purposes, no matter how legitimacy is defined.)

This characterization amounts to making a distinction between two kinds of alternatives (situations; possible worlds) among all the relevant ones. Some possibilities are excluded by what b knows. They are the ones that can legitimately be disregarded. Others are not so excluded. They are the ones b will have to heed. It should be emphasized that the specification of such a set of admitted situations can be made independently of the psychological, cognitive or sociological peculiarities of the knower in question. Hence epistemic logic does not necessarily involve any subjective or even pragmatic element.

Thus we can see what kinds of structures are to be used in the model theory of epistemic logic (see MODEL THEORY). They will be called 'model structures'. They are classes of models of the underlying language minus K. Let us consider one of them, say, w_0, in which a potential knower, b, exists. Each such w_0 is associated with a number of other models ('possible worlds') w_1 which are not excluded by what b knows in w_0. They will be called the epistemic b-alternatives to w_0. Thus the basic truth-condition of epistemic logic can be formulated as follows:

$K_b S$ is true in w_0 iff S is true in every epistemic b-alternative w_1 to w_0.

This definition is of course relative to a model structure. If the b-alternativeness relation is called R_b and Ω is the set of all possible worlds, the truth-condition can be expressed as follows:

$K_b S$ is true in $w_0 \in \Omega$ iff S is true in each $w_1 \in \Omega$ such that $w_0 R_b w_1$.

We can also introduce a notion of epistemic possibility, P. Then $P_b S$ means, roughly, 'It is possible, for all that b knows, that S'. Obviously the following pairs of sentences are logically equivalent: $\sim K_b S$ and $P_b \sim S$; $\sim P_b S$ and $K_b \sim S$. The truth-condition for epistemic possibility is the obvious one:

$P_b S$ is true in $w_0 \in \Omega$ iff S is true in some $w_1 \in \Omega$ such that $w_0 R_b w_1$.

Normally it is required that each $w_0 \in \Omega$ be an alternative to itself (for each b in w_0). This amounts to requiring that b can know (in w_0) that S only if it is true (in w_0) that S. Combined with the usual truth-conditions for propositional connectives, we can in this way obtain a semantic basis, complete with a truth-definition, for propositional epistemic logic.

The question of whether the alternativeness relation is transitive or not is equivalent to the question of the logical truth of sentences of the form:

(1) $(\forall x)(K_x S \supset K_x K_x S)$.

Unfortunately, in ordinary discourse, saying that one 'knows that one knows' has a number of different meanings, most of which have little to do with (1). Hence the question of whether 'knowing implies that one knows that one knows' needs a separate examination which falls only partially within the purview of epistemic logic.

On the basis of these semantic ideas, an epistemic propositional logic is easily developed. It admits of a complete Gentzen-style axiomatization. In such an axiomatization, the rules for '&' and '$\vee$' are the usual cut-free ones, while no transfer of formulas between the left-hand side and the right-hand side is allowed. (For simplicity, it is assumed here and in the following that the formulas considered are in negation normal form, that is, that all negation signs in them are prefixed to atomic formulas.) The epistemic rules can then be formulated as follows:

$$\frac{\Gamma, K(S_1 \& S_2) \to \Delta}{\Gamma, KS_1, KS_2 \to \Delta}$$

$$\frac{\Gamma \to \Delta, P(S_1 \vee S_2)}{\Gamma \to \Delta, PS_1, PS_2}$$

$$\frac{S_1, S_2 \to S_3}{\Gamma, KS_1, PS_2 \to \Delta, PS_3}$$

$$\frac{S_1 \to S_2, S_3}{\Gamma, KS_1 \to \Delta, KS_2, PS_3}$$

We also need, of course, suitable structural rules and axioms. The following can serve as such axioms.

$$S_1, \sim S_1 \to$$
$$\to S_1, \sim S_1$$
$$S \to S$$

A game-theoretic truth-definition is better suited for the purposes of epistemic logic than an ordinary (Tarski-type) one (see SEMANTICS, GAME-THEORETIC). In such a definition two players are involved: the proponent and the opponent. At each stage of the game, the two players are considering a sentence and a possible world. The game starts from the world w_0 in which a sentence S is to be evaluated. Such a game $G(S; w_0)$ is defined by the following rules:

(G.~) $G(\sim S; w_0)$ is like $G(S; w_0)$ but with the roles of the two players reversed. (That is, the proponent of $G(\sim S; w_0)$ is the opponent in $G(S; w_0)$, and vice versa.)

(G.&) $G((S_1 \, \& \, S_2); w_0)$ begins with a choice by the opponent of S_i ($i = 1$ or 2) and the rest of the game is as in $G(S_i; w_0)$.

(G.∨) $G((S_1 \vee S_2); w_0)$ likewise, except that the choice of S_1 or S_2 is made by the proponent.

(G.K) $G(K_b S; w_0)$ begins with a choice by the opponent of an epistemic b-alternative w_1 to w_0. The rest of the game is as in $G(S; w_1)$.

(G.P) $G(P_b S; w_0)$ likewise, except that the choice is made by the proponent.

(G.atom) Any play of a semantic game will come to an end in a finite number of moves with an atomic sentence or identity A and a model (world) w. Since the underlying language has been interpreted in w, A is either true or false. If the former, the proponent of A has won and the opponent lost. If the latter, vice versa.

The game-theoretic definition of truth and falsity says that S is true (false) in w_0 iff there exists a winning strategy for the proponent (opponent) in $G(S; w_0)$.

2 The semantics of quantified epistemic logic

When we move to *quantified* epistemic logic, we need individuals to serve as values of bound variables. Since we are dealing with a multiplicity of models (worlds), individuals must in principle be identifiable in more than one of them. ('No entity without identity', to quote Quine.) Hence an individual is, model-theoretically speaking, a 'world line' connecting the roles or embodiments of one and the same individual in several worlds. Less metaphysically expressed, given a model system Ω, an individual is logically speaking a function (an 'individuating function') from models $w \in \Omega$ to the members of the domain $do(w)$ of w (see INTENSIONAL LOGICS §2). (Since we want to keep our discussion as general as possible, we must allow individuating functions to be partial. In other words, an individual might not be identifiable in all possible worlds.)

A singular term likewise has as its value (bearer), in a given model w, a member of $do(w)$. However, these might not be the same individual in two different models. In other words, the values of a singular term c in two worlds might not be connected by a world line. The bearers of a singular term c in different models are said to be the values of the 'meaning function' associated with c. Individuating functions are a special case of meaning functions. Obviously, a meaning function is, like an individuating function, a (possibly partial) function from models $w \in \Omega$ to their respective domains $do(w)$. (In the interests of generality, a singular term must be allowed to be empty in some models.)

It cannot be assumed in epistemic logic that individuating functions are expressed in ordinary language by singular terms of any particular linguistic category, such as proper names, in the sense that the individuating function would coincide with the meaning function of such a 'rigid designator'. This impossibility is shown by the fact that one can meaningfully ask, using a proper name, for example, 'Do you know who John is?' or 'Who is John?' The idea that there are in natural language 'rigid designators' that express individuating functions hence does not work in epistemic contexts (see REFERENCE §3).

On the basis of these considerations, we can now formulate the additional game rules needed in epistemic first-order logic:

(G.∀) $G((\forall x)S(x); w_0)$ begins with the choice by the opponent of an individual from the domain of w_0. If it is stipulated that a new singular term c has the same meaning function as the identifying function of the chosen individual, the rest of the game is as in $G(S(c); w_0)$.

Even though it seems to restrict our treatment somewhat, we can also require that the chosen individual exists in w_0, that is, that its identifying function is defined for the argument w_0.

(G.∃) $G((\exists x)S(x); w_0)$ likewise, except that the proponent makes the choice.

In the epistemic first-order logic so far formulated, many interesting logical relationships can be expressed. However, a fully satisfactory logic of the concept of knowledge can be obtained only by extending our language in one important respect. For one thing, the interrelationship between our formal language and knowledge statements in ordinary language is made much more perspicuous by this extension.

The new element in our epistemic language is a

notation for informational independence, slightly extended. Moves are sometimes made by a player in ignorance of what has happened in certain specified earlier moves. Such moves are said to be independent of the earlier ones. This idea applies naturally to our semantic games. In them an application of the rules (G.&), (G.∨), (G.∀) or (G.∃) can be informationally independent of an earlier application of one of the rules (G.K) or (G.P). Actually, in much of epistemic logic, we need to consider only the possible independence of (G.∨) and (G.∃) of (G.K).

Independence will be indicated by a slash notation, for example, in $(\vee/K)$ and $(\exists x/K)$. However, the possibility of moving from one model to another necessitates a specification as to what the model w is in relation to which a move connected with, say, $(\exists x/K)$ is made. Here the obvious stipulation is that it must be made in relation to the model (world) which the rule application connected with K moved us away from. In brief, the slash indicates that the moves connected with K and with the existential quantifier $\exists x$ are made in the reverse order.

These stipulations imply that there is a difference in meaning, for example, between sentences of the following forms: $K(\forall x)S(x)$ and $(\forall x)KS(x)$. In the former, the choice of the values of x is between the individuals existing in an epistemic alternative chosen by the opponent. In the latter, the choice is between individuals existing in the world in which the sentence is evaluated.

It is our reliance on the notion of informational independence that forces us to use game-theoretic semantics. The reason is that the logic of informational independence cannot be handled by means of the usual Tarski-type truth-definitions.

By means of the slash notation, most of the usual types of knowledge, and most of the logical laws holding for these different types of knowledge, can be formulated. The value of a quantifier such as '$(\exists x/K_b)$' is chosen independently of the epistemic alternative selected by the opponent in applying the rule (G.K). Hence the value of x must be the same in all the situations compatible with what b knows, that is, must be known to b. Yet this value may depend on that of a universal quantifier which depends on K, wherefore no linear ordering can capture the dependence relations in question. Thus we have, for instance:

(2)   'b knows whether S' $= K_b(S(\vee/K_b)\sim S)$

(3)   'b knows whether S_1 or S_2' $= K_b(S_1(\vee/K_b)S_2)$

(4)   'b knows who satisfies the condition $S(x)$' $= K_b(\exists x/K_b)S(x)$

(5)   'b knows of everybody whether they satisfy the

condition $S(x)$' $= K_b(\forall x)(S(x)(\vee/K_b)\sim S(x))$

(6)   'b knows to whom each person bears the relation $S(x,y)$' $= K_b(\forall x)(\exists y/K_b)S(x,y)$.

Even more complex types of knowledge can be expressed in our notation. In these examples, it is assumed that the range of quantifiers consists of persons.

Of (2)–(6), the first three have equivalents in a slash-free notation, namely:

(7) $K_b S \vee K_b \sim S$

(8) $K_b S_1 \vee K_b S_2$

(9) $(\exists x)K_b S(x)$.

However, (5) and (6) do not have slash-free equivalents. For instance, (6) is not equivalent to:

(10) $(\forall x)(\exists y)K_b S(x,y)$.

This is seen from the following second-order equivalents to (6) and (10), respectively:

(11) $(\exists f)K_b(\forall x)S(x,f(x))$

(12) $(\exists f)(\forall x)K_b S(x,f(x))$.

This reduction of a large number of other constructions with 'knows' to the 'knows that' construction is evidence for the propositional character of knowledge.

3   Rules for quantified epistemic logic

In terms of the slash notation, deductive rules for quantified epistemic logic can be formulated.

First, the vaunted intensionality of knowledge can be understood and accounted for without postulating any special intensional entities to serve as 'objects of knowledge' (see INTENSIONAL ENTITIES). Intensionality is a matter of how meaning functions and identifying functions behave. It means that an identity which holds in one situation (model) need not hold in another one. In other words, we cannot have in our epistemic logic an unrestricted rule of the following form:

(13) $\dfrac{\Gamma, S(a), a = b, S(b) \rightarrow \Delta}{\Gamma, S(a), a = b \rightarrow \Delta}$

We can have such a rule only when S is required not to contain any intensional operators.

Second, rules for existential generalization and universal instantiation have to be changed. For instance, we cannot have the rule:

(14) $\dfrac{\Gamma, (\forall x)S(x), S(a) \rightarrow \Delta}{\Gamma, (\forall x)S(x) \rightarrow \Delta}$

for this inference presupposes that a is the same

individual in all the relevant models. If x occurs in $S(x)$ within the scope of only one epistemic operator, say, K (while $S(x)$ is in negation normal form), this rule can be restored by means of an additional premise.

$$(15) \quad \frac{\Gamma, (\forall x)S(x), K(\exists y/K)(a=y), S(a) \to \Delta}{\Gamma, (\forall x)S(x), K(\exists y/K)(a=y) \to \Delta}$$

This modification of the usual rules is eminently natural both 'intuitively' and model-theoretically. If I know that a did something, it does not follow that I know who did it, unless I know who a is. At the same time, the need of the extra clause shows that in a sense the objects of knowledge are not world-bound individuals, but individuals that can be identified in several possible situations. If this is what is meant by saying that knowledge is intentional, the saying is true.

Third, rules for existential instantiation and universal generalization also have to be changed. They no longer do their whole job. We cannot have merely:

$$(16) \quad \frac{\Gamma, S(a) \to \Delta}{\Gamma, (\exists x)S(x) \to \Delta}$$

where a does not occur anywhere in $S(x)$, Γ or Δ. Instead, we need a stronger rule of the form:

$$(17) \quad \frac{\Gamma, S_0(S_1(f(y_1, y_2, \ldots))) \to \Delta}{\Gamma, S_0((\exists x)S_1(x)) \to \Delta}$$

where S_0 is in negation normal form and $(\forall y_1), (\forall y_2), \ldots$ are all the universal quantifiers within the scope of which $(\exists x)S_1(x)$ occurs in $S_0 = S_0((\exists x)S_1(x))$, and where f is a function symbol which does not occur anywhere in S_0, Γ or Δ. Clearly (16) can be thought of as a special case of (17). Parallel sequent rules have to be modified analogously.

Fourth, negation behaves in quantified epistemic logic in an unwonted way. For instance, the law of excluded middle no longer holds. This is almost predictable on the basis of our definitions of truth and falsity in §1 above. They imply that the law of excluded middle is a determinacy assumption, that is, that it says that one or the other player always has a winning strategy in one of our epistemic games. From game theory it is known that such determinacy assumptions are very strong, and hence likely to fail.

In general, quantified epistemic logic thus exhibits several phenomena that have no counterpart in ordinary first-order logic. In spite of the failure of the law of excluded middle, one can formulate a complete disproof procedure for epistemic logic. It can also be shown that many standard metalogical results, such as compactness, and the separation and Löwenheim–Skolem theorems, can be extended to epistemic logic.

4 Wider perspectives

The epistemic logic outlined here can be extended and applied in several different directions.

First, epistemic logics have proved relevant to such branches of computer science as artificial intelligence and database theory. A growing number of results have been reached by scientists working in this area.

Second, an interpretational rule (game rule) must be associated also with nonlogical constants of different kinds, for instance, with singular terms such as names. Applications of such rules can be independent of epistemic rules, which create distinctions between sentences such as the following:

(18) $K_b S(d)$

(19) $K_b S((d/K))$

This distinction is nothing but the so-called *de re/de dicto* distinction (see DE RE/DE DICTO). This famous distinction turns out to be another independence phenomenon and not an irreducible contrast between two kinds of knowledge nor two kinds of reference.

Third, epistemic logic is the cornerstone of the logic of knowledge-seeking developed by Jaakko Hintikka and his associates and called by them the interrogative model of inquiry (Hintikka *et al.* 1997). In fact, we obtain the rules for such an inquiry by reversing Gentzen-type rules for epistemic logic and adding to them the following additional rule:

$$(R.Q) \quad \frac{\Gamma, S_0 \to \Delta}{\Gamma, S_0, S_1 \to \Delta}$$

where S_0 is the presupposition of any one question and S_1 the desideratum of the same question. In such interrogative inquiry, it must also be specified which questions are answerable. The applicability of (R.Q) then presupposes the answerability of the question.

Fourth, in epistemic contexts quantifiers have been shown to depend on a method of identifying individuals as members of different possible situations. Now it can be seen that individuals can be identified in two different ways. Then we have two sets of identifying functions and, corresponding to them, two pairs of quantifiers. The rules governing each of them separately are the same as have been explained. In one kind of identification, the knower uses their direct cognitive relations to objects (for example, their visual space) as a framework of identification. Such identification has been called 'perspectival'. In ordinary language, perspectival identification shows up in the form of the direct-object construction with 'knows', for example, 'Jack knows Jill', as distinguished from 'Jack knows who Jill is'. In the other, an impersonal (public) framework of identification is relied on. It can be shown that this duality is indeed realized in our actual conceptual practice with epistemic concepts. This results in an extremely important application of epistemic logic. In this application, questions concerning the interaction of the two kinds of quantifiers belong to the province of epistemology and cognitive science rather than epistemic logic.

This distinction between two kinds of identification is approximately instantiated by Bertrand Russell's distinction between knowledge by description and knowledge by acquaintance (see KNOWLEDGE BY ACQUAINTANCE AND DESCRIPTION), by neuroscientists' distinction between the what-system and where-system in cognition, by Endel Tulving's distinction between semantic and episodic memory, and so on. It is important to realize that these distinctions are not at bottom distinctions between two kinds of knowledge (or memory-knowledge), or between two kinds of objects within some one world, but between two kinds of principles of identification of individuals from one world to another. It is nevertheless tempting and even natural to speak of 'two kinds of objects' here. For instance, so-called phenomenological objects (including Russell's 'objects of acquaintance') are in effect individuals identified in a certain way.

Fifth, in natural language we are dealing with more than just one domain of individuals. Rather, we have at the very least a different domain corresponding to each different 'wh- question'. This distinction between different ranges of quantifiers (for that is what wh-words in effect express) is closely related to Aristotle's distinction between different categories.

Finally, a model-theoretic treatment of knowledge seems to lead to the paradox of logical omniscience, that is, to the consequence that everyone knows all the logical consequences of what they know. One natural explanation is that in their actual thinking humans articulate the possible worlds they are tacitly considering only to a certain depth. This notion of a world articulated only to a given depth can be captured by means of Rantala's (1975) notion of urn models, which hence offers a natural way out of the paradox.

See also: LOGIC AND MATHEMATICAL TERMS, GLOSSARY OF

References and further reading

Boh, I. (1993) *Epistemic Logic in the Later Middle Ages*, London: Routledge. (The prehistory of epistemic logic.)

Fagin, R., Halpern, J.Y., Moses, Y. and Vardi, Moshe Y. (1955) *Reasoning about Knowledge*, Cambridge, MA: MIT Press. (Synthesis of computer scientists' work on epistemic logic.)

Hintikka, J. (1962) *Knowledge and Belief*, Ithaca, NY: Cornell University Press. (First fully fledged treatment of the logic of knowledge.)

—— (1992) 'Independence-Friendly Logic as a Medium of Information Representation and Reasoning About Knowledge', in S. Ohsuga *et al.* (eds) *Information, Modelling and Knowledge Bases*, Amsterdam: IOS Press, vol. 3, 258– 65. (Develops the themes of §§2–3 of this entry.)

—— (1996) 'Knowledge Acknowledged: Knowledge of Propositions vs. Knowledge of Objects', *Philosophy and Phenomenological Research* 56: 251–75. (Knowledge of truths and knowledge of objects distinguished from each other.)

* Hintikka, J., Halonen, I. and Mutanen, A. (1997) 'Interrogative logic as a general theory of reasoning', in R. Johnson and J. Woods (eds) *Handbook of Applied Logic*, Dordercht: Kluwer. (Survey of the uses of epistemic logic in knowledge acquisition by questioning.)

Hintikka, J. and Hintikka, M.B. (1989) *The Logic of Epistemology and the Epistemology of Logic*, Dordrecht: Kluwer. (Essay 2 is an alternative survey of epistemic logic; essay 4 applies epistemic logic to the problem of the objects of knowledge; essay 5 treats the problem of logical omniscience; and essay 8 explores the connections between different modes of identification and their manifestations in cognitive science.)

Hintikka, J. and Sandu, G. (1989) 'Informational Independence as a Semantical Phenomenon', in J.E. Fenstad, I.T. Frolov and R. Hilpinen (eds) *Logic, Methodology and Philosophy of Science*, Amsterdam: North Holland, vol. 8, 571–89. (Introduces the idea of informational independence into logical semantics.)

Lenzen, W. (1978) *Recent Work in Epistemic Logic*, Acta Philosophica Fennica, vol. 30, number 1, Helsinki: Societas Philosophica Fennica. (Survey of the literature up to 1978.)

* Rantala, V. (1975) 'Urn Models', *Journal of Philosophical Logic* 4: 455–74. (Urn models defined.)

Wright, G.H. von (1951) *An Essay in Modal Logic*, Amsterdam: North Holland. (Von Wright began the first systematic treatment of epistemic logic.)

JAAKKO HINTIKKA
ILPO HALONEN

EPISTEMIC PARADOXES
see PARADOXES, EPISTEMIC

EPISTEMIC RELATIVISM

An account of what makes a system of reasoning or belief revision a good one is relativistic if it is sensitive to facts about the person or group using the system. It may then turn out that one system is best for one person or group, while a quite different system is best for another. Some of the most popular accounts of how systems of reasoning are to be assessed, including those based on reflective equilibrium and those based on the system's truth-generating capacity, appear to be relativistic. It is sometimes claimed that epistemic relativism leads to nihilism or that it severs the connection between good reasoning and true belief.

1   Relativism defined
2   Two relativistic accounts of cognitive assessment
3   Is epistemic relativism problematic?

1   Relativism defined

The term 'epistemic relativism' has been used in a bewildering variety of ways. Here, we focus on an account that takes epistemic relativism to be a species of normative cognitive pluralism (see COGNITIVE PLURALISM). Normative cognitive pluralism claims that there is no unique system of reasoning (or of forming and revising beliefs) that people ought to use, because various quite different systems can all be equally good. An account of what makes a system of reasoning a good one is relativistic if the assessments of cognitive systems it offers are sensitive to facts about the person or group using the system. If systems of reasoning are evaluated in this way, then in general it will make no sense to ask whether one system is better than another: rather, we must ask whether one system is better than another for a given person or group.

2   Two relativistic accounts of cognitive assessment

Though it often goes unnoticed, some of the most popular accounts of how systems of reasoning are to be assessed are, or at least might well turn out to be, relativistic. Here, two such accounts are considered: one based on reflective equilibrium, the other based on a system's truth-generating capacity.

Nelson GOODMAN claimed that general principles of inference were justified by their conformity with the particular inferences we make and accept, and that our acceptance of particular inferences was justified by their accord with general inferential principles. This, he noted, looked 'flagrantly circular' but, he continued:

> this circle is a virtuous one. The point is that rules and particular inferences alike are justified by being brought into agreement with each other. A rule is amended if it yields an inference we are unwilling to accept; an inference is rejected if it violates a rule we are unwilling to amend. The process of justification is the delicate one of making mutual adjustments between rules and accepted inferences; and in the agreement achieved lies the only justification needed for either.
>
> (Goodman 1965: 64)

John Rawls (1971) introduced the term 'reflective equilibrium' to label the endpoint of the process of 'delicate... mutual adjustments' that Goodman describes.

Although Goodman did not discuss the matter, other authors have noted that there is no guarantee that everyone who uses the process will end up at the same point. If two people begin with significantly different judgments rejecting or accepting particular inferences, or with different views about which rules they are willing to amend (or both), then it seems entirely possible that they will end up with quite different sets of rules, though each set will be in reflective equilibrium. If, as Goodman insists, the process of mutual adjustment is all that is needed for rules and inferences to be justified, then these people may end up reasoning in very different ways, each of which is justified for the person who reasons in that way.

Reliabilist accounts of how to assess systems of reasoning or belief revision link the assessment to the truth-generating capacity of the system (see RELIABILISM). Other things being equal, the better a system is at producing true beliefs and avoiding false one, the more highly a reliabilist will rank it. Though it is not often emphasized by reliabilists, this sort of assessment is quite sensitive to the environment in which people using the system find themselves. Thus it may well turn out that a given system of reasoning does an excellent job for one person and a very poor job for another. Imagine a pair of people who suddenly fall victim to Descartes' demon, and are from that time provided with systematically misleading or deceptive perceptual data. Suppose that one of the victims has been using cognitive processes quite like our own, and that these have done a good job in generating truths and avoiding falsehoods, while the other victim's cognitive processes have been (by our lights) quite mad, and have produced far more falsehoods and far fewer truths. In their new demon-infested environment, however, the 'normal' system of cognitive processes will yield a growing fabric of false beliefs. The other system, by contrast, may now do a much better job at generating truths and avoiding falsehoods, since what the evil demon is doing is providing his victims with radically misleading evidence – evidence that only a lunatic would take to be evidence for what actually is the case. So on an account of cognitive evaluation in which generating truths and avoiding falsehoods plays a central role, our system would be preferable in one environment, the mad system in another. Which system a person ought to use will depend on which environment the person is in.

Invocation of evil demons to make the point might suggest that this is a very peripheral phenomenon that is hardly worth worrying about. However, the Cartesian demon case is just the very small tip of a very large iceberg. Any reliabilist evaluation of cognitive processes is going to be acutely sensitive to the cultural, technological and epistemic setting in which the processes are to function. The likelihood that one system of cognitive processes will do a better job than another at generating truth, I suspect, will depend on such factors as the existence of a system of writing, the existence and the structure of disciplinary communities, and the relation of those communities to the political and economic arrangements of the wider society. It will also often depend on the level of conceptual, mathematical, scientific and technological sophistication that has been achieved. If these conjectures are right, it follows that reliabilist accounts of cognitive or epistemic evaluation will have a certain post-Hegelian historicist flavour. There will be no one ideal method of inquiry, no cognitive system that excels in all historical settings. Rather, we can expect that the assessment of a cognitive system will vary as its historical setting varies, and that, just as with technologies (and indeed with genes), it will sometimes happen that a successful system will undermine its own success by changing the environment in such a way that competing systems will now be more successful.

3 Is epistemic relativism problematic?

Many philosophers consider epistemic relativism a dangerous or troubling doctrine. It is, however, not easy to find plausible arguments justifying this negative attitude. This section briefly sketches two lines of argument that might motivate opposition to relativism, although I do not think either argument very persuasive.

The first charge against relativism is that it is nihilistic because it simply gives up on the project of distinguishing good reasoning from bad, and embraces a sort of epistemic anarchy. From our previous discussion, however, it should be clear that the 'anything goes' slogan is a singularly inappropriate one for many relativistic accounts of cognitive assessment. Many versions of reliabilism are relativistic. But reliabilists are certainly not epistemic anarchists – quite the contrary. Reliabilism offers an extremely demanding account of cognitive evaluation. For a given cognitive agent in a given historical setting, it will typically be the case that a reliabilist evaluation will rank one system of reasoning higher than another. Rarely will it be the case that reliabilism ranks all contenders on a par.

A second complaint against relativism is that it threatens the connection between cognitive inquiry and truth. For if the epistemic relativist is right, then there may be a pair of people whose systems of reasoning are very different from one another, though each system is optimal for the person using it. We can expect that on being exposed to essentially the same data these people will sometimes end up with very different sets of beliefs. When this happens it is unlikely to be the case that both sets are true; at least one set of beliefs will be substantially mistaken. Since at least one person will end up with false beliefs, and since *ex hypothesi* they are both using optimally good cognitive systems, it can not be the case that good cognition always leads to true beliefs.

What this argument shows is that if the epistemic relativist is right, then good reasoning does not guarantee truth. But it does not show that good reasoning and truth are unconnected. If, for example, we adopt a reliabilist account of cognitive evaluation, then people who reason well will do the best job possible at producing truths and avoiding falsehoods. To expect more than this seems unreasonable.

See also: RATIONAL BELIEFS; RELATIVISM

References and further reading

Daniels, N. (1980) 'Wide Reflective Equilibrium and Archimedean Points', *Canadian Journal of Philosophy* 10: 83–103. (Discussion of the virtues and shortcomings of reflective-equilibrium accounts of justification.)

Foley, R. (1987) *The Theory of Epistemic Rationality*, Cambridge, MA: Harvard University Press. (A sophisticated statement of an epistemic position that has some features of relativism.)

Goldman, A. (1986) *Epistemology and Cognition*,

Cambridge, MA: MIT Press. (Important statement of reliabilism.)

* Goodman, N. (1965) *Fact, Fiction and Forecast*, Indianapolis, IN: Bobbs-Merrill. (Referred to in §2 above. The classic statement of a reflective-equilibrium account of justification.)

Hollis, M. and Lukes, S. (eds) (1982) *Rationality and Relativism*, Cambridge, MA: MIT Press. (Collection of essays by philosophers, anthropologists and historians of science debating the evidence for descriptive pluralism and the merits of relativism.)

* Rawls, J. (1971) *A Theory of Justice*, Cambridge, MA: Harvard University Press. (Classic work in which reflective equilibrium is used to defend an account of justics.)

Stein, E. (1996) *Without Good Reason: The Rationality Debate in Philosophy and Cognitive Science*, Oxford: Clarendon Press. (Systematic study of the empirical and philosophical literature relevant to relativism.)

Stich, S. (1990) *The Fragmentation of Reason*, Cambridge, MA: MIT Press. (Expansion of the material of this entry; see especially chapters 1, 4 and 6.)

STEPHEN P. STICH

EPISTEMIC VIRTUES

see THEORETICAL (EPISTEMIC) VIRTUES; VIRTUE EPISTEMOLOGY

EPISTEMOLOGY

Epistemology is one of the core areas of philosophy. It is concerned with the nature, sources and limits of knowledge (see KNOWLEDGE, CONCEPT OF). There is a vast array of views about those topics, but one virtually universal presupposition is that knowledge is true belief, but not mere true belief (see BELIEF AND KNOWLEDGE). For example, lucky guesses or true beliefs resulting from wishful thinking are not knowledge. Thus, a central question in epistemology is: what must be added to true beliefs to convert them into knowledge?

1 The normative answers: foundationalism and coherentism

The historically dominant tradition in epistemology answers that question by claiming that it is the quality of the reasons for our beliefs that converts true beliefs into knowledge (see EPISTEMOLOGY, HISTORY OF). When the reasons are sufficiently cogent, we have knowledge (see RATIONAL BELIEFS). This is the normative tradition in epistemology (see NORMATIVE EPISTEMOLOGY). An analogy with ethics is useful: just as an action is justified when ethical principles sanction its performance, a belief is justified when epistemic principles sanction accepting it (see JUSTIFICATION, EPISTEMIC; EPISTEMOLOGY AND ETHICS). The second tradition in epistemology, the naturalistic tradition, does not focus on the quality of the reasons for beliefs but, rather, requires that the conditions in which beliefs are acquired typically produce true beliefs (see INTERNALISM AND EXTERNALISM IN EPISTEMOLOGY; NATURALIZED EPISTEMOLOGY).

Within the normative tradition, two views about the proper structure of reasons have been developed: foundationalism and coherentism (see REASONS FOR BELIEF). By far, the most commonly held view is foundationalism. It holds that reasons rest on a foundational structure comprised of 'basic' beliefs (see FOUNDATIONALISM). The foundational propositions, though justified, derive none of their justification from other propositions. (Coherentism, discussed below, denies that there are foundational propositions).

These basic beliefs can be of several types. Empiricists (such as HUME and LOCKE) hold that basic beliefs exhibit knowledge initially gained through the senses or introspection (see A POSTERIORI; EMPIRICISM; INTROSPECTION, EPISTEMOLOGY OF; PERCEPTION, EPISTEMIC ISSUES IN). Rationalists (such as DESCARTES, LEIBNIZ and SPINOZA) hold that at least some basic beliefs are the result of rational intuition (see A PRIORI; RATIONALISM). Since not all knowledge seems to be based on sense experience, introspection or rational intuition, some epistemologists claim that some knowledge is innate (see INNATE KNOWLEDGE; KNOWLEDGE, TACIT; KANT, I.; PLATO). Still others argue that some propositions are basic in virtue of conversational contextual features. That is, some propositions are taken for granted by the appropriate epistemic community (see CONTEXTUALISM, EPISTEMOLOGICAL).

Foundationalists hold that epistemic principles of inference are available which allow an epistemic agent to reason from the basic propositions to the non-basic (inferred) propositions. They suggest, for example, that if a set of basic propositions is explained by some hypothesis and additional confirming evidence for the hypothesis is discovered, then the hypothesis is justified (see INFERENCE TO THE BEST EXPLANATION). A notorious problem with this suggestion is that it is always possible to form more than one hypothesis that appears equally well confirmed by the total available data, and consequently no one hypothesis seems favoured over all its rivals (see INDUCTION, EPISTEMIC ISSUES IN; GOODMAN, N.). Some epistemologists have argued that this problem can be overcome by appealing to features of the rival hypotheses beyond their explanatory power. For example, the relative simplicity of one hypothesis might be thought to provide a basis for preferring it to its rivals (see SIMPLICITY; THEORETICAL(EPISTEMIC) VIRTUES).

In contrast to foundationalism, coherentism claims that every belief derives some of its justification from other beliefs (see KNOWLEDGE AND JUSTIFICATION, COHERENCE THEORY OF; PROBABILITY THEORY AND EPISTEMOLOGY; BOSANQUET, B.; BRADLEY, F.H.). All coherentists hold that, like the poles of a tepee, beliefs are mutually reinforcing. Some coherentists, however, assign a special justificatory role to those propositions that are more difficult to dislodge because they provide more support for the other propositions and are more supported by them. The set of these special propositions overlaps the set of basic propositions specified by foundationalism.

There are some objections aimed specifically at foundationalism and others aimed specifically at coherentism. But there is one deep difficulty with both traditional normative accounts. This problem, known as the 'Gettier Problem' (after a famous three-page article by Edmund Gettier in 1963), can be stated succinctly as follows (see GETTIER PROBLEMS): suppose that a false belief can be justified (see FALLIBILISM), and suppose that its justificatory status can be transferred to another proposition through deduction or other principles of inference (see DEDUCTIVE CLOSURE PRINCIPLE). Suppose further that the inferred proposition is true. If these suppositions can be true simultaneously – and that seems to be the case – the inferred proposition would be true, justified (by either foundationalist or coherentist criteria) and believed, but it clearly is not knowledge, since it was inferred from a false proposition. It is a felicitous coincidence that the truth was obtained.

One strategy for addressing the Gettier Problem remains firmly within the normative tradition. It employs the original normative intuition that it is the quality of the reasons that distinguishes knowledge from mere true belief. This is the defeasibility theory of knowledge. There are various defeasibility accounts but, generally, all of them hold that the felicitous coincidence can be avoided if the reasons which justify the belief are such that they cannot be defeated by further truths (see KNOWLEDGE, DEFEASIBILITY THEORY OF).

2   The naturalistic answers: causes of belief

There is a second general strategy for addressing the Gettier Problem that falls outside of the normative tradition and lies squarely within the naturalistic tradition (see QUINE, W.V.). As the name suggests, the naturalistic tradition describes knowledge as a natural phenomenon occurring in a wide range of subjects. Adult humans may employ reasoning to arrive at some of their knowledge, but the naturalists are quick to point out that children and adult humans arrive at knowledge in ways that do not appear to involve any reasoning whatsoever. Roughly, when a true belief has the appropriate causal history, then the belief counts as knowledge (see KNOWLEDGE, CAUSAL THEORY OF).

Suppose that I am informed by a reliable person that the temperature outside the building is warmer now than it was two hours ago. That certainly looks like a bit of knowledge gained and there could be good reasons provided for the belief. The normativists would appeal to those good reasons to account for the acquisition of knowledge. The naturalists, however, would argue that true belief resulting from testimony from a reliable source is sufficient for knowledge (see SOCIAL EPISTEMOLOGY; TESTIMONY).

Testimony is just one reliable way of gaining knowledge (see RELIABILISM). There are other ways such as sense perception, memory and reasoning. Of course, sometimes these sources are faulty (see MEMORY, EPISTEMOLOGY OF). A central task of naturalized epistemology is to characterize conditions in which reliable information is obtained (see INFORMATION THEORY AND EPISTEMOLOGY). Thus, in some of its forms, naturalized epistemology can be seen as a branch of cognitive psychology, and the issues can be addressed by empirical investigation.

Now let us return to the Gettier Problem. Recall that it arose in response to the recognition that truth might be obtained through a felicitous coincidence. The naturalistic tradition ties together the belief and truth conditions of knowledge in a straightforward way by requiring that the means by which the true belief is produced or maintained should be reliable.

3   Scepticism

The contrast between normative and naturalized epistemology is apparent in the way in which each addresses one of the most crucial issues in epistemology, namely, scepticism (see SCEPTICISM). Scepticism comes in many forms. In one form, the requirements for knowledge become so stringent that knowledge becomes impossible, or virtually impossible, to obtain. For example, suppose that a belief is knowledge only if it is certain, and a belief is certain only if it is beyond all logically possible doubt. Knowledge would then become a very rare commodity (see CERTAINTY; DOUBT).

Other forms of scepticism only require good, but not logically unassailable, reasoning. We have alluded to scepticism about induction. That form of scepticism illustrates the general pattern of the sceptical problem: there appear to be intuitively clear cases of the type of knowledge questioned by the sceptic, but intuitively plausible general epistemic principles appealed to by the sceptic seem to preclude that very type of knowledge.

Another example will help to clarify the general pattern of the sceptical problem. Consider the possibility that my brain is not lodged in my skull but is located in a vat and hooked up to a very powerful computer that stimulates it to have exactly the experiences, memories and thoughts that I am now having. Call it the 'sceptical hypothesis'. That hypothetical situation is clearly incompatible with the way I think the world is. Now, it seems to be an acceptable normative epistemic principle that if I am justified in believing that the world is the way I believe it to be (with other people, tables, governments and so on), I should have some good reasons for denying the sceptical hypothesis. But, so the argument goes, I could not have such reasons; for if the sceptical hypothesis were true, everything would appear to be just as it now does. So, there appears to be a conflict between the intuition that we have such knowledge and the intuitively appealing epistemic principle. Thus, scepticism can be seen as one instance of an interesting array of epistemic paradoxes (see PARADOXES, EPISTEMIC).

Of course, epistemologists have developed various answers to scepticism. Within the normative tradition, there are several responses available. One of them is simply to deny any epistemic principle – even if it seems initially plausible – that precludes us from having what we ordinarily think is within our ken (see COMMONSENSISM; CHISHOLM, R.M.; MOORE, G.E.; REID, T.). Another response is to examine the epistemic principles carefully in an attempt to show that, properly interpreted, they do not lead to scepticism. Of course, there is always the option of simply declaring that we do not have knowledge. Whatever choice is made, some initially plausible intuitions will be sacrificed.

Within the naturalistic tradition, there appears to be an easy way to handle the sceptical worries. Possessing knowledge is not determined by whether we have good enough reasons for our beliefs but, rather, whether the processes that produced the beliefs in question are sufficiently reliable. So, if I am a brain in a vat, I do not have knowledge; and if I am not a brain in a vat (and the world is generally the way I think it is), then I do have knowledge. Nevertheless, those within the normative tradition will argue that we are obliged to withhold full assent to propositions for which we have less than adequate reasons, regardless of the causal history of the belief.

4 Recent developments in epistemology

Some recent developments in epistemology question and/or expand on some aspects of the tradition. Virtue epistemology focuses on the characteristics of the knower rather than individual beliefs or collections of beliefs (see VIRTUE EPISTEMOLOGY). Roughly, the claim is that when a true belief is the result of the exercise of intellectual virtue, it is, ceteris paribus, knowledge. Thus, the virtue epistemologist can incorporate certain features of both the normative and naturalist traditions. Virtues, as opposed to vices, are good, highly prized dispositional states. The intellectual virtues, in particular, are just those deep dispositions that produce mostly true beliefs. Such an approach reintroduces some neglected areas of epistemology, for example, the connection of knowledge to wisdom and understanding (see WISDOM).

In addition, there are emerging challenges to certain presuppositions of traditional epistemology. For example, some argue that there is no set of rules for belief acquisition that are appropriate for all peoples and all situations (see COGNITIVE PLURALISM; EPISTEMIC RELATIVISM). Others have suggested that many of the proposed conditions of good reasoning, for example 'objectivity' or 'neutrality', are not invoked in the service of gaining truths, as traditional epistemology would hold, but rather they are employed to prolong entrenched power and (at least in some cases) distort the objects of knowledge (see FEMINIST EPISTEMOLOGY).

In spite of these fundamental challenges and the suggestions inherent in some forms of naturalized epistemology that the only interesting questions are empirically answerable, it is clear that epistemology remains a vigorous area of inquiry at the heart of philosophy.

See also: CHARITY, PRINCIPLE OF; CRITERIA; EPISTEMIC LOGIC; HERMENEUTICS; PHENOMENALISM; PHENOMENOLOGY, EPISTEMIC ISSUES IN; RORTY, R.M.; SOLIPSISM

References and further reading

Chisholm, R. (1966/1977/1989) *Theory of Knowledge*, Englewood Cliffs, NJ: Prentice Hall, 1st, 2nd and

3rd edns. (The successive editions contain a general introduction to many issues in epistemology and increasingly complex foundationalist accounts of knowledge, along with versions of the defeasibility account. The first edition is a good place to begin a study of contemporary epistemology.)

* Gettier, E. (1963) 'Is justified true belief knowledge?', *Analysis* 23 (6):121–3. (This article was responsible for focusing attention on the inadequacy of characterizing knowledge as true, justified belief. Many of the most interesting contemporary issues in epistemology can be traced directly or indirectly to this article.)

Lehrer, K. (1990) *Theory of Knowledge*, Boulder, CO: Westview Press. (An accessible introduction to the fundamental questions in epistemology that defends a version of coherentism as supplemented by the defeasibility account.)

Lucey, K. (1996) *On Knowing and the Known*, Buffalo, NY: Prometheus Books. (A collection of contemporary, fairly accessible articles on a wide variety of epistemic issues.)

Moser, P. and Vander Nat, A. (eds) (1987) *Human Knowledge: Classical and Contemporary Approaches*, New York and Oxford: Oxford University Press. (An accessible collection of classical and contemporary essays on a wide variety of issues in epistemology.)

Sosa, E. (ed.) (1994) *Knowledge and Justification*, vols 1 and 2, Brookfield, VT: Ashgate Publishing Company. (A comprehensive set of contemporary essays in epistemology.)

PETER D. KLEIN

EPISTEMOLOGY AND ETHICS

Epistemology and ethics are both concerned with evaluations: ethics with evaluations of conduct, epistemology with evaluations of beliefs and other cognitive acts. Of considerable interest to philosophers are the ways in which the two kinds of evaluations relate to one another. Philosophers' explorations of these relations divide into two general categories: examination of potential analogies between the two fields, and attempts to identify necessary or conceptual connections between the two domains.

There is little doubt that there are at least superficial similarities between ethics and epistemology: one might say that ethics is about the appraisal of social behaviour and agents, while epistemology is about the appraisal of cognitive acts and agents. On

the other hand, the widely held view that behaviour subject to moral evaluation is free and voluntary while beliefs are not, suggests one important disanalogy between the two fields.

1 **Epistemic and ethical evaluations**
2 **Naturalism**
3 **Universality, objectivity and subjectivity**
4 **Internalism and externalism**
5 **The 'ought-implies-can' principle**
6 **Conceptual connections**

1 Epistemic and ethical evaluations

People regularly evaluate actions as right or wrong, justified or unjustified, obligatory or prohibited, and they evaluate individuals as good or bad, virtuous or immoral. Ethics is the branch of philosophy that studies evaluations of these sorts. While ethicists do at times evaluate particular acts and agents, their concern is more typically with the general principles governing these evaluations and with the meaning and nature of the evaluations themselves. People make comparable judgments about beliefs and other cognitive acts, sometimes using the same evaluative language. They say that beliefs are justified or unjustified, that someone ought or ought not to believe a certain proposition. They also evaluate people as reasonable or unreasonable, as rational or irrational. Epistemology is the branch of philosophy that studies these sorts of evaluations of cognitive acts. Like ethicists, epistemologists are usually primarily concerned with the general principles governing epistemic evaluations and with their meaning and nature rather than with the status of particular beliefs or believers.

The evaluative nature of the central concepts of ethics and epistemology gives rise to intriguing philosophical questions. To say that an action is right, for example, seems to be to endorse or approve of the action, and it also seems to say something descriptive about the action, something that could be true or false. This suggests that there is a property or characteristic of actions, rightness, just as there are other causal, spatial or temporal properties of objects. But what sort of property is moral rightness? What connection does it have to the properties to which the natural sciences appeal? Are there universal standards of moral rightness or are standards in some sense determined individually or culturally? Can a person have an obligation to perform an action even if they do not see anything of value in the action? Analogous questions arise in epistemology. When we say that a belief is justified or that a body of evidence is good evidence for some conclusion, we seem to suggest that there is a real property – being justified – and a real relation – being good evidence for something. But what sort of property and relation are these? What connection do they have to the properties and relations of the natural sciences? Are there universal standards of justification and rationality or are standards determined individually or culturally? Can a person have good reasons to believe something even if they do not see the evidential merit of those reasons? Many philosophers have thought that there are important analogies between ethics and episte-mology and that the answers to these questions in one domain may shed light on the analogous questions in the other.

2 Naturalism

There has been considerable discussion concerning the connections of ethics and epistemology to the sciences. The debate has often focused on the plausibility of doctrines known as 'naturalism'. There are at least two distinct issues taken up under this heading, one of which has received a great deal of attention from ethicists while the other has been more prominent in epistemology. The discussion of natur-alism in ethics has concentrated on the plausibility of giving naturalistic definitions of ethical terms. The discussion of naturalism in epistemology has focused on the connection between empirical studies of cognition and epistemological theorizing.

Naturalistic definitions of ethical terms purport to define – or reduce – the concepts or terms of ethics to those of science. To make sense of reductionism, we first must acknowledge a distinction between two categories of properties or concepts: the evaluative properties of ethics on the one hand and the allegedly more fundamental properties of the sciences. These latter would, perhaps, include causal, structural, spatial and temporal properties. Reductionists about ethics think that the descriptive role of moral predicates – for example 'right' – is to express moral properties – the property 'moral rightness' – and that these moral properties are simply complexes of basic scientific properties. Further, they think that it is a conceptual or philosophical job to say which com-plexes of natural properties moral properties reduce to. To take a simple (and not very plausible) example, an ethicist might hold that the property of being a right action is the same as the property of having the approval of the majority of people in its agent's society. This amounts to a proposed reduction of the ethical notion of a right action to a social and psychological notion of majority approval. Reduc-tionists need not say that the entire meaning of evaluative terms is captured by these reductive definitions. They can say that there is also a prescriptive component of their meaning as well. Their contention is that their definitions bring out the core descriptive meaning of the terms, that they spell out in scientifically acceptable terms what moral properties are.

The open question argument, due to G.E. Moore, is a widely discussed objection to all proposed naturalistic definitions of ethical terms. It begins with the observation that for any proposed definitional equivalent of a term such as 'good' or 'right', it is an open (or significant) question whether things having the reductive property are always good or right. However, if the properties were identical, then it would not be an open question whether things having one would have the 'other'. Hence, no such definition is correct (see MOORE, G.E. §1).

Among ethicists who reject naturalistic definitions, on the basis of the open question argument or for other reasons, there are some who contend that moral predicates do not have descriptive meaning and are instead used to express approval or disapproval or to prescribe or proscribe behaviour. On this view, known as non-cognitivism, evaluative sentences do not say anything that can be true or false. Rather, they express the speaker's attitude (moral indignation or approba-tion). Others contend that moral properties are natural properties of objects, though they deny the possibility of any sort of definitional reduction to the concepts of, say, physics. Some versions of this non-reductive naturalism draw on the causal theory of reference. They hold that there is a natural property of objects which is causally related to our use of words such as 'right' in some appropriate way and that an action is right just in case it has that property. There is no need to assume, however, that philosophical reflection can reveal just what this property is or that there are any other terms of our language that refer to this property and would constitute a definition of 'right'. Another view, not widely endorsed, is non-naturalism, according to which ethical properties exist and are genuine properties of objects, but they are in some sense independent of the properties studied in the sciences. It strikes many philosophers as myster-ious how there could be any moral knowledge if non-naturalism is true.

One can see in the debate about naturalism in epistemology analogues of most of the views just described. There have been some attempts at natur-alistic definitions of epistemic terms. An example is reliabilism, which defines 'justified belief' roughly as 'belief caused by a reliable belief-forming process'. Non-cognitivism in epistemology has found some support. For example, J.L. Austin (1946) held that to say that I know some proposition is not to describe some striking cognitive feat, nor is it to describe anything else. It is, he held, to 'give one's word' that the proposition is true. It is something like promising that the proposition is true. Notably, however, non-cognitivism in epistemology has received far less attention and support than it has in ethics.

The view that epistemic properties are not reducible to naturalistic properties is not uncommon. On this view there are fundamental epistemic facts, facts that cannot be reduced to logical or empirical facts. To say that p is evidence for q is not, according to this view, to say that p implies q or that p has any other logical relationship to q, and it is not to say that it is an empirical fact that typically, when p is true, q is also true. Thus, for example, non-naturalists might say that certain sorts of perceptual experiences simply do provide evidence for certain truths about the world or that certain data provide evidence for a particular theory. According to a similar view, defended by Chisholm (1991), epistemic concepts are all ultimately to be understood in terms of the epistemic relation 'being more reasonable than', as in 'believing p is more reasonable than believing q'. As is the case in ethics, critics of this view wonder how we could have any access to epistemological properties and relations if they are not, in some sense, complexes of natural properties.

Another element of the debate about naturalism concerns the relationship of ethics and epistemology to the sciences. A primary source for discussions of this aspect of naturalism in epistemology is Quine's 'Epistemology Naturalized' (1969). There, Quine appears to hold that traditional epistemology ought to be replaced by empirical investigation of the ways in which people form beliefs. The analogous view in ethics has scarcely received attention from philosophers. While few epistemologists endorse Quine's replacement thesis, many agree that epistemology would benefit from closer ties to cognitive science. Epistemologists, who see epistemology as largely devoted to helping people to reason better, understandably think that their task can best be accomplished by paying attention to empirical discoveries about the ways people do reason and about their cognitive capacities. Lacking that sort of empirical information, epistemologists might recommend futile strategies that people cannot follow and attempt to correct errors that do not actually occur. The epistemological enterprise that seeks to make realistic recommendations about reasoning is in some ways comparable to efforts in applied ethics to ascertain the status of particular kinds of actions. Few would deny that empirical results have some implications for those efforts. For example, information about the deterrent effects of capital punishment surely has some bearing on its moral status. There is less clearly room for empirical input into debates about the conceptual analysis of epistemic or ethical terms. Accordingly, epistemologists and ethicists whose primary aim is to provide such analyses are less inclined to endorse naturalism (see NATURALISM IN ETHICS; NATURALIZED EPISTEMOLOGY).

3 Universality, objectivity and subjectivity

A second area in which the analogies between ethics and epistemology warrant careful scrutiny concerns the universality and objectivity of the judgments under discussion. It is common to wonder whether there are standards of proper conduct or rational belief that transcend particular cultural norms, and whether there are standards that exist independently of the values and practices of any particular culture. Negative answers to these questions have long been common in ethics, and they are becoming increasingly common in epistemology. Some philosophers have tried to make use of the more developed debate in ethics about these matters to shed light on the epistemological questions (see COGNITIVE PLURALISM; EPISTEMIC RELATIVISM).

People often wonder whether ethical evaluations are in any interesting sense 'objective'. Some of our conflicting intuitions about this possibly can be resolved by distinguishing two senses of evaluative terms. Consider a physician faced with a choice between two incompatible treatment plans for a patient with a serious disease. It seems clearly right for the physician to select the treatment plan that the evidence indicates would best serve the patient. If, however, that evidence is for some reason misleading and the other approach would in fact prove more successful, it also seems that it would be right for the physician to chose that other alternative. These judgments appear to conflict, but a plausible way out is to say that the former judgment concerns a subjective sense of 'right' and the latter concerns an objective sense of the term. More generally, we might say that the desired end of our actions is the overall well-being of those affected. An action is objectively right or good when it actually would have the best consequences among all available alternatives. It is subjectively right (for a person) when that person reasonably thinks that it would have the best consequences among the available alternatives. Some philosophers would recognize an even more radically subjective notion, according to which an action is right (for a person) provided they think, with or without good reason, that it would produce the most good. Note that the less extreme subjective notion makes at least one important ethical concept analysable in epistemic terms.

Some philosophers have suggested that there are analogous distinctions in the senses of epistemic terms, and this too may help resolve some apparent controversies in epistemology. It is unclear, however, exactly how to conceive of the distinction in the epistemic realm. One might say that the epistemic goal is true belief and that a belief is objectively epistemically justified when it achieves this goal. However, this has the plainly mistaken result that all true beliefs are objectively epistemically justified. A belief held solely on the basis of, say, wishful thinking, is not justified in any sense, even if it happens to be true. An alternative conception of the objective–subjective distinction in epistemology takes an objectively justified belief to be one held for what in fact are good reasons and a subjectively justified belief to be one held for what the believer has good reasons to think are good reasons. Again, one can say that there is an even more radically subjective notion, according to which a belief is justified provided the believer thinks, with or without good reason, that the reasons for it are good. This way of drawing the objective–subjective distinction makes even objective epistemic justification depend upon an individual's evidence or reasons, and thus it differs from objective ethical justification which has no such dependence on evidence. Hence, it seems that objective epistemic justification is perspectival or dependent upon individual factors in a way that objective ethical justification is not. In this area the analogy may be weaker than some philosophers have thought.

4 Internalism and externalism

Epistemology and ethics alike have seen extensive debate about views known as internalism and externalism. Internalists in ethics contend that the factors which determine moral rightness must be in some sense internal factors that are accessible to agents by reflection or introspection alone and that these factors must to some extent motivate agents. Externalists hold that a factor can make an action morally right for an agent even if the agent is not motivated by it or would not be motivated by it upon becoming aware of it (see MORAL MOTIVATION §1). Epistemology has experienced a similar split. Internalists hold that the factors which determine epistemic justification must be internal and accessible by reflection. Perceptual experiences, memories and other beliefs would thus qualify as potential sources of justification. Further, on at least some internalist views, the relation between evidence and what it justifies is in some important sense internally accessible. Externalists, in contrast, think that factors external to, and not directly accessible to, a mind can determine what is justified (see INTERNALISM AND EXTERNALISM IN EPISTEMOLOGY; RELIABILISM).

5 The 'ought-implies-can' principle

An area in which the analogy between ethics and epistemology seems to break down has to do with the voluntariness of the behaviour they are about. We regularly speak of how we ought to act or believe, and of our ethical and epistemic obligations. It is natural to slide readily from the claim that an act is justified or right to the claim that it ought to be done. Similarly, it is natural to take as equivalent the statements that a belief is justified and that it ought to be held or adopted. A closer look uncovers puzzles. A widely held principle in ethics is the 'ought-implies-can' principle: a person ought to perform an action only if the person can perform the action. This principle forms the basis for the powerful inclination to think that the inability to do things excuses people from doing those things and absolves them of charges of having failed to act as they ought.

Carrying the ought-implies-can principle into epistemology is problematic. In general, our beliefs do not seem to be things over which we have any sort of direct control. At best, we can set out to expose ourselves to influences that we think are likely to lead us to form desired beliefs. If the ought-implies-can principle is true and we have only this limited sort of control over our beliefs, then it less than clear how we can be justified in believing things that we do not believe or how any actual beliefs can be unjustified. Yet, it seems clear that there are examples of both kinds. A person presented with conclusive evidence for the occurrence of some dreaded event might be psychologically incapable of believing the conclusion justified by that evidence. They are then justified in believing something but cannot believe it. Considerations of this sort lead some philosophers to conclude that the ought-implies-can principle does not hold in the epistemological realm, others to conclude that the proper subject matter of epistemic evaluation is voluntary behaviour such as evidence gathering, yet others to conclude that talk of obligation about beliefs is misguided and that epistemic justification has nothing to do with obligations. Analogues of the first and third of these responses are less common in ethics.

There are, of course, numerous other areas in which one can explore similarities and differences between ethics and epistemology. Although much of ethics has explored the evaluation of individual actions, there has also been considerable discussion of the moral virtues. Here, emphasis is placed on identifying and understanding virtuous character traits, not on identifying conditions of right and wrong action. Some epistemologists have followed suit, investigating what they call the 'epistemic virtues' and developing a brand of epistemology known as 'virtue epistemology'. Epistemic virtues might include such traits of mind as a concern for the truth, impartiality, a desire to acquire relevant evidence and so on. The least revisionary versions of virtue epistemology attempt to analyse justification and knowledge in terms of epistemically virtuous belief. More radical versions argue that epistemologists ought to focus on the study of the intellectual virtues themselves, even though their connection to knowledge and justification might be indirect. Whether further investigation of the virtues reveals close analogies or notable differences between ethics and epistemology, such investigation is likely to prove fruitful (see VIRTUE EPISTEMOLOGY).

6 Conceptual connections

Some philosophers have argued that the relation between epistemology and ethics is not simply one of analogy, but rather of reducibility or interdefinability, claiming that the concepts of one domain can be defined or analysed in terms of the concepts of the other. Although the idea that the fundamental ethical concepts can be defined in epistemic terms has not received much support, it is widely held that there is an important ethical concept that can be partially defined in epistemic terms. Thus, many philosophers have held that a person is subjectively justified in performing a particular action provided they are epistemically justified in believing that the action satisfies some appropriate ethical standard. Philosophers will differ about exactly what that standard is, depending upon their basic perspective in ethics. This sort of connection between ethics and epistemology does not help to resolve any central ethical controversies. It simply acknowledges that there is a notion of ethical justification that features in an agent's epistemic perspective.

Perhaps of greater interest to philosophers have been questions about whether epistemic concepts can be understood in terms of ethical concepts. Roderick Firth (1959) and Roderick Chisholm (1991) long debated this question, Firth arguing that the connection between epistemic justification and ethical justification is merely that of analogy, and Chisholm contending that epistemic justification is a kind of ethical justification.

The simplest possible account of epistemic justification in ethical terms holds that 'S is justified in believing p' means something like 'It is morally right for S to believe p' or 'S has a moral duty to believe p'. On this view, beliefs and other actions are all appraised using the same standards, whether these be consequentialist, deontological or otherwise. Epistemic appraisal is thus taken to be ethical appraisal applied to belief. This simple theory is unsatisfactory. Assuming for the sake of argument that beliefs are the sort of thing for which ethical appraisal is appropriate, there seem to be numerous cases in which ethical evaluations of beliefs depart from epistemic evaluations. Sometimes, there are decisive moral considerations against a belief that is epistemically justified. For example, it may be that one is morally justified in believing the testimony of family and friends, even when the evidence seems to go against them. Perhaps the value of optimism in the face of adversity morally justifies beliefs that go against the evidence. Examples such as these convince many that epistemic justification is not simply ethical justification applied to beliefs. Of course, the failure of the simplest analysis of epistemic justification in ethical terms does not guarantee the failure of more complex analyses. However, Firth argues that no such 'categorical' analysis of epistemic justification in ethical terms can succeed. He claims that while the epistemic fact is determined by considerations of evidential support for the belief, these considerations always leave open the moral evaluation of the belief.

Another approach to analysing epistemic concepts in ethical terms appeals to the notion of *prima facie* ethical justification. The simplest version of such an analysis says that 'S is epistemically justified in believing p' means the same as 'S has a *prima facie* moral duty to believe p'. This implies that if a person is epistemically justified in believing a proposition, then they have a moral duty to believe it unless some other considerations override that duty. It also implies that if a person has a *prima facie* moral duty to believe a proposition, then they are epistemically justified in believing the proposition. This latter implication opens the analysis to convincing counterexamples. One can have *prima facie* moral duties to believe propositions arising from non-epistemic sources (on the assumption that we can have duties to believe at all). In such cases, there will be the *prima facie* duty, but no epistemic justification.

In addition to efforts to define epistemic terms in ethical terms, philosophers have argued for a weaker sort of necessary connection. The best known claim along these lines is due to W.K. Clifford: 'It is wrong, always, everywhere, and for every one, to believe anything upon insufficient evidence' (1866: 346). Given two assumptions, Clifford's assertion has implications for the connection between epistemology and ethics. One is that by 'wrong' he means 'ethically wrong'. The other is that one has epistemic justification for a belief if and only if one has sufficient evidence for it. Given those assumptions, Clifford's remark implies that if a person is not epistemically justified in believing a proposition, then it is morally wrong for them to believe the proposition. What Clifford says here does not amount to a full reductive analysis, since, for one thing, it does not make a claim about the meaning of epistemic statements. Furthermore, his words do not imply that if a person has sufficient evidence for a proposition, then it is morally wrong for them to fail to believe.

Most commentators take Clifford's thesis to be too strong, for reasons such as those mentioned above. Non-epistemic factors can make belief morally wrong, even though it is supported by the evidence. A more modest thesis along the lines of Clifford's suggestion holds that if a person is justified in believing a proposition, then they have a *prima facie* moral duty to believe it. It is difficult to envisage a decisive refutation of this claim, since it only asserts the existence of a *prima facie* moral duty. Objectors must contend that epistemic justification can fail to carry any moral significance at all. Some would agree with the general line suggested by Clifford, and by Chisholm, which holds that as rational beings we have a moral duty to believe as our evidence indicates, provided there are no stronger moral considerations imposing a conflicting obligation.

See also: CONFUCIAN PHILOSOPHY, CHINESE; JUSTIFICATION, EPISTEMIC; NORMATIVE EPISTEMOLOGY

References and further reading

All these items involve detailed argument but are not technical. All focus primarily on epistemological issues.

Alston, W. (1978) 'Meta-Ethics and Meta-Epistemology', in A.I. Goldman and J. Kim (eds) *Values and Morals*, Dordrecht: Reidel. (Explores the analogies between the two fields, with emphasis on issues concerning naturalism.)

—— (1989) *Epistemic Justification: Essays in the Theory of Knowledge*, Ithaca, NY: Cornell University Press. (Includes essays on internalism and externalism, subjective and objective conceptions of justification, the ought-implies-can principle, and other related topics.)

* Austin, J.L. (1946) 'Other Minds', in J.O. Urmson and G.J. Warnock (eds) *Philosophical Papers*, New York: Oxford University Press, 3rd edn, 1979, 76–116. (Defends a non-cognitivist account of sentences about knowledge.)

Chisholm, R. (1966) *Theory of Knowledge*, Englewood Cliffs, NJ: Prentice Hall, 2nd edn, 1977. (Defends a non-naturalistic account of epistemic concepts.)

* —— (1991) 'Firth and the Ethics of Belief', *Philosophy and Phenomenological Research* 51 (1): 119–28. (Defends the thesis that epistemic evaluations are a species of ethical evaluation.)

* Clifford, W.K. (1866) *Lectures and Essays*, London: Macmillan, 2nd edn. (Defends the thesis that it is always wrong to believe on the basis of insufficient evidence.)

Feldman, R. (1988) 'Epistemic Obligations', in J.E. Tomberlin (ed.) *Philosophical Perspectives* 2, Atascadero, CA: Ridgeview, 235–56. (Discusses the ought-implies-can principle in epistemology and defends an account of epistemic obligations.)

* Firth, R. (1959) 'Chisholm and the Ethics of Belief', *Philosophical Review* 68 (4): 493–506. (Firth's earliest defence of his view that epistemic concepts can not be defined in ethical terms.)

—— (1978) 'Are Epistemic Concepts Reducible to Ethical Concepts', in A.I. Goldman and J. Kim (eds) *Values and Morals*, Dordrecht: Reidel. (A later and more detailed account of Firth's view.)

Goldman, A. (1992) *Liaisons: Philosophy Meets the Cognitive and Social Sciences*, Cambridge, MA: MIT Press. (Collection of essays discussing several issues related to naturalism.)

Kvanvig, J.L. (1992) *The Intellectual Virtues and the Life of the Mind*, Savage, MD: Roman & Littlefield. (Argues that the cognitive virtues have a central place in epistemology.)

* Moore, G.E. (1903) *Principia Ethica*, Cambridge: Cambridge University Press, 1968. (Contains the classic statement of Moore's open question argument.)

* Quine, W.V.O. (1969) 'Epistemology Naturalized', in *Ontological Relativity and Other Essays*, New York: Columbia University Press, 69–90. (Classic statement of Quine's account of naturalistic epistemology.)

Sosa, E. (1991) *Knowledge in Perspective*, Cambridge: Cambridge University Press. (Defends an analysis of knowledge in which epistemic virtues figure prominently.)

Zagzebski, L. (1996) *Virtues of the Mind: An Inquiry into the Nature of Virtue and the Ethical Foundations of Knowledge*, Cambridge: Cambridge University Press. (Develops a unified virtue theory in ethics and epistemology.)

RICHARD FELDMAN

EPISTEMOLOGY, HISTORY OF

Epistemology has always been concerned with issues such as the nature, extent, sources and legitimacy of knowledge. Over the course of western philosophy, philosophers have concentrated sometimes on one or two of these issues to the exclusion of the others; rarely has a philosopher addressed all of them. Some central questions are:

(1) What is knowledge – what is the correct analysis or definition of the concept of knowledge?

(2) What is the extent of our knowledge – about what sorts of things is knowledge actually held?

(3) What are the sources of knowledge – how is knowledge acquired?

(4) Is there any genuine knowledge?

Concern with the first question has predominated in philosophy since the mid-twentieth century, but it was also discussed at some length in antiquity. Attention to the second question seems to have begun with Plato, and it has continued with few interruptions to the present day. The third question was also important in antiquity, but has also been a central focus of epistemological discussion through the medieval and early modern periods. The fourth question raises the issue of scepticism, a topic which has generated interest and discussion from antiquity to the present day, though there were some periods in which sceptical worries were largely ignored.

Various attempts to answer these questions throughout the history of philosophy have invariably served to raise additional questions which are more narrow in focus. The principal one which will be treated below can be stated as:

(5) What is a justified belief – under which conditions is a belief justified?

There has been but occasional interest in this last question in the history of philosophy; however, it has been a crucial question for many philosophers in the twentieth century.

1 **Ancient philosophy**
2 **Hellenistic philosophy**
3 **Medieval philosophy**
4 **Modern philosophy: Descartes**
5 **Modern philosophy: Spinoza and Leibniz**
6 **Modern philosophy: Locke and Berkeley**
7 **Modern philosophy: from Hume to Peirce**
8 **Twentieth century**
9 **Recent issues**

1 Ancient philosophy

The extant writings of the Presocratics primarily address issues in metaphysics and cosmology; epistemological concerns appear to arise first in Plato. In the *Meno* Plato tells the story of a slave boy who has had no formal education and in particular has never studied geometry. In a conversation with Socrates, the boy is led to answer questions about a geometrical figure and his answers turn out to be correct. The boy is led to assert that when given a square with side S, so that its area is S^2, then a square of exactly $2S^2$ is formed by taking as its side the diagonal of the original square. The boy could hardly have learned this earlier, since he is uneducated. Plato takes this example to show that the boy knew the geometrical truth all along and, more generally, that the boy's soul existed earlier in a state of knowledge. Indeed, he held that the boy's soul earlier knew all truths but had since forgotten them. What the boy was really doing in his conversation with Socrates was recollecting something he had forgotten. And this Plato takes to hold for everyone: what we think of as coming to know is really recollecting.

The soul or knower may have come into existence and so it would not have always had knowledge; or it may have always been in existence but at some time acquired its stock of knowledge; or it may have always been and always had knowledge. Plato certainly rejects the first option, especially in the *Phaedo* where he argues for the indestructibility and indefinite prior existence of the soul. He also appears to reject the second option (*Meno* 86b) so that his view would be that the soul always exists and earlier had a great deal of knowledge without having acquired this knowledge at some time.

The *Meno* also contains a distinction between true belief and knowledge (97d–98b). Knowledge, Plato says, is 'tied down' or tethered in a way that true opinion is not. This view, which seems to suggest that knowledge is justified true belief, is taken up again in the *Theaetetus*, where Plato suggests that knowledge is true belief plus an account or *logos* (201d). However, several attempts to explicate the notion of an account are rejected, and the dialogue ends inconclusively. It is not clear whether Plato rejects this account of knowledge outright, or whether he is best construed as rejecting this definition given the defective notions of an account (*Theaetetus* 210a–b).

In the *Republic*, especially in Book V, Plato addresses a version of our question pertaining to the extent of knowledge. There he distinguishes between knowledge at one extreme and ignorance at the other, and he roughly identifies an intermediate state of opinion or belief. Each of these states of mind, Plato says, has an object. The object of knowledge is what is or exists; the object of ignorance is what does not exist; and the object of belief is some intermediate entity, often taken as what is becoming or the sensible physical world of objects and their qualities (*Republic* 508d–e; *Cratylus* 440a–d). What truly exists for Plato are unchanging Forms, and it is these which he indicates as the true objects of knowledge. Moreover, knowledge is infallible, while belief is fallible (*Republic* 477e). In thus identifying knowledge with infallibility or certainty, Plato is departing widely from the view of knowledge given in *Meno* and *Theaetetus*. And, his account of the extent of our knowledge is also severely restricted: genuine knowledge is had only of the higher realm of immutable, ideal Forms (see CERTAINTY; FALLIBILISM; PLATO §§11, 15).

Aristotle discusses a special form of knowledge, scientific knowledge, in the *Posterior Analytics*. A science, as Aristotle understands it, is to be thought of as a group of theorems each of which is proved in a demonstrative syllogism. In the first instance, a demonstrative syllogism in science *S* is a syllogistic argument whose premises are first principles of *S*. These first principles, in turn, must be true, primary, immediate, better known than and prior to the conclusion, which is further related to them as effect to cause (*Posterior Analytics* 71b 21–22). First principles are primary and immediate when they are not themselves demonstrable. Still, such principles are known; indeed, they are better known than the demonstrated conclusion, a contention which may mean either that they are more familiar than the conclusion, or perhaps more certain than the conclusion. The first principles are also said to be prior to the conclusions in an epistemic way: knowledge of the conclusion requires knowledge of the first principles, but not conversely (*Taylor 1990: 121*). And the first principles must explain why it is that the demonstrated conclusion is true.

The science can be extended by taking theorems proved from first principles as premises in additional demonstrative syllogisms for further conclusions. Here, too, the premises must explain the truth of the conclusion. A science will be the sum of all such theorems, demonstrated either from first principles or from already-demonstrated theorems in appropriate syllogisms. And a person who carries through all these syllogisms with relevant understanding has knowledge of all of the theorems.

The first principles, however, are also known though they are not demonstrated as theorems. On this point Aristotle gives what may be the first statement of a regress argument in favour of a kind of foundationalist position (see FOUNDATIONALISM).

Some might hold that even the first principles must be demonstrated if they are to be known. This would lead to an infinite regress, as these first principles would themselves be conclusions of syllogisms whose premises were other first principles which, to be known, would have to be demonstrated. To avoid the infinite regress, one would need either to allow for circular demonstration, or to agree that the first principles are not themselves known but are mere suppositions. Aristotle rejects all these options in favour of the foundationalist view in which the first principles are known even though they are not demonstrated. For him, one has an immediate, intuitive grasp of the first principles. However, his foundationalism is to be distinguished from those discussed below, because his foundations are made up of fundamental principles of special sciences.

In *De Anima*, Aristotle discusses perception and perceptual knowledge. Among perceptible objects, he distinguishes between proper and common sensibles. Common sensibles are those objects that are perceivable by more than one sense, for example, the shape of a box which can be both seen and touched. Proper sensibles are those objects that are only perceivable by one sense, for example, colour can only be seen. With respect to these proper objects, Aristotle says that one cannot be in error, or one cannot be deceived (*De Anima* 418a 9–13; 428b 17–21). So, if a person sees a white cat, they can be deceived about whether it is a cat, but not in thinking that there is white present. The same would apply to proper objects of other senses. If we then assume, as Aristotle seems to have done, that the impossibility of being deceived about *X* is sufficient for having knowledge about *X*, then we reach the conclusion that we have certain perceptual knowledge about the proper objects of each sense. What is not clear is whether Aristotle felt that one could not be mistaken about actual qualities of physical objects, such as their colours; or rather about an object's perceived qualities. Clearly the former is much less plausible than the latter (see ARISTOTLE §6).

2 Hellenistic philosophy

The Hellenistic phase of philosophy occupies several centuries after Aristotle's death (322 BC), and is notable for its three schools of philosophy: Epicureanism, Stoicism, and Scepticism (see SCEPTICISM). The sceptical tradition, however, continued well into the second century AD.

The Epicurean school supported an even more thoroughgoing empiricism than we find in Aristotle, and is best known for its doctrine that all perceptions are true. In perception, Epicurus says, thin layers of atoms are emitted from external physical objects (*eídōla*) and reach our senses, which passively receive and register these *eídōla* exactly as they are. But this, *per se*, is not to have knowledge of the external causes of our experiences of *eídōla*. For that, we need to make well-grounded inferences to the existence and nature of the external objects. Epicurus, however, maintains that these inferences, doubtless causal ones, can be legitimately made, and thus that there is genuine perceptual knowledge of physical objects. The fact that these inferences may fare poorly under sceptical scrutiny is not a matter to which Epicurus paid special attention, probably because he did not think that the defeat of sceptical concerns was a necessary project within epistemology (see EPICUREANISM §§6–7).

The Stoic position is much less optimistic. Their central concept is that of a cognitive impression. In normal conditions a red object appears red, and one has the thought (cognitive impression) 'This is red'. Such a cognitive impression, Stoics held, cannot fail to be true. It is not, by itself, knowledge of the red object however, because the person might not assent to this impression. One has knowledge only if one assents to a cognitive impression and this assent is firm, the sort of assent that one cannot be persuaded to withhold. Ordinary people fall short of assent of this firm sort, and so really have mere opinions about objects. Only the wise man typically engages in firm assent to only cognitive impressions; so only the wise man truly has knowledge of such objects (see STOICISM §12).

In thus restricting knowledge, the Stoic position is actually close to a sceptical doctrine. The two schools of ancient scepticism, the Academic and the Pyrrhonian, had notable differences and each had points of development over nearly five centuries, ending with Sextus Empiricus in the late second century AD. A common feature of each school, though, is an attack on claims to knowledge. For any argument towards a conclusion which goes beyond sensory appearances, sceptics maintained that an equally strong counter-argument could be given. Other sceptical arguments point to the relativity of all perception, depending on changes in the percipient or in the observation conditions or perspectives, and conclude that we do not gain knowledge of external physical objects via perception. Also, if a criterion for knowledge-acquisition is relied upon – such as perception or causal inductive inference as in Epicurus – then this criterion could be questioned as itself far from evidently reliable. These sceptical arguments were properly taken to lead to the suspension of belief (*epochē*), rather than to the assertion that there is no knowledge. Moreover, the Pyrrhonian sceptics noted

that the ultimate goal of their arguments was a non-epistemic one, that of *ataraxía* or being undisturbed. This calm state is presumed achievable once beliefs have been suspended and one is content to carry on one's life dealing only with appearances (see PYRRHONISM; SEXTUS EMPIRICUS).

Scepticism was challenged in the early medieval period by Augustine in his *Contra Acadcemicos*, in which he dealt critically with the arguments of Cicero, the last of the great academic sceptics (see AUGUSTINE §2; CICERO). However, scepticism was not a major concern in the Middle Ages, and did not receive special philosophical attention again until the Renaissance.

3   Medieval philosophy

Medieval philosophy is concerned primarily with issues in metaphysics, logic and natural theology, less with epistemological topics. Aquinas and Ockham, however, were two thinkers for whom epistemological questions were of great interest and importance.

Aquinas closely followed Aristotle on many points, including Aristotle's account of scientific knowledge (see §1 above). Thus, *scientia* or genuine scientific knowledge is restricted to propositions proved in demonstrative syllogisms whose premises are themselves known. And, as in Aristotle, Aquinas holds that this account of *scientia* requires as premises in some demonstrative syllogisms, first principles that are known *per se*, immediately and without inference. That there must be such first principles is shown by the fact that otherwise one is faced with either an infinite regress of items of knowledge or with circularity. The former is ruled out because nobody can achieve an infinite number of inferential steps; and circularity, wherein one knows p on the basis of q and knows q on the basis of p, is dismissed because it allows that a single proposition, p, can both be and not be epistemically prior to q. For both Aquinas and Aristotle, the premises of a demonstrative syllogism are epistemically prior to their conclusions in the sense that one cannot know the conclusion without first knowing the premises, though not vice versa.

First principles of demonstrative syllogisms, for Aquinas, are necessary truths, propositions in which there is a necessary connection between the predicate and subject concepts. To grasp or know a first principle, then, requires that one grasp this necessary connection. To achieve this, one must first possess the general concepts expressed by the subject and predicate terms. Accordingly, Aquinas gives an account of how we may acquire such concepts. To do this, one must abstract the intelligible species or forms of objects from the sense impressions received in perception of them. Ultimately, then, knowledge of the first principles depends on perception, though it is not epistemically based on perception.

William of Ockham makes an interesting break with Aquinas' conception of knowledge. Part of the break concerns the fact that Ockham allows for knowledge of contingent truths, as opposed to restricting knowledge to necessary truths. Another difference concerns perception. Aquinas held that, in perception, one has an experience of an image or phantasm from which by some cognitive mechanism (called an agent intellect) one abstracts an intelligible species or form of the perceived object. By means of this abstracted item one knows some universal aspect of the perceived object (see AQUINAS, T. §11). Ockham disagrees with a number of these points. For him, in perception of an external physical object, there is no intermediary such as a phantasm or sensible species. Instead, the object is itself perceived directly, an experience which Ockham regards as an intuitive cognition. In this respect, Ockham's account is close to that of perceptual direct realism (see PERCEPTION, EPISTEMIC ISSUES IN). But he also holds epistemic direct realism, because he argues that the direct visual awareness of the external object suffices for one to acquire immediate and certain knowledge of the existence of the object and of some of its qualities. In this regard, one is 'knowing the singular' rather than something universal; and the proposition one comes to know in perception is a contingent truth. So, in perceiving a red box, one might come to know that there is a red box before one.

Sceptical worries could intrude, even here. One might see a red box and still be mistaken in one's resulting belief. One might think, therefore, that forming the belief as a result of a red-box visual experience does not suffice for knowledge. Ockham is aware of this objection, but he has a two-part answer to it. First, he notes that the mere possibility of mistaken belief does not rule out knowledge. He also notes that aligning the concept of certainty with the impossibility of mistaken belief is itself an error. Certainty, he says, requires only the absence of actual doubt or grounds for doubt. Certainty of this weaker sort, he holds, is all that is needed for knowledge (see WILLIAM OF OCKHAM §§4–5).

This is a decisive break with earlier views, both with respect to the concept of certainty and with respect to its relation to the concept of knowledge. But, with one or two notable exceptions, these ideas were not taken up by many writers until much later.

4 Modern philosophy: Descartes

It is customary to begin the story of modern philosophy with Descartes, but we need to start a little farther back with a discussion of scepticism. We have noted that ancient scepticism was hardly known during the Middle Ages. In the sixteenth century, however, the old sceptical texts of Cicero were re-published and works by Sextus Empiricus were translated into Latin and thus made available to scholars. These texts and their arguments became very important to those on both sides of disputes over the legitimacy and extent of religious knowledge, an issue given great currency by the Reformation and the Counter-Reformation. Under the direct influence of Sextus Empiricus, MONTAIGNE published his *Apology for Raimond Sebond* (1576) in which he set forth sceptical arguments and recommended suspension of belief on practically all topics. His disciple, Pierre Charron, popularized sceptical doctrines even further. This sceptical climate was well known to Descartes in the first half of the seventeenth century. Still later, Pierre Bayle's *Dictionary*, which contained a number of sceptical entries, was to have a great deal of influence on Berkeley and Hume (see BAYLE, P.).

Descartes was thoroughly aware of the sceptical writings and debates of his time, and of the development of sceptical literature since Montaigne. But Descartes himself was no sceptic; on the contrary, he set out to defeat scepticism on its own terms, that is, by finding some knowledge which is completely certain and thus immune to sceptical criticism.

To accomplish this, Descartes used the method of doubt, a method wherein a proposition is considered false provided there is even the slightest possible ground for doubting it. Whole classes of propositions would then be excluded as not known: everything which one believes on the basis of the senses is dubitable by this criterion, and so is not knowledge. The many propositions of science also qualify as dubitable, and so are not items of knowledge. Indeed, it is possible, Descartes reasons, that an evil demon systematically deceives us all, even with respect to the necessary truths of mathematics. If such a demon is even possible, then there is at least the possibility of grounds for doubt, and so virtually nothing would qualify as knowledge.

Descartes contends, however, that such an evil demon cannot deceive him in one case, namely when he thinks in any way. Even when the thinking in which he engages is a case of doubting, whenever Descartes thinks he must exist, and thus he affirms as certain '*Cogito, ergo sum*' – I think, therefore I exist. This is an item about which he cannot be deceived, and it is thus for Descartes indubitable or certain, and assuredly a case of knowledge.

Descartes' epistemological project then becomes one of seeing whether any other genuine certain knowledge can be derived from this very slender base. He finds first a criterion for certainty: those thoughts or ideas which are clear and distinct are also true. In fact, he says that clarity and distinctness of a thought or idea suffices to assure him of its truth. Using this criterion together with his certain knowledge that he exists, Descartes constructs a complex causal argument for the existence of God. The clarity and distinctness of the thoughts that God is not a deceiver and that God would not allow wholesale deception is then put to work to try to derive propositions formerly excluded as dubitable by the method. Especially important here are propositions concerning the existence of external physical objects.

Descartes' project is thus a foundationalist one of an austere sort. For him, the foundations are restricted to the propositions that he himself exists, that he has certain ideas, and that God exists. From these, utilizing the criterion of clarity and distinctness, the foundations can be augmented to include propositions about immediately experienced sensations. However, derivations of other propositions from these foundational ones have to be restricted to deductions that themselves can be seen to be clear and distinct. If the derivations were inductive, then grounds for doubting the conclusions would be possible. And even if the derivations were deductive, if one did not see that they were validly made from individually indubitable premises, once again the possibility of grounds for doubting the conclusions would arise. Only if the possibility of such grounds are eliminated can these derived conclusions count as items of knowledge.

Descartes, thus, perpetuates and even emphasizes the close conceptual connection between knowledge and the strictest sort of certainty (see CERTAINTY). He also gives currency to the problem of the external world, that is, the problem of deriving propositions concerning external physical objects from foundational propositions made up mostly of propositions concerning sensations. Of course, Descartes has propositions about a non-deceiving God in his foundations, unlike later writers who grappled with this problem. So armed, Descartes claims in the sixth Meditation that he can derive the general claims that there are external physical objects and that they have at most the so-called primary qualities. But even if these claims count as items of knowledge, so that to some extent scepticism is vanquished, it does not seem that Descartes secures knowledge of individual propositions about physical objects and their qualities. For he concedes that, with respect to these, error is possible in the best of circumstances, even with God's help (Williams 1978: 234, 249ff) (see DESCARTES, R. §§3–5).

5 Modern philosophy: Spinoza and Leibniz

It is customary to classify Spinoza and Leibniz along with Descartes as rationalists. In epistemology, rationalism is the view which stresses the role of reason in the acquisition of knowledge, and correspondingly downplays the role of experience or observation. A limiting case of rationalism, then, would be a position which held that only reason is operative in knowledge acquisition. It is perhaps Spinoza who comes closest to a rationalist position of this sort (see RATIONALISM).

For Spinoza, a true idea is one which must agree with its object (*Ethics* I: Ax.6). An adequate idea is one which, considered by itself, has an internal sign or intrinsic mark of a true idea (*Ethics* II: Def.4). Having an adequate idea, then, suffices to recognize it as true. There is no need of a clarity-and-distinctness criterion for determining which ideas are true. In this respect, Spinoza differs sharply from Descartes.

Spinoza distinguishes three levels of knowledge. The first is that which we receive in sense perception or from what he calls 'signs', as when the sight of some printed words causes one to remember something. First-level knowledge is not strictly knowledge, however, but rather opinion or imagination. Second-level knowledge or reason (*ratio*) is knowledge of the properties of objects and of relations between properties. Third-level knowledge is intuitive science, which Spinoza says 'advances from an adequate idea of the formal essence of certain attributes of God to the adequate knowledge of the essence of things' (*Ethics* II: pr.XL, schol. 2). Third-level knowledge proceeds from one thing to another in the sense that a person who has an adequate idea of the formal essence of one of God's attributes may logically infer to adequate knowledge of the essence of things.

Knowledge is adequate when one may logically infer, merely from having an adequate idea of x, to some general truth about x (second level), or to some truth about x's effects (third level). Thus, on the second level, from an adequate idea of body one may infer that all bodies are capable of motion, and thus knowledge of this proposition is adequate. And from the adequate idea of the essence of a divine attribute, one may infer to the essence or nature of objects, and thus the proposition concerning the essence of the objects is adequately known.

Spinoza certainly thinks we have adequate ideas, and so have adequate knowledge (*Ethics* II: pr.XXXIV). And he holds that the propositions known at the second and third levels are necessarily true (*Ethics* II: pr.XLI). So, it looks very much as if Spinoza is committed to the view that second- and third-level knowledge is a priori, that is, knowledge that need not rely on experience, and to this degree he would qualify as a rationalist (see SPINOZA, B. DE §§7–8).

Leibniz, the other great philosopher usually classified as a rationalist, did not develop a systematic view in epistemology. His classification as a rationalist is no doubt tied to two important strands of his thought. For simple subject-predicate propositions, fundamental for Leibniz, he proposed the predicate-in-notion principle. This is the thesis that the concept of the predicate in such a proposition is contained in the concept of the subject. It seems as though this principle implies that all subject-predicate propositions are necessarily true. For the conceptual-containment doctrine amounts to the claim that such propositions are true in virtue of their meanings or are conceptually true, and this would make them necessarily true. This has the twofold result that all truth is necessary truth, given that subject-predicate propositions are fundamental; and, that all knowledge is or can be a priori, the latter on the assumption that if a proposition is a necessary truth, then it is a priori knowable. If Leibniz held these views, his status as a rationalist is secure.

Leibniz strove to ward off these consequences, however, by an account of analysis. He held that in a necessary proposition, the concept-containment feature allows for the proposition to be analysed or reduced to an identity proposition in a finite number of steps. Contingent truths, however, cannot be so analysed, despite the concept-containment thesis. Instead, in an infinite number of steps of analysis, such propositions would converge on an identity proposition. (Sometimes Leibniz suggests that such propositions can be analysed into identity propositions by God.) So, not all truths are necessary, and thus neither is all knowledge a priori.

There is a strong rationalist side to Leibniz, however, which emerges in the second strand of his thought, namely, his defence of innate truths. In a dispute with Locke, Leibniz contended that there are numerous innate concepts and principles in pure mathematics, logic, metaphysics and ethics. These innate truths are all necessary truths, and they are all knowable a priori. The senses, Leibniz says, merely function as the occasions by and on which these truths are brought to attention (see LEIBNIZ, G.W. §§8–9).

6 Modern philosophy: Locke and Berkeley

Locke provides a strong empiricist contrast to both Spinoza and Leibniz. For Locke, the fundamental items of all cognitions are ideas, which divide into those of sensation and those of reflection. The former are acquired in perception, the latter in introspective attention to the contents and workings of one's own mind. Perception and reflection, for Locke, make up experience, and the fundamental empiricist thesis is that all ideas and all knowledge derive from experience. It follows from empiricism so construed that no ideas are innate. For Locke, the mind is a 'blank tablet' at birth, and it is only by experience that it acquires its stock of ideas.

Locke defines knowledge as the perception of the agreement or disagreement of two ideas (1689: IV, I, 1 and 5). This definition has the immediate effect of restricting all knowledge to ideas, something Locke recognizes and appears to accept (1689: IV, II, 1). It also seems to have the effect of restricting knowledge to relations between ideas. The definition and the restriction accord well with most of what Locke says about knowledge.

Intuitive knowledge is the perception of the agreement or disagreement between two ideas 'immediately by themselves, without the intervention of any other' (Locke (1689): IV, II, 1). Perception that white is not the same as black, for example, is immediate and requires no intermediate idea between those of white and black. Intuitive knowledge, for Locke, is the most certain: it is both irresistible and infallible.

Locke seems to desert his definition of knowledge in three important cases, however, and in two of these cases intuitive knowledge is at issue. One has, for instance, intuitive knowledge of individual ideas, as when one knows that some pain is very sharp (Locke 1689: IV, II, 1). Locke also maintains that one has intuitive knowledge of oneself. In such a case, even if an idea of reflection is had, self-knowledge is not a perception of an agreement or disagreement of two ideas. Moreover, it is knowledge about the self, which is not an idea or group of ideas. In this case, Locke departs not merely from his definition, but also from his explicit claim about the extent of our knowledge.

Demonstrative knowledge, for Locke, requires that each step in the demonstration be intuitively known, and that the relation between the premises and the conclusion also be intuitively known. Meeting these constraints on demonstrative knowledge assures that it is virtually as certain as intuitive knowledge. But meeting these constraints is not easy, especially in long demonstrations where one must keep in mind inferences made earlier. In such cases, Locke indicates, one's degree of certainty with respect to the conclusion will drop and one will not have demonstrative knowledge properly speaking.

Locke's account of sensitive knowledge marks a third point at which he seems to depart from his official definition of knowledge and the restriction of knowledge to our ideas. Sensitive knowledge is knowledge of the existence of external physical objects. It is not as certain as intuitive or demonstrative knowledge, yet it is still knowledge. And Locke clearly thinks that we have such knowledge, at least in those cases when an external physical object is actually present to one's senses (1689: IV, III, 5). Locke conceives of sensitive knowledge of presently perceived physical objects as inferential knowledge. From knowledge of presently experienced ideas one infers that there is an external physical object present as the cause of those ideas. Locke is untroubled by sceptical worries over whether such inferences can be legitimately made.

The distinction between intuitive and certain knowledge of ideas, and sensitive knowledge of physical objects, with the latter knowledge inductively based on the former, is indicative of Locke's foundationalist position. It differs from that proposed by Descartes, however, in two important ways. First, the propositions making up the foundations are different. For Locke, these are confined to propositions about individually experienced ideas, or to propositions describing a perceived agreement or disagreement between ideas. Thus, Locke's commitment to empiricism dictates what the foundations shall be. Another difference comes in the inferences from the foundational propositions which Locke finds acceptable. He allows for both deductive and inductive inferences, whereas for Descartes permissible inferences may only be deductive. Locke thus marks a liberalization of the foundationalist strictures imposed by Descartes (see LOCKE, J. §§2–3).

Berkeley was critical of Locke's account of knowledge of physical objects, as was Hume (though, unlike Berkeley, Hume did not mention Locke by name). Locke notes that inductive inferences from currently experienced ideas to physical objects will succeed only when there is a conformity between the ideas and the physical object (1689: IV, IV, 3). Ideas, that is, have to represent the physical objects in some way. Berkeley denies that ideas can serve this role. An idea, he says, can only be like or similar to another idea, not a physical object. Moreover, even allowing for this similarity, the needed inductive inferences depend on and so require that one establish that some ideas do adequately represent objects. To accomplish this, Berkeley argues, one must be in a position to compare the ideas and the physical object. However, as Berkeley notes, this is a position one cannot occupy given Locke's account of perception, which restricts immediate perception to ideas, and so never allows for immediate perception of physical objects. Locke's overall theory, according to Berkeley, really leads to scepticism about physical objects.

To avoid this, Locke could drop the demand that currently experienced ideas conform to or represent objects. Berkeley suggests that this manoeuvre is no help because Locke's theory still requires inductive inferences from the ideas to the physical objects. He notes that the inferences at issue would be explanatory – the supposition that there are physical objects present causally explains the ideas one experiences – but denies their cogency (Berkeley 1710: 19–20, 53). A simpler and thus better explanation of our ideas, Berkeley argues, would be the supposition that they are caused by a single powerful being such as God.

Locke's empiricist version of foundationalism is often attributed to Berkeley. However, Berkeley seems to reject such a theory in favour of a foundationalism both more expansive and more modest. It is more expansive because Berkeley allows that we have immediate and certain knowledge of physical object propositions as well as propositions about currently experienced ideas. Hence, while Berkeley accepts an empiricist version of foundationalism, the propositions he is willing to count as foundational include many more than are countenanced on Locke's theory. Berkeley's theory is more modest in regard to the concept of certainty. For him, a proposition is certain provided that one has no actual grounds for doubting it. It is not further required that mistaken belief is logically impossible. In this way, Berkeley is able to contend that physical object propositions are certain, and he can avail himself of a much more modest criterion of what is to count as a foundational proposition. On this point, Berkeley lines up with Ockham (see §3 above), and with certain twentieth century philosophers (see §8 below).

Berkeley also aimed to refute scepticism regarding the external world. He argues that this may be achieved provided one can find a way to allow for the immediate perception of physical objects. His thought is that if we perceive physical objects immediately, then we also have immediate and certain knowledge of them. He claims that these results are all achieved by abandoning realism regarding physical objects, and embracing instead a thesis which entails that objects exist if and only if they are perceived. Thus, he defends the phenomenalist thesis that a physical object is identical to a collection of ideas (see PHENOMENALISM). Objects which are collections are immediately perceivable so long as one immediately perceives some of their constituent members. So, the phenomenalist thesis regarding objects allows Berkeley to defend the view that physical objects are immediately perceivable, and hence to argue for the claimed refutation of scepticism and a more expansive foundationalism. In these respects, Berkeley claims, he is merely defending the views of common sense (see BERKELEY, G. §§5–9).

7 Modern philosophy: from Hume to Peirce

Both Locke and Berkeley accept the theory that in every perceptual experience, one is immediately aware of at least one idea. Hume follows them in this, but he distinguishes between impressions, which are our more lively and original perceptions, and ideas, which are less lively. In seeing a red cup, one experiences a red impression (or perhaps an impression of red), while in remembering the cup one attends to an idea of the red cup. Hume's fundamental principle is that all ideas are derived from impressions, and in this regard he is a thorough-going empiricist about concepts (ideas).

He also seems to accept epistemic empiricism, at least in the sense that a proposition about an object not currently present to one's senses would count as knowledge only if that proposition were derivable from propositions about currently experienced impressions. Hume denies that physical-object propositions can be deduced from propositions about impressions. He also notes that inductive inference is not something that can be given a non-circular justification. Hence, the inductive inferences from impression propositions to physical-object propositions are not justified, and so scepticism regarding physical objects results.

Hume does note, however, that nature or our psychological make-up does not allow us actually to accept scepticism, or to refrain from making inductive inferences, especially causal ones. He may mean that the fact that we are built in such a way, psychologically, that we make inductive inferences beyond our impressions to beliefs about physical objects itself constitutes being justified in having these beliefs and making these inferences. If so, then Hume is an early externalist about justification and knowledge (see INTERNALISM AND EXTERNALISM IN EPISTEMOLOGY). Or, he may mean that we can only describe the beliefs we have and the inferences we make; questions about the justification of these inferences and whether the beliefs count as knowledge cannot be settled. In that case, Hume accepts the sceptical results noted above (see HUME, D. §2).

Two very important critics of what they regarded as Humean scepticism were Reid and Kant. Reid argued that Hume's scepticism was generated by acceptance of the theory of ideas (impressions), arguing that no philosopher had ever given any good reason for accepting this theory, and that it gives a mistaken account of perception in any case. The correct account, for Reid, is a complex version of direct realism in which we gain immediate and certain knowledge of physical objects. The beliefs we gain in direct perception of objects are typically irresistible,

and it is a first principle for Reid, a matter of common sense, that perception is reliable and so such beliefs are justified and constitute knowledge (see REID, T. §§1, 7).

Hume's scepticism did not extend to what he called 'relations of ideas'. These included the necessary truths of mathematics, and of these Hume allowed we can have a priori knowledge (1748: IV, 1). It was only with respect to some statements of matters of fact that Hume was sceptical. For Kant, relations of ideas are analytic statements, while matters of fact are synthetic (see A PRIORI; A POSTERIORI; ANALYTICITY). He felt that there was a third category, however, which Hume had missed, namely synthetic a priori propositions. These are necessary truths in which the meanings of the predicate terms are not contained in the meanings of their subject terms; hence, they are synthetic. But Kant argued that the necessary truths of geometry and arithmetic are synthetic a priori, as are some very general principles of science, and these can all be known a priori. He argues that the a priori concepts he calls categories genuinely apply to objects we experience, and that our experience actually is objective in the sense that it is of real physical objects. Kant also held that having experience of objects suffices for having knowledge of such objects, and so scepticism regarding physical objects is incorrect (see KANT, I. §§4, 6).

Hegel's *Phenomenology of Spirit* (1807) contains an extended criticism of a doctrine often thought to be common to all empiricists, namely that there is immediate knowledge of something *given* in perception (for the classical empiricists, ideas), and that this knowing is passive in the sense that it is unmediated by concepts. This criticism, of course, would apply to any variant of empiricism, including a view which holds that physical objects and not subjective ideas are perceptually given and are objects of passive, immediate knowledge. Hegel's view is that there simply is no knowledge of this sort. Rather, all knowledge is conceptually mediated. Hegel seems to have drawn the conclusion that there is nothing at all which is given, a doctrine later given great currency in the twentieth century (see HEGEL, G.W.F. §5).

Charles Peirce was another important critic of foundationalism, both empiricist and Cartesian. Against the former, Charles Peirce held that no empirical belief is certain – we can be mistaken in any empirical belief – and neither is it unrevisable – we can be reasonably motivated to give up any empirical belief in the light of new evidence. These two points make up part of Peirce's fallibilism (see FALLIBILISM). The Cartesian programme is criticized on the grounds that wholesale doubt is not a psychologically possible action, so that Descartes' method of securing foundations for knowledge does not succeed (see PEIRCE, C.S. §2).

8 Twentieth century

The empiricist tradition continued into the twentieth century in sense-datum theories of the sort found in Russell, with special attention paid to knowledge of the external physical world. It was argued that, in any perceptual experience, one is immediately aware of sense-data rather than physical objects. Sense-data are taken to be phenomenal objects having qualities such as colour and shape (see SENSE-DATA). Immediate awareness of sense-data is acquaintance, itself a form of certain knowing, namely, knowing objects rather than propositions about objects. Propositional knowledge of objects is knowledge by description, and it is inferential, based upon acquaintance knowledge of sense-data (see KNOWLEDGE BY ACQUAINTANCE AND DESCRIPTION).

The needed inferences were to be underwritten by analytical phenomenalism, that is, the thesis that all physical-object sentences are analysable into, and so equivalent in meaning to, sets of sense-datum sentences. Given this equivalence, it was felt, inferences from sense-datum sentences to physical-object sentences would be secured as legitimate; thus the problem of the external world was solved.

Related theories were defended by AYER and C.I. LEWIS. Ayer dropped the notion of acquaintance. Sense-data were taken as items of immediate awareness, which typically issued in incorrigible propositional knowledge. Lewis dispensed with sense-data; he expressed the foundational sentences using ordinary idioms such as 'This seems red', but he made the same demands on these as Ayer did of sense-datum sentences. They are certain, and the basis of all other empirical knowledge. As in Russell, inferences from these were supposed sanctioned by analytical phenomenalism.

Interestingly enough, G.E. Moore also defended a sense-datum theory of perception, but did not couple it with an empiricist version of foundationalism. Rather, he defended common sense, which for him included the view that there are many particular material-object propositions which are known immediately and with certainty. For instance, Moore claimed to know, immediately and with certainty, that a certain mantelpiece was closer to his body than a specific bookcase. For Moore, knowledge of this proposition and of many other material-object propositions need not be based on more secure knowledge of sense-data. In this regard, then, Moore's view is more a version of epistemic direct realism than it is empiricist foundationalism (see MOORE, G.E. §3).

The programme of empiricist foundationalism and analytical phenomenalism was widely criticized. The alleged incorrigibility or certain knowledge of sense-data was influentially attacked by J.L. AUSTIN. All empirical sentences, he argued, are corrigible because in forming a belief about an object, such as is expressed by 'This is red', one is classifying the object as among the red things and so is relying on one's wholly fallible memory of other comparably red items. Moreover, certainty or incorrigibility is not needed for knowledge. Many critics argued that certainty in the sense of lack of actual grounds for doubt was a more adequate analysis of this concept, and in this sense many physical-object sentences would count as certain. Analytical phenomenalism was also criticized, principally by Chisholm (see PHENOMENALISM §2). He showed that physical-object sentences do not entail sense-datum sentences, and hence are not equivalent to them.

Ayer and Lewis also were in rough agreement on the definition of the concept of knowledge. They held that propositional knowledge is justified true belief, an account shared by many others. Edmund Gettier (1963) argued that this definition was incorrect. His idea was that one could have a true justified belief which is not knowledge in a situation in which one reasons from some already justified beliefs to a new belief that, as it happens, is coincidentally true. Since it would then be a matter of coincidence that one's belief was correct, it would not count as knowledge, even though it was a justified belief because it was knowingly inferred from already justified beliefs (see GETTIER PROBLEMS).

Gettier's 1963 article generated a great deal of interest. While some argued that his argument was unsatisfactory, a majority assumed that he was more or less right, and many new analyses of knowledge were proposed, including many which incorporated the justified true belief analysis as a part. What has emerged as perhaps the most promising and least prone to new counterexamples is the defeasibility analysis. The key idea is that of defeated justification: where one is justified in believing a proposition p on the basis of evidence e, one's justification is defeated when there is a true proposition q, such that the conjunction $(e\&q)$ does not justify p. The defeasibility analysis would then be that knowledge is justified, true, undefeated belief. Sophisticated versions of the defeasibility analysis have been worked out in detail by a number of authors, including Klein (1971), Lehrer (1974) and Swain (1972) (see KNOWLEDGE, DEFEASIBILITY THEORY OF).

Closely connected to the concept of knowledge is the concept of a justified belief, and a number of important theories of epistemic justification have been developed, the principal ones being foundational theories, coherence theories and reliability theories (see JUSTIFICATION, EPISTEMIC). We have already noted Cartesian and empiricist versions of foundationalism. In recent years some philosophers have defended modest versions of foundationalism. That is, they have defended the view that a belief would be justified if and only if either it were a basic, foundational belief, or were inferrable from basic beliefs. The modesty of the theory would then derive from the fact that basic beliefs need not be certain or incorrigible; it would suffice if the basic beliefs were to be non-inferentially justified. Beliefs are non-inferentially justified when their justification need not result from being based on or inferrable from other justified beliefs.

Many philosophers have found even modest foundationalism suspect, primarily because they have found problematic the notion of a basic, non-inferentially justified belief. Some have accordingly avoided this notion altogether, and developed coherence theories of justified belief. The core idea in all such coherence theories is that a belief is justified if and only if it is a member of a system of beliefs, and this system of beliefs is coherent. A number of different accounts of coherence have been proposed, but most favoured has been that of explanatory coherence. On such a view, some beliefs (explainees) in the coherent system are justified because they are explained by other beliefs in the system; the remaining beliefs in the system are justified in virtue of their role in explaining the explainees. A problem for these theories has been to provide a reasonable way of selecting those beliefs within the system which are to be explained (see KNOWLEDGE AND JUSTIFICATION, COHERENCE THEORY OF).

The most widely discussed reliabilist theory has been the reliable-process theory. The core idea here is that a belief is justified if and only if it is caused by, or causally sustained by, a reliable process. A process is reliable when it has a high truth-ratio; that is, when that process produces more true beliefs than false ones. Typical processes selected as reliable belief-forming or belief-sustaining ones are perception, memory, introspection, and inferring or reasoning.

A problem which has proved especially vexing for supporters of the reliable-process theory is that of generality. Any specific belief is produced (sustained) by a process token which is an instance of many different process types. The generality problem is essentially that of fixing how broadly to individuate the process types in question (see RELIABILISM).

9 Recent issues

In a reliable-process theory cognizers may have no knowledge or awareness of the processes which cause or causally sustain their beliefs, or of the reliability of these processes. Most foundational and coherence theories, however, construe the notion of justification in such a way that a person's belief is justified only if they have some access to, or awareness of, whatever it is that serves to justify that belief. Theories with this access condition are generally thought of as internalist theories; those which dispense with the access requirement are externalist. Though widely discussed, no fully adequate resolution of the question of whether an access requirement should be imposed on a theory of justification has yet gained general acceptance (see INTERNALISM AND EXTERNALISM IN EPISTEMOLOGY).

Proponents of reliable-process theories have typically tried to develop a naturalistic theory (see NATURALIZED EPISTEMOLOGY). Minimally, a naturalistic epistemological theory is one in which key epistemic concepts such as knowledge and justification are analysed or explained in a form which makes use only of non-epistemic concepts. A more radical form of naturalism in epistemology, proposed by Quine, dispenses outright with the normative elements of traditional epistemology, and reconceives the subject as a part of empirical psychology (see QUINE, W.V. §2). On this view, epistemology becomes a wholly descriptive discipline, one which studies how beliefs are formed, and how they are related to what we take evidence to be. Whether a minimal or more radical form of naturalized epistemology is acceptable is an open question at present.

Issues in social epistemology have also loomed large recently, as have topics in feminist epistemology. Within the former, two important questions are whether social factors play a role in determining whether a person has knowledge or justified belief, and whether non-individuals such as groups or institutions can be said to have knowledge or justified beliefs (see SOCIAL EPISTEMOLOGY). Within feminist epistemology a leading question has been whether women acquire knowledge in ways that differ from methods of knowledge acquisition open to men. Another important issue has been whether social and cultural factors as they affect women have a bearing on what it is that women know (see FEMINIST EPISTEMOLOGY).

All these recent developments in epistemology are being vigorously pursued and explored. They have served to expand and enrich the field in ways not appreciated just a few decades ago.

See also: CHINESE PHILOSOPHY; EPISTEMOLOGY, INDIAN SCHOOLS OF; EPISTEMOLOGY IN ISLAMIC PHILOSOPHY; KNOWLEDGE, CONCEPT OF; KNOWLEDGE, INDIAN VIEWS OF

References and further reading

Adams, M. (1987) *William Ockham*, Notre Dame, IN: University of Notre Dame Press. (Authoritative work; chapters 13 and 14 are especially relevant.)

Alston, W. (1989) *Epistemic Justification*, Ithaca, NY: Cornell University Press. (Defends a modest foundationalism.)

Aquinas, T. (1266–73) *Summa Theologiae*, trans. by Fathers of the English Dominican Province, Westminster: Christian Classics, 5 vols, 1981. (Particularly relevant to the matter of abstracting intelligible species from sense impressions, mainly in Questions 84–7.)

—— (1271–2) *Commentary on Aristotle's Posterior Analytics*, trans. F. Larcher, Albany, NY: Magi Books, 1970. (Contains Aquinas' account of genuine knowledge and demonstrative syllogism.)

* Aristotle (*c.* mid 4th century BC) *Posterior Analytics*, ed. and trans. J. Barnes, Oxford: Clarendon Press, 1975. (Contains Aristotle's account of scientific knowledge.)

* —— (*c.* mid 4th century BC) *De Anima*, ed. and trans. D. Hamlyn, Oxford: Clarendon Press, 1968. (Aristotle's account of perception and perceptual knowledge is found in Books 2 and 3.)

* Augustine (386) *Contra academicos* (Against the Academicians), ed. and trans. P. King, Indianapolis, IN: Hackett Publishing Company, 1995. (Augustine's extended criticism of academic scepticism, mainly that found in Cicero.)

Ayer, A.J. (1940) *Foundations of Empirical Knowledge*, London: Macmillan. (A defence of empiricist foundationalism and of analytical phenomenalism.)

—— (1956) *The Problem of Knowledge*, Baltimore, MD: Pelican. (An account of knowledge as roughly justified true belief.)

Ayers, M. (1993) *Locke: Epistemology and Ontology*, London: Routledge. (Authoritative, scholarly treatment of Locke on all matters pertaining to his epistemology.)

* Bayle, P. (1695–7) *Historical and Critical Dictionary, Selections*, trans. R. Popkin, Indianapolis, IN: Hackett Publishing Company, 1991. (Some of the *Dictionary* material strongly influenced Berkeley and Hume.)

* Berkeley, G. (1710) *A Treatise Concerning the Principles of Human Knowledge*, ed. K. Winkler, Indianapolis, IN: Hackett Publishing Company, 1982. (One of Berkeley's main writings on epistemological topics.)

—— (1713) *Three Dialogues Between Hylas and Philonous*, ed. R.M. Adams, Indianapolis, IN: Hackett Publishing Company, 1979. (Important for Berkeley's discussion of scepticism.)

BonJour, L. (1985) *The Structure of Empirical Knowledge*, Cambridge, MA: Harvard University Press. (Both an influential criticism of foundationalism and a defence of explanatory coherence.)

Broad, C.D. (1975) *Leibniz – an Introduction*, Cambridge: Cambridge University Press. (A fine introduction to Leibniz by a master expositor, but it is somewhat advanced.)

Burnyeat, M. (1980) 'Can the sceptic live his scepticism?', in M. Schofield, M. Burnyeat and J. Barnes (eds) *Doubt and Dogmatism*, Oxford: Clarendon Press. (Deals with the question of whether those Hellenistics professing scepticism can actually withhold belief in the relevant ways.)

Chisholm, R. (1948) 'The Problem of Empiricism', *Journal of Philosophy* 45 (19): 512–17. (A trenchant criticism of analytical phenomenalism.)

—— (1957) *Perceiving*, Ithaca, NY: Cornell University Press. (Contains an anti-sense-datum account of perception.)

—— (1966) *Theory of Knowledge*, Englewood Cliffs, NJ: Prentice Hall, 2nd edn, 1977. (General discussion which includes a defence of foundationalism.)

Code, L. (1991) *What Can She Know? Feminist Theory and the Construction of Knowledge*, Ithaca, NY: Cornell University Press. (Defence of feminist epistemology as a reorientation of the field of epistemology, by a leading researcher in the area.)

Cornman, J. (1980) *Skepticism, Justification, and Explanation*, Dordrecht: Reidel. (Careful discussion of scepticism and many varieties of theories of justification.)

* Descartes, R. (1641) *Meditations on First Philosophy*, in J. Cottingham, R. Stoothoff, D. Murdoch and A. Kenny (eds) *The Philosophical Writings of Descartes*, Cambridge: Cambridge University Press, 3 vols, 1984–91. (Now the standard English edition of the main philosophical works.)

Everson, S. (1990) 'Epicurus on the Truth of the Senses', in S. Everson (ed.) *Epistemology*, Cambridge: Cambridge University Press. (Especially helpful on Epicurus' relations to sceptical doctrines.)

Feldman, R. (1985) 'Reliability and justification', *The Monist* 68 (2): 159–74. (Penetrating statement of the generality problem for reliabilism.)

Fine, G. (1978) 'Knowledge and Belief in Republic V', *Archiv fur Geschichte der Philosophie* 58: 121–39.

(Deals with knowledge of Forms and the contrasts between knowledge and belief in Plato's *Republic*.)

Fogelin, R. (1985) *Hume's Scepticism in the Treatise of Human Nature*, London: Routledge. (Interprets Hume as an epistemological sceptic.)

Frede, M. (1983) 'Stoics and sceptics on clear and distinct ideas', in M. Burnyeat (ed.) *The Sceptical Tradition*, Berkeley, CA: University of California Press. (A very sympathetic examination of Stoic doctrines; particularly helpful in understanding the role of cognitive impressions.)

Fumerton, R. (1988) 'The internalism/externalism controversy', *Philosophical Perspectives* 2: 442–59. (Good discussion of the matters at issue in this dispute.)

* Gettier, E. (1963) 'Is justified true belief knowledge?', *Analysis* 23 (6): 121–3. (This brief paper stimulated more than two decades of work on the analysis of factual knowledge.)

Goldman, A. (1979) 'What is justified belief?', in G. Pappas (ed.) *Justification and Knowledge*, Dordrecht: Reidel. (Exceptionally lucid early statement of a reliable-process theory of justification.)

—— (1986) *Epistemology and Cognition*, Cambridge, MA: Harvard University Press. (Updated version of reliabilism, along with some attempt to solve the generality problem and a detailed look at the relevance of psychological theories and findings to epistemology.)

* Hegel, G.W.F. (1807) *The Phenomenology of Spirit*, trans. A.V. Miller, Oxford: Clarendon Press, 1977. (The introduction contains trenchant criticism of empiricism and Cartesian epistemology.)

Hookway, C.J. (1985) *Peirce*, London: Routledge & Kegan Paul. (Good account of Peirce's views of science and scientific method.)

* Hume, D. (1740) *A Treatise of Human Nature*, ed. P. Nidditch, Oxford: Clarendon Press, 2nd edn, 1978. (Hume's views on knowledge and scepticism are found in Book 1.)

* —— (1748) *Enquiry Concerning Human Understanding and Enquiry Concerning the Principles of Morals*, ed. L.A. Selby-Bigge, revised P. Nidditch, Oxford: Clarendon Press, 1975. (Hume here expresses his views in a more accessible manner than in the *Treatise*.)

Irwin, T. (1988) *Aristotle's First Principles*, Oxford: Clarendon. (A fine, detailed treatment of Aristotle's epistemological doctrines.)

Kant, I. (1781/1787) *Critique of Pure Reason*, trans. N. Kemp Smith, London: Macmillan, 1964. (This difficult work contains Kant's answer to both empiricists and rationalists. Most relevant is the 'Transcendental Analytic'.)

Kim, J. (1988) 'What is naturalized epistemology?', *Philosophical Perspectives* 2: 381–405. (Helpful discussion of Quine's view, and a defence of the idea that traditional epistemology should not be, and perhaps cannot be, given up.)

* Klein, P. (1971) 'A proposed definition of propositional knowledge', *Journal of Philosophy* 68 (16): 471–82. (An early defence of the defeasibility theory.)

* Lehrer, K. (1974) *Knowledge*, New York: Oxford University Press. (Contains a powerful criticism of explanatory coherence theories, and a defence of a subjective coherence theory.)

—— (1989) *Thomas Reid*, London: Routledge. (A comprehensive discussion of Reid's philosophy. It includes an excellent account of Reid's criticisms of Hume, and of Reid's defence of common sense.)

—— (1990) *Theory of Knowledge*, Boulder, CO: Westview Press. (Contains Lehrer's latest defence of defeasibility and much besides.)

Leibniz, G. (1765) *New Essays on Human Understanding*, trans. P. Remnant and J. Bennett, Cambridge: Cambridge University Press, 1981. (Comments on and responds to Locke; notable for Leibniz' discussion of innate truths.)

—— (1969) *Philosophical Papers and Letters*, ed. and trans. L.E. Loemker, Dordrecht: Reidel. (Contains most of Leibniz' important philosophical writings.)

Lewis, C.I. (1946) *Analysis of Knowledge and Valuation*, LaSalle, IL: Open Court Publishing. (Defence of a complex form of analytical phenomenalism, and of empiricist foundationalism without sense-data.)

* Locke, J. (1689) *An Essay Concerning Human Understanding*, ed. P. Nidditch, Oxford: Clarendon Press, 1975. (The best modern edition of Locke's classic. Most important are Books I, II, and IV.)

Long, A. and Sedley, D.N. (eds) (1987) *The Hellenistic Philosophers*, Cambridge: Cambridge University Press. (Contains relevant Epicurean and Stoic texts.)

MacDonald, S. (1992) 'Aquinas's Epistemology', in N. Kretzmann and E. Stump (eds) *Aquinas*, Cambridge: Cambridge University Press. (Comprehensive discussion of Aquinas' scattered epistemological remarks.)

* Montaigne, M. de (1576) *Apology for Raimond Sebond*, trans. D. Frame in *The Complete Works of Montaigne*, Stanford: Stanford University Press, 1958. (Very influential early modern text.)

Moore, G.E. (1953) *Some Main Problems of Philosophy*, London: Allen & Unwin. (Contains Moore's account of the common sense view of the world.)

—— (1959) *Philosophical Papers*, London: Allen &

Unwin. (This collection contains Moore's famous paper 'A Defence of Common Sense'.)

Moser, P. (1989) *Knowledge and Evidence*, New York: Cambridge University Press. (A defence of foundationalism.)

Pappas, G. (1991) 'Berkeley and Common Sense Realism', *History of Philosophy Quarterly* 8 (1): 27–42. (Discusses Berkeley's commitment to epistemic direct realism.)

Pappas, G. and Swain, M. (1978) *Essays on Knowledge and Justification*, Ithaca, NY: Cornell University Press. (Contains many papers on the analysis of knowledge and on foundational and coherentist theories of justified belief.)

Parkinson, G.H.R. (1954) *Spinoza's Theory of Knowledge*, Oxford: Clarendon Press. (Comprehensive treatment of Spinoza's doctrines about knowledge.)

Peirce, C. (1931–58) *Collected Papers of Charles S. Peirce*, ed. P. Weiss, C. Hartshorne and A. Burks, Cambridge, MA: Harvard University Press, 8 vols. (Volume 5 contains papers most relevant to epistemological issues.)

Pitcher, G. (1977) *Berkeley*, London: Routledge & Kegan Paul. (Penetrating analysis of Berkeley's thought, a modern classic which interprets Berkeley as an empiricist foundationalist.)

* Plato (427–347 BC) *The Collected Dialogues of Plato*, ed. E. Hamilton and H. Cairns, Princeton, NJ: Princeton University Press, 1961. (Contains all of Plato's dialogues in English translation. See especially the *Meno*, *Theaetetus*, *Cratylus* and *Republic*, discussed in §1 above.)

Popkin, R. (1979) *The History of Scepticism from Erasmus to Spinoza*, Berkeley, CA: University of California Press. (A great source of information, both historical and philosophical.)

Quine, W.V. (1969) 'Epistemology naturalized', in *Ontological Relativity and Other Essays*, New York: Columbia University Press. (Defends abandonment of traditional epistemology and the view that epistemology should be taken as a branch of empirical psychology.)

Reid, T. (1785) *Essays on the Intellectual Powers*, ed. B. Brody, Cambridge, MA: MIT Press, 1969. (Reid's systematic treatment of epistemological themes.)

Russell, B. (1912) *Problems of Philosophy*, London: Williams & Norgate. (Discusses and defends the sense-datum theory and empiricist foundationalism; also contains Russell's famous distinction between knowledge by acquaintance and knowledge by description.)

—— (1914) *Knowledge of the External World*, London: Allen & Unwin. (As with his 1912 work, this also discusses and defends the sense-datum theory and empiricist foundationalism; analytical phenomenalism is defended under the term 'logical constructions'.)

—— (1918) *Mysticism and Logic*, New York: Longmans. (Discusses and defends the sense-datum theory and empiricist foundationalism – see especially Essays 7, 8 and 10.)

Schmitt, F. (1994) *Socializing Epistemology*, Lanham, MD: Rowman & Littlefield. (Contains many important recent papers on social epistemology, with notable attempts to map out the field in Schmitt's introduction and in papers by Kornblith, Kitcher and Schmitt.)

Sellars, W. (1963) 'Empiricism and the philosophy of mind', in *Science, Perception and Reality*, New York: Humanities. (A most influential criticism of foundationalism.)

Sextus Empiricus (c. AD 200) *Outlines of Pyrrhonism* and *Against the Mathematicians*, ed. R. Bury, London: Heinemann, 4 vols, 1933–49. (Complete offering of Sextus' writings.)

Shope, R. (1983) *The Analysis of Knowing*, Princeton, NJ: Princeton University Press. (A most useful in-depth survey of a wealth of material on the concept of knowledge.)

* Spinoza, B. (1677) *Ethics* and *Treatise on the Improvement of the Intellect*, in *The Collected Works of Spinoza*, ed. E. Curley, Princeton, NJ: Princeton University Press, 2 vols, 1985. (The primary texts.)

Stroud, B. (1977) *Hume*, London: Routledge & Kegan Paul. (Fine discussion of all Hume's main ideas and arguments.)

* Swain, M. (1974) 'Epistemic defeasibility', *American Philosophical Quarterly* 11: 15–25. (The Klein and Swain papers deal with defeasibility and knowledge in roughly the same way; both are very polished complex discussions of the issues.)

* Taylor, C.C.W. (1990) 'Aristotle's Epistemology', in S. Everson (ed.) *Epistemology*, Cambridge: Cambridge University Press. (Very clear discussion, easily accessible to the non-specialist.)

William of Ockham (c.1287–1347) *Ockham: Philosophical Writings*, ed. P. Boehner, Indianapolis, IN: Bobbs-Merrill, 1964. (Good translations of major writings in philosophy.)

—— (1322–7) *Quodlibeta Septem*, in R. McKeon (ed.) *Selections from Medieval Philosophers*, New York: Charles Scribner's Sons, 1930. (The seven 'quodlibeta' are directly concerned with intuitive cognition.)

* Williams, B. (1978) *Descartes: The Project of Pure Enquiry*, Harmondsworth: Penguin. (Outstanding and detailed treatment of all of the main ideas in

Descartes' epistemology; this book is very helpful in understanding Descartes' relation to sceptical arguments.)

GEORGE S. PAPPAS

EPISTEMOLOGY IN ISLAMIC PHILOSOPHY

Muslim philosophers agree that knowledge is possible. Knowledge is the intellect's grasp of the immaterial forms, the pure essences or universals that constitute the natures of things, and human happiness is achieved only through the intellect's grasp of such universals. They stress that for knowledge of the immaterial forms, the human intellect generally relies on the senses. Some philosophers, such as Ibn Rushd and occasionally Ibn Sina, assert that it is the material forms themselves, which the senses provide, that are grasped by the intellect after being stripped of their materiality with the help of the divine world. However, the general view as expressed by al-Farabi and Ibn Sina seems to be that the material forms only prepare the way for the reception of the immaterial forms, which are then provided by the divine world. They also state that on rare occasions the divine world simply bestows the immaterial forms on the human intellect without any help from the senses. This occurrence is known as prophecy. While all Muslim philosophers agree that grasping eternal entities ensures happiness, they differ as to whether such grasping is also necessary for eternal existence.

1   **Nature of knowledge**
2   **Sources of knowledge**
3   **Logic and knowledge**
4   **The role of the mind**
5   **Philosophical and prophetic knowledge**

1   Nature of knowledge

Muslim philosophers are primarily concerned with human happiness and its attainment. Regardless of what they consider this happiness to be, all agree that the only way to attain it is through knowledge. The theory of knowledge, epistemology, has therefore been their main preoccupation and appears chiefly in their logical and psychological writings. Epistemology concerns itself primarily with the possibility, nature and sources of knowledge. Taking the possibility of knowledge for granted, Muslim philosophers focused their epistemological effort on the study of the nature and sources of knowledge. Their intellectual inquiries,

beginning with logic and ending with metaphysics and in some cases mysticism, were in the main directed towards helping to understand what knowledge is and how it comes about.

Following in the footsteps of the Greek philosophers, Muslim philosophers consider knowledge to be the grasping of the immaterial forms, natures, essences or realities of things. They are agreed that the forms of things are either material (that is, existing in matter) or immaterial (existing in themselves). While the latter can be known as such, the former cannot be known unless first detached from their materiality. Once in the mind, the pure forms act as the pillars of knowledge. The mind constructs objects from these forms, and with these objects it makes judgments. Thus Muslim philosophers, like ARISTOTLE before them, divided knowledge in the human mind into conception (*tasawwur*), apprehension of an object with no judgment, and assent (*tasdiq*), apprehension of an object with a judgment, the latter being, according to them, a mental relation of correspondence between the concept and the object for which it stands. Conceptions are the main pillars of assent; without conception, one cannot have a judgment. In itself, conception is not subject to truth and falsity, but assent is. However, it should be pointed out that *tasdiq* is a misleading term in Islamic philosophy. It is generally used in the sense of 'accepting truth or falsity', but also occasionally in the sense of 'accepting truth'. One must keep in mind, however, that when assent is said to be a form of knowledge, the word is then used, not in the broad sense to mean true or false judgment, but in the narrow sense to mean true judgment.

In Islamic philosophy, conceptions are in the main divided into the known and the unknown. The former are grasped by the mind actually, the latter potentially. Known conceptions are either self-evident (that is, objects known to normal human minds with immediacy such as 'being', 'thing' and 'necessary') or acquired (that is, objects known through mediation, such as 'triangle'). With the exception of the self-evident conceptions, conceptions are known or unknown relative to individual minds. Similarly, Muslim philosophers divided assent into the known and the unknown, and the known assent into the self-evident and the acquired. The self-evident assent is exemplified by 'the whole is greater than the part', and the acquired by 'the world is composite'. In *Kitab at-tanbih 'ala sabil as-sa'ada* (The Book of Remarks Concerning the Path of Happiness), AL-FARABI calls the self-evident objects: 'the customary, primary, well-known knowledge, which one may deny with one's tongue, but which one cannot deny with one's mind since it is impossible to think their contrary'. Of the objects of conception and assent, only the unknown ones are subject to inquiry. By reducing the number of unknown objects one can increase knowledge and provide the chance for happiness. But how does such reduction come about?

2 Sources of knowledge

In Islamic philosophy there are two theories about the manner in which the number of unknown objects is reduced. One theory stresses that this reduction is brought about by moving from known objects to unknown ones, the other that it is merely the result of direct illumination given by the divine world. The former is the upward or philosophical way, the second the downward or prophetic one. According to the former theory, movement from the known objects of conception to the unknown ones can be effected chiefly through the explanatory phrase (*al-qawl ash-sharih*). The proof (*al-burhan*) is the method for moving from the known objects of assent to the unknown ones. The explanatory phrase and proof can be either valid or invalid: the former leads to certitude, the latter to falsehood. The validity and invalidity of the explanatory phrase and proof can be determined by logic, which is a set of rules for such determination. IBN SINA points out that logic is a necessary key to knowledge and cannot be replaced except by God's guidance, as opposed to other types of rules such as grammar for discourse (which can be replaced by a good natural mind) and metre for poetry (which can be replaced by good taste).

By distinguishing the valid from the invalid explanatory phrase and proof, logic serves a higher purpose, namely that of disclosing the natures or essences of things. It does this because conceptions reflect the realities or natures of things and are the cornerstones of the explanatory phrase and proof. Because logic deals only with expressions that correspond to conceptions, when it distinguishes the valid from the invalid it distinguishes at the same time the realities or natures of things from their opposites. Thus logic is described as the key to the knowledge of the natures of things. This knowledge is described as the key to happiness; hence the special status of logic in Islamic philosophy.

3 Logic and knowledge

We are told that because logic deals only with the known and unknown, it cannot deal with anything outside the mind. Because it is a linguistic instrument (foreign in nature to the realities of things), it cannot deal with such realities directly, whether they exist in the mind or outside it, or are external to these two

realms of existence. It can only deal with the states or accidents of such realities, these states comprising links among the realities and intermediaries between the realities and language. Logic therefore deals with the states of such realities, as they exist in the mind. Such states are exemplified by 'subject' or 'predicate', 'universality' or 'particularity', 'essentiality' or 'accidentality'. In other words, logic can deal with realities only in that these realities are subjects or predicates, universal or particular, essential or accidental and so on.

Because the ultimate human objective is the understanding of the realities, essences or natures of things, and because the ultimate logical objective is the understanding of conceptions, logicians must focus on the understanding of those conceptions that lead to the understanding of the essences if they intend to serve humanity. Ibn Sina points out that since the essences are universal, such expressions are also universal in the sense of representing universal conceptions such as 'human being', not in the sense of being universal only in expression, such as 'Zayd'. A universal expression can be applied to more than one thing, as the last two examples show, but one must keep in mind Ibn Sina's distinction between these two types of universal expressions: the former represents reality, although indirectly, the latter does not. It is only the former with which the logician should be concerned (see LOGIC IN ISLAMIC PHILOSOPHY).

Considering that the discussion of universals occupies a central place in Arabic logic, it is important to focus briefly on this subject to ensure understanding of the proper objects of the knowledge of the natures of things. Muslim philosophers divide universal expressions into five types, known together as the five predicables: genus, species, difference, property and common accident. Genus refers to the common nature of all the species that fall under it, such as 'animality' for 'human being', 'dog', 'cat' and so on. As such, it tells us what the general nature of a thing is. Species refers to the common nature of all the individuals that fall under it, such as 'human being' for 'John', 'George' and 'Dorothy'. As such, it tells us what the specific nature of a thing is. Difference refers to that which differentiates the members of the genus, such as 'rational', which differentiates the species of being human from other animal species; it tells us which thing a being is. These three universals are essential to a thing; that is, without them the essence will not be what it is. Property and common accident are accidental, in that they attach to the thing but are not part of its essence. Property refers to something that necessarily attaches to one universal only, such as 'capacity for laughter' for 'human being'. Common accident refers to a quality that attaches to more than one universal, either in an inseparable manner, such as 'black' for 'crow', or in a separable manner, such as 'black' for 'human being'. The inseparability of the common accident, however, is only in existence.

Only the first three of the above universals constitute the essences of things. If one is to understand the essence of a thing, one must first understand its genus, species and difference or differences. The understanding of these three universals takes place through the explanatory phrase and proof, of which these universals are simple elements. The explanatory phrase is either definition or description. The definition is a phrase which mirrors the essence of a thing by indicating its general and specific essential qualities, that is, its genus, species and difference; the description is like the definition except that it indicates the property instead of the difference. Thus the description does not give a complete picture of the essence of a thing as does the definition. The proof is a set of propositions, which consist of conceptions joined or separated by particles. The proof that helps in the understanding of the essences of things is that which moves from known universal judgments to an unknown universal one.

The important question that concerned Muslim philosophers is how the universals or forms that are essential to the natures of things arrive at the human mind before it has the chance to employ the explanatory phrase and proof to compose known conceptions and known judgments from them. In order to answer this question, Muslim philosophers first discussed the structure of the human soul and then the steps through which the universals pass on their way to the place of knowledge (see SOUL IN ISLAMIC PHILOSOPHY). As stated above, conceptions come to the mind through either the philosophical way or the prophetic way. The philosophical way requires one first to use one's external senses to grasp the universals as they exist in the external world, mixed with matter. Then the internal senses, which like the external senses are a part of the animal soul, take in these universals and purify them of matter as much as possible. The imagination is the highest internal sense, in which these universals settle until the next cognitive move. It is from this point to the next step in the philosophical journey that the details seem particularly unclear.

4 The role of the mind

All Muslim philosophers believe that above the senses there is the rational soul. This has two parts: the practical and theoretical intellects. The theoretical intellect is responsible for knowledge; the practical intellect concerns itself only with the proper management of the body through apprehension of particular things so that it can do the good and avoid the bad. All the major Muslim philosophers, beginning with AL-KINDI, wrote treatises on the nature and function of the theoretical intellect, which may be referred to as the house of knowledge.

In addition to the senses and the theoretical intellect, Muslim philosophers include in their discussion of the instruments of knowledge a third factor. They teach that the divine world contains, among other things, intelligences, the lowest of which is what al-Kindi calls the First Intellect (al-'aql al-awwal), better known in Arabic philosophy as the 'agent intellect' (al-'aql al-fa''al), the name given to it by AL-FARABI (§3), or 'the giver of forms' (wahib as-suwar). They contend that the world around us is necessary for the attainment of philosophical knowledge. Some, such as IBN BAJJA, IBN RUSHD and occasionally IBN SINA, say that the mixed universals in the imagination that have been derived from the outside world through the senses are eventually purified completely by the light of the agent intellect, and are then reflected onto the theoretical intellect.

Al-Farabi's and Ibn Sina's general view, however, is that these imagined universals only prepare the theoretical intellect for the reception of the universals from the agent intellect that already contains them. When expressing this view, Ibn Sina states that it is not the universals in the imagination themselves that are transmitted to the theoretical intellect but their shadow, which is created when the light of the agent intellect is shed on these universals. This is similar, he says, to the shadow of an object which is reflected on the eye when sunlight is cast on that object. While the manner in which the universals in the imagination can prepare the theoretical intellect for knowledge is in general unclear, it is vaguely remarked by al-Farabi and Ibn Sina that this preparation is due to the similarity of these universals to the pure universals, and to the familiarity of the theoretical intellect with the imagined universals owing to its proximity to the imagination. In other words, the familiarity of this intellect with what resembles its proper objects prepares it for the reception of these objects from the agent intellect.

5 Philosophical and prophetic knowledge

The prophetic way is a much easier and simpler path (see PROPHECY). One need not take any action to receive the divinely given universals; the only requirement seems to be the possession of a strong soul capable of receiving them. While the philosophical way moves from the imagination upward to the theoretical intellect, the prophetic way takes the reverse path, from the theoretical intellect to the imagination. For this reason, knowledge of philosophy is knowledge of the natures of things themselves, while knowledge of prophecy is knowledge of the natures of things as wrapped up in symbols, the shadows of the imagination.

Philosophical and prophetic truth is the same, but it is attained and expressed differently. Ibn Tufayl's *Hayy Ibn Yaqzan* is the best illustration of the harmony of philosophy and religion (see IBN TU-FAYL). The so-called double truth theory wrongly views these two paths to knowledge as two types of truth, thus attributing to Ibn Rushd a view foreign to Islamic philosophy. One of the most important contributions of Islamic philosophy is the attempt to reconcile Greek philosophy and Islam by accepting the philosophical and prophetic paths as leading to the same truth.

Muslim philosophers agree that knowledge in the theoretical intellect passes through stages. It moves from potentiality to actuality and from actuality to reflection on actuality, thus giving the theoretical intellect the respective names of potential intellect, actual intellect and acquired intellect. Some Muslim philosophers explain that the last is called 'acquired' because its knowledge comes to it from the outside, and so it can be said to acquire it. The acquired intellect is the highest human achievement, a holy state that conjoins the human and the divine realms by conjoining the theoretical and agent intellects.

Following in the footsteps of ALEXANDER OF APHRODISIAS, al-Farabi, Ibn Bajja and Ibn Rushd believe that the theoretical intellect is potential by nature, and therefore disintegrates unless it grasps the eternal objects, the essential universals, for the known and the knower are one. Ibn Sina rejects the view that the theoretical intellect is potential by nature. He argues instead that it is eternal by nature because unless it is, it cannot grasp the eternal objects. For him, happiness is achieved by this intellect's grasping of the eternal objects, for such grasping perfects the soul. Muslim philosophers who believe that eternity is attained only through knowledge also agree with Ibn Sina that knowledge is perfection and perfection is happiness.

See also: EPISTEMOLOGY; ETHICS IN ISLAMIC PHILOSOPHY; AL-FARABI (§3); IBN BAJJA (§3); IBN RUSHD (§6); IBN SINA (§3); AL-KINDI; LOGIC IN ISLAMIC PHILOSOPHY; MEANING IN ISLAMIC PHILOSOPHY

References and further reading

Davidson, H.A. (1992) *Al-Farabi, Avicenna and Averroes on Intellect*, London: Oxford University Press. (Discusses the link between Greek and Arabic understanding of intellect and the various transformations the concept of intellect underwent in Islamic philosophy.)

Fakhry, M. (ed.) (1992) *Rasa'il Ibn Bajja al-ilahiyya* (Ibn Bajja's Metaphysical Essays), Beirut: Dar al-Jil. (Includes the most important of Ibn Bajja's philosophical treatises, *Tadbir al-mutawahhid* (Management of the Solitary), *Risalat al-ittisal al-'aql al-fa''al bil-insan* (Essay on the Conjunction of the Intellect with Human Beings) and *Risalat al-wada'* (Essay on Bidding Farewell).)

al-Farabi (c.870–950) *Risala fi al-'aql* (Essay on the Intellect), ed. M. Bouyges, Beirut: al-Maktab al-Katulikiyya, 1939. (One of the best known and most influential treatises on intellect in Islamic philosophy; it gives the different senses of 'intellect' known to al-Farabi.)

* —— (c.870–950) *Kitab at-tanbih 'ala sabil as-sa'ada* (The Book of Remarks Concerning the Path of Happiness), ed. J. Al-Yasin, Beirut: Dar al-Manahil, 1985. (Includes al-Farabi's definition of the self-evident objects.)

Ibn Rushd (1126–98) *Talkhis kitab an-nafs* (Epitome of Aristotle's *On the Soul*), ed. A.F. al-Ahwani, Cairo: Maktabat an-Nahda, 1950. (This edition also includes three other essays: Ibn Bajja's *Risalat al-ittisal* (Essay on Conjunction), Ishaq ibn Hunayn's *Kitab fi an-nafs* (Book on the Soul) and al-Kindi's *Risalat al-'aql* (Essay on Intellect).)

Ibn Sina (980–1037) *al-Shifa'* (Healing), ed. F. Rahman, London: Oxford University Press, 1959. (Standard account by Ibn Sina of his views on the soul, including the essays *at-Tabi'iyyat* (Physics) and *an-Nafs* (Psychology).)

—— (980–1037) *al-Isharat wa'l-tanbihat* (Remarks and Admonitions), part translated by S.C. Inati, *Remarks and Admonitions: Part One, Logic*, Toronto: Pontifical Institute for Mediaeval Studies, 1984. (The most comprehensive of Ibn Sina's logic and best representation of Arabic logic.)

* Ibn Tufayl (before 1185) *Hayy Ibn Yaqzan* (The Living Son of the Vigilant), ed. L. Gauthier, Beirut: Catholic Press, 1936; trans. L. Goodman, *Ibn Tufayl's Hayy Ibn Yaqzan, A Philosophical Tale*, New York: Twayne Publishers, 1972. (Expresses the harmony between reason and revelation in a literary form).

Nuseibeh, S. (1996) 'Epistemology', in S.H. Nasr and O. Leaman (eds) *History of Islamic Philosophy*, London: Routledge, ch. 49, 824–40. (Analysis of the main concepts of epistemology, along with discussion of how some of the main thinkers take up different positions.)

Rida, A. (ed.) (1950) *Rasa'il al-Kindi al-falsafiyya* (al-Kindi's Philosophical Essays), Cairo: Dar al-Fikr al-'Arabi. (These two volumes include four essays relevant to al-Kindi's theory of knowledge: *Risalat al-Kindi fi al-qawl fi an-nafs* (Al-Kindi's Essay on the Discourse Concerning the Soul), *Kalam lil-Kindi fi an-nafs* (Words for al-Kindi Concerning the Soul), *Risalat al-Kindi fi mahiyyat an-nawm warru'ya* (Al-Kindi's Essay on Sleep and Vision) and *Risalat al-Kindi fi al-'aql* (Al-Kindi's Essay on the Intellect). The last of these is the best known and seems to have been the first in a long and influential series of Arabic works on the intellect.)

Rosenthal, F. (1970) *Knowledge Triumphant: The Concept of Knowledge in Medieval Islam*, Leiden: Brill. (By far the best work on epistemology in Islamic thought, authoritative and always interesting.)

SHAMS C. INATI

EPISTEMOLOGY, INDIAN SCHOOLS OF

Each classical Indian philosophical school classifies and defines itself with reference to a foundational text or figure, through elaboration of inherited positions, and by disputing the views of other schools. Moreover, the schools have literatures that define them in a most concrete sense, literatures that in some cases stretch across twenty centuries and comprise hundreds of texts. And without exception, every school takes a stance on the nature of knowledge and justification, if only, as with the Mādhyamika Buddhist, to attack the positions of others. A blend of epistemology, ontology or metaphysics, and, sometimes, religious or ethical teachings constitutes the view of most schools, and sometimes only very subtle shifts concerning a single issue differentiate one school's stance from another's.

Relabelling schools of Indian epistemology using terminology forged in Western traditions ('foundationalism', 'coherentism', and so on) risks skewing the priorities of classical disputants and distorting classical debates. Nevertheless, there are positions shared across some of the schools, as well as refinements of position that apparently because of merit received greater attention in classical discussions and appear to deserve it still. Given the broad context of world philosophy, selectivity cannot be free from bias stemming from a sense of reverberation with non-Indian traditions of

thought. With these warnings in mind, we may proceed to examine three important approaches within classical Indian philosophy to questions of epistemology.

First, the late Yogācāra Buddhist philosophers, Dignāga (b. circa 480), Dharmakīrti (c.600–660) and followers, present a complex first-person approach to questions about knowledge that is constrained by an anti-metaphysical theme (found in earlier Buddhist treatises), along with a phenomenalism that grows out of a vivid sense of the real possibility of nirvāna experience as the supreme good. Their thought also exhibits an academic strand that is sensitive to non-Buddhist philosophical discussions. Second, a realism identifying sources of veridical awareness is the most distinctive, and most central, approach to epistemology within classical Indian philosophy as a whole. Even the Yogācāra first-person approach gets framed in terms of reliable sources (perception and inference as pramānas, 'sources of knowledge'). Philosophers of diverse allegiance make contributions to what may be called this field of thought (as opposed to an approach), since, to repeat, it is the philosophical mainstream. However, the Nyāya school (the 'Logic' school) leads in most periods. Finally, the Brahmanical school known as Mīmāṃsā ('Exegesis'), supplemented in particular by centuries of reflection under an Advaita Vedānta flag, develops what can be called an ethics of belief, namely, that we should accept what we see (for example) as real (and the propositional content of perceptual awarenesses as true), what we are told by another as true, what we infer as true, and so on, except under specific circumstances that prove a proposition false or at least draw it into question. The (Nyāya) epistemological mainstream is moved to incorporate a variation on this position; for Mīmāṃsā and Advaita, 'self-certification' (svataḥprāmāṇya), or the intrinsic veridicality of cognition, defines an alternative approach to questions about knowledge, awareness and a presumed obligation to believe.

1 **Buddhist pragmatism and coherentism**
2 **Nyāya reliabilism**
3 **Mīmāṃsā self-certificationalism**

1 Buddhist pragmatism and coherentism

The most important context for the epistemology of the late Yogācārins (c.450 on), sometimes called the Buddhist logicians, may well be non-Buddhist developments, or views about the criteria of successful debate mutually developed in both Buddhist and non-Buddhist circles. But Buddhist soteriology ('mystical enlightenment theory'), including an anti-metaphysical attitude, appears to determine much that is distinctive in Dignāga's school's approach to epistemology. The *summum bonum* is conceived within Buddhism as an immediate experience, a state of awareness attained through concentrated meditation (*samādhi*) that is free from such disturbances as the inner voice of thought and feelings of desire. Possibly through a confusion of thought as an occurrent psychological phenomenon with conceptualization in general, Buddhist teachings of meditative practice embrace, or come to embrace, a broad anti-intellectualism, especially concerning speculative efforts of philosophy. With thought devalued, sceptical arguments found a receptive audience among Buddhist practitioners. Immediate experience, in contrast, is highly regarded. Indeed, *nirvāṇa* is immediate experience purged of distractions, in particular thought and desire. The very designation 'Yogācāra' indicates those devoted to meditation and other yogic practices. The school's focus on phenomenal presentations thus need not be taken to stem from a radically empiricist approach to questions of evidence, as in Western phenomenalism. It appears to have moorings in meditative mysticism instead.

Now sense perception in its raw immediacy and stripped (if this is possible) of all relatings to previous experiences, seems to present unique particulars; at least, this contention is made by DIGNĀGA and other Yogācārins. The world of thought and desire is not the world of immediate experience, especially not the world of immediate experience purged of psychological defilements. The world of immediate experience is a world of ineffably interdependent and strictly unconceptualizable particulars, and perception accessible to thought and discussion is already infected with concepts, with desire-based, imaginational relatings (*kalpanās*) to other experiences. Thus the best we can do concerning generalities and concept formation (all concepts are general) and questions of warrant about the claims that purport to classify what are really unclassifiable particulars is to take a pragmatic attitude underpinned by a broad scepticism about what things are in reality. To best capture the exclusion (*apoha*) of generalities from particulars, Bessie's being a cow, for example, should be expressed as her not being a non-cow. We cognize things in accordance with what we want to do with them, and the success of actions based on our cognitions proves whether those cognitions are adequate (pragmatically true) or not.

Of course, success in action is itself made known to us through our own cognitions. The final touchstone of a cognition's veridicality is its agreement with other cognitions, or, in some formulations, lack of failure to agree. Incoherence is a cognitive dissonance that means that we hold something in error. We may well be in error about almost everything, but we do not notice it until there is a (jarring) cognitive failure of

agreement. Now satisfaction of desire is also mediated by sense experience, and so some scholars have seen an implicit foundationalism (knowledge as founded in sense experiences). But DHARMAKĪRTI at least is a coherentist in the sense that no empirical proposition is sacrosanct; any proposition can be defeated and overridden by considerations of overall coherence. Neither he, nor any Yogācārin, is a pure coherentist, however; it seems a judgment would, by virtue of being perceptual, be accorded warrant of at least a minimal sort.

The Yogācāra approach to logic appears to be broadly conventionalist, although sometimes logical principles are discussed as though they were discoveries. In the world of generalities, Bessie's not being a non-cow is always equivalent to her being a cow, for we set up our logic to have invariable rules. Again, the presentations of immediate experience do not obey logical principles. But when we worry about cognitive agreement, we reason according to rules. Dignāga concocts a table of inferential relations that is abstract and formal, unlike the treatment in Nyāya, where inference is thought to be underpinned by natural realities, by relations occurring in the world independently of us as cognizers.

Finally, much in the logical and epistemological texts of the late Yogācārins seems to grow out of a concern with criteria for proper debate, including, to be sure, what makes an argument cogent, but also criteria for appropriate procedure. In this and in many details of logic and debate theory – also even in the epistemology of sense perception – there is a lot of overlap with non-Buddhist texts. The extent to which academicism flourished among classical philosophers is underappreciated by modern scholars, who tend to look for something distinctively Buddhist in everything a Buddhist epistemologist says. But probably much or even most of Yogācāra epistemology was not considered to flow out of peculiarly Buddhist views. Dignāga, Dharmakīrti and company often seem to write simply as epistemologists, not as adherents to a Buddhist epistemological school.

2 Nyāya reliabilism

At the heart of the Nyāya ('Logic') approach to epistemology is the view that a proposition-laden awareness is to be counted veridical – for the purposes of resolving a doubt or an issue in dispute – just in case it is the result of a reliable cognitive process, *pramāṇa*. (According to Nyāya, what the veridicality of an awareness amounts to is, roughly, a reflecting of, or corresponding to, a fact; our concern, however, is not what it is for an awareness to *be* veridical, but why an awareness is to *be regarded as* veridical. This latter is a matter of reliabilism in the Logic approach, although a qualification concerning context of inquiry has to be made: see below.) Nyāya identifies four such reliable processes: perception, inference, vocabulary acquisition through an analogy drawn, and testimony. Other schools identify fewer *pramāṇas* as independent 'means of knowledge' (for example, Yogācārins accept only two, perception and inference); still others accept more (for example, Mīmāṃsā accepts six) (see KNOWLEDGE, INDIAN VIEWS OF).

Logic's reliabilism is a causal theory of knowing; it is articulated in the *Nyāyasūtra* (*c.* AD 150; although it did not reach its present form until about 400) and developed in commentaries and extra-commentarial literature stretching into modern times. We rely on our cognition to get what we want, and both our getting it and knowing it are natural, causal processes.

Logic philosophers may also be said to be empiricists in the precise sense of viewing perception as our principal cognitive link with the world. It is the process generating reliable awarenesses *par excellence*. When we acquire a new piece of vocabulary through someone drawing an analogy for us, we must have already acquired analogue terms experientially, by definitions given through ostension. Testimony is reliable only if the testifier (or the first in a chain of testifiers) knows through perception (or through an inference itself perceptually based) what is being testified. Not only may the result of an inference be defeated by perception, but the crucial general rule, or 'pervasion' (*vyāpti*, wherever *F* there *G*) is established by wide perceptual experience. And, of course, through sight of a single counterinstance (an *F* but no *G*) a putative pervasion would be disproved.

An ontological realism and a fallibilism about knowledge are also important in the overall epistemological approach of the Logic school. A pervasion is held to obtain in nature, and for this reason one could, strictly speaking, be grasped from a single exhibited connection. For example, from a single instance of the sight of smoke rising from fire, the pervasion 'wherever smoke there fire' could be grasped; or, from viewing a horse and a cow, one can know that a horse is not a cow and – to express the pervasion known, here a negative one – 'whatever is a cow is not a horse, and conversely'. Repeated experience of the connection (along with no experience of the presence of an *F* without a *G*) increases one's confidence. Perception, inference and the rest are natural causal process, and generally reliable, but on a particular occasion there may be no way of knowing whether we are right or wrong. Knowledge is a factual matter, and we may well not know that we know something or other when in fact we do know it. That is to say, a lower-order fact may be being

cognized ('That is a pot' as known), without one's becoming aware that one knows ('I am knowing "That is a pot"' as itself not known), just as there are plenty of other types of fact of which we are unaware. With the exception of apperception (see AWARENESS IN INDIAN THOUGHT §3), certification, according to Nyāya, is a process external to the knowledge episode that is certified – a position giving rise to disputes between Logicians and Exegetes (see §3).

The difference between inquiry about a cognition's source and ultimate certification appears to be a matter of context. Most generally, certification depends on the success of action undertaken on the basis of a (claim-laden) cognition, and sometimes we find out in action that, for example, what we thought was a veridical perception is an illusion (one cannot drink sand). But in a particular context of inquiry it may be enough to trace a cognition to its source, or to turn to the recognized sources for new information. The entire reliabilism programme of Nyāya is said to be grounded in the success of action undertaken on the basis of identified sources of knowledge. We know perception *et al.* are generally reliable by an inference based on the usual success of acts guided by perception *et al.*

3 Mīmāṃsā self-certificationalism

The Mīmāṃsā ('Exegesis') approach to epistemology emerges in the context of a challenge to religious practices and social mores now known as Hindu from, in particular, Buddhism. The teachings of the Vedas and Vedic literature were propagated by a hereditary class of priests, or Brahmans, comprising the highest of the traditional Hindu castes. Buddhism (also Jainism) rejects caste along with the Brahmanical canon. Buddhists claim that their religious teachings are founded on nothing other than experience (albeit mystical), the *nirvāṇa* experience that makes a *buddha* an expert about spiritual matters. Similar moves were made by some with regard to the Vedas. But the genius of Mīmāṃsā is to defend the Brahmanical canon by an appeal to the common practice of taking even unexamined beliefs to be correct. That the Vedas' truth is secured by a Divine Author is a position at odds with the Exegetes' polytheism and their sense of the Vedas as a moral authority superior to the gods. The Vedas are so holy and profound that no one, neither the greatest of mystics nor a god, could have composed them. The Vedas are *apauruṣeya*, 'without a person as author'. The ethics of belief that arises among Exegetes proposes more than a right to believe Vedic teachings; it proposes that we have a duty to follow Vedic injunctions to perform certain sacrifices and lead a certain form of life. Just as in perceiving an object such as a cow we require no certification extrinsic to the perception itself to act appropriately with respect to the cow, so in hearing Vedic injunctions we requires no extrinsic certification with respect to what we know we ought to do.

In classical epistemological debates, Exegetes, led by Kumārila (c.670) and Prabhākara (c.700), attend, like their rivals, to *pramāṇas*, 'knowledge sources'. The point of this focus, according to Logic philosophers, is to be able to trace a cognition or claim to a reliable source as a way of dispelling doubt and ending debate; Yogācārins turn to coherence considerations as the test of truth and veridicality, with perception as the source responsible for an initial credibility or warrant that by agreement or disagreement with other cognitions may be strengthened or overruled. In contrast, Exegetes insist that the initial credibility of a cognition is practically absolute. Strictly speaking, no awareness is nonveridical; no cognition is absolutely wrong, but is at worst a confusion. Error can and does occur. But what is called a perceptual illusion, for example, is a confusion, or blending, of a veridical perception and a correct memory in such a way that it appears that there is a single cognition (misrepresenting the world), whereas in fact there are two. Error results from a departure from a *pramāṇa*'s normal functioning and a failure, for example, to distinguish a perception and a memory (the error of seeing mother-of-pearl as silver combines a perception of an object that is indeed there – mother-of-pearl – and a memory of silver that one has indeed previously experienced).

Exegetes promote ideas of demarcation concerning legitimate spheres of *pramāṇa* operation and causal considerations with respect to each sphere. For example, sense experience is not a legitimate source of ethical knowledge, for only an existent object can be the cause of a perception, and ethics concerns future acts.

Such reflection as this is put forth to dispel confusion, not to establish a legitimate pedigree. Inquiry concerning legitimate epistemic pedigree is not itself normally legitimate: the absolutely central thesis of self-certification does not rule out *pramāṇa* inquiry, but it allows us to take a genial, nonsceptical and inclusivist attitude (finding as we do six sources of knowledge), and to get clear about distinctions concerning what is known and how we know it.

There are different versions of self-certification (*svataḥprāmāṇya*) among Exegetes. According to Prabhākara, every veridical cognition is known to be so intrinsically, just by the occurrence of the cognition itself. Nonveridicality, however, is known extrinsically. Thus the same causal nexus that produces a veridical cognition produces knowledge of its veridicality. But when we discover an error, we discover it on extrinsic grounds. On an alternative view deriving from Kumārila, veridicality is known through a process of inference: this is the same process of inference whereby a cognition itself is known as having occurred. A cognition, which is an act, produces a feature in the object it cognizes, namely 'cognizedness', and then from apprehension of this feature, both the original cognition and its veridicality are known. (Similarly, cooking is an act that produces a feature in its object, namely 'being cooked'.) Thus on Kumārila's view, too, there is no difference between knowing a cognition as a fact and knowing it as veridical. Certification is intrinsic to a cognition's occurrence, that is, with cognitions that are veridical. With respect to knowledge of nonveridicality, extrinsic certification is required – as in Prabhākara's view.

Briefly we may note a Logic rejoinder, which is that normally there is no call to wonder about a cognition's veridicality; normally we proceed to act without wondering, and rightly without wondering, whether the cognition guiding an act is reliable. An assumption of veridicality is the epistemological default. But under circumstances that call for reflection about certification, we do not find it in the cognition itself, for that would make nonveridical cognitions impossible. Logic philosophers also hold that there is an excellence (*guṇa*) in the causal process resulting in a veridical cognition that may be said to account for its veridicality, just as there is a reliability-undercutting fault (*doṣa*) in the process resulting in a cognition that is nonveridical. Exegetes have a pretty easy time showing that this is a cumbersome conception. On the score of what cognition reveals, both schools are realist and learn and borrow from one another.

Finally, Advaita Vedāntins, generally speaking, endorse the Mīmāṃsā approach to epistemology, especially that of the Prabhākara camp. Indeed, in disputes with Logic philosophers and others, Advaitins bring out new ramifications of self-certificationalism and interesting attacks on rival positions. However, in contrast to the common-sense realism of Mīmāṃsā concerning the pots and cows of the world, Advaitins are intent upon upholding the sole reality of the self, which is identified with the Absolute, Brahman. For Advaitins, self-certificationalism proves to be an immensely important mainstay in an overall idealist polemic (see MONISM, INDIAN §§1–2).

See also: BUDDHISM, YOGĀCĀRA SCHOOL OF §§1–4; ERROR AND ILLUSION, INDIAN CONCEPTIONS OF;

MĪMĀMSĀ §§2–3; NYĀYA-VAIŚEṢIKA §6; SĀNKHYA §4

References and further reading

Bhatt, G.P. (1962) *The Basic Ways of Knowing*, Delhi: Motilal Banarsidass, 2nd edn, 1989. (A helpful study of, in particular, Kumārila's Mīmāṃsā epistemology, although Bhatt makes the common mistake of rendering *jñāna* as 'knowledge' – instead of 'cognition' or 'awareness' – and thus speaks of true and false knowledges.)

Bhattacharyya, S. (1987) *Doubt, Belief and Knowledge*, New Delhi: Indian Council of Philosophical Research and Allied Publishers. (Lucid reflection on late developments within the Logic school.)

Dharmarāja (c. 1600) *Vedāntaparibhāṣā*, trans. and ed. S.S.S. Sastri, *Vedāntaparibhāṣā by Dharmarāja Adhvarin*, Madras: Adyar Library and Research Centre, 1971. (An excellent translation of an important late classical Advaita text with an epistemological slant.)

Hayes, R.P. (1988) *Dignāga on the Interpretation of Signs*, Dordrecht: Kluwer. (Provides a good sense of the overall Yogācāra epistemological approach.)

Kumārila (c. 670) *Ślokavārttika*, trans. G. Jha, Delhi: Sri Satguru, 1983. (The only available English translation of the work of the important Mīmāṃsaka philosopher; this is a reprint of a 1908 edition.)

Matilal, B.K. (1986) *Perception: An Essay on Classical Indian Theories of Knowledge*, Oxford: Oxford University Press. (Though Matilal defends Nyāya, his discussion ranges penetratingly over the whole of classical Indian theory of knowledge.)

Matilal, B.K. and Evans, R.D. (eds) (1986) *Buddhist Logic and Epistemology*, Dordrecht: Kluwer. (Contains several excellent papers on the Yogācāra logicians and epistemologists.)

Mohanty, J.N. (1966) *Gangeśa's Theory of Truth*, Delhi: Motilal Banarsidass, 1989. (Excellent investigation of, especially, the late Nyāya and Mīmāṃsā debate over certification.)

STEPHEN H. PHILLIPS

EPISTEMOLOGY, NORMATIVE *see* NORMATIVE EPISTEMOLOGY

EPISTEMOLOGY, SOCIAL
see SOCIAL EPISTEMOLOGY

EPISTEMOLOGY, YORUBA
see YORUBA EPISTEMOLOGY

EPOCHÉ *see* PHENOMENOLOGY, EPISTEMIC ISSUES IN

EQUALITY

Equality has long been a source of political and philosophical controversy. A central question about equality is how one might link empirical or moral claims about the extent to which persons are equal to judgements about the moral acceptability or unacceptability of social inequalities, and in particular how far considerations of equality license social action to bring about greater social equality. A traditional liberal argument holds that approximate equality of human strength makes it prudent for humans to place themselves under a common political authority, thus producing a justification for equality before the law. But any generalization of this argument ignores the cases where strength is unequal and the resulting balance of power unjust. Equality of worth is a principle recognized in many philosophical traditions, but its broad acceptance leaves open many problems of interpretation. In particular, it is not clear how far the principle calls for greater equality of social conditions. Persons may derive a sense of worth from enjoying the fruits of their labour, and this will legitimately block some redistribution; certain inequalities may work to everyone's advantage; and the impartial concern of the equality principle may be at odds with the sense of ourselves as persons with specific attachments. In this context, some have wanted to soften the interpretation of equality to mean equality of opportunity or merely that inequalities should not be cumulative, although how far these moves are justified is a matter for dispute. By contrast, challenges to the equality principle from considerations of incentives, desert or difference can more easily be met.

1 The idea of equality
2 Equality of strength
3 Equality of moral worth
4 Challenges to equality

1 The idea of equality

Nearly 2,500 years ago Aristotle remarked in *The Politics* (336–22 BC) that disputes over equality and inequality were generally behind the warfare within states. Nowadays in topics as diverse as the distribution of income and wealth, access to public services, the distribution of work and employment opportunities, the political representation of different social groups and the control of natural resources among nations, the issue of equality plays a central, but controversial, role.

The idea of equality occurs in political philosophy in three main ways. First, it has sometimes been used as a purported description of certain features of human life in society, most notably in the claim that human beings are approximately equal in strength. Second, it is used as a principle of action to the effect that persons should be treated as having equal moral worth. Third, it is used to indicate a supposedly desirable set of social conditions, for example 'one person, one vote' or a more equal distribution of income. A central issue is how far one can employ premises drawn from the first two senses of the term to evaluate social, economic and political inequalities in the third sense. In particular the question arises as to how far social inequalities are just, or at least justifiable (see JUSTICE §5).

To speak of equality without qualification is to speak elliptically. Strictly speaking, equality is a relation that holds between objects or persons in respect of some common characteristic that they share. In most respects, human beings are unequal: they exhibit differences of height, weight, intelligence, manual dexterity, earning capacity and so on. Moreover, if society or governments were to seek to equalize some goods or resources, for example income, they would render unequal some other aspect of social relations, for example hourly rates of pay when people work for different lengths of time.

The upshot of these logical points is that the idea of equality needs to be embedded within a broader theory of politics and society in order to be given a specific content. No political theory aims at equality pure and simple. It aims instead at specific types of equality thought to be morally or socially important.

2 Equality of strength

Given the diversity of human beings, can it ever be said that all human beings are equal in any respect? In *Leviathan* (1651), Hobbes suggested that, although differing in bodily and mental capacities, human beings were equal in that it would be always possible for one person to kill another, an idea picked up by Hume in the eighteenth century and H.L.A. Hart in the twentieth.

According to this tradition, such rough equality of strength makes it prudent or rational for human beings to place themselves under a common body of rules comprising a system of mutual forbearance and agreement. Thus, despite persistent differences in wealth and status in society, equality of obligation under the law flows from equality of strength in some hypothesized pre-legal situation. Political agents should therefore recognize a common system of authority not merely as wise but also as just.

This line of thought can be carried too far, however. For the equality of strength condition only holds under rather specific circumstances, and where it does not hold the weak are vulnerable. One intuitive idea of justice is that bargaining advantage should not be allowed to prevail where this would threaten certain fundamental interests of persons; political power will thus only be legitimate when it protects the vulnerable (see JUSTICE §4).

3 Equality of moral worth

If we cannot establish a normatively adequate theory of politics solely on the notion of an approximate equality of strength, the idea of equality will have to be given an irreducible moral content. This introduces the second sense of the idea: namely, equality means that all persons are to be thought of as having the same moral worth and are entitled to equal respect and consideration in the treatment of their interests. Although associated with contemporary liberal political thought, both in its utilitarian and its Kantian variants (see LIBERALISM), this idea has also found a place in many other philosophical and religious traditions, including Jewish and Christian political thought, the Stoic tradition, and the Confucianism associated with Mencius. Currents of thought within Islam, as well as breakaway sects from Hinduism, have also advanced the idea that there is an equal moral worth of all persons. However, can any specific implications about the ordering of social relations be derived from a principle that thinkers of such varying political and philosophical persuasions have endorsed?

One issue here concerns the terms in which we spell out the implications of greater equality. Greater social equality in principle leaves open the question of what exactly is to be equalized: should it be resources, welfare or some other aspect of human life? There are sound arguments for taking any one of these possibilities as the basis of public policy.

However the issue of measurement is resolved, the central justificatory arguments for equality claim that the principle of equal moral worth places limits on what actions a state may pursue (for example, it may not privilege the interests of some at the expense of others), and that a sense of personal worth depends upon the political, social and economic institutions in which members of society participate. Yet, it is easy to see that, although in general this claim may be true, there is no simple way in which the precise nature of these connections can be ascertained.

Suppose it is allowed that people's sense of self-worth depends upon the social institutions in which they participate, so that poverty and social deprivation will undermine a person's sense of self-worth. The extent to which this assumption will license a general equalization of social and economic resources is not obvious. Thus, some libertarians have claimed that such equalization will require practices of redistribution that in effect treat the wealthy as mere means to the attainment of some social goal, in a way that is inconsistent with the respect for persons that the principle of equal worth requires (see LIBERTAR-IANISM §3).

In this simple form the libertarian argument does not carry much conviction, since it does not show why requiring persons to fulfil putative obligations under a principle of justice is to treat them merely as means. However, it does at least indicate that there may be constraints on the way in which the practice of redistribution is accomplished and that persons should, by and large, enjoy the fruits of their own labour.

Quite apart from these libertarian objections to the equalization of property, it has also been argued that the principle of equality it should be recognized that there may be a general advantage in some forms of social inequality. Thus, Rawls (1972) has consistently argued that it would be irrational for persons seeking to advance their own interests to prefer a more equal distribution of resources to an unequal distribution of a larger stock that left the poorest persons better off than they would be under the scheme of equality. By this argument the principle of equal moral worth is seen to coexist with permissible inequalities in the allocation of resources or welfare in society.

Further complications stem from the notion of personality itself. It may be argued that the sense of ourselves as persons derives from the special attachments that we form to other persons, or particular places and institutions. Our sense of moral worth depends therefore on subjectively meaningful attachments that limit the extent to which we can take a general impartial concern in the interests of others. For example, if all people are of equal moral worth, it would seem that large-scale international redistribution is called for to realize the principle, but such a proposal could cut across the subjective attachments that persons form within the political communities of which they are members.

The distinctive feature of all three of these sorts of argument is that they do not simply counterpose the principle of equality to other principles of social organization, but seek instead to develop different aspects of that principle to cut the inference from equal moral worth to an equal allocation of rights and goods in society.

In response, one option is to weaken the implications of the principle of equality. For example, perhaps the principle of equal worth does not imply an equalization of rights and goods taken as a whole, but merely that there should be no discrimination in their allocation, so that relative advantages are not unfairly achieved. Similarly, it may be argued that the principle of equality merely requires that persons be given an equal opportunity to acquire unequal social and economic advantages. A particularly influential argument in this mode has been the claim that it is not social and economic inequality in itself that is objectionable, but the accumulation of social and economic inequalities across the different dimensions of social life. Related to this argument is the claim that it may be important to reduce or eliminate only certain social inequalities – in particular those that relate to access to health care or education – in order to be consistent with the principle of equal moral worth.

The most natural way to deal with this variety of interpretations is to allow that one can identify not one but a family of political positions, all of which claim to embody the principle of equal moral worth. The choice between these positions in part depends upon broader issues of social theory (for example, the extent to which one believes that inequalities in different dimensions can be kept separate) and in part depends upon the exercise of judgement (for example, the extent to which one judges that a sense of personal worth depends upon persons being able to retain the fruits of their labour as distinct from enjoying access to collectively shared rights and goods).

4 Challenges to equality

There have been a number of challenges to the moral claims of the equality principle. One familiar argument refers to the supposed disincentives to work that would be created by the practice of redistribution from the more productive to the less productive. From one point of view this can be regarded as a pragmatic question, with policy makers having to determine what the balance should be between greater productivity and greater equality. The Rawlsian difference principle, according to which inequalities should be allowed provided they raise the incomes of the least advantaged, can be interpreted here as one possible, but attractive, compromise on this question (see RAWLS, J. §1).

However, the issue of incentives also raises matters of principle, since one way to avoid disincentive effects would be to adopt a scheme of taxation based not on labour but on ability. Although difficult to operate, such a scheme would in principle impose a lump-sum tax (an inherited debt) upon the more able that they would have to work to pay off. Clearly, the problem of work incentives in this case leads straight back to some of the problems of combining equality with a sense of personal attachment that were identified in the previous section.

A second principle that is often set against that of equality is the principle of merit or desert. This principle does provide a direct challenge to equality, since it requires that goods be distributed in proportion to the merits of those receiving them – with the best flute players receiving the best flutes, as Aristotle put it. However, the notion of desert is not without its own problems, and it may be argued that its application only makes sense within the context of an ongoing practice, like an orchestra with its own standards of performance, and not across society as a whole (see DESERT AND MERIT).

The final challenge to the principle of equality has come from the appeal to the notion of difference. Here the argument is that equality implies a uniformity of treatment, whereas interests in society are in fact plural. Thus, instead of basing public decision making on the principle of one person, one vote, a principle of difference would require some groups to be given a special say in certain matters of public policy, for example women a veto over changes to the law on abortion.

The extent to which the appeal to difference mounts a serious challenge to the principle of equality is a matter for dispute, however. Requiring equal consideration of the interests of all persons is compatible with recognizing that over some questions the interests of certain groups are more deeply engaged than others, as can quite easily be seen in the protection of the rights of local communities to take decisions that affect them especially. Thus, to allow that there may be a special say for certain groups in matters of public policy may be compatible with the principle of equality, provided that the acknowledgement of the possibility is not unique to a particular group.

Despite these challenges, therefore, the principle of equality still remains as a central principle of modern political thought. But its very centrality means that continuing discussion over its exact interpretation and implications is likely for a long time to come.

References and further reading

* Aristotle (*c.* mid 4th century BC) *The Politics*, trans. H. Rackham, Cambridge, MA: Harvard University Press, London: Heinemann, 1932. (Book 5 offers Aristotle's thoughts on equality and inequality as the source of political revolution.)

Barry, B.M. (1989) *Theories of Justice*, London: Harvester Wheatsheaf. (An extended discussion of the implications for equality and social justice of the equality of strength argument and its weaknesses.)

Dworkin, R. (1981a) 'What is Equality? Part 1: Equality of Welfare', *Philosophy and Public Affairs* 10 (3): 185–246. (One of two articles arguing that equality should govern resources, not welfare.)

—— (1981b) 'What is Equality? Part 2: Equality of Resources', *Philosophy and Public Affairs* 10 (4): 283–345. (The second of Dworkin's articles arguing that equality should govern resources, not welfare.)

Goodin, R.E. (1985) *Protecting the Vulnerable*, Chicago, IL, and London: University of Chicago Press. (An analysis of the intuition that inequalities of strength should not be exploited.)

Hart H.L.A. (1962) *The Concept of Law*, Oxford: Clarendon Press. (Chapter 8 contains the best modern statement of the implications of the equal strength view discussed in §2.)

* Hobbes, T. (1651) *Leviathan*, ed. M. Oakeshott, Oxford: Blackwell. (States the argument that humans are approximately equal in strength and draws conclusions.)

Hume, D. (1742) *Enquiries Concerning Human Understanding and Concerning the Principles of Morals*, ed. L.A. Selby-Bigge and P.H. Nidditch, Oxford: Clarendon Press, 3rd edn, 1975. (Makes equality of strength one of the circumstances of justice.)

Kymlicka, W. (1990) *Contemporary Political Philosophy*, Oxford: Clarendon Press. (Argues that leading contemporary accounts of justice are all egalitarian in the sense that they conceive of persons as equals.)

Nagel, T. (1979) 'Equality', *Mortal Questions*, Cambridge: Cambridge University Press, 106–27. (Argues that equality is tied to social decision procedures that seek to reflect the view of all affected parties.)

—— (1991) *Equality and Partiality*, Oxford: Oxford University Press. (The source of the argument in §3 that equality may conflict with the subjective sense of personal attachments.)

Nozick, R. (1974) *Anarchy, State and Utopia*, Oxford: Blackwell. (Part 2 contains a statement of the libertarian case against equality of income and wealth, but on the basis of a Kantian understanding of persons.)

Nussbaum, M. and Sen, A. (1993) *The Quality of Life*, Oxford: Clarendon Press. (A useful collection reviewing the issue of what the metric of redistribution should be.)

* Rawls, J. (1972) *A Theory of Justice*, Oxford: Clarendon Press. (A classic of twentieth-century political philosophy which is the source of the argument in §3 that benefit to the least well-off might justify certain inequalities.)

Vlastos, G. (1962) 'Justice and Equality', in R.B. Brandt (ed.) *Social Justice*, Englewood Cliffs, NJ: Prentice Hall. (A beautifully lucid statement of the equal worth view.)

Walzer, M. (1983) *Spheres of Justice*, Oxford: Martin Robertson. (A statement of the view that it is cumulative inequalities, rather than inequality itself, that is morally objectionable.)

Williams, B. (1962) 'The Idea of Equality', in P. Laslett and W.G. Runciman (eds) *Philosophy, Politics and Society*, second series, Oxford: Blackwell. (A statement of the equal worth view, with some interesting claims about 'irrelevant' bases of treatment.)

Young, I.M. (1991) *Justice and the Politics of Difference*, Princeton, NJ: Princeton University Press. (A statement of the view that difference calls into question universalistic assumptions about equality of citizenship.)

ALBERT WEALE

EQUITY *see* JUSTICE, EQUITY AND LAW

ERASMUS, DESIDERIUS (*c.*1466–1536)

Although Erasmus was not a systematic philosopher, he gave a philosophical cast to many of his writings. He believed in the human capacity for self-improvement through education and in the relative preponderance of nurture over nature. Ideally, education promoted docta pietas, *a combination of piety and learning. Erasmus' political thought is dominated by his vision of universal peace and the notions of consensus and consent, which* he sees as the basis of the state. At the same time he upholds the ideal of the patriarchal prince, a godlike figure to his people, but accountable to God in turn. Erasmus' epistemology is characterized by scepticism. He advocates collating arguments on both sides of a question but suspending judgment. His scepticism does not extend to articles of faith, however. He believes in absolute knowledge through revelation and reserves calculations of probability for cases that are not settled by the authority of Scripture or the doctrinal pronouncements of the Church, the conduit of divine revelation. Erasmus' pioneering efforts as a textual critic of the Bible and his call for a reformation of the Church in its head and members brought him into conflict with conservative Catholic theologians. His support for the Reformation movement was equivocal, however. He refused to endorse the radical methods of the reformers and engaged in a polemic with Luther over the question of free will. On the whole, Erasmus was more interested in the moral and spiritual than in the doctrinal aspects of the Reformation. He promoted inner piety over the observance of rites, and disparaged scholastic speculations in favour of the* philosophia Christi *taught in the gospel. The term 'Christian humanism' best describes Erasmus' philosophy, which successfully combined Christian thought with the classical tradition revived by Renaissance humanists.*

1 **Life and works**
2 **Educational philosophy**
3 **Political thought**
4 **Scepticism**
5 **Philosophy of language**
6 *Philosophia Christi*

1 Life and works

Erasmus was born at Rotterdam, the illegitimate son of a priest. Orphaned at an early age, he was persuaded by his guardians to enter an Augustinian monastery. He became a canon regular and was ordained priest in 1492. In 1495 he was sent to Paris to study theology, but soon developed a strong distaste for the scholastic method taught there. When the financial help promised by his bishop did not materialize, Erasmus was obliged to support himself by tutoring well-to-do young men. In 1499 he accompanied one of his pupils to England. The visit led to important connections with future patrons (among them William Warham, Archbishop of Canterbury) and to lifelong friendships with Thomas More (see UTOPIANISM §1) and John Colet. Over the next two decades Erasmus travelled extensively. He returned to France, visited the Low Countries, made a second journey to England, and then spent three years (1506–9) in Italy. While in Turin he obtained a Doctorate of Theology *per saltum*, that is, without fulfilling the usual academic and residence requirements. For a year he lived in Venice, doing editorial work and research for the Aldine press. On the accession of Henry VIII in 1509 he returned to England and taught Greek at Cambridge, but his hopes for royal patronage were only modestly rewarded.

By this time Erasmus had made a name for himself as the author of the homiletic *Enchiridion Militis Christiani* (Handbook of the Christian Soldier) (1503) and the witty *In Praise of Folly* (1511), both calling for spiritual renewal of church and society. In 1515 he was appointed counsellor to Prince Charles of Burgundy (later Emperor Charles V) and through the generosity of his patrons in England and the Low Countries acquired sufficient wealth to live the life of an independent scholar. He took up residence at Louvain in 1517 and with short interruptions remained there until 1521. In 1516 he published his *magnum opus*, an edition of the New Testament containing a revised text of the Vulgate faced by the Greek original (the first printed Greek text of the New Testament to reach the market). Erasmus' pioneering work as textual critic was immediately attacked by the Louvain theologians, and his move to Basle in 1521 was partly motivated by a desire to escape their hostilities. However, geographical distance did not deter Erasmus' opponents in the Low Countries. Soon opposition to his work spread to France and Spain, involving Erasmus in bitter controversy and culminating in a formal condemnation by the faculty of theology at Paris in 1531. His critics accused Erasmus of attacking the principle of divine inspiration of Scripture, undermining the traditions of the Church, and providing the underpinning for the Lutheran 'heresy'. Erasmus denied these charges. He noted that his revision of the Vulgate text was not aimed at changing the words of the inspired evangelist, but at correcting the mistakes of an incompetent translator or a careless scribe. Although he occasionally challenged the traditional interpretation of a scriptural passage, he was willing in all instances to submit his views to the verdict of the Church. While he was no doubt sympathetic to the goals of the Reformation, he disapproved of the radical methods adopted by the reformers. Trying to maintain a scholarly detachment was difficult, however. Erasmus soon found himself attacked by both parties. Conservative theologians perceived him as Luther's inspiration; followers of Luther resented his refusal to endorse the reformer unequivocally and accused him of hypocrisy. Challenged to clarify his position, Erasmus reluctantly entered the arena against Luther

with a *Discourse on Free Will* (1524). The ensuing polemic led to a breach between the two men, but failed to convince Catholic critics of the orthodoxy of Erasmus' views. The controversy over Erasmus' commitment to the Catholic faith continued after his death in 1536. In the wake of the Council of Trent which imposed strict doctrinal norms, Erasmus' works were placed on the Index of Prohibited Books.

2 Educational philosophy

Erasmus' pedagogical theories are based on the anthropological optimism that characterizes Renaissance humanism. His philosophy of education is formulated in a number of treatises, dealing with curriculum, methods and objectives. Curriculum is discussed in *De ratione studii* (On the Method of Study) (1512) and *Ratio verae theologiae* (The Method of True Theology) (1518). Erasmus rejected the traditional emphasis on logic and speculative sciences in favour of language studies, history and moral philosophy. Such a curriculum was meant not only to develop skills and train the intellect, but also to provide moral instruction and promote civic virtue. *De pueris instituendis* (On the Education of Children) (1529) is a comprehensive statement of Erasmus' views on the goals of education and the respective roles played by parent, teacher and pupil in the process of education.

Erasmus believed in the human capacity for self-improvement through education and in the relative preponderance of nurture over nature. Indeed he believed that individuals are 'made human' through education. Although Erasmus placed the customary emphasis on imitation as the principal method of learning, he defined it in a wider sense as comprising the thorough understanding of a subject. Copying models was only a first step in the learning process. This must be followed by the judicious application of skills acquired by imitation, which includes choosing elements suitable to the subject, the occasion and the parties involved. Thus Erasmus acknowledged that mastering a subject required analysis, judgment, and a process of creative appropriation. Erasmus abhorred corporal punishment and insisted that positive reinforcement and healthy competition were the most effective means of motivating the learner. In the educational process Erasmus attached a disproportionate importance to the teacher, whom he held largely responsible for the success or failure of a pupil. Apparently he considered a pupil's negative attitude to learning or inability to benefit from instruction the direct result of inadequate teaching methods. While Erasmus asserted that everyone was capable of self-improvement, he grew up with the belief that females were less likely to benefit from education than males. He tells us that he revised his views when confronted with evidence to the contrary. All of Erasmus' pronouncements on education have a Christian subtext. He believed that the student must be transformed, not only into a learned person, but a learned Christian. In his estimate, St Jerome was the perfect scholar, embodying *docta pietas*, that is, combining erudition with piety.

3 Political thought

The main source for Erasmus' political thought is his *Institutio Principis Christiani* (The Education of a Christian Prince), published in 1516 and dedicated to the 16–year-old Prince Charles. In this essay the ruler appears as a father figure, who looks after the welfare of his people, dispenses justice and provides moral leadership. He is the representative of God and as such is owed unquestioning obedience by his people. The ruler in turn must render an account of his stewardship to God. 'He does not have the same rights over men as over cattle,' Erasmus notes. 'Government depends to a large extent on the consent of the people, which was what created kings in the first place' (*Collected Works*: vol. 27, p. 284). Consent and consultation are prominent themes in Erasmus' political writings. He saw consensus-building as an important process in the government of both state and church. Accordingly, he proposed to settle territorial conflicts among states by calling on a group of referees, and to determine dogmatic questions within the church by summoning a general council. His emphasis on consensus as a means of ensuring a correct decision also of course has epistemological implications (see §4).

The maintenance of peace and concord is another central theme of Erasmus' political writings. It is the subject of two essays, 'Dulce Bellum Inexpertis' (War is Sweet to the Inexperienced) (1515) and *Querela Pacis* (The Complaint of Peace) (1517). Erasmus' pacifism is informed by the classical ideal of *humanitas* and the Christian ideal of a universal fellowship. In *De bello Turcico* (On War Against the Turks) (1530) Erasmus accepts the concept of a 'just war' against the Ottoman Empire but disparages a military solution. Instead he promotes the idea of the Turks as a scourge of God, which calls for spiritual weapons rather than battle gear. A transfer from the political to the theological realm is apparent also in Erasmus' image of the Christian commonwealth with Christ surrounded by clergy, princes and common people in three concentric circles. This iconography is reminiscent of the traditional division of the polity into king and estates. It assigns to Christ a position analogous to that of the king and dispenser of power. In Christ's case, this is the power to purify those on earth from moral corruption. As heavenly king he delegates this power to the lower orders, enabling them to carry out his work of purification according to their own capacities (see SOVEREIGNTY).

4 Scepticism

Erasmus' moral integrity was questioned by his opponents when he declared that, although it was not permissible to 'go against' the truth, it might be expedient in some circumstances to conceal it. He also considered careful judgment and a fine sense of timing to be of prime importance in the deployment of truth. The notion that the truth needs husbanding is best understood as an aspect of Erasmus' scepticism. He believed that human beings were unable to grasp the absolute truth by their own intellectual efforts. Through discussing arguments on both sides of a question they could arrive at an approximation of the truth, but the investigation must necessarily end in *epoche*, the suspension of judgment. Erasmus' polemic with Luther over free will illustrates this method of investigation. His *Discourse on Free Will* consists of a comparison of biblical and patristic passages for and against the concept of free will. He concludes that the human will is exceedingly weak but able, with the help of divine grace, to choose the path of salvation. Erasmus does not assert this view, however, but presents it as the more likely to be true, emphasizing that his role was not to judge matters but to discuss them. It is important to note, however, that Erasmus set limits to scepticism in the religious sphere. He believed in absolute knowledge through revelation and resorted to calculations of probability only in cases that could not be settled by the authority of Scripture and had not been determined by the doctrinal pronouncements of the Church (see SCEPTICISM, RENAISSANCE §3).

5 Philosophy of language

As the author of several textbooks on style and composition, Erasmus took a substantial interest in language. However, he was concerned primarily with the practicalities of teaching language skills and does not seem to have a coherent philosophy concerning the nature, origin and function of language. Pronouncements such as 'In principle, knowledge as a whole seems to be of two kinds, of things and of words. Knowledge of words comes earlier, but that of things is the more important' (the opening sentence of *De ratione studii*) are isolated statements and do not lead to a fuller discussion of the underlying issues.

They suggest the metaphysical questions raised and discussed in Plato's *Cratylus*, Aristotle's *Metaphysics*, or Augustine's *On Christian Doctrine* (see PLATO §15; ARISTOTLE §11; AUGUSTINE §8), but are merely echoes of classical commonplaces. Indeed, Erasmus is concerned, not with philosophy, but with rhetoric, and more specifically, with effective methods of teaching rhetoric.

De ratione studii, a curriculum outline, continues appropriately with remarks of a pedagogical rather than a philosophical nature: 'But some people, while they hurry on to learn about things, neglect a concern for language.' Elsewhere, while discussing the relation between words and things, Erasmus claims that people who are unskilled in the use of language are 'short-sighted', 'deluded' and unable to form proper judgments about things. Once again, the philosophical implications are left unexplained. The statement therefore amounts to little more than a comment on the importance of effective communication. The subject of the dichotomy between words and things recurs in *De copia* (On the Abundance of Style) (1512). There it serves as an organizational principle (Book I deals with 'words', that is, style; Book II with 'things', that is, subject matter). As in *De ratione*, references to the dichotomy are linked with remarks on the effectiveness of communication: subject matter is obscured by the failure to organize words and expressions correctly. Indeed Erasmus seems to disavow any philosophical purpose. Considering distinctions between words and things to be a matter of theory rather than practice, he explained that the arrangement in his book had no philosophical basis, but was a 'teaching procedure'.

More significant in the context of a philosophy of language is a statement found in the prolegomena of Erasmus' edition of the New Testament. Defending his revision of the Vulgate translation, he argues that speech is made up of two things: words (which he relates to the body) and meaning (which is related to the soul). Similarly in *De copia*, a textbook on style, he writes of style being to thought what clothes are to the body. Like his remarks on the dichotomy of words and things, however, these statements operate on a rhetorical rather than a philosophical level and concern method rather than logic. He goes on, in one case, to discuss techniques of translation, in the other, to suggest techniques for varying expression. The overwhelming consensus of modern scholars is that it is futile 'to impute a philosophy of language to Erasmus' (O'Rourke Boyle 1977) on the basis of these and other isolated remarks, or at any rate, that his thinking on the subject is ill-disciplined and 'very imperfectly worked out' (Woodward [1904] 1964). Erasmus' comments on language bear out his propensity to focus on practical application rather than on theory, a propensity also found in his religious writings with their pronounced emphasis on Christian living rather than on doctrinal definitions (see LANGUAGE, RENAISSANCE PHILOSOPHY OF).

6 *Philosophia Christi*

Erasmus called his *Enchiridion Militis Christiani* a 'summary guide' to Christian living. In this work he developed the concept of a *philosophia Christi*, a term which is taken from patristic writings and develops Pauline notions: the dichotomy of spirit and flesh and the inferiority of visible to invisible things. Erasmus describes the human being as having a divine soul but the body of 'a brute beast'. He therefore places emphasis on the inner man rather than on the observance of rites, on faith rather than works. He does not reject the ceremonial aspect of religion out of hand, but reduces its role to that of a crutch aiding the weak in their progression towards a more perfect faith. Erasmus also takes a stand against scholastic theologians who place inordinate trust in Aristotelian dialectics (see MAJOR, J.). The philosophy of Christ advocated by him does not require scholarship, but manifests itself in the believer's heart and through the conduct of their life. The body of theological work published by Erasmus – editions and translations of patristic writings; an annotated edition of the New Testament; paraphrases and commentaries on Scripture – indicates the focal points of his religious thought. In Erasmus' view, the essence of the Christian faith could be discovered, not from the disputations of scholastic theologians, but from the life of Christ related by the evangelists and the interpretations of the divine word by the early Church Fathers.

Erasmus was not a systematic philosopher, but a keen observer of society, commenting on the questions that agitated his contemporaries and at the same time shaping the opinions of his own and future generations. His call for reform of church and society merited him the title of a 'forerunner' of the Reformation, and his pedagogical works had a pervasive influence on curriculum in his time. His criticism of the scholastic method and his scepticism in particular commended him to readers in the Age of Enlightenment. This induced a modest Erasmian renaissance after a decline in popularity during the seventeenth century, especially in areas where the Counter-Reformation had led to a strict enforcement of censorship laws. We find, however, that the positions taken by Erasmus on individual questions are not integrated into a whole: patriarchal government is advocated along with the egalitarian ideal of consensus and consent; scepticism is juxtaposed with devout and unquestioning belief; anthropological optimism with the reduction of the human will to a spark kindled by divine grace. Erasmus' ideas are clearly modified by the tenets of the Catholic Church. His belief in the human potential is tempered by the doctrine of God's omnipotence, his rationalism by the tenet of God's inscrutability, his intellectual curiosity is circumscribed by articles of faith, and his scholarly findings subjected to the verdict of the Church. The term 'Christian humanism' best describes Erasmus' brand of philosophy. It acknowledges that Erasmus' thought is firmly rooted in the Christian tradition and that he was a man of letters rather than a professional philosopher.

See also: EDUCATION, HISTORY OF PHILOSOPHY OF; FREE WILL; HUMANISM, RENAISSANCE; LUTHER, M.; SCEPTICISM; SCEPTICISM, RENAISSANCE

List of works

Erasmus, D. (1503–36) *Desiderii Erasmi Roterodami Opera Omnia* (Complete Works of Desiderius Erasmus of Rotterdam), ed. J. Leclerc, Leiden: Vander Aa, 1703–6; repr. Gregg Press, 1962. (The Gregg Press edition is a facsimile reprint.)

—— (1503–36) *Erasmi Opuscula: A supplement to the Opera Omnia*, ed. W. Ferguson, The Hague: Martinus Nijhoff, 1933. (Collection of Erasmus' short works.)

—— (1503–36) *Opus epistolarum Des. Erasmi Roterodami*, ed. P.S. Allen, Oxford: Clarendon Press, 1906–47. (Collection of Erasmus' letters.)

—— (1503–36) *Des. Erasmi Opera Omnia* (Complete Works of Desiderius Erasmus), Amsterdam: North Holland, 1969–. (New Critical Latin edition, in progress. It does not include Erasmus' correspondence.)

—— (1503–36) *The Collected Works of Erasmus*, Toronto, Ont.: University of Toronto Press, 1974–. (English edition in progress. *Ratio verae theologiae* and *De bello Turcico* are forthcoming; the other works mentioned in this article have appeared.)

—— (1503) *Enchiridion Militis Christiani* (The Handbook of the Christian Soldier), in *The Collected Works of Erasmus*, vol. 66, Toronto, Ont.: University of Toronto Press, 1988. (Develops Erasmus' concept of the *philosophia Christi*.)

—— (1511) *In Praise of Folly*, in R.M. Adams (ed.) *The Praise of Folly and Other Writings*, New York: W.W. Norton, 1990. (Includes *Paraclesis*, *Querela Pacis*, the foreword to the New Testament, a selection of colloquies and letters, and critical essays by modern scholars.)

—— (1512) *De copia* (On the Abundance of Style), in *The Collected Works of Erasmus*, vol. 24, Toronto, Ont.: University of Toronto Press, 1978. (One of Erasmus' many textbooks on style. Book 1 deals with style, Book 2 with subject matter.)

—— (1512) *De ratione studii* (On the Method of Study), in *The Collected Works of Erasmus*, vol. 24, Toronto, Ont.: University of Toronto Press, 1978. (A curriculum outline and approach to a philosophy of language from pedagogical standpoint.)

—— (1515) 'Dulce Bellum Inexpertis' (War is Sweet to the Inexperienced), in M. Mann Phillips (trans.) *Erasmus on his Times*, Cambridge: Cambridge University Press, 1967. (Outlines Erasmus' pacifism in the light of classical notions of humanity and the idea of Christian fellowship.)

—— (1516) *Institutio Principis Christiani* (The Education of a Christian Prince), in *The Collected Works of Erasmus*, vol. 27, Toronto, Ont.: University of Toronto Press, 1986. (Presents Erasmus' ideas on sovereignty and good government.)

—— (1517) *Querela Pacis* (Complaint of Peace), in *The Collected Works of Erasmus*, vol. 27, Toronto, Ont.: University of Toronto Press, 1986. (Concerned with the maintenance of peace and concord, appeals to Christian virtues in an argument against the necessity of war.)

—— (1518) *Ratio verae theologiae* (The Method of True Theology), in H. Holborn (ed.) *Desiderius Erasmus Roterdamus: Ausgewählte Werke*, Munich: C.H. Beck, 1933. (On the aims and methods of theological studies.)

—— (1524) *Erasmus–Luther: Discourse on Free Will*, trans. E. Winter, New York: Frederick Ungar, 1961. (Erasmus' investigation of the concept of free will, using biblical and patristic sources; part of a major dispute with Luther.)

—— (1529) *De pueris instituendis* (On the Education of Children), in *The Collected Works of Erasmus*, vol. 26, Toronto, Ont.: University of Toronto Press, 1985. (A comprehensive statement of Erasmus' views on the goals of education and the respective roles played by parent, teacher and pupil in the process of education.)

—— (1530) *De bello Turcico* (On War Against the Turks), in *Des. Erasmi Opera Omnia*, vol. 3, Amsterdam: North Holland, 1986. (Accepts the concept of a 'just war' against the Ottoman Empire but recasts it as a primarily spiritual conflict. *De bello Turcico* is partially translated into English in *The Erasmus Reader*.)

—— (1990) *The Erasmus Reader*, ed. E. Rummel, Toronto, Ont.: University of Toronto Press. (This collection includes a partial translation of *De bello Turcico*.)

References and further reading

Augustijn, C. (1991) *Erasmus: His Life, Works, and Influence*, Toronto, Ont.: University of Toronto Press. (Extensive bibliography.)

Hoffmann, M. (1994) *Rhetoric and Theology: The Hermeneutics of Erasmus*, Toronto, Ont.: University of Toronto Press. (Provides the best analysis of Erasmus' *Ecclesiastes* (The Preacher) available in English.)

Jardine, L. (1993) *Erasmus, Man of Letters: The Construction of Charisma in Print*, Princeton, NJ: Princeton University Press. (Documents Erasmus' skill as a publicist; serves as a comment on his philosophy of language.)

Mansfield, B. (1979, 1992) *Phoenix of his Age: Interpretations of Erasmus, 1550–1750*, vol. 1; *Interpretations of Erasmus, c.1750–1920: Man on His Own*, vol. 2, Toronto, Ont.: University of Toronto Press. (Two-volume work on Erasmus' influence.)

McConica, J.K. (1991) *Erasmus*, Oxford: Oxford University Press. (A concise, insightful examination of Erasmus' thought.)

O'Malley, J. (1988) 'Introduction', *The Collected Works of Erasmus*, vol. 66, Toronto, Ont.: University of Toronto Press. (This is the best discussion in English of Erasmus' *philosophia Christi* and contains further bibliographical references.)

* O'Rourke Boyle, M. (1977) *Erasmus on Language and Method in Theology*, Toronto, Ont.: University of Toronto Press. (Referred to in §5. An investigation of Erasmus' linguistic principles.)

—— (1983) *Rhetoric and Reform: Erasmus' Civil Dispute with Luther*, Cambridge, MA: Harvard University Press. (Includes a discussion of Erasmus' scepticism.)

Popkin, R. (1964) *The History of Scepticism from Erasmus to Descartes*, New York: Humanities Press. (Chapter 1 deals with Erasmus' scepticism.)

Rummel, E. (1989) *Erasmus and His Catholic Critics*, Nieuwkoop: de Graaf. (Examines Erasmus' biblical scholarship and Christian humanism in the context of his polemics.)

—— (1995) *The Humanist–Scholastic Debate in the Renaissance and Reformation*, Cambridge, MA: Harvard University Press. (Discusses Erasmus' role in this curricular/philosophical debate passim; chapter 6 explores his position as humanist and reformer.)

Tracy, J. (1970) *The Politics of Erasmus: A Pacifist Intellectual and His Political Milieu*, Toronto, Ont.: University of Toronto Press. (On Erasmus' political thought.)

—— (1972) *Erasmus: The Growth of a Mind*, Geneva: Droz. (An incisive study of Erasmus' thought.)

—— (1996) *Erasmus of the Low Countries*, Berkeley, CA: University of California Press. (An intellectual biography situating Erasmus in his political and cultural milieu; extensive bibliography.)

* Woodward, W.H. (1904) *Desiderius Erasmus: Concerning the Aim and Method of Education*; repr. New York: Columbia University Press, 1964. (Most recent reprint of a work first published in 1904; this remains the most comprehensive study of Erasmus' educational philosophy. Referred to in §5.)

ERIKA RUMMEL

ERETRIAN SCHOOL
see SOCRATIC SCHOOLS

ERIUGENA, JOHANNES SCOTTUS (*c.800–c.877*)

Johannes Scottus Eriugena is the most important philosopher writing in Latin between Boethius and Anselm. A Christian Neoplatonist, he developed a unique synthesis between the Neoplatonic traditions of Pseudo-Dionysius and Augustine. Eriugena knew Greek, which was highly unusual in the West at that time, and his translations of Dionysius and other Greek authors provided access to a theological tradition hitherto unknown in the Latin West. From these sources, Eriugena produced an original cosmology with Nature as the first principle. Nature, the totality of all things that are and are not, includes both God and creation, and has four divisions: nature which creates and is not created, nature which creates and is created, nature which is created and does not create, and nature which is neither created nor creates. These divisions participate in the cosmic procession of creatures from God and in their return to God. As everything takes place within Nature, God is present in all four divisions. Eriugena influenced twelfth-century Neoplatonists but was condemned in the thirteenth century for teaching the identity of God and creation.

1 **Life and writings**
2 **Sources**
3 **The divisions of nature**
4 **Influence and significance**

1 Life and writings

Little is known about Eriugena's life. His exact place and date of birth are unknown, but contemporary sources refer to him as *scottus*, meaning 'Irish', and he signed one of his manuscripts with the pleonasm 'Eriugena' (Irish born). No evidence of his education survives. Johannes joined the court of Charles the Bald, possibly in the 840s, and achieved recognition as a liberal arts master. Two partial commentaries on *De nuptiis Philologiae et Mercurii* (The Marriage of Philology and Mercury), the liberal arts handbook of the late Latin author Martianus Capella, survive from Eriugena's period as royal master (see ENCY-CLOPEDISTS, MEDIEVAL §4).

Eriugena was commissioned to refute a treatise by a Saxon monk, Gottschalk, who interpreted AUGUS-TINE as teaching a twofold predestination: of the elect and of the damned. Eriugena's reponse, *De divina praedestinatione* (On Divine Predestination), denied predestination by defending God's transcendence and goodness. God, being perfectly good, wants all humans to be saved. Humans, however, damn themselves through their own free choices. God, who is outside time, cannot be said to '*fore*-know' or to '*pre*-destine', terms which involve temporal predicates. Hence God does not predestine souls to damnation (see ETERNITY). Due to a perceived overemphasis on human free-will in the salvific process, Eriugena was accused of Pelagianism (the heresy that human beings can be saved through their own resources rather than by divine grace) (see PELAGIANISM), and *De divina praedestinatione* was condemned in France at the councils of Valence (855) and Langres (859). While purporting merely to interpret Augustinian texts, this early treatise is philosophically significant for its rationalistic, dialectical analysis of key theological concepts.

Despite the condemnations of *De divina praedestinatione*, Eriugena continued to have the patronage of Charles the Bald, who invited him to translate the writings of Dionysius the Areopagite, a mysterious Christian Neoplatonist, possibly of the sixth century, who imitated PROCLUS and purported to be Dionysius, the first convert of St Paul at Athens (see PSEUDO-DIONYSIUS). This author had been wrongly identified with St Denis, patron saint of France. For Dionysius, it is more true to say 'God is not' than 'God is', since God is 'above all the things that are and are not'. Eriugena adopted Dionysius' affirmative and negative theology, according to which denials concerning God are 'more true', 'better', 'more apt', than affirmations.

Eriugena's major dialogue, *Periphyseon* or *De divisione naturae* (On the Division of Nature) was completed around 867. He also wrote a commentary on Dionysius' *Celestial Hierarchy* (*Expositiones in hierarchiam coelestem*) and on Maximus' *Ambigua*. A fragmentary commentary on the Gospel of St. John and a sermon, *Homilia in Johannem* (Homily on the Prologue to St John's Gospel), were also written probably in the late 860s or 870s. A number of poems also survive. It is probable that Eriugena died sometime around 877; an apocryphal tale, dating from the twelfth century, records that he was stabbed to death by his students.

2 Sources

Eriugena had no direct knowledge of PLOTINUS, PORPHYRY or Proclus. He appears to have known Plato's *Timaeus* in Calcidius' translation (see PLATO). He knew the Pseudo-Augustinian paraphrase of Aristotle's *Categories*, Rufinus's Latin translation of Origen's *De principiis* (On First Principles), and Boethius' trinitarian tracts and *De consolatione philosophiae* (Consolation of Philosophy) (see BOETHIUS, A.M.S.; ORIGEN). His chief authorities were Augustine, Ambrose, Hilary of Poitiers and Jerome, among the Latin Fathers, but he more often expresses a preference for Eastern Church Fathers, in particular Dionysius and the Cappadocians, Basil, Gregory of Nazianzus and Gregory of Nyssa, whose *De hominis opificio* (The Creation of Man) he translated under the title of *De imagine* (On the Image of Good). He also translated Maximus Confessor's *Ambigua* (Difficult Questions of Interpretation [in Pseudo-Dionysius]) and *Quaestiones ad Thalassium* (Questions to Thalassius) and he may have translated Epiphanius's *Anchoratus (De fide)* (The Hermit State (On Faith)) (see PATRISTIC PHILOSOPHY).

Given the available resources, Eriugena was exceptionally learned, but his genius lay in being able to bring all these 'authorities' together in a new cosmological framework. Eriugena enthusiastically incorporated many Greek Christian theological concepts: God, the One, creates by self-emanation; creation is a timeless event and hence ongoing and always contemporary; human nature is originally a Platonic Idea in the mind of God. Humans fail to understand their true nature as image of God in God because they are distracted by created, temporal images (*phantasiai*), leading to a fall into the spatio-temporal realm of sense. However, through intellectual contemplation (*theoria*) and divine illumination (which is the divine self-manifestation, *theophania*), humans may achieve unification (*henosis*) with God, deification (theosis). God became man so that humans can become God (see PLATONISM, EARLY AND MIDDLE).

3 The divisions of nature

The *Periphyseon*, or *De divisione naturae* (On the Division of Nature), a long dialogue in five books between an anonymous teacher and his student, is Eriugena's major philosophical treatise. It opens with an all-encompassing definition of its subject matter. Nature is the general term 'for all things that are and all things that are not' (CXXII I.441a), including both God and creation. The first principle of nature is God, 'the cause of all things that are and that are not' (I.442b). Nature is divided into four 'species', echoing similar divisions in Augustine and MARIUS VICTORINUS: first, that which creates and is not created (that is, God); second, that which creates and is created (that is, Primary Causes or Ideas); third, that which is created and does not create (that is, Temporal Effects, created things); and fourth, that which is neither created nor creates (that is, non-being or nothingness).

Eriugena proceeds to list five ways (*quinque modi*) in which things may be said to be and not to be. According to the first mode, things accessible to the senses and the intellect are said to be, whereas those which – through their excellence – transcend our faculties are said not to be. According to this classification, God is said not to be; he is 'nothingness through excellence' (*nihil per excellentiam*). The second mode of being and non-being is based on the 'orders and differences of created natures', whereby if one level of nature is said to be, those orders above or below it are said not to be. According to this mode, to affirm 'man' is to negate 'angel' and vice versa. This mode invokes the medieval hierarchy of being and at the same time subverts it by relativising the notion of being: only one level of the hierarchy can at any time be said to be. The third mode asserts that *actual* things are, whereas *potential* things still caught up 'in the secret recesses of nature' are not. The fourth mode says that things which the intellect contemplates truly are, whereas material things caught up in generation do not truly exist. The fifth mode says that humans sanctified by grace are, whereas sinful humans are not.

Eriugena's discussion of being and non-being is subject to a dialectic of affirmation and negation. Being and non-being, then, are correlative categories; something may be said to be under one mode and not to be under another mode. These modes further must be taken into account when assessing Eriugena's metaphysical statements. Thus when Eriugena calls God 'nothing,' he means that God transcends all created being. Matter is called 'nothing through privation' (*nihil per privationem*), and created things are called 'nothing' because they do not contain in themselves their principles of subsistence (see BEING).

Periphyseon Book I examines the first division, God. The Aristotelian categories do not properly apply to God, who is not literally (*proprie*) substance or essence, does not possess quantity or quality, has no relations and is not in place and time. God transcends all. His 'being' is beyond being. God is a 'nothingness' whose real essence is unknown to all created beings, including the angels. Indeed, God's nature is unknown even to himself, since he is the 'infinity of infinities' and hence beyond all comprehension and circumscription. God does not know evil, and, in a real sense, God may be said not to know anything (see GOD, CONCEPTS OF).

However, for Eriugena, God also creates himself. He manifests himself in theophanies. This self-creation is God's self-manifestation and also the expression of the Word and the creation of all other things, since all things are contained in the Word. The Word enfolds in itself the Ideas or Primary Causes of all things. God is 'all in all'. All things are in God: '. . . the Creative nature permits nothing outside itself because outside it nothing can be, yet everything which it has created and creates it contains within itself, but in such a way that it itself is other, because it is superessential, than what it creates within itself' (III.675c). God's transcendent otherness above creatures is precisely that which allows creatures to be within God and yet other than God. Eriugena stresses both the divine transcendence and immanence in creation, which is at the same time the immanence of creatures within God (see CREATION AND CONSERVATION, RELIGIOUS DOCTRINE OF).

God and the creature are one and the same: 'It follows that we ought not to understand God and the creature as two things distinct from one another, but as one and the same. For both the creature, by subsisting, is in God; and God, by manifesting himself, in a marvellous and ineffable manner creates himself in the creature' (III.678c). Eriugena's assertion that God is the 'form of all things' (forma omnium) led to the accusation of heresy, an accusation which fixates on one side only of Eriugena's dialectical reasoning. Although Eriugena asserts the identity of God and creation, he explicitly rejects the view that God is the 'genus' or 'whole' of which the creatures are 'species' or 'parts'. Only metaphorically (*metaforice, translative*) can it be said that God is a 'genus' or a 'whole'. The immanence of God in creation is balanced by God's transcendence above all things. God is both form of all things and without form.

Periphyseon Book II discusses the Primary Causes located in the mind of God. This doctrine combines the Platonic theory of Forms, Dionysius's discussion of the divine names and the Stoic–Augustinian notion of eternal reasons. The number of causes is infinite and none has priority over the other; for example, Being is not prior to Goodness, or vice versa. Each is a divine theophany. The very nature of these Causes is to flow out from themselves, bringing about their Effects. This outflowing (*exitus*) creates the whole universe from the highest genus to the lowest species. In this causal procession, like produces like; incorporeal causes produce incorporeal effects (see CAUSATION). All created things are essentially incorporeal, immaterial, intellectual and eternal. Place and time are definitions which locate things, and since definitions are in the mind, then place and time are also in the mind. The sensible, corporeal spatio-temporal appearance of things is produced by the qualities or 'circumstances' of place, time, position and so on, which surround the incorporeal essence. The whole spatio-temporal world and our corporeal bodies are a consequence of the Fall, an emanation of the mind.

Book III discusses the nature of creation from nothing (*ex nihilo*). 'Nothing' has two meanings. The lowest rung in the hierarchy of being, unformed matter, is 'almost nothing' (*prope nihil*), 'nothingness through privation' (*nihil per privationem*). In contrast, God is non-being through excellence. Creation from nothing cannot mean creation from a principle outside God, since there is nothing outside God. *Ex nihilo* creation then means 'out of God's superabundant nothingness'. God creates out of himself and all creation remains within him.

Books IV and V discuss the return (*reditus*) of all things to God. Corporeal things will return to their incorporeal causes, the temporal to the eternal. The human mind will achieve reunification with the divine, and then the corporeal, temporal and material world will become essentially incorporeal, timeless and intellectual. Human nature will return to its Idea in the mind of God. This perfect human nature is paradise. There is a general return of all things to God. Humans who refuse to let go of the 'circumstances' remain trapped in their own phantasies, and this constitutes hell. The elect achieve a special deification whereby they will merge with God completely, as lights blend into the one light. Neither hell or heaven are localized; for Eriugena, they are intellectual states.

Eriugena's anthropology has been the focus of much philosophical interest in the twentieth century. For Eriugena, 'rational animal' does not adequately define human nature, nor is humanity a microcosm: humanity is an Idea eternally made in the mind of God. Perfect human nature is omniscient and omnipotent. Human nature is open to infinite possibility and perfectibility (see PERFECTIONISM).

4 Influence and significance

Eriugena had immediate influence in France, notably at the schools of Laon, Auxerre and Corbie. His translations of Dionysius were widely used into the thirteenth century. His *Vox spiritualis* (The Spiritual Voice) or *Homilia in Johannem* (often attributed to Origen) was widely read in the Middle Ages. The *Periphyseon* was popular in the twelfth century especially in the paraphrase of Honorius Augustodunensis; HUGH OF ST VICTOR, Alanus of Lille, Suger of St Denis and William of Malmesbury were all influenced by Eriugena. In the thirteenth century, the *Periphyseon* was associated with the writings of DAVID OF DINANT and Amaury of Bène, two theologians at the University of Paris, and was condemned with them in 1210 and 1225. According to Thomas Aquinas, Amaury of Bène was condemned for saying that God is the formal principle of all things, an accusation of pantheism, which recalled Eriugena's statement that God is the 'form of all things' (*forma omnium*). In the later Middle Ages both MEISTER ECKHART of Hochheim and NICHOLAS OF CUSA were sympathetic to Eriugena and familiar with his *Periphyseon*. Interest in Eriugena was revived by Thomas Gale's edition of *De divisione naturae* (1681). Hegel and his followers saw Eriugena as the father of German idealism (see GERMAN IDEALISM). Critical editions of his major works are only now being produced.

Eriugena is an original philosopher who articulates the relation between God and creation in a manner which preserves both divine transcendence and omnipresence. His theory of human nature is rationalist and intellectualist. His theory of place and time as defining structures of the mind anticipates Kant, and his dialectical reasoning prefigures Hegel. Eriugena is a mystic who emphasises the unity of human nature with God.

See also: AUGUSTINIANISM; CAROLINGIAN RENAISSANCE; PLATONISM, MEDIEVAL

List of works

Eriugena, Johannes Scottus (*c*.800–*c*.877) *Complete Works*, ed. H.-J. Floss, *Johannis Scoti Opera quae supersunt Omnia*, Patrologia Latina 122, Paris: 1853. (The complete edition of Eriugena's works in Latin.)

—— (*c*.840–60) *Iohannis Scotti Annotationes in Marcianum*, (Commentary on Martianus Capella's *The Marriage of Philology and Mercury*), ed. C. Lutz, Cambridge, MA: Medieval Academy of America, 1939. (Edition of the Latin text of one of Eriugena's commentaries on Martianus Capella's *The Marriage of Philology and Mercury*.)

—— (*c*.851) *De divina praedestinatione* (On Divine Predestination), ed. G. Madec, *Iohannis Scotti de divina praedestinatione*, Corpus Christianorum, Series Latina 50, Turnhout: Brepols, 1978. (Critical edition of the Latin text of Eriugena's *On Divine Predestination*.)

—— (*c*.865–70) *Expositiones in Ierarchiam coelestem* (Commentaries on Pseudo-Dionysius' *Celestial Hierarchy*), ed. J. Barbet, *Iohannis Scoti Eriugenae Expositiones in Ierarchiam coelestem*, Turnhout: Brepols, 1975. (The critical Latin edition of Eriugena's Commentary on the *De coelesti hierarchia* of Pseudo-Dionysius.)

—— (*c*.865–70) *Commentarius in Evangelium Iohannis* (Commentary on the Gospel of John), ed. E. Jeauneau, *Jean Scot: Commentaire sur l'Evangile de Jean*, Sources Chrétiennes 180, Paris: Éditions du Cerf, 1972. (Critical edition of the Latin text with French translation of Eriugena's incomplete Commentary on the Gospel of John.)

—— (*c*.865–70) *Homilia in Johannem* (Homily on the Prologue to the Gospel of St John), ed. E. Jeauneau, *Jean Scot: L'Homélie sur le Prologue de Jean*, Sources Chrétiennes 151, Paris: Éditions du Cerf, 1969. (Critical edition of the Latin text with French translation of Eriugena's homily on the Prologue to St. John's Gospel.)

—— (*c*.860–64) *Maximi Confessoris Ambigua ad Iohannem iuxta Iohannis Scotti Eriugenae latinam interpretationem* (Commentary on Maximus' *Ambigua*), ed. E. Jeauneau, Turnout: Brepols, Louvain: Leuven University Press, 1988. (Critical edition of the Latin text of Eriugena's translation of Maximus.)

—— (*c*.867) *Periphyseon, or De divisione naturae* (On the Division of Nature), ed. I.-P. Sheldon-Williams, *Johannis Scotti Eriugenae Periphyseon*, Dublin: Institute for Advanced Studies, 1968–95, 4 vols. (Critical edition of the Latin text of the first four books of Eriugena's *De divisione naturae*, together with English translation and notes. It should be noted that vol. 4 is edited by E. Jeauneau, and a fifth volume is in preparation also under the editorship of E. Jeauneau. The indispensable English translation of the complete text can also be found in I.-P. Sheldon-Williams and J.J. O'Meara, *Eriugena: Periphyseon* (The Division of Nature), Montreal and Paris: Bellarmin, 1987. A very useful abridged English translation of major sections of the work is M. Uhlfelder and J. Potter (1976) *John the Scot. Periphyseon. On the Division of Nature*, Indianapolis: Bobbs-Merrill.)

References and further reading

Brennan, M. (1977) 'A Bibliography of Publications in the Field of Eriugena Studies 1800–1975', *Studi Medievali* ser. 3a, 28: 401–47. (Lists all books and articles which treat aspects of Eriugena's work.)

—— (1986) 'Materials for the Biography of Johannes Scottus Eriugena', *Studi Medievali* ser. 3a, 27: 413–60. (Latin extracts and English translations of all the texts which give biographical information on Eriugena.)

—— (1989) *A Guide to Eriugenian Studies: A Survey of Publications 1930–87*, Paris: Éditions du Cerf. (Contains English-language summaries of all the major secondary literature on Eriugena published in the twentieth century.)

Cappuyns, M. (1933) *Jean Scot Erigène: sa vie, son oeuvre, sa pensée* (Johannes Scottus Eriugena: His Life, Works and Thought), Louvain: Abbaye de Mont Cesar. (The standard twentieth-century study on Eriugena.)

Gersh, S. (1978) *From Iamblichus to Eriugena*, Leiden: Brill. (A study of Eriugena in the context of late Greek Neoplatonism.)

Marenbon, J. (1981) *From the Circle of Alcuin to the School of Auxerre: Logic, Theology and Philosophy in the Early Middle Ages*, Cambridge: Cambridge University Press. (A study of Eriugena in the context of Latin philosophy of the early Middle Ages.)

Moran, D. (1989) *The Philosophy of John Scottus Eriugena: A Study of Idealism in the Middle Ages*, Cambridge: Cambridge University Press. (Philosophical interpretation of Eriugena which focuses on his negative dialectics and anthropology as a key to understanding his idealist metaphysics.)

—— (1990) 'Pantheism from John Scottus Eriugena to Nicholas of Cusa', *American Catholic Philosophical Quarterly* 64 (1): 131–52. (A study of the accusation of pantheism levelled against Eriugena and Nicholas of Cusa.)

—— (1992a) 'Time, Space and Matter in the *Periphyseon*: an Examination of Eriugena's Understanding of the Physical World', in F. O'Rourke (ed.) *At the Heart of the Real*, Dublin: Irish Academic Press. (A study of Eriugena's account of the spatio-temporal world.)

—— (1992b) 'Origen and Eriugena: Aspects of Christian Gnosis', in T. Finan and V. Twomey (eds) *The Relationship Between Neoplatonism and Christianity*, Dublin: Four Courts Press. (Shows Eriugena's debt to Origen's Platonism in the *On First Principles*.)

O'Meara, J.J. (1988) *Eriugena*, Oxford: Clarendon Press. (Contains a very useful summary of

Eriugena's *On the Division of Nature* together with a translation of some poems.)

Roques, R. (1975) *Libres sentiers vers l'érigénisme* (Free-Wheeling Paths Towards Eriugenian Thought), Rome: Edizioni dell'Ateneo. (A collection of Rene Roques's scholarly articles in French on Eriugena.)

Sheldon-Williams, I.-P. (1970) 'The Greek Platonist Tradition from the Cappadocians to Maximus and Eriugena', in A.H. Armstrong (ed.) *The Cambridge History of Later Greek and Early Medieval Thought*, Cambridge: Cambridge University Press. (Contains Sheldon-Williams' masterly account of the relation between Eriugena and the Greek Christian Platonist tradition.)

DERMOT MORAN

EROTIC ART

Erotic art is art with a sexual content, which may be more or less overt. The presence of sexual content, however, is not sufficient for a work of art to be considered erotic. Although there is more than one sense in which a work can be said to be erotic, an erotic work of art must aim at and to some extent succeed in evoking sexual thoughts, feeling or desires in the spectator, in virtue of the nature of the sexual scene it represents and the manner in which it represents it. This aim, definitive of erotic art, may be a work's principal aim, but need not be. Erotic art often tends to express the artist's interest in and attitude towards sexuality; and whether or not it does, seeing it as expressing the artist's sexuality is likely to contribute towards the spectator's sexual arousal. An erotic work of art has an intended audience of a more or less specific kind, most frequently men. Erotic art is distinguished from pornography in at least two ways. First, pornography lacks any artistic intent. Second, its main aim is not only to stimulate the spectator sexually but to degrade, dominate and depersonalize its subject, usually women. This article is restricted in scope in at least two ways. First, it concerns exclusively the visual arts. Second, its focus is Western art, and primarily art from the Renaissance onwards.

1 Main questions

The chief philosophical questions in the aesthetics of erotic art are: (1) What is the distinction, within art, between erotic and non-erotic art, and how sharp are the boundaries of this category? (2) What are the ideological implications, if any, of the different forms and manners of erotic art, and what, in particular, is the distinction between erotic art and pornography? (3) How can erotic art in fact be art, or something properly eliciting an aesthetic response that is traditionally characterized as disinterested, when it is also aimed at provoking sexual desire, the very paradigm of an interested reaction? (4) In what ways might the criteria for assessing erotic art differ from those appropriate to other sorts of art, and how does the degree of eroticism of erotic art connect, if at all, to its value or worth as art? This entry will be devoted almost exclusively to (1) and (2).

2 The concept of erotic art

A good proportion of the work of many great visual artists – Rubens, Ingres, Delacroix, Degas, Rodin, Gauguin, Matisse, Magritte, Munch, Klimt, Picasso, Modigliani – is unquestionably erotic. But what is it, precisely, for art to be erotic? It seems that, at a minimum, it must have sexual content. Though sexual content may be either overt or covert, let us first consider art with overt sexual content. Typically, this takes the form of depictions of unclothed or semi-clothed human beings, alone or accompanied, at rest or performing actions of a sexual nature. Yet for art to be accounted erotic, it must do more than represent the naked human body or otherwise make reference to sexual matters: not all art concerned in some way with sexuality is automatically erotic. Anatomical sketches of genitalia, a realistic study of a gynaecologist's examining room, or a modern comic strip featuring pneumatic bimbos, are not erotic, despite the sexual content they include. Rather, erotic art is art that treats its sexual content in a particular way or projects a certain attitude towards it. Erotic art is art aimed at arousing sexual interest, at evoking sexual thoughts, feelings or desires in viewers, in virtue of what it depicts and how it is depicted, and which achieves some measure of success in doing so. The intent to awaken and reward sexual interest through what is depicted can be taken as criterial of at least central cases of erotic art. The erotic work of art does more than refer to or acknowledge human sexuality; rather, it expresses an involved attitude towards it, whether of fascination, obsession or delectation, and in addition invites the viewer to engage their imagination along similar lines.

Erotic art typically aims not only to activate the viewer's sexuality but to reflect that of the artist. That is to say, erotic works usually embody a perspective on what is depicted that suggests sexual interest on the maker's part. Furthermore, the sense of sharing in what at least appears to have been sexually stimulating to the artist often plays a causal role in the viewer's own stimulation. It is worth emphasizing that the sexual response occasioned by erotic art occurs largely on the plane of imagination, consisting primarily of thoughts, images and feelings, and rarely goes as far as full physiological arousal; the upshot of engagement with erotic art is imagined desire as often as it is real desire.

As suggested above, the term 'erotic art', in its primary usage, covers art that is aimed at stimulating sexual thoughts and feelings in its target audience, and which at least minimally succeeds. But this gives way to two secondary usages, according to which fulfilling either the intentional condition or the success condition (somewhat modified) independently qualifies a work as erotic. On the first such usage, a work counts as erotic if it is ostensibly aimed at stimulating sexual thoughts and feelings, even when it does not succeed in doing so; on the second, a work counts as erotic if it succeeds noticeably in stimulating viewers sexually, even when it is not intended or even apparently intended to do so. In addition, for works of art that are erotic in the central sense, it is natural to employ 'erotic' as a comparative term as well as a classificatory one. There are works one describes as mildly erotic and those one describes as highly erotic, depending on the degree of sexual involvement they tend to sustain.

Finally, perhaps some works of art reasonably accounted erotic neither aim at nor achieve viewer arousal (in other words, sexual thoughts, feelings or sensations directed towards what is depicted), but are instead erotic merely in virtue of the fact that they facilitate the imagining of erotic states of others, without erotic involvement as such on the viewer's part – without the viewer identifying with or entering into those states, either in reality or in imagination.

3 Instrumentally erotic art and anti-erotic art

With some erotic art, the evocation of erotic feelings is a secondary aim, employed or manipulated by the artist in order to achieve some further end, such as wry humour (for example, Tom Wesslemann's caricatures of pulchritude, in his 'Great American Nudes' series, or Mel Ramos's exaggeratedly voluptuous pin-ups), social commentary (Degas's monotypes of brothel scenes), or psychological disorientation (Magritte's or Dali's recombinant sexual imagery). We might label such art 'instrumentally' erotic art. As a result of these secondary aims, the excitatory tendency of such works may be weakened or even wholly neutralized. In some limiting cases works are in effect *about* erotic art – they comment on or satirically appropriate the conventions and mechanisms of normal erotic art – but without being erotic in the primary sense, that is, without being ultimately aimed at sexually engaging the viewer. Such art may be accounted erotic in virtue of the fact that it leads the viewer to question the presuppositions and consequences, social and otherwise, of erotic responses, without inviting or even permitting viewers to have such responses.

Some other cases of works representing sexual matters without appearing clearly erotic serve to illuminate further the boundaries of the category:

(1) Lysippus' *Aphrodite*, Botticelli's *Birth of Venus*, or Cranach's images of Eve occasion some hesitation if classified as erotic. Probably this is because we take the primary intent of the artist to have been to embody ideals of the human form, male and female, and not to prompt imaginative erotic engagement on the part of viewers of either sex. But this may be ingenuous; at any rate, such a line could not plausibly be extended to exclude from the erotic Donatello's sensuous, almost coquettish *David*.
(2) Picasso's *Demoiselles d'Avignon* occasions hesitation of a different sort. Though the painting presents women who are not only nude but in fact prostitutes, they are depicted in a highly nonrealistic mode, which shortcircuits erotic involvement, as well as drawing attention primarily to the painting's formal and expressive dimension.
(3) Judy Chicago's *The Dinner Party*, an elaborate sculptural installation, uses female genital imagery in a celebratory though arguably not erotic way; its sexual content is of a sort that is purely symbolic, rather than sexually involving.
(4) Though displaying some of the hallmarks of erotic art, Lucian Freud's paintings of naked subjects are not obviously erotic, being more evocative of the *boucherie* than the *boudoir* – an observation even truer of the images of nudes in Francis Bacon's paintings. Philip Pearlstein's superrealist figure paintings or, in another vein, Dubuffet's quasi-paleolithic images of squashed and splayed humanity belong here as well.

These latter artists – Bacon, Freud, Pearlstein, Dubuffet – are not aptly described merely as non-erotic – as is, say, a Corot landscape or Chardin still life – but rather as anti-erotic. Thus in a broader sense they, unlike Chardin or Corot, are erotic after all, that is to say, concerned with sexuality in a way that reflects the sexual interests of the maker and engages those of the viewer, if not in a positive manner. De Kooning's raw and primitivist images of women also come naturally to mind in this connection as well, though the case can be made that those images project a more ambivalent attitude to human sexuality than those of, say, Bacon – an admixture of terror, awe and admiration.

4   Covertly erotic art

It is relatively easy to give plausible examples of erotic works of art that contain no explicit depictions of sexuality or nakedness: Georgia O'Keeffe's landscapes and still lifes, with their oblique evocation of female anatomy; Caravaggio's paintings of Bacchus or St John the Baptist, with their coded references to homosexual experience; or Bernini's marble of St Teresa in spiritual ecstasy, a state readily transposed by the viewer into its profane cousin. The criterion of covert sexual content, however, remains unclear. Depiction of objects recognized as sexually symbolic – umbrellas or fruit, for example – especially when juxtaposed with human subjects, may be a typical indication of such content, but can hardly serve as a general mark. According to some writers, virtually all art has covert sexual content in virtue of being the expression of unconscious wishes or fantasies of a sexual sort. Thus, for Wollheim (1987), Ingres' history paintings, Bellotto's landscapes with buildings, and Poussin's landscapes with water are as substantially imbued with sexuality as Goya's *Naked Maja* or Titian's *Venus of Urbino*.

Even so, it seems that not all covertly sexual art is usefully considered erotic, but only that which is plausibly aimed, if unconsciously, at exciting sexual thoughts or feelings in target viewers, and which succeeds in doing so. In putative cases of covert sexual content, the arousal of the viewer of intended orientation and appropriate background may be just what signals the presence of such content and justifies its ascription.

5   The relationality of erotic art

If a painting is erotic, this is in virtue of its being aimed at and to some extent its eliciting an erotic response *from a certain class of viewer* – the work's intended or target audience. Such classes may be delimited not only by the requirements of sensitivity and background knowledge but also by less acquirable ones of physiological make-up or sexual orientation. Thus, a painting may be erotic in virtue of its being designed to produce an erotic reaction in heterosexual males, elderly homosexual males, young heterosexual girls, homosexual women, or bisexuals

of either sex. There is a fact of the matter, albeit a hazy one, about whether a given painting is erotic, but it is an inherently relational one, whose nature is only fully evident when the group targeted for response is identified. Indeed, according to Nochlin (1988), '.... the very term "erotic art" is understood to imply the specification "erotic-for-men".' Still, once such implicit indexing has been made explicit, it may then be cancelled, so as to recognize art that is erotic relative to other target groups.

6   Social and political aspects of erotic art

Recent writers on erotic art stress the way in which entrenched genres and conventions of representation embody dominant ideas and assumptions about the nature of men and women and their proper relationship. Paintings such as Delacroix's *Death of Sardanapalus*, Gerome's *Oriental Slave Market*, Ingres' *The Turkish Bath* or *Jupiter and Thetis* lend themselves readily to such analysis. For example, Nochlin (1988) speaks of 'the power relations obtaining between men and women inscribed in visual representation' as a focus of her investigations.

Equally frequently noted is the element of voyeurism in erotic art. It is said that the spectator is a voyeur (at least fictionally), and that the work of art often reinforces or echoes this by depicting a spectator who, together with the viewer, regards the erotic object. Furthermore, the implicit or explicit voyeurism of erotic art is sometimes held to reflect the necessary impotence of the artist in respect of the imaginary and thus unattainable individuals depicted within their art.

Finally, the relationship of erotic art and pornography has been much debated. They may be distinguished, arguably, in at least two ways. First, pornography has, perhaps by definition, no significant artistic aspect. That is to say, pornography makes no credible appeal to viewers to consider the mode and means of depiction, as opposed merely to what is depicted; pornography, unlike art of any kind, is wholly transparent in both aim and effect. Second, pornography has, as a central intent and characteristic result, not only the stimulation of sexual feelings or fantasies in viewers, but the degradation, domination and depersonalization of what it depicts, usually women. Courbet's *Sleep*, which shows two beautiful nude women in the arms of Morpheus and each other, or Schiele's 1917 *Reclining Woman*, which presents its subject provocatively spread-legged and scarlet-nippled, perhaps court dismissal as pornography by some of these criteria, but on reflection they remain at a safe distance from it. Though the images in question are starkly arousing, even exploitative, the technique of their construction, the style in which they are rendered, the preceding art history they encapsulate, and the entrée they afford into their makers' psyches, are at least as absorbing as what they flatly represent, and conspire to redeem them as art.

See also: AESTHETIC ATTITUDE; AESTHETICS AND ETHICS; ART AND MORALITY; EMOTION IN RESPONSE TO ART §§1, 2, 6; FEMINIST AESTHETICS §3; FREEDOM OF SPEECH; PORNOGRAPHY

References and further reading

Berger, J. (1972) *Ways of Seeing*, London: Penguin. (A politically sensitive tour of the history of pictorial representation.)

Clark, K. (1956, 1972) *The Nude: A Study in Ideal Form*, Princeton, NJ: Princeton University Press. (The classic study of its subject, which highlighted the distinction between the naked and the nude.)

Devereaux, M. (1990) 'Oppressive Texts, Resisting Readers and the Gendered Spectator: The "New" Aesthetics', *Journal of Aesthetics and Art Criticism* 48: 337–47. (Examines issues of representation in art from a feminist perspective.)

Hess, T. and Nochlin, L. (eds) (1972) *Woman as Sex Object: Studies in Erotic Art, 1730–1970*, New York: Newsweek, Inc. (A collection of essays accompanying an exhibition.)

Kronhausen, P. (1968) *Erotic Art*, Copenhagen: Uniprint A/S. (Introduction to catalogue, briefly addressing the problem of definition or delimitation of the sphere of erotic art.)

Lucie-Smith, E. (1972, 1991) *Sexuality in Western Art*, London: Thames & Hudson. (The standard survey of eroticism in the visual art of the West, focusing on painting.)

Mulvey, L. (1989) *Visual and Other Pleasures*, Bloomington, IN: Indiana University Press. (Includes 'Visual Pleasure and Narrative Cinema', an influential essay in feminist psychoanalytical film theory.)

Nead, L. (1992) *The Female Nude: Art, Obscenity and Sexuality*, London: Routledge. (Politically up-to-date successor to Clark's 1956 study.)

* Nochlin, L. (1988) *Woman, Art, and Power and Other Essays*, New York: Harper & Row. (A collection of essays by the best known American feminist art historian.)

Pollock, G. (1988) *Vision and Difference: Femininity, Feminism and the Histories of Art*, London: Routledge. (A collection of essays by the best known British feminist art historian.)

Rose, J. (1986) *Sexuality in the Field of Vision*, London: Verso. (A study of sexuality in visual art by a prominent art critic.)

Scruton, R. (1986) *Sexual Desire: A Moral Philosophy of the Erotic*, New York: Free Press. (A wide-ranging treatment of the issues, with a valuable appendix on intentionality in general.)

Sircello, G. (1990) *Love and Beauty*, Princeton, NJ: Princeton University Press. (A philosophical study of its subjects, focusing on sexual love.)

Steinberg, L. (1972) 'Picasso's Sleepwatchers', in *Other Criteria*, London: Oxford University Press. (A brilliant essay on the erotic and other content of a particular slice of Picasso's oeuvre.)

* Wollheim, R. (1987) *Painting as an Art*, Princeton, NJ: Princeton University Press. (A masterly survey, with a number of elaborate case studies ascribing sexual content to the work of painters in whom such content is not obvious.)

JERROLD LEVINSON

ERROR AND ILLUSION, INDIAN CONCEPTIONS OF

From the earliest Indian speculation, illusion has been key in the exposition of Indian mysticism. In classical philosophy proper, all schools take positions concerning illusion (sometimes called error) early in their histories, and in some schools successive refinements are achieved over the centuries.

There is a wealth of reflection on illusion from different angles – for example, psychological treatments that differentiate seven, eight or ten types of illusion, identifying causal factors for each variety. Illusion is taken to have ontological and epistemological ramifications brought out in elaborations of one or another metaphysical system.

The sections of classical philosophical texts devoted specifically to illusion generally presuppose or smuggle in criteria of veridical awareness in the midst of causal analyses or systematic explanations of such stock examples as a snake appearing as a rope, a piece of shell appearing as silver, two moons, a 'red' crystal with a red flower behind it, a mirage, the 'blue' of the sky, and dreams. Arguments in support of a criterion, or set of criteria, of veridicality do appear, however. How we understand (1) what counts as a veridical and a nonveridical experience and (2) why individual cases of illusion occur are distinct issues, but positions taken on the former determine important parts of conceptions about why illusions occur. A peculiar stylistic feature of the later and more refined philosophic treatments is a polemical ordering, where a first view's inadequacy is shown to lead to a second view whose inadequacy, demonstrated in turn, leads on to a better theory, and so on, until we reach the right view, which is thus established by a sequence of arguments.

1 Illusion in Indian metaphysical systems
2 Criteria of veridicality
3 A polemical survey of conceptions

1 Illusion in Indian metaphysical systems

In proclaiming the supreme value of a mystical experience, both Upaniṣadic (*c.*800 BC and on) and Buddhist texts (*c.*300 BC and on) put illusion to use as an analogy. This is most dramatically exemplified in the epithet *buddha*, which in Sanskrit is the past passive participle of the common verb for 'to awaken': thus 'the Awakened', implying that those who do not have the *nirvāṇa* experience need to awaken from their all too unpleasant dreams to a blissful reality (see NIRVĀṆA). Similarly, in the Advaita Vedānta philosophy, which is one of two or three major classical systematizations of the thought of the early Upaniṣads, an illusion analogy is central to a teaching of an experience of Brahman, the Absolute and One, as supremely valuable (see BRAHMAN).

It is worth dwelling on illusion within the Advaita system. The use of illusion as a metaphor for mysticism is generalized to a metaphysical position: as the illusory snake is to the real rope, so the manifest universe, in its diversity, is to Brahman, the supreme reality, who is One and Nondual. Later Advaitins bring out the tension between diverse appearances and Brahman's unity. The great eighth-century philosopher ŚAṄKARA (§2) is more concerned with defending an understanding of mystical awareness of Brahman: like the experience of a rope sublating a snake appearance, Brahman-awareness sublates all other modes of experience.

Śaṅkara uses the term *adhyāsa*, commonly translated 'superimposition', to indicate the relation of the world to Brahman. But that is from our point of view. Strictly speaking, there is no relation of Brahman *to* the world (no two-way street), since (as maintained by the early interpreter Padmapāda), the snake simply does not exist. On our side, the world, like the snake, does of course appear. Consonantly, Advaitins say (again from 'our side', from the perspective of spiritual ignorance) that the world has a problematic ontic status 'impossible to explain' (*anirvacanīya*). Matching such a conception is the view (see §3) that the content of an illusory awareness cannot be explained (*anirvacanīya*) as real or not real. In applying to the world the category 'being impossible to explain' (*anirvacanīyatva*), Advaitins generate an

entire metaphysics. The world is not not-real because it appears (unlike the horn of a rabbit), but it should not be said to be real because it is (or is to be) sublated.

Illusion likewise plays a central role in Buddhist philosophy, both with the Mādhyamika of Nāgārjuna (*c.*150–200 CE) and his followers, and the Yogācāra of Vasubandhu (*c.*400), Dignāga (b. *circa* 480), Dharmakīrti (*c.*600–60) and company (see BUDDHISM, MĀDHYAMIKA: INDIA AND TIBET; BUDDHISM, YOGĀCĀRA SCHOOL OF). NĀGĀRJUNA says that his seeming to maintain positive philosophical positions in spite of his proclamation that everything is empty is to be understood as analogous to the unreal words of an imaginary, magical man. 'Everything is empty' is no exception to itself, since that statement too is empty, like statements in an illusion.

Nāgārjuna's appeal to this possibility seems integral to his entire outlook, but just what that outlook is (must a sceptic have an outlook?) is controversial among modern interpreters, as indeed it was in classical debates. A more straightforwardly theoretical approach to illusion is made by VASUBANDHU and his school. Though we may suspect peculiarly Buddhist motivations having to do with defending the possibility of *nirvāṇa* experience, the great Yogācārin launches a project known in the West from Cartesian epistemology – or from what is called the argument from illusion for phenomenalism, and a perceptual core common to illusion and veridical experience (see PERCEPTION, EPISTEMIC ISSUES IN §5). Vasubandhu embraces a phenomenalism of atomic awareness-events, events of colour, sound, feeling, and so on, arguing that these are what we directly experience, as is proved by illusion. There must be a phenomenal core common to both veridical and illusory awareness since illusions do occur that are indistinguishable from veridical experiences, at least at the time of their occurrence.

In subsequent philosophic discussion both within Buddhist traditions and outside, the term 'error' (Sanskrit, *bhrama*, *bhrānti*) is used to refer to perceptual illusion in a neutral, non-question-begging fashion. Usually the term is not used to refer to other types of cognitive failure, such as false claims or faulty logic. However, on some views – notably taken by some Yogācārins as well as proponents of an influential Mīmāṃsaka stance (to be explained) – the error in what is ordinarily taken to be perceptual illusion is attributed to nonexperiential factors. There is no nonveridical experience according to these views. Thus the explananda targeted by these theories are patterns of everyday speech and behaviour where we commonly take cases of (experiential) error, or illusion, to occur.

Later Yogācārins view illusion pragmatically, but Dignāga, an important theorist standing about midway in the history of the school, sees error as a matter of incorrect interpretation, with no illusion on the level of experience itself. Although he claims that his epistemological positions are independent of such considerations as whether things known are viewed as 'external' or (as Buddhists are wont to say) 'Void', it seems plausible that the metaphysics of atomic awareness-events contributed to his interpretationalist stance – for how with a phenomenal core seen as reality could there be illusion in experience?

Philosophers belonging to Indian realist schools are called upon to defend their views against objections based on the occurrence of illusions. The great names from the Mīmāṃsā and the Nyāya-Vaiśeṣika traditions forge positions on illusion in consonance with a realism about the objects revealed by veridical experiences – and, surprisingly, the objects of nonveridical experiences.

2 Criteria of veridicality

The question of the nature of veridicality – what veridicality is – connects with the question of how it is known, that is, how an awareness is known to be veridical. A centrepiece of Nyāya-Vaiśeṣika realism (henceforth, for convenience, simply 'Nyāya') is what may be called a correspondence view: facts are what they are independently of consciousness (about which there are other facts), and what it is for an awareness to be veridical is for it to reveal an object, or, more precisely, an objective complex. The simplest veridical awareness makes known an objective complex: 'a is F' just in case F (a qualifier) qualifies a (the qualificandum) – or, to suggest more explicitly the tie to Nyāya's ontology, just in case a has F-hood. In other words, an awareness' propositional content (Fa) must reflect what is in fact (a's being F) if the awareness is veridical, according to Nyāya. An awareness with the content Fa is erroneous just in case a is not qualified by F. The world contains both a and F even, as will be explained, in cases of error. Finally, to be accurate, the fourteenth century philosopher GAṄGEŚA (§2), a leader of the New Nyāya school, and others as well, criticize characterizations of veridicality as simply correspondence with fact (yāthārthya), demanding more precise formulations. But a correspondence view may be said to be the spirit of Nyāya throughout its two-millennia history (see NYĀYA-VAIŚEṢIKA §6).

The question of the marks whereby such a match is itself discernible is not an easy one for the realist, the Naiyāyika or any other. Before reviewing Nyāya's proposals, let us look at two other views about what

veridicality is, in Mīmāṃsā – specifically, the Prābhākara branch – and in Yogācāra.

Contrasting with the Nyāya position is Mīmāṃsā, a realist school that assumes an unexpected stance (see MĪMĀṂSĀ §2). Veridicality is identified with awareness itself: all awarenesses are veridical. The Buddhist argument from illusion to find a phenomenal core is met head on by the (Prābhākara) Mīmāṃsaka: the nature of all awareness is to reveal objects in a person's immediate environment. The question of how an awareness is known to be veridical is understood as asking how an awareness, our own awareness, is known to have occurred. (The Prābhākara answer is, like that of the Yogācāra Buddhist, that every awareness is self-aware, while also – a departure from the Buddhist position – making the self known: thus something about the world, the awareness itself and the cognizer are all made known by a single awareness.) Why take it as given, the Prābhākara asks, that any awareness misrepresents the world? It is natural for awareness to present things as they are, and so another source of error should be assumed. Common speech and other behaviour do of course show that error occurs; this is admitted by all disputants. But no criteria for differentiating the veridical and the nonveridical are needed. Nor need we say what veridicality is, apart from specifying what awareness is and how it is different from other realities.

Coherence, or agreement with other awarenesses, is both the nature of veridicality and the criterion whereby it is discerned, according to the later Yogācāra of DHARMAKĪRTI and others. To be sure, Dharmakīrti proposes that there are pragmatic criteria – whether action based on an (interpreted or proposition-laden) awareness leads to successful results – but since the results are themselves (proposition-laden) awarenesses, on his view, coherence seems to remain the criterion, as it clearly is with earlier members of his school.

Finally, as early as VĀTSYĀYANA (c.350), whose commentary on the Nyāyasūtra is the oldest extant – indeed in the very opening passage of Vātsyāyana's commentary and throughout the history of the school – a pragmatic criterion is proffered as the test of veridicality. Veridical awarenesses are proved so by their fruits; nonveridical awarenesses lead to error in action, preventing us from getting what we want and avoiding things to which we are averse.

Again, what it is for an awareness to be veridical is for it to reveal a fact; but we do not know from the occurrence of an awareness A itself that A is veridical (except in the case of an apperception, where what is known is a preceding awareness). We infer A's veridicality or nonveridicality – if circumstances call it into question – from whether it has proved workable in helping us get what we want and avoid our aversions.

The Nyāya pragmatism does not amount to a hidden coherentism, although to judge from the accounts given of particular types of illusion, coherence considerations are, as one might expect, appealed to. Veridical awarenesses are the results of reliable sources, and are themselves the foundations of warranted statements. If there is reasonable doubt about a statement's truth, then one turns to reliable sources of knowledge, such as perception, to resolve the doubt. According to Nyāya, it may be impossible to tell at the time of occurrence whether an ordinarily presumed veridical perception is in fact veridical, and if there is reasonable doubt about this it is here that the pragmatic criterion comes into play. Thus the epistemological default is a fallibilistic presumption of veridicality, and we are presumed not ordinarily to be called to wonder about error in our awarenesses.

3 A polemical survey of conceptions

An illuminating attempt to refute non-Naiyāyika views of error is made by the modern Nyāya philosopher Ramanuja Tatacharya in his *Pratyakṣatattvacintāmaṇi Vimarśa* (Consideration of the *Tattvacintāmaṇi*'s [Treatment of] Perception; 1992), which is based on the thought of Gaṅgeśa. The polemical ordering of his argument – whereby successive refinements or corrections of a view are shown to be inadequate until the correct one is arrived at – is typical of later classical philosophy.

Tatacharya starts by characterizing the Yogācāra view as *ātma-khyāti* ('illusion is "self-" or "internal" manifestation': *khyāti* means 'perception' or 'manifestation' and is used in a neutral way with respect to all theories considered; *ātma* means 'self', and since there is no self on the Buddhist view the term should be taken as 'internal'). With the error 'This is silver', when the object in front is instead a piece of shell, the Yogācārin holds, says Tatacharya, that the silver form that appears is an internal manifestation and that the correcting cognition 'This is a piece of shell' negates only the 'thisness' of the error. The silver form is uncorrected by the succeeding moment of consciousness (it has simply passed away, though also helping to give rise to the consciousness of a piece of shell, according to Yogācāra psychology). Illusion shows that the silver form has to be internal; 'thisness' with respect to silver cannot be external. Therefore, illusion is an internal manifestation (due, like all occurrences of consciousness, to dispositions, some common to other persons, some not).

However, if this view were correct, Tatacharya

continues, the error would be appropriately verbalized as 'I am silver', not 'This is silver'. Moreover, since it is held that the silver form is no illusion, we should be able to use it in the market. Clearly, the silver, which is the object of the illusion, does not exist, as the correcting cognition, 'Not (this-is-silver)', shows. The right view would then be *asat-khyāti*, 'manifestation of the nonexistent', a view attributable to the Mādhyamika school of Nāgārjuna. How the nonexistent can be the object of a cognition should not be asked, for cognitive objecthood is not to be understood causally, but in its own way; the existent and nonexistent are both within its range. Error is a cognition with a nonexistent object.

However, with reference to the error 'This is silver', the Nyāya philosopher asks whether what is nonexistent is just the silver or also the 'this'. It cannot be the latter, for the deluded person desiring silver reaches out to pick up the piece of shell (the 'this'), and no such action would be taken with respect to something nonexistent. And with regard to the silver, is it nonexistent everywhere or is it simply not at this locus or place? It cannot be the former, for the universally nonexistent does not appear (whereas silver is appearing in the illusion). The right view is that cognition reflects reality (*yāthārthya*); only the existent appears (*sat-khyāti*). Error is not a single cognition, but two cognitions, a perceiving and a remembering, with their distinctness unrecognized; this is *akhyāti*, 'nonmanifestation (of the distinctness between a perception and a memory)', a view attributable to the Prābhākara Mīmāṃsaka. What gets verbalized as 'this' is reflected by a (veridical) perception of an object in the perceiver's immediate environment; what gets verbalized as 'silver' is reflected by a (veridical) memory acquired from previous experience of silver. Due to a causal irregularity – various causal factors influence cognition – the class character of the piece of shell (namely, 'piece-of-shell-hood') is not apprehended, but its similarity to silverhood, along with the causal irregularity, triggers a silverhood memory. (Memories are stored associatively.) The two cognitions get fused, with no awareness of their distinctness. The deluded person thus reaches out to pick up what is presented experientially. The correcting cognition works with respect to the failure to grasp the distinctness. When that failure ceases, the activity based on it ceases. Error is just a matter of activity (including speech-behaviour) that can come to be corrected, not of a cognition's object or content. Neither perceiving nor remembering manifests anything except the real. All cognition reflects reality. Thus is the right view established.

However, from the Nyāya perspective, it is a person

looking to gain silver who moves to pick up the 'this' as indicated by the error 'This is silver', not a person who does not see it *as* silver. That someone simply fails to be aware – from not grasping a distinction between a memory and a perception – that the thing in front is not silver is insufficient to prompt the act of reaching out to pick it up. It must be cognized *as* silver. Therefore, the erroneous cognition is single but, like all verbalizable cognition, complex: what is verbalized as 'this' is the cognition's indicating a qualificandum, a bearer of properties, and what is verbalized as 'silver' is the cognition's predication content, a qualifier that the qualificandum is presented as having. This analysis gives us, finally, the truly right view, *anyathā-khyāti*, 'manifestation (of a qualifier) elsewhere (than where in fact it obtains)'. A causal story is indeed to be told of why a particular illusion occurs, and of how such-and-such a cognition, whose predication content does not qualify the qualificandum cognized, can be generated. Cognition is a complicated process, and the possibilities for something going wrong are numerous, depending on what is cognized, the sense organs, internal dispositions, and other factors.

See also: EPISTEMOLOGY, INDIAN SCHOOLS OF; KNOWLEDGE, INDIAN VIEWS OF; SENSE PERCEPTION, INDIAN VIEWS OF

References and further reading

Gaṅgeśa (first half of 14th century) *Tattvacintāmaṇi*, vol. 1, *pratyakṣa-khaṇḍa*, with the *Prakāśa* commentary by Rucidatta Miśra and a subcommentary by Rāmakṛṣṇādhvarin, ed. N.S.R. Tatacharya, Kendriya Sanskrit Vidypeetha Series 20, Tirupati: Kendriya Sanskrit Vidyapeetha, 1972. (Contains a section on *anyathā-khyāti-vāda*, elaborated in Tatacharya 1992.)

Matilal, B.K. (1986) *Perception: An Essay on Classical Indian Theories of Knowledge*, Oxford: Oxford University Press. (The best philosophical study to appear on issues surrounding perception as understood in classical Indian philosophies; highly readable and strongly recommended.)

Mohanty, J.N. (1966) *Gaṅgeśa's Theory of Truth*, Delhi: Motilal Banarsidass, 1989. (Contains an annotated translation of Gaṅgeśa's reflections on how the veridicality of an awareness is cognized.)

Phillips, S.H. (1995) *Classical Indian Metaphysics: Refutations of Realism and the Emergence of 'New Logic'*, La Salle, IL: Open Court. (Contains an annotated translation of Gaṅgeśa's reflections on how veridicality should be characterized or defined.)

Sinha, J. (1958) *Indian Psychology: Cognition*, Calcutta: Sinha Publishing. (Contains a wealth of information about classical conceptions of illusion; requires in places an understanding of Sanskrit philosophical terminology.)

* Tatacharya, N.S.R. (1992) *Pratyakṣatattvacintāmaṇi Vimarśa: A Comprehensive and Evaluative Study of the Pratyakṣakhaṇḍa of the Tattvacintāmaṇi*, Tirupati: Rastriya Samskrita Vidyapitha. (In Sanskrit; the principal source for §3, which takes one about halfway through Tatacharya's defence of the Nyāya position.)

STEPHEN H. PHILLIPS

ESCHATOLOGY

Eschatology is the study of or doctrine about the end of history or the last things. Eschatology is a branch of Christian theology, and the term still finds its primary home in that context, but it is also used broadly to cover any theory about the end of human life or of the world.

There are many types of eschatological theory. Some of the most important are those of Plato, Vedāntic Hinduism, Karl Marx and Christianity. The contemporary philosopher of religion who makes most use of eschatology in his thinking is doubtless John Hick. There are several issues that are of interest to philosophers in the area of eschatology. Among them are such questions as whether there is good reason to believe that human life and/or history are moving towards a final end; whether personal identity problems are solvable in the eschaton *(the end-state); whether eschatological considerations can help philosophers address other philosophical problems (for example, the problem of evil); whether the very notion of disembodied survival of death is coherent; and how (in Christian theology especially) immortality of the soul and bodily resurrection are related.*

1 Types and varieties of eschatological theory
2 John Hick on eschatology
3 Philosophical issues in eschatology

1 Types and varieties of eschatological theory

An eschatological theory can be either religious (as in Christianity) or secular (as in the classless society anticipated by Marx). But it is important to note that eschatology always presupposes a linear view of history. The common assumption of all eschatology is that human life and/or history are moving in a certain direction, towards a certain end or goal (see

413

HISTORY, PHILOSOPHY OF §§1–2). Accordingly, circular views of history, or even linear views of time with no envisaged afterlife or end-state, have no eschatology.

What we might call a theory of *individual eschatology* presupposes that there is life after death for human beings and deals with their postmortem fate. The three main options for those who affirm an individual eschatology are reincarnation, immortality of the soul, and bodily resurrection (see REINCARNATION; SOUL, NATURE AND IMMORTALITY OF THE; RESURRECTION). What we might call a theory of *cosmic eschatology* deals with the larger issue of the goal or end towards which (so it is claimed) history is moving and with what happens at the end of history or of the world.

PLATO (§13) is an example of a philosopher who argued for an individual eschatology but no cosmic eschatology. It is exceedingly difficult to combine into one coherent theory everything that Plato said in his dialogues about the soul and its life after death. Nevertheless, in both the *Phaedo* and the *Republic* he argued that the human soul, which he took to be the essence of the person, is indestructible and thus immortal. It survives death and faces judgment for its earthly deeds. Since Plato was convinced of the moral governance of the universe, he expected that this judgment would be just, with punishment for evil people and reward for the righteous. He did not dogmatize about the details of the afterlife, offering only 'possible' or mythic explanations. This much can certainly be said about Plato's individual eschatology. However, there seems to be no notion in his writings of history moving towards a goal or end.

Theories of reincarnation, at least those that posit a possible final escape from the cycle of life, death and rebirth, also typically suggest an individual eschatology, but no cosmic eschatology. The Vedāntic school of Hinduism affords an example. Ultimate reality is Brahman; it is pure being or pure consciousness and is beyond all qualities. The phenomenal world is *māyā*, the realm of illusion. *Māyā* is the product of the creative power of Brahman, not through conscious acts of creation, but through Brahman's emitting successive waves or emanations of reality. *Māyā* is unreal in the sense of not being ultimately real, of being temporary and contingent, unlike Brahman. One aspect of *māyā* is the existence of *jīvas*, individual souls that are incarnate as empirical selves. Limitless numbers of *jīvas* have always existed and are born in various bodies, both human and nonhuman. After the death of one body, they are reborn in another, a *jīva*'s station in life being a function of its deeds in previous lives.

Karma is an impersonal law to the effect that *jīvas*

reap in one life what they have sowed in previous lives. The karmic imprint is carried from one incarnation to the next by what is called the subtle body. Western philosophers would call it mental; it is a body in the sense that it is part of the realm of *māyā*. It registers and transmits the moral and spiritual influence of previous lives. Through a series of lives, it is possible for *jīvas* to be purged of ignorance (*avidyā*) and evil, and to attain true self-consciousness, which is consciousness of their own essential oneness with Brahman and of the illusoriness of all differentiation (reality for Vedāntists is non-dual). If *ātman* is the non-empirical self, the eternal and immutable spiritual reality of each *jīva*, then liberation (*mokṣa*) and escape from rebirth are achieved when one realizes that '*ātman* is Brahman'. In other words, an empirical self is an expression of a *jīva*, which is itself ultimately one with *ātman*, which is itself ultimately one with Brahman.

Karl MARX (§12) is an example of a philosopher who argued for a cosmic eschatology but no individual eschatology. Marx believed neither in God nor survival of death, but he did posit an end-state towards which history is irresistibly moving, namely increasing suffering of the workers, increasing contradictions in capitalism, world revolution, the dictatorship of the proletariat, and a final ideal society. In this society there will be common ownership of property and of the means of production; productivity will increase and prosperity will prevail; and there will be no wages, government or class structure.

Like most historical religions, Christianity posits both an individual and a cosmic eschatology. Christian eschatological notions are not easy to summarize, and eschatology is an area of great disagreement among theologians. The idea of personal survival of death arose late in the Hebrew Bible, but the hope of national and spiritual revival on the 'Day of the Lord', when God will judge the wicked, vindicate the righteous and restore the nation of Israel, was ancient. In the first century AD, the Pharisaical party accepted the idea of life after death while the Sadducees did not.

Jesus announced the end of the present age and the arrival of the kingdom of God, and the New Testament writers interpreted his life, death and resurrection as the defeat of all the forces that oppose God's rule. They also held that Jesus' resurrection from the dead is a promise of a general resurrection and of eternal life for those who believe in him. In one sense the kingdom of God arrived with the advent of Jesus; in another sense, the sense in which it arrives publicly and with power, it is postponed until the end-time. Thus Christian eschatology points to the end-time as the period when Jesus will return and the divine redemptive purposes for creation will be fulfilled. There will be a new heaven and a new earth. People will be raised from the dead and judged; the damned will live forever apart from the presence of God in hell, and the blessed will 'see God' in heaven (see HELL; HEAVEN).

2 John Hick on eschatology

Among contemporary philosophers of religion, John Hick has made the most sustained use of eschatology. In his earlier writings he introduced the notion of 'eschatological verification'. In response to critics such as Antony Flew who argued that theological statements like 'God exists' and 'Jesus is the Son of God' are unfalsifiable and thus without cognitive content, Hick argued that the mere possibility that such statements might be verified in some future *eschaton* (one day we might have, for example, an unambiguous experience of 'the reign of Christ in the kingdom of God') renders those statements cognitively meaningful here and now (1957: ch. 7).

Following ORIGEN (§4) and other theologians, Hick also posits an eschatological universalism in which every human person will eventually achieve full consciousness of God and thus salvation or liberation. There is no hell, at least no permanent hell. In *Death and Eternal Life* (1976), Hick argues for a possible afterlife in which this might occur, one involving various lives in different worlds. In the end-state, Hick says, personality is retained but egoicity is transcended. Hick also uses universalism as an important element in his soul-making theodicy. Unless everyone will eventually enter a limitlessly good end-state, he says, the problem of evil cannot be solved. Hick thus holds that there can be no successful theodicy apart from eschatology.

3 Philosophical issues in eschatology

There are many issues of interest to philosophers in eschatology. Four will be briefly noted, and a fifth discussed.

(1) Perhaps the most important issue is the question of whether there is any good reason to believe that human beings will survive death and/or whether history is moving towards a final end. This question obviously cannot be answered apart from larger questions about what sort of world we live in, and whether it can be fully described in entirely naturalistic terms or whether some sort of God or divine reality exists (see GOD, ARGUMENTS FOR THE EXISTENCE OF). As far as individual eschatology is concerned, most philosophers seem to have lost interest in the classic 'proofs' for survival of death, such as those of Plato or KANT (§11). Some look to such empirical or psychological phenomena as near-death experiences, psychical research or purported memories of previous lives. But in general the project of offering philosophical arguments for or against survival of death is not nearly as popular as it once was.

(2) One of the most interesting philosophical issues related to eschatology is that of personal identity in the afterlife, whether the denizens of the afterlife will be identical to the ante-mortem persons they will apparently claim to be. Will the traditional criteria of personal identity (see PERSONAL IDENTITY) suffice to establish that identity? If not, will 'closest continuer' or other notions less robust than identity satisfy the concerns of the religious systems in which most survival theories are embedded?

(3) Another important question is whether eschatological considerations can or should play any role in solving the problem of evil, as Hick insists that they can (see EVIL, PROBLEM OF §4). For Christian theodicists at least, Hick seems right. As the apostle Paul said, 'I consider that the sufferings of this present time are not worth comparing to the glory about to be revealed to us' (Romans 8: 18). Critics will respond that it is question-begging or in some other way unconvincing to 'solve' the problem by appealing to a future outcome that is hoped for but in no way assured. Theodicists like Hick can reply that it is rationally permissible and even essential that they respond to the problem of evil from the perspective of their own beliefs or those of their religious community, which may well include belief in an afterlife and eschatology.

(4) In an often-reprinted article (1953), H.H. Price argued for the coherence of the notion of a purely mental world, thus supporting the possibility of disembodied survival of death. Price posited a world of mental images (visual, auditory, telepathic, and so on) in which souls are aware of each other, live in a coherent 'world' (consisting of mental images rather than physical objects), communicate with each other telepathically, and have dreamlike (rather than bodily) perceptions of their world. According to Price, such a world may have different causal laws from our present world (for example, wish-fulfilment will be powerfully operative), but it will seem to its denizens just as real and even as 'solid' a world as ours does to us.

Some have detected problems in Price's argument. Hick, for example, notes that it is hard to combine Price's insistence on the public, non-solipsistic nature of the world he describes with his notion that the character of the world will be in large part a function of the wishes of its inhabitants (1976: 265–77). If it is a public world, sustained by telepathic contact between different individuals, how can wish-fulfilment be as potent a force in shaping it as Price suggests? Hick may well be correct here in detecting a tension in Price's account, but the problem seems solvable. And if it is solvable, then Price's main point – that disembodied survival of death is logically possible – is correct.

(5) A question relating specifically to Christian eschatology is that of the relationship between immortality of the soul and bodily resurrection. Traditional Christian theories, such as those of Aquinas, combine the two, arguing that after death there is an interim period during which we exist merely as disembodied souls, and that only later, at the end-time, will our bodies be miraculously raised by God and reunited with our souls, thus making us whole and complete persons again.

This picture now faces three quite different sorts of challenge. First, the two theories have been radically separated by the New Testament scholar Oscar Cullmann (1973). He argues that only resurrection is a genuinely Christian notion; immortality is an alien theory imported from Greek philosophy. It played no role in primitive Christian conceptions of the afterlife and ought not to be part of Christian belief today. Second, several contemporary philosophers (such as Antony Flew and Terence Penelhum) argue that the very concept of disembodied existence is either incoherent or deeply problematic. There are, however, other philosophers (such as John Hick and Richard Swinburne) who strongly defend the coherence of the concept. Third, many contemporary liberal Christian theologians (such as Hans Küng) are inclined to dismiss bodily resurrection in favour of a theory (usually only vaguely spelled out) called 'spiritual resurrection'. As with virtually all Christian theologians, their eschatological views presuppose certain views (in this case revisionist ones) of Jesus and of the reliability of the biblical witness to Jesus. They claim that bodily resurrection amounts to a superstitious and unchristian theory of resuscitation; what was raised was not Jesus' body but his person or self. On the other hand, there are contemporary philosophers and theologians who defend more traditional Christian notions of resurrection, both the resurrection of Jesus (for example, William Craig) and the general resurrection (for example, Stephen Davis).

Returning to Cullmann, he is entirely correct in differentiating immortality from resurrection. Immortal souls naturally survive death; for resurrected persons, on the other hand, survival of death occurs only because of a miraculous intervention by God. On the view of souls as naturally immortal, the human body is the intrinsically evil prison-house of the soul; on the view that bodies are resurrected, both body and soul were created good by God, are now equally corrupt due to sin, and are thus equally in need of redemption. On the first theory, death is a friend (at least, as Plato says, to the philosopher) precisely because it means escape from the body; on the second, death is a fearsome enemy that must be defeated.

Still, Cullmann seems too hasty in rejecting any notion of immortality as unchristian. The traditional or Thomistic notion of the bodiless interim state can easily be purged of the problematic aspects that Cullmann correctly sees in Plato's theory. The survival of death of even the soul can be attributed to a gracious and miraculous act of God; it can be affirmed that both body and soul are sinful and must be redeemed; and death can still be seen as an enemy. Furthermore, the traditional notion seems to offer a way of resolving a possible tension in the New Testament concerning the time of entry into eternal life. Pauline thought especially seems committed to the idea that the general resurrection occurs at the end-time (2 Thessalonians 2: 1–15); yet Jesus said to the 'good thief' on the cross, 'Today, you will be with me in paradise' (Luke 23: 43). The solution, then, is that the thief's soul went immediately to paradise, only much later in the end-time to be reunited with his body.

See also: FEMINIST THEOLOGY §2

References and further reading

Aquinas, T. (1259–64) *Summa contra gentiles*, Notre Dame, IN: Notre Dame University Press, 1975, Book IV. (A classic statement of the traditional Christian view of personal eschatology.)

Badham, P. and Badham, L. (1982) *Immortality or Extinction?*, London: Macmillan. (A clear discussion of various options in personal eschatology and an assessment of the relevant evidence for and against survival of death.)

Craig, W.L. (1989) *Assessing the New Testament Evidence for the Historicity of the Resurrection of Jesus*, Lewiston, NY: Edwin Mellen Press. (An energetic defence of the resurrection of Jesus by a philosopher who is also trained in theology.)

* Cullmann, O. (1973) 'Immortality of the Soul or Resurrection of the Dead?', in T. Penelhum (ed.) *Immortality*, Belmont, CA: Wadsworth Publishing Co. (An influential article in twentieth-century Christian eschatology.)

Davis, S.T. (1993) *Risen Indeed: Making Sense of the Resurrection*, Grand Rapids, MI: Eerdmans. (A defence of a fairly traditional notion of the resurrection of Jesus and of the general resurrection.)

Flew, A. (1987) *The Logic of Mortality*, Oxford: Blackwell. (Criticisms of survival-of-death theories.)

* Hick, J. (1957) *Faith and Knowledge*, London: Macmillan, 2nd edn, 1988. (Eschatological verification is explained in Chapter 7.)

—— (1966) *Evil and the God of Love*, New York: Harper & Row. (Although an early work, this book is the fullest statement of Hick's 'soul-making' theodicy. Later writings do not change the argument appreciably.)

—— (1976) *Death and Eternal Life*, New York: Harper & Row. (Part 5 is a clear statement of Hick's eschatological views in the 1970s. Some of them are updated in his later writings.)

Küng, H. (1976) *On Being A Christian*, New York: Doubleday. (A summary of Küng's liberal Catholic theology. Part A, chapter 5 discusses resurrection.)

Marx, K. and Engels, F. (1848) *The Communist Manifesto*, in L.S. Feuer (ed.) *Marx and Engels: Basic Writings on Politics and Philosophy*, Garden City, NY: Doubleday, 1959. (A brief statement of Marxism and of Marx's eschatology.)

Penelhum, T. (1970) *Survival and Disembodied Existence*, New York: Humanities Press. (The author no longer appears to agree with everything that he said in this book, but it is a clear and well-argued critique of the notion of disembodied existence.)

Phillips, D.Z. (1970) *Death and Immortality*, London: Macmillan. (A Wittgensteinian critique of traditional conceptions of immortality.)

* Plato (*c.*428–347 BC) *Phaedo*, in E. Hamilton and H. Cairns (eds) *The Collected Dialogues of Plato*, New York: Pantheon Books, 1961. (Concerned with immortality and the rewards of justice.)

* —— (*c.*428–347 BC) *The Republic*, in E. Hamilton and H. Cairns (eds) *The Collected Dialogues of Plato*, New York: Pantheon Books, 1961. (Book 10 deals with immortality and the rewards of justice.)

* Price, H.H. (1953) 'Survival and the Idea of "Another World"', *Proceedings of the Society for Psychical Research* 50 (182): 1–25. (A classic argument for the coherence of the notion of a purely mental postmortem world.)

Reichenbach, B. (1983) *Is Man The Phoenix? A Study of Immortality*, Washington, DC: University Press of America. (A helpful discussion of immortality and its relation to resurrection.)

—— (1990) *The Law of Karma*, London: Macmillan. (A Western philosopher analyses and criticizes aspects of karma and reincarnation in Hinduism and Buddhism.)

Swinburne, R. (1986) *The Evolution of the Soul*, Oxford: Oxford University Press. (A defence of what the author calls 'soft dualism'.)

STEPHEN T. DAVIS

ESSENCE *see* ESSENTIALISM

ESSENTIALISM

Essentialists maintain that an object's properties are not all on an equal footing: some are 'essential' to it and the rest only 'accidental'. The hard part is to explain what 'essential' means.

The essential properties of a thing are the ones it needs to possess to be the thing it is. But this can be taken in several ways. Traditionally it was held that F is essential to x if and only if to be F is part of 'what x is', as elucidated in the definition of x. Since the 1950s, however, this definitional conception of essence has been losing ground to the modal conception: x is essentially F if and only if necessarily whatever is x has the property F; equivalently, x must be F to exist at all. A further approach conceives the essential properties of x as those which underlie and account for the bulk of its other properties. This entry emphasizes the modal conception of essentiality.

Acceptance of some form of the essential/accidental distinction appears to be implicit in the very practice of metaphysics. For what interests the metaphysician is not just any old feature of a thing, but the properties that make it the thing it is. The essential/accidental distinction helps in other words to demarcate the subject matter of metaphysics. But it also constitutes a part of that subject matter. If objects have certain of their properties in a specially fundamental way, then this is a phenomenon of great metaphysical significance.

1   **Anti-essentialism**
2   **Grades of essential involvement**
3   **Essential epistemology**
4   **Applications of essentialism**
5   **Conceptions of the essential**

1   Anti-essentialism

Essentialists have two basic commitments: to the essential/accidental distinction as such; and to the existence of properties of both types. Accordingly there are two main schools of anti-essentialism. 'Sceptical anti-essentialists' reject the very idea of essential versus accidental, while 'trivializing anti-essentialists' insist that all or nearly all properties fall on the same side of the line.

Sceptics typically argue as follows. Whether x is essentially F is supposed to turn on whether it is necessary that x be F. But this leads to contradictions. Is nine essentially greater than seven? Yes, because nine is seven plus two, and it is necessary that seven plus two exceeds seven. Yet also no, for nine is the number of planets, and it need not have been that the numbers of planets exceeded seven. The only way out is to admit that nothing is essentially F as such but only as described in a certain way. So-called 'essential' properties are really just properties entailed by some currently salient description.

What ought to make us suspicious is that similar worries can be raised about intuitively quite innocent distinctions, such as that between the constant properties of a thing – those that it always possesses – and its temporary ones. While it is always the case that seven plus two exceeds seven, for example, the number of planets was (let us imagine) once six. Described one way, then, nine is constantly greater than seven, while described another it is only temporarily greater than seven.

Here the fallacy seems clear. For the purposes of assessing constancy, 'it is always the case that the D is F' must be read *de re*: 'concerning the object which is in fact the D, it is always F' (see DE RE/DE DICTO). Read *de re*, the objector's claim that at one time the number of planets was six is simply false because nine was never six. Might not a similar response be available to the essentialist? It certainly might, unless the sceptic can convince us that *de re* modal talk is less intelligible than its temporal analogue.

Sceptics have tried, complaining that there is nothing on the modal side to match our well-developed criteria of identity over time (see POSSIBLE WORLDS §I). But since temporal criteria have clear trans-world implications (that a thing can evolve in such-and-such ways shows it to be capable of such-and-such otherworldly careers), the latter cannot be *too* shapeless without dragging the former into similar disrepute. Anyway, few essentialists would grant the sceptic's assumption that without trans-world identity criteria, *de re* modal discourse becomes emptied of content. If anything, content flows in the other direction; to call a counterfactual object identical to x is just to say that its properties are *ipso facto* properties x could have possessed.

Now turn to the trivializer's claim that all, or nearly all, of the properties of a thing are accidental; or else that all, or nearly all, are essential. The second idea seems to be present in Leibniz, who holds that Adam would not have existed had Peter not gone on to deny Christ some thousands of years after his death. (Even today one encounters it in remarks such as 'If the pistol had been equipped with a silencer, a death would have resulted, but not the same death'.) This 'superessentialism' is often backed by a strikingly unconvincing line of argument, namely that the identity of indiscernibles (see IDENTITY) rules out a possible x differing from our actual x in any way. (G.E. Moore's 'External and Internal Relations' (1919) contains a devastating critique.) The first idea of trivialization is far more common.

Not every property can be accidental, because it is sometimes necessary just as a matter of logic that x be F. For every x whatsoever, logic tells us that x is round if round. Since what logic tells us is necessary, 'being round if round' is essential to x. But perhaps the trivializer will try to draw the line at these 'logically essential' properties, counting all other properties accidental.

Such an approach will seem more trivializing than it is if one supposes that a property logically essential to one thing is thereby logically essential to everything. 'Identity with x' is the obvious counter-example; it is logically necessary that $x = x$ but not that $y = x$, so 'identity with x' comes out essential to x alone.

Now, though, it becomes hard not to allow additional properties as essential. Without accidental identity, for example, how can there be accidental distinctness? Apparently, then, nine, in addition to being essentially identical to nine, should be reckoned essentially distinct from seven. But to be identical to seven, another number after all, would seem to be less contrary to the nature of nine than to be an entirely different kind of thing, such as a painting or person. Once we recognize non-membership in these other kinds as essential to nine, there seems little point in refusing to count it essentially a member of its actual kind, that is, essentially a number. By this point, we have shed our former colours and taken on a modest and unassuming essentialism.

2 Grades of essential involvement

Nearly all essentialists regard at least kind-properties as essential: Aristotle is essentially human, the set of horses is essentially a set, 'Cow's Skull' is essentially a painting, and so on. But it is common to go further and conceive a thing's kind as the key to its essential properties more generally. The simplest version of this 'priority of kinds' doctrine maintains that (ignoring identity-properties and other such trivia) the essential properties of a K are, first, to be a K, and, second, whatever being a K entails. Thus while Ks have different essences than things of other kinds, between themselves all Ks are essentially alike.

Yet there might be reasons for allowing essential differences within a kind. Does not each set, for instance, have its specific membership essentially, and is not each painting essentially due to its actual painter? Such a view may seem at odds with the priority of kinds doctrine; but the conflict is only superficial, for we can understand a thing's kind to dictate not the essentiality of this or that specific property, but the essentiality of its properties of such-and-such types, whatever those properties may in fact be. So, Kripke proposes that a person essentially derives from whatever gametes they in fact derive from: 'How could a person originating from different parents, from a totally different sperm and egg, be *this very woman*?' (1980: 113; original emphasis). Again, 'could *this table* have been made from a completely *different* block of wood, or even of water cleverly hardened into ice...?' (1980: 113; original emphasis). It could not, so the table essentially originated in this block of wood or one sufficiently like it.

Now that we are countenancing essential differences among conspecifics, we might wonder how deep these differences run; indeed, whether each object emerges with a uniquely identifying modal profile. By an 'individual essence' of x, let us mean a collection of properties such that

(1)   necessarily, whatever has these properties is x,

and

(2)   necessarily, whatever is x has these properties.

The second clause asks for properties necessitated by 'identity with x', that is, properties essential to x. But where shall we look for properties with the further feature, demanded by the first clause, that to possess them is *sufficient* for identity with x? Of course, the property of 'identity with x' handles the job easily. But a property whose identity itself depends on that of x seems ill-suited to the task of singling x out. Thus our problem becomes one of finding individual essences untainted by identity-properties and similar trivia. Essentialists of an Aristotelian bent call this impossible: 'to make clear which thing a thing is, it is not enough (*pace* the friends of logically particularized essence) to say however lengthily that it is *such*, or *so and so*' (Wiggins 1980: 104; original emphasis).

Opposing this pessimism are, first, the Leibnizian strategy of specifying which thing x is through a world-by-world catalogue of its properties and, second, Forbes' idea of identifying x as the unique entity of its kind originating in a certain way from certain other entities: its members if x is a set, its original matter if x is an artefact, its gametes if x is an organism, and so on (Forbes 1985: ch. 7).

Note that the second approach does not offer to identify objects in purely qualitative terms, but only in terms of prior objects. This is not objectionable in itself but it does leave a puzzle about items to which nothing is prior, say, coexistent eternal particles of the same kind. How will their essences differ? (Faced with a similar problem, Aquinas decided that each angel was a species unto itself.) Proponents of the first approach can say that, for each particle, there is a world where it exists all by itself. But since these worlds are not themselves distinguishable except in terms of their solitary inhabitants, this leaves us not much further ahead. Ultimately, then, the Aristotelian may have a point; at least some identity facts will have to be taken as primitive and unexplained.

3   Essential epistemology

Kant famously remarked that experience tells us how a thing is, but not that the thing could not have been otherwise. If this is true, how do we discover essential properties?

At least the outlines of an answer are set forth in Kripke's *Naming and Necessity* (1980). Suppose that the essential properties of x flow from its kind K in the following sense: x is essentially F if and only if x is F and F is a type of property that Ks possess essentially if at all. Then to know x's essential properties, it would be enough to know (1) its kind, (2) which types of properties things of that kind possess essentially, and (3) which properties of those types x actually possesses.

Can we claim access to this information? For at least many objects, it seems arguable that (2) is knowable a priori and (3) a posteriori. One knows a priori, for example, that paintings essentially derive from their actual painters, and a posteriori that Georgia O'Keeffe painted 'Cow's Skull'. As for (1) – in this case, the knowledge that 'Cow's Skull' is a painting, this involves a priori and a posteriori factors working together. Experience reveals that 'Cow's Skull' has a certain history, internal make-up and so on, and it is a priori that these features suffice to make it a painting.

4   Applications of essentialism

Apart from uses already mentioned, what is the essential/accidental distinction good for? From Descartes on, many have seen its potential as a counter to identity theses. The argument is simple. Identicals are indiscernible, so if x has a feature essentially that is at best accidental to y, then x and y are distinct. Allowing that my body is essentially a thing that takes up space and I am not, it follows that I am distinct from my body. If the tree in the quad can exist without my idea of it, then since the same cannot be said of my idea, my idea is not the tree.

Yet the argument might appear to prove too much. Imagine a statue that is always composed of the same hunk of clay, while the clay, for its part, always composes the statue. Given their overwhelming similarity, the statue and the clay might well seem identical. True, the statue is essentially humanoid in form while the clay would survive reshaping into a ball. But are we really to conclude, on the basis of such a subtle difference, that the statue and its clay are two distinct objects?

So-called 'one-thingers' suspect a fallacy of equivocation. Substituting 'the clay' for 'the statue' in 'The statue is essentially humanoid' reverses its truth-value, all right, but is this due to a change in subject matter or a change in what is said about that subject matter? Perhaps the substitution works to deflect attention from the property of having humanoid statue-counterparts to that of having humanoid clay-counterparts. That two separate properties are involved removes the need for a distinction between the objects (see Lewis 1971).

'Two-thingers' urge us to accept the distinction while rethinking its significance. If objects as similar as a statue and its clay can fail to be identical, then non-identity is not *per se* a very powerful conclusion. This makes life harder for philosophers promoting substantive forms of dualism; they must now explain what beyond mere non-identity they intend, and what they can offer as evidence beyond mere differences in essential properties. But life becomes easier for those struggling to understand the various intimate identity-like relations so important in recent metaphysics; for instance, the relations between material objects and their constituent matter, between actions and their associated bodily movements, between mental states and the physical states that realize them, and between fine-grained events occupying the same spatiotemporal region. The last example will be developed further since it sets up one final application of essentialism, to the problem of causation.

What is the relation between the Titanic's sinking so swiftly and its sinking at all? Both events were swift but only the first, arguably, had to be so. This comes out in the fact that the Titanic's sinking might have stretched out over days or weeks (suppose that certain hatches had held) whereas its *swiftly* sinking could not have been that prolonged. Of course it is not just in this respect that the events differ. That the hatches broke was crucial to the ship's swiftly sinking, but no factor at all in its sinking as such; and we can imagine that it was the ship's sinking as such (not its sinking so swiftly) that led to the navigator's dismissal. Is this only happenstance or can we find a theory of causation capable of 'predicting' the causal differences between the events from their essential differences? A counterfactual theory looks promising since the conditions under which an event would not have occurred are visibly sensitive to its essential properties.

5 Conceptions of the essential

So far we have been understanding an essential property of x as a property that x cannot exist without. But although this is the prevailing conception of essentiality, even its advocates admit that it suffers from certain anomalies. The first and best-known concerns the property of existence. Since it is impossible to exist without existing, the modal conception extends to absolutely everything a compliment normally reserved for God, namely essential existence. The problem arises because of the way we conditionalize on existence in the definition of an essential property. Suppose then that we drop the existence condition and define the essential properties of x simply as the ones it must possess, regardless of whether it exists or not. This has the desired effect of eliminating essential existence for contingent beings, but at a cost: no property presupposing existence can be essential to such beings either. So, since to be human one must exist, you and I are not essentially human; hence, perhaps, not human at all.

Now to a second and deeper problem. A thing's essential properties are supposed to be the properties that make it the thing it is. But the modal conception has no way of distinguishing the properties that make x the thing it is from the ones it has as a necessary result of being that thing; it cannot distinguish the *conditions* of x's identity from the *consequences* of its identity. This is clearest in the case of universally necessary properties such as that of 'being an element if gold', or 'being such that $2 + 3 = 5$'. Neither helps make Aristotle the thing he is, but since nothing can be Aristotle without them, the modal conception reckons them essential. Now consider Aristotle's not-universally-necessary property of being distinct from the Eiffel Tower. This is not a factor in Aristotle's identity either; or, to explain what Aristotle was, we would have to mention every other object, past, present and future. Nevertheless, the modal conception calls it essential to Aristotle to be distinct from the Eiffel Tower. A final example seems decisive. To go by the modal conception, Aristotle's membership of {Aristotle} (the set whose only member is Aristotle) is essential to man and set alike. But the truth is surely different: although it lies in the nature of the set to contain the man, the man's membership of the set is not a condition of his identity but a consequence of it. No purely modal account can deliver this result; the case presents no modal asymmetries whatever, hence none for a modal account to exploit.

Troubled by these anomalies, Fine has urged a revival of the definitional conception of essence. With each object x, he associates a proposition $D(x)$ to function as the 'real definition' of x. The properties essential to x are those that can be assigned to it just on the basis of $D(x)$, with no help from any other source. Assuming suitable definitions, this approach allows him to resist the unwelcome essential attributions of the last few paragraphs. Aristotle's definition makes no mention of the Eiffel Tower, so it cannot pronounce on the two objects' relations. Since {Aristotle}'s definition describes it as containing Aristotle, but not the other way around, their relationship will be essential to the set only (Fine 1994).

Not every modally essential property will be definitionally essential, but there is room for debate about the converse. Suppose I make a statue out of the one hunk of clay in my studio. Then in defining the statue – in explaining what it is – I will say that it was created out of this hunk of clay. I will say this despite the fact that a distinct but sufficiently overlapping hunk would have resulted in the very same statue. (In explaining what the statue *is*, why would I mention the various objects it *could* have been fashioned from?) So, 'originating in this hunk of clay' looks like an example of a definitionally essential property that is not modally essential. Yet it could equally be argued that since the statue did not need to originate in the given clay, originating in that clay is not a condition of identity with the statue; hence it should not be considered essential even on the definitional approach.

Disputes like this force a closer look at the phrase 'conditions of identity with x'. Due to a familiar ambiguity in 'condition', this can mean either the necessary *prerequisites* of identity with x (the properties a thing would have to have in order to be x) or the factors actually *constituting* its identity (the properties that x actually possesses by which it succeeds in being x). Deriving from this particular hunk of clay may not be required for identity with the statue, but it seems still to be essential in the constitutive sense. To have derived from the given clay is part of what it is, even if not part of what it had to be, to be that statue.

So we end up with three conceptions of essential property, depending on whether x's essential properties are understood as (1) the necessary prerequisites of identity with x, (2) the factors actually constituting x's identity or (3) the necessary consequences of being x. (3) expresses the modal conception of essentiality. (2) is a fully de-modalized version of the definitional conception. (1) lies somewhere between; it is the definitional conception but with a modal twist. Each of the three seems worthy of further study.

See also: ARISTOTLE §8; DEFINITION; LOCKE, J. §5; IDENTITY OF INDISCERNIBLES §2; LOGICAL AND MATHEMATICAL TERMS, GLOSSARY OF; NATURAL KINDS §3; SUBSTANCE §1

References and further reading

Adams, R. (1979) 'Primitive Thisness and Primitive Identity', *Journal of Philosophy* 76: 5–26. (Defends primitive identity against a Leibnizian position on individual essence; see §2.)

Carnap, R. (1947) *Meaning and Necessity*, Chicago, IL: University of Chicago Press, 2nd edn, 1956. (Attempts to explain *de re* necessity in terms of meaning relations.)

* Fine, K. (1994) 'Essence and Modality', *Philosophical Perspectives* 8: 1–16. (Basis for much of §§1, 5. Criticizes modal conception of essence and revives definitional conception.)

* Forbes, G. (1985) *The Metaphysics of Modality*, Oxford: Clarendon Press. (Cited in §2 as defending individual essences. Excellent overall treatise on *de re* modality.)

* Kripke, S.A. (1980) *Naming and Necessity*, Cambridge, MA: Harvard University Press. (Cited in §§2–3. Extremely important. Argues for essentiality of kinds and origins, and sketches a *de re* modal epistemology.)

* Lewis, D.K. (1971) 'Counterparts of Persons and Their Bodies', *Journal of Philosophy* 68: 203–11. (Defends 'one-thingism' using counterpart theory. See §4.)

* Moore, G.E. (1919) 'External and Internal Relations', repr. in *Philosophical Studies*, London: Routledge & Kegan Paul, 1922. (Cited in §2. Early statement of the modal conception of essence.)

Quine, W.V. (1954) 'Reference and Modality', repr. in *From a Logical Point of View: Nine Logico-Philosophical Essays*, Cambridge, MA: Harvard University Press, 2nd edn, 1980. (Classic presentation of sceptical anti-essentialism. See §1.)

Sidelle, A. (1989) *Necessity, Essence, and Individuation*, Ithaca, NY: Cornell University Press. (Defends a sophisticated conventionalism about essential properties.)

* Wiggins, D. (1980) *Sameness and Substance*, Cambridge, MA: Harvard University Press. (Cited in §2. Stresses essentiality of kinds and connections with trans-temporal identity.)

Yablo, S. (1987) 'Identity, Essence, & Indiscernibility', *Journal of Philosophy* 84: 293–314. (Expands on §§2, 4.)

STEPHEN YABLO

ETERNALITY *see* ETERNITY

ETERNITY

The distinctive, philosophically interesting concept of eternity arose very early in the history of philosophy as the concept of a mode of existence that was not only beginningless and endless but also essentially different from time. It was introduced into early Greek philosophy as the mode of existence required for fundamental reality (being) contrasted with ordinary appearance (becoming). But the concept was given its classic formulation by Boethius, who thought of eternity as God's mode of existence and defined God's eternality as 'the complete possession all at once of illimitable life'. As defined by Boethius the concept was important in medieval philosophy. The elements of the Boethian definition are life, illimitability (and hence duration), and absence of succession (or timelessness). Defined in this way, eternity is proper to an entity identifiable as a mind or a person (and in just that sense living) but existing beginninglessly, endlessly and timelessly.

Such a concept raises obvious difficulties. Some philosophers think the difficulties can be resolved, but others think that in the light of such difficulties the concept must be modified or simply rejected as incoherent. The most obvious difficulty has to do with the combination of atemporality and duration.

Special objections have arisen in connection with ascribing eternality to God. Some people have thought that an eternal being could not do anything at all, especially not in the temporal world. But the notion of an atemporal person's acting is not incoherent. Such acts as knowing necessary truths or willing that a world exist for a certain length of time are acts that themselves take no time and require no temporal location. An eternal God could engage in acts of cognition and of volition and could even do things that might seem to require a temporal location, such as answering a prayer.

The concept of God's eternality is relevant to several issues in philosophy of religion, including the apparent irreconcilability of divine omniscience with divine immutability and with human freedom.

1 **The concept**
2 **Difficulties associated with the concept**
3 **The history of the concept**
4 **Applications of the concept to issues in the philosophy of religion**

1 The concept

Eternality – the condition of having eternity as one's mode of existence – has been understood in more than one way. Sometimes 'eternal' has been associated with endless temporal existence (as in 'eternal life') or with beginningless temporal existence (as in the medieval debate over whether the world was eternal). In these senses the concept of eternality presents no distinctive philosophical difficulties. But there is another sense of 'eternality' in which the concept has been an issue in philosophy from the Greeks to the present. The concept was given its classic formulation in this sense by BOETHIUS (§5), who defined it as 'the complete possession all at once of illimitable life' (*The Consolation of Philosophy*, bk V, pr. 6).

Although the interpretation of the definition becomes controversial in its details, it pretty clearly identifies four elements of eternality. First, anything eternal in the Boethian sense has life. In this sense, then, eternality could not characterize numbers, truth or the world. Next, the life of whatever is eternal is illimitable – necessarily beginningless and endless. Sometimes this element has been interpreted as attributing to whatever is eternal a mode of existence that is illimitable in virtue of being absolutely unextended (like a single instant) and only in that way without a beginning or an end. But a more natural reading and one more consonant with other things Boethius and his successors say about eternity is that it is illimitable in virtue of its infinite duration. Duration is thus the (implicit) third element of eternality in Boethius' formulation. The fourth and last is conveyed by the phrase 'complete possession all at once'. Although living temporal persons may be said to possess their life, they do not possess it completely all at once because they live out their life successively. Past parts of their life they possess no longer, future parts not yet. Consequently, whatever is eternal is also not in time. Eternality thus combines atemporality and duration. (This apparent incoherence is discussed in §2 below.)

Eternity, then, is a real, atemporal mode of existence characterized by both the absence of succession and limitless duration. Nothing in that concept denies the reality of time or implies that temporal experiences are illusory. Boethius and others who use the concept suppose that reality includes time and eternity as two distinct modes of real existence, neither of them reducible to or incompatible with the other.

Temporal events are instructively ordered in terms of the A-series – past, present and future – and the B-series – earlier than, simultaneous with, later than (see McTaggart, J.M.E.). Because an eternal entity is atemporal, its life cannot be ordered successively in either of those series. Moreover, no temporal entity or event can be past or future with respect to, or earlier or later than, the whole life of an eternal entity, because otherwise the eternal entity would itself be part of a temporal series. But nothing in eternality's absence of successiveness entails that it cannot be characterized by *presentness*, or that an eternal entity's cognitive or causal relationship with temporal entities and events cannot be a kind of *simultaneity*. Of course, the presentness and simultaneity associated with an eternal entity could not be temporal presentness or temporal simultaneity. Taking the concept of eternality seriously involves recognizing that it introduces technical senses for several familiar words, including 'now', 'present', and 'simultaneous with', as well as the present-tense forms of many verbs.

In order to allow for real relationships between what is eternal and what is temporal it is particularly important to establish a special sense of 'simultaneous'. A relationship that can be recognized as a kind of simultaneity will of course be symmetric; but, since its relata have relevantly distinct modes of existence, it will be neither reflexive nor transitive. In this sense of 'simultaneous', each of two temporal events can be simultaneous – co-occurrent – with one and the same eternal event without being in any sense simultaneous with each other. This special sort of simultaneity has been called 'ET-simultaneity' (for 'simultaneity between what is eternal and what is temporal'). From a temporal standpoint, the temporal present is ET-simultaneous with the whole infinite extent of an eternal entity's life. From an eternal standpoint, every time is present to or co-occurrent with the whole infinite atemporal duration; that is, each instant of time as it is actually present temporally is ET-simultaneous with the one enduring present of an eternal entity, so that for an eternal entity all of time is present at once.

2 Difficulties associated with the concept

Many of the difficulties in the concept of eternality have been discussed in twentieth-century philosophical literature. The most obvious difficulty arises from the combination of atemporality with duration – the heart of the concept. Ordinarily, 'duration' means persistence through time, and the incoherence of atemporally persisting through time needn't be argued. But the philosophers who developed the concept of eternality were using ordinary terms in extraordinary ways in order to express their theoretical notion of an illimitable life possessed completely all at once. Of course, language is strained when it is stretched to accommodate things utterly outside the ordinary experience language is founded on, as in the black holes and the Big Bang of twentieth-century cosmology (see Cosmology §3). Serious attempts to show that eternity really is an incoherent concept require showing that the apparent incoherence persists when the technical interpretations of its terms are fully taken into account.

One attempt at doing just that involves taking atemporal duration as a species of extension and then arguing that any extension must be divisible and so cannot be all at once, or atemporal. The problem with such an attempt is that it uses an inductive survey of temporal and spatial extensions to reach the generalization that all extensions are divisible. But since eternity is neither temporal nor spatial, it will not be surprising if the properties attributed to extension as a result of such an induction fail to apply to what is eternal.

Still, this way of avoiding the ascription of divisibility to what is eternal seems to run into an old problem: insisting that terms cannot be used univocally of temporal and of eternal things looks like introducing equivocation into the description of eternity. Not only does 'duration' not have its ordinary sense when used of the eternal, but it is also difficult to say precisely what its extraordinary sense is. This sort of problem has become familiar in connection with discourse about God. It has often been pointed out that to use ordinary terms univocally of God and creatures is to deny the transcendence of God, but to use them equivocally masks a radical agnosticism about God's nature and activity. So discourse about God can use neither univocal nor equivocal predication (see Religious Language §4).

Analogical predication is the traditionally recognized solution to this dilemma, and it is also what is needed for interpreting the description of the eternal. Atemporal duration is *analogous* to temporal duration, enough like temporal duration to make using the term 'duration' helpful, but enough unlike it to mean that the definition of '(temporal) duration' will not apply. Eternal duration is fully actualized duration, none of which is already lost or not yet gained: beginningless, endless, non-successive existence possessed completely, all at once, present entirely to its possessor – a mode of existence consisting entirely in a present that is infinite rather than instantaneous.

Timeless duration might well be thought of as Plato thought of it, as the genuine duration of which temporal duration is only the moving image. Not all critics of the concept of eternity find such a response adequate, and the most persistent objections to the concept concentrate on the difficulties of ascribing duration to what is atemporal.

Because eternality in the sense at issue here is taken primarily to characterize God's mode of existence, other objections to the concept stem from combining it with traditional concepts of God. In this vein philosophers have objected that a God who is eternal could not act at all, and especially not in time. But this objection is based on a confusion. Of course, there are things an atemporal God could not do – such as remembering, or planning ahead. But not all cognitive and volitional acts require temporal location, and God could engage in those that do not. Furthermore, an atemporal God could not change the past or foreknow the future. Such actions, if possible at all, would require a temporal location, without which there can be neither past nor future. Still, eternal God, present at once to each temporal instant in its temporal presentness, could in the eternal present directly affect events that are past with respect to us and be directly aware of events future with respect to us. He could also act in time. He could, for example, will timelessly that something occur or come into existence at a particular time. By the same token, he could also do things that might appear to require a particular temporal location, such as answering a particular prayer. Because both the time of the prayer and the time at which the answer to it occurs are ET-simultaneous with the whole of eternity, an eternal God could be aware, timelessly, of a prayer prayed at one time, willing (ET-simultaneously) that the answer to that prayer occur at a later time.

Finally, some critics suppose that if God is eternal and creatures are temporal, then God could not be directly aware of creatures or interact with them directly and immediately as he is traditionally said to do. Such criticisms must presuppose that for one being to interact directly with another, the two must share a mode of existence. But traditional theists are already committed to rejecting this presupposition as regards space. God is traditionally described as non-spatial and thus as not sharing with creatures a spatial mode of existence, and yet that difference in modes of existence is generally thought to be no obstacle to God's being directly aware of or directly interacting with his creatures. If the presupposition is false as regards space, however, it is hard to see why it should be accepted as regards time.

3 The history of the concept

The earliest indisputable appearance of the concept of eternity is in Plato's *Timaeus*. Parmenides' description of the mode of existence of Being, or the One, in his *Way of Truth* is much older, but scholars disagree over whether Parmenides intended to ascribe atemporality to Being (see PARMENIDES §3). Whatever Parmenides meant, what Plato says about eternity is in several respects just what Parmenides says about Being's mode of existence, and to that extent at least Parmenides may be thought of as the inventor or discoverer of the concept of eternity.

Many scholars believe that Aristotle rejected Plato's notion of eternity, although there is also some textual evidence suggesting that, on the contrary, he accepted and made use of it in describing the life of the Prime Mover. Whether or not Aristotle himself accepted the concept of eternity, it is indisputable that the concept came into medieval philosophy through the Platonic rather than the Aristotelian tradition. PLOTINUS (§4), for instance, has a well-developed concept of eternity, and in *Enneads* III 7 he stresses the importance of duration in the concept. Boethius seems to have based his definition of eternity on the one Plotinus develops.

AUGUSTINE (§8), who was even more clearly in the Platonic tradition than Boethius was, understood and accepted the concept of eternity, which plays a significant part in two of his most important works, the *Confessions* (bk XI, ch. 11) and *The City of God* (bk XI, ch. 21). Like Boethius' formulations, Augustine's views of eternity were an important influence on later medieval philosophy.

In the Middle Ages, the concept of eternity was widely used and discussed. It can be found, for example, in Anselm's *Monologion* (ch. 24) and *Proslogion* (ch. 13), where it seems taken for granted, as a standard part of traditional theology. But it received its most sophisticated development in the work of Aquinas, who discussed and employed it in several of his works (for example, *Summa theologiae* Ia, q.10). After Aquinas, although many medieval philosophers and theologians continued to hold that God is eternal, they did not always mean by 'eternal' what Boethius (and Aquinas) had meant by it. Duns Scotus, for example, seems to have held that God's eternity is not co-occurrent with all of time.

In the modern period, with the rejection of the medieval synthesis in theology, the notion of eternity, in the special sense at issue here, was largely abandoned. Hobbes is still aware of it in the Boethian sense *'as a permanent now'* (1680: 435), but Locke, for example, takes eternity to be just an infinity of temporal duration: 'By being able to repeat any such

Idea of any length of time... and add them one to another, without ever coming to the end of such addition... we come by the *Idea* of *Eternity*' (1689, bk II, ch. 14).

4 Applications of the concept to issues in the philosophy of religion

Applying the concept of eternality makes a significant difference in considering various issues in philosophy of religion. Here we will concentrate on just two of the most important: omniscience and immutability, and foreknowledge and free will.

It has been argued that omniscience and immutability, two traditional divine attributes, are not compossible. An omniscient knower always knows what time it is (or precisely what is going on) now, and any knower who always knows what time it is now is a knower whose knowledge is always changing. Consequently, a knower could be omniscient and mutable, or immutable and not omniscient, but there could not be an omniscient, immutable knower (see IMMUTABILITY).

This argument presupposes that knowers are temporal. If omniscient God is eternal, however, the argument becomes more complicated. For example, in the claim that an omniscient knower always knows what time it is now, 'now' and the present tense of 'knows' can each be read as indicating either the temporal or the eternal present, thus allowing for four different interpretations of the claim. Not all of those interpretations make sense; for example, 'An omniscient knower always knows in the eternal present what time it is in the eternal present' incoherently attributes time to the eternal present. The most reasonable interpretation of the claim, on the supposition that the omniscient knower in question is eternal, is that the knower always knows in the eternal present what time it is in the temporal present. But on that interpretation it is much more difficult to show that such a knower could not be immutable.

Even if we suppose that the indexical 'now' is ineliminable, that there is an absolute temporal present as distinct from a present that is merely relative to some particular temporal entity, it is not clear that an eternal God could not know what time it is without constantly changing. On the view that the whole of eternity is ET-simultaneous with each temporal event as it is actually happening, an eternal omniscient knower will know all the events actually occurring at a particular time as well as the temporal location of that time and its being experienced as present by temporal entities at that time. Such a knower will also know that from the standpoint of eternity every temporal event is actually happening.

There is nothing further for an eternal entity to know about what time it is now, for either the eternal or the temporal now; and nothing in what it does know requires constant change or change of any sort. Thus, while the argument may show that no temporal knower can be both omniscient and immutable, it does not make its case if the omniscient, immutable knower is eternal.

Arguments that knowledge of future contingent events is irreconcilable with human freedom depend on the notion of *fore*knowledge, on someone's knowing ahead of time what someone else will 'freely' decide to do (see OMNISCIENCE §§3–4). On the face of it, then, the concept of eternity provides a solution to the problem of foreknowledge and free will, as Boethius maintained in introducing the concept. An eternal omniscient knower will be eternally aware of *all* contingent events as they are occurring, including those that occur in the temporal future, but he will not *fore*know them, since nothing eternal can be earlier than anything else. Consequently, arguments purporting to show that foreknowledge and free will are incompatible will not apply to eternal omniscient knowledge, which is evidently compatible with human free will.

But some philosophers have thought that eternality nonetheless fails to provide a solution to the problem of divine knowledge and human freedom, because the fixity and infallibility of divine knowledge seem enough by themselves to make God's knowledge of future contingents incompatible with free will. 'God knows in the eternal present that Paula mows her lawn in 2095' entails that Paula mows her lawn in 2095, and so God's eternal awareness of a future event seems to have the result that the event is inevitable *now*, before the event occurs, in a way incompatible with Paula's freedom of action. Consequently, the concept of eternity seems after all unhelpful for resolving the apparent incompatibility between divine knowledge and human freedom.

The idea of this line of argument is that a proposition such as 'God eternally knows that *p*' (where *p* is of the form 'Paula mows her lawn (at some date future with respect to us in the present)') entails 'It is now the case that *p*'. That is why eternal knowledge is supposed to have the result that the future is somehow fixed and inevitable now. But is there such an entailment? 'God eternally knows that *p*' does entail *p*, and *p* does seem equivalent to 'It is now the case that *p*'. But is it equivalent in a context involving eternity? In that context, God knows that *p* in virtue of being ET-simultaneous with the future events he is eternally aware of. In that context, furthermore, it is also true that God's knowledge that *p* is ET-simultaneous with the temporal now. That is why we can appropriately say such things as 'It is now (in the temporal present) true that God eternally knows that *p*'. But, as has already been pointed out, ET-simultaneity is not transitive. From the facts that the state of affairs that *p* is ET-simultaneous with eternity and that eternity is ET-simultaneous with the temporal present, it does not follow that it is *now* the case that *p*. Therefore, while it is true that God's knowing that *p* entails that *p*, the relationship between time and eternity is such that God's knowing that *p* does not entail that it is *now* the case that *p*. Hence, it seems that the concept of eternity can constitute the basis for an adequate solution to the problem of foreknowledge and free will.

See also: GOD, CONCEPTS OF; NECESSARY BEING; SIMPLICITY, DIVINE

References and further reading

Adams, M. (1987) *William Ockham*, Notre Dame, IN: University of Notre Dame Press, 1115–48. (Contains a helpful explanation of Duns Scotus' and Ockham's views on God's knowledge of future contingents and of how their views are related to Aquinas'.)

* Anselm (1076) *Monologion*, in J. Hopkins and H. Richardson (trans and eds) *Anselm of Canterbury*, vol. 1, Toronto, Ont. and New York: Edwin Mellen Press, 1974. (A classic of natural theology.)

* —— (1077–8) *Proslogion*, in J. Hopkins and H. Richardson (trans and eds) *Anselm of Canterbury*, vol. 1, Toronto, Ont. and New York: Edwin Mellen Press, 1974. (Anselm supposes that God's eternality can be proven from the basic idea of what God is.)

* Aquinas, T. (1266–73) *Summa theologiae* Ia, q.10, in P. Caramello (ed.) *S.Thomae Aquinatis Summa theologiae*, Turin: Marietti, 1952. (The classic scholastic formulation of the concept of eternity.)

* Augustine (397–401) *Confessions*, trans. W. Watts, Cambridge, MA: Harvard University Press, and London: Heinemann, 1968–70, vol. 2, bk XI, ch. 11. (Augustine's story of his conversion to Christianity, containing much important work in metaphysics and ethics.)

* —— (413–27) *The City of God*, trans. D.S. Wiesen, Cambridge, MA: Harvard University Press, and London: Heinemann, 1968, vol. 3, bk XI, ch. 21. (Contains presentations and applications of the concept that were influential in later medieval philosophy.)

* Boethius (521–4) *De trinitate*, in H.F. Stewart, E.K. Rand and S.J. Tester (eds) *Boethius: The Theological Tractates and The Consolation of Philosophy*, London: Heinemann, and Cambridge, MA: Harvard University Press, 1973. (A classic attempt to resolve philosophical problems in the concept of the Trinity.)

* —— (525–6) *The Consolation of Philosophy*, in H.F. Stewart, E.K. Rand and S.J. Tester (eds) *Boethius: The Theological Tractates and The Consolation of Philosophy*, London: Heinemann, and Cambridge, MA: Harvard University Press, 1973. (Boethius' presentation and applications of the concept became the *locus classicus* for later medieval discussion.)

Fitzgerald, P. (1985) 'Stump and Kretzmann on Time and Eternity', *Journal of Philosophy* 82: 260–9. (Argues that the notion of atemporal duration is incoherent.)

Hasker, W. (1989) *God, Time, and Knowledge*, Ithaca, NY, and London: Cornell University Press. (Contains a careful examination of the concept of eternity, finally rejecting it.)

* Hobbes, T. (1680) *Considerations upon the Reputation, Loyalty, Manners and Religion of Thomas Hobbes of Malmsbury, written by himself by way of Letter to a Learned Person*, London: Crooke. (Referred to in §3.)

Leftow, B. (1991) *Time and Eternity*, Ithaca, NY, and London: Cornell University Press. (An excellent discussion of all aspects of the concept of eternity, with some philosophically interesting modifications of it.)

* Locke, J. (1689) *An Essay Concerning Human Understanding*, ed. P. Nidditch, Oxford: Clarendon Press, 1975. (Referred to in §3.)

Nelson, H. (1987) 'Time(s), Eternity, and Duration', *International Journal for Philosophy of Religion* 22: 3–19. (An argument that duration cannot be part of a coherent concept of eternity.)

Pike, N. (1970) *God and Timelessness*, London: Routledge & Kegan Paul. (A helpful overview of eternality in philosophy of religion, raising many of the classic objections.)

Plantinga, A. (1986) 'On Ockham's Way Out', *Faith and Philosophy* 3: 235–69; reprinted in T. Morris (ed.) *The Concept of God*, Oxford: Oxford University Press, 1987, 171–200. (Argues that the concept of eternity does not constitute an adequate solution to the problem of foreknowledge and free will.)

* Plato (*c.*366–360 BC) *Timaeus*, trans. R.G. Bury, Cambridge, MA: Harvard University Press, and London: Heinemann, 1961, 37D–38C. (Plato's classic exposition of the concept of eternity.)

* Plotinus (*c.*250–66) *Enneads*, trans. A.H. Armstrong, London: Heinemann, and Cambridge, MA: Harvard University Press, 1967, vol. 3, III 7. (Plotinus'

definition of the concept of eternity and his argument that duration is part of the concept.)

Stump, E. and Kretzmann, N. (1981) 'Eternity', *Journal of Philosophy* 78: 429–57; reprinted in T. Morris (ed.) *The Concept of God*, Oxford: Oxford University Press, 1987, 219–52. (An exposition and defence of Boethius' concept of eternity.)

—— (1991) 'Prophecy, Past Truth, and Eternity', in J.E. Tomberlin (ed.) *Philosophical Perspectives (5): Philosophy of Religion*, Atascadero, CA: Ridgeview Publishing Company. (Argues that the concept of eternity provides an adequate solution to the problem of foreknowledge and free will.)

—— (1992) 'Eternity, Awareness, and Action', *Faith and Philosophy* 9: 463–82. (Argues that duration is a coherent part of the concept of eternity.)

Wierenga, E. (1989) *The Nature of God: An Inquiry into Divine Attributes*, Ithaca, NY, and London: Cornell University Press. (Includes detailed arguments against the concept of eternity.)

Zagzebski, L. (1991) *The Dilemma of Freedom and Foreknowledge*, New York: Oxford University Press. (Includes a careful examination of the concept of eternity and of objections to it.)

ELEONORE STUMP
NORMAN KRETZMANN

ETERNITY OF THE WORLD, MEDIEVAL VIEWS OF

The problem of the eternity of the world was much debated in Western philosophy from the twelfth through the fourteenth centuries, but its history goes back as far as Philo of Alexandria and the Church Fathers. The principal topic of controversy was the possibility of a beginningless and yet created world. The arguments that fashioned the medieval discussion rested upon assumptions concerning the concepts of eternity and creation. In addition, the issue of eternity intertwined with discussions of the relationship of God to creation, with proofs of the existence of God, with the nature of the material universe and with the nature of infinity. Some of the most ingenious ideas in these debates were obtained from pagan Greek, Islamic and Jewish traditions.

1   Early stages
2   The two sides

1   Early stages

According to Judaeo-Christian tradition, based in particular upon the opening words of Genesis ('In the beginning God created the heaven and the earth'), the universe had a beginning. From the fourth century onwards, however, Christian thinkers had to take into consideration accounts from antiquity, transmitted by authors such as Augustine and Boethius, according to which the existence of the material universe (*mundus*) was 'from eternity' (*ab aeterno*), that is, beginningless.

In its early stages, the medieval discussion of the eternity of the world was preoccupied with two types of questions, one asking whether the world had existed from eternity and the other examining the concept of eternity and its relation with time. In general, 'time' (*tempus*) was understood to imply having both a beginning and an end, and perpetuity (*aevum*) involved a beginning but not an end, whereas 'eternity' (*aeternitas*) had neither beginning nor end. 'Eternity' in this sense was understood as a temporal notion, meaning 'infinite temporal extension'. However as BOETHIUS pointed out in *De consolatione philosophiae* (The Consolation of Philosophy), 'eternity' could also be taken as atemporal. This conception of eternity, sometimes called 'eternity proper' by later authors, introduced the notion of timelessness within the notions of 'all at once' (*tota simul*) and of 'life', and referred to God's mode of existence.

Medieval thinkers all agreed that the universe was not coeternal with God. They were divided, however, over the question whether the universe had always existed in a temporal sense, and over how this question should be understood in the first place. Using a distinction derived from AUGUSTINE in *De civitate Dei* (The City of God) and *Confessiones* (Confessions), many medieval thinkers would observe that the world was created *together with* time, and in this sense had *always* existed: there was no past at the time of creation.

In the early thirteenth century, the discussion of the eternity of the world was raised to a higher level. Three events contributed to this. First, the Fourth Lateran Council (1215) declared the temporal beginning of the world to be an article of faith. Second, around that same time the *Sentences* by Peter LOMBARD, which included a statement (Book 2, distinction 1) about the world's eternity, became an official textbook in the faculty of theology. Third, the translation into Latin of Aristotle's books on natural philosophy (*Libri naturales*), especially *Physics* VIII, brought medieval thinkers in the arts faculty into routine contact with arguments proving the eternity of motion and generation (see ARISTOTLE). Aristotle's views on eternity, especially the question whether he had intended to prove the beginninglessness of the world, became an issue of debate that culminated in the condemnations of 1270 and 1277 by Bishop

Etienne Tempier (see ARISTOTELIANISM, MEDIEVAL). Aristotle's views were perceived through the interpretations offered by Averroes' *Commentary on Aristotle's Physics* and Maimonides' *Guide to the Perplexed*, works that had also been translated recently into Latin (see AVERROISM; IBN RUSHD; MAIMONIDES, M.).

The most important result of these events was that the issue to be debated came into sharper focus: could the world have been eternal, if God had so willed? In other words, must the beginning of the world be accepted as an article of faith, or can it also be proved by (demonstrative) arguments? In this way, the issue of the eternity of the world helped to determine the position philosophers held with regard to the relation between faith and reason.

2 The two sides

The various conceivable ways of responding to the question of the eternity of the world can be reduced to the following two positions. One group of thinkers, of whom BONAVENTURE is the archetype, claimed that it could be demonstrated that the world began to exist. Other adherents of this position were MATTHEW OF AQUASPARTA, HENRY OF GHENT, JOHN PECHAM, RICHARD OF MIDDLETON, Peter AUREOL, William of Alnwick, Henry Totting of Oyta and MARSILIUS OF INGHEN. The demonstrations hinged on two basic assumptions concerning creation and eternity.

The Christian view had come to be that God had created the world where before there had been nothing: in other words, creation from nothing. In an argument that goes back to RICHARD OF ST VICTOR, it was maintained that since creation from nothing (*ex nihilo*) is a transition from non-being (*nihil*) to being, non-being necessarily precedes being. Hence, creation necessarily implies a beginning in time. In sum, creation 'from nothing' was understood as creation 'after nothing' (*post nihil*).

Furthermore, an eternal world was conceived to imply the existence of an infinite series of past events. The contradictions that allegedly arose from this assumption were considered reasons why an eternal world is impossible. Most of the arguments were drawn from Aristotle's widely accepted theory of the infinite, but were here employed in a new context to substantiate the un-Aristotelian conclusion that the world is not eternal but had a beginning. In particular, the following generally accepted Aristotelian rules were considered to be violated by the idea of a beginningless world: first, that it is impossible to add to the infinite; second, that it is impossible to traverse what is infinite; third, that it is impossible for the infinite to be grasped by a finite power; and fourth,

that it is impossible that there be simultaneously an infinite number of things. In addition, the theory of a possible eternal world seemed to clash with self-evident principles such as that the whole is greater than the part (John Pecham) or that, since the infinite is *infinite*, one infinity cannot be greater than another, or that there is no order in the infinite because there is no first element (Bonaventure). Some of these alleged contradictions had already been pointed out by John PHILOPONUS in his *De aeternitate mundi contra Proclum* (On the Eternity of the World Against Proclus) and had circulated among Arabic authors such as Algazel in his *Metaphysica* before they were transmitted to the Latin West (see AL-GHAZALI; ISLAMIC PHILOSOPHY: TRANSMISSION INTO WESTERN EUROPE).

Another group of thinkers, including SIGER OF BRABANT, BOETHIUS OF DACIA, Thomas AQUINAS, GILES OF ROME, GODFREY OF FONTAINES, WILLIAM OF OCKHAM, HENRY OF HARCLAY, Thomas of Wylton and Thomas of Strasbourg, argued that the universe could have existed from eternity. In part, their argumentation rested on the rebuttal of those arguments that the proponents of a demonstrable beginning had invoked to refute the possibility of an eternal world. They concluded that since the beginning of the world could not be *demonstratively* proved, the universe could have existed without beginning to exist.

Proponents of the possibility of a beginningless universe interpreted creation out of nothing as creation not out of anything, that is, not out of any independently existing matter. Creation was understood as a relation of causal dependence of creatures upon God, and in this interpretation the status of being a creature was not necessarily inconsistent with being beginningless. The argument that the universe depends for its existence upon a superior principle that is not prior in time but prior in the order of things can be found in Avicenna's *Metaphysica*, and was at the heart of Aquinas' rebuttal of Bonaventure's interpretation of creation from nothing (see AQUINAS, T. §9; IBN SINA §4).

The infinity arguments in favour of a beginning were considered off the mark by the proponents of the possibility of an eternal world. With regard to the traversal argument, for instance (that is, the argument that if the world had always been, an infinite past time would have been traversed), they emphasized that the traversed infinite time was a successive and not a simultaneous infinity, and hence, that the contradictions that seemed to follow from the premise of an eternal world were not pertinent. There will always be only finitely many past days between this and any past day. A beginningless world does not imply that any past day was infinitely remote from this day.

In general, the adherents of a possible beginningless world held the same Aristotelian views on the infinite as their opponents. They disagreed only over the kind of infinity that was involved in a possible eternal world. Henry of Harclay was an interesting exception. He agreed with his opponents that a possible eternal world would entail an *actual* infinity, but he denied that the conclusions that followed from this stance were contradictory. Harclay argued that the infinite can be traversed, that it can be exceeded, and that not all infinites are equal (see INFINITY).

See also: ARISTOTELIANISM, MEDIEVAL; CREATION AND CONSERVATION, RELIGIOUS DOCTRINE OF; ETERNITY; NATURAL PHILOSOPHY, MEDIEVAL; RICHARD RUFUS OF CORNWALL; TIME

References and further reading

Boethius of Dacia (*c*.1275) *De aeternitate mundi* (On the Eternity of the World), trans J.F. Wippel, *On the Supreme Good, On the Eternity of the World, On Dreams*, Toronto, Ont.: Pontifical Institute of Mediaeval Studies, 1987. (An important text from the faculty of arts in the early 1270s.)

Brown, S.F. (1991) 'The Eternity of the World Discussion at Early Oxford', in A. Zimmermann and A. Speer (eds) *Mensch und Natur im Mittelalter* (Man and Nature in the Middle Ages), Berlin: de Gruyter, vol. 1, 259–80. (An examination of how the conception of theology influenced the discussion of the eternity of the world, with an edition of Richard Rufus of Cornwall II *Sent.* d.1 q.1.)

Bukowski, T. (1991) 'Understanding St. Thomas on the Eternity of the World: Help from Giles of Rome?', *Recherches de théologie ancienne et médiévale* 58: 113–25. (A contribution to the controversy over the interpretation of Thomas Aquinas' views, which at the same time clarifies some intricacies of the medieval debate concerning the eternity of the world in general.)

Dales, R.C. (1990) *Medieval Discussions of the Eternity of the World*, Leiden: Brill. (Assembles and discusses a wealth of source material and provides an extensive bibliographical guide.)

Dales, R.C. and Argerami, O. (1991) *Medieval Latin Texts on the Eternity of the World*, Leiden: Brill. (A dossier of medieval Latin texts extending from the 1220s to the second quarter of the fourteenth century, accompanied by brief introductions.)

Davidson, H.A. (1987) *Proofs for Eternity, Creation and the Existence of God in Medieval Islamic and Jewish Philosophy*, Oxford: Oxford University Press. (A brilliant typology of the medieval Islamic and Jewish arguments for eternity, many of which recur in the Latin West.)

Hoenen, M.J.F.M. (1992) 'The Eternity of the World according to Marsilius of Inghen with an Edition of the *Dubium* in II *Sent.* q.1 a.2', in H.A.G. Braakhuis and M.J.F.M. Hoenen (eds) *Marsilius of Inghen*, Acts of the International Marsilius of Inghen Symposium, Nijmegen: Ingenium, 117–43. (A presentation of the views of the late-fourteenth-century authors Thomas of Strasbourg, Henry Totting of Oyta, Marsilius of Inghen and Conrad of Soltau, whose discussions of the eternity of the world rest upon assumptions concerning the nature of God as an immeasurable spiritual quantity.)

John Pecham (1269–73) *Quaestiones de aeternitate mundi* (Questions on the Eternity of the World), trans. V.G. Potter, *Questions concerning the Eternity of the World*, New York: Fordham University Press, 1993. (Translation of a key text, reflecting the state of the debate in the 1270s.)

Kretzmann, N. (1985) 'Ockham and the Creation of the Beginningless World', *Franciscan Studies* 45: 1–31. (A philosophical analysis of Ockham's views on the eternity of the world and an extremely useful general introduction to the entire debate.)

MacIntosh, J.J. (1994) 'St Thomas and the Traversal of the Infinite', *American Catholic Philosophical Quarterly* 68: 157–77. (A consideration of the so-called traversal-of-the-infinite argument in its ancient, medieval and early modern versions, and a contemporary assessment of Aquinas' response to it.)

Sorabji, R (1983) *Time, Creation and the Continuum: Theories in Antiquity and the Early Middle Ages*, London: Duckworth. (A philosophical analysis of discussions of eternity and creation in Greek philosophy. Very important for understanding the medieval debates.)

Stump, E. and Kretzmann, N. (1981) 'Eternity', *Journal of Philosophy* 78: 429–70. (The most profound analysis to date of Boethius' atemporal notion of eternity.)

Vollert, C., Kendzierski, L.H. and Byrne, P.M. (eds) (1964) *On the Eternity of the World*, Milwaukee, WI: Marquette University Press. (A translation (by the editors) of three important texts under this title by Thomas Aquinas, Siger of Brabant and Bonaventure, which provide a useful catalogue of the arguments that played a role in the eternity debate.)

Wissink, J.B.M. (1990) *The Eternity of the World in the Thought of Thomas Aquinas and His Contemporaries*, Leiden: Brill. (Contains contributions by M.J.F.M. Hoenen about the discussion of the world's eternity in the *Correctoria* literature of the Dominican and Franciscan schools, and by

J.M.M.H. Thijssen about the reception of Aquinas' views concerning infinity in the works of the fourteenth-century thinkers Harclay, Alnwick and Wylton.)

J.M.M.H. THIJSSEN

ETHICAL NATURALISM

see NATURALISM IN ETHICS

ETHICAL SYSTEMS, AFRICAN

Ethical thought in sub-Saharan Africa grows largely out of traditions that are communalistic, not based in individual consent, anti-universalizing, naturalistic, and humanist. Within such thought, the general vocabulary of evaluation, like such English words as 'good' and 'bad', does not strongly differentiate between narrow moral assessments, on the one hand, and technical or aesthetic evaluation on the other. This is true of places where Islam has been present for many centuries. The substantial exposure, in the colonial and postcolonial periods, to European moral ideas (both through various forms of Christian missionary evangelism and as a result of contact with secular moral and political traditions from elsewhere), along with the changes produced by the modern economy, have produced a wide range of ethical ideas. However, the residue of precolonial ethical theory remains the most distinctive, if not always the most important, component and is the main topic of this entry.

1   **Defining the subject matter**
2   **Traditional cultures: general features**
3   **Traditional cultures: ethical education**
4   **Comparisons with 'modern' societies**
5   **Contemporary trends**

1   Defining the subject matter

Sub-Saharan Africa has a wide range of varied cultures. A standard audit (Greenberg 1970: 25) shows that more than one thousand languages are spoken on the continent. It is made up of more than fifty modern states which include peoples descended from hundreds of earlier societies, ranging, by degrees of political organization, from the hunter-gathering King Kung of central southern Africa, who were without a ruler, through to the hierarchical states of Buganda in the east and the Yoruba and Asante in the west, to the Islamic kingdoms, emirates and sultanates of the Sahel and northwest Africa.

Most contemporary sub-Saharan African cultures have grown out of interactions between the so-called 'traditional' systems of thought of these earlier societies, on the one hand, and Christianity, Islam and the many influences of the extensive colonial administrations of modern European and US cultures, on the other. Such colonial rule, which spanned more than a century, continued until the 1970s. Ethical theory in the Maghreb (the largely Arabic-speaking region of north Africa, which has been part of the literate Islamic world for more than a millennium), deserves separate consideration in the broader context (see ETHICS IN ISLAMIC PHILOSOPHY; ISLAMIC PHILOSOPHY). For similar reasons, Ethiopia's literate philosophical traditions are best considered separately (see ETHIOPIA, PHILOSOPHY IN). Contemporary moral philosophy in universities is largely an extension of ethics in the colonial metropolitan cultures, more particularly of the UK and France (see AFRICAN PHILOSOPHY, ANGLOPHONE; AFRICAN PHILOSOPHY, FRANCOPHONE). The ethical traditions of white settler populations in southern Africa are continuous with those of their European ancestors. This entry deals generally with those sub-Saharan African traditions that remain.

2   Traditional cultures: general features

To begin with traditional cultures, sociological and anthropological accounts suggest a number of generalizations about the ethical dimensions (in the broadest sense of practical reason) of their modes of thought and behaviour. A number of formal features related more to the kinds of moral systems there are, and less to the particular ends or values they endorse, must be considered.

First, it is widely agreed (Danquah 1944; Mbiti 1969) that these earlier societies were essentially *communitarian* or *communalistic* in their ethical ideas. This means that they held (like many pre-modern societies elsewhere) that prerogatives of rights to land use and property inheritance, for example, inhere in various corporate groups, such as families, lineages, villages and societies, rather than in individuals. These societies also maintained that the flourishing of corporate interests were superior to the projects of individuals. Thus, property rights – the claim to exclusive use of an area of land for farming for a period of time – were assigned by chiefs or kings in many cultures to lineages. The head and senior members of each such group would allocate responsibilities and a share of the crop to members of the group and would manage profits from sales or exchanges to cover the needs of individual members. Marriage and the attendant obligation to raise and support children would be a relationship between families in which control of children and their obedience often belonged to the family of one spouse. This was symbolically acknowledged by dowry payments for a future bride.

A second significant aspect of traditional ethical thought relates to the extended family or clan. This form of moral thought permits someone, the agent, to treat someone else, the patient, in a certain manner because the two are related, not because the patient has particular qualities or needs, for example, I might give shelter to someone 'because she is my kinswoman'. This produces a structure of thought that is, in a sense, *anti-universalizing*. The reasoning behind it is historical as well as indexical and relates to the agent's conviction that the patient can be treated in a certain way: 'because she's my kinswoman', although this is not consonant with some understandings of the Kantian demand for universalizability (see KANTIAN ETHICS). (However, it is possible to defend partiality towards, for example, one's close kin as a universalizable principle. It is a familiar idea in European societies that obligations to a parent or sibling should not depend on their intrinsic attributes: Europeans and Americans do not normally suppose that the reason we should care more for our siblings than for strangers is that they have general features that make them abstractly more deserving.) Such reasons for anti-universalizability are independent of the character and needs of the patient, and do not arise out of either obligations created through consent whose model is the contract in liberal political theory (for example, Hobbes, Locke and Rawls) or reciprocation (which might account for obligation) to those who bore and brought one up. This range of obligations, rooted in unchosen relationships to people from whom one has received nothing, is much more extensive in traditional Africa than in Europe or the USA.

In matrilineal societies, for example, the Akan of Ghana and the Ivory Coast, children 'belong' to their mothers' families, which are headed ideally by a maternal uncle or great-uncle. In patrilineal traditions, for example, the Yoruba, the child 'belongs' to their fathers' lineage, which is headed ideally by a father, paternal uncle or grandfather, although these are not the only forms of affiliation known in Africa. These differing ideas of kinship have profound consequences because they determine the range of familial obligation and define who retains custody of the children after divorce. At this point, relationships enter the anti-universalizing range of the indexical reason mentioned earlier: 'because they are my kin'.

A third aspect of traditional ethical thought deals with traditional religious ideas. These were *naturalistic*, conceiving of gods, spirits and ancestors as continuous with and continually operative within the natural world. These ideas did not make a sharp ontological distinction, of the kind central to Christian and Platonist thinking, between a realm of spirit and a realm of matter. Spiritual beings were supposed to be concerned with the flourishing of specific groups of people of certain places or lineages. Because of the centrality of the prescriptions of various spiritual forces in shaping behaviour, the separation of moral principles from principles of prudence is not always easy in such a setting. (Plato's discussion in the *Euthyphro* (*c*.386–*c*.380) of whether an act is right because the gods love it or they love it because it is right, raises an unanswerable question (see PLATO §2).) On the one hand, it seems clear that traditional peoples felt obligations to and wished to help others for reasons other than the spiritually-underwritten sanctions associated with not doing so (in the same way that most people do not commit murder simply because they know they would be punished if they did). On the other hand, certain proscriptions, of incest for example, that might be thought of as moral in some European societies, seem to have derived from beliefs about the consequences, as when the Azande understood leprosy to be caused by incest.

Many areas of life, such as food preparation, ritual practice in association with cults for spirits and ancestors, and everyday contact with others, generally involved the observance of taboos, for which the sanctions were often misfortunes, like hunting accidents, disease, or a failed crop visited upon an individual or the group to which they belonged. The avoidance of harm of this type was apparent in practical reasoning. Rarely was there an articulated notion of doing right that was distinct from doing what was appropriate and conformed to custom and prudence so that no taboos were violated. Indeed, one of the highest terms of commendation for conduct in many African societies was also used to describe both physical beauty and the aesthetic appeal in artefacts. Thus, in Twi, an Akan language, *fé* refers to physical beauty in people, to a well-made artefact and to commend good behaviour. A common criticism of a child's behaviour would be that it is not *fé* (see AKAN PHILOSOPHICAL PSYCHOLOGY).

Fourth, there is often no clear distinction between moral vocabulary and aesthetic or technical commendation. This reflects the low degree of linguistic division of labour within most pre-literate communities.

A further consequence of regular involvement with spirits of lineage and place is that, in the majority of cultures that recognize a high god associated with the heavens, this god is a *deus remotus* whose interest in peoples' affairs is minimal. The notion that one's conduct should be aimed at affecting an afterlife is unusual and concern for affairs after one's death focuses on questions of one's descendants performing cultish acts for their ancestors to conserve their memory. Such systems of thought are thus *anthropocentric* or *humanistic*, centring on the contemporary concerns of human beings, including ancestors (who are always with their kin), rather than on other-worldly considerations.

3 Traditional cultures: ethical education

The transmission of ethical ideas from one generation to the next in pre-literate societies was accomplished by counsel and correction, as well as in other important ways. In many cultures young people underwent periods of education removed from the community prior to the transition to adulthood. In these periods ideas about behaviour appropriate to one's gender and status, notions of what kind of person is worthy of respect, and conceptions of one's duties to others (including ancestors and other nonhuman spirits) were often inculcated.

It was common to recount the history (rather than the myth, as in contemporary usage myth connotes fictional status and these narratives are usually presented as true), of one's own people in terms that underwrote existing social arrangements. Ritual enactment of these histories provided a reinforcement for the broadly ethical understandings they underwrote. Another major source of moral instruction was through the various forms of *orature*, the verbal art that corresponds to the literature of literate societies. Among the most important of these are the folktale, a story told as fiction often with an Aesopian moral, and the proverb, a shorthand reference to history and the folktale. Proverbs have been seen as evidence of the moral notions of earlier African societies. Many of those who have written on this subject, including J.B. Danquah (1944), have relied on their interpretation to deduce traditional moral, and sometimes metaphysical, views. This process has its dangers: the interpretation of proverbs is a matter of context. In English, for example, it is easy to come up with two proverbs that might sound contradictory: 'more haste, less speed' and 'a stitch in time saves nine'. Which one is appropriate depends on whether the context refers to being timely or being careful. To infer from the first of these proverbs that UK culture values care over punctuality would be an error. Analogous mistakes have been made by observers interpreting African proverbs.

In African traditions the interpretation of proverbs is a difficult matter. Indeed, one Akan proverb says: 'if we tell a fool a proverb, we explain its meaning to him'. Many proverbs are less obvious in their application than the few with which most Europeans and Americans are familiar, because the language is densely figurative. A typical Akan proverb says: 'The drongo (bird) says: if he had known that the palm nuts were going to ripen, then he would not have married the raffia palm with a twisted leg'. Any contextual application of this proverb requires knowledge of the two plants in question: they are both palms, but one produces a valuable oil, while the other produces less valuable fibres. The knowledge that, before a certain stage of development, it is not obvious which is which, is also required. With this knowledge, it might be grasped that, in a particular context, the proverb was being used to express regret at having made the wrong choice in a situation of insufficient knowledge. In this context, the proverb could be said to be analagous to: 'more haste, less speed'. However, it would be wrong to infer that Akan culture values caution over efficacy. In fact, more can be learned about cultural values by exploring a proverb's presuppositions, than by the message it communicates.

There is an Akan proverb that says: 'when your child cheats your co-wife's child, it is not good; but when your co-wife's child cheats your child it is also not good'. It is often used in circumstances where the UK proverb, 'do as you would be done by', might be invoked. This proverb is used to make a point unconnected with marriage or family life and presupposes that men may have more than one wife at a time, that there is likely competition among co-wives and that this is something to be avoided. These presuppositions are communicated to young people as they grow up through the contextual and didactic use of such proverbs.

Proverbs are, therefore, an important source of ethical ideas in many cultures in Africa. As a result, the careful analysis of proverbs, especially where the analyst deals with their presuppositions, can reveal a culture's values.

4 Comparisons with 'modern' societies

In terms of content, there is less similarity among African traditions than at the level of the abstract formal features catalogued in §§2 and 3. The communitarian and anti-universalist character of ethical thought means that in most traditional African systems of ideas, public questions of practical reason, for example, in courts or in family decision making, rarely focused on the enforcement of individual rights. Instead, they concentrated on individual needs and a concern for corporate harmony. These tendencies remain in the areas where the influences of modernity (in the form of contemporary critiques by African intellectuals, of world religions and of Euro-American ideas), have not percolated. This is in contrast to formal juridical practice in most modern societies (including the modern sectors of most African states).

Another major contrast is with the central questions of propriety, reputation and status in practical reasoning. This is striking because in Euro-American culture, at least since the Enlightenment, such questions are related to the surface of action and a concern with them is seen as superficial in ways that contrast with genuine moral concerns.

In Akan cultures the notion of *animuonyam*, which comes close to the meaning of 'respect' or 'honour', plays a central role. The possibility of losing respect is very troubling for those who have it. (Well-known Akan proverbs such as the following show that respect is not something that belong to everybody: 'father soul and father slave Kyereme, neither of them has any respect'. This means that whatever you call him or her, a slave is still a slave.) But *animuonyam* is not just related to being thought well of: it is a matter of meriting a high opinion and being seen to merit it. One way of earning respect is by providing generously for one's fellow citizens through acts of munificence or serving one's country well in warfare.

A familiarity with European or Asian moral philosophy begs the question of how public ethical discourse relates to the inner language of private decision. The difficulty in understanding this relationship stems from the fact that access to such information in those cultures is a consequence of literacy. In pre-literate societies there is no record of ethical views except through the collective sphere of oral traditions, neither are there generic conventions, such as the confession (on the model of St AUGUSTINE), or the protestant diary (as the record of an individual conscience) to provide models of organized reflection on questions outside the public sphere. More than this, central genres such as the novel provide us with models of interiority in moral life that do not occur in the major genres of oral literature. To the extent that a nuanced language of private moral reflection, distinct from the discourse of collective decision making, is the product of the kind of privacy made possible through the conventions that constitute genres of writing such as autobiography and the novel, it can be said that there is no such private morality in the pre-literate cultures of precolonial Africa.

All of these latter facts lead anthropologists to speak of cultures of (external) shame as opposed to

(internal) guilt. In using such a classification, it is important to remember that shame, like guilt, requires a person to share the values that they have failed to live up to, rather than simply incurring embarrassment. Therefore, it would be misleading to think of African cultures without developed discourses of individualized (or private) morality being governed by the notion that it is only what is known publicly that is of any real ethical significance. In Asante, it is said that the man whose wife has had intercourse with another must be paid adultery fees even if intercourse occurred in a dream. This is because, in the Akante culture it is understood that dreams reflect the real experiences of one's *sunsum* and the idea that the dream is private does not exist. Thus, if a man dreams of intercourse with a woman she is assumed to have dreamed of intercourse with him. It is difficult to see how such a rule would come into being in a culture where people thought that what others did not know was of no ethical significance (see AKAN PHILOSOPHICAL PSYCHOLOGY).

The distinction between what I know and what others know is less crucial in cultures where everyone is supposed to be the subject of continuous surveillance by spirits of various sorts and where forms of divination and spiritual vision may allow others to discover what I have done by means other than witnessing or hearing about it.

A final difference, which is as a result of the lack of models of self-reflection provided in the major modern literary genres, is that certain moral ideas, such as the modern notion of authenticity, do not appear to have been present in most African moral traditions. There are notions of behaviour appropriate to one's status or role, and notions of honesty that come close to the idea of sincerity. However, the idea that a person can truly be defined as one thing or another beneath the masks that convention and ascribed status impose, is foreign. Instead, there are notions of destiny or fate. For example, in many west African traditions, along the whole of the Guinea coast, there is an idea that people are offered or given a fate by a high god before entering the world, and that this prenatal message shapes their life on earth. It is worthy of note that, the contrasts between African ethical ideas and those of modern Europe and the USA, do not necessarily distinguish African ethics from those of other traditional peoples who are outside the areas of influence of the literate ethical culture of the monotheistic world religions.

5 Contemporary trends

Against this background, it is possible to understand the ethical crises associated, on the one hand, with the growth of literacy, the development of the African novel, and access to Western literary forms, and on the other, with urbanization and the growth of commodity production and wage labour. Each of these changes contributes to undermining the compatibility of traditional ethical ideas of kinship and community and contemporary practical life. The problem of political corruption in many African states has arisen in part from the fact that state officials in the modern sector are paid salaries intended to support a family unit closer to a Euro-American nuclear model. These officials inherit obligations to corporate groups, such as lineages and places of origin, that they cannot sustain. Similarly, the question of nepotism or tribalism in the state bureaucracy should be seen in the context of a conflict between formal rights-based notions of the role of state agents and traditional corporate obligations.

As far as sub-Saharan ethical discourse is concerned, there is evidence of the influences of Islamic and Christian theory, as well as Marxist and liberal political and moral ideas introduced through European colonial education. These latter secular traditions are not too different from their Euro-American counterparts, although Marxist revolutionaries in Africa, such as Amílcar CABRAL have shared with Mao Zedong the problem of reshaping the ideas of Marx and Engels for predominantly nonindustrial societies.

With regard to major religious traditions, the contrast between traditional and contemporary ideas is less striking in Islamic areas. This is because, in many parts of sub-Saharan Africa, Islam was well-established before the period of European colonialism and existed for a long period as a literate tradition alongside the popular culture of a largely nonliterate populace. As a consequence, there was a mutual accommodation of Islamic ideas and the ethical thought of the pre-Islamic cultures into which they were introduced. It is said, therefore, that African Islam is highly syncretic, melding with local traditions in the various places it has been established. Just as Islam in other parts of the contemporary Muslim world has developed new secularizing traditions and new forms of fundamentalism, so has Africa. Secularization has tended to be the response of a literate intelligentsia with substantial familiarity with European culture, while fundamentalism has more of a popular, although literate, base. A consequence of the increasing flow of information through broadcast media and literacy, is that public ethical discourse in sub-Saharan Islamic Africa has grown closer to that of the rest of the Muslim world than it has been since the early period of African Islam.

The effect of Christianity has been to challenge the content of traditional ethical thought in many areas, such as objections to polygamy and caste-like hereditary status systems, and to appeal to ancestors and other spirits. (This latter conflict is less distinct because of the strong tradition of reference to saints, angels, devils and other 'principalities and powers' in European and north African Christian traditions whose spirits resemble African ones.) Furthermore, Christian otherworldliness and individualistic notions of merit and responsibility (deriving from contemporary economic relations) have penetrated many societies. It is reasonable to assume that the ethical thought of most contemporary African Christians is closer than it may appear to that of the precolonial period, especially in its communalism. To the extent that African Christians participate in formal literate ethical discourse, they do so within contemporary traditions that belong to European Christianity, with the exception of Coptic churches in Egypt and Ethiopia.

See also: AESTHETICS, AFRICAN; CONFUCIAN PHILOSOPHY, CHINESE; FAMILY, ETHICS AND THE; HONOUR; PRACTICAL REASON AND ETHICS; AFRICAN TRADITIONAL RELIGIONS

References and further reading

Ackah, C.A. (1988) *Akan ethics: a study of the moral ideas and the moral behaviour of the Akan tribes of Ghana*, Accra: Ghana University Press. (Discussion of Akan ethics in theory and practice.)

Beidelman, T.O. (1993) *Moral imagination in Kaguru modes of thought*, Washington, DC: Smithsonian Institution Press. (Exploration of the ethnography of Kaguru moral life.)

* Danquah, J.B. (1944) *The Akan Doctrine of God: A Fragment of Gold Coast Ethics and Religion*, London: Frank Cass, 1968. (A good source for the claim of the communitarian character of African traditions.)

Evans-Pritchard, E.E (1976) *Witchcraft, Oracles, and Magic Among the Azande*, abridged with introduction by E. Gillies, Oxford: Clarendon Press. (A classical discussion of how practical reasoning is affected by traditional religious beliefs.)

Fortes, M. (1983) *Oedipus and Job in West African religion*, Cambridge: Cambridge University Press. (Discusses the role of ideas about fate in the thought of a number of west African cultures.)

* Greenberg, J.H. (1970) *The Languages of Africa*, Bloomington, IN: Indiana University Press, 3rd edn. (The best source for material on African languages.)

Howard, R. and Donnelly, J. (1996) 'Human Dignity, Human Rights and Political Regimes', *American Political Science Review* 80: 801–17. (Makes the point that notions of dignity are more central than notions of rights in many African traditions.)

* Mbiti, J. (1969) *African Religions and Philosophy*, London: Heinemann, 2nd edn, 1990. (Covers a range of philosophical and religious ideas across Africa.)

Rattray, R.S. (1916) *Ashanti Proverbs*, Oxford: Clarendon Press. (An early collection of African proverbs which indicates their range and ethical significance.)

K. ANTHONY APPIAH

ETHICS

1 Ethics and meta-ethics

What is ethics? First, the systems of value and custom instantiated in the lives of particular groups of human beings are described as the ethics of these groups. Philosophers may concern themselves with articulating these systems, but this is usually seen as the task of anthropology.

Second, the term is used to refer to one in particular of these systems, 'morality', which involves notions such as rightness and wrongness, guilt and shame, and so on (see RECTIFICATION AND REMAINDERS). A central question here is how best to characterize this system. Is a moral system one with a certain function, such as to enable cooperation among individuals, or must it involve certain sentiments, such as those concerned with blame (see MORALITY AND ETHICS; MORAL SENTIMENTS; PRAISE AND BLAME; RECIPROCITY)?

Third, 'ethics' can, within this system of morality itself, refer to actual moral principles: 'Why did you return the book?' 'It was the only ethical thing to do in the circumstances.'

Finally, ethics is that area of philosophy concerned with the study of ethics in its other senses (see ETHICS IN ISLAMIC PHILOSOPHY). It is important to remember that philosophical ethics is not independent of other areas of philosophy. The answers to many ethical questions depend on answers to questions in metaphysics and other areas (see AESTHETICS AND ETHICS; METAPHYSICS; PRAGMATISM IN ETHICS). Furthermore, philosophers have been concerned to establish links between the ethical sphere of life itself and other spheres (see ART AND MORALITY; LAW AND MORALITY). Some philosophers have, for philosophical reasons, had doubts about whether philosophy provides anyway the best approach to ethics (see THEORY AND PRACTICE; WITTGENSTEINIAN ETHICS). And even those who believe philosophy has a contribution to make may suggest that ethical justification must refer outside philosophy to common sense beliefs or real-life examples (see EXAMPLES IN ETHICS; MORAL JUSTIFICATION).

A central task of philosophical ethics is to articulate what constitutes ethics or morality. This project is that of meta-ethics. What is it that especially constitutes the moral point of view as opposed to others? Some argue that what is morally required is equivalent to what is required by reason overall, whereas others see morality as providing just one source of reasons (see PRACTICAL REASON AND ETHICS). Yet others have suggested that all reasons are self-interested, and that concern for others is ultimately irrational (see EGOISM AND ALTRUISM). This has not been seen in itself to be inimical to the notion of morality, however, since a moral system can be seen to benefit its participants (see CONTRACTARIANISM; DECISION AND GAME THEORY).

The moral point of view itself is often spelled out as grounded on a conception of equal respect (see EQUALITY; RESPECT FOR PERSONS). But there is some debate about how impartial morality requires us to be (see IMPARTIALITY).

Another set of issues concerns what it is that gives a being moral status, either as an object of moral concern or as an actual moral agent (see MORAL AGENTS; MORAL STANDING; RESPONSIBILITY). And how do our understandings of human nature impinge on our conception of morality and moral agency (see MORALITY AND IDENTITY)?

Once we have some grip on what ethics is, we can begin to ask questions about moral principles themselves. Moral principles have often been put in terms of what is required by duty, but there has been something of a reaction against this notion (see DUTY). Some have seen it as outdated, depending on a conception of divine law with little relevance to the modern world (see ANSCOMBE, G.E.M.; SCHOPENHAUER, A.); while others have reacted against it as a result of a masculine overemphasis on rules at the cost of empathy and care (see FEMINIST ETHICS; WOLLSTONECRAFT, M.).

These doubts are related to general concerns about the role principles should play in ethical thought. Situation ethicists suggest that circumstances can lead to the abandonment of any moral principle, particularists arguing that this is because it cannot be assumed that a reason that applies in one case will apply in others (see MORAL PARTICULARISM; SITUATION ETHICS). The casuistical tradition has employed moral principles, but on the understanding that there is no 'super-principle' to decide conflicts of principles (see CASUISTRY). At the other end of the spectrum, some philosophers have sought to understand morality as itself constituted by a single principle, such as that not to lie (see WOLLASTON, W.).

Duties have been seen also as constituting only a part of morality, allowing for the possibility of heroically going beyond the call of duty (see SUPEREROGATION). This is a matter of the scope of the notion of duty within morality. There are also issues concerning the scope of moral principles more generally. Does a given moral principle apply everywhere, and at all times, or is morality somehow bounded by space or time (see MORAL RELATIVISM; UNIVERSALISM IN ETHICS)? This question is related to that concerning what is going on when someone allows morality to guide them, or asserts a moral principle (see EPISTEMOLOGY AND ETHICS; MORAL JUDGMENT; MORAL KNOWLEDGE). How is the capacity of moral judgment acquired (see MORAL EDUCATION)? The view that humans possess a special moral sense or capacity for intuition, often identified with conscience, is still found among contemporary intuitionists (see COMMON-SENSE ETHICS; CONSCIENCE; CUDWORTH, R.; HUTCHESON, F.; INTUITIONISM IN ETHICS; MORAL SENSE THEORIES; MOORE, G.E.; ROSS, W.D.; SHAFTESBURY). Scepticism about the claims of morality, however, remains a common view (see MORAL SCEPTICISM; NIETZSCHE, F.).

In recent centuries, a dichotomy has opened up between those who believe that morality is based solely on reason, and those who suggest that some nonrational component such as desire or emotion is also involved (see HUME, D.; MORALITY AND EMOTIONS; RATIONALISM). Denial of pure rationalism need not lead to the giving up of morality. Much work in the twentieth century was devoted to the question whether moral judgments were best understood as beliefs (and so candidates for truth and falsity), or as disguised expressions of emotions or commands (see ANALYTIC ETHICS; EMOTIVISM; HARE, R.M.; LOGIC OF ETHICAL DISCOURSE; PRESCRIPTIVISM; STEVENSON, C.L.). Can there be moral experts, or is each person entirely responsible for developing their own morality (see EXISTENTIALIST ETHICS; MORAL EXPERTISE)? These questions have been seen as closely tied to issues concerning moral motivation itself (see MORAL MOTIVATION). Moral judgments seem to motivate people, so it is tempting to think that they crucially involve a desire.

Moral principles can be understood to rest on moral values, and debate continues about how to characterize these values and about how many evaluative assumptions are required to ground ethical claims (see AXIOLOGY; CONSTRUCTIVISM IN ETHICS; MORAL PLURALISM; VALUES). Against the emotivists and others, moral realists have asserted the existence of values, some identifying moral properties with those properties postulated in a fully scientific worldview (see FACT/VALUE DISTINCTION; MORAL REALISM; NATURALISM IN ETHICS; VALUE, ONTOLOGICAL STATUS OF).

2 Ethical concepts and ethical theories

Some philosophical ethics is broad and general, seeking to find general principles or explanations of morality. Much, however, focuses on analysis of notions central to ethics itself. One such notion which has been the focus of much discussion in recent years is that of autonomy (see AUTONOMY, ETHICAL). The interest in self-governance sits alongside other issues concerning the self, its moral nature and its ethical relation to others (see AKRASIA; DETERMINISM AND INDETERMINISM; EVOLUTION AND ETHICS; FREE WILL; SELF-DECEPTION, ETHICS OF; SELF-RESPECT; WILL, THE); and the relations of these selves in a social context (see RECOGNITION; SOLIDARITY; VULNERABILITY AND FINITUDE). Other topics discussed include the nature of moral ideals, and the notions of desert and moral responsibility (see IDEALS; DESERT AND MERIT; MORAL LUCK).

The question of what makes for a human life that is good for the person living it has been at the heart of ethics since the Greek philosophers enquired into *eudaimonia* ('happiness') (see ARISTOTLE; EUDAIMONIA; HAPPINESS; LIFE, MEANING OF; PLATO; SOCRATES). Once again, a philosopher's theory of the good will almost always be closely bound up with their views on other central matters (see GOOD, THEORIES OF THE). For example, some of those who put weight on sense experience in our understanding of the world have been tempted by the view that the good consists entirely in a particular kind of experience, pleasure (see EMPIRICISM; PLEASURE). Others have claimed that there is more to life than mere pleasure, and that the good life consists in fulfilling our complex human nature (see PERFECTIONISM; SELF-REALIZATION). Nor have philosophers forgotten 'the bad' (see EVIL; SUFFERING; SUFFERING, BUDDHIST VIEWS OF ORIGINATION OF).

Moral philosophy, or ethics, has long been at least partly concerned with the advocacy of particular ways of living or acting. Some traditions have now declined (see ASCETICISM; MACINTYRE, A.); but there is still a large range of views on how we should live. One central modern tradition is that of consequentialism (see CONSEQUENTIALISM). On this view, as it is usually understood, we are required by morality to bring about the greatest good overall (see TELEOLO-GICAL ETHICS). The nature of any particular consequentialist view, therefore, depends on its view of the good. The most influential theory has been that the only good is the welfare or happiness of individual human and other animals, which, when combined with consequentialism, is utilitarianism (see BEN-THAM, J.; MILL, J.S.; UTILITARIANISM).

It is commonly said that consequentialist views are based on the good, rather than on the right (see RIGHT AND GOOD; RIGHTS). Theories based on the right may be described as deontological (see DEON-TOLOGICAL ETHICS). The towering figure in the deontological tradition has been the eighteenth-century German philosopher, Immanuel Kant (see KANT, I.; KANTIAN ETHICS). Such theories will claim, for example, that we should keep a promise even if more good overall would come from breaking it, or that there are restrictions on what we can intentionally do in pursuit of the good (see DOUBLE EFFECT, PRINCIPLE OF; PROMISING).

In the second half of the twentieth century there was a reaction against some of the perceived excesses of consequentialist and deontological ethics, and a return to the ancient notion of the virtues (see ARETĒ; THEOLOGICAL VIRTUES; VIRTUE ETHICS; VIRTUES AND VICES). Work in this area has consisted partly in attacks on modern ethics, but also in further elaborations and analyses of the virtues and related concepts (see CHARITY; FORGIVENESS AND MERCY; HELP AND BENEFICENCE; HONOUR; HOPE; INNOCENCE; LOVE; PRUDENCE; SELF-CONTROL; TRUST; TRUTHFULNESS).

3 Applied ethics

Philosophical ethics has always been to some degree applied to real-life. Aristotle, for example, believed that there was no point in studying ethics unless it would have some beneficial effect on the way one lived one's life. But, since the 1960s, there has been a renewed interest in detailed discussion of particular issues of contemporary practical concern (see AP-PLIED ETHICS).

One area in which ethics has always played an important role is medicine, in particular in issues involving life and death (see BIOETHICS; BIOETHICS, JEWISH; LIFE AND DEATH; MEDICAL ETHICS; SUI-CIDE, ETHICS OF). Recently, partly as a result of advances in science and technology, new areas of enquiry have been explored (see GENETICS AND ETHICS; REPRODUCTION AND ETHICS). In addition, certain parts of medical practice which previously lacked their own distinctive ethics have begun to develop them (see NURSING ETHICS).

This development is part of a wider movement involving research into the ethical requirements on those with particular occupations. Some of this research is again related to scientific advance and its implications for public policy (see INFORMATION TECHNOLOGY AND ETHICS; RESPONSIBILITIES OF SCIENTISTS AND INTELLECTUALS; RISK; TECHNOL-OGY AND ETHICS). But, again, attention has also been given to occupations not in the past subjected to much philosophical ethical analysis (see BUSINESS ETHICS; JOURNALISM, ETHICS OF; PROFESSIONAL ETHICS; SPORT AND ETHICS).

The planet, and those who live and will live on it, have in recent times become the focus of much political concern, and this has had its effect on philosophy (see AGRICULTURAL ETHICS; ANIMALS AND ETHICS; DEVELOPMENT ETHICS; ECOLOGICAL PHILOSOPHY; ENVIRONMENTAL ETHICS; FUTURE GENERATIONS, OBLIGATIONS TO; POPULATION AND ETHICS). But just as the scope of ethical enquiry has broadened, so there has been renewed interest in the specific details of human relationships, whether personal or between society, state and individual (see ECONOMICS AND ETHICS; MARKET, ETHICS OF THE; FAMILY, ETHICS AND THE; FRIENDSHIP; PATERNALISM; POLITICAL PHILOSOPHY; PORNOGRAPHY; SEXUALITY, PHILO-SOPHY OF).

See also: AUGUSTINE §§12–14; CHENG; CONFUCIAN PHILOSOPHY, CHINESE; DAOIST PHILOSOPHY; ETHICS IN ISLAMIC PHILOSOPHY; JIA YI; LI; MENCIUS; SELF-CULTIVATION IN CHINESE PHILOSOPHY; WATSUJI TETSURŌ; XIN (TRUSTWORTHINESS); ZHU XI

References and further reading

Rachels, J. (1986) *The Elements of Moral Philosophy*, New York: Random House. (A helpful introduction to metaethics and ethical theory, with good use made of real-life examples. Contains suggestions for further reading.)

Singer, P. (ed.) (1991) *A Companion to Ethics*, Oxford: Blackwell. (Contains short, pithy articles on central topics in ethics, including metaethics, ethical theory, and applied ethics. The articles include useful bibliographies.)

ROGER CRISP

ETHICS IN INDIAN PHILOSOPHY *see* DUTY AND VIRTUE, INDIAN CONCEPTIONS OF

ETHICS IN ISLAMIC PHILOSOPHY

*The study of Islamic ethics, whether philosophical or theological, grew out of early discussions of the questions of predetermination (*qadar*), obligation (*taklif*) and the injustices of temporal rulers, particularly the caliphs. Early writers on ethics from the Mu'tazila school were probably influenced by Greek philosophy. By the third century AH (ninth century AD) a clearly discernible current of philosophical ethics began to take shape, with strong influences from Greek ethics including Stoicism, Platonism and Aristotelianism.*

Al-Kindi, the first genuine philosopher of Islam, appears from his extant ethical writings to have been particularly influenced by Socrates and Diogenes the Cynic. Other classical influences can be seen in the work of Platonists such as Abu Bakr al-Razi, who followed Plato's division of the parts of the souls, and Neoplatonists such as al-Farabi, while Aristotelian influences can be seen in al-Farabi, who also discussed the problem of evil, Ibn Sina and Ibn Rushd. Ibn Sina developed a theory of the conjunction of the soul with the active intellect; with this conjunction is bound up the ultimate perfection of the soul which has attained the highest degree of wisdom and virtue.

Neoplatonism again surfaces in the work of Ibn Miskawayh and his followers, to whom we owe the groundwork of a whole ethical tradition which flourished in Persia well into the twelfth century AH (eighteenth century AD) and beyond. Onto Plato's threefold division of the soul, Ibn Miskawayh grafts a threefold division of virtue into wisdom, courage and temperance. His views were elaborated upon by al-Tusi and al-Dawwani, among others. A blend of philosophical and religious ethics is characteristic of the work of some later writers such as al-Ghazali and Fakhr al-Din al-Razi, in which the road to moral and spiritual perfection has mystical overtones.

1   Theological preludes
2   The rise of philosophical ethics: early Socratic and Stoic trends
3   The advent of Aristotle
4   Ibn Miskawayh and the Persian writers on ethics
5   Philosophical and religious ethics

1   Theological preludes

The earliest ethical discussions in the seventh and eighth centuries appear to have centred on the question of *qadar*, which could equally mean 'capacity', as predicated of man, or 'predetermination', as predicated of God. The early so-called Qadarites of

Damascus raised the question of *qadar* in the context of the moral responsibilities of the Umayyad caliphs, who justified their most oppressive policies on the ground that they were part of the divine decree (*qada' wa qadar*). Subsequently, the Mu'tazilite theologians of Basra and Baghdad refined upon the speculation of their Qadarite predecessors and attempted for the first time to give an adequate definition of right and wrong and its bearing on God's justice and his decrees in the world. This definition was expressed in essentially rationalist and deontological terms and was received with disapproval by their traditionalist and conservative rivals, who adhered to a voluntarist thesis according to which right is by definition what God commands and wrong is what he prohibits (see ASH'ARIYYA AND MU'TAZILA §5).

Other instances of Mu'tazilite rationalism include the espousal of the absolute identity of God's essence and his attributes, the irreversibility of his decrees and the freedom of the will as a precondition of moral responsibility. Mu'tazilite theologians also stressed God's wisdom and goodness and exonerated him of the responsibility for evil in the world, which was 'created' by humankind. The degree to which Mu'tazilite theological ethics was influenced by Greek philosophy cannot be fully determined from our present knowledge of the early sources, since the translation of philosophical texts had not been started by the time the founder of the school, Wasil ibn 'Ata, launched this radical theological movement in the second century AH (eighth century AD). However, contact with Christian theologians, such as JOHN OF DAMASCUS and his disciple Theodore Abu Qurrah, was definitely a factor in initiating the Qadarite theologians, the forerunners of the Mu'tazila, into the scholastic methods of discourse that Syriac-speaking Christian scholars had been applying to theological questions prior to the Arab conquest of Syria, Egypt and Iraq.

2   The rise of philosophical ethics: early Socratic and Stoic trends

AL-KINDI, the first genuine philosopher of Islam, was also the first writer on philosophical ethics, and it is significant that he was in sympathy with Mu'tazilite theology during the heyday of that movement. However, unlike his Mu'tazilite contemporaries, whose starting-point was the Qur'an and the Traditions (*hadith*) of Muhammad, al-Kindi's starting point was Greek philosophy. He is reported by the classical bibliographers to have written a number of ethical treatises reflecting a profound interest in Socratic thought. Thus, in addition to a treatise on *Ethics*, he is credited with a work on *Paving the Way to*

Virtue, as well as an extant tract, *Fi al-hila li-daf' al-ahzan* (On the Art of Dispelling Sorrows). Of his Socratic writings, a tract on the *Excellence of Socrates, A Dialogue between Socrates and Aschines* and a short collection, *Alfaz Sugrat* (Socratic Utterances), which has survived, are mentioned in the classical sources.

It is noteworthy, however, that in the last-mentioned collection the personalities of SOCRATES and Diogenes the Cynic (see DIOGENES OF SINOPE) are fused and both emerge as paragons of virtue and asceticism. However, in the more discursive *Fi al-hila li-daf' al-ahzan* the Stoic ideal of *apatheia* (freedom from passion) and the consequent indifference to the vicissitudes of fortune are set out in eloquent terms. The antidote of sorrow, which al-Kindi argues in Stoic fashion is inseparable from humanity's ephemeral condition in this world of generation and corruption, is to consider that sorrow results either from our actions or from the actions of others. In the first case, it is our duty as rational agents to refrain from doing that which is the cause of sorrow. In the second case, averting the sorrow which results from the actions of others is either in our power or it is not. If it is in our power, we ought certainly to avert it; if it is not in our power, we should not grieve at the prospect of injury in the hope that it might somehow be turned away. However, should we nevertheless be afflicted by sorrow resulting from actions over which we have no control, it is our duty as rational beings to bear this with fortitude. This view, and the exhortation to shun material possessions as temporary acquisitions of which we are mere borrowers and not real owners, reflect clearly the influences of the great second-century Stoic teacher EPICTETUS and appear to derive from his famous *Enchiridion*.

However, it was Socrates and his disciple Plato who were at the centre of the moral-ascetic speculation of the early Muslim ethical philosophers. Abu Bakr AL-RAZI, in his ethical treatise *al-Tibb al-ruhani* (The Spiritual Physic), refers to Plato as 'the master of the Philosophers and their leader', and to his teacher Socrates as 'the ascetic and godly' sage. He speaks of the three Platonic parts of the soul as the rational or divine, the irascible or animal and the concupiscent or vegetative souls, as these parts are designated by the Alexandrian physician–philosopher GALEN in a treatise on ethics (which has survived in Arabic translation only). He then proceeds to summarize Plato's teaching on the manner in which each of the parts or 'souls' should be 'managed' through reasoning and demonstration, a process which he labels 'spiritual physic' or therapy.

Another Socratic–Platonic theme which recurs in al-Razi's writings is the folly of the hedonistic life which turns man into a slave or a beast. Because so many of our pleasures are either ephemeral or unattainable, we are assailed by anxiety or grief. But the true philosopher will not succumb to grief, because he understands that nothing in this world of generation and corruption is ever permanent and that whatever cannot be turned away should be ignored or disregarded, since it is often the product of passion and not of reason: 'For reason summons us only to what is susceptible of bringing about profit sooner or later; grief does not bring any advantage.... That is why the perfectly rational man will only follow the summons of reason...and will never follow the summons of passion or allow himself to be led by it or get close to it' (*Rasa'il al-Razi al-falsafiya*: 69).

Like Socrates and Plato, al-Razi believed that the soul on leaving the body will return to its original abode in the intelligible world, after passing through an endless cycle of purifications. That, he argues, is why the fear of death is irrational, and like al-Kindi and other moral philosophers he admonishes the truly reasonable man to resign himself to the prospect of death as a logical consequence of our being human. As al-Kindi had written: 'Since the definition of man is that he is a living, dying, rational being, then if there was no death, there would be no man' (*al-Hila li-daf' al-ahzan*: 45), death being an essential part of the very definition of man.

However, al-Razi adds to this argument another argument which appears to derive from Epicurus, namely that death is the privation of sensation (see EPICUREANISM §13); in death, man is stripped of the sensations of pleasure or pain and thus is in a better condition than the living who are constantly subjected to pain, let alone the fact that pleasure sought by our concupiscent nature is really nothing but 'relief from pain' or return to the natural condition (as Plato has taught in the *Philebus*). Therefore, 'according to the judgment of reason the condition of death is better than the condition of life' (*Rasa'il al-Razi al-falsafiya*: 93).

3 The advent of Aristotle

The first systematic writer on philosophical questions in Islam was AL-FARABI, who had also contributed to ethical discussions. He is reported in the classical sources to have written a commentary on 'parts' of the *Nicomachean Ethics*, translated into Arabic by Ishaq ibn Hunayn. This commentary is lost, but judging from an extant collection of *Fusul muntaza'ah* (Excerpts on Ethics),which he is established as having written, he appears to have followed Aristotle's lead in dividing the virtues into moral (practical) and intellectual (see ARISTOTLE §§22–25). The former, he says, are the virtues or perfections of the concupiscent part or faculty of the soul; they include temperance, courage, liberality and justice. The latter are the perfections of the intellectual part and include practical reasoning, good judgment, sagacity and sound understanding.

In his discussion of justice, al-Farabi also follows Aristotle's lead, arguing that justice consists in the equitable distribution of 'common goods' in the city or the state. These goods include security, wealth, dignity and public office, of which every member of the city or state is entitled to a share. Another more general meaning of justice is given as 'man's exercise of virtuous actions in himself and in relation to others, whatever such a virtue might be'.

An interesting feature of al-Farabi's ethics which has no Aristotelian parallel is the discussion of evil. He starts in Neoplatonic fashion by asserting that 'evil has no existence as such in anything found in these worlds; that is generally in whatever does not exist through human volition. Everything therein is good' (*Fusul muntaza'a*: 81). Evil, then, is a predicate of human action, not of physical occurrences. However, al-Farabi disagrees with traditional Neoplatonists who identified being with the good and not-being with evil pure and simple, on the ground that 'being is good only when it is in conformity with justice (or merit); not-being is evil when it is not in conformity with justice' (*Fusul muntaza'a*: 81). This appears to reflect Heraclitus' concept of *dike* as chaos (see HERACLITUS §3).

Al-Farabi's successor and spiritual disciple IBN SINA (Avicenna) is the author of a very short tract on ethics which follows closely the Platonic model in psychology. Ibn Sina divides the soul into the rational, irascible and concupiscent, to which correspond the virtues of wisdom, courage and temperance respectively, and with justice being the 'summation' of all three. To ensure the enforcement of justice within the state, argues Ibn Sina, the existence of the caliph, as conceived of by the Shi'ites, is necessary as the sovereign of the world and God's vicegerent on earth.

More explicitly than al-Farabi, Ibn Sina develops in his psychological writings a theory of conjunction (*ittisal*) of the soul with the active intellect, that supermundane agency which according to the Muslim Neoplatonists governs the sublunary world (see NEOPLATONISM IN ISLAMIC PHILOSOPHY §2). With this conjunction, he argues, is bound up the ultimate perfection of the soul which has attained the highest degree of wisdom and virtue, becoming thereby a replica or a mirror of the higher intelligible world. Therein lies man's ultimate happiness while his soul is still in the body.

IBN RUSHD, the great Aristotelian philosopher and commentator, is known from the bibliographical sources to have written a paraphrase and a middle commentary on the *Nicomachean Ethics*, which have survived only in Hebrew and Latin, together with a paraphrase of Plato's *Republic* which is also relevant to his ethical theory. The principal virtues, according to Ibn Rushd, correspond to the perfection of the three parts of the soul, the rational, the irascible and the concupiscent. Justice is then described along Platonic lines as the 'harmony' of the three corresponding virtues of wisdom, courage and temperance; but it has, as Aristotle stated in the *Nicomachean Ethics*, two subdivisions which Ibn Rushd calls common or universal, corresponding to 'perfect virtue', and particular, whose further subdivisions are distributive and rectificatory. Contrary to expectations, however, Ibn Rushd does not identify happiness with the contemplative life, as ARISTOTLE (§26) had done, but rather with conjunction (*ittisal*) with the active intellect, which the Muslim Neoplatonists – with whom he was at loggerheads – had regarded as man's ultimate goal.

4 Ibn Miskawayh and the Persian writers on ethics

The most important writer on ethics in Islam, however, was an eclectic who inclined to Platonism, Ahmad ibn Muhammad IBN MISKAWAYH. He laid down in his *Tahdhib al-akhlaq* (The Cultivation of Morals) and other ethical writings the groundwork for a whole tradition of Persian ethical writing, the chief representatives of which were Nasir-i Khusraw (d. AH 467/AD 1074), Nasir al-Din AL-TUSI, Jalal al-Din AL-DAWANI, Hussain Kashifi (d. AH 910/AD 1504), Mulla Ahmad Nuraqi (d. AH 1244/AD 1828) among others.

The psychological basis of Ibn Miskawayh's ethics is clearly Platonic, as was generally the case in Islamic philosophical circles. Onto Plato's threefold division of the soul (see PLATO §14), as modified by GALEN, he grafts a threefold division of virtue into wisdom, corresponding to the rational part of the soul; courage, corresponding to the irascible part; and temperance, corresponding to the concupiscent part. Justice, which Ibn Miskawayh describes as a form of moderation (*i'tidal*) or proportion (*nisba*), arises when the three powers or parts of the soul are in harmony. This virtue is not part of virtue, but virtue entire, as ARISTOTLE (§22) had argued. Its subdivisions, according to Aristotle as interpreted probably by PORPHYRY, are then given as three: our duties to God, to our superiors or equals, and finally to our ancestors. Ibn Miskawayh, however, refers to the genuine Aristotelian twofold subdivisions of justice into distributive and rectificatory and predicates the exercise of this supreme virtue on submission to the holy law (*shari'a*), which emanates from God. He then assigns to the 'just imam' or caliph the function of warding off the different forms of violating justice. Ibn Miskawayh even attributes to Aristotle, quoting an apocryphal Aristotelian source in Arabic translation, the view that justice stipulates rendering God the kind of worship due to him as our beneficent creator.

However, the Neoplatonic element in Ibn Miskawayh's ethics is nowhere more pronounced than in his analysis of happiness. Its two subdivisions, according to him, are practical and theoretical. The latter consists in 'conjunction' with the active intellect, whereby man is able to join the 'higher intellectual' realm. However, Ibn Miskawayh recognizes beyond this intellectual perfection a 'divine' or supernatural condition whereby man partakes of divine perfection or achieves a condition of self-divinization which goes far beyond his worldly conditions. This 'divine condition' is also alleged to derive from an Aristotelian fragment *On the Virtues of the Soul*, which Ibn Miskawayh quotes in Arabic translation, but which is clearly different from the apocryphal tract of the Aristotelian corpus known as *De virtutibus et vitiis*.

Ibn Miskawayh's two best-known Persian followers are Nasir al-Din al-Tusi, author of *Akhlaq-i Nasiri* (Nasirean Ethics), and Jalal al-Din al-Dawani, author of *Lawami al-ishraq fi makarim al-akhlaq* (Flashes of Illumination on the Nobility of Character), known also as *Akhlaq-i Jalali*. Both al-Tusi and al-Dawani follow closely the lead of Ibn Miskawayh in the *Tahdhib al-akhlaq*. A fundamental difference between Ibn Miskawayh and the latter two authors is the addition of 'household management' and politics to the purely ethical part of their work by both al-Tusi and al-Dawwani. This may be viewed as a broadening, in Aristotelian fashion, of the scope of practical philosophy, which Ibn Miskawayh had tended to confine to ethical discourse only.

In the political section, inspired chiefly by al-Farabi, al-Tusi argues that orderly association is an essential precondition of the good life. Of the three forms of government, the monarchical, the tyrannical and the democratic (which he attributes to Aristotle), he favours the monarchical, identified like Plato's with the 'rule of the virtuous' or aristocrats. However, the true monarch is assisted by divine inspiration but is subordinate to the imam, who according to Shi'ite doctrine is in 'temporary concealment'. This monarch acts accordingly in a vicarious or interim capacity to ensure the administration of justice in the absence of the true head of the community or 'hidden imam'.

Al-Dawani's ethical treatise follows essentially al-Tusi's lead, but in genuine Shi'ite fashion he stresses more than his predecessor the position of humans as God's vicegerent (*khalifa*) on earth (Surah 2: 30). In mystical fashion, he then goes on to argue that people reflect in their capacity as God's vicegerent the dual character of the divine nature, the outer and the inner, the spiritual and the corporeal, and more than any other creatures, including the angels, can be described as the 'image' of God. The foremost duty of the ruler, he argues, is to preserve the ordinances of the divine law (*shari'a*) and to conduct the affairs of state in accordance with universal principles and the requirements of the times. The ruler is for that reason God's 'shadow' and the vicar of the Prophet.

5 Philosophical and religious ethics

A specific blend of philosophical and religious ethics is characteristic of the writings of some late authors, including al-Raghib al-Isfahani (d. AH 502/AD 1108), Abu Hamid AL-GHAZALI, Fakhr al-Din AL-RAZI and others. AL-GHAZALI is the foremost representative of this group, who in both his ethical treatise *Mizan al-amal* (The Balance of Action) and his religious summa, *al-Ihya' 'ulum al-din* (The Revival of the Religious Sciences), has developed an ethical theory in which Platonic psychology serves as the groundwork of an essentially Islamic and mystical worldview. In this theory, the table of the four cardinal virtues accords with the Platonic virtues but admits of a series of subdivisions or ramifications analogous to those of his predecessors. A good example of the combination of religious and philosophical ideas in al-Ghazali is the manner in which happiness can be achieved. Happiness, as the chief good, admits of two subdivisions, the worldly and the otherworldly. Otherworldly happiness, which is our ultimate goal, cannot be achieved without certain worldly goods. These include the four cardinal virtues of wisdom, courage, temperance and justice, the bodily virtues of health, strength, good fortune and a long life, the external virtues of wealth, kin, social position and noble birth, and finally the 'divine virtues' of guidance, good counsel, direction and divine support. Those virtues are referred to in the Qur'an and the *hadith*, al-Ghazali says, and the final virtue, 'divine support', is identified with the Holy Spirit (Surah 2: 87, 253) (see VIRTUES AND VICES).

The road to moral and spiritual perfection is described as the 'quest for God'. The seekers after God must satisfy two conditions: their actions must be governed by the prescriptions or ordinances of the 'divine law' (*al-shar'*), and they must ensure that God is constantly present in their hearts. By this presence al-Ghazali means genuine contrition, adoration and submission, born of the seeker's awareness of the beauty and majesty of God which al-Ghazali, like other Muslim mystics or Sufis, regards as analogous to human passion or love (*'ishq*) (see MYSTICAL PHILOSOPHY IN ISLAM).

See also: ARISTOTELIANISM IN ISLAMIC PHILOSOPHY; ETHICS; AL-GHAZALI; GREEK PHILOSOPHY: IMPACT ON ISLAMIC PHILOSOPHY; IBN MISKAWAYH; LOGIC IN ISLAMIC PHILOSOPHY; PLATONISM IN ISLAMIC PHILOSOPHY

References and further reading

Alon, I. (1991) *Socrates in Mediaeval Arabic Literature*, Leiden: Brill; Jerusalem: Magnes Press, The Hebrew University. (A reliable review of Socratic literature in Arabic.)

Arkoun, M. (1970) *Contribution à l'étude de l'humanisme arabe au IV/Xe siècle* (Contribution to the Study of Arab Humanism in the 4th–10th Centuries), Paris: Vrin. (A detailed account of Ibn Miskawayh's ethics and his philosophical impact.)

Donaldson, D.M. (1953) *Studies in Muslim Ethics*, London: SPCK. (Contains useful information on Arabic and Persian ethics, but is now somewhat out of date.)

Fakhry, M. (1994) *Ethical Theories in Islam*, Leiden: Brill, 2nd enlarged edn. (A systematic analysis of philosophical and religious ethical theories in Islam.)

* al-Farabi (c. 870–950) *Fusul muntaza'ah* (Excerpt on Ethics), ed. F. Najjar, Beirut, 1971. (Al-Farabi's work on ethics, showing the influence of Aristotle.)

Hourani, G. (1985) *Reason and Tradition in Islamic Ethics*, Cambridge: Cambridge University Press. (An important collection of ethical studies by an eminent writer on ethical questions in Islam.)

* Ibn Miskawayh (before 1030) *Tahdhib al-akhlaq* (The Cultivation of Morals), trans. C.K. Zurayk, *The Refinement of Character*, Beirut: American University of Beirut, 1966. (Reliable and annotated translation.)

Khadduri, M. (1984) *The Islamic Conception of Justice*, Baltimore, MD: Johns Hopkins University Press. (A discursive and informative account of this central ethical concept in Islamic thought.)

al-Kindi (before 873) *Rasa'il al-Kindi al-falsafiyah* (Al-Kindi's Philosophical Writings), ed. A.H. Abu Rida, Cairo, 1950. (Collected philosophical writings of al-Kindi.)

* —— (before 873) *al-Hila fi-daf' al-ahzan* (On the Art of Dispelling Sorrows), ed. H. Ritter and R.

Walzer, *Uno scritto morale de al-Kindi*, Rome, 1938. (Contains al-Kindi's account of Stoic ideals.)

Leaman, O. (1995) 'Christian Ethics in the Light of Muslim Ethics', in C. Rodd (ed.) *New Occasions Teach New Duties?*, Edinburgh: T. & T. Clark, 219–31. (Comparative study of the differing roles played by ethics in Islam and Christianity.)

* al-Razi (before 925) *Rasa'il al-Razi al-falsafiyah* (Al-Razi's Philosophical Writings), ed. P. Kraus, Cairo, 1939. (Collected philosophical writings of Abu Bakr al-Razi.)

* al-Tusi (1201–74) *Akhlaq-i Nasiri* (The Nasirean Ethics), trans. G.M. Wickens, London: Allen & Unwin, 1964. (Translation of al-Tusi's *Akhlaq-i Nasiri* from Persian. Reliable on the whole.)

MAJID FAKHRY

ETHIOPIA, PHILOSOPHY IN

Ethiopia is a unique phenomenon in Africa for three reasons. First, because of its historical continuity and political independence; second because of its written language and third because of its written philosophy. Ethiopian philosophy in the broadest sense is expressed in both oral and written language. In this entry only the written documents are dealt with. This methodological approach limits the investigation to linguistic and cultural phenomena as it deals with the ancient Semitic language known as Ethiopic and the Christian zones of influence on the high plateaus of Ethiopia.

There are five basic texts of Ethiopian philosophical literature: the Physiologue *(the Fisalg^{w}os) (c. fifth century AD), The Book of the Wise Philosophers (1510/22), The Life and Maxims of Skendes (c. eleventh century AD), The Treatise of Zar'a Ya'ecob (1667) and The Treatise of Wäldä Heywät (c. eighteenth century). The first three are adaptations of works transmitted from Greek sources through Arabic; the latter two (appearing in modern publications in a combined form) are original works of a rationalist flavour.*

1 **The basic texts**
2 **From wisdom to rationalism**
3 **Dialectical pattern**

1 The basic texts

The Ethiopic *Physiologue* (c. fifth century AD), a naturalistic-theological book of Christian symbolism, is a translation and adaptation from the Greek original. The Greek *Physiologue* seems to have been written between the end of the second century AD and the beginning of the third. There is near unanimity among scholars that Alexandria, Egypt was the place where it was revised. The Ethiopian translation was probably adapted around the beginning or middle of the fifth century. It was completed in Egypt by an Ethiopian living in a monastery of Skete where he had access to the Greek original.

The sixteenth century is particularly rich in the history of Ethiopic literature with a philosophical slant. At this time, Abba Mikael, an Egyptian, translated and adapted into Ethiopic *The Book of the Wise Philosophers* (1510/22). After its adaptation, an Ethiopian transcribed it into on parchment in Ethiopic. The Arabic text is thought to have been written by Hunain ibn Ishâq (*c.* 809–?), the son of a Nestorian Christian. The Arabic version is based on the lost Greek original. This original belonged to the later literature of apophthegm in the form in which it flourished during the Byzantine period (seventh to early ninth century). The Greek influence is evident throughout *The Book of the Wise Philosophers* in its allusion to Presocratic (sixth and fifth centuries BC), Socratic (469–399 BC), Aristotelian (384–322 BC), and especially Platonic (427–347 BC) and Neoplatonic (from third to sixth or seventh centuries AD) dialogues. *The Book of the Wise Philosophers* is a collection of sayings, or a *liber sententiarum*. It presents the quintessence of what various philosophers have said on a certain number of topics, the greater number of which are ethical.

The Life and Maxims of Skendes (*c.* eleventh century AD) was also translated and adapted from the Arabic into Ethiopic at this time, although the identity of the author is unknown. The Arabic story seems to have been based on a Greek original of the second century AD. A careful examination of the Ethiopic and the Arabic texts shows that the Ethiopian translator of this version of the Oedipus story is clearly a deeply thinking person with sensitive powers of perception. The Skendes story, as it is conveyed in Ethiopic, is the most perfect and morally chastened of all preserved accounts of this type.

A close comparison of the Arabic, Ethiopic and Greek texts (there are parallels of the lost Greek original in other Greek works) reveals that the Ethiopians never translate literally except for the Holy Scriptures. They adapt, modify, add and subtract. A translation therefore bears a typically Ethiopian stamp. Although the nucleus of what is translated is foreign, the way it is assimilated and transformed is typically Ethiopian. This phenomenon, which is not limited to philosophical works but also applies to other cultural areas like iconography, is known as 'creative incorporation'.

The Treatise of Zar'a Ya'ecob (1667) is original in many ways. The author begins the treatise with the story of his life. It is the only autobiography in Ethiopic literature. Zar'a Ya'ecob (1599–1692) was born in the environs of Aksum, northwest Ethiopia. He attended traditional Ethiopian schools and attained the highest learning levels. Afterwards he taught Holy Scriptures for ten years. Denounced before the king, he was compelled to flee for his life. On his way to Shoa in the south (Addis Ababa is the modern capital of the province of Shoa), he found an uninhabited cave at the foot of a valley, where he lived for two years. In peace and solitude he developed his philosophy. His philosophy is presented as the fruit of his own personal reflection and not as a translation-adaptation from foreign sources as is the case with most Ethiopic literature. It is clearly rationalistic in a religious (not scientific) sense. Rationalism is understood as the view which recognizes as true only that content of faith which can be made to appeal to reason. In Ethiopia, traditional philosophy in its written form is closely linked with Christianity in general and monasticism in particular. Zar'a Ya'ecob's rationalism, in contrast, insists precisely on the absolute and exclusive sufficiency of human reason and denies all dogmatic assertion that reason is unable to establish by its own means.

Through the application of his method, the light of reason, whose immediacy enlightened his investigation, Zar'a Ya'ecob discovered a basic principle: the goodness of created nature. From this foundation he moved towards theodicy, ethics and psychology. In his ethics, because he accepted the fundamental goodness of creation, he endorsed married life and the enjoyment of food, and rejected the time-honoured traditions of celibacy and fasting in Ethiopian monastic life. In his psychology he emphasized the freedom of the human and their superiority over the rest of creation.

As a contemporary of René Descartes, Zar'a Ya'ecob resembled him in many ways, although Ya'ecob did not make use of the method of universal doubt. In both these philosophers one finds a method, occasion for a critical inquiry and the discovery of a criterion that leads to the establishment of a basic principle, which is then applied in both authors to theodicy, ethics and psychology. Also in both, the method of inquiry is revolutionary, although its roots are deeply theological. The historical circumstances from which the rationalism of both philosophers originated are equally similar. They are based in the collapse of scholasticism, the harmony between faith and reason in Europe, and in Ethiopia, the confrontation with Western culture and violent religious discord (see DESCARTES, R. §1).

Zar'a Ya'ecob, unlike Descartes, was not a mathematical genius. His philosophy does not develop deductively as a linear growth from a first principle or original idea, but rather, like the unfolding of the sun's rays, it emanates from a single centre and safeguards the complexity and richness of reality.

After his death, Zar'a Ya'ecob's disciple Wäldä Heywåt wrote *The Treatise of Wäldä Heywåt* (*c.* eighteenth century) in which his master's last years are related and his thought is presented in a more pedagogical and accessible fashion.

2 From wisdom to rationalism

The five basic texts that have been presented span more than twelve centuries of literary production. They show a double evolution: from translation, the *Physiologue* (*c.* fifth century AD), with its frequent misunderstandings, *The Book of the Wise Philosophers* (1510/22), with its intuitions, *The Life and Maxims of Skendes* (*c.* eleventh century AD), with its sensitive, reflective perceptions) to originality, *The Treatise of Zar'a Ya'ecob* (1667), *The Treatise of Wäldä Heywåt* (*c.* eighteenth century); from wisdom to rationalism. The link with Christianity evolves from the Christian symbolism of the *Physiologue* to the theologically-oriented anthropocentrism of *The Book of the Wise Philosophers*, to the theistic pantheism of the first series of maxims in *The Life and Maxims of Skendes* to the anti-Christian, though mystical radicalism of Zar'a Ya'ecob and his disciple.

However, it is the very notion of philosophy, in both a broad and narrow sense, which shows the greatest evolution. In the widest sense it is synonymous with wisdom understood as involving knowledge and the ability, inclination and steady purpose of putting knowledge to good use. Thus evidence of wisdom in a person involves an end or purpose to be attained, an understanding of this purpose and an effort to achieve it in the best possible manner. Objectively, wisdom is the sum total of things worth knowing and ends worth working for.

The Book of the Wise Philosophers and *The Life and Maxims of Skendes* attempt, each in their own way, to express wisdom in the broad sense of philosophy. *The Book of the Wise Philosophers* presents the simplest and most common form of wisdom literature: the *angarä*, or saying. *The Life and Maxims of Skendes*, on the other hand, is a philosophical novel. The second and third sections, within the question and answer frame, cover the spectrum of forms of wisdom literature, including maxims, numbers, exhortations and the biographical portrait.

The Treatise of Zar'a Ya'ecob and *The Treatise of Wäldä Heywåt* are philosophy in a stricter sense. Each is the result of the reflection of one person, and each has a clearly defined method, characterized by criticism, inquiry (the name of the treatise in Ethiopic is *hatätä*, or inquiry), and the use of the criterion of the light of reason as a basis upon which the whole edifice is founded. But, within the same rationalistic approach, a clear distinction appears between the master and his disciple. Zar'a Ya'ecob is the only one of the two who presents in a complete, systematic and original way, the methodology of his philosophy. Although Wäldä Heywåt shares the ideas of his master, the starting point and the dialectical movement from this origin are not found in his treatise. In this sense, he is in line with Ethiopian traditional thought (see RATIONALISM).

Since the *Physiologue* is not a philosophical work, one may ask why it has been placed at the beginning of a series of texts on Ethiopian philosophical literature. The following quotation might indicate why:

> Seen from the vantage point of later developments in Ethiopian philosophy, especially the XVI, XVII and XVIII centuries, the Fisalg^wos (the Physiologue) affords a first glimpse into its rudimentary beginning. It is like observing a great river in its initial streamlets. Nearly all the main characteristics of Ethiopian philosophy that will flourish in Mäshafä fälasfa (The Book of the Wise Philosophers), The Life and Maxims of Skendes, and The Treatise of Zar'a Ya'ecob and of Wäldä Heywåt are already present in the Fisalg^wos, although in an inchoate way: its thought patterns, its archetypal images and symbolism, its world view..., its anthropology, its social approach and its set of ethical values. Without the later developments of Ethiopian philosophy, the Fisalg^wos is deprived of its significance; without the Fisalg^wos, Ethiopian philosophy is deprived of its roots.
>
> (Sumner 1985: 8–9)

3 Dialectical pattern

Like ancient and medieval philosophies in Europe, classical Ethiopian philosophical literature has a definite beginning and end. The history of Ethiopian philosophy appears as a dialectical process representing a curve rather than a straight line. This curve is also apparent within *The Life and Maxims of Skendes*, as it moves from the life of Skendes through the first series of maxims and into the second.

The thesis of the dialectical pattern is represented by Ethiopian philosophy of Greek origin. Just as Aristotelian thought was introduced into the Latin medieval world through translations made from the original Greek into Arabic and later into Latin, Greek Platonic and Aristotelian thought was introduced into Ethiopia during the sixteenth century by translations made from the original Greek into Arabic and later into Ethiopic. This stage can be seen in *The Book of the Wise Philosophers* and *The Life and Maxims of Skendes*. The Ethiopian response to this alien influence did not represent a slavish adherence to imported forms, but rather, a creative incorporation. These two works offer adaptations which are so free and original that they are practically the equivalent of an authentic Ethiopian work. The link with Christianity is also apparent in both works.

Zar'a Ya'ecob's work breaks the intimate link with Christianity in general and monasticism in particular, even though his thought remains profoundly theistic. Therefore, he represents an antithetic position to the works of his predecessors. The departure is even greater if one considers that his work is original, the product of personal reflection and not a translation or adaptation from foreign sources.

The treatise written by Wäldä Heywåt after his master's death attempted to synthesize Ya'ecob's ideas with the traditional wisdom literature represented by *The Book of the Wise Philosophers*. His treatise is interspersed with illustrations taken from this sixteenth-century work, although they are more dramatic and picturesque in Wäldä Heywåt than in their original models. The result of this synthesis is no less deep than his master's investigation, but does establish a rapport between the autobiographical insights of Ya'ecob and other practical and educational considerations.

Wäldä Heywåt represents a major contribution to Ethiopian philosophy with respect to ordinary human life. His treatise stresses the value of work, develops a social philosophy with its different practical applications, affirms the equality of all human beings whatever their beliefs, and insists on the beauty of marriage and family life. Yet looked at from the perspective of originality, critical rigour and methodological structure, the synthesis represented by Wäldä Heywåt's treatise is not the summit of the dialectical movement. The line that began with wisdom literature and ascended in an original arc curves back on itself.

References and further reading

Arefayne Hagos (1987) 'Where is the Spring of African Philosophy?', *The Ethiopian Herald* 48 (165): 3–6. (The precise meaning of the title of Sumner's book: *The Source of African Philosophy: The Ethiopian Philosophy of Man*, 1986.)

Littmann, E. (1909) 'Geschichte der Ethiopischen Literatur' (History of Ethiopian Literature), in C. Brockelmann (ed.) *Geschichte der christlichen Literaturen des Orients* (History of Christian Literature in the East), Leipzig: C.F. Zmelangs. (This book on oriental Christian literature contains a chapter on Ethiopian literary history.)

* Sumner, C. (1510/22) *Ethiopian Philosophy*, vol. 1, *The Book of the Wise Philosophers*, Addis Ababa: Ministry of Culture and Sports, 1974. (Large sections of text in English translation; analysis in English.)

* —— (1667; *c*.18th century) *Ethiopian Philosophy*, vol. 2, *The Treatise of Zar'a Ya'ecob and of Wäldä Heywåt*, Addis Ababa: Addis Ababa University, 1976. (Complete English translation of text and discussion of scholarship.)

* —— (1667; *c*.18th century) *Ethiopian Philosophy*, vol. 3, *The Treatise of Zar'a Ya'ecob and of Wäldä Heywåt: an Analysis*, Addis Ababa: Addis Ababa University, 1978. (Thorough analysis of preceding text.)

* —— (*c*.11th century AD) *Ethiopian Philosophy*, vol. 4, *The Life and Maxims of Skendes*, Addis Ababa: Addis Ababa University, 1978. (Analysis and complete English translation of text.)

* —— (*c*.5th century AD) *Ethiopian Philosophy*, vol. 5, *the Fisalg^wos*, Addis Ababa: Addis Ababa University, 1982. (Analysis and complete English translation of text.)

—— (1985) *Classical Ethiopian Philosophy*, Addis Ababa: Alliance Ethio-Française. (Complete English translation of texts contained in vols 1, 2, 3, 4 and 5. General introduction on Ethiopia and its culture and specific introductions for each of the five basic texts. Recommended as introductory reading.)

—— (1986) *The Source of African Philosophy: the Ethiopian Philosophy of Man*, Stuttgart: Franz Steiner Verlag Wiesbaden. (Analysis of the five basic texts. Recommended as a companion to *Classical Ethiopian Philosophy*, 1985.)

—— (1988) 'The Ethiopian Philosophy of Greek Origin', in S. Uhlig and Bairu Tafla (eds) *Collectanea Aethiopica*, Stuttgart: Franz Steiner Verlag Wiesbaden, 1988. (Comparative study of Greek, Arabic and Ethiopic texts.)

CLAUDE SUMNER

ETHNOPHILOSOPHY, AFRICAN

Ethnophilosophy refers to bodies of belief and knowledge that have philosophical relevance and which can be redescribed in terms drawn from academic philosophy, but which have not been consciously formulated as philosophy by philosophers. These bodies of belief and knowledge are manifested in the thoughts and actions of people who share a common culture.

Most of the literature on ethnophilosophy is written about African cultures. Ethnophilosophy's most immediate African antecedents include Leopold Senghor's philosophy of négritude and the writings of the Belgian missionary to the Congo (later Zaire), Placide Tempels. Ethnophilosophy examines the systems of thought of existing and precolonial African communities in order to determine what can be the ideal forms of 'authentic' African philosophy and praxis in the emerging postcolonial situation. In addition to the pioneering work of Senghor and Tempels, this school is represented in the writings of philosopher Alexis Kagamé (1956) and theologian John Mbiti (1969) among others, many of whom were regarded as Tempels's disciples.

The central themes of the work of these disciples include assertions that there is a unified 'Bantu philosophy' and that its fundamental categories are manifested in features of language such as grammar, or features of culture such as cosmology and ritual. According to many of these authors writing about Bantu philosophy, the boundaries between self and other are not as rigid as in Western philosophy. Also, interdependence rather than competition is a primary social value and the human and nonhuman world is animated by a 'vital force', which underlies the perception of reality.

1   **Defining ethnophilosophy**
2   **African ethnophilosophy**
3   **Ethnophilosophy and the politics of culture**

1   Defining ethnophilosophy

The literature defining African socialism can be included in the ethnophilosophical approach. This is a body of materials combining Marxist social and economic theories with *négritude*'s politics of difference. Two works by Nyerere (1968a, 1968b) reveal that these political accounts share with other works of ethnophilosophy the thesis that the central values of Africa are communal rather than individual (see ETHICAL SYSTEMS, AFRICAN). The definition of ethnophilosophy is complex and ambiguous because

it arises out of a basic ambiguity in the definition of philosophy itself. The idea of philosophy refers to two related but separable orders of discourse. The first order is located in the forms of talk and action found among the ordinary members of society and elaborated by them in the course of their everyday life and activities. In common parlance, a person, group, historical period or culture could be referred to as having a philosophy when the systematic nature of their moral judgments, the ontological notions that underlie their view of the world, the ways in which they argue and the criteria of evidence and truth that are exhibited in their arguments are under discussion. Usually the philosophy attributed to a person or social entity is not consciously held or espoused, but is part of the tacit set of conventions that make discourse intelligible.

The second order of discourse is dependent on the first order and uses first-order discourse to develop a self-consciously critical order of discourse that is philosophical in a narrower sense and is perceived as having the capacity to correct the flaws of first-order discourse. This is the critical aspect of second-order discourse, but it can also have a speculative side that has not always been acknowledged by the analytic movement which has dominated so much of the history of modern philosophy.

The second problem in defining philosophy as second-order discourse returns to the basic question of defining ethnophilosophy. In a sense all philosophy is culturally shaped and socially determined. It is doubtful that any form of discourse is independent of its cultural and social contexts. If that is so, then all thought, even second-order thought, is shaped by such aspects of the lives of thinkers as their identity, social relations and the culture they share in common with their audiences and interlocutors. From a sociological and anthropological point of view all philosophy is ethnophilosophy. The distinction between first- and second-order thinking, while useful as a means of distinguishing modes of thought used within a single setting, does not help a great deal in specifying the defining features of philosophy believed to transcend the cultural and historical contexts in which they were elaborated.

These observations suggest a second definition for ethnophilosophy which arises more from the practices of philosophers than from the definitions they themselves have offered: ethnophilosophy is a term used to describe the bodies of belief and knowledge defined by colonized people whose institutions cannot easily be assimilated into models derived from the Western experience in general and the Enlightenment in particular, notably those historical contexts out of which the modern discipline of (Western) philosophy emerged and from which it draws its specificity. From this point of view the ambiguity that created ethnophilosophy has little to do with the people to whom the term is applied and much to do with the social contexts from which a specialism such as philosophy is derived.

2 African ethnophilosophy

Both African socialism and more strictly philosophical works of ethnophilosophy celebrate the subordination of the individual to the community that they argue is central to African culture and philosophy. On the surface this position appears to be radically non-Western and opposed to the emphasis on the adversarial individual in Western thought and culture. Actually it accepts a distinct opposition between individual and community that is not only Western but profoundly rooted in nineteenth-century utilitarian thought. The primary difference between utilitarian thinkers and ethnophilosophers on the subject of the individual and community is that the direction of causation is reversed. In the philosophy of the social sciences, for example, the utilitarian position known as 'methodological individualism' asserts that collective and communal forms are reducible to calculating individuals. In ethnophilosophy, by contrast, individuals are reducible to (or explicable in terms of) communities (see HOLISM AND INDIVIDUALISM IN HISTORY AND SOCIAL SCIENCE).

A number of contradictions are exhibited in ethnophilosophical writings. First and foremost, they remain profoundly descriptive and nonjudgmental, that is noncritical, about African traditions and customs. But they are generally offered in the service of a discourse that is powerfully critical of colonial rule and culture. This is the basis for the reproach aimed at ethnophilosophy by the African philosophers Paulin Hontoundji (1983) and Kwasi Wiredu (1980), that critical discourse cannot exempt one side from the criticism it levels at the other side.

What is even more important, however, is the criticism that ethnophilosophy is oppositional without being radical. On the surface ethnophilosophy is robustly anti-colonial, yet it still accepts the basic categories in terms of which colonial culture defines other cultures and peoples. It attempts to re-evaluate them instead of seeking to criticize the grounds out of which colonial discourse emerges, such as the distinction between culture and civilization, or the primitive or 'traditional' and the 'modern'.

Thus, it appears that ethnophilosophy has two contradictory aspects. It is a critical discourse that defines itself in opposition to colonialism, yet it begins by accepting the colonial categories of tradi-

tional and modern. The most significant difference between the original colonial categories and their use in ethnophilosophy is that instead of treating them as diametrically opposed in the colonial fashion, ethnophilosophy tries to merge them by re-appraising indigenous values as worthy of attention and then accordingly discovering the traditional in the modern.

Ethnophilosophers tend to be scholars trained in the West who work on materials derived from outside the cultural contexts in which they were trained. The context and structure of their work engages them in an activity that is culturally hybridized. Since many of them are Africans, the hybridity also works in the other direction, from Africa to the West. Ethnophilosophers have occasionally used the hybrid nature of their cultural productions to create knowledge that is itself hybrid by arguing that characteristics of Western intellectual history can be found in African traditional thought. For example Alexis Kagamé (1956) argues that African thought utilizes Aristotelian and Thomistic elements. Placide Tempels (1959), arguably the father of ethnohistory, even founded a Catholic religious movement in the Congo (later Zaire) based on the convergence of Bantu philosophy and Christianity.

The literature on ethnophilosophy does not usually combine discussions of ethnophilosophy proper with accounts of the writings on African socialism and Afrocentricity. The notable exception is Anthony Appiah's *In My Father's House* (1982) which examines nationalist themes and assertions about the person found in pan-Africanism, the counter-hegemonic discourses on race and the literature on African philosophy (see PAN-AFRICANISM). Appiah's work represents a rare attempt to take a stance which acknowledges the ways in which philosophical discourse emerges from cultural and historical conditions and is manifested in a range of materials that include but are not limited to philosophy. By avoiding the increasingly sterile debate about whether African discourse has a second-order dimension, Appiah is able to discuss philosophical aspects of a broad range of materials in a way that has escaped the grasp of philosophers more concerned with the boundaries of their discipline.

Perhaps the most notable characteristic of the ethnophilosophy school was its characterization of philosophy as a kind of collective narrative. Ethnophilosophers treated African philosophy as a narrative whose content is revealed through various codes, such as myth, symbolic systems and religious and ordinary language. In this sense, although African philosophy was represented as an innate form of indigenous expression, it could only be recovered and re-evaluated from a hybridized postcolonial present.

This is another example of ethnophilosophers' ambivalent mediation between two points, the 'traditional' and the 'modern'.

3 Ethnophilosophy and the politics of culture

The political implications of ethnophilosophy are also displayed in the idea that traditional knowledge is or was collectively produced and appropriated. This central theme of ethnophilosophy suggests that individuals cannot be free; that in a society where knowledge is a collective product, cultural criticism is not possible. This in turn raises fundamental questions about personhood, agency and the possibility of change.

The idea that African thought is collective and unchanging has been accepted by some of the critics of ethnophilosophy. Hountondji (1983) and Wiredu (1980) argue that the capacity for change depends on three elements of Western Enlightenment inheritance lacking in traditional societies: individual freedom, abstract theory and openness to alternative theories and interpretation. In their view traditional philosophy appears to reject these features of thought. Wiredu (1980) identifies these with science and sees hope for this redemption in the application of analytic practice as people seek new methods and solutions to old problems. Hountondji (1983) proposes that this redemption takes as its foundation Althusserian neo-Marxist notions which he believes govern the mobility of knowledge through history. Both regard the individual as the agent of change through social and cultural criticism. In other words, Wiredu and Hountondji defend the colonial and postcolonial as the new spatial and temporal realities not to be ignored by Africa.

This countercritique ranks the West above the traditional as they separate the past from the present. This is because the influence of the past on the present should be minimized to avoid anachronism. In effect, it offers an alternative representation of the hybrid postcolonial social and cultural condition.

The critique of ethnophilosophy began around the 1960s after the first works of ethnophilosophy were published. Among the first critics of ethnophilosophy was Franz Crahay (1965). In his paper 'Le Décollage Conceptuel: Conditions d'une Philosophie bantoue' (Conceptual Launch: the Terms of a Bantu Philosophy) he argued that the colonial distinction between the traditional and the modern is analogous to the distinction between 'constructing myth' and 'practising philosophy'. This distinction is in turn similar to the metaphysical distinction between form and matter. Although form and matter make complementary contributions to the identity of things, they none

the less remain conceptually distinct in nature and function. According to this perspective philosophy like form is of the mind. It deals with those elements of thought in which experience as event and practice is presented in and to our minds. It deals with ideas, related to and distinct from the particulars from which they derive. Though it is a human practice, philosophy diverges from other human practices such as customary ways of living and traditional (or any) group behavioural patterns.

Like matter, myth, tradition, custom and mores are glued to the sensual mode of experience. Their language remains unabstracted from the metaphors and experiences of everyday life; they are sociologically immediate and concrete. In this sense Crahay (1965) argues that while philosophy frees itself from its conceptually limiting fixation with sociological conditions by 'taking-off' to a free, or universal conceptual level, ethnophilosophy remains trapped in the closed confines of sociological structures and relativism like anthropology. In anthropology the argument that African systems of thought have been closed was developed by Robin Horton (1967). He argues that the nature of African social structures prevents African thought treating society and nature as abstract rather than personalized. In his view social relations are the idiom for thinking about natural elements, not vice versa.

The difficulty with the critics of ethnophilosophy, as well as with the alternatives developed by scholars such as Horton, is that by reserving criticism for themselves, the authors of this literature also reserve the role of criticism for the Western trained philosopher. This position implicitly supposes that traditional African society is still collective and so cannot regenerate itself by means of social and cultural criticism. From a political point of view the strategy of constructing a subject who can only be represented by an other is characteristic of nationalist thought and assertion, where some political actor or writer sets themselves up as the voice and representative of an emerging collectivity which can not speak for itself. The parallel between ethnophilosophy and nationalist discourse is not accidental. The guiding assumption of ethnophilosophy, that philosophical notions can be held unconsciously, requires a conscious agent to represent and lead the mass of ordinary Africans to a different world and a better life. This political project shared by ethnophilosophy and many of its critics is unmistakably nationalist and modernist. It is organized by ideas about progress and divides the social world into two classes, citizens who are critically self-aware agents and subjects who have yet to acquire the cultural apparatus that would enable them to become citizens. The debate about whether Africans and others possess second-order modes of thought also exhibits modernist premises about critical self-awareness, but is more concerned with the relationship of philosophy (as an emergent profession) with society than with how cultures should be classified. Ethnophilosophy brings together two usually separate cultural arenas: professional discourse and cultural discourse. The result sheds light on unresolved issues in the definition of philosophy, as well as problems of how cultures are classified and ranked.

See also: AFRICAN PHILOSOPHY, ANGLOPHONE; AFRICAN PHILOSOPHY, FRANCOPHONE §5; AKAN PHILOSOPHICAL PSYCHOLOGY; YORUBA EPISTEMOLOGY

References and further reading

Abraham, W.E. (1962) *The Mind of Africa*, Chicago, IL: University of Chicago Press. (The first book on African philosophy, containing a sophisticated account of ethnophilosophy and a critique of colonialism.)

* Appiah, A.K. (1982) *In My Father's House: Africa in the Philosophy of Culture*, London: Methuen; Oxford: Oxford University Press, 1992. (A collection of essays on African culture, philosophy and pan-Africanism which uses analytical philosophy to examine changing definitions of race, problems of ethnophilosophy and the ideology of culture in Africa.)

Asante, K.M. and Kariamu, W.A. (1990) *African Culture: The Rhythms of Unity*, Trenton, NJ: New World Press. (One of many books on Afrocentricity. It is a broad-ranging exposition of Asante, a major figure, whose thinking exhibits many of the features of the literature in ethnophilosophy.)

* Crahay, F. (1965) 'Le Décollage Conceptuel: Conditions d'une Philosophie bantoue' (Conceptual Launch: the Terms of a Bantu Philosophy), in *Diogène* 52: 61–84. (The classic critique of ethnophilosophy discussed in the text in §3)

Fløistad, G. (1987) *Contemporary Philosophy*, vol. 5: *African Philosophy*, Boston, MA: Kluwer. (A collection of essays by major figures writing about African philosophy. Perhaps the best text in which to survey the range of work on the subject.)

* Horton, R. (1967) 'African Traditional Thought and Western Science', *Africa* 37 (1–2): 50–71, 155–87. (The most important modern essay by an anthropologist who compares the structure of African traditional thought to the structure of scientific thinking.)

—— (1982) 'Tradition and Modernity Revisited', in M. Hollis and S. Lukes (eds) *Rationality and Relativism*, Oxford: Basil Blackwell. (Influential articles by an anthropologist who examines African worldviews as forms of intellectual activity and compares them with the worldview of science. He finds many parallels and some significant differences, notably in the attitude to alternative explanations of the world found in each system.)

* Hountondji, P.J. (1983) *African Philosophy: Myth and Reality*, Bloomington, IN: Indiana University Press; 2nd edn, 1996. (A major work by an African philosopher trained in France. Hountondji writes in the tradition of Bachelard and Althusser and seeks to find the space in which to situate an 'epistemological break' in African worldviews.)

* Kagamé, A. (1956) *La philosophie bantu-rwandaise de l'être* (The Bantu-Rwandan Philosophy of Being), Brussels: Académie Royale des Sciences Coloniales. (Perhaps the most detailed and analytical study of an African system of thought from an ethnophilosophical point of view.)

Masolo, D.A. (1994) *African Philosophy in Search of Identity*, Bloomington, IN: Indiana University Press. (A thorough study of ethnophilosophy and its African critics. The book takes account of relevant anthropological literature.)

* Mbiti, J. (1969) *African Religions and Philosophy*, London: Heinemann, 2nd edn, 1990. (Ethnophilosophy is combined with Christian theology in this influential book.)

Mudimbe, V.Y. (1988) *The Invention of Africa: Gnosis, Philosophy, and the Order of Knowledge*, Bloomington, IN: Indiana University Press. (A major survey of what Mudimbe calls the 'colonial archive' of images about Africa. Special attention is paid to the literature on African philosophy.)

* Nyerere, J.K. (1968a) *Ujamaa: Essays on Socialism*, New York: Oxford University Press. (The classic exposition of African socialism, which examines African society to find socialist priciples.)

* —— (1968b) *Ujamaa: The basis of African Socialism*, Dar es Salaam: Oxford University Press. (The most influential writer on African socialism.)

Pearce, C. (1992) 'African Philosophy and the Sociological Thesis', in *Philosophy of the Social Sciences* 22 (4): 440–60. (An important review of African philosophy.)

Senghor, L.S. (1964) *Liberté 1: négritude et humanisme* (Liberty 1: négritude and humanism), Paris: Editions de Seuil. (An explanation of *négritude* by Senegal's president and distinguished poet.)

* Tempels, P. (1959) *Bantu Philosophy*, Paris: Présence Africaine. (The founding text of ethnophilosophy. Argues that Bantu philosophy is expressed in collective forms and that it perceives the world as animated by a vital force.)

* Wiredu, K. (1980) *Philosophy and An African Culture*, Cambridge: Cambridge University Press. (A rigorous examination of the ethnophilosophical point of view from the twin perspectives of analytical philosophy and pragmatism.)

IVAN KARP
D.A. MASOLO

EUCLIDEAN GEOMETRY

see GEOMETRY, PHILOSOPHICAL ISSUES IN; MEGARIAN SCHOOL; POSIDONIUS; PROCLUS; THALES

EUCLIDES *see* MEGARIAN SCHOOL

EUDAIMONIA

The literal sense of the Greek word eudaimonia *is 'having a good guardian spirit': that is, the state of having an objectively desirable life, universally agreed by ancient philosophical theory and popular thought to be the supreme human good. This objective character distinguishes it from the modern concept of happiness: a subjectively satisfactory life. Much ancient theory concerns the question of what constitutes the good life: for example, whether virtue is sufficient for it, as Socrates and the Stoics held, or whether external goods are also necessary, as Aristotle maintained. Immoralists such as Thrasymachus (in Plato's Republic) sought to discredit morality by arguing that it prevents the achievement of* eudaimonia, *while its defenders (including Plato) argued that it is necessary and/or sufficient for* eudaimonia. *The primacy of* eudaimonia *does not, however, imply either egoism (since altruism may itself be a constituent of the good life), or consequentialism (since the good life need not be specifiable independently of the moral life). The gulf between 'eudaimonistic' and 'Kantian' theories is therefore narrower than is generally thought.*

1　**Conventional morality and Aristotle**
2　**Attacks on conventional morality**
3　**Eudaimonistic and Kantian ethics**

1　Conventional morality and Aristotle

The word *eudaimonia* and the corresponding adjective *eudaimōn* are derived from *eu* 'good, well' and *daimōn*

'spirit', giving the literal sense 'having a good guardian spirit', hence being blessed, having the life of one who enjoys divine favour. To possess *eudaimonia* is to have a life which is objectively desirable, and thereby to have achieved the most worthwhile of conditions available to humans. It thus overlaps substantially with the modern concept of happiness (see HAPPINESS), where that is conceived, not as a (possibly short-lived) episode of feeling, but as a condition characterizing a whole life, or a substantial part of it, as when one wishes a newly married couple happiness in their life together. But even when thus conceived, happiness in the modern sense is determined primarily by one's subjective attitude to one's life; broadly, to be happy is to be content with one's life, whereas contentment with one's life, although arguably necessary for *eudaimonia*, is not sufficient for it. According to ARISTOTLE (§21) (*Nicomachean Ethics*, 1095a15–22) everyone agrees (1) that *eudaimonia* is the highest human good and (2) that the word means 'doing and living well', but there are substantive disagreements on what kind of life counts as doing and living well. Some kinds, such as the life devoted to bodily pleasure, are disqualified not on the ground that people who live like that are always dissatisfied, but because they fail to satisfy objective requirements for a worthwhile life, in particular that it should be an excellent realization of specifically human potentiality. Again, Aristotle asserts (1100a1–2) that a child is not *eudaimōn*, meaning not that no one has a happy childhood, but that the life of a child is not one in which human potential is realized to its highest bent.

In popular usage the term has strong connotations of material prosperity, traditionally regarded as one of the signal marks of divine favour. This conception is in tension with a more specifically ethical one, according to which the condition of the agent's personality or character is at least the primary determinant of living well. The latter conception, found already in DEMOCRITUS §§15–16 (fr. 171), finds its strongest expression in the Socratic thesis, later adopted as the cardinal tenet of Stoicism, that virtue is the only intrinsic human good and wickedness the only intrinsic evil (see STOICISM §15–16). Aristotle's treatment (*Nicomachean Ethics* I 7–10) is a characteristic exercise in reconciliation of these standpoints. On the one hand *eudaimonia* must be comprehensive and self-sufficient, requirements which seem to imply that it includes the gifts of fortune; on the other the achievement of the good life must be in our power. Aristotle's middle way is the thesis that excellence or virtue (see ARETĒ) of character and intellect is (1) indispensable for the good life, (2) although not totally invulnerable, less subject to the vicissitudes of fortune than anything else. Hence the achievement of excellence, although not strictly sufficient for *eudaimonia*, as Socrates arguably and the Stoics certainly claimed, comes as close to guaranteeing it as the limitations of human life permit.

2 Attacks on conventional morality

Since *eudaimonia* was universally agreed to be the good, critics of conventional morality such as ANTIPHON, CALLICLES (in Plato's *Gorgias*) and THRASYMACHUS (in Plato's *Republic*) sought to devalue morality by arguing that it hinders or prevents the achievement of *eudaimonia*, while defenders of morality sought to show that it is necessary and/or sufficient for *eudaimonia*. The attacks assume that *eudaimonia* is to be achieved through the gratification of desire, whereas morality requires resistance to or suppression of desire; the defences take different forms. One line of defence, seen in Democritus, Protagoras' myth (in Plato's *Protagoras*) and Glaucon's social contract account of morality in *Republic* II, stresses the benefits which the individual derives from social institutions, for the existence of which morality is necessary. In the *Republic* (see PLATO §14) Plato takes the more radical step of internalizing social morality; the 'individual' is in fact a community in miniature, and the requirements of morality are therefore reduced to the proper organization of that community: that is, to the harmonious organization of the 'individual' personality. Plato, and Greek philosophers generally, take the primacy of individual *eudaimonia* pretty well for granted; the possibility that morality might require the sacrifice of the agent's *eudaimonia* for the good of others, or of society, is hardly canvassed.

This raises the difficult problem of the extent to which Greek ethical theory allowed for altruism. Certainly, all the main writers and schools – Plato, Aristotle, Epicurus and the Stoics – stress the importance of one form or another of social life, whether that of the city, the Epicurean community or the cosmos as a whole, insisting that interpersonal ties of one or other kind are themselves essential constituents of individual *eudaimonia* (see ARISTOTLE §§27–8; EPICURUS §11; STOICISM §14). If the most worthwhile life is the most excellent one, and the most excellent thing to do is to sacrifice one's life for one's friend, as Aristotle recommends, or to take one's turn ruling instead of devoting oneself full-time to metaphysics, as Plato requires of his guardians in the *Republic*, then in sacrificing oneself one does not sacrifice, but perfects, one's *eudaimonia*. The primacy of *eudaimonia* is thus preserved, but at the cost of moralizing the concept of *eudaimonia* itself; the good life includes the moral (whether the just or the altruistic) life as an essential component. This in turn threatens the project of defending morality by showing it to be necessary and/or sufficient for the independently acknowledged good of *eudaimonia*.

3 Eudaimonistic and Kantian ethics

The primacy of *eudaimonia* in Greek ethical thought standardly leads to its being characterized as 'teleological', in opposition to 'deontological' theories of a Kantian type (see TELEOLOGICAL ETHICS; DEONTOLOGICAL ETHICS), in which the fundamental concept is that of obligation binding on all rational beings (see KANT §9). This contrast is superficial. As we have seen, 'eudaimonistic' theories need not be consequentialist, since the good life need not be specifiable independently of the moral life (see CONSEQUENTIALISM). Furthermore, the tendency of much Greek thought, notably that of Plato, Aristotle and the Stoics, to identify the real self with the rational self tends towards the identification of the achievement of *eudaimonia* with conformity to demands of reason. The Stoic community of all rational nature is the forerunner of the Kantian kingdom of ends.

See also: CYRENAICS §§3–4; WISDOM

References and further reading

Annas, J. (1993) *The Morality of Happiness*, Oxford and New York: Oxford University Press. (Aristotle and later Greek philosophers on happiness and the good.)

* Aristotle (c. mid 4th century BC) *Nicomachean Ethics*, trans. T. Irwin, Indianapolis, IN: Hackett, 1985. (Includes notes.)

Irwin, T. (1986) 'Stoic and Aristotelian Conceptions of Happiness', in M. Schofield and G. Striker (eds) *The Norms of Nature*, Cambridge: Cambridge University Press, 205–44. (An illuminating comparison of the two conceptions.)

—— (1995) *Plato's Ethics*, Oxford and New York: Oxford University Press. (Comprehensive treatment of the ethical theories of the early and middle dialogues, with brief discussion of the later dialogues.)

Kenny, A. (1992) *Aristotle on the Perfect Life*, Oxford: Clarendon Press. (Aristotle's treatments of virtue and the good life.)

Long, A.A. and Sedley, D.N. (1987) *The Hellenistic Philosophers*, vol. 1, Cambridge: Cambridge University Press. (Translates the principal sources for Stoicism and Epicureanism; includes commentary.)

* Plato (*c.*390s–380s BC) *Gorgias*, trans. T. Irwin, Oxford: Clarendon Press, 1979. (Includes notes.)

* —— (*c.*380s BC) *Protagoras*, trans. C.C.W. Taylor, Oxford: Clarendon Press, 2nd edn, 1991. (Includes notes.)

* —— (*c.*370s BC) *Republic*, trans. R. Waterfield, Oxford and New York: Oxford University Press, 1994. (See especially Books I, IV, VIII and IX.)

White, S.A. (1992) *Sovereign Virtue*, Stanford, CA: Stanford University Press. (Aristotle on the relation between happiness and prosperity.)

C.C.W. TAYLOR

EUDOXUS (*c.*390–*c.*340 BC)

Eudoxus of Cnidos was a Greek mathematician with wide-ranging philosophical and scientific interests. He was known in antiquity for his mathematical astronomy and his philosophical hedonism, and placed, if loosely, within the Pythagorean tradition. More recently, debate about the correspondence between mathematical models produced by astronomers and the physical motions of the astronomical bodies themselves has focused especially on Eudoxus, since he is generally regarded as the first to have used a mathematical model in astronomy.

Very little about Eudoxus' life and work is known with any certainty. Diogenes Laertius (VIII 86–91), in his biography of Eudoxus, reports that he was called 'Endoxus' ('illustrious') because of his brilliant reputation. None of his works survives, only accounts and fragments in other ancient authors. Even the long-standing belief that he was a leading member of Plato's Academy (see ACADEMY) is now in doubt. However, there is evidence that he founded a school at Cyzicus, on the Hellespont, which may have survived into the third century BC. Tantalizingly little is known about his relationships to such important contemporaries as his supposed teacher Archytas, Plato and Aristotle. Anecdotes relate his invention of a type of sundial, and his introduction of the practice of arranging furniture in a semi-circle to accommodate more people.

Eudoxus is mentioned, together with Anaxagoras, by Aristotle in his arguments against the theory of Platonic Forms (see ARISTOTLE §15). The reference is short and ambiguous; consequently scholars have debated whether Eudoxus actually had a 'theory' of Forms. Alexander of Aphrodisias, in his commentary on Aristotle, provides a lengthier discussion of what he understands as Eudoxus' views, including the idea

that forms are mixed together with and are 'homoeomerous' (of like parts) to those things they inform. Eudoxus can be understood as suggesting that forms are immanent (rather than transcendent), for they are physical ingredients in entities (Dancy 1991).

Eudoxus is particularly celebrated for his geometric model of planetary motion. According to the ancient story, he was the first to answer Plato's challenge to account for the apparently irregular motions of the celestial bodies by using only uniform, circular and regular motions in order to describe the phenomena or 'save the appearances'. He devised a separate system of nested homocentric spheres to describe the apparent motions of each of the heavenly bodies (reported by Aristotle in *Metaphysics* XII 8). Writing much later, Simplicius explained that according to Eudoxus the path of a planet describes a figure called a 'hippopede' or horse-fetter. Eudoxus was able to account for various phenomena and 'save the appearances' in an approximate way, although not all phenomena could be explained, including the changing brightness of planets. Aristotle mentions that Callipus (of Cyzicus) adopted Eudoxus' approach but added to the number of spheres, in order to explain the phenomena better. Aristotle objected to the number of spheres of both Eudoxus and Callipus, and offered his own improvements to the system. Although the ancient descriptions of Eudoxus' astronomy are brief, several nineteenth century scholars reconstructed in detail the geometry thought to underlie his solution.

Questions regarding the application of mathematical methods to the explanation of natural phenomena are of great interest to historians and philosophers of science, and Eudoxus' work often figures importantly in their discussions. Eudoxus played a key role in the history of science, according to Pierre DUHEM, who was himself a proponent of an instrumentalist view of science and, as a physicist, philosopher and historian of science, was interested in the relationship between mathematics and physics (Duhem 1908) (see SCIENTIFIC REALISM AND ANTIREALISM §1; PTOLEMY). According to instrumentalists, theories permit predictions which correspond to observations, but do not necessarily describe physical reality. Many, including Duhem, have assumed that Eudoxus did not believe that his geometric model had any physical reality. This would qualify Eudoxus as the first 'instrumentalist' in the history of science. However, the paucity of our knowledge of Eudoxus' work makes any statement regarding the intention underlying his astronomical solution purely speculative.

Within the broader context of early Greek astronomy, it has been suggested that Eudoxus' originality lay in providing the basis of a geometric explanation useful in accounts of problems of practical interest, namely the risings and settings of stars, in geographical studies, and in justifying a more mathematically sophisticated sundial (Goldstein and Bowen 1983). On this view, Eudoxus' work represents a synthesis of two existing activities, calendar-making and cosmological theorizing, and his introduction of a geometric model to explain celestial motions inaugurated a new phase in astronomy.

It is tempting to look for some connection between Eudoxus' astronomical work and his ethical philosophy. Both the science of music and cosmological speculation may have had an important influence on him: the Pythagoreans and Plato were already pointing to a moral order manifested in the circular motions of the heavenly bodies (see PYTHAGOREANISM §§2–3). Furthermore, there is evidence that theological concerns motivated the followers of Eudoxus in his school at Cyzicus (Sedley 1976).

As a hedonist, Eudoxus thought that pleasure was the good and the goal of life (see HEDONISM). Aristotle (*Nicomachean Ethics* X 2) explains Eudoxus' argument, which was based on the observation that all things aim towards pleasure. Because that which is the object of choice is excellent and that which is most the object of choice is most excellent, the fact that all things move towards the same goal indicates that for all things it is the good. Aristotle observes that Eudoxus' views regarding pleasure were taken seriously because of his good character, rather than on their own merits. Because he was regarded as remarkably self-controlled, it was thought that Eudoxus presented his views 'not simply as a friend of pleasure, but because the facts really were so'.

References and further reading

* Aristotle (*c.* mid 4th century BC) *Metaphysics*, trans. H. Tredennick, Loeb Classical Library, Cambridge, MA: Harvard University Press and London: Heinemann, 1933, 2 vols. (Parallel Greek text and English translation; Eudoxus' astronomy is covered in XII 8; his theory of Forms is described in I 9.)

* —— (*c.* mid 4th century BC) *Nicomachean Ethics*, trans. H. Rackham, Cambridge, MA.: Loeb Classical Library, Harvard University Press and London: Heinemann, 1982. (Parallel Greek text and English translation; X 2 discusses Eudoxus' hedonism.)

* Dancy, R.M. (1991) *Two Studies in the Early Academy*, Albany, NY: State University of New York. (Considers Eudoxus' theory of Forms.)

* Diogenes Laertius (*c.* 3rd century AD) *Lives of the Philosophers*, trans. R.D. Hicks, *Diogenes Laertius Lives of Eminent Philosophers*, Loeb Classical Library, Cambridge, MA: Harvard University Press and London: Heinemann, 1925, 2 vols. (A life of Eudoxus can be found at VIII 86–91.)

Dreyer, J.L.E. (1906) *History of the Planetary Systems from Thales to Kepler*, Cambridge: Cambridge University Press; 2nd edn, *A History of Astronomy from Thales to Kepler*, New York: Dover, 1953. (Gives a detailed account of Schiaparelli's reconstruction of Exodus' possible geometry.)

* Duhem, P. (1908) *ΣΩZEIN TA ΦAINOMENA, Essai sur la notion de théorie physique, de Platon à Galilée*, Paris: A. Hermann; repr. Paris: Vrin, 1990; trans. E. Dolan and C. Maschier *To Save the Phenomena: An Essay on the Idea of Physical Theory from Plato to Galileo*, Chicago, IL: University of Chicago Press, 1969. (Influential interpretation of the relationship between astronomy and physics.)

* Goldstein, B. and Bowen, A.C. (1983) 'A New View of Early Greek Astronomy', *Isis* 74: 330–40. (A reappraisal of the role of Eudoxus within the Greek astronomical tradition.)

Gosling, J.C.B. and Taylor, C.C.W. (1982) *The Greeks on Pleasure*, Oxford: Clarendon Press. (Chapter 14 discusses Eudoxus' hedonism.)

Guthrie, W.K.C. (1962–78) *A History of Greek Philosophy*, Cambridge: Cambridge University Press, 6 vols. (Volume 5 pages 447–57 covers Eudoxus.)

Lasserre, F. (1966) *Die Fragmente des Eudoxos von Knidos*, Berlin: de Gruyter. (Presents the evidence regarding Eudoxus.)

Lloyd, G.E.R. (1978) 'Saving the Appearances', *Classical Quarterly* 28: 202–22; repr. in *Methods and Problems in Greek Science*, Cambridge: Cambridge University Press, 1991. (Expresses important reservations about Duhem's interpretation.)

North, J. (1994) *The Fontana History of Astronomy and Cosmology*, London: Fontana, 1994. (A useful description of Eudoxus' geometric model.)

* Sedley, D. (1976) 'Epicurus and the Mathematicians of Cyzicus', *Cronache Ercolanesi* 6: 23–54. (Shows that Eudoxus' students built physical models of his system.)

* Simplicius, (6th century AD) *In Aristotelis de caelo commentaris*, ed. J.L. Heiberg, *Commentaria in Aristotelem Graeca VII*, Berlin: Reimer, 1894, 493–507; trans. G.V. Sciaparelli, *Scritti sulla storia della astronomia antica*, Bologna: Zanichelli, 3 vols, 1925–7, II, 95–112; trans. of major sections, T. Heath, *Aristarchus of Samos: The Ancient Copernicus*, New York: Dover, 1981, 201–2, 213, 221–3. (A late ancient account of Eudoxus' astronomy.)

LIBA TAUB

EURASIAN MOVEMENT

The Eurasian movement was a creation of émigré Russian intellectuals following the First World War and the October Revolution. The ideology of Eurasianism was formally proclaimed in 1921. It obtained considerable development, prominence, distinction and notoriety in the two following decades, essentially running its course by the time of the Second World War. Eurasianism attracts attention because of the novelty and originality of its central argument, proposing that the Russian Empire and later the Soviet Union constituted an independent organic entity separate from both Europe and Asia, called Eurasia (it was the complete separation from Europe that represented an explosive novelty), and because of the intellectual variety and abilities, at times brilliance, of its proponents. Also, as an extraordinary phenomenon in Russian intellectual history, it demands explanation.

1   **Eurasianism**
2   **The historical position of Eurasianism**

1   Eurasianism

Eurasianism emerged quite explicitly in 1921 when four young Russian intellectuals published a collective volume, *Iskhod k vostoku* (Exodus to the East). The four were Prince Nikolai Sergeevich Trubetskoi (1890–1938), later to earn fame as a linguistic scholar, Pëtr Nikolaevich Savitskii (1894–1968), an economist-geographer and specialist in many subjects, Pëtr Petrovich Suvchinskii (1892–1985), a gifted music critic and many-sided intellectual, and Georgii Vasilievich Florovskii (1893–1979), a theologian, intellectual historian, and a man of numerous interests with a remarkable breadth of knowledge. The anthology consisted of an introduction and ten essays.

The introduction spoke of a world cataclysm, of a catastrophic change of scenes, of a new age, of the dying of the West and of the imminent rise of the East. It concluded: 'Russians and those who belong to the peoples of "the Russian world" are neither Europeans nor Asiatics. Merging with the native element of culture and life which surrounds us, we are not ashamed to declare ourselves *Eurasians*' (1921: 7).

In the essays which followed Florovskii and Suvchinskii concentrated on a fundamental and sweeping criticism of the hopelessly rationalistic, war-devastated, and moribund West, as well as on the catastrophe of Russian history and society, which eventuated in the unparalleled disaster of communist revolution; Savitskii and Trubetskoi, however, paid major attention to the new redeeming concept of

Eurasia. In an essay on 'The Migration of Culture' Savitskii outlined how in world history cultural centres and leadership moved with each millennium to colder and colder climates; if the migration continued, the next step will transfer the world leadership to Canada and 'northern Minnesota' on the one hand, and on the other to 'parts of northern and central Russia together with all of eastern Russia, both eastern European Russia and Siberia'. And in another essay, 'Continent-Ocean (Russia and the World Market)', the economist and geographer insisted that because of its landlocked position and huge bulk Russia had to minimize recourse to oceanic trade routes and devote itself instead to the entirely feasible rich and varied development of its own continental economy. Trubetskoi's essay, 'The Upper and Lower Layers of Russian Culture (The Ethnic Base of Russian Culture)', sketched in effect cultural Eurasia: in contrast to the superficially and unsuccessfully Westernized upper classes, Russian masses and their culture were in no sense simply European, because proto-Slav dialects (and hence the Russian language) occupied a middle geographic position between the proto-Indo-Iranian and proto-Western-Indo-European ones, closer to the former than to the latter in essential characteristics; because Great Russian folk songs utilized the 'five-tone' or 'Indo-Chinese' scale; because Russian folk dance, in contrast to Western dance, was not based on a couple, a man and a woman, dancing together; because Russian material culture indicated the closest possible association with Ugrofinnic peoples; because Russians had Ugrofinnic and Turkic as well as Slav blood; because they were inclined to oriental contemplation and devotion to ritual, but also to *udal'*, extravagant daring or audacity, 'a purely steppe virtue, which the Turkic peoples understand, but neither the Romano-germans nor the Slavs can', and so on. The two Eurasias, Savitskii's geopolitical and Trubetskoi's cultural, became partners but also independent streams in the new ideology.

The first Eurasian symposium was followed by others, the seventh and last coming out in 1931. Also, twelve volumes of the *Evraziiskaia khronika* (Eurasian Chronicle) appeared between 1925 and 1937, and they were joined by numerous individual publications by participants in the movement. Indeed in the 1920s and 1930s Eurasianism acquired some prominence and attracted much attention among Russian exiles in Europe. Eurasian publications were supplemented by 'seminars', public lectures, formal debates and private disputations. Although Florovskii, one of the founders, rather quickly abandoned Eurasianism and in 1928 published a crushing critique of it, other émigré intellectuals, a few of them of great prominence, joined the movement. Thus Roman Osipovich Jakobson (1896–1982), another linguist of the first rank, followed Trubetskoi's lead to make some remarkable discoveries about languages in Eurasia, while Georgii Vladimirovich Vernadsky (1887–1973) became the prolific Eurasian historian, and, because he taught Russian history at Yale and published many books in English, the greatest propagandist of Eurasianism to the world outside Russian émigré circles. The movement also displayed a certain political bent, even aspiring to replace communism, regarded as a rival and undesirable ideocracy, in the government of Russia-Eurasia. Still, always confined to a small minority and essentially to one particular generation of exiles, the Eurasian movement ended with the new perturbations of the Second World War and the decline and death of the generation in question.

2 The historical position of Eurasianism

Eurasianism is both easy and difficult to understand and explain. It certainly belongs with other European doctrines of bitterness, suffering and despair, as well as at times apocalyptic hopes, which proliferated after the First World War and the disasters which attended and followed it. In the Russian case the October Revolution, civil war and famine could be considered even more horrible than the great War itself, and they all found rich response in Eurasianism. Still another major historical development, described by phrases like the rise of colonial peoples, the decline of imperialism, or the gradual loss by the so-called White race of its dominant global position, also found powerful response. In fact, Trubetskoi had published already in 1920, the year preceding the inauguration of Eurasianism, a brief book *Europe and Mankind*, which was a relentless indictment of imperialism and a declaration of essential Russian solidarity with colonial peoples.

The difficulty resides in the positive part of the Eurasian teaching, in the concept of Eurasia itself. More exactly, of the two main versions of that concept, Savitskii's geopolitical Eurasia found considerable understanding and some approval. But Trubetskoi's cultural Eurasia, the alleged Eurasian identity of the Russians, exploded among the émigrés like a bombshell. No Russian intellectual prior to the Eurasian movement had denied a fundamental Russian affiliation with Europe. Such severe critics of the West as the Slavophiles and Dostoevskii emphasized the very point that the West was guilty of not treating Russians like brothers. Nikolai Danilevskii, it is true, rejected the West, but his entire allegiance went to Slavdom and the coming Slav age in Europe (see PAN-SLAVISM §3). The new identity

was so revolutionary and so baffling that most critics totally failed to understand, let alone accept it. Where did this identity come from? A few disparate suggestions appear possible. As already indicated, the Eurasians reacted to the new phenomenon of the rise of the colonial peoples. Moreover, without doubting the sincerity of Eurasians, it seems clear that if Eurasia, organic and glorious, were also real, the Russian or the Soviet Empire, rebaptized Eurasia, would have perdured in the age when other empires crumbled. The Russian intellectual climate also made its contributions. Russian scholarship was in the process of discovering ever more about the character and the role of non-Slav peoples, whether Finnic tribes of the north or steppe inhabitants to the southeast, in Russian history and culture. Beyond that, on the eve of the appearance of Eurasianism a few poets, most notably Aleksandr Blok in a poem entitled 'The Scythians' written 30 January 1918, began to identify the Russians themselves as such an intermediate people between Europe and Asia. Finally, the personal circumstances of the Eurasians deserve consideration. They were gifted young intellectuals ready to participate in the cultural leadership of Russia, when Russia disappeared (and they found themselves permanently in exile). Eurasianism can be regarded as a desperate bid to compensate for that loss.

Essentially fantastic and certainly abortive, Eurasianism deserves attention because of its intellectual variety and richness and also as a sign of the times. Understandably it has attracted new interest with the collapse of the Soviet Union and the Russian search for identity.

List of works

Florovskii, G., Savitskii, P., Suvchinskii, P and Trubetskoi, N. (1921) *Iskhod k vostoku: Predchustviia i sversheniia. Utverzhdenie evraziitsev, Sofia: Tipografiia 'Balkan'*; translated in I. Vinkovetsky, N.V. Riasanovsky and C. Schlacks, Jr (eds), *Exodus to the East: Foreboding and Events: An Affirmation of the Eurasians*, Marina del Rey, CA: Charles Schlacks, Jr, in preparation. (This and other Eurasian publications are rare and usually exist only in Russian. At last, a scholarly translation is scheduled to appear.)
Trubetskoi, N.S. [Trubetzkoy] (1991) *The Legacy of Genghiz Khan and Other Essays on Russian Identity*, ed. and with postscript by A. Liberman, preface by V.V. Ivanov, Ann Arbor, MI: Michigan Slavic Publication.
Vernadsky, G. (1929) *A History of Russia*, New Haven, CT: Yale University Press.

—— (1953) *The Mongols and Russia*, New Haven, CT: Yale University Press.

References and further reading

Böss, O. (1961) *Die Lehre der Eurasier: Ein Beitrag zur Russischen Ideengeschichte des 20. Jahrhunderts* (The Teaching of the Eurasians: A Contribution to the Russian History of Ideas of the Twentieth Century), Wiesbaden: Otto Harrassowitz. (For a bibliography see 125–30.)

Riasanovsky, N.V. (1964) 'Prince N.S. Trubetskoi's "Europe and Mankind"', in *Jahrbücher für Geschichte Osteuropas, Neue Folge* 12 (2): 207–20.

—— (1967) 'The Emergence of Eurasianism' in *California Slavic Studies*, vol. 4, eds N.V. Riasanovsky and G. Struve, 39–72.

—— (1972) 'Asia through Russian Eyes' in *Russia and Asia: Essays on the Influence of Russia on the Asian Peoples*, ed. W. Vucinich, Stanford, CA: Hoover Institution Press, 3–29, 369–75.

NICHOLAS V. RIASANOVSKY

EUROPE: IMPACT OF ISLAMIC PHILOSOPHY ON WESTERN *see* ISLAMIC

PHILOSOPHY: TRANSMISSION INTO WESTERN EUROPE

EUSEBIUS (*c.* AD 264–*c.*339)

Eusebius, Bishop of Caesarea in Palestine from c.314, was the foremost Christian scholar of his age and wrote extensively on history, geography, chronology, apologetics and philosophical and biblical theology. He is best known for his pioneering History of the Church, *but philosophers may prefer to consult his* Preparation of the Gospel, *which argues that basic Christian doctrines had been foreshadowed by well-known philosophers and preserves valuable extracts from writers whose works have otherwise been lost. In his own philosophical ideas, Eusebius was strongly influenced by classical philosophy, especially Platonism, and sought to reconcile this with Christian theology.*

1 **Life, works and philosophical sources**
2 **Logic and ethics**
3 **The physical world**
4 **The world of Ideas, and theology**
5 **Providence and human freedom**

1 Life, works and philosophical sources

Eusebius was born *c.* AD 264 and became Bishop of Caesarea in Palestine *c.*314. The library at Caesarea contained books brought from Alexandria by Origen with additions by Eusebius' mentor Pamphilus. Eusebius became an enormously industrious and wide-ranging scholar with a good general knowledge of philosophy. His *Historia ecclesiastica* (History of the Church) appeared in successive editions from *c.*300 onwards. His *Praeparatio evangelica* (Preparation of the Gospel), in fifteen books, was written *c.*312–18; it argues that Christian doctrines were foreshadowed by the philosophers, and is an invaluable source-book, especially for Middle Platonist authors whose works have otherwise been lost. A companion work, the *Demonstratio evangelica* (Proof of the Gospel) appeared about the same time.

Eusebius was a conservative theologian, anxious to maintain clear distinctions between the three divine Persons. He had some sympathy with Arius, signed the Creed of Nicaea (325) with reluctance, and led a partially successful reaction against its extreme adherents. Yet he warmly approved of the Emperor's reforms and wrote an eloquent address in praise of Constantine (*Laus Constantini*). He died *c.*339.

Eusebius quotes PLATO very freely from original texts; but his knowledge of the Presocratics and of Aristotle, Epicurus and the Stoics is plainly derivative. He uses Philo of Alexandria and Plutarch, including some works not otherwise preserved, and is an important source for Atticus and Numenius. He quotes two books of Plotinus, now known as *Enneads* IV 7 and V 1, but not from Porphyry's edition. He uses Porphyry's *Philosophy from Oracles* and other writings, despite Porphyry's anti-Christian stance, but ignores his logical works.

2 Logic and ethics

Eusebius accepts the conventional division of philosophy into ethics, physics and logic (see STOICISM §2). But his treatment of logic is perfunctory; he ignores Plato's dialectic and does not use Albinus/Alcinous or Clement of Alexandria's *Stromateis* VIII, let alone Aristotle's or Chrysippus' logic. The 'logical skill' that he claims for Hebrew writers is identified with 'comprehension of the truth itself', which he finds in the Book of Proverbs; he also argues that Hebrew names correspond with realities, appealing to Genesis 2: 19 and adducing Plato's *Cratylus*.

His treatment of ethics, again, hardly goes beyond

discussion of the *summum bonum*. He adopts the conventional criticisms of Epicurus as making pleasure the sole good, and of Aristotle as teaching a 'triad of goods' which values health and prosperity as much as virtue. He does, however, cite Plato's *Philebus* 67a, which assigns a positive though limited value to pleasure. Stoic ethics pass almost unnoticed. Eusebius praises Plato for locating the good in the intelligible world and assimilates Hebrew piety to Platonism, describing God as the source of all good things, so that the 'God-loving' person alone lives a happy and blessed life. Eusebius does not discuss the Jewish law in detail, though his own moral axioms are shown indirectly in his repeated condemnation of polytheism.

3 The physical world

For Eusebius, physics includes the study of the intelligible, incorporeal world as well as perceptible things, a Platonic doctrine which he claims the Hebrews accepted. Plato agreed with Moses in regarding the world as created; and Eusebius repeatedly criticizes the doctrines of the 'physicists' – some of them were atheists, while others deified the material elements, or at least regarded matter as the ultimate reality. Anaxagoras revered a divine creative mind, but failed to explain its operations. Parmenides, however, rightly believed in unchanging reality, and Heraclitus in a divine *logos*. Aristotle's doctrine of the eternity of the cosmos is rejected in favour of the literalist interpretation of the *Timaeus* offered by Atticus; Eusebius ignores the common Platonist view that the myth of a divine creative act really signifies eternal dependence. Epicurus rejects any providential order, and his doctrine of atoms denies the unity of the cosmos, though Eusebius apparently ignores his view that the cosmos originated in an uncaused 'swerve' of free-falling atoms. The Stoics are blamed for explaining the universe in material terms, though their concept of God as 'intelligent fire' is defended, following Clement of Alexandria, as compatible with Scripture.

Apart from accepting Empedocles' doctrine of four elements, Eusebius says little about astronomy, geography and physics in its modern sense; he is content to reproduce a doxography from Pseudo-Plutarch. His claim of a biblical 'physiology' relies on Solomon's reputed expertise (1 Kings 4: 29–34), and is not further pursued.

4 The world of Ideas, and theology

Eusebius agrees with the 'dogmatic' Platonists in the importance he attaches to the Ideas, or intelligible reality; but like most Platonists before Plotinus he fails to include them in a consistent theory. He shows no serious interest in Plato's attempts to classify the Ideas by genera and species. He presents them as eternal and unchanging and adopts the prevalent view of them as thoughts in God's mind which function as prototypes for God's works in creation. But this view is presented mainly in relation to the species of things in the world, whereas a more consistent Platonist would begin the creative process with the highest genera: possibly the Idea of mutable being, or that of the living creature as such. Eusebius takes from Philo of Alexandria and Clement a Stoicized theory which gives first place to the cosmos and its elements. Yet he also presents the Ideas as intelligent beings, which so far from being changeless are capable of 'fall and divergence' from their original position as archangels, thus becoming demons. Eusebius quotes Plato's *Laws* in support; but an assimilation of Ideas to souls, based perhaps on *Phaedo* 79 and *Sophist* 248e–249a, was assumed by Philo and many Platonists. Eusebius of course accepts the immortality of the soul, and approves Plato's description of a judgment after death, but shows without difficulty that Plato offers inconsistent pictures of the soul's continued existence.

Eusebius also draws on Platonism for his description of God's being, presenting him not only as transcending the universe but also as incomprehensible. He claims that God is 'above all intelligence and beyond every concept and consideration', which recalls the Platonic phrase 'beyond mind and being' (*epekeina nou kai ousias*), based on Plato's *Republic* 509b (compare Aristotle fr. 46). He uses the human mind and its utterance (*logos*) as an analogy for God's being and self-disclosure, but (unlike Numenius) he seldom actually designates God as mind. He thinks of the divine Logos as a distinct personality, though in a later work he notes the unpopularity of the phrase 'a second God'. Opposing any theology which blurred the distinction between the divine Persons or envisaged their unity in material terms, he gave qualified support to the strongly subordinationist view of Arius; he accepted the Creed of Nicaea (325) only with reservations.

5 Providence and human freedom

Besides creation, Eusebius upheld the doctrine of divine providence against Epicurus and others, but was also concerned to establish the freedom of the human will, as presupposed by the concepts of moral effort and of praise and blame. He therefore attacked the determinism presupposed by the astrologers and pagan oracles, and condemned as inadequate the Stoics' attempt to reconcile determinism with moral freedom. In Eusebius' view, Chrysippus offered us a 'semi-slavery'. Eusebius appealed to our consciousness of freedom and correctly pointed out that future events are differently determined. Some events are bound to happen; others result unpredictably from a coincidence of natural causes. Nevertheless, the human will is a true cause, determining some events that would otherwise be undetermined or otherwise determined, and is not itself necessarily controlled either by physical causes or by social pressures. God's providence disposes the general laws of the universe, but also cooperates with our free wills to encourage us to virtue. Eusebius presents evil in terms of human wrongdoing, no doubt presupposing the Stoic doctrine that natural disasters are not evils unless feared or resented.

All this is intelligently argued; but Eusebius does not eliminate the problems presented by the predictive element in *Christian* prophecy and by the well-established doctrine of God's total foreknowledge. Nevertheless, his philosophical ability deserved more recognition than it received. The relatively open-minded approach that he inherited from Origen rapidly became unpopular in the Eastern Church. The Nicene Creed became the standard of orthodoxy, and Eusebius' coolness towards it was remembered; he was never canonized, and his reputation rested upon his much valued and repeatedly imitated *History of the Church*.

See also: PLATONISM, EARLY AND MIDDLE

List of works

A complete list is given by D.S. Wallace-Hadrill (1960 – see below).

Eusebius (*c.*300–24) *Historia ecclesiastica* (History of the Church), ed. E. Schwartz, *Eusebius Werke 2: Die Kirchengeschichte*, Leipzig: Hinrichs, 1903–8. (Massive edition containing all evidence; other useful editions include: Lake, K. (trans. and ed.) (1926, 1932) *Eusebius: The Ecclesiastical History*, London: Loeb Classical Library, Heinemann – Greek text with English translation; Lawlor, H.J. and Oulton, J.E.L. (trans. and eds) (1927–8) *Eusebius: The Ecclesiastical History*, London: SPCK – English translation with valuable notes; and Williamson, G.A. (trans. and ed.) (1965) *The History of the Church from Christ to Constantine*, Harmondsworth: Penguin – translation with introduction.)

—— (*c.*312–18) *Praeparatio evangelica* (Preparation of the Gospel), trans. and ed. E.H. Gifford, *Eusebii praeparatio evangelica*, Oxford: Oxford University Press, 5 vols, 1903. (Outstandingly good edition, with Greek text, English translation and valuable notes; see also Mras, K. (ed.) (1954, 1956) *Eusebius Werke 8: Die Praeparatio Evangelica*, Berlin: Akademie Verlag, 2 vols; 2nd edn ed. E. des Places, 1982 – authoritative Greek text.)

—— (*c.*312–18) *Demonstratio evangelica* (Proof of the Gospel), ed. I.A. Heikel, *Eusebius Werke 6: Die Demonstratio Evangelica*, Leipzig: Hinrichs, 1913. (Critical Greek text; see also Ferrar, W.J. (trans.) (1920) *Eusebius: The Proof of the Gospel*, London: SPCK, 2 vols – an English translation.)

—— (335–6) *Laus Constantini* (In Praise of Constantine), ed. I.A. Heikel, *Eusebius Werke I*, Leipzig: Hinrichs, 1902, 193–259. (Critical Greek text; see also Drake, H.A. (1975) *In Praise of Constantine*, Berkeley, CA: University of California Press – includes introduction, translation and notes.)

References and further reading

Des Places, E. (1982) 'Eusèbe de Césarée commentateur', *Théologie Historique* 63. (Catalogues Eusebius' use of Platonic, Platonist and scriptural texts.)

Dillon, J. (1977) *The Middle Platonists*, London: Duckworth. (Essential information on most philosophers immediately prior to Eusebius.)

Lyman, J.R. (1993) *Christology and Cosmology*, Oxford: Clarendon Press. (Well-written, simple account of basic themes in philosophical theology; see pages 82–123 for Eusebius.)

Stead, G.C. (1994) *Philosophy in Christian Antiquity*, Cambridge: Cambridge University Press. (Outline of Greek philosophy, and study of its use by Christians.)

Wallace-Hadrill, D.S. (1960) *Eusebius of Caesarea*, London: Mowbray. (Reliable introduction to Eusebius' life and works, a complete list of which can be found on pages 57–8.)

—— (1982) 'Eusebius von Caesarea', in G. Krause *et al.* (eds) *Theologische Realenzyklopädie*, Berlin: de Gruyter, vol. 10, 537–43. (Succinct and authoritative, with full bibliography.)

CHRISTOPHER STEAD

EUSTACHIUS A SANCTO PAULO *see* ARISTOTELIANISM IN THE 17TH CENTURY

EUTHANASIA *see* LIFE AND DEATH (§§3, 4)

EVANS, GARETH (1946–80)

Frege's notion of sense is a conception of content whose application is controlled by the idea of rationality. A Fregean outlook is often taken to imply that singular reference is always mediated by descriptions, and hence to be inconsistent with the insights that have motivated proponents of 'direct reference'. But in his major work, The Varieties of Reference *(1982), Gareth Evans showed how a treatment of singular reference on Fregean lines can accommodate those insights. This means that the semantics of singular reference need not be distanced from the philosophy of mind, in the way that proponents of 'direct reference' typically suppose. Within the framework provided by this synthesis, Evans gave detailed treatments of the different ways in which thought and speech are directed at particular objects. Particularly notable are his discussions of demonstrative thinking, which exploits the perceptible presence to the thinker of the object it concerns; of first-personal thinking; and of singular statements of nonexistence.*

1 Life
2 Historical background
3 Evans on Fregean sense
4 Varieties of reference

1 Life

Gareth Evans was a Fellow of University College, Oxford; in 1979 he became Wilde Reader in Mental Philosophy at the University of Oxford. His articles, on issues in metaphysics, philosophy of language and philosophy of mind, are assembled in his *Collected Papers* (1985), but his major contribution to philosophy is the posthumously published *The Varieties of Reference* (1982).

2 Historical background

In the Theory of Descriptions, Russell gave a precise account of one way in which the content of an episode of thinking or speaking can be targeted on an individual, in the sense that its truth-value depends on how things are in respect of that individual: the individual is singled out by uniquely fitting a specification that figures in the content – say, 'presently reigning over France' (see RUSSELL, B. §9; DESCRIPTIONS §§2–3). It is central to Russell's point that contents of this

shape are available to be entertained in an episode of thinking, whether or not anything conforms to the specification. If nothing does, the thought is simply false, not deprived of content.

Russell contrasts this kind of content with contents that are more intimately related to objects on whose properties their truth depends. A content of this second kind can be entertained only by a thinker 'acquainted with' the objects concerned, and the very existence of such a content depends on the existence of these objects. Contents of this second kind are expressed by forms of words containing what Russell calls 'logically proper names'. Compared with the first kind of content, contents of this second kind seem to be genuinely singular; and compared with definite descriptions, 'logically proper names' seem to be genuinely referring expressions.

However, Russell thinks there are hardly any 'logically proper names'. In his view one cannot entertain or express one of these genuinely singular contents if there is so much as a possibility, by the lights of hyperbolical Cartesian doubt, that one's conviction that a suitable object exists is an illusion. Thus almost all expressions that would ordinarily be classified as referring expressions (for instance ordinary proper names) must be interpreted as 'disguised descriptions' – that is, abbreviations for expressions of the specifications that figure in the other kind of content. This 'disguised description' picture became something of an orthodoxy, supposedly with referring as its subject matter, even though in Russell's own thinking the idea of referring seems more at home in connection with 'logically proper names', which Russell himself sets in contrast with 'disguised descriptions'.

Frege had argued that singular terms must be credited with senses as well as referents (see FREGE, G. §3; SENSE AND REFERENCE §1). The sense of a sentence is the thought expressible by it, and it is the sense rather than the referent of a singular term that contributes to determining the sense of a sentence in which the term figures. Frege's point here is to delineate a notion of content, thinkable or expressible, whose employment is controlled by the idea of rationality, in a way that can be illustrated as follows. Suppose two singular terms have the same referent; take a pair of sentences which are alike except that one contains one of those terms, where the other contains the other. If a rational subject can understand these sentences and take rationally opposed attitudes to them (for instance, endorsing one and rejecting the other), then the thoughts they express must differ; and this difference in the senses of the sentences can only trace back to a difference in the senses of the singular terms.

In the orthodoxy, the Fregean idea that singular terms have senses became assimilated to the neo-Russellian idea that they are 'disguised descriptions'; the assimilation set up a supposedly unified doctrine, against which Saul KRIPKE and others recoiled. Their alternative yields a liberalized analogue to Russell's conception of 'logically proper names'. In the new picture, various contextual relations between thinkers or speakers and objects play something like the role in which Russell cast 'acquaintance', and genuinely referring expressions are not as rare as Russell thought. With Frege assimilated into the orthodoxy, this new picture is conceived as rejecting the Fregean apparatus. If Fregean sense figures at all in the new picture, it is not as an aspect of the semantics of singular terms, but in a supposedly separate role, as an instrument for describing the configurations of thinkers' minds (see PROPER NAMES §1).

3   Evans on Fregean sense

Evans offers a reading of Frege that undermines this assimilation. There are three main claims. First, the assimilation is not required by the motivation for Frege's notion of sense. In the case of what singular terms contribute to thoughts, Frege's point is that if attributing propositional attitudes is to be controlled by the idea of rationality, then individuating the contents of the attitudes by the identity of the objects that figure in them is too coarse-grained. Evans insists that singular thoughts can be individuated more finely, as Frege required, but still be 'Russellian' – that is, depend for their very existence on the existence of the objects they are about.

Second, Frege himself evidently feels the attraction of such a conception. He maintains that a putative singular utterance with no referents for its putative singular terms has no truth-value. We can best make sense of that as an implication of the idea that there is no thought (of the appropriate kind) for such an utterance to express – since the thoughts that singular utterances express, when they do express thoughts, are 'Russellian'. Frege's own principles make it difficult, perhaps impossible, to make sense of the alternative idea that such an utterance does express a thought, but one with no truth-value.

Third, although Frege often seems to say that a singular term's possession of a sense does not depend on whether it has a referent, this can be explained away. Such claims belong in the context of Frege's thesis that in cases of reference-failure one lapses into fiction. In fiction, he says, one expresses apparent thoughts. This suggests that when he says that an apparent singular term can have a sense even though it lacks a referent, what he really means is that such a

term gives the appearance of having a sense, not that it genuinely has a sense.

It is not as important to settle what Frege himself held as to see that his basic principles allow for expressions whose semantics – possession of senses and all – qualify them to count, by quasi-Russellian lights, as genuine singular terms, rather than something on the lines of the 'disguised descriptions' that Russell contrasts with them. This means that a broadly Fregean conception of thought and its expression can accommodate the insights of the recoil from the 'disguised description' picture. We can acknowledge cases in which reference is not mediated by descriptions, but partly constituted by contextual relations between thinkers and objects, without needing to separate such reference from the characteristically Fregean topic, the rationally organized configurations of thinkers' minds.

4   Varieties of reference

Evans gives a general account of how 'informational' relations between thinkers and objects can enter into determining referential relations between thoughts and objects, even while the thoughts are conceived in a fundamentally Fregean way, as individuated by their positions in a space of possibilities open to a rational subject. He recommends his picture by contrasting it with 'the Photograph Model of mental representation', according to which relations of 'informational' type suffice for a mental state or episode to be about an object, without any need for a Fregean framework. In a transition from philosophy of mind to philosophy of language, he discusses at a general level how 'information-based' thoughts figure in the understanding that is required for some communication.

The general picture of 'information-based' thoughts is applied in detailed accounts of thoughts of three interdependent kinds: (1) thoughts in which objects are singled out demonstratively in a way that exploits their perceptible presence to the thinker; (2) thoughts about places or regions of space expressible by the use of words such as 'here'; and (3) first-personal thoughts. A central aim is to reconcile the fact that these thoughts single out their objects egocentrically with the claim that they are targeted on elements in the objective order. The capacities to think these thoughts belong to a subject who is experientially and practically placed in the objective world. Such a subject enjoys a course of experience understood as jointly determined by the way things are anyway and by the subject's trajectory through objective reality, and thereby knows what it is for egocentric identifications of objects (including places) to be directed at items that are also identifiable in more objective ways (for instance by map references). Evans thus displays first-personal thoughts, in particular, as being in their own way about particular objects (the human beings – animals of a certain distinctive kind – who self-consciously think them). This stands in radical contrast to the Cartesian position, in which at least some such thoughts involve reference to immaterial entities problematically related to certain animals: it also defuses a temptation to avoid the Cartesian position by denying that those thoughts involve reference to anything at all.

Evans' general account of 'informational' relations might lead one to expect discussions of thoughts linked to their objects by relations of testimony and memory, corresponding to his treatment of perceptually demonstrative thoughts. The book contains nothing answering to the former, however, and where one might expect the latter, a treatment of thoughts whose objects are singled out by the thinker's ability to recognize them. This is insightful about recognitional capacities, but arguably not well integrated into the overall structure of the book.

A problem for 'Russellian' conceptions of reference is posed by negative existential statements that appear to have singular terms in subject position (for example, 'The planet Vulcan does not exist'). The 'disguised description' picture has no difficulty here; such a statement simply says that the associated specification is not satisfied. Metalinguistic treatments are not satisfying; such a statement seems somehow to use, rather than talk about, the singular terms it contains. One would like to say: 'Such a statement says, of some specified thing (for example, the planet Vulcan), that it does not exist.' But that would describe the statement in a way that undermines what it tries to say. Evans gives an ingenious and original account of such statements, which allows us to get as close as possible to that desideratum without falling into nonsense. One can go through the motions of referring within the scope of a game of make-believe (as when one 'talks about' fictional characters); the idea is that a statement such as 'Vulcan does not exist' exploits such a game of make-believe for the serious purpose of declaring that that is all it is. The book concludes with a suggestive discussion of proper names, centring on different degrees of involvement in name-using practices.

See also: REFERENCE §§4, 8

List of works

Evans, G. (1982) *The Varieties of Reference*, ed. J. McDowell, Oxford: Clarendon Press. (Evans' major work; it places Frege and Russell with respect to more recent reflection about singular reference, and discusses the various ways in which thought and speech are targeted on particular objects. Rough in places, and occasionally technical, but well worth the effort.)

—— (1985) *Collected Papers*, Oxford: Clarendon Press. (Evans' shorter writings, ranging from technical philosophy of language to general metaphysics and philosophy of mind. Perhaps especially noteworthy is the brilliant paper 'Things without the Mind'.)

References and further reading

Frege, G. (1892) 'On Sense and Meaning', in *Collected Papers on Mathematics, Logic and Philosophy*, ed. B. McGuinness, Oxford: Blackwell, 1984. (Frege's introduction of the notion of sense. A classic.)

Kripke, S. (1980) *Naming and Necessity*, Oxford: Blackwell. (A brilliant and trenchant attack on the 'disguised description' picture of how proper names refer.)

McDowell, J. (1986) 'Singular Thought and the Extent of Inner Space', in P. Pettit and J. McDowell (eds) *Subject, Thought and Context*, Oxford: Clarendon Press, 137–68. (Discusses the significance, for philosophy of mind and metaphysics, of the way Evans synthesizes a basically Fregean outlook with rejecting the 'disguised description' picture.)

Russell, B. (1905) 'On Denoting', in *Logic and Knowledge*, ed. R.C. Marsh, London: Allen & Unwin, 1956, 39–56. (Another classic: Russell's announcement of the Theory of Descriptions. Not difficult, apart from a famously opaque section on Frege.)

—— (1918) 'The Philosophy of Logical Atomism', in *Logic and Knowledge*, ed. R.C. Marsh, London: Allen & Unwin, 1956, 177–281. (Lectures for nonspecialists: contains a lucid exposition of Russell's central doctrines about reference.)

JOHN McDOWELL

EVANS, MARY ANN *see* ELIOT, GEORGE

EVENTS

Events are entities like collisions and speeches, as opposed to things like planets and people. Many are changes, for example things being first hot and then cold. *All lack a thing's full identity over time: either they are instantaneous, or they have temporal parts, like a speech's words, which stop them being wholly present at an instant; whereas things, which lack temporal parts, are wholly present throughout their lives.*

Events may be identified with two types of entity: facts, like the fact that David Hume dies, corresponding to truths like 'Hume dies'; or particulars which, like things, correspond to names, for example 'Hume's death'. Which one they are taken to be affects the content of many metaphysical theories: such as that all particulars are things; that times, or causes and effects, or actions, are events; or that mental events are physical.

1   **Events and things**
2   **Events and facts**

1   Events and things

Many kinds of entity, from any cause or effect to everything a space-time region contains, have been called 'events'. But events usually so-called – deaths, collisions, speeches – form an apparently distinct kind, different from things like people, planets and books (see CONTINUANTS). What is the difference? Many events are changes, for example, human bodies being first alive and then dead. But this may not define events. For first, we may need events to distinguish intrinsic changes, like dying, from some relational ones, like being orphaned; the latter being mere entailments of the former, which are real events, with contiguous causes and effects (see CHANGE). Second, events that begin or end things, like the Big Bang and other explosions, cannot be changes in them and may not, if nothing precedes or survives them, be changes in anything else.

The difference between things and events, whether changes or not, may be that things keep a full identity over time, which events lack. First, some events may be instantaneous and lack any identity over time. Second, temporally extended events are deprived of full identity over time by their temporal parts, like a speech's spoken words, which stop them ever being wholly present at an instant; whereas people and other things have no temporal parts and are wholly present at every instant of their lives. This full identity over time will then distinguish one thing changing from successive things having different properties, thus explaining why only things can change and why changes, being events, are not things (Mellor 1981).

This difference may be denied by giving things temporal parts by definition, such as Hume-in-1739. But these are mere logical constructions from things

and times, not independent events like the words in a speech. Some apparent things might indeed be mere strings of contiguous and causally related events (it has been suggested, for example, that we are strings of experiences). But not all: unchanging elementary particles involve no independent events. Moreover, since contiguity and causation can always link one event or thing to two successors, as when a cell divides, they cannot entail a thing's identity over time (see PERSONAL IDENTITY). So, equating us to strings of experiences implies not that things can be strings of events but that we are not things. Events and things remain distinct types of entity.

2   Events and facts

Assuming there are things, are there also events? That may depend on whether events are facts, corresponding to truths like 'Hume dies in 1776', or particulars corresponding to names or descriptions like 'Hume's death' (see FACTS; PARTICULARS). Changes look like facts, for example the fact that a thing is first hot and then cold; and that things start and cease to exist at certain times are also facts. Thus events of both types mentioned above may be facts, and what many authors call 'events' certainly are: Kim (1976), for whom events are things having properties at times, like Hume being alive in 1775, is an example. Events in this sense are real entities if and only if facts are.

This being so, 'event' is best reserved, as by DAVIDSON, for particulars like Hume's death. Their reality is independent of that of facts, but equally contentious: after all, the only particular apparently referred to in 'Hume dies' is Hume. Yet Davidson argues that 'Hume dies' also entails that an event exists which is a death of Hume. For first, this shows how 'Hume dies slowly' entails 'Hume dies', since a slow death must be a death. Second, identifying actions with particular events satisfying different descriptions dissolves puzzles about their identity: for example my bid can be a purchase even though many bids are not purchases (see ACTION). Similarly, if mental events are particulars, they can also be physical brain events satisfying neurophysiological descriptions (see IDENTITY THEORY OF MIND). This explains, without invoking non-physical causes or effects, how events satisfying mental descriptions – such as 'is a decision to bid' – can have physical causes and effects, like hand movements (see ANOMALOUS MONISM). This explanation assumes moreover that causes and effects are particulars, not facts, and this requires particular events. For only if Hume's death exists can the effect of whatever caused Hume to die be a particular; otherwise the effect can only be the fact that Hume dies.

All these arguments have been disputed. Events remain more contentious than things, despite having identity criteria: for example, that a headache is a certain brain event if it has the same causes and effects as that event. Yet since such criteria may only relate particular events to each other, we may still need people and other things to identify some events to start with, as in 'Hume's death' (see STRAWSON, P.F.). This may explain scepticism about events, but cannot make them less real than things, or less able to be particulars. For to be a particular is just to be of a kind we make true first-order generalizations about (see QUINE, W.V.), many of which, like Newton's 'to every action there is always opposed an equal reaction', are about events as well as things.

See also: ADVERBS; CAUSATION; LOGICAL FORM; MOMENTARINESS, BUDDHIST DOCTRINE OF; MUJO; ONTOLOGY; REICHENBACH, H.; TIME; WHITEHEAD, A.N.

References and further reading

Bennett, J. (1988) *Events and Their Names*, Oxford: Clarendon Press. (An analytic assessment of rival views of events, concluding that they are facts.)

Davidson, D. (1980) *Essays on Actions and Events*, Oxford: Clarendon Press. (A collection of articles arguing for and applying the view that events are particulars.)

* Kim, J. (1976) 'Events as property exemplifications', in M. Brand and D. Walton (eds) *Action Theory*, Dordrecht: Reidel, 159–77. (Referred to in §2 above. Equates events with things having properties at times.)

Lombard, L.B. (1986) *Events: A Metaphysical Study*, London: Routledge & Kegan Paul. (Argues that events are changes.)

* Mellor, D.H. (1981) *Real Time*, Cambridge: Cambridge University Press. (Referred to in §1 above. Chapter 7 argues that events are particulars which differ from things in having temporal parts.)

D.H. MELLOR

EVIDENTIALISM *see* RELIGION AND EPISTEMOLOGY

EVIL

Evil is serious unjustified harm inflicted on sentient beings. Two types of evil can be distinguished: 'natural evil', which is the product of nonhuman agency, and 'moral evil', which is the product of human agency. Moral thinking tends to focus on moral evil, and three main interpretations of it have been made. One, initiated by Socrates, holds moral evil to be deviation from the good; another, favoured by Stoic-Spinozists, views it as illusory; the third, made originally by Leibniz, sees it as a contrast necessary for the existence of the good. A realistic account must face the fact that moral evil does exist, and much of it is due to common human vices, which coexist with virtues in human character. It is primarily the proportion of the mixture, not the knowledge and intentions of agents, that determines how much evil will be caused by specific individuals in specific contexts.

1   The nature of evil
2   Evil as deviation from the good
3   Evil as illusory
4   Evil as contrast necessary for the good
5   Facing evil

1   The nature of evil

Evil is the most severe condemnation our moral vocabulary allows. Murder, torture, enslavement and prolonged humiliation are some examples of it. Evil must involve harm, and it must be serious enough to damage its victims' capacity to function normally (see SUFFERING). Furthermore, the harm must be unjustified, since not even serious harm is in itself necessarily evil, as it may be just punishment for crimes committed or the only means of preventing even greater harm (see CRIME AND PUNISHMENT §2). What harm is justified is one of the fundamental questions of moral philosophy. The competing answers to it, however, share the key idea of a moral equilibrium. In general terms, harms that tend to maintain the moral equilibrium are justified, while those that tend to produce a disequilibrium are unjustified. The generality of this explanation allows for disagreements about what count specifically as harms, and about how the moral equilibrium can be best maintained.

Evil may be the product of human or nonhuman agency. Inclement weather that causes crop failure and widespread starvation is an example of the latter, and it is usually described as natural evil. Evil caused by human beings, such as torturing an innocent person, is moral. This traditional distinction between natural and moral evil is useful, but it should not be drawn too sharply because human beings may be natural agents, as carriers of a disease, for instance, and evil caused by natural agency may warrant moral opprobrium, if it was preventable and those responsible for doing so failed. Moral thinking nevertheless tends to focus on moral evil, since it is much more likely to be within human control than natural evil.

The primary subjects to which moral evil (simply 'evil' from now on) may be ascribed are human actions. Intentions, agents, and institutions may also be evil, but only in a derivative sense. For intentions are evil if they lead to evil actions; agents are evil if the preponderance of their actions are evil; and institutions are evil if they regularly prompt agents representing them to perform evil actions. In its primary sense, therefore, evil is connected essentially with causing serious unjustified harm to sentient beings, and since the means by which this is done are human actions, an account of evil should begin by concentrating on them.

It is clear that evil actions are widespread, and that they are responsible for much suffering. The obvious explanation of this fact is that human beings are motivated by greed, cruelty, envy, rage, hatred, and so forth, and evil actions are the manifestations of these vices. But this is unilluminating, unless it is combined with an explanation of why human beings possess and act on vices. To attribute vices to choice is a poor explanation, since many vices are the unchosen consequences of genetic predispositions and corrupting circumstances, and even if vices are the results of choices, the question of why vices rather than virtues are chosen remains (see VIRTUES AND VICES §4).

2 Evil as deviation from the good

The philosophically most influential explanation of evil is embedded in the Socratic view that no one does evil knowingly (see SOCRATES §6). The thought behind the apparently obvious falsehood of this claim is that human agents are normally guided in their actions by what seems to be good to them. The explanation of evil actions must therefore be either that the agents are ignorant of the good, and perform evil actions in the mistaken belief that they are good, or, while they know what the good is, they do evil unintentionally, through accident, coercion, or some incapacity (see MORAL KNOWLEDGE §1; AKRASIA). The remedy for evil, consequently, is moral education that imparts genuine knowledge of the good and strengthens the intention to act on it.

This Socratic view, however, is driven to rely on a metaphysical assumption about the nature of reality and its effect on human aspirations. For, since human experience of the world testifies that thorough knowledge of the good and good intentions are compatible with evil actions, it must be supposed that human experiences disclose only appearances, not reality. The metaphysical assumption that needs to be made, therefore, is: first, that beyond human experiences of the world that appears to contain chaos and evil, there is a suprasensible true reality, in which a moral order prevails; and second, that good lives for human beings depend on learning to live in conformity to this order, rather than being led astray by deceptive appearances. Plato's Socrates explains evil, therefore, as a deviation from the good due to a human defect in cognition or intention that leads to mistaking appearance for reality.

This metaphysical assumption and the explanation of evil implied by it has passed from Greek thought to Christian theology chiefly through the works of Augustine and Aquinas. Christianity attributes to an all-knowing, all-powerful, all-good God the creation of the moral order that permeates reality, and it explains the prevalence of evil by the corrupting influence of original sin, which leads human beings to choose evil over the good, and thereby wilfully or weakly pit themselves against God's moral order (see SIN §2). Although Christian thinking about evil has dominated Western thought between the Greeks' time and ours, it nevertheless must be seen, if we ignore some twists and turns of theological sophistication, as a particular adaptation and elaboration of the metaphysical assumption and explanation of evil first advanced by Plato's Socrates.

This metaphysical assumption, however, cannot be reasonably maintained in the light of well-known objections, which can only be stated here without elaboration. First, any evidence that may be cited in favour of the supposed existence of a moral order in a supposed suprasensible reality beyond the world as it appears to normal human observers must be derived from the world as it appears to normal human observers, since, as a matter of logic, there is no other possible source of evidence. The evidence derived from appearances, however, cannot reasonably be taken to point to any suprasensible order in reality because the most such evidence can imply is that human knowledge of the world as it appears is limited and fallible. It is logically impossible for evidence to support inferences about what may lie beyond all possible evidence. Second, if, undeterred by this logical obstacle, defenders of the metaphysical assumption pursue their speculations about the implications of the evidence, they must recognize that evidentially unsupported implications can be derived both in favour of and against their assumption. If the existence of a moral order in suprasensible reality is inferred from observed instances of apparent goodness, then the existence of an evil order in suprasensible reality must be analogously inferrable from observed instances of evil. There is, consequently, no more reason to think of evil as deviation from the good than there is to think of the good as deviation from evil. Third, even if it is assumed for the sake of argument that the metaphysical assumption is defensible, it accounts only for moral evil, caused by human failure, and not for natural evil, whose occurrence cannot be attributed to human agency.

3   Evil as illusory

The Stoic-Spinozistic view attempts to avoid these objections by denying the reality of evil. It acknowledges that evil appears to exist, but its appearance is said to be an illusion to which human beings succumb through misdirected desires (see Spinoza 1677). Such desires cannot be satisfied because they are contrary to the moral order of reality, which need not be supposed to be suprasensible. If the misdirection of these desires is recognized, then the unavoidable experience of frustration they cause will be seen as emotional detritus that has been misidentified as evil. The advantage of the Stoic-Spinozistic view is that if evil were indeed illusory rather than real, then the objection to the Socratic view that it is incapable of explaining the reality of evil would be met (see SPINOZA, B. DE §10; STOICISM §19).

The Stoic-Spinozistic view is undoubtedly right in that what appears to be evil may not be and that greater self-knowledge and self-control make it possible to avoid much unnecessary suffering caused by mistaking for evil the frustration of misdirected desires. This view, however, is advanced not merely as a proposal for alleviating some instances of evil, but as an explanation of all evil. And as such, it is a failure for several reasons.

First, it cannot reasonably be held that all desires are misdirected, for human nature requires having and satisfying some desires. Rightly directed desires, however, are often frustrated, their frustration often results in serious unjustified harm, and that is real evil which cannot be alleviated by growth in self-knowledge and self-control. Second, the distinction between real and illusory evil rests on moral beliefs, which may be true or false. This view is committed to holding that beliefs about the occurrence of evil are always false. For if some were true, not all evil could be illusory. If, on the other hand, beliefs about the occurrence of evil were always false, then the belief that torturing innocent people is evil, for instance, would also be false. It is, however, a precondition of morality, and indeed of civilized life, that such basic

moral beliefs are regarded as true. The view that all evil is illusory, therefore, is incompatible with human nature, morality, and civilized life.

4   Evil as a contrast necessary for the good

Another attempt to account for evil is the Leibnizian view that recognizes its reality, but argues that the evil that exists is the minimum necessary for the existence of the good, which far outweighs the amount of evil there is (see Leibniz 1710). Evil is thus seen as the cost of the great benefits the good provides (see LEIBNIZ, G.W. §3). The assumption behind this view is that the good could exist only in contrast with evil. But whatever is true of phenomena requiring contrasting aspects, it is not true of good and evil. It is absurd to suppose that there can be kindness only if there is cruelty, or freedom only if there is tyranny. Defenders of this view therefore tend towards an epistemological sense of the contrast: evil is said to be required so that the good could be appreciated as good. The difficulty with this is that even if a contrast were necessary for appreciation, drawing it would not require the existence of evil. The good could be properly appreciated even in contrast with imaginative depictions of evil. It is, for instance, unnecessary to have people actually drawn and quartered in order to maintain a lively appreciation of one's good health. Nor is it required for the appreciation of the good that it be contrasted with evil, since the neutral or the indifferent would serve as a contrast just as well. People's dying in their sleep, without being tortured to death, is sufficient to enhance one's appreciation of the good of being alive.

5   Facing evil

It will perhaps be apparent that the various attempts to account for evil are not among the highest achievements of Western philosophy. All the surveyed accounts begin with the assumption that the good is primary and then vainly struggle to explain the prevalence of evil. It is hard to avoid the conclusion that the history of this subject is riddled with bad arguments and sentimentalism. A reasonable account of evil must acknowledge the reality and prevalence of evil. It must recognize that much evil that prevents the wellbeing of humanity is caused by human beings who are not moral monsters but ordinary people going about their ordinary lives. The character of such people includes virtues and vices, and a struggle between them (see VIRTUES AND VICES §5). Depending on the hardships they face, the traditions and institutions that guide their conduct, and their capacity, opportunity, and motivation for moral reflection, sometimes their virtues and sometimes their vices prevail. Human nature is mixed; it is neither simply good, nor simply evil. It is primarily the proportion of the mixture, not the knowledge and intentions of agents, that determines how much evil will be caused by specific individuals in specific contexts. The search for a metaphysical explanation for this banal fact is a diversion from the morally necessary task of decreasing evil by improving the conditions and character of individual moral agents.

See also: EVIL, PROBLEM OF; HOLOCAUST, THE

References and further reading

Aquinas, T. (1266–73) *Summa theologiae* (Synopsis of Theology), trans. English Dominican Fathers, London: Dent, 1934, Ia.47–9. (A classic of the Christian approach to evil.)

Augustine (397–401) *Confessionum libri tredecim* (Confessions), trans. E.B. Pusey, London: Dent, 1907, book VII, chaps 3–5. (Another classic of the Christian approach to evil.)

Kant, I. (1793) *Die Religion innerhalb der Grenzen der blossen Vernunft*, trans. T.M. Greene and H.H. Hudson, *Religion Within the Limits of Reason Alone*, New York: Harper & Row, 1960. (An attempt to combine the Christian approach with a secular understanding of evil.)

Kekes, J. (1990) *Facing Evil*, Princeton, NJ: Princeton University Press. (A treatment of evil from a secular point of view.)

* Leibniz, G.W. (1710) *Essai de Theodicée sur la bonté de Dieu, la liberté de l'homme, et l'origine du mal*, trans. E.M. Huggard, *Theodicy: Essays on the Goodness of God, the Freedom of Man, and the Origin of Evil*, London: Routledge & Kegan Paul, 1952. (A classic statement of the view that evil is required by the good.)

Madden, E.H. and Hare, P.H. (1968) *Evil and the Concept of God*, Springfield, IL: Charles C. Thomas. (A criticism of the main Christian approaches.)

McCord Adams, M. and Adams, R.M. (eds) (1991) *The Problem of Evil*, New York: Oxford University Press. (A collection of articles and a bibliography representing recent work on the Christian problem of evil.)

Plato (*c.*386–380 BC) *Meno*, trans. W.K.C. Guthrie, in *The Collected Dialogues*, Princeton, NJ: Princeton University Press, 1961. (One source of the Socratic view.)

* Spinoza, B. de (1677) *Ethica Ordine Geometrico Demonstrata* (Ethics Demonstrated in a Geometrical Manner), trans. E. Curley, *Ethics*, Princeton, NJ: Princeton University Press, 1985, parts IV–V. (A classic statement of the view that evil is due to misdirected desires.)

JOHN KEKES

EVIL, PROBLEM OF

In this context, 'evil' is given the widest possible scope to signify all of life's minuses. Within this range, philosophers and theologians distinguish 'moral evils' such as war, betrayal and cruelty from 'natural evils' such as earthquakes, floods and disease. Usually the inescapability of death is numbered among the greatest natural evils. The existence of broad-sense evils is obvious and spawns a variety of problems, most prominently the practical one of how to cope with life and the existential one of what sort of meaning human life can have.

Philosophical discussion has focused on two theoretical difficulties posed for biblical theism. First, does the existence of evils show biblical theism to be logically inconsistent? Is it logically possible for an omnipotent, omniscient and perfectly good God to create a world containing evil? One classical response to this, following Leibniz, is to argue that such a God would create the best of all possible worlds, but that such a world may contain evil as an indispensable element. Alternatively, evil may be an unavoidable consequence of the boon of free will, or it may be part of a divine plan to ensure that all souls attain perfection.

The second difficulty for biblical theism is, even if we grant logical consistency, does evil (in the form, for instance, of apparently pointless suffering) nevertheless count as evidence against the existence of the Bible's God? One frequent theistic response here is to argue that the apparent pointlessness of evil may be merely a result of our limited cognitive powers; things would appear the same to us whether or not there were a point, so it is not legitimate to argue from the evidence.

1 **Problems of evil**
2 **Logically necessary connections with greater goods**
3 **Free-will defences**
4 **Divine goodness to creatures**
5 **Methodological notes**
6 **The evidential problem of evil**

1 Problems of evil

The so-called 'logical' problem of evil rests on the contention that the following two claims of biblical theism:

(I) God exists, and is essentially omnipotent, omniscient and perfectly good; and

(II) evil exists,

combine with the following plausible attribute analyses:

(P1) a perfectly good being would always eliminate evil so far as it could;

(P2) an omniscient being would know all about evils; and

(P3) there are no limits to what an omnipotent being can do,

to form an inconsistent quintet, so that the conjunction of any four entails the denial of the fifth; most notably the conjunction of (P1)–(P3) with either of (I) or (II) entails that the other is false.

Such an argument can be taken aporetically, as a challenge to propose more subtle alternatives to (P1)–(P3), but it has usually (in analytical philosophy of religion since the 1950s) been advanced 'atheologically' as an argument against the existence of God (see ATHEISM §4; NATURAL THEOLOGY §5). Likewise important is the distinction between the abstract problem, which takes 'evil' in (II) to refer generally to some evil or other (say the pain of a single hangnail), and the concrete problem, which construes (II) as shorthand for the existence of evils in the amounts and of the kinds and with the distribution found in the actual world. While the abstract problem raises a question of conceptual interest, it is the concrete version that gives the issue its bite.

Bold responses deny (P3), maintaining variously that God cannot overcome certain natural necessities (like Plato's Demiurge), that he cannot conquer his evil twin (as in Manichean dualism), or even that he lacks the power to compel at all (see PROCESS THEISM §2). Some reject (P2), observing that many evils arise from free choice, while future contingents are in principle unknowable (see OMNISCIENCE §4). (P1) is the most obviously vulnerable because it is contrary to the common intuition that ignorance and weakness excuse, and is best replaced with:

(P4) it is logically impossible for an omniscient, omnipotent being to have a reason compatible with perfect goodness for permitting (bringing about) evils.

Rebuttals seek to counterexemplify (P4) by identifying logically possible reasons available even to an omniscient, omnipotent God.

2 Logically necessary connections with greater goods

Since omnipotence is not bound by causally necessary connections, it is natural to look for reasons among the logically necessary connections of evils with greater goods. Because the piecemeal approach of correlating distinctive sorts of good with different kinds of evil (for example, courage with danger, forgiveness with injury) threatens to be endless, it seems advantageous to identify a single comprehensive good that logically integrates all ills. One promising strategy takes its inspiration from Leibniz and develops his 'best of all possible worlds' ('BPW') theodicy in terms of contemporary possible-worlds semantics (see LEIBNIZ, G.W. §3; MODAL LOGIC, PHILOSOPHICAL ISSUES IN §1). If a possible world is a maximal consistent state of affairs, each of infinitely many constitutive details is essential to the possible world of which it is a part. Assuming (P5) that possible worlds as wholes have values (P6) that can be ranked relative to one another and (P7) that the value scale has a maximum (P8) occupied by one and only one world, one can interpret divine creation in terms of actualizing a possible world and reason (P9) that necessarily an essentially omniscient, omnipotent and perfectly good God would actualize the best. Given the further controversial claim that:

(P10) the BPW contains instances of evil as logically indispensable components,

it follows that the desire to create the BPW is a reason compossible with perfect goodness for God not to prevent or eliminate all instances of evil.

(P10) contradicts our *prima facie* intuition that the BPW should be homogeneously good. Defenders of BPW approaches (see Chisholm 1968) distinguish two ways in which value-parts may be related to value-wholes. The one presupposed by the critics is simply additive: negatively and positively valued parts simply 'balance off' one another and the inclusion of any 'minuses' inevitably lowers the value total. By contrast, parts may be integrated into wholes by relations of organic unity, in such a way that the positive value of the whole may defeat the negative value of the part (for example, the way the beauty of Monet's design defeats the ugliness of some colour patches). (P10) envisages the defeat of evil within the context of the possible world as a whole.

Leibniz thought he could prove the necessity of (P10) on the basis of his a priori arguments for the necessity of (I) and (P9); he believed that (P10) followed from the fact that God had actualized this world. Yet (P10) seems to fall into that class of propositions that are logically possible if and only if logically necessary. Those who recognize no sound demonstrations of (I) are left to claim that (P10) is epistemically possible. Since the atheologian is in the same epistemic predicament with respect to (P10), this epistemic defence would be sufficient *ceteris paribus* to discharge the burden of proof imposed on the theist by the argument from evil.

This BPW approach makes several other debatable value-theory assumptions. Augustine's notion (*contra* P8) that many alternative worlds have maximum value imposes no damage. Aquinas' insistence (*contra* P7) that for every collection of creatures there is a better one would not be crippling if every possible world above a certain value-level included evil. The rejection of (P5) and (P6), however, would be fatal for BPW approaches. Some question whether our comparative evaluations of small-scale states of affairs (for example, Jones' enjoying a symphony as better than his experiencing excruciating pain) is good evidence that the values of maximal states of affairs form a hierarchy. More fundamentally, some have argued (*contra* P5) that states of affairs are not intrinsically good or bad, although they can be good or bad for certain persons or projects and can ground different moral evaluations by particular agents. Anti-consequentialists in ethics also challenge whether (P9) follows from (P5)–(P8) (see CONSEQUENTIALISM). Deontologists would let justice to individuals trump putative increases in the value of states of affairs (see DEONTOLOGICAL ETHICS). Could creating the BPW be a reason compossible with perfect goodness for permitting suffering and degradation for the relatively innocent? Even if such value-maximizing were compatible with perfect goodness, it is not obviously required. For example, divine goodness is often interpreted as grace, a disposition to show favour independently of merit.

Finally, this modified Leibnizian approach entails divine determinism, because in choosing which of infinitely many fully determinate possible worlds to actualize, God is deciding on each and every detail. Some find this theologically objectionable, either because it seems incongruous for God to hold created persons responsible to himself for actions he determined, or because it fails to put enough distance between evil and divine aims.

3 Free-will defences

The last-mentioned worries are well accommodated by the other main traditional theme – that (some or all) evil originates in the wrong or evil choices of free creatures. Free-will approaches contend that:

(A1) created free will is a very great good, whether intrinsically or as a necessary means to God's central purposes in creation;

(A2) God cannot fulfil his purposes for and with free creatures without accepting the possibility that some will misuse their freedom, thereby introducing evil into the world.

In classical developments of this defence, (A1) is supposed to be a reason compossible with perfect goodness for making free creatures, while (A2) is compatible with the claim that evil is not necessary to the perfection of the universe or any other divine purpose. Some or all evil is not something God causes or does, but something he allows, a (perhaps) known but unintended side effect of his aims. The introduction of evil into the world is explained by the doctrine of 'the Fall', according to which God made angelic and human free agents in naturally optimal condition and placed them in utopian environments. God wanted them freely to choose what is right or good, but some angels and the primordial humans Adam and Eve chose what is wrong, thereby actualizing the possibility of evil.

Contemporary attention (beginning with Plantinga) has turned away from free-will defences based on the principles of double effect and doing–allowing – the principle that agents are not as responsible for the known but unintended side effects of their actions as they are for their chosen means and ends; that they are not as responsible for what they allow as for what they do – to others that reconnect with possible-worlds semantics (see DOUBLE EFFECT, PRINCIPLE OF). Once again, God creates by actualizing a possible world, but freedom is now taken to be incompatible with determinism, with the consequence that God and free creatures collaborate in determining which possible world becomes actual. Created freedom does not so much 'distance' God from evils as limit which worlds God can create. As with BPW approaches, God evaluates possible worlds as to their global features – (P5) and (P6) are assumed true, although not necessarily (P7) and (P8) – but this time he evaluates those that are a function of created incompatibilist-free choice: for example, a very good world with the optimal balance of created moral goodness over moral evil.

In defence of (A2), both classical and possible-worlds approaches appeal first to the notion that not even God can cause someone else's incompatibilist-free choices. To the objection that God should use his foreknowledge to actualize only incompatibilist-free creatures who will never sin, free-will defenders reply that such foreknowledge is not prior in the order of explanation to God's decision to create. To the suggestion that God should use his middle knowledge of what free creatures would do in particular circumstances, some (notably Plantinga 1974) grant that such counterfactuals of freedom can be true, but argue that it is logically possible that all incompatibilist-free creatures be 'transworld depraved' – that is, that no matter which combinations of individuals and circumstances God actualized, each would go wrong at least once – and logically possible that any world containing as much moral goodness as the actual world would also include at least as much moral evil as the actual world contains. Thus, it is logically possible that God could not create a world with a better balance of moral good over moral evil – which would be a reason compossible with perfect goodness for his not doing so.

This ingenious argument is controverted both by those who agree and those who deny that counterfactuals of freedom can be true. Among the former, SUÁREZ (§1) defends middle knowledge but arguably finds transworld depravity impossible because of God's necessary resourcefulness, which he takes to have the following implication: necessarily, for any possible person and any situation in which they can exist, there are some helps of grace that would (should God supply them) win the creature over without compromising its incompatibilist freedom. Others (notably R.M. Adams 1977) wonder what could make such counterfactuals true about creatures considered as merely possible. Incompatibilist freedom rules out divine choices or any native features of the creative will. To appeal to a contingent condition (*habitudo*, or primitive property) independent of both is too close for comfort to the ancient doctrine of fate that falls alike on the gods and their creatures, and contradicts traditional Christian views of divine providence (see PROVIDENCE §1). To maintain that counterfactuals of freedom are true although there is nothing to make them true violates a correspondence theory of truth (see TRUTH, CORRESPONDENCE THEORY OF). Denying truth to such counterfactuals of freedom does not automatically put (A2) clear of the objection from omniscience, however, if God could know about merely possible creatures what they probably would do in any given circumstance. But the meaning and ground of such probability assessments is at least as problematic as that of the original counterfactuals (see R.M. Adams 1977, 1985).

Even if (A2) were unproblematic, it could still be asked whether (A1) necessarily constitutes a reason compossible with perfect goodness for allowing evils. Two dimensions of divine goodness may be distinguished: 'global' goodness and goodness to individual created persons. The possible-worlds approaches cite global features – 'the best of all possible worlds', 'a world a more perfect than which is impossible', 'a world exhibiting a perfect balance of retributive justice', 'a world with as favourable a balance as God can get of created moral good over moral evil' –

by way of producing some generic and comprehensive reason for allowing evil. But worlds with evils in the amounts and of the kind and with the distribution found in the actual world contain horrendous evils – evils the participation in (the doing or suffering of) which gives one *prima facie* reason to doubt whether one's life could (given their inclusion in it) be a great good to one on the whole – unevenly distributed among humans and uncorrelated with variations in desert. Even if horrors thus apportioned were epistemically compatible with global perfections, these defences of divine goodness as a producer of global perfection would not so much guarantee as raise doubts about God's goodness to individual participants in horrors. Divine goodness to them would require God to defeat the disvalue of horrors not only within the context of the world as a whole, but also within the framework of the individual participant's life. Nor will precise individual retribution fit this bill where the perpetrators of horrors are concerned. 'Balancing' horror with horror only deepens the difficulty. Some Christians bite this bullet, insisting that decisive defeat of evil is promised only to the obedient, while the wicked can expect the reverse, a decisive defeat of positive meaning in their lives in the form of eternal damnation. Others insist that the doctrine of hell only makes matters worse by giving rise to a specialized version of the problem of evil (see HELL).

4 Divine goodness to creatures

Soul-making theodicies try to fill the explanatory gap regarding divine goodness to individual created persons by adding further hypotheses as to what they might get out of existence in an environment in which they are so vulnerable to sin, suffering and horrors. Some versions stipulate:

(A3) God's purpose in creation culminates in a process of spiritual development in which autonomous created persons with their own free participation are perfected, and transformed from self-centred to other-centred, God-centred, Christlike or otherwise virtuous souls; and

(A4) environmental evils are permitted because they create an environment favourable to soul-making.

(A3) is compatible both with the notion that humans are initially created with mature unobstructed agency and so are fully responsible for their choices, and with the alternative idea (retrieved from Irenaeus by Hick (1966)) that human agency began immature, so that sin was to be expected in the course of the 'growing-up' process. The idea is that life in a world with evils such as this is, or with created cooperation can be, 'good for the soul'.

Establishing (A4) is difficult thrice over because: (i) the task shatters into piecemeal cataloguing, with separate demonstrations for each sub-type of environmental evil; (ii) relevant necessary connections with the soul-making environment can be hard to show; and (iii) experience makes it *prima facie* implausible that a world with evils such as ours is a good classroom for the soul. In response to (ii), some (notably Hick 1966) ingeniously contend that 'dysteleological' evils lend an air of mystery which is itself favourable to soul-making. Others (for example, Stump 1985) modify (A4) to acknowledge that some environmental evils are consequences of sin.

Where God's soul-making purpose succeeds, it is easy to see how the painful journey is worth the individual's while. What about where it fails? Some (especially Swinburne 1983) reply that the dignity of self-determination is enough, whatever the outcome. The credibility of this contention varies with one's estimate of the robustness of human nature as well as one's conception of the natural or punitive consequences of repeated bad choices. Pessimists argue that ante-mortem participation in horrors makes a mockery of human self-determination; *a fortiori*, so does decisive personal ruin in hell.

Others (notably Hick 1966) embrace a doctrine of universal salvation: if ante-mortem horrors remain undefeated between birth and the grave, education will continue after death, probably in a series of careers, until the soul is perfected and brought into intimacy with God. Thus, God does guarantee each created person an overall existence that is a great good to them on the whole, one in which participation in horrors is balanced by the incommensurate goodness of intimacy with God. Are such horrors likewise defeated within the context of the individual's existence? The stout of heart might say 'yes', because participation in horrors that remain undefeated within the individual's ante-mortem career contributes to the sense of mystery that makes a positive contribution to the soul-making of others. Since one is at least the agent-cause of the willy-nilly sacrifice of one's ante-mortem good, participation in horrors would constitute some sort of shift from self- to other- or God-centredness after all. Even if this putative positive dimension of participation in horrors is swamped by its negative aspect when considered within the framework of the individual's ante-mortem career, it provides a means for participation in horrors to be integrated into the overall development that gives positive meaning to the individual's life and thus defeated within the context of the individual's existence as a whole.

Some (notably M.M. Adams) contend, on the contrary, that divine goodness to created persons would do more to lend positive meaning to any careers in which they participate in horrors. The sacrifice involved in participation in horrors is pedagogically inept as a first lesson because it can damage the person so much as to make much further ante-mortem progress from self- to other- or God-centredness virtually impossible. This combines with the delay in gratification to another or perhaps many lives later to de-emphasize the importance of this life, leaving the impression that it would have been better skipped by those whose spiritual development was significantly set back through participation in horrors. To give this life, or any career involving participation in horrors, positive significance, some parameter of positive meaning other than contribution to soul-making must be found. Given two further assumptions – that divine metaphysical goodness is infinite, and that intimacy with God is incommensurably good for created persons – the mystical literature suggests several ways for participation in horrors to be integrated into the created person's relationship with God, ranging from divine gratitude for one's earthly career to various types of mystical identification between God and creatures in the midst of horrors. Because the identification occurs in this life and divine gratitude is for this life, they add positive significance to this life even where the creature has no ante-mortem but only postmortem recognition of these facts.

5 Methodological notes

Much contemporary discussion of BPW and free-will defences has addressed itself to the logical problem of evil because we seem epistemically in a better position to assess the compossibility of logically possible reasons with various conceptions of perfect goodness than to pronounce on what God's actual reasons are. In identifying logically possible defeaters, many of the earlier discussions (including those by Pike (1963) and Plantinga (1974)) confine themselves to a religion-neutral value theory, the better to answer the atheologian on their own turf. By contrast, soul-making, mystical and other explanatory theodicies draw on the resources of revelation for their speculations about God's actual reasons for the evils of this world and usually address their remarks in the first instance to the believing community. The distinction between these approaches blurs when attention is riveted on the concrete logical problem of evil – that is, on the logical compossibility of God with evils in the amounts and of the kinds and with the distribution found in the actual world. In so far as the consistency of actual religious belief is at stake, it becomes highly relevant to test the reasons supplied by revelation for logical compossibility with the existence of evils and the goodness of God. Where they pass, they can be advanced as solving the concrete logical problem of evil, whether or not their truth can be proved to the atheologian.

Once the wider resources of the religions under attack are allowed to interpret (I) and (II), it becomes clear that explanatory reasons come in two broad types: reasons why God causes or permits evils, and does not prevent or eliminate them; and explanations as to how God could be good to created persons despite their participation in evil. Reasons-why identify some great-enough good with which evils are necessarily connected, while reasons-how specify ways God could defeat evils in which the created person has participated and thus give that person a life that is a great good to them on the whole. Much philosophical discussion (Swinburne is particularly insistent on this point) presupposes that the problem cannot be solved without sufficient reasons-why. The criticized religions arguably take a mixed approach. Assuming that what perfect goodness can permit or cause is a function of what it can defeat, they combine partial reasons-why with elaborate scenarios by which God defeats even the worst horrors.

6   The evidential problem of evil

Recently many philosophers (notably Rowe, Alston, van Inwagen and Wykstra) have concluded that the most serious version of the problem of evil concerns not the logical but the evidential relation between (I) and (II). The mere logical possibility that a student has broken all four limbs and been hospitalized for a heart attack will win them no extension of essay deadlines if the tutor can see that the student is in fact physically sound. Likewise, the evidential argument contends, many actual evils – such as the slow, painful death of a fawn severely burned in a forest fire started by lightning – appear pointless, in the sense that our composite empirical evidence constitutes strong reason to believe they have no point. But an omniscient, omnipotent being could have prevented some of them, while a perfectly good being would not allow or cause any of them it could avoid. Therefore, (II) concretely construed constitutes decisive evidence against (I).

Once again, replies could take the piecemeal approach, trying to show for each type of very intense suffering that it has a discernible point after all. It would not be necessary to complete the process to undermine the evidential argument. Success with some important cases would increase

the probability that defeating goods are also present in other cases where we have not discovered any (see SUFFERING §4).

The favourite response (for example, by Wykstra, Alston and van Inwagen) attacks the argument at its epistemological foundations. The contention is that our composite empirical evidence could constitute strong reason to believe some actual evils pointless only if our cognitive powers would afford access to any point such evils might have were they to have one. If things would seem roughly the same to us (that is, if our evidence would be roughly the same) whether or not such evils had a point, the fact that we detect no point is not good evidence that there is no point. In particular, we are in no position to see that many instances of intense suffering are not explained by some of the reasons appealed to in traditional theodicies.

Defenders of the evidential argument (notably Rowe) grant the appeal of the underlying evidential principle, but relocate the disagreement in the richness of the theological hypothesis on which one draws. They argue that if one restricts oneself to a straightforward philosophical reading of (I), then it is likely that the situation with regard to intense suffering would be different in ways discernible by us. Expanded theism might import assumptions about the hiddenness of divine providence, mystical identification with suffering creatures, etc., but deploying these resources in the evidential debate carries a cost, because the prior probability of expanded theism is lower than that of (I).

This last point holds only if the richer theological theory is advanced as true. If instead it is used, as with the logical problem, to generate possible – this time not merely logically but epistemically possible – explanations, then no dilution in prior probabilities need be accepted. And once again, the more epistemically possible explanations there are, the greater the probability that the suffering in question is not pointless.

See also: EVIL; GOD, ARGUMENTS FOR THE EXISTENCE OF; GOODNESS, PERFECT; HOLOCAUST, THE; LIBERATION THEOLOGY; RELIGION AND EPISTEMOLOGY

References and further reading

Adams, M.M. (1989) 'Horrendous Evils and the Goodness of God', *Proceedings of the Aristotelian Society*, supplementary vol. 63: 297–310. (Argues that in view of horrendous evils, global and generic hypotheses do nothing to defend divine goodness to created persons.)

Adams, R.M. (1972) 'Must God Create the Best?', *Philosophical Review* 81: 317–32. (Elaborates the argument referred to in §2 that a perfectly good God would not be obliged to create the best.)

* —— (1977) 'Middle Knowledge and the Problem of Evil', *American Philosophical Quarterly* 14: 109–17. (Rejects middle knowledge and argues that counterfactuals of freedom cannot be true, as discussed in §3.)

* —— (1985) 'Plantinga on the Problem of Evil', in J.E. Tomberlin and P. van Inwagen (eds) *Profiles: Alvin Plantinga*, Dordrecht: Reidel, 225–55. (Criticizes Plantinga's treatment of the problem of evil, especially issues about counterfactuals and probability.)

Alston, W.P. (1991) 'The Inductive Argument from Evil and the Human Cognitive Condition', *Philosophical Perspectives* 5: 26–67. (Responds to evidential arguments by arguing that our composite empirical evidence does not constitute good reason to think none of the traditional theodicies are true.)

* Chisholm, R. (1968) 'The Defeat of Good and Evil', *Proceedings of the American Philosophical Association* 42: 21–38. (Distinguishes balancing-off from defeat and assesses its relevance to the problem of evil.)

Griffin, D.R. (1981) 'Creation out of Chaos and the Problem of Evil', in S. Davis (ed.) *Encountering Evil: Live Options in Theodicy*, Atlanta, GA: John Knox Press, 101–23, 125–36. (Draws on process philosophy to extend a free-will defence to natural evils.)

* Hick, J. (1966) *Evil and the God of Love*, San Francisco, CA: Harper & Row, 2nd edn, 1978. (Criticizes 'Augustinian' theodicies that rely on the doctrine of the Fall, and develops a soul-making theodicy in the spirit of Irenaeus.)

Mackie, J.L. (1955) 'Evil and Omnipotence', *Mind* 64: 200-12. (The most influential formulation of the atheological argument from evil, slightly modified in §1.)

* Pike, N. (1963) 'Hume on Evil', *Philosophical Review* 72: 180–97. (Articulates an epistemic defence using a BPW approach discussed in §2.)

* Plantinga, A. (1974) *The Nature of Necessity*, Oxford: Clarendon Press, ch. 9, §10, 191–3. (Develops the possible-worlds version of the free-will defence discussed in §3 of the present entry, with considerable attention to counterfactuals of freedom and the hypothesis of transworld depravity.)

Rowe, W.L. (1979) 'The Problem of Evil and Some Varieties of Atheism', *American Philosophical Quarterly* 16: 335–41. (Formulates the most discussed version of the evidential problem.)

—— (1984) 'Evil and the Theistic Hypothesis: A Response to Wykstra', *International Journal for the Philosophy of Religion* 16: 95–100. (Replies to Wykstra's objection.)

—— (1991) 'Ruminations about Evil', *Philosophical Perspectives*, 69–88. (Further reflections on his version of the evidential argument.)

* Stump, E. (1985) 'The Problem of Evil', with comment by M. Smith and Stump's reply, *Faith and Philosophy* 2: 392–435. (Develops a theodicy based on the doctrine of the Fall.)

* Swinburne, R. (1983) 'A Theodicy of Heaven and Hell', in A. Freddoso (ed.) *The Existence and Nature of God*, Notre Dame, IN: University of Notre Dame Press, 37–54. (Offers a free-will defence of annihilation or benevolent alternative environments for those who die with characters unfit for heaven.)

—— (1987) 'Knowledge from Experience and the Problem of Evil', in W.J. Abraham and S.W. Holtzer (eds) *The Rationality of Religious Belief: Essays in Honour of Basil Mitchell*, Oxford: Clarendon Press, 141–67. (Argues that natural evils contribute to a good environment for humans' self-determined choices of their own destinies.)

Van Inwagen, P. (1991) 'The Problem of Evil, the Problem of Air, and the Problem of Silence', *Philosophical Perspectives* 5: 135–65. (Develops a response to the evidential argument.)

Wykstra, S.J. (1984) 'The Humean Obstacle to Evidential Arguments from Suffering: On Avoiding the Evils of "Appearance"', *International Journal for the Philosophy of Religion* 16: 73–94. (Formulates a principle of epistemic access and uses it to attack Rowe's evidential argument.)

MARILYN McCORD ADAMS

EVOLUTION AND ETHICS

The fact that human beings are a product of biological evolution has been thought to impinge on the study of ethics in two quite different ways. First, evolutionary ideas may help account for why people have the ethical thoughts and feelings they do. Second, evolutionary ideas may help illuminate which normative ethical claims, if any, are true or right or correct. These twin tasks – explanation and justification – may each be subdivided. Evolutionary considerations may be relevant to explaining elements of morality that are culturally universal; they also may help explain why individuals or societies differ in the ethics they espouse. With respect to the question of justification, evolutionary considerations have sometimes been cited to show that ethics is an elaborate illusion – that is, to defend versions of ethical subjectivism and emotivism. However, evolutionary considerations also have been invoked to justify ethical norms. Although there is no conflict between using evolution both to explain traits that are universal and to explain traits that vary, it is not consistent to claim both that evolution unmasks ethics *and justifies particular ethical norms.*

1 Explanation
2 Genetic arguments
3 The is/ought distinction

1 Explanation

Before we can assess whether evolution helps explain why we have the ethical beliefs we possess, we need to be clear on what the phenotype in question is. What part of human culture is delimited by the term 'ethics'?

Some of the evaluations an organism may place on an action or a person or a motive may count as ethical in character. What makes an evaluation ethical? The question here is not the normative question, 'What standards *should* an individual use?' Rather, it is descriptive; its answer helps define a line of inquiry in the social and natural sciences. If we visited an alien society – either that of human beings or of some other species – how would we tell whether that society has an ethics?

Even if the individuals concerned have altruistic motives, this does not show that they possess an ethics. Parents may care for the welfare of their children, but feeling love and concern are not the same as possesing a morality. Closer to the mark is the idea that an ethics is a set of principles that possesses a certain sort of generality (see MORALITY AND ETHICS).

In his *Methods of Ethics* (1874), Sidgwick suggested that it is a self-evident truth of common-sense morality that if one person has a right to do something, then so does anyone else who is similarly situated. This normative claim has a descriptive analogue: an organism has a morality only if it possesses a set of principles that dictate what anyone fitting a certain qualitative description is entitled or required to do. These principles need not provide an algorithm for deciding which actions are morally right; they simply may specify a set of ethically relevant considerations. Nor does this idea require that a morality treat all human beings as having equal ethical standing. Tribal moralities, no less than universal moralities, state what individuals must be like to be entitled to perform various actions. Nor does the Kantian pedigree of the idea mean that

ethics focuses exclusively on disinterested reason and has nothing to do with engaged emotion (see KANT, I. §§9–10); an ethics of caring about personal relations may still find expression in a set of general principles.

Although generality is arguably a necessary feature of a morality, it is not sufficient. The hypothetical imperatives that specify rules for different aspects of cultural practice – of etiquette, of sports, and so on – may also be general. Ethics may be special because it dictates what individuals ought to care about, no matter what else they happen to want.

Even after we single out the aspect of a culture that falls under the rubric of 'ethics', we must take care to describe this phenotype accurately. A person's or a society's ethics may fail to coincide with the slogans that figure in public discourse. Aliens visiting Earth from another galaxy would make an enormous mistake if they thought that the people who pay homage to the Ten Commandments believe that the acts listed are always prohibited or always required. An ethics may be compared to a grammar; just as people speak a language without being able to articulate the grammatical principles their language obeys, so their ethical intuitions correspond to a set of principles that they often are unable to articulate. Descriptive ethics poses problems that are no less subtle than those addressed in theoretical linguistics.

Regardless of how exactly a morality is defined, the fact that moralities are so common in human societies raises a fundamental evolutionary puzzle. An individual may possess a mixture of selfish and altruistic motives without having a morality. Why, then, do moralities exist? It is worth considering the possibility that moralities began life and continue to exist because they perform a certain social function. The idea that there are obligations, prohibitions and entitlements that people must respect regardless of whatever else they happen to want obviously contributes to a well-functioning society. Perhaps everyone benefits from a society in which a morality is present; alternatively, it may be that some benefit at the expense of others. Each of these patterns can be accommodated in an evolutionary explanation of why morality emerged as a social form in ancestral populations.

In addition to asking why moralities exist, evolutionary theory can be asked to explain why moralities have the features they do. But here we must be careful. To ask whether evolution can explain 'our ethics' is to begin with a poorly formulated problem. There are many features of the ethical norms endorsed by a person or a society. Some of these may have important connections with evolutionary considerations; others may not.

In virtually every human society, killing a member

of one's own society is viewed as a morally more weighty act than killing a chicken. It is hard to believe that evolution is irrelevant to why this is so. On the other hand, the fact that many societies have changed their views about capital punishment in the last century may be explicable by cultural, rather than evolutionary, factors.

This is not to deny that having views about capital punishment requires an organism to have a big brain, and that having a big brain is a product of evolution. The point remains, a big brain is something that people of today share with their ancestors of a hundred years ago; thus it does not explain why our views on capital punishment differ from those held a few generations ago.

The present example about the ethics of killing should not be taken to imply that evolution can help explain only those features of ethics that are culturally universal. Evolution has endowed human beings with enormous behavioural plasticity; however, sometimes the details of an organism's plasticity are themselves dictated by evolution. For example, polar bears grow thick fur when it is cold and thinner fur when it is warm; natural selection has made the organism's phenotype respond to environmental changes in ways that maximize fitness. So the mere fact that human beings espouse different ethical systems in different cultures does not imply that evolution is irrelevant to understanding that variation. The question is whether the pattern of variation can be understood as a phenotypically plastic adaptation.

2 Genetic arguments

If morality emerged and persisted because it conferred some evolutionary benefit, then we may speculate that morality would have had this utility even if there really were no such things as the obligations and rights that people objectively possess. It is worth remembering that ethics and religion were closely connected in the histories of many societies. Although Western philosophy since the Greeks prominently featured the idea that ethical principles have a status independent of divine decree, this declaration of independence is hardly a cultural universal. If theism emerged and persisted for reasons having nothing to do with its objective correctness, one may ask whether the same is true of moral convictions.

Here we find the beginning of a genetic argument for ethical subjectivism. The idea is that the causes of a conviction – the factors that generated it – provide evidence about whether the conviction is true. Arguments to this effect are called genetic because they refer to an idea's genesis; they need have nothing

to do with chromosomes. The question we need to consider is whether the fact that ethical beliefs can be explained – either by evolution or by details concerning human culture – show that these beliefs are never true or right or correct.

We must be careful not to dismiss this suggestion simply by invoking the so-called 'genetic fallacy'. To be sure, one cannot deduce that a proposition is false just from information concerning why someone came to believe it. Even if Kekulé first thought of the benzene ring while he was hallucinating, this does not prove that benzene is not a ring.

Even so, facts about the genesis of a belief can provide non-deductive evidence about whether the proposition believed is true. If you form your belief concerning how many planets there are by drawing a number at random from an urn, then your belief is probably mistaken. The *process* of belief formation provides an indication of whether its *product* is likely to be correct.

If evolution produced some of the ethical convictions we have, what does that show about whether those convictions are likely to be true? Is this fact about their genesis evidence that the beliefs are false? It is easy to see how a genetic argument could show that a specific ethical belief is probably mistaken. If your belief about the number of planets can be cast in doubt by a genetic argument, there is no reason why your ethics should be immune from this challenge.

What is more puzzling is how the whole status of ethics as a subject can be undermined by genetic considerations. In the case of your belief about the number of planets, we assume that there is a fact of the matter concerning how many planets there are. We further assume that the process of drawing a number at random from an urn is not connected in the right way to that fact. This set of background assumptions explains why we are entitled to be confident that your belief about the number of planets is probably untrue.

For a genetic argument to support ethical subjectivism, it would have to be shown that the process of evolution is completely unrelated to the factors that make an ethical proposition true or false. But even if this could be demonstrated, it would not follow that no normative statements are true, only that the ones we happen to espouse are probably mistaken. How could a genetic argument support the conclusion that ethics, in its entirety, not just in the details we happen to believe now, is an illusion? Subjectivism and emotivism, if they are to be defended, must be defended by some other route (see MORAL SCEPTICISM).

3 The is/ought distinction

HUME (§4) famously observed that a normative conclusion cannot be deduced validly from purely descriptive premises. One cannot derive an *ought* from an *is*. This claim is not undermined by the fact that terms in natural languages sometimes combine normative and descriptive elements. To say that someone is cruel is both to describe and criticize the person in question. However, that does not affect the Humean thesis.

It follows from this Humean doctrine that descriptive facts about evolution cannot be sufficient to deduce normative conclusions. The fact that human beings in ancestral populations were omnivores does not provide an ethical justification for eating meat. It is 'natural' for human beings to eat meat, in the sense that this is a trait that is found in nature. Nothing normative follows from this point.

The Humean thesis concerns deduction. Even if an ought-statement cannot be deduced from purely is-premises, the question remains of whether descriptive premises provide non-deductive support for normative conclusions. Here the Humean thesis should be extended to the domain of non-deductive inference; purely is-premises do not, by themselves, provide evidence for an ought-conclusion.

It does not follow that evolutionary information is always irrelevant to ethical problems. Evolutionary facts may be relevant, even if they do not provide the whole story. Whether this is so depends on the specific ethical system one considers and on the details of the ethical problem at hand. In just the same way, human psychology is relevant to ethics only in so far as some ethical theory makes this so. For example, hedonistic utilitarianism says that an action's moral standing is determined by its propensity to cause pleasure and pain. If psychology tells us about the pains and pleasures that an action is apt to cause, this information is ethically relevant because utilitarianism (or some other ethical theory of interest) says that it is.

One ethical idea that has been thought to establish the relevance of evolution to ethics is the 'ought-implies-can' principle. This principle says that obligations encompass only what is possible; we are not obliged to perform actions that are impossible for us to perform. If evolutionary considerations establish that certain types of behaviour are outside the human repertoire, then the idea of requiring them would not only be hopelessly utopian – such reforms also would fail to be ethically imperative.

This concept sometimes surfaces in discussion of the idea that natural selection will lead females to evolve the inclination to be more choosy about their sexual partners than males; females may have more to lose in fitness terms by making a poor choice. If evolution has hard-wired a sexual double standard into our ethical intuitions, then it will be false that we ought to change the way we think. However, a moment's reflection shows that a double standard does not strike all people everywhere as obviously correct. For many species, natural selection has forged the details of behaviour; but for human beings, it has caused a big brain to evolve. This big brain allows us to reflect on what would be for many other species an automatic reflex. Paradoxically enough, natural selection has caused a trait to evolve in human beings that limits the hegemony of natural selection in determining human behaviour. The human brain is a monkey wrench of the first order; apparently, it frequently prevents the ought-implies-can principle from demonstrating that evolutionary theory has a great deal to say about what our obligations are.

Still, ethics since Aristotle has repeatedly found attractive the thought that reflection on the biological nature of human beings must yield important information concerning what human flourishing amounts to, and a conception of human flourishing must be an important tool in forging theories of the right and the good. The more appealing such theories become, the more relevant to ethics will evolutionary ideas appear. There is no way to settle, once and for all, what evolution can teach us about ethics. As ethical theory evolves, the relevance of evolution will also experience a continuing metamorphosis.

See also: HUMAN NATURE; SPENCER, H.; SOCIOBIOLOGY

References and further reading

Alexander, R.D. (1987) *The Biology of Moral Systems*, New York: de Gruyter. (A systematic argument for the fruitfulness of evolutionary explanations of moral practices.)

Huxley, T.H. (1894) *Evolution and Ethics*, Princeton, NJ: Princeton University Press, 1989. (Argues that evolution often produces morally repulsive outcomes, which human culture should attempt to modify.)

Kitcher, P. (1994) 'Four Ways of Biologicizing Ethics', in E. Sober (ed.) *Conceptual Issues in Evolutionary Biology*, Cambridge, MA: MIT Press, 2nd edn, 439–50. (A criticism of Ruse and Wilson (1986).)

Ruse, M. (1986) *Taking Darwin Seriously*, Oxford: Blackwell. (A systematic defence of the relevance of evolution to ethics and epistemology.)

Ruse, M. and Wilson, E. (1986) 'Moral Philosophy as Applied Science', *Philosophy* 61: 173–92; repr. in E.

Sober (ed.), *Conceptual Issues in Evolutionary Biology*, Cambridge, MA: MIT Press, 2nd edn, 1994, 421–38. (A defence of the relevance of evolution to both meta-ethics and normative ethics.)

* Sidgwick, H. (1874) *Methods of Ethics*, London: Macmillan. (A classic text, which examines intuitionism, egoism and utilitarianism.)

Sober, E. (1994) 'Prospects for Evolutionary Ethics', in *From a Biological Point of View*, Cambridge: Cambridge University Press. (Assesses how evolutionary theory bears on the tasks of explanation and justification in ethics.)

ELLIOTT SOBER

EVOLUTION, THEORY OF

The biological theory of evolution advances the view that the variety and forms of life on earth are the result of descent with modification from the earliest forms of life. Evolutionary theory does not attempt to explain the origin of life itself, that is, how the earliest forms of life came to exist, nor does it apply to the history of changes of the non-biological parts of the universe, which are also often described as 'evolutionary'. The mechanisms of natural selection, mutation and speciation are used in evolutionary theory to explain the relations and characteristics of all life forms. Modern evolutionary theory explains a wide range of natural phenomena, including the deep resemblances among organisms, the diversity of life forms, organisms' possession of vestigial organs and the good fit or 'adaptedness' between organisms and their environment.

Often summarized as 'survival of the fittest', the mechanism of natural selection actually includes several distinct processes. There must be variation in traits among the members of a population; these traits must be passed on from parents to offspring; and the different traits must confer differential advantage for reproducing successfully in that environment. Because evidence for each of these processes can be gathered independently of the evolutionary claim, natural selection scenarios are robustly testable. When a trait in a population has arisen because it was directly selected in this fashion, it is called an adaptation.

Genetic mutation is the originating source of variation, and selection processes shape that variation into adaptive forms; random genetic drift and various levels and forms of selection dynamic developed by geneticists have been integrated into a general theory of evolutionary change that encompasses natural selection and genetic mutation as complementary processes.

Detailed ecological studies are used to provide evidence for selection scenarios involving the evolution of species in the wild.

Evolutionary theory is supported by an unusually wide range of scientific evidence, gaining its support from fields as diverse as geology, embryology, molecular genetics, palaeontology, climatology and functional morphology. Because of tensions between an evolutionary view of homo sapiens *and some religious beliefs, evolutionary theory has remained controversial in the public sphere far longer than no less well-supported scientific theories from other sciences.*

1 **Basics of evolutionary theory**
2 **The nature of the supporting evidence**
3 **Scientifically contested issues**
4 **Philosophical worries – tautology**
5 **Philosophical worries – prediction**
6 **Philosophical worries – design**
7 **Progress and goals**

1 Basics of evolutionary theory

According to the biological theory of evolution the variety and forms of life on earth are the result of descent with modification from the earliest forms of life. The theory does not attempt to explain the origin of life itself (see LIFE, ORIGIN OF), nor does it apply to the history of changes of the non-biological parts of the universe, which are also often described as 'evolutionary'. A number of European thinkers in the seventeenth and eighteenth centuries advocated an evolutionary view of life, but it is Charles DARWIN and Alfred Russel WALLACE who offered the mechanism, *natural selection*, which is accepted as a primary process by which evolutionary change is effected.

At the time of the proposals of evolutionary theory presented in Darwin's book, *On the Origin of Species* (1859), and Wallace's article 'On the tendency of varieties to depart indefinitely from the original type' (1858), there was no adequate naturalistic (non-miraculous) explanation for the diversity of life forms, their adaptations to their environments, their possession of vestigial organs, the resemblances among them, or their history. Evolutionary theory gives unified and naturalistic explanations for these features of life and for a wide range of other biological phenomena.

The problem of mechanism in evolutionary biology is to explain how the originating group of organisms has led, through descent with modification, to other groups of organisms with very different characteristics from those of the ancestral group. The mechanism of natural selection requires a particular type of set-up: in the standard case, the organisms in a particular population must vary among themselves in some trait that is important to surviving and reproducing in their environment; the differences in that trait must be inheritable to some degree; and the different versions of the trait must actually make a difference in that environment to the success of reproducing and raising offspring to reproductively successful adulthood. Given this set-up, and given the continual importance of that feature of the environment which advantages some versions of the trait over others, the result is change in the traits of the population over time, that is, evolutionary change.

A simple illustration: take a population of brown bears living in the Arctic. They vary in the darkness of their fur, and their offspring tend to resemble their parents in fur colour. Most importantly, they are hunters living in an environment with little cover; prey find it more difficult to escape those with lighter fur, as they see these predators less well against the arctic landscape. Hence, those bears with lighter fur will on average be more successful in hunting, less likely to starve, more likely to reproduce and provide for their young than are those with darker fur. Over tens of thousands of generations of this cyclic process, this population of bears will become lighter and lighter in colour. Note that this explanation assumes a number of facts: heritable variations in fur colour continue to arise; the bears choose to stay in an arctic environment; the arctic environment itself remains snowy and icy for a significant portion of the year; and the prey populations continue to respond differently to lighter and darker predators.

The basic selection process incorporates several distinct biological processes, including heredity, reproduction and the production of variation, as well as the ecological and behavioural processes involved in differential survival and reproduction. Each of these components of evolutionary theory has been investigated, developed and empirically confirmed. Perhaps the most significant successes have been in the science of genetics, which gives accounts of mutation and genetic recombination as causes of the variation on which selection acts, as well as offering insight into the mechanisms and measurements of genetic drift. The most serious deficiency of Darwin's own view of evolutionary change was its lack of a well-confirmed theory of heredity and variation. Modern genetics has provided that theory, and has become a thriving science since the discovery of the structure of the hereditary material, DNA, by Francis Crick and James Watson in 1953. The discovery and investigation of the basic biochemistry of heredity, involving DNA and RNA, has confirmed the similarities among living things at the most fundamental levels, and has also led to huge bodies of

evidence that can be used to compare and differentiate lineages (see GENETICS; MOLECULAR BIOLOGY).

The modern view is not that every detail of evolutionary change can be attributed to natural selection within species; genetic drift, in which forms fluctuate or persist by chance, also leads to substantial genetic variation within and among species. Evolutionary phenomena, then, are understood as consequences of the actions of drift and selection on various levels of biological entities, including genes, organisms and groups of organisms.

Moreover, the existence of mutation and the operation of natural selection do not, by themselves, suggest that new species could arise, nor do they account for the increased diversification of species that we see in the history of life. Given only the facts mentioned in the scenario, our white bears, considered above, will not necessarily comprise a new species of bear. Thus, some attention to the nature of speciation is needed.

Darwin suggested that speciation occurred when there was relatively rapid change in the environment; these different environmental pressures, operating on variations that arose over the generations, could eventually result in a divergence of the descendent group from the ancestral one that was substantial enough that they could or would no longer interbreed. Thus, reproductive isolation is considered a primary cause and result of speciation in sexually reproducing species.

Ernst Mayr, a leading evolutionary biologist, has emphasized a crucial conceptual change (1982) that was involved in changing to the modern evolutionary view of life, namely, the switch from 'typological' thinking – or thinking of organisms and species in terms of their essences or basic types – to 'population' thinking, in which species are irreducible populations of unique individual organisms, and in which the variability among individuals is of the most fundamental importance. The difference between the evolutionary view of species and the essentialist view is thus not primarily that evolutionary species change over time, while essentialist species do not. Individual organisms in modern evolutionary theory are not members of their species in virtue of their sharing some basic group of properties or traits, or because they belong to a particular type or have certain features. On an evolutionary view of species, each organism is unique in its non-trivial properties, and there is no average type or typical specimen of any species. This is not to say that particular individuals cannot exhibit some calculated average height, colour or weight; the point is rather that all such averages over individuals must be interpreted as abstractions, and not even as temporary essential features of that species (see SPECIES).

Developments in evolutionary genetics helped to clarify the importance of thinking in terms of populations. Mathematical population genetics, first developed by R.A. Fisher, J.B.S. Haldane and Sewall Wright, explored mathematically the issue of which evolutionary changes are possible under what conditions and how quickly genetic change could occur. They examined the relative effectiveness and roles of mutation and selection in evolutionary change and, generally, developed models of evolution under a wide variety of conditions and assumptions.

In the late 1930s and early 1940s a general approach called 'the evolutionary synthesis' expressed the newly united views of population geneticists, systematists and palaeontologists. Genetic mutation was seen as the originating source of variation, and selection as the shaper of that variation into adaptive forms; random genetic drift and various levels and forms of selection dynamic developed by the geneticists were integrated into a general theory of evolutionary change that encompassed both natural selection and genetic mutation as complementary processes. Detailed ecological studies were used to provide evidence for selection scenarios involving the evolution of species in the wild. Subsequently, synthesis of the fields of population genetics and ecology created the field of population biology, which studies such phenomena as population dynamics and ecological diversity in their effects on the genetic characteristics of populations.

In sum, contemporary evolutionary biology addresses a broad range of issues, all involving processes that produce key aspects of living beings, including their history, forms, functions, distribution, and their ways of earning a living and reproducing. Evolutionary explanations involve an interlacing of theories and evidence from an array of scientific subfields, including molecular and population genetics, anatomy and morphology (the study of life forms), palaeontology and ecology.

2 The nature of the supporting evidence

Darwin's evolutionary claims involve two central theses: that present and past forms of life are all descended from one or few primitive life forms (descent with modification); and, second, that a primary mechanism of evolutionary change is the mechanism of natural selection. The major kinds of evidence supporting each of these claims are reviewed in this section.

Descent with modification. The field of palaeontology provides some of the most important evidence for descent with modification. In Darwin's time, geologists recognized that there are patterns of geological formations which are parallel the world over, each containing distinctive sets of fossil species; these patterns helped establish the progression of the history of life. Two features of the fossil record were especially important: the fact that each animal and plant form appeared at certain times and certain places only, showing a pattern of increased diversification of life forms; and the evidence that extinction occurred. Moreover, the more ancient a form was, the more markedly it differed from living forms, and fossils from adjacent formations resemble one another far more than those from formations remote in time. The geographical distribution of fossils was also significant; extinct forms on a continent are closely related to living forms there. All of these facts support the view that the extinct forms of life are the ancestors of the living ones, and that modifications in form resulted in the diversification of life.

Morphology, the study of plant and animal form, also provides vital support for descent with modification. All mammals share a common form – as do all birds, all fish and all insects. These basic anatomical similarities within groups are evidence that they descended from a common ancestor. Admittedly, there are variations within the basic form: a bat's arms now appear as wings, while a dog's forelegs and a chimpanzee's arms – defined as 'homologous' because they are derived from the same character of the mammalian ancestor – serve for running and climbing respectively. The fact that a wide variety of forms of forelimb are variations on a common pattern is evidence that a common ancestral population evolved and diversified. Microstructures of organisms can also serve as evidence for evolution. The fact that cells share many basic structural properties across all plants and animals provides evidence for genealogical affinities among organisms. Perhaps most powerfully, the structure of some macromolecules, for example, specific proteins, has been useful in determining the relations among different groupings of organisms; resemblances among proteins has been used to help reconstruct the history of the evolution and diversification of different forms of life, that is, phylogenetic trees.

Embryological morphology, especially, provided important evidence for common ancestors and a continuous process of branching. Darwin emphasized the differences between the embryonic and adult forms of many animals as well as the very close resemblances of embryos within the same class, arguing that 'community in embryonic structure reveals community of descent' (1859: 449). The fact that land-dwelling vertebrates all go through a gill-arch stage in embryo, for example, is explained by their having descended from fish. Vestigial organs similarly provided strong support for common descent. The presence of the remnants of a pelvis and hind limbs in whales, for example, was explicable through their descent from land mammals.

Finally, the facts of geographic distribution provided particularly important evidence for common ancestors. Darwin emphasized certain features of oceanic islands and their differences from continental islands; oceanic islands have many fewer species, and are typically missing certain types, such as terrestrial mammals and freshwater fishes. Oceanic island species also resemble most of the species from their nearest continent. The inhabitants of the Galapagos archipelago, for example, closely resemble species from the nearby tropical Americas, rather than those from similar temperate climates.

Natural selection. The details of the evidential support for the mechanism of natural selection need to be understood in terms of the structure of natural selection explanations. One remarkable feature of the theory of evolution by natural selection is its explanatory power; it seems that the basic selection framework can be used, when applied with imagination, to account for the emergence, transformation or elimination of *any* trait or population. This flexibility is, in fact, the source of the theory's capacity to underwrite so many hypotheses, and is a primary source of its fruitfulness as a scientific theory.

However, the *proposal* of a selectionist explanation of a trait or evolutionary change is never enough for its scientific acceptance; the hypothesis must be tested. Unfortunately, the traditional emphasis placed on prediction by philosophers of science has contributed to a widespread misperception of the scientific status of these selection hypotheses (Hempel 1965). Under a classical hypothetico-deductive view of theory testing, the theory is used to generate an *outcome* or prediction about the natural system being modelled. If the outcome turns out to hold in nature, the theory is confirmed (see CONFIRMATION THEORY). In the case of natural selection explanations, however, the outcome – the frequency or nature of the evolved traits – is standardly already known, and the substance of the selection hypothesis involves an account of how the population or trait *got* that way. It may seem, therefore, that all selection explanations could be successfully confirmed as predictions, whether they are true or not.

The logic of testing selection hypotheses was clarified by Darwin: the various empirical claims that appear in any selection explanation – about the existence of variation of reproductive success with the possession of different traits, about the existence and

character of environmental stresses, about the inheritance of the relevant variety of traits – must be *independently* confirmed empirically. This independent confirmation of the detailed empirical claims made in selection explanations comprises the chief form of empirical testing for specific evolutionary explanations (Lloyd 1994).

In evolutionary explanations, the abstract framework of selection is filled in with specific details of the particular population, traits and environments at issue; the *empirical content* of any explanation by selection consists of particular claims about particular organisms and their environments. These particular empirical claims are subject to robust evidential testing, independently of any selectionist explanation of which they are a part. There remains, however, a question about the evidential status of the selection framework itself: is it proper to consider the abstract framework well-confirmed, on the basis of its independently confirmed successes in accounting for particular cases of evolution by selection? We tend to regard general theories as well-confirmed if, taken in conjunction with particular facts, they are good at accounting for other particular facts (see §4).

We are now in a position to appreciate the range of evidence relevant to Darwin's theory of natural selection. Important empirical support for natural selection explanations comes from several of the fields that provide evidence for descent with modification. The investigation of homologies, from morphology for example, has provided significant instances of the evolution of special adaptations through natural selection. The bat forelimb – homologous to both the human arm and the canine foreleg – presents an intriguing problem for the theory: how and why did bat ancestors evolve from squirrel-like creatures without wings? The occurrence of random mutation in forelimb form, combined with strong selection on the resulting variation, is used to explain the divergence of bat species from other mammalian species. Similarly, special adaptations to local environments are found to explain a variety of specialized mammalian forelimb forms and functions. The evolution of hundreds of species of bat, all descended from a single ancestral population, is an example of adaptive radiation; specializations in particular prey and particular environments proved advantageous to the survival and reproduction of past bat groups. Even vestigial traits can support the effectiveness of natural selection. The mammalian ancestors of whales, who entered the water around 55 million years ago, experienced little or no selection pressure to maintain working hindlimbs: mutations and variations in which the hindlimbs were reduced or nonfunctional may have been advantageous, or may have been linked to traits that were advantageous in the new aquatic environments, and subsequently became fixed in the population.

Finally, evolutionary systematics has provided abundant evidence on evolutionary trends and patterns of adaptations, as well as detailing the types of evolutionary transformation that organisms' features undergo, and the patterns of variation within species (Futuyma 1979, ch. 1).

3 Scientifically contested issues

There are currently several areas of controversy within evolutionary biology. One of the most vigorous involves issues of macro-evolution, that is, changes in diversity, the distribution of traits across lineages, extinctions of major taxa, and trends in evolution, such as increase in average size of organisms. The key theoretical questions revolve around the tempo and mode of evolutionary change: when exactly does most evolutionary change occur? Do forms of life evolve mostly gradually, or is evolutionary change concentrated in speciation events? Under what is called the gradualist view, patterns of macro-evolutionary change are explained completely by patterns of gradual selection within species. An important alternative set of mechanisms, advocated since the 1970s by Stephen Jay Gould (1989), Niles Eldredge (1985), Steven Stanley, and other palaeontologists, involves phenomena higher than the species' level, for example, rates of speciation and extinction; under this approach, large-scale events of evolutionary history are explained as consequences of drift of species and species selection (seen as analogous to drift and selection of alleles within populations.)

Another debate about mechanism and the explanation of patterns involves the role of biological development and the ultimate sources of organismal structure. Developmental biologists have been concerned to explore how mutations in genes affect changes in form; some forms are much more likely to arise than others, due to the biochemistry of how organisms grow and change. Selection processes always require the presence of *variation* in traits that matter to the survival and reproduction of genes in an environment. Investigations into which variations are likely and which are even possible can provide information crucial to selection explanations. In addition, the fact that some traits vary along with other ones simply in virtue of how the organism grows makes it vital to incorporate information about the complexities of development into evolutionary explanations.

A very visible and important set of debates has revolved around the levels and units of selection.

Generally, disagreement concerns the relative importance of different mechanisms of selection that cause evolutionary change.

Finally, there are robust debates in phylogenetic systematics, some of which concern the detailed evolutionary history of particular species or groups of organisms, and some of which involve the proper role of evolution in phylogenetic systematics. Regarding the latter, Darwin made it clear that he thought that evolution could help systematics by making the classification of life fundamentally a genealogy (Mayr 1982) (see TAXONOMY).

4 Philosophical worries – tautology

There is a philosophical concern about modern evolutionary biology which seems to be quite serious: is evolutionary theory based on a tautology? A tautology is a statement that is necessarily true because of the meaning of its terms. Briefly: the theory of natural selection is based on 'the survival of the fittest'; but which organisms are the fittest, according to evolutionary theory? Answer: those that survive. This is the logical truism that is frequently taken to represent the core of evolutionary theory.

Although this objection about tautology has been raised and answered in different ways since the nineteenth century, it continues to cause confusion in each new generation of thinkers facing evolutionary theory. There are two general strategies in answering it. The first is to highlight that, as a matter of fact, the 'fittest' are not defined in terms of survival by evolutionists (Hull 1974). The term 'fitness' has a potentially confusing multiplicity of meanings in evolutionary theory: it can refer to the expected rate of survival and reproduction of a certain type (usually defined in terms of genes); it can also refer to the 'adaptedness' of a certain type of trait to the pressures of its local environment – here, adaptedness is analogous to being well-suited or well-engineered for a specific task. When using this latter meaning of 'fitness', an evolutionist appeals to the suitability of a certain character for coping with the challenges presented to its owner in the expected environments. (For example, the 'adaptedness' of being insulated by blubber in arctic environments depends on its effectiveness at maintaining body temperature in mammals compared to other available options, for example, faster metabolism.) Using this substantive notion of the 'fitness' of an organism possessing a particular trait in a particular environment thus involves no hint of tautology; not only is such a claim substantive, it may be independently testable. Hence, explanations of evolution by natural selection are not tautological.

The second approach to answering the tautology objection is to point out that, strictly speaking, many accepted scientific theories are in fact empirically empty, especially those expressed in mathematical form. A model of a system in Newtonian mechanics is, for example, purely mathematical, as are all predictions arising from the model. This does not prevent the theory from being scientific and empirical, because a proper understanding of the theory entails that the model *represents* some real system which it is used to explain. Similarly, models from mathematical population genetics may show that, as a matter of mathematical deduction, those organisms with higher fitness parameters will necessarily have a higher probability of surviving and contributing to future generations; the related empirical application of the model, however, is not guaranteed to be true. In other words, many mathematically expressed theories – from physics and from natural selection theory – are self-contained or tautologous when taken alone; when used in their scientific context, however, they have precise and testable empirical content (Sober 1993).

The tautology objection can be answered by calling attention to the role of the principle of natural selection – the survival of the fittest – within the rest of the theoretical and explanatory parts of evolutionary theory. When this is done, the objection appears to be based on a misunderstanding of how either the specific theory, or scientific theories generally, really do their work (see THEORIES, SCIENTIFIC).

5 Philosophical worries – prediction

One of the most common misperceptions of evolutionary theory is that it makes no predictions, concerning, as it does, the past history of life. But being about past events does not prevent a science from being predictive; there are numerous predictions from evolutionary biology which concern the fossil record. For example, whatever will be discovered in the fossil record in the future, mammals will not appear at a date prior to the evolution of bony fishes. Nor will hominids be found to coincide in time with the large dinosaurs. Nor will fossil birds predate the earliest amphibia. Evolutionary theory also underwrites many predictions about genetic findings; closely related species are predicted to share a larger percentage of their basic genetic material than less closely related species and groups. These genetic predictions, made on the basis of evidence preceding the discovery of DNA, have recently gathered abundant empirical confirmation.

There is a distinct concern about evolutionary explanations, which is that they depend so strongly on uncontrollable and, in most cases, unpredictable contingencies – such as environmental changes, chance mutations, or complex interactions among members of a species – that it is impossible for evolutionists to predict the direction that evolutionary processes will take a given population in the future. Evolutionists faced with the question, 'Which way is humankind evolving?', admit that evolutionary theory does not enable this type of prediction.

The mathematical models of modern population genetics do allow precise predictions to be made regarding, for example, the future frequencies of specific forms of genes (called 'alleles') in a population of laboratory fruitflies. These successes are very significant in their support of the efficacy of natural selection, random genetic drift or mutation rates, as causes of evolutionary change. However, population genetics does not presently have the capacity to predict changes over the periods of time involved in major evolutionary events such as speciation, which take place on the order of tens of thousands of years.

More generally (as reviewed in §2) the overemphasis on prediction in understanding scientific evidence has contributed to a failure to understand the evidential relations on the basis of which evolutionary claims are scientifically evaluated.

6 Philosophical worries – design

Design seems to be everywhere in nature; this fact supported the efforts of eighteenth and nineteenth century churchmen, such as William Paley, to encourage piety through the study of nature (see PALEY, W. §2). The existence of order, complexity and adaptedness in living things is still the most common reason given by those who believe in direct supernatural creation of the myriad forms of life on earth. As reviewed in §1, the presentation, development and broad, detailed evidential support of the theory of evolution have provided a scientific and empirically tested alternative to the hypotheses of direct supernatural design. The empirical successes of the modern theory, its compatibility and interdependence with other natural sciences, and its fruitfulness in facilitating scientific investigations into life, have led to its scientific acceptance as an adequate nonsupernatural account of the very features of life that were formerly taken to be explicable only by the actions of a supernatural creator (Dawkins 1986) (see GOD, ARGUMENTS FOR THE EXISTENCE OF §§4–5; RELIGION AND SCIENCE §§4–5).

The distinction between proximate and ultimate causes in biological explanations is useful in understanding goal-like states and the appearance of design. *Proximate* causes concern the functions of an organism and its parts, as well as its development. *Ultimate* or evolutionary causes concern why an organism is the way it is. Any biological phenomenon has two independent sets of causes, according to Ernst Mayr, 'because organisms have a genetic programme. Proximate causes have to do with the decoding of the programme of a given individual: evolutionary causes have to do with the changes of genetic programmes through time, and with the reasons for these changes' (1982: 68). Thus, for example, the proximate causes of sexual differences between male and female fruitflies may be hormonal, while the selective advantage of differential utilization of the food niche may be the ultimate cause of these differences. The design of the system is explained through evolution by natural selection over time, while its local functioning is explained through local conditions.

7 Progress and goals

The mechanisms of evolution seem especially mysterious in their capacity to generate what appears to be *progress*. Reviewing the increased cranial capacity of the hominid lines, for instance, it can appear that there was some goal towards which the hominid group was progressing. However, the appearance of 'upward progress' is, on the modern theory, misleading; there is no natural goal or state of perfection towards which any lineage has evolved (Gould 1989). The series of improvements manifested in any lineage is solely the produce of evolutionary processes operating locally. As Futuyma notes, 'future conditions cannot affect present survival. The enduring variations may increase the organism's complexity or behavioural repertoire, or they may decrease it. They may increase the likelihood of survival through subsequent environmental changes, or they may increase the likelihood of subsequent extinction' (1979: 7).

See also: AL-AFGHANI §2

References and further reading

* Darwin, C. (1859) *On the Origin of Species by Means of Natural Selection or the Preservation of Favoured Races in the Struggle for Life*, London: John Murray. (Revolutionary argument for both the evolution of varied forms of life from earlier ones, and the theory of evolution by natural selection. Accessible to general readers.)
* Dawkins, R. (1986) *The Blind Watchmaker*, London: Longman. (Accessible defence of the powers of natural selection to create adaptations.)

* Eldredge, N. (1985) *The Unfinished Synthesis*, New York: Oxford University Press. (Discussion and defence of operation of selection at levels above the organism.)
* Futuyma, D.J. (1979) *Evolutionary Biology*, Sunderland, MA: Sinauer. (Outstanding and accessible text, with abundant examples and careful discussion of conceptual issues.)
* Gould, S.J. (1989) *Wonderful Life*, New York: W.W. Norton. (Accessible discussion of the role of processes above the species level and of chance events in the evolution of life. Highly recommended.)
* Hempel, C.G. (1965) *The Structure of Scientific Explanations*, New York: Free Press. (Classic presentation of scientific explanation and scientific confirmation using a logical positivist framework. For upper-level philosophy students.)
* Hull, D.L. (1974) *Philosophy of Biological Science*, Englewood Cliffs, NJ: Prentice Hall. (Classic presentation and discussion of key philosophical issues in evolutionary theory; especially notable discussion of goal-orientated processes.)
—— (1980) 'Individuality and Selection', *Annual Review of Ecology and Systematics* 11: 311–32. (Extremely influential rethinking of conceptual issues in levels of selection debates. Intermediate level.)
Keller, E.F. and Lloyd, E.A. (eds) (1992) *Keywords in Evolutionary Biology*, Cambridge, MA: Harvard University Press. (Essays by biologists, historians, philosophers about evolutionary terms with multiple meanings. Suitable for novice to expert readers.)
* Lloyd, E.A. (1994) *The Structure and Confirmation of Evolutionary Theory*, Princeton, NJ: Princeton University Press. (Fairly advanced philosophical analysis of modern evolutionary theory.)
Maynard Smith, J. (1989) *Evolutionary Genetics*, Oxford: Oxford University Press. (Widely-used text, with interesting examples.)
* Mayr, E. (1982) *The Growth of Biological Thought: Diversity, Evolution and Inheritance*, Cambridge, MA: Harvard University Press. (Readable and comprehensive history of evolutionary biology; especially useful discussions of proximate and ultimate explanations, typological thinking, and a defence of evolutionary taxonomy.)
Ruse, M. (1979) *The Darwinian Revolution: Science Red in Tooth and Claw*, Chicago, IL: Chicago University Press. (Discussion of chief conceptual issues involved in the nineteenth-century context of Darwinism; excellent review of Darwin's evidence. Suitable for upper-level students.)
* Sober, E. (1993) *Philosophy of Biology*, Boulder, CO: Westview. (Sophisticated discussion of key philo-

sophical issues in evolutionary biology and systematics. Suitable for upper-level students.)

* Wallace, A.R. (1858) 'On the Tendency of Varieties to Depart Indefinitely from the Original Type', *Journal of the Proceedings of the Linnaean Society (Zoology)* 3: 53–62. (One of the original statements of the theory of evolution by natural selection.)

ELISABETH A. LLOYD

EVOLUTIONARY THEORY AND SOCIAL SCIENCE

Ideas from evolutionary theory impinge on the social sciences in two ways. First, there is the research programme of sociobiology, which attempts to demonstrate the impact of biological evolution on important features of human mind and culture. Second, there is the idea that biological evolution provides a suggestive analogy for the processes that drive cultural change. Both research programmes have tended to focus on the idea of natural selection, even though the theory of biological evolution considers processes besides selection. Sociobiology attempts to show that the following conditional helps explain psychological traits just as it applies to traits of morphology and physiology: if a trait varies in a population, makes a difference for the survival and reproduction of individuals, and is influenced by genetic factors, then natural selection will lead the trait to change its frequency in the population. Models of cultural evolution are built on an analogous conditional: if a set of alternative ideas are found in a culture, and people tend to find some of these ideas more attractive than others, then the mix of ideas in the culture will change. Sociobiology and the understanding of cultural change as an evolutionary process are approaches that have a history and both will continue to be explored in the future. Each is a flexible instrument, which may be better suited to some tasks than to others, and may be handled well by some practitioners and poorly by others. As a consequence, neither can be said to be 'verified' and 'falsified' by their track records to date.

1 **What is biological evolution?**
2 **Two approaches**
3 **The need for a piecemeal assessment**
4 **The explanation of variation in sociobiology**
5 **The meaning of fitness in evolutionary epistemology**
6 **Cultural evolution without selection**
7 **Philosophical connections**

1 What is biological evolution?

The term 'evolution' has a misleading etymology. It comes from the Latin *evolvere*, which means to unfold. In the eighteenth century, the term was used to name the process of ontogeny in which a single organism develops from a fertilized egg into an adult. Later, in the aftermath of Darwin's theory, the term itself underwent an evolution, shifting its application from ontogeny to phylogeny (see DARWIN, C.). It now no longer describes the development of an individual organism, but applies to the process of 'descent with modification', whereby new species emerge from ancestral forms.

This transposition in subject matter did not leave the meaning of the term intact. It is natural to think that important aspects of the development of an organism are 'preprogrammed'. Although the environment obviously influences the organism's phenotype in many ways, a great deal of the developmental sequence is relatively invariant over environmental changes. Organisms in the same species often share a fixed sequence of developmental stages, each marked by a special constellation of distinctive traits.

Darwin's theory of evolution entirely rejects this view when it is applied to phylogeny. Although organisms may have a preprogrammed ontogeny, species do not have a preordained phylogeny. There is no such thing as the developmental stages through which a species must pass. Rather, the Darwinian idea is that evolution by natural selection is 'opportunistic'; the trajectory of change is an adventitious consequence of the environmental conditions that the species experiences and the variation that the species happens to contain. There is no inherent tendency for species to evolve in the direction of greater complexity, specialization, or body size. Evolution often moves in those directions, but often it does just the reverse.

Contemporary evolutionary theory retains the twin Darwinian ideas of descent with modification and natural selection as an important cause of diversity. The former idea is usually formulated by saying that all living things on earth, both now and in the past, are part of a single genealogical tree. Current species may be closely related to each other or related only distantly, but all are related. The status of the latter idea is the focus of the debate about adaptationism: how important is natural selection as a cause of the similarities and differences we see within and among species?

When biologists apply this two-part theory, they use the term 'evolution' with a restricted and technical meaning. It does not mean mere change; planets change, but this is not evolution in the biologist's sense. And even when the change occurs in the traits of a population of organisms, the term may still fail to apply. If the organisms in one generation are taller than their parents, this may simply reflect a change in the nutrition available. If the population has not changed its genetic composition, this will be change without evolution. Biologists do not restrict the term 'evolution' to genetic changes; traits of morphology, physiology, and behaviour evolve in the strict sense. However, these phenotypic changes must reflect genetic changes, if they are to be genuinely evolutionary.

2 Two approaches

Biology recognizes other possible causes of evolution besides natural selection. Mutation, migration, systems of mating, recombination, and random genetic drift are examples. However, since natural selection is the factor that has been of greatest interest to the social sciences, it is well to explore its logic a bit further.

If natural selection is to produce biological evolution in a population of organisms, there must be variation in fitness and heredity. Let us explore a simple example to see what these twin requirements mean. Consider a population of zebras in which faster running speed evolves. If this is due to natural selection, then the population must contain variation. So let us suppose that some zebras run faster, others slower, and that this makes a difference in the organisms' fitness – their capacity to survive and reproduce. In particular, we may imagine that running speed affects fitness because faster zebras are better able to evade predators than are slower ones. In addition to these facts about fitness, there also must be a process of heredity: offspring tend to resemble their parents in running speed, and this resemblance, at least in part, is due to genetic factors. These assumptions permit the phenotypic trait to evolve in the population; we expect the average running speed of the organisms in the population to increase.

When the concept of natural selection is applied to the subject matter of the social sciences, these two elements are interpreted either literally or metaphorically. The literal application gives rise to the research programme called sociobiology; the metaphorical application leads to the idea that cultural change involves competition among ideas in which the 'best' ideas survive. A standard example of sociobiological explanation concerns the existence of an incest taboo. Human beings seldom reproduce with close genetic relatives. In addition to this regularity in behaviour, there is also the fact that societies often have norms of prohibition. Sociobiologists propose to explain both the behaviour and the taboo by describing the fitness

consequences of inbreeding and outbreeding. Reproduction with close relatives increases the chance that the offspring will possess two copies of deleterious recessive genes. As a result, there has been selection for avoiding such matings. The result is not just that human beings now avoid inbreeding, but that they have a genetic inclination to do so. The dual ideas of fitness and heredity are said to apply to incest avoidance in human beings just as literally as they apply to running speed in zebras.

A good example of the metaphorical application of the biological idea of natural selection is the economic theory of the firm (reviewed in Hirshliefer 1977). The problem is to explain why businesses are usually efficient profit maximizers. One hypothesis is that managers are rational and well-informed; they determine which strategies work best and then they adopt them. The theory of the firm offers an alternative explanation. Firms that are efficient stay in business; those that are not, go bankrupt. The economic market induces a selection process in which only the fit survive. Firms do not rationally adjust their behaviour; rather, the market adjusts the composition of the population of firms.

Notice how the concepts of fitness and heredity are interpreted in this theory. The idea is not that people who run efficient businesses live longer or have more children. The fitness of firms has nothing to do with the biology of survival and reproduction. In addition, the reason that firms in later years tend to resemble their former selves (that is, are relatively stable in the strategies they deploy) has nothing to do with genetic transmission. Although sociobiologists often suggest that incest avoidance is 'in the genes', theorists of the firm do not claim that economic behaviour is genetically encoded. The theory of the firm posits a selection process, but one that is related only metaphorically to the process of biological selection (see SOCIOBIOLOGY).

3 The need for a piecemeal assessment

Proponents and critics of sociobiology often treat that subject as a monolithic entity. Proponents defend sociobiology by emphasizing that human beings are the product of evolution; critics argue that human behaviour is enormously flexible and responsive to cultural context – so much so, that the human mind is said to liberate us from the 'tyranny of the genes'.

Although the interest of reaching a general assessment of the promise of sociobiology is undeniable, it is important to consider its merits and demerits on a case by case basis (Kitcher 1985). Perhaps some elements of human behaviour are adequately explained by the theory of natural selection while others are not. Even if sociobiologists are right about incest avoidance, it is a separate question whether other behavioural regularities can be explained similarly. We should not accept sociobiology because it is sometimes correct; nor should we reject it because it is sometimes mistaken.

Parallel remarks apply to metaphorical applications of the biological concept of natural selection. It is not inevitable that the theory of the firm is correct. But even if it is, the question remains of which other social regularities can be explained within an evolutionary framework. For example, it is often true that unemployment reduces inflation. The usual supply-and-demand explanation of this fact does not advert to different individuals deploying different strategies and, as a result, prospering to different degrees. Rather, the usual approach holds that all individuals are rational or approximately so. All individuals try to pay the lowest price they can. The social regularity is explained by the hypothesis that people are, in the relevant respect, always the same. This is not an explanation in which behavioural variation is sifted and winnowed.

4 The explanation of variation in sociobiology

Well posed problems about the evolution of behaviour concern the explanation of variation. It is all too easy to explain why human beings 'tend' to avoid incest by saying that this behaviour maximizes fitness. The word 'tend' is vague; how much incest would we have to observe to cast doubt on the evolutionary explanation? A better formulated problem would begin by measuring the amount of inbreeding that occurs in a range of species, our own included. Accounting for this quantitative data gives more structure to the problem.

Although sociobiologists often are interested in explaining features of human behaviour that they believe are cultural universals, they also are interested in explaining behavioural variation among human beings. Perhaps the most familiar context for this type of problem concerns differences between the sexes. Behavioural differences between men and women, they argue, can often be explained by the hypothesis that men and women have evolved in response to different selective pressures. A standard example is their claim that men tend to be more sexually promiscuous than women because selection placed a larger premium on being discriminating about sexual partners in females than it did in males. The claim is not that all men are more promiscuous than all women; rather, selection is said to be an important influence on the behaviour, the result of which is different averages for the two sexes.

Sociobiologists are often criticized for assuming that 'genetic determinism' is true – that human behaviour is rigidly controlled by genes and cannot be changed by environmental factors. There are two defects in this general criticism, correct though it may be in some instances. First, even when sociobiologists claim that genetic differences are a cause of the phenotypic variation under study, they are not committed to saying that this is the only cause. For example, even if there is a genetic basis for some behavioural differences between the sexes, this does not exclude the possibility that environmental causes also play a role.

The second defect in the charge of genetic determinism is that some sociobiological explanations of behavioural variation are purely environmental. Consider, for example, Alexander's (1979) proposed explanation of the kinship system known as the avunculate. In some societies, men provide more care for their sister's children than for the children of their own wives. Alexander argues that this behaviour will be selectively advantageous when there is considerable female promiscuity. The avunculate maximizes a man's inclusive fitness if he is more likely to have genes in common with his nephews and nieces than he is with his wife's children.

The point of interest here is not whether this explanation is empirically correct, but the role it assigns to genetic factors. Alexander is not saying that societies that deploy the avunculate are genetically different from societies that do not. Rather, his idea is that human beings have basically the same genetic endowment, one that leads them to behave in ways that maximize their fitness. A behaviour that maximizes fitness in one circumstance may not do so in another. According to Alexander's model, the within-species variation in behaviour is explained environmentally, not genetically.

5 The meaning of fitness in evolutionary epistemology

John Stuart Mill defended the value of freedom of thought and expression by describing a 'marketplace of ideas' in which ideas compete for acceptance (see MILL, J.S.). Consumers judge which ideas are best, and so the quality of ideas found in the market gradually improves. Evolutionary epistemologists, such as Karl POPPER, Donald Campbell, and David Hull, argue that this idea may be applied fruitfully to the scientific process itself (see Bradie 1994). Scientists are the consumers; they propose theories that compete with each other in an ideational environment. Successful theories persist; unsuccessful theories suffer extinction.

Literal applications of the concept of biological evolution by natural selection not only posit fitness differences among traits, but explain why the traits have the fitness consequences they do. In the mundane example of running speed in zebras, the claim was not just that fast zebras are fitter than slow ones, but that this is so because running speed enhances a zebra's ability to evade predators. It is important not to forget this further element when evolutionary epistemologists propose to use natural selection as a metaphor for scientific change.

It is harmless to say that theories differ in their (cultural) fitness. But what makes for a fitter theory? That is, which properties of a theory bear on its chances of surviving and spreading in the marketplace of ideas? There are many possibilities, as the ongoing dispute between internalists and externalists in the history of science attests. An extreme internalist might say that observational support is the only important factor influencing a theory's viability. An extreme externalist might say that ideological palatability is all that matters. In between these extremes are pluralistic theories which say that a variety of factors influence whether a theory will be accepted. The point is that in a model of ideational selection, everything depends on the substantive account of fitness. The model risks vacuity if fitness is left unexplained (see INTERNALISM AND EXTERNALISM IN EPISTEMOLOGY §4).

In developing a substantive model, the theorist must decide whether the goal is descriptive, or normative, or both. Is the point to describe how scientists actually evaluate theories or how they should do so? These two goals will coincide to the extent that the theorist believes that scientists are rational.

6 Cultural evolution without selection

The concept of natural selection is so striking an ingredient in evolutionary theory that it is easy to forget the theory's other resources. As noted earlier, a fundamental ingredient in current evolutionary theory is the idea of phylogenetic relationship. Current species have common ancestors, and a great deal of work in evolutionary biology is devoted to determining what the family trees are for various taxonomic groups. The detailed working out of ancestry is a quite separate task from the problem of identifying the adaptive significance, if any, of the traits that various species possess.

Social scientists have explored the idea that elements of culture are sometimes related to each other genealogically. For example, historical linguists attempt to determine which languages are closely related to each other and which are related only distantly. This enterprise leads them to postulate unobserved languages, such as proto-Indo European, which are said to be the ancestors of current languages. In similar fashion, philologists study the provenance of manuscripts and try to reconstruct an *Urtext* that lies at the root of a branching tree, the tips of which represent the variants of the manuscript they observe.

There is an important isomorphism between the biologist's problem of phylogenetic inference and the historian's problem of inferring the genealogy of cultural objects. What is observed, in the first instance, are species or artefacts that exist now. From the pattern of similarity and difference they exhibit, one postulates a branching tree, whose internal nodes and root represent species or artefacts that are not observed. The epistemological problem is how to judge this postulated tree in the light of available evidence. What makes one postulated tree more plausible than another? This common methodological problem is, and will continue to be, an arena for mutual influence between biology and the social sciences.

7 Philosophical connections

In addition to the relationships just sketched between evolutionary theory and the social sciences, there is considerable overlap in the philosophical questions pertinent to each.

The issue of reductionism arises in several forms. One involves sociobiology's attempt to 'reduce' certain social and psychological phenomena to biology. A second concerns whether biology and the social sciences are each 'reducible in principle' to physics. A third is occasioned by the fact that the relationship of wholes and parts is an important subject in both sciences; the dispute between methodological holism and individualism arises in both.

A second domain of philosophical overlap concerns the role of teleological concepts. Just as a biologist might say that the function of the heart is to pump blood, so a social scientist might say that the function of ideology is to preserve existing power relations. It is worth asking what such functional claims mean and what ramifications they have for the aims and methods of the sciences in which they occur.

Finally, both the social sciences and biology deal with systems on which a large number of different causes impinge. This makes especially important the project of understanding how real causes may be disentangled from spurious ones and what it means for one cause to be more important than another.

See also: EVOLUTION AND ETHICS; EVOLUTION, THEORY OF

References and further reading

* Alexander, R. (1979) *Darwinism and Human Affairs*, Seattle, WA: University of Washington Press. (An energetic defence of sociobiology.)

Barlow, J., Cosmides, L. and Tooby, J. (1992) *The Adapted Mind: Evolutionary Psychology and the Generation of Culture*, Oxford: Oxford University Press. (A collection of essays that aims to apply Darwinian ideas to cognitive structures, rather than directly to behaviour.)

Boyd, R. and Richerson, P. (1985) *Culture and the Evolutionary Process*, Chicago, IL: University of Chicago Press. (Discusses both the origin of culture and the changes in evolutionary processes occasioned by the emergence of culture.)

* Bradie, M. (1994) 'Epistemology from an Evolutionary Point of View', in E. Sober (ed.), *Conceptual Issues in Evolutionary Biology*, 2nd edn, Cambridge, MA: MIT Press, 453–76. (A useful survey article.)

Campbell, D. (1974) 'Evolutionary Epistemology', in P. Schilpp (ed.), *The Philosophy of Karl Popper*, Peru, IL: Open Court. (Elaborates a selective-retention model of scientific change and of problem solving generally.)

Cavalli-Sforza, L. and Feldman, M. (1981) *Cultural Transmission and Evolution: A Quantitative Approach*, Princeton, NJ: Princeton University Press. (Develops models that represent the simultaneous effects of biological and cultural evolution.)

* Hirshliefer, J. (1977) 'Economics from a Biological Viewpoint', *Journal of Law and Economics* 1: 1–52. (A useful review of attempts to develop evolutionary models in economics.)

Hull, D. (1988) *Science as a Process*, Chicago, IL: University of Chicago Press. (Argues that many of the group beneficial features of the scientific process are side effects of individuals seeking to maximize self interest.)

* Kitcher, P. (1985) *Vaulting Ambition: Sociobiology and the Quest for Human Nature*, Cambridge, MA: MIT Press. (A philosophical critique of sociobiology that leaves open the possibility that human sociobiology may evolve into a viable research programme.)

Popper, K. (1973) *Objective Knowledge*, Oxford: Oxford University Press. (Argues that the epistemology of conjectures and refutations can be thought of as a Darwinian selection process.)

Sober, E. (1993) *Philosophy of Biology*, Oxford: Oxford University Press. (An introduction to philosophy of biology that discusses adaptationism, sociobiology, models of cultural evolution, and the issue of phylogenetic reconstruction.)

ELLIOTT SOBER

EXAMPLES IN ETHICS

Philosophers often employ examples to illustrate how their favoured principles are to be applied to concrete cases, and sometimes even to show that principles are of no help in decision-making. Examples are also used to convince readers of the existence of moral dilemmas – unresolvable conflicts between moral obligations. But a variety of different philosophical questions concerning the role, status, and nature of examples used in ethics have also been raised. One such question concerns the role that examples should play in our moral experience: should this be a rhetorical, pedagogic role of persuading us to do what is right, as determined by pre-existing principle; or a stronger, logical role of helping to determine what is morally right? Another query relates to moral teaching: is exposure to and reflection on stories, tales, narratives and exemplars sufficient for moral education, or is there a further need for exposure to principles and theories of ethics? Third, in terms of the kinds of examples employed in moral philosophy and reflection, should such examples be culled from great literature or sacred texts? Alternatively, should they be actual case studies drawn from real life, or hypothetical but realistic examples constructed by theorists? Or should they be imaginary, highly improbable cases designed to test our intuitions? A fourth question asks how examples are best identified and described, and to what extent the examples used in ethics are themselves theory-laden or even theory-constituted.

1   A rhetorical or logical role?
2   Are examples enough?
3   What kind of examples?
4   How to identify and describe examples
5   Concluding remarks

1   A rhetorical or logical role?

There is widespread agreement among moral philosophers that relevant examples play an important role in persuading us to do what is morally appropriate and in encouraging us to try to become morally virtuous agents. The right kind of example, skilfully employed and presented, can bring home the moral point to us in ways that the abstractions of theories, principles, and rules often cannot. Vivid examples frequently possess a motivating power that principles lack.

But according to this familiar view, the standards of moral rightness (or courage, generosity, and so on) are always established antecedently by principle and theory. Examples, while important and necessary, particularly in the early stages of moral education, in bringing the abstractions of theory down to earth, thus remain the handmaiden of principle and theory. Kant's warning in *Grundlegung zur Metaphysik der Sitten* (*Groundwork of the Metaphysics of Morals*) ([1785] 1903: 409) that cogent examples, while serving to 'make perceptible what the practical law expresses more generally', must nevertheless always be judged by 'their true original, which resides in reason' is a classic expression of this position.

However, some philosophers advocate a stronger role for examples, one in which the examples themselves are held to play a logical role in determining what is morally appropriate. On this latter view, examples function not just as applications of rules or illustrations of principles but rather as challenges for moral judgment to respond to particular situations in a manner which goes beyond mere rule-following. Aristotle's doctrine of practical wisdom or *phronēsis*, which holds that the correct decision 'depends on the particular facts and on perception [of the particular facts]' (*Nicomachean Ethics* 1126b4, 1109b20–3) is the classic representative of this latter view (see ARISTOTLE §23; VIRTUE ETHICS §6). The medieval tradition of moral casuistry, particularly as elaborated by Aquinas, according to which individual circumstances may 'touch' or alter cases in important ways, represents a critical historical development of this Aristotelian perspective towards examples (see CASUISTRY).

2 Are examples enough?

Some philosophers argue that moral principles simply do not exist. According to ethical particularists, moral decisions should always be made case by case, without the false support or illusory guidance of moral principles (see UNIVERSALISM IN ETHICS §3; MORAL REALISM §5; LOGIC OF ETHICAL DISCOURSE §7). Others hold that moral rules and principles, while not illusory, are unhelpful and often harmful in determining what to do and how to live. Antitheorists in ethics attack the whole idea of a moral 'theory' which seeks to evaluate particular situations by reference to general principles. The intellectual ancestry of particularism and antitheory in ethics is diverse; such views have been imputed variously to Aristotle, Wittgenstein, and postmodernists such as FOUCAULT and LYOTARD (see VIRTUE ETHICS §6;

WITTGENSTEINIAN ETHICS §§2–3; POSTMODERNISM). But the upshot of both views is simply that examples are enough. The best approach to moral education and reflection, for adults as well as for children, is one that emphasizes not impersonal principles and abstract arguments but personal exemplars and concrete cases.

Opponents argue that the worthiness of any alleged moral exemplar or example must always be judged according to antecedently established and defended general norms. Here again, Kant is the classic advocate: 'Every example of...[morality] presented to me must first itself be judged by moral principles in order to decide if it is fit to serve as...a model: it can in no way supply the prime source for the concept of morality' ([1785] 1903: 408). Additionally, defenders of theory hold that a primary goal of moral education must always be critical, autonomous reflection concerning norms. Autonomous moral agents do not assent blindly to others' teachings, but strive continually to make the truths of moral exemplars their own by reflecting critically on the legitimacy and justifiability of these teachings.

3 What kind of examples?

Disagreement also exists concerning what kind of examples to use in ethics. Some prefer literary examples, on the ground that they characterize our moral situation more profoundly and precisely than the less engaging, schematic examples constructed by theorists. On this view, personal experience is, in comparison with fiction, too confined and too parochial. Well-crafted literary examples give readers data that is deeper, sharper, and more precise than much of what occurs in real life. Antitheory tendencies often prevail among strong defenders of literary examples as well, in so far as they are committed to the view that the process of understanding our moral situation is a task not for theory but for nonphilosophical genres.

Others hold that case studies from real life are preferable, for the simple reason that moral theories stand a better chance of guiding moral practices effectively if they draw their data from reality rather than fiction. Additionally, it is often held that such examples are less 'cooked' and have fewer hidden theoretical strings attached to them (see §4). Granted, the theorist's own life experience may well be too confined and too parochial to serve as a satisfactory resource, but examples drawn from, for instance, medical practice, environmental policy, or international relations present theorists with more than ample opportunities. Much recent work in applied and professional ethics is inspired by this desire to bring theory into closer contact with actual practice via real-life examples (see APPLIED ETHICS §§2, 6). The concern of many virtue ethicists to articulate a more realistic moral psychology by examining the personalities of real-life moral exemplars represents an analogous development.

A third, more traditional camp claims that hypothetical examples constructed by the theorists themselves are the best way to go, on the ground that a better fit between principle and example is thereby achieved. Theorists here are the creators of their examples, and can embellish them to suit their own purposes. Because they have more control over the examples, a clearer, less *ad hoc* picture of how moral choices are to be made can also supposedly be gained. Within this third category one also finds a wide range of hypothetical example-types, extending from bare, highly schematic accounts at one end to intensely detailed and finely nuanced accounts at the other.

Finally, a fourth kind of example which also has its philosophical defenders is what might be called the imaginary case. This type too is of course hypothetical, but more extremely or fantastically so: it frequently involves counterfactual scenarios quite removed from everyday life. Sometimes one senses a frustrated science fiction writer behind the philosopher who concocts such cases, but when skilfully constructed and presented they can serve to flesh out our moral intuitions in ways that less fantastic stories cannot. The idea is then to transfer these intuitions to relevant (more earthly) cases where our intuitions are confused.

4 How to identify and describe examples

Some authors have also pressed sceptical questions concerning the ways in which specific cases are conceptualized and singled out by moral theorists. Postpositivist philosophers of science are fond of slogans such as 'All facts are theory-laden' (see OBSERVATION §§3–4), but it would appear that the theory-ladenness of examples used in ethics is radically deeper. What counts as an important moral problem, and the ways and reasons why it counts, are strongly affected by the theory one advocates or presupposes, as well as the time and place in which one lives. Applied and professional ethicists who work closely with practitioners also run the danger of allowing their perspective to be unduly influenced by the concerns of various interest groups and bodies of professional opinion. When unchecked, the result is not a critical reflection on moral practices but merely a reiteration of them. Given the evident theory-ladenness and conventionalism of many examples in ethics, it has been argued that philosophers who employ examples in ethical discussion need to pay much closer attention to the ways in which their examples are chosen and described. Additionally, stronger justificatory strategies are needed to defend such choices and descriptions against possible alternative conceptualizations.

5 Concluding remarks

The kinds of question philosophers have raised about examples in ethics are diverse, and the above discussion does not claim to be exhaustive. At the same time, some commonality can be detected within this diversity. Simplifying somewhat, one can say that a unifying theme running through at least parts of §§1, 2 and 4 is an ethical variation on traditional metaphysical and epistemological themes concerning the relationship between universals and particulars (see NOMINALISM; UNIVERSALS). Within philosophical discussions of ethics, should we grant pride of place to universals or to particulars? Should moral reflection and theory construction proceed in a 'top-down' application of principle to problem, or in a 'bottom-up' manner which insists that all rules and principles must submit to the jurisdiction of specific examples and not the other way around? (Here too, however, one needs to remember to allow room for adamant 'bottom-dwellers' – particularists and antitheorists who dismiss principles altogether.)

Philosophers as a group are undoubtedly more constitutionally principle-prone and theory-inclined than are novelists, dramatists, story tellers, and others who provide moralists with their richest stores of examples. Nevertheless, when philosophers decide to philosophize about ethics they need to keep in mind that they are ultimately philosophizing not about timeless entities but rather about how agents should live and act – agents, that is, who live in a world not only of space, time, and causality, but of history, politics, culture, and assorted other contingencies as well. The philosopher's natural impulse towards abstraction needs to be continually checked in ethics if we are not to lose sight of our subject matter. At the same time, while ethical theory cannot realistically aspire to the same level of generality as, say, astrophysical theory, the perpetual need to reflect on, understand, and evaluate moral examples eventually necessitates the resources of normative theory.

See also: CONSCIENCE; CASUISTRY; MORAL EDUCATION; MORAL KNOWLEDGE; SITUATION ETHICS; THEORY AND PRACTICE

References and further reading

* Aquinas, T. (1266–73) *Summa theologiae* (Synopsis of Theology), London: Burnes, Oates, 1924, IaIIae.18.10–11. (Outlines the maxim that circumstances alter cases.)
* Aristotle (*c.* mid 4th century BC) *Nicomachean Ethics*, trans. W.D. Ross, revised by J.O. Urmson, Oxford: Oxford University Press, 1975, book VI 8–13. (Contains an extended discussion of phronēsis.)
  Clarke, S.G. and Simpson, E. (1989) *Anti-Theory in Ethics and Moral Conservatism*, Albany, NY: State University of New York Press. (Good source book on antitheory movement. See especially contributions by A. Baier, B. Williams, J. McDowell, and bibliographic essay by editors.)
  Dancy, J. (1983) 'Ethical Particularism and Morally Relevant Properties', *Mind* 92: 530–47. (Strong defence of ethical particularism.)
  Flanagan, O. (1991) *Varieties of Moral Personality: Ethics and Psychological Realism*, Cambridge, MA: Harvard University Press. (Develops exemplar issue within virtue ethics movement.)
  Jonsen, A.R. and Toulmin, S. (1988) *The Abuse of Casuistry: A History of Moral Reasoning*, London: University of California Press. (Excellent history and defence of moral casuistry tradition.)
* Kant, I. (1785) *Grundlegung zur Metaphysik der Sitten*, in *Kants gesammelte Schriften*, ed. Königlichen Preußischen Akademie der Wissenschaften, Berlin: Reimer, vol. 4, 1903; trans. with notes by H.J. Paton, *Groundwork of the Metaphysics of Morals* (originally *The Moral Law*), London: Hutchinson, 1948; repr. New York: Harper & Row, 1964. (References made to this work in the entry give the page number from the 1903 Berlin Akademie volume; these page numbers are included in the Paton translation. The work expounds the view that any alleged moral exemplar or example must always be judged according to antecedently established principles.)
  Larmore, C.E. (1987) *Patterns of Moral Complexity*, Cambridge: Cambridge University Press, ch. 1. (Presents the distinction between a rhetorical and a logical role for examples, and defends the logical role.)
  Louden, R.B. (1992) 'Go-carts of Judgment: Exemplars in Kantian Moral Education', *Archiv für Geschichte der Philosophie* 74: 303–22. (A close textual analysis of Kant's views on both the value and the danger of teaching morality by exemplification.)
  —— (1992) *Morality and Moral Theory: A Reappraisal and Reaffirmation*, Oxford: Oxford University Press. (A response to antitheorists and particularists which defends a more empirically informed model of ethical theory. Also argues that the moral theories of Aristotle and Kant have far more in common than is usually thought.)
  Nussbaum, M. (1990) *Love's Knowledge: Essays on Philosophy and Literature*, Oxford: Oxford University Press. (Strong defence of literary examples in ethics.)
  O'Neill, O. (1986) 'The Power of Example', in *Constructions of Reason: Explorations of Kant's Practical Philosophy*, Cambridge: Cambridge University Press, 1989. (A Kantian critique of various example-oriented approaches to ethics.)
  —— (1988) 'How Can We Individuate Moral Problems?', in D.M. Rosenthal and F. Shehadi (eds) *Applied Ethics and Ethical Theory*, Salt Lake City, UT: University of Utah Press. (Argues that the examples and cases discussed by contemporary ethicists are themselves heavily theory-laden.)

ROBERT B. LOUDEN

EXISTENCE

Philosophical problems concerning existence fall under two main headings: 'What is existence?' and 'What things exist?'. Although these questions cannot be entirely separated, this entry will concentrate on the first.

The question 'What is existence?' has produced a surprising variety of answers. Some hold that existence is a property that every individual has, others that it is a characteristic that some individuals have but other (for example, imaginary) individuals lack, while proponents of the thesis that 'existence is not a predicate' hold that existence is not a property or characteristic of individuals at all.

Other philosophical issues concerning existence include: disputes about whether there are abstract objects (for example, numbers, universals) as well as concrete ones, immaterial souls as well as bodies, possible objects as well as actual ones, and so on; and questions about which entities (if any) are the fundamental constituents of reality.

1 **Objects and existence**
2 **The quantifier account of existence**

1 Objects and existence

To the question 'What is existence?' it is tempting to respond: 'A property that belongs to everything'. However, this answer appears to have paradoxical consequences.

An ancient puzzle, traceable to Parmenides, concerns denials of existence. If existence is a property of everything, one cannot talk about anything that does not exist. But if one cannot talk about what does not exist, how can one truly deny the existence of anything? Yet it is obvious that there are true denials of existence (true negative existential statements): Santa Claus does not exist, nor do Henry VIII's seventh wife or talking tigers.

A second puzzle concerns assertions of existence (positive existential statements). If everything that can be talked about exists, how can a true assertion that something exists be other than trivial? Yet it is obvious that there can be true but non-trivial assertions of existence: 'Egg-laying mammals exist', for example, is not trivial; and 'Homer existed' would be informative if true.

One response to these puzzles consists in holding that as well as objects that exist, there are objects that do not exist. Theories of this type are called 'Meinongian' (see Meinong 1904), after the most famous exponent of such a theory (see MEINONG, A.). According to a Meinongian theory, the possibility of true negative existential statements is explained by the fact that Santa Claus, the seventh wife of Henry VIII and so on are objects which can be talked about and can possess various properties (such as driving reindeer and being married), but which lack existence. As for the second puzzle: if some objects are nonexistent, it can clearly be informative to be told, of an object, that it exists.

Such a theory may appear to offer an attractive account of discourse about fiction; one that allows us to take at face value the fact that both 'Pegasus has wings' and 'Pegasus does not exist' appear to be true. However, there are features of this Meinongian theory that many find unacceptable. For example, if we are to use the theory to explain all true negative existential statements, we must follow Meinong in admitting that there are impossible objects such as the round square (since 'The object that is both round and square does not exist' is evidently true). Also, the Meinongian theory implies that Pegasus, although nonexistent, is a horse, yet it is debatable whether the property of being a horse can belong to something nonexistent. Even the fundamental tenet of the theory – that we can distinguish being an object from being an existent object – is open to question. If we admit that Pegasus is an object, a possible subject of discourse and a bearer of properties, does it make sense to add that Pegasus does not exist? If the answer is that existence requires location in space and time, although being an object does not, we may ask why we should accept this distinction.

2 The quantifier account of existence

An influential rival to the Meinongian account holds that the puzzles described in §1 above arise from the mistaken assumption that the term 'exist(s)' attributes a property to individuals. This solution employs an account of existence given by Frege and elaborated by Russell (see FREGE, G. §2; RUSSELL, B. §9). The account is associated with the slogan 'existence is not a predicate', a dictum derived from the writings of Kant, who anticipated the Frege–Russell theory in claiming that the ontological argument for God's existence depends on the illegitimate assumption that existence is a property (see GOD, ARGUMENTS FOR THE EXISTENCE OF §§2–3).

According to the Frege–Russell theory, the superficial grammatical form of the sentence 'Egg-laying mammals exist' (according to which it appears to attribute a property of existence to egg-laying mammals) is misleading. Its true logical form is revealed by reading it as 'There are egg-laying mammals', which can be analysed using logical symbolism as '$(\exists x)x$ is an egg-laying mammal', where '$\exists x$' is the existential quantifier (to be read as 'There is some x such that...'). According to this 'quantifier' account of existence (or of the word 'exist(s)') the grammatical predicate 'exist(s)' disappears when the sentence is subjected to logical analysis, being replaced by the existential quantifier. As for 'Talking tigers do not exist', this is to be treated as equivalent to 'There are no talking tigers', which can be analysed as 'It is not the case that: $(\exists x)x$ is a talking tiger'. Frege and Russell combined this quantifier account of existence with a claim to the effect that although 'exist(s)' is not a first-order predicate (a predicate of individuals), it is a higher-order predicate: a predicate of properties. For example, although in 'Egg-laying mammals exist' the word 'exist' does not ascribe the property of existence to egg-laying mammals, it does ascribe a property – that of being instantiated ('having an instance') – to the property of being an egg-laying mammal.

Using his celebrated theory of descriptions, Russell (1918) argued that the quantifier account can be extended to existential sentences involving definite descriptions and proper names, thus providing an ingenious general solution to the puzzles described above (see DESCRIPTIONS). According to Russell, 'Henry VIII's seventh wife does not exist' and 'Santa Claus does not exist' should be construed not as saying, of certain objects, that they lack existence, but rather as saying that certain properties (for example, being a seventh wife of Henry VIII or being a unique white-bearded, reindeer-driving, gift-delivering inhabitant of the North Pole) are not instantiated; that nothing has these properties. Similarly, 'God does not exist' is to be interpreted as the claim that a certain property – perhaps that of being a uniquely powerful, wise and benevolent creator of the universe – is not possessed by anything. Finally, if, following Russell, we treat the proper name 'Homer' as equivalent to the description 'the author of the *Iliad* and the *Odyssey*', we can construe the assertion that Homer existed as the claim that one person wrote both of these poems, an item of information that would be far from trivial.

The quantifier account is widely accepted as an analysis of general existential statements. However, many philosophers have been reluctant to follow Russell in holding that all meaningful existential statements are to be analysed in terms of the existential quantifier. (A notable exception is Quine (1953).) One difficulty is that there appear to be meaningful statements asserting the existence of particular things that resist the quantifier treatment. Even if we accept Russell's (controversial) analysis of definite descriptions, and accept his descriptive analysis of proper names such as 'Santa Claus' and 'God', there are powerful reasons for thinking that most proper names are not equivalent to descriptions (see PROPER NAMES §§1–3). Hence it is doubtful whether 'Bertrand Russell existed' is equivalent to any claim that some set of properties is or was instantiated. Even more recalcitrant are existential statements involving demonstratives, such as 'This exists' or 'That elephant exists'. Unless we say, implausibly, that all such sentences are false or meaningless, we appear to be committed to the conclusion that there are, after all, some true sentences in which 'exist(s)' ascribes a property of existence to particular objects. Further, it has been argued that some statements saying that things have existed, will exist, or might not have existed cannot be given a satisfactory analysis without invoking a property of existence.

However, if existence is a genuine property, an account must be given of the relation between this property and the existential quantifier, since it is undeniable that some general existential sentences are closely related to, if not equivalent to, existential quantifications. Moreover, if 'exist(s)' can express a property of individuals, does it play this role in any of the negative and positive existential statements discussed in §1? If so, how – assuming that the Meinongian account is rejected – are the puzzles to be solved? And what, if anything, can be said about the alleged property of existence beyond the claim that it belongs to everything? There is at present no consensus about these issues.

See also: BEING; FICTION, SEMANTICS OF; FREE LOGICS; LOGICAL AND MATHEMATICAL TERMS, GLOSSARY OF; ONTOLOGY; ONTOLOGICAL COMMITMENT

References and further reading

Barnes, J. (1972) *The Ontological Argument*, London: Macmillan, ch. 3. (A succinct critical discussion of the thesis that existence is not a predicate, including many references to other works.)

Evans, G. (1982) *The Varieties of Reference*, Oxford: Clarendon Press, ch. 10. (Defends the thesis that existence is a property of everything, offering a sophisticated solution to some of the problems mentioned in §2.)

* Meinong, A. (1904) 'Über Gegenstandstheorie' ('The Theory of Objects'), in R.M. Chisholm (ed.) *Realism and the Background of Phenomenology*, New York: Free Press, 1960, 76–117. (A difficult work. Parsons' *Nonexistent Objects* is an easier introduction to Meinongian views.)

Parsons, T. (1980) *Nonexistent Objects*, New Haven, CT: Yale University Press. (A modern and thorough development of Meinong's views. Quite technical in places.)

* Quine, W.V. (1953) 'On What There Is', in *From a Logical Point of View: Nine Logico-Philosophical Essays*, Cambridge, MA: Harvard University Press, 2nd edn, 1980. (A classic piece of advocacy for the quantifier account of existence, introducing Quine's famous 'criterion of ontological commitment'.)

* Russell, B.A.W. (1918) 'The Philosophy of Logical Atomism', Lectures 5 and 6, in *Logic and Knowledge: Essays 1901–1950*, ed. R.C. Marsh, London: Routledge, 1992. (An informal presentation by Russell of his version of the quantifier account.)

Williams, C.J.F. (1981) *What is Existence?*, Oxford: Clarendon Press. (A wide-ranging discussion, including a defence of a version of the quantifier account against numerous objections.)

PENELOPE MACKIE

EXISTENTIAL INSTANTIATION

see QUANTIFICATION AND INFERENCE

EXISTENTIALISM

The term 'existentialism' is sometimes reserved for the works of Jean-Paul Sartre, who used it to refer to his own philosophy in the 1940s. But it is more often used as a general name for a number of thinkers in the nineteenth and twentieth centuries who made the concrete individual central to their thought. Existentialism in this broader sense arose as a backlash against philosophical and scientific systems that treat all particulars, including humans, as members of a genus or instances of universal laws. It claims that our own existence as unique individuals in concrete situations cannot be grasped adequately in such theories, and that systems of this sort conceal from us the highly personal task of trying to achieve self-fulfilment in our lives. Existentialists therefore start out with a detailed description of the self as an 'existing individual', understood as an agent involved in a specific social and historical world. One of their chief aims is to understand how the individual can achieve the richest and most fulfilling life in the modern world.

Existentialists hold widely differing views about human existence, but there are a number of recurring themes in their writings. First, existentialists hold that humans have no pregiven purpose or essence laid out for them by God or by nature; it is up to each one of us to decide who and what we are through our own actions. This is the point of Sartre's definition of existentialism as the view that, for humans, 'existence precedes essence'. What this means is that we first simply exist – find ourselves born into a world not of our own choosing – and it is then up to each of us to define our own identity or essential characteristics in the course of what we do in living out our lives. Thus, our essence (our set of defining traits) is chosen, not given.

Second, existentialists hold that people decide their own fates and are responsible for what they make of their lives. Humans have free will in the sense that, no matter what social and biological factors influence their decisions, they can reflect on those conditions, decide what they mean, and then make their own choices as to how to handle those factors in acting in the world. Because we are self-creating or self-fashioning beings in this sense, we have full responsibility for what we make of our lives.

Finally, existentialists are concerned with identifying the most authentic and fulfilling way of life possible for individuals. In their view, most of us tend to conform to the ways of living of the 'herd': we feel we are doing well if we do what 'one' does in familiar social situations. In this respect, our lives are said to be 'inauthentic', not really our own. To become authentic, according to this view, an individual must take over their own existence with clarity and intensity. Such a transformation is made possible by such profound emotional experiences as anxiety or the experience of existential guilt. When we face up to what is revealed in such experiences, existentialists claim, we will have a clearer grasp of what is at stake in life, and we will be able to become more committed and integrated individuals.

1 **Historical development**
2 **The human condition**
3 **Being-in-the-world**
4 **Freedom and responsibility**
5 **Everyday existence, anxiety and guilt**
6 **Authenticity**
7 **Criticisms and prospects**

1 Historical development

Although such earlier thinkers as Augustine, Montaigne, Shakespeare and Pascal have been called existentialists, the term should be reserved for a loosely connected group of thinkers in recent times who were responding to certain views that became widespread in the nineteenth century. These views include, first, the scientific picture of reality as a meaningless, value-free collection of material objects in causal interactions, and second, the modern sense of society as an artificial construct that is inevitably in conflict with the aspirations of the individual. German Idealism had attempted to counteract the implications of these new ideas, but idealism had collapsed by the 1840s, and the result was a growing feeling that the individual is ultimately alone and unsupported in a cold and meaningless universe (see IDEALISM).

Existentialism appeared in the nineteenth century alongside romanticism, but it was different from romanticism in important respects. For one thing, where romanticism tried to evoke a sense of the individual's participation in the larger context of nature, the first great existentialist, Søren KIERKE-GAARD, held that humans are at the most basic level solitary, 'existing individuals' with no real connections to anything in this world. Instead of suggesting that we are at home in this world, Kierkegaard tried to intensify the individual's feeling of anxiety and despair in order to bring about a 'leap of faith' that would bring the person into a defining relationship to the God-man (Christ).

The next figure usually included in the pantheon of existentialists, Friedrich NIETZSCHE, began from the assumption that the development of science and critical thinking in Western history has led to the result that people have lost the ability to believe in a transcendent basis for values and belief. When Nietzsche said that 'God is dead', he meant that all the things people previously thought of as absolutes – the cosmic order, Platonic Forms, divine will, Reason, History – have been shown to be human constructions, with no ultimate authority in telling us how to live our lives. In the face of the growing 'nihilism' that results from the death of God, Nietzsche tried to formulate a vision of a healthy form of life people can achieve once they have given up all belief in absolutes (see NIHILISM).

The translation of Kierkegaard's works and the discovery of Nietzsche's writings had an immense impact on German thought after the First World War. The psychiatrist and philosopher, Karl JASPERS, drew on these two figures to develop what he called a 'philosophy of existence'. Martin HEIDEGGER, influenced by Kierkegaard as well as by the movement called 'philosophy of life' (then associated with the names of Nietzsche, Wilhelm DILTHEY and Henri BERGSON), began his major work, *Being and Time* (1927), with an 'existential analytic' aimed at describing life from the standpoint of concrete, everyday being-in-the-world (see LEBENSPHILOSOPHIE). Heidegger's thought was also influenced by Edmund Husserl's phenomenology, an approach to philosophy that emphasizes description of our experience as it is prior to reflection and theorizing (see PHENOMENOLOGICAL MOVEMENT).

Working independently in France, Gabriel MARCEL was building on Bergson's philosophy to develop an alternative to the dominant idealist philosophy taught in the universities. Basing his reflections on his own experience of life, Marcel claimed that a human being must be understood as an embodied existence bound up with a concrete situation. Because the body and the situation can never be completely comprehended by the intellect, Marcel sees them as part of what he calls the 'mystery'. Maurice MERLEAU-PONTY took over Marcel's notion of embodied being-in-a-situation as basic for his own existential phenomenology. Jean-Paul SARTRE also drew on Marcel's thought, but he was especially influenced by the thought of Husserl and Heidegger. It seems that the term 'existentialism' was first used by critics of Sartre, but it came to be accepted in the 1940s by Sartre and Simone de BEAUVOIR as they replied to their critics. Merleau-Ponty and Albert CAMUS were initially associated with the movement called existentialism during its heyday after the Second World War, but both eventually rejected the term as they came to distance themselves from Sartre due to political differences.

There have been important developments outside Germany and France. The Spanish philosopher, José ORTEGA Y GASSET, influenced by Dilthey's philosophy of life, developed a number of ideas that closely parallel those of Heidegger and other existentialist thinkers. The novels and short stories of the Russian writer, Fëdor DOSTOEVSKII, were influential not only for Russian existentialists like Nikolai BERDIAEV, but for Heidegger, Sartre and Camus as well. Existentialism has also had a profound impact on other fields. The movement of existential theology remains influential today (see EXISTENTIALIST THEOLOGY), and existential psychoanalysis (especially Ludwig Binswanger, Medard Boss and Rollo May) continues to be of interest in psychotherapy. Though existentialism is no longer a central movement in philosophy, many of its principal exponents continue to be important in current philosophical discussions.

2 The human condition

Existentialists start out from the assumption that it is no longer possible to believe that there is some transcendent justification or underlying ground for our existence. If God is dead, then we find ourselves 'abandoned', 'forlorn', 'thrown' into a world, with no pregiven direction or legitimation. Though we seek some overarching meaning and purpose for our lives, we have to face the fact that there is no 'proper function of humans' or 'plan in God's mind' that tells us the right way to be human.

This picture of our predicament leads to a particular view of human existence that is accepted by many existentialists. In contrast to traditional theories, which think of a human as a thing or object of some sort (whether a mind or a body or some combination of the two), existentialists characterize human existence as involving a deep tension or conflict between two different aspects of our being. On the one hand, we are organisms among other living beings, creatures with specific needs and drives, who operate at the level of sensation and desire in dealing with the present. At this level, we are not much different from other animals. On the other hand, there is a crucial respect in which we differ from other organisms. One way to describe this difference is to say that, because we are capable of self-awareness, we are able to reflect on our own desires and evaluate ourselves in terms of some larger vision of what our lives are adding up to. In this sense we transcend our own being as mere things. What is characteristic of our being as humans is that we *care* about the kinds of beings we are, and we therefore take a stand on our basic desires. According to the existentialists, humans are unique among entities in that they form second-order desires about their first-order desires, and they therefore have aspirations that go beyond the immediacy of their sensual lives.

Heidegger and Sartre try to capture this reflexive dimension of human existence by saying that what is unique about humans is that their own being is 'in question' or 'at issue' for them. What kind of person I am matters to me, and because I am concerned about what I am and will be, I take some concrete *stand* on my life by assuming roles and developing a specific character through my actions. But this means that my existence is characterized by a fundamental tension or clash between my immediate sensations and desires on the one hand, and my long-range aims and projects on the other. As Sartre puts it, a 'rift' or a 'gap' – a 'nothingness' – is introduced into the fullness of being in the universe by human existence. Because consciousness makes us more than what we are as creatures with immediate sensations and desires, Sartre says that human reality 'is not what it is and is what it is not'.

The conception of human existence as a tension also appears in Kierkegaard's description of the self. For Kierkegaard, humans are both finite and infinite, temporal and eternal, contingent and free. What defines our identity as selves is the concrete way we relate ourselves to this tension. In a similar way, Nietzsche holds that we are both creatures and creators, and we have to embrace both these dimensions of ourselves in order to be fully human. Heidegger and Sartre refer to the two aspects of the self as 'facticity' (our mere givenness) and 'transcendence' (our ability to surpass our givenness through our interpretations and aspirations). In their view, life is a continuous tension between these elements, a tension resolved only in death. Finally, Jaspers seems to have a similar conception of humans in mind when he points out the polarity between our being as an empirical consciousness-as-such and our desire to grasp the general and realize our freedom as *Existenz*.

If we regard the self as a tension or struggle, it is natural to think of human existence not as a thing or object of some sort, but as an unfolding event or happening – the story of how the tension is dealt with. What defines my existence, according to this view, is not some set of properties that remain the same through time, but the 'event of becoming' through which I carry out the struggle to resolve the tension that defines my condition in the world. As an ongoing happening, I *am* what I make of myself throughout the course of my life as a whole. In Ortega's words, a human 'does not have a nature, but rather a history' (see ORTEGA Y GASSET, J.). What defines my existence as an individual is the ongoing story of what I accomplish throughout my life.

To think of a human as an unfolding story suggests that human existence has a specific sort of temporal structure. We are not like rocks and cauliflowers which continue to exist through an endless sequence of 'nows'. Instead, human temporality has a kind of cumulativeness and future-directedness that is different from the enduring presence of physical things. First, our existence is directed toward the future to the extent that we are striving to realize something for our lives. Heidegger calls this element of 'futurity' our 'being-*towards*-death,' understood as a movement toward realizing our own being by achieving certain things throughout our active lives. Second, the past shows up for us as something retained and carried forward for the purposes of our future. Depending on our projects at any given time, our past actions show up for us as assets or as liabilities in relation to what we are doing. Finally, our present appears as a point of intersection between our future projects and our past accomplishments. Because we are time-binding beings whose lives always reach out into the future and hold on to the past, we can never achieve the kind of direct presence of self to self that Descartes thought he had found in the *Cogito* ('I think').

To say that human temporality is cumulative is to say that everything we do is contributing to creating our 'being' as a totality. In this sense, we *are* what we *do* in living out our lives: we define our own identity through the choices we make in dealing with the world. Because there is no fixed essential nature which we have in advance, our 'essence' as individuals is defined and realized through our concrete existence in the world. Whatever capacities and traits I am born with, it is up to me to take them over and make something of them in what I do. Thus, whether aware of it or not, I am creating my own identity in my actions.

3 Being-in-the-world

Existentialists are deeply suspicious of the high-level, abstract theorizing about humans found in traditional philosophy and in the sciences. In their view, the concern with subsuming all particulars under concepts and building systems tends to conceal crucial features of our lives as individuals. For this reason, existentialists generally start out from a description of ourselves as agents in everyday contexts, prior to reflection and theorizing. These descriptions reveal that it is part of our 'facticity' that we are generally caught up in the midst of things, involved with others in trying to accomplish specific goals, and affected by moods and commitments that influence our perception and thoughts. Furthermore, we are embodied beings who encounter the world only from the standpoint of a particular bodily orientation that gives us a set on things: 'I am my body' Marcel wrote, and this theme of embodiment became central to the thought of Beauvoir and Merleau-Ponty. We are also bound up with contexts of equipment in practical situations where we are trying to accomplish certain goals. Finally, as social beings, we always find ourselves embedded in a particular cultural and historical milieu that conditions our outlook and determines our basic orientation toward the world. To say that we are 'factical' beings is to say that we are always 'being-in-a-situation', where our being as selves is inseparable from a shared, meaningful life-world.

If we are always embedded in a situation, then all inquiry must start out from an 'insider's perspective' on things, that is, from a description of the world *as it appears to us* – to beings who are participants in our forms of life, with our unique sort of bodily set, feelings and modes of perception. We have no choice but to begin from where we stand in the thick of our actual lives, with our local attachments and particular cares and concerns. But this means that there is no way to achieve the sort of global 'God's-eye view' on ourselves and our world philosophers have sought ever since Plato. Existentialists are critical of the philosophical ideal of achieving a totally detached, disinterested, disengaged 'view from nowhere' that will provide us with completely objective knowledge. The attempt to step back from our ordinary concerns in order to achieve a totally detached and dispassionate standpoint – the stance Marcel calls 'desertion' and Merleau-Ponty calls 'high-altitude thinking' – will always give us a distorted view of the world, because it bleaches out our normal sense of the significance and worth of the things we encounter around us. In order to be able to gain an insight into the way reality presents itself to us at the most basic level, then, we need to start from a description of what Heidegger calls our 'average everydayness', our ordinary, familiar ways of being absorbed in practical affairs.

The idea that our being-in-a-situation or being-in-the-world is fundamental and inescapable gives the existentialists a way of criticizing the idea, central to philosophy since Descartes, that we are at the most basic level *minds* receiving sensory inputs and processing information. Sartre, for example, rejects the idea that the self can be thought of as a 'thinking substance' or self-encapsulated 'field of consciousness' distinct from the world. In my pre-reflective activities, Sartre says, I encounter myself not as a bundle of beliefs and desires in a mental container, but as being 'out there' *with* the things I am concerned about. When I am chasing a bus, I encounter my *self* as a 'running-toward-the-bus'. My being is found not in my head, but with the bus. Sartre thinks that this follows from Husserl's view that consciousness is always 'intentional,' always directed *towards* entities in the world (see INTENTIONALITY). If Husserl is

right, according to Sartre, then the 'I' is not an object, not a 'something', but is instead sheer intentional activity directed towards things in the world. The totality of my intentional acts defines me; there is no residue of 'substantial thinghood' distinct from my acts.

The existentialist conception of our irreducible being-in-a-situation calls into question some of the dualisms that have dominated so much of Western thought. First, existentialists deny the romantic distinction between an outer self – what we *do* in the world – and an inner, 'true' self that embodies our genuine nature. If we just *are* what we *do*, as existentialists contend, then there is no basis for positing a substantive 'real me' distinct from the parts I play and the things I do. Second, the account of the primacy of being-in-the-world tends to undermine the traditional subject-object model of our epistemological situation. Existentialists suggest that the assumption that humans are, at the most basic level, subjects of experience trying to formulate beliefs about objects on the basis of their inner representations, distorts our situation. If it is true that we are initially and most basically already out there with things in the world, then there must be something wrong with traditional epistemological puzzles about how a knowing subject can 'transcend' its veil of ideas to gain knowledge of objects in the external world. Finally, the existentialist picture of our basic situation as always bound up with a practical life-world seems to raise questions about the traditional fact–value distinction. Existentialists hold that we always encounter the everyday life-world as a context of equipment bound up with our aims as agents in the world. If the things we encounter are initially and most basically functional entities tied up with our purposive activities, however, then it is an illusion to think that what is given 'at first' is a collection of brute objects we subsequently invest with subjective values. In our everyday lives, fact and value are inseparable.

In general, existentialists hold that traditional dualisms arise only when we try to adopt a cool, detached, theoretical stance towards things. But since such a stance is derivative from and parasitic on a more basic way of being in which we are inseparably bound up with things in practical contexts, it cannot be regarded as providing us with a privileged insight into the way things really are.

4 Freedom and responsibility

As being-in-the-world, we are already engaged in a shared life-world that gives us a prior sense of what is possible, and we find ourselves with choices in our past that carry weight in determining how we can act in the future. This is our 'facticity', and it makes up what is just 'given' in our lives. However, existentialists regard facticity as only one aspect of human existence, for they hold that humans always have the ability to transcend their given situation by taking a stand on their own lives. As 'transcendence' we are always taking over our situations and making something of them through our choices. This ability to transcend our facticity means that we have free will. Our choices are free in the sense that (1) no outside factors determine our will, (2) in any particular case we could have acted otherwise than we did, and (3) we are therefore responsible for our choices in a way that justifies moral praise and blame (see FREE WILL). (Nietzsche is inclined to reject the third sense because of its role in imposing feelings of guilt on people, but in other respects he seems to be committed to believing in human freedom.)

The existentialist belief in human freedom is based on a phenomenological description of our everyday lives. In confronting situations where I must make a choice, I find myself facing an open range of possible courses of action where nothing compels me to choose one course of action over the others. Even in cases where I am not aware of making choices, a moment's reflection shows that I am in fact deciding my own life. Suppose that I show up for work faithfully each day, and I believe that I am compelled to do this because I need to make money to support my family. Does this mean that I am forced to do what I do? An existentialist like Sartre would say that it is self-deception to think I am *compelled* to be a conscientious worker, for I *could* always walk away from it all and join a monastery or turn to a life of crime. If I am choosing to let considerations of duty or money be deciding factors for me in this way, then this is my choice. What this suggests is that even in my habitual and seemingly 'automatic' actions I am actually *assuming* a particular identity for myself through my own free choices, and am therefore responsible for what I do.

Sartre tries to capture this idea by saying that humans are 'condemned to be free'. Because our being is 'in question' for us, we are always taking it over and giving it some concrete shape through our actions. And this means that, whether we are aware of it or not, in continuing to act in familiar ways we are constantly renewing our decisions at every moment, for we could always change our ways of living through some radical self-transformation. Moreover, since all criteria or standards for evaluating our actions are also freely chosen, in our actions we are also deciding what sorts of reasons are going to guide our actions. With no higher tribunal for evaluating reasons for acting, we are entirely responsible for

what we do: we have 'no excuses behind us nor justifications before us'.

Existentialists generally hold that we are not only responsible for the direction our own lives take, but also for the way the world around us appears. This idea has its roots in Kant's view that the reality we experience is partly shaped by the constituting activity of our own minds, though existentialists differ from Kant in holding that our construction of reality depends on our own choices (see KANT, I. §5). Kierkegaard, for example, contends that one's sense of reality is determined by the 'sphere of existence' in which one lives, so that the person who lives the life of a pleasure-loving aesthete will experience a world that is quite different from that of the duty-bound follower of the ethical. Similarly, Nietzsche holds that reality is accessible to us only through some 'perspective' or other, that there is no way to get in touch with reality as it is in itself, independent of any point of view or framework of interpretation.

Sartre works out an especially strong version of this Kantian outlook by developing the theory of constitution in Husserl's phenomenology. Husserl held that the world we experience is constituted through the meaning-giving activity of consciousness. Sartre takes this account of constitution to mean that, because I shape the world around me through my meaning-giving activity, I am ultimately responsible for the way the world presents itself to me in my experience. Thus if I have had some painful experiences as a child, it is up to me to decide what these mean to me. I can use them as an excuse for going through life feeling cheated, or regard them as challenges that will make me stronger. Sartre's point is not that there are no constraints on the ways I interpret my situation, but that constraints and obstacles gain their meaning from me, and since there are indefinitely many possible meanings any situation can have, there is no way to identify any supposedly 'hard' facts that could be said to compel me to see things one way rather than another. But this means, according to Sartre, that in choosing my interpretation of myself, I simultaneously choose the world. It is our own freely chosen projects that determine how reality is to be carved up and how things are to count. Sartre even goes so far as to say that, if a war breaks out around me, then I am responsible for that war, because it is up to me to decide what the war is going to mean to me in my life.

Other existentialists have tried to formulate a more tempered conception of freedom. Kierkegaard argues that, because being human involves both necessity and possibility, the extreme sort of 'anything-goes' freedom (such as that later envisaged by Sartre) would lead to the 'despair of lack of necessity'. Both

Heidegger and Merleau-Ponty work towards a notion of 'situated freedom' according to which choice is always embedded in and dependent upon the meaningful choices disclosed by a specific social and historical situation. Beauvoir tries to show how institutions and social practices can cut off the choices open to women and oppressed groups. Finally, Nietzsche calls attention to the way biological and historical factors operate 'behind our backs,' influencing our decisions without our awareness. But even when such limitations are recognized, the belief that we can rise above our situations to be 'creators' remains fundamental to existentialist thought.

5 Everyday existence, anxiety and guilt

Though existentialists agree that people are free to choose their own fates, they also hold that most people are quite unaware of their freedom. This obliviousness results not from ignorance or oversight, but from the fact that we usually try to avoid facing up to our responsibility for our lives. For the most part we are 'fleeing' from ourselves, throwing ourselves into mundane concerns and drifting into standardized public ways of acting. Existentialists are generally quite critical of everyday social existence. As they see it, there is a strong temptation to let ourselves get swallowed up by the 'public', the 'they', the 'herd' or the 'masses'. We try to do what 'one does' in familiar situations, and we assume that our lives are justified so long as we are following the norms and conventions laid out in our social context. In throwing ourselves into the kinds of busy-ness characteristic of contemporary society, we become more and more effective at finding means to achieving socially accepted ends, but at the same time we lose the ability to understand what is at stake in existing. Life then becomes a disjointed series of episodes with no real coherence or direction, and we end up dispersed and distracted, lacking any basis for meaningful action.

Existentialists give similar accounts of how social existence undermines our ability to realize ourselves as individuals. Kierkegaard describes the way that being a well adjusted member of 'the public' levels everything down to the lowest common denominator, with the result that nothing can really *count* or *matter* to people anymore. Similarly, Nietzsche describes the way that our being as 'herd' animals domesticates us and deadens our creativity, and Heidegger points out the 'tranquilization' and 'alienation from ourselves' that results from our absorption in the familiar social world. Sartre presents an especially harsh picture of social relations. Since, in his view, people can only see each other as objects and not as free beings, the Look of the Other always objectifies me and pressures me into thinking I am just a brute thing. As each individual struggles to affirm their being as a free 'transcendence' against the objectifying Look of others, the result is inevitable conflict: in the words of a character in one of Sartre's plays, 'Hell is the others'.

But many existentialists also see a positive side to social life. Though Heidegger criticizes the temptation to self-loss in our participation in the 'they', he also holds that all our possible ways of interpreting ourselves ultimately come from the social context in which we find ourselves. For this reason, becoming authentic is not a matter of escaping society, but of embracing our social existence in the right way. Marcel's attitude toward social existence shows how different he is from Sartre. He criticizes the 'technocratic attitude' of mass society not because it leads to conformism, but because it breeds an 'atomic individualism' that robs us of our deep sense of connection and obligation to others. And Jaspers and BUBER both emphasize the importance of 'I–Thou' relations in realizing a full and meaningful life.

Although existentialists differ in their assessment of social existence, they agree in thinking that our ordinary, day-to-day existence is shot through with concealment and self-deception. What can free us from this distorted sense of things is not rational reflection, but a profound affective experience. This emphasis on the role of emotions or moods in giving us access to the truth about ourselves is one of the most characteristic features of existentialist thought. Kierkegaard and Heidegger, for example, focus on the disclosive role of anxiety in leading us to confront the fact that we exist as finite beings who must decide the content of our own lives. Jaspers' concept of 'limit-situations' refers to situations in which our ordinary ways of handling our lives 'founder' as we encounter certain inescapable 'antinomies' of life. For Sartre, the feeling of *nausea* shows us that it is up to us to impart a meaning to things, and *anguish* reveals our 'terrible freedom' to decide our own fates. Finally, Marcel refers to the experience of *mystery* in which we encounter that which defies our ability to gain intellectual mastery through our problem-solving skills.

Some existentialists also talk about an experience of the absurd that can come over us in our rationalistic age. Sartre claims that there are no ultimate grounds that validate our choices, so that any fundamental project we adopt must be absurd in the sense that it is ultimately unjustified. Camus' conception of the absurd is perhaps the best known of all, though it is not really representative of existentialist thought. In *The Myth of Sisyphus* (1942a), he describes the feeling of futility we can experience when we become aware of the repetitiveness and pointlessness of our everyday routines and rituals. For Camus, this feeling of the absurdity of existence, a feeling in which suicide begins to seem like a real possibility, is the most fundamental experience philosophy must confront.

Finally, many existentialists point to the experience of guilt as providing an insight into our own being. Existential guilt refers to something broader than the feeling we sometimes have when we have done something wrong. In its broadest significance, existential guilt refers to the fact that there is no pre-given legitimation or justification for our existence. Though we are creatures who feel the need for some 'reason for existing', we find ourselves thrown into a world where there is no higher court of appeals that could validate our lives. We are ultimately answerable only to ourselves. In a somewhat narrower sense, existential guilt can refer to the fact that, because we are always engaged in acting in concrete situations, we are implicated in whatever happens in the world, and so we always have 'dirty hands'.

6 Authenticity

Experiences like anxiety and existential guilt are important, according to existentialists, because they reveal basic truths about our own condition as humans. Everyday life is characterized by 'inauthenticity', and in our ordinary busy-ness and social conformism we are refusing to take responsibility for our own lives. In throwing ourselves into socially approved activities and roles, we disown ourselves and spin a web of self-deception in trying to avoid facing up to the truth about what we are. This picture of inauthentic existence is contrasted with a vision of a way of living that does not slide into self-loss and self-deception. Such a life is (using the term found in Heidegger and Sartre) 'authentic'. Authenticity suggests the idea of being true to yourself – of owning up to who you really are. However, it is important to see that authenticity has nothing to do with the romantic ideal of getting in touch with an 'inner self' that contains one's true nature, for existentialists hold that we have no pregiven 'nature' or 'essence' distinct from what we do in the world.

If authenticity is not a matter of being true to some core of traits definitive of the 'real me', what is it? For most existentialists, becoming authentic is first of all a matter of lucidly grasping the seriousness of your own existence as an individual – the raw fact of the 'I exist' – and facing up to the task of making something of your own life. Kierkegaard, for example, holds that the only way to succeed in becoming a 'self' (under-

stood as an 'existing individual') is by living in such a way that you have 'infinite passion' in your life. This kind of intensity is possible, he thinks, only through a total, life-defining commitment to something that gives your life an ultimate content and meaning. Nietzsche is also concerned with getting us to take hold of our own lives in a more intense and clear-sighted way. To free people from the attempt to find some overarching meaning for their lives, he proposes the idea of eternal recurrence: the idea that everything that happens in your life has happened before in exactly the same way, and will happen again and again, an endless number of times. If we accept this, Nietzsche suggests, we will be able to embrace our lives as they are, on their own terms, without regrets or dreams about how things could be different. Heidegger suggests that, in the experience of anxiety, one confronts one's own 'naked' existence as 'individualized, pure and thrown'. As we become aware of our 'being-towards-death' in this experience, we will grasp the weightiness of our own finite lives, and we will then be able to seize on our own existence with integrity, steadiness and self-constancy.

Many existentialists agree that owning up to one's own existence requires a defining commitment that gives one's life a focus and sense of direction. For Kierkegaard, a religious thinker, self-fulfilment is possible only for the 'knight of faith', the person who has a world-defining relation to a particular being which has infinite importance (the eternal being who has existed in time, the God-man). For Heidegger, authenticity requires 'resoluteness', a commitment to some specific range of possibilities opened up by one's historical 'heritage'. The fact that the ideal of commitment or engagement appears in such widely different existentialist works raises a question about the distinction, first made by Sartre, between 'religious' and 'atheist' existentialists. Kierkegaard, Marcel and Jaspers are often grouped together as religious existentialists, yet there are profound differences in their views of the nature of religious commitment. Where Kierkegaard emphasizes the importance of relating oneself to a concrete particular, Marcel and Jaspers speak of a relation to the 'mystery' or to 'transcendence' (respectively). At the same time, so-called 'atheist' existentialists like Heidegger and Sartre tend to agree with Kierkegaard's view that being 'engaged' or having a 'fundamental project' is necessary to achieving a focused, intense, coherent life. The distinction between atheist and religious existentialists becomes harder to maintain when we realize that what is important for religious thinkers is not so much the factual properties of the object of commitment as the inner condition of faith of the committed individual.

Thus, Kierkegaard says that what is crucial to faith is not the 'objective truth' about what one believes, but rather the intensity of one's commitment (the 'subjective truth').

The idea that intensity and commitment are central to being authentic is shared by all types of existentialists. Another characteristic attributed to an authentic life by most existentialists is a lucid awareness of one's own responsibility for one's choices in shaping one's life. For Sartre, authenticity involves the awareness that, because we are always free to transform our lives through our decisions, if we maintain a particular identity through time, this is because we are choosing that identity at each moment. Similarly, Kierkegaard and Heidegger talk about the need to sustain our identity at each moment through a 'repetition' of our choice of who we are. In recognizing our freedom to determine our own lives, we also come to accept our responsibility for who we are.

The notion of authenticity is supposed to give us a picture of the most fulfilling life possible for us after the 'death of God'. It calls on us to assume our own identities by embracing our lives and making something of them in our own way. It presupposes lucidity, honesty, courage, intensity, openness to the realities of one's situation and a firm awareness of one's own responsibility for one's life. But it would be wrong to think of authenticity as an *ethical* ideal as this is normally interpreted. First, becoming authentic does not imply that one adopts any particular moral code or follows any particular path: an authentic individual might be a liberal or a conservative, a duty-bound citizen or a wild-eyed revolutionary. In this respect, authenticity pertains not to *what* specific kinds of things you do, but *how* you live – it is a matter of the style of your life rather than of its concrete content. Second, in formulating their different conceptions of authenticity, many existentialists describe the ideal of authenticity in terms that suggest that it can be opposed to ethics as ordinarily understood. Kierkegaard, for example, says that it is possible that the knight of faith might have to 'transcend the ethical', and Nietzsche holds that authentic individuals will live 'beyond good and evil'. Thus, authenticity seems to have more to do with what is called the 'art of self-cultivation' than it does with ethics as traditionally understood.

7 Criticisms and prospects

Existentialism has been criticized from a number of different angles. One line of criticism holds that the emphasis on individual freedom and the rejection of absolutes in existentialism tends to undermine ethics; by suggesting that everyday life is 'absurd' and by denying the existence of fixed, binding principles for evaluating our actions, existentialists promote an 'anything-goes' view of freedom that exacerbates the nihilism already present in contemporary life. Camus' novel *The Stranger* (1942b), for example, has come under attack for glorifying immoral 'gratuitous acts' as a way of affirming one's own absolute freedom. In reply, supporters of existentialism have noted that the stance portrayed in the work is not at all typical of existentialist views, and that existentialism's ideal of freedom and its sense of the need for human solidarity after the 'death of God', far from undermining ethics, might provide a very good basis for a moral point of view in the modern world (see EXISTENTIALIST ETHICS).

Other critics have tried to show that the basic picture of reality presupposed by existentialism necessarily leads to nihilism. Hans Jonas (1966) argues that existentialism, despite its avowed goal of overcoming Cartesianism, tends to introduce a new kind of dualism with its sharp distinction between humans (who are thought of as absolutely free centres of choice and action), and an inert, meaningless 'being' that is on hand for humans to interpret and transform as they please. Not only does this extreme opposition exclude animals from the realm of beings with intrinsic worth, its view of humans as thrown into an indifferent universe seems to give us freedom only at the cost of making nothing really worthy of choice.

This line of criticism is closely connected to the claim, formulated by various postmodern theorists, that existentialism is still trapped within the assumptions of Humanism, a view now supposed to have been discredited. Humanism in this context means the view, central to modern philosophers from Descartes to Kant, that the human subject is immediately present to itself as a centre of thought and action, and that the rest of the universe should be thought of as a collection of things on hand to be represented and manipulated by the subject. Postmodern theorists claim that a number of intellectual developments in the last two centuries have made it impossible to accept this picture of the centrality of the subject. The semiotic theories of SAUSSURE, for example, have shown how language tends to work behind our backs, controlling our capacities for thought and speech, and Freudian theory has shown how unconscious drives and desires lie behind many of our conscious thoughts and actions. Given these developments, it is claimed, we can no longer accept the idea that humans are capable of the sorts of self-transparency and self-determination that seem to be presupposed by existentialists like Sartre (see POSTMODERNISM).

In reply to this objection, one might point out that

most existentialists have been very critical of the Cartesian belief in the transparency of consciousness to itself. Such themes as being-in-a-situation, 'thrownness', embodiment and mystery show the extent to which many existentialists think of humans as embedded in a wider context they can never totally master or comprehend. Moreover, the existentialist description of humans as temporal beings whose 'present' is always mediated by what is projected into the future and retained from the past undermines any Cartesian conception of the immediate presence of self to self in self-awareness. Finally, as Sonia Kruks (1990) argues, postmodern theorists seem to have run up against a wall in their attempts to 'de-centre the subject'. Having identified the pervasive background structures that influence the thoughts and actions of subjects, these theorists now find it difficult to give an account of the kind of critical thinking they see as central to the postmodern stance. In Kruks' view, existentialists have much to offer postmodern theory in formulating the conception of a 'situated subjectivity' that will fill this gap.

It is not clear what the future holds in store for existentialism understood as a philosophical movement. Many of the ideas that sounded so exciting in Paris in the 1940s now seem terribly old-fashioned. Many of the more viable themes in existentialism have been absorbed into new philosophical movements, especially into hermeneutics with its emphasis on humans as self-interpreting beings (see HERMENEUTICS). While some existentialist writers have faded from the scene, others have become more and more influential (though not always *as* existentialists). There has been an explosion of interest in Heidegger and Nietzsche recently, and the works of Kierkegaard, Sartre and Beauvoir are widely discussed.

Whether or not existentialism as such will continue to thrive, it seems that there will always be a place for the style of critique of society and the concern with the concrete realities of life that are central to existentialist thought. As a reactive movement, existentialism challenged the uncritical assumptions of mainstream philosophy as well as the complacency of everyday social existence. In its more positive side, it attempted to counteract the tendency to self-loss in contemporary life by formulating a vision of the kind of coherent, focused way of living that would provide a basis for meaningful action. These certainly seem to be valuable aims, and it is likely that existentialist writers will always have important contributions to make toward realizing them.

See also: EXISTENTIALIST THOUGHT IN LATIN AMERICA

References and further reading

Blackham, H.J. (1952) *Six Existentialist Thinkers*, New York: Harper Torchbooks, 2nd edn, 1959. (Dependable introductions to Kierkegaard, Nietzsche, Jaspers, Marcel, Heidegger and Sartre.)

* Camus, A. (1942a) *Le Mythe de Sisyphe*, trans. J. O'Brien in *The Myth of Sisyphus and Other Essays*, New York: Knopf, 1955. (A classic account of the 'absurdity' of everyday life.)

* —— (1942b) *L'Etranger* (*The Stranger*), trans. S. Gilbert, New York: Knopf, 1973. (Description of the kind of 'gratuitous act' discussed in §7 above.)

Cooper, D.E. (1990) *Existentialism: A Reconstruction*, Oxford: Blackwell. (An up-to-date and thorough survey of existentialist thought. Helpful bibliography.)

Dilman, Ì. (1993) *Existentialist Critiques of Cartesianism*, Lanham, MD: Barnes & Noble Books. (Clear and interesting account of how existentialism criticizes ideas inherited from Descartes; focuses primarily on Sartre and Marcel.)

Golomb, J. (1995) *In Search of Authenticity: From Kierkegaard to Camus*, London: Routledge. (Clearly written survey of existentialist conceptions of authenticity.)

Guignon, C. and Pereboom, D. (eds) (1995) *Existentialism: Basic Writings*, Indianapolis, IN: Hackett Publishing Company. (Core texts by Kierkegaard, Nietzsche, Heidegger and Sartre, with extensive introductions by the editors.)

* Heidegger, M. (1927) *Sein und Zeit* (*Being and Time*), trans. J. Macquarrie and E. Robinson, New York: Harper & Row, 1962. (A seminal work: the first systematic presentation of such existentialist themes as death, guilt, conscience, authenticity and being-in-the-world.)

* Jonas, H. (1966) 'Gnosticism, Existentialism and Nihilism', in *The Phenomenon of Life*, New York: Harper & Row. (Interesting criticisms of existentialism and especially of Heidegger.)

Kierkegaard, S. (1843a) *Enten-eller* (*Either/Or*), trans. H.V. Kong and E.H. Kong, Princeton, NJ: Princeton University Presss, 1987. (Develops the idea of different 'spheres of existence' in which humans live.)

—— (1843b) *Frygt og Baeven*, trans W. Lowrie in *Fear and Trembling and The Sickness Unto Death*, Garden City, NY: Doubleday, 1954. (Kierkegaard's poetic evocation of the 'Knight of Faith'.)

* Kruks, S. (1990) *Situation and Human Existence: Freedom, Subjectivity and Society*, London: Unwin Hyman. (Excellent study of the relevance of French existentialist thought to current postmodern devel-

opments. Covers Marcel, Sartre, Beauvoir and Merleau-Ponty.)

Macquarrie, J. (1972) *Existentialism*, Philadelphia, PA: Westminster. (A dependable and clear survey of existentialist thought. Extensive bibliography listing older works on existentialism.)

McBride, W.L. (ed.) (1997) *Sartre and Existentialism: Philosophy, Politics, Ethics, The Psyche, Literature, and Aesthetics*, New York: Garland, 8 vols. (Collections of classic essays in English on existentialism, with volumes on its background and development.)

May, R., Angel, E. and Ellenberger, H.F. (eds) (1958) *Existence: A New Dimension in Psychiatry and Psychology*, New York: Basic Books. (Collection of classic readings in existential psychoanalysis.)

Nietzsche, F. (1892) *Also Sprach Zarathustra* (*Thus Spoke Zarathustra*), trans. W. Kaufman in *The Portable Nietzsche*, New York: Viking, 1954. (Nietzsche's vision of the *Übermensch* or 'superman'.)

Sartre, J.-P. (1943) *L'Être et le Néant: Essai d'ontologie phénoménologique* (*Being and Nothingness: An Essay on Phenomenological Ontology*), trans. H.E. Barnes, New York: Philosophical Library, 1956. (The most representative work of the existentialist tradition.)

—— (1946) *L'Existentialisme est un humanisme*, trans. B. Frechtman as *Existentialism*, New York: Philosophical Library, 1946. (Influential, brief statement of Sartre's existentialist views.)

Schrag, C.O. (1961) *Existence and Freedom: Towards an Ontology of Human Finitude*, Evanston, IL: Northwestern University Press. (A classic synthesis of different existentialist philosophers and themes.)

Solomon, R.C. (1972) *From Rationalism to Existentialism: The Existentialists and Their Nineteenth-Century Backgrounds*, New York: Harper & Row. (The best account of existentialism in its historical context.)

Wahl, J. (1969) *Philosophies of Existence: An Introduction to the Basic Thought of Kierkegaard, Heidegger, Jaspers, Marcel, and Sartre*, London: Routledge & Kegan Paul. (Difficult but trustworthy introduction by a respected French scholar.)

Warnock, M. (1970) *Existentialism*, Oxford: Oxford University Press. (Clear exposition of the basic concepts.)

Yalom, I.D. (1980) *Existential Psychotherapy*, New York: Basic Books. (Well written and insightful study of existentialist themes and their relevance to psychotherapy.)

CHARLES B. GUIGNON

EXISTENTIALIST ETHICS

Central to existentialism is a radical doctrine of individual freedom and responsibility. On the basis of this, writers such as Sartre have offered an account of the nature of morality and also advanced proposals for moral conduct. Important in that account are the claims that (a) moral values are 'created' rather than 'discovered', (b) moral responsibility is more extensive than usually assumed, and (c) moral life should not be a matter of following rules. Existentialist proposals for conduct derive from the notion of authenticity, *understood as 'facing up' to one's responsibility and not 'fleeing' it in 'bad faith'. Authenticity, many argue, entails treating other people so as to encourage a sense of freedom on their part, although there is disagreement as to the primary forms such treatment should take. Some have argued that we promote a sense of freedom through commitment to certain causes; others that this is best achieved through personal relationships.*

1   **Existential freedom**
2   **Values, responsibility and rules**
3   **Authenticity**
4   **Reciprocal freedom**

1   Existential freedom

Existentialism has been described as a 'philosophy for living', an engagement with the realities of the human predicament. But some have argued that an existentialist ethics is impossible, on the grounds that the existentialist understanding of moral choice and value precludes advocating any particular choices and values. This charge is sometimes supported by citing (a) the variety of personal commitments – Christian, communist, even fascist – among writers in this tradition, and (b) the reluctance of some of these writers to express their commitments in moral terms (KIERKEGAARD sometimes seems to commend the person-of-faith's 'suspension of the ethical', and NIETZSCHE the 'higher' person's going 'beyond good and evil'). To assess these competing views, we need to understand (a) the existentialist emphasis on freedom and responsibility, (b) the resulting account of moral choice, values and rules, and (c) the ideal of authenticity.

Existentialism is not a sharply defined tradition. Here, we are concerned primarily with the views of Jean-Paul SARTRE, but also with those of predecessors and contemporaries – including Kierkegaard, HEIDEGGER and Gabriel MARCEL – to the extent that these have affinities with Sartre's position. Central to the tradition is the idea of radical individual freedom and responsibility to which, as human beings, we are 'condemned'. This is not freedom in the sense of absence of constraints, for this varies from society to society. Nor is it simply the freedom to will which actions to perform. Rather, it is a person's freedom to 'make himself... since nothing foreign has decided what we are' (Sartre 1943: 554). We are responsible, therefore, for our characters and emotional make-up, and even for the situations in which we 'find ourselves', since circumstances only constitute a *situation* when interpreted by us in a certain way. Someone who interprets the mountain as a challenge is in a different situation from one who sees it merely as an obstacle. Such interpretations of the world are embedded in purposes for which we are responsible. Neither human beings nor the world, therefore, have a given nature or 'essence': it is through purposive activities that they become what they are.

Sartre spoke of our 'choosing' to be what we are, but others identify existential freedom with a capacity to stand back from our lives and change them. I may not have chosen my social situation, but I could reflect upon it, 'refuse' it and 'begin something else' (Merleau-Ponty 1945: 452). Although 'thrown' into an already interpreted world, we can, with 'resoluteness', become 'released' from the prevailing interpretations (Heidegger 1927: 163).

2 Values, responsibility and rules

From such accounts of freedom, existentialists have drawn conclusions concerning moral values, responsibility, and the place of rules in moral life.

(a) Values are, in a sense, 'subjective' functions of our interpretative activity rather than features of an independent reality. They are not, wrote Sartre, 'strewn in our path', but 'created' or 'invented'. This does not mean, however, that existentialists insist on a 'gap' between facts and values. Nietzsche (1886) denied that there are moral facts, arguing there are no facts at all, independent of human 'perspectives'. Values are *no more* 'subjective' than other features of the world, for even 'factual' descriptions are inseparable from evaluation. Values, as Heidegger stressed (1927), are not 'stuck on' to a world first articulated in a value-free manner, since all articulation reflects human 'projects' which are shaped by what matters to us, what we find worth pursuing.

It follows from this that the existentialist view of values is 'anti-foundationalist' (though see §4). There can be no final justification for a particular value, since all justification presupposes an interpretative stance which is itself imbued with values. Some writers dramatize this 'predicament' by referring to the 'absurdity' which thereby infects our lives. It is not moral values themselves which are absurd, but the discrepancy between the serious commitment they require and the recognition that they lack any final foundation. (This 'absurd' discrepancy is distinct from the one, discussed by Albert Camus (1943), between our aspirations to knowledge and the world's 'refusal' to supply it – see CAMUS, A.).

(b) The existentialist view of moral responsibility is predictably demanding. First, for some writers, notably Kierkegaard, adoption of the moral point of view is itself an individual decision that cannot be dictated by reasons, since any such reasons would presuppose a commitment to that point of view. Even after it has been adopted, there remains a choice as to the *kind* of morality to follow. Sartre's wartime student, who must decide between joining the Free French and looking after his mother, is in effect having to choose between the 'collective' good and a 'morality of... personal devotion' (1946: 36).

Second, our responsibility allows for much less mitigation than is usually thought. We are, according to Sartre, 'without excuses' (1946: 34). The 'villains' in existentialist fiction often excuse their behaviour by citing their 'character' or the exigencies of their job, failing to admit that their 'character' and the demands incumbent on them are of their own making. Nor is my responsibility confined to what I *do*, for by *failing* to oppose a war, say, I have 'dirty hands' and share responsibility with those actually waging the war. Neither is it to the results of what *I* do that my responsibility is limited. By acting in a certain way, I give a green light to others to act in the same way, and hence bear responsibility for the results of their doing so.

It might be thought that for 'religious existentialists' our responsibility is reduced by the obligation to obey God's commands. But the tendency of these writers is to emphasize that faith itself is a free commitment and one, moreover, which reflects, rather than constrains, a person's moral values. My perception that it is God's command that I am obeying is therefore one for which I am accountable.

(c) Existentialists generally reject the familiar picture of morality as a system of rules or principles. This is not due to a predilection for motiveless *actes gratuits*, but for two other reasons. First, the familiar picture encourages people to go along with conventions and to respond to situations mechanically. One can 'do anything "on principle" and avoid all personal responsibility', Kierkegaard complained (1846: 85). Adherence to rules, moreover, detracts from the task of identifying what these situations really are, something that itself calls for moral deliberation since situations are functions of how circumstances are interpreted and evaluated (see §1). An obsession with following rules, then, implies abdication from responsible appraisal of our situations and deeds.

Second, the feasibility of basing decisions upon rules is much exaggerated. Moral rules are typically vague and, in many contexts, speak ambiguously. Sartre's student (see §2 (b)) can easily cite rules which, suitably construed, would endorse either of the courses of action contemplated. By their very nature, moreover, moral rules are tailored to recurrent, everyday situations, and are useless, therefore, in what JASPERS calls 'boundary situations'. How I should confront my death, for instance, is an issue so individual to me that the precedents set by other people can have no automatic bearing. Even much less dramatic circumstances can have a complexity and uniqueness which render the application of rules hazardous. As one of Simone de Beauvoir's characters puts it, 'I can't tell you [what to have done]...because I wasn't in your place' (1954: 646).

3   Authenticity

These claims about the nature of morality do not themselves provide practical guidance to the values and goals people should adopt. 'Anti-foundationalism' and hostility to rules may even seem to preclude this. If existentialism is to furnish a practical ethics, this will be on the basis of a notion, already visible in Kierkegaard's and Nietzsche's sketches of the 'subjective existing individual' and the 'overman' respectively, which later writers call 'authenticity'.

The authentic person is one who lives in clear, honest recognition of existential freedom. This is best understood in contrast with the various ways of being inauthentic that Sartre calls 'bad faith'. These are strategies for denying or disguising one's freedom and responsibility in order to minimize the 'anxiety' which full appreciation of these would induce. Inauthentic life, as Heidegger puts it, 'tranquillizes'. One such strategy is to regard oneself as being in the grip of unconscious drives; another is illustrated by the woman, in Sartre's example, who pretends that her seduction by a man is something that is merely 'happening' to her (1943: 55–6).

The most common and insidious strategy, however, is that of identifying too closely with one's 'being-for-others', with the images and expectations that other people have of one. Simone de Beauvoir (1949) complained of women's tendency to match themselves with the image men have of them and then behave as women are 'supposed' to do (see BEAUVOIR, S. DE). More generally, I surrender my 'ownmost being', as Heidegger calls it, when I do what 'one does', when I tailor my values and attitudes to those expected of me. I have surrendered to the anonymous 'Them', to

Kierkegaard's 'Public' or Nietzsche's 'Herd'. 'Authentic' is the translation of the German *eigentlich*, from a word meaning 'own'. The authentic individual 'owns' and 'owns to' their life.

4   Reciprocal freedom

When Sartre says that an authentic decision cannot be 'judged', this seems to confirm the charge that authenticity is at best a recipe for how to 'think and feel', not for what 'we ought to *do*' (Warnock 1970: 125; original emphasis). But he also holds, qualifying his 'anti-foundationalism' apparently, that freedom is 'the foundation of all values' (1946: 51). This refers us to a theme stated succinctly by Jaspers, that 'man becomes free only in so far as the other becomes free' (1957: 85). This theme is inherited from German Idealists, like Johann FICHTE, rather than from Kierkegaard and Nietzsche, whose heroes engage in solitary self-cultivation to the relative exclusion of concern for 'the other'.

In contrast with his earlier view that people assert their own freedom at the expense of that of others, Sartre came to hold that 'my freedom impl[ies] mutual recognition of others' freedom' (1983: 487). Although he writes that, in oppressing others, 'the oppressor oppresses himself', the point is not primarily a political one. The idea is that unless I recognize the freedom of others, I cannot properly appreciate my own and so live authentically. This is because my conception of myself is indelibly coloured by how I take other people to view me. Now I cannot suppose that they regard me as free unless I regard *them* as free. Hence my obligation to cultivate an authentic sense of myself as a free person commits me to cultivating in others a similar sense of their freedom. In Heidegger's language, people exist authentically when each 'frees the other in his freedom for himself' (1927: 159).

But how is this cultivation of other people's sense of their own freedom to proceed? For Sartre, it is primarily through commitment to large causes, such as resistance to fascism. But for others, it is in personal relationships of love and friendship that, in Marcel's words, I 'apprehend' another person as free, 'help him to be freed, [and] collaborate with his freedom' (1935: 107).

The ideal of authenticity, it seems, does have broad implications for the treatment of other people, in which case the charge that existentialism cannot furnish a practical ethics is misplaced. That existentialists differ as to the precise implications of the ideal may reflect a human dilemma rather than confusion on their part. It is, in effect, the dilemma confronting Sartre's student, for either of the actions he considers could be seen as honouring the freedom of others (in a way that his going off to peddle heroin to children could not). Existentialists, like the student himself, have no short answer to the question of which kind of concern – one for people at large, or one for those to whom one is intimately related – is the better expression of an authentic life. That is hardly cause for concluding that existentialism cannot make 'any contribution to moral philosophy at all' (Warnock 1970: 125).

See also: AUTONOMY, ETHICAL; EXISTENTIALISM; EXISTENTIALIST THEOLOGY

References and further reading

Baldwin, T. (1986) 'Sartre, Existentialism and Humanism', in G. Vesey (ed.) *Philosophers Past and Present*, Cambridge: Cambridge University Press. (Acute analysis of Sartre's lecture, with useful discussion of the later Notebooks (1983).)

* Beauvoir, S. de (1949) *Le deuxième sexe, tome I, Les faits et les mythes, tome II, L'expérience vécue*, Paris: Gallimard; trans. H.M. Parshley, *The Second Sex*, London: New English Library, 1962. (Classic feminist text, which emphasizes women's own responsibility for accommodating themselves to men's image of them.)

* —— (1954) *Mandarins*, Paris: Gallimard, 2 vols; trans. L.B. Friedman, London: Fontana, 1982. (Massive novel of human relationships and betrayals. A fictional vehicle for its author's views on ethics.)

* Camus, A. (1943) *Le Mythe de Sisyphe*, Paris: Gallimard; trans. J. O'Brien, *The Myth of Sisyphus*, Harmondsworth: Penguin, 1986. (Famous discussion of absurdity, different from Sartre's.)

Cooper, D.E. (1990) *Existentialism: A Reconstruction*, Oxford: Blackwell. (Revisionary account, but suitable as an introduction. Defends prospects for an existentialist ethics.)

* Heidegger, M. (1927) *Sein und Zeit*, trans. J. Macquarrie and E. Robinson, *Being and Time*, Oxford: Blackwell, 1962. (Difficult but seminal twentieth-century work. Essential reading on authenticity and anxiety.)

* Jaspers, K. (1957) 'Philosophical autobiography', in P. Schilpp (ed.) *The Philosophy of Karl Jaspers*, La Salle, IL: Open Court. (A leading and usually verbose existentialist's briefest statement of his position.)

* Kierkegaard, S. (1846) *The Present Age*, trans. A. Dru, London: Fontana, 1962. (A bitter attack on the 'Public's suppression of individuality.)

Macquarrie, J. (1977) *Existentialism: An Introduction, Guide and Assessment*, Harmondsworth: Penguin. (Focuses on 'religious existentialism'.)

* Marcel, G. (1935) *Être et Avoir*, trans. K. Farrer, *Being and Having*, London: Dacre, 1949. (Sensitive exploration of personal relationships by a neglected thinker.)

* Merleau-Ponty, M. (1945) *Phénoménologie de la perception*, Paris: Gallimard; trans. C. Smith, *The Phenomenology of Perception*, London: Routledge & Kegan Paul, 1962. (Classic work of existential phenomenology; presents the most plausible account of existential freedom.)

* Nietzsche, F. (1886) *Jenseits von Gut und Böse*, trans. W. Kaufmann, *Beyond Good and Evil*, New York: Vintage, 1966. (One of Nietzsche's most important and closely structured works. Contains essential chapters on religion, the history of morals, 'free spirits' and nobility.)

Olafson, F. (1967) *Principles and Persons: An Ethical Interpretation of Existentialism*, Baltimore, MD: Johns Hopkins University Press. (Full and penetrating discussion of existentialist ethics. Usable as a sophisticated introduction.)

* Sartre, J-P. (1943) *L'Être et le Néant: Essai d'ontologie phénoménologique*, Paris: Gallimard; trans. H. Barnes, *Being and Nothingness: An Essay on Phenomenological Ontology*, London: Methuen, 1957. (*The* classic existentialist tome, as difficult as its title suggests; includes discussion of 'bad faith', which is essential reading.)

* —— (1946) *L'Existentialisme est un humanisme*, Paris: Nagel; trans. P. Mairet, *Existentialism and Humanism*, London: Methuen, 1966. (Punchy, readable lecture, but not always a reliable expression of Sartre's views. Contains the example of the student torn between joining the Free French and looking after his mother.)

* —— (1983) *Cahiers pour une morale*, Paris: Gallimard; trans. D. Pellauer, *Notebooks for an Ethics*, Chicago, IL: University of Chicago Press, 1992. (These posthumously published notes from the 1940s for a book which was never to be give Sartre's fullest account of reciprocal freedom.)

* Warnock, M. (1970) *Existentialism*, Oxford: Oxford University Press. (Introductory and not very sympathetic account of main existentialist figures. Rejects possibility of existentialist ethics.)

DAVID E. COOPER

EXISTENTIALIST THEOLOGY

Existentialist theology is a term used to describe the work of a number of theologians, chiefly from the twentieth century, whose writings were strongly influenced by the literary and philosophical movement known as existentialism. Because of the diversity of the movement, it is difficult to say much that is illuminating about existentialist theology as a whole. In general, however, these theologians attempt to understand God in relation to the situation of the concretely existing human individual. Their analysis of human existence is one that emphasizes the freedom of individuals to shape their own identities through choices, and the paradoxical, ambiguous or even absurd character of the reality that humans encounter. Religious faith is seen as closely related to feelings of alienation and despair; faith may grow out of such emotions or it may provide the key to overcoming them, or both these relations may be present at once.

Though the designation of any particular theologian as 'existentialist' is a controversial matter, Karl Barth, Rudolf Bultmann and Paul Tillich are among the more important thinkers whose work exhibits existentialist themes. The entire movement has been strongly influenced, directly or indirectly, by the nineteenth-century Danish philosopher-theologian Søren Kierkegaard, while the works of the Russian novelist Fëdor Dostoevskii and the German philosopher Friedrich Nietzsche, both from the late nineteenth century, have also been important.

1 **Kierkegaard's critique of Enlightenment-inspired theologies**
2 **Insights of Kierkegaard and other nineteenth-century thinkers**
3 **Twentieth-century existentialist theologians**
4 **Critical problems and lasting contributions**

1 Kierkegaard's critique of Enlightenment-inspired theologies

Though KIERKEGAARD lived from 1813 to 1855, his writings were not widely known outside Denmark until the end of the nineteenth century. As these works were translated, Kierkegaard became increasingly influential, both directly and indirectly through his impact on people such as Heidegger. Much of his influence stemmed from devastating criticisms of nineteenth-century liberal Protestant thought.

Kierkegaard was a Christian writer who saw himself as a kind of missionary, whose task was to 'reintroduce Christianity into Christendom' (1967,

vol. 1: 160). He believed that the established churches of Europe had departed from genuine Christianity, which required a risky commitment to and willingness to suffer with the crucified Christ. These churches had instead developed a complacent religion that identified Christian faith with conventional ethical virtue. Kierkegaard felt that what was needed was the abolition of 'Christendom', the easy assumption that all born in Christian countries become Christians as a matter of course; Christianity requires a decisive commitment on the part of the individual. Kierkegaard believed that the rationalistic theologies that had come out of the Enlightenment provided a justification for 'Christendom' because of their underlying optimistic view of human nature. Such theologies assumed that humans had a natural capacity to gain religious truth on their own, and so the necessity of historical revelation as the foundation of faith was eliminated. They also de-emphasized human sinfulness by a tendency to reduce the religious life to a form of morality.

KANT (§11), for example, had attempted to develop a 'religion within the limits of reason alone', in which the essential tenets of Christian faith, a pure moral religion, could be derived from practical reason. HEGEL (§8) had constructed a philosophical system in which the content of Christianity was supposedly justified by being philosophically developed and articulated. SCHLEIERMACHER (§7) had developed a theology in which the general religious experience of dependence became the foundation of faith. Though all of these thinkers attempted to find some continued role for historical revelation, the truth of any such revelation was for them something to be vindicated by showing that the revelation was in agreement with the conclusions of critical reflection. Revelation was thus subordinated to reason. In contrast, Kierkegaard attempted to make the categories of faith and revelation once again central for religious understanding.

2 Insights of Kierkegaard and other nineteenth-century thinkers

In *Fear and Trembling* (1843), Kierkegaard tries to show that the life of faith, exemplified for both Jews and Christians by Abraham, cannot be understood solely in ethical terms, since Abraham's faith was shown by an action that could not be ethically justified, namely his willingness to obey God by sacrificing his son Isaac. In *Philosophical Fragments* (1844), he goes on to argue that the 'Socratic' assumption that humans can achieve religious truth on their own is incompatible with the Christian view that humans are sinners who must be transformed and given the truth by God himself. This perspective is developed further in *Concluding Unscientific Postscript* (1846), in which Kierkegaard describes Christian faith as involving a particular kind of inward passion, or 'subjectivity', that cannot be the result of philosophical reflection. The *Postscript* contains a thoroughgoing critique of the Hegelian claim to have achieved a systematic understanding of the whole of reality; it emphasizes the unfinished, historical character of human existence and the failure of thinking to reach objective certainty on existential concerns. The Hegelian system has difficulties both at the beginning and at the end: it cannot really begin, as it claims, with no presuppositions, because of the situated, interested character of human existence; and it cannot finally be completed, which means that it cannot be a system. A system requires a completeness and finality that human existence does not allow.

Kierkegaard does not deny objective truth; he affirms that reality is a system for God (that is, from God's point of view, reality is a system). When it comes to what he calls essential truth, however, he affirms that this truth can only be achieved by the existing thinker through passionate commitment. The person whose life is qualified by the right kind of 'subjectivity' may be said to be living truly even if that person believes things that are not objectively true. The truth of Christianity, which assumes that humans cannot achieve this kind of subjective truth on their own, is grasped in the passion of faith that is created by God within the person who encounters God in the historical figure of Jesus of Nazareth.

The centre of Christian faith for Kierkegaard is the incarnation. Far from wishing to prove historically that Jesus of Nazareth was God incarnate, Kierkegaard insists that faith does not require objective certainty; in fact, it thrives on the risk generated by objective uncertainty (see FAITH §5). The idea of God becoming incarnate is, to us humans, the absolute paradox; as such it cannot be an object of proof. We come to believe in Christ only when we receive at first hand from him an awareness of our sinfulness and need of revelation. Since the object of faith is paradoxical, it necessarily appears 'absurd' and constitutes a 'possibility of offence' to the sinful self, which insists on holding on to its own autonomy. The believer, however, is not offended. To believers, Christ as the God-man is the truth, the truth that is at the same time 'the way and the life'. Thus, the true Christian does not seek speculatively to understand the incarnation, but to live as a follower of Jesus, who is for the believer both the redeemer and 'the pattern'. The believer must be willing to suffer with Christ and break with the established patterns of the world.

Though Kierkegaard provides the most important

nineteenth-century background for existentialist theology, the figures of DOSTOEVSKII and NIETZSCHE also deserve mention. Though independent of Kierkegaard, both emphasize the idea that human thinking is passionate and interested rather than completely objective and disinterested, and both emphasize the ways in which the universe does not appear to make sense to existing human beings. In *Notes from Underground* (1864), Dostoevskii highlights the way in which choice, even irrational choice, preserves our individuality and humanity, and in *The Brothers Karamazov* (1879–80), he powerfully presents the ways in which human suffering and evil seem to make no sense in a world God has created. Yet in such an ambiguous world our freedom is preserved, a freedom which God honours by approaching us in the humble figure of Christ.

Nietzsche not only emphasizes the interested character of human thought, but provides a challenge for theology by reinterpreting Christian morality as a morality of weakness, based on resentment and envy. He challenges the Christian to examine the unconscious motives that may lie beneath what is presented as Christian love, and poses the question as to whether God is a threat to human freedom and autonomy.

3 Twentieth-century existentialist theologians

Karl BARTH (1886–1968) is both the earliest and the most influential of twentieth-century theologians indebted to existential thought. Barth's first major work, a commentary on Romans (1919), was forged in the disillusionment created by the First World War and clearly shows the influence of Kierkegaard and Dostoevskii. In this work, Barth challenged the optimism of liberal Protestant thought by attacking its assumptions that human beings could develop a natural knowledge of God and that Christianity could be vindicated as a higher evolutionary stage in the natural development of such knowledge.

Barth stressed instead the 'infinite qualitative difference' between a God who is 'wholly other' and human beings. The knowledge of God cannot be achieved through human religious experience, but is completely dependent on God's self-revelation. This revelation can be given no philosophical foundation, but is understood as true in the existential situation in which human beings encounter God. The Church must listen to the word of the living God, before whom human religious systems and institutions are judged and found wanting.

Barth's emphasis on the transcendence of God won great respect because of his opposition to the Nazi attempt to give a theological justification of their racist and nationalist policies. Barth clearly saw the idolatrous character of National Socialism and became a leading figure in the protest of the Confessing Church. He largely authored the 'Barmen Declaration' (1934), which argued strongly that the lordship of Christ over the state must be acknowledged and that Nazi ideology must be judged in the light of God's transcendent revelation.

In his later writings, notably the massive *Church Dogmatics* (1939–67), which occupied most of the rest of Barth's life, there is a movement away from any overt reliance on Kierkegaard or other existentialist thinkers. In his later work, Barth emphasizes not only the 'no' that God pronounces against autonomous human religious and political striving, but the 'yes' that God graciously grants in Christ. All of the classic Christian doctrines are reinterpreted in a Christocentric manner, since the eternal Word of God has become incarnate in Jesus of Nazareth. That Word is still seen as a call to decision and commitment.

Rudolf BULTMANN (1884–1976) was linked to Barth early on, but the two quickly distanced themselves from each other. Bultmann is equally renowned as a theologian and New Testament scholar, and his theological work reflects his insights as an inventor of form criticism, a discipline that studies the New Testament in the light of the situation of the early Church. Bultmann agreed with Barth that the 'quest for the historical Jesus' carried on by liberal Protestantism had failed to provide a foundation for faith, and that it was imperative to hear again the message of God as proclaimed by the Church. Unlike Barth, however, he saw the need for a radical translation of the message of the New Testament if it was to be heard by twentieth-century people.

As Bultmann saw it, the New Testament message is presented in mythical language that reflects the prescientific cosmology of the day. That message must be demythologized if it is to be meaningful to contemporary persons, and the key to this reinterpretation is provided by the analysis of human existence found in the early writings of Martin Heidegger. When the New Testament is read in this way, the offer of salvation is understood as an offer of a new form of authentic existence. Human persons must face the limits of human existence, especially their own death, without fleeing to some form of inauthenticity in which their being is identified with some objective entity in the world. Instead, humans must recognize that their authentic being lies in possibility, in their potentiality-to-be. In a way that is not completely clear, even to many of Bultmann's followers, this form of authentic existence is offered to humans in the historical figure of Jesus of Nazareth. History must here be understood as meaningful

narrative (*Geschichte*), rather than as 'what actually happened', the object of scholarly investigation (*Historie*). What is important about Jesus is the 'historic' significance of the narrative, its meaning for the individual facing a decision, not the 'historical' (factual) accuracy of the narrative, regarding which Bultmann takes a critical, sceptical view.

Paul TILLICH (1886–1965) differs from both Barth and Bultmann in being less tied to biblical exegesis and more overtly engaged in philosophical reflection. Tillich practised what he termed a 'method of correlation', in which the questions posed by human existence philosophically interpreted and the answers provided by religious revelation (also philosophically interpreted) were to be understood as mutually illuminating. In his analysis, God is understood as 'being-itself' or 'the ground of being' rather than as a supernatural being. The modern religious task in the West is to discover the power of being-itself, to find the 'God above the God of theism'. It is the 'God above the God of theism' who appears when the traditional God, understood as a distinct personal being, has died.

Tillich reflects the concerns of Nietzsche, Sartre and other existentialists that the traditional God of theism would limit human freedom and autonomy. The human task is therefore to confront a world of meaninglessness and discover 'the courage to be', the power that allows us to accept ourselves even when there is no personal God who accepts us.

For Tillich, the power of being-itself is mediated through 'symbols' that are said to participate in the power of being. For Christians, the story of Jesus can be such a symbol, but Tillich does not claim that the Christian symbols are unique or universal, and their truth does not lie in depicting the way things are objectively. The power of a symbol depends partly on the ability of a community for which that symbol functions to perceive that power.

4   Critical problems and lasting contributions

The diversity of views found in existentialist theology demonstrates that it cannot be defined in terms of particular conclusions. In relation to Christianity, it is useful to distinguish between thinkers such as Kierkegaard and Barth, who reformulated Christian themes to show their relevance to the human predicament, from those such as Bultmann and Tillich, who use Christian language to present 'existentialist' views radically different from traditional religious faith. Kierkegaard and Barth use new thought-forms creatively to express and make sense of classical religious convictions, while Bultmann and

Tillich use traditional language to express very nontraditional views.

While some would argue that such theologies simply reflect the cultural and political situation of twentieth-century Europe, the attempt to relate religious concerns to the human existential predicament cannot be dismissed so easily. Existentialist theology reflects the perennial encounter between philosophical reflection and religious commitment and illustrates the power of each to shape the other. The existentialist theologian challenges the philosopher by highlighting the 'interested' character of human thinking, while the philosopher challenges the theologian to make sense of religious commitments in the light of all that humans know and experience.

See also: BERDIAEV, N.A.; BRUNNER, E.; BUBER, M.; EXISTENTIALISM; EXISTENTIALIST ETHICS

References and further reading

* Barth, K. (1919) *The Epistle to the Romans*, trans. E.C. Hoskyn, Oxford: Oxford University Press, 1933. (A translation of the sixth edition. This work shattered classical liberal theology and initiated existential or 'dialectical' theology in twentieth-century Europe.)
* —— (1934) 'The Barmen Theological Declaration', trans. D.S. Bax, in E. Jungel (ed.) *Christ, Justice and Peace*, Edinburgh, T. & T. Clark, 1992. (Issued by the German Evangelical Church, this strongly repudiated the Nazi attempt to justify their programme on theological grounds.)
* —— (1939–67) *Church Dogmatics*, trans. and ed. G.W. Bromiley and T.F. Torrance, Edinburgh: T. & T. Clark, 1956–69. (In four volumes, with each volume published in several books. This is Barth's *magnum opus*, arguably the most significant work of systematic theology of the twentieth century.)
Brunner, E. (1937) *Man in Revolt*, trans. O. Wyon, London: Lutterworth, 1939. (Provides a theology of the human person heavily shaped by existential philosophy.)
Bultmann, R. (1957) *History and Eschatology*, Edinburgh: Edinburgh University Press. (Develops the distinction between what is historic as existentially meaningful and what is merely historical in the sense of being the object of historical science.)
—— (1984) *New Testament and Mythology*, trans. and ed. S. Ogden, Philadelphia, PA: Fortress Press. (A collection of some of Bultmann's most important writings.)
* Dostoevskii, F. (1864) *Notes from Underground*, trans. A.R. MacAndrew, New York: New American Library, 1961. (This volume also contains *White Nights, The Dream of a Ridiculous Man* and selections from *The House of the Dead*.)
* —— (1879–80) *The Brothers Karamazov*, trans. D. Magarshack, London: Folio Society, 1964. (A rich and complex novel that resists any brief summation, but deals with the conflict between faith and unbelief, the anxieties linked to freedom, and whether it is true that 'if God does not exist, then everything is permitted'.)
* Kierkegaard, S. (1843) *Fear and Trembling*, trans. H.V. Hong and E.H. Hong, Princeton, NJ: Princeton University Press, 1983. (Kierkegaard's argument that faith is not reducible to morality, developed through reflection on the story of Abraham and Isaac. This edition also includes his *Repetition* of the same year.)
* —— (1844) *Philosophical Fragments*, trans. H.V. Hong and E.H. Hong, Princeton, NJ: Princeton University Press, 1985. (Develops the idea of the incarnation as the absolute paradox that must be accepted through faith received directly from God.)
* —— (1846) *Concluding Unscientific Postscript*, trans. H.V. Hong and E.H. Hong, Princeton, NJ: Princeton University Press, 1992. (Kierkegaard's philosophical critique of Hegel, with the development of his own analysis of human existence.)
* —— (1967) *Journals and Papers*, trans. and ed. H.V. Hong and E.H. Hong, Bloomington, IN: Indiana University Press. (Entry 388 contains the famous phrase about reintroducing Christianity into Christendom, although the idea is present in many places in Kierkegaard's writings.)
Tillich, P. (1951–63) *Systematic Theology*, Chicago, IL: University of Chicago Press. (A three-volume comprehensive statement of Tillich's theological views.)
—— (1952) *The Courage to Be*, New Haven, CT: Yale University Press. (Connects religious faith to a form of courage that struggles with meaninglessness and despair.)
—— (1957) *The Dynamics of Faith*, New York: Harper & Rowe. (Looks at faith from the viewpoint of existential philosophy and psychology.)

C. STEPHEN EVANS

EXISTENTIALIST THOUGHT IN LATIN AMERICA

In Latin America the thought and teaching of José Ortega y Gasset have been very influential. Their influence leaves an important mark on the substance of existentialism. The most effective aspect of Ortega y

Gasset's philosophical conception was his thesis that humans do not have a nature, only a history. It is this concept that encouraged Latin American thinkers to create their own original thought as a product of their concrete historical circumstances. This entry will deal with Latin American existence, unique in its historical concreteness, and from this general view will attempt to construct a metaphysical theory of Latin America's historical endeavour.

Given that all historicist conception involves values that are objective in nature, it is not surprising that Latin American existentialism was profoundly influenced by Max Scheler and Nicolai Hartmann, together with the existential analysis of Martin Heidegger. Consequently, in opposition to the phenomenologists with a Husserlian orientation, implicit in Latin American existentialism, there is a phenomenological methodology in the interpretation of history as culture in accordance with the analysis of the dialectics of the structure of history. This opposes all possible perceptions of pure essences which might precede existence. The essence of existence is seen as progressive, constructing itself as it is bypassed by historical events.

Both in terms of the search for an original philosophy, which could be reduced to a philosophy of history (for example in the Orteguian philosophy of life) and in terms of a Heideggerian approach, Latin American philosophy applies a phenomenological method in its analysis. This would explain the fusion of phenomenology and existentialism in the works of Latin American philosophers. All Latin American phenomenological-existentialist philosophical effort is a struggle between the analysis and interpretation of the European currents and their search for the historical realization of the autonomous Latin American being.

1   **Existentialism and literature**
2   **Relevant thinkers: Argentina**
3   **Relevant thinkers: Brazil**
4   **Relevant thinkers: Mexico**
5   **Relevant thinkers: Peru**
6   **Relevant thinkers: Venezuela**

1   Existentialism and literature

Existentialist thought centres its philosophical speculation around concrete human existence, focusing on lived experiences, or *Erlebnisse*, and emphasizing the freedom of choice and the subsequent responsibility of the human being as self, or *être-en-soi*. The statement given by Jean-Paul SARTRE that man is condemned to be free implies the necessity of 'engagement' with one's own life project. Because of these principles, many existentialist thinkers chose literature as a vehicle through which they could better express the search for the authentic self. This choice often caused some confusion between philosophy and literature, for example in the work of Sartre and Miguel DE UNAMUNO, the latter undoubtedly the precursor of the trend of thought that can be identified as strictly existentialist. In fact, novelist and thinker, de Unamuno, coined the definition 'El hombre de carne y hueso' (the man of flesh and bone).

In Latin America, the existentialist search for authenticity was similar to the quest for an authentic national identity. Specific examples can be found in Puerto Rico, with its special political situation and the continuous intellectual struggle to defend Puerto Rican and Latin American culture in its development as Hispanic culture, set against North American culture, which is held to be alien and imposed on Puerto Rico by colonial imperialism. Hence, the existentialist vision of both humanity and life has been influential for writers, such as Edelmira González Maldonado (1923–) and Emilio Díaz Valcárcel (1929–).

González Maldonado is a well-known and well-respected short story writer, although her literary work is not very extensive. Her most important short story collections include, *Crisis* (1973), *Soledumbre* (Solitude) (1976) and *Alucinaciones* (Hallucinations) (1981). Her literary work has focused on the themes of humankind's loneliness and the limitations and ambiguities of language and the problem of interpretation between speaker and listener.

Crisis (1973) was the first attempt to express the concept and feeling of existentialist anguish. Argentine thinker Angel Casares who wrote the prologue for the book states: 'This book is, then, a piece of life, a life'. The title of *Soledumbre* is the deliberate use of an ancient word meaning both solitude and remoteness. *Soledumbre* is clearly an existentialist writing as it focuses on the concrete *hic et nunc*, the space and time of the literary work of art. Vital space and time are set against radical loneliness representing the horizon of the self. One of González Maldonado's short stories (1976), whose title is a quote from Martin HEIDEGGER's *Unterwegs zur Sprache* (On the Way to Language) (1959), *Die Sprache spracht* (language speaks), shows with its play on words, the impossibility of communication between human beings and establishes the dark dimension of existentialism. This dimension is the alienation which occurs with the loss of self and identity and the way in which the quality of being unique and authentic is lost within humdrum existence. In *Alucinaciones* (Hallucinations) (1981) the writer searches for the solution to metaphysical anguish in the realm of dazzling fantasy.

Emilio Díaz Valcárcel felt a deep commitment to

his country and its problematic future. Díaz Valcárcel believed that the solution must begin with the construction of the self as a Puerto Rican Latin American, although he considered that Puerto Rican writers such as himself are trapped in the gap between cultural and national identity and political identity. His most important novel with the striking title of *Figuraciones en el mes de marzo* (Representations in the month of March) (1972), is considered to rank alongside the works of García Márquez, Fuentes and Vargas Llosa. In this novel the protagonist, a mask for the author himself, struggles with two of the most significant existentialist concepts: freedom and authenticity. He is incapable of accomplishing the task of the construction of the self and is dominated by feelings of solitude and impotence in the face of his existence. He escapes by entering a realm of strange and often frightening fantasy in which he is persecuted by something monstrous, bizarre and terrible. He tries to maintain the ties that bind him to his country and his family, but the conflict between dreams, patriotism, love and the necessity of writing drive him towards a fantasmagoric fantasy, the parody of literature, and worse, solipsism. At this point, his writing falls into the existentialist black abyss of nothingness.

2 Relevant thinkers: Argentina

Carlos Astrada (1894–1970) used the ontology of Heidegger as a starting point and addressed many Marxist issues. He centred his thought on the idea of the risk implied by all metaphysical speculation. The game unleashes its own process within an existential scope. Astrada (1942) concerned himself with certain structures which were not thoroughly developed in the work of Heidegger, such as, the concrete composition of the 'Dasein' (being-here) and the relation of the 'Dasein' to things, before moving towards the Marxist dialectic in the latter stages of writing (1970).

Jorge Casares was professor at the University of Buenos Aires from 1953 to 1964 and after moved to the University of Puerto Rico. Mostly concerned with Heidegger, he emphasized three fundamental points in Heideggerian metaphysics: the loss of being as domination of thought, being in its totality and the loss by and for humans of their essence. These three points, tied in with other existentialist themes, are thoroughly explored in his work *Sobre la esencia del hombre* (On the Essence of Man) (1979).

Vicente Fatone (1903–62) was professor of cosmology and metaphysics at the National University of Litoral and of the history of religion at the National University of La Plata. He mostly concerned himself with the mystical experience and philosophical

thought in India. He focused on the theme of liberty, which he interpreted from different existentialist viewpoints (1952; 1972). Fatone maintained: 'I am nothing but my freedom; but I am not my freedom because I am not: I have to be' (1948: 25). For Fatone, humanity is not free, but creates its own freedom, because liberty is not a property of the human being. It is a condition by virtue of which man becomes man and woman becomes woman. Towards the end of his life, he took up the theme of mysticism again.

Eugenio Pucciarelli's existentialist roots lay in his interest in ontological, historical and aesthetic topics. A student of Alejandro Korn and Francisco Romero he was preoccupied with the sciences of the spirit. He was more distinguished for his teaching than for his written work. He maintained that metaphysical testimony – perception of the a priori conditions that make experience and morality feasible – is perceived through experience and morality.

Ismael Quiles (1958) was professor of philosophy at the University of Buenos Aires. A Jesuit priest, he edited the journal *Ciencia y fe* (Science and Faith) (1944–64). His thought is known as the philosophy of insistence. He was not a strict existentialist, but took advantage of certain Heideggerian concepts featured in *Being and Time* (1927) in his metaphysics of interiority in which humans are fulfilled through the knowledge of the world (be-in), of others (be-with) and of God as the absolute transcendence of all finitude.

Anibal Sánchez Reulet (1910–) wrote extensively on Husserl and Nicolai Hartmann. He followed, in part, Romero's direction and was influenced by Ortega y Gasset. He was interested in the aspiration to transcendence in human existence as an affirmation of freedom through objective value judgments. For Sánchez Reulet this transcendence, in the end, becomes a question of transcending the historical conditions which determine the finitude of existence.

Miguel Angel Virasoro (1900–66) was professor at the University of Buenos Aires and at the Universities of Córdoba, Bahía Blanca and Mendoza. Virasoro (1942) was influenced by Hegel and later, Heidegger. His work was thus an existentialist synthesis of Hegelian dialectics (1957). His starting point was the intuition of the finitude in the concreteness of existence (see ARGENTINA, PHILOSOPHY IN).

3 Relevant thinkers: Brazil

Gerd A. Bornheim is not very well known internationally. He distinguished himself among scholars of existentialism in Brazil with *Sartre: metafisica e existencialismo (Sartre: Metaphysics and Existentialism)* (1971). He dealt with problems of an ontological nature and, to a certain degree, reaffirmed Hegelian ontology. He showed deep insight in unravelling the metaphysical aspect of Sartre's thought as he tried to expose the metaphysical underpinnings of the phenomenon of being.

Euryalo Cannabrava (1908–91), like many other Latin American thinkers, was attracted by the phenomenological-existentialist movement. He drifted towards logical neopositivism as he was interested in the philosophy of language and in the attempt to reduce philosophy to a method. His most important existential writings were *Descartes e Bergson* (Descartes and Bergson) (1938) and *Seis temas de espírito moderno* (Six Themes of Modern Spirit) (1941). In *Descartes e Bergson*, he attempted to surpass rationalism and vitalism. In 1956 he published *Elementos de metodología filosófica* (Elements of Philosophical Methodology) in which he revealed his increasing distance from Heidegger.

Vicente Ferreira da Silva's philosophical endeavours raised consciousness about the need for philosophizing in Brazil. He was one of the most important and enthusiastic followers of the existentialist movement. He wrote *Ensaios filosóficos* (Philosophical Essays) (1964) (see BRAZIL, PHILOSOPHY IN).

4   Relevant thinkers: Mexico

Adolfo Menéndez y Samara (1908–54) was deeply influenced by Heidegger and his question of being and its constant emergence from nothingness. In his youth he wrote *Dos ensayos sobre Heidegger* (Two Essays on Heidegger) (1939), which reveals a preoccupation with ontology. His early death did not allow the metaphysical-existentialist aspect of his work to develop fully.

José Romano Muñoz (1953) was one of the first disseminators of Orteguian thought in Hispanic America. His principal preoccupation was with finding answers to the questions of those who are more interested in wisdom than in science, such as: Who are we? What role do we play in the world? What is our fate? These questions brought him to the field of ethics which became his major preoccupation under the influence of Max Scheler and Nicolai Hartmann. His book, *Hacia una filosofía existencial: al margen de la nada, de la muerte y de la náusea metafísica* (Towards an Existential Philosophy: at the Edge of Nothingness, Death and Metaphysical Nausea) (1953) had a strictly existentialist perspective.

José Sánchez Villaseñor (1950) was a Catholic thinker, who worked on the thought of Sartre from a critical perspective, particularly with respect to the assertion of the absurd nature of existence. He was also a critic of the thought of Ortega y Gasset (1949) (see MEXICO, PHILOSOPHY IN).

5   Relevant thinkers: Peru

Luis Felipe Alarco was a student of Alejandro Deústua (1849–1945), professor of philosophy at the University of San Marcos, Lima. Deústua (1967) defended a philosophy of creative freedom in which liberty is the basis of all social and moral values. Alarco is considered to be the initiator and catalyst of the philosophical movement in Peru. He was principally interested in the thought of Nicolai Hartmann. His inclination towards the philosophy of Hartmann was owing to his interest in overcoming the propaedeutic character of Heideggerian phenomenological analysis. His three most representative writings are *Nicolai Hartmann y la idea de la metafísica* (Nicolai Hartmann and the Idea of Metaphysics) (1943), *Lecciones de metafísica* (Lessons in Metaphysics) (1947) and *Ensayos de filosofía prima* (Essays on Prime Philosophy) (1951).

Alberto Wagner de Reyna (1939) studied in Berlin with Nicolai Hartmann and in Freiburg with Heidegger. His first work focused on the thought of Heidegger. Later, in an approximation to Gabriel Marcel (1889–1973), he became interested in several existentialist themes, including the priority of existence over essence and commitment and engagement in one's own historical reality, that were useful to Catholic thought. He was one of the first to propagate the thought of Heidegger in Hispanic America. He focused his attention on themes that are typically Heideggerian such as death and care. He attempted to demonstrate that existential analysis meant to clarify beings as such and that temporality is the ontological condition of human existence.

6   Relevant thinkers: Venezuela

Ernesto Mayz Vallenilla (1925–) is a phenomenologist who deals with existentialist thought (1966), influenced by Dilthey and Heidegger. One of the themes that has interested him most is technology as a means of overcoming the finitude imposed by nothingness from a temporal perspective. For Mayz Vallenilla, technology has an ontological foundation in its utility, one of the ingredients of existence according to Heidegger, but also in the will to dominate.

See also: EXISTENTIALISM; HEIDEGGER, M.; HUSSERL, E.; LITERATURE, PHILOSOPHY IN LATIN AMERICAN; ORTEGA Y GASSET, J.; PHENOMENOLOGY IN LATIN AMERICA

References and further reading

* Alarco, L.-F. (1943) *Nicolai Hartmann y la idea de la metafísica* (Nicolai Hartmann and the Idea of Metaphysics), Lima: Librería e Imprenta D. Miranda. (Alarco tries to overcome the propaedeutic character of Heideggerian phenomenology.)
* —— (1947) *Lecciones de metafísica* (Lessons in Metaphysics), Lima: Universidad Nacional Mayor de San Marcos, 4th edn, 1965. (A description of Alarco's view of metaphysics.)
* —— (1951) *Ensayos de filosofía prima (Essays on Prime Philosophy)*, Lima: Imprenta Santa María. (An overview of philosophy by the the initiator of the philosophical movement in Peru.)
* Astrada, C. (1942) *El juego metafísico (para una filosofía de la finitud)* (The Metaphysical Game (for a Philosophy of Finitude)), Buenos Aires: El Ateneo. (Astrada concerns himself with certain structures which were not thoroughly developed in the work of Heidegger.)
  —— (1970) *Martin Heidegger: de la analítica ontológica a la dimensión dialéctica* (Martin Heidegger: From Analytical Ontology to the Dialectical Dimension), Buenos Aires: Juárez Editor. (Includes bibliographical references to all the works of Heidegger.)
* Bornheim, G.A. (1971) *Sartre: metafísica e existencialismo* (Sartre: Metaphysics and Existentialism), São Paulo: Editora Perspectiva. (A distinguished work among scholars of existentialism in Brazil.)
* Cannabrava, E. (1938) *Descartes e Bergson* (Descartes and Bergson), São Paulo: Amigos de Livro. (His most important existential work.)
* —— (1941) *Seis temas do espírito moderno* (Six Themes of Modern Spirit), São Paulo: S.E. Panorama. (Another important work in the area of existentialism.)
* —— (1956) *Elementos de metodología filosófica* (Elements of Philosophical Methodology), São Paulo: Companhia Editora Nacional. (Cannabrava establishes his distance from Heidegger.)
* Casares, J. (1979) *Sobre la esencia del hombre* (On the Essence of Man), Rio Piedras: Editorial de la Universidad de Puerto Rico. (Concerned with Heideggerian metaphysics.)
* Deústua, A. (1967) *Ensayos escogidos de filosofía y educación nacional* (Selected Essays on Philosophy and National Education), Huancayo: Concejo Provincial De Huancayo, Inspección de Cultura. (Defends a philosophy of creative freedom.)
* Díaz Valcárcel, E. (1972) *Figuraciones en el mes de marzo* (Representations in the month of March), Barcelona: Seix Barral. (A novel which ranks alongside the works of García Márquez.)
* Fatone, V. (1948) *El existencialismo y la libertad creadora: una crítica al existencialismo de Jean-Paul Sartre* (Existentialism and Creative Freedom: a Critique of the Existentialism of Jean-Paul Sartre), Buenos Aires: Argos. (A discussion opposing the views of Sartre.)
* —— (1952) *Introducción al existencialismo* (Introduction to Existentialism), Buenos Aires: Columba. (A general introduction to his own views of existentialism.)
* —— (1972) La existencia humana y sus filósofos (Human Existence and its Philosophers), in *Obras completas* (Complete Works), Buenos Aires: Editorial Sudamericana. (A discussion of the view that humanity is not free, but creates its own freedom.)
* Ferreira da Silva, V. (1964) *Ensaios filosóficos* (Philosophical Essays), in *Obras Completas* (Complete Works), São Paulo: Instituto Brasileiro de Filosofia. (Ferreira da Silva attempts to raise consciousness about the need for philosophizing in Brazil.)
* González Maldonado (1973) *Crisis*, Río Piedros: Edil. (Expresses the concept and feeling of existentialist anguish.)
* —— (1976) *Soledumbre* (Solitude), San Juan: Instituto de Cultura Puertorriqueña. (A novel which focuses on the space and time of the literary work of art.)
* —— (1981) *Alucinaciones* (Hallucinations), San Juan: Instituto de Cultura Puertorriqueña. (A novel in which the writer searches for the solution to metaphysical anguish.)
* Heidegger, M. (1927) 'Sein und Zeit', *Jahrbuch für Philosophie und phänomenologische Forschung* 8: 1–438; *Sein und Zeit*, Halle an der Salle: Max Niemeyer; trans. J. Macquarrie and E. Robinson, *Being and Time*, New York: Harper & Row, 1962; trans. J. Stambaugh *Being and Time*, Albany, NY: State University of New York Press, 1996. (Heidegger's most famous work. The unpublished second half of the work was to have shown that the meaning of being is time.)
* Mayz Vallenilla, E. (1966) *Del hombre y su aliencación* (Of Man and his Alienation), Venezuela: Instituto Nacional de Cultura y Bellas Artes. (Existentialism and alienation are discussed.)
* Menéndez y Samara, A. (1939) *Dos ensayos sobre Heidegger* (Two Essays on Heidegger), Mexico: Letras de México. (Reveals a preoccupation with ontology.)
* Quiles, I. (1958) *Más allá del existencialismo (filosofía in-sistencial: una filosofía del ser y dignidad del hombre)* (Beyond Existentialism (In-sistential Philosophy: a Philosophy of the Being and the

Dignity of Man)), Barcelona: Luis Miracle. (Influenced by Heideggerian concepts.)

* Romano Muñoz, J. (1953) *Hacia una filosofía existencial: al margen de la nada, de la muerte y de la náusea metafísica* (Towards an Existential Philosophy: at the Edge of Nothingness, Death and Metaphysical Nausea), Mexico: Imprenta Universitaria. (A strictly existentialist perspective.)

Sánchez-Reulet, A. (ed.) (1954) *Contemporary Latin American Philosophy: a Selection, with an Introduction and Notes*, trans. W.R. Trask, Albuquerque: University of New Mexico Press. (An anthology of Latin American existentialist thought.)

* Sánchez Villaseñor, J. (1949) *Ortega y Gasset, existencialista: un estudio crítico de su pensamiento y sus fuentes* (Ortega y Gasset, Existentialist: A Critical Study of his Thought and its Sources), Chicago, IL: H. Regnery Co. (An extensive study of Ortega y Gasset.)

* —— (1950) *Introducción al pensamiento de Jean-Paul Sartre* (Introduction to the Thought of Jean-Paul Sartre), Mexico: Editorial Jus. (Wrote about Sartre from a critical perspective.)

* Virasoro, M.A. (1942) *La libertad, la existencia y el ser* (Freedom, Existence and Being), Buenos Aires: Imprenta López. (His starting point was the intuition of the finitude in the concreteness of existence.)

* —— (1957) *Existencialismo y moral: Heidegger–Sartre* (Existentialism and Morality: Heidegger–Sartre), Sante Fe, NM: Librería y Editorial Castellvi. (An existentialist synthesis of Hegelian dialectics.)

* Wagner De Reyna, A. (1939) *La ontología fundamental de Heidegger: su motivo y significación* (The Fundamental Ontology of Heidegger: its Motivation and Meaning), Buenos Aires: Editorial Losada, repr. 1945. (The author's first work.)

MARÍA TERESA BERTELLONI

EXPERIMENT

Experiment, as a specific category of scientific activity, did not emerge until the Scientific Revolution of the seventeenth century. Seen primarily as an arbiter in theory choice, there was little, if any, analysis of experimental techniques or, the ways in which data become transformed into established facts. Philosophical analysis of experiment was typically simplistic, focusing on the role of observation alone as the foundation for experimental facts. This was challenged by Thomas Kuhn who stressed the importance of background theory and beliefs in all perception, including (its role in) scientific experiment. This interconnection between theory and experiment severely undermined the idea that experiment could stand as an independent and objective criterion for judging the merits of one theory over another.

In the 1980s new philosophical analyses of experiment began to emerge, emphasizing the ways in which experiment could be seen to have a life of its own embodying activities that could supposedly be understood without recourse to theory. Factors important in the evaluation of experimental results as well as the ways in which laboratory science differs from its theoretical counterpart became the focus for a new history and philosophy of experiment. Consequently, further debates arose regarding the relationship of experiment to theory, and whether it is possible to provide a methodological framework within which experimental practice can be evaluated.

1 **Historical overview**
2 **Experiment as distinct but subordinate**
3 **The rise of experimentalism**

1 Historical overview

Although the use of trial and error methods to establish scientific results can be traced back to the Greeks, experiment as a specific category of scientific activity did not emerge until the Scientific Revolution of the seventeenth century. This occurred partly in response to the development of precision instruments like the telescope, microscope and pendulum clock, but also as a result of the growth of scientific academies that provided laboratory environments. Galileo's work on hydrostatics was perhaps the first instance of what we now think of as the experimental method. He showed how experiments on bodies floating in water could be used to confirm Archimedes' principles and refute those of Aristotle. Francis Bacon was the first to provide a classification for various kinds of experiment including the concept of a crucial experiment, which came to be thought of as a decisive test of one theory over its rival (see CRUCIAL EXPERIMENTS).

Even though experimental demonstration was an important component of the Scientific Revolution its primary function was thought to be that of an arbiter in theory choice. There was little, if any, analysis of experimental techniques. Issues about the epistemic status of experiment were typically assimilated to debates about the nature of experience in general. Emphasis on experiment was associated with empiricism; consequently, not everyone saw experiment as the foundation for scientific knowledge. Descartes, for example, relied heavily on experiment in his scientific work; yet in his philosophical writings deduction from first principles or innate ideas took precedence over empirical inquiry as the ultimate ground for knowledge.

2 Experiment as distinct but subordinate

Although experiment occupied a role distinct from theory, at least in historical and philosophical writing on science, theory continued to hold the dominant position. Even the most respected physicists, such as James Clerk Maxwell and Albert Einstein, devoted little if any attention to experiment in their writings about science (even though Maxwell was a gifted experimenter and Einstein emphasized the role of thought experiments in the development of relativity theory (see THOUGHT EXPERIMENTS). Philosophical and historical accounts focused either on crucial experiments, such as Fresnel's diffraction experiments which decided in favour of the wave over the corpuscular theory of light (see OPTICS §1), or experiments that were associated with important discoveries, for instance those that led Roentgen to the discovery of X-rays, or Millikan's measurements of the charge on the electron.

Although these kinds of experiment were discussed in articles and textbooks, much of the intricate detail that represents such an important part of experimental work, detail that is extracted from notebooks and investigations of laboratory practices, was excluded. As a result, the experiments were characterized in a highly idealized way, embodying none of the difficulties often encountered by working scientists in establishing specific results.

Philosophical analysis of experiment also presented a simplistic view of its function and its relationship to theory. Twentieth-century positivism (or logical empiricism) emphasized the importance of observation as the secure foundation for science, but provided no analysis of experiment itself. Nor did it question the authority of observational reports. For the positivists, the meaning of a particular term was its method of verification, and many considered simple observation reports entered in a log book or protocol to be the ultimate basis of science (see MEANING AND VERIFICATION; THEORIES, SCIENTIFIC §§1–2; LOGICAL POSITIVISM §4). Because all of science had to be understood in terms of empirical concepts, experimental procedures were sometimes appealed to as providing meanings for theoretical terms. One way of doing this was to identify terms like 'electric force', which is not empirically observable, specifically the operations necessary to measure the force, with the instrument or pointer readings that indicated its presence. This particular method of assigning mean-

ings or values to scientific concepts was known as operationalism (see OPERATIONALISM). Despite the importance of testability and observation reports for establishing meaning there was no analysis of how experimental results and procedures became stabilized and validated.

The emphasis on definitive observational reports was challenged most influentially by Thomas KUHN in *The Structure of Scientific Revolutions* (1962) (see also HANSON, N.R.; POPPER, K.R.). He argued that not only scientific experiments but also the interpretation of all experience was heavily dependent on background theoretical knowledge (see OBSERVATION §§3–4). Kuhn's thesis, known as the theory-ladenness of observation, entails that two individuals, such as Kepler and Tycho Brahe, who hold different theories about the sun literally see different things when they observe it. One of them sees a stationary body around which the earth moves while the other sees a moving body rotating around the earth. As a result neither simple experience nor experiments (including crucial experiments) can provide a neutral ground for theory choice. The analysis of experiment that Kuhn provides is really an account of how psychological factors influence perception. Consequently, theory becomes the focal point from which the interpretation and relevance of all experimental data is assessed.

In response to theory-ladeness, sociologists of science denied that appeals to nature in the form of experiment were ever decisive in deciding between competing theories. Such decisions, and even the interpretation of data, were made simply on the basis of social and political factors that often stood outside the laboratory domain. Philosophers responded by accepting that observation was theory-laden while maintaining that those theories nevertheless corresponded to a determinate world, which, if characterized correctly, would reveal its true nature.

3 The rise of experimentalism

The emphasis on experiment as a distinct field of philosophical inquiry began with the work of Ian Hacking (1983). He urged philosophers to focus on activities like the building and operation of instruments, calculation and measurement, the creation of phenomena and manipulation of entities in the laboratory, all of which are part of an experimental culture that is distinct from the theoretician's world and from questions that have traditionally dominated philosophy. As a result, a new set of philosophical issues arose: for example, how should we characterize the relationship of experiment to theory in light of Hacking's claim that 'experiment has a life of its own'; is there a methodology of experiment that can furnish validating procedures and constraints for evaluating results; and how do the credibility of particular instruments and the theories implicit in their operation bear on the integrity of laboratory events?

Hacking stressed the independence from theory of various aspects of experimental practice, such as viewing and manipulating microscopic images and specimens, the manipulation of entities such as electrons using electron guns, and the creation of particles in accelerators. He claimed that most of these images and entities are robust and survive even radical theory change. Knowledge of them derives from their low-level causal properties (for example, mass, charge, and so on) that are involved in the design and operation of devices used to measure, observe and create them. However, it is not simply the fact that these entities can be experimented on that attests to their reality; they must be capable of being manipulated and used as tools in the investigation of other aspects of nature, not simply observed or detected in the laboratory. Hence, the goal is not just understanding the nature of these entities, but using them to transform nature. As Hacking (1983) remarked about electrons – 'If you can spray them then they are real'.

Despite the importance of isolating experimental practice in this way, questions have arisen concerning the interplay of experiment and theory and whether Hacking's reliance on manipulation can underwrite the realistic status of experimental entities. A much greater theory than that of low-level causal generalization is needed to differentiate, for example, between specific kinds of particle interactions that take place, even in a straightforward case like the identification of a particle in a cloud chamber. In this context one must appeal to a scaffolding of theoretical knowledge that comes from electrodynamics, mechanics and so on, in order to distinguish an electron from a negatively charged pion. Similarly, when a beam is produced using a simple ruby laser, the apparatus utilizes causal properties such as the mass and charge of the electron, but in order to understand simulated emission, the very basis of laser action, we need the quantum theory of the electron. A great deal of theory, over and above the theory about how the apparatus produces the beam, is required before one can meaningfully say that one is producing laser light by the manipulation of electrons.

In addition to simply describing the activity of manipulating particles, interpretive controversies often arise in cases where different groups evaluate experimental results and practices in different ways. Experiments done in the late 1970s to investigate the existence of charmed quarks involved photon, neutrino and hadron beams. One group of physicists thought that quarks were the constituents of hadrons, and that, in that sense, quarks were being manipulated in order to investigate charm. Another group, who thought quarks were merely fictional entities that provided a mathematical description of hadron collisions, saw the manipulation of the beams as having nothing to do with quarks; still another group with a different account of quarks also had a different interpretation of the practice of manipulating hadron beams.

What the examples show, and indeed what an emphasis on experiment has clarified, is the degree of complexity involved in the relationships among experiments, phenomena, instruments and theories. The idea that an experiment can serve as an independent judge in a theoretical dispute is not necessarily vindicated by showing how experiment has a life distinct from theory. Very often an analysis of experimental work exposes subtle theoretical influences not obviously present in textbook histories. When Heinrich HERTZ successfully produced electromagnetic waves in his laboratory in 1888, it was against the backdrop of competing views about electromagnetism from Maxwell and Helmholtz. The experiment acquired a different meaning and had different implications for British scientists (who saw it as definitive confirmation of Maxwell's electrodynamics) than it did for Hertz. There was no ambiguity about what were produced were electromagnetic waves, but the velocities of the waves contradicted a fundamental component of Maxwell's theory, a result ignored by the British, but which caused Hertz great concern. It was not as though the British could explain away the experimental anomaly, or that Hertz had reasons unknown to the British causing him to distrust his results. Hertz saw the experiments as proving that electrical action is propagated in space rather than at a distance, but did not sanction any particular account of how that process took place. Although Hertz's anomalous results were never explained, similar experiments done by others established the velocities predicted by Maxwell's theory, to Hertz's satisfaction. As we can see, the transition from laboratory event to experimental fact is one that involves more than 'reading the book of nature'.

Establishing an experimental fact also involves evaluating the interpretation of an experiment; this involves determining the legitimacy of a particular result, together with assessing the validity of background assumptions that are brought to bear in understanding the meaning and significance of experimental outcomes. There are competing philosophical views about the justification of an experimental result and the role it plays in the broader theoretical context. The evidence model emphasizes the connection between a particular result as the manifestation of a determinate world and a theory that attempts to describe that world. Thus Allan Franklin (1986) suggests that there is a set of strategies explicated in terms of Bayesian confirmation theory that determines the validity of an experimental outcome and the role it plays in deciding between competing theories (see CONFIRMATION THEORY; INDUCTIVE INFERENCE §3). On this view, it is simply a fact whether or not a particular outcome occurs and whether it is relevant in a theoretical context. In contrast, the social model advocated by Andrew Pickering (1984) and others proposes that the way a piece of evidence is interpreted and judged relevant depends on sociological and political factors including the interests of specific groups of scientists who wish to promote particular theoretical views, rather than on its reflecting a determinate way the world is. Consequently there is no unique characterization of experimental evidence. Others like Peter Galison (1987) recognize a role for both natural and social constraints. By showing how experiment involves not just the work of a single scientist or group, but a complex community of subgroups, each with its own goals and standards, Galison shows the diversity that constitutes experimental work and the various levels at which the interplay between natural and social concerns emerges.

The philosophy of experiment recognizes that experimental practice is an autonomous part of a broader scientific culture with distinct problems and issues. The literature has focused primarily on two kinds of concern: first, the 'how to' of experiment, which emphasizes laboratory practices and techniques that differentiate it from theoretical work; and, second, the epistemological debate about the proper characterization of experiment and its implications for scientific realism and theory confirmation. The latter presents two options. One involves attempts to provide a framework within which to understand and codify that practice – a 'theory' of experiment. The other focuses on the local nature of experimental practice by presenting it in a way that defies a unitary view or method describing how specific results are reached and legitimated. Emphasis on experiment has thus produced a new theoretical debate about what a proper philosophy of experiment and science ought to be.

See also: EXPERIMENTS IN SOCIAL SCIENCE; SCIENTIFIC REALISM AND ANTIREALISM

References and further reading

Ackerman, R. (1985) *Data, Instruments and Theory*, Princeton, NJ: Princeton University Press. (A discussion of the role of instruments in providing stable data. Ackerman argues that experimental practice provides continuity in the face of theoretical change.)

Bogen, J. and Woodward, J. (1983) 'Saving the Phenomena', *Philosophical Review* 97: 302–52. (Introduction of distinction between data and phenomena that brings the complexities of experimentalism into distinctions of explanation, testing and theory structure, which should be understood as encompassing phenomena only.)

* Franklin, A. (1986) *The Neglect of Experiment*, Cambridge: Cambridge University Press. (See Franklin 1990.)

—— (1990) *Experiment, Right or Wrong*, Cambridge: Cambridge University Press. (Both books discuss the role experiments and their results play in scientific practice, the difficulties that arise in interpreting results and the methods involved in their justification. Some of the case studies are fairly technical. Both books expand on the arguments mentioned in §3.)

* Galison, P. (1987) *How Experiments End*, Chicago, IL: University of Chicago Press. (An account of how historical, philosophical and sociological factors play a role in laboratory science. Technical in parts, but with a helpful introduction.)

Gooding, D., Pinch, T. and Schaffer, S. (1989) *The Uses of Experiment*, Cambridge: Cambridge University Press. (A collection of essays on a variety of topics in the history, philosophy and sociology of experiment. Some involve intricate detail but most are not technically difficult.)

* Hacking, I. (1983) *Representing and Intervening*, Cambridge: Cambridge University Press. (The first systematic treatment of the role of experiment in philosophy of science. The history of theory-dominated philosophy is discussed in a clear and comprehensive way. Also expands on material in §3.)

Latour, B. and Woolgar, S. (1986) *Laboratory Life*, Princeton, NJ: Princeton University Press. (The book presents a sociological account of how scientific facts are established and is based on field work done at the Salk Institute.)

Morrison, M. (1990) 'Theory, Intervention and Realism', *Synthèse* 82: 1–22. (A critical discussion of some of the issues in philosophy of experiment, particularly Hacking's view that experiment and theory can be successfully separated.)

* Pickering, A. (1984) *Constructing Quarks*, Chicago, IL: University of Chicago Press. (A detailed account of sociological factors in the practice of elementary particle physics, particularly the accep-

tance of the quark model and interpretation of important experiments. Technical in parts.)

Woodward, J. (1989) 'Date and Phenomena', *Synthèse* 79: 393–472. (Like the article with Bogen but in a more detailed discussion, the distinction between data and phenomena cautions against confused philosophical understanding of data as directly relevant to explanation and theory testing, which really concerns phenomena. Data, with their experimental dimension, play the role of observation but only in witness for claims about phenomena.)

MARGARET C. MORRISON

EXPERIMENTS, CRUCIAL
see CRUCIAL EXPERIMENTS

EXPERIMENTS IN SOCIAL SCIENCE

Within social science the experiment has an ambiguous place. With the possible exception of social psychology, there are few examples of strictly experimental studies. The classic study still often cited is the Hawthorne experiments, which began in 1927, and is used mainly to illustrate what became known as the 'Hawthorne Effect', that is, the unintended influence of the research itself on the results of the study. Yet, experimental design is often taken within social research as the embodiment of the scientific method which, if the social sciences are to reach the maturity of the natural sciences, social research should seek to emulate. Meeting this challenge meant trying to devise ways of applying the logic of the experiment to 'non-experimental' situations where it was not possible directly to manipulate the experimental conditions. Criticisms have come from two main sources: first, from researchers who claim that the techniques used to control factors within non-experimental situations are unrealizable with current statistical methods and, second, those who reject the very idea of hypothesis-testing as an ambition for social research.

1 **The logic of the experiment**
2 **Variable analysis**
3 **Problems with the experimental model**

1 The logic of the experiment

The intention of the experiment is to organize inquiry so that it bears decisively on hypotheses and the theories from which they are deduced. The classic means of achieving this is to set up a controlled comparison between two groups which are as alike as possible at the outset of the experiment. Only one of the groups is subjected to the experimental treatment. Thus, if there is a difference in the experimental outcome, then this can only be due to the experimental treatment. Control is typically achieved by matching subjects and randomizing their allocation to the experimental or to the control group so that possible confounding factors are excluded as possible explanations of the outcome.

John Stuart Mill's formalization of the general logic of the experiment (Mill 1843) was used as a framework for Durkheim's efforts to formulate sociology as a discipline with a properly scientific method. In his *The Rules of Sociological Method* (Durkheim 1895), he proposed the 'method of concomitant variation' as the means by which the causes of 'social facts' can be identified (see MILL, J.S. §2). In his later study, *Suicide* (Durkheim 1897), applying this logic to relevant official statistics, he identified variations in the suicide rate among various subgroups and, by eliminating alternative explanations, arrived at what he regarded as the social causes of different types of suicide.

Distinctive about Durkheim's work was his attempt to exploit the logic of the experiment in non-experimental situations; that is, situations in which it is impossible directly to manipulate causal and possible confounding factors. His own procedure, using official statistics, was to identify variations in the suicide rate among ever finer delineated subgroups, and a precursor of what became known as 'variable analysis' which is now one of the standard social research methods (see DURKHEIM, É.).

2 Variable analysis

However, the refinement of what became known as variable analysis owes more to the work of Lazarsfeld and his colleagues than directly to Durkheim (Lazarsfeld and Rosenberg 1955; Campbell and Stanley 1963; Stouffer 1950). Immediately after the Second World War, mainly in the USA, considerable effort was devoted to developing research methods which, though used in non-experimental situations, would provide a means of approximating to experimental designs and so make empirical research more decisive for social theory. This period led to the refinement of social survey and questionnaire design, measurement techniques and statistical multivariate methods for the analysis of social survey data.

Unike the classic experimental design which directly allocates subjects to control and experimental groups, in variable analysis, typically using survey data, the grouping of respondents takes place after the data have been collected. In place of matching and randomization, relationships of interest to the researcher are examined by holding constant other factors which may influence such relationships. For example, suppose a researcher is interested in the effects of ethnicity on voting choice, then the task is to isolate the effects of ethnicity given that other factors, such as occupation, gender, age, income, level of education, and more, may also have an effect on voting. Grouping the respondents into such other categories, and then determining the strength of the association between ethnicity and voting within each of them, is seen as holding constant any effects on voting choice which may arise from factors other than ethnicity. However, there is a limit to the number of factors which can be handled in this way before the statistical measures used to determine the relationship become unstable and, of course, only those factors on which data have been collected can enter into the analysis.

3 Problems with the experimental model

More seriously, the procedures of variable analysis depend heavily upon the random selection of respondents in order to neutralize the effects of possible confounding factors, whereas in the classic experimental design control is done through matching and the random allocation to control and experimental groups. In non-experimental research, the random selection of cases is an approximation to experimental randomization if it can be assumed that the population from which the sample is drawn is homogeneous; a reasonable assumption when dealing with a population of seeds, plants or germs, but less secure when dealing with populations of human beings. Indeed, one of the founding presuppositions of social science is that individuals are not isolated but related in a myriad of ways. It becomes harder to make the assumption that samples of individuals – which is the typical method employed in survey research – selected for their distinctiveness on one variable will vary randomly on others. Indeed, Lieberson makes the point that although most data in social research are non-experimental in origin, they are 'treated as if they were truly experimental data...sliced, chopped, beaten, molded, baked, and finally artificially coloured until the researcher is able to serve us proudly with a plateful of mock experiment' (Lieberson 1985: 4). The

burden of this critique of the use of the experimental model in social research, is that controlling fails to deal adequately with selectivity in the control variables. That is, social research deals with situations in which people, apart from their birth, have not been randomly assigned to their respective social worlds. Social processes of selectivity operate throughout life among subgroups, with varying effects and with different magnitudes, with the result that controlling in social research is not a 'benign procedure' since it takes little account of these selectivity processes.

Lieberson's arguments direct attention to what it is matching and randomization are intended to provide, namely, a basis for sustaining the *ceteris paribus* conditions which govern any theoretical hypothesis. Selectivity processes, under current practices of social research, cannot be controlled which means that such *ceteris paribus* assumptions cannot be sustained. Similar considerations, though from a very different perspective, emerge in consideration of even laboratory experiments using human subjects. It was noted earlier that one of the claims to fame of the Hawthorne experiments was the discovery of 'reactive effects', that is, effects of the experiment itself on its results. Although this was not a standard laboratory experiment, none the less, it did provoke serious considerations of the ways in which the very organization of experimental situations could itself violate *ceteris paribus* assumptions by introducing uncontrolled 'reactive effects' (Rosenthal and Rosnow 1969, especially the paper by Boring who suggests that such 'reactive effects' were originally the rationale underlying the idea of the control group). Among such 'reactive effects' are the meanings and understandings that subjects themselves bring to the experimental situation. As Cicourel (1964) points out, experimenters have to make assumptions about basic social processes in order to select subjects, organize their experimental activities, give them directions, and so on, but which are not explicated, let alone controlled. Rarely is the question of what is commonly perceived by subjects and experimenter as invariant about the social scene of the experimental situation addressed. As Milgram's (1974) experiments on obedience show, subjects themselves give meanings to experimental situations, for example, as normal, as involving legitimate activities and trusting in the experimenters that they will come to no harm, and so on. So much so that they are 'willing' to engage in actions, such as supposedly inflicting intense pain on others, out of obedience to what is perceived as the normative structure of the experimental situation.

A broader issue of debate relevant to the experiment in social science is the nature of the social sciences themselves; a debate which, of course, enters into epistemology. The experimental model is very much a hypothesis-testing procedure and, in this respect, intended as a means of building general theories. However, as discussed earlier, in social science research the direct manipulation of the factors and the experimental conditions is not possible. There are approaches which question whether this model is appropriate given that the experiment presumes that a great deal is known about the phenomena in question in order that the method may be brought to bear decisively on hypotheses. Approaches which draw their inspiration from less positivistic theories of knowledge, such as symbolic interactionism and ethnomethodology, emphasize the importance of studying the social world as a naturally occurring world without the intervention of experimental or quasi-experimental methods (Hughes 1990).

See also: EXPERIMENT; STATISTICS AND SOCIAL SCIENCE

References and further reading

* Campbell, D.T. and Stanley, J.C. (1963) *Experimental Designs and Quasi-experimental Designs for Research*, Chicago, IL: Rand McNally. (A valuable discussion of the efforts to incorporate the logic of the experiment into social research.)
* Cicourel, A.V. (1964) *Method and Measurement in Social Research*, New York: Free Press. (A serious critique of the foundations of orthodox social research methods, including the experiment.)
* Durkheim, É. (1895) *The Rules of Sociological Method*, ed. G.E.G. Catlin, trans. S.A. Solovay and J.H. Mueller, New York: Free Press, 1938. (A classic effort to formulate the methodological framework for a scientific sociology using Mill's specification of the experimental method. First published in French.)
* —— (1897) *Suicide: A Study in Sociology*, trans. J.A. Spaulding and G. Simpson, London: Routledge & Kegan Paul, 1952. (An early and classic investigation using multivariate analysis. First published in French.)
* Hughes, J.A. (1990) *The Philosophy of Social Research*, London: Longman, 2nd revised and enlarged edn. (A discussion of some of the philosophical problems arising from social research methods, including the experiment.)
* Lazarsfeld, P.F. and Rosenberg, M. (eds) (1955) *The Language of Social Research*, New York: Free Press. (A pioneering collection of readings setting out the procedures of variable analysis.)
* Lieberson, S. (1985) *Making it Count: The Improvement of Social Research and Theory*, Berkeley, CA: University of California Press. (An 'insider's' critique of the assumptions of experimental thinking in social research.)
* Milgram, S. (1974) *Obedience to Authority: An Experimental View*, London: Tavistock. (A discussion of Milgram's much misunderstood experiments.)
* Mill, J.S. (1843) *System of Logic*, London: Longman, 1970. (The classic formulation of the logic of the experiment.)
Roethlisberger, F.J. and Dickson, W.J. (1939) *Management and the Worker*, Cambridge, MA: Harvard University Press. (A presentation of the famous Hawthorne studies.)
* Rosenthal, R. and Rosnow, R.L. (eds) (1969) *Artifact in Behavioural Research*, New York: Academic Press. (A collection of papers dealing with 'reactive effects' in social research.)
* Stouffer, S. (1950) 'Some Observations on Study Designs', *American Journal of Sociology* 53: 355–61. (A classic statement on the need for experimental and quasi-experimental design in social research.)

JOHN A. HUGHES

EXPLANATION

Philosophical reflections about explanation are common in the history of philosophy, and important proposals were made by Aristotle, Hume, Kant and Mill. But the subject came of age in the twentieth century with the provision of detailed models of scientific explanation, prominently the covering-law model, *which takes explanations to be arguments in which a law of nature plays an essential role among the premises. In the heyday of logical empiricism, philosophers achieved a consensus on the covering law model, but, during the 1960s and 1970s, that consensus was challenged through the recognition of four major kinds of difficulty: first, a problem about the relation between idealized arguments and the actual practice of explaining; second, the difficulty of characterizing the underlying notion of a law of nature; third, troubles in accounting for the asymmetries of explanation; and, four, recalcitrant problems in treating statistical explanations.*

Appreciation of these difficulties has led to the widespread abandonment of the covering-law model, and currently there is no consensus on how to understand explanation. The main contemporary view seeks to characterize explanation in terms of causation, that is, explanations are accounts that trace the causes of the events (states, conditions) explained. Other philosophers believe that there is no general account of explanation, and offer pragmatic theories. A third option sees explanation as consisting in the unification of the phenomena. All of these approaches have associated successes, and face particular anomalies.

Although the general character of explanation is now a subject for philosophical debate, some particular kinds of explanation seem to be relatively well understood. In particular, functional explanations in biology, which logical empiricists found puzzling, now appear to be treated quite naturally by supposing them to make tacit reference to natural selection.

1   **Early history**
2   **The covering-law model**
3   **Four kinds of difficulty**
4   **Picking up the pieces**
5   **Functional explanation: a recent success story**

1   Early history

Thinking about explanation goes back at least to Aristotle, whose discussion of four kinds of causation in the *Posterior Analytics* can properly be viewed as distinguishing modes of scientific explanation (see ARISTOTLE §9). In the modern period, the writings of Hume, Kant and Mill offer many insights on causation, laws and regularities in nature that, sometimes explicitly, sometimes implicitly, propose doctrines about the character of scientific explanation (see HUME, D. §2; KANT, I. §§4–7; MILL, J.S. §5). However questions about scientific explanation became sharply focused in the mid-twentieth century, with the emergence of an orthodoxy about scientific explanation, which, despite its later demise, stands as one of the most significant achievements of the movement known as 'logical empiricism' (see LOGICAL POSITIVISM §4). The writings of Karl Popper (1959), R.B. Braithwaite (1953), Ernest Nagel (1961) and especially, C.G. Hempel (1965), articulate an influential conception. Namely, scientific explanations are viewed as arguments in which a statement describing the fact (or regularity) to be explained is derived from premises, at least one of which is a law of nature (see HEMPEL, C.G. §3). The underlying idea is that scientific explanations provide understanding by showing that the phenomena to be explained should be expected as a consequence of the general laws of nature.

2   The covering-law model

One important and much-discussed species of scientific explanation according with this general conception is *deductive-nomological* explanation (D-N explanation). In cases of this type, the argument is deductive, so that the statement describing the phenomenon to be explained (the *explanandum*) is a deductive consequence of the premises advanced in giving the explanation (the *explanans*). D-N explanations may be provided for explananda that describe particular facts or for explananda that announce general regularities. In the former case, there is a simple schema which exhibits the form of the explanation

$$\frac{C_1, C_2, \ldots, C_n}{L_1, L_2, \ldots, L_m}$$
$$E$$

where the statement E is the explanandum, describing the fact to be explained, the statements $L_1, L_2, \ldots, L_m$ are laws of nature, and the statements $C_1, C_2, \ldots, C_n$ describe particular facts (such as initial conditions). It is not hard to construct arguments that accord with this schema and which seem to explain their conclusions: derivations in classical Newtonian dynamics that deduce the trajectories of bodies from force laws and initial conditions supply many examples.

Not all explanatory arguments are deductive. The logical empiricist orthodoxy admitted *inductive-statistical* explanations (I-S explanations) as well as D-N explanations. In an I-S explanation, the explanandum is inferred inductively from premises at least one of which is a probabilistic law, for example a statement that assigns a value to the probability with which a particular trait is found among members of a specific class. Thus, to cite a famous example of Hempel's, we may explain why a child, Henrietta, contracted measles, by noting that she has been in contact with another child, Henry, who has measles, and that a large percentage of children who come into contact with measles' patients (say 99 per cent) subsequently come down with measles. Imitating the schema for D-N explanation, we can present this modest derivation as follows:

Henrietta has been in contact with Henry, and Henry has measles.

The frequency with which children in contact with measles' patients subsequently acquire measles is 99 per cent.

$$\frac{(0.99)}{\text{Henrietta has measles}}$$

Here, the rule indicates that the inference from premises to conclusion is inductively strong, rather than deductively valid; the figure in brackets (0.99) reveals the strength of the inference. I-S explanations have to meet several requirements. First, the numerical strength of the inductive inference must be high (close to 1). Second, the explanans must meet a requirement of maximal specificity: there must not be known further premises which, if added to the explanans, would change the strength of the inference – as, for example, the inductive reasoning would be modified if we knew that Henrietta had received a measles' shot, and that children given such shots have a very low probability of acquiring measles.

Plainly, the explanations that scientists and others actually put forward do not look much like these stripped-down arguments. The logical empiricists claimed only that the everyday provision of explanations could be reconstructed by identifying arguments of D-N or I-S form, and that these reconstructions brought into the open what it was about the explanations that enabled them to fulfil their function. In the 1940s and 1950s, many scholars were happy to concede that the covering-law model of explanation, which assimilated explanations to arguments with laws among their premises, worked well as a reconstruction of explanations in the natural sciences – especially in physics and chemistry – but there were important debates about the application of the model to the social sciences and to explanation in everyday life. Controversy focused in particular on the activity of historical explanation. Historians construct detailed narratives that appear to explain particular events – the outbreak of the American Civil War or Henry VIII's dissolution of the monasteries. If the covering-law model is correct, then a proper reconstruction of these accounts must expose general laws. Are there indeed general laws in history? Or are the general laws that underlie historical explanation simply psychological laws that connect the motivations of historical actors with their actions (see EXPLANATION IN HISTORY AND SOCIAL SCIENCE)?

3 Four kinds of difficulty

Troubles with history aside, the covering-law model appeared remarkably successful, a rare example of a convincing solution to a philosophical problem. Yet, in the 1960s, it came under sustained attack, and, by the end of the decade, it had been almost entirely abandoned. Four separate kinds of consideration contributed to this swift reversal of fortune.

First was a complaint, articulated by Michael Scriven (1962), that perfectly satisfactory explanations can be given, and understood, by people who are quite ignorant of the covering-laws that are essential to the supposed reconstruction. It is easy to explain to a friend why there is a mess on the floor by pointing out that your arm knocked the open ink bottle off the desk at which you were writing. Perhaps

it would be possible for a knowing philosopher of science to cite the general laws that govern the behaviour of the bottle and the spilled ink, but this knowledge seems entirely irrelevant to the episode in which the chagrined mess-maker explains what has occurred. At the heart of Scriven's complaint lay the recognition that the covering-law model had failed to show how the idealized derivations that supposedly highlight how the explanatory work is done are adapted, in specific local situations, to transmit understanding from one person to another. Without a *pragmatics* of explanation, an account of how the ideal arguments that fit particular logical forms relate to what people actually do in giving explanations, it was possible to challenge the claim that the structures exposed by the logical empiricists reveal the crucial features that make the explanation successful.

A second difficulty resulted from continued inability to provide a satisfactory account of natural laws. From the earliest formulations of the covering-law model, its champions had insisted that not every generalization counts as a law. So-called *accidental* generalizations cannot discharge any explanatory function: it may be a timeless truth about the universe that all ball games played by a red-haired left-hander who forgoes lunch are won by the opposite team, but that accidental generalization sheds no light on the outcome of any particular game (see LAWS, NATURAL §2). Prior to Nelson Goodman's formulation of a cluster of difficulties surrounding counterfactuals, induction and laws (1956), the problem of distinguishing laws from accidental generalizations appeared an interesting challenge to the logical empiricist project (see GOODMAN, N. §3). Once the depth of Goodman's 'new riddle of induction' had become apparent, it seemed impossible to find a solution within the constraints that empiricists allowed themselves (see INDUCTION, EPISTEMIC ISSUES IN).

A third trouble emerged from the recognition that, even if the distinction between laws and accidental generalizations could be drawn, the covering-law model would still be too liberal. Introducing an example that was to become famous, Sylvain Bromberger (1966) pointed out that the model is blind to certain asymmetries in explanation. We can explain the length of the shadow cast by a flagpole by deriving a statement ascribing the pertinent numerical value from premises identifying the height of the pole and the angle of elevation of the sun, together with the law of the rectilinear propagation of light. This derivation fits the D-N schema beautifully. The trouble, however, is that we can produce a modified argument, according equally well with the D-N schema, by interchanging the premise that identifies the height of the pole with the conclusion: the height of the flagpole is deducible from the length of the shadow, the elevation of the sun and the law of rectilinear propagation of light. This new derivation does not seem explanatory, for it appears wrong to explain the heights of poles (or, more generally, the sizes of physical objects) in terms of the measurements of the shadows they cast. Scrupulous about appealing to causation, logical empiricism had tried to construct an account of explanation without invoking causal notions that would offend Humean sensibilities (hence, in part, the difficulty of characterizing natural laws). Bromberger's critique suggests that the omission of causal concepts assimilates cases that are importantly different: after all, it is tempting to characterize the difference between the two derivations by pointing out that the height of the flagpole *causes* the shadow to have the length it does, but that the length of the shadow does not cause the flagpole to have the height it does.

Perhaps the most influential difficulty, was the fourth, which focused on the failure of the account of statistical explanation. Alberto Coffa (1974) probed the conditions required of I-S explanation, revealing that they involved an essential reference to the state of knowledge, which made it impossible to develop a concept of a true inductive explanation. Coffa's critique complemented the work of Richard Jeffrey (1969), who had earlier argued that it is possible to explain individual events that do not have high probability in the light of background conditions, and thus that the high probability requirement was also defective. At the same time, Wesley Salmon (1970) worked out, in considerable detail, an account of statistical explanation that, like Jeffrey's, rejected the thesis that explanations are arguments. Central to Salmon's account was the idea that we explain by citing probabilistically relevant information. In the early versions of his model of statistical explanation, Salmon proposed that probabilistic explanations gain their force from the recognition that the probability that an individual has a property has been raised. Schematically, the information that a is F helps explain why a is G when the probability of something's being G is increased if that thing is F (more exactly: $P(G/F) > P(G)$). In this way, Salmon was able to respond to a difficulty noted earlier by Scriven – we may explain the fact that the mayor has paresis by noting that he previously had untreated syphilis, even though the frequency with which untreated syphilitics contract paresis is small (around 15 per cent). On Salmon's account, noting that the mayor had untreated syphilis gives an enormous boost to the probability of his having paresis, raising it from the baseline figure of close to 0 to about 15 per cent.

4 Picking up the pieces

Salmon's account of explanation was deliberately motivated by the felt need to allow for explanations in the indeterministic contexts of contemporary physics. His approach dovetailed neatly with attempts, like those of Patrick Suppes (1970), to fashion a conception of causality that would no longer be restricted to deterministic situations (see CAUSATION §4; DETERMINISM AND INDETERMINISM). From 1970 to the present, one important strand in contemporary theories of explanation has taken explanation to consist in delineating the causes of events, and has tried to honour Humean concerns about the invocation of causality by providing a theory of causation that will define causal relations in statistical terms. The simplest account of probabilistic causality would propose that A is causally relevant to B just in case $P(B/A) \neq P(B)$. Unfortunately, this account is too simple. As Hans Reichenbach pointed out in the 1950s the inequality will obtain when A and B are both effects of a common cause (Reichenbach 1956). Thus further conditions must be imposed to identify the statistical relations constitutive of probabilistic causation.

Since the 1970s a number of different proposals have competed to inherit the position of orthodoxy once occupied by the covering-law model. Most popular have been causal approaches to explanation, and, initially, proposals to ground explanation in a detailed conception of probabilistic causality promised to answer (or sidestep) the four principal difficulties outlined above. However, it has proved remarkably difficult to work out a satisfactory account of explanation along these lines, and a number of critiques, most notably that by Nancy Cartwright (1983), have cast doubt on the viability of the enterprise. Faced with powerful objections, champions of causal approaches to explanation have pursued one of two options. One is to continue to honour Humean concerns about the causal relation, and to seek an analysis of causation that will not make use of metaphysical notions that empiricists consider dubious. The most thorough attempt to carry out this programme has been undertaken by Wesley Salmon (1984), who has attempted to develop Reichenbach's account of causation in terms of the fundamental notion of mark transmission. The alternative approach is to declare victory by taking some causal notion as an unanalysed primitive, resisting Humean scruples about how we might know how to apply this notion as misguided (perhaps the proposals of Humphreys (1992) and Cartwright (1989) should be viewed as embodying this approach).

One evident attraction of the causal programme is

that it provides an immediate response to the problem posed by the asymmetries of explanation. However, not all current theories view explanation as a matter of tracing causes. In recent years, Bas van Fraassen (1980), Peter Achinstein (1983) and Peter Railton (1981) have all made important contributions to the pragmatics of explanation, and the first two authors have defended the view that the enterprise of seeking substantive necessary conditions that apply across all contexts in which people seek and give explanations is misguided. The danger is that such pragmatic theories of explanation reduce the enterprise to triviality. For any explanation-seeking question and any proposition we choose, it seems that we can construct a context in which that proposition is licensed as an adequate (or even a perfect) explanatory answer to that question (see Kitcher and Salmon 1987, and, for a response, Lloyd and Anderson 1994).

A third cluster of positions stays close to the covering-law model's conception of explanations as arguments, proposing that explanatory arguments are not distinguished singly but emerge from the best way of systematizing our body of knowledge. Michael Friedman (1974) and Philip Kitcher (1981) have developed (different) accounts of explanation that take arguments to be explanatory if they belong to a system of arguments that best unifies our beliefs. One virtue of this approach is its ready provision of an analysis of theoretical explanation; its principal difficulties lie in formulating appropriate criteria for unification and for addressing the asymmetries of explanation.

The present debate echoes themes from earlier chapters in the history of philosophy. Hume's scruples about causation loom behind some efforts to articulate causal theories of explanation, those who oppose Hume on causation (like Cartwright) sometimes seem to harken back to Aristotle, and the unification approach has made an explicit connection with Kant. Perhaps these affinities suggest that contemporary debates about scientific explanation turn on larger metaphysical questions that need to be confronted directly (see UNITY OF SCIENCE).

5 Functional explanation: a recent success story

Ironically, after the fragmentation of the consensus on the covering-law model of explanation, considerable progress has been made on studying a species of explanation that, despite careful studies by Hempel and Nagel, was always somewhat difficult for logical empiricist orthodoxy. Biologists often appear to explain the presence of a trait or structure by identifying its function, and it is not clear how such explanations should be assimilated to a D-N (or an I-S) schema. Thanks to pioneering work by Larry Wright (1976), contemporary philosophers of biology are largely agreed on a central idea: functional explanations are abridged versions of explanations in terms of natural selection. The identification of the function is thus seen as picking out the kind of selection pressure that causes the trait (or structure) to become originally established (or, maybe, to be maintained). The details of this idea are worked out in different ways by different authors, but the selectionist (or etiological) account of functional explanation appears to provide a philosophically satisfactory reconstruction of parts of biological practice (see EVOLUTION, THEORY OF; FUNCTIONAL EXPLANATION).

A possible moral of the comparative success in studying functional explanation is that philosophers may be too ambitious in seeking general theories of explanation. Pragmatists, like van Fraassen, sometimes suggest that there are many different kinds of successful explanation, and that there may be no interesting general conditions that all must meet. Perhaps the most fundamental issue confronting the theory of explanation today is whether it is reasonable to seek a theory of explanation across all contexts and all epochs or whether the study of scientific explanation should be more local, concentrating on specific types of explanation.

See also: MEYERSON, É.

References and further reading

* Achinstein, P. (1983) *The Nature of Explanation*, New York: Oxford University Press. (See §4. A sophisticated exploration of the practices of asking for and giving explanations.)
* Braithwaite, R.B. (1953) *Scientific Explanation*, Cambridge: Cambridge University Press. (See §1. A major work from the heyday of logical empiricism.)
* Bromberger, S. (1966) 'Why-Questions', in R. Colodny (ed.) *Mind and Cosmos*, Pittsburgh, PA: University of Pittsburgh Press. (See §3. An important critique of covering-law models.)
* Cartwright, N. (1983) *How the Laws of Physics Lie*, New York: Oxford University Press. (See §4. A sustained attack on traditional conceptions of law, cause and explanation.)
* —— (1989) *Nature's Capacities and their Measurement*, New York: Oxford University Press. (See §4. A defence of approaching causation and explanation in non-Humean terms.)
* Coffa, J.A. (1974) 'Hempel's Ambiguity', *Synthèse* 28: 141–63. (See §3. A penetrating critique of Hempel's views about statistical explanation.)

* Fraassen, B. van (1980) *The Scientific Image*, Oxford: Oxford University Press. (In particular, chapter 5. An important work on theory and explanation in science. See §4.)

* Friedman, M. (1974) 'Explanation and Scientific Understanding', *Journal of Philosophy* 71: 5–19. (See §4. An important presentation of the unificationist approach to explanation.)

* Goodman, N. (1956) *Fact, Fiction, and Forecast*, Indianapolis, IN: Bobbs-Merrill. (See §3. The classic source of the difficulties faced by logical empiricists in explicating the notion of a law of nature.)

* Hempel, C.G. (1965) *Aspects of Scientific Explanation and Other Essays*, New York: Free Press. (Contains the *locus classicus* of the covering-law model. See §§1– 2.)

* Humphreys, P. (1992) *The Chances of Explanation*, Princeton, NJ: Princeton University Press. (See §4. An articulation of a causal approach to explanation.)

* Jeffrey, R. (1969) 'Statistical Explanation vs Statistical Inference', in N. Rescher (ed.) *Essays in Honor of Carl G. Hempel*, Dordrecht: Reidel, 104–13. (See §3. An important critique of covering-law models of explanation.)

* Kitcher, P. (1981) 'Explanatory Unification', *Philosophy of Science* 48: 507–31. (See §4. An account of explanation in terms of unification.)

* Kitcher, P. and Salmon, W. (1987) 'Van Fraassen on Explanation', *Journal of Philosophy* 84: 315–30. (See §4. A critique of van Fraassen's pragmatic theory of explanation.)

* Lloyd, E. and Anderson, C. (1994) 'Empiricism, Objectivity, and Explanation', *Midwest Studies in Philosophy* 18: 121–31. (See §4. A defence of van Fraassen's pragmatic approach to explanation.)

* Nagel, E. (1961) *The Structure of Science*, New York: Harcourt Brace. (See §1. A classical logical empiricist text that takes explanation to be central to scientific practice.)

Pitt, J. (1989) *Theories of Explanation*, New York: Oxford University Press. (A collection containing many important contemporary articles.)

* Popper, K. (1959) *The Logic of Scientific Discovery*, New York: Basic Books. (See §1. A seminal logical empiricist work, containing an account of explanation as subsumption under law.)

* Railton, P. (1981) 'Probability, Explanation, and Information', *Synthèse* 48: 233–56. (See §4. An important contribution to the pragmatics of scientific explanation.)

* Reichenbach, H. (1956) *The Direction of Time*, Berkeley, CA: University of California Press. (See §4. A work containing a seminal discussion of probabilistic causation.)

Rubin, D.-H. (1994) *Explanation*, Oxford: Oxford University Press. (A collection explicitly designed to complement the Pitt volume.)

* Salmon, W. (1970) 'Statistical Explanation', in R. Colodny (ed.) *The Nature and Function of Scientific Theories*, Pittsburgh, PA: University of Pittsburgh Press, 173–231. (See §3. A thorough scrutiny of Hempel's views about statistical explanation, together with an important rival theory.)

* —— (1984) *Scientific Explanation and the Causal Structure of the World*, Princeton, NJ: Princeton University Press. (See §4. The *locus classicus* for one of the leading contemporary accounts of scientific explanation.)

* Scriven, M. (1962) 'Explanations, Predictions and Laws', in H. Feigl and G. Maxwell (eds) *Minnesota Studies in the Philosophy of Science*, vol. III, Minneapolis, MN: University of Minnesota Press. (See §3. An important early critique of covering-law models.)

* Suppes, P. (1970) *A Probabilistic Theory of Causality*, Amsterdam: North Holland. (See §4. A pioneering study of probabilistic causation.)

* Wright, L. (1976) *Teleological Explanation*, Berkeley, CA: University of California Press. (See §5. The major source of the most widely accepted current account of functional explanation.)

PHILIP KITCHER

EXPLANATION, FUNCTIONAL *see* FUNCTIONAL EXPLANATION

EXPLANATION IN HISTORY AND SOCIAL SCIENCE

Historians and social scientists explain at least two sorts of things: (a) those individual human actions that have historical or social significance, such as Stalin's decision to hold the show trials, Diocletian's division of the Roman Empire, and the Lord Chief Justice's attempt to reform the English judicial system; (b) historical and social events and structures ('large-scale' social phenomena), such as wars, economic depressions, social customs, the class system, the family, the state, and the crime rate. Philosophical questions arise about explanations of both kinds (a) and (b).

Concerning (b), perhaps the most pressing question is whether explanations of this sort can, ultimately, be understood as merely explanations of a large number of individual human actions, that is, as a complex set of explanations of the first kind, (a).

A causal explanation is an explanation of something in terms of its event-cause(s). Some explanations under (b) appear not to be causal explanations in this sense. There are two ways in which this appears to happen. First, we sometimes seem to explain a social structure or event by giving its function or purpose. This seems to be an explanation in terms of its effects rather than by its causes. For example, it might be claimed that the explanation for a certain social custom in a tribal society is the way in which it contributes to social stability or group solidarity. An explanation of a thing in terms of its effects cannot be a causal explanation of that thing. Second, we sometimes seem to cite social structure as the explanation of something. Whatever a social structure is, it is not itself an event, and since only (it is often said) events can be causes, such a 'structural' explanation does not seem to be a causal explanation.

A second question, then, about explanations of kind (b) is whether some of them, at any rate, are genuinely non-causal explanations, or whether functional and/or structural explanations of this sort can be seen as special sorts of causal explanation.

Explanations of kind (a) are a proper subset of explanations of human actions generally. Although some of the discussion of these issues began life as a distinct literature within the philosophy of history, it has now been absorbed into philosophical action theory more generally. Even so, a question that remains is just which proper subset of human actions are the ones of interest to the historical and social sciences: how can we discriminate within the class of human actions between those in which historians or social scientists have a legitimate interest and those outside their purview?

1 **Holistic explanation**
2 **Functional and structural explanation**
3 **Individual action explanation**
4 **In virtue of what is an action of interest to the historian or social scientist?**

1 Holistic explanation

Many explanations in history and social science are explanations of large-scale events or structures such as wars, invasions, economic depressions, social customs, the class system, the family, the state, and the crime rate. A plausible thought is that these large-scale phenomena are merely patterns, or complexes, of individual actions, that the former are, in principle,

ontologically reducible to the latter. This idea is sometimes captured by using the terminology of wholes and parts (see MEREOLOGY). Large-scale social events or structures are wholes, whose parts are the individual actions which constitute them. If this is so, then explanations of such large-scale social and historical phenomena are nothing more than complexes of explanations of those constituent actions of individuals which are the former's parts.

The term 'methodological individualism' is ambiguous (see Ruben 1985). Sometimes it is said to be the view that social wholes are nothing more than sums of their parts. In this sense, it is not a thesis about language, that is, about the translatability without remainder of the language of social science into the language of individual psychology, although some writers have expressed it in this form. Nor is it a thesis about the methodology of social scientific practice, as its name might misleadingly suggest. It is a metaphysical thesis about what social phenomena really are, namely that they are just, or are wholly constituted by, individual persons with beliefs, desires, and other mental states, who stand in various relations with one another. This states the metaphysical thesis both in terms of identity and constitution. It is controversial whether the numerical identity and constitution relations are the same relation, and no statement of methodological individualism carefully delineates these two alternatives.

At other times, methodological individualism is described as a view about explanation: that the explanation of social facts is ultimately in terms of individual psychological facts (perhaps with purely physical facts added to the psychological ones). Stated in this way, one needs an account of social fact, in order to clarify the scope of the claim. What makes a fact a *social* fact? Presumably, social facts are not only facts about large-scale social phenomena: the fact that LaGuardia was a mayor is a social fact, because a social property, being a mayor, was true of that person. LaGuardia was himself not a large-scale social event or structure, and being a mayor is a property, neither an event nor a structure, large-scale or otherwise. Presumably, the fact that he was a mayor is a social fact, because being a mayor is a social property. So, in the end, methodological individualism as a view about explanation will need a perspicuous account of social property.

The important point, though, is that the metaphysical doctrine of methodological individualism does not, by itself, warrant any conclusion about the explanation of social facts. No such inference, from a metaphysical premise to an epistemological conclusion, could be valid without the addition of further premises. The methodological individualist thesis about the explanation of social facts in terms of facts about individuals would require some additional argument independent of the metaphysical thesis, in order to claim credibility.

So even if it were true that social wholes were nothing more than the 'sums' of individual actions, nothing immediately follows about the explanation of the former in terms of the latter. This point is further strengthened by the reminder that, whereas full constitution (and identity, if this is a distinct relation) is an extensional relation, explanation is non-extensional. That is, if {a and b} fully constitute w, and if a = d, b = e, and w = x, then {d and e} fully constitute x. How we describe constituents and what they constitute is not relevant to the truth of constitution (or identity) claims.

But this is not the case for explanation. With explanation, description matters: something can be explanatory or get explained when described in one way but not in another (see EXPLANATION). Even though red is the colour of ripe strawberries, one might be able to explain why bulls charge at certain flags waved in front of them by the fact that the flags are red, but not by the fact that the flags are the colour of ripe strawberries. So it may well be that even if a social whole, say a war or an economic slump or the state, is nothing more than, is wholly constituted by, the actions of individuals, no explanation of the war or the slump or the state, could be adequate, even in principle, if expressed in the language of individual action. The relationship between the metaphysical truth of methodological individualism (if it were one) and the parallel methodological individualist thesis about ultimate explanation in the social sciences seems far more complicated than writers on these issues have typically assumed (see METHODOLOGICAL INDIVIDUALISM §2, 3).

2 Functional and structural explanation

There is a 'strong' view that all explanations of large-scale social phenomena are functional explanations. Even if this view is false, it seems undeniable that there are at least some functional explanations in history and the social sciences (see FUNCTIONALISM IN SOCIAL SCIENCE §1). Certain customs, practices or institutions in a society might be explained by the role they play: religion; etiquette; bureaucracy; education or the state might be explained by their function for a society or for a specific group within the society in question. There seem to be functional explanations in biology as well, but the parallel between biology and social science on this issue is controversial, and it is better, therefore, to consider functional explanation in social science and history on its own, without

considering the issue in biology and attempting to establish a general account of functional explanation, equally applicable to both fields.

Functional explanation in social science should be sharply distinguished from purposive (or intentional) explanation of individual human action. In the latter case, explanation is by way of the beliefs and desires or intentions of the agent. It has sometimes been alleged that functional explanation in social science also requires reference to mental states such as belief and desire, but mental states attributable to a group as a whole rather than to individual persons. Such an implausible view, with its notorious idea of a group mind, seems unnecessary, if we refuse to assimilate functional and purposive explanation. The former does not require reference to any mental states whatever, whether of an individual or of a group.

Are functional explanations a type of causal explanation? It might seem not, since such explanations seem to be in terms of the beneficial effects of a thing rather than in terms of its cause(s). But one plausible suggestion is that, for an adequate functional explanation, there must be some causal 'feedback' loop: if education is to be explained by the way in which it helps a certain group retain power, then it is insufficient that education merely leads to the group's retaining power. If that were all there were to it, we would have an ordinary causal explanation of the group's power retention by the existence of the system of education.

On the contrary, what we had hoped for was the explanation of the education system in terms of the group's retaining power. On one view of the matter, to have the latter explanation, the group retaining its power must itself lead, by a causal loop, to further expansion or entrenchment of education. As such, we can see how the fact that education has the result of a group's power-retention is explanatory of the education itself, since education having this effect is itself a cause of more such education. Perhaps the stronger the group gets, the more it reinforces and develops the educational system. Education's effect further strengthens the system of education itself. We can also see, on this account of functional explanation, that functional explanation is merely a more complicated kind of causal explanation, involving a feedback loop in the causal chain (Elster 1983).

What about explanations in which social structure of some sort is cited as what does the explaining? How could these be causal explanations? For example, the kinship structure in a specific society might be said to explain why certain persons do and do not marry other persons to whom they are related in certain ways. One way in which to understand these cases might be to distinguish more carefully just what it is that one is explaining. Does the social structure explain some token event, like Tom marrying Rita, or does it explain some more general structural fact, like the fact that men must marry their dead brother's male-childless wife? If the former, then presumably the kinship system by itself cannot explain the specific marriage of Tom to Rita: the beliefs and wants of Tom and Rita, at the very least, will have to be included. Social structure cannot have an effect on the agents' behaviour directly; its effect must be mediated through, or combined with, the psychology of the agents. These mental states must figure in the explanation, and they will ensure that the explanation of the specific marriage is an ordinary causal explanation (see STRUCTURALISM IN SOCIAL SCIENCE §1).

On the other hand, if what we are explaining is the structural fact about levirate marriage, then that feature of the kinship structure might follow from certain other features of the kinship structure, in the sense that the fact can be derived, or follows, from them. Writers in this tradition of explanation, basing themselves on themes and modes of explanation in the philosophies of Hegel and Marx, often speak of the underlying 'logic' of the social structure working itself out, thereby signifying that such explanations are akin to logical deductions (Zeleny 1980). In something like this sense, we could 'explain' some theorem of Euclidean geometry by deriving it from axioms and definitions. In the case of structural explanations in the social sciences, social structures are sometimes said to have their own dynamic, based on what they essentially are, and to develop according to their own inner laws or tendencies. If the concept of explanation were to be extended in this way, then there may well be structural explanations in social science which are not causal explanations. Even so, the thought that all explanations of events are causal explanations remains undisturbed; whatever such structural explanations are explanations of, they do not seem to be events in any sense.

3 Individual action explanation

Even if history and social science sometimes explain structures or events which are irreducible to individual actions and events, it is undeniable that they sometimes at least do engage in explanation of the actions of specific individual persons. What kind of explanations are these action explanations?

There are two 'grand' traditions in the philosophy of history and social science that supply an answer to this question, one represented (*inter alia*) by John Stuart Mill and Carl Hempel, the other by Wilhelm Dilthey, William Dray, and Peter Winch. The tradi-

tions' conventional names conjure up too many other views, which bear no logical connection to their views on action (see ACTION), so one can call the first tradition simply 'the causal tradition', and the second, 'the non-causal tradition'. By the former, the thesis intended is that every human action is to be explained by its causes, which are to be found, at least in part, in the mental states of the agents; by the latter, one understands any thesis which gives some other account of action explanation. This latter tradition is something of a catch-all. It is sometimes called 'hermeneutic', because many non-causal theorists liken explaining human action to interpreting a text. It is also sometimes called the 'interpretative' view, since it tends to stress the way in which action needs to be interpreted in order to be rendered intelligible. A specific version of this view is called 'contextualism', since it focuses on the societal norms or rules in the social setting in which the agent acts, with which we can interpret what he is doing as an action of one kind or another. For example, it is only because there exist certain religious rules, or rules about banking, that we can say of someone that what they are doing is celebrating mass or cashing a cheque.

There are at least three distinctions required, in order to make any progress in deciding between these views. The first is between a mere bodily movement and an action. A person's hand may move, or their finger bend, without them moving their hand or bending their finger. The former may not be actions, things they do, and their explanation may not include any of their mental states at all. They might, for example, be merely reflex 'actions'. Even if mental states are included in their explanation, it may still not be actions which are being explained. Fear may cause my pupils to dilate; St Thomas' example is that of lust causing a man's erection. Neither the dilation nor the erection are the actions of a person. These latter explanations are not within the scope of social science at all, but rather of biology.

The second and third distinctions both have to do with what is sometimes called 'explaining under a description'. Explanation is, as claimed above, non-extensional; how something is described matters to whether it explains or is explained by something else.

The second distinction is between the intentional and non-intentional descriptions of action. On one plausible account of action individuation, what we explain are not just actions, but actions under some specific description or other. For example, every action will have an indefinitely large number of unintended effects, and the action can always be redescribed as the action having such-and-such an unintended effect. Theories of action explanation focus on explanation of actions under their intended descriptions. Once an explanation of action under its intended description is found, an explanation under its unintended description will be quickly forthcoming: it is just that the action as intended happened to have such a causal consequence.

The third distinction is between the action under its basic and its non-basic descriptions. (Non-basic descriptions can be either intentional or unintentional.) A man flexes his finger, pulls the trigger, shoots the gun, kills Smith, and executes a criminal. He executes the criminal by killing Smith; he kills Smith by shooting the gun; he shoots the gun by pulling the trigger; he pulls the trigger by flexing his finger. 'Flexing his finger' is the basic description of the action, if there is no other description of the action such that he flexes his finger by doing the action described under that other description.

The causal tradition, deriving from Hobbes and Hume, is the view that every action is to be explained, *inter alia*, by the mental states that cause it. The mental states may be only part of the full explanation of the action, but they are a necessary part. Metaphysically, this view about explanation is consistent with, but does not entail, physicalism: such rationalizing mental states may or may not be physical states (see MATERIALISM §1).

On the causal view, the item that is explained is an action only if the mental causes not only cause the movement but also rationalize it, make it the rational thing to have done in the circumstances, relative to the agent's beliefs and desires. Rationalizing and causing are two distinct relations and provide two distinct requirements. On the causal view, the mental states that explain an action must both cause and rationalize it. On the traditional causal view, such a mental state must include a belief and a desire. This is the old Humean view of rationality as instrumental: an action is rationalized if it can be 'justified' in terms of what the agent believes they need to do in order to satisfy their desires (see HUME, D. §3). On other accounts, such a mental state may be an intention rather than a belief and desire pair. An agent's doing A can be explained by their intention to do so, if such an intention both causes their doing that action and makes it rational for them to do it (Ayer 1967; Gardiner 1978).

Since the non-causal tradition is, as has been described, something of a ragbag, let us select one strand from many possible ones. Often, non-causal theories focus on explanation of action occurring in an alien culture. How can we understand, or make sense of, what someone from such a society is doing, if it makes no obvious sense in our own terms? The answer surely is that we must know the rules and norms of that society, in order to interpret what they are doing, to endow their movements with sense and significance. We must, as it were, go native. If we are seeking to explain action under its intentional description, then we must know what the intentions of the agent are, and one can know the latter only by knowing the rules and norms of the society which give rise to, or at least make possible, the having of such intentions. Movements of one's body can only be given meaning in terms of such rules; one's hand movements can only constitute a writing of a cheque, in the light of regulations about banking. And what is true of alien societies is true of our own; our own behaviour only acquires social meaning or significance, in the light of our own social rules and conventions (Dilthey 1976; Winch 1958).

The non-causal view seems plausible as a view about at least some non-basic action. So-called social actions are just actions under non-basic social descriptions. A person moves their hand (if they are acting, then it is not just that their hand moves). To understand their moving of their hand as their writing a cheque, one must cite, *inter alia*, the rules and regulations of banking. In order to do that, the explainer will need to cite, or suppose, the existence of a social institution, that is, banking. Social rules and institutions may only be relevant to action explanation at the level of non-basic descriptions of action. The non-causal view explains the possibility of giving social descriptions of action.

The causal theory, on the other hand, seems to be doing at least two different things. First, it accounts for the differences between mere bodily movement and intentional action. Second, given that the action performed was of a certain kind, it offers an explanation of why the agent acted in that way.

4 In virtue of what is an action of interest to the historian or social scientist?

Some actions will be of no possible interest to the social scientist. On 17 July 1995, I went into my garden and picked some sour cherries. Such an action certainly has an explanation: I desired some sour cherries and I believed that by picking some fruit from a specific tree in my garden, I could obtain some. Given the circumstances, it is hard to see how an explanation of that action could be of any interest to the social scientist. Other cherry pickings might be, in different circumstances. But that picking was not. Why should that be so?

It is important to see that this question is not the same as another question, with which it is sometimes conflated: which actions are social actions? Whether or not an action is a social action (as so described) can be determined a priori. Some action descriptions are social: writing a cheque, celebrating a marriage, witnessing a will. That is, it is logically or conceptually necessary for there to be a society, and certain rules or conventions, in order for persons to engage in actions of that description. Some philosophical disputes can be understood as disputes about whether certain action descriptions are social, for example, 'speaking a language'.

We need here another distinction: between action types and singular action tokens. An action type is a universal, which has many possible instances. Stalin moving his left thumb is an action type, since there could have been many such movings by him. An action token is an individual instance; it is an unrepeatable, dated item. Stalin moving his left thumb at a specific time is an action token.

Do social scientists explain action types or action tokens? One might suppose that to explain why Hitler annexed Austria in 1938 is to explain an action token; to explain why investors withdrew their bank deposits in 1929 is to explain why some action type had many instances. However, another way to consider this might be to say that social scientists only ever explain types, but that sometimes they explain why an action type had at least one instance (why there was at least one annexing of Austria by Hitler in 1938), and at other times why an action type had many instances (why there were many withdrawals of bank deposits by investors in 1929).

Now, not all social action, whether type or token, is of any interest to the social scientist. Not only will they be uninterested in explaining why I picked those sour cherries, they might be equally uninterested in explaining the social action token, my writing a cheque at a particular time for sour cherries. Further, they may have no interest in explaining why the social action type, writing a cheque for sour cherries, has many instances. They might be interested in explaining the origins and development of the system of capitalist agriculture, but that is not the same as an explanation of any action, type or token, one or many, made possible by that institution (unless, perhaps, methodological individualism is true).

So only some social actions and only some non-social actions (whether types or tokens) are of interest to the social scientist. Which ones are they? Those, presumably, which are thought to have consequences of social significance. But what kinds of consequences are those? I do not think that one can ultimately make sense of the idea of 'consequences of social significance' except via an account of 'consequences for the wellbeing or ill-being of a large number of individuals'. That latter concept has itself nothing irreducibly social about it. This is not to deny that the social scientist will also be interested in giving explanations

of historical and social events and structures, nor is it to argue that such explanations must be in principle reducible to explanations of individual actions of significance. It is merely to say that there is no way in which to circumscribe which sorts of actions the social scientist will want to explain other than by using an ultimately ethical notion of the wellbeing of individuals. It is, of course, consistent with this that the wellbeing of an individual will itself include the satisfaction of their need for relationships with other persons.

See also: FUNCTIONAL EXPLANATION; HOLISM AND INDIVIDUALISM IN HISTORY AND SOCIAL SCIENCE

References and further reading

* Ayer, A.J. (1967) 'Man as a subject for science', in P. Laslett and W.G. Runciman (eds), *Philosophy, Politics and Society*, Oxford: Blackwell, 3rd series. (A good discussion of the compatibility of the interpretative and causal approaches to the explanation of human action.)
* Dilthey, W. (1976) *Selected Writings*, ed. by H.P. Rickman, Cambridge: Cambridge University Press. (A major contribution to the hermeneutic tradition of action explanation.)
* Elster, J. (1983) *Explaining Technical Change*, Cambridge: Cambridge University Press. (A presentation of the causal feedback loop account of functional explanation.)
* Gardiner, P. (ed.) (1978) *The Philosophy of History*, Oxford: Oxford University Press. (A useful collection of the literature in the philosophy of history on the explanation of action. Essays by William Dray, Carl Hempel, and others are included.)
Hempel, C. (1942) 'The function of general laws in history', repr. in *Aspects of Scientific Explanation*, New York: Free Press, 1965. (A major contribution to the causal tradition of action explanation, although Hempel himself eschews explicit use of the concept of causation.)
—— (1959) 'The logic of functional analysis', repr. in *Aspects of Scientific Explanation*, New York: Free Press, 1965. (An alternative to the causal feedback loop account of functional explanation.)
Mill. J.S. (1843) *System of Logic: Ratiocinative and Inductive*, London: Longman, 1970. (A classical statement of the causal position.)
* Ruben, D.-H. (1985) *The Metaphysics of the Social World*, London: Routledge. (A discussion of the varieties of methodological individualism and an assessment of their plausibility.)
—— (1990) 'Singular explanation and the social sciences', in P. French, T. Uehling, Jr., and H.

Wettstein (eds), *Midwest Studies in Philosophy: The Philosophy of the Human Sciences*, Notre Dame, IN: University of Notre Dame Press, vol XV. (The volume as a whole is well worth browsing.)

Ryan, A. (1973) *The Philosophy of Social Explanation*, Oxford: Oxford University Press. (A somewhat dated but still useful collection of articles on a range of issues about explanation in the social sciences.)

* Winch, P. (1958) *The Idea of a Social Science*, London: Routledge. (A well-known statement of the non-causal view of action explanation.)

Wright, G.H. von (1971) *Explanation and Understanding*, London: Routledge & Kegan Paul. (An unrivalled, insightful discussion of the contrasting merits of the two great traditions of explanation.)

* Zeleny, J. (1980) *The Logic of Marx*, Oxford: Blackwell. (A defence and elaboration of the method of structural explanation.)

DAVID-HILLEL RUBEN

EXPRESSION, ARTISTIC

see ARTISTIC EXPRESSION

EXTERNAL WORLD SCEPTICISM *see* SCEPTICISM

EXTERNALISM IN EPISTEMOLOGY

see INTERNALISM AND EXTERNALISM IN EPISTEMOLOGY

F

FA

Fa is a technical term in a variety of Chinese philosophical traditions. As a noun it means 'standard' or 'norm', and, by extension, 'law'. As a verb it means 'to be in accord with'. The disagreements among the various indigenous schools tended to focus on the origin and nature of fa, whether it is an order or pattern within things or an external pattern to which things conform. When Buddhism entered China, translators often used fa for rendering the Sanskrit term dharma. Depending on context, the Buddhist term could refer to true teachings, moral duty, phenomenal reality or rule.

Like other philosophical terms, *fa* originally had an ordinary use in the Chinese language. As such, *fa* appears as a noun or a verb, suggesting either a standard to be met or the action of meeting that standard. Chinese philosophers differed over the external or internal nature of *fa*. Some maintained it is internal to things, part of their natural expression. Others held that *fa* is an external standard to which things normatively conform. Daoist philosophy tended to favour the internalist view; for example, Laozi used *fa* as a verb in maintaining that the *dao* itself 'accorded with' things as they naturally are (see DAODEJING). Most other classical Chinese philosophers, however, used the term primarily as a noun to express a norm or standard.

Because the social, moral and political dimensions of human experience were central to Chinese systems of thought, philosophers often analysed norms relevant to the harmony of the state. Generally, the Chinese thinkers assumed the ruler to be responsible for setting and enforcing these standards. In such contexts, the term *fa* assumed a meaning close to that of the English term 'law' or, more specifically, 'penal law' (see LAW, PHILOSOPHY OF; LAW AND RITUAL IN CHINESE PHILOSOPHY). The Confucians and Legalists were especially inclined to view *fa* in such a manner.

For Confucius, social order arises from the practice of 'ritual' or 'propriety' (*li*) rather than law. Social harmony derives from each person's following the appropriate forms of basic human relations. If the conditions are right and the ruler is a person of sufficient charismatic virtue, Confucius maintained, then the society will organize itself harmoniously

without legal sanctions. However, the Confucians also recognized that such ideal conditions do not necessarily prevail. When harmony breaks down, the ruler must enforce certain minimal standards of social behaviour through penal law (*fa*). In short, *fa* compensates for the inadequate practice of ritualized human interaction (see CONFUCIAN PHILOSOPHY, CHINESE).

The Legalists, as represented by HAN FEIZI for example, characterized the role of *fa* differently. For them, *fa* is not a last resort, but instead the very foundation of the harmonious state. According to the Legalists, the state evolves out of the authority of the ruler and that ruler's capacity to establish a system of laws enforced by sanctions. For the Legalists, therefore, *fa* is neither part of the natural order (as the Daoists generally maintained) nor a back-up system for the virtuous charisma of the ruler (as the Confucians held).

The Legalist philosophy was perhaps the first systematic attempt in China to deal with the state independently of discourse about virtue or morality (see LEGALIST PHILOSOPHY, CHINESE). It stressed rule by law rather than rule by virtuous people. The Legalists argued for a universal legal system applying even to the ruler who originally established the laws. In a pragmatic vein, the Legalists maintained that government office should be assigned on the grounds of the candidates' practical talents and skills rather than education or virtue. This was, however, a strict totalitarian system of penal law in which offenders were not re-educated but were immediately (and by modern standards severely) punished. Although the strict Legalist philosophy was generally discounted as too harsh and inflexible, its ideal of *fa* endured as a central philosophical category within Chinese political theories and practices.

Buddhism brought a new layer of meanings to the term. When the Chinese began to translate Indian Buddhist texts two thousand years ago, they used the Chinese word *fa* to render the Sanskrit term *dharma*. The Buddhist term itself has several facets of meaning, including 'real (that is, non-delusory) phenomenon', 'true teachings', 'moral duty' and 'rule'. The match between the two terms was not perfect. At the time of its introduction, Buddhism was understood by the Chinese to be a philosophy akin to Daoism (see BUDDHIST PHILOSOPHY, CHINESE). It is helpful, therefore, to consider how the Daoist notion of *fa* relates to the Buddhist *dharma*.

Both Daoism and Buddhism aim to understand phenomena for what they are in themselves, without their being coloured by human or personal ideas of 'usefulness'. There are vast differences between Daoist and Buddhist practice, however. In Daoism, the focus is on observing the natural pattern or way (*dao*) of things, of seeing human beings as part of a larger natural process (see DAO; DE). In Buddhism, on the other hand, the focus is on introspection and the eradication of the ego-centred projection of delusory contexts that lead one to interpret phenomena as 'mine', as 'permanent' and as 'desirable.' The Daoists and Buddhists share, however, the idea that if one sets right one's relation with the world, social morality will follow spontaneously. Specifically, for the Chinese Buddhists, if one eradicates the ego, one can experience the phenomena (*fa*) as they are in their own contexts without distortion. This experience will confirm the true teachings (*fa*) of Buddhism. Without ego, one will enact a spontaneous morality (*fa*). To achieve the proper attitude for the introspection leading to the eradication of ego, the monastic community sets social rules or laws (*fa*) that nurture detachment. When viewed in this light, we see how the different meanings of *dharma* in Buddhism are related and how the Buddhist term *dharma* could be construed as being consistent with aspects of the term fa, especially in its Daoist sense.

See also: BUDDHIST PHILOSOPHY, CHINESE; LEGALIST PHILOSOPHY, CHINESE; CONFUCIAN PHILOSOPHY, CHINESE; DAOIST PHILOSOPHY; DUTY AND VIRTUE, INDIAN CONCEPTIONS OF; LAW AND RITUAL IN CHINESE PHILOSOPHY; LAW, PHILOSOPHY OF

References and further reading

Ames, R.T. (1983) *The Art of Rulership: A Study in Ancient Chinese Political Thought*, Honolulu, HI: University of Hawaii Press. (Chapter 4, pages 108–41, is a thorough discussion of pre-Buddhist uses of the term *fa* in Chinese philosophy.)

Chan Wing-tsit (1963) *A Source Book in Chinese Philosophy*, Princeton, NJ: Princeton University Press. (A useful, inclusive definition of *fa* is found in the appendix, page 786; this index is generally useful in finding key uses of the term in various Chinese philosophies by following references to either 'law' or '*dharma*'.)

Hansen, C. (1994) '*Fa* (standards: laws) and meaning changes in Chinese philosophy', *Philosophy East and West* 44 (3): 433–88. (Discussion of the mean-

ing of *fa* within the context of a broader discussion of the philosophical issue of what it means for a word to change its meaning.)

Wu, J.C.H. (1967) 'The Status of the Individual in the Political and Legal Traditions of Old and New China', in C.A. Moore (ed.) *The Chinese Mind: Essentials of Chinese Philosophy and Culture*, Honolulu, HI: University of Hawaii Press, 213–37. (Helpful overview of key philosophical motifs in traditional Chinese conceptions of law.)

THOMAS P. KASULIS

FABRI, H. *see* ARISTOTELIANISM IN THE 17TH CENTURY

FACKENHEIM, EMIL LUDWIG (1916–)

Fackenheim is best known for his account of authentic philosophical and Jewish responses to the Nazi Holocaust. Fackenheim's thought, indebted to German philosophy, always had a practical, existential purpose. He aimed, consistently, to show how philosophical and theological thought could pay attention to lived experience in order to gain the understanding it sought. In this way, he exposed the varied ways in which thought and life, ideas and history, are interdependent. Philosophical and religious thought are grounded in historical experience and give direction to that experience; life is the ground of reflection and derives its meaning from it.

Fackenheim was born in Halle, Germany. Although aware of the dangers of Nazi persecution, he left Halle for Berlin, where in 1935 he began rabbinic studies at the Hochschule für die Wissenschaft des Judentums. After *Kristalnacht*, Fackenheim fled to Scotland and finally to Toronto, where he completed his doctorate with a dissertation on the doctrine of substance in the thought of the medieval Islamic authors known as the Sincere Brethren of Basra (see IKHWAN AL-SAFA'). Four years later, having served as a congregational rabbi in Hamilton, Ontario, he began to teach philosophy at Toronto. He spent the post-war years studying German Idealism. This period culminated with the publication of a book on Hegel's treatment of religion. In this early period he defended faith and revelation. Understanding revelation and the faith it engendered as a divine-human encounter, Fackenheim took that encounter to be the ground of genuine religious life. After 1966–7, Fackenheim turned his attention to the memory of the Nazi death camps. He came to see the radical evil that erupted there as a threat both to reason and to faith. His defence of reason and faith became increasingly historical as he interpreted the continuity of religious faith as part of an authentic philosophical and religious response to the Nazi atrocities. Fackenheim remained in Toronto until his retirement and subsequent emigration to Israel in 1982.

Fackenheim's work and thought are united by several interrelated themes. The first of these is the existential relevance of philosophical and theological thought. This was a central attraction of existential philosophy: thinking is not detached from life; it arises in a concrete situation and is a committed response to that situation. Fackenheim shunned antiquarianism as he immersed himself in the great philosophers of the past, from PLATO and ARISTOTLE and PLOTINUS to KANT, FICHTE, SCHELLING, HEGEL and HEIDEGGER. His aim was to grasp and grapple with the central issues of the present.

One of those issues is the conflict between reason and revelation. Stimulated by the thinking of Soren KIERKEGAARD, Martin BUBER, and later Franz ROSENZWEIG, Fackenheim struggled with the challenges made by modernity and modern philosophy to the very possibility of faith and revelation. First, there is modern secular philosophy and thought, the challenge of figures like FEUERBACH and FREUD. Then there is the philosophical overcoming of revelation in Schelling and ultimately in Hegel, where a genuine divine-human encounter is transformed into an expressive monism and religion is superseded by philosophy. Finally, there is the existential, historical challenge of an evil unprecedented and radical, the evil of the Holocaust and the Nazi death camps. Throughout his career, in the face of each wave of attack, Fackenheim held firm to the banner of revelation and defended it philosophically – early on as the possibility of a fundamental commitment that is no more an act of sheer faith than are the secularism or naturalism that denied it, later as a possible and even necessary response to the deepest vector of Nazi evil and hence as an expression of hope.

The final theme that pervades Fackenheim's career is a life-long reflection on the complex relationships between thought and life. It is this issue that leads him to Hegel. If any modern philosopher succeeded in articulating how reason and thought, while doing justice to all of history and life, still tame them, it was Hegel. If Hegel failed, perhaps the project cannot succeed. Perhaps, ultimately, life is intractable to

thought; perhaps thought must unavoidably go to school with life.

As Fackenheim, in 1966 and after, makes the important, even heroic decision to confront the Nazi Holocaust in all its darkness and its horror, the interdependence of thought and life emerges as central to his thinking (see HOLOCAUST, THE). In the essays of 1967 and 1968 Fackenheim's analysis proceeds this way. The thinker, whether philosopher, theologian, historian, or social theorist, confronts Naziism and the death camps with the desire to understand. This desire is quite natural, an expression of aspiration to transcendence that is characteristic of all thought. But probity requires a sense of unease and even humility. The cognitive capacity is paralyzed by the enormity of the event; what can thought do? It can recognize that meaning and purpose are one thing, response another. The elicitation of meaning here may be impossible. But the response is unavoidable. Hence the thinker, seeking guidance, comes to the realization that real, living Jews have all along been responding in their own ways. In order to understand how one ought to respond and why, the thinker turns to actual response and engages in a 'transcendental' analysis of what makes such response necessary and possible. It is this analysis that leads to Fackenheim's momentous and famous conclusion – that for Jews, whether religious or non-religious, the Divine Commanding Voice was present at Auschwitz and that the imperative which it 'spoke' (and still speaks) was a commandment to resist Nazi purposes, not to give Hitler posthumous victories. This command becomes a means of identifying the ground and content of the necessity for contemporary Jewish existence.

But if authentic post-Holocaust existence – here, Jewish existence – is necessary, is it possible? In the essays of 1967–8, Fackenheim had relied on the Kantian conviction that ought implies can. Paralleling this is the neo-orthodox faith that a God who commands at the same time graciously gives the freedom to respond. By the late 1970s and early 1980s, if not before, these strategies had come to seem inadequate. Indeed, they seemed to belittle the heroism of those who had resisted, as well as the grim courage of those who had not. In the central sections of *To Mend the World* (1982) Fackenheim attempts to rectify the fault. Thought, he acknowledges, tries to comprehend the evil, the pain, the horror, the agency, but as it moves from victim to victim and from agent to agent it acknowledges its own inadequacy. As it tries to grasp why the perpetrators of genocide committed their many crimes, thought fails and fails again until, in a shocking resolution, it grasps the death camps as a whole that is greater than its parts, a whole of horror, a world of evil, and thought is surprised. But the surprise is not neutral; it is recognition, amazement, and horrified recoil, all at once, and while it contains a kind of cognitive grasp, it registers as well a compulsion to oppose. Fackenheim finds this conjunction, this attitude, realized in the actions of some who lived that recognition and that opposition, victims who at the moment of truth resisted and tell us how their resistance was born out of a recognition of the evil, its intent, and the sense of obligation that they felt. In this way, an ontological possibility is grounded in an ontic reality, and in this way too theory and praxis, realized in the event itself as a synthetic whole, lead to action. The theory is incomplete without the praxis, the praxis impossible without the theory.

See also: HOLOCAUST, THE; JEWISH PHILOSOPHY, CONTEMPORARY

List of works

Fackenheim, E.L. (1961) *Metaphysics and Historicity*, Milwaukee, WI: Marquette University Press. (Aquinas Lecture on the universality of philosophical thought and a defence of existential, situated selfhood against the charge of historicism.)

—— (1967) *The Religious Dimension in Hegel's Thought*, Bloomington, IN: Indiana University Press. (Systematic examination of the role of religion in Hegel's thought, from the youthful works and the Phenomenology of Spirit through the *Encyclopedia of the Philosophical Sciences*.)

—— (1970) *God's Presence in History*, New York: New York University Press. (Deems Lectures on Jewish theology in midrashic literature, the challenges of modernity and the Enlightenment, and exposure to the Holocaust.)

—— (1973) *Encounters Between Judaism and Modern Philosophy*, New York: Basic Books. (Philosophical confrontations between Judaism and modern empirical and ananlytical philosophy, Kantian thought, Hegel and existential philosophy.)

—— (1982) *To Mend the World*, New York: Schocken Books; 3rd edn, 1994. (Systematic recovery of Jewish thought through encounters with Spinoza, Rosenzweig, Hegel and Heidegger; justification for the necessity and possibility of post-Holocaust response by Judaism, Christianity, philosophers and others.)

—— (1996) *The God Within: Kant, Schelling and Historicity, Essays by E.L. Fackenheim*, ed. J. Burbidge, Toronto: University of Toronto Press.
(Collection of Fackenheim's essays on Kant, Schelling, Hegel and German philosophy.)

References and further reading

Greenspan, L. and Nicholson, G. (eds) (1992) *Fackenheim: German Philosophy & Jewish Thought*, Toronto: University of Toronto Press. (Essays on philosophical and theological themes in Fackenheim's work; includes a complete bibliography.)

Morgan, M.L. (ed.) (1987) *The Jewish Thought of Emil Fackenheim*, Detroit: Wayne State University Press. (Comprehensive anthology with introductions and complete bibliography.)

—— (1996) *Jewish Philosophers and Jewish Philosophy: Essays by Emil Fackenheim*, Bloomington, IN: Indiana University Press. (Essays on Jewish philosophers and post-Holocaust Jewish philosophy.)

—— (1996) 'The Central Problem of Fackenheim's *To Mend the World*', *The Journal of Jewish Thought and Philosophy* 5: 297–312. (Analysis of Fackenheim's argument for the ground of the possibility of post-Holocaust response.)

MICHAEL L. MORGAN

FACTS

The existence and nature of facts is disputed. In ordinary language we often speak of facts ('that's a fact') but it is hard to take such talk seriously since it can be paraphrased away. It is better to argue for the existence of facts on the basis of three connected theoretical roles for facts. First, facts as the referents of true sentences: 'the cat sat on the mat', if true, refers to the fact that the cat sat on the mat. Second, facts as the truth-makers of true sentences: the fact that the cat sat on the mat is what makes 'the cat sat on the mat' true. Third, facts as causal relata, related in such sentences as 'Caesar died because Brutus stabbed him'. The so-called 'slingshot' argument aims to show that these roles are misconceived.

1   Roles for facts
2   The slingshot argument

1   Roles for facts

We often speak of facts in ordinary discourse. For example, we append 'the fact' to an indirect sentential clause in sentences such as 'Smith was surprised at the fact that Brown's wife left him'. It is controversial whether this talk of facts is to be taken at face value since the apparent commitment to facts disappears under analysis, becoming 'Smith heard with surprise that Brown's wife left him. Brown's wife left him', in which no mention is made of any fact. Other ordinary talk of facts is also subject to paraphrase: 'It is a fact that p' is equivalent to 'It is true that p', 'That is a fact' is equivalent to 'That is true'. This last style of paraphrase has been taken in two ways: either as showing that facts do not exist, or that they exist but can be identified with the true bearers of truth-values. Following the second course, the bearers of truth-values are commonly taken to be propositions, that is, the meanings of sentences, and facts are then identified with true propositions.

Rather than squeeze ontological juice from ordinary language, we can argue for the existence of facts on the basis of theoretical demands. First, there is a role for facts within semantic theory, as the worldly referents of true sentences. So a true sentence such as 'The cat sat on the mat' refers to the fact that the cat sat on the mat, sometimes called the situation or state of affairs of the cat sitting on the mat.

A related second role for facts lies within a correspondence theory of truth (see TRUTH, CORRESPONDENCE THEORY OF). The unworkable correspondence theory of logical atomism, in which correspondence consists in a structural isomorphism between a true atomic sentence and the fact to which it corresponds, is replaced with a truth-maker principle of the form 'every true sentence has a truth-maker' (see LOGICAL ATOMISM). This principle retains the doctrine that the world is independent of linguistic description and must be a certain way for a given sentence to be true of it. The intuitive idea is that a truth-maker grounds the truth of a sentence, where the grounding can be spelled out in a modal fashion: entity E is a truth-maker for the sentence S just in case necessarily, if E exists, then S is true. Facts are introduced as the required truth-makers. Neither the particular cat nor the property of sitting on the mat makes 'The cat sat on the mat' true; each might exist even if the sentence is false. But the fact that the cat sat on the mat, consisting of the cat instantiating the property of sitting on the mat, will do the job. Facts as worldly referents or truth-makers of true sentences are best conceived as composite entities, having particulars and properties or relations as constituents, and as themselves parts of the actual world, unlike true propositions which belong to the abstract and other-worldly realm of sense.

Composite worldly facts may play a third role as causal relata (see CAUSATION §6). One way of reporting singular causation uses the sentential connective 'because' (as in 'Caesar died because Brutus stabbed him'), which is true only if the flanking sentences are true. And if the truth-maker principle is right, these sentences need facts as truth-makers, and so the original sentence can be understood as reporting a causal relation between these facts. This account of causal relata has been criticized by Davidson (1967) using the so-called slingshot argument.

2 The slingshot argument

The aim of the slingshot argument is to show that a causal 'because' would have to be truth-functional: that is, the truth-value of a sentence containing the causal 'because' is preserved if one of the sentences flanking the 'because' is replaced by another which shares its truth-value. But it cannot be truth-functional, so the assumption that there is a causal 'because' must be rejected (see DAVIDSON, D.).

In more detail, suppose we are given a true sentence featuring the purported causal 'because': for example, 'Caesar died because Brutus stabbed Caesar'. The idea of the slingshot is to show that this sentence entails a sentence such as 'Caesar died because Caesar had a big nose', which differs from the first only in that a true sentence is substituted for a true sentence flanking the 'because'. So we have reached the absurd result that the causal 'because' is truth-functional.

The steps of the argument are licensed by two premises: that a necessarily equivalent sentence can be substituted for a sentence flanking the 'because' without change of truth-value; and that a co-referential singular term can be substituted for a singular term occurring in one of the flanking sentences without change of truth-value. Here is one way to construct a slingshot argument.

(1) Caesar died because Brutus stabbed Caesar.

(2) Caesar died because $\{x: x$ is a natural number and Brutus stabbed Caesar$\} = \{x: x$ is a natural number$\}$.

(3) Caesar died because $\{x: x$ is a natural number and Caesar had a big nose$\} = \{x: x$ is a natural number$\}$.

(4) Caesar died because Caesar had a big nose.

The move from (1) to (2) is justified by the first premise. The singular term '$\{x: x$ is a natural number and Brutus stabbed Caesar$\}$' names the set which contains every object to which the predicate '...is a natural number and Brutus stabbed Caesar' applies; similarly for '$\{x: x$ is a natural number$\}$'. So 'Brutus stabbed Caesar' is necessarily equivalent to '$\{x: x$ is a natural number and Brutus stabbed Caesar} = {x: x is a natural number}'.

The move from (2) to (3) is justified by the second premise. We replace the singular term '{x: x is a natural number and Brutus stabbed Caesar}' with the co-referential '{x: x is a natural number and Caesar had a big nose}'; these are guaranteed to be co-referential given that 'Brutus stabbed Caesar' and 'Caesar had a big nose' have the same truth-value. The move from (3) to (4) is justified by the first premise and the fact that '{x: x is a natural number and Caesar had a big nose} = {x: x is a natural number}' and 'Caesar had a big nose' are necessarily equivalent.

We have thus shown that a causal 'because' would have to be truth-functional. But it cannot be, so there is no such 'because'. The slingshot argument is valid, so at least one of the premises must be rejected if facts are to be causal relata. Indeed the slingshot argument also threatens facts in their roles as referents of true sentences and truth-makers for true sentences. For the argument can be used to establish the truth-function-ality of 'sentence S refers to the fact that P' and 'sentence S is made true by the fact that P', by operating on the sentence following 'the fact that'. This yields the undesirable result that a true sentence refers to and is made true by any fact. The slingshot argument cannot be dismissed as logical trickery, for it exposes a critical lacuna in the theory of composite facts. Any motivated criticism of the argument must rely on an account of the identity conditions of facts, and these remain undecided.

See also: EVENTS; NEGATIVE FACTS IN CLASSICAL INDIAN PHILOSOPHY; ONTOLOGICAL COMMITMENT

References and further reading

Armstrong, D.M. (1989) *Universals: An Opinionated Introduction*, Boulder, CO: Westview Press. (An introductory guide to the theory of properties, with facts – or states of affairs as Armstrong calls them – as worldly composites in their role as truth-makers.)

Barwise, J. and Perry, J. (1983) *Situations and Attitudes*, Cambridge, MA: MIT Press. (Advocates of a formal semantic theory, situation semantics, based on the idea that true sentences refer to worldly facts or 'situations'.)

* Davidson, D. (1967) 'Causal Relations', in *Essays on Actions and Events*, Oxford: Clarendon Press, 1980, 149–62. (Contains the slingshot argument against facts as causal relata.)

—— (1984) *Inquiries into Truth and Interpretation*, Oxford: Clarendon Press. (Chapters 2 and 3 contain further uses of the slingshot argument, under-

mining the theoretical roles of worldly facts by showing that every true sentence refers to the same fact and that a given true sentence corresponds to every fact.)

Geach, P.T. (1963) 'Aristotle on Conjunctive Propositions', in *Logic Matters*, Oxford: Blackwell, 1972. (Facts as 'a dream of our language'. §1.2, 21–3 is especially relevant.)

Mellor, D.H. (1987) 'The Singularly Affecting Facts of Causation', in *Matters of Metaphysics*, Cambridge: Cambridge University Press, 1991, 201–24. (A friend of facts as truth-makers and causal relata; criticises Davidson's slingshot argument by denying its second premise.)

Olson, K.R. (1987) *An Essay on Facts*, CSLI Lecture Notes Number 6, Stanford, CA: Center for the Study of Language and Information, Stanford University. (A detailed appraisal of rival accounts of facts and a history of the slingshot argument.)

Russell, B.A.W. (1918) 'The Philosophy of Logical Atomism', in *Logic and Knowledge*, ed. R.C. Marsh, London: Allen & Unwin, 1956, 177–281. (Facts as constituents of the world corresponding to true *and* false sentences within the framework of logical atomism.)

ALEX OLIVER

FACT/VALUE DISTINCTION

According to proponents of the fact/value distinction, no states of affairs in the world can be said to be values, and evaluative judgments are best understood not to be pure statements of fact. The distinction was important in twentieth-century ethics, and debate continues about the metaphysical status of value, the epistemology of value, and the best characterization of value-judgments.

A fact is an actual state of affairs (see FACTS). A value is either something good (pleasure, for example), or a belief that something is good (to say that pleasure is one of my values is to say that I believe pleasure to be good) (see VALUES). The fact/value distinction was of great importance in twentieth-century moral philosophy, a distinction being drawn between actual states of affairs and values in both senses (each sense not always being clearly distinguished from the other).

On one version of the fact/value distinction, there are no values 'in the world'. John Mackie (1977), for example, argued that such items were too peculiar to be fitted into any decent metaphysics or epistemology, and that the nonexistence of values was the best way to explain disagreements in evaluations. According to existentialist ethics, the non-factuality of value leaves us in a position of radical freedom to choose (see EXISTENTIALIST ETHICS §§1–2).

The distinction understood as concerning evaluations suggests evaluations are not pure attempts to state facts. One famous and influential version of this view is that of Hume (1739/40), who claimed that 'ought' conclusions do not follow logically from 'is' statements (see HUME. D. §4; LOGIC OF ETHICAL DISCOURSE §§1–3). So if you claim successfully that something ought to be done (this may be one of your values) on the basis of an argument apparently referring only to facts, it must be the case that one of your 'factual' statements involves a covert 'ought'.

This version of the fact/value distinction, allied to a narrow conception of what can count as a factual statement, has been of great importance. If facts are, for example, restricted to purely neutral descriptions, such as those found in natural science, moral judgments may be seen as other than fact-stating. (It has been argued by some that science itself is an evaluative enterprise, so that the fact/value distinction is spurious – see ANALYTIC ETHICS §2.) Words such as 'good' or 'right' can then be claimed to have special, non-descriptive roles. According to emotivism, to claim that X is good is to express a pro-attitude towards it, and perhaps to encourage others to adopt that attitude; according to prescriptivism, the claim is to be understood as imperatival (see EMOTIVISM; PRESCRIPTIVISM). On such views, certain words, such as 'courageous' for example, may have some factual content; but this can always be distinguished, at least conceptually, from the evaluative content.

Those who have claimed that values are part of the world and that evaluations are fact-stating include advocates of moral realism (see MORAL REALISM). This comes in at least two varieties. Ethical naturalism states that values are natural facts, 'natural' meaning that such facts are to be identified with, or seen as constituted by, facts open to investigation by natural science. Ethical non-naturalism sees values as facts *sui generis*, any attempt to identify them with natural facts being to commit what G.E. Moore (1903) called the 'naturalistic fallacy' (see NATURALISM IN ETHICS; MOORE, G.E. §1).

See also: LOGIC OF ETHICAL DISCOURSE

References and further reading

Ayer, A.J. (1936) *Language, Truth and Logic*, London: Gollancz; 2nd edn, 1946, ch. 6. (An early and influential statement of emotivism.)

Foot, P.F. (1978) *Virtues and Vices*, Oxford: Blackwell, esp. ch. 8. (Collection of essays by an influential ethical naturalist.)

Hare, R.M. (1952) *The Language of Morals*, Oxford: Oxford University Press. (Key exposition of prescriptivism.)

* Hume, D. (1739/40) *A Treatise of Human Nature*, ed. L.A. Selby-Bigge, revised by P.H. Nidditch, Oxford: Clarendon Press, 2nd edn, 1978, book 3, part I, section 1. (Contains 'Hume's Law' concerning 'is' and 'ought'.)

* Mackie, J.L. (1977) *Ethics: Inventing Right and Wrong*, Harmondsworth: Penguin. (Claims that values are not facts, but that moral language attempts to state facts.)

* Moore, G.E. (1903) *Principia Ethica*, Cambridge: Cambridge University Press. (Critique of naturalism and defence of non-naturalism.)

ROGER CRISP

FAITH

Faith became a topic of discussion in the Western philosophical tradition on account of its prominence in the New Testament, where the having or taking up of faith is often urged by writers. The New Testament itself echoes both Hellenistic concepts of faith and older biblical traditions, specifically that of Abraham in the Book of Genesis.

The subsequent attention of philosophers has been focused primarily on three topics: the nature of faith, the connection between God's goodness and human responsibility, and the relation of faith to reason. Discussions on the nature of faith, from Aquinas to Tillich, have tried to examine the subject in terms of whether it is a particular form of knowledge, virtue, trust and so on. Regarding divine goodness, the argument has primarily focused on the relationship between faith and free will, and whether lack of faith is the responsibility of the individual or of God. Concerning the relation between faith and reason, there are two quite separate issues: the relation of faith to theorizing, and the rationality of faith. Aquinas in particular argued that faith is a necessary prerequisite for reasoning and intellectual activity, while later, John Locke explored the relationship between faith, reason and rationality, and concluded that faith can be reached through reason. This latter viewpoint was later heavily criticized by Wittgenstein and his followers.

1   The New Testament background
2   The nature of faith
3   Faith, volition and responsibility

4 Faith and reason: the relation of faith to theorizing
5 Faith and reason: the rationality of faith

1 The New Testament background

In the course of everyday life we speak of persons as having faith in one thing and another – in themselves, in other persons, in causes, in the ability of themselves or others to carry out some project, and so forth. One can imagine some philosopher undertaking, in disinterested fashion, to uncover the nature and role in human life of this phenomenon of having faith; and others then taking up the topic in response to his discussion. There have in fact been a few such discussions. But that is not how faith became a prominent topic of discussion in Western philosophy. It became that because of its prominence in the New Testament; more precisely, because of the prominence the New Testament gives to faith in its description of the mode of life that it advocates. The context is, of course, that the New Testament belongs to the canon of the Christian Church and that Christianity has been powerfully formative of philosophy in the West.

Various writers of the New Testament record Jesus as having urged his hearers to take up the stance of faith. Likewise, those and other New Testament writers urge their own readers to take up this stance. Indeed, they urge their readers to take it up towards Jesus himself. It is clear that when the writers urged this on their readers, and when Jesus urged it on his hearers, they and he saw themselves as doing so on behalf of God.

Sometimes when the New Testament writers represent God as requiring faith of us, they are thinking of faith as one among other things that God requires of us. Faith is then one among other 'virtues'. Paul, in the famous thirteenth chapter of his first letter to the Christians in Corinth, urges on his readers hope and charity along with faith; he concludes that of the three, charity is greatest – on the ground that whereas in the New Age there will no longer be any need for faith and hope, the relevance of charity will abide forever. In other passages, however, the New Testament writers appear to use 'faith' to refer to that total stance towards God to which, on behalf of God, they call us. Then faith in things not seen, hope and charity are three of the requisite *manifestations* of faith. As Rudolf Bultmann remarks, 'In Primitive Christianity, *pistis* became the leading term for the relation of man to God' (1968: 205).

Bultmann observes that in both classical and Hellenistic Greek, the root meaning of *pistis* and its grammatical variants is 'trust' (reliance, belief in, confidence). The objects of *pisteuein* are characteristically such things as contracts and oaths, laws,

armaments and persons. Likewise the words of a person can be the object of trust, in which case the sense of *pisteuein* shades towards that of our 'believe'. And sometimes, not surprisingly, *pisteuein* has the nuance of 'to obey'.

In the New Testament as well, the root meaning of the term, when used for that comprehensive stance towards God to which God calls us, is 'trust'. That is especially clear in the famous discourse on faith in the eleventh chapter of Hebrews. The chapter opens with a crisp definition of faith: 'faith is the *hypostasis* of things hoped for, the *elenchos* of things not seen'. In older translations, *hypostasis* and *elenchos* were translated, literally and straightforwardly, as 'substance' and 'evidence' respectively. The authors of the Revised Standard Version, in recognition of the fact that both words are here being used eccentrically, translate the passage as 'the assurance of things hoped for, the conviction of things not seen'. After giving his definition of faith, and indicating its importance by adding that 'by it the men of old received divine approval', the writer cites examples. His first example is a case of 'conviction of things not seen', not of 'assurance of things hoped for': 'By faith we understand that the world was created by the word of God, so that what is seen was made out of things which do not appear'. All the other examples are cases of both. And in each case, the ground of the assured hope is trust in God's promise to save and bless. It was on account of hope thus grounded that men and women of old 'received divine approval'.

Not only has the Western intellectual tradition been influenced by this general picture of faith and its proper role in human life, but some of the specifics of the New Testament discussion have been influential as well. That is especially true for the discussion of faith in Paul's letter to the Roman Christians. The topic in hand is how to understand theologically the relation of the Christian Church, with its mixture of Jews and Gentiles, to the people of Israel, given that in Genesis it says that God's covenant was with Abraham and all his descendants. The issue was of intense existential concern to Paul, since he was both ethnically Jewish and a Christian. A corollary of the theological issue was the practical issue of whether Christians should be required to follow the ritual practices of Judaism.

The first move in Paul's solution is to refer to Genesis 15: 3, where it says, using Paul's near-paraphrase, that 'Abraham believed God, and it was reckoned to him as righteousness' (Romans 4: 3). From this, along with certain ancillary considerations, Paul draws two conclusions. First, that the divine promise (covenant) is not with those who are descendants of Abraham 'after the flesh' but with those who are descendants of Abraham 'according to the Spirit' – that is to say, not with those who happen to be ethnically Jewish but with those who share Abraham's faith in God and God's promises. Though Paul never offers a definition of faith in the manner of the writer of the book of Hebrews, it is clear that for him, too, trusting in the promises of God is the core, if not the whole, of what he has in mind. The second conclusion Paul draws is that what makes persons pleasing to God is not their performance of some array of ethical and ritual 'works', but simply faith. In the language Paul uses, we are 'justified by faith'. To suppose that one's performance of certain ethical and ritual 'works' would make one just before God would be to suppose that one could achieve that status on one's own — that one could earn it. But we cannot earn it, since we all inevitably in one way or another fail to perform the full panoply of 'works' prescribed in the manner prescribed. Yet Abraham was declared to be righteous before God – that is, just (justified). It follows that having the status of being just before God is a gift on God's part, a status God accords one – on the ground of one's faith. If we are not to fall into contradictions, we must also then understand faith itself as a gift of God, rather than as a 'work' which earns the status of being righteous (justified) before God.

2 The nature of faith

The philosophical discussions of faith almost all fall under one or the other of three headings. In the first place, there is a long history of discussions on the nature of faith. Of what genus is faith a species? Is it a species of believing propositions on say-so? Is it a species of loyalty to some person or cause? Is it a species of trusting someone? Is it a species of believing what someone has promised? Is it a species of 'concern'? Is it a virtue of a certain sort? Is it a species of knowledge? If so, of what sort: *agnitio* (recognition, acknowledgement), *cognitio*, or what? An exceptionally fine example of a philosophical discussion concerning the nature of faith is that by Thomas AQUINAS (§14) in *Summa theologiae* IIaIIae, qq.1–7.

The disputes which have arisen among those who propound different analyses of faith have no doubt often had a large component of purely verbal disagreement; if one looks beneath the surface, however, usually one will find a great deal more at stake than just how the word 'faith' should be used. What is customarily at stake is how to understand the fundamental character of a person's proper relation to God; what is often also at stake is the nature of God and of the human being. To give an example: the twentieth-century German-American theologian Paul

TILLICH (§4) argued that faith is 'ultimate concern'. That proposal was in good measure motivated by Tillich's traditional view that faith is the core of a person's proper relation to God, combined with his very nontraditional conviction that God is the impersonal 'Ground of Being'. The latter conviction made it impossible for him to think of faith as trusting in God's promises – an impersonal entity cannot make promises. Another example: there was a wide-ranging and highly diffuse dispute in the twentieth century as to whether faith has propositional content. The quick way with the dispute would have been to say that on one concept of faith it does, and on another it does not. But once again, what was actually under dispute, in the context of the shared conviction that faith constitutes the fundamental character of the Christian life, was the nature of divine revelation. Those who held out for faith as having propositional content were of the view that God reveals truths, and that faith consists in part in accepting those truths. Those who held that faith does not have propositional content were of the view that divine revelation consists simply in God manifesting God's self, and that propositions enter the picture only when we human beings interpret the divine self-manifestation. Many other examples could be cited to make the same point: for example, the dispute between the Reformers, who insisted that faith at bottom is *fiducia* (belief *in*), and their medieval opponents, who customarily defined faith as *fides* (belief *that*).

3 Faith, volition and responsibility

Paul's theology of faith in his letter to the Roman Christians has spawned an enormous quantity of theological reflections and controversies. These – the second major type of discussion on faith – have repeatedly spilled over into philosophy. The reason is obvious. Paul interpreted Judaism as a religion of 'works righteousness'. That is to say, he interpreted Judaism as holding that the satisfactory performance of prescribed ethical and ritual 'works' would earn one the status of being righteous (justified) before God. To forestall Christianity becoming Judaism under another guise, with the 'work' that earns justification now being faith, he went on to argue that faith itself is not a 'work' of the person, in which that person can 'glory', but a 'work' of God. Some of the questions this picture poses are subtle; others are obvious. If faith is entirely a gift of God and not a 'work' of the human being, how can anyone other than God rightly be held accountable for a given human being's lack of faith? How can it be just of God to punish a person for lacking faith? Indeed, how can it be just of God to grant it to some and not to others – since presumably the gift of faith itself can no more be earned than can the status of being justified before God? If faith is a good, how can it be good of God to withhold it from certain human beings? To say that the Pauline view posed profound issues of responsibility, free agency, and justice would be to understate the matter. It can scarcely be doubted that the depth of the discussion of these issues in the philosophical tradition of the West is in good measure due to the Pauline inheritance.

4 Faith and reason: the relation of faith to theorizing

The bulk of the remaining discussions of faith, in the philosophical tradition of the West, have been concerned with faith and reason, to use the traditional nomenclature. The nomenclature in fact covers issues of two quite different sorts: the role of faith in theorizing, and the rationality of faith itself.

Issues surrounding the role of faith in theorizing arose out of the confluence between the Bible on the one hand and the texts of classical Greek philosophy on the other. Both Plato and Aristotle held that the ideal human life is the life devoted to theorizing. Though their understanding of theorizing was different in various ways, both regarded it as the acquisition of knowledge, *episteme*, this being understood as awareness or insight; and Plato especially was emphatic in his insistence that the acquisition of *episteme* requires turning away from opinion or belief (*doxa*). Almost everybody in the Christian tradition of late antiquity and the Middle Ages agreed with the classical Greeks that rational insight is a human ideal. Yet none of them thought of faith as *episteme* – or, to use the Latin, *scientia*; all were vividly aware of Paul's statement, in 1 Corinthians 13, that 'now we see in a mirror dimly, but then face to face. Now I know in part; then I shall understand fully'. Hence the problem: as Christians they could not forswear faith, nor regard it as unimportant. Yet, as inheritors of the Greek tradition, they found themselves incapable of renouncing the ideal of rational insight into reality. The 'faith and reason' problem of late antiquity and the Middle Ages was the problem of how to resolve this tension.

Rather than offering at this point a rapid taxonomy of the various attempts at resolution, the main contours of a representative and influential formulation – that of Thomas AQUINAS (§11) – will be sketched. Since the deepest happiness of a rational being is found in, and to be derived from, rational activity of the noblest sort, and since God is the one who, above all, is worth our being in rational contact with, our deepest happiness is to be achieved by gaining rational, intellectual contact with God. In

general, it is not just the *activity* of exercising reason that gives us happiness, but the *love* of the object known, which is the intrinsic accompaniment of achieving the goal of the activity – namely, coming to know.

One way of gaining intellectual contact with God is by the practice of Aristotelian *scientia*: one starts from propositions which some rational being has seen to be true, and then proceeds to deduce consequences. In the ideal case, one's premises are propositions that one has oneself seen to be true. Given our human limitations, however, that is often not possible. *Scientia* in its actuality is a communitarian enterprise in which one practitioner often takes it on the say-so of another that they, the latter, have constructed a demonstration of *P* starting from propositions which they personally saw to be true, and in which the first practitioner then takes *P* as a premise for their own work, without trying to prove it independently for themselves. It was Aquinas' conviction that it is possible to prove certain things about God in the ideal fashion; it is possible to construct a natural theology – a *scientia* of God (see NATURAL PHILOSOPHY, MEDIEVAL §§3, 7).

This *scientia* has its limitations, however, especially when assessed by reference to the happiness it contributes to human life. Prominent among the deficiencies, though by no means exhaustive of them, is the fact that, relative to the fullness of God's reality, there is not very much that one can prove about God. Natural theology, as Aquinas saw and practised it, was as subtle and complex in its argumentation and as rich in its results as any other natural scientific enterprise; yet, when one surveys the whole, one notices that nowhere does it yield knowledge of the nature (essence) of God. All that is provable is various relations of God to other things, various consequences of God's activity, and various things that God is not.

Now suppose we understand faith as belonging to the genus of 'believing something on someone's say-so' – specifically, on God's say-so. Faith thus understood also puts us in rational, intellectual contact with God. And when compared to natural theology, it proves advantageous in a number of ways. Prominent among them is the fact that the content of faith extends, at various points, beyond the reach of natural theology; belief that God is trinitarian in nature is an example. On the other hand, there is one serious and undeniable deficiency in faith when compared to natural theology. Whereas the practitioner of natural theology comes to 'see' various things to be true of God, the believer is confined to the inferior mental state of believing things about God on say-so. It is indeed God's say-so; and that makes faith more than mere opinion. Though like opinion in being belief, faith is unlike opinion in being utterly reliable belief, since God is the one believed. None the less, there is no gainsaying the fact that the mental act of 'seeing' a proposition to be true is distinctly better than that of believing it on say-so. It follows that even for a believer there is an advantage in the pursuit of natural theology – given that the believer in question has the time, the intelligence and the training necessary. By the practice of natural theology, the believer 'transmutes' that mode of intellectual contact which they have with regard to various propositions about God, from believing them on say-so to 'seeing' them to be true.

In this precise way, Aquinas would be happy to affirm the Augustinian formula, 'faith seeking understanding' (*fides quaerens intellectum*). He would, in his own way, also be willing to affirm Augustine's other formula, bequeathed to him by CLEMENT OF ALEXANDRIA, 'I believe in order that I may know' (*credo ut intelligam*). AUGUSTINE (§11) not only held that believers should strive to understand those things about God which they already believe, but also, conversely, that a condition of their coming to understand those things is that first they believe them. Augustine's thought was that faith is intertwined with love; and that there is no hope of attaining genuine understanding of God until one loves God. The theme is picked up and expressed in plaintive language by Anselm in the opening pages of his *Proslogion*, where he says that 'the smoke of our wrongdoing' will prohibit us from knowledge of God until that smoke is dissipated by faith. And it is picked up by Aquinas in his teaching that faith and charity are prerequisite for the achievement of such intellectual states as *scientia* and *sapientia* (wisdom).

5 Faith and reason: the rationality of faith

What strikes us in reading Aquinas and other medieval thinkers is that virtually no attention is paid to the question whether faith is itself rational. That question – the other 'faith and reason' topic – first became a matter of concern in the early Enlightenment. Again, rather than attempting a rapid taxonomy of positions held, it will be useful to develop the thought of a representative and influential figure – John LOCKE (§7).

Locke was living at a time when the traditional medieval view, that the great bulk of the texts bequeathed us together contain a unified body of highly articulate wisdom on moral, religious and philosophical matters, no longer seemed plausible. The textual tradition was now seen as fractured into incompatible components. Furthermore, though the Aristotelian concept of *scientia* remained part of Locke's conceptual repertoire, he himself was of the view that human knowledge in general, and *scientia* in particular, comes to very little. Thus it was that the main question to which Locke addressed himself was this: how should opinion (belief, *doxa*) be regulated? His proposal was that on those matters where we are obliged to do our best to find out the truth of the matter, we ought to employ the following practice: first, collect satisfactory evidence concerning the truth or falsity of the proposition in question, this evidence consisting of things of which one is certain because one 'sees' them to be true; then determine the probability of the proposition in question on that evidence; and then believe or disbelieve the proposition with a firmness proportioned to its probability on that evidence. Locke believed that every normal adult is obliged to do their best on matters of religion – hence, to employ his proposed method on such matters. And since it was his view that no substantive propositions about God can be 'seen' to be true, it followed straightforwardly that he was an 'evidentialist' concerning theistic belief. One is entitled to believe things about God only if one believes them on propositional evidence. Evidentialism concerning theistic belief has been a prominent position in the West ever since Locke.

Locke's own concept of faith was exactly the same as Aquinas': faith is believing things on God's say-so. Locke did not, however, follow Aquinas in holding that faith, thus understood, is a thing between knowledge and opinion; faith is just a species of opinion. Even more importantly, Locke differed from Aquinas in his emphatic insistence that it is irresponsible to believe something on the ground that God has said or revealed it unless one has good reason, of the indicated sort, for the assumption that God has indeed said or revealed it. Locke himself was of the view that only the occurrence of miracles provides good evidence for divine speech or revelation. In summary: believing something on God's say-so is responsible only if one has first established in the specified way that there indeed exists a God who is capable of speaking or revealing, and then established, secondly, that there is good evidence of the specified sort for the conclusion that God has said that particular thing.

The way in which Locke connected reason, responsibility and faith has proved enormously influential in the modern world. A great many believers have attempted to meet the Lockean requirement for responsible faith by a combination of collecting evidence of the requisite sort and narrowing the scope of their faith until it contains nothing that the evidence does not justify. A great many nonbelievers have tried to show that the attempts all fail – and that faith is accordingly irresponsible. And a helpful way to look at the project of the Oxford philosopher Richard Swinburne is to look at it as a rigorous and far-ranging attempt to resuscitate the Lockean project in the twentieth century (see Swinburne 1984).

In recent years, however, Locke's epistemology of religious belief has itself come under persistent attack. Wittgensteinian philosophers of religion, represented especially by D.Z. Phillips (1971, 1976), have argued that religion has its own unique criteria for acceptable belief, and that the flaw in Locke's argument is that he attempts to impose criteria of acceptability on religious belief which are alien thereto. By contrast, the so-called 'Reformed epistemologists' – Alston, Plantinga and Wolterstorff being prominent representatives – while vigorously affirming the propriety of formulating a general epistemology and working at doing so, have gone on to contend that Locke's foundationalist epistemology as a whole is seriously flawed; and that, in particular, it is often the case that a person who believes some theistic proposition immediately (or basically – that is, not on the basis of propositional evidence) is entirely within their rights in so doing. It is Locke's universalizing insistence on the need for propositional evidence concerning religious beliefs that is misguided (see RELIGION AND EPISTEMOLOGY).

It should be noted that neither the Wittgensteinians nor the Reformed epistemologists espouse the view that the rationality of faith is irrelevant to whether or not it is acceptable to embrace it. That position has traditionally gone under the name of 'fideism', and such thinkers as TERTULLIAN, WILLIAM OF OCKHAM (§9), Pierre BAYLE (§1), Søren KIERKEGAARD (§§4–5) and Leo SHESTOV (§§3–4) have regularly been classified as fideists. However, when one digs into the thought of the five thinkers mentioned on the topic of faith and reason, one not only finds it to be in each case subtle, and the various positions taken diverse, one also becomes less and less convinced of the propriety of describing any of them as a defender of irrationality in matters of faith. The difficulty lies in good measure in the protean character of our word 'rational'. If one accepts the Lockean paradigm of rationality, then the Wittgensteinians and the Reformed epistemologists will also be regarded as defenders of irrationality in matters of faith – a characterization which both parties themselves, however, would firmly reject. In short, interwoven with different positions on the rationality of faith are different positions on the nature of rationality – as, indeed, on the nature of faith.

See also: JUSTIFICATION, RELIGIOUS; NATURAL THEOLOGY; NEGATIVE THEOLOGY; RELIGIOUS EXPERIENCE; THEOLOGICAL VIRTUES

References and further reading

Alston, W.P. (1991) *Perceiving God*, Ithaca, NY: Cornell University Press. (An extended 'Reformed epistemological' treatment of religious experience.)

Aquinas, T. (1259–65) *Summa contra gentiles* I, trans. A.C. Pegis, Notre Dame, IN: University of Notre Dame Press, 1975. (The best introduction to Aquinas' understanding of the *scientia* of theology and its relation to faith; though see also the opening of his later *Summa theologiae*.)

* —— (1266–73) *Summa theologica* IIaIIae, qq. 1–7, trans. Dominican Brothers, New York: Benziger Brothers, 1947. (Aquinas' fullest and most mature discussion of faith.)

* Bultmann, R. (1968) *'pisteuo'*, in G. Kittel (ed.) *Theological Word Book of the New Testament*, Grand Rapids, MI: Eerdmans, vol. 6, 174–228. (Though Bultmann has his own theological axe to grind, this remains a classic discussion of the various understandings of faith operative in the Bible.)

Kenny, A. (1992) *What Is Faith?*, Oxford: Oxford University Press. (This, along with Swinburne's book below, is a good entry into contemporary philosophical discussions concerning faith.)

Locke, J. (1689) *Essay Concerning Human Understanding*, ed. P.H. Nidditch, Oxford: Clarendon Press, 1975. (Locke's account of the relation between faith and reason is developed in Book IV.)

Matczak, S.A. (1967) 'Fideism', in W.J. McDonald (ed.) *New Catholic Encyclopedia*, New York: McGraw-Hill. (An authoritative Catholic treatment of fideism.)

* Phillips, D.Z. (1971) *Faith and Philosophical Inquiry*, New York: Schocken Books. (This and the following work are the best examples of the Wittgensteinian philosophy of religious belief.)

* —— (1976) *Religion without Explanation*, Oxford: Blackwell. (See previous annotation.)

Plantinga, A. (1993) *Warrant*, Oxford: Oxford University Press, 2 vols. (A detailed treatment of the general epistemological theory underlying Plantinga's 'Reformed epistemology'.)

Plantinga, A. and Wolterstorff, N. (eds) (1983) *Faith and Rationality*, Notre Dame, IN: Notre Dame University Press. (The articles by Alston, Plantinga and Wolterstorff are seminal examples of 'Reformed epistemology'.)

Popkin, R.H. (1972) 'Fideism', in Edwards, P. (ed.) *Encyclopedia of Philosophy*, New York: Macmillan.

(A good, traditional philosophical treatment of fideism.)

* Swinburne, R. (1984) *Faith and Reason*, Oxford: Oxford University Press. (Swinburne's corpus as a whole can be seen as an attempt to revive the Lockean vision in the twentieth century; this is perhaps the best point of entry.)

Wolterstorff, N. (1995) *Divine Discourse: Philosophical Reflections on the Claim that God Speaks*, Cambridge: Cambridge University Press. (A treatment of biblical interpretation by a 'Reformed epistemologist'.)

NICHOLAS P. WOLTERSTORFF

FALLACIES

Fallacies are common types of arguments that have a strong tendency to go badly wrong, or to be used as deceptive tricks when two parties reason together. In some instances they are simply careless errors in thinking, while in other cases they are techniques of argumentation used by one arguer more or less deliberately to try to fool another into accepting a false conclusion. Fallacies have been described in logic textbooks since the time of Aristotle; their study, long neglected, has begun to be revived in recent years, as its practical importance in natural l   *become apparent.*

Many fallacies have been recogni   major ones that are unquestionably very common and influential in familiar thinking on all subjects have been emphasized in logic textbooks and manuals since the time of Aristotle – see Hamblin (1970) for a survey of these and their historical background. Fallacies were first systematically studied by Aristotle in his book *De Sophisticis Elenchis* (*On Sophistical Refutations*) and many of the textbook treatments have basically followed Aristotle's, except that more fallacies have been added along the way. Below, some of the traditionally most important fallacies are briefly charac

The '*ad hom* attack to try to und argument. Broadly, this takes two forms. The 'abusive *ad hominem*' consists of a direct attack on the arguer's character, and in particular, honesty. The 'circumstantial *ad hominem*' alleges some form of conflict between the arguer's personal circumstances and the argument. For example, it might be the charge that the arguer 'does not practise what he preaches', or that the arguer is biased because of having something to gain financially by advocating the argument in question.

The '*ad verecundiam* fallacy' is the use of appeal to expert opinion to support one's argument in such a way as to take advantage of one's opponent's respect for authority, allowing no room to question the pronouncement of an expert. Appeal to expert opinion is a common, and in principle legitimate, type of argumentation, but one that is easily abused by being pressed too heavily in an argumentative exchange. Experts can be (spectacularly) wrong in some cases, and their views can be misquoted, or otherwise distorted, especially when they use technical language.

The '*ad ignorantiam* fallacy' is the exploitation of ignorance (lack of knowledge) by one party in a dialogue to try to shift the burden of proof unjustifiably onto the other party. This type of argument takes two forms: (1) It is not known that proposition A is true; therefore A is false; (2) it is not known that A is false; therefore A is true. An example would be: 'This supposed theorem has never in fact been proved to be true, therefore it must be false'. In such a case, it could be that the conjecture has just been very difficult to prove, and no one has succeeded so far, but that somebody will prove it in the future. The fallaciousness of such an argument is indicated by the fact that there is such a thing as an incompleteness proof in logic; a proof that some propositions cannot be proved (see GÖDEL'S THEOREMS).

The '*ad baculum* fallacy' is the use of threat or, more broadly, scaremongering, to try to exploit the insecurity of one's opponent to get them to accept some proposition, instead of justifying the proposition by good evidence. Instances of the *ad baculum* fallacy often take the form of covert threats, for example, 'I wouldn't say that if I were you – the last person who said it wound up on the bottom of the river wearing cement boots!'

The '*ad misericordiam* fallacy' is the blowing up out of proportion of an appeal to pity to cover up for lack of evidence to support a claim; or to brush aside other considerations that should be given more importance in arriving at a conclusion. There are many instances of quite reasonable arguments based on appeals to compassion or sympathy, but it is easy to blow such emotional appeals out of proportion to the slender weight of evidence that should be attached to them (within a larger evidential picture).

The '*ad populum* fallacy' is committed when an arguer suggests that someone's argument is wrong or unacceptable in so far as it deviates from popular opinion, or the conventionally accepted view. When pursued with rhetorical enthusiasm, this type of argumentation is called 'mob appeal'.

'Begging the question' is a kind of fallacious circular reasoning in which the conclusion is itself required as a premise to support the argument being advanced to justify the conclusion. Many cases of this type of fallacy are disguised by being quite complex arguments – see Walton (1991) – but a simple case would be the following argument: someone asked to prove that God is benevolent replies, 'God has all the virtues, therefore God is benevolent.' Since benevolence is presumably a virtue, the premise requires the prior assumption that God is benevolent.

'Equivocation' is the fallacy whereby an argument contains an ambiguous word or phrase that means one thing in one premise, but something different in another premise or in the conclusion. As a consequence of this shift of meaning, one may be fooled into thinking one has been presented with a single argument, which looks pretty good.

The 'straw man fallacy' is committed when one arguer misrepresents another's position to make it appear less plausible than it really is, in order more easily to criticize or refute it. For example, an environmentalist position may be exaggerated by saying, 'They are trying to make this country a paradise on earth, by barring all industrial development. They will cause all of us to become unemployed.'

The 'fallacy of affirming the consequent' appears to be valid because of its superficial similarity to the valid form of argument *modus ponens*. An example of this valid form would be: 'If it is raining, the streets are wet. It is raining. Therefore, the streets are wet.' The comparable argument in the form of affirming the consequent may have the superficial appearance of also being valid: 'If it is raining, the streets are wet. The streets are wet. Therefore, it is raining.' (But maybe the streets are wet because a water main has burst.) It is perhaps because of our tendency to reverse the first premise in some instances that we can be deceived by this kind of fallacious reasoning.

See also: FORMAL AND INFORMAL LOGIC; LOGIC, ANCIENT §1; LOGICAL AND MATHEMATICAL TERMS, GLOSSARY OF

References and further reading

* Aristotle (*c.*330 BC) *De Sophisticis Elenchis*, trans. E.S. Forster, *On Sophistical Refutations*, Loeb Classical Library Edition, Cambridge, MA: Harvard University Press, 1938. (Historical.)
* Hamblin, C.L. (1970) *Fallacies*, London: Methuen; repr. Newport News, VA: Vale Press, 1993. (Still extremely useful, especially on historical aspects.)
* Walton, D.N. (1991) *Begging the Question*, New York: Greenwood Press. (On circular arguments.)
—— (1995) *A Pragmatic Theory of Fallacy*, Tuscaloosa, AL: University of Alabama Press. (Up to date and comprehensive.)

DOUGLAS WALTON

FALLIBILISM

Fallibilism is a philosophical doctrine regarding natural science, most closely associated with Charles Sanders Peirce, which maintains that our scientific knowledge claims are invariably vulnerable and may turn out to be false. Scientific theories cannot be asserted as true categorically, but only as having some probability of being true. Fallibilists insist on our inability to attain the final and definitive truth regarding the theoretical concerns of natural science – in particular at the level of theoretical physics. At any rate, at this level of generality and precision each of our accepted beliefs may turn out to be false, and many of them will. Fallibilism does not insist on the falsity of our scientific claims but rather on their tentativity as inevitable estimates: it does not hold that knowledge is unavailable here, but rather that it is always provisional.

1   The fallibilist perspective
2   Grounds for fallibilism
3   Approximation and its problems
4   Scientific versus everyday knowledge
5   Ethical ramifications of fallibilism

1   The fallibilist perspective

Fallibilism is the view that we have no assurance that our scientific theories or systems are definitely true; they are simply the best we can do here and now. New theoretical knowledge does not just supplement but generally upsets our knowledge-in-hand. A scientific theory or system – like any product of human contrivance be it a house or a knowledge-claim – is ultimately bound to encounter conditions that its constructors did not and could not anticipate and which render its ultimate failure likely. Changed social conditions destabilize social systems; changed physical conditions destabilize physical structures; changed experiential (that is, experimental and observational) conditions – changed scientific technology, if you will – destabilize scientific theories. Rational inquiry links the products our understanding to the experienced conditions of a world in which chance and chaos plays an ineliminable role, so that there will always be new conditions and circumstances that ultimately threaten our rational contrivances. Thomas Kuhn's picture of scientific progress, which envisages a repetitive cycle of periods of normal science punctuated by revolutionary revisions, lends itself naturally to such a construction (see KUHN, T. §§2–3).

Peirce, the most prominent exponent of fallibilism, has not been alone. Other recent thinkers who have espoused scientific fallibilism include Gaston BACHELARD, Rudolf CARNAP, Pierre DUHEM, and Karl POPPER. In antiquity, the mitigated sceptics of the middle academy were the precursors of this position, since they taught that we can never achieve certain knowledge (*epistēmē*) in matters regarding the world's ways, but have to make do with what is merely probable or plausible (*to pithanon*) (see CARNEADES §4).

2 Grounds for fallibilism

Why should we see all of our claims to knowledge of the world – even our best state-of-the-art scientific theories – as vulnerable? One of the most basic lessons of modern epistemology is that the available observational data underdetermine theories. For observations are always discrete, finite in number, and episodic. They deal in specific information-yielding episodes that occur at particular times and places. Theories, on the other hand, are general and non-finite: they deal in how certain features of a generic sort characterize situations of a certain kind always and everywhere. Accordingly, theories transcend the data and reach beyond them, so that there is always an evidential gap between the claims of a theory and the particular facts that are its supporting data. (The fitting of a continuous curve to discrete data points provides a somewhat oversimplified analogy.) Theories – as Pierre Duhem emphasized – lie beyond the possibility of definitive confirmation by data.

This data-transcendence of all theoretical claims means that there will always be various alternative ways of rounding the data off into generalized theories. The available data themselves can never constrain unique theoretical resolutions. Observed data are finite, possible hypotheses infinite, and the finite cannot constrain the infinite. The concrete realities we experience observationally are always to some extent ambiguous. They always admit, in principle, of alternative theoretical rationalizations. Theorizing without data is futile. But even theorizing on the basis of data involves interpretation, and thus carries in its wake the prospect of ambiguity, diversity and discord. The experiential realities determine and canalize the work of theorizing reason, but they cannot impose altogether unique resolutions upon it.

In sum, theories are always informatively underdetermined by data (see INFERENCE TO THE BEST EXPLANATION; UNDERDETERMINATION).

There is much in this picture of the cognitive situation that rings true. The fact is that the equilibrium achieved by natural science at *any* given stage of its development is always an unstable one. The subject's history indicates that scientific theories have a finite life span; they come to be modified or replaced under various innovative pressures, in particular the enhancement of observational and experimental evidence (through improved techniques of experimentation, more powerful means of observation and detection, superior procedures for data-processing, and so on). As C.S. Peirce and, subsequently, Karl Popper have insisted, we must acknowledge an inability to attain the final and definitive truth in the theoretical concerns of natural science – in particular at the level of theoretical physics. Our present science cannot plausibly claim to deliver a definitive picture of physical reality. We would like to think of our science as something safe, solid and reliable. Unfortunately, however, history militates against this comfortable view. In science, new knowledge does not just supplement but generally upsets our knowledge-in-hand.

We learn by empirical inquiry about empirical inquiry, and one of the key things we learn is that at no actual stage does science yield a final and unchanging result. We have no responsible alternative to supposing the imperfection of what we take ourselves to know. (And there is no reason to see the posture of our successors as fundamentally different from our own in this respect.) We occupy the predicament of the 'Preface Paradox' exemplified by the author who apologizes in his preface for those errors that have doubtless made their way into his work, and yet blithely remains committed to all those assertions he makes in the body of the work itself. We know or must presume that (at the synoptic level) there are errors, though we certainly cannot say where and how they arise (see PARADOXES, EPISTEMIC §1).

3 Approximation and its problems

To protect scientific realism in the face of the prospect of unending scientific change, it is tempting to adopt Peirce's stratagem of a resort to *convergent approximation*. This calls for envisaging a situation where, with the passage of time, the theories we successively arrive at grow increasingly concordant and their claims less and less differentiated. In the face of such a course of successive changes of ever-diminishing significance, we could proceed to maintain that the world really is not as *present* science claims it to be, but rather is as the ever-more clearly emerging science-in-the-limit claims it to be. The reality of ongoing change is now irrelevant, as with the passage of time the changes matter less and less. We increasingly approximate an essentially stable picture. This prospect is certainly a theoretically possible one. But neither historical experience nor considerations of general principle provide reason to think that it is actually possible.

Any theory of convergence in science, however carefully crafted, will shatter against the *conceptual innovation* that continually brings entirely new, radically different scientific concepts to the fore, carrying in its wake an ongoing wholesale revision of 'established fact'. Investigators of an earlier era not only did not *know* what the half-life of californium was, but they would not have *understood* it even if this fact had been explained to them. The questions we can pose are limited by our conceptual horizons. It did not appear to be a realistic prospect to all those late nineteenth-century physicists who investigated the properties of the luminiferous ether that no such medium for the transmission of light and electromagnetism might exist at all. Ongoing scientific progress is not simply a matter of increasing accuracy by extending the numbers in our otherwise stable descriptions of nature to a few more decimal places. Significant scientific progress is genuinely revolutionary in involving a fundamental change of mind about how things happen in the world. Progress of this calibre is generally a matter not of adding further facts, like filling in a crossword puzzle, but of changing the framework itself. And this blocks the theory of convergence.

Accordingly, we should temper our claims to scientific knowledge with a Cognitive Copernicanism. The original Copernican revolution made the point that there is nothing *ontologically* privileged about our own position in space. The fallibilistic doctrine now at issue effectively holds that there is nothing *cognitively* privileged about our own position in time. A kind of intellectual humility is in order – a diffidence that abstains from the hubris of pretensions to cognitive finality or centrality. Such a position calls for the humbling view that just as we think our predecessors of a hundred years had a fundamentally inadequate grasp on the furniture of the world, so our successors of a hundred years hence will almost certainly take the same view of *our* purported knowledge of things. The facts of epistemic life require us to recognize that, as concerns our scientific understanding of the world, our most secure knowledge is very likely no more than presently acceptable error. Such a view of scientific progress enjoins an even more modest position than Peircean convergentism.

In any convergent process, later is lesser. But since scientific progress on matters of fundamental importance is generally a matter of replacement rather than mere supplementation, there is no reason to see the later issues of science as lesser issues in the significance of their bearing upon science as a cognitive enterprise – to think that nature will be cooperative in always yielding its most important secrets early on and reserving nothing but the relatively insignificant for later on. The fact is that a very small-scale effect – even one that lies very far out along the extremes of a 'range exploration' in terms of temperature, pressure, velocity, or the like – can force a far-reaching revolution and have a profound impact by way of major theoretical revisions. (Think of special relativity in relation to etherdrift experimentation, or general relativity in relation to the perihelion of Mercury.) Given that natural science progresses mainly by substitutions and replacements that go back to first principles and lead to comprehensive overall revisions of our picture of the phenomena at issue, it seems sensible to say that the shifts across successive scientific 'revolutions' maintain the same level of overall significance – it is neither a convergent nor a divergent process. Thus if we are to be realistic fallibilists we must hold a position more radical than that of Peirce. His approximationism cannot offset the sceptical impetus of fallibilism. There are, however, mitigating circumstances.

4 Scientific versus everyday knowledge

Fallibilists are prepared to concede that the claims of descriptive astronomy or of human anatomy are true enough. But they insist that the frontiers of theorizing are very different. With any sort of estimate, there is always a characteristic trade-off relationship between the evidential *security* of the estimate on the one hand (as determinable on the basis of its probability or degree of acceptability), and its contentual *definiteness* (exactness, detail, precision, and so on) on the other. But technical science forswears the looseness of vague generality: its law claims are strict and unshaded. In making the assertion 'The melting point of lead is 327.5°,' we mean to assert that *all* (not most) pieces of (pure) lead will unfailingly melt at *exactly* (not somewhere around) this temperature. In technical science we always aim at the maximum of universality, precision, accuracy and exactness. And this commitment to generality and detailed precision renders the claims of science highly vulnerable. We realize that none of the hard claims of present-day frontier natural science will move untouched down the corridors of time.

The interesting fact is that fallibilism is a more

plausible doctrine with respect to scientific knowledge than with respect to the less demanding 'knowledge' of everyday life. Ordinary-life generalizations are such as to allow one who asserts (say) that peaches are delicious, to be asserting something like, 'Most people will find the eating of suitably grown and duly matured peaches a rather pleasurable experience'. Such statements have all sorts of implicit safeguards, that can be cashed in through such guarding locutions as 'more or less', 'in ordinary circumstances', 'by and large' and so on. They are thus so well hedged that it is eminently implausible that contentions such as these should be overthrown.

In science, however, we willingly accept greater cognitive risks because we ask much more of the project. Here the objectives are primarily theoretical and governed by the aims of disinterested inquiry. Accordingly, the claims of informativeness – of generality, exactness, and precision – are paramount. We deliberately court risk by aiming at maximal definiteness and thus at maximal informativeness and testability. Aristotle's view that terrestrial science deals with what happens ordinarily and in the normal course of things has long ago been left by the wayside. The theories of modern natural science have little interest in what happens generally or by and large; they seek to transact their explanatory business in terms of strict universality – in terms of what happens always and everywhere and in all kinds of circumstances. We therefore have little choice but to acknowledge the vulnerability of our scientific statements, subject to the operation of the security-definiteness trade-off. Ironically, then, the 'common sense' of everyday life is securer than the more sophisticated claims of frontier science.

This distinction between the rougher but more secure level of 'schoolbook science', as it were, and the more demanding (but destabilizing) level of technical science at the frontiers of research, enables one to hold the realistic view that science does actually describe the real world, while accepting the implications of ongoing change in our scientific view of the world. The point is not that our pursuit of truth in science is futile, but rather that the information we obtain is to be seen as no more (but also no less) than the best available *estimate* of the truth that is available to us in the circumstances. Fallibilism is something very different from nihilistic scepticism.

5 Ethical ramifications of fallibilism

Some philosophers (Peirce included) see fallibilism as having ethical implications. They project an ethics of belief, according to which we have no right to claim definitive truth for our current scientific claims, a view

which they combine with a purported duty for the community of thinkers to pursue inquiry to the greatest extent possible in the circumstances. Accordingly, they insist that the fallibilism of our cognitive endeavours must emphatically *not* be construed as an open invitation to a sceptical abandonment of the scientific enterprise. Instead, it is an incentive to do the very best we can. In human inquiry, the cognitive ideal is correlative with the striving for definitive systematization. And this is an ideal that, like other ideals, is worthy of pursuit despite the fact that we must recognize that its full attainment lies beyond our grasp.

See also: Commonsensism; Epistemology and ethics; Scepticism

References and further reading

Kuhn, T. (1962) *The Structure of Scientific Revolutions*, Chicago, IL: University of Chicago Press. (Classic statement of scientific revisionism which stresses the dynamism of scientific change.)

Peirce, C.S. (1931) 'Principles of Philosophy', in *Collected Papers of C. S. Peirce*, Vol. 1, ed. C. Hartshorne and P. Weiss Cambridge, MA: Harvard University Press. (Classic statement of fallibilism by the father of the doctrine. Section 1.120 'The Uncertainty of Scientific Results' is especially relevant.)

Popper, K.R. (1959) *The Logic of Scientific Discovery*, New York: Basic Books. (Forceful attack on claims to definitive finality in science. Depicts Popper's 'conjection and refutation' theory of cognitive progress.)

Rescher, N. (1984) *The Limits of Science*, Berkeley and Los Angeles, CA: University of California Press. (A synoptic examination of scientific fallibilism. Extensive bibliographic information.)

NICHOLAS RESCHER

FALSIFICATION *see* Crucial Experiments; Fallibilism; Popper, Karl Raimund

FAMILY, ETHICS AND THE

Do obligations to children take priority over filial and other family obligations? Do blood kin have stronger moral claims than relatives acquired through marriage?

Whatever their origin, do family obligations take precedence over obligations to friends, neighbours, fellow citizens? Do family moral ties presuppose specific family feeling, love, or loyalty? Is the traditional family of a married, heterosexual couple with biological offspring morally preferable to families formed by adoptive, single, remarried or same-sex parents, or with the help of gamete donors or gestational ('maternal') surrogates? On what grounds may friends, neighbours or government agencies intrude upon 'family privacy'?

To simplify the complexity and diversity of family life, reasoned answers to such questions may stress a single dimension. A metaphysical *approach draws on the commands of a deity or the needs of a nation. A* biological *approach appeals to physical resemblance, blood or genes. An* economic *approach focuses on family property, income, division of work and resources, and inheritance. A related* political *approach attends to power, subordination, and rights within a family, as well as to their regulation by the state. A* psychological *approach takes affection, identification, intimacy, and emotional needs as morally decisive. A* narrative *approach makes recalling and revision of family stories the basis of moral education and the definition of family ties.*

Although mutually compatible, these approaches do each tend to favour particular moral theories.

1   **Metaphysical conceptions of families**
2   **Biological conceptions of families**
3   **Economic conceptions of families**
4   **Political conceptions of families**
5   **Psychological conceptions of families**
6   **Narrative conceptions of families**
7   **Conclusion**

1   Metaphysical conceptions of families

As in the major religions of Middle Eastern origin, parents may be regarded as recipients of God's gifts of newly created life. As such they are deputized guardians, not creators with powers of life and death over their creatures. Or, parents and children are seen as dutiful representatives of generations of long dead, but still attentive and demanding ancestors. In some versions or secular analogues, it is the nation or race that married couples must preserve and serve through the children they bear and rear. Accordingly, decisions about suitable marriage partners, or family size and comportment are decided by authorities speaking in the name of the transcendental agent or group, not by romantic couples or family-planning individuals.

Each of these theories prompts questions about the existence and moral authority of the metaphysical agent or collective invoked, such as: How can long dead ancestors continue to make demands of service or obedience on the living? How can a racial or national identity require those to whom it is ascribed to marry and procreate within its socially constructed limits? Answers to such questions often suppose that individuals are defined by particular relational properties (for instance, children of God the Father, sons of Erin, descendants of slaves). By contrast, Kantian and Utilitarian moral theories presuppose a metaphysical individualism of persons, each defined by nonrelational capacities for reason, good will, interests, or preferences (see KANTIAN ETHICS; UTILITARIANISM). Accordingly, children are not conceived as belonging to their parents, clan, or God, but as dependent on others for gradual development of their autonomy.

2   Biological conceptions of families

On a biological view, family ties are defined primarily through reproductive and genetic links. We distinguish between 'real' or 'true' mothers and adoptive, 'social' or step-mothers, full brothers and half-brothers, first cousins and distant cousins. Such traditional distinctions are accompanied by different levels of priority within families: the saying that 'blood is thicker than water' (and than diluted blood) indicates that blood kin have greater obligations to one another than to other relatives, but presumably find those greater demands less onerous in virtue of a natural sympathy that sociobiologists attribute to gene-preserving strategies (see SOCIOBIOLOGY).

However enshrined in legal and moral sentiment, this biological-based approach has problems of gradation, derivation and scope. Whatever genetic links or tendencies, do we owe half-sisters less loyal support? Do adoptive parents have more excuse for failing in their parental duties of care and comfort? Do adopted children have less obligation to 'honour' their parents, or more? If the moral gradations set out in such questions are indefensible, it would seem that an appeal to more than Darwinian notions would be needed to bridge Hume's gap between *is* and *ought* (see LOGIC OF ETHICAL DISCOURSE §§1–3).

But even if such prescriptive norms for family composition and conduct can be drawn from evolutionary or any other biological theory, there is an issue of scope. Whatever the value ascribed to biological connections, they are only a fraction of the ties by which families are formed and maintained. Biological considerations may govern marital and reproductive choices but have little or no bearing on many other family obligations, such as those of parents to their in-laws, or to one another, or to their children once they have become adult (grandchildren aside). Non-biological bases must be found for these other familial ties.

3 Economic conceptions of families

For many social scientists, a family is a household, a group of cohabitants who stand in various kinds of economic relationships, actual or potential. Kant and other family traditionalists have claimed male heads of family to have property rights in their wives and children (see PROPERTY). In many cultures, parents regard early support as an investment that children repay by working in or outside the home, by suitable marriages, and eventual care in old age. Adult children often regard their grandparents and parents as stewards of family assets to be used and distributed with due regard for the next generation (see FUTURE GENERATIONS, OBLIGATIONS TO). So viewed, a family produces, consumes, accumulates and transmits economic goods.

This approach focuses on what for most families are principal sources of distress and dispute, namely, distribution of labour, goods, and economic responsibilities. It also helps expose unexamined divisions of family labour, for example, the unpaid labour of women who maintain the home and care for the young, ill and elderly family members who otherwise would need public services. In some areas of family life, economic assessment of women's traditional work is explicit, for example, in the hiring of substitute home childcare workers or gestational ('maternal') surrogates – practices often criticized for having a financial aspect that subverts the natural affection that ideally motivates the bearing and rearing of children.

Economic analyses are most compatible with utilitarian moral theories: both share the ideal of a quasi-calculus (of costs and benefits, or positive and negative utilities) for reaching principled decisions on actions or policies, for individuals or for groups with disparate interests or preferences (see UTILITARIANISM; RATIONAL CHOICE THEORY). In general, however, both approaches seem to ignore or discount a variety of morally relevant factors (fairness, needs, altruistic and selfish motives) that seem important in family matters. Moreover, both seem to presuppose individuals, with clearly distinguishable preferences and interests. But those families that do satisfy this requirement are not likely to have the solidarity, or intimacy, or communal history that other accounts of the family take to be definitive or primary (see SOLIDARITY). Families composed of rational, self-interested, negotiating utility-maximizers seem like temporary roommates, not people who share a life over their lifetimes. This criticism does not, however, count against economic analyses less reliant on a calculus of individual interests.

4 Political conceptions of families

As in society generally, economic relationships reflect and produce within the family differences of power and subordination. Families are political in at least two senses: they are the 'basic units of society' in which social values are inculcated, enforced, or subverted; and they are also mini-realms in which power is distributed and exercised among and over its members. In some political theories, families have been the model for the larger polity, rulers cast as fathers and their subjects as their children.

John Locke (1689) attacked such patriarchy, both political and domestic, limiting the scope and duration of parents' authority over their children. Contemporary egalitarian critics view the traditional family as exploiting gender and age inequalities, as well as fostering unjust disparities of wealth. Some family theorists have found a remedy in Kantian notions of autonomy or in Rawls' 'difference principle', applied to families taken to be part of the basic structure of a society (see AUTONOMY, ETHICAL; RAWLS, J. §1). This principle allows differences in wealth, opportunities, and other 'primary social goods' only to the extent that they make the worst off members better than they would otherwise be.

Some feminist critics think that this principle still allows for traditional gender divisions of family labour (see FEMINIST POLITICAL PHILOSOPHY §5); communitarian critics find it too individualistic to do justice to the shared interests that sustain family life and obligation (see COMMUNITY AND COMMUNITARIANISM). Both types of critic tend to see the notion of individual rights as essentially adversarial, needed only when family feeling and harmony are failing. On the other hand, family harmony and feeling may depend on the weaker members' confidence that conflicts of interest will be resolved equitably, a confidence that requires explicit recognition and respect of their individual rights of liberty and reciprocity.

5 Psychological conception of families

Neither the political nor the other approaches take much thought for the complex emotions that give families their peculiar fraught unity. In most modern cultures families are supposed to begin in love, or at least the hope of love, and be sustained by the love that grows among its members. Maternal love especially – whether connected with gestation and birth – is taken to be a deep, abiding base for self-sacrificial care and forgiveness (see FEMINIST ETHICS §2); brotherly love is supposed to be a model for relationships outside the family. But these emotional stereotypes ignore the variety and complexity of maternal or sibling sentiments.

To correct such sentimental simplicities, there is a growing philosophical literature on various intimate relationships and their emotions from which to draw. And, of course, any philosophically adequate phenomenology of family feeling must draw freely and widely from the world of plays, poetry, and novels in which familial emotional ties, both preserving and abusive, are central.

6 Narrative conceptions of families

Literature aside, families tend to create and recreate their own stories that serve to inspire loyalty, pride and identification with one another and with selected ancestors. By such stories of courageous grandparents, generous uncles, devoted sisters, good and bad in-laws, notions of family honour are defined and family trees are selectively pruned and shaped, thereby setting the moral parameters within which family members are expected to move, even if at odds with wider social mores.

This narrative approach is far from the Kantian conception of morality as based on general principles, applied impersonally across family and cultural boundaries (see UNIVERSALISM IN ETHICS). For any moral philosopher who insists that moral principles or lists of virtues and vices be derived from or constitute a human nature, to give moral weight to such family stories might seem to endorse a kind of idiosyncratic, asocial moralism without sufficient concern for the role of families in a civic culture. There is, however, nothing inherently asocial in a moral education that appeals to ancestral deeds and family tradition. Family heroes and villains are often remembered for their public as well as their private acts, virtues, and vices. Told and retold with revisions, these family litanies are akin to the common law, or much religious moral pedagogy (see MORAL EDUCATION). Philosophically, this narrative approach to family morality can find a framework in the existentialist ethics of thinkers such as Sartre, de Beauvoir, and Marcel (see EXISTENTIALIST ETHICS).

Such literary approaches would favour an ethics of precedent rather than an ethics of principles, not unlike the common law and the teachings of the major Middle Eastern religions.

7 Conclusion

Each approach may yield reasoned answers to some of the various questions a comprehensive ethics of the family would pose. Whether we should expect any single approach to answer all such questions is debatable, especially in cultures for whom 'the family' no longer refers to a single, well-defined and widely-accepted norm. The diversity of families, as well as each family's complexity, may require a plurality of approaches, perhaps even greater than the six sketched here. What we should hope for, perhaps, is not a systematic ethics of the family, but a conceptually enriched capacity for moral reflection on family matters as they arise in context at different stages of our lives.

See also: FRIENDSHIP; GENETICS AND ETHICS; IMPARTIALITY; LOVE; REPRODUCTION AND ETHICS; SEXUALITY, PHILOSOPHY OF

References and further reading

Blustein, J. (1982) *Parents and Children: The Ethics of the Family*, New York: Oxford University Press. (An analysis that draws on Locke and Rawls for an analysis of parental obligations to meet a child's needs for 'primary goods' and to foster a child's autonomy.)

Bubeck, D. (1995) *Care, Gender, and Justice*, Oxford: Clarendon Press. (An economic and political analysis of women's traditional work of care in the family and elsewhere.)

* Locke, J. (1689) *Two Treatises of Civil Government*, ed. P. Laslett, Cambridge: Cambridge University Press, 1963, esp. *Second Treatise*, ch. 6. (A political analysis of the limited scope and duration of parental authority and children's duty of obedience.)

Okin, S.M. (1989) *Justice, Gender, and the Family*. New York: Basic Books. (A liberal theory of justice meant to address women's inequalities within the traditional family more adequately than other theories of justice.)

O'Neill, O. (1988) 'Children's Rights and Children's Lives', *Ethics* 98: 445–63; repr. in *Constructions of Reason: Explorations of Kant's Practical Philosophy*, Cambridge: Cambridge University Press, 1989. (A shift from political focus on children's rights to parental obligations of care, kindness, and other contributions to 'the genial play of life'.)

Ross, J.J. (1994) *The Virtues of the Family*, New York: Free Press. (A biologically-based defence of the traditional nuclear family.)

Sartre, J-P. (1964) *Les Mots*, trans. B. Frechtman, *The Words*, New York: Random House, 1981. (Autobiographical reflections on early relationships to his parents and grandparents, informed by his existentialist theories of authenticity and bad faith. An example of a narrative approach.)

Schoeman, F. (1980) 'Rights of Children, Rights of Parents, and the Moral Basis of the Family', *Ethics* 91: 6–19. (A psychological approach to family commitments in terms of intimacy.)

Anthologies of original and reprinted philosophical essays, as well as useful bibliographies:

Aiken, W. and LaFollette, H. (eds) (1980) *Whose Child? Children's Rights, Parental Authority, and State Power*, Totowa, NJ: Rowman & Littlefield. (A collection of journalists' and philosophers' essays on child abuse and children's moral and legal rights.)

Archard, D. (1993) *Children: Rights and Childhood*, London: Routledge. (A concise critique of the 'liberal standard' for parental privacy, child abuse and state intervention, with a 'modest collectivist proposal' for children's sexual and voting rights. A compendious bibliographic essay.)

Ekman, R. (ed.) (1996) *Children's Rights Re-Visioned: Philosophical Readings*, Belmont, CA: Wadsworth. (A collection of philosophical essays examining the distinct interests and justified claims children have in regard to parental and state control and resources.)

Houlgate, L. (ed.) (1998) *Family Values: Issues in Ethics, Society and the Family*, Boulder, CO: Westview. (A collection of classic and current philosophic commentaries on ethical problems in marriage and family relations.)

Ladd, R.E. (ed.) (1996) *Children's Rights Re-Visioned: Philosophical Readings*, Belmont, CA: Wadsworth. (A collection of philosophical essays examining the distinct interests and justified claims children have in regard to parental and state control and resources.)

Meyers, D.T., Kipnis, K. and Murphy, Jr, C. (eds) (1993) *Kindred Matters: Rethinking the Philosophy of the Family*, Ithaca, NY: Cornell University Press. (Papers by philosophers and lawyers drawn mostly from the 1988 AMINTAPHIL conference on the family in moral and legal theory.)

Nelson, H. (1996) *Feminism and Families*, New York: Routledge. (A collection of critiques of, and various alternatives to, the 'traditional family'.)

O'Neill, O. and Ruddick, W. (eds) (1979) *Having Children: Philosophical and Legal Reflections on Parenthood*, New York: Oxford University Press. (A collection of philosophic essays and US legal decisions on the bearing and rearing of children.)

Scarre, G. (1989) *Children, Parents, and Politics*, Cambridge: Cambridge University Press. (A collection of philosophical and other essays on various conceptions of childhood and their bearing on parental and state rights and responsibilities in liberal democracies.)

WILLIAM RUDDICK

FANON, FRANTZ (1925–61)

Fanon's views (and often various misinterpretations of them) on the nature of colonialism, racism and the role of violence in Third-World revolutions were enormously influential. The main themes of all his writing are the critique of ethnopsychiatry and the Eurocentrism of psychoanalysis, the critique of négritude and the development of a political philosophy for Third-World liberation.

Frantz Fanon was born in the French Antilles on the island of Martinique and was educated there and in France. He served in the Free French army during the Second World War, both in north Africa and in Europe. He went on to study medicine and psychiatry at the University of Lyons between 1947 and 1951. In 1953 he was appointed chief of service of the psychiatry department of a hospital in Algeria (which was then still a French territory). He joined the Algerian liberation movement in 1954 and began to work for its underground newspaper El Moudjahid *a few years later. His political activities caused him to leave his job, after which he moved to Tunisia where he practised psychiatry from 1957 to 1959. In 1961 he was appointed ambassador to Ghana by the Algerian provisional government. He died of leukaemia in 1961.*

1   *Black Skin, White Masks*
2   **Other works**

1   *Black Skin, White Masks*

Fanon's work is profoundly shaped both by his (largely psychoanalytic) training as a psychiatrist and his response to the work of European ethnopsychiatrists trying to understand the psychology of non-European peoples. But, like all African and Afro-Caribbean intellectuals in the Francophone world in the 1950s, he was also shaped (if only in reaction) by the ideas of the *négritude* movement (see AFRICAN PHILOSOPHY, FRANCOPHONE §4). In his first book *Black Skin, White Masks* (1952), Fanon asserted that 'the black soul is a white man's artefact'. He claimed that the purportedly essential qualities of the negro spirit celebrated by the writers of *négritude* were a European fantasy. Fanon also argued against *négritude* that its assumption of a natural solidarity of all black people in the Caribbean and Africa was a political error; that far from needing to return to an African past, black intellectuals needed to adapt to modern European culture and that the movement had done nothing to change the everyday life of ordinary black people.

Yet even in this work (and more so later) he conceded that *négritude* could play an important role in freeing native intellectuals of dependence on metropolitan culture. This position which combined a critique of the theoretical claims of *négritude* with an account of it as a historically progressive movement, has affinities with Sartre's account of *négritude* in his essay 'Orphée noir' (1948) (see SARTRE, J.-P.). Fanon's vehement attack on Sartre is surprising, therefore, in which he says that Sartre has undermined black fervour in his account of *négritude* as the 'minor term' of a dialectical progression from racism to humanism.

In *Black Skin, White Masks* Fanon developed an account of the psychological effects of racism. However, he did not acknowledge that he was referring to a racism that was based on the experiences of the black middle class in the French Caribbean. The dominant colonial culture, he argued, identifies the black skin of the negro with impurity. The Antilleans accept this association and have come to despise themselves. For example, colonial women exhibit their identification with whiteness by attempting neurotically to avoid black men and to get close to (and ultimately cohabit with) white men. This process Fanon dubbed 'lactification'.

This self-contempt manifests itself in other ways, for example, as anxiety in the presence of whites about revealing one's 'natural' negro inferiority; in a pathological hypersensitivity that Fanon dubbed 'affective erethism'; in existential dread and in a neurotic refusal to face up to the fact of one's own blackness. ('Erethism' is a medical word for pathologically irritable tissue: 'affective erethism', by analogy, is pathological irritability of the feelings.) Black children raised within the colonial system where racist cultural assumptions were prevalent can partially resolve the tension between contempt for blackness and their own dark skins by coming to think of themselves, in some sense, as white (hence the 'white masks' of the title). This fantasy can only be maintained away from direct exposure to Europeans: once the Antillean reaches metropolitan France, Fanon says, this illusion is destroyed with consequent damage to the ego.

2 Other works

Fanon's approach in *Black Skin, White Masks* focuses on the problems of identity created for the colonial subject by colonial racism. In the course of the book he not only develops this account, but also criticizes the alternative accounts of the 'native mind' in the ethnopsychiatry of Octave Mannoni, proposing that his *Prospero and Caliban* (1964) is an apology for colonialism. He argues, too, that psychoanalytic theory (in the Adlerian and Jungian forms he draws on most heavily) requires substantial revision if it is to give an adequate account of the psychological development of non-European peoples.

In *Toward the African Revolution* (1964), Fanon developed an account of the ways in which the colonial system and its ideology over time adapted themselves to the changed economic realities. He argued that colonial racism begins as 'vulgar' racism. The aim of this racism is to prove the inferiority of colonial subjects by appealing to anatomy or physiology and especially to notions of the inferiority of their nervous systems. A later form of 'cultural' racism proposes that it is the culture of the native that is inferior. Fanon argued that the shift from vulgar to cultural racism reflected changes in the economic character of colonialism. As the colonial system developed it created a new class of colonial subjects trained in European methods and who, in collaborating with the colonizer, profited from the colonial system.

The changes associated with the creation of this new colonial class are characterized in *The Wretched of the Earth* (1961) as a transition from 'extractive' to 'consumer' colonialism. Whereas his earlier work had focused on a primary distinction between colonizer and the colonized, Fanon (1961) introduced, for the first time, a class analysis of colonialism which offered a more detailed account of the internal divisions of colonial societies.

In the extractive phase of colonialism there exists a peasantry, a traditional ruling group and a small number of native traders. In the transition from extractive to consumer colonialism a native petty bourgeoisie, a landed bourgeoisie, a proletariat and a lumpen-proletariat develop. However, Fanon rejects a conventional Marxist account of the colonial situation because he believed that the association of whiteness with money and power meant that the ruling class was identified by race, not by its relation to the means of production. Therefore, conventional class analysis and accounts of the role of ideology fail, power relations are crudely fixed and no ideology conceals the reality of the situation (see MARX, K.).

Instead, Fanon offers an account in which the peasantry are the revolutionary class who have escaped the total devastation of the traditional culture that has overtaken the bourgeoisie and the proletariat.

Their revolutionary urge derives from their bid for land. Such a bid leads them to reject the colonizers' expropriation of the colonial territory. While Fanon expressed some ambivalence towards the revolutionary ardour of the peasantry, what was seen as his celebration of their revolutionary potential, rooted in their resistance to colonial cultural domination, was taken up by many Third-World intellectuals in the 1960s.

As Fanon died young and his last book was written under great pressure of time, there is no final attempt to bring consistency to the many strands of his work. For example, the psychological analysis of questions of identity begun in *Black Skin, White Masks* is never fully integrated with the increasingly political analysis of later essays and books.

See also: AFRICAN PHILOSOPHY, FRANCOPHONE §7; CULTURAL IDENTITY; MARGINALITY

List of works

Fanon, F. (1952) *Black Skin, White Masks*, London: Pluto Press, 1986. (His first major work.)

—— (1959) *Studies in a Dying Colonialism*, London: Earthscan, 1989. (Essays mostly on the psychological harm done in Algeria by colonialism.)

—— (1961) *The Wretched of the Earth*, London: Penguin, 1983. (His final book written over a ten-week period with the knowledge of his impending death from leukaemia.)

—— (1964) *Toward the African Revolution*, London: Writers and Readers, 1980. (A collection of essays written between 1952 and 1959. The essay 'Racism and Culture' of 1956 is of special interest.)

References and further reading

Caute, D. (1970) *Fanon*, London: Fontana. (A brisk intellectual biography.)

* Mannoni, O. (1964) *Prospero and Caliban*, trans. P. Powesland, New York, NY: Praeger. (A classic of ethnopsychiatry to which Fanon responded in *Black Skin, White Masks*.)

McCulloch, J. (1983) *Black Soul, White Artifact*, Cambridge: Cambridge University Press. (A careful discussion of Fanon's intellectual development that focuses on the connection between the clinical psychology and the political theory.)

* Sartre, J.-P. (1948) 'Orphée noir', *Situations III*, Paris: Gallimard; trans. 'Black Orpheus', *Présence Africaine*, 1963. (Sartre's influential essay on the *négritude* movement.)

K. ANTHONY APPIAH

AL-FARABI, ABU NASR (*c.*870–950)

Al-Farabi was known to the Arabs as the 'Second Master' (after Aristotle), and with good reason. It is unfortunate that his name has been overshadowed by those of later philosophers such as Ibn Sina, for al-Farabi was one of the world's great philosophers and much more original than many of his Islamic successors. A philosopher, logician and musician, he was also a major political scientist.

Al-Farabi has left us no autobiography and consequently, relatively little is known for certain about his life. His philosophical legacy, however, is large. In the arena of metaphysics he has been designated the 'Father of Islamic Neoplatonism', and while he was also saturated with Aristotelianism and certainly deploys the vocabulary of Aristotle, it is this Neoplatonic dimension which dominates much of his corpus. This is apparent in his most famous work, al-Madina al-fadila *(The Virtuous City) which, far from being a copy or a clone of Plato's* Republic, *is imbued with the Neoplatonic concept of God. Of course,* al-Madina al-fadila *has undeniable Platonic elements but its theology, as opposed to its politics, places it outside the mainstream of pure Platonism.*

In his admittedly complex theories of epistemology, al-Farabi has both an Aristotelian and Neoplatonic dimension, neither of which is totally integrated with the other. His influence was wide and extended not only to major Islamic philosophers such as Ibn Sina who came after him, and to lesser mortals such as Yahya ibn 'Adi, al-Sijistani, al-'Amiri and al-Tawhidi, but also to major thinkers of Christian medieval Europe including Thomas Aquinas.

1 Life and works
2 Metaphysics
3 Epistemology
4 Political philosophy
5 Influence

1 Life and works

Abu Nasr Muhammad ibn Muhammad ibn Tarkhan ibn Awzalagh al-Farabi was born in approximately AH 257/AD 870. He may rightly be acclaimed as one of the greatest of Islamic philosophers of all time. While his name tends to be overshadowed by that of IBN SINA, it is worth bearing in mind that the latter was less original than the former. Indeed, a well-known story tells how Ibn Sina sought in vain to understand Aristotle's *Metaphysics*, and it was only through a book by al-Farabi on the intentions of the *Meta-*

physics that understanding finally came to him. However, unlike Ibn Sina, al-Farabi has left us no autobiography and we know far less about his life in consequence. Considerable myth has become attached to the man: it is unlikely, for example, that he really spoke more than seventy languages, and we may also query his alleged ascetic lifestyle. We do know that he was born in Turkestan and later studied Arabic in Baghdad; it has been claimed that most of his books were written here. He travelled to Damascus, Egypt, Harran and Aleppo, and in the latter city the Hamdanid ruler Sayf al-Dawla became his patron. Even the circumstances of his death are not clear: some accounts portray him dying naturally in Damascus while at least one holds that he was mugged and killed on the road from Damascus to Ascalon.

Al-Farabi became an expert in philosophy and logic, and also in music: one of his works is entitled *Kitab al-musiqa al-kabir* (The Great Book of Music). However, perhaps the book for which he is best known is that whose title is abbreviated to *al-Madina al-fadila* (The Virtuous City), and which is often compared, misleadingly in view of its Neoplatonic orientation, to Plato's *Republic*. Other major titles from al-Farabi's voluminous corpus included the *Risala fi'l-'aql* (Epistle on the Intellect), *Kitab al-huruf* (The Book of Letters) and *Kitab ihsa' al-'ulum* (The Book of the Enumeration of the Sciences).

2 Metaphysics

Majid Fakhry (1983) has described al-Farabi as 'the founder of Arab Neo-Platonism and the first major figure in the history of that philosophical movement since Proclus'. This should be borne in mind as we survey the metaphysics of the philosopher whom the Latin Middle Ages knew as Abunaser and whom the Arabs designated the 'Second Master' (after Aristotle). It should be noted that al-Farabi was an Aristotelian as well as a Neoplatonist: he is said, for example, to have read *On the Soul* two hundred times and even the *Physics* forty times. It should then come as no surprise that he deploys Aristotelian terminology, and indeed there are areas of his writings that are quite untouched by Neoplatonism. Furthermore, al-Farabi tried to demonstrate the basic agreement between Aristotle and Plato on such matters as the creation of the world, the survival of the soul and reward and punishment in the afterlife. In al-Farabi's conception of God, essence and existence fuse absolutely with no possible separation between the two. However, there is no getting away from the fact that it is the Neoplatonic element which dominates so much else of al-Farabi's work. We see this, for example, in the

powerful picture of the transcendent God of Neoplatonism which dominates *al-Madina al-fadila*. We see this too in al-Farabi's references to God in a negative mode, describing the deity by what he is not: he has no partner, he is indivisible and indefinable. And perhaps we see the Neoplatonic element most of all in the doctrine of emanation as it is deployed in al-Farabi's hierarchy of being.

At the top of this hierarchy is the Divine Being whom al-Farabi characterizes as 'the First'. From this emanates a second being which is the First Intellect. (This is termed, logically, 'the Second', that is, the Second Being). Like God, this being is an immaterial substance. A total of ten intellects emanate from the First Being. The First Intellect comprehends God and, in consequence of that comprehension, produces a third being, which is the Second Intellect. The First Intellect also comprehends its own essence, and the result of this comprehension is the production of the body and soul of *al-sama' al-ula*, the First Heaven. Each of the following emanated intellects are associated with the generation of similar astral phenomena, including the fixed stars, Saturn, Jupiter, Mars, the Sun, Venus, Mercury and the Moon. Of particular significance in the emanationist hierarchy is the Tenth Intellect: it is this intellect which constitutes the real bridge between the heavenly and terrestrial worlds. This Tenth Intellect (variously called by the philosophers the active or agent intellect in English, the *nous poiétikos* in Greek, the *dator formarum* in Latin and the *'aql al-fa''al* in Arabic) was responsible both for actualizing the potentiality for thought in man's intellect and emanating form to man and the sublunary world. With regard to the latter activity, it has been pointed out that here the active intellect takes on the role of Plotinus' Universal Soul (see PLOTINUS).

In Farabian metaphysics, then, the concept of Neoplatonic emanation replaces that of Qur'anic creation *ex nihilo* (see NEOPLATONISM IN ISLAMIC PHILOSOPHY §2). Furthermore, the Deity at the top of the Neoplatonic hierarchy is portrayed in a very remote fashion. Al-Farabi's philosophers' God does not act directly on the sublunary world: much is delegated to the Active Intellect. However, God for al-Farabi certainly has an indirect 'responsibility' for everything, in that all things emanate from him. Yet we must also note, in order to present a fully rounded picture, that while it is the Neoplatonic portrait of God which dominates al-Farabi's writings, this is not the only picture. In some of his writings the philosopher *does* address God traditionally, Qur'anically and Islamically: he *does* invoke God as 'Lord of the Worlds' and 'God of the Easts and the Wests', and he asks God to robe him in splendid clothes, wisdom and humility and deliver him from misfortune. Yet the overwhelming Neoplatonic substratum of so much else of what he writes fully justifies Fakhry's characterization of al-Farabi, cited earlier, as 'the founder of Arab Neo-Platonism'.

3 Epistemology

Farabian epistemology has both a Neoplatonic and an Aristotelian dimension. Much of the former has already been surveyed in our examination of al-Farabi's metaphysics, and thus our attention turns now to the Aristotelian dimension. Our three primary Arabic sources for this are al-Farabi's *Kitab ihsa' al-'ulum*, *Risala fi'l-'aql* and *Kitab al-huruf*.

It is the second of these works, *Risala fi'l-'aql*, which provides perhaps the most useful key to al-Farabi's complex theories of intellection. In this work he divides *'aql* (intellect or reason) into six major categories in an attempt to elaborate the various meanings of the Arabic word *'aql*. First, there is what might be termed discernment or prudence; the individual who acts for the good is characterized by this faculty, and there is clearly some overlap with the fourth kind of intellect, described below. The second of al-Farabi's intellects is that which has been identified with common sense; this intellect has connotations of 'obviousness' and 'immediate recognition' associated with it. Al-Farabi's third intellect is natural perception. He traces its source to Aristotle's *Posterior Analytics*, and it is this intellect which allows us to be certain about fundamental truths. It is not a skill derived from the study of logic, but it may well be inborn. The fourth of the six intellects may be characterized as 'conscience': this is drawn by the philosopher from Book VI of Aristotle's *Nicomachean Ethics*. It is a quality whereby good might be distinguished from evil and results from considerable experience of life (see ARISTOTLE §§18–21).

Al-Farabi's fifth intellect is both the most difficult and the most important. He gives most space to its description in his *Risala fi'l-'aql* and considers it to be of four different types: potential intellect, actual intellect, acquired intellect and agent or active intellect. *'Aql bi'l-quwwa* (potential intellect) is the intellect which, in Fakhry's words, has the capacity 'of abstracting the forms of existing entities with which it is ultimately identified' (Fakhry 1983: 121). Potential intellect can thus become *'aql bi'l-fi'l* (actual intellect). In its relationship to the actual intellect, the third subspecies of intellect, *'aql mustafad* (acquired intellect) is, to use Fakhry's words again, the 'the agent of actualization' to the actualized object. Finally, there is the *'aql al-fa''al* (agent or active intellect), which was described in §2 above and need not be elaborated upon again.

The sixth and last of the major intellects is Divine Reason or God himself, the source of all intellectual energy and power. Even this brief presentation of Farabian intellection must appear complex; however, given the complexity of the subject itself, there is little option.

The best source for al-Farabi's classification of knowledge is his *Kitab ihsa' al-'ulum*. This work illustrates neatly al-Farabi's beliefs both about what can be known and the sheer range of that knowledge. Here he leaves aside the division into theological and philosophical sciences which other Islamic thinkers would use, and divides his material instead into five major chapters. Through all of them runs a primary Aristotelian stress on the importance of knowledge. Chapter 1 deals with the 'science of language', Chapter 2 formally covers the 'science of logic', Chapter 3 is devoted to the 'mathematical sciences', Chapter 4 surveys physics and metaphysics, and the final chapter encompasses 'civil science' (some prefer the term 'political science'), jurisprudence and scholastic theology. A brief examination of these chapter headings shows that a total of eight main subjects are covered; not surprisingly, there are further subdivisions as well. To give just one example, the third chapter on the mathematical sciences embraces the seven subdivisions of arithmetic, geometry, optics, astronomy, music, weights and 'mechanical artifices'; these subdivisions in turn have their own subdivisions. Thus al-Farabi's epistemology, from what has been described both in this section and §2 above, may be said to be encyclopedic in range and complex in articulation, with that articulation using both a Neoplatonic and an Aristotelian voice.

4 Political philosophy

The best known Arabic source for al-Farabi's political philosophy is *al-Madina al-fadila*. While this work undoubtedly embraces Platonic themes, it is in no way an Arabic clone of Plato's *Republic*. This becomes very clear right at the beginning of al-Farabi's work, with its description of the First Cause (Chapters 1–2) and the emanation of 'the Second' from 'The First' (Chapter 3). Later in the work, however, al-Farabi lays down in Platonic fashion the qualities necessary for the ruler: he should be predisposed to rule by virtue of an innate disposition and exhibit the right attitude for such rule. He will have perfected himself and be a good orator, and his soul will be, as it were, united to the active intellect (see §3). He will have a strong physique, a good understanding and memory, love learning and truth and be above the materialism of this world. Other qualities are enumerated by al-Farabi as well, and it is clear that here his ideal ruler is akin to Plato's classical philosopher-king (see PLATO §14).

Al-Farabi has a number of political divisions for his world. He identifies, for example, three types of society which are perfect and grades these according to size. His ideal virtuous city, which gives its name to the whole volume, is that which wholeheartedly embraces the pursuit of goodness and happiness and where the virtues will clearly abound. This virtuous city is compared in its function to the limbs of a perfectly healthy body. By stark contrast, al-Farabi identifies four different types of corrupt city: these are the ignorant city (al-madina al-jahiliyya), the dissolute city (al-madina al-fasiqa), the turncoat city (al-madina al-mubaddala) and the straying city (al-madina al-dalla). The souls of many of the inhabitants of such cities face ultimate extinction, while those who have been the cause of their fall face eternal torment. In itemizing four corrupt societies, al-Farabi was surely aware of Plato's own fourfold division of imperfect societies in the Republic into timarchy, oligarchy, democracy and tyranny. The resemblance, however, is more one of structure (four divisions) rather than of content.

At the heart of al-Farabi's political philosophy is the concept of happiness (sa'ada). The virtuous society (al-ijtima' al-fadil) is defined as that in which people cooperate to gain happiness. The virtuous city (al-madina al-fadila) is one where there is cooperation in achieving happiness. The virtuous world (al-ma'mura al-fadila) will only occur when all its constituent nations collaborate to achieve happiness. Walzer reminds us that both Plato and Aristotle held that supreme happiness was only to be gained by those who philosophized in the right manner. Al-Farabi followed the Greek paradigm and the highest rank of happiness was allocated to his ideal sovereign whose soul was 'united as it were with the Active Intellect'. But Walzer goes on to stress that al-Farabi 'does not confine his interest to the felicity of the first ruler: he is equally concerned with the felicity of all the five classes which make up the perfect state' (Walzer, in introduction to al-Madina al-fadila (1985: 409–10)). Farabian political philosophy, then, sits astride the saddle of Greek eudaimonia, and a soteriological dimension may easily be deduced from this emphasis on happiness. For if salvation in some form is reserved for the inhabitants of the virtuous city, and if the essence of that city is happiness, then it is no exaggeration to say that salvation is the reward of those who cooperate in the achievement of human happiness. Eudaimonia/sa'ada becomes a soteriological raft or steed.

5 Influence

The impact of al-Farabi's work on IBN SINA was not limited merely to illuminating Aristotle's *Metaphysics*. It was with good reason that al-Farabi was designated the 'Second Master' (after Aristotle). One modern scholar recently acknowledged the dependence of Ibn Sina on al-Farabi in a book dealing with both which he entitled *The Two Farabis* (Farrukh 1944). And if AQUINAS (§9) did not derive his essence–existence doctrine from al-Farabi but from the Latinized Ibn Sina, as is generally assumed, there is no doubt that Farabian concepts of essence and existence provided a base for the elaborated metaphysics of Ibn Sina and thence of Aquinas. Finally, the briefest of comparisons between the tenfold hierarchy of intellection produced by al-Farabi and the similar hierarchy espoused by Ibn Sina, each of which gives a key role to the Tenth Intellect, shows that in matters of emanation, hierarchy and Neoplatonic intellection, Ibn Sina owes a considerable intellectual debt to his predecessor.

Al-Farabi influenced many other thinkers as well. A glance at the period between AH 256/AD 870 and AH 414/AD 1023 and at four of the major thinkers who flourished in this period serves to confirm this: Yahya IBN 'ADI, Abu Sulayman AL-SIJISTANI, Abu 'l-Hasan Muhammad ibn Yusuf AL-'AMIRI and Abu Hayyan AL-TAWHIDI may all be said to constitute in one form or another a 'Farabian School'. The Christian Monophysite Yahya ibn 'Adi studied in Baghdad under al-Farabi and others. Like his master, Yahya was devoted to the study of logic; like his master also, Yahya held that there was a real link between reason, ethics and politics. Al-Sijistani was a pupil of Yahya's and thus at one remove from al-Farabi; nonetheless, he shared in both his master's and al-Farabi's devotion to logic, and indeed was known as al-Sijistani al-Mantiqi (The Logician). In his use of Platonic classification and thought, al-Sijistani reveals himself as a true disciple of al-Farabi. Although al-'Amiri appears to speak disparagingly of al-Farabi at one point, there can be no doubt about al-Farabi's impact on him. Indeed, al-'Amiri's works combine the Platonic, the Aristotelian and the Neoplatonic. Finally, Abu Hayyan al-Tawhidi, a pupil of both Yahya and al-Sijistani, stressed, for example, the primacy of reason and the necessity of using logic. Like others of the Farabian School outlined above, al-Tawhidi contributed towards a body of thought the primary constituents of which were the soteriological, the ethical and the noetic.

See also: ARISTOTELIANISM IN ISLAMIC PHILOSOPHY; GREEK PHILOSOPHY: IMPACT ON

ISLAMIC PHILOSOPHY; IBN SINA; LOGIC IN ISLAMIC PHILOSOPHY; NEOPLATONISM IN ISLAMIC PHILOSOPHY; POLITICAL PHILOSOPHY IN CLASSICAL ISLAM

List of works

al-Farabi (c.870–950) *al-Madina al-fadila* (The Virtuous City), trans. R. Walzer, *Al-Farabi on the Perfect State: Abu Nasr al-Farabi's Mabadi' Ara Ahl al-Madina al-Fadila*, Oxford: Clarendon Press, 1985. (Revised with introduction and commentary by the translator.)

—— (c.870–950) *Risala fi'l-'aql* (Epistle on the Intellect), ed. M. Bouyges, Beirut: Imprimerie Catholique, 1938. (A seminal text for the understanding of Farabian epistemology.)

—— (c.870–950) *Kitab al-huruf* (The Book of Letters), ed. M. Mahdi, Beirut: Dar al-Mashriq, 1969. (Modelled on Aristotle's *Metaphysics*, but of interest to students of linguistics as well as of philosophy.)

—— (c. 870–950) *Kitab ihsa' al-'ulum* (The Book of the Enumeration of the Sciences), ed. and trans. A. González Palencia, *Catálogo de las Ciencias*, Arabic text with Latin and Spanish translation, Madrid: Imprenta y Editorial Maestre, 1953. (A survey of the learned sciences of the day, of encyclopedic range.)

—— (c.870–950) *Kitab al-musiqa al-kabir* (The Great Book of Music), ed. G.A. Khashab and M.A. al-Hafni, Cairo: Dar al-Katib al-'Arabi, 1967. (Al-Farabi's major contribution to musicology.)

References and further reading

Alon, I. (1990) 'Farabi's Funny Flora: Al-Nawabit as Opposition', *Arabica* 37: 56–90. (Highly creative discussion of the links between the philosophical terminology of Ibn Bajja and al-Farabi, which brings out the complexity of the theological and political ramifications of such language.)

Black, D. (1996) 'Al-Farabi', in S.H. Nasr and O. Leaman (eds) *History of Islamic Philosophy*, London: Routledge, ch. 12, 178–97. (Account of the thought and main works of al-Farabi.)

* Fakhry, M. (1983) *A History of Islamic Philosophy*, London: Longman; New York: Columbia University Press, 2nd edn. (An excellent standard introduction to the field. See especially pages 107–128.)

* Farrukh, U. (1944) *Al-Farabiyyan* (The Two Farabis), Beirut. (Ibn Sina's dependence on al-Farabi, as mentioned in §5.)

Galston, M. (1990) *Politics and Excellence: The Political Philosophy of Alfarabi*, Princeton, NJ: Princeton University Press. (A major analysis of an important aspect of Farabian philosophy.)

Netton, I.R. (1989) *Allah Transcendent: Studies in the Structure and Semiotics of Islamic Philosophy, Theology and Cosmology*, London and New York: Routledge. (Contains a wide-ranging chapter on al-Farabi, see pages 99–148. This volume was later published in paperback by Curzon Press in 1994.)

—— (1992) *Al-Farabi and His School*, Arabic Thought and Culture Series, London and New York: Routledge. (Assesses the philosopher through an epistemological lens.)

IAN RICHARD NETTON

FARDELLA, MICHELANGELO (*c.*1646–1718)

Fardella was one of the first and most famous Italian Cartesians. Influenced by Malebranche and Leibniz, he rejected materialism in metaphysics, and endorsed a strongly Augustinian form of Cartesian dualism in philosophy of mind. In mathematics, he popularized Descartes' analytic method. An insufficiently radical thinker, the cultural significance of his work rests on his defence of the Cartesian method against scholasticism.

The Italian Michelangelo Fardella was educated by the Franciscans. Introduced by Giovanni Alfonso Borelli to mathematics and the Galilean method, he soon acquired an everlasting dislike for scholasticism. In Paris (1678–80), he became acquainted with the Cartesian movement and possibly MALEBRANCHE, whose writings affected his Augustinianism. He taught in Rome, Modena and Padua (1694–1710), where he was an influential advocate of Cartesianism. Between 1690 and 1714 he corresponded with LEIBNIZ, and published his three major works: *Universae philosophiae systema* (1691), a methodological treatise presenting a critical combination of themes from the Logic of PORT-ROYAL and DESCARTES; *Universae usualis mathematicae theoria* (1691), a presentation of the various branches of mathematics based on Descartes' method; and *Animae humanae natura ab Augustino detecta* (1698), a long, erudite commentary on Augustine's works, meant to demonstrate that the mind or soul is incorporeal and eternal (see AUGUSTINE §§5–6). In 1710 he became theologian and mathematician to Charles III in Barcelona. He died leaving most of his ambitious projects uncompleted.

Fardella celebrates Descartes as the first philosopher to have provided a proper method of philosophical investigation: as in mathematics, truth must be pursued by following only clear and certain inferences. Not only the rationality of Christianity, but also Descartes' metaphysics itself could profit from a firm application of the method. For, on its basis, it is possible to argue against the existence of the material world, as Fardella argues in the second appendix to *Universae philosophiae systema*. The mind is acquainted only with its ideas which are more like conceptual dispositions than images, and can be innate (God and mathematical principles) or acquired. Ideas are not different from their references, but since they could be exactly the same even if their ontological source were only another mind – Fardella denies any distinction in this respect between primary and secondary qualities – there is no reason to postulate an unlimited domain of independent, material bodies on the basis of a limited perception of appearances. This does not mean that only minds are real. The notion of a material substance is epistemologically redundant, but God still guarantees the existence of physical bodies, a conclusion that BERKELEY explicitly criticized in his *Notebooks*. It does imply, however, that we should refrain from endorsing the Cartesian equation between *res extensa* and matter, and the subsequent mechanical physics of vortex.

Fardella interprets mathematics like GALILEO, as the art whereby God created the universe, and infers that the world is intrinsically mathematical and that a science of nature must be quantitative. But then, instead of material substance we should speak of geometrical points, unextended atoms somewhat similar to Leibniz's monads, acting as the source of extension. The mind itself, whose actions Fardella places in the brain, is a mathematical point, immaterial and unextended. How this ontology might be possible, Fardella never made completely clear. Leibniz and BAYLE objected that such geometrical points could not be material, or they would divisible, but could not be purely mathematical either, otherwise they would not give rise to extension.

Fardella's critique of our belief in the necessary existence of an external world remains nevertheless original. It differs both from Malebranche's position (Fardella does not provide probabilistic arguments for an external world), and from that of Berkeley (Fardella does not deny the existence of a mind-independent world). Unlike Descartes, Fardella maintains that God leaves us free to withhold our assent to any impression, and that our belief in the existence of material bodies is justified only by our faith in the revelation of the Holy Scriptures. Fardella's ontology is based on a weak understanding of the principle of sufficient reason, resembling the one endorsed by Samuel CLARKE in his correspondence with Leibniz, according to which God's will is a sufficient *ratio essendi* of the external world.

See also: AUGUSTINIANISM

List of works

The first three works were meant to be part of a larger and very ambitious system of 'philosophia architectonica' which Fardella never completed.

Fardella, M. (1691) *Universae philosophiae systema*, Venice. (A textbook of philosophical logic in five sections: on the origin of error, the theory of perception and judgment, the principles of reasoning and the method of investigation. The second of two appendices contains Fardella's anti-materialist argument.)

—— (1691) *Universae usualis mathematicae theoria*, Venice. (The first comprehensive presentation of the various branches of mathematics to be written by an Italian according to the Cartesian method.)

—— (1698) *Animae humanae natura ab Augustino detecta in libris de Animae Quantitate, decimo de Trinitate, et de Animae Immortalitate*, Venice; partial Italian trans. R. Venza (1991–2) as 'L'Opera Filosofica di Michelangelo Fardella', pts 1 and 2, *La Fardelliana* 10: 107–49 and 11: 107–64. (Meant to show how Cartesian rationalism combined easily with Augustinian spiritualism. The mind or soul is represented in Leibnizian terms, as a metaphysical point. Epicurus and Lucretius are the main polemical targets of Fardella's anti-materialism.)

—— (1691–1709) *Lettere ad Antonio Magliabechi*, Cassino: Editrice Garigliano, 1978. (Sixty-nine letters on disparate topics written by Fardella to the famous Florentine librarian.)

—— (1698) *Pensieri Scientifici e Lettera Antiscolastica*, Naples: Bibliopolis, 1987. (A critical edition of two previously unpublished manuscripts. The *Lettera Antiscolastica* is a powerful and detailed attack against scholasticism in all fields of knowledge, from logic to physics and metaphysics.)

References and further reading

Barbata, A. and Corso, C. (1993) "'Fra' Michelangelo Fardella – Trapanese "in fuga" tra XVII e XVIII sec. nella Repubblica delle Lettere d'Europa', *La Fardelliana* 12: 65–159. (Detailed reconstruction of Fardella's life and intellectual biography; contains further bibliography.)

* Berkeley, G. (1707–8) *Philosophical Commentaries*, in *The Works of George Berkeley, Bishop of Cloyne*, vol. 1, ed. A.A. Luce and T.E. Jessop, Edinburgh: Thomas Nelson. (Berkeley's notebooks, first published in 1871. On page 15 Berkeley criticizes Fardella for being an immaterialist.)

Femiano, S. (1979) *Ricerca su Michelangelo Fardella, Filosofo e Matematico, in appendice due editi non conosciuti*, Cassino: Tipografia 'S. Benedetto'. (A historical reconstruction of Fardella's intellectual development and scientific production, which however does not discuss his philosophy.)

Garin, E. (1933) 'Michelangelo Fardella', *Giornale Critico della Filosofia Italiana* 14: 394–408. (A philosophical analysis of Fardella's thought and his intellectual position within Italian Cartesianism.)

Lauria, D. (1974) *Agostinismo e Cartesianesimo in Michelangelo Fardella*, Catania: Niccolò Gannotta Editore. (A brief introduction to Fardella's Augustinian Cartesianism including correspondence between Fardella and Matteo Giorgi about Descartes' theory of material substance).

McCracken, C.J. (1986) 'Stages on a Cartesian Road to Immaterialism', *Journal of the History of Philosophy* 24: 19–40. (Places Fardella's immaterialism in relation to the theories of Malebranche, Norris, Collier, Berkeley and Bayle.)

Meschini, F.A. (1994) 'Fardella, Michelangelo', in *Dizionario Biografico degli Italiani*, vol. 44, Rome: Istituto dell'Enciclopedia Italiana, 776–81. (A good synthesis of Fardella's life and works, with an extended bibliography.)

Pepe, L. (1982) 'Notes on the dissemination of Descartes' Geometrie in Italy in the 17th century', *Bollettino di Storia delle Scienze Matematiche* 2: 249–88. (An interesting evaluation of Fardella's work in mathematics.)

Predaval Magrini, M.V. (1986) 'Problemi connessi all'edizione di un epistolario sei-settecentesco. La corrispondenza Leibniz-Fardella', in G. Canziani and G. Paganini (eds) *Le Edizioni dei Testi Filosofici e Scientifici del '500 e '600*, Milan: Angeli, 183–91. (A well-documented overview of the correspondence between Leibniz and Fardella.)

Sasso, R. (1980) 'Fardella et la Philosophie comme discours systématique', *Recherches sur le XVIIème Siècle* 4: 115–25. (Focuses on Fardella's conception of philosophy as an encyclopedic system of knowledge.)

LUCIANO FLORIDI

FARRER, AUSTIN MARSDEN (1904–68)

Austin Farrer is widely regarded as the Church of England's most brilliant philosophical theologian of the twentieth century. His elegant, sometimes difficult, writings aim more at synthesis and the elaboration of images than at analytical rigour; they characteristically take the form of a running debate between opposing positions. He focuses on the relations between divine and creaturely action in the spheres of nature, revelation and grace.

In the foreword to *The Freedom of the Will*, Austin Farrer writes:

> A host of able men, their wits sharpened by logical training, have written ingenious papers lately in the philosophical journals, each discussing voluntary freedom within the area of a carefully limited question. I could not hope to vie with their detailed thoroughness, or formal elegance. If I was to contribute anything, it would have to be by aiming at greater completeness, and at a synthesis of topics. So that is what I have done, well or ill.
>
> (1958: v)

This statement could aptly serve as a description of Farrer's entire philosophical output. He had an acute awareness of the metaphorical character of much apparently literal thinking, and an unrivalled deftness in penetrating and extending those metaphors, as his sermons and exegetical writings bear witness. And he was loath to take up any issue piecemeal. These features of Farrer's thought perhaps explain why his writing seems to lack rigour in comparison with those 'ingenious papers... in the philosophical journals'. They certainly make impossible the task of summarizing his thought in a short space. (Readers who want a quick introduction to Farrer's mature thinking on natural theology and on human freedom can do no better than to read his summaries at the end of *Faith and Speculation* and *The Freedom of the Will*.) So this entry will focus on an issue that was central to Farrer's thought: the relation between divine and human action.

The bare assertion of the existence of God, Farrer says, is 'of metaphysical interest only'. Practical importance attaches instead to assertions about God's particular actions. Since religion is precisely the voluntary association of one's own action with the divine, there can be no religion without some conception of how God acts in the world. And so a central problem for Farrer is how to conceive the relation between divine and creaturely action. Surprisingly, though, he insists that the 'causal joint' between infinite and finite action cannot be of any practical concern to us. The Christian holds that the divine action embraces whatever happens. But every event in our world is an immediate act of natural agents – otherwise it would be no part of our world. So:

God's agency must actually be such as to work omnipotently on, in, or through creaturely agencies without either forcing them or competing with them. But as soon as we try to conceive it in action, we degrade it to the creaturely level and place it in the field of interacting causalities. The result can only be (if we take it literally) monstrosity and confusion.

(1967: 62)

Given this position, the problem of human freedom and divine predestination in the achievement of salvation disappears. 'We know that the action of a man can be the action of God in him; our religious existence is an experimenting with this relation' (1967: 66). But since we cannot conceive the manner in which God acts, we cannot pose the question of the relation between his action and ours. Similarly, there is no room for a special concept of grace. 'Grace is an action of the Creator in the creature. He acts in the creature everywhere; when he acts in the rational creature he is pleased to act in that creature's mental and voluntary life, bringing them into his own' (1967: 67).

Farrer's understanding of revelation also depends on this conception of divine and human action. When we try to understand the experience of receiving a divine communication, we are often preoccupied with trying to locate the 'point of punctuation' between the divine and the human. But no such question should arise. God's will is always taking effect in the actions of his creatures. The events that make up revelation are simply those actions of God for the eternal salvation of his rational creatures 'in which the relation of human instrument to divine act becomes transparent' (1967: 103). 'God reveals himself effectively through fallible minds and takes care that their imperfections shall not frustrate his purpose' (1967: 102).

See also: GRACE; REVELATION

List of works

Farrer, A.M. (1943) *Finite and Infinite*, London: Dacre Press. (An early work of natural theology, sketching a voluntarist metaphysics.)
—— (1948) *The Glass of Vision*, London: Dacre Press. (An investigation of the nature of revelation, with

particular attention to the role of images in metaphysics, poetry and Scripture.)
—— (1958) *The Freedom of the Will*, London: Adam & Charles Black; 2nd edn, New York: Charles Scribner's Sons, 1960. (The second edition includes a 'Summary of the Argument'. Farrer defends an incompatibilist account of human freedom and relates that account to empirical psychology, action theory and natural theology.)
—— (1961) *Love Almighty and Ills Unlimited*, London: Collins. (An essay in theodicy, strictly philosophical in its discussion of physical disasters and animal suffering, but explicitly appealing to Christian revelation for the explanation of human suffering.)
—— (1967) *Faith and Speculation*, London: Adam & Charles Black. (Farrer's mature thinking in natural theology, synthesizing his work on a great range of topics.)
—— (1972) *Reflective Faith: Essays in Philosophical Theology*, ed. C.C. Conti, London: Society for Promoting Christian Knowledge. (A collection of essays spanning Farrer's whole career.)

References and further reading

Conti, C. (1995) *Metaphysical Personalism: An Analysis of Austin Farrer's Metaphysics of Theism*, Oxford: Clarendon Press. (Conti emphasizes the influence of process theology and personalism in the development of Farrer's thought and highlights the central role played by his notion of divine action.)
Eaton, J.C. and Loades, A. (eds) (1983) *For God and Clarity: New Essays in Honor of Austin Farrer*, Allison Park, PA: Pickwick Publications. (Chiefly valuable for its bibliography of works by and about Farrer.)
Hebblethwaite, B. and Henderson, E. (eds) (1990) *Divine Action: Studies Inspired by the Philosophical Theology of Austin Farrer*, Edinburgh: T. & T. Clark. (A collection of essays on divine action, most of which explore and extend Farrer's work. Contains an index to several of Farrer's books.)

THOMAS WILLIAMS

FASCISM

'Fascism' is a term referring both to a political ideology and to a concrete set of political movements and regimes. Its most prominent examples were the Italian and German regimes in the interwar period. Fascist

ideology is sometimes portrayed as merely a mantle for political movements in search of power, but in reality it set forth a new vision of society, drawing on both left- and right-wing ideas. Fascists stressed the need for social cohesion and for strong leadership. They were more concerned to revitalize nations by cultural change than to propose institutional changes, but they saw themselves as offering a third way between capitalism and communism. There was no fascist philosophy as such, but fascist ideology drew inspiration from earlier philosophers, most notably Nietzsche and Sorel, and was supported by several contemporary philosophers, including Heidegger, Gentile and Schmitt.

There has always been a small number of philosophers and historians willing to concede that fascism has a serious intellectual pedigree. Some have traced its origins to Rousseau's concept of the 'general will' or Hegel's defence of the state. More commonly, the focus has been on the new nationalism which became prominent during the late nineteenth century, and which is best epitomized by the writings of Barrès or the German *völkisch* (blood nationalist) theorists such as de Lagarde. Whereas the nationalism associated with the French revolutionary doctrine of 'sovereignty of the people' tended to be universalistic and humanistic, the new strand was more emotive, stressing the bonds which linked the holistic community (see NATIONS AND NATIONALISM §2). This in turn was often linked to the rise of a more systematic form of racist thinking, inspired both by developments in science – especially Darwinism – and by a reading of history which saw nation and race as the main engine of change and conflict (see RACE, THEORIES OF).

Other major sources of influence which have often been highlighted are the writings of NIETZSCHE, with his emphasis on the 'will to power', leadership and the total decadence of European bourgeois society, or Sorel's belief in the importance of myths as a means of motivating the masses (see SOREL, G.). These philosophical developments were reinforced by new ideas in the social sciences emerging at the turn of the twentieth century. Of particular importance was the work of elite theorists like Michels and Pareto, who argued that democracy was an impossibility, and the theories of psychologists like FREUD and Le Bon, who pointed to the essential irrationality of much human behaviour.

These precursors were not, however, fascists in the full sense. Nietzsche, for instance, was opposed to anti-Semitism and emotive German nationalism – yet these were to be central elements in Nazism. Sorel was a revisionist socialist concerned with the problem of how to achieve a revolutionary working class, whereas

the *völkisch* thinkers were nothing if not conservative. The First World War provided the impetus for fascism to develop as a more coherent ideology, synthesizing a variety of elements in pre-fascist thought.

Fascism took its name from the *fasci di combattimento*, a movement founded in 1919 by Mussolini, an ex-socialist attracted to nationalism as a means of uniting the people and promoting economic development which could fund radical social reform. Similar movements emerged elsewhere, sharing a set of ideological dispositions, although some, like the Nazis, did not normally refer to themselves as fascist.

The starting point was a view of human nature: fascists like Valois reversed Rousseau in the sense that they believed that 'man' was a savage until given a purpose by strong leaders. The need for a new fascist man was linked to a cyclical view of history, which saw conflict as inherent in the world: Hitler argued that it was necessary to ensure that the nation was sufficiently revitalized to withstand challenges from outside. Social cohesion required the destruction of deleterious humanistic or individualistic influences, like religion and liberalism, whilst the need to forge social unity made fascist theorists like Gentile and SCHMITT hostile to the class analysis preached by much of the left (see GENTILE, G. §3). In general, fascists paid little attention to specific institutional forms, preferring to talk vaguely about a Third Way (neither left nor right, rather lying between capitalism and communism), or the need to find a new sense of being – a major reason for Heidegger's conversion to fascism (see HEIDEGGER, M. §1). The main focus was on changing culture and on the propaganda that was seen as necessary to do this, for fascism held that people were essentially swayed by myths and symbols rather than by rational argument – although some fascists, such as De Man and Mosley, were capable of developing serious economic and political programmes based on a form of authoritarian and statist corporatism.

There were important differences between specific national manifestations of fascism. Nazism, for instance, saw the basis of the community as lying in 'blood', whereas Italian Fascism saw nationalism more in terms of culture. Thus, early fascism had no serious anti-Semitic side, or developed racial theory (although it had an ethnocentric commitment to colonial expansion). Most Nazis also placed far less emphasis on the role of the state than Italian Fascists, seeing the state as a repository for reactionary elements and a source of division between the people and its leader. Moreover, some fascist intellectuals, like Drieu La Rochelle, were more concerned with the threat (from both internal decadence and more virile external enemies) to European rather than specifically national culture.

Linking all true examples of fascism, however, was a broad desire to revitalize society by forging a *holistic–national–radical–Third Way*. This characterization is flexible enough to embrace diverse examples of fascism like Nazism and Italian Fascism, while excluding other alleged cases such as General Franco's Spain as too conservative. It is also capable of encompassing the more subtle form of post-war intellectual fascism, such as the writings of the key *nouvelle droite* theorist, de Benoist.

See also: ANTI-SEMITISM; TOTALITARIANISM

References and further reading

Aschheim. S. (1993) *The Nietzsche Legacy in Germany, 1890–1990*, Berkeley, CA: University of California Press. (Shows how Nietzsche's legacy was manipulated, but also clearly illustrates the affinities between aspects of Nietzsche's thought and fascism.)

Bendersky, J.W. (1983) *Carl Schmitt. Theorist for the Reich*, Princeton, NJ: Princeton University Press. (Shows that Schmitt was largely an authoritarian conservative opportunist – albeit one capable of producing a brilliant defence of statist fascism.)

Eatwell, R. (1996) 'On Defining the "Fascist Minimum": The Centrality of Ideology', *Journal of Political Ideologies* 1 (3): 303–19. (Focusing especially on a critique of the notable interpretations of Griffin, Payne and Sternhell, this article moves on to offer an expanded version of the definition offered above.)

Gregor, A.J. (1979) *Young Mussolini and the Intellectual Origins of Fascism*, Berkeley, CA: University of California Press. (Views Mussolini as a relatively serious thinker, and traces fascism to left-wing roots; sees the resulting fascist ideology as being as coherent as liberalism or Marxism.)

Griffin, R. (1995) *Fascism: A Reader*, Oxford: Oxford University Press. (Excellent set of texts – coming up to the 1990s – which seek to illustrate the author's thesis that fascism is a form a 'palingenetic, populist, ultranationalism', but cover other interpretations as well.)

Mosse, G. (1966) *The Crisis of German Ideology*, New York: Grosset & Dunlap. (Important study of the origins of Nazism in Romantic and *völkisch* thought; plays down more left-wing influences on Nazism seeing the Nazi revolution as threatening 'none of the vested economic interests of the middle class'.)

—— (1978) *Toward the Final Solution*, New York: Howard Fertig. (History of ideas approach to the rise of racism, showing its centrality to late nineteenth- and early twentieth-century European thought.)

Payne, S. (1980) *Fascism: Comparison and Definition*, Madison, WI: University of Wisconsin Press. (Important comparative typological book, written by a historian who defines fascism in terms of: its style, such as mass rallies; its negations, such as anti-communism; and its positive points, such as nationalism and authoritarianism.)

Popper, K. (1945) *The Open Society and Its Enemies*, London: Routledge & Kegan Paul, 2 vols. (Classic work which seeks to trace the roots of fascism – and communism – to important developments in Western thought. In the case of fascism, Hegel is seen as the main challenge to the liberal Western tradition of pluralism and tolerance.)

Rockmore, T. (1992) *On Heidegger's Nazism and Philosophy*, London: Harvester. (One of several books to appear during the 1980s and 1990s which accepts that Heidegger can reasonably be considered a fascist.)

Sternhell, Z. (1986) *Neither Right Nor Left*, Berkeley, CA: University of California Press. (Argues both that fascism was a serious ideology and that French fascism, by not having to deal with the problems of office, produced the purest form of fascist theory; part of a trilogy, beginning in the late nineteenth century with Barrès.)

Sternhell, Z., Sznajder, M. and Asheri, M. (1994) *The Birth of Fascist Ideology*, Princeton, NJ: Princeton University Press. (Sternhell sees fascism as based on nationalism and socialism. Covers both France and Italy, and pays particular emphasis to the impact of Sorel and anti-Marxist socialism. Sternhell does not consider Nazism to be fascist on account of its biological racist core).

ROGER EATWELL

FATALISM

'Fatalism' is sometimes used to mean the acceptance of determinism, along with a readiness to accept the consequence that there is no such thing as human freedom. The word is also often used in connection with a theological question: whether God's supposed fore-knowledge means that the future is already fixed. But it is sometimes explained very differently, as the view that human choice and action have no influence on future events, which will be as they will be whatever we think or do. On the face of it this is barely coherent, and invites

the assessment that fatalism is simply an expression of resigned acceptance.

Taken as meaning exactly what it says, the dictum that human choice and action have no influence on future events is absurd, since any action must make some aspects of some future events different from how they would have been had that action not been performed. If I leave the house, then *something* happens in the future which would not have happened had I not left it, even if that just turns out to be my rapid return to where I would have been had I stayed at home. Likewise, unless we are to deny that how we decide to behave ever has any effect on how we actually do behave, we must agree that our choices of action frequently affect future events. So if fatalism is not to fall into immediate incoherence, it must be understood rather differently, perhaps as saying only that there are *certain* things destined to happen irrespective of what we do. (Usually these will be events of particular significance: the soothsayer's prediction will come true, regardless of any attempts we may make to ensure that it does not.)

It follows that fatalism, in this form, cannot be supported by any argument which, if it worked at all, would apply to all future events. Any argument for thoroughgoing causal determinism would fall into this category. So would the notorious argument from the sea-battle: if there will be a sea-battle tomorrow, it is true now that there will be; if there will not, it is true now that there will not be. So since one of these is true now, there is nothing we can do to influence whether there will be a battle or not. If this reasoning works, it works for every future event. But in any case, although this argument and variants of it are found, it faces a severe difficulty. For it will have to address the crucial question about the direction of dependence: does the occurrence of the battle depend on the truth of today's statement, or the truth of today's statement on tomorrow's events? The fatalist conclusion calls for the former, but the latter is far more plausible and the basic argument does nothing to refute it.

Fatalism can appear more coherent if seen against a certain kind of background. Whether it appears more plausible depends on the reader's attitude to the background, which many will find rather too superstitious for their taste. We are to think of powers, watching over human life, who have decreed that certain things shall happen to certain people (that a particular individual will die young, that Oedipus will kill his own father), and are bent on manipulating the world, and perhaps also the fated individual's state of knowledge, so as to bring their decrees about. Imagine a rat in a maze, from which you have decided that it will never find its way out. If it turns left (which leads to the exit), you take out a piece from somewhere else in the maze and slot it in round the next corner, turning the chosen route into a dead end. If it turns right, you do nothing, since the right turn leads to a dead end anyway.

It should be noted that fatalism, understood in this way, has very little to do with problems about the freedom of the will. In choosing which way to turn, our rat can be free in the strongest sense that any libertarian has ever dreamed of; the fates make their move after it has made its choice. Oedipus may be equally free; the fates make sure that he does not know who the obstructive old man at the crossroads really is. Had he known that, no doubt he would have made his free choice differently, leaving the fates to outwit him in another way on another occasion.

See also: DETERMINISM AND INDETERMINISM; FREE WILL; ŁUKASIEWICZ, J. §3 ; MANY-VALUED LOGICS, PHILOSOPHICAL ISSUES IN §1; PREDESTINATION; STOICISM §§20–1

References and further reading

Aristotle (*c.* mid 3rd century BC) *De Interpretatione*, in *The Complete Works of Aristotle* ed. J Barnes, Princeton, NJ: Princeton University Press, 1984, vol. 1, 25–38. (Chapter 9 introduces the notorious sea-battle example. Aristotle appears to be arguing that to avoid fatalism we must give up the idea that the law of excluded middle applies to statements about the future. However, the passage has given rise to a great deal of conflicting interpretation.)

Cicero (44 BC) *De Fato* (On Fate), with trans. and commentary by R.W. Sharples, Warminster: Aris & Phillips, 1991. (Sections 28–30 offer an account of Stoic views on fatalism, which they appear to have understood both as determinism and in the sense emphasized in this entry.)

Taylor, R. (1963) *Metaphysics*, Englewood Cliffs, NJ: Prentice Hall. (Chapter 5 is on fatalism. It presents a version of the sea-battle argument, with the usual concealed defect.)

EDWARD CRAIG

FATALISM, INDIAN

Indian speculation about the vicissitudes of human life has a long and complex history. Life in the early Vedic period was considered to be largely hostage to the 'fate' of natural and psychic forces controlled by various gods (devas). Fate was what proceeded 'from the gods' (daiva), who were considered to be the guardians of the cosmic order and the ultimate source of prosperity. Sacrifice and prayer were the principal means to win their favour.

Later the idea arose that one's present lot is due, not to the whim of some god, but to karma, the effect of one's own actions performed in this or previous lives. On this view, humans do have some scope or 'freedom' to change themselves and the environment in which they live. This more individual potential is called puruṣakāra, which, to varying degrees, may modify daiva. The literal meaning of this term is 'human action' (from the Sanskrit for 'man' and a verbal root meaning 'to act'). With the increasing popularity of the karma theory, daiva tended to become equated with the effects of past behaviour.

Finally, in the context of the spiritual ascent towards a unifying vision of existence, the status of human agency itself became an issue. As long as the seeker remains blinded by false notions of 'I', the ego must experience a sense of agency and a modicum of freedom to chart its course of life. However, from the perspective of enlightenment, or mokṣa, all is 'fate' in the hands of a personal God or a Supreme Self.

1   Background
2   Fate in the *Mahābhārata*
3   Subsequent elaborations

1   Background

The concept of 'fate' (*daiva*) is already well known in the *Ṛg Veda* (completed before 800 BC), the earliest of the sacred texts of modern Hinduism. Here fate is simply the favours obtained from the gods in return for praise or sacrifice. Sacrifices are performed to ensure the good order of the world, to secure a boon or to remove impurity associated with 'sin' (for example, disease). This seeming dependence on the whims of the gods changes rather dramatically, however, at the somewhat later period of the Brāhmaṇa texts (no later than 600 BC), when the priests take control of the gods themselves through their knowledge of the sacrifice. Power is understood to reside in the ritual itself rather than in the gods (who are virtually forced to act). The belief also arises that the cosmic powers can be harnessed by means of ascetic practices known as *tapas*, and by the appropriate use of incantations or mantras. This new magical tradition received its orthodox stamp of approval in the *Atharva Veda*.

There is still little at this period to suggest the existence of a 'person' in the modern sense of an autonomous, self-directing centre of willing and doing. The human agent remains at the mercy, as it were, of external forces. Plans to shape one's own future 'destiny' (in the form of prosperity, progeny, and so on) rely less on an inner sense of agency than on the power of gods, ritual or magic to exert control over the general order of the world. Furthermore, the esoteric knowledge on which this control is based is not in the hands of the individual, but remains a closely guarded secret of the priestly caste.

A shift towards the assertion of more distinctly human powers is signalled by the emergence of a doctrine of moral causality, subsequently known as the karma doctrine. First presented in the Bṛhadāraṇyaka Upaniṣad, this doctrine came to represent the hard facts of human life not as fate, but as the inevitable result of past behaviour. The results of all deeds, good or bad as the case may be, must ultimately bear fruit in one form or another. There is no such thing as chance or luck, and even the intervention of God himself becomes problematic in certain traditions. We are punished not *for* our sins but *by* them.

The doctrine drew its logic from the companion belief in reincarnation. Eventually, life itself, including character, the circumstances of birth, the span of life, and even the daily alternation of pleasure and pain, came to be regarded as the maturation of attitudes and actions in this and previous existences. In sum, the cumulative effects of the past are seen progressively to take the place of fate as the source of human character and circumstances.

2   Fate in the *Mahābhārata*

The *Mahābhārata* (probably compiled between 200 BC and AD 300–400) is a great repository of ideas on fate in the Indian context, moving from those reminiscent of the early Vedas to concepts of divine grace and the mature doctrines of karma. A humanization of divine powers is implicit in the circumstances surrounding the central subject of this epic, a great fratricidal war whose roots are anchored in a conflict of gods and demons for control of heaven. For example, the difference between gods and humans is blurred by the fact that the battle is being waged on the earth, where human 'sons' of the divine prototypes battle for control of a dynastic succession. More importantly, this divine infusion has evidently sired in humans a sense of an inherent power of their own.

The most common Sanskrit term for this human capacity for self-effort is *puruṣakāra* (literally 'human action'). Only what is preordained by universal consensus of the heavenly gods is now sure to prevail on the Earth. Humans are otherwise at liberty to challenge the gods, although they do so at their peril since these gods may be jealous, or even fearful, of human aspirations. Indra, the king of the gods himself, can feel threatened by the fierce austerities of some power-hungry sage. The best-laid human plans may thus be blunted or bent by a *daiva* that confronts the individual either from within, as an eruption of doubt, inner conflict or irrational behaviour, or from without, in the form of some untoward reversal of fortune. The respective spheres and strengths of these two forces is a popular topic of learned discussion in the epic.

From the macrocosmic perspective, the fate of the cosmos is in the hands of Viṣṇu-Nārāyaṇa in his supreme aspect. It is he who controls the Wheel of Time (*kālacakra*), the immense temporal cycle of creation (activity) and destruction (quiescence) of the seven worlds (*lokas*). It is he too who must provide the superordinate backing to settle the difficult or contentious rulings of Brahmā, the epic arbiter of heavenly disputes. At the human level, the fate of society is governed by a 'morality' of world ages (*yugas*) that repeat themselves with chronological precision as long as the universe is in being. The crisis that arises at each low point of moral decay can only be resolved by the eschatological destruction of the old order of society by the Divinity in his lower, human, aspect (*avatāra*). The *Mahābhārata* is essentially the (quasi-) history of one such intervention, which follows upon a prearranged heavenly accord between the old Vedic gods and Viṣṇu-Nārāyaṇa, incarnated as Kṛṣṇa. He does no actual fighting, but it is his strategic guidance that leads the human 'sons' of these gods to eventual victory.

As events escalate towards their momentously regenerative climax, the fate of individuals becomes ever more hopelessly caught up in the chain of events. Not surprisingly, the protagonists tend to rail against fate, as their own ambitions encounter inexplicable reversals in the world around them. This is particularly true of blind King Dhṛtarāṣṭra. As Kaurava losses mount, he becomes more and more convinced that he is the victim of a fate opposed to reason and human volition. *Puruṣakāra* appears increasingly ephemeral, inconsequential or futile as he is dragged from one disaster to another by his own emotional attachment to his son. These feelings are expressed in an endless litany of complaints against cosmic justice.

The more widely held belief, however, is that human planning can succeed through *puruṣakāra*, provided the undertaking is in accord with the prescribed order of *dharma* (see DUTY AND VIRTUE, INDIAN CONCEPTIONS OF §§1–2). *Puruṣakāra* is considered a particularly vital quality for a king, whose *dharma* is to protect the all-important Brahmans and his subjects as a whole. The important watchword 'Victory is where the *dharma* [or Kṛṣṇa]

is', is not only a harbinger of victory on the battlefield; it also has important spiritual overtones. Whatever the challenges of the world, it is believed, these can only be successfully met if individuals are able to change themselves for the better through self-control and spiritual insight. The epic expresses this notion in the well-known imagery of the chariot: one must learn to control the chariot of the body by taming the wild horses of the senses with the reins of the intellect.

This mastery of the unruly senses through the intellect (*buddhi*) underlines the epic, and subsequent Hindu, idea that volition is not a separate act in itself, but follows automatically upon an act of spiritual insight. However, while *puruṣakāra* is an important element in this process it must not be confused with 'free will' or the modern concept of freedom. What is regarded as free is not the executive function of an empirical self (*jīvātman*) but the *puruṣa* or *ātman*, the self-realized transcendental Self (see SELF, INDIAN THEORIES OF §1). The great problem of human life is precisely the bondage caused by the ego-centred self and its 'will'. Even full control of the chariot is not true freedom, since the very need for control implies that the unruly senses are still drawn by various desires to their worldly objects. The empirical self may identify with particular motives and will them to the extent that it casts its lot in with them. But in doing so, it effectively squanders its freedom, since it is precisely the identification of the *ātman* with these various dispositions and impulses that constitutes what the *Bhagavad Gītā* regards as the false notion of 'I' (*ahaṃkāra*), with its sense of agency.

These ideas can only be fully understood in the broader context of the ascent of life through many lives and life forms (exemplified in an epic story of a lowly worm that finally becomes Brahmā). Humanity is regarded as a sort of bridge between the animals and the gods, the point at which instinct gives way to the need for self-control, and where consciousness becomes the possibility of knowledge of the Self. On the one hand, a human birth is the envy of the lower orders of being. On the other hand, the soul now finds itself in a difficult predicament. It no longer automatically follows the *dharma* of its species (like the animals), but it is also not yet able consciously to follow the imperatives of *dharma* as if they were its own (like God himself). Instead, it faces the arduous task of battling the atavistic forces of desire, aversion and anger that constantly seek to usurp the throne of the higher values and ideals that point the way to its own transcendence. The fratricidal war itself is a fitting metaphor for this human struggle on the 'field of *dharma*' between a lower nature experienced as the 'fate' of the gods or past karma as the case may be and a higher nature acting as a proxy for the spirit (Kṛṣṇa) that takes no active part in the conflict.

The protagonists face further complications over the many branches of *dharma* itself. Conflicts of values cause confusion and heartache, making it even more difficult to know what course to take. King Yudhiṣṭhira, the son of the god Dharma no less, is notably torn between the *dharma* of Brahmanical world-renunciation (*nivṛttidharma*) and the active *dharma* (*pravṛttidharma*) of the warrior king. Arjuna too, the main hero of the epic, is moved by caste and family values to avoid his moral obligation as a warrior chieftain to 'get up and fight' this war. It takes Kṛṣṇa himself to resolve this issue by transforming the traditional Brahmanical practice of renunciation into its inner form. Any undertaking, says Kṛṣṇa, including the most inhuman violence against one's own kith and kin, can be 'right' for the world and for the individual (that is, can be *dharma*), provided it is performed with no thought of personal gain (*karmayoga*), and in a spirit of devotion to Kṛṣṇa (*bhaktiyoga*). This suggests that *puruṣakāra* is no longer judged for its outward function or form, or even for the results to which it leads, but for the spirit that animates it from within.

3 Subsequent elaborations

The later commentaries generally treat the problem of fate in the context of discussions about *mokṣa* or spiritual freedom, the final goal of this spiritual journey. This is due to the fact that, psychologically, *mokṣa* involves a quantum shift in self-identity, in which the human ego, together with its sense of agency, is transcended in favour of a larger system of identity described in the *Bhagavad Gītā* as 'the self of the self of all beings'. Since *puruṣakāra* is based on ideas of 'I' and 'mine', it is fated to dissolve with the ego into the larger 'fate' of the will of God. This interplay between the individual and God raises the issue of the identity of the real agent of action. The consensus in the principal philosophical schools is that, ultimately, it is the Supreme Divinity (*puruṣottama*) who is the agent. ŚAṄKARA and RĀMĀNUJA both approach the issue in the context of their respective theories. Arguing from the relative standpoint in *Brahmasūtrabhāṣya* 2.3.42, Śaṅkara reverts to the traditional mode of thinking that the soul (*jīva*) is driven by a god, in this case the personalized form of the Supreme Reality (*īśvara*) acting in accord with the previous efforts of the soul itself. In *Śrībhāṣya* 1.3.41, Rāmānuja too argues that the Lord is the source of all agency. However, being more conscious of preserving the integrity of the Vedic injunctions, he manages to salvage some

responsibility for the individual by falling back on his theory of qualified difference. Since the embodied soul (*jīvātman*) is independent of the Supreme Self it can act on its own. However, the latter is still given the final word in 'granting permission' for the soul to act.

Later views on fate thus develop along the lines of subsequent religious beliefs. Ascetic traditions such as Vedānta accept self-effort as a practical fiction that dissolves with the advent of true knowledge, at which point one would no doubt view all of creation as moved by fate. However, in devotional sects for whom the permission, assistance or 'grace' of a personal God is called for, the devotee in some sense remains separate from God. In this case, the soul surrenders to the higher Divine Agency and itself becomes an instrument of fate. An example of this would be Kṛṣṇa's exhortation to Arjuna to be his chosen instrument of cosmic destruction.

In the last analysis, therefore, fate is all. In terms of the tasks and responsibilities of everyday life, humans may be regarded as enjoying a modicum of freedom to chart their own course of life, thereby modifying their individual fates. However, from the perspective of the higher freedom of *mokṣa*, this self-concept is inherently flawed, the sense of 'action' and freedom being nothing but fate in disguise.

See also: KARMA AND REBIRTH, INDIAN CONCEPTIONS OF; PREDESTINATION

References and further reading

No comprehensive analysis of Indian approaches to the problem of fate has been published to date. The issue is often raised in discussions concerning karma and related themes, or in more general works related to Indian mythology, the Dharmaśāstras or the epic literature; see, for example, Hopkins 1915 and O'Flaherty 1980.

Bedekar, V.M. (1961) 'The Doctrines of *Svabhāva* and *Kāla* in the *Mahābhārata* and other Old Sanskrit Works', *Journal of the University of Poona (Humanities)* 13: 17–28. (Discusses fate in the form of 'own nature' and time (*kāla*).)

* *Bhagavad Gītā* (*c.*200 BC – AD 300–400), trans. W. Sargeant, ed. C. Chapple, Albany, NY: State University of New York Press, revised edn, 1984. (This text contains the Sanskrit with both literal and more readable English translations, plus grammatical notes on the Sanskrit vocabulary.)

Bharadwaj, S. (1992) *The Concept of 'Daiva' in the Mahābhārata*, Delhi: Nag Publishers. (A compendium of the concepts and the Sanskrit words used to convey the notion of fate in the *Mahābhārata*.)

Bhattacharyya, K. (1967) 'The Status of the Individual in Indian Metaphysics', in C.A. Moore with the assistance of A.V. Morris (ed.) *The Indian Mind: Essentials of Indian Philosophy and Culture*, Honolulu, HI: East–West Center Press and University of Hawaii Press, 299–319. (Indian views of the human being as the subject of fate.)

—— (1971) 'The Indian Concept of Freedom', *Bulletin of the Ramakrishna Mission, Institute of Culture* 22 (9): 348–60. (Argues the case for determinism in Indian thought, with reference to Western and later Indian philosophical literature.)

De Smet, R.V. (1972) 'Early Trends in the Indian Understanding of Man', *Philosophy East and West* 22 (3): 259–68. (A brief but informative survey of Indian self-understanding from the early Vedic period to the rise of *bhakti* devotionalism.)

Divanji, P.C. (1946) '*Puruṣārtha, Daiva* and *Niyati*', parts 1–2, *Annals of the Bhandarkar Oriental Research Institute* 26: 142–51. (A discussion of the factors that influence the human capacity to pursue the traditional Indian goals of life.)

Hiriyanna, M. (1952) 'Karma and Free Will', in *Popular Essays in Indian Philosophy*, Mysore: Kavyalaya Publishers. (Discusses the relationship of karma to fate and free will.)

Hopkins, E.W. (1915) 'The Gods Collectively as Fate', in *Epic Mythology*, Strasbourg: Verlag von Karl J. Trübner. (A review of the various Sanskrit references to fate in the two major Indian epics, the *Mahābhārata* and the somewhat older *Rāmāyaṇa*.)

—— (1906–7) 'Modifications of the Karma Doctrine', *The Journal of The Royal Asiatic Society* 38: 581–93; 39: 397–401, 665–72. (Hopkins was one of the first to note the plethora of seemingly conflicting notions about fate, chance, luck, karma, grace, and so on in Indian traditions.)

* *Mahābhārata* (*c.*200 BC – AD 300–400), trans. K.M. Ganguli, *The Mahābhārata of Krishna Dwaipayana Vyasa*, Calcutta: Oriental Publications Co., 2nd edn, 1952–62, 12 vols; Books 1–5 trans. J.A.B. van Buitenen, *The Mahābhārata*, Chicago, IL: University of Chicago Press, 1973–8, 3 vols. (Ganguli's translation, originally published in eighteen volumes in 1887–96, is the best complete English translation to convey the flavour of this Hindu epic; however, Buitenen's is the most faithful English rendition of the first five books.)

O'Flaherty, W.D. (ed.) (1980) *Karma and Rebirth in Classical Indian Traditions*, Berkeley, CA: University of California Press. (A useful collection of articles by well-known authorities on the subject of karma in Hinduism, Buddhism, Jainism and various Indian philosophical traditions.)

* Rāmānuja (11th century) *Śrībhāṣya*, ed. and trans.

R.D. Karmarkar, *Śrībhāṣya of Rāmānuja: Edited with a Complete English Translation, Introduction, Notes and Appendices*, Poona: University of Poona Sanskrit and Prakrit Series, 1964, 3 vols. (An English-language translation of Rāmānuja's commentary on the *Brahmasūtra* of Bādarāyaṇa.)

* Śaṅkara (early 8th century) *Brahmasūtrabhāṣya*, trans. Swami Gambhirananda, *Brahmasūtrabhāṣya of Śrī Śaṃkarācārya*, Delhi: Advaita Ashrama, 3rd edn, 1977. (An English-language translation of the philosopher Śaṅkara's commentary on the Brahmasūtra of Bādarāyaṇa.)

Sharma, A. (1980) 'Fate and Free Will in the *Bhagavadgītā*', *Religious Studies* 15: 531–7. (An attempt to reconcile the conflicting statements about fate and 'free will' in the *Bhagavad Gītā*.)

Walli, K. (1977) *Theory of Karma in Indian Thought*, Varanasi: Bharata Manisha. (A wide-ranging attempt to trace the development of the karma doctrine in Hindi, Buddhist and Jaina thought, based on the author's doctoral thesis at the University of Allahabad.)

Woods, J.F. (1988–9) 'The Doctrine of Karma in the *Bhagavadgītā*', *The Journal of Studies in the Bhagavadgītā* 8–9: 47–81. (An examination of the views of Śaṅkara and Rāmānuja with respect to action (*karma, karmayoga*) in their respective commentaries on the *Bhagavad Gītā*.)

JULIAN F. WOODS

FA-TSANG *see* FAZANG

FAZANG (643–712)

The monk-scholar Fazang is one of China's great Buddhist thinkers. Drawing on Buddhist scriptural literature and exegetical and systematic works of his predecessors, he fashioned a highly elaborate philosophy that served to provide a rational explanation of his vision of the way things really are. Huayan philosophy is an attempt to show rationally and systematically how the many phenomena that make up existence abide harmoniously in a double relationship of identity and interpenetration. Fazang was credited by his successors with being the third patriarch of the Huayan school.

Fazang was born in Changan (modern Xian), at that time the capital of China. He left home in his mid-teens to study Buddhism, and after several years met

Zhiyan, who became the second Huayan patriarch. With Zhiyan he became acquainted with the *Huayan Sūtra* and its depiction of the cosmic identity and interpenetration of the many individual entities that constitute existence. Fazang became a monk in his mid-twenties and settled in a monastery in Changan as a scholar. He assisted Diksānanda in the latter's translation work, where he became intimately acquainted with the Mahāyāna Buddhist texts and doctrines that later would be cited in support of his portrayal of reality. Along with his translation work and his exegetical and commentarial writings, he composed several treatises that attempt to communicate the Huayan world view.

Fazang's more important works include the *Huayan wujiaozhang* (Huayan Treatise on the Five Doctrines). Ostensibly a work on doctrinal classification, this text is the most important source of the complete Huayan system. He also composed the *Huayanjing tanxuanji* (Notes on Searching for the Profundities of the Huayan Sūtra), an enormous phrase-by-phrase commentary on the sixty-volume version of the Huayan Sūtra. His *Huayan jinshizizhang* (Huayan Essay on the Golden Lion) is a demonstration of identity and interpenetration using the image of a golden lion as a device. The *Banluoboluomituo xinjing liushu* (Brief Commentary on the Sūtra of the Heart of Prajñāpāramitā) is a phrase-by-phrase commentary on the extremely influential Sūtra on the Heart of the Perfection of Wisdom. In the *Qixinlun yiji* (Notes on the Meaning of the Treatise on the Awakening of Mahāyāna Faith), he provides a commentary on the enormously influential text mentioned in the title.

The Huayan philosophy is the result of Fazang's attempt to provide a reasoned, coherent description of what he believed to be the enlightened vision of the Buddha. This grasp of reality reveals a cosmos in which each individual particular is identical with all other particulars and at the same time interpenetrates with them. No thing exists in and of itself but rather is both the conditioned result of the many and a condition for all others. Consequently, the real cosmos is a place where all things of whatever nature are bound together intimately in a vast net of relationships.

This description of the true state of things is presented as the highest, final teaching of Mahāyāna Buddhism, and since Fazang's time, most Mahāyāna schools have accepted it as the high water mark of Buddhist thought. It was assembled from several parts that were central and foundational to Mahāyāna Buddhist thought and practice. One element is the doctrine of emptiness (*śūnyatā*) which, as a critique of things, is the denial that individuals exist autonomously by virtue of substances or essences. Primarily a critique of language but also secondarily a critique of the material world, 'emptiness' means that anything exists solely as the result of a vast array of conditions that generate and maintain the individual (see BUDDHIST CONCEPT OF EMPTINESS).

Another source of Huayan is the doctrine of the 'womb (or matrix) of Buddha' (*tathāgatagarbha*). In its simplest form, this is the doctrine that human beings are like wombs in which the seed or embryo of Buddhahood grows. In its most radical form, it teaches that everything, animate and inanimate, contains the Buddha and is thus both an ordinary, mundane individual and the body of the Buddha. Fazang also drew heavily on his predecessors in China, such as the Dilun School and the Shelun School, and on influential texts such as the *Awakening of Mahāyāna Faith* (see BUDDHIST PHILOSOPHY, CHINESE; AWAKENING OF FAITH IN MAHĀYĀNA).

Huayan thought should be seen as Fazang's attempt to unpack and develop the basic teaching of emptiness. If things are empty of independent existence, then if we examine any individual x in its relationship with the total environment, it will be seen that x arises out of a vast array of conditions and remains dependent on them. However, by the same token, because all things are simultaneously empty and existent, x in its capacity of being an actual entity acts as a condition for the others. In this way, each item of existence is at once an actual fact of existence and empty. As conditions for others, all things retain their unique characteristics and qualities; as empty results of others, all things are identical. As a concrete individual with its own peculiar characteristics, the conditioning entity is simply one phenomenal item among myriads; as an instantiation of emptiness, it is the noumenous body of the Buddha Vairocana. The deluded see only the ordinary and phenomenal; the enlightened see the Buddha in each thing.

The Huayan cosmos is fundamentally and essentially a dynamic and creative place. Each individual is the focal point of vast number of causes and conditions that impinge on it and modify it from moment to moment. The ever-changing individual simultaneously acts creatively on its environment, for to be an existent being is necessarily to possess conditioning power. Such a situation has great implications for how the human individual grasps his or her own status and function in the world and for how one should act in a world where the fundamental fact is codependence.

See also: BUDDHIST PHILOSOPHY, CHINESE; BUDDHIST CONCEPT OF EMPTINESS

List of works

Fazang (643–712) *Huayan wujiaozhang* (Huayan Treatise on the Five Doctrines), trans. F.H. Cook, 'Fa-tsang's Treatise on the Five Doctrines: An Annotated Translation', unpublished Ph.D. dissertation, University of Wisconsin, 1970; text in *Taishō Shinshū Daizōkyō* 45, no. 1866. (Fazang's most complete discussion of the intricacies of Huayan philosophy; he was the chief architect of Huayan thought.)

— (643–712) *Huayanjing tanxuanji* (Notes on Searching for the Profundities of the *Huayan Sūtra*), text in *Taishō Shinshū Daizōkyōō* 35, no. 1733. (An exhaustive phrase-by-phrase commentary on the *Huayan Sūtra* (Sanskrit title, *Avatamsaka Sūtra*, translated into Chinese in sixty volumes by Buddhabhadra). The *sūtra* or scripture is an important source for Huayan thought.)

— (643–712) *Huayan jinshizizhang* (Huayan Essay on the Golden Lion), text in *Taishō Shinsh Daizōkyō* 45, no. 1880. (Fazang's attempt to demonstrate the relationship of absolute and relative, and individual and totality, by the use of a small golden statue of a lion.)

— (643–712) *Banluoboluomituo xinjing liushu* (Brief Commentary on the Sūtra of the Heart of Prajñāpāramitā), text in *Taishō Shinshū Daizōyō* 33, no. 1712. (Fazang's Huayan interpretation of the *Prajñāāramitā Heart Sūtra*, a basic source for the Huayan teaching of emptiness as interdependence.)

— (643–712) *Qixinlun yiji* (Notes on the Meaning of the *Treatise on the Awakening of Mahāyāna Faith*), text in *Taishō Shinshū Daizōkyō* 44, no. 1846. (A discussion of the teachings of the *Awakening of Mahāyāna Faith*, a fertile source of ideas for Chinese innovators such as Fazang.)

References and further reading

Cook, F.H. (1977) *Hua-Yen Buddhism: The Jewel Net of Indra*, University Park: Pennsylvania State University Press. (An accessible interpretive study of key philosophical ideas.)

Liu Ming-wood (1979) 'The Teaching of Fa-tsang: An Examination of Buddhist Metaphysics', unpublished Ph.D. dissertation, University of California, Los Angeles. (The only Western-language critical study of Huayan metaphysics; in the course of commenting critically on the Huayan system, the author provides the reader with a thorough understanding of difficult Huayan concepts.)

FRANCIS H. COOK

FECHNER, GUSTAV THEODOR (1801–87)

Fechner was a pioneer in experimental psychology and the founder of psychophysics, the speciality within psychology devoted to quantitative studies of perception. In his foundational Elemente der Psychophysik *(Elements of Psychophysics) (1860), he defined the mission of the new science to be the development of an 'exact theory of the functionally dependent relations of . . . the physical and the psychological worlds'. It is in this work that Fechner developed the law of sensation-magnitudes (Fechner's Law): the strength of a sensation is proportional to the logarithmic value of the intensity of the stimulus. Among his contemporaries he was well known not only for basic research in the field of electricity, but also as the author of a number of satirical works under the name 'Dr Mises'.*

1 Life
2 Fechner's law
3 Panpsychism

1 Life

Fechner was born in Saxony, in the village of Grossärchen, son and grandson of Protestant clergymen. Seventy years of his life were spent in Leipzig, many of them at the University, first as a medical student, then as an instructor, and finally as a professor.

Although trained in medicine, Fechner first distinguished himself in physics. While still a student he published translations of Biot's *Textbook of Physics* and Thénard's *Textbook of Theoretical and Practical Chemistry*. Under the pseudonym 'Dr Mises' he also published satirical and poetical works, the first appearing in 1821 as a *Proof That the Moon Is Made of Iodine*. It was his research on electrical currents that earned him a salaried ('Ordinarius') professorship when he was 33. But later experiments on visual afterimages resulted in temporary blindness which, coupled with a harrowing nervous exhaustion, resulted in his resignation from the Leipzig faculty in 1840. A period of exile and depression followed for several years, whereupon recovered vision and restored strength permitted him to resume a productive life of research and writing.

2 Fechner's law

Elemente der Psychophysik (Elements of Psychophysics) (1860) is at once a defence of scientific approaches to the study of mind and a detailed treatise on the proper methods of experimental research in perception. Moreover, it contains the mathematical rationale for the derivation of what might be regarded as the first general law of perception, 'Fechner's Law', which declares the magnitude of sensations to grow as a logarithmic function of the intensity of physical stimuli.

The starting point for this derivation had been provided by the research of E.H. Weber, under whom Fechner had studied physiology and mathematics at Leipzig. Weber had shown that a constant ratio obtained between a stimulus and the amount by which it must be increased or diminished for the change to be just perceptible. Thus, a standard weight of, say, ten units might have to be increased by two units to be judged as 'just heavier'. In this case, on average, a weight of twenty units would have to be increased by four; one of thirty units by six. The general law, which Fechner named 'Weber's law', is expressed, '$\Delta S/S = C$', where S refers to the magnitude of the standard stimulus, ΔS to the difference or change in the magnitude of the standard stimulus sufficient to be just perceptible, and C to the constant fraction discovered for a given class of stimuli. It should be noted that this constant ratio obtains where the standard and the comparison stimuli are just noticeably different. Thus, for any value of the standard stimulus, the amount by which a comparison must differ to result in a just-noticeable difference (the 'jnd') is a constant fraction of the magnitude of the standard stimulus.

Weber's law is a law of discrimination, not a law relating the physical intensity of stimuli to the magnitude of the resulting sensations. To derive the latter from the former Fechner adopted a number of assumptions, chief among them that a given sensation represents (or may be taken as representing) the summation of an indefinitely large number of just-noticeable differences. He reasoned that the law of sensation-magnitude could be found by mathematical integration. Thus, by integrating the Weber ratio over all values of S, Fechner derived the general expression relating sensation-magnitude (R) to stimulus-magnitude (S): '$R = k \log_e S$'. Transforming this to the base-10 system through the appropriate constant then yields '$R = k \log S$', the familiar form of Fechner's law.

Fechner developed the central ideas of his *Elements of Psychophysics* in a number of subsequent publications and extended the general perspective to the domain of aesthetics in his *Vorschule der Aesthetik* (*Propaedeutic to Aesthetics*) (1876). His defence of experimental approaches to the study of mental processes and his development of methods useful for

the purpose place him among the most influential figures in the history of psychology.

3 Panpsychism

Although the psychophysical research and theory were rich in mathematical and experimental content, their underlying rationale was drawn from cosmological and metaphysical conceptions somewhat misleadingly referred to as Fechner's 'panpsychism'. In a number of books and articles Fechner defended the thesis that the cosmos itself has a life – an inner life not unlike human consciousness and not to be confused with its mere externals. The parallel is clear between this view and his distinction between 'inner' and 'outer' psychophysics. Inner psychophysics refers to the inner dynamics of the relations between the psychic and the physiological; outer psychophysics to the relations between stimulation and immediate experience. So too is the balance of nature impelled by animating principles not discernible in the mere outward appearances of things. A relentlessly materialistic science is doomed to ignore such principles and thus to arrive at a conception of nature that is literally meaningless (see PANPSYCHISM).

In *Über die Seelenfrage* (*On the Soul*) (1861), Fechner criticized the conventional scientific perspective that divorced the earth from the diverse lives that arise from and return to it, rather than recognizing all living things as aspects of the earth's own inward development. A decade earlier in *Zend-Avesta* he had argued for the view that consciousness permeates all, but in a manner not accessible to prosaic modes of experience. It was only when he could once again look without pain at the flowers in his garden that he conceived of *Nanna, oder Über das seelen-leben der pflanzen* (*Nanna, The Soul Life of Plants*) (1848) in which he attributed the beauty of nature to inner principles of an irreducibly psychic sort. As he said in the conclusion of this work, 'Indeed, one will hardly believe how new and vivid is the nature which meets the man who himself comes to meet it with new eyes'.

See also: PSYCHOLOGY, THEORIES OF §§1–2

List of works

Fechner, G.T. (1836) *Das Büchlein vom Leben nach dem Tode*, Leipzig: Insel-verlag; trans. M. Wadsworth, *Life after Death*, New York: Pantheon, 1943. (Fechner's little book of eschatological theories emphasizes the indestructibility of the psychic.)
—— (1848) *Nanna, oder Über das seelen-leben der pflanzen*, Leipzig: Voss; trans. W. Lowrie, *Nanna,*

the *Soul-Life of Plants*, in *Religion of a Scientist: Selections from Gustav Th. Fechner*, New York: Pantheon, 1946. (Fechner again emphasizes the life-principle of creation, absorbing both plant and animal forms into an organic and creative cosmos.)

—— (1860) *Elemente der Psychophysik*, Leipzig: Breitkopf & Hartel; trans. H. Adler, *Elements of Psychophysics*, New York: Holt, Rinehart & Winston, 1960. (Fechner's major contribution to experimental psychology in which a precise methodology is developed and its rationale defended productively and with rigour. It is one of the classical works in the history of psychological thought. Chapter 7 contains Fechner's mathematical rationale for his law. A list of 175 of Fechner's publications, including those under the name 'Dr Mises', was compiled by R. Müller and furnished by Wilhelm Wundt in the third German edition.)

—— (1861) *Über die Seelenfrage*, Leipzig: C.F. Amelang; trans. W. Lowrie, *On the Soul*, in *Religion of a Scientist: Selections from Gustav Th. Fechner*, New York: Pantheon, 1946. (The tension between science and religion is acknowledged but Fechner insists that it is only through a consideration of spirit that the material transactions of the physical world become intelligible.)

—— (1863) *Die drei Motive und Gründe des Glaubens*, Leipzig: Breitkopf & Hartel; trans. W. Lowrie, *The Three Motives and Grounds of Faith*, in *Religion of a Scientist: Selections from Gustav Th. Fechner*, New York: Pantheon, 1946. (More on 'the religion of a scientist'.)

—— (1876) *Vorschule der Aesthetik* (Propaedeutic to Aesthetics), Leipzig: Breitkopf & Hartel. (Fechner's place in the history of experimental aesthetics begins with this work, but as the speciality itself has progressed little beyond where Fechner left it, this remains something of a promissory history.)

—— (1906) *Zend-Avesta, oder Über die Dinge des Himmels und des Jenseits* (Zend-Avesta, or that Concerning Matters of Heaven and the Future Life), collected in 2 vols by K. Lasswitz, Leipzig: L. Voss, 3rd edn. (The collection in these volumes offers Fechner's views on religion and philosophy, on immortality and the divine, with acknowledged debts to Eastern religion and thought.)

References and further reading

Boring, E.G. (1950) *A History of Experimental Psychology*, New York: Appleton, Century, 2nd edn. (Boring's chapter on psychophysics and the debt of experimental psychology to Fechner is nontechnical and historically accurate.)

James, W. (1909) *A Pluralistic Universe*, New York: Longmans, Green. (Chapter 7 of this work is a retrospective appreciation of Fechner.)

DANIEL N. ROBINSON

FEDERALISM AND CONFEDERALISM

Federative arrangements involve two or more governments ruling over the same territory and population. They have been of interest to political philosophers because they challenge, or at least complicate, some fundamental political concepts like authority, sovereignty, democracy and citizenship. Like citizens in actual federations, philosophers do not treat the terms of federation as a merely technocratic matter: they believe that there are morally legitimate and illegitimate ways of, among other things, dividing powers between governments, determining the representation of the subunits (for example, provinces) within federal institutions and amending the constitution. Philosophers also see in federalism a means of securing a degree of self-determination for ethnic minorities who cannot realistically expect to have their own homogeneous nation-states.

Most writers call a political arrangement federal if it has: (1) two or more levels or orders of government ruling over the same territory and citizens; (2) a division of legislative or administrative powers between these orders of government, with at least some areas of exclusive responsibility at each level; and (3) a constitutional guarantee that this division of powers cannot be changed without the agreement of governments of all orders. Contemporary federal theorists usually characterize the implications of these three conditions in a way that most philosophers prior to the twentieth century would have thought logically impossible. The combination of (1) and (2) implies that citizens of federal states are members of more than one political community and hence have a special kind of multiple citizenship; (2) and (3) imply that sovereignty in federations is divided.

An arrangement is likely to be called confederal rather than federal if effective sovereignty rests with the constituent units. In practice this is the case if the governments of the member states can unilaterally alter the terms of the arrangement, including the division of powers, or if member states can unilaterally secede from the union.

The development of federal and confederal theories in the modern era has always been closely linked to actual experiences with these sorts of political arrangements. Just before the predominance of the unitary nation-state there was widespread experimentation with leagues and confederations, including the Holy Roman Empire (800–1806), the Hanseatic League in Germany (1158–1669), the Swiss Confederation (1291–1848) and the United Provinces in Holland (1567–1798). Within these territories theorists attempted to work out a political and legal philosophy of confederation. So parallel to what was to become the mainstream tradition of political philosophy for the unitary nation-state, which begins with Bodin and Hobbes, is another philosophy which is much more receptive to federative arrangements and to what we would now call cultural and political pluralism. It starts with Althusius and PUFENDORF in the seventeenth century and runs through the Abbé de Saint Pierre, MONTESQUIEU, ROUSSEAU, KANT, Madison and Hamilton, TOCQUEVILLE, Proudhon and Carl Schmitt, among others.

From Althusius to Kant, confederal arrangements were advocated primarily as a means of achieving international order and peace. What they contemplated in various forms was a permanent association of independent sovereign states that would delegate limited powers to a common council. Philosophical debates generally focused on three issues. The first concerned whether confederations violated the supposed indivisibility of sovereignty (see SOVEREIGNTY). Following Pufendorf, most theorists employed a distinction between sovereignty-in-itself, which remained indivisible, and the 'marks' of sovereignty – such as judicial and legislative power and powers of peace and war – which could be divided and shared within confederations. Second, there were debates about which forms of international cooperation were necessary and sufficient to realize the idea of international law. Kant's own views on this question evolved considerably in the 1780s and 1790s: as he became more optimistic about the possibility of international law for states sending delegates to a peace congress, he came to see confederations, and in particular a worldwide confederal state, as less essential for the preservation of peace. Third, there were disputes about what kinds of states could enter into the same confederation. Early writers found no objections to unions involving a mixture of feudal and republican states. But from Montesquieu and Rousseau onwards, most republicans insisted on the need for common forms of government. They saw confederation as a necessary feature of republicanism, since to be just and effective republics must be small; yet being small, they have to band together to defend themselves against larger enemies (see REPUBLICANISM). An analogous argument for the desirability of smaller political units within a larger economic union is still popular today.

The idea of federalism, as outlined above, was not seriously developed by anyone, even in theory, until the American Confederation began to founder shortly after the thirteen colonies' seceded from Britain. Its constitution was replaced in 1789 by one setting up the first modern federation. In their brilliant defence of the new constitution, Madison, Jay and Hamilton (Hamilton *et al.* 1787–8) followed continental republicans in stressing the possibility of achieving within a federation the advantages enjoyed by both large states (security and economic strength) and small states (liberty and active democracy), without the usual disadvantages of either. Unlike Montesquieu and Rousseau, however, they paid careful attention to institutional design and argued for a strong central government responsible to a nation of equal citizens as well as to a union of states. They persuaded Tocqueville and J.S. Mill as well as the Swiss, who reconstructed their 500-year-old confederation on federal lines in 1848. Successful constitutional designs in the dozens of federations born since the late nineteenth century have all been guided by the idea of finding a division of powers and a system of federal representation that will protect diversity while encouraging a panfederal patriotism and stability (see CONSTITUTIONALISM).

Concern for stability in a federation tends to introduce a number of normative considerations because in democracies political arrangements will be unstable if perceived to be unfair or illegitimate. Regional groups find an arrangement unjust if, for example, it imposes disproportionate economic burdens on them; denies them adequate representation in central institutions, such as the parliament or the supreme court; does not give them sufficient control over matters of cultural importance; or fails to recognize in an appropriate way their existence as distinct national communities. Many of these concerns involve group rights and identity politics – issues largely absent from federal debates before the twentieth century, and largely neglected by political philosophers until recently.

See also: MULTICULTURALISM

References and further reading

Carney, F.S. (ed.) (1964) *The Politics of Johannes Althusius*, Boston, MA: Beacon Press. (Includes a translation of the third edition of Althusius's *Politica* from 1614.)

Forsyth, M. (1981) *Unions of States: The Theory and Practice of Confederation*, Leicester: Leicester University Press. (An excellent and accessible introduction to the history of federal and confederal thought.)

Friedrich, C.J. (1968) *Trends of Federalism in Theory and Practice*, New York: Praeger. (Includes a short, useful survey of the history of federal and confederal thought.)

* Hamilton, A., Madison, J. and Jay, J. (1787–8) *The Federalist Papers*, New York: New American Library, 1961. (See papers 3–5, 9, 14 and 39 for some of their more explicit discussions of the classic republican case for federalism over confederalism.)

Mill, J.S. (1863) *Considerations on Representative Government*, New York: Dutton, 1904. (See chapter 17, on federal government.)

Montesquieu, C.-L. de S. (1748) *The Spirit of Laws*, trans. A. Cohler, B.C. Miller and H.S. Stone, Cambridge: Cambridge University Press, 1989. (Discusses republican confederation in book IX, chapters 1–3.)

Norman, W. (1994) 'Towards a Philosophy of Federalism' in J. Baker (ed.) *Group Rights*, Toronto, Ont.: University of Toronto Press. (An exploration of criteria relevant to the design and evaluation of federal constitutions.)

Pufendorf, S. (1672) *The Law of Nature and Nations*, trans. C.H. Oldfather and W.A. Oldfather, Oxford: Clarendon Press, 1934. (See books V1 and VII for discussion of confederal structures and divisions of powers, as well as the challenges these raise for the concept of sovereignity.)

Reiss, H. (ed.) (1991) *Kant's Political Writings*, Cambridge: Cambridge University Press, 2nd edn. (Kant discusses confederal arrangements and international law in *Perpetual Peace*, *Idea of a Universal History*, the essay on *Theory and Practice* and in *Metaphysical Elements of Justice*.)

Riker, W.H. (1964) *Federalism: Origin, Operation, Significance*, Boston, MA: Little, Brown & Company. (The definition of 'federalism', above, is adapted from this philosophically literate, if somewhat dated, introduction to the idea and practice of federalism.)

Rousseau, J.-J. (1761) *Abstract of the Abbé de Saint Pierre's Project for Perpetual Peace*, in M. Forsyth *et al.* (eds) *The Theory of International Relations*, London: Allen, 1970. (Rousseau's most extensive discussion of confederation, apart from a manuscript on the subject which was apparently destroyed during the French Revolution.)

Tocqueville, A. de (1835–40) *Democracy in America*, trans. H. Reeve, New York: Knopf, 1966. (See especially volume I, chapter 8.)

Vernon, R. (1987) 'The Federal Citizen', in R.D. Olling and M. Westmacott (eds) *Perspectives on Canadian Federalism*, Scarborough, Ont.: Prentice Hall. (A provocative analysis of the way federalism complicates the notion of citizenship.)

WAYNE NORMAN

FËDOROV, NIKOLAI FËDOROVICH (1829–1903)

Like many other major figures in the nineteenth-century Russian tradition of speculation, Fëdorov was not an academic philosopher, but an unsystematic religious thinker who sought working answers to the fundamental questions of life. Fëdorov's basic question was: 'Why do the living die?' His answer, in short, was that we die because we neglect our God-given duty to regulate nature. Fëdorov's life work was to formulate an activist approach to the problem of death, a 'common task' in which all people living on earth, all religions and all sciences would eventually be united in a universal project to resurrect all the dead.

Born in southern Russia near Tambov as an illegitimate son in the princely Gagarin family, Nikolai Fëdorovich Fëdorov always wrote from the viewpoint of the outsider looking in, the unlearned addressing the learned, raising for serious discussion the 'naïve' questions that philosophy had previously failed to answer: Why do we kill? Why do we hunger? Why are some people kin and others strangers? Why do we die?

With support from the Gagarin family, Fëdorov received a sound education, first at the Tambov gymnasium, and then at the respected Richelieu Lyceum in Odessa. In 1851, upon the death of the uncle who was his benefactor, Fëdorov left the Lyceum without a degree, ending his formal education. For the next several years, he wandered from village to village through central and southern Russia, serving as a teacher of elementary history and geography in such places as Lipetsk, Bogorodsk, Uglich and Podolsk. As a teacher, Fëdorov seems to have been loved by his pupils but viewed by headmasters as an overzealous nuisance. Narratives from people who knew him in those years depict a devoted, saintly, eccentric educator who engaged his pupils in unusual group research projects and who on one occasion even gave up his own teacher's uniform to pay for the burial of an indigent pupil's father.

In 1869, Fëdorov took a position as assistant librarian at the Rumiantsev Museum in Moscow, where he became a legend among writers and scholars over the next thirty years. Living alone as an ascetic vegetarian, sleeping on a humpback trunk in a tiny rented room, wearing the same overcoat winter and summer, giving away most of his meagre salary to the poor, always the first to arrive at work and the last to leave, he was said to know not only the location and title but also the contents of every book in the vast library. When a scholar would order books on an obscure research topic, it was said that Fëdorov would usually bring double that number, including titles that the scholar had been unaware of but that gave new depth or direction to the research.

His writing was done for the most part in collaboration with disciples, late at night, on work holidays, and in his last years after retirement from the library. His great work, published in two posthumous volumes under the title *Filosofiia obschago dela* (The Philosophy of the Common Task) (1907?–13), is essentially a 1,200-page miscellany of long and short essays, unfinished drafts, fragments and inspired jottings, all variations on a single theme. In the world as it is, ruled by nature, the universe of matter and man is disintegrating into isolated particles; in the world as it ought to be, regulated by human reason, eternal unity and harmony will prevail. Therefore the human task, our common duty, is to join a universal project to guide our own evolution to the point where we may exercise benign control over nature and complete the perfection of ourselves and our universe.

Knowledge, in Fëdorov, is neither subjective nor objective, but 'projective', action guided by reason towards the realization of an ideal. The 'project' is the bridge between the real and ideal, and between all other opposite poles in Western dualism.

By uniting all to overcome the only true enemy of all, namely death, Fëdorov believed that the project of resurrection would also solve the social, economic and other problems of his day. Energies and resources now directed towards war or commercial exploitation would be redirected towards resurrection. Historical enemies would find mutual assistance not only possible but necessary. Unbelievers, who in theory might find Christianity unacceptable, would, by resurrecting the dead, become in practice followers of Christ.

The first steps towards resurrection might consist of little more than the brief, temporary resuscitation of a person who had just died. But, as all scientific technology, sociopolitical organization – indeed, all human knowledge and action – gradually became directed towards the goal of resurrection, more than brief and temporary resuscitation would become possible. Eventually the synthesizing of bodies should be feasible, and ultimately, Fëdorov believed, whole persons could be recreated from the least trace. To recover particles of disintegrated ancestors, Fëdorov imagined, research teams would have to travel to the moon, the planets, and to distant points throughout the universe. Eventually these outer points of the cosmos would be inhabited by the resurrected ancestors, whose bodies might be synthesized so as to live under conditions that could not now support human life as it is known.

Fëdorov published almost nothing during his lifetime, and his posthumous works were circulated haphazardly in tiny editions. Nevertheless, his ideas had a strong impact on both late nineteenth- and early twentieth-century Russian intellectuals. In varying ways and to varying degrees, Dostoevskii, Tolstoi and Vladimir Solov'ëv all incorporated Fëdorov's ideas into their work. In the twentieth century, Fëdorov's influence is apparent in the works of the rocket scientist Tsiolkovskii, the writers Briusov, Belyi Maiakovskii, Khlebnikov, Platonov and Pasternak, the religious thinkers Bulgakov, Florenskii and Berdiaev, and the natural scientists Vernadskii, Chizhevskii, Kholodnyi, Kuprevich and Maneev.

Viewed strictly as a philosopher, Fëdorov was an amateur who contributed little to the history of the discipline, but as an imaginative thinker his bold, comprehensive project of resurrection represents a unique coalescence of several previously divergent tendencies in Russian thought, Slavophile and Westernist, scientific and religious, traditionalist and futurist, probably making him, as Berdiaev observed, 'the most Russian' of Russian thinkers.

List of works

Fëdorov, N.F. (1982) *Sochineniia* (Works), ed. S.G. Semenova, Moscow: Mysl'. (Consists mainly of selections from *Filosofiia obschago dela*. Includes bibliographical references and indexes.)

—— (1907?–13) *Filosofiia obschago dela. Stat'i, mysli i pis'ma Nikolaia Fëdorovicha Fëdorova* (The Philosophy of the Common Task. Essays, Thoughts and Letters of Nikolai Fëdorovich Fëdorov), ed. V.A. Kozhevnikov and N.P. Peterson, vol. 1, Verny, vol. 2, Moscow, 1970; repr. Farnborough: Gregg International.

—— (1990) *What Was Man Created For? The Philosophy of the Common Task. Selected Works*, trans. E. Koutaissoff and M. Minto, UK: Honeyglen and Switzerland: L'Age d'Homme. (The first English translation of extensive selections from Fëdorov's major essays.)

Edie, J., Scanlan, J., Zeldin, M. and Kline, G. (eds) (1965) *Russian Philosophy*, Chicago: Quadrangle

Books, vol. 3, 16–54. (Translation of part of the opening essay in Fëdorov's collected works.)

Schmemann, A. (ed.) (1965) *Ultimate Questions: An Anthology of Modern Russian Religious Thought*, New York, 175–223. (Translation of selected passages from the collected works.)

References and further reading

Hagemeister, M. (1989) *Nikolaj Fëdorov: Studien zu Leben, Werk und Wirkung* (Nikolai Fëdorov: A Study of his Life, Work and Influence), Munich: Otto Sagner. (Detailed and thorough, with special attention to Fëdorov's twentieth-century followers.)

Koehler, L. (1979) *N.F. Fëdorov: The Philosophy of Action*, Pittsburgh, PA: Institute for the Human Sciences. (Special attention to Fëdorov's relationship to twentieth-century Russian religious thinkers.)

Lukashevich, S. (1977) *N.F. Fedorov (1828–1903): A Study in Russian Eupsychian and Utopian Thought*, Newark, NJ: University of Delaware Press. (An interpretive study.)

Masing-Delic, I. (1992) *Abolishing Death: A Salvation Myth of Russian Twentieth-Century Literature*, Stanford, CA: Stanford University Press. (Gives special attention to Fëdorov's impact on twentieth-century Russian literature.)

Semenova, S.G. (1990) *Nikolai Fëdorov: Tvorchestvo zhizni*, Moscow: Sovetskii Pisatel'. (A thorough study of the life and works using information from archives available only in Russia.)

Young, G.M. (1979) *Nikolai Fedorov: An Introduction*, Belmont, MA: Nordland. (A general introduction to the life and thought.)

Zenkovsky, V.V. (1948–50) *Istoriia russkoi filosofii*, Paris: YMCA-Press, 2 vols; 2nd edn, 1989; trans. G.L. Kline, *A History of Russian Philosophy*, London: Routledge & Kegan Paul and New York: Columbia University Press, 1953.

GEORGE M. YOUNG

FEMINISM

Feminism is grounded on the belief that women are oppressed or disadvantaged by comparison with men, and that their oppression is in some way illegitimate or unjustified. Under the umbrella of this general characterization there are, however, many interpretations of women and their oppression, so that it is a mistake to think of feminism as a single philosophical doctrine, or as implying an agreed political programme. Just as there are diverse images of liberation, so there are a number of feminist philosophies, yoked together not so much by their particular claims or prescriptions as by their interest in a common theme.

In the earlier phases of feminism, advocates focused largely on the reform of women's social position, arguing that they should have access to education, work or civil rights. During the latter half of the twentieth century, however, feminists have become increasingly interested in the variety of social practices (including theoretical ones) through which our understandings of femininity and masculinity are created and maintained. As a result, the scope of feminist enquiry has broadened to include, for example, jurisprudence, epistemology and psychoanalysis.

Despite its diversity, this work characteristically draws on and grapples with a set of deeply-rooted historical attempts to explain the domination of women. Aristotle's claim that they are mutilated males, together with the biblical account of the sin of Eve, gave rise to an authoritative tradition in which the weakness, irrationality and ineducability of women, the inconstancy, inability to control their emotions and lack of moral virtue, were all regularly cited and assumed as grounds for controlling them and excluding them from the public realm.

1 **Feminism and feminisms**
2 **Renaissance and early-modern forerunners**
3 **Claims of right**
4 **Sexual oppression and emancipation**
5 **The pervasiveness of male domination**
6 **Second- and third-wave feminism**

1 Feminism and feminisms

While there have been, throughout the history of philosophy, writers who challenge the sexual stereotype and offer different pictures of women, their works do not contribute to a single story. It can therefore be misleading to assimilate them too quickly to the philosophical literature and political campaigns which initiated later feminist movements, or to contemporary feminist positions. Only at the end of the eighteenth century did a stream of philosophical arguments aimed at the emancipation of women begin to gather force. Only at the end of the nineteenth century did the term *la féminisme* appear, put into circulation after the fact in France during the 1890s, and rapidly taken up in the rest of Europe and then in America. The label 'feminist' thus arose out of, and was in many ways continuous with, the sequence of diverse campaigns for female emancipation fought throughout the nineteenth century – campaigns for the vote, for access to education and the professions, for the right of married women to own property and have custody of their children, for the abolition of laws about female prostitution which assumed the double standard. While the character and success of these movements varied from country to country (for example, women's suffrage was introduced in New Zealand in 1893, Finland in 1906 and Britain in 1918) they all drew upon, and generated, arguments about the nature and capacities of women and the character of their oppression, and entertained, explicitly or implicitly, images of what a better condition would be like. Many of the most influential philosophical defences of women's emancipation dating from this period were in fact written by people involved in political work – to name only two, John Stuart MILL, the author of *The Subjection of Women*, proposed to the British parliament in 1867 an amendment to the Reform Bill designed to give votes to women, while Emily Davies, author of *The Higher Education of Women*, was the foundress of Girton College, Cambridge, the first women's college of higher education in England.

We have no difficulty in retrospectively classifying works such as these as feminist, although this is not a description their authors would have used, because they contain analyses of women's oppression and proposals for overcoming it which mesh easily with analyses and proposals later regarded as central to the feminist cause. However, there are also significant divergences between feminist writers, past as well as present. Different interpretations of the disadvantages to which women are subject, allied to different conceptions of what would constitute an improvement, gave rise to distinctive and sometimes irreconcilable feminisms. Compare, for example, the broadly liberal view that the oppression of women consists in their lack of political equality with men and can be alleviated by giving women and men the same political rights, with the separatist view that women's oppression lies principally in their sexual subordination to men and can only be overcome in societies that are, as far as possible, exclusively female. As these examples indicate, there are many feminisms, each with a history of its own.

Historians are bound to select their material in the light of the kind or kinds of feminism that concern them, and to work with interpretations that are used to distinguish texts and movements that qualify as feminist from those that are merely about women. To pursue the examples already discussed, historians whose interest in feminism focuses on the quest for equality between the sexes may identify certain writers as feminists *avant la lettre*. For example, they may include in their canon Poulain de la Barre, author of *De L'Égalité des deux sexes* (1673), or Mary Wollstonecraft. By contrast, a history of feminism understood as the quest for a separate society of women is more likely to pick out Mary Astell's proposal that ladies should retire from the society of men who debar them from realizing the natural desire to advance and perfect their being, or Charlotte Perkins Gilman's utopia *Herland* about an isolated society of women who are able to have children without male assistance. As long as there is more than one interpretation of feminism, feminism will not have a unified history.

2 Renaissance and early-modern forerunners

Although female inferiority is the dominant note that sounds through the Western philosophical tradition, its character was never a matter of consensus. Long drawn out theological debates about whether woman is a human being, whether she is made in the image of God, whether she is a perfect creation of God or an imperfect version of man, and whether men and women are equal before God, all appeal to classical authorities, to the Bible and to the Church Fathers, and rumble on through the Middle Ages and into the Renaissance. Complementing them are a series of more secular discussions, of which one of the most consistent focuses on women's learning. In her *Livre de la cité des dames* (1405) CHRISTINE DE PIZAN extols the advantages of educating women, a theme subsequently taken up by Renaissance writers for whom it played a part in the so-called *Querelle des Femmes* – a sequence of philosophically repetitive, interwoven disputes about whether fidelity in marriage should be demanded of both sexes, whether and to what extent women should be educated, and whether women were entitled to the respect and gratitude of men for the services they rendered them. On one side of these debates, women's inferiority was reasserted by appeal to example, authority and reason. On the other, their superiority was defended in a variety of genres. Some writers – for example Cornelius Agrippa – employed the rhetorical device of the paradoxical encomium, attempting to entertain and impress by ingeniously reversing conventional evaluations of men and women (see AGRIPPA VON NETTESHEIM). Others drew on a well-tried stock of cases to illustrate women's superior virtue, intelligence or judiciousness. The choice of these genres contributes to the impression that, while these champions of women sometimes propose certain social reforms, they are on the whole anxious not to unsettle the status quo. Their aim is to entertain – to tease men and flatter women, and perhaps in doing so to make both reconsider their roles – rather than to foment social change.

Traces of this style endured well into the seventeenth century and are visible even in writers who in other ways broke with the terms of the *querelle*. A particularly striking change is the move away from debates about the relative inferiority or superiority of women, to works purporting to show that the sexes are equal. Marie de Gournay, who claimed that she was the first to take this view, published her *Égalité des hommes et des femmes* in 1622, and the same theme was taken up with a new determination later in the century. In France, Poulain de la Barre adopted a fresh approach when he appealed to Cartesian scientific method: a clear and distinct understanding of the issue can be arrived at, he insists, by rational demonstration. Although his *De l'égalité des deux sexes* (1673) sometimes lapses into the older style of argument – women are more decorous and discreet than men, women's work is more valuable than that of men, and so on – Poulain is remarkable for the forthright manner with which he asserts that the relations between mind and body and the capacities of the mind are the same in both sexes, and even more for the consequences he draws from this claim. There is no reason, in his view, why women should not occupy all the public roles currently held by men. Since they are capable of equalling men in understanding all the sciences (including both civil and canon law) they could, if educated, teach in the universities, be legislators, rulers, generals of armies, judges and – most radical of all – preachers and ministers of the Church.

Poulain's willingness to contemplate such dramatic social change is unusual, but less so is his emphasis on intellectual equality and downplaying of the significance of the bodily differences between men and women. This is shared by a number of women writing in the second half of the seventeenth century, who criticize men for depriving them of learning and education, and imply that women are quite capable of ruling themselves, and indeed men. In the Netherlands, Anna Maria VON SCHURMAN writes in favour of the education of girls. In England, women such as Margaret CAVENDISH and Mary ASTELL are by turns bitter and witty in their undermining of women's subjection to men.

3 Claims of right

As early as 1673, Poulain de la Barre argued that women and men possess an equal right to knowledge, conferred on them by nature. All humans pursue happiness; no one can achieve happiness without knowledge; so everyone needs knowledge. To ensure that people are able to pursue their proper end, nature has supplied the necessary means in the form of a right. We find here the beginnings of an appeal to rights which became progressively more central until, a century or so later, it dominated debate. In the immediate wake of the French Revolution, Olymphe de Gouges presented the French Assembly with a Declaration of the Rights of Women (which it declined to ratify). Women, she argued, should have rights to employment, legal rights within the family, a right to free speech and a separate assembly in which they could represent themselves. The same theme was taken up in England by Mary WOLLSTONECRAFT, who in 1792 published *A Vindication of the Rights of Women*. Challenging Rousseau, Wollstonecraft argued that the education and emancipation of women are conditions of a truly civilized society. God has endowed all humans with reason so that they can use it to govern their passions and attain knowledge and virtue. To deprive women of the opportunity to perfect their nature and increase their capacity for happiness is to treat them as less than human and render them 'gentle, domestic brutes'. It is to trample on their rights and keep them in a state of subjection which damages both them and their male captors.

Far from being natural, Wollstonecraft explains echoing the arguments of Mary Astell, the presumed inferiority of women stems primarily from their lack of education. Cut off from learning and encouraged to care only for love and fashion, they are unable to cultivate any solid virtues, and do indeed display the flightiness and stupidity for which they are criticized. However, as well as damaging themselves, women in this condition diminish others. First, they damage men. To treat a fellow human despotically shows a lack of virtue, and just as kings are corrupted by their excessive power, so men are corrupted by the tyranny they exercise over their sisters, daughters and wives. Second, ignorant and powerless women are unfitted to instil virtue into their children. 'To be a good mother – a woman must have sense and that independence of mind which few women possess who are taught to depend entirely on their husbands ' (Wollstonecraft [1792] 1995: 243).

Although Wollstonecraft's argument hinges on her claim that women are as rational as men, she has no sympathy for what she calls 'masculine women'. The aim of educating women is, in her view, to make them into virtuous wives and mothers who, by fulfilling these natural duties, will become useful members of society. Freed from male subjection, educated women would not usurp the roles of men but would freely and virtuously pursue their domestic lives to the benefit of society as a whole. The claim that men and women are intellectual equals is here allied to the view that there are natural differences between them which fit them for distinct ways of life: rational women will see that their place is in the home.

This easy division of labour was put under increasing pressure during the nineteenth century, as feminist thinking became less concerned with women's overarching moral right to liberty and focused instead on particular legal entitlements such as the right to own property, to enter the professions, and above all to vote. Nevertheless, arguments which appeal simultaneously to the equality and difference of the sexes, and sustain the view that women excel in certain domestic virtues, remained common. The US suffragist, Elizabeth Cady Stanton, demanded the vote for women from the New York legislature during the 1850s on the grounds that 'the rights of every human being are the same and identical'. But she also argued that, if women were able to represent themselves by voting, they would make a distinctive contribution which would balance that of men.

The wish to reconcile the demands of equality and difference is also evident in John Stuart Mill's *The Subjection of Women* (1869). Mill argues that women are entitled to the same rights as men and should be able to hold public office, to work, to own property and to vote. He also argues that married women should not be required to obey their husbands and should have custody over their children. His primary ground for these conclusions is that women and men are equal, but he supplements this argument with further claims about the benefits that the freedom of women would bring. Like Wollstonecraft, he claims that the power of men over women 'perverts the whole manner of existence of the man, both as an individual and a social being', and reiterates her view that there can be no true affection between spouses who have nothing in common. It is only once women are educated that there can be the solid, enduring friendship between the sexes that heralds the moral regeneration of mankind. However, two further lines of thought appeal to assumed differences. Mill first argues that women possess a distinctive aversion to war and addiction to philanthropy, of which they would make better use if they were better informed. In addition, although women should have the right to work, Mill takes it that when they marry they make 'a choice of the management of a household, and the bringing up of a family' as the first call on their exertions. Older women who have completed this task may decide to direct their energies to public life, for instance by standing for parliament. But the first place of married women is, once again, in the home.

4 Sexual oppression and emancipation

The view that the oppression of women could be overcome once they had the same rights as men was therefore compatible with a conventional understanding of the division of male and female labour. But doubt was cast on this whole approach to emancipation by the fact that, once the vote was won, women did not on the whole use their new-found political power to press for further reform. Many suffragists were keenly disappointed, and feminists of more radical political persuasions were strengthened in their conviction that the source of women's oppression did not lie in their lack of political rights. Reforms such as the married women's property act and the right to higher education, they pointed out, benefited middle-class more than working women. More important still, the root of women's subordination lay not in their civic but in their private lives – in their roles as wives and mothers.

This latter view was partly derived from Engels' *Origins of the Family, Private Property and the State* (1884) in which he argued that women's oppression is primarily sexual. There is nothing natural about the patriarchal family. Rather, this institution came into existence at a particular point in history together with private property. To be able to hand down their property to their sons, men needed complete sexual possession of the mothers of their children, and to this end they reduced women to servitude. In capitalist society, women's subjection consists not in their lack of legal rights, but in their weak position in the labour market which in turn forces them into marriage. Women face a choice between lives of near-destitution as workers or lives of slavery as wives and mothers, or in the case of working class women, both exploitation at work and subjection in marriage. Only once capitalism is overthrown will they escape this plight and be freed from dependence.

In Russia, the predicament diagnosed by Engels was confronted by the revolutionary Alexandra Kollontai (1872–1952), who insisted in *The Social Basis of the Woman Question* (1909) that proletarian women must refuse to cooperate with the bourgeois feminist movement and attack capitalism, the source of their oppression. As Commissar of Social Welfare in the Russian Revolutionary Government of 1917, Kollontai oversaw the drafting of far-reaching legal reforms designed to revolutionize the family and sexual relations between men and women, and to relieve women of the 'triple load' of wage worker, housekeeper and mother. These reforms were organized around a distinction between productive and non-productive labour, and were based on the view that women should be relieved of the burden of non-productive domestic labour (cleaning, cooking, washing, caring for clothes, and many aspects of child-rearing) to engage in productive labour alongside men. In this way they would achieve economic independence. At the same time, women's work was to take account of their productive childbearing role. The work of carrying and bringing up children was no longer to be seen as the responsibility of individual families but as a task for the state, since it was in the interest of the workers' collective that children should be born and that they should grow up to be able-bodied and good revolutionaries.

In the early years of the Bolshevik government, Kollontai began to implement a series of radical though short-lived reforms. Women were to have full civil rights; civil marriage and divorce laws were introduced; legitimate and illegitimate children were to have the same legal rights; and in 1920 abortion was legalized. As far as labour was concerned, women's work was to take account of childbearing. They were not to do heavy work which might damage their health or work long hours or night shifts. They were to have paid maternity leave and health care during pregnancy. As for their children, once out of infancy they were to be cared for in crèches, kindergartens and schools which would also provide meals and clothing.

According to Kollontai, the dictatorship of the proletariat will abolish the family and with it bourgeois sexual morality. For though the state must, in her view, concern itself with children, it did not have any more extended interest in the relations between their parents. Conventional notions of romantic love must not undermine comradeship; yet Kollontai stresses that solidarity can only exist between those who are capable of love and sympathy, and envisages a society in which people are emotionally educated to feel many forms of love for different people.

In the USA, Engels' view that women's oppression is rooted in the family was used by the anarchist, Emma Goldman (1869–1940), to ground a different set of conclusions. Access to education and work, for which emancipationists had fought so hard, produced women who were 'professional automatons' and lacked 'the essence that enriches the soul'. By entering the public sphere, women had joined an impure State which prevents both women and men from developing the inner qualities that spring from sexual intimacy and constitute freedom, but is particularly distorting for women, for whom love is even more important than it is for men. The question of how to become free is therefore a question about how to foster sexual self-expression, and Goldman is adamant that this can only happen once women cease to be the sexual possessions of their husbands. As well as eschewing the public sphere, women must reject the private institution of marriage in which, driven by economic

need, they purchase financial security at the price of their independence. They must learn instead to recognize and follow what Goldman calls their instinct.

Goldman and Kollontai share with some of their liberal forebears and contemporaries the premise that an institution of marriage in which women are sexually dominated by, and economically dependent on, their husbands, makes them unfree. More radically, both claim that these evils can only be overcome by sweeping away conventional notions of marriage and family. Beyond this, however, they diverge sharply. For Kollontai, liberty consists in productive labour in which both women and men must engage if they are to be equal and equally free. In the case of women, however, productive labour can take the distinctive form of bearing children. Motherhood (women's difference), is subordinated to an overall conception of equality according to which men and women are not treated in the same way, but make the same kind of contribution by working productively. Goldman, by contrast, conceives freedom as a state of individual exploration and self-expression which needs to be pursued outside the impurity and corruption of the State and has little to do with work. Both men and women need love in order to become free, but for women, sexual intimacy plays a particularly important part in this process. While Kollontai separates reproductive sex from other erotic relations, Goldman tips the balance away from motherhood. Unconstrained love, which may or may not be the love of mothers for their children, is what enables women to fulfil themselves and become free.

5 The pervasiveness of male domination

It has become customary to distinguish a first wave of feminism, dating from the mid nineteenth century to the 1930s, from a second wave, breaking in the 1970s. This chronology is designed to highlight the absence of specifically feminist political campaigns in the intervening period, but is misleading if applied more generally, since one of the most influential works of modern feminist philosophy, Simone de Beauvoir's *The Second Sex*, was published in 1949 (see BEAU-VOIR, S. DE). Dissatisfied with existing accounts of women's subordination to men, Beauvoir confronted the question 'What is Woman?' by exploring the limited answers offered by historical materialism and psychoanalysis. Both these theories, she claims, beg the question. In *The Origin of the Family*, Engels asserts that the institution of private property results in the enslavement of women, but offers no means of explaining why this should have been so. Equally,

Freud's account of sexual differentiation fails to say what previous evaluation of virility makes boys proud of their penises and makes girls attribute special significance to their lack of this bodily part. To explain women's oppression, in which women themselves are complicitous, it is not enough to appeal merely to economic categories or patterns of psychological development already imbued with the evaluations that constitute male power. What is needed is a theory grounded on dynamics of consciousness running deeper than physiological, psychological or economic forces, capable of doing justice to the vast variety of practices that contribute to women's subordination.

Beauvoir derives her analysis of woman from the existentialist view of consciousness articulated by Sartre in *Being and Nothingness* (see SARTRE, J.-P.). Each consciousness faces the world alone, and must create itself through its own choices by responding to the things around it, whether these are passive natural objects or other consciousnesses. Adapting Hegel's account of the relations between master and slave, Sartre portrays the meeting of one consciousness with another as profoundly disturbing (see HEGEL, G.F.W. §5). In the gaze of the Other, a consciousness recognizes a point of view which is different from its own and unattainable, a mark of its own incompleteness. At the same time, the gaze of the Other threatens to destroy it by turning it into an object. In response, the consciousness can choose to retaliate – to objectify the Other. But in doing so it destroys an external view of itself and must resign itself to the incompleteness of its self-understanding. The consciousness is therefore caught: it can dominate the Other, or live with the threat it poses.

It is through woman, Beauvoir argues, that male consciousness alleviates this conflict. Like men, women are conscious beings capable of returning the male gaze, and yet they allow themselves to be dominated. By possessing them, men are able to control the Other without destroying it, to withstand a gaze which is not unbearably threatening. Why do women occupy this position? Why do they not try to dominate men? Although Beauvoir suggests that the comparative passivity of women originates in childbearing, she is more interested in analysing the multitude of social practices which conspire to keep women in the position of the Other and prevent them from seeking their own transcendence. These practices, she argues, are sustained both by men, who encourage and reward female passivity, and by women, who cooperate in their own domination. The latter, however, is an example of bad faith. To allow oneself to be treated as an object is to fail to realize one's being by making ones own choices, and

to shirk the painful project of becoming free. How, then, are women to liberate themselves? To avoid becoming Other, Beauvoir suggests, women must abandon the roles of wives and mothers in which they are most easily objectified and compete with men through work. Once they begin to exercise the assertiveness and courage essential to freedom, conceptions of what it is to be a woman will alter, and women and men will find ways to treat one another as equals.

One of Beauvoir's most profound contributions to feminist philosophy lay in her insistence that women are dominated in all aspects of their lives. Their comparative lack of freedom does not consist merely in lack of civic rights, or in particular institutions of motherhood and marriage, although these are contributory factors. Rather, they are kept in their inferior place by 'the whole of civilization' – by a multitude of evaluations and social practices (tellingly described in chapters on childhood, the young girl, sexual initiation and so on) which shape our understandings of male and female, masculine and feminine. As she indicates in her celebrated remark, 'One is not born, but rather becomes, a women', Beauvoir holds that it is through social practices that bodies come to be understood as sexually differentiated, and through these same practices that the differences between them are invested with evaluative significance. Becoming a woman is a cultural and historical process which is never completed. Although Beauvoir allows that there will always be differences between women and men deriving from their bodily distinctions and the effect these have on their sensuality, there is no one thing that women intrinsically or naturally are. Correspondingly, there is no discernible limit to what they may become.

6 Second- and third-wave feminism

Many of the critical and constructive themes discussed by Beauvoir were taken up again in the late 1960s and 1970s (though often without much reference to *The Second Sex*) by a generation of women who struggled, in the light of their personal experience, to revise the social and psychological theories around which academic debate revolved. On a critical plane, they enlarged Beauvoir's objections to Marxism and psychoanalysis and added criticisms of other sociological approaches such as functionalism, sometimes engendering debates which remained lively throughout the next twenty or so years. For feminists concerned with Marxism, the key issues were whether women could be satisfactorily accommodated within the class structure of society, and whether women's oppression could be adequately explained in terms of their place in the relations of production and the ideologies to which these gave rise. Studies of domestic labour and of women's sexual subordination suggested that, while Marxist analyses of women in capitalist societies remained valuable, the answer to these questions was negative. Turning their attention to psychoanalysis, a number of writers launched an influential attack on what they saw as Freud's construction of femininity as a passive, masochistic, narcissistic and intellectually limited condition. These readings of Freud and his successors gave feminists pause, and initiated a series of fruitful reinterpretations and modifications within psychoanalytic theory (see FEMINISM AND PSYCHOANALYSIS; IRIGARAY, L.; KRISTEVA, J.).

This critical work was also the vehicle for a number of important innovations in feminist thinking which raised fresh questions and consolidated novel approaches. Writers such as Kate Millett and Shulamith Firestone argued in the early 1970s that the forms of domination isolated by feminists are all relatively superficial in comparison with patriarchy – the sexual power that men exercise over women, primarily within the family, but also in social, economic and political institutions. In a wide range of societies, it was pointed out, men's sexuality is the source and justification of their power, the purportedly natural characteristic that gives them the right to rule women. The workings of patriarchy are evident not just in erotic relations between the sexes, but in the manifold means by which men and women are socialized as to temperament, role and status, men being taught to regard themselves as potent and active, women to perceive themselves as subordinate and sexually impure.

Patriarchy, then, relies not so much on the biological differences between men and women as on deep-seated cultural interpretations that give them value and significance. In the early 1970s this distinction came to be regarded as crucial, and writers such as Millett and Ann Oakley took over the terms 'sex' and 'gender' to mark it: sex refers to the biological traits that make a person male or female, gender to culturally variable conceptions of masculinity and femininity. Taken together, the notions of patriarchy, sex and gender provided an Anglo-American articulation of many of the themes announced by Beauvoir, and gave rise to a series of theoretical debates, some of which are still going on. Is sex really separable from gender, or is our experience and theorizing so mediated by culture that the idea of the simply biological ceases to make sense? Is patriarchy a useful analytical category, or is it either unduly general, or unduly reductionist? How, in any case, is patriarchal power related to other forms of political and economic power? And is it really as strong and pervasive as its exponents claim?

Regardless of the fate of these questions, the belief that men's domination of women may be sustained by all sorts of practices had a vast impact on the Academy, as feminists began to take a fresh look at the texts and theories they studied professionally. This approach proved fruitful when applied to literary texts – Simone de Beauvoir had included a study of 'The Myth of Woman in Five Authors' in *The Second Sex*, and Millett's *Sexual Politics* opens with striking readings of Henry Miller, Norman Mailer and Jean Genet (see FEMINIST LITERARY CRITICISM). It was soon adopted by philosophers, who started to analyse the conceptions of gender embedded in the great works of the philosophical tradition. Genevieve Lloyd's *The Man of Reason* (1984) and Carole Pateman's articles on contractarian political theory are notable early examples of this kind of work, and were rapidly followed by critical scrutinies both of the various areas of philosophy and particular positions within them (see FEMINIST AESTHETICS; FEMINIST EPISTEMOLOGY; FEMINIST ETHICS; FEMINIST JURISPRUDENCE; FEMINIST POLITICAL PHILOSOPHY; FEMINISM AND SOCIAL SCIENCE; FEMINIST THEOLOGY).

While the results of this academic flowering have been extremely diverse, two themes stand out. First, some of the most impressive contributions to this recent work have shown how philosophical standards and doctrines that have claimed for themselves an objective and universal status reflect particular interests, values and priorities attuned to broader conceptions of masculinity. In this way, philosophy contributes to the cultural constructions of gender that play a part in legitimating and maintaining men's power over women. Second, the third-wave feminism of the 1980s and 1990s has turned its critical techniques back on feminism's own long-standing habit of making claims on behalf of 'women'. These purportedly universal pronouncements, it is now pointed out, fail to take account of the differences between women of diverse races, sexual orientations, nationalities or classes. Moreover, if gender is not a natural category, there is nothing to be said about women as such, and we must become more sensitive to the many conceptions of femininity found in different societies. This anti-essentialism has profound implications for feminism, both as an academic preoccupation and as a political movement, and marks an important shift away from its own origins towards new themes and questions.

See also: GENDER AND SCIENCE; LANGUAGE AND GENDER

References and further reading

Aristotle (*c.* mid 4th century BC) *Generation of Animals*, in J. Barnes (ed.) *The Complete Works of Aristotle*, vol. 1, Princeton, NJ: Princeton University Press, 1984, 1111–218. (Aristotle's discussion of male and female roles in procreation.)

* Beauvoir, S. de (1949) *The Second Sex* , trans. and ed. H.M. Parshley, Harmondsworth: Penguin, 1972. (The classic existentialist interpretation of masculinity and femininity and a path-breaking analysis of the social construction of gender.)

* Davies, E. (1866) *The Higher Education of Women*, London: Hambledon, 1988. (The case for women's education put by a pioneer.)

* Engels, F. (1884) *The Origin of the Family, Private Property and the State*, intro. M. Barrett, Harmondsworth: Penguin, 1985. (A vastly influential discussion of the family by one of the founders of Marxism.)

* Firestone, S. (1970) *The Dialectic of Sex*, London: The Women's Press, 1979. (Firestone argues that women's oppression lies in their reproductive role and that the goal of feminist revolution is the elimination of sexual difference.)

Goldman, E. (1972) *Red Emma Speaks. Selected Speeches and Writings of the anarchist and feminist Emma Goldman*, ed. A. Kates Shulman, New York: Random House. (Includes selections from Goldman's writing on the individual and the state, woman's emancipation, prostitution and marriage.)

* Gouges, O. de (1782) *The Rights of Women*, trans. V. Stevenson, London: Pythia, 1989. (An impressive early statement of women's rights.)

* Gournay, M. Le Jars de (1622) *Égalité des Hommes et des Femmes*, Paris: Côté-Femme, 1989. (A brief defence of the equality of the sexes by a woman whom Montaigne described as his adopted daughter. This edition includes the *Grief des Dames*, a defence of women of letters.)

Griffith, E. (1984) *In her own Right. The life of Elizabeth Cady Stanton*, New York: Oxford University Press. (A biography of one of the best-known US suffragists.)

Kollontai, A. (1977) *Selected Writings*, trans. and intro. A. Holt, London: Allison & Busby. (Includes selections from Kollontai's writing on women and work, work and motherhood, communism, the family and marriage.)

* Lloyd, G. (1984) *The Man of Reason*, London: Methuen. (Innovative analysis of the prevalence of the association of women and irrationality within the philosophical tradition.)

Maclean, I. (1977) *Woman Triumphant. Feminism in French literature 1610–1652*, Oxford: Clarendon Press. (A study of works by and about women in seventeenth-century France. Includes a chapter on the *Querelle des femmes*.)

* Mill, J.S. (1869) *On the Subjection of Women*, in S. Collini (ed.) *On Liberty and other Writings*, Cambridge: Cambridge University Press, 1989. (A classic, nineteenth-century account of the advantages of giving women the same access to education and work, and the same civil rights, as men.)

* Millett, K. (1969) *Sexual Politics*, London: Virago, 1977. (A formative analysis of the construction of femininity in twentieth-century literature and in social theory.)

* Oakley, A. (1972) *Sex, Gender and Society*, London: Temple Smith. (An influential discussion of the biological and social aspects of sexuality.)

Pateman, C. (1989) *The Disorder of Women*, Cambridge: Polity Press. (Includes seminal essays on the place of women in contractarian political theories.)

* Perkins Gilman, C. (1919) *Herland*, London: Women's Press, 1979. (Utopian novel by a leading American feminist about a community of women who live without men.)

* Pizan, C. de (1405) *The Book of the City of Ladies*, trans. E.J. Richards, New York: Persea Books, 1982. (An exchange between Christine and the figures of Reason, Rectitude and Justice, who reassure her that women are not evil and instruct her to build a city for ladies.)

* Poulain de la Barre, F. (1673) *The Equality of the Sexes*, trans. D.M. Clarke, Manchester: Manchester University Press, 1990. (An early defence, along Cartesian lines, of the equality of the sexes.)

* Sartre, J.-P. (1943) *Being and Nothingness*, trans. H. Barnes, London: Methuen, 1958. (Sartre's classic work, mentioned in §5 above.)

* Wollstonecraft, M. (1792) *A Vindication of the Rights of Women*, in S. Tomaselli (ed.) *A Vindication of the Rights of Man and A Vindication of the Rights of Women*, Cambridge: Cambridge University Press, 1995. (A classic defence of the view that women and men have the same rights though different social roles.)

SUSAN JAMES

FEMINISM AND PSYCHOANALYSIS

Broadly speaking, there have been two main types of philosophical response to psychoanalysis. The first sets out to assess the scientific status of Freud's hypotheses; the second uses the insights of psychoanalytic theory to re-evaluate the status and foundations of philosophy. Feminists in philosophy have overwhelmingly adopted the second stance, which in practice turns the first on its head, since the epistemological basis of science itself becomes a problem from the vantage point of psychoanalytic accounts.

Although in the popular imagination feminism and psychoanalysis are sworn enemies, and many feminists continue to be hostile to Freud, serious feminist engagement with psychoanalysis began with post-1970 feminism in the work of Juliet Mitchell, Luce Irigaray, Dorothy Dinnerstein and Nancy Chodorow. Feminists in philosophy turned to psychoanalysis in an attempt to understand what they perceived as the masculinism of philosophy and its attempt to exclude the feminine. Since psychoanalysis is specifically concerned with issues such as the formation of masculine and feminine identity at the level of the unconscious, it provides a framework for arguing that rationality and knowledge are always unconsciously gendered, thus challenging the self-proclaimed neutrality and universality of philosophy, a claim which feminists had come to see as increasingly suspect.

1 Trends in psychoanalytic feminism
2 Theoretical issues in psychoanalytic feminism

1 Trends in psychoanalytic feminism

To understand the thrust of psychoanalytic interventions in philosophy, it is helpful to make a comparison between psychoanalytic approaches to literary theory and psychoanalytic approaches to philosophy. Because psychoanalysis looks at *the effects of desire in language*, psychoanalysis and literary criticism are allies in a way that psychoanalysis and philosophy are not (see FEMINIST LITERARY CRITICISM). Whereas psychoanalysis has given literary criticism a new lease of life, it has, on the contrary, tended to destabilize philosophy as traditionally understood.

Psychoanalytic criticism examines texts with a view to locating literary or rhetorical strategies analogous to psychic mechanisms. It takes into account relationships both between author and text, and reader and text. It may often extrapolate from the strategies of the text to the strategies of the culture in general. Using Wright's classification as a guide (1984), one can distinguish five main types of approach: (1) psychobiography or psycho-critique (analysing the psyche of the author or the characters); (2) reader-response theory (analysing the psyche of the reader, or the relationship between reader and writing); (3) analysis of psyche as text, starting from the Lacanian assumption that psychic mechanisms are analogous to linguistic ones; (4) analysis of the text as psyche,

starting from the Derridean assumption that textual mechanisms are analogous to psychic ones; (5) analysis of the ideology of psychoanalysis, an approach inspired by Foucault which sees psychoanalysis as a discourse which produces effects of power, both positive and negative (see LACAN, J.; DERRIDA, J.; FOUCAULT, M.).

Because mainstream English-language philosophy has been reluctant to see itself as 'text', that is as in any way 'literary', and has often been resistant to structuralist and post-structuralist philosophy, feminist work here has tended to remain within the first kind of approach, psychobiography or psychocritique, which is also the most vulnerable to the charge of reductivism. In its early attempts to use psychoanalytic theory in philosophy, there was a certain lack of theoretical clarity concerning the analysand or 'patient' whose psyche or psychopathology was up for scrutiny. The analysand was seen variously as the individual philosopher (Plato, Descartes and Hobbes were typical examples), the philosophical system each had produced, or Western culture in general. All of these were in turn subject to analysis. The definition put forward by Naomi Scheman (1993: 7) of the analysand as 'the normative philosophical subject', 'the epistemically authoritative modern subject', would probably now be generally accepted.

Feminist English-language philosophy relies on the strand of psychoanalytic theory known as object-relations theory and associated with the post-Kleinians: Winnicott and Fairbairn in Britain, Guntrip in the USA. Object-relations theory differs both from classical Freudianism and also from (post-)structuralist psychoanalysis. Whereas the focus of classical Freudianism was primarily on the conflict between instinctual drive and the frustrations of external reality, object-relations theory focuses more on the child's relations with its real or fantasied 'others'. It thus provides a more intersubjective and socially-orientated account of psychic reality. Similarly, whereas Lacanian theory stresses the internal splitting and division of the self, object-relations theory is more likely to stress the integration of different parts of the self in healthy development, with 'splitting' as a mark of pathology. Emphasis once more is placed on the child's social and familial environment, which assists or militates against psychic integration. Object-relations theory plays down the drives in favour of social reality; this makes it readily accessible to feminist theory which already has a predominantly social orientation. It is argued, for example, that the sexual division of labour, both within the family and also between public and private worlds, creates a pathogenic environment, reproducing the distortions of masculinity and femininity which have been the target of feminist critique (Chodorow 1978).

In the continental tradition, psychoanalytic critique has been more far-reaching. There was a convergence between the feminist critique of the claims of philosophy, and the structuralist and post-structuralist critiques of the primacy accorded to consciousness. Feminism's argument that there was no possibility of an Archimedean point anchoring knowledge found common ground with the claim of psychoanalysis that complete self-possession or self-awareness is impossible, that the knowing, rational, speaking subject is dependent on structures outside conscious control and which are impossible *in principle* to grasp in their entirety. For feminists in the continental tradition, the aim is to rethink what is understood by subjectivity, given the hypothesis of the unconscious: 'The subject of the unconscious demands that the subject of philosophy... faces his/her incompleteness, recognises the libidinal bodily roots of intelligence, and accepts the partiality of his/her modes of thinking' (Braidotti 1991: 35). In displacing the centrality of consciousness, a challenge is raised to the project of philosophy as previously understood.

Continental philosophy refers to a different set of psychoanalytic theorists. Lacan's reading of Freud has dominated, but Klein has also been influential (in the work of J. KRISTEVA), as have Abraham and Ferenczi (see PSYCHOANALYSIS, POST-FREUDIAN). There is also a flourishing French tradition of psychoanalysts with an interdisciplinary orientation, who have read Nietzsche, Hegel, Heidegger and the phenomenologists, and are acquainted with surrealism, as well as structural linguistics (Saussure) and structural anthropology (Lévi-Strauss) (Roudinesco 1986). Unlike object-relations theory, French psychoanalysis has retained and developed Freud's controversial notion of the death drive; it remains suspicious of the US stress on the integration of the ego, and is much more likely to emphasize the decentred subject, a notion which had already been introduced in French philosophy.

Structuralism and post-structuralism have made it clear that there is more than one way of reading Freud: there is the Enlightenment Freud, committed to science and rational mastery; there is also a more deconstructive Freud, whose drive theory introduces a permanent threat of destabilization to the constructions of the rational ego. Feminist theorists in the continental tradition have been more interested in the deconstructive Freud, since they perceive the constructions of the rational ego as hostile to the feminine. While this has produced some undoubtedly powerful theoretical work, the links to feminism as a social movement remain on the whole more tenuous and less programmatic than for more ego-orientated philosophy (see STRUCTURALISM; POST-STRUCTURALISM).

2 Theoretical issues in psychoanalytic feminism

Two levels of theoretical problem can be identified in the encounter between feminism, psychoanalysis and philosophy. To the first level belong the objections to the use of psychoanalytic theory *per se*, made from a feminist but not necessarily philosophical perspective. One can distinguish four types of argument here. First, it was held that psychoanalytic theory was organized around male desire (represented by the centrality of the phallus) and that its central concepts, implicitly or explicitly, maintained women as inferior. This argument is associated with the view that psychoanalysis is inevitably prescriptive rather than primarily descriptive. Psychoanalytic feminists accept that psychoanalytic theory is often phallocentric; however, masculine bias may also be seen, not as a reason for rejecting psychoanalysis *in toto*, but rather for rethinking its concepts (Brennan 1992; Flax 1990; Kofman 1980; Schneider 1980). Even in his own lifetime, Freud's account of women's psycho-sexuality had been challenged by women analysts. Second, it was thought that psychoanalytic theory (particularly in the work of French feminists) equated the feminine with the irrational, so that the celebration of the feminine was in effect promoting irrationalism. However, it was not so much that objectivity or rationality were thrown out, which would have been self-defeating; it was more that they were displaced. Psychoanalytic feminists wanted to discuss issues such as objectivity as a mechanism of defence (involving splitting, or the attempt to distance oneself from unacceptable or unbearable feelings by projecting them elsewhere) and the consequences of this, especially for women (Bordo 1987; Keller 1985).

Third, it was further pointed out that it was reductive to read philosophical texts in terms of the hypothetical psychopathology of their – often long-dead – authors. In practice, this argument has been generally accepted, and has led to more sophisticated textual readings. It is a critique which has less bite when one adopts the more literary technique of taking the 'author' to be an extrapolation of the text rather than an actual individual. The fourth and perhaps most telling objection was that major tenets of Freudian theory, such as the Oedipus complex, were presented as though they were universal and ahistorical data, rather than hypotheses generated in a particular social, cultural and historical era. This critique of ethnocentrism was difficult to evade; in response there has been an attempt to distinguish

585

between the content of unconscious fantasies, which may be culturally specific, and the inevitability of certain types of mental processes occurring during the development and socialization of children. These processes have greater claim to universality and it seems legitimate to accept them provisionally as cross-cultural, although the distinction between form and content is not always easy to make in psychoanalytic theory, so that the problem of universality remains a controversial one.

We now turn to the second level, where the arguments taking place within the three-way debate between feminism, philosophy and psychoanalysis are more conceptual. At this fundamental level, central issues include the status of psychoanalytic theory and the limits of philosophy.

It is recognized that Freud's account of the mind (and the elaboration of this account in subsequent and not always mutually compatible theories) provides an immanent critique of its own constructions. Psychoanalytic theory explicitly recognizes that all theory, including its own, is indebted to unconscious determinants. For example, one of the problems of psychoanalytic theory has to do with the representation of the drives and the way in which fantasies, images and words become attached to what are in origin somatic impulses. Since no correspondence can ever be established between the drive and its representation (there is no possible position from which the drive can be observed, one can only observe the representation), it is argued that the representation has a structuring effect on the drives (Irigaray 1974). Arguments of this type have major implications for theoretical formulations in psychoanalysis, which are claimed to *produce* as well as derive from the objects which are their field of study. This gives a particularly passionate edge to theoretical arguments.

It also means that questions about the status of psychoanalytic concepts can be raised without necessarily implying a complete rejection of psychoanalytic findings. Such questions are major philosophical issues in contemporary feminist theory. For example, Judith Butler (1990), drawing on Foucault, analyses the power-effects of psychoanalytic discourse. According to Butler, psychoanalytic theory maintains the irreducibility of the binary (and heterosexist) structure of gender as though this were foundational. It accepts that masculine and feminine identities are constructions, but it continues to build on the bedrock of the castration complex which divides human beings into men and women. In so doing it takes culture to be nature. In Butler's view, the sexual binary reinforces male primacy and makes heterosexuality normative. She puts forward an alternative account of the construction of gender

designed to allow for the possibility of multiplicity where previously there had only been a hierarchical dualism.

Feminists in more activist traditions such as socialist feminism are also concerned that psychoanalytic feminism, with its emphasis on unconscious determinants, does away with any useful notion of agency; they are concerned about its apparent lack of strong social orientation. At the same time, they accept that materialist theory has no adequate account of subjectivity and that psychoanalysis might be a source of indispensable insights here (Sayers 1986).

Drawing on the psyche-text analogy, the mental operations described by psychoanalysis – projection, introjection, identification, splitting, repression, disavowal, unconscious fantasy, and so on – are identified in the text of the culture at large (following the precedent set by Freud who thought social phenomena could be described in psychoanalytic terms). They are seen as functions of a text, a discourse, or a culture in general, so that a whole culture, or subsection of it, may be said to be projecting (for example, projecting men's gender-specific fears on to women) or splitting, or disavowing (for example, disavowing the debt to the mother, or the bodily origins of language). This leads on to an analysis of the cultural imaginary (that is the unconscious fantasies of a whole culture), a task undertaken by many feminists who do not define themselves as philosophers, but who use psychoanalytic premises. Outstanding studies include work by Parveen Adams, Teresa Brennan, Elisabeth Bronfen, Teresa De Lauretis, Jane Gallop, Mary Jacobus, Rosalind Krauss, Griselda Pollock, Ellie Ragland-Sullivan, Jacqueline Rose, and Kaja Silverman. (For a survey of the range of work in feminism and psychoanalysis, see Wright (ed.) 1992). There are particularly incisive analyses in meta-psychological theory, literary theory, film theory and art criticism. If one accepts the argument put forward by Michèle Le Doeuff – that the traffic between philosophy and the wider culture is not all one-way, that it is not just a question of philosophy clarifying culture, but also of philosophy depending on influences and understandings from other disciplines – then it is hard to draw clear boundaries between what is philosophically relevant and what is not. The issue of what is internal to the text/psyche being analysed and what is external, and how/whether one establishes the boundaries in any instance becomes one of the theoretical issues up for debate.

Feminists are interested in psychoanalysis because of a felt necessity for change. They take from psychoanalysis the recognition that intellectual understanding does not in itself effect unconscious transformation, for which the shifts of desire in transference are necessary. Such transformations are evidently subject neither to conscious decision nor to the exercise of either will, reason or force. This indicates the limits of philosophy for feminists, but also the dilemmas with which psychoanalysis confronts the feminist project.

See also: FEMINIST EPISTEMOLOGY; PSYCHOANALYSIS, POST-FREUDIAN; PSYCHOANALYSIS, METHODOLOGICAL ISSUES IN

References and further reading

Benjamin, J. (1988) *The Bonds of Love: Psychoanalysis, Feminism and the Problem of Domination*, New York: Pantheon; London: Virago. (Work by a psychoanalyst influenced by German political philosophy, with a strong social theory orientation, making it a reference-point for feminist philosophers.)

—— (1995) *Like Subjects, Love Objects: Essays on Recognition and Sexual Difference*, New Haven, CT, and London: Yale University Press. (Recent theory which attempts to integrate psychoanalytic and social perspectives. Both sophisticated and accessible.)

* Bordo, S. (1987) *The Flight to Objectivity: Essays on Cartesianism and Culture*, Albany, NY: SUNY Press. (A psychocultural narrative of the birth of Cartesian rationalism.)

* Braidotti, R. (1991) *Patterns of Dissonance: A Study of Women in Contemporary Philosophy*, trans. E. Guild, New York: Routledge; Cambridge: Polity Press. (An account of the relation between feminist and structuralist/post-structuralist philosophy. Chapter 2 is particularly relevant.)

Brennan, T. (ed.) (1989) *Between Feminism and Psychoanalysis*, New York and London: Routledge. (A collection representing a range of theoretical approaches. Not for the beginner.)

* Brennan, T. (1992) *The Interpretation of the Flesh: Freud and Femininity*, New York and London: Routledge. (Densely argued analysis of contradictions in Freud's account of gender.)

* Butler, J. (1990) *Gender Trouble: Feminism and the Subversion of Identity*, New York and London: Routledge. (Difficult work which includes a critique of psychoanalytic feminism from a Foucauldian perspective.)

* Chodorow, N. (1978) *The Reproduction of Mothering: Psychoanalysis and the Sociology of Gender*, Berkeley, CA: University of California Press. (Subject to considerable debate but still one of the most influential psychoanalytic works for feminist philosophers in the USA.)

Corradi Fiumara, G. (1992) *The Symbolic Function: Psychoanalysis and the Philosophy of Language*, Cambridge, MA and Oxford: Blackwell. (Its central argument – that there is no cognition without affect – is fundamental to the feminist contribution to philosophy.)

Dinnerstein, D. (1976) *The Mermaid and the Minotaur*, New York: Harper & Row; published in the UK as *The Rocking of the Cradle and the Ruling of the World*, London: Souvenir Press, 1978. (An influential psychocultural critique, drawing on Freud and Klein.)

Di Stefano, C. (1991) *Configurations of Masculinity: A Feminist Perspective on Modern Political Theory*, Ithaca, NY: Cornell University Press. (Readings of Hobbes, Marx and Mill in the light of object-relations theory.)

Ferrell, R. (1996) *Passion in Theory: Conceptions of Freud and Lacan*, New York and London: Routledge. (An excellent discussion of the implications of Freud and Lacan for philosophy.)

* Flax, J. (1990) *Thinking Fragments: Psychoanalysis, Feminism, and Postmodernism in the Contemporary West*, Berkeley, CA: University of California Press. (Clear and accessible, with a distinct bias towards object-relations theory. A useful work which shows how feminism, psychoanalysis and postmodern philosophers can each contribute to, interrogate or critique the other.)

Grosz, E. (1990) *Jacques Lacan: A Feminist Introduction*, New York and London: Routledge. (A clear and accessible assessment of Lacan's value for feminist theory.)

—— (1994) *Volatile Bodies: Toward a Corporeal Feminism*, Bloomington and Indianapolis, IN: Indiana University Press. (Psychoanalytic theory is presented as one of several possible narratives conceptualizing the body. An important, accessible contribution to recent debates in feminist philosophy.)

* Irigaray, L. (1974) *Speculum of the Other Woman*, trans. G.C. Gill, Ithaca, NY: Cornell University Press, 1985. (A psychoanalytic critique, influenced by Lacan and Derrida, both of Freud and of the history of philosophy. Important but difficult.)

—— (1984) *An Ethics of Sexual Difference*, trans. C. Burke and G.C. Gill, Ithaca, NY: Cornell University Press; London: Athlone Press, 1993. (A major psychocultural reading of the history of philosophy in the continental tradition. Difficult.)

* Keller, E.F. (1985) *Reflections on Gender and Science*, New Haven, CT: Yale University Press. (An influential feminist critique, based on object-

relations theory, of the ideology of scientific objectivity.)

* Kofman, S. (1980) *The Enigma of Woman: Woman in Freud's Writing*, trans. C. Porter, Ithaca, NY: Cornell University Press, 1985. (The work of a philosopher who reads text as psyche, turning the tools of psychoanalysis on itself. Quite specialized.)

Kristeva, J. (1986) *The Kristeva Reader*, ed. T. Moi, New York: Columbia University Press; Oxford: Blackwell. (An introduction to the work of a theorist who has been particularly influential for feminist philosophers in the continental tradition.)

—— (1987) *Black Sun: Depression and Melancholia*, trans. L. Roudiez, New York: Columbia University Press, 1989. (Brilliant and challenging psychocultural theory. Difficult.)

Laplanche, J. and Pontalis, J.-B. (1967) *The Language of Psychoanalysis*, trans. D. Nicholson-Smith, New York: W. W. Norton; London: The Hogarth Press, 1973. (An indispensable reference work for finding one's way around the Freudian corpus.)

Le Doeuff, M. (1989) *Hipparchia's Choice: An Essay Concerning Women, Philosophy, Etc.*, Cambridge, MA and Oxford: Blackwell, 1991. (Lucid and accessible account of relations between feminism and philosophy.)

Minsky, R. (1996) *Psychoanalysis and Gender: An Introductory Reader*, New York and London: Routledge. (Lucid and accessible account. An ideal introduction.)

* Mitchell, J. (1974) *Psychoanalysis and Feminism*, London: Allen Lane; New York: Pantheon. (A major reference point for all further work in this area.)

* Roudinesco, E. (1986) *Jacques Lacan & Co.: A History of Psychoanalysis in France 1925–1985*, trans. J. Mehlman, Chicago, IL: University of Chicago Press; London: Free Association, 1990. (Essential background reading for an understanding of the French psychoanalytic context.)

* Sayers, J. (1986) *Sexual Contradictions: Psychology, Psychoanalysis and Feminism*, New York and London: Tavistock. (A lucidly-written socialist-feminist assessment of the strengths and limitations of psychoanalytic theory.)

* Scheman, N. (1993) *Engenderings: Constructions of Knowledge, Authority and Privilege*, New York and London: Routledge. (A psychoanalytically informed account of the relation of gender to epistemology.)

* Schneider, M. (1980) *La Parole et l'Inceste*, Paris: Aubier-Montagne. (In French. Uses French but non-Lacanian psychoanalytic theories, showing the defences against the feminine in Freudian theory.)

* Wright, E. (1984) *Psychoanalytic Criticism: Theory in Practice*, New York and London: Methuen. (Highly recommended for its account of the implications of psychoanalysis for texts in general, written for the non-specialist reader.)

* —— (ed.) (1992) *Feminism and Psychoanalysis: A Critical Dictionary*, Cambridge, MA and Oxford: Blackwell. (An indispensable reference work, mapping out a field of theoretical intersections.)

MARGARET WHITFORD

FEMINISM AND SOCIAL SCIENCE

Feminists have two sorts of interest in the social sciences. With the advent of the second-wave women's movement, they developed wide-ranging critiques of gender bias in the conceptual framework and methodology, as well as in the goals, institutions and practice of virtually all the social sciences; they argue that the social sciences both reflect and contribute to the sexism of the larger societies in which they are embedded. Alongside these critiques feminist practitioners have established constructive programmes of research that are intended to rectify the inadequacies of existing traditions of research and to address questions of concern to women. In this they are committed both to improving the disciplines in which they participate and to establishing a sound empirical and theoretical basis for feminist activism. This engagement of feminists with social science, as commentators and practitioners, raises a number of philosophical issues that have been addressed by feminist social scientists and philosophers. These include questions about ideals of objectivity and the role of contextual values in social scientific inquiry, the goals of feminist research, the forms of practice appropriate to these goals, and the responsibilities of feminist researchers to the subjects of inquiry and to those who may otherwise be affected by its conduct or results.

1 Feminist critiques of the social sciences
2 Constructive initiatives
3 Philosophical implications

1 Feminist critiques of the social sciences

Feminist critics of the social sciences make the case, usually with respect to specific examples, that often even the most rigorous and conscientious research in the social sciences has been androcentric or sexist or both: it embodies a male-centred view of its subject matter, and sometimes explicit assumptions of male superiority. These critiques began to appear regularly in most fields in the early 1970s and quickly gained wide currency. They frequently coincided with the founding of committees on the status of women which undertook to document and to counteract inequities in the recruitment, training, employment and professional recognition of women within the social sciences. Although there are important differences in the form that feminist critiques take and in the impact they have had in various fields and subfields of the social sciences, they follow similar lines of development and converge on four broad areas of concern (Wylie *et al.* 1989).

Often the first issues raised by feminist critics have to do with the goals of the social sciences. They object that the questions central to much mainstream research reflect androcentric interests in the social world; women's activities, roles and contributions have been largely ignored, as have issues of particular concern to women (for example, violence against women, the history of domestic technologies, gender segregation in the workplace). At the very least this line of criticism suggests that the scope of social scientific inquiry should be expanded. In addition, however, feminists ask how adequate our understanding can be, even of the subjects that are typically considered, if substantial dimensions of social life have been left out of account.

A second family of objections, content critiques, draws attention to ways in which social research is compromised when its subjects are conceptualized in terms that reflect sexist or androcentric presuppositions. These include implicit, 'taken-for-granted' assumptions about gender categories and relations – about the typical (or 'natural') roles and capabilities of women and men. Male experience, behaviour, interests and attributes may be treated as normative, with the result that gender differences are ignored. In some cases the whole subject domain is characterized in male-specific terms or, when women are considered, it is exclusively in relation to men (Eichler describes these as errors of overgeneralization and gender insensitivity). Some widely cited cases include ethnographic studies in which 'hunter-gatherer societies' are characterized in terms of the hunting activities of men (Rosaldo and Lamphere 1974), and the 'man the hunter' theories of evolution informed by these accounts (Dahlberg 1981; Hager 1997), historical periodization schemes which reflect a preoccupation with the fortunes of (elite) men (Kelly-Gadol 1976), and theories of human psychological development based exclusively on male samples (Gilligan 1982; see MORAL DEVELOPMENT). Gender stereotypes may also be reflected in the converse assumption that men and women are categorically different. In this case, similar and overlapping traits are either ignored or are characterized in different terms when associated with men rather than women (in Eichler's terms these are errors that arise from imposing a 'double standard' and from 'sexual dichotomism', 1988); sex difference research abounds with examples of this practice (Fausto-Sterling 1985). The central point feminist critics make is that the background assumptions underlying such 'distortions' of content should be made explicit and subjected to critical empirical scrutiny.

These critiques both generate and depend upon 'remedial' research; the study of 'women worthies', 'women's contributions' and 'women victims' (Harding 1986) has been crucial in establishing, in concrete terms, what androcentric social science has left out of its account. But wherever such compensatory strategies have been adopted, autocritiques have appeared which made it clear that they are not sufficient on their own. To take one example among many that could be cited, through the 1970s and early 1980s feminist anthropologists, historians and political scientists argued (often independently) that a central limitation of their respective fields of study is a preoccupation with a male-identified 'public' domain (for example, public figures, public exercises of power, politics in a juridical sense); they urged that feminists turn their attention to the neglected, private, domestic spheres in which women are to be found. Critical reflection shows, however, that simply inverting the emphasis of previous research leaves intact precisely the gender categories and stereotypes that feminists had insisted should be called into question (Rosaldo 1980; Tomm and Hamilton 1988). To rectify the androcentrism operating at this deeper level it is necessary, not just to add considerations of (for example) the work women do, the symbolic universes they construct and the forms of power they exercise in domestic and other contexts, but to more fundamentally reconceptualize what counts as work or as power, and as the 'domestic' or private sphere both in its own terms and in relation to 'public' life.

By the mid-1980s it was widely noted that the effects of androcentric goals and presuppositions were pervasive in two senses. Deepening critiques of content suggested that all aspects of research may be affected, not just the formation of questions or the interpretation of results, but also domain-defining assumptions that determine the design of research, the selection of methodologies and the formulation of categories of description and analysis. Moreover, androcentric bias of one kind or another had been identified in virtually all the fields of social research in which feminists had undertaken critical analyses. A third type of critique, of research methodologies, arises when feminists ask how it is possible that androcentric bias in the goals and content of inquiry could be as deeply rooted and persistent as their collective analyses suggest.

The point of departure for methodological critiques is a suspicion that the forms of inquiry typical in the social sciences may be responsible, in some part, for the production and persistence of androcentric bias. Some feminists maintain that established methods for evaluating knowledge claims are adequate as they stand, but that they have simply not been applied as widely or as systematically as they should have been; this constitutes a form of feminist empiricism (Harding 1986). Others insist that we should reassess our faith in the capacity of these methods to expose systematic bias. They may be powerful tools for assessing the empirical adequacy, reliability and scope of specific knowledge claims within a frame of reference, but will often simply reproduce error if it is rooted in the fundamental presuppositions of inquiry. Still others suggest that some methods may actually generate androcentric and sexist bias. For example, in many contexts a central theme in feminist critiques has been a rejection of the 'naturalist' conviction that social research must conform to models of natural scientific practice (Mies 1983; Nielsen 1990; Stanley and Wise 1983) (see NATURALISM IN SOCIAL SCIENCE). Especially when formulated in terms of positivist theories of science, this enforces a preoccupation with quasi-experimental and quantitative methodologies which may systematically obscure devalued subordinate perspectives (for example, of women) that do not conform to the conventions of dominant ideology. Although few endorse this thesis in its strongest form – few maintain that research methods are intrinsically sexist or androcentric – it is clear that, in order to recover dimensions of social life ignored by mainstream research, feminist practitioners frequently and increasingly turn to forms of evidence considered ephemeral (for example, diaries, private papers, material culture, as opposed to archives of public record) and rely on methodologies that are nonstandard or marginal by the conventions of their fields (for example, open-ended qualitative methodologies in fields dominated by naturalism).

A fourth and final type of feminist critique is also inspired by reflection on the ways in which research is typically conducted in the social sciences, especially when informed by objectivist and positivist ideals (Fonow and Cook 1991; Nebraska Collective 1983; see the summary discussions in Reinharz 1992). A recurrent theme is concern that human subjects, especially those who are disempowered by established

social hierarchies, may be demeaned and exploited by research practices which require that they be 'objectified' or treated like objects (Stanley and Wise 1983) (see OBJECTIVITY). In this feminists join many other social scientists who have insisted on the need to take responsibility for the effect of their research practice on subjects, and to scrutinize the ways in which they, and their research enterprises, function as agents of social manipulation and control (Smith 1987).

2 Constructive initiatives

These critiques by no means exhaust feminist interests in the social sciences. As insiders to the social sciences (Westcott 1979; Collins in Fonow and Cook 1991), feminist practitioners actively work against the sexism and androcentrism they identify in extant traditions of research; in this they are concerned to improve the research enterprises in which they are engaged. In addition, as feminists, many have a strong commitment to change conditions of life that are oppressive for women and they recognize that, if they are to be effective in realizing these goals, it is necessary to understand with accuracy, subtlety and explanatory precision the nature and sources of the inequities that disadvantage women. Whatever their limitations, social-scientific modes of inquiry are among the most powerful tools available for doing this. Feminists also have an interest, then, in developing programmes of research which address questions relevant to women and promise a secure empirical and conceptual foundation for feminist activism.

In taking up these constructive projects, feminists immediately confront the questions of how research should be conducted if it is to avoid the pitfalls of androcentric practice, and whether there is any distinctively 'feminist' mode of inquiry. Consensus emerged by the late 1980s that the quest for a 'feminist method' or 'feminist science' is misguided; it bespeaks a faith in methodological solutions that feminists have long cautioned against, and presupposes an implausible unity of feminist interests. It is more fruitful to ask what it means to 'do [social] science as a feminist' (Harding 1987; Longino 1987, 1994). In this spirit feminist practitioners have typically formulated quite general guidelines for ensuring that research practice is nonsexist, and is otherwise consistent with feminist ideals (Eichler 1988; Mies 1983; Reinharz 1992). These may be characterized in terms of responses to the four types of criticism described above.

First, feminists have insisted that, at the very least, the goals of social scientific inquiry should include consideration of women and gender. In addition, many feminist social scientists advocate research that has (potential) practical import: research that addresses questions of concern to women, and that promises an understanding relevant for improving their lives.

Second, a persistent, if controversial, theme is the recommendation that feminist research should be 'grounded in' women's experience (Mies 1983; Stanley and Wise 1983). This principle is interpreted in widely divergent ways. In some cases it is understood to mean that feminist research should take women's lives and experience as a primary subject of inquiry; it should redress the silencing and devaluation of women's perspectives that is reproduced by male-normative thinking in the social sciences. Many consider this too restrictive a mandate for feminist researchers, and urge that the experience and understanding of women should serve as a basis for identifying new questions, formulating new categories of description and analysis, and expanding our interpretive repertoire; it represents a standpoint from which the limitations of androcentric thinking may be discernible in all areas, not just those in which women predominate (see Harding 1991 on 'thinking from women's lives').

Third, feminist practitioners frequently insist on thoroughgoing 'reflexivity': they hold that the theoretical and methodological presuppositions of their research should be subject to the same sort of critical scrutiny as they apply to mainstream research (Longino's 'provisionalism', 1994).

Finally, by extension of these three principles, feminist social scientists are actively concerned with issues of accountability to research subjects and to others who may be affected by the practice or results of their research. They insist that, as a minimum requirement, research practices should not, themselves, exploit or oppress women. Often they urge that research be designed, as far as possible, as interventions that may benefit research subjects and they recommend collaborative models of inquiry.

Consistent with the requirement for reflexivity, there is active ongoing debate about all these recommendations and their implications for practice.

3 Philosophical implications

These constructive guidelines for doing research as feminists, and the critiques from which they arise, pose a number of philosophical problems, foundational and epistemic. In the process of interrogating entrenched assumptions about women and gender, feminist social scientists have contributed to wider debates that substantially destabilize the assumption that these constitute coherent categories which can be presupposed as the basis either for feminist activism

or feminist scholarship. As critics of the inherent elitism, racism, and ethnocentrism of second-wave feminism point out, women's experience is so diverse and gender categories and roles so deeply structured by other systems of social differentiation, it is untenable to treat 'gender' as an autonomous category for analysis or to presume a unitary 'women's' standpoint (Anderson and Collins 1995; Mohanty, Russo and Torres 1991). This reinforces the commitment to reflexivity; it is a thoroughly contingent, empirical question how gender should be conceptualized and whether it is a relevant category for critical or constructive analysis. The interests of feminists in the social sciences thus converge on those of critics working from innumerable other subordinate standpoints.

In addition to these foundational issues, feminist critiques of and contributions to the social sciences raise fundamental epistemic questions about entrenched ideals of objectivity and the relationship of 'external' contextual values and interests to the 'internal' epistemic values generally assumed to be constitutive of scientific inquiry (Longino 1990). The extent and depth of androcentric bias identified by feminist critics makes it increasingly implausible that the difficulty lies only with instances of 'bad science'; it suggests that good science, 'science as usual', even our best science, is more deeply infused with the values and interests of its practitioners than has generally been acknowledged (Harding 1986). Moreover, where feminists working from an explicitly interested standpoint have made important contributions to the social sciences, even judged by quite traditional standards, it seems that contextual values should not always be regarded as a contaminant of inquiry (Alcoff 1987). Standpoint theorists argue, on the basis of such observations, that 'contextual' values play an irreducible role in all research practice, and postmodern critics are frequently identified as drawing strong relativist conclusions on this basis (see Harding 1986 for a summary of these positions). In practice, however, few feminist practitioners are prepared to embrace such conclusions (di Leonardo 1991; Hawkesworth 1989). This is not just a strategic stance motivated by concern that feminists' insights should be taken seriously as offering an improved rather than just an alternative understanding of the social world. It reflects, as well, an appreciation, often born of activist engagement, that it is possible to be (disastrously) wrong even about subjects as enigmatic as the cultural, intentional systems studied by social scientists. As is often observed, only the most powerful could imagine that the world is as they construct it; for feminists much depends on establishing an empirically and explanatorily accurate understanding of the world in which they hope to intervene.

The epistemological challenge posed by feminist research is to develop an account of epistemic values and ideals, such as empirical adequacy, explanatory power, objectivity, which makes sense of the nuanced judgments social scientists (including feminists) routinely make about the relative credibility of knowledge claims without requiring untenable conditions of value-neutrality or empirical foundationalism (see FOUNDATIONALISM). In taking up these questions, feminists engage issues which are central to postpositivist philosophy of science (Alcoff and Potter 1993; Lloyd 1995).

See also: FEMINISM; FEMINIST EPISTEMOLOGY; FEMINIST ETHICS; FEMINIST JURISPRUDENCE; FEMINIST POLITICAL PHILOSOPHY; GENDER AND SCIENCE; LOGICAL POSITIVISM; SCIENTIFIC METHOD; SOCIAL SCIENCES, PHILOSOPHY OF

References and further reading

* Alcoff, L. (1987) 'Justifying Feminist Social Science', *Hypatia*, special issue on 'Feminism and Science', 2: 107–27. (An excellent survey of epistemological issues raised by feminist work in the social sciences.)

* Alcoff, L. and Potter, E. (eds) (1993) *Feminist Epistemologies*, New York: Routledge. (Provides a good introduction to the issues in feminist epistemology and philosophy of science discussed in §3.)

* Anderson, M.L. and Collins, P.H. (eds) (1995) *Race, Class, and Gender*, Belmont, CA: Wadsworth. (An excellent anthology on the intersections between dimensions of oppression, cited in §3.)

* Dahlberg, F. (ed.) (1981) *Woman the Gatherer*, New Haven, CT: Yale University Press. (Includes examples of feminist critiques of androcentrism in theories of evolution and ethnographies of foraging societies, as cited in §1.)

* Eichler, M. (1988) *Nonsexist Research Methods*, Boston, MA: Allen & Unwin. (A comprehensive summary of the feminist critiques discussed in §1.)

* Fausto-Sterling, A. (1985) *Myths of Gender*, New York: Basic Books. (Includes a review of feminist critiques of sex-difference research, as cited in §1.)

* Fonow, M.M. and Cook, J.A. (eds) (1991) *Beyond Methodology: Feminist Scholarship as Lived Research*, Bloomington, IN: Indiana University Press. (A useful collection of essays on feminist contributions to the social sciences with an excellent introductory summary of the principles that inform feminist research.)

* Gilligan, C. (1982) *In a Different Voice: Psychological Theories and Women's Development*, Cambridge, MA: Harvard University Press. (A critique of Kholberg's theory of moral development, cited in §1.)

* Hager, L. (1997) *Women in Human Evolution*, London: Routledge. (A selection of essays on feminist research on evolution, cited in §1.)

* Harding, S. (1986) *The Science Question in Feminism*, Ithaca, NY: Cornell University Press. (Includes an influential discussion of feminist empiricism, standpoint theory and postmodernism.)

* —— (ed.) (1987) *Feminism and Methodology: Social Science Issues*, Bloomington, IN: Indiana University Press. (Includes influential examples of feminist research in the social sciences and a useful introduction to the epistemological issues they raise.)

* —— (1991) *Whose Science? Whose Knowledge?*, Ithaca, NY: Cornell University Press. (Includes discussion of concepts of objectivity relevant to §3.)

* Hawkesworth, M.E. (1989) 'Knowers, Knowing, Known: Feminist Theory and Claims of Truth', *Signs* 14: 533–57. (A useful summary of feminist epistemologies, including a critique of feminist postmodernism. Cited in §3.)

* Kelly-Gadol, J. (1976) 'The Social Relations of the Sexes: Methodological Implications of Women's History', *Signs* 1: 809–23. (Cited in §1, a feminist critique of underlying assumptions that structure historical inquiry.)

* Leonardo, M. di (1991) *Gender at the Crossroads of Knowledge: Feminist Anthropology in the Postmodern Era*, Berkeley, CA: University of California Press. (A valuable selection of feminist research in anthropology with an excellent introductory essay, cited in §3.)

* Lloyd, E.A. (1995) 'Objectivity and the Double Standard for Feminist Epistemologies', *Synthèse* 104: 351–81. (An account of the relationship between feminist critiques of objectivity and central themes in postpositivist philosophy of science. Cited in §3.)

* Longino, H. (1987) 'Can there Be a Feminist Science?', *Hypatia* 2: 51–64. (An excellent summary of and response to the debates about 'feminist method'. Cited in §2.)

* —— (1990) *Science as Social Knowledge: Values and Objectivity in Scientific Inquiry*, Princeton, NY: Princeton University Press. (Provides a sophisticated introduction to the philosophical issues discussed in §3.)

* —— (1994) 'In Search of Feminist Epistemology', *The Monist* 77: 472–85. (An overview of values that inform feminist research, cited in §§2 and 3.)

* Mies, M. (1983) 'Toward a Methodology of Feminist

Research', in G. Bowles and R.D. Klein (eds) *Theories of Women's Studies*, New York: Routledge & Kegan Paul. (An influential and controversial proposal for feminist research that focuses on epistemological issues. Cited in §§1 and 2. See also Mies' contribution to Fonow and Cook 1991.)

* Mohanty, C.T., Russo, A. and Torres, L. (eds) (1991) *Third World Women and the Politics of Feminism*, Bloomington, IN: Indiana University Press. (An anthology of critiques of the elitism of much first world feminist scholarship and activism with an excellent introductory analysis by Mohanty. Cited in §3.)

* Nebraska Feminist Collective (1983) 'A Feminist Ethic for Social Science Research', *Women's Studies International Forum* 6: 535–45. (A classic statement of ethical issues addressed by feminist social scientists. Cited in §§2 and 3.)

* Nielsen, J.M. (ed.) (1990) *Feminist Research Methods: Exemplary Readings in the Social Sciences*, Boulder, CO: Westview Press. (A collection of essays that both describe and exemplify principles of feminist research with a useful introduction to these principles and the epistemological issues they raise. Cited in §§2 and 3.)

* Reinharz, S. (1992) *Feminist Methods in Social Research*, Oxford: Oxford University Press. (The most comprehensive account available of feminist research practice in the social sciences.)

Reinharz, S., Bombyk, M. and Wright, J. (1983) 'Methodological Issues in Feminist Research: A Bibliography of Literature in Women's Studies, Sociology and Psychology', *Women's Studies International Forum* 6: 437–54. (An excellent guide to the first decade of feminist research in the social sciences; includes references to much of the literature cited in §1.)

Roberts, H. (ed.) (1981) *Doing Feminist Research*, London: Routledge & Kegan Paul. (Includes important critiques of traditional research methodologies, as described in §1.)

* Rosaldo, M.Z. (1980) 'The Use and Abuse of Anthropology: Reflections on Feminism and Cross-Cultural Understanding', *Signs* 5: 389–417. (An example of internal feminist critiques that call into question 'remedial' research, as described in §§1 and 2.)

* Rosaldo, M.Z. and Lamphere, L. (eds) (1974) *Women, Culture and Society*, Stanford, CA: Stanford University Press. (An anthology of early and widely influential feminist critiques of anthropology of the sort cited in §1.)

* Smith, D. (1987) *The Everyday World as Problematic: A Feminist Sociology*, Toronto, Ont.: University of Toronto Press. (An influential feminist critique of

sociological technologies of control, informed by Marxist and ethnomethodological critiques of sociology.)

* Stanley, L. and Wise, S. (1983) *Breaking Out: Feminist Consciousness and Feminist Research*, London: Routledge & Kegan Paul. (One of the most radical and influential epistemological critiques of traditional research, cited in §1.)

* Tomm, W. and Hamilton, G. (eds) (1988) *Gender Bias in Scholarship: The Pervasive Prejudice*, Waterloo, Ont.: Wilfrid Laurier University Press. (A useful collection of essays summarizing feminist critiques of and contributions to the social sciences.)

* Westkott, M. (1979) 'Feminist Criticism of the Social Sciences', *Harvard Educational Review* 49: 422–30. (Provides a review of feminist critiques discussed in §1.)

* Wylie, A., Okruhlik, K., Thielen-Wilson, L. and Morton, S. (1989) 'Feminist Critiques of Science: The Epistemological and Methodological Literature', *Women's Studies International Forum* 12: 379–88. (A general guide to feminist critiques of science which includes sections on the social sciences. Provides references to much of the literature considered in §1.)

ALISON WYLIE

FEMINIST AESTHETICS

Feminist perspectives in aesthetics and philosophy of art have emerged not only from the discipline of philosophy but also from cognate fields such as literary theory, film studies and art history. Like other feminist philosophy, feminist aesthetics is founded upon critiques of fundamental assumptions that have traditionally governed this area of study. Such staple concepts as aesthetic value, disinterested attention, aesthetic perception and fine art have been analysed for biased perspectives that explicitly or covertly favour masculine gender.

Gender bias has been located, for example, in theories of aesthetic attention and appreciation. Feminist analyses have speculated that the traditional, ideal, 'disinterested' aesthetic perceiver covertly stands in a position of masculine privilege encouraging desire and control of the object of contemplation. Calling attention to the masculine position of the perceiver goes hand in hand with analyses of visual arts and literature that focus on their representations of gender – formalist interpretive methods that ignore the portrayal of women and sexuality have been especially criticized. The paucity of female artists on lists of acknowledged geniuses and the relative absence of their work from canons of art has occasioned speculation that the concept of art itself is biased in so far as it excludes the creations of most women.

Feminist analyses stress the social contexts within which theories develop. Not only do concepts basic to aesthetics manifest ideas about gender that derive from formative traditions, but notions of beauty and art are themselves influential components of culture and contribute to the shape and perpetuation of gender roles.

1   **Historical critiques**
2   **Creativity and art**
3   **Perception and the male gaze**
4   **Style**

1   Historical critiques

Feminist challenges to academic disciplines begin with critiques of the basic assumptions of a field and often consist of examinations of canonical texts for any gender-related implications. In philosophy, this involves demonstrating that theories that purport to be universalist, that is, to pertain generically to all human beings, are in fact models of ideal masculine nature. The gender biases of Western philosophy are often related in some way to the fundamental reliance of philosophical views on the centrality of reason. Reason is the standard faculty of knowledge and of moral responsibility, and it operates in most theories as the chief essential characteristic of being human. Reason raises the human creature above nature, making possible creation beyond what nature has given. But rationality is also a trait that is employed to contrast male with female dispositions, for the nonrational domains of emotion, sense and the body are widely associated with femininity. Thus many theories that at first glance seem to be general views about all people may be discovered to refer standardly to men, and sometimes actually to exclude women. In the history of aesthetics, reason is often not the chief faculty governing artistic creativity or aesthetic experience. However, still operative in aesthetic theory are the binary correlations that link reason to masculinity and the transcendence of nature, and that associate emotion, the body, femininity and rootedness in nature. Two examples that illustrate this phenomenon are provided by the notion of artistic genius and the concepts of the beautiful and the sublime.

Though the idea of genius has taken a variety of forms throughout its long history, none has countenanced a female genius. The sensitivity, intuition and even madness sometimes associated with genius contravene rationality; nonetheless genius is preserved

as a masculine domain by its bold originality and by the ability of the creative artist to transcend what is given by nature or culture. In the Romantic period – arguably the time when genius was of the greatest importance in aesthetic theory – the exclusion of women from the company of geniuses was especially marked; Kant, Nietzsche and Schopenhauer are among those who discuss genius in exclusively masculine terms. (Kant notoriously remarked that a woman who aspired to higher learning, let alone genius, might as well wear a beard.) The presumption of the masculinity of genius effectively screens out women from the ranks of the most important producers of art; however skilful their creations, lacking genius, they can presumably produce little more than derivative versions of the works that define and vivify a culture.

In the formative period of eighteenth-century European theory, the category of the aesthetic itself was becoming established, and this period framed views of perception, beauty and criticism upon which contemporary theories rest. At this time, beauty and sublimity were important theoretical categories, and the language of analysis directed to these topics is consistently gendered. The experience of the sublime – unbounded, vast, awesome – was cast in terms that not only stress the adventurous masculinity of the experience but also suggest that its grasp exceeds the capacity of the female mind. Beauty was conceived as a pleasurable, bounded, controllable object of enjoyment and described by terms such as 'graceful' or 'delicate'. In fact, the bodies of women figured as examples of objects of beauty more often than females were invoked as aesthetic perceivers. Implicitly, the ideal critic was male (indeed, a heterosexual male), and judgments of beauty and taste remained masculine activities.

2   Creativity and art

Since the greatest geniuses were conceived to be masculine, it was correspondingly difficult to make room for the works of female artists in the lists of important art. The degree to which women have been hindered from practising art varies according to genre: arts such as painting and music have been highly exclusionary; literature and dance less so. Philosophically, the most important issue regarding the absence of women from the canon is the effect of this on the concept of art itself. Here conceptual analysis merges with social history: the idea of fine art includes the production of objects that are conceived not only to have enduring value, but to be public objects that are products of individual talent. Throughout the history of Western art, few women have had the access to education and studio training that men have enjoyed, and furthermore many of them have chiefly been assigned domestic roles. What they created in such an ambience were not the sorts of objects that could easily join the category of fine art, but were rather objects of domestic crafts, designed as much for practical function as for beauty or expressivity. Moreover, products such as quilts are often the work of many hands, making the creative talents of individuals hard to discern. Thus the limitations of education and social roles are not the sole explanation for the scant presence of women in the history of Western painting, music and sculpture. The reigning concept of art and its attendant notion of creative genius is blind to the objects that most women in fact have created during much of recorded history. In recognition of this fact, many feminist scholars of the arts are expanding the scope of their enquiries to include hitherto neglected genres, such as domestic arts and crafts or private diaries and letters, in order to bring the art of women of the past into full view.

3 Perception and the male gaze

Above it was noted that formative eighteenth-century theories of the beautiful frequently mention women as objects of beauty and aesthetic attention. This fact needs to be placed in context with one of the most influential ideas that has governed the idea of the aesthetic in Euro-American theory: that of disinterested attention. (Several terms are employed to express this notion, including distanced appreciation and aesthetic contemplation.) For two centuries this idea has formed the heart of theories of the aesthetic; indeed, it has virtually defined the notion. The aesthetic is classically defined as the realm of pleasure or enjoyment that is contrasted to practical, moral, religious or political interests. The desires of the individual perceiver are set aside in aesthetic enjoyment, which is a receptive state of appreciation of presentational qualities of an object of art or nature.

Such a description of a mental state makes it seem generic, that is, to be the same whoever is looking; gender difference would not be seem to play any role in the concept of aesthetic attention. However, feminist critics have juxtaposed this ideal mental state with standard examples of works of art: the history of art, sculpture and literature is rife with seductions and rapes, nude figures of odalisques and prostitutes. Sceptical about the figurative distance that the notion of the aesthetic puts between the viewer and the object, feminist theorists have speculated that the disinterested viewer actually assumes a position of power over the object viewed. Especially when the object is a (real or portrayed) female character or figure, the aesthetic attitude is one that assumes a kind of prerogative on the part of a viewer and passivity on the part of the object, whose chief purpose is to be posed for the enjoyment of the viewer. In place of the notion of disinterested aesthetic attention, feminists have introduced the notion of the 'male gaze'.

While the general point is made for all art forms, the critique of aesthetic perception has been especially strong in discussion of the visual arts of film and painting. (The work of film-maker and theorist Laura Mulvey has been particularly influential.) The term 'male gaze' sums up an analysis of the privileged art connoisseur, who embodies a perspective of social dominance and particularly of traditional, patriarchal authority. Psychoanalysis provides a theoretical scaffolding congenial to many theorists of the gaze, because it fosters an understanding of how perception and pleasure become gendered. It is important to note that the viewer is in an imaginative masculine position, but need not actually be male. Male or female, socially powerful or marginal, the viewer assumes this position in order to appreciate art according to accepted norms. Nevertheless, identifying the ideal aesthetic position as masculine and patriarchal also raises questions about the critical, appreciative and interpretive act, and about the uniformity of aesthetic responses.

4 Style

Given the above analysis of the history of aesthetic theory as gender-biased, and the suspicion that many of the central concepts and terms with which theory is conducted retain the mark of gender, what positive remedies are available to feminist theorists? Are there distinctions between the art works of females and those of males that might be developed into a 'feminine' aesthetic theory that offers fruitful alternatives to customary aesthetic values? Is there a discernible female creative tradition? Does feminist analysis suggest gender differences in looking, reading, listening or appreciating?

There are proponents of both affirmative and negative positions on all of these issues. A particular problem that must be addressed in answering any of these questions affirmatively is the problem of essentialism, by which is meant the view that all women at all times share certain common aesthetic responses or stylistic traits – identifiably feminine qualities that are manifest in spite of their social differences.

As feminist theory developed in the 1970s, some theorists argued that there are certain common themes and styles in women's art works. Since women regularly share experiences that are different from those of men, the case might be made that their common social histories yield similar artistic themes, such as childbirth and domesticity. Some tied thematic focus to speculations about style, surmising that fluidity and softness are more characteristic of feminine style than are rigid boundaries and divisions. Perhaps the strongest and certainly the most sophisticated suggestions regarding the feminine style have come from francophone theorists such as Julia KRISTEVA, Luce IRIGARAY and Hélène CIXOUS. Pursuing suggestions made by Lacan and Derrida that language represents the feminine only in terms of absence, these thinkers (in their different ways) introduce the possibility of writing that disrupts patriarchal, symbolic order. *L'écriture féminine* – one of the concepts that has issued from this work – is posited as women's writing that rejects patriarchal discourse and inscribes a distinctively feminine voice. This type of theory is both a deep critique of language that inscribes a patriarchal order in which women have no subject position of their own, and a visionary prescription for women's language once these fetters are recognized and broken.

Against these views lie the objections that such categorization merely mimics stereotyped notions of femininity; that women's social circumstances often vary; and that historical periods, positions of social class, race, ethnicity, nationality and religion are all factors that distinguish women from one another. According to this view, to look for a common 'feminine style' is to assume wrongly that there is some essential femininity to be discovered. An emphasis on variety in gender identities and fluidity of social roles undermines the search for distinctively feminine voices and styles. However, the search for common feminine aesthetic qualities needs to be distinguished from the empirical search for the work that women have created outside traditionally recognized art forms. Such a search presumes no female essence, but acknowledges that if one is going to study the work of women, one must look in the right places.

Not only have feminist perspectives in aesthetics been developed to re-examine assumptions and basic concepts and to envision alternatives, but it is also the case that aesthetics contributes to projects of feminist theory. Art, language and representation are powerful components of the formation of subjectivities and self-concepts, as well as of public culture; they perpetuate cultural norms and provide imaginative space for violating or transcending these norms. Thus the aesthetic and its pleasures, art, style and representation are locations for the investigation of gender and the boundaries of masculinity and femininity.

See also: BEAUTY; DERRIDA, J.; FEMINISM; FILM, AESTHETICS OF §1; LACAN, J.; SUBLIME, THE

References and further reading

Battersby, C. (1989) *Gender and Genius: Towards a Feminist Aesthetic*, London: The Women's Press. (An analysis of the concept of genius from classical antiquity to the present.)

Brand, P.Z. and Korsmeyer, C. (eds) (1994) *Feminism and Tradition in Aesthetics*, University Park, PA: Penn State Press. (This anthology investigates philosophical issues in art from the perspective of feminism.)

Feski, R. (1989) *Beyond Feminist Aesthetics*, Cambridge, MA: Harvard University Press. (This work reviews feminist theories of the arts, especially literature, arguing that there is no property common to the work of women.)

Hein, H. and Korsmeyer, C. (eds) (1993) *Aesthetics in Feminist Perspective*, Bloomington, IN: Indiana University Press. (Collection of articles exploring aesthetics in the light of feminist theory.)

Korsmeyer, C. (1996) 'Perceptions, Pleasures, Arts: Considering Aesthetics', in J. Kouraney (ed.) *Philosophy in a Feminist Voice*, Princeton, NJ: Princeton University Press. (Expansion of the material of this entry.)

Marks, E. and de Courtivron, I. (eds) (1980) *New French Feminisms*, Amherst, MA: University of Massachussetts Press. (This collection contains selections from works of various francophone theorists.)

Mulvey, L. (1988) *Visual and Other Pleasures*, Basingstoke: Macmillan. (Essays analysing film and exploring psychoanalysis, gender and perpetual pleasures.)

Pollock, G. (1988) *Vision and Difference*, London: Routledge. (An art historian analyses painting and the male gaze.)

Wolff, J. (1990) *Feminine Sentences: Essays on Women and Culture*, Cambridge: Polity Press. (This work by a sociologist places problems of aesthetics in historical and social context.)

CAROLYN KORSMEYER

FEMINIST EPISTEMOLOGY

The impact of feminism on epistemology has been to move the question 'Whose knowledge are we talking about?' to a central place in epistemological inquiry. Hence feminist epistemologists are producing conceptions of knowledge that are quite specifically contextualized and situated, and of socially responsible epistemic agency. They have elaborated genealogical/ interpretive methods, have advocated reconstructions of empiricism, have articulated standpoint positions and have demonstrated the potential of psychosocial and post-structural analyses to counter the hegemony of epistemological master narratives. In these reconfigured epistemologies, feminists have argued that the cognitive status and circumstances of the knower(s) are central among conditions for the possibility of knowledge. They have demonstrated the salience, in evaluating any epistemic event, of the social arrangements of power and privilege by which it is legitimated or discredited.

Feminists are engaged at once in critical projects of demonstrating the privilege-sustaining, androcentric character of 'the epistemological project' in most of its received forms, and in transformative projects of reconstructing methodologies and justificatory procedures so as to eradicate their oppressive, exclusionary effects. They have shown that, in late-twentieth-century western philosophy, the circumstances of mature white men continue to generate prevailing ideals and norms of 'human nature', while the ideals of reason, objectivity and value-neutrality around which most mainstream theories of knowledge are constructed, like the knowledge they legitimate, tacitly validate affluent male experiences and values. Scientific knowledge, which is still an overwhelmingly male preserve, stands as the regulative model of objective epistemic authority; and the experiences and values of non-male, non-white and otherwise differently placed knowers typically have to accommodate themselves, Procrustean-style, to an idealized scientific and implicitly masculine norm, or risk dismissal as inconsequential, aberrant, mere opinion.

In engaging with these issues, most feminists – like many other participants in 'successor epistemology' projects – retain a realist commitment to empirical evidence, while denying that facts or experiences 'speak for themselves' and maintaining that most truths are as artefactual as they are factual. Questions of cognitive authority and answerability thus figure as prominently as issues of epistemic warrant in these projects, where feminists are concentrating less on formal, universal conditions for making and justifying knowledge 'in general' than on the specificities of knowledge construction. Hence these inquiries are often interdisci-plinary, producing detailed analyses of everyday knowledge-making and of scientific or social scientific inquiry; drawing out their gendered and other locational implications. In these projects feminists are showing that avowedly engaged, politically committed investigations can yield well-warranted conclusions.

1 **Epistemologies of privilege**
2 **Feminism and empiricism**
3 **Standpoints, interpretations, genealogies**
4 **Implications**

1 Epistemologies of privilege

Feminist epistemologies, like many other post-Enlightenment, post-colonial epistemological projects, have grown out of critical interrogations of the universalistic presumptions of the theories of knowledge of the Western philosophical tradition. Sceptical about the very possibility of developing a theory of knowledge 'in general', whose claims to universal validity are premised on its abstraction from the specificities of human circumstances, feminist epistemologists have insisted on the constitutive part that epistemic location plays in the making and evaluating of knowledge claims. Many of the best-established post-positivist and neo-rationalist theories of knowledge – together with the conceptions of reason, epistemic agency, objectivity, experience and knowledge itself that comprise their core – tacitly draw their conceptual and theoretical apparatus from an idealized view of the knowledge produced and validated by the (male) occupants of the dominant social, political and economic positions in white Western societies. The consequent distribution of epistemic authority perpetuates a hierarchical order in which women and other 'others' occupy the least authoritative positions. Eschewing traditional a priori approaches with their normative goal of determining what an ideal knower ought to do, feminists are producing critical and self-critical analyses of what variously embodied, historically and materially 'situated' knowers (in Donna Haraway's (1991) phrase) actually do, deriving normative conclusions from critical-constructive readings of epistemic practice.

The dominant epistemologies of modernity, as they have developed out of the Enlightenment with a later infusion of positivist-empiricist principles, have defined themselves around ideals of objectivity and value-neutrality. Ideal objectivity, in post-positivist times, has come to mean a detached, neutral and disinterested approach to a subject matter that exists in a publicly observable space, separate from knowers/ observers and making no personal claims on them. Value-neutrality elaborates this disinterested aspect to insist that knowers must have no vested interest in the object of knowledge and are responsible only to the evidence. Such ideals are best suited to govern evaluations of the knowledge claims of persons whose situations allow them to assume that theirs is a 'view from nowhere', that through the autonomous exercise of their reason they can transcend particularity and contingency and the accidents of gendered embodiment. Such persons have usually tended, within the social arrangements of affluent Western societies, to be white and male, though the specificity of their identity and circumstances are usually effaced in their self-presentation as 'representative' human subjects.

Ideals of Reason, both in theories of knowledge, and in their trickle-down effects in everyday discourse, have been consistent even across centuries of historical variation in yielding a regulative conception of rationality in which, as Genevieve Lloyd ([1984] 1993) has shown, traits, values and activities commonly associated with 'the feminine' are systematically suppressed. Analogously, feminists such as Evelyn Fox Keller (1985) and Susan Bordo (1987) have shown that the psychosocial characteristics that affluent, white, male children in such societies have commonly been nurtured to embody have been just those that prepare them for a lifetime of detached, objective control in everyday and scientific knowledge-seeking, and in a public world of work and deliberation. Instrumental reason and a science-derived ideal of knowledge have shaped conceptions of good epistemic practice, with consequences that are often exclusionary not just of women's knowledge, but of the knowledgeable activities of other marginalized people. The point is not that women and other 'others' cannot emulate the ideal, but rather (as Lloyd has shown) that the symbolisms out of which the ideal acquires its (historically mutable) content work simultaneously to validate the knowledge and epistemic status of would-be knowers whose socioculturally fostered character traits coincide with the ideal, and to suppress those whose subjectivities are differently produced. In short, feminist genealogies and deconstructions of these ideals have shown that, despite their proclaimed neutrality, they derive from, naturalize and normalize the experiences and social positions of privileged European men and their (male) descendants.

No simple taxonomy of feminist epistemologies classified as distinct or self-contained categories could present an accurate, state-of-the-art picture of these ongoing projects. Yet certain strands run through them, sometimes separately but usually intertwined. Here I elaborate the principal features of an empiricist strand in feminist theories of knowledge, of standpoint positions, and of genealogical and interpretive practices (see FEMINISM AND SOCIAL SCIENCE; GENDER AND SCIENCE §§1–2, 6).

2 Feminism and empiricism

The relationship between feminism and empiricism, both classical and post-positivist, has been uneasy. Feminists have to work with empirical evidence if they are to move knowledgeably about the physical world and engage effectively with the social, political and 'natural' realities that sustain hierarchical social structures. Yet, classical and many contemporary versions of empiricism are constructed around assumptions that are inimical to feminist emancipatory projects (see EMPIRICISM). They are as androcentered as the liberal moral-political theories that they inform (see LIBERALISM). A woman can claim space within them only in so far as she is prepared and able to be 'more like a man' – that is to say, a privileged, able-bodied white man.

It is with the abstract individualism of empiricist orthodoxy, and its residues within everyday conceptions of knowledge in Anglo-American societies, that many feminists take issue. Individualist assumptions yield a picture of knowers as interchangeable in their autonomous epistemic projects, where they are at once sceptical of testimony and unswayed by emotion. Such knowers are 'individuals' in their placeholder status as units of analysis, yet they are never individuated. Correlatively, knowledge is objective, universally valid, available impartially and indiscriminately to everyone in identical observation conditions; and observation often reduces to simple, atomic givens, reportable in discrete propositions of the form '*S* knows that *p*' ('Sara knows that it is raining'). The apolitical character of such utterances, together with their paradigm (and often foundational) status in theories of knowledge, generates an assumption that all knowledge claims worthy of the title will be equivalently apolitical; and that propositional knowledge alone merits the (honorific) title 'knowledge'.

Yet many classical versions of empiricism and their latter-day analogues come apart around a paradox: for all their alleged grounding in experience, that experience is itself an abstraction. Orthodox empiricists are not equipped, conceptually or theoretically, to deal with real, idiosyncratic, specifically located experiences. Historical, gendered, locational differences reduce to bias, aberration, errors, to be eradicated and thence discounted in justificatory procedures. When empiricist claims are upheld within social-political structures that deploy a rhetoric of formal equality, yet depend upon structural inequalities to maintain themselves (as do liberal, capitalist societies), the elusiveness of their democratic egalitarianism is apparent. None the less, committed to eradicating uneven distributions of epistemic power and privilege – where gendered unevenness always intersects with the unevenness of race, class, ethnicity and other disprivileged locations – feminists have drawn, albeit critically and selectively, on the resources of many of these same theories to enlist them in transformative and emancipatory projects.

For feminist empiricists, then, the goal of inquiry, both secular and scientific, is to produce knowledge that is neither androcentric nor marked by sexist, racist, classist or other biases. They contend that an unabashedly value-laden yet rigorous empiricism can yield more adequate knowledge than methods whose practitioners are ignorant of their specificity, and of their complicity in a sex/gender system, can yield. Objectivity, in these feminist projects, is disconnected from the universalist assumptions on which analyses of knowledge 'in general' depend, and reconfigured around a requirement to take the subjectivity of the inquirers as seriously into account as the objects of inquiry. Thus for feminist empiricists, investigators cannot function as anonymous, isolated and silent spectators. They become answerable for their interventions and epistemic negotiations, as much to the epistemic community as to the evidence; and details about an inquirer's epistemic location and interests are likewise subject to empirical scrutiny. The central idea is that politically-informed inquiry fosters a better empiricism, and what Sandra Harding (1991) calls a 'strong objectivity' that is more objective than an objectivity that defines itself by bypassing the conditions of its own possibility.

According to Lynn Nelson (1990), Quinean empiricism demands neither the stark individualism nor the theory-neutrality of the classical theories; hence it lends itself to feminist reconstructions in which communities, not individuals, are knowers and knowledge claims are entangled in and shaped by webs of belief, testable always against (communal) experience (see QUINE, W.V. §2). For Nelson, communities are knowers in a strong sense, for which 'individual' experience and knowledge are possible only within a community. The point recalls Wittgenstein's private language argument: it amounts to a contention that there could be no knowledge, no appropriately justified beliefs, without communal standards of justification and critique (see PRIVATE LANGUAGE ARGUMENT). In a radical rereading of Quinean 'naturalized' epistemology, Nelson finds a rich resource for feminist successor epistemology projects (see NATURALIZED EPISTEMOLOGY). Departing from preoccupations with determining whether knowledge is possible, naturalized epistemologies start from an assumption that people can and do have knowledge.

Appealing to scientific psychology, they abandon transcendence to examine how people actually know, individually and socially. Yet because they adhere to principles of empirical objectivity and retain a realist commitment to 'the evidence', they are effective in producing reliable knowledge of the physical and social world. For Nelson, the value of these inquiries for feminist epistemologies depends on their being 'socialized' to focus on questions about how knowledge is made and adjudicated in gender-inflected social groups. Lorraine Code argues that it also depends on their taking an appropriately critical stance towards residues of a positivistic orthodoxy that informs much of present-day cognitive psychology, with the individualistic, tacitly masculine conception of 'human nature' it often presupposes. Jane Duran (1991) contests that conception by advocating a justificatory approach that is both naturalized and gynocentric, appealing to 'essentially feminine' principles. Object relations theory, psychoanalysis read through French feminist theory, and cognitive science will inform its studies of how gendered knowers are psychologically produced and reproduced, she maintains.

In the contextual empiricism that Helen Longino (1990) elaborates, evidential reasoning is context-dependent, and data count as evidence only in relation to background assumptions and hypotheses. Knowledge construction is a thoroughly social practice; hence acknowledging the constitutive role of values and ideology in inquiry does not require an indiscriminate tolerance of individual subjective preferences. Objectivity is ensured by high standards of social criticism, which all epistemic products must satisfy. Such criticism can unmask androcentricity and other 'centricities' even in 'good' science and inquiry, even from an admittedly interested position that is at once open to scrutiny and rigorously committed to working within the limits and multiple possibilities of empirical evidence.

Lorraine Code's position is residually empiricist in its realism. Yet it departs from canonical versions of empiricism in its conception of socially constructed and interactive subjectivities, located and enacted within uneven structures of power and privilege; and in situating issues of responsibility firmly within epistemological inquiry. Here the monologic individualism of post-positivist theories gives way to a picture of situated, socially embedded knowers conducting epistemic negotiations across the multiply configured rhetorical spaces of the social-political world. Code proposes that knowing other people is as exemplary an epistemic activity as knowing medium-sized physical objects, and that testimony is as crucial a source of knowledge as perception and memory. She advocates an ecologically modelled epistemology that draws on narrative analyses to position human knowing within interconnected systems of social, natural and other environmental relations.

3 Standpoints, interpretations, genealogies

Feminist standpoint theorists such as Patricia Hill Collins, Sandra Harding, Nancy Hartsock and Hilary Rose contend that neither orthodox nor feminist empiricists can adequately address the historical and material conditions that produce both epistemic agency and knowledge itself. Because the authoritative, standard-setting knowledge in western societies is derived from and tested against the social experiences and material circumstances of white, middle-class, educated men, women (like the proletariat of Marxist theory) are oppressed in marginal, underclass epistemic positions. Science as practice has created an esoteric discourse to which few women and non-white men gain ready access. It explains their limited success with 'scientifically proven facts' about their natural intellectual inferiority: facts that have been established by a methodology not explicitly designed to oppress, but whose oppressive consequences are manifold. Yet it is possible to transform oppression into epistemic advantage. Just as Marxist inquiry started from within the lives of the proletariat to produce historically-materially located analyses that offered a sharply focused lens through which to inspect the social system as a whole, shorn of its naturalistic ideology, so starting from the diverse and often contradictory lives of women casts a critical frame around taken-for-granted epistemic hierarchies and practices of disempowerment. Collins (1990) claims, for example, that a Black feminist standpoint rooted in the everyday experiences of African-American women resonates with the epistemologies of subordinate groups in a multitude of disparate locations. It 'makes strange' the taken-for-granted practices of rejecting concrete experiences and testimony in favour of standardized abstractions, and it values wisdom over knowledge more conventionally (propositionally) conceived. And Rose (1983, 1994) maintains that an epistemology that bypasses the hands-on, affectively engaged labour that attests to a profound knowledge of the nature of things cannot hope to be adequate to the knowledge that enables people to work and live well.

A standpoint is more than merely a perspective, one among many. It is an achieved intellectual and embodied political position, forged out of painstaking analyses of the systems that legitimate oppressive practices, and firmly located *in media res*. Standpoints are neither guaranteed innocence, nor are they immune from criticism: their affinities with the consciousness-raising practices of the 1970s work to preserve a critical interpretive stance for which even first-person experiential claims have often to be interrogated, albeit responsibly, in mutually respectful debate.

Some critics claim that because there is no single, unified feminist position, standpoint theory obliterates differences and hence fails by its own feminist standards. Others argue that its 'locatedness' merely produces a perspective that is as limited as any other. Yet few self-identified standpoint theorists would assume that there can be a single privileged speaking position or one unified epistemic voice. Because they work from within the specificities of women's lives and are resistant to the reductivism that obliterates lived, practical differences, they take limitation and partial perspective as facts within which epistemologies must be produced, not as obstacles they must seek to overcome. Points of commonality from one material, embodied location to another produce sites of feminist solidarity and opportunities for strategic coalition-building; points of difference confirm the necessity of ongoing critical negotiation.

In the interpretive and genealogical projects of postmodernity, feminists such as Linda Alcoff and Susan Hekman have found critical-constructive tools that work sometimes in concert with empiricist and standpoint theories, sometimes in tension with them. Interpretive strategies, with their origins in Gadamerian hermeneutics, contest any claim to the effect that experience, evidence or texts speak for themselves (see GADAMER, H.-G.). It is philosophy's task to interpret the cultural-historical prejudgments out of which knowledge necessarily comes into being: prejudgments which are neither pernicious nor escapable, but which have to be confronted if the knowledge that they inform is to be adequate. Hekman (1990), for example, argues that all knowledge is interpretive; and Alcoff (1996) proposes a coherentist, 'immanent epistemology' that contrasts with transcendent, observational theories of knowledge in revealing connections between power-infused political issues and epistemic justification.

Genealogical inquiry, with its Nietzschean origins and later Foucauldian elaborations, situates knowledge-production within historically changing structures of power, maintaining the radical contingency of currently hegemonic modes of understanding, legitimating, and establishing knowledge claims (see GENEALOGY). Some theorists, such as Kathy Ferguson, see a tension between interpretation with its presumed quest for one true original meaning, and genealogy with its commitment to unearthing a multiplicity of meanings which gain hegemonic status through complex power structures and strategies.

Again, some self-identified feminist empiricists and/or standpoint theorists resist making common cause with these postmodern projects because they fear that such resistance to totalizing, stabilizing theory initiates a slide into a pernicious form of relativism. Others, such as Haraway, Code and Alcoff, see interpretation and genealogy as mutually informative; they draw on these strategies from within feminist inquiries that resist exclusive alignment with any single category or strand.

In their concentration on the real-world effects of knowledge-making within a community of inquirers, many of these feminist positions demonstrate affinities with the epistemological preoccupations that Charlene Siegfried discerns in the thought of the American pragmatists. Siegfried (1996) shows how feminism and pragmatism might make common cause as social movements inspired by the emancipatory potential of the everyday experiences of real, embodied and active knowers.

4 Implications

If feminist critiques are taken seriously, then epistemologists cannot assume that 'reason is alike in all men'; nor can they represent knowers as mere place-holders in an infinitely replicable process, whose minds convert information, mechanically and indifferently, into knowledge. Many of the dichotomies around which Western philosophy has been built are pulled apart under feminist scrutiny. Feminists have shown that such hierarchically ordered pairs as reason/emotion, mind/body, abstract/concrete, objective/subjective, theory/praxis, universal/particular – and of course male/female – with their persistent veneration of the first and devaluation of the second term, have sustained conceptions of knowledge and subjectivity that are neither dictated by natural necessity, nor exhaustive of the available options. Knowledge is as much body-dependent as it is mind-dependent; fostered as much by well-schooled emotions as by a well-honed reason; at once subjective and objective; its universal and abstract claims are only as good as their concrete and particular manifestations allow. Working across the territory opened out by the revealed instability of these dichotomies, feminists have resituated knowledge-constructing practices within human lives. They have reclaimed testimony as a source of knowledge as valuable (and as fallible) as perception and memory (see TESTIMONY); and have challenged the divide that is often thought to separate 'knowing how', 'folk wisdom', and narrative knowledge from 'knowledge properly so called'. Feminists have demonstrated the effectiveness of dialogic, negotiated epistemic deliberation and the integrity of local knowledge, contrasted with monologic or reductive pronouncements and projects designed to affirm the unity of science. Feminists are not alone in articulating these challenges: neo-pragmatists, deconstructionists and hermeneuticists, naturalistic epistemologists, Marxists, narrative theorists and reassessors of relativism, to mention only a few, often make good scholarly allies (see COGNITIVE PLURALISM; EPISTEMIC RELATIVISM). But few of their projects are explicitly gender-sensitive to the extent that feminist inquiry has to be: hence feminist voices cannot simply speak in chorus with these other voices. Theirs are distinctive, and often necessarily dissident, speaking parts.

None the less, most late-twentieth-century feminists resist affirming simplistic, across-the-board alignments, say of men with objectivist, distanced, positivistic, scientific methods and women with subjectivist, connected, interpretive, non-scientific methods. Nor do they opt for an essentialism that would identify quantitative methodologies as male, qualitative ones as female; positivism as male, interpretation as female. Few would endorse a wholesale science-bashing that smacks more of ideological excess than of a genuine quest for knowledge. Even feminists who are wary of the oppressive effects of scientific and other authoritative knowledge rely upon its (intermittent) successes. Yet feminists are also convinced, on good evidence across a range of disciplines and areas of inquiry, that feminist research makes a difference. Hence questions about 'method', which are central to feminist epistemological debates become, in effect, questions about what difference feminism makes, and how. Its answers come from as many directions as there are epistemic practices. They are not reducible to a single, closed set of ideals and principles, for the era of theoretical and methodological monotheism has passed. But they provide nodal points for ongoing deliberation and active engagement with social and material issues.

See also: FEMINISM AND PSYCHOANALYSIS; FEMINIST POLITICAL PHILOSOPHY

References and further reading

* Alcoff, L. (1996) *Real Knowing: New Versions of the Coherence Theory*, Ithaca, NY: Cornell University Press. (Breaks down the analytic–continental divide in a normative epistemology that takes power and desire as epistemically salient.)

Alcoff, L. and Potter, E. (eds) (1993) *Feminist Epistemologies*, New York: Routledge. (Elaborations and refinements of most of the principal approaches to feminist epistemology in the early 1990s.)

Antony, L. and Witt, C. (eds) (1993) *A Mind of One's Own: Feminist Essays on Reason and Objectivity*, Boulder, CO: Westview Press. (Critical responses to contentions that the domain of reason is masculine.)

* Bordo, S. (1987) *The Flight to Objectivity: Essays on Cartesianism and Culture*, Albany, NY: State University of New York Press. (A psycho-historical reading of the development of the role of Cartesian doubt in modern philosophy.)

Code, L. (1987) *Epistemic Responsibility*, Hanover, NH: University Press of New England. (Discussion of responsibility issues in epistemic communities.)

—— (1991) *What Can She Know? Feminist Theory and the Construction of Knowledge*, Ithaca, NY: Cornell University Press. (Analysis of the androcentric character of traditional epistemologies, an examination of the politics of knowledge, and a sketch of new directions for theory of knowledge.)

—— (1995) *Rhetorical Spaces: Essays on (Gendered) Locations*, New York: Routledge. (Addresses questions about testimony, empathy, knowing other people, and epistemic authority in specific, power-infused situations.)

Collins, P.H. (1990) *Black Feminist Thought: Knowledge, Consciousness, and the Politics of Empowerment*, London: HarperCollins. (Analysis of the social construction of Black feminist thought and of Black feminist standpoint epistemology.)

* Duran, J. (1991) *Toward a Feminist Epistemology*, Savage, MD: Rowman & Littlefield. (A discussion of the resources of 'naturalized' epistemology and a proposal for a gynocentric epistemics.)

Ferguson, K. (1993) *The Man Question: Visions of Subjectivity in Feminist Theory*, Berkeley, CA: University of California Press. (Critical reading of interpretive and genealogical strategies.)

* Haraway, D. (1991) 'Situated Knowledges: The Science Question in Feminism and the Privilege of Partial Perspective', in *Simians, Cyborgs and Women: The Reinvention of Nature*, New York: Routledge. (Argues for an embodied, specifically situated, critical feminist approach to knowledge questions.)

Harding, S. (1986) *The Science Question in Feminism*, Ithaca, NY: Cornell University Press. (Classifies feminist epistemologies as empiricist, standpoint, and postmodern.)

—— (1991) *Whose Science? Whose Knowledge? Thinking from Women's Lives*, Ithaca, NY: Cornell University Press. (Elaborates a conception of strong objectivity, and refines the 1986 account of standpoint theory.)

Hartsock, N. (1983) *Money, Sex, and Power: Toward a Feminist Historical Materialism*, Boston, MA: Northeastern University Press. (Develops a standpoint epistemology from a Marxist starting point.)

Harvey, E. and Okruhlik, K. (eds) (1992) *Women and Reason*, Ann Arbor, MI: University of Michigan Press. (Critical feminist rereadings of Western ideals of reason and rationality.)

* Hekman, S. (1990) *Gender and Knowledge: Elements of a Postmodern Feminism*, Boston, MA: Northeastern University Press. (Advocates a postmodern, deconstructive and genealogical epistemological approach.)

Keller, E.F. (1985) *Reflections on Gender and Science*, New Haven, CT: Yale University Press. (Exposes the masculine assumptions in the history of western science.)

Lennon, K. and Whitford, M. (eds) (1994) *Knowing the Difference*, London: Routledge. (Postmodern essays on feminism and epistemological questions.)

* Lloyd, G. (1984) *The Man of Reason: 'Male' and 'Female' in Western Philosophy*, Minneapolis, MN: University of Minnesota Press; 2nd edn, 1993. (Traces the symbolisms that construct dominant conceptions of reason and masculinity throughout the history of western philosophy.)

* Longino, H. (1990) *Science As Social Knowledge*, Princeton, NJ: Princeton University Press. (Shows that background assumptions shape scientific knowledge, and that communities are the principal knowers.)

* Nelson, L.H. (1990) *Who Knows: From Quine to a Feminist Empiricism*, Philadelphia, PA: Temple University Press. (Argues that Quinean empiricism is a valuable resource for a feminist-informed empiricism in which communities are the primary knowers.)

* Rose, H. (1983) 'Hand, Brain and Heart: A Feminist Epistemology for the Natural Sciences', *Signs: Journal of Women in Culture and Society* 9 (1): 73–90. (Argues for a praxis-based feminist standpoint approach to knowledge issues.)

* —— (1994) *Love, Power and Knowledge: Towards a Feminist Transformation of The Sciences*, Cambridge: Polity Press. (Expands and elaborates standpoint theory.)

* Seigfried, C.H. (1996) *Pragmatism and Feminism: Reweaving the Social Fabric*, Chicago, IL: University of Chicago Press. (Sets up a dialogue between American pragmatism and feminist epistemology.)

LORRAINE CODE

FEMINIST ETHICS

Critics greet feminist ethics with suspicion, alleging that it is biased towards the interests of women. Feminist ethicists reply that it is traditional ethics which is biased. As they see it, for centuries traditional ethicists claimed to speak for all of humanity, when they were speaking only or primarily for men, and the most privileged of men at that. In contrast, although feminist ethicists openly admit that they proceed from the perspective of women's experience, their paramount goal is simply to reconstruct traditional ethics so that it becomes more universal and objective by including women's as well as men's moral voices.

Far from being monolithic, feminist ethics encompasses a wide variety of woman-centred approaches to the moral life. Feminine *approaches to ethics, with their stress on personal relationships and an ethics of care, put a premium on the value of human connection.* Maternal *approaches focus on one relationship in particular, that between mothers and children, as the paradigm for moral interaction.* Lesbian *approaches stress choice rather than duty, aiming to define the conditions in which lesbian women can flourish. Finally, specifically* feminist *approaches to ethics emphasize the political task of eliminating systems and structures of male domination and female subordination in both the public and the private domains.*

1 **Feminine ethics**
2 **Maternal ethics**
3 **Lesbian ethics**
4 **Feminist ethics**

1 Feminine ethics

Woman-centred approaches to ethics, as well as debates about gender and morality, are hardly new. Thinkers like Mary WOLLSTONECRAFT, John Stuart MILL, Harriet TAYLOR , Catherine Beecher, Charlotte Perkins Gilman, Elizabeth Cady Stanton and others considered the 'woman question' in the eighteenth and nineteenth centuries. They asked whether morality is gendered, and whether moral and psychological traits come from culture or biology. Such thinkers paved the way for twentieth-century debate about whether women's biology and maternal experience predispose them to espouse an ethics of care, while men's biology and public experiences predispose them to espouse an ethics of justice.

For centuries, men wrote most of the great books of ethics, speaking, as might be expected, from a male perspective. The response of those developing feminine approaches to ethics has been to offer the traditionally 'feminine' characteristics of care, com-passion, benevolence, nurturing and kindness as no less morally significant than the traditionally 'masculine' characteristics of rationality, justice and independence. Among others, psychologist Carol Gilligan (1982) has claimed that women, for whatever reasons, tend to speak in a voice of care that focuses on concrete relationships, rather than in a voice of justice that focuses on abstract rules (see VIRTUE ETHICS §6). In the personal narratives of women contemplating abortion, for example, Gilligan heard more concerns expressed about the personal and professional needs of particular people than about a foetus' right to life or a woman's right to choose. Although Gilligan denies that she regards women's and men's respective moralities as decidedly separate, many of her critics still view her approach to morality not only as a deeply gendered ethics, but also as a highly femininized ethics meant to counter the supposedly 'masculinist' morality of psychologist Lawrence Kohlberg.

Kohlberg, who mentored Gilligan early in her career, constructed a six-stage scale of moral development: while men tend to ascend to at least stage five on this ladder, 'the social contract legalistic orientation', women tend to stop at stage three, 'the interpersonal concordance of "good boy-nice girl" orientation' (1971: 164–5). Doubting that women are in any way men's moral inferiors, Gilligan hypothesized that women did poorly on Kohlberg's scale simply because it was calibrated to gauge male, rather than human moral development. As such, she proclaimed it an inappropriate scale for judging female moral development. Whereas men typically interpret their greater independence and reliance on an ethics of justice as signs of their moral growth, Gilligan speculated that women tend to regard their greater interdependence and reliance on an ethics of care as signs of their moral growth (see MORAL DEVELOPMENT; MORAL EDUCATION §1).

Nell Noddings' relational ethics is another example of a 'feminine' approach to ethics. In any good human relationship, says Noddings (1984), there is the 'one-caring' and the 'cared-for'. The one-caring should engross themselves in the cared-for, focusing on their needs, actions and thoughts. In return, the cared-for should welcome the one-caring's attention and willingly share their own needs, hopes and accomplishments with the one-caring. Noddings believes that caring consists more in specific obligations to particular people than in general duties to human kind. Concrete actions, far more than abstract intentions, define real caring.

There is reason to suspect, however, that Noddings – like Gilligan – makes caring the special province of women. Although Noddings claims that caring should be the responsibility of all humans, in most of her examples the carers are women, some of whom push their acts of caring to the point where their own identity, needs, and even existence are sacrificed. Thus, many critics fault Noddings as well as Gilligan for over-stressing women's role as carers. As Sheila Mullett points out (1988), since equality of care between men and women is unlikely in a still patriarchal society, caring remains dangerous for women. Until full social, political and psychological equality between the sexes exists, men will be inclined to let women take care of them without reciprocating the favour.

2   Maternal ethics

Critics also express reservations about maternal ethics, another feminine approach to ethics. Virginia Held (1993), Caroline Whitbeck (1974/5) and Sara Ruddick (1980) all offer a good mother–child relationship as a promising paradigm for any relationship. They find the traditional rational-contractor model inadequate (see CONTRACTARIANISM). After all, most human connection and interaction does not take place between equally autonomous, powerful and informed adults (typically men). Instead it occurs between unequals, such as parent–child, student–professor, professional–client, doctor–patient, and employer–worker. Therefore, a caring, although unequal, mother–child relationship provides a normative standard for the assessment of relationships that are inevitably imbalanced. Presumably, mothers have their children's best interests at heart. They try to protect and teach them, and make them socially acceptable and successful. In the process, they teach both themselves and their children to be sensitive, responsible people, aware of others' needs (Ruddick 1984) (see FAMILY, ETHICS AND THE §5).

Both feminists and non-feminists challenge maternal approaches to ethics, however. Non-feminist critics object to using one relationship in particular as a moral paradigm for all relationships in general, especially a relationship that seems to exclude all men and non-reproducing women. Feminist critics also challenge the adequacy of the mother–child relationship. As they see it, in a patriarchal society, mothers are already laden with guilt, expectations and demands. They doubt that anyone, but especially women, should seek to emulate the all-sacrificing mother who denies her own needs to serve those of her child. Instead people should pattern their relationships on a good friendship relationship (see FRIENDSHIP). Like the mother–child paradigm, a friendship paradigm rings truer with our moral experience than the abstract rational-contractor relationship; unlike

the mother–child paradigm, however, it comes closer to signalling the kind of give-and-take only equals can achieve.

3   Lesbian ethics

The women-centred approach to ethics most specifically tailored for women is clearly the lesbian one. Lesbian ethicists focus unapologetically not simply on women, but on women-loving women. Lesbian approaches are varied and complex, and generalizations are difficult, but most lesbian approaches seem to replace the traditional moral question, 'Is this action good?' with, 'Does this action help my quest for freedom and self-identity?' Although lesbian ethicists stress choice rather than duty, they are not relativists (see DUTY; MORAL RELATIVISM). As Sarah Lucia Hoagland asserts (1988), lesbian ethics concerns community: when a lesbian chooses for herself, she chooses for other lesbians, and those lesbians in turn will choose for her. Ethics, on this view, involves not an individual lesbian doing what she believes is absolutely right, but a community of lesbians weaving moral values together. Moral value and meaning is born and sustained in the spaces between oneself and others. Lesbian ethicists seek to become persons 'who are not accustomed to participating in relationships of domination and subordination' (1988: 241), but who are 'playful' beings with 'the ability to travel in and out of each other's world' (Lugones 1987: 13). To the degree that lesbians learn to move among and delight in a variety of worldviews, they lose interest in using ethics as what Hoagland has termed a 'tool of control' (1988: 246).

4   Feminist ethics

What makes specifically feminist approaches to ethics different? The answer is their strong emphasis on politics. Susan Sherwin aptly comments that a feminist approach to ethics 'applies a specifically political perspective and offers suggestions for how ethics must be revised if it is to get at the patterns of dominance and oppression as they affect women' (1992: 42). Feminist ethicists focus not so much on goodness as on power. They emphasize the ways in which traditional approaches to ethics maintain a status quo oppressive to women.

Many feminists discuss ways in which traditional ethics support women's subordination. Alison Jaggar, for example, discusses five specific ways in which this occurs, in her essay, *Feminist Ethics* (1992). First, traditional ethics focuses on men's rights and interests at the expense of women's. Indeed, traditional ethics has even encouraged women to develop supposed 'virtues' like patience and self-sacrifice that tend to further women's subordination. Second, traditional ethics justifies its neglect of women's interests by claiming that important moral questions rarely arise in women's world, the domestic sphere. Thus, women's double-workday, reproductive burdens, and sexual vulnerabilities, for example, are often dismissed as 'private' matters of little genuine moral significance. Third, traditional ethics often adds insult to injury by alleging that women are men's moral inferiors. Since the time of Aristotle and Plato, to Freud and the present day, (male) philosophers have described women as capable of only limited moral thought and action. Fourth, traditional ethics tends to overrate traditionally masculine traits such as 'independence, autonomy, intellect, will, wariness, hierarchy, domination, culture, transcendence, product, asceticism, war, death', and to undervalue traditionally feminine traits, such as 'interdependence, community, connection, sharing, emotion, body, trust, absence of hierarchy, nature, immanence, process, joy, peace and life' (Jaggar 1992: 364). Finally, traditional ethics tends to employ a 'masculine' way of thinking characterized by rules, abstraction, and impartiality, eschewing 'feminine' ways of thinking as 'emotional', rooted as they are in relationships, particularity, and partiality.

As a remedy for the sexism in traditional ethics, Jaggar suggests a feminist approach to ethics that does at least the following: (1) begins by acknowledging that men and women have different experiences and situations in life; (2) provides guides to action 'that will tend to subvert rather than reinforce the present systematic subordination of women'; (3) offers action guides and approaches to handle issues in both the public and the private realms; and (4) 'takes the moral experience of all women seriously, though not, of course, uncritically' (Jaggar 1992: 366). Thus, feminist approaches to ethics – unlike feminine and maternal approaches – do not call upon women to become exemplary carers. Nor do they, like lesbian approaches, ask women to develop meaning and value only for women-loving women. Instead, feminist approaches call upon women *and* men to overcome gender inequality and oppression. Therefore, they offer something of value to all human beings – for care, justice, and moral value can flourish only in a truly equal and balanced world.

See also: FEMINISM; FEMINIST EPISTEMOLOGY; FEMINIST JURISPRUDENCE; FEMINIST POLITICAL PHILOSOPHY; NURSING ETHICS; SEXUALITY, PHILOSOPHY OF

References and further reading

* Gilligan, C. (1982) *In a Different Voice: Psychological Theory and Women's Development*, Cambridge, MA: Harvard University Press, 76–92. (Claims that, on the average, and for a variety of cultural reasons, women tend to espouse an ethics of care that stresses relationships and responsibilities, whereas men tend to espouse an ethics of justice that stresses rules and rights.)
* Held, V. (1993) *Feminist Morality: Transforming Culture, Society, and Politics*, Chicago, IL: University of Chicago Press. (Argues that society would be more moral if the ideal of the 'autonomous man' were replaced with the ideal of the 'relational woman'.)
* Hoagland, S.L. (1988) *Lesbian Ethics*. Palo Alto, CA: Institute of Lesbian Studies. (Argues that choice, not duty, is the basis of lesbian ethics.)
* Jaggar, A.M. (1992) 'Feminist Ethics', in L. Becker and C. Becker (eds) *Encyclopedia of Ethics*, Lawrence, KS: University Press of Kansas. (Identifies the necessary conditions for a feminist ethics.)
* Kohlberg, L. (1971) 'From Is to Ought: How to Commit the Naturalistic Fallacy and Get Away With It in the Study of Moral Development', in T. Mischel (ed.) *Cognitive Development and Epistemology*, New York: Academic Press, 164–5. (Proposes a six-stage interpretation of moral development, which is taken to be universal, invariant and hierarchical.)
* Lugones, M. (1987) 'Playfulness, "World"-Travelling, and Loving Perception', *Hypatia* 2: 13. (Argues that we cannot be moral unless we are willing to see reality through eyes different from our own.)
* Mullett, S. (1988) 'Shifting Perspectives: A New Approach to Ethics', in L. Code, S. Mullett, C. Overall (eds) *Feminist Perspectives: Philosophical Essays on Method and Morals*, Toronto: University of Toronto, esp. 119. (Presents the moral agent as constructing a moral perspective within the context of a collective endeavour to transform an oppressive *status quo*.)
* Noddings, N. (1984) *Caring: A Feminine Approach to Ethics and Moral Education*, Berkeley, CA: University of California Press, esp. 9. (Argues that ethics concerns caring relationships between particular individuals.)
* Ruddick, S. (1980) 'Maternal Thinking', *Feminist Studies* 6 (2); shortened version repr. in J. Trebilcott (ed.) *Mothering: Essays in Feminist Theory*, Totowa, NJ: Rowman & Allanheld, 1983, 213–30. (Describes the three fundamental goals of maternal practice as being the preservation, growth, and making acceptable of children.)

* Sherwin, S. (1992) *No Longer Patient: Feminist Ethics and Health Care*, Philadelphia, PA: Temple University Press. (Shows how raising the 'woman question' makes a moral difference in the world of medicine.)

Tong, R. (1993) *Feminine and Feminist Ethics*, Belmont, CA: Wadsworth. (Explains the difference between a 'feminine' ethics of care and a 'feminist' ethic of power.)

* Whitbeck, C. (1974/5) 'The Maternal Instinct', *Philosophical Forum* 6 (2, 3); repr. in J. Trebilcott (ed.) *Mothering: Essays in Feminist Theory*, Totowa, NJ: Rowman & Allanheld, 1983, 185–98. (Suggests that men's and women's different biological experiences typically affect the intensity of their respective attachments to their children.)

ROSEMARIE TONG

FEMINIST JURISPRUDENCE

The diversity of feminist philosophy and theory is represented in feminist jurisprudence, but two models of feminist jurisprudence predominate: the parity model, according to which women should be given legal parity with men; and the transformative model, which proposes the transformation of male legal categories and concepts to address women's experiences. The parity model has also been identified by the terms 'the male monopoly of law', or 'law as male bias'. The transformative model has sometimes been equated with feminist jurisprudence per se, *sometimes more specifically with US feminist jurisprudence. The two models differ primarily in their response to the claim of liberal jurisprudence – a claim made by law itself – that law is a neutral, rational and fair institution which defends individual liberty and treats people equally. The models also differ over the analysis of rights, and over the place of feminist jurisprudence in the legal curriculum. Both models have been subjected to a subversionist critique of any form of feminist jurisprudence.*

The parity model supports the values of liberal jurisprudence as imputed to law, but identifies a discrepancy between those liberal values and legal practice, such that women are not accorded parity with men. It follows either that law must be persuaded to apply these standards more rigorously in the case of women or that liberal values must be revised to recognize gender as a source of social injustice. The objective is to give women genuine, as opposed to nominal, equal rights or, where their special social situation demands it, special rights. On this model, courses in feminist jurisprudence comprise what have come to be known as 'women and law' studies which generally promote the visibility of women in jurisprudence. These studies may include documentation of law's discrimination against women, analyses of law's male bias against women, and reviews of all liberal jurisprudence which omits reference to gender.

The transformative model also notes the discrepancy between the liberal values imputed to law and law's treatment of women but recognizes the limitations of attempting to close the gap between liberal jurisprudence and legal practice either by making law apply liberal principles more scrupulously in the area of gender or by revising liberal principles. Instead, feminists working with this model argue that liberal jurisprudence can make no impact on law's treatment of women so long as legal categories, such as crime or family law, and legal concepts, such as provocation or marriage, embody male norms and accordingly fail to address women's experiences. It follows that such legal categories and concepts must be transformed to address women's social position and experiences. In so far as rights discourse embodies male norms, it too must be transformed. On this view, courses in feminist jurisprudence comprise the transformation of broad legal categories and specific legal concepts so that they engage with the reality of women's lives.

The subversionist critique seeks to undermine both the parity model and the transformative model. This critique questions the value of feminist jurisprudence for feminist politics. The reason given is that to work within the paradigm of jurisprudence is to legitimate the strategy of recourse to law as the proper means of solving social problems, the very strategy which both the parity model and the transformative model have exposed as inadequate. The subversionist critique recommends instead that feminists subvert the paradigm of jurisprudence, if necessary by abstaining from engagement with it. The use of rights discourse becomes a tactical calculation, and the inclusion of feminist jurisprudence in the law curriculum is a dubious strategy for feminists. The subversionist critique has been criticized in its turn for undervaluing the achievements of liberal legal systems and liberal jurisprudence.

1   The parity model
2   The transformative model
3   The subversionist critique

1   The parity model

Central to the parity model of feminist jurisprudence is the theory of law as an institution for the defence of individual liberty and the resolution of disputes between individuals which upholds the values of neutrality, rationality and fairness, all individuals being equal before the law. This doctrine is fundamental to law's conception of itself, as expressed in the ideology of the rule of law, and it provides the rationale for the introduction of equality legislation, such as anti-discrimination and equal pay legislation. It is also typical of contemporary jurisprudence dedicated to the development of liberal theories of justice. For example, Rawls (1972) is a major exponent of the liberal jurisprudential doctrine of justice as fairness. Similarly, Dworkin (1978) is concerned to develop a jurisprudence according to which all people have the fundamental right to be treated as equals (see DWORKIN, R.; RAWLS, J. §1).

The parity model of feminist jurisprudence subscribes to such liberal doctrines, but identifies a discrepancy between liberal principles and legal practice such that, in failing to uphold the values of neutrality, rationality, fairness, and liberty and equality in their treatment of women, neither the law nor contemporary liberal jurisprudence ascribes parity to women (see LAW AND MORALITY §2). The parity model offers two main types of argument to support that claim: the socio-legal and the philosophical.

First, Sachs and Wilson (1978) have amassed a wealth of socio-legal materials to show that the law has systematically operated as a male monopoly. They examine the 'persons' cases in the UK and the 'monopoly cases' in the USA, which focus on the law's resistance to extending the category of the legal person to include women. They argue that, through the biased use of judicial discretion, the judiciary has pursued male interests in maintaining obstacles to women's entry into public spheres of citizenship and the professions, notably medicine and law.

The work of Sachs and Wilson has provided the impetus for many similar socio-legal studies revealing the discrepancy between anti-discrimination legislation, such as the principle of equal pay for work of equal value, and the actual benefits experienced by women (see DISCRIMINATION). Feminists have identified sex stereotyping as a key mechanism for maintaining this discrepancy. For example, Atkins and Hoggett (1984) argue that the law has consistently worked on the assumption that women are primarily dependent on men, and that their lives are defined by their domestic and sexual roles. These socio-legal materials are the basis for the parity model's claim that, in its failure to uphold its own proclaimed values of equality and neutrality, the law continually fails to accord parity to women.

Here, the parity model urges ever more vigilance in the pursuit of genuine equality for women and their unbiased treatment in legal practice. The strategies include general vigilance for discrepancy between law's stated values and intentions and its actual practice in relation to women, political pressure for improved anti-discrimination legislation, the introduction of gender issues into legal education, and reform of the judiciary and parliament so that women's issues are given greater recognition.

Second, feminist philosophers have challenged liberal jurisprudence for its articulation of the values of liberty and equality in ways which neglect the inferior social status of women. For example, Pateman (1988) has criticized Rawls' theory of the social contract, in particular his use of the 'original position'. She argues that Rawls' attempt to justify our intuitions about contemporary society incorporates implicit but unjustifiable assumptions about gender and sexual relations, thereby obscuring 'the sexual contract' which provides the foundation of modern patriarchy and the political right of men over women. Similarly, Okin (1989) has pointed to the omission of family justice and gendered family structures from contemporary theories of social justice. This omission reinforces the notion of justice as a public virtue, and, in perpetuating women's exclusion from social justice, impedes progress towards a just and democratic society (see JUSTICE).

The parity model of feminist jurisprudence here requires revision of liberal jurisprudence so that the social significance of gender inequalities is given due recognition. Of particular importance is the need to extend the scope of liberal jurisprudence so that it is not restricted to the public sphere of social justice but extends also to the private sphere. By pointing to the limitations of liberal jurisprudence in this regard, feminists hope to undermine the assumption that the attribution of formal equality to women is sufficient to ensure that women enjoy material equality with men. Working within the parity model, feminists have identified the discrepancy between women's formal equality, for example in labour legislation, and their material inequality, for example through financial disadvantage incurred by their assumption of domestic and child-rearing responsibilities.

This concern with the neglect of the private sphere is typically expressed in terms of rights. For while the parity model accepts the claim of liberal jurisprudence that rights are the inalienable moral possessions of equal individuals, feminists have pointed out that many rights have not been fully enjoyed by women. While liberal jurisprudence articulates concepts of rights situated in the public sphere, such as civil rights, the parity model emphasizes rights which should be enjoyed in the private sphere, such as the right to protection against domestic violence (see PRIVACY §4).

A corollary of this view is scepticism about campaigns for women's rights expressed in terms of equal rights when these are inappropriate to women's social situation. Here supporters of the parity model argue that women need special rights in recognition of their different social position from men's, particularly in the sphere of reproductive rights and in the institution of the family. Yet there are difficulties in determining when special rights are more appropriate than equal rights. Accordingly, some feminists within the parity model have become disillusioned with the potentially divisive nature of rights and argue that rights discourse must be transcended in order to achieve the goals of a communitarian society in which persons can live as genuine equals with respect for their different talents (see RIGHTS).

On the parity model, courses in feminist jurisprudence comprise what has come to be known as 'women and law' work: cataloguing the failures of anti-discrimination law and equality legislation, the operation of male bias and sexist stereotypes (for example, in family law), the shortcomings of legislation and legal practice in the areas of abortion, rape and domestic violence, and exposure of the legal profession's exclusion of women. The parity model of feminist jurisprudence also includes the revision or adaptation of liberal jurisprudence to produce analyses which draw attention to gendered social institutions, such as the family, as major sources of social injustice.

The parity model has been subject to the criticism that the discrepancy between liberal principles and legal practice cannot be made good either by exhorting law to uphold them more scrupulously or by revising liberal principles. The reason given is that, by concentrating on the discrepancy between liberal principles and legal practice, and by giving prominence to 'women's issues', the parity model leaves intact existing categories of law, such as crime and family law, and existing concepts of law, such as provocation and marriage. These criticisms are more fully developed by feminists working within the framework of the transformative model of feminist jurisprudence.

2   The transformative model

The transformative model follows the parity model in noting the discrepancy between the liberal values imputed to law and law's actual treatment of women. But feminists working with the transformative model argue that the attempt to make good that discrepancy either by reforming legal practice or by amending liberal jurisprudence is doomed. The attempt is doomed because it leaves undisturbed broad legal categories and legal concepts which embody male norms and which consequently fail to address the

reality of women's social position and experiences. It follows that these legal categories and concepts must be transformed so as to address the concrete reality of women's lives. There are two main versions of the transformative model of feminist jurisprudence: the systematic and the thematic.

The systematic version is associated almost exclusively with the work of MacKinnon (1989). She argues that the legal manifestation of the liberal state is institutionalized male power based on male sexual dominance of women. She identifies two main ways in which law effects male domination. The first is by the eroticization of sexual abuse, so that legislation on rape, prostitution and obscenity is proposed ostensibly for the protection of women but works in practice to protect men's sexual power over women. The second is by law's claim to the standard of neutrality. Here MacKinnon argues that it is futile and dangerous for feminists to demand that law apply this standard. For this legal standard is itself male. Furthermore, the greater the *prima facie* neutrality of law – for example, in equality legislation governing paid work – the more effectively 'neutrality' works as a key mechanism for masking the law's defence of male domination, for example, by requiring women to fit into an economic system which denies them substantive equality.

For these reasons, MacKinnon believes that feminists have wrongly made their demands in terms of rights, whether equal or special, because the pursuit of rights requires women to aspire – in vain – to men's rights. Rights are little more than the expression of institutionalized male power. Consequently, MacKinnon advocates the development of a feminist jurisprudence, namely the systematic inversion of the complete and comprehensive institutionalization of male power and ideology, all derived from male sexuality. This feminist jurisprudence would have a central place in legal education.

Other feminists working with the transformative model, however, have reservations about the project of an exclusively feminist jurisprudence. They suspect that it is a form of essentialism, namely the view that masculine law and feminine law are discrete and unitary spheres. On this view, MacKinnon's feminist jurisprudence is essentialist because it theorizes women as the permanent victims of male sexual power. Instead, these feminists have advocated the development of thematic feminist jurisprudence through the strategic transformations of key areas of law. This exercise is characterized by two linked approaches: first, the transformation of legal categories; and second, the transformation of legal concepts.

Key exponents of the transformation of legal

categories are Graycar and Morgan (1990). They show how it is not possible to consult a traditional legal textbook for the collected legal rules and regulatory practices concerning, for example, domestic violence. Relevant material will be found in textbooks on criminal law, family law, housing and social security rules, tort law, and in some jurisdictions constitutional law. These classifications, however, are meaningless for women who experience domestic violence. They and their lawyers typically need to identify an immediate practical remedy, one which can be rapidly selected from a compendium of legal doctrines and rulings related specifically to domestic violence. Graycar and Morgan accordingly engage in a fundamental recategorization of law according to themes such as women's sources of financial income, legal responses to motherhood, and gendered injuries to women, such as rape.

The transformation of legal categories may well involve the transformation of specific legal concepts. For example, feminist scrutiny of criminal law from the point of view of women's experiences has focused on provocation as a partial defence open to women and men charged with murder. For the charge to be reduced to one of manslaughter, the accused needs to prove that the act of killing followed a sudden and temporary loss of control, such as might be experienced by a person goaded beyond endurance. Feminists have argued that this concept of provocation embodies male norms of physical strength and anger. One feminist response, articulated by the pressure group Rights of Women (1992), has been to recommend the introduction of a new partial defence to murder, namely self-preservation. This defence would be open to persons who kill someone who has subjected them to continuing sexual and/or physical abuse and intimidation, to the extent that they honestly believe they have reached a point where there is no protection or safety from the abuse and that they will die if the aggressor remains alive.

A further example of the transformation of a specific legal concept to reflect women's lives is Howe's use of the term 'social injury' (1991). This concept has had an established use in criminology, where it was used to broaden the definition of crime to include injury to the state, thereby bringing white-collar crime within the scope of criminology. Howe appropriates this concept for feminist jurisprudence with the identification of social injuries which are gender-specific, or social injuries by gender stereotype. The transformed concept can then be used to theorize not only offences such as rape, sexual assault and domestic violence but also superficially gender-neutral offences under anti-discrimination legislation and divorce law reform.

The scrutiny of legal categories and concepts for the extent to which they embody male norms will also include the investigation of rights discourse in law-oriented feminist campaigns. Unlike the systematic transformative model, however, the thematic transformative model makes no a priori judgment about whether feminists should continue to use appeals to rights. Rather, each instance of rights discourse requires evaluation. Sometimes the appeal to a right has great popular appeal for a specific cause; none the less it may have damaging implications. For example, justifying abortion as a woman's right to choose has been a powerful slogan for law reform. At the same time, it invites the assertion of counter-rights, such as fathers' rights and foetal rights, which are potentially damaging to women. Instead, feminists have argued, rights discourse in the context of abortion needs to be transformed into 'safe strategies' which emphasize not the individual choice of a pregnant woman but social responsibility for women in a state of emotional distress and economic need.

The principle that feminist jurisprudence should transform legal categories and concepts to reflect the reality of women's lives is carried into the legal curriculum. At Dahl's law school in Oslo, there are specialist courses in women's law (1987). These organize materials from existing law into collections which follow the typical pattern of women's experience, such as money law, law surrounding birth, and housewives' law. Further, all mandatory courses in the law school are required to include feminist legal analyses. Where such radical measures are not possible, however, feminists have also seen the merits of a process of 'infecting' the traditional legal curriculum with feminist perspectives.

The main criticism of the transformative model, whether in its systematic or thematic form, is that feminist jurisprudence is of questionable value for feminist politics. This is because, however much feminists seek to transform legal categories and concepts, feminist jurisprudence remains a form of jurisprudence. As such it will retain the notion, common to all forms of jurisprudence, that law is the proper site for the resolution of social conflicts. Yet feminist analysis has shown that this strategy has been unreliable for the achievement of feminist goals. This criticism constitutes the subversionist critique.

3   The subversionist critique

This critique does not comprise a third model of feminist jurisprudence; rather it constitutes a warning to feminists about the impressive resilience of jurisprudence in the face of critical analyses in and from other disciplines. Of special note is its capacity to absorb and redefine interventions issuing from feminist analyses.

On this view, every engagement with law, either as an object of theoretical analysis or as a political reality, needs to be reprimanded by the reminder that, by entering on to the terrain of law, and by implication the field of jurisprudence, the endeavour may be, and probably is, conceding territory for law's hegemony. To the extent that it is incorporated within the paradigm of jurisprudence, feminist jurisprudence will reproduce the assumption that law is the proper terrain for feminist politics. Feminist jurisprudence is therefore in danger of collusion with jurisprudence. For example, according to the subversionist critique, the feminist recommendation that criminal law introduce self-preservation as a new partial defence to murder is helpful to women only when they are already embroiled in certain criminal law procedures; it leaves unanswered the question of whether the courts are the appropriate context for solving problems of domestic violence.

A further example of the subversionist critique draws attention to feminist engagement with the policy debate on how women should be supported financially after divorce. Smart (1984) shows that the policy debate is constructed so that the policy options are reduced to only two alternatives: support by former husbands or support by the state. Smart has argued that neither option permits a satisfactory answer, because feminists have argued both for women's financial independence from men and for recognition of the value to their husbands of women's unpaid domestic labour in the fixing of maintenance payments.

It follows easily from this example of the subversionist critique that formulating feminist politics in terms of equal rights, or indeed in terms of special rights, is unlikely to produce justice for women. For rights are law's preferred language, and they are tainted with law's claim to sole authority to adjudicate disputes between individuals who advance competing rights claims. Similarly, the inclusion of feminist jurisprudence into legal education carries all the risks of assimilation – the depoliticization of feminism in the academic sphere.

The subversionist critique has itself been criticized for its tendency to undervalue the genuine achievements of liberal legal systems and of liberal jurisprudence. For example, it undervalues relatively liberal abortion legislation, anti-discrimination legislation, and greater awareness on the part of the judiciary of the need to strengthen the position of vulnerable female cohabitants. Similarly, the subversionist critique misguidedly undermines the success of feminists working with the transformative model of feminist jurisprudence in forcing liberal jurisprudence to acknowledge gender as a significant social division impeding progress to greater social justice.

See also: CRITICAL LEGAL STUDIES §5; FEMINIST POLITICAL PHILOSOPHY; LAW, PHILOSOPHY OF

References and further reading

* Atkins, S. and Hoggett, B. (1984) *Women and the Law*, Oxford: Blackwell. (The classic text of the parity model of feminist jurisprudence.)
* Dahl, T.S. (1987) *Women's Law: an Introduction to Feminist Jurisprudence*, Oslo: Norwegian University Press. (Pioneering exponent of the thematic transformation model of feminist jurisprudence.)
* Dworkin, R. (1978) *Taking Rights Seriously*, London: Duckworth. (Criticized by Okin for neglect of family justice.)
* Graycar, R. and Morgan, J. (1990) *The Hidden Gender of Law*, Annandale, New South Wales: The Federation Press, also available through The Blackstone Press. (The most extensive collection of legal materials exemplifying the thematic transformation model of feminist jurisprudence.)
* Howe, A. (1991) 'The Problem of Privatised Injuries: Feminist Strategies for Litigation', in M.A. Fineman and N.S. Thomadsen (eds), *At the Boundaries of Law: Feminism and Legal Theory*, London: Routledge. (A key example of the feminist transformation of a legal concept.)
  Kingdom, E.F. (1991) *What's Wrong with Rights? Problems for Feminist Politics of Law*, Edinburgh: Edinburgh University Press. (Text documenting limitations of rights discourse for feminist politics.)
* MacKinnon, C.A. (1989) *Toward a Feminist Theory of the State*, Cambridge, MA: Harvard University Press. (The definitive statement of the systematic transformation model of feminist jurisprudence.)
  Naffine, N. (1990) *Law and the Sexes: Explorations in Feminist Jurisprudence*, London: Allen & Unwin. (A most accessible account of feminist discourses and law, focusing on gender and class bias in legal constructions of the individual.)
* Okin, S.M. (1989) *Justice, Gender and the Family*, New York: Basic Books. (Thoroughgoing criticism of the failure of liberal jurisprudence to address gendered relations in the family.)
* Pateman, C. (1988) *The Sexual Contract*, Cambridge: Polity Press. (Influential text revealing the gendered assumptions of Rawls.)
* Rawls, J. (1972) *A Theory of Justice*, Oxford: Oxford University Press. (Criticized by Pateman for omission of gender in his account of social justice.)
* Rights of Women (1992) *Proposals for Amending the*

1957 Homicide Act: Including a New Defence of Self Preservation, submission to the Royal Commission on Criminal Justice, London: Rights of Women. (A key example of the development of a feminist transformation of legal defences to murder.)

* Sachs, A. and Wilson, J.H. (1978) *Sexism and the Law: A Study of Male Beliefs and Legal Bias in Britain and the United States*, Oxford: Martin Robertson. (A landmark text of the parity model of feminist jurisprudence.)

* Smart, C. (1984) *The Ties that Bind: Law, Marriage and the Reproduction of Patriarchal Relations*, London: Routledge & Kegan Paul. (An early statement of the subversionist critique.)

—— (1989) *Feminism and the Power of Law*, London: Routledge. (The most influential account of feminist discourses and law. A critique of feminist jurisprudence in chapter 4 and a summary of feminist theories of rights.)

—— (1991) 'Feminist Jurisprudence', in P. Fitzpatrick (ed.) *Dangerous Supplements*, London: Pluto Press. (The best exposition of the subversionist critique.)

E. F. KINGDOM

FEMINIST LITERARY CRITICISM

Feminist literary criticism looks at literature assuming its production from a male-dominated perspective. It re-examines canonical works to show how gender stereotypes are involved in their functioning. It examines (and often rediscovers) works by women for a possible alternative voice. A study of the social suppression and minimalization of women's literature becomes necessary. These questions emerge: What is sexual difference and how has it been represented? How has the representation of woman relied on a presupposition of inequality between the sexes? Is there a feminine essence, biological or otherwise, that produces 'women's writing'? Feminists who believe that a 'woman' is culturally or socially constructed look for evidence of that process in literature. The socio-cultural and politico-economic construction of sexual difference is 'gender.' A study of the difference between sexual and gender difference can establish alliances with gay and lesbian studies. Feminist criticism sometimes relates to psychoanalysis and/or Marxism, criticizing their masculinism and using their resources. It expands into film/ video as well as social-scientific or philosophical texts. Feminists sensitive to racism and imperialism demonstrate the culture-specificity of all of the above.

1 History
2 Theory

1 History

Although the remote antecedents of feminist literary criticism may be located in many ways, the source-texts of modern feminist criticism are Virginia Woolf in Britain and Simone de BEAUVOIR in France. The generations that came of age during the Vietnam War found evidence of discrimination against women within the New Left Anti-War movement in the USA. In Britain, a comparable dissatisfaction with Marxism is to be found in works such as Sheila Rowbotham, Lynne Segal and Hilary Wainwright's *Beyond the Fragments* (1979). Women of the 'baby-boom' generation (born at the end of the Second World War), though not necessarily involved in political struggle, became increasingly dissatisfied with the treatment of women at home and in the workplace. This combination of protest and dissatisfaction worked to produce the first wave of feminist literary criticism in the USA and Britain. The first important texts are Elaine Showalter's A *Literature of Their Own* (1977) – echoing Woolf's title *A Room of Her Own* – and Sandra Gilbert and Susan Gubar's *The Madwoman in the Attic* (1979) – establishing Charlotte Brontë's *Jane Eyre* as the model feminist text (see FEMINIST POLITICAL THEORY §2).

British feminist criticism was, at its inception, more marked by a sociological and psychoanalytic stance (see FEMINISM AND SOCIAL SCIENCE; FEMINISM AND PSYCHOANALYSIS). Two path-breaking texts in this mode are *Women Take Issue* (1978) and Juliet Mitchell's *Psychoanalysis and Feminism* (1974). In the field of literary criticism proper, British feminists were reading US books such as Mary Ellmann's *Thinking About Women* (1968).

Although Simone de Beauvoir's *The Second Sex* (1949) was internationally influential as a source-text of feminist consciousness, it had little acknowledged influence on French feminist literary criticism. In France, feminist literary criticism was less disciplinary, more imbricated in the general social field than in the USA, where the professionalization of the academy is more systematic, and the apparent possibility of resistance more academically tolerated. The bringing together of Marx and Freud, or the feminization of philosophy, was the agenda of interventionist intellectual French feminism. The events of May 1968, when workers and students came together and almost toppled the State, were a motive force of French feminism. The groups *Psych et po* (psychoanalysis and politics) and *Cheveux longues*

611

idées courtes (long hair short ideas) convey an idea of these characteristics of the French scene.

By the 1990s, Julia KRISTEVA, with her new readings of Freudian psychoanalysis, and Helène CIXOUS, with her writerly assimilation of the philosophy of deconstruction, had come to dominate the French feminist literary-critical scene. (It should be noted that the word 'feminism' denotes a particular group-politics in France, and therefore would not necessarily be acknowledged as a description by either of these women.)

In the USA and Britain, the impact of French feminist theory has divided the feminist literary-critical scene into two broad camps. (The work of the philosopher Luce IRIGARAY must also be counted as a French influence on literary criticism written in English.) This division is charted in Toril Moi's *Sexual/Textual Politics* (1985). In the field of feminist literary, film and cultural criticism the work of bell hooks (Gloria Watkins) has been a sustained combative voice. Black feminist criticism is in many ways at the cutting edge of British and US feminist thought.

As mentioned earlier, *Women Take Issue* was one of the early texts of British feminist cultural and literary intervention. Emerging as it did from the Birmingham School of Cultural Studies, it was a statement from postcolonial Black British women. (Hazel Carby, one of the chief spokeswomen of that group, has since moved to the USA and works both in the area of restoring the history of literature by African-American women as well as laying down ground-rules for a cultural critique of the representation of Black women, using some of the categories established by the philosopher Louis ALTHUSSER and the sociologist Stuart Hall.) In the USA, where the history of slavery, 'settlement' of indigenous peoples and immigration is complex and multi-layered, 'multiculturalist' feminist literary criticism began to appear in the 1980s, although the label is of later provenance. Cherrié Moraga and Gloria Anzaldua's *This Bridge Called My Back* (1983), with its focus on Chicana feminism, was an important early text of cultural criticism. As a result of a change in US Immigration Law in 1965, the influx of Asian immigration increased 500 per cent. It was among second-generation women of this group that a specifically 'postcolonial' multiculturalist feminism took root (see MULTICULTURALISM §3). A not uncritical but fruitful exchange between the former British and French colonies and the metropolitan countries has been the result. In the British and French context might be mentioned Buci Emecheta from sub-Saharan Africa, Assia Djebar and Nawal el-Saadawi from North Africa, and Meenakshi Mukherjee from India. Feminist literary criticism from Japan and the Philippines is closely interactive with feminist criticism in the USA.

The relationship between feminist literary and cultural critique and the women's movement in the various countries mentioned here is a subject that must be taken into consideration in any extended study. Luce Irigaray (and Michel Foucault) in France, cultural workers such as Pratibha Parmar in Britain, and theorists such as Judith Butler in the United States have shown how an apparently empirical positioning outside heterosexuality can provide new presuppositions for general ethical, social, legal and cultural speculation. Their work is important for those feminists who feel that the alliance with gay and lesbian studies means a fuller critique of the assumption that the historico-legally sanctioned 'male' perspective is objective and just.

In colloquial academic parlance, and taking mainstream Britain and the USA as our examples, 'sixties feminism' was marked by protest and 'consciousness-raising' (collective self-education through sharing personal experience), 'seventies feminism' was Eurocentric and essentialist (emphasizing benevolent middle-class women as women as such); 'eighties feminism' was obliged to take race-class-gender and 'theory' into account; and 'nineties feminism' was marked by a post-feminist and/or multiculturalist impatience by the generation that grew up on, or on the other side of, the gains of 'white' feminist struggle. Feminist literary criticism relates to this general movement. A vade mecum for the twenty-first century is yet to be established.

2 Theory

If the feminine is ungeneralizable as the human, what is the validity of the human sciences? This is the first question of feminism. All methods that question the validity of the apparently reasonable can therefore potentially be its ally. This is how Marxism, psychoanalysis, the general critique of 'humanism', multiculturalism and multi-ethnicity (questioning 'Europe's claim to the culture of Reason), and gay theory (questioning the heterosexual male as the model of man), have contributed their methodological resources to feminism. At the same time, their theory and practice have also been questioned for participating in masculinism. Mainstream feminism, which builds on the strengths of liberal humanism, adopts Marxism via the Engelsian narrative of the origin of the family (Friedrich Engels, *The Origin of the Family and Private Property*; Gayle Rubin, 'The Traffic in Women') or the theory of the modes of production (Christine Delphy, *Close to Home*); psychoanalysis via its Oedipal storyline (Nancy Chodorow, *The Repro-*

duction of *Mothering*), and multiculturalism as liberal pluralism with an enlightened civil society at the centre. Feminist literary and cultural criticism are related to these moves.

Lively controversies within feminist literary and cultural criticism are a sign of its strength. The main line of debate is between 'essentialism' and 'anti-essentialism,' although sometimes the rubrics used are different. Is woman a special kind of human being by nature (or essence)? Or is what is understood by the word corresponding to 'woman' in English, a cultural and social construction? These seem to be the broad lines of the controversy.

There is a smaller group of more radical 'anti-essentialist' feminists who presume that the necessary focusing or centring of the thinking and acting subject may not be accessible to direct analysis. Whether such feminist literary and cultural critique can be 'politically engaged' is a question that is not without consequence.

If the non-'European' feminine is ungeneralizable as woman, socio-culturally constructed or otherwise, what is the validity of Eurocentric feminism? (The 'European' here is of Northwest Europe or its legacy: Euro-US, Euro-Australia, Euro-Canada.) The poignancy of this question is that it can only be asked for global attention by women marked by the modern university – an institution developed within the European tradition – or by migrancy – a Eurocentric phenomenon. Testimonies obtained from non-academic Third-World women are sometimes used in an effort to bypass this problem.

See also: FEMINISM; FEMINIST AESTHETICS

References and further reading

* Beauvoir, S. de (1949) *Le deuxième sexe* (*The Second Sex*), trans. H.M. Parshley, New York: Alfred A. Knopf, 1953. (Womanhood considered from a number of theoretical angles, followed by a contemporary account of woman's life. Source-text of Western feminism.)

* Brontë, C. (1969) *Jane Eyre*, ed. J. Jack and M. Smith, Oxford: Oxford University Press. (The classic feminist story of the social and psychological development of a gifted orphan girl.)

Butler, J. (1990) *Gender Trouble: Feminism and the Subversion of Identity*, New York: Routledge. (Source book of lesbian feminist theory.)

* Chodorow, N. (1978) *The Reproduction of Mothering: Psychoanalysis and the Sociology of Gender*, Berkeley, CA: University of California Press. (Source book of US-style feminist psychoanalytic theory.)

* Delphy, C. (1984) *Close to Home: A Marxist Analysis of Women's Oppression*, trans. D. Leonard, London: Hutchinson. (Considers the economic dimensions of patriarchy.)

Djébar, A. (1980) 'Regard interdit, son coupé' ('Forbidden Gaze, Severed Sound') in *Femmes d'Alger dans leur appartement* (*Women of Algiers in their Apartment*), trans. M. de Jaegar, Charlottesville, VA: University of Virginia Press, 1992, 133–51. (Combines psychoanalytic and postcolonial feminist theory.)

* Ellmann, M. (1968) *Thinking About Women*, New York: Harcourt, Brace & World. (Outstanding analysis of common-sense sexism, written in the style of the familiar essay.)

Emecheta, B. (1983) *The Rape of Shavi*, London and Ibuza: Ogwugu Afor. (Fictional allegory of the relationship between cultural construction of African and British women.)

* Engels, F. (1884) *Der Ursprung der Familie, des Privateigentums und des Staats* (*The Origin of the Family, Private Property and the State*), ed. E.B. Leacock, New York: International Publishers. (Powerful communist classic of a broad spectrum of influence connecting economic history to gender through nineteenth-century anthropology.)

Gates, H.L. (ed.) (1990) *Reading Black, Reading Feminist: A Critical Anthology*, New York: Meridian Books. (Primary and secondary texts of and on black women writing, suitable for introductory as well as advanced work, for students as well as teachers.)

* Gilbert, S.M. and Gubar, S. (1979) *The Madwoman in the Attic: The Woman Writer and the Nineteenth-Century Literary Imagination*, New Haven, CT: Yale University Press. (Path-breaking discussing of *Jane Eyre* as feminist allegory.)

hooks, b. (1992) *Black Looks: Race and Representation*, Boston, MA: South End Press. (African-American feminist cultural theory with the greatest international currency.)

Landry, D. and McLean, G. (1993) *Materialist Feminisms*, Cambridge, MA: Blackwell. (Broad analytic summary of Western feminism.)

* Mitchell, J. (1974) *Psychoanalysis and Feminism*, London: Allen Lane. (Unpolemical account of Freud, attempting to make him useful for feminism.)

* Moi, T. (1985) *Sexual/Textual Politics: Feminist Literary Theory*, London: Methuen. (A representative collection of essays from the 1950s to the 1980s.)

—— (1987) *French Feminist Thought: A Reader*, Oxford: Blackwell. (Introduces the important anti-essentialist debate within feminist literary theory.)

* Morraga, C. and Anzaldua, G. (1983) *This Bridge*

Called My Back: Writings by Radical Women of Color, New York: Kitchen Table. (Mixed-form classic feminist text by women of colour in the USA, antedating today's diasporic feminism.)

Mukhejee, M. (1993) 'Story, History and Her Story', *Studies in History* 9 (1): 72–85. (Variations in the construction of woman as hero in Indian nationalist historiography, literature and autobiography.)

Mulvey, L. (1973) 'Visual Pleasure and Narrative Cinema', in *Visual and Other Pleasures*, London: Macmillan, 14–26. (Lays out principles of feminist psychoanalytic film criticism.)

* Rowbotham, S., Segal, L. and Wainwright, H. (1979) *Beyond the Fragments: Feminism and the Making of Socialism*, London: Merlin Press, 2nd edn. (Account of British feminism's disaffection from Marxism in a compelling activist style.)

* Rubin, G. (1975) 'The Traffic in Women: Notes on the Political Economy of Sex', in R. Reiter (ed.) *Toward An Anthropology of Women*, New York: Monthly Review Press, 157–210. (Source-text of gender theory.)

Saadawi, N. (1980) *The Hidden Face of Eve: Women in the Arab World*, London: Zed Press. (Hortatory and descriptive text for and about the past, present and future of women of the eastern Arab world. Extensive documentation.)

* Showalter, E. (1977) *A Literature of Their Own: British Women Novelists from Brontë to Lessing*, Princeton, NJ: Princeton University Press. (Introduction to feminist literature, establishing the difference between 'female', 'feminine' and 'feminist'.)

Spivak, G.C. (1987) *In Other Worlds: Essays in Cultural Politics*, New York: Methuen. (Source book of postcolonial feminist theory.)

* Women's Studies Group, Centre for Contemporary Cultural Studies, University of Birmingham (1978) *Women Take Issue: Aspects of Women's Subordination*, London: Hutchinson. (Early and practical intervention by gays and women of colour in the field of Womens Studies. Excellent example of British Althusserian feminism.)

GAYATRI CHAKRAVORTY SPIVAK

FEMINIST PHILOSOPHY OF SCIENCE *see* GENDER AND SCIENCE

FEMINIST POLITICAL PHILOSOPHY

In all its forms, feminism asserts that social and political structures in society discriminate against women. Feminist political philosophy aims to show how traditional political philosophy is implicated in that discrimination and how the resources of political philosophy may nevertheless be employed in the service of women. Sometimes, feminist political philosophy extends the arguments of traditional political philosophy to indicate that women are unjustly treated and to propose ways in which that injustice might be removed. This is clearest in liberal feminism, where it is argued that since women are essentially the same as men in being rational creatures, they are entitled to the same legal and political rights as men: arguments which defend the rights of man also support the rights of women. Similarly, Marxist and socialist feminism extend the insights of Marxism and socialism in an attempt to expose and remove the oppression of women: Marxist emphasis on the exploitation of labour under capital is supplemented by Marxist feminist emphasis on the exploitation of women under patriarchy.

However, there are also forms of feminist political philosophy which are more critical of traditional political philosophy and which question the very distinctions upon which it is premised. Thus, radical feminist philosophers question the scope of the term 'political' as it is usually used by political philosophers, and argue that by excluding domestic concerns, traditional political philosophy excludes many of the things which are most important to women. The aim here is not to extend the insights of political philosophy, but rather to highlight the ways in which political philosophy itself shows a distinct gender bias.

Yet more radically, the postmodernists have been critical of philosophy's emphasis on truth and objectivity, and some feminists have extended their arguments to suggest that the very language of philosophy, and by extension of political philosophy, is 'man-made'.

Feminist political philosophy is therefore not one thing but many, and feminist political philosophers are deeply divided as to whether traditional political philosophy may be modified so as to include women's interests, or whether it is itself one of the ways in which women's politically disadvantaged position is legitimized and perpetuated.

1 **The scope of feminist political philosophy**
2 **The history of feminist political philosophy**
3 **Liberal feminism**
4 **Marxist and socialist feminism**
5 **Radical feminism**

6 Postmodernism and feminism
7 Recent feminist political philosophy

1 The scope of feminist political philosophy

Political philosophy is primarily concerned with the justification of the state. It raises questions about what the state may demand of citizens and what citizens, in turn, owe to the state. Feminist political philosophy addresses those same concerns as they affect women. It asks whether and why there are differences between the ways in which men and women are treated by the state. Thus, in the nineteenth century, feminist political philosophers questioned the laws which dictated that men but not women were allowed to vote, and similarly they questioned the laws which prevented married women from retaining rights over their property. Here, feminist political philosophy emphasized the equality of men and women and demanded a justification for their different political and legal treatment.

More recently, feminist political philosophers have noted that even where the laws are gender neutral, women remain at a disadvantage: in most Western liberal democracies there are no longer laws which prevent women from being politically active, but nevertheless there are far fewer women than men in positions of political power or influence. This suggests that attaining full, as distinct from formal, political equality may require something more than laws which are gender neutral. As a result, feminist political philosophers have been concerned to argue for an understanding of the concept of equality which goes beyond the formal equality of gender-neutral laws (see EQUALITY).

These two schools of thought exemplify distinct feminist approaches to political philosophy. In the first case, political philosophy's concern for equality is shown to be incompatible with laws which give women fewer political rights than men. In the second case, political philosophy's formalistic interpretation of equality is questioned. The two examples show how different forms of feminist political philosophy relate to traditional political philosophy: feminist political philosophers sometimes argue for the consistent application of the central concepts of political philosophy; sometimes for a reconsideration of those concepts.

The latter strategy manifests the more subversive character of some feminist political philosophy: traditional concern for justice and equality is often premised on a distinction between public and private life, and concern about the justice of political institutions and practices does not, in general, extend to the private world. But if political philosophy takes

as its central concern the justice of political institutions, it needs to explain which institutions count as political and why. In particular, it needs to explain the grounds on which domestic affairs are deemed to be private and outside the domain of the political, outside the scope of theories of justice: for feminists, the decision to differentiate between public and private, between an area which is and an area which is not the legitimate concern of the state, is itself a political decision of some consequence (see PRIVACY §4). Hence the feminist claim that 'the personal is political', for what is meant by this is precisely that the decision as to what will and what will not count as the proper business of the state is a decision which itself has a political dimension.

Feminists who argue that the personal is political may take a further and yet more radical step, questioning the privileged position accorded to the concepts of justice and equality in traditional political philosophy. In private life, concern and compassion may be more important than justice, and if the distinction between the private world and the political world is undermined, then it seems to follow that concern and compassion should be more prominent, and justice and equality less prominent, than they usually are in political philosophy.

The views outlined above indicate that the term 'feminist political philosophy' covers a wide range of arguments. Some feminists argue for the consistent application of terms like 'justice' to women; others argue for the revision of those concepts; while yet others demand their replacement. At its most radical, feminist political philosophy is highly subversive of political philosophy, since it denies the existence of a separate, political realm or insists that the concept of the political is itself 'male'. Nevertheless, in all its forms, feminist political philosophy seeks to identify the causes of women's political disadvantage and to suggest remedies for it.

2 The history of feminist political philosophy

Feminist political philosophy may plausibly be said to begin in the late eighteenth century, with the publication in 1792 of Mary Wollstonecraft's *A Vindication of the Rights of Woman* (see WOLLSTONECRAFT, M.). Wollstonecraft's arguments owe much to Enlightenment philosophy and she champions vigorously the extension of the rights of man to women. One of her most important and controversial claims is that both men and women are essentially rational beings. Since they are alike in this respect, and since it is this which justifies the ascription of political rights, women should be accorded the same political rights as men. In its time, Wollstonecraft's assertion that women are rational was highly controversial and had been denied by many of the great philosophers. Most importantly for her, it was denied by ROUSSEAU, J.-J., her contemporary and one of the foremost philosophers of the Enlightenment. On Rousseau's account, men were rational, whereas women were intuitive and emotional. *A Vindication* is in large part an attack on Rousseau's political philosophy, and especially on its assertion that women lack the capacity for rationality.

Although it is somewhat anachronistic to refer to Mary Wollstonecraft as a feminist (the term was not used in England until 1894), *A Vindication* does nevertheless display both the critical and the constructive aims of feminist political philosophy: it exposes the ways in which traditional political philosophy excludes women and it presents a vigorous argument in favour of the extension of political rights to women.

However, Wollstonecraft also insists that, although men and women are equally rational and therefore equally entitled to be citizens of the state, they will express their citizenship in different ways. While men will occupy public positions, women will remain primarily within the private or domestic realm, and will express their citizenship in that context. Opinions differ as to the worth of Wollstonecraft's thought in this area: some see her insistence on women's role in the home as inappropriately conservative, while others argue that she is in fact a radical before her time, acknowledging the political importance of the domestic sphere. Whatever the correct judgment, we can see in her writings several of the most important features of feminist political philosophy: Wollstonecraft shows a keen awareness of the legal and political disadvantages which women suffered in the later eighteenth century, she identifies the cause of those disadvantages as being the belief that women and men have different natures, and she argues for the extension of political rights to women. Perhaps also she goes further, questioning the division between political and private on which political philosophy is premised, but even if she does not, her insistence on the common nature of men and women is still a central feature of feminist political philosophy and was taken up by other philosophers in the nineteenth century.

Chief among these were J.S. MILL and Harriet TAYLOR. Like Wollstonecraft, Mill presented an argument which was both critical and constructive. In *The Subjection of Women* (1869), he attacked those, like Rousseau, who argued that woman's political exclusion was justified by her different nature, insisting instead that women had been so repressed by social and political discrimination that it was impossible to tell what their true nature was. In so far

as woman's nature appeared different from man's this was most likely to be a result of an education and upbringing which was distorting and repressive.

However, in his positive proposals, Mill appears less radical than either Mary Wollstonecraft or Harriet Taylor, who also wrote extensively on the subject of women's political position, most notably in her essay *The Enfranchisement of Women* (1851). For while Mill is eager to emphasize the fact that woman's nature has been deformed by her poor treatment, he also predicts that when women are granted equal legal and political rights with men, they will nevertheless not choose to exercise those rights in the public arena, but will prefer to remain within the home, pursuing the occupations traditionally reserved for women. And, contrary to his official position, he sometimes implies that this is because women are more emotional and intuitive than men and therefore better suited to domestic than to political occupations.

We have already seen that Mary Wollstonecraft favoured equal legal and political rights for women, yet also argued that men and women would express their citizenship differently. J.S. Mill also inveighs against women's inequality in legal and political contexts, but he sometimes implies that men and women are by nature the same, sometimes that they are different. His uncertainty about whether the differences between men and women are of political significance, and whether they spring from nature or from nurture, recur in the disputes which characterize much twentieth-century feminist political philosophy.

What is overwhelmingly clear, however, is that Wollstonecraft, Mill and Taylor set the agenda of modern feminist political philosophy. At a time when the rights of man were being declared in France and in the USA, Wollstonecraft raised the question of why those legal and political rights had not been extended to women. She argues in terms of justice and equality. Similarly, Mill and Taylor emphasize justice and equality in their discussion of women's subjection. In so doing, they provide the framework for modern liberal feminism, but it is arguable that they do more, and in some ways also anticipate the more radical forms of feminism which have become prominent in the late twentieth century.

3 Liberal feminism

The difficulties inherent in defining liberal feminism arise in part from the difficulties in defining liberalism itself, but in general we can identify the salient features of liberalism as being its individualism, its emphasis on justice and equality, and its understanding of the state ideally as a neutral arena within which people should be left to pursue their own interests in their own way (see LIBERALISM; NEUTRALITY, POLITICAL). For liberals, the most important function of the state is to protect individuals from interference by others. Liberalism takes as its premise the freedom and equality of all human beings and construes the state as justified in so far as it preserves that freedom and equality. Accepting these central premises, liberal feminism also emphasizes the rights of women as individuals; specifically, their right to equal treatment under the law and the responsibility of the state to ensure their freedom to develop as autonomous individuals.

Liberal feminism is primarily concerned with the legal and political rights of women and with the justice of political arrangements. Thus, members of the suffrage movement emphasized the injustice of denying the vote to women, and nineteenth-century campaigns for married women to be allowed to own property were also based on liberal premises: they appealed to the equality of men and women and to the consequent injustice of denying women the rights accorded to men.

More recently, liberal feminism has been concerned to argue for women's rights in the workplace: rights to equal pay and to equal opportunities more generally. These issues, however, raise doubts about the scope of liberalism in general, and liberal feminism in particular. The first doubt arises in connection with the individualism of liberal political philosophy: as we have seen, early liberal feminists argued for the essential sameness of men and women as rational beings. For liberal political philosophy, human beings are essentially rational creatures, and physical differences between people should not be used to justify differential treatment. Obviously, this argument was important in, for example, the Civil Rights movement in the USA. In similar vein, modern liberal feminists argue that since women are, like men, essentially rational beings, they should be accorded all the legal and political rights of man. But in the case of women, it is far from clear that physical differences can be so easily disregarded, much less that it is just to disregard them. In this respect, it has been argued, liberal political philosophy is gendered, since it assumes the centrality of rationality and thereby ignores the important differences which spring from woman's role as child-bearer and child-rearer. Connectedly, liberal feminism has been criticized for being altogether too willing to comply with the denial of difference and the characterization of human beings as essentially rational.

These reflections on woman's different physical and biological nature can either inform or undermine liberal feminism and liberalism generally. Some have argued that differences can be incorporated within the liberal understanding of justice, while others have insisted that the differences cast doubt upon the very concepts of justice and equality themselves and their centrality to traditional political philosophy. Thus, Susan Okin (1990) argues that John Rawls' theory of justice may be extended in such a way that the justice of a society is partly determined by the justice of domestic arrangements. Others have argued that the extension of justice to the domestic realm is inconsistent with central liberal principles, while yet others have cast doubt upon the importance which liberalism places on justice (see JUSTICE §5).

4 Marxist and socialist feminism

Where liberal feminism emphasizes justice and equality and locates the source of women's oppression in their unjustified exclusion from the political and legal rights accorded to men, Marxist and socialist feminism see women's oppression as springing from their socio-economic condition, arguing that it will end only when social and economic circumstances change. The terms 'Marxist feminism' and 'socialist feminism' require elucidation because they are not used uniformly in the literature: sometimes they are used interchangeably, while at other times Marxist feminism is used to refer strictly to those who base their analysis on Marxist theory, and socialist feminism to refer to the more general belief that the liberation of women requires the transformation of the socio-economic system. Rather differently, socialist feminism is often used to refer to the synthesis of Marxist feminism and radical feminism. In general, however, we may take both Marxist and socialist feminism to be characterized by their belief that the causes of women's oppression are rooted in the socio-economic system and by their proposals for remedies for that oppression – namely, the transformation of the system.

Orthodox Marxist feminism aims to extend the concepts and insights of Marx's writings to the situation of women (see MARX, K.; MARXISM, WESTERN). In the past, this involved an understanding of women's oppression as a special case of the quite general exploitation of workers within capitalist societies, and the remedy was to treat women's work simply as one form of necessary labour under capitalism. This certainly seems to have been Engels' position (see ENGELS). However, the analysis raises a number of problems: it is unclear whether housework should remain a 'private' matter, but shared equally between men and women or whether it should itself become a form of labour which attracts recompense. For many Marxist feminists, housework, or domestic labour, should not be seen as a personal service to an individual man, but as a more general presupposition of capitalism, one which is necessary if the workforce is to be reproduced. Additionally, and crucially, feminists have argued that housework is an area in which women are not merely exploited by men as capitalists, but by men as husbands. Put bluntly, Marxist feminism must account for the fact that it is not only capitalists who benefit from the oppression of women, but men generally. This argument undermines the ability of Marxist feminism to reduce all exploitation to class exploitation. For women, there is, or appears to be, a double exploitation – one rooted in class, the other rooted in gender. In consequence, there is reason to believe that women's oppression will survive the demise of capitalism: there is no simple Marxist solution to the problem of patriarchy unless the Marxist understanding of production is extended to include reproduction.

These problems have generated a more general 'socialist' feminism which acknowledges the separate and distinct forms which oppression may take and which is reluctant to see all oppression as rooted in class. Here it is argued that women experience the dual oppressions of class and gender differently. Potential unities of class are disrupted by conflicts of gender (see SOCIALISM §4).

But if this point holds, it signals not only the demise of Marxist feminism, narrowly construed, but also the possibility that different kinds of oppression will require different, and perhaps conflicting, remedies. This possibility, implicit in the denial of a single source of oppression, is problematic for feminist political philosophy because it undermines the attempt to identify a single source of women's oppression, suggesting instead that for different women there will be multiple and conflicting sources, not easily reconcilable one with another.

5 Radical feminism

Where liberal feminism traces the oppression of women to unjust laws, and Marxist and socialist feminism traces it to socio-economic structures, radical feminism identifies the cause of women's oppression as men. It is to radical feminism that we owe the central feminist term, 'patriarchy', and the feminist slogan, 'the personal is political'. As the name implies, it is also in radical feminism that we find the most vigorous attacks on the aims and preoccupations of traditional political philosophy. For whereas liberal feminism, Marxist feminism and socialist feminism all subscribe to political philosophies which they believe can be modified to include women's interests, radical feminism is inherently critical of political philosophy itself, seeing it as one

of the many ways in which male power is legitimized. On this account, socialism, Marxism and liberalism all misidentify the cause of women's oppression by interpreting it as a specific case of a more general problem. But for radical feminists, the oppression of women is a distinctive form of oppression in itself: it transcends other forms of oppression and in order to combat it women must unite as women against men as the oppressors.

From the perspective of political philosophy, the importance of radical feminism lies in its reconstruction of the concept of the political. Where liberal feminism emphasizes the injustice of existing laws, and urges the extension of the rights of man to woman, radical feminists construe the injustice of existing laws as part of an all-pervasive structure of male domination which begins in the family and spreads outward to political institutions. Hence the claim that 'the personal is political'. On this account, changes to existing laws governing divorce, property ownership and suffrage are merely cosmetic devices which conceal, and sometimes even perpetuate the injustice which exists in the structure of the family itself, and about which liberalism and liberal feminism, are largely silent. Similarly, the socialist and Marxist emphasis on the economic basis of women's oppression overlooks the important respects in which oppression may take non-economic, specifically sexual, forms. Thus, the ways in which women are disadvantaged in the workplace, and the problems associated with the status of domestic work, are but symptoms of a wider problem – the problem of women's sexual subordination to men.

But if the causes of women's oppression are as identified by radical feminists, what are the remedies? Here, radical feminists disagree profoundly: some claim that the demise of the family itself, and of women's role as child-bearers is what is required; others argue that what is needed is the re-evaluation of those roles and institutions. Expressed more generally, this is a disagreement about whether woman's biological nature is an inconvenient encumbrance obstructing her liberation, or whether it is the source of values which are currently unrecognized in politics but which, if cultivated, could provide a richer and more humane understanding of the political.

An example of the former strategy is to be found in the work of Shulamith Firestone, who argues in *The Dialectic of Sex* (1970) that the source of woman's oppression lies in her child-bearing capacity, in her 'fundamentally oppressive biological condition'. However, reproductive technology may enable woman to break free of the burden of her biology. If, therefore, women can control reproductive technology, they will, for the first time, be able to overcome oppression. Adapting Marx's arguments, Firestone argues that, like workers under capitalism, women must seize the means of (re)production with the ultimate aim of eliminating sex power and the sex distinction itself. By contrast, other radical feminists have asserted the value of reproduction and child-rearing, and have argued that women should not aspire to free themselves of those roles, but should rather emphasize the importance of the qualities which are developed through child-bearing and rearing. Thus, Sara Ruddick (1990) argues that distinctive ways of thinking may grow out of the work that mothers do. These ways of thinking are not, however, the unique preserve of women: they are developed via 'woman's work', but they are not rooted in woman's nature. They are, moreover, qualities which could have a political use in, for example, our dealings with conflict, but political philosophy's emphasis on justice and equality tends to disguise their significance.

In radical feminism, therefore, we find not so much a political philosophy as a critique of political philosophy. For this reason, radical feminism's lack of a theory of the state is not an indication that it is apolitical. On the contrary, its emphases on sexuality and child-bearing are themselves a political statement. For radical feminists, the identification of a separate, political realm is a mechanism for disguising the vast operations of power within the private world of the family. Until these latter are explained and removed, attempts to secure the liberation of women via the 'political' methods advocated by liberal feminists, or the social and economic methods advocated by socialist and Marxist feminists, will be doomed to failure.

6 Postmodernism and feminism

In recent years, feminist political philosophy has been much influenced by the postmodernists. The term 'postmodern' covers a very wide range of thinkers, including the poststructuralists, deconstructionists, French theorists and psychoanalytic thinkers (see POSTMODERNISM AND POLITICAL PHILOSOPHY). However, from a feminist perspective, the important feature of all these thinkers is, as the name implies, their rejection of the modernism of Enlightenment philosophy. In the Enlightenment tradition, philosophy aims at the rational pursuit of truth, certainty and objectivity. We have already seen how some feminist philosophers reject the Enlightenment emphasis on reason and subvert traditional political philosophy by drawing attention to the 'maleness' of its central concepts. Thus, in moral and political philosophy, some radical feminists have argued that care and compassion should supplement, or even

replace, justice and equality as core terms (see FEMINIST ETHICS). However, postmodernism goes further: its rejection of the Enlightenment search for truth is part of a general denial that truth or objectivity can be attained. Postmodernism is therefore at odds with both liberal feminism and Marxist feminism, since both, in their different ways, are committed to the possibility of certainty and objectivity. For postmodernists, all such commitment is itself a form of domination and therefore cannot form any part of a feminist project.

In addition, for postmodernists, the denial that there can be objective truth or certainty is often linked with an emphasis on the importance of language as a mediator between individuals and the world. Here, feminists sympathetic to postmodernism have emphasized the ways in which language itself is 'man-made' and thus constitutes a form of oppression for women. For many 'French feminists' such as Cixous and Irigary, the removal of patriarchy requires that we think as women, but thinking as a woman requires a recognition of the extent to which the language in which we think is itself man-made. The question which now arises is whether there can be such a thing as 'thinking as a woman' or whether there are simply different subjectivities and no unified category of woman.

Although postmodernism has found enthusiastic support among many feminists, it is not without difficulties. For one thing, there is an air of paradox about its confident assertion that there can be no such thing as certainty. But even ignoring that problem, postmodernism threatens to leave feminism as a rebel without a cause, for if there is no certainty or objectivity, what is the status of women's oppression? Is it also simply a feature of different subjectivities and not an objective fact? By denying the possibility of objectivity, postmodernist feminists appear to be depriving feminism of its central tenet – its claim that women as a group suffer systematic political disadvantage – and reducing it to little more than an analysis of different subjectivities. And this threatens to undermine both the possibility of, and the motivation for, feminist political action.

7 Recent feminist political philosophy

The categories of feminist political philosophy are, in part, artificial. The distinctions between socialist, Marxist and radical feminism are often blurred and controversial. Moreover, many writers resist categorization in this way – unsurprisingly, since one of the main aims of much feminist political philosophy is to indicate the ways in which the traditional branches of political philosophy themselves contribute to the oppression of women. In recent years, therefore, attention has shifted away from the distinct categories of feminist political philosophy towards the ways in which the insights of feminism, however categorized, may inform our understanding of political arrangements.

One important area here is feminist discussion of democracy and of the way in which democracy may involve a recognition of differences between people (see DEMOCRACY). In the history of political philosophy, and in the history of feminist political philosophy, individual rights have usually been asserted on the basis of the similarities between men and women. Mary Wollstonecraft, J.S. Mill and Harriet Taylor all emphasized the essential sameness of men and women as rational beings, and concluded that since women were the same as men in this respect, they should be accorded equal rights. However, the argument from sameness has its limitations. There are many important respects in which women are not the same as men, and these differences affect women's ability to make full use of their political rights, even when such rights are granted. For this reason, feminist political philosophers have turned their attention to the ways in which equality and justice between men and women may be guaranteed through a recognition of difference, rather than through its denial or removal. One of the main proponents of this argument is the US writer, Iris Marion Young, who argues for the recognition of differences between different groups of people and for the differential treatment of those groups, in the name of fairness. Justice, she maintains, must not be interpreted as requiring abstraction from the particular circumstances of one's life (Young 1990). On the contrary, it requires a recognition and accommodation of those circumstances.

Young's argument against abstraction and universalism can, however, appear to license a special pleading at odds with an understanding of citizenship as essentially a relationship between equals. Thus, Mary Dietz argues that citizenship is about getting beyond one's immediate sphere, and dealing as a citizen with other citizens (Dietz 1985). In this respect she appears to insist upon precisely the abstraction and universalism of which Young is deeply suspicious. But the differences between them are less important than the similarities, since both insist on the importance of difference and on the need to find ways of acknowledging difference in political contexts (see CITIZENSHIP §3).

From Wollstonecraft to Dietz, feminist political philosophy has been concerned with the political significance of differences between men and women, and the ways in which those differences may be rendered compatible with political justice and equal-ity. Often, that project has been pursued through a critique of the central concepts of political philosophy, and sometimes through a critique of political philosophy itself. In these respects, feminist political philosophy serves not only as a mechanism for drawing attention to the injustices of political arrangements as they affect women, but also as a means of revising our understanding of what political philosophy is.

See also: FEMINISM; FEMINIST ETHICS; FEMINIST JURISPRUDENCE

References and further reading

Bryson, V. (1992) *Feminist Political Theory*, London: Macmillan. (An excellent introductory text, clear and comprehensive, containing an extensive bibliography.)

* Dietz, M. (1985) 'Citizenship with a Feminist Face. The Problem with Maternal Thinking', *Political Theory* 13 (1): 19–37. (A critique of the political importance of maternal thinking; referred to in §7 of this entry.)

* Firestone, S. (1970) *The Dialectic of Sex*, New York: William Morrow. (A highly controversial and provocative book; discussed in §5 of this entry.)

* Mill, J.S. (1869) *The Subjection of Women*, P, 1983. (The most important nineteenth-century argument for the enfranchisement of women; discussed in §2 of this entry.)

* Okin, S. (1990) *Justice, Gender and the Family*, New York: Basic Books. (An incisive discussion of the gendered nature of modern political philosophy; referred to in §3 of this entry.)

Pateman, C. (1988) *The Sexual Contract*, Oxford and Cambridge: Polity Press. (A highly influential critique of contract theory, covering much of the history of political philosophy. A difficult but rewarding book.)

Phillips, A. (1991) *Engendering Democracy*, Oxford and Cambridge: Polity Press. (A clearly written and accessible account of the ways in which democratic theory is gendered.)

* Ruddick, S. (1990) *Maternal Thinking. Towards a Politics of Peace*, London: Women's Press. (A clearly written and influential book emphasizing the importance of ways of thinking developed through 'women's work'; discussed in §5 of this entry.)

* Taylor, H. (1851) *The Enfranchisement of Women*, London: Virago, 1983. (Contemporary with J.S. Mill's *Subjection of Women*, the text arguably more radical but less influential than Mill's work; discussed in §2 of this entry.)

* Wollstonecraft, M. (1792) *A Vindication of the Rights of Woman*, Harmondsworth: Penguin, 1978. (The first significant philosophical argument for the rights of women; discussed in §2 of this entry.)

Young, I.M. (1990) *Justice and the Politics of Difference*, Oxford: Princeton University Press. (A very influential discussion of the shortcomings of traditional democratic theory. Young argues for the affirmation rather than the suppression of social group difference. Discussed in §7 of this entry.)

SUSAN MENDUS

FEMINIST THEOLOGY

Feminist theology began as a reaction to the exclusion of women and women's concerns from traditional Christian theology, but it soon incorporated constructive as well as critical elements. Originating 'from the margins' of women's exclusion, it now is a major force within Christian theological thought. The issue it raised initially was the cultural and social suppositions that inform all theological thinking and that enter into theologies as 'universals'. In response to such universals, a feminist 'hermeneutic of suspicion' seeks out the hidden norms and biases within religious texts.

Feminist theology is diverse, but it is characterized by pervasive themes. Immanence is valued over transcendence, relation over substance, change over immutability, liberation over salvation, and ecological concerns over traditional Christian eschatological concerns. As could be expected from its hermeneutic of suspicion, feminist theology is also characterized by its insistence on the social location of all thinking. Feminist theologians uniformly use gender-inclusive language not only in reference to humanity, but also in reference to God. Finally, all feminist theologians manifest a concern for liberation from every type of oppression, environmental as well as social, and not just liberation from the oppression women have experienced.

1   A brief history of contemporary feminist theology
2   Feminist themes

1   A brief history of contemporary feminist theology

Feminist theology began modestly in April 1960 with the appearance of Valerie Saiving's article 'The Human Situation: A Feminine View'. Saiving raised a critical question concerning the work of the prominent theologian Reinhold NIEBUHR. In Niebuhr's monumental *The Nature and Destiny of Man* (1941–3), he analysed sin as pride and sensuousness, with pride clearly being the greater sin. Saiving suggested that perhaps pride was the distinctive sin of men; perhaps women's experience suggested a different understanding of sin as triviality, shallowness, and a deficiency of pride, which hindered women's self-development. Although it was eight years before the first major feminist work appeared (Mary Daly's *The Church and the Second Sex* (1968)), distinctive themes of feminist theology are already apparent in Saiving's article. These are: the particularity and social location of all theology; the marginality of women within male theology; and the social framework of patriarchy as the mediator of values, and the negative effect of these values upon women. These three themes formed the matrix of feminist theology in its early years. Feminist theology was a largely critical theology, aimed at exposing the pretensions to universality and the inherent sexism of all Western Christian thought.

Feminist theology moved towards constructive thought with Mary Daly's second book, *Beyond God the Father* (1973). Daly redefined the Christian doctrines of God, humanity, sin, salvation, Christology and ecclesiology by casting them within the framework of feminist values. She rejected the traditional notion of God as Being, and developed 'God the Verb' (see GOD, CONCEPTS OF §§1–3). Humanity was depicted as distorted by patriarchy, so that any ideal of humanity could only be developed in separation from patriarchy. Women unfolding their potential in response to the call of God the Verb were presented as the model for anthropology. Daly identified the primal sin as 'stolen energy', or men's systemic victimization of women together with the attribution of blame for this victimization to women themselves. Salvation is not through a Christ figure (for no male can save women), but through women reclaiming their energy and answering death-oriented male values with life-oriented female values. With regard to ecclesiology, Daly called for a new sisterhood of humanity governed by the vision of a community of women living in harmony with the world of animals and nature, beyond the reaches of the evil patriarchy. The work had a catalytic effect within the feminist religious community.

Two other major feminist theologians in the 1970s were Rosemary Radford Ruether and Letty Russell. Ruether's first major feminist work was *Liberation Theology* (1973), which was quickly followed by *New Woman, New Earth* (1975). In the first text, Ruether related feminist theology to the emergent liberation theologies of African-Americans and South Americans (see LIBERATION THEOLOGY); in the second work, she developed what was to become a dominant feminist theme concerning the connections between women and the earth in patriarchal theology. The earth, like woman, becomes object to man's subject; the earth, like woman, is exploitable for man's purposes. Thus the revaluation of woman entails a revaluation of earth as well. The redemption of women and men from patriarchy will result not only in new possibilities for women, but new possibilities for the earth.

Letty Russell's work focuses upon the implications of feminist theology for the redevelopment of the Church. Unlike Daly (and like Ruether), Russell argues that Christianity contains the seeds of its own redemption. The prophetic strain of Christianity always offers a critique of every present state of affairs, and the role of women in the present is to call Christianity to a more faithful expression of itself in communities of justice. A dominant motif for Russell is 'partnership', which signifies women and men together transforming the patriarchal Church into a newly redemptive community of wellbeing.

Daly, Ruether and Russell continued to have a major influence on feminist theology through the 1980s and into the 1990s. Following *Beyond God the Father*, however, Daly abandoned Christianity entirely and devoted her subsequent works to feminist philosophy rather than theology. Ruether's major subsequent works are *Sexism and God-talk* (1983) and *Gaia and God* (1992). In both works Ruether continues to develop her earlier themes, exploring reconceptualization of Christian doctrines, further analysing the intertwined history of sexism and the disregard of nature, and proposing a transforming synthesis of Christian notions of God with ecological notions of the earth as Gaia. Ruether maintains that only through such a reconceptualization can we address the almost irreversible destruction of the earth's biosphere that has been brought about by patriarchy.

Other major feminist voices are Rebecca Chopp, author of *The Power to Speak* (1989), and Elizabeth Johnson, author of *She Who Is* (1992). Both focus on the doctrine of God in relation to communities of justice and wellbeing, with Chopp developing the traditional language of God as 'Word' into the notion of a 'perfectly open sign' that cannot be restricted within one image. She contrasts 'Word' as perfectly open sign with the restrictive metaphor of 'father', arguing that because of the latter's patriarchal limitations, it is no longer an adequate portrayal of the God whose very being is directed towards emancipation for the oppressed.

Johnson develops a new understanding of the Trinitarian God, both drawing from the tradition and transforming it through explicitly putting feminist theology and classical theology in dialogue with one another. In the process, she shows that feminist

sensitivities can illuminate much in the ancient concept of God – particularly through revision of concepts such as 'omnipotence' and 'impassivity'. She also argues that feminist theology is given increased depth through incorporating aspects of the tradition.

In the decades since Saiving's initial article, it has become apparent that feminist theology can no more be reduced to a single voice than traditional theology. Not only is feminist theology itself diverse, but it has led to such alternative modes of theology as Womanist Theology, Mujerista Theology, Asian Women's Theology and Goddess Thealogy. The first three criticize the implicit and sometimes explicit racism of feminist theologians, who are seen to speak only for white middle- or upper-class women. These modes of theology go beyond critique, however, and create constructive theology by building upon insights developed through the distinctive ethnicities of (respectively) African-American women, Hispanic/ Latina women and women from the various countries in Asia. Goddess Thealogy criticizes the orientation towards God and/or Christianity of feminist theologians, claiming that Christianity, in large part by virtue of its notion of God, is the primary perpetrator of sexism and should therefore be abandoned. Despite its diversity, however, feminist theology tends to be characterized by the themes described below.

2   Feminist themes

Immanence over transcendence. Traditional theologies claim both of these categories, but the emphasis is clearly on transcendence. Feminists either retain both, but reverse the valuation, or eliminate or ignore transcendence in favour of immanence. Carter Heyward, in *The Redemption of God* (1982), falls into the latter category. For Heyward, God is wholly immanent, and is defined as the power of relationships between persons. Whether or not there is a transcendent locus to this power is irrelevant; the issue is our ability to relate to one another in constructive ways that value not only the individual but also the community. The power that generates this form of relation is also generated by this form of relation, so that, in a sense, the God who empowers relation is also strengthened by the dynamism of the resultant relations.

While Heyward comes close to collapsing the notion of God into the notion of community, other feminists, such as Mary Daly, retain the sense of transcendence in balance with immanence. Daly's naming of God moves successively from 'God the Verb' in *Beyond God the Father* to 'Goddess the Verb', the 'Unfolding Verb', 'Be-ing' and 'Meta-being' in her later works. The transcendent aspect of this 'Be-ing' functions as a power of the future. Patriarchal theologians such as Wolfhart Pannenberg also named God the power of the future, but in Daly's treatment the deity's transcendence acts as a lure to women who are freed from, or seek to be freed from, the powers of patriarchy. This dynamic 'Be-ing' calls women into a new future; hence this divine reality transcends the present moment. As a new future, this transcendent reality is also a transformative reality, calling women into a mode of being that has never before been achieved. Thus, in its transformative mode, 'Be-ing' is immanent as well as transcendent. 'Be-ing' becomes the other side of woman's self as a kind of meta-self, or, in Daly's capitalized version, the Self. It is the transcendent 'Be-ing' of the future become immanent, empowering woman's transformation. Thus in feminist theology, transcendence becomes a temporal rather than a spatial term, and immanence becomes an inward 'otherness' that is more than the self, yet intimately connected to it.

Relation over substance. The major category of Western theology is arguably 'substance' (see SUBSTANCE). Substance is that which requires nothing other than itself in order to exist, with the understanding, of course, that only God conforms perfectly to this ideal. Feminists roundly repudiate the notion of an independent substance, capable of existing apart from any relation, and argue instead that existence is itself profoundly relational. To exist is to be in relation; thus substance as that which requires nothing other than itself in order to exist is an absurdity.

The feminist value of relation over substance is not unique in late twentieth-century theology; process theologians, who follow Alfred North WHITEHEAD (§4), have long argued that process is reality, and that process is a dynamic movement in which every existent reality comes into being through integrating the influence of its predecessors into its own becoming (see PROCESS THEISM). Feminist theologians have generally not developed the metaphysical basis of relationships; rather, they tend to assume the primacy of relationships. In many respects, the appeal is simply to women's experience. Who one is develops in and through the relationships in which one participates. Relationships can be negative when one is subsumed into subservience to another, as in the sexist attempt to 'own' another person, or relationships can be positive, as in the richness of mutual relation. But that existence is formed in and through relationships tends to function as a given in feminist theology.

Change over immutability. Traditional theology tended to attribute immutability to God and mutability to the world, with mutability being the clearly subordinate and dependent state (see IMMUTABILITY).

Given the feminist assertion of the primacy of relation over substance, feminists likewise value mutability over immutability. The latter is regarded as an abstraction, merely posited as the antithesis of what is considered to be universal movement, process or change.

A major implication of the feminist rejection of immutability is the redefinition of perfection. Classical theology related perfection to immutability, holding that if a subject could change, it was either better or worse than the state from which it changed; hence perfection required immutability. The feminist rejection of immutability entails a change in the understanding of perfection. In feminist hands, perfection is a dynamic condition that requires change in order continuously to manifest itself. Far from being a subordinate category, change is essential to existence.

Liberation over salvation. Traditional theology maintained that there were both historical and everlasting aspects to salvation, but feminist theologians focus almost entirely on the historical. For them, salvation is not a change of state before God, an imputed righteousness covering one's sins, or an individual affair. But since 'salvation' connotes all these things, feminists eschew the word and speak instead of 'liberation'. Far from being individualistically oriented, liberation bespeaks a transformation of the social/symbolic system of one's culture from patriarchal exclusiveness to communities of inclusive wellbeing. In *The Power to Speak*, Rebecca Chopp describes such communities as existing through 'emancipatory transformation'.

Many feminist theologians envisage such communities of liberation as already existing through para-Church organizations such as 'women-church' (Ruether 1985). These small group communities are both inside and outside the Church. Inside, they function to bring about change within congregations; outside, they function as small worship and support groups for like-minded feminists. Other feminists, such as Russell (1993), focus more clearly on the existing Church as a community of liberation, finding congregations within the Church that are willing to experiment with new modes of inclusive wellbeing. But all feminists call for transformation not only within the Church, but within society, with the aim of achieving more just and sustainable conditions of life. This is liberation, and like the symbol of 'salvation' before it, it is both the goal and the process of Christian life.

Ecology over eschatology. As implied in the preceding section, feminist concerns focus on the wellbeing of this world, both the many-cultured world of peoples and the many-splendoured world of nature.

As early as the 1970s, feminists pointed out the symbolic connections between women and nature, and argued that the liberation of one entails the liberation of the other. For example, Ruether in *Gaia and God* contrasts the feminist ecological concern with Christian eschatology (see ESCHATOLOGY §1). While the latter dealt in temporal as well as eternal salvation, it tended to include an end of the world, along with other-worldly redemption and spiritualized bodies. Feminist adaptation of this eschatology also speaks about an end of the world, but through human wastefulness rather than through divine judgment. The apocalypse often associated with eschatology becomes the natural disasters resulting from deforestation, ozone depletion, air, ground and water pollution, and the rapid extinction of species. This feminist adaptation of eschatology into ecology decries eschatology's depiction of the loss of this world in favour of another, calling instead for social and individual conversion in order to realize responsible, just and sustainable communities of wellbeing.

The above five themes characterize feminist theology. Emphasis and development vary, depending upon the perspective of the particular theologian. But the impact of feminist theology as a new genre within theological discourse is raising awareness of these issues within all modes of contemporary theology.

See also: FEMINISM; FEMINIST ETHICS

References and further reading

* Chopp, R. (1989) *The Power to Speak: Feminism, Language, God*, New York: Crossroad Publishing. (Replaces the notion of 'God' with 'Word' as the 'perfectly open sign', open for its own and for society's transformation.)

Chopp, R. and Taylor, M.L. (eds) (1994) *Reconstructing Christian Theology*, Minneapolis, MN: Fortress Press. (Collection of essays juxtaposing traditional Christian doctrines with contemporary challenges and reconstructing the doctrines accordingly.)

* Daly, M. (1968) *The Church and the Second Sex*, Boston, MA: Beacon Press. (Uncovers the history of misogyny in the Church.)

* —— (1973) *Beyond God the Father*, Boston, MA: Beacon Press. (Redevelops the major doctrines of Christianity according to feminist criteria.)

* Heyward, C. (1982) *The Redemption of God: A Theology of Mutual Relation*, Lanham, MD: University Press of America. (A theology of immanence, stressing the power of God within and for human relationships.)

* Johnson, E. (1992) *She Who Is: The Mystery of God in Feminist Theological Discourse*, New York: Crossroad Publishing. (Redevelops the notion of the trinity through the centrality of Sophia-Spirit, with implications developed for human communities involving just and liberating relationships.)

McFague, S. (1993) *The Body of God: An Ecological Theology*, Minneapolis, MD: Fortress Press. (A revision of theology developed around the central metaphor of the world as God's body.)

* Niebuhr, R. (1941) *The Nature and Destiny of Man*, vol. 1, *Human Nature*, New York: Charles Scribner's Sons. (An investigation of what it is to be human, including consideration of finitude, freedom and sin.)

* Ruether, R.R. (1973) *Liberation Theology*, New York: Paulist Press. (An exploration of the issues raised in Black theology and in the emerging feminist theology of the 1960s and early 1970s in America.)

* —— (1975) *New Woman, New Earth*, New York: The Seabury Press. (An analysis of the formation of images of women in religion through study of the ideologies and structures of sexism, racism and capitalism.)

* —— (1983) *Sexism and God-Talk: Toward a Feminist Theology*, Boston, MA: Beacon Press. (Argues that Christianity has a prophetic stream within it that works towards its own transformation, and redevelops major Christian doctrines accordingly.)

* —— (1985) *Women-Church: Theology and Practice of Feminist Liturgical Communities*, New York: Harper & Row. (Practical analysis of the historical and theological understanding of the Church as a community of liberation. Offers guidelines for developing a feminist renewal movement within the Church.)

* —— (1992) *Gaia and God: An Ecofeminist Theology of Earth Healing*, San Francisco, CA: Harper. (Outlines the history of human destruction of the earth, relating this destruction to social symbol systems. Proposes a new symbolism to catalyse healing of the earth and its communities.)

* Russell, L. (1993) *The Church in the Round: Feminist Interpretation of the Church*, Louisville, KY: Westminster/John Knox Press. (Uses a paradigm of partnership to develop an ecclesiology that lessens distinctions between clergy and laity, and that interprets the Church in terms of its mission of liberation both within the Church and in society.)

* Saiving, V. (1960) 'The Human Situation: A Feminine View', *Journal of Religion* 40: 100–12. (A consideration from the point of view of women of Niebuhr's analysis of sin as pride and sensuousness. Argues that Niebuhr concentrates overly on the sin of pride, which peculiarly defines male experience, and neglects the issues problematic to women, such

as triviality and a failure to have enough pride in oneself and one's work.)

Thistlethwaite, S.B. and Potter, M.E. (eds) (1990) *Lift Every Voice: Constructing Christian Theologies from the Underside*, New York: Crossroad Publishing. (A collection of essays treating major Christian doctrines from the point of view of oppression and liberation.)

MARJORIE SUCHOCKI

FEMINIST THOUGHT IN LATIN AMERICA

Any analysis of feminist thought in Latin America is burdened by the task of combatting the frequent assumption that feminism is an ideology imported from the USA or Europe. One could begin by arguing that in certain senses autocthonous feminist thought has existed in Latin America for centuries. The thought of Sor Juana Inés de la Cruz, a seventeenth-century Mexican writer and nun, had certain qualities, themes and perspectives that can be called feminist. Her autobiographical essay, 'Reply to Sor Filotea de la Cruz', is a brilliant defence of a woman's right to engage in intellectual pursuits and includes many feminist strategies and dimensions.

Among the Latin American feminists through the centuries, exemplary passages are easily found, such as the following from the Peruvian Flora Tristán, who said 'Without liberation of woman, there will be no liberation of man' (1843). Revisionist reappraisals of underappreciated women thinkers have grown more common. Venezuelan Teresa de la Parra's important writings which have been re-examined as texts by women continue to be rescued from relative obscurity. Rosario Castellanos, Rigoberta Menchú and Domitila Barrios de Chungara count among those whose work has enjoyed increased critical attention. Concurrently, the voices of traditionally voiceless women are being heard through expanding oral history projects, such as those of domestic workers in Bogotá: 'It is not enough to have rights. We must raise consciousness and organize ourselves to defend those rights'.

In recent years, particularly after the international year of the woman in 1975 and the decade of the woman sponsored by the United Nations from 1976 to 1985, women and men have continued to develop feminist philosophies appropriate for Latin American contexts.

Professional feminist philosophy has been practised in Latin America since the early part of the twentieth century. Perhaps surprisingly, a theoretically sophisticated feminist philosophy was practised in Uruguay at this time by male social philosopher, Carlos Vaz Ferreira (1871–1958). His work had significant impact on women's rights in Latin America. Vaz Ferreira was a pioneer in feminist theory.*

1 **The early twentieth century: Carlos Vaz Ferreira**
2 **Recent trends**

1 The early twentieth century: Carlos Vaz Ferreira

The ideas of this seminal Latin American social thinker and his thought-provoking study of gender and family have stood the test of time since they were first delivered in Uruguay in 1914. *Sobre feminismo* (On Feminism) (1933) was written between 1914 and 1922 in the form of lectures which were delivered at the University of Montevideo where Vaz Ferreira was an academic. The book is concerned primarily with examining 'factual' differences between the sexes and 'normative' issues, such as the political, civil rights, their social life and the organization of the family within society. Vaz Ferreira analyses the disproportion between the ideas and faculties of women and the scope which society allows to their activity. He advocates the right of women to participate in all that makes life valuable to the individual human being. The ideas he expresses in *Sobre feminismo* (On Feminism) are poignant, relevant and innovative in the light of contemporary social debates throughout the Americas.

Sobre feminismo (On Feminism) is the Latin American counterpart of John Stuart Mill's *The Subjection of Women* (1869) in terms of content and tone, and more importantly, its impact on elite thinking. *Sobre feminismo* (On Feminism), however, reflects the social changes that could be expected more than fifty years later. Vaz Ferreira's early influence on the suffrage movement was significant and his contributions are particularly noteworthy given that in general Hispanic men of his culture and age were not renowned for their progressive attitudes towards women. In Latin American intellectual circles in the early part of the twentieth century, an effect of the pervasive *machismo* and its complementary femininity was to marginalize women so thoroughly that thought about gender and family roles only had widespread impact when expressed by powerful men.

As one of Latin America's most influential social philosophers in the early twentieth century, Vaz Ferreira's complete works were collected in twenty-five volumes (1957–63). *Sobre feminismo* (On Feminism), set within the Latin American experience, presents cogent arguments against the marginalization of women, the infringement of their political rights and their second-class status in marriage. Vaz

625

Ferreira outlined a theory of cooperation between men and women which privileged monogamy, the family and the equitable division of household tasks. He studied the ways in which pregnancy can be a disadvantage for women and suggested remedies to compensate for what he viewed as biological inequity. Ahead of his time, Vaz Ferreira reflected on divorce, artificial insemination and abortion. He was a painstaking, self-consciously philosophical craftsman who clearly grappled with what evidence he could muster to support what was essentially cultural and social criticism of the intimate dealings of men and women. He was avid in avoiding contradiction so as to insist on a certain philosophical probity which was not expected in Latin American discourses on women's roles at that time. Because of this insistence, he was considered a model of anthropologically-sensitive social philosophy.

The first print-run of *Sobre feminismo* (On Feminism) (1933) coincided with the year in which Uruguayan women's suffrage was enacted. Since Uruguay was one of the first Latin American countries in which women's suffrage was achieved, the lengthy gestation period and public lectures which led to its publication reveal both its timeliness within Uruguayan society and Vaz Ferreira's role as an influential public thinker.

These dates are historically significant because they show that serious feminist thought has been going on in Latin America since the early part of the twentieth century. However, the theories of Vaz Ferreira have not received the critical attention they deserve. *Sobre feminismo* (On Feminism) is still a relatively unknown work, while European and North American analyses of feminism remain privileged and widely disseminated. One distinguishing feature of Vaz Ferreira's work is that it includes analysis of justice for women within the context of the family while many contemporary theories of justice omit consideration of women in families (see FAMILY, ETHICS AND THE; JUSTICE).

Sobre feminismo (On Feminism) is an analysis of the social situation of the woman 'of flesh and bone' in the context of 'feminism' and 'antifeminism'. In Vaz Ferreira's words, 'those terms "feminism" and "antifeminism", "feminist" and "antifeminist", in reality, do more harm than good, and they complicate the many and sometimes enormous difficulties of the problems: they complicate them further with questions of words and with confusions derived from the words' (1933: 14). He believed that a false polarization is produced by the terms 'feminism' and 'antifeminism' because there are those who believe 'we are the true feminists because we want to preserve the distinctive traits of the female sex. You want to

make men of women; your true name ought to be "hominists" and not "feminists"' (1933: 17). In Vaz Ferreira's view, the issues are neither so polarized nor so simple and this kind of resentment impedes serious analysis of the situation in which modern woman finds herself. Nevertheless, considering the various connotations implicit in the term 'feminism', contemporaries run the risk of being misunderstood when calling themselves 'feminist'. Vaz Ferreira recognized the importance of clarifying language usage and tried to extract concrete meanings when discussing feminism.

He felt the best strategy for confronting the problem of the social situation of women is to examine, on the one hand, the possible questions relating to the similarities and differences between the two sexes and, on the other, examine normative problems. Vaz Ferreira distinguished factual questions from normative ones in *Lógica viva* (Living Logic) (1910). Such factual questions relate to knowledge and verification and the normative questions relate to action, preference and choice. The latter are most relevant in terms of the female condition.

Among the questions of similarities and differences between the sexes, Vaz Ferreira maintains that there are debatable and undebatable data. The important undebatable fact, radical for his time is: 'From the union between a man and a woman, the woman can become pregnant; nothing happens to the man'. He argued that, 'finding this fact to be satisfactory is to be "antifeminist"' (1933: 25). The factual data are of three types: biological, physiological and psychological. A recurring debate is that of 'the comparative intelligence of the two sexes, a special case in the category of comparative psychology' (1933: 12). However, in his treatment of the intelligence and mental aptitudes of women, Vaz Ferreira takes seriously the possibility that it could be verifiable that women might be less intelligent than men as he ponders why there have been no female Beethovens or Darwins, for example. This is the weakest point in his argument and one of the rare occasions when he fails to take socialization into account when trying to explain differences between social groups and their roles.

More convincing is his treatment of normative problems in *Sobre feminismo* (On Feminism) (1933). The normative problems for Vaz Ferreira are women's political rights, their activity in society, their access to public office, careers, professions and education; civil rights, the relations between the sexes and the organization of the family.

The basic idea in his analysis of these problems is to maintain the difference between 'feminism of equality' and 'feminism of compensation'. The former, according to Vaz Ferreira, is based on the idea that 'jobs and careers should be open to women as they are to men; that women should have the same civil capacity as men, the same level of education; that, in general, the sexes should be equalized by diminishing the difference between them and by placing women in the same situation as men, making them more like men' (1933: 16). For him, 'feminism of equality' does not merit much attention because of the mere fact that women are biologically mistreated by the likelihood of pregnancy in their unions with men and therefore it is not possible to speak of 'equalization'. The only acceptable feminism to Vaz Ferreira is that of 'compensation', based on the idea that it is necessary to compensate physiological injustice given that it will never be possible to equalize it and that it would be counterproductive to attempt to do so. Thus, 'Antifeminism takes as its guide that fact (women's biological disadvantage). Bad feminism does not even take it into account. Good feminism strives to correct it and compensate for it' (1933: 38).

With respect to the civil and political rights and social participation of women, Vaz Ferreira had a decisive impact in favour of women in the Uruguayan legislature. Suffrage in Uruguay was enacted in 1933, following the USA (1920) and Ecuador (1929). Vaz Ferreira also proposed a bill, the law of unilateral divorce, which passed into law in the form he had conceived it. The law gave women the power to obtain a divorce at will 'without giving cause, while men have to show just cause' (1933: 83). This law is consistent with his theory that the situations of men and women are fundamentally different. When the law was passed, 'opponents of divorce did not like it because of their need to preserve the family as the basis of society. Proponents of the right to a divorce did not like it either because they framed the question as one of "equality"' (1933: 83). Vaz Ferreira's position can be criticized as a case of reverse sexism in which men do not have the same rights as women. It can also be placed in the context of his theory of 'feminism of compensation' in the way he seems to propose replacing patriarchy with matriarchy to correct historical inequities. To some extent Vaz Ferreira also believed that matriarchy deserved a turn in beginning the long process of compensation.

The normative problem which most concerned Vaz Ferreira was that of relations between the sexes and the organization of the family. His analysis of marriage and divorce was a curious mix of obsolete and progressive ideas. He asserted that roles outside the home are for men and those inside the home are for women; that it is possible that women are less intelligent than men because most great cultural figures are men and that 'free love' is a destructive social force.

At the same time, Vaz Ferreira was a pioneer of feminist ideas which became widespread much later. For example, although he believed that relationships are ideally constituted as monogamous marriages, he also indentified marriage as an institution which unfairly regulates and limits the role of women both in professions and as part of a workforce, and therefore needed modification. Vaz Ferreira wrote, 'A woman's capacity to live for herself, which has to do with power, ability, and opportunity, should not depend wholly on marriage, as it seems to in mainstream society, which is one of the saddest and most unpleasant aspects of traditional society' (1933). He also criticized the arguments of opponents of divorce who 'reason as if those who support the right to a divorce maintained that divorce is a good' (1933: 81). He believed that it was unfair that women have been expected to change their names when they marry while men do not modify theirs. He asked: 'Isn't this a relic of antiquated social structures in which the man owned the woman, or she was subordinate to him?' (1933: 141).

2   Recent trends

Women's suffrage did not immediately translate into social change. After 1933, although suffrage spread throughout Latin America, with Paraguay being the last country to enact it in 1961, philosophy continued to be practised almost exclusively by men. However, feminist concerns sometimes arose tangentially in other philosophical discussions. The Mexican philosopher Leopoldo Zea (1912–) focused on women, indigenous peoples and children as early as 1952 in his analyses of marginality (see MARGINALITY; MEXICO, PHILOSOPHY IN). Similarly, theories of liberation often selfconsciously advocated the rights of women (see LIBERATION PHILOSOPHY).

Since the 1980s Latin American women have entered the academy in greater numbers, many of whom have become actively engaged in feminist philosophy in addition to other philosophical areas of expertise. Scholars of literature and the social sciences have increasingly drawn philosophers into their debates about feminist theory. There has been an increase in the number of feminist conferences, books and journals, most notably in Mexico and Argentina, as well as throughout Latin America. *Fem* (1975–) and *Debate feminista* (1988–) are journals of feminist thought published in Mexico. *Feminaria* has been published in Argentina since 1988.

One of the key points of debate among feminist thinkers has centred on the primordial nature of gender and class. While some have maintained a traditional socialist idea that women must work towards justice with men rather than emphasize differences between men and women, others have argued that patriarchy must be subverted before there can exist a society unconstrained by divisions of gender. Thus, the former believe that class is primordial, while the latter privilege gender-based social order in their analyses.

Feminist thought in Latin America can be differentiated from many of its North American and European counterparts by an almost ever-present concern for the family and certain forms of Latin social life and relationships. Although alternative lifestyles do exist among women in Latin America, feminist philosophy has commonly attempted to end discrimination against women while simultaneously accepting the family as the fundamental social unit. Many translations of North American and European feminist thought are published in Latin America and read widely, despite the fact that their emphasis on the individual rather than the family is not easily adapted to Latin American contexts and is often seized on as evidence of fundamental cultural difference.

Feminist thought in Latin America continues to focus on the pressing concerns of Latin American societies first, without necessarily concerning itself with questions of its applicability to other regions of the world. Rather than being a separatist movement, feminist thought is often well-served by connections forged with other areas of contemporary thought in Latin America, such as the development of democracy, equality and socialism, religious and secular ethics and liberation philosophy.

See also: FEMINISM; FEMINIST POLITICAL PHILOSOPHY

References and further reading

* Barrios de Chungara, D. (1978) *Let Me Speak! Testimony of Domitila, a Woman of the Bolivian Mines*, trans. V. Ortiz, New York: Monthly Review Press. (Written with M. Viezzer.)
* Castellanos, R. (1973) *Mujer que sabe latín* (A Woman Who Knows Latin), Mexico: Secretaría de Educación Pública. (Counts among some of the feminists whose work has been rescued from relative obscurity.)
  Cruz, J. Inés de la (c.1700) *A Woman of Genius: the Intellectual Autobiography of Sor Juana Inés de la Cruz*, trans. and intro. M. Sayers Peden, Salisbury, CT: Lime Rock Press, 1982. (Contains her autobiographical essay, 'Reply to Sor Filotea de la Cruz'.)

  Hierro, G. (1985) *La naturaleza feminina: tercer coloquio nacional de filosofía* (Feminine Nature: Third National Convention on Philosophy), Mexico: Universidad Nacional Autónoma de México. (Anthology of articles by feminist philosophers in Mexico, many of which centre on the question of the existence of feminine nature.)
  —— (1990) *Ética y feminismo* (Ethics and Feminism), Mexico: Universidad Nacional Autónoma de México. (Analysis of the ethics of 'being for others'.)
* Menchú, R. (1984) *I, Rigoberta Menchú, an Indian Woman in Guatemala*, ed. with intro. E. Burgos-Debray, trans. A. Wright, London and New York: Verso. (An account of being a woman in a country where women traditionally have been voiceless.)
  Patai, D. (1988) *Brazilian Women Speak: Contemporary Life Stories*, New Brunswick, NJ: Rutgers University Press. (Tales of women in Brazil.)
  Schutte, O. (1993) *Cultural Identity and Social Liberation in Latin American Thought*, Albany, NY: State University of New York Press. (The chapter on cultural identity, liberation and feminist theory provides an excellent overview of this topic.)
* Tristán, F. (1843) *La emancipación de la mujer* (The Emancipation of Woman), trans. M.E. Mur de Lara, Lima: Editorial P.T.C.M., 1948. (A posthumous work completed from her notes by A. Constant.)
* Vaz Ferreira, C. (1910) Lógica viva (Living Logic), in *Obras: Homenaje*, 25 vols, Montevideo: Cámara de Representantes de la República Oriental de Uruguay, 1957–63. (Vaz Ferreira distinguishes factual questions relating to knowledge from normative ones.)
* —— (1933) *Sobre feminismo* (On Feminism), Buenos Aires: Editorial Losada, 2nd edn. 1957, 3rd edn. 1963. (A collection of lectures on feminism that constitute the foundations of feminist theory in twentieth-century Latin America.)
* —— (1957–63) *Obras: Homenaje* (Complete Works: Homage), 25 vols, Montevideo: Cámara de Representantes de la República Oriental de Uruguay. (All of his original Spanish works are included.)
* Zea, L. (1952) *Conciencia y posibilidad del mexicano* (Consciousness and Possibilities of the Mexican Citizen, Mexico: Porrúa. (Analysis of the Mexican condition of marginality which includes discussion of women's treatment.)

AMY A. OLIVER

FÉNELON, FRANÇOIS DE SALIGNAC DE LA MOTHE (1651–1715)

Fénelon is best-known for his utopian political novel Aventures de Télémaque fils d'Ulysse *(Telemachus, Son of Ulysses) (1699), which contrasts the rustic simplicity of Greek antiquity with the corrupt luxuriousness of Louis XIV's Versailles. The crucial philosophical works of Fénelon are the* Refutation of Malebranche *(c.1686–7) and the* Maxims of the Saints *(1697).*

Fénelon came from a provincial aristocratic family (Périgord) which had long served the French crown. First noticed by Bishop Bossuet in the 1670s, Fénelon spent that decade ministering to the 'new Catholics' (ex-Huguenots) in Northern France. He was made tutor to the grandson of Louis XIV in 1689, then Archbishop of Cambrai in 1695.

Although Fénelon is best-known for his utopian political novel *Aventures de Télémaque fils d'Ulysse* (Telemachus, Son of Ulysses) (1699), which contrasts the rustic simplicity of Greek antiquity with the corrupt luxuriousness of Louis XIV's Versailles, the *Réfutation du système du Pére Malebranche* (c.1686–7) is the best evidence of his philosophical abilities. MALEBRANCHE had argued in his controversial *Traité de la nature et de la grace* (1680) that God governs the realms of nature and of grace equally by 'simple' and 'general' invariable laws; that these laws are the product of divine 'general will' or *volonté générale*; that nature is 'nothing but the general laws which God has established in order to construct or to preserve his work by the simplest means'. God, according to Malebranche, 'does not act at all' by *volontés particulières*, by lawless *ad hoc* volitions, as do 'limited intelligences'; and the generality and simplicity of the divine operation even explains the origin of evil in an imperfect world: if, Malebranche says, 'rain falls on certain lands, and if the sun roasts others... this is not at all because God wanted to produce those effects by *volontés particulières*; it is because he has established [general] laws... whose effects are necessary consequences'. Those who claim that God *ought*, through special *volontés particulières*, to suspend general laws if their operation will harm the innocent, or that he ought to confer grace particularly only on those who will be saved by it, fail to understand that it is unworthy of a wise being to abandon general rules. Those who want God to act through particular wills, simply 'imagine that God at every moment is performing miracles in their favour'. But this 'self-love', Malebranche insists, rests on 'ignorance' of the fact that God 'rarely' departs from generality and simplicity (unless 'order' permits the departure), that he acts 'not often' through anything as *particulier* as a miracle.

In his *Réfutation*, Fénelon challenged the whole Malebranchian notion of a 'general' and 'simple' universe, and thought that he had found a fatal flaw in Malebranche's admission that God acts only *usually*, but not invariably, through general wills and general laws – that God sometimes, though 'rarely', acts through volontés particulières. 'In what', Fénelon demands, 'consists that which the author calls "rarely"? These words signify nothing, unless they mean that there is a certain small number of *volontés particulières* which order permits to God outside the general laws, after which he can will nothing particularly'. But if order permits God a small number of particular wills, then 'it follows not only that these *volontés particulières* do not harm in the slightest the simplicity of God's ways, but even that it is more perfect of God to mix some *volontés particulières* in his general plan, than to limit himself absolutely to his *volontés générales*'. Fénelon imagines a hypothetical case in which 'order' has permitted God to have a hundred 'particular wills'; and asks the rhetorical question: 'What, then, is this "simplicity" which is able to accommodate a hundred [particular] wills, which even requires them, but which invincibly rejects the hundred and first?' Fénelon responds in an effective passage: 'If God did not have these hundred *volontés particulières*, he would cease to be God; for he would violate the order which requires them... [but] if he had the hundred and first *volonté*, he would also cease to be God, for he would destroy the simplicity of his ways'. Finally, Fénelon inquires, triumphantly and sarcastically, whether there is 'a fatal number of exceptions which God is obliged to use up, after which he can will nothing except according to general laws?' No one who takes divine omnipotence seriously, Fénelon insists, would 'dare' to say this.

In 1697, Fénelon wrote the book which caused his banishment by Louis XIV, the *Maximes des saints* (Maxims of the Saints) – the 'quietist' work arguing for the 'disinterested' or 'pure' love of God which got Fénelon into such trouble with the Church. In the *Maxims*, Fénelon argued for five degrees of 'purity' or 'disinterestedness' in human love of God. At the lowest end of the scale one finds 'purely servile love': the love of God, not for himself but for 'the goods which depend on his power and which one hopes to obtain'. One small notch above this Fénelon places loving God, not for 'goods' which he can provide but as the 'instrument' of our salvation; even this 'higher' love, however, is still 'at the level of self-love'. At the

629

third and fourth levels Fénelon finds a mixture of self-love and true love of God; but what really interests him is the fifth and highest degree, the 'pure love' of God that one finds only in 'saints': 'One can love God', Fénelon urges, 'from a love which is pure charity, and without the slightest mixture of self-interested motivation'. In such a love, neither the 'fear of punishment' nor the 'hope of reward' plays any part at all. To achieve this love, one must 'go out of oneself' (*sortir de soi*), even 'hate oneself' (*se haïr*). Malebranche, in his *Traité de l'amour de Dieu* (date?), argued that Fénelon's 'disinterested' love excluded all hope of salvation, as well as all fear of justified punishment, and thus subverted Christianity; and Fénelon's work was finally placed on the Index. Only LEIBNIZ (among important contemporaries) continued to urge that Fénelon's version of 'quietism' was well-meant.

In 1713, near the end of his life, Fénelon wrote *De l'existence de Dieu*, which is not as original and controversial as it is lucid and graceful; its object was to turn back Jansenism as a form of demi-Calvinism. The sheer orthodoxy of this work left it unattacked – an uncommon event in Fénelon's life. But it is the works on Malebranche and on 'quietism' which are still taken seriously – together with *Aventures de Télémaque fils d'Ulysse*, which became the most read book in eighteenth-century France after the Bible.

See also: PIETISM

List of works

Fénelon, F. de S. de la M. (1699) *Aventures de Télémaque fils d'Ulysse*, ed. and trans. P. Riley, *Telemachus, Son of Ulysses*, Cambridge: Cambridge University Press, 1994. (Fénelon's political utopian novel.)
—— (1835) *Oeuvres de Fénelon*, Paris, 3 vols. (All the works of Fénelon mentioned are most conveniently to be found in this collection. Including (c.1686–7) *Réfutation du système du Père Malebranche*; (1697) *Maximes des saints*; (1699) *Telemachus* and (1713) *De l'existence de Dieu*.)

References and further reading

Goré, J.L. (1957) *L'Itinéraire de Fénelon: humanisme et spiritualité*, Paris.
Gouhier, H. (1977) *Fénelon philosophe*, Librairie Philosophique, Paris: Vrin.
* Malebranche, N. (1680) *Traité de la nature et de la grace*, in *Oeuvres complètes de Malebranche* (Complete works of Malebranche), ed. A. Robinet, Paris: Vrin, 1958–65, vol. 5; trans. P. Riley as *Treatise on Nature and Grace*, Oxford: Oxford University Press, 1992. (Malebranche's theodicy and account of human freedom.)
* —— (1697) *Traité de l'amour de Dieu*, in *Oeuvres complètes de Malebranche* (Complete works of Malebranche), ed. A. Robinet, Paris: Vrin, 1958–65, vol. 14. (Criticism of Fénelon's 'disinterested love'.)

PATRICK RILEY

FERGUSON, ADAM (1723–1815)

Rarely mentioned by philosophers except as companion of David Hume and Adam Smith, Ferguson contributed a political consciousness to the moral philosophy of eighteenth-century Scotland. In An Essay on the History of Civil Society *(1767), Ferguson used a comparative method to reflect on a commercial society distinguished by refined division of labour and to caution against its political dangers. With his intentionally elevated rhetoric he sought to counter his philosophical contemporaries' analytical aloofness from the negative effects of the civility, commerce, security and critical philosophy they prized. Ferguson's textbooks and Roman history deserve philosophical attention for their help with interpreting his distinctive social diagnosis of the liberal political constitution.*

Ferguson's Highlands birth and Gaelic made him unique among the figures prominent in the 'Scottish Enlightenment' (see ENLIGHTENMENT, SCOTTISH), but he was unexceptionally Whig in politics and Moderate in Church affairs. Born 1723 in Logierait near Perth, Ferguson moved to Edinburgh for divinity studies after an MA from the then provincial St Andrews. An intimate of the circle around David HUME, he early abandoned a clerical career. Ferguson served five years as professor of natural philosophy in the University of Edinburgh, thanks to political patrons of the literary set, and then, in 1765, began a popular twenty years as professor of pneumatics and moral philosophy. The professorial position was more didactic than scholarly, as was clear from Ferguson's effectiveness in the science chair; but Ferguson's *Essay on the History of Civil Society* (1767) gained him recognition beyond the lecture room and salon. There were French and German translations, and attention from philosophers on the Continent. In addition to four pamphlets on political controversies, Ferguson published two textbooks for his course, the second a retrospective work, in which he systematized the changes he made during his years of teaching and a long-standard, but largely derivative, *History of the Progress and Termination of the Roman Republic* (1785). He died in 1815. His books were staples of instruction in American colleges well into the nineteenth century.

Neither Hume nor Adam SMITH was impressed by Ferguson as a theorist. Philosophers have left his work to on the one hand intellectual historians, who find there the epitome of republican misgivings – perhaps conditioned by a pre-Romantic Highlands sensibility – about the Scottish race to modernity after the Jacobite Rising of 1745, and on the other hand to sociologists, who honour Ferguson as a science-minded progenitor of sociological theories of modernity. With his invocation of classical models and his alarms against corruption in nations dedicated to individual gain rather than heroic action, Ferguson amplifies the discourse of 'civic humanism' or 'Machiavellian moralism', as many historians emphasize; but he also fits in with a wider class of didactic rhetoricians who sought to bolster a religiously latitudinarian moral community in eighteenth-century Scotland. Sociologists' claims to Ferguson are no less justified, first and especially by Ferguson's insistence that the study of human nature is an empirical study of humans in civil societies differing in design from one developmental stage to another, and second by his conjectural reconstruction of these designs to recognize not only political, economic and ideological differences, in the manner of MONTESQUIEU, but also sociological mechanisms such as integration through conflict, stratification, and diverse forms of sociation. Karl Marx's incidental commendation of Ferguson as a materialist thinker with original insights into the harm done to workers by a refined division of labour (see MARX, K.) stimulated a tradition of commentary that emphasizes – and exaggerates – the extent to which Ferguson first identifies each historical period with a distinctive mode of subsistence, second, rationalizes the respective schemes of stratification, property, mentality, political formation by reference to this feature, and, third, identifies a potentially explosive tension in the latest stage – a commercial society whose political order is progressively undermined by its own socio-economic arrangements.

Although modest about the originality and rigour of his efforts, Ferguson counted himself a participant in the philosophical debates of his time and, indeed, as Adam Smith's competitor in addressing what George Davie calls 'the central problem of Scottish philosophy', namely, reconciling material advance with traditional moral standards in a 'teachable philosophy of civilization' (Davie 1976). Viewed from this perspective, Ferguson's writings appear as exercises in complementarity, in which their author is seeking a reasonable strategy for co-ordinating two distinct modes of reflection. On one side is an analytical model of the progressive development of the human species through a sequence of stages in the history of civil society, with each stage conceived as a configuration of diversely formed productive, legal, moral, intellectual and hierarchical relations, some more systematic than others. On the other side is the evocation of a practical capacity to act in the diverse historical contexts, with the quality of actions assessed by standards of active virtue, especially manifest in political practice.

Ferguson submits the first level of study to Newtonian rules of method, in principle; and his work often varies themes from Hume and Smith. The second type of knowledge he distinguishes from the first as the knowledge appropriate to actors, not spectators; and he attacks Smith for neglecting this dimension and for allowing moral psychology or economic laws to stand in for responsible decisions. Moral conduct is opaque without a science of the facts of human existence, but incoherent without practical understanding. Historical stages constitute scenes for actions subject to principles derived from a practical philosophy of elevated happiness. Political arrangements express modes of action designed to counter the negative effects of adventitious social circumstances. The essay form bypasses philosophical difficulties in interrelating these levels, but Ferguson's experiment gains in philosophical seriousness from his astute reflection on literary forms like the essay.

In his moral philosophy class, as documented in the Institutes of *Moral Philosophy* (1768) and the retrospective *Principles of Moral and Political Science* (1792), Ferguson grounded the 'history of the species' in a psychological theory of the individual, and elaborated a distinction between explanatory and normative theories. Although his decisive construct, of 'man's progressive nature', has the wobble of improvisation, the effort to constitute a structured connection between the distinct domains marks an advance in the literature of Common Sense responses (see COMMON SENSE SCHOOL) to Hume. Put in the context of his view of constitutions as imperfect syntheses of conflicts, Ferguson's designs are suggestive for a period of philosophical experimentation.

See also: HUMAN NATURE, SCIENCE OF IN THE 18TH CENTURY; SOCIAL SCIENCE, HISTORY OF PHILOSOPHY OF

List of works

Ferguson, A. (1767) *An Essay on the History of Civil Society*, ed. and intro by D. Forbes, Edinburgh: Edinburgh University Press, 1966 (reprint of first edition, with collation of the variants in the seventh); ed. D. Forbes with intro. L. Schneider, New Brunswick, NJ, and London: Transaction, 1980. (Forbes 1966 edition is a reprint of the first edition, with a collation of the variants in the seventh edition of 1814. Ferguson's best-known work, presenting the moral and political issues of the time as a function of the 'advancement of civil and commercial arts' and emphasizing the threat of civic corruption in a 'polished and commercial' society.)

—— (1768) *Institutes of Moral Philosophy*, New York: Garland, 1978. (1773 edition, 1785 edition is expanded; contemporary translations in French, German, and Russian. A textbook in which Ferguson elaborates the claim of a natural congruence between the optimal workings of human impulses to pursue happiness, as established by a science of human nature avowedly Baconian in method, and Ciceronian moral teachings.)

—— (1785) *The History of the Progress and Termination of the Roman Republic*; new edition, Edinburgh: Bell & Bradfute, 1825. (Enlarged and revised in 1793; several nineteenth-century American editions. A narrative history, covering the period from the beginning of the First Punic Wars to the end of the reign of Augustus. Ferguson punctutates the text with moralizing set-pieces on Caesar, Brutus and others, but he also makes a contribution to the problem of' 'republican' historiography, interweaving the actions of leading actors with the operation of social forces, moral climates and political institutions.)

—— (1792) *Principles of Moral and Political Science*, preface L. Castiglione, New York: AMS Press, 1973. (A philosophically more ambitious reaction of Ferguson's textbook teachings, now divided into a separate volume on 'the facts' and another on the 'excellences or defects' of human nature. The unifying theme is a conception of man's 'progressive' nature.)

Philip, W. (1986) *The Unpublished Essays of Adam Ferguson*, ed. and commentary W.M. Philip, Kilberry, Argyll: [W.M. Philip]. (Ferguson's brief essays, written in old age, range from mildly pious meditations to astute political analyses. A pugnacious essay challenges Adam Smith's conception of moral theory.)

Ferguson, A. (1995) *The Correspondence of Adam Ferguson*, ed. V. Merolle, Brookfield, VT: William Pickering. (Ferguson's correspondence is of interest mainly from the standpoint of biography and political history.)

References and further reading

Allen, D. (1993) *Virtue, Learning and the Scottish Enlightenment*, Edinburgh: Edinburgh University Press. (A discussion of Ferguson and other Enlightenment historians in the context of a century of 'self-consciously edificatory discourse'.)

Brewer, J. (1986) 'Adam Ferguson and the Theme of Exploitation', *British Journal of Sociology* 37: 461–87. (Ferguson is viewed as a precursor of post-Marxist sociology, realistically insightful about class relations, without reducing the theory of exploitation to a mechanical economic determinism. Author rejects the emphasis on 'virtue' in the standard interpretations.)

Broadie, A. (1990) *The Tradition of Scottish Philosophy: A New Perspective on the Enlightenment*, Edinburgh: Polygon. (Useful re-analysis of issues between Common Sense philosophers and Hume.)

* Davie, G. (1976) 'Berkeley, Hume, and the Central Problem of Scottish Philosophy', in D.F. Norton *et al.* (eds), *McGill Hume Studies*, San Diego, CA: Austin Press. (The eighteenth-century problem constellation is defined by the conflict between the insights of Mandeville and Hutcheson, and this sets Hume and his circle the task of a theory of civilization that recognizes the realism of the one without abandoning the social idealism of the other.)

—— (1990) *The Scottish Enlightenment and Other Essays*, Edinburgh: Polygon, 1991. (The philosophical problem constellation.)

Emerson, R.L. (1990) 'Science and Moral Philosophy in the Scottish Enlightenment', in M.A. Stewart (ed.) *Studies in the Philosophy of the Enlightenment*, Oxford: Clarendon Press, 11–36. (Representative study by prolific intellectual historian, here cautioning against over-emphasis on political discourse in interpreting Ferguson, among others.)

Hamowy, R. (1987) *The Scottish Enlightenment and the Theory of Spontaneous Order*, Carbondale, IL: Southern Illinois University Press. (A short monograph on an analytical figure developed by F. Hayek.)

Hont, I. and Ignatieff, M. (1983) *Wealth and Virtue*, Cambridge: Cambridge University Press. (Contains several statements of the 'civic humanist' thesis.)

Jack, M. (1989) *Corruption and Progress: The Eighteenth-Century Debate*, New York: AMS Press. (Introductory, comparing Ferguson with Mandeville and Rousseau.)

Kettler, D. (1965) *The Social and Political Thought of Adam Ferguson*, Columbus OH: Ohio State University Press. (A sociology of knowledge approach, with special emphasis on Ferguson as a representative 'intellectual'; as well as university teacher and popular moralist.)

—— (1977) 'History and Theory in Ferguson's *Essay on the History of Civil Society*: A Reconsideration', *Political Theory* 5 (4): 437–60. (A challenge to the interpretation that Ferguson's theory is derived from his conception of historical stages. Instead, a theory of human action is seen as complementary to the proto-sociological theory of a developmental process, corresponding to Ferguson's distinction between the point of view of actors and spectators.)

—— (1978) 'Ferguson's Principles: Constitution in Permanence', *Studies in Burke and His Time* 19 (3): 208–22. (An application of Kenneth Burke's concept of 'constitution' to Ferguson's integration of the complementary elements in his social and political thought.)

Lehman, W. (1930) *Adam Ferguson and the Beginnings of Modern Sociology*, New York: Columbia University Press. (The classic of the sociological thesis.)

Meek, R. (1976) *Social Science and the Ignoble Savage*, Cambridge: Cambridge University Press. (The four stages and history of the Americas.)

Sher, R. (1990) 'Professors of Virtue: The Social History of the Edinburgh Moral Philosophy Chair in the Eighteenth Century', in M.A. Stewart (ed.) *Studies in the Philosophy of the Enlightenment*, Oxford: Clarendon Press. (Highlights didactic functions of professorship.)

DAVID KETTLER

FERREIRA, CARLOS VAZ

see FEMINIST THOUGHT IN LATIN AMERICA; ANTI-POSITIVIST THOUGHT IN LATIN AMERICA

FERRIER, JAMES FREDERICK (1806–64)

Ferrier represents the transition within nineteenth-century Scottish philosophy from the tradition of common-sense realism begun by Thomas Reid, the last major exponent of which was Ferrier's mentor, Sir William Hamilton, to versions of idealism influenced by German philosophers, especially Hegel. Although he is largely forgotten, Ferrier merits study for at least two reasons. First, he had a role in importing Hegelian ideas into British thought; and second there are parallels between his arguments and those advanced by anti-realist philosophers in the analytical tradition.

Ferrier was born in Edinburgh into a Scottish legal family. He studied at Edinburgh University (1825–7) and at Magdalen College, Oxford (1828–32), then began a short-lived legal career before turning to writing. In 1834 he toured Germany and in Berlin was taken with the ideas and cultural influence of Hegel who had died there three years previously. In 1837 Ferrier married and around that time began writing and publishing philosophical work. His first and most accessible publication was 'An Introduction to the Philosophy of Consciousness' which appeared in seven parts in *Blackwood's Magazine* during 1838–9. Subsequent works included 'Berkeley and Idealism' (1842); his *magnum opus*, the *Institutes of Metaphysics* (1854); and 'Scottish Philosophy, the Old and the New' (1856). Further material was published posthumously, such as the 'Lectures on Greek Philosophy' (1875) and 'Criticism of Adam Smith's Ethical System' (1986). Ferrier began his academic career as Professor of Civil History at Edinburgh (1842–6) but failed in his efforts to succeed Sir William Hamilton (1791–1856) in the Chair of Logic and Metaphysics there. In 1845, however, he was appointed Professor of Moral Philosophy at St Andrews, where he remained until his death.

Although much indebted to the teaching and writings of William HAMILTON, who had edited the works of Thomas REID, the 'father' of the Scottish 'common sense' tradition, Ferrier rejected the doctrines and methods of the 'Scottish Philosophy', as that tradition had come to be titled (see COMMON SENSE SCHOOL). In an effort to refute Humean scepticism, Reid and his followers had argued that in cognition the mind is directly engaged with reality and not with mental intermediaries such as 'impressions' or 'ideas'. This cognitive power was taken to be a constitutive feature of the human mind, and the study of it and of other mental faculties had come to be a major focus of interest for Reid's realist contemporaries and successors, who sought thereby to develop a 'Science of the Human Mind'.

As this study became more empirical a new form of scepticism began to emerge, since it was realized that all the method could reveal is how things appear to consciousness. Given a different empirical constitution, however, it might be that a subject's experiences would be quite unlike those taken to be common among human beings as they actually are. The

633

resulting conception of the 'Relativity of Knowledge', as it came to be called, also drew upon Kantian themes which suggested the possibility that we are not even acquainted with the world and the self as they are *in themselves*, but only with subjectively conditioned *appearances*. Ironically, then, by the time of Hamilton, the anti-sceptical realist tradition initiated by Reid had come to the point of finding our knowledge of self and of reality problematic.

Ferrier's rejection of this tradition was due in part to its tendency to generate scepticism, which he judged to be ultimately incoherent, but also to what he saw as its disastrous substitution of empirical psychology for a priori reasoning. Following in the tradition of the Rationalists, in particular Descartes, Ferrier sought to show that philosophy is able to determine the necessary limits and structure of reality, showing what can and must be so and not restricting itself to what contingently exists. In the *Institutes of Metaphysics* he even goes as far as to claim that his entire philosophical system, comprised of 'epistemology' (a term of which Ferrier was the author), 'agniology' and 'ontology' (the theories of knowledge, ignorance and being, respectively) is derivable by deduction from the law of identity: 'that a thing must be what it is. A is A'.

Ferrier's charge against his predecessors is related to the objection made by later writers to the psychologizing of logical reasoning. One aspect of this is his observation that empirical study is incapable of refuting philosophical arguments such as those taken to imply scepticism. His own response to the sceptic is unmistakably aprioristic, involving the claim that epistemological and metaphysical relations between the subject of cognition, the act of cognitive consciousness and the object of cognition are internal or non-contingent. All 'subjects' and all 'objects' are, as such, necessarily terms of actual or possible cognitive relations. Even ignorance ensures the possibility of knowledge inasmuch as one can only fail to know that which can be known. Thus, anticipating arguments of later phenomenologists and antirealists, he concluded that the idea that reality might in principle transcend our capacity to know it is an incoherent one: the real is the knowable.

Among his contemporaries, other than those within the sphere of his immediate influence in Edinburgh and St Andrews, Ferrier's idealist system was not well-received. Those who knew his work recognized his ability but were unpersuaded by his doctrines. In part that was probably due to the fact that the temper of the period was increasingly one of empiricism and naturalism, approaches opposed to that of a priori metaphysics. Set against this, however, there are interesting parallels between aspects of Ferrier's philosophical system and ideas developed within analytical philosophy by writers such as Michael Dummett and Hilary Putnam, concerning the extent to which 'reality' is a function of our ways of thinking, (see REALISM AND ANTIREALISM), and there is certainly scope for useful scholarship exploring these points of similarity. Indeed, the time is overdue for a proper assessment of Ferrier's philosophical contribution.

See also: SCEPTICISM; RATIONALISM

List of works

Ferrier, J.F. (1854) *Institutes of Metaphysics*, Edinburgh: Blackwood. (Ferrier's definitive presentation of his version of Absolute Idealism. It is markedly rationalist in method, attempting to derive important claims about knowledge and reality from the 'law of identity' – that a thing must be what it is.)

—— (1875) *Philosophical Works of the late James Frederick Ferrier*, ed. A. Grant and E.L. Lushington, Edinburgh: Blackwood, 3 vols. (Comprises the *Institutes* (vol. 1), *Lectures on Greek Philosophy* (vol. 2) and *Philosophical Remains* (vol. 3), the last containing 'Introduction to the Philosophy of Consciousness'. This edition of Ferrier's works has been reprinted by Garland Press.)

—— (1986) 'The 1849–1850 Lectures of J.F. Ferrier: Criticism of Adam Smith's Ethical System', ed. A. Thomson, *Edinburgh Review* 74: 100–7. (Two short essays in which Ferrier expounds Smith's account of moral judgment as resting upon natural sympathy and then argues that such sympathy is acquired, not innate.)

References and further reading

Davie, G. (1967) 'J. Ferrier', in *Encyclopedia of Philosophy*, ed. P. Edwards, New York: Macmillan. (A brief account of Ferrier's life and work emphasizing the interest of Ferrier's earlier 'phenomenological' writings.)

Haldane, E. (1899) *James Frederick Ferrier*, Edinburgh: Oliphant. (Notwithstanding a more recent study by Thomson (see below), this remains the most comprehensive and reliable introduction to Ferrier's life and work.)

Mayo, B. (1969) *The Moral and Physical Order: A Reappraisal of James Frederick Ferrier*, St Andrews: University of St Andrews. (A short but interesting discussion of aspects of Ferrier's epistemology and moral psychology which argues that they anticipate ideas associated with twentieth-century analytical philosophy).

Thomson, A. (1964) 'The Philosophy of J.F. Ferrier', *Philosophy* 39: 46–62. (An account of Ferrier's thought, as presented in the 'Introduction to the Philosophy of Consciousness', which holds that among Scottish philosophers he is second only to Hume in the originality and value of his ideas.)

—— (1985) *Ferrier of St Andrews: An Academic Tragedy*, Edinburgh: Scottish Academic Press. (Although much more detailed in biographical aspects than Haldane (1899), like Thompson's *Philosophy* article (1964) this exaggerates Ferrier's philosophical importance. It also makes controversial claims concerning his private life.)

JOHN J. HALDANE

FEUERBACH, LUDWIG ANDREAS (1804–72)

Ludwig Feuerbach, one of the critical Young Hegelian intellectuals of the nineteenth century, has become famous for his radical critique of religious belief. In Das Wesen des Christentums *(*Essence of Christianity*) (1841) he develops the idea that God does not exist in reality but as a human projection only, and that the Christian principles of love and solidarity should be applied directly to fellow humans rather than being regarded as an indirect reflection of God's love. In religion, the believer 'projects his being into objectivity, and then again makes himself an object of an object, another being than himself'. Religious orientation is an illusion and is unhealthy, as it deprives and alienates the believer from true autonomy, virtue and community, 'for even love, in itself the deepest, truest emotion, becomes by means of religiousness merely ostensible, illusory, since religious love gives itself to man only for God's sake, so that it is given only in appearance to man, but in reality to God' (Feuerbach 1841: 44, 48). In* Grundsätze der Philosophie der Zukunft *(*Principles of the Philosophy of the Future*) (1843) he extends his criticism to all forms of metaphysics and religion: 'True Dialectics is not the Monologue of the sole Thinker, rather the Dialogue between I and Thou', he writes in paragraph 62 (1846–66 II: 345), criticizing in particular his former teacher Hegel. The philosophy of the future has to be both sensual and communal, equally based on theory and practice and among individuals. In an anonymous encyclopedia article (1847) he defines his position: 'the principle from which Feuerbach derives everything and towards which he targets everything is "the human being on the ground and foundation of nature"', a principle which 'bases truth on sensuous experience and thus replaces previous particular and* abstract philosophical and religious principles' (1964–III: 331). Feuerbach's sensualism and communalism had great influence on the young Karl Marx's development of an anthropological humanism, and on his contemporaries in providing a cultural and moral system of reference for humanism outside of religious orientation and rationalistic psychology. In the twentieth century, Feuerbach influenced existential theology (Martin Buber, Karl Barth) as well as existentialist and phenomenological thought.*

1 **Philosophy of the I and the Thou**
2 **Critique of religion**
3 **Individual emancipation versus political revolution**

1 Philosophy of the I and the Thou

Born in Landshut, son of the legal scholar and Bavarian diplomat Anselm von Feuerbach, Ludwig Andreas Feuerbach studied theology with Karl Daub in Heidelberg and philosophy with HEGEL in Berlin. He became lecturer in philosophy at the Bavarian university of Erlangen in 1829, but retired into private life after his marriage in 1837. His later years were without much communication and social activities; he died a poor and sick man in Rechenberg, near Nuremberg.

The interaction between the individual and the worlds of facts and thought, and the interrelatedness of individuals, were the central topics in Feuerbach's thinking. His dissertation *De infinitate, unitate atque communitate rationis* (On the infinity, unity and universality of reason) (1828) concerns the relationship between the individual and the general, the subjective and the objective; here his answer is that panlogic rationality is the universal individual as well as the general mode of essence and existence. Two years later he published his fiercest critique of Christian belief in immortality and eternal life after death in *Gedanken über Tod und Unsterblichkeit* (*Thoughts on Death and Immortality*) (1830). Here he holds that the mystical experience of sensual love and interpersonal community has infinity and eternity in itself, and that the neglect of this world and its riches in favour of the anticipated eternal world to come causes unhappiness and great discontent. Both studies mark two different attempts at a non-religious, humanistic transformation of traditional mystical insights concerning the unity of object and subject into, first, panlogical rationalism and, second, sensualistic realism. The publication of the critique of immortality, even though it appeared anonymously, made it impossible for Feuerbach to get a permanent salaried position as professor of philosophy in Christian Bavaria; he quit his teaching post after nine years of only moderately successful academic teaching at the University of Erlangen.

Feuerbach's existentialist concept of philosophy is explicated in *Abelard and Heloise* (1834) and *Pierre Bayle* (1838), as well as in his selected studies on Spinoza and Leibniz. In *Grundsätze der Philosophie der Zukunft* (*Principles of the Philosophy of Future*) (1843) he asserts that the philosophy of the future is 'the complete, coherent, and absolute resolution of theology into anthropology', into the 'unity of the I and the Thou': 'The essence of man is contained only in community, in the unity of man with man – a unity which however is founded only in the reality of the differences between I and Thou'. Thus, the new philosophy 'replaces religion…contains the essence of religion…truly is religion'. Epistemologically, reality resides in human rational and sensuous perception, in the rational, sensuous and passionate nature of man; 'Truth, reality, and sensation are identical. Only the sensuous being is a true and real being' (Feuerbach 1846–66 II: 344, 346). In critically reconstructing the history of religious systems of reference, Feuerbach finds in references to God the believers' complex reference to themselves. Thus his method of critical reconstruction of previous systems of reference and self-reference reveals, as Wartofsky (1977) observes, a mode of self-revelation and self-articulation which represents the essential pattern of human consciousness and self-understanding, a consequent application of the existentialist interpretation of Hegel's *Phenomenology of Spirit* in Feuerbach's anthropological interpretation: 'the true critique lies in the development itself'.

This unorthodox approach to traditional metaphysics and anthropology influenced twentieth-century theologians and philosophers such as Martin BUBER, Karl BARTH, Karl Loewith, Henri Arvon and Louis ALTHUSSER. Feuerbach's influence on the young MARX also played an important role in the post-Leninist interpretation of the humanism of the young Marx as an alternative to Marxism-Leninism and Stalinist interpretation of political economy.

In his last period in *Über Spiritualismus und Materialismus* (On Spiritualism and Materialism) (1866) Feuerbach developed an eudaimonistic and utilitarian ethics on the basis of the I–Thou anthropology, and a critique of perverted forms of seeking happiness and community in religion: 'Good is the acceptance, bad the rejection of the drive to happiness. Happiness, but not reduced into one single person, rather disseminated among different persons, I and Thou integrating, therefore not one-sided but dual-sided and all-sided, is the principle of morality'. Sexual happiness is his paradigm for 'the human drive to happiness, which can only be fulfilled in and through the happiness of the other' (Feuerbach 1846–66 X: 62). The individual moral conscience thus works on the basis of reciprocity in assessing moral norms and attitudes: 'The conscience is nothing else than the I which looks at things from the perspective of the vulnerable Thou, nothing else than the proxy for the happiness of the other on the basis and on the calling of one's own happiness' (Feuerbach 1846–66 X: 65).

2 Critique of religion

Feuerbach's humanist approach prevented his philosophy of religion from merely rejecting religion as unrealistic and unfounded. On the contrary, he believed that religion contains the dreams and visions of individuals and cultures in an indirect way, a human product of self-transcending and visualizing oneself and humanity in ideal terms, not a divine inspiration: religion is the 'knowledge of the infinite, it is therefore and can be nothing else than the consciousness which man has of his own – not finite and limited – but infinite nature' (Feuerbach 1846–66 VII: 26). Feuerbach therefore rejects the notion that he is a promoter of atheism; he calls himself 'a natural philosopher in the domain of the mind', an 'anthropocentric' thinker: 'the mystery of theology is anthropology, that of the divine being the human being' (Feuerbach 1846–66 V: xiv–xv). This was exactly the interpretation of religion used by Hegel to interpret Greek and Roman mythology and religion as centred around the human world and simply transposing human characters, virtues and vices into the gods and goddesses. While Hegel's main interest in the philosophy of religion was dialectically and speculatively to harmonize Christian tradition with speculative idealism, for Feuerbach all religious references are models of 'alienation' of man from himself, as God is nothing else but the artificially created outside nature of man's own inside nature (see ALIENATION §2). Feuerbach rejects religion to the extent that it separates God and humans, and deprives humans of their best by making them a part of the divine; but he accepts religion to the extent that it recognizes divine powers and challenges which are genuinely human.

Feuerbach originally intended to entitle *Das Wesen des Christentums* (*Essence of Christianity*) (1841) as 'Critique of Pure Unreason' in order to set it alongside Kant's *Critique of Pure Reason*; and indeed the composition of his book mirrors that of Kant. Its first part characterizes religion as a human product and its positive content (that is, the 'true and anthropological essence of religion' which understands God as 'love' in the New Testament or as 'a moral being or law' in the Old Testament), just as Kant in the first part of the *Critique of Pure Reason* develops the positive capacities of epistemology in his transcendental analytics and aesthetics. The second part deconstructs religious speculation and metaphysics as being unrealistic and inhuman (that is, 'the false or theological essence of religion'), just as Kant destroys the arguments for metaphysics and the existence of God independently of human projection and existence (see KANT, I. §8). Thus, in making Christian monotheism his predominant object of critique, he presents an anthropological reduction of what in Hegel's interpretation still had the form of speculative transcendentalism. The human being is not a bearer of reason, subordinated to as well as participating in the 'idea', but a natural being existing in relationship with others. The revised second edition (1843) moves away from the dominance of the 'species being' model of human religious projection and alienation, which was still strongly influenced by Hegel, towards a more naturalistic sensualistic approach under the influence of reading LUTHER.

Later, in a short essay on the nature of religion, *Das Wesen der Religion* (Essence of Religion) (1845), Feuerbach additionally identifies angst and fear of unknown natural elements as the prime sources of religious projection. This generalizes his earlier theory into the explanation of religion as a response to social as well as natural environmental challenges based in feelings of dependence of and exposure to nature: 'man's original dependence and the feelings of dependency relates to nothing else than nature'; therefore, '"spirit" is nothing other than a general term to name essences, things, utensils which man is confronted with and which are different to his own products, he also uses the collective term "nature"' (Feuerbach 1964– X: 4).

In his widely read *Vorlesungen über das Wesen der Religion* (Lectures on the Essence of Religion) (1851), originally delivered publicly in the revolutionary year 1848 on the invitation of students and citizens of Heidelberg, Feuerbach describes the cultural and social implications and consequences of religion and belief. Here, as in the *Essence of Religion*, the true object of religion and religious self-articulation or alienation is not primarily the individual and the social environment, but nature all-encompassing, the sum of powers and forces on which the individual feels absolutely dependent while simultaneously seeking freedom and self-determination.

His final exercise in promoting the thesis that 'man created God' is the voluminous book *Der Ursprung der Götter nach den Quellen des classischen, hebräischen und christlichen Altertums* (Theogony following the Sources of the Classical, Hebrew, and Christian Past), written between 1852 and 1857, with an even greater arsenal of quotes and references from a broad variety of religious literature. Different forms of religion demonstrate different attitudes of humans towards themselves and towards nature. While polytheism expresses the subordination of man under a multitude of external powers in nature, monotheism suppresses those many forces and powers in nature under one single rule or ruler, indirectly under man, who has created this divine supreme power after his own human image.

It is this analytical and educational drive to 'transform friends of God into friends of man, believers into thinkers, devotees of prayer into devotees of work, candidates for the hereafter into students of this world' and the I-and-Thou which became instrumental in shaping modern existentialist theology, both Jewish (Martin Buber) and Protestant (Karl Barth). Despite being religious believers, Buber and Barth were nevertheless struck by Feuerbach's suggestion that all previous forms of theology and dogmatics, including Hegel's philosophy of religion, were nothing other than 'esoteric psychology', and they themselves became critics of religious fundamentalism. Most of Feuerbach's theological critics agree that the importance of religion as a mode of reference to oneself, to others and to the social and natural world rarely has been grasped as comprehensively as it was by Feuerbach.

3 Individual emancipation versus political revolution

Feuerbach refused to accompany Marx, RUGE and other political revolutionaries and liberals into the course of direct political argumentation and action. He held that the time was not yet right for a political revolution because individual emancipation and the development of a culture of self-determination had not run its course in Germany. Therefore he chose the emancipatory and educative approach, analysing and criticizing traditional models of orientation in religion, philosophy and ideology in order to promote political change by promoting self-understanding and self-determination based on the principles of enlightenment. Contrasting his method to that of socialist political action, he compares his philosophical methodology to the methods of medical diagnosis, prognosis and therapy: 'I have, determined by internal and external factors, decided to assess the diseases of the head and of the heart of mankind'.

Feuerbach's belief that the grounds for a true revolution lay in the liberation of human sensuousness and feeling in interpersonal relations, not primarily in the externalities of political life, had an enormous influence on the more radical former disciples of Hegel, the Young Hegelians Bruno BAUER, Karl Marx, Friedrich ENGELS, and Max STIRNER. Instead of becoming a member of the 1848 revolutionary parliament in Frankfurt, he chose to lecture publicly in Heidelberg where he declared religion to be closely related to politics, emphasizing that his lectures were focused on practical rather than theoretical politics. He maintained that 'individualism in practical consequence is socialism, but not in the sense of French individualism'; for him 'the dissolution of theology into anthropology in the realm of thinking is the dissolution of the monarchy into the republic in the realm of practice, of life....Imagination is the power of religion and imagination is the power of the monarchy. Only so long will monarchs rule over humans as humans will be ruled by imagination. Despots rule only where phantasies rule' (Feuerbach 1846–66 VIII: 460). It has been stressed in the literature (Arvon 1964; Cabada 1975; Kamenka 1970; Sass 1972) that Feuerbach is not merely a transitional figure towards Marx and Marxism-Leninism, but an alternative to the concept of political revolution and party elites.

Thus Feuerbach gave his own meaning to the term 'communist', in direct opposition to that employed by Marx and the socialist movement, when answering Max Stirner's question 'where does Feuerbach stand?': 'neither a materialist, nor an idealist, nor an identity philosopher is Feuerbach. So, what is he? He is in thought what he is in his deeds, in spirit what he is in flesh, in essence what he is in his senses – human being [mensch]; for Feuerbach only sees the essence of man in community: communal being, communist' (Feuerbach 1846–66 V: 359).

In his *Grundsätze der Philosophie der Zukunft* (*Principles of the Philosophy of the Future*) (1843) Feuerbach uses the image of the ellipse having two focal points, as compared to the circle having only one centre, to compare the purely intellectual philosophy of Hegel and other schools of rationalism and metaphysics with his own approach of 'head and heart', rationality and sensuality, as the two commanding principles for theory and practice (Feuerbach 1846–66 II: 344). Marx took this image of the two centres of the ellipse from Feuerbach in 1844 in order to identify philosophy and proletariat as 'head and heart' of the emancipatorial process of history, this time in terms of political revolution, not educational and critical evolutionary emancipation as Feuerbach had done.

See also: HEGELIANISM

List of works

Feuerbach, L. (1846–66) *Ludwig Feuerbach's Sämtliche Werke*, Leipzig: Otto Wigand. (This is the edition of collected works published by Feuerbach himself, with revised versions of earlier articles and new works.)

—— (1903–11) *Ludwig Feuerbach Sämtliche Werke*, ed. W. Bolin and F. Jodl, Stuttgart, 10 vols; reprint 1959–64; 3 suppl. vols, ed. H.M. Sass, 1962–4. (Collected works, with a bibliography in volume 11.)

—— (1964–) *Historical-critical edition: Ludwig Feuerbach Gesammelte Werke*, ed. W. Schuffenhauer, Berlin: Akademie Verlag, vols 1–12; 17; 19 published. (This edition is also available in electronic form on disk or CD-ROM, eds M. Neumann and S.T. Stoler, Georgetown University Washington DC: Center for Text and Technology, 1994.)

—— (1828) *De infinitate, unitate atque communitate rationis* (On the infinity, unity and universality of reason), University Archives Erlangen. (Dissertation manuscript, first published in 1962 in volume 11 of the 1846–66 *Sämtliche Werke*, pages 11–62.)

—— (1830) *Gedanken über Tod und Unsterblichkeit* (*Thoughts on Death and Immortality*), ed. and trans. J.A. Massey, Berkeley, CA: University of California Press, 1980. (Originally published anonymously in Nürnberg.)

—— (1834) *Abelard und Heloise*, Ansbach: Brügel. (Outlines Feuerbach's existentialist concept of philosophy.)

—— (1838) *Pierre Bayle*, Ansbach: Brügel. (Another explication of Feuerbach's existentialist concept of philosophy.)

—— (1839) 'Zur Kritik der Hegelschen Philosophie'; trans. Z. Hanfi, 'Towards a Critique of Hegelian Philosophy', in Z. Hanfi (ed.) *The Fiery Brook: Selected Writings of Ludwig Feuerbach*, New York: Anchor Books. (This work established Feuerbach's position as a spokesman for the Hegelian Left.)

—— (1841) *Das Wesen des Christentums*, trans. M. Evans (George Eliot) as *Essence of Christianity*, 1854; new edn, intro. K. Barth, foreword H.R. Niebuhr, New York: Harper & Row, 1957. (Feuerbach's most influential work.)

—— (1842) *Vorläufige Thesen zur Reformation der Philosophie* (Provisional Theses Towards the Reform of Philosophy). (Develops Feuerbach's humanistic materialism.)

—— (1843) *Grundsätze der Philosophie der Zukunft*, trans. and intr. M.H. Vogel as *Principles of the Philosophy of Future*, Indianapolis, IN and New York: Hackett Publishing Company, 1966. (Sketches the new philosophy of 'I and thou'.)

—— (1844) *Das Wesen des Glaubens im Sinne Luthers,*

ein Beitrag zum Wesen des Christentums, trans. M. Cherno as *The Essence of Faith according to Luther*, New York: Harper & Row, 1967.

—— (1845) *Das Wesen der Religion* (Essence of Religion), in *Die Epigonen I*, Leipzig: Wigand, 117–78. (An essay on the nature of religion)

—— (1851) *Vorlesungen über das Wesen der Religion, nebst Zusätzen und Anmerkungen*, trans. R. Manheim as *Lectures on the Essence of Religion*, New York: Harper & Row, 1967. (Originally delivered at the invitation of students in Heidelberg during the revolutionary year of 1848.)

—— (1857) *Der Ursprung der Götter nach den Quellen des classischen, hebräischen und christlichen Altertums* (Theogony following the Sources of the Classical, Hebrew, and Christian Past), in *Ludwig Feuerbach's Sämmtliche Werke* IX, Leipzig: Otto Wigand, 1846–66. (A most extensive scholarly analysis of modes of religious thought.)

—— (1866) *Über Spiritualismus und Materialismus*, in *Ludwig Feuerbach's Sämmtliche Werke* X, Leipzig: Otto Wigand, 1846–66. (Develops a eudaimonistic and utilitarian ethics on the basis of I–Thou anthropology.)

—— (1972) *The Fiery Brook. Selected Writings of Ludwig Feuerbach*, trans. Z. Hanfi, New York: Anchor Press. (Contains, among other selections, translations of 'Zur Kritik der Hegelschen Philosophie' (1839, 1657–), *Vorläufige Thesen zur Reform der Philosophie* (1843, vol. 2, 62–), and *Grundsätze der Philosophie der Zukunft* (1843).)

References and further reading

Amengual, G. (1980) *Critica de la religion y antropologia en Ludwig Feuerbach* (Ludwig Feuerbach's critique of religion and anthropology), Barcelona: Laia. (Comprehensive interpretation of Feuerbach's anthropology and critique of religion.)

* Arvon, H. (1964) *Ludwig Feuerbach ou la transformation du sacre* (Ludwig Feuerbach, on the transformation of the sacred), Paris: PUF. (An existentialist interpretation of Feuerbach as one of the sources of modern existentialism.)

Barata-Moura, J. and Marques, V.S. (eds) (1993) *Pensar Feuerbach*, Lisbon: Edicoes Colibri. (Collection of Portuguese essays from 1991, commemorating the 150th anniversary of Feuerbach's *Essence of Christianity*.)

Braun, H.J., Sass, H.-M., Schuffenhauer, W. and Tomasoni, F. (eds) (1990) *Ludwig Feuerbach und die Philosophie der Zukunft* (Ludwig Feuerbach and the Philosophy of the future), Berlin: Akademie Verlag. (Collection of essays originally contributed to the Second International Feuerbach Conference in 1989.)

Braun, H.J. (ed.) (1994) *Solidarität oder Egoismus. Studien zu einer Ethik bei und nach Feuerbach* (Solidarity or Egoism: Studies toward an ethics with and after Feuerbach), Berlin: Akademie Verlag. (Collection of conference papers from 1992.)

* Cabada Castro, M. (1975) *El Humanismos Premarxista de Ludwig Feuerbach* (The pre-marxist humanism of Ludwig Feuerbach), Madrid: Bibliotheka des Autores Christianos. (Detailed interpretation of Feuerbach's humanism and his influence on Marx.)

Cesa, C. (1972) *Studi sulla sinistra hegeliana (Studies on the left Hegelianism)*, Urbino: Argalia Editore (Interpretation of Feuerbach's historiography (167–84) and philosophy of religion (185–248) within the context of Young Hegelian thought.)

Harvey, Van A. (1995) *Feuerbach and the Interpretation of Religion*, Cambridge: Cambridge University Press. (Classic study of Feuerbach's epistemology and interpretation of religion in the context of the philosophical and theological disputes on the validity of Feuerbach's critique of religion.)

Jaeschke, W. (ed.) (1992) *Sinnlichkeit und Rationalität. Der Umbruch in der Philosophie des 19. Jahrhunderts* (Sensibility and rationality: the revolution in nineteenth century philosophers), Berlin: Akademie Verlag. (Collection of essays, with an English-language bibliography, 1873–1991, compiled by Scott Stebelman.)

* Kamenka, E. (1970) *The Philosophy of Ludwig Feuerbach*, New York: Praeger. (Focuses mainly on the interpretation of Feuerbach's humanist I–Thou philosophy.)

Loewith, K. (1964) *From Hegel to Nietzsche. The Revolution in Nineteenth Century Thought*, trans. D. Green, New York: Holt, Rinehart & Winston. (Classic study of Young Hegelians and Feuerbach's role in promoting the radicalization of critical theory.)

Luebbe, H. and Sass, H.-M. (1975) *Atheismus in der Diskussion. Kontroversen um Ludwig Feuerbach* (Atheism in debate: Controversies concerning Ludwig Feuerbach), Munich: Kaiser. (Collection of essays, originally contributions to the First International Feuerbach Conference in 1973.)

Rawidowitz, S. (1964) *Ludwig Feuerbach*, Berlin: de Gruyter. (An elaborate scholarly interpretation (in German) of Feuerbach and his influence in the history of ideas.)

* Sass, H.-M. (1972) *Ludwig Feuerbach*, Reinbek bei Hamburg: Rowohlt, 4th edn, 1994. (Illustrated intellectual biography (in German) using as yet

unpublished material; Korean translation by Moon-Gil Chung, 1986.)

—— (1983) 'The Transition from Feuerbach to Marx. A Reinterpretation', *Studies of Soviet Thought* 26: 123–42. (Analyses the conceptual differences between Feuerbach and Marx from a post-Leninist perspective.)

Sass, H.-M. and Wartofsky, M.W. (eds) (1978) *Feuerbach, Marx and the Left Hegelians*, special issue of *The Philosophical Forum*. (Contains English translations of minor works by Feuerbach and of some correspondence.)

Tomasoni, F. (1986) *Ludwig Feuerbach e la natura non umana* (Ludwig Feuerbach and the non-human nature), Florence: La Nuova Italia Editrice. (An interpretation of Feuerbach's philosophy of nature (in Italian), based on previously unpublished text edited by Tomasoni.)

* Wartofsky, M.W. (1977) *Ludwig Feuerbach*, Cambridge: Cambridge University Press. (Classic epistemological interpretation of Feuerbach's ideas.)

HANS-MARTIN SASS

FEYERABEND, PAUL KARL (1924–94)

Feyerabend was an Austrian philosopher of science who spent most of his academic career in the USA. He was an early, persistent and influential critic of the positivist interpretation of science. Though his views have some affinities with those of Thomas Kuhn, they are in important ways more radical. Not only did Feyerabend become famous (or notorious) for advocating 'epistemological anarchism' – the position that there is no such thing as scientific method, so that in advancing scientific research 'anything goes' – he also argued that the scientific outlook is itself just one approach to dealing with the world, an approach that is not self-evidently superior in all respects to other approaches. This radicalism led to his being widely attacked as an irrationalist though perhaps he might better be seen as a sceptic in the humane and tolerant tradition of Sextus Empiricus and Montaigne.

Paul Feyerabend was born and educated in Austria. His studies were interrupted by the Second World War, in which he served as an infantry officer in the German army and was awarded the Iron Cross. His wartime service ended when a bullet in the spine left him with injuries from which he never fully recovered. After the war, he resumed his education, eventually switching from physics to philosophy of science. His academic career, which began in England and included a year working with Karl POPPER, was spent mostly in the USA.

Feyerabend was an early and persistent critic of the once-dominant logical positivist interpretation of science. Like other such critics – Thomas KUHN and N.R. HANSON for example – Feyerabend insisted on paying close attention to the history of science and to contemporary scientific debates. Again like them, he thought that such attention showed standard philosophical accounts of science to be wildly at variance with actual scientific practice.

Feyerabend is perhaps best remembered for two views. First, he was an early advocate of the view that competing theories are often 'incommensurable', meaning that there is no common standard by which their respective merits can be judged. Positivist philosophers of science sought such a standard in the 'basic' or 'protocol' statements of a purely observational language, uncontaminated by theoretical preconceptions (see LOGICAL POSITIVISM §4). But according to Feyerabend – and this aspect of his thought goes all the way back to his doctoral dissertation – there is no such language. The meanings of the observation-terms that figure in statements relevant to the confirmation and disconfirmation of scientific theories are affected by the theories in which they are embedded. This can be disguised by the retention of the same words, as when both classical mechanics and special relativity talk about 'length'. But classical and relativistic length are different quantities, so that the measurement of 'length' is a different operation, depending on which theory we are working with (see INCOMMENSURABILITY; OBSERVATION).

Feyerabend argued further that, even if there were a pure observation language, this would not guarantee commensurability, since competing theories typically address themselves to different ranges of data. It is rarely, if ever, the case that a new theory explains everything an old theory explains and more besides. In consequence, choosing a new theory over an old one will typically involve explanatory loss as well as gain. For example, after Newton, theories of the heavens no longer attempt to explain the number of the planets, though it was previously thought essential to do so.

The second idea for which Feyerabend became famous – or notorious – is his 'epistemological anarchism'. Feyerabend denied that there is such a thing as 'scientific method': there are no universally valid methodological precepts by which scientific practice either is or should be governed. If we insist that there must be some such precept, the only defensible candidate is 'anything goes' (see PLURALISM).

One of Feyerabend's reasons for taking this position was that methodology can no more be abstracted from substantive, theoretical ideas than can observation. (The quest for a permanent, theory-neutral, observation language is just one way of trying to force science into a methodological straightjacket.) But, even if it could, strict adherence to abstract methodological rules (such as Popper's critical rationalism, with its emphasis on attempts to falsify theories via severe tests) would spell the death of scientific progress. The history of science shows that all theories, even the most successful, swim in a sea of anomalies; but this is reason to develop them, even with the aid of *ad hoc* hypotheses, not a reason for going back to the drawing board. Furthermore, old, well-developed theories typically do better than new theories by just about any methodological standard one cares to name. In part, this reflects the 'law of uneven development': a persuasive defence of a new theory in one area may depend on theoretical advances in various ancillary domains, and there is no guarantee that these will appear on cue. New ideas therefore need breathing space if we are to appreciate their full potential. But granting them this breathing space can involve violating any and every canon of 'rationality'. Feyerabend did not deny that, if a new idea turns out to be a good one, it will be possible – after the fact – to demonstrate its superiority according to one's favourite methodological prescriptions. His point, however, was that such prescriptions provide no guidance whatsoever to the practice of research. Whatever story one tells about the merits of an idea that worked out well, there will be alternatives that, in their undeveloped state, look worse but which, in their turn, could prove to be better. One simply never knows, which is why there are no rules to guide our efforts (see SCIENTIFIC METHOD §2).

Feyerabend's views have clear affinities with Kuhn's. Nevertheless, while he admired Kuhn, he criticized him for remaining in thrall to the idea of method. According to Feyerabend, Kuhn's distinction between 'normal' and 'revolutionary' science applies to different *aspects* of scientific research but not, contrary to Kuhn himself, to separable *phases*. However, Feyerabend did not only see Kuhn's model as failing to correspond to the actual workings of science: he also regarded it as a disastrous normative ideal. This shows that, his professed anarchism notwithstanding, Feyerabend did have methodological advice to offer. Where Kuhn commends working within a dominant theoretical tradition, until it collapses from internal strains, Feyerabend held that progress depends on the constant proliferation of theoretical ideas, hence continuous 'philosophical' criticism of entrenched views. He saw the desirability of proliferation as a consequence of the fact that observation-terms and methodological preferences do not float free of background theoretical ideas, so that the experiments that supposedly *confirm* such ideas are often better seen as *illustrating* them. To be fully understood, hence seriously tested, a theory needs to be criticized from the outside, not just the inside. And since there is no neutral standpoint, beyond all theoretical preconceptions, this means criticized from the perspective of some alternative theory. Feyerabend differed from Popper in many ways, but his epistemological views, with their scepticism about justification and stress on the importance of critical argument, retained a distinctly Popperian coloration.

At the time of their publication, Feyerabend's writings, especially his book *Against Method* (1975), enjoyed a considerable *succes de scandale*. They have come to seem less outrageous. While some of his views may strike some philosophers as overstated, their general spirit has some claim to be seen as today's conventional wisdom. However, there is a way in which Feyerabend differed from most academic philosophers of science of his generation and which sets him apart even now. This is that he did not recommend proliferation merely as the best way of proceeding within science. On the contrary, he held that modern science is itself just one approach to dealing with the world and should not simply be assumed to be superior to alternative approaches.

By being willing to argue that, say, witchcraft could usefully be studied with the degree of seriousness currently reserved for science, Feyerabend acquired a reputation for irrationalism. This is hardly surprising, for when Feyerabend recommended studying witchcraft, he did not mean studying it in a scientific manner, as a detached observer: he meant immersing oneself in its practices, with a view to becoming a witch. In fact, it is not easy to gauge how seriously Feyerabend himself took the nonscientific outlooks he so often commended. He enjoyed playing the *enfant terrible* and, as he remarked in response to criticism of his supposed beliefs, 'argument is not confession'. But the main point is that what he opposed was not science as such but – our according any outlook, the scientific outlook included – authoritative status. His epistemological aim was to sharpen our critical sense by making us more keenly aware of the ways in which all outlooks have their weaknesses as well as their strengths, their costs as well as their benefits. Not surprisingly, then, he rejected the 'irrationalist' label. What he objected to, he claimed, was all petrified conceptions of rationality, together with the orthodoxies they support. He can thus usefully be seen as a late representative of the classical sceptical tradition – the urbane and tolerant tradition of SEXTUS EMPIRICUS and M. de MONTAIGNE – in which the sceptic explores and counterposes all manner of competing ideas without regarding any as definitely established. The sceptic of this stamp need not deny his own *preferences*, including theoretical preferences, but he will not see them as singled out for approval by some extra-human authority: reason, for example. His scepticism thus grows out of the acuteness of his critical faculties. To the sceptic, his dogmatist opponents are the real irrationalists.

Feyerabend's distrust of authority led him to argue that a truly humane society would make room for the greatest possible variety of what Mill called 'experiments in living' (see MILL, J.S. §12). But although his philosophy took an increasingly political turn, he never gave serious thought to the question of how this conception of society might be given institutional expression under the conditions of modern life. In consequence, the political dimension of his thought amounts only to a vague and romantic utopianism.

See also: INCOMMENSURABILITY

List of works

Feyerabend, P. (1975) *Against Method*, London: New Left Books. (Feyerabend's best known book, in which he defends the position that the only generally valid methodological maxim for science is 'anything goes'.)

—— (1978) *Science in a Free Society*, London, New Left Books. (Collection of essays containing responses to several reviews of *Against Method*.)

—— (1981) *Philosophical Papers*, vols 1 and 2, Cambridge: Cambridge University Press. (Feyerabend's earlier and more standardly 'philosophical' essays on scientific method and the philosophy of physics.)

—— (1991) *Three Dialogues on Knowledge*, Oxford: Blackwell. (Late defence of epistemological anarchism.)

—— (1995) *Killing Time*, Chicago, IL: University of Chicago Press. (Feyerabend's autobiography, completed just before his death.)

References and further reading

Anderssen, G. (1994) *Criticism and the History of Science: Kuhn's, Lakatos' and Feyerabend's Criticisms of Critical Rationalism*, Leiden, and New York: Brill. (Critical evaluation of Feyerabend *et al.* from a Popperian standpoint.)

Couvalis, G. (1989) *Feyerabend's Critique of Foundationalism*, Aldershot: Avebury. (Sympathetic

account of Feyerabend's views drawing mainly on his earlier (pre-*Against Method*) essays.)

Munevar, G. (ed.) (1991) *Beyond Reason: Essays on the Philosophy of Paul Feyerabend*, Dordrecht, and Boston, MA: Kluwer. (Essays on Feyerabend by various contemporary philosophers of science.)

Stove, D. (1982) *Popper and After: Four Modern Irrationalists*, Oxford, Pergamon Press. (Traces the alleged irrationalism of Feyerabend and others to the mistaken 'deductivism' the author claims to be in Hume's original argument for inductive scepticism.)

MICHAEL WILLIAMS

FICHTE, JOHANN GOTTLIEB (1762–1814)

Fichte developed Kant's Critical philosophy into a system of his own, which he named 'Theory of Science' or Wissenschaftslehre. *Though Fichte continued to revise this system until the end of his life, almost all of his best known and most influential philosophical works were written in first portion of his career, when he was a professor at the University of Jena.*

The task of philosophy, as understood by Fichte, is to provide a transcendental explanation of ordinary consciousness and of everyday experience, from the standpoint of which philosophy must therefore abstract. Such an explanation can start either with the concept of free subjectivity ('the I') or with that of pure objectivity (the 'thing in itself'), the former being the principle of idealism and the latter that of what Fichte called 'dogmatism' (or transcendental realism). Though neither of these first principles can be theoretically demonstrated, the principle of freedom possesses the advantage of being practically or morally certain. Moreover, according to Fichte, only transcendental idealism, which begins with the principle of subjective freedom and then proceeds to derive objectivity and limitation as conditions for the possibility of any selfhood whatsoever, can actually accomplish the task of philosophy.

One of the distinctive features of Fichte's Jena system is its thoroughgoing integration of theoretical and practical reason, that is, its demonstration that there can be no (theoretical) cognition without (practical) striving, and vice versa. Another important feature is Fichte's demonstration of the necessary finitude of all actual selfhood. The 'absolute I' with which the system seems to begin turns out to be only a practical ideal of total self-determination, an ideal toward which the finite I continuously strives but can never achieve. Also emphasized in Fichte's Jena writings is the social or intersubjective character of all selfhood: an I is an I only in relationship to other finite rational subjects. This insight provides the basis for Fichte's political philosophy or 'theory of right', which is one of the more original portions of the overall system of the Wissenschaftslehre, a system that also includes a foundational portion (or 'first philosophy'), a philosophy of nature, an ethics and a philosophy of religion.

1 **Life and works I: Jena**
2 **Life and works II: Berlin**
3 **The project of a *Wissenschaftslehre***
4 **Idealism versus dogmatism**
5 **Foundations of the Jena *Wissenschaftslehre***
6 **Philosophy of nature and ethics**
7 **Political philosophy and philosophy of religion**

1 Life and works I: Jena

Born in the village of Rammenau in the Oberlausitz area of Saxony, Fichte was the eldest son in a family of poor and pious ribbon weavers. At the age of 9 his extraordinary intellectual talents brought him to the attention of a local baron, who sponsored his education, first at the Pforta school and then at the Universities of Jena and Leipzig. With the death of his patron, Fichte was forced to discontinue his studies and earn his livelihood as a private tutor, a profession the proud young man quickly came to detest.

After several years of such employment, including a long sojourn in Zurich, where he met his future wife, Johanna Rahn, Fichte returned to Leipzig to pursue a literary career. All his projects failed, however, and he was again forced to survive as a tutor. This time he was asked by a university student to give lessons in the Kantian philosophy (see KANT, I.). This encounter with Kant's writings in the summer of 1790 proved to be decisive, and Fichte became an instant convert to a philosophy he described as having 'occasioned a revolution in my way of thinking'. Eventually he made his way to Königsberg, where he lived for a few months. After his first disappointing interview with Kant, he resolved to demonstrate his mastery of the new philosophy by writing a treatise on a theme as yet unaddressed by Kant: namely, the question of the compatibility of the former with any concept of divine revelation. In just a few weeks Fichte composed a remarkable manuscript in which he concluded that the only revelation consistent with the Critical philosophy is the moral law itself. Suitably impressed, Kant helped to arrange the publication of Fichte's manuscript, which was published by Kant's own publisher in 1792 under the title *Versuch eine Kritik aller Offenbarung* (Attempt at a Critique of All Revela-

tion). For reasons that have never been satisfactorily explained, the first edition appeared without the author's name and preface. Not surprisingly, the book was hailed as a product of Kant's own pen and was widely praised as such. When the true identity of its author was revealed, Fichte was immediately catapulted from total obscurity to philosophical celebrity.

At the time that this stroke of fortune occurred Fichte was again employed as a private tutor, this time in Poland, where he was also working on several political tracts, including the provocatively entitled *Reclamation of the Freedom of Thought from the Princes of Europe, who have Hitherto Suppressed it* (1793). In the summer of 1793, however, he returned to Zurich where he married his fiancée and oversaw the publication of the first two instalments of his spirited *Contribution to the Rectification of the Public's Judgment of the French Revolution* (1793 and 1794), a work in which he outlined his own democratic view of legitimate state authority and insisted passionately on the right of revolution. Even though both of these political tracts were published anonymously, Fichte was widely known to be their author and thus acquired an early reputation as a political – as well as a religious and philosophical – radical.

In Zurich, Fichte's time was increasingly occupied by his efforts to construct for himself a systematic revision of what he still took to be Kant's Critical philosophy. It was while he was so engaged that he received an invitation to assume the recently vacated chair of Critical Philosophy at the University of Jena, which was rapidly emerging as the capital of the new philosophy and, together with nearby Weimar, as one of the liveliest intellectual centres in the German-speaking world.

Fichte arrived in Jena in May of 1794, and enjoyed tremendous success there for the next six years, during which time he laid the foundations and developed the first systematic articulations of his new system (the *Wissenschaftslehre* or 'Theory of Science'). Even as he was engaged in this tremendous theoretical labour, he also tried to address a larger, popular audience and also threw himself into various practical efforts to reform university life. As one bemused colleague accurately remarked, 'His is a restless spirit; he thirsts for some opportunity to act in the world. Fichte wants to employ his philosophy to guide the spirit of his age'. This passionate striving to address the pressing needs of his own time is plainly evident in the text of the enormously popular public lectures that he began to deliver immediately upon his arrival in Jena and published under the title *Einige Vorlesungen über die Bestimmung des Gelehrten* (Some Lectures concerning the Scholar's Vocation) (1794c).

The first hint of Fichte's new philosophical project and strategy came in his 1794a review of G.E. Schulze's *Aenesidemus*, which was soon followed by a brief but important manifesto for the new system, *Über den Begriff der Wissenschaftslehre* (Concerning the Concept of the Wissenschaftslehre) (1794b). The first full – albeit still provisional – presentation of the first or 'foundational' portion of the new system was presented in the so-called private lectures that Fichte delivered during the 1794–5 academic year, lectures he arranged to have printed in fascicles for the convenience of his students, to whom these printed sheets were distributed in instalments over the course of the year. Eventually, these same pages were bound together and offered to the public under the title *Grundlage der gesamten Wissenschaftslehre Wissenschaftslehre* (Foundations of the Entire Wissenschaftslehre) (Parts I and II, 1794; Part III, 1795), supplemented by the *Grunriß des Eigenthümlichen der Wissenschaftslehre in Rüchsicht auf das theoretishce Vermögen* (Outline of the Distinctive Character of the *Wissenschaftslehre* with Respect to the Theoretical Faculty) (1795), though each of these publications still bore on its title page the words 'a manuscript for the use of his listeners'.

Dissatisfied with many features of this initial presentation and surprised and shocked by the virtually universal misunderstanding of his published Foundations, Fichte immediately set to work on an entirely new exposition of the same, which he repeated three times in his private lectures on 'The Foundations of Transcendental Philosophy (*Wissenschaftslehre*) *nova methodo*' (1796–7, 1797–8, 1798–9). Though he intended to revise these lectures for serial publication under the title *An Attempt at a New Presentation of the Wissenschaftslehre in the Philosophisches Journal einer Gesellschaft Teutscher Gelehrten*, of which he himself was by then co-editor, the only portions of this projected New Presentation that ever appeared were the 'First and Second Introductions to the *Wissenschaftslehre*' (1797) and Chapter One of the same (1798).

At the same time that Fichte was revising the presentation of the foundational portion of his system he was also elaborating its various subdivisions or branches – first in private lectures and then in published treatises on *Foundations of Natural Right Based on the Wissenschaftslehre* (1796–7) and *Das System der Sittenlehre nach den Principien der Wissenschaftslehre)* (System of Ethical Theory Based on the *Wissenschaftslehre*) (1798a). Fichte's intention was then to turn to the development of the remaining subdivision of his system and to expound a philosophy of religion 'in accordance with the principles of the Wissenschaftslehre', but before he had a chance to

do this he published a brief essay *Ueber den Grund unsers Glaubens an eine göttliche Weltregierung* (On the Basis of Our Belief in a Divine Governance of the World) (1798b), in which he attempted to sketch some of his preliminary ideas on this topic. This essay, along with another by K.L. Forberg, that was contained in the same issue of the *Philosophisches Journal*, provoked an anonymous author to publish a pamphlet charging Fichte with atheism, which eventually led to the official suppression of the offending issue of the journal and to public threats by various German princes to prevent their students from enrolling at the University of Jena. The crisis produced by these actions and the growing number of publications for and against Fichte – which included an intemperate *Appeal to the Public* by Fichte himself (1799) – quickly assumed a life and even a name of its own: 'the Atheism Controversy' or *Atheismusstreit*. In the end, Fichte badly miscalculated his own position and was finally forced to resign from Jena and flee to Berlin, where he arrived in the summer of 1799 and where the final phase of his career largely unfolded.

2 Life and works II: Berlin

In Berlin, which was not yet home to a university, Fichte supported himself by giving private lectures on his philosophy and by a new flurry of literary production, increasingly aimed at a large, popular audience. The first of these new writings was a brilliant popular presentation of some of the characteristic features and conclusions of Fichte's system, with a strong emphasis upon the moral and religious character of the same. This work, *Die Bestimmung des Menschen* (The Vocation of Man) (1800b), which is perhaps Fichte's greatest literary achievements, was published in 1800, the same year that he also published a typically bold foray into political economy, *The Closed Commercial State*, in which he propounds a curious blend of socialist political ideas and protectionist economic principles. Defending his own philosophy against misunderstanding remained a primary concern for Fichte, however, as is attested by the publication in 1801 of the poignantly titled *Sonnenklarer Bericht an das größere Publikum über das eigentliche Wesen der neuesten Philosophie. Ein Versuch, die Leser zum verstehen zu zwingen* (Sun-Clear Report to the Public at Large on the Actual Character of the latest Philosophy: An Attempt to Force the Reader to Understand).

At the same time that he was addressing the public, Fichte was deeply engrossed in yet another effort to rethink and to restructure the foundations of his system. Hardly a year went by that he did not produce, either for his own use, or else for use in conjunction with the private lectures he was delivering in Berlin, yet another completely new version of the *Wissenschaftslehre*, each of which differed more and more dramatically from the familiar published version of 1794–5. (By 1804, for example, most references to 'the I' had been replaced with references to 'the absolute' and its various 'appearances'.) Having learned a lesson from the public reception of his 1794–5 presentation, Fichte resolved never to publish any of these new versions of his system (of which more than a dozen survive in manuscript), explaining in an official pro memoria of 3 January 1804 that the author of the *Wissenschaftslehre* 'wishes to confine himself to oral communication, so that misunderstanding can thereby be detected and eliminated on the spot'. Consequently, the sole public hint of Fichte's new understanding of his system was a brief and enigmatic *Die Wissenschaftslehre, in ihrem allgemeinen Umrisse dargestellt* (General Outline of the Wissenschaftslehre) published in 1810, as well as whatever hints in this direction readers might glean from the popular works published during this period.

In 1805 Fichte spent a semester lecturing at the University of Erlangen, but returned in the autumn to Berlin, where, in 1806, he published in rapid succession three popular and well-received books, all of which were based upon earlier lectures: *On the Essence of the Scholar* (a reworking of some of the same themes first addressed in the similarly titled lectures of 1794); *Der Grundzüge des gegewärtigen Zeitalters* (Characteristics of the Present Age) (1806a) (an attempt to show the implications of his 'system of freedom' for a speculative philosophy of history); and *Guide to the Blessed Life* (an eloquent and rather mystical treatise on philosophy and religion). With the entry of the French army into Berlin in 1806, Fichte joined the Prussian government in exile in Königsberg, where he held yet another course of lectures on the *Wissenschaftslehre* and wrote an important short work on *Machiavelli as Author* (1807), in which he defends a form of Realpolitik that appears to contrast starkly with the liberalism and political idealism of his earlier writings. Eventually, however, he returned to Berlin, where, under the eyes of the occupying forces, he delivered his celebrated *Reden an die deutsche Nation* (Addresses to the German Nation) (1808). Though these lectures later obtained a place of dubious honour as founding documents in the history of German nationalism, they are mainly concerned with the issue of national identity – and hence with the question of national education (which is the main topic of the work) – as a means to a larger, cosmopolitan end.

Fichte had always had a lively interest in pedago-

gical issues and hence took a leading role in planning the new Prussian university to be established in Berlin. Appropriately, when the new university finally opened in 1810, Fichte himself served as the first head of the philosophical faculty as well as the first elected rector of the entire university. His final years saw no diminution in the pace either of his public activity or of his philosophical efforts. He continued to produce new lectures on the foundations and first principles of his system, as well as new introductory lectures on philosophy in general ('Logic and Philosophy' (1812) and 'The Facts of Consciousness' (1813)), political philosophy ('System of the Theory of Right' (1812) and 'Theory of the State' (1813)) and ethics ('System of Ethical Theory' (1812)). As presaged by the book on Machiavelli, these late forays into the domain of practical philosophy paint a far darker picture of human nature and defend a much more authoritarian view of the state than anything to be found in the earlier, published writings on these subject.

In 1813 Fichte cancelled his lectures so that his students could enlist in the 'War of Liberation' against Napoleon, of which Fichte himself proved to be an indirect casualty. Through his wife, who was serving as a volunteer nurse in a Berlin military hospital, he contracted an infection of which he died on 29 January 1814.

3 The project of a *Wissenschaftslehre*

The primary task of Fichte's system of philosophy is to reconcile freedom with necessity, or, more specifically, to explain how freely willing, morally responsible agents can at the same time be considered part of a world of causally conditioned material objects in space and time. Fichte's strategy for answering this question was to begin simply with the ungrounded assertion of the subjective spontaneity and freedom (infinity) of the I and then to proceed to a transcendental derivation of objective necessity and limitation (finitude) as a condition necessary for the possibility of the former. Hence, in his 'First Introduction to the *Wissenschaftslehre*' (1797), he describes philosophy's task as that of 'displaying the foundation of experience', that is, 'explaining the basis of the system of representations accompanied by a feeling of necessity'. Fichte owed this conception of the task and strategy of philosophy entirely to his reading of Kant, and no matter how far his own presentation of his system seemed to diverge from 'the letter' of Kant's own presentation, he always maintained that it remained true to 'the spirit' of the same – which, for Fichte, lay entirely in its uncompromising insistence upon the practical indubitability of human freedom and its thoroughgoing dedication to the project of giving a transcendental account of ordinary experience that could explain the objectivity and necessity of theoretical reason (cognition) in a manner consistent with the affirmation of human liberty. For this reason Fichte sometimes referred to his own presentation of this same philosophy as 'the system of human freedom'.

In accordance with this conception of philosophy's task, Fichte insisted firmly upon the sharp distinction between the 'standpoint' of natural consciousness (which it is the task of philosophy to somehow 'explain') and that of transcendental reflection (from which alone such a philosophical explanation can be conducted – if at all). Thus there is no possible conflict between transcendental idealism and every-day realism; on the contrary, the whole point of the former is to demonstrate the necessity and unavoid-ability of the latter.

However 'Kantian' in spirit Fichte's enterprise might have been, he was at the same time all too keenly aware of certain glaring weaknesses and inadequacies in Kant's own execution of this project. Taking to heart the criticisms of such contemporaries as F. JACOBI, Salomon MAIMON and G.E. Schulze, Fichte realized, first, that the doctrine of the thing in itself, understood as an external cause of sensations, was indefensible on Critical grounds, and second, that Kant's denial of the possibility of 'intellectual intuition', though certainly justified as a denial of the possibility of any non-sensory awareness of objects, was nevertheless difficult to reconcile with certain other Kantian doctrines regarding the subject's presence to itself both as a (theoretically) cognizing subject (the doctrine of the transcendental apperception) and as a (practically) striving moral agent (the doctrine of the categorical imperative).

Fichte was also persuaded by his reading of the works of K. L. REINHOLD that the systematic unity of the Critical philosophy – specifically, the unity of theoretical and practical reason, of the First and Second *Critiques* – was insufficiently apparent in Kant's own presentation of his philosophy. His study of Reinhold also convinced him that the most promising way to display the unity in question would be to provide both theoretical and practical philo-sophy with a common foundation. The task, then, was to discover a single, self-evident starting point or first principle from which one could then somehow deduce or 'derive' both theoretical and practical philosophy. Not only would such a method guarantee the systematic unity of philosophy itself, but, more importantly, it would also display what Kant hinted at but never demonstrated: namely, the underlying unity of reason itself.

Since it is a central task of philosophy, so

construed, to establish the very possibility of any knowledge or science (*Wissenschaft*) whatsoever, Fichte proposed to replace the disputed term 'philo-sophy' (or 'love of wisdom') with the new term *Wissenschaftslehre* or 'Theory of Science' – a name that clearly designates the distinctively 'second order' character of philosophical reflection. Though Fichte's proposal never caught on as a general name for what was once called 'philosophy', it did become the universally acknowledged name for his own distinc-tive version of transcendental idealism. It is, however, important to note that *Wissenschaftslehre* is not the name of any particular Fichtean treatise, but is instead the general name for his entire system or project – a larger system that consists of a number of interrelated parts or systematic subdisciplines and an overarching project that could be expounded in a series of radically different presentations and a bewildering variety of systematic vocabularies. In fact, Fichte spent his entire life demonstrating this last point: that is, expounding and re-expounding what he himself took to be the same philosophy ('the *Wissenschaftslehre*') in a number of radically different forms and guises (*The Foundations of the Entire Wissenschaftslehre* of 1794–5, *Wissenschaftslehre nova methodo*, 'the *Wissenschaftslehre* of 1801–2', 'the 1804 *Wissenschaftslehre*', 'the *Wissenschaftslehre* of 1805', and so on) – more than a dozen in all between 1794 and 1814.

4 Idealism versus dogmatism

In order to construct any genuine philosophy of freedom, thought Fichte, the reality of freedom itself must simply be presupposed and thus treated as an incontrovertible 'fact of reason' in the Kantian sense. This, of course, is not to deny the possibility of raising theoretical objections to such claims; on the contrary, it was the very impossibility of any theoretically satisfactory refutation of scepticism concerning the reality of freedom that led Fichte to the recognition of the inescapable 'primacy of the practical' with respect to the selection of any philosophical starting point.

In so far as any proposed first principle of philosophy is really supposed to be the 'first principle' of all knowledge and hence of all argument, it clearly cannot be derived from any higher principle and hence cannot be established by any sort of argument. Furthermore, Fichte maintained that there are two and only two possible starting points for the philo-sophical 'explanation' of experience sketched above: namely, the concept of pure selfhood (freedom) and that of pure thinghood (necessity) – neither of which can be warranted, qua philosophical starting point, by a direct appeal to experience, and both of which can be arrived at only by a selfconscious act of philosophical abstraction from ordinary experience (within which freedom and necessity, subject and object, are invariably joined).

The two rival philosophical strategies made possible by these opposed starting points are unforgettably limned by Fichte his two 1797 *Introductions to the Wissenschaftslehre*, where he characterizes the sort of philosophy that begins with the pure I as 'idealism' and that which begins with the thing in itself as 'dogmatism'. Since, according to Fichte's earlier argument in *Concerning the Concept of the Wissenschaftslehre*, a unified system of philosophy can have one and only one first principle, and since there are two and only two possible first principles, then it follows that no 'mixed' system of idealism/dogmatism is possible. Moreover, since dogmatism, as understood by Fichte, unavoidably implies a strict form of determinism or 'fatalism', whereas idealism is, from the start, committed to the reality of human freedom, it is also practically impossible to reach any sort of 'compromise' between two such radically opposed systems.

Though Fichte conceded that neither dogmatism nor idealism could directly refute its opposite and also recognized that the choice between philosophical starting points could not be resolved philosophically, he nevertheless denied that any dogmatic system – any system that started with the concept of sheer objectivity – could ever succeed in accomplishing what was required of all philosophy. Dogmatism, he argued, could never provide a transcendental deduction of ordinary consciousness, for, in order to accomplish this, it would have to make an illicit leap from the realm of things to the realm of mental ideas or 'representations' (*Vorstellungen*). Idealism, in contrast, at least when correctly understood as the sort of Critical idealism that recognizes that the intellect itself most operate in accordance with certain necessary laws, could – at least in principle – accomplish the prescribed task and explain our experience of objects ('representations accompanied by a feeling of necessity') in terms of the necessary operations of the intellect itself, without having to make an illicit appeal to things in themselves. To be sure, one cannot decide in advance whether or not any such deduction of experience from the mere concept of free selfconsciousness is *in fact* possible. This is something that can be decided only after the construction of the system in question. Until then, it remains a mere hypothesis that the principle of human freedom, for all of its practical certainty, is also the proper starting point for a transcendental account of objective experience.

Returning to the question of the starting point,

however, it still must be granted that the truth of the latter cannot be established by any philosophical means, including its utility as a philosophical first principle. On the contrary, one must be convinced, on wholly extraphilosophical grounds, of the reality of one's own freedom before one can enter into the chain of deductions and arguments that constitute the system of transcendental idealism. This is the meaning of Fichte's oft-cited assertion that 'the kind of philosophy one chooses depends upon the kind of person one is'.

In the end, the only reason why transcendental idealists come to a stop with – and thus begins their philosophy with – the proposition 'the I freely posits itself' is not because they are unable to entertain theoretical doubts on this point nor because they cannot continue the process of reflective abstraction. Instead, as Fichte explains in his essay *On the Basis of Our Belief in a Divine Governance of the World*, 'I cannot go beyond this standpoint because I am not permitted to do so'. Of course I could think of myself as determined by things, but still 'I ought to begin my thinking with the thought of the pure I, and I ought to think of this pure I as acting with absolute spontaneity – not as determined by things, but rather, as determining them'. It is precisely because the categorical imperative is in this way invoked to secure the first principle of his entire system that Fichte can make the rather startling claim that the '*Wissenschaftslehre* is the only kind of philosophical thinking that accords with duty'.

5 Foundations of the Jena *Wissenschaftslehre*

The published presentation of the first principles of the Jena *Wissenschaftslehre* commences with the proposition 'the I posits itself'; more specifically, 'the I posits itself as an I – that is, as positing itself'. To be sure, this starting point is somewhat obscured in the *Foundations of the Entire Wissenschaftslehre* by a difficult and somewhat forced attempt to connect this starting point to the logical law of identity, as well as by the introduction of two additional 'first principles', corresponding to the logical laws of noncontradiction and sufficient reason. (Significantly, this distraction is eliminated entirely in the 1796–9 lectures on *Wissenschaftslehre nova methodo*.)

'To posit' (*setzen*) means simply 'to be aware of', 'to reflect upon', or 'to be conscious of', and thus the principle in question simply states that the essence of selfhood lies in the assertion of ones own self-identity. Such immediate self-identify, however, cannot be understood as a 'fact', no matter how privileged, nor as an 'accident' of some previously existing substance or being. Instead, it must be understood as an *activity*, albeit an activity of a most extraordinary, auto-productive type: in Fichte's own language, it is a *Tathandlung* or 'fact/act', a unity that is presupposed by and contained within every fact and every act of empirical consciousness, though it never appears as such therein.

This same 'identity in difference' of self-consciousness might also be described as an 'intellectual intuition', since it involves the immediate presence of the I to itself, prior to and independently of any sensory content. Understood in this way, this original intellectual intuition is merely the reflectively realized presupposition for the possibility of actual consciousness and does not designate any act or state of actual, empirical consciousness – including the consciousness of the philosopher. Fichte himself, however, confuses matters by sometimes using the term 'intellectual intuition' to designate the act of philosophical reflection through which the philosopher arrives at the former concept or, on still other occasions, to indicate our direct, practical awareness within everyday life of our moral obligations (categorical imperative *qua* 'real intellectual intuition'). Given the subsequent abuse of this term by SCHELLING and the romantics, it is important to recognize its systematic ambiguity in Fichte's own writings. Significantly, the term 'intellectual intuition' does not even occur in the 1794–5 *Foundations*.

A fundamental corollary of Fichte's understanding of selfhood as a kind of act is his denial that the I is originally any sort of 'substance'. Instead, the I is simply what it posits itself to be, and thus its 'being' is, so to speak, a consequence of its self-positing. The first principle of the Jena *Wissenschaftslehre* is thus equally 'practical' and 'theoretical', insofar as the act described by this principle is a 'doing' as well as a 'knowing', a deed as well as a cognition. Thus the problematic unity of theoretical and practical reason is guaranteed from the start, inasmuch as this very unity is a condition for the possibility of selfconsciousness.

After establishing the first principle and conceiving the act expressed therein, the philosophical task is then to discover what other acts must occur as conditions for the possibility of the original, 'simply posited', first act and then to do the same for each of these successively discovered acts (or the theorems in which they are formulated). By continuing in this manner, one will finally arrive at a complete deduction of the a priori structure of ordinary experience – or, what amount to the same thing, a complete inventory of the 'original acts of the mind'. This is precisely the task of the first or 'foundational' portion of the Jena system.

Just as we are never directly aware of the original

act of self-positing with which the system commences, so we are also unaware – except, of course, from the artificial standpoint of philosophical reflection – of each of these additional 'necessary but unconscious', acts that are derived as conditions necessary for the possibility of this first act. Furthermore, though we must, due to the discursive character of reflection itself, distinguish each of these acts from the others that it is conditioned by and that are, in turn, conditioned by it, none of these individual acts can actually occur in isolation from all of the others. Thus what transcendental philosophy actually does is to *analyse* what is in fact the single, *synthetic* act through which the I posits for itself both itself and its world, thereby becoming aware in a single moment of both its freedom and its limitations, its infinity and its finitude. The result of such an analysis is a clear realization on the part of the transcendental philosopher that, although 'the I simply posits itself', its freedom is never 'absolute' or 'unlimited'; instead, freedom proves to be conceivable – and hence the I itself proves to be 'possible' – only as limited and finite. Despite widespread misunderstanding of this point, the *Wissenschaftslehre* is not a philosophy of the absolute I. Instead, the conclusion of both the *Foundations of the Entire Wissenschaftslehre* and of the *Wissenschaftslehre nova methodo* is that the 'absolute I' is a mere abstraction and that the only sort of I that can actually exist or act is a finite, empirical, embodied, individual self.

An I must posit itself in order to be an I at all; but it can posit itself only insofar as it posits itself as limited (and hence divided against itself). Moreover, it cannot even posit for itself its own limitations, in the sense of producing or creating these limits. Instead, according to Fichte's analysis, if the I is to posit itself at all, it must simply discover itself to be limited, a discovery that Fichte characterizes as a 'check' or *Anstoß* to the free, practical activity of the I. Such an original limitation of the I itself is first posited as a mere 'feeling', then as a 'sensation', then as an 'intuition' of a thing, and finally as a 'concept'. The *Anstoß* thus provides the essential occasion that first sets in motion the entire complex train of activities that finally result in our conscious experience both of ourselves as empirical individuals and of a world of spatio-temporal material objects.

Though this doctrine of the *Anstoß* may seem to play a role in Fichte's philosophy not unlike that which has sometimes been assigned to the thing in itself in the Kantian system, the fundamental difference is this: the *Anstoß* is not something foreign to the I. Instead, this term signifies the I's original encounter with its own finitude. Rather than claim that the Not-I is the cause or ground of the Ansto, Fichte argues that the former is posited by the I in order to explain to itself the latter. Though the *Wissenschaftslehre* demonstrates that such an *Anstoß* must occur if selfconsciousness is to be actual, philosophy itself is quite unable to 'deduce' or to 'explain' the actual occurrence of such an *Anstoß* – except as a condition for the possibility of consciousness. Accordingly, there are strict limits to what can be expected from any a priori deduction of experience. Though transcendental philosophy can explain, for example, why the world has a spatio-temporal character and a causal structure, it can never explain why objects have the particular sensible properties they happen to have. This is something that the I simply has to 'discover' at the same time that it discovers its own freedom, and indeed, as a condition for the latter.

But there remains much that can be demonstrated within the foundational portion of the *Wissenschaftslehre*. For example, it can be shown that the I could not become conscious of its own limits in the manner required for the possibility of any self-consciousness unless it also possessed an original and spontaneous ability to synthesize the finite and the infinite. In this sense, the *Wissenschaftslehre* deduces the power of productive imagination as an original power of the mind. Similarly, it can be shown that the I could not be 'checked' in the manner required for the possibility of consciousness unless it possessed, in addition to its original 'theoretical' power of productive imagination, an equally original 'practical' power of sheer willing, which, once 'checked', is immediately converted into a capacity for endless striving. The *Wissenschaftslehre* thus also includes a deduction of the categorical imperative and of the practical power of the self. For Fichte, therefore the Kantian principle of 'the primacy of practical reason' means not simply that philosophy must recognize a certain autonomous sphere within which practical reason is efficacious and practical considerations are appropriate; instead, it implies something much stronger: namely, the recognition that 'the practical power is the innermost root of the I' and thus that 'our freedom itself is a theoretical determining principle of our world'. The *Wissenschaftslehre* demonstrates from the very start that reason could not be theoretical if it were not also practical – at the same time, to be sure, that it also demonstrates the converse of this proposition, that reason could not be practical if were not also theoretical.

Freedom, according to Fichte's argument, is possible and actual only within the context of natural necessity, and thus it is never 'absolute', but always limited and finite. On the other hand, just as surely as a free subject must posit its freedom 'absolutely' – that is to say, 'purely and simply' (*schlechthin*) or 'for

no reason' – so must it never identify itself with any determinate or limited state whatsoever. Instead, a finite free self must constantly strive to transform both the natural and the human worlds in accordance with its own freely-posited goals. The sheer unity of the self posited in the starting point of the *Foundations* is thereby transformed into an idea of reason in the Kantian sense: the actual I is always finite and divided against itself, and hence always striving for a sheer self-determinacy that it never achieves. Between the original abstraction of pure selfhood as pure *Tathandlung* and the concluding ideal of a self that is only what it determines itself to be, in which 'is' and 'ought' wholly coincide, lies the entire realm of actual consciousness and experience.

6 Philosophy of nature and ethics

Having established the foundations of his new system, Fichte then turned to the task of erecting a fully-articulated transcendental system according to a plan that is perhaps most clearly outlined in 'The Deduction of the Subdivisions of the *Wissenschaftslehre*', with which the lectures on *Wissenschaftslehre nova methodo* conclude. At least as conceived during the Jena years, the entire *Wissenschaftslehre* consists of four parts: (1) first philosophy, which is to say, the 'foundational' portion of the system; (2) 'theoretical philosophy' or 'philosophy of nature', the latter understood in a sense corresponding to Kant's *Metaphysical First Principles of Nature*; (3) 'practical philosophy' or ethics; and (4) 'philosophy of the postulates', which includes the subdisciplines of political philosophy or 'theory of right' and philosophy of religion.

The closest Fichte himself ever came to developing a philosophy of nature according to transcendental principles is the compressed account of the same presented in the *Outline of the Distinctive Character of the Wissenschaftslehre with Respect to the Theoretical Faculty* (1795), in which, however, the domain of specifically 'theoretical' philosophy is not rigorously distinguished from the 'theoretical' portion of the *Foundations*, which also includes a discussion of the a priori structure of the objective world. In fact, the kind of theoretical philosophy of nature made possible by the *Wissenschaftslehre* turns out to be even more modest than Kant's and more closely resembles what later came to be called the philosophy of (natural) science than it does the speculative *Naturphilosophie* of Schelling and HEGEL.

In contrast to Fichte's rather cursory treatment of purely theoretical philosophy, ethics or 'practical philosophy', which analyses the determinate ways in which willing and acting are determinable by principles of pure reason, constitutes a major portion of the Jena system, and the *System of Ethical Theory* (1798a) is Fichte's longest single book. Whereas theoretical philosophy 'explains how the world is, and the result is the same as pure experience', practical philosophy 'explains how the world ought to be constructed by rational beings, and its result is something ideal'. Ethics thus considers the object of consciousness not as something given or even constructed by necessary laws of consciousness, but rather as something to be produced by a freely acting subject, consciously striving to establish and to accomplish its own goals. The specific task of Fichte's ethics is therefore to deduce from the general obligation to determine oneself freely the particular obligations of every finite rational being.

Viewed from the perspective of practical philosophy, the world really is nothing more than what Fichte once described as 'the material of our duty made sensible', which is precisely the viewpoint adopted by the morally engaged, practically striving subject. On the other hand, this is not the only way the world can be viewed, and, more specifically, it is not the only way in which it is construed by transcendental philosophy. For this reason it is somewhat misleading to characterize the *Wissenschaftslehre* as a whole as a system of 'ethical idealism'. As noted above, Fichte certainly does succeed in constructing an account of consciousness that fully integrates the imperatives and activities of practical reason into the very structure of the latter, but this integration is always balanced by a recognition, first, of the constitutive role of theoretical reason, and secondly, of the sheer 'giveness' of the I's original determinacy (doctrine of the *Anstoß*).

7 Political philosophy and philosophy of religion

The final portion of the Jena system is devoted to 'the philosophy of the postulates', a discipline conceived as occupying the middle ground between purely theoretical and purely practical philosophy. In this portion of the system the world is considered neither as it simply is nor as it simply ought to be; instead, the moral world is itself considered from the perspective of the natural world (that is, one considers the postulates that theoretical reason addresses to the practical realm) or else, alternatively, the natural world is considered from the perspective of the moral world order (that is, one considers the postulates that practical reason addresses to the realm of theory). The first of these perspectives is that of political philosophy, or what Fichte calls 'theory of right' or sometimes the domain of 'natural right'; the latter is that of the philosophy of religion.

A transcendental theory of right proceeds from the general principle that one must limit one's own freedom in accordance with an a priori concept of the other free beings with whom one comes into contact, and goes on to consider the precise conditions under which such a postulated society of free and equal individuals is in fact possible. Ultimately, this leads Fichte to the formulation of his own version of the contract theory of political legitimacy.

If one is to posit one's own freedom, then one must posit the freedom of others and limit one's own freedom accordingly. It follows that a just political order is a demand of reason itself, since 'the concept of justice or right is a condition of selfconsciousness'. This passage, from the *Foundations of Natural Right*, points to what is perhaps the most original feature of Fichte's political philosophy: its attempt to demonstrate the intrinsically social character of reason itself and thus to deduce the concept of right from the 'reciprocal concept' of an individual free being. The strategy of Fichte's deduction of intersubjectivity is to establish, first, that an I can posit itself only as an individual and, second, that it can posit itself as an individual only insofar as it recognizes other free individuals – a recognition facilitated by the presence, within selfconsciousness itself, of an immediate awareness of oneself as 'summoned' by the other to limit oneself freely in recognition of the latter's freedom. This a priori deduction of intersubjectivity is so central to the conception of selfhood developed in the Jena *Wissenschaftslehre* that Fichte, in his lectures on *Wissenschaftslehre nova methodo*, incorporated it into his revised presentation of the very foundations of his system.

The theory of natural right developed by Fichte during his Jena period is clearly quite different from the kind of theories that have traditionally gone by this name. The task of Fichte's theory of right is to consider the specific ways in which the freedom of each individual must be restricted so that several individuals can live together with the maximum amount of mutual freedom. Furthermore, it derives its a priori concepts of the laws of social interaction entirely from the sheer concept of an individual I, as conditions for the possibility of the latter. The concept of right obtains its binding force not from the ethical law, but rather from the general laws of thinking and from enlightened self-interest, and the force of such considerations is hypothetical rather than categorical. The theory of right examines how the freedom of each must be externally limited if a free society of equals is to be possible.

Unlike Kant, Fichte does not treat political philosophy merely as a subdivision of moral theory, but as an independent philosophical discipline with a topic and laws of its own. Whereas ethics analyses the concept of what is *demanded* of a freely willing subject, the theory of right describes what such a subject is *permitted* to do; and whereas ethics is concerned with the inner world of conscience, the theory of right is concerned only with the external, public realm, though only insofar as the latter can be viewed as an embodiment of freedom. If the *Wissenschaftslehre* as a whole can be described, in Fichte's words, as a 'system of freedom', then the spirit of such a system is perhaps best reflected in the distinctively liberal political philosophy based thereupon.

In addition to the postulates addressed by theoretical to practical reason, there are also those addressed by practical reason to nature itself. The latter is the domain of the transcendental philosophy of religion, which is concerned solely with the question of the extent to which the realm of nature can be said to accommodate itself to the aims of morality. The questions dealt with within such a philosophy of religion are those concerning the nature, limits, and legitimacy of our belief in divine providence.

As it happened, Fichte never had a chance to develop this final subdivision of his Jena system and, somewhat ironically, he was prevented from doing so by a controversy that erupted in the wake of the publication, in 1798, of a tentative foray into this very domain in his essay *On the Basis of Our Belief in a Divine Governance of the World*. In this essay Fichte seems to contend that, so far as philosophy is concerned, the realm of the divine is wholly coextensive with that of the moral law itself and that no further inference to a 'moral lawgiver' is theoretically or practically required or warranted. In this same essay Fichte also sought to draw a sharp distinction between religion and philosophy (a distinction parallel to the crucial distinction between the 'ordinary' and 'transcendental' standpoints) and to defend philosophy's right to postulate something like a 'moral world order'. Philosophy of religion would thus include a deduction of the postulate that our moral actions really do make some difference in the world. The argument of the essay *On the Basis of Our Belief* is, nevertheless, primarily a negative one, designed to deny that any postulate of the existence of a God independent of the moral law is justifiable on philosophical grounds. In the wake of the atheism controversy, Fichte returned to this subject and, in his *From a Private Letter* (1800) and in Part III of *The Vocation of Man* (1800b), attempted to restate his position in a manner that at least appeared to be more compatible with the claims of theism.

See also: ENLIGHTENMENT, CONTINENTAL; IDEALISM; KANTIAN ETHICS

List of works

Fichte, I. H. (ed.) (1834–5) *Johann Gottlieb Fichtes nachgelassene Werke*, Bonn: Adolph-Marcus, 3 vols.
—— (1845–6) *Johann Gottlieb Fichtes sämmtliche Werke*, Berlin: Veit, 8 vols. (Taken together, these 11 volumes, edited by Fichte's son, constitute the first attempt at a complete edition of his works and are still widely cited and reprinted.)
Fichte, J.G. (1792) *Versuch einer Kritik aller Offenbarung* (Attempt at a Critique of All Revelation), trans. G. Green, New York: Cambridge University Press, 1978.
—— (1794a) '[Rezension:] *Aenesidemus*' (Aenesidemus Review), in D. Breazeale (trans. and ed.) *Early Philosophical Writings*, Ithaca, NY: Cornell University Press, 1988.
—— (1794b) 'Ueber den Begriff der Wissenschaftslehre' (Concerning the Concept of the Wissenschaftslehre), in D. Breazeale (trans. and ed.) *Early Philosophical Writings*, Ithaca, NY: Cornell University Press, 1988.
—— (1794c) 'Einige Vorlesungen über die Bestimmung des Gelehrten' (Some Lectures Concerning the Scholar's Vocation), in D. Breazeale (trans. and ed.) *Early Philosophical Writings*, Ithaca, NY: Cornell University Press, 1988.
—— (1794/5) 'Grundlage der gesamten Wissenschaftslehre' (Foundations of the Entire Science of Knowledge), in P. Heath and J. Lachs (eds) *Science of Knowledge (Wissenschaftslehre)*, trans. P. Heath, New York: Appleton-Century-Crofts, 1970; 2nd edn., Cambridge: Cambridge University Press, 1982. (An adequate translation of Fichte's most famous work, despite the retention of the traditional and misleading title 'Science of Knowledge'.)
—— (1795) 'Grundriß des Eigenthümlichen der Wissenschaftslehre in Rücksicht auf das theoretische Vermögen' (Outline of the Distinctive Character of the Wissenschaftslehre with respect to the Theoretical Faculty), in D. Breazeale (trans. and ed.) *Early Philosophical Writings*, Ithaca, NY: Cornell University Press, 1988.
—— (1796–99) 'Wissenschaftslehre nova methodo (student lecture transcripts)', (Foundations of Transcendental Philosophy (*Wissenschaftslehre*) *nova methodo*), trans. and ed. D. Breazeale, Ithaca, NY: Cornell University Press, 1992.
—— (1796/7) *Grundlage des Naturrechts nach Principien der Wissenschaftslehre* (The Science of Rights), trans. A.E. Kroeger, Philadelphia, PA: Lippincott, 1869. (Very unreliable translation.)

—— (1797/8) 'Versuch einer neuen Darstellung der Wissenschaftslehre ('Erste' und 'Zweite Einleitung,' 1797; Erste Capitel,' 1798)', (Attempt at a New Presentation of the Wissenschaftslehre), in D. Breazeale (trans. and ed.) *Introductions to the Wissenschaftslehre and Other Writings (1797 – 1800)*, Indianapolis, IN: Hackett, 1994.

—— (1798a) *Das System der Sittenlehre nach den Principien der Wissenschaftslehre* (The Science of Ethics as Based on the Science of Knowledge), trans. A.E. Kroeger, London: Kegan Paul, 1897. (Very unreliable translation.)

—— (1798b) 'Über den Grund unsers Glaubens an eine göttliche Weltregierung' (On the Basis of our Belief in a Divine Governance of the World), in D. Breazeale (trans. and ed.) *Introductions to the Wissenschaftslehre and Other Writings (1797 – 1800)*, Indianapolis, IN: Hackett, 1994.

—— (1800a) 'Aus einem Privatschreiben' (From a Private Letter), in D. Breazeale (trans. and ed.) *Introductions to the Wissenschaftslehre and Other Writings (1797 – 1800)*, Indianapolis, IN: Hackett, 1994.

—— (1800b) *Die Bestimmung des Menschen* (The Vocation of Man), trans. P. Preuss, Indianapolis, IN: Hackett, 1987.

—— (1801) 'Sonnenklarer Bericht an das größere Publikum über das eigentliche Wesen der neuesten Philosophie. Ein Versuch, die Leser zum Verstehen zu zwingen' (A Crystal Clear Report to the General Public Concerning the Actual Essence of the Newest Philosophy: An Attempt to Force the Reader to Understand), in E. Behler (ed.) *Philosophy of German Idealism*, trans. J. Botterman and W. Rash, New York: Continuum, 1987.

—— (1806a) 'Der Grundzüge des gegewärtigen Zeitalters' (The Characteristics of the Present Age), in *The Popular Works of Johann Gottlieb Fichte*, trans. W. Smith, London: Chapman, 2 vols, 1848/49; 4th edn, 1889.

—— (1806b) 'Über des Wesen des Gelehrten, und seine Erscheinungen im Gebiete der Freiheit' (On The Nature of the Scholar and Its Manifestations), in *The Popular Works of Johann Gottlieb Fichte*, trans. W. Smith, London: Chapman, 2 vols, 1848/49; 4th edn, 1889.

—— (1806c) 'Die Anweisung zum seeligen Leben, oder auch die Religionslehre' (The Way Towards the Blessed Life; or, the Doctrine of Religion), in *The Popular Works of Johann Gottlieb Fichte,* trans. W. Smith, London: Chapman, 2 vols, 1848/49; 4th edn, 1889.

—— (1808) *Reden an die deutsche Nation* (Addresses to the German Nation), trans. R. F. Jones and G. H. Turnbull, eds G. Armstrong Kelly, New York: Harper & Row, 1968.

—— (1810) 'Die Wissenschaftslehre, in ihrem allgemeinen Umrisse dargestellt' (The Science of Knowledge in its General Outline), trans. W.E. Wright, *Idealistic Studies* 6: 106–17, 1976.

Lauth, R., Jacobs, H. and Gliwitzsky, H. (eds) (1964–) *J. G. Fichte: Gesamtausgabe der Bayerischen Akademie der Wissenschaften*, Stuttgart-Bad Cannstatt: Frommann, 25 vols to date. (Organized into four separate series – writings published by Fichte, unpublished writings, correspondence and student lecture transcripts – this monumental critical edition, though still incomplete, supersedes all earlier editions.)

References and further reading

(See too the journal *Fichte-Studien* (1990–) Amsterdam and Atlanta, GA: Editions Rodopi, which appears roughly once a year and publishes papers, most of them in German, on every aspect of Fichte's life and thought.)

Adamson, R. (1881) *Fichte*, Edinburgh: Blackwood. (Though seriously out of date, this remains the only full-scale treatment of Fichte in English.)

Baumanns, P. (1974) *Fichtes Wissenschaftslehre. Probleme ihres Anfangs*, Bonn: Bouvier. (Useful exposition of various ways of interpreting the starting point of the first *Wissenschaftslehre*.)

—— (1990) *J. G. Fichte: Kritische Gesamtdarstellung seiner Philosophie*, Freiburg: Alber. (A useful and critical overview of Fichte's philosophical development.)

Baumgartner, M. and Jacobs, W.G. (1968) *J. G. Fichte: Bibliographie*, Stuttgart-Bad Cannstatt: Frommann. (A complete bibliography. Supplemented by Doyé's bibliography.)

Breazeale, D. and Rockmore, T. (eds) (1993) *Fichte: Historical Context/Contemporary Controversies*, Atlantic Highlands, NJ: Humanities Press. (A collection of essays on various aspects of Fichte's philosophy. Includes a complete bibliography of works in English by and about Fichte.)

Doyé, S. (ed.) (1993) *J. G. Fichte-Bibliographie (1969–1991)*, Amsterdam and Atlanta, GA: Editions Rodopi. (An essential addition to the bibliography by Baumgartner and Jacobs.)

Gueroult, M. (1930) *L'evolution et la structure de la doctrine de la science chez Fichte*, Paris: Société de l'édition, 2 vols. (A pioneering developmental study of the *Wissenschaftslehre*.)

Everett, C.C. (1884) *Fichte's Science of Knowledge: A Critical Exposition*, Chicago, IL: Griggs. (The only monograph in English devoted entirely to the 'Foundations of the Entire Wissenschaftslehre'.)

'Fichte and Contemporary Philosophy' (1988) special issue of *Philosophical Forum* 19 (2 and 3).

Fuchs, E. (ed.) (1978–92) *J. G. Fichte im Gespräch: Berichte der Zeitgenossen*, Stuttgart-Bad Cannstatt: Frommann, 6 vols. (An encyclopedic collection of contemporary reports on Fichte and his writings. An invaluable research tool.)

Henrich, D. (1967) *Fichtes ursprüngliche Einsicht*, Frankfurt: Klostermann; trans. D. Lachterman, 'Fichte's Original Insight', *Contemporary German Philosophy* 1: 15–52, 1982. (An influential reading of Fichte's alleged movement beyond a 'reflective theory of consciousness'.)

Janke, W. (1970) *Fichte: Sein und Reflexion – Grundlagen der kristischen Vernunft*, Berlin: de Gruyter. (A hermeneutic reading of Fichte, with an emphasis upon the later writings.)

Lauth, R. (1984) *Die transzendentale Naturlehre Fichtes nach den Prinzipien der Wissenschaftslehre*, Hamburg: Meiner. (A masterly exposition of Fichte's transcendental approach to the philosophy of nature.)

—— (1987) *Hegel vor der Wissenschaftslehre*, Stuttgart: Steiner-Verlag. (A vigorous and convincing defence of Fichte against the familiar criticisms of Hegel.)

—— (1989) *Transzendentale Entwicklungslinien von Descartes bis zu Marx und Dostojewski*, Hamburg: Meiner. (A collection of essays, most of them on Fichte, by the leading Fichte scholar of the age.)

Léon, X. (1922, 1927) *Fichte et son temps*, Paris: Armand Colin, 3 vols. (Though outdated, this remains the best study of Fichte's 'life and thought'.)

Neuhouser, F. (1990) *Fichte's Theory of Subjectivity*, Cambridge: Cambridge University Press. (A good example of a contemporary appropriation of Fichte's thought and of an analytically sensitive exposition of the same.)

'New Studies in the Philosophy of Fichte' (1979) special issue of *Idealistic Studies* 6 (2). (A collection of essays on Fichte in English.)

Pareyson, L. (1976) *Fichte. Il sistema della liberté*, Milan: Mursia, 2nd edn. (Along with Philonenko, Pareyson's exposition of the early system as a 'system of freedom' is one of the most influential works on Fichte of the post-war period.)

Philonenko, A. (1966) *La liberté humaine dans la philosophie de Fichte*, Paris: Vrin; 2nd edn, 1980. (A tremendously original and influential study of Fichte's early philosophy, interpreted as a 'philosophy of human finitude'. Essential.)

Radrizzani, I. (1993) *Vers la fondation de l'intersub-jectivité chez Fichte: des Prinzipes à la Nova Methodo*, Paris: Vrin. (Argues for the continuity of Fichte's development within the Jena period and for the centrality therein of the *Wissenschaftslehre nova methodo*.)

Renaut, A. (1986) *Le système du droit: Philosophie et droit dans la pensée de Fichte*, Paris: Presses Universitaires de France. (A powerful reading of the Foundations of Natural Right. Argues that political philosophy is the keystone of the Jena *Wissenschaftslehre*.)

Rockmore, T. (1980) *Fichte, Marx, and the German Philosophical Tradition*, Carbondale, IL: Southern Illinois University Press. (The first successful effort in English to liberate Fichte's philosophy from the shadow of Hegel's.)

Seidel, G.J. (1993) *Fichte's Wissenschaftslehre of 1794: A Commentary on Part I*, Lafayette, IN: Purdue University Press. (An elementary introduction to the early system. Written with the beginning student in mind.)

Widmann, J. (1977) *Der Grundstrukture des transzen-dentalen Wissens nach J. G. Fichtes Wissenschaftslehre 1804*, Hamburg: Meiner. (A elaborate formal analysis of what is widely considered to be the most successful and complete presentation of the later Wissenschaftslehre.)

Wundt, M. (1929) *Fichte-Forschungen*, Stuttgart: Frommann. (Another pioneering study of the development of Fichte's thought, with an emphasis upon the 'spirits' of the various Wissenschaftslehren.)

DANIEL BREAZEALE

FICINO, MARSILIO (1433–99)

With Giovanni Pico della Mirandola, Marsilio Ficino was the most important philosopher working under the patronage of Lorenzo de' Medici, 'Il Magnifico', in the Florence of the High Renaissance. Ficino's main contribution was as a translator of Platonic philosophy from Greek into Latin: he produced the first complete Latin version of the works of Plato (1484) and Plotinus (1492) as well as renderings of a number of minor Platonists. He supplied many of his translations with philosophical commentaries, and these came to exercise great influence on the interpretation of Platonic philo-sophy in the Renaissance and early modern periods. Ficino's most important philosophical work, the Theologia platonica de immortalitate animae *(Platonic Theology, On the Immortality of the Soul) (1474) aimed to use Platonic arguments to combat the Averroists, 'impious' scholastic philosophers who denied that the immortality of the soul could be proven by reason. The most famous concept associated with his name is that of 'Platonic love'.*

1 Life and mission
2 The 'ancient theology'
3 The immortality of the soul
4 Platonic love

1 Life and mission

Marsilio Ficino was born in 1433 in Figline Valdarno, a small town in the territory of Florence; his father, Dietifeci, was a doctor who worked in the city of Florence and served as private physician to Cosimo de'Medici, then the *de facto* ruler of Florence. Dietifeci intended that his son should follow him in the medical profession, and the young Marsilio was sent to the University of Florence to hear the lectures on Aristotelian logic and natural philosophy that would fit him for his medical studies. Though Ficino retained a lifelong interest in medicine, he eventually left the university without taking his degree. He had discovered that his true bent was for philosophy and theology, especially the Platonic and Augustinian theology he met in his confraternity, led by the priest and theologian Lorenzo Pisano. Thanks to the indulgence of Cosimo de'Medici, Ficino was able to study Greek so as to have direct access to Plato's works, only a few of which were available in Latin at the time (see PLATONISM, RENAISSANCE). Ficino's desire to return to the original Greek text was also a symptom of his ties with the humanist movement; he had enjoyed something of a classical education under two minor humanist schoolmasters, and was surrounded in later life by friends, patrons and pupils who were deeply involved in the movement for 'good letters' (see HUMANISM, RENAISSANCE).

In addition to supporting his Greek studies, Cosimo de'Medici had lent the young Ficino a precious manuscript containing the complete works of Plato, and Ficino's first large translation project was a Latin version of ten dialogues of Plato, dedicated to Cosimo de'Medici a few weeks before the latter's death in 1464. Before 1469 Ficino had drafted a translation of all thirty-six dialogues in the Thrasyllan canon, though the final version was not printed until 1484. All of these dialogues were provided with short 'arguments', philosophical in character, and several were also supplied with full-scale philosophical commentaries. Ficino eventually wrote commentaries on the *Timaeus*, *Symposium*, *Philebus*, *Phaedrus*, *Parmenides*, *Sophist*, and on the mysterious passage in Book VIII of the *Republic* on the 'Platonic number'; these were published together

in 1496. In addition to his work on Plato, Ficino also produced an exceptionally fine translation and commentary on Plotinus' *Enneads* (published 1492), a version of PSEUDO-DIONYSIUS (dedicated 1492), and versions of texts by the Platonists Iamblichus, Proclus, Porphyry, Synesius, Michael Psellus, Priscianus Lydus, Albinus, pseudo-Pythagoras, Speusippus and pseudo-Xenocrates (collection published 1499). Ficino's work of translation and commentary makes him by far the most important conduit for the transmission of the ancient Platonic tradition to Renaissance and early modern Europe.

Ficino was able to devote himself to his scholarly and philosophical labours thanks largely to the support of the Medici family over four generations as well as of other wealthy Florentine aristocrats. Cosimo de' Medici had given Ficino a house in Florence and a small farm near his own villa at Careggi; Cosimo's son Piero gave Ficino a brief appointment as a lecturer at the Florentine *studio*; Piero's son, the great Lorenzo, arranged for Ficino to have two small ecclesiastical benefices after the philosopher was ordained a priest in 1473 and in 1487 had him made a canon of the Cathedral of Florence. Before receiving this major benefice Ficino supplemented his income by tutoring wealthy pupils in rhetoric, philosophy and other subjects. He referred to his pupils collectively as his *gymnasium* or *academy* and, since most of his students concurrently attended the University of Florence (also called a gymnasium or academy by contemporary humanists), the confusion of terminology led later scholars to elaborate the rich fable of Ficino's 'Platonic Academy' (an expression not documented before 1638). In fact, Ficino's closest, though informal, institutional link was with the University of Florence.

Though Ficino was not the leader of a Platonic Academy at the centre of Florentine intellectual life, his influence went far beyond what might be expected of a private scholar and teacher. Thanks to his position as a protégé of the Medicis, his own wide circle of pupils and friends, his numerous publications and an extensive, Europe-wide correspondence, Ficino became the leader of a philosophical counter-culture that challenged in a small but significant way the dominance of Aristotelian school philosophy (see ARISTOTELIANISM, RENAISSANCE). Ficino saw himself as an educational and cultural reformer. A sincere Christian, he believed that religious belief in his day was under threat from the growing estrangement of piety from philosophy. On the one hand were priests and other religious authorities, too ignorant of philosophy to defend Christianity; on the other hand were impious university philosophers, chiefly those whom Ficino labelled the 'Averroists' and 'Alexandrists' (that is, followers of Averroes' and Alexander of Aphrodisias' interpretations of Aristotle's psychology), who denied the ability of philosophy to prove central tenets of the faith like the immortality of the soul. In Ficino's view the great medieval project to integrate Christianity and Aristotelian philosophy had ended in intellectual disaster. But Ficino believed the best way to combat the growing autonomy of philosophy from religion in the schools was neither to retreat to fideism nor to seek a more successful Christian interpretation of Aristotle, but to replace Aristotle with Plato as the primary philosophical authority of Christendom. It was Ficino's belief that Plato, who had believed in creation and in the immortality of the soul, would provide a better foundation for Christian belief than Aristotle, who had believed in the eternity of the world and had been fatally unclear on the immortality question. In this Ficino was supported by the authority of AUGUSTINE, who in a much-quoted passage of *De civitate Dei* (The City of God) had declared Plato to be the pagan philosopher closest to Christianity. Indeed, Ficino (who also thought himself to have prophetic powers) declared that he had personally been appointed by divine providence to bring about a rebirth of Platonic theology in order to save the Christian faith from impious intellectuals.

Ficino's other sharp difference from contemporary scholasticism was his interest in the therapeutic side of ancient philosophy. This interest grew out of his early medical training, which helped him recognize the close connection between medicine and philosophy in Plato, Aristotle and the Hellenistic philosophers. Psychic health for Ficino involved both the cultivation of moral virtue and the achievement of a proper equilibrium between states of the body and states of the soul. The former theme is mostly explored in Ficino's letters; the latter in his major work on magic, the *De vita* (*On Life*). In this work Ficino tries to find magical remedies for scholar's melancholy, in particular psychosomatic remedies that work on the *spiritus* – the *tertium quid* linking soul and body. It was once believed on the authority of Frances Yates that the sources of Ficino's magic were to be found in Hermes Trismegistus, but this has recently been shown to be an error; Ficino's actual sources were the same late ancient Platonic texts that guided his interpretation of Plato (see HERMETISM).

2 The 'ancient theology'

Ficino's real interest in 'Thrice-Great Hermes' was theological rather than magical. Ficino believed that the texts going under the names of Hermes Trismegistus and Orpheus, as well as the Chaldean Oracles which he (following Pletho) attributed to Zoroaster, were theological writings of extreme antiquity, belonging roughly to the time of Moses. (In fact they were late ancient forgeries.) For him, they represented a tradition of gentile theology, parallel to the Hebrew Old Testament, that culminated in the writings of Plato. Like the Old Testament, they were inspired but obscure writings whose full meaning only became clear with the advent of Christ. Following Eusebius and Lactantius, Ficino held that the writings of the ancient theologians had prepared the gentiles for Christianity as the Old Testament writings had prepared the Jews. In Christian times the writings of the pagan philosophers and theologians in the Platonic tradition retained value for a variety of reasons. They provided a model for the kind of *pia philosophia* or *docta religio*, combining religious belief and philosophical wisdom, that Ficino wished to see revived in his own time. If Platonism could be successfully reconciled with Christian faith, the latter's credibility would be much enhanced among people educated by humanists for whom ancient authority was paramount. Platonism could also act as an introductory credo preparing the philosophically minded for the higher truths of Christianity, as it had in the case of Origen and Augustine. It could serve as an apologetic weapon against sceptical intellectuals: Ficino said as much in a letter praising Pico della Mirandola as a 'fisher of men' for having used Plato as a net to draw 'Averroists and Epicureans' back to Christianity.

It may be asked what could have led Ficino and his circle to promote so unusual a view of the role of ancient theology and Plato within Christianity. It must be remembered that the efforts of those in the Renaissance movement to revalue all things classical led to a certain cognitive dissonance between classical and Christian values. While most Christian writers in antiquity were anxious to distinguish Christianity from the surrounding pagan culture, in the Renaissance many humanist writers wished to emphasize the common ground between Christian doctrine and the best pagan thought. Ficino's interpretation of the historical role of Platonism integrated the greatest of ancient philosophers into the Christian tradition, and strengthened the humanist hope that Christendom could renew itself from ancient sources without alienating itself wholly from pagan culture. The 'ancient theology' also presupposed Ficino's wider belief in natural religion: that religion was natural to all men, and that all manifestations of religion were in some degree good as expressions of the natural desire of man for God. Though Ficino did not declare all religions equal – he held that each species of belief should be arranged hierarchically with Christianity holding the first place in the genus – his attitude to religions other than Christianity stands in marked contrast with older medieval attitudes. While traditional church teachings declared Islam, for example, to be a demonic invention or a divinely-ordained scourge of sinful Christians, Ficino (like NICHOLAS OF CUSA) regards Islam as a sincere though misguided form of worship. Ficino's conception of natural religion and the 'ancient theology' continued to retain a certain appeal throughout the later Renaissance; it has been shown that as late as the seventeenth century the Jesuits in China were attempting to convince their catechumens that the 'ancient theology' of the Chinese was a foreshadowing of the truths of Christianity.

3 The immortality of the soul

The question of the soul's immortality was perhaps the most hotly debated philosophical issue of the later fifteenth and early sixteenth century. After a long period in which 'the common doctrine of the philosophers' (that is, Averroism) had reigned almost unchecked in Italian universities (see AVERROISM), the 1470s saw a revival, in the religious orders and among secular thinkers like Ficino and Apollinaris Offredi, of attempts to establish rational proofs for the immortality of the soul. The campaign culminated with the Fifth Lateran Council (1512–7), summoned by Ficino's former pupil Leo X, which denounced 'those who assert that the intellective soul is mortal or is one for all mankind'. Ficino, like Thomas AQUINAS and many others who argued for immortality, held that those who denied personal immortality were undermining the traditional belief in rewards and punishments in the afterlife, and thus removing a key sanction against immoral behaviour. In his argument to the tenth book of Plato's Laws Ficino went so far as to say that the immortality of the soul was the main foundation for religion.

This historical background does not however account fully for Ficino's preoccupation with human immortality. Ficino was the first philosopher to give the immortality of the soul the central place in his thought, a prominence indicated by the full title of his principal work, Theologia platonica de immortalitate animae (Platonic Theology, On the Immortality of the Soul) (1474). In his classic study of Ficino's thought (1943), P.O. Kristeller maintained that immortality was central to Ficino's work because of its close connection with contemplative experience. For Ficino, the experience of God which may be attained in contemplation constitutes the highest human act of consciousness, and it therefore both defines the essence of humanity and establishes the end of human existence. Since the contemplative experience of God in this life is only partial and transitory, the soul must be capable of some form of separate incorporeal existence in which its natural appetite for the knowledge and enjoyment of God may be fulfilled. Ficino does not seem to realize that this is at best an argument for the soul's survival after death and not necessarily for eternal existence, since he admits elsewhere that souls are created in time. But in fact, many of the dozens of immortality arguments that fill the last thirteen books of the Theologia platonica begin from similar subjective analyses of acts, habits, faculties, appetites and affinities of soul. The arguments from affinity, drawn in the first instance from Plato's Phaedo, are of particular importance, but Ficino also employs the argument from self-motion found in the Phaedrus, while the arguments from appetitus naturalis have Augustinian and Thomistic antecedents.

The immortal soul is also central to Ficino's philosophy in a broader metaphysical context. The early books of the Theologia platonica lay out an ontological hierarchy of five substances, God, angel, soul, quality and matter. This hierarchy was probably taken from Proclus, though the hypostasis of quality seems to be original with Ficino. Within the hierarchy soul functions as the central link: what is above soul is eternal, immaterial, unchanging, intelligible; what is below it is temporal, material, mutable and sensible. It is soul that binds the two spheres together and makes them a unity. Paradoxically, the unifying functions of soul within total metaphysical reality mean that the soul is radically divided within itself. It contains within itself two separate and opposing impulses. It has a natural desire for God which drives it to cut itself off from the body and empirical reality, to turn within and upwards to the source of its being through rational activity. In addition to this contemplative nisus, obviously inspired by Plotinus, Ficino posits another which leads the soul to 'care for' lower things such as the body, for which it has a natural affection. To these two natural tendencies or affections there correspond the higher parts of the soul, pre-eminently the reasoning and noetic powers, and the lower parts of the soul such as sensation and vegetation which are responsible for its empirical activity.

Ficino's definition of the soul, partly in consequence of this radical division within the soul, is not entirely satisfactory. In some passages he asserts, following Aristotle and Aquinas, that it has a hylomorphic relationship to the body, that is, it is the substantial form of the body. He rejects the Plotinian formulation of the relation of soul to body, in which the soul, while remaining separate from body, controls it by means of a physis or reflection of itself which it projects into the body. He also will not endorse the implausible solution of some medieval Augustinians, which calls for the soul to be a distinct substance, though composed of form and 'spiritual matter'. Yet in most contexts Ficino does speak of the soul in Platonic terms as though it were an independent substance and not subject to material potencies. He infers from the fact that we form simple concepts and can conceive of pure simplicity that the soul itself is simple; he uses many of the old Platonic analogies, such as that the soul is imprisoned in the body, that the soul is to the body as the person at the helm is to the ship, and so forth.

Plato's doctrine of the pre-existence and transmigration of souls presented Ficino with a major interpretative challenge, since it threatened the Florentine's larger project of demonstrating the compatibility of Platonism and Christianity. The doctrine had been confidently attributed to Plato by PLOTINUS, AUGUSTINE, the standard commentary on the Bible (where King Herod is also said to have believed in it) and Thomas AQUINAS. Several of Ficino's contemporary opponents, such as the Dominicans Savonarola and Dominic of Flanders, used it to discredit Ficino's Platonic revival and the doctrine was, significantly, condemned by the Inquisition in articles published at the University of Pisa in 1490. Ficino's response was to deny that Plato had ever really held the doctrine. Metempsychosis as referred to in Plato and the other ancient theologians was to be understood as a mystery; to understand it in a literal sense was a vulgar error first put about in the late Academy. In reality the doctrine of transmigration must be taken as an allegory of the return of the soul to the One in contemplative experience, or typologically as a prophecy of the resurrection of the body, or as an obscure, proto-Christian premonition of the doctrine of purgatory. Ficino also employed the not wholly consistent argument that when Plato discussed transmigration in his works he was simply retailing a Pythagorean doctrine to which he was not himself necessarily committed. To the metaphysical problem of explaining how an eternal substance could have been created in particular souls at particular moments of time, Ficino argues that creation in this instance is to be understood as the ontological dependence of the temporal manifestations of soul on their eternal source, not as the production *ex nihilo* of new substances in time.

4 Platonic love

If the *Theologia platonica* was Ficino's most substantial independent work of philosophy, his most influential work was his commentary on Plato's *Symposium*, known as *De amore* (*On Love*) (1469). Unlike Ficino's other commentaries, the *De amore* was cast in the form of a literary dialogue, set in the villa of Lorenzo de'Medici, with Ficino's friends and patrons as the interlocutors. Each interlocutor gives a speech which is effectively a Neoplatonic reading of the several speeches in Plato's *Symposium*. It was this work, and translations of it into Italian, French and German, that popularized the concept of 'Platonic love', a concept that became a popular poetical conceit in the later Renaissance and is still used in a debased sense in modern colloquial speech (see LOVE).

Ficino is usually credited as the inventor of this concept, and the expression *amor platonicus* actually occurs in one of his letters (though not in the *De amore*). Ficino's account of love, however, is closely based on Plotinus (in particular *Enneads* 3.5), and a similar Plotinian reading of the *Symposium* can be found in Cardinal Bessarion's *In Calumniatorem Platonis* (Against Plato's Calumniator), printed within a few months of the publication of Ficino's *De amore* in 1469 (see PLATONISM, RENAISSANCE §3). Nevertheless, it was certainly Ficino who gave the concept its currency in Renaissance Europe and invested it with the philosophical richness that gave it its wide appeal. As Kristeller (1943) points out, the concept combines a Plotinian reading of love with the will of St Augustine, the charity of St Paul, and ideas on friendship found in Aristotle, the Stoics, and Cicero's *Laelius*.

Ficino's basic move is to interpret our experience of love in terms of the spiritual dynamics of the Neoplatonic cosmos. A true experience of love awakens one to the natural desire of the soul for union with God. It may begin with a sensual element but that is a mere preparation for genuine love, which is the love of God. The instantiations of beauty or goodness that kindle mutual desire between human beings are to be understood as reflections of the divine beauty and goodness. What we love in others rightly belongs to God; to give love to another without at the same time giving love to God, as Ficino says in a striking formulation, is 'nothing but robbery'. Yet the true basis of active love is not the unconscious dependence of attributes on their divine source, but a conscious striving of souls together towards God in contemplative experience. It is the active search for truth in the philosophical life which is the true basis of love and forms a genuine union between lovers. Real, divine love is thus independent of the sex of the lovers and can exist between members of the same or opposite genders. Ficino's concept of love in this way subsumes the Pauline and Augustinian concept of charity; it also absorbs the classical pagan concept of friendship. In the *Nicomachean Ethics*, for example, Aristotle argues that true friendship is necessarily between equals and has as its subject common pursuits. Ficino understands this to mean that souls united in contemplation of the same object are *eo ipso* equal. Such souls are always present to each other even when separated, and love even has the power to transform the lover into the image of the beloved.

Ficino insists that the biblical command to love one another has a metaphysical basis; he argues that unrequited love is, so to speak, spiritually defective. Mutual love which constitutes a concrete communion between persons is the only true and perfect form of love; it is not only a moral obligation but a cosmic necessity. If love is based on a similarity or equality between the souls of lovers and has the same divine source, then it must exist in both souls equally. A failure of charity is a denial of one's essential nature. It has recently been suggested that Ficino's emphasis on Platonic love has a political meaning, that it was meant as a cure for the endemic divisions in Florentine civil society. It has also been argued that Ficino feared criticism of Plato on account of the numerous scenes of homosexual gallantry depicted in the dialogues, and that the doctrine of Platonic love was in part intended as an exegetical device to protect Plato from this charge. Both statements may well be true. But the doctrine of Platonic love is one that grows naturally from the central themes of Ficino's philosophy, especially his emphasis on the special dignity of contemplative noesis among human cognitive powers and his belief in the unitive functions of soul within creation.

See also: HERMETISM; PLATO; PLATONISM, RENAISSANCE

List of works

Ficino, M. (1433–99) *Opera omnia* (Complete Works), Basle: Heinrich Petri, 1576; repr. Turin: Bottega d'Erasmo, 1959. (The only widely available edition for many of Ficino's Latin works; most of those not included here are given in Kristeller's *Supplementum Ficinianum*.)

—— (1469) *De amore*, ed. and trans. R. Marcel, *Commentaire sur le Banquet de Platon*, Paris: Les Belles Lettres, 1956; trans. S. Jayne, *Commentary on Plato's Symposium On Love*, Dallas, TX: Spring Books, 1985. (Referred to in §4. Marcel's edition gives the Latin text with French translation; Jayne has a useful introduction describing the influence of *De amore* on Renaissance literature.)

—— (1474) *Theologia platonica de immortalitate animae* (Platonic Theology, On the Immortality of the Soul), ed. and trans. R. Marcel, *Théologie platonicienne de l'immortalité des âmes*, Paris: Les Belles Lettres, 1964–79, 3 vols. (Referred to in §3. Edition of the Latin text with a French translation; the third volume also contains most of Book 2 of Ficino's *Letters*.)

—— (1489) *De vita libri tres*, ed. and trans. C.V. Kaske and J.R. Clark, *Three Books On Life*, Binghamton, NY: Center for Medieval and Early Renaissance Studies, 1989. (Referred to in §1. Critical edition of the Latin text of the *De vita* with English translation and notes.)

—— (1496) *Commentaria in Platonem* (Commentaries on Plato), Florence: Lorenzo di Francesco da Venezia; ed. M.J.B. Allen, *The Philebus Commentary*, Berkeley, CA: University of California Press, 1975; *Marsilio Ficino and the Phaedran Charioteer*, Berkeley, CA: University of California Press, 1981; *Icastes: Marsilio Ficino's Interpretation of Plato's Sophist*, Berkeley, CA: University of California Press, 1989; *Nuptial Arithmetic: Marsilio Ficino's Commentary on the Fatal Number in Book VIII of the Republic*, Berkeley, CA: University of California Press, 1994. (The 1496 edition is the final Latin text of the commentaries; now largely superseded by M.J.B. Allen's critical editions of the Latin text, which also provide English translations, monographs and notes.)

—— (1937) *Supplementum Ficinianum: Marsilii Ficini... opuscula inedita et dispersa*, ed. P.O. Kristeller, Florence: Olschki. (Contains most of the Latin works not included in Ficino's *Opera* of 1576; gives textual improvements to, and the textual history of, many of the works included in the *Opera*.)

—— (1975–88) *The Letters of Marsilio Ficino*, trans. by Members of the Language Department of the School of Economic Science, London: Shepheard-Walwyn, 4 vols to date. (Referred to in §1. English translation of the first five of Ficino's twelve books of philosophical letters.)

—— (1990) *Lettere. I. Epistolarum familiarium liber I* (First Book of Familiar Letters), ed. S. Gentile, Florence: Olschki. (Referred to in §1. Critical edition of the Latin text of Book I of Ficino's *Epistolarum familiarium*, with important biographical material in the introduction.)

References and further reading

Allen, M.J.B. (1984) *The Platonism of Marsilio Ficino: A Study of His Phaedrus Commentary, Its Sources and Genesis*, Berkeley, CA: University of California Press. (Supplements Kristeller 1943 for a number of themes in Ficino's philosophy.)

Hankins, J. (1990) *Plato in the Italian Renaissance*, Leiden: Brill. (A study of Ficino as a translator and interpreter of Plato.)

—— (1991) 'The Myth of the Platonic Academy of Florence', *Renaissance Quarterly* 44: 429–75. (Expansion of material in §1; disproves the myth of Ficino's 'Platonic Academy'.)

* Kristeller, P.O. (1943) *The Philosophy of Marsilio Ficino*, New York: Columbia University Press; revised edn, *Il pensiero filosofico di Marsilio Ficino*, Florence: Le Lettere, 1988. (Referred to in §§3–4. The classic study of Ficino's philosophical thought. Revised edition was published in Italian with an updated bibliography.)

—— (1987) *Marsilio Ficino and His Work after Five Hundred Years*, Istituto Nazionale di Studi sul Rinascimento, *Quaderni di 'Rinascimento'* 7, Florence: Olschki. (Contains an exhaustive bibliography of secondary literature on Ficino as well as additions and corrections to Kristeller's *Supplementum Ficinianum* (1937).)

Marcel, R. (1958) *Marsile Ficin*, Paris: Les Belles Lettres. (The standard biography, not very critical.)

JAMES HANKINS

FICTION, SEMANTICS OF

Taken at face value, 'Anna Karenina is a woman' seems true. By using Tolstoi's name 'Anna Karenina' and the predicate 'is a woman' we appear to refer to the character Anna and to attribute to her a property which she has. Yet how can this be? There is no actual woman to whom the name refers. Such problems of reference, predication and truth also arise in connection with representational art and with beliefs and other attitudes.

Meinong distinguishes the 'being' of objects (including fictional objects) from the 'existence' of actual objects such as Napoleon. 'Anna Karenina' refers to a concrete, particular, nonexistent object that has the property of womanhood. However, Meinong's distinction seems to many ontologically suspect. Perhaps, then, being is existence and 'Anna Karenina is a woman' is actually false because 'Anna Karenina' has no referent. Russell in 'On Denoting' (1905) agrees. But how can we explain the apparent contrast in truth between this sentence and the unquestionably erroneous 'Anna Karenina is from Moscow'? Or is it that being is existence but 'Anna Karenina' refers to an abstract, not a concrete, thing – an existent, abstract thing that does not have the property of being a woman but has merely the property of being said, by Tolstoi's novel, to be a

woman? Then, however, the meaning of our sentence about Anna no longer parallels that of 'Emily Dickinson is a woman'. Perhaps, as many argue, we only pretend that 'Anna Karenina' refers and that the sentence is true. This position may not adequately explain the intuitions that support Anna Karenina as a genuine object of reference and predication, however.

1 Meinongian and abstract-object views
2 Pretence and make-believe
3 Further questions

1 Meinongian and abstract-object views

Meinong distinguishes the 'being' of objects (including fictional objects) from the 'existence' of actual objects such as Napoleon. Although Meinong's position at first blush respects our face-value understanding of sentences about fiction, it encounters difficulties (see MEINONG, A.). Fictional characters normally are incomplete: it is not true, according to the novel, that Anna is right-handed; and it is not true, according to the novel, that Anna is not right-handed. Yet how, without violating the law of excluded middle, can there be such a thing? Again, some fictions are inconsistent: in a story, a wood sprite squares the circle. Does the realm of being then include an object that infringes the law of contradiction?

Contemporary Meinongians suggest answers to such difficulties. Thus Parsons (1980) distinguishes sentence negation ('*x* is not *P*') from predicate negation ('*x* is non-*P*'). He correlates existent objects one to one with the sets of ordinary properties that they have and extends the correlation by introducing nonexistent objects as entities that are correlated one to one with the sets of ordinary properties that are not correlated with existent objects. No object is contradictory, that is, no object satisfies a formula of the form '*x* is *F* and not (*x* is *F*)'. But objects may have impossible properties – for example, being *P*-and-non-*P* – without implying the truth of any contradictions. (Such objects are impossible objects and cannot exist.) Objects also may be incomplete without violating excluded middle: the lack both of being-*P* and of being-non-*P* does not contradict the fact that an object either is *P* or is not *P*.

Such theories show that Meinongian views can be defended with far more plausibility than has been thought by philosophers heavily influenced by Russell's and others' identification of being and existence. Nevertheless, these views do not easily capture all aspects of sentences relating to fiction. For one thing, there are problems specific to particular Meinongian approaches. Thus in Parsons' theory, as in non-

Meinongian theories that regard characters as collections of properties (for example, Wolterstorff 1980), it is difficult to allow that a novel may introduce two distinct characters assigned the same properties. Again, our epistemic situation and that of Sherlock Holmes are relevantly similar: Holmes senses and reasons about objects in the world, and so do we. How then can we know (as we do) that we exist, given that he – a nonexistent thing – cannot know that he exists? For another thing, the 'face-value' understanding just sketched of sentences relating to fiction – in which in saying 'Anna Karenina is a woman' we state a truth, refer to the character Anna, and attribute to her the property of womanhood – is over simple.

Thus although 'Anna Karenina is a woman' may be true *in the story*, so also is 'Anna Karenina exists'; and if we grant that the same character may occur in different stories and be described contradictorily by them, then it may be true that the character both is *P* (in one story) and is not *P* (in another story). On pain of contradiction, Meinongians cannot understand such claims as together implying that objects both have and do not have the relevant properties. Complex Meinongian treatments of these claims can be devised. But it seems simpler to allow story-relative properties and then take fictional names to designate abstract, but existent, things that have properties such as being-*P*-according-to-story-*s* and being-not-*P*-according-to-story-*t* without having the non-relative properties of being-*P* and of being-not-*P*. We can thus proceed without having to introduce mysterious Meinongian nonexistent, particular things at all. As discussed in §§2–3 below, there are still further alternatives to considering claims relating to fiction as simple, literal truths in which objects of reference are assigned properties. Many writers would say that unless all these alternatives fail, it is unreasonable to commit ourselves to the perplexities of the Meinongian approach.

The one alternative that is clearly unsatisfactory is the unsupplemented Russellian view that a claim such as 'Anna Karenina is a woman' is false (or lacks truth-value, as Fregeans hold). Perhaps such a claim, taken on its own, is indeed false (or expresses no proposition at all, given direct-reference theories of proper names). But such a view leaves unexplained the contrast between that claim and 'Anna Karenina is from Moscow'. Nor does it explain our inclination to ascribe truth to further claims such as 'Sherlock Holmes is a fictional detective', 'Odysseus is the same as Ulysses' and 'Sherlock Holmes is far more famous than any real detective' (Howell 1979; Parsons 1980; van Inwagen 1977). Unsupplemented Russellian views suggest nothing about the semantic or pragmatic factors which may enter into the understanding and acceptance of these further claims. (With qualifications, a similar point also holds for proposals such as that made by Woods (1974) to understand the truth of claims about fiction by appeal to the specific words or sentences that actually occur in the fictions themselves.)

The abstract-existent-object position allows for the further claims just noted, and that fact together with its non-Meinongian way of accepting genuine fictional entities makes it attractive. In van Inwagen's version of this position, characters of fiction are theoretical entities of literary criticism. Sentences in a work of fiction that describe a character must be distinguished from our own sentences about that character. As part of the novel, Tolstoy's sentence 'Anna took the tray' is not about anything, expresses no proposition, is not used by Tolstoy as a vehicle of an assertion. But my description of the novel, using the same sentence, expresses a true proposition about Tolstoy's character: the proposition that the property of taking a tray is ascribed to that character in *Anna Karenina*. Like all entities, that character exists and obeys the laws of excluded middle and of contradiction. The evidence for the existence of characters is provided by sentences such as 'Anna is the principal character of *Anna Karenina*' or 'There is a character in a nineteenth-century novel who is presented in greater physical detail than are any characters in eighteenth-century novels'. We accept these sentences as true, and it seems impossible to paraphrase them in ways that say the same thing yet involve no quantification over characters. Yet these and other sentences can be straightforwardly represented using van Inwagen's apparatus: 'Anna Karenina has the property of being the principal character in *Anna Karenina*'; or (roughly) 'There is a character *c* and a nineteenth-century novel *n* such that there are properties ascribed to *c* in *n* and some of those properties imply more physical detail than any properties ascribed to any characters in any eighteenth-century novels'.

The abstract-existent-object theory provides the most plausible account so far that recognizes genuine fictional objects without accepting Meinongianism. But the theory has never been presented in full detail. Moreover, as used by us the name 'Anna Karenina' (unlike 'Emily Dickinson') is not the usual proper name that, according to direct-reference theories of proper names, refers directly to its bearer through an initial act of baptism. Rather, we refer to the theoretical entity via the name ascribed to it in the novel. As noted, we also attribute to this entity the property of having the property of womanhood ascribed to it in the novel, rather than the simple property of womanhood. Yet the theory by itself offers no particularly plausible explanation why, when we are really treating Tolstoi's character in this way, we none the less use language appropriate to the reference and predication that concern ordinary concrete particulars ('Anna Karenina is a woman').

2 Pretence and make-believe

Instead of directly attacking questions about fictional reference, predication, truth and ontology, perhaps we should focus on the fictional use of language. Clearly (to ignore issues about fictional names), sentences in fiction or about characters in fiction are not distinguished from ordinary literal sentences by special lexical meanings or grammatical constructions. Like ordinary literal sentences, such sentences also may be true (as are various of Tolstoi's claims about Napoleon in *War and Peace*) and may be vehicles of assertion (as, again, are various of Tolstoi's claims). Perhaps, however, as some speech-act theorists have suggested, fictional claims are specially marked out by their use in communication, for example, by possessing a special illocutionary force (see SPEECH ACTS §1).

In one version of this suggestion, in producing fiction the author performs no new illocutionary act analogous to ordinary acts of asserting, questioning or requesting. Instead, authors pretend, in a non-deceptive way, to perform such acts; for example, pretend to be making assertions about events of which they have knowledge. This suggestion fails, for not all pretences to assert produce fiction (for example, putting on an illustrative performance of making a silly claim), and not all productions of fictional sentences are pretences to assert (typing out one's story and mailing it to a publisher).

In another version of the suggestion, the author performs a special new sort of illocutionary act. For example (as Currie (1990) proposes), the author produces sentences with the intention that the audience will *make believe* the content of those sentences (that there is someone named 'Anna Karenina' who is a woman, and so on) through the audience's recognition of the author's intention. Like other pretence and make-believe approaches (including Walton's, described below, which has influenced Currie), this suggestion explains why both Tolstoi and we produce the sentence 'Anna Karenina is a woman' even while we recognize that 'Anna Karenina' denotes no actual person. We do so because that sentence gives the content that we are to make believe is true. (Because the sentence mimics claims describing real persons, we can also easily use it in making believe that there is a real person whom it truly describes.)

One might object that the notion of fiction includes nonlinguistic items such as representational paintings and sculptures as well as sentences. However, its defenders argue that the preceding suggestion can be generalized to cover such items.

A deeper objection derives from Walton's non-linguistic theory of fiction. For Walton (1990), individuals and groups play games of make-believe, the rules of which require the participants to imagine various matters to be true. Props generate fictional truths in such games. (Thus in a game in which the rule is that stumps are to be imagined to be bears, a stump by its presence generates the fictional truth that a bear is present.) Fictions – including linguistic fictions, representational paintings and sculptures – serve as props in games of make-believe. A text constitutes a fiction when, roughly, there is a rule in force that we are to make believe that there are objects such that the words of that text refer to and describe those objects. (Thus we make believe that 'Anna Karenina' is a genuine proper name that directly refers to a Russian woman of whom the story is telling us, and so on.) In Walton's account, the fact that words constitute a fiction depends on their thus being a prop in a game of make-believe, not on the fact that an author intends the audience to make believe that the propositional content expressed by the words is true. For Walton, fiction has nothing special to do with communicative acts of intentional agents; naturally occurring cracks in a rock can spell out a story.

These last points are controversial. (Perhaps the cracks are only treated by us as fiction, without really being so, as Currie argues.) But the basic idea, developed in detail by Walton, that our claims about fiction are to be understood in terms of make-believe provides a deep, powerful explanation of much that concerns those claims. Quite possibly, and as both Walton's and Currie's views suggest, we only make believe that through Tolstoi's sentences about Anna Karenina we get genuine reference, predication and truth.

3 Further questions

Nevertheless, questions remain: about the content of our make-believe, about non-make-believe claims concerning fiction, and about ontology. If we make believe that 'Anna Karenina is a woman' is true, what exact proposition do we make believe is true? If in a piece of literary criticism I assert that Anna is from St Petersburg – or if I compare her with real persons or with other characters ('Anna Karenina is a stronger, more developed personality than is Theodor Fontane's Effi Briest') – then I seem to be stating a sober, literal truth rather than simply making believe that something is true. If you and I independently remark that Tolstoi's character Anna is from St Petersburg, our remarks seemingly concern the selfsame character. But how can they, if, without having any particular object in mind, we each independently merely make believe that 'Anna Karenina' is a genuine name that refers to some real entity?

Writers such as Walton and Currie suggest somewhat different answers to such questions. Common to their answers, however, is the view that the most we can make believe – in propositional content – is the existential general claim that there is a woman who is named 'Anna Karenina', and so on. We cannot literally make believe *of* a concrete, particular fictional character that *it* is so-and-so because, actually, there are no such characters. This last point can be supported by an argument of Kripke's in *Naming and Necessity* (1980). Our make-believe is not *of* any actual, concrete, particular entity genuinely referred to by 'Anna Karenina'. Nor (to ignore inconsistent fictions) can it be *of* any purely possible thing that exists in all the possible worlds compatible with what is said in the novel and is picked out from each such world by the properties that the novel assigns to Anna. There is no way to decide which of the many possible entities that have all those properties is the unique, particular referent of the name.

Again, writers in the make-believe tradition may understand our non-make-believe claims to indicate or allude to practices of make-believe. Thus, as Walton suggests, my sober, literal assertion that Anna Karenina is from St Petersburg may in effect claim that to say such a thing in the appropriate game of make-believe is fictionally to speak truly. Finally, when both you and I independently talk of Anna Karenina, or when I compare Anna Karenina to Effi Briest, then, Walton urges, we engage in a shared game of make-believe, or I simply combine the games individually appropriate to *Anna Karenina* and *Effi Briest*. (About such literal assertions and comparisons, Currie offers somewhat different treatments, involving what he holds are further, 'metafictive' and 'transfictive' uses of fictional names.)

Some of these suggestions may succeed. But in the end they deny that there can be a single fictional character – a single entity created by the author – that in actual fact two people independently refer to and describe. They also turn out to deny that it is literally and actually true that one and the same character – one single entity – can occur in different works of fiction (or can be the common focus of different games of make-believe; or of different dreams, illusions and beliefs). If we take seriously the idea that there actually are such characters of fiction, then we are forced back into accepting characters as objects of genuine reference and true predication. If so, then unless some Meinongian or similar view is adopted, it seems that we should combine the abstract-existent-object theory with the make-believe approach. Or perhaps (swallowing popular objections to Lewis's modal realism) we should accept a version of Lewis's counterpart theory (see LEWIS, D.K.). We might hold, for example, that 'Anna Karenina' refers to various concrete, particular, non-actual individuals that exist in the possible worlds in which Tolstoi's novel is told as known fact. Those would be the individuals that have all the properties the novel attributes to Anna and that (while not strictly identical to one another) are enough alike to function as counterparts (see MODAL LOGIC, PHILOSOPHICAL ISSUES IN §4). It remains to be seen, however, whether these proposals, or any other ideas for countenancing genuine reference to and predication of characters of fiction, can be successfully defended.

See also: FICTIONAL ENTITIES; PROPER NAMES; REFERENCE

References and further reading

Adams, F., Fuller, G. and Stecker, R. (forthcoming) 'The Semantics of Fictional Names', *Pacific Philosophical Quarterly*. (Proposes forgoing fictional characters in favour of talk of fictional names, using the notion of a partial proposition.)

Crittenden, C. (1991) *Unreality*, Ithaca, NY, and London: Cornell University Press. (Defends a Meinongian view against competing theories.)

* Currie, G. (1990) *The Nature of Fiction*, Cambridge: Cambridge University Press. (A comprehensive, well-argued make-believe account of the semantics of fiction and related issues. Many valuable references to the earlier literature. Technical in places. Discussed in §§2–3.)

* Howell, R. (1979) 'Fictional Objects: How They Are and How They Aren't', *Poetics* 8: 129–77. (Presents difficulties for views rejecting fictional objects. Technical in places.)

* Inwagen, P. van (1977) 'Creatures of Fiction', *American Philosophical Quarterly* 14: 299–308. (A forceful defence of an abstract-existent-object view. Discussed in §1.)

* Kripke, S.A. (1980) *Naming and Necessity*, Cambridge, MA: Harvard University Press. (A centrally important discussion of reference in general with application to fictional terms such as 'unicorn' and 'Sherlock Holmes'.)

Kroon, F. (1994) 'Make-Believe and Fictional Reference', *Journal of Aesthetics and Art Criticism*

52: 207–14. (Presents problems for make-believe accounts of fictional names; suggests a counterpart theory.)

Lewis, D.K. (1978) 'Truth in Fiction', in *Philosophical Papers*, New York and Oxford: Oxford University Press, 1983, vol. 1, 261–76, with 'Postscripts', 277–80. (A classic pretence account of truth in fiction, with analyses of 'in fiction *f*, so-and-so is the case' claims.)

* Parsons, T. (1980) *Nonexistent Objects*, New Haven, CT, and London: Yale University Press. (A careful defence of a Meinongian theory. Technical in parts but with excellent nontechnical discussions. Discussed in §1.)

Routley, R. (1980) *Exploring Meinong's Jungle and Beyond*, Canberra: Research School of Social Sciences, Australian National University. (A broad discussion of Meinongian theories and their applications. Technical in places.)

* Russell, B. (1905) 'On Denoting', *Mind* 14: 479–93; repr. in *Logic and Knowledge: Essays 1901–1950*, ed. R.C. Marsh, London: Routledge, 1992. (A classic treatment of reference and description.)

* Walton, K. (1990) *Mimesis as Make-Believe*, Cambridge, MA: Harvard University Press. (A rich, highly original development of a make-believe theory of all aspects of verbal and nonverbal fictions. Excellent references to the earlier literature. Offers a subtle account of how fictional truths are generated – implicit truths such as 'Anna Karenina has a cerebral cortex' as well as explicit ones. Discussed in §§2–3.)

* Wolterstorff, N. (1980) *Works and Worlds of Art*, Oxford: Clarendon Press. (Treats characters as collections of properties. Regards works of fiction as vehicles of special illocutionary acts.)

* Woods, J. (1974) *The Logic of Fiction*, The Hague: Mouton. (Treats fictional claims via the sentences occurring in fiction, utilizing substitutional quantification. Technical.)

ROBERT HOWELL

FICTIONAL ENTITIES

By 'fictional entities', philosophers principally mean those entities originating in and defined by myths, legends, fairy tales, novels, dramas and other works of fiction. In this sense unicorns, centaurs, Pegasus, the Time Machine and Sherlock Holmes are all fictional entities.

A somewhat different category of fictional entities is associated with empiricist philosophy. It includes entities apparently assumed by common discourse but which admit of no direct empirical experience. Thus Jeremy Bentham classified as 'fictitious entities' motion, relation, power and matter, as well as, notoriously, rights, obligations and duties. David Hume called substance, the self, even space and time 'fictions' and Bertrand Russell thought ordinary things, such as Piccadilly or Socrates, were fictions, on the grounds that they are 'constructed' out of simpler, more immediate objects of acquaintance.

Philosophical interest in fictional entities thus covers a surprisingly wide area of the subject, including ontology and metaphysics, epistemology, logic, philosophy of language, and aesthetics. The first question that arises is how the distinction should be drawn between fictional and nonfictional entities. As the examples from Bentham, Hume and Russell show, this is by no means a straightforward matter. The next question concerns what to do with fictional entities once they have been identified. Here the primary philosophical task has been to try to accommodate two powerful yet apparently conflicting intuitions: on the one hand, the intuition that there are no such things as fictional entities, so that any seeming reference to them must be explained away; on the other hand, the intuition that because 'things' like Sherlock Holmes and Anna Karenina are so vividly drawn, so seemingly 'real', objects of thoughts and emotions, they must after all have some kind of reality. Broadly speaking, we can discern two kinds of philosophical approach: those which incline towards the latter intuition, being in some way hospitable to fictional entities; and the less hospitable kind, which incline towards the former and seek only to show how fictional entities can be eliminated altogether in the strict regime of rational discourse.

1 **Distinguishing the fictional from the nonfictional**
2 **Deflationary theories**
3 **Hospitable theories**

1 Distinguishing the fictional from the nonfictional

It might be supposed that what determines whether an entity is fictional or not is whether it exists. Perhaps fictional just means nonexistent. Certainly it is commonplace to contrast what is fictional with what is real. The crucial difference between Socrates and Sherlock Holmes is that the one existed and the other did not. The trouble comes when we find serious philosophers, such as Russell, describing even beings like Socrates as 'fictions'. That invites the thought that there are different kinds of fiction and even different kinds of nonexistence. If that is right it compromises any simple identification of the fictional with the nonexistent. Also philosophers in the twentieth century have become increasingly wary of unqualified talk about what exists and what does not. Among logicians and philosophers of science there has been a pronounced shift away from asking what entities exist (or are real) towards asking what entities particular theories are committed to. Underlying this shift and acting as a constraint on theory construction is the heuristic principle called Ockham's razor (after the medieval logician WILLIAM OF OCKHAM), namely 'Do not multiply entities beyond necessity'.

In seeking to refine the association of the fictional with the nonexistent it is helpful to distinguish the role of fictional entities in logic, epistemology and literary narrative. There is no compulsion to suppose that some uniform account of fictional entities must span these three applications. Indeed it becomes evident that different criteria for distinguishing the fictional from the nonfictional operate in each case.

First of all, fictions in logic are most commonly associated with eliminability by logical paraphrase. The idea is roughly this: that a fictional entity is the purported referent of an eliminable singular term. It relies on a distinction between apparent reference and genuine reference; the object of a genuine reference must exist, or be assumed to exist by a theory, while apparent but non-genuine reference is that which is eliminable by paraphrase without loss of content. The conception probably originated with Bentham, who thought that rights, for example, were fictitious entities, precisely because sentences containing 'rights' as a noun (such as 'The people demanded their rights') can be paraphrased into sentences in which no such noun or singular term appears (such as 'The people demanded fair treatment under the law'). As long as the paraphrase captures the significant content of the original it shows that the apparent reference in the original (to a specific class of entities) is not a genuine reference: thus are the entities 'fictional'.

Bentham's theory was a clear forerunner of the school of twentieth-century logical analysis epitomized by such philosophers as Bertrand Russell, Rudolf Carnap and W.V. Quine. Russell's Theory of Descriptions eloquently showed that singular descriptive phrases, such as 'the highest prime' or 'the golden mountain', do not need to function logically as naming expressions (that is, having, in our earlier terminology, 'genuine reference') in order to be meaningful (see RUSSELL, B. §9). Quine extended the thesis to all singular terms, including proper names, arguing that each is eliminable by logical paraphrase, in favour of quantifiers and predicates. Only bound variables, for Quine, are the true bearers of referential commitments (see QUINE, W.V. §5). We will return to Russell's and Quine's theories in the next section, for they have been highly influential in deflationary accounts of fictional entities.

While fictions in logic connect with reference and paraphrase, fictions in epistemology rest on the idea of 'construction'. Ordinary objects can be thought of as fictions, in epistemological theories, just to the extent that they are thought of as 'constructed' (by the human mind) out of more basic, perhaps more real, elements. A characteristic kind of empiricism equates what is real with what is knowable and what is knowable with what is given in experience. For those empiricists who hold that the only immediate objects of experience are subjective entities like 'impressions' (Hume) or 'sense-data' (Russell), it is a short and natural step to the idea that enduring objects in space and time are mere 'constructs' or posits of the mind that round out the flux of experience. Quine, albeit rejecting any privileged foundation of knowledge, has famously compared physical objects with the gods of Homer and spoken of both as 'myths'.

No doubt for those who think of fictional characters in legend or literature as paradigmatic fictional entities, it will seem tendentious, even paradoxical, to describe physical objects as 'fictions'. However, etymology associates fiction more with 'making' or 'feigning' than with nonexistence and empiricist epistemologists can be taken to be emphasizing the different kinds of 'making', or imaginative invention, involved in human knowledge. Nelson Goodman has described knowledge itself as a species of 'worldmaking'. None of these philosophers wants to collapse the distinction between a fictional character, in the familiar literary-critical sense, and a real person.

So what sets apart the characters of literary narratives from the 'fictions' in logic and epistemology? One common idea is that fictional entities such as the Time Machine and Sherlock Holmes are logically rooted in the narratives in which they are first introduced; their very conception derives from the descriptive content of those narratives. To find out about Holmes one must read the Holmes stories. This already hints at a fundamental difference from nonfictional objects, for the latter do not derive their existence and nature from any narrative; to find out about them we must investigate the world, not merely a source text. Fictional entities of the literary type are 'made' or 'made up' precisely by being described in an act of storytelling, under the appropriate conventions. The fact that they do not exist in the real world can be seen to be as much a consequence of their origin (real objects are not made up by storytellers) as a defining feature of their fictionality.

2 Deflationary theories

The intuition that there are no such things as fictional entities, so that any apparent ontological commitment to them must be removed, is powerful among philosophers. The logical analysis of Russell and Quine provides a striking example of how such a commitment can be avoided. The eliminative strategy applied to logical fictions can be applied to more familiar literary fictions as well. When we describe the exploits of Sherlock Holmes or the properties of Pegasus we appear to be referring to, or speaking about, entities which have some kind of existence. But this is an illusion, according to deflationary theories. In fact we are not referring to any such things.

Russell's Theory of Descriptions sets the standard for deflationary theories. Suppose, regarding a character in a novel, we want to assert, 'The invisible man could see but not be seen.' For Russell, a logical analysis of our assertion would be somewhat as follows: 'There is one and only one thing that is a man, is invisible, and can see without being seen'. The latter sentence removes the apparent naming expression 'the invisible man' and asserts only that something or other satisfies a collection of predicates. The sentence turns out to be false (for there is no such thing) but is perfectly meaningful.

Quine showed that the analysis could be generalized to eliminate all singular terms, proper names included. He suggested that, from a logical point of view, names can be turned into predicates purely formally. Thus he analyses the seemingly true sentence 'Pegasus does not exist' as 'Nothing pegasizes'. By losing the troublesome singular term 'Pegasus' and speaking only of the instantiation (or lack of it) of a complex, albeit artificial, predicate, the analysis neatly shows how it is possible to deny the existence of a fictional entity without incurring any ontological commitment to that entity. It is a lesson, for example, that atheists can usefully apply in their denials of the existence of God (for it might seem that even to use the name 'God' is to admit that there is such a being).

To the extent that the logical problem of fictional entities is that of how to discriminate apparent reference from genuine reference the Russell/Quine deflationary theory is highly effective. But it also has serious drawbacks in accounting for other intuitions concerning ordinary talk 'about fictional characters'. For one thing it has the consequence that all sentences containing singular terms for fictional characters turn out to be false (because they involve false existence claims). Yet is there not a sense in which the assertion 'Sherlock Holmes is a detective' is true, in contrast, say, to 'Sherlock Holmes is a ballet dancer', which is clearly false? On the Russell/Quine view they are both

false. What needs to be captured is the fact that the claims are *about the Holmes stories*, not about persons in the real world. What is meant is something like: 'Within the Holmes stories, as told by Conan Doyle, Holmes is a detective (and not a ballet dancer)'. It is a further question how assertions of that kind are to be analysed. In some deflationary theories they are said to refer only to novels and their component sentences. That has the advantage that it too removes unwelcome ontological commitments, but is surprisingly difficult to sustain in practice (not least because truths about the content of fictional stories extend beyond the explicit content of the stories' sentences: for example, it is surely true that Holmes did not travel in a rocket, though that is never made explicit by Conan Doyle).

Another drawback of the Russell/Quine view is that it fails to distinguish storytelling discourse from discourse about stories. If the sentence 'Holmes returned to London' occurs in a Holmes story it seems inappropriate to analyse it as a false assertion about the real world. Conan Doyle, the author, is not asserting, or attempting to assert, facts about the world; he is making up a story. If on the other hand readers report the content of the story by using the same sentence they, in contrast to the author, are making an assertion (true or false), but one about the story, and again not about the world.

There are other deflationary theories, which attempt to remove commitment to fictional entities. Two deserve particular mention. The first is that of Nelson Goodman (§2), who defends a strict nominalist ontology. Given that there are no unicorns and no centaurs, the predicates 'is a unicorn' and 'is a centaur' have the same extension, according to Goodman, namely, a null extension: the set of unicorns is identical to the set of centaurs because it is the empty set. Yet surely unicorns and centaurs are different? Goodman seeks to explain the difference, not by invoking fictional entities, but by appeal to further predicates that do differ in extension. For example, a unicorn-picture, as he puts it, is different from a centaur-picture and can be recognized as such. While normally 'X is a picture of Y' is a two-place predicate, relating a picture and an object (for example, a portrait and the Duke of Wellington), in 'fictional' cases, such as 'This is a picture of Sherlock Holmes', there is only a one-place predicate involved, namely 'is a Holmes-picture'. Pictures can be sorted into 'Holmes-pictures', 'unicorn-pictures', etc., without commitment to a separate class of 'fictional entities'. Pictures, after all, are unproblematically real.

Another deflationary strategy comes from Kendall Walton, for whom works of fiction are 'props in games of make-believe'. Readers of *Don Quixote* seem to be introduced to a dreamy knight, who tilts at windmills, crusades against Evil, and so forth. Furthermore, they seem to think about him, refer to him and even feel sympathy for his predicament. However, for Walton it is only make-believe that they do such things. It is all pretence; they are playing a game with the novel as prop. In Walton's alternative idiom, 'it is fictional that' they describe him, refer to him and respond emotionally to him. There is not even any such proposition that Don Quixote tilted at windmills. Walton offers a systematic theory which locates all 'relations with fictional characters' in imaginative games; to speak 'about characters' is just an elliptical way of speaking about the relevant games.

3   Hospitable theories

A presupposition behind deflationary theories is that if there is no such thing as X then X cannot (literally) be referred to or spoken about. The focus in all cases is in removing the appearance of reference. Some philosophers, notably Richard RORTY, find this association between reference and ontological commitment unjustified. Referring, for Rorty, is just 'talking about' and he claims we can talk about Holmes, the number three, the beauty of a landscape or moral values, for instance, without engaging any deep issues in ontology. Rorty views the very idea of 'ontological commitment' as pointless.

A more widely held view is that 'referring to fictional entities' does have ontological significance but that different kinds of *being* are involved. Fictional entities are, after all, entities. If Russell's Theory of Descriptions is the starting point for (modern) deflationary theories, then Alexius Meinong's Theory of Objects (*Gegenstandstheorie*) is the starting point for (modern) hospitable theories (see MEINONG, A. §§2–4). Meinong postulated a realm of objects of which only a tiny subset are existent objects. He seems at least partially to have worked with a syntactic criterion for objecthood: any expression functioning as a singular term in a well-formed sentence designates an object. Notoriously, Meinong held that even 'the round square' denotes an object (albeit one that does not, and could not, exist in reality). Although Meinong's theory was strongly attacked by Russell, it has proved remarkably resilient, with defences by, for example, Terence Parsons and Charles Crittenden. The point, again, is not to collapse the distinction between Socrates and Sherlock Holmes but only to claim they are both objects, the one existent, the other nonexistent. An added difference, for Parsons, is that Holmes, unlike Socrates, is an 'incomplete' object, in the sense that for any given property it is not always determinate whether Holmes has that property or not. But what is to be gained by saying that *there are* nonexistent objects? Principally, it makes sense out of common ways of speaking, without the need for paraphrase: we refer to Holmes, we distinguish him from Dr Watson, we ascribe properties to him. What could be more natural than saying there is an *object* here?

Other theorists sympathetic to fictional entities attribute to them existence as *abstract* objects. Nicholas Wolterstorff has argued that fictional characters are kinds (the character Holmes is a person-kind, though not a kind of person), Peter van Inwagen views them as 'theoretical entities of literary criticism', comparable in status to plots, metres and rhyme schemes. A consequence for Wolterstorff is that characters not only exist (as kinds) but do so eternally; a writer 'selects' but does not strictly create characters, for the properties ('being a detective', 'solving mysteries', etc.) that constitute the relevant kinds are not themselves created. If fictional characters exist as abstract objects, what properties do they possess? Holmes, it seems, is a detective, yet no abstract object could be a detective. Van Inwagen responds by distinguishing those properties 'ascribed' to characters (such as 'being a man', 'smoking a pipe') that they do not literally possess and those which characters 'exemplify' (such as 'being introduced in Chapter 29', 'being wittily conceived'). The intuition that fictional characters are in some such way real is further supported by other common modes of speech, as when we say, for example, that Dostoevsky's characters are more realistic than those of Cervantes. It is difficult for deflationary theories to paraphrase away such references.

The debate about fictional entities goes to the heart of methodological issues in philosophy. It highlights the status and role of logical analysis, the nature of ontological commitment, and above all the remarkable indifference of ordinary language to philosophical worries about what does and does not exist.

See also: CARNAP, R.; EMOTION IN RESPONSE TO ART §3; FICTION, SEMANTICS OF; ONTOLOGICAL COMMITMENTS; REFERENCE; RIGHTS; SEMANTICS

References and further reading

* Crittenden, C. (1991) *Unreality: The Metaphysics of Fictional Objects*, Ithaca, NY, and London: Cornell University Press. (Mentioned in §3. Good general introduction to the subject, with a point of view sympathetic to that of Meinong.)

Currie, G. (1990) *The Nature of Fiction*, Cambridge: Cambridge University Press. (Presents a detailed logical theory of all aspects of fictionality. Quite technical.)

* Goodman, N. (1968) *The Languages of Art*, New York: Bobbs-Merrill. (Referred to in §2. A strict eliminative theory of fictional entities applied to all art forms.)

Howell, R. (1979) 'Fictional Objects: How They Are and How They Aren't', *Poetics* 8: 129–77. (Careful, critical exposition of the main logical approaches.)

* Inwagen, P. van (1977) 'Creatures of Fiction', *American Philosophical Quarterly* 14: 299–308. (Referred to in §3. Attributes some reality to fictional entities.)

Lamarque, P.V. and Olsen, S.H. (1994) *Truth, Fiction and Literature: A Philosophical Perspective*, Oxford: Clarendon Press. (Useful introduction to logical, epistemological and literary conceptions of fiction, as outlined in §1.)

* Meinong, A. (1960) 'Theory of Objects', in R.M. Chisholm (ed.) *Realism and the Background of Phenomenology*, Glencoe, IL: Free Press. (Referred to in §3. Classic statement of the case for nonexistent objects as well as existent objects.)

* Ogden, C.K. (ed.) (1932) *Bentham's Theory of Fictions*, London: Kegan Paul, Trench, Trubner & Co., Ltd. (Referred to in §2. Bentham's theory of fictions and paraphrase was a strong influence on twentieth-century logical analysis.)

* Parsons, T. (1980) *Nonexistent Objects*, New Haven, CT: Yale University Press. (Referred to in §3. A sophisticated defence and development of Meinong's theory. Technical in parts.)

* Quine, W.V.O. (1953) 'On What There Is', in *From a Logical Point of View*, Cambridge, MA: Harvard University Press. (Referred to in §2. Classic statement of the logical criterion of ontological commitment.)

* Rorty, R. (1982) 'Is There a Problem About Fictional Discourse?', in *Consequences of Pragmatism*, Brighton: Harvester Wheatsheaf. (Referred to in §3. Dismisses the whole approach of analytic philosophy to fictional entities.)

* Russell, B. (1956) *Logic and Knowledge*, ed. R.C. Marsh, London: Allen & Unwin. (Includes 'On Denoting' and 'The Philosophy of Logical Atomism', where Russell develops and applies his Theory of Descriptions and conception of logical fictions. See §2.)

* Walton, K.L. (1990) *Mimesis as Make-Believe: On the Foundations of the Representational Arts*, Cambridge, MA: Harvard University Press. (Referred to in §2. Presents an eliminative theory of fictional entities, in terms of 'games of make-believe'.)

* Wolterstorff, N. (1980) *Works and Worlds of Art*, Oxford: Clarendon Press. (Referred to in §3. At times difficult; but a powerful case for fictional characters as eternal kinds.)

PETER LAMARQUE

FICTIONALISM

'Fictionalism' generally refers to a pragmatic, antirealist position in the debate over scientific realism. The use of a theory or concept can be reliable without the theory being true and without the entities mentioned actually existing. When truth (or existence) is lacking we are dealing with a fiction. Thus fictionalism is a corollary of instrumentalism, the view that what matters about a theory is its reliability in practice, adding to it the claim that science often employs useful fictions. Perhaps the fullest expression of fictionalism occurs in Vaihinger's once popular philosophy of 'as if'.

Fictionalism is allied to instrumentalism, the brand of pragmatism associated with Dewey's 'Chicago School of Thought' (see DEWEY, J.; PRAGMATISM). There is also fictionalism in the philosophy of logic and of mathematics (see ANTIREALISM IN THE PHILOSOPHY OF MATHEMATICS). Dewey coined the term 'instrumentalism' (sometimes also 'experimentalism') to describe his pragmatic treatment of 'how thought functions in the experimental determination of future consequences' (Dewey 1943: 463). According to instrumentalism what we look for in all the various contexts of inquiry, whether around the house or in the laboratory, is instrumental reliability; that is, we want our theories or concepts to be useful in all the practical and theoretical endeavours for which we try them out. Such usefulness or reliability does not imply that the theory is true nor that the 'entities' involved actually exist. In such a case the 'entities' mentioned by the theory are in fact useful *fictions*.

Perhaps the fullest expression of fictionalism occurs in Vaihinger's once popular philosophy of 'as if' (see VAIHINGER, H.). According to Vaihinger (1911) thinking by means of fictions is a fundamental cognitive process, as basic and pervasive as deductive or inductive thought themselves. Vaihinger makes a primary distinction between 'scientific' and the 'unscientific' fictions: that is, between those that actually prove useful (scientific) and those that do not. He cites atoms as an example of a scientific fiction, believing that they rest on the concept of point masses and the vacuum, neither of which he regards as real. Newton's laws would be another scientific fiction (see MECHANICS, CLASSICAL). By contrast the infamous 'dormitive virtue' proposed by

667

the doctors in Molière's *Le Misanthrope* would be an example of an unscientific fiction. Vaihinger goes on to classify many different types of fiction and to document their occurrence in virtually every scientific discipline. The fundamental distinction for Vaihinger's account, as for any version of fictionalism, is that between a fictional proposition and a scientific hypothesis. For Vaihinger, scientific hypotheses are verifiable by observation and are chosen over rivals according to the probability that they are true. Fictions on the other hand are justifiable only in terms of their utility (not truth or probability) and are chosen over rivals as being the most expedient means to the ends we have in mind.

Vaihinger's work, and fictionalism in general, enters the debate over scientific realism by challenging the inference from something's being useful to its being real, from utility to reality. A fiction is precisely a useful construct that is not real. In terms of recent debates (see SCIENTIFIC REALISM AND ANTIREALISM) fictionalism challenges the explanationist argument for scientific realism, which holds that only the truth of a scientific theory and the actual existence of the entities occurring in the theory could account for the theory's instrumental success. Fictionalism's challenge to realism is to point out that we can account for success quite well by supposing nothing more than this, that at the observable level it is just *as if* the scientific theory were actually true. This may not seem satisfactory to the realist who will accept no explanation short of the literal truth of science and will therefore press the question as to why our theories possess this dispositional property of instrumental reliability (the 'as if'). Pragmatists, however, point out that requests for explanation have to stop somewhere and that stopping here, with the fundamental reliability of our theories, is the right place (indeed the only place) if we want to align our beliefs with our epistemological practice, since that practice all along is pitched to reliability. Whatever the final verdict, it does seem that we can respond to the realist and explain scientific success by treating successful scientific stories as, roughly speaking, scientific fictions.

Idealizations and approximations play an essential role in science (see IDEALIZATIONS). These are paradigm examples of scientific fictions. Moreover if we think of models as maps, useful tools for navigating our way around but always and necessarily false to reality, then the idea of a scientific fiction encompasses models as well. In the present era of computer simulations and virtual reality, a dominant picture is the image of science as the builder of useful models. Thus one productive way to appreciate fictionalism is to see it as concerned with how models are articulated and work in scientific thought. In that light it may have more to offer than just another twist in the realism debate. Rather we might think of fictionalism as the beginning of a more comprehensive philosophical treatment of modelling (see MODELS).

See also: BENTHAM, J.; MAXWELL, J.C.

References and further reading

Cohen, M.R. (1923) 'On the Logic of Fictions', *Journal of Philosophy* 20: 477–88. (Questions Vaihinger's concept of a genuine fiction.)

Dewey, J. (1916) *Essays in Experimental Logic*, Chicago, IL: University of Chicago Press. (Introduces 'instrumentalism'.)

* —— (1943) 'The Development of American Pragmatism', in D.D. Runes (ed.) *Twentieth Century Philosophy*, New York: Philosophical Library, 451–67. (Definitive account of the Chicago School.)

Fine, A. (1993) 'Fictionalism', *Midwest Studies in Philosophy* 18: 1–18. (Expansion of the material of this essay that traces the historical connections between fictionalism and logical positivism.)

Frank, J. (1970) *Law and the Modern Mind*, Gloucester, MA: Peter Smith. (Applies fictionalism to the law.)

Schaper, E. (1966) 'The Kantian Thing-In-Itself as a Philosophical Fiction', *Philosophical Quarterly* 16: 233–43. (Traces the Kantian roots of fictionalism.)

Scheffler, I. (1963) *The Anatomy of Inquiry*, New York: Alfred A. Knopf. (Treats fictionalism as a thesis about the language of a regimented science.)

* Vaihinger, H. (1911) *Die Philosophie des Als Ob*, Leipzig: Felix Meiner Verlag; trans. C.K. Ogden, *The Philosophy of 'As If'*, London: Routledge & Kegan Paul, 1924. (First publication of Vaihinger's philosophy. Contains significant introduction for the English translation.)

ARTHUR FINE

FIELD THEORY, CLASSICAL

A physical quantity (such as mass, temperature or electrical strength) appears as a field if it is distributed continuously and variably throughout a region. In distinction to a 'lumped' quantity, whose condition at any time can be specified by a finite list of numbers, a complete description of a field requires infinitely many bits of data (it is said to 'possess infinite degrees of freedom'). A field is classical if it fits consistently within the general framework of classical mechanics. By the start of the twentieth century, orthodox mechanics had evolved to a state of ontological dualism, *incorporating a worldview where massive matter appears as 'lumped' points which communicate electrical and magnetic influences to one another through a continuous intervening medium called the electromagnetic field. The problem of consistently describing how matter and fields function together has yet to be fully resolved.*

Initially, most of the fields considered in mechanics were *material*: they possess mass and can be acted upon by forces. Simple examples are flexible strings, membranes, fluids (which include gases) and elastic spheres (as long as these objects are treated as continuously distributed and not merely as swarms of point masses). Derivative kinds of field can depend upon these material underpinnings – for example, the distribution of a temperature field. The laws for such material 'continua' can be rather tricky to formulate (see MECHANICS, CLASSICAL).

By the end of the nineteenth century, massless fields independent of particulate matter began to be considered in classical mechanics. When J.C. Maxwell originally proposed his equations for electromagnetism, he believed that this field was composed of an 'ether' that was similar in many respects to a common elastic solid (see MAXWELL, J.C. §2). After the Michelson–Morley experiment of 1887, this material interpretation was abandoned and the electromagnetic field became regarded as a physical entity *sui generis*. It was now a substance without mass that could store and transmit energy as ably as matter.

In this respect, electromagnetism differs from what is loosely dubbed 'the classical gravitational field'. On the Newtonian account, if a massive particle is wiggled, any distant particle will instantly feel a gravitational tug due to an 'action-at-a-distance' force acting directly between the matter (see NEWTON, I. §§3–4). No intervening medium is needed to transmit the force between the particles or to store the tug's energy while in passage. If the gravitational attraction of a massive body is approximated as an 'external force', a so-called 'field of the gravitational potential' can be introduced which, mathematically, proves a great convenience, but this 'field' does not qualify as an independent entity because it transmits all effects instantaneously and its state is always entirely conditioned by the state of the originating particles. In electromagnetism, by contrast, one could know the 'initial condition' of all matter in the universe, yet be unable to determine how the universe will behave. The condition of the field apart from the matter must also be specified, for significant amounts of energy might be traversing the field in the form of electromagnetic waves.

A basic problem tends to plague all forms of particle–field duality. If the two entities subsist independently, the field created by a bit of matter ought to affect that bit of the matter itself according to the same laws as govern the coupling between the field and any other body. The reaction of matter to a field that it itself initiates is called the back action of the field. If the matter is concentrated within an isolated point, as often happens in classical theories, it will usually create too strong a field within its own locality, leading to infinite amounts of back action against itself.

A variety of strategies have been proposed to rectify this problem: regard the 'field' as merely a mathematical convenience – retain a 'monism' of particles only. A careful look at how gravitational 'fields' are introduced into 'point mass' mechanics reveals that no overall gravitational field is ever defined by standard arguments, but merely a set of so-called 'other fields' that codify the forces exerted upon a given mass by the other bodies in the universe. 'Other fields', by their very definition, exert no back action and they should not be regarded as truly independent of the matter. Another strategy would be to smear out the mass, charge, and so on, of the particle over a finite volume, so that the total back action of its component points never becomes infinite. 'Other fields' are thus avoided, although this kind of field will still transmit all effects instantaneously and cannot sustain gravitational waves. In the 1890s, H.A. Lorentz tried to resolve the difficulties of electromagnetic dualism in a 'smeared out' manner also. A mechanism for creating a resistant stress becomes necessary to prevent the finite back action from quickly collapsing or inflating the particle. Suitable candidates for this 'stress' are hard to find. A third strategy could be to remove the dualism by converting the 'particle' into a singularity within the field – this supplies a 'monism' of fields. Examples of the approach are (William Thomson) Lord Kelvin's proposal that ordinary atoms represent the centres of vortices twisting in the ether and William Clifford's suggestion that particles are geometrical singularities within a non-Euclidean space.

In electromagnetism, none of these alternatives works very well. Because of field energy storage, one cannot easily retreat to the simple 'monism' permitted in the case of gravitation. An interesting effort at electromagnetic particle monism was proposed by Feynmann and Wheeler, based upon the work of Gustav Mie. Philosophers sometimes claim that this theory, despite its distinct ontology, is 'observationally equivalent' to standard electromagnetism. In the author's opinion, such claims do not survive scrutiny. In any case, since a measurable electromagnetic back action is experimentally detectable, the simple 'Lorentz law' treatment of field–particle coupling described in most textbooks is too simple to be correct. The more refined classical treatment articulated by P.A.M. Dirac in the 1930s turns out to have very bizarre consequences with respect to causality and the like.

Related problems of back action continue to trouble quantum versions of field theory as well.

See also: ELECTRODYNAMICS; FIELD THEORY, QUANTUM

References and further reading

Hesse, M. (1965) *Forces and Fields*, Totowa, NJ: Littlefield, Adams. (Readable survey of the historical struggle between field and action-at-a-distance perspectives.)

Maxwell, J.C. (1873) *Treatise on Electricity and Magnetism*, Oxford: Clarendon Press, 2 vols. (The classic work.)

Parrott, S. (1987) *Relativistic Electrodynamics and Differential Geometry*, New York: Springer. (Detailed exploration of the problems of dualism in electromagnetism. Requires university level mathematics.)

Whittaker, E. (1951) *A History of the Theories of Aether and Electricity*, London: Nelson. (Despite its grudging attitude towards Einstein, still the best general history.)

MARK WILSON

FIELD THEORY, QUANTUM

Quantum field theory extends the basic ideas of quantum mechanics for a fixed, finite number of particles to systems comprising fields and an unlimited, indefinite number of particles, providing a coherent blend of field-like and particle-like concepts. One can start from either field- or particle-like concepts, apply the methods of quantum mechanics, and arrive at the same theory. The result inherits all the puzzles of conventional quantum mechanics, such as measurement, superposition and quantum correlations; and it adds a new roster of conceptual difficulties. To mention three: the vacuum seems not really to be empty; the particle concept clashes with classical intuitions; and a method called 'renormalization' gets the best predictions in physics, apparently by dropping infinite terms.

1   Approaches to quantum field theory
2   Puzzles in quantum field theory

670

1   Approaches to quantum field theory

There are three conceptually distinct ways of introducing quantum field theory. We grasp the theory best by taking note of all three.

Classical objects have degrees of freedom, independent ways they can move – a locomotive confined to its tracks has one degree of freedom, a baseball has three (ignoring spin). We start with the classical picture of a system of discrete particles, each with three degrees of freedom, each degree of freedom in turn described with a pair of (conjugate) variables, typically position and momentum (see MECHANICS, CLASSICAL). Conventional quantum mechanics 'quantizes' such a system by replacing each pair of variables with a pair of operators (satisfying a commutation relation) that transform vectors in a vector space. These vectors describe the quantum states, and a simple formalism involving the operators and a state gives the values for quantities in the state. Unlike a classical system, the states do not in general give exact values for quantities, but only probabilities for what values will be found if a measurement is made. At most, one of a pair of quantities, such as position and momentum, can take on an exact value in a given state (see QUANTUM MECHANICS, INTERPRETATION OF).

The first approach to quantum field theory applies this procedure to a classical field conceived of as a system with an infinite number of degrees of freedom (see FIELD THEORY, CLASSICAL). In classical field theory one associates a field value, such as a value of the electric field, with each point in space. Think of such a field value as a 'position' in an abstract space. A standard (Lagrangian) formalism associates a second 'momentum' variable with each of these 'position' variables. So the field has been described as a system with infinitely many degrees of freedom, one at each spatial point, and each described with a 'position' and a 'momentum' variable. To quantize, one replaces each pair of variables with a pair of operators, all acting on a giant vector space. As before, vectors represent states, in general giving only probabilities on measurement for observed field values. The classical field equation, describing the relation between classical field values at neighbouring places and times, generalizes to an operator equation constraining the probabilities for field values at neighbouring points.

So far we see the theory's connection with fields but not with particles: a second approach allows us to see the latter connection. Quantum descriptions of 'particles' depart from classical descriptions in never assigning exact spacetime trajectories and in recognizing no 'individuality' distinct from qualitative properties. To mark the differences we will talk about *quanta* instead of particles. To reveal the theory's commitment to quanta, start with a classically described field, but redescribe it as a sum of simple waves – called 'harmonic modes' – of various frequencies. Each mode has the form of a harmonic oscillator – something behaving like a pendulum or oscillating spring – so that the field has been redescribed formally as a collection of independent harmonic oscillators. Now apply the quantization procedure to each of the (formal) harmonic oscillators.

A quantized harmonic oscillator has evenly spaced, exact energy states, beginning with a lowest, inviting us to interpret them as a state with zero quanta, a state with one quantum, a state with two quanta, and so on, each quantum with the same momentum. Different momenta go with different oscillators so that any 'excitation' state of the collection of oscillators can be reinterpreted as a collection of various number of quanta with various momenta. So far the account describes only Bosons, quanta of which there can be any whole number in a given state; but with an adjustment in the operators used in quantizing the oscillators (changing commutators to anticommutators) one gets a description of Fermions, quanta of which there can be only zero or one quantum in a given state.

In this formulation the collection of possible quantum states, called 'Fock space', is described in terms of basis states, written '$| n_1, n_2, n_3, \ldots n_k \rangle$', in which, for each n_i, there are n_i quanta described by some maximal list of properties, and each n_i a non-negative integer for Bosons, or zero or one for Fermions. Fock space includes weighted sums (superpositions) of these basis vectors, introducing an element not found in conventional quantum mechanics, states with an indefinite number of quanta and temporal change from states with one number of quanta into states with another number. Manipulation of the formalism is facilitated by special (non-Hermitian) *raising* and *lowering* operators which transform a Fock space state into one describing, respectively, one more or one less quantum. Often these are called 'creation' and 'annihilation' operators, but since arguably they do not describe processes of creation and annihilation the alternative 'raising' and 'lowering' operator terminology is recommended.

Approaching the theory via quantized harmonic oscillators yields a formulation which seems to talk about quanta. But a simple redescription (a transformation very like the conventional Fourier transform from the momentum to the position basis) restores a field-theoretic appearance. After redescription one has raising and lowering operators, $\Psi^\dagger(x)$ and $\Psi(x)$,

indexed by a spatial variable. (To facilitate relativistic description practitioners generally use a spacetime variable.) Often one informally describes $\Psi^\dagger(x)$ and $\Psi(x)$ as 'creating and annihilating quanta at x'. But the raising and lowering operators do not describe creation and annihilation events, and the quanta associated with such operators are concentrated around a point, x, but not strictly localized at it.

Given the operators indexed by spatial (or spacetime) variables, people often talk of an 'operator valued field', as if the theory specified values of a physical quantity to spatial points by providing operators indexed with a spatial variable. This is misleading: an operator does not correspond to a value of a quantity, but to the whole spectrum of values which the quantity can assume. One sees the field-theoretical aspect more accurately in the assignment of probabilities of values to spatial points or, better yet, in the connection with classical field theory through the first form of field quantization.

The two methods described above are called *field quantization*. An extension of the technique starts with a spacetime description of the state from conventional or *first quantized* quantum mechanics and applies the quantization procedure to this state function, or *second quantizes* it, treating it as if it were itself a classical field. Field quantization of the classical electromagnetic field results in a theory of photons. Second quantization of a first quantized theory of particles produces a theory of quanta such as electrons and protons.

A third approach to quantum field theory starts with the quanta themselves. One assumes a state to be completely described by specifying the number of quanta described by each possible maximal list of properties: one cannot get a new state description by switching around 'which' quanta have which properties. But these are just the basis states of the Fock space from the last approach. Taking the full Fock space to include the weighted sums (superpositions) of these basis states gives a theory including indefinite and variable number of quanta; and by generalizing on the assumption that the quanta individually obey conventional quantum mechanics, one gets the same theories generated by field quantization and its second quantization analogue.

2 Puzzles in quantum field theory

In the *vacuum*, the state with no quanta, one would expect all quantities to have a null value. But many have a positive expected average on measurement (expectation value). A second problem concerns any detector designed to register 'no quanta' when it is non-accelerating in the vacuum state. If one accelerates this detector through the vacuum it will react as if it were moving through a thermal bath of so-called *Rindler quanta*! So is the vacuum a state with no quanta or is it not?

Both these problems turn out to have the same formal basis as the fact from conventional quantum mechanics that a state which has an exact value for either position or momentum will have no exact value for the other quantity. The vacuum is exact for the quantity, *number of quanta*, and inexact for (complementary) field quantities. Consequently the vacuum definitely has zero quanta and has no actual values for field quantities, though this state has positive *probability* for finding non-null values for field quantities on measurement. Then field quantities such as energy, which have only positive values, can still have a positive average (expectation value) for the results of measurement. Formally analogous considerations apply to Rindler quanta. Interpreters disagree as to whether these considerations resolve the puzzle. There are further puzzles about the free vacuum in a relativistic theory, involving distant correlations which suggest that any quantal concept must, strictly speaking, be a global concept, not a local one.

The presentation to this point has described only free quantum field theory, a theory of non-interacting quanta. But different kinds of quanta interact with one another: free quantum field theory is a severe idealization since, as physicists say, 'we cannot turn off the interaction'. One transforms the free theory into interacting quantum field theory by adding the effects of interaction into the equations of motion, resulting in a theory vastly more complex and laden with difficulties. Calculation requires approximation methods which, if not to be interpreted instrumentalistically, introduce new interpretive problems.

A common method of approximation (perturbation expansion) results in divergent integrals arising from quanta interacting with themselves. An ingenious scheme, known as *renormalization*, allows the offending terms to be grouped systematically with terms describing the quanta's mass and strength of interaction. By substituting the observed values of the mass and 'coupling constants' for these 'renormalized' terms the approximation method produces startlingly good predictions. This procedure has shocked many who gloss it as 'discarding infinities'.

Physics texts make clear that renormalization involves no mathematical sleight of hand. The theory must break down at very high momenta, if only because not all interactions have been taken into account. In effect one substitutes observed values for masses and coupling constants where the theory breaks down, ensuring mathematical honesty by

making the substitutions before taking the limits on the offending integrals. It is a little like using an observed value for Hooke's spring constant where one could not calculate the constant from first principles. (While most endorse the foregoing, two of the subject's giants, Dirac and Feynman, thought renormalization could not be so easily resolved.)

Many likewise accept resolution of puzzles surrounding *virtual quanta*. The terms of an approximation expansion can be presented by a graphic technique called *Feynman diagrams*. These diagrams depict a network of creation and annihilation of 'virtual' quanta thought of as 'mediating' the interactions, tempting people to think that the virtual quanta actually exist. But they exist only as elements of a gigantic sum (superposition), so that they exist as do component simple waves whose sum is a complicated actually occurring wave pattern.

Quantum field theory as used by working physicists is not a formally exact theory. There is a version, axiomatic quantum field theory, which achieves rigour at the expense of most practical application. Within axiomatic quantum field theory one can prove (Haag's theorem) that in the interacting theory observed states of quanta are not related by intermediate states in the way usually assumed by the working theory, again suggesting that the theory recognizes only a global concept of quanta. Most working physicists simply dismiss these and related problems: after all (precise) axiomatic quantum field theory and (imprecise) working quantum field theory are not the same theory. But some maintain that Haag's theorem signals important formal and interpretive problems.

Description of electrons involves an arbitrary element (the absolute phase) superficially similar to an arbitrary choice of unit of length. Setting this element arbitrarily at each point in space seems to force the assumption of a 'compensating' field, interpretable as the photon field, which describes electromagnetic forces. Generalization of this idea of *gauge theories* extends quantum field theory: internal degrees of freedom of quanta involve similar 'arbitrary' elements again appearing to require assumption of further quantized fields, interpretable as the agents of the weak and strong forces. The resulting theory, known as the *standard model*, provides our most detailed picture of the internal structure of matter with the electro-weak theory and quantum chromodynamics. But the quarks of chromodynamics apparently cannot exist in a free state. Is that a problem? The fact that deep inelastic scattering experiments are interpretable as extremely indirect detection of quarks probably means that such quark confinement should not worry us. But at the time of writing the nature of the argument for the existence of gauge fields stands to be better understood.

See also: BELL'S THEOREM; QUANTUM MEASUREMENT PROBLEM

References and further reading

Each of the following include extensive further bibliography.

Auyang, S.Y. (1995) *How is Quantum Field Theory Possible?*, New York: Oxford University Press. (A Kantian interpretation of contemporary field theories.)

Redhead, M.L.G. (1983) 'Quantum Field Theory for Philosophers', in P.D. Asquith and T. Nickles (eds) *PSA 1982*, East Lansing, MI: Philosophy of Science Association, vol. 2, 57–99. (A relatively accessible introduction to some of the basic ideas and interpretive problems of quantum field theory.)

—— (1988) 'A Philosopher Looks at Quantum Field Theory', in H. Brown and R. Harre (eds) *Philosophical Foundations of Quantum Field Theory*, Oxford: Clarendon Press. (Review and elaboration on material in the 1983 article.)

Teller, P. (1995) *An Interpretive Introduction to Quantum Field Theory*, Princeton, NJ: Princeton University Press. (A general introduction to the elementary formalism and interpretive problems of quantum field theory, accessible to anyone who knows a little quantum mechanics.)

PAUL TELLER

FILM, AESTHETICS OF

Film aesthetics has been dominated by issues of realism. Three kinds of realism attributable to film may be distinguished: (1) the realism inherent in film because of its use of the photographic method (realism of method); (2) realism as a style which approximates the normal conditions of perception (realism of style); (3) realism as the capacity of film to engender in the viewer an illusion of the reality and presentness of fictional characters and events (realism of effect). Some theorists have argued that realism of method requires us to avoid realist style, others that it requires us to adopt realist style. Most have agreed that realist style makes for realism of effect; they disagree about whether this is a desirable goal. It is argued here that these realisms are independent of one another, that realism of style does not entail any kind of metaphysical realism, and that realism of effect is irrelevant to understanding

the normal experience of cinema. Realism of style suggests a way of making precise the claim that cinema is an art of time and of space, because this kind of realism is partially explicated in terms of the representation of time by time and of space by space. Psychological theorizing about the cinema has been strongly connected with realism of effect, and with the idea that an illusion of the film's reality is created by the identification of the viewer's position with that of the camera. Another version of illusionism has it that the experience of film-watching is significantly similar to that of dreaming. Such doctrines are undermined when we acknowledge that realism of effect is an insignificant phenomenon.

1   History
2   Realism of method and of style
3   Space, time and film
4   The camera, the eye and realism of effect

1   History

The first period of serious writing on film aesthetics (roughly from the 1920s to the 1950s) was devoted to the problems raised by the photographic method, and to the accusation that film was merely the automatic recording of reality. The second period, still under way, has been dominated by attempts to elaborate a theory about the role of the camera as spectator, participant and the object or vehicle of the viewer's identification. But issues of realism have continued to be influential.

Two opposing tendencies were evident in the first period. One sought to show that what was distinctive about cinema, and therefore to be encouraged, was the means, notably editing, by which the product deviated from a mere recording of the real world (realism of method). This view was often combined with an opposition to the use of integrated sound, on the grounds that its use resulted in a hybridized and weakened medium. In film practice this tendency was evident in the montage style of the early Soviet cinema, which emphasized the juxtaposition of objects and events by quick cuts, close-ups and striking camera angles. Thus realism of method was made the grounds for preferring an unrealistic style. The contrary and somewhat later tendency was to celebrate the dependence of film on the process of automatic recording, to argue that the medium of film is reality itself, and that in consequence developments like sound and colour are to be seen as fulfilling the historical destiny of cinema because they are additions to the realism of film. Central to this view was an endorsement of so-called 'long-take, deep-focus' style, thought to provide a visual experience approximating to our visual experience of the real world, and enabling different actions to take place within the same frame – a capacity later enhanced by the introduction of wide screen. Thus realism of style was justified by an appeal to realism of method.

Both tendencies exhibit a high degree of concern for prescriptive issues about film-making. The writing that initiated the second period during the 1960s rejected this approach and sought a new, ostensibly more scientific attitude to cinema through the articulation of a supposed language of film, which would enable us to analyse film technique and the viewer's strategies for understanding film. But this approach soon abandoned its structuralist and quasi-scientific impetus in favour of a psychologically oriented approach that sought to analyse the way that film, especially the mimetic cinema of Hollywood, engages the viewer, and to characterize the experience of engagement as a species of entrapment. Thus the second period has generally been hostile to the realist tendency of the first period. Film theory in this second period has had a distinctly political agenda, drawing on Marxism and psychoanalysis to explore the role of film in reinforcing the viewer's subjective identity. Feminist theorists have argued that conventional film-making is geared to the satisfaction of male voyeuristic desire (Mulvay 1976).

2 Realism of method and of style

The idea behind realism of method seems to be that the photographic medium enables us to see things themselves rather than representations of them; in this respect photographs are said to be akin to lenses and mirrors, in contrast to paintings (and, presumably, animated cartoons) which give us mere representations of things (see PHOTOGRAPHY, AESTHETICS OF). Even assuming that realism of method is correct, no theorist has adequately explained how this purely descriptive claim entails the evaluative claim that long-take style is preferable to montage style. And those who sought to justify realist style in terms of realism of method overlooked a crucial distinction between what the camera literally records – actors, props and sets – and the fictional objects and events it presents. Realism of method applies only to the first of these, whereas realism of style is primarily a vehicle for the presentation of the second. Further, if realism of method unequivocally favours realist style, we must endorse what are generally agreed to be rather problematic developments: 3D, smellorama, and the ultra-long-take method of Hitchcock's *Rope*.

Some writers have denied that long-take, deep-focus style is realistic. In fact, a defence of the realism of that style is possible. Let us say that a mode of

representation is realistic when, or to the degree that, we employ the same capacities in recognizing its representational content that we employ in recognizing the (kind of) objects its represents. A good-quality, well focused, middle-distance photograph of a horse is realistic in this sense: we employ our capacity to recognize horses visually so as to determine that this is, indeed, a photograph of a horse. Many paintings would count as realistic by the same criterion. A linguistic description of a horse, by contrast, is not realistic, for the capacity to recognize horses visually is not sufficient to enable you to recognize this as a representation of a horse; that requires a knowledge of the conventions of language. (There may be other senses in which the description is realistic.) Realism of style is a matter of degree; some aspects of the content of a representation may be recognized by deploying the capacity for object-recognition, while others are not.

By this criterion, long-take, deep-focus style is (relatively) realistic. Watching a film in this style, we judge the spatial and temporal relations between the objects (and their parts) and the events that the image represents by using the capacity visually to judge spatial and temporal relations between real things. We judge the spatial relations between objects visible in the same frame by seeing that they are spatially related thus and so within the visual field; we judge the temporal properties of and relations between events within the take by noting that this event took (roughly) so long to observe, while this one was experienced as occurring later than or earlier than that one. That is just how we perceive the spatial and temporal properties of things and events in the real world. With montage style, by contrast, where there is quick cutting between very distinct spatial (and sometimes temporal) perspectives, these properties and relations have to be judged, with greater frequency, by means of inference from the overall dramatic structure of the film.

It has been said that deep-focus style is unrealistic in that it presents us with an image in which objects at considerably different distances from the camera are simultaneously in sharp focus, whereas objects at comparable distances from the eye could not be seen in focus together (Ogle 1972). This does not seriously detract from the realism of deep focus. Deep focus, particularly when used in conjunction with wide screen, enables us to concentrate our attention on one object, and then to shift our attention at will to another object, just as we are able to do when perceiving the real world. Since we are usually not very conscious of refocusing our eyes, the similarities between viewing deep-focus style and perceiving the real world are more striking than the differences. With montage style, on the other hand, we are severely limited, by shot length and depth of field, in our capacity to shift our attention from one object to another at will – though this feature is not entirely absent in montage style.

Explicating the idea of realism of style in this way helps us to avoid an error that has dogged theorizing about the cinema: that realism in film can be attacked on metaphysical grounds because it postulates a real, observer-independent world, an idea that some theorists then further associate with a politically conservative agenda of submission to prevailing conditions. But realism of style as I have explicated it here appeals to no such postulate of an observer-independent world (though one might argue that such a postulate is both philosophically respectable and politically neutral). The claim of stylistic realism is not the claim that cinema presents objects and events isomorphic to those that exist in an observer-independent world. It is the claim that, in crucial respects, the experience of film-watching is similar to our ordinary perceptual experience of the world, irrespective of whether and to what extent that world is independent of our experience of it.

3 Space, time and film

We can now see an important sense in which film is both a spatial and a temporal medium. Film represents space by means of space, and time by means of time. It is the spatial (temporal) properties of the cinematic representation that we observe and rely upon in order to figure out what spatial (temporal) properties of the fictional characters and events are portrayed. It is correctly said that painting and still photography are capable of representing the temporal: by inference, by juxtaposition of distinct static images, by transforming temporal properties into spatial ones (where, say, being further to the right represents being later in time), and by special techniques such as blurring and multiple exposure. But these possibilities do not constitute grounds for calling painting and still photography arts of time in the way that cinema is, for they do not represent time by means of time.

So far we have considered untensed temporal properties of duration and precedence. What about the representation of tensed temporal properties: pastness, presentness and futurity? Theorists have often argued that film represents fictional events as occurring now, in the sense that viewers are to think of those events going on in the present as they watch. This is one consequence of the doctrine of realism of effect, according to which film typically creates an illusion in viewers' minds that the fictional events

represented on screen are real, and that they, the viewers, are present (spatially and temporally) at their occurrence. Realism of effect will be discussed in the next section; here we concentrate on the claim of temporal presentness. One problem with the view that film represents fictional events as occurring in the viewer's present is that it then becomes difficult to make sense of the idea of 'anachrony' in film – the flashback or flashforward. If viewers are to think of the image they see as representing something occurring now, an anachronous sequence would require them to imagine travelling in time, viewing what is objectively past or future in their subjective present. But this is neither plausible psychologically, since viewers of anachronous material do not seem to imagine themselves travellers in time, nor helpful in maintaining the integrity of the action, since time travel introduces an element of fantasy that would be unwelcome in our experience of many naturalistic films that none the less display anachrony in their narratives.

If, on the other hand, we say that film does not represent fictional events as present to the viewer, but merely as standing in untensed relations of precedence and simultaneity to one another, how shall we explain anachrony? After all, anachronous representations seem to be ones that represent the past (as in flashback) and the future (as in flashforward). In fact, we can explain anachrony in untensed terms as follows: we have anachrony when an event occurring earlier in fictional time than another occurs later in the time of narrative exposition; here we appeal only to untensed notions of precedence. Such a tenseless approach implies a certain relativity and even arbitrariness in the application of the notions of flashback and flashforward; a film's narrative structure, or part of it, could sometimes equally well be described as employing the one as the other. If, on the other hand, we could appeal to tense and identify non-anachronous material as temporally present, we would have an absolute distinction between flashback (past) and flashforward (future). But this relativity in the tenseless account of anachrony is arguably no drawback. The fact that one of the two labels (flashforward, flashback) often seems more natural than the other may be accounted for by appeal to the fact that one of them allows a simpler, and therefore preferable, description of the film's temporal structure. It may also be that one or other description accords better with the dramatic structure of the film at that point, which may involve an episode of memory (in which case the description in terms of flashback will seem preferable) or premonition (which favours flashforward). There will, on this view, be occasions when there is nothing to choose between the two descriptions; and indeed there are films (*Last Year at Marienbad*, for example) of which it seems right to say that there is no uniquely correct description of their temporal structure. In that case, while anachrony itself is a notion definable in temporal but tenseless terms, the direction of anachrony needs to be defined in pragmatic and dramatic terms.

4   The camera, the eye and realism of effect

Many theorists have argued that the mechanism or 'apparatus' of cinema encourages and perhaps requires the viewer to think of cinematic images as corresponding to the perceptual states of an observer whose eye is the lens of the camera itself (Aumont 1989: 2). This idea is reinforced by the doctrine of realism of effect, in the following way. If viewers are victims of an illusion created by the film, then presumably they must think that the reality supposedly seen is seen from their point of view, by means of their visual organs. Since film manifestly works by presenting events from another, independent position – that of the camera – illusion-dominated viewers must come to think of themselves as occupying that position.

There are two objections to the idea that film induces the illusion that fictional events are real and that the viewer is directly witnessing them. The first is that there is little evidence that film typically creates, even temporarily or in part, the false beliefs necessary to sustain such an illusion; film watchers do not behave like people who believe, or even suspect, that they are in the presence of axe murderers, world-destroying monsters or nuclear explosions. Second, this theory is at odds with much of the experience of film-watching; identification with the camera would frequently require us to imagine ourselves in peculiar or impossible locations, undertaking movements out of keeping with the natural limitations of our bodies, and peculiarly invisible to the characters. None of this seems to be part of the ordinary experience of film-watching. In the attempt to identify the camera with some observer within the world of the action with whom the viewer can in turn identify, theorists have exaggerated the extent to which shots within a film can be thought of as point-of-view shots, and have sometimes postulated, quite ad hoc, an invisible narrator from whose position the action is displayed. It would be better to acknowledge that cinematic shots are only rarely from a psychological point of view, and abandon the thesis that the viewer identifies with an intelligence whose point of view is the camera.

A variant of illusionism says that the situation of the film watcher approximates to that of a dreamer, in that both situations present us with a strong impression of the reality of that which is actually unreal (Metz 1970). In that case the camera would correspond to a supposed 'inner eye' by means of which we perceive the images of dreams. This analogy has been a powerful stimulus to the development of psychoanalytic theories of film and film experience. In fact the analogy with dreaming fails to compare like with like. Dreamers, like film watchers, are usually physically passive while watching or dreaming. But the experience of dreaming is usually one that involves action – sometimes ineffectual – on the dreamer's part, while the experience of film-watching, our reflex responses aside, rarely involves physical action. And it is the experience of film-watching and the experience of dreaming that are claimed by the advocates of the dream/film analogy to be alike. In dreams, our own actions and sufferings are of central concern to us; the experience of film-watching makes us largely forgetful of ourselves while we concentrate on the fate of the characters.

See also: SEMIOTICS

References and further reading

Arnheim, R. (1958) *Film as Art*, London: Faber & Faber. (A translation of essays written in German between 1933 and 1938. An antirealist statement from the first period.)

* Aumont, J. (1989) 'The Point of View', trans. A. Denner, *Quarterly Review of Film and Video* 11: 1–22. (On the supposed subjectivity of the camera.)

Bazin, A. (1967) *What is Cinema?*, vol. 1, trans. H. Gray, Berkeley, CA, and Los Angeles, CA: University of California Press. A translation of selected essays from *Qu-est-ce que le cinéma?*, 4 vols, Paris: Éditions du Cerf, 1958–65. (The classic statement of realism.)

Bordwell, D. and Carroll, N. (eds) (1995) *Post-Theory: Reconstructing Film Studies*, Madison, WI: University of Wisconsin Press. (A collection of writings by philosophers and theorists opposed to the dominant models of the second period.)

Carroll, N. (1988) *Philosophical Problems of Classical Film Theory*, Princeton, NJ: Princeton University Press. (A useful discussion of expressionist and realist tendencies.)

—— (1990) *Mystifying Movies*, Ithaca, NY: Cornell University Press. (An attack on the film theory of the second period from the perspective of contemporary Anglo-American philosophy.)

Cavell, S. (1971) *The World Viewed*, New York: Viking Press. (A statement of the realist view.)

Currie, G. (1995) *Image and Mind. Film, Philosophy,*

and *Cognitive Science*, New York: Cambridge University Press. (A theory of film which rejects semiotic and psychoanalytic models in favour of Anglo-American philosophy of mind and cognitive science.)

Metz, C. (1977) *Le signifiant imaginaire. Psychoanalyse et cinéma*, Paris: Union Générale d'Éditions; trans. C. Britton *et al.*, *The Imaginary Signifier*, Bloomington, IN: Indiana University Press, 1982. (Represents a semiotician's turn to psychoanalytic and especially Lacanian ideas.)

* Mulvay, L. (1976) 'Visual Pleasure and Narrative Cinema', *Screen* 16, reprinted in G. Mast, M. Cohen, and L. Braudy (eds). (An account of the viewer's relation to the screen image, influenced by Lacan.)

Nichols, B. (ed.) (1976, 1985) *Movies and Methods*, 2 vols, Berkeley and Los Angeles, CA: University of California Press. (An anthology in which Marxist, semiotic and feminist perspectives are well represented.)

* Ogle, P. (1972) 'Technological and Aesthetic Influences on the Development of Deep-Focus Cinematography in the United States', *Screen* 13, reprinted in Nichols (ed.), vol. 2. (A historical account of deep-focus style.)

Wilson, G. (1986) *Narration in Light*, Baltimore, MD, and London: Johns Hopkins University Press. (This work by a philosopher develops an account of narration in film through close analysis of five films.)

GREGORY CURRIE

FILMER, SIR ROBERT (1588–1653)

Filmer was one of the most important political thinkers in seventeenth-century England, and the author of Patriarcha. *Locke replied to this and other works by Filmer in the* Two Treatises of Government – *perhaps the most famous of all works of liberal political theory. Filmer argued that notions of mixed or limited government were false and pernicious, and that the powers of all legitimate rulers were derived not from the people but directly from God, to whom alone rulers were accountable. Filmer's contemporaries commonly held that the authority of a father and husband over his family stemmed not from the consent of his wife and children but from the natural and divinely appointed order of things. Filmer harnessed such ideas to the cause of royal absolutism by arguing that the state and the family were essentially the same institution.*

1 Life and works
2 Political theory
3 Posthumous debate on his ideas

1 Life and works

Filmer was born in 1588 into a large and wealthy Kentish family. He was an eldest son, and upheld political beliefs which took it for granted that primogeniture in the male line was the proper means of succession in families and states. After attending Trinity College, Cambridge, and Lincoln's Inn, in 1613 he was called to the bar. He married a bishop's daughter and the couple settled in lodgings at Westminster Abbey. In 1619 Robert was knighted. A decade later he inherited his father's estate in Kent.

Sir Robert had connections with the royal court (where a brother held office) and with the upper ranks of the church (through his wife and through his friend Peter Heylin, the chaplain and biographer of William Laud, Archbishop of Canterbury). The ideological stance which Filmer adopted in his writings was strongly influenced by attitudes common among courtiers and high-ranking clerics. It is unclear when he began to write, but not long before 8 February 1632 he brought to the relevant royal official 'a Discourse to bee licensed for printing, written of Government and in praise of Royaltie and the supreme authority thereof'. The official asked the king himself whether it would be expedient to publish the book, and on 8 February Charles I examined the work and decided to forbid publication. The book was almost certainly *Patriarcha. The Naturall Power of Kinges Defended Against the Unnatural Liberty of the People*: the text of one manuscript of *Patriarcha* is dateable on internal evidence to between 1628 and 1631, and it is plausible that parts of the work are from much earlier still. Charles refused to license Filmer's treatise for the press, probably because he feared that it would foment unnecessary strife as its political doctrines were so uncompromising and so trenchantly expressed. Filmer later revised the book and drew on it in his published pamphlets, but *Patriarcha* itself was printed only in 1680.

In the Civil War between Charles and parliament (1642–6), Filmer's eldest son left Kent and sided actively with the king, but the ageing Sir Robert stayed at home. Kent quickly fell into the hands of parliament, and for a while Filmer was imprisoned. In 1648 the leading royalist publisher Richard Royston brought out two pamphlets by Filmer, *The Freeholders Grand Inquest Touching Our Soveraigne Lord the King and His Parliament* and *The Anarchy of a Limited or Mixed Monarchy* (Filmer's authorship of *The Free-holders* has been challenged but is generally accepted). Royston also published another work, *The Necessity of the Absolute Power of All Kings: and in particular, of the King of England*, compiled by Filmer from the writings of BODIN (§§2–3). Internal evidence suggests that the two former texts were written around 1644. Until Charles I's final defeat in 1646, most royalist pamphlets attempted to win support for the king by stressing the moderation of his cause, but Filmer's writings were outspokenly absolutist; this may explain why they (like other trenchantly absolutist writings such as Hobbes' *Elements of Law*) were not published until later (see ABSOLUTISM). Two final political writings by Filmer appeared in 1652, the year before his death. One, *Observations Concerning the Originall of Government*, criticized the ideas of HOBBES (§§6–8), Milton and GROTIUS. The other, *Observations upon Aristotles Politiques, Touching Forms of Government*, included an appendix, 'Directions for Obedience to Governours in Dangerous and Doubtfull Times', in which Filmer argued that limited obedience to the usurping government of the Rump parliament was justifiable, but that no usurpation – however lengthy – could extinguish the right of the true rulers (contradicting his earlier views on usurpation). Some other brief political writings have been attributed to Filmer, but on insufficient grounds. Filmer did, however, write short published works on witchcraft and usury, and a manuscript essay 'In Praise of the Vertuous Wife'.

2 Political theory

Filmer's political writings were intended to refute ideas of legitimate resistance and limited or mixed monarchy which circulated among critics of royal policy in the early seventeenth century (these included the Catholics SUAREZ (§4) and Bellarmine, and a number of parliamentarian pamphleteers). The cardinal error of most political theorists, Filmer argued, was their supposition that people were born free and equal. From this false premise they drew the erroneous conclusions that states had originally arisen by the consent of their members, that political power had at first grown out of the community as a whole (for if all were equal, no one had any more right to exercise such power than anyone else), and that the powers of rulers were therefore derived from the community, which could discipline and perhaps even depose them if they failed to abide by the conditions upon which authority had been transferred to them.

Filmer claimed that this whole line of reasoning was faulty since people were in fact born into subjection to their fathers. He argued that Adam (the first father of all) had held authority over his children and their descendants, and over all property in the world. Adam's authority arose from his position as the ultimate ancestor of the group. Filmer claimed that Adam's power was fully political, and that it included the right to execute his subjects. By nature, he held, children remained subject to their fathers throughout their lives, although a father could decide to free them from subjection. If a son were freed in this way, he would then be able to wield full fatherly/political power over his own descendants. The ordinary means of succession to a father's power and property was by primogeniture in the male line, but a ruler could alter this arrangement (Noah, for example, divided the earth among his sons). Sovereigns could also hand over authority to someone else, and God might providentially intervene in human affairs by changing the ruling family or even the form of government (although monarchy was the best form). Filmer did not argue that the whole world should be ruled by Adam's heir (whoever that might be), for he recognized that Adam's original empire had been split into a large number of states. His central contention was that the rulers in all of these states exercised the same powers that Adam had – powers which were sovereign and independent of the consent of the people.

Filmer frequently quoted scripture (particularly the book of Genesis), the Civil Law, Aristotle and Bodin. His patriarchal theory of the origins and nature of government is, however, not easy to find in these sources. Bodin did indeed assert that by nature fathers have the power of life and death over their wives and children, but the Adamite elements of Filmerian patriarchalism are not present in his writings. They are present in the works of some English authors, notably Hadrian Saravia, who put forward views which are virtually indistinguishable from Filmer's in the 1593 Latin text, *De imperandi authoritate*. Like Filmer, Saravia argued that the family and the state were not merely analogous but identical institutions. Filmer, throughout his political writings, stressed that sovereignty in every state must be unlimited (except by the laws of God and nature) and indivisible, ideas which he took unaltered from Bodin (see SOVEREIGNTY §1).

Arguably Filmer was at his most effective and most original in his criticisms of theories of original popular sovereignty and the contractual origins of political power. He argued that contract theory was unconvincing on both historical and philosophical grounds and claimed that contract theorists themselves inconsistently adopted patriarchalist principles – for example, to argue that women and children were bound by political arrangements to which they had not consented (see CONTRACTARIANISM).

3 Posthumous debate on his ideas

In 1680 *Patriarcha* was published as a contribution to the debate over the nature and extent of royal power which accompanied the Exclusion Crisis. Filmer's other political works had been reissued in the previous year. His writings soon attracted responses from James Tyrrell, Algernon Sidney and John Locke. For many years it was almost universally accepted that Locke had refuted Filmer's theory, successfully exposing his opponent's absurdities (Locke 1690). More recently, some feminist scholars have argued that this verdict is only partially justified and that Locke (and other liberal theorists) did not adequately meet Filmer's criticisms of contract theory, since they tacitly and inconsistently accepted patriarchalist assumptions.

List of works

Filmer, Sir R. (1648a) *The Free-holders Grand Inquest Touching Our Soveraigne Lord the King and His Parliament*, London: Royston. (A long historical account of English constitutional development, arguing that parliament is subordinate to the king.)
— (1648b) *The Anarchy of a Limited or Mixed Monarchy*, London: Royston. (Attacks the claim of the parliamentarian pamphleteer, Philip Hunton, and others that England is a mixed and limited monarchy by asserting that such a monarchy is impossible.)
— (1648c) *The Necessity of the Absolute Power of All Kings: and in particular, of the King of England*, London: Royston; compiled from J. Bodin, *The Six Bookes of a Commonweale*, trans. R Knolles, London: Bishop, 1606. (A collection of extracts from Bodin on absolute power and sovereignty.)
— (1652a) *Observations Concerning the Originall of Government*, London: Royston. (Attacks Hobbes, Grotius and Milton. Agrees with Hobbes on the nature of sovereign power, but denies that it is rooted in popular consent.)
— (1652b) *Observations upon Aristotles Politiques, Touching Forms of Government*, London: Royston. (Argues that Aristotle's *Politics* supports absolute monarchy.)
— (c.1628–31) *Patriarcha. The Naturall Power of Kings Defended Against the Unnatural Liberty of the People*, London: Davis, 1680. (Presents the fullest version of Filmer's theory. First published a s Tory propaganda long after his death.)
— (1991) *Patriarcha and Other Writings*, ed. J.P. Sommerville, Cambridge: Cambridge University Press. (Includes the writings listed above, edited from the manuscripts and original editions.)

References and further reading

Daly, J. (1979) *Sir Robert Filmer and English Political Thought*, Toronto, Ont.: Toronto University Press. (The fullest account, but overestimates Filmer's originality.)
* Saravia, H. (1593) *De imperandi authorite, et Christiana obedientia* (On the Authority to Command, and Christian Obedience), London: Barker. (A vigorously absolutist work on the origins and nature of political power.)
Laslett, P. (1949) *Patriarcha and Other Political Works of Sir Robert Filmer*, Oxford: Blackwell. (Informative but a little dated.)
Locke, J. (1690) *Two Treatises of Government*, ed. P. Laslett, Cambridge: Cambridge University Press, 1960. (Replies in detail to Filmer's theory, especially in the first treatise.)
Pateman, C. (1988) *The Sexual Contract*, Stanford, CT: Stanford University Press. (Includes discussion of the theories of Filmer and his critics from a feminist perspective.)
Schochet, G.J. (1975) *Patriarchalism and Political Thought*, Oxford: Blackwell. (Contains much important background information and two useful chapters on Filmer.)
Sommerville, J.P. (1986) *Politics and Ideology in England, 1603–1640*, Harlow: Longman. (Discusses the political and ideological context of *Patriarcha*. Chapter 1 is especially relevant.)

JOHANN P. SOMMERVILLE

FINCH, ANNE *see* CONWAY, ANNE

FINITUDE *see* VULNERABILITY AND FINITUDE

FINLAND, PHILOSOPHY IN
see SCANDINAVIA, PHILOSOPHY IN

FIRST CAUSE ARGUMENT
see GOD, ARGUMENTS FOR THE EXISTENCE OF

FLORENSKII, PAVEL ALEKSANDROVICH (1882–1937)

A figure of genius in the history of twentieth-century Russian religious philosophy, Florenskii did much to influence the directions of subsequent Russian thought, both within the Soviet Union and abroad in the Russian diaspora. Florenskii's originality is most noticeable in his chief philosophical work, Stolp i utverzhdenie istiny *(The Pillar and Foundation of Truth) (1914), a somewhat eclectic and romantic work in which he sets forth his basic tenets in epistemology and sophiology. The work, which was his doctoral dissertation, represents a decisive rejection of rationalist and Western-orientated religious philosophy and theology in favour of a more concrete and experiential methodology.*

1   Life
2   Theodicy: epistemology and sophiology
3   Anthropodicy: aesthetics and philosophy of language

1   Life

Florenskii was born in 1882 in Yevlakh, Azerbaijan, to a Russian father and an Armenian mother, both of a liberal secular orientation indifferent to religion. His own personal journey to devout religious practice, which culminated in theological studies (1904–8) and ordination to the Orthodox priesthood (1911), came only gradually and began, as he states in his memoirs, with an early fascination with the aesthetic form of nature that matured in a lifelong interest in natural science and mathematics. Declining an offer to pursue advanced studies in mathematics upon graduation from Moscow University (1904), where he studied under the noted mathematician N.V. Bugaev, Florenskii, to the dismay of family and friends, chose to enrol at the Moscow Theological Academy whose faculty he himself was to join (1908).

Bolshevik repression after the Russian Revolution brought about a change of direction in both his professional activities and his philosophical thought. With the forced closure of the Moscow Theological Academy, Florenskii was, owing to his scientific talents, still able to collaborate in various Soviet undertakings, including the Commission for the Electrification of Soviet Russia. His 1927 invention of a noncoagulating machine oil was even called 'dekanite' by the Soviets, in commemoration of the tenth anniversary of the Bolshevik Revolution. It was during this time that Florenskii shifted his philosophical interest to aesthetics and the philosophy of language. Refusing to renounce the priesthood, he was exiled in 1933 to Siberia and then in 1934 to the Solovki Island concentration camp in the White Sea, where he was executed by firing squad in 1937, contrary to official Soviet data which for decades listed the year of his death as 1943.

2   Theodicy: epistemology and sophiology

The first period of Florenskii's philosophical development reaches its climax in his already noted masterwork, which, even according to his critic G. Florovskii, is the most characteristic work of the religious renaissance during Russia's short-lived Silver Age at the beginning of this century (see RUSSIAN RELIGIOUS-PHILOSOPHICAL RENAISSANCE). Florenskii subtitled his study 'The Experience of Orthodox Theodicy in Twelve Letters', indicating the root motivation inspiring the development of his reflections. One might say that *Stolp i utverzhdenie istiny* constitutes a form of intellectual autobiography in which Florenskii's own inner struggle for truth is articulated and justified. Indeed, the justification of the mind's claims to know truth lies at the core of Florenskii's own unique understanding of theodicy. After an initial discussion of his point of departure – concrete experience – he considers the divisions characteristic of a fallen world (along with the partial truths about the world) as facts crying out for Ultimate Truth that can undergird reality, imparting integrality to it.

Postulating 'living religious experience as the sole legitimate method for understanding dogma', Florenskii seeks to rejuvenate intellectual thought beyond confessional Orthodox lines towards a true existential appreciation of the whole of reality. Orthodox theologians as diverse as S.N. BULGAKOV, J. Meyendorff and A. Schmemann have all followed his lead on this point. His stress on the immediateness of concrete experience also influenced other Russian philosophers like A.F. LOSEV, whose own work has similarities to Husserlian phenomenology.

Florenskii's aim is to foster dialectical thinking, which he conceives as living, unmediated thought unlike the 'schooled', rationalistic variety that prescinds from concrete experience. His emphases in cognition are an offshoot of the Slavophile theory of integral knowledge, first developed by I.V. Kireevskii and A.S. Khomiakov, then continued by V.S. Solov'ev (see SLAVOPHILISM §1; SOLOV'ËV, V.S. §1). The whole thrust of Florenskii's epistemological query is to shed light on the experience of truth as gained in lived contact with reality. He approaches the topic from various angles, finally defining truth as an 'intuition-discursion' in which the immediate givenness of truth is not blunt or blind, but is instead infused with intelligibility and *ratio*. Florenskii in this fashion offers a dynamic understanding of the principle of identity, making 'otherness' constitutive of identity through a process of adoption (*usvoenie*) and assimilation (*upodobenie sebe*), thus grounding it in the principle of sufficient reason. Comparative analysis reveals similar (although subsequent and independent) insights on these themes in the work of such diverse and seminal thinkers as Heidegger and Whitehead.

Florenskii's epistemological study of the experience of truth sets the stage for his metaphysical worldview, which, borrowing a term from the history of patristic theology, he fashions as *homoousian* philosophy or a philosophy of consubstantiality in opposition to a *homoiousian* one of mere similarity. The whole thrust of Florenskii's metaphysics is to lay out the fundamental truth of pan-unity (*vseedinstvo*) at the root of all being. All created beings are not atomized units in isolation, but are consubstantial with one another. Cognition thereby enjoys an ontological moment in which knower and known are truly united in opposition to all representationalist theories of knowledge.

Florenskii transcribes his metaphysics into a sophiological key, holding all being to be nothing but a symbol of Sophia, which, for him, is an all-embracing reality linking both Creator and creature together and is considered variously as the 'great root of the total creature', the 'guardian angel of creation' and the 'eternal spouse of the Word of God', among other designations. As an attempt to address the ontological problem of the relations obtaining between Creator and creature, Florenskii's sophiology, however, raises a host of problems on its own. In particular, critics (for instance N.O. Lossky and J. Meyendorff) have charged him with both Gnosticism and pantheism, since his conception of Sophia as a 'fourth hypostatic element' seems to compromise God's freedom in creation as well as efface the ontological difference between God and creation (see GNOSTICISM; PANTHEISM). Others (for instance Slesinski) more sympathetic to Florenskii suggest that a more careful analysis of love as a central category of his metaphysics of consubstantiality can obviate these difficulties.

3 Anthropodicy: aesthetics and philosophy of language

If the major concern of *Stolp i utverzhdenie istiny* is the justification of the claims of truth, Florenskii makes the specific truth about the human person the focus of his later works, which he dedicates to concrete metaphysics or 'anthropodicy'. The centrality of art and language for the meaning of the human person is the main theme of this endeavour, the human person and the world being expressions of the spiritual in the sensual or empirical order of being. Being for Florenskii is no longer Sophia, but rather 'symbol' or 'icon', ontologically conceived as a dynamic interchange between the knower and symbolized reality, visually in the case of art and verbally in that language, wherein the symbol is not a sign of an absent reality, but its very presence. Florenskii defines symbol as 'being which is greater than itself', and thus understands it as a manifestation or energy of being without exhausting its essence.

An heir to the linguistic school of W. von HUMBOLDT, Florenskii centred his studies on the dynamic aspect of language as a pining of the spirit to express itself and, accordingly, was sympathetic to avant-garde poetic theory. From his university years, he enjoyed a close friendship with Russian Symbolist poets, A. Belyi in particular. There were also theological roots to Florenskii's philosophy of language. The controversy (1912) over the 'glorification of the name' (*imiaslavie*) among Athonite monks regarding the immediate presence of God in his name had a decisive bearing on the development of Florenskii's thought. Theological concerns also motivated his studies in aesthetics and the philosophy of cult in which the meaning of iconography and the significance of liturgical action are primary themes.

The chief works in which he explores these ideas are *U vodorazdelov mysli* (At the Watersheds of Thought) (1990), *Ikonostas* (Iconostasis) (1972), and a series of lectures on the philosophy of cult now published under the heading of *Iz bogoslovskogo naslediia sviashchennika Pavla Florenskogo* (From the Theological Heritage of the Priest Pavel Florenskii). Not published during Florenskii's lifetime because of the political climate, these studies largely lay dormant even after his posthumous rehabilitation (1956). *Glasnost'* and the fall of communism reversed this situation. A complete publication of all his works remains to be achieved.

List of works

Florenskii, P.A. (1914) *Stolp i utverzhdenie istiny* (The Pillar and Foundation of Truth), Moscow: Izdatel'stvo 'Pravda', 1990, 2 vols; trans. B. Jakim, *The Pillar and Ground of the Truth*, Princeton, NJ: Princeton University Press, 1997. (Florenskii's best-known work, detailing his epistemology and sophiology.)

—— (1915) *Smysl idealizma* (The Meaning of

Idealism), Sergiev Posad. (Provides Florenskii's original reading of Plato.)

—— (1922) *Mnimosti v geometrii* (The Imaginary in Geometry), Moscow: Pomor'e; repr. Munich: Otto Sagner, 1985. (Florenskii offers a defence of the Ptolemaic cosmological worldview of Dante's *Divine Comedy* in the last section of this work.)

—— (1972) *Ikonostas* (Iconostasis), in *Bogoslovskie trudy* (Theological Studies) 9: 80–148; integral trans., Crestwood, NY: St Vladimir's Seminary Press, 1996. (A key work in the aesthetics of iconography. The previously unpublished manuscript dates to 1922.)

—— (1977) *Iz bogoslovskogo naslediia sviashchennika Pavla Florenskogo* (From the Theological Heritage of the Priest Pavel Florenskii) in *Bogoslovskie trudy* (Theological studies) 17: 85–248. (Written from 1918 to 1922, this work treats the philosophy of cult.)

—— (1990) *U vodorazdelov mysli* (At the Watersheds of Thought), Moscow: Izdatel'stvo 'Pravda'. (The original manuscript, itself incomplete, was written over 1917–22, and comprises various studies on the philosophy of language. It includes his noted monograph on inverse perspective. Another volume with the same title was published by YMCA-Press, Paris, 1985, but contains only articles on art, including his monographs on inverse perspective and the *Ikonostas*.)

—— (1992) *Detiam moim: vospominan'ia proshlykh dnei* (To My Children: Reminiscences of Past Days), Moscow: Moskovskii rabochii, 1992. (The original manuscript was written intermittently between 1916 and 1925. Appended to this autobiography are Florenskii's own genealogical investigations and his letters to his family written from imprisonment.)

—— (1993) *Analiz prostranstvennosti i vremeni v khudozhestvenno-izobrazitel'nykh proizvedeniiakh* (An Analysis of Space and Time in Works of Fine Art), Moscow: Izdatel'skaia gruppa 'Progress'. (This contains his lectures at the Higher Artistic-Technical Studios [VKHUTEMAS], 1924–5.)

—— (1994) *Sochineniia v chetyrekh tomakh* (Compositions in Four Volumes), vol. 1 Moscow: Izdatel'stvo 'Mysl'". (A collection of his articles from 1903–9 along with Florenskii's résumé (c.1925–6) of his own thought. Volume 2 is to include subsequent articles from 1903–33 with volumes 3 and 4 containing *Stolp i utverzhdenie istiny* and *U vodorazdelov mysli* respectively.)

References and further reading

Bychkov, V. (1990) *Ėsteticheskii lik bytiia: Umozreniia Pavla Florenskogo*, Moscow: Znanie; trans. R.

Pevear and L. Volokhonsky, *The Aesthetic Face of Being: Art in the Theology of Pavel Florensky*, Crestwood, NY: St Vladimir's Seminary Press, 1993. (An overview of Florenskii's aesthetics and his understanding of classical iconography in particular.)

* Florovskii, G. (1937) *Puti russkogo bogosloviia* (The Ways of Russian Theology), Paris: n.p.; 2nd edn, Paris: YMCA-Press, 1981. (For his critical commentary on Florenskii, see 493–8.)

Isupov, K.G. (ed.) (1996) *P.A. Florenskii: Pro et Contra*, St Petersburg: Izdatel'stvo Russkogo Khristianskogo Gumanitarnogo Instituta. (An anthology of critical reviews of Florenskii written by leading past and contemporary Russian philosophers.)

* Lossky, N. (1951) *History of Russian Philosophy*, New York: International Universities Press, 176–91. (A critical synopsis of Florenskii's metaphysics and sophiology.)

* Slesinski, R. (1984) *Pavel Florensky: A Metaphysics of Love*, Crestwood, NY: St Vladimir's Seminary Press. (The most extensive commentary on Florenskii in English.)

Trubachev, A. (1989) '*K 100-letiiu so dnia rozhdeniia sviashchennika Pavla Florenskogo. Ukazatel' pechatnykh trudov*' (In Commemoration of the Centenary of the Birth of the Priest Pavel Florenskii. Index of Published Works) in *Bogoslovskie trudy* (Theological Studies) 23: 264–309. (Lists all Florenskii's works published in Russia and the Soviet Union from 1901–82; 338 entries.)

Zenkovsky, V.V. (1948–50) *Istoriia russkoi filosofii*, vol. 2, Paris: YMCA-Press, 413–30; 2nd edn 1989; trans. G.L. Kline, *A History of Russian Philosophy*, London: Routledge & Kegan Paul and New York: Columbia University Press, 2 vols, 1953. (A digest of the metaphysics of pan-unity, along with an outline of Florenskii's epistemology and metaphysics.)

ROBERT SLESINSKI

FLUDD, ROBERT (1574–1637)

Fludd is a marginal figure in the mainstream development of philosophy in seventeenth-century England, but of some importance in the development of an esoteric and mystical philosophy which took the form of an 'underground' movement, Rosicrucianism. Rejecting the various types of scholastic philosophy that were still dominant in his day, Fludd drew on Neoplatonist and Renaissance sources in an effort to redirect learning in what he took to be a Christian direction. His writings centre around a search for hidden connections between a purely intelligible realm and the realm of sensation.

Robert Fludd was born in Kent in the south of England. After a period at St John's College, Oxford, he studied medicine, chemistry and the occult sciences in continental Europe, where he was employed as a tutor to noble families. He returned to England in 1604 and studied medicine at Christ Church, Oxford. Despite his rejection of the current Galenist orthodoxies, he was admitted a Fellow of the Royal College of Physicians, and pursued a form of holistic medicine in which magnetism and psychic healing played a significant role. From 1619 onwards he was engaged in various controversies with GASSENDI, KEPLER, MERSENNE and others.

Fludd assumed a continuity or even an identity between ancient and Christian thought, to the extent that the whole of ancient thought must be shown to anticipate Christianity, even down to points of detail such as the doctrine of the Trinity. In setting out this account he relies very extensively on Hermetic texts, which he maintains date from remote antiquity, despite the fact that Isaac Casaubon had shown in 1614 that they were actually composed well into the Christian era. Much of his work takes its bearings from commentary on the book of Genesis, having as its aim the reconciliation of Scripture with natural philosophy. Fludd pursued this project in a way which had two distinctive features. First, he read Genesis as showing that light and dark are the two basic principles from which everything else follows. God created the universe by contracting into himself, thereby creating darkness, then expanding outwards again in the form of light. Fludd relied heavily on the metaphorical connotations of light and dark, associating them directly with God and Satan. The second distinctive feature of his approach is that it depends as much, if not more, on pictorial representation as on verbal description. The latter is insufficient if we are to capture the deep, hidden relations between the world of sensation and the intelligible reality that underlies it, and pictorial representation is able to capture such mysteries as the Trinity in a way that verbal description is not. Here Fludd believed he had discovered the key to knowledge that Kabbalists, Rosicrucians and various Hermetist sects had been seeking (see HERMETISM; KABBALAH).

With this key, Fludd proceeded to unlock hidden antipathies and sympathies, using pairings of terms that mirrored the fundamental dichotomy between light and darkness in his exploration of various harmonic and magnetic phenomena. All natural phenomena are to be construed ultimately as manifestations of the one light–dark contrast, but Fludd

interpreted this claim sometimes reductively (for example, in terms of a contrast between heat and cold, the universal effects of which were displayed by means of a primitive thermometer), and sometimes metaphorically and analogically, seeking parallels and similarities rather than simply trying to explain one thing in terms of another.

See also: ALCHEMY; NEOPLATONISM; PARACELSUS; THEOSOPHY

List of works

Fludd, R. (1617) *Tractatus Theologico-Philosophicus in Libros tres...* (Theological-Political Treatise in three books), Oppenheim: Johann Theodore de Bry. (Fludd's most extensive theological tract, written from a Hermetic and Neoplatonic perspective.)

—— (1617/21) *Utriusque Cosmi Maioris scilicet et Minoris Metaphysica, Physica atque Technica Historia...* (History of the Microcosm and Macrocosm), Oppenheim/Frankfurt: Johann Theodore de Bry, 2 vols. (Fludd's account of the two worlds, the microcosm – the human being – and the macrocosm – God and the rest of his creation.)

—— (1621) *Veritatis Proscenium...* (First Reply to Kepler), Frankfurt: Johann Theodore de Bry. (The first reply to Kepler sets out Fludd's defence of his application of the principles of harmony to the study of the heavens.)

—— (1622) *Monochordum mundi symphoniacum...* (The second reply to Kepler), Frankfurt: Johann Theodore de Bry. (Continues the theme of the 'First Reply'.)

—— (1623) *Anatomiae amphitheatrum...* (The Amphitheatre of Anatomy), Frankfurt: Johann Theodore de Bry. (An account of anatomy and physiology on the basis of dissections, alchemical experiments and mystical principles.)

—— (1633) *Clavis Philosophiae et alchymiae...* (The key to Philosophy and Alchemy), Frankfurt: Wilhelm Fitzer. (Fludd's defence of alchemy and the principal response to Gassendi's criticisms of alchemy from the point of view of atomism.)

—— (1640) *Philosophia Moysaica...*, Gouda: Petrus Rammazenius; trans. as *Mosaicall Philosophy: Grounded upon the Essentiall Truth or Eternal Sapience*, London: Humphrey Moseley, 1659. (Summary of Fludd's cosmology, setting out a theory of universal attraction and repulsion.)

References and further reading

Debus, A.C. (1966) *The English Paracelsians*, New York: Franklin Watts, 105–27. (Good general account of Fludd's work, paying special attention to his work in alchemy and medicine.)

Hutin, S. (1971) *Robert Fludd (1574–1637): alchimiste et philosophe rosicrucian* (Robert Fludd: alchemist and rosicrucian philosopher), Paris: Alchimie et Alchimistes, vol. 8. (The only book-length treatment of Fludd that can be recommended without major qualification: available only in French.)

STEPHEN GAUKROGER

FODOR, JERRY ALAN (1935–)

Jerry Fodor has been one of the most influential figures in the philosophy of mind, the philosophy of psychology, and 'cognitive science' through the latter part of the twentieth century. His primary concern has been to argue (vigorously) for a certain view of the nature of thought. According to this view, thinking is information processing within 'the language of thought'. The mind can be understood as a computer, which directs action with the aid of internal representations of the world.

1 Fodor's view of the mind
2 Debates

1 Fodor's view of the mind

Like several other philosophers, Fodor in the 1960s and 1970s defended a functionalist view of the mind (Fodor 1968; see FUNCTIONALISM). Functionalism makes possible a physicalist worldview but does not seek simply to reduce sciences such as psychology to physics. The computer model of the mind has been central to functionalism. Fodor, however, developed a more literal application of this model than other functionalists.

For Fodor, the value of the computer model lies in the light it sheds on reasoning, belief, planning and other intelligent thought-processes. (He does not see functionalism as a way of explaining the first-person 'feel' of experience.) Fodor claims that thinking is performing computational operations on mental representations. These inner representations form a system with many of the basic properties of a language, so the system can be called 'the language of thought' (Fodor 1975). This inner language is not identical to any public language, such as English. Rather, it is used in learning public languages. Thus the language of thought is innate (see LANGUAGE OF THOUGHT).

Fodor holds that to believe that limes contain

vitamin C, for example, is to have in one's head a certain sentence-like formula in the language of thought. A formula is a belief that limes contain vitamin C in virtue of both its internal causal role, which makes it a belief rather than a hope or desire, and also in virtue of connections to the external world, which determine its content. These formulas are made up of mental 'terms' with their own properties of meaning and reference. The terms combine to generate the truth-condition of the whole. There are also 'implicit' beliefs which follow trivially from the explicitly represented ones, but only explicitly represented beliefs contribute to thought processes.

Though the inner formulas have semantic properties, their causal contributions to thought depend only on their formal or 'syntactic' properties; these are the properties relevant in computational processes. Indeed, these semantic properties depend partly on the nature of the thinker's environment, and what is outside the head cannot directly affect the production of behaviour. None the less, Fodor insists that there are many psychological generalizations that are naturally and perhaps necessarily expressed in terms of the semantic content of thoughts.

For some time Fodor posited an inner code with representational properties, but did not have a theory of how such representation was possible. He has tried to solve this problem with his 'asymmetric dependence' theory of meaning (Fodor 1990). This is a variety of informational or indicator semantics, based on causal and law-like connections between thoughts and their objects (see SEMANTICS, INFORMATIONAL). We cannot simply say that whatever can cause a representational state is represented by that state, since then error would be impossible. Fodor's proposal is that an inner symbol 'horse' represents horses if occurrences of this symbol are reliably caused by horses, and the only other things that can cause occurrences of this symbol do so *because* of the connection between the 'horse' and horses.

These are the central elements of Fodor's view, but he has contributed to many other topics. He has defended the 'automomy' of higher-level sciences against reductionism (Fodor 1975). He has outlined a 'modular' view of mind, in which specialized and partially autonomous mental faculties are responsible for perception and some other features of cognition (Fodor 1983). Recently he has also attacked the holism influential in much twentieth-century epistemology and semantics (Fodor and LePore 1992; see HOLISM: MENTAL AND SEMANTIC; MODULARITY OF MIND).

2 Debates

Fodor's programme is so ambitious that nearly every aspect of his view has been controversial. Some have found the idea of an inner language to be either incoherent (as languages are essentially public) or empirically unmotivated. For others more sympathetic to the representationalist approach, Fodor has never resolved a tension between his stress on the 'syntactic' nature of mental processes, and his insistence on the importance of semantic properties in psychological explanation.

This problem is magnified by his acceptance of the view that the semantic properties of thought depend on factors external to the agent's body. For some years Fodor and others tried to develop a purified 'narrow' way of ascribing thoughts which would not distinguish physically identical agents who happen to inhabit different environments. More recently he has argued that there is no real problem here after all; intentional laws are 'implemented' in computational processes, and these are two distinct levels of description. For some, however, Fodor has never resolved this problem (Loewer and Rey 1991; see CONTENT: WIDE AND NARROW).

Another problem, which Fodor himself has explored, concerns learning (Fodor 1981). Psychologists have often seen various types of learning as hypothesis testing. Fodor adopts a realist interpretation of this view: such theories must posit internal representations of hypotheses and the evidence used to choose between them. But how then can new *concepts* be learned? To test hypotheses about the concept 'cigar' we must already be able to represent internally the various possibilities for its meaning. Consequently we cannot acquire genuinely new representational capacities from experience; all we can do is rearrange and rename concepts we already have. So the representational approach, in Fodor's hands, leads to a view in which much of what appears to be learning is actually nothing of the sort (see NATIVISM §3; CONCEPTS).

Fodor's 'asymmetric dependence' theory of meaning has not been widely accepted. (Loewer and Rey 1991). Some have raised problem cases, while others (like the present author) are more generally sceptical about the counterfactuals that Fodor's theory posits. Fodor says that the inner symbol 'horse' represents horses if it is reliably caused by the presence of horses, and other things only produce occurrences of the symbol because of the connection between the symbol and horses. This dependence is present-tense rather than historical. But why is it the connection between 'horse' and horses that explains the other connections? As a consequence of physical facts about the wiring connecting the symbol to the senses, some horses can cause occurrences of the symbol. These same facts explain why other objects, such as cows, sometimes cause occurrences of the symbol. The connection which explains the others is a connection between the symbol and a certain sensory appearance. If so, the connection between the symbol and horses is not fundamental in the way that Fodor claims. These debates are complex, however, and no naturalistic theory of meaning has generated wide acceptance.

For many years Fodor claimed that, with the demise of behaviourism, the computational, symbolic approach was the only genuine research programme we had for studying cognitive processes. Hence it was 'the only game in town' as a theory of the general nature of thought. The rise of connectionism during the 1980s partially undermined this claim. The connectionist model of thought is based upon parallel and simultaneous interactions, of a very simple nature, between neuron-like elements. Connectionism has closer links to the brain sciences than Fodor's more abstract approach, and it does not posit language-like inner symbols. Fodor has been an outspoken critic of connectionism (Fodor and Pylyshyn 1988), but there are now other games in town, and in this new context there is ongoing debate over the merits of the symbolic approach (see CONNECTIONISM).

List of works

Fodor, J.A. (1968) *Psychological Explanation*, New York: Random House. (Presents a functionalist view of mind and defends it against reductionism and behaviourism.)

—— (1975) *The Language of Thought*, New York: Thomas Crowell. (Probably Fodor's most influential book. Outlines and defends the hypothesis of a language of thought, utilizing both philosophical and psychological evidence with great ingenuity.)

—— (1981) *Representations*, Cambridge, MA: MIT Press. (Mostly a collection of reprinted articles, including 'Methodological Solipsism...', which influenced many discussions of 'narrow psychology'. Also includes Fodor's most detailed discussion of innate concepts.)

—— (1983) *The Modularity of Mind*, Cambridge: MIT Press. (An interdisciplinary work positing a range of specialized and partly independent mental faculties or 'modules' for certain cognitive tasks. Expresses pessimism about our chances of understanding mental capacities which do not have modules.)

—— (1984) 'Semantics, Wisconsin Style', *Synthèse* 58: 231–50. (An influential article outlining the problem that the asymmetric dependence theory was intended to solve.)

—— (1987) *Psychosemantics*, Cambridge, MA: MIT Press. (A systematic statement of Fodor's view of the mind. Defends common-sense 'folk psychology', introduces the asymmetric dependence theory, criticizes meaning-holism, and defends the language of thought.)

Fodor, J.A. and Pylyshyn, Z. (1988) 'Connectionism and Cognitive Architecture', *Cognition* 28: 3–71. (An attack on connectionism.)

Fodor, J.A. (1990) *A Theory of Content, and Other Essays*, Cambridge, MA: MIT Press. (Contains his most detailed discussion of the asymmetric dependence theory of meaning, also 'Semantics, Wisconsin Style' and various other articles.)

Fodor, J.A. and LePore, E. (1992) *Holism: A Shopper's Guide*, Cambridge, MA: MIT Press. (A criticism of holist positions in philosophy of mind, semantics and epistemology.)

Fodor, J.A. (1994) *The Elm and the Expert*, Cambridge, MA: MIT Press. (Attempts to reorient the debates about individualism and 'narrow psychology'.)

References and further reading

* Loewer, B. and Rey, G. (1991) *Meaning in Mind: Fodor and his Critics*, Oxford: Blackwell. (A collection of essays on Fodor's work, with replies by Fodor.)

Dennett, D.C. (1978) 'A Cure for the Common Code', in *Brainstorms*, Cambridge, MA: Bradford Books. (A critical notice of *The Language of Thought*.)

PETER GODFREY-SMITH

FOLK PSYCHOLOGY

There is wide disagreement about the meaning of ordinary mental terms (such as 'belief', 'desire', 'pain'). Sellars suggested that our use of these terms is governed by a widely shared theory, 'folk psychology', a suggestion that has gained empirical support in psychological studies of self-attribution and in a growing literature concerning how children acquire (or, in the case of autism, fail to acquire) ordinary mental concepts. Recently, there has been a lively debate about whether people actually 'theorize' about the mind, or, instead, engage in some kind of 'simulation' of mental processes.

Traditionally, it was thought that the meanings of mental terms such as 'thought', 'desire', 'pain' were provided by people's direct acquaintance with the 'inner' mental states to which these terms referred. This raised a number of puzzles: about how such inner states could interact with the outer, physical world, and about how anyone could ever know about the inner states of others given that they only observed their outer physical behaviour (see OTHER MINDS).

Under the influence of Ryle (1949) and Wittgenstein (1953), many philosophers have argued that this traditional picture of the 'inner' is an illusion and that the meaning of mental terms involves their use to describe publicly observable behavioural dispositions (see BEHAVIOURISM, ANALYTIC). Another suggestion is that the meaning of mental terms is provided by a theory that people unselfconsciously believe. This view was originally proposed by Wilfrid SELLARS (1956), but has come to play an increasingly influential role in both philosophy and psychology.

A central theme in Sellars' philosophy is a sustained attack on 'the myth of the given' – the idea that some of our beliefs or claims have a privileged epistemic status because the facts that make them true are given to us by experience. To counter the idea that our claims about our own mental states are underwritten by a special, introspective faculty that guarantees the truth of those claims, Sellars constructs an alternative story, which he presents as a 'myth' involving three stages: first, we go back to a time in prehistory when our ancestors used a 'Rylean language' whose descriptive vocabulary is restricted to terms for public properties of public objects located in space and enduring through time, with no terms for inner mental episodes (see RYLE, G.; PRIVACY; PRIVATE STATES AND LANGUAGE).

The second stage in the myth begins with the appearance of a genius named Jones who proposes a theory to account for the intelligent behaviour of his fellow humans. Sometimes, he notes, people explicitly state detailed arguments leading to a conclusion about what they should say or do. But most intelligent behaviour is not accompanied by any overt verbal behaviour. To account for these cases, Jones hypothesizes a process of 'inner speech' that is modelled on overt verbal behaviour, and that can lead to conclusions or action in much the same way that publicly stated arguments can. These inner episodes are what Jones calls 'thoughts'. At this stage of Sellars' myth, the theory is only applied to other people. But in the third stage Jones and his compatriots learn to apply the theory to themselves. At first they apply it to themselves in much the same way that they apply it to others. They infer various theoretical claims by attending to their own behaviour. Later, they discover a new way of applying the language of the theory to themselves. For it turns out that they can be trained to give reasonably reliable self-descriptions, using the language of the theory, without having to observe their own behaviour. At the conclusion of Sellars' myth, our ancestors begin to speak of the privileged access each of us has to his own thoughts. What began as a language with a purely theoretical use has gained a reporting role.

The important point about this myth is that, if it were true, we would talk just as we now do about inner mental states. But this talk would be both theoretical and fallible: indeed, folk psychology might turn out to be entirely false (see ELIMINATIVISM). Once we appreciate the point, the myth is irrelevant: Sellars has freed us from the uncritical introspectionism that was traditionally assumed.

Actually, Sellars' speculation has received some independent support, not only from 'language of thought' theories (see LANGUAGE OF THOUGHT), but also from recent psychological research on the topic of 'self-attribution'. In an influential article, Nisbett and Wilson (1977) reviewed a mass of experiments that seem to show that people's 'introspections' may often involve not so much any direct acquaintance, but rather the imposition upon themselves of the views of popular psychology (see INTROSPECTION, PSYCHOLOGY OF).

However, if there is a folk psychology, what are its principles? Asked to state them, most people would have no idea what to say. However, it is important to note that, while most of us have difficulty in articulating the principles of folk psychology, there are lots of common-sense psychological platitudes, such as 'People whose bodies are injured generally feel pain', that we immediately recognize as correct when they are proposed. Moreover, as CHOMSKY and his followers have argued in explaining our ability to understand natural language, people can 'tacitly' know elaborate rules that they might be unable to articulate or recognize. Perhaps much of our knowledge of the principles of folk psychology is tacit in the same way.

'Simulation theory' poses another objection to the idea that we rely on a theory when we attribute mental state terms to others. According to simulation theory, we attribute mental states to others by taking a part of our own psychological system 'off-line' and then pretending that we are in the situation of the other person. We then simply note the mental states that this exercise in imagination provokes in us, and attribute those states to the other person. Thus, simulation theorists maintain, there is no need for the hypothesis that people have knowledge of a rich set of folk psychological principles (see Gordon 1986).

References and further reading

Baron-Cohen, S. (1995) *Mindblindness*, Cambridge, MA: MIT Press. (A recent discussion of the links between autism and the failure to acquire folk psychology.)

Churchland, P.M. (1981) 'Eliminative Materialism and the Propositional Attitudes', *Journal of Philosophy* 78: 67–90. (A well-known defence of the eliminative materialist position.)

Fodor, J. (1987) *Psychosemantics*, Cambridge, MA: Bradford Books/ MIT Press. (Defends both the importance and the scientific viability of folk psychology.)

* Gordon, R. (1986) 'Folk Psychology as Simulation', *Mind and Language* 1: 158–71. (Suggests that our knowledge of another's mind is based not on theoretical inferences, but on 'simulating' what it would be like for ourselves to be in the other person's place.)

Nisbett, R. and Wilson, T. (1977) 'Telling More Than We Can Know: Verbal Reports on Mental Processes', *Psychological Review* 84 (3): 231–59. (Influential review of a large number of experiments that seem to show that people have much less introspective access to their minds than they suppose.)

* Ryle, G. (1949) *The Concept of Mind*, London: Hutchison. (Classic statement of the behavioural analyses of ordinary mental terms.)

* Sellars, W. (1956) 'Empiricism and the Philosophy of Mind', in *Science, Perception and Reality*, London and New York: Routledge & Kegan Paul, 1963, 127–96. (A detailed exposition of the myth of Jones and its implication.)

Stich, S. and Nichols, S. (1992) 'Folk Psychology: Simulation or Tacit Theory?', *Mind and Language* 7: 35–71. (An assessment of the debate between the simulation theory and the folk psychology hypotheses.)

Stich, S. and Ravenscroft, I. (1994) 'What Is Folk Psychology?', *Cognition* 50: 447–68. (Expansion of the material in this entry.)

* Wittgenstein, L. (1953) *Philosophical Investigations*, Oxford: Blackwell, esp. §§230–308. (An extremely influential attack on the idea that the meaning of mental terms involves reference to private inner states.)

STEPHEN P. STICH
GEORGES REY

FONSECA, PEDRO DA
(1528–99)

*Called in his own time 'the Portuguese Aristotle', Pedro da Fonseca was a sixteenth-century Jesuit philosopher and theologian. Schooled as a Thomist, Fonseca was a master of the Greek, Arabic and scholastic traditions, which enabled him to pursue his own independent line on various issues dealt with by Aquinas and Aristotle. As reflected in his publications, his chief accomplishments were in logic and metaphysics. He authored two very important and widely used works: a clear, comprehensive and systematic textbook in logic (*Institutionum dialecticarum*) and an edition of Aristotle's* Metaphysics *with translation plus explanation and commentary. A third shorter work of introduction to logic (*Isagoge philosophica*) was also influential.*

1   Life
2   Logic
3   Metaphysics

1   Life

Pedro da Fonseca (Petrus Fonseca) was born at Cortiçada (now Proença-a-Nova) in Portugal. He entered the Society of Jesus in 1548. After a period of noviciate, in 1551 he enrolled at the newly founded University of Évora, where between 1552 and 1555 he studied theology and also taught philosophy in 1552–3. From 1555 to 1561, he taught philosophy in the Jesuit-directed College of Arts at the University of Coimbra. During this last period, Fonseca promoted the idea of a *Cursus Conimbricensis* which later became a reality through the efforts of fellow Jesuits at Coimbra (see COLLEGIUM CONIMBRICENSE). From 1561 to 1564 he served the Jesuits in various administrative roles. In 1570 he received his doctorate in theology at Évora and became chancellor there. From 1572 to 1582 he served in Rome as general assistant for the Jesuit Province of Portugal. While in Rome, he worked with others on a 'Plan of Studies' (*Ratio studiorum*) which was later adopted by the Society of Jesus. Returning to Portugal in 1582, he became a Jesuit superior in Lisbon and then a visitor for the province. In 1592, he was again in Rome, a delegate to the fifth General Congregation of the Society, which among other things legislated that the Jesuits should follow Aristotle in philosophy. He died in Lisbon.

2   Logic

Fonseca's contribution to philosophy is in two main parts, logical and metaphysical. In logic, he authored two important works. The first was *Institutionum dialecticarum libri octo* (Eight Books of Dialectical Instructions). Published at Lisbon in 1564 and re-edited fifty-two more times by 1625, it was adopted as a textbook, especially by the Jesuits, throughout Europe, America and the Far East. The second work was a much shorter *Isagoge philosophica* (Philosophical Introduction), which was published initially in 1591 and re-edited eighteen times up to 1623. More than a simple commentary on the *Isagōgē* of PORPHYRY (§§2, 5), Fonseca's book was a new introduction to the Organon of ARISTOTLE (§4). After a brief preface and a proem, he devoted six chapters to a general treatment of universals, particulars and the abstraction of one from the other. Then over five chapters he treated the five universals (genus, species, difference, property and accident) of Porphyry. Finally, in Chapter 12 he treated 'certain other species of universals [connected with the logic of the Trinity and the Incarnation] which pagan philosophers did not know' (*Isagoge philosophica*: 61).

The *Institutionum dialecticarum* is a systematic presentation of Aristotelian formal logic. Book 1 consists of thirty-two chapters in which Fonseca treats successively of the necessity, the names and the nature of logic. He distinguishes it from dialectic as Aristotle speaks of this in his *Topics* and then goes on to discuss nouns, verbs and signs (formal and instrumental as well as natural and conventional). After discussion of concepts as signs, he treats terms as equivocal (including analogical) and univocal, concrete and abstract, connotative and absolute, common and singular, transcendent and supertranscendent, positive and negative, contradictory and non-contradictory, as well as of first and second intention, and so on. Book 2 concerns the universal and covers much of the same matter (for example, genus, species and so on) treated in his Isagoge, plus the ten categories of Aristotle. Book 3 deals with various types of proposition. Book 4 covers division and Book 5 treats of definition. Book 6 deals with consequence, argumentation, invention and judgment, syllogisms, enthymemes, and induction. Book 7 is concerned with demonstration, dialectical reasoning, 'places' (or seats of argument), teaching procedure and the art of disputation. Book 8 mainly concerns fallacies, but Fonseca also treats supposition, ampliation, restriction and appellation in detail. As for the Aristotelian character of the *Institutionum dialecticarum*, Ferreira Gomes ([1564] 1964: xlvi–xlvii) notes that in them Aristotle is cited 600 times and he quotes a 1597 editor to the effect that Fonseca's work covers the Aristotelian logic so well that it makes Aristotle's own work, apart from its historical value, almost useless (see LOGIC, RENAISSANCE).

3 Metaphysics

Comprising four quarto volumes, Fonseca's *In libros Metaphysicorum Aristotelis Stagiritae* (Commentary on the Books of Aristotle's *Metaphysics*) contains a critical Greek text which he himself established from the best available manuscripts and printed editions. Through the four volumes, in a right-hand column matching the Greek to the left, he has given a fine Latin translation. An explanation of the text follows each chapter and then commentary 'by way of question' (*per modum quaestionis*) on most of the chapters through the first nine books of the *Metaphysics*. Published posthumously, Books 10, 11, and 12 continue to give the Greek and Latin plus the explanation, while Books 13 and 14 give only the text in the two languages. The questions, which contain Fonseca's own thought on subjects metaphysical, were developed in scholastic fashion. After asking a particular question, Fonseca, through a series of 'sections', presents objections and opinions, clarifies terms and concepts, gives and proves his own answer, and then returns to answer the objections raised in support of other views. Extraordinarily well versed in the earlier Greek, Arabic and scholastic traditions, Fonseca wherever possible follows the lead of Aristotle and Thomas AQUINAS, but with a decided independence.

After rejecting opinions which hold that the subject of metaphysics is God, Aristotelian 'separate substances', or being in the categories, Fonseca says that the first and adequate subject of metaphysics is being in so far as it is common to God and creatures (*In libros Metaphysicorum* IV c.1 q.1 s.3). Understood in this way, being is analogous, although as said of species within one genus or of individuals within one species it is univocal. Between God and creatures, between created substance and accidents, between different classes of accident, and between real being and being of reason, being is analogous by analogies both of proportion and of attribution. As God is related to his being, so in proportion a created substance is related to its being. Likewise, as created substance and its being are related, so in proportion is an accident related to its being. Again, as one kind of accident is disposed to its existence so is each other kind of accident to its existence. And as real beings are disposed to their being, so beings of reason are to theirs (*Metaphysicorum* IV c.2 q.1 s.5, 7). An analogy of attribution obtains among accidents as an analogy of two things to a third (that is, created substance), while between accidents and substance it is analogy of one to the other. The same is true of beings of reason among themselves and then in comparison with real being; for beings of reason do not depend less upon

real beings than do accidents upon substance. Again, a creature is being only by attribution or reference to God. Pursuing this, Fonseca distinguishes between formal and objective concepts. A formal concept is an 'actual likeness' (*actualis similitudo*) of a thing that is understood, produced by the intellect in order to express that thing. An objective concept is that thing which is understood in so far as it is conceived through the formal concept. Both the formal and the objective concept of being are one, but not perfectly so for the reason that they do not prescind perfectly from the concepts of the members which divide being. Being as such is transcendent as are also the concepts of thing, something, one, true and good (*Metaphysicorum* IV c.2 q.2 s.1, 4–5; q.5 s.2) (see BEING).

In God alone there is a perfect identity of essence and existence. In every creature, essence is distinct from existence, but not as one thing from another. Rather, says Fonseca, a created essence is as distinct from its existence as a thing from its ultimate intrinsic mode. In this doctrine, he tells us, he is following ALEXANDER OF HALES and DUNS SCOTUS (§12) (*Metaphysicorum* IV c.2 q.3 s.4). It is possible that here Fonseca has also to some extent anticipated the Suárezian doctrine of modes.

Excluded from the subject of metaphysics are accidental beings (*entia per accidens*) and beings of reason. An accidental being, in the sense excluded, is a juxtaposition of two or more beings which lack any (intrinsic) relation to one another (*Metaphysicorum* IV c.1 q.1 s.3). Beings of reason are those which exist only inasmuch as they are objects of understanding. Within such beings of reason, as they stand in contrast with mind-independent real beings, Fonseca distinguishes a proper being of reason from one which is fictitious. Properly taken, a being of reason is one whose being depends upon the understanding in such way that it can still be said of real beings, for example, the concepts of genus, species, and the like. A fictitious being as such is a being whose essence depends upon the understanding in such way that it cannot be said of any real being, for example, a chimera, a goat-stag, or the like (*Metaphysicorum* IV c.7 q.6 s.5).

See also: ARISTOTELIANISM, RENAISSANCE; LANGUAGE, RENAISSANCE PHILOSOPHY OF; LOGIC, RENAISSANCE

List of works

Fonseca, P. da (1564) *Institutionum dialecticarum libri octo* (Eight Books of Dialectical Instructions), Coimbra, 1575; ed. and trans. J. Ferreira Gomes, *Pedro da Fonseca: Instituições dialécticas*, Coimbra: Universidade de Coimbra, 1964, 2 vols. (This edition of Fonseca's main logical work includes introduction, critical Latin text, notes and Portuguese translation. Ferreira Gomes' introduction lists the editions of this work and also those of the *Isagoge* and commentary on Aristotle's *Metaphysics*.)

—— (1591) *Isagoge philosophica* (Philosophical Introduction), Lisbon; ed. and trans. J. Ferreira Gomes, *Pedro da Fonseca. Isagoge filosófica*, Coimbra: Universidade de Coimbra, 1965. (Fonseca's introduction to Aristotelian logic; with introduction and Portuguese translation.)

—— (1615–29) *In libros Metaphysicorum Aristotelis Stagiritae. Tomi quatuor* (Four Books on Aristotle's *Metaphysics*), Coloniae; repr. Hildesheim: Olms, 1964. (Fonseca's Greek text of the *Metaphysics* with Latin translation, explanation and commentary. The complete text was published posthumously.)

References and further reading

Ashworth, E.J. (1974) *Language and Logic in the Post-Medieval Period*, Dordrecht and Boston, MA: Reidel. (A general study which includes discussion of Fonseca's logic.)

Ceñal, R. (1943) 'Pedro da Fonseca (1528–1599). Su crítica del Texto de la "Metaphysica" de Aristóteles' (His Textual Criticism of Aristotle's *Metaphysics*), *Revista de Filosof—a* 2 (4): 124–46. (Treats Fonseca as a textual critic of Aristotle's *Metaphysics*.)

Giacon, C. (1944) *La seconda scolastica* (The Second Scholasticism), Milan: Bocca, vol. 2, 31–66. (Fonseca treated, along with Toletus and Pereira, within the sixteenth-century revival of scholasticism.)

Lohr, C.H. (1987) *Latin Aristotle Commentaries. II Renaissance Authors*, Florence: Olschki, 150–1. (Contains bibliographical information on Fonseca.)

Risse, W. (1964) *Die Logik der Neuzeit* (The Logic of the Modern Period), Stuttgart and Bad Cannstatt: Frommann, vol. 1, 361–72. (Fonseca's logic treated within its historical context.)

Solana, M. (1940) *Historia de la filosofía española. Época del renacimiento (siglo XVI)* (History of Spanish Philosophy. The Time of the Renaissance (16th Century)), Madrid: Asociación Española para el Progreso de las Ciencias, vol. 3, 339–66. (A good introductory overview of Fonseca.)

JOHN P. DOYLE

FONSECA, PETRUS *see* FONSECA, PEDRO DA

FONTENELLE, BERNARD DE (1657–1757)

Despite his considerable historical importance and vast output of literary, critical and philosophical works, Fontenelle did not make original contributions to philosophy. He popularized a modern view of nature, and raised doubts about institutionalized religions and unexamined theistic beliefs. As a champion of science and secularization, Fontenelle was extremely influential; his Entretiens *(Conversations) of 1686 were quickly translated into many languages and became one of the basic texts of the early Enlightenment.*

1 Life and work
2 Philosophy of nature
3 Philosophy of religion

1 Life and work

Bernard Le Bovier ('Boyer') de Fontenelle was born in Rouen, France, and received a Jesuit education at the Collège de Bourbon. Early literary fame and the support of Pierre and Thomas Corneille, his uncles, gained him access to the intellectual and social circles of Paris. He was elected to the Académie Française in 1687 and became its perpetual secretary ten years later. He died in Paris shortly before his one-hundredth birthday.

Fontenelle wrote poems, tragedies, novels, comedies and libretti for operas (set to music by Jean-Baptiste Lully). The pieces written for the stage met with only moderate success. Apart from satires, dialogues and critical essays, he composed so-called 'lettres galantes' and maintained a far-reaching correspondence with the leading thinkers of his time.

As a historian of science, Fontenelle distinguished himself through his exhaustive report of the Academy's work since its inception, the *Histoire de l'Académie royale des sciences depuis 1666 jusqu'en 1699* (1720–33). Several multivolume sequels followed at regular intervals. Parallel to these chronicles, Fontenelle drafted almost seventy eulogies on deceased members, the *Éloges des académiciens* (1708, 1722 and following), reviewing and summarizing their achievements.

Interested in the infinitesimal calculus, Fontenelle wrote a preface to a work by d'Hôpital and an account of recent mathematical research, the *Élé-*

ments de la géometrie de l'infini (1727). In his philosophy of nature, Fontenelle defended theories developed by others instead of developing new ideas; in his philosophy of religion, he was a sceptic inspired by de Huet, Thomassin and Spinoza (see HUET, P.-D. §2; SPINOZA, B. DE §14). But as a popularizer and advocate, Fontenelle became an influential champion of science and secularization, and the leading pioneer of the early French Enlightenment.

2 Philosophy of nature

Fontenelle's most famous work is the 1686 *Entretiens sur la pluralité des mondes habités* (Conversations on the Plurality of the Inhabited Worlds). This popular account of astronomy and natural philosophy consists of five dialogues, to which a sixth dialogue was added in a revised edition of 1687. The conversations begin with the assertion that our planetary system is not the only one in the universe: there are others whose suns are the fixed stars. Earth and the planets revolve around the sun; the celestial motions are described by the Copernican model and explained by Cartesian vortices. The second dialogue touches on the corpuscular theory of light, an explanation of solar eclipses and the possibility of space flight, and turns into a discussion about the moon. An examination of lunar features reveals the moon to resemble Earth in significant respects. Considering this, Fontenelle speculates that Earth's satellite is inhabited. This claim is expanded in the third dialogue. The microscope reveals a compelling ubiquity of life even in the tiniest water droplet and on the smallest stone in our world. Since Earth and other heavenly bodies are alike in their appearances, we can treat them alike in what is not apparent as well, as long as evidence to the contrary is lacking. Operating with this strong principle of analogical reasoning, Fontenelle argues for the possibility of life on other worlds. The fourth and fifth dialogues are imaginative summaries of the current knowledge about planets and stars. The supplementary sixth dialogue contains an update of recent astronomical and geological discoveries and a reflection on probability and analogical reasoning.

What makes this work interesting is Fontenelle's persuasive presentation of an entirely modern world-view. Anthropocentrism is obsolete; humans do not reside at the centre of a small enclosed universe, but are just one among many possible civilizations in a boundless cosmic ocean in which worlds are scattered like so many islands. It is doubtful that humans are the pinnacle of creation; far more advanced beings may exist. Anthropomorphism fails to fathom how such extraterrestrials might look; the universe is too fertile and diverse for even the boldest imagination.

But despite its diversity, the cosmos is a well-ordered system: a principle of order generates a maximum of effects with a minimum of means. These means are mechanical and law-governed, and modern science can account for them. The *Entretiens* proved to be extremely influential in the European thought of the eighteenth century; Fontenelle's conception of nature was picked up by subsequent *philosophes* and even influenced Kant's cosmology.

Throughout his life, from the *Entretiens* to the *Lettre à Basnage de Beauval* (1699) to his last work, the *Théorie des tourbillons cartésiens* (1752), Fontenelle defended Cartesian vortices against the rise of Newton's universal gravitation. Since whirls of matter presuppose a medium, Fontenelle argued for the existence of a cosmic ether in which heavenly bodies move. Apart from that, however, Fontenelle did not feel much allegiance to Cartesianism. Whereas Descartes excluded teleology, Fontenelle emphasized purposive explanations of nature. Fontenelle rejected Malebranche's occasionalist interpretation of Descartes in the *Doutes sur le système physique des causes occasionelles* (1686b), favouring a physical influx model of causality (see OCCASIONALISM).

3 Philosophy of religion

On the surface, God seems to be an indispensable part of Fontenelle's universe, but it remains unclear what God is. Like Spinoza, Fontenelle subscribed to the idea that there is a fundamental conformity between the order of reason and the order of nature (see SPINOZA, B. DE §§5–6). This conformity permits humans to know nature but does not lead to knowledge of God. Like the Deists, in his correspondence with Leibniz (1701–4) Fontenelle took the principle of order to be immanent to nature: matter, not God, determines the laws of motion (see DEISM). The nature of God's existence cannot be known; at the very least, the Cartesian proofs do not work (*Sur l'existence de Dieu* 1724). Fontenelle remained evasive about these issues through fear of censorship and persecution. At any rate, the utopian society envisaged in the clandestine novel *Histoire des Ajaoiens* (c.1680, attributed to Fontenelle) is devoid of institutionalized monotheism, and instead embraces pantheism.

Continuing themes of Fontenelle's work were his impatience with superstition and his criticisms of religious credulity. He derided pagan superstition in the *Dialogues des morts* (1683), and in *La Comète* (1681), a comedy written after the appearance of Halley's comet in 1680, ridiculed the widespread belief that passing comets have negative effects. According to *De l'origine des fables* (1679, published 1724 as part of *Sur l'histoire*) and the *Histoire des oracles* (1686c), religions stem from an anthropological and a social source. Human imagination triggered by an ignorance of natural phenomena, and successful imposters exploiting human gullibility were the first causes of religious beliefs.

In the essay *Traité de la liberté de l'âme* (written 1700, seized and burnt on parliamentary order, republished anonymously in the 1743 collection *Nouvelles libertés de penser*), Fontenelle raised even more serious questions. Not only is God unknowable, not only do religions derive from human imagination, but it also appears that divine foreknowledge and human freedom are incompatible. Although Fontenelle makes an ostensible attempt at their reconciliation, the actual result of his examination is different: divine foreknowledge implies fatalism; human freedom is possible only without a prescient God.

See also: CLANDESTINE LITERATURE

List of works

Fontenelle, B. de (1742–6) *Oeuvres*, Paris: Brunet; repr. 1758–66, Amsterdam, 12 vols. (The first edition of collected works, published during Fontenelle's lifetime, originally in eleven volumes. The subsequent Amsterdam edition was augmented by an additional volume.)

—— (1818) *Oeuvres complètes*, ed. G.-B. Depping, Paris; repr. Geneva: Slatkine, 1968, 3 vols. (The second edition of Fontenelle's works; not complete, despite its title. Arranged by categories: science and mathematics in volume 1, philosophy and history in volume 2, poetry and fictional works in volume 3.)

—— (1989–) *Oeuvres complètes*, ed. A. Niderst, Paris: Arthème-Fayard, 7 vols. (The supposedly definitive edition. Fontenelle's works are arranged chronologically as well as topically.)

—— (1970) *The Achievement of Bernard Le Bovier de Fontenelle*, ed. L. Marsak, New York and London: Johnson Reprint Corporation. (The only English anthology of Fontenelle's works. Contains photographic reproductions of the first English editions of Fontenelle's *Plurality of Worlds* (London 1688) and *The History of Oracles* (London 1688). It also contains a new translation of the *Discourse Concerning the Ancients and the Moderns* and short selections from other works.)

—— (1679) *De l'origine des fables* (On the origin of myths), in *Oeuvres complètes* ed. G.-B. Depping, vol. 2; ed. A. Niderst, vol. 3. (An attack of religious superstitions in the form of a brief essay.)

—— (c.1680) *Histoire des Ajaoiens* (History of the Ajaoiens). (Novel with antireligious overtones, the fictional account of a benevolent and atheist society.)

—— (1681) *La Cométe* (The comet), in *Oeuvres complètes* ed. G.-B. Depping, vol. 3; ed. A. Niderst, vol. 4. (Comedy written after the appearance of Halley's Comet in 1680.)

—— (1683) *Dialogues des morts anciens et modernes* (Dialogues of the dead in antiquity and modernity), in *Oeuvres complètes*, ed. G.-B. Depping, vol. 2. (Thirty fictional dialogues, some among ancient figures, such as Anacreon and Aristotle, others between ancients and moderns, such as Socrates and Montaigne, and again others among moderns, such as Cortez and Montezuma.)

—— (1686a) *Entretiens sur la pluralité des mondes habités*, in *Oeuvres complètes*, ed. G.-B. Depping, vol. 2; trans. H. Hargreaves, *Conversations on the Plurality of Worlds*, Berkeley and Los Angeles, CA: University of California Press, 1990. (Fontenelle's main work, which has appeared in almost one hundred editions since its first publication. The 1990 translation contains an introduction by N.R. Gelbart.)

—— (1686b) *Doutes sur le système physique des causes occasionelles* (Doubts on the physical system of the occasional causes), in *Oeuvres complètes*, ed. G.-B. Depping, vol. 1; ed. A. Niderst, vol. 1. (Philosophical treatise; a defence of Cartesianism and a critique of Malebranche and Arnauld.)

—— (1686c) *Histoire des oracles* (History of oracles), in *Oeuvres complètes*, ed. G.-B. Depping, vol. 2; ed. A. Niderst, vol. 2. (One of Fontenelle's main works in the philosophy of religion. Consists of two parts, 'That Oracles were not at all given by demons', and 'That Oracles did not cease to exist at the coming of Jesus Christ'. A characteristic work of the early French Enlightenment and a sequel to *De l'origine des fables*.)

—— (1699) *Lettre de M. Fontenelle à M. Basnage de Beauval* (Letter from Fontenelle to Basnage de Beauval), in *Oeuvres complètes*, ed. A. Niderst, vol. 3. (Fontenelle defends himself against the critic of Entretiens, and insists that the sun rotates around its own axis. Both observational and theoretical evidence support the hypothesis of solar rotation: the movement of the sun spots and the fact that the vortical centre of a revolving cosmic liquid cannot remain at rest.)

—— (1700) *Traité de la liberté de l'âme* (Treatise on the freedom of the soul), in *Oeuvres complètes*, ed. G.-B. Depping, vol. 2; ed. A. Niderst, vol. 3. (Short philosophical essay, published anonymously, involving implicit objections to Church doctrine.)

—— (1701–4) 'Correspondence with Leibniz', in *Oeuvres complètes*, ed. A. Niderst, vol. 3. (An exchange of eleven letters touching on astronomy, chemistry, the composition of fire, mathematics, Leibniz's *Essai de Science Numerique* and Fontenelle's own works.)

—— (1708, 1722–) *Éloges des académiciens* (Eulogies of the Members of the Academy), in *Oeuvres complètes*, ed. G.-B. Depping, vol. 1. (Fontenelle eulogized sixty-nine Academicians, among them Bernoulli, Boerhaave, d'Hôpital, Leibniz, Malebranche, Newton and Tschirnhaus.)

—— (1720–33) *Histoire de l'Academie royale des sciences depuis 1666 jusqu'en 1699* (History of the Royal Academy of Sciences from 1666 to 1699). (A multivolume work published in Paris 1720–33. Fontenelle explains the research and discoveries of the new generation of scientists and natural philosophers in a non-technical language. The preface to the *Histoire* is reprinted in Depping, volume 1.)

—— (1724) 'Sur l'existence de Dieu' (On the existence of God), in *Oeuvres complètes*, ed. A. Niderst, vol. 3. (A short philosophical essay. It is unlikely that matter caused life and thus, the existence of life suggests that God exists. None the less, metaphysical proofs of God's existence aspiring to certitude, such as the argument from design, are problematic.)

—— (1727) *Éléments de la géométrie de l'infini* (Elements of the geometry of the infinite), in *Oeuvres complètes*, ed. G.-B. Depping, vol. 1; repr. Paris: Editions Klincksieck, 1995. (Book-length treatise on the philosophy of mathematics that contains a systematic theory of the infinite. The 1995 edition is a photographic reproduction of the 1727 text, with Fontenelle's responses to objections; also has new introduction by M. Blay and A. Niderst.)

—— (1752) *Théorie des tourbillons cartésiens* (A Cartesian Vortex Theory), in *Oeuvres complètes*, ed. G.-B. Depping, vol. 1. (A longer philosophical treatise. Fontenelle's defence of the Cartesian vortices involves general reflections on physics, an attempt at coming to terms with Descartes' theory, and arguments to support a solar vortex and the ethereal atmosphere enveloping celestial objects.)

References and further reading

Carré, J.-R. (1932) *La Philosophie de Fontenelle ou le sourire de la raison*, Paris: F. Alcan; repr. Geneva: Slatkine, 1970. (A general survey of Fontenelle's views.)

Ekstein, N. (1996) 'Appropriation and Gender: the Case of Catherine Bernard and Bernard de Fontenelle', *Eighteenth Century Studies* 30: 59–81. (A historical-feminist study: no philosophical content. The author argues that Fontenelle's tragedy *Brutus*, as well as certain other plays, was not written by the author alone, but in collaboration with Catherine Bernard.)

Fayol, A. (1961) *Fontenelle*, Paris: Debresse. (A readable but superficial essay.)

Grégoire, F. (1947) *Fontenelle, une 'philosophie' désabusée*, Paris: J. Vrin. (A study emphasizing Fontenelle's philosophy of nature.)

Howells, R. (1992) 'The principle of mobility in Fontanelle's 'Entretiens sur [*sic*] la Pluralité des Mondes", *French Studies* 46: 129–44. (A literary-interpretative study; no philosophical content. The author investigates how the multiplicity of points of view contained in the *Entretiens* can be subsumed under the heading of mobility.)

James, ED. (1990) 'Fontenelle's *Entretiens sur la pluralité des mondes* and their Intellectual Context', in *Actes de Columbus Racine; Fontenelle: 'Entretiens sur la pluralité des mondes', histoire et littérature: actes du XXI Colloque de la North American Society for Seventeenth-Century French Literature*, Paris: Papers on French Seventeenth Century Literature, 133–47. (A careful account of the background of the *Entretiens*.)

Maigron, L. (1906) Fontenelle, l'homme, l'oeuvre, l'influence, Paris: Librairie Plon. (The earliest and standard monograph on Fontenelle.)

Niderst, A. (1972) *Fontenelle. A la recherche de lui-même (1657–1702)*, Paris: Nizet. (A well-researched study of the early Fontenelle and his intellectual growth.)

—— (1989) *Fontenelle. Actes du colloque tenu à Rouen du 6 au 10 octobre 1987*, Paris: Presses universitaires. (A useful compendium of the results of recent research on Fontenelle's philosophy.)

MARTIN SCHÖNFELD

FORCE, ILLOCUTIONARY
see PRAGMATICS; SPEECH ACTS

FORCING

The method of forcing was introduced by Paul J. Cohen in order to prove the independence of the axiom of choice (AC) from the basic (ZF) axioms of set theory, and of the continuum hypothesis (CH) from the accepted axioms (ZFC = ZF + AC) of set theory (see SET THEORY, AXIOM OF CHOICE, CONTINUUM HYPOTHESIS*). Given a model M of ZF and a certain*

$P \in M$, it produces a 'generic' $G \subseteq P$ and a model N of ZF with $M \subseteq N$ and $G \in N$. By suitably choosing P, N can be 'forced' to be or not be a model of various hypotheses, which are thus shown to be consistent with or independent of the axioms. This method of proving undecidability has been very widely applied. The method has also motivated the proposal of new so-called forcing axioms to decide what is otherwise undecidable, the most important being that called Martin's axiom (MA).

1   The method: three basic lemmas

Let M be a countable transitive model of ZFC (see SET THEORY §7, terminology and notation from which will be used throughout). Let $P \in M$. Then $p, q \in P$ are called compatible if there is an $r \in P$ with $p \subseteq r$ and $q \subseteq r$. $D \subseteq P$ is dense if it is nonempty and for every $p \in P$ there exists a $q \in D$ with $p \subseteq q$. If F is a set of dense sets, G is generic for F if: (1) $q \in G$ whenever $q \subseteq p$ and $p \in P$, (2) any $p, q \in G$ are compatible, and (3) for any $D \in F$, $G \cap D \neq \emptyset$. G is generic for M if G is generic for $F = \{D \subseteq P \mid D \text{ dense}$ and $D \in M\}$ (which appears uncountable to M but is really countable). If $F = \{D_0, D_1, D_2, \ldots\}$ is countable, choosing $p_0 \subseteq p_1 \subseteq p_2 \subseteq \ldots$ with $p_k \in D_k$, as is possible since each D_k is dense, $G = \{q \in P \mid q \subseteq p_k$ for some $k \in \omega\}$ is generic. A generic G generally cannot be an element of M.

For example, let P be the set of all functions p with domain a finite subset of ω and range a subset of 2. (Recall that an ordinal is identical with the set lesser ordinals, so $2 = \{0, 1\}$, $\omega = \{0, 1, 2, \ldots\}$.) Then p, q are compatible unless they 'disagree' in the sense that there is an $n \in \text{dom}(p) \cap \text{dom}(q)$ with $p(n) \neq q(n)$. For each $n \in \omega$, $D_n = \{p \in P \mid n \in \text{dom}(p)\}$ is dense, since any function p not already defined on n can be extended to a function q that is. Likewise, for any function $f \in M$ from ω to 2, $D_f = \{p \in P \mid p(n) \neq f(n)\}$ is dense, since any function p with a finite domain that does not already disagree with f can be extended to a function q that does. In the example, if all the $D_n, D_f \in F$ for all n and f as above, then $g = \cup G$ will be a function g from ω to 2 disagreeing with each $f \in M$. Hence $g \notin M$.

Cohen's method associates to any given countable transitive model M of ZFC, and any given $P \in M$, and any given $G \subseteq P$ generic for M another countable transitive model $N = M[G]$ of ZFC, with $M \subseteq M[G]$

and $G \in M[G]$, in such a way that three basic lemmas stated below hold. For various choices of P the three basic lemmas can be used to show that $M[G]$ will be a model of various hypotheses Δ. Before stating the three basic lemmas it should be remarked that the best way to gain an intuitive understanding of their rather technical content is to see how they are used in applications (as in §§2,3).

Minimality lemma The $b \subseteq M$ with $b \in M[G]$ will be precisely those $b \subseteq M$ of the form $\delta_G(c) = \{x \mid (p, x) \in c$ for some $p \in G\}$ for some $c \in M$. Note that such a $\delta(c)$ would certainly have to belong to *any* countable transitive model N with $M \subseteq N$ and $G \subseteq N$. It is sometimes said that while M cannot 'know' about which p will get into G or about which $b \subseteq M$ will get into $M[G] - M$ (since G and such b simply do not exist in M), M does contain 'codes' c for such b, which can immediately be 'decoded' by δ_G once G is given. Especially important are the *canonical* code $x^{\#} = P \otimes x$ for any $x \in M$, and the *canonical* code $\Gamma = \{(p, p) \mid p \in P\}$ for the generic set. It is fairly easily checked that for any generic G, $\delta_G(x^{\#}) = x$ and $\delta_G(\Gamma) = G$.

Truth lemma If $\Phi(\delta_G(a), \delta_G(b), \ldots)$ holds inside $M[G]$, then there is some $p \in G$ such that $\Phi(\delta_H(a), \delta_H(b), \ldots)$ holds inside $M[H]$ for *any* H generic for M with $p \in H$. Such a p is said to *force* $\Phi(a, b, \ldots)$ over M.

Definability lemma To every formula Φ there may be associated a formula $\Phi^{\dagger}$ such that given any $p \in P$ and any $a, b, \ldots \in M$, then $\Phi^{\dagger}(p, a, b, \ldots)$ holds in M if and only if p forces $\Phi(a, b, \ldots)$ over M. Note that it follows, by the axiom of separation, that for any set A that is an element of M, the set $\{(p, a, b, \ldots) \mid u, v, \in A$ and p forces $\Phi(a, b, \ldots)\}$ is an element of M. It is sometimes said that though M cannot 'know' which p will get into G or whether a given Φ will come to hold in $M[G]$, at least Φ will come to hold in $M[G]$ only if it is forced to hold by some p that gets into G, and M 'knows' which p will, if they get into G, force Φ to hold in $M[G]$.

2   Application to the continuum hypothesis

To treat CH, let now ξ, η be the ordinals inside M that appear to M to be ω_1, ω_2 (really, they are, like M itself, countable), and vary the example of §1 by letting P be the set of all functions p with domain a finite subset of $\eta \otimes \omega$ and range a subset of 2. If G is generic, $g = \cup G$ will be a function from $\eta \otimes \omega$ to 2, and there will be functions g_ρ from ω to 2 for $\rho < \eta$, given by $g_\rho(n) = g(\rho, n)$. Since for distinct $\rho, \sigma < \eta$, $D_{\rho,\sigma} = \{p \in P \mid (\rho, n), (\sigma, n) \in \text{dom}(p)$ and $p(\rho n) \neq p(\sigma n)\}$ is dense, these functions will be distinct not only from any function in M, but from each other.

So ~CH will hold inside $M[G]$ provided ξ, η still appear to $M[G]$ to be ω_1, ω_2.

The proviso means there is no function e or f in $M[G]$ with dom $(e) = \omega$, $\xi \subseteq \mathrm{ran}(e)$ or $\mathrm{dom}(f) = \xi$, $\eta \subseteq \mathrm{ran}(f)$. Cohen showed that for this it suffices that P should appear to M to have a certain property, the *countable chain condition* (CCC). Here an *antichain* is an $A \subseteq P$ such that p, q are incompatible for any two $p, q \in A$, and CCC is the property that any antichain is countable. (It ought logically to be called the '*no* countable *anti*chain condition', but the illogical terminology is well established.) To sketch why this suffices to rule out the existence of an e as above (the case of an f as above being similar), suppose $e \in M[G]$ is a function with $\mathrm{dom}(e) \subseteq \omega$.

By the minimality lemma, $e = \delta_G(c) \in M$ for some $c \in M$. By the truth lemma there is a $p_0 \in G$ forcing 'c is a function with $\mathrm{dom}(c) = \omega^{\#}$ and $\xi^{\#} \subseteq \mathrm{ran}(c)$', and by restricting attention to those $p \in P$ such that $p_0 \subseteq P$, we may suppose that every $p \in P$ forces this. By the definability lemma $E = \{(p, n, \rho) \in P \otimes \omega \otimes \xi \mid p$ forces 'the value of function c for argument $n^{\#}$ is ρ'$\} \in M$.

Now consider how things appear inside M, where P appears CCC. For each $n \in \omega$ let $C_n = \{\rho < \xi \mid (p, n, \rho) \in E$ for some $p \in P\}$, and let $C = \cup\{C_0, C_1, C_2, \ldots\}$. Intuitively, C_n is the set of 'candidates' to become the output of the function for input n, while C is the set of 'candidates' to belong to the range of the function. For each $n \in \omega$ and $\rho \in C_n$ choose a $p(n, \rho)$ with $(p(n, \rho), n, \rho) \in E$, and let $A_n = \{p(n, \rho) \mid \rho \in C_n\}$. Note that if (p, n, ρ), $(q, n, \sigma) \in E$ and $\rho \neq \sigma$, then p, q are incompatible (since they force things which cannot both hold in $M[G]$ for any G). Hence any two elements of any A_n are incompatible. By CCC, each A_n, hence each C_n and hence C are all countable. Since $\xi = \omega_1$ (or so it appears inside M), C is bounded by some $\sigma < \xi$. Back outside M this means that $e = \delta_G(c)$ will be a function with $\mathrm{ran}(e) \subseteq \sigma < \xi$, contrary to assumption that $\mathrm{ran}(e) = \xi$.

To show that the set of functions p with domain a finite subset of $\omega_2 \otimes \omega$ and range a subset of 2 (which set is what P appears inside M to be) is CCC, the *delta system theorem* from combinatorial set theory is used (see SET THEORY §4): given an uncountable set A of incompatible elements of P, there must be a finite b and an uncountable $B \subseteq A$ such that $\mathrm{dom}(p) \cap \mathrm{dom}(q) = b$ for all $p, q \in B$. Thus the restrictions of the $p \in B$ to b give uncountably many distinct functions from b to 2. But if k be the number of elements in b, the number of such functions is just 2^k, which is finite, a contradiction.

3 Other applications

Among many other uses of the method of forcing, the following may be cited: If CH fails, the number of cardinals between $\aleph_0$ and $\mathbf{c}$ can be almost anything from one (hypothesis CH') to $\mathbf{c}$ (hypothesis CH$^{\#}$). Moreover, as regards the function $\exp \alpha = 2^{\alpha}$, all kinds of combinations are possible: One can have $\exp \aleph_0 = \exp \aleph_1 = \aleph_2$, or one can have $\exp \aleph_0 = \aleph_2$ and $\exp \aleph_1 = \aleph_3$, and so on.

Cohen himself proved the independence of AC from ZF, combining forcing with an earlier construction used to prove independence of AC from a variant of ZF allowing 'individuals'. Indeed, Cohen's proof established the independence of the weaker axiom of dependent choice DC. The independence of AC from ZF+DC can similarly be established. Indeed, a whole range of implications of AC have been studied and questions as to which imply which and which are independent of which have been settled.

Many undecidability results have also been obtained by forcing in combinatorial set (see SET THEORY §4). For instance, any combination of CH or ~CH with SH or ~SH is consistent, where SH is Suslin's hypothesis.

Many undecidability results have also been obtained by forcing in the related areas of descriptive set theory and large cardinal theory (see SET THEORY §§5,7). In particular, adding the hypotheses IC, MC, ... of the existence of inaccessible, measurable, ... cardinals to ZFC does not decide CH (or SH or any other such combinatorial hypothesis).

As for the hypothesis AM (resp. PM) that all (resp. all projective) sets of reals are Lebesgue measurable, in a noteworthy early extension of Cohen's work, Robert Solovay established consistency relative to ZF+IC for DC+AM and AC+PM. (Also projective uniformization PU fails in one of the models involved.) For the related hypothesis RM (resp. RSM) that there is a measure with all the properties of Lebesgue measure except invariance (resp. with all the properties of Lebesgue measure except invariance, plus superadditivity), Solovay proved the consistency of RSM (which is known to imply CH$^{\#}$) relative to ZFC+MC, and of MC relative to ZFC+RM (which is known to imply ~CH and ~CH').

In many applications, it is convenient to work with a generalization of the notions of §1: one starts with an arbitrary set P and an arbitrary partial order $\leqslant$ on it, and defines p, q to be compatible if there is an $r \in P$ with $p \leqslant r$ and $q \leqslant r$, $D \subseteq P$ to be dense if it is nonempty and for every $p \in P$ there exists a $q \in D$ with $p \leqslant q$, and so on. In §1 only the special case where $\leqslant$ is the subset relation $\subseteq$ was considered, but the general case easily reduces to this special case,

695

since setting $[p] = \{r \in P \mid r \leqslant p\}$ one has $[p] \subseteq [q]$ if and only if $p \leqslant q$.

4 Martin's axiom

D.A. Martin and Solovay, by a method involving reduction of several successive applications of forcing by $P \in M$, $Q \in M[G]$, $R \in M[G][H] \ldots$ to a single application, showed the consistency with ~CH (indeed with CH′) of a consequence of CH called *Martin's axiom* (MA). MA is the most basic example of a *forcing axiom*, asserting that anything of a certain kind that could be forced to hold already does hold. MA asserts that for any P that is CCC and any set F of fewer than continuum many ($< \mathbf{c}$) dense subsets of P, there exists a G generic for F. (Assuming CH, $< \mathbf{c}$ amounts to $\leqslant \aleph_0$, and the existence of G in this case was essentially proved in §1.)

To give at least one example, consider the usual order on the reals $\mathbf{R}$ (as in SET THEORY, end of §4, beginning of §5): $S \subseteq \mathbf{R}$ is *open dense* if for every rational a, c with $a < c$ there are rational d, e with $a \leqslant d < e \leqslant c$ such that $b \in S$ for every real b with $d \leqslant b \leqslant e$. It is easily proved that the intersection of finitely many open dense sets is open dense and hence not empty. It is an important theorem of modern analysis and topology that the intersection of countably many open dense sets is not empty. It is an interesting consequence of MA that an intersection of fewer than continuum many open dense sets is not empty.

To derive this consequence, let X be a set of fewer than continuum many open dense sets, to prove $\cap X \neq \emptyset$. Consider the set P of triples (a, c, Y) where $Y \subseteq X$ is finite, where a, c are rational with $a < c$, and where $b \in \cap Y$ for every real b with $a \leqslant b \leqslant c$. Consider the partial order on P given by $(a, c, Y) \leqslant (d, e, Z)$ if and only if $Y \subseteq Z$ and $a \leqslant d < e \leqslant c$. Then (a, c, Y) and (a', c', Y') are compatible if and only if $\max(a, a') < \min(c, c')$. For then letting $Z = Y \cup Y'$, using the fact that $\cap Z$ is open dense, there are rational d, e with $\max(a, a') \leqslant d < e \leqslant \min(c, c')$ such that $b \in \cap Z$ for every real b with $d \leqslant b \leqslant e$, and so $(a, c, Y), (a', c', Y') \leqslant (d, e, Z)$.

In particular, (a, c, Y) and (a', c', Y') are always compatible if $d = d'$ and $e = e'$, and since there are only countably many possibilities for d, e, any set of pairwise incompatible elements of P must be countable, and the partial order is CCC. Also, for any $(a, c, Y) \in P$ and any $S \in X$, letting $Z = Y \cup \{S\}$ and using the fact that $\cap Z$ is open dense, there are rational d, e with $a \leqslant d < e \leqslant c$ such that $b \in \cap Z$ for all real b with $d \leqslant b \leqslant e$, and so $(a, c, Y) \subseteq (d, e, Z)$ and $S \in Z$. Thus for each $S \in X$ the set $Q_S = \{(d, e, Z) \mid S \in Z\}$

is dense in P. A similar argument shows that for each $n = 1, 2, 3, \ldots$, the set $R_n = \{(d, e, Z) \mid d - e < 1/n\}$ is dense in P. Applying MA, there is a $G \subseteq P$ generic for $\{Q_S \mid S \in X\} \cup \{R_n \mid n = 1, 2, 3, \ldots\}$.

Let α be the least upper bound of $\{a \mid (a, c, Y) \in G$ for some $c, Y\}$ and let γ be the greatest lower bound of $\{c \mid (a, c, Y) \in G$ for some $a, Y\}$. Since any elements $(a, c, Y), (a', c', Y') \in G$ are compatible, and so have $\max(a, a') < \min(c, c')$, one has $\alpha \leqslant \gamma$. For any n there is an $(a, c, Y) \in G \cap R_n$, whence $(\alpha - \gamma) \leqslant (a - c) < 1/n$, and since this holds for all $n = 1, 2, 3, \ldots$, one has $\alpha = \gamma$. For any $S \in X$ there is an $(a, c, Y) \in G \cap Q_s$, and since $a \leqslant \alpha \leqslant \gamma$ one has $\alpha \in S$, and since this holds for all $S \in X$, one has $\alpha \in \cap X$, completing the proof.

Of the most interesting consequences of CH, about half follow from MA alone, about half are refutable assuming MA+~CH, which also has other interesting consequences (Σ_2^1-measurability, SH). By contrast, ~CH by itself has few interesting consequences. MA+~CH thus provides a rather attractive alternative to CH, though there is no generalization of MA+~CH to higher cardinals comparable to the generalized continuum hypothesis (GCH) generalizing CH. Saharon Shelah has introduced forcing axioms considerably strengthening MA+~CH and implying CH′.

5 On the proofs of the three basic lemmas

Only the briefest sketch of the highly technical proofs of the three main lemmas may be given here. It cannot be emphasized strongly enough that the best way to gain an intuitive understanding of the three main lemmas is to see how they are used in applications (as in §§2,3), which hardly ever refer back to details of their proofs.

First, while the notion of coding given in §1 is that generally needed in applications, for the proofs a different notion of coding is needed, one providing codes for *all* elements of M[G] and not just for those that are subsets of M. Correspondingly, a different notion of decoding is needed: $\delta_G(c) = \{\delta_G(b) \mid (p, b) \in c$ for some $p \in G\}$. This definition appears circular but is really an instance of a legitimate method of definition of operations on sets by $\in$-recursion, a generalization of the method of definition of operations on ordinals by $<$-recursion (or transfinite recursion, as in SET THEORY §4): As an operation on ordinals may be defined by defining its value for ρ in terms of its values for $\sigma < \rho$, so an operation on sets may be defined by defining its value for c in terms of its values for $b \in c$. With this alternate definition of decoding, M[G] is simply defined to be

$\{\delta_G(c) \mid c \in M\}$, and to establish the minimality lemma what remains to be proved is that M[G] so defined is a model of ZFC. To prove this, one makes heavy use of various necessary and sufficient conditions for being a model of this or that axiom of set theory (see SET THEORY §7). For instance, to handle the axiom of pairing, one must show that M[G] is closed under the operation of pairing: One must show that if $a, b \in M$, then there is a $c \in M$ such that $\delta_G(c) = \{\delta_G(a), \delta_G(b)\}$. In this case it is easily checked that the required c is provided by $P \otimes \{a, b\}$.

Second, while the definition of forcing given in §1 is that generally needed in applications, for the proofs a different definition is needed initially, though the two definitions will be proved equivalent *eventually*. This alternate definition of p forces Φ is by induction on the complexity of the formula Φ: (i) p forces 'not Φ' if and only if no q with $p \subseteq q$ forces Φ; (ii) p forces 'Φ and Ψ' if and only if p forces Φ and p forces Ψ; (iii) p forces 'for all x, $\Phi(x)$' if and only if for all c, p forces $\Phi(c)$; and so on. What is most difficult is to define p forces Φ for the *simplest* formulas '$c = d$' and '$c \in d$': The definition for these simplest formulas requires a highly technical $\in$-recursion. With the alternate definition of forcing, the definability lemma is almost immediate.

Towards establishing the truth lemma, and with it the equivalence of the alternate definition of forcing to the definition given in §1, one notes that it follows from clause (i) of the alternate definition of forcing that the set $D = \{p \mid p \text{ forces } \Phi \text{ or } p \text{ forces } \sim\Phi\}$ is dense, and it follows from the definability lemma that $D \in M$. Hence for any generic G there will be a $p \in G \cap D$. What remains to be proved is that if $p \in G$ and p forces $\Phi(a, b, \ldots)$, then $\Phi(\delta_G(a), \delta_G(b), \ldots)$ holds in M[G]. This is proved by induction on the complexity of the formula Φ.

See also: LOGICAL AND MATHEMATICAL TERMS, GLOSSARY OF

References and further reading

Burgess, J. (1977) 'Forcing', in K.J. Barwise (ed.) *Handbook of Mathematical Logic*, Amsterdam: North Holland, 403–52. (A survey in a standard reference, derived from lectures of Solovay and emphasizing consistency proofs for combinatorial principles.)

Cohen, P.J. (1966) *Set Theory and the Continuum Hypothesis*, New York: Benjamin. (The original source for forcing, now mainly of historical interest, having been superseded in technical aspects by later, streamlined treatments.)

Jech, T. (1978) *Set Theory*, New York: Academic Press. (A comprehensive treatise, covering the applications mentioned and many more besides, with attributions to their original authors and references to the original technical literature.)

—— (1986) *Multiple Forcing*, Cambridge: Cambridge University Press. (A semi-popular account of the forbiddingly technical work of Shelah.)

Martin, D.A. and Solovay, R. (1970) 'Internal Cohen Extensions', *Annals of Mathematical Logic* 2: 143–78. (The original, and a highly readable, source for Martin's axiom.)

JOHN P. BURGESS

FOREKNOWLEDGE

see OMNISCIENCE

FORGERY, ARTISTIC

see ARTISTIC FORGERY

FORGIVENESS AND MERCY

Forgiveness and mercy are regarded as virtues in many moral and religious traditions, although different traditions will emphasize different aspects. The Christian tradition, for example, tends to emphasize purity of heart as the core of the virtue of forgiveness, whereas the Judaic tradition gives priority to the social dimension of reintegration into the covenanted community. Forgiveness involves the overcoming of anger and resentment, and mercy involves the withholding of harsh treatment that one has a right to inflict. Both allow for healing, but some critics would say that this healing may come at too high a price. Forgiveness, if carried to extremes, can lapse into servility, entailing a loss of self-respect. There are similar paradoxes associated with mercy, particularly in the context of punishment; too strong an emphasis on mercy can lead to a departure from justice. Clearly, though both forgiveness and mercy are obvious virtues, there are difficulties in putting them into practice in the complex situations that make up everyday reality.

1   **Forgiveness and mercy analysed**
2   **Forgiveness and self-respect**
3   **Mercy and justice**

1 Forgiveness and mercy analysed

Forgiveness and mercy are typically regarded as virtues. As virtues, they represent moral demands that may not be satisfied by actions alone, but require certain motives or dispositions of character. Obligations are different; the obligation to keep a promise has been discharged when the promise is kept, whatever the motive. The virtue of mercy is not manifested merely in an act of leniency, however, but only if that act flows from a character motivated by compassion or some other appropriate motive (love of God, perhaps). The forgiving or merciful person will typically respond to others in characteristic ways, of course, and the person receiving the response might well claim to have been forgiven or shown mercy. Ordinary language is not always precise here. What has been done exemplifies a virtue, however, only if it is the product of a merciful or forgiving heart.

With respect to forgiveness, the disposition of heart may be all that is required. Bishop Butler, one of the most insightful of all philosophical writers on forgiveness, characterized the forgiving person simply as one who has, on moral or religious grounds, forsworn resentment – forsworn the very personal response of anger or sometimes even hatred that one naturally (and perhaps properly) initially feels when one believes that one has been wronged by another. The person who no longer resents will obviously avoid certain actions – namely, those without any basis other than resentment. Since grounds other than resentment may be the basis for harsh treatment of a wrongdoer, however, the demand for harsh treatment may well survive even a sincere and complete act of forgiveness. It would be consistent, for example, for a rape victim to forgive the person who has assaulted her – to harbour no resentment at all – but still demand that he be legally punished. She might make this demand not because of any residual anger or hatred that she personally feels, but rather because she believes that punishment (for reasons of crime control, perhaps) is a socially necessary response to such serious rights violations. The person truly manifesting the virtue of forgiveness is not to be confused with the unvirtuous person who is indifferent to or complicitous in wrongdoing, and who is willing to cooperate in the further corruption of the wrongdoer or of the life of the community.

Although a good case can be made that forgiveness may be understood solely in terms of such internal dispositions as the forswearing of resentment, mercy seems different in at least two important ways: first, the person in a position to bestow mercy (for example, a judge) need not have been personally wronged and thus need not have any feelings of resentment to overcome through forgiveness; and second, although mercy as a virtue necessarily involves dispositions of character (such as compassion), it also requires – in a way that forgiveness does not – a public manifestation. One can forgive another in one's heart of hearts, but one cannot show mercy to another in one's heart of hearts. This is because mercy has its primary life in an institutional context (typically, but not necessarily, legal) where one has the right or duty to inflict a certain level of harsh treatment on another, but refuses to do so, imposing instead a less harsh treatment or no harsh treatment at all.

Because mercy necessarily involves a mitigation or abandonment of hard treatment, it may easily be confused with mere leniency. When the fallen knight begs for mercy, he knows that the rules of chivalric combat give the victor the right to kill the vanquished and he is asking that the victor waive that right. If the victor does waive it, and spares the life of the vanquished, we may say – speaking casually – that mercy was shown, because ordinary language often allows us to confuse mercy with leniency. Surely, however, the victor reveals the *virtue* of mercy only if he acts from such an appropriate motive as compassion or love of God. Or consider, in a legal context, an example from Shakespeare's *Measure for Measure*: when Isabella begs Angelo to show mercy to her brother Claudio, Angelo's false promise to free Claudio in exchange for sexual intercourse with Isabella is an insincere offer of leniency, but no kind of an offer of mercy in any sense in which mercy may be regarded as a virtue.

But are forgiveness and mercy properly regarded as virtues? They are both responsive, in a moral or legal context, to genuine cases of wrongdoing for which the wrongdoer is responsible. In this they are unlike both excuse and justification, concepts with which they are sometimes confused. The person with a valid excuse (insanity, perhaps) is not responsible for wrongdoing. The person with a valid justification (self-defence, perhaps) establishes that, initial appearances to the contrary, there was (all things considered) no ultimate wrongdoing. In these cases there is nothing to resent and nothing for which to demand punishment or other harsh treatment, and thus the avoidance of resentment and demands for harsh treatment is obviously required by elementary rationality and justice. Forgiveness and mercy, however, get their main life in cases where there *is* wrongdoing for which the wrongdoer is responsible, and thus where either resentment or the demand for punishment might well seem justified. But this is what makes both forgiveness and mercy problematic candidates for moral virtues: they demand that we avoid psychological responses and actions that seem not only understandable, but perhaps actually justified by a proper respect for rights and justice.

2   Forgiveness and self-respect

There are, of course, many things to be said in favour of forgiveness: it allows us to show our genuine commitment to love and compassion (central virtues in the Christian tradition) in really hard test cases, cases where we have been personally wronged or injured; it allows us to check excessive self-importance or self-love, tendencies that incline us to overdramatize some of the wrongs done to us (a point well made by Simone Weil and others); it allows us to avoid the self-poisoning effects of resentment itself (a poison graphically described by NIETZSCHE (§§8–9)); it may confer considerable social benefits, such as the avoidance of feuds and vigilante activities; and it allows us to maintain our most valued personal relationships. This last benefit arises from the fact that, since each of us will sometimes wrong the people that mean the most to us, there will be times when we will want to be forgiven by those whom we have wronged. Seeing this, no rational person would desire to live in a world where forgiveness was not seen as a healing virtue.

In spite of all these splendid fruits that may be born of forgiveness, it is hard to regard it as an unqualified virtue. Although one of course wants to guard against excessive self-importance or self-love, are not certain assertions of the value of the self – the assertion of one's moral rights, for example – morally permissible, perhaps even morally mandatory? If one thinks that self-respect, in contrast to servility, is a virtue, is it not plausible to argue that one important way in which this self-respect may sometimes be shown is through resenting those persons who maliciously inflict wrongs upon us? We show our moral respect for others in feeling indignation when they are wronged. May we not show moral respect for ourselves by feeling resentment when we are wronged? And if we do not, what does this show? That we are manifesting the virtues of love and forgiveness, or simply that we are servile persons with low self-esteem, unable to demand the respect that we deserve?

Forgiveness thus creates a problem: can it be conceptualized as a virtue in such a way that it does not immediately collapse into the vice of servility? One way out of this tension, perhaps, is to make forgiveness conditional on a change in the wrongdoer: namely, repentance. When we are wronged, one of the things most threatening to our self-respect is the symbolic message that the wrongdoer seems to be conveying about us: the message that we matter less than the wrongdoer and thus may simply be used, like an object, for the wrongdoer's own purposes. This is a message that one's own self-respect prompts one to resist, and resentment of the wrongdoer is our primary emotional way of expressing such resistance. As much as we might like to follow Augustine's counsel that we should 'hate the sin and not the sinner', it is difficult to follow this counsel when the wrongdoer remains attached to the wrongdoing. But what if the wrongdoer seeks to break this attachment – as shown by sincere repentance? Then there is no longer an endorsement of the insulting and humiliating message contained in the wrongful conduct, and the wronged person can now forgive and join with the wrongdoer in condemning the act from which the wrongdoer is now severed. In this case forgiveness and self-respect seem obviously compatible. For this reason it is not surprising that repentance, which opens the door to forgiveness by allowing the wronged person a self-respecting retreat from resentment, has loomed large in the moral literature on forgiveness. It is also not surprising that repentance (and the purity of heart at which it aims) has been regarded within some (but not all) religious traditions as a precondition of God's forgiveness of sinners.

Of course, not everyone would agree that resentment of wrongdoers is essentially tied to human self-respect. (The whole conceptual framework of resentment and self-respect may not even apply to God, of course, and thus divine forgiveness may have to be understood in totally different terms.) A person who grounds their self-respect in something other than the regard of other people will perhaps see resentment as a natural response but also as a dangerous temptation – a temptation to rely on something that is an improper basis for self-respect. Such a person may well see forgiveness – even in the absence of repentance on the part of the wrongdoer – as a way of restoring full and properly founded self-respect. Persons who do not derive their self-respect from treatment by other people may, of course, rely on a variety of different sources and worldviews to support a sense of their own worth – for example, the moral elitism of a Socrates ('Why should I care if the ignorant seek to harm me?') or the belief of Christians that their self-respect is grounded in the fact that God loves them.

3   Mercy and justice

Mercy is also a concept that is capable of generating tension and paradox; this is particularly so in the context of punishment, where it initially seems most at home. If a certain punishment is required by justice, representing what the wrongdoer in justice deserves, then it would seem to be an injustice to depart from that punishment. We are fond of using the slogan that 'justice should be tempered with mercy', yet it is unclear that such a slogan represents morally wise counsel. If it is simply a somewhat misleading way of demanding proper individuation to guarantee that justice is finely tuned and thus truly done, then one can hardly have any deep quarrels with it. If it counsels an actual departure from justice (an injustice), however, then what it counsels seems manifestly unvirtuous. It is for this reason that Kant feared the role of compassion in the criminal law and argued that the sovereign's power of pardon (a dramatic kind of legal mercy) is one of the most dangerous of all sovereign powers because it might tempt the sovereign, out of compassion, to avoid a genuine duty: namely, the doing of justice. It is manifestly illegitimate, Kant argues, for the sovereign or judge to pursue personal and private commitments to compassion when such individuals have explicitly taken on the public responsibility of administering justice.

The tension – perhaps even contradiction – between justice and mercy produces paradoxes even with respect to the idea of divine mercy. Anselm, for example, found it paradoxical that God, who is committed to justice, could through his mercy spare the wicked from the eternal punishment that they deserved.

Perhaps the way out of this paradox, at both the human and the divine level, is to distinguish between two different models of mercy: the criminal law model and the private law model. On the criminal law model, a judge has an obligation (a role responsibility) to enforce just laws by imposing the just sanctions specified. The responsibility of the office precludes appeals to personal compassion, since the very essence of the job is defined in terms of certain specified duties. This criminal law model would, of course, have serious problems as a model for divine justice. God is presumably not like a judge in a criminal case, having the duty to enforce rules that are independent of his will, but is in some sense the author of the rules that are enforced. God is thus not accountable to a constituency in the way a human judge is, and thus does not experience anything that might plausibly be regarded as role responsibility or role conflict. Anselm, however, may have been tempted to see God occupying such a role; his paradox seems to depend upon seeing God caught in the very kind of dilemma that might plague a human judge in a criminal case.

A private law model of mercy, however, might allow us to avoid some of the tensions between mercy and justice at both the human and the divine level.

According to this model, mercy is best illustrated not by a judge in a criminal case, but by a private party in a private lawsuit. Shakespeare's *The Merchant of Venice* nicely illustrates this private law model in its portrayal of Portia pleading with Shylock to show mercy to Antonio, a man who has defaulted on a contract and who now, according to the terms of the contract, owes Shylock 'a pound of flesh'. Unlike a judge, Shylock has no duty to enforce any legal rules. Rather, the legal rules of contract give him certain rights, rights that he is free to waive if he chooses. And it is such a waiver, motivated by compassion, that Portia is asking him to consider – a waiver that, since he has only rights and no duties in this situation, could not open him up to a valid charge of injustice or dereliction of duty.

So too, one might say, for God. If God is properly conceived as a being who mainly has rights over his creatures rather than external (non-self-imposed) duties to them, then perhaps he may show mercy – waiving his right to consign a person to eternal damnation – without being validly charged with injustice. We may now begin to see our way out of at least one paradox about mercy. Others, however, may still be present – for example, what might be called the 'equal protection' paradox raised by Anselm when he wondered how God, a rational being, can consistently show mercy to some who are unworthy while punishing others who are equally unworthy.

Both forgiveness and mercy, because of the tensions they generate, will no doubt remain problematic concepts that will continue to generate rich philosophical and theological discussion. It is an obvious truth, of course, that the virtuous person is one lacking in neither charity (the primary foundation of mercy and forgiveness) nor justice (the primary foundation for resentment and punishment). What is by no means obvious, however, is how these virtues are to be brought into harmony in all the actual complex cases that arise in the moral lives of individuals and communities.

See also: ATONEMENT; GRACE; JUSTIFICATION, RELIGIOUS; RECTIFICATION AND REMAINDERS; SALVATION; SELF-RESPECT; SIN; VIRTUE ETHICS; VIRTUES AND VICES

References and further reading

Adams, M.M. (1991) 'Forgiveness: A Christian Model', *Faith and Philosophy* 8 (3): 277–304. (Criticizes the work of Jeffrie Murphy and others who have argued that forgiveness may be incompatible with self-respect.)

* Butler, J. (1722) *Sermons*, Oxford: Clarendon Press,

1897. (Sermon VIII, 'Upon Resentment', and Sermon IX, 'Upon Forgiveness of Injuries', present the essence of Butler's account of forgiveness.)

Card, C. (1972) 'On Mercy', *Philosophical Review* 81: 182–207. (Argues that mercy is a part of justice (on a sophisticated theory of justice) and not an autonomous moral virtue.)

Hill, T.E., Jr (1973) 'Servility and Self-respect', *The Monist* 57: 87–104. (Argues, on Kantian grounds of duty to self, that servility is a moral vice.)

* Kant, I. (1797) *The Metaphysics of Morals*, trans. M. Gregor, Cambridge: Cambridge University Press, 1991, 140–45, 168–9. (Develops Kant's theory of justice and employs it to defend retributive punishment and to oppose pardons for those convicted of crime.)

Kolnai, A. (1973–4) 'Forgiveness', *Proceedings of the Aristotelian Society* 74: 91–106. (Argues that forgiveness can be a virtue only if it does not involve complicity in wrongdoing.)

Moore, K.D. (1989) *Pardons: Justice, Mercy, and the Public Interest*, Oxford: Oxford University Press. (Presents, in a generally Kantian framework, a theory of when legal pardons may be justified.)

Murphy, J.G. (1997) 'Repentance, Punishment and Mercy', in A. Brien (ed.) *The Quality of Mercy*, Value Inquiry Book Series, Amsterdam: Rodopi; also in A. Etzioni (ed.) *Repentance*, Lanham, MD: Rowman & Littlefield. (Presents a detailed analysis of the concept of repentance and argues that repentance can be relevant not simply to mercy and the reduction of punishment, but to the justification of punishment itself.)

Murphy, J.G. and Hampton, J. (1988) *Forgiveness and Mercy*, Cambridge: Cambridge University Press. (Hampton's two chapters seek to develop, with philosophical rigour, a Christian defence of forgiveness and mercy, while Murphy's three chapters explore the sceptical case against the claim that forgiveness and mercy are virtues.)

Murphy, J.G. and Morris, H. (1988) 'Exchange: Forgiveness and Mercy', *Criminal Justice Ethics* 7 (2): 3–22. (Murphy summarizes the view of forgiveness and mercy he develops in *Forgiveness and Mercy* and Morris builds his case against this from remarks on unjustified self-importance made by Simone Weil in her book *Gravity and Grace*.)

Newman, L.E. (1987) 'The Quality of Mercy: On the Duty to Forgive in the Judaic Tradition', *Journal of Religious Ethics* 15: 155–72. (Stresses the idea that, in the Judaic tradition, forgiveness is more a matter of community reintegration than purity of heart.)

Nietzsche, F. (1887) *On The Genealogy of Morals*, trans. W. Kaufmann, New York: Random House, 1967. (Explores, among many other things, the destructive role that resentment (*ressentiment*) plays in the moral life. See, for example, pages 36–9.)

Nussbaum, M. (1993) 'Equity and Mercy', *Philosophy and Public Affairs* 22 (2): 83–125. (Builds a case for mercy and empathetic individuation from Seneca's essays 'On Anger' and 'On Clemency'.)

Quinn, P.L. (1978) *Divine Commands and Moral Requirements*, Oxford: Oxford University Press. (Contains, in the last chapter, a fine discussion of Saint Anselm's paradoxes of divine mercy.)

Twambley, P. (1976) 'Mercy and Forgiveness', *Analysis* 36: 84–90. (Introduces the distinction between the criminal law and private law models of mercy.)

JEFFRIE G. MURPHY

FORMAL AND INFORMAL LOGIC

Formal logic abstracts the form of an argument from an instance of it that may be encountered, and then evaluates the form as being valid or invalid. The form is the important thing, rather than the concrete instance of the form. Informal logic, on the other hand, evaluates how an argument is used in a given context of conversation. This more practical, real-world orientation requires more judgment in interpreting what a given text of discourse should be taken to argue.

Formal logic abstracts from the context of use of an argument by seeing an argument as an instance of a form of argument, composed of constants and variables. The constants are defined in a precise way that makes any reference to context unnecessary (see LOGICAL CONSTANTS). The variables are blanks that are filled in by the component parts of the argument under consideration. Take the argument 'Jane and Dick will not both be elected; Jane will be elected; therefore Dick will not be elected'. In the modern formal logic of propositions, 'and' and 'not' are defined as constants, and 'Jane will be elected' and 'Dick will be elected' are represented using propositional variables, A and B. The constants 'and' and 'not' are defined as follows:

'A and B' is true only if both A and B are true; otherwise it is false.

'not A' is true if A is false; and false if A is true.

Symbolized thus, the argument above about Jane and Dick has the following form:

not(*A* and *B*)

A
_____

Therefore not *B*.

This form of argument is 'valid', meaning that every single instance of it is such that if both premises are true, the conclusion must also be true. Thus formal logic guarantees that a valid argument will never take you from true premises to a false conclusion. This is simply a matter of the form of the argument and the way the constants have been defined. Hence formal logic is an abstract, mathematical discipline – a study of forms.

Formal logic of this mathematical sort, using constants and variables, is a relatively modern development, but the roots of it can be traced back to Aristotle's theory of the syllogism (see ARISTOTLE §5; LOGIC, ANCIENT §§1–3). A 'syllogism' is an argument made up of three propositions put together in a particular form, of which the following is an example: 'All bears climb trees; all grizzlies are bears; therefore, all grizzlies climb trees'. This kind of argument was ruled valid in Aristotle's theory: *if* the premises are true, then the conclusion must be true too. This does not imply that the premises *are* true. Validity, you could say, is a conditional concept in Aristotle's theory, and the same can be said in modern logic.

Modern formal logic has been centrally concerned with two kinds of arguments. Propositional logic has to do with arguments that are valid or not by virtue of certain constants, such as 'and', 'not' and 'if..., then...', which function as connectives between propositions. Quantifier logic is a sophisticated and powerful system of formal logic that not only encompasses the limited varieties of arguments treated in Aristotle's theory of the syllogism, but also many other more complex arguments depending on 'all' and 'some' (see QUANTIFIERS; PREDICATE CALCULUS).

Informal logic was also founded as a systematic subject by Aristotle, principally in his *Topics* and *Sophistical Refutations* (see *Topica et Sophistici Elenchi*), but never received the same consistent and more serious attention that formal logic did in the subsequent history of logic. Consequently, it was never developed as a scientific subject in the way that formal logic was. However, it survived in a practical form, in logic textbooks and manuals used for instruction in universities throughout the Middle Ages and into the modern period. Only recently, with the advent of argumentation theory, has there come to be a relatively serious and sustained scholarly attempt to develop informal logic as a subject of research. Yet even at the end of the twentieth century, informal logic is a more practical subject which addresses contextual factors of how arguments are actually used in everyday conversation in a given discourse. Unlike formal logic, informal logic cannot abstract from the context of use of an argument, and must evaluate it as subject to an interpretation of the speaker's discourse as a part of a conversational exchange.

Both formal and informal logic are concerned primarily with the task of evaluating arguments as correct or incorrect, according to standards. Formal logic, as noted above, works by identifying forms and proving them valid or invalid by means of some method of calculation independent of the context in which the argument was used. Applying the formal test to a real argument does involve some informal determining of what kind of argument was meant by the speaker, what its most precise form is, and so forth. But in informal logic such questions of interpretation are a much more central part of the task of evaluation.

Informal logic has to do with the use of an argument in a conversational setting where participants are supposed to contribute to the conversation by making moves appropriate to the current stage of the conversation (see Grice 1975; PRAGMATICS; IMPLICATURE). Different types of conversation can be recognized. For example, van Eemeren and Grootendorst (1984) cite one very important type where the purpose is to resolve a conflict of opinions by verbal means, using arguments. Generally an argument is correct if it contributes to the goal of the conversation, and incorrect if it fails to do so. Some particularly deceptive or misleading types of arguments can even actively interfere with the goal of a conversation, and the most common and dangerous of these are called fallacies (see FALLACIES).

See also: LOGICAL AND MATHEMATICAL TERMS, GLOSSARY OF

References and further reading

* Aristotle (*c.*330 BC) *Topica et Sophistici Elenchi* (Topics and Sophistical Refutations), trans. W.A. Pickard-Cambridge, ed. W.D. Ross, New York: Oxford University Press, 1958. (Historical.)
* Eemeren, F.H. van and Grootendorst, R. (1984) *Speech Acts in Argumentative Discussions*, Dordrecht: Foris. (Account of argumentation theory.)
* Grice, H.P. (1975) 'Logic and Conversation', in D. Davidson and G. Harman (eds) *The Logic of Grammar*, Encino, CA: Dickenson. (Account of implicature.)
Jeffrey, R.C. (1967) *Formal Logic: Its Scope and*

Limits, New York: McGraw-Hill, 2nd edn, 1981. (General introduction to formal logic.)

Walton, D. (1989) *Informal Logic*, Cambridge: Cambridge University Press. (General introduction to informal logic.)

DOUGLAS WALTON

FORMAL LANGUAGES AND SYSTEMS

Formal languages and systems are concerned with symbolic structures considered under the aspect of generation by formal (syntactic) rules, that is, irrespective of their or their components' meaning(s). In the most general sense, a formal language is a set of expressions. The most important way of describing this set is by means of grammars. Formal systems are formal languages equipped with a consequence operation yielding a deductive system. If one further specifies the means by which expressions are built up (connectives, quantifiers) and the rules from which inferences are generated, one obtains logical calculi of various sorts, especially Frege–Hilbert-style and Gentzen-style systems.

1 **Expressions and grammars**
2 **Deductive systems**
3 **Logical calculi**

1 Expressions and grammars

A formal language is a set $\mathcal{L}$ of expressions. Expressions are built up from a finite set Σ of atomic symbols or atoms (the 'alphabet' of the language) by means of certain constructors. Normally one confines oneself to linear association (concatenation) '∘' as the only constructor, yielding 'strings' of atoms, also called 'words' (over Σ), starting with the empty word ϵ. Mathematically, the structure obtained is the semigroup freely generated by the alphabet Σ. When $a_1 \circ a_2 \circ \ldots \circ a_n$ with atoms $a_1, a_2, \ldots, a_n$ is written in the usual way as $a_1 a_2 \ldots a_n$, it is assumed that the decomposition of this expression into atoms is unique.

It should be noted that languages based on more than one constructor may well be considered. An example would be Frege's two-dimensional *Begriffsschrift*, which may be viewed as a formal language based on constructors for horizontal and vertical alignment (see Frege 1879). However, since any constructor can be written linearly as a function symbol applied to arguments, the notion of formal

languages as based on linear concatenation is sufficiently general. The atomic symbols which form the basis of a formal language are themselves abstract entities, in contrast to the tokens which constitute their individual realizations.

A formal language $\mathcal{L}$ can be investigated from various points of view. One possibility is to specify a device $\mathcal{A}$ that recognizes exactly those words over Σ which belong to $\mathcal{L}$, that is, which enters a certain state if and only if a word of $\mathcal{L}$ is given as an input. When this occurs we say that $\mathcal{A}$ *accepts $\mathcal{L}$*. Such a device is called an 'automaton' (in the mathematical, not the physical sense). The relationship between languages and automata accepting them is studied in automata theory.

A formal grammar $\mathcal{G}$ for $\mathcal{L}$ describes a way to generate the words of $\mathcal{L}$ by means of formal rules, beginning with a special start symbol S. A rule (also called a 'production') has the form $u \rightarrow v$, which expresses that in any word of the form $w_1 u w_2$ the part u may be replaced by v, yielding $w_1 v w_2$. In addition to the atoms of the alphabet Σ under consideration (which are called 'terminals' in formal language theory), rules may contain variables (called 'nonterminals'), among which S is distinguished. For example, the grammar

$$S \rightarrow ASA$$
$$S \rightarrow a$$
$$A \rightarrow b$$

generates all words $b \ldots bab \ldots b$ over the alphabet $\{a, b\}$ with equally many instances of b on each side of a.

Formal languages may be classified by the type of grammar generating them. For example, a language $\mathcal{L}$ is called 'context-free' if it can be generated by a context-free grammar, which is one whose productions always have just a single variable on the left side (as in the example just given). Context-free grammars play a distinguished role in the construction of artificial languages (such as programming languages). However, for the study of (fragments of) natural languages, more complicated ('context-sensitive') types of grammar must be considered. Formal grammars have the same expressive power as computable functions: the computation by a Turing machine can be described by means of a formal grammar; and the generation of words in a formal grammar can be simulated by a Turing machine.

2 Deductive systems

A formal system is based on a formal language $\mathcal{L}$, endowing it with a 'consequence operation' C. This operation can be specified at different levels of abstraction. In the most general sense, $\mathcal{C}$ is just an arbitrary function transforming subsets of $\mathcal{L}$ into subsets of $\mathcal{L}$. $\mathcal{C}$ is said to be an 'inference operation' if the set of consequences of a set X comprises at least X.

$$X \subseteq \mathcal{C}(X) \text{(inclusion)}$$

The pair $\langle \mathcal{L}, \mathcal{C} \rangle$ is then called an 'inference system'. It is called a 'closure system' if furthermore

$$\mathcal{C}(\mathcal{C}(X)) \subseteq \mathcal{C}(X) \text{(idempotence)}$$

and

$$X \subseteq Y \Rightarrow \mathcal{C}(X) \subseteq \mathcal{C}(Y) \text{(monotonicity)}$$

are fulfilled. It is called a 'deductive system' if the consequences of a set X can be obtained from the finite subsets of X, that is, if in addition to the three conditions mentioned,

$$\mathcal{C}(X) \subseteq \cup \{\mathcal{C}(Y): Y \subseteq X, Y \text{ finite}\} \text{(compactness)}$$

holds. Equivalently, formal systems can be described by a consequence relation $X \vdash A$ between subsets of $\mathcal{L}$ and expressions of $\mathcal{L}$. The four conditions mentioned then become

$$X \cup \{A\} \vdash A$$
$$X \vdash A \Rightarrow X \cup Y \vdash A$$
$$(X \vdash A \text{ for all } A \in Y \text{ and } Y \cup Z \vdash B) \Rightarrow X \cup Z \vdash B$$
$$X \vdash A \Rightarrow Y \vdash A \text{ for some finite } Y \subseteq X.$$

If we confine ourselves to consequences of finite sets X, Y, Z, which in the case of deductive systems is appropriate, these conditions are equivalent to

$\{A\} \vdash A$	(identity)
$X \vdash A \Rightarrow X \cup \{B\} \vdash A$	(thinning)
$(X \vdash A \text{ and } \{A\} \cup Z \vdash B) \Rightarrow X \cup Z \vdash B$	(cut)

which are the basic structural (that is, logic-free) principles of Gentzen-style sequent systems (see Gentzen 1935).

Deductive systems can be given by means of a set Δ of inference rules R, where an inference rule is an $(n+1)$-ary relation $R \subseteq \mathcal{L}^n \times \mathcal{L}$. Any $(A_1, \ldots, A_n, B) \in R$ (also written as $A_1, \ldots, A_n \Rightarrow B$) is called an instance of R, and $A_1, \ldots, A_n$ are said to be the premises and B the conclusion of that instance. If $n = 0$ then the rule $\Rightarrow A$ is called an axiom. If we define $\mathcal{C}_\Delta(X)$ to be the smallest set of expressions in $\mathcal{L}$ containing X and closed under the rules in Δ (that is, if $\{A_1, \ldots, A_n\} \subseteq \mathcal{C}_\Delta(X)$, then $B \in \mathcal{C}_\Delta(X)$ for any instance $A_1, \ldots, A_n \Rightarrow B$ of a rule in Δ), then $\langle \mathcal{L}, \mathcal{C}_\Delta \rangle$ is a deductive system, called the rule-based system with respect to Δ.

Conversely, the consequence relation of any deductive system defines a set of rules with respect to

which this system can be viewed as a rule-based system. Like grammars, rule-based systems are as powerful as Turing machines: they can be used to express any algorithm.

3 Logical calculi

In logic one considers deductive systems over a language $\mathcal{L}$ whose expressions, called formulas, are built up from certain basic expressions by means of functions, predicates and logical operators. In propositional logic, which for reasons of simplicity is considered here, formulas are built up from a subset $\mathcal{P}$ of $\mathcal{L}$ (the set of propositional letters or propositional variables) and a finite set $\mathcal{S}$ of symbols of the alphabet Σ of $\mathcal{L}$ (the set of propositional connectives). Prominent connectives are 'not' ($\sim$), 'and' ($\wedge$), 'or' ($\vee$) and 'implies' ($\supset$). The two principal ways of specifying a consequence operation $\mathcal{C}$ for such a system are (1) by presenting it as a rule-based system and (2) by formally describing its consequence relation $\vdash$. Other approaches modify or extend the notion of consequence by considering (3) multiple consequences, (4) consequence relations with restricted structural principles ('substructural logics') or (5) the fine structure of proofs.

(1) For a *rule-based system* a set of axioms and a set of inference rules are given. Axioms for a fragment of propositional logic based on conjunction and implication (the so-called 'positive implication–conjunction logic') are, for example, all formulas of the form

$$A \supset (B \supset A)$$
$$(A \supset (B \supset C)) \supset ((A \supset B) \supset (A \supset C))$$
$$(A \supset (B \supset C)) \supset ((A \wedge B) \supset C)$$
$$((A \wedge B) \supset C) \supset (A \supset (B \supset C)).$$

Inference rules are all instances of the following schema.

$$A, A \supset B \Rightarrow B(\textit{modus ponens})$$

Rule-based systems of this kind are often called Frege–Hilbert-style systems. Typically, they include a relatively long list of axioms and just a few inference rules (in ordinary propositional logic, just *modus ponens*). The consequence relation '$X \vdash_\mathcal{C} A$' corresponding to the consequence operator $\mathcal{C}$ is called 'derivability from assumptions'.

(2) In contradistinction to this approach, Gentzen-style sequent systems formulate the desired properties of a consequence relation '$X \vdash_\mathcal{C} A$' as formal rules of inference. In a sequent system of propositional logic based on the connectives '$\wedge$' and '$\supset$' the above rules of identity, thinning and cut are typically postulated

as logic-free structural rules, in addition to the following logical rules.

$$X \cup \{A\} \vdash B \Rightarrow X \vdash A \supset B \quad \text{($\supset$-introduction right)}$$
$$X \vdash A, \, X \cup \{B\} \vdash C \Rightarrow X \cup \{A \supset B\} \vdash C$$
$$\text{($\supset$-introduction left)}$$
$$X \vdash A, \, X \vdash B \Rightarrow X \vdash A \wedge B \quad \text{($\wedge$-introduction right)}$$
$$X \cup \{A, B\} \vdash C \Rightarrow X \cup \{A \wedge B\} \vdash C$$
$$\text{($\wedge$-introduction left)}$$

Formally, this is just a specification of a rule-based system with respect to a more complicated language. Rather than a set of formulas $\mathcal{L}$ over $\mathcal{P}$ and $\mathcal{S}$ one considers a language $\mathcal{L}'$, whose expressions are 'sequents' of the form '$X \vdash A$', where $A \in \mathcal{L}$ with X finite. The deductive system $\mathcal{C}'$ over $\mathcal{L}'$ is then given by the rules stated. (Actually, to capture the idea of finite *sets* X in *expressions* '$X \vdash A$', one has to consider lists instead and to add special inference rules.) Intuitively, $\langle \mathcal{L}', \mathcal{C}' \rangle$ states features of the relation $\vdash_C$ which are intended to describe properties of the connectives of $\mathcal{S}$. So a Gentzen-style sequent system is a rule-based system with a consequence relation $\vdash_{C'}$ that can be viewed as a description of a deductive system with a consequence relation $\vdash_C$ such that $X \vdash_C A$ if and only if $\emptyset \vdash_{C'} (X \vdash A)$.

(3) In the Gentzen tradition, more complicated types of consequence relations '$\vdash$' have been investigated that do not completely fit the pattern described. One such approach is to consider consequence relations with a set of formulas appearing on the right side of '$\vdash$' ('multiple-conclusion logics' or, sometimes, 'Scott consequence relations'; see MULTIPLE-CONCLUSION LOGIC). The intended reading is disjunctive: '$X \vdash Y$' means that under the assumptions X at least one element of Y holds (although that cannot be formally derived!). Gentzen (1935) has proposed this idea to formulate sequent calculi for classical logic in which each connective obtains a 'natural' meaning via introduction rules for it on the right or left side of the turnstile without the need to consider special axioms or rules to guarantee the validity of, for example, $A \vee \sim A$ or $\sim\sim A \supset A$. Negation and disjunction rules in this system can be formulated as follows.

$$X \cup \{A\} \vdash Y \Rightarrow X \vdash Y \cup \{\sim A\}$$
$$\text{($\sim$-introduction right)}$$
$$X \vdash Y \cup \{A\} \Rightarrow X \cup \{\sim A\} \vdash Y$$
$$\text{($\sim$-introduction left)}$$
$$X \vdash Y \cup \{A, B\} \Rightarrow X \vdash Y \cup \{A \vee B\}$$
$$\text{($\vee$-introduction right)}$$

$$X \cup \{A\} \vdash Y, \, X \cup \{B\} \vdash Y \Rightarrow X \cup \{A \vee B\} \vdash Y$$
$$\text{($\vee$-introduction left)}$$

(Note the duality between these $\vee$-rules and the $\wedge$-rules formulated above, the right and left sides of the sequents being interchanged.) The *tertium non datur* (excluded middle) $\{\vdash A \vee \sim A\}$ is then obtained from $\{A\} \vdash \{A\}$ via $\vdash \{A, \sim A\}$. It is obvious that this notion of consequence has strong elements of symmetry which are characteristic of classical logic.

(4) Another approach is to restrict the structural principles underlying deductive systems. If in $X \vdash A$ we consider X no longer as a set but as a list of formulas, we may discuss whether in all cases we want to assume that elements of X are 'permutable' (that is, whether $Y, A, B, Z \vdash C \Rightarrow Y, B, A, Z \vdash C$ holds), or whether two identical formulas in X may be 'contracted' to a single one (that is, whether $Y, A, A, Z \vdash B \Rightarrow Y, A, Z \vdash B$ holds), or whether we want to assume or reject the principle of thinning (see above).

Such considerations, which apply analogously to the multiple-conclusion case, lead to so-called 'substructural' logics, which have become important in computer science and linguistics (but not only there); in particular, relevance logics (logics without thinning), contraction-free logics (in which the multiplicity of formulas counts), linear logics (without thinning and contraction) and Lambek logics (without thinning, contraction and permutation). If at the level of general consequence relations we consider logics without monotonicity, we enter the general field of non-monotonic logics, which is of special interest in artificial intelligence, since it helps to frame many common forms of reasoning (see NON-MONOTONIC LOGIC).

(5) In proof theory (see PROOF THEORY) one is often interested in the structure of the derivation that leads from a set of assumptions X to a conclusion A and in criteria for when two proofs of the same 'derivability fact' $X \vdash A$ are to be seen as identical – rather than in whether $X \vdash A$ holds or not. Significant cases are calculi of natural deduction (see NATURAL DEDUCTION, TABLEAU AND SEQUENT SYSTEMS). With respect to derivability, they can be described as Gentzen sequent systems in the sense above. However, crucial features of the fine structure of derivations, such as the fact that different occurrences of the same formula as an assumption may be treated differently, cannot be captured in that way.

One should be aware that in cases (3)–(5), as well as in other cases, in which extensions or modifications of the usual concept of a deductive system are considered with respect to some 'object logic', the system in which this object logic is described has itself the structure of a deductive system in the ordinary sense. Sequent calculi for a multiple-conclusion consequence relation '⊢', perhaps with substructural features, are themselves rule-based systems. Even the structure of natural deduction proofs can be characterized by a rule-based system, namely a system of type assignment for λ-terms. Therefore, it is not so much the specific type of consequence relation studied which makes logical systems formal systems, but rather the fact that the variety of logical systems can be described in terms of formal systems in the very specific sense of a rule-based system.

See also: GENTZEN, G.K.E.; LOGICAL AND MATHEMATICAL TERMS, GLOSSARY OF; TURING MACHINES

References and further reading

Došen, K. and Schroeder-Heister, P. (eds) (1993) *Substructural Logics*, Oxford: Clarendon Press. (Overview of logics with restricted structural rules.)

* Frege, G. (1879) *Begriffsschrift, eine der arithmetischen nachgebildete Formelsprache des reinen Denkens*, Halle: Nebert; trans. J. van Heijenoort, 'Begriffsschrift, a Formula Language, Modelled Upon That of Arithmetic, for Pure Thought', in J. van Heijenoort (ed.) *From Frege to Gödel: A Source Book in Mathematical Logic 1879–1931*, Cambridge, MA: Harvard University Press, 1967. (The first formulation of a complete axiom system for first-order logic.)

* Gentzen, G. (1935) 'Untersuchungen über das logische Schließen', *Mathematische Zeitschrift* 39: 176–210, 405–565; repr. Darmstadt: Wissenschaftliche Buchgesellschaft, 1969; trans. 'Investigations into Logical Deduction', in *The Collected Papers of Gerhard Gentzen*, ed. M.E. Szabo, Amsterdam and London: North Holland, 1969. (Gentzen's doctoral thesis, in which he created the notions of natural deduction and sequent calculus.)

Harrison, M.A. (1978) *Introduction to Formal Language Theory*, Reading, MA: Addison-Wesley. (Like Salomaa (1973), an advanced textbook of formal language theory.)

Hopcroft, J.E. and Ullman, J.D. (1979) *Introduction to Automata Theory, Languages and Computation*, Reading, MA: Addison-Wesley. (Elementary textbook of formal language theory.)

Kleene, S.C. (1952) *Introduction to Metamathematics*, Amsterdam: North Holland, 1974. (Classic textbook of mathematical logic with emphasis on logical calculi.)

Salomaa, A. (1973) *Formal Languages*, New York: Academic Press. (Like Harrison (1978), an advanced textbook of formal language theory.)

Takeuti, G. (1975) *Proof Theory*, Amsterdam: North Holland. (Textbook of Gentzen-style proof theory.)

Tarski, A. (1956) *Logic, Semantics, Metamathematics: Papers from 1923 to 1938*, trans. and ed. J.H. Woodger, Oxford: Clarendon Press; repr. Indianapolis, IN: Hackett Publishing Company, 2nd edn, 1983. (Includes Tarski's basic logical papers, particularly 'On Some Fundamental Concepts of Metamathematics' (1930), in which he defined the abstract notion of consequence for the first time.)

Troelstra, A.S. and Schwichtenberg, H. (1996) *Basic Proof Theory*, Cambridge: Cambridge University Press. (Textbook of Gentzen-style natural deduction and sequent systems.)

Wójcicki, R. (1988) *Theory of Logical Calculi: Basic Theory of Consequence Operations*, Dordrecht: Kluwer. (A comprehensive development of the theory of consequence relations.)

HEINRICH HERRE
PETER SCHROEDER-HEISTER

FORMALISM *see* HILBERT'S PROGRAMME AND FORMALISM

FORMALISM IN ART

Formalism in art is the doctrine that the artistic value of a work of art is determined solely by the work's form. The concept of artistic form is multiply ambiguous, however, and the precise meaning of formalism depends upon which sense of form it operates with. There are two main possibilities. The first understands form as the structure of a work's elements, the second as the manner in which it renders its 'content'. If form is understood as structure, formalism is still ambiguous: understood one way, it has never been denied; understood another way, it is untenable. If form is understood as manner, formalism is false.

1   **Formalism and artistic value**
2   **Form as structure**
3   **Form as manner**

1   Formalism and artistic value

Formalism as an artistic doctrine is a claim about the value of a work of art *as* a work of art. Let us call this 'artistic value' (see ART, VALUE OF §2). Formalism is the thesis that the artistic value of a work of literature, music, architecture or any other art is determined by the work's form, and by nothing else. This thesis presupposes that any work of art has two or more aspects, a formal aspect and one or a number of non-formal aspects, and implies that artistic appreciation should be focused exclusively on the form of the work. Note that it does not follow from the thought that a work's artistic value is determined solely by its form that all other aspects of the work are irrelevant to its value. For some or all of these other aspects may determine or contribute to form. If so, formalism does not require the aesthetic spectator to ignore them; rather, it requires the spectator to attend to them only in so far as it is necessary to perceive the work's form – only for this reason, and not for their own sakes.

But what is the form of a work of art? Is there a unitary notion of form, or does the idea of form change from art to art, or even from genre to genre?

2 Form as structure

'Form' often signifies the way in which the elements of an object are related to one another, that is to say, the structure of the elements. If 'form' is understood in this sense, formalism maintains the aesthetic irrelevance of the nature of the elements of a work of art, locating a work's value only in how it structures these elements: it does not matter what the elements of a work are, except in so far as only those elements, or elements of a similar kind, can be combined in the precise structure of the work. This version of formalism requires that a work of art is a composition of elements. But what are supposed to be the elements that compose works of art in the various art forms? The most obvious candidates for the elements of poems and musical works are, respectively, the words, and the notes, chords and rests that compose them. But it is not so clear what the elements of a play, a dance, a picture or a building might be supposed to be.

Let us shelve this difficulty, however, and concentrate on poetry and music. Given that a poem is a composition of words, and a piece of music a composition of notes, chords and rests, the crucial question is whether a work's form is separable from its elements. If a work's form is *its elements as concatenated in the work*, its form is not separable from its elements. Understood in this way, it is undeniable that a work's artistic value is determined not by its elements considered in themselves, but by its elements as related to one another in the work, that is, by its form. This variety of formalism is harmless. If, on the other hand, the form of a work of art can be shared with another work which has different elements, it is uncertain what the form of a work is,

and there is no plausible candidate that would make formalism acceptable. To see this, consider what the form common to two poems or two symphonies might be. Whatever answer you give, it should be clear that the artistic value of a poem or symphony is not determined solely by its form.

3 Form as manner

The idea of artistic form as a structure of elements is not, however, the sole or even principal conception of form at work in the doctrine of formalism. Usually formalists allege the aesthetic irrelevance of one particular aspect of a work of art, which aspect changes from art form to art form. In architecture, form is principally opposed to function; in music, to the expression of emotion and other affective states; in the pictorial arts, to pictorial content (what is depicted); in poetry, to meaning or what is said. Accordingly, formalism in architecture maintains the artistic irrelevance of a building's function, except in so far as it contributes to the building's form; in music, of the expressive aspects of a work; in the pictorial arts, of what a picture depicts; in poetry, of what is said, as opposed to how it is said. So it is the manner in which a function is realized, a subject depicted, an emotion or thought expressed – not the function, subject, emotion or thought – that determines the value of a work. Or so formalists claim.

What might lead one to embrace formalism? Let us call the non-formal aspect of a work of art that formalism dismisses F. A train of thought that often underlies formalism is this. A fine work of art can lack F. A poor one can possess F. Therefore, the value of a work of art that possesses F cannot be in any way due to its possessing F. For example: there are good paintings that do not depict significant subjects; there are poor paintings that do; hence, the significance of a painting's subject is irrelevant to its artistic value. Again: there are fine buildings that are not churches; there are poor buildings that are; hence, a building's being a church is irrelevant to its value as a work of art. But this line of thought is fallacious, as can be most easily seen by considering a parallel argument: there are good soccer players who lack a powerful kick; there are poor soccer players who do not; hence, the possession of a powerful kick is irrelevant to being a good soccer player. On the contrary, someone who possesses a powerful kick might be a good player partly because of that ability – it might be one of his strengths. The formalist argument mistakenly concludes from the fact that a certain feature – which it usually calls 'content' – is neither necessary nor sufficient for artistic value, that it is irrelevant to artistic value.

Formalists are motivated by a concern to preserve the autonomy of artistic value, but mistakenly believe that the only way to achieve this is by insulating artistic value from any aspect of a work – function, subject, emotion, thought – that has an extra-aesthetic reference. It is true that any aspect of a work of art contributes to the work's artistic value only as it is realized in the work. For example, the depicted content of a picture does not itself determine the picture's artistic value, which can easily be seen from the fact that two pictures can depict the same state of affairs but have unequal artistic values. But it does not follow from this that it is only how a picture depicts its content, not what that content is, that is relevant to its value as a picture. The consideration licences no stronger claim than that it is a picture's content *as depicted* that determines its value as art. Likewise, the fact that two buildings of unequal value can have the same function, two musical passages express the same emotion or mood, or two poems say the same thing shows no more than that a work's artistic value is determined not by its non-formal aspect, considered in itself, but only as realized in the building's structure, as expressed in the music's notes or in the arrangement of words that constitutes the poem. The truth of the matter is that the value of Pope's poetry is inseparable from the quality of the thought it expresses; the value of Poussin's *Echo and Narcissus* is inseparable from its being a depiction of that mythological story; and so on.

See also: HANSLICK, E.; KANT, I. §12

References and further reading

Bell, C. (1961) *Art*, London: Arrow Books. (The best-known statement of formalism with respect to visual art.)

Bradley, A.C. (1909) 'Poetry for Poetry's Sake', in *Oxford Lectures on Poetry*, London: Macmillan. (A sophisticated attempt to undermine the debate about formalism as applied to poetry.)

Hanslick, E. (1885) *Vom Musikalisch-Schönen*, 7th edn, trans. G. Cohen, *The Beautiful in Music*, London and New York: Novello, Ewer & Co, 1891. (The classic statement of a formalist view of music.)

Isenberg, A. (1973) 'Formalism', in *Aesthetics and the Theory of Criticism*, Chicago, IL, and London: University of Chicago Press. (An incisive critique of formalism.)

Kant, I. (1790) *The Critique of Judgment*, trans. J.C. Meredith, Oxford: Clarendon Press, 1957. (Part I contains Kant's celebrated account of aesthetic judgment, which emphasizes the form of the object

of the judgment. It is a contentious matter how formalistic Kant's treatment of art is.)

MALCOLM BUDD

FORMALISM IN ETHICS
see UNIVERSALISM IN ETHICS

FORMALISM, RUSSIAN
see RUSSIAN LITERARY FORMALISM

FORMS, THEORY OF *see* PLATO

FOUCAULT, MICHEL (1926–84)

Michel Foucault was a French philosopher and historian of thought. Although his earliest writings developed within the frameworks of Marxism and existential phenomenology, he soon moved beyond these influences and developed his own distinctive approaches. There is no overall methodological or theoretical unity to Foucault's thought, but his writings do fall into several main groups, each characterized by distinctive problems and methods. In his early studies of psychiatry, clinical medicine and the social sciences, Foucault developed an 'archaeology of knowledge' that treated systems of thought as 'discursive formations' independent of the beliefs and intentions of individuals. Foucault's archaeology displaced the human subject from the central role it played in the humanism which had been dominant since Kant. While archaeology provided no account of transitions from one system to another, Foucault later introduced a 'genealogical' approach, which seeks to explain changes in systems of discourse by connecting them to changes in the non-discursive practices of social power structures. Like Nietzsche's, Foucault's genealogies refused all comprehensive explanatory schemes, such as those of Marx or Freud. Instead he viewed systems of thought as contingent products of many small, unrelated causes. Foucault's genealogical studies also emphasize the essential connection between knowledge and power. Bodies of knowledge are not autonomous intellectual structures that happen to be employed as Baconian instruments of power. Rather, they are essentially tied to systems of social control. Foucault first used his genealogical approach to study the relations between modern prisons and the psychological and sociological knowledge on which they are based. He next proposed a similar analysis of modern practices and 'sciences' of sexuality, but eventually decided that such a study had to begin with an understanding of ancient Greek and Roman conceptions of the ethical self. This study was published in two volumes that appeared just before his death.

1 Biography

Foucault was born on 15 June 1926 in Poitiers, where his father was a prominent physician. In 1946, after preparatory studies with Jean Hyppolite at the Lycée Henri IV, he entered the École Normale Supérieure. He completed advanced degrees in both philosophy and psychology, working with, among others, Maurice Merleau-Ponty (see MERLEAU-PONTY, M. §2). Dissatisfied with French culture and society, Foucault held various academic posts in Sweden, Poland and Germany from 1955 to 1960, while he also completed his thesis (on madness in the Classical Age) for the *doctorat ès lettres*, which he published in 1961. During the 1960s, Foucault held a series of positions in French universities, culminating in 1969 with his election to the Collège de France, where he was Professor of the History of Systems of Thought until he died. Throughout the 1970s and until his death, Foucault was active politically, helping to found the Groupe d'Information sur les Prisons and supporting protests on behalf of homosexuals and other marginalized groups. He also frequently lectured outside France, particularly in the USA, and in 1983 had agreed to teach annually at the University of California at Berkeley. One of the first victims of AIDS, Foucault died in Paris on 25 June 1984.

Contrary to common views of authorship as self-expression, Foucault said that he wrote to escape from himself, to become other than he was. Correspondingly, there is no methodological or theoretical unity of Foucault's thought that will support any single comprehensive interpretation. His writings instead fall into several main groups, each characterized by a distinctive problematic and method of approach. It is fruitful to follow certain themes through some or all of these groups, but the core of his effort at any point is defined by what is specific to the problems then engaging him.

2 The history of madness

Foucault's earliest publications dealt with psychology and mental illness. His initial approach, developed in a long introduction to the French translation of Ludwig Binswanger's *Traum und Existenz* (1954), was through existential phenomenology, particularly that of the early Heidegger. His 1954 book, *Maladie mentale et personnalité* (Mental Illness and Psychology), combined this approach with a Marxist analysis (which, however, Foucault soon decisively rejected). His first major work, *Folie et déraison: histoire de la folie à l'âge classique* (Madness and Civilization) (1961), tried to combine the experiential emphasis of his earlier phenomenological discussions with an essentially historical approach.

Folie et déraison is a challenge to the modern use of the terms 'mad' and 'mentally ill' as synonyms. Beginning in the early nineteenth century, doctors and other therapists rejected such traditional conceptions of madness as divine ecstasy or diabolical possession in favour of the 'enlightened' view that madness is mental illness. Standard histories of psychiatry canonize this view, telling the story of how brave and compassionate men such as Tuke and Pinel replaced superstitious cruelty with scientific treatment of the mad. Foucault's rejection of this view is based on a detailed analysis of the 'experience' of madness that prevailed in the Classical Age (roughly, 1650 to 1800). Then, he maintains, madness was regarded not as mental illness but as a fundamental choice in favour of unreason (*déraison*), where unreason is any basic rejection of the norms of rationality constituting the boundaries of bourgeois social life. Among the various forms of unreason (including sexual promiscuity and deviancy, irreligion and idleness) madness was distinguished by its embracing the animal aspect of human nature at the expense of all higher aspects. The mad were those who had stripped themselves of everything distinctive of their humanity and had chosen to live like beasts. Since, on the classical view, madness was defined by its rejection of reason, the only rational reaction to it was rejection and exclusion. (Foucault regards Descartes' dismissal of his possible madness as grounds for doubt as a paradigm of this point.) Since the Classical Age had no coherent way of giving the mad a place in society, the only alternative was to exclude them from rational society, an exclusion epitomized by the Great Confinement of 1656.

The implication of Foucault's analysis is that there was, even in the relatively recent past of our own culture, a view of madness which was radically different from our own and no less defensible. This alone, he suggests, should begin to undermine our idea that there is something inevitable about our conception of madness. Foucault drives home his point through an analysis of the development of the modern (post-French-Revolution) 'experience' of madness as mental illness. This experience restores a social locus to madness, seeing it as a deviation from norms (an illness), not a rejection of the entire framework of rationality that defines these norms. He takes particular pains to show that, in spite of its veneer of scientific objectivity, the modern view is based more on a moral disapproval of the values implicit in madness than on any objective scientific truth. Similarly, he argues that the modern treatment of the mad (in asylums) was not so much a matter of medical compassion as a concerted effort to bring the mad back beneath the yoke of bourgeois morality. Initiating a theme further developed in various literary essays during the 1960s, *Folie et déraison* continually evokes the lives and works of artists haunted by madness (Van Gogh, Roussel, Artaud, Nietzsche) as precious expressions of a truth suppressed by both classical and modern experiences of madness.

3 The archaeological method

The second major division of Foucault's work begins with his history of the origins of modern medicine, *Naissance de la clinique: une archéologie du régard médical* (The Birth of the Clinic) (1963). Its first pages suggest that it is an extension of Foucault's ethical critique of the concept of mental illness to that of physical illness. But very soon the study becomes an analysis of the linguistic and conceptual structures underlying the modern practice of medicine; or, in the phrase of its subtitle, 'an archaeology of medical perception'.

Foucault's development of his 'archaeological method' synthesized three fundamental lines of influence on his thought: the history and philosophy of science of Gaston Bachelard and Georges Canguilhem (see BACHELARD, G. §2; FRENCH PHILOSOPHY OF SCIENCE §§1–6); the modernist literature of (especially) Raymond Roussel, George Bataille and Maurice Blanchot; and the historiography of Fernand Braudel and his *Annales* School. The point of convergence of these influences was the elimination of the subject as the centre of historical and philosophical analysis. Bachelard and Canguilhem challenged what Foucault called the 'transcendental narcissism' of existential phenomenology through a philosophy of objective concepts opposed to the existentialists' philosophy of subjective experience. Bachelard worked primarily on the physical sciences and Canguilhem on the biological and medical

sciences, but Foucault extended their viewpoint to the strongholds of the modern conception of subjectivity: the 'human sciences'. Modernist writing excited Foucault by its potential for, in Bataille's terminology, 'transgressing' the limits of standard knowledge and experience. As illustrated in his essay, 'What Is an Author?' (1969a), Foucault was particularly impressed with the modernists' decentring of the author and their constitution of language itself as the essence of literature. Braudel and his school had obtained extremely interesting results by varying the historiographical perspective; that is, by writing history not in terms of individuals' experience but from the broader standpoint of long-term factors such as geography, climate and natural resources. Foucault's archaeology did not take over any of Braudel's specific results or methods but tried to effect a parallel change of perspective in the history of thought: a move away from the individual thinker and towards more fundamental categories and structures.

Foucault's fullest deployment of his archaeological method was in *Les mots et les choses: une archéologie des sciences humaines* (The Order of Things) (1966), where he analysed the linguistic systems ('epistemes') characteristic of certain periods of thought. In particular, Foucault delineated the linguistic systems underlying the classical disciplines of general grammar, natural history and analysis of wealth, as well as those of the modern disciplines of philosophy, biology and economics that replaced them. He argued that there were strong structural similarities among the three classical disciplines and among the three modern disciplines, but a sharp break between classical and modern modes of thought taken as wholes. On this basis he rejected, for example, the common view that the work of nineteenth-century biologists such as Darwin was a continuous development of the work of eighteenth-century natural historians such as Lamarck. Specifically, he maintained that there is no hint of the Darwinian concept of evolution in Lamarck or any other classical thinker. He took such results as illustrative of the superiority of his archaeological approach to standard history of ideas, which focused on the specific concepts and theories of particular thinkers and not on the linguistic structures underlying them.

L'archéologie du savoir (The Archaeology of Knowledge) (1969b) systematically articulated the methodology Foucault had gradually forged in his preceding historical studies. It did this through an account of discourse, based on his notion of the statement (*l'énoncé*), which described a level of linguistic structure prior to and determining the range of objects, concepts, methodological resources and theoretical formulations available to individuals who speak and write. This account provided a theoretical elucidation of the decentring of the subject effected by Foucault's histories.

4 Genealogy

Foucault's writings during the 1970s constitute a third major division of his work. Although archaeological method is not abandoned in this period, it is subordinated to a new style of analysis that Foucault, with a bow to Nietzsche, dubs 'genealogical'. A genealogical analysis explains changes in systems of discourse by connecting them to changes in the non-discursive practices of social power structures. Foucault recognizes the standard economic, social and political causes of such changes, but he rejects the efforts of many historians to fit these causes into unitary, teleological schemata, such as the rise of the bourgeoisie or Napoleonic ambition. Rather, he sees changes in non-discursive practices as due to a vast number of minute and unconnected facts, the sorts of 'petty causes' that Nietzsche evoked in his genealogies (see GENEALOGY).

Foucault's genealogical studies emphasize the essential connection between knowledge and power. Bodies of knowledge are not autonomous intellectual structures that happen to be employed as instruments of power. Rather, precisely as bodies of knowledge, they are tied (but not reducible) to systems of social control. This essential connection of power and knowledge reflects Foucault's view that power is not merely repressive but a creative, if always dangerous, source of positive values. Although systems of knowledge may express objective truth in their own right, they are none the less always tied to current regimes of power. Conversely, regimes of power necessarily give rise to bodies of knowledge about the objects they control; but this knowledge may – in its objectivity – go beyond and even ultimately threaten the project of domination from which it arises.

Surveiller et punir: naissance de la prison (Discipline and Punish) (1975) is the best example of Foucault's genealogical approach. Here Foucault applies his conception of knowledge/power to the connection between modern disciplinary practices and modern social scientific disciplines. His primary example is the relation of the practice of imprisonment to such disciplines as criminology and social psychology. But imprisonment quickly becomes a model for the entire range of modern disciplinary practices, as employed in schools, factories, the military and so on. *Discipline and Punish* is a genealogical study in the precise sense that it shows how fundamental changes in thought (the emergence of new social scientific disciplines)

were causally connected with changes in non-discursive practices (characteristically modern means of controlling the body).

Foucault's *Histoire de la sexualité* (History of Sexuality) (1976–84) was initially conceived as a straightforward extension of the genealogical approach to sexuality. His idea was that modern bodies of knowledge about sexuality (the 'sciences of sexuality', including psychoanalysis) have an intimate association with the power structures of modern society. Volume 1, published in 1976, was intended as the introduction to a series of studies on particular aspects of modern sexuality (children, women, perverts and population), outlining the basic viewpoint and methods of the project. A central contention was that the history of sexuality is distorted by our acceptance of the 'repressive hypothesis': the proposition that the primary attitude towards sex during the last three centuries was one of opposition, silencing and, as far as possible, elimination. Foucault argues that in fact this period produced a 'discursive explosion' regarding sex, beginning with the rules of the Counter-Reformation governing sacramental confession. These rules emphasized the need for penitents to examine themselves and articulate not just all their sinful sexual actions, but all the thoughts, desires and inclinations behind these actions. The distinctive modern turn is the secularization (in, for example, psychoanalysis) of this concern for knowing and expressing the truth about sex.

Foucault emphasizes the similarities in our views of sex and crime. Both are objects of allegedly scientific disciplines, which simultaneously offer knowledge and domination of their objects. In the case of sexuality, however, control is exercised not only through others' knowledge of individuals but also through individuals' knowledge of themselves. We internalize the norms laid down by the sciences of sexuality and monitor our own conformity to these norms. We are controlled not only as *objects* of disciplines but also as self-scrutinizing and self-forming *subjects*. Foucault thus sees our apparently liberating focus on our sexuality as just a reinforcement of the mechanisms of social control. The self-scrutiny that overcomes psychic repression to reveal our deep sexual nature is merely a subtle means of shaping us to the norms of modern society.

5 Sexuality and ethics

Foucault planned the second volume of his history of sexuality as a study of the origins of the modern notion of the subject in the practices of Christian confession. He wrote such a study, 'Les aveux de la chair' (The Confessions of the Flesh), but did not

711

publish it because he decided that a proper understanding of the Christian development required a comparison with ancient conceptions of the ethical self. This led to two volumes on Greek and Roman sexuality: *L'usage des plaisirs* (The Use of Pleasure) (1984a) and *Le souci de soi* (The Care of the Self) (1984b). These two volumes mark the fourth and final period of Foucault's work, a period most striking for its emphasis on the individual self: the 'problematization' of its world and actions and the 'aesthetics of existence' whereby it makes its life a work of art. It might seem that Foucault has finally rejected the derivative and ephemeral status of the individual. But this would be doubly mistaken. On the one hand, he still sees our history as strongly structured by discursive and non-discursive practices operating at much deeper levels than that of human consciousness. On the other hand, every stage of Foucault's work was directed towards overcoming the limitations of individuals (himself and others). Previously, his effort was the negative one of dissolving the apparently necessary constraints of society and its discourses. In this final turn to what he calls 'ethics', he began to explore the positive possibilities of self-creation.

In *The Use of Pleasure* and *The Care of the Self*, Foucault compares ancient pagan and Christian ethics through studies of the test case of sexuality. He notes that the moral codes of pagans and Christians were similar, but maintains that there were fundamental differences in the ways in which individuals were subordinated to the codes (in the 'forms of subjectification'). The Greeks of the fourth and fifth centuries BC, unlike the early Christians, did not regard the domain of sexual acts (*ta aphrodisia*) as evil in its own right, but as natural and necessary. The Greeks did see sexual acts as objects of moral concern because of their animality and their great intensity. What was dangerous, however, was not sex in itself but its excesses. Therefore, the Greek mode of subjection to the code of sexual ethics was a matter of the proper use (*chresis*) of pleasures. Unlike the Christians, the Greeks allowed the full range of sexual activities (heterosexual, homosexual, in marriage, out of marriage) with proper moderation. Properly used, sex was a major part of an aesthetics of the self: the self's creation of a beautiful and enjoyable existence.

The Use of Pleasure analyses a variety of primary texts (for instance, those of Plato and Xenophon) in order to understand the classical Greek conception of an aesthetics of existence. *The Care of the Self* continues with studies (of Galen, Artemidorus and Plutarch, for example) showing how later antiquity gradually moved away from this aesthetics towards a hermeneutics of the self. The latter, fully developed only by Christianity, replaced the ideal of aesthetic self-creation with that of a deep understanding of a hidden 'real self'. Foucault regards this Christian conception as the root of our domination by the sciences of sexuality he discussed in *The History of Sexuality I*. Although insisting that there can be no question of 'going back to the Greeks', he suggests that reflection on the aesthetics of existence may help us devise liberating alternatives to the traps of modern sexuality (see SEXUALITY, PHILOSOPHY OF §3).

6 Conclusion

It is impossible to understand Foucault's work in the typical manner of histories of philosophy. There is not only no system, but no sustained vision, message or project (which we find even in such mavericks as Nietzsche, Kierkegaard and Wittgenstein). For Foucault, philosophy is always just a means of overcoming some specific set of historical limits. It has no final goal, no specific truth or effect, of its own. It is merely a set of intellectual techniques, tied to a consciousness of the historical enterprise that has been known as philosophy. If philosophy ever transforms its self-conception along the lines of Foucault's practice, then he will be recognized as a great philosopher (or, more likely, as someone who played a major role in eliminating philosophy as it had been understood since Plato). Otherwise, he will in all likelihood remain a minor figure, interesting for his odd historical perspectives and his quirky social criticism.

List of works

Foucault, M. (1954) *Maladie mentale et personnalité*, Paris: Presses Universitaires de France; revised as *Maladie mentale et psychologie*, Paris: Presses Universitaires de France, 1962; trans. A. Sheridan, *Mental Illness and Psychology*, Berkeley, CA: University of California Press, 1987. (Foucault's first book, showing the strong influence of existentialist phenomenology and of Marxism. The 1962 revision (the version used in the translation) eliminates most of the Marxist discussions and develops a view much closer to that of *Folie et déraison*.)

—— (1961) *Folie et déraison: Histoire de la folie à l'âge classique*, Paris: Plon; 2nd edn, with new preface and appendices, *Histoire de la folie à l'âge classique*, Paris: Gallimard, 1972; trans. R. Howard, *Madness and Civilization*, New York: Pantheon, 1965. (A critical history of the origins of modern psychiatry. The English translation is greatly abridged, amounting to less than half of the original.)

—— (1963) *Naissance de la clinique: une archéologie*

du régard médical, Paris: Presses Universitaires de France; trans. A. Sheridan, *The Birth of the Clinic*, New York: Vintage, 1973. (An analysis of the linguistic and conceptual structures underlying the modern practice of medicine.)

—— (1966) *Les mots et les choses: une archéologie des sciences humaines*, Paris: Gallimard; trans. A. Sheridan, *The Order of Things*, New York: Random House, 1970. (A critical history of the origins of the modern social sciences.)

—— (1969a) 'Qu'est-ce qu'un auteur?', *Bulletin de la Societé française de Philosophie* 63: 73–104; trans. 'What is an Author?', in D. Bouchard and S. Simon (eds) *Language, Countermemory, and Practice: Selected Essays and Interviews [of M. Foucault]*, Ithaca, NY: Cornell University Press, 1977. (Foucault's influential essay on the 'death of the author'.)

—— (1969b) *L'archéologie du savoir*, Paris: Gallimard; trans. A. Sheridan, *The Archaeology of Knowledge*, New York: Pantheon, 1972. (Reflections on Foucault's method of archaeological analysis.)

—— (1975) *Surveiller et punir: naissance de la prison*, Paris: Gallimard; trans. A. Sheridan, *Discipline and Punish*, New York: Pantheon, 1977. (A genealogical study of the modern prison and, more generally, of the disciplinary practices of modern society. The work introduces Foucault's influential views on knowledge and power.)

—— (1976) *Histoire de la sexualité I: la volonté de savoir*, Paris: Gallimard; trans. R. Hurley, *The History of Sexuality, Volume I: An Introduction*, New York: Pantheon, 1978. (An introduction to a projected, but never completed, series of studies on aspects of modern sexuality.)

—— (1984a) *L'usage des plaisirs: histoire de la sexualité, tome 2*, Paris: Gallimard; trans. R. Hurley, *The Use of Pleasure*, New York: Pantheon, 1985. (A study of texts by Plato, Xenophon and others, with a view to understanding the Classical Greek conception of an aesthetics of existence.)

—— (1984b) *Le souci de soi: histoire de la sexualité, tome 3*, Paris: Gallimard; trans. R. Hurley, *The Care of the Self*, New York: Pantheon, 1985. (Studies of texts from late antiquity, tracing the move from an aesthetics of existence to a hermeneutics of the self.)

—— (1994) *Dits et écrits, 1954–1988, tomes 1–4*, ed. D. Defert and F. Ewald with J. Lagrange, Paris: Gallimard. (A comprehensive collection of Foucault's essays, lectures and interviews.)

References and further reading

Armstrong, T.J. (ed. and trans.) (1991) *Michel Foucault, Philosopher*, New York: Routledge. (A collection of papers presented at a major international conference on Foucault.)

* Binswanger, L. (1954) *Le rêve et l'existence*, trans. from the German by J. Verdeaux, Bruges: Desclée de Brouwer. (Foucault's long introductory essay shows the early influence of Sartre and Heidegger.)

Deleuze, G. (1988) *Michel Foucault*, trans. S. Hand, Minneapolis, MN: University of Minnesota Press. (An analysis of Foucault's work by a friend and major French philosopher.)

Dreyfus, H. and Rabinow, P. (1983) *Michel Foucault: Beyond Structuralism and Hermeneutics*, Chicago, IL: University of Chicago Press, 2nd edn. (A very influential early interpretation of Foucault's work.)

Gutting, G. (1989) *Michel Foucault's Archaeology of Scientific Reason*, Cambridge: Cambridge University Press. (A detailed study of Foucault's writings from the early works to the *Archaeology of Knowledge*.)

—— (ed.) (1994) *The Companion to Foucault*, Cambridge: Cambridge University Press. (Essays covering most of the main areas of Foucault's thought.)

Hoy, D. (ed.) (1986) *Foucault: A Critical Reader*, Oxford: Blackwell. (A collection of some of the best essays on Foucault.)

McNay, L. (1994) *Foucault: A Critical Introduction*, New York: Continuum. (An excellent introductory survey of Foucault's work.)

Macey, D. (1993) *The Lives of Michel Foucault: A Biography*, New York: Pantheon. (The best of the several biographies of Foucault.)

Rajchman, J. (1985) *Michel Foucault: The Freedom of Philosophy*, New York: Columbia University Press. (A perceptive discussion of Foucault's 'scepticism of our modernity'.)

GARY GUTTING

FOUCHER, SIMON (1644–96)

Simon Foucher, Canon of Dijon, was a sceptical thinker, active in intellectual circles in Paris. His main philosophical project was the revival of Academic scepticism, and he emerged as an important and influential critic of Cartesian philosophy, questioning the consistency of the Cartesians' commitment both to mind–body dualism and to the claims that ideas in the mind represent and make known external bodies, and that mind and body interact. He was generally concerned to undermine the Cartesian pretension to know the real essences of mind and body. Foucher was also an early constructive critic of Leibniz's system of pre-established harmony.

1 Life and works

Foucher was born on 1 March 1644, in Dijon, France. He was ordained to the Roman Catholic priesthood while still quite young, and made an honorary canon of the Sainte Chapel of Dijon. Although he received a bachelor's degree in theology from the Sorbonne, and earned a small salary as the chaplain of a religious house in Paris, his real interests were philosophical. He spent the rest of his life in Paris, and quickly became known as a formidable critic of Cartesian philosophy. His first serious contacts with Cartesianism probably came in 1667–8 through the weekly lectures on physics given by Jacques ROHAULT. (There is an apocryphal story that Rohault asked Foucher to deliver a funeral oration when Descartes' remains were returned to Paris for burial in 1667). It was probably Rohault's lectures (and subsequent arguments between the two) that stimulated Foucher's interest in experimental physics, and in 1672 he published a letter describing various instruments for measuring air humidity. By that time, he had also developed a passion for Academic scepticism, not just as a means for criticizing what he perceived as Cartesian dogmatism, but also as a useful and important propaedeutic for Christian belief. In 1673, he published the first of three dissertations on the Academic philosophy, *Dissertation sur la recherche de la vérité, ou sur la logique des academiciens*. It was Foucher's belief that Nicolas Malebranche's *De la recherche de la vérité*, was a response to this work that led him to compose his *Critique de La recherche de la vérité* (1675), in which he criticizes Malebranche in particular and Cartesian metaphysics and epistemology generally. This was only the opening salvo in what would be an extended (and acrimonious) public polemic between Foucher and the Cartesians, especially MALEBRANCHE and Dom Robert DESGABETS (who rallied to Malebranche's defence). Foucher also found himself engaged in a fruitful, twenty-year philosophical correspondence with LEIBNIZ (whom he had met when Leibniz resided in Paris from 1672 to 1676). Foucher's early critical remarks on Leibniz's metaphysics forced Leibniz to clarify and develop his views, which Foucher helped get published. Foucher died (some said of overwork) on 27 April 1696.

2 Academic scepticism

In his assault on the Cartesian system, Foucher employed the weapons of classical scepticism. He looked, in particular, to the thinkers of the New Academy, such as Antilochus and PHILO, although he also saw Academic scepticism as a perfectly Augustinian tool that promotes Christian faith (see ACADEMY; PLATONISM, EARLY AND MIDDLE). Foucher's scepticism was of the moderate variety. He sought to steer a middle course between dogmatism and extreme Pyrrhonism (see PYRRHONISM). While there are, to be sure, many things that cannot be known, there are also some that can be known with certainty. The sincere sceptic does not doubt all things. Rather, the goal of the Academic sceptic is precisely to distinguish that which can be known from that which cannot. Philosophy just is the search for those *veritez evidentes* and *connoissances certaines* that lead to new knowledge.

According to Foucher, the criterion of truth is absolutely certain evidence, complete indubitability, particularly as detected by application of the law of non-contradiction. One should thus admit as true and as known only that which is evidently true, or that which cannot be denied without contradiction. On this criterion, it turns out that the most evident truths are mathematical and conceptual, along with introspective claims concerning states of mind. This class of self-evident truths gives us our first principles, from which we can then seek out further knowledge, particularly concerning the soul, God and the existence of the world. As long as we start from incontestable first principles and draw from them only necessary consequences, we will not be led into error and falsehood. Foucher thus sums up the Academic method in five simple principles: (1) in the matter of science, proceed only by demonstration; (2) do not concern oneself with problems that clearly cannot be resolved; (3) admit that one does not know those things that one effectively does not know; (4) distinguish those things that can be known from those that cannot be known; and (5) always seek new knowledge.

While the evidence of introspection does provide knowledge of our internal states – states of the soul, such as pleasure, pain, heat and cold sensations, and other sensible qualities as sensed – and we can infer the *existence* of external bodies in the world from the testimony of sensation, we cannot have real knowledge of the natures or essences of external things, how they are 'in themselves'. The senses, he insists, can tell us nothing about the truth of things; they provide only phenomenal appearances, and we can never know whether those appearances represent to us things are they really are. Immediately-known appearances are only 'ways of being' (*façons d'être*) or 'modifications' of the soul, which we can never compare with the things themselves, to which we have no direct access. Similar considerations apply to our knowledge of the soul. We can be certain that the soul exists, and we have immediate knowledge of the modifications or properties of the soul – that it is a thinking thing – but we cannot have certain knowledge of what the soul is in its being or nature.

In the case of the particular sciences, which are based on sense experience, Foucher insists that one can attain many probabilities, as long as one follows proper (that is, academic) method. Speculation about the causes of our sensations can lead to a kind of knowledge about the world, and will even produce many useful and practical results. But one should be properly modest (and not dogmatic) about the status of the results thereby obtained.

3 Critique of Cartesianism

Academic scepticism gave Foucher the means to criticize the Cartesians. When Descartes and his followers claim to know the essence of matter and the essence of mind, and to know therefore that these are two substances that are radically different in nature, they go beyond what is evident and certain. While Foucher, in his dissertations on *les Academiciens*, contrasts in a general way the Academic philosophy with the Cartesian philosophy, the particular occasion for him to compose a detailed critical investigation into the principles of Cartesianism was the publication in 1674 of the first volume (the first three books) of Malebranche's *Recherche*. Foucher took this to be a complete work in its own right, and this led him to misunderstand some important features of Malebranche's system. (Malebranche himself testily replied that 'when one criticizes a book, it seems one ought at least to have read it'). But although Foucher may occasionally miss the mark with respect to Malebranche, he none the less scores some important points, later to prove influential, against a more orthodox version of the Cartesian system. Foucher, in fact, takes himself to be examining not just Malebranche's work, but at the same time *une partie des principes de M. Descarte*s.

Foucher composed his *Critique* in 1674, and it was published in early 1675. His real object of attack, in this and subsequent critical works, is the confidence of Cartesians that they know the essences of mind (thought) and matter (extension). Two themes running throughout the *Critique* are, first, that these are matters for investigation, and are not to be assumed at the outset of one's inquiries; and, second, for all we

know there may be something material about the mind. Perhaps, for example, our mental operations consist in certain brain activities. Moreover, if mind–body dualism is true, Foucher argues, then there are some serious internal and sceptical problems facing Cartesian epistemology and metaphysics.

Cartesians say (and Foucher agrees) that what the mind always immediately perceives is a representative idea: external bodies are perceived only by means of ideas. But then Cartesians also want to draw a distinction between quantitative ideas (of extension and motion) that truly represent features of external bodies and qualitative sensory ideas (colours, light, heat and so on) which do not. Foucher claims that they are not entitled to this distinction. For the Cartesian, he insists, *all* ideas are only modes of being of the soul and all are caused in the mind by bodies in the same way (here he misreads Malebranche, for whom ideas properly speaking are not modes of the soul but are in God (see MALEBRANCHE, N. §§2–3). On what grounds, therefore, can one say that some mental modes represent features of external bodies and others do not? Either both kinds of ideas represent, or neither does.

In the course of his arguments in the *Critique* and other works (in effect, arguments against the difference in epistemological value granted by philosophers to 'primary quality ideas' and 'secondary quality ideas'), Foucher introduced considerations that would prove to be influential in the history of sceptical objections to the so-called 'way of ideas'. Cartesians say that we know colours, light and other such qualities through the senses; that is, that they just are sensations and properties of the mind. But if this is an argument that there is nothing like colour in external bodies, it follows that it is equally an argument that there is nothing like extension in bodies, since we also know extension through the senses. Thus, extension and figure would have to be no less 'in us' than are light and colours and heat. Moreover, if one grants that sensory qualities such as colour are in us, then it is difficult not to admit that the mathematical qualities are in us as well. First, the sceptical arguments that appeal to variations in sensory appearances to show that such qualities as heat and cold are in us and not in bodies can be used to demonstrate the same thing about all the other qualities, such as shape and size. Second, how could one claim that colours are in us without also recognizing that extension must be in us as well, since the extension of a colour, its shape, is obviously and undeniably where the colour is? Thus, once again, either both kinds of ideas represent, or neither does.

Foucher, however, raises an even deeper question

for the Cartesian theory of ideas. How can *any* mental being such as an idea represent and thus make known something material? Since, as the Cartesians insist, 'the soul has nothing at all in it that is like matter and extended beings', a mode of the soul cannot be like a material body. And if there is no likeness between an idea and a body, then an idea cannot represent a body. *None* of our ideas, for the Cartesian, should be capable of giving us knowledge of objects outside us. To save their system, Foucher believes, Cartesians deny that representation requires resemblance; words, for example, represent objects without resembling them. Foucher replies that the notion of non-resembling representative ideas is incomprehensible. On that assumption, any idea could arbitrarily represent any object and all of our ideas could represent one and the same object. Furthermore, representation (at least in its primary signification) essentially involves resemblance. Words can represent objects they do not resemble only because they excite in the mind ideas that do represent things in a primary (that is, a resembling) manner. Foucher's conclusion is that since representation requires resemblance, to posit representational ideas in the mind is to admit that mind and matter cannot be as different as the Cartesians say they are. Either our ideas do not represent material things at all, or they do so because they are like those material things – in which case the Cartesians do not really know the essences of mind and matter.

The same general sceptical conclusion is drawn from a consideration of the question of mind–body interaction. Foucher claims that Cartesians are committed to a causal principle according to which there must be an essential or substantial likeness between a cause and its effect. But for Cartesians there is no respect whatsoever in which mind and body are alike. So they must, by their own principles, deny that mind and body causally interact. But, Foucher continues, mind and body obviously *do* interact; and the causal principle is self-evident. It follows that Cartesians cannot really know the essences of mind and matter.

4 Correspondence with Leibniz

In 1676, Foucher began a correspondence with Leibniz that lasted until the end of his life. Its interest lies both in Leibniz's own comments on his constantly developing metaphysics and in Foucher's insightful constructive criticisms. The extracts published in the *Journal des sçavans* between 1692 and 1696 constitute Leibniz's first public presentation of the principles of his *nouveau système*. There is much common ground between the correspondents. They agree, for example,

on the value of Academic scepticism for philosophical inquiry, although Leibniz is the more insistent that the philosopher should seek to establish metaphysical and physical truths by building up a system from first principles. What Foucher seems to find most attractive about Leibniz's system is the critique of Cartesianism and the alternative to a strict dualism which it offers. He agrees with Leibniz, for example, that the essence of matter does not consist in extension, as the Cartesians had asserted.

Part of Leibniz's project in the 1680s and 1690s was to explain 'the communication of substances and the union of mind and body' without postulating either real causal interaction between them, or the continuous, quasi-miraculous agency of God (as Malebranche and, perhaps, if more equivocally, Descartes had done). Every individual substance, Leibniz claimed, spontaneously generates (from an inner principle of action) its own sequence of states, and God has so set up things from the start that there is, in the unfolding of the states of things over time, a 'grand concommitance' (what Leibniz later called the 'pre-established harmony') (see LEIBNIZ, G.W. §6).

Foucher grants that God could adjust things in such a way that the body could produce by itself all the movements that the soul joined to the body would produce, without giving to the soul any power to effect motion in the body; and, conversely, that the thoughts and modifications of the soul that correspond to these bodily motions could arise successively at the precise moments when the body undergoes its movements. But what, he asks, is gained by such a 'grand artifice'? As much as Malebranche's occasionalism, it has God go to a great deal of trouble to make it seem as though substances causally interact when in truth they do not (see OCCASIONALISM). God might as well dispense with material bodies altogether and simply produce thoughts and modifications in the mind directly. Bodies, on Leibniz's (and the occasionalist) view, are useless anyway, since the mind can neither move nor know them. What Foucher really wants, however, is an explanation of *how* mind and body do interact, and not the implausible claim that the appearance of interaction is misleading.

Foucher is surprised by Leibniz's account. It is clear to him that Cartesians are forced into their metaphysical contortions by their commitment to dualism: since mind and body are so unlike each other, real interaction is not possible; thus, the recourse to a *deus ex machina*. But Leibniz rejects the conception of two utterly different kinds of substance, and he puts active force in things. So what, Foucher wonders, prevents mind and body from really interacting? But perhaps, he suggests in fine sceptical manner, these are questions that we simply cannot yet resolve, at least not until all philosophers agree on the infallible criterion of truth.

5 Influence

Unlike Descartes, Malebranche and Leibniz, Foucher was not a system-builder. His philosophical talents were mainly critical and analytical in nature. Yet he is, for that reason, important and influential in the history of seventeenth and early eighteenth century philosophy, particularly through the epistemological criticisms he directed at the Cartesian theory of ideas. His sceptical arguments against the distinction between ideas which represent features of external bodies and sensations which do not, were picked up by such contemporary and later thinkers as BAYLE (*Dictionnaire historique et critique*, article on Pyrrho, remark B; article on Zeno, remarks G and H), BERKELEY (*Principles of Human Knowledge*, 8–15, and *Three Dialogues* I) and HUME (*A Treatise on Human Nature* I.4.ii).

See also: DESCARTES, R.; DUALISM; PYRRHO

List of works

Foucher, S. (1673) *Dissertation sur la recherche de la vérité, ou sur la logique des academiciens* (Dissertation on the search after truth or on the logic of the academics), Dijon. (A presentation of the principles of Academic scepticism, including a comparison with Cartesian philosophy.)

—— (1675) *Critique de La recherche de la vérité*, Paris; trans. R. A. Watson and M. Greene in *Malebranche's First and Last Critics*, Carbondale, IL: Southern Illinois University Press, 1995. (A critique of Malebranche's *Recherche de la vérité* in particular, and of Cartesian philosophy in general.)

—— (1676a) *Réponse à la Critique de la Critique de La Recherche de la vérité* (Response to the critique of the critique of the search after truth), Paris. (Foucher's response to Desgabets, who had rallied to Malebranche's defence.)

—— (1676b) *Réponse pour la Critique à la Preface du second volume de La recherche de la vérité* (Response to critique in the preface of the second volume of the search after truth), Paris. (Foucher's direct response to Malebranche's response to Foucher's original Critique.)

—— (1693) *Dissertations sur la recherche de la vérité, contenant l'histoire et les principes de la philosophie des academiciens. Avec plusiers réflexions sur les sentimens de M. Descartes* (Dissertation on the search after truth containing the history and the principles of the philosophy of the academics with

several reflections on M. Descartes' sentiments), Paris. (A compilation of the material presented in Foucher's three treatises on the Academic philosophy.)

—— (1693) 'Extrait d'une lettre de M. Foucher, chanoine de Dijon, pour repondre à M. de Leibniz sur quelques axiomes de philosophie' (Extract from a letter of M. Foucher Canon of Dijon to respond to M. Leibniz on some axioms of philosophy), *Journal des sçavans* 21 (16 March): 365–9. (Some remarks on philosophical method.)

—— (1695) 'Reponse de M. S. F. à L. B. Z. sur son nouveau sisteme de la communication des substances, proposé dans les journaux du 27 juin & 4 juillet 1695' (Response of M.S.F. à L.B.Z. on his new system of the communication of substances proposed in the journals of 27 June and 4 July 1695), *Journal des sçavans* 23 (12 September): 639–45. (Further remarks on Leibniz's metaphysics.)

References and further reading

* Bayle, P. (1696) *Dictionnaire historique et critique*, ed. and trans. R. Popkin, *Pierre Bayle, Historical and Critical Dictionary*, Indianapolis IN: Hackett, 1995. (Bayle's most important philosophical work, influenced by Foucher.)

* Berkeley, G. (1710/1713) *A Treatise concerning the Principles of Human Knowledge* and *Three Dialogues between Hylas and Philonous*, in *The Works of George Berkeley, Bishop of Cloyne*, ed. A.A. Luce and T.E. Jessop, vol. 2, Edinburgh: Thomas Nelson, 1948–57. (Both works bear Foucher's influence.)

Gouhier, H. (1927) 'La Première Polémique de Malebranche' (Malebranche's first polemic), *Revue d'histoire de la philosophie* 1: 23–48, 168–91. (Examines Foucher's criticisms of Malebranche and Malebranche's responses.)

* Hume, D. (1740) *A Treatise on Human Nature*, ed. P.H. Nidditch, Oxford: Clarendon, 1978. (Foucher's influence is evident here at I.4.ii.)

* Malebranche, N. (1674–5) *De la recherche de la vérité*, trans. T. Lennon and P.J. Olscamp as *The Search After Truth/Elucidations of the Search After Truth*, Columbus, OH: Ohio State University Press, 1980. (Malebranche's major philosophical work.)

Popkin, R. (1957) 'L'Abbé Foucher et le problème des qualités premières' (The Abbé Foucher and the problem of primary qualities), *XVIIe Siècle* 33: 633–47. (Discusses Foucher's arguments against distinguishing between ideas that represent the quantitative features of things, and ideas of sensible qualities that do not.)

—— (1980) *The High Road to Skepticism*, San Diego,

CA: Austin Hill Press; repr. as *The High Road to Pyrrhonism*, Indianapolis IN: Hackett Publishing, 1993. (A collection of essays, the first of which places Foucher's scepticism in its historical and philosophical context.)

Rabbe, F. (1867) *Étude philosophique. L'Abbé Simon Foucher chanoine de la Sainte Chapelle de Dijon* (Philosophical study: Abbé Simon Foucher Canon of the holy church of Dijon), Paris: Didier. (Foucher's life and work.)

Watson, R.A. (1987) *The Breakdown of Cartesian Metaphysics*, Atlantic Highlands, NJ: Humanities Press. (Contains a reissue of *The Downfall of Cartesianism*, which analyses Foucher's critique of Cartesian philosophy and Cartesian responses to that critique.)

—— (1991) 'Foucher's Mistake and Malebranche's Break: Ideas, Intelligible Extension and the End of Ontology', in S. Brown (ed.) *Nicolas Malebranche: His Philosophical Critics and Successors*, Van Assen: Gorcum. (Examines, in the context of the Foucher–Malebranche debate, the issue of whether epistemological questions about ideas could or should have ontological answers.)

STEVEN NADLER

FOUNDATIONALISM

Some foundationalists are rationalists who rely on intuition and deduction. Others are empiricists, in a broad sense, and accept observation and induction or abduction or yet other ways to support beliefs by means of other beliefs. What they have in common is that they are all willing to hazard a positive view about what in general makes a belief epistemically justified in the way required for it to be a case of knowledge; and they all propose something of the following general form: belief b is justified if and only if either b is foundationally justified through a psychological process of direct apprehension p (such as rational intuition, observation, introspection, and so on) or else b is inferentially justified through a psychological process of reasoning r (such as deduction, induction, abduction, and so on) ultimately from beliefs all of which are acquired or sustained through p. If one rejects all forms of such foundationalism, then a question remains as to what distinguishes in general the cases where a belief is epistemically justified from the cases in which it is not. Can anything general and illuminating be said about what confers epistemic justification on a belief, and what gives a belief the epistemic status required for it to constitute knowledge (provided it is true)?

1 Formal foundationalism versus substantive foundationalism

The foundationalism controversy in the late twentieth century can be clarified by a distinction between 'formal foundationalism' and 'substantive foundationalism'. Substantive foundationalism is opposed to coherentism; formal foundationalism is opposed not to coherentism but to what is here called (epistemic) 'pessimism'.

Formal foundationalism may be held with respect to the study of normative or evaluative principles of any sort. For instance, it may be held in ethics as well as in epistemology. Formal foundationalism in ethics tries to fix the goodness of events or states, or the rightness of actions, perhaps recursively. Thus a simple utilitarian theory might say that:

(1) every event of someone undergoing pleasure is good,

(2) every event that causes a good event is good, and

(3) every event that is good is so in virtue of (1) or (2).

(This is of course absurdly simple but it will serve as an example of a foundationalist ethical theory.)

Analogously, formal foundationalism in epistemology would say that:

(1) every belief with a certain non-epistemic property g is justified,

(2) if a belief bears relation r to a set of justified beliefs then it is itself justified, and

(3) every belief that is justified is so in virtue of (1) or (2)

There are various familiar candidates for the role of property g or of relation r. Thus property g may be indubitability or infallibility of belief, and relation r may hold between a belief b and a set α of further beliefs when b is deductively based on α. But these are only some examples.

Is there an alternative to foundationalism thus understood? If there is a class of justified beliefs at all, must it be specifiable in some illuminating way, at least recursively, or can it just be the class of justified beliefs and that is that? There is no obvious reason to think that the class of blue things must be recursively specifiable in terms of a basis and a generator that are colour-neutral. Why should we think that the class of justified beliefs must be recursively specifiable in terms of a basis and a generator that are epistemically neutral?

The main reason in favour of formal foundationalism – antecedent to an actual, compelling foundationalist theory – is the apparently supervenient or consequential character of the evaluative generally and of epistemic justification in particular. For example, an apple may be a good apple in virtue of certain non-evaluative properties: in virtue, say, of being sweet, juicy, large and so on. If so, then its evaluative property of being a good apple 'supervenes' upon its complex of non-evaluative properties that include being sweet, juicy, large and so on. And this means that any sweet, juicy, large, apple would also be a good apple. This example introduces the concept of the 'supervenient' to be defined in what follows. According to the doctrine of supervenience, evaluative and normative properties always supervene upon or derive from non-evaluative, non-normative properties, in the way the goodness of an apple might supervene upon or derive from its juiciness, sweetness and so on (see SUPERVENIENCE).

An acceptable formal foundationalist theory would specify a particular non-epistemic basis and generator, which would give more precise content to the doctrine of supervenience or consequentialism, and would fulfil its promise. Such a formal foundationalism would assure us that for every case of a justified belief, its being justified is supervenient on a set of non-epistemic facts involving only the basis property of the recursion and its generating relation. (The very same defence can be given for foundationalism in ethics, where, of course, utilitarianism is only one example of such foundationalism.)

It should be noted that formal foundationalism does not entail a doctrine of objectively unique foundations for empirical knowledge. For there might be several alternative recursive specifications of the class of justified beliefs, making use of different bases and generators, without any evident criterion for selecting one as objectively correct. If so, there might be different bases determining different foundations, none objectively prior or superior to the others.

That being so, if (for the sake of example) we presuppose a definition of the justified using indubitability as the basis and deduction as the generator, we may then think of the set of indubitable beliefs as the foundation of empirical knowledge. If so, we will be right only relative to our definition. For if the foundation is what is picked out by the basis property, then the indubitable is the foundation only relative to the definition that uses indubitability as the basis property. And so long as other definitions, using other

bases, are equally possible and on a par with ours, the relativity is ineliminable.

2 Epistemic supervenience and formal foundationalism

Pessimism is to be distinguished from the more radical position that simply rejects supervenience. The 'doctrine of supervenience' for an evaluative property f is simply that, for every x, if x has ϕ then there is a non-evaluative property (perhaps a relational property) ψ such that:

(1) x has ψ, and

(2)   necessarily, whatever has ψ has ϕ.

The denial of this for an evaluative property ϕ is a doctrine of the *autonomy* of ϕ. It holds that ϕ can be exemplified even though it does not supervene on any non-evaluative properties of what exemplifies it.

Formal foundationalism entails the doctrine of supervenience for epistemic justification, but is also considerably stronger. It requires in addition a certain faith in our intellectual powers, or a certain confidence in the manageable simplicity of the sphere of the relevant values (that is, epistemic if the foundationalism is epistemic, ethical if it is ethical, aesthetic if it is aesthetic, and so on). After all, formal foundationalism requires not just supervenience but *explicable, comprehensible* supervenience: supervenience at least surveyable by the human mind.

Accordingly, since pessimism is the denial of formal foundationalism and *not* of the weaker doctrine of supervenience, pessimism is a weaker claim than the doctrine of autonomy. Pessimism is compatible with supervenience and requires only a certain scepticism about our ability to comprehend the principles that underlie such supervenience, perhaps because they are infinite in number or degree of complexity.

Far from being pessimist, the coherence theory in epistemology is a kind of formal foundationalism, for it does try to provide principles that specify the conditions within which beliefs are justified. Thus a coherentist might choose coherence within a set of a certain sort as basis and deduction as generator. For example, a coherentist may hold that a belief is justified if and only if *either* it coheres within a large and diverse set of beliefs held by the subject *or* it is deduced by the subject from a set of such beliefs. In fact the coherentist usually has an all-encompassing basis that absorbs all generators, but this is quite compatible with formal foundationalism, though it is a limiting case (see KNOWLEDGE AND JUSTIFICATION, COHERENCE THEORY OF).

Coherentism is opposed not to formal foundationalism but at most to substantive foundationalism. The conflict here is over what basis to choose in the recursive definition of justification. Obviously, there are grades of coherentism and of foundationalism. Radical coherentism holds that *only* coherence can serve as a basis. Radical foundationalism holds that coherence *never* serves as a basis, that the basis property which gives a belief B access to the foundation never makes reference to *other* beliefs of the subject, except of course such beliefs as B itself may refer to. And various intermediate positions are clearly possible.

An infinite regress of justification is incompatible neither with formal foundationalism nor even with radical foundationalism. Consider the infinite sequence:

(P1) That there is at least one real number in the interval (0–1)

(P2) That there are at least two real numbers in the interval (0–1)

⋮

I can think of no compelling reason why there could not be a sequence of justified dispositional beliefs in (P1), (P2), . . . such that each member of the sequence is justified in the following sense (J1) by its successor: (J1) *p justifies (would justify) q if and only if that p is justified is sufficient for q to be justified.* This sense is not ruled out by formal foundationalism, nor does formal foundationalism rule out the possibility of a sequence of dispositional beliefs in (P1), (P2), ... What formal foundationalism would require of such a sequence, however, is that for each of its members there be a possible finite epistemic account or explanation of how its justification supervenes on the non-epistemic (such an explanation to be carried out perhaps by means of a non-epistemic basis g and a non-epistemic generator r).

It seems, therefore, that foundationalists misplace their objection when they focus on the infinite regress of justification. What they really oppose is pessimism. Their fundamental thesis is formal foundationalism, which we have found to be a form of the doctrine of supervenience.

G.E. Moore was optimistic enough about the possibility of a normative ethics (that is, of an ethical theory or system) to write as follows in *Principia Ethica*:

When A asks B what school he ought to send his son to, B's answer will certainly be an ethical judgment. And similarly all distribution of praise or blame to any personage or thing that has existed, now exists, or will exist, does give some answer to the question 'What is good?' . . . But this

is not the sense in which a scientific Ethics asks the question. Not one, of all the many million answers of this kind, which must be true, can form a part of an ethical system; although *that science must contain reason and principles sufficient for deciding on the truth of all of them.*

(Moore 1903: 3; emphasis added)

For Moore, a scientific ethics must have a kind of completeness which, given that it is comprehensible, it can have only if pessimism is false and formal foundationalism true.

By way of contrast, compare W.D. Ross' opposing view (1930: 41): 'For the estimation of the comparative stringency of . . . *prima facie* obligations no general rules can, so far as I can see, be laid down.' Ross' view is pessimist, but it may well be true, not only for ethics but also for epistemology. It seems unrealistic to suppose that either subject admits of the kind of completeness required by Moore. Only an evaluative monist, perhaps Mill, could reasonably believe otherwise. Mill himself was well aware of this, and made it the basis of scorn for pluralist 'intuitionism'. The pluralist must abandon all hope of attaining Moorean completeness, for there is no *general* answer accessible to our limited intellects to the question of how to resolve value conflicts or moral dilemmas.

Here we must distinguish between a general *method* for resolving such conflicts or dilemmas and its *application*. The value monist can have a method, even if it may be difficult to apply. Thus it may be difficult to tell whether a certain action would lead to more pleasure than any alternative, but at least the monist radical hedonist can tell us that it is right if and only if it does in fact do so.

Even if it turns out that one must in the end yield to pessimism, moreover, one can still reject autonomism. Suppose one resigns oneself to the fact that given epistemic pluralism (several different *basic* sources of justification) there is no possibility of a complete epistemology, such that every correct attribution of justification to a belief would follow logically from the principles of our complete epistemology and certain non-epistemic facts about the belief. Even so, one might still reasonably reject autonomism and accept supervenience by holding that for every justified belief there must be a property ψ (perhaps a very complex relational property) such that:

(1)   that belief has ψ,

(2) ψ is not a normative epistemic property, and

(3)   necessarily, whatever belief has ψ is a justified belief.

Here again the foundationalist and the coherentist could turn out to be allies. For each could surely carry on despite pessimism in an attempt to specify *as completely as possible* the conditions within which beliefs are justified. Each could retain formal foundationalism as an ideal which we might approach but probably could never reach.

Formal foundationalism leaves open the viability of coherentism even in its most radical forms, therefore, which means that *substantive* foundationalism requires additional support beyond that provided by *formal* foundationalism. We need not rehearse in detail the familiar arguments against radical coherentism, since we are not assessing the merits of that doctrine. But, these objections to coherentism should be detached from the alleged impossibility of an infinite regress of justification.

3 An argument for classical foundationalism

We turn now to the controversy between classical foundationalism (a sort of substantive foundationalism) and epistemic coherentism. Often when we are adequately justified in believing something, *p*, we are so justified on the basis of some inference or argument or adduced reasons. In such cases our belief is *mediately* justified. The foundationalistic thesis might then be put as follows:

(F) If a subject *S* has (epistemically) justified beliefs, not all of the beliefs held by *S* can be only mediately justified: *S* must (sometime) have beliefs that are immediately justified.

What is it for *S* to hold a belief *b* at least partly on the basis of another belief *b'*? What is it for the 'basing relation' *r* to hold thus from *b* to *b'*? One thing seems clearly involved: *S* must hold *b* at least partly because it holds *b'*: the latter must contribute causally to the former. More is presumably involved, but that much is enough to start a foundationalist argument as follows:

(1) There is at least one justified belief held by *S*.

(2) *r*, the basing relation among beliefs, is irreflexive.

(3) *r* is transitive.

(4) There is no infinite sequence of justified beliefs of *S*'s each member of which has a predecessor that bears *r* to it (on which it is based).

(5) Therefore, at least one justified belief held by *S* is based on no belief held by *S*.

The foundationalist concludes that there must be some way for a belief to be justified that does not involve its being based on some *other* already justified belief. Such 'immediately justified' beliefs would hence constitute a foundation on which one could erect one's system of beliefs. One could base *other* beliefs on those that are foundationally, immediately justified.

That argument for foundationalism depends crucially on the premise that the basing relation, *r*, is irreflexive (premise 2). That premise is questionable, however, as follows. The relatively clear core of the basing relation is constituted by the causal contribution relation *c*, and *c* provides a good approximation to *r*. Consider now the 'ancestral' of that relation, c^* (roughly the relation that *x* bears to *y* if and only if either *x* bears *c* to *y* or *x* bears *c* to x_1 which bears *c* to x_2 which ... which bears *c* to x_n which bears *c* to *y*). So long as we allow not only immediate or direct but, *also*, mediate and indirect basing, c^* provides an even better approximation to the basing relation than does *c*. Is c^* irreflexive? Consider two rigid cards c_1 and c_2 that support each other by each standing on end on a flat surface and leaning on the other. And suppose God creates these, already arranged thus, at a time *t*. In that case, is it not true that, for every *e*, c_1's being positioned as it is during the interval $[t$ to $(t + \varepsilon)]$ *partly results* from c_2's being positioned as it is during that interval, *and conversely*? Take then the relation of causal contribution *c* (the converse of the relation of partial resultance). From the fact that, as we have seen, *c* is not asymmetrical, it follows that c^* is not asymmetrical. Obviously, moreover, c^* is transitive. And it follows that c^* is *not* irreflexive. In our particular example what we are forced to say is that c_1's being positioned as it is during the interval $[t$ to $(t + \varepsilon)]$ *results in part* from its being so positioned during that very interval. For this contributes to supporting c_2 which, being thus supported, can return the favour coincidentally.

The case for the irreflexivity of the belief-basing relation presumably rests at least in part on the supposed irreflexivity of the causal contribution relation (or its ancestral c^*). In any case, once the latter is abandoned this is bound to weaken our intuitive support, such as it is, for accepting the former. And that intuitive support can also be attacked directly in terms of examples such as one in terms of the following five propositions:

(P1) It is drizzling.

(P2) Expanding circles are constantly forming in the puddles.

(P3) There is a pitter-patter on the window panes.

(P4) There was a forecast of drizzle or rain by now.

(P5) Car wipers are on.

If, at a given time, *t*, I believe all five of these, what is wrong with supposing each to be based in part (perhaps in *small* part) on the others?

4 Foundationalism versus coherentism

The beliefs supporting a belief p_1 held by a subject S might be thought to form one of at least three possible structures: (1) first, a 'tree' that branches infinitely upwards from the 'root' node constituted by S's belief p_1; (2) second, a pyramid with foundational beliefs on which rest level after level of beliefs supported by reasoning and leading ultimately to S's belief p_1 at the tip of the pyramid; (3) third, a raft, one of whose planks is S's belief p_1, where each of the many planks is held in place by its ties of coherence with the other planks.

So far the foundationalist has ruled the tree out of the question for limited human minds, and argued against the raft by supposing that such belief structures must be built by means of some causal belief-basing relation that must be both irreflexive and transitive. Given these assumptions, it follows that any justified set of beliefs held by a limited subject must take the form of a foundational pyramid. As we have seen, however, it is questionable whether the relevant causal-contribution and belief-basing relations must be indeed irreflexive. And doubt on the irreflexivity assumption undermines the foregoing line of reasoning for pyramidal foundations of knowledge. We do well to consider another approach.

A belief may be both true and justified without being knowledge. This is shown by any Gettier example in which someone is justified in believing some falsehood f from which in turn they deduce a truth, t. Their belief that t is then both true and justified without being knowledge (see GETTIER PROBLEMS). A particularly striking Gettieresque case is that of the victim of an evil demon who is allowed a *true* belief that he faces a fire, along with a set of necessarily associated truths – one, however, that is minuscule by comparison with the falsehood that massively surrounds it in our victim's belief set. Concerning the experiences, memories, introspections and reasonings of the victim, there is not the slightest flaw: the victim is, internally, as cognitively worthy as the best of us (see INTERNALISM AND EXTERNALISM IN EPISTEMOLOGY). In that sense, therefore, the victim is perfectly well justified in believing that they face a nearby fire. And there is indeed such a fire there. But clearly our victim has no knowledge of that fact, despite the fact that the belief is true and well justified, not if their supporting web of beliefs, and their broader belief system, is almost entirely a tissue of falsehoods; so that, for example, their visual, auditory and other experiences as of a fire before them are entirely unaffected by the fire there, and so on.

What is involved in such internal justification? Classical coherentism and foundationalism are best understood, it seems, as accounts of such justification. According to coherentism, one's belief b is thus justified if and only if b coheres well enough with one's system of beliefs. Let us explore this briefly before turning to foundationalism.

Coherence involves the logical, explanatory, and probabilistic relations among one's beliefs. However, it would not do to attain a tightly interrelated system by merely lopping off whatever beliefs may refuse to fit. Theoretically, it would be possible (perhaps with the aid of advanced cognitive technology) to perform such drastic surgery on one's belief system. But that would not necessarily yield epistemic justification. Thus take arbitrary beliefs p (that the moon is made of cheese) and q (that clouds are cotton wool) and surround those beliefs with the likes of $(p \supset q)$, $(q \supset (p \supset q))$, $(q \supset p)$, $(p \supset (q \supset p))$, and so on. (The '$\supset$' stands for material implication; so an expression of the form '$x \supset y$' is shorthand for 'either not-x or y'.) The result will be a set that is not only tightly coherent but also as large as one may like. Yet it will obviously lack a desirable sort of scope or comprehensiveness none the less. Such comprehensiveness is hence not just a matter of numerosity; scope of subject matter also counts.

Such comprehensiveness, even when tightly coherent, still will not suffice for justification, however. Take one's I/now perspective. Suppose one replaces one's concepts of (1) oneself, and (2) the present, wherever they may figure in one's vast system of object level beliefs, by corresponding concepts of (1′) the holder of passport number n, and (2′) 18 May 1998. This system will nearly match one's original system in true comprehensiveness and in interlocking coherence. Yet there is little semblance of justification in it. One will be wildly unjustified in attributing to the holder of passport number n, as of 18 May 1998, the vast set of things that one attributes to oneself now. The coherentist needs to require interlocking comprehensiveness not only with regard to the object level of beliefs, but also in a way that reaches up to meta-levels, where one takes note, at least implicitly, of the sources of one's beliefs and of how reliable these are, and so on. Once this is required, the transformation from the I/now system to the passport number n/18 May 1998 system is blocked.

Even that seems insufficient, however, if it is conceivable that such a comprehensively coherent system of beliefs could still fail to mesh properly with the subject's sensory experience. This failure of mesh might occur in either or both of two ways. Someone might experience as if p and might have no reason to question or resist such prompting to believe that p, but might none the less believe something, that q, incompatible with the proposition that p, and might even believe that $\sim p$ for good measure. In addition they might have a conspicuous experience e – a splitting headache, say – and might none the less believe that they do *not* have such an experience. If such failure of mesh is indeed possible, then it could preclude even a highly coherent and comprehensive system of beliefs from rendering its member beliefs justified.

Coherentism seems well advised to adopt such requirements of (1) comprehensiveness, (2) perspectival content, and (3) mesh with experience. With such needful qualifications and improvements, coherentism is on a rapprochement course with classical foundationalism as accounts of (internal) justification. This seems especially clear in light of the fact that foundationalism, for its part, seems forced to withdraw its objections to mutually supportive beliefs, and must willingly allow that the appropriate internal coherence of a body of beliefs can indeed account for much of the justification that resides in the member beliefs. The potential for a meeting of the minds is evident if we put it this way: the coherence required for epistemic justification in a system of beliefs requires that the system of beliefs be appropriately comprehensive. And this in turn requires that the system of beliefs should include an epistemic (meta) perspective, *and* a suitable complement of *foundational* beliefs! Once it is put thus, the game is obviously up. Both sides score significant points. Coherentism scores for its emphasis on appropriately comprehensive (and perspectival) coherence, an indispensable component of our concluding view. And foundationalism scores for its emphasis on the extrabelief components that are clearly needed in an appropriately justified system: especially the need for appropriate mesh with experience.

See also: CERTAINTY; EMPIRICISM; JUSTIFICATION, EPISTEMIC; KNOWLEDGE, CONCEPT OF; RATIONALISM; REASONS FOR BELIEF

References and further reading

Alston, W. (1990) *Epistemic Justification: Essays in the Theory of Knowledge*, Ithaca, NY: Cornell University Press. (Influential essays by a distinguished epistemologist.)

Audi, R. (1993) *The Structure of Justification*, Cambridge: Cambridge University Press. (Collected essays by an important defender of a moderate foundationalism.)

Chisholm, R.M. (1982) *The Foundations of Knowing*, Minneapolis, MN: University of Minnesota Press. (Influential defence of foundationalism, especially in chapters 1 and 6.)

Kuhn, T. (1977) *The Essential Tension*, Chicago, IL: University of Chicago Press. (See especially 'Objectivity, Value Judgment, and Theory Choice' for a case in favour of the reality and importance of epistemic dilemmas.)

Lewis, C.I. (1946) *An Analysis of Knowledge and its Valuation*, La Salle, IL: Open Court. (Thorough defence of a radical form of foundationalism by a major figure.)

Mill, J.S. (1861) *Utilitarianism*, London: Dent, 1971. (Classic account of right action unified under its single overarching principle of utility. Many editions are available.)

* Moore, G.E. (1903) *Principia Ethica*, Cambridge: Cambridge University Press, 1930. (Main work in ethics by a major founding-figure of analytic philosophy.)

Moser, P. (1989) *Knowledge and Evidence*, Cambridge: Cambridge University Press. (Sophisticated booklength development of strong foundationalism, the most thorough and unified.)

Reid, T. (1785) *Essays on the Intellectual Powers of Man*, ed. B. Brody, Cambridge, MA: MIT Press, 1969. (Classic work whose importance is growing steadily.)

* Ross, W.D. (1930) *The Right and the Good*, Oxford: Clarendon Press. (Important work that defends radical pluralism.)

Sosa, E. (1991) *Knowledge in Perspective*, Cambridge: Cambridge University Press. (Detailed discussion of the foundationalism-coherentism controversy, especially in parts II and III.)

ERNEST SOSA

FRANCIS OF MEYRONNES (d. after 1325)

Francis of Meyronnes, the doctor illuminatus (Enlightened Doctor), was called the 'Prince of the Scotists' for his work in systematizing and propagating the philosophy of Duns Scotus in the fourteenth century. His work in metaphysics and theology, while heavily dependent on Scotus, shows originality and independence of mind, and is characterized by his dedication to finding rational defences of Catholic doctrine. His discussion of Ideas includes a critique of Aristotelian metaphysics, and he argues instead for a position based on his conception of Platonism.

Born in Provence, Francis joined the Franciscan order and studied theology at the University of Paris, where he was probably a pupil of John DUNS SCOTUS some time between 1304 and 1307. In 1323 he was awarded the degree of Master of Theology. Prior to this, in the academic year 1320–21, he represented the Scotist school in a spirited debate with the Thomist Peter Roger (later Pope Clement VI) over Trinitarian theology. However, Francis was never merely Scotus' mouthpiece, but was an original and creative thinker. He often addressed philosophical issues in ways Scotus did not, and criticized Scotus when he found the latter lacking. Francis's written work, which shows the influence also of AUGUSTINE, PSEUDO-DIONYSIUS and Avicenna (see IBN SINA), includes sermons, commentaries on the Bible, studies of theology, metaphysics and moral philosophy, and commentaries on the works of ARISTOTLE, Pseudo-Dionysius and Augustine. His writings became very popular in the later Middle Ages, in particular his *Conflatus*, a revision of his commentary on Book I of Peter Lombard's *Sentences* (see LOMBARD, P.).

Francis argues that theologians cannot demonstrate the doctrine of the Trinity, but they can defend it against objections. According to this doctrine, as Francis understands it, God is a Trinity of three persons – Father, Son and Holy Spirit – three things, each of which is the same as the divine essence (see TRINITY). Francis recognizes that this doctrine is vulnerable to criticism. For instance, the Father begets the Son, and the Son is begotten by the Father. However, the divine essence, which is the same as the Father, does not beget; nor is it begotten, although it is the same as the Son. Either the principle of non-contradiction does not apply to God, or each divine person must be distinct in some way from the divine essence.

Accepting the first alternative would, of course, put an end to all rational inquiry about God. Francis holds instead that each person of the Trinity is distinct in some way from the divine essence. These are not real distinctions, for real distinctions hold between things, and the doctrine of the Trinity maintains that God is three things, not four. Nor, he argues, are the distinctions purely conceptual: mental constructs that do not reflect any distinction in the Trinity itself. The sort of distinction that holds between a person and the divine essence lies between the real and the purely conceptual. Following Scotus, Francis calls this the *formal* distinction.

Scotus makes the formal distinction a cornerstone of his philosophy, and Francis builds on that cornerstone. To say of *x* and *y* that they are formally distinct is to say that they are really the same – they are not two things – but that *x* can be characterized differently than *y*, and the different characterizations accurately capture facts about *x* and *y* and are not simply mental constructs. By appealing to the formal

distinction in order to explain how each divine person is rightly characterized in a way different from the essence, Francis attempts both to defend the orthodox doctrine of the Trinity and to preserve the possibility of rational theology. Furthermore, Francis argues, this solution carries the weight of authority. Examining the history of Trinitarian theology, Francis finds that orthodox theologians such as BONAVENTURE and AQUINAS had been working toward this solution, though they had not fully articulated it.

Francis's originality displays itself in the *Conflatus*, in a series of articles on Ideas. He begins by asking whether there are Ideas in the mind of God. Ideas conceived in this way – the way theologians conceive of them – are the eternal, immutable archetypes of created things. Francis, however, does not see any necessity for concluding that there are such Ideas in God's mind. He explores Augustine's reasons for maintaining that there are Ideas in God, but finds them inconclusive. Nevertheless, he finds the view that there are Ideas in God's mind a plausible one, and he is willing to concede this point on the authority of Augustine.

According to Francis, when metaphysicians discuss Ideas, they are referring not to divine, immutable archetypes, but to the quiddities, or defining characteristics, of things. Are these Ideas, as Plato argues, separated from particulars? Francis recounts the commonly held view that the quiddities are conjoined to individuating conditions in particular things, but the intellect can abstract a quiddity from its individuating condition. According to this view, there are indeed separated Ideas, but only in intellects. Francis rejects this view, offering instead what he takes to be Plato's position: there are separated Ideas prior to any activity of the intellect, and in fact it is the Idea's separation that grounds its abstractability by the intellect. Ideas are separated not only from the individuating conditions, but also from potentiality and actuality, existence, time and place. The Idea *equinity*, for example, is not actual or potential, existent or nonexistent, located in any place or at any time. It is, as Avicenna maintains, just equinity.

The reason so few philosophers have subscribed to Plato's view, Francis suggests, is that Aristotle misrepresented it to posterity. According to Francis – who had almost no direct access to Plato's works – Aristotle ascribes to Plato the ridiculous view that the Ideas are bizarre particulars which exist in the air. Francis thinks that Aristotle, motivated by jealousy, tried to sabotage Plato's reputation. Otherwise we would have to say that although Aristotle was the best natural philosopher, he was the worst metaphysician, because he did not understand abstraction. Plato, Francis supposes, never held that Ideas are separated from particulars locally, but only formally. On Francis' view, the formal distinction is a cornerstone not just of Scotism, but of Platonism as well (see NOMINALISM; REALISM AND ANTIREALISM).

See also: PLATONISM, MEDIEVAL

List of works

Francis of Meyronnes (1320–1) *In libros sententiarum* (Commentary on the *Sentences*), first printed edition Venice, 1520; repr. Frankfurt: Minerva, 1966. (An extensive discussion of a vast array of philosophical and theological issues raised in or suggested by Peter Lombard's *Sentences.*)
—— (1323–25?) *Quodlibeta* (Quodlibetal Questions), first printed edition Venice, 1520; repr. Frankfurt: Minerva, 1966. (Records Francis' answers to a series of questions originally posed during disputations by members of the academic community. The questions concern diverse issues ranging from Trinitarian theology to the obedience owed by secular rulers to the church.)

References and further reading

Maurer, A. (1990) *Being and Knowing: Studies in Thomas Aquinas and Later Medieval Philosophers,* Toronto, Ont.: Pontifical Institute of Medieval Studies. (Contains two earlier articles by Maurer, one on Francis' epistemology and his disagreements with Ockham and Aureol (311–31) and the second on Francis' account of infinity as the primary mode of being in God (333–59).)
Roth, B. (1936) *Franz. von Mayronis, O.F.M. Sein Leben, seine Werke, seine Lehre vom Formalunterschied in Gott* (Francis of Meyronnes, OFM: His Life, Works and Teaching on the Formal Distinction in God), Werl-in-Westfalen: Franziskus-Druckerei. (The most complete study of Francis's life and works.)
Vignaux, P. (1962) 'L'être comme perfection selon François de Meyronnes' (Being as Perfection according to Francis of Meyrones), *Études d'histoire littéraire et doctrinale,* Publications de l'Institut d'Études Médiévales, Paris: Vrin, and Montreal: Institut d'Études Médiévales, 259–318. (An excellent but technical essay focusing on Francis's differences from Scotus, in particular his Platonism.)

JEFFREY HAUSE

FRANCIS SYLVESTER OF FERRARA *see* SILVESTRI, FRANCESCO

FRANCISCO DE TOLEDO *see* TOLETUS, FRANCISCUS

FRANCISCUS PATRITIUS *see* PATRIZI DA CHERSO, FRANCESCO

FRANK, JEROME (1889–1957)

Jerome Frank was a significant contributor to the 'realist' movement in US legal theory. He is most closely associated with 'fact scepticism', the view that legal processes, especially court processes, are afflicted with pervasive uncertainty and unpredictability because of the difficulties of finding out with certainty or even strongly justified confidence what happened in the past.

Frank himself distinguished 'fact scepticism' from rule scepticism. By contrast with doubt arising from uncertainty in interpreting rules, 'fact scepticism' concerns the difficulties of finding out about past events, difficulties inevitably exacerbated by the adversarial character of legal processes conducted under common law, most notably where a jury is involved. Since 'facts' in the legal sense are both uncertain and malleable, the personal predilections and intuitions of the trier of fact come to be primary determinants of the practical outcomes of trials and litigations (see LEGAL EVIDENCE AND INFERENCE §1; LEGAL REASONING AND INTERPRETATION §§1,2).

Frank's theoretical views about law arose from his engagement in legal practice and in New Deal politics, and finally from experience as a Federal appellate judge in the USA. Although he taught occasionally at Yale in his later years, he was never a full-time academic lawyer. His philosophical contributions are the reflections of a legal practitioner, not of a philosopher of law. In fact, he came to legal practice with considerable reluctance and under pressure from his family. This may account for the fact that quite early in his career he underwent psychoanalysis, becoming in consequence an advocate of the relevance of Freud's theories to legal understanding. Humans' delusory belief in and search for certainty in law he likened to the search in life for a father-figure as a repository of unquestionable authority. The process of achieving adulthood was the process of abandoning the myths of certainty and acknowledging the irreducible indeterminacy and negotiability of practical life. This case was put vigorously in his *Law and the Modern Mind* (1930), which achieved some standing as an account of realist ideas accessible to the general reader. His later work, culminating in *Courts on Trial* (1949), carried forward his critique of adversarial processes and over-reliance on juries and other characteristic institutions of the common law.

Despite his scepticism concerning the determinability of past facts, he retained an ideal of a legal system that could function more objectively and predictably than the one in which he worked and to which he contributed a great deal both intellectually and judicially. As a judge of the Courts of Appeals for the Second Circuit (a position to which he was appointed by President Roosevelt in 1941), he showed himself to be a friend of civil liberties and a proponent of judicial activism especially in favour of individuals under threat from encroachment by the state. While many commentators have found his doctrines somewhat overstated, and indeed they do contain elements easy to caricature, there is no doubt that Frank left an important mark upon jurisprudence. After him, it has been impossible for serious thought about the judicial process to ignore the crucial elements of fact-finding, evidence and proof, and the special problems attendant on these subjects.

See also: LAW, PHILOSOPHY OF; LEGAL REALISM §§2–3

List of works

Frank, J. (1930) *Law and the Modern Mind*, Birmingham, AL: Legal Classics Library, 1985. (This is a reprint of the original edition, including a useful introduction by Julian Mack.)
—— (1949) *Courts on Trial*, Princeton, NJ: Princeton University Press. (This collection of papers expresses Frank's mature thought on the wide range of subjects about administering justice that his life's work focused on.)

References and further reading

Chase, A. (1979) 'Jerome Frank and American Psychoanalytic Jurisprudence', *International Journal of Law and Psychiatry* 2: 329–48. (A useful account of the influence of psychoanalytic thought on Frank, and of his application of it to law.)
Duxbury, N. (1991) 'Jerome Frank and the Legacy of Legal Realism', *Journal of Law and Society* 18:

175–205. (A particularly helpful and balanced summary of Frank's thought and influence.)
Glennon, R.J. (1985) *The Iconoclast as Reformer: Jerome Frank's Impact on American Law*, Ithaca, NY: Cornell University Press. (Valuable, constructively critical, biography and account of Frank's work and influence.)

NEIL DUXBURY
NEIL MacCORMICK

FRANK, SEMËN LIUDVIGOVICH (1877–1950)

The philosophy of S.L. Frank was one product of the renewed interest in epistemology, speculative metaphysics and religion among educated Russians in the quarter-century preceding the Revolution of 1917. Frank published the first volume of his philosophical system in 1915, but most of his major works were written after the Revolution, in European exile.

Influenced by tendencies in turn-of-the-century European thought that criticized the exaggerated pretensions of scientific reason, Frank formed the conviction that abstract, conceptual thought was inherently incapable of mastering ultimate reality. A valid metaphysics was nevertheless possible, founded on our capacity for direct, intuitive apprehension of reality in its living concreteness.

In intuitive knowledge, reality discloses itself as a 'total-unity' – an all-embracing unity in which the dualities with which conceptual thought wrestles are overcome without being dissolved. Ultimate reality is itself grounded in, and embraced by, a principle Frank termed 'Divinity', one that manifests itself in religious experience as the personal God of Christian faith. The rootedness of the human person in this divine principle is the condition of possibility of all spiritual creativity – of art, science, morality and law, and religion.

1 Life; sources of his thought
2 First philosophy (epistemology, logic, metaphysics)
3 The metaphysics of human nature; the doctrine of Godmanhood
4 Social philosophy

1 Life; sources of his thought

Semën Liudvigovich Frank was born in Moscow, of Jewish parentage. Converted to Marxism at the age of 16, he chose to devote his studies at Moscow University (1894–8) to political economy. In 1899, he was briefly detained by the tsarist police for his involvement in revolutionary activities. He subsequently attended lectures on economics and philosophy at the universities of Berlin and Heidelberg. By 1901, he had ceased to consider himself a Marxist, but remained a proponent of social as well as political democracy for Russia. In 1903, he began his long, intimate journalistic collaboration with P.B. Struve, a pioneer of the philosophical revival and a leading figure in the emerging Russian liberal movement. As a supporter of constitutional government, Frank initially hailed the Russian Revolution of 1905 with enthusiasm; its ultimate failure precipitated major changes in his views. After 1906, Frank was an unsparing critic of socialism; of the many articles he wrote criticizing the beliefs and mentality of the Russian left, the most famous is his contribution to the 1909 *Vekhi* (*Signposts*) symposium (see SIGNPOSTS MOVEMENT §1–3). At this time, he also abandoned the Fichtean idealism professed in his early philosophical writings in favour of the spiritualist metaphysics characteristic of his mature works.

Although Frank now became the advocate of a religious outlook on life, he never returned to Judaism. In 1908, he married a Gentile; in 1912, he was baptized into the Russian Orthodox Church.

Soon after his marriage, Frank resolved upon a career as a professional philosopher. After passing his master's examination at the University of St Petersburg, he was appointed, in 1912, as an unsalaried lecturer there. He subsequently held professorships at the universities of Saratov and Moscow.

Frank was one of many prominent anti-Marxist academics arrested in 1922 and deported from Soviet Russia. He spent the first fifteen years of his exile in Berlin, where he taught at various émigré educational institutions, and, briefly, at the University. His Jewish ancestry led to his dismissal from his posts after Hitler came to power, but he was not able to escape from Germany until 1937. The final dozen years of his life, during which he wrote his last three books, were passed in France and Britain.

In exile, Frank styled himself a 'Christian Platonist', claiming PLOTINUS and NICHOLAS OF CUSA as his 'masters' in philosophy. But his mature thought was actually shaped by a great variety of philosophical influences. The Kantian tradition, with which he associated himself in his earliest philosophical writings, impressed a permanent stamp on his thinking about epistemology (see NEO-KANTIANISM). Other, countervailing influences on his mature epistemological views were the writings of Goethe, Bergson, N.O. Lossky and Husserl. Frank's thought on logic was indebted to both Hegel and Hermann Cohen. While his mature metaphysical system bears a broad resemblance to that of Vladimir SOLOV'ËV (who

popularized the term 'total-unity' in Russia), the extent of Solov'ëv's actual impact on Frank has arguably been overstated by historians of Russian philosophy.

2 First philosophy (epistemology, logic, metaphysics)

In his first major work, *Predmet znaniia* (*The Object of Knowledge*) (1915), Frank maintained that epistemology, logic and metaphysics constitute a single philosophical discipline, to which (following Aristotle) he gave the name 'first philosophy'. Neither epistemology nor logic could claim the rank of an autonomous branch of philosophy, since a correct solution to their fundamental problems could only be attained through an inquiry which brought the problem of knowledge into relation with the problem of being. Metaphysics was not an independent discipline either, since an understanding of the true character of ultimate reality could only be reached by way of an analysis of human knowledge.

Frank distinguished three different modes of knowledge: 'abstract' or 'conceptual' knowledge; 'intuition'; and 'living knowledge'. Abstract knowledge, which relates particular concepts to each other in judgments, is generally thought to be the only kind of knowledge there is: both our everyday understanding of the world and organized science are systems of conceptual judgments. But Frank contended that we cannot explain how abstract knowledge is possible unless we recognize that it is dependent upon a prior form of cognitive access to reality: a direct intuition of being as an integral whole, unmediated by concepts.

The concepts with which abstract knowledge operates are fixed 'determinations', subject to the logical laws of identity, contradiction and the excluded middle. To account for our ability to affirm, in the judgment 'A is B', a necessary connection between two discrete, mutually exclusive conceptual contents, the philosopher must concede that we already 'possess' both A and B in a form in which they are not discrete determinations, but moments of a 'metalogical unity' to which these logical laws do not apply. Valid conceptual knowledge becomes possible only after we have intuited the necessary connection between A and B as nondiscrete elements in a continuous whole. This continuous whole is the 'total-unity', the all-encompassing unity outside of which nothing is conceivable. All particular knowledge is partial knowledge of this whole; abstract knowledge can be systematic only because the elements of the total-unity constitute a system.

We can possess the total-unity prior to the cognitive acts that engender conceptual knowledge because the total-unity transcends the opposition between being and knowledge; it is not simply 'being' but also 'thought'; it is not objective being (being for a subject) but absolute being, a reality that reveals itself to itself. As existent entities, we humans belong to being; our being is the being of the total-unity. Accordingly, we participate, albeit imperfectly, in the knowledge reality has of itself. This ontological communion we enjoy with the reality we seek to know is the supreme condition of possibility of all knowledge.

In abstract knowledge, and even in intuition, our ontological communion with the object of knowledge is imperfect: the knowing subject remains enclosed in itself and merely sends out 'rays' which illuminate its object. Living knowledge, the third mode of knowing distinguished by Frank, involves a much deeper kind of communion with the object: a mutual penetration, as a result of which the knower merges with the thing known and, as it were, experiences it from inside. Living knowledge was not, for Frank, a rare or esoteric phenomenon; it is instanced in every genuine encounter with another 'I'; in the uncanny insights of the real expert dealing with the objects of their passionate concern; and in all aesthetic, moral and religious experience.

Philosophy itself, as Frank conceived it, is 'transcendental thinking': living knowledge of absolute being as the ground of rational, conceptual thought. Since absolute being transcends the oppositions between concepts which are ultimate for abstract knowledge, philosophy can find verbal expression only in the form of 'antinomian knowledge'. In speaking of the total-unity, the philosopher must couple every affirmative judgment with a negative judgment that logically contradicts it, but in uttering these judgments does not affirm any contradiction within the total-unity itself.

3 The metaphysics of human nature; the doctrine of Godmanhood

Frank's metaphysics of total-unity provided him with a philosophical framework within which to examine a wide range of questions relating to our place, as human beings, in the universe and to the meaning and purposes of human life. His second book, *Dusha cheloveka* (*Man's Soul*) (1917) shows that most of the principles which guided his mature thinking on these subjects had been formulated before the Revolution; but his 'metaphysics of human nature' and philosophy of religion were fully elaborated only in his writings of the 1930s and 1940s.

The foundation of all Frank's thinking about human life was a conception of the 'person' as a

'divine-human' entity. Frank labelled this conception – a complex amalgam of Neoplatonic, Romantic and Christian ideas – the doctrine of 'Godmanhood'.

According to Frank, when we contemplate our own inner life – prescinding from the varied interactions with the external world which usually monopolize our conscious attention – we encounter an elusive mode of being which he terms 'psychic life' or 'immediate self-being'. 'Pure' psychic life may be characterized as a restless chaos of formless potentiality; but we almost always experience psychic being as 'formed' by active forces which penetrate it, organize it and direct its flow into particular channels. Some of the forces which shape psychic life have their origin in this sphere of being itself. But the most exalted of them – those which direct the soul in its highest creative activities – emanate from a sphere of being that lies beyond the threshold of the individual self, the sphere of supra-individual 'spiritual life'. The true 'centre' of the *person* lies outside the individual human self, in the realm of spirit, and through spirit is rooted in the divine principle which grounds all things. To conceive the person as an isolated individuality is the great error of modern humanism, an error which takes its revenge upon humanism in fascist and communist ideology and practice.

True philosophy, for Frank, must therefore be 'religious' philosophy. He believed that the eternal truths of religion had found their most perfect historical embodiment in the Christian faith. But a philosophy which is religious, while harmonizing with the essential teachings of Christianity, will rest on universal truths revealed in the philosopher's own religious and metaphysical experience; it need not derive its premises from the positive revelation preserved by the Church.

4 Social philosophy

Frank outlined the fundamental theses of his social philosophy in *Dukhovnye osnovy obshchestva* (*The Spiritual Foundations of Society*) (1930); in *Svet vo t'me* (*The Light Shineth in Darkness*) (1949), he discussed the dilemmas posed for a Christian social ethics by the power of evil in human affairs.

On the empirical plane, society presents itself to us as an aggregate of competing individuals, who accept a measure of subordination to a guiding social will in the form of personal 'power' or impersonal 'law'. The error of liberal social theory is to suppose that the inner essence of society coincides with this, its external manifestation. In its essence, apparent only to living knowledge, society is a primary ontological reality, no less 'real' than the individuals who constitute it, a spiritual communion founded on the shared obligation of service to divine truth. The impossibility of fully realizing the essential nature of human social life in a world subject to sin expresses itself in the unresolvable tension between the demands of inner moral life and the imperatives of law and outward social morality.

Since the late 1980s, many of Frank's works have been reprinted in Russia. Until then, his influence was largely confined to Russian émigré circles. There, his achievement was much esteemed; V.V. Zenkovsky ranked him as the most eminent of all Russian philosophers. Frank wrote a philosophical prose remarkable for its clarity and concision.

See also: RUSSIAN RELIGIOUS-PHILOSOPHICAL RENAISSANCE §4

List of works

Frank, S. (1909) 'Ètika nigilizma', in *Vekhi: Sbornik statei o russkoi intelligentsii*, Moscow: M. Sablin; trans. M. Shatz and J. Zimmerman, 'The Ethic of Nihilism: A Characterization of the Russian Intelligentsia's Moral Outlook', *Vekhi (Landmarks): A Collection of Articles about the Russian Intelligentsia*, Armonk, NY: M.E. Sharpe, 1994, 131–55. (Frank's extremely influential critique of the Russian revolutionary left's incoherent ethical outlook; the English translation supplies historical background helpful in understanding the essay.)

—— (1915) *Predmet znaniia: Ob osnovakh i predelakh otvlechënnogo znaniia* (The Object of Knowledge: On the Grounds and Limits of Abstract Knowledge), Petrograd: R.G. Shrëder; abridged French trans. Kaffi, Oldenbourg and Fedotoff, *La connaissance et l'être*, Paris: Aubier, 1937. (Frank's fundamental work: a dense, technical and closely argued exposition of his 'first philosophy'.)

—— (1917) *Dusha cheloveka: Opyt vvedeniia v filosofskuiu psikhologiiu*, Petrograd: Sakharov & Leman; trans. B. Jakim, *Man's Soul: An Introductory Essay in Philosophical Psychology*, Athens, OH: Ohio University Press, 1993. (A subtle and complex analysis of human psychic life and its relation to other modes of being. 'Foreword' by P. Swoboda sets the work in its historical and philosophical context.)

—— (1930) *Dukhovnye osnovy obshchestva: Vvedenie v sotsial'nuiu filosofiiu*, Paris: YMCA-Press; trans. B. Jakim, *The Spiritual Foundations of Society: An Introduction to Social Philosophy*, Athens, OH: Ohio University Press, 1987. (A short, fairly accessible treatise.)

—— (1939) *Nepostizhimoe: Ontologicheskoe vvedenie v filosofiiu religii*, Paris: Dom Knigi & Sovremennye

zapiski; trans. B. Jakim, *The Unknowable: An Ontological Introduction to the Philosophy of Religion*, Athens, OH: Ohio University Press, 1983. (A tour of the entire system of reality, often regarded as Frank's most important book; skilfully written and challenging to read.)

—— (1946) *God With Us: Three Meditations*, trans. N. Duddington, London: Jonathan Cape; *S nami Bog: Tri razmyshleniia*, Paris: YMCA-Press, 1964. (A presentation of Frank's philosophy of religion, first published in translation, intended for the general reader.)

—— (1949) *Svet vo t'me: Opyt khristianskoi ètiki i sotsial'noi filosofii*, Paris: YMCA-Press; trans. B. Jakim, *The Light Shineth in Darkness: An Essay in Christian Ethics and Social Philosophy*, Athens, OH: Ohio University Press, 1989. (An eloquent philosophical meditation on the struggle with evil in the world; very accessible.)

—— (1956) *Real'nost' i chelovek: Metafizika chelovecheskogo bytiia*, Paris: YMCA-Press; trans. N. Duddington, *Reality and Man: An Essay on the Metaphysics of Human Nature*, New York: Taplinger, 1965. (Covers much the same ground as *Nepostizhimoe* on a more popular level.)

References and further reading

Boobbyer, P. (1995) *S.L. Frank: The Life and Work of a Russian Philosopher, 1877–1950*, Athens, OH: Ohio University Press. (The first full-length biography of Frank; some discussion of his philosophy; good bibliography.)

Copleston, F. (1986) *Philosophy in Russia: From Herzen to Lenin and Berdyaev*, Tunbridge Wells: Search Press. (Chapter 13 offers a very brief but eminently readable account of Frank's philosophy.)

Edie, J., Scanlan, J., Zeldin, M. and Kline, G. (1976) *Russian Philosophy*, Knoxville, TN: University of Tennessee Press, vol. 3, 277–304. (Contains a brief sketch of Frank's life and thought, and two well-chosen excerpts from his late writings.)

Frank, V. (1980) *Bibliographie des oeuvres de Simon Frank*, Paris: Institut d'Études Slaves. (Helpful, although not altogether complete.)

Lossky, N. (1951) *History of Russian Philosophy*, New York: International Universities Press, 266–92. (A detailed and generally critical summary of the contents of *Predmet znaniia* and *Nepostizhimoe*; fairly difficult.)

Swoboda, P. (1995) 'Windelband's Influence on S.L. Frank', *Studies in East European Thought* 47: 259–90. (A discussion of the enduring influence of Neo-Kantianism on Frank's thinking; fairly difficult.)

* Zenkovsky, V.V. (1948–50) *Istoriia russkoi filosofii*, Paris: YMCA-Press, 2 vols; 2nd edn 1989; trans. G.L. Kline, *A History of Russian Philosophy*, vol. 2, London: Routledge & Kegan Paul and New York: Columbia University Press, 1953, 852–72. (The standard history; both admiring and critical in its treatment of Frank; ignores the Western influences on his thought; somewhat challenging for non-specialists.)

PHILIP J. SWOBODA

FRANKFURT SCHOOL

The origins of the circle of philosophers and social scientists now known as the Frankfurt School lie in the 1920s when a number of critics and intellectuals were attempting to adapt Marxism to the theoretical and political needs of the time. The distinguishing feature of the approach adopted by the Frankfurt School lies less in its theoretical orientation than in its explicit intention to include each of the disciplines of the social sciences in the project of a critical theory of society. The objectives of this theoretical innovation vis-à-vis all the traditional Marxist approaches were established by Max Horkheimer in various articles written in the 1920s and 1930s. His critique of neo-idealist philosophy and contemporary empiricism sought to develop a philosophy of history which would comprehend the evolution of human reason; in so doing, he drew on empirical research. Thus the Institute of Social Research, conceived as a way of realizing this plan, was founded in 1929. Its work drew on economics, psychology and cultural theory, seeking to analyse, from a historical perspective, how a rational organization of society might be achieved.

However, after the National Socialists came to power and drove the Institute into exile, historical/philosophical optimism gave way to cultural/critical pessimism. Horkheimer and Adorno now saw it as the function of a critical theory of society to try, by returning to the history of civilization, to establish the reasons for the emergence of Fascism and Stalinism. Their Dialectic of Enlightenment, *which bears some resemblance to Heidegger, impressively testifies to this change of orientation: it asks why totalitarianism came into being and it identifies a cognitive and practical perspective on the world which, because of its concern with the technical control of objects and persons, only allows for an instrumental rationality.*

But there was some opposition to this critique of reason which tended to view totalitarianism as a consequence of an inescapable cycle of instrumental reason and social control. The concept of total reification was called into question by some of the more marginal members of the Institute working under Adorno and Horkheimer. These were far more interested in asking whether, even under totalitarian conditions, they could determine the remains of a desire for communicative solidarity. The work of philosopher Walter Benjamin constitutes an analysis of the interrelation of power and the imagination; Franz Neumann and Otto Kirchheimer inquired into legal consensus culture and social control; while Erich Fromm conducted a psychoanalytic investigation of communicative needs and their potential for resistance.

After the core members of the School had returned from exile, the Institute resumed its work in Frankfurt and embarked on large-scale empirical projects. From the very beginning, however, a considerable gap existed between the empirical investigations which focused on the industrial workplace and the philosophical radicalization of negativity on which Adorno and Horkheimer worked, albeit with differing emphasis. This gap was bridged only when Habermas began to challenge the systematic bases of critical theory, causing the basic philosophical concepts and the intentions of empirical social research once again to correspond. The central idea, with which Habermas introduced a new phase in the history of the Frankfurt School, was his understanding of a form of rationality which would describe the communicative agreement between subjects rather than the instrumental control of things. The concept of communicative rationality which emerged from this idea has since formed the basis for the moral grounds and democratic application of critical theory.

1 **Origins and aims of critical theory: Horkheimer and Marcuse**

2 **The turn to a negative philosophy of history: Theodor W. Adorno**

3 **Neglected margins: Benjamin, Kirchheimer, Neumann, Fromm**

4 **Continuation and revision of critical theory: Jürgen Habermas**

1 Origins and aims of critical theory: Horkheimer and Marcuse

Critical theory stands out from the various attempts to develop a productive model of Marxism which took place between the World Wars. It differed from comparable approaches primarily in its methodological objectives rather than its theoretical principles. These objectives derived from an unquestioned and programmatic acknowledgement of the sciences. Critical theory's fundamental aim was to include all the disciplines of the social sciences in the project of a materialist theory of society. It thereby overcame the theoretical purism which had long persisted in historical materialism, and made space for the fruitful integration of academic social science and Marxist theory. This methodological vision was most ably represented by Max HORKHEIMER in whose hands the project of a more broadly interdisciplinary Marxism developed during the 1920s.

When Horkheimer succeeded Grünberg as Director of the Institute for Social Research in 1930, an opportunity presented itself for the realization of this project. He revealed, for the first time, the theoretical programme of a critical theory of society in his inaugural speech (Horkheimer 1972). In *Zeitschrift für Sozialforschung* (Journal for Social Research), founded in 1932 and which, until 1941, represented the intellectual centre of the Institute's work, he attempted to develop this approach in collaboration with Herbert MARCUSE. The idea of overcoming the scientific and historical gulf which had arisen between factual research and philosophy formed the methodological framework. Following a Hegelian model of history, both branches of knowledge were again to be fused in a single form of reflection to such a degree that the empirical analysis of reality could coincide with the philosophical determination of reason. To achieve this, one needed a theory of history which would be able to determine the powers of reason as they operated within the historical process. Although their interpretative approaches differed, both Horkheimer and Marcuse inherited these basic philosophical-historical conceptions from the tradition of Marxist thought.

In the 1930s, Horkheimer and Marcuse continued to represent the classical Marxist theory of history. According to this, the central mechanism of social progress lies in the development of the forces of production, and as the domination of nature moves through increasingly technical stages, these determine new stages in the relations of production (Horkheimer 1932). Thus critical theory was to enter into this historical development not merely as a cognitive example of the work process, as was the case in the empirical sciences, but as a critical example of society's self-knowledge. It is by critical theory, according to Marcuse and Horkheimer, that we are made conscious of the possibilities which are already developing within the historical situation itself (Marcuse 1937). They no longer believed, however, that rationality, as embodied in the contemporary forces of production, simultaneously finds expression in the revolutionary awareness of the proletariat. From the very beginning they were conscious that, because of the increasing integration of the working classes into the social system of late capitalism, a

strictly Marxist theory had lost its social relevance. Hence the empirical analyses, which are regarded as an immanent part of the theory of society which was evolving, should also aim to explain precisely those social and psychic mechanisms by which all potential social resistance has become integrated.

Horkheimer's and Marcuse's preliminary philosophical reflections, not unlike those of their contemporaries LUKÁCS and Korsch, continued along the general lines of a productivist philosophy of history, and the openness of their methodology to empirical social research enabled them to formulate something new. The idea of including all the social sciences in the development of a critical theory of society, as well as the subjects of their empirical research, led them far beyond other contemporary attempts to revive Marxism. As a point of reference for the entire research of the Institute, Horkheimer sought the origin of the psychic mechanisms that prevent the outbreak of conflict between social classes which would otherwise result from the tension due to their economic differences (Horkheimer 1932). This question represents a soberly empirical change in the problem of the revolutionary subject which until this time had been fraught with philosophical and historical difficulty. The focus of the Institute's interdisciplinary investigations throughout the 1930s was now clear, and the projects to which each member contributed their specialist knowledge were to elucidate the specific form of social integration which capitalism had systematically constructed in its post-liberal phase.

To Horkheimer belongs the credit of having defined the form and content of a critical theory of society. He used his position as director to acquire specialists for the wide-ranging tasks of the interdisciplinary research projects, and the Institute's programme emerged from the interconnection of three disciplines. Horkheimer continued to regard the research as being fundamentally based on the economic analysis of the post-liberal phase of capitalism. He entrusted his friend Friedrich Pollock with the task of implementing this analysis and answering the question of whether a different principle of capitalist organization was beginning to emerge from the new, planned economy. The psychological study of the individual's integration into society represented the next stage of inquiry. Erich Fromm, who at this time still spoke for the Freudian Left and the fusion of historical materialism and psychoanalysis, was to implement this project. He started with the proposition that the integration of individuals into the capitalist system of social domination took place alongside the formation and socialization of their psycho-sexual characteristics. Hence he made it his task to investigate the consequences of capitalism's structural change for socialization within the family and individual personality formation. Cultural theory and its analysis of the operations of mass culture completed the Institute's programme of inquiry. Horkheimer's definitions of the object of this cultural analysis were ambivalent, even contradictory (Honneth 1991: 1.1), but within a short time it was focusing on the ways in which adaptations in behaviour were brought about by the media of the new culture industry. Theodor W. Adorno and Leo Löwenthal were entrusted with the study of this pivotal cultural dimension of the capitalist process of integration.

Horkheimer and his colleagues were able to bring a theoretical unity to this range of subjects by employing a very simple functionalism. This guaranteed a conceptual fusing of the individual studies only because every social process was examined according to its function in the reproduction and development of work within the context of society (see FUNCTIONALISM IN SOCIAL SCIENCE). The reasons for this reduction to functionalism were the very historical-philosophical premises which consistently underwrite the thoughts of Marcuse, Adorno and Horkheimer. Because no other type of social activity was allowed other than work, even on the level of social theory only the instrumental forms of social praxis could be considered. But in the face of this functionalism one necessarily loses sight of that very dimension of everyday praxis by which the socialized subjects communicatively reproduce, and creatively learn to direct, their common action (see Honneth 1987).

2 The turn to a negative philosophy of history: Theodor W. Adorno

Within the Institute itself, however, the concept of interdisciplinary social research only existed in a vital and constructive form until the beginning of the 1940s. The articles which Horkheimer contributed to the last issue of the *Zeitschrift für Sozialforschung* in 1941 announced a general change of orientation affecting both the philosophical-historical premises of critical theory and its political conception of itself. While the Institute's sense of resignation in the face of Fascism increased throughout the 1930s, its work was still sustained by hopes of progress theoretically founded on the Marxist conception of history. In spite of scepticism about the established workers' parties, Horkheimer still regarded the research of the Institute as an intellectual reflection of the workers' movement. At the end of the 1930s, however, the world represented by the Institute finally collapsed. The practical-political experience of the closed circle of Fascism, Stalinism and capitalist mass culture,

which seemed to have become a totalitarian whole, led Horkheimer and his colleagues to abandon all Marxist conceptions of social progress. It was the change from a positive to a negative concept of work which reshaped critical theory and introduced a new phase in the history of the Institute. Thus a critique of reason and progress, so radical that it could not but cast general doubt on the potential for political revolution within social relations, replaced the conception of progress founded on production.

The outstanding representative of this new conception of critical theory is not Horkheimer but Theodor W. Adorno. His thinking, more than that of anyone else, is marked by the historical experience of Fascism as the fate of civilization. This made him sceptical of the Institute's original historical-materialist ideas of progress. Moreover, the interests of his intellectual development were so predominantly artistic that he was bound quite naturally to doubt the limited rationalism of the Marxist theoretical tradition. Under the influence of Walter Benjamin he had already started to develop effective methods of aesthetic interpretation for a materialist philosophy of history. In his collaboration with Horkheimer (which intensified during the late 1930s), whose earlier reading of Schopenhauer had prepared him for critical reflections on civilization, Adorno's scepticism about progress came to the fore. The *Dialectic of Enlightenment* (1947), which they wrote together in the early 1940s, articulated this new theme within a negative philosophy of history. In its philosophical-historical approach this work undoubtedly surpasses the Institute's earlier efforts. The totalitarian condition which the rise of Fascist systems was bringing to the world was no longer to be explained as a consequence of the conflict between forces and relations of production, but as a consequence of the inner dynamic of the development of human consciousness. Horkheimer and Adorno abandoned the theoretical framework of capitalism and made the process of civilization as a whole their frame of reference. Hence Fascism came to be seen as the final historical stage in a logic of disintegration which is intrinsic to the original form of survival of the species itself. The prehistorical efforts of instrumental thought, by which mankind learns to survive and suppress the diversity of nature, gradually reproduce themselves in the disciplining of mankind's natural impulses, in the impoverishment of its sensory faculties, and in the development of social power relations. Thus an increasing reification, set in motion by the first acts of domination of nature and reaching its logical conclusion in Fascism, shapes the process of civilization.

Even this philosophical-historical thesis, which

implicitly rests on a series of anthropological and ethnological studies and their more recent interpretations, relies on Marxist premises. The prehistory of the human species is reduced to the single dimension of nature's manipulation by mankind, and thus the development of civilization is interpreted according to a pattern of the domination of nature. But the motifs of Romanticism and *Lebensphilosophie*, which Horkheimer and Adorno take up again in their research, reveal the process of the adaptation of nature in a completely different light (see ROMANTICISM, GERMAN; LEBENSPHILOSOPHIE). If humankind's freedom is seen to lie in its ability to devote itself directly to natural life, every act of instrumental control over nature must be interpreted as one step towards the self-alienation of the species.

Two different points arise from this negative turn in the Marxist philosophy of history. On the one hand the consideration of the process of civilization so categorically excludes the whole sphere of everyday communicative praxis that the social advances which may have occurred can no longer be accommodated. Consequently, the *Dialectic of Enlightenment* is compelled to ignore another dimension of civilization's progress, namely one which is not expressed in the intensification of the forces of production, but in the extension of legal freedoms and the scope for individual action. The second consequence is of a political nature and of no less importance for the development of critical theory: every kind of political praxis is interpreted as a form of coercive action and is therefore excluded from the range of available positive alternatives. Thus Horkheimer and Adorno ultimately deny themselves the possibility of mobilizing their own research activity in the real political sphere. While this conclusion might not lead to complete political self-destruction, it necessitates a conception of revolution which no longer sees even the slightest possibility of political emancipation through the radical overthrow of social relations – instead, it looks toward messianic intervention in the process of civilization. Hence in conclusions such as these, drawn in fact by Horkheimer himself in his essay the 'Authoritarian State' (1942), the *Dialectic of Enlightenment* corresponds with the ideas explored in Benjamin's 'Theses on the Philosophy of History' in which he was attempting to criticize the model of social democratic progress.

3   Neglected margins: Benjamin, Kirchheimer, Neumann, Fromm

The only alternative which could have emerged within the Institute to counter such negativistic theories would have been found within the kind of research practised by Franz Neumann and Otto Kirchheimer. They formed a group, together with Walter BENJAMIN and later Erich Fromm, who both only briefly or indirectly contributed to the Institute's research. Independently, the work of each of these authors stands for an anti-functionalist impulse which could have called into question the image of a totally administrated society, an image which would inevitably have led to the dual impasse of political self-destruction or revolutionary messianism. But the dominating philosophical position of Adorno, Horkheimer and Marcuse never allowed such alternative theoretical approaches to be properly represented within the Institute (Honneth 1987).

Neumann and Kirchheimer, who were both trained in jurisprudence and had come of political age in German social democracy, contributed legal and constitutional investigations to the work of the Institute from their New York exile. Their scholarly and political background convinced them from the outset that the Law is a central medium of control in bourgeois society. Within the rules of constitutional law they recognized the social substance of a political compromise which the different classes, variously empowered by the conditions of private capitalism, all agreed upon. This social-theoretical premise provided the background for the analyses in which Neumann and Kirchheimer examined the changes in constitutional law which accompanied the structural change of the economy under capitalism (Neumann 1978; Kirchheimer 1976). Thus they are far better able to account for the political and legal mediations of capitalist rule than Adorno and Horkheimer who, following Pollock's state capitalism thesis, had been bound to the model of a centrally controlled society.

What also makes Neumann and Kirchheimer's conception superior are the social-theoretical ideas which tacitly influence their investigations. From the outset they perceived the social order from a different perspective than that which prevailed in Horkheimer's circle. For them, social integration represents a process which does not just take place over and above the always unconscious fulfilment of the functional imperatives of society, but via political communication between the social groups. Dealing with questions concerning the constitutional state had brought Neumann and Kirchheimer up against the phenomenon of political legitimacy; thence arose the view that the constitutional order of society is always the expression of a general compromise or consensus between the political powers. Active interest in class disputes, characteristic of the Weimar Republic, led to a realistic assessment of the power relations of social interests; the power which arose from private-capitalist control of the means of production could not be overestimated. The compromise character of the social order as a whole was finally revealed to them through their work on Austro-Marxism: the institutional structures of a society must be understood as nothing other than momentary determinations of social contracts in which the various interest groups are implicated according to their particular power potential.

Within Neumann's and Kirchheimer's thinking this all makes for a concept of society at the centre of which stands the overarching process of communication between social groups. If this concept had been used to direct the Institute's theoretical inquiries, it would not only have prevented the uncritical adoption of ideas of the total integration of society, but could also have opened up new modes of political orientation for its own research.

4 Continuation and revision of critical theory: Jürgen Habermas

When the Institute for Social Research re-opened in Frankfurt in 1950, it resumed its research activities without direct reference to its socio-philosophical identity of the previous two decades. During the post-war years, the unifying theoretical line which could have linked the empirical research and philosophical reflection was broken. The unity and coherence of the Frankfurt School no longer existed.

While scarcely any common denominator could be found for the empirical research projects of the Institute, the idea of a 'totally administrated world' came to represent a standard (if temporary) point of reference for the socio-philosophical work. This idea runs through the cultural-critical writing of Horkheimer, Adorno and Marcuse like a leitmotif; the central premise of the state-capitalism theory became the general framework for an analysis of post-war capitalism. Hence the theoretical perspective on totalitarianism, which had already shaped the image of society in the *Dialectic of Enlightenment*, also determined the current investigations. Because administrative social control and the individual's readiness to adapt were meshed seamlessly together, the life of society seemed to be integrated in a stable and now unassailable system of coercion. The three authors drew quite different conclusions for the project of a critical theory of society from their common diagnoses of the present. Horkheimer's thinking was affected by a deepening Schopenhauerian pessimism until it turned to negative theology (Horkheimer 1985). Adorno continued to pursue a self-critique of conceptual thought in which the idea of a mimetic rationality, vicariously preserved in the work of art, remained the normative point of reference (Adorno

1973). Marcuse alone reacted to the pessimistic diagnosis of the present situation with an impulse to save the lost idea of revolution, thereby repositioning reason below the social threshold, in the sphere of the natural libidinal needs of mankind (Marcuse 1955).

In spite of their different objectives, the common background to these three approaches remained a philosophy of history in which historical development is interpreted as a process of technological rationalization which reaches its conclusion in the closed system of rule of contemporary society. Only one theory, at first scarcely recognizable as a point of departure within critical theory, relinquished the philosophical premises of this diagnosis. Jürgen Habermas had emerged from the Institute of Social Research as Adorno's assistant. Yet his theoretical origins and orientation had never had much in common with the philosophical tradition of critical theory; more significant for the development of his thought were the theoretical movements of philosophical anthropology, hermeneutics, pragmatism and linguistic analysis, to which the older generation remained hostile. Nevertheless, from the work of Habermas a theory gradually took shape which was so clearly motivated by the original aims of critical theory that it counts today as the only serious attempt at theoretical renewal.

The insight into the linguistic intersubjectivity of social action forms the basis of this theory. Habermas arrived at his central premise through studying hermeneutic philosophy and the linguistic analysis of WITTGENSTEIN, from which he learned that human subjects are always already linked through the medium of language. The human form of life is distinguished by an intersubjectivity embodied in the structures of language; linguistic communication between subjects constitutes an absolutely fundamental prerequisite for the reproduction of social life. Habermas gives this thesis socio-theoretical weight by making it the starting point of a debate with the socio-philosophical and sociological tradition. He is critical of the tendency of modern social philosophy gradually to reduce all practical intersubjective interests to decisions based on technical criteria (Habermas 1968). Against sociological functionalism he asserts that a society's tasks of reproduction are always fixed by the normative self-conceptions of the socialized communicative subjects. Consequently the necessary functions of life as such are nowhere to be found in the relations of human life (Habermas 1963). He is therefore also led to a critique of Marxism which results in an expanded conception of the theory of action within history. If the human form of life is distinguished by the medium of linguistic communication, then social reproduction cannot be reduced, as it was in the theoretical writings of Marx, to the single dimension of work. Rather, the praxis of linguistically-mediated interaction must be regarded as no less fundamental a dimension of the history of mankind than the activity of manipulating nature (Habermas 1971).

But the decisive step taken by Habermas towards his own theory of society, and hence a revision of critical theory, came about through his investing both concepts of action (work and interaction) with different categories of rationality. Within the subsystem of rationalized action in which the social tasks of work and political administration are organized, the species develops through the accumulation of technical and strategic knowledge. But within the institutional frame, in which the integrating norms of society are reproduced, it continues to develop by means of the liberation of communicative constraints (Habermas 1970). During the 1970s, Habermas' ramifications of his theory follow this concept of society, whereby rationalized systems are differentiated from the sphere of everyday communicative praxis, and separate forms of rationalization are postulated for each social sphere. A universal pragmatism further elucidates the linguistic infrastructure of communicative action; a theory of social evolution is to help resolve the logic of the development of social knowledge and thus the dual process of rationalization; and finally, the further development of systematic theoretical conceptions is intended to determine the mechanisms through which areas of social activity evolve into rationalized systems.

Although these theoretical endeavours reach into the most diverse fields of knowledge, they all aim to establish a critique of society with a basis in the theory of communication. Thus in seeking to prove that the rationality of communicative action is so fundamental a condition of social development, Habermas' work constitutes a critique of Adorno's and Horkheimer's biased thesis, revealing their diagnoses of the tendencies of instrumental reification to be forms of social rationalization wholly defined by functionalism. In the *Theory of Communicative Action* (1987) this programme is systematized for the first time. The fruits of the various studies are brought together to reconstruct the rationality of communicative action within the context of a speech-act theory, to develop it into the basis of a theory of society by going through the history of sociological theories, and finally, to make it the point of reference for a critical diagnosis of the present (see COMMUNICATIVE RATIONALITY).

One of Habermas' most recent studies can be understood as an answer to the pessimistic thesis in which claims are made for a tendency towards the colonization of the living world. In *Between Facts and Norms* (1992) he reconstructs, in the form of a critical legal philosophy, the legal and cultural conditions under which the project of a further democratization of our society can be continued today.

See also: CRITICAL THEORY

References and further reading

* Adorno, T.W. (1973) *Negative Dialectics*, London: Verso. (Adorno's final statement on the nature of philosophical analysis in which he attacks identity thinking, replacing it with the notion of the dialectics of non-identity.)
—— (1986) *Aesthetic Theory*, trans. C. Lenhardt, London and New York: Routledge & Kegan Paul. (Unfinished and published posthumously, this links Adorno's critique of human domination over nature with a critique of the administered society. As such it represents a continuation of the earlier dialectics of Enlightenment.)
Arato, A. and Gebhardt, E. (eds) (1978) *The Essential Frankfurt School Reader*, Oxford: Blackwell. (Excellent selection of articles on the central concerns of critical theory by members of The Frankfurt School, with additional explanatory commentaries by the editors.)
Benhabib, S. (1986) *Critique, Norm and Utopia*, New York: Columbia University Press. (A major work which analyses the notion of critique within the Frankfurt School up to Habermas.)
Benjamin, W. (1968) 'Theses on the Philosophy of History', in *Illuminations*, ed. H. Arendt, trans. H. Cohn, New York: Harcourt, Brace & World. (Essential for an understanding of Adorno's thought on the nature of history as developed in *The Dialectic of Enlightenment* and after.)
—— (1978) *Reflections. Selected Works: Essays, Aphorisms, Autobiographical Writings*, trans. E. Jenncott, New York: Harcourt Brace Jovanovitch. (Good selection of Benjamin's works, with extracts from his reflections on cities and his autobiographical writings.)
Fromm, E. (1992) *The Revision of Psychoanalysis*, ed. R. Funk, Boulder, CO: Westview Press. (Important essays by early and influential Frankfurt-School thinker, linking the works of Marx and Freud.)
* Habermas, J. (1963) *Theorie und Praxis*, Darmstadt: Hermann Luchterand Verlag; trans. J. Viertal as *Theory and Practice*, Boston, MA: Beacon Press, 1973. (Contains important essays on modern political theory, including several on Hegel.)
* —— (1968) *Erkenntnis und Interesse*, Frankfurt: Suhrkamp Verlag; trans. J.J. Shapiro as *Knowledge*

and Human Interests, Boston, MA: Beacon Press, 1971. (An important interpretation of philosophy from Kant to the pragmatists, arguing that epistemology must now be pursued as social theory.)

* —— (1970) *Zur Logik der Sozialwissenschaft*, Frankfurt: Suhrkamp Verlag; trans. S. Nicholson and J. Stark as *On the Logic of the Social Sciences*, Cambridge MA: MIT Press, 1988. (Early sketch of Habermas' interpretive approach and his critique of Gadamer's philosophical hermeneutics.)

* —— (1971) 'Technology and Science as Ideology', trans. J.J. Shapiro in *Toward a Rational Society: Student Protest, Science and Politics*, Boston, MA: Beacon Press, 1971. (Important essay which formulates a method for studying the relationship between technology, science and ideology.)

* —— (1987) *Theory of Communicative Action*, Cambridge: Polity Press, 2 vols. (Habermas' central work which attempts to provide a normative basis and conceptual framework for a new critical theory.)

* —— (1992) *Faktizät und Geltung. Beiträge zur Diskurstheorie des Rechts und des demokratischen Rechtsstaates* (Between Facts and norms: Contributions to a Discourse Theory of Law and Democracy), trans. W. Rehg, Cambridge: Polity Press, 1996. (Works out the legal and political implications contained in the earlier *Theory of Communicative Action* and presents a sociologically informed conceptualization of law and rights, together with a normative account of the rule of law and the constitutional state.)

Held, D. (1980) *Introduction to Critical Theory*, London: Hutchinson. (Detailed and judicial treatment which clearly explores the central and substantive concerns of the first generation of Critical Theorists.)

* Honneth, A. (1987) 'Critical Theory', in A. Gidden and J. Turner (eds) *Social Theory Today*, Cambridge: Polity Press. (Clear exposition of Critical Theory in the light of Habermas' theory of communicative action, highlighting possible future directions.)

—— (1987) *Critique of Power: Stages of Reflection of a Critical Theory of Society*, trans. K. Baynes, Cambridge, MA: MIT Press. (Offers an interpretation of the history of Critical Theory focusing largely on Adorno and Horkheimer and debating their work on the nature of power within the context of the later debate between Foucault and Habermas.)

Honneth, A. and Joas, H. (eds) (1991) *Communicative Action*, Cambridge: Polity Press. (Collection of articles debating the strengths and limitations of Habermas' theory of communicative action.)

* Horkheimer, M. (1932) 'Geschichte und Psychologie' (History and Psychology), *Zeitschrift für Sozialforschung* 1: 125–44. (Horkheimer's first discussion of the role of psychic mechanisms within the historical and social realm, later implemented by Fromm in his empirical analysis of the political and psychic attitudes of German workers in the 1930s.)

* —— (1941a) 'The End of Reason', *Zeitschrift für Sozialforschung* 9: 36–304. (This early essay introduces key distinctive concepts which distinguished Critical Theory from orthodox Marxism – the domination of nature, the decline of the individual and the role of technology in Western culture.)

* —— (1941b) 'Art and Mass Culture', *Zeitschrift für Sozialforschung* 9: 290–304. (Early articulation of what was to become the orthodox view of Critical Theorists on the potential critical function of art in relation to 'mass culture'.)

* —— (1942) 'The Authoritarian State', in *The Essential Frankfurt School Reader*, ed. A. Arato and E. Gerbhardt, trans. People's Translation Service, Oxford and New York: Blackwell, 1982. (Radical statement linking working-class organizations and orthodox Marxism to the notion of an 'authoritarian state'; puts into political context Horkheimer's analysis of 'The End of Reason'.)

—— (1968) *Kritische Theorie* (Critical Theory), ed. A Schmidt, Frankfurt: Fischer, 2 vols. (Seminal essays from the 1930s.)

* —— (1972) 'Die gegenwärtige Lage der Sozialphilosophie und die Aufgaben eines Instituts für Sozialforschung' (The Current Situation in social Philosophy and the Tasks of an Institute for Social Research), in W. Brede (ed.) *Sozialphilosophische Studien* (Social-philosophical Studies), Frankfurt: Fischer, 33–46. (Inaugural speech of 1930, laying out the theoretical programme to be followed by The Frankfurt School in subsequent years.)

* —— (1985) *Gesammelte Schriften* (Collected Writings), ed. A. Schmidt and G. Schmid Noerr, Frankfurt: Fischer. (Collected writings of Horkheimer in fourteen volumes covering the period from 1914 to 1972.)

* Horkheimer, M. and Adorno, T.W. (1947) *Dialektik der Aufklärung. Philosophiche Fragmente* (The Dialectic of Enlightenment), trans. J. Cummings, London: Verso, 1979. (Seminal work in which a new Benjamin-inspired philosophy of history is introduced, moving Critical Theory away from an orthodox Marxian concept of history to one that places power and the domination of nature at the centre.)

Jay, M. (1973) *The dialectical Imagination: A History of the Frankfurt School and the Institute of Social Research, 1923–50*, London: Heinemann. (A model of intellectual clarity and accuracy, perhaps the best and most accessible introduction to the early work of the Frankfurt School available in English.)

* Kirchheimer, O. (1976) *Von der Weimarer Republik zum Faschismus: Die Auflösung der demokratischen Rechtsordnung* (From the Weimar Republic to Fascism: The Dissolution of the Democratic Rule of Law), ed. W. Luthard, Frankfurt: Suhrkamp. (Account of the transformation of the German legal system with the rise of fascism. Demonstrates the ideological nature of Nazi political theory in its claim that it had brought together the spheres of law and morality.)

* Marcuse, H. (1937) 'Philosophie und kritische Theorie' (Philosophy and Critical Theory), *Zeitschrift für Sozialforschung* 6: 632–47. (Early, important essay by Marcuse which maps out the relationship of Critical Theory to traditional forms of bourgeois philosophy.)

* —— (1955) *Eros and Civilisation. A Philosophical Inquiry into Freud*, Boston, MA: Beacon Press. (Radical re-reading of Freud which produces a dialectically inspired account of Freudian instinct theory. Combines an analysis of a historicized and liberatory set of instincts with a Marxist inspired theory of historical development.)

* Neumann, F. (1978) *Wirtschaft, Staat, Demokratie. Aufsätze 1930–1954* (Economy, State, Democracy. Essays 1930–1954), ed. A. Sollner, Frankfurt: Suhrkamp. (Collected essays of Neumann covering his significant contribution to Critical Theory's work on political economy during the fascist period of German history.)

Wiggershaus, R. (1994) *The Frankfurt School: Its History, Theories and Political Significance*, trans. M. Robertson, Cambridge, MA: MIT Press. (The most comprehensive history available, providing a thorough analysis and overview of the intellectual development of The Frankfurt School, a wealth of biographical detail and an analysis of internal politics and conflicts within the Institute.)

Translated by Bridget Thomson
Bibliographical annotations by Michael Bull

AXEL HONNETH

FRANKLIN, BENJAMIN (1709–1770)

Benjamin Franklin was a candlemaker's son who became a successful businessman, politician, diplomat, scientist, philosopher, writer, and social reformer. He played a major role in winning American independence and in American intellectual history. In philosophy Franklin was a deist, and struggled much with problems of morality and determinism.

Benjamin Franklin was born on 17 January 1706 in Boston, Massachusetts. He was apprenticed to his brother James to become a printer. James Franklin was a freethinker, under whose influence Benjamin became a deist (see DEISM). After his brother's arrest, Benjamin went to Philadelphia in 1723. In 1725 he went to England, and while there published *A Dissertation on Liberty and Necessity, Pain and Pleasure* (1725). In this work, Franklin adopted an extreme deism based on Newtonian mechanics (see NEWTON, I.); he asserted a total determinism, which, together with the claim that God is perfect, led to the conclusion that whatever is is right, and to a complete denial of a self-determining human will. He viewed people as machines governed by pain and pleasure, the latter defined as the absence of pain, and claimed that since all pain ends at death, the amounts of pain and pleasure in life are always equal. He denied the existence of an afterlife or any difference in merit or demerit among creatures; all are equal since all do what God ordains.

Returning to Philadelphia in 1726, Franklin became a successful printer, and revised his earlier extreme views. By 1732 the belief that God commands prayers, which, according to the necessitarian view he had espoused, would be pointless, led Franklin to conclude that God has endowed us with free will, and does directly intervene in human affairs. The admission of free will introduced virtue and vice, and, influenced by the benevolence morality of the time, Franklin concluded that virtue consists in doing good to others. He believed this could best be done by helping others to become able to provide for themselves. This he thought was possible through the universal ownership of property; thus property had a moral function for him. Such ownership would make people free to engage in disinterested benevolence, serving the public good. Franklin was thus a believer in the doctrine of civic virtue, which he practiced through social reform and politics, particularly after he retired from business in 1748.

In 1747 Franklin began working on electricity. He was the foremost American scientist of his century. His one-fluid theory of electricity, his law of the conservation of electric charge, and his demonstration of the electrical character of lightning, made him an international celebrity and won him honorary degrees from Oxford and Cambridge. Franklin capitalized on his fame to serve first Pennsylvania and then the Colonies as their representative in England and subsequently in France. He was a member of the committee that drafted the Declaration of Independence in 1776. The treaty with France, which he negotiated in 1778, gave the colonies the French support necessary to achieve independence. He was a negotiator of the peace treaty with England, and served in the convention that drafted the Constitution of the United States.

See also: AMERICAN PHILOSOPHY IN THE 18TH AND 19TH CENTURIES; JEFFERSON, T.

List of works

Franklin, B. (1840) *The Works of Benjamin Franklin*, ed. J. Sparks, Boston, MA: Tappan, Whittemore & Mason, 10 vols. (An old edition, but covering the span of Franklin's life.)

—— (1709–70) *The Papers of Benjamin Franklin*, ed. L.W. Labaree *et al.*, New Haven, CN: Yale University Press, 1960–, 30 vols; vols 1–14, vols 15–26, ed. W. Willcox, vol. 27 ed. C. Lopez, vols. 28–30 ed. B. Oberg. (The best modern scholarly edition of Franklin's writings in chronological order, but still in progress; the last volume issued is for 1779).

—— (1725) *A Dissertation on Liberty and Necessity, Pleasure and Pain*, London: Samuel Palmer's Printing House. (Addressed to his friend James Ralph, the pamphlet advances an extreme form of mechanisitic Deism designed to prove that 'all is right'.)

—— (1790) *Autobiography*, ed. D. Aaron, New York, Vintage, 1990. ed. J.A. Leo Lemay and P.M. Zoll, *The Autobiography of Benjamin Franklin: A Genetic Text*, Knoxville: University of Tennessee Press, 1981. (The textual and publication history of the *Autobiography* is very complex, with portions of it appearing as early as 1790. Franklin's best statement of his views on virtue.)

References and further reading

Cohen, I. B. (1956) *Franklin and Newton*, Philadelphia, PN: American Philosophical Society. (Excellent study of Franklin's scientific work.)

Flower, E. and Murphey, M.G. (1977) *A History of Philosophy in America*, New York: Putnam, vol. 1, ch. 2. (Brief treatment of Franklin's philosophical views.)

MURRAY G. MURPHEY

FREE LOGICS

We often need to reason about things that do not – or may not – exist. We might, for example, want to prove that there is no highest prime number by assuming its existence and deriving a contradiction. Our ordinary formal logic, however (that is, anything including standard quantification theory), automatically assumes that every singular term used has a denotation: if you can use the term 'God' – if that term is part of your language – automatically there is a denotation for it, that is, God exists. Some logicians have thought that this assumption prejudges too many important issues, and that it is best to get rid of it. So they have constructed logics free of this assumption, called 'free logics'.

A 'free logic' is a system of quantification theory, with or without identity, that allows for non-denoting singular terms. In other words, some of the expressions that may be considered singular terms – individual constants, free variables, definite or indefinite descriptions – are not assigned any object in some of the models of the system. In a system of *standard* quantification theory, schemata such as $\exists x(x = a)$ are logical truths; not so in free logics. Free logics reject the 'principle of particularization', $A(t/x) \supset \exists x A$, and all equivalent principles or rules, among them the 'principle of specification', $\forall x A \supset A(t/x)$, and the rules of existential generalization and universal instantiation.

Historically, contemporary logicians since Frege have tended to dispense with non-denoting singular terms, adopting either Frege's device of assigning them an arbitrary denotation or Russell's of denying them singular term status (via his theory of descriptions; see DESCRIPTIONS). It was Henry Leonard (1956) who first proposed that standard quantification theory be revised to allow for non-denoting singular terms. Subsequently, Hailperin, Leblanc, Hintikka, Lambert and Smiley proposed various formal systems to this effect (between 1959 and 1967 – see Lambert 1991). But, until the mid-1960s, no semantic interpretation of these systems was provided, for good reason.

Standard semantics is based on the 'correspondence theory of truth': a statement such as 'Socrates is wise' is true if and only if the object corresponding to 'Socrates' has the property corresponding to 'wise'. But this scheme has no natural application to statements such as 'Pegasus is white', relating to nonexistent objects. So a semantics for a free logic (a 'free semantics') should provide for some alternative (or extension) to the correspondence theory, to account for those cases in which a singular term 'corresponds to' nothing – a problem for which it is difficult to find an uncontroversial solution.

There are currently three main kinds of free semantics. An 'outer domain' semantics adds to the ordinary domain of quantification a second ('outer') domain and allows singular terms to be interpreted on either domain. Intuitively, the outer domain is constituted by nonexistent objects and the reason why 'Pegasus is white', say, is true is that the nonexistent object corresponding to 'Pegasus' has the property corresponding to 'white'. A 'conventional' free semantics assigns a single truth-value (usually False) to all atomic formulas containing non-denoting singular terms, and then evaluates complex formulas accordingly. Both conventional and outer domain semantics are bivalent, and strong soundness and completeness theorems can be proved for them; that is, not only the set of logically true formulas but also the set of valid arguments can be axiomatized. Not so with the third kind of free semantics, 'supervaluational' semantics, due principally to Bas van Fraassen. This assigns truth-values to formulas containing non-denoting singular terms (relative to a model M), either by convention or by extending the domain, and then defines a 'supervaluation' (on M) that makes a formula true if it is true under all such assignments, false if it is false under all such assignments, and truth-valueless otherwise.

For illustration, suppose a is non-denoting in the model M, and consider the following formulas:

(1) Pa

(2) $\sim Pa$

(3) $Pa \vee \sim Pa$

(4) $Pa \mathbin{\&} \sim Pa$.

There will be conventions on M (or extensions of its domain) that make (1) true, and others that make it false, and similarly for (2); so the supervaluation on M will leave both (1) and (2) truth-valueless. But *all* these conventions (or extensions) will make (3) true and (4) false; so the supervaluation on M will agree on assigning them these truth-values. Intuitively, supervaluational semantics makes a statement containing non-denoting singular terms true (false) if it would be true (false) were its atomic components containing non-denoting singular terms to have *any* combination of truth-values (or its non-denoting singular terms to have *any* combination of denotations) – a 'counterfactual' theory of truth, as it is sometimes called.

Free logics have been applied in other parts of logic and to the formalization of scientific theories. Most typical of an application of the first kind is modal quantification theory, where a free logic base is quite natural (for consider: in the presence of the rule of 'necessitation', the theorem $\exists x(x = a)$ of standard quantification theory can be strengthened to $\Box\exists x(x = a)$ – that is, whatever we can name not only exists, but exists necessarily). Most typical of an application of the second kind is set theory, where a free logic base will let us use the *name* of, say, the Russellian set $\{x\colon x \notin x\}$ without being committed to its *existence* – indeed, while being able to prove that it does not exist (it cannot, by Russell's paradox).

Finally, free logics must be distinguished from 'inclusive' logics, that is, logics that allow for an empty domain of quantification. Though it is natural to require inclusiveness of a free logic, and though indeed most free logics are also inclusive, the definitions of the two are distinct, and independent of one another.

See also: EXISTENCE; FREE LOGICS, PHILOSOPHICAL ISSUES IN; LOGICAL AND MATHEMATICAL TERMS, GLOSSARY OF

References and further reading

Bencivenga, E. (1986) 'Free Logics', in D. Gabbay and F. Guenthner (eds) *Handbook of Philosophical Logic*, Dordrecht: Reidel, vol. 3, 373–426. (An ample survey of the subject.)

Lambert, K. (ed.) (1991) *Philosophical Applications of Free Logic*, New York: Oxford University Press. (A collection of articles illustrating various uses of free logic.)

* Leonard, H. (1956) 'The Logic of Existence', *Philosophical Studies* 7: 49–64. (The first proposal that standard quantification theory be revised to allow for non-denoting singular terms.)

ERMANNO BENCIVENGA

FREE LOGICS, PHILOSOPHICAL ISSUES IN

The expression 'free logic' is a contraction of the more cumbersome 'logic free of existence assumptions with respect to both its general terms (predicates) and its singular terms'. Its most distinctive feature is the rejection of the principle of universal specification, a principle of classical predicate logic which licenses the logical truth of statements such as 'If everything rotates then (the planet) Mars rotates'. If a free logic contains the general term 'exists', this principle is replaced by a restricted version, one which licenses the logical truth only of statements such as 'If everything rotates then

Mars rotates, provided that Mars exists'. If the free logic does not contain the general term 'exists', but contains the term 'is the same as', the principle is replaced by a version which licenses only statements such as 'If everything rotates then Mars rotates, provided that there is an object the same as Mars'.

Most free logicians regard the restricted version of universal specification as simply making explicit an implicit assumption, namely, that Mars exists. Indeed, free logic is the culmination of a long historical trend to rid logic of existence assumptions with respect to its terms. Just as classical predicate logic purports to be free of the hidden existence assumptions which pervaded the medieval theory of inference with respect to its general terms, so free logic rids classical predicate logic of hidden existence assumptions with respect to its singular terms.

There are various kinds of free logic, with many interesting and novel philosophical applications. These cover a wide range of issues from the philosophy of mathematics to the philosophy of religion. In addition to the issue of how to analyse singular existence statements, of the form '3 + 7 exists' and 'That than which nothing greater can be conceived exists', of special importance are issues in the theory of definite descriptions, set theory, the theory of reference, modal logic and the theory of complex general terms.

1 Kinds of free logic
2 Philosophical semantics
3 Implications and applications

1 Kinds of free logic

Though there are various historical antecedents of free logic, it is a relatively recent development in the logic of terms – that is, in the development of predicate logic with or without identity. In fact, serious technical and philosophical study of this alternative to classical predicate logic originated only in the second half of the twentieth century with Henry Leonard's 1956 paper, 'Logic of Existence'. The technical rudiments of free logic were then worked out in the subsequent decade and a half, the expression 'free logic' being first coined in 1960 (by Karel Lambert). Since then many studies discussing or employing free logic in general philosophy, philosophical logic and in the philosophy of science have appeared.

'Free logic' is short for 'logic free of existence assumptions with respect to both its general terms (predicates) and its singular terms'. It restricts the principle of universal specification (which licenses the logical truth of statements such as 'If everything rotates then (the planet) Mars rotates') to a version which licenses only statements such as 'If everything

rotates then Mars rotates, provided that Mars exists' (if the logic contains the general term 'exists') or such as 'If everything rotates then Mars rotates, provided that there is an object the same as Mars' (if the free logic does not contain the general term 'exists', but contains the term 'is the same as').

When a free logic also entertains the empty universe of discourse, it is called a universally free logic. In such comprehensive free logics, statements (perhaps without singular terms) such as 'There is an object which is tall or is not tall' and 'There is an object which is self-identical' – statements which Russell (§§9, 11) regarded as impure logical truths because of the evidently factual implication that there exists at least one thing – are also excluded from the class of logical truths.

In any free logic, universal or otherwise, the quantifier context 'There is an object...' has existential force just as it does in classical predicate logic. So in any free logic containing the general term 'is the same as' (the identity symbol), a statement such as 'Mars exists' can be taken as shorthand for the statement 'There is an object the same as Mars'. Indeed, statements of the latter form can be false in free logic with identity, and hence, in contrast to classical predicate logic with identity, are not logically true. An example is the false statement 'There is an object the same as (the planet) Vulcan'.

Free logics may be divided into three classes depending on the treatment of atomic (or simple) statements containing at least one singular term t such that the statement 't exists' is false. For example, the statement 'Vulcan rotates' is an atomic statement containing a singular term, 'Vulcan', such that 'Vulcan exists' is false. Those which count all such statements as false are called 'negative', those which regard some such statements as true are called 'positive', and those which assign no truth-value at all to such statements – except perhaps statements of the form 'Mars exists'(or 'Vulcan exists') – are called 'neutral'.

In virtue of these different views about the truth-value of atomic statements with singular terms that refer to no existent object there is a significant inferential difference between the different kinds of free logic. For only in negative free logic does a version of the classical principle of particularization hold. In a negative free logic, the principle of particularization licenses the logical truth of the conditional statement 'If Vulcan rotates then there is an object which rotates' because the antecedent, 'Vulcan rotates', is an atomic statement. This does not alter the falsity of the conditional 'If Vulcan is not an object then there is an object which is not an object' because its (true) antecedent, 'Vulcan is not an object', is not atomic.

The kind of free logic one adopts has epistemological significance. For instance, when Descartes' declaration 'I think, therefore I am [exist]' is construed as an argument and formulated in a positive free logic it is invalid. For when the singular term 'I' is replaced by the singular term 'Sherlock Holmes', and the general term 'think' is replaced by the general term 'is self-identical', the resulting premise 'Sherlock Holmes is self-identical' is true in virtually any positive free logic but the resulting conclusion 'Sherlock Holmes exists' is false. On the other hand, if formulated in a negative or neutral free logic, Descartes' argument is valid because the premise is either false or without truth-value when 'I' is replaced by a singular term such as 'Sherlock Holmes', no matter what general term is substituted for 'thinks'.

2 Philosophical semantics

It is a common misunderstanding that in free logics some singular terms need not refer. There do exist, however, semantic developments of free logics which entertain disjoint (and possibly empty) universes of discourse. Usually (though not always) these are philosophically interpreted as sets of existent objects and sets of nonexistent objects, after Alexius MEINONG. In such developments, a singular term *always* refers, but not always to an existent object – the singular term, 'Sherlock Holmes', for example, may be taken to refer to a nonexistent (fictional) object. On the other hand, there also exist semantic treatments of free logic with a single (and possibly empty) universe of discourse. This is virtually always interpreted philosophically as the set of existent objects, after Russell. In such developments, a singular term can fail to refer to an existent object, and hence to any thing at all. Since free logics can be based on either Meinongian or Russellian ontologies, it is only correct to say that in such logics a singular term may fail to refer to an *existent* object. In free logics, successful or failed reference is explained as follows. Let 'X' be a place-holder for the name of a singular term, and let '___' be a place-holder for the singular term named. Then a statement of the form 'X refers (to an existent object)' is true if and only if a statement of the form '___ exists' is true – hence, when the language contains identity, if and only if a statement of the form 'There exists an object the same as ___' is true. For example, the statement 'The satellite of the Earth refers (to an existent object)' is true if and only if the statement 'The satellite of the Earth exists' is true (or, if the language contains identity, if and only if the statement 'There is an object the same as the satellite of the Earth' is true).

The quantifiers of free logic can be interpreted either objectually or substitutionally (see QUANTIFIERS, SUBSTITUTIONAL AND OBJECTUAL); if interpreted in the latter way, then it is necessary to say in the clause for a quantifier context of the form 'There is an object such that it ___' that it is true just in case a sentence of the form 'it ___' becomes true when 'it' is replaced by some name 'n' such that 'n exists' is true. This condition is needed to give the quantifier context in question the requisite existential force. In current parlance, quantifier contexts of the form 'There is an object such that it ___' in free logic are 'actualist'. Treatments seeking to preserve classical predicate logic by interpreting the quantifier context in question substitutionally while nevertheless admitting singular terms that refer to no existent object are not free logics because that quantifier context has no existential force; it is, in other words, 'non-actualist' in such treatments.

3 Implications and applications

Free logics are not committed to the philosophical doctrine that existence is a 'predicate' (see EXISTENCE) – indeed, there are free logics without identity or an existence symbol. Neither are they committed to the philosophical doctrine that proper names are truncated definite descriptions. They are not even committed to the doctrine that the reference of most grammatically proper names is determined by the reference of some description, a view often attributed to Frege and Russell (see PROPER NAMES §1). But an important result in the proof theory of positive free logic does bear on the traditional problem of defining (and, hence, explaining away) existence. Since it can be shown that, in the otherwise classical formal idiom minus identity, statements of the form 'Mars exists' (or 'Vulcan exists') are not definable in positive free logics, then, if one chooses to couch one's logic of an existence predicate in positive free logic, that predicate cannot be eliminated save by means of the complex general term (predicate) 'is the same as something' or its equivalents.

Applications of free logic to important philosophical concerns are numerous. They range from the philosophy of mathematics to the philosophy of religion. Of special philosophical importance are the topics of definite descriptions, modality, the notion of reference, set theory and the theory of complex predicates.

In contrast to the Fregean tradition, which assigns an existent, sometimes arbitrarily, as referent to 'unfulfilled' definite descriptions such as 'the planet Vulcan', in contrast to the Russellian tradition which treats all definite descriptions as grammatical but not as genuine singular terms, and in contrast to the

Hilbert–Bernays tradition which regards unfulfilled definite descriptions as formally ungrammatical (ill-formed), free theories of definite descriptions hold all definite descriptions to be genuine singular terms, but do not regard unfulfilled definite descriptions as referring to existents if they refer at all (see DESCRIPTIONS). More precisely, in free theories of definite descriptions, if the noun or noun phrase following the word 'the' in a definite description is not true of exactly one existent thing, then it refers to no existent thing if it refers at all.

Free theories of definite descriptions are all based on the basic principle that

> Everything is such that *it* is the same as *the* ___ if and only if *it* and *it only* is ___.

This principle is known as Lambert's Law in the literature. Free theories of definite descriptions form a continuum. At one end there is a Russell-like theory which counts all atomic statements having at least one unfulfilled definite description as false, and contains scope distinctions *à la* Russell. At the other end there is a Frege-like theory which counts all atomic identity statements having only unfulfilled definite descriptions as true, and collapses all scope distinctions held to be dependent on definite descriptions. There are also a multitude of intermediate cases in the literature which, in contrast to the other traditions, is dramatic evidence of the fecundity of free logic in the logical treatment of definite descriptions.

In many, if not most, treatments of the logic of singular and general terms, supplemented by the logical modalities 'it is necessary that' and 'it is possible that', the purely quantificational fragment is free. For in such developments, the conditional

C   If every (existent) thing exists, then Mars exists,

an instance of the classical principle of universal specification, is rejected on the ground that it leads, via unimpeachable modal principles, to the conditional

C*   If necessarily every (existent) thing exists, then necessarily Mars exists.

But C* is false because though 'Necessarily every (existent) thing exists' is true, 'Necessarily Mars exists' is false. In contrast, the principle of restricted universal specification yields only the innocent and trivial

C⁺   If necessarily every (existent) thing exists then necessarily Mars exists, *provided that* necessarily Mars exists.

The various treatments of free logic can influence the relationship between the meta-logical notion of

reference and the logical notion of identity, the relationship reflected in the traditional adequacy condition that, for example, the singular term 'the planet causing the perturbations in the orbit of Mercury' refers to Vulcan if and only if the planet causing the perturbations in the orbit of Mercury is the same as Vulcan. To clarify the point, suppose the singular term 'the planet causing the perturbations in the orbit of Mercury' is replaced throughout the adequacy condition by the singular term 'Vulcan'. Then one obtains the special case that 'Vulcan' refers to Vulcan if and only if Vulcan is the same as Vulcan. Clearly the traditional adequacy condition is sustained in negative free logics because both the reference claim and the identity claim are false since there exists no such object as Vulcan. Similarly, if the free logic is positive, but treats all singular terms as referring, in the spirit of Meinong, then the traditional adequacy condition is also sustained because both the identity claim and the reference claim will be true. However, if the free logic is positive and it recognizes that some singular terms do not refer, in the spirit of Russell, the traditional adequacy condition may have to be altered; in such a version of free logic, it is false that 'Vulcan' refers to Vulcan if Vulcan does not exist, but usually it is true that Vulcan is identical with Vulcan. In such a treatment of positive free logic the relationship between reference and identity is expressed in the following way: 'the planet causing the perturbations in the orbit of Mercury' refers to Vulcan if and only if Vulcan exists and the planet causing the perturbations in the orbit of Mercury is the same as Vulcan.

Free logic also exerts an influence in set theory; in free set theory, for instance, the naïve axiom of set abstraction, from which Russell deduced his famous paradox, is assertible without condition (see PARADOXES OF SET AND PROPERTY §4). Because of the replacement of universal specification by the restricted version of that principle, the most that can be deduced from the statement 'Everything is a member of the set of sets which are not members of themselves if and only if it is not a member of itself', an instance of the naïve principle of set abstraction, is that the set of all sets which are not members of themselves does not exist.

A final application of free logic concerns the important topic of complex general terms. In certain developments of free logic, both positive and negative, devices exist for generating complex general terms out of 'open' sentences, which are expressions without truth-value of the form 'it rotates'. For instance, the open sentence in question can be turned into the complex general term 'object such that it rotates' by prefixing to it the general term-forming operator 'object such that'. Then applying that complex general term to the singular term 'Vulcan' yields an expression capable of having a truth-value, the statement 'Vulcan is an object such that it rotates'. In some developments this statement is equivalent to the statement 'Vulcan rotates' if and only if it is true that Vulcan exists. The result is a free logic in which scope distinctions with respect to the connective 'it is not the case that' can be made over the whole class of singular terms and not just with respect to the class of definite descriptions. For instance, in the developments in question, 'Vulcan is an object such that it does not rotate' may be false, although 'It is not the case that Vulcan is an object such that it rotates' may be true. If, however, 'Vulcan' is replaced by 'Mars', the distinction between negation in the general term and negation over the whole statement collapses because the resulting statements have the same truth-value in virtue of the existence of Mars. Indeed, the means are available in these augmented free logics to make a distinction in general between *de re* and *de dicto* predicates or properties (see DE RE/DE DICTO). In such treatments, '*t* exists' can now be defined even if identity is not present – as Arthur Prior once anticipated. The requisite definition is that '*t* exists' means 'For any general term *G*, it is *not* the case that *t* is an object such that it is *G* if and only if *t* is an object such that it is *not* the case that it is *G*'. More idiomatically, the definition says that an object exists just in case denying it is *G* is tantamount to asserting it is *non-G*, and vice versa, for any *G*.

See also: FREE LOGICS; LOGICAL AND MATHEMATICAL TERMS, GLOSSARY OF

References and further reading

Bencivenga, E. (1989) 'Why Free Logic?' in *Looser Ends*, Minneapolis, MN: University of Minnesota Press. (A very readable and distinctive philosophical explanation of free logic.)

Evans, G. (1979) 'Reference and Contingency', *The Monist* 62: 161–89. (An argument that Kripke's doctrine of contingent a priori statements presupposes free logic.)

Lambert, K. (1983) *Meinong and the Principle of Independence*, Cambridge: Cambridge University Press, esp. ch. 5. (An informal account of the varieties of free logic and its connection with issues in the theory of predication.)

* Leonard, H. (1956) 'The Logic of Existence', *Philosophical Studies* 7: 49–64. (The essay which initiated the development of free logics.)

KAREL LAMBERT

FREE WILL

'Free will' is the conventional name of a topic that is best discussed without reference to the will. Its central questions are 'What is it to act (or choose) freely?', and 'What is it to be morally responsible for one's actions (or choices)?' These two questions are closely connected, for freedom of action is necessary for moral responsibility, even if it is not sufficient.

Philosophers give very different answers to these questions, hence also to two more specific questions about ourselves: (1) Are we free agents? and (2) Can we be morally responsible for what we do? Answers to (1) and (2) range from 'Yes, Yes' to 'No, No' – via 'Yes, No' and various degrees of 'Perhaps', 'Possibly', and 'In a sense'. (The fourth pair of outright answers, 'No, Yes', is rare, but appears to be accepted by some Protestants.) Prominent among the 'Yes, Yes' sayers are the compatibilists, *who hold that free will is compatible with determinism. Briefly, determinism is the view that everything that happens is necessitated by what has already gone before, in such a way that nothing can happen otherwise than it does. According to compatibilists, freedom is compatible with determinism because freedom is essentially just a matter of not being constrained or hindered in certain ways when one acts or chooses. Thus normal adult human beings in normal circumstances are able to act and choose freely. No one is holding a gun to their heads. They are not drugged, or in chains, or subject to a psychological compulsion. They are therefore wholly free to choose and act even if their whole physical and psychological make-up is entirely determined by things for which they are in no way ultimately responsible – starting with their genetic inheritance and early upbringing.*

Incompatibilists *hold that freedom is not compatible with determinism. They point out that if determinism is true, then every one of one's actions was determined to happen as it did before one was born. They hold that one cannot be held to be truly free and finally morally responsible for one's actions in this case. They think compatibilism is a 'wretched subterfuge..., a petty word-jugglery', as Kant put it (1788 : 189–90). It entirely fails to satisfy our natural convictions about the nature of moral responsibility.*

The incompatibilists have a good point, and may be divided into two groups. Libertarians answer 'Yes, Yes' to questions (1) and (2). They hold that we are indeed free and fully morally responsible agents, and that determinism must therefore be false. Their great difficulty is to explain why the falsity of determinism is any better than the truth of determinism when it comes to establishing our free agency and moral responsibility. For suppose that not every event is determined, and that some events occur randomly, or as a matter of chance. How can our claim to moral responsibility be improved by the supposition that it is partly a matter of chance or random outcome that we and our actions are as they are?

The second group of incompatibilists is less sanguine. They answer 'No, No' to questions (1) and (2). They agree with the libertarians that the truth of determinism rules out genuine moral responsibility, but argue that the falsity of determinism cannot help. Accordingly, they conclude that we are not genuinely free agents or genuinely morally responsible, whether determinism is true or false. One of their arguments can be summarized as follows. When one acts, one acts in the way one does because of the way one is. So to be truly morally responsible for one's actions, one would have to be truly responsible for the way one is: one would have to be causa sui, *or the cause of oneself, at least in certain crucial mental respects. But nothing can be* causa sui – *nothing can be the ultimate cause of itself in any respect. So nothing can be truly morally responsible.*

Suitably developed, this argument against moral responsibility seems very strong. But in many human beings, the experience of choice gives rise to a conviction of absolute responsibility that is untouched by philosophical arguments. This conviction is the deep and inexhaustible source of the free will problem: powerful arguments that seem to show that we cannot be morally responsible in the ultimate way that we suppose keep coming up against equally powerful psychological reasons why we continue to believe that we are ultimately morally responsible.

1 **Compatibilism**
2 **Incompatibilism**
3 **Pessimism**
4 **Moral responsibility**
5 **Metaphysics and moral psychology**
6 **Challenges to pessimism**

1 Compatibilism

Do we have free will? It depends what you mean by the word 'free'. More than two hundred senses of the word have been distinguished; the history of the discussion of free will is rich and remarkable. David Hume called the problem of free will 'the most contentious question of metaphysics, the most contentious science' (1748: 95).

According to *compatibilists*, we do have free will. They propound a sense of the word 'free' according to which free will is compatible with *determinism*, even though determinism is the view that the history of the universe is fixed in such a way that nothing can happen otherwise than it does because everything that happens is necessitated by what has already gone before (see DETERMINISM AND INDETERMINISM).

Suppose tomorrow is a national holiday. You are considering what to do. You can climb a mountain or read Lao Tse. You can mend your bicycle or go to the zoo. At this moment you are reading the *Routledge Encyclopedia of Philosophy*. You are free to go on reading or stop now. You have started on this sentence, but you don't have to... finish it.

In this situation, as so often in life, you have a number of options. Nothing forces your hand. It seems natural to say that you are *entirely* free to choose what to do. And, given that nothing hinders you, it seems natural to say that you act entirely freely when you actually do (or try to do) what you have decided to do.

Compatibilists claim that this is the right thing to say. They believe that to have free will, to be a free agent, to be free in choice and action, is simply to be free from *constraints* of certain sorts. Freedom is a matter of not being physically or psychologically forced or compelled to do what one does. Your character, personality, preferences, and general motivational set may be entirely determined by events for which you are in no way responsible (by your genetic inheritance, upbringing, subsequent experience, and so on). But you do not have to be in control of any of these things in order to have compatibilist freedom. They do not constrain or compel you, because compatibilist freedom is just a matter of being able to choose and act in the way one prefers or thinks best *given how one is*. As its name declares, it is compatible with determinism. It is compatible with determinism even though it follows from determinism that every aspect of your character, and everything you will ever do, was already inevitable before you were born.

If determinism does not count as a constraint or compulsion, what does? Compatibilists standardly take it that freedom can be limited by such things as imprisonment, by a gun at one's head, or a threat to the life of one's children, or a psychological obsession and so on.

It is arguable, however, that compatibilist freedom is something one continues to possess undiminished so long as one can choose or act in any way at all. One continues to possess it in any situation in which one is not actually panicked, or literally compelled to do what one does, in such a way that it is not clear that one can still be said to choose or act at all (as when one presses a button, because one's finger is actually forced down on the button).

Consider pilots of hijacked aeroplanes. They usually stay calm. They *choose* to comply with the hijackers' demands. They act responsibly, as we naturally say. They are able to do other than they do, but they choose not to. They do what they most want to do, all things considered, in the circumstances in which they find themselves.

All circumstances limit one's options in some way. It is true that some circumstances limit one's options much more drastically than others; but it does not follow that one is not free to choose in those circumstances. Only literal compulsion, panic, or uncontrollable impulse really removes one's freedom to choose, and to (try to) do what one most wants to do given one's character or personality. Even when one's finger is being forced down on the button, one can still act freely in resisting the pressure, and in many other ways.

Most of us are free to choose throughout our waking lives, according to the compatibilist conception of freedom. We are free to choose between the options that we perceive to be open to us. (Sometimes we would rather not face options, but are unable to avoid awareness of the fact that we do face them.) One has options even when one is in chains, or falling through space. Even if one is completely paralysed, one is still free in so far as one is free to choose to think about one thing rather than another. Sartre (1948) observed that there is a sense in which we are 'condemned' to freedom, not free not to be free.

Of course one may well not be able to do everything one wants – one may want to fly unassisted, vapourize every gun in the United States by an act of thought, or house all those who sleep on the streets of Calcutta by the end of the month. But few have supposed that free will, or free agency, is a matter of being able to do everything one wants. That is one possible view of what it is to be free; but according to the compatibilists, free will is simply a matter of having genuine options and opportunities for action, and being able to choose between them according to what one wants or thinks best.

It may be said that dogs and other animals can be free agents, according to this basic account of compatibilism. Compatibilists may reply that dogs can indeed be free agents. And yet we do not think that dogs can be free or morally responsible in the way we can be. So compatibilists need to say what the relevant difference is between dogs and ourselves.

Many suppose that it is our capacity for self-conscious thought that makes the crucial difference, because it makes it possible for us to be explicitly aware of ourselves as facing choices and engaging in processes of reasoning about what to do. This is *not* because being self-conscious can somehow liberate one from the facts of determinism: if determinism is true, one is determined to have whatever self-conscious thoughts one has, whatever their complexity. Nevertheless, many are inclined to think that a creature's explicit self-conscious awareness of itself as chooser and agent can constitute it as a free agent in a fundamental way that is unavailable to any unself-conscious agent.

Compatibilists can agree with this. They can acknowledge and incorporate the view that self-conscious awareness of oneself as facing choices can give rise to a kind of freedom that is unavailable to unself-conscious agents. They may add that human beings are sharply marked off from dogs by their capacity to act for reasons that they explicitly take to be moral reasons. In general, compatibilism has many variants. According to Harry Frankfurt's version, for example, one has free will if one wants to be moved to action by the motives that do in fact move one to action (Frankfurt 1988). On this view, freedom is a matter of having a personality that is harmonious in a certain way. Freedom in this sense is clearly compatible with determinism.

Compatibilism has been refined in many ways, but this gives an idea of its basis. 'What more could free agency possibly be?', compatibilists like to ask (backed by Hobbes (1651), Locke (1690), and Hume (1748), among others). And this is a very powerful question.

2 Incompatibilism

Those who want to secure the conclusion that we are free agents do well to adopt a compatibilist theory of freedom, for determinism is unfalsifiable, and may be true. (Contemporary physics gives us no more reason to suppose that determinism is false than to suppose that it is true – though this is contested; for further discussion see DETERMINISM AND INDETERMINISM.) Many, however, think that the compatibilist account of things does not even touch the real problem of free will. They believe that all compatibilist theories of freedom are patently inadequate.

What is it, they say, to define freedom in such a way that it is compatible with determinism? It is to define it in such a way that a creature can be a free agent even if all its actions throughout its life are determined to happen as they do by events that have taken place before it is born: so that there is a clear sense in which it could not at any point in its life have done otherwise than it did. This, they say, is certainly not free will. More importantly, it is not a sufficient basis for true moral responsibility. One cannot possibly be truly or ultimately morally responsible for what one does if everything one does is ultimately a deterministic outcome of events that took place before one was born; or (more generally) a deterministic outcome of events for whose occurrence one is in no way ultimately responsible.

These anti-compatibilists or *incompatibilists* divide into two groups: the *libertarians* and the *no-freedom theorists* or *pessimists* about free will and moral responsibility. The libertarians think that the compatibilist account of freedom can be improved on. They hold (1) that we do have free will, (2) that free will is not compatible with determinism, and (3) that determinism is therefore false. But they face an extremely difficult task: they have to show how *indeterminism* (the falsity of determinism) can help with free will and, in particular, with moral responsibility.

The pessimists or no-freedom theorists do not think that this can be shown. They agree with the libertarians that the compatibilist account of free will is inadequate, but they do not think it can be improved on. They agree that free will is not compatible with determinism, but deny that indeterminism can help to make us (or anyone else) free. They believe that free will, of the sort that is necessary for genuine moral responsibility, is provably impossible.

The pessimists about free will grant what everyone must: that there is a clear and important compatibilist sense in which we can be free agents (we can be free, when unconstrained, to choose and to do what we want or think best, given how we are). But they insist that this compatibilist sense of freedom is not enough: it does not give us what we want, in the way of free will; nor does it give us what we believe we have. And it is not as if the compatibilists have missed something. The truth is that nothing can give us what we (think we) want, or what we ordinarily think we have. All attempts to furnish a stronger notion of free will fail. We cannot be morally responsible, in the absolute, buck-stopping way in which we often unreflectively think we are. We cannot have 'strong' free will of the kind that we would need to have, in order to be morally responsible in this way.

The fundamental motor of the free will debate is the worry about moral responsibility (see RESPONSIBILITY). If no one had this worry, it is doubtful whether the problem of free will would be a famous philosophical problem. The rest of this discussion will therefore be organized around the question of moral responsibility.

First, though, it is worth remarking that the worry about free will does not have to be expressed as a worry about the grounds of moral responsibility. A commitment to belief in free will may be integral to feelings that are extremely important to us independently of the issue of moral responsibility: feelings of gratitude, for example, and perhaps of love. One's belief in strong free will may also be driven simply by the conviction that one is or can be *radically self-determining* in one's actions (in a way that is incompatible with determinism) and this conviction need not involve giving much – or any – thought to the issue of moral responsibility. It seems that a creature could conceive of itself as radically self-determining without having any conception of moral right or wrong at all – and so without being any sort of moral agent.

3 Pessimism

One way of setting out the no-freedom theorists' argument is as follows.

(1) When you act, you do what you do, in the situation in which you find yourself, because of the way you are.

It seems to follow that

(2) To be truly or ultimately morally responsible for what you *do*, you must be truly or ultimately responsible for the way you *are*, at least in certain crucial mental respects. (Obviously you don't have to be responsible for the way you are in all respects. You don't have to be responsible for your height, age, sex, and so on. But it does seem that you have to be responsible for the way you are at least in certain mental respects. After all, it is your overall mental make-up that leads you to do what you do when you act.)

But

(3) You cannot be ultimately responsible for the way you are in any respect at all, so you cannot be ultimately morally responsible for what you do.

Why is that you cannot be ultimately responsible for the way you are? Because

(4) To be ultimately responsible for the way you are, you would have to have intentionally brought it about that you are the way you are, in a way that is impossible.

The impossibility is shown as follows. Suppose that

(5) You have somehow intentionally brought it about that you are the way you now are, in certain mental respects: suppose that you have intentionally brought it about that you have a certain mental nature N, and that you have brought this about in such a way that you can now be said to be ultimately responsible for having nature N. (The limiting case of this would be the case in which you had simply endorsed your existing mental nature N from a position of power to change it.)

For this to be true

(6) You must already have had a certain mental nature N$_{-1}$, in the light of which you intentionally brought it about that you now have nature N. (If you did not already have a certain mental nature, then you cannot have had any intentions or preferences, and even if you did change in some way, you cannot be held to be responsible for the way you now are.)

But then

(7) For it to be true that you and you alone are truly responsible for how you now are, you must be truly responsible for having had the nature N$_{-1}$ in the light of which you intentionally brought it about that you now have nature N.

So

(8) You must have intentionally brought it about that you had that nature N$_{-1}$. But in that case, you must have existed already with a prior nature, N$_{-2}$, in the light of which you intentionally brought it about that you had the nature N$_{-1}$.

And so on. Here one is setting off on a potentially infinite regress. In order for one to be truly or ultimately responsible for *how one is*, in such a way that one can be truly morally responsible for *what one does*, something impossible has to be true: there has to be, and cannot be, a starting point in the series of acts of bringing it about that one has a certain nature – a starting point that constitutes an act of ultimate self-origination.

There is a more concise way of putting the point: in order to be truly morally responsible for what one does, it seems that one would have to be the ultimate cause or origin of oneself, or at least of some crucial part of one's mental nature. One would have to be *causa sui*, in the old terminology. But nothing can be truly or ultimately *causa sui* in any respect at all. Even if the property of being *causa sui* is allowed to belong (unintelligibly) to God, it cannot plausibly be supposed to be possessed by ordinary finite human beings. 'The *causa sui* is the best self-contradiction that has been conceived so far', as Nietzsche remarked in *Beyond Good and Evil*:

it is a sort of rape and perversion of logic. But the extravagant pride of man has managed to entangle itself profoundly and frightfully with just this nonsense. The desire for 'freedom of the will' in the superlative metaphysical sense, which still holds sway, unfortunately, in the minds of the half-educated; the desire to bear the entire and ultimate responsibility for one's actions oneself, and to absolve God, the world, ancestors, chance, and society involves nothing less than to be precisely this *causa sui* and, with more than Baron Münchhausen's audacity, to pull oneself up into existence by the hair, out of the swamps of nothingness.

(1886: §21)

In fact, nearly all of those who believe in strong free will do so without any conscious thought that it requires ultimate self-origination. Nevertheless, this is the only thing that could actually ground the kind of strong free will that is regularly believed in, and it does seem that one way in which the belief in strong free will manifests itself is in the very vague and (necessarily) unexamined belief that many have that they are somehow or other radically responsible for their general mental nature, or at least for certain crucial aspects of it.

The pessimists' argument may seem contrived, but essentially the same argument can be given in a more natural form as follows. (i) It is undeniable that one is the way one is, initially, as a result of heredity and early experience. (ii) It is undeniable that these are things for which one cannot be held to be in any way responsible (this might not be true if there were reincarnation, but reincarnation would just shift the problem backwards). (iii) One cannot at any later stage of one's life hope to accede to true or ultimate responsibility for the way one is by trying to change the way one already is as a result of one's heredity and previous experience. For one may well try to change oneself, but (iv) both the particular way in which one is moved to try to change oneself, and the degree of success in one's attempt at change, will be determined by how one already is as a result of heredity and previous experience. And (v) any further changes that one can bring about only after one has brought about certain initial changes will in turn be determined, via the initial changes, by heredity and previous experience. (vi) This may not be the whole story, for it may be that some changes in the way one is are traceable to the influence of indeterministic or random factors. But (vii) it is foolish to suppose that indeterministic or random factors, for which one is *ex hypothesi* in no way responsible, can in themselves contribute to one's being truly or ultimately responsible for how one is.

The claim, then, is not that people cannot change the way they are. They can, in certain respects (which tend to be exaggerated by North Americans and underestimated, perhaps, by members of many other cultures). The claim is only that people cannot be supposed to change themselves in such a way as to be or become truly or ultimately responsible for the way they are, and hence for their actions. One can put the point by saying that the way you are is, ultimately, in every last detail, a matter of luck – good or bad.

4 Moral responsibility

Two main questions are raised by the pessimists' arguments. First, is it really true that one needs to be self-creating or *causa sui* in some way, in order to be truly or ultimately responsible for what one does, as step (2) of the pessimists' argument asserts? Addressing this question will be delayed until §6, because a more basic question arises: What notion of responsibility is being appealed to in this argument? What exactly is this 'ultimate' responsibility that we are held to believe in, in spite of Nietzsche's scorn? And if we do believe in it, what makes us believe in it?

One dramatic way to characterize the notion of ultimate responsibility is by reference to the story of heaven and hell: 'ultimate' moral responsibility is responsibility of such a kind that, if we have it, it *makes sense* to propose that it could be just to punish some of us with torment in hell and reward others with bliss in heaven. It makes sense because what we do is absolutely up to us. The words 'makes sense' are stressed because one certainly does not have to believe in the story of heaven and hell in order to understand the notion of ultimate responsibility that it is used to illustrate. Nor does one have to believe in the story of heaven and hell in order to believe in ultimate responsibility (many atheists have believed in it). One does not have to have heard of it.

The story is useful because it illustrates the *kind* of absolute or ultimate responsibility that many have supposed – and do suppose – themselves to have. It becomes particularly vivid when one is specifically concerned with moral responsibility, and with questions of desert; but it serves equally well to illustrate the sense of radical freedom and responsibility that may be had by a self-conscious agent that has no concept of morality. And one does not have to refer to the story of heaven and hell in order to describe the sorts of everyday situation that seem to be primarily influential in giving rise to our belief in ultimate responsibility. Suppose you set off for a shop on the eve of a national holiday, intending to buy a cake with your last ten pound note. Everything is closing down. There is one cake left; it costs ten pounds. On the steps of the shop someone is shaking an Oxfam tin. You stop, and it seems completely clear to you that it is entirely up to you what you do next. That is, it seems clear to you that you are truly, radically free to choose, in such a way that you will be ultimately responsible for whatever you do choose. You can put the money in the tin, or go in and buy the cake, or just walk away. (You are not only completely free to choose. You are not free not to choose.)

Standing there, you may believe that determinism is true. You may believe that in five minutes' time you will be able to look back on the situation and say, of what you will by then have done, 'It was determined that I should do that'. But even if you do believe this, it does not seem to undermine your current sense of the absoluteness of your freedom, and of your moral responsibility for your choice.

One diagnosis of this phenomenon is that one cannot really believe that determinism is true, in such situations of choice, and cannot help thinking that the falsity of determinism might make freedom possible. But the feeling of ultimate responsibility seems to remain inescapable even if one does not think this, and even if one has been convinced by the entirely general argument against ultimate responsibility given in §3. Suppose one accepts that no one can be in any way *causa sui*, and yet that one would have to be *causa sui* (in certain crucial mental respects) in order to be ultimately responsible for one's actions. This does not seem to have any impact on one's sense of one's radical freedom and responsibility, as one stands there, wondering what to do. One's radical responsibility seems to stem simply from the fact that one is fully conscious of one's situation, and knows that one can choose, and believes that one action is morally better than the other. This seems to be immediately enough to confer full and ultimate responsibility. And yet it cannot really do so, according to the pessimists. For whatever one actually does, one will do what one does because of the way one is, and the way one is is something for which one neither is nor can be responsible, however self-consciously aware of one's situation one is.

The example of the cake may be artificial, but similar situations of choice occur regularly in human life. They are the experiential rock on which the belief in ultimate responsibility is founded. The belief often takes the form of belief in specifically moral, desert-implying responsibility. But, as noted, an agent could have a sense of ultimate responsibility without possessing any conception of morality, and there is an interesting intermediate case: an agent could have an irrepressible experience of ultimate responsibility, and believe in objective moral right and wrong, while still denying the coherence of the notion of desert.

5 Metaphysics and moral psychology

We now have the main elements of the problem of free will. It is natural to start with the compatibilist position; but this has only to be stated to trigger the objection that compatibilism cannot possibly satisfy our intuitions about moral responsibility. According to this objection, an incompatibilist notion of free will is essential in order to make sense of the idea that we are genuinely morally responsible. But this view, too, has only to be stated to trigger the pessimists' objection that indeterministic occurrences cannot possibly contribute to moral responsibility: one can hardly be supposed to be more truly morally responsible for one's choices and actions or character if indeterministic occurrences have played a part in their causation than if they have not played such a part. Indeterminism gives rise to unpredictability, not responsibility. It cannot help in any way at all.

The pessimists therefore conclude that strong free will is not possible, and that ultimate responsibility is not possible either. So no punishment or reward is ever truly just or fair, when it comes to moral matters.

This conclusion may prompt a further question: What exactly is this 'ultimate' responsibility that we are supposed to believe in? One answer refers to the story of heaven and hell, which serves to illustrate the *kind* of responsibility that is shown to be impossible by the pessimists' argument, and which many people do undoubtedly believe themselves to have, however fuzzily they think about the matter. A less colourful answer has the same import, although it needs more thought: 'ultimate' responsibility exists if and only if punishment and reward can be fair without having any pragmatic justification.

Now the argument may cycle back to compatibilism. Pointing out that 'ultimate' moral responsibility is obviously impossible, compatibilists may claim that we should rest content with the compatibilist account of things – since it is the best we can do. But this claim reactivates the incompatibilist objection, and the cycle continues.

There is an alternative strategy at this point: quit the traditional metaphysical circle for the domain of *moral psychology*. The principal positions in the traditional metaphysical debate are clear. No radically new option is likely to emerge after millennia of debate. The interesting questions that remain are primarily psychological: Why do we believe we have strong free will and ultimate responsibility of the kind that can be characterized by reference to the story of heaven and hell? What is it like to live with this belief? What are its varieties? How might we be changed by dwelling intensely on the view that ultimate responsibility is impossible?

A full answer to these questions is beyond the scope of this entry, but one fundamental cause of our belief in ultimate responsibility has been mentioned. It lies in the experience of choice that we have as self-conscious agents who are able to be fully conscious of what they are doing when they deliberate about what to do and make choices. (We choose between the Oxfam box and the cake; or we make a difficult, morally neutral choice about which of two paintings to buy.) This raises an interesting question: Is it true that any possible self-conscious creature that faces choices and is fully aware of the fact that it does so must experience itself as having strong free will, or as being radically self-determining, simply in virtue of the fact that it is a self-conscious agent (and whether or not it has a conception of moral responsibility)? It seems that we cannot live or experience our choices as determined, even if determinism is true. But perhaps this is a human peculiarity, not an inescapable feature of any possible self-conscious agent. And perhaps it is not even universal among human beings.

Other causes of the belief in strong free will have been suggested. Hume stressed our experience of serious indecision, as above. Spinoza (1677: 440) proposed that one of the causes is simply that we are not conscious of the determined nature of our desires. Kant (1793: 93n.) held that our experience of moral obligation makes belief in strong free will inevitable. P. F. Strawson (1962) argued that the fundamental fact is that we are irresistibly committed to certain natural reactions to other people, like gratitude and resentment. Various other suggestions have been made: those who think hard about free will are likely to become convinced that investigation of the complex moral psychology of the belief in freedom, and of the possible moral and psychological consequences of altering the belief, is the most fruitful area of research that remains. New generations, however, will doubtless continue to launch themselves onto the old metaphysical roundabout.

6 Challenges to pessimism

The preceding discussion attempts to illustrate the internal dynamic of the free will debate, and to explain why the debate is likely to continue for as long as human beings can think. The basic point is this: powerful logical or metaphysical reasons for supposing that we cannot have strong free will keep coming up against equally powerful psychological reasons why we cannot help believing that we do have it. The pessimists' or no-freedom theorists' conclusions may seem irresistible during philosophical discussion, but they are likely to lose their force, and seem obviously irrelevant to life, when one stops philosophizing.

Various challenges to the pessimists' argument have been proposed, some of which appear to be supported by the experience or 'phenomenology' of choice. One challenge grants that one cannot be ultimately responsible for one's mental nature – one's character, personality, or motivational structure – but denies that it follows that one cannot be truly morally responsible for what one does (it therefore challenges step (2) of the argument set out in §3).

This challenge has at least two versions. One has

already been noted: we are attracted by the idea that our capacity for fully explicit self-conscious deliberation, in a situation of choice, suffices by itself to constitute us as truly morally responsible agents in the strongest possible sense. The idea is that such full self-conscious awareness somehow renders irrelevant the fact that one neither is nor can be ultimately responsible for any aspect of one's mental nature. On this view, the mere fact of one's self-conscious presence in the situation of choice can confer true moral responsibility: it may be undeniable that one is, in the final analysis, wholly constituted as the sort of person one is by factors for which one cannot be in any way ultimately responsible; but the threat that this fact appears to pose to one's claim to true moral responsibility is simply obliterated by one's self-conscious awareness of one's situation.

The pessimists reply: This may correctly describe a strong source of *belief* in ultimate (moral) responsibility, but it is not an account of something that could *constitute* ultimate (moral) responsibility. When one acts after explicit self-conscious deliberation, one acts for certain reasons. But which reasons finally weigh with one is a matter of one's mental nature, which is something for which one cannot be in any way ultimately responsible. One can certainly be a morally responsible agent in the sense of being aware of distinctively moral considerations when one acts. But one cannot be morally responsible in such a way that one is ultimately deserving of punishment or reward for what one does.

The conviction that fully explicit self-conscious awareness of one's situation can be a sufficient foundation of strong free will is extremely powerful. The no-freedom theorists' argument seems to show that it is wrong, but it is a conviction that runs deeper than rational argument, and it survives untouched, in the everyday conduct of life, even after the validity of the no-freedom theorists' argument has been admitted.

Another version of the challenge runs as follows. The reason why one can be truly or ultimately (morally) responsible for what one does is that one's *self* – what one might call the 'agent self'– is, in some crucial sense, independent of one's general *mental nature* (one's character, personality, motivational structure, and so on). One's mental nature *inclines* one to do one thing rather than another, but it does not thereby *necessitate* one to do one thing rather than the other. (The distinction between inclining and necessitating derives from Leibniz (1686. 1704–5).) As an agent-self, one incorporates a power of free decision that is independent of all the particularities of one's mental nature in such a way that one can, after all, count as truly and ultimately morally

responsible in one's decisions and actions even though one is not ultimately responsible for any aspect of one's mental nature.

The pessimists reply: Even if one grants the validity of this conception of the agent-self for the sake of argument, it cannot help to establish ultimate moral responsibility. According to the conception, the agent-self decides in the light of the agent's mental nature but is not determined by the agent's mental nature. The following question immediately arises: *Why* does the agent-self decide as it does? The general answer is clear. Whatever the agent-self decides, it decides as it does because of the overall way it is; and this necessary truth returns us to where we started. For once again, it seems that the agent-self must be responsible for being the way it is, in order to be a source of true or ultimate responsibility. But this is impossible, for the reasons given in §3: nothing can be *causa sui* in the required way. Whatever the nature of the agent-self, it is ultimately a matter of luck (or, for those who believe in God, a matter of grace). It may be proposed that the agent-self decides as it does partly or wholly because of the presence of indeterministic occurrences in the decision process. But it is clear that indeterministic occurrences can never be a source of true (moral) responsibility.

Some believe that free will and moral responsibility are above all a matter of being governed in one's choices and actions by reason – or by Reason with a capital 'R'. But possession of the property of being governed by Reason cannot be a ground of radical moral responsibility as ordinarily understood. It cannot be a property that makes punishment (for example) ultimately just or fair for those who possess it, and unfair for those who do not possess it. Why not? Because to be morally responsible, on this view, is simply to possess one sort of motivational set among others. It is to value or respond naturally to rational considerations – which are often thought to include moral considerations by those who propound this view. It is to have a general motivational set that may be attractive, and that may be more socially beneficial than many others. But there is no escape from the fact that someone who does possess such a motivational set is simply lucky to possess it – if it is indeed a good thing – while someone who lacks it is unlucky.

This may be denied. It may be said that some people struggle to become more morally responsible, and make an enormous effort. Their moral responsibility is then not a matter of luck; it is their own hard-won achievement.

The pessimists' reply is immediate. Suppose you are someone who struggles to be morally responsible, and make an enormous effort. Well, that, too, is a matter of luck. You are lucky to be someone who has a character of a sort that disposes you to make that sort of effort. Someone who lacks a character of that sort is merely unlucky. Kant is a famous example of a philosopher who was attracted by the idea that to display free will is to be governed by Reason in one's actions. But he became aware of the problem just described, and insisted, in a later work (1793: 89), that 'man *himself* must make or have made himself into whatever, in a moral sense, whether good or evil, he is to become. Either condition must be an effect of his free choice; for otherwise he could not be held responsible for it and could therefore be *morally* neither good nor evil'. Since he was committed to belief in ultimate moral responsibility, Kant held that such self-creation does indeed take place, and wrote accordingly of 'man's character, which he himself creates' (1788: 101), and of 'knowledge [that one has] of oneself as a person who...is his own originator' (1793: 213). Here he made the demand for self-creation that is natural for someone who believes in ultimate moral responsibility and who thinks through what is required for it.

In the end, luck swallows everything. This is one way of putting the point that there can be no ultimate responsibility, given the natural, strong conception of responsibility that was characterized at the beginning of §4. Relative to that conception, no punishment or reward is ever ultimately just or fair, however natural or useful or otherwise humanly appropriate it may be or seem.

The facts are clear, and they have been known for a long time. When it comes to the metaphysics of free will, André Gide's remark is apt: 'Everything has been said before, but since nobody listens we have to keep going back and beginning all over again.' It seems that the only freedom that we can have is compatibilist freedom. If – since – that is not enough for ultimate responsibility, we cannot have ultimate responsibility. The only alternative to this conclusion is to appeal to God and mystery – this in order to back up the claim that something that appears to be provably impossible is not only possible but actual.

The debate continues; some have thought that philosophy ought to move on. There is little reason to expect that it will do so, as each new generation arises bearing philosophers gripped by the conviction that they can have ultimate responsibility. Would it be a good thing if philosophy did move on, or if we became more clear-headed about the topic of free will than we are? It is hard to say.

See also: ACTION; CRIME AND PUNISHMENT; MENTAL CAUSATION; DESERT AND MERIT; MORAL AGENTS; MORAL PSYCHOLOGY; WILL, THE

References and further reading

Alexander of Aphrodisias (*c.* AD 200) *On Fate*, with translation and commentary by R.W. Sharples, London: Duckworth, 1983. (Incompatibilist defence of free will against the Stoics, by an Aristotelian.)

Aristotle (*c.* 384–322 BC) *Nicomachean Ethics*, trans. J.A.K. Thomson, Harmondsworth: Penguin, 1953. (Combines compatibilist points with the view that we can be in some sense ultimately responsible for how we are. See book III, chapter V.)

Augustine (AD 388–395) *De Gratia et Libero Arbitrio*, trans. R. P. Russell, in L. Schopp, R. J. Deferrari *et al.* (eds) *Fathers of the Church*, Catholic University of America Press, 1968, vol. 59. (Attempts, hesitantly and controversially, to show that free will is compatible with divine grace.)

Campbell, C. A. (1967) 'In Defence of Free Will', in *In Defence of Free Will*, London: Allen & Unwin. (Famous statement of the libertarian position that finds scope for exercise of free will especially in situations of moral conflict.)

Chisholm, R. (1964) 'Human Freedom and the Self', in G.Watson (ed.) *Free Will*, Oxford: Oxford University Press, 1982. (Libertarian who argues that free agency involves a distinct kind of causation called 'agent-causation'.)

Cicero (43–late 50s BC) *On fate*, trans. and commentary R.W. Sharples, Warminster: Aris & Phillips, 1991 with Latin text. (Critique, by an Academic, of Stoic and Epicurean views on determinism; sole source for the outstanding defence of incompatibilism by Carneades, the second-century BC Academic philosopher.)

Dennett, D. (1984) *Elbow Room*, Oxford: Oxford University Press. (Vivid defence of compatibilism.)

Double, R. (1993) *The Non-Reality of Free Will*, New York: Oxford University Press. (Thorough, full-length study whose title is self-explanatory.)

Fischer, J.M. (1994) *The Metaphysics of Free Will*, Oxford: Blackwell. (Tightly argued study of the ramifications of compatibilism.)

* Frankfurt, H. (1988) *The Importance of What We Care About*, Cambridge: Cambridge University Press, essays 1–5. (Essay 1 is an influential challenge to the view that free will requires the ability to do other than one does. Essays 3 and 5 develop the view referred to in §1 of this entry.)

Hobart, R.E. (1934) 'Free Will as Involving Determinism and Inconceivable without It', *Mind* 43. (Influential rehearsal of a Humean compatibilist position.)

* Hobbes, T. (1651) *Leviathan*, Cambridge: Cambridge

University Press, 1996. (Uncompromising 'necessitarian' compatibilism.)

Honderich, T. (1988) *The Consequences of Determinism*, Oxford: Clarendon Press. (Determinist who argues against both compatibilism and incompatibilism and considers three responses to determinism: dismay, intransigence and affirmation.)

Hume, D. (1748) *Enquiry Concerning Human Understanding*, Oxford: Clarendon Press, 1975, §VIII. (Famous statement of the case for compatibilism, following Hobbes and Locke.)

Kane, R. (1996) *The Significance of Free Will*, New York: Oxford University Press. (Contains a careful statement of the 'free willist', libertarian case, and a general survey of the debate.)

Kant, I. (1781) *The Critique of Pure Reason*, trans. N. Kemp Smith, London: Macmillan, 1933. (Kant grounds human freedom in a 'noumenal' self not subject to the laws of causality, and holds that it requires that one be responsible for one's character: he believes that we cannot understand how freedom is possible, although we can know that it exists.)

—— (1785) *Groundwork of the Metaphysic of Morals*, in *Practical Philosophy*, trans. M.J. Gregor, Cambridge: Cambridge University Press, 1996. (Kant grounds human freedom in a 'noumenal' self not subject to the laws of causality, and holds that it requires that one be responsible for one's character: he believes that we cannot understand how freedom is possible, although we can know that it exists.)

* —— (1788) *The Critique of Practical Reason*, trans. L.W. Beck, Indianapolis, IN: Bobbs-Merrill, 1956. (Kant grounds human freedom in a 'noumenal' self not subject to the laws of causality, and holds that it requires that one be responsible for one's character: he believes that we cannot understand how freedom is possible, although we can know that it exists.)

* —— (1793) *Religion within the Limits of Reason Alone*, in *Religion and Rational Theology*, trans. A.W. Wood, Cambridge: Cambridge University Press, 1996. (Kant grounds human freedom in a 'noumenal' self not subject to the laws of causality, and holds that it requires that one be responsible for one's character: he believes that we cannot understand how freedom is possible, although we can know that it exists.)

* —— (1993) *Opus Postumum*, trans. E. Förster and M. Rosen, Cambridge: Cambridge University Press.

* Leibniz, G. (1686) *Discourse on Metaphysics*, trans. R. Martin, D. Niall and S. Brown, Manchester: Manchester University Press, 1988. (Adapts the astrological tag 'the stars incline but do not necessitate' in an account of how free will is compatible with the fact that there is always a reason why we act as we do.)

* —— (1704–5) *New Essays on Human Understanding*, trans. P. Remnant and J. Bennett, Cambridge: Cambridge University Press, 1981. (Adapts the astrological tag 'the stars incline but do not necessitate' in an account of how free will is compatible with the fact that there is always a reason why we act as we do; see Book II, Chapter 21.)

* Locke, J. (1690) *An Essay Concerning Human Understanding*, Oxford: Clarendon Press, 1975. (Brief statement of compatibilist position.)

Long, A.A. and Sedley, D.N. (1987), *The Hellenistic Philosophers*, Cambridge: Cambridge University Press, 2 volumes. (The contributions of the incompatibilist Epicureans and Academics and of the – perhaps – compatibilist Stoics are documented in sections 20, 38, 55, 62 and 70.)

Lucretius (*c.*90–*c.*50 BC) *On the nature of things*, trans. W.H.D. Rouse, revised M.F. Smith, Cambridge, MA: the Loeb Classical Library, 1975 with Latin text. (II 216–93 is a classic Epicurean incompatibilist argument for physical indeterminism as a necessary condition of free will, and contains the earliest occurrence of the expression 'free will'.)

Mele, A. (1995) *Autonomous Agents*, New York: Oxford University Press. (Subtle defence of a form of libertarianism.)

Nietzsche, F.W. (1886) *Beyond Good and Evil*, trans. W. Kaufman, New York: Random House, 1966. (Disbeliever in free will who recommends 'love of fate'.)

O'Connor, T. (1995) *Agents, Causes and Events*, New York: Oxford University Press. (Useful collection of essays on the prospects for indeterministic accounts of free will.)

* Sartre, J.-P. (1948) *Existentialism and Humanism*, London: Methuen. ('Existentialist' defence of human beings' radical and self-instituted freedom of choice.)

* Spinoza, B. de. (1677) *Ethics*, in *The Collected Works of Spinoza*, trans. E. Curley, Princeton, NJ: Princeton University Press, 1985. (Determinist who argues that to be free is to be conscious of the necessities that compel one.)

Strawson, G. (1986) *Freedom and Belief*, Oxford: Clarendon Press. (Puts the case for disbelief in free will and discusses the 'cognitive phenomenology' of belief in free will.)

* Strawson, P.F. (1962) 'Freedom and Resentment', in *Freedom and Resentment*, London: Methuen, 1974. (Develops the view mentioned in §4 of this entry, suggesting that the traditional debate about free

will may be rendered unnecessary by proper attention to facts about human psychology.)

Van Inwagen, P. (1983) *An Essay on Free Will*, Oxford: Clarendon Press. (Contains an exhaustive statement of the objection to compatibilism.)

Wolf, S. (1990) *Freedom Within Reason*, New York: Oxford University Press. (Develops the view that the freedom necessary for responsibility involves the ability to act in accordance with one's values and to form or revise one's values in accordance with what 'right reason' recommends.)

GALEN STRAWSON

FREEDOM AND LIBERTY

There are at least two basic ideas in the conceptual complex we call 'freedom'; namely, rightful self-government (autonomy), and the overall ability to do, choose or achieve things, which can be called 'optionality' and defined as the possession of open options. To be autonomous is to be free in the sense of 'self-governing' and 'independent', in a manner analogous to that in which sovereign nation states are free. Optionality is when a person has an open option in respect to some possible action, x, when nothing in the objective circumstances prevents them from doing x should they choose to do so, and nothing requires them to do x should they choose not to. One has freedom of action when one can do what one wills, but in order to have the full benefit of optionality, it must be supplemented by freedom of choice (free will), which consists in being able to will what one wants to will, free of internal psychological impediments. Autonomy and optionality can vary independently of one another. A great deal of one can coexist with very little of the other.

Perhaps the most controversial philosophical question about the analysis of freedom concerns its relation to wants or desires. Some philosophers maintain that only the actual wants that a person has at a given time are relevant to their freedom, and that a person is free to the extent that they can do what they want, even if they can do very little else. Other philosophers, urging that the function of freedom is to provide 'breathing space', insist that freedom is a function of a person's ability to satisfy possible (hypothetical) as well as actual wants. A third group consists of those who hold a 'value-oriented' theory according to which freedom is not merely the power of doing what one wants or may come to want, rather it is the capacity of doing something 'worth doing or enjoying', something that is important or significant to the person said to be free, or to others.

1   Freedom and liberty

These two terms are often used interchangeably, but on those occasions when they are not taken to be synonyms, the basis of the distinction between the two is usually clear. 'Freedom', when applied to persons and their actions, refers to the *ability* of a person in a given set of circumstances to act in some particular way. 'Liberty' refers to authoritative *permission* to act in some particular way. The contrast is a basis for the grammatical distinction between 'can' and 'may', between the *de facto* and the *de jure* perspectives, or between (overall) ability and permission.

The concept of a liberty is an important part of juridical systems. A set of governing rules can impose *duties* on those who are subject to their authority. But when the rules remain silent about a given type of activity, x, then they are said to leave the subjects *at liberty* to x or not to x, or however they see fit. To be at liberty to x is simply to have no duty not to x (see RIGHTS §2).

So conceived, freedom and liberty can vary independently. For example, when a statute is only sporadically enforced, if at all, it may leave a person's *de facto* ability to do what it prohibits virtually unimpaired. Thus a cohabiting unmarried couple in Arizona is perfectly capable of doing what the law prohibits only because the law in question is hardly ever enforced. Cohabiting couples have almost perfect *de facto* freedom to cohabit because police indifference makes the risk of detection and conviction minimal. Not only are we sometimes free (to some degree or other) to do what we are not at liberty to do; conversely, we may be at liberty to do what we are not free to do, as when circumstances other than enforced rules prevent us from doing what we are legally permitted to do.

2   Freedom as autonomy

Judgments of freedom are made not only about individual persons but also about their political communities. Many nation states at some point in their histories have had occasion to declare their independence or, what amounts to the same thing, their sovereignty or status as free states. At the same time, other countries may have lost their freedom (independence) and become mere colonies of stronger nation states. When a political state becomes unfree in this way, each citizen can think of themselves as also deprived of the same kind of freedom, or something analogous to it, for few of them remain entirely self-governed when their own country is governed from afar by masters who simply impose their directives by force. 'None of us are truly free so long as our nation is not', a local patriot might say, even while conceding that the colonial power that governs them has treated them decently, allowing them many freedoms. The question of who rightly governs them, as Sir Isaiah Berlin puts it, is logically distinct from the question of how their governors – foreign or domestic, legitimate or not – protect their liberties (Berlin 1958). The first question concerns autonomy; the second concerns optionality.

Autonomy and optionality also can vary independently. National autonomy can produce its own tyranny, as when a newly independent nation, free of its colonial repressors, refuses to govern democratically and recognizes no civil rights in its subjects. In such a case the native populace may feel as badly mistreated, if not worse, by their own government as before by the colonizers.

Autonomy or self-government can consist of sharing with one's fellow citizens political independence, or can consist of self-direction by that element of the self authorized by nature to rule (often identified with reason). To be self-governed requires that we not be governed by illegitimate outsiders and equally not by alien forces from within.

Note the close analogy to slavery. One slave owner, *A*, is very severe with his only slave, *S1*, permitting him only minimal free movement, no choice in deciding what his off-duty conduct shall be, or what he shall read, how he dresses and so on. Another slave-owner, *B*, is very easy-going. He treats his only slave, *S2*, as if he were a valued friend, and allows him to do anything short of harming others or leaving the plantation. It is clearly understood that *S2* may do all these things only because *B* permits him to, not as a matter of right. The only rights in this situation are *B*'s property rights. The rules of property ownership permit *B* to be as tough with *S2* as he wishes, but he prefers to be kind. So there is in *S2*'s situation a predominance of heteronomy (government by others) conjoined with high optionality (*de facto* freedom). It seems clear then that one can have little or no autonomy, and yet live a contented life with a high standard of living, something resembling friendship and respect, and most important – options left open for one's own choice to exercise, though not as a matter of right.

Suppose that in respect to a certain choice there are two possibilities left open for *S2*. His master can restore his autonomy and turn him loose into an unfriendly world where other human beings, even

though they lack authority over him, treat him badly, effectively closing many key options that would have been left open for him by his earlier beneficent master. Should he accept this offer at the expense of much *de facto* freedom? If the question is a difficult one, it shows that it is not clear to which of the two contending values, independence or optionality, he attaches the greater importance (see AUTONOMY, ETHICAL).

3 Negative and positive freedom

Philosophical advocates of 'positive freedom' are often reacting to a tradition among English empiricists that extends from HOBBES to J.S. MILL and RUSSELL. Hobbes intended his definition to apply to the most essential of the common elements in free action and free movement generally. He defined 'free' as the absence of external impediments, to apply equally well, for example, to free-flowing (undammed) streams of water as to the purposeful conduct of human beings. Subsequent empiricists, including LOCKE (§10) and HUME (§3), also held that all freedom is essentially something negative; namely, the absence of restraint or impediment to our actions.

The family of theories to which Berlin attached the label 'positive liberty' are those that identify freedom (or liberty) with personal autonomy or self-government. One version of that theory emphasizes the internal forum that is the agent's self and the legitimate claim of the rational self to rule over the self's lesser elements. The second of the autonomy theories is less individualistic and more political. It holds that no individual can live their life autonomously except as a member of a free political community, a state that is not only independent of other states, but one that is itself organized democratically so that all citizens can share in its governance, and in that sense, at least, be self-governing.

The nineteenth-century idealist philosopher T.H. GREEN (§3) summed up these requirements in his definition of 'freedom' as a 'positive power or capacity of doing or enjoying something worth doing or enjoying, and that too, something that we do or enjoy in common with others' (1888: 371). Green's definition also expresses a second conception of positive freedom as more than the mere absence of impediment to our desires, even more than the absence of impediment to our 'worthy' desires. In addition to the absence of constraint, genuine freedom must provide full opportunity beyond the mere non-interference of the police and other people. If a person desires above all things to own and enjoy a Mercedes, and there are no external impediments, legal or nonlegal, in the community to such ownership, then both the legal code and the neighbours leave them free to do as they desire. But if that person has no money, then that negative freedom is effectively useless. To have true freedom, say supporters of positive freedom, one must have what is required for the satisfaction of worthwhile wants, and that will usually include at least minimal wealth, physical health, talent and knowledge, including the sorts of knowledge normally imparted by formal education. The more we are able to do the things worth doing, they insist, the freer we are.

The positive freedom theorists may go on to charge that the negative theorist cannot explain why the laudatory title of freedom should ever characterize the person who is paralyzed, insane, infantile, impoverished and ignorant, as generally free. It must be ironic, they claim, to say that such an unfortunate person is well off in the manner implied by the term 'free'. Negative freedom theorists argue that to be free does not mean to be well off; one may be free but discontented, unhappy, ignorant, hungry or in pain. An individual may have freedom but find that in their circumstances it is not worth much. What this shows is that freedom is the kind of good whose worth fluctuates, or in the words of John RAWLS (§§1–2): 'the worth of liberty is not the same for everyone' (1971: 204).

The pauper is *unable* to buy the Mercedes, but according to the negative freedom advocate, this is not through being *unfree* to buy one. Most writers within the negative freedom tradition deny that all inabilities are also 'unfreedoms'. The inabilities that constitute unfreedoms, they insist, are those that can be traced directly or indirectly to the deliberate actions or policies of other human beings, in particular legislators and police offers, who can intervene directly and forcefully in other persons' lives. Sometimes the relevant explanation of some other person's incapacity (for example, to earn a decent living) can be linked indirectly to various social influences. The impoverished person might be so because of a lack of technical skill, and that lack, in turn, could be a product of a poor education traceable, however obscurely, to the inequities of a national system of racial segregation, which in turn was supported as deliberate policy by an apartheid government. In that case we could say not only that they are unable to do x, but also that they are unfree, given the circumstances, to do so.

The gap between the positive and negative theorists can be further decreased by a theory which has a wider conception of 'restraint' and 'impediment.' Such a theory would have a place both for negative constraints like lack of money, and internal constraints like intense headaches. Such a theory could

support negative freedom (that all freedom consists of the absence of impediments, whether positive, negative, internal or external), yet also encompass the important point made by positive freedom (that there is a lot more to freedom than simple non-interference from police officers and other persons, important as that is).

A large number of philosophers now reject the view that there are two irreducibly distinct concepts of freedom, one positive and the other negative (MacCallum 1967; Feinberg 1973; Rawls 1971). These 'single concept' theorists do not contend that one of the pair of allegedly distinct concepts is 'the only, the "truest", or the "most worthwhile"' (MacCallum 1967: 312), but rather that it is a mistake to make the distinction between positive and negative concepts in the first place. According to MacCallum, there is only one concept of liberty and that is best understood as 'always one and the same triadic relation' between a person (subject or agent), an intended action (actual or possible) and what MacCallum calls a 'preventing condition' (barriers, compulsions and constraints) (1967: 312, 314). Freedom, in his view, is always *of* someone, *from* something, *to* do, have or be something. Disputes about the nature of freedom like that which divided adherents of positive freedom from adherents of negative freedom are, according to MacCallum, really disagreements over the proper range of one or more of the three variables in a single analytic model: what the term 'person' is to stand for, what is to count as an obstacle, or impediment, or forceful interference, and what is to count as a wanted or intended action.

4 Freedom as optionality

Among the controversies that still divide writers about freedom is the question of whether freedom (in the sense of optionality alone) should be conceived of as simply the absence of present frustration or whether it is best understood as the absence of wider opportunities to do more than one wants to do now. We can call the former concept the 'actual-want satisfaction' theory and the latter the 'hypothetical-want' or 'dispositional' theory. The former allows a person to be called free to the extent that they can satisfy their present wants, without hindrance or frustration. The dispositional concept, however, will not consider them free unless they can also do things that they do not want to do at that present moment, but could, for all they now know, come to want to do at some future time. Why, one might ask, would added dispositional freedom be of value to the person whose actual wants are always permitted their satisfaction? Why should a person miss merely hypothetical want-satisfaction when they can do everything they want without frustration? The usual answer to this question points out that the love of freedom can be a love of breathing space, or room to manoeuvre, of frequent opportunities to change one's mind. The hypothetical account of optionality, therefore, can also be called the 'breathing space' theory.

The most influential spokesmen for the 'actual-wants' concept were the ancient Stoics (see STOICISM §17). According to Stoic teaching, there are two ways a person can increase the degree of their want-satisfaction. One is to leave their wants as they are and work for the means to satisfy them. The second is to avoid trying to change the world – that is the path to misery – but instead to develop the techniques for changing desires so that they always accord with what happens. The Stoic does not need any breathing space. Whatever happens will please them because their only desire is that God's will be done, and since Zeus is believed to be omnipotent, that desire cannot be frustrated.

Consider Dorothy Doe, who can choose among 1,000 things at time t, but is prevented from choosing, or actually doing, the one thing she wants most to do. Richard Roe, on the other hand, can only do one thing at time t, but it happens to be the one thing he wants most to do. Richard Roe, one should say, is not simply 'comparatively' or 'largely' unfree; rather, he is totally unfree, for to say that he can do only one thing is to say that he is forced or made to do that thing. And it is beyond controversy that one cannot be both free and compelled to do the same thing. It may be the case, however, that Richard Roe will be entirely content with the arrangement, and actually welcome the compulsion, which if so, shows again that one can sometimes find more contentment in being unfree than in being free. This at least is the message derived from the example by the hypothetical-wants theorist. The actual-wants theorist will deny that Roe is truly unfree; after all, Roe *can* do what he most wants to do.

Dorothy Doe, on the other hand, may have just lost her last chance to pursue a career as a medical researcher, or her last chance to marry the man she loves, or to find a cure for her child's disease. But she does 'enjoy' thousands more options than Richard Roe. She might seem to be freer in respect (say) to prospective marriage partners (one hundred philosophers are eager to marry her tomorrow, but she loathes them all). But her greater freedom is of no significant use. She will be unhappier but more free than Roe. This example may please the breathing space theorist more than the actual-wants theorist, but it may give still more support to the value-oriented philosopher of freedom considered next.

Is Dorothy Doe really more free simply by having more open options? Does not the superior desirability, in her judgment, of some of the options count as well as the sheer number of them? The proponent of the hypothetical-wants theory of freedom often baulks at permitting desirability into our determinations, partly because of the danger that philosophers will reduce the issue to a purely normative question to be settled by considering which definition of the word 'free' links its meaning to something that is worthy of the value we associate with the word.

The problem of counting options remains a difficulty for all the above theories. Berlin had earlier written that 'the method for counting [possibilities] can never be more than impressionistic. Possibilities of action are not discrete entities like apples, which can be exhaustively enumerated' (1958: 130, footnote 1) But individuating possible actions is not the only problem for the philosopher who would apply quantitative measures to freedom's many dimensions, including comprehensiveness, fecundity, and diversity. And one does not exhaust the relevant possibilities by dividing all action into 'possible' and 'impossible.' There are also the component categories – difficult and easy, possible at great cost and possible at small cost, statistically probable and statistically improbable, multiple choices and either/or choices.

It is hard enough to deal with these problems of measurement, but they are almost equally difficult to evade, especially if we continue to speak of one individual or one society having more freedom than another. Moreover, if a philosopher maintains that both the number and the significance, importance or value of open options determines how free one is (and probably most philosophers take such a combination view), then the difficulties begin all over again when they leave off option-counting and begins option-evaluating.

See also: COERCION; FREE WILL; FREEDOM OF SPEECH; LAW, LIMITS OF; LIBERALISM

References and further reading

Arneson, R.J. (1985) 'Freedom and Desire', *Canadian Journal of Philosophy* 15 (3): 425–48. (Considers the question whether amounts of freedom can be measured, and if so, what role the free person's desires play in the process.)

Benn, S.I. and Weinstein, W.L. (1971) 'Being Free to Act and Being a Free Man', *Mind* 80 (3): 194–211. (Argues that the concept of freedom presupposes a concept of autonomy; that is, the concept of the free person as chooser.)

* Berlin, I. (1958) 'Two Concepts of Liberty', in *Four*

Essays on Liberty, Oxford: Oxford University Press, 1969; repr. in D. Miller (ed.) *Liberty* Oxford: Oxford University Press, 1991. (Classic source of the distinction between positive and negative liberty.)

Dworkin, G. (1982) 'Is More Choice Better than Less?', in P.A. French, T.E. Uehling, Jr, and H.K. Wettstein (eds) *Midwest Studies in Philosophy, VII*, Minneapolis, MN: Minnesota University Press, 47–61. (Considers the question of whether more choices are always preferable to fewer for a rational individual, concluding that more is not always better.)

* Feinberg, J. (1973) *Social Philosophy*, Englewood Cliffs, NJ: Prentice Hall. (This introduction to social and philosophy concentrates on the concept and limits of freedom, the distinction between legal and moral rights, and the concept of social justice.)

—— (1980) 'The Interest in Liberty on the Scales', and 'The Idea of a Free Man', in *Rights, Justice, and the Bounds of Liberty*, Princeton, NJ: Princeton University Press. (The former deals with the problem of weighing the interest in liberty against other interests in the effort to minimalize social harms; the latter probes for conceptual linkages between the idea of a free person and of a free society by considering how the word 'free' has come to apply to both.)

Gray, J.N. (1980) 'On Negative and Positive Liberty', *Political Studies* 28 (4): 507–26. (Important critique of the theory of Isaiah Berlin.)

* Green, T.H. (1888) 'Liberal Legislation and Freedom of Contract', in *Works of Thomas Hill Green*, vol. 3, ed. R.L. Nettleship, London: Longmans Green; abridged by D. Miller (ed.) *Liberty*, Oxford: Oxford University Press, 1991. (The author defines freedom as 'a positive power or capacity of doing or enjoying something worth doing or enjoying, and that too, something that we do or enjoy in common with others'.)

* MacCallum, G.C. (1967) 'Negative and Positive Freedom', *Philosophical Review* 76 (3): 312–34; repr. in D. Miller (ed.) *Liberty*, Oxford: Oxford University Press, 1991. (Argues that there is only one concept of liberty; namely, that expressed in the schema *x* (the actor) is free from *y* (constraining condition) to do or become *z*.)

Miller, D. (ed.) (1991) *Liberty*, Oxford: Oxford University Press. (The most useful bibliography of philosophical analyses of freedom. Contains, among other things, influential articles by T.H. Green, Isaiah Berlin, Gerald C. MacCallum and G.A. Cohen.)

Pelczynski, Z.A. and Gray, J.N. (eds) (1984) *Conceptions of Liberty in Political Philosophy*, London: Athlone Press. (Contemporary authors discuss the differing conceptions of freedom that appear throughout the history of philosophy, from the ancient Greeks to John Rawls. A major theme is the comparison of the various views with Berlin's distinction between positive and negative freedom.)

* Rawls, J. (1971) *A Theory of Justice*, Cambridge, MA: Harvard University Press, 201–10. (Claims that the usual debates about liberty are not properly conceived of as disputes about the proper definition of 'liberty'. Instead, the concern is with the relative values of several distinct liberties, which can conflict.)

Swanton, C. (1992) *Freedom: A Coherence Theory*, Cambridge: Hackett Publishing Company. (Argues that a properly conceived coherence model can provide a theory of freedom that reconciles a wide variety of views on freedom while retaining the strengths of each.)

JOEL FEINBERG

FREEDOM, DIVINE

In the theistic tradition, many thinkers have held that God is infinitely powerful, all-knowing, perfectly good and perfectly free. But since a perfectly good being would invariably follow the best course of action, what can be meant when it is said that God acts freely? Two different views of divine freedom have emerged. According to the first view, God acts freely provided nothing outside him determines him to act. So when we consider God's action of creating a world, it is clear that on the first view he acts freely since there is nothing outside him to determine him to do as he does. The difficulty with this view is that it neglects the possibility that God's own nature might require him to create one particular world rather than another or none at all. According to the second view, God is free in an action provided it was within his power not to perform that action. Unlike the first view, on this view God acts freely only if nothing beyond God's control necessitates his performing that action. The problem for this view is that since it is impossible for God, being perfectly good, not to choose to follow the best course of action, it is difficult to see how God could be free in such an action.

1 Two views of God's freedom
2 The first view and its chief difficulty
3 The second view and its chief difficulty
4 Possible solutions to the difficulties

1 Two views of God's freedom

In traditional theism, God is understood to be an omnipotent, omniscient, perfectly good creator of all things other than himself. But what of divine freedom? Is the God of traditional theism also free with respect to creating things other than himself? If God were not free not to create what he does create then it seems we could make no sense of thanking him or praising him for creating what he did. He would not merit our gratitude and praise for the simple reason that he would create of necessity and not freely. So in addition to his other attributes, traditional theism has insisted on ascribing freedom to God (see GOD, CONCEPTS OF §6).

How are we to understand divine freedom? Two different views have emerged. According to the first view, God is free in creating a world or in acting within the world he has created provided nothing outside him determines him to create the world he creates or determines him to act in a particular way in the world he has created. According to the second view, God is free in creating or acting within his creation provided it was in his power not to create what he did or not to act within his creation as he did.

How are these two views of divine freedom connected? If it was in God's power not to create the world he did create, then there was nothing outside God that absolutely determined him to create the world he did create. So God's having the power not to create what he did create implies the absence of something outside him that absolutely determined him to create what he did. But the reverse is not true. The absence of something outside a being that determines that being to act in a certain way does not imply that the being has the power not to act in that way. For something within that being may absolutely determine it to act in a certain way. And if something within a being necessitates that it act in a certain way, then, unless the presence or absence of that necessitating factor is within the being's control, that being lacks the power not to act in that way.

2 The first view and its chief difficulty

The first of these two views has the advantage of establishing beyond question that God possesses freedom from external forces with respect to his selection of a world to create. For given that he is omnipotent and the creator of all things other than himself, it is evident that nothing outside him determines him to create whatever he does create. And given that whatever he creates is within his control, it would seem that he is completely at liberty to act as he sees fit within the world he has created. So

the fact that nothing outside God determines him to create or act as he does clearly shows that God is an autonomous agent; he is self-determining in the sense that his actions are the result of decisions determined only by his own nature. But is this sufficient to establish that God is genuinely free? We believe that a human being need not be free in performing a certain action even when it is clear that they were not determined to perform that action by external forces. Perhaps the person was in the grip of some internal passion or irresistible impulse that necessitated the performance of that action, overcoming their judgment that the action is wrong or unwise. With respect to human beings, the defender of the first view of divine freedom can agree that the mere absence of determining external agents or forces is not sufficient for an individual's action to be free. But in the case of God, as opposed to humans, the defender can argue that it is sufficient. For in God there is no possibility of his passions overcoming the judgment of reason. As Leibniz remarks:

> The Stoics said that only the wise man is free; and one's mind is indeed not free when it is possessed by a great passion, for then one cannot will as one should, i.e. with proper deliberation. It is in that way that God alone is perfectly free, and the created minds are free only in proportion as they are above passion.
>
> (1704: 175)

The chief objection to this view of divine freedom is that it does not sufficiently recognize the importance of agents having control over their free acts. An action that an agent performs freely is an action the agent was free to perform and free not to perform; it was up to the agent whether to perform or not perform that act. If some external force or internal passion was beyond the control of the agent, and the agent's action was inevitable given that external force or internal passion, then the agent did not act freely in performing that action. Since God is a purely rational being and not subject to uncontrollable passions, which sometimes compel human agents to act, it is tempting to conclude that God enjoys perfect freedom of action. But this will be so only if there are no other features in God that both necessitate his actions and are not within his control. Because human beings are generally thought to have the power to act against the counsel of reason, we regard their acts due to reason – as opposed to their acts due to irresistible impulses – as acts they perform freely. For we believe they were free to reject the counsel of reason and act otherwise. But what if God cannot reject the counsel of his reason as to what action to perform? A human being who is morally good and rational may yet have the power to refrain from acting as his goodness and reason direct. But can this be true of God? And if it cannot be, how can we then say that God acts freely? Thus, it has seemed to many philosophers and theologians that the first view of divine freedom fails to capture an essential element in the idea of freedom, whether human or divine.

3 The second view and its chief difficulty

The second view of divine freedom embraces the idea that agents, whether divine or human, act freely only if they have the power to refrain from so acting. Although the idea of 'power to refrain from so acting' is not particularly clear, the proponents of the second view are united in rejecting any conditional account such as 'power to refrain from so acting if the agent wills to refrain', for such an account does not require that it was in the agent's power to will to refrain. So, according to the second view, God was free in creating the world he did create only if it was unconditionally in his power either to create some other world instead or to refrain from creating any world at all.

The chief difficulty facing this second view of divine freedom arises when we consider some of God's other attributes and ask whether they leave God with any significant degree of freedom. It has already been noted that the theistic God is a being of infinite power and perfect goodness. These perfections are generally regarded as *essential* to God. They constitute part of his very nature. That being so, we can ask whether God is ever free to do an evil (morally wrong) act. The answer seems to be no. Of course, being perfectly good, omnipotent and omniscient, God will never in fact do an evil act. No being who knowingly and willingly performs an evil act is perfectly good. Since being free to do an evil act is consistent with never in fact doing an evil act, it may seem that God could be free to perform such an act. But if God is free to perform an evil act, then he has it in his power to perform that act. And if God has it in his power to perform an evil act, then he has it in his power to deprive himself of one of his essential attributes (perfect goodness), to change his nature. But no being has the power to deprive itself of one of its essential attributes. Therefore, it would seem that God does not have it in his power to perform an evil act (see GOODNESS, PERFECT §2).

The fact that God cannot do evil does not severely limit God's freedom so long as there remains a sufficient range of actions that are open to God. For example, it has long been held that God's action in creating the world was a free action, that God was free to create a world and free not to create a world. Moreover, it has been held that among worlds God

can create, God is free to select the one he will create. Of course, since he cannot do what is evil he cannot create a bad world. But presumably there are many good worlds from which he is free to select the one he wishes to create. Even here, however, there are serious problems in reconciling God's freedom with his omnipotence, omniscience and perfect goodness.

Suppose among creatable worlds there is one that is better than all others. Is God free to create some world other than this best world? If God creates some world that is less than the best world he can create, it would seem to be possible for there to be a being better than God. For it is the nature of perfect goodness to create the best it can. Therefore, since God is perfectly good, a being whose goodness is unsurpassable, it follows that if there is a unique best world among worlds he can create, it is impossible for him to create a world inferior to it. For then he would not be a being whose goodness is unsurpassable (see Quinn 1982).

What if there is no best world among creatable worlds? This could be true in two ways. First, it might be that for any creatable world there is a better world God could create. Second, it might be that there is no unique best world. Perhaps instead there are many equally best worlds among the worlds God can create. Let us consider these two cases in turn.

On the assumption that for any world God might create there is a better world he could create instead, it is clear that it is impossible for God to do the best that he can. Whatever he does, he could have done better. This being so, it seems only reasonable that God's perfect goodness would be fully satisfied should he create a very good world. Presumably there are a large number of such worlds from which he can choose one to create. So long as he creates one of these worlds it seems he will have satisfied the demands of his perfect nature. For the idea that he should create the best world he can is an idea that logically cannot be realized. Hence, on the assumption that there is no best world among the worlds God can create, it would seem that God's perfect goodness is fully compatible with his freely creating any one of a number of good worlds that lie in his power to create. To complain that God cannot then be perfect because he could have created a better world is to raise a complaint that no creative action God took would have enabled him to avoid. Thus it appears that if for any creatable world there is a better creatable world, God would be free to select among an infinite number of good worlds to create. (Thomas Aquinas, for example, thought that no matter what world God created he could have created a better world in the sense of a world with a greater amount of good in it.) But the difficulty with this position is that it conflicts with the principle that if a being creates a world when there is a better world that it could have created, then it is possible that there be a being better than it. For it would be possible that there be a being whose degree of goodness is such that it would choose to create a better world. So if for every creatable world there is a better creatable world, it is not clear that the traditional theistic God could be perfectly good and be the creator of a world (see Rowe 1993).

Let us now consider the second way in which it could be true that no creatable world is better than all others. Suppose that among the worlds God can create there are a number of worlds that are equally best. It is plausible to think that if a perfectly good being creates a world, he cannot create a world that is inferior to some other that he can create, at least provided that there is a world than which none is better. Therefore, if there are a number of equally best worlds among the worlds he can create, then if he creates at all he must create one of those worlds. But unlike the case when there is exactly one best world among the worlds he can create, here some degree of divine freedom can exist in harmony with God's perfect goodness. For God would seem to be free to create any one of the equally best worlds. In any case, God's absolute perfection imposes no requirement on his creation from among those equally best worlds.

Is God free not to create a world at all? Here we may limit our inquiry to the possibility that there is exactly one best world among the worlds creatable by an omnipotent being. As we have seen, in this case there is some reason to think that God is not free to select any other world to create. Our present question is whether in this situation God is free not to create at all.

What world would be actual if God exists but does not create at all? Apart from God and whatever necessarily existing entities there are, in a world God inhabits but does not create, no other being would exist. To answer our question of whether God is free not to create a world at all, we must compare the best world God can create with a world whose inhabitants are simply God and whatever necessarily existing entities there are. Assuming such a world would not be incommensurate with the best among worlds God can create, there is reason to think that God is not free with respect to whether he will not create at all. For either the world he inhabits but does not create is better than the best world he can create or it is not. If it is better, then he is not free to create a world, and thus necessarily refrains from creating. If it is worse, then he is not free not to create a world, and thus necessarily creates a world. For it is plausible to hold that if a being can but does not create a world that is better than the one it merely inhabits, then it is

possible that there be a being better than it. Would the world he inhabits but does not create be just as good as the best world among those an omnipotent being can create? If so, then, as in the case where there are a number of equally best worlds omnipotence can create, we again have room for some degree of divine freedom. But in this situation, God's freedom would be restricted to creating the best world or not creating at all.

4 Possible solutions to the difficulties

The difficulty with the first view of divine freedom is that it fails to satisfy our basic conviction that a free action requires the freedom to have done otherwise. Once we see that God's nature would necessitate his action of creating the best of all creatable worlds, the failure to satisfy this basic conviction becomes apparent. The proponent of the first view may try to solve this difficulty by arguing that the intention behind emphasizing the freedom to have done otherwise is not to exclude all necessitating factors, only those for which the agent bears no responsibility. If by freely engaging in strenuous moral effort Mahatma Gandhi developed his moral nature to such a degree that in certain situations he was not capable of acting unkindly towards others, we would still view his acts of kindness as free in a derivative sense since the virtuous nature now necessitating his acts of kindness was itself brought about, at least in part, by his own free moral striving. The difficulty with this suggestion, however, is that God's properties of omnipotence, perfect goodness, and omniscience are not properties he acquired by any kind of striving. In fact, he did not acquire them at all, but had them from all eternity. Thus it seems that although we may describe God as perfectly free in the sense that his actions are never determined by agents or factors outside him, this perfect freedom does not by itself ensure that his actions are free in the sense required if he is to be thanked and praised for performing those actions.

The chief difficulty confronting the second view of God's freedom is that his attributes of omnipotence, omniscience and perfect goodness appear to impose significant restrictions on his freedom in creating a world and in acting within the world he creates. As we saw, it seems that it is not in God's power to do evil or to create less than the best that he can create. Proponents of the second view have tried to solve this problem by distinguishing the necessity imposed on his actions by God's absolute perfections from the sort of necessity that deprives an agent of the power to act otherwise. While admitting that the inflamed passions may causally necessitate an agent's action, thus depriving the agent of the power to do otherwise, some proponents of the second view hold that rational motives are not causes at all. In their view, rational motives do not deprive the agent of the power to act against their counsel. On the other hand, God's essential attributes of omnipotence and perfect goodness make it truly impossible that God should fail to follow what he sees to be the best course of action. How, then, can God be free in carrying out what he sees to be the best course of action? How can the fact that he cannot do other than choose the best not be seen as a limit on his freedom? The answer traditionally given is that power extends only to what is logically possible. A being who is essentially omnipotent and perfectly good cannot possibly fail to choose the best course of action. But this implies no lack of power, for power is lacking only when an agent cannot do what is possible to be done. Thus Samuel CLARKE (§1) concludes his discussion of divine freedom by remarking:

> It is no diminution of power not to be able to do things which are no object of power. And it is in like manner no diminution either of power or liberty to have such a perfect and unalterable rectitude of will as never possibly to choose to do anything inconsistent with that rectitude.
>
> ([1706] 1738: 122)

The solution proposed by Clarke and others is promising. That it is not within God's power to weaken himself does not mean that his power is less than infinite. For it is logically impossible that an essentially omnipotent being should weaken itself. Hence, since power extends only to what is possible, the fact that it is not within God's power to weaken himself does not imply any diminution of power. And perhaps the same can be said for it not being within God's power to refrain from following what he sees as the best course of action. This too may not imply any diminution of power. But for God to act freely in following the best course of action it must be within his power not so to act. The fact that it is not within his power not so to act may not imply any diminution of power, but it remains unclear why it does not imply a diminution of freedom.

See also: CREATION AND CONSERVATION, RELIGIOUS DOCTRINE OF; FREE WILL; LEIBNIZ, G.W. §§3, 7; OMNIPOTENCE §5; SIMPLICITY, DIVINE §2

References and further reading

Adams, R.M. (1972) 'Must God Create the Best?', *Philosophical Review* 81 (3): 317–32. (An important discussion of God's obligations with respect to what he creates.)

* Clarke, S. (1706; 9th edn 1738) *A Discourse Concerning the Being and Attributes of God, the Obligations of Natural Religion, and the Truth and Certainty of the Christian Revelation*, British Philosophers and Theologians of the 17th and 18th Centuries, New York: Garland, 1978. (Contains Clarke's account of how God's inability to do less than the best is no diminution of his perfect power or his perfect freedom; the Garland reprint is of the ninth (1738) edition.)

Garcia, L.L. (1992) 'Divine Freedom and Creation', *Philosophical Quarterly* 42 (167): 191–213. (Defends a Thomistic view of God's perfect freedom with respect to creation against some recent challenges to it.)

Kretzmann, N. (1990) 'A General Problem of Creation', in S. MacDonald (ed.) *Being and Goodness*, Ithaca, NY, and London: Cornell University Press. (Discusses Aquinas' theory of God's freedom with respect to creating a world or not creating at all.)

—— (1990) 'A Particular Problem of Creation', in S. MacDonald (ed.) *Being and Goodness*, Ithaca, NY and London: Cornell University Press. (Discusses Aquinas' theory of God's freedom in selecting among worlds the one he will create.)

* Leibniz, G.W. (1704) *New Essays on Human Understanding*, trans. and ed. P. Remnant and J. Bennett, Cambridge: Cambridge University Press, 1982. (Contains Leibniz's discussion of Locke's account of free will.)

—— (1710) *Theodicy*, trans. E.M. Huggard, ed. A. Farrer, La Salle, IL: Open Court, 1985. (Contains Leibniz's extended treatment of divine freedom and the problem of evil.)

Morris, T.V. (1993) 'Perfection and Creation', in E. Stump (ed.) *Reasoned Faith*, Ithaca, NY, and London: Cornell University Press. (Argues that if it is impossible for God to do the best he can, his perfection is not impaired by his creating a world when he could have created a better world.)

Morriston, W. (1985) 'Is God Significantly Free?', *Faith and Philosophy* 2 (3): 257–64. (Argues that God lacks the freedom to refrain from doing what is morally obligatory.)

* Quinn, P. (1982) 'God, Moral Perfection, and Possible Worlds', in F. Sontag and M. Darrol Bryant (eds) *God: The Contemporary Discussion*, New York: The Rose of Sharon Press. (Somewhat technical discussion of the principles governing God's freedom in relation to creation.)

* Rowe, W.L. (1993) 'The Problem of Divine Perfection and Freedom', in E. Stump (ed.) *Reasoned Faith*, Ithaca, NY, and London: Cornell University Press.

(Argues that God is not free to create a given world if there is a better world he can create.)

WILLIAM L. ROWE

FREEDOM OF SPEECH

Freedom of speech is one of the most widely accepted principles of modern political and social life. The three arguments most commonly offered in its defence are that it is essential for the pursuit of truth, that it is a fundamental constituent of democracy, and that it is a liberty crucial to human dignity and wellbeing. Its advocates also plead the dangers of allowing govern-ments to control what may be said or heard. Yet there is also general agreement that speech should be subject to some limits. Most contemporary controversies about free speech concern those limits; some focus upon what should count as 'speech', others upon the harms that speech may cause.

1 **Definitions**
2 **Justifications**
3 **Limits**

1 Definitions

In discussions of free speech, 'speech' is typically given a meaning that is both more and less inclusive than in ordinary usage. It includes written as well as spoken words and it may include nonverbal forms of communication such as pictures, symbols and ges-tures. That is why the phrase 'freedom of expression' is sometimes preferred to 'freedom of speech'. On the other hand, certain forms of speech fall outside this privileged domain; despite involving speech, perjury and blackmail, for example, receive no privileged treatment.

The 'freedom' that is most commonly of concern is legal freedom – the absence of legal restraints upon speech. But other sorts of freedom may also be at issue, for example freedom from inhibiting social pressures or economic threats, such as loss of trade or employment. Questions of free speech can also arise in matters such as the editorial policy of an academic journal or the purchasing policy of a library. The reality of people's opportunities to air their views through the media is another important matter for free speech, particularly in contexts of economic inequality or government-controlled media and in relation to competitive speech such as political argument (see FREEDOM AND LIBERTY).

Freedom of speech is typically asserted as a 'right',

which therefore has a privileged moral and political status, and it has become a standard ingredient of constitutional bills of rights and declarations of human rights. The right to unfettered speech is most commonly claimed for those who wish to *speak*, but it may also be claimed for those who wish to *hear* and the right to *hear* what others wish to say may be no less important.

Analysts sometimes try to give content to freedom of speech as a right by dissecting the meanings of 'speech' and 'freedom', but philosophically it is impossible to divorce the proper content of the right from its justification. Only when we have considered why freedom of speech matters are we in a position to identify what sort of speech the right should encompass, what sort of freedom it should imply, and what sort of status that freedom should enjoy.

2 Justifications

The pursuit of truth. Freedom of speech has been commonly defended as an instrument of truth. That was the claim central to Milton's *Areopagitica* (1644) and to Mill's *On Liberty* (1859) – the two most celebrated defences of free speech in the English language (see MILL, J.S. §12). If there is to be progress in knowledge and understanding, people must be free to present, criticize and discuss ideas and information. Only in such a free and open exchange will the truth have maximum opportunity to emerge. Once the truth has emerged, we might suppose that free speech has done its job and can be safely abandoned. But the fallibility of our beliefs has always figured strongly in this defence: we may believe that the opinion we suppress is false, but history shows how often truth has been mistaken for error and error for truth. Moreover, as Mill argued, even if an opinion is true, we can be confident of its truth only so long as it can withstand challenge, and even a true belief is liable to become a 'dead dogma' rather than a genuine conviction if immured from challenge.

Powerful though this defence is, it encounters a number of objections. First, it makes free speech valuable only in so far as truth is valuable. In general, we are unlikely to deny that truth is better than error and knowledge better than ignorance, but on occasion truth and knowledge may conflict with other goods such as public security and peace of mind. Some doubt whether truth should always be the overriding value.

Second, the argument supposes that free speech will actually foster truth and understanding. Sceptics find such a claim unduly optimistic and doubt the ability of ordinary people to distinguish truth from error and irrational prejudice from sober reasoning. In assessing that objection, however, we must be alive to the alternatives. The relevant question is not whether truth will always emerge from the market-place of ideas but whether it will be better served by open and unfettered discussion than by government censorship.

Third, some forms of expression, such as some types of art, are not concerned with truth and cannot therefore be defended as its instruments. On the other hand, in those cases there are often other goods, such as creativity, which can take the place of truth in a similarly structured consequentialist defence of free expression.

Democracy. The fundamental idea of democracy is that of a people governing itself. This cannot be done if the members of a people are unable to present their views to one another. Democratic decision making requires discussion and debate as well as voting, and a significant limit upon its deliberative process will significantly limit its democratic character. Moreover, democracy implies that no one is authorized to limit a people's freedom of discussion, except perhaps the people itself. Democracy in ideal form also entails that each person who is subject to its decisions should be entitled to participate equally in its processes, and hence that each should enjoy equal rights of free expression (see DEMOCRACY).

Given the indirect character of modern democracy, freedom of speech is also important politically for ensuring that rulers are aware of the wishes and opinions of the ruled, for enabling the conduct of opposition and for preventing abuses of power. Indeed, as a check upon the abuse of power, the case for free speech extends beyond democratic forms of government.

Democracy is sometimes thought to afford an unsafe haven for free speech. Suppose a majority wishes to silence a minority; does democracy not then sanction the removal of that minority's freedom of speech? The answer depends in part on what sort of speech is at issue. Since democracy requires that all members of a demos should enjoy equal political rights, democracy itself cannot justify a majority's removing or reducing the democratic rights – includ-ing democratic rights of free expression – of some members of the demos. However, the speech that can be defended by appealing to democracy is limited to that which is essential to participation in a democratic process. That does not encompass every form of speech. For example, if we wish to defend the right of scientists to challenge the orthodoxies of their peers, the prerequisites of democratic participation do not provide the most convincing foundations for that right – although it is not possible to state in a simple a

priori fashion what sorts of speech will be relevant to a democratic process and what will not.

Individual liberty. Free speech is often valued as a constituent of individual liberty rather than only as an instrument of social purposes or as a specifically political institution. Sometimes what is emphasized is the moral standing of persons. To prevent people from communicating their beliefs and opinions is to violate the respect and standing to which they are entitled as persons. Equally, not allowing them to hear the views of others and to reach their own conclusions is inconsistent with their moral status as persons. Sometimes the emphasis shifts from the 'rightness' to the 'goodness' of free speech. The ability to communicate freely with one's fellows, it is claimed, is essential to human development and human fulfilment. Free speech is a crucial feature of a society whose institutions and ethos enable individuals to shape their lives, to exercise meaningful choices and to achieve wellbeing in its fullest human sense.

3 Limits

Nowadays, controversy over free speech centres mainly upon its limits. Debates about those limits focus on two matters: the scope of speech and the harms that might be wrought by speech.

What some seek to protect as speech, others deny is speech in any credible sense. For example, attempts to incorporate pornographic displays within the free speech principle have met with the objection that those displays have no communicative content and are not speech in any reasonable sense (see PORNO-GRAPHY). In addition, some of what would ordinarily be termed speech may not qualify as speech of a privileged kind. Advertisers, for instance, are engaged in intentional communication but arguably justifica-tions of free speech provide no case for including commercial advertising in the category of privileged speech. Equally, there are acts, such as flag-burning or wearing a symbolic armband, which would not ordinarily be described as speech but which may be encompassed by the free speech principle because of their expressive or communicative character. In some measure, then, the limits of free speech are set by what its justifications imply should count as speech.

Second, speech is often limited because it proves harmful. It is sometimes held that speech, because it is speech and not action, cannot harm; but that is clearly not so. Defamation damages a person's reputation and that harm is usually accepted as reason enough for proscribing libellous speech, provided that what is said is neither true nor 'fair comment'. Speech which invades privacy is also a candidate for proscription where no genuine public interest is at stake; here even 'truth' is no defence – there are some things that a public has no right to know. Other types of speech that are often outlawed because of their alleged harmfulness are obscenity and pornography, incitements to violence and other sorts of illegal conduct, and speech which incites hatred, particularly racial hatred.

Four types of controversy surround claims about the harmfulness of speech. One is the essentially empirical question of whether a particular form of speech actually causes the harm it is alleged to cause. Many people, for example, believe that pornographic material encourages sex crimes, while others claim it has no such effect and may even provide a catharsis which reduces criminality. A second issue is whether an alleged harm is really a harm. If a speaker incites others to overthrow a political system or to defy a law, is that harmful? Clearly, the answer will depend, in part, upon our estimate of the political system or the law at stake (see LAW, LIMITS OF §4).

A third matter is whether an acknowledged harmful effect is sufficiently harmful to justify restricting speech. Should we, for instance, outlaw blasphemous statements so that people with religious convictions are spared offence? Given the weight of the free speech principle, a harm will have to be significant and substantial to justify curtailing speech. On the other hand, in making that assessment it is reasonable also to take into account the nature of the speech involved, even when it is speech whose subject falls within the privileged realm. For example, the case against prohibiting offensive religious statements will be less strong if those statements are merely scurrilous and aim only to cause distress than if they form part of a serious disquisition.

In most cases in which we restrict harmful speech, we are delimiting the right of free speech. For example, in accepting laws of libel we are accepting that people have no right to engage in defamatory speech. But there is a fourth area of debate concerning harm that is about overriding rather than defining the right of free speech. Suppose someone addresses a hostile audience; they say nothing they are not entitled to say but the audience starts to react violently; the authorities, anxious to prevent a riot and to protect life and limb, step in and silence the speaker. In these circumstances, we might accept that, all things considered, the authorities rightly silenced the speaker even though the speaker had committed no wrong. In such cases, we are not setting the boundaries of the right of free speech; rather we are accepting that there are circumstances in which the right may be justifiably overridden.

Not every wrong that is cited as a reason for limiting speech is readily described as a 'harm'.

'Indecency' and 'obscenity', for example, are sometimes condemned for reasons other than the injury they do to others. Generally, there is a reluctance nowadays to accept that statements should be prohibited merely because they are false. After all, fallibility and uncertainty about truth figure prominently in the case for free speech. One current and controversial exception is the Holocaust, denial of which is now outlawed in some countries. Even that measure, however, is often justified as a way of combating racism and of preventing affronts to victims of the Holocaust, rather than as a simple endeavour to uphold truth by law.

Not all rules which govern speech should be conceived as restricting it. For example, orderly discussion of issues in a legislature requires rules of debate and, taken in the round, those rules regulate rather than restrict speech. Similarly, there is a difference (although one that is often controversial) between regulating and restricting street demonstrations.

In all cases in which speech is limited, determining where precisely the boundary should fall can prove difficult. Legislators and judges need precise distinctions between the tolerable and intolerable, yet general philosophical arguments often fail to supply those sharp distinctions. In addition, debates about the moral limits of free speech need not be wholly identical with debates about its proper legal limits. Because there is reason to fear political power and the clumsiness of law, the legal right of free speech may be cast more generously than the moral right. Thus, morally, there may be things that we ought not to say, even though, legally, we are and ought to be free to say them.

References and further reading

Baker, C.E. (1989) *Human Liberty and Freedom of Speech*, Oxford: Oxford University Press. (A comprehensive study which integrates philosophical and legal issues.)

Fish, S. (1994) *There is No Such Thing as Free Speech, and It's a Good Thing Too*, Oxford: Oxford University Press. (A sceptical appraisal of enthusiasm for free speech.)

MacKinnon, C.A. (1994) *Only Words*, London: HarperCollins. (An impassioned attack upon attempts to defend pornography and racism through free speech.)

Meiklejohn, A. (1965) *Political Freedom*, New York: Oxford University Press. (A democratic defence of free speech.)

* Mill, J.S. (1859) *On Liberty*, London: Dent, 1972.

(Probably the most influential defence of free speech ever written.)

* Milton, J. (1644) Areopagitica, in K. Barton (ed.) *Prose Writings of Milton*, London: Dent, 1970. (A classic early defence of free speech.)

Scanlon, T. (1972) 'A Theory of Freedom of Expression', *Philosophy and Public Affairs* 1 (2): 204–26. (A defence of free expression grounded in autonomy and rationality.)

Schauer, F. (1982) *Free Speech: A Philosophical Enquiry*, Cambridge: Cambridge University Press. (A comprehensive philosophical study.)

PETER JONES

FREGE, GOTTLOB (1848–1925)

A German philosopher-mathematician, Gottlob Frege was primarily interested in understanding both the nature of mathematical truths and the means whereby they are ultimately to be justified. In general, he held that what justifies mathematical statements is reason alone; their justification proceeds without the benefit or need of either perceptual information or the deliverances of any faculty of intuition.

To give this view substance, Frege had to articulate an experience- and intuition-independent conception of reason. In 1879, with extreme clarity, rigour and technical brilliance, he first presented his conception of rational justification. In effect, it constitutes perhaps the greatest single contribution to logic ever made and it was, in any event, the most important advance since Aristotle. For the first time, a deep analysis was possible of deductive inferences involving sentences containing multiply embedded expressions of generality (such as 'Everyone loves someone'). Furthermore, he presented a logical system within which such arguments could be perspicuously represented: this was the most significant development in our understanding of axiomatic systems since Euclid.

Frege's goal was to show that most of mathematics could be reduced to logic, in the sense that the full content of all mathematical truths could be expressed using only logical notions and that the truths so expressed could be deduced from logical first principles using only logical means of inference. In this task, Frege is widely thought to have failed, but the attempted execution of his project was not in vain: for Frege did show how the axioms of arithmetic can be derived, using only logical resources, from a single principle which some have argued is, if not a logical principle, still appropriately fundamental. In addition, Frege contributed importantly to the philosophy of mathematics through his trenchant critiques of alternative conceptions of mathematics, in particular those advanced by John Stuart Mill and Immanuel Kant, and through his sustained inquiry into the nature of number and, more generally, of abstract objects.

In the course of offering an analysis of deductive argument, Frege was led to probe beneath the surface form of sentences to an underlying structure by virtue of which the cogency of inferences obtains. As a consequence of his explorations, Frege came to offer the first non-trivial and remotely plausible account of the functioning of language. Many of his specific theses about language – for instance, that understanding a linguistic expression does not consist merely of knowing which object it refers to – are acknowledged as of fundamental importance even by those who reject them.

More generally, three features of Frege's approach to philosophical problems have shaped the concerns and methods of analytic philosophy, one of the twentieth century's dominant traditions. First, Frege translates central philosophical problems into problems about language: for example, faced with the epistemological question of how we are able to have knowledge of objects which we can neither observe nor intuit, such as numbers, Frege replaces it with the question of how we are able to talk about those objects using language and, once the question is so put, avenues of exploration previously invisible come to seem plausible and even natural. Second, Frege's focus on language is governed by the principle that it is the operation of sentences that is explanatorily primary: the explanation of the functioning of all parts of speech is to be in terms of their contribution to the meanings of full sentences in which they occur. Finally, Frege insists that we not confuse such explanations with psychological accounts of the mental states of speakers: inquiry into the nature of the link between language and the world, on the one hand, and language and thought, on the other, must not concern itself with unshareable aspects of individual experience.

These three guiding ideas – lingua-centrism, the primacy of the sentence, and anti-psychologism – exercised a commanding influence on early analytic philosophers, such as Wittgenstein, Russell and Carnap. Through them, these ideas have been spread far and wide, and they have come to create and shape analytic philosophy, with whose fathering Frege, more than anyone else, must be credited.

1 **Life and work**
2 **Language and ontology**
3 **Sense and reference**
4 **Thought and thinking**
5 **Objectivity and privacy**
6 **Contributions to logic**

1 Life and work

Gottlob Frege, a German philosopher and mathematician, is the father of modern logic and one of the founding figures of analytic philosophy. Trained as an algebraic geometer, he spent his professional life at the University of Jena, where, because his views about logic, mathematics and language were generally at odds with the dominant trends of the time, he laboured independently on his central philosophical project.

Frege's main work consists of his *Begriffsschrift* (*Conceptual Notation*, 1879), in which he first presents his logic; *Die Grundlagen der Arithmetik* (*The Foundations of Arithmetic*, 1884), in which he outlines the strategy he is going to employ in reducing arithmetic to logic and then goes on to provide the reduction with a philosophical rationale and justification; *Grundgesetze der Arithmetik* (*Basic Laws of Arithmetic*, volumes 1, 1893, and 2, 1903), in which he seeks to carry out the programme in detail (a planned third volume was aborted following Bertrand Russell's communication to Frege in 1902 of his discovery of paradox in Frege's logic); and a series of philosophical essays on language, the most important of which are *Funktion und Begriff* ('Function and Concept', 1891), 'Über Sinn und Bedeutung' ('On Sense and Reference', 1892a), 'Über Begriff und Gegenstand' ('On Concept and Object', 1892b) and 'Der Gedanke: eine logische Untersuchung' ('Thoughts', 1918).

In general, Frege was not philosophically intrigued by what was specific to the human condition; for instance, he sought neither to probe the nature and limits of human knowledge nor to understand how humans actually reason. Yet he pursued his non-parochial philosophical interests by attending carefully to natural language and to the way it serves to express our thoughts. Frege's approach, in conjunction with his powerful tool of linguistic analysis (logic) and the collection of subtle, innovative and interwoven theses about language which he elaborated, spurred in others not only an intense interest in language as an object of inquiry but also adherence to a distinctive methodology which has come to characterize much analytic philosophy past and present.

2 Language and ontology

Frege's short book *Begriffsschrift* revolutionized the study of deductive inference. In the course of explaining how his 'conceptual notation' relates to natural language, Frege illuminates important features of language's underlying structure. He recognized that traditional grammatical categories have no logical significance and he urged the consideration instead of the categories of 'singular terms' (which he calls 'proper names') and of 'predicates' (which he calls 'concept-words'). For Frege, a singular term is a complete expression, one which contains no gaps into which another expression may be placed; for example, 'Virginia Woolf', 'the third planet from the Sun' and 'the largest prime number' are all singular terms according to Frege.

By contrast, a predicate such as '( ) was written by Virginia Woolf' is something incomplete; it is a linguistic expression which contains a gap and which becomes a sentence once this gap is filled by a singular term. (The parentheses are not part of the predicate but are intended only to indicate the location of the gap.) Thus, if we fill the gap with 'the third planet from the Sun', we get a complete sentence. This example shows that the resulting sentence may be false or perhaps even nonsense; what is important is that a complete sentence does result. Other examples of predicates are 'Leonard Woolf married ( )', '( ) orbits Jupiter' and '( ) is an even prime number greater than two'; there are infinitely many predicates in any natural language.

Frege distinguishes more finely between predicates, depending on how many gaps they contain and on the types of linguistic expressions that can fill them. The predicates we have so far considered each have just one gap and are known as 'one-place' predicates. '( ) is the mother of ( )' is an example of a 'two-place' predicate, for it contains two gaps, each to be filled by a singular term. Predicates whose gaps are to be filled by one or more singular terms, as is the case with all those mentioned so far, are said to be 'first-level'. Predicates whose gaps are to be filled by first-level predicates are said to be 'second-level', and so on. For example, when properly analysed, 'All [ ] are mammals' is seen to be a second-level predicate: its structure is really 'Everything is such that if it [ ], then it is a mammal', which makes it plainer that the gap is to be filled by a predicate of first-level. (We use square brackets to distinguish such gaps, which must be filled by first-level predicates, from those occurring in first-level predicates, which must be filled by singular terms.) And, for Frege, 'There is at least one thing which [ ]' is likewise a second-level predicate: as we shall see in a moment, this corresponds to his view that existence is not a concept that applies to objects but rather to concepts. This finer classification will not be discussed further here. Nor will the issue of how precisely to understand the incompleteness of predicates, and the corresponding completeness of singular terms, a question that continues to be debated.

The following two points, however, are not in dispute: first, Frege discerns in the categories of reality counterparts to the linguistic categories of singular term and predicate; he calls these ontological categories 'object' and 'concept', respectively. Second, Frege understands concepts on the model of functions as they are commonly encountered in mathematics.

A singular term refers to, or designates, an object. A predicate refers to, or designates, a concept. (We shall use 'designate' and 'refer' and their cognates interchangeably; in some discussions of Frege, 'denote' and 'mean' are also used.) Corresponding to the fact that a first-level predicate yields a complete sentence upon its gap being filled by a singular term, we have the fact that a first-level concept is true or false of an object – or, as Frege puts it, that an object 'falls under' or fails to fall under a concept. For this reason, Frege calls concepts 'unsaturated': unlike objects, they await completion, whereupon they yield one of the two truth-values, which Frege takes to be objects: the True and the False (1891: 6). For example, the concept designated by '( ) is an Oxonian' yields the value the False when completed with the object designated by 'Gottlob Frege' and the value the True when completed with the object designated by 'John Locke'.

Concepts are incomplete in the way that functions in mathematics are. For example, the function designated by '2+ ( )' yields the value 8 when completed with the object 6, or, as we might more simply say, it yields that value for the argument 6. The function '2+ ( )' is not an object, but yields one upon completion by an argument. On Frege's view, concepts are a kind of function, namely those that take as their only values the True or the False.

In describing this congruence of linguistic and ontological categories, Frege is not confusing use and mention (see USE/MENTION DISTINCTION AND QUOTATION); indeed, Frege exhibited an understanding of the distinction between words and what they designate not witnessed again until well into the twentieth century. Though linguistic expressions are claimed to slot into a certain set of categories and reality into another, an intimate connection obviously exists between the two categorial schemes. Whether Frege takes the linguistic scheme or instead the ontological one as fundamental is a subject of debate and bound up with the question of whether and in what sense Frege sees philosophical reflection on language as the foundation of philosophy.

Regardless of this debate's resolution, we know that Frege takes the categories of concept and object to be fundamental ontologically, ones not amenable to further analysis. In addition, basic structural features of language raise insurmountable obstacles to expressing certain truths about these categories. This can be demonstrated by considering the obvious claim (1) seeks to articulate:

(1)   The concept designated by '( ) is a horse' is a concept.

This seems patently correct. Yet Frege recognizes in 'On Concept and Object' (1892b) that we must judge (1) to be false. This is because the expression 'The concept designated by "( ) is a horse"' is a singular term and hence refers to an object, not to a concept. (The expression does not contain a gap, though it does mention one.) So (1) does not succeed in expressing what we intended. To do this, we need to fill the gap in '( ) is a concept' by an expression that refers to a concept. But the straightforward way of doing this yields (2):

(2)   ( ) is a horse is a concept,

which is not even a sentence. In trying to articulate our thought, we are led either to falsity or to something that makes no claim at all. This 'awkwardness of language', as Frege calls it, has been the subject of much controversy, but it seems clear that Frege draws the lesson that there are elemental facts about language and the world that perforce escape expression (1892b: 196).

3   Sense and reference

How do what words refer to (concepts and objects) relate to our understanding of language? In his seminal essay 'On Sense and Reference' (1892a), Frege considered whether the 'sense' of an expression – what it is that we know when we understand the expression – is simply identical to what it designates (the 'reference'). Frege offers the following argument, as famous as it is simple, to show that our understanding of singular terms cannot consist just of knowing their reference:

(3)   (a) If two singular terms t and t' have the same sense and C is any (first-level) predicate, then $C(t)$ has the same sense as $C(t')$.

(b) 'The evening star = the morning star' does not have the same sense as 'The evening star = the evening star'.

(c) 'The evening star' does not have the same sense as 'the morning star'.

[This follows from (a) and (b): let C in (a) be 'The evening star = ( )'.]

(d) 'The evening star' refers to the same object as 'the morning star'.

(e) The reference of 'the evening star' is not identical with its sense.

[This follows from (c) and (d).]

So the sense of an expression – that which must be known in order for a speaker to understand it – cannot be identified with its reference (see SENSE AND REFERENCE). (A terminological digression: in this essay of 1892, Frege used the words '*Sinn*' and '*Bedeutung*', respectively. There is, however, no consensus on how these should be rendered in English. More importantly, there is not yet agreement about how precisely to understand these notions and how they are related to more everyday notions, such as meaning.)

Frege's justification for premise (a) relies on a 'compositionality thesis': the sense of a sentence is determined by the senses of its components (and by the way in which the sentence is constructed from them; see COMPOSITIONALITY). Premise (b) is justified by noting that an alert speaker would find the one sentence obvious, but not the other: 'The evening star = the evening star' is an uninformative statement of self-identity, whereas 'The evening star = the morning star' may impart hitherto unsuspected information. This difference in what Frege called 'cognitive value' suffices, according to him, to register distinct senses (1892a: 25). Finally, premise (d) follows from the observation that both singular terms designate the planet Venus, an astronomical discovery that was not made for some time.

If sense is not reference, then what is it? To this, Frege provides no clear answer. He writes that the sense of an expression is 'the mode of presentation of that which is designated' (1892a: 26), but he does not offer any elaboration regarding the nature of these modes (see PROPER NAMES §1). Frege does, however, advance a number of other theses concerning the relation between sense and reference. In the first place, the sense of an expression determines the identity of its reference, but not vice versa. For instance, the expression 'the author of *Begriffsschrift*' designates a particular individual, Frege, and any expression with the same sense designates the same individual; yet the expression 'the author of *Die Grundlagen der Arithmetik*', which also refers to Frege, has a different sense. Likewise, though 'George Orwell' and 'Eric Blair' both designate the same person (they have the same reference), the two singular terms have distinct senses.

Second, expressions can be formed which, while possessing a sense, lack a reference. For example, 'Sherlock Holmes' is a singular term that has a sense but lacks a reference, for Holmes does not exist. This is not in conflict with saying that sense determines reference, for what this means is that if two expressions have the same sense, then they have the same reference. One might wonder, though, whether this thesis is at odds with Frege's description of sense as the way 'that which is designated' is presented: how can there be such a way when that which is designated, the reference, does not exist? (See Evans 1981.)

Many have found in the distinction between sense and reference relief from the philosophical distress that follows upon assuming, first, that we understand an expression by directly associating a reference with it and, second, that we understand expressions that fail to refer. Holding both of these assumptions has led philosophers to extravagant claims about the reality that is actually designated by our expressions, for instance that Holmes must exist in some fashion if we are to speak of him intelligibly (if only to deny his existence). Frege's distinction between sense and reference, and his thesis that an expression can have a sense while lacking a reference, simply dissolves the problem by rejecting the first assumption (see DESCRIPTIONS §1).

The argument (3) concerns singular terms, but Frege believed that other kinds of expressions have sense and reference. The distinction can also be drawn in the case of predicates:

(4) Something is a bottle of claret if and only if it is a bottle of claret.

(5) Something is a bottle of claret if and only if it is a bottle of Hume's favourite wine.

(4) does not have the same sense as (5): no one would deny the first, but the second might come as something of a gastronomic discovery. Though '( ) is a bottle of claret' and '( ) is a bottle of Hume's favourite wine' are predicates that refer to the same concept, they have different senses. (Frege identifies two concepts if an object falls under the one if and only if it falls under the other.)

What is the reference of a whole sentence? Frege answers this by observing what remains unchanged about a sentence when we substitute coreferring expressions (that is, expressions that have the same reference) in it. Assuming a compositionality thesis for reference (that the reference of a sentence is determined by the reference of its components), we then have some reason to take whatever remains unchanged to be the sentence's reference. Consider (6) and (7):

(6)   George Orwell wrote *1984*.

(7)   Eric Blair wrote *1984*.

What remains unchanged? Not the 'thought' expressed by each sentence: someone might believe one sentence to be true, but not the other. Rather, it is the truth-value of the sentences that is constant: (6) and (7) are either both true or both false. This leads Frege to identify the reference of a sentence with its truth-value; a sentence refers to one of the two truth-values. Frege takes the two truth-values to be objects and he observes that on his view all true (false) sentences are really singular terms that refer to the same object, the True (the False).

Because the sciences are interested in what is true, we can see why Frege holds that reference 'is thus shown at every point to be the essential thing for science' ([1892–5] 1979: 123). Natural language permits the formation of expressions that lack reference, and so Frege judged it unsuitable as a tool of rational inquiry. For this purpose, it was inferior to his *Begriffsschrift*, a formal language he designed with the intention that no expression without reference could be constructed in it.

Frege notes that if his thesis that the reference of a sentence is its truth-value is correct, then we would predict (again on the basis of the compositionality thesis for reference) that if a subordinate sentence is replaced by a coreferential one (which will have the same truth-value), the reference of the entire containing sentence (that is, its truth-value) will remain unchanged. For instance, consider:

(8)   Ronald Reagan was elected President in 1984 and George Orwell wrote *1984*.

(9)   Ronald Reagan was elected President in 1984 and Eric Blair wrote *1984*.

(8) and (9) have the same truth-value, as predicted if the reference of a sentence is its truth-value. But now consider:

(10)   Stimpson believes that George Orwell wrote *1984*.

(11)   Stimpson believes that Eric Blair wrote *1984*.

If Stimpson does not realize that George Orwell and Eric Blair are one and the same person, (10) and (11) might have different truth-values, that is, they might differ in reference. And yet one is obtained from the other merely through substitution of what, on Frege's hypothesis, are the coreferring sentences (6) and (7).

Frege defends his hypothesis by claiming that in certain contexts expressions refer not to their ordinary reference but rather to an 'indirect' reference (1892a: 28). And, he adds, the indirect reference of an expression is just its ordinary sense. Because 'Stimpson believes that ( ) wrote 1984' is just such a context and because 'George Orwell' has a different sense from 'Eric Blair' (and so, in this context, a different reference), the compositionality thesis for reference no longer forces us to the conclusion that (10) and (11) have the same truth-value. Frege's response inaugurated a long, fruitful and continuing debate about the nature of such linguistic contexts. (For further discussion, see INDIRECT DISCOURSE; SENSE AND REFERENCE §5; PROPOSITIONAL ATTITUDE STATEMENTS.)

And what about the sense of a complete sentence? Given the compositionality thesis for sense, it will be preserved upon substitution of one expression in a sentence by another with identical sense. Frege says that such a substitution preserves the thought expressed by the sentence and he consequently identifies this thought with the sentence's sense. So, because 'to lie' has the same sense as 'to express something one believes to be false with the intention of deceiving', Frege would predict that the following two sentences express the same thought:

(12)   Everyone has lied.

(13)   Everyone has expressed something he believes to be false with the intention of deceiving.

And this prediction does seem to be borne out. But what precisely is the thought expressed by a sentence?

4   Thought and thinking

When one thinks the thought that lemons are sour, many different kinds of psychological events may transpire; certain memories, images or sensations may be triggered. These events, according to Frege, belong to the psychological world of the subject and, as such, are not fully shareable with others: much as one may try, one cannot experience what another does. It is a serious error, Frege says, to confuse such private events as may accompany our grasping of a thought with the thought that is grasped. One commits the sin of 'psychologism' if one does not sharply distinguish between the psychological process of thinking and the thoughts that are, as a consequence of this private activity, apprehended.

Thoughts then, in contrast to what Frege calls 'ideas', are fully shareable. When you and I grasp the sense of 'Lemons are sour', we arrive at the very same thought: there are not two different, related thoughts (as we might, for example, have two different mental images of lemons), but just the one that, through perhaps idiosyncratic and private paths, we both succeed in apprehending. And so it is in general with senses: they are not of the mental world, but objective in that different individuals can grasp them and associate them with their words. To stray from this perspective, according to Frege, is simply to abandon the view that communication is possible; that two speakers can understand a linguistic expression in the same way.

To grasp a thought is not to hold it true. For though one grasps a thought in the course of asserting it, it is no less grasped in the acts of assuming it to be true, wishing that it were true, commanding that it be made true, questioning whether it is true, and so on. These acts correspond to the different kinds of 'force' that may be attached to a thought. This is not quite Frege's position, but it is an influential one closely related to his views (1892a: 38–9). It has been attractive to many students of language because it divides the daunting project of giving an explanation of linguistic understanding and use into two potentially more tractable components. The first task, the articulation of a 'theory of sense' or 'theory of meaning', is to explain how the sense of a sentence is determined by the senses of its parts. The second task, the articulation of a 'theory of force' (sometimes also called 'pragmatics'), is to explain, taking for granted an account of the thoughts expressed by sentences, the different speech acts into which they may enter. For example, it falls to the theory of meaning to describe the content of 'Lemurs are native to London' and to show how that thought is determined by the senses of the sentence's constituent components. It falls to the theory of force to discover what, beyond the apprehension of that thought, is involved in asking 'Are lemurs native to London?', in wishing 'Oh, would that lemurs were native to London!', and so on. Should the theory of force need to make reference to the mental states of agents, then it is not merely helpful to divide an account of linguistic understanding and use into these two components but, Frege would insist, essential if we are to keep psychology from intruding into an account of sense (see PRAGMATICS; SPEECH ACTS §1).

5 Objectivity and privacy

In the previous section, we saw that Frege insists on the objectivity of thoughts (and senses generally), intending by this that different speakers can attach the very same thoughts to their sentences. There is a second way in which Frege takes thoughts to be objective. To say that thoughts are shareable is compatible with saying that their existence and properties are dependent upon human activity. Frege's view seems to be that thoughts are also objective in that they exist independently of human activity. Thoughts are not created or shaped by the process of thinking; they exist regardless of whether we have apprehended them, regardless of whether we shall ever apprehend them. Thoughts await our grasp in somewhat the way that physical objects await our observation, though the latter are located in space and time whereas thoughts are not.

These two kinds of objectivity, shareability and independence, are taken by Frege to apply to truth as well, which he considers a property of thoughts. There are not different properties – say, 'true-for-you' and 'true-for-me' – which are private unto individuals. There is just one property, being true, which some thoughts have and others lack. Furthermore, whether a thought possesses this property is in no way dependent upon our capacity to recognize that it does. A thought's being true must be sharply distinguished from our believing it to be true or our being justified in taking it to be true. On Frege's view, the truth of a thought is not dependent upon our beliefs, not even upon our beliefs in some ideal epistemic situation. Truth is one thing, our recognition of truth something else entirely. This position regarding the independence of truth, present throughout Frege's writings, is a robust realist motif in his thought, the evaluation of which has occupied centre-stage of much contemporary philosophy of language (see REALISM AND ANTIREALISM §4).

Since on Frege's view a sentence is true if and only if it refers to the value the True, his realism amounts to saying that a sentence refers to what it does independently of our recognition of this fact. But a sentence refers to an object only via its sense (the thought it expresses), which is what determines its reference. And its sense is not something that it has independently of speakers (after all, an expression – like 'chat', for example – can have one sense in one language and another in another), but is associated with it through human activity. Putting all this together, we see that, according to Frege, humans associate senses with linguistic expressions – this is what their understanding of language consists of – on account of which those expressions take on references whose identity may remain forever unknown.

That such a realism should follow from the senses attached to expressions forces our attention not only to Frege's notion of sense but, relatedly, to his conception of what it is to grasp a sense and associate it with an expression. Frege's anti-psychologism with regard to sense is not extended by him to an account of the grasping of sense, for in his few remarks about the subject he appears to avow a psychological picture of the process of apprehending a thought, of judging it to be true and so on (see [1897a] 1979: 145). Given his view of the privacy of mental events, it might seem that for Frege one cannot always determine which thought another has associated with a sentence: not that one cannot apprehend the same thought as another (for one feature of the objectivity of thoughts, that they can be grasped by all alike, guarantees that one can); but that one cannot always ascertain that one has.

That a speaker's linguistic understanding might remain private is a view that has troubled many, especially those influenced by the work of Ludwig Wittgenstein (see PRIVATE LANGUAGE ARGUMENT). Michael Dummett, the most influential interpreter of Frege's philosophy (see Dummett 1973), argues that, while much remains of lasting value in Frege's views on language, they should be modified in such a way that not only must senses be graspable by all, something on which Frege already insists, but the attachment of senses to expressions must be accessible as well; that is, the nature of a speaker's linguistic understanding must be a thoroughly public affair (see PRIVATE STATES AND LANGUAGE). Once these modifications are made, Dummett claims, important consequences will follow about which senses can be coherently grasped: if the only intelligible senses are those the grasp of which is subject to public inspection, then we must be sceptical of any analysis of linguistic understanding in terms of senses that underwrite realism and we should instead consider seriously analyses employing senses that do not countenance the possibility of sentences being true independently of all potential human knowledge. Both Dummett's argument and his assumptions have been disputed, and the controversy continues to be a lively one. This is not an issue about which Frege explicitly said much, but it is among the many deep debates on the nature of language and thought which his work has made possible.

6 Contributions to logic

Infamous for using a notation difficult to learn to read, Frege's *Begriffsschrift* is one of the greatest logical works ever written. (Its full title in English is *Conceptual Notation: a Formula Language, Modelled Upon That of Arithmetic, for Pure Thought*.) It contains a number of major innovations, two of which are of foundational importance for contemporary logic: a satisfactory logical treatment of generality and the development of the first formal system. *Begriffsschrift* also introduces (what are essentially) truth tables, contains Frege's definition of the ancestral (§9) and sows the seeds of his philosophy of language (§§2–5).

Let us first discuss Frege's treatment of generality, that is, his logical analysis of sentences containing such words as 'everything', 'something', 'no one' and the like. The foundation for this is Frege's predicate–singular term analysis of simple sentences (§2). Sentences such as 'Tony is alive' contain a singular term, 'Tony', and a predicate, '( ) is alive'. We can extend this analysis to such sentences as 'Everything is alive' by drawing 'upon [the formula language of] arithmetic'. In arithmetic, a sentence containing a variable, 'x', is taken to be true if and only if a true sentence results no matter what x is supposed to be. For example, '$x + 2 = 2 + x$' is true if and only if, no matter what x may be, $x + 2 = 2 + x$. So, if we allow the argument of '( ) is alive' to be a variable, the resulting sentence 'x is alive' may be taken to express the generalization of 'Tony is alive'; it will be true if and only if, no matter what x may be, x is alive. Similarly, 'Everything is not alive' may be represented as 'x is not alive'. For, given the convention just explained, this will be true if and only if, no matter what x may be, x is not alive. But, as a little experimentation will show (and as can be proven), it is impossible to represent such sentences as 'Not everything is alive', so long as we use variables in this way alone. Nor can one so express 'If everything is alive, then snow is black'. One could try to represent it as 'If x is alive, then snow is black'. But this actually represents 'Everything is such that, if it is alive, then snow is black' (1879: §11).

What is required here is some way of confining the generality expressed by the variable to a part of the sentence. In his informal discussions, Frege uses the phrase 'no matter what x may be' to do this (for example, 1879: §12). We may then represent 'Not everything is alive' as 'It is not the case that, no matter what x may be, x is alive'; and 'If everything is alive, then snow is black' as 'If, no matter what x may be, x is alive, then snow is black'. The phrase 'no matter what x may be', and its placement in the sentence, is said to delimit the 'scope' of the variable (see SCOPE). Frege's most vital discovery is not that variables may be used to indicate generality, but that variables have scope; his most significant innovation, the development of a notation in which scope can be represented, that is, his introduction of the *quantifier*.

Frege's second fundamental contribution was his construction of the first formal system. A formal system, as Frege conceives it, has three parts: first, a highly structured 'language' in which thoughts may be expressed; second, precisely specified 'axioms', or basic truths, about the subject matter in question; and third, 'rules of inference' governing how one sentence may be inferred from others already established. Frege believed that there were a number of advantages to carrying out proofs in such formal systems, for example, that giving a proof in a formal system would better one's understanding of the proof, by revealing precisely what principles it employs. Suppose, for example, that one wants to show that a given theorem can be proven without using the axiom of choice: the obvious method would be to prove the theorem without using the axiom. But how can one be sure that the axiom has not tacitly been employed (as it was in Richard Dedekind's proof of Theorem 159 in *Was sind und was sollen die Zahlen?* in 1888)? Proving the theorem in a formal system makes this possible: the axioms which may be used are clearly specified and steps in the proof may be taken only in accordance with certain rules. (Compare 1879: Preface; 1884: §2. Formal systems are important in contemporary logic for related reasons; see MODEL THEORY.)

The formal system of *Begriffsschrift* does not actually live up to the standards Frege imposes upon it: not all its rules of inference are explicitly stated. However, this complaint cannot be made about the system presented in Part I of his *Grundgesetze der Arithmetik* (1893). (The first-order fragment of this system is complete; the second-order fragment is a formulation of standard, second-order logic.) The rigour of Frege's formulation was not equalled until Kurt Gödel's work in the early 1930s, almost forty years later.

It is arguable that Frege goes even further and, in *Grundgesetze*, presents a semantics for his system; that is to say, he attempts to explain, rigorously, how the formal system is to be interpreted; how its symbols are to be understood. Using these explanations, he attempts to prove that the axioms of the system, so interpreted, are true and that the rules of the system, so interpreted, preserve truth (that is, in technical parlance, to prove the system's soundness). If these controversial claims are correct, then Frege may also be credited with having anticipated, to a limited extent, the development of model theory.

7 *Die Grundlagen der Arithmetik*: three fundamental principles

In the Preface to *Begriffsschrift*, Frege announced his interest in determining whether the basic truths of arithmetic could be proven 'by means of pure logic'. Kant's answer had been negative. According to Kant, the truths of arithmetic are synthetic a priori: for example, knowledge of '7 + 5 = 12' requires appeal to intuition (see KANT, I. §§4–5). One of Frege's main goals in his *Die Grundlagen der Arithmetik* (*The Foundations of Arithmetic*) was to refute this view by giving purely logical proofs of the basic laws of arithmetic, thereby showing that arithmetical truths can be known independently of any intuition. Frege

conceived the formal system of *Begriffsschrift* as an important prerequisite for this project: without it, it would be impossible to determine whether the complex proofs required do indeed depend only upon axioms of 'pure logic'.

There has been some controversy about what motivated Frege's logicism – his view that the truths of arithmetic are truths of logic (see LOGICISM §1). Frege says that his project is inspired by both mathematical and philosophical concerns (1884: §§1–3). Some, notably Paul Benacerraf (1981), have defended the view that Frege was interested in philosophical problems only in so far as they were susceptible of mathematical resolution. However that may be, Mark Wilson (1992) and Jamie Tappenden (1995) have argued that there are important connections between Frege's work on arithmetic and then recent developments in geometry to which he would have been exposed during his graduate career.

Grundlagen is important for a number of reasons. The philosophy of arithmetic developed in the book is of continuing interest. Moreover, a large number of more specific theses propounded there have had a profound influence on later philosophers, including Ludwig Wittgenstein, W.V. Quine and Michael Dummett, to name but three. More generally, *Grundlagen* is arguably the first work of analytic philosophy. At crucial points in the book, Frege makes 'the linguistic turn': that is, he recasts an ontological or epistemological question as a question about language. Unlike some 'linguistic' philosophers, his purpose is not to dissolve the philosophical problem – to unmask it as a 'pseudo-problem' – but to reformulate it so that it can be solved.

According to Frege, his work in *Grundlagen* is guided by 'three fundamental principles' he states in the Preface:

> always to separate sharply the psychological from the logical, the subjective from the objective;
>
> never to ask for the meaning of a word in isolation, but only in the context of a proposition;
>
> never to lose sight of the distinction between concept and object.
>
> (1884: x)

All of these are sufficiently important to warrant separate discussion. The first, which announces Frege's opposition to 'psychologism', has been discussed in §§4–5; the second, which is called 'the context principle', will be discussed in §8 below.

The third principle, which distinguishes the sorts of things singular terms denote – objects – from the sorts of things predicates denote – concepts – has already been discussed in §2. Of present interest is the application Frege makes of this distinction in *Grundlagen* §§45–54. Just prior to these sections, Frege has been concerned with what numbers are, his results having been almost entirely negative: numbers are neither physical objects; nor collections or properties of such; nor subjective ideas. Frege now suggests that progress may be made by asking to what, exactly, number is ascribed. The crucial observation is that different numbers seem to be assignable to the same thing: of a pack of cards, for example, one could say that it was one pack or fifty-two cards. Frege realizes that this might suggest that ascription of number is subjective; dependent upon our way of thinking about the object in question (1884: §§25–6). But what is different in our way of regarding the pack is, specifically, the 'concept' we choose to employ: that denoted by '( ) is a pack' in the one case, or by '( ) is a card' in the other. If, with Frege, we insist that concepts, and facts about them, can be just as objective as objects and facts about them (1884: §48; 1891), there is no need to regard number as subjective. Rather, we must acknowledge that number is ascribed not to objects, nor to collections thereof, but to concepts:

> If I say 'Venus has 0 moons', there simply does not exist any moon or agglomeration of moons for anything to be asserted of; but what happens is that a property is assigned to the *concept* 'moon of Venus', namely that of including nothing under it. If I say, 'the King's carriage is drawn by four horses', then I assign the number four to the concept 'horse that draws the King's carriage'.
>
> (1884: §46; emphasis added)

(Note that we will use '"moon of Venus"' and '( ) is a moon of Venus' to denote the same concept.) As Frege famously puts the point in §55: 'the content of a statement of number is an assertion about a concept'.

Observe here how Frege's interest in what numbers are has led him to an interest in the nature of ascriptions of number and, in particular, to an investigation of the 'logical form' of such statements. According to Frege, the most fundamental way of referring to a number is by means of an expression of the form 'the number belonging to the concept *F*'; for example, 'the number belonging to the concept "moon of the earth"' refers to the number one, for there is just one object that is a moon of the earth. This seemingly innocuous linguistic claim plays a crucial role in Frege's account of what numbers are.

8 *Die Grundlagen der Arithmetik*: the context principle

Frege denied both that numbers are physical objects and that they are objects of intuition, in Kant's sense. In *Grundlagen* §62, he therefore raises the question of how 'numbers [are] given to us, if we cannot have any ideas or intuitions of them'. This question is plainly epistemological, concerning how we can have knowledge of the objects (and so the truths) of arithmetic. What is astonishing is how Frege sets about answering it: 'Since it is only in the context of a proposition that words have any meaning, our problem becomes this: to define the sense of a proposition in which a number word occurs.' As Michael Dummett has emphasized, Frege here makes 'the linguistic turn' in a profound way: what was plainly an epistemological problem is converted into one about language (Dummett 1991: 111–12). The question of how we can have knowledge about numbers becomes the question of how we refer to – that is, succeed in talking about – numbers.

Frege suggests that this question can be answered by examining whole sentences in which names of numbers occur. It is here that the second of Frege's fundamental principles, the context principle, is at work. Frege rejects any requirement that he should point out or, in some other way, display numbers for his audience. He has already asserted that this would be impossible, since numbers cannot be encountered in perception (we have no 'ideas' of them) or in intuition. Rather, Frege insists, one's ability to refer to numbers should be explained in terms of one's understanding of complete sentences in which names of numbers are employed. That is to say, Frege refuses to say what 'zero' refers to except to say what such sentences as 'Zero is the number belonging to the concept "moon of Venus"' mean. More precisely, he insists that to explain the meanings of such sentences is to say what 'zero' refers to.

Frege intends this view to be generalized: indeed, his own discussion of it does not concern numbers directly, but the analogous case of directions. So-called abstract objects pose serious philosophical problems, both ontological and epistemological. Frege's strategy for defending their existence and for defusing worries about our cognitive access to them is appealing and may well seem the only workable option. His general idea, that our capacity to refer to objects of a given kind may be explained only in terms of our understanding of sentences containing names of them, has been of continuing influence.

To return to our main thread, the immediate goal is to explain the meaning of sentences in which reference is made to numbers. Frege claims that, when we are concerned with names of *objects*, the most important such sentences are those asserting an identity. Because Frege takes numbers to be objects, he focuses upon such sentences as 'The number belonging to the concept "plate on the table" is the same as that belonging to the concept "guest at dinner"'. Frege observes that this sentence will be true if and only if there is a way of assigning plates to guests such that each guest gets exactly one plate and each plate, exactly one guest; that is, if and only if there is a one-to-one correlation between the plates and the guests. More generally, say that the concept F is equinumerous with the concept G if and only if there is a one-to-one correlation between the objects falling under F and those falling under G. Then the thought is this: the number belonging to the concept F = the number belonging to the concept G if and only if the concept F is equinumerous with the concept G. Since Frege introduces it with a quotation from Hume, this is sometimes called 'Hume's Principle' (1884: §§55–63). The principle had been known for some time, but it was only in the work of Georg Cantor (1897) that its mathematical significance was fully realized (see SET THEORY §2).

Of course, if Hume's Principle is to play any role in Frege's attempt to prove the axioms of arithmetic from logical principles alone, the notion of equinumerosity must be definable in purely logical terms. But Frege shows that it is, if the general theory of relations is accepted as part of logic (1884: §§70–2).

For reasons which are not entirely clear, Frege rejects the claim that Hume's Principle suffices to explain numerical identities. His stated reason (1884: §66; compare §56) is that it fails to decide whether Julius Caesar is the number zero! But there is little agreement about the point of this complaint or about its force. Still, Hume's Principle continues to be important to Frege, since he insists that any correct explanation of numbers must have Hume's Principle as a (relatively immediate) consequence. He himself settles upon an explicit definition of names of numbers: the number belonging to the concept F is to be the extension of the second-level concept '[ ] is a concept equinumerous with the concept F'. (Roughly, the extension of a concept is the collection of things that fall under that concept.) Frege shows how Hume's Principle may be derived from this definition (1884: §73). To make the definition and proof precise, however, he has to appeal to some axiom concerning extensions. Frege's idea, developed in *Grundgesetze*, was that extensions could be characterized by means of a principle analogous to Hume's Principle, namely, his Basic Law V: the extension of the concept F is the same as that of the concept G if and only if the very same objects fall under the concepts F and G (1893: §§3, 20). Famously and unfortunately, however,

Bertrand Russell showed Frege, in 1902, that the resulting theory of extensions is inconsistent, since Russell's paradox can be derived from Basic Law V in (standard) second-order logic (see PARADOXES OF SET AND PROPERTY §4).

9 Frege's formal theory of arithmetic

The story of Frege's work on arithmetic might well have ended there. In *Grundlagen*, Frege does sketch proofs of axioms for arithmetic (1884: §§70–83) and, in *Grundgesetze*, offers formal versions of them (1893: §§78–119). But little attention was paid to these proofs for almost a century, on the ground that Frege gave his proofs in an inconsistent theory, and anything can be proven in an inconsistent theory. Frege himself decided in about 1906 that no suitable reformulation of Basic Law V was forthcoming and, his wife having died in 1904, appears to have become deeply depressed. He published nothing at all between 1908 and 1917 and only three further articles after that.

Closer attention to the structure of Frege's proofs reveals something interesting, however. As already stated, Frege requires that his explicit definition of names of numbers imply Hume's Principle, and he shows that it does (given Basic Law V). But neither the explicit definition nor Basic Law V is used essentially in the proof of any other arithmetical theorem; these other theorems are proven using only second-order logic and Hume's Principle. Thus, Frege in fact proves that axioms for arithmetic can be derived in second-order logic from Hume's Principle alone. Frege himself knew as much, but, sadly, never appreciated the philosophical and mathematical significance of this result, now known as Frege's Theorem.

The details of Frege's proof of this result are beyond the scope of this discussion. But a few points are worth mentioning. First, one cannot actually prove each of the infinitely many truths of arithmetic from logical principles, or from anything else. So any attempt to show that all truths of arithmetic follow from logical principles, or from Hume's Principle, will depend upon the identification of some finite number of basic laws, or axioms, of arithmetic from which we are confident all other arithmetical truths will follow. The most famous such axioms are those due to Dedekind (though widely known as the Peano axioms; see NUMBERS §6). Frege employs his own axiomatization which, while similar, is importantly different and arguably more intuitive (1893: §§128–57).

Second, Frege's hardest task is to prove that there are infinitely many numbers, and his method of doing so is extremely elegant. The basic idea is as follows.

Begin by noting that 0 is the number belonging to the concept 'object not the same as itself' and then that 1 is the number belonging to the concept 'identical with 0'. Further, 2 is the number belonging to the concept 'identical with 0 or 1', and so on. More generally, if n is finite, then the number of the concept 'natural number less than or equal to n' is always one more than n, which implies that every finite number has a successor and (in the presence of the other axioms) that there are infinitely many numbers (1884: §§82–3; 1893: §§114–19).

Third, Frege needs, for a variety of reasons, to define the notion of a finite, or natural, number. He also needs to prove the validity of proof by induction, since one of his (and Dedekind's) axioms is, essentially, that such proofs are legitimate. Induction is a way of proving that all natural numbers fall under a concept F; a proof by induction proceeds by showing (1) that 0 falls under F and (2) that, if a number n falls under F, $n + 1$ must also fall under F. In essence, Frege *defines* the natural numbers as those objects for which induction works. According to Frege's definition, a number is a natural number if and only if it falls under every concept F which is a concept (1′) under which 0 falls and (2′) which is 'hereditary in the number series', that is, under which $n + 1$ falls whenever n does. It then follows, immediately, that proof by induction is valid: if F is a concept satisfying (1) and (2), then, since F is then a concept satisfying (1′) and (2′), every natural number must fall under it, by definition.

It is possible to see, intuitively, that this is a good definition, that is, that what Frege calls 'the natural numbers', the things that fall under every concept satisfying (1′) and (2′), *really are* the natural numbers. Certainly, if x is a natural number, then it falls under every concept satisfying (1′) and (2′). Conversely, suppose that x falls under every concept satisfying (1′) and (2′). Well, the concept 'natural number' is such a concept: for (1″) 0 certainly falls under it, and (2″) whenever a number n falls under it, $n + 1$ also falls under it. So, since x falls under *every* concept satisfying (1′) and (2′), it must fall under this one, that is, it must be a natural number. Thus, falling under every concept satisfying (1′) and (2′) is both necessary and sufficient for being a natural number. (Objections can be made to this argument, chiefly on the grounds of its 'impredicativity'; see PROPERTY THEORY §1.)

This method of definition may be generalized to furnish a definition of the 'ancestral' of any given relation. Frege's definition of the ancestral, introduced in *Begriffsschrift* (and independently discovered by Dedekind), is of quite general importance in mathematics.

Frege's formal work in *Grundgesetze* does not end with his proof of the arithmetical axioms. He goes on to develop purely logical definitions both of finitude and of infinitude; he proves the so-called categoricity theorem, that any two structures which satisfy his axioms for arithmetic are isomorphic; and he proves the validity of definition by induction. (These last two results were first proven by Dedekind.) There is also some reason to believe that Frege was interested in proving results now known to depend upon the axiom of choice and that his investigations led him to discover – though not to communicate – this axiom some years before Ernst Zermelo's formulation of it in 1904 (see AXIOM OF CHOICE). Finally, in later parts of *Grundgesetze*, Frege proves a number of preliminary results required for a logicist development of the theory of real numbers, but a projected third volume, which would have completed that part of the project, was abandoned in the wake of Russell's paradox.

10 The fate of Frege's logicism

Frege proved Frege's Theorem, that is, that axioms for arithmetic are (second-order) logical consequences of Hume's Principle. Of course, this would be of little interest but for the fact that, unlike Basic Law V, Hume's Principle is consistent. If, therefore, Hume's Principle could be argued to be a truth of logic, then the truths of arithmetic, being logical consequences of a truth of logic, would all be truths of logic and logicism would be vindicated! Work on Frege's philosophy of arithmetic has therefore tended to abstract from Frege's ill-fated explicit definition and to concern itself with the view Frege himself rejected, namely that names of numbers may be defined, or explained, by means of Hume's Principle.

No one nowadays really thinks that Hume's Principle is a truth of logic. Still, one might think that Hume's Principle is suitable as some kind of definition, or philosophical explanation, of names of numbers. And, or so argues Crispin Wright (1983), if the truths of arithmetic turn out to be logical consequences of an explanation, is that not almost as good as if they were truths of logic? This view is appealing precisely because Hume's Principle does seem to capture something very fundamental about (cardinal) numbers: saying that the number belonging to the concept F is the same as that belonging to G if and only if the concepts F and G are equinumerous just does seem a good way of explaining what (cardinal) numbers are. Still, there are serious worries. Saying that the extension of F is the same as the extension of G if and only if the same objects fall under F and G also *seems* to be a good way of explaining what extensions are – until one realizes this explanation is inconsistent. Hume's Principle is not inconsistent, of course, but one might wonder whether it can rightly be viewed as explanatory of what numbers are if such a kindred principle cannot rightly be viewed as explanatory of what extensions are. It is in the debate over this, the 'bad company objection' raised by George Boolos (1987) and Michael Dummett (1991), that the fate of Frege's logicism will be decided.

See also: LOGIC IN THE 19TH CENTURY; LOGIC IN THE EARLY 20TH CENTURY; LOGICAL AND MATHEMATICAL TERMS, GLOSSARY OF; MEANING AND TRUTH; INTUITIONISTIC LOGIC AND ANTIREALISM

List of works

Frege, G. (1952) *Translations from the Philosophical Writings of Gottlob Frege*, ed. P.T. Geach and M. Black, Oxford: Blackwell, 3rd edn, 1980. (The page numbers of the original publications appear in the text.)

—— (1984) *Collected Papers on Mathematics, Logic and Philosophy*, ed. B. McGuinness, Oxford: Blackwell. (This includes translations of almost all of Frege's published papers; the page numbers of the original publications appear in the margins.)

—— (1879) *Begriffsschrift, eine der arithmetischen nachgebildete Formelsprache des reinen Denkens*, Halle: Nebert; trans. '*Begriffsschrift*, a Formula Language, Modelled Upon That of Arithmetic, for Pure Thought', in J. van Heijenoort (ed.) *From Frege to Gödel: A Source Book in Mathematical Logic, 1879–1931*, Cambridge, MA: Harvard University Press, 1967, 1–82. (Includes the first formulation of Frege's system of logic, and discussion of its importance for philosophical reflection on language and thought.)

—— (1884) *Die Grundlagen der Arithmetik: eine logisch-mathematische Untersuchung über den Begriff der Zahl*, Breslau: Koebner; trans. J.L. Austin, *The Foundations of Arithmetic: A Logico-Mathematical Enquiry into the Concept of Number*, Oxford: Blackwell, 2nd edn, 1980. (Includes criticism of then extant views about the nature of arithmetic, motivation for Frege's own proposal and informal proofs of the laws of arithmetic. One of Frege's most central texts.)

—— (1891) *Funktion und Begriff*, Jena: Pohle; trans. P.T. Geach, 'Function and Concept', in *Translations* and *Collected Papers*. (Important paper in which Frege offers his analysis of concepts as functions whose values are restricted to the two truth-values.)

—— (1892a) 'Über Sinn und Bedeutung', *Zeitschrift für Philosophie und philosophische Kritik* 100: 25–50;

trans. M. Black, 'On Sense and Meaning', in *Translations* and *Collected Papers*. (Frege's most famous and seminal paper in which he argues for the distinction between the sense and reference of expressions and presents a number of important theses regarding the two notions.)

—— (1892b) 'Über Begriff und Gegenstand', *Vierteljahrsschrift für wissenschaftliche Philosophie* 16: 192–205; trans. P.T. Geach, 'On Concept and Object', in *Translations* and *Collected Papers*. (Expands on what Frege takes to be the fundamental distinction between concepts and objects.)

—— (1892–5) 'Ausführungen über Sinn und Bedeutung', trans. P. Long and R. White, 'Comments on Sense and Meaning', in *Posthumous Writings*, ed. H. Hermes, F. Kambartel and F. Kaulbach, Oxford: Blackwell, 1979, 118–25. (Expands some of the themes in Frege 1892a and discusses the importance of the sense/reference distinction in connection with predicates.)

—— (1893, 1903) *Grundgesetze der Arithmetik: begriffsschriftlich abgeleitet*, Jena: Pohle, 2 vols; repr. as *Grundgesetze der Arithmetik*, Hildesheim: Olms, 1966; Part 1 of vol. 1 trans. M. Furth, *Basic Laws of Arithmetic: An Exposition of the System*, Berkeley, CA: University of California Press, 1964; no complete translation of vol. 2 exists, though fragments, trans. M. Black and P.T. Geach, appear as 'Frege on Definitions', 'Frege Against the Formalists' and 'Frege on Russell's Paradox', in *Translations*. (Gives a rigorous exposition of Frege's mature logic, with some philosophical discussion of its importance and an extended discussion of psychologism. Also includes formal proofs of the laws of arithmetic within this system, and the beginnings of a development of a theory of real numbers.)

—— (1894) Review of Edmund Husserl's *Philosophie der Arithmetik*, *Zeitschrift für Philosophie und philosophische Kritik* 103: 313–32; trans. H. Kaal, in *Collected Papers*. (One of the most important of Frege's discussions of 'psychologism'.)

—— (1897a) 'Logik', in *Nachgelassene Schriften und Wissenschaftlicher Briefwechsel* (Posthumous Writings), ed. H. Hermes, F. Kambartel and F. Kaulbach, Hamburg: Meiner, 1969–76. (A philosophical treatise on notions fundamental to logic, such as assertion, thought, sense and the like. A predecessor of Frege 1918.)

—— (1897b) 'Über die Begriffsschrift des Herrn Peano und meine eigene', *Berichte über die Verhandlungen der königlich Sächsischen Gesellschaften der Wissenschaften zu Leipzig, mathematisch-physische Klasse* 48: 362–8; trans. V. Dudman, 'On Mr. Peano's Conceptual Notation and My Own', in

Collected Papers. (A comparison of Frege's logic with that of Peano, bringing out certain of the advantages of the former.)

—— (1903, 1906) 'Über die Grundlagen der Geometrie' (first and second series), *Jahresbericht der Deutschen Mathematiker Vereinigung* 12: 319–24, 368–75 and 15: 293–309, 377–403, 423–30; trans. E.-H. Kluge, 'The Foundations of Geometry: First Series' and 'The Foundations of Geometry: Second Series', in *Collected Papers*. (A critical discussion of David Hilbert's work on the foundations of geometry, frequently cited in connection with Frege's attitude towards early work in model theory.)

—— (1918) 'Der Gedanke: eine logische Untersuchung', *Beiträge zur Philosophie des deutschen Idealismus* 1: 58–77; trans. P.T. Geach and R. Stoothoff, 'Thoughts', in *Collected Papers*. (Late paper of Frege's in which he focuses on the nature of thoughts, that is, the senses of complete statements, and emphasizes their objectivity and their independence of psychology.)

—— (1969–76) *Nachgelassene Schriften und Wissenschaftlicher Briefwechsel*, ed. H. Hermes, F. Kambartel and F. Kaulbach, Hamburg: Meiner; trans. *Posthumous Writings*, ed. H. Hermes, F. Kambartel and F. Kaulbach, Oxford: Blackwell, 1979. (Translations of Frege's extant unpublished writings, most of which were destroyed during the bombing of Münster in the Second World War.)

References and further reading

* Benacerraf, P. (1981) 'Frege: The Last Logicist', in P. French *et al.* (eds) *Midwest Studies in Philosophy* vol. 6, Minneapolis, MN: University of Minnesota Press, 17– 35; repr. in Demopoulos 1995, 41–67. (Mentioned in §7, this paper discusses the mathematical motivations for Frege's logicism and contrasts them with the epistemological motivations of the logical positivists.)

* Boolos, G. (1987) 'The Consistency of Frege's Foundations of Arithmetic', in J.J. Thomson (ed.) *On Being and Saying: Essays in Honor of Richard Cartwright*, Cambridge, MA: MIT Press, 3–20; repr. in Demopoulos 1995, 211–33. (Raises the 'bad company objection' discussed in §10 and also includes a proof of the consistency of Hume's Principle.)

* Cantor, G. (1897) *Beiträge zur Begründung der transfiniten Mengenlehre, 2er artikel*, Halle; trans. P. Jourdain, *Contributions to the Founding of the Theory of Transfinite Numbers*, London: Open Court, 1915; repr. New York: Dover, 1955. (This is mentioned in §7.)

* Dedekind, R. (1888) *Was sind und was sollen die Zahlen?*, Braunschweig: Vieweg; trans. W. Beman, 'The Nature and Meaning of Numbers', in R. Dedekind, *Essays on the Theory of Numbers*, New York: Dover, 1963. (Referred to on a number of occasions, this is a classic in the philosophy of mathematics and a useful contrast to Frege's approach.)

Demopoulos, W. (ed.) (1995) *Frege's Philosophy of Mathematics*, Cambridge, MA: Harvard University Press. (This work collects most of the classic papers on the subject, not all of which are mentioned here.)

* Dummett, M. (1973) *Frege: Philosophy of Language*, London: Duckworth, 2nd edn, 1992. (This is a long, difficult, but superb and seminal study of Frege's views on language and logic which is relied upon heavily throughout the above.)

—— (1978) 'Frege's Distinction Between Sense and Reference', in *Truth and Other Enigmas*, London: Duckworth, 116–44. (This offers a detailed reconstruction of Frege's arguments.)

—— (1981) *The Interpretation of Frege's Philosophy*, London: Duckworth. (This is an extended defence of Dummett's exegesis of Frege together with a critical assessment of other interpretations.)

* —— (1991) *Frege: Philosophy of Mathematics*, London: Duckworth; repr. 1995. (Mentioned in §§8, 10, this raises the 'bad company objection'; a sequel to *Frege: Philosophy of Language*, it is somewhat more accessible but perhaps not as definitive.)

—— (1993) *The Seas of Language*, Oxford: Clarendon Press. (This is a collection of essays some of which first forcefully raised the issues discussed in §5.)

* Evans, G. (1981) 'Understanding Demonstratives', in H. Parrett and J. Bouveresse (eds) *Meaning and Understanding*, Berlin: de Gruyter, 280–303; repr. in *Collected Papers*, Oxford: Clarendon Press, 1985, 291–321. (Puts forward an important interpretation of Frege's views on sense and reference; mentioned in §3.)

Heck, R.G., Jr (1993) 'The Development of Arithmetic in Frege's *Grundgesetze der Arithmetik*', *Journal of Symbolic Logic* 58: 579–601; repr. in Demopoulos 1995, 257–94. (This paper includes an extended, technical discussion of Frege's formal work on arithmetic.)

Parsons, C. (1965) 'Frege's Theory of Number', in M. Black (ed.) *Philosophy in America*, Ithaca, NY: Cornell University Press, 180–203; repr. in Demopoulos 1995, 182–210. (This is a classic, accessible paper on Frege's philosophy of arithmetic, that raises many central issues.)

Ricketts, T. (1986) 'Objectivity and Objecthood: Frege's Metaphysics of Judgment', in J. Hintikka and L. Haaparanta (eds) *Frege Synthesized*, Dordrecht: Reidel, 65–95. (This is a dense work that discusses the question, mentioned in §6, of whether Frege anticipated modern semantics.)

* Tappenden, J. (1995) 'Frege on Extending Knowledge and "Fruitful Concepts"', *Nous* 29: 427–67. (Mentioned in §7, it discusses the relation between Frege's work on arithmetic and developments in geometry with which he would have been familiar.)

* Wilson, M. (1992) 'Frege: The Royal Road from Geometry', *Nous* 26: 149–80; repr. in Demopoulos 1995, 108–59. (Mentioned in §7, it presents an interpretation of Frege's work relying heavily on connections with work in geometry.)

* Wright, C. (1983) *Frege's Conception of Numbers as Objects*, Aberdeen: Aberdeen University Press. (Mentioned in §9, it includes important discussions of logicism and the context principle and the first post-Fregean proof of Frege's Theorem.)

ALEXANDER GEORGE
RICHARD HECK

FREI, HANS (1922–88)

Frei was concerned with two particular questions: why had the traditional Christian mode of biblical interpretation collapsed in the modern world, and how could it be recovered? He argued that, while the traditional interpretation of the Bible treated it as realistic narrative, in the modern period it had become accepted to treat the events described in it as myths and allegories. He argued for a more literal interpretation of the Gospels, which could lead to a more realistic interpretation of the person and nature of Jesus.

Hans Frei was an American theologian who fled his native Germany before the Second World War, and spent almost all of his teaching career at Yale University. He was of the view that, until the modern period, there had been near-consensus in the Church around the convictions that the Bible must be interpreted as one book, that the Gospels must be given priority in that unified interpretation, and that the Gospels as a whole must be interpreted literally. It was especially the collapse of consensus over the third element that drew Frei's attention. In the modern world, the Gospels are regularly interpreted as allegories, myths or moral tales.

Frei argued that there is something very strange about this. The Gospels are narratives. If one looks at the sort of narratives they are, it seems obvious that they are very different from paradigmatic examples of allegorical, mythical or moral narratives. The genre that fits them best is that of realistic narrative. Frei delineated various hallmarks of this genre, emphasizing especially that a realistic narrative, by tracing persons' actions and their reactions to features and events in their situation, renders the narrative identity of persons. It tells us who they are. The application of this point to the Gospels is that they render the narrative identity of Jesus.

One can summarize that identity in various ways: they narrate Jesus' enactment of his Messiahship, they narrate Jesus' enactment of the coming of God's kingdom, and so forth. What one cannot say, however, is that they are about such things as 'the coming of God's kingdom' or 'divine–human reconciliation'. To interpret them thus is to overlook their realistic narrative character and turn them into allegories or myths about some abstraction. The point – or, as Frei usually called it, the 'meaning' – of a realistic narrative is not something outside the narrative but the narrative itself, with its thematic core.

If, then, the literary genre of the Gospels is realistic narrative, why in the modern world have they been interpreted as allegories, as myths, as moral tales? Frei's answer is that interpreters confused 'meaning' with 'reference'. They assumed that the point of these narratives lies in something outside the narrative rather than in the narrative itself. They furthermore confused *history-likeness* in a narrative with the *historicity* of the narrative. Putting these points together: they assumed that the point of these narratives was to put us in touch with events in ancient history. But then scepticism set in as to whether the events really did occur. Yet most interpreters resisted concluding that these narratives lack 'meaning'. So they searched for aspects of reality other than ancient historical events which these narratives might be 'about'; and they construed the narratives as allegories of or myths about those aspects. Thus there occurred, to quote the title of Frei's best-known book, an 'eclipse of biblical narrative'.

Frei repudiated the assumption that meaning is reference in the case of the Gospels. The meaning of the Gospel narratives is what they say. The narrative interpretation that he called for finds literary criticism of far more use than historical studies. Frei's *The Eclipse of Biblical Narrative* (1974) is open to the antirealist interpretation that the important thing in the case of the Gospels is nothing but the story. When Frei's other major book, *The Identity of Jesus Christ* (1975), published almost simultaneously with *Eclipse*, is brought into the picture, it becomes clear that that was not his view. The Gospels – provided we interpret them as realistic narratives – present to us an actual

historical person, Jesus of Nazareth, in his fundamental identity. They constitute the best access we
have to that person; and, for religious purposes, an
entirely adequate access. It is true that we do not have
a proof of this. The situation is rather that some
people, upon reading the Gospels, find themselves
believing that they are in the 'presence' of Jesus of
Nazareth, and are entitled to so believe.

It comes as no surprise to learn that after the
publication of *Eclipse* and *Identity*, Frei began to
emphasize the legitimacy and importance of what
some have called 'Anselmian theology'; that is,
theology that from the beginning is conducted as an
exposition of Christian belief, in contrast to theology
that develops natural or foundational theology before
it sets about expounding Christian belief.

See also: HERMENEUTICS, BIBLICAL; REVELATION §3

List of works

Frei, H. (1974) *The Eclipse of Biblical Narrative: A
Study in Eighteenth and Nineteenth Century Hermeneutics*, New Haven, CT: Yale University Press.
(Frei's classic study of biblical hermeneutics;
densely written.)
—— (1975) *The Identity of Jesus Christ: The
Hermeneutical Bases of Dogmatic Theology*, Philadelphia, PA: Fortress Press. (Considerably less
difficult than *Eclipse*; corrects the impression of
antirealism conveyed by *Eclipse*.)
—— (1992) *Types of Christian Theology*, New Haven,
CT: Yale University Press. (Frei had been working
for some years before his death on this typology of
Christian theology.)
—— (1993) *Theology and Narrative*, ed. G. Hunsinger
and W.C. Placher, New York: Oxford University
Press. (A very helpful collection of Frei's most
important articles, collected after his death by
former students.)

References and further reading

Green, G. (ed.) (1987) *Scriptural Authority and
Narrative Interpretation*, Philadelphia, PA: Fortress
Press. (As yet, no full-length treatment of Frei's
work has been published. However, a good many
articles have appeared; this is a representative
collection.)

NICHOLAS P. WOLTERSTORFF

FRENCH MORALISTS
see MORALISTES

FRENCH PHILOSOPHY OF SCIENCE

*A distinctively French tradition in the philosophy of
science began with Descartes, continued through the
Enlightenment in works such as D'Alembert's* Discours
préliminaire *and the* Encyclopédie, *and flowered in the
nineteenth and the early twentieth century with the work
of Comte, Duhem, Meyerson and Poincaré. Throughout
the twentieth century, the dominant fashions in French
philosophy derived more and more from German
influences, especially idealism and phenomenology
(Hegel to Heidegger). But amidst these developments,
there persisted an essentially autonomous tradition of
French philosophy of science that offered an indigenous
alternative to the Germanic imports. Here the key
figure was Gaston Bachelard (1884–1962), for many
years professor at the Sorbonne and director of the
Institut d'Histoire des Sciences et des Techniques. His
work was continued and modified by Georges Canguilhem (1904–95), his successor at the Institute, who
himself was an important influence on philosophers such
as Louis Althusser, Michel Foucault and Michel Serres.
Jean Cavaillès' critique of Husserl's philosophy of
mathematics and his effort to develop a neo-Hegelian
alternative to it had deep affinities with Bachelard's
work and was also an important influence on Canguilhem.*

*The most important general features of twentieth-
century French philosophy of science appear if we
contrast it with its two major rivals: existential
phenomenology and logical positivism. Existential
phenomenology is a 'philosophy of the subject',
maintaining that ultimate truth resides in the immediacy of lived experience. Bachelard and his followers,
by contrast, proposed a 'philosophy of the concept', for
which experiential immediacy is subordinate to and
corrected by concepts produced by rational reflection.
This process of rational reflection is, moreover,
embodied in science, which is not, as existential
phenomenology maintains, a derivative and incomplete
form of knowing, but the very paradigm of knowledge.
In giving science a privileged epistemic position, the
French philosophers of science are like the logical
positivists. But, unlike the positivists, they treat science
as essentially historical, irreducible in either method or
content to the rigour of a formal system. They also
opposed the positivists' effort to find the foundions of
scientific knowledge in sense experience, maintaining*

that there are no simply given data and that all experience is informed by conceptual interpretation.

1 **Bachelard's philosophy of science: epistemology and method**
2 **Bachelard's philosophy of science: metaphysics**
3 **Canguilhem on concepts and theories**
4 **Rationality and norms**
5 **Michel Foucault: the influence of Bachelard and Canguilhem**
6 **Michel Foucault: beyond Bachelard and Canguilhem**
7 **Michel Serres**
8 **Conclusion**

1 Bachelard's philosophy of science: epistemology and method

Bachelard accepts Descartes' view that knowledge derives from the methodical questioning of accepted beliefs (see DESCARTES, R. §4). But he is explicitly anti-Cartesian in rejecting the idea that, from this questioning, there emerge intuitive certainties that provide an unshakeable foundation for knowledge. Descartes' absolute certainty requires an entirely simple object (lest there be any hidden complexity misleading our judgment) and a subject that is entirely transparent to itself (lest we be deceived by unexamined prejudices or other distortions). But Bachelard maintains that such simplicity and transparency are not available; as the history of science amply shows, future generations always discover complexities and prejudices unnoticed by previous inquirers.

Scientific inquiry, therefore, never attains the entirely clear path Descartes sought but is always blocked, in some key respects, by *epistemological obstacles*. These are ways of thinking and perceiving, typically tied to common sense or past scientific theories, that prevent us from seeing truths essential for the further progress of science. Early chemistry, for example, had to overcome faulty intuitions based on the animism of primitive common sense; twentieth-century physics had to break through inadequate concepts of space, time and causality implicit in classical physics. Because of the need, at every stage, to overcome such obstacles, the development of science is not a continuous progress but a series of *epistemological breaks*, whereby scientists attain new conceptions of nature and of the methods required to study it.

In Bachelard's view the development of science is not continuous, but it is progressive. This is so in two respects: first, some scientific results are permanently valid and must be preserved in all subsequent formulations; second, successive scientific theories in a given domain provide a more general perspective from which the claims of previous theories can be assessed and, to the extent they are found valid, incorporated into current thinking.

Given his anti-Cartesian stance, the methodology of Bachelard's philosophy of science must be historical. The nature of scientific thinking cannot be determined from a priori principles but must be discerned from a close examination of actual scientific practice. However, within this historical approach, current science holds a privileged position as the best available account of nature. It alone is a basis for judging the degree of descriptive and methodological success attained by previous scientific efforts. In Bachelard's terminology, contemporary science allows us to judge which parts of scientific history are valid (*l'histoire sanctionée*) and which outdated (*l'histoire périmée*). Thus, in contrast to ordinary political history, the history of science does not aim at a narration of objective facts that refrains from judging past events by contemporary standards. History of science essentially involves normative judgments of the past it studies.

As science develops, then, so too does the philosophy of science. (Bachelard in fact thinks that all domains of philosophy, not just the philosophy of science, develop in tandem with science.) He sees his own philosophy of science, in particular, as developing out the 'new scientific spirit' that gave rise to the relativistic and quantum revolutions at the beginning of the twentieth century. For example, Bachelard's notions of epistemological obstacle and epistemological break reflect the self-consciously revolutionary character of twentieth-century physics. Similarly, physicists' derivation of classical laws as limiting cases of the principles of relativity and quantum theory are the model for Bachelard's account of the way later theories contain the truth of earlier ones.

2 Bachelard's philosophy of science: metaphysics

The influence of current science on Bachelard's philosophy of science is particularly evident in his treatment of the reality of scientific entities. He vigorously opposes what he calls 'realism', by which he means the view that the middle-sized objects of ordinary sense experience are the fundamental realities of the world. According to Bachelard, the development of science has amply demonstrated that accounts based on such objects are entirely unequal to the task of explaining the facts of experience and must, therefore, be replaced by the more adequate ontology of theoretical science.

Although Bachelard thinks the explanatory power of science establishes the ontological priority of its theoretical postulations, he also maintains that a proper understanding of contemporary physics excludes metaphysical realism, which would see scientific entities as mind-independent substances. First, the metaphysics underlying the mathematical formalisms of the new physics are of mutually interdependent processes, not autonomous substances. More importantly, Bachelard maintains that the way in which contemporary physics constructs its objects reveals that they cannot be regarded as entirely independent of mental processes. Any particular scientific object (for example, Bohr's atom) is a construction of theoretical reason. Nonetheless, Bachelard does not accept the idealist claim that objects are simply the creations of mind. Any particular act of theoretical construction operates on an object pregiven to it.

Bachelard characterizes his position as an 'applied rationalism' that mediates between the metaphysical poles of realism and idealism. It is a 'rationalism' because it maintains the active role of the mind in the constitution of its objects and the priority of theoretical conceptualization over sense experience. The mind's activity, however, is not an autonomous creation but an application of its concepts to an object already given to it (through, of course, previous conceptualizations). Bachelard further separates himself from classical forms of idealism by giving scientific instruments an essential role in the constitution of scientific objects. Instruments are the material realization of theories, and such realization is necessary for the constitution of a scientific object. The mind constitutes objects only through the material intermediary of technical (instrumental) intervention in the world (see SCIENTIFIC REALISM AND ANTIREALISM §§3–4).

Bachelard's applied rationalism is very nicely illustrated by his account of how a modern scientist would undertake the investigation of the nature of wax suggested by Descartes in his *Second Meditation*. Descartes focuses on a piece of wax in its natural state, fresh from the hive, describes its appearance under various everyday circumstances (warmed by the sun, rolled between the fingers, and the like), and derives the essential nature of wax (as an extended body) from intellectual reflection on these descriptions. A modern scientist, by contrast, systematically transforms the 'natural' wax through experimental procedures that theory tells us will allow the observation of its characteristic features. It is purified, melted and methodically reshaped, X-rayed to obtain diffraction patterns, and so on. Its qualities appear not as simple givens to our intuition but as products of our rational experimental techniques (see EXPERIMENT; OBSERVATION).

Bachelard's philosophy of science obviously relies on a sharp distinction between the scientific and the nonscientific (see DEMARCATION PROBLEM). He sees the history of thought as a long struggle of scientific reason to overcome obstacles posed by nonscientific modes of thought and experience. For Bachelard, the fundamental epistemological break is the one that separates science from the illusions of the senses and the imagination. Bachelard does not, however, deny all positive significance to the nonscientific realm of sense and imagination. He makes room for this realm in a series of studies on the 'poetics' of human thought. Here he introduces the project of a 'psychoanalysis' of reason that would uncover the unconscious significance of primitive images (such as those of earth, air, fire and water). He continues to deny that such images have any role in the objective description of what the world is like, resisting, as he says, 'the ontological temptation of beauty'. But he insists on the irreducible value of the subjective realm of poetic images as a necessary aesthetic complement to scientific knowing.

3 Canguilhem on concepts and theories

Georges Canguilhem succeeded Bachelard as director of the Institut d'Histoire des Sciences et des Techniques. Although he starts from an essentially Bachelardian view of science, the foci of his work are different from Bachelard's: philosophical history rather than historical philosophizing, the biological and medical sciences rather than physics and chemistry. Further, his results suggest a number of important modifications to Bachelard's position.

Canguilhem's most important methodological contribution is his distinction between concepts and theories. In much twentieth-century philosophy of science, concepts are functions of theories, deriving their meaning from the roles they play in theoretical accounts of phenomena (see THEORIES, SCIENTIFIC). Newtonian and Einsteinian mass, for example, are regarded as fundamentally different concepts because they are embedded in fundamentally different physical theories. This subordination of concept to theory derives from the view that the interpretation of phenomena (that is, their subsumption under a given set of concepts) is a matter of explaining them on the basis of a particular theoretical framework. For Canguilhem, by contrast, there is a crucial distinction between the interpretation of phenomena (via concepts) and their theoretical explanation. According to him, a given set of concepts provides the preliminary descriptions of a phenomenon that allow the formulation of questions about how to explain it. Different theories (all, however, formulated in terms of the same set of basic concepts) will provide competing answers to these questions. Galileo, for example, introduced a new conception of the motion of falling bodies to replace the Aristotelian concept. Galileo, Descartes and Newton all employed this new conception in their descriptions of the motion of falling bodies and in the theories they developed to explain this motion. Although the basic concept of motion was the same, the explanatory theories were very different. This shows, according to Canguilhem, the 'theoretical polyvalence' of concepts: their ability to function in the context of widely differing theories. His own historical studies (for example, of reflex movement) are typically histories of concepts that persist through a series of theoretical formulations.

Taken seriously, Canguilhem's emphasis on the history of concepts as opposed to the history of theories requires important modifications to Bachelard's view of science. Epistemological breaks, for example, must be construed as due to conceptual rather than theoretical innovation. Since successful conceptualizations tend to reappear in even quite diverse theories, epistemological breaks are, for Canguilhem, less frequent and, in many cases, less radical than Bachelard had suggested. The priority of concepts also requires us to rethink the notion of an epistemological obstacle. The same piece of scientific work may be an obstacle in terms of the theoretical context in which it is formulated and a creative breakthrough in terms of some of its conceptual content. Thus Black, even though working in the now outdated context of phlogiston theory, introduced the enduring concept of specific heat. The notion of an epistemological obstacle is more ambivalent than Bachelard suggests. Canguilhem makes particularly effective use of this ambivalence in his discussion of vitalism, so often abused as an enemy of progress in biology. Canguilhem admits that vitalistic theories have generally impeded the development of more adequate mechanistic accounts, but he maintains that the concept of vitalism, through its insistence on the uniqueness of biological phenomena, has served as a valuable protection against unfortunate reductionist tendencies of mechanistic theories (see VITALISM).

Canguilhem's refinement of the notions of epistemological breaks and obstacles also suggests a weakening of Bachelard's sharp distinction between science and nonscience. Science is what overcomes epistemological obstacles and effects epistemological breaks. To the extent that the notions of obstacle and break have become ambivalent, so has the notion of science. As a result, Canguilhem is reluctant to say more than that – in a given context – a given idea or approach is 'more scientific' than another (that is, more fully integrated into current experimental

procedures). Further developing this line of thought, Canguilhem (influenced here by his students, Althusser and Foucault) introduced the notion of *scientific ideology* as an intermediary between science and nonscience.

A scientific ideology (Herbert Spencer's philosophy of evolution is a good example) is scientific in the sense that it models itself on a successful scientific theory. It is ideological, however, because it makes claims about the world that go beyond what the science contemporary with it is able to establish; it has, in other words, pretensions that are not scientifically grounded. Such pretensions may very well function as obstacles to the development of science. But Canguilhem also sees a positive role for scientific ideologies: they provide an essential, if not entirely responsible, dimension of intellectual adventure, without which many scientific advances would not occur. Scientific ideologies are a prime example of the ambivalence of epistemological obstacles.

4 Rationality and norms

Like other antifoundational philosophers of science, Bachelard and Canguilhem must pay particular attention to the problem of rationality and objectivity. If there are no Cartesian certainties grounding science, if its development is a contingent historical process, what guarantee do we have that it is a reliable source of truths about the world? The historicist turn in Anglo-American philosophy of science, which is in many ways a later parallel to the French development, encountered these same questions.

Bachelard tried to ground the objectivity of science through social norms. Contrary to Descartes, he holds that objectivity is not found in the individual self's intuitions (which will always remain obstacles to scientific progress) but in a move to considerations that convince not just a given individual but all rational minds. This move, which Bachelard characterizes as from the isolated *cogito* (I think) to the social *cogitamus* (we think), takes us, he maintains, from the subjectivity of the merely psychological to the objectivity of the epistemological.

Canguilhem offers a much more extensive treatment of norms, rooted in his analysis of biological norms. He notes that, whereas modern physics has rejected any distinction between normal and pathological states of its entities, biological systems (organisms) require a distinction between states that enhance their functioning and those that impede it; in other words, a distinction between health and disease. However, Canguilhem maintains, we cannot define health as simply life in accord with the relevant biological norms. In any state, even one that is clearly pathological, there will be norms specifying the proper functioning of the organism in that state. (For example, a person who has lost a kidney is in a pathological state, even though the norms for proper functioning in this state are the same as for someone with both kidneys.) The pathological must, accordingly, be understood rather as a reduction in the range of circumstances in which an organism can function properly. Correspondingly, health is a state in which an organism is not only able to survive in its current circumstances but is capable of surviving in a significant range of varying circumstances.

Canguilhem emphasizes that, according to his account, biological norms are not objective in any scientific sense. Physiology can describe the states that we call 'normal' or 'pathological', but their normative status as such derives not from the physiological description but from the meaning of those states for the organism. Put another way, biological norms are subjective in the sense that they are constituted by the organism itself. On the other hand, this constitution is not a matter of individual idiosyncrasy but corresponds to the essential nature of the organism in question. Biological norms are not objective in the sense of being derived from value-neutral scientific inquiry, but they are rooted in the biological reality of the organisms that they regulate.

Turning to the question of social norms, such as those Bachelard sees as governing scientific practice, Canguilhem notes that there are important ways in which societies are similar to organisms and that social norms can have the same sort of necessary force that biological norms have. The biological analogy works, however, only for so-called 'traditional' societies, where there is a set of norms that defines, once and for all, the essential nature and purpose of the society. Modern societies have no such 'intrinsic finality', since the question of what should be their fundamental direction is contested in principle. A distinguishing feature of a modern society is dissent regarding basic norms. Canguilhem does not conclude, however, that a consensus, no matter how formed, would legitimately establish norms in a modern society. He criticizes, for example, Thomas Kuhn's account of scientific norms because, in his view, it derives them from a contingent, merely psychological, agreement that has no genuine regulative force. Canguilhem makes a similar criticism of Bachelard, who, he suggests, poses but does not solve the problem of finding a middle ground between grounding scientific norms in the illusion of Cartesian foundations and reducing them to the merely descriptive realm of empirical psychology. Unfortunately, Canguilhem himself never provides a solution to this problem and, after all the subtlety of his analysis of norms, they are still left without a philosophical basis.

5 Michel Foucault: the influence of Bachelard and Canguilhem

It would be a serious mistake to read Michel Foucault's work as simply another stage of the historical approach to philosophy of science developed by Bachelard and Canguilhem. Foucault is too original a thinker to be confined to any school, and his work is informed by numerous currents far removed from and even opposed to Bachelard's applied rationalism or Canguilhem's history of concepts. But there was considerable influence on Foucault by both Bachelard and, especially, Canguilhem, who supervised his doctoral thesis on the history of madness. Because of this influence some aspects of Foucault's work must be understood in the context defined by these two predecessors.

Foucault accepted many of the key claims of Bachelard and Canguilhem's philosophy of science. These included the essentially historical character of science and the central role of epistemological breaks or discontinuities. On an even deeper level, Bachelard's notion of epistemological obstacle foreshadows Foucault's project of showing the historical, contingent nature of concepts and practices that present themselves as ahistorical necessities. Just as Bachelard spoke of a psychoanalysis of knowledge, Foucault characterized his own work as an effort to discover the unconscious of our knowledge.

Canguilhem's strongest influence on Foucault is through his history of concepts. Foucault employed this approach both as an alternative to what he saw as the excessive subjectivism ('transcendental narcissism') of phenomenology and as a way of de-emphasizing the role of individual 'great minds' in the history of science. *The Birth of the Clinic* (1963) and *The Order of Things* (1966) are particularly influenced by Canguilhem, offering, respectively, a history of the concept of disease in modern medicine and a history of the concept of man in the modern social sciences. The history of concepts is an essential tool of Foucault's famous archaeology of knowledge.

6 Michel Foucault: beyond Bachelard and Canguilhem

Foucault's major differences with Bachelard and Canguilhem can best be understood through two of his most important epistemological distinctions: that between *savoir* and *connaissance* and that between the threshold of scientificity and the threshold of epistemologization. By *connaissance* Foucault means, in accord with standard French usage, any given domain of knowledge, such as biology, economics or philology. *Savoir* he uses to refer to the underlying epistemic conditions that, in a given period, make various domains of *connaissance* (various scientific disciplines) possible. For example, eighteenth-century knowledge (*connaissance*) of natural history was, according to Foucault, based on a fundamental conception of natural entities as representable through tables of timeless genera and species. In the nineteenth century, he maintains, the new discipline (*connaissance*) of biology was, on the contrary, based on the fundamental concept of the organism as an essentially historical entity (see TAXONOMY §1). Such fundamental concepts belong to what Foucault calls *savoir*. They correspond to the 'unconscious' of knowledge that his archaeological method is designed to excavate.

From Foucault's standpoint, Bachelard and Canguilhem treat science only at the level of *connaissance*. They take as givens the bodies of knowledge produced by scientific disciplines and remain unaware of the epistemic realm of *savoir* that underlies this knowledge. This prevents them from discerning the common ground between apparently diverse sciences (for example, the epistemic structure – in Foucault's terminology, *episteme* – shared by modern biology and economics). It also keeps hidden important connections between scientific and nonscientific forms of knowledge.

Foucault distinguishes (in *The Archaeology of Knowledge*, 1969) four thresholds in the development of a body of knowledge. At one extreme is the threshold of positivity (the initial emergence of an autonomous body of discourse) and at the other the threshold of formalization (formulation in axiomatic terms). Between these two are the thresholds of epistemologization and of scientificity. The threshold of epistemologization is crossed when a body of discourse (what Foucault calls a 'discursive formation') comes to be governed by epistemic norms that provide criteria (logical coherence, support from observed facts) for evaluating knowledge claims. The threshold of scientificity is crossed when these norms are extended to include the specific principles of a scientific methodology. Such principles introduce a kind of rigour and precision far beyond that of ordinary discourse and define the special form taken by scientific objectivity.

Foucault's studies of science, in contrast to those of Bachelard and Canguilhem, deal with *savoir* rather than *connaissance* and operate on disciplines that have passed the threshold of epistemologization but not that of scientificity. The 'epistemological history' of Bachelard and Canguilhem begins with disciplines well-established as scientific and reflects only on the methodological and empirical content of their concepts and theories. As a result, Bachelard and Canguilhem simply accept the norms of current science as given and use them to evaluate the content of earlier science as well as the content of nonscientific discourses (for example, poetry or ideology) insofar as the latter implies a description of the natural world. By focusing on the *savoir* presupposed by scientific concepts and theories and on disciplines, such as psychiatry and the human sciences, that are not fully entrenched as scientific, Foucault is able to study scientific norms as the products of historical processes. Canguilhem (1967), reviewing *Les mots et les choses* (Foucault 1966), wrote that 'there is today no philosophy less normative than that of Foucault'. This is true in the sense that Foucault, unlike his two predecessors, writes the history of scientific (or would-be scientific) disciplines without presupposing the norms of these very disciplines. On the other hand, Foucault's archaeological analysis of science is fundamentally concerned with norms, in the sense of understanding their precise role in the historical development of scientific practices.

What might Foucault's approach contribute to the problem of the objectivity of scientific norms? His contribution is not so much a solution as a transformation of the problem. The issue, he suggests, is not how to provide a philosophical basis for objective norms. There is nothing outside of a given scientific community and its practices that can intelligibly underwrite its objectivity. A widely accepted, successful and enduring scientific enterprise has, of itself, *prima facie* status as a source of objective knowledge. But although scientific claims cannot, and need not, be grounded by philosophical argument, they can be undermined by the special sort of historico-philosophical inquiry that Foucault practised in his historical studies. Specifically, a careful untangling of the structure of the *savoir* underlying a given discipline and a tracing of the historical development of this structure can demonstrate the arbitrariness or contingency of principles that the discipline presents as objectively necessary. Foucault's studies of psychiatry (in *The History of Madness*), of criminology and related disciplines (in *Discipline and Punish*), and of the modern 'sciences' of sexuality (in the first volume of *The History of Sexuality*) are all attempts at such demonstrations.

Foucault's critiques are not intended as rejections of scientific objectivity as such. He is concerned with only specific disciplines and never, for example, subjects physics or chemistry to his critique. Moreover, his critiques never conclude that the discipline under scrutiny entirely lacks objective validity. Even the modern psychiatry that he denounces with such virulence in *The History of Madness* he acknowledges to have a certain validity. This eschewal of global scepticism is just the inverse of his rejection of foundationalism. Doubting everything and justifying everything are both totalizing epistemological enterprises entirely contrary to the spirit of Foucault's work (see FOUNDATIONALISM; OBJECTIVITY).

7 Michel Serres

Michel Serres is even less a disciple of Bachelard and Canguilhem than Foucault. Nonetheless, there are important ways in which his work is a continuation and transformation of theirs. Like Bachelard, Serres emphasizes the dispersed, regional character of scientific work. Each domain is like a Leibnizian monad, with a life and intelligibility of its own. (The comparison to Leibniz is far from superficial. Serres wrote his thesis on the Leibnizian system, and his subsequent work can very fruitfully be read as a twentieth-century reformulation of Leibniz's philosophy.) But, like Foucault, Serres sees also a structural unity that connects independent scientific domains. He explicates this unity in terms of the concept of communication, which he employs as a formalized and secularized version of Leibniz's pre-established harmony (see LEIBNIZ, G.W. §6; UNITY OF SCIENCE). Serres also goes much further than Canguilhem and Foucault in questioning Bachelard's sharp demarcation of science from nonscience. He maintains that domains conventionally regarded as nonscientific, such as art and literature, share the structures of scientific disciplines and must be regarded as their epistemic peers. In this regard, Serres makes some particularly striking claims; for example, that Emile Zola discovered thermodynamics before it was explicitly formulated by physicists.

Serres's own writings are an often disconcerting – but also stimulating – mixture of the philosophical and the artistic. He tries to show the structural identity of Descartes' *Meditations* and La Fontaine's fables, argues that 'Turner translates Carnot', and presents Lucretius' *De Rerum Natura* as a contribution to twentieth-century physical theory. His style correspondingly combines close philosophical analysis with poetic evocation; casual readers may be in doubt as to whether they have picked up a philosophical treatise or a prose poem. Serres would, of course, maintain that such apparent incongruities simply reflect the limitations of conventional intellectual categories and that the pursuit of truth requires violating artificial disciplinary boundaries.

8 Conclusion

The history of French philosophy of science in the twentieth century is a history of the radicalization of Bachelard's insight that science and our philosophical reflection on it are historical phenomena. Bachelard's original formulations try to make this insight consistent with traditional views of the autonomy, progressiveness and normativity of scientific knowledge. Canguilhem, Foucault and Serres in turn raise fundamental questions about the viability of such views in the face of a full acceptance of the historicality of science. The issues emerging from this line of development parallel those familiar to Anglo-American philosophers of science in the years since Thomas Kuhn's *The Structure of Scientific Revolutions*. Like Bachelard, KUHN (writing over twenty-five years later) tried to take seriously the historical nature of science while still maintaining traditional views about its epistemic status. Post-Kuhnian discussions, from Feyerabend through late twentieth-century sociology of science, have raised questions very similar to those posed by Bachelard's successors. Despite formidable obstacles, both rhetorical and conceptual, there is much that each of these traditions could learn from the other.

References and further reading

Bachelard, G. (1934) *Le nouvel esprit scientifique*, Paris: Alcan; trans. A. Goldhammer, *The New Scientific Spirit*, Boston, MA: Beacon Press, 1984. (An important early statement of Bachelard's approach to the philosophy of science.)

—— (1938) *La psychoanalyse du feu*, Paris: Gallimard; trans. A.C.M. Ross, *The Psychoanalysis of Fire*, Boston, MA: Beacon Press, 1964. (A study of the poetic images at the origins of our thought about nature.)

—— (1949) *Le rationalisme appliqué*, Paris: Presses Universitaire de France. (An important late formulation of Bachelard's philosophy of 'applied rationalism'.)

Canguilhem, G. (1966) *Le normale et le pathologique*, Paris: PUF; trans. C. Fawcett, *The Normal and the Pathological*, New York: Zone Books, 1991. (A study of the concept of the normal in biology and medicine; the English translation also includes an important essay on Canguilhem by Michel Foucault.)

* —— (1967) 'Mort de l'homme ou épuisement du cogito?', *Critique* 24: 599–618; trans. C. Porter, 'The Death of Man, or Exhaustion of the Cogito?', in G. Gutting (ed.) *The Cambridge Companion to Foucault*, Cambridge: Cambridge University Press,

1994. (Canguilhem's review of Foucault's *Les mots et les choses* (The Order of Things).)

—— (1983) *Etudes d'histoire et de philosophie des sciences* (Studies in History and Philosophy of Science), Paris: Vrin, 5th edn. (A collection of some of Canguilhem's most important historical and philosophical articles, including his interpretive essays on Bachelard.)

* Foucault, M. (1963) *Naissance de la clinique*, Paris: Presses Universitaires de France; trans. A. Sheridan, *The Birth of the Clinic*, New York: Vintage, 1973. (A history of the concept of illness, written for a series edited by Canguilhem.)

* —— (1966) *Les mots et les choses*, Paris: Gallimard; trans. A. Sheridan, *The Order of Things*, New York: Random House, 1970. (A study of the origins of the fundamental concepts of the modern human sciences, from the Renaissance through the nineteenth century.)

* —— (1969) *L'archéologie du savoir*, Paris: Gallimard; trans. A. Sheridan, *The Archaeology of Knowledge*, New York: Pantheon, 1972. (A systematic reflection on the 'archaeological method' employed in Foucault's previous historical studies.)

Gutting, G. (1989) *Michel Foucault's Archaeology of Scientific Reason*, Cambridge: Cambridge University Press. (A study of Foucault's earlier work, with emphasis on his connections to Bachelard and Canguilhem; chapter one provides an overview of the work of Bachelard and Canguilhem.)

Lecourt, D. (1972) *Pour une critique de l'épistémologie (Bachelard, Canguilhem, Foucault)*, Paris: Maspero; trans. B. Brewster, *Marxism and Epistemology: Bachelard, Canguilhem, and Foucault*, New York: New Left Books, 1975. (A critical discussion from a Marxist viewpoint.)

Saint-Sernin, B. (ed.) (1985) 'Canguilhem', *Revue de la métaphysique et de morale* 90. (A special issue of the journal with essays on various aspects of Canguilhem's work, along with a comprehensive bibliography.)

Serres, M. (1968) *Le système de Leibniz et ses modèles mathématiques* (Leibniz's system and its mathematical models), Paris: Presses Universitaires de France. (Serres's doctoral thesis on Leibniz.)

—— (1969–80) *Hermès I–V*, Paris: Editions de Minuit; trans. J.V. Harari and D.F. Bell, *Hermes: Literature, Science, Philosophy*, Baltimore, MD: Johns Hopkins University Press, 1982. (A series of collections of Serres's essays; the English translation selects some of the more important pieces from the five original volumes.)

Tiles, M. (1984) *Bachelard: Science and Objectivity*, Cambridge: Cambridge University Press. (An analysis of Bachelard's work, emphasizing its relevance to problems of Anglo-American philosophy of science.)

GARY GUTTING

FREUD, SIGMUND (1856–1939)

Freud developed the theory and practice of psychoanalysis, one of the most influential schools of psychology and psychotherapy of the twentieth century. He established a relationship with his patients which maximized information relevant to the interpretation of their behaviour, and this enabled him to find explanations of dreams, symptoms and many other phenomena not previously related to desire. In consequence he was able radically to extend our common-sense psychology of motive.

On Freud's account everyday actions are determined by motives which are far more numerous and complex than people realize, or than common-sense understanding takes into account. The most basic and constant motives which influence our actions are unconscious, that is, difficult to acknowledge or avow. Such motives are residues of encounters with significant persons and situations from the past, often reaching back to early childhood; and they operate not to achieve realistic satisfaction, but rather to secure a form of pacification through representation. When we interpret what others say and do we apply these patterns of satisfaction and pacification to explain their behaviour; and in so far as we succeed in understanding others in this way we support the patterns as empirical generalization. While we recognize that pacification consequent on genuine satisfaction is deeper and more lasting than that effected by representation alone, we also know that human desire outruns opportunities for satisfaction to such an extent that pacification via imagination is common. This is a view which psychoanalysis radically extends.

This understanding of the mind enabled Freud to give psychological accounts of neurosis and psychosis, and to explicate how the past gives significance to the present in normal mental functioning. Past desires, even those of infancy, are not psychologically lost; rather they are continually re-articulated through symbolism, so as to direct action towards their representational pacification throughout life. In this Freud provides both a radically holistic account of the causation of action and a naturalistic description of the generation of meaning in life. New goals acquire significance as representatives of the unremembered objects of our earliest and most visceral passions; and the depth of satisfaction we feel in present accomplishments flows from their unac-

knowledged pacification of unknown desires from the distant past. Thus, paradoxically, significant desires can remain forever flexible, renewable and satisfiable in their expressions, precisely because they are immutable, frustrated and unrelenting at the root.

1 **Early life and research**
2 **Collaboration with Breuer**
3 **Investigation of sexual abuse**
4 **Dreams and wish-fulfilment**
5 **Transference, childhood conflict and sexuality**
6 **Fantasy and primary process**
7 **Psychology and the brain**
8 **Psychic structure and function**
9 **Social psychology**

1 Early life and research

Freud was born in Freiburg, Moravia, the first son of the third wife of a travelling wool merchant. In 1861, the year after Austria abolished legal restrictions on Jews, the family settled in Vienna, where Freud remained until the Nazi occupation. As a student at the Medical School of the University of Vienna he attended lectures by the physiologist Ernst Bruke, which set out the Darwinian and physicalistic approach to nature associated with the school of Helmholtz. Shortly afterwards Freud began research in Bruke's laboratory, and within a year published the first of many articles on the nervous system.

On becoming engaged Freud found that he could not support a family through neurological research. He prepared for medical practice at the General Hospital of Vienna, working also in Meynert's Institute of Cerebral Anatomy. His publications on disorders of the nervous system led to an appointment as Lecturer in Neuropathology, and in 1885 he was awarded funds to study in Paris under Charcot, whose work on hysteria included the use of hypnosis for producing and removing symptoms. Here Freud made his first characteristic psychological observation, noting that the regions of the body liable to hysterical paralysis or anaesthesia did not correspond to real functional demarcations. Hysteria, it seemed, knew nothing of anatomy.

2 Collaboration with Breuer

Freud's psychoanalytic work was based on a discovery by his senior colleague Joseph Breuer. Breuer's patient Anna O, diagnosed as hysterical, was an exceptionally intelligent and articulate woman, who enquired with him into her symptoms in great detail. They found that each symptom had meaningful connections with significant but forgotten events,

related to feelings which she had neither expressed nor mastered. When she recovered these her symptoms were eased. Thus one symptom was an aversion to drinking: despite 'tormenting thirst', she would push away a glass of water 'like someone suffering from hydrophobia' (Freud 1953–74: vol. 2, 34). Under hypnosis she traced this to an episode in which she had remained silent while a companion let a dog, a 'horrid creature', drink water from a glass. After reliving this and expressing her disgust she drank without difficulty. Again, a range of symptoms – hallucinations, paralyses and disturbances of speech – were similarly related to experiences which had distressed her while she nursed her father in his terminal illness; when she went through these with Breuer the symptoms were relieved.

The research of Charcot and others had indicated that hysterical symptoms could be understood in psychological terms, and were sometimes related to emotional trauma. Although Breuer's patient relapsed before finally recovering, his observations suggested two further more specific hypotheses: first, that symptoms expressed memories and feelings associated with significant forgotten events; and second, that symptoms could be relieved by a cathartic therapy, which enabled patients to relive these events, thereby working through feelings connected with them. So Freud followed Breuer's example, and began questioning his patients about their lives and feelings in great detail. In this he abandoned hypnotism, and for a time substituted a technique, derived from Bernheim, of pressing patients to remember significant events. His experience corroborated Breuer's sufficiently for them to publish a series of case reports arguing that 'hysterics suffer mainly from [unconscious] reminiscences' (Freud 1953–74: vol. 2, 7).

3 Investigation of sexual abuse

As his research progressed, Freud found that an important range of the memories connected with symptoms were sexual, and went back in time. Under the pressure of his technique, indeed, a number of his patients recovered apparent memories of sexual abuse from early childhood. As he pressed further, in a series of female patients, the role of abuser was consistently assigned to the father. (This experience has been repeated by a number of therapists in the USA.) In considering these scenes of seduction, however, Freud finally concluded that while parental abuse could be a factor in causing neurosis, it was not as widespread as suggested by the readiness of patients to recollect it. For, as he noted, there seemed to be 'no indications of reality in the unconscious', so that 'one cannot distinguish between truth and [emotionally charged] fiction', where this could include 'sexual fantasy [which] seizes on the theme of the parents' (Freud 1953–74: vol. 1, 260; also see Masson 1985: 265). Hence, it seemed, the primary cause of symptoms might be found in activity of the imagination.

These events also led Freud to change his therapeutic technique. It had became apparent both that he had to guard against effects of suggestion, and also that the most relevant and reliable material tended to emerge not when patients were pressed for memories, but rather when they expressed their thoughts and feelings spontaneously. So he began asking his patients simply to communicate each idea or thought which occurred to them as fully as possible, and without regard to whether it seemed significant, sensible or morally acceptable. This kind of immediate and unconstrained self-description, which Freud called free association, led both to the topics previously found important by questioning, and to others not yet investigated. Since this procedure maximized the data relevant to understanding his patients, Freud made it the fundamental rule of psychoanalytic treatment (see UNCONSCIOUS MENTAL STATES).

4   Dreams and wish-fulfilment

During this period Freud observed that dreams, like symptoms, could be understood as related to memories and motives which emerged in free association. In investigating dreams, moreover, he could make use of his own case. He thus began his self-analysis, applying to himself the interpretive techniques which he applied to his patients. As this progressed, Freud saw that his and Breuer's findings about symptoms were better understood on the model that he was developing for dreams. In consequence he was able to frame an account of both dreams and symptoms which was relatively simple and unified, and which he published in *The Interpretation of Dreams* (1900). Further, as he soon saw, this account could be extended to other products of the mind, including slips and errors, jokes and works of art.

Freud's discussion of dreams thus constituted a paradigm by which he consolidated his first phase of psychoanalytic research. We can see some main features of this by considering the first dream he analysed, his own dream of Irma's injection. In this dream Freud met Irma, a family friend whose pains he had diagnosed as hysterical and treated by analysis. He told her that if she still felt pains, this was her own fault, for not accepting his 'solution' to her problems. He became alarmed, however, that he had failed to diagnose an organic cause of her suffering, and this

turned out to be so. A senior colleague, M, examined Irma, and found that she was organically ill. The cause of her illness also became manifest: another of Freud's colleagues, his family doctor Otto, had given her a toxic injection. As the dream ended Freud censured Otto firmly, saying, 'Injections of that kind ought not to be made so thoughtlessly' and 'probably the syringe had not been clean'.

On the surface this dream dealt with topics which were unpleasant to Freud, such as the continued suffering of a friend and patient, and the possibility that he had misdiagnosed an organic illness, which he described as 'a constant anxiety' to a doctor offering psychological therapy. Freud's associations, however, made clear that the dream represented these things in a way which was actually in accord with various of his desires or wishes. For Freud remembered that on the day before the dream he had discussed Irma with Otto, who had recently visited Irma's family. Otto had been called away to give an injection while at Irma's, and had told Freud that Irma was looking 'better, but not yet well'. Freud imagined that he detected a professional reproof in this remark, considered it thoughtless, and felt vaguely annoyed. That night, in order to justify his treatment of Irma, he had started to write up her case to show to M, who was respected by both himself and Otto, and who appeared in the dream as diagnosing Irma's illness and realizing that it was Otto's fault. (Also, as it happened, Freud had just had news indicating that another of his female patients had been given a careless injection by some other doctor, and had been contemplating how safe his own practice with injections was.)

In considering this dream Freud noted that his desire to justify himself in respect of Irma's case – and in particular not to be responsible for her continued suffering – was apparent from the beginning, in which he told Irma that her pains were now her own fault. Also, he felt that his alarm at her illness in the dream was not entirely genuine. So, as he realized, it seemed that the dream-situation, in which Irma was organically ill, actually served to fulfil a wish on his account: for as he undertook to treat only psychological complaints, this would mean that despite what he had taken Otto thoughtlessly to imply, he and his mode of treatment could not be held responsible for Irma's continued illness. This theme, moreover, seemed carried further in the rest of the dream, in which M found that Otto, not Freud, bore responsibility for Irma's suffering. It thus emerged that the dream could be seen as a deeply wishful response to Otto's remark. For as the dream represented matters, Freud bore no responsibility whatever for Irma's condition. Rather, Otto was the sole cause of her suffering; and this was the result of Otto's thoughtless practice with injections, a matter about which Freud himself, as he had been considering, was particularly conscientious and careful. The dream thus repaid what Freud felt to be Otto's professional reproof with a charge of serious malpractice on Otto's part. So Freud concluded that the dream was a wish-fulfilment, that is, that it was caused by certain of his desires (or irresponsible wishes derived from these desires) and expressed these by representing them as fulfilled.

We can bring out the nature of Freud's proposal here by contrasting the way his desire to be clear of responsibility for Irma's suffering operated in his dream as opposed to his intentional action. Schematically, the role of a desire that P in intentional action is to bring about (cause) a situation that P, which both satisfies the desire and pacifies it, that is, causes the desire to cease to operate. Action on a desire that P (that one be cleared of responsibility) should ideally satisfy the desire, that is, should bring it about that P (that one is cleared of responsibility). This, in turn, should cause one to experience and believe that P (that one has been cleared of responsibility); and this, perhaps acting together with the satisfying situation, should pacify the desire that P, so that it ceases to govern action. This is roughly the sequence of results which Freud was seeking to produce, in accord with standard medical practice, in writing up Irma's case history on the night of the dream to discuss with M, his respected senior colleague. M would be able to offer an independent and authoritative opinion on Freud's treatment of Irma; so his judgment could partly serve to put Freud, and his mode of therapy, in the clear.

In Freud's dream the same motive was apparently also at work, but in a quite different way. There it produced no rational action, but rather gave rise to a (dreamt) representation of a situation in which Freud was cleared of responsibility, and by M. This representation, moreover, was extravagantly wishful – Irma was made physically ill, Freud was cleared in a great number of ways, Otto was elaborately blamed, and so on. So we can contrast the causal role of desire, as between intentional action and what Freud called wish-fulfilment, as follows. In intentional action a desire that P serves to bring about a situation that P, and this a (justified and true) belief that P, so that the desire is pacified. In Freudian wish-fulfilment, by contrast, the desire that P causes a wishful representation that P which, although perhaps exaggerated and unrealistic, is experience- or belief-*like*, so that it serves to pacify the desire directly, at least temporarily. So in rational action we find both the real satisfaction and also the pacification of desire, with the latter a rational and causal consequence of

the former; whereas in wish-fulfilment we find only imaginary satisfaction, and the pacification which is consequent on this.

It seems intelligible that the mind (or brain) should operate in accord with both these patterns, for in both desire is ultimately pacified by the representation of satisfaction. On reflection, indeed, the latter pattern seems almost as familiar as the former. We are aware that our response to a desire or lack is often simply to imagine it satisfied; and this process seems clearly to have other forms. Children, for example, often pacify desires which arise from their being small and immature by representing themselves as various sorts of admired or impressive figures in play. Also it seems clear that many books, films, video games and so on enable people to imagine gratifying desires which they could not (and often would not) otherwise satisfy. In such cases we speak of make-believe, suspension of disbelief and virtual reality, thereby indicating the way the kind of representation involved is comparable to experience or belief in serving to pacify desire (see ACTION; DESIRE).

5 Transference, childhood conflict and sexuality

Freud found that the motives expressed in dreams and symptoms could be retraced to the past. Also, he noted that in the course of analysis his patients were liable to experience towards himself versions of motives and feelings which they had felt towards earlier objects of love and hate, in particular their parents. Freud called this phenomenon 'transference'. Thus a main symptom of his patient the Rat Man was involuntarily to imagine his father being punished, by being eaten into from behind by hungry rats. This caused him anxiety and depression, from which he protected himself by the rituals of an obsessional neurosis. He insisted that this symptom did not show hostility towards his father, with whom he had been the best of friends. He could not remember his father having punished him; but as the treatment progressed, he developed a fear that Freud would punish him – would beat him and throw him out because of the dreadful things he said in his free associations.

In discussing these matters with Freud the patient went down to the end of the room, saying that he did so from delicacy of feeling for Freud, to whom he was saying such dreadful things. Freud interpreted, however, that he had moved away because, as he had previously been saying, he was afraid that Freud would beat him. To this he responded like 'a man in desperation and one who was trying to save himself from blows of desperate violence; he buried his head in his hands, rushed away, covered his face with his arms, etc.' (Freud 1953–74: vol. 10, 284). He was reliving an episode from his childhood, in which, while lying between his parents in bed, he had urinated, and his father had beaten him and thrown him out. He thus recovered a buried image of his father as a terrifying, punishing figure in relation to whom he felt helpless and hostile. This in turn made it possible to understand his involuntary imaginings, in which his father suffered such cruel punishments, as wish-fulfilments fitting the same pattern as Freud's dream above. Just as Freud's dream could be seen as a wishful and extravagant reversal of the feelings of responsibility prompted by Otto's remark, so this patient's symptom of imagining his father cruelly punished could be seen as a wishful and extravagant reversal of his own feelings as a punished child. But these childhood feelings were re-experienced towards Freud in the transference before being consciously remembered as relating to his father.

The childhood motives revealed by analysis characteristically included sensual love for one parent combined with rivalry and jealous hatred for the other, a constellation Freud called the 'Oedipus complex'. It now appeared that little children were liable to intense psychical conflict, as between desires to harm or displace each parent, envied and hated as a rival for the love of the other, and desires to preserve and protect that same parent, loved sensually and also as a caretaker, helper and model. Further, children apparently attached great emotional significance to their interactions with their parents in such basics of disciplined and cooperative activity as feeding and the expulsion and management of waste. These activities also involved the first use, and hence the first stimulation, of bodily organs or zones – particularly the mouth, genitals and anus – which would later figure in the emotionally significant activities of normal and abnormal sexuality. Analysis indicated that the feelings related to the early uses of these organs had significant continuity with those aroused by their later uses; and on this basis Freud framed an account which systematically linked normal and abnormal sexual phenomena in the development of the individual.

In normal development, weaker and less acceptable childhood feelings were subjected to a process of repression, which removed them from conscious thinking and planning, so that they could achieve pacification only indirectly. Apart from causing dreams or symptoms, such motives could undergo a process of sublimation, whereby they provided symbolic significance for everyday activities, and could thus be pacified in the course of them. This achievement can be illustrated by a relatively successful teacher and writer, who had been surprised when one of his pupils – who had made a special effort to be taught by him, and was trying hard to master his ideas – had unexpectedly offered to suck his penis. He had not accepted this offer, but that night dreamed that a lamb had come to suck milk from his finger. On waking he realized that the lamb represented the pupil who had come to imbibe his ideas, and his milk-giving finger the penis his pupil had wanted to suck. So the dream could be seen as representing the fulfilment, in a more acceptable and symbolic form, of a sexual wish which had arisen on the day before.

The symbolism, however, went deeper, for the dreamer also represented himself as a mother nursing a child. In this he represented his finger/penis in the role of a feeding breast, and his writing and teaching as the production of milk as well as semen. He thus represented himself as enjoying a combination of feminine nurture and masculine potency which was impossible in real life, and his desires for which had been repressed in early childhood. Still, these same desires could to some degree be pacified in his adult work, owing to the symbolic significance which he attached to it. In writing or teaching he could with some justice see himself – to use more familiar metaphors – as potent and seminal, and at the same time as giving others food for thought.

6 Fantasy and primary process

Psychoanalysts now commonly describe the kind of imaginative representational activity which serves to pacify unconscious desire as fantasy. Fantasies can be shown not only in dreams or symptoms, but any form of activity which has representational significance; and fantasies characteristically realize the psychological mechanisms and processes described in psychoanalytic theory. Thus the fantasy of Freud's patient above – that Freud was about to give him a beating – simultaneously implemented his transference onto Freud of emotions originally felt towards his father; the repression of his memory of an episode in which his father had punished and terrified him; and the projection into Freud of his own desire to punish, which was apparently related to the episode with his father, and otherwise expressed in his symptom of imagining his father punished. Again, persons form permanent life-shaping fantasies of themselves on the model of others, thereby establishing identifications with those persons, which process Freud took to be central to the constitution of the self.

Freud held that the pattern of wish-fulfilling representation, in which a desire that P produces a pacifying (and perhaps symbolic) representation that P, marks a primary process in the pacification of desire, whereas the pattern of intentional action, in which a desire that P gives rise to a real action or situation that P, marks a secondary process, to be seen both as developing from the first and occurring in the context of it. We can understand this as the claim that present action characteristically stands in a representational and pacificatory relation to desires from the past. Thus Freud's patient above consciously desired to go to the end of the room partly in response to his unconscious fantasy that Freud, representing his father, was about to beat him; and the author who dreamed of a sucking lamb consciously desired to teach and write partly because these activities unconsciously realized fantasies of taking the role of a feeding mother. That is to say, a person acting in the present may thereby be representing himself as satisfying, and so may thereby now actually be pacifying, desires which have remained unsatisfied from early childhood.

7 Psychology and the brain

Freud's initial research was on the nervous system, and in his *Project for a Scientific Psychology* (1895) he sketched a version of physicalism – an account of psychological processes as neural processes – which could accommodate his psychological findings. He took the brain to operate by transferring excitation through networks of neurons, so that information was stored in the form of facilitations or inhibitions of the interneural links. Hence, as he put it, 'psychic acquisition generally', including memory, would be 'represented by the differences in the facilitations' of neural connections (Freud 1953–74: vol. 1, 300). In this he anticipated the contemporary conception of the brain as a computational device whose knowledge is 'in the connections' among neuronal processing units, and also the associated view of mental processes as forms of neural activation, and mental states as dispositions to these, or structures determining them (see Glymour 1992; CONNECTIONISM).

In Freud's model the signalling of a bodily need – say, for nutrition in an infant – causes a disequilibrium in neural excitation. This at first results in crying and uncoordinated bodily movements, which have at best a fleeting tendency to stabilize it. Better and more lasting equilibration requires satisfaction, for instance, by feeding; and this causes the facilitation of the neural connections involved in the satisfying events. The brain thus constantly lays down neural records, or prototypes, of the sequences of perceptions, internal changes, bodily movements and so on, involved in the restoration of equilibrium by satisfaction. Then when disequilibrium again occurs – such as when the infant is again hungry – the input signals engage previously facilitated pathways, so that the records of the best past attempts at coping with

comparable situations are naturally reactivated. This, Freud hypothesized, constitutes early wish-fulfilment.

Freud thus identified the wish-fulfilling pacification of infantile proto-desire with a form of neural prototype activation (see Churchland 1995). He took it that this served to stabilize and organize the infant's responses to need, by reproducing those previously associated with satisfaction. Then, as the infant continued to lay down prototype upon prototype, the original wishful stabilizations evolved towards a system of thought, while also coming to govern a growing range of behaviour, increasingly coordinated to the securing of satisfaction. This, however, required the brain to learn to delay the activation of prototypes of past satisfactions until present circumstances were perceptually appropriate – that is, to come into accord with what Freud called the reality principle. This in turn depended upon a tolerance of frustration, and the absence of a satisfying object, which permitted reality-testing, and hence the binding of the neural connections involved in the securing of satisfaction to perceptual information about the object, and later to rational thought. This benign development could, however, be blighted, if frustration (or intolerance of it) led to the overactivation of inappropriate prototypes, and this to greater frustration. Such a process could render the mind or brain increasingly vulnerable to disequilibrium and delusion, and hence increasingly reliant on wish-fulfilling modes of stabilization, in a vicious circle constitutive of mental illness.

8 Psychic structure and function

Freud allocated the task of fostering the sense of reality to a hypothetical neural structure, or functional part of the mind, which he called 'das Ich', or the *ego*. (The literal meaning of Freud's phrase is 'the I'; but the Latin pronoun used in the English translation has now acquired a life of its own.) In his final conceptualizations he linked this structure with two others, the 'super-ego', which judged or criticized the ego, and which included the ego-ideal, representing the ideals or standards by which the ego was judged; and the primitive 'it', or *id*, the natural matrix of basic and potentially conflicting instincts or drives – that is, structures which would yield basic emotions and motives for action – out of which these others developed. His late discussions of these notions are particularly difficult, partly because they combine differing modes of explanation.

Overall the ego, super-ego and id are neural systems described in a functional way, that is, in terms of the goals which their operation secures and the information upon which they operate. This kind of explanation has been refined in contemporary cognitive science, in which distinct functional units are often represented by boxes, in a flow chart which describes the contribution of each boxed unit to psychological functioning overall. In his later work Freud sought to combine this mode of explanation with the empirical claim that the main functional systems of the human mind are partly constituted by the mind's internalized representations of significant persons in the environment, particularly the parents. Hence the working of these systems is partly felt, and can partly be described, via the motives, feelings or actions of the imagos of persons which they embody (see FUNCTIONALISM).

Freud took the drives constituting the id as divisible into two main categories: those which engender motives which are creative and constructive, such as affection, love and care, which he called the life instincts; and those which yield motives linked to aggression, such as envy and hate, which he called the destructive or death instincts. The sexual drives (or motives), together with those aimed at self-preservation, were among the life instincts generally; but owing to their great plasticity they were liable to be mixed with aggression, as in the case of sadism, masochism, devaluation of the object of love, and so on. His final view was thus that the primary conflicts in a person's life – those which necessitated repression and could become constitutive of mental illness – might involve sexuality, but were ultimately to be seen as holding between impulses to create or destroy.

On Freud's account the ego and super-ego develop out of the id, mainly through the child's formative identifications with others, particularly the parents. The child ordinarily begins to advance towards self-control by laying down prototypical images of the parents, in their role as regulators of socially significant primitive bodily activities, particularly, as noted, those involved in feeding and the elimination of waste. These 'earliest parental imagos' (Freud 1953: vol. 22, 54) provide the basis of the super-ego. This self-critical faculty embodies the child's aggression in a projected form, and so tends to be far more punitive than the actual parents. Hence it can be a source of great anxiety or guilt, or even, in the extreme, of suicide. (Compare the material in §5 above, which might also be described as involving projection of the patient's punitive super-ego.)

The child further constitutes its ego by identifying with the parents as agents, that is, as desirers and satisfiers of desire. A main step in normal development is identification with the parent of the same sex, which has the consequence that sexual (and other) desires are rendered non-incestuous, heterosexual and reproductive. For this to occur, however, the child must renounce the goal of replacing the envied parent with that of becoming like him or her. Hence the final establishment of the ego and super-ego coincides with what Freud called the dissolution of the Oedipus complex.

9 Social psychology

Freud held that the cohesiveness of many groups results from their members identifying with one another by putting a common idealized figure (or cause or creed) in the place of the ego-ideal. Groups may likewise be identified by the projection of their bad aspects – and in particular their own hostile and destructive motives – into some common locus, which thereby becomes a focus of collective and legitimated hate. This may be a particular figure, such as the devil, or another family, race or nation, the leaders of which may also be denigrated or demonized.

People who identify themselves with the same idealized object, or who represent a common object as hateful, can thereby feel purified, unified and justified in cooperating in destructive activities validated by common ideals. Identification by the projection of good or bad aspects into a common locus thus serves systematically to organize persons into groups which represent themselves as unrealistically good and others as unrealistically bad; and this in turn allows aggressive and destructive motives to be entertained and satisfied with a minimum of indirectness and guilt. This pattern of good us/bad them is shared by most participants in the great variety of human conflicts which it encourages. Where groups are organized on this basis their rational disagreements tend to be underpinned and exaggerated by suspicions and hatreds which can be seen to be irrational, but which remain none the less intractable, in so far as they are integral to group cohesion.

See also: JUNG, C.G.; NIETZSCHE, F.; PSYCHOANALYSIS, METHODOLOGICAL ISSUES IN; PSYCHOANALYSIS, POST-FREUDIAN

List of works

Freud, S. (1953–74) *The Standard Edition of the Complete Psychological Works of Sigmund Freud*, trans. and ed. J. Strachey *et al.*, London: Hogarth Press, 24 vols. (The standard English edition of Freud's works.)

—— (1979) *The Pelican Freud Library*, Harmondsworth & New York: Penguin. (A slightly abridged version, this omits Freud's original case notes on the Rat Man, from which the description of treatment in section 5 is taken.)

—— (1895) *Project for a Scientific Psychology*, in Freud 1953–74: vol. 1, 283–. (Freud's physiological hypotheses about the mind, sketched but not published while he was formulating his account of dreams. He took mental processes to be realized by the passing of excitation through networks of neurons, which also altered neural connections so as to store information for later use. The mind/brain thus naturally laid down neural records of its activities relating to the satisfaction of desire, and these prototypes were automatically reactivated so as to guide action, and receive further modification, in comparable situations later. Freud expressed a number of his basic ideas in these terms, and his later discussions are consistent with them.)

—— (1900) *The Interpretation of Dreams*, in Freud 1953–74, vols 4–5. (Freud's account of dreams and symptoms as wish-fulfilments, that is, as serving to pacify desires by representing them as satisfied. Freud later applied this paradigm to other kinds of representation, and extended it to everyday intentional action through his account of the sublimation of infantile sexual and aggressive desires. These hypotheses explain present desires by mapping them to objects and situations desired in the past, and hence in accord with the role assigned past neural prototypes in the Project.)

References and further reading

Cavell, M. (1993) *The Psychoanalytic Mind*, Cambridge, MA: Harvard University Press. (Relates Freud's work to Donald Davidson's philosophy of mind.)

* Churchland, P. (1995) *The Engine of Reason, The Seat of the Soul*, Cambridge, MA, and London: MIT Press. (Enthusiastic account of the connectionist understanding of the brain foreshadowed by Freud's *Project* of 1896; does not mention Freud, hence usefully consulted together with Gill and Pribram 1976, and Glymour 1992.)

Clark, P. and Wright, C. (eds) (1988) *Mind, Psychoanalysis and Science*, Oxford: Blackwell. (Essays by philosophers and psychologists, including summary and discussion of Grunbaum 1984.)

Erwin, E. (1996) *A Final Accounting: Philosophical and Empirical Issues in Freudian Psychology*, Cambridge, MA, and London: MIT Press. (Critique which follows Grunbaum in arguing against the role assigned to clinical data in supporting psychoanalytic theory.)

Gardner, S. (1993) *Irrationality and the Philosophy of Psychoanalysis*, Cambridge: Cambridge University Press. (Discusses psychoanalysis and the explanation of irrationality.)

Gay, P. (1988) *Freud, A Life for Our Time*, London and Melbourne: J.M. Dent. (Biography which contains accounts of Freud's main ideas and a comprehensive Bibliographical Essay.)

Gill, M. and Pribram, K. (1976) *Freud's 'Project' Reassessed*, London: Hutchinson. (Early appreciation of the contemporary relevance of Freud's understanding of the brain.)

* Glymour, C. (1992) 'Freud's Androids', in J. Neu (ed.) *The Cambridge Companion to Freud*, Cambridge: Cambridge University Press. (Sketches relation of Freud to recent work in computational cognitive science.)

Grunbaum, A. (1984) *The Foundations of Psychoanalysis: A Philosophical Critique*, University of California Press. (Most influential of recent empiricist critiques of Freud's work, arguing against the role assigned by Freud and his successors to clinical data in support of psychoanalytic theory. Summarized and discussed, with criticisms, in Clark and Wright 1988; carried forward in Erwin 1996.)

—— (1993) *Validation in the Clinical Theory of Psychoanalysis*, Madison, CT: International Universities Press. (Further discussions of themes raised in Grunbaum 1984.)

Hopkins, J. and Savile, A. (eds) (1992) *Psychoanalysis, Mind, and Art: Perspectives on Richard Wollheim*, Oxford: Blackwell. (Includes philosophical essays explicating and making use of psychoanalytic concepts.)

Kitcher, P. (1992) *Freud's Dream: A Complete Interdisciplinary Science of Mind*, Cambridge, MA, and London: MIT Press. (Discusses Freud's systematic psychology in comparison to contemporary cognitive science.)

Kline, P. (1984) *Psychology and Freudian Theory: An Introduction*, London: Methuen. (Clear introduction to the literature on empirical testing of Freudian concepts and theories.)

Laplanche, J. and Pontalis, J.B. (1973) *The Language of Psychoanalysis*, London: Hogarth Press. (Basic explanations of psychoanalytic concepts.)

Lear, J. (1990) *Love and Its Place in Nature*, New York: Farrar, Strauss & Giroux. (Philosophical discussion centred on the concept of love in psychoanalysis.)

* Masson, J. (ed.) (1985) *The Complete Letters of Sigmund Freud to Wilhelm Fliess 1887–1904*, Boston, MA: Harvard University Press. (Personal letters in which Freud describes his developing ideas, including his self-analysis.)

MacDonald, C. and MacDonald, G. (eds) (1995) *Philosophy of Psychology: Debates on Psychological Explanation*, Oxford: Blackwell. (Discussions of psychoanalysis in the context of other debates in the philosophy of psychology.)

Neu, J. (ed.) (1992) *The Cambridge Companion to Freud*, Cambridge: Cambridge University Press. (Philosophical essays on Freud and psychoanalysis.)

Wollheim, R. (1984) *The Thread of Life*, Cambridge, MA: Harvard University Press. (Philosophical and psychoanalytic approach to the concept of the life of a person.)

—— (1991) *Freud*, London: Fontana, 2nd edn. (Lucid and philosophically informed account of Freud's work).

—— (1993) *The Mind and Its Depths*, Cambridge, MA: Harvard University Press. (Psychoanalytically informed philosophical essays on the mind.)

Wollheim, R. and Hopkins, J. (1982) *Philosophical Essays on Freud*, Cambridge: Cambridge University Press. (Essays discussing psychoanalytic concepts and modes of explanation.)

JAMES HOPKINS

FRIENDSHIP

Philosophical interest in friendship has revived after a long eclipse. This is due largely to a renewed interest in ancient moral philosophy, in the role of emotion in morality, and in the ethical dimensions of personal relations in general. Questions about friendship are concerned with issues such as whether it is only an instrumental value (a means to other values), or also an intrinsic value – a value in its own right; whether it is a mark of psychological and moral self-sufficiency, or rather of deficiency; and how friendship-love differs from the unconditional love of agape. *Other issues at stake include how – if at all – friendship is related to justice; whether the particularist, partialist perspective of friendship can be reconciled with the universalist, impartialist perspective of morality; and whether friendship is morally neutral.*

1 Ancient philosophy
2 Medieval Christian philosophy
3 Modern philosophy
4 Twentieth-century philosophy

1 Ancient philosophy

Ancient moral philosophy devoted considerable attention to understanding friendship (*philia*) and passionate love (*eros*) (see LOVE §§2–3). In its widest sense, *philia* covers both amicable relations among casual acquaintances, and intimate, loving relationships within and beyond the family. Plato's *Lysis* is the first serious philosophical treatment of friendship, and sets the stage for subsequent treatments. The dialogue is largely inconclusive, but some of the claims made in it re-emerge in Plato's later dialogues: we love people, like other objects of love, because of some lack in ourselves, and we love them only in so far as they are useful in pursuing our final end or *eudaimonia*, achieved with knowledge of Goodness (see PLATO; EUDAIMONIA). Thus, the notion of friendship as an enduring and reciprocal love between equals, and as a mark of self-sufficiency rather than deficiency, remains absent from Plato's account.

These lacunae are made good in Aristotle's writings. A flourishing (*eudaimōn*) human life, a life that is complete and self-sufficient (lacking in nothing), includes friendship – reciprocal affection and goodwill – because human flourishing is relational. People can be loved for their pleasure- or utility-value, or for their good character; accordingly, there are pleasure-friendships, utility-friendships and character-friendships. Character-friendships include pleasure and utility, because good character is both pleasurable and useful. Here friends love (*philein*) each other for who they are, their character, and 'not coincidentally' (*Nicomachean Ethics* 1156b11–12); hence, they wish each other 'to be' and to flourish for their own sakes (1166a3–20). Character-friendship requires virtuous activity, and a choice (*prohairesis*) of 'another self' (1170b6–7). Such a choice presupposes genuine self-love, which only virtuous people possess; hence, only they can choose another self. Moreover, virtue is best exercised in pleasurable and beneficial activities with and towards friends, so it is virtuous people who most *want* friends.

A much-discussed problem in Aristotle's account is that he first makes non-instrumental concern – goodwill – a distinguishing feature of *all* friendships (1155b29–1156a5), but subsequently restricts it to character-friendships (1156b10–11, 1167a11–14). He does not attempt to reconcile these claims; nor does he explain *why* we cannot have goodwill towards utility- or pleasure-friends, given his belief that we *can* towards strangers. So perhaps we should take Aristotle to mean simply that active and *enduring* goodwill is found only in character-friendships.

Aristotle also discusses friendship in the wider sense of relations of mutual goodwill and justice among people, including strangers. The general claim is that friendship, justice and community are coextensive, and so all humans capable of community, including slaves, have a sort of friendship with each other (1159b25–30, 1161b6). This belies the widespread view that Aristotle's ethics is parochial. Also noteworthy is Aristotle's insistence that the claims of justice increase with the closeness of the friendship, a claim that runs contrary to many contemporary depictions of friendship as being 'beyond justice' (see ARISTOTLE §25).

The Aristotelian idea that noninstrumental concern is essential to friendship is central to Hellenistic accounts of friendship, though sometimes uneasily so. Thus, Epicurus recognizes friendship as an intrinsic good which necessarily involves loving our friends as we love ourselves, yet insists that every act of friendship must aim at our *eudaimonia* (see Mitsis 1988). But this insistence, conjoined with his conception of *eudaimonia* as a static end-state of unhindered pleasure (*ataraxia*, tranquillity), rather than as pleasurable activity, makes friendship simply instrumental to *eudaimonia*, and so not an intrinsic good. Another problem arises from Epicurus' conception of *eudaimonia* as invulnerable and up to us (*par' hemas*). *Eudaimonia* is achieved through a rational control of the strength and range of one's desires, a control that makes it relatively immune to chance. But what if the desire that one's friend live and flourish is frustrated? Epicurus must either insist that we can and should eliminate such desires in the interests of *eudaimonia*, thereby rendering his conception of friendship rather shallow, or acknowledge that *eudaimonia* is not entirely *par' hemas* or invulnerable (see EPICUREANISM §11).

Laelius, De amicitia (Laelius: On Friendship) by Cicero (106–43 BC) was largely responsible for transmitting Aristotle's conception of friendship to Christian philosophers, notably St Augustine (354–430) and Aelred of Rievaulx (1109–66), exemplifying his aim of using rhetoric to disseminate philosophical ideas (see CICERO §§4–5). Building on Aristotle's account, Cicero stressed the internal component of self-sufficiency – a sense of security and self-confidence – as a necessary condition of friendship, and made explicit the centrality of mutual respect in perfect friendship, a factor only implicit in Aristotle. In addition, he emphasized rationality by the admonition to base friendship on careful observation and occasional testing of a person's character, and continual self-scrutiny.

2 Medieval Christian philosophy

Friendship raises new questions and problems in the context of the Christian conception of perfect love, *agape* or charity (see CHARITY; LOVE §2). For *agape* is universal and unconditional, directed at saint and sinner alike, whereas friendship is preferential and conditional on the friend's goodness (see UNIVERSALISM IN ETHICS). Does not the exclusiveness of

friendship, then, contradict the inclusiveness of *agape*? Augustine's answer is 'no', so long as we recognize that friendship is a gift of divine *agape*, and use it – like all earthly loves – as a means to perfect love for God, the only love to be enjoyed for its own sake. To love persons as ends is to seek infinite satisfaction in them, and this is idolatory, a violation of the commandment of total devotion to God. As in Plato, so in Augustine, personal love ultimately seeks, and finds satisfaction in, a good that transcends any earthly good (see AUGUSTINE §12).

Not all Christian philosophers, however, see personal love as a mere means to a divine end. Like Augustine, Aelred believed that only Christians can have true ('spiritual') friendship, because true friendship requires agreement on both human and divine affairs and a mutual wish for both temporal and eternal happiness. However, Aelred agreed with Cicero that friendship is its own 'fruition and reward' (*De spiritali amicitia* 1:45). For spiritual friendship combines the joys of intimate, trusting, mutual openness with justice, prudence, fortitude, and temperance, which are forms of charity. And, since God is charity, 'he that abides in friendship, abides in God, and God in him' (1:70).

Likewise, the Aristotelian Aquinas (c.1224–74) saw the true friend as one who is loved 'simply and for itself', not 'from any extrinsic cause' (*Summa theologiae* IaIIae.26.4, IaIIae.28.2). So exalted is friendship in Aquinas' eyes, that it even serves as a model for charity-love of God. Thus, charity involves communication with God the friend, a communication that enables us to achieve our 'ultimate end' of becoming more like God (*Summa contra gentiles* III.1.3, c.19). What remains unexplained is how friendship can have value for God, given that his perfect self-sufficiency renders external goods superfluous (see AQUINAS §13).

3 Modern philosophy

Medieval Christian thinkers see *agape* as predicated on the good or God in everyone, even the sinner, and friendship as predicated on the friend's good character. Martin LUTHER, however, regarded all conditional-on-goodness love as instrumental, and reinterpreted *agape* as a spontaneous, gratuitous love, unmotivated by goodness. This turn had a profound influence on later philosophers, both secular and Christian, notably, Immanuel Kant (1785, 1797) and Søren Kierkegaard (1847).

In Kant's discussion, the Lutheran influence was curiously intermingled with the influence of ancient accounts. Like Aristotle, Kant distinguished friendships based on a shared moral attitude – perfect friendships – from lesser sorts and, like Cicero, he emphasized equality and mutuality of love and respect in perfect friendship. Contrary to Aristotle, however, Kant denied emotions any intrinsic moral worth: emotions are subject to natural laws, whereas morality requires freedom or autonomy (self-governance) (see KANT, I. §9). Hence, intrinsic moral worth accrues only to respect and 'practical' love (*agape*'s secular analogue), which can be willed, and their object, the friend's 'humanity' – the purely rational capacity for moral self-legislation that makes rational beings ends in themselves. Emotional love, and its object, the friend's good character, have, at best, instrumental moral worth. Furthermore, Kant regarded the desire for our friends' happiness as a mere means to our own. Hence, emotional love is inevitably instrumental self-love. Finally, the view that emotions are involuntary implies that it is *morally* inconsequential whether we love virtuous or vicious people. These counter-intuitive consequences raise the question of whether Kant's view of emotion and emotional love – later echoed by Kierkegaard – can do justice to friendship.

This question, and the utilitarian worry about how to justify the differential concern of friendship if morality requires impartial concern for all, dominate twentieth-century discussions of friendship.

4 Twentieth-century philosophy

The Kantian view of emotion, and its contribution to philosophers' neglect of friendship, is discussed thoroughly by Lawrence Blum in *Friendship, Altruism, and Morality* (1980), the first philosophical book on friendship since Aelred's. In this work, Blum argues that love and concern require thought and choice, are crucial to moral perception and motivation, and can be non-instrumentally (though conditionally and preferentially) directed at friends' good (see VIRTUE ETHICS §4). Hence, friendship-love is morally significant.

The idea of the moral significance of friendship is also central to discussions of friendship inspired by Aristotle. Thus, several philosophers have emphasized the importance of friendship to self-knowledge and moral growth. Since friends share the same basic values, each gains greater self-awareness by observing the other's actions and responses, and since friends differ in important ways, each grows through emulation of the other's admirable qualities.

Elizabeth Telfer (1970/1) addresses the utilitarian worry about justifying differential concern (see UTILITARIANISM §3; IMPARTIALITY §2). Telfer's solution is that unequal concern is justified because we are more effective producers of utility (the good)

when we concentrate our energies on the needs of the few we know best. However, if utilitarians must justify their friendships as instrumental means to utility, their moral commitments seem psychologically incompatible with friendship's commitments. The usual response to this is that utility-maximization is only a *standard* of right action, not its primary *motivation*. Indeed, utilitarians *should* cultivate the motivations of friendship, subject to the (background) proviso that if, overall, these motivations failed to maximize utility, they would seek to change them. But this is just to say that utilitarians' motivations are, ultimately, shaped by instrumental considerations. So, even if they are *psychologically* compatible with dispositions of friendship, they seem *logically* inconsistent with them.

The theme of preferential concern is salient in feminist and communitarian writings. Feminists emphasize the 'care perspective' as a moral perspective independent of justice, and friendship as a caring relationship that is particularly valuable because of its voluntariness, mutuality and equality. But like most contemporary philosophers on friendship, including communitarians, who oppose justice to friendship, most feminists also oppose the universalist, impartialist justice perspective to the particularist, partialist care perspective (see FEMINIST ETHICS; COMMUNITY AND COMMUNITARIANISM). Some, however, recognizing that there is no inherent tension between these perspectives, and deploring the frequent inequality of caring work in female–male friendships, have argued for the reconciliation of the two perspectives, and for the importance of justice in friendship.

But more needs saying. Our particularity cannot exist, or be understood, independently of our common humanity. Hence, caring for someone implies seeing their particularity as a distinctive expression of common aspirations and needs. Conversely, justice implies giving due weight to the particular expressions of people's commonalities. Sensitivity to these aspects requires both justice and care. Justice and care are thus mutually dependent, and equally important in friendship. Indeed, in so far as justice depends on perceptiveness and imaginative effort, and the rightful expectation of these is greater within friendship, friendship *intensifies* the claims of justice.

See also: MORALITY AND EMOTIONS; SEXUALITY, PHILOSOPHY OF; TRUST

References and further reading

* Aelred of Rievaulx (1148) *De spiritali amicitia*, trans. E. Laker, *Spiritual Friendship*, Kalamazoo, MI: Cistercian Publications, 1974. (The original title

shows the influence of Cicero's *De amicitia* on Aelred. In a true friendship, which is necessarily spiritual, the friends are willing to die for each other, love each other unconditionally and never-endingly, and hold all possessions in common. The only alternative to true friendship is sinful friend-hip.)

* Aquinas, T. (*c*.1259–65) *Summa contra gentiles* (Synopsis [of Christian Doctrine] Directed Against Unbelievers), trans. V.J. Bourke, Notre Dame, IN: University of Notre Dame Press, 1975, III.1.3, c.19. (Expresses the view that our 'ultimate end' is to become more like God.)

* —— (1266–73) *Summa theologiae* (Synopsis of Theology), trans. Fathers of the English Domini-can Province, Glencoe, MN: McGraw-Hill, 1947. (IaIIae.26–8 discuss love as an emotion; IaIIae.26.4 distinguishes friendship based on friendship-love (friendship proper) from friendships based on love of concupiscence or desire (friendships of pleasure and utility). IIaIIae.23–46 discuss charity as friend-ship with God.)

* Aristotle (*c*. mid 4th century BC) *Nicomachean Ethics*, trans. W.D. Ross, revised by J.O. Urmson, in J. Barnes (ed.) *The Complete Works of Aristotle*, vol. 2, Princeton, NJ: Princeton University Press, 1984. (In addition to the issues discussed in this entry, books VIII–IX on friendship also discuss the justification of friendship, conflicts among friends, when friendships should be dissolved, civic friend-ship, and other topics.)

* Augustine (397–401) *Confessionum libri tredecim*, trans. F.J. Sheed, *Confessions*, Indianapolis, IN: Hackett Publishing Company, 1993, IV, 4–12. (Describes Augustine's grief on the death of a friend, and his later reflection that he had mistakenly loved his friend as an end in himself.)

* —— (396–426) *De doctrina christiana* (On Christian Doctrine), trans. D.W. Robertson, Jr, New York: Liberal Arts Press, 1958. (See book I: section iv, passage 4 and xxii, 20–1, for the view that all earthly loves, including neighbour-love, are instru-mental or utility loves, and love of God alone an end love to be enjoyed for its own sake.)

* Blum, L. (1980) *Friendship, Altruism, and Morality*, London: Routledge & Kegan Paul. (The first book on friendship since Aelred's *De spiritali amicitia*, and probably the best-known single contemporary work on the topic. Argues that sympathy, compas-sion and concern are cognitive emotions that are intentionally diverted at others' good and since friendship is a locus of these emotions, it is an intrinsically moral phenomenon.)

* Cicero, M.T. (mid-44 BC) *Laelius, De amicitia* (Laelius: On Friendship), Latin text with trans.

and notes by J.G.F. Powell, Warminster: Aris & Phillips, 1990. (A somewhat unsystematic, but historically influential, dialogue on friendship. Gaius Laelius (186 BC–?), who studied philosophy under the Stoics, is the main speaker.)

* Kant, I. (1785) *Grundlegung zur Metaphysik der Sitten*, trans. M.J. Gregor, *Groundwork of the Metaphysics of Morals*, in *Practical Philosophy*, Cambridge: Cambridge University Press, 1993, esp. 389–401, 401 note. (Presents Kant's sharp dichot-omy between the moral-rational and the natural-emotional realms, and his view that emotional love is instrumental self-love.)

* —— (1797) *Metaphysische Anfangsgründe der Tugen-dlehre*, trans. M.J. Gregor, *The Doctrine of Virtue*, in *Practical Philosophy*, Cambridge: Cambridge University Press, 1993, 469–73. (Contains the only extended discussion of friendship in Kant's devel-oped philosophical works.)

* Kierkegaard, S.A. (1847) *Kierlighedens Gjerninger*, trans. H. Hong and E. Hong, *Works of Love*, New York: Harper & Row, 1962. (Kierkegaard follows Luther in regarding friendship as essentially irreconcilable with *agape*, and echoes Kant in declaring that friendship-love and *eros* 'contain no ethical task', both because they are forms of self-love, and because, as natural inclinations, they cannot be willed or, therefore, commanded by God's law.)

* Mitsis, P. (1988) *Epicurus' Ethical Theory: The Pleasures of Invulnerability*, Ithaca, NY: Cornell University Press, ch. 3. (Expands on Epicurus' interpretation of friendship, particularly his con-ception of *eudamonia* as invulnerable.)

* Plato (*c*.380–367 BC) *Lysis*, trans. S. Lombardo, in *Complete Works*, ed. J.M. Cooper, Indianapolis, IN: Hackett Publishing Company, 1997. (The only Platonic dialogue devoted entirely to friendship.)

Railton, P. (1984) 'Alienation, Consequentialism, and the Demands of Morality', *Philosophy and Public Affairs* 13 (2): 134–71; repr. in N.K. Badhwar (ed.) *Friendship: A Philosophical Reader*, Ithaca, NY: Cornell University Press, 1993. (Expands on the idea that commitment to utilitarianism or conse-quentialism is psychologically compatible with personal commitments.)

* Telfer, E. (1970/1) 'Friendship', *Proceedings of the Aristotelian Society*, supplementary volume: 223–41. (Examines the nature, duties and values of friendship, arguing that friendship is valuable because it is useful, pleasurable and life-enhancing. The article marks the revival of friendship as an important philosophical topic in this century.)

NEERA K. BADHWAR

FRIES, JACOB FRIEDRICH (1773–1843)

Fries was a German post-Kantian philosopher, active chiefly in Jena and Heidelberg. He was a personal as well as a philosophical enemy of Hegel. Fries' version of Kantian philosophy opposed the speculative idealism of Fichte, Schelling and Hegel, developing an 'anthropological critique of reason'. Fries also emphasized subjectivity in ethics and religion. In politics he was a republican and a German nationalist. For his participation in the Wartburg Festival of 1817 (a gathering of radical student fraternities), Fries was removed from his professorship at Jena in 1820, but restored in 1824. He wrote both scholarly and popular treatises on metaphysics, logic, ethics and politics, as well as mathematics and natural science. His continuing influence early in this century was mediated chiefly by the Göttingen Neo-Kantian Leonard Nelson and by Rudolf Otto's theory of religious experience.

Fries accepted Kant's distinction between sensibility and understanding, the transcendental ideality of empirical objects and the consequent unknowability of things-in-themselves (see KANT, I. §5). Early in his career he defended a critical Kantian position against the emerging speculative idealism in the polemical essay *Reinhold, Fichte und Schelling* (1803). In his *Neue Kritik der Vernunft* (New Critique of Reason) (1807, revised in 1838 under the title *Anthropologische Kritik der Vernunft* (Anthropological Critique of Reason)). Fries was critical of Kant's strategy of arguing for a priori principles by transcendental deduction from the possibility of experience; Fries claimed that a priori principles must instead be known 'anthropologically'. Accordingly, he admitted that we cannot prove the objective validity of Kantian principles such as substance and causality, but only that such principles are indispensable for our own cognitive activities. Fries' approach is sometimes described as psychologism; it does not deny the Kantian a priori, however, but claims that it is knowable through the observation of our faculties.

In ethics, Fries placed primary emphasis on an agent's possession of a 'pure will', one which follows the dictates of conscience and acts solely from the motive of duty (see KANTIAN ETHICS). In his *Handbuch der praktischen Philosophie* (Manual of Practical Philosophy) (1818), Fries maintained that we know our duty through the exercise of moral sentiments leading to conscientious 'convictions'; but conscience is always 'educable', and moral judgment fallible. Erring moral judgment, however, does not imply that conscience itself is fallible. An agent whose convictions are objectively wrong still has a pure will, and is therefore to be esteemed rather than blamed. Hence, when judging the acts of others, the standard should always be their convictions, rather than objectively right convictions.

Like Kant, Fries based religion on a faith in divine providence which is rationally justifiable on moral grounds (see KANT, I. §11). But Fries' religious upbringing in Moravian pietism led him to emphasize far more than Kant both the specifically Christian and the experiential aspects of religion. Fries drew the categories of the beautiful and the sublime from Kantian aesthetic theory and – again like Kant – he interpreted these aesthetic experiences as having a moral-religious significance (see KANT, I. §12). For such experiences Fries coined a special term, with a deliberately archaic spelling: '*Ahndung*'; it might be translated 'presentiment', 'divination' or 'inkling'. Inklings do not count as empirical cognitions of any kind, but they do reveal, through feeling, the limitation of the sensible world by the supersensible, and thus count as a kind of experiential awareness of a higher spiritual reality. Fries' philosophy of religion was first expounded in *Wissen, Glauben und Ahndung* (Knowledge, Faith and Inkling) (1805), but later popularly presented in his dialogue *Julius und Evagoras: ein philosophischer Roman* (Julius and Evagoras: A Philosophical Novel) (1813, revised 1822).

Fries is sometimes described as a 'liberal' in opposition to the 'conservatism' of Hegel. This terminology certainly involves a grosser distortion of Hegel's thought than of Fries', but it is oversimplified and misleading in his case too. Fries was a defender of individual rights and liberty, and an egalitarian in economic as well as political matters; he hated the fact that modern society is unified by a cash nexus rather than by moral ties, and he was outraged by the exploitation of the poor by the rich. Fries' views on both points have a German nationalist as well as a communitarian bent, which the term 'liberal' is not well suited to capture. In *Von deutschem Bund und deutscher Staatsverfassung* (German Federation and German Constitution) (1816), Fries advocated the unification of all German states into a single federated constitutional republic – which entailed the abolition of the various monarchical forms of government prevailing in all of them at the time. His German cultural nationalism, however, made him as hostile to the French Republic and the ideals of the French Revolution as any ultra-reactionary monarchist. While Fries was a social egalitarian, like Kant he favoured a representative republic with a voting franchise limited by property and occupational restrictions (as well as by those of age and gender).

Hence he was hostile to the idea of a democratic government, which he equated with mob rule.

Fries was also an anti-Semite, as appears in his pamphlet: *Über die Gefährung des Wohlstandes und Characters der Deutschen durch die Juden* (On the Danger Posed by the Jews to German Well-Being and Character) (1816). He did not recognize Judaism as a religion at all, but saw Jewry as a politico-economic state within a state, one founded on ancient and barbarous principles and hostile alike to individual freedom, moral universality and human dignity. Blaming Jews for the rule of money in society, he opposed any toleration of Judaism, as well as the extension of political and civil rights to Jews. To qualify for such rights, Fries maintained, Jews must first declare their allegiance to the German state (requiring that they renounce Judaism). Judaism was to be 'extirpated root and branch' from German society.

In later life Fries wrote on mathematics and natural science. In general he took Kantianism in a moralistic and empiricist direction, in opposition to the speculative tendencies of German idealism.

See also: GERMAN IDEALISM

List of works

Fries, J.F. (1967–76) *Sämtliche Schriften* (Collected Writings), Aalen: Scientia Verlag. (The standard collected works, in six divisions, itemized below.)
—— (1967–71) *Schriften zur reinen Philosophie* (Writings on Pure Philosophy), *Sämtliche Schriften* (Collected Writings) Div. 1, Aalen: Scientia Verlag, 5 vols. (Contains the *Neue Kritik der Vernunft* (New Critique of Reason) (1807), revised in 1838 under the title *Anthropologische Kritik der Vernunft* (Anthropological Critique of Reason).)
—— (1969) *Schriften zur Geschichte der Philosophie* (Writings on the History of Philosophy), *Sämtliche Schriften* (Collected Writings) Div. 4, Aalen: Scientia Verlag, 3 vols. (Contains Fries' works on the history of philosophy.)
—— (1970–1) *Schriften zur angewandten Philosophie 1* (Writings on Applied Philosophy 1), *Sämtliche Schriften* (Collected Writings) Div. 2, Aalen: Scientia Verlag, 4 vols. (Contains *Wissen, Glauben und Ahndung* (Knowledge, Faith and Inkling) (1805).)
—— (1973a) *Schriften zur angewandten Philosophie 2* (Writings on Applied Philosophy 2), *Sämtliche Schriften* (Collected Writings) Div. 3, Aalen: Scientia Verlag, 1 vol. (Contains *Handbuch der praktischen Philosophie* (Manual of Practical Philosophy) (1818), *Von deutschem Bund und deutscher Staatsverfassung* (German Federation and German Constitution) (1816) and *Julius und Evagoras: ein philosophischer Roman* (Julius and Evagoras: A Philosophical Novel) (1813, revised 1822).)
—— (1973b) *Populäre Schriften* (Popular Writings), *Sämtliche Schriften* (Collected Writings) Div. 5, Aalen: Scientia Verlag, 3 vols. (Contains occasional writings of a popular nature.)
—— (1976) *Polemische Schriften* (Polemical Writings), *Sämtliche Schriften* (Collected Writings) Div. 6, Aalen: Scientia Verlag, 1 vol. (Contains, among other writings, some of Fries' attacks on Hegel.)
—— (1982) *Dialogues on Morality and Religion*, ed. D.Z. Phillips, trans. D. Walford, Totowa, NJ: Barnes & Noble. (The recent translation of Fries, an abridged version of *Julius and Evagoras*. The editor emphasizes the affinity of Fries' philosophy of religion with Wittgensteinian Fideism.)

References and further reading

Nelson, L. (1962) *Fortschritte und Rückschritte der Philosophie* (Steps Forward and Backward in Philosophy), Frankfurt: Suhrkamp. (Contains a polemical defence of Fries by the leading twentieth-century German exponent of his philosophy.)
Otto, R. (1931) *The Philosophy of Religion Based on Kant and Fries*, trans. E.B. Dickler, London: Allen & Unwin. (The author is an influential twentieth-century philosopher of religion, whose classic study *The Idea of the Holy* was strongly influenced by Fries' theory of religious experience.)
Wood, A.W. (1990) *Hegel's Ethical Thought*, New York: Cambridge. (Chapter 10 focuses on a discussion of Fries' 'ethics of conviction' and Hegel's critique of it.)

ALLEN W. WOOD

FROMM, ERICH *see* FRANKFURT SCHOOL

FUJIWARA SEIKA (1561–1619)

In Tokugawa intellectual historiography, Fujiwara Seika has been traditionally deemed the founding father of the Zhu Xi school of neo-Confucianism in Japan. He emphasized seiza (quiet-sitting) in order to perceive the ethical essence of human nature, and asserted the priority of principle, moving away from dualism towards a more rationalistic monism.

Prior to the Tokugawa period (1600–1868), Zhu Xi's commentaries on the Four Books – the *Daxue* (Great Learning), the Analects, the Mengzi and the *Zhongyong* (Doctrine of the Mean) – had long circulated among Rinzai Zen monks (see ZHU XI; DAXUE; CONFUCIUS; MENCIUS; ZHONGYONG). They were understood, however, as ingredients in a syncretic, religio-philosophical system combining Buddhism, neo-Confucianism, and Shintō. Only in the Tokugawa period did scholars who were keenly interested in neo-Confucianism break away from Rinzai temples to make neo-Confucianism the independent, anti-Buddhist philosophy that Zhu Xi had intended it to be (see NEO-CONFUCIAN PHILOSOPHY; CONFUCIAN PHILOSOPHY, JAPANESE). Seika played a cardinal role in this process because he, though initially a Rinzai monk, quit Buddhism to study and teach neo-Confucianism as a purely secular scholar in Kyoto, the imperial capital.

One of Seika's students, Hayashi Razan (1583–1657), also severed his links with Buddhism to pursue a purer neo-Confucian teaching. Razan studied only briefly under Seika, who later recommended him to Tokugawa Ieyasu (1543–1616), the *samurai*-unifier of Japan as of 1600. The Hayashi family, having established itself in Edo (now Tokyo), the shogun's capital, became hereditary scholars serving the Tokugawa regime; they later praised Seika for initiating the neo-Confucian break with Buddhism in Japan, which they continued wholeheartedly. With the Hayashi family, neo-Confucians increasingly came to serve the Tokugawa in ways that Buddhist scholars had served other earlier military regimes (see BUDDHIST PHILOSOPHY, JAPANESE).

Some historians, however, have questioned the extent to which Seika (1) broke with Buddhism, and (2) taught Razan. Some suggest that Razan, a largely self-educated scholar, was legitimizing his family's teachings by tracing them to Seika, a reclusive scholar of aristocratic lineage. It is true that Seika's ideas were developed most faithfully not in Edo, but instead within the confines of Kyoto, an aristocratic haven surrounded by the *samurai*-dominated world of the Tokugawa shogunate (see BUSHI PHILOSOPHY §3). Seika's longest standing, most respected disciple was not Razan but Matsunaga Sekigo (1592–1657), who remained in Kyoto and founded an academy which flourished after Seika's death, largely dedicated to propagating Seika's teachings.

Seika's thought was, unlike Razan's, rather Buddhistic. Seika emphasized *seiza* or 'quiet-sitting', a neo-Confucian meditative practice outwardly similar to *zazen*, or 'sitting-in-Zen meditation', but aimed at perceiving the ethical essence of human nature. Razan had no use for *seiza*. Metaphysically, Seika asserted the priority of principle, skewing Zhu Xi's dualism of principle and material force towards a more rationalistic monism (see QI). Razan's thinking tended towards materialism and activism. Like Rinzai syncretism, Seika's teachings were eclectic, accommodating critics of Zhu Xi like WANG YANGMING, and elements of Buddhism and Shintō as well; Razan disliked Seika's easy eclecticism. Seika and his disciples mostly refused to serve *samurai*, but Razan's family became scholar-servants *par excellence* of the *samurai* estate.

See also: CONFUCIAN PHILOSOPHY, JAPANESE; JAPANESE PHILOSOPHY; NEO-CONFUCIAN PHILOSOPHY; SHINTŌ; ZHU XI

List of works

Fujiwara Seika (1561–1619) *Fujiwara Seika shū* (Complete Works of Fujiwara Seika), Tokyo: Kokumin seishin bunka kenkyūjo, 1938–9; ed. Ishida Ichirō and Kanaya Osamu, *Fujiwara Seika/ Hayashi Razan*, Nihon shisō taikei vol. 28, Tokyo: Iwanami shoten, 1975. (The Complete Works includes essays discussing Seika's works; analyses the *Kana seiri* (Neo-Confucianism for Japanese Readers), traditionally attributed to Seika and part of his Complete Works, and explores questions about its authenticity. This Ishida and Kanaya edition includes Seika's *Suntetsu roku* (Philosophical Apothegms), *Daigaku yōryaku* (Essential Teachings of the Great Learning) and selections from the *Fujiwara Seika bunshū*, as well as analytic essays by the editors. The *Kana seiri* is included, along with the similar, anonymous text, *Shingaku gorinsho* (Ethical Teachings of the Learning of the Mind).)

References and further reading

de Bary, W.T. and Bloom, I. (eds) (1979) *Principle and Practicality: Essays in Neo-Confucianism and Practical Learning*, New York: Columbia University Press. (An anthology including sophisticated essays, many pertaining to Seika, by leading Japanese and American scholars.)

Boot, W.J. (1982) 'The Adoption and Adaptation of Neo-Confucianism in Japan: The Role of Fujiwara Seika and Hayashi Razan', unpublished Ph.D. dissertation, University of Leiden. (Traces Razan's ideas to pre-Tokugawa Japanese thinkers, scrutinizing the real impact of Razan's tutelage under Seika.)

Imanaka Kanshi (1973) *Kinsei Nihon seiji shisō no seiritsu: Seika gaku to Razan gaku* (The Establishment of Early Modern Japanese Political Thought: The Learning of Fujiwara Seika and Hayashi

Razan), Tokyo: Sōbunsha. (Questions traditional accounts regarding the Seika–Razan relationship.)

Ota Seikyū (1985) *Fujiwara Seika*, Tokyo: Yoshikawa kōbunkan. (The most recent biography of Seika in Japanese.)

JOHN ALLEN TUCKER

FULLER, LON LOUVOIS (1902–78)

Lon Louvois Fuller was a leading US legal philosopher and contracts lawyer who in his controversies with H. L. A. Hart and with US 'legal realists' advanced a version of 'procedural natural law' deriving an 'inner morality of law' from the formal properties of law. At the same time, through his insistence that legal interpretation must always consider the essentially purposive character of legal activity, he forms an intellectual bridge between earlier pragmatist accounts of law and the late twentieth-century interpretivist approach associated particularly with Ronald Dworkin.

Soon after Fuller's birth in Hereford, Texas, his family moved to California, where Fuller received his education, partly at Berkeley, but finally, both in economics and law, at Stanford University. In 1926 he took up a post in the Law School of the University of Oregon, subsequently moving to Illinois, to Duke University, and finally to Harvard in 1940, retiring in 1972.

Anti-formalism is the leading theme in Fuller's theoretical work. It is expressed primarily in giving attention to the extra-statal forms of law, to what he calls 'implicit law', and to extrajudicial and extra-legislative forms of production of law, for instance contracts (his speciality) and industrial relations. Law was for him not just the outcome of decisions by authorities, but also and especially of agreements, compromises and mediations, if not indeed of spontaneous and in a certain sense unconscious harmonization of interests and wills. Fuller's anti-formalism was, moreover, expressed not just in the area of the theory of sources of law. The area dearest to him, to which he devoted special attention in his years of maturity, was that of the relation between law and ethics. Formalists were in his view all those who denied that relation, isolating the law in a sphere made either of forms of various types or of acts of authorities or mere external behaviour, or of meanings of linguistic propositions. It was not just legal positivist doctrine that in his view was guilty of this sort of formalism, but also the realism of such jurists

as Karl LLEWELLYN and the pragmatism of philosophers like John DEWEY.

He wrote, 'For its meaning any rule of law is tragically dependent upon an understanding of the purpose pursued and this in turn usually requires a feeling for the extra-legal community and its problems.' But legal positivists and 'realists' denied the need for this reference to purposes and to extra-legal problems in order to understand and explain legal norms. These purposes and problems are not included among the conditions for the validity or existence of a norm, whether by legal positivists like Hans KELSEN or Hart, or realists like Llewellyn or Jerome Frank (see FRANK, J.; LEGAL REALISM §1; LEGAL POSITIVISM). For all these the jurist's ethos is broadly identical with the scientists' ethos, and is value-free. There is no 'role morality' that binds the jurist's activity and conditions the possible contents of their social function. But for Fuller the problem is just that without reference to values one cannot even identify the scope of what is legal.

The values that Fuller refers to in this connection are not those of good morality. They do not entirely and at every point coincide with ethical values. He wrote to his adversary, Llewellyn, 'You say that there are obviously bad rules which exist. I don't deny that.' Saying, then, that a legal norm exists does not mean preaching its morality (goodness). But in order for a legal norm to exist it has to pursue certain purposes, derived from law's external character, that are separate from the specific content of the norms. Thus Fuller's finalism proves to be a formalist approach, but a deliberately *sui generis* formalism, quite different from the imperativist and legal positivist variety. His formalism is essentially Kantian (see KANTIAN ETHICS; LEGAL IDEALISM §2), since the specific purposes of law also define a procedural scope to be respected, without which the legal norm would be an arbitrary act or a mere instrumental measure. Fuller thus seems to anticipate the distinction recently made familiar by John RAWLS between 'right' and 'good'. For him, the law is largely equal to just what Rawls today (along with Habermas) would call the sphere of 'right': a series of formal and procedural principles within which each subject can pursue their own purposes and develop their own conception of the good. Fuller identifies in this connection eight fundamental qualities of legal acts, understood as elements in a value-laden legal order: (1) the generality of the act; (2) its publicity; (3) its orientation towards future behaviour; (4) its comprehensibility; (5) the noncontradictoriness of the provision; (6) consistency and constancy in time; (7) not demanding the impossible; and finally (8) an interpretation and application that are sufficiently respectful of the text and of its ordinary meaning. Failing such requirements, a legal act would not be called 'nonexistent' or 'invalid' by Fuller; it would however be denied the possibility of acting as a justificatory basis for any legally relevant conduct (a judicial decision or a contract between private individuals, for instance). These eight aspects define the 'inner morality of law' or 'procedural natural law' for which Fuller contended in his great debate with H.L.A. HART and in his greatest book, *The Morality of Law* (1964).

See also: LAW, PHILOSOPHY OF; NORMS, LEGAL; RULE OF LAW/RECHSSTAAT §2

List of works

Fuller, L.L. (1940) *The Law in Quest of Itself*, 2nd edn, Cambridge, MA: Harvard University Press, 1966. (This is Fuller's earliest work of legal theory, in which he stresses the significance of the purposive approach to law and its interpretation.)
—— (1964) *The Morality of Law*, 2nd revised edn, New Haven, CT: Yale University Press, 1969. (The great work which establishes the thesis of the 'inner morality of law' in opposition to the version of legal positivism proposed by H.L.A. Hart.)
—— (1967) *Legal Fictions*, Stanford, CA: Stanford University Press. (Three essays giving a lucid account of the development and significance of 'fictions' in law.)
—— (1968) *Anatomy of the Law*, New York: Praeger. (A short overview of jurisprudence and legal system, cast in Fuller's characteristic line of thought.)

References and further reading

Summers, R.S. (1984) *Lon L. Fuller*, London: Edward Arnold. (A very thorough account of Fuller's work, with full bibliography, by an author who started as an opponent but became (with qualifications) a supporter of Fuller's doctrine.)

MASSIMO LA TORRE

FUNCTIONAL EXPLANATION

Explanations appealing to the functions of items are common in everyday discourse and in science: we say that the heart pumps blood because that is its function, and that the car fails to start because the ignition is not functioning. Moreover, we distinguish the functions things perform from other things they do: the heart makes a noise, but that is not one of its functions. Philosophical discussions in this area attempt to specify conditions under which it is appropriate to ascribe functions to items and under which it is appropriate to appeal to those functions in explanations. Difficulties arise because functions are normative: there is some sense in which items ought to perform their functions; failure to perform is a kind of error. Philosophical discussions investigate whether and how this normativity can be understood in scientifically respectable terms. This is important, because biological entities are among the most characteristically functional items. This issue gives rise to differing views as to what it is that functional explanations explain. One view is that they explain how a containing system achieves some goal or effect. Another is that functional explanations explain causally why the functional item exists.

1 **Historical context**
2 **Explaining the accomplishment of real goals**
3 **Explaining the presence of the functional item**
4 **Explaining interesting capacities**

1 Historical context

Science and explanatory practice prior to the modern age was based on the Aristotelian view that explanation is by appeal to causes, and that the primary sense of 'cause' is final cause – *telos* or purpose (see ARISTOTLE §9). Activities of things which are parts of wholes were understood as subserving the final causes of the wholes of which they are parts. Their activities, insofar as understood, are their functions. With the discovery of precise mathematically formulable laws of dynamics for general application to all types of inanimate motion, appeal to purposes falls not just out of service but into disrepute. Contemporary science generally conceives nature as the realm of law-like regularity, devoid of irreducible purpose and design. Explanation is still appeal to causes, but these are now conceived in terms of regularity and mechanism. The advent of genetics, the means by which Darwinian natural selection can account for the origins of complex animate behaviour, gives further weight to this conception (see EVOLUTION, THEORY OF).

Yet despite its apparent appeal to purposes and its lack of overt appeal to natural laws, functional discourse and explanation has persisted and been of great utility, especially in the biological sciences. Contemporary discussions seek to provide for these practices a basis which is naturalistic in the modern sense. Three interrelated problems beset such attempts. First, not all effects are functional (the heart has the mere effect, but not the function, of making sound); so functional must be distinguished from 'mere' effects. Second, items may have functions which they do not perform. A heart in fibrillation, and the eyes of a congenitally blind person, still have their functions. Third is the specification of what functional explanations explain.

2   Explaining the accomplishment of real goals

Some philosophers distinguish functional from mere effects by taking functions to be contributions to real goals of containing systems, whose accomplishment is partially explained by the resulting function ascription. Ernest Nagel and Morton Beckner, among others, have offered naturalistic criteria for such goals. Roughly, systems are goal-directed if and only if they maintain some feature (possibly a developmental tendency) in relative homeostasis through varying conditions, where that relative homeostasis is achieved by the combined operation of multiple components of the system, whose states are logically independent of one another but causally related. The goal of the system may then be understood as the maintenance of the homeostatic feature (or the state towards which the development tends).

Nagel himself recognized that such non-directed objects as elastic solids and chemical systems in thermodynamic equilibrium are not obviously ruled out by his proposed definition. Moreover, nothing in this approach helps to solve the second, 'malfunction', problem, for, unless more is said, a system which ceases to behave in a goal-directed manner ceases to have a goal, and its subparts cease to have a function. Efforts to solve this difficulty generally specify system types in terms of typical members. Since tokens of a type can fail to be typical, token systems can have typical goals they do not accomplish, and their components typical functions they do not perform. However, attempts to distinguish typical members have generally seemed either arbitrary or else to appeal, implicitly or explicitly, to their proper functioning, rendering the account circular for present purposes.

3   Explaining the presence of the functional item

Following claims of sociologists such as Malinowski and Merton that functional explanation is a distinctive method in sociology (see FUNCTIONALISM IN SOCIAL SCIENCE), positivist philosophers, notably Hempel and Nagel, attempted to assimilate functional explanation to the deductive-nomological model thought to characterize all explanation. On the deductive-nomological (D-N) model, explanation is a species of inference: from the relevant laws of nature

and further facts and relevant background conditions, explananda can be deduced or, in the case of statistical laws, induced (see EXPLANATION §2). Function ascriptions are here taken as equivalent to arguments in which the presence of the functionally characterized item is inferred from a containing system's having certain effects, and from the need for an item of that sort to produce those effects.

It is rarely if ever the case, however, that the only means by which a system can have a given effect is by means of a single specific item. For example, the pumping of blood may be achieved by means of an artificial device. For this reason, plausible function ascriptions will fail as D-N explanations, because the inference from the effect to the presence of the item in question will typically be unsound. This problem has been generally regarded as fatal to any attempt to accommodate function ascription to the D-N model.

The demand that explanations support valid or strong statistical inferences has been generally attacked as too strict. Understanding explanation more modestly, some philosophers continue to maintain that legitimate function ascription explains the presence of functionally characterized items. In a highly influential analysis, Larry Wright (1973) claims that 'the function of I is F' means

(a) I is there because it Fs;
(b) F is a result (or consequence) of I's being there.

The first, etiological requirement is designed to eliminate mere effects, but is clearly too weak to do the job. To cite a well-known example, suppose a pebble has the effect of propping up a rock in a stream. But for the presence of the rock, the pebble would be washed away. Hence the pebble is where it is because it has the effect of propping up the rock. On Wright's analysis, then, the pebble has the function of propping up the rock, which is surely a misapplication of the concept of function. The account also seems under-inclusive, as the second clause demands that the item actually have the functional effect, eliminating mal- and non-functioning items.

The most plausible efforts to refine Wright's basic etiological framework attempt to solve these two problems at once, holding that the etiologies which mark out functional effects are selectional, understood roughly on the model of selectional explanation in evolutionary biology. Importantly, selection always involves the relative replicative or reproductive success of objects with a given feature as compared with competing objects without that feature. The function of the feature is the effect it had in virtue of which objects possessing it were selected. The 'malfunction problem' is supposedly solved by the fact that the function of an item is not identified with any of its actual or even possible effects, but rather with selected-for effects of some predecessor items.

Whether selection history, even in the biological case, actually provides a genuine etiology for particular items is disputed. Robert Cummins (1975) and Elliott Sober (1984), for example, each deny that it does, holding that the etiology of a biological trait is exclusively a matter of the genetic plan inherited by the containing organism. Proponents of the selection view counter that selection accounts for the increased incidence of the item in the population, thereby explaining the fact that the token system in issue possesses it.

Appeal to original selection etiology seems in any event to give rise to further counterexamples, since the effects for which an item has been selected may intuitively be non-functional or positively disfunctional in subsequent generations of the containing systems, and items may have effects in systems that are plausibly regarded as functional, even where their etiologies are either non-selectional, or involve selection for some other effects. Ruth Millikan (1984), whose influential selectional theory of 'proper functions' is intended for use in a naturalized semantics (see SEMANTICS, TELEOLOGICAL), has attempted to deflect such counter-examples by claiming that her account is a theoretical definition, rather than an analysis of our ordinary concept of 'function'; failure of overlap with our intuitive function ascriptions is beside the point. However, actual selection histories are generally difficult if not impossible to determine, and the boundaries of the theoretical concept, from an instrumental or operational point of view, are no sharper than those of the intuitive. Moreover, Millikan's account is intended to capture not just biological functions, but others as well, and it is not clear that the notions of ancestry and replication it requires are applicable outside of the biological context (or perhaps even within it).

Notice that the types of counterexample mentioned above involve the temporal dimension (items can lose functions they once had, and can gain functions after having been selected for other effects). Peter Godfrey-Smith (1994) and Paul Griffiths (1992, 1993), each concerned particularly with biological function, have suggested that these counterexamples can be avoided if only recent or proximal selection history is regarded as relevant to function ascription. The viability of such accounts depends upon whether the notions of 'recent' or 'proximal' history can be made precise. This is turn depends upon empirical assumptions about likely mutation rates and the incidence and nature of competitors, as well as the assumption that evolution is efficient in the sense that, if an item is not providing some fitness benefit to an organism, then the incidence of that item in the population will decline. Though not implausible, such assumptions are far from clearly warranted. Any attempt similarly to refine a selectional account of function for general application beyond the context of biology would involve a more dubious generalization of these assumptions. Finally, some biological items with selectional etiologies, notably, so-called 'segregation distorters', provide no benefit to containing systems, and are even positively harmful. Unless we wish, counter-intuitively, to regard these effects as functional, some non-arbitrary means of ruling them out of the analysis is needed.

4 Explaining interesting capacities

Because of difficulties of these kinds, some philosophers deny that the distinction between functional and mere effects is ultimately real and that function ascriptions do or can operate as explanations of the presence of the functional item. Robert Cummins has offered a well-known account along these lines, on which ascriptions of functional properties to items are always relative to an analytical account of some capacity of some containing system, that is, to an account which breaks down the net capacity into sub-processes which, taken together, are sufficient to explain the capacity. On this view, any capacity of a containing system which results from contributions of its parts is subject to functional analysis, and such parts could conceivably be ascribed innumerable distinct, even incompatible functions (though because of the relativization of function ascription to analysis, no inconsistency results). Cummins' analysis is thoroughly instrumental, holding that our explanatory interests determine which effects we single out in the sciences for this kind of analysis, hence our ascriptions of functions to particular items, and also which tokens we take as typical, hence what we treat as malfunctional.

There is little doubt that Cummins' functions are naturalistically respectable, so long as the particular analyses offered are themselves naturalistic, and that they capture much of the actual practice of functional explanation. However, function ascription along Cummins' lines seems inadequate to account for those cases in which selectional or other etiological accounts adverting to function can be given, notably in the case of artifacts. Moreover, Cummins' functions are plainly inadequate for service in broader philosophical projects, such as naturalized semantics and epistemology, which require a robustly realist conception of the normativity of function.

See also: CAUSATION; TECHNOLOGY, PHILOSOPHY OF; TELEOLOGY

References and further reading

Beckner, M. (1959) *The Biological Way of Thought*, New York: Columbia University Press. (See chapters 6 and 7. Moderately technical accounts of functions as contributions to goals and of goal-directed systems, in the biological context.)

Bigelow, J. and Pargetter, R. (1987) 'Functions', *Journal of Philosophy* 84: 181–97. (Functions as contributions to goals).

* Cummins, R. (1975) 'Functional Analysis', *Journal of Philosophy* 72: 741–65. (Detailed critique of positivist and etiological theories of function; presentation of instrumental account.)

Godfrey-Smith, P. (1993) 'Functions: Consensus Without Unity', *Pacific Philosophical Quarterly* 74: 196–208. (Highly readable presentation of the etiological and instrumental accounts as distinct and equally important.)

* —— (1994) 'A Modern History Theory of Functions', *Nous* 27: 344–62. (Attempts to accommodate loss and gain of functions within the selection etiology framework, along with a discussion of segregation distortion.)

* Griffiths, P. (1992) 'Adaptive Explanation and the Concept of a Vestige', in P. Griffiths (ed.) *Trees of Life*, Dordrecht: Kluwer, 111–31. (Somewhat technical attempt to accommodate loss and gain of function within the selection etiology framework.)

* —— (1993) 'Functional Analysis and Proper Functions', *British Journal of Philosophy of Science* 44: 409–22. (As above, with a discussion of segregation distortion and an extension to artifacts.)

Hempel, C.G. (1965) 'The Logic of Functional Analysis', in *Aspects of Scientific Explanation*, New York: Free Press. (Classic discussion of functional explanation as a species of D-N explanation.)

Kitcher, P. (1988) 'Function and Design', *Midwest Studies in Philosophy* 18: 379–97. (Attempts to unify function under the concept of design; moderately difficult.)

Manning, R.N. (1997) 'Biological Function, Selection, and Reduction', *British Journal for the Philosophy of Science* 48: 69–82. (Rejecting reductive status of selectional accounts of function; moderate difficulty.)

* Millikan, R.G. (1984) *Language, Thought, and Other Biological Categories*, Cambridge, MA: MIT Press. (Influential theory of 'proper functions' for use in naturalized semantics; technical but rewarding.)

Nagel, E. (1953) *The Structure of Science*, New York: Harcourt Brace. (See chapter 12. A typical account, in a positivist framework, of goal-directedness for systems; somewhat technical.)

* Sober, E. (1984) *The Nature of Selection*, Cambridge, MA: MIT Press. (See chapter 5. Argues that selection does not explain the presence of biological items; moderately difficult.)

* Wright, L. (1973) 'Functions', *Philosophical Review* 82: 139–68. (An etiological theory of function; highly readable.)

RICHARD N. MANNING

FUNCTIONALISM

The term 'functionalism' means different things in many different disciplines from architectural theory to zoology. In contemporary philosophy of mind, however, it is uniformly understood to stand for the view that mental states should be explained in terms of causal roles. So, to take a simple example, a functionalist in the philosophy of mind would argue that pains are states which are normally caused by bodily damage, and tend in turn to cause avoidance behaviour.

Functionalism is often introduced by an analogy between mental states and mechanical devices. Consider the notion of a carburettor, say. For something to be a carburettor it need not have any particular physical make-up. Carburettors can come in many different materials and shapes. What makes it a carburettor is simply that it plays the right causal role, namely that it mixes air with petrol in response to movements of the accelerator and choke. Similarly, argue functionalists, with the mind. The possession of mental states does not depend on the physical make-up of the brain; it depends only on its displaying the right causal structure. Since organisms with very different sorts of biological make-up, like octopuses and humans, can have states with the causal role of pain, say, it follows from functionalism that octopuses and humans can both be in pain.

There exists a number of different subspecies of functionalism. One important division depends on how the relevant causal roles are determined. 'Common-sense' functionalists take them to be fixed by common-sense psychology; 'scientific' functionalists take them to be fixed by the discoveries of scientific psychology. So, for example, common-sense functionalists will hold that emotions play the causal role that common-sense psychology ascribes to emotions, while scientific psychologists will argue that scientific psychology identifies this causal role.

Functionalism, of whatever subspecies, is open to a number of well-known criticisms. One central objection is that it cannot accommodate the conscious, qualitative aspect of mental life. Could not a machine share the causal structure of someone who was in pain, and thereby satisfy the functionalist qualification for pain, and yet have no conscious feelings?

It might seem that functionalists can respond to this difficulty by being more stringent about the requirements involved in the causal role of a given human sensation. But there is a danger that functionalism will then lose much of its appeal. The original attraction of functionalism was that its 'liberal' specification of causal roles allowed that humans could share mental states with non-humans. This feature is likely to be lost if we switch to more 'chauvinist' specifications designed to explain why non-humans do not share our conscious life.

Another objection to functionalism is that it cannot account for mental representation. Functionalism focuses on the way mental states enter into causal structure. But it is doubtful that mental representation can be explained in purely causal terms.

Some philosophers argue that the issue of mental representation can be dealt with by adding some teleology to functionalism, that is by considering the biological purposes for which mental states have been designed, as well as their actual structure of causes and effects. However, once we do appeal to teleology in this way, it is not clear that we still need a functionalist account of representational states, for we can now simply identify such states in terms of their biological purposes, rather than their causal roles.

1 **Origins of functionalism**
2 **Common-sense and scientific functionalism**
3 **Roles and realizers**
4 **Inverted spectra**
5 **Responses to inverted spectra**
6 **Absent qualia**
7 **Representational content**

1 Origins of functionalism

Originally functionalism was a response to philosophical behaviourism. The behaviourists rejected the traditional Cartesian picture of the mind as an essentially private realm accessible only to the conscious subject (Descartes 1641). Instead they argued that mental states are dispositions to behaviour, and so are publicly accessible. To desire an ice cream, said the behaviourists, is to be disposed to eat one when the opportunity presents itself (see BEHAVIOURISM, ANALYTIC; PRIVATE STATES AND LANGUAGE).

The functionalists argued that behaviourism fails to distinguish sufficiently between mental cause and behavioural effect. They argued that there is no simple pairing of mental states with pieces of behaviour, since which behaviour issues from any given mental state will depend on the agent's other mental states. My desire for an ice cream will make me walk to the fridge if I believe it contains an ice cream, but it will make me walk down the street to the shop if I believe I can buy an ice cream there.

Because of this, functionalists argued that mental states are inner causes distinct from their behavioural effects. In saying this, however, they did not want to return to the Cartesian conception of mental events as essentially private states. In their view, mental states are part of the public world of causes and effects studied by science. They are 'inner' only in the sense that they are unobservable causes of overt behaviour, in the same way as atomic structures are unobservable causes of chemical reactions.

Because they take mental states to be unobservable, functionalists think that we only have an indirect grasp of their nature, as playing a certain causal, or 'functional', role in a cognitive system. One important consequence of this is that different physical states might play the relevant role in different beings, or even in the same being at different times. (Indeed functionalism as such leaves it open that this role could be played by some special non-physical state. In this sense functionalism is compatible with dualism (see DUALISM). However, most functionalists also hold, for independent reasons, that mental roles are in fact filled by physical states. I shall simplify the following discussion by adopting this assumption.)

Some early functionalists, most notably Hilary Putnam (see Block 1980), appealed to an analogy with computers to add precision to the idea of a causal role. Putnam pointed out that any programmed computer can be abstractly characterized as a Turing machine, independently of its 'hardware' or physical make-up; he then argued that any two systems will share mental states as long as they have the same Turing machine description (see PUTNAM, H. §6; TURING MACHINES). Today, however, it is more common to elaborate functionalism in terms of the analogy with scientific unobservables.

Unobservable entities of any kind pose a *prima facie* problem which has been much discussed in the philosophy of science. How should we understand terms like 'ionized', 'radioactive', 'diatomic', and so on, given that we have no direct access to their referents? Frank Ramsey argued that our grasp of such terms derives from our theories about the relevant unobservables. If we have a theory $T(P_1 \ldots P_n, O)$, about how various unobservable properties, $P_1 \ldots P_n$, relate to each other and to observables O, then we can read claims involving these properties as claims about whichever properties happen to play the relevant theoretical roles. More precisely, a claim attributing property Π, to individual $\underline{a}$, say, can be read as the claim $(\exists F_1 \ldots F_n)(T(F_1 \ldots F_n, O)\&F_i\underline{a})$. (In words: 'There exist properties $F_1 \ldots F_n$, which are related to each other and to observables as T says, and $\underline{a}$ has the ith one.') Note that this way of understanding claims about the Ps does not credit us with any prior understanding of these terms, but only with an understanding of existential quantification and of the observable terms O (see RAMSEY, F.P. §5).

Functionalists take an analogous attitude to terms for mental states, like 'belief', 'desire', 'jealousy', 'pain', and so on. Suppose that our psychological theory contains such assumptions as that: anybody faced with an ice cream will believe there is an ice cream in front of them; anybody who is hungry and hot will desire an ice cream; anybody who desires an ice cream and believes one is in front of them will reach out for it; and so on. Then we can understand ascriptions of desires and beliefs to particular people as claims that there are states which behave as this theory claims, and that the people in question have them.

2 Common-sense and scientific functionalism

There are various brands of functionalism. One division depends on whether the theory T used to introduce mental terminology derives from common-sense psychology or from scientific research. This issue also determines whether functionalism can claim to give an account of the *meaning* of everyday mental terms like 'desire' and 'pain'.

If the theory T is derived from common-sense psychology, then it is open to functionalists to argue that the resulting Ramsey-style account of mental discourse explicates what everyday people mean by terms like 'desire' and 'pain'. That is, they can argue that these terms, in everyday discourse, simply signify 'the causal roles specified by T'.

On the other hand, if the theory T used to introduce mental terminology is not part of everyday thinking, but rather some new scientific theory, then it cannot plausibly be argued that everyday thinkers derive their grasp of terms like 'desire' and 'pain' from this theory. So functionalists who want to replace common-sense psychology by some new scientific theory need to view the Ramsey-style account as fixing the meaning of new technical terms, which signify the causal roles specified by the new scientific theory. It is then open to them to argue that the states

picked out by their technical terms are in fact the same states as referred to by the everyday terms 'desire' and 'pain'. But, from the point of view of this kind of scientific functionalism, this will be a synthetic matter, to be supported by empirical evidence, and not a matter of definition.

The former kind of functionalism, which I am calling common-sense functionalism, is sometimes also called 'analytic' functionalism, in recognition of the fact that it makes it a matter of definition that everyday mental terms stand for certain theoretical roles. It is perhaps worth pointing out, however, that the common-sense theory T involved in these definitions will not itself be analytic. What is analytic is this claim: *if* there are states which play the roles specified by T, *then* these states are desires, pains, and so on. But the further claim, that there are in fact such states linking sensory inputs with behavioural outputs, is obviously synthetic.

One issue facing both common-sense functionalists and scientific functionalists is how *much* of the relevant theory to count as contributing to the meanings of mental terminology. It is obviously unsatisfactory to include all the many assumptions of everyday or scientific psychology in our Ramsey-style definitions of mental terms. For it would then follow that, if any single one of these assumptions turns out to be false, then all these terms will fail to refer to anything (since there will not then be any states which play the precise causal roles specified by the original incorrect theory).

The obvious remedy is to argue that only some core set of assumptions from the relevant theory plays a part in fixing the meanings of its terms. This would in effect make it an analytic requirement that desires, or pains, or whatever other mental states are at issue, satisfy the relevant core assumptions, while leaving it synthetic that they satisfy any further assumptions. However, there are general doubts about any sharp analytic-synthetic distinction of this kind. What principled reason could there be for picking out certain theoretical assumptions as constitutive of the meaning of 'desire', say, while excluding others? Perhaps the best solution for the functionalist would be to postulate some more-or-less vague distinction between the central and non-central assumptions of the relevant theory, and then take it to be a matter of meaning that the various mental terms will satisfy most of these assumptions. This will admittedly make it a vague matter whether the relevant mental terms apply to states which do not satisfy all the central assumptions; but this vagueness is arguably a feature of all theoretical terminology in science, and not necessarily vicious.

3 Roles and realizers

A further division among functionalists depends on whether they identify mental states with 'roles' or 'realizers'. Should we equate pain, say, with the property of having-some-state-which-plays-the-requisite-causal-role; or should we equate it with whichever physical state in fact realizes that role? Suppose, to adopt the usual philosophical oversimplification, that the pain role is realized in human beings by C-fibres firing. The question is then whether our term 'pain' picks out the 'realizer' property *C-fibres firing*, or whether it picks out the 'role' property *having-some-physical-state-which-plays-the-pain-role*. Note that the role answer implies that humans and octopuses, say, share the same mental state when they are in pain, for it is true that they are both in a physical-state-which-plays-the-pain-role, even if octopus pains are realized by a quite different physical state from C-fibres firing. The realizer answer, by contrast, implies that in this case human pains are different states from octopus pains, since the physical states which realize these roles are different.

The issue here is whether mental properties are first-order properties or second-order properties. By way of comparison, consider the property of being coloured. This is a second-order property, since you have it if you have some first-order property (red, blue, . . .), which in turn has the property of being a colour. Role functionalists maintain that mental states are second-order properties in this sense, in that you have them if you have some first-order physical property, which in turn has the property of playing a given causal role.

The obvious argument in favour of the role answer is precisely that it does allow humans and other beings to share pains. It seems odd to hold that the state of pain can only be present in those beings that possess C-fibres. Indeed one of the original attractions of functionalism was that, by detaching mentality from physical make-up, it seemed to allow beings of quite different physiologies to share the same mental state.

Those functionalist philosophers who favour the realizer view will allow that there is a role property common to humans and other beings with different physiologies, and that we understand the concept 'pain' by associating it with this role property. But they nevertheless argue that this term still refers to different realizer states in application to the two species. By analogy, consider the word 'eye'. All eyes have a common role feature (namely, that they are sense organs which respond to visible light), in virtue of which they are all eyes, despite their different physical realization in different species. Nevertheless, when we use the term 'eye' in application to some individual organism, we seem clearly to use it to refer to a physical part of that individual, not to the individual's instantiation of some abstract property.

In the end the debate between role and realizer versions of functionalism hinges on whether we take physical instantiation or causal role to be the essential feature of states like pain. Does difference in physical instantiation, or only difference in role, imply that we have a different state? This may seem an overly nice metaphysical issue. But it matters to the question of whether functionalism supports the identity theory of mind. The identity theory argues that mental states are identical with physical states (see MIND, IDENTITY THEORY OF). The realizer version of functionalism agrees with this identity theory, since it identifies human pains, say, with the physical state of C-fibres firing. But role functionalism denies the identity theory, since it equates human and other pains with the second-order role states.

Of course, this does not mean that role functionalism is not 'physicalist' in some broader sense. For the role properties it identifies with mental properties are still *realized* by physical properties. We should not think of the role properties as akin to substantial nonphysical properties, like the properties a Cartesian dualist would ascribe to mental substance. Rather, they are simply second-order properties – in particular second-order properties that are guaranteed by the possession of physical properties with certain causal roles.

4 Inverted spectra

Now to criticisms of functionalism: one family of objections focuses on functionalism's ability to deal with conscious, qualitative states – states that it is 'like something to have', in Thomas Nagel's (1974) phrase. These states include sensory experiences, pains, itches, and emotions, and so on, but arguably do not include such propositional attitudes as belief and desire (see QUALIA; PROPOSITIONAL ATTITUDES).

Let us start with the 'inverted spectrum' argument against functionalism. Suppose that baby Matthew has an operation performed on his retina at birth which switches the 'red' and 'green' messages from his retina to his visual cortex: the central physiological state produced in Matthew by red things is thus the state normally produced by green things in other people, and vice versa. From then on Matthew is brought up normally, learning how to discriminate between red and green things, to call them 'red' and 'green' respectively, and so on. Consider now the state (let us call it A) produced in Matthew by red things. It seems likely, given Matthew's normal upbringing, that

A will play the same causal role as the physiologically different state which arises when other people are presented with red things. Now let us ask: what kind of conscious experience will Matthew have when he is in state A? Despite A's sharing a causal role with the state normally produced by red things, it seems intuitively plausible that A will be consciously like the state normally produced by green things. After all, when Matthew has A, his brain is physiologically just like a normal brain presented with a green thing.

But this now presents a *prima facie* problem for functionalism. For if the functional role of A classifies it with the state normally produced by red things, but it feels like the state which is normally produced by green things, then functionalism has failed to capture the conscious aspect of this state.

Note how this thought experiment differs from the simpler, traditional 'inverted spectrum', which postulates an individual – Millie, say – who is normal in all physical respects but still has her colour experiences 'inverted'. The physical state which gives normal people the conscious experience of red gives her the conscious experience of green. Millie is incompatible with the general physicalist assumption that there cannot be mental differences without physical differences of some sort. The 'retinal operation' version of the inverted spectrum thought experiment, by contrast, does not require us to deny this general physicalist assumption. There are physical abnormalities in Matthew to account for his abnormal colour experiences. The point of the retinal operation thought experiment is rather that Matthew's abnormality is only at the physical level, and not at the functional level. Because of this, the retinal operation thought experiment poses a problem specifically for functionalism, which is committed to explaining mental differences in terms of functional differences, but not necessarily for other versions of physicalism.

5   Responses to inverted spectra

There are various responses to the retinal operation thought experiment open to both 'role' and 'realizer' functionalists. Let us consider them in turn, starting with role functionalism.

(1) The most direct response open to role functionalism is simply to deny the intuition that Matthew will have different conscious experiences from normal people. That is, role functionalists can argue that if Matthew's state A plays the same functional role as the state produced in normal people by red things, then it will feel the same, even if it is physiologically different. After all, they can point out, by hypothesis this state will make Matthew react in just the way that normal people react to red experiences, both in his behaviour and in

forming further beliefs and desires. If this is so, they will ask, then what substance is there to the hypothesis that the experience is nevertheless consciously different?

However, this answer is less than wholly convincing. Maybe some qualitative states, like pain, can plausibly be argued to depend on nothing but functional role (if a state creates a pressing and intense desire to move some part of your body, does that not show it is a pain?). But other qualitative states, of which colour experiences are the paradigm, do not seem to be nearly so closely tied to functional role (there is no specific desire or behaviour which is typically prompted by an experience of green). So if we take some such state, like normal people's experience of green, and imagine its functional role switched while its physiology stays the same, as in Matthew, then most philosophers have a strong intuition that will still feel the same, despite the fact this runs counter to role functionalism.

(2) Other role functionalists adopt a different tack. They simply admit that their theory of mind cannot deal with 'qualia' – that is, with the qualitative aspects of colour and similar conscious experiences. Instead they accept that these aspects are fixed by physical realization rather than functional role. Role functionalists of this stripe can continue to maintain a role functionalist account of non-qualitative states like belief and desire, and indeed of the non-qualitative aspects of qualitative states. But their role functionalism will be incomplete, in that they admit that qualia themselves are not fixed by their functional role. In particular, they concede that an individual who is functionally normal but physically abnormal, like Matthew, will not experience normal qualia.

(3) The 'retinal operation' thought experiment is much less of a problem for realizer functionalism than for role functionalism. After all, realizer functionalists take mental terms to refer to physical states from the start: they distinguish between human pains (one physiological state) and octopus pains (a different physiological state), even though both states play the pain role. Similarly, they can distinguish between Matthew's experience of red, which is one physical state, and a normal person's experience, which is a different physical state. True, both states play the same functional role. But nevertheless the realizer functionalist counts them as distinct mental states, and to this extent need not be disturbed by intuitions that they are also qualitatively distinct.

(4) Both the realizer functionalist of the last paragraph, and the incomplete role functionalist of the previous one, take qualia to be fixed by physical realization. Different physics, different qualia. However, some philosophers argue that this principle is excessively 'chauvinist', since it implies that beings

who lack human physiology cannot share human experiences. Surely, more 'liberal' philosophers argue, we want to allow that dolphins, say, or the inhabitants of Proxima Centauri's third planet, might be functionally organized in such a way as to experience pain and sadness, say, even if they have non-human physiologies.

David Lewis has devised an ingenious version of functionalism, which allows this kind of liberalism while still respecting the intuition that Matthew's experience when he is faced with something green is like a normal person's experience of red. Lewis argues that terms for mental states ('belief', 'desire', 'pain', 'sadness', 'experience of green' and so on) should be understood, in their application to any given being, to refer to the first-order state that realizes the relevant functional role *in normal members of the species* (or other group to which the being belongs). Matthew is a human being, so 'experience of green' as applied to him refers to the physical state that is produced by green things and plays the corresponding functional role in normal human beings. In Matthew, of course, this physical state (state A) plays the functional role that relates to red things. But classified mentally it is still an experience of green, because in normal people it plays the role appropriate to green things.

If we are talking about a Proxima Centaurian, by contrast, then 'experience of green' does not refer to the physical state produced by green things in humans, but rather to the physical state (if there is one) produced by green things in Proxima Centaurians. So it is possible for a Proxima Centaurian to have an experience of green, Lewis argues, as long as it is in the physical state that plays the relevant role in its normal conspecifics, even if that is different from the state A that plays this role in humans. (Note that there could also be an abnormal Proxima Centaurian in whom the experience of green does not play the green functional role, as long as it is the state that plays that functional role in normal Proxima Centaurians.)

So, according to Lewis, qualitative experiences vary with physical realizer states within a given group, but with functional role states across groups. His theory thus accommodates the intuition that Matthew is qualitatively different from normal humans, while avoiding the chauvinist implication that animals and extraterrestrials cannot share our experiences.

Lewis is normally classified as a realizer functionalist. But in one respect the mixed theory just outlined goes beyond realizer functionalism. A different physical state realizes experiences of green in humans and Proxima Centaurians. Yet Lewis counts them alike in respect of their qualitative nature. This makes him different from the realizer functionalists described in (3) above, who take the difference in physical

realization to lead to a difference in qualitative feel. Still, this only shows that Lewis is not a straightforward realizer functionalist, not that he is wrong.

A more serious difficulty for Lewis' theory is that it makes the qualitative classification of peoples' mental states depend on which species or group we assign them to. Suppose a minority subspecies of humans evolves a different pain mechanism from other humans. And suppose Jane belongs to this subspecies. *Qua* member of the subspecies, Jane will be in pain when her mechanism is activated, for she will be in the state that plays the pain role in normal members of the subspecies. But *qua* human *simpliciter*, she will not be in pain, for she is not in the state that plays the pain role in normal humans. Lewis accepts that there will sometimes be no unique answer to the question of which group an individual belongs to, and consequently that it will be indeterminate what qualitative mental states it has. This is, to say the least, a surprising consequence of his theory.

(5) Some role functionalists argue that the way to deal with the inverted spectrum problem is to distinguish extra levels of functional organization. Standard discussions only consider two levels — 'macroscopic' functional role and physical realization. Because of this, standard discussions face a dilemma: they either tie qualia to 'macroscopic' functional role, and fail to accommodate the intuition that Matthew is qualitatively abnormal; or they tie qualia to physical realization, and end up 'chauvinistically' denying pains to Proxima Centaurians. Lewis' mixed theory offers one way out. But another way out would be to uphold role functionalism, but identify some intermediate level of 'micro-functional' organization, which will distinguish Matthew from other humans, yet be common to humans and members of different species. By hypothesis, Matthew's states coincide with normal human states in respect of such 'macroscopic' role features as which actions they give rise to, which beliefs and desires they prompt, and so on. But they need not coincide in more 'microscopic' respects such as the light reflectance profile being computed, the firing pattern of the relevant neural units, and so on. The important point is that these microscopic features are still functional, in that they can be realized in systems of different physical composition. So they could be shared by humans and physically different species, while at the same time serving to distinguish Matthew from normal humans.

Note that this 'microfunctional' solution is open to scientific functionalists, but not to common-sense functionalists. Assumptions about reflectance profiles and neuronal firing are not part of common-sense psychology. Common-sense functionalism is therefore forced to count Matthew as functionally normal, and so unable to explain his intuitive qualitative difference by reference to functional factors. Scientific functionalism is not so constrained, as there are many possible levels of functional organization in the brain which might distinguish Matthew from normal humans. The only question is whether this is an embarrassment of riches. For once we have opened up the possibility that qualitative features might be fixed by any level of functional organization, what could possibly decide which level does in fact fix it? It is no good appealing to the subject's introspective reports, since they are part of macro-functional role, which is already agreed not to fix qualia (thus Matthew will describe state A as 'seeing red', yet nearly everybody agrees he is experiencing green). On the other hand, it seems highly unlikely that intuition can resolve the issue, for intuition is surely not fine-grained enough to decide such questions as whether somebody who is computing the normal reflectance profile for green things, but using an abnormal pattern of neuronal firing to do so, is experiencing green or not.

6 Absent qualia

The inverted spectrum thought experiment is consistent with the idea that appropriate functional organization guarantees conscious states of some kind. The only issue raised by the inverted spectrum argument is whether functional identity suffices to fix the qualitative identity of those conscious states. A more radical form of argument asks whether functional organization can guarantee consciousness at all. Are there not always going to be systems that display the appropriate functional organization yet lack qualia altogether?

Clearly, answers to this question will depend crucially on what qualifies as 'appropriate functional organization'. Recall that earlier the notion of a functional role was introduced via Ramsey's strategy for defining unobservable terms in terms of a theory. On this conception, you have mental states with a certain functional role if you have a set of states which interact in the way specified by some psychological theory $T(M_1 \ldots M_n, O)$.

A number of thought experiments aim to show that any such notion of functional role must yield too 'liberal' an account of qualitative states, in that it will imply the presence of qualia in systems that in fact lack them. Imagine that the sensory messages into your brain and the motor messages going out are disconnected from your brain and instead linked by radio to a complicated structure made of old beer cans. This system of beers cans is arranged in such a way that its properties relate to each other and to your sensory and motor messages in just the way that psychological theory T says your brain states did before they were disconnected. Then the system consisting of your debrained body plus beer cans will have exactly the same functional organization as you had before your brain was disconnected. Yet it seems implausible that this system would be conscious, that there is something that it would be like to be a debrained body plus beer cans.

Even so, a significant number of functionalist philosophers are prepared to bite this bullet, and maintain that the beer can system would be conscious. After all, if some diseased part of your brain were replaced by some microscopic silicon-based circuitry, this would not necessarily stop you being conscious. What is the difference in principle, it could be asked, between this and the beer can case?

The beer can thought experiment starts with a normal human being, and then assumes the alteration of this human being's brain. But there are further arguments which query whether even behavioural similarity to human beings is necessary for the relevant kind of functional organization. These arguments focus on the contribution of the observational terms O to the specification of functional roles. Note that it is essential to any plausible functionalism that these terms somehow be independently understood. For, if the O terms are themselves defined in terms of theory, T, there will be far too many systems the properties of which satisfy T. Indeed, given a completely uninterpreted theory $T(M_1 \ldots M_n, O)$, it is arguable that *any* physical system – the air molecules in your house, say – will display *some* set of properties that are related to each other as T says the Ms and O are related. So some prior understanding of the O terms is needed to give us any chance of ensuring that only conscious systems have the functional organization specified by T.

The natural way to do this is to equate O terms with terms for perceptual inputs (for example, 'receiving visual stimuli from an ice cream') and behavioural outputs (for example 'moving your arm towards an ice cream'). But this, then, has the disadvantage of implying that some presumably conscious human beings, such as experimental subjects whose optic nerves are being stimulated by brain scientists, or paralyzed people who display no behavioural outputs, will lack the relevant functional organization.

The natural response to this difficulty (for a scientific functionalist at least, even if not for a common-sense functionalist) is to appeal to physiology to specify less peripheral inputs (kinds of stimulation of the optic nerve, say) and less peripheral outputs (kinds of activity in the motor cortex). But this physiological move threatens chauvinism. For it will exclude from the category of conscious beings any extraterrestrials and animals whose non-human physiologies do not include optic nerves and motor cortexes.

There remains some room for functionalists to manoeuvre here. One possibility would be to return to Lewis' mixed theory, which would imply that the experimental subject and the paralyzed person are conscious because they are in the states that play the requisite causal role in their normal conspecifics, even if not in themselves. Another increasingly popular response is to appeal to teleological considerations, and understand 'functional organization' as not only specifying a causal structure but requiring in addition that this structure be a product of biological design. By appealing to this further sense of 'function', such 'teleofunctionalists' can specify that beings with different physiologies can nevertheless share the same functional organization, in virtue of having causally similar structures which have been designed for similar biological purposes.

7 Representational content

This further teleological sense of 'function' is also relevant to the difficulties functionalists face in accounting for content. Many mental states, and in particular such non-qualitative propositional attitudes as belief and desire, represent states of affairs other than themselves. It is unclear whether the functionalist theory of mental states can account for such representational contents.

One immediate difficulty is that many representational contents are 'broad', in the sense that the content of many propositional attitudes seems to depend not just on the thinker's physical make-up but also on features of the context (see CONTENT: WIDE AND NARROW). For example, it is arguable that the possession of beliefs about natural kinds depends not just on the organization of the believer's brain, but also on features of the believer's social context and on which natural kinds are present in the believer's world. This raises a *prima facie* problem for functionalism. For functionalism makes the possession of mental states depend on the subject's brain having a certain causal structure. Yet by hypothesis the possession of broad propositional attitudes is not fixed by facts about brains.

However, functionalism has an obvious remedy. There is no obvious reason why functionalism should only consider causal structures inside the head. Why not have a 'broad' functionalism, which recognizes 'broad' causal structures in which mental states interact, not only with each other and with sensory inputs and motor outputs but also with such external factors as the social environment and objectively existing natural kinds? This would then open the way to a theory which makes the possession of broad propositional attitudes depend on broad causal structures.

So perhaps broad contents present no special problem for functionalism. A more radical criticism of functionalism, however, queries its ability to account for representational contents of any kind, broad or not. Functionalism identifies mental states as items that have certain causes and effects. Yet it is doubtful whether representation can be explained in any simple causal terms.

It might seem that, once we are allowed to appeal to 'broad' causal structures, we can identify the contents of beliefs as those external circumstances that typically cause them, and the contents of desires as those external states of affairs to which they typically give rise. But this simple strategy is afflicted by the problem of 'disjunctivitis'. Take the belief with the content that an ice cream is in front of you. This can be caused, not only by a real ice cream, but also by a plastic ice cream, or a hologram of an ice cream, and so on. Similarly the results which follow any given desire will include not only the real content of the desire, but also various unintended consequences.

So, even if we are allowed broad causal roles that include external causes and effects, we still need somehow to identify, among the various causes that give rise to beliefs, and the various results that eventuate from desires, those which comprise the beliefs' and desires' real contents. There are a number of possible ways of doing this. One of the most promising is to appeal to teleological considerations once more. For then we can pick out a desire's content as that effect which it is the desire's biological purpose to produce. And, similarly, we can pick out a belief's content as that condition with which it is the biological purpose of the belief to be co-present (see SEMANTICS, TELEOLOGICAL).

One question raised by this appeal to teleology is whether the original functionalism is still doing any work. We started with the functionalist idea that mental states can be identified by their causal roles. But it now seems that, for contentful mental states at least, causal roles are not enough, and need to be supplemented by biological purposes. The obvious question is whether biological purposes would suffice by themselves. Perhaps we can identify contentful mental states by their purposes alone. The answer depends on whether a common biological purpose, but different causal roles, implies different representational states, and relates to a number of currently controversial questions in the philosophy of representation.

See also: MATERIALISM IN THE PHILOSOPHY OF MIND;
REDUCTIONISM IN THE PHILOSOPHY OF MIND

References and further reading

* Block, N. (ed.) (1980) *Readings in the Philosophy of Psychology*, London: Methuen, vol. 1. (The section on functionalism contains many important articles, including early versions of functionalism by H. Putnam, D. Lewis and D.M. Armstrong. See also Block's Introduction to this section, and the difficulties he raises in 'Troubles with Functionalism'.)

* Descartes, R. (1641) *Meditations on First Philosophy* in *The Philosophical Writings of René Descartes*, trans. J. Cottingham, R. Stoothoff, D. Murdoch, Cambridge: Cambridge University Press, vol. 2 1984. (Classic statement and defence of dualism.)

Lewis, D. (1980) 'Mad Pain and Martian Pain', in N. Block (ed.), *Readings in the Philosophy of Psychology*, London: Methuen, 1980, vol. 1; repr. with a postscript in D. Lewis *Philosophical Papers*, Oxford: Blackwell 1983, vol. 1. (Lewis' 'mixed' version of functionalism.)

Millikan, R. (1986) 'Thoughts without Laws', *Philosophical Review* XCV: 47–80. (Argues that mental states should be analysed in terms of biological purposes rather than causal roles.)

* Nagel, T. (1974) 'What is it like to be a Bat?', *Philosophical Review* 83: 435–50, repr. in Block (1980). (Argues that the subjective character of experience is not captured by physicalist theories.)

Papineau, D. (1991) 'Teleology and Mental States', *Aristotelian Society Supplementary Volume* LXV: 33–54. (Argues that functionalism without teleology cannot account for representation.)

Ramsey, F.P. (1931) 'Theories' in *Foundations of Mathematics*, London: Routledge & Kegan Paul. (The original statement of Ramsey's account of theoretical terms.)

Rosenthal, D.M. (ed.) (1991) *The Nature of Mind*, London: Oxford University Press. (Good general collection on contemporary philosophy of mind. Papers by W.G. Lycan and E. Sober argue for 'microfunctionalism' (Lycan) and 'teleofunctionalism' (Lycan and Sober).)

Shoemaker, S. (1984) *Identity, Cause and Mind*, Cambridge: Cambridge University Press. (This collection of Shoemaker's papers includes discussions of the different species of functionalism and of the inverted spectrum and absent qualia objections.)

DAVID PAPINEAU

FUNCTIONALISM IN SOCIAL SCIENCE

In the social sciences, functionalists are theorists who give an especially prominent role to functional explanations. One of the most influential self-defined functionalists, Malinowski (1926), summed up this view: the functionalist 'insists... upon the principle that in every type of civilisation, every custom, material object, idea and belief fulfils some vital function, has some task to accomplish, represents an indispensable part within a working whole'. As an example of a functionalist explanation, one might consider the hypothesis, as argued for instance by Evans-Pritchard in his work on the Azande in Africa, that belief in witches generally plays a role in maintaining social stability (1937).

In the last few decades of the twentieth century, postmodern, or post-structuralist, sociologists have largely disavowed the pursuit of functional explanations. The extremism of some functionalist theses has been matched by an equal extremism in postmodern antitheses. In denying that everything must be explained functionally, some go so far as to say that nothing should ever be explained functionally.

Yet there is liveable logical space between the modernist's 'There has always got to be a reason, the real reason, for everything', and the postmodernist's 'There is never any real reason for anything'. We do not have to be card-carrying functionalists to suspect that functional explanations might be found for at least some of the bewildering things that some people do in various parts of the world. New models of functional explanation are emerging from recent ferment in the biological sciences, and these new models may suggest new ways of approaching functional explanations in the social sciences.

1   **Apparent limits of rational choice explanations**
2   **Functionalists and their influence**
3   **Critiques of functionalism**
4   **Social functions compared with biological functions**
5   **New tools from the biological sciences**

1   Apparent limits of rational choice explanations

When European explorers made first contact with various different cultures, they were sometimes at a loss to understand many of the practices they witnessed. Potlatch for instance: this was a spectacular practice among the indigenous peoples of north-western North America of the giving and then almost immediate destruction of extremely impressive gifts.

After the initial shock of the exotic, some anthropologists then began to imagine how many of their own practices might appear to strangers. Then familiar things in their own lives began to cry out for explanation. In a similar way, Americans may have been prompted to wonder (in, say, the 1980s): why do businessmen wear ties, and business women shoulder pads, for instance?

There is often a common thread running through those things that seemed especially difficult to understand: it is initially difficult to see goals which you could believe the agents to have, and which you could believe that the agents were thinking they could achieve by the actions they were performing. You ask the agents themselves why they do these things, and either they say they do not know, or they do their best to tell you their motives but somehow you still feel that there is more to be explained.

Research in the social sciences is often driven by a sense of bewilderment at some of the things people do. When our common sense (individualistic, rational choice theoretic) explanatory strategies fail to get a grip, functional explanations naturally emerge to fill the explanatory vacuum.

Functional explanations are not the only sorts of explanations that present themselves as rivals to rational choice theoretic explanations. Functionalism emerged from a range of competing explanatory strategies, as for instance: causal/historical explanations, diffusionism, evolutionary theories of the sort typified by Frazer's *The Golden Bough* (1890), and the possibility of explaining some social phenomena by reference to instincts. But functional explanations have had a tendency to become peculiarly pervasive, as soon as we move beyond rational choice explanations.

If you wonder why a person holds a particular belief, or engages in a particular practice, then one answer that is worth pondering is this: perhaps they believe or act as they do just because that is what other people believe and do. But then we are slipping into a regress: why do those other people hold this belief and engage in this practice? You might speculate that this regress ends with a person who, once upon a time, introduced this belief and associated practices for reasons that were perfectly comprehensible at the time, easily explicable by common-sense rational choice theory. Then this belief and associated practices have been replicated through the ages even though people have forgotten the initial rationale behind them, just because it is, in certain contexts, individually rational to conform to the beliefs and practices of others. In brief, one way to explain something through rational choice theory is by tracing it back to its origins.

This sort of explanation is problematic, however, for several reasons. Often, there are too few empirical constraints on speculations about the origins of a practice. And even if one were confident about the origin of a practice, there remains something to be explained in the fact that while other practices die out, this one persists. Malinowski said: 'There are no survivors' (1922). This may be an overstatement: there may be some practices which really are explained by there having been a rational choice by some originator, and then transmission by rational imitation from there on. Nevertheless, it is arguable that our default assumption should be in the spirit of Malinowski's dictum; usually, there is something important left unexplained by the theory of rational origin followed by rational imitation.

When our default explanations of behaviour, by common-sense rational choice theory, fail to satisfy, we are at a loss for understanding, and functional explanations in the social sciences aim to fill this explanatory gap. This is the first step towards functionalism. The second step towards functionalism is taken when social scientists begin to look more sceptically at cases that used to seem straightforwardly explicable in terms of common-sense rational choice theory. A suspicion begins to grow, that the veneer of rationality is always just rationalization or, to take a phrase from Marxism, false consciousness. An analogy can be drawn with psychoanalysis. Some sorts of bizarre behaviour seem difficult to explain by common-sense rational choice theory, so extraordinary modes of explanation are introduced, that posit unconscious beliefs and desires. Then the psychoanalyst looks back at superficially rational choices of everyday life and begins to suspect that our 'real' reasons are never the conscious reasons. Likewise, the extreme functionalist always looks for 'latent' functions behind whatever 'manifest' functions there may be, if any.

2 Functionalists and their influence

Many theorists, some less outspoken than Malinowski, have been collected under the label of functionalism because of family resemblances, acknowledged indebtednesses, and affiliations to others travelling under that label. Famous names in the family are predominantly anthropologists: Marcel Mauss, Émile Durkheim, Talcott Parsons, E.E. Evans-Pritchard, Arnold Radcliffe-Brown, Franz Boas, Ruth Benedict, Margaret Mead, Edward Sapir.

Some theorists, like Claude Lévi-Strauss, broke away from some (though not all) of the distinctive doctrines of the self-defined functionalists and travelled under the label of structuralism (see Lévi-Strauss, C.; Structuralism in social science). But the relationship between structuralism and functionalism is often far from clear, and it is not clear whether structuralism is a friend or a foe of functionalism. Structuralists aim to understand a social phenomenon by describing a network of interdependent phenomena within which the thing to be explained is located. The whole network is then seen to be a structure that, at a sufficiently high level of abstraction, is instantiated in every human society. The metaphors guiding structuralism are more often drawn from grammar than from biology; the natural bedfellow of this sort of theory is what is known as systems theory. The supposed universality of certain deep structures suggests that they are in some important sense innate. Structuralism may thus be seen as a sophisticated version of social explanation by reference to human instincts. And this is often seen as a rival to explanation by reference to functions.

Nevertheless, the structuralists' explanatory strategy does still have a close kinship with functional explanations. Systems theory embodies much of what is distinctive of functional explanations, and is applied across a wide range of research in the social sciences: in politics, social psychology, agrarian studies, and in sociology generally. Much of structuralism can be absorbed into what is called structural-functionalism (this label attaches especially to Talcott Parsons (1952)), and much of systems theory can be construed as raw materials for a more complete functional explanation. A description of 'how a system works' can be construed as a description of 'the functions' which the elements are playing in the whole.

3   Critiques of functionalism

Yet, as with the posits of psychoanalysis, a social scientist's attributions of functions can be clouded by logical and epistemological miasmas. It is sometimes unclear just what it means to say that some practice has a certain function. And while it is often relatively easy to think up a story about what function some practice might have, it is often hard to know what sort of evidence would count for or against that hypothesis: verification or falsification are not so straightforward.

For instance, Cohen used the tools of the logical positivists, especially Hempel's model of scientific explanation (1965), to articulate the logic of functional explanations. He also drew heavily on what was a novel idea at that time: feedback loops. In *Karl Marx's Theory of History: A Defence* (1978), he brought all this to bear on political examples of special interest to Marxists. This brought the nature of functional explanation into sharp focus, and thereby helped to define some of the growing unease about these sorts of explanations. In an influential critique, in *Ulysses and the Sirens* (1979) and else-where, Jon Elster (another Marxist) argued that the required postulations of feedback loops are almost never empirically testable. Hence functional explanations are just as empirically unconstrained as fanciful speculations about origins, which they were supposed to supplant. Much can be said in defence of Cohen, but the kinds of worries expressed by Elster have led many people to retreat from the functionalist bandwagon.

4   Social functions compared with biological functions

To get a grip on the nature of functional explanation in general, it may be useful to consider some of the most successful functional explanations outside the social sciences. Think first of functional explanations of features of artefacts, as for instance when we are puzzled by one of the attachments on a Swiss army knife. However these functional explanations seem to draw us back towards the intentions of a designer, and this is not a model which helps us with the kinds of puzzle-cases which mostly cry out for functional explanation in the social sciences.

Functional explanation in the social sciences can be more profitably compared with functional explanation in the biological sciences. Just as an anthropologist is puzzled by a practice like potlatch, so too a biologist is puzzled by something like the peacock's tail. Adaptationism is the name given to the default assumption, for every feature of an animal which catches your interest, that it must be serving a function. The functionalism of Malinowski's dictum, that 'there are no survivors', is like an extreme adaptationism that would look for a current function not only for say the pancreas, but even for the human appendix.

In the biological sciences, it used to be thought that any references to functions and purposes would presuppose the intentions of a creator. There are analogous viewpoints that could be held in the social sciences. It might be thought that the attribution of social functions would presuppose the intentions of some agent: either the intentions of the human or deity who invented the practice, or the unconscious intentions of the people who engage in the practice, or else intentions embodied in some sort of group mind. For various reasons, the prospects for functional explanation in the social sciences would be slim if they carried that much metaphysical baggage with them.

Fortunately, however, it has become apparent that sense can be made of biological functions without presupposing any conscious processes of design or selection or intention. A biologist may undertake to find a purely biological explanation of the presence of the pancreas for instance, or of the peacock's tail. One way to do so is by finding that this thing has had a propensity to bring about certain characteristic effects, which in turn have contributed to the reproductive capacities of the animals which possessed it. One key concept in evolutionary thinking is that of 'inclusive fitness': this is taken to be the propensity of an organism to reproduce other organisms with this same propensity.

Thus, a biologist who wants to explain the presence of something biological can legitimately do so by reference to its functions, and can do so without thereby incurring a theological commitment. And this is a relief: it does seem obvious that one reasonable way of explaining the presence of, say, the pancreas is by identifying some of its functions, and that this is not tantamount to belief in a creator.

According to what is called the etiological theory of biological functions, for something to have a biological function is for it to have an evolutionary history that explains its current existence by reference to those of its past effects which have contributed to its reproductive fitness and subsequent survival and replication.

The application of the etiological theory of functions to the social sciences generates some interesting results. One example is provided by Marvin Harris in *Cows, Pigs, Wars and Witches* (1974). Here, some of the puzzling activities of people in New Guinea are explained by attributing to these practices the function of population control.

It is not implied by Harris that the people engaging in various social practices in New Guinea are either consciously or unconsciously aiming at population control. It is not implied that any person or deity designed the practices with the intention that this would result in population control, or that there was any intention on behalf of something you might call a group mind. Yet Harris meant more than just that these puzzling practices resulted in population control. He meant that these practices existed in these social groups precisely because they have a propensity to result in population control. What he hypothesizes is that, over the ages, those social groups which engaged in such practices prospered. Furthermore, those groups prospered because these practices resulted in population control, which in turn ensured that the social group did not exceed the carrying capacity of their environment. If Harris were right about this sort of evolutionary past for the relevant social groups, then the etiological theory of functions would license the attribution of functions to those practices.

Functional explanations of this sort, however, will seldom be well supported by evidence. It is seldom that we will have good reason to believe that the practices we seek to explain have the kind of history which would be called for by the etiological theory of functions.

Consider an example. Some witch beliefs and practices are pandemic, and one might reasonably suppose them to have had enough evolutionary history to justify an etiologically grounded attribution of functions. But the case is different with the large scale European witch-hunts that began a little before 1492, and periodically flared up or smouldered on until the last of these horrific witch-hunts, in Salem in 1692. This is just the sort of case in which explanation by common-sense rational choice theory seems to be missing something of underlying importance, and hence in which we might hope to find some more satisfying functional explanations. Yet the European witch-hunts also constitute a case in which it seems doubtful that we could ever establish the kind of evolutionary history that Harris postulates for the New Guinea case.

There is a striking feature of early functionalism that can be seen to arise naturally out of an etiological conception of functions. There used to be a propensity of early functionalists to attribute to every practice the very same function: that of promoting social stability. There was a tendency to see every belief and every practice as cogs in a social machine for suppressing change. Later functionalists have tried to explain change as well as stability. But if we are using an etiological theory of functions, then functional explanations of change do not rest easily on those etiological foundations.

There is an instructive parallel in biology. On the etiologist's conception, biological functions cannot contribute to an explanation of an increasing frequency of some brand new feature: with no evolutionary history there can be no etiological function. The etiologist's functions can only explain the presence of a feature which has contributed to fitness over a significant period of time. So for the etiologist, functional explanations can only get a grip when there is stability rather than change.

Likewise in the social sciences, the etiologist's functions cannot explain change but only the existence of 'survivors'. This is a disappointment, because among the things that a functionalist was hoping to explain were, not just 'where do we come from?', but also 'what is going on here?' and 'where are we going?'

5 New tools from the biological sciences

Some functional explanations appeal to an intelligent creator, others to Darwinian evolution; both of these kinds are of limited use in social theory. It is thus worth asking whether there may be other logical forms which functional explanations might take, and which might better serve the needs of the social sciences. Here are some models which have been emerging in the biological sciences.

Instead of wondering about why a characteristic is present in an animal, a biologist might take an interest in the fitness of the animal in some particular environment. Overall fitness may then be analysed as the product of several distinct components, somewhat as a physicist analyses a resultant force as deriving from several distinct component forces. Whenever some feature of an organism is currently contributing to the propensity for survival and replication, it is natural to speak of this feature as serving a function. This may be so, even if there is not yet any history during which this propensity has actually contributed to survival and replication. Not yet having enough history, the relevant feature cannot 'have a biological function' according to the etiologist. Nevertheless, if something is currently contributing to overall fitness, then there is already a clear enough non-etiological sense in which it makes sense to speak of it as serving some biological function.

This construal of functions might be instructively applicable to various problem cases in the social sciences. It is more likely that a sociologist could establish that something is currently contributing to success, than that it has an etiology which explains its current existence in terms of past successes. In the case of the European witch-hunts, for instance, the spread of witch-hunts did not happen by magic; there must have been something about witch-hunts that explained their alarming propensity for replication. This sort of explanation would speak more directly to our bewilderment, than would the backward-looking etiologist's search for an evolutionary history behind the witch-hunts. What is especially puzzling about witch-hunts, after all, what is crying out for explanation, is the way they spread and kept recurring, their replicatory fitness so to speak. And what a non-etiological functional explanation can hope to offer is an identification of the component functions which contributed to that overall replicatory fitness.

In recent biology, there has been heated debate about the so-called units of selection. There have been interesting challenges to the narrowly Darwinian assumption that biologically functional features of an organism must always enhance the inclusive fitness of the individual organism which carries that feature. In opposition, it has been argued that in special circumstances it can sometimes happen that a gene will increase in frequency even if it lowers the survival and reproductive prospects for the organism which carries it. This is, for instance, the point of the Dawkins' 'selfish gene' theory (1976). Others have argued that patterns can evolve in groups of individuals, or even in 'developmental systems' or 'ecologies' that blur the boundaries between organisms and environment, and that these patterns can evolve in a way which is to some degree autonomous from any contributions that are being made to the fitness of the individuals involved. Whether or not the empirical evidence in biology backs up these less narrowly Darwinian biological theories, the logic of these debates over units of selection can teach lessons of value for functional explanation in the social sciences.

If we model social science functional explanations exclusively on narrowly Darwinian evolutionary theory, then the only things with social functions will be things that 'benefit' the particular societies in which they appear. Yet consider again the example of the European witch-hunts. On the face of things, they had a high propensity to replicate themselves even though it was far from obvious what 'benefits' if any they conferred on the social groups in which they occurred. Thus, it is desirable to at least try out the hypothesis that witch-hunts were analogous to an epidemic, which has a propensity to spread and persist even though it does nothing but harm to its victims. It is therefore of theoretical interest if we can find ways of articulating functional explanations of things like the witch-hunts without presupposing that whatever is functionally explainable has to be socially beneficial.

Functionalism in the social sciences has had a troubled history. It arose out of an urgent need for explanations of various bewildering things people do; and at least in some cases it is very tempting to explain these things by reference to social functions rather than to rational choices, instincts, or other explanatory candidates. Arguably, functionalists overplayed their hand in demanding functional explanations for everything. They also had difficulty getting a secure grip on the logic and epistemology of functional explanations. And they had trouble understanding how functional explanations could account for change as well as stability. However, similar difficulties also beset functional explanations in the biological sciences, and progress has been made in overcoming these difficulties. It is premature to conclude, as some postmodernists have done, that functional explanations can have no place in the social sciences (see POST-STRUCTURALISM IN THE SOCIAL SCIENCES; POSTMODERNISM).

See also: EVOLUTIONARY THEORY AND SOCIAL SCIENCE; EXPLANATION IN HISTORY AND SOCIAL

SCIENCE; FUNCTIONAL EXPLANATION; SOCIAL
SCIENCE, METHODOLOGY OF

References and further reading

* Cohen, G.A. (1978) *Karl Marx's Theory of History: A Defence*, Princeton, NJ: Princeton University Press. (For its time, one of the most careful and penetrating analyses and applications of the concept of function as it occurs in social explanations, presenting a clearly defined target for Elster's (1979) influential epistemological critique.)

* Dawkins, R. (1976) *The Selfish Gene*, Oxford: Oxford University Press. (An influential critique of individualistic presuppositions of many Darwinians, proposing the controversial thesis that features of organisms serve the function of benefiting, not the individual, but the individual's genes.)

Durkheim, E. (1915) *The Elementary Forms of the Religious Life*, trans. J.W. Swain, London: Allen & Unwin, 1971. (A classic work in sociology, portraying societies as more like organisms than like mere aggregates of rational individuals.)

* Elster, J. (1979) *Ulysses and the Sirens*, Cambridge: Cambridge University Press. (An influential Marxist critique of functional explanations, especially Cohen (1978).)

* Evans-Pritchard, E.E. (1937) *Witchcraft, Oracles and Magic Among the Azande*, Oxford: Clarendon Press. (A functionalist classic in anthropology, seeking the social functions served by apparently irrational magical beliefs.)

* Frazer, J.G. (1890) *The Golden Bough*, London: Macmillan, 3rd edn, 1925–36. (An 'evolutionary theory' in anthropology, laden with stories of strange beliefs and practices from all over the world.)

* Harris, M. (1974) *Cows, Pigs, Wars and Witches*, New York: Random House. (The chapter on 'Primitive War' is especially interesting, pp. 61–80, proposing to explain puzzling practices in New Guinea as serving the function of population control.)

* Hempel, C.G. (1965) *Aspects of Scientific Explanation*, New York: Free Press. (A classic in the broadly logical positivist tradition, including an influential analysis of scientific explanation in general, and functional explanations in particular.)

* Malinowski, B. (1922) *Argonauts of the Western Pacific: An Account of Native Enterprises and Adventure in the Archipelagoes of Melanesian New Guinea*, London: Routledge. (A functionalist classic in anthropology, seeking a functional explanation for every social phenomenon.)

* —— (1926) 'Anthropology' in *Encyclopaedia Britannica*, London: Encyclopaedia Britannica

Inc, 13th edn, supplement I. (A manifesto for an extreme functionalist thesis: that there is a functional reason for everything social.)

Mauss, M. and Humbert, H. (1899) *Sacrifice: Its Nature and Function*, trans. W.D. Halls, London: Cohen & West, 1964. (A functionalist classic in anthropology, seeking the social function of rituals of sacrifice.)

Merton, R.K. (1957) *Social Theory and Social Structure*, Glencoe, IL: Free Press. (Contains an influential essay on 'Manifest and Latent Functions': functionalists are especially concerned with uncovering 'latent' functions.)

Midelfort, C.E. (1872) *Witch Hunting in Southwestern Germany 1562–1684*, Stanford, CA: Stanford University Press. (Excellent material, with critical commentson early functionalism, and reasons for thinking witch hunting in Europe did not function to maintain social stability.)

Parijs, P. van (1981) *Evolutionary Explanation in the Social Sciences*, Totowa, NJ: Rowman & Littlefield. (Clear and comprehensive exposition and further references.)

* Parsons, T. (1952) *The Social System*, London: Routledge & Kegan Paul. (A sociological classic in 'structural-functionalism', construing functions both as essential elements within the structures which constitute any human society ('structuralism'), and as processes which meet the needs of the societies in which they occur ('functionalism').)

Radcliffe-Brown, A.R. (1922) *The Andaman Islanders*, London: Cambridge University Press. (A functionalist classic in anthropology.)

Summers, M. (1971) *The Malleus Maleficarum of Heinrich Kramer and James Sprenger*, New York: Dover. (Source material on early witch-hunts in Europe, full of expressions of and exhortations to apparently irrational and socially dysfunctional beliefs and practices.)

Thomas, K. (1971) *Religion and the Decline of Magic*, London: Weidenfield and Nicolson. (A classic on a topic on the interface between history, sociology and anthropology, seeking explanations for things which are not easy to understand just by reference to rational choices of individuals.)

Weber, M. (1922) *Die protestantische Ethik und der Geist des Kapitalismus* (The Protestant Ethic and the Spirit of Capitalism), trans. T. Parsons, London: Allen & Unwin, 1930. (A classic in sociology, seeking to explain various features of religion by reference, neither to reason not to revelation, but to the functions they serve in a capitalist society.)

Wilson, E.O. (1975) *Sociobiology*, Cambridge, MA: Harvard University Press. (An influential attack on the individualistic presuppositions of many Darwinists in biology, arguing like Dawkins (1976), that many things serve functions other than those of benefiting individuals.)

JOHN C. BIGELOW

FUNDAMENTALISM, ISLAMIC *see* ISLAMIC FUNDAMENTALISM

FUTURE GENERATIONS, OBLIGATIONS TO

There are at least three different views concerning obligations to future generations. One is that morality does not apply here, future generations not being in any reciprocal relationship with us. Another is that, though we are not obliged to do anything for future generations, it would be praiseworthy to do so. A third view is that justice demands that we respect the interests of future generations.

Philosophers and others have discussed obligations in three main areas: the environment, and the damage inflicted upon it in pursuit of profit; savings and the accumulations of capital; and population policy.

Different theoretical approaches have been taken. According to utilitarianism, the interests of people count equally with those of present people, and all interests are to be satisfied maximally. This may have very demanding implications. Contractarianism rests morality on the agreement of all affected parties. But whose views will be considered in the case of future generations? Perhaps the most plausible approach is communitarianism, according to which obligations can rest on a sense of community which stretches into the future.

1 **Areas of debate**
2 **Utilitarianism**
3 **Contractarianism**
4 **A communitarian theory**

1 Areas of debate

The idea that one generation should regard itself as having duties to succeeding generations is not new. We find the following story, for instance, in the Talmud. A a young man once saw an old man planting a carob tree. Knowing that the tree would bear fruit only seventy years later, the young man asked him whether he was sure that he would live long enough to eat the fruit, only to be answered, 'When I came into the world I found it planted with carob trees. Just as my ancestors planted for me, so shall I plant for posterity.' Discussions of the issue in Christian and secular Western philosophy can also be found in the works of Bacon, Kant and others (Passmore 1974). And yet, only in the 1970s did a few scholars start to discuss the issue in depth (Rawls 1971; Sikora and Barry 1978; Parfit 1984).

Relations between distant generations involve important political and moral issues in three areas. The first is the environment. To what extent do contemporary people have the right to deplete resources, to leave 'time-bombs' such as radioactive waste for future persons, and to change the environment while seeking to improve their own material welfare? The treatment of such problems as the depletion of non-renewable natural resources, the pollution of the soil, the contamination of water, the production of toxic and radioactive waste, the destruction of rare species, conservation, and preservation represents the neglect of our duties not only to other contemporaries and, perhaps, to the environment itself, but also to the people of the future. Failure on our side to fulfil these duties incurs much economic cost and considerable difficulties in terms of health and quality of life for future people (thus the optimistic view that technology and science will solve all environmental problems is rejected) (see ENVIRONMENTAL ETHICS.)

The second area in which inter-generational issues are at stake is savings and the multi-generational accumulation of capital. Should we save for future people, even though this prevents us from improving the welfare of the most disadvantaged among contemporaries? Should our governments be allowed to take very long-term loans, assuming that future people will repay the loan plus interest (without necessarily enjoying the fruits of these loans)? The third area is population policies, which also involves the issue of inter-generational distribution and the ever-growing demands for such goods as energy and food (see POPULATION AND ETHICS).

2 Utilitarianism

The question of the grounds for our obligations to future generations raises many theoretical difficulties. The most obvious is that this kind of relationship is different from the usual intra-generational relationship. For example, relevant information is absent. And so, although environmental policies may be seen in terms of inter-generational distribution of access to goods, such as clean air and beautiful landscape, and although we may assume that a certain act or policy will affect future generations, we do not know precisely how bad the consequences of our actions will be, what future generations will want or need, what will bring them happiness, and how many people will be affected (indeed, the very existence and identity of future generations depends on our actions today, and, at least theoretically, we can decide not to reproduce).

These are the difficulties faced by consequentialist theorists such as utilitarians when constructing a theory of inter-generational justice (see CONSEQUENTIALISM; UTILITARIANISM). It seems impossible to measure or to calculate accurately the personal utilities of the not-yet-born. Moreover, if the time at which people exist cannot affect the value of their happiness, how far should we consider the interests of posterity when they seem to conflict with those of existing persons? A utilitarian who is committed to temporal universalism (that is, regarding the utilities of all persons as equal, whatever the period in which they live) will find it impossible to achieve an equilibrium between our obligations to posterity and the necessity to improve the welfare of contemporaries. If we assume that an investment is productive and is used wisely by subsequent generations, the bigger the initial investment is, the larger the total utility will be. Thus, we may infer that we should reduce our standard of living to a minimum; but then, the next generation will find itself in the same situation, with the same moral demands. Are we then to assume that each generation should save and conserve as much as it can, consuming as little as possible, or almost nothing? While some radical Greens find this idea appealing, many people would find it unreasonable and perhaps impossible to put into practice (see GREEN POLITICAL PHILOSOPHY §4). In addition, there is a serious question about which generation should break the chain and enjoy the fruits of savings by past generations.

3 Contractarianism

Perhaps a contractarian theory could avoid some of these problems (see CONTRACTARIANISM). The basic idea of contractarianism is that a policy is approved if all concerned people would have approved it had they been asked. Therefore, the first question which arises is who will be 'invited' to decide upon the principles of justice between generations: one's contemporaries, all possible people, or all actual people? The difficulty is that our decisions and policies will also affect the identity and number of future people. Do we first decide upon the policies (that will determine the identity of future people), or upon the identity of the

parties to the contract (who will decide upon the policies)?

There are other difficulties with the contractarian theory. It is widely agreed that a contract will be reached in 'circumstances of justice', that is, a rough equality in the powers and capacities of the parties concerned, a situation of moderate scarcity, and a conflict of interests, which is moderated by a sense of potential mutual benefit from social and economic cooperation. But it is not certain that, when applied to the inter-generational context, these circumstances still exist. The second and third conditions are a matter of information which is not now available; and it is certain that the first – equality of powers between generations – does not exist, both because the current generation has the capacity and power to decide not to reproduce, and also because it is we who decide about every matter which concerns our relationship with future generations. Even a sense of mutual advantage is lacking: it seems quite reasonable, from the point of view of self-interest, to suppose that, after benefiting from a contract with previous generations, a generation will change the terms of the contract, and hence of its obligations to future generations.

It has thus been suggested that an inter-generational contract should be based on the idea of impartiality rather than on mutual advantage (Barry 1989) (see IMPARTIALITY). Justice is an impartial identification with the interests of everyone, and thus in deciding upon principles of justice we should not be influenced by our knowledge of what makes us different from others (such as the fact that we are contemporaries). This contractarian theory is strongly related, however, to the idea of neutrality about the good, and the theorist must then explain, for example, why one should care about the distant future or the conservation of ecosystems rather than show greater concern for the welfare of disadvantaged contemporaries (is the environment, or nature, being unjustifiably assumed as part of the good?).

4 A communitarian theory

Perhaps our obligations to future generations can be derived from the sense of a community that stretches and extends over generations and into the future (see COMMUNITY AND COMMUNITARIANISM; SOLIDARITY). However, unlike the backward-looking Burkeian notion of a trans-generational community that grounds an obligation to continue the heritage of previous generations, this notion of trans-generational community would be based on the argument that, just as many people regard the past as part of what constitutes their 'selves', so they regard the future as part of their 'selves' (see BURKE, E.). These, then, would be the relationships that form the trans-generational community, which constitute the source of our obligations to future generations.

Often, the concept of community is related to face-to-face interaction. It goes without saying that such interaction does not exist in relations between distant generations. But community is arguably a level of relationships standing beyond contractual or legal relations. As such, the trans-generational community is defined not geographically but rather as a moral entity which does not have to rely on face-to-face interactions. Instead, it is constituted by a framework from which people draw their values and derive their cultural and moral identities. It is within this framework that the discourse about the moral and political ideas constituting social life and identity takes place. This discourse is carried on through critical discussion, mass-media, art, literature, academic research, and so on. But is there an interaction of this kind between distant – and not necessarily overlapping – generations?

The answer seems to be affirmative: the moral discourse extends beyond one's lifetime. There is no reason why, if I want to do something because I think it is good, I should be indifferent to its value if it turns out that it could only be accomplished after my death (compare Rolston 1981; Barry 1977). When we conceive an idea or create something, we reflect on its relevance not only to the political and moral environment in which we live, but also to the political and moral environment of the future. This is illustrated in many spheres of human activity. For example, what is pure mathematics today may become applied mathematics within a few generations; several technological inventions that are utilized now will still be useful in a generation or more. The same applies to the humanities and arts, and also to political theory and reflections on the values a society holds. Thus, philosophers consider how the future will view their ideas, and politicians do certain things because they wish to be remembered in the future in a certain way. Just as contemporaries study and reflect on the ideas of Plato, Kant or Hume, so will future people discuss ideas which were conceived by our contemporaries. Distant generations do reflect on each other's cultural and moral ideas, and these reflections are always directed towards the future. In that sense, even our notion of the present is future-oriented. This constructs the multi-generational community which extends into the future, and is the source of our obligations to other members of this community (future generations).

All these theories offer explanations of the moral grounds for our obligations to future generations. We are still left with questions such as how much we should save and what we should conserve. The answers to these questions depend partly on the value we attach to natural resources, rare species, and objects of conservation, and are thus related to Green theory and environmental philosophy.

See also: AGRICULTURAL ETHICS; DEVELOPMENT ETHICS; RECIPROCITY; TECHNOLOGY AND ETHICS

References and further reading

* Barry, B. (1977) 'Justice Between Generations', in P.M.S. Hacker and J. Raz (eds) *Law, Morality and Society*, Oxford: Clarendon Press. (An analysis of the contractarian approach to inter-generational justice.)

* —— (1989) *Theories of Justice*, London: Harvester Wheatsheaf, ch. 5. (Uses the idea of inter-generational relations to illustrate the two different contractarian traditions and the advantage of the theory of impartiality.)

de-Shalit, A. (1994) *Why Posterity Matters*, London: Routledge. (Expounds a communitarian theory of justice between generations.)

Gauthier, D. (1986) *Morals By Agreement*, Oxford: Clarendon Press, ch. 9. (Tries to turn the issue into a matter of making a contract between a chain of overlapping generations.)

Laslett, P. and Fishkin, J. (eds) (1992) *Justice Between Age Groups and Generations*, New Haven, CT: Yale University Press. (A collection of essays which considers both familiar and newer theoretical questions as well as the application of the theories and their implementation.)

* Parfit, D. (1984) *Reasons and Persons*, Oxford: Clarendon Press. (An important and provocative book which attacks person-regarding morality, partly as applied to inter-generational relations.)

Partridge, E. (ed.) (1981) *Responsibilities to Future Generations*, Buffalo, NY: Prometheus Books. (A collection of essays which mainly discusses theoretical questions. Very good as an introduction.)

* Passmore, J. (1974) *Man's Responsibility for Nature*, London: Duckworth. (Focuses specifically on the theme of responsibility for the natural world.)

* Rawls, J. (1971) *A Theory of Justice*, Cambridge, MA: Harvard University Press. (Discusses our obligations to future generations mainly with regard to savings and the accumulation of capital.)

* Rolston, H., III (1981) 'The River of Life: Past, Present, Future', in E. Partridge (ed.) *Responsibilities to Future Generations*, Buffalo, NY: Prometheus Books. (The issue is treated by this environmental philosopher as another way – in

addition to non-anthropocentric ethics – of justifying environmental policies.)

Sen, A. (1961) 'On Optimising the Saving Rate', *Economic Journal* 71: 479–97. (A pioneering work of an economist in this field.)

* Sikora, R.I. and Barry, B. (eds) (1978) *Obligations to Future Generations*, Philadelphia, PA: Temple University Press. (An excellent collection of essays dealing both with population policies and with the question of inter-generational distribution.)

AVNER DE-SHALIT

FUZZY LOGIC

The term 'fuzzy' refers to concepts without precise borders. Membership in a 'fuzzy' set – the set of things to which a 'fuzzy' concept (fuzzily) applies – is to be thought of as being a matter of degree. Hence, in order to specify a fuzzy set, one must specify for every item in the universe the extent to which the item is a member of the set. The engineer Lotfi Zadeh developed a theory of fuzzy sets and advocated their use in many areas of engineering and science. Zadeh and his zealous followers have attempted to develop fuzzy systems theory, fuzzy algorithms and even fuzzy arithmetic. The phrase 'fuzzy logic' has come to be applied rather imprecisely to any analysis that is not strictly binary. It does not refer to any particular formal logic, in the sense in which the term 'logic' is used by philosophers and mathematicians. ('Fuzzy logic' is sometimes used anachronistically to refer to any many-valued logic.)

1 Philosophy
2 Vague concepts
3 Fuzzy theory

1 Philosophy

Fuzzy theory has, paradoxically, tended to partition the intellectual community into true believers and unbelievers. Early fuzzy researchers sometimes ignored or failed to credit properly ideas and similar approaches in other areas, resulting in much duplication of work. Simplistic condemnations of bivalent thinking and everything based on it (virtually all of science) were made, along with broad, often unsupported, claims for the utility of a fuzzy approach. These factors together with the intellectual conservatism of the engineering community led to the unwarranted view in some quarters that fuzzy theory was a fringe development designed only to appeal to those unable to measure up to the rigours of higher mathematical techniques. As a result, fuzzy theory was often ridiculed, frequently ignored, and sometimes excluded from conferences and publications. This situation resulted in some circling of the intellectual wagons and the founding of several conferences and journals devoted solely to fuzzy theory.

Some advocates have attributed the schism to philosophical differences, suggesting that a fuzzy world view has roots in eastern philosophies while western thinking has been dominated by bivalence. The fuzzy world view may be summed up by saying that everything is a matter of degree; that nothing real has any property to the complete exclusion of its negation. Fuzzy advocates criticize bivalent thinking as too simplistic.

Advocates of the fuzzy world view claim that bivalent thinking leads to paradoxes, such as the sorites paradox (see VAGUENESS §2). (If we pluck one hair from the face of a bearded man, he is still bearded; applying this argument many times over, there is no real difference between a bearded man and one without a beard.) They claim that we can avoid such paradoxes by recognizing that most predicates apply only to some degree. (If we pluck one hair from a man's face, then he is simply slightly less bearded than before: any sharp line drawn between having a beard and not having a beard is completely artificial.)

Critics respond that progress in science is usually the result of abstracting or idealizing: maps are useful because they leave out a lot of detail; computation of pressure/temperature/volume relationships does not require, and would be hindered by, the details of molecular positions, masses and velocities. Further, (western) science has developed mathematical techniques for dealing with matters of degree that do not require a fundamental change of logic. With regard to the paradoxes, critics point out that the specification of precise numerical degrees for concepts such as 'bearded' is artificial and impossible to carry out in any meaningful way. Further, there is no reason to think that we can linearly order the universe in terms of degree of 'beardedness'; some individuals are just not comparable. And if fuzzy advocates avoid drawing artificial distinctions, the paradoxes will simply reappear. For example, let 'really-bearded' apply 100% to those individuals whose degree of beardedness is 0.5 or greater and 0% to those whose degree of beardedness is less than 0.5. Unless fuzzy theorists are going to draw some very artificial fine distinctions, then it seems that removing one facial hair should not change one from being 'really-bearded'. If fuzzy advocates draw fine distinctions to avoid the paradox, then they can hardly criticize bivalent logic for drawing such distinctions.

2 Vague concepts

Most of the concepts which we employ are vague rather than sharp. Vague concepts (see VAGUENESS) are extremely useful for getting around in the world and for communication. Suppose you have been told to look for a tall, bald man with a beard, wearing a flowered shirt and walking with a limp. You do not need to have the criteria for the term 'tall' specified to within a millimetre; you do not need criteria for baldness spelled out in terms of percentage of coverage of scalp; and so on. If we tried to make these terms very precise, we would have more difficulty applying them. It seems that the more precise a term, the more difficult it is to determine whether it applies.

Classical logic makes the simplifying assumption of bivalence: every sentence is either true or false. But consider the concept of baldness. Certainly there are clear cases in which we would agree that 'X is bald' is true, and others in which we would agree that 'X is bald' is false. But there are also a lot of cases on the borderline. Instead of just 'true' or 'false', it is tempting to use locutions such as 'partially true', 'more true than not', and so on. Classical logic does not seem suited to reasoning with vague concepts. Such observations are cited as a motivation for many-valued logic (see MANY-VALUED LOGICS).

Max Black (1937) was the first to publish systematic suggestions for formalizing reasoning with vague concepts. Suppose our universe is human beings, and consider the predicate 'bald'. We may think of the predicate as standing for the set of objects which have the property. In classical logic we would have to decide all borderline cases arbitrarily. Classically, we may identify the set with its two-valued 'characteristic' function: $b(x) = 1$ if x is bald, and $b(x) = 0$ if x is not bald.

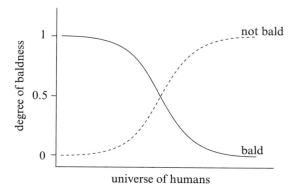

universe of humans

Black suggested that instead of taking the characteristic function to be two-valued, we should allow it to take any value in the closed real interval $[0, 1]$. Ordering the universe in terms of degree of baldness, we could plot a 'baldness' curve as shown.

Black advocated treating the negation of a concept as the complement with respect to 1, that is, $\sim b(x) = 1 - b(x)$. He noted that the curve for a vague concept and its negation would cross at the 0.5 position. He further noted that for items in the grey area between 0 and 1, it made sense to say that the item both did and did not have the property. Black recognized the rather arbitrary nature of assigning precise numerical degrees to the membership relation. He suggested using statistical surveys and assigning $b(x)$ to be the percentage of the linguistic community that would agree that x has property b. Paradoxically, this procedure is based on the possibility of forcing vague concepts into a binary ideal that Black's analysis was intended to avoid.

3 Fuzzy theory

In name, fuzzy set theory was first developed by Lotfi Zadeh (1965, 1975), though the content is strikingly similar to Black's earlier analysis. However, Zadeh took the theory much further.

Assume some universe, U; identify each fuzzy set f with its characteristic function $f : U \to [0, 1]$. Zadeh suggested the following definitions.

union:	$(f \cup g)(x) = \max\{f(x), g(x)\}$
intersection:	$(f \cap g)(x) = \min\{f(x), g(x)\}$
complement:	$f'(x) = 1 - f(x)$
universal set:	$u(x) = 1$
empty set:	$\emptyset(x) = 0$

These definitions reduce to the classical notions if we restrict characteristic functions to being two-valued. Union and intersection so defined are commutative, associative, idempotent and mutually distributive, and De Morgan's laws are satisfied. (Zadeh's definitions are not the only ones to satisfy these properties.) However, if there is an x in U for which $0 < f(x) < 1$, then $f \cup f' \neq u$ and $f \cap f' \neq \emptyset$. These observations correspond well with our intuition that we cannot draw a sharp line between, for example, 'bald' and 'not bald'.

Difficulties arise when trying to treat fuzzy set theory as a basis for a logic of vagueness. There is a simple correspondence between classical set theory on a universal set and classical logic. We may think of the universe as the domain of a model, with sets corresponding to predicates; and union, intersection and complement corresponding to disjunction, conjunction and negation, respectively. The same sort of correspondence exists between Zadeh's fuzzy set theory and the infinite-valued logic of ŁUKASIEWICZ (§3). But the quantificational version of infinite-valued Łukasiewicz logic is not finitely axiomatizable. Further, trying to assign a precise numerical degree to the extent to which each person is bald seems even more artificial than simply assigning True or False to each attribution.

Finally, Łukasiewicz logic is not expressively strong enough to allow one to express in the object language the fundamental semantic concepts which served as the motivation. We want our formal language to contain 'autodescriptive' operators J_i for each truth-value i, such that, in any particular model, the sentence $J_i(E)$ takes the value 1 if E takes the value i in that model, and 0 otherwise. But if we include autodescriptive operators in the syntax, it is not possible to give a finitary proof theory for even the propositional logic. So, either the object language must be inadequate to express the notions fundamental to fuzzy theory, or there can be no finitary proof theory.

Zadeh's response to such criticisms was to fuzzify even the metatheory. He suggested that a fuzzy logic should be regarded as a complex association of some formal base logic (for example, that of Łukasiewicz) with fuzzy linguistic structures. Semantic attributions such as 'true', 'very true', 'somewhat true' and so on are to be treated as fuzzy sets. He claimed that all rules of inference are only approximate, criteria for good arguments can be given only semantically, and that the standard metatheoretical notions such as consistency and completeness are not relevant to fuzzy logic.

In spite of the difficulties of developing a formal logic based on fuzzy principles, a fuzzy analysis has led to some elegantly simple techniques for mathematical approximation of complex systems. As a result there have been some impressive systems developed in areas of expert systems and control engineering.

See also: LOGICAL AND MATHEMATICAL TERMS, GLOSSARY OF

References and further reading

* Black, M. (1937) 'Vagueness: An Exercise in Logical Analysis', *Philosophy of Science* 427–55. (Original analysis of vague concepts; referred to in §2.)

Dubois, D. and Prade, H. (1980) *Fuzzy Sets and Systems*, New York: Academic Press. (Excellent formal development and review of the literature of the theory of fuzzy sets and related matters.)

Kosko, B. (1992) *Neural Networks and Fuzzy Systems*, Englewood Cliffs, NJ: Prentice Hall. (Formal development of important results in fuzzy systems theory, along with partisan philosophical commentary on the fuzzy world view.)

—— (1993) *Fuzzy Thinking*, New York: Hyperion. (A much less formal version of the previous item with some intellectual history.)

Morgan, C.G. and Pelletier, F.J. (1976) 'Some Notes concerning Fuzzy Logics', *Linguistics and Philosophy* 1: 79–97. (Problems finding proof theory for fuzzy logic.)

Scarpellini, B. (1962) 'Die Nicht-Axiomatisierbarkeit des unendlichwertigen Prädikatenkalküls von Łukasiewicz', *Journal of Symbolic Logic* 27: 159–70. (Quantified infinite-valued Łukasiewicz logic is not axiomatizable; see §3.)

* Zadeh, L.A. (1965) 'Fuzzy Sets', *Information and Control* 8: 338–53. (Classic paper on fuzzy set theory; referred to in §3.)

* —— (1975) 'Fuzzy Logic and Approximate Reasoning', *Synthese* 30: 407–28. (Rejection of formal proof theory for fuzzy logic; referred to in §3.)

CHARLES G. MORGAN

G

GADĀDHARA (1604–1709)

Gadādhara Bhaṭṭācārya was a seventeenth-century Indian philosopher belonging to a school of thinkers, Navya-Nyāya, noted for its extreme realism and its contributions to philosophical methodology. Though Gadādhara's commentaries on the school's key texts are recognized as among the latest, most detailed and innovative, his greater claim to fame is due to his composition of a number of independent tracts on topics in philosophy of language, philosophy of mind, ethics and legal theory. He may be credited in particular with the discovery of a version of the pragmatic theory of pronominal anaphora. His work on case grammar and inferential fallacies is highly admired in India, while recent translations into English have begun to make him better known outside.

1 Life and work
2 Philosophy of language
3 Legal theory

1 Life and work

Gadādhara Bhaṭṭācārya lived from 1604 to 1709. He was a native of Bengal, and became a student of the 'celebrated Naiyāyika' Harirāma Tarkavāgīśa at Navadvīpa, the famous centre for philosophical studies in the district of Nadia, northwest of Calcutta. The late medieval philosophical school to which he belonged, Navya-Nyāya, was especially noted for its contributions to logical theory (quantification, propositional laws, soundness of argumentative schema, negation), epistemology (perception, testimony, casual/reliabilist theory of knowledge), and for developing a quasi-formal technical language capable of great exactness.

Gadādhara is known first as a masterly Nyāya commentator, and second for having written a large number of celebrated tracts on particular philosophical concepts. His subcommentary on Raghunātha's *Tattvacintāmaṇidīdhiti* (Ray in the Jewel of Knowledge) soon became a standard and authoritative work, gaining wide popularity throughout India. Gadādhara's principal contributions to Indian logical theory are to be found within this commentary, notably his remarks on the proper analysis of the 'pervasion' (*vyāpti*) relation between an inferential

sign and the property to be inferred (Ingalls 1951: 154–61), and his study of the inferential fallacies. Among his philosophical tracts, which are always illuminating and often brilliant, the ones which brought him greatest fame are those on the philosophy of language (the *Śaktivāda* and *Vyutpattivāda* (Theory of the Analysis of Sentence Meaning)), the philosophy of mind (the *Viṣayatāvāda*), and ethical and legal theory (the *Muktivāda*, *Vidhisvarūpavādārtha* and *Vivāhavādārtha*).

2 Philosophy of language

Gadādhara's contribution to the study of language in India is of particular importance. His influence here lies in his move away from the earlier Nyāya epistemic conception of language, of language as essentially an instrument for communication of knowledge, towards a conception more influenced by semantic theory and linguistics. When an expression is indexical its meaning, according to Gadādhara, is not to be identified with its reference, but rather with what is called the *śakyatāvacchedaka* or 'limiter-of-the-property-of-being-a-referent'. Gadādhara supposes that an ordinary nominal, such as '(the) cow', is an indexical referring expression, whose limiter is the property cowhood. Introducing an important semantic distinction related to Kripke's distinction between reference-fixing and meaning-giving (see KRIPKE, S.A. §2), he asks whether this property is an 'indicating' property (*upalakṣaṇa*) or a 'qualifying' property (*viśeṣaṇa*). According to Gadādhara's definition, cowhood is here a qualifying property just in case one correctly understands an utterance of the word 'cow' only if one thinks of the referent under the mode or sortal 'cowhood'. In the Nyāya technical language, cowhood is then the 'limiter-of-the-property-of-being-the-object-of-the-hearer's-thought' (*viṣayatāvacchedaka*). Gadādhara argues that the limiter of an ordinary noun-phrase must be a qualifying property, for otherwise two coextensive nominals would be synonymous, but that as there is no single conventionally fixed way of thinking about the reference of a proper name, the limiter of a name merely 'indicates' its reference.

Extending this approach to other types of expression, Gadādhara says that the meaning, that is, limiter of reference, of the first person pronoun 'I' is the property 'being the speaker', which here functions merely to 'indicate' the reference. In constructions such as

(1)   The teacher said: 'I am not coming today',

Gadādhara distinguishes between 'dependent' and 'independent' occurrences of 'I', a dependent occurrence being defined as one in which the first person is embedded in a sentence or noun-phrase dominated by a verb-phrase. Such occurrences are governed by a coreference rule of the form: 'I' corefers with the principal noun-phrase. Another construction involving pronominal anaphora is examined at great length by Gadādhara:

(2)   There is a pot next door – bring it!

Here, however, Gadādhara rejects a coreference rule in favour of a pragmatic account of anaphora: the reference of the pronoun is determined by the speaker's referential intentions.

Pāṇini, the fourth-century BC Indian grammarian, is renowned for his introduction of a *kāraka* or deep-level analysis of sentence structure, which permits one to say that

(3)   Rāma cooks rice for Sitā, and

(4)   Rice is cooked by Rāma for Sitā

have the same deep structure, the inflected noun 'Rāma' in both sentences designating the logical 'agent', even though it has nominative case inflexion in (3) but instrumental case inflexion in (4). In his *Vyutpattivāda* Gadādhara adapts this method of sentence analysis, interpreting the *kārakas* in a manner akin to the 'participant roles' of modern case grammar, and making them the basis for a compositional account of the relation between word-meaning and sentence-meaning.

3   Legal theory

Like many late Indian logicians, Gadādhara wrote also on philosophy of law, reflecting the political importance of Hindu legal theory in Islamic, and later in British, India. Raghunātha, for example, argued that the older definition of property (*svatva*) as the capacity of a thing to be used at pleasure hid a circularity, for even if an object is owned there are still restrictions on its use, and these restrictions cannot be explicated without appeal to the notion of property itself. Raghunātha (?1500–50) proposed instead that property is a *sui generis* ontological category. Some later Naiyāyikas (apparently including Gadādhara) rejected this 'category' view in favour of a subjectivist definition of property as a legally grounded disposi-

tional judgment 'this is mine', a definition which was itself subjected to further refinement (see Derrett 1956).

See also: ANAPHORA; LANGUAGE, INDIAN THEORIES OF; NYĀYA-VAIŚEṢIKA; PROPER NAMES

List of works

Gadādhara Bhaṭṭācārya (1604–1709)*The Gādādharī*, ed. V.P. Dvivedi *et al.*, Varanasi: Chowkhamba Sanskrit Series Office, 1970. (A commentary on the *Tattvacintāmaṇidīdhiti*.)

—— (1604–1709) *Vādavāridhi*, ed. B. Mishra and D. Shastri, Varanasi: Chowkhamba Sanskrit Series Office, 1933. (The collected tracts.)

—— (1604–1709) *Vyutpattivāda* (Theory of the Analysis of Sentence Meaning), trans. V.P. Bhatta, Delhi: Eastern Book Linkers, 1990. (Gadādhara's account of sentential semantic structure).

—— (1604–1709) *Viṣayatāvāda*, trans. S. Bhattacharya, *Gadādhara's Theory of Objectivity, Containing the Text of Gadādhara's Viṣayatāvāda with an English Translation and Explanatory Notes*, Part II, Delhi: Motilal Banarsidass, 1990. (A clear presentation of Gadādhara's work on mental content and intentionality.)

—— (1604–1709) *Vivāhavādārtha*, trans. J.D.M. Derrett, 'The Discussion of Marriage by Gadādhara: A Preliminary Investigation', *The Adyar Library Bulletin* 27 (1): 171–99, 1963. (Includes a study of the text; see also Derrett 1956.)

References and further reading

Annaṃbhaṭṭa (18th century) *Tarkasaṃgrahadīpikā on Tarkasaṃgraha* (Commentary on the Compendium of Logic), ed. and trans. G. Bhattacharya, Calcutta: Progressive Publishers, 1983. (An introduction to Navya-Nyāya, sometimes called the *Bālagādādharī* or 'Gadādhara for Beginners'.)

Bhattacharya, D.C. (1951) *Bāngalīr Sarasvat Avadīn, pratham bhāg, Bange Navyanyāyacarccā* (History of Navya-Nyāya in Bengal), Calcutta, 182–3. (Biographical details; in Bengali.)

* Derrett, J.D.M. (1956) 'An Indian Contribution to the Study of Property', *Bulletin of the School of Oriental and African Studies* 18 (3): 475–98.

Ganeri, J. (forthcoming) *Meaning, Realism & Testimony: Philosophy of Language in Classical India*, Oxford: Oxford University Press. (A study of Gadādhara's theory in the context of contemporary philosophy of language.)

* Ingalls, D.H.H. (1951) *Materials for the Study of Navya-nyāya Logic*, Cambridge, MA: Harvard

University Press. (A work which marked the beginnings of the modern study of Navya-Nyāya.)

Tarkatīrtha, V. (1992) 'The Nyāya on the Meaning of some Words', *Journal of Indian Philosophy* 20 (1): 41–88. (A summary of Gadādhara's views on meaning.)

JONARDON GANERI

GADAMER, HANS-GEORG (1900–)

Hans-Georg Gadamer is best known for his philosophical hermeneutics. Gadamer studied with Martin Heidegger during his preparation of Being and Time *(1927). Like Heidegger, Gadamer rejects the idea of hermeneutics as merely a method for the human and historical sciences comparable to the method of the natural sciences. Philosophical hermeneutics is instead about a process of human understanding that is inevitably circular because we come to understand the whole through the parts and the parts through the whole. Understanding in this sense is not an 'act' that can be secured methodically and verified objectively. It is an 'event' or 'experience' that we undergo. It occurs paradigmatically in our experience of works of art and literature. But it also takes place in our disciplined and scholarly study of the works of other human beings in the humanities and social sciences. In each case, understanding brings self-understanding.*

Philosophical hermeneutics advocates a mediated approach to self-understanding on the model of a conversation with the texts and works of others. The concept of dialogue employed here is one of question and answer and is taken from Plato. Such understanding never becomes absolute knowledge. It is finite because we remain conditioned by our historical situation, and partial because we are interested in the truth that we come to understand. By grounding understanding in language and dialogue as opposed to subjectivity, Gadamer's philosophical hermeneutics avoids the danger of arbitrariness in interpreting the works of others.

Gadamer's most important publication is Wahrheit and Methode *(Truth and Method) (1960). He has also published four volumes of short works,* Kleine Schriften *(1967–77), containing important hermeneutical studies of Plato, Hegel, and Paul Celan among others. His many books and essays are collected into ten volumes (*Gesammelte Werke*). Gadamer is widely known as a teacher who practises the dialogue which is at the core of his philosophical hermeneutics.*

1 **Life**
2 *Truth and Method* **and Kant's aesthetics**
3 **Basic concepts of philosophical hermeneutics**
4 *Truth and Method* **and Heidegger's existential phenomenology**
5 **Criticisms and self-criticism**

1 Life

Gadamer was born in Marburg and brought up in Breslau, and his academic life mirrors the most important philosophical movements in Germany in the twentieth century. He encountered Neo-Kantianism when he studied philosophy at Marburg from 1918 to 1922, completing his doctoral dissertation in 1922 under the direction of Nicolai Hartmann and Paul Natorp (see NEO-KANTIANISM §§3–5). In 1923 he transferred to Freiburg to study phenomenology with Edmund HUSSERL and Martin HEIDEGGER, whom he followed to Marburg in 1924. Gadamer completed his habilitation under Heidegger's sponsorship in 1929, just two years after Heidegger had published his existential phenomenology in *Being and Time* (1927). Gadamer was a precocious student, obtaining his doctorate and his habilitation at the unusually early ages of 22 and 29 respectively. While at the University of Marburg, Gadamer also studied classical philology and completed his state examination in philology in 1927. Gadamer's doctoral dissertation and habilitation were both on Plato. He published the latter, *Platos dialektische ethik*, in 1931.

Gadamer began teaching while still at Marburg. He also taught at Leipzig (1938–47), Frankfurt (1947–9), and Heidelberg, where in 1949 he assumed the chair in philosophy previously occupied by Karl JASPERS. After his retirement in 1968, Gadamer continued to lecture at the University of Heidelberg and began teaching part of the year in the USA, notably at Boston College.

In 1952 Gadamer and Helmut Kuhn founded the *Philosophische Rundschau*, which quickly became one of Germany's most important philosophy journals. Gadamer published relatively little after 1931, until he produced *Wahrheit und Methode* (Truth and Method) in 1960. Like Kant's *Critique of Pure Reason*, which was also published late in the author's life (Kant was 57), Gadamer's book immediately established its author's reputation. *Truth and Method* and *Being and Time* were recognized as the most important contributions to hermeneutics in the twentieth century. In the 1960s Gadamer became engaged in a lively debate with Jürgen HABERMAS and the Frankfurt School about hermeneutics and critical theory. In the 1970s, and in connection with his second teaching career in the USA, Gadamer was able to expand on the contribution that *Truth and Method* had made to practical philosophy, a move that brought him into contact with Americans influenced by pragmatism, such as Richard Bernstein and Richard RORTY. Later, in the 1980s, Gadamer initiated a debate with Jacques DERRIDA on hermeneutics and deconstruction.

2 *Truth and Method* and Kant's aesthetics

Even in the earliest stages of his philosophical journey, when he was writing on Plato, Gadamer remained convinced that the experience of art was connected to philosophy. But it was not until *Truth and Method*, his late and mature work, that Gadamer makes this connection philosophically explicit. Gadamer maintains that the experience of art is an experience of truth as an 'event' that 'happens to us over and above our wanting and doing' ([1960] 1975: xvi). This event structure of truth is, Gadamer believes, a universal characteristic of human understanding. The phenomenon of understanding – *Verstehen* – that concerns Gadamer should not be confused with *Verstand*, which is also translated as 'understanding'. *Verstand*, most notably in Kant's *Critique of Pure Reason*, is objectifying and means the natural scientific understanding subjects have of something other than themselves, namely, spatiotemporal objects (see KANT, I. §6). The phenomenon of understanding that Gadamer takes up in *Truth and Method* is that introduced by Heidegger in §32 of *Being and Time* (see HEIDEGGER, M. §3). Understanding as *Verstehen* is non-objectifying. It is ontological and concerns a subject's very being in the world. Understanding is once again of something other than oneself, but in this case it is of other possibilities for oneself as a being in the world.

Truth and Method begins when Gadamer takes up the question of truth as it emerges from the experience of art. The target of Gadamer's criticism is Kant's aesthetics and the abstraction of the art work from its original world and from our own concrete historical situation when we experience a work aesthetically. Gadamer's goal in the first part of *Truth and Method* is to transform aesthetics by transcending the limits placed upon what counts as aesthetic experience and opening up the truth-claims made on us in this experience by works of art and literature. Gadamer shows how Kant's *Critique of Judgment* subjectivizes aesthetics by narrowing the concept of aesthetic experience to the experience (*Erlebnis*) of the subject's pleasurable 'state of mind' (the free play of the mental faculties) (see KANT, I. §12). Gadamer contrasts this narrowing to the role played earlier by judgment and taste in connection with culture and the formation of a *sensus communis* ('common sense'). Gadamer

proposes that we think instead of aesthetic experience on the model of *Erfahrung*, Hegel's concept of experience. *Erfahrung* gives us something to understand. It challenges us so that we must 'change our minds'. The subjective universality or 'disinterested interest' that Kant claims for aesthetic experience and the judgments we make about it cuts us off, Gadamer concludes, from the interest we take in the truth of works of art and literature in so far as they challenge us to change our minds and therefore our lives.

The experience of art offers Gadamer a model for how truth happens in human experience generally. Gadamer models human experience not on the sense perception of what is immediately given but on the experience of reading and understanding a text which has become historically distant from us. He reminds us of the practice of hermeneutics or interpretation in the reading and understanding of legal and religious texts that are temporally distant. These texts remain 'classical' (like those literary texts, 'the classics', that admit of no final interpretation) so long as they continue to challenge present-day readers to produce new interpretations of them. According to Gadamer, we understand these texts when we understand them to be making a true claim about how we are to understand something that is an issue for us in our own world and historical age. Like the experience we undergo with art, the event of understanding these texts changes our minds. Despite the prominent role played in *Truth and Method* by the experience of art, this book turns out not to be a work in aesthetics. Instead, *Truth and Method* transforms Kantian aesthetics into a philosophical hermeneutics, a general theory of understanding and interpretation that is also an ontology of ourselves as historical beings (see HERMENEUTICS §5).

3 Basic concepts of philosophical hermeneutics

Four interrelated concepts define Gadamer's philosophical hermeneutics. The first of these is 'effective-historical consciousness' (*wirkungsgeschichtliches Bewusstsein*), which means that consciousness is at once 'affected by history' and 'open to the effects of history'. Gadamer's philosophical hermeneutics preserves Heidegger's central insight in *Being and Time* that the understanding of oneself and one's possibilities as a being in the world is temporal and situated historically. Understanding is therefore constituted in a positive way by its own historicity instead of being threatened by it, as Enlightenment thinkers after DESCARTES had feared. To be affected by history means that there can be no unmediated starting-point of the kind Descartes sought. To be open to the effects of history means to allow one's present horizon of understanding to be called into question by texts and works of art handed down to us by tradition.

Gadamer retains Heidegger's concept of the 'hermeneutical circle' to express the way understanding is always mediated. Understanding is always circular, but in a non-vicious sense. Anticipation of meaning, preconceptions or prejudgments ('prejudices') play a constitutive role as we use them to project wholes out of the parts of the text or art work that we are interpreting. Gadamer's claim that prejudgments enable understanding, that is, positively condition it, has been mistaken to mean that he affirms prejudice blindly. But Gadamer does not mean that we must remain uncritical of those prejudices that block or distort our understanding of a text or art work. Rather, since we cannot get out of the hermeneutical circle of understanding and assume an unprejudiced view from nowhere, we must aim instead at becoming more conscious of our particular hermeneutical situatedness so that new and more appropriate judgments can play the role of older and less appropriate prejudices in conditioning our understanding of the text or art work.

The third concept is that of 'play' (*Spiel*), which Gadamer borrows and transforms from Kant's aesthetics (the free play of the mental faculties). 'Play' or 'game' is used at two crucial points in *Truth and Method* to describe how his philosophical hermeneutics transcends the subjectivism of aesthetics and of modern philosophy in general. Gadamer speaks first of the game we play with art to show how individual subjects most lose themselves to experience the truth claimed by the art work, just as an individual player must in order to become absorbed in the game. And when, in Part 3, Gadamer turns to focus upon language as the medium of hermeneutical experience, he grounds language not in the consciousness of an individual subject but in the language game we call dialogue or conversation.

Language in the form of conversation leads us to the fourth concept, the 'fusion of horizons'. The understanding of a text or art work involves a challenge in so far as the truth claimed by the text or art work is at variance with what the interpreter believes to be the truth about the matter at issue ('*die Sache*'). The interpreter's horizon of understanding first excludes the truth claimed by the text or art work. The interpreter opens up to the horizon of the other (the text or art work) by allowing it to question the interpreter's own prejudgments about the matter at issue. What ensues is a dialogue of question and answer where the interpreter not only questions the truth claimed by the work but also allows what the interpreter prejudges to be true to be put into question by the work. The fusion of horizons that

ends the dialogue occurs when the interpreter understands differently. This may require altering the interpreter's prejudgments in line with what has been learned from the text or art work. But it may also mean reaffirming the original prejudgments for different reasons since they have survived the challenge by another way to judge the matter at issue.

4 *Truth and Method* and Heidegger's existential phenomenology

Truth and Method also takes up the existential phenomenology of Heidegger's *Being and Time* and transforms it into a philosophical hermeneutics, and here too the experience of art is pivotal. Gadamer has always acknowledged that Heidegger's *The Origin of the Work of Art* (1936) played a vital role in his first formulation of the idea of a philosophical hermeneutics in the 1930s. In this essay, Heidegger asserts that the truth which an art work discloses emerges out of the strife between 'earth' and 'world'. What strikes Gadamer as so insightful about Heidegger's characterization of the experience of art as the 'event of truth' is that 'earth' becomes a 'necessary determination of Being of the work of art' (1994: 100). 'World', Gadamer notes, is a familiar concept from *Being and Time*. 'Earth', however, introduces an altogether new conceptuality, one drawn from the poetry of Friedrich HÖLDERLIN. 'Earth' (*Erde*) does not mean 'matter' (*Stoff*), but that which continues to conceal itself even though it is that out of which everything emerges and into which everything retires.

Although Gadamer underplays this, Heidegger concentrates almost exclusively on the poetry of Hölderlin in the Nazi period, because he believes it to be history-making, that is, capable of inaugurating a new epoch of European history, one identified from now on as German, just as poetry had inaugurated the Greek beginning of European history. Gadamer nowhere shares Heidegger's belief in the need to inaugurate a new beginning. On the contrary, what is necessary is a creative renewal of the truth-claims made by the tradition and history of Europe's past. Gadamer aims, therefore, both to retain what is insightful about Heidegger's turn to art, poetry and language in his works after *Being and Time*, and to redirect it to the past. Accordingly, Gadamer reinterprets 'earth', which in Heidegger is associated with the German country and land, so that it takes on the meaning of the European tradition in which Gadamer finds himself embedded. This tradition is like 'earth' in that it continues to conceal resources within itself. But for Gadamer these become resources for renewal instead of unmediated sources of the altogether new.

Not surprisingly, we find that Hölderlin's poetry

plays only a minor role in Gadamer's thinking, compared to the importance Gadamer continues to attach to the Plato's dialogues and Aristotle's practical philosophy. Plato's concept of dialogue, for example, lives on in Gadamer's concept of language in and as a conversation with the text. And Aristotle's concept of practical wisdom (*phronesis*) survives and flourishes in Gadamer's solution to the problem of the application of our understanding of a text to our particular situation (see ARISTOTLE §23; PLATO §4).

5 Criticism and self-criticism

Gadamer has continued to define his hermeneutical philosophy in response to questions raised about *Truth and Method*. Emilio Betti (1980) and E.D. Hirsch (1967) were the first to object to Gadamer's philosophical hermeneutics in the belief that it failed to provide a method for validating interpretation. Habermas questioned instead Gadamer's rehabilitation of prejudice and the authority of tradition (see FRANKFURT SCHOOL §4). Derrida has raised doubts about Gadamer's reliance on a hermeneutics of good will after Nietzsche's hermeneutics of suspicion (see NIETZSCHE, F. §7). In each case, Gadamer has used these objections as an occasion to expand upon the scope of his hermeneutical philosophy and clarify its potential.

In 1992, in reflecting on his philosophical journey during the better part of the twentieth century, Gadamer acknowledges the validity of the following criticisms of *Truth and Method*. He admits that his concept of scientific method did not reflect the nuanced and complex concept of method that had grown up in the natural sciences between the 1930s and 1960. He grants that *Truth and Method* did not sufficiently differentiate the historian's work of interpreting a historical text from the philologist's work of interpreting a literary and classical text. Finally, he recognizes a potential problem with his concept of play or game. In conversation, the game of language that mediates understanding, we transcend our subjectivity dialogically by changing our self-understanding along with changing our understanding of the truth claimed by the other. In the experience of art, however, we seem to transcend subjectivity in a more one-sided way. The game we engage in with art challenges us to change our minds and ourselves without apparently being able at the same time to reciprocate and challenge the work's claim to truth.

Gadamer's own self-criticism has led him to renew the question of the relation between philosophy and art or literature. Gadamer argues that there is indeed reciprocity in the game that we engage in with art. Just as the art work challenges us to change our minds, so too our interpretation of the art work challenges it to produce a response to our questions. By interpreting the art work, we do not merely reproduce the truth claimed by the art work but we produce a different understanding of its claim to truth.

Ironically, once play and gaming became associated with post-structuralist theories of interpretation, especially that of Derrida, Gadamer's attempt to rethink his earlier concept of the game we play with the art work risks being misunderstood as an affirmation of the very subjectivity in understanding and interpretation that *Truth and Method* sets out to deny. Gadamer attempted but failed to engage successfully in a dialogue with Derrida on the concept of the interpretation of a text that appears to divide the hermeneutical renewal of tradition from its deconstruction (Michelfelder and Palmer 1989). The confrontation of hermeneutics and deconstruction, both legacies of Heidegger's later philosophy, remains a task for the future.

List of works

Gadamer, H.-G. (1985–) *Gesammelte Werke*, Tübingen: J.C.B. Mohr (Paul Siebeck), 10 vols. (Gadamer's *Collected Works*: vols 1 and 2 are on hermeneutics; vols 3 and 4 on recent philosophy; vols 8 and 9 on aesthetics and poetics; vol. 10 on hermeneutics in retrospective.)

—— (1931) *Platos dialektische Ethik: Phänomenologische Interpretationen zum Philebos*, in *Platos dialektische Ethik*, Hamburg: Felix Meiner, 1968; trans. R.M. Wallace, *Plato's Dialectical Ethics*, New Haven, CT: Yale University Press, 1991. (Gadamer's 1931 habilitation, a phenomenological interpretation of Plato's *Philebus*.)

—— (1960) *Wahrheit und Methode*, Tübingen: J.C.B. Mohr (Paul Siebeck); trans. *Truth and Method*, New York: Sheed & Ward, 1975; 2nd edn, rev. trans. J. Weinsheimer and D.G. Marshall, 1989. (Gadamer's philosophical hermeneutics. The original translation was edited by G. Barden and J. Cumming in 1975. The later, revised translation is preferred.)

—— (1967a) *Hegels Dialektik*, Tübingen: J.C.B. Mohr; trans. P. Christopher Smith, *Hegel's Dialectic*, New Haven, CT: Yale University Press. (Five hermeneutical studies.)

—— (1967b) *Kleine Schriften I: Philosophie, Hermeneutik*, Tübingen: J.C.B. Mohr (Paul Siebeck). (These essays address early formulations and further developments of Gadamer's philosophical hermeneutics.)

—— (1972) *Kleine Schriften III: Idee und Sprache*, Tübingen: J.C.B. Mohr (Paul Siebeck), 2nd edn.

(These essays interpret the thought of Plato, Husserl, Heidegger and Hegel, among others.)

—— (1972) *Kleine Schriften IV: Variationen*, Tübingen: J.C.B. Mohr (Paul Siebeck), 2nd edn. (These essays respond to further questions about the philosophical hermeneutics presented in *Truth and Method*.)

—— (1976) *Philosophical Hermeneutics*, trans. D. Linge, Berkeley, CA: University of California Press. (Essays developing Gadamer's hermeneutics.)

—— (1979) *Kleine Schriften II: Interpretationen*, Tübingen: J.C.B. Mohr (Paul Siebeck), 2nd edn. (These essays exemplify the practice of hermeneutics in the domain of aesthetics.)

—— (1980) *Dialogue and Dialectic*, trans. P. Christopher Smith, New Haven, CT: Yale University Press. (Eight hermeneutical studies of Plato.)

—— (1981) *Reason in the Age of Science*, trans. F.G. Lawrence, Cambridge, MA: MIT Press. (Essays on practical philosophy.)

—— (1986) *The Relevance of the Beautiful*, trans. N. Walker, ed. R. Bernasconi, Cambridge: Cambridge University Press. (Essays on art, literature and philosophy.)

—— (1994) *Heidegger's Ways*, trans. J. Stanley, Albany, NY: State University of New York Press. (Essays on Heidegger.)

References and further reading

* Betti, E. (1980) 'Hermeneutics as the General Methodology of the *Geisteswissenschaften*', in *Contemporary Hermeneutics*, ed. J. Bleicher, London: Routledge & Kegan Paul. (Criticism of Gadamer's hermeneutics.)

Grondin, J. (1982) *Hermeneutische Wahrheit?*, Königstein: Forum Academicum. (Gadamer's concept of truth.)

Habermas, J. (1977) 'A Review of Gadamer's *Truth and Method*', in *Understanding and Social Inquiry*, ed. F. Dallmayr and T. McCarthy, Notre Dame, IN: Notre Dame University Press. (Discussion from the perspective of critical theory.)

* Heidegger, M. (1927) *Being and Time*, New York: Harper & Row, 1962. (The first major contribution to hermeneutics in the twentieth century.)

* —— (1977) 'The Origin of the Work of Art', in *Basic Writing*, ed. D.F. Krell, New York: Harper & Row. (A major influence on Gadamer's hermeneutics.)

* Hirsch, E.D. (1967) *Validity in Interpretation*, New Haven, CT: Yale University Press. (Criticism of Gadamer's hermeneutics.)

Hoy, D. (1978) *The Critical Circle*, Berkeley, CA: University of California Press. (On Gadamer and Hirsch, Habermas and Derrida.)

* Michelfelder, D. and Palmer, R. (eds) (1989) *Dialogue and Deconstruction*, Albany, NY: State University of New York Press. (The 1981 encounter between Gadamer and Derrida.)

Palmer, R. (1969) *Hermeneutics*, Evanston, IL: Northwestern University Press. (The interpretation theory of Schleiermacher, Dilthey, Heidegger and Gadamer.)

Wachterhauser, B. (ed.) (1986) *Hermeneutics and Modern Philosophy*, Albany, NY: State University of New York Press. (Important essays on Gadamer.)

Warnke, G. (1987) *Gadamer: Hermeneutics, Tradition and Reason*, Stanford, CA: Stanford University Press. (Gadamer, Frankfurt School, and pragmatism.)

Weinsheimer, J. (1985) *Gadamer's Hermeneutics: A Reading of Truth and Method*, New Haven, CT: Yale University Press. (A useful commentary.)

Wright, K. (ed.) (1990) *Festivals of Interpretation*, Albany, NY: State University of New York Press. (Essays on concepts central to Gadamer's philosophical hermeneutics.)

KATHLEEN WRIGHT

GAIUS (*c.110–c.180*)

Gaius was a great but not a typical classical Roman jurist. His Institutes *(c. AD 161), an introductory textbook, is the first known attempt to see Roman law as a systematic whole. His scheme was used by Justinian and so played a central role in subsequent European thought on the classification of law.*

Little is known of the Roman jurist Gaius apart from his writings. An adherent of the Sabinian school at Rome, he seems to have lived in the provinces. Gaius was not typical of the jurists of the classical age (c. 50 BC–c.AD 250), who do not cite his opinions. Unlike them, he held no political office. Evidently a teacher of law rather than a practising lawyer, his writings show an interest in legal history, Greek philosophy and the classification of law. None of these was characteristic of the other jurists, who clung to a tradition of clever argument in individual cases, the casuistic approach.

Extracts from his many works in the *Digest* show that Gaius was also a master of practical legal reasoning in this sense. But his *Institutes*, a short introductory textbook written about AD 161, is unique. The only classical law book to have survived complete and unaltered by Justinian (see JUSTINIAN), a manuscript of it was found by the German historian Niebuhr in 1816. After some opening remarks on the sources of law, Gaius presents his famous tripartite division of private law into persons (personal status), things (property, succession and obligations) and actions (forms of action and procedure). There are many subdivisions until, for example, the level of individual contracts is reached. Out of a great heap of statutes, edicts, opinions and actions Gaius produced for his students a clear map of the law.

Was Gaius an original thinker? Some have argued that he borrowed his system from an earlier legal work, but no such book is known to exist. And when, for example, Gaius deals with the classification of obligations, he sounds like someone breaking new ground. His debt to Greek philosophy raises a different question. That he was familiar with some common philosophical ideas is suggested, for instance, by his many reference to what is 'natural' in relation to law. But even if he did sometimes adapt and apply classifications he found in Aristotle and elsewhere to the intricacies of actual Roman law, this in itself was an original achievement. Gaius deserves to be considered a great lawyer, an excellent teacher and a brilliant inventor.

Gaius' merits were eventually recognized in the later Empire, when his *Institutes* became a standard work in the law schools. Justinian calls him 'our Gaius' and based his own *Institutes* squarely on the work of Gaius. In this way Gaius became the teacher of Europe. The institutional scheme was not perfect, but it was there. Through it, Gaius can claim to be the father of systematic legal thinking in the West.

See also: LAW, PHILOSOPHY OF; LEGAL CONCEPTS §1; ROMAN LAW

List of works

Gaius (*c.*AD 161) *The Institutes of Gaius*, F. de Zulueta (ed.), Oxford: Oxford University Press, 1946, 1953; W.M. Gordon and P.F. Robinson (eds), London: Duckworth, 1988. (In the former part 1 is the text with critical notes and a translation, part 2 an extensive and useful commentary. The latter edition has the text with a readable, modern translation.)

References and further reading

Honoré, A.M. (1962) *Gaius*, Oxford: Oxford University Press. (Brilliant but speculative account of Gaius' life. Technical in places.)

Jolowicz, H.F. and Nicholas, B. (1972) *Historical Introduction to the Study of Roman Law*, Cambridge: Cambridge University Press, esp. 374–94, 405–20. (An accessible account, with extensive references to the literature, of Gaius and the classical Roman jurists.)

Justinian (AD 533) *The Digest of Justinian*, T. Mommsen, P. Krueger and A.Watson (eds), Philadelphia, PA: University of Pennsylvania Press, 1985. (Contains excerpts from Gaius' other works. The Latin text by Mommsen and Krueger with a readable translation by various writers edited by A. Watson.)

—— (AD 533) *Justinian's Institutes*, P. Birks and G. McLeod (eds), London: Duckworth, 1987. (The Latin text by Krueger with a good modern translation and useful introduction.)

GRANT McLEOD

GALEN (AD 129–*c.*210)

Galen was the most influential doctor of late Greco-Roman antiquity. But he was also a notable philosopher, who desired to effect a synthesis of what was best in the work of his predecessors, not only in medicine but also in logic, epistemology, philosophical psychology and the philosophy of science and explanation. In logic he made use of both Aristotelian and Stoic material, but supplemented them with his own treatment of relational logic. His epistemology, while resolutely anti-sceptical on the grounds that nature could not have furnished us with systematically delusive sense-organs, was none the less sober and cautious: some philosophers' questions are simply unanswerable. He attacked the Stoics' unitary psychology, establishing by means of detailed experiments that the brain was the source of voluntary action. Finally, drawing on the philosophical and medical tradition, he crafted a theory of cause and explanation sophisticated enough to rebut the sceptical challenges to such notions, and rich enough to enable him to construct a comprehensive physiology and pathology on its basis.

1 Life and work
2 Galen's intellectual inheritance
3 Theory of causation
4 Reason and experience

1 Life and work

Galen is best known to history as a doctor, the systematizer of a Hippocratism (see HIPPOCRATIC MEDICINE) which became the foundation of medicine for more than 1,500 years. But he was also a considerable philosopher in his own right, writing extensively on logic and language, and scattering philosophical remarks, arguments and controversies throughout his vast medical *oeuvre*. And this is no mere accidental collocation of interests, to be explained by the fact that he trained first in philosophy before turning to medicine. He wrote a short pamphlet *That the Best Doctor is Also a Philosopher*, which survives, stressing the intimate connections between the two disciplines, and never tired of pointing out the errors made by his medical colleagues caused by their insufficient attention to logical detail and their ethical shortcomings.

Galen was born into a well-to-do family in Greek Asia Minor, and received an extensive liberal education, learning philosophy from leading Platonists and Peripatetics, as well as Stoic logic. He had little time for atomism in any of its forms (see ATOMISM, ANCIENT), and is scathing about the inability of the atomists, and doctors influenced by them, to give satisfying explanations of complex phenomena in purely material terms without recourse to teleological explanation. For Galen, teleology was an essential part of any rationally acceptable explanation of the world and its contents.

Galen travelled widely in pursuit of his education, absorbing both Empiricist and Rationalist views (see HELLENISTIC MEDICAL EPISTEMOLOGY), which conspired to nurture his distinctively eclectic views in methodology, as well as a syncretism in philosophical outlook typical of the times (although original enough in its elaboration). He moved to Rome in 162, making (on his own account, in *On Prognosis*) an immediate impact upon the cultural and aristocratic elite for his competence as a doctor and for the soundness of his logical reasoning.

He wrote at a furious pace, dictating to relays of scribes, and his output of treatises medical and philosophical, in the form of original monographs or of commentaries on the masters was correspondingly enormous (see §2 below). Some of this *oeuvre* was destroyed by fire in his own lifetime, and much else has been lost since. But a great deal survives in Greek (Kühn's monumental edition runs to about 10,000 pages of text), and much else in other languages, notably Arabic, Latin and Hebrew, a fact ensured by his early acceptance in the Islamic world as the great repository of medical wisdom. His influence on the subsequent history of medicine was enormous, his views in physiology and anatomy not being superseded until the sixteenth century, his medicine itself surviving even longer.

2 Galen's intellectual inheritance

Galen's chief sources of inspiration were Hippocrates and Plato, his *On the Doctrines of Hippocrates and Plato* being a typically syncretistic attempt to demonstrate their basic agreement on all important issues. His theory of disease is fundamentally Hippocratic in conception: an illness consists in the impediment to or destruction of one of the crucial functions of the body, while treatment involves restoring that function to its proper state. These impediments can take the form of imbalances in the fundamental four humours, blood, phlegm, and yellow and black bile, which regulate the body; and each of the four humours is itself associated with one pair of the four basic qualities, hot, cold, wet and dry, which may by distempered either individually, or in their humoral pairs. Furthermore, there are four types of disease of the organic parts, plus a general category he terms 'loss of cohesion' (this scheme forms the basis of *On the Therapeutic Method*). However, for Galen, Hippocrates was important not so much as a medical gospel, but rather for having exemplified a methodology of investigation, theorizing, and testing, which, if competently pursued, would in time reveal the whole of medical truth.

Galen's greatest philosophical debt to Plato is his adoption and elaboration of the type of creationist natural teleology sketched in the latter's *Timaeus* (see PLATO §16; TELEOLOGY). For Galen, this time in agreement with the Stoics (see STOICISM §5), the idea that the world, in all its structural regularity, might be a spontaneous efflorescence of blind mechanical forces was simply anathema: no mechanical theory could possibly account for the complexity and organization of the world and its inhabitants. Moreover, the artifice of such a world demands an actual Creator: Aristotelian purely immanentist teleology is equally unsatisfactory. Galen calls his own great teleological account of biological structure and function, *On the Function of the Parts*, a 'hymn to Nature' and the Creator. Those (such as Erasistratus; see HELLENISTIC MEDICAL EPISTEMOLOGY), who have dared to say that Nature on occasion does something in vain have simply failed to appreciate the subtlety and complexity of her works, which are only apparent to the skilled and conscientious investigator.

Galen also seeks in *On the Doctrines of Hippocrates and Plato* to ground the Platonic hypothesis of a tripartite soul, with reason in the brain, emotion in the heart and desire in the liver, upon detailed anatomical investigation and experiment. He subjects the unitary psychology of the Stoics (see STOICISM §19) to a withering attack, accusing them of logical incompetence as well as blindness to the evidence. Yet Galen was equally powerfully influenced by the Peripatetic tradition in natural science: while the underlying pattern to his teleology is Platonic, the great model for his practical work in the investigation of function is Aristotle's biology. And he admired Aristotle's logic, sometimes troubling to cast his arguments in syllogistic form (but see §4 below).

3 Theory of causation

Equally, Galen happily adopts the basic model of Aristotle's four causes (*Physics* II 3) and deploys it in his own analysis (see ARISTOTLE §9). There is ample room for the final cause in nature given his commitment to teleology; efficient causes clearly have a role in explaining how things come to be what they are; while a just appreciation of the importance of the material cause will help to evade some of the stronger sceptical attacks (notably again those of Erasistratus) upon the coherence of the notion of causation in the first place. The reason why different things respond differently to the same influences (the prime empirical weapon in the sceptical armoury) is that they are differently constituted, and so differently susceptible (a view perfectly consistent with Hippocratism: the different constitutions, at least in the case of animals, will be humoral in structure).

Yet Galen's use of Aristotle is selective and creative. He has very little use for the formal cause (or indeed for Platonic hypostasized Forms) as such, although he is perfectly well aware of the importance of form for function. He simply does not regard it as a properly separate explanatory category; instead he adopts the Middle Platonist category of the instrumental cause.

Equally, his treatment of efficient causes is unorthodox, since he happily embraces the Stoic (or at least Stoic-influenced) treatment of causal agency as involving categorially distinct stages. There are antecedent causes, external influences brought to bear on objects (or physical systems), which may, if they are suitably disposed, trigger in them a sequence of events leading to the establishment of some further condition (for example, disease). But antecedent causes are not on their own sufficient for their effects; they operate only on patients in a suitable condition, and even then their progress may, if caught early enough, be arrested. For they set in motion processes within the organism, a sequence of preceding causes, which then culminate (unless appropriate action has been taken) in a set of conditions both necessary and sufficient for the disease in question, as well as being contemporary with it: the so-called 'containing', or sustaining, cause.

Thus Galen's detailed account of causal efficiency involves a wholly un-Aristotelian concentration on the sequential nature of causation as a temporal phenomenon; and, in addition to being of sufficient complexity and sophistication to defuse sceptical objections, it allows him to build up a detailed theoretical account of the structure of human pathology.

4 Reason and experience

Galen's commitment to theory places him in the Rationalist camp (see HELLENISTIC MEDICAL EPISTEMOLOGY); but he insisted with the Empiricists upon the importance of testing, and sought to effect a reconciliation: theory without experience was empty, but experience without theory, blind. He emphasizes the importance of practical engagement in physiology and medicine; of regular, repeated observation and experiment; but he also believes that such observation is hamstrung unless it can be placed within its appropriate theoretical context. Students of medicine must make repeated dissections and vivisections in order to learn the structure and arrangement of things in the body; but they must also learn to sytematize those observations by attending to logic, and to understand them in nature's teleological light.

The basic theoretical categories he adopts, the four qualities, while not directly equivalent to their phenomenal counterparts, are still susceptible of empirical appreciation. Chilled white wine is, surface indications notwithstanding, hot and dry, since its effect is to heat and desiccate. Empirical testing, the main tool in the Empiricist context of discovery, is equally essential for Galen, but rather in the context of justification. The theories elaborated by reason on the basis of observation must themselves answer at the tribunal of experience.

Galen never abandons his belief (stated in the opening books of *On the Therapeutic Method*) that medicine can be made into an Aristotelian demonstrative science, where necessarily true theorems flow ineluctably from indubitable axioms, which include definitions stating the essence of things as well as fundamental logical and metaphysical principles, such as the law of the excluded middle and the principle of causality. Yet for such a science to be of practical use, it must be applicable to contingent circumstances, and pass stiff empirical tests. Moreover, given the diversity of circumstances, practical medicine will never be infallible; but if it is probabilistic, it is so not because of any intrinsic uncertainty in nature itself, but only because of our own inabilities to see clearly or accurately enough into it.

Galen insisted on the importance of training in logic, for systematizing empirical evidence and exposing others' fallacies. He made use of Stoic as well as Aristotelian argument schemata (although not uncritically: he rejects the Stoic third 'indemonstrable' (see STOICISM §11) as incapable of delivering necessary conclusions); and he saw more clearly than either school that neither system could handle relations properly, a deficiency he sought, albeit rather naïvely, to remedy with an account of 'relational syllogisms'.

Galen was not overly sanguine about knowledge; indeed he held that many of the disputes of the theoretical philosophers and cosmologists, over the nature of the soul or the existence of an extra-mundane void, were simply undecidable, since reason alone cannot decide them and neither is there any relevant experience to be won regarding them. But where they can operate, the sense-organs are 'natural criteria'; and nature does nothing in vain. Thus animals must naturally be able to assimilate perceptible form, and no inductive problem of the sort which plagues empiricist accounts of concept-formation arises. Equally, scepticism is refuted by teleology. It is by analysis of these naturally arising conceptions that we may, if we are able and conscientious enough, arrive at the real, definitional principles of things upon which all genuine, scientific knowledge is based.

List of works

Galen (c. AD 150–210) *Opera omnia*, ed. C.G. Kühn, Leipzig: Knoblauch, 1821–33. (Greek text with Latin translation; Galen is standardly cited by volume and page number from this edition.)

—— (c. AD 150–210) *Selected Works*, trans. P.N. Singer, Oxford and New York: Oxford University Press, 1997. (A broad range of works.)

—— (c. AD 170) *On the Function of the Parts*, trans. M.T. May, *Galen on the Usefulness of the Parts of the Body*, Baltimore, MD: Johns Hopkins University Press, 2 vols, 1967. (Translation with useful notes of Galen's defence of natural teleology.)

—— (c. AD 175) *On the Therapeutic Method, Books I and II*, trans. R.J. Hankinson, Oxford: Oxford University Press, 1991. (Translation and commentary, with introduction and notes, of Galen's most extended discussion of scientific method.)

—— (c. AD 175) *On Antecedent Causes*, trans. R.J. Hankinson, Cambridge: Cambridge University Press, 1998. (New edition, with translation, commentary and general introduction, of Galen's important short treatise on causation.)

—— (c. AD 175) *On the Doctrines of Hippocrates and Plato*, trans. P.H. De Lacy, *Galeni de Placitis Hippocratis et Platonis*, in *Corpus Medicorum Graecorum* V 4 2 1, Berlin: Akademie-Verlag, 3 vols, 1978–83. (Magisterial edition and translation, with short commentary, on Galen's great text.)

—— (c. AD 178) *On Prognosis*, trans. V. Nutton, *Galeni de Praecognitione*, in *Corpus Medicorum Graecorum* V 4 2 1, Berlin: Akademie-Verlag, 1979. (Fine edition, with commentary, of an interesting text in which Galen recounts many of his early medical triumphs in Rome.)

—— (c. AD 190, 195, 150) *Three Treatises on the Nature of Science: On the Sects for Beginners, An Outline of Empiricism, On Medical Experience*, trans. M. Frede, Indianapolis, IN: Hackett Publishing Company, 1985. (Clear translations of three key short works on medical methodology, with an excellent introduction.)

—— (c. AD 195) *On Anatomical Procedures*, trans. C. Singer, Oxford: Oxford University Press, 1956; later books trans. W.H.L. Duckworth, Cambridge: Cambridge University Press, 1962. (Complete English version of Galen's major treatise on anatomy.)

References and further reading

Barnes, J. (1991) 'Galen on Logic and Therapy', in R. Durling and F. Kudlien (eds) *Galen on the Method of Healing*, Leiden: Brill, 50–102. (A magisterial account of the philosophical basis of Galen's medical theory.)

Frede, M. (1982) 'On Galen's Epistemology', in V. Nutton (ed.) *Galen: Problems and Propects*, London: Wellcome Institute, 65–86. (A brief, comprehensive overview.)

Hankinson, R.J. (1989) 'Galen and the Best of All Possible Worlds', *Classical Quarterly* 39: 206–27. (Discussion of Galen's creationist teleology; see §2.)

—— (1992) 'Galen's Philosophical Eclecticism', in W. Haase (ed.) *Aufstieg und Niedergang der römischen Welt*, Berlin and New York: de Gruyter, II 36 5: 3,505–22. (Brief, general account of Galen's philosophy and its sources.)

—— (1994a) 'Galen's Anatomical Procedures', in W. Haase (ed.) *Aufstieg und Niedergang der römischen Welt*, Berlin and New York: de Gruyter, II 37 2: 1,834–55. (An account of the theoretical basis of Galen's anatomy, and its relation to his teleology.)

—— (1994b) 'Galen's Theory of Causation', in W. Haase (ed.) *Aufstieg und Niedergang der römischen Welt*, Berlin and New York: de Gruyter, II 37 2: 1,757–74. (Expanded version of §3.)

Temkin, O. (1973) *Galenism*, Ithaca, NY: Cornell University Press. (A good general account of Galen's medical views and their afterlife.)

R.J. HANKINSON

GALILEI, GALILEO
(1564–1642)

Galileo Galilei, one of the most colourful figures in the long history of the natural sciences, is remembered best today for two quite different sorts of reason. He has often been described as the 'father' of modern natural science because of his achievements in the fields of mechanics and astronomy, and for what today would be called his philosophy of science, his vision of how the practice of science should be carried on and what a completed piece of natural science should look like. While none of the elements of that philosophy was entirely new, the way in which he combined them was so effective that it did much to shape all that came after in the sciences. In the popular mind, however, as a continuing stream of biographies attest, it is his struggle with Church authority that remains the centre of attention, symbolic as it is of the often troubled, but always intriguing, relationship between science and religion.

1   Life and works
2   The practice of natural science
3   The conception of science
4   Theology and science

1   Life and works

Born in Pisa, Galileo enrolled in 1581 in medicine at the University of Pisa. But his interests lay rather in mathematics and he left the university without completing a degree. He continued his work in mathematics, however, and obtained a teaching post in mathematics and natural philosophy at Pisa in 1589. To aid his teaching, he composed several commentaries on standard logical topics in the Aristotelian curriculum of the day, drawing heavily (as Wallace (1992a) has persuasively argued) on class-notes from lectures at the Jesuit Collegio Romano. Around this time, he also composed a treatise on motion which departed from Aristotle in some significant respects, but supported Aristotelian doctrine against its critics in the main, holding, for example, that the speed of natural fall, after a brief initial period, is constant and that the motion of a body on a frictionless plane will eventually cease.

In 1592, he gained a teaching position at the University of Padua, then perhaps the leading centre in natural philosophy. There he continued his work in mechanics along lines that diverged more and more from Aristotelian norms. Aided by experiments with an inclined plane, he concluded that free fall is uniformly accelerated. The mathematics of uniform acceleration had already been explored by the Merton school at Oxford (see OXFORD CALCULATORS); Galileo applied this mathematics to falling motion, with the crucial proviso that the motion be idealized by supposing the resistance of the medium to be removed. There is evidence, as Drake and others have shown, that he also discovered the parabolic shape of projectile motion by empirical means at this time.

In 1609, Galileo turned his newly constructed telescope to the skies and in the short space of a few years made a series of remarkable discoveries that altogether changed the direction of his researches and of his life generally. He announced the earth-like nature of the lunar surface, the existence of sunspots and the apparent axial rotation of the sun, the four moons of Jupiter (which he named the 'Medicean' planets in honour of the Medici ruler of Florence, Cosimo II) and the phases of Venus which showed it to revolve around the sun. His first book-length publication, the *Sidereus Nuncius* (The Starry Messenger) (1610), was an instant best-seller, provoking heated debate. His new-found fame led to the appointment he had so eagerly sought, as court mathematician and philosopher to Cosimo.

Galileo's discoveries definitively undermined the Aristotelian geocentric world-system (see COSMOLOGY). Though he took this to affirm its Copernican rival, there was, in fact, another alternative, the Tychonic model which had the planets orbit the sun and the sun in turn revolve around an immobile earth. Galileo's intuitions led him to reject this model as dynamically absurd, but it was greeted warmly by those who wanted to maintain the stability of the earth either for physical or for theological reasons.

Galileo soon found himself opposed not only by his beleaguered Aristotelian colleagues but by the theologians whose aid the latter solicited. A number of biblical passages referred, directly or indirectly, to the motion of the sun or the stability of the earth. In a letter to his former student Benedetto Castelli, and in a much longer *Letter* (1615) addressed nominally to Cosimo's mother, the dowager Grand Duchess Christina, Galileo formulated a set of hermeneutic principles addressed to cases where science and Scripture appear to clash. All of the principles found a precedent, he emphasized, in St Augustine's *De Genesi ad litteram*. But his arguments were in vain. In 1616, the Roman Congregation of the Index banned Copernicus' *De revolutionibus*, until the passages implying the reality of the earth's motion and the sun's rest should be 'corrected', and asserted in passing that the Copernican theses, taken literally, were 'contrary to Scripture'. Galileo was summoned before Cardinal Bellarmine and warned to abandon the Copernican claims. Whether he also received the further injunction not to teach, defend or even discuss the Copernican theses, which was to be delivered only if he proved recalcitrant, has been much debated; the documentary evidence on this issue is clouded.

Burdened by recurrent illness, Galileo returned to the astronomical topics he had already addressed in his *Letters on Sunspots* (1613). He turned now to comets and engaged in an increasingly contentious dispute about their nature with the Jesuit natural philosopher Orazio Grassi, culminating in the publication of *The Assayer* (1623). It was here that Galileo broke entirely with Aristotelian natural philosophy, maintaining that the Book of Nature is written in the language of mathematics, that the qualitative properties of sensible objects are merely subjective, and that matter is composed of imperceptible corpuscles.

In 1623, Galileo's friend, Maffeo Barberini, was elected Pope as Urban VIII. In a series of interviews with the new Pope, Galileo won an evidently reluctant permission to proceed with a treatise on the Copernican system, provided it be treated as a hypothesis. The traditional understanding of mathematical astronomy was that mathematical 'hypotheses', like those of Ptolemy and Copernicus, were to be regarded as convenient predictive devices only. Furthermore, for theological reasons rooted in the earlier nominalist-voluntarist tradition, Urban himself maintained that the underlying causes of a physical phenomenon could never be established demonstratively, as the Aristotelian notion of science required, since God could always bring about the phenomenon by other hidden means. But Galileo evidently considered himself licensed by Urban to argue for the possible *truth* of the Copernican claims, understanding 'hypothesis' now in a very different sense, a sense closer to the modern one. And so he began work on a treatise that would make the best case possible for Copernicanism, stopping short only of claiming it had been demonstrated. After a lengthy struggle with the ecclesiastical censors in Rome and in Florence, he was finally permitted to publish the *Dialogue Concerning the Two Chief World Systems* in 1632.

The book immediately encountered strenuous opposition from Roman theologians, most particularly from the Pope himself, principally on the grounds that it contravened the decree of 1616 declaring the Copernican doctrine to be contrary to Scripture. The Pope ordered Galileo to be brought to trial before the Holy Office in 1633. Found 'suspect of heresy', he was ordered to recant. After his recantation he was sentenced to imprisonment, commuted to house arrest.

Deeply discouraged and forced to abandon his cherished project of showing that the Church had nothing to fear from Copernicanism, Galileo returned to the treatise on motion he had commenced long before in Padua. It still needed to be given a literary form, and a properly axiomatic structure had to be found for the two laws of motion. The completed manuscript was smuggled to Holland and the *Two New Sciences* was finally published in 1638. It announced 'a brand new science concerning a very old subject', and set forth in elegant geometrical form his two laws of motion. It was his final testament, one that would 'open wide a gateway' for the labours of others, as he prophesied that it would.

2 The practice of natural science

The most striking feature of Galilean science was its emphasis on *mathematization*. Not only did it treat quantity to the exclusion of quality, but quantity itself was assumed to be expressible in purely geometric terms. Time was represented as a line, and velocity, instead of being treated in the traditional way as an irreducible ratio between distance covered and time taken, was presented as a mathematical quantity in its own right. Galileo's two laws were both purely kinematic; they simply described motion. Quantities like mass or force would not have lent themselves to the simple sort of geometrization that length and time allowed. (Descartes achieved a similar geometrical reduction by equating matter with extension.) Furthermore, the axiomatic mode of presentation customary for geometry encouraged Galileo (as it later did Newton) to adopt a similar mode for mechanics. Galileo's success in dispensing with weight and resistance of the medium, the two non-geometrical factors determining velocity in older accounts of falling motion, may have led him to be over-optimistic about the prospects for a reductively geometric science of motion. But his resolute move to mathematically expressible quantities as the proper basis of physics was to prove its long-term worth.

What made both of his laws possible was his decision to *idealize*, that is, to extrapolate to the (at the time empirically unachievable) case of *in vacuo* fall. The medium invariably present in actually observed fall was to be treated as an 'impediment', a complicating factor that should as far as possible be eliminated, in order to focus on the 'pure' case of fall. Though conceptual idealization was not new in natural philosophy, finding a precedent especially in the work of Archimedes, the construction of deliberately simplified material situations was a distinctively Galilean contribution to the science of motion. Galileo was convinced that it would lead to the mathematically simple laws that lie hidden beneath the complexities of natural process. This aspect of his practice has often been described as 'Platonic', but it runs contrary to the Platonic conviction that the sense-world, far from being 'written in the language of mathematics' as Galileo's famous slogan ran, lends itself only imperfectly to the intelligibility of mathematics.

Idealization of this sort, opposed even more to Aristotle's way with nature, finds material expression in *experiment*. Galileo had to contrive situations that would reveal how selected physical factors would relate to one another in the absence of disturbing causal influences, such as friction. Though his inclined-plane experiment became a model for later emulation, it must be added that he could, on occasion, manifest a rather casual attitude towards experimental warrant. His allusions to experiments sometimes appear as rhetorical devices rather than as reports of actual performance. Koyré (1940) claimed, indeed, that Galileo rarely performed the experiments he describes, that these were no more than thought-experiments resting on his own powerful intuitions (see THOUGHT EXPERIMENTS). Recent work on Galileo's work-notes has shown this to be exaggerated. Galileo undoubtedly sought support for his new science in repeated observation.

This in turn required specially-designed *instruments* to supplement the testimony of the unaided senses. The new emphasis on mathematically expressible quantities meant that a degree of precision would be needed that the senses alone could never achieve. Furthermore, instruments such as the telescope and the microscope could extend the very notion of observation to realms the senses could not reach. Instruments could even be devised to measure quantities, like the 'strength' of magnets, that escape the senses entirely. A significant part of Galileo's success lay in his talent for improving instruments already in use, or for constructing instruments of entirely novel kinds. The new science would depend heavily on technological skills, a feature entirely alien to natural philosophy in the Greek tradition (see EXPERIMENT; SCIENTIFIC METHOD).

This novel complex of practices gave the new science an immediate degree of autonomy relative to the rest of philosophy. Thus began the long and often painful process of separation between two disciplines that had up to this point been considered as one. The ridicule that Galileo often directed to 'the philosophers' was clearly meant for Aristotelian philosophers, not for philosophy itself. He had, after all, insisted on the title of 'Philosopher' when he joined the Medici court, in part to ensure that his work would not be dismissed as mere 'mathematics'. How would he have regarded the redefinition of philosophy itself that his work did so much to set in train, had

this been presented to him? Despite what some historians have claimed, he was not a positivist in the making. His conception of science as a structure of 'necessary demonstrations' leant as much to a past when the principles of natural philosophy carried their own intuitive self-evidence as to a future when scientific theories would be warranted primarily by their observational consequences.

3 The conception of science

Given the marked shift in scientific practice represented by Galileo's mature work, one might have expected that his conception of what makes a knowledge-claim truly scientific would have altered correspondingly. But in this respect, he stayed close to the Aristotelian ideal absorbed in his youth. His new science departed in one important respect, of course, from the earlier conception: it was mathematical, not syllogistic, in form. But this made it *more* scientific in his eyes, not less. Indeed, it made it equal in certainty to God's own knowledge. His opening promise was that his science 'would prove demonstratively, and not just persuade by probable arguments' (1638: 16). And the familiar Aristotelian phrase, 'necessary demonstration', is dotted throughout his writings. He contrasts the probable mode of argumentation characteristic of the humanities with the demonstration proper to the natural sciences 'whose conclusions are true and necessary, and have nothing to do with human will' (1632: 53).

But how could he make good on this claim? In demonstration, the inference proceeds deductively from the premises, which must be seen to be true and necessary in their own right; whereas in an observational science the order is reversed, since inferences proceed backwards, as it were, from observed particulars to (universal) premises. The warrant for the postulated premises lies in the consequences drawn from them, not in their own self-evidence. Such an inference cannot be deductive, it would seem, unless the observed particulars can somehow prompt the mind to formulate a universal principle. This had been Aristotle's doctrine of *epagōgē*, extensively elaborated by Galileo's predecessors in Padua as a 'demonstrative regress' from observation to principle and back down to observation. Could an investigation relying on experiment fit this model? Galileo seems, at times at least, to have thought so.

Contrary to a once-popular presumption, Galileo was no inductivist. He would never have supposed that, for example, observation alone could establish as a *principle* that projectile motion follows a parabolic path. The material world, he remarks, is too full of potentially disturbing factors, and observation itself is always subject to correction. Instead, one would have to show either that the parabolic law is a principle in its own right or that it follows from other such principles. Primary among these latter, of course, would be the law of free fall, described as 'the simplest and most evident rule' (1638: 154). But how can one be sure that nature actually follows this rule? Galileo concedes that this has to be 'confirmed' by experiment. But if that is so, can the supposed 'principle' exhibit the necessity that the starting point of strict demonstration demands? Galileo was well-aware of this difficulty and hedged his claim in phrases like 'little short of necessary demonstration', 'worthy of being conceded as if demonstrated' (1638: 162, 164). The tension here between two very different conceptions of science, one demonstrative, the other hypothetical, is evident.

The axiomatic structure of his mechanics undoubtedly encouraged him, if encouragement was needed, in his retention of the language of demonstration. Regarded purely as mathematics, his mechanics could be called 'demonstrative', though admittedly in a weaker sense of that term, a sense that Galileo often exploited. In response to critics after the publication of *Two New Sciences*, he could claim to have 'demonstrated conclusively' what the properties of uniformly accelerated motion were, 'on the supposition' (*ex suppositione*) that falling motion actually *is* uniformly accelerated in nature. This allowed him to affirm that the reasoning would remain 'demonstrative' even if experiment were to show that downward motion does not quite conform to the supposition (Letters to Baliani and de Carcavi, *Opera*, XVIII: 12–13; XVII: 90). The retreat to an *ex suppositione* claim, however, was equivalently, to open the possibility that his mechanics, considered as *physics* rather than just as mathematics, could claim only a hypothetical warrant. Or else it was to assume that experimental discrepancies can be disregarded in such a case because of the inherent messiness of the causal order impeding the operation of the 'pure' physical principles. But *ought* one to rely on intuition in this way, especially in the face of counter-evidence? This was the challenge that defenders of the traditional regress model of proof had never really been able to handle.

The question of *why* bodies fall as they do was expressly laid aside; had it been acknowledged, even the appearance of demonstration could hardly have been maintained. But elsewhere in his inquiries, notably in his cosmology, the quest for agent-causes could not be avoided. What was the nature of the lunar surface, of comets, of sunspots? The only way to answer questions like these about natures that were not immediately accessible was to postulate in hypothetical fashion causes that would explain the observed effects. This sort of inference could never fit the mould of strict demonstration. The natures of these distinct objects could not become the subject of self-authenticating principle, and effect-to-cause reasoning inevitably leaves open the possibility of alternative explanations that might fit the data equally well. Galileo tried to limit this latter difficulty by proposing that for any given effect there should be one unique 'true cause'. But it was difficult to deny that in practice, in his detailed argument for the earth-like character of the lunar surface, for example, he was proposing a plausible hypothesis whose epistemic status depended on its being confirmed by the verification of consequences drawn from it (see INFERENCE TO THE BEST EXPLANATION).

Galileo's attachment to the notion of demonstration was such that he never really came to terms with the notion of hypothesis. Unlike others of his day (Kepler, Descartes and Boyle immediately come to mind), he did not concern himself with the question, urgent in a science that argues from observed effects to unobserved agent-causes, of how the credentials of an explanatory hypothesis are to be assessed. This was to prove a critical weakness in his attempts to prove the reality of the earth's double motion, the key to the Copernican debate. His opponents, both the Aristotelian philosophers and the Roman theologians, insisted, for different reasons, on the standards of demonstration. And Galileo on his own account was not disposed to challenge these standards. But lacking demonstration of these motions, as he rather evidently did, what lesser status could he claim for the Copernican theses? The hesitant language in which he couches his conclusions in *Two Chief World Systems* betrays not only the theological dilemma in which he found himself, but also a lifelong reluctance to allow properly 'scientific' status to anything less than demonstration.

4 Theology and science

In conclusion, something should be said about his theological dilemma. What the Church was at pains to defend throughout the Galileo affair was not so much the Aristotelian worldview, as has often been supposed, as the authority of Scripture and the Church's own authority as its interpreter. Had the handful of references in Scripture to the motion of the sun or the stability of the earth not been present, as they might well not have been, the Church would have been unlikely to become so forcefully involved in the Copernican debate. Furthermore, had the debate itself come a century earlier or a century later, a major confrontation might well have been avoided. But this was the age of the Counter-Reformation, when one of the principal issues in dispute between Protestants and Catholics involved hermeneutics: how was Scripture to be interpreted, and who had the authority to interpret it? And here was a layman affirming on his own authority (so it would have seemed in Rome) a nonstandard interpretation of biblical passages. No matter that he could advance good arguments in favour of his interpretation and even cite the authority of one of the greatest of the Church's own theologians on behalf of the principles of interpretation he employed, it was still not to be borne that such a challenge should go unanswered.

Galileo's *Letter to the Grand Duchess* has been described as one of the most effective pieces of theological writing of its century, an ironic assessment, given the lay status and the later fate of its author. Had its arguments been heeded, the fateful 1616 decree of the Congregation of the Index, effectively outlawing the Copernican theses as contrary to Scripture might never have been penned. Or would it? There was a hidden tension between the hermeneutic principles Galileo advanced, a tension to be found likewise in the Augustinian principles he appealed to. On the one hand, Scripture, was held to have no bearing on matters of natural science; these latter were said to lie outside its concerns entirely. On the other hand, where the literal reading of Scripture appears to conflict with a scientific finding, his principles implied that this latter finding has to have the status of demonstration in order to warrant the search for a different reading of Scripture.

The implications of these two directives were quite different for the Copernican debate. Were one to be guided by the first, the status of the scientific arguments for the Copernican theses would be irrelevant; the debated biblical passages mentioning sun and earth would have no scientific standing in the first place. Were one to be guided by the second, the Copernican theses would have to be demonstrated. How crucial the difference is needs no emphasis. Galileo's opponents, notably Cardinal Bellarmine in 1616, adhered to the second and more traditional directive, and demanded demonstration before they would consider a reinterpretation of the Scriptural passages along less literal lines. Galileo himself evidently favoured the first principle, which would have absolved him from the necessity of providing a demonstration of the earth's motion that he simply did not have. To defenders of the second approach (the probable arguments Galileo advanced) arguments that carried weight, though admittedly not conclusive weight with his fellow scientists, were of no avail. And Galileo's own hesitations about the epistemic status of such arguments complicated matters further.

The complexities of character and political circumstance that propelled the Galileo affair continue to fascinate modern readers. But it should also be said that this event, one of the greatest moments in human affairs, hinged to no small extent around an issue in philosophy of science.

See also: ARISTOTELIANISM, RENAISSANCE; EXPLANATION; IDEALIZATIONS; INDUCTIVE INFERENCE; MECHANICS, ARISTOTELIAN; MECHANICS, CLASSICAL; PLATONISM, RENAISSANCE

List of works

Galilei, G. (1610) *The Starry Messenger*; ed. and trans. S. Drake, *Discoveries and Opinions of Galileo*, New York: Doubleday, 1957. (Includes a helpful narrative by the translator, situating this and the following two works that marked Galileo's early involvement in the Copernican debate.)

—— (1613) *Letters on Sunspots*; ed. and trans. S. Drake, *Discoveries and Opinions of Galileo*, New York: Doubleday, abridged, 1957.

—— (1615) *Letter to the Grand Duchess Christina*; ed. and trans. S. Drake, *Discoveries and Opinions of Galileo*, New York: Doubleday, 1957.

—— (1623) *The Assayer*; in C.D. O'Malley and S. Drake (eds), trans. S. Drake, *The Controversy on the Comets of 1618*, Philadelphia, PA: University of Pennsylvania Press, 1960. (Where Galileo lays out some of his most characteristic philosophic theses in the context of an increasingly bitter dispute about the nature of comets with the Jesuit natural philosopher Orazio Grassi.)

—— (1632) *Dialogue Concerning the Two Chief World Systems*; trans. S. Drake, Berkeley, CA: University of California Press, 1953. (The classic work in which Galileo undermines the Aristotelian arguments against the Copernican proposal, refutes Aristotle's own concentric world-system, and advances a number of arguments in support of the Copernican alternative.)

—— (1638) *Two New Sciences*; trans. S. Drake, Madison, WI: University of Wisconsin Press, 1974. (The foundational work in modern mechanics, proposing Galileo's two laws of motion. The 'new science' concerns the strength of materials.)

—— (1890–1909) *Edizione Nazionale delle Opera di Galileo Galilei*, ed. A. Favaro, Florence: Barbera; repr. 1968. (Definitive 20-volume edition of Galileo's works and correspondence.)

—— (1989) *The Galileo Affair*, ed. and trans. M. Finocchiaro, Berkeley, CA: University of California

Press. (Useful collection of documents bearing on the 'Galileo affair'. Includes the *Letter to the Grand Duchess Christina*, selected correspondence, and Holy Office files.)

References and further reading

Biagioli, M. (1993) *Galileo, Courtier: The Practice of Science in the Culture of Absolutism*, Chicago, IL: University of Chicago Press. (Critical of the 'idealism' of the traditional approaches to Galileo's science in terms of arguments advanced, evidence presented and methods followed; suggests that when faced with controversy Galileo relied for legitimation to a significant extent on princely patronage. Employing the methods of cultural anthropology, the author focuses on the dynamics of princely patronage that made possible Galileo's 'self-fashioning' as a 'new philosopher' and contributed to his ultimate downfall.)

Butts, R.E. and Pitts, J. (eds) (1978) *New Perspectives on Galileo*, Dordrecht: Reidel. (Detailed essays dealing primarily with Galileo's scientific methods and his notion of what constitutes science.)

Drake, S. (1978) *Galileo at Work: His Scientific Biography*, Chicago, IL: University of Chicago Press. (Detailed chronicle, year by year, of Galileo's scientific work.)

Fantoli, A. (1994) *Galileo: For Copernicanism and for the Church*; trans. G. Coyne, Rome: Vatican City Publications, 2nd revised and enlarged edn, 1996. (With 180 pages of footnotes and extensive bibliography, an amply documented account of Galileo's protracted attempt to convince the church authorities in Rome of the merits of the Copernican system, the dramatic failure of his efforts, and the aftermath in Rome up to the mid-1990s.)

Finocchiaro, M.A. (1980) *Galileo and the Art of Reasoning: Rhetorical Foundations of Logic and Scientific Method*, Dordrecht: Reidel. (Immensely detailed analysis of *Dialogue Concerning the Two Chief World Systems*, dividing it into sixteen main arguments and 229 sub-arguments. The author claims this work as the book of choice for anyone who wants to see critical reason at its best.)

* Koyré, A. (1940) *Etudes Galiléennes*, Paris: Hermann; trans. J. Mepham, *Galileo Studies*, Atlantic Highlands, NJ: Humanities Press, 1978. (Groundbreaking analyses of Galileo's science, situating it within the Archimedean tradition, and strongly contesting the nineteenth-century view of Galileo as the model empiricist.)

Machamer, P. (ed.) (1998) *Cambridge Companion to Galileo*, Cambridge: Cambridge University Press. (A set of essays from recent contributors to Galileo scholarship that effectively illustrates how diverse that scholarship's findings still remain.)

McMullin, E. (ed.) (1967) *Galileo: Man of Science*, Notre Dame, IN: University of Notre Dame Press. (A collection of twenty-three studies of Galileo's scientific achievements, including classical essays by notable scholars of an earlier generation: Koyré, Olschki, Tannery, Cassirer. Comprehensive bibliography covering 1940–64.)

—— (1985) 'Galilean Idealization', *Studies in the History and Philosophy of Science*, 16: 247–73. (Analysis of six different modes of idealization employed by Galileo in his scientific work.)

* Wallace, W.A. (1992a) *Galileo's Logical Treatises*, Dordrecht: Kluwer. (Translation of, and commentary on, two unpublished treatises Galileo evidently composed as aids in his early teaching duties c.1590. They deal with two themes in Aristotle's *Posterior Analytics*: demonstration and prior knowledge. Wallace has shown by dint of patient research that these treatises almost certainly derive from the 1588 class-notes of Paulus Vallius, a professor at the Jesuit Collegio Romano.)

—— (1992b) *Galileo's Logic of Discovery and Proof*, Dordrecht: Kluwer. (Culmination of a series of works analysing the background and content of Galileo's early commentaries on Aristotelian logical themes. Argues cogently for the influence of these doctrines on the logical structure of Galileo's later writings on motion.)

ERNAN McMULLIN

GALILEO *see* GALILEI, GALILEO

GAME THEORY *see* DECISION AND GAME THEORY; SEMANTICS, GAME-THEORETIC

GAME-THEORETIC SEMANTICS *see* SEMANTICS, GAME-THEORETIC

GANDHI, MAHATMA *see* GANDHI, MOHANDAS KARAMCHAND

GANDHI, MOHANDAS KARAMCHAND (1869–1948)

Gandhi was called Mahatma *(the Great Soul) by Rabindranath Tagore and many in the West, while Gandhi's followers often simply called him* Bapuji *(Father). His confrontation with racism in South Africa provided a challenging context for the development of his idea of* satyāgraha *(holding fast to the truth), a method of nonviolent, noncooperative resistance to the authorities. Influenced by several religious traditions, such as Hinduism (especially Vaishnava), Jainism, Islam and Christianity, Gandhi was both a religious thinker and practical reformer. While in jail on several occasions, he wrote prolifically. He was murdered on 30 January 1948 by a Hindu zealot.*

1   Life and career
2   Truth, religion and politics

1   Life and career

Gandhi was born on 2 October 1869 in Porbandar, Kathiawad to a politician father, Karamchand Uttamchand and a religiously devout mother, Putalibai. At the age of thirteen an arranged marriage took place between Gandhi and Kasturbai, although he was later to oppose child marriage. Educated in India and London, Gandhi passed his bar examination with ease, enrolled at the High Court on 11 June 1891 and sailed for India the following day. After a brief and unsuccessful attempt at law in India he went to South Africa, initially to represent the interests of a Muslim firm. From 1893–1914 Gandhi struggled against racism in South Africa.

Gandhi returned to India in 1915 to engage in a struggle with the British for *swarāj* (self-rule). He lived a life of simplicity and renunciation and used the method of fasting to the brink of death as a way of persuading opponents.

The Amritsar massacre of 1919 was decisive in Gandhi's rejection of British colonial rule in any form. *Khādī*, white home-spun cotton clothes and *charkha*, the spinning wheel, became Gandhian symbols. *Charkhas* were difficult to find, as they were rare among the professional elite in Gandhi's time, and the making of *khādīs* had to be learned.

2   Truth, religion and politics

Gandhi made his first public speech on truth in business dealings in Pretoria, South Africa. He believed in both 'truth of statement' and the notion of 'truth of being'. He was preoccupied with truth and felt it must be expressed in a life of *ahiṃsā*, or non-injury (which entails vegetarianism). He always saw the divine in the less fortunate (for instance by opposing untouchability). Gandhi believed that a *satyāgrahī*, one 'steadfast in truth', ideally must exemplify celibacy (following the vow of *brahmacarya*). Only then could the *satyāgrahī* rise above all passionate attachments and generate enough internal 'heat' (*tapas*) to do battle with untruth. Gandhi's goal was one of serving the public rather than only achieving his individual salvation. He was motivated by the ideal of *sarvodaya*, the welfare of all (see DUTY AND VIRTUE, INDIAN CONCEPTIONS OF).

Gandhi appropriated the term *sadāgraha* and changed it to *satyāgraha* (holding fast to the truth), with *satya* representing truth and *āgraha* firmness. In *An Autobiography, or the Story of My Experiments with Truth* (1927) Gandhi spoke of truth as an underground mine holding many opportunities for service. Proposing that 'there is no other God than truth', Gandhi understood divinity as immanently realizable through dedicating one's work to God. In Hindu tradition this idea is *karma yoga*. For Gandhi *karma yoga* meant a dedication to truth in each particular case, rather than in mystical contemplation of an abstract Godhead. He often appealed to 'the Voice' of conscience wherein God speaks. Accepting the principle of *karma* and the doctrine of transmigration, Gandhi hoped to be reborn an untouchable to be of further service.

In *An Autobiography, or the Story of My Experiments with Truth* (1927), Gandhi revealed that he was not well-versed in Sanskrit and the Hindu classics at the time when the role of guru was thrust upon him by the public. His 'philosophy of religion' was confessional in form, not analytical. He thought at a metareligious level, believing that all religions participate in truth. The Sermon on the Mount, the *Bhagavad Gītā* (which Gandhi himself translated) and the writings of TOLSTOI were sources of particular fascination for him. The Jain doctrine of *ahiṃsā* (non-injury) was one of his main tenets and provided the background to his vegetarianism (see JAINA PHILOSOPHY). His close friend C.F. Andrews supplied a Christian stimulus in his life, but Gandhi found deeper inspiration in his native *Bhagavad Gītā*. Self-purification and dedication to God through service to humanity provided the basis for religiosity according to Gandhi. For Gandhi, religion must bind together humankind and include politics. There were no particular religious images in Gandhi's *ashram*. With the knowledge that God has many names, several scriptures were recited in the daily routine. In this way Gandhi's practice exemplified the tolerance of Jain *syādvāda*, the view that all judgments of nonomniscient beings must be qualified by 'somehow' or 'perhaps' (see MANIFOLDNESS, JAINA THEORY OF). Gandhi was influenced by Jainism from early on. Philosophically, his position expressed a reverence for life characteristic of both Jainism and Buddhism. He disputed the notion that Buddhism is atheistic, preferring to interpret Buddhist *dharma* in the sense of 'truth' as representing God. In his view, religion at its best is concerned with human community and the transcendence of cultural tribalism and parochialism.

Gandhi's goals were the achievement of *sarvodaya*, sovereignty and self-sufficiency in India, encompassing the idea of teaching in native languages. Although untouchability and child marriage were vigorously opposed as they oppressed the less fortunate and defenceless, Gandhi defended stratification in terms of *varna* in the limited sense of the division of labour. He was also opposed to individualistic capitalism. Education was important to Gandhi, and he thought that colleges should be linked to particular industries. Like Martin Luther King, he did not offer a theory of justice, but believed, as King was later to say: 'injustice anywhere is a threat to justice everywhere'.

See also: DUTY AND VIRTUE, INDIAN CONCEPTIONS OF; POLITICAL PHILOSOPHY, INDIAN; TAGORE, R.

List of works

Gandhi, M.K. (1958–) *The Collected Works of Mahatma Gandhi*, New Delhi: Ministry of Information and Broadcasting, 100 volumes to date. (This voluminous work is the authoritative edition of Gandhi's collected works.)
—— (1927) *An Autobiography, or the Story of My Experiments with Truth*, trans. M. Desai, Boston, MA: Beacon Press, 1957. (This book is the single most important work by Gandhi for understanding his philosophy of life.)

References and further reading

Carter, A. (1996) *Mahatma Gandhi: A Selected Bibliography*, Bibliographies of World Leaders 2, Westport, CT: Greenwood Press. (This work is an up-to-date, indispensable bibliography.)
Chatterjee, M. (1983) *Gandhi's Religious Thought*, London: Macmillan. (This is the best single work on Gandhi from a theological viewpoint currently available.)
Herman, A.L. (1990) *The Ways of Philosophy*, Atlanta, GA: Scholars Press. (Chapters 11–12 describe the link between the ideas of Gandhi and Martin Luther King.)
Hick, J. and Hempel, L. (1989) *Gandhi's Significance*

for Today, New York: St Martin's Press. (This volume constitutes an important collection of essays on Gandhi, his religion, ethics, politics and economics.)
Iyer Raghavan, N. (1986–7) *The Moral and Political Writings of Gandhi*, Oxford: Oxford University Press, 3 vols. (This volume is a major scholarly study of Gandhi's moral and political thought.)
Jack, H.A. (1956) *The Gandhi Reader*, Bloomington, IN: Indiana University Press. (This source book is ideal for classes and study groups on Gandhi.)
Juergensmeyer, M. (1984) *Fighting with Gandhi*, San Francisco, CA: Harper & Row. (This work is an engaged, thoughtful study of Gandhian *satyāgraha* that includes both case studies and confrontations with the intellectual currents of Marx, Freud and Niebuhr.)
Rani, A. (1981) *Gandhian Non-Violence and India's Freedom Struggle*, Delhi: Shree Publishing House. (This work offers a detailed insider's view of Gandhi's philosophy-in-practice, amply researched from Indian archives.)
Richards, G. (1982) *The Philosophy of Gandhi: A study of his Basic Ideas*, London: Curzon Press. (This is an excellent philosophical study of Gandhi's · thought.)

FRANK J. HOFFMAN

GAṄGEŚA (*fl. c.*1325)

Gaṅgeśa launched and solidified advances in logic and epistemology within the classical Indian school of Logic, Nyāya. He is traditionally taken to have inaugurated the 'New' school, Navya-Nyāya. Nyāya, both Old and New, is a multidimensional system that belies the stereotype of Indian philosophy as idealist and mystical in orientation. Gaṅgeśa worked with a realist ontology of objects spoken about and experienced every day. He articulated what may be called a reliabilist theory of knowledge: under specified conditions, sense-mediated and inferential cognitions (along with two other types) are reliable sources of information about reality.

Gaṅgeśa was a pivotal figure in classical Indian philosophy; most later debate both within his school and outside it presupposed cognitive analyses that he standardized. These analyses focus on properties exhibited by things known, properties central to the processes whereby they are known. Properties relating the cognized to the cognizer are especially important. Though Gaṅgeśa had a lot to say about the ontological status of these properties, others in his school found them problematic. Such controversy appears to have contributed to New Logic's success: proponents of rival views were able to utilize Gaṅgeśa's formulas and definitions without abandoning their own positions on what is real.

1   Historical particulars
2   Perception and inference
3   Ontology

1   Historical particulars

Gaṅgeśa Upādhyāya lived in the first half of the fourteenth century, in Mithilā, in northern India, where he was a prominent teacher. Gaṅgeśa's school of New Logic remained a Mithilā monopoly for almost two hundred years; students travelled there to learn the system and returned with it to their own regions. Within another century, New Logic came to dominate late classical thought all over India, influencing jurisprudence and aesthetics as well as shaping the philosophical scene. But unfortunately we know Gaṅgeśa the person almost exclusively as the author of a single work, the *Tattvacintāmaṇi* (Jewel of Reflection on Reality).

The *Tattvacintāmaṇi* is New Logic's root text. Numerous commentaries were written on it, and all later New Logic writers presupposed its acquaintance. It is without question one of the premier works of the whole of classical Indian thought. The *Tattvacintāmaṇi* contains the distilled reflections of generations of earlier philosophers, mainly within the sister schools of Nyāya and Vaiśeṣika (see NYĀYA-VAIŚEṢIKA), but also arguments of historic opponents of these two complementary realist views. Gaṅgeśa's originality is in fact less than one might expect given the acclaim for his *Tattvacintāmaṇi*. He himself recognizes UDAYANA (*fl. c.*1000), and rightly so, as the innovator of positions characteristic of the New Logic movement. But Gaṅgeśa does refine the Logic understanding of the cognitively veridical and nonveridical (among other things), and it is here that he has his greatest influence on subsequent Indian thought.

The *Tattvacintāmaṇi* comprises four chapters, each devoted to a separate source of right cognition: veridical perception, cogent inference, analogical vocabulary acquisition, and reliable testimony. Within each chapter there are clearly delineated sections on various subtopics, including reflections, mainly in the first chapter, concerning cognition and veridicality in general, considered independently of particular instruments. Gaṅgeśa is lucid and precise; he argues forcefully, ingeniously leading the reader into positions by careful examination of alternatives.

2   Perception and inference

Cognition (*jñāna*, often translated 'awareness') is the most important item in Gaṅgeśa's philosophy. Ontologically, cognitions are short-lived, episodic attributes or qualities of the self or soul, and, in the case of sensory awarenesses, are causally continuous with physical realities as a result of the relations between sense organ and object. A cognition may be understood as a mental event, but it is a product or state rather than an act. Cognitions are intentional; they are invariably *of* some object or objects, or, more precisely, objective complex(es).

Gaṅgeśa posits sensory cognitions below the level of what we can consciously articulate; these are called indeterminate cognitions, by contrast with the determinate. Every determinate cognition is verbalizable, but indeterminate cognitions are not. Even the simplest verbalizable cognition has an object that is ontologically complex: that is, a qualificandum is cognized through one of its qualifiers in the case of a veridical awareness. It is to avoid an infinite regress of qualification that Gaṅgeśa posits indeterminate cognition, where qualifiers are directly known. Otherwise, there would be the problem of how a qualifier$_1$ of qualificandum$_1$ is known; that is, if the qualifier had to be itself a qualificandum, qualificandum$_2$, to be known through another qualifier, qualifier$_2$, for anything to be known, there would have to be an infinite series of qualifiers and qualificanda. Thus some qualifiers are cognized directly though indeterminately.

Indeterminate cognition is said to give rise to determinate cognition through a causal process. Although acquaintance with an individual is determinate, it should be thought of as causally direct: perception is a causal process spread over time, and indeterminate cognition may be viewed as a first phase. Verbalizable cognition of an individual is mediated by – or, better, fused with – what the individual appears as. Only determinate cognition is verbalizable, in that its content is expressible in propositional form as something, *a*, being an *F* (*Fa*).

All simple (non-doubly, triply, and so on) qualificative or determinate cognitions have a content that exhibits a common structure: qualificandum, qualificative relation, qualifier (*a–R–b*). Qualification is a relational property that obtains in the world, but it is used to talk about cognitions. The simplest veridical sensory cognition reflects a fact or state of affairs, an individual cognized (the qualificandum) as related to a qualifier. With the veridical awareness '(A) pot', for example, we would have the particular pot–inherence–potness as the objective complex (*a–R–b*) cognized as something appearing as a pot. The qualificandum is the bearer or possessor of properties; with the veridical awareness '(A) pot', the particular pot is the subject of qualification and possesses the property of potness. The awareness '(A) pot' has 'potness' as its predication content.

With this apparatus, Gaṅgeśa is able to analyse nonveridical sensory awareness as a cognition whose predication content does not qualify the object cognized, that is, the object that stands in relation to the sense organ. A causal story is to be told why there is such a foul-up, why something appears as other than it is, a story that will vary with the circumstances of individual instances of error (see ERROR AND ILLUSION, INDIAN CONCEPTIONS OF §3).

Inferential knowledge is defined by Gaṅgeśa as the cognition arising as the result of the perceptual cognition of something *a* as possessing a property *F* that is understood as pervaded by (or invariably concomitant with) another property *G* (*F* as invariably co-located with *G*). To quote Gaṅgeśa: 'Inferential knowledge is cognition generated by cognition of a property-belonging-to-a-locus-and-qualified-by-a-pervasion' (*Tattvacintāmaṇi*, 1982: 5; the dashes in the translation are to indicate that the cognition has to have all this as content). Logicians throughout the history of their school are concerned with inference only in so far as it provides knowledge of the world. Thus any correct inference must have a perceptual premise, which is its starting point, so to speak: for example, 'There is smoke on yonder hill', as known perceptually. (Perceptual cognition may be said to be the premier knowledge source in another way as well: inferential cognitions that are *prima facie* correct can be overridden by sensory awareness.) But of course it is not just any perceptual awareness that leads to inferential knowledge: for example, the smoke, or smokiness, as a qualifier of a locus or qualificandum must be seen as invariably related to another property called technically the property to be proved; it must be qualified by pervasion, or co-locatedness, with the property of being-fiery. Throughout New Logic it is the nature of the relation called pervasion (*vyāpti*, often translated 'invariable concomitance') that is the main focus of reflection under the general rubric of inference. Gaṅgeśa considers and rejects a total of twenty-one definitions of pervasion. He accepts a total of five.

Among other important aspects of Gaṅgeśa's epistemology is fallibilism, which feeds his response to scepticism concerning how a pervasion in its full generality can by known (occurrence of *G wherever* there is occurrence of *F*: how can this be known?). The answer is wide experience, but future experience could prove us wrong.

Gaṅgeśa shows a pragmatic orientation in his final response to scepticism on this score. The sceptic's behaviour gives the lie to the complaint: does the sceptic not, for example, in voicing the complaint, assume a *vyāpti* between speaking and others' comprehension?

3 Ontology

Like all Nyāya ontology, that of Gaṅgeśa's *Tattvacintāmaṇi* is realistic in the sense of a commitment to entities whose existence is independent of consciousness. Realism led the philosophers of Gaṅgeśa's Nyāya school to embrace fallibilism, because the transcendence, so to speak, of a physical object with respect to the instruments of knowledge means that the possibility of error cannot be ruled out. Gaṅgeśa's definitional projects are attempts at philosophical characterization as opposed to linguistic analysis, because the various definienda (veridical awareness, inference-grounding pervasion, and so on) are realities in the world, not linguistic items. Then regarding the backbone of Nyāya ontology – its categorial system – all individuals of whatever fundamental type (substances, qualities, motions, natural kinds, inherence, ultimate individuators, and absences) are viewed as reals.

Gaṅgeśa's ontological labours are generally in the service of epistemology. Consonantly, his treatment of six 'operative relations in sense experience' is extensive. So also are his reflections on *vyāpti*, inference-underpinning pervasion. The material on *vyāpti* received an enormous measure of attention from later Logicians.

Depending on what is cognized – individual substance, quality, natural-kind character, an absence (for example, of my glasses on the table), a previous cognition (as in apperception), and so on – the relationality between the grasping and the grasped varies. Moreover, the different sense organs relate to objects differently. And there are special problems about the 'operative relation' in a perception of an absence, as well as with what in the West is known as the 'Bradley problem' of a possible infinite regress of relations centring on inherence as joining a quality to a substance (for example) – what then joins the inherence? The importance of the ontology of absence looms especially large because the acceptable characterizations of pervasion require mention of certain general types of absence. That characterization project also involves Gaṅgeśa in explaining ontologically what 'co-locatedness' amounts to.

Gaṅgeśa takes very seriously a principle of ontological parsimony (*lāghavatva*), and so his reasoning through all the complexities of a variety of desiderata and principles potentially in tension is at times tortuous. But it is invariably tight, and though later Logicians abandon some of his positions (Gaṅgeśa sometimes appears too conservative, too intent on defending Udayana's ontological stances), his arguments form the problem space for later reflection.

See also: EPISTEMOLOGY, INDIAN SCHOOLS OF §2; KNOWLEDGE, INDIAN VIEWS OF; ONTOLOGY IN INDIAN PHILOSOPHY

List of works

Gaṅgeśa (first half of 14th century) *Tattvacintāmaṇi* (Jewel of Reflection on Reality), with the *Māthurī* commentary of Mathurānātha (or others where that is not extant), ed. K. Tarkavagish, Calcutta: Asiatic Society, 5 vols, 1884–1901; repr. Delhi: Chowkhambha Sanskrit Pratisthan, 1990. (The reprint has made Gaṅgeśa easily available to the Sanskrit-reading community in India, whose numbers are considerable.)

—— (first half of 14th century) *Tattvacintāmaṇi* (Jewel of Reflection on Reality), vol. 1, *pratyakṣa-khaṇḍa*, with the *Prakāśa* commentary by Rucidatta Miśra and a subcommentary by Rāmakṛṣṇādhvarin, vol. 2, *anumāna-khaṇḍa*, with the *Prakāśa* commentary by Rucidatta Miśra and a subcommentary by Dharmarājādhvarin, ed. N.S. Ramanuja Tatacharya, Kendriya Sanskrit Vidypeetha Series 20 and 33, Tirupati, 1972, 1982. (The commentary and subcommentary, as well as the alternative readings and punctuation supplied by the editor, make these volumes invaluable to scholars.)

References and further reading

Bhattacharya, D.C. (1958) *History of Navya-nyāya in Mithilā*, Darbhanga: Mithila Institute. (Informative historical research.)

Bhattacharya, K. (trans.) (1977, 1978, 1980, 1982, 1984) 'Le *Siddhāntalakṣaṇaprakaraṇa* du *Tattvacintāmaṇi* de Gaṅgeśa avec la *Dīdhiti* de Raghunātha Śiromaṇi et la *Ṭīkā* de Jagadīśa Tarkālaṃkāra', *Journal Asiatique*, 1977: 97–139, 1978: 97–124, 1980: 275–322, 1982: 401–13, 1984: 47–82. (Elegant translation of difficult materials; the commentaries are important in their own right.)

Bhattacharyya, S. (1993) *Gaṅgeśa's Theory of Indeterminate Perception*, New Delhi: Indian Council of Philosophical Research. (Lucid explanation of key concepts of Gaṅgeśa's epistemology and philosophy of perception.)

Goekoop, C. (1967) *The Logic of Invariable Concomitance in the Tattvacintāmaṇi*, Dordrecht: D. Reidel. (A translation and explanation of a portion of the *Tattvacintāmaṇi* devoted to defining 'pervasion', *vyāpti*.)

Ingalls, D.H.H. (1951) *Materials for the Study of Navya-Nyāya Logic*, Cambridge, MA: Harvard University Press. (Though now a little dated, this is a masterly exploration of the analytic weaponry of New Logic.)

Matilal, B.K. (1968) *The Navya-Nyāya Doctrine of Negation*, Cambridge, MA: Harvard University Press. (Matilal's long introduction to a translation of a *Tattvacintāmaṇi* section – the section on the ontology of absence – is an excellent overall introduction to the central concepts and claims of Gaṅgeśa's system.)

Mohanty, J.N. (1966) *Gaṅgeśa's Theory of Truth*, repr. Delhi: Motilal Banarsidass, 1989. (Though Mohanty renders *pramātva* as 'truth' instead of 'veridicality', his investigation of epistemological views belonging to Gaṅgeśa's opponents as well as to the great Logician himself is excellent philosophy.)

Phillips, S.H. (1995) *Classical Indian Metaphysics: Refutations of Realism and the Emergence of 'New Logic'*, La Salle, IL: Open Court. (Contains elaboration of, in particular, what is discussed §2 of the present entry.)

Phillips, S.H. and Tatacharya N.S.R. (trans.) (1998) *Gaṅgeśa's 'Jewel of Reflection on Reality', the Perception Chapter*, Delhi: Motilal Banarsidass. (Translation, interspersed with the translators' commentary, of the entire first chapter of Gaṅgeśa's 'Jewel'.)

Potter, K.H. (ed.) (1977) *Encyclopedia of Indian Philosophies*, vol. 2, *Nyāya-Vaiśeṣika*, Princeton, NJ: Princeton University Press. (The best introduction to the philosophies and philosophers that most inform Gaṅgeśa's reasonings.)

Potter, K.H. and Bhattacharyya, S. (eds) (1994) *Encyclopedia of Indian Philosophies*, vol. 6, *Nyāya-Vaiśeṣika from Gaṅgeśa to Raghunātha Śiromaṇi*, Princeton, NJ: Princeton University Press. (Contains summaries of most of the *Tattvacintāmaṇi* written by a group of scholars and philosophers; should prove a landmark publication.)

STEPHEN H. PHILLIPS

GANS, EDUARD *see* HEGELIANISM

GARRIGOU-LAGRANGE, RÉGINALD (1887–1964)

Garrigou-Lagrange was a French Dominican who for decades adorned the Angelicum in Rome, where in his courses he commented closely on the Summa theologiae. *The spiritual life was a principal interest of Garrigou-Lagrange, and many of his books are devoted to the theology and practice of mystical union with God. Impatient with theological novelty, Garrigou-Lagrange came to be caricatured by the champions of innovators. His own work, solid, careful, illuminating, is a monument to a golden period of the Thomistic revival.*

Garrigou-Lagrange was an influential figure in the second phase of the revival of Thomism initiated by Pope Leo XIII's 1879 encyclical *Aeterni Patris.* He first studied medicine, then entered the Order of Preachers, where, after studying philosophy and theology, he began in 1905 a teaching career which was to last sixty years. He taught at Le Saulchoir, Belgium, until, in 1909, he was assigned to the Dominican university in Rome, the Angelicum.

Mentor of Jacques Maritain, *bête noire* of Étienne Gilson and Henri de Lubac, Garrigou-Lagrange was a Thomist of the strict observance. His writings, vast in number, fall into three main classes: philosophical, theological and spiritual. His theological work consists of commentaries on Aquinas, in which he follows the lead of the great commentators of the Dominican Order – Cajetan, John of St Thomas and Báñez – as well as original work in a Thomistic key. His spiritual writings deal with the progressive appropriation of the life of grace leading to mystical union with God. His philosophical works are of particular interest to the philosopher of religion.

In theory of knowledge, Garrigou-Lagrange was an ardent defender of the doctrine of Aquinas which, while taking due account of the contribution of our mind to the object of intellectual knowledge, sees that contribution as modal rather than substantive. The essences or quiddities that are the object of intellectual knowledge are those of really existing things. These essences are individuated in material substances and are universal and immaterial (modally) as known (see AQUINAS, T. §11).

Garrigou-Lagrange's Thomism can best be sampled in the lengthy article he contributed to the *Dictionnaire de théologie catholique,* which became the basis for his book *La Synthèse thomiste* (The Thomist Synthesis, 1946). After a bibliographical introduction to the philosophical and theological works of Aquinas, Garrigou-Lagrange significantly discusses the Thomistic commentators. He saw his own efforts as a continuation of a tradition that had been broken and was to be renewed. The 'metaphysical synthesis of Thomism' concentrates on act and potency. The bulk of the work deals with Aquinas' explicitly theological doctrines, following the general plan of the *Summa theologiae.* It ends with a section devoted to the 'Twenty-Four Theses', a list of key tenets of Thomism which had been drawn up by several professors and approved by the Congregation of Sacred Studies as an adequate summary of Thomas' teaching, and a discussion of epistemological realism.

Garrigou-Lagrange's magisterial *Dieu, son existence et sa nature* (*God: His Existence and His Nature,* 1915) is a running debate with post-Kantian thought. Thus he defends the epistemological assumptions of proofs for the existence of God before giving a detailed analysis of Aquinas' Five Ways and discussing the divine attributes. Throughout, Garrigou-Lagrange indicates how Aquinas' views differ from those of major modern philosophers. The work ends with a discussion of the principle of inertia and conservation of energy, an indication of the author's concern to deal with apparent difficulties for the assumptions of the traditional proofs of God's existence. He also argues that agnosticism leads to atheistic evolutionism.

Other works of interest to philosophers of religion are *De de uno* (The One God, 1937), *La prédestination des saints et la grâce* (The Predestination of the Saints and Grace, 1936) and *Providence et la confiance en Dieu* (Providence and Confidence in God, 1935). *Le Sens commun* (Common Sense, 1921) is at once a defence of realism and an extended engagement with the thought of Bergson and with the Scottish Common-Sense school. Throughout, Garrigou-Lagrange recommends Thomistic positions as preferable to those of the rivals he examines. The work ends with criticism of the modernist interpretation of dogmatic formulas. *Le Réalisme du principe de finalité* (The Realism of the Principle of Finality, 1932) compares knowledge of natural and supernatural truths. The motto on the title page reads thus: 'Every being acts for an end, from the grain of sand to God. Our intellect knows its own finality: to judge in conformity with the nature and existence of things and to raise itself to their first cause and ultimate end.'

The style and approach of Garrigou-Lagrange have been deplored by some post-conciliar Catholics. This is in many ways unjust. He is an engaging writer, a thinker of great power, a Thomist who takes the thought of his master to be the answer to some of the twentieth century's more vexing philosophical divagations. But that, of course, was the message of *Aeterni Patris.*

See also: THOMISM

List of works

Garrigou-Lagrange, R. (1915) *Dieu, son existence et sa nature*, trans. Dom B. Rose, *God: His Existence and His Nature*, St Louis, MO: Herder, 2 vols, 1934, 1935. (Proof of the demonstrability of God; treats the Five Ways of St Thomas, and various divine attributes and their interrelationship.)
—— (1921) *Le Sens commun* (Common Sense), Paris: Nouvelle Librairie Nationale. (An examination of whether the immortality of the soul and the first principles are known by common sense, and the role of common sense in proving the existence of God.)
—— (1932) *Le Réalisme du principe de finalité* (The Realism of the Principle of Finality), Paris: Desclée de Brouwer. (A discussion of being, change and finality, with reference to chance, and the application of of the principle of finality to epistemological realism.)
—— (1933) *Le Sauveur et son amour pour nous*, Paris: Éditions du Cedre; trans. A. Bouchard, *Our Savior and His Love for Us*, St Louis, MO: Herder, 1951. (A discussion based on *Summa theologiae* IIIa: the personality of Christ and his redemptive act.)
—— (1935) *Providence et la confiance en Dieu*, Paris: Desclée de Brouwer; trans. Dom B. Rose, *Providence*, St Louis, MO: Herder, 1937. (A practical rather than theoretical treatment of providence from the point of view of philosophy, Scripture and providence, and religious submission to providence.)
—— (1936) *La Prédestination des saints et la grâce*, Paris: Desclée de Brouwer; trans. Dom B. Rose, *Predestination*, St Louis, MO: Herder, 1953. (Comparison of Thomas' teaching on predestination and the later disputes between Jesuits and Dominicans that are summed up under the tag *de auxiliis*.)
—— (1937) *De de uno*, Paris: Desclée de Brouwer; trans. Dom B. Rose, *The One God*, St Louis, MO: Herder, 1951. (A commentary on questions 1–26 of *Summa theologiae* Ia.)
—— (1938) *Les Trois Âges de la vie intérieure*, Paris: Éditions du Cerf, 2 vols; trans. Sister M.T. Doyle, O.P., *The Three Ages of the Interior Life*, St Louis, MO: Herder, 2 vols, 1948, 1952. (The sources and end of the interior life; a statement of the classical conception of degrees of spirituality. This masterpiece in mysticism treats grace, the gifts of the Holy Spirit, the indwelling of the Trinity, purification and illumination.)
—— (1946) *La Synthèse thomiste*, Paris: Desclée de Brouwer; trans. P. Cummins, *Reality: A Synthesis of Thomistic Thought*, St Louis, MO: Herder, 1950. (An examination of the nature of theology, proofs of God's existence, his nature, Trinity, angels, humanity and morals.)
—— (1948) *De unione sacerdotis cum Christo sacerdote*, Turin: Marietti; trans. E. Hayden, *The Priesthood and Perfection*, Westminster, MD: Newman Press, 1955. (Treats the pursuit of perfection, the spirituality fitting for priests, mental prayer, cultivation of the virtues, and the Eucharist.)

References and further reading

Gilson, É. and Maritain, J. (1990) *Étienne Gilson, Jacques Maritain, Deux approches de l'Être: Correspondance, 1923–1971*, ed. G. Prouvost, Paris: J. Vrin. (The two leading Thomists correspond over the years; their estimates of the work of Garrigou-Lagrange differ fundamentally, Maritain defending it, Gilson criticizing it.)
* Leo XIII (1879) *Aeterni Patris* (Of the Eternal Father), in J. Maritain, *Le Docteur angélique*, Paris: Desclée de Brouwer, 1930; trans. J. Evans and P. O'Reilly, *St Thomas Aquinas*, New York: Meridian, 1958. (Includes a discussion of the encyclical, as well as its text.)
Lubac, H. de and Gilson, É. (1988) *Letters of Étienne Gilson to Henri de Lubac*, ed. H. de Lubac, San Francisco, CA: Ignatius Press. (Gilson's letters deftly used to win arguments with various departed foes of de Lubac. Garrigou-Lagrange subjected to much bantering and some serious criticism.)

RALPH McINERNY

GASSENDI, PIERRE (1592–1655)

Pierre Gassendi, a French Catholic priest, introduced the philosophy of the ancient atomist Epicurus into the mainstream of European thought. Like many of his contemporaries in the first half of the seventeenth century, he sought to articulate a new philosophy of nature to replace the Aristotelianism that had traditionally provided foundations for natural philosophy. Before European intellectuals could accept the philosophy of Epicurus, it had to be purged of various heterodox notions. Accordingly, Gassendi modified the philosophy of his ancient model to make it conform to the demands of Christian theology.

Like Epicurus, Gassendi claimed that the physical world consists of indivisible atoms moving in void space. Unlike the ancient atomist, Gassendi argued that there exists only a finite, though very large number of atoms, that these atoms were created by God, and that the resulting world is ruled by divine providence rather than blind chance. In contrast to Epicurus' materialism, Gassendi enriched his atomism by arguing for the existence of an immaterial, immortal soul. He also believed in the existence of angels and demons. His theology was voluntarist, emphasizing God's freedom to impose his will on the Creation.

Gassendi's empiricist theory of knowledge was an outgrowth of his response to scepticism. Accepting the sceptical critique of sensory knowledge, he denied that we can have certain knowledge of the real essences of things. Rather than falling into sceptical despair, however, he argued that we can acquire knowledge of the way things appear to us. This 'science of appearances' is based on sensory experience and can only attain probability. It can, none the less, provide knowledge useful for living in the world. Gassendi denied the existence of essences in either the Platonic or Aristotelian sense and numbered himself among the nominalists.

Adopting the hedonistic ethics of Epicurus, which sought to maximize pleasure and minimize pain, Gassendi reinterpreted the concept of pleasure in a distinctly Christian way. He believed that God endowed humans with free will and an innate desire for pleasure. Thus, by utilizing the calculus of pleasure and pain and by exercising their ability to make free choices, they participate in God's providential plans for the Creation. The greatest pleasure humans can attain is the beatific vision of God after death. Based on his hedonistic ethics, Gassendi's political philosophy was a theory of social contract, a view which influenced the writings of Hobbes and Locke.

Gassendi was an active participant in the philosophical and natural philosophical communities of his day. He corresponded with Hobbes and Descartes, and conducted experiments on various topics, wrote about astronomy, corresponded with important natural philosophers, and wrote a treatise defending Galileo's new science of motion. His philosophy was very influential, particularly on the development of British empiricism and liberalism.

1 **Life and works**
2 **Gassendi's Epicurean project**
3 **Logic**
4 **Physics**
5 **Ethics and political philosophy**

1 Life and works

Pierre Gassendi was born in Champtercier, a village near Digne in Provence, France. He received his early education in Digne and Riez and was admitted to the clerical state in 1604. The remainder of his formal education was supervised by the Church, as it formed part of his preparation for the priesthood. From 1604 through 1611 he studied Aristotelian philosophy and Catholic theology at the college of Aix-en-Provence. Upon receiving his doctorate in theology at Avignon in 1614, he was appointed official diocesan teacher of theology and superintendant of theological education. In 1616 he assumed the chair of philosophy at Aix-en-Provence, where he taught Aristotelian philosophy for the next six years. He voiced his dissatisfaction with Aristotelianism in his first published work, *Exercitationes Paradoxicae Adversus Aristoteleos* (Paradoxical Exercises against the Aristotelians) (1624), in which he claimed to have taught his students the principles of Aristotelianism, only to refute them with sceptical arguments. When the college at Aix was turned over to the Jesuits in 1622, Gassendi and the rest of the faculty were forced to leave their positions. Since his student days, he had been a member canon of the Cathedral of Digne. He was appointed provost of the Cathedral in 1634, a position which he held for the rest of his life.

Apart from his administrative position at the Cathedral of Digne, Gassendi relied on patronage for his scholarly work. His first patron was the polymath and humanist Nicolas-Claude Fabri de Peiresc (1580–1637), councillor of the Parlement of Aix and patron of arts and letters. Gassendi and Peiresc conducted scientific experiments together and corresponded about astronomy and philosophy. During the years until Peiresc's death, Gassendi divided his time among Aix, Digne, and Paris. During the winter of 1628, he travelled with his friend the *libertin érudit* François Lullier (*c.*1600–51) to Holland where he met a number of important intellectual figures, including the atomist Isaac Beeckman (1588–1637), who reinforced his resolve to restore the philosophy of Epicurus, an enterprise that became his life's work.

In 1630, Gassendi published two works not directly related to his Epicurean project. In the *Epistolica exercitatio, in qua principia philosophiae Roberti Fluddi, medici, reteguntur* he responded to Marin Mersenne's request for an evaluation of the natural philosophy of the Paracelsian Robert FLUDD (see MERSENNE). In the *Parhelia, sive soles quat[u]or qui circa verum apparuerunt Romae, die XX mensis martii anno 1629* he gave an account of a strange appearance of parhelia (or the appearance of multiple suns and patches of shimmering light around the sun). Two years later, in *Mercurius in sole visus et Venus invisa Parisiis anno 1631*, he confirmed Kepler's prediction of Mercury's transit of the sun.

Gassendi suffered a major loss when Peiresc died in

1637. Losing not only his patron but also a close and valued friend, he wrote little for the next four years. In 1641 he published a memorial to his friend, *Viri illustris Nicolai Fabricii de Peiresc Senatoris Aquisextiensis vita*. Having returned to Provence to perform his clerical duties, Gassendi was invited by Louis-Emmanuel de Valois, count of Alais, a man closely connected to the royal family, 'to wait upon' him, that is, to enter a client–patron relationship which continued until Valois' death in 1653.

Gassendi was deeply involved in the major developments in natural philosophy in his day. He published an exposition of Galileo's new science of motion, *De motu impresso a motore translato* (1642), which contains the first correct statement of the principle of inertia in print (see GALILEO, G.). Prior to the publication of Descartes' *Meditations* in 1641, Mersenne invited Gassendi, among other philosophers and theologians, to comment on the manuscript of the work. These comments, first published as the fifth set of 'Objections', were enlarged in Gassendi's *Disquisitio metaphysica, seu dubitationes et instantiae adversus Renati Cartesii metaphysicam et responsa* (Metaphysical disquisition, or doubts and instances against the metaphysics of René Descartes and responses) (1644), which contains Gassendi's objections to the *Meditations*, Descartes' replies, and Gassendi's rejoinders (see DESCARTES, R.). He also published an account of the new astronomy in *Institutio astronomica juxta hypotheseis tam veteram quam Copernici et Tychonis Brahei* (1647).

In 1645, Gassendi received an appointment as professor of mathematics at the Collège Royal. In 1653, after Valois' death, Gassendi came under the protection of Henri-Louis Habert, lord of Montmor, a patron of natural philosophy, with whom he lived until his own death in 1655.

During the last decade of his life, Gassendi published the products of his extensive work on the life and philosophy of EPICURUS. The three major Epicurean works include *De vita et moribus Epicuri libri octo* (1647), *Animadversiones in decimum librum Diogenis Laertii, qui est de vita, moribus, placitisque Epicuri* (Observations on Book X of Diogenes Laertius, Which is about the Life, Morals, and Opinions of Epicurus) (1649), and the *Syntagma Philosophicum*, published posthumously in 1658.

2 Gassendi's Epicurean project

The unifying theme of Gassendi's work was his project to restore the philosophy of Epicurus, making it acceptable to orthodox Christians. He envisaged this Christianized Epicureanism as a complete philosophy that would replace Aristotelianism, which had been dominant in the universities for centuries (see ARISTOTELIANISM IN THE 17TH CENTURY; EPICUREANISM).

Gassendi's rejection of Aristotelianism is the theme of his 1624 *Exercitationes Paradoxicae Adversus Aristoteleos*. Drawing on the Pyrrhonian scepticism of SEXTUS EMPIRICUS, Gassendi attacked the epistemological and metaphysical foundations of Aristotelianism (see PYRRHONISM). He rejected Aristotle's philosophy of matter and form, as well as his ideal of demonstrative certain knowledge as the epistemological goal of natural philosophy (see ARISTOTLE). Rather than sinking into sceptical despair, however, Gassendi adopted what Popkin (1979) has happily called 'mitigated scepticism', advocating a science of appearances which can attain at best probable knowledge of things based on their appearances. He denied the possibility of knowing essences and explicitly allied himself with the nominalists (see NOMINALISM). An empiricist epistemology and a nominalist metaphysics were central themes in his philosophical writings. In this early work as well as in correspondence from the second half of the 1620s, he expressed a growing interest in Epicureanism as a substitute for Aristotelianism.

Although there is evidence that Gassendi was attracted to the philosophy of Epicurus from the mid-1620s, he did not defend Epicureanism in print until the 1640s. During the intervening years, his Epicurean project grew from the straightforward humanist task of translating Book X of Diogenes Laertius' *Lives of Eminent Philosophers*, one of the major sources for knowledge of Epicurus' writings, to a full-fledged rehabilitation of Epicureanism (see DIOGENES LAERTIUS). During the early 1630s, Gassendi produced a manuscript of his Epicurean commentary, which he shared chapter-by-chapter with Peiresc and some other friends. By 1634, he completed a draft of what would later be published as *De vita et moribus Epicuri* (1647). During 1641 and 1642, he wrote a series of letters containing a sketch of his Epicurean project to his patron, the new governor of Provence, Louis-Emmanuel de Valois. In *De vita et moribus Epicuri*, Gassendi defended Epicurus against the allegations of decadence and immorality that had dogged his reputation since antiquity. In 1649, he published *Animadversiones in decimum librum Diogenis Laertii*, a book still conceived in the humanist format as a commentary on an ancient text. The posthumous *Syntagma Philosophicum* (1658) was the culmination of Gassendi's Epicurean project, incorporating material from contemporary natural philosophy into an exposition of Epicureanism.

At every stage of his Epicurean project, Gassendi was concerned to modify certain of the ancient philosopher's doctrines in order to make his philosophy consistent with Christian orthodoxy. He rejected the theologically objectionable components of Epicureanism: polytheism, a corporeal conception of the divine nature, the negation of all providence, the denial of Creation *ex nihilo*, the infinitude and eternity of atoms and the universe, the plurality of worlds, the attribution of the cause of the world to chance, a materialistic cosmogony, the denial of all finality in biology, and the corporeality and mortality of the human soul. Gassendi replaced these doctrines with a Christianized atomism which asserted the creation of the world and its constituent atoms by a wise and all-powerful God who rules the world providentially, the existence of a large but finite number of atoms in a single world, the evidence of design throughout the Creation, a role for final causes in natural philosophy, and the immortality and immateriality of the human soul.

Gassendi's theology was thoroughly voluntarist. Voluntarism is an interpretation of God's relationship to the Creation which insists on God's omnipotence and his absolute freedom of will. Nothing exists independently of him, and nothing that he creates can bind or impede him. Emphasizing the contingency of the world on God's will, Gassendi believed that God's omnipotence is in no way constrained by the Creation, which contains no necessary relations that might limit God's power or will. 'There is nothing in the universe that God cannot destroy, nothing that he cannot produce, nothing that he cannot change, even into its opposite qualities' (1658 vol 1: 308). Consequently there are no universal or eternal essences of created things. Even the laws of nature lack necessity. 'He is free from the laws of nature, which he constituted by his own free will' (1658 vol 1: 381). The laws of nature have no existence apart from serving as descriptions of the regularities we observe in the operations of nature. In contrast to Descartes, Gassendi never identified any particular propositions as laws. Like everything else God created, he can negate them. He could have created an entirely different natural order if it had pleased him to do so. Similar to other voluntarists, for example OCK-HAM, Gassendi believed that God's will was constrained only by the law of non-contradiction and that nothing God creates can prevent him from acting directly on the Creation. God does not directly produce all the motions of bodies, nor does he simply create bodies in the beginning, leaving them to act in accordance with their individual natures as bodies. He makes use of second causes – that is, natural causes that he has created. But he can always intervene and act directly if he wants. Nothing he creates constrains him in any way. 'God . . . is the most free; and he is

not bound, as he can do whatever . . . he wishes' (1658 vol 1: 309). Nominalism was one important implication of Gassendi's voluntarism. The existence of universals, even universals created by God, would limit God's freedom of action. Gassendi's voluntarism and anti-essentialism played a central role in his debate with Descartes over the *Meditations*. These assumptions infused every part of his version of Epicureanism.

Gassendi employed humanist methods in philosophy. That is, he insisted on finding an ancient model for his philosophical views, and he wrote in a style marked by frequent allusions to and quotations from classical authors. Each section of his massive *Syntagma Philosophicum* begins with a summary of all existing views on the subject at hand. Only after having rehearsed all the traditional views did he embark on his own account of a subject. He articulated his own views in dialogue with his ancient model, Epicurus. In this respect, he was traditional, even though the content of his philosophy in many ways broke from traditional ideas. He claimed that he chose Epicurus as his model because his atomistic physics and hedonistic ethics could be more readily reconciled with 'the Sacred Faith' than any of the other ancient schools of philosophy. Presented as a complete philosophy to replace Aristotelianism, the *Syntagma Philosophicum* is divided into three large sections, entitled 'Logic', 'Physics', and 'Ethics'.

3 Logic

The first part of the *Syntagma Philosophicum*, entitled 'Logic', is the culmination of Gassendi's lifelong considerations of this subject. He proposed to substitute the canonic of Epicurus for Aristotelian dialectic which he judged to be useless for obtaining knowledge of nature. He considered logic to be the art of thinking well. He developed it as a theory of knowledge and a primitive psychology to explain how ideas get into the mind rather than simply a study of the forms of syllogism and the relationships among propositions, although he discussed these topics as well. He advocated an empirical approach to knowledge of the world, one modelled on the Epicurean canonic.

In his early *Exercitationes Paradoxicae Adversus Aristoteleos*, Gassendi attacked Aristotelian dialectic as overly complex and abstruse, useless as a method for making new discoveries. He used the classical sceptical arguments to question the reliability and validity of sensory experience. Since Aristotelian demonstration requires premises based on experience, Gassendi argued that the syllogisms involved cannot produce certain knowledge about the world. Moreover, since the conclusion of a syllogism contains no information not already present in the premises, syllogistic demonstration is incapable of producing new knowledge. Gassendi concluded that the entire method of Aristotelian demonstration is without foundation or utility. Not satisfied with the suspension of judgment advocated by the ancient sceptics, he opted for a middle way, 'mitigated scepticism'. He based this approach on a series of rules or canons, which he drew from the Epicurean Canonic. These canons defined sensations, ideas, propositions and syllogisms. Gassendi then elaborated a criterion of truth, based on empiricist assumptions.

Adopting the fundamental empiricist doctrine that all ideas contained in the mind derive from the senses, Gassendi distinguished between two sorts of truth, what he called 'truth of existence' and 'truth of judgment'. Truth of existence refers to the content of sensation itself. That it is what it is must be true. In this respect the senses are infallible. The sensation of gold is a sensation of gold, whether or not the object sensed is really gold or even exists. Truths of judgment, in contrast to truths of existence, are truths about the judgments we make about sensations. They are fallible, since they can assert statements about the world which might not be true. An example of such a judgment would be the proposition that this object is gold.

On the basis of this distinction, Gassendi argued that sensations, which are truths of existence that he called 'appearances', provide the basis for our knowledge of the world. This knowledge cannot penetrate to the inner natures of things precisely because it is knowledge of how they appear to us. On the basis of the appearances, however, it is possible to seek causal explanations, with the understanding that such reasoning is always conjectural and subject to revision in the face of further knowledge. This science of appearances can never achieve certainty, only probability, but such probability is adequate for our needs. In settling for probability rather than certainty as the epistemic goal of natural philosophy, Gassendi was rejecting the traditional Aristotelian and Scholastic conception of *scientia* or demonstrative knowledge. His redefinition of the goals of natural philosophy influenced the conceptions of later natural philosophers such as Robert BOYLE John LOCKE and Isaac NEWTON.

4 Physics

The 'Physics' is by far the longest part of Gassendi's *Syntagma Philosophicum*. Here he laid down the basic principles of his natural philosophy. He claimed that the fundamental components of the natural world are atoms and the void.

Gassendi began his account of the nature of things in general with a discussion of the void, since he thought that the entire universe is contained in empty space. In accordance with traditional discussions, Gassendi classified the void into three categories: the separate, extra-cosmic void; the interparticulate, interstitial, or disseminated void; and the *coacervatum*, produced by collecting a number of interstitial voids, usually by means of some kind of mechanical device. The question of the existence of void led him into a discussion of space and time more generally. Borrowing from the Renaissance Platonist Francesco PATRIZI, Gassendi argued that space is neither substance nor accident but, rather, a kind of incorporeal extension. He thus avoided Aristotle's error of confounding dimensionality and corporeality. Space, according to Gassendi, continues to exist even when the matter contained in it moves away or ceases to exist.

The large extramundane void is the space in which God created the universe. It is boundless, incorporeal extension. Following Epicurus, Gassendi argued that the existence of interstitial void is a necessary condition for motion; for without void spaces, there would be no place into which particles of matter could move. Other Epicurean arguments included the saturation of water with salt, the dissemination of dyes through water, the penetration of air by light, heat and cold, all of which he assumed to be corpuscular. These phenomena seemed to require empty spaces between the particles composing material bodies. Gassendi also borrowed several arguments from Hero of Alexandria (*fl.* 62 AD), who had drawn an analogy between the matter composing bodies and a heap of grain or sand. Just as the individual grains are separated from each other by air or water, so the particles composing bodies are separated by small void spaces. The compressibility of air, which Hero had demonstrated by means of several inventions, including the pneumatic cannon and the aeolipile (a prototype of the steam engine), seemed to call for the existence of interstitial void between the material particles composing air.

Gassendi drew on contemporary natural philosophy to argue for the existence of the *coacervatum* void, especially the barometric experiments of Torricelli and Pascal. Gassendi accepted the mechanical explanation of the suspension of mercury in the barometer, as the result of atmospheric pressure, thereby rejecting the Aristotelian explanation which appealed to the paradigmatic occult quality, the *horror vacui*. He argued that the space in the tube above the mercury is void.

Gassendi's atoms are perfectly full, solid, hard, indivisible particles, so small that they fall below the threshold of sense. Following LUCRETIUS, the Roman expositor of Epicureanism, Gassendi noted several commonly observed phenomena that lend support to the existence of such atoms. Wind is evidence that invisible matter can produce visible, physical effects. So is the fact that paving stones and ploughshares wear away because of constant rubbing, even though individual acts of rubbing produce no discernible change. The passage of odours through the air can be explained in terms of tiny particles travelling from the source of the odour to the nose.

Atoms possess only a few primary qualities: magnitude and figure, resistance or solidity, and heaviness. Gassendi appealed to observations using the new instrument, the microscope, to provide evidence for their small size. He also cited traditional observations such as the dispersion of pigment in water and the large quantity of smoke emanating from a smouldering log. He argued for the indivisibility of these atoms by appealing to Zeno's paradoxes, which he interpreted as implying the absurdity of the idea of the infinite divisibility of matter (see ZENO OF ELEA).

Matter, in the form of atoms, is the material principle in Gassendi's world. The efficient principle explains the causal structure of the world. The first cause is God, who created the world, including the atoms. Second causes, the natural causes operating in the physical world, are reduced to collisions among atoms moving in void space. In contrast to Epicurus who had claimed that an endless series of worlds is being produced by an eternal series of chance collisions among an infinite number of uncreated atoms, Gassendi argued that the world and its constituent atoms – a large, but finite number of them – had been created by God, who continues to rule the world providentially, with special providence for humankind. Rejecting the atomic swerves or *clinamen* that Epicurus had introduced to account for the collision of atoms that would otherwise only fall downward in parallel paths, Gassendi maintained that the motions of atoms had been caused by God at the beginning. Gassendi argued for God's providential relationship to the creation on the basis of an extended argument from design.

Having established the material and efficient principles of things, Gassendi proceeded to argue that all the qualities of bodies can be explained in terms of the motions and configurations of their constituent atoms. He gave mechanical, atomistic explanations of the whole range of qualities, including rarity and density, transparency and opacity, size and shape, smoothness and roughness, heaviness and lightness, fluidity and firmness, moistness and dryness, softness and hardness, flexibility and ductility, flavour and odour,

sound, light, and colour. He concluded his account of qualities with a chapter on the so-called occult qualities, in which he argued that there is no action at a distance and that even apparently occult qualities such as magnetism and the sympathies and antipathies favoured by the Renaissance naturalists can be explained in mechanical terms.

In this first section of the 'Physics', Gassendi created the blueprint for his version of a mechanical philosophy of nature, a Christianized version of Epicurean atomism, designed to replace Aristotle's *Physics* and consonant in spirit, if not detail, with that of his contemporary Descartes (see DESCARTES, R. §11). In the remaining sections of the 'Physics', Gassendi tried to explain all the phenomena of the world in these terms. His work paralleled Aristotle's treatises *De caelo*, *Meteorologica*, *De partibus animalium*, and *De anima*; but he took account of recent developments in natural philosophy. His intentions to mechanize notwithstanding, he wrote eclectically, often appealing to concepts and terms drawn from traditions such as Aristotelianism, Renaissance naturalism and even alchemy (see ALCHEMY).

Having considered the universal principles of physics, Gassendi proceeded to consider the created world, starting with celestial things. He discussed the following questions: the substance of the sky and stars; the variety, position, and magnitude of the stars; the motions of the stars; the light of the stars; comets and new stars; and the effects of the stars. In his youth, Gassendi had endorsed the new Copernican astronomy enthusiastically. The condemnation of Galileo in 1633 dampened his enthusiasm, at least in print, where he expressed sceptical doubts about being able to prove any of the three main world systems – Ptolemaic, Copernican, and Tychonic – conclusively. In the *Syntagma Philosophicum*, he proposed the system of Tycho Brahe as a compromise approved by the Church, but not before having stated that the Copernican theory was 'more probable and evident'.

As for the effects of the stars, Gassendi thought astrology 'inane and futile.' He rejected the possibility that the stars cause terrestrial and human events. Sidereal and planetary configurations may be signs of some events on earth, such as the seasons or the weather, but they are not their causes. Moreover, the ability to prognosticate the future is the prerogative of God alone. Gassendi found horoscopes based on the moment of nativity ridiculous. Why, he asked, should the heavenly bodies have more influence at the moment of birth than at any other moment in a person's life? He thought that the principles of astrology were based on insufficient evidence, and that astrologers often resort to deception.

Having discussed the heavens, Gassendi turned his attention to terrestrial phenomena, considering inanimate things first. He described the properties of Earth, the distribution of water and land, the tides, subterranean heat and the saltiness of the sea. He then turned to 'meteorological' phenomena, which included winds, rain, snow, ice, lightning and thunder, rainbows and parhelia, and the Aurora Borealis. Shifting his attention to smaller things, he wrote about stones and metals, paying particular attention to recent observations of the magnet and to the question of the transmutation of gold, which he considered possible. Finally, among inanimate things, he discussed plants which, he claimed, Epicurus had believed to be inanimate, that is, lacking soul. Gassendi discussed the varieties of plants and their parts, considering their various physiological processes, including grafting, nutrition, germination, growth, and death.

The final section of the 'Physics' was devoted to terrestrial living things, or animals. This section contains discussions of the varieties of animals, the parts of animals – which he described in explicitly finalistic terms, and various physiological topics including generation, nutrition, respiration and motion. Gassendi devoted about half of this lengthy section to the topics of sensation, perception and the immortality of the human soul.

Gassendi's argument for the immortality of the soul was a key factor in his Christianization of Epicureanism. Epicurus, in order to eliminate fear of death and anxiety about punishment and reward in the afterlife as major sources of human distress, claimed that the soul is material and mortal (see EPICURIANISM §13). In addressing the nature of the soul, Gassendi said that the soul is what distinguishes living things from inanimate things. Adopting the distinction between *anima* and *animus* directly from Lucretius, Gassendi argued that the *anima* or sentient soul is material and present throughout the body but that the *animus* or rational soul is incorporeal. Like animals, humans possess an *anima*, but the possession of an *animus* distinguishes them from animals.

The *anima* was thought to be composed of very fine and intensely active atoms, 'like the flower of matter'. It is the principle of organization and activity for the organism and the source of the animal's vital heat. It is also responsible for perception, forming the imagination or 'phantasy', a physical organ which forms images derived from perception. The *anima* is transmitted from one generation to the next at the moment of conception.

The *animus* or rational soul is an incorporeal substance, created by God, infused in the body and functioning like an informing form. Gassendi argued

on several traditional grounds for the incorporeality of the rational soul. We know that it is distinct from the corporeal imagination or phantasy, because we can understand some things of which we cannot form images, for example, that the sun is 160 times larger than the earth. Moreover, unlike corporeal things, the rational soul is capable of reflecting on itself. It is also able to reflect on the nature of universality *per se*, whereas animals, possessing only the corporeal *anima*, are limited to forming universal concepts without having the ability to reflect on them abstractly. Gassendi's claim that the rational soul, in contrast with the animal soul, is incorporeal established one of the boundaries of his mechanization of the world.

Having established the immateriality of the rational soul, Gassendi proceeded to argue for its immortality. He wrote of this topic as the 'crown of the treatise' and the 'last touch of universal physics'. Although he knew of the soul's immortality on the basis of 'the Sacred Faith', he supported this article of faith using philosophical and physical arguments, his response to the Fifth Lateran Council's call on philosophers in 1513 'to use all their powers, including natural reason, to defend the immortality of the soul'. Epistemologically similar to all reasoning in natural philosophy, the conclusions drawn from physics and philosophy could at best be highly probable. Nevertheless Gassendi was certain of the soul's immortality which was ultimately grounded in faith.

Gassendi argued on the basis of physics that the soul is immortal because it is immaterial. Lacking matter, an immaterial thing 'also lacks mass and parts into which it can be divided and analyzed.' This argument was similar to arguments used by Kenelm DIGBY, Henry MORE and others. Another approach, which he called 'moral', argued for immortality on the grounds that the afterlife is necessary in order to compensate for various injustices in this life. Gassendi went on to argue against many detractors of the soul's immortality, especially Epicurus against whose arguments he devoted an entire chapter of the *Syntagma Philosophicum*.

Gassendi's argument that the rational soul is immaterial and immortal provides evidence that he was not a materialist, despite arguments to the contrary by some scholars, notably O.R. Bloch. Bloch (1971) bases his claim that Gassendi defended the immateriality of the rational soul only in deference to the Church on two claims: that Gassendi ascribed many aspects of cognition to the material *anima*; and that he did not fully articulate his arguments for an immaterial *animus* until 1642. Bloch's interpretation of Gassendi as a clandestine materialist belies the fact that Gassendi's assertion of the existence of God, angels, demons and an immaterial immortal soul is to be found throughout his Epicurean writings. These topics appear as early as a manuscript outline of his Epicurean project which he sent to Peiresc in 1631 at the inception of his project, in his letters to Valois in the 1640s, and in the posthumous *Syntagma Philosophicum*.

Gassendi's Christianized Epicureanism had significant influence on natural philosophy in the latter half of the seventeenth century. Brought to England in Walter Charleton's translation in the 1650s, Gassendi's ideas influenced the thinking of Robert Boyle and Isaac Newton. His epistemology was also important for the thought of John Locke.

5 Ethics and political philosophy

The 'Ethics' comprises the third and final part of the *Syntagma Philosophicum*. Here, Gassendi fulfilled his youthful determination to Christianize all parts of Epicureanism. Epicurean ethics was founded on the principle that pleasure is the end of life (see HEDONISM). Pleasure, according to Epicurus, consists of freedom from bodily pain and freedom from mental turmoil. The greatest pleasure is associated with the absence of both anxiety and physical pain, a state of tranquillity. The achievement of tranquillity gives individuals self-sufficiency, so that they are free to pursue their own pleasures. Epicurus recognized that not all pleasures are of equal value, and gave reason the role of calculating pleasure and pain. In this way, he could claim that long-term pleasure was of greater value than short-term pleasure that might lead to long-term pain. The freedom humans need to implement the calculus of pleasure and pain was insured by the random swerve of atoms, the *clinamen*, which added a dimension of indeterminism to the human soul which Epicurus believed to be composed of atoms. Epicurean hedonism did not receive a good press, either in antiquity or in the Christian Middle Ages. Dogged by Epicurus' reputation for atheism and moral decadence, this philosophy needed to be restored and Christianized in order to be acceptable to orthodox intellectuals in the seventeenth century. Gassendi addressed this task in the 'Ethics'.

Although Gassendi accepted the Epicurean principle that equated pleasure with the good, he reinterpreted the concepts of pleasure and human action, thereby creating a Christian hedonism which found a natural place in his providential worldview. Gassendi described four kinds of pleasure: the instinctive desire for pleasure that even irrational creatures possess; the calculated strategy of maximizing physical pleasure; the prudence of the wise who understand that true pleasure consists of tranquillity and the absence of pain; and finally the sublime pleasure of the beatific vision of God. The prudence of the wise is based on understanding the vanity of most human desires. The wise person will employ the calculus of pleasure and pain to achieve the state of tranquillity. Gassendi united this hedonistic ethics with his providential worldview by claiming that God has instilled in humans a natural desire for pleasure and a natural aversion to pain. In this way, God guides human choices, without negating free will. The prudent pursuit of pleasure will ultimately lead to the greatest pleasure of all, presence with God in heaven.

Consistent with the voluntarist theology that informed all of Gassendi's philosophy, the 'Ethics' presumed both divine and human freedom. Human freedom is a necessary concomitant of voluntarism, for if human actions are inexorably determined, that determinism will limit God's freedom to intervene in their lives. Gassendi considered true freedom, *libertas*, to be the freedom of indifference, the ability of the mind to make judgments and take action without being determined in one direction or another. This kind of freedom gives reason a central role in moral deliberation. Gassendi contrasted *libertas* with *libentia* – spontaneity or willingness – which is characteristic of boys, brutes and stones, creatures that are impelled to move in certain ways, but not on the basis of judgments deriving from the freedom of indifference.

Gassendi's emphasis on freedom, both human and divine, led him to consider the question of predestination, which was the main context for discussions of freedom and determinism in the post-Reformation setting. How can human action be free if God has foreknowledge of who will be saved and who will be damned? Influenced by the Jesuit Luis de Molina's moderate stance on the question of predestination (see MOLINA, L. DE; PREDESTINATION), Gassendi argued that God created people free to choose, even though he knows from his eternal viewpoint how they will choose. Gassendi, following Molina, claimed that divine foreknowledge does not interfere with human freedom. Similar concerns with free will led Gassendi to reject both Stoic fatalism and astrology.

Gassendi's hedonism led him to formulate a political philosophy based on the idea of *pactum* or contract (see CONTRACTARIANISM). Starting from the idea of a hypothetical state of nature in which there was no secure ownership of property, a state which would inevitably degenerate into turmoil and conflict, Gassendi argued that individuals could secure greater happiness for themselves by forming societies. These societies are based on pacts or contracts in which both individual rights and property rights are defined and in which the weaker are protected from the stronger. The contracts establish rights, which Gassendi considered natural in the sense that they follow from the calculus of pleasure and pain. Civil society is thus a natural outcome of human nature. A system of justice comes into being to restore rights that have been violated and to prevent further violations. Gassendi favoured monarchy as simpler and more efficient than the other traditional forms of government. However, he argued that the power of the monarch remains answerable to the consent of the governed who first established the contract. He was therefore opposed to absolutism on the grounds that the absolute monarch had severed his relationship with the governed and was consequently answerable to no one. Gassendi developed his political philosophy in close contact with Thomas HOBBES, and his ideas had a profound influence on John Locke, who is usually named as the founder of the liberal tradition in political philosophy (see LIBERALISM).

See also: ATOMISM, ANCIENT; BERNIER, F.; DEMOCRITUS; FREEDOM, DIVINE; SCEPTICISM, RENAISSANCE; WILL, THE

List of works

Gassendi, P. (1658) *Opera Omnia* (Collected works), Lyon; repr. Stuttgart-Bad Canstatt: Friedrich Frommann Verlag, 1964. (The most easily accessible edition of Gassendi's works.)
—— (1972) *The Selected Works of Pierre Gassendi*, trans. C. Brush, New York: Johnson Reprint. (English translations of selections from *Exercitationes paradoxicae adversus Aristoteleos*, *De motu impressu*, *Rebuttals to Descartes* from the *Disquisitio metaphysica*, and *Syntagma philosophicum*.)
—— (1624) *Exercitationes Paradoxicae Adversus Aristoteleos* (Paradoxical Exercises against the Aristotelians); Books I and II ed. and trans. B. Rochot as *Dissertations en forme de paradoxes contre les Aristotéliciens*, Paris: Vrin, 1959. (French translation with facing pages in Latin of Gassendi's first published work.)
—— (1630a) *Epistolica exercitatio, in qua principia philosophiae Roberti Fluddi medici, reteguntur* (An Epistolary Exercise, in which the principles of the philosophy of the physician Robert Fludd are brought to light), in *Opera omnia*, vol. 3. (Critical response to Robert Fludd's alchemical philosophy of nature.)
—— (1630b) *Parhelia, sive soles quat[u]or qui circa verum apparuerunt Romae, die XX mensis Martii anno 1629* (Parhelia, or the four suns which appeared real at Rome on 20 March 1629), in *Opera omnia*, vol. 3 as *Parhelia, sive soles Quatuor Spurii, qui circa verum apparverunt Romae Anno*

MDCXXIX, Die XX Martij (Parhelia or four spurious suns...). (Deals with optical illusions in astronomy.)
—— (1632) *Mercurius in sole visus et Venus invisa Parisiis anno 1631* (Mercury seen in the sun and Venus unseen at Paris in 1631), in *Opera omnia*, vol. 4. (On observations of Mercury's transit of the Sun.)
—— (1632–3) *Lettres Familières à François Lullier pendant l'hiver 1632–1633* (Familiar letters to François Luillier during the winter of 1632–1633), ed. B. Rochot, Paris: Vrin, 1944. (Discusses his reading and travels during this year.)
—— (1641) *Viri illustri Nicolai Fabricii de Peiresc Senatoris Aquisextiensis vita* (The Life of the famous Senator of Aix, Nicholas Fabri de Peiresc), in *Opera omnia*, vol. 5; French trans. R. Lasalle and A. Bresson as *Peiresc, 1580–1637. Vie de l'illustre Nicolas-Claude Fabri de Peiresc*, Paris: Belin, 1992. (Biography of Gassendi's patron, the polymath Peiresc.)
—— (1642) *De motu impresso a motore translato* (On motion impressed by the moved mover), in *Opera omnia*, vol. 3. (An exposition of Galileo's new science of motion and contains the first correct statement of the principle of inertia in print.)
—— (1644) *Disquisitio Metaphysica seu dubitationes et instantiae adversus Renati Cartesii Metaphysicam et responsa* (Metaphysical disquisition, or doubts and instances against the metaphysics of René Descartes and responses), ed. and trans. B. Rochot, Paris: Vrin, 1962. (French translation with facing pages in Latin of Gassendi's objections to Descartes' *Meditations*, Descartes' replies, and Gassendi's rejoinders.)
—— (1647) *Institutio astronomica juxta hypotheseis tam veteram quam Copernici et Tychonis Brahei* (Astronomical instruction according to the ancient hypotheses as well as those of Copernicus and Tycho Brahe), in *Opera omnia*, vol. 4. (An account of the astronomical theories of Ptolemy, Copernicus and Tycho Brahe.)
—— (1649) *Animadversiones in decimum librum Diogenis Laertii, qui est de vita, moribus, pacitisque Epicuri* (Observations on Book X of Diogenes Laertius, Which is about the Life, Morals, and Opinions of Epicurus), repr. New York and London: Garland, 3 vols, 1987. (Translation of and commentary on Book X of Diogenes Laertius, *Lives of Eminent Philosophers*. Not in *Opera omnia*.)
—— (1658) *Syntagma philosophicum* (Philosophical treatise), in *Opera omnia*, vols 1 and 2. (Final version of Gassendi's Epicurean project, first published in the *Opera omnia*.)
Jones, H. (1981) *Pierre Gassendi's Institutio Logica,*

1658, Assen: Van Gorcum. (English translation of Part IV of the 'Logic' of Gassendi's *Syntagma Philosophicum*, his major statement on method.)

Murr, S. (1993) 'Pierre Gassendi – Préliminaires à La Physique *Syntagma Philosophicum,' Dix-septième Siècle*', 45 (2): 353–85. (French translation of the introductory section of Gassendi's *Syntagma Philosophicum*.)

Peiresc, N.C.F. de (1888–98) *Lettres de Peiresc*, ed. P.T. de Larroque in *Documents inédits sur l'histoire de France*, 7 vols, Paris: Imprimerie Nationale. (Contains Gassendi's correspondence with Peiresc.)

References and further reading

* Bloch, O.R. (1971) *La philosophie de Gassendi: Nominalisme, matérialisme, et métaphysique* (Gassendi's philosophy: nominalism, materialism and metaphysics), The Hague: Martinus Nijhoff. (The major modern study of Gassendi's philosophy. Argues that Gassendi was a materialist.)

Brundell, B. (1987) *Pierre Gassendi: From Aristotelianism to a New Natural Philosophy*, Dordrecht: Reidel. (Argues that Gassendi sought to replace Aristotelianism with a modified Epicureanism, which would then serve as a complete philosophy of nature.)

* Descartes, R. (1641) *Meditations on First Philosophy and Objections and Replies*, in *The Philosophical Writings of Descartes*, trans. J. Cottingham, R. Stoothoff, D. Murdoch, and A. Kenny, Cambridge: Cambridge University Press, 1984. (Gassendi wrote the fifth set of *Objections*.)

Jones, H. (1981) *Pierre Gassendi 1592–1655. An Intellectual Biography*, Nieuwkoop: B. de Graaf. (A biography of Gassendi which focuses on his philosophy but pays little attention to his scientific interests.)

Joy, L.S. (1987) *Gassendi the Atomist: Advocate of History in an Age of Science*, Cambridge: Cambridge University Press. (Interprets Gassendi's atomism in light of his use of the history of philosophy.)

Michael, F. (1992) 'La place de Gassendi dans l'histoire de la logique' (Gassendi's place in the history of logic), *Corpus* (Corpus des oeuvres de philosophie en langue française) 20/21: 9–36. (Discusses the historical background to and influence of Gassendi's writings on logic.)

Osler, M.J. (1994) *Divine Will and the Mechanical Philosophy: Gassendi and Descartes on Contingency and Necessity in the Created World*, Cambridge: Cambridge University Press. (Examines the influence of voluntarist theology on Gassendi's articulation of the mechanical philosophy. Contains extensive bibliography.)

* Popkin, R.H. (1979) *The History of Scepticism from Erasmus to Spinoza*, Berkeley, CA: University of California Press. (Situates Gassendi's epistemology in the context of the sceptical crisis of the early modern period.)

Rochot, B. (1944) *Les travaux de Gassendi sur Épicure et sur l'atomisme, 1619–1658* (Gassendi's works on Epicurius and atomism), Paris: Vrin. (Thorough examination of the development of Gassendi's project to Christianize Epicurean philosophy. A basic work.)

Sarasohn, L.T. (1996) *Gassendi's Ethics: Freedom in a Mechanistic Universe*, Ithaca, NY: Cornell University Press. (Study of Gassendi's moral and political philosophy in relation to his physics.)

MARGARET J. OSLER

GAUDĪYA VAIṢṆAVISM

The philosophical school encompassing the Bengali devotees of the god Viṣṇu is traditionally known as the Gauḍīya Vaiṣṇava school. Caitanya is considered to be the founder of this school in the sense that he led a revival of Kṛṣṇa devotionalism in Bengal during the early sixteenth century, inspiring a number of contemporary intellectuals to some original speculations of a metaphysical nature. Some of these were directly related to Vedānta, others were not. Since the eighteenth century the school has also become associated through Baladeva Vidyābhūṣaṇa with the Madhva school. However, the latter propounded a dualistic doctrine, while the Gauḍīyas are believers in the inconceivable simultaneous difference and oneness of the Supreme and his creation.

1 Kṛṣṇa Caitanya (1486–1534)
2 The Gosvāmins of Vṛndān
3 Later Gauḍīya Vaiṣṇavas

1 Kṛṣṇa Caitanya (1486–1534)

Born in Nabadwip, Bengal as Viśvambhara Miśra, Caitanya was first a precocious student and then worked as a teacher of Sanskrit grammar until becoming possessed by unusually strong devotional impulses at the age of twenty-three. He took the name Kṛṣṇa Caitanya when taking monastic vows in 1510. Despite entering a Śaṅkarite order, Caitanya had a deep-rooted distaste for the conclusions of exclusive nondualism (see ŚAṄKARA). He thus reversed Śaṅkara's interpretation of the essential statements of the Vedānta, taking 'Thou art that' (*tat tvam asi*) as 'Thou art his (servant)'. After his renunciation, Caitanya travelled throughout India before retiring to Puri in Orissa where he remained fully absorbed in devotional acts until his death. Caitanya's influence was born primarily of his charisma and he himself wrote nothing more than a few devotional verses (*Śikṣāṣṭaka* (Eight verses of instruction)) which encapsulate his doctrine: by singing the names of God one can be liberated from material suffering and reunite with him.

2 The Gosvāmins of Vṛndān

The brothers Sanātana (d. 1556) and Rūpa Gosvāmin (d. 1566) and their nephew Jīva Gosvāmin (d. 1612) are considered to be the foremost thinkers of the school. Sanātana's commentary on the tenth book of the *Bhāgavatapurāṇa* and his *Bhāgavatamṛta* (Essence of the *Bhāgavata*) are primarily concerned with the descriptions of the avatar Kṛṣṇa and the distinctions made between the various personal manifestations of Viṣṇu (or Kṛṣṇa) and giving them a hierarchical classification. This same preoccupation is found in all the Gauḍīya writers. Rūpa Gosvāmin is notable for his utilization of the theories of Sanskrit poeticians, the writers on literature and rhetoric, in particular that of aesthetic experience (*rasa*). Viśvanātha Kavi-rāja (fourteenth century) had identified aesthetic experience as *brahma-sahodara*, the 'twin of spiritual experience' and Rūpa adapted the current taxonomy of *rasa* as given in Siṅgabhūpāla's *Rasasudhākara* to the *līlā* of Rādhā and Kṛṣṇa. His justification for such a jump was as follows: of the three features of the Supreme, existence (*sat*), consciousness (*cit*) and joy (*ānanda*), joy is the highest. It is to realize this joy that the Supreme creates, as joy cannot exist in a nonmanifold state. The highest truth is thus revealed in emotional experience which is reflected in our personal human relations. Just as these experiences are distilled and experienced transcendentally in works of drama or poetry, so too is an even higher transcendental emotional relation experienced with the Supreme. Just as sexual love is the most intense and dominating of the varieties of human relation-ships, its spiritual counterpart is also the preeminent amongst those experienced with God. Because this relationship is found in its most relishable form exclusively in God's manifestation as Kṛṣṇa, Kṛṣṇa is the highest form of God. The monistic view of God, in which personal relationships are denied, is con-sidered a partial and defective view of the Supreme. Its monotheistic counterpart – the concept of God as possessing only certain attributes of omniscience and omnipresence – is conducive to the mood of devotion known as the 'peaceful' (*śānta*) which is also considered to be inferior to the filial and servile (*dāsya*), the friendly (*sākhya*) or protective (*vātsalya*) moods.

Jīva attacked more basic questions of doctrine in his *Bhāgavatasandarbha* (Treatise on the *Bhāgavata*), a systematic treatment of the theology of the *Bhāgavatapurāṇa*. As with the other Vedāntists, Jīva accepts the three sources of knowledge (*pramāṇas*): direct perception, logical reason and revelation (see KNOWLEDGE, INDIAN VIEWS OF). However, Jīva considers the *Bhāgavata* to be the most perfect source of revelation which gives the clearest explanation of the *Vedāntasūtras*. Many of his key concepts are derived from the *Viṣṇupurāṇa* and a great deal of his thought concurs with that of RĀMĀNUJA. For Jīva the problem of unity and difference is resolved through the concept of *śakti* (power): all creation is a product of God's power or energy which is innate in him. God's energies form a unity with him just as the heat, light and sparks of a fire form a unity with the fire. God's energies are divided into three categories: internal, external and marginal. The temporal crea-tion is external to God, comparable to a shadow which, although devoid of light depends on light for its existence and is unconscious. The internal energy is the world of God's grace; it has three aspects according to the Vedāntic categories of eternity, consciousness and bliss. The marginal energy (*taṭasthaśakti*) is the living being, a spark of consciousness who is conditioned by association with matter. The conditioned soul possesses limited free-dom to choose between the internal and external energies. This ability to choose is awakened by association with God's devotees who give him a taste of the joy of the perfections available in the internal realm. Through such association, an individual becomes aware that relations in the conditioned existence are partial and unsatisfying and he learns to seek the essential relationship that he possesses with the root of all existence, the Supreme soul. Through the purifying process of devotion in practice (*sādhanābhakti*), the specific character of this emo-tional relationship is awakened in him. Love of God (*premabhakti*) is the ultimate goal of perfection.

3 Later Gauḍīya Vaiṣṇavas

Prominent later members of the school include Viśvanātha Cakravartī (seventeenth century) and Baladeva Vidyābhūṣaṇa (early eighteenth century). Baladeva's main contribution is his commentary on the *Vedāntasūtra*, the *Govindabhāṣya*, in which he arranges the ideas of his predecessors according to the sūtras. He also introduced certain elements of Madhvācārya's thought into the tradition, despite the fact that Madhvācārya (fourteenth century) propounded a dualist (*dvaita*) doctrine, while the Gauḍīyas style themselves as believers in the inconceivable simultaneous difference and oneness of the Supreme and his creation (*acintyabhedābhedavādins*).

See also: GOD, INDIAN CONCEPTIONS OF; MADHVA; VEDĀNTA

References and further reading

Bhaktivedanta Swami, A.C. (1970) *The Teachings of Lord Caitanya*, New York: Bhaktivedanta Book Trust. (A good summary of the essential teachings found in Caitanya's biographies.)

Bhaktivedanta Swami, A.C. and H. Goswami (1972–85) *Śrīmad-Bhāgavatam*, Los Angeles, CA: Bhaktivedanta Book Trust, 41 vols. (A complete multivolume work.)

Brahmachari, M.N.B. (1974) *Vaiṣṇava Vedānta: The Philosophy of Śrī Jīva Gosvāmī*, Calcutta: Das Gupta and Co. (A useful introduction to some epistemological questions.)

Chakravarty, R. (1985) *Bengal Vaiṣṇavism, 1486–1900*, Calcutta: Sanskrit Pustaka Bhandar. (An excellent history of the school.)

Chaudhuri, R. (1975) *Ten Schools of the Vedānta*, Calcutta: Rabindra Bharati University. (Vol. 3: 241–365 gives a detailed account of the philosophy of Baladeva Vidyābhūṣaṇa.)

De, S.K. (1943) *Early Vaishnava Faith and Movement in Bengal*, Calcutta: Firma K.L. Mukhopadhyay, 2nd edn, 1962. (A wide-ranging and thorough study.)

Delmonico, N. Gorton (1990) 'Sacred Rapture: A Study of the Religious Aesthetic of Rūpa Gosvāmin', unpublished doctoral dissertation, University of Chicago, IL. (The best study of Rūpa Gosvāmin's religious aesthetic.)

Eidlitz, W. (1968) *Kṛṣṇa-Caitanya: Sein Leben und Seine Lehre*, Stockholm: Almqvist & Wiksell. (One of the earliest scholarly works on the Caitanya movement, it still provides a good introduction to its thought and literature.)

Elkman, S. (1985) *The Tattvasandarbha of Jīva Gosvāmīn*, Delhi: Motilal Banarsidass. (Deals with the first volume of Jīva's oeuvre which sets the stage for accepting the *Bhāgavatapurāṇa* as the main source of knowledge and the analysis of the tripartite understanding of the Supreme as *Brahma, paramaātman, bhagavān*.)

Kapoor, O.B.L. (1983) *The Religion and Philosophy of Śrī Caitanya*, Delhi: Motilal Banarsidass. (Provides insight into major theological issues in Gauḍīya Vaiṣṇavism.)

Masson, J. and Patwardhan, M.V. (1970) *Aesthetic Rapture*, Poona: Deccan College, 2 vols. (A more general discussion of *rasa*.)

JAN K. BRZEZINSKI

GAUTAMA, AKṢAPĀDA

'Akṣapāda Gautama' (or 'Gotama') stands for the legendary founder of the Nyāya ('Logic') school of Indian philosophy, who is reputed also to be the author of its basic text, the Nyāyasūtra. *This compilation of roughly 500 mnemonic sentences reached its first defined form around AD 400. Its oldest core preserves a manual of philosophical debate supplemented by elements of an early philosophy of nature and a basic soteriology. The later parts of the text deal with the number and nature of the means of valid cognition; they further treat the objects of valid cognition and discuss basic questions of metaphysical content.*

Pakṣilasvāmin VĀTSYĀYANA (*circa* second half of the fifth century AD), the author of the first preserved commentary on the *Nyāyasūtra*, refers to the founder of Nyāya as the sage Akṣapāda. This name, meaning 'the one with eyes on his feet', appears repeatedly in the school's older tradition. Later anecdotes current among Indian pandits connect it with the sage's deep philosophical contemplation and the superiority of Nyāya over its critics from the more orthodox camp, who held the Vedic revelation to be the most authoritative means of valid cognition. From the tenth century onward, the personal name Gotama or clan name Gautama ('descendant of Gotama') is connected with the school's basic teachings; both names become more current in the eleventh and following centuries, often appearing next to the older 'Akṣapāda'. The identity of this Akṣapāda Gautama/ Gotama – if there ever was a historical personage of that name – remains a matter of speculation, as does his possible role in the formation of the Nyāya school and its basic text.

The *Nyāyasūtra*, divided into five chapters, reflects in its textual history the origin and early development of Nyāya itself. The ancient core of the text is preserved in chapters one and five, and could stem in this or a similar form from the second century AD. It is actually a manual of debate (*vāda*) which enumerates and concisely defines sixteen categories (*padārtha*) relevant to the orderly and successful conduct of a public philosophical debate. These are: (1) means of valid cognition, (2) objects of valid cognition, (3) doubt, (4) purpose, (5) generally accepted fact, (6) tenets, (7) members of proof, (8) reasoning, (9) decision, (10) friendly debate, (11) wrangle, (12) dispute involving mere criticism by one party, (13) fallacious reasons, (14) distortions, (15) sophistries and (16) points of defeat. An early philosophy of nature and a rudimentary soteriology were integrated into the category of objects of valid cognition (*prameya*); these are: (1) self, (2) senses, (3) body, (4) sense objects, (5) cognition, (6) 'internal instrument', (7) linguistic, mental and physical activity, (8) emotional and intellectual faults that instigate activity, (9) rebirth, (10) the result of activity and faults – that is, the experience of pleasure and pain, (11) suffering and (12) release. The text's initial sentence proclaims that adequate knowledge of all sixteen categories effects the attainment of the highest good – namely, release from suffering, or liberation. In the Indian context, the school's teachings could not be presented as a complete philosophical doctrine without this soteriological component.

Owing to its origin in a tradition concerned with methodical and sound argumentation, logical and epistemological issues are prominent in Nyāya from early on. In chapter two of the *Nyāyasūtra*, the very possibility of means of valid cognition (*pramāṇa*) is defended against attacks by an opponent who professes a functional essentialism; related attacks are also found in works ascribed to NĀGĀRJUNA (§2). Subsequently, the four means of valid cognition accepted in Nyāya are examined in detail and established as distinct; these are sensory perception, inference, analogy or comparison, and verbal testimony (see KNOWLEDGE, INDIAN VIEWS OF). Further means accepted by other schools, such as traditional lore, circumstantial evidence or presumption, coincidence or inclusion, and absence or negation, are shown to be included in verbal testimony and inference. The examination of sensory perception entails an exposition and defence of the doctrine of the whole as distinct from its parts (contested by Buddhist opponents), which is taken up again in chapter four and expanded with a defence of the atom as the ultimate partless constituent of matter (see MATTER, INDIAN CONCEPTIONS OF §2; SENSE PERCEPTION, INDIAN VIEWS OF §§4–5). In this context, the realistic outlook of Nyāya, as opposed to Buddhist idealism, is maintained. The topic of verbal testimony, instruction by a trustworthy person which may have visible or invisible objects, occasions a defence of the authority of the Veda. This places Nyāya within the larger Brahmanical tradition, although it differs from the orthodox Mīmāṃsā school in assuming a personal authorship of these texts and denying their eternity

(see MĪMĀṂSĀ §2). A digression on the impermanence of articulated sound and a refutation of its eternity underscores the difference between their philosophies of language, as does the concluding section on the referent of the word.

Like chapter two, chapters three and four proceed in a dialogical-dialectical manner, treating mainly the objects of valid cognition. The existence of a self or soul (*ātman*) is proved by various arguments; arguments based on innate dispositions imply its previous existence in other bodies. Cognition, which is momentary, is shown to be a quality of the soul, not of the body or of the 'internal instrument' called the *manas* (often misleadingly rendered as 'mind'); the *manas* functions in non-sensory cognitive events, such as recollection, and regulates cognitions in general. The senses are argued to be material, of the nature of the five elements earth, water, fire, wind and 'ether', whose specific qualities they grasp – these are smell, taste, colour, temperature and sound respectively. Sight receives special treatment as consisting in fiery rays issuing from the eyes to make contact with objects. Finally, several sections address soteriological issues, the possibility of release and the knowledge eventually leading to it. This knowledge chiefly concerns the true nature of the sense objects and can be attained by meditative contemplation and yogic practices aided by self-restraint. Friendly debate with disciples, teachers, fellow students and others striving for salvation serves the same purpose. Disputations with opponents protect one's nascent ascertainment of the truth.

See also: NYĀYA-VAIŚEṢIKA

List of works

Nyāyasūtra (c.400 AD), trans. G. Jha, *The Nyāya-Sūtras of Gautama with the Bhāṣya of Vātsyāyana and the Vārtika of Uddyotakara*, Indian Thought 4–11, 1912–19; repr. Delhi: Motilal Banarsidass, 4 vols, 1984. (Complete translation together with the first preserved commentary and its subcommentary; contains profuse notes from further commentaries. However, the translation of the *Sūtra* is heavily influenced by the commentaries.)

Nyāyasūtra (c.400 AD), trans. W. Ruben *Die Nyāyasūtra's. Text, Übersetzung, Erläuterung und Glossar* (The *Nyāyasūtras*: Text, Translation, Commentary and Glossary), Abhandlungen für die Kunde des Morgenlandes 18, 2, Leipzig: Deutsche Morgenländische Gesellschaft, 1928. (Standard critical edition and still by far the best annotated translation of the complete text. Contains useful index and glossary.)

References and further reading

Frauwallner, E. (1984) 'Erkenntnistheorie und Logik der klassischen Zeit' (Epistemology and Logic of the Classical Period), in *Nachgelassene Werke*, vol. 1, *Aufsätze, Beiträge, Skizzen* (Posthumous Works, vol. 1, Essays, Contributions, Outlines), ed. E. Steinkellner, Österreichische Akademie der Wissenschaften, phil.-hist. Klasse, Sitzungsberichte 438, Veröffentlichungen der Kommission für Sprachen und Kulturen Südasiens 19, Wien: Verlag der österreichischen Akademie der Wissenschaften, 66–87. (Traces the development from debate to epistemology and logic by demonstrating the refinement of the Nyāya categories from an early manual of debate that survives – explained for the needs of physicians – in a classical compilation on Indian medicine.)

Junankar, N.S. (1978) *Gautama: The Nyāya Philosophy*, Delhi: Motilal Banarsidass. (Detailed account and extensive discussion of the *Nyāyasūtra* and the two earliest commentaries, concentrating on the theory of cognition and the concept of proof and inference.)

Meuthrath, A. (1996) *Untersuchungen zur Kompositionsgeschichte der Nyāyasūtras* (Investigations into the Compositional History of the *Nyāyasūtras*), Religionswissenschaftliche Studien 36, Würzburg: Echter Verlag, and Altenberg: Oros Verlag. (Discusses the entire *sūtra*-text with a view to its philological-historical stratification.)

Oetke, C. (1988) *'Ich' und das Ich. Analytische Untersuchungen zur buddhistisch–brahmanischen Ātmankontroverse* ('I' and the Self. Analytical Investigations into the Controversy over Ātman between Buddhists and Brahmans), Alt- und Neu-Indische Studien 33, Stuttgart: Franz Steiner, 247–77, 288–98. (Penetrating analytical study of the arguments for the existence of a self or soul and for cognition being its quality in the *Nyāyasūtra* and its earliest commentary.)

—— (1991) Zur Methode der Analyse philosophischer Sūtratexte. Die Pramāṇa Passagen der Nyāyasūtren (On the Method of Analysis of Philosophical *Sūtra*-Texts. The Passages on *Pramāṇa* in the *Nyāyasūtra*), Studien zur Indologie und Iranistik, Monographie 11, Reinbek: Dr Inge Wezler. (Excellent philological-philosophical analysis of the key passages on the possibility of means of valid cognition, also of consequence for the text's relation to early Madhyamaka works.)

Preisendanz, K. (1994) *Studien zu Nyāyasūtra III.1 mit dem Nyāyatattvāloka Vācaspati Miśras II.*, Alt- und Neu-Indische Studien 46, 1–2, Stuttgart: Franz Steiner. (Combined diachronic and synchronic study of the *Nyāyasūtra* on the soul, senses, body and sense objects, together with a fifteenth-century commentary.)

Randle, H.N. (1930) *Indian Logic in the Early Schools*, Oxford: Oxford University Press; repr. Delhi: Oriental Books Reprint Corporation, 1976. (Study of the epistemology and logic of the *Nyāyasūtra* in its wider historical context; although partially outdated, it is still valuable for the understanding of these topics in the *Nyāyasūtra* itself.)

Saha, S. (1987) *Perspectives on Nyaya Logic and Epistemology*, Calcutta/New Delhi: K P Bagchi & Company. (Although the author makes some use of later materials, he concentrates on the *Nyāyasūtra* and follows the text's order in his clear presentation.)

ELI FRANCO
KARIN PREISENDANZ

GEDANKENEXPERIMENTE
see THOUGHT EXPERIMENTS

GENDER AND ETHICS
see FEMINIST ETHICS

GENDER AND LANGUAGE
see LANGUAGE AND GENDER

GENDER AND SCIENCE

Gender-based analyses of philosophies of science have arisen at the conjunction of two other movements. First, in the 1960s it became increasingly the accepted position that scientific claims failed to reflect only an external reality. Scientific processes are not transparent; they necessarily permit cultural and social values and interests to contribute to the descriptions and explanations of nature's order. Thus gender values and interests, too, could have shaped scientific practices and claims. Second, women's movements developed powerful gender analyses of all other aspects of social relations. What resources could such accounts provide to illuminate also the practices and cultures of the sciences?

Consequently, diverse analyses have appeared showing how sexist and androcentric values and interests have shaped scientific projects, and shaped them with unfortunate results not only for gender relations, but also for the advance of both sciences and philosophy. They also examine how other values and interests, ones that are gender-neutral and ones that draw on resources found in women's lives, can have beneficial effects. Concern has been raised in the following issues. Is correcting 'bad science' sufficient to eliminate sexist and androcentric results of research? How has the exclusion of women from those groups that select what will count as scientific problems resulted in narrow and distorted representations of nature's order? How has excessive reliance on gendered meanings of nature, the scientist, and scientific method – gender coding – shaped scientific claims? If the subject of science remains coded masculine, how can women claim positions as speakers/authors of scientific research – as scientific subjects? In what ways have research procedures (technologies) been gender-coded and how has their use directed the development of subsequent sexist and androcentric technologies and applications of science? Why have standards for maximizing objectivity and good method been too weak to prevent of knowledge-decreasing values and interests from shaping the results of research?

1   **Origins and scope**
2   **Bad science or standard science?**
3   **Whose problems?**
4   **Gender coding**
5   **Technology**
6   **Objectivity and method**

1   Origins and scope

By the late 1960s, the Enlightenment vision of science had been undermined by views that observations are theory-laden, our beliefs form a network such that none are in principle immune from revision, and our best theories are underdetermined by any possible collection of evidence (see OBSERVATION §§3–4; UNDERDETERMINATION). Thus empirical evidence could no longer be regarded as foundational. Slack in the procedures of the scientific system of belief-sorting permits the play of local values and interests across the entire fabric of scientific practices and claims – values and interests that can advance as well as retard the growth of knowledge. Moreover, there are no longer good grounds for assuming the unity of science, since neither physics' formally expressed laws of nature, nor the logic supposed to ground them, can be regarded as foundational in the sense of being assumed to have escaped the play of values and interests (see UNITY OF SCIENCE). Sciences are embedded in their surrounding cultures – or, as the point was later made, co-constituted with them.

These findings made it difficult to reserve a subject matter for the philosophy of science that was safe from the legitimate gaze of historians and, later, sociologists, anthropologists, political theorists and even literary critics. After all, what is the point of philosophies of science that cannot account for the successes of science? In this first stage of post-Enlightenment philosophy of science, feminists raised issues about how gender relations, too, had shaped the sciences and their philosophies.

A second stage focused on one or another specific science, since it was thought that science in general had turned out to be too complicated to permit any comprehensive philosophical claims. Participation in this stage included Evelyn Fox Keller's works on, and in, physics and biology and Helen Longino, Elisabeth Lloyd and others in, and on, biology. Ethnographies of scientific practices and culture meanwhile were produced by historians, sociologists and anthropologists (for example, Donna Haraway's on twentieth-century primatology (1989) and Sharon Traweek's on contemporary physics (1988)). Feminist political theorists' questions about philosophical issues in the social sciences were understood often to be relevant also to the natural sciences. By the late 1980s, a third stage had produced a revival of more general philosophic concerns. These analyses have been able to draw on both earlier stages, and on the resources of literary and other cultural analyses of representation, narrative, discourse and rhetoric.

Feminism does not introduce gender into science or the philosophy of science, for it is already there. Instead, feminism introduces gender as an analytic category (parallel to economic or Christian categories) into the philosophy and social studies of science discourses. As Keller puts the point, feminism tries to locate the scientific subject in *his* (masculine) practices and *his* rhetoric of neutrality that deny *his* very existence (Fox Keller 1983: 16–). Determining where this occurs is an empirical project. Moreover, in these accounts, gender is understood as socially constructed, not as determined by sex differences. As such, gender is not only a property of individuals but, far more importantly, of institutions and of symbolic systems. Thus science and the military are more masculine than are nursing or social welfare in their gendered divisions of activities and social meanings.

Feminist science studies were initially focused on six distinct areas. One, where have women been located in sciences' institutions, and what have been the obstacles to their entrance, retention and advancement? What are the particular consequences for the content of knowledge in each scientific field of the exclusion or restriction of women? Two, in what ways are scientific applications and technologies sexist or androcentric? Are these only 'misuses and abuses', or are blueprints for them provided by research methods themselves? Three, where are there sexist or androcentric silences and distortions in the results of research in biology and the social sciences? How do these biases reflect back on 'logics' of research and explanation for the natural sciences? Four, how do gendered models and meanings of nature, the scientist and the research process distort scientific representations of nature and social relations? Five, how are central epistemological regulatory notions – objectivity, good method, rationality, the abstract individual knower – conceptualized to favour the values and interests of the dominant groups? And six, what is the role of science education in exacerbating these problems?

Feminist work in other disciplines has been self-transforming. Women of colour in the West, working-class women, third-world women, sexual minorities and others marginalized by the dominant discourses have all challenged the centring of concerns and perspectives characteristic primarily of privileged women in the West. Thinking from the margins has become a crucial theoretical and empirical strategy for many 'centre' women, too. This work has only begun for the philosophy and social studies of science. Nevertheless, outlines for such projects have already been sketched out in the work of a few thinkers such as Harawayand Harding, and Shiva (1989) (see POSTCOLONIAL PHILOSOPHY OF SCIENCE). The serious attention to issues of self-reflexivity characteristic of feminist work more generally provides stimulus and resources for the philosophy and the social studies of science also.

Finally, feminist philosophies of science draw on diverse disciplinary and theoretical resources. There is not now, nor will there ever be, a single feminist philosophy of science. Philosophical issues have been raised within the conceptual frameworks of the special sciences studied, disciplinary and theoretical frameworks of the social studies of science, and diverse political philosophies (see FEMINISM AND SOCIAL SCIENCE; FEMINIST POLITICAL PHILOSOPHY). This entry will focus on five issues that surface repeatedly in these diverse approaches.

2 Bad science or standard science?

Are sexist and androcentric silences and distortions in the results of research in biology and the social sciences the consequence merely of bad science or, worse, also of standard science? The line between the empiricists and the post-empiricists, as we can refer to those who prefer one or the other of these positions, is

not always hard and fast. Nevertheless, it is useful to characterize in such a way the two poles of the continuum on which feminists think about this question. Those who are satisfied with the first choice believe that there is nothing wrong with existing principles of good research in each disciplinary area, or with an empiricist logic of explanation. The problem is that researchers have not carefully or thoughtfully enough followed them. Basing generalizations about humans only on data about men, assuming that women's biology normally functions in immature or pathological ways, or that only males have evolved – such claims are examples only of bad science. Philosophers in this group often go on to criticize conventional assumptions that knowers are abstract individuals and to stress the importance of accountability to an epistemic community. Whatever their concerns, this group is marked by its vigorous intention to keep its projects firmly located within the empiricist tradition. For them, feminism raises new issues that enlarge the scope of research and reveal cause for greater care in its conduct and philosophic formulations, but leaves fundamentally unchallenged an empiricist logic of research and explanation.

A diverse group think gender problems in the natural sciences cannot adequately be understood or resolved by empiricist approaches: standpoint theorists such as Hilary Rose (1983), Dorothy Smith (1987) and Nancy Hartsock, standpoint theorists who also draw on post-structuralist resources; Donna Haraway (1991) and Sandra Harding (1986), and others like Evelyn Fox Keller who do not give their distinctive analyses a special name.

These feminist post-empiricists differ among themselves on the whole range of issues that divide the rest of post-empiricists; philosophically some feminist post-empiricists are more conservative and others more radical. All share the suspicion that there is something wrong with the standard 'logics' of both research and explanation. Androcentric values and interests are not just contingently present in the results of research; they also play a role in the cognitive, technical core of science that, in the Enlightenment vision, was held to be immune to all social fingerprints. If such values and interests can permeate the cognitive core of science – its 'method' and collection of formal claims – then it is not sufficient simply to more carefully follow existing methods, theories and norms of science; instead these features must be transformed if the results of research are to escape distortion. Nor are remedies that rely on the critical effectiveness of a community of experts – an epistemic or scientific community – sufficient, since it is precisely such communities that have been unable to detect their own shared androcentric assumptions. There are problems with standard science that post-empiricists think require more radical kinds of resolution (see SCIENTIFIC METHOD §§2–3).

3   Whose problems?

Androcentric biases enter sciences at every stage of the research process, including the selection of problems. Just which array of problems scientists will pursue at any moment is far less due to scientists' individual choices to 'pursue the truth wherever it may lead' than it is to priorities of their sponsors and culture. However, the prevailing view has been that the selection of problems has no effect on the cognitive, technical core of science, that there is no logic of discovery, and thus that any attempt to regulate science prior to the context of justification is not only futile, but an infringement on sciences' creative potential (see DISCOVERY, LOGIC OF).

There is something odd about this protection of problem selection from responsibility for distortion in the results of research. The post-Kuhnian histories and ethnographies of science have revealed in great detail exactly how cultural assumptions and politically interested decisions made prior to the context of justification, the ones that constitute scientific projects and select methods to test hypotheses, preclude the possibility of the results of this research achieving cultural neutrality. If the problem is conceptualized as how to identify the proximate biological causes of cancer, one can be sure of a very different picture of nature and social relations in the results of that research than if the problem were conceptualized as how to identify the environmental carcinogens that are known to be the most powerful of the many causes of cancer. Focusing on proximate causes supports the interests and values of medical researchers, the tobacco, junk food and meat industries, and industrial and military polluters; focusing on environmental causes supports the interests and values of their critics and environmental researchers. Neither approach can be interest-free.

Feminists have argued that our collective knowledge about the natural and social worlds disproportionately represents the kinds of question of interest to the dominant social institutions – those interested in increasing profit, maximizing social control, legitimating hierarchical authority and the *status quo* and thereby advancing the values and interests of men in the advantaged groups, frequently at the expense of the values and interests of the poor, women, racial and ethnic minorities, and 'have nots' in other parts of the world. The patterns and contents of what sciences tend to discover about nature's order disproportionately reflect what the dominant groups both have and have not wanted to know.

Faced with this problem, all feminists have recommended that scientific communities become more inclusive for scientific reasons as well as ones of social justice. Since the victims tend to be more sensitive to less obvious expressions of discrimination and devaluing of their concerns, their presence and critical analyses would be likely to improve the ability of the sciences to arrive at less partial and distorted representations of nature. However, such strategies are of dubious effectiveness by themselves; the concerns of marginalized people tend to remain marginalized when individuals from such groups are simply inserted into dominant and often resisting institutions that make no other changes.

Some feminists have proposed an additional strategy that could systematically help eliminate distortions in sciences' representations of nature that are produced by androcentrism, Eurocentrism, or other values and interests that are shared by research communities (and, often, their cultures). They propose a strategy of conceptualizing scientific projects in the first place from outside the conceptual frameworks of dominant social institutions and research disciplines, namely from the standpoint of the lives of those who bear a disproportionate share of the costs of how such institutions and disciplines function. Standpoint epistemologies thus direct researchers to start research from women's lives ('lives' plural, since 'women' is as heterogeneous a category as is 'humans') to generate scientific problems that are ones for women too, rather than only problems for the dominant institutions and the disciplines that work up knowledge for them. This 'method' is a collective and political process – a social and scientific achievement rather than an automatic outcome of women's experience or of living a woman's life. In a sense, they are proposing a kind of logic of discovery for more accurate, because interest-balanced, representations of nature and social relations.

4   Gender coding

What should one make of gendered metaphors and models of nature, the scientist and the research process that have been prevalent throughout the history of modern science? Historians and philosophers have pointed to the 'nature, she; scientist, he' language so familiar from Bacon and Machiavelli's writings to those of contemporary science texts. Susan Bordo (1987) Evelyn Fox Keller (1984) and Carolyn Merchant (1980) show how invoking images of the hyper-masculinity of science provided solace for the loss of the organicist 'mother-world' in early modern science. Such metaphors and models have helped to constitute the cognitive content of scientific claims, they and others argue.

The interactionist theory of metaphors and models holds that such forms of socially-meaningful language and concepts are a necessary part of every scientific theory. 'Nature is a machine' is not only heuristically or pedagogically useful; it also tells scientists how to develop their theories into new domains and where to revise when observations prove recalcitrant. As machines become more familiar, more natural, so too nature is experienced as more mechanical. And as the metaphor becomes more familiar, its regulatory functions shift from explicit plans into tacit knowledge. Similarly, conceptualizing nature as a wild and unruly woman who must be tamed if man is to be able to control his fate, as did Machiavelli, simultaneously directs scientists to favour certain kinds of interaction with nature and naturalizes certain ways of treating women. Enlightenment sciences have been directed by the illusion that there is a 'bare nature' at which scientists can gaze if they strip away the veils under which she hides her true features. But this metaphor distorts our understanding of how nature-as-an-object-of-knowledge is always already socially constructed, and yet also not agreeable to just any old fears, fantasies or desires that cultures choose to project on to its order. Humans speak in diverse metaphors, models and conceptual frameworks, but nature does answer back with as much (and only as much) precision as human interactions with it demand.

Such gender coding appears in ancient dichotomizing practices evident from Parmenides to the present day that construct self–other schemas coded masculine–feminine: rational–irrational, logic–emotions/passions, culture–nature, dynamic–static, mind–body, adult–infant, abstract–concrete, autonomous–dependent/relational/contextual, and so forth. Reliance on these symbolic systems can lead to oppressive social relations and distorted understandings of nature's order. After all, the dichotomies are empirically false of men and women's natures. Our understanding of nature can benefit from a broader array of metaphors and scientific processes than containment within such androcentric metaphors permits.

A persistent feminist concern has been with the modern coding of neutrality as masculine. If maximizing objectivity and rationality are conceptualized as requiring neutrality, and masculinity is defined partially in terms of its neutrality (even to gender, since 'man' and 'he' are taken to represent the generically human), then it is a kind of contradiction in terms to imagine that women can be objective and rational. This remains so even when their achievements are indistinguishable from men's. There is no speaking position available to women as rational, objective thinkers since that position has been fully occupied by the masculine. Moreover, those areas of science that are thought least shaped by social values and interests thus are the most vigorously masculine. Precisely because they are thought to be the most neutral, physics, mathematics and logic are the most masculine intellectual areas.

It should be stressed that these arguments about the role of gender metaphors and models in science are no more about individuals' idiosyncratic motivations than are arguments about the role of mechanistic or organicist metaphors. Androcentric individuals are not the issue: cultural assumptions, fears, desires, values and interests are. The metaphors and models used by Plato, Machiavelli, Bacon and Descartes are interesting because of what they reveal of the cultures within which these individuals constructed their texts for imagined audiences.

What should be done about these distorting conceptual frameworks? One widely shared proposal is to recover and revalue the feminine in nature, scientific practice, and the history and philosophy of science in order to enlarge sciences' conceptual resources. If hierarchical models of nature are preferred by cultures seeking to legitimate gender or other social hierarchies, then we lose the chance to understand those 'democratic' aspects of nature's order that are often coded feminine. If masculine models of research are preferred, we lose the chance to understand those aspects of nature's order that could be revealed by methods associated with the feminine. If reason must be divorced from the emotions and objectivity from cultural location, we lose the chance to understand the positive role that emotions and cultures can play in the growth of knowledge.

Another proposal is to seek metaphors and models that do not emphasize the importance of gender difference, and point out the limitations of those that do. We would thus have the chance to grasp heretofore less visible aspects of nature's order as well as undermine the oppressive rule of hegemonic gender difference.

5 Technology

Like the science discussions, feminist approaches to technology have drawn upon recent constructivist tendencies to show how artefacts have politics: technological change is a site for gender struggles over the meanings of and access to technological literacy, the use of new technologies and control over their consequences (see CONSTRUCTIVISM). Judy Wajcman's (1988) important analysis focuses on such issues as they occur in the organization of work, reproduction, the built environment, militarism, and computer culture. Research technologies, too, are gendered. Since modern science is often distinguished from other more speculative science traditions precisely by its reliance on experimental methods' technologies of intervention in nature, these studies show yet another way in which the social consequences of sciences are a direct result of features of their cognitive core. If one learns about genes or extra-uterine forms of reproduction by manipulating them, one creates blueprints for how to change them. Technological uses of sciences are partially directed by successful research methods.

These accounts are also valuable because they provide rich resources for understanding how Western claims to scientificity are used to impose technologically oppressive social relations on women in developing countries. Here too, feminist standpoint approaches reveal why philosophies and other social studies of technology should start off their projects from the lives of those who have suffered from Western sciences and technologies, in order to gain a less partial and distorted understanding of their strengths and weaknesses (see TECHNOLOGY AND ETHICS).

6 Objectivity and method

Feminist reflections on the goal of objectivity, the neutrality ideal and methods to achieve these are part of a more general discomfort with the West's assumed authority about the nature of reality and desirable forms of social relations. Five analyses will suggest the range of proposals here.

The first of these was referred to in §4. If objectivity requires neutrality, and neutrality is coded masculine, how can a woman – or a feminism that speaks on behalf of women – ever claim objectivity for women's speech? And how can sciences' claims to objectivity avoid continuing to overvalue manliness? Many feminists have found these objections compelling and have recommended adopting some other language –for example, subjectivism or relativism – for discussing the reliability of our understandings of nature and social relations. However, others have sought to clarify or transform the concept.

Helen Longino (1990) sets out to show how even though science is socially constructed, it already has good procedures for achieving objectivity. The relevance of evidence to a theory is determined by the context of inquiry, by background beliefs. All too often, social or practical interests (contextual values),

including gendered ones, in background beliefs have functioned as the cognitive values (constitutive ones) that determine what counts as a good scientific judgment. However, she argues that we can identify these background beliefs independently, and thus show how certain states of affairs have been rightly or wrongly taken as evidence for a hypothesis. Such processes are social and thus public, for they depend upon a scientific community sharing a common language with which to describe experience and intersubjective agreement that screens out idiosyncratic and subjective elements. Most importantly, since the scientific community rather than the individual scientist is the knower, enhanced attention to the role of criticism is crucial for overcoming power imbalances within such a community that can result in the devaluation of legitimate criticisms. Objectivity requires a transformative criticism such that the community adjusts its assumptions and processes in light of criticism by all of its qualified members.

Evelyn Fox Keller draws on psychoanalytic theory to argue that objectivity is best reconceptualized as profiting from the use of subjective experience rather than as opposed to it. This 'dynamic objectivity' contrasts with the prevailing philosophical preference for 'static objectivity' through which the knower must take a basically adversarial relation to the objects of study. Such a science, with its rhetoric of domination and coercion, attracts individuals who find emotional and cognitive comfort in such ways of relating to nature and other people to the exclusion of other, at least equally revealing styles, methods and theories of such relations. 'Good science' gets defined in an excessively narrow way. Dynamic objectivity 'grants to the world around us its independent integrity but does so in a way that remains cognizant of, indeed relies on, our connectivity with that world... dynamic objectivity is not unlike empathy' (Keller 1984). Dynamic objectivity's long history can be detected in the thought of the many scientists who have seen their work primarily as an erotic rather than adversarial activity.

Sandra Harding has argued (1991) that the neutrality ideal can usefully be detached from the goal of objectivity; methods for maximizing 'strong objectivity' can be substituted for it. Androcentrism, Eurocentrism and the like have been shared by virtually entire research communities; they are not the kind of subjective, idiosyncratic values that the research methods activated in the context of justification are capable of detecting. The neutrality ideal is an obstacle to detecting the conceptual practices of power since it categorizes as political only the critics of power, not those who claim the 'view from nowhere' within its protective normalizing assumptions and procedures. Standpoint epistemologies, that direct one to formulate questions in the first place from outside the dominant institutions, practices and culture, and to start instead from disadvantaged lives, can provide systematic resources – a 'strong method' – for philosophies of the natural and social sciences. Abjuring both epistemic foundationalism and relativism, and careful neither fully to identify with nor to appropriate the voice of the other, standpoint theories insist that only socially situated knowledge, only partial perspectives, are possible. Those issuing from disadvantaged social locations can provide less partial and distorted understandings of nature and social relations.

Donna Haraway's rethinking of objectivity occurs in the context of her incisive questions about the relation between the production of science ('technoscience') and of culture. She develops the ethical and political implications of standpoint theory further, stressing the need for a notion of objectivity that initiates, instead of closing off, issues of responsibility for science's images of nature and the rational knower. She argues that the objects of knowledge, too, must be reconceptualized:

> A corollary of the insistence that ethics and politics covertly or overtly provide the bases for objectivity in the sciences as a heterogeneous whole, and not just in the social sciences, is granting the status of agent/actor to the 'objects' of the world.... Accounts of a real world do not, then, depend on a logic of 'discovery', but on a power-charged social relation of 'conversation'.
>
> (Haraway 1991)

Such an agent could be pictured as the Coyote or Trickster, she proposes, embodied in American southwest Indian accounts, for this figure 'suggests our situation when we give up mastery but keep searching for fidelity, knowing all the while we will be hoodwinked' by nature.

In conclusion, it is striking how little attention has been paid to the philosophic effects of gender relations by even the most radical of mainstream philosophies and social studies of science. In effect they exclude such relations from the realm of the social that otherwise is a major concern. Feminist accounts are more objective in this respect, as well as in their attention to the conceptual effects of race/imperial relations and more rigorous understanding of self-reflexivity issues.

In their attention to relations between power and knowledge, feminist science analyses both reflect and promote the widespread critical re-examination of Enlightenment ideals and their political consequences. Their diverse attempts to envisage post-Enlightenment sciences and philosophies of science join widespread global projects to bring Western sciences under democratic control. And yet the feminist projects also are fully inside Western traditions, for they emerge from and advance one long-standing project there of criticizing the favoured beliefs of the powerful in order to block 'might makes right' in the domain of knowledge production.

See also: FEMINISM; FEMINIST EPISTEMOLOGY; OBJECTIVITY

References and further reading

* Bordo, S.R. (1987) *The Flight to Objectivity: Essays on Cartesianism and Culture*, Albany, NY: State University of New York Press. (Important analysis of issues in §4.)

* Haraway, D. (1989) *Primate Visions: Gender, Race and Nature in the World of Modern Science*, New York: Routledge. (Primatology's role in the production of androcentric and Eurocentric culture, and vice versa. Early classic accounts of how gender and race shaped the choice and conceptual frameworks of scientific projects.)

* —— (1991) 'Situated Knowledges: The Science Question in Feminism and the Privilege of Partial Perspective', in *Simians, Cyborgs and Women: The Reinvention of Nature*, New York: Routledge. (Widely cited analysis of the non-absolutist and non-relativistic epistemology emerging from philosophies of science. Originated as a review of Harding 1986.)

* Harding, S. (1986) *The Science Question in Feminism*, Ithaca, NY: Cornell University Press. (Expansion of the material of §§1 and 2. Mapped the feminist empiricist and standpoint philosophies of science that were being developed by practising scientists and science theorists in philosophy and the social sciences, and the challenges to them emerging from feminist poststructuralism.)

* —— (1991) *Whose Science? Whose Knowledge?*, Ithaca, NY: Cornell University Press. (Expansion of the material of §§3 and 6. Develops programme for 'strong objectivity' to replace conventional neutrality requirement.)

—— (1998) *Is Science Multicultural? Postcolonialism, Feminism and Epistemology*, Bloomington, IN: Indiana University Press. (Shows how feminist philosophies of science and two decades of multicultural and postcolonial science studies can inform each other.)

Harding, S. and Hintikka, M. (eds) (1983) *Discovering Reality: Feminist Perspectives on Epistemology, Metaphysics, Methodology and Philosophy of*

Science, Dordrecht: Reidel. (Earliest collection of philosophically focused papers, including standpoint theory essay by Nancy Hartsock.)

* Keller, E.F. (1983) 'Feminism as an Analytic Tool for the Study of Science', *Academe* September–October: 15–21. (A concise discussion of themes from her 1984 publication.)

* —— (1984) *Reflections on Gender and Science*, New Haven, CT: Yale University Press. (Important arguments for §§4, 6. Classic early analyses of gender and method, objectivity, Plato's epistemology, Baconian science, contemporary physics and biology.)

* Longino, H. (1990) *Science as Social Knowledge: Values and Objectivity in Scientific Inquiry*, Princeton, NJ: Princeton University Press. (Analysis of issues in §6. How gendered meanings infuse not only modern sciences' background beliefs, but also their constituting values.)

* Merchant, C. (1980) *The Death of Nature: Women, Ecology and the Scientific Revolution*, New York: Harper & Row. (Important history of early modern science; arguments for §4. How modern sciences came to reflect and help to shape shifting gender relations of fifteenth- through seventeenth-century Europe.)

Nelson, L.H. and Nelson, J. (eds) (1996) *Feminism, Science, and the Philosophy of Science*, Dordrecht: Kluwer. (Thirteen philosophers – men and women – discuss a range of issues that feminist scholars have raised in philosophy of science. Diverse topics and philosophical approaches.)

* Rose, H. (1983) 'Hand, Brain and Heart: A Feminist Epistemology for the Natural Sciences', *Signs: Journal of Women in Culture and Society* 9: 1. (Important development of standpoint theory; argument of §3.)

* Shiva, V. (1989) *Staying Alive: Women, Ecology and Development*, Atlantic Highlands, NJ: Zed Books. (Critique of Western science, its patriarchal conceptions of nature, rationality and objectivity by an Indian physicist and environmental activist.)

* Smith, D.E. (1987) *The Everyday World as Problematic: A Feminist Sociology*, Boston, MA: Northeastern University Press. (Important standpoint theory essays by the most eminent feminist philosopher–sociologist writing from the perspective of concerns about research methodologies.)

* Traweek, S. (1988) *Beamtimes and Lifetimes: The World of High Energy Physics*, Cambridge, MA: Harvard University Press. (Ethnography of physics, including its gender relations.)

* Wajcman, J. (1991) *Feminism Confronts Technology*, University Park, PA: Pennsylvania State University Press. (Analysis of issues in §5. A pathbreaking constructivist analysis of technology that enables development of a distinctive and influential philosophy of technology.)

Wylie, A., Okruhlik, K., Morton, S. and Thielen-Wilson, L. (1990) 'Philosophical Feminism: A Bibliographic Guide to Critiques of Science', *RFR/DRF New Feminist Research* 19 (2): 2–36. (The most comprehensive guide to the first two decades of the literature.)

SANDRA G. HARDING